THE NEW GROVE
DICTIONARY OF MUSIC AND MUSICIANS®

Volume Eighteen

The New
GROVE
Dictionary
of Music and
Musicians®

EDITED BY

Stanley Sadie

18

Spiridion–Tin whistle

GROVE

MACMILLAN PUBLISHERS LIMITED, LONDON
GROVE'S DICTIONARIES OF MUSIC INC., NEW YORK, NY
MACMILLAN PUBLISHERS (CHINA) LIMITED, HONG KONG

First Edition of *A Dictionary of Music and Musicians*, planned and edited by SIR GEORGE GROVE, DCL, in
four volumes, with an Appendix edited by J. A. Fuller Maitland, and an Index by Mrs Edmond
Wodehouse, 1878, 1880, 1883, 1890.
Reprinted 1890, 1900

Second Edition, edited by J. A. FULLER MAITLAND, in five volumes, 1904–10

Third Edition, edited by H. C. COLLES, in five volumes, 1927

Fourth Edition, edited by H. C. COLLES, in five volumes, with Supplementary Volume, 1940

Fifth Edition, edited by ERIC BLOM, in nine volumes, 1954; with Supplementary Volume, 1961
Reprinted 1961, 1973, 1975

American Supplement, edited by WALDO SELDEN PRATT, in one volume, 1920
Reprinted with new material, 1928; many later reprints

The New Grove Dictionary of Music and Musicians,®
edited by STANLEY SADIE, in twenty volumes, 1980

The New Grove and *The New Grove Dictionary of Music and Musicians* are registered trademarks
in the United States of Macmillan Publishers Limited, London.

Macmillan Publishers Limited, London and its associated companies are the proprietors of the trademarks
Grove's, *The New Grove*, and *The New Grove Dictionary of Music and Musicians* throughout the world.

First published 1980 in hardback edition.
Reprinted with minor corrections, 1981, 1984, 1985, 1986, 1987, 1988, 1989, 1990, 1991, 1992, 1993, 1994, 1995.
Reprinted 1995 in paperback edition.

Published by Macmillan Publishers Limited, London. Both editions are distributed outside the United
Kingdom and Europe by Macmillan Publishers (China) Limited, Hong Kong, a member of the Macmillan
Publishers Group, and by its appointed agents. In the United States of America and Canada, Macmillan
Publishers (China) Limited, Hong Kong have appointed Grove's Dictionaries of Music Inc., New York,
NY, as sole distributor.

Text keyboarded, corrected, page-made-up and filmset by
Richard Clay (The Chaucer Press) Ltd, Bungay, Suffolk, England

Illustrations originated by Fletcher & Son Ltd, Norwich, England

Music examples processed by Halstan & Co.Ltd, Amersham, England

Printed and bound in the United States of America by R. R. Donnelley & Co., Crawfordsville, Indiana

British Library Cataloguing in Publication Data
The New Grove dictionary of music and
musicians.®
A catalogue record for this book is available
from the British Library.
ISBN 0–333–23111–2 (hardback)
ISBN 1–56159–174–2 (paperback)

Library of Congress Cataloging in Publication Data
Main entry under title:
The New Grove dictionary of music and musicians.®
Includes bibliographies.
1. Music-Dictionaries.
2. Music-Bio-bibliography.
I. Grove, George, Sir, 1820–1900.
II. Sadie, Stanley.
ML100.N48 780'.3 79-26207

ISBN 0–333–23111–2 (hardback)
ISBN 1–56159–174–2 (paperback)

Contents

Executive Committee

Stanley Sadie
Editor

Ian D. Bent   Nigel Fortune   Lewis Lockwood
Senior Consulting Editors

Gerard Béhague
Stanley Boorman
Howard Mayer Brown
George J. Buelow
Geoffrey Chew
Peter Cooke
Charles Cudworth
Paul Doe
Vincent H. Duckles
Peter Evans
Paul Griffiths
James Haar
Daniel Heartz
H. Wiley Hitchcock
Mantle Hood
Peter le Huray

Alec Hyatt King
Kenneth Levy
Mark Lindley
Hugh Macdonald
Diana McVeagh
Jeremy Noble
Edward Olleson
Claude V. Palisca
Andrew Porter
Harold S. Powers
Michael Tilmouth
John Tyrrell
Klaus P. Wachsmann
John M. Ward
John Warrack
Charles Warren

Advisory Board

Gerald Abraham
Nicolas Barker
Donald J. Grout
Mantle Hood
Alec Hyatt King
Edward N. Waters
The Editor and Senior Consulting Editors

National Advisers

John Beckwith
Ludwig Finscher
Masakata Kanazawa
François Lesure
Andrew McCredie
Genrikh Orlov
Pierluigi Petrobelli

General Abbreviations

A	alto, contralto [voice]	Bte	Benedicite
a	alto [instrument]	Bucks.	Buckinghamshire (GB)
AB	see BA	Bulg.	Bulgarian
ABC	American Broadcasting Company; Australian Broadcasting Commission	BVM	Blessed Virgin Mary
Abt.	Abteilung [section]	BWV	Bach-Werke-Verzeichnis [Schmieder, catalogue of J. S. Bach's works]
acc.	accompaniment, accompanied by		
AD	anno Domini		
add, addl	additional		
add, addn	addition	c	circa [about]
ad lib	ad libitum	Calif.	California (USA)
Ag	Agnus Dei	CanD	Cantate Domino
all	alleluia	carn.	Carnival
AM	see MA	CBC	Canadian Broadcasting Corporation
a.m.	ante meridiem [before noon]	CBE	Commander of the Order of the British Empire
amp	amplified		
AMS	American Musicological Society	CBS	Columbia Broadcasting System (USA)
Anh.	Anhang [appendix]	CBSO	City of Birmingham Symphony Orchestra
anon.	anonymous(ly)	CeBeDeM	Centre Belge de Documentation Musicale
ant	antiphon	cel	celesta
appx	appendix	CEMA	Council for the Encouragement of Music and the Arts [now the Arts Council of Great Britain]
arr.	arrangement, arranged by/for		
ASCAP	American Society of Composers, Authors and Publishers		
		cf	confer [compare]
attrib.	attribution, attributed to	c.f.	cantus firmus
Aug	August	CH	Companion of Honour
aut.	autumn	chap.	chapter
		Chin.	Chinese
		chit	chitarrone
		Cie	Compagnie
B	bass [voice]	cimb	cimbalom
B	Brainard catalogue [Tartini]	cl	clarinet
b	bass [instrument]	clvd	clavichord
b	born	cm	centimetre(s)
BA	Bachelor of Arts	CNRS	Centre National de la Recherche Scientifique (F)
Bar	baritone [voice]		
bar	baritone [instrument]	Co.	Company; County
BBC	British Broadcasting Corporation	Cod.	Codex
BC	British Columbia (Canada)	col.	column
BC	before Christ	coll.	collected by
bc	basso continuo	collab.	in collaboration with
Bd.	Band [volume]	comm	communion
Berks.	Berkshire (GB)	conc.	concerto
Berwicks.	Berwickshire (GB)	cond.	conductor, conducted by
bk	book	Conn.	Connecticut (USA)
BLitt	Bachelor of Letters/Literature	cont	continuo
BM	British Museum	Corp.	Corporation
BMI	Broadcast Music Inc. (USA)	c.p.s.	cycles per second
BMus	Bachelor of Music	Cr	Credo, Creed
bn	bassoon	CSc	Candidate of Historical Sciences
Bros.	Brothers	Ct	countertenor
Bs	Benedictus	Cz.	Czech

D	Deutsch catalogue [Schubert]; Dounias catalogue [Tartini]
d.	denarius, denarii [penny, pence]
d	died
Dan.	Danish
db	double bass
DBE	Dame Commander of the Order of the British Empire
dbn	double bassoon
DC	District of Columbia (USA)
Dec	December
ded.	dedication, dedicated to
DeM	Deus misereatur
Dept	Department
Derbys.	Derbyshire (GB)
dir.	director, directed by
diss.	dissertation
DLitt	Doctor of Letters/Literature
DMus	Doctor of Music
DPhil	Doctor of Philosophy
DSc	Doctor of Science/Historical Sciences
ed.	editor, edited (by)
edn.	edition
e.g.	exempli gratia [for example]
elec	electric, electronic
EMI	Electrical and Musical Industries
Eng.	English
eng hn	english horn
ens	ensemble
esp.	especially
etc	et cetera [and so on]
ex., exx.	example, examples
f, ff	following page, following pages
f., ff.	folio, folios
f	forte
facs.	facsimile
fasc.	fascicle
Feb	February
ff	fortissimo
fff	fortississimo
fig.	figure [illustration]
fl	flute
fl	floruit [he/she flourished]
fp	fortepiano
Fr.	French
frag.	fragment
FRAM	Fellow of the Royal Academy of Music, London
FRCM	Fellow of the Royal College of Music, London
FRCO	Fellow of the Royal College of Organists, London
FRS	Fellow of the Royal Society, London
Gael.	Gaelic
Ger.	German
Gk.	Greek
Gl	Gloria
Glam.	Glamorgan (GB)
glock	glockenspiel
Glos., Gloucs.	Gloucestershire (GB)

GmbH	Gesellschaft mit beschränkter Haftung [limited-liability company]
govt.	government [district in USSR]
grad	gradual
GSM	Guildhall School of Music and Drama, London
gui	guitar
H	Hoboken catalogue [Haydn]; Helm catalogue [C. P. E. Bach]
Hants.	Hampshire (GB)
Heb.	Hebrew
Herts.	Hertfordshire (GB)
HMS	His/Her Majesty's Ship
HMV	His Master's Voice
hn	horn
Hon.	Honorary; Honourable
hpd	harpsichord
HRH	His/Her Royal Highness
Hung.	Hungarian
Hunts.	Huntingdonshire (GB)
Hz	Hertz [c.p.s.]
IAML	International Association of Music Libraries
ibid	ibidem [in the same place]
i.e.	id est [that is]
IFMC	International Folk Music Council
Ill.	Illinois (USA)
IMS	International Musicological Society
Inc.	Incorporated
inc.	incomplete
incl.	includes, including
Ind.	Indiana (USA)
inst	instrument, instrumental
int	introit
IPEM	Institute for Psycho-acoustics and Electronic Music, Brussels
ISCM	International Society for Contemporary Music
ISM	Incorporated Society of Musicians (GB)
ISME	International Society of Music Educators
It.	Italian
Jan	January
Jap.	Japanese
Jb	Jahrbuch [yearbook]
Jg.	Jahrgang [year of publication/volume]
jr	junior
Jub	Jubilate
K	Kirkpatrick catalogue [D. Scarlatti]; Köchel catalogue [Mozart; no. after / is from 6th edn.]
kbd	keyboard
KBE	Knight Commander of the Order of the British Empire
KCVO	Knight Commander of the Royal Victorian Order
kHz	kilohertz
km	kilometre(s)
Ky	Kyrie
Ky.	Kentucky (USA)

£	libra, librae [pound, pounds sterling]
L	Longo catalogue [D. Scarlatti]
Lancs.	Lancashire (GB)
Lat.	Latin
Leics.	Leicestershire (GB)
lib	libretto
Lincs.	Lincolnshire (GB)
lit	litany
LittD	Doctor of Letters/Literature
LlB	Bachelor of Laws
LlD	Doctor of Laws
LP	long-playing record
LPO	London Philharmonic Orchestra
LSO	London Symphony Orchestra
Ltd	Limited

M.	Monsieur
MA	Master of Arts
Mag	Magnificat
mand	mandolin
mar	marimba
Mass.	Massachusetts (USA)
MBE	Member of the Order of the British Empire
Mez	mezzo-soprano
mf	mezzo-forte
mic	microphone
Mich.	Michigan (USA)
Minn.	Minnesota (USA)
Mlle	Mademoiselle
mm	millimetre(s)
Mme	Madame
MMus	Master of Music
mod	modulator
Mon.	Monmouthshire (GB)
movt	movement
MP	Member of Parliament (GB)
mp	mezzo-piano
MS	manuscript
MSc	Master of Science(s)
Mt	Mount
MusB, MusBac	Bachelor of Music
MusD, MusDoc	Doctor of Music
MusM	Master of Music

NBC	National Broadcasting Company (USA)
n.d.	no date of publication
NJ	New Jersey (USA)
no.	number
Nor.	Norwegian
Northants.	Northamptonshire (GB)
Notts.	Nottinghamshire (GB)
Nov	November
n.p.	no place of publication
nr.	near
NSW	New South Wales (Australia)
Nunc	Nunc dimittis
NY	New York State (USA)

ob	oboe
obbl	obbligato
OBE	Officer of the Order of the British Empire

Oct	October
off	offertory
OM	Order of Merit
Ont.	Ontario (Canada)
op., opp.	opus, opera
op cit	opere citato [in the work cited]
opt.	optional
orch	orchestra, orchestral
orchd	orchestrated (by)
org	organ
orig.	original(ly)
ORTF	Office de Radiodiffusion-Télévision Française
OUP	Oxford University Press
ov.	overture

P	Pincherle catalogue [Vivaldi]
p.	pars (1p. = *prima pars*, etc)
p., pp.	page, pages
p	piano
p.a.	per annum
PC	number of chanson in A. Pillet and H. Carstens: *Bibliographie der Troubadours* (Halle, 1933)
Penn.	Pennsylvania (USA)
perc	percussion
perf.	performance, performed (by)
pf	piano
PhD	Doctor of Philosophy
pic	piccolo
pl.	plate; plural
p.m.	post meridiem [after noon]
PO	Philharmonic Orchestra
Pol.	Polish
Port.	Portuguese
posth.	posthumous(ly)
POW	prisoner of war
pp	pianissimo
ppp	pianississimo
pr.	printed
PRO	Public Record Office, London
prol	prologue
PRS	Performing Right Society (GB)
Ps	Psalm
ps	psalm
pseud.	pseudonym
pt.	part
ptbk	partbook
pubd	published
pubn	publication

qnt	quintet
qt	quartet

R	[in signature] editorial revision
R.	number of chanson in G. Raynaud: *Bibliographie des chansonniers français des XIIIe et XIVe siècles* (Paris, 1884) and H. Spanke: *G. Raynauds Bibliographie des altfranzösischen Liedes* (Leiden, 1955)
R	response
R	Ryom catalogue [Vivaldi]
R	photographic reprint
r	recto

RAF	Royal Air Force
RAI	Radio Audizioni Italiane
RAM	Royal Academy of Music, London
RCA	Radio Corporation of America
RCM	Royal College of Music, London
re	response
rec	recorder
recit	recitative
red.	reduction, reduced for
repr.	reprinted
Rev.	Reverend
rev.	revision, revised (by/for)
RIdIM	Répertoire International d'Iconographie Musicale
RILM	Répertoire International de Littérature Musicale
RISM	Répertoire International des Sources Musicales
RMCM	Royal Manchester College of Music
RNCM	Royal Northern College of Music, Manchester
RO	Radio Orchestra
Rom.	Romanian
RPO	Royal Philharmonic Orchestra (GB)
RSFSR	Russian Soviet Federated Socialist Republic
RSO	Radio Symphony Orchestra
Rt Hon.	Right Honourable
RTE	Radio Telefís Eireann (Ireland)
Russ.	Russian
RV	Ryom catalogue [Vivaldi]
S	San, Santa, Santo, São [Saint]; soprano [voice]
S.	south, southern
$	dollars
s	soprano [instrument]
s.	solidus, solidi [shilling, shillings]
SACEM	Société d'Auteurs, Compositeurs et Editeurs de Musique (F)
San	Sanctus
Sask.	Saskatchewan (Canada)
sax	saxophone
Sept	September
seq	sequence
ser.	series
sf, sfz	sforzando, sforzato
sing.	singular
SJ	Societas Jesu (Society of Jesus)
SO	Symphony Orchestra
SPNM	Society for the Promotion of New Music (GB)
spr.	spring
SS	Saints
Ss	Santissima, Santissimo
SSR	Soviet Socialist Republic
St	Saint, Sint, Szent
Staffs.	Staffordshire (GB)
Ste	Sainte
str	string(s)
sum.	summer
Sup	superius
suppl.	supplement, supplementary
Swed.	Swedish
sym.	symphony, symphonic
synth	synthesizer

T	tenor [voice]
t	tenor [instrument]
TeD	Te Deum
Tenn.	Tennessee (USA)
timp	timpani
tpt	trumpet
Tr	treble [voice]
tr	tract; treble [instrument]
trans.	translation, translated by
transcr.	transcription, transcribed by/for
trbn	trombone
U.	University
UHF	ultra-high frequency
UK	United Kingdom of Great Britain and Northern Ireland
unacc.	unaccompanied
unattrib.	unattributed
UNESCO	United Nations Educational, Scientific and Cultural Organization
unperf.	unperformed
unpubd	unpublished
US	United States [adjective]
USA	United States of America
USSR	Union of Soviet Socialist Republics
$\bar{V}$	versicle
v, vv	voice, voices
v., vv.	verse, verses
v	verso
va	viola
vc	cello
vcle	versicle
VEB	Volkseigener Betrieb [people's own industry]
Ven	Venite
VHF	very high frequency
vib	vibraphone
viz	videlicet [namely]
vle	violone
vn	violin
vol.	volume
W.	west, western
Warwicks.	Warwickshire (GB)
Wilts.	Wiltshire (GB)
wint.	winter
Wisc.	Wisconsin (USA)
WoO, woo	Werke ohne Opuszahl [works without opus number]
Worcs.	Worcestershire (GB)
WQ	Wotquenne catalogue [C. P. E. Bach]
ww	woodwind
xyl	xylophone
Yorks.	Yorkshire (GB)
z	Zimmerman catalogue [Purcell]

Bibliographical Abbreviations

All bibliographical abbreviations used in this dictionary are listed below, following the typography used in the text of the dictionary. Broadly, *italic* type is used for periodicals and for reference works; roman type is used for anthologies, series etc (titles of individual volumes are italicized).

Full bibliographical information is not normally supplied in the list below if it is available elsewhere in the dictionary. Its availability is indicated as follows: D – in the article 'Dictionaries and encyclopedias of music'; E – in the article 'Editions, historical'; and P – in the list forming §III of the article 'Periodicals' (in this case the number in that list of the periodical concerned is added, in brackets). For other items, in particular national (non-musical) biographical dictionaries, basic bibliographical information is given here; and in some cases extra information is supplied to clarify the abbreviation used.

Festschriften and congress reports are not, in general, covered in this list. Although Festschrift titles are usually shortened in the dictionary, sufficient information is always given for unambiguous identification (dedicatee; occasion, if the same person is dedicatee of more than one Festschrift; place and date of publication; and where the dedicatee has an entry the editor's name may be found); for fuller information on musical Festschriften up to 1967 see W. Gerboth: *An Index to Musical Festschriften and Similar Publications* (New York, 1969). The only congress report series listed below are those of the international and the German musicological associations; for others cited in the dictionary, sufficient information is always given for identification (society or topic; place; date of occurrence); full information may be found in J. Tyrrell and R. Wise: *A Guide to International Congress Reports in Music, 1900–1975* (London, 1979).

AcM	*Acta musicologica* P [Intl 5]
ADB	*Allgemeine deutsche Biographie* (Leipzig, 1875–1912)
AM	Antiphonale monasticum pro diurnis horis (Paris, Tournai and Rome, 1934)
AMe (AMeS)	*Algemene muziekencyclopedie* (and suppl.) D
AMf	*Archiv für Musikforschung* P [D776]
AMI	L'arte musicale in Italia E
AMP	Antiquitates musicae in Polonia E
AMw	*Archiv für Musikwissenschaft* P [D552]
AMZ	*Allgemeine musikalische Zeitung* P [D32, 154, 170]
AMz	*Allgemeine Musik-Zeitung* P [D203]
AnM	*Anuario musical* E
AnMc	*Analecta musicologica* (some vols. in series Studien zur italienisch-deutschen Musikgeschichte), Veröffentlichungen der Musikabteilung des Deutschen historischen Instituts in Rom (Cologne, 1963–)
AnnM	*Annales musicologiques* P [F638]
AntMI	Antiquae musicae italicae E
AR	Antiphonale sacrosanctae romanae ecclesiae pro diurnis horis (Paris, Tournai and Rome, 1949)
AS	Antiphonale sarisburiense, ed. W. H. Frere (London, 1901–25/R1967)
Baker 5, 6	*Baker's Biographical Dictionary of Musicians* (5/ 1958 and 1971 suppl., 6/1978) D
BAMS	*Bulletin of the American Musicological Society* P [US540]
BeJb	*Beethoven-Jahrbuch* [1953–] P [D925]
BJb	*Bach-Jahrbuch* P [D434]
BMB	Biblioteca musica bononiensis E
BMw	*Beiträge zur Musikwissenschaft* P [D1013]
BNB	*Biographie nationale* [belge] (Brussels, 1866–)
BordasD	*Dictionnaire de la musique* (Paris: Bordas, 1970–76) D
Bouwsteenen: JVNM	*Bouwsteenen: jaarboek der Vereeniging voor Nederlandsche muziekgeschiedenis* P [NL20]
BrownI	H. M. Brown: *Instrumental Music Printed before 1600: a Bibliography* (Cambridge, Mass., 2/1967)
BSIM	*Bulletin français de la S[ociété] I[nternationale de] M[usique]* [previously *Le Mercure musical*; also other titles] P [F364]

BUCEM	*British Union-catalogue of Early Music*, ed. E. Schnapper (London, 1957)
BurneyH	C. Burney: *A General History of Music from the Earliest Ages to the Present* (London, 1776–89) [p. nos. refer to edn. of 1935/R1957]
BWQ	*Brass and Woodwind Quarterly* P [US756]
CaM	Catalogus musicus E
CEKM	Corpus of Early Keyboard Music E
CEMF	Corpus of Early Music in Facsimile E
CHM	Collectanea historiae musicae (in series Biblioteca historiae musicae cultores) (Florence, 1953–)
CM	Le choeur des muses E
CMc	*Current Musicology* P [US747]
CMI	I classici musicali italiani E
CMM	Corpus mensurabilis musicae E
CMz	*Cercetări de muzicologie* P [R29]
CS	E. de Coussemaker: Scriptorum de musica medii aevi nova series (Paris, 1864–76/R1963)
ČSHS	*Československý hudební slovník* D
CSM	Corpus scriptorum de musica E
CSPD	Calendar of State Papers (Domestic) (London, 1856–1972)
Cw	Das Chorwerk E
DAB	*Dictionary of American Biography* (New York, 1928–)
DAM	*Dansk aarbog for musikforskning* P [DK88]
DBF	*Dictionnaire de biographie française* (Paris, 1933–)
DBI	*Dizionario biografico degli italiani* (Rome, 1960–)
DBL	*Dansk biografisk leksikon* (Copenhagen, 1887–1905, 2/1933–)
DBP	*Dicionário biográfico de musicos portuguezes* D
DČHP	*Dějiny české hudby v příkladech* E
DDT	Denkmäler deutscher Tonkunst E
DHM	Documenta historica musicae E
DJbM	*Deutsches Jahrbuch der Musikwissenschaft* P [D980]
DM	Documenta musicologica E
DNB	*Dictionary of National Biography* (London, 1885–1901, suppls.)
DTB	Denkmäler der Tonkunst in Bayern E
DTÖ	Denkmäler der Tonkunst in Österreich E

EDM	Das Erbe deutscher Musik E		*JbMP*	*Jahrbuch der Musikbibliothek Peters* P [D336]
EECM	Early English Church Music E		*JEFDSS*	*The Journal of the English Folk Dance and Song Society* P [GB341]
EIT	*Ezhegodnik imperatorskikh teatrov* P [USSR17]		*JFSS*	*Journal of the Folk-song Society* P [GB183]
EitnerQ	R. Eitner: *Biographisch-bibliographisches Quellen-Lexikon* D		*JIFMC*	*Journal of the International Folk Music Council* P [Intl 10]
EitnerS	R. Eitner: *Bibliographie der Musik-Sammelwerke des XVI. und XVII. Jahrhunderts* (Berlin, 1877)		*JMT*	*Journal of Music Theory* P [US683]
EKM	English (later Early) Keyboard Music E		*JRBM*	*Journal of Renaissance and Baroque Music* P [US590]
EL	The English Lute-songs		*JRME*	*Journal of Research in Music Education* P [US665]
EM	The English Madrigalists E		*JVNM*	see *Bouwsteenen: JVNM* P [NL20]
EM	*Ethnomusicology* P [US664]			
EMDC	*Encyclopédie de la musique et dictionnaire du Conservatoire* D			
EMN	Exempla musica neerlandica E		*KJb*	*Kirchenmusikalisches Jahrbuch* P [D284]
EMS	The English Madrigal School E		*KM*	*Kwartalnik muzyczny* P [PL35, 64]
ES	*Enciclopedia dello spettacolo* D			
ESLS	The English School of Lutenist-songwriters E			
			LaborD	*Diccionario de la música Labor* D
FAM	*Fontes artis musicae* P [Intl 16]		*LaMusicaD*	*La musica: dizionario* D
FasquelleE	*Encyclopédie de la musique* (Paris: Fasquelle, 1958–61) D		*LaMusicaE*	*La musica: enciclopedia storica* D
			LM	*Lucrări de muzicologie* P [R27]
FCVR	Florilège du concert vocal de la renaissance E		*LSJ*	*The Lute Society Journal* P [GB487]
FétisB (*FétisBS*)	F.-J. Fétis: *Biographie universelle des musiciens* (2/1860–65) (and suppl.) D		*LU*	*Liber usualis missae et officii pro dominicis et festis duplicibus cum cantu gregoriano* (Solesmes, 1896; many later edns., incl. Tournai, 1963)
GerberL	R. Gerber: *Historisch-biographisches Lexikon der Tonkünstler* D			
GerberNL	R. Gerber: *Neues historisch-biographisches Lexikon der Tonkünstler* D		*MA*	*The Musical Antiquary* P [GB240]
GfMKB	*Gesellschaft für Musikforschung Kongressbericht* [1950–]		MAB	Musica antiqua bohemica E
			MAM	Musik alter Meister E
GMB	*Geschichte der Musik in Beispielen*, ed. A. Schering (Leipzig, 1931) E		MAP	Musica antiqua polonica E
			MAS	[publications of the British] Musical Antiquarian Society E
GR	*Graduale sacrosanctae romanae ecclesiae* (Tournai, 1938)		MB	Musica britannica E
Grove 1(–5)	G. Grove, ed.: *A Dictionary of Music and Musicians*, 2nd–5th edns. as *Grove's Dictionary of Music and Musicians* D		MC	Musica da camera E
			MD	*Musica disciplina* P [US590]
			ME	*Muzïkal'naya entsiklopediya* D
Grove 6	*The New Grove Dictionary of Music and Musicians* D		MEM	Mestres de l'escolania de Montserrat E
			Mf	*Die Musikforschung* P [D839]
GS	*Graduale sarisburiense*, ed. W. H. Frere (London, 1894/R1967)		*MGG*	*Die Musik in Geschichte und Gegenwart* D
			MH	Musica hispana E
GS	M. Gerbert: *Scriptores ecclesiastici de musica sacra* (St Blasien, 1784/R1963)		*MJb*	*Mozart-Jahrbuch des Zentralinstituts für Mozartforschung* [1950–] P [A254]
GSJ	*The Galpin Society Journal* P [GB415]		*ML*	*Music and Letters* P [GB280]
			MLMI	Monumenta lyrica medii aevi italica E
			MM	*Modern Music* P [US488]
			MMA	*Miscellanea musicologica* [Australia] P [AUS19]
HAM	*Historical Anthology of Music*, ed. A. T. Davison and W. Apel, i (Cambridge, Mass., 1946, rev. 2/1949); ii (Cambridge, Mass., 1950) E		MMB	Monumenta musicae byzantinae E
			MMBel	Monumenta musicae belgicae E
			MMC	*Miscellanea musicologica* [Czechoslovakia] P [CS191]
HawkinsH	J. Hawkins: *A General History of the Science and Practice of Music* (London, 1776) [p. nos. refer to edn. of 1853/R1963]		MME	Monumentos de la música española E
			MMFTR	Monuments de la musique française au temps de la renaissance E
HJb	*Händel-Jahrbuch* P [D712, 968]		*MMg*	*Monatshefte für Musikgeschichte* P [D188]
HM	Hortus musicus E		MMI	Monumenti di musica italiana E
HMT	*Handwörterbuch der musikalischen Terminologie* D		MMN	Monumenta musicae neerlandicae E
HMw	Handbuch der Musikwissenschaft, ed. E. Bücken (Potsdam, 1927–) [monograph series]		MMP	Monumenta musicae in Polonia E
			MMR	*The Monthly Musical Record* P [GB75]
HMYB	*Hinrichsen's Musical Year Book* P [GB381]		MMRF	Les maîtres musiciens de la renaissance française E
HPM	Harvard Publications in Music E		MMS	Monumenta musicae svecicae E
HR	*Hudební revue* P [CS80]		*MO*	*Musical Opinion* P [GB90]
HRo	*Hudební rozhledy* P [CS176]		*MQ*	*The Musical Quarterly* P [US447]
HV	*Hudební věda* P [CS204]		*MR*	*The Music Review* P [GB376]
			MRM	Monuments of Renaissance Music E
			MRS	Musiche rinascimentali siciliane E
IIM	*Izvestiya na Instituta za muzïka* P [BG14]		*MS*	*Muzïkal'nïy sovremennik* P [USSR37]
IMa	Instituta et monumenta E		MSD	Musicological Studies and Documents, ed. A. Carapetyan (Rome, 1951–)
IMi	Istituzioni e monumenti dell'arte musicale italiana E		*MT*	*The Musical Times* P [GB33]
IMSCR	*International Musicological Society Congress Report* [1930–]		MVH	Musica viva historica E
			MVSSP	Musiche vocali strumentali sacre e profane E
IMusSCR	*International Musical Society Congress Report* [1906–11]		Mw	Das Musikwerk E
IRASM	*International Review of the Aesthetics and Sociology of Music* P [Intl 32]		*MZ*	*Muzikološki zbornik* P [YU37]
IRMO	S. L. Ginzburg: *Istoriya russkoy muzïki v notnïkh obraztsakh* D		*NA*	*Note d'archivio per la storia musicale* P [I186]
IRMAS	*The International Review of Music Aesthetics and Sociology* P [Intl 32]		*NBJb*	*Neues Beethoven-Jahrbuch* P [D636]
IZ	*Instrumentenbau-Zeitschrift* P [D806]		*NBL*	*Norsk biografisk leksikon* (Oslo, 1921–)
			NDB	*Neue deutsche Biographie* (Berlin, 1953–)
			NM	Nagels Musikarchiv E
JAMS	*Journal of the American Musicological Society* P [US613]		*NNBW*	*Nieuw Nederlandsch biografisch woordenboek* (Leiden, 1911–37)
			NÖB	*Neue österreichische Biographie* (Vienna, 1923)

NOHM	*The New Oxford History of Music*, ed. E. Wellesz, J. A. Westrup and G. Abraham (London, 1954–)
NRMI	*Nuova rivista musicale italiana* P [I 282]
NZM	*Neue Zeitschrift für Musik* P [D75, 1088]
OHM	*The Oxford History of Music*, ed. W. H. Hadow (Oxford, 1901–5, enlarged 2/1929–38)
QM	*Opus musicum* P [CS222]
ÖMz	*Österreichische Musikzeitschrift* P [A233]
PalMus	Paléographie musicale (Solesmes, 1889–) [see entry SOLESMES]
PAMS	*Papers of the American Musicological Society* P [US543]
PÄMw	Publikationen älterer praktischer und theoretischer Musikwerke E
PBC	Publicaciones del departamento de música de la Biblioteca de Catalunya E
PG	*Patrologiae cursus completus*, ii: Series graeca, ed. J.-P. Migne (Paris, 1857–1912)
PGfM	Publikationen der Gesellschaft für Musikforschung E
PIISM	Pubblicazioni dell'Istituto italiano per la storia della musica E
PL	*Patrologiae cursus completus*, i: Series latina, ed. J.-P. Migne (Paris, 1844–64)
PM	Portugaliae musica E
PMA	*Proceedings of the Musical Association* P [GB80]
PMFC	Polyphonic Music of the Fourteenth Century E
PNM	*Perspectives of New Music* P [US724]
PRM	*Polski rocznik muzykologiczny* P [PL85]
PRMA	*Proceedings of the Royal Musical Association* P [GB80]
PSB	*Polskich słownik biograficzny* (Kraków, 1935)
PSFM	Publications de la Société française de musicologie E
Quaderni della RaM	*Quaderni della Rassegna musicale* P [I 272]
Rad JAZU	*Rad Jugoslavenske akademije znanosti i umjetnosti* (Zagreb, 1867–)
RaM	*La rassegna musicale* P [I 197]
RBM	*Revue belge de musicologie* P [B126]
RdM	*Revue de musicologie* P [F462]
ReM	*La revue musicale* [1920–] P [F475]
RHCM	*Revue d'histoire et de critique musicales* [1901]; *La revue musicale* [1902–10] P [F320]
RicordiE	*Enciclopedia della musica* (Milan: Ricordi, 1963–4) D
RiemannL 12	*Riemann Musik Lexikon* (12/1959–75) D
RIM	*Rivista italiana di musicologia* P [I 280]
RISM	*Répertoire international des sources musicales* [see entry under this title]
RMARC	*R[oyal] M[usical] A[ssociation] Research Chronicle* P [GB496]
RMFC	*Recherches sur la musique française classique* P [F677]
RMG	*Russkaya muzïkal'naya gazeta* P [USSR19]
RMI	*Rivista musicale italiana* P [I 84]
RMS	Renaissance Manuscript Studies E
RN	*Renaissance News* P [see US590]
RRMBE	Recent Researches in the Music of the Baroque Era E
RRMR	Recent Researches in the Music of the Renaissance E

SartoriB	C. Sartori: *Bibliografia della musica strumentale italiana stampata in Italia fino al 1700* (Florence, 1952–68)
SBL	*Svenska biografiskt leksikon* (Stockholm, 1918–)
SchmidlD (SchmidlDS)	C. Schmidl: *Dizionario dei musicisti* (and suppl.) D
SCMA	Smith College Music Archives E
SeegerL	H. Seeger: *Musiklexikon* D
SEM	[University of California] Series of Early Music E
SH	*Slovenská hudba* P [CS192]
SIMG	*Sammelbände der Internationalen Musik-Gesellschaft* P [Intl 2]
SM	*Studia musicologica Academiae scientiarum hungaricae* P [H49]
SMA	*Studies in Music* [Australia] P [AUS20]
SMd	Schweizerische Musikdenkmäler E
SML	*Schweizer Musiker Lexikon* D
SMM	Summa musicae medii aevi E
SMN	*Studia musicologica norvegica* P [N45]
SMP	*Słownik muzyków polskich* D
SMw	*Studien zur Musikwissenschaft* P [D536]
SMz	*Schweizerische Musikzeitung/Revue musicale suisse* P [CH4]
SOB	Süddeutsche Orgelmeister des Barock E
SovM	*Sovetskaya muzïka* P [USSR66]
STMf	*Svensk tidskrift för musikforskning* P [S46]
TCM	Tudor Church Music E
TM	Thesauri musici E
TVNM	*Tijdschrift van de Vereniging voor Nederlandse muziekgeschiedenis* P [NL26]
UVNM	Uitgaven der Vereniging voor Nederlandse muziekgeschiedenis E
VMPH	Veröffentlichungen der Musik-Bibliothek Paul Hirsch E
VMw	*Vierteljahrsschrift für Musikwissenschaft* P [D282]
VogelB	E. Vogel: *Bibliothek der gedruckten weltlichen Vocalmusik Italiens, aus den Jahren 1500 bis 1700* (Berlin, 1892); rev., enlarged, by A. Einstein (Hildesheim, 1962); further addns in *AnMc*, nos.4, 5, 9 and 12; further rev. by F. Lesure and C. Sartori as *Bibliografia della musica italiana vocale profana pubblicata dal 1500 al 1700* (?Geneva, 1978)
WaltherML	J. G. Walther: *Musicalisches Lexicon oder Musicalische Bibliothec* D
WDMP	Wydawnictwo dawnej muzyki polskiej E
WE	Wellesley Edition E
WECIS	Wellesley Edition Cantata Index Series E
YIFMC	*Yearbook of the International Folk Music Council* P [Intl 31]
ZfM	*Zeitschrift für Musik* P [D75]
ZHMP	Zrodła do historii muzyki polskiej E
ZI	*Zeitschrift für Instrumentenbau* P [D249]
ZIMG	*Zeitschrift der Internationalen Musik-Gesellschaft* P [Intl 3]
ZL	*Zenei lexikon* D
ZMw	*Zeitschrift für Musikwissenschaft* P [D556]

Library Sigla

The system of library sigla in this dictionary follows that used in its publications (Series A) by Répertoire International des Sources Musicales, Kassel, by permission. Below are listed the sigla to be found; a few of them are additional to those in the published RISM lists, but have been established in consultation with the RISM organization. Some original RISM sigla that have now been changed are retained here.

In the dictionary, sigla are always printed in *italic*. In any listing of sources a national sigillum applies without repetition until it is contradicted. For German sigla, the intermediate *brd* and *ddr* are excluded; the list below shows in which part of Germany or Berlin each library is located.

Within each national list, entries are alphabetized by sigillum, first by capital letters (showing the city or town) and then by lower-case ones (showing the institution or collection).

A: AUSTRIA

Ee	Eisenstadt, Esterházy-Archiv
Eh	——, Haydn Museum
Ek	——, Stadtpfarrkirche
F	Fiecht, Benediktinerordensstift St Georgenberg
Gd	Graz, Diözesan Archiv
Gk	——, Hochschule für Musik und Darstellende Kunst
Gl	——, Steiermärkische Landesbibliothek am Joanneum
Gmi	——, Musikwissenschaftliches Institut der Universität
Gu	——, Universitätsbibliothek
GÖ	Furth bei Göttweig, Benediktinerstift
GÜ	Güssing, Franziskaner Kloster
H	Herzogenburg, Chorherrenstift
HE	Heiligenkreuz, Zisterzienserstift
Ik	Innsbruck, Konservatorium
Imf	——, Museum Ferdinandeum
Imi	——, Musikwissenschaftliches Institut der Universität
Iu	——, Universitätsbibliothek
Iw	——, Prämonstratenser-Chorherrenstift Wilten
KN	Klosterneuburg, Augustiner-Chorherrenstift
KR	Kremsmünster, Benediktinerstift
L	Lilienfeld, Zisterzienser-Stift
LA	Lambach, Benediktinerstift
LEx	Leoben, Pfarrbibliothek St Xaver
LIm	Linz, Oberösterreichisches Landesarchiv
LIs	——, Bundesstaatliche Studienbibliothek
M	Melk an der Donau, Benediktinerstift
MB	Michaelbeuern, Benediktinerabtei
MÖ	Mödling, Pfarrkirche St Othmar
MZ	Mariazell, Benediktiner-Priorat
N	Neuburg, Pfarrarchiv
NS	Neustift, Pfarrarchiv
R	Rein, Zisterzienserstift
Sca	Salzburg, Museum Carolino Augusteum
Sd	——, Dom-Musikarchiv
Sk	——, Kapitelbibliothek
Sm	——, Internationale Stiftung Mozarteum
Smi	——, Musikwissenschaftliches Institut der Universität
Sn	——, Nonnberg, Benediktiner-Frauenstift
Ssp	——, St Peter Benediktiner-Erzabtei
SB	Schlierbach, Stift
SCH	Schlägl, Prämonstratenser-Stift
SE	Seckau, Benediktinerabtei
SEI	Seitenstetten, Benediktinerstift
SF	St Florian, Augustiner-Chorherrenstift
SH	Solbad Hall, Franziskaner-Kloster
SL	St Lambrecht, Benediktiner-Abtei
SP	St Pölten, Diözesanarchiv
SPL	St Paul, Stift
ST	Stams, Zisterzienserstift
STE	Steyr, Stadtpfarrarchiv
TU	Tulln, Pfarrkirche St Stephan
Wd	Vienna, Stephansdom
Wdo	——, Zentralarchiv des Deutschen Ordens
Wdtö	——, Gesellschaft zur Herausgabe von Denkmälern der Tonkunst in Österreich
Wgm	——, Gesellschaft der Musikfreunde
Wh	——, Pfarrarchiv Hernals
Whb	——, Hauptverband des Österreichischen Buchhandels
Wk	——, Pfarrkirche St Karl Borromäus
Wkann	——, Hans Kann, private collection
Wkh	——, Kirche am Hof
Wkm	——, Kunsthistorisches Museum
Wl	——, Archiv für Niederösterreich (Landesarchiv)
Wm	——, Minoritenkonvent
Wmg	——, Pfarre, Maria am Gestade
Wmi	——, Musikwissenschaftliches Institut der Universität
Wmk	——, Akademie für Musik und Darstellende Kunst
Wn	——, Österreichische Nationalbibliothek, Musiksammlung
Wögm	——, Österreichische Gesellschaft für Musik
Wp	——, Musikarchiv, Piaristenkirche Maria Treu
Wph	——, Wiener Philharmoniker, Archiv und Bibliothek
Wps	——, Priesterseminar
Ws	——, Schottenstift
Wsa	——, Stadtarchiv
Wsp	——, St Peter, Musikarchiv
Wst	——, Stadtbibliothek, Musiksammlung
Wu	——, Universitätsbibliothek
Ww	——, Pfarrarchiv Währing
Wweinmann	——, Alexander Weinmann, private collection
Wwessely	——, Othmar Wessely, private collection
WAY	Waydhofen an der Ybbs, Pfarre
WE	Wels, Stift
WIL	Wilhering, Zisterzienserstift
Z	Zwettl, Zisterzienserstift

B: BELGIUM

Aa	Antwerp, Stadsarchief
Aac	——, Archief en Museum voor het Vlaamse Culturleven
Ac	——, Koninklijk Vlaams Muziekconservatorium
Ak	——, Onze-Lieve-Vrouwkathedraal
Amp	——, Museum Plantijn–Moretus
Apersoons	——, Guido Persoons, private collection
As	——, Stadsbibliotheek
Asa	——, Kerkebestuur St-Andries
Asj	——, Collegiale en Parochiale Kerk St-Jacob
Averwilt	——, F. Verwilt, private collection
AN	——, Anderlecht, St-Guiden Kerk
Ba	Brussels, Archives de la Ville
Bc	——, Conservatoire Royal de Musique
Bcdm	——, Centre Belge de Documentation Musicale [CeBeDeM]
Bg	——, Eglise de Ste Gudule
Bi	——, Institut de Psycho-acoustique et de Musique Electronique

Br	——, Bibliothèque Royale Albert 1er/Koninklijke Bibliotheek Albert I
Brtb	——, Radiodiffusion-Télévision Belge
Bsp	——, Société Philharmonique
BRc	Bruges, Stedelijk Muziekconservatorium
D	Diest, St Sulpitiuskerk
Gar	Ghent [Gent, Gand], Stadsarchief
Gc	——, Koninklijk Muziekconservatorium
Gcd	——, Culturele Dienst Province Ost Vlaanderen
Geb	——, St Baafsarchief med Bibliotheek Van Damme
Gu	——, Rijksuniversiteit, Centrale Bibliotheek
K	Kortrijk, St Martinskerk
Lc	Liège, Conservatoire Royal de Musique
Lu	——, Université de Liège
LIc	Lier, Conservatoire
LIg	——, St Gummaruskerk
LV	Louvain, Dominikanenklooster
LVu	——, Université de Louvain
M	Mons, Conservatoire Royal de Musique
MA	Morlanwelz-Mariemont, Musée de Mariemont
MEa	Mechelen, Archief en Stadsbibliotheek
MEs	——, Stedelijke Openbare Bibliotheek
OU	Oudenaarde, Parochiale Kerk
Tc	Tournai, Chapitre de la Cathédrale
Tv	——, Bibliothèque de la Ville
TI	Tienen, St Germanuskerk
Z	Zoutleeuw, St Leonarduskerk

BR: BRAZIL

Rem	Rio de Janeiro, Escola de Música, Universidade Federal do Rio de Janeiro
Rn	——, Biblioteca Nacional

C: CANADA

E	Edmonton, University of Alberta
Fc	Fredericton, Christ Church Cathedral
Ku	Kingston, Queens University, Douglas Library
Lu	London, University of Western Ontario, Lawson Memorial Library
Mc	Montreal, Conservatoire de Musique et d'Art Dramatique
Mfisher	——, Sidney T. Fisher, private collection [in *Tu*]
Mm	——, McGill University, Faculty and Conservatorium of Music and Redpath Libraries
On	Ottawa, National Library of Canada
Qc	Quebec, Cathédrale de la Sainte-Trinité
Qul	——, Université Laval
SAu	Sackville, Mt Allison University
SJm	St John, New Brunswick Museum
Tb	Toronto, Canadian Broadcasting Corporation
Tm	——, Royal Ontario Museum
Tolnick	——, Harvey J. Olnick, private collection
Tp	——, Toronto Public Library, Music Branch
Tu	——, University of Toronto, Faculty of Music
Vu	Vancouver, University of British Columbia Library, Fine Arts Division
W	Winnipeg, University of Manitoba

CH: SWITZERLAND

A	Aarau, Aargauische Kantonsbibliothek
AShoboken	Ascona, Anthony van Hoboken, private collection
Bchristen	Basle, Werner Christen, private collection
Bm	——, Musikakademie der Stadt
Bmi	——, Musikwissenschaftliches Institut der Universität
Bu	——, Öffentliche Bibliothek der Universität, Musiksammlung
BA	Baden, Historisches Museum (Landvogtei-Schloss)
BEk	Berne, Konservatorium
BEl	——, Schweizerische Landesbibliothek
BEms	——, Musikwissenschaftliches Seminar der Universität
BEsu	——, Stadt- und Universitätsbibliothek; Bürgerbibliothek
BI	Biel, Stadtbibliothek
C	Chur, Kantonsbibliothek Graubünden
D	Disentis, Stift
E	Einsiedeln, Benediktinerkloster
EN	Engelberg, Stift
Fcu	Fribourg, Bibliothèque Cantonale et Universitaire
Ff	——, Franziskaner-Kloster
Fk	——, Kapuziner-Kloster
Fsn	——, Kapitel St Nikolaus
FF	Frauenfeld, Thurgauische Kantonsbibliothek
Gamoudruz	Geneva, Emile Amoudruz, private collection
Gc	——, Conservatoire de Musique
Gpu	——, Bibliothèque Publique et Universitaire

GLtschudi	Glarus, A. Tschudi, private collection
Lmg	Lucerne, Allgemeine Musikalische Gesellschaft
Ls	——, Stiftsarchiv St Leodegar
Lz	——, Zentralbibliothek
LAc	Lausanne, Conservatoire de Musique
LAcu	——, Bibliothèque Cantonale et Universitaire
LU	Lugano, Biblioteca Cantonale
Mbernegg	Maienfeld, Sprecher von Bernegg, private collection
MO	Morges, Bibliothèque de la Ville
MÜ	Müstair, Frauenkloster
N	Neuchâtel, Bibliothèque Publique
R	Rheinfelden, Christkatholisches Pfarramt
S	Sion, Bibliothèque Cantonale du Valais
Sa	——, Staatsarchiv
Sk	——, Kathedrale
SA	Sarnen, Bibliothek des Kollegiums
SAf	——, Frauenkloster
SCH	Schwyz, Kantonsbibliothek
SGs	St Gall, Stiftsbibliothek
SGv	——, Stadtbibliothek
SH	Schaffhausen, Stadtbibliothek
SM	St Maurice, Bibliothèque de l'Abbaye
SO	Solothurn, Zentralbibliothek, Musiksammlung
TH	Thun, Stadtbibliothek
W	Winterthur, Stadtbibliothek
Wpeer	——, Peer private collection
Zi	Zurich, Israelitische Kulturgemeinde
Zjacobi	——, Erwin R. Jacobi, private collection
Zk	——, Konservatorium und Musikhochschule
Zma	——, Schweizerisches Musik-Archiv
Zms	——, Musikwissenschaftliches Seminar der Universität
Zp	——, Pestalozzianum
Zz	——, Zentralbibliothek
ZG	Zug, Stadtbibliothek
ZO	Zofingen, Stadtbibliothek
ZU	Zuoz, Gemeindearchiv

CO: COLOMBIA

B	Bogotá, Catedral

CS: CZECHOSLOVAKIA

Bb	Brno, Klášter Milosrdných Bratří [in *Bm*]
Bm	——, Ústav Dějin Hudby Moravského Musea, Hudebněhistorické Oddělení
Bu	——, Státní Vědecká Knihovna, Universitní Knihovna
BA	Bakov nad Jizerou, pobočka Státní Archívu v Mladé Boleslavi
BEL	Bělá pod Bezdězem, Městské Muzeum
BER	Beroun, Okresní Archív
BRa	Bratislava, Okresní Archív
BRe	——, Evanjelícka a. v. Cirkevná Knižnica
BRhs	——, Knižnica Hudebného Seminara Filosofickej Fakulty University Komenského
BRnm	——, Slovenské Národné Muzeum, Hudobné Oddělenie
BRsa	——, Štátny Ústredný Archív Slovenskej Socialistickej Republiky
BRsav	——, Slovenská Akadémia Vied
BRu	——, Univerzitná Knižnica
BREsi	Březnice, Děkanský Kostel Sv Ignáce
BSk	Banská Štiavnica, Farský Rímsko-Katolícky Kostol, Archív Chóru
CH	Cheb, Okresní Archív
CHOd	Choceň, Děkanský Úřad
CHOm	——, Městské Muzeum
H	Hronov, Muzeum Aloise Jiráska
HK	Hradec Králové, Muzeum
HOm	Hořice, Vlastivědné Muzeum
J	Jur pri Bratislave, Okresní Archív, Bratislava-Vidick
JIa	Jindřichův Hradec, Státní Archív
JIm	——, Vlastivědné Muzeum
K	Český Krumlov, Pracoviště Státního Archívu Třeboň, Hudební Sbírka
KL	Klatovy, Okresní Archív
KO	Košice, Městsky Archív
KOL	Kolín, Děkanský Chrám
KRa	Kroměříž, Státní Zámek a Zahrady, Historicko-Umělecké Fondy, Hudební Archív
KRA	Králíky, Děkanský Úřad
KRE	Kremnica, Městsky Archív
KU	Kutná Hora, Oblastní Muzeum
KVd	Karlovy Vary, Děkanský Úřad
KVso	——, Karlovarský Symfonický Orchestr
L	Levoča, Rímsko-Katolícky Farský Kostol
LIa	Česká Lípa, Okresní Archív

LIT	Litoměřice, Státní Archív
LO	Loukov, Farní Úřad
Mms	Martin, Matica Slovenská, Oddělenie Hudobných Pamiatok
Mnm	——, Slovenské Národné Muzeum, Archív
MB	Mladá Boleslav, Okresní Archív
ME	Mělník, Okresní Archív
MH	Mnichovo Hradiště, Vlastivědné Muzeum
N	Nítra, Státní Archív
ND	Nové Dvory, Farní Úřad
NM	Nové Mesto nad Váhom, Rímsko-Katolický Farský Kostol
OLa	Olomouc, Státní Oblastní Archív v Opava
OLu	——, Státní Vědecká Knihovna, Universitní Knihovna
OP	Opava, Slezské Muzeum
OS	Ostrava, Československý Rozhlas, Hudební Archív
OSE	Osek, Klášter
Pa	Prague, Státní Ústřední Archív
Pak	——, Archív Metropolitní Kapituly
Pdobrovského	——, Knihovna Josefa Dobrovského
Ph	——, Československá Církev Holešovice
Pis	——, Československo Hudební Informační Středisko
Pk	——, Archív Státní Konservatoře v Praze
Pnm	——, Národní Muzeum, Hudební Oddělení
Pp	——, Archív Pražského Hradu
Ppp	——, Památník Národního Písemnictví na Strahově
Pr	——, Československý Rozhlas, Hudební Archív Různá Provenience
Pra	——, Rodinní Archív Karla Kovařovice
Ps	——, Strahovská Knihovna [in *Ppp*]
Psf	——, Kostel Sv Franciscus
Psj	——, Kostel Sv Jakuba
Pu	——, Státní Knihovna ČSSR, Universitní Knihovna
PLa	Plzeň, Městsky Archív
PLm	——, Západočeské Muzeum
PLA	Plasy, Okresní Archív
POa	Poděbrady, pobočka Státní Archívu Nymburk
POm	——, Helichovo Muzeum
PR	Příbram, Okresný Muzeum
PRE	Prešov, Rímsko-Katolický Farský Kostol
RA	Rakovník, Státní Archív
RAJ	Rajhrad, Klášter [in *Bm*]
RO	Rokycany, Okresný Muzeum
ROZ	Rožnava, Biskupsí Archív
RY	Rychnov, Muzeum Orlicka
Sk	Spišská Kapitula, Katedrálny Rímsko-Katolický Kostol, Knižnica Spišskej Kapituly
SNV	Spišská Nová Ves, Rímsko-Katolický Farský Kostol
SO	Sokolov, Státní Archív
TC	Třebíč, Městsky Archív
TN	Trenčín, Okresní Archív
TR	Trnava, Dóm Sv Mikuláša
TRB	Třebenice, Klášter
TRE	Třeboň, Státní Archív
TU	Turnov, Okresný Muzeum
VE	Velenice, Farní Úřad
VM	Vysoké Mýto, Okresný Muzeum
ZA	Zámrsk, Státní Archív

CU: CUBA

Hn	Havana, Biblioteca Nacional
Hse	——, Biblioteca de la Sociedad Económica de Amigos del País

D: GERMANY

Aa	Augsburg, BRD, Kantoreiarchiv St Annen
Af	——, Bibliothek der Fuggerschen Domänenkanzlei
Ahk	——, Dominikanerkloster Heilig-Kreuz
As	——, Staats- und Stadtbibliothek
Asa	——, Stadtarchiv
AAd	Aachen, BRD, Bischöfliche Diözesanbibliothek
AAg	——, Kaiser Karl-Gymnasium, Lehrerbibliothek
AAm	——, Domarchiv
AAst	——, Stadtbibliothek
AB	Amorbach, BRD, Fürstlich Leiningische Bibliothek, private collection
ABG	Annaberg-Buchholz, DDR, Pfarramt, Kirchenbibliothek
ABGa	——, Kantoreiarchiv St Annen
AD	Adolfseck bei Fulda, BRD, Schloss Fasanerie, Bibliothek der Kurhessischen Hausstiftung
ALa	Altenburg, DDR, Landesarchiv (Historisches Staatsarchiv)
ALs	——, Stadtarchiv

ALt	——, Bibliothek des Landestheaters
AM	Amberg, BRD, Staatliche Provinzialbibliothek
AN	Ansbach, BRD, Regierungsbibliothek
AÖ	Altötting, BRD, Kapuziner-Kloster St Konrad
ARk	Arnstadt, DDR, Kirchenbibliothek
ARsk	——, Stadt- und Kreisbibliothek
ARsm	——, Schlossmuseum
ASh	Aschaffenburg, BRD, Hofbibliothek
ASm	——, Stadtbücherei
ASsb	——, Stiftsbibliothek
B	Berlin, Staatsbibliothek Preussischer Kulturbesitz [W]
Ba	——, Amerika-Gedenkbibliothek (Berliner Zentralbibliothek) [W]; Deutsche Akademie der Künste [E]
Bch	——, Musikbücherei Charlottenburg [W]
Bdhm	——, Deutsche Hochschule für Musik Hanns Eisler [E]
Bds	——, Deutsche Staatsbibliothek (formerly Königliche Bibliothek; Preussische Staatsbibliothek; Öffentliche Wissenschaftliche Bibliothek), Musikabteilung [E]
Bdso	——, Deutsche Staatsoper [E]
Be	——, Institut für Musikerziehung der Humboldt-Universität [E]
Bgk	——, Streit'sche Stiftung [in *Bs*] [E]
Bhbk	——, Staatliche Hochschule für Bildende Kunst [W]
Bhesse	——, A. Hesse, private collection [E]
Bhm	——, Staatliche Hochschule für Musik und Darstellende Kunst [W]
Bim	——, Staatliches Institut für Musikforschung Preussischer Kulturbesitz [W]
Bk	——, Staatliche Museen Preussischer Kulturbesitz [W]
Bko	——, Komische Oper [E]
Blk	——, Bezirks-Lehrerbibliothek Kreuzberg [W]
Bm	——, Marienkirche [E]
Bmb	——, Internationale Musikbibliothek, Verband Deutscher Komponisten und Musikwissenschaftler [E]
Bmi	——, Musikwissenschaftliches Institut der Freien Universität [W]; Musikwissenschaftliches Institut der Humboldt-Universität [E]
Bmm	——, Märkisches Museum [E]
Bn	——, Nikolaikirche [E]
Bp	——, Pädagogisches Zentrum [W]
Br	——, Deutscher Demokratischer Rundfunk, Notenarchiv [E]
Bs	——, Berliner Stadtbibliothek [E]
Bst	——, Stadtbücherei, Hauptstelle Berlin-Wilmersdorf [W]
Btu	——, Universitätsbibliothek der Technischen Universität [W]
Btum	——, Lehrstuhl für Musikgeschichte der Technischen Universität [W]
Bu	——, Universitätsbibliothek der Freien Universität [W]
Buh	——, Universitätsbibliothek der Humboldt-Universität [E]
BAa	Bamberg, BRD, Staatsarchiv
BAf	——, Franziskaner-Kloster
BAs	——, Staatsbibliothek
BAL	Ballenstedt, DDR, Stadtbibliothek
BAR	Bartenstein, BRD, Fürst zu Hohenlohe-Bartensteinsches Archiv, private collection
BAUd	Bautzen, DDR, Domstift und Bischöfliches Ordinariat
BAUk	——, Stadt- und Kreisbibliothek
BB	Benediktbeuren, BRD, Pfarrkirche
BD	Brandenburg an der Havel, DDR, Domstift
BDH	Bad Homburg von der Höhe, BRD, Stadtbibliothek
BE	Berleburg, BRD, Fürstlich Sayn-Wittgenstein-Berleburgsche Bibliothek, private collection
BEU	Beuron, BRD, Benediktiner-Erzabtei
BEV	Bevensen, BRD, Superintendantur, Ephoratsbibliothek und Bibliothek Sursen
BFa	Burgsteinfurt, BRD, Gymnasium Arnoldinum
BFb	——, Fürstlich Bentheimsche Bibliothek [in *MÜu*]
BG	Beuerberg über Wolfratshausen, BRD, Pfarramt, Stiftskirche
BGD	Berchtesgaden, BRD, Katholisches Pfarramt
BH	Bayreuth, BRD, Stadtbücherei
BI	Bielefeld, BRD, Städtisches Ratsgymnasium
BIB	Bibra, DDR, Pfarrarchiv
BIR	Birstein über Wächtersbach, BRD, Fürst von Ysenburgisches Archiv und Schlossbibliothek, private collection

BIT	Bitterfeld, DDR, Kreismuseum
BK	Bernkastel-Kues, BRD, Cusanusstift
BKÖ	Bad Köstritz, DDR, Pfarrarchiv
BMek	Bremen, BRD, Bücherei der Bremer Evangelischen Kirche
BMs	—, Staats- und Universitätsbibliothek
BNba	Bonn, BRD, Beethoven-Haus und Beethoven-Archiv
BNek	—, Gemeindeverband der Evangelischen Kirche
BNms	—, Musikwissenschaftliches Seminar der Universität
BNu	—, Universitätsbibliothek
BO	—, Bollstedt, Pfarramt
BOCHb	Bochum, BRD, Bergbaumuseum
BOCHmi	—, Musikwissenschaftliches Institut der Ruhr-Universität
BOCHs	—, Stadtbibliothek, Musikbücherei
BORp	Borna, DDR, Pfarrkirche
BS	Brunswick, BRD, Stadtarchiv und Stadtbibliothek
BTH	Barth, DDR, Kirchenbibliothek
BÜ	Büdingen, BRD, Fürstlich Ysenburg- und Büdingisches Archiv und Schlossbibliothek
BW	Burgwindheim über Bamberg, BRD, Katholisches Pfarramt
Cl	Coburg, BRD, Landesbibliothek
Cm	—, Moritzkirche
Cv	—, Kunstsammlung der Veste Coburg
CA	Castell, BRD, Fürstlich Castell'sche Bibliothek
CD	Crottendorf, DDR, Kantoreiarchiv
CR	Crimmitschau, DDR, Stadtkirche St Laurentius
CZ	Clausthal-Zellerfeld, BRD, Kirchenbibliothek
CZu	—, Universitätsbibliothek
Dhm	Dresden, DDR, Hochschule für Musik Carl Maria von Weber
Dkh	—, Katholische Hofkirche
Dl	—, Bibliothek und Museum Löbau [in *Dlb*]
Dla	—, Staatsarchiv
Dlb	—, Sächsische Landesbibliothek
Dmb	—, Musikbibliothek
Ds	—, Staatstheater
DB	Dettelbach über Kitzingen, BRD, Franziskanerkloster
DEl	Dessau, DDR, Universitäts- und Landesbibliothek
DEs	—, Stadtarchiv, Rathaus
DI	Dillingen an der Donau, BRD, Kreis- und Studienbibliothek
DIp	—, Bischöfliches Priesterseminar
DIN	Dinkelsbühl, BRD, Katholisches Pfarramt St Georg
DIP	Dippoldiswalde, DDR, Evangelisch-Lutherisches Pfarramt
DL	Delitzsch, DDR, Museum und Bibliothek
DM	Dortmund, BRD, Stadt- und Landesbibliothek
DO	Donaueschingen, BRD, Fürstlich Fürstenbergische Hofbibliothek, private collection
DÖ	Döbeln, DDR, Pfarrbibliothek St Nikolai
DÖF	Döffingen über Bölingen, BRD, Pfarrbibliothek
DS	Darmstadt, BRD, Hessische Landes- und Hochschulbibliothek
DSim	—, Internationales Musikinstitut
DSk	—, Kirchenleitung der Evangelischen Kirche in Hessen und Nassau
DT	Detmold, BRD, Lippische Landesbibliothek
DÜgg	Düsseldorf, BRD, Staatliches Görres-Gymnasium
DÜha	—, Hauptstaatsarchiv
DÜk	—, Goethe-Museum
DÜl	—, Landes- und Stadtbibliothek
DÜmb	—, Stadtbüchereien, Musikbücherei
DÜR	Düren, BRD, Stadtbücherei, Leopold-Hoesch-Museum
Ek	Eichstätt, BRD, Kapuzinerkloster
Es	—, Staats- und Seminarbibliothek
Ew	—, Benediktinerinnen-Abtei St Walburg
EB	Ebrach, BRD, Katholisches Pfarramt
EBS	Ebstorf, BRD, Kloster
EF	Erfurt, DDR, Wissenschaftliche Bibliothek der Stadt
EFd	—, Dombibliothek
EFs	—, Stadt- und Bezirksbibliothek
EIa	Eisenach, DDR, Stadtarchiv
EIb	—, Bachhaus und Bachmuseum
EIl	—, Landeskirchenrat
EIHp	Eichtersheim, BRD, Pfarrbibliothek
EL	Eisleben, DDR, Andreas-Bibliothek
EM	Emden, BRD, Grosse Kirche
EMM	Emmerich, BRD, Staatliches Gymnasium
EN	Engelberg, BRD, Franziskanerkloster
ERms	Erlangen, BRD, Musikwissenschaftliches Seminar der Universität
ERu	—, Universitätsbibliothek
ES	Essen, BRD, Musikbücherei der Stadtbücherei
EU	Eutin, BRD, Kreisbibliothek
F	Frankfurt am Main, BRD, Stadt- und Universitätsbibliothek
Fkm	—, Museum für Kunsthandwerk
Fmi	—, Musikwissenschaftliches Institut der Johann Wolfgang von Goethe-Universität
Fsg	—, Philosophisch-Theologische Hochschule St Georgen
Fsm	—, Bibliothek für Neuere Sprachen und Musik
FBa	Freiberg, DDR, Stadtarchiv
FBb	—, Bergakademie, Bücherei
FBo	—, Geschwister-Scholl-Oberschule, Historische Bibliothek
FBsk	—, Stadt- und Kreisbibliothek
FF	Frankfurt an der Oder, DDR, Stadt- und Bezirksbibliothek
FG	Freyburg, DDR, Pfarrarchiv
FLa	Flensburg, BRD, Stadtarchiv
FLs	—, Staatliches Gymnasium
FRcb	Freiburg im Breisgau, BRD, Collegium Borromaeum
FRms	—, Musikwissenschaftliches Seminar der Universität
FRu	—, Universitätsbibliothek
FRIs	Friedberg, BRD, Stadtbibliothek
FRIts	—, Theologisches Seminar der Evangelischen Kirche in Hessen und Nassau
FS	Freising, BRD, Dombibliothek
FUf	Fulda, BRD, Kloster Frauenberg
FUl	—, Hessische Landesbibliothek
FUp	—, Bischöfliches Priesterseminar, Bibliothek der Philosophisch-Theologischen Hochschule
Ga	Göttingen, BRD, Staatliches Archivlager
Gb	—, Johann Sebastian Bach-Institut
Gms	—, Musikwissenschaftliches Seminar der Universität
Gs	—, Niedersächsische Staats- und Universitätsbibliothek
GA	Gaussig bei Bautzen, DDR, Schlossbibliothek
GAH	Gandersheim, BRD, Stiftsbibliothek
GAM	Gau-Algesheim, BRD, Stadtarchiv
GAR	Gars am Inn, BRD, Philosophisch-Theologische Ordenhochschule der Redemptoristen
GBB	Grossbrembach, DDR, Pfarrarchiv
GBR	Grossbreitenbach bei Arnstadt, DDR, Pfarrbibliothek
GD	Gaesdonck über Goch, BRD, Collegium Augustinianum
GE	Gelenau, DDR, Pfarrarchiv
GERk	Gera, DDR, Kirchenarchiv
GERs	—, Stadtmuseum
GERsb	—, Stadt- und Bezirksbibliothek
GEY	Geyer, DDR, Kirchenbibliothek
GF	Grossfahrer, DDR, Pfarrarchiv Starcklof-Eschenberger
GHk	Geithain, DDR, Evangelisch-Lutherisches Pfarramt
GHNa	Grossenhain, DDR, Archiv
GHNk	—, Kirche
GI	Giessen, BRD, Justus Liebig-Universität
GL	Goslar, BRD, Marktkirchenbibliothek
GLA	Glashütte, DDR, Pfarrarchiv
GM	Grimma, DDR, Göschenhaus, Johannes Sturm, private collection
GMl	—, Landesschule
GO	Gotha, DDR, Evangelisch-Lutherische Stadtkirchengemeinde
GOa	—, Augustinerkirche
GOg	—, Gymnasium
GOl	—, Forschungsbibliothek [former Landesbibliothek]
GOs	—, Stadtarchiv
GOsk	—, Stadt- und Kreisbibliothek
GÖp	Görlitz, DDR, Evangelischer Parochialverband
GÖs	—, Stadtbibliothek
GÖsp	—, Pfarramt St Peter
GOL	Goldbach bei Gotha, DDR, Pfarrarchiv
GRim	Greifswald, DDR, Institut für Musikwissenschaft
GRk	—, Konsistorialbibliothek
GRu	—, Ernst-Moritz-Arndt-Universität
GRÜ	Grünhain, DDR, Pfarramt
GÜ	Güstrow, DDR, Heimatmuseum
GZ	Greiz, DDR, Stadt- und Kreisbibliothek
GZbk	—, Staatliche Bücher- und Kupferstichsammlung

Mcg	——, Georgianum, Herzogliches Priesterseminar
Mdm	——, Deutsches Museum
Mh	——, Staatliche Hochschule für Musik
Ml	——, Evangelisch-Lutherisches Landeskirchenamt
Mmb	——, Städtische Musikbibliothek
Mms	——, Musikwissenschaftliches Seminar der Universität
Msl	——, Süddeutsche Lehrerbücherei
Mth	——, Theatermuseum der Clara-Ziegler-Stiftung
Mu	——, Universitätsbibliothek
Mwg	——, Wilhelms-Gymnasium, Lehrerbibliothek
MAk	Magdeburg, DDR, Kulturhistorisches Museum, Klosterbibliothek
MAkon	——, Konsistorialbibliothek
MAl	——, Landeshauptarchiv
MAs	——, Stadt- und Bezirksbibliothek
MB	Marbach an der Neckar, BRD, Schiller-National-museum
MBG	Miltenberg am Main, BRD, Franziskanerkloster
MCH	Maria Laach über Andernach, BRD, Benediktiner-abtei
ME	Meissen, DDR, Stadt- und Kreisbibliothek
MEIk	Meiningen, DDR, Evangelisch-Lutherische Kirchen-gemeinde
MEIl	——, Staatsarchiv
MEIo	——, Opernarchiv
MEIr	——, Staatliche Museen mit Reger-Archiv
MEL	Meldorf, BRD, Joachimsche Bibliothek, Dithmarsches Landesmuseum
MERa	Merseburg, DDR, Domstift
MERr	——, Regierungsbibliothek
MERs	——, Stadt- und Kreisbibliothek
MERz	——, Deutsches Zentral-Archiv, Historische Abteilung
MFL	Münstereifel, BRD, St Michael-Gymnasium
MGmi	Marburg an der Lahn, BRD, Musikwissenschaftliches Institut der Philipps-Universität
MGs	——, Staatsarchiv und Archivschule
MGu	——, Universitätsbibliothek der Philipps-Universität
MH	Mannheim, BRD, Wissenschaftliche Stadtbibliothek und Universitätsbibliothek
MHrm	——, Reiss-Museum
MHR	Mülheim, BRD, Stadtbibliothek
MI	Michelstadt, BRD, Evangelisches Pfarramt West
MK	Markneukirchen, DDR, Gewerbemuseum
MLHb	Mühlhausen, DDR, Blasiuskirche
MLHr	——, Ratsarchiv im Stadtarchiv
MMm	Memmingen, BRD, Evangelisch-Lutherisches Pfarramt St Martin
MMs	——, Stadtbibliothek
MÖ	Mölln, BRD, Evangelisch-Lutherische Kirchen-gemeinde St Nikolai
MOSp	Mosbach, BRD, Pfarrbibliothek
MR	Marienberg, DDR, Kirchenbibliothek
MS	Münsterschwarzach über Kitzingen am Main, BRD, Abtei
MT	Metten über Deggendorf, BRD, Abtei
MÜd	Münster, BRD, Bischöfliches Diözesanarchiv
MÜms	——, Musikwissenschaftliches Seminar der Universität
MÜp	——, Bischöfliches Priesterseminar und Santini-Sammlung
MÜrt	——, Seminar für Reformierte Theologie
MÜs	——, Santini-Bibliothek [in *MÜp*]
MÜsa	——, Staatsarchiv
MÜu	——, Universitätsbibliothek
MÜG	Mügeln, DDR, Pfarrarchiv
MWR	Marienweiher über Kulmbach, BRD, Franziskanerkloster
MZfederhofer	Mainz, BRD, Hellmut Federhofer, private collection
MZgm	——, Gutenberg-Museum
MZgottron	——, Adam Gottron, private collection
MZmi	——, Musikwissenschaftliches Institut der Universität
MZp	——, Bischöfliches Priesterseminar
MZs	——, Stadtbibliothek und Stadtarchiv
MZsch	——, Musikverlag B. Schotts Söhne
MZu	——, Universitätsbibliothek der Johannes-Gutenberg-Universität
Ngm	Nuremberg, BRD, Germanisches National-Museum
Nla	——, Landeskirchliches Archiv
Nst	——, Stadtbibliothek
NA	Neustadt an der Orla, DDR, Pfarrarchiv
NAUs	Naumburg, DDR, Stadtarchiv
NAUw	——, Wenzelskirche
NBsb	Neuburg an der Donau, BRD, Staatliche Bibliothek
NBss	——, Studienseminar
NEhz	Neuenstein, BRD, Hohenlohe-Zentral-Archiv
NEschumm	——, Karl Schumm, private collection
NERk	Neuenrade, BRD, Kirchenbibliothek
NEZp	Neckarelz, BRD, Pfarrbibliothek
NGp	Neckargemünd, BRD, Pfarrarchiv
NIw	Nieheim über Bad Driburg, BRD, Weberhaus
NL	Nördlingen, BRD, Stadtarchiv, Stadtbibliothek und Volksbücherei
NLk	——, Kirchenbibliothek St Georg
NM	Neumünster, BRD, Schleswig-Holsteinische Musik-sammlung der Stadt [in *KII*]
NO	Nordhausen, DDR, Humboldt-Oberschule
NS	Neustadt an der Aisch, BRD, Evangelische Kirchen-bibliothek
NSg	——, Gymnasialbibliothek
NT	Neumarkt-St Veit, BRD, Pfarrkirche
NW	Neustadt an der Weinstrasse, BRD, Heimatmuseum
OB	Ottobeuren, BRD, Benediktiner-Abtei
OF	Offenbach am Main, BRD, Verlagsarchiv André
OH	Oberfrankenhain, BRD, Pfarrarchiv
OLl	Oldenburg, BRD, Landesbibliothek
OLns	——, Niedersächsisches Staatsarchiv
OLH	Olbernhau, DDR, Pfarrarchiv
ORB	Oranienbaum, DDR, Landesarchiv–Historisches Staatsarchiv
OS	Oschatz, DDR, Ephoralbibliothek
OSa	Osnabrück, BRD, Niedersächsisches Staatsarchiv
OSm	——, Städtisches Museum
Pg	Passau, BRD, Gymnasialbibliothek
Pk	——, Bischöfliches Klerikalseminar
Po	——, Bischöfliches Ordinariat
Ps	——, Staatliche Bibliothek
PA	Paderborn, BRD, Erzbischöfliche Akademische Bibliothek
PI	Pirna, DDR, Stadtarchiv
POh	Potsdam, DDR, Pädagogische Hochschule
PR	Pretzschendorf über Dippoldiswalde, DDR, Pfarr-archiv
PU	Pulsnitz, DDR, Nikolaikirche
PW	Pesterwitz bei Dresden, DDR, Pfarrarchiv
Q	Quedlinburg, DDR, Stadt- und Kreisbibliothek
QUh	Querfurt, DDR, Heimatmuseum
QUk	——, Stadtkirche
Rim	Regensburg, BRD, Institut für Musikforschung [in *Ru*]
Rp	——, Bischöfliche Zentralbibliothek
Rs	——, Staatliche Bibliothek
Rtt	——, Fürstlich Thurn und Taxis'sche Hofbibliothek, private collection
Ru	——, Universitätsbibliothek
RAd	Ratzeburg, BRD, Domarchiv
RB	Rothenburg ob der Tauber, BRD, Stadtarchiv und Rats- und Konsistorialbibliothek
RE	Reutberg bei Schaftlach, BRD, Franziskanerinnen-Kloster
REU	Reuden, DDR, Pfarrarchiv
RH	Rheda, BRD, Fürst zu Bentheim-Tecklenburgische Bibliothek [in *MH* and *MÜu*]
RIE	Riesa, DDR, Heimatmuseum
RL	Reutlingen, BRD, Stadtbücherei
RMmarr	Ramelsloh über Winsen, BRD, G. Marr, private collection
ROmi	Rostock, DDR, Institut für Musikwissenschaft der Universität
ROs	——, Stadt- und Bezirksbibliothek
ROu	——, Universitätsbibliothek
RÖ	Röhrsdorf über Meissen, DDR, Pfarrbibliothek
RÖM	Römhild, DDR, Pfarrarchiv
ROT	Rotenburg, BRD, Predigerseminar
ROTTd	Rottenburg an der Neckar, BRD, Diözesanbiblio-thek
ROTTp	——, Bischöfliches Priesterseminar
RT	Rastatt, BRD, Friedrich-Wilhelm-Gymnasium
RUh	Rudolstadt, DDR, Hofkapellarchiv
RUl	——, Staatsarchiv
RÜ	Rüdenhausen über Kitzingen, BRD, Fürst Castell-Rüdenhausen Bibliothek
Seo	Stuttgart, BRD, Bibliothek und Archiv des Evangelischen Oberkirchenrats
Sh	——, Staatliche Hochschule für Musik und Darstellende Kunst
Sl	——, Württembergische Landesbibliothek
SAh	Saalfeld, DDR, Heimatmuseum
SAAmi	Saarbrücken, BRD, Musikwissenschaftliches Institut der Universität

SAAu	——, Universitätsbibliothek
SBg	Straubing, BRD, Johannes Turmair-Gymnasium
SBj	——, Kirchenbibliothek St Jakob
SBk	——, Karmeliter-Kloster
SCHhv	Schwäbisch Hall, BRD, Historischer Verein für Württembergisch-Franken
SCHm	——, Archiv der St Michaelskirche
SCHr	——, Ratsbibliothek im Stadtarchiv
SCHEY	Scheyern über Pfaffenhofen, BRD, Benediktinerabtei
SCHM	Schmölln, DDR, Archiv der Stadtkirche
SCHMI	Schmiedeberg bei Dresden, DDR, Pfarramt
SCHWherold	Schwabach, BRD, Herold collection
SCHWk	——, Kirchenbibliothek
SDF	Schlehdorf, BRD, Katholische Pfarrkirche
SF	Schweinfurt-Oberndorf, BRD, Kirchen- und Pfarrbibliothek des Evangelisch-Lutherischen Pfarramts
SFsj	——, Pfarramt St Johannis, Sakristei-Bibliothek
SGh	Schleusingen, DDR, Heimatmuseum
SHk	Sondershausen, DDR, Stadtkirche
SHs	——, Stadt- und Kreisbibliothek
SHsk	——, Schlosskirche
SI	Sigmaringen, BRD, Fürstlich Hohenzollernsche Hofbibliothek, private collection
SLk	Salzwedel, DDR, Katharinenkirche
SLm	——, J. F. Danneil-Museum
SLmk	——, Marienkirche
SNed	Schmalkalden, DDR, Evangelisches Dekanat
SNh	——, Heimatmuseum Schloss Wilhelmsburg
SO	Soest, BRD, Stadtbibliothek im Stadtarchiv
SÖNp	Schönau bei Heidelberg, BRD, Pfarrbibliothek
SPlb	Speyer, BRD, Pfälzische Landesbibliothek, Musikabteilung
SPlk	——, Bibliothek des Protestantischen Landeskirchenrats der Pfalz
SPF	Schulpforta, DDR, Heimoberschule
SSa	Stralsund, DDR, Bibliothek des Stadtarchivs
ST	Stade, BRD, Predigerbibliothek [in *ROT*]
STO	Stolberg, DDR, Bibliothek
SUa	Sulzenbrücken, DDR, Pfarrarchiv
SUH	Suhl, DDR, Stadt- und Bezirksbibliothek Martin Andersen Nexö
SWl	Schwerin, DDR, Wissenschaftliche Allgemeinbibliothek [former Mecklenburgische Landesbibliothek]
SWs	——, Stadt- und Bezirksbibliothek, Musikabteilung
SWsk	——, Schlosskirchenchor
SWth	——, Mecklenburgisches Staatstheater
SZ	Schleiz, DDR, Stadtkirche
Tes	Tübingen, BRD, Evangelisches Stift
Tl	——, Schwäbisches Landesmusikarchiv [in *Tmi*]
Tmi	——, Musikwissenschaftliches Institut der Eberhard-Karls-Universität
Tu	——, Universitätsbibliothek
Tw	——, Bibliothek des Wilhelmstiftes
TAB	Tabarz, DDR, Pfarrarchiv, Evangelisch-Lutherisches Pfarramt
TEG	Tegernsee, BRD, Pfarrkirche, Katholisches Pfarramt
TEI	Teisendorf, BRD, Katholisches Pfarramt
TH	Themar, DDR, Pfarramt
TIT	Tittmoning, DDR, Kollegiatstift
TO	Torgau, DDR, Johann-Walter-Kantorei
TOek	——, Evangelische Kirchengemeinde
TOs	——, Stadtarchiv
TRb	Trier, BRD, Bistumarchiv und Dombibliothek
TRp	——, Priesterseminar
TRs	——, Stadtbibliothek
Us	Ulm, BRD, Stadtbibliothek
Usch	——, Von Schermar'sche Familienstiftung
UDa	Udestedt über Erfurt, DDR, Pfarrarchiv, Evangelisch-Lutherisches Pfarramt
V	Villingen, BRD, Städtische Sammlung
VI	Viernau, DDR, Pfarramt
W	Wolfenbüttel, BRD, Herzog August Bibliothek
Wa	——, Niedersächsisches Staatsarchiv
WA	Waldheim, DDR, Stadtkirche St Nikolai
WAB	Waldenburg, DDR, Kirchenmusikalische Bibliothek von St Bartholomäus
WB	Weissenburg, BRD, Stadtbibliothek
WBB	Walberg, BRD, Albertus-Magnus-Akademie, Bibliothek St Albert
WD	Wiesentheid, BRD, Musiksammlung des Grafen von Schönborn-Wiesentheid, private collection
WE	Weiden, BRD, Pfannenstiel'sche Bibliothek, Evangelisch-Lutherisches Pfarramt

WEH	Weierhof, BRD, Mennonitische Forschungsstelle
WEL	Weltenburg, BRD, Benediktinerkloster
WER	Wernigerode, DDR, Heimatmuseum, Harzbücherei
WERk	Wertheim am Main, BRD, Evangelisches Pfarramt
WERl	——, Fürstlich Löwenstein'sche Bibliothek, private collection
WEY	Weyarn, BRD, Pfarrkirche [in *FS*]
WF	Weissenfels, DDR, Heimatmuseum
WFg	——, Heinrich-Schütz-Gedenkstätte
WGk	Wittenberg, DDR, Stadtkirche
WGl	——, Reformationsgeschichtliches Museum, Lutherhalle
WGp	——, Evangelisches Predigerseminar
WH	Windsheim, BRD, Stadtbibliothek
WIl	Wiesbaden, BRD, Hessische Landesbibliothek
WILd	Wilster, BRD, Stadtarchiv (Doos'sche Bibliothek)
WL	Wuppertal, BRD, Wissenschaftliche Stadtbibliothek
WM	Wismar, DDR, Stadtarchiv
WO	Worms, BRD, Stadtbibliothek
WRdn	Weimar, DDR, Deutsches Nationaltheater
WRgm	——, Goethe-National-Museum
WRgs	——, Goethe–Schiller-Archiv und Franz-Liszt-Museum
WRh	——, Franz-Liszt-Hochschule
WRhk	——, Herderkirche
WRiv	——, Institut für Volksmusikforschung
WRl	——, Landeshauptarchiv
WRs	——, Stadtbücherei, Musikbücherei
WRtl	——, Thüringische Landesbibliothek, Musiksammlung
WRz	——, Zentralbibliothek der Deutschen Klassik
WS	Wasserburg am Inn, BRD, Chorarchiv St Jakob, Pfarramt
WÜms	Würzburg, BRD, Musikwissenschaftliches Seminar der Universität
WÜsa	——, Stadtarchiv
WÜu	——, Universitätsbibliothek
X	Xanten, BRD, Stifts- und Pfarrbibliothek
Z	Zwickau, DDR, Ratsschulbibliothek
Zmk	——, Domkantorei der Marienkirche
Zsch	——, Robert-Schumann-Haus
ZE	Zerbst, DDR, Stadtarchiv
ZEo	——, Bücherei der Erweiterten Oberschule
ZGh	Zörbig, DDR, Heimatmuseum
ZGsj	——, Pfarramt St Jacobi
ZI	Zittau, DDR, Stadt- und Kreisbibliothek
ZIa	——, Stadtarchiv
ZL	Zeil, BRD, Fürstlich Waldburg-Zeil'sches Archiv, private collection
ZW	Zweibrücken, BRD, Bibliotheca Bipontina, Wissenschaftliche Bibliothek am Herzog-Wolfgang-Gymnasium
ZZ	Zeitz, DDR, Heimatmuseum
ZZs	——, Stiftsbibliothek

DK: DENMARK

A	Århus, Statsbiblioteket
Dschoenbaum	Dragør, Camillo Schoenbaum, private collection
Hfog	Hellerup, Dan Fog, private collection
Kc	Copenhagen, Carl Claudius Musikhistoriske Samling
Kh	——, Københavns Kommunes Hovedbiblioteket
Kk	——, Det Kongelige Bibliotek
Kmk	——, Det Kongelige Danske Musikkonservatorium
Km(m)	——, Musikhistorisk Museum
Ks	——, Samfundet til Udgivelse af Dansk Musik
Kt	——, Teaterhistorisk Museum
Ku	——, Universitetsbiblioteket 1. Afdeling
Kv	——, Københavns Universitet, Musikvidenskabeligt Institut
Ol	Odense, Landsarkivet for Fyen, Karen Brahes Bibliotek
Ou	——, Universitetsbibliotek
Rk	Ribe, Stifts- og Katedralskoles Bibliotek
Sa	Sorø, Sorø Akademis Bibliotek

E: SPAIN

Ac	Ávila, Catedral
Asa	——, Monasterio de S Ana (Real Monasterio de Encarnación)
Ast	——, Monasterio del S Tomás, Archivo de la Iglesia
AL	Alquezar, Colegiata
ALB	Albarracín, Colegiata
AS	Astorga, Catedral
Ba	Barcelona, Real Academia de Ciencias y Artes
Bac	——, Corona de Aragón

Bc	——, Biblioteca de Cataluña
Bca	——, Catedral
Bcapdevila	——, Felipe Capdevila Rovira, private collection
Bcm	——, Conservatorio Superior Municipal de Música
Bih	——, Instituto Municipal de Historia (formerly Archivo Histórico de la Ciudad)
Bim	——, Instituto Español de Musicología
Bit	——, Instituto del Teatro (formerly Museo del Arte Escénico)
Boc	——, Biblioteca Orfeó Catalá
Bsm	——, S María del Mar
Bu	——, Biblioteca del Universidad
BA	Badajoz, Catedral
BUa	Burgos, Catedral
BUlh	——, Monasterio de Las Huelgas
BUm	——, Museo Arqueológico
BUp	——, Biblioteca Provincial
BUse	——, Parroquia de S Esteban
C	Córdoba, Catedral
CA	Calahorra, Catedral
CAL	Calatayud, Colegiata de S María
CAR	Cardona, Archivo Comunal
CU	Cuenca, Catedral
CUi	——, Instituto de Música Religiosa
CZ	Cádiz, Archivo Capitular
E	El Escorial, Real Monasterio de S Lorenzo
G	Gerona, Biblioteca Catedralicia
Gm	——, Museo Diocesano
Gp	——, Biblioteca Pública
Gs	——, Seminario Gerundense
GRc	Granada, Catedral
GRcr	——, Capilla Real
GU	Guadalupe, Real Monasterio de S María
H	Huesca, Catedral
J	Jaca, Catedral
JA	Jaén, Catedral
LPA	Las Palmas, Catedral de Canarias
La	León, Catedral
Lc	——, Colegiata de S Isidoro
Lp	——, Biblioteca Pública Provincial
LEc	Lérida, Catedral
LEm	——, Museo Diocesano
Ma	Madrid, Real Academia de Bellas Artes de S Fernando
Mah	——, Archivo Histórico Nacional (Real Academia de la Historia)
Mam	——, Biblioteca Musical Circulante
Mat	——, Museo-Archivo Teatral
Mc	——, Conservatorio Superior de Música
Mca	——, Casa de Alba, private collection
Mcns	——, Congregación de Nuestra Señora
Mic	——, Instituto de Cultura Hispánica, Sección de Música
Mit	——, Ministerio de Información y Turismo
Mlg	——, Fundación Lazaro Galdiano
Mm	——, Biblioteca Municipal
Mmc	——, Casa Ducal de Medinaceli, Bartolomé March Servera, private collection
Mn	——, Biblioteca Nacional
Mp	——, Palacio Real
Mpm	——, Patronato Marcelino Menéndez y Pelayo del Consejo Superior de Investigaciones Científicas
Mrt	——, Radio Nacional de España-Televisión
Msa	——, Sociedad General de Autores de España
Msi	——, Ciudad Universitaria, Facultad de Filosofía y Letras, Biblioteca de S Isidro
MA	Málaga, Catedral
MO	Montserrat, Monasterio de S María
MON	Mondoñedo, Catedral
OL	Olot, Biblioteca Popular
OR	Orense, Catedral
ORI	Orihuela, Catedral
OS	Osma, Catedral
OV	Oviedo, Catedral Metropolitana
P	Plasencia, Catedral
PAc	Palma de Mallorca, Catedral
PAp	——, Biblioteca Provincial
PAMc	Pamplona, Catedral
PAMm	——, Museo Sarasate
PAS	Pastrana, Iglesia Parroquial
RO	Roncesvalles, Monasterio de S María
Sc	Seville, Catedral
Sco	——, Biblioteca Capitular Colombina [in *Sc*]
SA	Salamanca, Catedral
SAcalo	——, José López-Calo, private collection
SAu	——, Universidad Pontificia, Biblioteca Universitaria

SAuf	——, Universidad Pontificia, Facultad de Filosofía y Letras
SAN	Santander, Biblioteca de Menéndez y Pelayo
SC	Santiago de Compostela, Catedral
SCu	——, Biblioteca Universitaria
SD	Santo Domingo de la Calzada, Archivo
SE	Segovia, Catedral
SEG	Segorbe, Catedral
SI	Silos, Monasterio Benedictino (Abadía) de S Domingo
SIG	Sigüenza, Catedral
SIM	Simancas, Archivo General
SO	Soria, Biblioteca Pública
Tc	Toledo, Archivo Capitular
Tp	——, Biblioteca Pública Provincial y Museo de la Santa Cruz
TAc	Tarragona, Catedral
TAp	——, Biblioteca Pública
TO	Tortosa, Catedral
TU	Tudela, Colegiata (formerly Catedral) de S María
TZ	Tarazona, Catedral
U (also SU)	Seo de Urgel, Catedral
V	Valladolid, Catedral
Vp	——, Parroquia de Santiago
VAa	Valencia, Archivo, Biblioteca y Museos Municipales
VAc	——, Catedral
VAcm	——, Conservatorio Superior de Música
VAcp	——, Colegio y Seminario del Corpus Christi del Patriarca
VAim	——, Instituto Valenciano de Musicología
VAu	——, Biblioteca Universitaria
VI	Vich, Museo Episcopal
VIT	Vitoria, Catedral
Zac	Saragossa, Archivo de Música del Cabildo
Zcc	——, Colegio Calasanci
Zfm	——, Facultad de Medicina
Zp	——, Biblioteca Pública
Zs	——, Biblioteca Capitular de la Seo
Zsc	——, Seminario de S Carlos
Zu	——, Biblioteca Universitaria
Zvp	——, Iglesia Metropolitana [in *Zac*]
ZA	Zamora, Catedral

EIRE: IRELAND

C	Cork, University College
Da	Dublin, Royal Irish Academy
Dam	——, Royal Irish Academy of Music
Dcb	——, Chester Beatty Library
Dcc	——, Christ Church Cathedral
Dm	——, Marsh's Library
Dmh	——, Mercer's Hospital
Dn	——, National Library and Museum of Ireland
Dpc	——, St Patrick's Cathedral
Dtc	——, Trinity College
Duc	——, University College

ET: EGYPT

S	Mt Sinai

F: FRANCE

A	Avignon, Bibliothèque Municipale, Musée Calvet
Aa	——, Archives Départementales de Vaucluse
AB	Abbeville, Bibliothèque Municipale
AG	Agen, Archives Départementales de Lot-et-Garonne
AI	Albi, Bibliothèque Municipale
AIXc	Aix-en-Provence, Conservatoire
AIXm	——, Bibliothèque Municipale, Bibliothèque Méjanes
AIXmc	——, Maîtrise de la Cathédrale
AL	Alençon, Bibliothèque Municipale
AM	Amiens, Bibliothèque Municipale
AN	Angers, Bibliothèque Municipale
ANG	Angoulême, Bibliothèque Municipale
ANN	Annecy, Bibliothèque Municipale
APT	Apt, Cathédrale Ste Anne
AR	Arles, Bibliothèque Municipale
AS	Arras, Bibliothèque Municipale
ASO	Asnières-sur-Oise, François Lang, private collection
AU	Auxerre, Bibliothèque Municipale
AUT	Autun, Bibliothèque Municipale
AV	Avallon, Société d'Etudes d'Avallon
AVR	Avranches, Bibliothèque Municipale
B	Besançon, Bibliothèque Municipale
Ba	——, Bibliothèque de l'Archevêché
Be	——, Ecole Nationale de Musique
BD	Bar-le-Duc, Bibliothèque Municipale
BE	Beauvais, Bibliothèque Municipale
BER	Bernay, Bibliothèque Municipale

BG	Bourg-en-Bresse, Bibliothèque Municipale et Musée de l'Ain
BL	Blois, Bibliothèque Municipale
BO	Bordeaux, Bibliothèque Municipale
BOI	Boisguillaume, Musée Boieldieu
BOU	Bourbourg, Bibliothèque Municipale
BR	Brest, Bibliothèque Municipale
BS	Bourges, Bibliothèque Municipale
BSM	Boulogne-sur-Mer, Bibliothèque Municipale
C	Carpentras, Bibliothèque Inguimbertine et Musée de Carpentras
CA	Cambrai, Bibliothèque Municipale
CAc	——, Cathédrale
CAD	Cadouin, Bibliothèque de l'Abbaye
CAH	Cahors, Bibliothèque Municipale
CAL	Calais, Bibliothèque Municipale
CC	Carcassonne, Bibliothèque Municipale
CF	Clermont-Ferrand, Bibliothèque Municipale et Universitaire, Section Centrale et Section Lettres
CH	Chantilly, Musée Condé
CHA	Châteauroux, Bibliothèque Municipale
CHE	Cherbourg, Bibliothèque et Archives Municipales
CHM	Chambéry, Bibliothèque Municipale
CHR	Chartres, Bibliothèque Municipale
CN	Caen, Bibliothèque Municipale
CNc	——, Conservatoire National de Musique
CO	Colmar, Bibliothèque Municipale
COs	——, Consistoire de l'Eglise de la Confession d'Augsbourg à Colmar
COUm	Coutances, Bibliothèque Municipale
COUs	——, Grand Séminaire
CSM	Châlons-sur-Marne, Bibliothèque Municipale
CV	Charleville, Bibliothèque Municipale
Dc	Dijon, Bibliothèque du Conservatoire
Dm	——, Bibliothèque Municipale (Bibliothèque Publique)
DI	Dieppe, Bibliothèque Municipale
DO	Dôle, Bibliothèque Municipale
DOU	Douai, Bibliothèque Municipale
E	Epinal, Bibliothèque Municipale
EP	Epernay, Bibliothèque Municipale
EV	Evreux, Bibliothèque Municipale
F	Foix, Bibliothèque Municipale
G	Grenoble, Bibliothèque Municipale
Ge	——, Ecole Régionale de Musique, de Danse et d'Art Dramatique
GAP	Gap, Archives Départementales des Hautes-Alpes
H	Hyères, Bibliothèque Municipale
Lc	Lille, Conservatoire
Lfc	——, Facultés Catholiques
Lm	——, Bibliothèque Municipale
LA	Laon, Bibliothèque Municipale
LB	Libourne, Bibliothèque Municipale
LG	Limoges, Bibliothèque Municipale
LH	Le Havre, Bibliothèque Municipale
LM	Le Mans, Bibliothèque Municipale
LO	Louviers, Bibliothèque Municipale
LP	Le Puy-en-Velay, Bibliothèque Municipale
LR	La Rochelle, Bibliothèque Municipale
LV	Laval, Bibliothèque Municipale
LYc	Lyons, Conservatoire National de Musique
LYm	——, Bibliothèque Municipale
Mc	Marseilles, Conservatoire de Musique et de Déclamation
Mm	——, Bibliothèque Municipale
MAC	Mâcon, Bibliothèque Municipale
MD	Montbéliard, Bibliothèque Municipale
MEL	Melun, Bibliothèque Municipale
MH	Mulhouse, Bibliothèque Municipale
MIL	Millau, Bibliothèque Municipale
MIR	Mirecourt, Bibliothèque Municipale
ML	Moulins, Bibliothèque Municipale
MLN	Montluçon, Bibliothèque Municipale
MO	Montpellier, Faculté de Médecine de l'Université
MOv	——, Bibliothèque de la Ville et du Musée Fabre
MON	Montauban, Bibliothèque Municipale
MZ	Metz, Bibliothèque Municipale
Nd	Nantes, Bibliothèque du Musée Dobrée
Ne	——, Ecole Nationale de Musique, d'Art Dramatique et de Danse
Nm	——, Bibliothèque Municipale
NAc	Nancy, Conservatoire
NAm	——, Bibliothèque Municipale
NAR	Narbonne, Bibliothèque Municipale
NI	Nice, Bibliothèque Municipale
NIc	——, Conservatoire de Musique

NO	Noyon, Bibliothèque Municipale
NS	Nîmes, Bibliothèque Municipale
NT	Niort, Bibliothèque Municipale
O	Orleans, Bibliothèque Municipale
Pa	Paris, Bibliothèque de l'Arsenal
Pal	——, American Library in Paris
Pbf	——, Centre de Documentation Benjamin Franklin
Pc	——, Conservatoire National de Musique [in *Pn*]
Pcf	——, Comédie-Française, Bibliothèque
Pcrs	——, Centre National de la Recherche Scientifique
Pe	——, Schola Cantorum (Ecole Supérieure de Musique, Danse et Art Dramatique)
Pgérard	——, Yves Gérard, private collection
Pi	——, Bibliothèque de l'Institut
Pim	——, Institut de Musicologie de l'Université, Bibliothèque Pierre Aubry
Pis	——, Institut Supérieur de Musique Liturgique
Pm	——, Bibliothèque Mazarine
Pma	——, Musée Nationale des Art set Traditions Populaires
Pmeyer	——, André Meyer, private collection
Pmg	——, Musée Guimet
Pmh	——, Musée de l'Homme
Pn	——, Bibliothèque Nationale
Po	——, Bibliothèque–Musée de l'Opéra
Pphon	——, Phonothèque Nationale, Bibliothèque et Musée
Ppincherle	——, Marc Pincherle, private collection [dispersed 1975]
Ppo	——, Bibliothèque Polonaise de Paris
Prothschild	——, Germaine, Baronne Edouard de Rothschild, private collection
Prt	——, Office de Radiodiffusion-Télévision Française
Psc	——, Société des Auteurs et Compositeurs Dramatiques
Pse	——, Société des Auteurs, Compositeurs et Editeurs de Musique
Psg	——, Bibliothèque Ste Geneviève
Pshp	——, Bibliothèque de la Société d'Histoire du Protestantisme
Psi	——, Séminaire Israélite de France
Pthibault	——, Geneviève Thibault, private collection
PAU	Pau, Bibliothèque Municipale
PE	Périgueux, Bibliothèque Municipale
PO	Poitiers, Bibliothèque Municipale
POu	——, Faculté des Lettres de l'Université de Poitiers, Section de Musicologie
Rc	Rouen, Conservatoire
R(m)	——, Bibliothèque Municipale
RE	Rennes, Bibliothèque Municipale
RO	Roanne, Bibliothèque Municipale
RSc	Rheims, Bibliothèque de la Cathédrale
Sc	Strasbourg, Conservatoire
Sg(sc)	——, Grand Séminaire (Séminaire Catholique)
Sim	——, Institut de Musicologie de l'Université
Sm	——, Archives et Bibliothèque Municipale
Sn	——, Bibliothèque Nationale et Universitaire
Ssa	——, Société des Amis des Arts de Strasbourg
Ssp	——, Séminaire Protestant
SA	Salins, Bibliothèque Municipale
SAU	Saumur, Bibliothèque Municipale
SCL	St-Claude, Bibliothèque Municipale
SDE	St-Denis, Bibliothèque Municipale
SDI	St-Dié, Bibliothèque Municipale
SE	Sens, Bibliothèque Municipale
SEL	Sélestat, Bibliothèque Municipale
SERRANT	Serrant, Château
SO	Solesmes, Abbaye St-Pierre
SOI	Soissons, Bibliothèque Municipale
SQ	St-Quentin, Bibliothèque Municipale
T	Troyes, Bibliothèque Municipale
TH	Thiers, Bibliothèque Municipale
TLc	Toulouse, Conservatoire
TLd	——, Musée Dupuy
TLm	——, Bibliothèque Municipale
TO	Tours, Bibliothèque Municipale
TOgs	——, Grand Séminaire
TOul	——, Bibliothèque Universitaire, Section Lettres
TOur	——, Centre d'Etudes Supérieures de la Renaissance
TOU	Toulon, Ecole Nationale de Musique
TOUm	——, Bibliothèque Municipale
TOUs	——, Société des Amis du Vieux Toulon
TU	Tulle, Bibliothèque Municipale
V	Versailles, Bibliothèque Municipale
VA	Vannes, Bibliothèque Municipale
VAL	Valenciennes, Bibliothèque Municipale
VE	Vesoul, Bibliothèque Municipale
VN	Verdun, Bibliothèque Municipale

GB: GREAT BRITAIN

A	Aberdeen, University Library, King's College
AB	Aberystwyth, National Library of Wales
AM	Ampleforth, Abbey and College Library, St Lawrence Abbey
Bp	Birmingham, Public Libraries
Bu	——, University of Birmingham, Barber Institute of Fine Arts
BA	Bath, Municipal Library
BEas	Bedford, Bedfordshire Archaeological Society
BEcr	——, Bedfordshire County Record Office
BEp	——, Public Library Music Department
BENcoke	Bentley (Hants.), Gerald Coke, private collection
BEV	Beverley, East Yorkshire County Record Office
BO	Bournemouth, Central Library
BRb	Bristol, Baptist College Library
BRp	——, Public Libraries, Central Library
BRu	——, University of Bristol Library
Ccc	Cambridge, Corpus Christi College
Cchc	——, Christ's College
Cclc	——, Clare College
Cfm	——, Fitzwilliam Museum
Cgc	——, Gonville and Caius College
Cjc	——, St John's College
Cjec	——, Jesus College
Ckc	——, Rowe Music Library, King's College
Cmc	——, Magdalene College
Cp	——, Peterhouse
Cpc	——, Pembroke College
Cpl	——, Pendlebury Library of Music
Ctc	——, Trinity College
Cu	——, University Library
Cumc	——, University Music Club
Cus	——, Cambridge Union Society
CA	Canterbury, Cathedral
CAR	Carlisle, Cathedral
CDp	Cardiff, Public Libraries, Central Library
CDu	——, University College of South Wales and Monmouthshire
CF	Chelmsford, Essex County Record Office
CH	Chichester, Diocesan Record Office
CHc	——, Cathedral
DRc	Durham, Cathedral
DRu	——, University Library
DU	Dundee, Public Libraries
En	Edinburgh, National Library of Scotland
Enc	——, New College Library
Ep	——, Public Library, Central Public Library
Er	——, Reid Music Library of the University of Edinburgh
Es	——, Signet Library
Eu	——, University Library
EL	Ely, Cathedral
EXc	Exeter, Cathedral
EXcl	——, Central Library
EXed	——, East Devon Area Record Office
EXu	——, University Library
Ge	Glasgow, Euing Music Library
Gm	——, Mitchell Library
Gsma	——, Scottish Music Archive
Gtc	——, Trinity College
Gu	——, University Library
GL	Gloucester, Cathedral
H	Hereford, Cathedral
HAdolmetsch	Haslemere, Carl Dolmetsch, private collection
Lam	London, Royal Academy of Music
Lbbc	——, British Broadcasting Corporation
Lbc	——, British Council
Lbm	——, British Library, Reference Division (formerly British Museum) (= *Lbl*)
Lcm	——, Royal College of Music
Lco	——, Royal College of Organists
Lcs	——, Vaughan Williams Memorial Library (Cecil Sharp Library)
Ldc	——, Dulwich College
Lgc	——, Gresham College (Guildhall Library)
Lkc	——, University of London, King's College
Llp	——, Lambeth Palace
Lmic	——, British Music Information Centre
Lmp	——, Marylebone Public Library
Lpro	——, Public Record Office
Lsc	——, Sion College
Lsm	——, Royal Society of Musicians of Great Britain
Lsp	——, St Paul's Cathedral
Ltc	——, Trinity College of Music
Lu	——, University of London, Music Library

Lva	——, Victoria and Albert Museum
Lwa	——, Westminster Abbey
Lwcm	——, Westminster Central Music Library
LA	Lancaster, District Central Library
LAu	——, University Library
LEbc	Leeds, University of Leeds, Brotherton Collection
LEc	——, Leeds Public Libraries, Music Department, Central Library
LF	Lichfield, Cathedral
LI	Lincoln, Cathedral
LVp	Liverpool, Public Libraries, Central Library
LVu	——, University Music Department
Mch	Manchester, Chetham's Library
Mcm	——, Royal Northern College of Music
Mp	——, Central Public Library, Henry Watson Music Library
Mr	——, John Rylands University Library, Deansgate Branch
Mrothwell	——, Evelyn Rothwell, private collection
Mu	——, John Rylands University Library
NO	Nottingham, University Library
NW	Norwich, Central Library
NWr	——, Norfolk and Norwich Record Office
Ob	Oxford, Bodleian Library
Obc	——, Brasenose College
Och	——, Christ Church
Ojc	——, St John's College
Olc	——, Lincoln College
Omc	——, Magdalen College
Onc	——, New College
Ooc	——, Oriel College
Oqc	——, Queen's College
Ouf	——, University, Faculty of Music
Oumc	——, University Music Club and Union
P	Perth, Sandeman Music Library
R	Reading, University, Music Library
RI	Ripon, Cathedral
RO	Rochester, Cathedral
SA	St Andrews, University Library
SB	Salisbury, Cathedral
SH	Sherborne, Sherborne School Library
SHR	Shrewsbury, Shropshire County Record Office
SOp	Southampton, Public Library
SR	Studley Royal, Fountains Abbey MS 23 [in *LEc*]
STb	Stratford-on-Avon, Shakespeare's Birthplace Trust
STm	——, Shakespeare Memorial Library
T	Tenbury, St Michael's College [Toulouse–Philidor collection now largely in *F-Pn*, *V*]
W	Wells, Cathedral
WB	Wimborne, Minster
WC	Winchester, Chapter Library
WCc	——, Winchester College
WI	Wigan, Public Library
WO	Worcester, Cathedral
WRch	Windsor, St George's Chapter Library
WRec	——, Eton College
Y	York, Minster
Yi	——, Borthwick Institute of Historical Research

GR: GREECE

Ae	Athens, Ethnike Biblioteke tes Hellados
AT	Mt Athos, Koutloumousi Monastery
ATSch	——, Chilandari Monastery
ATSdionision	——, Dionision Monastery
ATSgreat lavra	——, Monastery of the Great Lavra
ATSiviron	——, Iviron Monastery
ATSserbian	——, Serbian Monastery
ATSvatopedi	——, Vatopedi Monastery
LA	Lavra
P	Patmos

H: HUNGARY

Ba	Budapest, Magyar Tudományos Akadémia Régi Könyvek Tára és Kézirattár
Ba(mi)	——, Magyar Tudományos Akadémia Zenetudományi Intézet Könyvtára
Bb	——, Bartók Béla Zeneművészeti Szakközépiskola Könyvtára
Bev	——, Evangélikus Országos Könyvtár
Bf	——, Belvárosi Föplébániatemplom Kottatára
Bj	——, Józsefvárosi Evangélikus Egyházközség Kottatára
Bl	——, Liszt Ferenc Zeneművészeti Főiskola Könyvtára
Bm	——, Budavári Nagyboldogasszony Templom Kottatára

Bn	——, Országos Széchényi Könyvtára
Bo	——, Állami Operaház
Bp	——, Piarista Gimnázium Könyvtára
Br	——, Ráday Gyűjtemény, Könyvtár és Levéltár
Bs	——, Központi Szemináriumi Könyvtár
Bst	——, Szent István Bazilika Kottatára
Bu	——, Egyetemi Könyvtár
BA	Bártfa, church of St Aegidius [in *Bn*]
CSg	Csurgó, Csokonai Vitéz Mihály Gimnázium Könyvtára
DR	Debrecen, Tiszántúli Református Egyházkerület Nagykönyvtára
DRm	——, Déri Múzeum
DRu	——, Kossuth Lajos Tudományegyetem Könyvtára
Ea	Esztergom, Komárom Megyei Levéltár
Efko	——, Főszékesegyházi Kottatár
Efkő	——, Főszékesegyházi Könyvtár
Em	——, Keresztény Múzeum Könyvtára
EG	Eger, Főegyházmegyei Könyvtár
EGb	——, Bazilika Kottatára
Gc	Győr, Püspöki Papnevelő Intézet Könyvtára
Gk	——, Székesegyházi Könyvtár
Gm	——, Xántus János Múzeum
Gz	——, Zeneművészeti Szakközépiskola Könyvtára
GGn	Gyöngyös, Országos Széchényi Könyvtár, Bajza József Műemlékkönyvtár
GYm	Gyula, Múzeum
KE	Keszthely, Országos Széchényi Könyvtár Helikon Könyvtára
KI	Kiskunhalas, Református Egyházközség Könyvtára
KŐ	Kőszeg, Plébániatemplom Kottatára
KŐm	——, Jurisich Múzeum
MOp	Mosonmagyaróvár, 1. sz Plébániatemplom Kottatára
NY	Nyiregyháza, Református Városi Egyházközség Könyvtára
P	Pécs, Székesegyházi Kottatár
PA	Pápa, Dunántuli Református Egyházkerület Könyvtára
PH	Pannonhalma, Szent Benedekrend Központi Főkönyvtára
Se	Sopron, Evangélikus Egyházközség Könyvtára
Sg	——, Berzsenyi Dániel Gimnázium Könyvtára
Sl	——, Liszt Ferenc Múzeum
Sp	——, Szentlélekről és Szent Mihályról Nevezett Városplébánia Kottatára
Sst	——, Storno Gyűjtemény
SA	Sárospatak, Tiszáninneni Református Egyházkerület Nagykönyvtára
SD	Szekszárd, Balogh Ádám Megyei Múzeum
SFk	Székesfehérvár, Püspöki Könyvtár
SFm	——, István Király Múzeum
SFs	——, Székesegyházi Kottatár
SG	Szeged, Somogyi Könyvtár
SGm	——, Móra Ferenc Múzeum
SGu	——, Szegedi Orvostudományi Egyetem Könyvtára
SY	Szombathely, Püspöki Könyvtár
SYb	——, Berzsenyi Dániel Megyei Könyvtár
SYm	——, Smidt Múzeum
T	Tata, Plébániatemplom Kottatára
V	Vác, Székesegyházi Kottatár
VE	Veszprém, Püspöki Könyvtár
VEs	——, Székesegyházi Kottatár

I: ITALY

Ac	Assisi, Biblioteca Comunale
Ad	——, Cattedrale S Rufino
Af	——, S Francesco
AC	Acicatena, Biblioteca Comunale
AG	Agrigento, Biblioteca Lucchesiana
AGI	Agira, Biblioteca Comunale
AGN	Agnone, Biblioteca Emidiana
AL	Albenga, Cattedrale
ALEa	Alessandria, Archivio di Stato
ALEi	——, Istituto Musicale Antonio Vivaldi
AN	Ancona, Biblioteca Comunale
ANcap	——, Biblioteca Capitolare
ANd	——, Archivio della Cappella del Duomo
AO	Aosta, Seminario Maggiore
AP	Ascoli Picena, Biblioteca Comunale
AQ	Aquileia, Archivio della Basilica
ARc	Arezzo, Biblioteca Consorziale
ARd	——, Duomo
ASc(d)	Asti, Archivio Capitolare (Duomo)
ASi	——, Istituto Musicale Giuseppe Verdi
ASs	——, Seminario Vescovile

AT	Atri, Museo della Basilica Cattedrale, Biblioteca Capitolare
Baf	Bologna, Accademia Filarmonica
Bam	——, Biblioteca della Casa di Risparmio (Biblioteca Ambrosini)
Bas	——, Archivio di Stato
Bc	——, Civico Museo Bibliografico Musicale
Bca	——, Biblioteca Comunale dell'Arciginnasio
Bl	——, Conservatorio di Musica G. B. Martini
Bof	——, Oratorio dei Filippini
Bpm	——, Facoltà di Magistero dell'Università degli Studi, Scuola di Perfezionamento in Musicologia
Bsd	——, Convento di S Domenico
Bsf	——, Convento di S Francesco
Bsm	——, Biblioteca Conventuale S Maria dei Servi
Bsp	——, Basilica di S Petronio
Bu	——, Biblioteca Universitaria
BAca	Bari, Biblioteca Capitolare
BAcp	——, Conservatorio di Musica Nicola Piccinni
BAgiovine	——, Alfredo Giovine, private collection
BAn	——, Biblioteca Nazionale Sagarriga Visconti-Volpi
BAR	Barletta, Biblioteca Comunale Sabino Loffredo
BDG	Bassano del Grappa, Biblioteca Civica
BE	Belluno, Biblioteca del Seminario
BEc	——, Biblioteca Civica
BGc	Bergamo, Biblioteca Civica Angelo Mai
BGi	——, Civico Istituto Musicale Gaetano Donizetti
BI	Bitonto, Biblioteca Comunale Vitale Giordano
BRa	Brescia, Ateneo di Scienze, Lettere ed Arti
BRd	——, Duomo
BRi	——, Istituto Musicale A. Venturi
BRp	——, Archivio di S Maria della Pace
BRq	——, Biblioteca Civica Queriniana
BRs	——, Seminario Vescovile
BRsg	——, S Giovanni Evangelista (Cappella del Ss Sacramento)
BRsmg	——, Madonna delle Grazie
BRss	——, S Salvatore
BRE	Bressanone, Seminario Vescovile Vicentinum
BRI	Brindisi, Biblioteca Pubblica Arcivescovile Annibale de Leo
BV	Benevento, Archivio Capitolare
BVa	——, Archivio di Stato
BVam	——, Biblioteca e Archivio Storico Provinciale Antonio Mellusi
BVT	Borgo Val di Toro, Biblioteca Comunale Manara
BZa	Bolzano, Archivio di Stato
BZc	——, Conservatorio di Musica Claudio Monteverdi
BZd	——, Duomo
BZf	——, Biblioteca dei Minori Francescani
BZtoggenburg	——, Count Toggenburg, private collection
CAc	Cagliari, Biblioteca Comunale
CAcon	——, Conservatorio di Musica Giovanni Pierluigi da Palestrina
CAsm	——, Cattedrale S Maria
CAu	——, Biblioteca Universitaria
CAP	Capua, Museo Provinciale Campano
CARcc	Castell'Arquato, Chiesa Collegiata
CARc(p)	——, Archivio Capitolare (Archivio Parrocchiale)
CATa	Catania, Archivio di Stato
CATc	——, Biblioteche Riunite Civica e Antonio Ursino Recupero
CATm	——, Museo Belliniano
CATss	——, Società di Storia Patria per la Sicilia Orientale
CC	Città di Castello, Duomo
CCc	——, Biblioteca Comunale
CDA	Codogna, Biblioteca Civica Popolare L. Ricca
CEb(sm)	Cesena, Badia S Maria del Monte
CEc	——, Biblioteca Comunale Malatestiana
CEN	Cento, S Biagio
CF	Cividale del Friuli, Archivio Capitolare
CFm	——, Museo Archeologico Nazionale
CHR	Chieri, Facoltà Teologica dei Gesuiti
CHT	Chieta, Biblioteca Provinciale Angelo Camillo de Meis
CHV	Chiavenna, Biblioteca Capitolare Laurenziana
CLE	Corleone, Biblioteca Comunale Francesco Bentivegna
CLO	Corlono, Chiesa della Reggia Ducale
CMac	Casale Monferrato, Archivio Capitolare
CMbc	——, Biblioteca Civica
CMs	——, Seminario Vescovile
CMI	Camogli, Biblioteca Comunale Nicolo Cueno
CMO	Camerino, Biblioteca Valentiniana e Comunale
COc	Como, Biblioteca Comunale
COd	——, Duomo

CORc	Correggio, Biblioteca Comunale
COS	Cosenza, Biblioteca Civica
CPa	Carpi, Archivio Paolo Guaitoli della Commissione di Storia Patria de Carpi
CPc	——, Biblioteca Comunale
CR	Cremona, Biblioteca Statale
CRd	——, Duomo
CRE	Crema, Biblioteca Comunale
CREi	——, Istituto Musicale L. Folcioni
CT	Cortona, Biblioteca Comunale e dell'Accademia Etrusca
CZorizio	Cazzago S Martino, Orizio private collection
DO	Domodossola, Biblioteca e Archivio dei Rosminiani di Monte Calvaro
E	Enna, Biblioteca Comunale
Fa	Florence, Ss Annunziata
Faq	——, Pius XII Institute, Graduate School of Fine Arts, Aquinas Library
Fas	——, Archivio di Stato
Fc	——, Conservatorio di Musica Luigi Cherubini
Fd	——, Duomo
Ffabbri	——, M. Fabbri, private collection
Fl	——, Biblioteca Medicea-Laurenziana
Fm	——, Biblioteca Marucelliana
Fn	——, Biblioteca Nazionale Centrale
Folschki	——, Olschki private collection
Fr	——, Biblioteca Riccardiana e Moreniana
Fs	——, Seminario Arcivescovile Maggiore
Fsa	——, Biblioteca Domenicana, Chiesa S Maria Novella
Fsm	——, Convento S Marco
Fu	——, Università degli Studi, Facoltà di Lettere e Filosofia
FA	Fabriano, Biblioteca Comunale
FAd	——, Duomo
FAN	Fano, Biblioteca Comunale Federiciana
FBR	Fossombrone, Biblioteca Civica Passionei
FEbonfigliuoli	Ferrara, Bonfigliuoli private collection
FEc	——, Biblioteca Comunale Ariostea
FEd	——, Duomo
FEmichelini	——, Bruto Michelini, private collection
FELc	Feltre, Biblioteca Comunale
FELd	——, Duomo
FELm	——, Museo Civico
FEM	Finale Emilia, Biblioteca Comunale
FERc	Fermo, Biblioteca Comunale
FERd	——, Duomo
FERl	——, Liceo Musicale Girolamo Frescobaldi
FERmichelini	——, Bruno Michelini, private collection
FOc	Forlì, Biblioteca Comunale Aurelio Saffi
FOd	——, Duomo
FOG	Foggia, Biblioteca Provinciale
FOLc	Foligno, Biblioteca Comunale
FOLd	——, Duomo
FOSc	Fossano, Biblioteca Civica
FZac(d)	Faenza, Archivio Capitolare (Duomo)
FZc	——, Biblioteca Comunale
FZsavini	——, Ino Savini, private collection
Gc	Genoa, Biblioteca Civica Berio
Gf	——, Biblioteca Franzoniana
Ggrasso	——, Lorenzina Grasso, private collection
Gi(l)	——, Conservatorio di Musica Nicolò Paganini
Gim	——, Istituto Mazziniano
Gsc	——, S Caterina
Gsmb	——, S Maria della Castagna
Gsmd	——, S Maria di Castello, Biblioteca dei Domenicani
Gu	——, Biblioteca Universitaria
GA	Ganna, Badia Benedittina
GE	Gemona, Duomo
GN	Giulianova, Biblioteca Comunale Vincenzo Bindi
GO	Gorizia, Seminario Teologico Centrale
GR	Grottaferrata, Badia Greca
GUA	Guastalla, Biblioteca Municipale Maldotti
GUBsp	Gubbio, Biblioteca Comunale Sperelliana
I	Imola, Biblioteca Comunale
IE	Iesi, Archivio Comunale
IV	Ivrea, Biblioteca Capitolare
La	Lucca, Archivio di Stato
Lc	——, Biblioteca Capitolare Feliniana
Lg	——, Biblioteca Statale
Li	——, Istituto Musicale Luigi Boccherini
Ls	——, Seminario Vescovile
LA	L'Aquila, Biblioteca Provinciale Salvatore Tommasi
LE	Lecce, Biblioteca Provinciale Nicola Bernardini
LI	Livorno, Biblioteca Comunale Labronica Francesco Domenico Guerrazzi
LOc	Lodi, Biblioteca Capitolare
LOcl	——, Biblioteca Comunale Laudense
LT	Loreto, Archivio Storico della Cappella Lauretana
LU	Lugo, Biblioteca Comunale Fabrizio Trisi
Ma	Milan, Biblioteca Ambrosiana
Malfieri	——, Trecani degli Alfieri, private collection
Mb	——, Biblioteca Nazionale Braidense
Mc	——, Conservatorio di Musica Giuseppe Verdi
Mca	——, Archivio della Curia Arcivescovile
Mcap(d)	——, Cappella Musicale del Duomo
Mcom	——, Biblioteca Comunale
Md	——, Archivio della Cappella Musicale del Duomo
Mdonà	——, Mariangelo Donà, private collection
Mr	——, Archivio Storico Ricordi (Casa Editrice)
Ms	——, Biblioteca Teatrale Livia Simoni
Msartori	——, Claudio Sartori, private collection
Mt	——, Biblioteca Trivulziana
Mvidusso	——, Carlo Vidusso, private collection
MAa	Mantua, Archivio di Stato
MAad	——, Archivio Storico Diocesano
MAav	——, Accademia Virgiliana di Scienze, Lettere ed Arti
MAc	——, Biblioteca Comunale
MAi	——, Istituto Musicale Lucio Campiani
MAp	——, Duomo S Pietro
MAs	——, Seminario Vescovile
MAC	Macerata, Biblioteca Comunale Mozzi-Borgetti
MACa	——, Archivio di Stato
MC	Monte Cassino, Biblioteca dell'Abbazia
ME	Messina, Biblioteca Universitaria
MEmeli	——, Alfonso Meli, private collection
MEnicotra	——, Arturo Nicotra, private collection
MEs	——, Biblioteca Painiana del Seminario Arcivescovile
MFc	Molfetta, Biblioteca Comunale Giovanni Panunzio
MFsr	——, Pontificio Seminario Regionale Pio XI
MFsv	——, Seminario Vescovile
MOa	Modena, Accademia Nazionale di Scienze, Lettere ed Arti
MOd	——, Duomo
MOdep	——, Deputazione di Storia Patria per le Antiche Province Modenesi
MOe	——, Biblioteca Estense
MOf	——, Archivio Ferni
MOl	——, Liceo Musicale Orazio Vecchi
MOs	——, Archivio di Stato
MTventuri	Montecatini-Terme, Antonio Venturi, private collection
MV	Montevergine, Biblioteca del Santuario
MZ	Monza, Insigne Basilica di S Giovanni Battista
MZc	——, Biblioteca Civica
Na	Naples, Archivio di Stato
Nc	——, Conservatorio di Musica S Pietro a Majella
Nf	——, Biblioteca Oratoriana dei Filippini
Nlp	——, Biblioteca Lucchesi-Palli [in Nn]
Nn	——, Biblioteca Nazionale Vittorio Emanuele III
Ns	——, Seminario Arcivescovile
Nsn	——, Società Napoletana di Storia Patria
Nu	——, Biblioteca Universitaria
NO	Novacello, Biblioteca dell'Abbazia
NON	Nonantola, Seminario Abbaziale
NOVc	Novara, Biblioteca Civica
NOVd	——, Archivio Musicale Classico del Duomo
NOVg	——, Archivio e Biblioteca di S Gaudenzio
NOVi	——, Civico Istituto Musicale Brera
NOVsg	——, Archivio Musicale di S Gaudenzio
NT	Noto, Biblioteca Comunale
Oc	Orvieto, Biblioteca Comunale Luigi Fumi
Od	——, Biblioteca dell'Opera del Duomo
OR	Oristano, Seminario Arcivescovile
ORT	Ortona, Biblioteca Comunale
OS	Ostiglia, Biblioteca Musicale Greggiati
OSI	Osimo, Biblioteca Comunale
Pbonelli	Padua, E. Bonelli, private collection
Pc	——, Biblioteca Capitolare
Pca	——, Biblioteca Antoniana, Basilica del Santo
Pci	——, Museo Civico, Biblioteca Civica e Archivio Comunale
Pi(l)	——, Istituto Musicale Cesare Pollini
Ppapafava	——, Novello Papafava dei Carreresi, private collection
Ps	——, Seminario Vescovile
Pu	——, Biblioteca Universitaria
PAac	Parma, Archivio Capitolare
PAas	——, Archivio di Stato
PAc	——, Conservatorio di Musica Arrigo Boito
PAi	——, Istituto di Studi Verdiani
PAsg	——, S Giovanni Evangelista
PAst	——, Madonna della Steccata

PAt	——, Teatro Regio
PAL	Palestrina, Biblioteca Comunale Fantoniana
PAVc	Pavia, S Maria del Carmine
PAVi	——, Civico Istituto Musicale Franco Vittadini
PAVs	——, Seminario Vescovile
PAVsm	——, S Michele
PAVsp	——, S Pietro in Ciel d'Oro
PAVu	——, Biblioteca Universitaria
PCa	Piacenza, Collegio Alberoni
PCc	——, Biblioteca Comunale Passerini Landi
PCcon	——, Conservatorio di Musica G. Nicolini
PCd	——, Duomo
PCsa	——, Biblioteca e Archivio Capitolare di S Antonino
PCsm	——, S Maria di Campagna
PEc	Perugia, Biblioteca Comunale Augusta
PEd	——, Cattedrale
PEl	——, Conservatorio di Musica Francesco Morlacchi
PEsp	——, S Pietro
PEA	Pescia, Biblioteca Comunale Carlo Magnani
PESc	Pesaro, Conservatorio di Musica Gioacchino Rossini
PEScerasa	——, Amadeo Cerasa, private collection [now *VTcerasa*]
PESd	——, Duomo
PESo	——, Biblioteca Oliveriana
PIa	Pisa, Archivio di Stato
PIarc	——, Biblioteca Arcivescovile Cardinale Pietro Maffi
PIc	——, Museo Nazionale di S Matteo
PIca	——, Biblioteca Cateriniana
PIcc	——, Archivio e Biblioteca Certosa di Calci
PIp	——, Archivio Musicale dell'Opera della Primaziale
PIr	——, Biblioteca Raffaelli
PIraffaelli	——, Raffaelli private collection
PIs	——, Fondo Simoneschi
PIst	——, Chiesa dei Cavalieri di S Stefano
PIN	Pinerolo, Biblioteca Comunale Camillo Allinudi
PLa	Palermo, Archivio di Stato
PLcom	——, Biblioteca Comunale
PLcon	——, Conservatorio Vincenzo Bellini
PLd	——, Duomo
PLi	——, Istituto di Storia della Musica, Facoltà di Lettere, Università degli Studi
PLm	——, Teatro Massimo
PLn	——, Biblioteca Nazionale
PLpagano	——, Roberto Pagano, private collection
PLs	——, Baron Pietro Emanuele Sgadari di Lo Monaco, private collection [in Casa di Lavoro e Preghiera Padre Massini]
PLsd	——, Archivio Storico Diocesano
PO	Potenza, Biblioteca Provinciale
POa	——, Archivio di Stato
POd	——, Duomo
PR	Prato, Duomo
PS	Pistoia, Cattedrale
PSc	——, Biblioteca Comunale Forteguerriana
Ra	Rome, Biblioteca Angelica
Rac	——, Accademia di Francia
Raf	——, Accademia Filarmonica Romana
Ras	——, Archivio di Stato
Rc	——, Biblioteca Casanatense
Rcg	——, Curia Generalizia dei Padri Gesuiti; Pontificio Collegio Germano-Ungarico
Rchristoff	——, Boris Christoff, private collection
Rcns	——, Archivio della Chiesa Nazionale Spagnuola
Rco	——, Congregazione dell'Oratorio
Rcsg	——, Oratorio di S Girolamo della Canità
Rdi	——, Discoteca di Stato
Rdp	——, Archivio Doria-Pamphili, private collection
Rf	——, Archivio dei Filippini
Rgiazotto	——, Remo Giazotto, private collection
Ria	——, Istituto Nazionale di Archeologia e Storia dell'Arte
Rif	——, Istituto di Fisiologia dell'Università
Rig	——, Istituto Storico Germanico
Rims	——, Pontificio Istituto di Musica Sacra
Rla	——, Biblioteca Lancisiana
Rli	——, Accademia Nazionale dei Lincei e Corsiniana
Rlib	——, Basilica Liberiana
Rn	——, Biblioteca Nazionale Centrale Vittorio Emanuele III
Rp	——, Biblioteca Pasqualini [in *Rsc*]
Rps	——, Pio Sodalizio di Piceni
Rsc	——, Conservatorio di Musica S Cecilia
Rsg	——, S Giovanni in Laterano
Rsgf	——, Arciconfraternità di S Giovanni dei Fiorentini
Rslf	——, S Luigi de' Francesi
Rsm	——, Archivio Capitolare di S Maria Maggiore [in *Rvat*]
Rsmm	——, S Maria di Monserrato
Rsmt	——, S Maria in Trastevere
Rsp	——, Santo Spirito in Sassia
Rss	——, S Sabina (Venerabile Convento)
Rv	——, Biblioteca Vallicelliana
Rvat	——, Biblioteca Apostolica Vaticana
RA	Ravenna, Duomo
RAc	——, Biblioteca Comunale Classense
RAs	——, Seminario Arcivescovile dei Ss Angeli Custodi
REas	Reggio Emilia, Archivio di Stato
REc	——, Archivio e Biblioteca Capitolare del Duomo
REd	——, Archivio Capitolare del Duomo
REm	——, Biblioteca Municipale
REsp	——, Archivio Capitolare di S Prospero
RIM	Rimini, Biblioteca Civica Gambalunga
RO	Rosate, S Stefano
RVE	Rovereto, Biblioteca Civica Girolamo Tartarotti
RVI	Rovigo, Accademia dei Concordi
Sac	Siena, Accademia Musicale Chigiana
Sas	——, Archivio di Stato
Sc	——, Biblioteca Comunale degli Intronati
Sd	——, Archivio Musicale dell'Opera del Duomo
Smo	——, Biblioteca annessa al Monumento Nazionale di Monte Oliveti Maggiore
SA	Savona, Biblioteca Civica Anton Giulio Barrili
SAL	Saluzzo, Archivio del Duomo
SAS	Sassari, Biblioteca Universitaria
SDF	San Daniele del Friuli, Biblioteca Civica Guarneriana
SE	Senigallia, Biblioteca Comunale Antonelliana
SI	Siracusa, Biblioteca Comunale
SML	Santa Margherita Ligure, Biblioteca Comunale Francesco Domenico Costa
SO	Sant'Oreste, Collegiata di S Lorenzo
SON	Sondrio, Biblioteca Civica Pio Rajna
SPc	Spoleto, Biblioteca Comunale
SPd	——, Duomo
SPE	Spello, Collegiata S Maria Maggiore
ST	Stresa, Biblioteca Rosminiana
SUsb	Subiaco, Biblioteca S Benedetto
SUss	——, Monumenta Nazionale dell'Abbazia di S Scolastica
Ta	Turin, Archivio di Stato
Tb	——, Convento di Benevagienna
Tci	——, Biblioteca Civica Musicale Andrea della Corte
Tco	——, Conservatorio Statale di Musica Giuseppe Verdi
Td	——, Duomo
Tf	——, Accademia Filarmonica
Ti	——, Istituto Salesiano Valsalice
Tmc	——, Museo Civico
Tn	——, Biblioteca Nazionale Universitaria
Tr	——, Biblioteca Reale
Trt	——, Archivio Musicale Radiotelevisione Italiana
TE	Terni, Istituto Musicale G. Briccialdi
TEc	——, Biblioteca Comunale
TI	Termini-Imerese, Biblioteca Liciniana
TLP	Torre del Lago Puccini, Museo di Casa Puccini
TOD	Todi, Biblioteca Comunale Lorenzo Feoni
TOL	Tolentino, Biblioteca Comunale Filelfica
TRa	Trent, Archivio di Stato
TRc	——, Biblioteca Comunale
TRmd	——, Museo Diocesano
TRmn	——, Museo Nazionale
TRmr	——, Museo del Risorgimento
TRE	Tremezzo, Count Gian Ludovico Sola-Cabiati, private collection
TRN	Trani, Biblioteca Comunale G. Bovio
TRP	Trapani, Biblioteca Fardelliana
TSci(com)	Trieste, Biblioteca Civica
TScm	——, Civici Musei di Storia ed Arte
TScon	——, Conservatorio di Musica G. Tartini
TSmt	——, Civico Museo Teatrale di Fondazione Carlo Schmidl
TSsc	——, Fondazione Giovanni Scaramangà de Altomonte
TSsg	——, Archivio della Cappella della Cattedrale S Giusto
TVca(d)	Treviso, Biblioteca Capitolare (Duomo)
TVco	——, Biblioteca Comunale
Us	Urbino, Cappella del Sacramento (Duomo)
Usf	——, S Francesco [in *Uu*]
Uu	——, Biblioteca Universitaria
UD	Udine, Duomo
UDa	——, Archivio di Stato

UDc	——, Biblioteca Comunale Vincenzo Joppi
UDi	——, Istituto Musicale Jacopo Tomadini
URBc	Urbania, Biblioteca Comunale
URBcap	——, Biblioteca Capitolare (Duomo)
Vas	Venice, Archivio di Stato
Vc	——, Conservatorio di Musica Benedetto Marcello
Vcg	——, Biblioteca Casa di Goldoni
Vgc	——, Biblioteca e Istituto della Fondazione Giorgio Cini
Vlevi	——, Fondazione Ugo Levi
Vmarcello	——, Andrighetti Marcello, private collection
Vmc	——, Museo Civico Correr
Vnm	——, Biblioteca Nazionale Marciana
Vqs	——, Accademia Querini-Stampalia
Vs	——, Seminario Patriarcale
Vsf	——, Conventuale di S Francesco
Vsm	——, Procuratoria di S Marco
Vsmc	——, S Maria della Consolazione detta Della Fava
Vt	——, Teatro la Fenice
VAa	Varese, Archivio Prepositurale di S Vittore
VAc	——, Biblioteca Civica
VCc	Vercelli, Biblioteca Civica
VCd	——, Duomo (Biblioteca Capitolare)
VCs	——, Seminario Vescovile
VD	Viadana, Biblioteca Civica
VEaf	Verona, Società Accademia Filarmonica
VEas	——, Archivio di Stato
VEc	——, Biblioteca Civica
VEcap	——, Biblioteca Capitolare (Cattedrale)
VEs	——, Seminario Vescovile
VEsg	——, S Giorgio in Braida
VG	Voghera, Collegiata di S Lorenzo
VIb	Vicenza, Biblioteca Civica Bertoliana
VId	——, Duomo
VImc	——, Museo Civico
VImr	——, Museo del Risorgimento
VIs	——, Seminario Vescovile
VIGsa	Vigévano, Duomo S Ambrogio
VIGsi	——, S Ignazio
VIM	Vimercate, S Stefano
VO	Volterra, Biblioteca Guarnacci
VTc	Viterbo, Biblioteca Comunale degli Ardenti
VTcarosi	——, Attilio Carosi, private collection
VTcerasa	——, Amadeo Cerasa, private collection
VTp	——, Biblioteca Pio XII, Pontificio Seminario Regionale
VTs	——, Seminario Diocesano
VTM	Ventimiglia, Civica Biblioteca Aprosiana

IL: ISRAEL

J	Jerusalem, Jewish National and University Library
Jp	——, Patriarchal Library
S	Mt Sinai
SS	St Sabas, Monastery

IS: ICELAND

Rn	Reykjavik, National Library

J: JAPAN

Tm	Tokyo, Musashino Ongaku Daigaku
Tma(Tmc)	——, Bibliotheca Musashino Academia Musicae
Tn	——, Nanki Music Library, Ohki private collection

N: NORWAY

Bo	Bergen, Offentlige Bibliotek
Bu	——, Universitetsbiblioteket
Oic	Oslo, Norwegian Music Information Centre
Oim	——, Institutt for Musikkvitenskap, Universitet
Ok	——, Musik-Konservatoriet
Onk	——, Norsk Komponistforening
Or	——, Norsk Rikskringkastings
Ou	——, Universitetsbiblioteket
Oum	——, Universitetsbiblioteket, Norsk Musikksamling
T	Trondheim, Kongelige Norske Videnskabers Selskab
Tmi	——, Musikkvitenskapelig Institutt

NL: THE NETHERLANDS

Ad	Amsterdam, Stichting Donemus
At	——, Toonkunst-Bibliotheek
Au	——, Universiteitsbibliotheek
Avnm	——, Bibliotheek der Vereniging voor Nederlandse Muziekgeschiedenis [in *At*]
AN	Amerongen, Archief van het Kasteel der Graven Bentinck, private collection

BI	Bilthoven, Stichting Gaudeamus
D	Deventer, Stads- of Athenaeumbibliotheek
DHa	The Hague, Koninklijk Huisarchief
DHgm	——, Gemeentemuseum
DHk	——, Koninklijke Bibliotheek
DHmw	——, Rijksmuseum
G	Groningen, Universiteitsbibliotheek
Hs	Haarlem, Stadsbibliotheek
HIr	Hilversum, Radio Nederland
L	Leiden, Gemeentearchief
Lml	——, Museum Lakenhal
Lt	——, Bibliotheca Thysiana [in *Lu*]
Lu	——, Bibliotheek der Rijksuniversiteit
Lw	——, Bibliothèque Wallonne
LE	Leeuwarden, Provinciale Bibliotheek van Friesland
R	Rotterdam, Gemeentebibliotheek
'sH	's-Hertogenbosch, Archief van de Illustre Lieve Vrouwe Broederschap
Uim	Utrecht, Instituut voor Muziekwetenschap der Rijksuniversiteit
Usg	——, St Gregorius Vereniging, Bibliotheek [in *Uim*]
Uu	——, Bibliotheek der Rijksuniversiteit

NZ: NEW ZEALAND

Ap	Auckland, Public Library
Au	——, University Library
Dp	Dunedin, Public Library
Wt	Wellington, Alexander Turnbull Library

P: PORTUGAL

AN	Angra do Heroismo, Biblioteca Pública e Arquivo Distrital
AR	Arouca, Museu Regional de Arte Sacra do Mosteiro de Arouca
AV	Aveiro, Museu de Aveiro, Mosteiro de Jesus
BA	Barreiro, Biblioteca Municipal
BRp	Braga, Biblioteca Pública e Arquivo Distrital
BRs	——, Sé de Braga
C	Coimbra, Biblioteca Geral da Universidade
Cm	——, Biblioteca Municipal
Cmn	——, Museu Nacional de Machado de Castro
Cs	——, Sé Nova
Cug	——, Biblioteca Geral da Universidade
Cul	——, Faculdade de Letras da Universidade
CA	Cascais, Museu-Biblioteca Condes de Castro Guimarães
Em	Elvas, Biblioteca Públia Hortênsia
EVc	Évora, Arquivo da Sé
EVp	——, Biblioteca Pública e Arquivo Distrital
F	Figuera da Foz, Biblioteca Pública Municipal Pedro Fernandes Tomás
G	Guimarães, Arquivo Municipal Alfredo Pimenta
La	Lisbon, Palácio Nacional da Ajuda
Laa	——, Academia de Amadores de Musica (Conservatorio Municipal)
Lac	——, Academia das Cieñcias
Lan	——, Arquivo Nacional de Torre do Tombo
Lc	——, Conservatorio Nacional
Lcg	——, Fundação Calouste Gulbenkian
Lf	——, Fábrica da Sé Patriarcal
Lif	——, Instituto de Franca
Ln	——, Biblioteca Nacional
Lr	——, Emissora Nacional de Radiodifusão
Ls	——, Sociedade de Escritores e Compositores Portugueses
Lt	——, Teatro Nacional de S Carlos
LA	Lamego, Biblioteca da Sé
LE	Leiria, Biblioteca Erudita e Arquivo Distrital (Biblioteca Pública)
Mp	Mafra, Palácio Nacional
Pa	Oporto, Ateneu Comercial
Pc	——, Conservatorio de Musica
Pcom	——, Biblioteca Comunale
Peh	——, Museu de Etnografia e Historia
Pf	——, Clube Fenianos Portuenses
Pm	——, Biblioteca Pública Municipal
PD	Ponta Delgada, Biblioteca Pública e Arquivo Distrital
PL	Ponte de Lima, Arquivo da Misericórdia
PO	Portalegre, Arquivo da Sé
Va	Viseu, Arquivo Distrital
Vm	——, Museu Grão Vasco
Vs	——, Arquivo da Sé
VV	Vila Viçosa, Casa da Bragança, Museu-Biblioteca

	PL: POLAND
B	Bydgoszcz, Biblioteka Miejska
BA	Barczew, Archiwum Kościoła Parafialnego
Cb	Cieszyn, Biblioteka Śląska, Oddział Cieszyn
Cp	——, Biblioteka Tschammera w Kościele Ewangelickim
CZp	Częstochowa, Klasztor OO. Paulinów na Jasnej Górze
GD	Gdańsk, Biblioteka Polskiej Akademii Nauk
GNd	Gniezno, Archiwum Archidiecezjalne
GR	Grodzisk, Klasztor OO. Cystersów
Kc	Kraków, Biblioteka Czartoryskich
Kcz	——, Biblioteka Czapskich
Kd	——, Klasztor OO. Dominikanów
Kj	——, Biblioteka Jagiellońska
Kk	——, Kapituła Metropolitalna
Kp	——, Biblioteka Polskiej Akademii Nauk
Kpa	——, Archiwum Państwowe
Kz	——, Biblioteka Czartoryskich
KA	Katowice, Biblioteka Śląska
KO	Kórnik, Polska Akademia Nauk, Biblioteka Kórnicka
Lk	Lublin, Biblioteka Katolickiego Uniwersytetu
Lw	——, Biblioteka Wojewódzka i Miejska im. H. Łopacińskiego
ŁA	Łańcut, Muzeum
ŁO	Łowicz, Biblioteka Seminarium
MO	Mogiła, Klasztor OO. Cystersów
OB	Obra, Klasztor OO. Cystersów
Pa	Poznań, Biblioteka Archidiecezjalna
Pr	——, Miejska Biblioteka Publiczna im. Edwarda Raczyńskiego
Pu	——, Biblioteka Uniwersytecka
PE	Pelplin, Biblioteka Seminarium Duchownego
PŁp	Płock, Biblioteka Towarzystwa Naukowego
R	Raków, Archiwum Kościelne
SA	Sandomierz, Seminarium Duchownego
SZ	Szalowa, Archiwum Parafialne
Tu	Toruń, Biblioteka Uniwersytecka
TA	Tarnów, Archiwum Archidiecezjalne
Wm	Warszawa, Biblioteka Muzeum Narodowego
Wn	——, Biblioteka Narodowa
Wp	——, Biblioteka Publiczna
Ws	——, Biblioteka Synodalna Ewangelicka
Wtm	——, Biblioteka Warszawskiego Towarzystwa Muzycznego
Wu	——, Biblioteka Uniwersytecka
WL	Wilanów, Biblioteka, Oddział Muzeum Narodowego Warszawy
WRol	Wrocław, Biblioteka Ossolineum Leopoldiensis
WRu	——, Biblioteka Uniwersytecka
	R: ROMANIA
Ab	Aiud, Biblioteca Documentară Bethlen
Ba	Bucharest, Biblioteca Academiei Republicii Socialiste România
Bc	——, Biblioteca Centrală de Stat
BRm	Brașov, Biblioteca Municipală
Sb	Sibiu, Muzeul Brukenthal
TMt	Tîrgu Mureș, Biblioteca Documentară Teleki
	S: SWEDEN
A	Arvika, Folkliga Musikskolan
E	Enköping, Samrealskolans Arkiv
ES	Eskilstuna, Stadsbiblioteket
Gem	Göteborg, Etnografiska Museet
Ghl	——, Hvitfeldtska Högre Allmänna Läroverket
Gu	——, Universitetsbiblioteket (formerly Stadsbiblioteket)
GÄ	Gävle, Vasaskolans Bibliotek
Hfryklund	Hälsingborg, D. Daniel Fryklund, private collection [in *Skma*]
Hs	——, Stadsbiblioteket
J	Jönköping, Per Brahegymnasiet
K	Kalmar, Stifts- och Gymnasiebiblioteket
KA	Karlstad, Stadsbiblioteket
KAT	Katrineholm, Stadsbiblioteket
KH	Karlshamn, Museums Biblioteket
L	Lund, Universitetsbiblioteket
Lbarnekow	——, Barnekow private collection
LB	Leufsta Bruk, De Geer private collection
LI	Linköping, Stifts- och Landsbiblioteket
M	Malmö, Stadsbiblioteket
N	Norrköping, Stadsbiblioteket
Ö	Örebro, Karolinska Skolans Bibliotek
ÖS	Östersund, Jämtlands Läns Bibliotek
Sdt	Stockholm, Drottningholms Teatermuseum
Sic	——, Stims Informationscentral för Svensk Musik
Sk	——, Kungliga Biblioteket
Skma	——, Kungliga Musikaliska Akademiens Bibliotek
Sm	——, Musikmuseet
Smf	——, Stiftelsen Musikkulturens Främjande
Sn	——, Nordiska Museet
Ssr	——, Sveriges Radio
St	——, Kungliga Teaterns Bibliotek
SK	Skara, Stifts- och Landsbiblioteket
STd	Strängnäs, Domkyrkobiblioteket
STr	——, Roggebiblioteket
Uifm	Uppsala, Institutionen för Musikforskning vid Uppsala Universitetet
Uu	——, Universitetsbiblioteket
V	Västerås, Stadsbiblioteket
VII	Visby, Landsarkivet
VIs	——, Stadsbiblioteket
VX	Växjö, Landsbiblioteket
	SF: FINLAND
A	Turku [Åbo], Sibelius Museum Musikvetenskapliga Institutionen vid Åbo Akademi, Bibliotek & Arkiv
Aa	——, Åbo Akademis, Bibliotek
Hko	Helsinki, Helsingin Kaupunginorkester
Hmt	——, Musiikin Tiedotuskeskus
Hr	——, Oy Yleisradio AB, Nuotisto
Hs	——, Sibelius-Akatemian Kirjasto
Hy	——, Helsingin Yliopiston Kirjasto
Hyf	——, Helsingin Yliopiston Kirjasto, Department of Finnish Music
TA	Tampere, Tampereen Yliopiston Kansanperinteen Laitos
	US: UNITED STATES OF AMERICA
AA	Ann Arbor, University of Michigan Music Library
AB	Albany, New York State Library
AL	Allentown (Penn.), Muhlenberg College, John A. W. Haas Library
AM	Amherst (Mass.), Amherst College, Robert Frost Building
ATu	Atlanta (Georgia), Emory University Library
AU	Aurora (NY), Wells College Library
AUS	Austin, University of Texas
Ba	Boston, Athenaeum Library
Bbs	——, Bostonian Society
Bc	——, New England Conservatory of Music
Bco	——, American Congregational Society, Congregational Library
Bfa	——, Fine Arts Museum
Bge	——, School of Fine Arts, General Education Library
Bh	——, Harvard Musical Association
Bhh	——, Handel and Haydn Society
Bhs	——, Massachusetts Historical Society
Bl	——, Grand Lodge of Masons in Massachusetts, A. F. and A. M. Library
Bm	——, University, Mugar Memorial Library
Bp	——, Public Library, Music Department
Bth	——, University, School of Theology
BAep	Baltimore, Enoch Pratt Free Library, Fine Arts and Music Department
BAhs	——, Maryland Historical Society
BApi	——, City Library, Peabody Institute
BAu	——, Johns Hopkins University Libraries
BAw	——, Walters Art Gallery
BAT	Baton Rouge, Louisiana State University Library
BE	Berkeley, University of California, Music Library
BER	Berea (Ohio), Baldwin-Wallace College, Ritter Library of the Conservatory
BETm	Bethlehem (Penn.), Archives of the Moravian Church in Bethlehem
BETu	——, Lehigh University, Lucy Packer Lindeman Memorial Library
BG	Bangor (Maine), Public Library
BK	Brunswick (Maine), Bowdoin College, Department of Music
BLl	Bloomington, Indiana University, Lilly Library
BLu	——, Indiana University, School of Music Library
BO	Boulder, University of Colorado Music Library
BRc	Brooklyn, Brooklyn College Music Library
BRp	——, Public Library
BU	Buffalo, Buffalo and Erie County Public Library
Charding	Chicago, W. N. H. Harding, private collection [in *GB-Ob*]
Chs	——, Chicago Historical Society Library
Cn	——, Newberry Library

Cu	——, University Music Library
CA	Cambridge, Harvard University Music Libraries
CAR	Carlisle (Penn.), Dickinson College
CDhs	Concord, New Hampshire Historical Society
CDs	——, New Hampshire State Library
CG	Coral Gables (Florida), University of Miami Music Library
CHua	Charlottesville, University of Virginia, Alderman Library
CHum	——, University of Virginia Music Library
CHH	Chapel Hill, University of North Carolina Music Library
CIhc	Cincinnati, Hebrew Union College
CIu	——, University of Cincinnati College-Conservatory of Music
CLm	Cleveland, Museum of Art, Cantatorium
CLp	——, Public Library, Fine Arts Department
CLwr	——, Western Reserve University, Freiberger Library and Music House Library
COu	Columbus, Ohio State University Music Library
CR	Cedar Rapids, Iowa Masonic Library
Dp	Detroit, Public Library, Music and Performing Arts Department
DB	Dearborn (Mich.), Henry Ford Museum and Greenfield Village
DE	Denver (Colorado), Public Library, Art and Music Division
DM	Durham (North Carolina), Duke University Libraries
DN	Denton, North Texas State University Music Library
DO	Dover (New Hampshire), Public Library
Eg	Evanston (Ill.), Garrett Theological Seminary
Eu	——, Northwestern University, Music Library
ECstarr	Eastchester (NY), Saul Starr, private collection
EXd	Exeter (New Hampshire), Phillips Exeter Academy, Davis Library
EXp	——, Public Library
FW	Fort Worth, Southwest Baptist Theological Seminary
G	Gainesville, University of Florida Library, Rare Book Collection
GA	Gambier (Ohio), Kenyon College Divinity School, Colburn Library
GB	Gettysburg, Lutheran Theological Seminary
GR	Granville (Ohio), Denison University Library
GRE	Greenville (Delaware), Eleutherian Mills Historical Library
Hhs	Hartford, Connecticut Historical Society Library
Hm	——, Case Memorial Library, Hartford Seminary Foundation
Hp	——, Public Library, Art and Music Department
Hs	——, Connecticut State Library
Hw	——, Trinity College, Watkinson Library
HA	Hanover (New Hampshire), Dartmouth College, Baker Library
HB	Harrisonburg (Virginia), Eastern Mennonite College, Menno Simons Historical Library and Archives
HG	Harrisburg, Pennsylvania State Library
HO	Hopkinton, New Hampshire Antiquarian Society
HU	Huntingdon (Penn.), Juniata College, L. A. Beechly Library
I	Ithaca (NY), Cornell University Music Library
IO	Iowa, University of Iowa Music Library
K	Kent (Ohio), Kent State University Library
Lu	Lawrence, University of Kansas Libraries
LAu	Los Angeles, University of California, Walter H. Rubsamen Music Library
LAuc	——, University of California, William Andrews Clark Memorial Library
LAusc	——, University of Southern California School of Music
LB	Lewisburg (Penn.), Bucknell University, Ellen Clark Bertrand Library
LChs	Lancaster (Penn.), Lancaster County Historical Society
LCm	——, Lancaster Mennonite Historical Library and Archives
LCts	——, Theological Seminary of the United Church of Christ
LEX	Lexington, University of Kentucky, Margaret I. King Library
LOs	Louisville (Ky.), Southern Baptist Theological Seminary, James P. Boyce Centennial Library
LOu	——, University, School of Music Library

LU	Lincoln University (Penn.), Vail Memorial Library
M	Milwaukee, Public Library, Art and Music Department
MI	Middletown (Conn.), Wesleyan University, Olin Memorial Library
MORduncan	Morgantown, Richard E. Duncan, private collection
MSp	Minneapolis, Public Library
MSu	——, University of Minnesota Music Library
MV	Mt Vernon (Virginia), Mt Vernon Ladies Association of the Union Collection
Nf	Northampton (Mass.), Forbes Library
Nsc	——, Smith College, Werner Josten Music Library
NAZ	Nazareth (Penn.), Moravian Historical Society
NBs	New Brunswick, Theological Seminary, Gardner A. Sage Library
NBu	——, Rutgers University Library
NEm	Newark (NJ), Newark Museum
NEp	——, Public Library
NH	New Haven, Yale University, School of Music Library
NORts	New Orleans, Theological Seminary
NORtu	——, Tulane University, Howard Tilton Memorial Library
NP	Newburyport (Mass.), Public Library
NYcc	New York, City College Library, Music Library
NYcu	——, Columbia University Music Library
NYfo	——, Fordham University Library
NYfuld	——, James J. Fuld, private collection
NYgo	——, University, Gould Memorial Library
NYgr	——, Grolier Club
NYhc	——, Hunter College Library
NYhs	——, New York Historical Society
NYhsa	——, Hispanic Society of America
NYj	——, Juilliard School of Music
NYlateiner	——, Jacob Lateiner, private collection
NYma	——, Mannes College of Music, Clara Damrosch Mannes Memorial Library
NYmc	——, City Museum, Theatre and Music Department
NYmm	——, Metropolitan Museum of Art, Thomas J. Watson Library
NYp	——, Public Library at Lincoln Center, Library and Museum of the Performing Arts
NYpm	——, Pierpont Morgan Library
NYq	——, Queens College of the City University, Paul Klapper Library, Music Library
NYts	——, Union Theological Seminary
OA	Oakland (Calif.), Public Library
OAm	——, Mills College, Margaret Prall Music Library
OB	Oberlin, Oberlin College Conservatory of Music
Pc	Pittsburgh, Carnegie Library
Pfinney	——, Theodore M. Finney, private collection [in *Pu*]
Ps	——, Theological Seminary, Clifford E. Barbour Library
Pu	——, University of Pittsburgh, Theodore Finney Music Library
PD	Portland, Maine Historical Society
PER	Perryville (Missouri), St Mary's Seminary
PHbo	Philadelphia, St Charles Borromeo Theological Seminary
PHbs	——, William Bacon Stevens Library
PHchs	——, American Catholic Historical Society of Philadelphia
PHci	——, Curtis Institute of Music
PHem	——, Eric Mandell Collection of Jewish Music
PHf	——, Free Library of Philadelphia
PHhs	——, Historical Society of Pennsylvania
PHkm	——, Lutheran Theological Seminary
PHlc	——, Library Company of Philadelphia
PHma	——, Musical Academy
PHphs	——, Presbyterian Historical Society
PHps	——, American Philosophical Society
PHr	——, Philip H. and A. S. W. Rosenbach Foundation
PHtr	——, Trinity Lutheran Church of Germantown
PHts	——, Westminster Theological Seminary
PHu	——, University of Pennsylvania, Otto E. Albrecht Music Library
PIlevy	——, Pikesville (Maryland), Lester S. Levy, private collection
PL	Portland (Oregon), Library Association of Portland, Music Department
PO	Poughkeepsie, Vassar College, George Sherman Dickinson Music Library
PRs	Princeton, Theological Seminary
PRu	——, University, Harvey S. Firestone Memorial Library

PROhs	Providence, Rhode Island Historical Society
PROu	——, Brown University Libraries
R	——, Rochester, University, Eastman School of Music, Sibley Music Library
RI	Richmond, Virginia State Library
Sp	Seattle, Public Library
Su	——, University of Washington Music Library
SA	Salem (Mass.), Essex Institute, James Duncan Phillips Library
SB	Santa Barbara, University of California, Library
SFp	San Francisco, Public Library, Fine Arts Department, Music Division
SFs	——, Sutro Library
SFsc	——, San Francisco State College Library, Frank V. de Bellis Collection
SHE	Sherman (Texas), Austin College, Arthur Hopkins Library
SLc	St Louis, Concordia Seminary
SLf	——, Fontbonne College
SLkrohn	——, Ernst C. Krohn, private collection
SLug	——, Washington University, Gaylord Music Library
SLC	Salt Lake City, University of Utah Library
SM	San Marino (Calif.), Henry E. Huntington Library and Art Gallery
SPmoldenhauer	Spokane (Washington), Hans Moldenhauer, private collection
STu	Stanford, University, Division of Humanities and Social Sciences, Music Library
SW	Swarthmore (Penn.), Swarthmore College Library
SY	Syracuse, University Music Library and George Arents Research Library
Tm	Toledo, Toledo Museum of Art
TA	Tallahassee, Florida State University, Robert Manning Strozier Library
U	Urbana, University of Illinois Music Library
Ufraenkel	——, Fraenkel collection
UP	University Park, Pennsylvania State University Library
Wc	Washington, DC, Library of Congress, Music Division
Wca	——, Cathedral
Wcu	——, Catholic University of America Music Library
Wgu	——, Georgetown University Libraries
Ws	——, Folger Shakespeare Library
Wsc	——, Scottish Rite Masons, Supreme Council
Wsi	——, Smithsonian Institution, Music Library
WA	Watertown (Mass.), Perkins School for the Blind
WC	Waco (Texas), Baylor University Music Library
WE	Wellesley (Mass.), Wellesley College Library
WELhartzler	Wellman (Iowa), J. D. Hartzler, private collection
WGc	Williamsburg (Virginia), College of William and Mary
WGw	——, Colonial Williamsburg Research Department, historical collection
WI	Williamstown (Mass.), Williams College, Chapin Library
WM	Waltham (Mass.), Brandeis University Library, Music Library, Goldfarb Library
WOa	Worcester (Mass.), American Antiquarian Society
WS	Winston-Salem (North Carolina), Moravian Music Foundation

USSR: UNION OF SOVIET SOCIALIST REPUBLICS

J	Jelgava, Muzei
Kan	Kiev, Tsentral'naya Naukova Biblioteka, Akademiya Nauk URSR
Kk	——, Biblioteka Gosudarstvennoy Konservatoriy imeni P. I. Chaykovskovo
KA	Kaliningrad, Oblastnaya Biblioteka
KAg	——, Gosudarstvennaya Biblioteka
KAu	——, Universitetskaya Biblioteka
KI	Kishinev, Biblioteka Gosudarstvennoy Konservatoriy imeni G. Muzichesku
Lan	Leningrad, Biblioteka Akademii Nauk SSSR
Lia	——, Gosudarstvennïy Tsentral'nïy Istoricheskïy Arkhiv
Lil	——, Institut Russkoy Literaturï
Lit	——, Leningradsky Gosudarstvennïy Institut Teatra, Muzïki i Kinematografii
Lk	——, Biblioteka Leningradskoy Gosudarstvennoy Konservatoriy imeni N. A. Rimskovo-Korsakova
Lph	——, Muzïkal'naya Biblioteka Leningradskoy Gosudarstvennoy Filarmonii
Lsc	——, Gosudarstvennaya Ordena Trudovovo Krasnovo Znameni Publichnaya Biblioteka imeni M. E. Saltïkova-Shchedrina
Lt	——, Leningradskiy Gosudarstvennïy Teatral'nïy Muzey
Ltob	——, Tsentral'naya Muzïkal'naya Biblioteka Gosudarstvennovo Akademicheskovo Teatra Operï i Baleta imeni S. M. Kirova
LV	L'vov, Biblioteka Gosudarstvennoy Konservatoriy imeni N. V. Lysenko
Mcl	Moscow, Gosudarstvennïy Tsentral'nïy Literaturnïy Arkhiv
Mcm	——, Gosudarstvennïy Tsentral'nïy Muzey Muzïkal'noy Kul'turï imeni M. I. Glinki
Mk	——, Gosudarstvennaya Konservatoriya imeni P. I. Chaykovskovo, Nauchnaya Muzïkal'naya Biblioteka imeni S. I. Taneyeva
Ml	——, Gosudarstvennaya Ordena Lenina Biblioteka SSSR imeni V. I. Lenina
Mm	——, Gosudarstvennïyi Istoricheskïyi Muzei
Mt	——, Gosudarstvennïyi Teatral'nïyi Muzei imeni A. Bakhrushina
MI	Minsk, Biblioteka Belorusskoy Gosudarstvennoy Konservatoriy
O	Odessa, Biblioteka Gosudarstvennoy Konservatoriy imeni A. V. Nezhdanovoy
R	Riga, Biblioteka Gosudarstvennoy Konservatoriy Latviyskoy imeni J. Vitola
TAu	Tartu, Universitetskaya Biblioteka
TAL	Tallinn, Biblioteka Gosudarstvennoy Konservatoriy
TB	Tbilisi, Biblioteka Gosudarstvennoy Konservatoriy imeni V. Saradzhisvili
V	Vilnius, Biblioteka Gosudarstvennoy Konservatoriy Litovskoy SSR

YU: YUGOSLAVIA

Bn	Belgrade, Narodna Biblioteka N. R. Srbije
Dsd	Dubrovnik, Knjižnica Samostana Dominikanaca
Dsmb	——, Franjevački Samostan Mala Braća
La	Ljubljana, Knjižnica Akademije za Glasbo
Lf	——, Knjižnica Frančiškanskega Samostana
Ls	——, Škofijski Arhiv in Biblioteka
Lsa	——, Slovenska Akademija Znanosti in Umjetnosti
Lsk	——, Arhiv Stolnega Kora
Lu	——, Narodna in Univerzitetna Knjižnica
MAk	Maribor, Glazbeni Arhiv Katedrale
MAs	——, Knjižnica Škofijskega Arhiva
NM	Novo Mesto, Knjižnica Frančiškanskega Samostana
NMc	——, Glazbeni Arhiv Katedrale
O	Ohrid, Narodno Museum
Sk	Split, Glazbeni Arhiv Katedrale
Ssf	——, Knjižnica Samostana Sv Frane
Za	Zagreb, Jugoslavenska Akademija Znanosti i Umjetnosti
Zda	——, Državni Arhiv
Zha	——, Hrvatski Glazbeni Zavod
Zk	——, Glazbeni Arhiv Katedrale
Zs	——, Glazbeni Arhiv Bogoslovnog Sjemeništa
Zu	——, Nacionalna i Sveučilišna Biblioteka

Volume Eighteen

Spiridion–Tin whistle

A Note on the Use of the Dictionary

This note is intended as a short guide to the basic procedures and organization of the dictionary. A fuller account will be found in the Introduction, vol.1, pp.xi–xx.

Abbreviations in general use in the dictionary are listed on pp.vii–x; bibliographical ones (periodicals, reference works, editions etc) are listed on pp.xi–xiii.

Alphabetization of headings is based on the principle that words are read continuously, ignoring spaces, hyphens, accents, bracketed matter etc, up to the first comma; the same principle applies thereafter. 'Mc' and 'M'' are listed as 'Mac', 'St' as 'Saint'.

Bibliographies are arranged chronologically (within section, where divided), in order of year of first publication, and alphabetically by author within years.

Cross-references are shown in small capitals, with a large capital at the beginning of the first word of the entry referred to. Thus 'The instrument is related to the BASS TUBA' would mean that the entry referred to is not '**Bass tuba**' but '**Tuba, bass**'.

Work-lists are normally arranged chronologically (within section, where divided). Italic symbols used in them (like *D-Dlb* or *GB-Lbm*) refer to the libraries holding sources, and are explained on pp. xiv–xxx; each national sigillum stands until contradicted.

S

CONTINUED

Spiridion [Pater a Monte Carmelo; Nenning, Johann] (*b* Neustadt an der Saale, Bavaria, 16 July 1615; *d* Bamberg, 21 Nov 1685). German composer and organist. He entered the Carmelite order at the age of 17 and in 1643 was organist of the Seminario Germanico, Rome. He then spent a few years in Belgium, returning to Germany in 1650. In 1658 he was vicar of the convent at Neustadt an der Saale. In 1660 he was a preacher and 'adiutor musicorum' in Prague and in 1664 was transferred to Bamberg. He carried out duties for his order at Fährbrück, near Würzburg, in 1667 and then at Obergriesheim, near Heilbronn, before returning to the monastery at Bamberg in 1670. In his *Nova instructio* he stated that he had received his musical education from Abbot Francesco of Spezia. His *Musica romana* is a product of this Italian influence; it is a collective volume including 13 works by Carissimi, Francesco Foggia and Bonifazio Graziani and a *Salve regina* of his own. His masses of 1668 are in the concertato style. The *Nova instructio pro pulsandis organis, spinettis, manuchordiis* (vols.i and ii, Bamberg, 1669–71; vol.iv, Gerbstedt, 1675) is a manual offering important evidence about performing and composing techniques in the second half of the 17th century.

WORKS
Musica romana, 3vv, 2 vn ad lib (Nuremberg, 1665³)
Musica theo-liturgica ... complectens 4 missas, 5vv, 2 vn ad lib (Würzburg, 1668)

BIBLIOGRAPHY
A. Göhler: *Verzeichnis der in den Frankfurter und Leipziger Messkatalogen der Jahre 1564 bis 1759 angezeigten Musikalien* (Leipzig, 1902/R1965)
F. W. Riedel: *Quellenkundliche Beiträge zur Geschichte der Musik für Tasteninstrumente* (Kassel, 1960)

AUGUST SCHARNAGL

Spirito da Reggio. *See* PRATONERI, GASPERO.

Spiritoso (It.: 'vivacious', 'alcoholic', 'ingenious'). Spirited, lively. As a tempo mark and as a qualification it has several forms, including *spirituoso, con spirito* ('with vivacity'), the adverb *spiritosamente* and the French adverb *spirituellement*. Two meanings have been current. The first is the slower one described by Brossard (1703): '*Spiritoso* or *spirituosò*; one also says *con spirito* or *con spirto*. It means with spirit [*esprit*], with soul, with judgment and discretion. It is also rather like *affettuoso*'. Similar definitions appear in Rousseau (1768) and Escudier (1844), both of whom placed it in the hierarchy between *adagio* and *andante*; and several early 18th-century uses (*largo spiritoso, adagio spiritoso*) suggest this same meaning.

The second meaning is most clearly expressed by Mozart, who in a letter of 7 August 1782 wrote of the *allegro con spirito* opening to his Haffner Symphony: 'Das erste Allegro muss recht feurig gehen' ('The first *allegro* must go with real fire'). That meaning, which is the one most commonly used today, stretches back well into the 18th century: there are several movements in Domenico Scarlatti and Rameau, for instance, that are so marked and must be fast. Alessandro Scarlatti's *Genuinda* (1694) includes the tempo mark *allegrissimo e spiritoso*.

For bibliography *see* TEMPO AND EXPRESSION MARKS.

DAVID FALLOWS

Spiritual. A type of folksong which originated in American revivalist activity between 1740 and the close of the 19th century. The term is derived from 'spiritual songs', a designation used in early publications to distinguish the texts from metrical psalms and hymns of traditional church usage.

I. White. II. Black.

I. White. The category 'white spiritual' includes the 'folk hymn', the 'religious ballad' and the 'camp-meeting spiritual', which is the counterpart of the 'negro spiritual' and shares with it certain musical elements, symbolism and probably a common origin.

This extensive genre was unnoticed in the USA until George Pullen Jackson, a professor at Vanderbilt University in Nashville, Tennessee, published *White Spirituals in the Southern Uplands* (1933), the first of a series of studies which documented its existence both in oral tradition and in its published form in the 'shape-note' tune books of rural communities (*see* SHAPE-NOTE HYMNODY). The existence of the spirituals among English Primitive Methodists was described by Anne Gilchrist (1927).

1. The folk hymn and the religious ballad. 2. The camp-meeting spiritual.

1. THE FOLK HYMN AND THE RELIGIOUS BALLAD. The folk hymn has been defined by Irving Lowens as 'basically a secular folktune which happens to be sung to a religious text'. The religious ballad, with a narrative text, may be similarly described. Folk hymns were the first spirituals to appear in the USA. Following the religious revival in the early 18th century called the Great Awakening, which was led by George Whitefield, Jonathan Edwards, James Davenport and others, converts from Congregationalist and Presbyterian churches formed 'new light' or 'new side' churches while remain-

ing within the organized denominations. Their musical expression was confined principally to settings of Watts's hymn and psalm texts. A more radical group of converts called 'Separatists' formed independent congregations. In New England they eventually merged with another disenfranchised sect, the Baptists, and it was in this religious tradition that the earliest folk-hymn texts and music originated.

Separatist Baptists believed that their musical texts, like all religious expression, should be intensely personal, exuberant, experiential and free from doctrinal restraints. James Davenport, an early Separatist evangelist, published a text in 1742 which was a prototype:

> Then should my soul with angels feast
> On joys that always last
> Blest be my God, the God of Joy
> Who gives me here a taste.

John Leland (1754–1841), a Baptist minister, wrote (1799):

> Come and taste along with me
> Consolation running free
> From my Father's wealthy throne
> Sweeter than the honeycomb.

Publications containing texts of Separatist Baptist music began to appear in the 1780s in the frontier areas of New England. The most popular was that of Joshua Smith: *Divine Hymns or Spiritual Songs for the Use of Religious Assemblies and Private Christians* (1794), which contains texts by Watts and the English evangelicals but also includes texts of American folk origin. Some texts have added refrains and tag lines, the principal characteristic of the camp-meeting spiritual of the early 19th century.

The tunes used for the early texts are much more difficult to document. The first reliable source was *The Christian Harmony* (Exeter, New Hampshire, 1805) by Jeremiah Ingalls, a singing master and composer in the tradition of William Billings and Andrew Law. He included among his fuging-tunes and set pieces a number of melodies which apparently were popular among his Baptist neighbours, harmonized in the style of the New England composers. The principal feature of the melodies of Ingalls and the many compilers who followed him is their relationship to secular folktunes of the British Isles. Some can be identified as appropriations of entire melodies, while others are clearly related in terms of contour, intervallic motifs, ornamentation and musical form. The tunes use scales other than the conventional heptatonic major and minor, and 'gapped scales' are frequently found (ex.1). They exist in both oral and printed forms.

Revivalist converts were encouraged to 'testify' or 'witness' in their singing to the joy that religion had

brought them. Some recounted their experiences in narrative, giving birth to a related form called the 'religious ballad'. Examples were *Wayfaring Stranger*, *Romish Lady* and *Wicked Polly*. These ballads became a means of witnessing to and teaching the young. Early examples of the genre first appeared in Anna Beeman's *Hymns on Various Subjects* (1792) and in John Peak's compilation *A New Collection of Hymns . . . and Spiritual Songs . . . Some Entirely New* (1793). The following example from Peak is typical:

> I hear the gospel's joyful sound
> An organ I shall be
> To sound aloud redeeming love
> And sinner's misery.

The religious ballads are the white spirituals most closely related to secular folktunes. Jackson transcribed many of the ballads found in oral tradition for *Spiritual Folk-songs of Early America* and *Another Sheaf of White Spirituals*, and related them to specific secular tunes. Ingalls and John Wyeth, whose *Repository of Sacred Music, Part Second* appeared in 1813, provided conclusive evidence that the early converts drew on their knowledge of folk and popular tunes to give musical expression to their new religious feeling. An example from *The Christian Harmony* of secular music appropriated for a religious text is *Christ the Appletree*, set to *Handel's Quick March*, a popular fife tune of the 18th century (see ex.2). This practice was not unknown

Ex.2

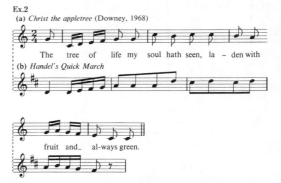

(a) *Christ the appletree* (Downey, 1968)

The tree of life my soul hath seen, la – den with

(b) *Handel's Quick March*

fruit and_ al-ways green.

in previous religious movements, and it continued in the USA as an outstanding characteristic of the later camp-meeting spiritual, the gospel songs of the Moody–Sankey era (late 19th century), and the 20th-century Christian folk-rock musical.

2. THE CAMP-MEETING SPIRITUAL. This is closely related to the folk hymn but is characterized by simplicity of text, frequent repetition, refrains and tag lines. Its music is related to existing folktunes, but is not entirely derivative. It resulted from a new wave of revivalistic activity beginning in 1800 in the areas of pioneer settlement (the 'Great Revival').

The camp meeting, an open-air religious service lasting several days, brought together thousands of settlers of all denominations. At similar Baptist services as early as 1770 hymns with added refrains were sung, although James McGready was credited with initiating the practice in 1800 in Logan County, Kentucky. Diversity of belief and practice was secondary to the religious fervour which permeated the preaching, singing, baptisms and Communion rites. The event was primarily social, giving settlers a release from the isolation and hardship

Ex.1 *Pisgah*, transcr. G. P. Jackson

Je – sus, thou art the sin – ner's friend As_

such I look to thee_____ Now in the bowels

of thy love, O Lord re-mem-ber_ me.

which characterized their daily lives; it provided occasions for religious frenzy, fed by evangelists of all persuasions and by the constant singing in the encampment. Out of this came the camp-meeting spiritual, directly prompted by the emotional fervour of the participants, and as varied in text and tunes as the diverse religious practices represented by the meeting.

Within the camp, particularly in the southern states, Negroes, both slaves and free men, mingled with whites, but conducted their religious meetings separately. The similarity of texts and tunes between white and black spirituals indicates a free exchange of musical elements and influences (see §II).

In the camp meetings, texts by Watts and from the collections of Joseph Hart and John Rippon were fragmented and supplied with tag lines and refrains. Tunes of the simplest order were improvised by the congregations. Participants drew on the musical sources of their denomination, but the religious expression of the Separatists, now institutionalized among Baptists, prevailed. Methodists readily adopted the practice. Repetition of text and music was characteristic:

> Where, O where are the Hebrew Children?
> Where, O where are the Hebrew Children?
> Where, O where are the Hebrew Children?
> Safe in the promised land.

Refrains were often added to existing texts:

> Whither goest thou, pilgrim stranger
> Passing through this darksome vale
> Knowest thou not 'tis full of danger
> And will not thy courage fail
> I am bound for the kingdom
> Will you go to glory with me
> Hallelujah, praise the Lord.

Tag lines were frequently inserted into a couplet:

> I know that my Redeemer lives,
>   Glory hallelujah!
> What comfort this sweet sentence gives,
>   Glory hallelujah!

In simpler form a couplet was followed by a refrain:

> O when shall I see Jesus
> And dwell with him above
>   And shall hear the trumpet sound
>   In that morning
>
> And from the flowing fountain
> Drink everlasting love
>   And shall hear the trumpet sound
>   In that morning

The repetition, tag lines, and refrains provided for participation in 'call and response' performances between evangelist and people. The most popular forms were four-line arrangements of *AAAB*, and the couplet with tag line, *A* (tag) *B* (tag). Refrains followed similar arrangements, and used the melody of the verse or a new tune with a higher tessitura (see §II, ex.4*a*).

The texts of the camp-meeting spiritual appeared first in pocket 'songsters' without music, compiled by ministers and enterprising laymen and sold on the site. Camp meetings became a community tradition in the 19th century and still occur in isolated areas of the southern states. After the Civil War (1861–5) there were only two significant publications for camp meetings: the *Revival and Camp Meeting Minstrel* (1867), popularly known as 'The Perkinpine Songster', and Joseph Hillman's *The Revivalist* (*c*1868).

The tunes of the folk hymns, religious ballads and spirituals persist in the rich oral tradition of the southern states (described by Jackson, Cecil Sharp and others in the early 20th century) and they retain much of the modal character of the original secular melodies. Printed sources of the folk hymns and spirituals are the shape-note tune books of the rural 'singing school' choral tradition. Wyeth's *Repository of Sacred Music, Part Second* (1813) was the first of a series of tune books used by itinerant music teachers who composed works in the style of Billings and Law, and in imitation of their models added treble, alto and bass parts to the melodies they transcribed from common usage (see ex.3, taken from the *Original Sacred Harp, Denson Revision*, where the tune is in the tenor part and is in the 'natural minor' or A mode; the harmonization – even the alto part added in the early 20th century – stays within this modal scheme, and emphasizes two-note rather than triadic harmony, particularly open 5ths and octaves).

Ex.3 *Kedron* (Denson, 1936)

Harry Eskew (1966) traced the history of these publications, identified the folk hymns and spirituals in each, and described their movement into the southern states. In particular, he documented the work of Ananias Davisson, who published the *Kentucky Harmony* (1816, suppl. 1820–25). William Walker's *The Southern Harmony and Musical Companion* (1835), and Benjamin F. White and E. J. King's *The Sacred Harp* (1847) both contain folk hymns and spirituals. Levi C. Myers's *Manual of Sacred Music* (1853) shows the strong preference for the camp-meeting songs.

An attempt to publish camp-meeting songs and other music for revivals in the cities of the northern states was made by Joshua Leavitt with *The Christian Lyre* (1830–31), but white spirituals never became popular in urban areas. From 1875, the main impetus of the revival movement was provided by the urban crusades of Dwight L. Moody and Ira Sankey and, later, the work of Billy Sunday and Homer Rodeheaver. The musical products of this era of revivalism, the gospel hymns and songs (*see* GOSPEL MUSIC), were popular in style, and, in many instances, their music was taken directly from contemporary music-hall and parlour songs.

A revival of interest in the folk hymns and spirituals among choral directors and composers in recent years is evident in the increased number of choral arrangements and orchestral works in which the tunes are used; and compilers of hymnals, particularly those of Baptist and Methodist denominations, have made use of many of the tunes and texts in their publications.

II. Black

1. Early collections. 2. African and European sources. 3. Texts. 4. After 1870.

1. EARLY COLLECTIONS. Black spirituals constitute one of the largest bodies of American folksong that have survived to the 20th century, and are probably the best known. They are principally associated with Afro-American church congregations of the American deep south. Although Afro-American singing, whether in the fields or in the churches, was remarked upon by many writers in the 18th and early 19th centuries, few commented upon the songs in detail. The English actress Fanny Kemble, wife of a slave-owner, noted in her diary in 1839 'how they all sing in unison, having never, it appears, attempted or heard anything like part-singing' (p.159). She described how at a funeral 'the whole congregation uplifted their voices in a hymn, the first high wailing notes of which – sung all in unison . . . sent a thrill through all my nerves' (p.140). She did not, however, note the words she heard. In the early 1860s Colonel Thomas Wentworth Higginson, in command of a black regiment, carefully wrote down the texts of songs he heard his men sing. Some of these were later included in his published memoirs of 1870, for example:

> I know moon-rise, I know star-rise,
>   Lay dis body down.
> I walk in de moonlight, I walk in de starlight,
>   To lay dis body down. (p.209)

This form was typical of a great many spirituals: an alternating line and refrain which permitted endless extemporisation. To the soldiers such songs were, he wrote, 'more than a source of relaxation; they were a stimulus to courage and a tie to heaven' (p.221). In 1867, William Francis Allen, Charles Pickard Ware and Lucy McKim Garrison published their *Slave Songs of the United States*, a collection which included some of the spirituals best known and still surviving in the 1970s, including *Old ship of Zion*, *Lay this body down*, *Michael, row the boat ashore* and *We will march through the valley*, as well as many lesser-known songs. The authors confirmed the absence of part-singing but added, 'yet no two appear to be singing the same thing'. The lead singer, who would frequently improvise, was generally supported by 'basers' who provided a vocal groundwork and interpolations. The singing they heard abounded in 'slides from one note to another, and turns and cadences not in articulated notes'. In presenting their collection they regretted their inability to convey in notation 'the odd turns made in the throat, and the curious rhythmic effect produced by single voices chiming in at different irregular intervals'.

2. AFRICAN AND EUROPEAN SOURCES. That the spirituals were collected from slaves and ex-slaves led to much speculation on possible African elements in the songs. Allen and others considered them 'to have become imbued with the mode and spirit of European music – often, nevertheless, retaining a distinct tinge of their native Africa' (1867). Wallaschek in *Primitive Music* (1893) denied that the songs had African elements, to which Krehbiel, after analysing some 500 collected spirituals, replied that his observations on the use of scales and on rhythmic elements showed that the spirituals were essentially Afro-American in character and origin. Both positions have had innumerable supporters since then. Few have questioned, however, the African nature of the plantation 'walk-around' or 'ring-shout', a shuffling circular dance to chanting and hand-clapping which accompanied the more joyous spirituals. Often viewed with alarm by Southern whites, such ring-shouts were still being performed in the 1930s. Their ecstatic and trance-inducing nature had evident links with African custom. Other elements which might be evidence of African retention in this type of spiritual, such as improvised antiphonal singing, shouting, chanting, stamping, and the involuntary spasms of 'possessed' members of the congregations, have also been observed in fundamentalist white churches, and may be related to the highly emotional forms of religious expression developed in the Great Awakening of the early 18th century. The English writer Isaac Watts (1674–1748) and others had published large numbers of hymns during this period, which were learnt by 'lining out' (the singing of a line by a precentor and its repetition by the congregation). The 1820 edition of Watts's hymns had wide circulation throughout the southern USA and 'Dr. Watts songs' were popular among blacks. The closeness of lining out to the traditional African work song form of leader-and-chorus antiphonal singing undoubtedly contributed to the popularity of this style. And many of the hymn texts were used, in whole or in part, as the basis for spirituals.

Ex.4

(a) *Roll Jordan*, white camp-meeting spiritual (Jackson, 1964)

He comes, he comes, The Judge se – vere,
The sev – enth trum – pet speaks him near,

Roll Jor-dan roll; I want to go to
Roll Jor-dan roll.

heav'n, I do; Hal – le – lu – jah, Lord; We'll

praise the Lord in heav'n a–bove, Roll Jor-dan roll.

(b) *Roll Jordan*, black spiritual; transcr. G. P. Jackson

O brothers, you ought t'ave been there, Yes, my_ Lord, A-

- sit-ting in the king-dom To hear Jor-dan roll.

Roll Jor-dan roll, roll Jor-dan roll, I want to go to

hea-ven when I die To hear Jor-dan roll.

Some doubt exists as to the origin of the black spiritual as a form; John Lovell jr contended with Krehbiel that the spirituals were the innovation of black slaves, but considerable evidence has been brought by Newman I. White, Guy B. Johnson and George Pullen Jackson to support the contention that both the black spiritual and the white originated from a common source in the camp meetings and the white Southern rural churches. In his article 'Spirituals' (*Grove 5*), Jackson included two examples of the same spiritual, *Roll Jordan*, first as a white camp-meeting song, and second as collected in oral tradition from blacks (ex.4*a* and *b*). The white version maintains a simple steady rhythm using only two note values; its scale is anhemi-pentatonic throughout. The black version shows much rhythmic complication (shifted accents, dotted rhythms), and though the scale used retains some pentatonic emphasis, it is actually heptatonic and includes a characteristic flexible seventh degree (bars 11 and 12). Jackson pointed out that the tune itself also entered 19th-century American popular music, as Stephen Foster's minstrel-show song *Camptown Races*. Johnson contended that even the themes of *Old ship of Zion* and *Give me that old time religion*, favourites with black congregations, were borrowed from whites (1930, p.117f), while Jackson (1933, p.266f) said that another popular song of the black church, *I'm a soldier in the army* or *I'm a soldier of the Cross*, was derived from the *Sacred Harp* of 1844 (where it is called *Service of the Lord*). While blacks were not extensively taught the shape-note musical notation used in the *Sacred Harp*, they undoubtedly learnt many of the songs orally (*see also* SHAPE-NOTE HYMNODY, §2).

It can thus be assumed that the exchange between black and white traditions was considerable: slaves had to learn to speak English and to become accustomed to plantation ways; and succeeding generations were further acculturated. Slaves were often permitted in the whites' churches where they heard the same services as their owners; whites heard slaves singing on the levees, the plantations, the riverboats. Yet the slaves were not a part of white society; in brush arbour meetings or at baptisms, or even in the work gang (where spirituals were also sung), the independent growth of the black spiritual was nurtured. In 1845 a new wave of religious fervour swept through the South. The Evangelical teaching and open-air preaching of the whites were imitated by black preachers with a 'call' but no church. The black spirituals created at this time provided a source of strength, and expressed many aspects of the black condition during slavery and just after its abolition.

3. TEXTS. Many writers have commented on the spirituals as 'sorrow songs' because of their strong vein of melancholy. Intensely moving slow spirituals such as *Sometimes I feel like a motherless child*, *He never said a mumblin' word*, *Where were you when they crucified my Lord?* or *Nobody knows the trouble I seen* reveal the singers' own trials and identification with the suffering of Jesus Christ. The theme of death runs through many spirituals; some, like *Toll the bell angel*, *I jus' got over*, suggest a spirit that has already left this earth. Some writers (e.g. Miles Mark Fisher) maintain that virtually all spirituals were codified songs of protest. The runaway ex-slave and black leader Frederick Douglass (*c*1817–95) wrote of singing spirituals when a slave: 'A keen observer might have detected in our repeated sing-

ing of "O Canaan, sweet Canaan, I am bound for the land of Canaan" something more than a hope of reaching heaven. We meant to reach the *North*, and the North was our Canaan' (p.157). Spirituals such as *Steal away, Children, we all shall be free* or *Didn't my Lord deliver Daniel?* must have been seen as incitements to escape from bondage, while *We'll stand the storm* and *We shall walk through the valley in peace* were reassuring to faltering spirits.

Often the imagery of the spirituals included vivid juxtapositions of phrases and literal interpretations of metaphoric biblical texts. The book of *Revelation* provided an important source of images for songs. But to quote spirituals out of context tends to emphasize their naivety; it is in the course of the singing that their beauty and freshness is most apparent.

4. AFTER 1870. The publication of collections in the 1860s increased interest in black spirituals. But they were brought to an international audience through the appearances from 1871 of the Jubilee Singers from Fisk University, Nashville, Tennessee (*see* JUBILEE SINGERS, (FISK)). The group's purpose was to raise funds for the university, which was intended for black students, but they were unsuccessful until they included a number of spirituals in their programmes. Thereafter they performed concert arrangements of spirituals both in the USA and in Europe, and awakened an abiding interest in this form. The Jubilee Singers and later the Hampton Singers from the Hampton Institute in Virginia were the inspiration for Frederick J. Work, R. Nathaniel Dett, T. P. Fenner and Clarence Cameron White (who all conducted both groups) to arrange and publish their songs as sheet music. From a folk form the spirituals rapidly became a part of the repertory of concert pianists, cathedral choirs and even symphony orchestras. Many of the performers and composers who popularized the spirituals in concerts all over the world were black, among them Roland Hayes (1887–1976), Paul Robeson (1898–1976), William Grant Still (1895–1978) and James Weldon Johnson (1871–1938). Publication ensured lasting respect for the spirituals and conservation of their words and melodies, but transcription for voice and piano, written arrangement for orchestras and the use of art-music singing techniques destroyed the spontaneity and unpredictable quality which the spiritual had had as a folk form.

Although the popularity of the spirituals on the concert platform increased through the 20th century, their appeal had already begun to wane in the black churches by the late 19th century. Gospel song began to replace the spiritual, especially among urban congregations (*see* GOSPEL MUSIC, §II). However, older forms of the spiritual survived in the remoter backwaters of black culture and particularly in the more conservative churches of the South. Many hundreds of recordings of these rural spirituals were made between 1933 and 1942 for the Archive of Folk Song of the Library of Congress. By far the most important pockets for conservation of the early spirituals and the ring-shout were in the Sea Islands of Georgia and South Carolina, as demonstrated by Lydia Parrish in 1942. Recordings made 20 years later from this region, and from elsewhere in the South such as Georgia and Alabama, emphasize the persistence of the tradition in isolated communities unassailed by outside influences. In one example of a ring-shout from Jennings, Alabama, *Run old Jeremiah* (recorded by J. W.

The Fisk Jubilee Singers in 1875

Brown and A. Coleman, Library of Congress L3, 1934), there is a train-like accompaniment of stamping feet. Another shout, *Eli you can't stand*, was performed with hand-clapping accompaniment to chanted lead-singing by Willis Proctor and others on St Simon's Islands (Prestige International 25002, 1959). Two singers who recorded spirituals extensively for the Library of Congress during the 1930s and early 1940s were Vera Hall and Dock Reed. Field recordings of these two a decade later included two examples of the simplest form of additive spiritual, *Dead and gone* and *Free at last* (1950, reissued on FE 4418, 1960), the latter dating from the mid-1860s. The complexity of the early shouting spirituals is suggested in *Rock chair, tol' you to rock* (*Rock chariot*, 1950), performed by Rich Amerson, Earthy Ann Coleman and Price Coleman at Livingston, Alabama, which includes a counter-chant sung against the main theme (FE 4418, 1960). Recreations of the Sea Islands spiritual songs with drum, fife and banjo accompaniment were made by Bessie Jones and a mixed group, including fine versions of *Before this time another year* and *Beulah Land* (Prestige International 25001, 1959). An outstanding example of the early form of the spiritual with unison singing and moaning is *Father I stretch my hands to Thee* (Folkways FP 2656, 1956), performed by Jake Field, Eastman Brand and Arthur Holifield. This is one of many recordings which show the relationship between black spirituals and white hymns, since the text used is one written by Charles Wesley (1707–88). Several spirituals with Watts texts were sung by John and Lovie Griffin of Perry County, Alabama, including *When I can read my title clear* (Folkways FP 2656, 1956). For comparison, there is a dramatic, though unfortunately truncated, example of the black style of hymn 'lining out' by the Reverend R. C. Crenshaw and congregation

called *I love the Lord* (Atlantic 1351/London LTZ-K15214, 1959). Early recordings were made of the Fisk Jubilee Singers, such as *Roll Jordan roll* (*c*1913, reissued on RBF5, 1962), and show the concert-style spiritual. Some of the better-known of these arrangements of spirituals, including those published by the Fisk Jubilee Singers themselves in 1876, have remained as favourites in black churches where gospel song has otherwise replaced the older traditions. Versions of the concert spirituals also appear among recordings made by many leading gospel singers and groups.

Thus, although the spiritual as a folk form has declined in popularity among blacks during the 20th century because of its association with slavery, extensive collecting, recording and scholarly study have ensured that the tradition will not be lost to future generations.

See also UNITED STATES OF AMERICA, §II, 7.

BIBLIOGRAPHY

WHITE SPIRITUAL
(*collections*)

All are reproduced on microcard in C. Skipton, ed.: *Early American Imprints* (Worcester, Mass., 1966).

J. Davenport: *A Song of Praise* (Boston, 1742)

S. Occom: *A Choice Collection of Hymns and Spiritual Songs Intended for the Sincere Christians of all Denominations* (New London, Conn., 1774)

A. Beeman: *Hymns on Various Subjects* (Norwich, 1792)

J. Peak: *A New Collection of Hymns . . . and Spiritual Songs . . . Some Entirely New* (Windsor, Vermont, 1793)

J. Smith: *Divine Hymns or Spiritual Songs for the Use of Religious Assemblies and Private Christians* (Norwich, Conn., 2/1794, 9/1799)

J. Ingalls: *The Christian Harmony* (Exeter, New Hampshire, 1805)

J. Wyeth: *Repository of Sacred Music, Part Second* (Harrisburg, Penn., 1813/R1964 with introduction by I. Lowens)

A. Davisson: *Kentucky Harmony* (Harrisonburg, Virginia, 1816)

——: *A Supplement to the Kentucky Harmony* (Harrisonburg, Virginia, 1820–25)

J. Leavitt: *The Christian Lyre* (New York, 1830–31)

W. Walker: *The Southern Harmony and Musical Companion*

(Spartenburg, South Carolina, 1835–54)
B. F. White and E. J. King: *The Sacred Harp* (Philadelphia, 1847)
L. C. Myers: *Manual of Sacred Music* (Mountain Valley, Penn., 1853)
J. G. McCurry: *The Social Harp* (Philadelphia, 1855)
Revival and Camp Meeting Minstrel (Philadelphia, 1867)
J. Hillman: *The Revivalist* (Troy, NY, c1868)

(*literature*)
A. Gilchrist: 'The Folk Element in Early Revival Hymns and Tunes', *JFSS*, viii (1927–31), 61–95
G. P. Jackson: *White Spirituals in the Southern Uplands* (Chapel Hill, North Carolina, 1933/R1964)
P. and T. J. Denson, eds.: *Original Sacred Harp, Denson Revision* (Haleyville, Alabama, 1936, rev. 4/1971)
G. P. Jackson: *Spiritual Folk-songs of Early America* (New York, 1937)
A. M. Buchanan: *Folk Hymns of America* (New York, 1938)
G. P. Jackson: *Down-east Spirituals, and Others* (New York, 1939)
——: *White and Negro Spirituals* (New York, 1943)
——: *Another Sheaf of White Spirituals* (Gainesville, Florida, 1952)
G. Chase: *America's Music: From the Pilgrims to the Present* (New York, 1955)
J. N. Sims: *The Hymnody of the Camp Meeting Tradition* (diss., Union Theological Seminary, NY, 1960)
H. L. Eskew: *Shape-note Hymnody in the Shenandoah Valley, 1816–1860* (diss., Tulane U., New Orleans, 1966)
J. C. Downey: *The Music of American Revivalism, 1740–1800* (diss., Tulane U., New Orleans, 1968)
D. D. Bruce jr: *And They All Sang Hallelujah: Plain-folk Camp-meeting Religion 1800–1845* (Knoxville, Tenn., 1974)

BLACK SPIRITUAL
F. A. Kemble: *Journal of a Residence on a Georgian Plantation in 1838–1839* (New York and London, 1863, rev. 1961)
W. F. Allen, C. P. Ware and L. McKim Garrison: *Slave Songs of the United States* (New York, 1867/R1929)
T. W. Higginson: 'Negro Spirituals', *Army Life in a Black Regiment* (Boston, 1870), 197ff
J. B. T. Marsh: *The Story of the Jubilee Singers with their Songs* (London, 1876)
F. Douglass: *Life and Times of Frederick Douglass* (Hartford, Conn., 1882), 157
R. Wallaschek: *Primitive Music* (London, 1893)
H. E. Krehbiel: *Afro-American Folksongs: a Study in Racial and National Music* (New York and London, 1914)
J. W. and J. R. Johnson: *The Book of American Negro Spirituals* (New York and London, 1925–7)
N. I. White: *American Negro Folk-songs* (Cambridge, Mass., 1928)
G. B. Johnson: *Folk Culture on St. Helena Island, South Carolina* (Chapel Hill, North Carolina, 1930), 117f
G. P. Jackson: 'Tunes of the White Man's Spirituals Preserved in the Negro's Religious Songs', 'White Man's and Negro's Spiritual Texts Compared', *White Spirituals in the Southern Uplands* (Chapel Hill, North Carolina, 1933/R1964), 242–302
R. N. Dett: *The Dett Collection of Negro Spirituals* (Chicago, 1936)
M. J. Herskovits: 'The Contemporary Scene: Africanisms in Religious Life', *The Myth of the Negro Past* (New York and London, 1941), 207–60
L. Parrish: *Slave Songs of the Georgia Sea Islands* (New York, 1942)
G. P. Jackson: *White and Negro Spirituals* (New York, 1943)
M. M. Fisher: *Negro Slave Songs in the United States* (Ithaca, NY, 1953)
G. P. Jackson: 'Spirituals', *Grove 5*
F. Ramsey jr: 'Music from the South, vi–vii: Elder Songsters', FP 2655–6 [disc notes]
A. Lomax: 'Georgia Sea Islands', INT 25001–2 [disc notes]
W. H. Tallmadge: 'Dr. Watts and Mahalia Jackson—the Development, Decline, and Survival of a Folk Style in America', *EM*, v (1961), 95
H. Courlander: 'Anthems and Spirituals as Oral Literature', *Negro Folk Music, U.S.A.* (New York and London, 1963), 35–79
P. Oliver: 'Gospel Songs and Spirituals', *Jazz on Record*, ed. A. McCarthy and others (London, 1968), 325ff
J. Lovell jr: *Black Song: the Forge and the Flame* (New York, 1972)
JAMES C. DOWNEY (I), PAUL OLIVER (II)

Spirituellement. *See* SPIRITOSO.

Spisak, Michał (*b* Dąbrowa Górnicza, 14 Sept 1914; *d* Paris, 29 Jan 1965). Polish composer. He studied at the Katowice Conservatory, where in 1937 he took a diploma in the violin and composition, and also took composition lessons with Sikorski in Warsaw (1935–7). In 1937 he went to Paris, where he studied with Boulanger and remained until his death, while maintain-ing constant contact with his native country. Also in 1937 he became vice-president of the Association of Young Polish Musicians in Paris. In Poland he had appeared as a violinist, but from 1937 he gave his attention exclusively to composition. He twice received the Lili Boulanger Prize (1945 and 1946) and was also twice winner of the Grand Prix of the Queen Elisabeth Competition (1953 for the orchestral Serenade, 1957 for the *Concerto giocoso*). In 1964 he was awarded the annual prize of the Polish Composers' Union.

Spisak was among the most outstanding Polish composers of his generation. His music, almost exclusively instrumental and emotionally rich and varied, shows an assurance of technique which is particularly apparent in his craftsmanlike writing for instruments, his transparent polyphony and his extraordinary feeling for orchestral colour. Throughout his career he remained faithful to the ideals of Boulanger and to the aesthetic of Stravinsky, whom he sometimes imitated to the extent of plagiarism. Undoubtedly his best compositions were modelled on Stravinsky's rejuvenated Classical and Baroque designs. Sometimes he attempted to reach beyond these influences by means of a neo-Romantic style, but this type of composition, exemplified by the String Quartet, is rather rare. More commonly his works are dominated by pre-Classical counterpoint, motor movement, a simple handling of form and traditionally accomplished facture. He avoided conventionality through his architectural mode of thought, which enabled him to construct the large-scale forms of such works as the Symphonie concertante no.2 and the Sonata for violin and orchestra. Most of his few vocal works were occasional; the *Anthem* for chorus and orchestra (1947), for example, was composed for Boulanger's 60th birthday.

WORKS
(*selective list*)

ORCHESTRAL
Serenade, 1939; Cl Concertino, 1940–41; Aubade, small orch, 1943; Bn Conc., 1944; Suite, str, 1945; Pf Conc., 1947; Toccata, 1947; 2 symphonies concertantes, 1947, 1956; Divertimento, 2 pf, orch, 1950; Divertissement (Musique légère no.1), 1950; Sonata, vn, orch, 1950; Melos (ballet, M.-L. de Noailles), 1951; Trbn Concertino, 1951; Andante et allegro, vn, str, 1954; Conc. giocoso, 1957; Allegro de Voiron [after work of 1943], 1957
Educational pieces: 5 Studies, str, 1948; Studies, vn ens, 1949–50

CHAMBER AND INSTRUMENTAL
2 caprices, vn, pf, 1937; Qt, ob, 2 cl, bn, 1938; Sonata, vn, pf, 1946; Sonatine, ob, cl, bn, 1947; Wind Qnt, 1948; Duetto concertante, va, bn, 1949; Musique légère no.2, 2 vn, vc, db, pf, 1951; Str Qt no.1, 1953; Andante et allegro [red. orch work], vn, pf, 1954; Suite, 2 vn, 1958; Suite, 2 va, 1959; Improvvisazione, vn, pf, 1962
Pf: Conc., 2 pf, 1942; Suite, 1943

VOCAL
Choral: 2 Psalms, chorus, orch, 1938; Anthem, chorus, orch, 1947; Christmas Mass, chorus, 1953; Olympic Anthem (Pindar), chorus, orch, 1955; Pędrek Wyrzutek (S. Themerson), cantata, Tr, B, reciter, choruses, 1962
Solo vocal: 3 Preludes, S, fl, 1953

Principal publisher: Polskie Wydawnictwo Muzyczne

BIBLIOGRAPHY
B. Frydrychowicz: ' "Allegro de Voiron" Michała Spisaka', *Ruch muzyczny* (1961), no.21, p.11
S. Jarocinski: 'Sztuka bez autobiografii (o Michale Spisaku)', *Ruch muzyczny* (1965), no.14, p.3
A. Mitscha: 'Michał Spisak (wspomnienie)', *Zeszyty naukowe PWSM w Katowicach* (1969), no.10, p.5
BOGUSŁAW SCHÄFFER

Spitta, Julius August Philipp (*b* Wechold, nr. Hoya, 7 Dec 1841; *d* Berlin, 13 April 1894). German music historian. His father was Philipp Spitta (1801–59), theologian and author of the Protestant hymn collection *Psalter und Harfe*. His musical education began early with piano, organ and composition lessons. He entered the University of Göttingen in 1860, first studying theology and then classical philology. In Göttingen he also continued to compose, wrote a brief biography of Schumann and began a lifelong close friendship with Brahms. He took the PhD in 1864 with a dissertation on Tacitus and became a Gymnasium teacher of Greek and Latin in Reval (now Tallinn), Sondershausen and finally Leipzig. While still in Reval he had begun lecturing at the museum on music history, and soon Bach research became his main interest. The first volume of his epoch-making study of Bach appeared in 1873; two years later he was appointed professor of music history at the University of Berlin and director of the Berlin Hochschule für Musik, positions he held until his death.

Spitta's approach in the Bach biography reflected the traditional concept of art history as the history of individual artists, but was tempered with a strong, fresh emphasis on historical context. The introductory chapters, for example, present the first detailed study of 17th-century German choral and keyboard music. In subsequent works his concern became increasingly the refinement of musicological research. By his rigorous application of source-critical studies (his aesthetic judgments were strongly influenced by neo-Kantian philosophy), he laid the foundations of a system of historical criticism. He was exceptionally active and productive as a researcher, teacher, writer and editor, and he developed an interest in almost every period of music history, from the early Middle Ages to the music of his own time.

As one of the leading figures of later 19th-century musicology, he made a lasting impression on the new academic discipline: together with Chrysander and Adler, he founded in 1885 the *Vierteljahrsschrift für Musikwissenschaft*, among the first scholarly music periodicals, and without his support the Denkmäler deutscher Tonkunst could not have been published. During his term of office at Berlin University he educated a whole generation of scholars, among them Oskar Fleischer, Max Friedlaender, Carl Krebs, Max Seiffert, Peter Wagner and Johannes Wolf.

WRITINGS

Ein Lebensbild Robert Schumanns (Leipzig, 1862)
Der Satzbau bei Tacitus (diss., U. of Göttingen, 1866)
Johann Sebastian Bach (Leipzig, 1873–80, 5/1962; Eng. trans., 1884–5, 2/1899/R1951)
'Sperontes "Singende Muse an der Pleisse" ', *VMw*, i (1885), 35
'Die Musica enchiriadis und ihr Zeitalter', *VMw*, v (1889), 443
Zur Musik (Berlin, 1892/R1975) [16 essays, incl. 'Kunstwissenschaft und Kunst', 'Vom Mittleramte der Poesie', 'Die Wiederbelebung protestantischer Kirchenmusik auf geschichtlicher Grundlage', 'Händel, Bach, Schütz', articles on Weber, Gade, Brahms]
'Denkmäler deutscher Tonkunst', *Grenzboten*, lii/2 (1893), 16
Musikgeschichtliche Aufsätze (Berlin, 1894) [collected essays, incl. 'H. Schütz's Leben und Werke', 'Die Anfänge madrigalischer Dichtung in Deutschland', 'Bachiana', 'Über R. Schumanns Schriften', 'Ballade']
'Palestrina im 16. und 19. Jahrhundert', *Deutsche Rundschau*, lxxix (1894), 74

EDITIONS

D. Buxtehude: Orgelwerke (Leipzig, 1876–7)
H. Schütz: Sämtliche Werke (Leipzig, 1885–94)
Friedrich II von Preussen: Musikalische Werke (Leipzig, 1889)

BIBLIOGRAPHY

RiemannL 12
J. Rodenberg: Obituary, *Deutsche Rundschau*, lxxix (1894), 468
H. Riemann: *Philipp Spitta und seine Bach-Biographie* (Berlin, 1900)
C. Krebs, ed.: *Johannes Brahms: Briefwechsel*, xvi (Berlin, 1920) [correspondence between Brahms and Spitta]

W. Gurlitt: 'Der Musikhistoriker Philipp Spitta', *Musik und Kirche*, xiv (1942), 27
F. Blume: *Johann Sebastian Bach im Wandel der Geschichte* (Kassel, 1947)
H. Spitta: 'Spitta, Julius August Philipp', *MGG*

CHRISTOPH WOLFF

Spitzflöte (Ger.). An ORGAN STOP.

Spitzharfe (Ger.). ARPANETTA.

Spitzmüller(-Harmersbach), Alexander, Freiherr von (*b* Vienna, 22 Feb 1894; *d* Paris, 12 Nov 1962). Austrian composer. The son of the last finance minister of the Austro-Hungarian Empire, he was originally intended for the legal profession and took a doctorate in law at Vienna in 1919. His first music studies were with Kanitz at the New Conservatory, Vienna; later he studied informally under Berg and Apostel. In 1928 he emigrated to Paris where he was appointed a professor at the Schola Cantorum, and where he remained until the end of his life. From 1946 to 1953 he was director of French broadcasts to Germany and Austria, conducting some performances himself. As a critic he championed the cause of new Austrian music, particularly that of Berg, in France; his commentaries frequently appeared under the pseudonym Jean Cartier, or under his hyphenated family name. He was a long-standing member of the International Society for Contemporary Music, which was instrumental in giving many of his own compositions their first performances. He also served as president of the Centre Culturel Autriche and as a representative of the Austrian Autorenschutzgesellschaft. In 1959 he was awarded the music prize of the city of Vienna, and in the following year the Paris Conservatoire library organized an exhibition devoted exclusively to his works. His music embraces tonal and 12-note methods of organization, frequently reflecting his interest in Les Six.

WORKS
(selective list)

Stage: L'impasse, ballet, 1956; Le journal, ballet, 1957; Construction humaine, ballet, A. Silbermann, 1959; Fabrik der Illusionen, opera satire, Silbermann, inc.
Orch: Sinfonietta ritmica, 1933; 2 pf concs., 1937, 1953; Sym., 1939; Der 40. Mai, suite, chamber orch, 1941; 3 Friedenshymnen, 1943; Concert dans l'esprit latin, 1951; Sym., str, 1954
Choral: Te Deum, chorus, orch, org, 1940; Beati mortui, 1947; Salve regina, S, female chorus, chamber orch, 1947; Psalm cxxix, 1950; Les heures d'automne (cantata, Verhaeren), female chorus, str, 1958
Radio melodramas: Léonce et Léna (after Büchner), 1947; Ainsi va le monde (Meran-Mellerio), Weh dem, dir lügt (Grillparzer)

Principal publishers: Boosey & Hawkes, Bote & Bock, Universal

JOHN MORGAN

Spivacke, Harold (*b* New York, 18 July 1904; *d* Washington, DC, 9 May 1977). American music librarian and administrator. At New York University he took the BA in 1923 and the MA in 1924. He later studied at the University of Berlin, where he received the PhD in 1933 with a dissertation on aspects of tonal intensity. His private teachers included Eugen d'Albert and Hugo Leichtentritt. After working in New York as a research assistant to Olin Downes (1933–4), he joined the staff of the music division of the Library of Congress in 1934; he was assistant chief of the division from 1934 to 1937 and chief from 1937 until his retirement in 1972. During his long tenure in the music division Spivacke was active with a number of governmental agencies and departments in addition to the Library of Congress. His activities in professional organizations included a term as president of the Music Library Association (1951–3) and offices in the National Music Council, the International Association of Music Libraries and the American Musicological Society.

WRITINGS

Über die objektive und subjektive Tonintensität (diss., U. of Berlin, 1933)

ed.: *Berkshire Festivals of Chamber Music, 1918–1938* (Pittsfield, Mass., 1938)

The Archive of American Folk Song in the Library of Congress (Pittsburgh, 1941)

Paganiniana (Washington, DC, 1945)

'The Brahms and Chausson Manuscripts Presented by Mr. Fritz Kreisler', *Library of Congress Quarterly Journal*, vi/3 (1949), 57

'The Preservation and Reference Services of Sound Recordings in a Research Library', *HMYB*, xi (1961), 99

'The CMS Amidst National Societies', *College Music Symposium*, ii (1962), 9

BIBLIOGRAPHY

C. Sprague Smith: 'Harold Spivacke (1904–1977)', *MQ*, lxiii (1977), 425

PAULA MORGAN

Split (It. Spalato). Town in Yugoslavia on the Adriatic coast. Originally it developed round the ruins of the palace of Emperor Diocletian; later with the rest of Dalmatia it was a part of the Venetian Republic. After the fall of the republic and after the Napoleonic wars it belonged to the Austro-Hungarian Empire, until the formation of Yugoslavia in 1918.

The cathedral church of St Doimus and the Franciscan monastery (founded *c*1213) were the centres of musical activity from the Middle Ages. At the beginning of the 17th century several native and Italian composers associated with the cathedral as *maestri di cappella* and organists (e.g. T. Cecchino, I. Lukačić) introduced the new monodic style into the local sacred and secular music. This was a relatively brief period of remarkable prosperity when musical activity seemed to keep pace with developments in Venice. The second half of the 17th century was a period of stagnation, and then in the 18th century musical standards improved again. C. A. Nagli, who later became *maestro di cappella* at the Chiesa dei Frari, Venice, was in charge of the music between 1710 and 1725; later in the century the post was occupied by J. Bajamonti.

The cathedral continued to appoint the directors of music in the 19th century, but this period was generally characterized by a decline in standards. In the mid-19th century opera became increasingly popular; between 1859 and 1881 visiting opera companies appeared regularly in the Teatro Bajamonti. The new Municipal Theatre was opened in 1893 (capacity 500). The permanent resident company was established in 1922; its repertory consists mainly of the standard Italian 19th-century operas and works by Yugoslavs, especially those associated with Split (Jakov Gotovac, Josip Hatze, Ivo Tijardović). The opera orchestra also gives symphony concerts. The summer festival Splitske Ljetne Priredbe, founded in 1955, chiefly presents opera.

BOJAN BUJIĆ

SPNM. See SOCIETY FOR THE PROMOTION OF NEW MUSIC.

Spofforth, Reginald (*b* Southwell, between 1768 and 1770; *d* Kensington, London, 8 Sept 1827). English composer. His uncle, Thomas Spofforth, was organist of Southwell Minster and took care of his early musical instruction. Sir Richard Kaye, a prebendary of Southwell who was also Dean of Lincoln, encouraged

him to go to Lincoln, where for a time he acted as deputy organist at the cathedral. He then moved to London, where he studied composition with Benjamin Cooke and piano with Steibelt. When in 1793 he won two prizes for glees from the Noblemen's and Gentlemen's Catch Club, his successful career as a composer had begun. His earliest publications had been of solo songs, but from about 1796 he published numerous glees, many of which also appeared in anthologies. He contributed various songs and glees to productions at Covent Garden Theatre, where he appears to have been chorus master for a time; but he declined Harris's invitation to succeed Shield as musical director there in 1797. He was at one time organist of Fitzroy Chapel, and later at Eltham parish church; much of his time was spent in teaching.

Spofforth was one of the leading glee composers. His glee *Hail, smiling morn*, no.6 of *Six Glees* (1810), was possibly the most popular glee in the entire repertory. It was one of the first in what Barrett termed the 'part-song' style: melodious, flowing and sentimental, but lacking the dramatic treatment of the text that was a feature of the earlier glee. Classical instrumental music played a part in this trend towards a more balanced structure: some of his glees, indeed, are in strict sonata form. Three charming books of nursery rhyme settings appeared, some as glees for two sopranos and bass, others as solo songs. Spofforth composed many songs and duets but, as far as is known, no instrumental or sacred music.

Reginald's brother Samuel Spofforth (1780–1864) was organist of Peterborough Cathedral and from 1807 of Lichfield Cathedral; he was a composer of cathedral music and chants.

WORKS

(all published in London)

75 glees (according to Baptie), pubd singly and in 18th- and 19th-century anthologies; also in Spofforth's collections: 6 Glees, Bk the First (*c*1796); 6 Glees (1810); A Collection of Glees, compiled from the unpublished MSS, ed. W. Hawes (1830)

Nursery rhyme settings: The Newest Christmas Box, op.2, 1–3vv, pf, bk 1 (*c*1797), bk 2 (*c*1805); The Twelfth Cake, a Juvenile Amusement, op.3 (1807)

Songs and duets: 6 Canzonets (1790); others pubd singly and in 18th- and 19th-century anthologies

Songs in Covent Garden stage works: The Pirates, 1792; Mago and Dago, 1794; Windsor Castle (J. P. Solomon), 1795; The Witch of the Wood, 1796

BIBLIOGRAPHY

R. Spofforth: Memoir, *A Collection of Glees*, ed. W. Hawes (London, 1830)

Biographical sketch, *The Harmonicon*, xi (1833), 186

W. A. Barrett: *English Glee and Madrigal Writers* (London, 1877), 36

[J. Bayley]: *A Sketch of the Life of Reginald Spofforth* (London, 1880)

D. Baptie: *Sketches of the English Glee Composers* (London, 1896), 74ff

NICHOLAS TEMPERLEY

Spohr, Louis [Ludewig, Ludwig] (*b* Brunswick, 5 April 1784; *d* Kassel, 22 Oct 1859). German composer, violinist and conductor. He was one of the leading composers of instrumental music of the early Romantic period, and in his operas he made stylistic developments that anticipated Wagner's music dramas in two important respects, *Durchkomponierung* and the use of leit-motifs.

1. LIFE. Spohr's ancestors can be traced back to the 17th century in the region of the foothills of the western Harz mountains, where his father, Karl Heinrich Spohr (1756–1843), was a doctor. In 1786 the family moved to Seesen. Spohr's first musical encouragement came

from his parents: his mother was a gifted singer and pianist, and his father played the flute. The Seesen musicians J. A. Riemenschneider and (after about 1790) Dufour gave him his earliest instruction on the violin, and soon he was able to join his parents in evenings of chamber music, playing trios by Christian Kalkbrenner. His first attempts at composition also date from the early 1790s, and Dufour, recognizing the boy's musical talents, persuaded his parents to send him to Brunswick for further instruction.

In Brunswick Spohr had violin lessons with the chamber musician Gottfried Kunisch and later from the Konzertmeister C. L. Maucourt. His studies were supplemented by a theory course given by the organist K. A. Hartung; this was his only theoretical training. He often took part in student and subscription concerts, sometimes performing his own works. The failure of his first concert tour, a badly planned venture to Hamburg in 1799, caused him to ask Duke Karl Wilhelm Ferdinand of Brunswick for financial help. A successful concert at the court impressed the duke so much that he engaged the 15-year-old Spohr as a chamber musician. In this post he became acquainted mainly with the French operas then in the repertory; but performances of *Die Zauberflöte* and *Don Giovanni* made Mozart Spohr's 'idol and model'. In 1802, through the good offices of the duke, he became the pupil of Franz Eck and accompanied him on a concert tour which took him as far as St Petersburg. Eck, who completely retrained Spohr in violin technique, was a product of the Mannheim school, and Spohr became its most important heir.

Having matured as a virtuoso and composer, Spohr returned to Brunswick in 1803. A concert by Pierre Rode impressed him so much that he virtually copied Rode's style of playing during the next years. Soon after Rode's concert Spohr made his official début as a soloist, which was brilliantly received and resulted in his re-employment in the court orchestra with a threefold increase in salary. A concert tour of Magdeburg, Halle, Leipzig (with sensational success at the Gewandhaus), Dresden and Berlin established his fame in Germany as a violinist, and, again through the generosity of the Duke of Brunswick, Spohr was offered and accepted the post of Konzertmeister in Gotha.

During his years in Gotha (1805–12) Spohr developed from a virtuoso into a versatile composer and conductor. His early attempts at opera were not particularly successful, but they brought him experience and understanding which later proved beneficial. His participation in the music festivals in Frankenhausen and Erfurt (1810–12) consolidated his reputation as a virtuoso and brought him recognition as a conductor, in which capacity his use of a baton (unusual for the time) lent precision to the performances. These festivals also inspired the Symphony no.1, the Clarinet Concerto no.2 and the oratorio *Das jüngste Gericht*. In 1806 Spohr married Dorette Scheidler (1787–1834), a virtuoso harpist, and proceeded to compose numerous works for the violin and harp for their joint concert tours. From 1807 to 1821 the couple undertook many tours to Vienna, Rome, London and Paris which were as successful artistically as they were financially. Among the musical highlights of the journeys were an appearance in Vienna at which Spohr successfully competed with Rode, the first performance of the Violin Concerto no.8 at La Scala and a concert at the Ruspoli Palace in

Rome; Spohr also made a successful appearance at the Philharmonic Concerts in London in 1820. Moreover, without having bribed the press beforehand, as was customary, he had an enthusiastic reception at his Paris début at the Opéra.

These years of travel were interrupted only twice by firm engagements. From 1813 to 1815 Spohr directed the orchestra of the Theater an der Wien, where his wife was engaged as principal harpist. His activity as a composer reached its first climax during this period, when many of his most important chamber works (including the Octet and Nonet) as well as his first important opera (*Faust*, 1813) were written, largely as well-paid commissions. He became friendly with Beethoven, whose influence showed itself in the increased concentration of the thematic material and in more intensive expression. The second hiatus during these concert-giving years was spent in Frankfurt am Main (1817–19), where Spohr directed the Opera. The nature of his activity there is shown in such events as the revival of *Faust*, the successful production of his opera *Zemire und Azor* and numerous public quartet concerts which characterized the current musical life. He was also engaged to write an opera *Der schwarze Jäger*, on a libretto by Georg Döring based on the ghost story by J. A. Apel; but when he heard that Weber was treating the subject (*Der Freischütz*) he stopped work on it. He never regretted this; in his *Lebenserinnerungen* he remarked: 'With my music, which is not designed to make a big hit and amuse the general masses, I should never have enjoyed the unprecedented success of *Der Freischütz*'. Increasing differences of opinion, brought about by an artistic sense of responsibility on the one hand and the commercial interests of a shareholder theatre on the other, arose between Spohr and the management and caused him to resign in 1819, to the disappointment of the Frankfurt public; in addition, he had been denied the life engagement which had originally been promised to him.

In 1821 he settled in Dresden, where he rested from his long journeys, contemplated new projects including *Jessonda* and renewed his acquaintance with Weber. When Weber was offered the post of Kapellmeister in Kassel but did not wish to accept, he suggested Spohr. A little later Spohr also received an offer from Gotha, but he came to an agreement with the Kassel theatre manager Carl Feige. The appointment would be for life, with an annual salary of 2000 thalers (Weber had been offered 2500), an annual holiday of six to eight weeks and (a point which he had learnt from his experience in Frankfurt) a voice in the composition of the programmes; he could claim a pension to the value of half his salary if unable to work, provided that he had been in service 'for a reasonable length of time'. The contract was signed on 4 February 1822.

The appointment fulfilled Spohr's long-cherished wish to settle down to a permanent post. The Elector Wilhelm II, who had come to power the year before, was anxious to make his theatre one of the most important in Germany and proved generous in granting subsidies, 60,000 thalers annually. The orchestra consisted of 55 musicians, a large number compared to other orchestras of the period, and first-rate singers worked with the ensemble. Spohr continued the subscription concerts initiated by his predecessors and founded a Cäcilienverein to encourage the city's choral activity. The revival of *Zemire und Azor* was a promising prelude to his work; the premières of *Jessonda* (1823), the oratorio *Die letzten Dinge* (1826) and the Symphony no.4 (1832) were major achievements. Apart from performances of works by other Kassel composers (Moritz Hauptmann, K. F. Curschmann, J. J. Bott and others), Spohr made a noteworthy contribution to the cultivation of interest in Bach: from 1832 to 1851, in the series of so-called Good Friday Concerts, he conducted five performances of the *St Matthew Passion*. He also made a stand in favour of Wagner's works with performances of *Der fliegende Holländer* (1843) and *Tannhäuser* (1853). He won social improvements for his musicians, including a firm ruling on salary support for their dependents.

His violin method, completed in 1831, documents his importance as a teacher. Numerous violinists from all over the world came to him for instruction, the most famous being Hubert Ries, Ferdinand David and Spohr's grandson August Wilhelmj.

The period after 1830 brought Spohr several personal hardships and professional difficulties. In November 1834 his wife died. Political unrest in Kassel led to the closing of the Opera in 1832, and on reopening the next year it had to operate on a considerably smaller subsidy, 35,000 thalers annually. Spohr also had occasional differences with the future elector, Friedrich Wilhelm, in power as co-regent from 1831, but these differences did not basically cloud the relationship between prince and musician. Spohr had been allowed an exceptional degree of personal freedom by Feige, and in 1851, two years after Feige's retirement, he was reprimanded for an unpermitted absence of several weeks by order of the general director Herringen and was forced to pay a fine of 550 thalers. He protested against the fine, but lost the case.

All kinds of honours and artistic successes outside Kassel brought Spohr a certain consolation. He was made an honorary member of 38 musical societies in Germany and abroad, and was awarded an honorary doctorate from the University of Marburg and several orders. He was enthusiastically received at the music festivals in Aachen (1840), Brunswick (1844) and Bonn (1845). The acclaim which greeted him in England was even greater: he was a guest in Norwich in 1839 and made four trips to London 1843–53, where the performances of his oratorios and the première of the revised version of *Faust* enjoyed a brilliant reception; after Mendelssohn, he was the most popular German composer in England. He married the pianist Marianne Pfeiffer in 1836 and undertook concert tours of Germany with her, renewing the glories of earlier days; for these journeys he also wrote a few works for violin and piano.

In 1847 Spohr was made Generalmusikdirektor at Kassel, and not merely for court prestige: for despite occasional disagreements the elector never lost his respect and affection for Spohr. The assistant Kapellmeister Bott gave him some respite from 1852 on; Bott was succeeded by Carl Reiss in 1856. In 1857, after 35 years' service, Spohr was retired with an annual pension of 1500 thalers. This was inevitable at his age, considering his weakening strength, and was not, as has often been maintained, the result of any animosity. His retirement conformed entirely with the regulations established in Hesse in 1831. No one seriously thought ill of him for his differences of opinion with the directorship, nor indeed for the fact, well known at court, that as a liberal he was opposed to the interests of small states.

1. Louis Spohr: self-portrait (c1807) in the Landesmuseum, Brunswick

Spohr's activity as a composer, so vigorous up to the beginning of the 1850s, declined in his last years. His memoirs, a striking and entertaining (if sometimes inaccurate) picture of his life and times up to 1838, were begun in 1847 but were left incomplete. He was buried in the new cemetery in Kassel amid great public mourning; his grave still survives.

2. WORKS. Spohr's origins in the early Romantic period, together with his unmistakable devotion to Mozart, were the determining factors in his musical style. This may explain why, despite a capacity for free expression, he adhered to the discipline of Classical form and only occasionally exceeded its limits in experimentation, not all of which was successful. Also characteristic of his music is its thorough craftsmanship, a trait which showed itself early in his career and in which sensitivity and an aversion to popular effects combined with a fondness for the elegiac. Besides the Viennese Classical composers, Méhul, Cherubini, Spontini and the Parisian violin virtuosos (especially Rode) had an influence on Spohr. His use of chromaticism, which anticipated Wagner's, was in turn influenced by the example of Cherubini.

Spohr first displayed his individuality in his violin concertos. He achieved mastery over the French forms by having the orchestra participate symphonically, not merely provide a framework, and by an unprecedented lyric sensitivity in the slow movements, e.g. the Siciliano of no.3 and the Adagio of no.7. Rapid bravura pieces, on the other hand, are by no means lacking, as evidenced by the 'alla spagnola' of no.6 and the finale to no.14 with its ironic allusion to 'Ole Bull'. Whereas Concerto no.7 best embodies Spohr's ideal in the genre, no.8, 'in the form of a vocal scena', displays an interesting exception: intended for Italy, it develops the use of recitative into a full assumption of operatic style, with the violin replacing the heroine. Although Spohr's concertos were far more popular in the 19th century than even Beethoven's, only no.8 is occasionally heard today. The clarinet concertos, on the other hand, have retained their popularity and, next to Mozart's and Weber's, may be considered the most important in the genre. Like the violin concertos they display a happy balance of substance and virtuosity. Spohr owed his knowledge of clarinet technique to Johann Simon Hermstedt, the soloist at the première of each of the four concertos.

Spohr also took up the double concerto and the sinfonia concertante, both of which had become rare in the 19th century. Apart from opp.48 and 88 for two violins and orchestra, which he enjoyed performing with his pupils, the Quartet Concerto op.131 is noteworthy.

As a symphonist Spohr was given an initial stimulus by the Kantor G. F. Bischoff, organizer of the Frankenhausen festivals. His ten symphonies can be divided into two groups, the first of which (comprising nos.1, 2, 3, 5 and 6) derives in style directly from the Classical period, including Beethoven. In this group, of which no.3 is the most successful, Spohr avoided using contrasting ideas in Beethovenian manner, without giving up a certain measure of grandeur; his melodious themes lend themselves more to an epic method of treatment. Inner balance and shapeliness of form combine with an often emotional contemplativeness, and, true to Romantic expression, the instruments are either scored in clearly distinguished, individual tone-colours or welded into a homogeneous body. The later group of symphonies is characterized for the most part by attempts to vary the traditional form with programmatic elements. Although there are formal and instrumental innovations, fundamentally the music lacks substance and is often eclectic. Though the Symphony no.4 found general favour, no.6 met particularly violent criticism for its misplaced satire of modern music. Moreover, these works are not really interesting in the history of programme music, since they do not progress beyond a primitive stage of programmatic association. Contemporary criticism praised their sound craftsmanship but pointed to their paucity of invention.

In the history of the string quartet Spohr assumes an important position. As Beethoven's middle and late quartets were regarded as exceptional and Schubert's remained unknown, composers of the stature of the two Rombergs, Danzi, J. P. Pixis, A. E. Fesca and Ferdinand Ries commanded the scene. Early in the 19th century, chamber music among the upper middle class and the nobility was replaced by a cultivation of the quartet in the planning of public concerts. Composers were no longer expected to make allowances for modest technical standards, and the *quatuor brillant* which had originated in France prospered on fertile ground. The first violinist, usually a travelling virtuoso, was given soloistic prominence while the other parts, played by resident musicians, merely constituted an accompanying ensemble. Many of Spohr's quartets, as well as variations and potpourris, are shaped by these considerations; and although he designated some of his works with the title *Quatuor brillant*, others, such as op.27 and op.30, are virtually violin concertos with string trio accompaniment. This tendency towards virtuosity was nevertheless compensated for by a scrupulously

2. Louis Spohr

Mozartian or Beethovenian construction and by adherence to sonata form, often with strikingly successful passages. The slow movements are particularly characteristic of Spohr in their elegiac sweetness; and Beethoven can be recognized as the model for the lively scherzos. By contrast, the finales are often rather pale.

Of the string quintets, the middle group, opp.69, 91 and 106, are the most noteworthy. In them a chamber music style is braced with considerable intellectual content, while technical effects, such as the harmonics in the third and fourth movements of op.106, are not ignored. The remaining quintets rather resemble the *quatuors brillants*.

Spohr's own inclination to extend the forms of art is well displayed in the four double quartets. The principle of a double chorus, which is most thoroughly cultivated in the last work in this genre, distinguishes them from the Octet. According to Spohr, the idea of these works looks back to Anton Romberg; and within the history of the genre it had no lasting effect.

Among Spohr's best works are the chamber music with wind instruments; the Octet and Nonet are among the leading works in the repertory. The concert tours with his first wife prompted the compositions for the harp; the six sonatas for violin and harp, though conceived only for Nadermann's simple pedal harp, are landmarks in the early development of idiomatic writing for the harp.

Interest in oratorio was one of the main activities of the musical bourgeoisie during Spohr's lifetime. Historical material emphasizing the heroic and biblical themes emphasizing the apocalyptic were especially favoured. Spohr's oratorios are distinguished from those of his contemporaries by the originality of their harmony and orchestration; they are the earliest to have a truly Romantic conception of sound. But the stylistic ideal of older church music up to the time of Handel, even though Spohr incorporated further artistic advancement and expressive means, led the composer into the blind alley of the period piece. What his contemporaries still found pleasing became unacceptable to later generations, and when Mendelssohn's oratorios came to the public's attention Spohr's works quickly fell into oblivion. His other choral works suffered a similar fate. Sacred compositions such as the Mass op.54, whose composition was encouraged by Thibaut, show an obvious eclecticism; many of the secular choruses became the favourites of singing groups but died out when these groups disbanded.

Spohr's solo songs, more than 90 in all, show him to be a composer whose strength lay in the creation of poetic moods, particularly in the gently melancholic type and the ballad that evokes the feeling of twilight. The variety of forms extends from the simple strophic lied to the *durchkomponiert* ballad. By occasionally employing an obbligato instrument, e.g. a clarinet in op.103, or four-hand accompaniment, Spohr attempted to enrich the genre, but these, like many other of his innovations, were superficial and are of only historical interest.

Three of Spohr's operas, *Faust*, *Zemire und Azor* and *Jessonda*, are important not only in Spohr's development as a composer but in the history of the genre itself, where Spohr's influences are traceable as late as in Wagner's music dramas. After a few early trials of little significance, Spohr's first success as an opera composer came with *Faust*, composed in 1813 though not produced until 1816. An important aspect of the music was recognized by Weber, its conductor at the Prague première, who described it as 'a few melodies, carefully and felicitously devised, which weave through the whole work like delicate threads, holding it together intellectually'. Its associative system of leitmotifs, which function here as symbols of psychic content, was consolidated in the 1852 revision of the opera, which Spohr provided with recitatives. Here he referred to 'reminiscences' and 'harmonies of then and now'. This anticipatory, almost prophetic function of the leitmotif had a strong influence on Wagner.

The system of reminiscence motifs and leitmotifs was developed further in *Zemire und Azor* (1818–19). Here, in the garb of fairy-tale opera, the Romantic concept of redemption achieved central importance. Harmony and orchestration were used to create the atmosphere, as, for example, the oscillations of *Rheingold*-like natural triads in the Prelude to Act 1.

Several favourable circumstances came together to make *Jessonda* (1822) Spohr's greatest operatic success. The librettist Gehe had profited from having studied earlier treatments of the subject and was able to create a text that was both poetically acceptable and satisfactory on dramatic grounds. The local colour of India fascinated the opera's first audiences. And the composer found ample opportunity to show off his gifts in the lyrical idiom in their best light, the introduction to Act 1 and the scenes with Jessonda, Amazili and Nadori making up the highpoints of the opera. Spohr's chromaticism, elsewhere used in only a haphazard fashion, is transformed poetically into a symbolical language of the soul, with almost Wagnerian sensitivity.

In his operas Spohr made significant attempts to step beyond the bounds of number opera by bringing recitative up to the level of arioso and thus making opera *durchkomponiert*. He was aware of the importance of his procedure and called upon his German colleagues to continue making developments in this direction, and the technical advances he had developed in these three operas were later taken up by other composers. Spohr himself made only a few advances in his later operas. For instance, he induced the librettist of *Berggeist* (1824), Döring, to abandon rhymed verse. It is also fascinating to note that, in *Der Alchymist* (1829–30), he included 'Tristan' chords in his more advanced harmonic language.

But these features are merely of historical interest; the reasons for the limited success of the later operas are many-sided and not always attributable merely to defects in the librettos: certainly the texts of *Der Alchymist* and *Pietro von Abano* are thoroughly workable on the stage. The real difficulties in the dramaturgy are probably the result of Spohr's clinging to a Classical aesthetic that remained tied to formal conventions, where only a Wagnerian ruthlessness would have sufficed. In addition, it would have been contrary to Spohr's natural inclination to have sought after popular effects, an inclination which developed primarily from his reaction to Meyerbeer's operas and made him increasingly hardened against everything indecent or shocking or requiring a starker effect than he could offer in his operas.

But even this does not entirely explain why Spohr was at first so highly esteemed and later so completely forgotten. The reasons for this are not due simply to the works themselves but also to the changing attitudes towards life and art in the first half of the 19th century. Spohr's artistic rise coincided with the bourgeoisie winning social independence from the nobility, to whom the privilege of music-making had primarily belonged. As a travelling composer and virtuoso, as well as a conductor at music festivals throughout Germany, Spohr won and maintained the reputation of artistic idol of the middle-class musical public; by 1820 his fame had spread throughout Europe and in 1823, with the successful production of *Jessonda*, it reached its highest point. His assumption of the post in Kassel marks the beginning of his downfall from this lofty position: he was no longer a free virtuoso or cosmopolitan, but an officially appointed conductor and a middle-class citizen in a small capital city. His life and works prospered and developed along a byway of Romanticism.

Partly from exhaustion after the Napoleonic wars, partly under the pressure of political restoration, increasing numbers of the German bourgeoisie turned to an independent livelihood and the sober, contemplative, culture-orientated sphere of Biedermeier. They were not concerned with accomplishing new ideals but merely preserving traditional values; and the ageing Spohr became a representative of these ideas. It is therefore not surprising that the following generation did not reckon him as a companion in their struggle; Wagner, a representative of this generation, described him sympathetically as 'an old man worthy of the highest honour ... whose youthful spirit is still directly illuminated by the radiant sunlight of Mozart'.

Like his younger contemporaries Marschner and Loewe, Spohr was fated to outlive a musical epoch of which he was a leading figure, and after his death only a few musicians – Brahms, Joachim, Bülow – defended his work. There is a contemporary trend towards the selective revival of his instrumental works and songs; the Louis Spohr Gesellschaft in Kassel, with its new editions, has been particularly active in initiating this revival.

WORKS

(* – autograph; vs – vocal score)

STAGE

Die Prüfung (operetta, 1, E. Henke), Gotha, 1806, ov. pubd as op.15 (Bonn, 1809), *D-Ksp
Alruna, die Eulenkönigin (romantic opera, 3), 1808, unperf., ov. pubd as op.21 (Offenbach, 1812), *US-Bp
Der Zweikampf mit der Geliebten (singspiel, 3, J. F. Schink), 1810–11, Hamburg, 15 Nov 1811, vs (Hamburg, n.d.)
Faust (opera, 2, J. K. Bernhard), 1813, Prague, 1 Sept 1816, vs (Leipzig, 1822), ov. pubd as op.60 (Leipzig, 1857); rev. 1852 as 3-act opera, London, 4 April 1852, vs (Leipzig, 1853)
Zemire und Azor (opera, 2, J. J. Ihlee, after Marmontel), 1818–19, Frankfurt am Main, 4 April 1819, vs (Hamburg, n.d.)
Jessonda (opera, 3, E. Gehe, after A. M. Lemierre: La veuve de Malabar), Kassel, 28 July 1823, vs, op.63 (Leipzig, 1824), full score (Leipzig, 1881)
Der Berggeist (opera, 3, G. Döring), 1824, Kassel, 24 March 1825, vs, op.73 (Leipzig, 1825)
Macbeth (incidental music, S. H. Spiker, after Shakespeare), 1825, ov. pubd as op.75 (Leipzig, 1827), *D-Bds
Der Sturm von Missolunghi (incidental music, C. Ehlers), 1826, 1 male chorus pubd (Hersfeld, 1826)
Pietro von Abano (romantic opera, 2, K. Pfeiffer, after L. Tieck), Kassel, 13 Oct 1827, vs, op.76 (Berlin, 1828)
Der Alchymist (opera, 3, F. G. Schmidt [pseud. of Pfeiffer], after W. Irving), 1829–30, Kassel, 28 July 1830, vs (Berlin, 1831)
Der Matrose (incidental music, K. Birnbaum), 1838, Kassel, 9 Jan 1839, collab. M. Hauptmann; *Km
Die Kreuzfahrer (opera, 3, L. and M. Spohr, after Kotzebue), 1843–4, Kassel, 1 Jan 1845, vs (Hamburg, 1845)

ORCHESTRAL

op.
12   Overture, c, 1807 (Bonn, 1808)
20   Symphony no.1, Eb, 1811 (Leipzig, 1811)
34   Notturno, C, wind insts, Turkish band, 1815 (Leipzig, 1816)
—   Grand Concert Overture, F, 1819, *GB-Lbm
49   Symphony no.2, d, 1820 (Leipzig, 1820)
—   Fackeltanz, D, 53 tpt, 4 timp, 1825
—   Festival March, D, 1825 (Kassel, 1882)
78   Symphony no.3, c, 1828 (Berlin, 1828)
86   Symphony no.4 'Die Weihe der Töne', F, 1832 (Vienna, 1834)
89   Waltz 'Erinnerung an Marienbad', A, 1833 (Vienna, c1835)
102   Symphony no.5, c, 1837 (Vienna, 1840)
116   Symphony no.6 'Historische Sinfonie im Stil und Geschmack vier verschiedener Zeitabschnitte', G, 1840 (Vienna, 1842)
121   Symphony no.7 'Irdisches und Göttliches im Menschenleben', C, 2 orch, 1841 (Hamburg, 1843)
137   Symphony no.8, G, 1847 (Leipzig, 1854)
142   Concert Overture 'im ernsten Stil', D, 1842 (Leipzig, 1846)
143   Symphony no.9 'Die Jahreszeiten', b, 1850 (Hamburg, 1853)
—   Symphony no.10, E, 1857, inc., *D-Bds

VIOLIN CONCERTOS

1   Violin Concerto no.1, A, 1802–3 (Leipzig, 1803)
2   Violin Concerto no.2, d, 1804 (Leipzig, 1805)
—   Violin Concerto, e, 1804, *Kl
7   Violin Concerto no.3, C, 1806 (Leipzig, 1806)
10   Violin Concerto no.4, b, 1805 (Bonn, 1808)
17   Violin Concerto no.5, Eb, 1807 (Zurich, 1810)
28   Violin Concerto no.6, g, 1809 (Vienna, 1813)
38   Violin Concerto no.7, e, 1814 (Leipzig, 1816)
47   Violin Concerto no.8 'in modo di scena cantante', a, 1816 (Leipzig, 1820)
55   Violin Concerto no.9, d, 1820 (Offenbach, 1823)
62   Violin Concerto no.10, A, 1810 (Leipzig, 1824)
70   Violin Concerto no.11, G, 1825 (Leipzig, 1827)
79   Violin Concerto no.12 (Concertino no.1), A, 1828 (Berlin, 1829)
92   Violin Concerto no.13 (Concertino no.2), E, 1835 (Leipzig, 1837)
110   Violin Concerto no.14 (Concertino no.3) 'Sonst und Jetzt', a, 1839 (Vienna, 1840)
128   Violin Concerto no.15, e, 1844 (Hamburg, 1846)

OTHER CONCERTOS

—   Concerto, C, vn, vc, 1803, *Kl
—   Concerto, f, vn, harp, 1807
—   Concerto, vn, harp, 1807
26   Clarinet Concerto no.1, c, 1808 (Leipzig, 1812)
48   Concerto, A, 2 vn, 1808 (Leipzig, 1820)
57   Clarinet Concerto no.2, Eb, 1810 (Leipzig, 1822)
—   Clarinet Concerto no.3, f, 1821 (Leipzig, 1884)
—   Clarinet Concerto no.4, e, 1828 (Leipzig, 1884)
88   Concerto, b, 2 vn, 1833 (Bonn, 1834)
131   Concerto, a, str qt, 1845 (Leipzig, 1847)

VIRTUOSO SOLO WORKS

(str trio acc., unless otherwise stated)

Potpourris for vn: no.1, G, on themes from Gaveaux's Le petit matelot, op.5 (Leipzig, c1806); no.2, Bb, on themes by Mozart, op.22 (Offenbach, 1812); no.3, G, on themes by Mozart, op.23 (Offenbach, 1812); no.4, B, on themes by Mozart, op.24 (Offenbach, 1812); E, on themes from P. von Winter's Das unterbrochene Opferfest, orch acc., op.56 (Leipzig, c1822); A, on Irish themes, orch acc., op.59 (Leipzig, 1823)
Other works for vn: 2 variation sets, d, op.6 (Leipzig, c1807), A, op.8 (Leipzig, 1807); 2 fantasias, c, on themes by Handel and Vogler, pf/harp acc., 1815, op.118 (Hamburg, 1845), D, on themes from Der Alchymist, pf acc., 1841, op.117 (Vienna, n.d.); 3 rondos, Bb, harp acc., 1813, E, pf acc., op.46 (Vienna, 1821); C 'alla spagnuola', pf acc., op.111 (Vienna, 1839); Polonaise, a, orch acc., op.40 (Leipzig, 1817); cadenzas for Beethoven's Violin Concerto (London, 1897)
For cl: Variations, Bb, on a theme from Alruna, orch acc., 1809 (Heilbrunn, c1888); Potpourri, F, on themes by P. von Winter, orch acc., 1811, op.80 (Berlin, c1829); Fantasia and Variations, Bb, on a theme of Danzi, str qt acc., 1814, op.81 (Berlin, 1829)
For vn, vc, orch acc.: Potpourri, Ab, on themes from Jessonda, op.64 (Leipzig, 1824)

STRING QUARTETS

op.
4   Two Quartets, C, g, 1807 (Leipzig, 1807)
11   Quatuor brillant, d, 1807 (Bonn, 1808)
15   Two Quartets, Eb, D, 1808 (Leipzig, before 1814)
27   Quartet, g, 1812 (Vienna, 1813)
29   Three Quartets, Eb, C, f, 1813–15 (Vienna, 1815)
30   Quartet, A, 1814 (Vienna, before 1819)
43   Quatuor brillant, E, 1817 (Leipzig, 1818)
45   Three Quartets, C, e, f, 1818 (Leipzig, 1819)
58   Three Quartets, Eb, a, G, 1821–2 (Leipzig, 1823)
61   Quatuor brillant, b, 1819 (Leipzig, 1823)
68   Quatuor brillant, A, 1823 (Leipzig, 1825)
74   Three Quartets, a, Bb, d, 1826 (Leipzig, 1827)
82   Three Quartets, E, G, a, 1828–9 (Berlin, 1829)
83   Quatuor brillant, Eb, 1829 (Berlin, 1830)
84   Three Quartets, d, Ab, b, 1831–2 (Offenbach, 1834)
93   Quatuor brillant, A, 1835 (Vienna, 1838)
132   Quartet, A, 1846 (Leipzig, 1847)
141   Quartet, C, 1849 (Kassel, 1849)
142   Quartet, Eb, 1855 (Leipzig, 1856)
146   Quartet, G, 1851 (Leipzig, 1856)
[155]   Quartet, Eb, 1856, unpubd, *D-Ksp
[157]   Quartet, g, 1857, unpubd, *Ksp

OTHER CHAMBER MUSIC WITHOUT PIANO OR HARP

Nonet, F, fl, ob, cl, hn, bn, vn, va, vc, db, 1813, op.31 (Vienna, 1815)
Octet, E, cl, 2 hn, vn, 2 va, vc, db, 1814, op.32 (Vienna, 1814)
4 double string quartets, d, 1823, op.65 (Leipzig, 1825); Eb, 1827, op.77 (Berlin, 1828); e, 1832–3, op.87 (Bonn, 1833); g, 1847, op.136 (Kassel, 1849)
Sextet, C, 2 vn, 2 va, 2 vc, 1848, op.140 (Kassel, 1850)
7 quintets, 2 vn, 2 va, vc, Eb, g, 1813–14, op.33 (Vienna, 1815); b, 1826, op.69 (Leipzig, 1827); a, 1833–4, op.91 (Bonn, 1834); g, 1838, op.106 (Dresden, 1839); e, 1845, op.129 (Leipzig, 1847); g, 1850, op.144 (Leipzig, 1855)
Duo, e, vn, va, 1808, op.13 (Leipzig, 1808)
14 duets, 2 vn, Eb, A, op.3 (Leipzig, c1805); C, A, 1808, op.9 (Leipzig, 1808); d, Eb, E, 1816, op.39 (Leipzig, 1816); a, D, g, 1824, op.67 (Leipzig, 1825); F, 1854, op.148 (Leipzig, c1855); D, 1854, op.150 (Leipzig, c1855); C, 1855, op.153 (Leipzig, c1855)

CHAMBER MUSIC WITH PIANO

Septet, a, fl, cl, hn, bn, vn, vc, pf, 1853, op.140 (Leipzig, c1855)
Piano Quintet, D, 1845, op.130 (Hamburg, 1846)
Quintet, c, fl, cl, hn, bn, pf, 1820, op.52 (Leipzig, 1821); arr. for str qt, pf, 1820, op.53 (Leipzig, 1821)
5 piano trios, e, 1841, op.119 (Hamburg, 1842); F, 1842, op.123 (Hamburg, ?1844); a, 1842, op.124 (Hamburg, ?1844); B, 1846, op.133 (pubd Hamburg); g, 1849, op.142 (Hamburg, ?1850)
Vn, pf: 3 duos concertants, g, 1836, op.95 (Leipzig, 1837), F, 1836, op.96 (Bonn, n.d.), E, 1837, op.112 (Dresden, 1840); 6 Duettinen, 1843, op.127 (Hamburg, 1844); 6 Salon Pieces, 1845–7, op.135 (Hamburg, 1848); 6 Salon Pieces, 1851, op.145 (Leipzig, n.d.); Salon Piece, D (New York, 1890)

CHAMBER MUSIC WITH HARP

6 sonatas, vn, harp, c, 1805, ed. (Leipzig, 1917); Bb, 1806, op.16 (Bonn, 1809); Eb, 1806, op.113 (Hamburg, 1841); Ab, 1809, op.114 (Hamburg, 1841); Eb, 1811, op.115 (Hamburg, 1841); Ab,

1819
Trio, f, vn, vc, harp, 1807, *Km

WORKS FOR ONE INSTRUMENT

Pf: Sonata, A♭, 1843, op.125 (Vienna, 1843); Rondoletto, G, 1848, op.149 (Leipzig, n.d.)

Harp: 2 fantasias, no.1, 1805, no.2, c, 1807, op.35 (Bonn, 1816); 2 variation sets, no.1, on Méhul's 'Je suis encore dans mon printemps', 1807, op.36 (Bonn, 1816), no.2, E♭, 1808

Vn: Violin-Schule, 1830–31 (Vienna, 1832)

CHORAL

Oratorios (for solo vv, chorus, orch): Das jüngste Gericht (A. Arnold), 1812, *Kl; Die letzten Dinge (F. Rochlitz), 1825–6, vs (Bonn, 1836); Des Heilands letzte Stunden (Rochlitz), 1834–5, vs (Hamburg, 1846); Der Fall Babylons (E. Taylor), 1839–40, vs (Leipzig, 1842)

Other sacred: Offertory, C, S, chorus, vn solo, orch, 1815, *Kl; Mass, C, 5 solo vv, double chorus, 1820, op.54 (Leipzig, 1822); Hymn to St Cecilia (P. von Calmberg), S, chorus, pf, 1823, op.97 (Kassel, c1860); Vater unser (S. A. Mahlmann), 4 solo vv, chorus, orch, 1829 (Berlin, 1831); 3 Psalms (M. Mendelssohn), solo vv, double chorus, 1832, op.85 (Bonn, 1834)

Ps xxiv, 4 solo vv, chorus, pf, 1836, op.97a (Berlin, c1888); Gott, du bist gross (J. F. Rohdmann), hymn, 4vv, chorus, orch, 1836, op.98 (Bonn, 1838); Vater unser (Klopstock), 2 male choruses, pf/wind insts, 1838, op.104, *Ksp, unpubd; Ps lxxxiv (M. Broadley), 4 solo vv, chorus, orch, 1846–7, op.134 (Hamburg, n.d.); Requiem, 1857, inc., *Bds

Secular: Das befreite Deutschland (K. Pichler), cantata, 1814, *Bds; 6 Songs, 4 male vv, 1817, op.44 (Leipzig, 1818); 2 Songs, 4 male vv, 1820 (Leipzig, c1820); Hessens Feiergesang (K. Wolf), unison vv, orch, 1830, *Bds; Es schwebt im lichten Strahlenkranze, festival song, 3 S, chorus, vn, pf, 1832, with new text (Leipzig, c1888) 6 Songs 4 male vv, 1833, op.90 (Hamburg, n.d.); Schill, male vv, pf 4 hands, 1840 (Leipzig, 1844); Festival Song, Alto, chorus, pf 4 hands, 1850 (Leipzig, c1888); 6 Songs, 4vv, 1855, op.151 (Hamburg, n.d.)

PARTSONGS

3 Duets, S, T, pf, op.107 (Bonn, 1839); 3 Duets, 2 S, pf, op.108 (Bonn, 1839); Jenseits, 2 S, pf (Leipzig, 1839); 6 Songs, S, A, T, B, pf, 1841–2, op.120 (Kassel, n.d.); 3 Songs, 2 S, 1849 (Leipzig, 1854); others, pubd individually or unpubd

SOLO SONGS

With orch: Oscar, S, 1805, *Kl; Torni scrina l'alma, T, vn solo, 1811; Tu m'abbandoni, ingrato, S, 1823, op.71 (Leipzig, 1827)

With pf: 6 German Songs, op.25 (Heidelberg, 1810); 6 German Songs, op.37 (Leipzig, 1816); 6 German Songs, op.41 (Leipzig, 1818); 6 German Songs, op.72 (Leipzig, 1826); 6 German Songs, A/Bar, op.94 (Bonn, 1837); 6 German Songs, 1v, pf 2 and 4 hands, op.101 (Leipzig, 1837); 5 Songs, 1836–48, op.139 (Kassel, n.d.); 6 German Songs, with cl, op.103 (Leipzig, 1838); 6 Songs, S/T, 1838, op.105 (Halle, n.d.); 6 Songs, Bar, vn, pf, 1856, op.154 (Kassel, 1857); others pubd individually or unpubd

BIBLIOGRAPHY

AUTOBIOGRAPHY, LETTERS, MEMOIRS

L. Spohr: Selbstbiographie, i–ii (Kassel and Göttingen, 1860–61; Eng. trans., 1865/R1969, 2/1878); ed. E. Schmitz (1954–5) [abridged adaptation of Lebenserinnerungen, autograph MS, lost]

——: 'Briefe L. Spohr's an das Haus Peters in Leipzig', AMZ, new ser., ii (1867), 290

A. Schöne, ed.: Briefe von Moritz Hauptmann an Franz Hauser, i–ii (Leipzig, 1871)

I. Moscheles: Aus Moscheles Leben: nach Briefen und Tagebüchern, ed. C. Moscheles, i–ii (Leipzig, 1872–3)

F. Hiller, ed.: Briefe von Moritz Hauptmann an Louis Spohr und andere (Leipzig, 1876)

La Mara [pseud. of M. Lipsius]: Musikerbriefe aus fünf Jahrhunderten (Leipzig, 1886)

——: 'Aus Spohrs Leben', Klassisches und Romantisches aus der Tonkunst (Leipzig, 1892)

W. J. von Wasilewski: Aus 70 Jahren (Stuttgart, 1897)

E. Istel: 'Fünf Briefe Spohrs an Marschner', Festschrift . . . Rochus Freiherrn von Liliencron (Leipzig, 1910), 110

E. Speyer: Wilhelm Speyer der Liederkomponist (Munich, 1925)

F. Göthel, ed.: Louis Spohr: Briefwechsel mit seiner Frau Dorette (Kassel, 1957)

F. Göthel, ed.: L. Spohr: Lebenserinnerungen (Tutzing, 1968)

GENEALOGIES AND BIOGRAPHICAL STUDIES

W. H. Riehl: 'Zwanzig Jahre aus der Geschichte der romantischen Oper, III: Spohr, Weber und Meyerbeer', Musikalische Charakterköpfe, i (Stuttgart, 1853, 8/1899), 332

W. Neumann: Louis Spohr (Kassel, 1854)

H. Giehne: Zur Erinnerung an Louis Spohr (Karlsruhe, 1860)

A. Malibran: Louis Spohr (Frankfurt am Main, 1860)

H. M. Schletterer: 'Spohr, Louis', ADB

——: L. Spohr (Leipzig, 1881) [incl. work-list]

W. Altmann: 'Spohrs Beziehungen zur Generalintendanz der königlichen Schauspiele zu Berlin', NZM, lxxi (1904), 199

E. Rychnowsky: 'Louis Spohr und Friedrich Rochlitz', SIMG, v (1903–4), 253–313

L. Spohr: Spohrsches Familienbuch (Karlsruhe, 1909–19)

O. Spohr: Die Nachfahren des Christoph Spohr (Leipzig, 1926)

H. Eberhart: Die ersten deutschen Musikfeste in Frankenhausen und Erfurt (Jena, 1934)

E. Preussner: Die bürgerliche Musikkultur (Hamburg, 1935)

P. Heidelbach: 'Louis Spohrs Prozess gegen den Kurfürsten von Hessen', AMz, lxiii (1936), 544, 563

E. Schmitz: 'Zu Louis Spohrs Selbstbiographie', Deutsche Musikkultur, ix (1944), 45

F. Uhlendorff: 'Kasseler Kapelle, Kapellmeister und Konzertmeister im Zeitraum 1814–1852', Festschrift 450 Jahre hessischer Staatskapelle (Kassel, 1952)

H. J. Becker: 'Meyerbeer in seinen Beziehungen zu Louis Spohr', Mf, x (1957), 479

H. Homburg: 'Louis Spohrs erste Aufführung der Matthäus-Passion in Kassel', Musik und Kirche, xxviii (1958), 49

E. Wolff zu Gudenberg: Beitrag zur Musikgeschichte der Stadt Kassel unter den beiden letzten Kurfürsten (diss., U. of Göttingen, 1958)

F. Uhlendorff: 'Chronik des Kasseler Musiktheaters 1814–1944', Theater in Kassel (Kassel, 1959)

H. Heussner: 'Spohr der Künstler und seine Welt', Hessische Heimat, ix (1959–60), 7

H. Homburg: 'Louis Spohr und die Bach-Renaissance', BJb, xlvii (1960), 65

R. Lebe: Ein deutsches Hoftheater in Romantik und Biedermeier, Kasseler Quellen und Studien, ii (Kassel, 1964)

H. Homburg: Louis Spohr: Bilder und Dokumente seiner Zeit (Kassel, 1968)

MUSICAL STUDIES

I. J. Ebers: Spohr und Halévy (Breslau, 1837)

F. Hand: Ästhetik der Tonkunst, ii (Jena, 1841)

A. Kahlert: Einige Gedanken über Louis Spohr (Stuttgart, 1841)

P. Spitta: 'Jessonda', Zur Musik (Berlin, 1892/R1975)

A. Schering: Die Geschichte des Instrumental-Konzerts (Leipzig, 1905, 2/1927/R1965)

R. Wassermann: Louis Spohr als Opernkomponist (diss., U. of Rostock, 1909)

L. Hirschberg: 'Louis Spohr als Balladenkomponist', Die Musik, xi/4 (1911), 212

A. Schering: Geschichte des Oratoriums (Leipzig, 1911/R1966)

A. Schmitz: 'Louis Spohrs Jugendoper Alruna', ZIMG, xiii (1911–12), 293

H. Glenewinkel: Louis Spohrs Kammermusik für Streichinstrumente (diss., U. of Munich, 1912)

A. Moser: Geschichte des Violinspiels (Berlin, 1923, rev., enlarged 2/1966–7)

G. Becking: Der musikalische Rhythmus als Erkenntnisquelle (Augsburg, 1928)

H. Rosenwald: Das deutsche Lied zwischen Schubert und Schumann (diss., U. of Heidelberg, 1929)

F. Göthel: Das Violin-Spiel Louis Spohrs, unter Berücksichtigung geigentechnischer Probleme seiner Zeit (diss., U. of Berlin, 1935)

E. Bücken: 'Romantik und Realismus: zur Periodisierung der Romantischen Epoche', Festschrift Arnold Schering (Berlin, 1937), 46

S. Goslich: Beiträge zur Geschichte der deutschen romantischen Oper (Leipzig, 1937)

H. J. Moser: Geschichte des deutschen Liedes (Berlin and Zurich, 1937)

E. Schmitz: 'Louis Spohrs erster Opernversuch', AMf, vii (1942), 84

A. Jacobs: 'Spohr and the Baton', ML, xxxi (1950), 307

H. Heussner: Die Symphonien Louis Spohrs (diss., U. of Marburg, 1956)

——: 'Louis Spohr und W. A. Mozart', MJb 1957, 199

F. Göthel: 'Louis Spohr als Pädagoge', Musik im Unterricht, 1 (1959), 301

——: 'Tragik des Mozartnachfolger', Acta mozartiana, vi (1959), 58

P. Michael: 'Die Pädagogischen Ansichten Louis Spohrs und ihre Beziehungen zum Philanthropismus', Louis Spohr-Festschrift (Weimar, 1959)

W. Lidke: 'Übereinstimmung und Gegensatz der Violin-Schulen von Leopold Mozart und Louis Spohr', Louis Spohr-Festschrift (Weimar, 1959)

F. Göthel: 'Zur Wiedergabe von Werken Louis Spohrs', Das Orchester, viii (1960), 36

D. Greiner: Louis Spohrs Beiträge zur deutschen romantischen Oper (diss., U. of Kiel, 1960)

A. A. Abert: 'Webers "Euryanthe" and Spohrs "Jessonda" als grosse Opern', Festschrift für Walter Wiora (Kassel, 1967), 35

J. Záloha: 'Několik zhudebnění známých Goethových veršů z románu Wilhelm Meisters Lehrjahre' [Some musical settings of well-known poems from Goethe's novel *Wilhelm Meisters Lehrjahre*], *HV*, vi (1969), 495

S. K. Johnston: *The Clarinet Concertos of Louis Spohr* (diss., U. of Maryland, 1972)

C. Brown: 'Spohr's "Jessonda" ', *MT*, cxxi (1980), 94

MARTIN WEYER

Spohrer, Thomas. *See* SPORER, THOMAS.

Spoleto. Italian town in the Umbrian region. It is the scene of the annual Festival of Two Worlds, founded by Menotti in 1958 with the purpose of giving young European and American artists an opportunity to appear in opera, drama, plays and concerts. Performances are given in a number of venues, notably the 17th-century Teatro Nobile (reconstructed in 1830 and renamed the Teatro Caio Melisso) and in the Teatro Nuovo (opened August 1864). Thomas Schippers was the festival's first musical director (1958–70); he was succeeded by Christopher Keene. Menotti, himself a gifted producer, has been responsible for staging several operas, and until his death in 1976 Visconti was also a regular visitor. The first festival opened with Visconti's production of Verdi's *Macbeth*, and in 1959 he was responsible for staging Donizetti's *Il duca d'Alba*, for which the designs of the original production (Rome, 1882) were used; both these works were conducted by Schippers. The Schippers–Visconti team was also responsible for productions of *Salome* (1961) and *Manon Lescaut* (1973 and 1974). Schippers and Menotti collaborated on *La bohème* (1960), *Carmen* (1962; with the young Shirley Verrett as Carmen and George Shirley as Don José), *Don Giovanni* (1967; with designs by Henry Moore) and *The Saint of Bleecker Street* (1968).

Menotti and his colleagues have also revived a number of neglected works, including Donizetti's *Il furioso all'isola di San Domingo* (1967), Mercadante's *Il giuramento* (1970), Marco da Gagliano's *La Dafne* (1973) and Salieri's *Prima la musica, dopo le parole* (1974). 20th-century works produced have included the world premières of Hoiby's *The Scarf* (1958), Hollingsworth's *La madre* (1963) and Berio's *Laborintus II* (1968), as well as productions of Prokofiev's *Fiery Angel* (1959), Henze's *Der Prinz von Homburg* (1960), Barber's *Vanessa* (1961), Weill's *Aufstieg und Fall der Stadt Mahagonny* (1972), Berg's *Lulu* (1974; produced by Polansky) and several of Menotti's own works.

HAROLD ROSENTHAL

Sponga, Francesco. *See* USPER, FRANCESCO.

Sponga, Gabriel. *See* USPER, GABRIEL.

Spongia, Francesco. *See* USPER, FRANCESCO.

Sponsel, Johann Ulrich (*b* Muggendorf, Upper Franconia, baptized 5 Dec 1721; *d* Burgbernheim, Middle Franconia, 10 Jan 1788). German clergyman and writer. He attended the Gymnasium Casimirianum Academicum in Coburg (but not until 1741–4), and studied philosophy, theology and oriental languages at Erlangen University until 1746. In 1747 he was appointed an *adiutor* at the Gymnasium in Bayreuth and received in 1748 the position of preacher at St George's Church there. On 22 January 1753 he was made an honorary member of the Lateinische Gesellschaft in Jena, and in April of that year became pastor in Lenkersheim. Finally in 1766 he moved to Burgbernheim as pastor and church superintendent. Among many publications, largely concerning church matters, his only musical work is *Orgelhistorie* (Nuremberg, 1771/*R*1968), a modest publication of 167 pages which originated as the sermon given for the dedication of the rebuilt organ in his church. In it Sponsel attempted to trace the history of the organ from ancient times, though he disclaimed any goal of completeness. His history is faulty and undependable, and heavily indebted to books on the organ by Praetorius, Printz, Werckmeister and Adlung. Most significant, however, and of continuing value, is a fairly detailed description of 26 important Franconian and Regensburg organs, with data compiled through correspondence.

GEORGE J. BUELOW

Sponsus, Play of. A play of the late 11th century on the theme of the wise and foolish virgins (*Matthew* xxv.1–13) found in a St Martial manuscript (now *F-Pn* lat.1139). It is remarkable for its early use of vernacular words (Provençal, from the district of Périgord) mixed with Latin, and for its non-liturgical melodies. The latter are notated in Aquitanian neumes heighted around a single line of unnamed pitch; there are no mensural indications in the manuscript. Four melodies suffice for the whole play.

For further information and bibliography *see* MEDIEVAL DRAMA, §III, 2(ii), esp. Coussemaker (1860); Monaci (1910) [facs.]; Liuzzi (1930); Young (1933), ii, 361; Ursprung (1938); Thomas (1951) [edn.]; Chailley (1952); Machabey (1959); Avalle (1965) [edn.].

JOHN STEVENS

Spontini, Gaspare (Luigi Pacifico) (*b* Maiolati, nr. Iesi, 14 Nov 1774; *d* Maiolati, 24 Jan 1851). Italian opera composer and conductor, the central figure in French serious opera in the first two decades of the 19th century.

1. Early career: Italy. 2. Middle years: Paris. 3. Later career: Berlin. 4. Final years: Paris. 5. Style. 6. Works.

1. EARLY CAREER: ITALY. Spontini was one of five children of poor parents. He, like his brothers, had first been intended for the priesthood, but early gave evidence of a musical talent and in 1793, at a rather advanced age for a beginning student, he entered the Conservatorio della Pietà dei Turchini at Naples. Among his teachers there were Nicola Sala and Giacomo Tritto. In August 1795 he failed to win the post of *maestrino* and in October left the conservatory without permission. His first opera, *Li puntigli delle donne*, was produced in Rome during Carnival 1796. This began a series of operas, all but one comic, written in the next few years for Venice, Florence and Naples.

Many of Spontini's Italian operas are lost, and the dates and places of performance of some of them have not been satisfactorily determined. The events of his life in these years are equally vague and much coloured by unverified legend. All this reflects the fact that he never achieved more than modest success, and therefore little public attention, in his Italian years. The dictionary of Choron and Fayolle, using materials probably supplied by Spontini himself, reports, for example, that with the performance of *L'eroismo ridicolo* in Naples in 1798 'he gained the esteem of Cimarosa, whose disciple he became and with whom he spent five years (until his departure for Palermo)'. In his early years in Paris Spontini was to call himself a pupil of Cimarosa. Whether he really deserved that distinction, or was trading on a famous name, is uncertain, but two years, not five, separated *L'eroismo ridicolo* from his departure for Palermo in 1800.

At the end of 1798 the Bourbon court had taken refuge in Palermo from the Revolution in Naples and remained there until the summer of 1801. It has been suggested that Spontini left Naples with the court, but there is no evidence of his presence in Palermo before the spring of 1800. (His *opera buffa La finta filosofa* was performed in Naples in the summer of 1799, and he was under contract to the Teatro del Fondo there as *maestro di cappella* for the following Carnival season.) After putting on three operas in Palermo in 1800, he returned to the mainland in 1801, a love affair with a high-born lady sometimes being given as the reason for his departure. After writing operas for Rome and Venice, he left for France in 1802.

2. MIDDLE YEARS: PARIS. In Paris, where he arrived early in 1803, he began humbly by giving singing lessons, but he soon received the patronage of Joséphine, who perhaps arranged for, and was in attendance at, a production of a revised version of *La finta filosofa* on 11 February 1804. This was a success, and Spontini took advantage of it by writing an *opéra comique*, *La petite maison*. Here, however, he came up against the faction that resented the inroads of Italian musicians in Paris. There was a disturbance at the opening night, 12 May 1804, and the opera received only three performances. Its one positive result was that it led Etienne de Jouy, on the day after the stormy première according to his own account, to ask Spontini to compose his libretto *La vestale*, which he had already offered unsuccessfully to Boieldieu, Cherubini and Méhul.

Before beginning *La vestale* Spontini composed two more *opéras comiques*, *Milton* (27 November 1804) and *Julie, ou Le pot de fleurs* (12 March 1805). *Julie* is a comedy, whereas *Milton* has a more serious subject and was Spontini's first attempt at a more elevated style in the French manner. From 1805 on, he also held the office of composer of Joséphine's private music, which he discharged with occasional works, among them an Italian cantata, *L'eccelsa gara*, in honour of the battle of Austerlitz, performed on 8 February 1806 at the Théâtre de l'Impératrice (Salle Louvoise), and the music for two vaudevilles, one entitled *Tout le monde a tort*, performed at Malmaison by members of the court, including Napoleon's sisters, on Joséphine's name day, 17 March 1806. *Milton* was also dedicated to Joséphine.

La vestale is said to have been composed in the summer of 1805, but it did not reach the stage of the Opéra until 15 December 1807, and only then with Joséphine's insistent support. Three times, at least, Napoleon ordered other operas to be put ahead of it, and it was only because Le Sueur's *La mort d'Adam* was not ready in time that *La vestale* at last received its chance. With its triumphant success Spontini became one of the foremost opera composers in Europe.

The government now seems to have tried to take advantage of this success by making Jouy's and Spontini's next opera, *Fernand Cortez*, a work of political significance. The subject is said to have been suggested by Napoleon himself, who wanted Cortez's conquest of Mexico implicitly compared with his own intended invasion of Spain, and Jouy was given as collaborator the poet, censor and police spy Esmenard to ensure that this comparison was clearly made. Given a gala première on 28 November 1809 with Napoleon and the King of Saxony present, *Fernand Cortez* did not achieve a lasting success in its first version. It is said that the members of the audience did not identify Cortez with Napoleon, but were demoralized by the courage of the ancestors of their present foes, and that this caused the government to suppress the work, which thus received only 24 performances in this version. It was the second version – drastically reconstructed to remove some of the dramatic weaknesses that critics had pointed out, and first performed on 8 May 1817 – that achieved a lasting place in the repertory, being given more than 200 times at the Opéra alone. In February 1832 Spontini produced in Berlin yet a third version, with changes in the final scene.

Although Spontini had become an important musical figure, he was always a controversial one. His technical equipment was attacked as faulty. It was said, incorrectly it seems, that Cherubini had made major changes in *La vestale* before its performance, and there was much opposition to awarding him the *prix décennal* in 1810 for the best grand opera of the previous decade. Berlioz later recalled that for years during his own student days he had heard in the classes of the Conservatoire, the centre of this opposition, that Spontini's 'melody lay on the accompaniment like a handful of hair on a soup'.

In February 1810, the year of his marriage to Céleste Erard, he was appointed director of the Théâtre-Italien. He threw himself into this work, performing 34 operas by 19 composers in 418 performances, and had considerable artistic success, but his proud and truculent personality created problems that led to his dismissal in 1812. His open devotion to Joséphine, even after her divorce in 1809, probably also did not help his career. Resentment against Napoleon may explain why he, almost alone among the important opera composers of Paris, did not collaborate on the patriotic operas performed to bolster public morale as the Allies neared Paris early in 1814, while hastening to celebrate the Restoration in August of that year with a new opera, *Pélage*. On 16 April he had petitioned Louis XVIII for the directorship of the king's private music and of the Théâtre-Italien, complaining that he was 'the only composer in Paris lacking a position and an assured existence'. On 9 September these requests were granted, but he soon sold his privilege to the Théâtre-Italien to the soprano Catalani.

Spontini sought the favour of the Bourbons assiduously during the rest of his stay in France, most notably by arranging the collaboration of four composers, himself included, on the *opéra-ballet Les dieux rivaux*, performed on 21 June 1816 in honour of the marriage of the Duc de Berry, heir to the throne. On 29 November 1817 he was naturalized by the king, and in the following May awarded a pension. This course separated him from Jouy, who had become an ardent liberal and opponent of the regime. He therefore had different collaborators, Dieulafoy and Briffaut, the authors of *Les dieux rivaux*, for his last *tragédie lyrique*, *Olimpie*. This work, begun in 1815, was not finished and performed until 1819. While he had great successes at the Opéra in 1817 with the revised *Cortez* and the numbers that he contributed to the revival of Salieri's *Les danaïdes*, the exaggerated expectations aroused by reports of the new opera's expensive spectacle, the frustrations aroused by his numerous postponements of its première, the political factionalism surrounding it and personal dislike of the composer, all resulted in the colossal failure of the most grandiose and ponderous work that he had yet written, when the management of the Opéra finally forced it onto the stage on 22 December 1819. There were only six performances.

3. LATER CAREER: BERLIN. From 1814 Spontini had been in intermittent negotiation for a post in Berlin. Eventually, in August 1819, he learned that the king, Friedrich Wilhelm III, a passionate admirer of his music, would give him a ten-year contract as General-musikdirektor on very good terms. He left Paris for Berlin in May 1820, having already begun a revision of *Olimpie* to remove the tragic conclusion, which he believed responsible for its failure. E. T. A. Hoffmann undertook some of the revision of the text and the German translation. The new version received its première in Berlin on 14 May 1821. Its success was great but short-lived, since on 18 June came the more successful première of *Der Freischütz*. Spontini found himself in the middle of even stronger currents of artis-tic nationalism and political factionalism than in Paris. The able and highly cultured theatre intendant, Count von Brühl, had bitterly opposed his appointment and resented the wide powers he had been given, which he felt impinged upon his own. A great admirer of Weber, for whom he had several times tried to get an appoint-ment in Berlin, Brühl was successful in the ensuing disputes in identifying his side with the cause of German art and Weber. Spontini saw the situation in terms of a personal cabal headed by Brühl and Weber, which he had to oppose with all his Italian powers of intrigue. The situation came to a head in 1824–5 in the *Euryanthe* affair. The Brühl party accused Spontini of trying to prevent or to sabotage the performance in Berlin of Weber's new work, and Spontini was not able to justify himself completely. As a result he lost what remained of the goodwill that had greeted his arrival. During the rest of his stay in Berlin he was never to be free of con-troversy and of criticism, sometimes high-minded and judicious, like that of A. B. Marx, sometimes vicious and personal, like that of Ludwig Rellstab. This succes-sion of controversies was fed by his eccentric, autocratic and often overbearing personality. His position would have been untenable had he not enjoyed the continued support of the king.

While he was maintaining this difficult position, his artistic hold on the European public was loosening. *La vestale* and *Fernand Cortez* were becoming super-annuated and losing their places in the repertory. *Olimpie* held the stage in Berlin only because Spontini was there, and he succeeded in getting it performed in only two other cities, Dresden in 1825, a kind of payment ex-tracted from Weber for the performance of *Euryanthe* in Berlin, and Paris in 1826, where it was again unsuc-cessful. He had largely created this situation himself by writing works of a complexity and grandiosity beyond the range of most theatres' time and money, and by holding to the older formulae of the *tragédie lyrique* at a time when the newer styles of Rossini and later Meyerbeer, as well as of Weber, were sweeping Europe. Once again he tended to see this as a plot, one directed

1. *Gaspare Spontini: portrait, French school (? Luigi Hersent), 19th century, in the Civica Galleria d'Arte Moderna, Milan*

2. Design by Schinkel for Act 1 of Spontini's 'Olimpie', first performed at the Paris Opéra on 22 December 1819 (Bibliothèque et Musée de l'Opéra, Paris)

by Meyerbeer, for whom he developed a pathological hatred; this attitude, which was to endear him to Wagner, reached its zenith when Meyerbeer replaced him in Berlin in 1842.

None of his other Berlin operas was ever performed in his time outside his own theatre, and only the first of them, *Nurmahal* (1822), was published. This opera is based on a story from Moore's *Lalla Rookh*. Spontini had written music to accompany a series of *tableaux vivants* drawn from this work, and it had been performed at court, before the première of *Olimpie*, on 27 January 1821. The success of the piece must have led him to turn one of its stories into a full-length opera. *Alcidor* (1825) has a similar fairy-tale subject.

Spontini's most important German opera was the last, *Agnes von Hohenstaufen*, to an inept libretto by Raupach, a dramatist who at that time dominated the Berlin stage. He began writing it in 1826. The first act alone, lasting more than two hours, was performed on 28 May 1827 as part of the festivities surrounding a royal wedding, the rest not being finished. It was not well received, and it had been considerably revised by the time of the first performance of the complete opera on 12 June 1829. Again the work was not entirely successful, and in 1832–3 the composer made a thorough revision, aided by his friend and subordinate Baron von Lichtenstein. It did not reach the stage until 6 December 1837 because of Spontini's difficulties in finding singers for the Opéra, and particularly for his own works, because of their reputation of being ruinous to the voice. The revision was not successful in Berlin, and Spontini, hoping to get the opera performed in Paris, was not even able to obtain an interview with the director of the Opéra.

The death of the king in June 1840 removed Spontini's main support in Berlin, though he seems at first not to have realized the profound alteration in his situation. Embroiled in bitter disputes with the theatre intendant Count von Redern, who had replaced Brühl in 1828, he made statements in print that in January 1841 caused him to be formally charged in criminal court with *lèse majesté*, an ironic fate for one as reverent of royalty as Spontini. When he dared to conduct again (*Don Giovanni* on 2 April) there was a riot in the hall,

and he was forced to leave the rostrum after the overture, never to return. In July he was sentenced to nine months in prison. Friedrich Wilhelm IV soon after relieved him of his duties, while allowing him to retain his title and full salary. When his sentence was upheld by an appeals court in May 1842, the king pardoned him. In June, just before leaving Berlin, he had the ultimate humiliation of seeing his arch-enemy Meyerbeer appointed his successor.

4. FINAL YEARS: PARIS. From Paris, to which he returned permanently in July 1842, he continued to carry on manoeuvres designed to bring himself back to power in Berlin or at the Opéra in Paris. The rebuffs or indifference which met these intrigues were partly balanced by moments of glory, such as the visit to Dresden in 1844 for the production of *La vestale*, described with such ironic relish by Wagner, or, the culmination of his hopes, the pope's raising him in the same year to the papal nobility as the Conte di San Andrea, a title he always insisted upon thereafter. By 1847 he was becoming feeble and deaf, and his activities were much curtailed. He returned to his birthplace in 1850, where he was royally received. He died there on 24 January 1851.

5. STYLE. In his essay on Spontini, Berlioz tried to create a Romantic image of a great original, a prototype of Berlioz himself perhaps, by claiming complete originality for the style of the operas beginning with *La vestale*:

The score of *La vestale* is, to my mind, in an entirely different style from that which had been adopted in France by the composers of that period.... It has been said that Spontini derived from Gluck. As regards dramatic inspiration, character portrayal, accuracy and vehemence of expression, this is true. But as regards melodic and harmonic style, scoring and musical colouring, Spontini proceeds from himself alone. His music has an individual look which it is impossible to mistake.

In one way Berlioz was right: Spontini's style had no single source. But neither did it proceed entirely from himself alone. The style of *La vestale* was a synthesis of French and Italian elements, as its contemporaries clearly saw, and Spontini can be regarded as one of that long succession of Italian émigrés who periodically

3. Autograph MS of the beginning of Act 2 scene v of Spontini's 'Fernand Cortez', first performed 28 November 1809 (F-Pn Opéra Rés.A.418.a.II)

revitalized French music with transfusions from the Italian. In this synthesis itself lay much of the reason for the success of *La vestale* and for the revolutionary impression that it made on its first audiences.

In the melodramatic *opéras comiques* of the 1790s

French composers had begun to move beyond Gluck's Winckelmannian ideal of passion presented in a setting of noble simplicity towards a style of more extreme emotional expression and contrast. They had sought expanded means of musical expression, sometimes in highly original experiments with harmony, orchestration and accompaniment figures, but also in striking but obvious effects that easily became clichés, such as diminished-7th chords, fast chromatic scales and strong accents off the beat. Orchestral performance reached a high degree of excellence at this time, particularly in the control of dynamic levels, and the orchestra often took on a more elaborate and independent role in its accompaniments than it had possessed in the works of Gluck. In the early 1800s these new trends were being felt in the much more conservative atmosphere of the Opéra as well.

Spontini absorbed all these tendencies. But Italianate lyricism, a quality not much stressed in the music of most serious French operas at this time, is also very apparent in *La vestale*, especially in the slow tempos, but adapted to the French taste and style of singing in that ornamentation and departures from a syllabic setting of the text are kept within strict bounds. In the fast arias Spontini tended to place a declamatory vocal line against an orchestral background made up of the patterned repetition of short motifs. This was a technique that came from the parlando arias of Italian opera, but it had already been used in French opera before Spontini, particularly by Cherubini and Méhul. He intensified the rhythmic aspect of these pieces, the regularity of the motivic repetitions reinforcing a pattern of strong accents that work to achieve an exciting forward momentum. The other elements of the piece were kept simple in order not to impede the effect. The harmony tends to swing between tonic and dominant, often over a pedal point. The principle is that of the so-called Rossini crescendo. Much of Spontini's popular appeal lay with his use of these effects, which at this time were novelties in the French serious opera. The device can be seen on its broadest scale in the stretta of the ensemble finale. Such finales had begun to make their way from *opera buffa* into *opera seria* in Italy in the late 1780s. In French serious opera they were still very rare, and that ending Act 2 of *La vestale* was the first to make an overwhelming impression.

Spontini implanted these new elements into the traditional framework of French opera. His operas abound with the triumphal processions, temple rituals, oath-swearings and other public ceremonies beloved by French composers because of the opportunity they afforded for large choral groupings and spectacular stage tableaux. His music is permeated with march rhythms, a reflection of the martial atmosphere of the Revolutionary and Napoleonic periods.

Spontini's operas tend, moreover, to be a series of sudden and unexpected dramatic strokes, providing the pivotal points of the action, new thrusts of dramatic energy and the opportunity for strong musical contrasts, often underlined by striking harmonic progressions, in 3rds, which stand out strongly from the simplicity and predictability of their surroundings. In *La vestale* these progressions occur mainly in recitatives as part of solemn public pronouncements. They are grand rhetorical gestures, the harmonic equivalent of the wide melodic leaps or pompous dotted rhythms of these recitatives. They are also musical metaphors, usually illustrating a text referring in some way to physical movement: 'La vierge impie est bannie à jamais', 'Cette heure auguste et solennelle vous met en presence des dieux', 'Vont-ils dans le chaos replonger l'univers?'. In *Cortez* Spontini learnt to absorb these effects into the more formal structure of arias and other set pieces, and in his later operas they often occur as the climactic gesture of a stretta.

He also liked to juxtapose contrasting musical forces simultaneously, sometimes with distance effects as well. In the trio in *Fernand Cortez*, the three soloists on stage sing of their foreboding at the refusal of the Aztecs to release their prisoners, while at a distance the chorus, mistakenly believing the prisoners to have been released, sings its joy. As the anxiety of the soloists increases, the chorus gradually draws nearer (in one of Spontini's favourite effects) until it finally appears on stage with the trio for a climax of opposing expressions. This kind of effect reaches its *ne plus ultra* in the second act finale of *Agnes von Hohenstaufen*. There he combined simultaneously a storm in the orchestra, a sextet of soloists disagreeing violently on stage, an unseen chorus of nuns singing a Latin hymn accompanied by another part of the orchestra imitating an organ, a second offstage chorus of peasants pleading for shelter from the storm, thunder and lightning and a tocsin ringing intermittently.

Spontini's operas were thus a series of somewhat calculated musical *coups de théâtre*, but they were held together and made to work, often brilliantly, by his remarkable sense of musical–dramatic continuity and pacing. Berlioz wrote that 'one might almost say that the second act of *La vestale* taken as a whole is just one gigantic crescendo, the *forte* of which does not come until the final scene with the veil'. As with Gluck, one cannot usually grasp Spontini's achievement as an opera composer from individual numbers. Even when these are weak, the overall dramatic shaping is often very effective. Further, one must try to imagine his operas as he himself produced them in Berlin, where he had a free hand and was often attacked by hostile critics for neglecting the works of others in favour of his own. In Berlin he conducted his operas himself. In these performances the musical aspects most important to him were tempo, rhythmic energy, precision of attack and strong accent, all qualities essential to producing the proper pacing and thus the cumulative dramatic effect that was his central concern. To achieve these ends he exercised a degree of control over his large orchestra unusual for the time, as this passage from the memoirs of A. B. Marx illustrates:

When, immediately after his appearance on the rostrum, his flashing dark eyes, in a quick sweep from left to right, captured the gaze of everyone, his arm with the baton rose, reached out and, pausing a moment, seemed to turn to stone. Then everyone felt that here his will was absolute, making all the participants completely an expression of himself; all of them were one body, and he its life force. There has been, in his time and later, finer, freer, perhaps more imaginative conducting, but never any more definitely all of a piece.

Under his direction every aspect of the production, not only music, but also acting, stage movement, spectacle and décor, was a part carefully calculated to contribute to the total dramatic effect. Each opera was staged with the utmost magnificence and rehearsed until all its parts worked together with the same precision that he demanded from his orchestra. Such a performance of *Fernand Cortez* in 1836 was a landmark in Wagner's early artistic life. In *Mein Leben* he wrote of the strong impression made on him by the 'wonderful precision and almost alarming effect' of the crowd movements, and it may be that this vivid experience of Spontini's mastery of such effects, and of the long-range dramatic shaping to which they contributed, provided a lesson for a composer who in his own work was to evince the same mastery to so high a degree.

6. WORKS. Spontini's non-operatic music is of little interest or consequence. It consists mostly of a large body of songs in the popular and ephemeral style of the French salon *romance* and of *oeuvres de circonstance* written for Berlin. The most important of the latter is the first, the *Preussischer Volksgesang* (1818), a bombastic hymn to Prussia, written for chorus and, ideally, an orchestra of 170, including 50 trumpets. Nor do the Italian operas, those that survive, give much hint of what he was to become with *La vestale*. According to legend, it was the first experience of Gluck's operas that sparked him to that unexpected achievement, and he may be considered an individualistic member of Gluck's school. Through him the most vital line of descent in that tradition passed, leading to Berlioz, at least in the opinion of Berlioz himself, who revered *La vestale* and *Fernand Cortez* as the two great masterpieces of the French opera in the generations after Gluck.

La vestale represents the Gluckian *tragédie lyrique* adapted to the taste of Empire audiences with stronger melodrama and a larger amount of stage spectacle. *Fernand Cortez* belongs to a different genre. It is less a psychological drama, as *La vestale* still is, than a historical pageant. The action is externalized into a series of spectacular tableaux, such as, in the first version, the mutiny of Cortez's army, the cavalry charge using 17 horses, the burning of the Spanish fleet, the dive by the heroine into a lake, the panoramic view of Cortez's army on the march, the Aztec temple scene in which the captives are almost, but not quite, sacrificed and the destruction of the temple itself in the final battle. Musically, *Cortez* relies largely on march music for the Spaniards and exotic (Turkish) effects for the Aztecs. The chorus, representing these two peoples, is in a sense the central character of the opera.

Olimpie is a *tragédie lyrique* based on a tragedy by Voltaire, but on this foundation Spontini placed as much spectacle as he could, including almost every device that had been in vogue in the French opera in his time – a triumphal procession, a bacchanal, a battle, a final apotheosis. Further, the set pieces tend to be longer than before. Thus, while the format of Act 2 seems to be modelled closely on the example of Act 2 of *La vestale*, it is about half as long again. As a result, the opera as a whole seems overloaded, even though it contains some of Spontini's best music and shows an advance in aspects of style and form.

The exoticism, supernaturalism and fairy-tale atmosphere of *Nurmahal* suggest that in it Spontini was attempting to compete with the German Romantic opera and so to accommodate himself to the taste of his Berlin audience. But *Nurmahal* does not really come close to being a German Romantic opera. Rather, it is a disguised French *opéra-féerie*, a traditional genre which was undergoing a new vogue in France at that time and which emphasized sensuous and exotic entertainment rather than the Romantic tone and attitude towards nature that the Germans infused into their fairy-tale settings. The libretto of *Nurmahal* is poor, and musically much of it is a pastiche, with numbers drawn from earlier works stretching back from *Lalla Rûkh* to Spontini's Italian period. These borrowings can partly be explained by his haste to finish the work in time for the royal wedding that it was to celebrate, but the result-

ing mixture of styles also seems to have been part of his artistic conception. Reflecting its occasional purpose, *Nurmahal* is a festive entertainment, one that mixes together different kinds of scenes, some serious or even tragic, others lighter, also scenes of suspense, the supernatural and love. This is mirrored by a musical mixture of florid vocal numbers, simple strophic songs and weighty declamatory pieces in the style of the big French operas. Dancing has an important role, a characteristic that did not endear it to its German audiences, which disliked ballets as much as the French insisted upon having them. The overall construction is simpler than in the French operas. Here Spontini did not usually group movements into large scenic complexes; neither are there elaborate ensembles.

Much the same can be said of *Alcidor*. Its French character is even more evident, since it is actually based on an *opéra-féerie* libretto of the 18th century reworked by the dramatist Théaulon (who was imported from Paris specially for the purpose). More of the music is new, although there are several borrowings, most notably the prologue, which is adapted from *Les dieux rivaux*. The same mixture of musical styles occurs in *Alcidor* as in *Nurmahal*, with the difference that in *Alcidor* there seems to be an attempt in some numbers to emulate the style and forms of the most recent Italian music, particularly of Rossini. The scenic construction remains simple, while the spectacle is even more extravagant than in *Nurmahal*, but there is a frequent linking of different parts of the opera by musical reminiscences.

Wagner quoted Spontini as having said to him in 1844:

After Gluck it was I who made the great revolution with *La vestale*; . . . with *Cortez* I took another step forward; then I took three steps with *Olimpie*. *Nurmahal*, *Alcidor*, and all that I did while I was first in Berlin, those were occasional works, I grant you; but then I took a hundred steps forward with *Agnes von Hohenstaufen*.

Wagner's purported quotes from Spontini must always be suspected of exaggeration, but this one represents the substance of his thinking. He never doubted that *Agnes* was his masterpiece, and it does return to the line of development that he had partly abandoned in *Nurmahal* and *Alcidor*.

In *Agnes*, as in *Olimpie*, there is a movement away from solo numbers to massive ensembles and an attempt to achieve a more continuous construction. This is done in two different ways, both already found to some extent in the French operas. One is that of massing together independent movements into large formal complexes with little or no recitative between the movements; the other is that of extending the fluid construction of the finale to cover a large part of an act, so that the sense of individual formal units is almost lost in a nearly unbroken continuity. This attempt is carried much farther in the 1837 version than in the earlier ones.

The lighter elements of style found in the previous two operas were abandoned in *Agnes*, although florid vocal writing is still present. In its medieval German subject matter Spontini was perhaps again trying to approach the taste of his Berlin audience, and again unsuccessfully. There are also in *Agnes* similarities to the Scribe type of grand opera that began in 1828 with *La muette de Portici*. Spontini himself recognized these similarities, in a letter published in 1837 without his knowledge, when he angrily claimed priority for the use of 'organs, churches, monks and masked balls' in *Agnes*, but he recognized as well that the essence of the Scribe–Meyerbeer opera was very different from that of his own and denounced it as 'demagogic, obscene and antireligious', equating the new grand opera with the wave of political liberalism resulting from the Revolution of 1830, which he equally abhorred. Just as he remained a political reactionary, he never renounced his devotion to the classic ideals of the Gluckian school, and these can still be clearly seen in *Agnes*, however much the surface may disguise them.

WORKS

OPERAS

Title and genre	Text	First performance	Sources and remarks
Li puntigli delle donne, farsetta	1	Rome, Pallacorda di Firenze, carn. 1796	autograph *I-Nc*
Il finto pittore		? Rome, 1797/8	lost
Adelina Senese, o sia L'amore secreto, dramma giocoso	2, G. Bertati: La principessa d'Amalfi	Palermo, S Cecilia, 1800 Venice, S Samuele, 10 Oct 1797	Act 1 autograph, see Albrecht (1953), 277
L'eroismo ridicolo, farsa	1, D. Piccinni	Naples, Nuovo, carn. 1798	*I-Nc*
Il Teseo riconosciuto, dramma per musica	2, C. Giotti	Florence, Intrepidi, spr. 1798	*Fc*
La finta filosofa, commedia per musica	2, ?D. Piccinni	Naples, Nuovo, sum. 1799	3 arias *Nc*, lib *Bc*; expanded from L'eroismo ridicolo
2nd version: dramma giocoso per musica	3	Paris, Théâtre-Italien (Salle Favart), 11 Feb 1804	*D-Dlb, US-Bp*
La fuga in maschera, commedia per musica	2, G. Palomba	Naples, Nuovo, carn. 1800	1 aria pubd with pf acc. and orch parts *B-Bc*, lib *I-Bc*
I quadri parlante, melodramma buffo		Palermo, S Cecilia, 1800	lost
Gli Elisi delusi, melodramma serio	2, M. Monti	Palermo, S Cecilia, 26 Aug 1800	ov., Act 1, extant
Gli amanti in cimento, o sia Il geloso audace, dramma giocoso	2	Rome, Valle, 3 Nov 1801	lost
Le metamorfosi di Pasquale, o sia Tutto è illusione nel mondo, farsa giocosa	1, G. Foppa	Venice, S Samuele, carn. 1802	lost, lib *Bc*
?Che più guarda meno vede		? Florence, 1798 (Fétis) ? Venice, 1802	probably never existed
La petite maison, opéra comique	?1, A. M. Dieulafoy, N. Gersaint	Paris, Opéra-Comique (Feydeau), 12 May 1804	ov., 7 nos. pubd, pf acc. (Paris, ?1804), all but 1 *GB-Lbm*
Milton, opéra comique	1, E. de Jouy, Dieulafoy	Paris, Opéra-Comique (Feydeau), 27 Nov 1804	(Paris, ?1804)
Julie, ou Le pot de fleurs, opéra comique	1, A. G. Jars	Paris, Opéra-Comique (Feydeau), 12 March 1805	(Paris, ?1805)
La vestale, tragédie lyrique	3, Jouy	Paris, Opéra, 15 Dec 1807	(Paris, ?1807/*R*), autograph *F-Po*
Fernand Cortez, ou La conquète du Mexique, tragédie lyrique	3, Jouy, J. A. d'Esmenard	Paris, Opéra, 28 Nov 1809 2nd version: Paris, Opéra, 8 May 1817 3rd version: Berlin, Opera, Feb 1832	(Paris, ?1809), autograph (Paris, ?1817/*R*), autograph *US-Eu* vocal score (Leipzig, *c*1832)
Pélage, ou Le roi et la paix, opéra	2, Jouy	Paris, Opéra, 23 Aug 1814	vocal score (Paris, ?1814), score *F-Po*
Les dieux rivaux ou Les fêtes de Cythère, opéra-ballet	1, Dieulafoy, C. Briffaut	Paris, Opéra, 21 June 1816	collab. Kreutzer, Persuis, Berton; excerpts (Berlin, n.d.), score *Po*
Olimpie, tragédie lyrique	3, Dieulafoy, Briffaut, after Voltaire	Paris, Opéra, 22 Dec 1819	vocal score (Paris, 1820), *US-STu*
Olympia, grosse Oper [2nd version of Olimpie]	3, Dieulafoy, Briffaut, rev., trans. E. T. A. Hoffmann	Berlin, Opera, 14 May 1821	vocal score (Berlin, ?1823); slightly rev., Fr.: Paris, Opéra, 28 Feb 1826 (Paris, ?1827/*R*), autograph *F-Po*
Nurmahal, oder Das Rosenfest von Caschmir, lyrisches Drama	2, C. A. Herklotz, after T. Moore: Lalla Rookh	Berlin, Opera, 27 May 1822	vocal score (Berlin, 1824), autograph *Po*
Alcidor, Zauberoper	3, G. M. Théaulon de Lambert, after Rochon de Chabannes; Ger. trans. Herklotz	Berlin, Opera, 23 May 1825	autograph *Po*
Agnes von Hohenstaufen 1st version: lyrisches Drama	2, S. B. E. Raupach	Berlin, Opera, 28 May 1827 [Act 1 only]	autograph fragments *US-Wc*
2nd version: grosse historisch-romantische Oper	3, Raupach	Berlin, Opera, 12 June 1829	inc. autograph *Wc*
3rd version: grosse historisch-romantische Oper	3, Raupach, rev. Lichtenstein	Berlin, Opera, 6 Dec 1837	autograph *F-Po*

OTHER DRAMATIC WORKS

L'eccelsa gara (cantata, L. Balocchi), Paris, L'Impératrice (Salle Louvoise), 8 Feb 1806, lost

Tout le monde a tort (vaudeville), Malmaison, 17 March 1806, *F-Pn*

Lalla Rûkh (Festspiel, S. H. Spicker, after T. Moore), Berlin, Royal Palace, 27 May 1822, vocal score (Berlin, ?1822)

Qui vive, qui spiro la bella che adoro, aria, cl obbl, *I-Gi(l)*, in ?Fioravanti: Il furbo contro il furbo, Genoa, 1798

Sentimi, o padre amato, scena, aria, autograph *Mc*, in Anfossi: Sofronia ed Olindo, ? Palermo, 1800

Se non piange un infelice, aria; Immagini funeste, duet (both Metastasio: L'isola disabitata), autograph sketches *F-Pn*; Choron and Fayolle

(1811) mention an otherwise unrecorded performance of this libretto in Parma

Parlami Eurilla mia, duet, *Nc*, *Mc*; as Parla Chiarella mia, *Nc*, pubd with pf acc. (London, ?1806), as inserted in La serva astuta; as Parla Lisetta mia, in Spontini: Le metamorfosi di Pasquale

Grand Bacchanale, orch, in Salieri: Les danaïdes, Paris, Opéra, 22 Oct 1817, *F-Po*; arr. wind band (Paris, n.d.)

SONGS AND DUETS
(published in Paris unless otherwise stated)

Consiglio a Nice (Bordese), arietta (*c*1804)

Sensations douces, mélancoliques et douleureuses (*c*1804): 1 Toi dont l'amour, 2 Les graces, la beauté, 3 Vous n'êtes rien, 4 Viens o divine

mélodie, 5 Jours fortunés, 6 Depuis l'instant affreux
3 romanze (c1804): 1 Chant du troubadour, 2 Etre aimé, 3 Les regrets
3 romances (c1805): 1 Le songe du prisonnier, 2 Le premier jour, 3
Romance
3 duos italiens (c1806): 1 Due bell'alme innamorati, 2 Ninfe, se liete
vivar bramate, 3 Oh dio, non sdegnarti
Les adieux d'un jeune croisé (c1806)
Les riens d'amour (c1806)
Flambeau d'amour (c1811)
3 nocturnes (Metastasio), 2 solo vv (c1811), repr. as Drei Nocturni
(Berlin, ?1836): 1 Fra tutte le pene, 2 Parto, si parto, 3 Basta, cosi
intendo
La nouvelle Valentine: stances élégiaques sur la mort de . . . Monseigneur le Duc de Berry (1820)
Tout deuil: romance sur la mort du Duc de Berry (1820)
Stances sur la mort de S. A. R. Mons. le Duc de Berry (Desaugiers)
(1820)
Les pleurs de Béarnais: romance sur la mort du Duc de Berry
(Delagarde) (1820)
Mignon's Lied (Goethe) (Berlin, ?1830)
4 romances (Berlin, c1831): 1 La petite sorcière, chansonette
(Bétourné), 2 L'heureux gondolier, barcarolle, 3 Il reviendra, 4 Salut,
vertes campagnes, nocturne, S, T
Zephir und die Träume (Berlin, n.d.)
6 oeuvres nouvelles (?1839): 1 Il faut mourir, 2 Le départ, 3 Le rêve
d'Orient (Escudier), 4 Mignon (E. Deschamps, after Goethe), 5 Les
regrets, 6 Arietta
L'adieu (1840)
Che non mi disse un di (Metastasio), arietta; Es blühte ein Blümchen
(J. F. L. Duncker), romanza: both in Album neuer Original-Compositionen für Gesang und Piano (Berlin, c1840)
Spontini's Lebewohl an seine Freunde in Berlin (Spontini) (Berlin,
1842)
A quinze ans (Gayrard) (Berlin, c1840–50)
L'orphelin du malheur (Berlin, c1840–50)
Ben mio ricordati (Metastasio), in Les cantilènes: album de chant (n.d.)
La charité (c1855)

L'inconstance, Le retour (both n.d.); Canzonetta tarantina, S, bc, c1795,
autograph F-Pn; La pêche de l'ambre: chant de Prusse orientale, duet,
1832, autograph D-Bds; Ma dernière plainte au bord de mon tombeau, 1838, autograph F-Pn

CHORAL

Leta voce et fide vera, motetto pieno, S, S, T, 4vv, orch, c1794–5, parts
I-Nc
Preussischer Volksgesang (Borussia) (J. F. L. Duncker), vv, orch, 1818
(Berlin, n.d.); arr. orch as Grosser Sieges- und Festmarsch (Berlin,
n.d.)
Gebet, Duetto und Hymnus, cantata, solo vv, 6vv, orch, for visit of Tsar
to Berlin, 1826, I-IE, inc.
Gott segne den König (Herklotz), cantata, perf. Halle, 12 Sept 1829
An den Frieden, T, vv, orch, 1831
Les cimbres, chant de guerre, TTB, pf (Berlin, n.d.)
Begrüsst den Tag, Festhymne, 1840
Domine salvum fac regem nostrum, solo vv, chorus, org, vcs, dbs, for
coronation of Friedrich Wilhelm IV, 1840, I-IE, inc.
Jesu Christe Domine, offertory, male vv, double chorus, org (Paris,
1854)
Domine Jesu, 3vv, vv, org (Paris, n.d.)

INSTRUMENTAL

Notturno, orch, Naples, 1795, autograph F-Pn
Ballo marziale, military band: 1 Evoluzioni militari, 2 Preludio ai
combattimenti ed alla vittoria sul campo di Marte, I-Mc
Geschwindmarsch, military band, in Sammlung von Märschen für
türkische Musik zum bestimmten Gebrauch der königlichen preussischen Armée (Berlin, n.d.)
4 Fackeltänze, for Prussian royal weddings, 1822, 1823, 1825, 1829,
orch (Berlin, n.d.); all 4 arr. pf (Berlin, n.d.)
Les charmes d'un fête, divertissement, pf (Vienna, n.d.)

PEDAGOGICAL WORKS

Ristretto di esercizi per apprendere la maniera di cantare, autograph
F-Pn

WRITINGS

Rapporto intorno alla riforma della musica sacra (MS, I-Rsc, 1838)
with H. Berton and M. Carafa: Reconstruction de la Salle Favart:
observations à MM les membres de la Chambre des députés (Paris,
?1839)
Opinion de M. Spontini sur les changements à introduire dans le règlement du concours de grand prix de composition musicale tels qu'ils
avaient été proposés par le même académicien et adoptés par la
commission spéciale designée par l'académie, Aug 1839 (Paris, n.d.)
'Rapport à l'Académie royale des beaux arts de l'Institut de France', pr.
in J. G. Prod'homme and A. Dandelot: Gounod (1818–1893): sa vie et
ses oeuvres, i (1911), 253ff [report, dated 17 Sept 1841, on Gounod's
Prix de Rome compositions]

Mes propositions pour la réorganisation des musiques militaires de
France, 1845 (?Paris, 1850)

BIBLIOGRAPHY

SOURCE MATERIAL

Des dramatischen Leib-Compositeurs, kgl.-preuss. General-Musikdirectors . . . Herrn Ritters Gasparo Spontini Klagen über den
Verfall der dramatischen Musik: aus dem Französischen übersetzt
und mit erläuternden Anmerkungen begleitet von einer Gesellschaft
von Kunstfreunden und Verehren des grossen Meisters (Leipzig,
1837)
G. Radiciotti: Lettere inedite di celebri musicisti a Pietro, Giovanni e
Rosa Morandi (Milan, 1897)
J. S. Shedlock: 'Letters from Weber to the Abbé Vogler and to Spontini',
Studies in Music by Various Authors (London, 1910)
J. Tiersot: 'Lettres de musiciens écrites en français du XVe au XXe
siècle', RMI, xxi (1914), 52–84; pubd separately (Turin, 1924)
E. Pfeiffer: 'Lettere inedite di Spontini', Musica d'oggi, xi (1929), 199
J. Heugel: 'Une lettre inédite de Spontini', Le ménestrel, xcii (1930),
344; Eng. trans., MMR, lxii (1932), 199 [the same letter as (Leipzig,
1837)]
G. Radiciotti and E. Pfeiffer: 'Lettere inedite di G. Spontini', NA, ix
(1932), 23
R. Sassi: 'Lettere inedite di Gaspare Spontini', NA, xii (1935), 165
M. Pincherle: Musiciens peints par eux-mêmes: lettres de compositeurs
écrites en français (Paris, 1939), 64ff
O. Albrecht: A Census of Autograph Music Manuscripts of European
Composers in American Libraries (Philadelphia, 1953), 276f
A. Belardinelli: Documenti spontiniani inediti (Florence, 1955)
F. Schlitzer: Frammenti biografici di Gaspare Spontini con lettere
inedite, Accademia musicale chigiana: settimane musicali senesi,
xxxiii (Siena, 1955)
——: Circonstanze della vita di Gaspare Spontini con lettere inedite,
Accademia musicale chigiana: settimane musicale senesi, xxxvii
(Siena, 1958)

BIOGRAPHY AND CRITICISM

FétisB
St Victor: Réflexions d'un amateur sur l'opéra La Vestale (Rouen,
1809)
A. Choron and F. Fayolle: 'Spontini, Gaspare', Dictionnaire historique
des musiciens, ii (Paris, 1811/R1971)
E. T. A. Hoffmann: 'Nachträgliche Bemerkungen über Spontinis Oper
Olympia', Zeitung für Theater und Musik, i/23–38 (1821); repr. in
Schriften zur Musik: Nachlese (Munich, 1963), 354ff
L. Rellstab: Über mein Verhältnis als Kritiker zu Herrn Spontini als
Componist und General Musikdirektor (Leipzig, 1827)
——: 'Spontinis Oper Agnes von Hohenstaufen', Berliner allgemeine
musikalische Zeitung, iv (1828)
A. B. Marx: 'Eine Betrachtung über den heutigen Zustand der deutschen
Oper, angeknüpft an Nurmahal von Spontini und Oberon von
Weber', Caecilia, vii (1828), 135–82
E. M. Oettinger: Spontini (Leipzig, 1843)
[L. L. de Loménie]: 'Spontini', Galerie des contemporains illustres par
un homme de rien, x (Paris, ?1847)
A. Gathy: 'Berlioz über Spontini', Neue Berliner Musikzeitung, v
(1851), 88, 97
H. Berlioz: Les soirées de l'orchestre (Paris, 1852; Eng. trans., 1965),
12e, 13e soirées
H. Krigar: 'Spontini', Almanach für Freunde der Schauspielkunst, xvi
(1852), 136
D. Raoul-Rochette: Notice historique sur la vie et les oeuvres de M.
Spontini (Paris, 1852)
C. von Ledebur: 'Spontini', Tonkünstler-Lexicon Berlin's (Berlin,
1861/R1965)
L. Rellstab: Aus meinem Leben (Berlin, 1861)
K. Varnhagen von Ense: Aus dem Nachlass Varnhagen's von Ense:
Tagebücher (Leipzig, 1862–70)
A. B. Marx: Erinnerungen (Berlin, 1865)
H. Dorn: Aus meinem Leben: musikalische Skizze, i (Berlin, 1870)
R. Wagner: 'Erinnerungen an Spontini', Gesammelte Schriften, iii
(Leipzig, 1872; Eng. trans., 1894), 86
T. de Lajarte: Curiosités de l'opéra (Paris, 1883)
C. Robert: Spontini: eine biographische Skizze (Berlin, 1883)
A. Jullien: Paris dilettante au commencement du siècle (Paris, 1884)
P. Spitta: 'Spontini in Berlin', Zur Musik (Berlin, 1892), 291–353
W. Altmann: 'Spontini an der Berliner Oper', SIMG, iv (1902–3), 242–
92
R. Wagner: Mein Leben (Munich, 1911; Eng. trans., 1911), 331ff
A. Pougin: 'Les dernières années de Spontini', RMI, xxix (1922), 54,
236
A. Maecklenburg: 'Der Fall Spontini–Weber: ein Beitrag zur
Vorgeschichte der Berliner Erstaufführung der Euryanthe', ZMw, vi
(1924–5), 449
C. Bouvet: Spontini (Paris, 1930)

K. Schubert: *Spontinis italienische Schule* (Strasbourg, 1932)
G. Abraham: 'The Best of Spontini', *ML*, xxiii (1942), 163
A. Ghislanzoni: *Gaspare Spontini* (Rome, 1951)
I° congresso internazionale di studi spontiniani: Iesi, Maiolati, Fabriano, Ancona 1951
P. Fragapane: *Spontini* (Bologna, 1954)
H. Engel: 'Wagner und Spontini', *AMw*, xii (1955), 167
H. Mueller von Asow: 'Gasparo Spontinis Briefwechsel mit Wolfgang von Goethe', *Chronik des Wiener Goethe-Vereins*, lxi (1957), 42
F. Schlitzer: *La finta filosofa di Gaspare Spontini* (Naples, 1957)
H. Becker: *Der Fall Heine-Meyerbeer: neue Dokumente revidieren ein Geschichtsurteil* (Berlin, 1958), 81ff, 118ff
A. Ghislanzoni: 'Un opera di Spontini rintracciata: *Gli Elisi delusi*', *Musica d'oggi*, new ser., ii (1959), 10
F. Schnapp: 'E. T. A. Hoffmanns Textbearbeitung der Oper "Olimpia" von Spontini', *Jb des Wiener Goethe-Vereins*, lxvi (1962), 126
A. Vander Linden: 'Notes de Madame Gaspare Spontini sur la vie et l'oeuvre de son mari', *RBM*, xxviii–xxx (1974–6), 222

DENNIS LIBBY

Spontone, Alessandro (*b* Bologna, baptized 1 June 1549; *d* Bologna, *c*1590). Italian composer and musician, brother of BARTOLOMEO SPONTONE, whose pupil he was. He held at least two appointments: in 1569 he was a member of the *concerto palatino* of the senate of Bologna and in 1585 was *maestro di cappella* of Forlì Cathedral. He earned at least local regard as a practical musician, for Ercole Bottrigari, whose friend he was, referred to him as 'assai buon musico pratico'.

WORKS

Il primo libro de [13] madrigali, 5, 6vv (Venice, 1585)
2 canzoni, 1582[13], 1 canzone, 1582[14], 1 madrigal, 1590[13]

BIBLIOGRAPHY

E. Bottrigari: *Il Trimerone de' fondamenti armonici* (MS, *I-Bc* B.44), f.137*v* f
G. Gaspari: 'Dei musicisti bolognesi al XVI secolo e delle loro opere a stampa', *Atti e memorie della R. Deputazione di storia patria per le provincie di Romagna*, 2nd ser., i (1875); repr. in *Musica e musicisti a Bologna* (Bologna, 1970), 334

FRANK TIRRO

Spontone, Bartolomeo (*b* Bologna, baptized 22 Aug 1530; *d* Treviso, ?1592). Italian composer and singer, brother of ALESSANDRO SPONTONE. He was a pupil of Nicolò Cavallari, *maestro di cappella* of S Petronio, Bologna, and continued his musical education with Giaches de Ponte and Morales in Rome. His own most famous pupil was Ercole Bottrigari; he also taught his brother Alessandro. He sang in the choir of S Petronio in 1551–2. From 1553 to 1582 he was a member of the *concerto palatino* of the senate of Bologna and apparently held other posts simultaneously. He was elected *maestro di cappella* of S Petronio in May 1577 and held the post until May 1583. He was *maestro di cappella* at S Maria Maggiore, Bergamo, from 1584 to 1586; at Verona Cathedral from 1586 to 1588; and at Treviso Cathedral in 1591–2. The inclusion of a seven-part dialogue by him in a collection of madrigals by Rore, Andrea Gabrieli, Palestrina and others in 1568 suggests that even at this comparatively early date his contemporaries held his music in high regard. The lack of a complete edition of his works makes it hard to assess his achievement, but of his few works in modern editions, the six-part *Missa 'Così estrema è la doglia'* displays rich harmonic writing in the context of superb contrapuntal craft. The Ciro Spontone who edited his madrigal collection of 1583 was his elder son.

WORKS

Il primo libro di madrigali, 4vv (Venice, 1558)
Il primo libro de madrigali et canzoni, 5vv, con uno dialogo, 8vv (Venice, 1561)
Il secondo libro de madrigali, 5vv, con una canzone (Venice, 1567)
Libro terzo de madrigali, 5vv, ed. C. Spontone (Venice, 1583)
Missarum, 5–6, 8vv, liber primus (Venice, 1588); Missa 'Così estrema è

la doglia', ed. in AMI, ii (1897/*R*), 31
2 madrigals each in 1568[12], 1586[12], 1590[13]; 1 madrigal each in 1566[17], 1568[19], 1570[15], 1574[8], 1576[5], 1577[7], 1582[5], 1584[4], 1585[19], 1586[1], 1586[9], 1589[6], 1590[17], 1590[20], 1592[13], 1592[15], 1593[3], 1594[6], 1594[8], 1596[12], 1597[13], 1600[7], 1600[8], 1600[9], 1604[10], 1611[12], 1629[8]; 8 madrigals, *I-Mc*
1 villotta in 1557[18]; 1 gregesca in 1564[16], ed. S. Cisilino, Celebri raccolte musicali venete del cinquecento, i (Padua, 1974); 2 dialoghi in 1590[11]
1 motet in 1615[2]; 6 motets, 8 psalms, *A-Wn*; 1 motet, *I-TVca*

BIBLIOGRAPHY

G. Gaspari: 'Memorie riguardanti la storia dell'arte musicale in Bologna al XVI secolo', *Atti e memorie della R. Deputazione di storia patria per le provincie di Romagna*, 2nd ser., i (1875); repr. in *Musica e musicisti a Bologna* (Bologna, 1970), 186ff

FRANK TIRRO

Spontoni, Ludovico (*b* Bologna, baptized 2 March 1555; *d* Bologna, before 1609). Italian composer and priest. Son of Costanzo and grandson of Benedetto Spontoni, he may have been related to the composers ALESSANDRO and BARTOLOMEO SPONTONE, who were active in Bologna at the same time. He studied in Forlì and called himself 'da Forlì' in the dedication of his madrigal collection of 1586, but he was certainly born in Bologna. His madrigals are similar in style to those of Rore in that expressive devices used to depict the text do not break the smooth flow of the part-writing. His surviving motets are for double chorus and continuo.

WORKS

Il primo libro de madrigali, 5vv (Venice, 1586)
Mottetti, 8vv, bc, libro secondo (Venice, 1609)
1 motet in 1611[1]; 1 motet in 1612[3]

FRANK TIRRO

Sponza, Francesco. *See* USPER, FRANCESCO.

Sponza, Gabriel. *See* USPER, GABRIEL.

Spoorenberg, Erna (*b* Yogyakarta, Java, 11 April 1926). Dutch soprano. She studied in the Netherlands with, among others, Julius Röntgen (piano and violin) and Aaltje Noordewier-Reddingius (singing). She made her concert début at Hilversum in 1947, and her opera début shortly afterwards. She toured extensively throughout Europe, the USA, where she made her début at Lincoln Center, New York, in 1967, South Africa and the USSR, and for many years formed a duo with the composer and pianist Géza Frid. In opera she was active with the Netherlands Opera, the Deutsche Oper am Rhein and at the Vienna Staatsoper (début, 1949), where she sang mainly Mozart. Among her finest roles was Mélisande, for which her charming appearance and clear, limpid vocal timbre were well suited (she took part in Ansermet's second recording of Debussy's opera). She also achieved wide renown in oratorio.

BIBLIOGRAPHY

E. Spoorenberg: *Daar lig je dan* (The Hague, 1962)

TRUUS DE LEUR

Sporck, Count Franz Anton (*b* Lysá nad Labem, Bohemia, 9 March 1662; *d* Lysá nad Labem, 30 March 1738). Bohemian nobleman, viceroy of Bohemia from 1691, and patron of the arts. He played a prominent role in establishing the Austro-Bohemian horn tradition. While at Versailles in about 1680 he came to know the French hunting-horn (*cor de chasse*) and had two of his retainers taught to play it. On their return to Bohemia they passed on the art of horn playing to their countrymen, and the first Nuremberg horns, built in the 1680s, were probably modelled on the instruments which Sporck's horn players had brought back from

Versailles. According to Sporck's Kapellmeister, Tobias Seemann, the horn was used in ensembles with other instruments in Sporck's house orchestra (at Prague, Kuks and Lysá) from the earliest years.

The Venetian opera troupe which Count Sporck introduced on the stage of his private theatres at Kuks and Prague in 1724 marked the beginning of regular operatic performances in Bohemia. That Sporck was sent a copy of the Sanctus of the B minor Mass (the copy does not survive) suggests that he may have known J. S. Bach. In the bass aria no.16 of the *Peasant Cantata* BWV212 Bach used Sporck's favourite hunting tune, derived from a horn call. Sporck set up his own printing press for the dissemination of his own philosophical and theological writings and translations. He sponsored the publication of an influential Czech songbook, *Slavíček rajský*, compiled by J. J. Božan (Hradec Králové, 1719). The monastery of the Merciful Brethren, founded by Sporck at Kuks, gathered a valuable collection of music during the 18th century (now in *CS-Pnm*). Sporck was also a patron of the graphic arts.

Count Johann Wenzel (Joseph) Sporck (1724–1804) was a distant relative of F. A. Sporck. A lawyer, he was also director of the imperial court music and theatre at Vienna from 1764 to 1775, as successor of Count Durazzo; he later made his home in Prague an important musical centre (he was a skilful cellist), and in 1803 became the first patron of the Prague Tonkünstler-Sozietät.

BIBLIOGRAPHY

Jahrbuch der Tonkunst von Wien und Prag (Prague, 1796), 108, 133, 141

G. J. Dlabacž: *Allgemeines historisches Künstler-Lexikon*, iii (Prague, 1815), 142, 178f

C. von Wurzbach: *Biographisches Lexikon des Kaiserthums Oesterreich*, xxxvi (Vienna, 1878), 219ff, 245ff

O. Teuber: *Geschichte des Prager Theaters*, i (Prague, 1883)

H. Benedikt: *Franz Anton Graf von Sporck* (Vienna, 1923)

J. Krupka: 'F. A. Sporck a jeho opera v Praze a Kuksu', *Dalibor*, xxxix (1922–3), 77, 89, 105, 145; xl (1923–4), 15, 113, 125

P. Nettl: 'F. A. Sporcks Beziehungen zur Musik', *Mf*, vi (1953), 324

J. Machovský: *Český překlad Šporkova tisku 'Hexenlieder'* (diss., Prague U., 1956)

R. Quoika: *Die Musik der Deutschen in Böhmen und Mähren* (Berlin, 1956)

P. Kneidl: 'Libreta italské opery v Praze v 18.století', *Strahovská knihovna*, i (1966), 97–131

H. Fitzpatrick: *The Horn and Horn-Playing and the Austro-Bohemian Tradition from 1680 to 1830* (London, 1970) [also review by A. C. Baines, *ML*, lii (1971), 438]

O. Michtner: *Das alte Burgtheater als Opernbühne* (Vienna, 1970), 18

MILAN POŠTOLKA

Sporer [Sporrer, Spohrer], **Thomas** (*b* Freiburg, *c*1490; *d* ?Strasbourg, 1534). German composer. On 27 February 1506 he matriculated at Freiburg University. He may have been a son of Heinrich Sporer, who in 1482 was living in Strasbourg, or of Sebastian Sporer, who was a drummer in the Innsbruck court chapel from 1478 to 1479. Sporer may have taught Matthias Greiter and Johannes Heugel, who also studied at Freiburg. On 11 October 1513 the university appointed Sporer, then living at Lindau am Bodensee, as warden of a student hostel. He appears subsequently to have lived in Strasbourg and to have died there; a five-part *Epicedion Thomae Sporeri musicorum principis*, composed by Dietrich (Strasbourg, 1534), contains the names only of Strasbourg humanists. Heugel also wrote two epitaphs in 1534 on the death of Sporer. The respect in which Sporer was held, according to the *Epicedion*, appears scarcely justifiable, judging by the few compositions of his that survive (a three-voice motet and eight songs, ed.

H. J. Moser, *T. Sporer: die erhaltenen Werke des Alt-Strassburger Meisters*, Kassel, 1929), even though his songs have a very individual style influenced by the French chanson, which sets him apart from the other German composers active at that time.

BIBLIOGRAPHY

R. Eitner: 'Das alte deutsche mehrstimmige Lied und seine Meister', *MMg*, xxvi (1894), 48

M. Vogeleis: *Quellen und Bausteine zur Geschichte der Musik und des Theaters im Elsass 500–1800* (Strasbourg, 1911)

W. Gurlitt: 'Johann Kotter und sein Freiburger Tabulaturbuch von 1513', *Elsass-Lothringisches Jb*, xix (1941), 216

G. Reichert: 'Die Preces primariae-Register Maximilians I. und seine Hofkapelle um 1508', *AMw*, xi (1954), 103

M. Staehelin: 'Zum Egenolff-Diskantband der Bibliothèque Nationale in Paris', *AMw*, xxiii (1966), 93

HANS-CHRISTIAN MÜLLER

Sportonio, Marc'Antonio ['Il Bolognese'] (*b* ?Bologna, *c*1631; *d* ?Palermo, after 1680). Italian singer and composer. He was a pupil of Carissimi at the German College, Rome, from July 1644 (the libretto of his opera *Elena* calls him 'romano'), and in 1645 he nominally entered the service of the Duke of Modena as a singer; he was a mezzo-soprano. In that capacity he went to Paris with Venanzio Leopardi at the end of 1646 to take part in the performance of Luigi Rossi's *Orfeo* (spring 1647); he remained there in the service of the French queen.

From 1653 Sportonio was at Palermo: in that year he sang in an 'attione tragica', *Costantino* (Jesuit College, Palermo; stage music by G. B. Fasolo). In 1655, together with other singers of Palermo, the 'Musici accademici sconcertati', he organized the first opera performance at Palermo, Cavalli's *Giasone*, in which he sang the comic role of Delfa. He was the leading figure in public theatre life at Palermo (where women's voices were introduced rather late). In Carnival 1661 he appeared as the composer of *Elena* (text by N. Minato; music originally by Cavalli). *La Flavia imperatrice* (text by F. Beverini), performed at the theatre of the impresario Pietro Rotino in March 1669, was described as his fourth opera; in 1675 he signed the libretto of *Caligola* and in 1678 composed one of the few operas of local origin, *La Fiordispina*, to a text by the Palermo writer Antonio Salamone (it was repeated at the viceregal court in February 1680 and at the Teatro S Bartolomeo, Naples, in Carnival 1683). Sportonio also made use of his international theatrical experience at the court of the viceroy: in February 1659 he sang, in a flying carriage, the introduction to a dancing festivity at the court at Palermo. He was a friend of the Scarlatti family (he was a witness to the marriage of the parents of Alessandro on 5 May 1658) and among the first members of the 'Unione dei musici' of Palermo in 1679–80. Two of his cantatas (or arias) survive in manuscript (in *GB-Och*).

BIBLIOGRAPHY

H. Prunières: *L'opéra italien en France avant Lulli* (Paris, 1913), 91, 101, 136, 377

R. Pagano: 'La vita musicale a Palermo e nella Sicilia del Seicento', *NRMI*, iii (1969), 448, 455

T. Culley: 'The Influence of the German College in Rome on Music in German-speaking Countries during the Sixteenth and Seventeenth Centuries', *AnMc*, no.7 (1969), 24; no.9 (1970), 32, 39

T. D. Culley: *Jesuits and Music*, i: *A Study of the Musicians Connected with the German College in Rome* (Rome, 1970), 219, 226

R. Pagano: *Alessandro Scarlatti: biografia* (Turin, 1972), 10, 19, 34, 56

L. Bianconi: 'Funktionen des Operntheaters in Neapel bis 1700 und die Rolle Alessandro Scarlattis', *Colloquium Alessandro Scarlatti: Würzburg 1975*

L. Bianconi and T. Walker: 'Dalla *Finta pazza* alla *Veremonda*: storie di Febiarmonici', *RIM*, x (1975), 393, 404

R. Pagano: 'Le origini ed il primo statuto dell'Unione dei musici intitolata a Santa Cecilia in Palermo', *RIM*, x (1975), 561
                                                    LORENZO BIANCONI

Spouge. A popular dance music style, arising in the eastern British Caribbean (primarily Barbados) in the early 1970s, related to a number of English-language folk and popular music styles, notably CALYPSO and REGGAE. It is in a simple quadruple metre, with a persistent rhythmic pattern.

Sprechgesang [Sprechstimme] (Ger.: 'speech-song' ['speech-voice']). A type of vocal enunciation intermediate between speech and song. Notated Sprechgesang was introduced by Humperdinck in his opera *Königskinder* (1897), though in the edition of 1910 he replaced it by conventional singing. The innovation was probably an attempt to prescribe means of articulation that were already being used by singers of both lieder and popular song. It was exploited most extensively by Schoenberg in the *Gurrelieder* (notation shown in ex.1a), *Die glückliche Hand* and *Pierrot lunaire* (ex.1b), and *Moses und Aron* (ex.1c, the notation

Ex.1

also used by Humperdinck). The preface to *Pierrot* is Schoenberg's most explicit statement on Sprechgesang, which should 'give [the pitch] exactly, but then immediately leave it in a fall or rise'; the performer is also instructed that Sprechgesang should neither resemble natural speech nor recall true singing. These directions have given rise to various interpretations, largely because of the difficulty in speaking the range and exactness of pitch required. In his last two compositions with Sprechgesang, the *Ode to Napoleon* and *A Survivor from Warsaw*, Schoenberg reduced the compass demanded and, while still indicating interval size (ex.1d), left the pitch level of the vocal line to be determined by the performer. Berg used *Pierrot*-type Sprechgesang in *Wozzeck* and *Lulu*, and at the same time introduced a new shade, 'half sung' (notated as in ex.1e), between Sprechgesang and song. A further refinement was made by Boulez in *Le visage nuptial*, where the two varieties used by Berg are joined by 'spoken intonation at the indicated pitch' (notated as in ex.1c), a median between speech and Sprechgesang.

BIBLIOGRAPHY

R. Wood: 'Concerning "Sprechgesang" ', *Tempo* (1951), no.17, p.3

H. Keller: 'Whose fault is the speaking voice', *Tempo* (1965–6), no.75, p.12

W. Austin: *Music in the 20th Century* (New York, 1966), 196ff

P. Boulez: 'Note sur le Sprechgesang', *Relevés d'apprenti* (Paris, 1966; Eng. trans., 1968; It. trans., 1968; Ger. trans., 1972), 262
                                                    PAUL GRIFFITHS

Sprechstimme. *See* SPRECHGESANG.

Sprenger, Eugen (*b* Stuttgart, 7 Jan 1882; *d* Frankfurt am Main, 25 Aug 1953). German string instrument maker. He was the son of Anton Sprenger the younger, with whom he served an apprenticeship, first in Stuttgart and then in Mittenwald, subsequently working for a year for his older brother, Adolf, who had taken over the Stuttgart workshop in 1897. In 1900, following his father's death, Eugen left Stuttgart to gain broader ex-

perience. Thereafter he worked in Munich, Switzerland, France and England. He later returned to Germany and in 1907 opened the Eugen Sprenger Workshop in Frankfurt am Main. After a suspension of business in World War I when he was called to service, he reopened in 1919 on the Hochstrasse in Frankfurt. Sprenger established an enviable reputation for his violins, violas da gamba, lutes and guitars, and for his restoration and reconstruction of historical instruments. Like his father and brother, he copied the old Italians, especially the Stradivari and Guarneri. His instruments are extremely well built, the tone full and powerful; the viols and lutes are especially sought after. In 1930 Sprenger patented his own model of viola, and later he wrote *Die Streichinstrumente und ihre Behandlung* (Kassel and Basle, 1951). His labels read 'Eugen Sprenger/Lauten-und/Geigenmacher in Frankfurt a.M.' or 'Eugen Sprenger. Fecit/Frankfurt a.M. Anno 19...', followed by a printed monogram. His son Eugen Sprenger (*b* Frankfurt, 26 Nov 1920) was an apprentice with his father, and took over the Frankfurt workshop in 1950. Under his direction the firm began to specialize in the restoration and reconstruction of historical instruments of all kinds.
                                                    MURRAY LEFKOWITZ

Sprezzatura. Term used in early 17th-century Italy to denote concepts of expressiveness and rubato in the composition and performance of monodic music. The use of the word originated outside music with Castiglione: 'this virtue . . . contrary to affectation which we now call *sprezzatura* . . . [is] the true source of grace'; and Shearman defined it as 'courtly grace revealed in the effortless resolution of all difficulties . . . [a] kind of well-bred negligence born of complete self-possession'.

Caccini was the first to apply the word to music. In the preface to *Euridice* (Florence, 1600) he wrote that he had 'employed a certain *sprezzatura*, which I consider to have something noble about it, believing that by means of it I approach that much closer to the essence of speech'. Shortly afterwards, in the preface to *Le nuove musiche*, he wrote of 'negligently' – that is, naturally – introducing dissonances to relieve the blandness of concord, and he directed that bars 15–17 of the madrigal *Deh, dove son fuggiti* be performed 'without regular rhythm, as if speaking in tones, with the aforesaid negligence' – an idea close to rubato. He finally returned to the question in the preface to his *Nuove musiche e nuova maniera di scriverle* (Florence, 1614).

The music that Caccini discussed is all for solo voice and continuo, and some Italian monodists and singers at least must have remembered his views when writing or performing recitatives, ariosos and other pieces 'without regular rhythm' during the ensuing few decades; for example, in the preface to *Dafne* (1608), Marco da Gagliano used the word 'sprezzatura' during a detailed discussion about the expressive performance of the prologue of his opera. Caccini's ideas might also be applied in, for example, the freer types of keyboard music.

BIBLIOGRAPHY

B. Castiglione: *Il libro del cortegiano* (Venice, 1528); ed. C. Cordié, La letteratura italiana, xxvii (Milan, 1960), 48ff; Eng. trans. (Harmondsworth, 1967), 67f

G. Caccini: *Le nuove musiche* (Florence, 1601/2); ed. H. W. Hitchcock, RRMBE, ix (1970), 44f, 54

J. Shearman: *Mannerism* (Harmondsworth, 1967), 21f, 96

H. W. Hitchcock: 'Vocal Ornamentation in Caccini's *Nuove musiche*', *MQ*, lvi (1970), 389ff

E. Schwandt: 'Caccini's *Sprezzatura di canto*: Some Seventeenth-century Applications', *Abstracts of Papers Read at the Thirty-seventh Annual Meeting of the American Musicological Society* (Chapel Hill and Durham, North Carolina, 1971), 43f

NIGEL FORTUNE

Springbogen (Ger.). SAUTILLÉ.

Springer (Ger.). JACK.

Spring Opera. Experimental opera company established in San Francisco in 1960; *see* SAN FRANCISCO, §1.

Spruch. A term used in German literary history to denote two different categories of medieval poetry.

(1) The verbal *Spruch*. Normally in rhyming couplets and of didactic content, it was written for spoken delivery. It is similar in nature to the *Priamel*, the *Bispel*, the *Epigramm* and the *Wappendichtung* (a description of a coat-of-arms in poetry). Important contributors to the tradition of the verbal *Spruch* are Freidank (13th century), Heinrich der Teichner and Peter Suchenwirt (14th century).

(2) The lyric *Spruch*. A form of Middle High German song, together with the Minnelied (*see* MINNESANG) and the *Leich* (*see* LAI). It is easily distinguished from the *Leich*, which is a more extended form made up of irregular sections and built on the principles of symmetry and repetition. The distinction between *Spruch* and Minnesang is, however, less clear.

In this context the term 'Spruch' is perhaps misleading, since it implies spoken delivery. Nevertheless it has been adopted by German literary historians since its introduction in 1833 (by Simrock). The definitions are not always watertight, and Moser's attempt to reclassify Middle High German lyric poetry remains questionable. So modern scholars recognize a terminology which is ambiguous in the following respects. (i) The distinction between courtly and bourgeois poetry does not coincide with that suggested between the Minnelied and the *Spruch*. (ii) The early *Spruch* has a stanza form quite different from that of the Minnelied, which is normally in the so-called canzona form, or BAR FORM. Later, however, the *Spruch* tended more and more to use this form, though sometimes in a rather freer manner. (iii) Earlier scholars stressed the single stanza of the *Spruch* as against the many stanzas of the Minnelied. This is not always the case. Although most *Sprüche* consist of a single stanza, there are also *Spruch* series – a number of stanzas in the same TON and belonging together (the *Sprüche* of Frauenlob, for instance, seem mostly to fall into coherent groups of three). Even here each stanza is usually complete within itself; but they can be seen as a series in terms of the unity of their content. Contemporary usage – which did not distinguish between *Spruch* and Minnelied – was to refer to a single stanza as *daz liet* ('the song') and a number of stanzas as *diu liet* ('the songs') irrespective of whether the stanzas belonged together.

Thus the distinction between the *Spruch* and the Minnelied is now seen less in formal terms and is drawn principally on the basis of content and of performance: the *Spruch* is didactic and pragmatic where the Minnelied is a love-song; the *Spruch*, by its nature, was addressed to a wider public. This different attitude of the poet or the performer of the *Spruch* seems to be reflected in the nature of the music: so far as the surviving melodies allow comparison, those for the *Spruch* tend more towards recitation in their manner.

The *Spruch* treats predominantly of rational, didactic and pragmatic issues. Its wide range of reference includes, for example, socio-political commentary, topics related to religion, morals and philosophy, practical wisdom, biographical material, praise of patrons, begging and much else besides. The genre seems to go back to the earliest tradition of the German lyric and probably became more widespread from the middle of the 12th century. Influence from goliard poetry and from the Provençal sirventes seems likely.

The earliest surviving *Sprüche* are connected with the name of Älterer Spervogel. Writers of *Sprüche* can be seen as representatives of an early literary profession. Originally they were not normally of noble stock, but travelling singers from the bourgeois classes; on the other hand, their refined artistic sense and considerable education gained them more respect in the courts than was accorded to the lesser wandering musicians. WALTHER VON DER VOGELWEIDE raised the status of the *Spruch* to a recognized genre of the courtly tradition; he developed its initial simplicity to perfection of content and artistic form. In his works, the *Spruch* clearly reflects the political situation of his time.

After Walther von der Vogelweide the *Spruch* was primarily cultivated by bourgeois poets, not by noble Minnesinger. Its subject matter remains mainly political and didactic, but scholarly topics are also found. On the whole the quality of the content sinks to bland flattery in the begging poems or, where the poet has suffered disappointment, to selfish and aggressive invective. Although they were originally concentrated in southern Germany, a later generation of *Spruch* poets was also to be found in the north (Reinmar von Zweter, Bruder Werner etc). FRAUENLOB marks a late culmination in the tradition and an end to the *Spruch* of the Minnesinger. At the same time he constitutes the springboard for the later Meistersinger tradition. Besides his Minnelieder and his three *Leiche*, he is represented by almost 300 *Sprüche*.

BIBLIOGRAPHY

K. Simrock: *Gedichte Walthers von der Vogelweide* (Berlin, 1833), i, 175ff
H. Schneider: 'Spruchdichtung', *Reallexikon der deutschen Literaturgeschichte*, iii (Berlin, 1928–9), 287
H. Tervooren: *Einzelstrophe oder Strophenbindung? Untersuchungen zur Lyrik der Jenaer Handschrift* (diss., U. of Bonn, 1967)
H. J. Moser, ed.: *Mittelhochdeutsche Spruchdichtung*, Wege der Forschung, cliv (Darmstadt, 1972) [21 essays with extensive bibliography]
B. Wachinger: *Sängerkrieg: Untersuchung zur Spruchdichtung des 13. Jahrhunderts* (Munich, 1973)
H. Brunner: *Die alten Meister: Studien zu Überlieferung und Rezeption der mittelhochdeutschen Spruchdichter im Spätmittelalter* (Munich, 1975)
E. Pickerodt-Uthleb: *Die Jenaer Liederhandschrift: metrische und musikalische Untersuchung* (Göppingen, 1975)

For further bibliography *see* MINNESANG.

BURKHARD KIPPENBERG

Squarcialupi, Antonio [Antonio degli Organi, Antonio di Bartolomeo, Antonio del Bessa] (*b* Florence, 27 March 1416; *d* Florence, 6 July 1480). Italian organist and composer. The son of a Florentine butcher named Bartolomeo di Giovanni, Antonio adopted the name Squarcialupi from a well-known Tuscan family at least as early as 1457. His teachers may have been Giovanni Mazzuoli (*see* JOVANNES DE FLORENTIA) and Matteo di Pagolo da Prato. In January 1431 he became organist at Orsanmichele in Florence. He left there in 1433, having been appointed organist at the Florentine cathedral S Maria del Fiore in 1432. He remained at this position until his death and was succeeded by his son Francesco (*b* 1457). In 1437 he joined the fraternity of Laudesi at S Zanobi and in 1453 entered the same order at Orsanmichele.

Antonio Squarcialupi was the most famous Italian organist of his time. In his *Diario fiorentino dal 1450 al 1516*, Landucci wrote of him as equivalent in stature to the architect Donatello and the painter Pollaiuolo, and Christoforo Landino mentioned him in his preface (1481) to Dante's *Divina commedia*. He was closely associated with Lorenzo the Magnificent and with Guillaume Dufay: in a letter of 1 May 1467 Squarcialupi wrote to Dufay on Lorenzo's behalf, and his epitaph in Florence Cathedral gives further evidence of his connection with Lorenzo. The claim that he was Heinrich Isaac's teacher is, however, no longer tenable, for Isaac can have arrived in Florence no earlier than 1484. Squarcialupi undoubtedly composed as well, but as yet no compositions ascribed to him have been found.

The celebrated early 15th-century MS (now *I-Fl* Med.Pal.87; ed. J. Wolf, Lippstadt, 1955) known as the 'Squarcialupi Codex (or MS)' became so called because he owned it; he did not compile it.

See also SOURCES, MS, §VIII, 2.

BIBLIOGRAPHY

N. Valorius: *Vita Laurentii Medicei*, ed. L. Mehus (Florence, 1749), 45f
L. Landucci: *Diario fiorentino dal 1450 al 1516*, ed. J. dal Badia (Florence, 1883), 3
O. Kade: 'Biographisches zu Antonio Squarcialupi, dem Florentiner Organisten im XV. Jahrhundert', *MMg*, xvii (1885), 1, 13
J. Wolf: *Geschichte der Mensuralnotation von 1250–1460* (Leipzig, 1904/*R*), i, 229ff
H. Kühner: 'Ein unbekannter Brief von Guillaume Dufay', *AcM*, xi (1939), 114
B. Beccherini: 'Un canto in panca fiorentino, Antonio di Guido', *RMI*, 1 (1948), 241
L. Parigi: *Laurentiana, Lorenzo dei Medici cultore della musica* (Florence, 1954), 49ff
B. Beccherini: 'Antonio Squarcialupi e il codice Mediceo-Palatino 87', *L'ars nova italiana del trecento I: Certaldo 1959*, 141–96
F. A. D'Accone: *A Documentary History of Music at the Florentine Cathedral and Baptistry during the Fifteenth Century* (diss., Harvard U., 1960), 39ff
——: 'Heinrich Isaac in Florence: New and Unpublished Documents', *MQ*, xlix (1963), 464–83
——: 'Antonio Squarcialupi alla luce di documenti inediti', *Chigiana*, xxiii/3 (1966), 3

KURT VON FISCHER

Squarcialupi Codex (*I-Fl* Med.Pal.87). *See* SOURCES, MS, §VIII, 2.

Square [swarenote, sqwarenote]. English musical term of the 15th and 16th centuries. The evidence currently available suggests that a square is a bottom part derived from a polyphonic composition of the late 14th century onwards in order to be used (usually via monophonic storage) in a later composition. The source need not be sacred, but all known later uses are. No further refinements to this definition are available. Compositions using squares may place the borrowed material at any pitch, in any voice part. The square may migrate between parts, be presented literally, or appear with considerable rhythmic and melodic elaboration. The number of voice parts is variable, and the compositions include keyboard settings. Baillie confined the term to the Mass Ordinary, but this now seems to have been too cautious. The style and compositional technique of such compositions cover a wide range.

Archival references between 1463 and 1564 permit a further broadening of the term. 'Sqwarenote' was taught (along with plainsong, polyphony and techniques that imply quasi-improvisation or rudimentary composition) and sung; squares were copied (in one case into graduals, in another 'upon' the eight tones); books of squarenote (including an 'old' one in 1465) are in some cases identified as polyphonic, or as being in sets (?part-books), and compositional references include a mass 'de squarenote'. The principal references come from Durham, Wells, Worcester, Warwick, Louth, Oxford, Cambridge and London, particularly St Paul's Cathedral (the presumed provenance of the Gyffard books, see below), where they continue to be associated with post-Reformation rites and English words.

Three masses in the Marian Gyffard books (*GB-Lbm* Add.17802–5), one by William Whitbroke and two by William Mundy, are described there as 'apon the square'. In these masses each movement is based on a different cantus firmus, though all three use the same Credo melody, and Mundy's second mass shares its Gloria, Sanctus and Agnus cantus firmi with Whitbroke's. These cantus firmi are hence assumed to be the squares on which the masses are composed. All three Kyrie squares, and one of the two Sanctus squares are found in a monophonic collection of such isolated tenor parts on the flyleaves of a Sarum gradual (*GB-Lbm* Lansdowne 462) which is in turn assumed to be a collection of squares such as those to which archival evidence attests. Other smaller repositories of such tenors establish a modest network of concordances and extend the repertory of potential squares. In many cases, further concordances for these tenors also exist in polyphonic works composed nearer 1400 (in the Old Hall Manuscript and elsewhere) and in one case in a French-texted ballade (*Or me veut*) which had a busy career on the Continent. Even where concordances have not survived, it can sometimes be demonstrated that the source of a square must have been a discant setting of a Sanctus chant (sometimes with migrant cantus firmus) or a strict faburden tenor to a non-Ordinary chant. In some cases no monophonic stage has survived, but direct concordances exist between 15th-century bottom parts and 16th-century settings. The repertory of squares is therefore likely to increase as further concordances come to light, since any bottom part is potentially available for use in this way.

Other polyphonic compositions based on such cantus firmi of the late (or even mid-) 15th century to the mid- (or even late) 16th are therefore assumed also to be composed on squares, and other cantus firmi used in related compositions (as in the set of seven Lady masses by Nicholas Ludford) are presumed to be further squares. Evidence suggests that the early Tudor practice of composition on the faburden of a chant rather than on the chant itself should be included within the procedure of composition on squares, since some such 'faburdens' are in fact bottom parts of non-faburden settings in discant style (e.g. *Magnificat* settings on the first tone which may relate to the archival reference to the eight tones), and since faburdens occur in company with squares of various derivations apparently for use in composition or impromptu techniques. Squares were sometimes described in association with their parent compositions, and it is clear that their subsequent use was not always confined to the same text or genre. These procedures suggest far-reaching analogies with continental techniques and with the use to which some melodies were put, though no actual links with authenticated squares have appeared. The term should probably be confined to English cases related as above until there is reason to extend it. It may even be necessary to regard the term merely as a local name for a much more widespread range of compositional approaches.

BIBLIOGRAPHY
M. F. Bukofzer: 'A Polyphonic Basse Dance of the Renaissance', *Studies in Medieval and Renaissance Music* (New York, 1950), 190ff
F. Ll. Harrison: *Music in Medieval Britain* (London, 1958, 2/1963)
H. Baillie: 'Squares', *AcM*, xxxii (1960), 178
J. Bergsagel: 'An Introduction to Ludford', *MD*, xiv (1960), 105
——: 'On the Performance of Ludford's *alternatim* Masses', *MD*, xvi (1962), 35
F. Ll. Harrison: 'Faburden in Practice', *MD*, xvi (1962), 11
R. D. Bowers: *Choral Institutions within the English Church, 1340–1500* (diss., U. of East Anglia, 1975)

MARGARET BENT

Square-dance. A dance performed by sets of four couples facing each other in a square. It evolved in the USA from the French QUADRILLE and other popular ballroom dances during the mid-19th century. As a less formal type of social dance, it became common particularly in the rural areas of New England, the Appalachian Mountains and the south-western USA, and is still danced in schools, at festivals and by folkdance societies; it was briefly popular in Europe in the mid-20th century. The basic movements – the *allemande, chassez, promenade, dos à dos* etc – reflect French origins, and their execution and variety change from region to region. The sequence of movements is sung or chanted by a 'caller', often in rhymed verse, to the accompaniment of a piano, fiddle, guitar, banjo, double bass, accordion or wind instrument, or any combination of these. As with the American quadrille, the music is usually borrowed from popular Anglo-American songs (e.g. *Soldier's Joy, Turkey in the Straw*); the duple-metre tunes have lively, rhythmic themes of eight or 16 bars, with heavily accented downbeats and simple, repetitive harmonies.

BIBLIOGRAPHY
B. Tolman and R. Page: *The Country Dance Book* (Weston, Vermont, 1937)
A. S. Duggan, J. Schlottmann and A. Rutledge: *Folk Dances of the United States and Mexico*, The Folk Dance Library, v (New York, 1948)
R. G. Kraus: *Square Dances of Today* (New York, 1950)
D. N. and H. Kennedy: *Square Dances of America* (n.p., n.d., rev. 2/1965 as *American Square Dancing*)

DEANE L. ROOT

Square pianoforte (Fr. *piano carré*; Ger. *Tafelklavier*; It. *fortepiano a tavola*). A piano in a horizontal rectangular case. It is the direct descendant of the clavichord, the shape and layout of 18th- and early 19th-century square pianos being identical with that of 18th-century clavichords. It was the most common domestic keyboard instrument for most of the 19th century, and was only gradually superseded by the space-saving and generally superior upright. Although the early square pianos were of modest size (*see* PIANOFORTE, figs.8, 10, 14, 25) the instrument eventually grew to enormous proportions, particularly in the USA, acquiring in the process some of the excessive decorative features of other 19th-century furniture.

The chief historical importance of the square piano lies in its having been the principal vehicle for the development of the piano in Germany in the mid-18th century; also, such important 19th-century improvements as cast-iron framing and overstringing were first developed in American square pianos (*see* PIANOFORTE, fig.27).

EDWIN M. RIPIN

Squillante (It.: 'harshly'; present participle of *squillare*, to ring, peal, blare). An expression mark found in the orchestral postlude to the 'Rataplan' of Verdi's *La forza del destino*.

Squire, W(illiam) H(enry) (*b* Ross, Herefordshire, 8 Aug 1871; *d* London, 17 March 1963). English cellist and composer. He was a pupil of his father and a foundation scholar at the RCM, London, where he studied the cello with Edward Howell and composition under Parry. His London début was at a concert given by Albéniz in 1891; in 1895 he performed the Saint-Saëns A minor Concerto at the Crystal Palace. He played in the Queen's Hall Orchestra, led the cellos at Covent Garden, toured frequently with Clara Butt, recorded Elgar's Concerto under Harty in 1930, and taught at both the RCM and the Guildhall. A generous player with warm, full tone, he received the dedication of Fauré's *Sicilienne*; among his compositions are a cello concerto, much light music and two operettas.

ROBERT ANDERSON

Squire, William Barclay (*b* London, 16 Oct 1855; *d* London, 13 Jan 1927). English musicologist and librarian. Educated privately and in Frankfurt, Squire graduated in law at Pembroke College, Cambridge, in 1879. He had intended to enter the Church, but because he had doubts about the Thirty-nine Articles he entered a firm of solicitors. Soon, however, his interest in music, which had been stimulated at Cambridge by his close friendship with Stanford, led him away from the law; his first musical writings were as a contributor to the early parts of *Grove 1*. When a vacancy for the charge of the printed music at the British Museum occurred in 1885, Squire was appointed, supported by testimonials from George Grove, A. D. Coleridge, Leslie Stephen, W. H. Husk, W. S. Rockstro and J. F. Bridge. Their enthusiasm was not misplaced. Working almost single-handed until 1900 (when William C. Smith joined him), Squire made extensive improvements to the catalogue, built up the collections with continually increasing purchases of old and new works, and devoted all his energy to preparing the two-volume catalogue of printed music before 1800 which the trustees issued in 1912. He next read through the whole of the general catalogue of printed books (then consisting of four million entries) searching for opera librettos; he indexed some 10,000.

It was during Squire's term of office that the King's Music Library was deposited on permanent loan in the British Museum. It had long been housed in Buckingham Palace, where difficulty of access was an obstacle to scholars. Moreover, there was no catalogue. Squire began protracted negotiations to acquire the collection for the museum during the reign of Edward VII. His persistence was rewarded soon after George V's accession and the transfer took place in 1911. Squire was appointed its first honorary curator, and after his retirement in 1920 began work on its catalogue. For his services he was appointed MVO in 1926. As his list of works shows, he was long active as a cataloguer outside the British Museum. Likewise, the list of what he edited shows the range of his sympathies. He served on the committee of the Folk Song Society from its inception in 1898, and was for some years secretary of the International Musical Society. He was secretary of the Purcell Society from 1879 to 1922. He played an active part in planning the Historical Music Loan Exhibition held at the Albert Hall in 1885, and later in preparing for the press the sumptuous catalogue of the exhibition of music and instruments held at Fishmongers' Hall in 1904. He found time to work as music critic to four journals between 1890 and 1904 – the *Saturday Review*, *Westminster Gazette*, the *Globe* and the *Pilot*. He was a competent geographer and a connoisseur of paintings.

Squire's work as critic, editor and scholar was equal to the highest standards of his day. As a librarian, he was a fast and accurate worker, guided by a strong sense of purpose and remarkable foresight, and is worthy to rank with such distinguished contemporaries as Wotquenne, Mitjana and Sonneck.

CATALOGUES

'Musik-Katalog der Bibliothek der Westminster-Abtei in London', *MMg*, xxxv (1903), Beilage, 1–45
Catalogue of Printed Music in the Library of the Royal College of Music (London, 1909)
Catalogue of Printed Music published between 1487 and 1800, now in the British Museum (London, 1912/*R*1968)
Catalogue of the King's Music Library: I. Handel Manuscripts (London, 1927)
Catalogue of the Manuscripts in the Library of the Royal College of Music (typescript, *GB-Lcm, Lbm* and elsewhere, 1931)

WRITINGS

'On an Early Sixteenth Century Manuscript of English Music in the Library of Eton College', *Archaeologia*, lvi (1889), 89
'Notes on Early Music Printing', *Bibliographica*, iii (1897), 99
'Notes on an Undescribed Collection of English 15th Century Music', *SIMG*, ii (1900–01), 342–92, 719 [on Old Hall MS]
'Purcell's Dramatic Music', *SIMG*, v (1903–4), 489–564
'Purcell as Theorist', *SIMG*, vi (1904–5), 521–67
'Pearsall on Chanting', *SIMG*, viii (1906–7), 166–220
'An Index of Tunes in the Ballad Operas', *Musical Antiquary*, ii (1910), 1
'Publishers' Numbers', *SIMG*, xv (1913–14), 421
'Gluck's London Operas', *MQ*, i (1915), 397
'Music', *Shakespeare's England*, ii (London, 1916), 15
'Some Novello Correspondence', *MQ*, iii (1917), 206–42 [incl. correspondence with Samuel Wesley]
'Musical Libraries and Catalogues', *PMA*, xlv (1918–19), 96
'Handel's Clock Music', *MQ*, v (1919), 538 [with the tunes]
'Letters of Robert Lucas Pearsall', *MQ*, v (1919), 264–97; vi (1920), 296
'Letters of Robert Franz', *MQ*, vii (1921), 278
'The Music of Shadwell's Tempest', *MQ*, vii (1921), 656
'A Spurious Mozart Portrait', *MQ*, ix (1923), 211
'L'iconographie musicale', *Actes du congrès d'histoire d'art*, ii (Paris, 1924), 731
'Beethoven's Appearance', *ML*, viii (1927), 122

EDITIONS

H. Purcell: Works, vi [Harpsichord Music] (London, 1895), xxii [Catches and Rounds] (London, 1922)
with J. A. Fuller Maitland: *The Fitzwilliam Virginal Book* (London and Leipzig, 1894–9/*R*1963)
Purcell: Suites, Lessons and Pieces for Harpsichord (London, 1918)
with J. A. Fuller Maitland: *B. Cosyn: Twenty-five pieces for Keyed Instruments* (London, 1923)
——: *G. F. Handel: Stücke für Clavicembalo* [The 'Aylesford' pieces] (Mainz, 1928)

Squire also edited over 100 English and Italian madrigals, partly in various series, and partly for some groups of singers with which he was connected.

BIBLIOGRAPHY

E. J. Dent: 'The Rewards of Scholarship' [obituary], *The Times* (22 Jan 1927)
A. H. King: 'The Music Room of the British Museum, 1753–1953', *PRMA*, lxxix (1952–3), 65
——: 'William Barclay Squire, 1855–1927: Music Librarian', *The Library*, 5th ser., xii (1957), 1

ALEC HYATT KING

Sqwarenote. *See* SQUARE.

Srb [Debrnov, Srb-Debrnov], **Josef** (*b* Debrno, nr. Kralupy nad Vltavou, 18 Sept 1836; *d* Prague, 1 Sept 1904). Czech writer on music. He was educated in Prague at the Malá Strana grammar school and Prague University (1858–63), where he studied history and Slavonic philology. As a youth he sang alto at the St Štěpán and Týn churches and later also sang at the Žofín Academy. He was a member of the St Cecilia Society, and while at the university ran first his own quartet and then an octet. From 1863 to 1879 he held posts successively as assistant teacher, tutor and clerk, but then decided to renounce a secure income and devote his energies to the cause of Czech music. He took a leading part in the organization of the Prague Hlahol Choral Society (1864–5, 1876–91) and was on excellent terms with the leading Czech musicians; he was Smetana's most intimate friend during the composer's last five years. For his literary work Srb adopted the name Josef Debrnov. He provided German translations for *Prodaná nevěsta* ('The bartered bride') and three other operas by Smetana, as well as Bendl's *Lejla*, and many of Dvořák's songs and duets. He contributed significantly to the Czech musical literature of his time; his most important writing, *Slovník hudebních umělců slovanských* ('Dictionary of Slavonic musical artists'), on which he worked for 25 years, remains unpublished.

WRITINGS

Dějiny konservatoře pražské [History of Prague Conservatory] (Prague, 1878)
'Friedrich Smetana', *Allgemeine deutsche Musikzeitung*, no.16 (1879)
'Hudba a umění' [Music and art], *Dalibor*, i (1879), 59, 67, 123
'Smetanovo smyčcové kvarteto "Z mého života"', [Smetana's string quartet 'From my Life'], *Dalibor*, i (1879), 69
'Varhanická škola v Praze' [The Prague Organ School], *Dalibor*, i (1879), 147, 171, 179
'Návštěva v Jabkenicích' [A visit to Jabkenice], *Dalibor*, iii (1881), 213
'Antonín Dvořák', *Kalendář českých hudebníků* (1882)
Instrumentace, stručný návod ku poznání nástrojů s dodatkem o hudbě komorní [Instrumentation: concise manual . . . with an appendix on chamber music] (Prague, 1883)
'Poslední rok života B. Smetany' [Smetana's last year], *Dalibor*, vii (1885), 177
'Smetanovy styky s Hlaholem' [Smetana's relations with the Hlahol choir], *Dalibor*, viii (1886), 176
Dějiny hudby v Čechách a na Moravě [A history of music in Bohemia and Moravia] (Prague, 1891)
'Čechy, v: dějiny hudby' [Bohemia, v: music history], *Ottův slovník naučný*, vi (Prague, 1893), 361
Z deníků Bedřicha Smetany [From Smetana's diaries] (Prague, 1902)
ed. L. Dolanský: *Paměti starého musikanta na Smetana a Dvořáka* [An old musician's reminiscences of Smetana and Dvořák] (Prague, 1930)
Slovník hudebních umělců slovanských [Dictionary of Slavonic musical artists] (MS, *CS-Pnm*)

BIBLIOGRAPHY

V. Balthasar: *Bedřich Smetana – dopisy B. Smetany na J. Srba-Debrnova* [Bedřich Smetana – letters of Smetana to Srb] (Prague, 1924)
F. Bartoš, ed.: *Smetana ve vzpomínkách a dopisech* (Prague, 1939, enlarged 4/1941, 9/1954; Eng. trans., 1955 as *Smetana: Letters and Reminiscences*)
J. Čeleda: *Smetanův druh sděluje: život a dílo Josefa Srba-Debrnova* [Smetana's companion communicates: the life and work of Srb] (Prague, 1945)
J. Plavec: *Smetanova tvorba sborová* [Smetana's choral works] (Prague, 1954), 222, 289, 308, 325, 337
B. Large: *Smetana* (London, 1970)
J. Clapham: *Smetana* (London, 1972)

JOHN CLAPHAM

Srebotnjak, Alojz (*b* Postojna, Slovenia, 27 June 1931). Yugoslav composer. He studied composition at the Ljubljana Academy of Music (1958) with Škerjanc, in Rome with Porrena (1958–9), in London with Fricker (1960–61) and in Paris (1963). After teaching at the Pedagogic Academy (1964–70) he was appointed to teach composition at the Ljubljana Academy. Among composers of his generation, Srebotnjak has the most distinctively expressionist style, despite the diversity of his techniques.

WORKS
(selective list)

Orch: Music for str, 1955; Sinfonietta in due tempi, 1958; Monologues, fl, ob, hn, timp, str, 1962; Antifona, 1964; The Karst Suite, 1964; Episodes, 1967; Bagatelles, 1969; Harp Conc., 1971; Vn Conc., 1975; Slovenica, 1976; Lamento, 1976; Balade, 1977
Chamber and inst: Fantasia notturna, 3 vn, cl, harp, 1956; 3 sonatinas, vn, pf, 1957, 1966, 1968; Invenzione variata, pf, 1961; Serenata, fl, cl, bn, 1961; Dnevnik [Diary], pf trio, 1972; 2 movimenti, gui, 1976
Cantatas: Mati [Mother], 1955; Vojne slike [Images of war], 1957; Microsongs, 1964; Ekstaza smrti [Ecstasy of death], 1966
Songs, choruses, music for the theatre and cinema

Principal publisher: G. Schirmer

ANDREJ RIJAVEC

Sri Lanka. Island in the Indian Ocean, known until 1972 as Ceylon; its area is about 65,000 sq km. A republic, it became independent in 1948 and is a member of the British Commonwealth.

1. Introduction. 2. Song and dance genres. 3. Instruments.

1. INTRODUCTION. Sri Lanka's estimated population in 1972 was 13 million, comprising two main linguistic groups, the Sinhalese and the Tamils. The official religion is Buddhism, introduced from India in the 3rd century BC (with approximately 7 million adherents in 1963); but there are also large numbers of Hindus (approximately 2 million), Muslims (approximately 750,000), Christians (900,000) and several minority religions, such as Parsees (totalling approximately 11,500). The majority of the population is rural, with about 20% living in the main cities. Although the official language is Sinhala, in 1966 Tamil was sanctioned by the government for some official purposes; English is widely learnt as a second language. Social stratification is determined by the caste system, as well as by linguistic, religious and ethnic divisions.

Sri Lanka's history may be divided into three periods: the pre-Aryan (prehistoric), the Aryan (historic) and the post-Aryan (from the 16th century). In the pre-Aryan period one of the main ethnic groups consisted of the Vedda who, through repeated conquest, acculturation and intermarriage, and the destruction of the jungles where they lived, had almost disappeared as a distinct group by the mid-20th century. The first Aryans to arrive from north India in 543 BC were reputedly Vijaya and his followers, ancestors of the present Sinhalese population; the influx of Tamils from southern India has continued into the 20th century. The *Mahāvamsa*, a 5th-century AD chronicle of the Sinhalese kings from 540 BC, indicates that Sri Lanka had a hierarchical polyethnic society with a primary ethnic distinction between Sinhalese and Tamils (it also defines the important position of Buddhism). In the 8th century and again in the 13th century the Tamils forced the Sinhalese to move their seat of power, which was finally established at Kandy, in the hills 97 km northeast of Colombo. Sinhalese folk art flourished in this kingdom, which was the last region to surrender totally to foreign invasion. The traditions of Sri Lanka have been influenced by bitter conflict between the Tamils and the Sinhalese, by the ensuing influx of supporters from south and north India, by the settlement and influence of the Portuguese (1505–1656) and Dutch (1602–1796), and by British rule (1796–1948).

2. SONG AND DANCE GENRES. Sri Lanka's music, like its population, has multiple origins, which are revealed through its legends. In the prehistoric era Sri Lanka was inhabited by people referred to in the *Mahāvamsa* as Yakkha, and Yakkhinī, probably ancestors of the Vedda. According to Buddhist scriptures the Yakkha had both song and dance. The Vedda (despite influence from both Sinhalese and Tamils), the Kinnarayā, the Rodiyā (beggars) and the Ahikuntakayā (gypsies) provide the nearest links to the pre-Aryan, pre-Buddhist music of Sri Lanka. The Seligmanns reported that those Vedda least affected by outside contact had no musical instruments, body percussion being the main rhythmic accompaniment for ceremonial dance. Other Vedda, however, have adopted the drum from the Sinhalese to accompany charms and invocations, lullabies and entertainment songs. Invocations are also accompanied by dance.

Working from a sample of 34 Vedda songs recorded by Seligmann, C. S. Myers (see Seligmann, chap.13) classified songs into three groups. The first (12 songs) has nine songs with two pitches and three with two pitches and grace notes; the range in this group does not exceed a major 2nd (ex.1). The 12 songs of the second

Ex.1 Commemoration song (Seligmann, 1911)

group each contain three pitches and in all but two the maximum range is a minor 3rd (ex.2). In the third group (ten songs) nine have four pitches, and one has five; with

Ex.2 Amusement song (Seligmann, 1911)

one exception, no song's range exceeds a 4th (ex.3). The intervals of Vedda music vary. The melodies have regular rhythm but lack regular accent; they are usually in duple metre, although bars with three or five beats

Ex.3 Lullaby (Seligmann, 1911)

occur. Isolated examples of songs in triple metre exist, but Seligmann suggested on textual grounds that they are a late development. Notes are attacked precisely, without glissandos, and the tonic is almost always clearly established. It is relatively certain that the Vedda are descendants of the Yakkha, and the 'devil' or masked dancers of the low-country Sinhalese (see fig.1a) and the Kandyan Sinhalese dancers possibly retain elements that originated with the Yakkha.

Music in Sri Lanka has always been associated with dance. The ancient Sinhalese treatise *Saṅgīta-śāstra* defined music as a threefold art including *nacca* (dancing), *gīta* (singing) and *vādita* (instrumental music). With the establishment of Theravada Buddhism in the 3rd century BC and subsequent Buddhist control of the educational system, especially in the *pirivena* (monastically sponsored centres of higher education), music and drama were seriously curtailed. The degree to which puritanical Buddhism was practised, however, varied with the religious disposition of the ruling king; patronage of the arts by the king and the aristocracy was common and there is evidence that Vedda women were employed as dancers in the Kandyan court. Kings of the later Kandyan period were from south India and introduced Carnatic instruments such as the *vīnā* and genres such as *nādagam* (folk music drama) and the lyrics in the *vannama* and *viraha* (mostly love poems, adopted by the Sinhalese in about the 18th century). The *paramparā*, a school that taught religious rituals involving song and dance, primarily performed by men, developed at the same time as the *pirivena*; each *paramparā* was different and keen competition between the schools perpetuated highly developed forms of dance and drumming.

The performing arts of Sri Lanka in the 20th century typically combine song, dance and drama with mime, acrobatics, costume and prose dialogue. Although most genres (e.g. *kōlam* folk drama) derive from south India, they have been transformed over the centuries into characteristically Sinhalese expressions. *Kandyan* dance, which flourished under the Kandyan kings (16th to 19th centuries), is often considered the national dance of Sri Lanka and has four distinct styles: *panteru*, *naiyadi*, *udākki* and *ves*. In addition to these basic styles 18 *vannam* (dance enactments), adaptations of the south Indian melodic formulae (*varnam*), depict various creatures, for example *hanuma vannama* (the monkey), *mayura vannama* (the peacock) and *gajaga vannama* (the elephant). The original subjects of *kandyan* dance were the Hindu myths, particularly the crossing of Rama into Lanka, but gradually other legends were added to the repertory. Under the Kandyan kings the genre was admitted to the Buddhist temple and it is still

performed every August as part of the annual Perahera festival during which the Buddha's tooth, enshrined in the Temple of the Tooth at Kandy, is carried in a street procession escorted by costumed elephants, palanquins, drummers, singers, dancers and robed Buddhist monks. Traditionally, certain styles of *kandyan* dance were secular (e.g., the *udākki* and *panteru*) and others were sacred (such as the *ves*, a ritual dance of the Kohomba Kankariya ceremony); in the 20th century this distinction is no longer clear and the *ves* is also performed in secular contexts.

Kandyan dance is typically performed by a team of five or six performers, each of whom sings and dances; formerly women did not participate except in the *digge netuma*, a ritual dance now rarely performed. The basic dance posture, similar to the south Indian kathakali, is strenuous, with knees bent outwards, widely separated and aligned with the torso; facial gesture and elaborate footwork are integral parts of the energetic choreography. The *udākki* is particularly demanding as the performer must simultaneously sing, dance and accompany himself on a small drum; in *panteru* the dancer, accompanied by a drum, passes a circular metal frame like a tambourine from hand to hand (see fig.1*b*). The *ves*, often considered the most spectacular of the styles, is accompanied by intricate drum rhythms (taught by a system of mnemonics), the *tālampota* (a pair of hand cymbals) and the rattling of the dancer's hollow ankle bracelets filled with metal pellets.

Ruhunu ritual dance is most common in the southern and western coastal areas of Sri Lanka. Some forms of *ruhunu* are now performed for entertainment (*sudda matra*, *giri devi*, *kumara pelapali*, *talan gurube raksha*, *naga raksha*). The choreography of *sabaragamuwa*, performed in the hilly region of southern Sri Lanka, is similar to *kandyan* dance and is regarded by some scholars as a blending of *kandyan* and *ruhunu* styles. In addition to these prevalent classical styles, numerous

(*a*) (*b*)

1. (a) Devil dancer accompanied by gäta bera (double-headed cylindrical drum); (b) panteru dancers, accompanied by drums, passing tambourine-like metal frames from hand to hand

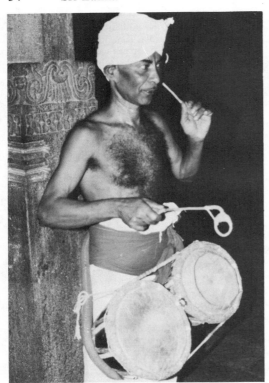

2. *Tammāṭṭama (double kettledrum) player in a Kandy temple*

3. *Uḍākki (hourglass drum)*

folk forms including *lee keli* (stick dance) and the *kalagedi* (pot dance) are common in rural areas. Some dances and accompanying song have been maintained during the 20th century by professional caste groups; perhaps the oldest are the devil or mask dances, which are concerned with exorcism and are accompanied by chanted poetry and drums (usually the cylindrical double-headed *gāṭa bera*, see fig.1*a* above). The *bali* and *tovil*, possibly of ancient origin, are other surviving forms of demonological ritual that use chanted poetry. The devil dance, an expression of pre-Buddhist belief, is performed to heal, to remove bad luck or to propitiate evil spirits.

Despite many foreign influences in the 20th century,

Sri Lanka retains it indigenous music and dance. Portuguese song genres have mostly been rejected since their texts are alien to native concepts. The influence of both north and south India, in contrast with Western influences, has been considerable and is most obvious in the Sinhalese adaptation of Indian forms such as *nāḍagam* (folk drama from south India) and *viraha* (lovesongs). However, Sri Lanka had traditional dramatic forms such as *kōlam* (a masked folk drama with chanted poetry, dialogue, song and dance) and *sokari* (a mimed story performed by masked dancers) before the introduction of *nāḍagam*. The *maddala* (Tamil drum) and a Tamil singing style were introduced to Sri Lanka together with the *nāḍagam*.

During the first half of the 20th century *nurtiya*, a north Indian theatre style, was introduced to Sri Lanka through the Elphinstone theatre group. This genre, related to the north Indian *rāgadhāri* system of music, had new melodies which were rapidly accepted. Indian influence increased with the teaching of Hindustani classical music in Sinhalese schools and of Carnatic music in Tamil schools. But few foreign instruments, except drums, have been adopted.

The culture and music of Sri Lanka are undergoing rapid change in the 20th century. Surviving folksongs, such as those of carters, boatmen, fishermen, miners and watchmen, are normally characterized by their four-line structure and simple rhythmic and melodic arrangement, but many traditional occupational songs have almost completely disappeared, with the traditional occupations they accompanied. However, the country's new national consciousness has prompted serious endeavours to revive and maintain older musical forms.

3. INSTRUMENTS. The drum has been particularly important in the music of Sri Lanka. The *Mahāvaṃsa* refers to the combination of drum and song in describing a wedding feast supposedly seen by Vijaya, and 80 different types of drum are mentioned in Sinhalese literature. According to Amaradeva, drums named in early manuscripts and still used include the *tammāṭṭama*, *magul bera*, *uḍākki*, *ḍavula* and *rabana*. The *tammāṭṭama*, formerly used to announce social events and Buddhist ritual, is a double kettledrum (see fig.2). Sound is produced by striking the head with two sticks that are bent at one end and turned back into a loop called the *kaḍuppuva*. The head of the right drum is larger and less taut than that of the left. The *magul bera* (also known as the *gāṭa bera*), like all drums of the *bera* group, is double-headed and tubular. The right-hand membrane is more taut than the left, and produces a louder, higher pitch; it is held at the waist with a sling and played with both hands. The *uḍākki* is a small double-headed hourglass drum. One hand is used to play the instrument, while the other varies the pitch by squeezing straps which are threaded through rings around the drumheads, thereby altering the tension (see fig.3). The *ḍavula* is a double-headed cylindrical drum suspended horizontally from the waist. It is struck on the right head with the palm of the hand. At Buddhist functions the *ḍavula* is played with the *tammāṭṭama* and *horanäva* in an ensemble known as *hevisi* (see fig.4). The *rabana* is a small single-headed frame drum used for entertainment and domestic rituals.

As Amaradeva noted, historical records indicate that the ancient orchestra of Sri Lanka consisted of 75 musical instruments in five categories: *ātata* (single-headed drums), *vitata* (double-headed drums), *ātata-vitata* (chordophones whose sounding chamber is covered with skin or parchment), *ghana* (struck metal idiophones) and *susira* (aerophones). 26 membranophones are mentioned; the chordophones include eight types of *vīṇā*, varying in number of strings (3, 5, 6, 12, 13 or 21); the 26 aerophones are of bamboo and wood; the 15 metal idiophones are hand cymbals, metal bells and tinkling anklets. Aerophones still in use include the large and small *horanä* (singular, *horanäva*), *nāgasinnam*, *ransinnam*, *vas daṇḍu* and conch shells. The *horanäva* has six to eight finger-holes and is made of wood, ivory or buffalo horn (see fig.4). A cone of bronze or brass is attached to one end of the central portion and a reed is fixed to the other. The reed is fitted into a narrow tube, with a disc of metal, against which the lips are pressed when blowing. Metal idiophones still played include the *tālampoṭa* (hand cymbals), *mini kikini* (small bells), *atgigiri* and *pāgigiri*.

BIBLIOGRAPHY
M. Wertheimer: 'Musik der Wedda', *SIMG*, xi (1909–10), 300
C. G. and B. Z. Seligmann: *The Veddas* (London, 1911)
B. Ryan: *Caste in Modern Ceylon* (New Jersey, 1953)
E. R. Sarachchandra: *The Sinhalese Folk Play and Modern Stage* (Colombo, 1953)
Devar Surya Sena: 'Folk Songs of Ceylon', *JIFMC*, vi (1954), 11
W. B. Makulloluwa: 'Music Education in Ceylon', *Composer*, no.19 (1966), 50
E. R. Sarachchandra: *The Folk Drama of Ceylon* (Ceylon, 1966)
M. D. Raghavan: *Siṅhala nāṭum: Dances of the Sinhalese* (Colombo, 1967)
W. D. Amaradeva, 'Sinhalese Music Through the Ages and Its Modern Trends', *The Musics of Asia*, ed. J. Maceda (Manila, 1971), 174
KATHY SCHOLZ ATWOOD

Srnka, Jiří (*b* Písek, south Bohemia, 19 Aug 1907). Czech composer. He studied with Mařák and Feld (violin, 1922–4) and with Šín (composition, 1924–8) at the Prague Conservatory, where he also attended the master classes given by Novák (composition, 1928–32) and Hába (quarter-tone composition, 1934–7). His first appointment was in Ježek's orchestra at the Osvobozené Divadlo, Prague (1929–35), after which he played in the orchestras of the National Theatre and of Radiojournal. From the beginning of the 1930s, however, he turned his attention almost completely to film music, becoming, with Trojan and Lucký, one of the leading Czech composers in the field. He lectured on film music at the Prague Academy of Music from 1950 to 1953.

Srnka's stylistic development was initiated under Hába's aegis. In early works he applied athematicism and atonality (the Suite and the Fantasia for piano), 12-note serialism (the Suite for violin and piano) and quarter-tones (the Two Piano Compositions), while the Symphonic Fantasia makes use of motor rhythm as a structural framework. At the end of the 1930s, however, Srnka drew close to Czech folksong in style, simplified his language and returned to tonality, largely as a result of his involvement with films. He has written more than 120 film scores, almost half of them for full-length works. Characteristic of his style are his lapidary, epigrammatic manner (as in *Jan Hus* and *Jan Žižka*) and his melodic invention, which is well displayed even where complicated harmonic relationships or an emphasis on colour exist (e.g. *Krakatit*). The folksong of

4. *Buddhist initiation dance, accompanied by a hevisi ensemble, with ḍavula (double-headed cylindrical drums), tammäṭṭama (double kettledrums) and horanäva (double-reed instruments)*

south Bohemia, whose atmosphere Srnka approaches most closely, has influenced the broad arching of his melodic lines, the symmetry of his motif construction and his expressive lyricism – features which are shown in *Stříbrný vítr* ('The silver wind') and *Měsíc nad řekou* ('The moon over the river'). Srnka has received the National Prize (1940, for *Ohnivé léto*, 'A fiery summer') and State Prizes in 1948, 1949 (for *Němá barikáda*, 'The silent barricade') and 1954 (for *The Moon over the River*).

WORKS
(*selective list*)

Film scores: Ohnivé léto [A fiery summer], 1939; Pohádka máje [The fairy tale of May], 1940; Nezbedný bakalář [The mischievous bachelor], 1946; Krakatit, 1948; Němá barikáda [The silent barricade], 1949; Vstanou noví bojovníci [New warriors arise], 1951; Měsíc nad řekou [The moon over the river], 1953; Stříbrný vítr [The silver wind], 1954; Jan Hus, 1955; Jan Žižka, 1955; Proti všem [Against everything], 1957; Praha – matka měst [Prague – mother of cities], 1958

Orch: Sym. Fantasia, 1932–5; Vn Conc., 1957; Historické obrázky [Historic pictures], str, 1962

Vocal: Songs (K. H. Mácha), Mez/Bar, pf, 1936; Dětský rok [The children's year] (F. Hrubín), choral cycle, 1951

Chamber: 2 str qts, 1928, 1936; Wind Qt, 1928; Suite, vn, pf, 1929; Str Qnt, str qt, vc, 1930; 3 Compositions, vn, pf, 1961; Partita, vn, chamber orch, 1962

Pf: Suite, 1933; Fantasia, 1934; 3 Pf Compositions, 1937; 2 Pf Compositions, 1938

Principal publishers: Československý Filmové Nakladatelství [songs and melodies from films], Československý Státní Film [film scores], Československá Televize Praha [film scores], R. A. Dvorský, Melantrich

BIBLIOGRAPHY

A. Hába: 'Jiří Srnka', *Program D37*, iv (1937), 2
'Jiří Srnka: profil skladatele' [Srnka: profile of the composer], *Rytmus*, ix (1943–4), 110
J. Pilka: 'Hudba k filmům Jan Hus a Jan Žižja', *HRo*, ix (1956), 223, 269
——: 'Jubileum Jiřího Srnky', *HRo*, x (1957), 638
——: *Filmová hudba Jiřího Srnky*, Knihovna hudebních rozhledů, iii/5 (Prague, 1957) [incl. list of works and bibliography]

OLDŘICH PUKL

Šrom, Karel (*b* Plzeň, 14 Oct 1904). Czech composer, writer on music and administrator. A private composition pupil of Zelinka and Karel Hába, he worked for many years as an administrator. He was also drama director of the Free Theatre of Voskovec and Werich and a music critic concentrating on contemporary work. In 1945 he was made chief of the music section of Czech Radio. He was editor-in-chief for the state music publishers and first director of the Český Hudební Fond (1954–60); after 1961 he devoted his attentions to composing and writing. As a composer he began as a disciple of Alois Hába's atonal, athematic style, moving later in the direction of greater clarity and balance. His later music includes large-scale works and small, witty pieces based on folktales; the style is fresh and inventive, particularly in instrumentation and rhythm, with a tendency towards grotesque humour.

WORKS
(*selective list*)

Orch: 2 syms., 1930, 1951; Suita, 1934; Plivník, scherzo, 1953; Vzdech na bruslích [The sigh on skates], sym. allegretto after Morgenstern: Galgenlieder, 1957; Hajaja, suite, 1961; Pf Conc., 1961; Study, 1970; Malá suita, chamber orch, 1972

Inst: 2 str qts, 1923, 1943; Scherzové trio, str trio, 1943; 7 kousků [7 pieces], pf, 1943; Vynajítka, 9 insts, 1952; Soumrak [Twilight], pf cycle, 1965

Vocal: Tvář [Countenance] (F. Halas), A, pf, 1936

WRITINGS

Orchestr a dirigent (Prague, 1960)
Záhudbi [Beyond music] (Prague, 1965)
Karel Ančerl (Prague, 1968)

JAN TROJAN

Ssugh. A sign indicating the shortening of the duration of a note in Armenian EKPHONETIC NOTATION.

St – alphabetized as 'Saint'.

Stabat mater dolorosa (Lat.: 'sorrowfully his mother stood'). A poem used in the Roman liturgy as both a sequence and a hymn.

1. General and history to 1700. 2. Settings since 1700.

1. GENERAL AND HISTORY TO 1700. The poem *Stabat mater dolorosa* was once ascribed to Jacopone da Todi (*d* 1306); though unlikely to be his, it is at any rate considered to be of 13th-century Franciscan origin. The text was apparently not intended as a sequence for the Mass, but it has the verse form of the later metrical sequence (i.e. pairs of versicles in 887 trochaic metre, with the rhyme scheme *aab aab*; *see* SEQUENCE (i), §9). At least three other medieval texts belong to the same general type: *Stabat mater speciosa*, *Stabat iuxta Christi crucem* and *Stabat virgo mater Christi*. The first of these is an imitation of the *Stabat mater dolorosa* intended for Christmas, the second is found as a sequence as early as the Dublin Troper (*c*1360, *GB-Cu* add.710; facs. in Monumenta Musicae Sacrae, iv, Rouen, 1970) where it is set to the melody of *Salvatoris mater pia*; it occurs, set by John Browne, in the Eton Choirbook as a votive antiphon. Browne also set the poem *Stabat virgo mater Christi*, which is otherwise unknown.

Stabat mater dolorosa came into use as a sequence in the late 15th-century, in connection with the new Mass of the Compassion of the Blessed Virgin Mary (though not in the English uses); the plainsong melody assigned to the sequence (*Liber usualis*, p.1634*v*) appears to be of the same date, although its melodic elements can be found in earlier sequences. It was removed from the liturgy by the Council of Trent (1543–63) but revived by Pope Benedict XIII in 1727 for use on the Feast of the Seven Dolours (15 September). The use of the *Stabat mater* as an Office hymn on the Friday after Passion Sunday is apparently a post-Tridentine practice, and in the Roman Breviary it is divided into the following sections: 'Stabat mater' (Vespers), 'Sancta mater istud agas' (Matins) and 'Virgo virginum praeclara' (Lauds). Stäblein (1956) gave four hymn melodies from 17th- and 18th-century sources; the *Liber usualis* melody (p.1424) seems to be a late 18th-century version resembling two of these. It was well established in this form by the end of the century; it appears with a bass in *Motetts or Antiphons* (1792) by Samuel Webbe (ii), and from there has passed into modern hymnals.

The text (with some variants) was set as a votive antiphon in the 15th century by such English composers as John Browne, Thomas Cornish, Richard Davy and Robert Hunt, the first three settings being in the Eton Choirbook (*GB-WRec* 178). The work by John Browne is indeed one of the great masterpieces of its period. Other settings before 1700 include those by Innocentius Dammonis, Josquin, Gaffurius, Gaspar van Weerbeke, Gregor Aichinger, Palestrina, Lassus, Agostino Steffani and Alessandro Scarlatti. The setting by Dammonis is a strophic four-part *laude* published by Petrucci in 1508. Josquin's five-part setting is based on similar material, which has led Reese (*Music in the Renaissance*, p.253) to conjecture a 'lost' melody, and uses the tenor of Binchois' *Comme femme desconfortée* as a tenor cantus firmus. Weerbeke's simple and moving five-voice setting uses a version of the responsory *Vidit speciosam* as cantus firmus. Only one of the three settings of *Stabat mater* included in Haberl's edition of Palestrina's works is authentic, the celebrated eight-part work, remarkable for its sensitive declamation, rhythmic fluidity, harmonic expressiveness and subtle use of varied textures within a double-chorus framework. The *Stabat mater* by Lassus is an eight-part work added at the end of his second book of four-part *Sacrae cantiones* (1585).

2. SETTINGS SINCE 1700. The *stile antico* exerted its influence on polyphonic settings of the *Stabat mater* well into the 18th century, especially in Rome. Domenico Scarlatti's ten-part setting, probably composed between 1715 and 1719 when he was *maestro* of the Cappella Giulia, follows the best traditions of Roman choral writing, though with a decidedly modern feeling for harmony and tonality. Settings with orchestral accompaniment in which choruses alternate with solo arias and duets are more typical of 18th-century practice. A good example is the little-known but expressive *Stabat mater* by Antonio Maria Bononcini for SATB, chorus, strings and continuo. Caldara's impressive setting adds to these vocal and orchestral forces the sepulchral tones of two trombones. They usually merely double the altos and tenors of the chorus, but in the tenor solo 'Tui nati vulnerati' they are given independent parts. Italian composers normally imposed some kind of tonal unity upon the *Stabat mater* by beginning and ending in the same key and by pursuing a logical course through a series of related keys for the rest of the work (treating it much like a chamber cantata). Caldara reinforced his return to the home key by recalling the opening theme in the short fugal passage ('Fac, ut animae donetur paradisi gloria') which ends the work.

Outside Rome the sequence was sometimes set for solo voices only, with instrumental accompaniment. Pergolesi's setting, completed shortly before his death in 1736, was evidently intended to replace Alessandro Scarlatti's, which had been performed annually at Naples during Lent for many years. Both works are for soprano, alto, two violins and continuo and both are influenced by the secular cantata and the chamber duet. Scarlatti's setting is the more substantial, falling into 18 sections of which five are duets. Pergolesi's rather shorter composition achieved immediate popularity and appeared in print many times during the 18th century, often extensively rearranged. John Walsh (i) published an edition in London in 1749, and 12 years later the Walsh firm brought out *An Ode of Mr Pope's adapted to the Principal Airs of the Hymn Stabat Mater compos'd by Signor Pergolesi*. An edition more representative of the 'improvements' effected by later hands is J. A. Hiller's of 1776, described on the title-page as 'improved in harmony, with added parts for oboes and flutes and arranged for four voices'. Even today authentic performances are very rare.

The *Stabat mater* did not figure prominently among the church compositions of the Viennese school. Mozart's early setting (K33c, 1766) is lost, and Haydn's (c1773) is not representative of his best work. Schubert's setting (D175, 1815) uses only the first 12 lines of the poem, which are then repeated to slightly different music. Like his setting of Klopstock's German

paraphrase (D383, 1816), it is accompanied by an orchestra which includes three trombones. In the 19th century the sequence was often composed for concert rather than liturgical use. Rossini's setting, completed in 1841, vacillates between impressive choral sections and frankly operatic arias that too often show little regard for the meaning of the text. It was first performed, significantly enough, not in a church but at the Salle Ventadour, Paris, in 1842, when it was received with tremendous enthusiasm. It has remained one of the most popular settings of the text in the modern repertory. Dvořák expanded his *Stabat mater* (1877) to the proportions of an oratorio by rather tiresome repetition of both words and music and the use of unremittingly slow tempos. Liszt's setting, part of his monumental oratorio *Christus* (1862–6), is of particular interest for its structural use of part of the plainsong melody, heard at the opening and again at various points later in the work. Using a large orchestra, Liszt succeeded in combining grandiose gestures with passages of restrained, austere devotion.

Liszt's is among the most successful 19th-century settings, but the greatest is undoubtedly Verdi's (1898), published as the second of his *Quattro pezzi sacri*. Commentaries on it have tended to overstress the influence that Verdi's study of Palestrina had on the sacred works of his last years. It is more significant that in the *Stabat mater* Verdi was able to achieve a deep sincerity of utterance (as he did also in the Requiem) without renouncing a style perfected through years of experience in the opera house. As in *Falstaff* and *Otello*, the expressive points are made with the utmost economy and there is no textual repetition. The result is probably the shortest setting of the *Stabat mater* composed in the 19th century, and Verdi's example has been followed by most 20th-century composers, although their orchestral requirements often rule out performance in church. Karol Szymanowski's (1925–6), Lennox Berkeley's (1947) and Poulenc's (1950) are outstanding settings. Another is Penderecki's (1962) for three unaccompanied choirs, which uses only six of the poem's 20 stanzas; the composer later incorporated it into his *St Luke Passion*. Bitter listed over 100 settings of the *Stabat mater* composed between 1700 and 1883, including those of Charpentier, Agostino Steffani, Tartini, Boccherini and Gounod. Among the many written since then may be mentioned those of Dohnányi, Kodály, Persichetti, Stanford and Virgil Thomson.

BIBLIOGRAPHY

C. H. Bitter: *Eine Studie zum Stabat Mater* (Leipzig, 1883)
J. Kayser: *Beiträge zur Geschichte und Erklärung der ältesten Kirchenhymnen*, ii (Paderborn, 1886), esp. 110–92
J. Julian: *A Dictionary of Hymnology* (London, 1892, rev. 2/1907, repr. 1915)
C. Carbone: *L'inno del dolore mariano* (Rome, 1911)
E. Schmitz: *Das Madonnenideal in der Tonkunst* (Leipzig, 1920)
B. Stäblein, ed.: *Die Hymnen (I)*, Monumenta Monodica Medii Aevi, i (Kassel and Basle, 1956)
F. Haberl: 'Stabat mater', *Musica sacra*, lxxvi (1956), 33
F. Ll. Harrison: *Music in Medieval Britain* (London, 1958, 2/1963)
A. Robertson: *Requiem: Music of Mourning and Consolation* (London, 1967), chap.11

JOHN CALDWELL (1), MALCOLM BOYD (2)

Stabile, Annibale (*b* Naples, *c*1535; *d* Rome, April 1595). Italian composer. The name 'Annibale' is recorded as that of a boy singer at St John Lateran from 1544 until 1545, and 'Annibale contralto' was a singer there from December 1555 until at least the end of

1556. Either or both of these references might have been to Stabile. The latter identification is particularly likely, since Stabile called himself a pupil of Palestrina, who was *maestro di cappella* there in 1555–6. Stabile was in the service of King Sigismund III of Poland at some time: a work of his appeared in an anthology of motets by the king's musicians (*RISM* 1604²). He probably held this position before 1575, since his career in Rome is documented from that year. From October 1575 until 6 January 1578 he was *maestro di cappella* of St John Lateran. He held the same position at the Collegio Germanico from July 1578 until 1590 (probably 6 February), during which time he was ordained (in 1582), and at S Maria Maggiore from 18 or 19 February 1591 until December 1594. He held several benefices, including that of S Lorenzo di Coll'Alto in the diocese of Nocera; he was a member of the Confraternità dei Musicisti de Urbe, which was officially founded in 1585. As a composer of sacred music Stabile is usually regarded as a follower of Palestrina. The style of his secular music is lyrical and sentimental, with supple rhythms and long smooth melodic lines. His later madrigals were moderately influenced by the lighter style that was popular in the last quarter of the 16th century. His music shows strong harmonic orientation and, in many cases, tonal organization.

His brother Pompeo Stabile (*b* Naples, mid-16th century) was from 1582 to 1583 organist at the Ss Annunziata, Naples. The dedication of his only publication, *Il primo libro de madrigali a sei voci* (Venice, 1585³²), is signed from Genoa; he contributed works to two collections (*RISM* 1585³¹ and 1591¹²).

WORKS

SACRED

Sacrarum modulationum . . . liber secundus, 5, 6, 8vv (Venice, 1585)
Sacrarum modulationum . . . liber tertius, 5, 6, 8vv (Venice, 1589); 1 ed. in Musica sacra, xvi (Berlin, 1839)
Hymnus de gloria paradisi, 4vv (Dillingen, 1590)
Litanie, 4vv (Venice, 1592), lost
Motets, incl. reprs. from earlier books, 1583², 1588², 1590⁵, 1596², A. Gualtieri: Motecta . . . liber primus (Venice, 1604), 1604², C. Sacchi: Missa, motecta, magnificat (Rome, 1607), 1611¹
Missa 'Ung gay bergier', 4vv, Warsaw Cathedral archives
Missa 'Vestiva i colli', 5vv, Warsaw Cathedral archives
Missa cantantibus organis, 12vv, *I-Rsg* [Ky, Cr, Cruxifixum only; collab. Palestrina and others]; ed. in Monumenta polyphoniae italicae, i (Rome, 1930)

SECULAR

Il primo libro de madrigali, 5vv (Venice, 1572, rev. 2/1586)
Madrigali di G. M. Nanino e di A. Stabile, 5vv (Venice, 1581¹⁰)
Il terzo libro de madrigali, 5vv (Venice, 1585)
Works in 1582⁴; 1582⁵; 1583¹⁰; 1583¹¹; 1583¹²; 1583¹⁴; 1585²⁹, 1585³²; 1589⁷; 1589¹¹; 1590¹⁵; 1591¹², 1 ed. C. H. Parry, Arion, iii (London, 1899); 1592¹¹; 1593³

BIBLIOGRAPHY

R. Casimiri: ' "Disciplina musicae" e "mastri di capella" ', *NA*, xix (1942), 103
T. D. Culley: *Jesuits and Music* (Rome, 1970)
J. Gołos: 'Liber missarum z Archiwum Kapituły Warszawskiej', *Muzyka*, xviii/1 (1973), 40
——: 'Le opere sconosciute di Annibale Stabile', *Istituto di studi musicali e teatrali Bologna 1973*

RUTH I. DeFORD

Stabile, Mariano (*b* Palermo, 12 May 1888; *d* Milan, 11 Jan 1968). Italian baritone. He studied at the S Cecilia Conservatory of Rome under Cotogni and made his début in 1911 at the Teatro Biondo, Palermo, as Marcello in *La bohème*. During the following years he appeared in several other Italian opera houses, but he was still unknown to the larger public when he was chosen by Toscanini to sing the title part in Verdi's *Falstaff* for the opening of the 1921–2 season at La Scala, Milan. This occasion, for which he was thoroughly coached both by Toscanini and by de Luca, proved to be the turning-point of Stabile's career: he scored a great success, and remained a Falstaff without peer. He sang the part in London during his first Covent Garden season in 1926, appearing also as Iago with Zenatello and Lotte Lehmann, and as Don Giovanni with Leider, Lehmann and Schumann. During the next five years he was a frequent visitor to London, adding to his Covent Garden repertory Gianni Schicchi, Scarpia, Rigoletto, Marcello and the Comte de Nevers in *Les Huguenots*.

Mariano Stabile in the title role of Verdi's 'Falstaff'

Stabile often sang with the Glyndebourne Opera; he sang at Glyndebourne itself between 1936 and 1939 as Mozart's Figaro and as Dr Malatesta in *Don Pasquale*, and during the 1948 Edinburgh Festival as Don Alfonso in *Così fan tutte*. He took part extensively in Jay Pomeroy's prolonged seasons at the Cambridge and the Stoll Theatres between 1946 and 1949, when he sang Malatesta, Scarpia, Falstaff and, on one occasion, Rossini's Figaro. In Italy he sang about 50 other parts, including Beckmesser.

Stabile's vocal powers were not exceptional, and his great artistic attainments were the result of a spontaneous dramatic exuberance schooled by a fine sense of style. His enunciation was unusually clear, and his mastery of dramatic inflection and gesture never failed him, whether in the cajolery of Don Giovanni, the brutality of Scarpia, the bland complacency of Falstaff or the mercurial egotism of Malatesta. His infectious sense of fun found full scope in *Don Pasquale* and *Così*, and in both these operas his relish of the approaching discomfiture of his victims always delighted the audience. Malatesta's 'Bella siccome un angelo' has been more smoothly vocalized by other singers, but there was something irresistibly comical in the gusto with which Stabile would arouse Don Pasquale's desires by his account of Norina's charms while at the same time holding him at arm's length by imperious gestures of restraint; and, whether with Baccaloni or with Martin Lawrence, the patter duet in the third act never failed to provoke an encore. Stabile's make-up as Falstaff was somewhat grotesque by English ideas, but in all other respects he was an ideal exponent of the part. Among countless delightful touches let one small detail be mentioned: the half-submerged gurgle of pleasure with which he received Ford's compliment 'Voi siete un uom' di mondo'.

DESMOND SHAWE-TAYLOR

Stabile, Pompeo. Italian musician, brother of ANNIBALE STABILE.

Stabinger [Stabingher, Staubinger], **Mathias** [Mattia] (*b* c1750; *d* Venice, c1815). Composer, conductor and instrumentalist, probably of German origin. In 1772 he appeared as a flautist and clarinettist in Lyons; in the same year he appeared in Paris, where he soon published his first instrumental works. In 1777 he left Paris for Italy, and shortly thereafter composed ballets for Milan. His *Le astuzie di Bettina*, produced in Genoa in 1780, achieved considerable success, and was performed in other European centres throughout the decade. After serving in 1781 as *maestro al cembalo* at the Warsaw Opera, he went to Russia, first to St Petersburg as a member of the Mattei-Orecia operatic troupe (1782) and then to Moscow, where he directed a small Italian troupe at the Petrovsky Theatre and produced an oratorio *Betulia liberata* (1783). He returned to Italy for two years, but in 1785 was again in Moscow where until 1799 he directed the orchestra of the Petrovsky theatre, composed many successful ballets, operas (some in Russian) and other works, and took an active part in the city's musical life, even undertaking a programme of educating the serfs in the arts. Stabinger left Russia for Italy just after the turn of the century, and his creative activity ceased. In 1805 in Naples he announced the publication of a music periodical or periodical collection, but it seems never to have appeared. By 1814 he had settled in Venice.

WORKS

STAGE

Calipso abbandonata, Milan, La Scala, c1777
Avventure d'Ircana (ballet), Milan, Canobbiana, 1779
La sconfitta delle amazone (ballet), Milan, Canobbiana, 1779
Le astuzie di Bettina (opera buffa, 2), Genoa, S Agostino, 1780; score, *F-Pn*
Il finto pazzo per amore (opera buffa, 2, ?T. Mariani), Moscow, 25 Oct 1782
La morte d'Arrigo, Bologna, 1784
Schastlivaya Tonia [Lucky Tonia] (comic opera, 4, D. Gorchakov), Moscow, Petrovsky, 14 Jan 1786
Baba Yaga (comic opera, 3, D. Gorchakov), Moscow, 2 Dec 1786
Pigmalion, ili Sila Lyubvï [Pygmalion, or The power of love] (drama, 1, Maykov, after Rousseau), Moscow, 20 Dec 1787
Zhenit'ba neudachnaya [The unfortunate marriage] (Russ. ?or It. opera), Moscow, 19 Feb 1788
Les époux infortunés, ou L'heureuse rencontre (ballet, F. Morelli), Moscow, Petrovsky, 1791
Orphée traversant l'enfer à la recherche d'Eurydice, ?cantata, Moscow, 22 Feb 1792
Ballet music to J. Kozłowski's Zelmira i Smelon ili Vzyatiye goroda Izmaïla [Zelmira and Smelon, or The capture of the town of Izmaïl] (lyric drama, 3, P. S. Potyomkin), Ostankino, 22 July 1795

VOCAL

Betulia liberata (oratorio, Metastasio), Moscow, 26 March 1783
La prise d'Ismaïl, composition allégorique, St Petersburg, 1793

La réconciliation de l'Europe, cantata, ?Moscow, 1801

INSTRUMENTAL

op.
1 Six duos, 2 fl (Paris, n.d.)
2 Six quatuors, fl, vn, va, vc (Paris, 1773)
– Six sonates, pf, vn acc., advertised 1786
3 Six trios, 2 vn, vc (Paris and Lyons, c1790)
4 Six quatuors concertants, fl, 2 vn, vc (Venice, 1792)
5 Sextuors concertants, fl, 2 vn, vc, 2 hn (Venice, 1792)
7 Six duos concertants, 2 fl (Venice, 1792)

Fl duets, *I-Mc, Pc*; 6 trios, 2 vn, vc, *Pc*; qt, fl, vn, va, vc, *A-Wn*

BIBLIOGRAPHY

EitnerQ; *GerberL*; *GerberNL*
Mercure de France (Aug, Sept 1772)
Letter to Tamburini (MS, 1790, *GB-Lbm* Add.29300)
R.-A. Mooser: *Annales de la musique en Russie au XVIIIe siècle*, ii (Geneva, 1951), esp. 406f
——: *Opéras, intermezzos . . . joués en Russie durant le XVIIIe siècle* (Basle, 3/1964)

ROGER COTTE

Stäblein, Bruno (*b* Munich, 5 May 1895; *d* Erlangen, 6 March 1978). German musicologist. He studied musicology from 1914 with Sandberger and Kroyer at the University of Munich, where he took his doctorate in 1918 with a dissertation on 16th-century instrumental music. At the same time he completed his studies in composition, the piano and conducting at the Munich Academy. After he had spent a year as a répétiteur at the Munich National Theatre (1918–19), his operatic and concert conducting career took him to the Innsbruck Stadttheater (1919–20) and to the Coburg Staatstheater (1920–26); he also directed the Ernst-Albert-Oratorien Verein (1920–29). In 1927 and 1929 he passed examinations qualifying him to teach music in places of higher education, and took up schoolteaching. From 1931 to 1945 he was a probationary schoolmaster at the Altes Gymnasium in Regensburg, where from 1939 he was an assistant master. During this period he became deeply interested in medieval music, making extensive visits to libraries and building up a collection of photographic copies of source materials.

In 1945 he founded the institute of musical research at the Philologisch-theologische Hochschule, becoming director in 1953. He completed his *Habilitation* in musicology in 1946 at the University of Erlangen with a work on hymnology, and subsequently lectured at the Regensburg Hochschule. In 1956 he was appointed to the new chair of musicology at the University of Erlangen. Here he instituted his extensive collection of microfilm reproductions of medieval manuscripts as an international centre of research (in 1973 it comprised about 4000 manuscripts). He also founded and edited Monumenta Monodica Medii Aevi which aims to realize from its sources European monodic song from early times up to the end of the Middle Ages. Although he retired in 1963 Stäblein continued his activities as director of the film archive and editor of Monumenta. He was also an executive member of the Gesellschaft für Musikforschung, a member of the music history committee of the Bavarian Academy of Sciences and chairman of the Gesellschaft für Bayerische Musikgeschichte. Stäblein was an authority on medieval music, particularly on monodic music and the chorale. His work combined an attempt at comprehensive presentation and ordering of source materials with interpretative insight. These qualities are typified in his articles for *MGG* (about 60), e.g. 'Psalm', 'Saint-Martial', 'Sequenz', 'Tropus' and 'Versus'.

Stäblein's wife, Hanna Stäblein-Harder (*b* Altona, 14

Jan 1929) studied with Gerber in Göttingen (1949–51), Gurlitt in Freiburg (1951–2) and Handschin in Basle (from 1952), where in 1956 she took the doctorate with a dissertation on 14th-century French mass ordinaries. She has pursued this area of research in publishing studies and editions of medieval music for the Mass.

WRITINGS

Musicque de Joye: Studien zur Instrumentalmusik des 16. Jahrhunderts (diss., U. of Munich, 1918)
'Die zwei St. Emmeramer Kantatorien aus dem 11. Jahrhundert (Clm 14322 und Clm 14083)', *13. Jahresbericht des Vereins zur Erforschung der Regensburger Diözesangeschichte 1939*, 231
Hymnenstudien (Habilitationsschrift, U. of Erlangen, 1946)
'Von der Sequenz zum Strophenlied: eine neue Sequenzenmelodie "archaischen" Stiles', *Mf*, vii (1954), 257
'Zur Frühgeschichte der Sequenz', *AMw*, xviii (1961), 1–33
'Notkeriana', *AMw*, xix–xx (1962–3), 84
'Modale Rhythmen im Saint-Martial-Repertoire?', *Festschrift Friedrich Blume* (Kassel, 1963), 340
'Zur archaischen ambrosianischen (Mailänder) Mehrstimmigkeit', *A Ettore Desderi* (Bologna, 1963), 169
'Zum Verständnis des "klassischen" Tropus', *AcM*, xxxv (1963), 84
'Die Sequenzmelodie "Concordia" und ihr geschichtlicher Hintergrund', *Festschrift Hans Engel* (Kassel, 1964), 364
'Der "altrömische" Choral in Oberitalien und im deutschen Süden', *Mf*, xix (1966), 3
'Zur Musik des Ludus de Antichristo', *Zum 70. Geburtstag von Joseph Müller-Blattau* (Kassel, 1966), 312
'Zur Stilistik der Troubadourmelodien', *AcM*, xxxviii (1966), 27
'Kann der gregorianische Choral im Frankenreich entstanden sein?', *AMw*, xxiv (1967), 153
' "Psalle symphonizando" ', *Festschrift für Walter Wiora* (Kassel, 1967), 221
' "Gregorius Praesul", der Prolog zum römischen Antiphonale', *Musik und Verlag: Karl Vötterle zum 65. Geburtstag* (Kassel, 1968), 537
'Nochmals zur angeblichen Entstehung des gregorianischen Chorals im Frankenreich', *AMw*, xxvii (1970), 110
'Oswald von Wolkenstein, der Schöpfer des Individualliedes', *Deutsche Vierteljahrsschrift für Literaturwissenschaft und Geistesgeschichte*, xlvi (1972), 113–60
'Zwei Melodien der altirischen Liturgie', *Musicae scientiae collectanea: Festschrift Karl Gustav Fellerer* (Cologne, 1973), 590
'Die Entstehung des gregorianischen Chorals', *Mf*, xxvii (1974), 5
'Oswald von Wolkenstein und seine Vorbilder', *Oswald von Wolkenstein*, ed. E. Kühebacher, Innsbrucker Beiträge zur Kulturwissenschaft, Germanistische Reihe, i (Innsbruck, 1974), 285
Schriftbild der einstimmigen Musik, Musikgeschichte in Bildern, iii/4 (Leipzig, 1975)
Further articles in *IMSCR*, v *Utrecht 1952*, *IMSCR*, viii *New York 1961* and in Festschriften for Schenk (1962), Fellerer (Regensburg, 1962), Smits van Waesberghe (1963), Senn (1975) and Haberl (1976)

EDITIONS

F. Cavalli: Vier Marianische Antiphonen (1586), Musica divina, i–iv (Regensburg, 1950)
Hymnen I: die mittelalterlichen Hymnenmelodien des Abendlandes, Monumenta monodica medii aevi, i (Kassel, 1956)
Die Gesänge des altrömischen Graduale (Vat.lat. 5319), Monumenta monodica medii aevi, ii (Kassel, 1970)

BIBLIOGRAPHY

M. Ruhnke, ed.: *Festschrift Bruno Stäblein* (Kassel, 1967) [incl. list of publications to 1967]
                   HANS HEINRICH EGGEBRECHT

Stabreim (Ger.: 'bar-rhyme', 'alliteration'). Alliteration was the oldest German verse-forming principle, used for both euphony, cohesion and as a means of emphasizing conceptual connections. It was revived by Wagner in *Tristan und Isolde* but with especial rigour in *Der Ring des Nibelungen*, as an answer to his need for a heightened poetic utterance that could link the sensuous and the conceptual: 'the poet . . . has sought by the consonantal *Stabreim* to bring [his row of words] to the feeling's understanding in an easier and more sensuous form' (*Oper und Drama*). Wagner's *Stabreim* normally consists of two or three alliterated *Hebungen* (strong beats, or *arses*) with freely arranged, non-alliterative *Senkungen* (weak beats, or *theses*). Despite precedents in 14th-century English verse (*Piers Plowman*), the use

of the device in English opera has not been effective, whether in translation of Wagner (H. and F. Corder) or in original texts (Holst's *Sita*); nor has it proved fruitful in German opera after Wagner.

BIBLIOGRAPHY

R. Wagner: *Oper und Drama*, Gesammelte Schriften (Leipzig, 1871–80, 5/1911, ed. H. von Wolzogen and R. Sternfeld; Eng. trans., London, 1892–9), iv
E. Sievers: *Altgermanische Metrik* (Halle, 1892, 2/1905)
R. Pischel: *Der Vers in R. Wagners Ring des Nibelungen* (Vienna, 1912)
H. Wiessner: *Der Stabreimvers in R. Wagners Ring des Nibelungen* (diss., U. of Berlin, 1923)
                   JOHN WARRACK

Staccato (It.: 'detached'). A term meaning separated with not only a very perceptible silence of articulation but a certain emphasis which may be nearly though not quite so marked as an extreme MARCATO, or may be much less (the antonym of LEGATO). The French 'détaché' is not quite equivalent. In notation, a dot, and also a vertical dash or wedge, came into increasing use through the later Baroque period, and remain standard; there is not necessarily any gradation between these markings, but when there is the vertical dash or wedge indicates a greater degree of separation and emphasis than the dot. The marking appears, at convenience, either above or below the note affected. When a series of notes so marked appears grouped under a slur, the implication may be technical: e.g. for bowed strings, one bowstroke to each group, either *spiccato*, with a bouncing bow, usually shown by dots; or normal staccato, with a continuously pressed bow, usually shown by dashes or wedges. (For the piano, a portato is intended; for the clavichord, the *Bebung*.) (For a special Baroque use of the dot implying rhythmic alteration, *see* NOTES INÉGALES.)

Since the Baroque period the vertical dash or wedge, though still in use, has for many purposes been replaced by a horizontal dash. Where this is distinguished from the vertical dash or wedge, the intention of the horizontal dash is less separation but heavier emphasis. When a series of notes (commonly two, and not often more than four) bearing the horizontal dash appears grouped under a slur, the intention for bowed instruments is a particular massive staccato employing only a short portion of the bow for each note, and stopping the vibrations of the string very forcibly between the notes; whereas the dot in this and other situations, even if not taken *spiccato*, will have a lighter separation, with the bow not pressed hard enough to stop the vibrations of the string completely, so that the sound rings slightly through. The heaviest staccato for bowed strings is sometimes called *martelé* ('hammered'), where the bow is raised from the string and dropped on it with the full weight of the arm, generally at the frog end: a stroke for which (alone) there is no contemporary evidence whatsoever in connection with Baroque music, though it is often used in modern performance (always to bad and unauthentic effect).

The Baroque staccato was variable, as is that of the present day, but always more inclined to crispness than to heaviness. For the Baroque tendency to take an ordinary movement, other things being equal, neither legato (as is now the practice) nor staccato, but in a moderately articulated style somewhere in between, *see* LEGATO.
                   ROBERT DONINGTON

Stachel (Ger.). ENDPIN.

Stachowicz, Damian [Damianus a Ss Trinitate] (*b* Sokołow, nr. Przemyśl, 1658; *d* Łowicz, nr. Warsaw, 27 Nov 1699). Polish composer. He was a member of the order of Piarists for 25 years and lectured on poetics and rhetoric at the college at Łowicz; he also published a few panegyrics. At his death he was vice-rector of the college, and he also directed the music in the college chapel. His compositions were chiefly intended for the chapel but were performed in other churches as well. According to his monastic obituary he was recognized by his contemporaries as an outstanding composer. His extant works are uneven: some show signs of haste and are deficient technically; others, on the contrary, show a masterly technique – e.g. the solo concertato *Veni consolator*, which resembles the trumpet arias of the Venetian operatic school and is now frequently performed. An essential feature of Stachowicz's music is his frequent use of homophony, with polyphony confined to a few passages, and his extensive application of concertato technique. Fanfare-like melodies are also characteristic of him: they stem from his partiality for clarini, which appear in nearly all of his extant compositions.

WORKS

Missa requiem, 5vv, 2 vn, 2 tpt, bc, *PL-R*
Beata nobis gaudia, several vv, 2 vn, 2 tpt, bc, *SA*
Laudate pueri, several vv, 2 vn, 2 tpt, bc, *Wtm*
Veni consolator, 1v, tpt, bc (org), ed. in WDMP, xiii (3/1966)
Litaniae della BMV, 4vv, 2 vn, bc, *R*
Completorium solemne, Requiem ex B (? = Missa requiem): lost, mentioned in 1751 inventory of Piarist chapel, Wieluń
Other sacred works, now lost, extant in A. Chybiński's pre-war transcrs.

BIBLIOGRAPHY

A. Chybiński: 'Przyczynki bio- i bibliograficzne do dawnej muzyki polskiej' [Biographical and bibliographical notes on early Polish musicians], *Przegląd muzyczny*, v/2 (1929), 5
Z. M. Szweykowski: 'Sylwetka kompozytorska Damiana Stachowicza', *Muzyka*, vii/1 (1962), 14
J. Buba and Z. M. and A. Szweykowski: 'Kultura muzyczna u pijarów w XVII i XVIII wieku', *Muzyka*, x (1965), no.2, p.15; no.3, p.20
Z. M. Szweykowski: preface to WDMP, xiii (3/1966)
ZYGMUNT M. SZWEYKOWSKI

Stachowski, Marek (*b* Piekary Śląskie, 21 March 1936). Polish composer. He studied theory and composition with Penderecki at the Kraków Conservatory, and in 1968 he won a prize at the Malawski Competition with *Neusis II*. At first strongly influenced by Penderecki's earlier works, he went on to work with broad planes and overlapping layers of periodic material, as in *Irisation*.

WORKS
(*selective list*)

Str Qt no.1, 1965; Musica con una battuta del tam-tam, orch, 1966; Neusis II, vocal ensembles, perc, vcs, dbs, 1968; Sequenze concertanti, orch, 1968; Chant de l'espoir (Eluard), narrator, S, Bar, chorus, orch, 1969; Audition, fl, vc, pf, 1970; Irisation, orch, 1970; Słowa ... [Words...], S, B, chorus, orch, 1971; Str Qt no.2, 1972; Musique solonnelle, 1973; Thakurian Chants, chorus, orch, 1974; Poème sonore, orch, 1975; Birds, S, ens, 1976; Divertimento, str, 1978

Principal publisher: Polskie Wydawnictwo Muzyczne
MIECZYSŁAWA HANUSZEWSKA

Stade, Frederica von. *See* VON STADE, FREDERICA.

Stadelmayer [Stadelmaier, Stadelmeyer], **Johann.** *See* STADLMAYR, JOHANN.

Staden, Adam. German composer and poet, son of JOHANN STADEN.

Staden, Johann (*b* Nuremberg, baptized 2 July 1581; *d* Nuremberg, buried 15 Nov 1634). German composer and organist, father of SIGMUND THEOPHIL STADEN. He was a distinguished and versatile composer, and one of the outstanding German musicians of his day. In his later years he was the leading musician in Nuremberg and established the so-called Nuremberg school of the 17th century.

1. LIFE. Staden's father married Elisabeth Löbele as his second wife in December 1574, and Johann was born of this marriage. The year of his birth is given on his portrait (see illustration) as 1581; the Nuremberg baptismal records show that a son called Johannes was born on 2 July to Hans and Elisabeth Starnn, this surname undoubtedly being a scribal error for 'Staden'. Doppelmayr wrote that Staden had become celebrated as an organist in Nuremberg by the age of 18. This reputation, and perhaps also experience as an assistant organist at one of the Nuremberg churches, led to his first traceable appointment, as court organist at Bayreuth; he is described thus in the Nuremberg city record of his marriage on 16 April 1604. After a big fire at Bayreuth in 1605, Margrave Christian moved his court to Kulmbach, where it remained until 1610. The only traces of Staden during these years are the baptismal records of his children and the dedications of his works. Three baptisms at Kulmbach in 1606, 1607 and 1608 identify him as court organist. The dedications of his *Neue teutsche Lieder* and *Neue teutsche geistliche Gesäng* (both 1609) are signed from Kulmbach and that of his *Venus Kräntzlein* from Bayreuth on 1 May 1610.

Staden must soon have returned to Nuremberg, for a daughter was baptized there on 10 January 1611, and two others in 1614 and 1615. It is not known what position he held there at this time. His name does not appear in the city records until 1616, when he dedicated a work to the city council, and the council promised him the next organist's post to become vacant. That occurred on 20 June 1616 at the Spitalkirche, and on 19 November of the same year Staden moved to St Lorenz to succeed Kaspar Hassler as organist. In 1618 he was appointed organist of St Sebald, the most important musical position in Nuremberg, which he held for the rest of his life.

That Staden had a wide reputation as an organist is suggested by Margrave Christian's invitation to him in 1618 to join Michael Praetorius, Scheidt and Schütz in testing a new organ at Bayreuth. As Nuremberg's leading musician he was often asked by the city council to judge new music that composers dedicated to the city. Among such works passed on to him were the second part of Schein's *Opella nova* (1626), Melchior Franck's *Suspirium Germaniae* (1628) and Scheidt's second set of *Geistliche Concerten* (1634); the letters of dedication of these three works are in the Nuremberg Staatsarchiv (Rechnungsbelege nos.702 and 783; those of Scheidt and Schein ed. in Zirnbauer, 1959). With great devotion and energy Staden established the direction that the so-called Nuremberg school was to take during the rest of the 17th century. Among his pupils were Kindermann, two lesser Nurembergers, Paul Grimmschneider and Daniel Dietel and probably David Schedlich. A teacher–pupil tradition runs uninterruptedly from Staden and Kindermann through Schwemmer and Wecker to Johann Krieger and Pachelbel at the beginning of the next century.

Staden also taught his four sons. They included not

JOHANNES STADEN, MUSICUS RELIGIOS, SYMPHŌISTA
ET ORGANISTA, AD D. SEBALDI NORIB. NAT, 1581. Obiit 1634.

Johann Staden: engraving (1640) by Johann Pfann

only Sigmund Theophil Staden, but two others who wrote some music: Johann (1606–27) by whom there are two pieces in his father's *Hauss-Music* (*RISM* 1628⁶ and 1634⁴, both reprinted in 1646⁵); and Adam (1614–59), who is known by three funeral songs (in *D-Nst*) and who wrote the texts of two of them as well as those of five other pieces, two by his brother Sigmund Theophil and three by Schedlich.

2. WORKS. About half of Staden's extant works have survived in incomplete form. Except for some instrumental pieces in two manuscripts, his music exists in printed partbooks (without bar-lines and with traces of mensural notation such as ligatures and blackened notes). His first printed work was *Neue teutsche Lieder* (1606), which was soon followed by two other collections of polyphonic secular songs, *Neue teutsche Lieder* (1609) and *Venus Kräntzlein* (1610); all three have instrumental pieces appended. Closely related stylistically to these secular works are the various collections of sacred songs: *Neue teutsche geistliche Gesäng* (1609), *Drey christliche Betgesäng* (1622), the four parts of *Hauss-Music* (1623–8), *Musicalischer Freuden- und Andachtswecker* (1630), the 12 strophic songs in *Hertzens Andachten* (1631) and the 12 songs appended to his son Sigmund Theophil Staden's new edition of Hans Leo Hassler's *Kirchen Gesäng* (1637). These collections provide a total of 65 secular and 180 sacred polyphonic songs by Staden. His models, as for other composers of the Nuremberg school such as H. C. Haiden, Melchior Franck and Jeep, were the songs of Lechner and especially Hassler (*Neue teutsche Gesäng*, 1596, and *Lustgarten*, 1601). Most of Staden's songs are in four parts (though many are in three or five parts), all are without basso continuo, and, as Staden wrote in

the foreword to part iv of his *Hauss-Music*, they can also be performed on instruments. The style is predominantly note-against-note, but one does find imitative counterpoint, especially in *Venus Kräntzlein*. The texts are by earlier and contemporary poets, including Staden himself; chorale texts are rare. The songs are distinguished by folklike melodies and simple rhythms.

Staden published no further secular vocal music after leaving the Bayreuth court about 1610. His major sacred works are a mixture of old and new styles: some motets without basso continuo, some with continuo as well as other instruments, and choral and solo concertos. His first major work, *Harmoniae sacrae* (1616), contains all these types and is of considerable historical interest. The first 21 pieces are five- to eight-part motets without continuo, modelled after Lassus; an appendix consists of six pieces for two to five voices with continuo (some also have other instrumental parts) in the style of Viadana's *Cento concerti ecclesiastici* (1602). Furthermore, the eighth partbook has all the parts in open score for the organist, which appears to be the earliest German instance of this Italian practice. Along with Aichinger's *Cantiones* (1607–9), Michael Praetorius's *Urano-Chorodia* (1613), the first part of Schein's *Opella nova* (1618) and Schütz's *Psalmen* (1619), Staden's *Harmoniae sacrae* offers some of the earliest sacred concertos in Germany; through it he introduced to Nuremberg an obligatory basso continuo (in the style of Viadana), independent instrumental accompaniment, the solo concerto and the modern score. Nevertheless, the basic style is still that of the motet; melodically and harmonically there is no trace of the *seconda prattica* anywhere in Staden's output. Other collections that can be grouped stylistically with *Harmoniae sacrae* are *Harmoniarum sacrarum continuatio* (1621), which also contains open scores, *Harmoniae novae sacrarum cantionum* (1628, 'cum & sine Basso ad Organum') and *Harmoniae variatae sacrarum cantionum* (1632), though the continuo part of all three is usually a *basso seguente*.

Staden's first major work with German texts is *Kirchen-Music* (1625–6), which contains several examples of concerted writing for solo voices, chorus and mixed vocal and instrumental groups. Part i makes extensive use of chorale texts, whose melodies often serve as cantus firmi in the manner of the chorale motets of Senfl and Finck a century earlier; in general, however, chorales play a minor role in Staden's music. The texts of part ii are psalms and other biblical verse, usually set in concerto style. The careful attention to declamation and pictorial aspects of the texts makes *Kirchen-Music* Staden's most expressive work. The basso continuo partbook of part ii contains his well-known 'brief and simple introduction' to 'basso ad organum' (see Arnold, 100ff, and the foreword to edn. of pt.i, DTB, xii, Jg.vii/1, p.xlii). He added nothing to the theories of Viadana, Agazzari and Praetorius, but he provided a clear summary of these earlier writings and showed his thorough understanding of the various types of basso continuo (see Eggebrecht). His *Hertzens Andachten* (1631) and *Geistliche Music-Klang* (1633) also contain solo concertos, and his lost *Davids Harpffe* (1643) probably did too. With his *Hertzentrosts-Musica* (1630) he introduced the solo continuo song to Nuremberg, and along with Schein and Franck he was an early composer of motet dialogues, two of which appear in *Hauss-Music* (1628).

Staden's instrumental music, with Hassler's *Lustgarten* as its model, ranks with that of Haussmann and Franck as among the most important in the Germany of his time. In addition to the instrumental pieces appended to his collections of secular songs of 1606, 1609 and 1610 and five pieces in a manuscript tablature, there are three printed collections by him, which appeared in 1618, 1625 and 1643 respectively. This gives a total of 196 pieces, many of which were probably written for a Nuremberg Musikkränzlein, a group of amateur performers (see Nagel, 1895, and Martin). The pieces include many and various dance movements, not grouped by key, as well as symphonias, sonatas (which are among the first published German examples of the form), intradas, canzonas and fantasias. Occasionally one finds a thematic relation between single pieces.

To sum up, Staden was one of Germany's earliest exponents of the concertato style (both choral and solo) and the continuo. But his maxim, according to Herbst and Walther, was: 'the Italians do not know everything, the Germans can also do something'. And indeed his output shows neither a complete surrender to, nor a stubborn evasion of, new Italian styles, forms and textures such as concertato, monody and recitative, based on the continuo, but a conservative interpolation of them with the German traditions of syllabic treatment of the text, unadventurous harmony and counterpoint and the dominating sacred songs with their restricted melodic flow and limited forms.

WORKS

(all printed works published in Nuremberg, unless otherwise stated)
Editions: *J. Staden: Ausgewählte Werke*, i, ed. E. Schmitz, DTB, xii, Jg.vii/1 (1906) [S i]
    J. Staden: Ausgewählte Werke, ii, ed. E. Schmitz, DTB, xiv, Jg.viii/1 (1907) [S ii]
    Chorbuch, ed. F. Jöde (Wolfenbüttel and Berlin, 1927–31) [J]

SACRED VOCAL
Neue teutsche geistliche Gesäng, 3–8vv (1609)
Harmoniae sacrae pro festis praecipuis totius anni, 4–8vv, quibus . . . adjectae sunt . . . novae inventionis italicae cantiones, 1–5vv, bc (1616); Angelicus hymnus, no.11, pubd separately (1615); 7 in S i; 1 in J ii
Jubila sancta Deo per hymnum et echo (1617)
Harmoniarum sacrarum continuatio, 1–12vv, bc (1621); 3 in S i; 3 in S ii
Drey christliche Betgesäng, 4vv (1622)
Harmonicae meditationes animae, 4vv (1622)
Hauss-Music, geistliche Gesäng, 3, 4vv: vol.i (1623, 2/1634⁴), 4 in S i; vol.ii (1628), 2 in S i, 1 in J ii; vol.iii (1628), 9 in S i, 6 in J v; vol.iv (1628⁵), 4 in S i; 4 vols. pubd together (1646⁵), 2 in S i
Kirchen-Music, geistliche Gesang und Psalmen: vol.i (1625), 1 in S i, 1 in S ii; vol.ii, 1–7vv/insts, bc (1626), 5 in S ii; incl. in bc of vol.ii, *Kurz und einfältig Bericht für die jenigen, so im Basso ad Organum unerfahren*; pr. in *AMz*, xii (1877), 99; extracts trans. in Arnold, 100ff
Harmoniae novae sacrarum cantionum, 3–12vv, bc (1628); 4 in S ii
Hertzentrosts-Musica, geistliche Meditationen, 1v (1630); copy in *D-Nst* incl. MS organ tablature of nos.1–9; 1 in S ii
Musicalischer Freuden- und Andachtswecker oder Geistliche Gesänglein, 4–6vv (1630); 3 in S i; 2 in J iv
Hertzens Andachten, geistliche Gesänglein, 1, 4vv, bc (1631); 2 in S ii
Harmoniae variatae sacrarum cantionum, 1–12vv, bc (1632); 1 in S ii
Plausus Noricus praecelsissimo atque potentissimo principi ac domino, domino Gustavo Adolpho, 9vv/insts, bc (1632)
Geistliche Music-Klang, 1, 3vv, 2, 3 viols, bc (1633); 1 in S ii
Davids Harpffe, 1v, bc (1643), lost
Ach bleib bey uns, song, 8vv (n.d.)

1 Magnificat, 1620⁹, incl. in Kirchen-Music, i
12 songs, 4vv, 1637²
5 motets, 1672², 4 from Harmoniae novae

Lamb Gottes, das du weg nimbst Sünd der Welt, response, 4vv, *D-Nla*

SECULAR VOCAL
Neue teutsche Lieder nach Art der Villanellen beyneben etlicher Baleti oder Tantz, 3–5vv (1606)

Neue teutsche Lieder mit poetischen Texten samt etlichen Galliarden, 4vv (1609); 3 in S ii; 1 in J iv; 4 ed. in W. Vetter, *Das frühdeutsche Lied*, ii (Münster, 1928), 20ff
Venus Kräntzlein, newer musicalischen Gesäng und Lieder, 4, 5vv (1610); 7 in S ii; 1 in J iv; 15 ed. in NM, cxix (1936, 2/1959)
Orpheus redivivus, MS, lost (see Zirnbauer, 1960, 346)

INSTRUMENTAL
Neue Pavanen, Galliarden, Curanten, a 4, 5 (1618) [incl. 1 repr. from 1616²⁴]; 6 in S ii; 6 ed. in NM, lxxx (1932, 2/1955); 2 balletti ed. in E. Mohr, *Die Allemande*, ii (Zurich and Leipzig, 1932), nos.46–7
Opusculum novum, a 4 (1625)
Operum musicorum posthumorum pars prima, a 3–8 (1643); 8 in S ii; 3 ed. in W. Hillemann, *Im Trio* (Mainz, 1954)
Inst pieces in secular vocal collections, see above
5 suite movts, a 3, Nuremberg, Staatsarchiv (score)
21 pieces incl. 4 toccatas, kbd, and org transcrs. of inst works, *I-Tn* (see Mischiati)

WRITINGS
Letter, 4 Dec 1626, Nuremberg, Staatsarchiv
Kurz und einfältig Bericht, see *Kirchen-Music*, ii (1626)

BIBLIOGRAPHY
WaltherML
J. A. Herbst: *Musica moderna prattica* (Frankfurt am Main, 1653, 2/1658)
J. G. Doppelmayr: *Historische Nachricht von den nürnbergischen Mathematicis und Künstlern* (Nuremberg, 1730)
R. Eitner: 'Johann Staden: eine Bio- und Bibliographie', *MMg*, xv (1883), 101, 119
W. Nagel: 'Die Nürnberger Musikgesellschaften (1588–1629)', *MMg*, xxvii (1895), 1
——: 'Zur Biographie Johann Stadens und seiner Söhne', *MMg*, xxix (1897), 53
A. Werner: 'Samuel und Gottfried Scheidt', *SIMG*, i (1899–1900), 401–45
E. Schmitz: Introduction to DTB, xii, Jg.vii/1 (1906)
F. T. Arnold: *The Art of Accompaniment from a Thorough-bass* (London, 1931/R1965), 100ff
H. Eggebrecht: 'Arten des Generalbasses', *AMw*, xiv (1957), 61
U. Martin: 'Die Nürnberger Musikgesellschaften', *Mitteilungen des Vereins für die Geschichte der Stadt Nürnberg*, xlix (1959), 185–225
H. Zirnbauer: *Der Notenbestand der Reichstädtischen Nürnbergischen Ratsmusik* (Nuremberg, 1959)
——: 'Lucas Friedrich Behaim', *Mitteilungen des Vereins für die Geschichte der Stadt Nürnberg*, i (1960), 330
F. Blume: 'Die Handschrift T 131', *Festschrift Karl Gustav Fellerer* (Regensburg, 1962), 51
O. Mischiati: 'L'intavolatura d'organo tedesca della Biblioteca nazionale di Torino', *L'organo*, iv (1963), 1–154
HAROLD E. SAMUEL

Staden, Sigmund Theophil [Gottlieb] (*b* Kulmbach, baptized 6 Nov 1607; *d* Nuremberg, buried 30 July 1655). German composer, instrumentalist, organist and theorist, son of Johann Staden. He was a leading musician in Nuremberg, and though a lesser composer than his father he is perhaps, as the composer of the first extant Singspiel, historically more important.

1. LIFE. The German form, 'Gottlieb', of Staden's middle name appears in part iv of the *Frauenzimmer Gesprächspiele* (1644) of GEORG PHILIPP HARSDÖRFFER, who was a crusader for the purification of the German language; Staden himself used 'Theophil'. His early musical studies with his father were so successful that in July 1620, some ten years after the family returned to Nuremberg from Kulmbach and Bayreuth, Johann Staden petitioned the city council for an expectant's salary for his 13-year-old son. This request was apparently denied, but in December 1620 the council granted the boy 150 gulden a year for board, room and lessons with Jakob Paumann in Augsburg. Johann Staden could teach his son composition, the organ and the violin, whereas Paumann, a well-known instrumental teacher, who from 1591 to 1596 had been in the Munich Hofkapelle under Lassus, could offer instruction on the

cornett, trombone, bassoon and viola, as well as on keyboard instruments and in composition. Hans Leo Hassler was in Augsburg at the same period. The young Staden returned to Nuremberg in 1623 and was granted an expectant's salary, thus beginning his lifelong service to the city. He again studied away from home between February and August 1627, when the city council paid for him to study string instruments (probably viola da gamba and viola bastarda) in Berlin with Walter Rowe (i). Before leaving Nuremberg he was appointed a city instrumentalist. In 1634 he received the further appointment of organist of St Lorenz. With this double salary, which he enjoyed for the rest of his life, he was Nuremberg's highest-paid musician.

Staden was often called on to perform duties normally assigned to a Kapellmeister, a position which in Nuremberg was seldom held by the city's outstanding musician. In 1649, for example, at a large banquet in honour of the peace treaty ending the Thirty Years War, music was performed under his direction by a group of 43 musicians (21 singers, 18 instrumentalists and four organists). Another elaborate concert conducted by him, which probably involved the entire musical forces of Nuremberg, was a programme of music of all types and from all times down to the year in which it took place, 1643. The printed programme is extant: *Entwerfung dess Anfangs, Fortgangs, Aenderungen, Brauchs und Missbrauchs der edlen Music* ('An outline of the beginning, continuation, developments, use and misuse of the noble art of music'). Most of the music performed at this historical concert, which included music of the angels, music that sounded at the beginning of the world and music of the Hebrews, was from Staden's imagination, though actual works by Lassus, Hassler, Giovanni Gabrieli and Johann Staden were either performed or referred to (see Kahl). There is a posthumous engraved portrait of Staden done in 1669 (see illustration).

Sigmund Theophil Staden: engraving (1669) by Joachim von Sandrart after Michael Herr

2. WORKS. The Singspiel *Seelewig* appeared in 1644 in part iv of the magazine *Frauenzimmer Gesprächspiele*, edited by Georg Philipp Harsdörffer. The complete series of eight parts (1642–9) contains 300 works, nine of which include either music or instructions for music, apparently all by Staden. *Seelewig* is the only one that is through-composed. It is designated as 'in the Italian manner' and is modelled on the school dramas of the 16th and 17th centuries. The recitatives lack the freedom of their Italian counterparts, and the emphasis on strophic songs, a trait still common in J. P. Krieger's operas 50 years later, retards the dramatic movement. The music in the other eight *Gesprächspiele* consists of one or more strophic songs and instrumental interludes which appear between sections of spoken dialogue. The oratorio-like religious plays which Staden produced in collaboration with Johann Klaj, a teacher in the Nuremberg schools, are related to the Singspiels. All the roles – biblical characters, the people, good and bad angels and the Lord – were read by Klaj, and Staden's solo, choral and instrumental sections were interspersed with the declamation. Six such works were reportedly performed in 1644 and 1645 at St Sebald following Sunday vesper services.

Staden published only two collections of vocal music, a modest contribution compared with the 20 collections (both vocal and instrumental) published by his colleague Kindermann. The 35 songs of *Seelen-Music* can be performed by four voices and continuo, or the latter can assume the lower parts as an accompaniment for the soprano voice. The outmoded melodic style of these pieces enjoyed a popularity long after Staden's death: all of them were included in *Geistliche Seelen-Music*, collected by CHRISTIAN HUBER, which appeared in nine editions between 1682 and 1753. Staden's second collection, *Musicalischer Friedens-Gesänger*, contains some of the music performed at the peace festival of 1649. Of the 12 sacred and secular compositions in it, nine are strophic songs; the other three are through-composed, of considerable length, and with a greater use of melodic ornamentation than is to be found in Staden's other compositions. A number of his other strophic songs with continuo were published in anthologies, and he wrote 19 for funerals, 11 of which are four-part chorales, note-against-note and without a separate continuo part. No other 17th-century Nuremberg composer wrote so often in this form. In 1637, when other German composers were experimenting with the new Italian style, Staden brought out a new edition of Hassler's *Kirchen Gesäng*, adding six of his own and 12 of his father's four-part strophic songs to the 69 of Hassler's 1608 edition. Although he did not stubbornly evade the new style, as can be seen in *Seelewig* by his adding of recitative to the strophic-song tradition of school plays, Staden, like his father, preferred the German traditions of syllabic treatment of the text, unadventurous harmony and counterpoint and the dominating sacred songs with their restricted melodic flow and limited forms. Of the large amount of instrumental music that one would have expected from one of Nuremberg's leading instrumentalists, there is only a single suite movement.

The pointedness and clarity of *Rudimentum musicum*, an elementary manual for schools which went through four editions, can serve now as an introduction to the basic theoretical practice of the 17th century. But despite this theoretical work, his printed collections, the renowned concerts under his direction and his reputation as a performer, there is no evidence that Staden influenced German music in the middle of the 17th century or that his fame was more than local. There is no record of his having had any pupils: it is known that in Nuremberg young musicians studied with Kindermann, who in contrast to Staden's conservatism could offer his pupils thorough, devoted training in the new Italian style.

WORKS

(all printed works published in Nuremberg unless otherwise stated)

DRAMATIC
(all published in Frauenzimmer Gesprächspiele, 1642–9)

Das geistliche Waldgedicht oder Freudenspiel genant Seelewig, Singspiel, in vol.iv (1644); ed. in *MMg*, xiii (1881), 65–147; extract ed. in GMB
Incidental music in other vols.:
vol.i: 1 song in Die Gedächtnisskunst
vol.ii: 4 songs in Vom halben Umbkreiss; 2 songs in Das Schauspiel teutscher Sprichwörter
vol.iii: 7 songs and 2 interludes, 3 str, in Von der Welt Eitelkeit
vol.iv: 1 song in foreword; 2 songs in Die Poeterey
vol.v: 1 song in Die Reimkunst; 8 songs and 7 interludes, 3, 4 insts, in Die Tugendsterne
vol.vii: 1 interlude in Das Schauspiel zu Ross

OTHER VOCAL

Seelen-Music . . . geist- und trostreicher Lieder, 1 or 4vv, bc (1644–8) (2 vols.); pt.ii lost; both vols. in Christian Huber: Geistliche Seelen-Music (St Gall, 1682)
Musicalischer Friedens-Gesänger, 3vv, 2 vn, vc, bc (1651)
6 lieder, 4vv, 1637[2]
18 occasional lieder, mostly for funerals, 4vv (1637–58)
1 funeral lied, 1647[6]
12 lieder, 1v, bc, in D. Wülffer: Zwölff Andachten (1648)
10 lieder, 1v, bc, in J. Rist: Neuer himlischer Lieder, i (Lüneburg, 1651)
5 lieder in L. Erhard: Harmonisches Chor- und Figural Gesang-Buch (Frankfurt am Main, 1659), incl. 4 from Seelen-Music

INSTRUMENTAL

Volta, suite movt, a 3, Nuremberg, Staatsarchiv

LOST WORKS
(oratorio texts extant and published in Nuremberg)

Der leidenden Christus (J. Klaj), oratorio, 1645
Incidental music for oratorios, probably by Staden (texts by Klaj): Aufferstehung Jesu Christi, 1644; Engel- und Drachen-Streit; Höllen- und Himmelfahrt Jesu Christi, 1644; Weyhnacht-Liedt der heiligen Geburt Jesu Christ, 1644; Herodes der Kindermörder, 1645; Der seligmachenden Geburt Jesu Christi, 1650
2 occasional lieder

WRITINGS

Rudimentum musicum, das ist Kurtze Unterweisung dess Singens für die liebe Jugend (3/1648); 1st edn. (1636), 2nd edn. (n.d.), 4th edn. (1663), all lost
Entwerfung dess Anfangs, Fortgangs, Aenderungen, Brauchs und Missbrauchs der edlen Music (1643, 2/1650); repr. in Clemen
4 letters, 1637, ?1639, 1644: Nuremberg, Staatsarchiv
Accentus L. habraicae . . . 1651, formerly in D-Nst, now lost (see Will, viii, 279)

BIBLIOGRAPHY

J. G. Doppelmayr: *Historische Nachricht von den nürnbergischen Mathematicis und Künstlern* (Nuremberg, 1730)
G. A. Will: *Nürnbergisches Gelehrten-Lexikon* (Nuremberg and Altdorf, 1755–8)
W. Nagel: 'Zur Biographie Johann Stadens und seiner Söhne', *MMg*, xxix (1897), 53
T. Norlind: 'Ein Musikfest zu Nürnberg im Jahre 1649', *SIMG*, vii (1905–6), 111
E. Schmitz: 'Zur musikgeschichtlichen Bedeutung der Harsdörfferschen "Frauenzimmergesprächspiele"', *Festschrift . . . Rochus Freiherrn von Liliencron* (Leipzig, 1910), 254
E. A. Krückeberg: 'Ein historisches Konzert zu Nürnberg im Jahr 1643', *AMw*, i (1918–19), 590
G. A. Narciss: *Studien zu den Frauenzimmergesprächspielen* (Leipzig, 1928)
O. Clemen: 'Das Programm zu einem Musikfest in Nürnberg im Mai 1643', *Otto Glauning zum 60. Geburtstag* (Leipzig, 1936), 18
H. Druener: *Sigmund Theophil Staden 1607–1655* (diss., U. of Bonn, 1946)
W. Körner: 'Zum Gedächtnis des Nürnberger Komponisten, und Organisten Sigmund Theophil Staden', *Gottesdienst und Kirchenmusik* (1955), 177
W. Kahl: 'Das Nürnberger historische Konzert von 1643 und sein Geschichtsbild', *AMw*, xiv (1957), 281
J. Haar: 'Astral Music in Seventeenth-century Nuremberg: the Tugendsterne of Harsdörffer and Staden', *MD*, xvi (1962), 175
H. E. Samuel: *The Cantata in Nuremberg during the Seventeenth Century* (diss., Cornell U., 1963)
P. Keller: *Stadens Oper 'Seelewig'* (diss., U. of Zurich, 1970)

HAROLD E. SAMUEL

Stader, Maria (*b* Budapest, 5 Nov 1911). Swiss soprano. She moved to Switzerland as a refugee and studied singing with Hans Keller and Ilona Durigo. In 1939 she won the singing prize at the Geneva International Music Competition, and at the end of the war began a career as a concert singer, and also taught at the Zurich Academy of Music. She gave numerous concert tours in the USA, Japan and Africa and sang at the principal festivals. Her fame is based chiefly on her interpretations of Mozart. Though she rarely appeared in the opera house – she did perform the Queen of Night at Covent Garden in the 1949–50 season – she sang many operatic roles in concerts, and on gramophone records (mainly with Fricsay). Her clean technique and flexible, powerful, though not large voice made her much in demand for the concert repertory, from Bach's Passions to Verdi's Requiem. She gave an indication of her working methods in her book *Gesang* (*Lektion*) *Arie 'Aus Liebe will mein Heiland sterben': Matthäus-Passion* [*von*] *Joh*(*ann*) *Seb*(*astian*) *Bach* (Wie Meister üben, iii, Zurich, 1967; Eng. trans., 1968) which contains a discography and two records. She was honoured with the Salzburg Lilli Lehmann Medal (1950), the Mozart silver medal (1956) and the Hans Georg Nägeli Medal of Zurich (1962). She retired from the concert platform in 1969 after a series of farewell concerts.

JÜRG STENZL

Stadlen, Peter (*b* Vienna, 14 July 1910). English pianist and writer on music of Austrian birth. He studied at the Vienna Akademisches Gymnasium and Hochschule für Musik, where his principal teachers were Paul Weingarten (piano), Joseph Marx and Max Springer (composition) and Alexander Wunderer (conducting); he also studied philosophy at Vienna University. From 1929 to 1933 he was at the Berlin Hochschule für Musik, under Leonid Kreutzer (piano), Josef Gmeindl (composition) and Julius Prüwer (conducting). In 1934 he embarked on a career as a concert pianist, specializing in the Viennese Classics and contemporary piano music, particularly that of the Second Viennese School, and playing widely in Europe; in 1937 he gave the première of Webern's op.27 Variations, and at the Venice Biennale in the same year he directed from the keyboard a performance of Schoenberg's op.29 Suite whose reception created a notorious scandal. Stadlen settled in England before World War II; after the war he introduced a number of important 12-note works, including Schoenberg's Piano Concerto, to audiences in Germany, Austria and England, and played under the composer in the premières of Hindemith's *Four Temperaments* and *Konzertmusik* for piano, brass and harp (Vienna, 1947), also supervising a master class in modern piano music at the Darmstadt summer courses (1947–51). In 1952 he was awarded the Austrian government Schoenberg medal.

During the mid-1950s Stadlen turned away from a career in practical music to one in research, criticism and broadcasting. He was appointed a music critic on the *Daily Telegraph* in 1959; in 1965–9 he was also a lecturer in music at the University of Reading, and in 1967–8 a visiting fellow of All Souls College, Oxford. His writings, and particularly his criticism of contemporary music, were much affected by his disillusionment with serialism. He gave a series of lectures 'The Rise and Decline of Serialism' at the British Institute of Recorded Sound in 1960. He has also worked extensively on the autograph and sketch material of Mozart and Beethoven, and has devoted particular attention to Beethoven's use of the metronome and the question of Schindler's forgeries in Beethoven's conversation books. His critical writings show his strongly committed standpoint on controversial matters and an unusually allusive style.

WRITINGS

'Serialism Reconsidered', *Score* (1958), no.22, p.12; Ger. trans., *Musica*, xiii (1959), 89 as 'Kritik am Seriellen'
'No Real Casualties?', *Score* (1958), no.24, p.65 [reply to articles by R. Gerhard, R. Sessions and W. Piston]
'Thoughts on Musical Continuity I', *Score* (1960), no.26, p.52
'The Webern Legend', *MT*, ci (1960), 695; Ger. trans., *Musica*, xv (1961), 66
'The Aesthetics of Popular Music', *British Journal of Aesthetics*, ii (1962), 351
'Beethoven and the Metronome I', *ML*, xlviii (1967), 330
'Possibilities of an Aesthetic Evaluation of Beethoven's Sketches', *Internationaler Beethoven-Kongress: Bonn 1970*, 111
'Das pointillistische Missverständnis', *5. Internationaler Webern-Kongress: Wien 1972*, 173; repr. in *ÖMz*, xxvii (1972), 152
'Schönberg und der Sprechgesang', *1. Kongress der Internationalen Schönberg-Gesellschaft: Wien 1974*, 202
'Schindler's Beethoven Forgeries', *MT*, cxviii (1977), 549
'Beethoven und das Metronom', *Beethoven-Kolloquium: Vienna 1977*, 57
'Schindler and the Conversation Books', *Soundings*, vii (1978), 2 [Ger. version in *ÖMz*, xxxiv (1979), 2]

STANLEY SADIE

Stadler, Anton (Paul) (*b* Bruck an der Leitha, 28 June 1753; *d* Vienna, 15 June 1812). Austrian clarinettist and basset-horn player famed for his association with Mozart. Stadler had a brother, Johann (Nepomuk Franz) (1755–1804), also a clarinettist and basset-horn player. They first performed together as soloists for the Vienna Tonkünstler-Sozietät in 1773, and about that time were employed by Count Dmitry Golitsïn, Russian ambassador to Vienna. The Viennese court engaged them from 1779 on a freelance basis, and in 1782 both were given salaried posts in the imperial wind band. In 1787 they were transferred to the court orchestra to become its first regular clarinettists. Anton played second to Johann's first, not because he was a lesser performer, but because of his partiality for low notes, which led him to experiment with a downward extension of four semitones to his instrument. It was for this 'basset clarinet' that Mozart wrote his Quintet K581 and Concerto K622. Other composers, notably Süssmayr and Paer, also wrote for the instrument, but it was not generally adopted and no example survives. Mozart's Quintet and Concerto were published in altered form to suit a clarinet of normal compass.

Like Mozart, Stadler became a freemason and a close, lasting friendship existed between the two musicians although Stadler seems to have taken advantage of Mozart in money matters. They played together in the first performance in 1784 of the Quintet K452, and Stadler took the solo part in the first performance of the Clarinet Quintet in 1789. Mozart wrote the clarinet and basset-horn obbligatos in nos.9 and 23 of *La clemenza di Tito* for Stadler, who accompanied the Mozarts to Prague in September 1791 for the first performances of the opera. His playing, reported to be

soft and voice-like, received an ovation. Encouraged by this success, he asked leave from court duties to go on an extended tour. This began with a benefit concert at Prague in October 1791. He then visited Berlin, the Baltic towns and St Petersburg, and only returned to Vienna, via Frankfurt and Nuremberg, in July 1796.

In 1799 Stadler was pensioned from the court orchestra, but continued to play in the opera orchestra for several years. He gave his last solo performance for the Tonkünstler-Sozietät in 1806. One of Stadler's pupils was Count Johann Karl Esterházy. In 1800 the Hungarian Count Georg Festetics commissioned Stadler to write a 'Musick Plan' for a new music school at Keszthely. The count intended to instal him as director of chamber music, an appointment he never took up, though he did execute a 'Plan' (now in *H-Bn*). In it he stated that he would write a tutor, but none has come to light. The 'Plan' is a well-formulated piece of writing, embodying sound principles of musicianship and high standards of professional conduct.

WORKS

10 sets of variations, cl (Vienna, 1810)
12 ländlerische Tänze, 2 cl (Vienna, before 1824)
3 caprices, cl (Vienna, after 1824)
6 progressive duets, 2 cl (Vienna, after 1826)
18 trios, 3 basset-hn, *A-Wgm*; 6 duettinos, 2 csákány [Hungarian wind insts]/csákány, vn, and 3 caprices, csákány, *D-B*; partitas, 6 wind insts (see Deutsch, p.226)

BIBLIOGRAPHY

G. Dazeley: 'De clarinettist van Mozart', *Symphonia*, xvii (1934), 170
E. Anderson, ed.: *The Letters of Mozart and his Family* (London, 1938, rev. 2/1966)
G. Dazeley: 'The Original Text of Mozart's Clarinet Concerto', *MR*, ix (1948), 166
M. Kingdon-Ward: 'Mozart's Clarinettist', *MMR*, lxxxv (1955), 8
E. Hess: 'Anton Stadlers "Musick Plan"', *MJb 1962–3*, 37
O. E. Deutsch: *Mozart: a Documentary Biography* (London, 1965)
E. Hess: 'Die ursprüngliche Gestalt des Klarinettenkonzertes KV 622', *MJb 1967*, 18
W. Maynard: 'Anton Stadler, Composer', *Woodwind World*, viii (1968)
A. Hacker: 'Mozart and the Basset Clarinet', *MT*, cx (1969), 359
G. Croll and K. Birsak: 'Anton Stadlers "Bassettklarinette" und das "Stadler-Quintett" KV 581', *ÖMz*, xxiv (1969), 3
K. M. Pisarowitz: ' "Müasst ma nix in übel aufniehma . . ." ': Beitragsversuche zu einer Gebrüder-Stadler-Biographie', *Mitteilungen der Internationalen Stiftung Mozarteum*, xix/1–2 (1971), 29
P. Weston: *Clarinet Virtuosi of the Past* (London, 1971)

PAMELA WESTON

Stadler, Johann Wilhelm (*b* Repperndorf, nr. Kitzingen, 8 Oct 1747; *d* Eltersdorf, nr. Erlangen, 26 June 1819). German composer. The son of a teacher, he received his first musical instruction from his grandfather and later from a Kantor in Heilsbronn near Ansbach. He began his study of theology in Erlangen in 1770, and went on to obtain a master's degree; for a time he was a pupil of Johann Balthasar Kehl, whom he succeeded as municipal Kantor in Bayreuth (1778) and tutor (in 1805 headmaster) at the college there. The culmination of his activity as a musician was probably the series of choral and orchestral concerts given there under his direction. He had to give up his position as Kantor in 1815 and subsequently became a teacher at the Gymnasium. In 1817 the University of Erlangen conferred a doctorate of philosophy on him. He retired in November 1818.

His 'musical genius', attested to by his many beautiful vocal pieces' and his 'excellent musical library' were praised as early as 1788 in Meusel's *Museum für Künstler*. According to the obituary notice written in his honour by the board of the Bayreuth Gymnasium, he was a 'learned connoisseur of music' who had trained 'a considerable number of excellent vocal artists in several areas of Germany'. Of his compositions the setting of Klopstock's funeral song *Auferstehn, ja auferstehn wirst du* was long popular in Bavaria. A few songs are extant in anthologies, among them a setting of Spiegel's *Die Sehnsucht* (in *Musen Almanach für 1782*) also attributed to Maximilian Stadler, but his many cantatas, choral pieces and the oratorio *Die Kreuzfahrer* are lost.

BIBLIOGRAPHY
GerberL
J. G. Meusel, ed.: *Museum für Künstler und für Kunstliebhaber*, iii (Mannheim, 1788), 56
F. J. A. Muck: *Biographische Notizen über die Componisten der Choralmelodien im Baierischen neuen Choral-Buche* (Erlangen, 1823), 74ff
J. Zahn: *Die Melodien der deutschen evangelischen Kirchenlieder*, vi (Gütersloh, 1893/*R*1963), 399f [incl. 2 melodies by Stadler]
K. Hartmann: 'Kunstpflege in Bayreuth nach der Residenzzeit (1769–1806)', *Archiv für Geschichte und Altertumskunde von Oberfranken*, xxxiii/2 (1937), *passim*
G. Schmidt: 'Johann Balthasar Kehl und Johann Wilhelm Stadler', *Archiv für Geschichte von Oberfranken*, xlvi (1966) [with list of works]

GÜNTER THOMAS

Stadler, Abbé **Maximilian** [Johann Karl Dominik] (*b* Melk, 4 Aug 1748; *d* Vienna, 8 Nov 1833). Austrian composer, music historian and keyboard performer. He received his earliest musical training from Johann Leuthner, bass at the Benedictine abbey of Melk. In 1758 he went as a choirboy to Lilienfeld, where he learnt the violin, clavichord and organ and made his first attempts at composition. During vacations he revisited Melk to study the music of the new organist J. G. Albrechtsberger. Stadler continued his formal education after 1762 at the Jesuit College in Vienna. In November 1766 he entered Melk as a novice, took his vows the following year and was ordained on 13 October 1772. After directing the abbey's theological studies for eight years he served briefly as chaplain in Wullersdorf in 1783. He was elected prior of Melk on 17 November 1784.

Favoured by Emperor Joseph II during the suppression of the Austrian monasteries, Stadler was appointed abbot of Lilienfeld in April 1786. In Kremsmünster, where he held the same post from May 1789, his administration was marked by his support of secular music, including performances of operas by Paisiello, Salieri and Umlauf. He moved to Linz in January 1791, acted as consistorial adviser to the bishop and was awarded an annual pension of 1000 florins from Kremsmünster for the next 12 years. In 1796 he settled in Vienna, was secularized in 1803 and received the titular canonry of Linz. He was given duties as parish priest in Alt-Lerchenfeld (1803) and Grosskrut (1810), near Vienna. Resigning this last post in November 1815, he made Vienna his permanent residence and remained active there until his death.

Stadler's musical activities were many-sided. He experimented with a type of 18th-century aleatory music, composition by throwing dice, and even developed an interest in ethnic music, as shown by his arrangements of chants of the Mevlevi dervishes. His more conventional essays in composition spanned almost three-quarters of a century. He wrote primarily vocal music, especially sacred compositions on German texts. The performances of his oratorio, *Die Befreyung von Jerusalem* (from 1813), established his reputation internationally. This success was followed by the publication of a number of his works in Vienna (by Mechetti, Steiner & Co., Diabelli and others).

After moving to Vienna in 1796, Stadler became musical adviser to Mozart's widow Constanze. Along with Nissen he was the first to order and catalogue the manuscripts in Mozart's estate (1798–9). The number of his completions of fragments and sketches left by Mozart remains to be determined. He made copies of the Requiem (K626), and when its authenticity was questioned by Gottfried Weber in 1825 Stadler published a series of articles in a successful defence. By 1819, according to the Beethoven conversation books, he was working on the *Materialien zur Geschichte der Musik unter den österreichischen Regenten*, now considered to be the first history of music in Austria. Long believed to be lost, this significant document was rediscovered in Vienna in 1969.

Stadler was considered a leading 'erudite composer' and an accomplished interpreter of keyboard music by his Viennese contemporaries. He held honorary memberships in both the Steiermarkischer Musikverein (after 1821) and the Gesellschaft der Musikfreunde in Vienna (1826). He was a prominent figure in Viennese musical life, maintaining relationships not only with the Mozart family, but with Haydn, Beethoven and Schubert as well. There are two engravings of him by J. B. Pfitzer (1813, 1818) in the Bild Archiv of the Austrian National Library, Vienna.

WORKS
(printed works published in Vienna unless otherwise stated)

SACRED
Masses: nos.1–2, G, B♭, 4vv, orch (1824), *A-M, Wn*; D, before 1790, *M, SEI, Wn*; 2, d, d, before 1790, *Wn, D-Dkh*; C, ?1763–7, lost; 2, 1772, lost; Requiem, c, 1820, *A-GÖ, M, Wn, Wst, D-Dkh*; Requiem, F (1821), *A-M, Wn, D-Bds*
Other liturgical: Asperges me, Ecce sacerdos magnus, Tantum ergo, Vidi aquam, 4vv, org (1818); Libera me Domine, 4vv, org (1821–2), *A-M*; 10 vesper psalms, 4vv, org (1826), *Wn*; Alma Redemptoris, Ave regina, Regina coeli, Salve regina, 4vv, org (1826); Magna et mirabilia, Salvum fac populum tuum, 4vv, orch (1829–30), *M, Wgm, Wn*; Delectare in Domino, Si Deus pro nobis, 4vv, orch (1831–2), *M*; 5 Magnificat, 4vv, *Wn*, 3 lost; Te Deum, *M, SEI*; 3 litanies, 1 in *Wgm* (frag.), 2 lost; 9 Salve regina, 8 in *M*, 1 lost; 3 Ave regina, 4 antiphons for Corpus Christi, 2 Christmas motets, Regina coeli, 2 Alma Redemptoris, O quam metuendus, Miserere, Omnipotens: all *M*; Exaltabo, *Wn*; Veni Sancte Spiritus, responsories for Holy Week, lost
Other sacred: 14 Trauergesänge (U. Petrack), 4vv, org (1805); Vater unser, 4vv (after 1810), *GÖ*; Der 111te [112] Psalm (trans. M. Mendelssohn), 4vv, orch, 1814 (1831–2), *M*; 24 Psalmen Davids (trans. Mendelssohn), Tr, pf (1815–c1817), *Wst, D-Bds*; Neue Messgesänge mit Melodien, Tr, org (1816), 4vv/org, *A-Wgm*; Der 50te Psalm (trans. Mendelssohn), 4vv (1819), *D-Bds*; Deutsches Salve regina, Tr, pf (1822); Gott! (H. W. Gerstenberg), hymn, after 1810, *A-M, Wgm, Wn*; Lobliedl, ?1810–21, *M*; Ps xxiv, c1821, *M, Wgm*; Ps xxix, 1832, *Wgm*; Ps lxiii, *Wgm*; Ps lxxxiv, 1831, *M*; 7 other psalm settings (trans. Mendelssohn), *M, Wgm, Wn, Ws, D-Bds*; chorales for Redemptorist nuns, c1832, lost

OTHER VOCAL
Dramatic: Das Studenten-Valete (Singspiel, Petrack), Melk, 6 Sept 1781, *A-M*; incidental music to Polyxena (H. von Collin), 4vv, orch, U. of Vienna, 15 Dec 1811, *M, Wgm, Wn*; Die Befreyung von Jerusalem (H. and M. von Collin), oratorio, U. of Vienna, 9 May 1813 (1821), *M, Wgm, D-Bds*
Secular cantatas: Cantate auf die zwote Primiz Seiner Hochwürden und Gnaden Urbans [Hauer] (Petrack), Melk, 5 April 1785, lost; O Tonkunst, Tochter der Erfindung, soloists, chorus, orch, 1789, *A-KR*; cantata (J. F. Ratschky), 4vv, orch, Linz, 1791–6, lost; Die Frühlingsfeyer (F. G. Klopstock), 5vv, orch, 1813, *M, Wgm, CH-Zz*
Lieder: Die Sehnsucht (Spielberg), Tr, pf (1782); Jung und schön bin ich (?Petrack), Tr, pf (1783); 12 Lieder von Gellert [= Petrack, Goethe], Tr, pf (c1785); 5 It. arias (Metastasio), S/B, orch, 1790–1803, lost; 2 scenes from Polyxena (Collin), Tr, pf (c1806); 2 Lieder (D. L. Witte), Tr, pf (Berlin, 1819); Die Liebe (F. L. Stolberg), Tr, pf (1821); 13 other lieder
Other secular: Hoch du mein Oesterreich, hymn, 4vv, wind insts (1818); An die Versöhnung (C. Kuffner), 4vv, pf/org (1820–21), *A-M*; Glaube, Hoffnung und Liebe (Kuffner), 4vv, pf/org (1820–21),

M, *Wgm*; Es ist ein Gott (C. A. Tiedge, from Urania), 4vv, orch, after 1810, *Wgm*; 2 melodramas (J. M. Denis, K. Mastalier), Tr, pf, *c*1770, ?1780–85, *M*; canons, 3–6vv, *KR*, *Wst*, private collection of L. Koch

INSTRUMENTAL

Kbd: 6 sonatinas, hpd/pf (1794); 3 fugues, org/pf, op.1 (1798–1803); Sonata, F, hpd/pf (1799); 2 sonatas, 1 fugue [= op.1 no.3], pf (Zurich, 1803); 12 Eng. dances, pf (*c*1809); Prelude and Fugue, E, pf (1818); variation on a waltz by Diabelli, pf, in Vaterländischer Künstlerverein (*c*1824); Fugue, c, on the name Schubert, org/pf, 1829 (1829), *Wgm*; 3 sonatas, hpd, 1763–7, lost; 6 variations, 1767–72, 3 Galanterie-Menuette, 1803–10, Fugue, 1828, *Wgm*; Minuet, 3 trios, Rondo, Variations, *c*1803, *GB-Lbm*; 7 sonatas, 1772, *A-Wgm*, *D-Bds*; 8 preludes, org, 1773, *Bds*

Other inst: 3 str trios, 1763–7, lost; Divertimento, fl, 4 str, 1772–86, *A-M*; 12 minuets, orch, *c*1782–5, *M*; 2 str qts, 1 divertimento, vn, va d'amore, va, vc, before 1790, *M*; 2 vc concs., before 1790, lost; Sonata, E♭, hn, pf, 1803–10, lost

COMPLETIONS AND ARRANGEMENTS

Completions: G. Benda: Mass (Cr–Ag), *Wn*; F. L. Gassmann: Requiem (Off, San, Bs, Ag), 1790, *KR*; J. Haydn: Hin ist alle meine Kraft, canon, as last movt of str qt, op.103, HIII:83 (1807), *Wgm*, as Musikalische Visitkarte des . . . Joseph Haydn, S, T, pf (1807), as An Joseph Haydn, 2 S, pf, *c*1809, *M*; W. A. Mozart: K372, 402/385e, 403/385c, ed. in Neue Ausgabe sämtlicher Werke, viii/23, Bd.2 (Kassel, 1965), suppl.ii; Mozart: Larghetto and Allegro, E♭, *CS-KRa*, ed. in Neue Ausgabe sämtlicher Werke, x/31, suppl. (in preparation), see Croll (1962–3) and 'Zu Mozarts Larghetto und Allegro' (1964); Mozart: K293/416f, 322/296a, 323/Anh.15, 348/382g, 355/576b, 396/385f, 400/372a, 401/375e, 442, 443/404b; Mozart–Bach: Das wohltemperirte Clavier, ii/22, for str qt, see Croll, 'Eine neuentdeckte Bach-Fuge' (1966)

Arrs.ed.: [M] Original-Chöre der Derwische Mewlevi (trans. V. von Hussar), unison chorus/1v, pf (*c*1822); L. van Beethoven: Septet, op.20, for pf; L. Cherubini: Médée, Lodoiska, Eliza, N. M. Dalayrac: Thurm von Gottenburg, C. W. Gluck: Orfeo, W. A. Mozart: Idomeneo, Der Schauspieldirektor, all for str sextet; Mozart: Menuetti ed Tedeschi, K361/370a, for str sextet, K492 for pf, str qt, before 1800, *A-Wn*, K429/468a for pf, *H-Bn*; works by Ammerbach, Caldara, Conti, Josquin Desprez, Ebner, Mouton, Obrecht, Ockeghem

WRITINGS

Anleitung zur musikalischen Composition durch Würfelspiel (autograph, MS, *A-Wgm*, *c*1780)

Erklärung, wie man aus . . . Ziffer- und Notentabellen eine Menuet herauswürfeln könne (Vienna, 1781)

Priorats-Ephemeriden (MS, *A-M*, 1784–6)

Beschreibung der Fragmente aus Mozart's Nachlass (MS, formerly *D-Bds*, *c*1798, ?lost)

Fragmente von Singstücken [from Mozart's estate] (MS, *A-Wgm*, *c*1798)

Fragmente einiger Mozartischen Klavierstücke, die von einem Liebhaber der Musik [Stadler] *vollendet worden* (MS, *Wn*); ed. in *ÖMz*, xxi (1966), 250

Materialen zur Geschichte der Musik unter den österreichischen Regenten (MS, *Wn*, *c*1816–25); ed. K. Wagner (Kassel, 1974)

Eigenhändig geschriebene Selbst-Biographie des Hochwürdigen Herrn Maximilian Stadler (MS, *Wgm*, *c*1816–26); ed. in *MJb* 1957, 78

'Musikalische Kunstschätze', *Wiener allgemeine musikalische Zeitung*, iii (1819), col.605, suppls.viii, ix

Vertheidigung der Echtheit des Mozartischen Requiem (Vienna, 1826)

Nachtrag zur Vertheidigung (Vienna, 1827)

Zweyter und letzter Nachtrag zur Vertheidigung . . . sammt Nachbericht über die Ausgabe . . . durch Herrn André in Offenbach, nebst Ehrenrettung Mozart's und vier fremden Briefen (Vienna, 1827)

'Verzeichniss der in Mozart's Verlassenschaft gefundenen musikalischen Fragmente und Entwürfe', in G. N. von Nissen: *Biographie W. A. Mozart's*, appx iii (Leipzig, 1828)

'Kurzer Auszug aus einer noch ungedruckten Geschichte der österreichischen Musik', *Monatsbericht der Gesellschaft der Musikfreunde*, xii (1829), 176

Biographische Notizen über Abbé Maximilian Stadler von ihm selbst aufgezeichnet (MS, *A-GÖ*, *c*1833); ed. in *MJb* 1964, 175

Letters concerning G. N. von Nissen, F. Artaria, C. Mozart (MS, *Wst*); G. N. von Nissen, I. F. von Mosel (MS, *Wn*); D. Artaria (MS, *GB-Lbm*)

BIBLIOGRAPHY

EitnerQ; *FétisB*; *GerberL*; *GerberNL*
'Bericht über den Musikzustand des löbl: Stiftes Mölk in alter und neuer Zeit', *Wiener allgemeine musikalische Zeitung*, ii (1818), col.365
I. F. von Mosel: 'Nekrolog: Abbé Maximilian Stadler', *Wiener Zeitschrift für Kunst, Literatur, Theater und Mode* (1833), nos.149–50, cols.1213, 1221
G. Schilling, ed.: *Encyclopädie der gesammten musikalischen Wissenschaften* (Stuttgart, 1835–42/*R*1973)
Oesterreichische National-Encyclopädie (Vienna, 1835)
H. Sabel: *Maximilian Stadlers weltliche Werke und seine Beziehungen zur Wiener Klassik* (diss., U. of Cologne, 1941)
——: 'Maximilian Stadler und Wolfgang Amadeus Mozart', *Neues Mozart-Jb*, iii (1943), 102
A. Kellner: *Musikgeschichte des Stiftes Kremsmünster* (Kassel, 1956)
R. Haas: 'Abt Stadlers vergessene Selbstbiographie', *MJb* 1957, 78
L. Finscher: 'Maximilian Stadler und Mozarts Nachlass', *MJb* 1960–61, 168
F. Blume: 'Requiem but no Peace', *MQ*, xlvii (1961), 147
H. Hellmann-Stojan: 'Stadler', *MGG*
G. Croll: 'Ein überraschender Mozart-Fund', *MJb* 1962–3, 108
——: 'Eine zweite, fast vergessene Selbstbiographie von Abbé Stadler', *MJb* 1964, 172
——: 'Zu Mozarts Larghetto und Allegro Es-dur für 2 Klaviere', *MJb* 1964, 28
——: 'Eine neuentdeckte Bach-Fuge für Streichquartett von Mozart', *ÖMz*, xxi (1966), 508
——: 'Zu den Verzeichnissen von Mozarts nachgelassenen Fragmenten und Entwürfen', *ÖMz*, xxi (1966), 250
——: 'Briefe zum Requiem', *MJb* 1967, 12
O. E. Deutsch: 'Eine merkwürdige Schubert-Handschrift', *Musamens–musici: im Gedenken an Walther Vetter* (Leipzig, 1969), 283
K. Wagner: 'Abbé Stadlers Musikgeschichte', *ÖMz*, xxiv (1969), 709
R. N. Freeman: *The Practice of Music at Melk Monastery in the Eighteenth Century* (diss., U. of California, Los Angeles, 1971)
K. Wagner: *Abbé Maximilian Stadler* (Kassel, 1974)

ROBERT N. FREEMAN

Stadlmayr [Stadlmair, Stadelmaier, Stadelmayer, Stadelmeyer], **Johann** (*b* ?Freising, Bavaria, *c*1575; *d* Innsbruck, 12 July 1648). German composer. The title-page and dedication of his *Sacrum Beatissimae Virginis Mariae canticum* (1603) report that he came from Freising. The date of his birth, given as 1560 by Fétis and others, was probably closer to 1580, for in 1619 he was called a 'rather young and lively man'. The earliest documented reference to him is in Georg Draudius's catalogue *Bibliotheca classica* (Frankfurt, 1611, 2/1625), where a collection of eight-part masses by him is said to have been published in 1596 (misprinted as 1569 but corroborated elsewhere). In 1603 he was a musician in the service of the Archbishop of Salzburg. In 1604, the year of his first marriage, he became vice-Kapellmeister and then Kapellmeister there, a post he held until 1607, when he was appointed to a similar position at the court of the Habsburg Archduke Maximilian II of the Tyrol at Innsbruck. Though later offered other positions he chose to remain in Innsbruck for the rest of his life.

Maximilian, who was Grand Master of the Teutonic Order and specially interested in serious music, apparently held Stadlmayr in great esteem, for he bought him a house and included him in his will. After Maximilian's death in 1618, the Innsbruck chapel was disbanded because his successor, Archduke Leopold V, kept his own musicians at his former Alsatian residence. Stadlmayr presented several petitions for employment so that he and his large family need not leave Innsbruck, where, as he said in 1620, he had 'spared no effort in 13 of the best years of his life'. During this period, which also saw the death of his first wife (in 1619) and his remarriage (in 1621), he added to his income by working as government meat inspector. Not until 1624, after he had sought leave to apply for a post in Vienna, was he reappointed Kapellmeister, with an appropriate salary. Leopold also wanted to make him a member of the nobility, but he refused (as he had also done when Maximilan made him a similar offer some years before) because he lacked sufficient funds to maintain such a position. The court chapel now attained its greatest brilliance, and after Leopold died in 1632 his widow, Claudia de' Medici, continued to support Stadlmayr despite financial difficulties caused by the Thirty Years War, which was ravaging neighbouring countries; part of her support was to help finance the publication of some of Stadlmayr's works.

Stadlmayr's renown went far beyond the Innsbruck of his day. Michael Praetorius praised him in his *Syntagma musicum*, iii (1618); W. C. Printz in his *Historische Beschreibung* (1690) counted him among the best-known composers of the 17th century. A number of his works were included in anthologies used from Italy to the Netherlands, or appeared in widely dispersed keyboard intabulations; some were still performed in the 18th century. But he is little known today. All his music shows solid musical craftsmanship and an ability to create varied works from unassuming material and with simple means.

Stadlmayr was almost exclusively a composer of Catholic church music, and a prolific one. 16th-century traditions as well as 17th-century innovations inform his style. He achieved clear articulation of the liturgical texts, as required by the Council of Trent, with short phrases of generally syllabic declamation that follow natural speech inflections. In imitative sections he highlighted the texts by frequent repetitions of a few words, and he often used stereotyped figures for expressive emphasis. His publications up to about 1628 continue 16th-century traditions of carefully handled polyphony and effectively treated homophonic chordal blocks in the Venetian manner. In some works the two kinds of texture are set against each other. In others one texture may predominate: the polychoral idiom does so in the masses and *Magnificat* settings for two and three choirs, while the textures of the fifth and ninth items in the *Magnificat* collection of 1603 are exclusively contrapuntal. Stadlmayr also continued to make use of plainchant in long notes for cantus firmi as well as of parody technique for many masses and *Magnificat* settings, which are based mainly on Italian works.

In the earlier works the new style intrudes only in added bass lines for the organ which merely double the lowest vocal notes. It is more pronounced with the substitution of instrumental ritornellos for the odd-numbered verses of the works forming the second part of the *Hymni* of 1628. From then on ensembles for widely varying combinations of solo voices, often with added instruments (usually two violins or cornetts), are increasingly deployed in imitative, often florid, concertato fashion, contrasted with homophonic sections for the tutti groups. While the earlier works are still modal, the later ones are tonal and diatonic.

WORKS

MASS COLLECTIONS

Missae, 8vv, 2 bc (org) (Augsburg, 1596), no known copy; cited in Draudius: Bibliotheca classica (Frankfurt am Main, 1611, 2/1625)

Missae, 8vv, 2 bc (org) (Augsburg, 1610): Missae super: 'Dies est laetitia', 'Donna la pure luce', 'Fuggi pur se sai', 'Ingredimini omnes', 'Jubilate Deo'

Missae, 12vv, 3 bc (org) (Vienna, 1616); Missae super: 'Exultate justi', 'Hor che nel suo bel seno'; Missa sine nomine

Missae concertatae, 6vv, 2 cornetts/vn, 4 trbn, bc (Innsbruck, 1631); Missae: Austriace alias Peltica, Diligam te Domine, super 'Bone Jesu' (12vv); 2 other masses

Missae breves, 4vv, cum una pro defunctis et alia, 5vv (Innsbruck, 1641); 3 masses, 4vv; 1 requiem mass, 4vv; 1 mass, 5vv (all with bc)

Missae concertatae, 10 et 12 vocibus et instrumentis cum 4 partibus pro secundo choro (Cantus, 8vv, 2 cornetts/vn, 3 trbn/va, 2 bc) (Innsbruck, 1642); Missae: 'Coelo rores', 8vv, 'Jesum omnes diliget', 12vv (with 2 additional vns), 'Quasi arcus', 10vv; 1 other mass, 12vv

Missae, 9vv primo choro concertante a 5vv, secundo pleno et necessario cum symphoniis ad libitum, 9vv, 3 cornetts/vn, 3 trbn/va, bc (Antwerp, 1643); Missa 'Dulcis Jesu'; 2 masses a 12

MAGNIFICAT COLLECTIONS

Edition: *Eight Magnificat Settings*, ed. H. H. Junkermann (Madison, 1974) [includes 4 from the 1603 collection, 1 from 1608, 2 from 1614, 1 from 1641]

Sacrum Beatissimae Virginis Mariae canticum, 5–8vv (Munich, 1603); Magnificat super: 'Benedictus Deus', 6vv, 'D'un si bel fuoco', 6vv, 'E viver è morire', 6vv, 'Hor che suave Laura', 5vv, 'Leggiadre ninfe', 6vv, 'Lucilla io vo morire', 7vv, 'Spuntavan gia', 5vv; 1 other Magnificat, 7vv; 2 others, 8vv

Magnificat, 4vv, super octo tonos, quibus accesserunt litaniae, antiphonae Mariales, 8vv (Passau, 1608); 8 Magnificat settings, one on each of the 8 tones; litany and 4 Marian antiphons (also pubd in Antiphonae, 1636)

Super magnae matris divino carmine Magnificat, symphoniae variae . . . 8, 12vv, 2, 3 bc (org) (Innsbruck, 1614); Magnificat super: 'Affrettiamoci', 'Buccinate', 'Ecco nuncio di gioia', 'Ego sum qui sum', 'Ingredimini omnes', 'Laudans exultans', 'Lieto Godea', all 8vv, 2 bc (org); Magnificat on the first tone, 8vv, 2 bc (org); another on the first tone, 12vv, 3 bc (org)

Cantici Mariani septies variati, liber quartus, 12vv, 3 bc (org), op.6 (Innsbruck, 1618); Magnificat: on the sixth tone, on the seventh tone, on the eighth tone; Magnificat: 'Laudate Dominum', 'Qual vive', 'Quam pulchra es', 'Tiridola'

Psalmi vesperini (1640) and Psalmi integri (1641) also contain Magnificat settings

OTHER COLLECTIONS

Musica super cantum gregorianum . . . pars prima missarum dominicalium introitus complectitur . . . 5vv, bc ad lib (Ravensburg, 1625); 52 introits, 9 Gloria Patri settings; for contents see R. Mitjana (1911–15)

Musicae super cantum gregorianum pars secunda: festa proprium et commune sanctorum, 5vv, bc (Ravensburg, 1626); 50 introits for feasts; for contents see Mitjana

Hymni quibus totius anni decursu . . . 4vv . . . accomodi, quibus et alii hymni pro festis solemnioribus . . . accesserunt, 4–8vv, 2 cornetts/vn, bc (Innsbruck, 1628); 4-part hymns of part i, ed. in DTÖ, v, Jg. iii/1 (Vienna, 1896/R)

Moduli symphoniaci in augustissima Christi nati celebritate et ceteris deinceps natalibus et Purificationis virginis feriis, 5–7 et pluribus vv (Innsbruck, 1629⁴); 5 compositions by other composers, 9 by Stadlmayr: Beata immaculata, 8vv, Dies est laetitiae, 6vv, Dulcis Jesu, 8vv, Exulta parva Bethlehem, 6vv, Geboren ist uns ein Kindlein, 5vv, Jure plaudunt omnia, 6vv, Puer natus, 6vv, Puer nobis nascitur, 6vv, Resonet in laudibus, 10vv (all with bc)

Antiphonae vespertinae . . . cum tribus litaniis Lauretanis duabus salutationibus angelicis, 2–8vv, bc (org) (Innsbruck, 1636); 6 Alma redemptoris settings, 7 Ave regina, 8 Regina coeli, 9 Salve regina, 3 litanies, 2 Ave Maria settings

Odae sacrae Jesu Christo . . . 5vv et totidem instrumentis si placet (2 vn, 3 va, bc) (Innsbruck, 1638²); 4 compositions by A. Reiner, 13 by Stadlmayr: Ad sanctam Mariam, Canite caelites, Coelo rores, Deponite me, Dum virgo vagientem, Gaudete Christiani, Gaudete cum mortalibus, Laetare virgo, O puer delectissime, Qui ad statis aspiratis, Quis mutuas amores, Quod solatium, Resurrexit salus noster

Salmi, 2, 3vv, 2 vn/cornetts (Innsbruck, 1640); Beatus vir, Confitebor, Credidi, Dixit Dominus, In convertendo, Laetatus sum, Lauda Jerusalem, Laudate Dominum, Laudate pueri, Nisi Dominus

Psalmi vespertini omnes cum 2 Magnificat concertationibus musicis per 6vv, bc (Innsbruck, 1640); Beati omnis, Beatus vir, Confitebor (2 settings), Credidi, De profundis, Dixit Dominus, Domine probasti, In convertendo, In exitu Israel, Lauda Jerusalem, Laudate Dominum, Laudate pueri, Laetatus sum, Memento, Nisi Dominus; 2 Magnificat settings: one on the first tone, the other on the sixth

Psalmi integri a 4vv concertantibus, 4 aliis accessoriis ad lib . . . 2 cornetts/vn, bc (Innsbruck, 1641); Beatus vir, Confitebor, Credidi, De profundis, Dixit Dominus (2 settings), Domine probasti, In convertendo, In exitu Israel, Lauda Jerusalem, Laudate Dominum, Laudate pueri, Laudate sit nomen Domini, Laetatus sum, Memento, Nisi Dominus; Magnificat primi toni; Magnificat super Magnificat Orlandi [Lassus]

Apparatus musicus sacrarum cantionum . . . 6–24 vocibus et instrumentis (Innsbruck, 1645); 44 vocal and 6 inst compositions; a 6: Aspice Domine, Benedicam Dominum, Canzon, Ego mater, Eructavit, Salve regina, Spiritus Domini; a 7: Benedicam Dominum; a 8: Audite gentes, 2 Canzons (tertii toni, quinti toni), Deus in nomine Deus, Estote fortes, Exaltabo te, Exultate Deo, O virum mirabilum, Peccavimus, Sanctum Benedictum, Sub tuum praesidium; a 9: Dominus illuminatio; a 10: Ascendo ad Patrem, 2 Canzons (quarti toni, octi toni); a 12: Deus qui glorificantes, Domine quis habitabit, Dum complementur, Sonata, Tribus miraculis; a 13: Laetamini in Domino, Sonata; a 14: Ave gratia, Canzon, Dies sanctificatus, Exultate Deo, Laudemus Dominum; a 15: Venite filii; a 16:

Domine Dominus noster, Domini est terra, Sonet vox; a 18: Cantantibus organi, Exultate Deo, Jubilate Deo, Regina coeli; a 20: Cantate Domino, Isti sunt viri; a 22: Te Deum laudamus, Veni Sancte Spiritus; a 24: Benedicam Dominum

Psalmus quinquagesimus Davidis . . . 4–6, 8vv cum secundo choro et instrumentis senis si placet (Innsbruck, 1646); 8 Miserere settings, 2 each for 4, 5, 6, 8vv (with 6 insts ad lib, except in 1 setting, 8vv, with 6 insts obbl); 4 settings of Miserere in falsibordoni, 3 for 2 solo vv and insts, 1 for 8vv

WORKS IN ANTHOLOGIES

Antiphon, 4vv, bc, in 1628[5]
Bonitatem fecisti, 2vv, bc, in 1622[2]
Cantate Domino, 2vv, bc, in 1623[2]
Canzon [without text], 3vv, bc, in 1624[1]
Dixit Dominus, reprinted from Salmi (1640), in 1659[3]
Maria klar, du bist fürwahr, 4vv, in 1604[7]
3 Salve regina settings: 2vv, bc; 9vv, bc; 12vv, bc; in 1629[1]

BIBLIOGRAPHY

J. Peregrinus [J. P. Hupfauf]: *Johann Stadlmayr* (Salzburg, 1885)
O. Kinkeldey: *Orgel und Klavier in der Musik des 16. Jahrhunderts* (Leipzig, 1910), 187ff
R. Mitjana: *Catalogue critique et descriptif des imprimés de musique des XVIᵉ et XVIIᵉ siècles conservés à la Bibliothèque de l'Université royale d'Upsala* (Uppsala, 1911–15)
F. Daniel: *Die konzertanten Messen Johann Stadlmayrs* (diss., U. of Vienna, 1928)
B. Hinterleitner: *Die Vokalmessen Stadlmayrs* (diss., U. of Vienna, 1930)
K. A. Rosenthal: 'Zur Stilistik der Salzburger Kirchenmusik von 1600 bis 1730', *SMw*, xvii (1930), 77; xix (1932), 3–32
K. F. Gress: *Die Motetten Johann Stadlmayrs im Lichte der Entwicklung der Motette im beginnenden siebzehnten Jahrhundert* (diss., U. of Vienna, 1931)
H. Spies: 'Die Tonkunst in Salzburg in der Regierungszeit des Fürsten und Erzbischofs Wolf Dietrich von Raitenau (1587–1612)', *Mitteilungen der Gesellschaft für Salzburger Landeskunde*, lxxi (1931), 1–64; lxxii (1932), 65–136
C.-H. Illing: *Zur Technik der Magnificat-Kompositionen des 16. Jahrhunderts* (Wolfenbüttel, 1936)
W. Senn: *Aus dem Kulturleben einer süddeutschen Kleinstadt: Musik, Schule und Theater der Stadt Hall in Tirol* (Innsbruck, 1938)
——: *Musik und Theater am Hof zu Innsbruck* (Innsbruck, 1954), 187–294
D. Calingaert: *Rosetum Marianum (1604): a Collection of German Marian Songs* (diss., U. of Rochester, NY, 1955)
H. Federhofer: 'Graz Court Musicians and their Contributions to the Parnassus musicus Ferdinandaeus (1615)', *MD*, ix (1955), 167–244
W. H. Schempf: *Polychoral Magnificats from H. Praetorius to H. Schütz* (diss., U. of Rochester, NY, 1960)
F. W. Riedel: 'Musikpflege im Benediktinerstift Göttweig (Niederösterreich) um 1600', *KJb*, xlvi (1962), 83
H. H. Junkermann: *The Magnificats of Johann Stadlmayr* (diss., Ohio State U., 1966)

HILDE H. JUNKERMANN

Stadtfeld, (Christian Josef Anton Franz) Alexander (*b* Wiesbaden, 28 April 1826; *d* Brussels, 4 Nov 1853). Belgian composer of German birth. The son of a military bandmaster, as a child prodigy he attracted the attention of the Belgian King Leopold I, who made it possible for him to attend the Brussels Conservatory. From 1839 to 1849 he studied there under the personal supervision of the director, Fétis. As winner of the Prix de Rome in 1849 he went to Paris, where several of his works were successfully performed. His numerous male choruses and songs, some of them published, are completely in accord with contemporary taste. His only grand opera *Hamlet* (1851–3; libretto by Jules Guillaume), which was performed posthumously in Darmstadt (1857), was strongly influenced by Meyerbeer. His first three symphonies and his two concert overtures show a talent for instrumentation as well as a serious attempt to come to grips with Beethoven's techniques of thematic development. In his fourth symphony, the *Symphonie triomphale* (1852), he succeeded in an independent synthesis of these achievements with elements of French Revolutionary music, but his early death from tuberculosis prevented the full development

of his individuality. His works, almost all in manuscript, are in the library of the Brussels Conservatory.

BIBLIOGRAPHY

FétisB
A. Wotquenne, ed.: *Catalogue de la Bibliothèque du Conservatoire de musique de Bruxelles*, iii (Brussels, 1908), 450ff
M. Weber: *Alexander Stadtfeld: Leben und Werk* (diss., U. of Bonn, 1969)

MAGDA MARX-WEBER

Städtisches Fachinstitut für Neue Musik. Original title (1947–9) of the Internationales Musikinstitut in DARMSTADT.

Stadtpfeifer (Ger.: 'town piper'). A professional musician employed by civic authorities. The term has been used in German-speaking countries since the late 14th century (*der statt pfiffer*, 1378, Berne) along with *Ratsmusicus* (*Ratsmusikant*), *Stadtmusicus* (*Stadtmusikant*), *Instrumentist*, *Kunstpfeifer* and *Zinkenist* and is equivalent to the English 'wait'. Earlier titles include *speleman dere stat* (1227, 1265, Brunswick), *figellatori consulum* (1335, Lüneburg), *des Rades Trometer* (1339, Bremen), *Stadtspielman* or *Stad spellude* (before 1401, Lüneburg). From the 17th century the *Prinzipal* of a town band was sometimes also given the title *Director der instrumentalen Musik* or *Stadtmusikdirektor*. While in smaller communities the position was usually held by a master together with his apprentices and journeymen, the larger cities had up to ten civic musicians of equal rank.

1. Employment and duties. 2. Training and skills.

1. EMPLOYMENT AND DUTIES. The earliest evidence of musicians being taken into civic employment in Germany dates from the 14th century: 1335, Lüneburg, and 1348, Frankfurt am Main (outside Germany there is slightly earlier evidence: *tubatores del comune*, 1291, Florence; 1297, Ieper). The musicians were usually minstrels and their appointment was of a temporary nature; service was for a specific occasion, or at least was paid by the event. Proper written appointments began in the 15th century and were an essential element in the establishing of town musicians. In these the contractual duties as well as the rights of the musicians were laid down, and the mayor and council of the town guaranteed the musician a yearly or half-yearly fixed salary (*salarium fixum*). The list of duties of the Stadtpfeiferei included performance at official celebrations, festival parades, royal visits, civic weddings or baptisms, participation in church services and church and school festivities, as well as the education of musical apprentices. In return the musicians were guaranteed the exclusive privilege of providing music within the city boundaries. Rural districts were frequently included in their domain, hence the title *Stadt- und Landmusicus*. They were often entitled to expenses for instruments, music or clothes, collections at Martinmas and the New Year, donations towards fuel and grain, and privileges such as exemption from taxes or watch duty. When players were disabled, substitutes were often engaged.

The town musician's social status depended mainly on the size of his income. On a fixed salary he generally earned less than the cantors and organists of an area's principal churches. Details of musicians' resources and revenue can be gathered from personal account books. Both social position and range of musical work depended largely on the size and nature of the city (whether it was the seat of a bishopric, a court residence,

The Nuremberg Stadtpfeiferei announcing the New Year: coloured pen and ink drawing by an unknown 16th-century artist from a collection of drawings depicting the social life of Nuremberg (D-B MS.Germ.Fol.442, f.91v–92r)

a university or garrison town, a free imperial city, municipal republic, or small town) and the amount of ceremony it had to provide. In smaller places the Stadtpfeifer would also have to assume the burden of tower or watch duty, and often combined his official post with a job as organist, schoolteacher, instrument maker or even a totally non-musical post. His counterparts in larger cities, on the other hand, were able to confine themselves to more artistic tasks commensurate with their position as musicians: directing or participating in operas, concerts, musical evenings, feast day masses etc. Hanseatic cities such as Hamburg, Lübeck, Rostock and Danzig also had, besides their privileged town musicians, *Chor- und Köstenbrüder* or *Rollmusikanten* – musicians who were organized according to the statutes of the various guilds and entrusted with providing music for the middle and lower classes. The eight city musicians (*Ratsmusikanten*) were appointed exclusively to play for patrician families and members of the upper class. As a rule the move from city to court musician meant a rise in social position.

The Stadtpfeifer waged a constant battle to retain their exclusive right to provide music. In order to preserve their professional privileges and to prevent competition from untrained musicians (*Pfuscher, Böhnhasen*), town musicians from northern and central

Germany formed in 1653 a provincial association of mutual interest whose statutes were ratified by Emperor Ferdinand III. But when free exercise of trade followed in the wake of the French Revolution, and with it the introduction of free competition, the legal basis for the town musicians' privileges disappeared, and with them many of the traditional town bands. Other factors contributed, notably the technical demands made on instrumentalists in music after 1790 which led to the replacement of the old Stadtpfeifer – the all-round musician – by a new type, the specialist, whose education was provided by the newly established conservatories of music.

2. TRAINING AND SKILLS. In many places, anyone wishing to begin study under a Stadtpfeifer was required to present proof of 'honourable and lawful birth'. After a five- or six-year period of study in which he had to master a large number of wind and string instruments he was ceremoniously released and became a journeyman. As a trained 'Musikant' he then chose either to continue working for his master or to undertake several years of travel. A proficient journeyman could obtain a position as Stadtpfeifer (*Prinzipal*), when one fell vacant, by means of an audition and selection by the local council. As in other trades, it was possible to become a Stadtpfeifer by marriage and to pass on the post

within a family. This was how the Bach family held posts for generations as Thuringian town musicians.

The Stadtpfeifer, as a rule, was a practising musician. From the mid-18th century he mastered and taught the newly fashionable piano and guitar, as well as wind and string instruments. A number of exceptional town musicians became famous as instrumental virtuosos: Nathaniel Schnittelbach (1633–67) and Thomas Baltzar (c1630–63) as violinists in Lübeck, and the Leipzig trumpeter Gottfried Reiche (1667–1734), whom J. S. Bach valued highly and who was also prominent as a composer of four-part *Turmmusik* ('tower music'). To match the wide variety of tasks assigned him, the Stadtpfeifer had a wide repertory. It embraced signal pieces, chorales, dance movements, conversational and representational music, and from the 18th century onwards included sinfonias and concertos as well. Among the better-known composers who developed through training as town musicians or were active as Stadtpfeifer or directors of *Stadtmusik* the following are noteworthy: Susato (Antwerp, 1531–49), Brade (Hamburg, 1608–10, 1613–15), Hassler (Augsburg, 1600; Nuremberg, 1601–4), Schop (Hamburg, 1621–67), Staden (Nuremberg, 1623–55), Pezel (Leipzig, from 1664; Bautzen, 1680–94), Zachow (Eilenburg, from 1676), Telemann (Frankfurt am Main, 1712–21; Hamburg, 1721–67), Quantz (Radeberg and Pirna, 1714; Dresden, 1716), Zelter (Berlin, from 1774) and Lumbye (Copenhagen, from 1829).

See GUILDS and WAIT; *see also* GERMANY, §I, 2.

BIBLIOGRAPHY

O. Nielsen: 'Om stadsmusikanter i København under Frederik d. IV. 1699–1730', *Københavns historie og beskrivelse*, vi (1892), 243

H. Waltz: *Die Lage der Orchestermusiker in Deutschland mit besonderer Berücksichtigung der Musikgeschäfte ('Stadtpfeifereien')* (Karlsruhe, 1906)

G. Wustmann: 'Die sächsischen Musikantenartikel von 1653', *Neues Archiv für sächsische Geschichte und Altertumskunde*, xxix/1–2 (1908), 104

K. Nef: 'Die Stadtpfeiferei und die Instrumentalmusiker in Basel (1385–1814)', *SIMG*, x (1908–9), 395

F. Wellmann: 'Die Bremer Stadtmusikanten: ein Beitrag zur bremischen Musikgeschichte (aus den Akten des Staatsarchivs)', *Jb der bremischen Sammlungen*, iv (1911), 79

F. Brönnimann: *Der Zinkenist und Musikdirektor Johann Ulrich Sultzberger und die Pflege der Musik in Bern in der zweiten Hälfte des XVII. Jahrhunderts* (Zopfingen, 1920)

A. Schering: 'Die Leipziger Ratsmusik von 1650 bis 1775', *AMw*, iii (1921), 17–53.

O. Spreckelsen: *Die Stader Ratsmusikanten* (Stade, 1924)

F. Rollberg: 'Johann Ambrosius Bach, Stadtpfeifer zu Eisenach von 1671–1695', *BJb*, xxiv (1927), 133

H. Rauschning: *Geschichte der Musik und Musikpflege in Danzig: von den Anfängen bis zur Auflösung der Kirchenkapellen* (Danzig, 1931)

H. Techritz: *Sächsische Stadtpfeifer: zur Geschichte des Stadtmusikwesens im ehemaligen Königreich Sachsen* (Dresden, 1932)

L. Krüger: *Die Hamburgische Musikorganisation im 17. Jahrhundert* (Strasbourg, 1933)

A. Werner: *Vier Jahrhunderte im Dienste der Kirchenmusik: Geschichte des Amtes und Standes der evangelischen Kantoren, Organisten und Stadtpfeifer seit der Reformation* (Leipzig, 1933)

F. Ernst: 'Die Spielleute im Dienste der Stadt Basel im ausgehenden Mittelalter (bis 1550)', *Basler Zeitschrift für Geschichte und Altertumskunde*, xliv (1945), 80–236

H. Federhofer: 'Die Grazer Stadtmusikanten und die privilegierte Stadtmusikantenkompagnie', *Zeitschrift des Historischen Vereines für Steiermark*, xli (1951), 91

L. G. Langwill: 'The Waits', *HMYB*, vii (1952), 170

G. Hempel: 'Das Ende der Leipziger Ratsmusik im 19. Jahrhundert', *AMw*, xv (1958), 187

T. Volek: 'Pražké muzikantské cechy, městští hudebníci a trubači v druhé polovině 18. století' [Prague musicians' guilds, town musicians and trumpeters in the 2nd half of the 18th century], *MMC*, vi (1958), 75

E. A. Bowles: 'Tower Musicians in the Middle Ages', *Brass Quarterly*, v (1961–2), 91

H. P. Detlefsen: *Musikgeschichte der Stadt Flensburg bis zum Jahre 1850*, Schriften des Landesinstituts für Musikforschung Kiel, xi (Kassel, 1961)

A. Downs: 'The Tower Music of a Seventeenth-century Stadtpfeifer: Johann Pezel', *Brass Quarterly*, vii (1963–4), 3–33

H. W. Schwab: 'Zunftwesen', *MGG*

H. Federhofer and D. M. Schmeiser: 'Grazer Stadtmusikanten als Komponisten vorklassischer Klavierkonzerte', *Historisches Jb der Stadt Graz*, iv (1971), 73

H. W. Schwab: 'Zur sozialen Stellung des Stadtmusikanten', *Der Sozialstatus des Berufsmusikers vom 17. bis 19. Jahrhundert*, ed. W. Salmen (Kassel, 1971), 9

——: *Das Einnahmebuch des Schleswiger Stadtmusikanten Friedrich Adolph Berwald*, Kieler Schriften zur Musikwissenschaft, xxi (Kassel, 1972)

——: 'Die Institutionen der Lübecker Stadtmusik und die Einführung der Musikantenordnung von 1815', *Zeitschrift des Vereins für Lübeckische Geschichte und Altertumskunde*, lii (1972), 62

HEINRICH W. SCHWAB

Staehelin, Martin (*b* Basle, 25 Sept 1937). Swiss musicologist. He trained in Basle as a secondary school instructor in music and classics, at the same time taking a flute teacher's certificate under Joseph Bopp (1962). He studied musicology under Schrade and Schmitz (1963–7), with Latin and Greek philology as secondary subjects, and received the doctorate at Basle University in 1967 with a dissertation on the masses of Isaac. With a scholarship from the Schweizerischer Nationalfonds (1968–71), he completed his *Habilitation*, also on Isaac's masses, under Kurt von Fischer at the University of Zurich in 1971. He became director of the Schweizerisches Volksliederarchiv in 1963 and has served on the board of directors of the Schweizerische Musikforschende Gesellschaft (president of the Basle chapter 1971–3). From 1972 to 1977 he represented Switzerland on the IMS committee. In 1976 he moved to Bonn and became director of the Beethoven-Archiv and the Beethoven-Haus; that year he won the Edward J. Dent medal for musicology.

Staehelin's research centres on the music of Josquin's period and is distinguished (e.g. in his exemplary edition of Isaac's masses) by its precision and by his knowledge and analysis of sources. His recent work includes articles on 18th-century music and the preparation of a comprehensive monograph on Nägeli.

WRITINGS

'Altgriechische Musikinstrumente', *Schweizerisches Jb 'Die Ernte'* (1959), 76

'Basels Musikleben im 18. Jahrhundert', *Schweizerisches Jb 'Die Ernte'* (1963), 116

'Musikvetenskap i Schweiz', *Musikrevy*, xviii (1963), 46

'Vertonte Chorlied-Zudichtungen zur Aulularia des Plautus aus der Basler Humanistenzeit: Untersuchungen zur Musikhandschrift F.II.35 der Universitätsbibliothek Basel', *Crustula Basiliensia* (Basle, 1965), 125–63

'Zum Egenolff-Diskantband der Bibliothèque Nationale in Paris', *AMw*, xxiii (1966), 93

'Quellenkundliche Beiträge zum Werk von Johannes Ghiselin-Verbonnet', *AMw*, xxiv (1967), 120

Quellenstudien zu Heinrich Isaac und seinem Messen-Oeuvre (diss., U. of Basle, 1967; Berne, 1974 in *Studien zu den Messenkompositionen von Heinrich Isaac*)

'Der sogenannte Musettenbass: Forschungen zur schweizerischen Instrumenten- und Musikgeschichte des späten 18. und frühen 19. Jahrhunderts', *Jb des Bernischen historischen Museums in Bern*, xlix/1 (1969–70), 93

'Pierre de la Rue in Italien', *AMw*, xxvii (1970), 128

'Zum Schicksal des alten Musikalien-Fonds von San Luigi dei Francesi in Rom', *FAM*, xvii (1970), 120

Der Grüne Codex der Viadrina: eine wenig beachtete Quelle zur Musik des späten 15. und frühen 16. Jahrhunderts in Deutschland (Mainz, 1971)

'Zur Echtheitsproblematik der Mozartschen Bläserkonzertante', *MJb 1971–2*, 56

Studien zu Werk- und Satztechnik in den Messenkompositionen von Heinrich Isaac (Habilitationsschrift, U. of Zurich, 1971; Berne, 1974 in *Studien zu den Messenkompositionen von Heinrich Isaac*)

'Eine Florentiner Musik-Handschrift aus der Zeit um 1500', *Schweizer Beiträge zur Musikwissenschaft*, i (1972), 55

'Neues zu Bartholomäus Frank', *Festschrift Arnold Geering* (Berne, 1972), 119

'Möglichkeiten und praktische Anwendung der Verfasserbestimmung an anonym überlieferten Kompositionen der Josquin-Zeit', *TVNM*, xxiii (1973), 79

'Zum Phänomen der Tradition in der Musikgeschichte des 15. und 16. Jahrhunderts', *Studien zur Tradition in der Musik: Kurt von Fischer zum 60. Geburtstag* (Munich, 1973), 85

'Beschreibungen und Beispiele musikalischer Formen in einem unbeachteten Traktat des frühen 15. Jahrhunderts', *AMw*, xxxi (1974), 237

'Obrechtiana', *TVNM*, xxv/1 (1975), 1

'Aus "Lukas Wagenrieders" Werkstatt: ein unbekanntes Lieder-Manuskript des frühen 16. Jahrhunderts in Zürich', *Formen und Probleme der Überlieferung mehrstimmiger Musik im Zeitalter Josquins Desprez: Wolfenbüttel 1976*

Many contributions to *Grove 6*, *BordasD*

EDITIONS

H. Isaac: Messen, Musikalische Denkmäler, vii–ix (Mainz, 1970–) [rev. edn. of Birtner's inc. MS edn.]

JÜRG STENZL

Staempfli, Edward (*b* Berne, 1 Feb 1908). Swiss composer. After studying medicine in Berne for two years he turned to music. He studied in Cologne under Jarnach and Maler (1929–30), and was then a pupil of Dukas in Paris for a year. There he was soon attached to the circle of Beck, Mihalovici, Martinů and Harsányi, who had some influence on him. In 1935 he attended Scherchen's conducting course in Brussels, where he was awarded the Le Boeuf Prize for the *Musique pour 11 instruments*. He was so deeply impressed by hearing the first performance of Berg's Violin Concerto (Barcelona, 1936) that 12-note technique became a constant concern until, in 1949, he was satisfied that it was the right method for him. The outbreak of World War II drove him from Paris back to Switzerland, where he lived in Basle and then, from 1944, in Lugano. In 1951 he moved to Heidelberg and in 1954 to Berlin. He made an extended visit to the USA in 1962, lecturing on contemporary Swiss music and having works performed. The influence of Staempfli's various places of residence is evident in his music. French impressionism and the radical polyphony of early Hindemith led him to produce first a series of chiefly concertante scores containing lyrical elements. His time in Switzerland coincided with a transitional period of approximately ten years, at the end of which he decided to use 12-note technique and later extended serial procedures. His writing has continued to be strict and fully determined, though also colourful. He has often appeared as a conductor or pianist, particularly in his own works.

WORKS
(selective list)

STAGE AND VOCAL

Operas: Ein Traumspiel (Strindberg), 1944; Medea (Grillparzer), 1954

Ballets: Le pendu, 1935; Choreographisches Divertimento, 1942; Die Prinzessin und der Schweinehirt (Kreis, after Andersen), 1943; Spannungen, 1961

Oratorios and cantatas: Filles de Sion (Jouve), chorus, orch, 1933; 6 Sonette (Barrett-Browning), S, chamber orch, 1942; Liberté (Eluard), solo vv, chorus, wind, timp, pf, 1944; 6 Liebesgedichte (Huch), A, orch, 1945; Der Spiegel der Welt (oratorio, Ecclesiastes, Baroque texts), solo vv, chorus, orch, 1950; Lyrische Kantate (Kafka), Bar, female chorus, orch, 1955; Divertimento (Arp, Kandinsky, Klee), S, 8 insts, 1958; Wenn der Tag leer wird (N. Sachs), solo vv, chorus, orch, 1969; Zion's Klage und Tröstung, oratorio, S, A, Bar, speaker, chorus, orch, 1970; L'avventura d'un povero christiano (oratorio, Silone), S, A, T, B, male speaker, female speaker, 2 choruses, orch, 1972

Other vocal works: La musique (Baudelaire), A, harp, str qnt, 1946; 5 poèmes (P. Patocchi), A, harp, cel, pf, 1948; Les 7 poèmes d'amour en guerre, chorus, 1948; 3 Lieder, Mez, orch, 1963; Traumschalmei (A. Valangin), S, pf, 1969; Solo la muerte (Neruda), Bar, chorus, 7 insts, 1971; Gedanken über die Zeit (Fleming), S, fl, ob, perc, pf,

1972; Jenseit (Kaschnitz), S, ob, cl, va, vc, harp, perc, pf, 1973; many other songs

INSTRUMENTAL

Orch: 4 konzertante Sym., 1931, 1932, 1933, 1934; 4 pf concs., 1932, 1933, 1954, 1963; 3 mouvements, str, 1935; 3 vn concs., 1936, 1939, 1941; 3 syms., 1938, 1942, 1945; Conc., 2 pf, 1940; Concertino, cl, str, 1941; Praeludium und Variationen über ein Tessiner Volkslied, 1945; Concertino, pf, chamber orch, 1947; Mouvements concertantes, 1947; Epitaphe pour Paul Eluard, 1954; Fantasie, str, 1955; Fl Concertino, 1957; Strophen, 1958; Orch Werk, 1960; 5 Nachtstücke, 1961; Musik für 16 Str, 1968; Tripartita, 3 pf, 23 wind, 1969; Sätze und Gegensätze, vib, pf, perc, 15 str, 1972

Chamber: 6 str qts, 1926, 1935, 1939, 1945, 1954, 1962; Qt, fl, str trio, 1932; 2 pf trios, 1932, 1956; Wind Qnt, 1934; Musique pour 11 insts, 1935; Trio, fl, vn, pf, 1935; Str Trio, 1937; 5 Pieces, ww, 1946; 4 Pieces, brass, 1946; Konzertante Fantasie, 2 tpt, 2 pf, timp, 1947; Wind Trio, 1949; 5 Stücke, fl, pf, 1954; Ornamente, 2 fl, cel, perc, 1960; Duo, cl, pf, 1970

Pf: 6 Pieces, 1932; 5 Characteristic Pieces, duet, 1939; 10 kleine Klavierstücke, 1944; 7 Klavierstücke, 1954; 3 Sätze, 1959

Principal publishers: Bote & Bock, Gerig

BIBLIOGRAPHY

E. Staempfli: 'Edward Staempfli', *Musik der Zeit* (1955), no.10, p.42

H. Ehinger: 'Edward Staempfli', *40 schweizer Komponisten der Gegenwart* (Amriswil, 1956), 185

H. H. Stuckenschmidt: 'Edward Staempfli sechzig', *SMz*, cviii (1968), 117

FRITZ MUGGLER

Staes, Ferdinand(-Philippe-Joseph) (*b* Brussels, baptized 16 Dec 1748; *d* Brussels, 23 March 1809). South Netherlands harpsichordist, organist and composer. The son of Guillaume Staes, an organist at the Brussels royal chapel from 1758, he studied with his father and later with Ignaz Vitzthumb. As a harpsichordist he was accompanist at the Grand Théâtre, Brussels, by 1767 and the following year was appointed assistant to his father (second court organist at that time); he also took part in *concerts de table* at court and performed successfully at the concerts of the academy and Concert Bourgeois in 1771. In January 1772 he gained the reversion for his father's post of principal court organist but (despite Fétis and later sources) he never filled this appointment, for his father was still active when the royal chapel was dissolved in 1794. By 1772 Staes was an organist at the Madeleine church, where Burney heard him and wrote that 'the organ was played in a masterly manner, by M. Straze [sic], who is esteemed the best performer upon keyed instruments in Brussels'. Staes was a member of the Masonic Lodge 'L'heureuse rencontre à l'Orient', Brussels, by 1786, but does not seem to have written masonic music. His compositions include several keyboard works (mainly sonatas for the harpsichord or piano) with instrumental accompaniment.

WORKS

5 sets of 3 sonatas, hpd/pf, vn, vc, opp.1–5 (Brussels, n.d.)

Concerto, solo hpd/pf, orch, op.6 (Brussels, n.d.)

Idées de campagne, hpd/pf, vn, vc, 2 hn (Brussels, n.d.)

Other kbd works in contemporary anthologies, and pf transcrs. of contemporary works by other composers

Nouvelle marche bruxelloise, military band (Brussels, 1790)

BIBLIOGRAPHY

FétisB

C. Burney: *The Present State of Music in Germany, the Netherlands and United Provinces* (London, 1773, 2/1775); ed. P. Scholes as *Dr. Burney's Musical Tours* (London, 1959)

A. Choron and F. Fayolle: *Dictionnaire historique des musiciens* (Paris, 1810–11/R1971)

E. Gregoir: *Galerie biographique des artistes-musiciens belges du XVIIIe et du XIXe siècle* (Brussels, 1862)

E. vander Straeten: *La musique aux Pays-Bas avant le XIXe siècle*, iv (Paris, 1878/R1969)

P. Bergmans: 'Staes (Ferdinand-Philippe-Joseph)', *BNB*

B. van der Schelden: *La franc-maçonnerie belge sous le régime autrichien (1721–1794): étude historique et critique* (Louvain, 1923)

S. Clercx: *Henri-Jacques de Croes*, ii (Brussels, 1940)
R. Vannes: *Dictionnaire des musiciens (compositeurs)* (Brussels, 1947)
PAUL RASPÉ

Staff [stave] (Fr. *portée*; Ger. *Liniensystem, System*; It. *sistema, rigo*). A set of lines on, between, above and below which notes of music are written. A five-line staff has been the most widely used type since north French manuscripts of the early 13th century containing polyphony. A four-line staff has been used for plainchant since the 12th century. Staves are also used in TABLATURE: in music for string and wind instruments they represent the strings or holes of the instrument, and have digits denoting which fingers are to touch the strings or holes; in keyboard tablature the lines denote specific pitches. Except in tablature for string and wind instruments, the staff carries low notes on its lowest line, high notes on its highest, and may be supplemented above and below by leger lines. Notes are prefaced by a clef indicating the pitch of the line on which it is placed (and hence of the other lines of the staff). Two or more staves, joined by a brace, form a system.

1. The staff in early theoretical writing. 2. Early plainchant notation and Guido of Arezzo. 3. Polyphonic music.

1. THE STAFF IN EARLY THEORETICAL WRITING. The earliest surviving examples of a staff date from the end of the 9th century. In *Musica enchiriadis* (*c*860 according to Handschin and Dronke, *c*900 according to Smits van Waesberghe; *see* MUSICA ENCHIRIADIS, §4) a set of lines called *chordae* ('strings' – an interesting link with tablature) are used, one for each pitch, a 2nd apart. To the left of each line appears a Daseian letter giving its pitch. The letter 'T' or 'S' to the left of each space denotes the interval of a tone or semitone between each *chorda*. Syllables of a chant text are set on the lines, indicating the pitch at which they are to be sung. The manuscript *F-VAL* 337, probably the earliest surviving copy (not later than 900), uses an eight-line staff (see fig.1).

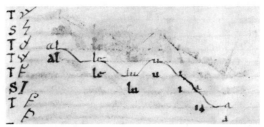

1. Lines (called 'chordae') forming a staff in the treatise 'Musica enchiriadis', 9th century (F-VAL 337, f.45r); Daseian letters indicate the pitch of each line, the letters 'T' and 'S' the intervals between the lines

Hucbald's *De harmonica institutione* (*c*900) contains an example of a six-line staff, bearing syllables of chant text in the same way as *Musica enchiriadis*, with the spaces designated tone or semitone but without Daseian letters. Hucbald specifically equated the lines with the strings of the cithara: 'Porro exemplum semitonii advertere potes in cithara sex chordarum, inter tertiam et quartam chordam' (Gerbert, in *GS*, i, 109, omitted the lowest line; *B-Br* 10078–95 f.87r, facs. in Smits van Waesberghe, 1969, p.107, shows that the text syllables should touch the lines, although the modern reproductions that appear to equate a syllable with an interval do have predecessors in medieval manuscripts: see Apel,

p.205). The link with early hexachord theory is unclear.

Such diagrammatic staves were also used in the organum instruction of *Musica enchiriadis, Scolica enchiriadis* and their successors throughout the Middle Ages, sometimes necessitating staves of 18 lines, as many as there were Daseian letters. But this system of notation was a teaching aid not used in functional liturgical manuscripts.

2. EARLY PLAINCHANT NOTATION AND GUIDO OF AREZZO. All cheironomic notations contained an element of the distinction between high and low notes in the very shape of their neumes. By the turn of the millennium Beneventan and Aquitanian notations were diastematic, i.e. individual neumes were placed higher or lower on the page relative to one another, though not clearly enough for completely certain modern transcription. By the mid-11th century Aquitanian notation regularly used a single dry-point (scratched) line, whose pitch varied according to the mode of the piece (a table is given in Stäblein, p.41). The author of the *Quaestiones in musica* suggested a mode-linked technique of using a single coloured line, with different colours for different modes; but he wrote half a century after and in knowledge of Guido of Arezzo's teaching.

Guido of Arezzo, in *Aliae regulae* (*c*1030), recommended that lines should be drawn for every other pitch, a 3rd apart, so that notes of a scale would be set alternately on a line or in a space. He further recommended that one or more of the lines be coloured to denote its pitch (he preferred a red F line and a yellow C line), or that a letter be set in front of at least one of the lines to denote its pitch (*see* CLEF, fig.1b). His principles, in one variant or another, were gradually adopted all over Europe, at different times in different places. Central Italy took up the coloured-line scheme quickly (Smits van Waesberghe, 1951, cites 17 manuscripts written by *c*1100). Coloured lines were slightly less common elsewhere, but use of the Guidonian staff with a clef spread rapidly through advanced European centres of music, especially those of the Low Countries. The Beneventan and west Aquitanian areas did not adopt it until nearer 1200. German Switzerland was particularly conservative; although isolated earlier manuscripts use it (e.g. *CH-E* 366, 12th century, possibly an importation, with four dry-point lines, red F line, F and C clefs; facs. in Stäblein, p.187), the staff was not generally used there until the 15th century. Smits van Waesberghe (1951) showed that references to lines in use at Corbie Abbey in the 10th century (*F-AM* 524; M. Gerbert: *De cantu et musica sacra*, St Blasien, 1774, ii, 61) and in the prologue of Odo's *Dialogus de musica* are both post-Guidonian.

Lines of different colours were not often used after the 13th century (German scribes again being the most conservative in this respect). Most surviving manuscripts have four-line staves (Guido did not specify a number), for which a four-nibbed pen would have been used. Often all four might be coloured red. These characteristics of chant books persisted into the age of printing and to the present day.

3. POLYPHONIC MUSIC. The more extended range of each voice in polyphonic music led to the general adoption of a five-line staff, as in *GB-Lbm* Add.36881 (*c*1200), where the lower part (with the chant) frequently has a four-line staff and the organal voice a five-line one (dry-point lines; see fig.2). The north

2. Four- and five-line staves (with dry-point lines) for the lower and organal parts in two-part polyphony, c1200 (GB-Lbm Add.36881, f.4r)

French sources of polyphony of the 13th century consistently use red or black five-line staves. Exceptions to a practice that has been standard ever since are the use of a six-line staff by scribes of Italian trecento music and a few later Italian-influenced repertories (*F-CH* 564, *I-Bc* Q15, *TRmr* 89), and the use of six or more lines for keyboard music (the florid upper line of the music of the Buxheim Organbook, *D-Mbs* Cim.352b, is written on a seven-line staff; *see* NOTATION, fig.108). Again, this was to cope with parts of generally more extended range. Occasionally the left hand had more lines than the right hand (Frescobaldi's *Toccate e partite d'intavolatura di cembalo*, 1614, left hand eight lines, right hand six; *see also* BAR, illustration). Frequently both had a middle C line (Fitzwilliam Virginal Book, *GB-Cfm* 32.g.29, two six-line staves). Staves of more than five lines were not generally used after the 17th century.

See also NOTATION, §III, 3(i), 4(v), and SCORE.

BIBLIOGRAPHY

J. Wolf: *Handbuch der Notationskunde* (Leipzig, 1913–19)
W. Apel: *The Notation of Polyphonic Music 900–1600* (Cambridge, Mass., 1942, rev. 5/1953/R1961)
J. Smits van Waesberghe: 'The Musical Notation of Guido of Arezzo', *MD*, v (1951), 15–53 [Eng. trans. of pp.47–85 of *De musicopaedagogico et theoretico Guidone Aretino*, 1953]
——: *Musikerziehung*, Musikgeschichte in Bildern, iii/3 (Leipzig, 1969)
B. Stäblein: *Schriftbild der einstimmigen Musik*, Musikgeschichte in Bildern, iii/4 (Leipzig, 1975)

DAVID HILEY

Staffa (It.). A TRIANGLE resembling a medieval stirrup.

Staffani, Agostino. *See* STEFFANI, AGOSTINO.

Stage design. *See* OPERA, §VIII.

Staggins, Nicholas (*d* Windsor, 13 June 1700). He was granted the post of musician-in-ordinary at court as a violinist to date from Michaelmas 1670 by a warrant of December 1671, and warrants of January and June 1673 also granted him a post as flautist. He suddenly achieved prominence in 1674 on his appointment, from 29 September, as Master of the King's Musick in succession to Grabu, a post which he continued to hold under James II and William and Mary. In 1682 he became MusD of Cambridge, though he did not perform the customary exercise at the time. Some criticism of this caused him to perform it in 1684 and to have the fact and its consequence announced in the *London Gazette* (no.1945):

Dr Nicholas Staggins, who was some time since admitted to the degree of Dr. of music, being desirous to perform his exercise upon the first opportunity for the said degree, has acquitted himself so much to the satisfaction of the whole University this Commencement, that by a solemn vote they have constituted him to be a public professor of music there.

The Grace appointing him first professor of music at Cambridge is dated 2 July 1684. In 1686 he was described as of 'Little Chelsey in the parish of Kensington', from which address he wrote his will in 1690. He died at Windsor and was buried at St George's Chapel there. He was unmarried. A reference in *Tom Brown's Letters from the Dead to the Living* (London, 1700) suggests that Nicholas Staggins was bandy-legged, and even contemptuously regarded.

As a composer he is of no significance, and he held no composing appointment at court. His most important work was the music for the court masque *Calisto, or The Chaste Nymph* of 1675, which was extravagantly praised by the librettist, John Crowne, in the published edition of the words. Seven of the songs are in *GB-Lbm* Add.19759, and some of the dances, attributed to 'Sgr. Callisto', are in *EIRE-Dtc*. There are traces of three odes for the birthday of William III, the words of two of which were printed in the *Gentleman's Journal* for 1693 and 1694, while the *London Gazette* in March 1697 referred to his 'Consort of Musick . . . which was performed at St James on His Majesty's Birthday' – presumably in November 1696. One air from the 1693 ode was printed in *Comes amoris*, book 5 (1694), and the solo 'Song on the King's Birthday' in *GB-Lbm* Add.19759 may come from the 1696 ode. There are 11 songs by Staggins in the printed collections of the period, including the following to words found in the contemporary theatre (dates quoted are those of first performance, not publication): 'How unhappy a lover' (Dryden, *Conquest of Granada*, 1671); 'While Alexis lay pressed' (Dryden, *Marriage à la mode*, 1672); 'How pleasant is mutual love' (Shadwell, *Epsom Wells*, 1672); 'How severe is fate' and 'Let business no longer' (Lee, *Gloriana*, 1676); 'As Amoret with Phyllis sate' (words by Scrope) and 'When first Amintas' (Etheridge, *The Man of Mode*, 1676). A few fragmentary instrumental pieces survive in *GB-Lbm* and *Och*, and Playford's *Dancing Master* (1679) includes 'Staggin's Jig', presumably his work.

WATKINS SHAW

Stahel [Stahl], **Johann** (*fl* 2nd quarter of the 16th century). German composer. Possibly the son of Johann Stahel, a singer in Maximilian's court, he ranks among the lesser of the Reformation composers strongly influenced by Franco-Netherlands procedures. He is known principally from the publications of Georg Rhau. In most of his works (such as those in *Vesperarum precum*) the cantus firmus is presented simply and in long, isometric note values. The pieces for festal occasions are in a more florid and imitative style; in these the cantus firmus is frequently ornamented.

WORKS

Editions: *G. Rhau: Newe deudsche geistliche Gesenge*, ed. J. Wolf, DDT, 1st ser., xxxiv (1908) [W]
    G. Rhau: Vesperarum precum officia, ed. H. J. Moser, Musikdrucke aus den Jahren 1538 bis 1545 in praktischer Neuausgabe, 1st ser., iv (Kassel, 1960) [M]

Missa super 'Winken ghy syt grone', 4vv, 1541[1]
Benedictus qui venit, 2vv, 1549[16]
Motets: In pace, in id ipsum dormiam, 5vv, 1568[7]; Oblatus est quia ipse voluit, 4vv, 1538[1]; Quam pulchra es, 4vv, *D-Rp* 940–41; Unam pety a Domino, 4vv, *RP* 940–41
39 antiphons, 4vv, M
Hymns, 4vv: Ne mens gravata, M 70; Veni Redemptor omnium, *D-ERu* 473, *ROu* Mus.Saec. XVI
Chorales: Nu lasst uns den Leib begraben, 5vv, 1544[21], W 182; Vater unser im Himmelreich, 4vv, W 75
Polyphonic songs: Ich wil zu Land ausreiten, 2vv, 1545[6]; Unser liebe Frawe vom kalten brunnen, 5vv, 1556[29]

BIBLIOGRAPHY

L. Hoffmann-Erbrecht: 'Das Opus musicum des Jacob Praetorius von 1566', *AcM*, xxviii (1956), 96

V. H. Mattfeld: *Georg Rhaw's Publications for Vespers* (Brooklyn, 1966)

VICTOR H. MATTFELD

Stählin, Jacob von (*b* Memmingen, Swabia, 9 May 1709; *d* St Petersburg, 25 June 1785). German historian and writer. He was educated at the Lateinschule in Memmingen and after 1728 at the Gymnasium in Zittau; here he also studied privately with a certain Montallegro, an Italian master of fireworks display. In 1732 he entered Leipzig University, and during this period became a friend of J. S. Bach's sons, playing flute duets with them. He was also a member of the circle surrounding the most famous literary critic of the day, J. C. Gottsched. His career as fireworks designer and professor of poetry and rhetoric took him in 1735 to Russia, where he held numerous positions in St Petersburg and at the imperial court. He edited a fortnightly German-language journal in St Petersburg, where he reported extensively on court activities and introduced a wide variety of materials related to the German Enlightenment. His *Original-Anekdoten Peters des Grossen* (1785) was known throughout Europe in various translations. His detailed accounts of cultural life in Russia and at court are the earliest historical documents for Russian theatre, music and dance. His *Nachrichten von der Musik in Russland* was published in J. J. Haigold: *Beylagen zum neuveränderten Russland* (Riga and Leipzig, 1769–70); see also *Muzïka i balet v Rossii XVIII veka*, translated from German (Leningrad, 1935).

BIBLIOGRAPHY

K. Stählin: 'Jacob von Stählin: ein biographischer Beitrag zur deutsch-russischen Kulturgeschichte des 18. Jahrhunderts', *Quellen und Aufsätze zur russischen Geschichte*, i (Leipzig, n.d.)

R.-A. Mooser: *Annales de la musique et des musiciens en Russie au XVIIIme siècle* (Geneva, 1948–51)

GEORGE J. BUELOW

Stahlspiel (Ger.). (1) BELL-LYRA.
　(2) [Stahlstäbe] GLOCKENSPIEL.

Staimitz. *See* STAMITZ family.

Stainer, Jacob [Jakob] (*b* Absam, nr. Hall, Tyrol, ?1617; *d* Absam, late Oct or early Nov 1683). Austrian violin maker. He received a good education as a chorister (serving in either a church choir – perhaps in Hall –

Violin by Jacob Stainer, Absam, Tyrol, c1670 (private collection)

or the Innsbruck court chapel); surviving letters from later years suggest he was a well-educated man. He is traditionally said to have learnt his craft in Cremona, but he was in fact apprenticed to a German violin maker resident in Italy. He based his style on an earlier German model, developing it to perfection. Hart wrote: 'I am satisfied that Stainer was assisted by neither the Brothers Amati nor Nicholas Amati, and I am strengthened in this opinion by the steadfastly German character of a model which no pupil of Amati could have persisted in using'. His oldest known violin is dated Absam, 1638.

Until 1655 Stainer made visits to monasteries, church choirs and court chapels in order to sell instruments and carry out repairs; his travels took him to Salzburg, Munich, Venice, Brixen, Bozen and elsewhere. In 1656 he acquired a house in Absam. Ferdinand Karl, the reigning prince of Tyrol, appointed him 'archprince's servant' (i.e. purveyor to the court) in 1658; this was not a salaried position, but involved promotion to the rank of a court employee. Meanwhile, he had become so well known that he was receiving commissions by post; about 1658 he carried out a commission for the Spanish court. A denunciation for suspected heresy in 1669, though hotly denied by Stainer, brought him into conflict with the Church. At that time, he had commissions for instruments from Italy, Nuremberg, the monasteries at Rottenbuch and Lambach and from the Bishop of Olomouc. From about 1675 he suffered from bouts of temporary insanity, probably acute manic depression, but in succeeding years he created some of his finest instruments, surpassing even the best products of his middle period. His last violin is dated 1682 (now in the Tiroler Landes-Museum Ferdinandeum, Innsbruck).

Besides violins, Stainer also made alto and tenor viols, cellos and double basses; for tenor gambas, he used as his model an English instrument by the virtuoso William Young, who was employed at the Innsbruck court from 1651 to 1662. Distinctive features of his violins are the relatively broad lower back and the modified contour of the corners at the waist. At first he worked with a highly arched model, but after about 1665 he also made rather less arched instruments. The wood and varnish are of the best quality, and the accuracy of his craftsmanship ranks close to Stradivari's. The silvery tone (*voce argentina*) of the Stainer violin was regarded as ideal for more than 150 years; literary sources confirm the high esteem in which his instruments were held, even in comparison with those of the Cremona masters. Hawkins, for example, wrote: 'The violins of Cremona are exceeded only by those of Stainer ... whose instruments are remarkable for a full and piercing tone'. The *Encyclopédie méthodique* states that 'the violins with the greatest reputation are those of Jacob Steiner'. And Stainer heads a list of distinguished violin makers compiled by Francesco Galeazzi. For a long time his model influenced violin making not only in German areas, but also in Italy (where only Brescia and Cremona stuck to their own tradition) as well as several other countries. Distinguished copiers included Gabrielli, Gobetti, the Caracassi brothers, Stadlmann, Widhalm and William Forster (ii). There are countless instruments that contain a forged label with Stainer's name, and even standard works, such as those by Lütgendorff, Vannes and Hamma include illustrations of labels that have proved to be forgeries. Towards the end of the 18th century there was a change in what was considered to be the ideal tone, and the smooth, clarinet-like timbre, characteristic of the instruments of the Cremona school, began to be preferred. Further, the greater volume obtainable from a Cremona instrument could meet the demands now made of the violin in concert-hall performance. During the 19th century the Cremona violin completely superseded the Absam, though Stainer's instruments still have a special value for historic performances.

A Markus [Marcus] Stainer (*b* Hallein, Salzburg, *c*1633; *d* Laufen, Upper Bavaria, 27 Nov 1693), an Austrian violin maker and player often described as Jacob's brother, was not in fact related to him. In 1655 he applied for citizenship at Laufen, granted in 1656. His few known instruments are unusually fine and are signed 'Marcus Stainer, Bürger und Geigenmacher in Kufstein'; there is no record of a violin maker of this name in Kufstein, however.

BIBLIOGRAPHY

HawkinsH

Encyclopédie méthodique: arts et métiers mécaniques, iv (Paris, 1785), 23

F. Galeazzi: *Elementi teorico-pratici di musica*, i (Rome, 1791), 80

G. Hart: *The Violin, its Famous Makers and their Imitators* (London, 1875)

P. O. Apian-Bennewitz: *Die Geige, der Geigenbau und die Bogenverfertigung* (Weimar, 1892)

P. de Wit: *Geigenzettel alter Meister* (Leipzig, 1902, 2/1910)

W. L. von Lütgendorff: *Die Geigen- und Lautenmacher vom Mittelalter bis zur Gegenwart* (Frankfurt am Main, 1904, rev. 6/1922/R1968)

R. Vannes: *Essai d'un dictionnaire universel des luthiers* (Paris, 1932, 2/1951/R1972 as *Dictionnaire universel des luthiers*, suppl. 1959)

F. Hamma: *Meister deutscher Geigenbaukunst* (Stuttgart, 1948, 2/1961)

I. G. Cozio di Salabue: *Carteggio*, ed. R. Bacchetta (Milan, 1950)

W. Senn: *J. Stainer, der Geigenmacher zu Absam: die Lebensgeschichte nach urkundlichen Quellen* (Innsbruck, 1951)

W. Henley: *Universal Dictionary of Violin and Bow Makers*, ed. C. Woodcock (Brighton, Sussex, 1959–60)

WALTER SENN

Stainer, Sir John (*b* London, 6 June 1840; *d* Verona, 31 March 1901). English musicologist and composer. His father, William Stainer, was parish schoolmaster of St Thomas, Southwark, and had a small chamber organ on which he gave the boy lessons from an early age. John lost the sight of his left eye through an accident when he was five years old. In 1848 he became a probationer and in 1849 a chorister at St Paul's Cathedral, where he was soon one of the leading solo boys. In 1854 he became organist of St Benedict and St Peter, Paul's Wharf; two years later Ouseley heard him deputizing at the organ at St Paul's and promptly offered him the post of organist at his recently founded College of St Michael, Tenbury; Stainer used to ascribe his later success to Ouseley's guidance during his years at Tenbury.

He entered Christ Church, Oxford, in 1859, and graduated BMus (1860), BA (1864), DMus (1865) and MA (1866). In 1860 he was appointed organist of Magdalen College and in 1861 organist to the university. He founded the Oxford Philharmonic Society and conducted its first concert in 1866. His supreme opportunity came in 1872, when he succeeded Goss as organist of St Paul's Cathedral. Long overdue reforms had been begun through the efforts of a minor canon, Robert Gregory; Stainer hastened them by means of tactful persuasion. The number and salaries of the choir were increased; rehearsals, processions, and weekly choral celebrations of communion were soon introduced. The musical repertory was greatly expanded and altered. Stainer soon gained a pre-eminent position as church musician, scholar and composer. In 1874 he helped Ouseley found the Musical Association. In 1876 he became organist and in 1881 principal of the National Training School for Music. He was knighted in 1888, but in the same year had to resign his position at St Paul's because of failing eyesight. In 1889 he returned to Oxford as professor of music. He was also vice-president of the Royal College of Organists, and president of the Musical Association, the Plainsong and Mediaeval Music Society and the London Gregorian Association. He died suddenly while on a visit to Italy.

In his lifetime and for a considerable period after his death, Stainer was known primarily as a composer of cathedral music. His services and anthems, most of them written for St Paul's, were fashionable throughout the Anglican communion and beyond it. They are superficially attractive, but their melodic and harmonic resourcefulness is spoilt by an inadequate sense of rhythm and accent: Stainer's fine literary feeling in his choice of texts was not matched by an ability to set them appropriately to music. He himself came to regret that he had published his compositions, and said to Fellowes that he knew they were 'rubbish'; they have been so judged by the severe critics of more recent times. Nevertheless, a few works remain favourites: *The Crucifixion* is usually broadcast every Passiontide, the *Sevenfold Amen* closes many an English country service and several of the hymn tunes can be heard in churches of almost every denomination.

Today Stainer is venerated not as a composer but as a pioneer of English musicology. His edition of *Early Bodleian Music*, completed shortly before his death, was the first serious effort by an English scholar to explore music before Palestrina and Tallis. Also of value is his edition, with the Rev. H. R. Bramley, of Christmas carols. His professorial lectures at Oxford, and his papers to the Musical Association (six of which are printed in *PMA*), were excellent models for younger scholars, often venturing into almost unexplored musical territory. Stainer was a noted collector of music, specializing in 18th-century songbooks. His elder daughter, Eliza Cecilia, who helped him with *Early Bodleian Music*, published a *Dictionary of Violin Makers* (London, 1896/R1977), and contributed, along with her father and a brother, John F. R. Stainer, to earlier editions of *Grove*.

WORKS
(all printed works published in London)

Gideon, oratorio, Oxford, 1865 (1875)
The Daughter of Jairus, cantata, Worcester Festival, 1878 (1878)
St Mary Magdalen (W. J. Sparrow-Simpson), cantata, Gloucester Festival, 1887 (1883)
Jubilee, cantata (1887)
The Crucifixion (Sparrow-Simpson), oratorio, St Marylebone Parish Church, 24 Feb 1887 (1887)
The Story of the Cross (E. Monro), cantata (1893)

3 communion services: A (1865), F (1887), C (1901)
2 evening services: E (1870), D, male vv (1898)
3 full services: E♭ (1874), A/D (1877), B♭ (1884)
12 Sacred Songs (E. Oxenford) (1893)
Benedicite, D (1894)
4 chant services (1895–7)
Sevenfold Amen (1897) [arr. of Dresden Amen]
[150] Hymn Tunes (1900)
*c*40 anthems, org works, madrigals, partsongs, songs

EDITIONS
with H. R. Bramley: *Christmas Carols, New and Old* (London, 1871)
with S. Flood Jones and others: *The Cathedral Psalter* (London, 1874)
Six Italian Songs (London, 1896)
The Church Hymnary (Edinburgh, 1898)
with J. F. R. and E. C. Stainer: *Early Bodleian Music* (London and New York, 1901/R1967)

with W. H. Frere and H. B. Briggs: *A Manual of Plainsong* (London, 1902)

WRITINGS
A Theory of Harmony (London, 1871)
with W. A. Barrett: *A Dictionary of Musical Terms* (London, 1876)
The Organ (London, 1877)
Music of the Bible, with an Account of the Development of Modern Musical Instruments from Ancient Types (London, 1879, 2/1914 with suppl. by F. W. Galpin)
Music in Relation to the Intellect and Emotions (London, 1892)
Dufay and his Contemporaries (London, 1898/R1963)

BIBLIOGRAPHY
W. S. Simpson: *A Year's Music in St Paul's Cathedral*, i–viii (London, 1879–86)
[C. Stainer, ed.:] *Catalogue of English Song Books, forming a Portion of the Library of Sir John Stainer* (London, 1891/R1977)
F. G. Edwards: 'John Stainer', *MT*, xlii (1901), 297
W. G. McNaught: 'Some Reminiscences of the Late Sir John Stainer', *RAM Magazine*, no.4 (1901), 1
——: 'Stainer, Sir John', *DNB*
E. H. Fellowes: 'Sir John Stainer', *English Church Music*, xxi (1951), 4
A. H. King: *Some British Collectors of Music c1600–1960* (Cambridge, 1963)
B. Rainbow: *The Choral Revival in the Anglican Church 1839–1872* (London, 1970)
P. Charlton: *The Life and Influence of Sir John Stainer* (diss., U. of East Anglia, 1976)

NICHOLAS TEMPERLEY

Stainer, Markus. Austrian violin maker, formerly thought to be a brother of JACOB STAINER.

Stainer & Bell. London music publishing firm. It was founded in 1907 by a group of composers as an outlet for British compositions (the names 'Stainer' and 'Bell' were chosen merely for euphony). The firm's reputation was quickly established, and it published the later music of Stanford, as well as works by Holst (*Hymn of Jesus*, 1919), Vaughan Williams (*A Sea Symphony*, 1918; *London Symphony*, 1920), Bantock and Boughton. In 1917 it was appointed by the Carnegie Trust to publish the Carnegie Collection of British Music. Since then the firm has undertaken the publication of several major scholarly series, notably E. H. Fellowes's editions of the English Madrigal School (1913–24), the Complete Works of William Byrd (1937–50), and the English School of Lutenist Song Writers (1920–31), which was taken over from the firm of Winthrop Rogers in 1924. Revised editions of all three series were published under the supervision of Thurston Dart, musical adviser to the firm from 1953 until his death in 1971. In 1951 the firm was entrusted with the publication of the Musica Britannica series for the Royal Musical Association, and a further important series, Early English Church Music, has been published for the British Academy since 1963. In addition the firm has published many sheet editions in its series Choral Library, Church Choir Library, Unison Songs, Organ Library, and Modern Church Services, all originally devoted to new works by British composers and latterly noted for fine editions of older music. In February 1971 the firm entered a partnership with GALLIARD LTD; with its purchase of that firm in November 1972 titles published by AUGENER, JOSEPH WILLIAMS and Joseph Weekes entered the catalogue. In 1968 Bernard Braley became the firm's managing director, succeeding his grandfather Ellis R. Howard (1920–48) and father Arthur E. Braley (1948–57). In 1978 Allen Percival became editorial director.

PETER WARD JONES

Staingaden, Constantin. *See* STEINGADEN, CONSTANTIN.

Stalder, Joseph Franz Xaver Dominik (*b* Lucerne, baptized 29 March 1725; *d* Lucerne, 4 Jan 1765). Swiss composer. After attending the Jesuit college in Lucerne he studied moral theology in Milan (1748–9) and also took up composition. In 1750, again in Milan, he became a pupil of Sammartini and Galimberti, at the recommendation of Meyer von Schauensee. In 1752 he was appointed provisor at St Leodegar monastery, Lucerne. In the following year, however, he moved to London, and in 1754 to Paris, where he began a productive career as a composer and as a conductor with the Prince of Monaco and the Prince of Conti. Probably of a sickly disposition, he returned to St Leodegar monastery in 1762 with a prebendary organist's post. As an instrumental composer Stalder stands between his Swiss contemporaries Meyer von Schauensee and Constantin Reindl. Saladin listed 48 symphonies by him which appeared in Paris between 1757 and 1759; the few of these that are extant show a remarkable freshness of style, particularly in their first movements.

WORKS

Dramatic (mostly written for Jesuit Theatre, Lucerne; all lost): Hans und Trini (operetta, 2); incidental music to: Marienspiel, 1745, Froyla, 1748, Athemenes Cretensis, 1749, Henricus Calvensis, 1751, Zeleux der König von Lokrien, incl. Der Einsiedler (Singspiel, 2)

Sacred vocal (all in *CH-E*): Magnificat, 4vv, insts, 1757; In te Domine speravi (Ps lxxi), 4vv, insts, org; In exitu Israel (Ps cxiv), 4vv, org

Syms.: 6 sonate a 3 con tutti l'orchestra, op.4, lost; 6 for 4 str (Paris, n.d.); 6 a 4, hns ad lib (Paris, n.d.); 6 simphonies italiennes, 4 str, hns ad lib, op.5 (Paris, n.d.) [also pubd as 6 simphonies à 4 (Paris, n.d.)]; 6 a 4, with hns (Paris, ?1759); 12 a 4, with hns, ?lost; 8 a 6, *F-Pc*; Sinfonia, *CH-EN*

Other inst: Ov., *Zz*; Fl Conc., *EN*; 6 str qts (London, c1770); 6 trio concertati, 2 vn, b, op.2 (Paris, n.d.), lost; Pf Sonata, *E*

BIBLIOGRAPHY

J. A. Saladin: *Die Musikpflege am Stift St. Leodegar in Luzern* (Stans, 1948), 65f, 91ff [incl. list of works]

W. Jerger: *Constantin Reindl (1738–1799)* (Fribourg, 1955); also in *Der Geschichtsfreund*, cvii–cviii (1954–5)

——: 'Zur Musikgeschichte der deutschsprachigen Schweiz im 18. Jahrhundert', *Mf*, xiv (1961), 303

WILHELM JERGER

Stamaty, Camille (Marie) (*b* Rome, 13 or 23 March 1811; *d* Paris, 19 April 1870). Graeco-French pianist, composer and teacher. He was the son of a Greek father and a musical French mother. After the death of his father in 1818 his mother returned to France, lived for some time at Dijon and eventually went to Paris. There Stamaty studied literature and, after long fluctuation between music and business as a profession, took a post in the Prefecture of the Seine in 1828. But music retained its hold on him, and under A. C. Fessy and Frédéric Kalkbrenner (from about 1830) he became a remarkable pianist. An attack of rheumatism forced him from playing to the study of composition. In March 1835, however, he made his first public appearance, playing a programme that included a concerto and other pieces of his composition. This led to his being much sought after as a teacher. In September 1836 he went to Leipzig where he studied briefly with Mendelssohn. He returned to Paris early in 1837 and introduced much more classical music – Bach, Mozart, Beethoven – into his programmes. In 1848 he married; in 1862 he was made a Chevalier of the Légion d'honneur. His pupils included Gottschalk and Saint-Saëns.

Stamaty's best-known works are educational; his *L'école du pianiste classique et moderne* (Paris, 1854–62) is a five-part set containing many transcriptions (of works by Rameau, Haydn, Mozart, Beethoven and others) and several volumes of studies. His Piano Concerto in A minor op.2, Piano Trio op.12, piano sonatas and other works (running to at least op.48 and including many salon pieces and some *airs*) were much esteemed by his contemporaries. The concerto and some brilliant variations on an original theme (op.3) were reviewed favourably by Schumann.

BIBLIOGRAPHY

FétisB

R. Schumann: *Gesammelte Schriften über Musik und Musiker* (Leipzig, 1854, 5/1914/*R*1969, ed. M. Kreisig; Eng. trans., 1877)

GEORGE GROVE/R

Stamegna [Stamigna], **Nicolò** [Nicolaus] (*b* Spello, nr. Perugia, c1615; *d* Loreto, 13 Sept 1685). Italian composer. He was a priest. From 1635 to 1638 he was *maestro di cappella* of Spoleto Cathedral and then, according to Pitoni, held a similar post at Fabriano. On 6 June 1639 he was named organist at the collegiate church of S Maria Maggiore, Spello, but had left by 10 September 1639. He was *maestro di cappella* at Orvieto Cathedral until 1658 and then at Perugia (according to Pomponi). On 31 January 1659 he took up the post of *maestro di cappella* at S Maria Maggiore, Rome, and then moved to S Giacomo degli Spagnoli, where he remained from 1667 to 1684. In 1670 he described himself as a canon, and on 17 October 1682 he obtained a benefice at Spello. According to Tebaldini and Schmidl he was *maestro di cappella* in Rome at the Cappella del Gesù and the Seminario Romano, both from 1665, but this may stem from a misreading of Gaspari (1892). On 14 July 1684 he went to the Santa Casa, Loreto, and remained there until his death.

Stamegna's *Sacrae modulationes* shows characteristics of the early concertato motet, while the pieces in his *Sacri concentus* of 33 years later are more akin to true sacred cantatas. His stylistic development cannot be traced in detail because of the apparent large gap in his production from the late 1630s to the 1660s. In 1665 he produced a new edition of Guidetti's *Directorium chori*, occasioned by changes in the Roman Breviary made by Pope Urban VIII. Pitoni listed him in his *Guida armonica* (MS, *I-Rvat*, c1685) and used an extract from one of his two-voice motets to illustrate a point of contrapuntal technique.

WORKS

Sacrarum modulationum, liber 1, 2–4vv (Rome, 1637)

Sacrorum concentuum, liber 1, 2–4vv (Rome, 1670)

Motets, psalms, 1–4vv, bc: 1662², 1664¹, 1665¹, 1667¹, 1668¹, 1672¹, 1683¹

Missa, 12vv, org, *I-Rsg*, *Rvat*

S Tomaso d'Aquina (S. Lazarini), oratorio, lost [text pubd Rome, 1678]

Messa 'Benedicamus Domino', 5, 9vv, insts, lost [catalogued in MS inventory of a Roman church in *Bc*, bound with Gaspari's *Miscellanea musicale*]

Missa Febea, 16vv, *Rvat* [arr. by Stamegna of Carissimi's Missa 'L'homme armé', 12vv, see Feininger]

ed.: G. Guidetti: *Directorium chori* (Rome, 1665)

BIBLIOGRAPHY

SchmidlD

G. O. Pitoni: *Notitia de contrapuntisti e de compositori di musica* (MS, *I-Rvat* C.G., I/1–2, c1725)

G. Gaspari: *Catalogo della biblioteca del Liceo musicale di Bologna*, ii (Bologna, 1892/*R*1969), 352

——: *Miscellanea musicale* (MS, *I-Bc* UU.12), iii, between pp.493 and 494 [MS inventory]

G. Tebaldini: *L'archivio musicale della Cappella Lauretana* (Loreto, 1921)

L. Fausti: 'La cappella musicale della collegiata di S. Maria di Spello', *NA*, x (1933), 141f

R. Casimiri: ' "Disciplina musicae" e "mastri di cappella" ', *NA*, xv (1938), 101

L. Pomponi: 'Memorie musicali della collegiata di S. Maria Maggiore di Spello', *NA*, xvii (1940), 182ff, 197, 212

L. Feininger: 'La scuola policorale romana del Sei e Settecento', *CHM*, ii (1957), 193

J. M. Llorens: *Le opere musicali della Cappella Giulia*, i: *Manoscritti e edizioni fino al '700* (Vatican City, 1971)

JUDITH NAGLEY

Stamitz [Stamic]. Bohemian family of musicians. The family can be traced back to Marburg an der Drau in Styria (now Maribor, Yugoslavia). From there Martin Stamitz emigrated to the Bohemian town of Pardubice, where his name is first recorded in 1665. About 1710 Martin's son Antonín Ignác moved to Německý Brod, where he was appointed organist and choirmaster of the Dean's church and later became a wealthy landowner and town councillor. In 1714 he married Rozina (Rozyna) Boëm; the third of their 11 children was (1) Johann Stamitz.

The spelling of the name in contemporary sources is extraordinarily erratic, the most common variants being Stamiz, Steinmetz, Steinmez, Stammiz, Stametz, Stammitz, Staimitz, Stamits and Stammetz. Every known signature by a member of the family uses the form Stamitz, even in documents in which the language and the forms of the first names are Czech.

(1) Johann (Wenzel Anton) [Jan Waczlaw (Václav) Antonin (Antonín)] **Stamitz** (*b* Německý Brod [now Havlíčkův Brod], baptized 19 June 1717; *d* Mannheim, ?27 March, buried 30 March 1757). Composer, violinist and teacher. He ranks among the most important early Classical symphonists and was influential in making the court of the Elector Palatine at Mannheim a leading centre of orchestral performance and composition.

1. Life. 2. Works. 3. Problems of attribution.

1. LIFE. Stamitz received his early schooling in Německý Brod, though his first musical instruction doubtless came from his father. From 1728 to 1734 he attended the Jesuit Gymnasium in Jihlava; the Jesuits of Bohemia, whose pupils included the foremost musicians in Europe, maintained high standards of musical education during this period. Stamitz is known to have spent the following academic year, 1734–5, at Prague University. His activities during the next six years, however, remain a mystery. It seems logical to assume that his decision to leave the university was prompted by a desire to establish himself as a violin virtuoso, a goal that could be pursued in Prague, Vienna or countless other centres.

The precise circumstances surrounding Stamitz's engagement by the Mannheim court are unclear. The date of his appointment was probably 1741 (i.e. when he was 24), for he remarked in a letter of 29 February 1748 to Baron von Wallbrunn in Stuttgart that he was in his eighth year of service to the elector. The most likely hypothesis is that Stamitz's engagement resulted from contacts made late in 1741 during the Bohemian campaign and coronation in Prague of the Bavarian Elector Carl Albert (later Carl VII), one of whose closest allies was the Elector Palatine. In January 1742 Stamitz performed at Mannheim as part of the festivities surrounding the marriage of Carl Theodor, who succeeded his uncle Carl Philipp as Elector Palatine less than a year later; Carl Albert of Bavaria was a guest at the wedding. The earliest known reference to a public appearance by Stamitz occurs in an advertisement for a concert in Frankfurt am Main on 29 June 1742, at which he was to perform on the violin, viola d'amore, cello and double bass.

At Mannheim Stamitz advanced rapidly: in 1743, when he was first violinist at the court, he was granted an increase in salary of 200 gulden; in payment lists from 1744 and 1745 his salary is given as 900 gulden, the highest of any instrumentalist at Mannheim; in 1745 or 1746 he was evidently awarded the title of Konzertmeister; and in 1750 he was appointed to the newly created post of director of instrumental music. Stamitz's principal responsibilities at court were the composition and performance of orchestral and chamber music, although he may also have composed sacred music for the court chapel. As leader of the band and conductor Stamitz developed the Mannheim orchestra into the most renowned ensemble of the time, famous for its precision and its ability to render novel dynamic effects.

In 1744 Stamitz married Maria Antonia Lüneborn. They had five children: the composers (2) Carl and (3) Anton, a daughter Maria Francisca (1746–99) and two children who died in infancy. In 1749 Stamitz and his wife journeyed to Německý Brod to attend the installation of Stamitz's younger brother Antonín Tadeáš as dean of the Dean's church. In February 1750, while the family was still in Bohemia, Stamitz's brother Václav Jan (*b* 1724; *d* after 1771), also a musician, was in Mannheim. Johann Stamitz returned to Mannheim in March 1750, but his wife remained temporarily in Německý Brod, where (3) Anton Stamitz was born on 27 November 1750.

In late summer 1754 Stamitz undertook a year-long journey to Paris, appearing there for the first time at the Concert Spirituel on 8 September 1754. (At least one work by Stamitz, a symphony with horns, trumpets and timpani, had already been performed in Paris, at the Concert Spirituel on 12 April 1751.) While in Paris Stamitz lived at Passy in the palace of A.-J.-J. Le Riche de la Pouplinière, a wealthy amateur whose private orchestra he conducted. He was also active in public concerts in Paris, appearing with particular success at the Concert Italien. Performances of his compositions were frequent, and his Mass was given on 4 August 1755. Stamitz's success in Paris induced him to publish his 'orchestral trios' op.1, for which he received a royal privilege on 29 August 1755, and possibly also to plan further publications with various Parisian houses. He probably returned to Mannheim in autumn 1755, dying there less than two years later at the age of 39.

2. WORKS. Stamitz's most important compositions are his symphonies, some 58 of which are extant, and his ten orchestral trios. The latter works, though frequently classed as symphonies, actually occupy a position midway in style between the symphony and chamber trio, and may be played with or without doubling of parts. Stamitz was also a prolific composer of concertos. These include, in addition to his numerous violin concertos, at least two for harpsichord (only one of which can be identified with certainty), 11 for flute, one for oboe, and one for clarinet, possibly the earliest solo concerto for that instrument. He also composed a large amount of chamber music for various instrumental combinations, as well as eight vocal works, including his widely circulated Mass in D.

Owing to the complete lack of autograph manuscripts

and the extreme paucity of dated sources, firm conclusions cannot yet be drawn about Stamitz's evolution as a composer. His pre-Mannheim compositions probably comprise several of the extant symphonies for strings alone and most of the eight lost symphonies listed in a thematic catalogue from Brtnice (Pirnitz) in Moravia. Certain of his chamber works and concertos may also have originated from this period, providing him with material for use in performance, as may many of the vocal works that still survive in Czech collections. However, the great majority of his compositions obviously date from after his arrival in Mannheim. The somewhat conservative style of most of the concertos and sonatas, together with evidence regarding the chronology of his orchestral trios and advanced symphonies, suggests that Stamitz's interest gradually shifted away from the composition of music intended for his personal use as a performer to the substantially different stylistic demands of the symphony and orchestral trio.

The principal innovation in Stamitz's symphonic works is their adoption of the cycle of four movements, with a minuet and trio in third place followed by a Presto or Prestissimo. While isolated precedents for this succession exist, Stamitz was the first composer to use it consistently: well over half of his symphonies, and nine of his ten orchestral trios, are in four movements. The chief exceptions among the symphonies are the three-movement works characteristic of his early period (to c1745–8).

Stamitz's early symphonies and most of his concertos are scored for strings alone or for strings and two horns. His more advanced symphonies generally call for a pair of horns and either oboes, flutes or (in several late works) clarinets, to which on five occasions he added a pair of trumpets and timpani. In conjunction with this expansion of the orchestra Stamitz gradually began to give more distinctive treatment to the wind instruments, for example handling them as sustaining instruments capable of providing a chordal background and support for the strings. The late symphonies place considerable emphasis upon striking dynamic effects, most notably the crescendo. Extended crescendo passages, almost certainly modelled on those of Nicolò Jommelli, occur in 14 of Stamitz's symphonies, primarily works in his most advanced (and familiar) style. Stamitz's treatment of orchestration and dynamics, combined with his forceful and vigorous rhythmic drive, represented a decisive new phase for the style of the concert symphony: the approach became manifestly orchestral rather than relying upon Baroque concerto style or the *galant* chamber idiom. Yet neither Stamitz nor the other Mannheim composers actually invented this style; it had already characterized a large number of Italian opera overtures from about 1730 to 1755 by such composers as Vinci, Leo, Jommelli and Galuppi, works that were staples of the operatic repertory at Mannheim during the 1740s and 1750s. In the process of adaptation, however, Stamitz unquestionably extended and deepened every element of the overture style. For instance he often introduced conspicuous passages for solo woodwind or horns in the first movements of all but his early symphonies, a rarity in the Italian opera overture of the time.

Stamitz's phrase structure shows a gradual expansion from an early hierarchy based on half-bar motifs and two-bar phrases (in 4/4 metre and *allegro* tempo) to a mature one containing most of the essentials of later Classical phrase syntax, founded on four-bar phrases, eight-bar sentences or periods and 16-bar double periods. On a larger scale, the structure of the individual movements of Stamitz's symphonies and orchestral trios has its basis in binary form, frequently modified in the later works by omission of the central double bar (and consequently of the repeats) and expansion of the second half of the movement. Thematic development of the type usually associated with later composers appears in Stamitz's symphonies from every period. By contrast, he never consistently employed the principle of full recapitulation, although enough examples of this procedure exist to demonstrate his awareness of its pos-

1. Johann Stamitz: engraving from the frontispiece of 'L'art du violon' (1789) by Jean Baptiste Cartier

sibilities. Perhaps by way of compensation, most of Stamitz's first movements among his later works return towards the end of the movement to thematic material originally presented near the beginning. This material normally consists of a crescendo passage, but in a few instances the primary theme itself recurs. The occasional appearance of primary material near the end of a movement has sometimes given rise to the belief that Stamitz and the other Mannheimers normally used 'reversed' or 'mirror' recapitulations. That is not statistically accurate; nor does it take account of the fact that the reorganization of the recapitulations in Stamitz's advanced first movements nearly always amounts to far more than the mere reversal of primary and secondary themes, which represents only one of many types of recapitulation procedures in his symphonies.

Although Stamitz's slow movements, dance movements and early finales are mostly homogeneous in style, the expositions of his first movements and more advanced finales regularly introduce contrasting thematic material – including, in just over half of these movements, a clearly articulated and differentiated secondary theme. This approach also originated in the Italian opera overture, which had used polythematic expositions since at least the 1730s. Once again, though, Stamitz went well beyond his model, often scoring his secondary themes for wind and, in his late works, increasing their lyricism substantially.

In sum, Stamitz's contribution in the particular areas of thematic differentiation, orchestration and dynamics may be defined as the transfer and adaptation of Italian overture style to the concert symphony, rather than as actual innovation. Charles Burney, writing some 15 years after Stamitz's death, stated this viewpoint:

It was here [in concerts at Mannheim] that Stamitz, stimulated by the productions of Jomelli, first surpassed the bounds of common opera overtures, which had hitherto only served in the theatre as a kind of court cryer, with an 'O Yes' in order to awaken attention, and bespeak silence, at the entrance of the singers.

To recognize Stamitz's debt to Italian overture style is not to belittle his achievement, for in the process of adaptation he greatly enriched and refined every element of that style; but it enables Stamitz's symphonies to be placed in a more valid historical context than that proposed by Riemann and others. Moreover, the imagination, vitality and craftsmanship evident in Stamitz's symphonies and orchestral trios were rarely surpassed by either contemporary symphonists or his more stylized followers at Mannheim. To quote Burney again:

He [Stamitz], like another Shakespeare, broke through all difficulties and discouragements; and, as the eye of one pervaded all nature, the other, without quitting nature, pushed art further than any one had done before him; his genius was truly original, bold, and nervous; invention, fire, and contrast, in the quick movements; a tender, graceful, and insinuating melody, in the slow; together with the ingenuity and richness of the accompaniments, characterise his productions; all replete with great effects, produced by an enthusiasm of genius, refined, but not repressed by cultivation.

3. PROBLEMS OF ATTRIBUTION. Because at least five other musicians of the 18th century bore the surname Stamitz – four from Stamitz's immediate family – and because few manuscripts of the time supplied first names, any attempt to enumerate Stamitz's authentic works is hazardous at best, particularly in view of the many variations in spelling. The relationship of the names 'Steinmetz' and 'Stamitz' has caused particular confusion, as at least two other musicians called 'Steinmetz' lived in the 18th century. The list of works below includes most of those compositions attributed in the sources to 'Steinmetz', because, first, the two names were constantly interchanged in the 18th century, as seen both in the numerous references to Stamitz (even at Mannheim) in the form 'Steinmetz' and in the large number of works indisputably by Johann Stamitz attributed to 'Steinmetz' in concordant sources; second, the notion that Johann Erhard Steinmetz, an oboe player in the Dresden hunting band, was a composer of symphonies derives primarily from J. G. I. Breitkopf, whose reliability on this point is demonstrably low; and third, analysis of the style of those works ascribed to 'Steinmetz' for which no concordant sources exist generally reveals an unmistakable connection to authentic works of Johann Stamitz in his relatively unfamiliar early style.

WORKS

All printed works were published in Paris unless otherwise stated. For thematic catalogue see Gradenwitz: *Johann Stamitz*, ii; the symphonies and orchestral trios have also been catalogued with incipits by Riemann (DTB, iv, Jg.iii/1, 1902/*R*) and Wolf (1972), and the chamber music by Riemann (DTB, xxviii, Jg.xvi, 1915/*R*).

ORCHESTRAL

Syms.: 6 as op.2 (1757), reissued as op.3 (1757), 2 ed. in DTB, iv, Jg.iii/1 (1902); 4 [and 2 orch trios] as op.4 (1758), 1 ed. in DTB, xiii, Jg.vii/2 (1906); 2 [and orch trio] in Six symphonies . . . de différents auteurs, op.5 (1759), 1 ed. in DTB, xiii, Jg.vii/2 (1906); 6 as op.7 (1763); 6 as op.8 (1763) [1 by F. X. Richter, ed. in DTB, iv, Jg.iii/1 (1902)]; 3 as op.11 (*c*1771–2) [first pubd in VI sinfonie . . . intitolate

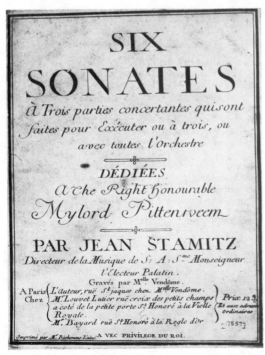

2. Title-page and first page of music from Johann Stamitz, 'Six Sonates à trois parties concertantes' (Orchestral Trios, op.1; Paris: Author, 1755)

La melodia germanica . . . da vari autori, op.11 (1758)], 1 ed. in
DTB, iv, Jg.iii/1 (1902), 1 ed. in DTB, xiii, Jg.vii/2 (1906); 1 as
Simphonie périodique, pubd La Chevardière no.12 (1760); 1 as
Simphonia, pubd Huberty no.9 (1762); 30 in MS, incl. *A-LA, ST,
Wgm, B-Bc, CH-Bu, CS-Pnm, D-Bds, DO, DS, HR, Rtt, SWl,
S-Skma, US-Wc*, 2 ed. in Corona, xxxviii (1957)
10 orch trios: 6 sonates à 3 parties concertantes, 2 vn, bc, op.1 (1755),
ed. in Collegium musicum, i–vi (Leipzig, 1903), 1 ed. in DTB, iv, Jg.
iii/1 (1902); 1 in VI sinfonie . . . da vari autori, op.9 (1757), ed. in
Collegium musicum, xlix (Leipzig, 1911); 2 in Six symphonies, op.4
(1758), 1 ed. in Collegium musicum, xlviii (Leipzig, 1911); 1 in Six
symphonies . . . de différents auteurs, op.5 (1759), ed. in Collegium
musicum, vii (Leipzig, 1904)
Concs.: 6 for vn (*c*1764), 3 lost; 11 for vn, *A-ST, CS-K, D-Dlb, DO,
EB* (arr. va), *S-Skma, US-Wc*; 1 for fl (London, *c*1770); 10 for fl, *A-
LA, CH-EN, D-KA, Rtt, RH, F-Pc*, 1 ed. W. Lebermann, EDM, 1st
ser., li (1964); 1 for ob, 1 for cl, *D-Rtt*; ?4 for kbd in Six Concertos . . .
by J. Stamitz (London, *c*1775) [no.1, D (The Hague, *c*1767), no.4 by
J. J. Agrell, no.6 by J. G. Lang], probably incl. 2 hpd concs. listed by
La Chevardière (*c*1763–4)
Other orch: 2 pastorellas, *Rtt*; 12 minuets, 13 polonaises, *A-Wn, CS-
TR*, doubtful

CHAMBER

Trios: 6 for vn, fl, bc (n.d.); 1 for vn, fl, bc, *B-Bc*; 4 for 2 vn, bc, *CS-
Pnm, D-DS, KA, S-Skma*; 2 for 2 fl, bc, *B-Bc, D-HR*; 1 for ob, vn,
bc, *US-Wc*
Sonatas: 6 sonate da camera, vn, bc, op.6 (*c*1759) [also as 6 Solos
(London, *c*1767)], 1 ed. in DTB, xxviii, Jg.xvi (1915); 2 for vn, bc, *B-
Bc, F-Pc*; 6 for vc, bc, *D-SWl*, doubtful; ?1 for vn, hpd (London,
*c*1770), also attrib. C. H. Graun, J. G. Neruda
Other chamber: 2 divertissements en duo, vn solo (1762); 6 fl duets
(London, *c*1775); caprices, vn solo, *A-Wgm, Wn, D-Bds*, Rome,
Fondo Monachesi, doubtful; 8 minuets, 1 polonaise, *D-DS*, doubtful

VOCAL

Liturgical: Mass, D, 4vv, chorus, orch, org, *A-Gd, D-Bds, I-MOe*;
Kyrie–Gloria, 4vv, orch, org, *CS-ME*; Litanie lauretanae, D, 4vv, 2
vn, 2 clarini, b, org, *Pnm*; Lytaniae lauretanae (Solenne), C, 4vv, 2
vn, b, org, *Mms, ME, Pnm*; Offertorium [Motetto] de venerabili
sacramento, 4vv, orch, org, *Pak, Pnm, Psj*
Other vocal: Cantata, B solo, orch, *D-F*; Aria de omni tempore, S, orch,
CS-Pnm
Lost works incl. at least 10 syms.; 5 partitas; 1 pastorella, vn obbl; 10
vn concs.; fl conc.; ?1 hpd conc.; 5 vn sonatas; vn sonata, hpd obbl;
Omni die, aria, B solo, orch

BIBLIOGRAPHY
C. Burney: *The Present State of Music in Germany, the Netherlands
and United Provinces* (London, 1773, 2/1775); ed. P. Scholes as *Dr.
Burney's Musical Tours* (London, 1959)
F. Walter: *Geschichte des Theaters und der Musik am kurpfälzischen
Hofe* (Leipzig, 1898/R1968)
M. Brenet: *Les concerts en France sous l'ancien régime* (Paris,
1900/R1969)
H. Riemann: Forewords, DTB, iv, Jg.iii/1 (1902/R); xiii, Jg.vii/2
(1906/R); xxviii, Jg.xvi (1915/R)
L. Kamieński: 'Mannheim und Italien', *SIMG*, x (1908–9), 307
G. Cucuel: *La Pouplinière et la musique de chambre au XVIII*e *siècle*
(Paris, 1913)
P. Gradenwitz: *Johann Stamitz*, i: *Das Leben* (Brno, 1936); ii:
Thematischer Katalog (MS, microfilm copies at *US-NYp* and Kassel,
RISM)
——: 'The Symphonies of Johann Stamitz', *MR*, i (1940), 354
A. Pospíšil: *Kolem Jana Václava Stamice* (Havlíčkův Brod, 1947)
P. Gradenwitz: 'The Stamitz Family: some Errors, Omissions, and
Falsifications Corrected', *Notes*, vii (1949–50), 54
P. Nettl: *Der kleine Prophet von Böhmisch-Broda* (Esslingen, 1953)
R. Schaal: 'Johann Stamitz' Mannheimer Bestallung von 1750', *Mf*, vi
(1953), 158
P. Gradenwitz: 'Stamitz, Johann', *Grove 5*
——: 'Johann Stamitz als Kirchenkomponist', *Mf*, xi (1958), 2
E. Schmitt: *Die kurpfälzische Kirchenmusik im 18. Jahrhundert* (diss.,
U. of Heidelberg, 1958)
F. Noack: 'Die Steinmetz-Manuskripte der Landes- und
Hochschulbibliothek Darmstadt', *Mf*, xiii (1960), 314
J. P. Larsen: 'Zur Bedeutung der "Mannheimer Schule" ', *Festschrift
Karl Gustav Fellerer* (Regensburg, 1962), 303
W. S. Newman: *The Sonata in the Classic Era* (Chapel Hill, 1963,
rev. 2/1972)
B. Štědroň: 'Zur Nationalität von Jan Václav Stamic', *BMw*, vi (1964),
16
P. Gradenwitz: 'Stamitz, Johann Wenzel Anton', *MGG*
J. Sochr: 'Dokumenty vydávají svědectví' [Documents as testimony],
HRo, xix (1966), 718–19
——: *Jan Václav Stamic: život a dílo* [Life and works] (Havlíčkův
Brod, 1967) [exhibition catalogue]
H.-R. Dürrenmatt: *Die Durchführung bei Johann Stamitz* (Berne, 1969)
H. Hell: *Die neapolitanische Opernsinfonie in der ersten Hälfte des 18.
Jahrhunderts* (Tutzing, 1971)
E. K. Wolf: *The Symphonies of Johann Stamitz: Authenticity,
Chronology, and Style* (New York, 1972)
E. Wellesz and F. Sternfeld, eds.: *The Age of Enlightenment, 1745–
1790*, NOHM, vii (1973)
H. Scharschuch: 'Johann Stamitz', *AMw*, xxxiii (1976), 189
E. K. Wolf: 'Authenticity and Stylistic Evidence in the Early Symphony:
a Conflict in Attribution between Richter and Stamitz', *A Musical
Offering: Essays in Honor of Martin Bernstein* (New York, 1977),
275
——: 'On the Origins of the Mannheim Symphonic Style', *Studies in
Musicology in Honor of Otto E. Albrecht* (Kassel, 1977)
——: *The Symphonies of Johann Stamitz: a Study in the Formation of
the Classic Style* (Utrecht, in preparation)

(2) Carl (Philipp) Stamitz (*b* Mannheim, baptized
8 May 1745; *d* Jena, 9 Nov 1801). Composer and violinist, viola player and viola d'amore player, son of (1)
Johann Stamitz. He was a leading member of the second
generation of Mannheim orchestral composers, a widely
travelled performer and a major contributor to the literature of the symphonie concertante.

1. LIFE. Carl Stamitz received his earliest musical training in Mannheim from his father, but was only 11 when
his father died. Subsequent teachers were other court
musicians: Christian Cannabich, Ignaz Holzbauer and
F. X. Richter. Extant orchestral lists include Stamitz as
a second violinist with the electoral orchestra from
1762 to 1770, a position that enabled him to learn the
contemporary Mannheim repertory and master a brilliant performing technique.

In 1770 Stamitz went to Paris, stopping en route to
perform in Mons. By 1771 he was court composer and
conductor for Duke Louis of Noailles in Paris, where he
came in contact with such musicians as Gossec, Leduc,
Sieber and Beer. In addition to publishing many new
compositions in Paris, both Stamitz and his brother (3)
Anton were active performers in the Concert Spirituel
in the 1770s. Between 1771 and 1773 the *Mercure de
France* reported appearances of both brothers as well
as performances of their compositions, but often without distinguishing clearly between Carl and Anton. In
summer 1772 Stamitz lived at Versailles, where he
composed *La promenade royale*, the first of several
programme symphonies. During his tenure with the
Duke of Noailles, journeys as a virtuoso took him in
1772 to Vienna, in 1773 to Frankfurt am Main, and in
1774 to Augsburg, Vienna and also Strasbourg, where
he published six quartets and delivered compositions to
Ignaz von Beecke for Prince Kraft Ernst of Oettingen-
Wallerstein. Either Carl or Anton performed again at
the Concert Spirituel on 2 February, 25 March and 7
April 1775; the *Mercure de France* described a concert
on 24 December 1775 at which a 'grande symphonie
nouvelle de M. Stamitz l'aîné' was performed with the
composer himself as one of the brilliant violinists. Additional references occur until March 1777. Stamitz's
years of relative security had come to a close; henceforth he lived the life of a travelling virtuoso, never
holding an important permanent position.

Stamitz's departure from Paris has not been precisely
documented, but Pohl stated that he was in London
from 1777 until at least 1779. There he published many
compositions, especially chamber works, continuing to
list himself as composer to the Duke of Noailles.
Some time after 1779 he moved to The Hague, where
between May 1782 and July 1784 he appeared,
primarily as a viola soloist, in no fewer than 28 concerts
at the court of William V, Prince of Orange. The concert on 23 November 1783 featured not only Stamitz

but Beethoven (aged 12), who played the piano and received a higher payment than his older colleague. Many compositions written by Stamitz during this period were published by B. Hummel of The Hague.

By April 1785 Stamitz had arrived in Hamburg, where he gave two academies. In August he performed in Lübeck, returning to Hamburg for two final concerts in the autumn. On 17 April 1786 he was in Magdeburg, then went to Leipzig and to Berlin, where on 19 May 1786 he joined J. A. Hiller in directing a performance of Handel's *Messiah* in the cathedral. At this time, according to Gerber, Stamitz negotiated a contract (as yet undiscovered) with the King of Prussia that guaranteed payment for any work composed by him for the Berlin court. Nor is there conclusive evidence to support Gerber's claim that in 1787 Stamitz held the title of Kapellmeister to the Prince of Hohenlohe-Schillingsfürst, although it is found on a printed concert announcement of 1792 and in his death notice.

In 1787 Stamitz travelled widely, performing as a violist in Dresden, Prague and Halle, and appearing in Nuremberg on 3 November 1787 for a performance of his musical allegory on the occasion of Blanchard's balloon ascent. Concert reviews from 1788 and 1789 report his appearance as a violist in Kassel. In 1789 he became director of the Liebhaber concerts there, a position he retained until April 1790.

Some time before 1790 Stamitz married Maria Josepha Pilz (*b* 1764; *d* Jena, 17 Jan 1801), and they settled in Greiz, Voigtland, where their first son was born in August 1790. The birth of a daughter by July 1792 and the illness of his wife prevented him from travelling extensively, and he tried unsuccessfully to obtain a permanent court position from Friedrich Franz I, Duke of Mecklenburg-Schwerin. He continued to earn what little he could by sending compositions to the King of Prussia, the Prince of Orange, the court at Schwerin and the court of Oettingen-Wallerstein, and succeeded in arranging two concerts, one on 12 November 1792 at the Hoftheater in Weimar, the other on 19 March 1793 in Leipzig. Letters to Breitkopf on 30 April and 6 May 1793 seeking help in producing operas and concerts or in finding a permanent position in Leipzig were of no avail.

A trip back to Mannheim before spring 1795 brought a variety of commissions, as mentioned in Stamitz's letter to Breitkopf of 28 May 1795 from Jena, where he had moved with his family to become Kapellmeister and teacher of music at the university. This post was not sufficient to settle his affairs, however, and he sent compositions as far as Wales and Russia in hopes of compensation. Stamitz even planned a concert tour to St Petersburg, but the letter sanctioning the trip did not arrive until after his death. Two sons born in Jena, like Stamitz's other children, died in childhood.

Despite Stamitz's earlier fame and his plans for grandiose concerts and travels – and even attempts at alchemy – his debts at the time of his death were so great that his possessions had to be auctioned. A printed catalogue of his music manuscripts was published for a separate auction in 1810, but the mode of the times had changed, and the music was neither bid for nor bought privately. The collection remained in Jena until 1812, but since then has disappeared.

2. WORKS. Stamitz composed nearly as many chamber as orchestral works, but his reputation as a composer derives principally from the latter. His 51 or more symphonies, 38 symphonies concertantes and more than 60 concertos make him the most prolific orchestral composer from Mannheim. On the whole his compositions reflect his Mannheim heritage, as seen in their idiomatic treatment of the orchestra, dynamic effects, homophonic texture, contrasting thematic types and specific Mannheim melodic clichés. Yet his years in Paris and London fostered the bulk of his compositions – in particular the popular symphonie concertante – and such characteristics of his style as pervasive lyricism and ease of melodic flow (often bordering on the superficial) place his music in a more cosmopolitan context than that of Mannheim alone.

Stamitz's instrumentation is standard for the time, but exceptions to the norm do occur: the Masquerade Symphony (*c*1781) employs an expanded percussion section to simulate Turkish music, and there are two works for double orchestra. Unlike his father, over half of whose symphonies are in four movements, Stamitz adopted the three-movement Italian pattern (fast–slow–fast) in almost all his extant orchestral works: only four symphonies use a minuet and trio as third movement (two others are programmatic works with relatively free structure), and eight of the 28 surviving symphonies concertantes are in two movements, a plan common in this genre, rather than three.

Stamitz's earliest symphonies date from his Mannheim years, and the last from Greiz in 1791. Like his contemporaries at Mannheim, he generally cast his first movements and finales in extended binary form (like sonata form but with only partial recapitulation),

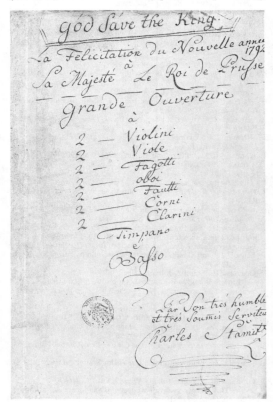

3. Title-page, in the composer's hand, of the 'Grande overture: God Save the King' (1791) by Carl Stamitz (D-Bds Königl.Hausbibl. M 5308)

often without repeat signs. 12 of his symphonies have slow introductions. In the early and middle-period symphonies there is often a rhythmic or motivic relationship between the introduction and first movement. In first movements Stamitz made relatively consistent use of contrasting secondary themes in the dominant, commonly set off by a reduction in orchestration and often featuring wind instruments in 3rds. Development sections are seldom extensive, and they do not consistently rework material from the exposition; instead, they are closely linked formally to the recapitulation and frequently introduce episodic material. A few symphonies omit developments entirely. Most of Stamitz's recapitulations begin with the second theme, though examples of full recapitulation can be found in symphonies throughout his career.

Stamitz's second movements were highly praised by his contemporaries for their lyricism and expressiveness. Sentimental appoggiaturas are frequent, and over a quarter of these movements are in minor keys. Simple and extended binary structures are typical. Stamitz's last movements resemble his first in form except in the case of seven symphonies that close with rondos.

Of Stamitz's 38 known symphonies concertantes, 30 call for two solo instruments (most often a pair of violins, a violin and cello, or a violin and viola), the others as many as seven. First movements follow the basic ritornello structure common in the 18th-century solo concerto, with three or four tutti sections in various keys framing modulatory solo sections. Stamitz used two types of finale: the norm is a rondo, but in five works there are minuets and trios, adapted in various ways to incorporate the soloists. He used rondos in his orchestral works more often than other Mannheim composers, presumably a result of his extensive contact with French music during the 1770s.

Stamitz wrote solo concertos for a wide range of instruments, including violin (15), clarinet (10), flute (7) and bassoon (7); many of these works are lost. His orchestral and chamber compositions for viola d'amore, an instrument with which he was especially identified, are historically important for their use of all seven strings, double and triple stops, left-hand pizzicato and harmonics.

WORKS
ORCHESTRAL

Syms. [thematic catalogues in DTB, iv, Jg.iii/1 (1902), xiii, Jg.vii/2 (1906)]: 3 as op.2 (Paris, 1768); 6 as op.6 (Paris, 1771) [also as opp.15, 16]; 6 as op.9 (Paris, 1772); La chasse (Paris, 1772) [with added movt, *D-Rtt*]; 3 as op.13 (Paris, 1776); 6 as op.16 (London, 1777) [also as op.16], 2 ed. in DTB, xv, Jg.viii/2 (1907); 3 as op.24 (Amsterdam, 1786); 3 as op.25 (Amsterdam, c1787); 4 in anthologies (Paris and Liège, 1773–6); 11 further syms., incl. La promenade royale, 1772, Masquerade, c1781, Sinfonia a due cori, *B-Bc, D-DS, SWl, W*; 3 lost, incl. 1 advertised 1775

Symphonies concertantes (all printed works published in Paris; only solo insts indicated): 9 for 2 vn: 8 (1774–81), incl. 1 as op.18 no.2 (c1776) and 3 lost, 1 in *Bds*; 1 for vn, vn/vc (1774); 8 for vn, vc (1773–4); 2 for vn, va, 1 in *BFb*, 1 lost; 5 for ob, bn (1781), lost, but 3 extant in arrs.: 2 for cl, bn, *Rtt, PL-WRu*; 1 for vn, va, *CH-Bu*; 1 for bn, hn (1781), lost; 1 for cl, cl/vn (1778); 2 for vn va (1774), 1 as op.18 no.1 (c1776); 1 for vn, va, vc (1774); 1 for 2 vn, vc (1773); 1 for 2 vn, va, vc, ?1774, *D-Rtt*; 1 for vn, ob/vn, va, bn/vc, op.14 (?1776); Echo symphony (Divertimento a 2 chori), ob/vn, vn, bn/vc, 2 hn, 1780, *Bds, DS, Rtt*; Concerto per 7 stromenti principali, fl, ob, cl, 2 hn, vn, vc, *A-Wgm, D-Bds, SWl*; 3 further works lost, known only from catalogues

Concs. (printed works published in Paris unless otherwise stated): 15 for vn: 2 as op.12 (1774), 1, A (1776), nos.4, 5, 7 (1777), 4 in *Mbs, I-Mc*, 5 lost [6 further vn concs. doubtful]; 3 for va: 2, D, B♭ (1774), 1 in *D-Dlb*; 3 for va d'amore, *A-Wgm, D-B, SPlb*; Sonata, va d'amore, orch, *GB-Lbm*; 6 for vc: 1, C (1777), ed. P. Gradenwitz (Wiesbaden, 1964), 3 in *D-Bds*, 1 in HM, lxxix, civ, cv (1951–2), 2 lost; 7 for fl: 1, D (1777), ed. in EDM, 1st ser., li (1964), 1, G, op.29 (The Hague, n.d.), ed. in Concertino (Mainz, 1964), 1 in *Rtt*, 4 lost [8 further fl concs. doubtful]; 2 for ob, lost; 10 for cl: 2, F, B♭ (1777),

no.5 (1779) [also for ob, *HR*, ed. J. Wojciechowski (Hamburg, 1962)], no.6 (c1780), 1, E♭ (Berlin, 1793), 2 in *A-Wn*, 1 ed. J. Wojciechowski (Frankfurt am Main and London, 1957), 1 ed. J. Michaels (Hamburg, 1958), 1 in *D-DS*, ed. H. Boese as Darmstädter Konzert (Leipzig, 1956), 1 in *Rtt*, ed. J. Wojciechowski (Hamburg, 1953), 1 formerly *DS*, ed. Schlenker arr. pf (Leipzig, 1956); 7 for bn: 1 in *SWl*, ed. J. Wojciechowski (Hamburg, 1956), 6 lost, advertised 1778–82 [1 = vc conc., C]; 3 for hn: 1, E (c1782) [attrib. G. Punto, c1789, apparently based on works by Stamitz], ed. in Concertino (Mainz, 1968), 2 lost; 2 for pf: 1 F, 1783, *CS-Pnm*, ed. G. Rhau (Wiesbaden, 1948), 1 (1779), lost; 2 for harp, lost

Other orch: A Grand Overture (London, 1790 or 1792); Grande ouverture: God Save the King, 1791, *D-Bds*; 8 orch qts: 6 as op.1 (Paris, 1770), 2 in 6 Str Qts (Strasbourg, 1774), 1 ed. in DTB, xxviii, Jg.xvi (1915)

CHAMBER
(thematic catalogue in DTB, xxviii, Jg.xvi, 1915)

Larger ens: 7 parties, 2 fl, 2 ob, 2 cl, 2 bn, 2 hn, *Dlb*; 6 minuets, 2 fl, 2 hn, 2 vn, b (London, c1777); 4 divertissements, 2 cl, 2 bn, 2 hn, op.21 (The Hague, n.d.), lost; 2 sextets, 2 hn, 4 str, *HR, SWl*; 4 quintetti concertanti, str (Amsterdam, 1774) [3 also as op.10, 3 with alternative wind insts as op.11]; 4 serenades, 2 fl, bn, 2 hn, op.28 (The Hague, 1786) [also as op.26; arr. kbd (The Hague, 1789)], ed. W. Lebermann (Hamburg, 1962); 5 str qnts, qnt for harp, 2 hn, 2 va, lost; 19 works, 10 wind insts, 1795, 16 works, wind insts, perc, 1801, 16 marches, 12 wind insts, all lost

Qts: 6 for cl, vn, va, b, op.8 (Paris, 1773), 1 ed. in HM, cix (1954), 1 ed. in DTB, xxvii, Jg.xv (1914), 2 ed. K. Janetki (London, 1958); 6 Str Qts (Strasbourg, 1774) [incl. 2 orch qts, 2 qts for fl/ob/cl/vn, vn, va, vc; also as opp.4, 11, 14], 1 ed. in Concertino (Mainz, 1961), 2 ed. in Antiqua (Mainz, 1963); 6 quartets concertantes, vn, 2 va, vc, op.15 (Paris, 1774) [also as opp.2, 10, 12; incl. arrs. of 4 quintetti concertanti]; 3 quartetti concertante, cl/vn, vn, va, b, op.12 (Paris, 1775); Qt, D, vn, 2 va, vc (London, c1775); 6 as op.19 (Paris, 1779) [4 for cl, str, 2 for bn, str], no.2 ed. D. Lasocki (London, 1971), no.3 ed. J. Kurtz (London, 1970), nos.5 and 6 ed. W. Waterhouse (London, 1968); 6 quatuors concertant, op.22 (The Hague, 1783)

Trios: 6 for 2 vn, b (Paris, 1768) [also as op.2], 1 ed. in DTB, xxviii, Jg.xvi (1915); 6 for 2 vn, b, op.2 (Paris, 1770); 6 Pf Trios, op.15 (Paris, 1776); 6 for 2 vn, b, op.7 (Paris, 1777) [also as op.1]; 6 for fl/vn, vc, op.14 (Amsterdam, 1777) [also as op.11], 1 ed. in NM, xxxiii (1928/R), 1 ed. in Collegium musicum, lxx (Leipzig, 1938); Sonate, hpd/pf, vn, op.20 (The Hague, c1779); 6 for fl/vn, vc (London, c1785); 2 for 2 vn, vc, op.16 (London, c1785) [with 4 earlier trios; also as op.21]; 1 for fl/vn, vn, b, op.25 (Amsterdam, 1785) [with 2 earlier trios]; 6 divertissements ou airs, arr. fl, vn, b (The Hague, n.d.); 1 for fl, fl/vn, vc, MS, ed. F. Schnapp (Kassel, 1939); 1 for 2 vn, vc, *A-Wgm*; 1 for hn, vn, vc, *CS-Pnm*, ed. in Diletto musicale, cxcvii (Vienna and Munich, 1970)

Duos: 30 for vn, va: 6 as op.10 (Paris, c1773) [also as opp.1, 8], 2 ed. in Diletto musicale, cviii, cix (Vienna and Munich, 1963), 3 as op.12 (Amsterdam, 1777), 6 as op.19 (Paris, c1778) [also for vn, vc; also as op.18], 6 as op.34 (London, c1785) [also as op.19], 6 as op.23 (The Hague, 1786) [also for 2 vn], 2 Duos (London, n.d.), Grand duo (Offenbach, c1803); 15 sonatas, vn, kbd: 6 as op.15 (London, c1778) [also as op.20], 3 as op.17 (Paris, c1778), 6 in *D-Dlb*; 6 fl/vn duets (London, ?1772); 6 Sonatas, vn/fl, vn (London, 1776); 6 vn duos (Amsterdam, c1778); Sonata, kbd, va obbl (London, c1778) [also as op.6]; 3 Duets, vc, vn/vc (London, c1780); 6 fl/vn duos, op.27 (The Hague, 1785), ed. in NM, lxii, clxxviii (1930, 1954); Duett, kbd (London, c1790); 6 va duos, B, ed. W. Lebermann (Mainz, 1955); Duetto, 2 fl, MS; Duo, va d'amore, vn/va, B [also with orch conclusion]; Sonata, va d'amore, b, *A-Wgm*, ed. in DTB, xxviii, Jg.xvi (1915); 6 further vn duets, doubtful

VOCAL

Dramatic: Der verliebte Vormund (Singspiel), before 1787, lost; Dardanus [Dardanens Sieg, oder Der Triumph der Liebe und Tugend] (grand opera), c1800, lost

Other vocal: Mass, D, *D-EB*; 3 cantatas, solo vv, chorus, orch, music lost: Ein grosses allegorisches Stück (Nuremberg, 1787) [on the occasion of Blanchard's balloon ascent], Teutsche Gefühle am Schluss des kriegevollen Jahrs 1794 (C. L. Schübler), Festgesang, 23 March 1801 [on the occasion of Tsar Alexander I's accession]; 4 ariettas or scenas, S, orch, *A-Wgm, D-HR, SWl*; 2 soprano arias with variations, lost

BIBLIOGRAPHY

F. Walter: *Geschichte des Theaters und der Musik am kurpfälzischen Hofe* (Leipzig, 1898/R1968)

H. Riemann: Forewords, DTB, xv, Jg.viii/2 (1907/R); xxvii, Jg.xv (1914/R)

F. Waldkirch: *Die konzertanten Sinfonien der Mannheimer im 18. Jahrhundert* (Ludwigshafen, 1931)

A. Schering: 'Fünf Briefe von Karl Stamitz: Bruchstücke einer Selbstbiographie', *Festschrift Fritz Stein* (Brunswick, 1939), 57

P. Gradenwitz: 'The Stamitz Family: some Errors, Omissions, and Falsifications Corrected', *Notes*, vii (1949–50), 54

F. C. Kaiser: *Carl Stamitz (1745–1801): biographische Beiträge, das symphonische Werk, thematischer Katalog der Orchesterwerke* (diss., U. of Marburg, 1962)

H. Heussner: Review of H. J. Schaefer and others: *Theater in Kassel* (Kassel, 1951), *Mf*, xv (1962), 287
W. S. Newman: *The Sonata in the Classic Era* (Chapel Hill, 1963, rev. 2/1972)
F. C. Kaiser: 'Stamitz, Carl', *MGG*
J. LaRue: 'Symphonie', §BI–IV, *MGG*
J. Záloha: 'Drei unbekannte Autographe von Karl Stamitz in der Musikaliensammlung in Český Krumlov', *Mf*, xix (1966), 408
M. Rosenblum: 'The Viola d'amore and its Literature', *The Strad*, lxxviii (1967), 250, 277
E. Wellesz and F. Sternfeld, eds.: *The Age of Enlightenment, 1745–1790*, NOHM, vii (1973)
M. de Smet: *La musique à la cour de Guillaume V, Prince d'Orange (1748–1806)* (Utrecht, 1973)
D. Thomason: *A Discussion of the Viola d'Amore Music of Karl Stamitz* (n.p., 1979)

(3) Anton (Thadäus Johann Nepomuk) Stamitz (*b* Německý Brod [now Havlíčkův Brod], 27 Nov 1750; *d* Paris or Versailles, between 1789 and 1809). Composer, violinist and viola player, son of (1) Johann Stamitz; he should not be confused with a brother, Johann Baptista (*b* Mannheim, 25 Nov 1754; buried 20 Dec 1755). Anton was born during a family visit to Německý Brod. Johann Stamitz had returned to Mannheim in late March 1750, and his wife and new son presumably joined him there in 1751. Anton grew up at the electoral court and as a youth received violin instruction from his brother (2) Carl and Christian Cannabich. He became a second violinist with the Mannheim orchestra in 1764, but resigned in 1770 to move to Paris with Carl. There, in addition to performing during at least the next 20 years, Anton composed the main body of his works – principally concertos (many for his own use), quartets and duos. The first specific mention of Anton in Paris occurs in a report in the *Mercure de France* of the Concert Spirituel on 25 March 1772, when he played a violin and viola duo with Carl. Anton may also have appeared at other concerts between 1772 and March 1777 for which the *Mercure de France* gives only the surname 'Stamitz'.

With Carl's departure for England in 1777 (there is no evidence that Anton ever left France), Anton figured more prominently in Parisian musical circles, appearing twice at the Concert Spirituel in 1778 as soloist in his own viola concertos. Between 18 May 1777 and 24 December 1787 three more of his works (and four other Stamitz works with no clear attribution) were played at these concerts. Mozart, who was in Paris in 1778, was evidently not favourably impressed with either Anton or Carl, for he wrote to his father from there (9 July):

Of the two Stamitz brothers only the younger one is here, the elder (the real composer à la Hafeneder) is in London. They indeed are two wretched scribblers, gamblers, swillers and adulterers – not the kind of people for me. The one who is here has scarcely a decent coat to his back.

Mozart's statements of this sort cannot always be taken at face value; but there is evidence that Anton had numerous debts, at least during the 1780s. Between September 1778 and 31 January 1780 Stamitz was violin instructor to Rodolphe Kreutzer of Versailles, receiving 18 livres monthly for 12 lessons. His many duos for string instruments were no doubt written in conjunction with his teaching, and as an instructor he gained fame when Kreutzer, aged 13, made a successful début playing a violin concerto of Anton's at the Concert Spirituel on 25 May 1780.

In 1782 the *Almanach musical* provided an address in Paris for Stamitz, but in the same year he probably moved to Versailles, for court records list him as a violinist with the *musique du roi* there from 1782 to 1789; at the same time various publications give Anton the title *ordinaire de la musique du roi*. With the Revolution in 1789 all trace of Stamitz disappeared. He may have died as early as 1789, for two letters from his widow, N. Bouchet de Grandpré, written in Paris in June and November 1809, explain that she is no longer receiving the pension of 800 livres granted at the death of her husband.

WORKS

All printed works were published in Paris unless otherwise stated; names of publishers are included only when identification is ambiguous.

ORCHESTRAL

Syms. (thematic catalogue in DTB, iv, Jg.iii/1, 1902): 3 as op.1 (n.d.); 3 as op.2 (n.d.); 6 as op.3 (n.d.); 2 symphonies concertantes: 1 for vn, vc (*c*1775), 1 for 2 fl (n.d.), ed. in Concertino (Mainz, 1967)
Vn concs.: 9 pubd Sieber: nos.1–2, 7–8, 15 (n.d.), no.3 (1775), no.4 (*c*1777), no.5 (*c*1782), no.6 (*c*1786); 4 pubd La Chevardière: no.1 (1776), nos.2–3 (*c*1778–9), no.4 (*c*1780–81); op.3 (*c*1777–8); 2 as op.2 (The Hague, 1779); 1 pubd Bérault (*c*1780); op.7 (*c*1781); op.12 (*c*1786–7); no.5, pubd Leduc (*c*1787–91); no.6, pubd Imbault (n.d.); 1 pubd Durieu (n.d.)
Other concs.: 1 for vn/va (*c*1778–9); 3 for va: no.2 (*c*1778–9), nos.3–4 (*c*1786), 1 ed. in Concertino (Mainz, 1970); 5 for kbd: 3 as livre 1 (1783), nos.4–5 (n.d.); 1 for fl (n.d.) [listed in Breitkopf catalogue, 1781], ed. in EDM, 1st ser., li (1964); 1 for ob (*c*1778–9)

CHAMBER
(thematic catalogue in DTB, xxviii, Jg.xvi, 1915)

Str qts (pubd in sets of 6): op.30 (*c*1776–9); op.1 (The Hague, 1779); livre 4, pubd La Chevardière (*c*1780–81); livre 4, pubd Sieber (n.d.), 1 ed. in DTB, xxvii, Jg.xv (1914); livre 5 (1782); livre 6 (1782); op.29 (*c*1782); livre 7 (n.d.); livre 8 (1785); livre 9 (n.d.), 1 ed. in DTB, xxvii, Jg.xv (1914); op.28 (n.d.)
Trios (pubd in sets of 6): 24 for 2 vn, b: op.1 (*c*1772), op.2 (n.d.), op.4 (*c*1775), 1 ed. in DTB, xxviii, Jg.xvi (1915), livre 3 (1787) [3 for orch]; 12 for fl, vn, b: op.17 (*c*1777), livre 1 (*c*1782)
Duos (pubd in sets of 6): 30 for 2 vn: op.1 (1776) [also arr. 2 fl (Mainz, n.d.)], livre 8 (1777), op.9 (*c*1777), livre 15 (1787), 6 (n.d.); 24 for vn, va: 6 (*c*1779), livre 3 (*c*1781), livre 4 (1786), livre 19 (1788); 24 for vn, vc: livre 1 (*c*1780), livre 3, pubd Boyer (1785), livre 3, pubd Louis (n.d.), op.5 (n.d.) [also arr. vn, va (*c*1778–9)]; 18 for fl, vn: op.4 (1785), op.7 (n.d.), 6 (n.d.); 30 for 2 fl: livre 1 (*c*1781), livre 3 (1783), op.3 (The Hague, ?1784), op.7 (n.d.), 6 (*c*1786)
Other chamber: 6 sonatas, 2 vn, op.1 (n.d.); 12 sonates, vn, vc: 6 as op.6 (n.d.), 6 as op.11 (1775); Nocturnes ou airs variés, vn, vc (1782); Airs variés, vn (1776); harp sonata, listed in Breitkopf catalogue, 1781

BIBLIOGRAPHY

M. Brenet: *Les concerts en France sous l'ancien régime* (Paris, 1900/R1969)
J. Hardy: *Rodolphe Kreutzer* (Paris, 1910)
M. Pincherle: 'La veuve d'Antoine Stamitz', *Bulletin de la Société 'Union musicologique'*, iv (1924), 29
——: 'Antoine Stamitz et sa veuve', *Feuillets d'histoire de violon* (Paris, 1927), 110
J. Sochr: *Jan Václav Stamic: život a dílo* [Life and works] (Havlíčkův Brod, 1967) [exhibition catalogue]
For further bibliography see (2) Carl Stamitz.

EUGENE K. WOLF (2, 3, with JEAN K. WOLF),
FRITZ KAISER (work-list for 2)

Stampiglia, Silvio (*b* Civita Lavinia [now Lanuvio], nr. Rome, 14 March 1664; *d* Naples, 26 Jan 1725). Italian librettist. His creative life was mainly spent collaborating with G. Bononcini (in 1692–6, 1706–13, 1719) and A. Scarlatti (1697–1706, 1720). In 1690 he was a founder-member of the Accademia dell'Arcadia (in which his name was Palemone Licurio), and presumably shared its purifying ideals. His first productions were in Rome: three oratorios (1687, 1690, 1693), about eight serenatas (1692–6), and revisions of Venetian operas for the Teatro di Tordinona (1692–5). These revisions simplify plot, structure and language; they and his own operas retain and often add to the comic delights present in Venetian models.

He wrote his first five operas for Naples (1696–

1702), but his residence there ended with the War of the Spanish Succession. He moved to Rome and wrote for various cities until called to the emperor's Viennese court, for which he produced five operas, nine serenatas and one oratorio (1707–13). He asked to be relieved of his Viennese duties in 1714 and spent most of his last 11 years in Rome and Naples, where, as an 'imperial poet' for life, he received commissions mainly from Viennese representatives. His most popular operas, *Il trionfo di Camilla* (1696) and *Partenope* (1699), were still performed long after his death.

Excluding revisions, he wrote texts for at least 14 operas, 8 oratorios and 26 shorter dramatic works. The composers who first set them include G. Aldrovandini, A. Ariosti, C. Badia, P. Bencini, A. Bononcini, G. Bononcini, J. Fux, F. Lanciani, L. Leo, S. di Luca, L. Mancia, G. Perroni, F. Pistocchi, N. Porpora, N. Sabini, A. Scarlatti and M. Ziani.

BIBLIOGRAPHY

P. Zeno: 'Elogio di Silvio Stampiglia Romano', *Giornale de' letterati d'Italia*, xxxviii/2 (1733), 117

M. Fabbri: *Alessandro Scarlatti e il Principe Ferdinando de' Medici* (Florence, 1961)

H. Powers: 'Il Serse trasformato', *MQ*, xlvii (1961), 481; xlviii (1962), 73

A. Mondolfi: 'Stampiglia, Silvio', *ES*

K. Hortschansky: 'Stampiglia, Silvio', *MGG*

R. Freeman: 'The Travels of *Partenope*', *Studies in Music History: Essays for Oliver Strunk* (Princeton, 1968), 356–85

L. Lindgren: *A Bibliographic Scrutiny of Dramatic Works set by Giovanni and his brother Antonio Maria Bononcini* (diss., Harvard U., 1972)

D. Grout, ed.: *A Scarlatti: Eraclea*, The Operas of Alessandro Scarlatti, i (Cambridge, Mass., 1974)

LOWELL LINDGREN

Stamps, V(irgil) O(liver) (*b* nr. Gilmer, Texas, 18 Sept 1892; *d* Dallas, 19 Aug 1940). American music publisher (*see* SHAPE-NOTE HYMNODY, §5). In 1926 he established with J. R. Baxter the Stamps–Baxter Music Co., located from 1929 in Dallas, which became one of the largest publishers of gospel hymns in seven-shape notation; the company promoted gospel music further by sponsoring vocal quartets. His brother Frank Stamps founded the Stamps Quartet Music Co. in Dallas in 1945.

BIBLIOGRAPHY

M. L. Smith, ed.: *Give the World a Smile: a Compilation of Songs by Frank H. Stamps with a Story of his Life by Mrs Frank Stamps* (Wesson, Mississippi, 1969)

Mrs J. R. Baxter jr and V. Polk: *Gospel Song Writers Biography* (Dallas, 1971)

HARRY ESKEW

Stancheva-Brashovanova, Lada. *See* BRASHOVANOVA, LADA.

Stanchinsky, Alexey Vladimirovich (*b* Vladimir govt., 1888; *d* Crimea, 6 Oct 1914). Russian composer. He studied the piano with Lhévinne, and then entered the Moscow Conservatory, where he took lessons from Igumnov. He began to compose seriously at the age of 16, studying with Zhilyayev and Taneyev; both recognized Stanchinsky's remarkable gifts, though Taneyev was puzzled by the compositions which Stanchinsky brought to him. Whereas his early music (simple and direct in style) suggests the influence of Musorgsky, his mature works reflect an admiration for Skryabin and Grieg: they comprise a series of short, impressionistic piano pieces, free in form, and using chromatic harmonies and brief snatches of melody, which conjure up a strange, twilit world of half-perceived images and dreamlike visions. It came as no surprise to Taneyev when, on the death of his father in 1908, the 20-year-old composer succumbed to an apparently hereditary schizophrenic illness. For a year he was confined to a clinic and suffered from religious mania and hallucinations, interspersed with periods of comparative lucidity. He developed a violent dislike of his earlier works and succeeded in destroying many of them; some, however, were reconstructed from memory by friends, and Zhilyayev was able to rescue other manuscripts before they were burnt. He was eventually pronounced incurable, discharged from the clinic, and for the remaining few years of his life composed sporadically. He became obsessed by formal ideas, and turned from almost improvisatory sketches and studies to sonatas, fugues and canons, experimenting with a variety of polyphonic techniques combined with harsh, often polytonal harmonies. His subjective approach to composition was replaced by a strictly objective one, and the fantasy world of his earlier music gave way to technical feats combined with a certain dry humour not unlike the young Prokofiev. His manuscripts were circulated among the musical cognoscenti of Moscow, and Stanchinsky became something of a cult figure. In 1914 the journal *Muzïka* devoted an issue to young composers, and foretold a bright future for Stanchinsky. Zhilyayev obtained a performance of some of his compositions, and even the more reactionary critics were impressed by the young man's talents. These favourable reviews provoked a new burst of activity but it was short-lived. In the autumn of 1914 Stanchinsky paid a visit to a friend's country estate in the Crimea; he was found dead beside a stream. The cause of death remains a mystery, though suicide has been suggested. In 1916 Zhilyayev and Alexandrov began to prepare Stanchinsky's works for publication (only his op.1 had appeared during his lifetime) but their work was interrupted by the war and the Revolution. However, they were able to carry out their scheme during the following decade, and most of Stanchinsky's extant compositions were published between 1926 and 1931. Metner dedicated his Three Pieces op.31 (1916) to Stanchinsky's memory.

WORKS

(all for solo pf)

8 Sketches, op.1, 1908 (Moscow, 1914); 5 sonatas, incl. eb, 1906, no.1, F, 1911–12 (Moscow, 1926); 3 studies, B, 1906, f, 1907, g, 1907; Nocturne, 1907; 5 preludes, 1907–12; Canon, 1908; Prelude, 1908; Prelude in the Lydian mode, 1908; Prelude and Fugue, g, 1909; Allegro, F, 1912 [orig. 1st movt of Sonata no.1]; 3 Preludes, set 1, 1913; 3 Preludes, set 2, 1913; Prelude in 2-pt. canon, 1913–14; 3 Preludes in canonic form, 1913–14; 3 Preludes

BIBLIOGRAPHY

A. N. Alexandrov: 'A. V. Stanchinsky', *Sovremennaya muzïka*, iv (1927)

L. L. Sabaneyev: *Modern Russian Composers* (London, 1927), 190

M. Montagu-Nathan: 'Was he a Genius?', *Tempo* (1953), no.28, p.23

JENNIFER SPENCER

Ständchen. The German equivalent of SERENADE. The term first appeared in 1618 in Praetorius's *Syntagma musicum* (iii, 18) and later in Walther's *Musicalisches Lexicon* (1732). At the beginning of the 19th century it became a fashionable term for songs with a piano accompaniment which tended to imitate figures characteristic of the guitar. Schubert's *Leise flehen meine Lieder* is a famous example, and several more are found in the works of Brahms and Richard Strauss. The term was also applied to movements for male-voice chorus.

HUBERT UNVERRICHT

Standford, Patric [Gledhill, John Patrick Standford] (*b* Barnsley, 5 Feb 1939). English composer and teacher. He was educated at Ackworth School and the Guildhall School of Music, where he studied composition with Rubbra. A Mendelssohn Scholarship enabled him to pursue his studies with Malipiero in Italy, and he worked with Lutosławski at Dartington in 1964 and 1965. He was appointed professor of composition at the GSM in 1967 and became a fellow in 1972.

Under the influence of Lutosławski, Standford's most progressive music was written during his late 20s, as in the Nocturne and *Notte*, both of which consist exclusively of material for improvisation. His music has always been remarkable more for its craftsmanship, however, than for its adherence to any one style. Within four or five years his writing was precisely determinate as in the first movement of his finely constructed First Symphony. Characteristically, in the long and boldly diverse *Christus-Requiem*, his major work, he puts more faith in creative intuition than in stylistic unity.

WORKS

Ballet: Celestial Fire, 1968, also orch suite
Orch: Epigrams, chamber orch, 1964; Saracinesco, poem, 1966; Suite, small orch, 1966; Nocturne, small orch, 1967; Concertante, pf, small orch, 1967; Notte, chamber orch, 1968; Preludio ostinato, 1968; 3 Studies, 1970; Antitheses, 15 str, 1971; Sym. no.1, 1972; Vc Conc., 1973; Sym. no.2, 1973; Vn Conc., 1975; Pf Conc., 1979
Vocal: Gitanjali, 4 songs, 1v, ens, 1964; Wayward Thoughts, 5 songs, 1v, pf, 1968; Cantico delle creature, 1v, str, 1969; A John Clare Cantata, 1v, chorus, orch, 1971; Christus-Requiem, solo vv, chorus, orch, 1972; Nursery Songs, S, Bar, ob, pf, 1979
Chamber: Suite française, wind qnt, 1964; Str Qt no.1, 1966; Bagatelles, str qt, 1969; Pf Trio, 1970; Sonata, brass qnt, 1973; Str Qt no.2, 1973
Inst: Suite, hn, 1964; Nocturnal, va, harp, 1967; Metamorphosis, org, 1969; Variations, pf, 1969; Sonatine, rec, hpd, 1970; 6 Preludes, pf, 1970; 4 Preludes, bn, pf, 1970; Peasant Songs, vn, pf, 1970; 3 Pieces, vc, pf, 1971; Sonata, vn, 1971; Recitative, Aria and Postlude, eng hn, pf, 1972; Pf Sonata no.1, 1974; Taikyoku, 2 pf, perc, 1975–6; Serenade, vn, gui, 1977; Meditation on the Birth of the Holy Infant, org, 1977; Pf Sonata no.2, 1979

Principal publisher: Novello

BIBLIOGRAPHY
G. Larner: 'Patric Standford', *MT*, cxiv (1973), 253

GERALD LARNER

Standfuss, J(?ohann) C. (*d* after *c*1759). German composer. He was a violinist and répétiteur with G. H. Koch's theatre company about 1750, wrote what is often regarded as the earliest German Singspiel and, despite Gerber's report that he died in a Hamburg hospital in 1756, was presumably still alive in 1759, in which year two further Singspiels by him were first performed. Although the term Singspiel had long been used in Germany for both comic and serious works, and by this period a flourishing Viennese tradition had been established, Standfuss's setting of C. F. Weisse's first version of Charles Coffey's *The Devil to Pay, or The Wives Metamorphos'd* (London, 1731) opened an era in the German musical theatre. Under the title *Der Teufel ist los, oder Die verwandelten Weiber* it was performed for the first time on 6 October 1752 in Leipzig by Koch's company. Coffey's original in a translation by the former Prussian Ambassador to London, C. W. von Borck, had been given in Berlin nine years earlier, probably with the original English tunes; works on the subject were frequent in the 18th century. As Koch had some good singers in his company it is reasonable to assume that *Der Teufel ist los* was well performed. Not the least significant aspect of its success was the battle of pamphlets to which it gave rise, Gottsched and his adherents objecting in vain to the demise of good taste evinced by the comic Singspiel. A sequel, *Der lustige Schuster, oder Der zweyte Theil vom Teufel ist los*, based on Coffey's *The Merry Cobbler* (London, 1735), appeared seven years later. Both parts of *Der Teufel ist los* were revised by C. F. Weisse and J. A. Hiller at Leipzig in 1766 and were published in vocal score there in 1770 and 1771 respectively.

Although Standfuss's scores have not survived, Hiller took over many of Standfuss's numbers into his own versions; in his preface to *Der lustige Schuster* Hiller spoke appreciatively of 'a certain gaiety, a not infelicitous expressiveness in the low comic vein, and now and again a witty touch' in Standfuss's music, the historical importance of which he clearly realized. The last of Standfuss's known works, the (lost) Singspiel *Jochem Tröbs, oder Der vergnügte Bauernstand*, to a libretto by an actor in Koch's company, was given in Hamburg on 17 September 1759. Two motets by Standfuss are in *A-Wn*; Gerber mentioned a third formerly owned by Rellstab, in Berlin.

WORKS

Der Teufel ist los, oder Die verwandelten Weiber (C. F. Weisse), Leipzig, 6 Oct 1752
Der lustige Schuster, oder Der zweyte Theil vom Teufel ist los (C. F. Weisse), Lübeck, 18 Jan 1759
Jochem Tröbs, oder Der vergnügte Bauernstand (J. C. Ast), Hamburg, 17 Sept 1759, music and text lost [also known as Der stolze Bauer Jochem Tröbs]

Two motets in *A-Wn*; a third, now lost, mentioned in *GerberNL*

BIBLIOGRAPHY
GerberNL
C. F. Weisse: *Selbstbiographie*, ed. C. E. Weisse and S. G. Frisch (Leipzig, 1806)
C. H. Schmid: *Chronologie des deutschen Theaters*, ed. P. Legband, Schriften der Gesellschaft für Theatergeschichte, i (Berlin, 1902), 102, 128, 157, 175
G. Calmus: 'Die ersten deutschen Singspiele von Standfuss und Hiller', *Publikationen der Internationalen Musikgesellschaft, Beihefte*, 2nd ser., vi (Leipzig, 1908), 1

PETER BRANSCOMBE

Standing, Frank H. *See* CELLI, FRANK H.

Standish, Orlando [Rowland] [Stephenson, Rowland]. Eldest son of EDWARD STEPHENSON.

Standley [Standly, Sandley] (*fl c*1450). ?English composer. He is presumed to be English on grounds of name, musical style and technique, and the manuscript context of his work. The two five-movement mass cycles both have Kyries that are untroped and too short to have been troped. Both have Credos with substantial (but apparently unsystematic) text omissions that do not easily lend themselves to restoration by telescoped setting. The composer avoided rhythmic differentiation between the voices; if the Strahov mass is based on a cantus prius factus, this is so assimilated by decoration to the style of the other parts that it resists identification. Consonant 3rd-based duet writing is fundamental to the moderately florid style of all these pieces. All this, together with the dates of the manuscripts, suggests that Standley belongs to the generation of Frye and Bedingham. The Trent cycle employs an unprecedented canonic technique. Two parts only are notated; the lower is labelled both 'tenor' and 'contra', and the contra entry is cued by a *signum congruentiae*. But the canonic contra has to omit all notes below a certain (unspecified) pitch. The motet *Que est ista* is composed according to the same scheme and is in all ways a twin to the cycle. It seems reasonable to assign it to Standley. Its text contains the words 'electa ut sol', which Loyan interpreted as a clue to this pitch exclusion. *Virgo prefulgens* is a setting of an otherwise unknown antiphon; the ascription of a false start to Binchois in a Trent manuscript (*I-TRmn* 92) can be set aside in favour of the strong stylistic and manuscript evidence supporting the Modena attribution (*MOe* α.x.1.11).

WORKS

Mass cycle, 3vv, ascribed 'Standley', *I-TRmn* 88, ed. in Loyan, pp.44ff; tenor and contratenor canonic
Mass cycle, 3vv, ascribed 'Standly', *CS-Ps* D.G.IV.47, ed. in Snow, pp.252ff; 3rd Agnus missing
Que est ista, motet, 3vv, anon. but constructed as the cycle in *I-TRmn* 88, *I-TRmn* 89, ed. in Loyan, pp.40ff
Virgo prefulgens avia, ant, 3vv, ascribed 'Sandley', *I-MOe* α.x.1.11, ed. in Marix, pp.227ff; survives inc. in *I-TRmn* 92 ascribed 'Winchois'

BIBLIOGRAPHY

J. Marix, ed.: *Les musiciens de la cour de Bourgogne au XVe siècle (1420–1467)* (Paris, 1937)

R. Loyan, ed.: *Canons in the Trent Codices*, CMM, xxxviii (1967)
R. Snow: *The Manuscript Strahov D.G.IV.47* (diss., U. of Illinois, 1968)

MARGARET BENT

Stane. Composer mentioned by John Hothby, probably identifiable with STONE.

Stanesby. English woodwind instrument makers, working in London in the first half of the 18th century. With Bressan, the Stanesbys were responsible for most of the finest surviving English Baroque woodwind instruments. Thomas Stanesby (i) (*b* c1668; *d* London, 1734) was the son of John Stanesby, yeoman of Moorly Lyme, Derbyshire. In 1682 he was apprenticed to Thomas Garrett. He married Mary Kilpin on 4 May 1690, and received the Freedom of the Turners' Company in 1691, whereupon he set up a modest establishment in Stonecutter Street, which led from Shoe Lane to the Fleet Market in the middle precinct of the parish of St Bride's. Stanesby and his son were registered as freemen in 1716. Surviving instruments bearing the

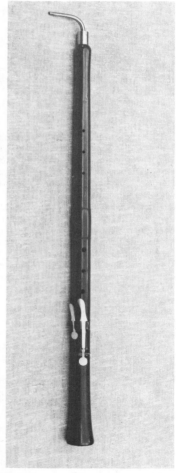

(a)   (b)

1. (a) Trade card of Thomas Stanesby (ii), engraved by George Bickham (Heal Collection, GB-Lbm); (b) tenor oboe by Thomas Stanesby (ii), London, first half of the 18th century (Victoria and Albert Museum, London)

father's mark include nine recorders and five oboes.

Hawkins wrote of Stanesby's unsuccessful attempt to make a racket from details given by Mersenne, and in Burney's *Account of the Musical Performances . . . in Commemoration of Handel* one reads that a 'Double Bassoon . . . was made with approbation of Mr Handel, by Stanesby the flute-maker, for the coronation of . . . George the second (1727) . . . but . . . no use was made of it at that time'. Unfortunately neither this instrument nor any bassoon of the elder Stanesby has survived.

Thomas Stanesby (ii) (*b* London, 1692; *d* London, March 1754) was apprenticed to his father in 1706 and set up his own establishment over the Temple Exchange in Fleet Street near St Dunstan's Church. In 1716 he was registered, with his father, as a freeman. In 1734 he inherited all his father's tools and a seal ring. His first apprentice was William Sheridan, who came to him in 1737. The second, Caleb Gedney, joined him in 1743, and finished his apprenticeship in 1750. Stanesby married, but his wife died before him without bearing children. He left all his tools, materials and unfinished work to Gedney, who appears to have continued the business at the same address.

About 1732 Stanesby, sensing the impending eclipse of the recorder in professional music circles, issued *A New System of the Flute A' Bec or Common English Flute* wherein he argued vigorously for the use of the 'C Flute' (tenor recorder in C) and presented a 'full and perfect' fingering chart. The demand for the transverse flute increased, however, and Stanesby made a considerable number of these. Halfpenny wrote that Stanesby signed himself 'junior' only up to 1732. He marked his instruments in several ways; the mark 'MURAEUS' is added to the only surviving bassoon, which is dated 1747.

The only surviving double bassoon is dated 1739 and is now in the National Museum in Dublin. The *London Daily Post* for 6 August 1739 announced '2 Grand or Double Bassoons' at the evening concert at Marylebone Gardens 'made by Mr Stanesby junior by the greatness of whose sound surpasses that of any other Bass instrument whatsoever'. F. G. Rendall (*Grove 5*) wrote that Stanesby seems to have reintroduced the tenor oboe, for which he issued a scale of fingerings. Only one of these made by Stanesby has survived, and is now in the Victoria and Albert Museum, London. Other surviving instruments listed by Halfpenny include 18 flutes (of which ten are ivory), 12 recorders and three oboes.

Stanesby's later instruments show a simplification of the older Baroque exterior following the general trend toward the classical woodwind design. Typical examples are a few recorders showing a slender profile with a footpiece similar to those of transverse flutes of the time, omitting the bulbous bottoms of recorders made by himself, his father, and others a generation earlier. But this exterior change is not matched by a change in acoustical properties. His transverse flutes mostly follow the English design established by Bressan and his father; that is, all sockets open toward the headpiece. Makers in the rest of Europe had the head socket alone opening toward the foot, which facilitates the making of *corps de rechange* so frequently found with continental design flutes.

One of Stanesby's interesting trade cards has survived (Heal Collection, *GB-Lbm*) and is reproduced in fig.1*a*. It suggests that Stanesby enjoyed a reputation outside his own country.

BIBLIOGRAPHY

HawkinsH

C. Burney: *An Account of the Musical Performances . . . in Commemoration of Handel* (London, 1785)

E. Halfpenny: 'The English 2- and 3-keyed Hautboy', *GSJ*, ii (1949), 10

——: 'The "Tenner Hoboy"', *GSJ*, v (1952), 17

——: 'Stanesby, Major and Minor', *ML*, xxiv (1953), 41

——: 'The English Baroque Treble Recorder', *GSJ*, ix (1956), 82

——: 'Biographical Notices of the Early English Woodwind-making School, *c.*1650–1750', *GSJ*, xii (1959), 44

——: 'Further Light on the Stanesby Family', *GSJ*, xiii (1960), 59

L. G. Langwill: *An Index of Musical Wind-instrument Makers* (Edinburgh, 1960, 3/1972)

——: *The Bassoon and Contrabassoon* (London, 1965)

FRIEDRICH VON HUENE

Stanford, Sir Charles Villiers (*b* Dublin, 30 Sept 1852; *d* London, 29 March 1924). British composer, teacher and conductor.

1. Life. 2. Works, influence.

1. LIFE. He was the only child of John James Stanford, a distinguished lawyer, and his second wife, Mary. His father was a keen amateur cellist and singer, and from his earliest days Stanford was exposed to cultured musical influences and a brilliant circle of judicial, medical and ecclesiastical intellectuals who frequented his home. He received a sound classical education at Henry Tilney Bassett's school, Dublin, and a firm foundation in the piano, the organ, the violin and composition from Michael Quarry, Robert Stewart (at St Patrick's Cathedral and the Royal Irish Academy of Music), Joseph Robinson, and Arthur O'Leary (with whom he studied in London). From Quarry in particular he gained a lasting regard for the music of Bach, Schumann and Brahms, little known in Ireland at that time. He is credited with the composition of a song, *The Venetian Dirge*, at the age of four, and with giving a piano recital of pieces by Handel, Beethoven, Mendelssohn, Mozart and Bach when he was nine.

Stanford had been intended for the legal profession, but in 1870 his father permitted him to follow a musical career on condition that he first receive a university education and then study music abroad. In that year he entered Queen's College, Cambridge, as a choral scholar. His talent before he reached his 18th birthday may be judged from a Concert Overture for full orchestra dated 30 July 1870 (almost his earliest surviving autograph). At Cambridge he achieved such distinction that by 1873 he had been appointed organist of Trinity College and conductor of two societies which he now combined under his leadership – the Cambridge Amateur Vocal Guild and the Cambridge Musical Society which had been a male choir up to that time; these were unprecedented achievements for an undergraduate. In 1874 he took the BA with third-class honours in the classical tripos.

During the second half of 1874 and of each of the two years following, Trinity College granted him leave of absence to study abroad. In the first two years he went to Leipzig to study composition under Reinecke and the piano under Papperitz. Surviving from this time is a commemoration anthem, *In memoria aeterna erit*, possibly written for the commemoration of benefactors at Trinity College. Then in 1876, at the instigation of Joachim, he studied under Friedrich Kiel in Berlin. Stanford travelled widely, visiting many musical centres in Germany and France; he met both Brahms and Offenbach and other leading figures, and was present at the opening of the Bayreuth Festival Theatre.

Charles Villiers Stanford: portrait (c1920) by William Rothenstein in the National Portrait Gallery, London

His reputation in Cambridge, both as composer and as conductor of the university musical society (CUMS), steadily increased and his name soon spread. In 1875 his First Symphony gained second prize in the Alexandra Palace competition for British composers, he published his Suite op.2 and Toccata op.3, and for the CUMS he composed and performed an extensive work for soloists, choir and orchestra, *The Resurrection*. Stanford attracted attention in London in 1876 through his incidental music to Tennyson's *Queen Mary*, composed at Tennyson's request for the Lyceum production. His *Festival Overture* was performed at the 1877 Gloucester Festival, and in the same year he wrote his first opera, *The Veiled Prophet of Khorassan*, first performed in Hanover. To this early period belong the now well-known Morning, Communion and Evening Services in Bb op.10 which set a higher standard in English church music than had been achieved for 200 years. In 1882 he conducted his Second Symphony with the CUMS and the Serenade in G op.18 at the Birmingham Festival.

Stanford possessed unbounded energy and his reputation kept pace with this untiring activity in promoting his highest ideals in music; soon he was offered the leading appointments in Britain. At the opening of the Royal College of Music in 1883 he was made professor of composition and orchestral playing (concurrently with Parratt's appointment as professor of organ), and in 1885 he became conductor of the London Bach Choir, a post he held until 1902. He was elected professor of music at Cambridge in 1887 – a signal honour for a man of 35. Through this post, and more particularly through his post at the RCM, both of which he held until his death, he exercised more influence in the teaching of composition than any other

musician in Britain throughout his tenure. In 1882 he resigned his organistship at Trinity College and moved to London because of ever-increasing demands on his time and energy. From 1901 to 1910 he was conductor to the Leeds Triennial Festival, and was associated as composer, conductor or both with every British festival of his time.

On 6 April 1878 he had married Jane Anna Maria (Jennie) Wetton at Ockley parish church, Surrey; they had two children, Guy and Geraldine Mary. He received many honours, including the honorary degrees of DMus (Oxford, 1883), MusD (Cambridge, 1888), DCL (Durham, 1894) and LlD (Leeds, 1904). He was knighted in 1902. Stanford died two days after Parratt and his ashes are buried in the north choir aisle of Westminster Abbey, next to those of Purcell.

2. WORKS, INFLUENCE. Stanford's name is linked with those of Parry, Parratt and Elgar in referring to the late 19th-century renaissance in English music. It is arguable both that Stanford made the greatest contribution to this renaissance, and that the labels of 'Victorian' and 'Edwardian' apply less to his music than to that of the others. His heritage of Irish folklore, folk music and mysticism was latent beneath the training and experience he gained abroad; it saved him from that insularity of outlook which had pervaded English music since Handel's time. This outward-looking characteristic was fostered by his friendship and meetings with such leading figures as Brahms, Joachim, von Bülow and Saint-Saëns, and linked with his encyclopedic knowledge of the whole field of musical literature, past and present. His contacts with the leading European musicians are attested by the collection of 177 letters and papers in his 'Autograph book' (*GB-Lcm*).

A prolific composer in almost all musical forms and for all combinations of forces, he set apart a portion of each day for composition, developing the ability to set down his final thoughts in ink without a preliminary sketch, even when this involved a full orchestral score. Most of his works received one or more performances shortly after their composition, although there were no regular repetitions of his major works, largely because of the late 19th-century convention which paid greater attention to first performances. *Grove 2* and *Grove 3* testify to the popular acclaim he received during 'his paramountcy as a composer' as Howells described it, going on to speak of the period 1911–24 as 'the days of his increasing neglect, a neglect he continually felt'. Styles and techniques in composition were changing radically and Stanford could not accept these developments other than as ephemeral, after which 'sanity' would prevail.

Nevertheless, Stanford's achievements and influence were prodigious; they may be summarized under four headings. First, he swept away the empty conventions and complacencies which had debased English church music since Purcell. In his Service in Bb and later settings he introduced a symphonic-cyclic treatment and gave the organ a vital and significant part. These, and his fine anthems and motets, enriched cathedral music and have maintained their place in the repertory. Second, he set a new standard in choral music with his oratorios and cantatas, which provided an incentive for amateurs and professionals alike at every major British festival. Of these *The Revenge*, the *Stabat mater*, *Songs of the Sea* and *Songs of the Fleet* have a perfection of workmanship and a rare beauty which are rewarding in performance. Third, in his partsongs, and still more in his solo songs with piano, he reached near perfection both in melodic invention and in capturing the mood of the poem; Plunket Greene (1921) gave some illuminating analyses.

But it was in the fourth capacity that Stanford exercised the most powerful influence on British music and musicians, that of the paramount teacher of composition. The memorial tributes of 16 of his pupils (*ML*, v) provide not only a balanced assessment of Stanford the teacher at first hand, but also a revealing character study. All smarted initially under the intolerant, autocratic lash of damning criticism of slovenliness, vulgarity, dubious material or workmanship, vagueness of attitude and the like; all acknowledged his ability to seize on the solution to every technical difficulty, and testified to the effectiveness and lasting worth of such teaching. Stanford's tuition benefited almost every British composer from Charles Wood to Lambert. The list includes Vaughan Williams, Holst, Coleridge-Taylor, Boughton, Ireland, Bridge, Butterworth, Bliss, Howells, Benjamin and Moeran, to quote only a few of the best-known names.

Stanford had a greater faith in the value of opera than had most of his countrymen at the time. Of his ten such works two received their first performances in Germany, some have not been performed, others have been performed once or twice, and it is only *Shamus O'Brien* that can claim success with 50 performances in its initial run at the London Opéra-Comique in 1896. After Howells's centenary address to the Royal Musical Association, Vaughan Williams gave his opinion that a composer of Stanford's calibre, if he had been German or Italian, would have been celebrated in every opera house in his country.

In the supplement to *Grove 4* Colles stated that the time was not ripe for a thorough re-evaluation of his music, commenting that the rare appearances of his major works in popular concert programmes 'cannot be taken as the measure of what survives of his art. The life of a large proportion of it may be held to be latent; because conditions have not been favourable it has never been presented to the public'. Such views had even greater force 12 years later at the centenary celebrations, when a scattering of his works was revived briefly to mark the occasion. One may sympathize (though not necessarily concur wholly) with similar views expressed by the composer's son Guy in letters to his cousin Susan Stanford: 'My reactions to all accounts of his life are *chiefly* that far too much emphasis has been given to his teaching and far too little on his composition' (7 November 1952) and 'One got tired to death of the same list of pupils – entirely ignoring the fact that he was a great *composer* first and foremost ... one now hopes more performances are given and less just lip-service' (6 December 1952). 50 years after his death conditions were even less favourable. Ivor Gurney's words (*ML*, v) provide an apt epitaph: 'He was a stiff master, though a very kind man; difficult to please and most glad to be pleased. England will bury many in the Abbey of Westminster much lesser than he'.

WORKS

ORATORIOS AND CANTATAS

op.
5   The Resurrection (Klopstock, trans. C. Winkworth), T, chorus, orch, org, Cambridge, 1875

—   The Golden Legend (Longfellow), solo vv, chorus, orch, ?Cambridge, 1875, unpubd
8   God is our Hope and Strength (Psalm xlvi), S, A, T, Bar, B, chorus, orch, Cambridge, 1877
17   Three Cavalier Songs (Browning), Bar, male chorus, 1880
21   Elegiac Ode (Whitman), solo vv, chorus, orch, Norwich, 1884
22   The Three Holy Children (Bible), solo vv, chorus, orch, Birmingham, 1885
24   The Revenge: a Ballad of the Fleet (Tennyson), chorus, orch, Leeds, 1886
26   Carmen saeculare (ode, Tennyson), S, chorus, orch, London, Buckingham Palace, 11 May 1887
27   O praise the Lord of Heaven (Psalm cl), S, chorus, orch, Manchester, 1887
34   The Voyage of Maeldune (ballad, Tennyson), solo vv, chorus, orch, Leeds, 1889
40   Eden (Bridges), 6 solo vv, chorus, orch, Birmingham, 1891
41   The Battle of the Baltic (ballad, T. Campbell), chorus, orch, Hereford, 1891
—   Installation Ode, 1892
46   Mass, G, 4 solo vv, chorus, orch, London, Brompton Oratory, 1893
50   The Bard (Gray), B, chorus, orch, Cardiff, 1895
52   East to West (ode, Swinburne), chorus, orch, London, 1893
62   Phaudrig Crohoore (ballad, J. S. Le Fanu), chorus, orch, Norwich, 1896
63   Requiem, solo vv, chorus, orch, Birmingham, 1897
66   Te Deum, solo vv, chorus, orch, Leeds, 1898
68   Our enemies have fallen (Tennyson) [from partsong, op.68 no.8], chorus, orch (1890)
75   Last Post (W. E. Henley), chorus, orch, Hereford, 1900
83   The Lord of Might (R. Heber), chorus, orch, London, 1903
91   Songs of the Sea (Newbolt), Bar, male chorus, orch, Leeds, 1904
96   Stabat mater, sym. cantata, solo vv, chorus, orch, Leeds, 1907
—   Choric Ode (J. H. Skrine), chorus, orch, 1907, unpubd
100   Ode to Wellington (Tennyson), S, Bar, chorus, orch, Bristol, 1908
107   A Welcome Song (Duke of Argyll), chorus, orch, 1908
—   Ode to Discord (C. L. Graves), chorus, orch, 1908
114   Ave atque vale (choral ov., Ecclesiasticus), chorus, orch, 1909
117   Songs of the Fleet (Newbolt), Bar, chorus, orch, Leeds, 1910
131   Fairy Day (3 idylls, Allingham), female chorus, chamber orch, 1913
172   Merlin and the Gleam (Tennyson), Bar, chorus, orch (1920)
177   At the Abbey Gate (Judge Darling), Bar, chorus, orch, London, 1921

CHURCH MUSIC

—   Magnificat and Nunc dimittis, F, 4vv, org, 1872, unpubd
—   Magnificat and Nunc dimittis, Eb, 6vv, org, 1873, unpubd
—   In memoria aeterna erit, commemoration anthem, S, A, T, B, SATB, org, 1874 unpubd
—   In memoria aeterna erit, commemoration anthem, S, A, T, B, S, A, T, B, 1876, unpubd
10   Morning, Communion and Evening Services, Bb, 4 solo vv, chorus, orch/org, 1879, additional Benedictus qui venit and Agnus Dei, 1910
12   Morning, Communion and Evening Services, A, chorus 4vv, orch/org, 1880
16   Awake my Heart (motet, Klopstock), Bar, chorus, org, 1881
—   If ye then be risen with Christ, Easter anthem, 1883
—   The Lord is my Shepherd (anthem, Ps xxiii), chorus, org, 1886
—   Blessed are the Dead, anthem, chorus, org, 1886
36   Morning, Communion and Evening Services, F, chorus, org, 1889; additional Benedictus qui venit and Agnus Dei, 1909
37   Two Anthems, chorus, org, c1885
38   Three Motets, 4–8vv (1905)
81   Morning, Communion and Evening Services, G, chorus, org, 1904
—   Arise, shine, for thy light is come, anthem, chorus, org (1905)
98   Magnificat & Nunc dimittis, chorus, org, 1907; additional Te Deum, Benedictus, Kyrie (1921)
—   For all the saints, choral hymn (1908)
—   O Living Will, motet (1908)
113   Six Hymns (1910)
115   Morning, Communion and Evening Services, C, chorus, org, 1909
—   I heard a voice from Heaven, anthem, 4vv (1910)
—   We bow our heads, anthem, chorus, org, from final chorus of Bach: St Matthew Passion (1910)
120   Come, ye thankful people, come, harvest anthem, 1910
123   Ye Choirs of New Jerusalem, Easter anthem, 1910
128   Festal Communion Service, Bb, chorus, orch/org, 1911
134   Blessed City, Heavenly Salem, anthem, c1913
—   St Patrick's Breastplate (anthem, Mrs Alexander) (1913)
135   Three Motets, 4–8vv (1913)
143   Thanksgiving Te Deum, Eb, 4vv, orch (1914)
145   For lo, I raise up, anthem, 1914
—   The Aviators' Hymn (A. C. Ainger) (1917)
—   Sing unto God, anthem, chorus, org (1918)

164 Magnificat, B♭, 8vv, 1918
169 Mass, d, 4vv, n.d., unpubd
173 Mass 'Via victrix', S, A, T, B, chorus, orch, org, 1919
176 Mass, 4vv, n.d., unpubd
—   Veni Creator, anthem, chorus, org (1922)
—   How beauteous are their feet, anthem (1923)
—   Morning, Communion and Evening Services, D, unison vv, org (1923)
192 Three Anthems, 4–8vv, org (1923)
—   When God of old, anthem, chorus, org (1923)
—   The Earth is the Lord's, anthem (1924)
—   Be merciful unto me, anthem (1928)
—   How long wilt thou forget me, anthem (1929)
—   Offertory Sentences (1930)

STAGE

6   Queen Mary (incidental music, Tennyson), London, Lyceum, 1876; arr. pf duet
—   The Veiled Prophet of Khorassan (opera, W. B. Squire, after Moore: Lalla Rookh), 1877; Hanover, Hoftheater, 6 Feb 1881
—   Savonarola (opera, G. A. A'Beckett), Hamburg, Stadttheater, 18 April 1884, unpubd
—   The Canterbury Pilgrims (opera, A'Beckett), London, Drury Lane, 23 April 1884
23   The Eumenides (incidental music, Aeschylus), Cambridge, 1885
29   Oedipus tyrannus (incidental music, Sophocles), Cambridge, 1887
48   Becket (incidental music, Tennyson), London, Lyceum, 1893, unpubd
55   Lorenza (opera), c1894, unperf., unpubd
61   Shamus O'Brien (opera, G. H. Jessop, after Le Fanu), London, Opéra-Comique, 2 March 1896
69   Christopher Patch (The Barber of Bath) (opera, B. C. Stephenson, G. H. Jessop), c1897, unperf., unpubd
76a Much Ado about Nothing (The Marriage of Hero) (opera, J. R. Sturgis, after Shakespeare), London, Covent Garden, 30 May 1901
102 Attila the Hun (incidental music, L. Binyon), London, His Majesty's, 1907, unpubd
130 Drake (incidental music, L. N. Parker), c1912, ?unperf., unpubd
—   The Spanish Student (incidental music, Longfellow), n.d., ?unperf., unpubd
144 The Critic (An Opera Rehearsed) (opera, L. C. James, after Sheridan), London, Shaftesbury, 14 Jan 1916
146 The Travelling Companion (opera, Newbolt, after H. Andersen), 1919; Bristol, Theatre Royal, 25 Oct 1926
—   The Miner of Falun (opera, Squire, H. F. Wilson), Act 1 only, unperf., unpubd

ORCHESTRAL

—   Rondo, vc, orch, 1869, unpubd
—   Concert Overture, 1870, unpubd
—   Symphony no.1, B♭, 1875, unpubd
—   Festival Overture, Gloucester, 1877, unpubd
18   Serenade, G, Birmingham, 1882, arr. pf duet
—   Symphony no.2 'Elegiac', d, Cambridge, 1882, unpubd
28   Symphony no.3 'Irish', f, London, 27 May 1887
—   Queen of the Seas, ov., Armada tercentenary, 1888, unpubd
31   Symphony no.4, F, Berlin, 14 Jan 1889
32   Suite, D, vn, orch, Joachim, Berlin, 14 Jan 1889
56   Symphony no.5 'L'allegro ed il penseroso', D, 1894; London, 1895
58   Suite of Ancient Dances [version of 5 movts from pf work, op.58], London, 28 Aug 1895
59   Piano Concerto no.1, G, London, 1896, unpubd
71   Concert Variations on 'Down among the dead men', c, pf, orch, London, March 1898
78   Irish Rhapsody no.1, d, 1901
80   Clarinet Concerto, a, 1 movt, 1902 (1977)
84   Irish Rhapsody no.2, f, c1903, unpubd
74   Violin Concerto no.1, D, 1904
89   Four Irish Dances [version of pf work, op.89], 1903
90   Overture in the Style of a Tragedy, 1904, unpubd
94   Symphony no.6 'In memoriam G. F. Watts', E♭, c1905, unpubd
108 March, wind, Cambridge, 1908, unpubd
109 Three Military Marches, unpubd
124 Symphony no.7, d, 1911
126 Piano Concerto no.2, c, Norfolk, Conn., 3 June 1915
137 Irish Rhapsody no.3, vc, orch, c1915, unpubd
141 Irish Rhapsody no.4, a (1914)
147 Irish Rhapsody no.5, g, London, 18 March 1917, unpubd
160 Ballata and Ballabile, vc, orch, 1918; London, 3 May 1919, unpubd
161 Irish Concertino, vn, vc, orch, 1919, unpubd
162 Violin Concerto no.2, g, 1918, unpubd
168 A Song of Agincourt, c1919, unpubd
171 Piano Concerto no.3, 1919, unpubd
180 Variations, vn, orch, 1921, unpubd; arr. vn, pf

191 Irish Rhapsody no.6, vn, orch, c1923, unpubd; arr. vn, pf (1923)

CHAMBER

Sonata no.1, A, op.9, vc, pf, c1878; Sonata no.1, D, op.11, vn, pf, c1880; 3 Intermezzi, op.13, cl, pf (1880); Pf Qt no.1, F, op.15, ?1879; Pf Qnt, d, op.25, 1887; Pf Trio no.1, E♭, op.35, 1889; Sonata no.2, d, op.39, vn, pf, 1893; Str Qt no.1, G, op.44, ?1891; Str Qt no.2, a, op.45, 1891; Legend, vn, pf, 1893; Irish Fantasies, op.54, vn, pf, 1894; Str Qt no.3, d, op.64, 1897; Sonata no.3, G, op.70, vn, pf, c1898, unpubd
Pf Trio no.2, g, op.73. 1899; Str Qnt no.1, F, op.85, 1903; Str Qnt no.2, c, op.86, c1903, unpubd; 3[?4] Irish Dances, op.89, arr. vn, pf (1917–24) [? no.2 not arr.]; 5 Characteristic Pieces, op.93, vn/vc, pf, 1905; Serenade, op.95, F, nonet, c1906, unpubd; Str Qt no.4, g, op.99, c1907, unpubd; Str Qt no.5, B♭, op.104, 1908; Str Qt no.6, a, op.121, 1910, unpubd; Sonata, op.129, cl/va, pf, c1912; Pf Qt no.2, op.133, c1912, unpubd; 6 Irish Sketches, op.154, vn, pf, c1917; 6 Easy Pieces, op.155, vn, pf, c1917
Pf Trio no.3, A, op.158 (1918); Sonata no.2, op.165, vn, pf, 1919, unpubd; Str Qt no.7, c, op.166, c1919, unpubd; Str Qt no.8, e, op.167, c1919, unpubd; 5 Bagatelles in Valse Form, op.183, vn, pf (1921); 6 Irish Dances, arr. vn, pf (1930); 6 Irish Marches, arr. vn, pf, n.d., unpubd; An Ancient Melody, A♭, arr. vn, pf, n.d., unpubd; Planxty Sudley, B♭, vn, pf, n.d., unpubd

PIANO

Suite, op.2 (1875); Toccata, op.3 (1875); Sonata, D♭, op.20, c1884, unpubd; 6 Pieces, op.42, c1887, unpubd; 10 Dances, Old and New, op.58; 4 Irish Dances, op.89, 1903; 3 Rhapsodies from Dante, a, B, C, op.92, 1875; 6 Characteristic Pieces, op.132, 1875; 5 Capriccios, op.136 (1913); Night Thoughts, op.148, 1917
Scènes de ballet, op.150 (1917); 6 Sketches (Children's Pieces) (1918); Preludes in all the Keys, nos.1–24, op.163 (1919); Ballade, g, op.170, 1919; Scherzo, b, unpubd; 3 Fancies, unpubd; A Toy Story (1920); 3 Waltzes, a, d, F, op.178 (1923); Preludes in all the Keys, nos.25–48, op.179 (1921); Fuga a 3, c, 1922, unpubd; Fuga à 4, b, 1923, unpubd; 2 pieces in The Young People's Music Portfolio, i (n.d.); 3 airs, ibid, ii (n.d./?1922); 12 Irish Airs Easily Arranged, pf (1922)

ORGAN

Jesu dulcis memoriae, prelude, 1899, unpubd; Fantasia and Toccata, d, op.57, 1894; 6 Preludes, op.88, c1903; 6 Short Preludes and Postludes, op.101, c1907; Fantasia and Fugue, d, op.103, 1907; 6 Short Preludes and Postludes, op.105, c1908; Installation March, op.108 [from orch work, op.108] (1908); Te Deum and Canzona, op.116, c1909; Idyll and Fantasia, op.121, c1910; Sonata no.1, F, op.149, 1917; Sonata no.2 'Eroica', op.151, 1917, 2nd and 3rd movts orchd
Sonata no.3 'Britannica', op.152, 1917; Sonata no.4 'Celtica', op.153, 1918; Sonata no.5 'Quasi una Fantasia', A, op.159 (1921); 6 Occasional Preludes, op.182 (1930); Fantasia upon a Tune by C. H. Parry, op.187, 1922; 4 Intermezzi, op.189 (1923); 3 Preludes and Fugues, op.193, 1922; Chorale Prelude [in A Little Organ Book, c1920]; 3 Idylls, op.194 (1930)

PARTSONGS

6 Part-songs, op.33, c1889, unpubd; 4 Part-songs, op.47, 1892; 6 Elizabethan Pastorales, op.49, 1892; A Ballad of the Ranks (Conan Doyle), female chorus 2vv (1893); Worship, 4vv (1893); The Frontier Line (Conan Doyle), female chorus 2vv (1893); As with gladness, 4vv (1894); 6 Elizabethan Pastorales op.53, 1894; 6 Elizabethan Pastorales, op.67, 1897; A Cycle of 9 Qts, op.68 (Tennyson: The Princess) (1898); Out in the windy west (A. C. Benson) [in Choral Songs in Honour of Queen Victoria (1899)]; 6 Irish Folksongs, op.78 (Moore), 1901; The Lark's Grave (Westwood), female chorus 2vv (1906)
A March Landscape (Wordsworth), female chorus 2vv (1906); Robin Redbreast (Allingham), female chorus 2vv (1907); The Echoing Green (Blake) (1907); 4 Part-songs, op.106, male chorus 4vv (1908); 4 Part-songs, op.110, 1908; 3 Part-songs, op.111, 1908; The Shepherd's Sirena (Drayton), female chorus 2vv (1909); 8 Part-songs, op.119, 1910; God and the Universe (choral song, Tennyson) [from song, op.97] (1906)
8 Part-songs, op.127, 1910; My Land (T. O. Davis), female chorus 2vv (1911); On Time, op.142 (ode, Milton), 8vv, 1914; 10 Part-songs, op.156, c1917, unpubd; The Rose upon my Balcony (Thackeray), female chorus 2vv (1918); Allen-a-dale (Scott), female chorus 3vv (1922); 6 Irish Airs (Moore), 4vv (1922); Virtue (G. Herbert), female chorus 2vv (1923); Lady May (H. Chappell), female chorus 3vv (1924)

SOLO SONGS

(for 1v, pf unless otherwise stated)

My boat is ready (C. Stephenson) (n.d.); A Valentine (A.D. 1560) (anon.) (1876); Irish Eyes (A. P. Graves) (1876); From the Red Rose (A. P. Graves) (n.d.); 2 Songs (Tennyson: Queen Mary) (1876); To Carnations (Herrick) (1877); 3 Ditties of the Olden Times (Suckling)

(1877); La Belle Dame sans merci (Keats) (1877); 8 Songs, op.1 (G. Eliot: Spanish Gypsy) (1877–8); 6 Songs, op.14 (1882); Hands all Round (Tennyson) (1882); Prospice (Browning) (1884); 6 Songs, op.19 (1884); Carmen Familiare Sanctae Colegii (1888); Ould Doctor Mack (A. P. Graves) (1890); We wander by the waves (1890); For ever mine [in 12 New Songs by British Composers (1891)]; The Tomb, 1891; A Child's Garland of Songs, op.30 (Stevenson) (1892); A Message to Phillis (Heywood) (1893); The Old Navy (Marryat) (1893); The Flag Union (A. Austin) (1893); Crossing the Bar (Tennyson) (1893)
May's Love (E. B. Browning) (1893); A Corsican Dirge (trans. A. Strettell) (1893); 6 Songs, op.4 (Heine) (1893); 6 Songs, op.7 (Heine) (1893); Prince Madoc's Farewell (F. Hemans) (1894); Parted (1896); The Calico Dress (Jessop) (1896); The Rose of Kilarney (A. P. Graves) (1896); O Fondest and Truest (1896); 3 Songs, op.43 (Bridges) (1897); Clown's Songs from 'Twelfth Night', op.65 (1897); The Battle of Pelusium (1897); Is it the wind of dawn?, duet (1898); Die Wallfahrt nach Kevlaar, op.72 (Heine) (1899); Jack Tar (Tennyson) (1900); An Irish Idyll in 6 Miniatures, op.77 (M. O'Neill) (1901); Sea Wrack (O'Neill) (?1902); The Linnet (1902); 5 Sonnets, op.82 (E. Holmes: Triumph of Love) (1903)
6 Songs of Faith, op.97 (Tennyson, Whitman) (1908); 4 Songs, op.112 (Tennyson) (1908); 6 Bible Songs, op.113, 1v, org (1909); Cushendall, op.118 (song cycle, J. Stevenson) (1910); 4 Songs, op.125 (1911); A Fire of Turf, op.139 (cycle of Irish songs, Letts) (1913); Lullaby (Sherman), duet (1913); The King's Highway (1914); 6 Songs, op.138, 2S, pf (1914); A Sheaf of Songs from Leinster, op.140 (Letts) (1914); A Carol of Bells (L. N. Parker) (1915); Devon Men (P. Hasleden) (1916); St George of England (C. F. Smith) (1917); The Grand Match (1917); A Japanese Lullaby (E. Field) (1918); St Andrew's Land (C. F. Smith) (1918); The Fair Hills of Ireland (1918); Wales for Ever (C. F. Smith, with Welsh trans. by E. Lewis) (1918)
Songs of a Roving Celt, op.157 (M. Maclean) (1919); There is no land like England (Tennyson: The Foresters) (1919); 6 Songs, op.174 (O'Neill: The Glens of Antrim) (1920); 6 Songs, op.175 (1921); Elegia maccheronica (C. L. Graves), 1921; A Runnable Stag (J. Davidson) (1923); Satyr's Song (Fletcher) (1923); The Hoofs of the Horses (1923); Fairy Lures ('H. F.') (1923); Songs (H. D. Adams: The Elfin Pedlar) (1925); The Merry Month of May (T. Dekker) (1927); The Sower's Song (T. Carlyle) (1927); Witches' Charms (Jonson) (1928); Nonsense Rhymes (Lear) (1960)

EDITIONS AND ARRANGEMENTS

Songs of Old Ireland (A. P. Graves), 1v, pf (London, 1882)
Blarney Ballads (C. L. Graves), 1v, pf (London, 1889)
Irish Songs and Ballads (A. P. Graves), 1v, pf (London, 1893)
Moore's Irish Melodies Restored, op.60, 1v, pf (London, 1895)
H. Purcell: Ten Sonatas of Four Parts, The Works of Henry Purcell, vii (London, 1896)
God Save the Queen (London, 1897)
J. S. Bach: Sleepers, Wake (London, 1898)
God Save the King (London, 1901)
Songs of Erin, op.76, 1v, pf (London, 1901)
The Petrie Collection of Irish Music (London, 1902–5)
The National Song Book (London, 1906)
The Organ Library (London, c1907–)
J. S. Bach: St Matthew Passion (London, 1910)
with W. Parratt: *Class Singing for Schools* (London, n.d.)
A. Goring Thomas: The Swan and the Skylark, orchd, unpubd

Principal publishers: Boosey & Hawkes, Curwen, Novello, Stainer & Bell

WRITINGS

'Defence of Richard Wagner: Reply to Rowbotham', *Nineteenth Century*, xxiv (1888), 727
'Mr Hubert Parry's "Judith"', *Fortnightly Review*, l (1888), 537
'Ernst Frank', *Murray's Magazine*, vii (1890), 202
'Verdi's "Falstaff"', *Fortnightly Review*, liii (1893), 455; also in *Shakespearia*, x (1893), 86
'On Musical Criticism in England', *Fortnightly Review*, lv (1894), 826
'On Joseph Robinson', *Cornhill Magazine*, v (1898), 795
Studies and Memories (London, 1908)
Musical Composition: a Short Treatise for Students (London, 1911, 6/1950)
Brahms (London, 1912)
Pages from an Unwritten Diary (London, 1914)
'Folk-song and Nationality', *MQ*, i (1915), 232
'Music and War', *Quarterly Review* (1915), 393
'Government and Music', *Musical Standard* (8 Jan 1916), 32
with C. Forsyth: *A History of Music* (London, 1916, 4/1951)
'William Sterndale Bennett', *MQ*, ii (1916), 628–57
'Sanity (?) in Composition', *Musical Herald* (1917), March, 78
'War and Music: Plea for an Art which has Enriched the World', *Musical Standard* (12 May 1917), 913
Interludes, Records and Reflections (London, 1922)

BIBLIOGRAPHY

'Tennyson's "Crossing the Bar" set to Music by Stanford', *English Illustrated Magazine*, vii (1890), 651
'Dr. Stanford and his "Eden"', *MT*, xxxii (1891), 599
F. Klickman: 'C. V. Stanford', *Sylvia's Journal* (1893), Aug, 458
J. F. Runciman: 'East to West', *Magazine of Music*, x (1893), 154
'The Veiled Prophet', *New Quarterly Musical Review* (1893), Aug, 63
Portrait and biography, *Cabinet Portrait Gallery*, i/2 (London, 1894), 25
Pitt: 'Shamus O'Brien', *Magazine of Music*, xiii (1896), 249
Biography, *Magazine of Music*, xiii (1896), 398
Portrait, *Strand*, xiv (1897), 685
Biographical notes, *MT*, xxxix (1898), 785
Review of *Pages from an Unwritten Diary*, *Spectator*, cxiii (1914), 595
Reviews of *The Critic*, *MO*, xl (1916), 320; *MT*, lvii (1916), 85; *Saturday Review* (29 Jan 1916), 106; *Spectator*, cxvi (1916), 257
H. Plunket Greene: 'Stanford's Songs', *ML*, ii (1921), 94
J. F. Porte: *Sir Charles V. Stanford* (London and New York, 1921/R1976)
W. Lyle: 'A Personal Impression', *Musical News*, xxviii (1922), 74
H. Orsmond Anderton: 'The Irish Minstrel: Sir Charles V. Stanford', *MO*, xlvi (1922), 413
W. J. Turner: 'Why we have no English Music', *New Statesman*, xxiii (5 April 1924), 41
'A Double Bereavement', *Saturday Review* (5 April 1924), 343
Obituary, *The Times* (31 March 1924)
'Charles Villiers Stanford by some of his Pupils', *ML*, v (1924), 193
T. F. Dunhill: 'C. V. Stanford: some Aspects of his Life and Works', *PMA*, liii (1927–8), 42
E. Markham Lee: 'Some Stanford Songs', *MO*, liii (1929), 722
'The Autograph MS of Stanford's "Revenge"', *British Museum Quarterly*, iii (1929), 77
J. A. Fuller Maitland: *The Music of Parry and Stanford* (Cambridge, 1934)
D. Hussey: 'C. V. Stanford', *Spectator*, clv (1935), 233
H. Plunket Greene: *Charles Villiers Stanford* (London, 1935)
D. F. Tovey: 'C. V. Stanford: Clarinet Concerto in One Movement, op. 80', *Essays in Musical Analysis*, iii (London, 1936), 197
A. H. Fox Strangways: *Music Observed* (London, 1936/R1968), 57ff
J. Baird Ewens: 'C. V. Stanford', *The Choir* (1937), 250, 278
T. F. Dunhill: 'Stanford, Charles V.', *DNB*
R. Aldrich: 'C. V. Stanford', *Concert Life in New York, 1902–23* (New York, 1941), 193
R. R. Ottley: 'Six Professors', *National Review*, cxxiii (1944), 428
G. F. Brockless: 'Two Irish Minstrels: Thomas Moore and C. V. Stanford', *The Choir* (1952), 163
A. J. E. Lello: 'Brief Account of Stanford's Music', *MO*, lxxvi (1952), 659
H. Howells: 'An Address at the Centenary of C. V. Stanford', *PRMA*, lxxix (1953–4), 19
G. Brown: 'Re-valuations: (V) Charles Stanford', *Quarterly Record of the Incorporated Association of Organists*, xlvii (1962), no.187, p.67; no.188, p.99; no.189, p.19
F. Hudson: 'C. V. Stanford: nova bibliographica', *MT*, civ (1963), 728
——: 'A Catalogue of the Works of Charles Villiers Stanford (1852–1924)', *MR*, xxv (1964), 44
——: 'C. V. Stanford: nova bibliographica II', *MT*, cv (1964), 734
——: 'Stanford, (Sir) Charles Villiers', *MGG*
——: 'C. V. Stanford: nova bibliographica III', *MT*, cviii (1967), 326
——: 'A Revised and Extended Catalogue of the Works of Charles Villiers Stanford (1852–1924)', *MR*, xxxvii (1976), 106
G. Norris: *Stanford, the Cambridge Jubilee and Tchaikovsky* (Newton Abbot, 1980)

FREDERICK HUDSON

Stanislav, Josef (*b* Hamburg, 22 Jan 1897; *d* Prague, 5 Aug 1971). Czech composer, pianist and administrator. His father was an orchestral player at various European opera houses, but Stanislav began his studies in Prague, with Jeremiáš and Foerster for composition and with Mikeš and Veselý for the piano. He graduated from the Prague Conservatory master classes as a pupil of Novák (composition, 1922) and Hoffmeister (piano, 1929). At the university he was a pupil of Zdeněk Nejedlý. In the inter-war period he was a leading figure in the organization of Prague musical life. As a communist he was employed in the amateur actors' union (Svaz DDOČ) and wrote music for Prague performances of plays by Russian and left-wing German writers. He was also active in the Přítomnost contemporary music association. In 1933 he was a delegate to the Olympiad of

Workers' Theatre and Music (MORT) in Moscow, and he took part in cultural activities associated with the formation in Czechoslovakia of a popular anti-fascist front (1935). His works were banned during the German occupation. After 1945 he helped to re-establish Czech musical life: he participated in the formation of the Czech Composers' Union and his mass political songs were widely disseminated. In 1948 he was appointed professor in the popular creative art department of the Prague Academy, and in 1953 he was made director of the institute for ethnography and folklore of the Czech Academy of Sciences. He received several state awards for his artistic and public work.

WORKS
(selective list)

Orch: Symfonické vypravování [Sym. narration], n.d.; Rudoarmějská symfonie [Red army sym.], G, 1942
Cantatas: Hledání ztracené hudby [Looking for lost music], 1930; Píseň o Granadě [Song about Granada], 1936; Bílé kříže [White crosses], 1937; Pochod úrody [March of the crop], 1937, rev. 1949; Malá kantata [Little cantata], 1941; Lidice, 1947; Matka země [Mother earth], 1950; Stalin bohatýr [Stalin the warrior], 1952
Inst: Sonata, E♭, va, pf, 1920; 3 pf sonatas, E, 1921, e, 1929, 'To jsou Vaši bratři' [Those are your brothers], 1944; Suita 1931, jazz ens, 1931; Sonata, vn, pf, 1933; Str Qt, C, 1935
Numerous songs and choruses, incidental music

WRITINGS

O té lidové a vážné hudbě a lidových hudebnících [Folk music, art music and folk musicians] (Prague, 1939)
Hudební kultura, umění a život [Musical culture, art and life] (Prague, 1940)
ed. J. Macek: *Soubor kritik a statí o hudbě* [Collection of reviews and essays on music] (Prague, 1957)
Ludvík Kuba (Prague, 1963)

BIBLIOGRAPHY
ČSHS
M. Koubková and M. Příhoda: *Soupis vydaných skladeb a článků* [Catalogue of published compositions and articles] (Prague, 1961)
JIŘÍ MACEK

Stanislavsky [Alexeyev], **Konstantin Sergeyevich** (*b* Moscow, 5 Jan 1863; *d* Moscow, 7 Aug 1938). Russian theatre and opera director, actor and theorist. He directed and performed in operettas in his family's private theatre and prepared for an opera career with the tenor Fyodor Komisarzhevsky. He turned to drama only because his voice proved unsuitable for opera. In 1898 he and Vladimir Nemirovich-Danchenko founded the Moscow Art Theatre, where they encouraged new playwrights such as Chekhov and Gorky and experimented with naturalistic staging. Out of this distinguished ensemble developed the Stanislavsky system, the theatre's most widespread approach to acting and directing. According to the system an actor prepares his role from within instead of concentrating on external presentation; he determines his character's psychological and social background, even extending beyond the specific dramatic situation. Combined with the actor's self-awareness and 'emotion memory', this leads to complete identification with the character, in turn resulting in an intensely realistic performance. Stanislavsky approached setting, costume, movement, light and sound with similarly studied concern for detail and accuracy. His early musical training and Shalyapin's influence left him especially sensitive to tempo and rhythm, and he proposed classes in music for his actors. He was among the first producers to 'orchestrate' serious dramatic scenes with music and sound-effects to support underlying moods and ideas. He believed that dramatic art was moving towards 'the synthesis of music and drama, of words and sound'.

Stanislavsky's last 20 years were devoted more to opera than to theatre. In 1918 he organized the Bol'shoy Theatre Opera Studio whose aims were to set up a laboratory for research in the art of lyric drama; to renovate archaic traditions of opera production; to apply the system to opera acting; and to fuse in performance music, singing, words and movement. He maintained that the score, not the libretto, must be the point of departure in producing opera, and he depended upon the music to supply his motivation and truth, as well as tempo and rhythm. Immediately successful and ultimately influential, his studio productions were noted for narrative clarity and consistency, convincing acting and unmannered singing. By 1926 the studio, detached from the Bol'shoy, was renamed the Stanislavsky Opera Theatre. Illness prevented Stanislavsky from taking sole responsibility for productions after 1928, but he continued planning and supervising opera until his death. His studio productions included: Tchaikovsky's *Eugene Onegin*, 1919 (Act 1), 1922 (complete); Massenet's *Werther*, 1921; Cimarosa's *Il matrimonio segreto*, 1925; Rimsky-Korsakov's *Tsar's Bride*, 1926; Puccini's *La bohème*, 1927; Rimsky-Korsakov's *May Night*, 1928; Musorgsky's *Boris Godunov*, 1929; Tchaikovsky's *The Queen of Spades*, 1930; Rimsky-Korsakov's *The Golden Cockerel*, 1932; Rossini's *Il barbiere di Siviglia*, 1933; Bizet's *Carmen*, 1935; Donizetti's *Don Pasquale*, 1936; Puccini's *Madama Butterfly*, 1938; and, posthumously produced, Verdi's *Rigoletto*, 1939.

WRITINGS

My Life in Art (London, 1923; Russ. orig., *Moya zhizn' v iskusstve*, 1926)
An Actor Prepares (London, 1936; Russ. orig., *Rabota aktyora nad soboy*, i, 1938)
Rabota aktyora nad soboy, ii (Moscow, 1948; Eng. trans., 1949 as *Building a Character*)
Creating a Role (London, 1949; Russ. orig., *Rabota aktyora nad rol'yu*, 1957)
ed. D. Magarshack: *Stanislavsky on the Art of the Stage* (London, 1950)
ed. M. N. Kedrov: *K. S. Stanislavsky: sobraniye sochineniy* [Collected works] (Moscow, 1954–61)

BIBLIOGRAPHY
K. E. Antarova, ed.: *Besedï K. S. Stanislavskovo v Studii Bol'shovo v 1918–22 gg.* [Conversations with Stanislavsky at the Bol'shoy Studio during the years 1918–22] (Moscow, 1939, rev. 3/1952)
P. I. Rumyantsev: 'Rabota Stanislavskovo nad *Borisom Godunovïm*' [Stanislavsky's work on *Boris Godunov*], *Teatral'niye al'manakh* (1946), no.1, p.120
——: 'Sistema Stanislavskovo v opernom teatre' [Stanislavsky's system in the opera theatre], *Ezhegodnik M.Kh.T* (1947), 471
G. V. Kristi: *Rabota Stanislavskovo v opernom teatre* [Stanislavsky's work in the opera theatre] (Moscow, 1952)
P. I. Rumyantsev: *Rabota Stanislavskovo nad opernoy Rigoletto* [Stanislavsky's work on *Rigoletto*] (Moscow, 1955)
I. N. Vinogradskaya, ed.: *Zhizn' i tvorchestvo K. S. Stanislavskovo: letopis'* [The life and work of Stanislavsky: a chronicle], iii (Moscow, 1973)
E. R. Hapgood, ed.: *Stanislavsky on Opera* (New York, 1975) [incl. recollections by P. I. Rumyantsev of Stanislavsky's productions]
PAUL SHEREN

Stanley, John (*b* London, 17 Jan 1712; *d* London, 19 May 1786). English composer and organist. He became blind as the result of a domestic accident at the age of two, and began to study music as a diversion when he was seven. Little progress was made under his first teacher, John Reading, but he got on so well under Maurice Greene at St Paul's Cathedral that before he was 12 he was appointed organist at the nearby church of All Hallows, Bread Street. In 1726 he obtained a

John Stanley: engraving by Mary Ann Scott after Thomas Gainsborough

similar post at St Andrew's, Holborn, 'in preference to a great number of candidates' (Burney), and in 1734 he was made organist to the Honourable Society of the Inner Temple, having resigned his All Hallows appointment in 1727. According to Burney, Stanley's playing of voluntaries at the Temple used to attract musicians, including Handel, from all over London. He was also an excellent violinist and for several years directed the subscription concerts at the Swan tavern, Cornhill, and the Castle, Paternoster Row. In 1729 he became the youngest person ever to gain the BMus degree at Oxford University.

Stanley was married in 1738 to Sarah, the elder daughter of Captain Edward Arlond (not 'Arnold', as is sometimes seen) of the East India Company, who brought him a dowry of £7000. In the same year the couple took up residence in Walbrook, and Sarah's sister Ann, who lived with them, later acted as amanuensis to the blind composer. Shortly after his marriage Stanley became friendly with the future music historian, John Hawkins, who supplied him with texts for solo cantatas, and who later lived opposite the house in Hatton Garden to which Stanley moved in 1751. Thanks largely to his remarkable memory, Stanley was able to enjoy a comfortable living as an organist and teacher and to join in music-making and card-playing with a large circle of friends. He was also able to direct several Handel oratorios during the 1750s, and after Handel's death in 1759 he assumed responsibility for the Lenten oratorio seasons at Covent Garden (and later Drury Lane), first with the younger J. C. Smith and from 1776 with Thomas Linley. His own oratorios, which he modelled on Handel's, were included in the same seasons. In 1770 he was elected a governor of the Foundling Hospital and until his death took a keen

interest in its musical affairs, directing the annual *Messiah* performances in 1775–7, and selecting and composing music for the chapel services. He also took part in charitable performances at the Magdalen Hospital. In 1779 he succeeded Boyce as Master of the King's Band of Musicians, in which capacity he composed a number of New Year and birthday odes, the music of which has not survived. His collection of music, books and instruments was auctioned at Christie's in June 1786.

Stanley is chiefly remembered today for his three published sets of organ voluntaries, which include pieces dating from the 1730s, and perhaps earlier. They are mostly in the two-movement form established by his teachers, Reading and Greene, consisting of a preludial Adagio for the diapasons and a quick movement which features some solo stop such as the cornet or the trumpet. Each volume ends with three or four preludes and fugues for full organ. Even more interesting, however, are the concertos and the cantatas, which illustrate the part played by Stanley's music in the transition from the Handelian Baroque to the *galant* style associated in England with J. C. Bach. The six concertos op.2 are among the finest English string concertos in the Corelli–Handel tradition, and they were popular enough to be reissued in arrangements for organ and also as solos for violin, flute or harpsichord. The sixth of them (with one movement omitted) reappeared as the third of the op.10 set of keyboard concertos, published some 33 years later, but the later concertos tend much more towards the newer, pre-Classical style. He abandoned fugues in favour of ritornello–sonata movements and elegant, symmetrical dances, and the keyboard writing (especially of no.6) seems to have been designed more for the late 18th-century fortepiano than for the early 18th-century organ or harpsichord.

A similar, though perhaps less radical, change of style can be observed in the two sets of six solo cantatas. The first of these, dating from 1742, shows a command of the da capo aria which is rare among Stanley's English contemporaries, and each cantata includes at least one example of the form. In the later set, published in 1748, there are none at all, most of the arias being in a binary form with repeats, often with instrumental symphonies to separate the two main vocal sections. (Binary forms also predominate in the two sets of instrumental solos, opp.1 and 4.) *The Choice of Hercules*, *Pan and Syrinx* and *The Power of Musick*, though often described as cantatas, are larger-scale works and represent a rather different genre, requiring orchestral accompaniment and in one case a chorus as well. Except that their recitatives consist of narrative rather than dialogue they resemble the pastoral, *Arcadia, or The Shepherd's Wedding*, that Stanley wrote for Drury Lane in celebration of George III's marriage to Queen Charlotte in 1761. This is the only extant example of the music he composed for the theatre, and if it seems to lack any strong dramatic instinct this is not surprising in view of the librettist's own admission that he 'paid but little attention to the nature of dramatic composition in the conduct of this piece'. Stanley may also be credited with the composition of a full-length opera, *Teraminta*, to a libretto by Henry Carey; there is no record of any performance but the attribution to him of the only surviving score (a manuscript in *GB-Lcm*) seems well founded (see Williams, 1979).

WORKS

STAGE

Oroonoko (incidental music, J. Hawkesworth, adapted from T. Southerne), Drury Lane, 1 Dec 1759, lost

The Tears and Triumphs of Parnassus (masque, R. Lloyd and A. Murphy), Drury Lane, 17 Nov 1760, lost

Arcadia, or The Shepherd's Wedding (dramatic pastoral, Lloyd), Drury Lane, 26 Oct 1761, *GB-Lcm*

Teraminta (opera, 3, H. Carey), not perf., *Lcm*

ORATORIOS

Jephtha (J. Free), ?1751–2, *GB-Lcm, D-Hs*

Zimri (Hawkesworth), Covent Garden, 12 March 1760, pubd (London, 1760)

The Fall of Egypt (Hawkesworth), Drury Lane, 23 March 1774, *GB-Lcm*

CANTATAS ETC

6 Cantatas, 1v, insts, op.3 (London, 1742): Marcus the young, the noble (J. Hawkins), 1v, vn, fl, bc; To wisdom's cold delights (Hawkins), 1v, vn, bc; Teach me Venus every art (Hawkins), 1v, bc; Whilst others barter ease for state (Hawkins), 1v, vn, 2 hn, bc; Compell'd by sultry Phoebus' heat (Hawkins), 1v, vn, bc; The god Vertumnus lov'd Pomona fair (F. Webb), 1v, vn, bc

6 Cantatas, 1v, insts, op.8 (London, 1748) [all texts by Hawkins]: Who'll buy a heart, 1v, vn, bc; Aloft and near her highest noon, 1v, 2 vn, va, bc; Cease Eugenio thus to gaze, 1v, vn, fl, ob, bc; Cymon, a rough unpolish'd swain, 1v, 2 vn, bc; Alas, my Julia, now no more, 1v, 2 vn, va, bc; No sooner had my infant face, 1v, 2 vn, 2 fl, bc

3 Cantatas, 1v, insts, op.9 (London, 1751): As in a pensive form Myrtilla sate, 1v, bc; As Delia (blest with ev'ry grace), 1v, bc; Long had fair Delia slighted, 1v, vn, ob/fl, bc

As once a gentle redbreast [The Redbreast] (cantata, McClellan), 1v, 2 vn, bc (London, 1784)

Great Hercules, Jove's warlike son [The Choice of Hercules] (ode), SAB, 2 tpt, 2 hn, 2 ob, bn, 2 vn, bc, *GB-Ckc, Lbm*

Rise harmony [The Power of Musick] (?cantata), A, SATB, 2 ob, bn, 2 vn, va, vc, db, org, *GB-Ckc*

The gay nymph Syrinx [Pan and Syrinx] (?cantata), S, 2 ob, bn, 2 vn, va, vc, db, bc, *GB-Ckc*

COURT ODES

(*music lost; librettos by W. Whitehead unless otherwise stated*)

Let Gallia mourn! th' insulting foe, birthday, 4 June 1779; And dares insulting France pretend, New Year, 1 Jan 1780; Still o'er the deep does Britain reign, birthday, 5 June 1780; Ask round the world, from age to age, New Year, 1 Jan 1781; Still does the rage of war prevail?, birthday, 4 June 1781; O wond'rous power of inborn worth, New Year, 1 Jan 1782; Still does reluctant Peace refuse, birthday, 4 June 1782; Ye nation, hear th' important tale, New Year, 1 Jan 1783; At length the troubled waters rest, birthday, 4 June 1783; Enough of arms, to happier ends, New Year, 1 Jan 1784; Hail to the day, whose beams again, birthday, 4 June 1784; Delusive is the poet's dream, New Year, 1 Jan 1785; Amid the thunder of the war [True Glory seems the pride of war] (T. Warton), birthday, 4 June 1785; Dear to Jove, a genial isle (Warton), New Year, 1 Jan 1786; When Freedom nurs'd her native fire (Warton), birthday, 5 June 1786

SACRED VOCAL

Hear me when I call (anthem), A, SAB, org, 1734, *EIRE-Dcc, GB-Ob*

My strength will I ascribe (anthem), S, A, SATB, org, *EIRE-Dcc, GB-Ob*; rev. with new final chorus, S, A, SA, Thomas Coram Foundation, London

Praise the Lord, O Jerusalem (anthem), A, B, SATB, org, 1740, *EIRE-Dcc, GB-Ob*

Arise, pour out thine heart (anthem), S, A, SAB, org, c1774, Thomas Coram Foundation, London

Hearken unto me my people (anthem), S, A, SA, org, c1774, Thomas Coram Foundation, London

Jehovah Lord, how great, how wondrous great (anthem), S, A, SA, org, Thomas Coram Foundation, London

Give praises unto God (hymn), SSB; With one consent (hymn), SSB, org; both *GB-Ob*; others pubd in 18th-century anthologies

INSTRUMENTAL

(*all published in London*)

op.

1 Eight Solo's, (fl/vn, bc)/hpd (1740); ed. G. Pratt (London, 1973); ed. J. Caldwell (London, 1974)

2 Six Concerto's in 7 parts, str (1742); ed. G. Finzi (London, 1949); arr. org, str (c1745); arr. (fl/vn, bc)/hpd (c1745)

4 Six Solo's, (fl/vn, bc)/hpd (1745); ed. G. Pratt (London, 1973); ed. J. Caldwell (London, 1974)

5 Ten Voluntarys, org/hpd (1748/R1957); ed. in Tallis to Wesley, xxvii (New York and London, 1967)

6 Ten Voluntarys, org/hpd (1752/R1957); ed. in Tallis to Wesley, xxviii (New York and London, 1967)

7 Ten Voluntaries, org/hpd (1754/R1957); ed. in Tallis to Wesley, xxix (New York and London, 1967)

10 Six Concertos, org/hpd/pf (1775)

Miscellaneous songs and inst pieces pubd in 18th-century anthologies; MSS in the following libraries: *EIRE-Dn, GB-Cfm, Ckc, Cpl, CDp, DRc, Gm, Lam, Lbm, Lco* [see Johnstone, 1967], *Mch, Mp, Oumc, P*

BIBLIOGRAPHY

BurneyH

'Some Account of John Stanley, Esq.', *European Magazine and London Review*, vi (1784), 171

W. Coxe: *Anecdotes of George Frederick Handel and John Christopher Smith* (London, 1799)

L.-M. Hawkins: *Anecdotes, Biographical Sketches and Memoirs* (London, 1822)

H. Davey: 'Stanley, John', *DNB*

G. Finzi: 'John Stanley (1713–1786)', *PRMA*, lxxvii (1950–51), 63

M. Sands: 'The Problem of Teraminta', *ML*, xxxiii (1952), 217

C. Cudworth: 'The English Organ Concerto', *The Score* (1953), no.8, p.51

G. Finzi: 'John Stanley', *Tempo* (1953), no.27, p.21

P. A. Scholes: *The Life and Activities of Sir John Hawkins* (London, 1953)

E. Bell: 'New Light on John Stanley', *New Beacon*, xli (1957), 193

J. Wilson: 'John Stanley: some Opus Numbers and Editions', *ML*, xxxix (1958), 359

H. D. Johnstone: 'An Unknown Book of Organ Voluntaries', *MT*, cviii (1967), 1003

——: 'English Solo Song, c.1710–1760', *PRMA*, xcv (1968–9), 67

M. Boyd: 'English Secular Cantatas in the Eighteenth Century', *MR*, xxx (1969), 85

T. Frost: 'The Cantatas of John Stanley (1713–86)', *ML*, liii (1972), 284

R. Fiske: *English Theatre Music in the Eighteenth Century* (London, 1973)

M. Boyd: 'John Stanley's Voluntaries', *MT*, cxv (1974), 598

S. Hemstead: *John Stanley, Six Concertos in Seven Parts, Op.2, 1742* (diss., U. of London, 1974)

B. Cooper: 'New Light on John Stanley's Organ Music', *PRMA*, ci (1974–5), 101

M. Boyd: 'John Stanley and the Foundling Hospital', *Soundings*, v (1975), 73

G. Williams, H. D. Johnstone and M. Boyd: 'New Light on Stanley', *MT*, cxvii (1976), 810

G. Williams: *The Life and Works of John Stanley (1712–86)* (diss., U. of Reading, 1977)

A. G. Williams: 'Stanley, Smith and "Teraminta"', *ML*, lx (1979), 312

MALCOLM BOYD

Stannar, William. English composer, possibly identifiable with WILLIAM STONARD.

Stansby, William (*d* 1638). English music printer. He was apprenticed to John Windet in 1591 and made free of the Stationers' Company in 1597. He succeeded to Windet's business in 1611, and in 1628 he acquired some of the music copyrights of Thomas Snodham. In this way Stansby inherited two of the most important music-printing businesses in 17th-century London, yet he made little use of them, printing only eight music volumes in his relatively long career. Stansby's press was astonishingly variable in the standard of its printing. Whereas Thomas Leighton's *Teares or Lamentacions of a Sorrowful Soule*, published over Stansby's imprint in 1614, is an elaborate, almost virtuoso piece of printing, his other publications appear slapdash and untidy. In fact, Stansby was severely taken to task by the Stationers' Company over the low standard of his work, and his relations with the company deteriorated so badly, over his unruly behaviour as much as his printing, that in 1627 his share of the English stock was sequestered, and he was banned from entering Stationers' Hall. Stansby cannot be described as either a distinguished or an enthusiastic music printer, yet the importance of his output is such that it seems likely he was the only printer in London who had the requisite materials to print music at that time. In 1629, for example, he printed *French Court-aires*, a volume of songs by Pierre Guédron and Antoine Boësset, originally published in Paris by Pierre Ballard, but appearing in England *with their Ditties Englished . . . Collected, Translated, Published by Ed. Filmer*. This volume marks the first appearance of a slur in English music printing, and in Martin Peerson's *Motets* of 1630 Stansby printed the first figured bass to appear in a printed volume in England. The year after he died his widow assigned his business to Richard Bishop. At the beginning of his career Stansby appears to have worked at the Cross Keys, St Paul's Wharf, which was his old master John Windet's address; he later moved to his own shop in St Dunstan's Churchyard, Fleet Street.

BIBLIOGRAPHY

C. Humphries and W. C. Smith: *Music Publishing in the British Isles* (London, 1954, rev. 2/1970)

C. Hill: 'William Stansby and Music Printing', *FAM*, xix (1972), 7

MIRIAM MILLER

Stantipes (Lat.). ESTAMPIE.

Stappen, Crispin van (*b* c1470; *d* Cambrai, 10 March 1532). Composer probably of Flemish birth. The first extant reference to him is a record dated 18 August 1492 of his leaving the royal chapel. As he is described as a tenor, it is unlikely that he was born much after 1470. Since he spent much of his later life at Cambrai he may be the 'Crasponnet' mentioned in the cathedral accounts in 1474 as a chorister, in which case a birthdate nearer 1465 is likely. From October 1492 he was *maestro di cappella* of Padua Cathedral for three months. During 1493 he became a member of the papal chapel, remaining there until 1507, except for six months from August 1498, spent in his old post at Padua, and periods at 's-Hertogenbosch in 1497, 1498 and 1506–7. In 1504 he had been appointed to a non-resident canonry at Cambrai; he was there in December 1504, but was in Rome by September 1507. From July 1509 until his death he stayed at Cambrai except for a recruiting expedition for the papal chapel in 1509, a pilgrimage to Rome and Padua in 1521, and a short period as *maestro di cappella* in Loreto (1524–5).

Stappen's few extant compositions, all apparently written by 1508, suggest that his style was already slightly old-fashioned. *Ave Maria*, *Beati pacifici* and *Virtutum expulsus* use cantus firmi in long notes: the first is in a chordal style with short passing phrases in the free voices; the second employs the chanson *De tous bien plaine* as well as the antiphon melody *Beati pacifici*. His frottola-like *Ave verum corpus* and *Vale, vale de Padoa* were doubtless written in Italy; both are in an MS perhaps written for van Stappen's own use.

WORKS

Ave Maria, 4vv; ed. A. Smijers, *Van Ockeghem tot Sweelinck* (Amsterdam, 1952), 109
Ave verum corpus, 3vv, *I-MOe* α.F.9.9.
Beati pacifici, 4vv, 1504³
Exaudi me, 5vv, 1508¹
Non lotis manibus, 4vv; ed. H. Albrecht, *G. Rhau: Symphoniae jucundae*, Musikdrucke aus den Jahren 1538 bis 1545, iii (Kassel and Basle, 1959), 170
Virtutum expulsus, 4vv, 1504³
Gentil, galans, 4vv, 1504³
Vale, vale de Padoa, 3vv, *I-MOe* α.F.9.9

BIBLIOGRAPHY

M. Brenet: *Les musiciens de la Sainte-Chapelle du palais* (Paris, 1910), 41f
A. Pirro: 'Dokumente über Antoine Brumel, Louis van Pullaer und Crispin van Stappen', *ZMw*, xi (1928–9), 349
R. Casimiri: 'Musici e musicisti nella cattedrale di Padova nei sec. xiv, xv, xvi', *NA*, lxviii (1941), 166
G. Reese: *Music in the Renaissance* (New York, 1954, rev. 2/1959) [see also K. Jeppesen: Review, *MQ*, xli (1955), 384]
C. Wright: 'Musiciens à la cathédrale de Cambrai 1475–1550', *RdM*, lxii (1976), 204

STANLEY BOORMAN

Starck, Ingeborg. Swedish pianist and composer, wife of HANS BRONSART VON SCHELLENDORF.

Stárek, Jiří (*b* Mocovice, 25 March 1928). Czech conductor. He studied the violin, clarinet, piano and conducting at the Prague Conservatory and College of Music to 1950. In 1953 he became conductor of the Czech RSO, a post he held for 15 years; during this time he was also principal conductor of the Prague Musical Theatre, 1961–2, director of the Collegium Musicum Pragense, 1963–8, and principal conductor of the Prague RO, 1964–8. He appeared at the 1967 ISCM festival in Prague and the 1968 Salzburg Festival, and has toured European cities as a guest conductor, particularly in broadcast concerts. In 1969 he began a regular association with the Trondheim SO and in 1973 with the Stuttgart Südfunk SO and the orchestra of Radio Sender Freies, Berlin. He was appointed a professor and conductor at the Musikhochschule in Frankfurt in 1973, and in 1974 became principal conductor of the Frankfurt RSO. His repertory contains much Romantic music, notably by Brahms, Mahler, Bruckner and Strauss, and Czech music, particularly Dvořák; partly because of the Mozart tradition in Prague, he is also a capable conductor of Classical works. His conducting is notable for attention to detail and a fresh, lively approach. He has made a number of gramophone records, mainly of Czech music.

KARI MICHELSEN

Starer, Robert (*b* Vienna, 8 Jan 1924). American composer of Austrian birth. He studied the piano from the age of four and entered the Vienna Academy in 1937. In 1938 he left Vienna and continued his studies at the Jerusalem Conservatory. A postgraduate scholarship took him to the Juilliard School in 1947; he received his diploma in 1949 and remained in New York, eventually as professor of music at Brooklyn College of the City University. In 1957 he took US citizenship. Among the awards he has received are two Guggenheim Fellowships and a Fulbright grant. His music is direct in expression, using dissonance coherently within clear forms. Often he employs wedge-like harmonic progressions, parallel chords and quartal harmonies; his melodies frequently have a plaintive, poignant lyricism, with small intervals and motivic repetitions. Some works use 12-note serialism, a particularly beautiful example being the Trio (1964). Starer's Prokofiev-like piano style is full and declamatory; the choral works are practical and dramatically effective, sometimes mingling song and speech. He has received commissions for ballet scores from Martha Graham, CBS television and National Educational Television.

WORKS
(*selective list*)

STAGE AND CHORAL

The Intruder, opera, 1, 1956; The Dybbuk, ballet, 1960; The Story of Esther, ballet, 10 insts, 1960; Samson Agonistes, ballet, 1961; Phaedra, ballet, 1962; The Lady of the House of Sleep, ballet, 1968; Pantagleize, opera, 1966–70; The Last Lover: Pelagia, chamber opera, 1977

5 Proverbs on Love, Bar, SATB, org (1950); Kohelet (Ecclesiastes), S, Bar, chorus, orch, 1952; Ariel, Visions of Isaiah, S, Bar, chorus, orch, 1959; Joseph and his Brothers, narrator, S, T, Bar, B, chorus, orch/org, 1966; Sabbath Eve Service, S, A, T/Bar, SATB, org, 1967; On the Nature of Things, SATB, 1968

OTHER WORKS

Orch: Fantasy, str, 1945; 3 pf concs., 1947, 1953, 1972; 3 syms., 1950, 1951, 1969; Prelude and Rondo giocoso, 1953; Conc. a 3, cl, tpt, trbn, str, 1954; Conc., va, str, perc, 1958; Samson Agonistes, sym. portrait, 1963; Mutabili, 1965; Conc., vn, vc, orch, 1967; Stone Ridge Set, band, 1973

Inst: Str Qt, 1947; Concertino for 2 Voices or Insts, vn, pf, 1948; 5 Miniatures, brass, 1948; 2 pf sonatas, 1948, 1965; Fantasia concertante, pf duet, 1959; Dialogues, cl, pf, 1961; Sketches in Color, pf, 1963; Variants, vn, pf, 1963; Trio, cl, vc, pf, 1964; Evanescents, pf, 1975

Songs, band music, pieces for student orch

Principal publishers: Israeli Music Publishers, Marks, MCA, Mercury, Presser, Southern

MSS in *US-Wc*, *NYp*

BRUCE ARCHIBALD

Staricius, Johann [Johannes] (*b* Schkeuditz, nr. Leipzig; *fl* 1609). German ?composer, poet and organist. His place of birth and the only other known facts about him – that he was a poet laureate and an organist at Frankfurt am Main – are given in his only publication: *Newer teutscher weltlicher Lieder nach Art der welschen Madrigalen neben etzlichen teutschen Tänzen* (Frankfurt am Main, 1609²⁹); the first six pieces are for five voices, the remaining 17 for four. He himself certainly wrote the texts, which include words in the Saxon dialect and are prefaced by Latin mottoes. The pieces include canzonas, canzonets, ballettos, madrigals and allemandes, though none is labelled as such. Bohn established that for no.2 Staricius borrowed no.7 of Morley's book of five-part balletts of 1595, and that nos.7–13 are identical with nos.7–9, 12 (which he used twice), 13 and 1 respectively of Morley's four-part madrigals of 1594. This unacknowledged borrowing encourages the assumption that he took other foreign pieces, perhaps including further English ones, as the basis of the other numbers and raises doubts as to whether he was a composer at all. Certain maladroit features of the texts suggest that he found it difficult to fit his words to the pre-existing music. He was probably a friend of Valentin Haussmann, whom he addressed in no.11 as 'the composer to whom the gods are so closely related' and who, significantly, brought out at Nuremberg in 1609 a German edition of Morley's balletts of 1595, properly attributed.

BIBLIOGRAPHY

E. Bohn: *50 historische Konzerte in Breslau 1881–92, nebst einer bibliographischen Beigabe: Bibliographie des gedruckten mehrstimmigen weltlichen deutschen Liedes vom Anfang des 16. Jahrhunderts bis ca. 1640* (Breslau, 1893)

J. Kerman: *The Elizabethan Madrigal: a Comparative Study* (New York, 1962), 137f

FRIEDRICH BASER

Stark. Bohemian family of organ builders. Abraham Stark (*b* Elbogen, Bohemia, 1659; *d* Elbogen, 18 March 1709) was trained by his father (an organist and organ builder) and later travelled, particularly to southern Germany. On his return he founded his own business in Elbogen, which after his death was carried on by his brother Wenzel Stark (*b* Elbogen, 1670; *d* Elbogen, 16 Sept 1757). Abraham Stark built the White Organ at St Niklas, Eger (1695; two manuals, 14 stops), and the organs of the Cistercian abbey at Goldenkron (Zlata Koruna) (1698; two manuals, 20 stops; still extant), the Premonstratensian abbey at Tepl (1700; one manual, ten stops; still extant), and St Jakub and St Franz, Prague (after 1705; both two manuals, 26 and 14 stops; both extant). In about 1700 he renovated the large organ in Prague Cathedral (four manuals, 71 stops). Wenzel Stark built organs in the town church in Brüx (1741; two manuals, 26 stops; still extant) and the parish church of Zlonitz (1746). Abraham Stark (frequently known as 'Meister Abraham') and the leading builders of his school (L. Burckhardt, A. Gartner, T. Schwarz, F.

Semrad, J. Pleyer, A. W. Schmied and F. Fassmann) further developed the style of specification already practised by the PUTZ family. The diapason choruses more often include 1⅓' and 1' registers, and there is often a Sesquialtera, while the Zimbel stop appears less often. The group of foundation stops is considerably enlarged; as in the neighbouring lands of Saxony and Silesia, stops such as Viola da gamba, Salicet, Fugara, Gemshorn, Quintaton and flutes of various kinds frequently appear. The pedal Mixtur stop is often replaced by a Cornet. The organ at Prague Cathedral, restored by Abraham Stark, is said to have been admired by J. A. Silbermann. The character of Abraham, the organ builder in E. T. A. Hoffmann's *Kreisleriana*, was probably modelled on Abraham Stark.

BIBLIOGRAPHY

V. Němec: *Pražské varhany* [Prague organs] (Prague, 1944)

R. Quoika: *Die altösterreichische Orgel der späten Gotik, der Renaissance und des Barock* (Kassel, 1953)

——: 'Ein Beitrag zum deutschböhmischen Orgelbau', *KJb*, xl (1956), 102

——: *Der Orgelbau in den Sudetenländern* (Mainz, 1963)

HANS KLOTZ

Starker, Janos (*b* Budapest, 5 July 1924). American cellist of Hungarian birth. He entered the Budapest Academy at the age of seven and made his début as a soloist there four years later. After graduating he was principal cellist of the Budapest Opera and PO (1945–6), but decided to leave Hungary. In 1948 he settled in the USA, where he became principal cellist of the Dallas SO (1948–9), the Metropolitan Opera Orchestra (1949–53), and the Chicago SO (1953–8). In 1958 he was appointed professor of cello at Indiana University, Bloomington, where he made his home. He has toured frequently throughout the world as a cellist of outstanding distinction, setting new standards in recordings and performances of Bach's cello suites which, though more restrained in character, were widely compared with those of Casals in intellectual grasp and command of line and technique.

Starker's playing has long been admired for its silken richness of tone and an expressive purpose governed by deep musical sensibility, to which more than 60 records also testify. He was the dedicatee and first performer of concertos by Bernard Heiden (1967) and Miklos Rosza (1968), and has been active in chamber ensembles, including the Roth String Quartet (1950–53), and a piano trio with Josef Suk and Julius Katchen for two years before Katchen's death in 1969. Starker has published teaching methods for all string instruments and an edition of Bach's cello suites. He owns a Matteo Gofriller cello (Venice, 1706), known as the 'Star'.

NOËL GOODWIN

Starkie, Walter (Fitzwilliam) (*b* Ballybrack, nr. Dublin, 9 Aug 1894; *d* Madrid, 2 Nov 1976). Irish writer on music. He studied classics, history and politics at Dublin University. He also studied the violin at the Royal Irish Academy of Music, and won many prizes. In 1920 he was appointed lecturer in Romance languages, and in 1926 professor of Spanish, at Trinity College, Dublin; during the 1930s he also lectured in Chicago and London. From 1940 he was in Madrid, where he was director of the British Institute. In 1959 he lectured at New York University, and from 1961 to 1970 at the University of California at Los Angeles. He was awarded many honours, in Britain, Ireland and elsewhere (notably CBE, 1948; CMG, 1954; and Chevalier of the Légion d'honneur).

Starkie's musical writings date from the 1920s, when he first began to write criticism in Irish newspapers. Most of his writings at this period were literary, in periodicals and elsewhere; they include books on Jacinto Benavente, 1924, and Luigi Pirandello, 1926. He became better known with his books on musical tours of adventure, notably *Raggle-Taggle* (London, 1933, 2/1964), which tells of his travels as a fiddler, particularly in the Balkans, and its continuation in *Spanish Raggle-Taggle* (London, 1934, 2/1961). Among his other books are *Spain: a Musician's Journey through Time and Space* (London, 1958) and his autobiographical *Scholars and Gypsies* (London, 1963).

ERIC BLOM/R

Staromieyski, J. (*fl c*1740). Polish composer. In 1743 he was a member of the Dominican chapel at Lwów; before that he may have been active in the Jesuit chapel in Kraków, for its inventories of 1737–41 mention 12 of his works for voices and instruments. Four of his compositions are extant, all of them derived from the musical heritage of the south Polish chapels – Mogiła (near Kraków), Sandomierz, and Raków (near Sandomierz). Staromieyski belonged to the generation of composers who, using a simplified technique, depended on expressive melodic lines, especially in cantata arias, and introduced popular dance rhythms in the instrumental sections, giving a certain local character to their compositions. Items from his *Vesperae de Sanctis* have been published in *Muzyka w dawnym Krakowie* (Kraków, 1964) and the Florilegium Musicae Antiquae series (xvi, 1965; xxvi, 1968).

BIBLIOGRAPHY
A. Chybiński: 'Z dziejów muzyki krakowskiej', *KM*, ii (1913), 24–62
Z. M. Szweykowski: 'J. Staromieyski – przedstawiciel okresu saskiego', *Ruch muzyczny*, ix/3 (1965), 15
ZYGMUNT M. SZWEYKOWSKI

Starowolski [Starovolscius], **Szymon** (*b* Stara Wola, Volhynia [now Belorussia] 1588; *d* Kraków, 4 or 27 April 1656). Polish historian and music theorist. He studied at Kraków Academy. From 1614 he travelled round Europe as a tutor to the sons of Polish princes, visiting and living in France, the south Netherlands (Louvain), Germany and Italy (mainly Padua and Rome). In 1639 he took holy orders and was appointed cantor at Tarnów. In 1653 he settled at Kraków, where in 1655 he became a canon of the cathedral chapter at Wawel Castle. Music was among his many interests, and he discussed it in three of his numerous publications. His collection of biographical sketches *Scriptorum polonicorum Hecatontas* includes those of two 16th-century Polish composers, Marcin Leopolita and Wacław Szamotuły, and he added notes on other composers too. He returned to them in *Monumenta sarmatorum*. These were the first indication of a conscious search for, and establishment of, a Polish musical tradition; his work includes both errors and factual historical information (stressed by Chybiński and Jachimecki respectively). His treatise *Musices practicae erotemata*, dedicated to Lilius, director of music of Kraków Cathedral, has the character of a school textbook. It leans heavily on the writings of Lossius, Ornithoparchus and Johann Spangenberg and testifies to the author's wide, but at the same time superficial, knowledge of music theory.

WRITINGS
(*only those on music*)
Scriptorum polonicorum Hecatontas, seu centum illustrium Poloniae scriptorum elogia et vitae (Frankfurt, 1625, Venice, 2/1627, Frankfurt, 3/1644, Breslau, 4/1733; Pol. trans. J. Starnawski as *Setnik pisarzów polskich albo pochwały i żywoty stu najznakomitszych pisarzów polskich*, Kraków, 1970)
Musices practicae erotemata in usum studiosae iuventutis breviter et accurate collecta (Kraków, 1650)
Monumenta sarmatorum viam universae carnis ingressorum (Kraków, 1655)

BIBLIOGRAPHY
EitnerQ; *SMP*
A. Sowiński: *Les musiciens polonais et slaves* (Paris, 1857; Pol. trans., 1874)
Z. Jachimecki: *Wpływy włoskie w muzyce polskiej* [Italian influences in Polish music] (Kraków, 1911), 71f
A. Chybiński: 'Wacław z Szamotuł', *KM* (1948), nos.21–2, pp.13, 34; no.23, pp.9–10, 13; no.24, p.124
Z. Jachimecki: *Muzyka polska w rozwoju historycznym* [Polish music in its historical development], I/i (Kraków, 1948), 212ff; I/ii (Kraków, 1951), 6
A. Chybiński: *Słownik muzyków dawnej Polski* [Dictionary of early Polish musicians] (Kraków, 1948–9)
F. Bielak: *Działalność naukowa Szymona Starowolskiego* [The scientific activity of Szymon Starowolski] (Warsaw, 1957)
K. Budzyk, ed.: *Bibliografia literatury polskiej 'Nowy Korbut'*, iii (Warsaw, 1965), 282ff
H. Feicht: 'An Outline of the History of Polish Religious Music', *Poland's Millennium of Catholicism*, ed. M. Rechowicz (Lublin, 1969), 523
M. Pamuła: 'Pojęcie tonów i śpiewu kościelnego w "Musicae practicae erotemata" Starowolskiego' [The concept of tones and ecclesiastical chant in Starowolski's *Musicae practicae erotemata*], *Muzyka*, xix/1 (1974), 54
MIROSŁAW PERZ

Starr, Ringo [Starkey, Richard] (*b* Liverpool, 7 July 1940). English pop singer, member of the BEATLES.

Starting transient. The initial sound produced when one vibrating system begins to drive another (e.g. string and soundboard, or reed and pipe). Although the time between the initiation and the emergence of a regular vibration may be very short, the starting transient produced in that time is one of the important characteristics distinguishing the sound of one type of musical instrument from that of another. *See also* SOUND, §6.

Starý, Emanuel (*b* Pardubice, 27 July 1843; *d* Prague, 1 Aug 1906). Czech music publisher. In 1867 he founded a lithographic works with Antonín Vítek in Prague, taking sole charge in November 1870. He was on friendly terms with the leading Czech composers and published a series of works by Smetana, Dvořák, Bendl, Fibich, Foerster and others. His collection of male choruses, *Hlahol*, was important in the development of Czech choral songs. He published *Dalibor* (1873–5) and *Hudební a divadelní věstník* ('Music and theatre bulletin', 1877–8). He was active in a number of artistic societies in Prague. After his death his son Emanuel (*b* Prague, 18 Jan 1874; *d* Prague, 20 April 1928) took over the firm. In 1908 he reorganized it and introduced engraving and note printing on the Leipzig pattern. Apart from choral and solo vocal compositions, he published a number of instrumental works, particularly Foerster's and Ostrčil's. After his death his widow, Růžena Stará, née Meruňková, ran the firm until 1949. In addition to Foerster's Cello Concerto and Second Violin Concerto (with piano arrangement) she brought out a series of Foerster's choral works and reprints of earlier publications of choral music.

ZDENĚK CULKA

Staryk, Steven (*b* Toronto, 28 April 1932). Canadian violinist and teacher. After studying in Canada and New York, he played with the Toronto SO and became leader of the CBC SO in Toronto. He was chosen by Beecham in 1956 as leader of the RPO, and was appointed leader of the Concertgebouw Orchestra in 1960, and leader of the Chicago SO in 1963. He held positions as professor at the Amsterdam Conservatory, Northwestern University in Evanston, Illinois, and the Oberlin College Conservatory in Ohio (1968–72). He became head of the string department at the Community Music School of Greater Vancouver in 1972 and artist-in-residence at the University of Ottawa in 1975. His pupils include leaders of many European and North American orchestras. As a soloist and recording artist, he is notable for brilliant technique and versatility of style; his extensive repertory covers all periods. He has appeared as a soloist in Europe, North America and the orient. He has owned a number of fine violins, including the 'Muntz' Stradivari of 1736.

BIBLIOGRAPHY
J. Creighton: *Discopaedia of the Violin, 1889–1971* (Toronto, 1974)

T. BROWN

Starzer, Joseph (?Franz) (*b* 1726 or 1727; *d* Vienna, 22 April 1787). Austrian composer, violinist and administrator.

1. LIFE. He joined the orchestra of the newly formed Burgtheater in Vienna as a violinist probably by 1752. A *Repertorium* of the theatre for 1752–7, published in 1757, gives him special recognition as a composer of ballet music, a career he was to pursue for the next 20 years with outstanding success. In winter 1758–9 he followed the Vienna ballet-master F. A. Hilverding to the Russian imperial court. There he also worked with the choreographers Calzevaro, Cesare and Granger, gave concerts (in 1760 he performed with the flautist Le Clerc in the Tsarkoié-Sélo Palace), and accepted a post as Konzertmeister and later as deputy Kapellmeister and composer of ballet music. In 1763 he bore the title *maître de chapelle et directeur des concerts*. Though obliged by contract (along with Gassmann) to compose for the Kärntnertortheater in Vienna from 1765 to 1767, he apparently returned to Vienna only in 1768.

In the following years in Vienna Starzer composed several major ballets for both the opposing great masters of the art – Noverre (*Roger et Bradamante*, *Adèle de Ponthieu* and *Les Horaces et les Curiaces*) and Angiolini (*Il Cid* and *Teseo in Creta*). Both apparently expected advantage and success from their collaboration with Starzer, and preferred him to other ballet composers such as his exact contemporary Franz Asplmayr.

Together with Gassmann, Starzer was actively involved in the founding of the Viennese Tonkünstler-Sozietät (1771), serving from that year as *Assessor* among the society's *Seniores* and frequently composing for its concerts (the society's first programme opened with a symphony by Starzer, and he later produced his oratorio *La passione di Gesù Christo* and his arrangement of Handel's *Judas Maccabaeus* there). In 1779 Starzer petitioned for health reasons to be relieved of playing the violin in the orchestra, though he remained active as *Directeur bei der Battuta* until 1783. In 1785 he asked to be discharged from his duties for the society.

He led a performance of his arrangement of *Judas Maccabaeus* the following year in a private concert at Baron von Swieten's. There he renewed his acquaintance with Mozart, whom he had earlier engaged for a Tonkünstler-Sozietät concert (3 April 1781). At his death Mozart succeeded him as director, and as Handel arranger, at van Swieten's concerts.

2. WORKS. Starzer's chamber and orchestral music was held by Adler (along with Monn's) to be superior to that of any Austrian composer of the period. He was equally highly regarded by his contemporaries, above all as a ballet composer, as Burney's judgment and Mozart's statements and his sketches for the first ballet in *Lucio Silla* (K Anh.109/135a) show; Heinse (*Hildegard von Hohenthal*, ii) pronounced him 'the classic master in this field'. Starzer was especially versatile in adapting his music to dance figures and stage action, and in accommodating choreography and settings; the abundance and variety of the principal ideas, often highly compressed, in his many dance pieces (a full-length ballet comprised 30 or more separate numbers) reveal a strikingly wide range of abilities. Many of his pieces depart from customary dance forms, and were freely composed to follow the action on stage and the representation through pantomime; this variety and adaptability of his talent as a ballet composer drew him to Noverre, as Gluck was drawn to Angiolini. Many folk themes appear in his works – a tendency derived from Hilverding, but equally consonant with his own artistic character. Like other Viennese ballet composers, Starzer frequently reused his pieces, both within a work and in later ballets. Occasionally (as in *Adèle de Ponthieu*) he used other composer's works; Mozart likewise noted down entire series of numbers from Starzer's *Le gelosie del serraglio*, *Les cinque soltanes* and *Nation* in connection with his *Lucio Silla*.

Starzer's symphonies were highly esteemed in Vienna in the 1770s (as can be seen for example in the Tonkünstler-Sozietät programmes), but they have yet to be fully studied. His string quartets merit comparison with Haydn's early and middle works in the genre, not only for dispensing with thoroughbass practice, but also for introducing polyphonic techniques and forms into the genre and for departing from the Italianate *galant* style by means of extended passages of 'obbligato accompaniment'. Besides two 'divertimentos' for string quartet (with a minuet as second movement and a slow third movement), whose varied scoring and highly developed treatment of thematic material and modulation have been traced by Finscher to the influence of Haydn's op.9, Starzer wrote two incomplete quartet sonatas as well as a complete quartet in B♭ (all in *CS-Pnm*) that are noteworthy for their polyphonic writing in all movements.

Apart from his ballets Starzer wrote only a single stage work – the Singspiel *Die drei Pächter* (a Russian prologue *Novyia lavry* is probably identical with the ballet *Les nouveaux lauriers*); the work is sometimes confused with the similarly named Singspiel translated by W. G. Becker from Monvel's French and produced at the Kärntnertor Theater in 1785. Each of its two acts has an instrumental introduction and ensembles, and the Act 2 finale is an 'Invitation to the Dance' with four-part chorus, soloists and orchestra. Starzer's *La passione di Gesù Christo* (to Metastasio's text) brought him substantial fame as an oratorio composer, as did in greater measure his arrangement of *Judas Maccabaeus*, though his many added expression marks tend to disguise the contours of Handel's original.

Starzer's orchestral music is often in 15 or 16 parts, and is noteworthy for its unusual instruments and combinations, such as the parts for chalumeaux and for english horn in *Roger et Bradamante*, and for four horns in *Les cinque soltanes*. He showed a special inclination for the picturesque in works with programmatic titles: a piece for wind band entitled *Le matin et le soir* depicts a bucolic landscape from dawn to dusk, imitating, among other effects, the bleating of lambs. Janissary music plays an especially large role in those ballets with exotic subjects or episodes. Late in his career he also composed works for the clarinet, including a lost concerto (or symphonie concertante) performed for the Tonkünstler-Sozietät by the brothers Anton and Johann Stadler (1780).

At least two of Starzer's siblings were also musicians. Karl Starzer (*b* c1733; *d* Vienna, 30 Dec 1789), was maker of Waldhorns to the court, and was perhaps the 'Starzer *père*' who in 1761 performed with his son as horn player at the Kärntnertor Theater. Katharina Starzer (*d* before 1787) was a notable contralto who in the 1750s performed in the concerts and opera productions of the Prince of Saxe-Hildburghausen in Vienna and at the Schlosshof castle, where in 1754 she sang Tangia in Gluck's *Le cinesi*. Another sister, Rosalia, married the composer Balthasar Ulbrich, and according to Eitner was also a singer.

WORKS

Tr. cat. – *lost, listed in Traeg catalogue (Vienna)*
Br. cat. – *lost, listed in Breitkopf catalogue (Leipzig)*

BALLETS

Diane et Endimione, Vienna, ?1754, 1759, *CS-K*
? Les bergers, Laxenburg, 1755, to Gluck: La danza (Metastasio)
Le misantrope (?F. A. Hilverding), Vienna, 1756, *K*
L'amour vengé (? = Les bergers), Laxenburg, 1759, *K*
L'asile de la vertu (Hilverding), St Petersburg, 1759, collab. H. F. Raupach
Les nouveaux lauriers (? = Novyia lavry) (Hilverding), St Petersburg, ?1759, 1764, collab. Raupach
La victoire de Flore sur Borée (Hilverding), St Petersburg, 1760, ?identical with Le triomphe du printemps
Siroe (Hilverding), St Petersburg, 1760, to Raupach: Siroe (Metastasio)
Le jugement de Paris (F. Calzevaro), St Petersburg, 1761, *K*
Prométhée et Pandore (Calzevaro), St Petersburg, 1761
Le pauvre Yourka (G. Cesare), Moscow, 1762
Le seigneur de village moqué (Hilverding), Moscow, 1762, to Manfredini: Olimpiade (Metastasio)
La vengeance du dieu de l'amour (Hilverding), Moscow, 1762, to Manfredini: Olimpiade (Metastasio)
Apollon et Daphne, ou Le retour d'Apolon au Parnasse (P. Granger), St Petersburg, 1763, to Manfredini: Carlo Magno
Apollon et Diane (G. Angiolini), Vienna, 1763, to G. Scarlatti: Artaserse (Metastasio)
Le retour de la déesse du printemps en Arcadie (Hilverding), Moscow, 1763
Les fêtes hollandoises (Ballo olandese) (Angiolini), Vienna, 1763, to Scarlatti: Artaserse (Metastasio), *K*
Pygmalion, ou La statue animée (Hilverding), St Petersburg, 1763
Acis et Galatée (Les amours d'Acis et Galatée) (Hilverding), St Petersburg, 1764
Le triomphe du printemps (Hilverding), St Petersburg, 1766, *K*, ?identical with La victoire de Flore
Don Quichotte (?J. G. Noverre), Vienna, ?1768, *A-Wn*
Les moissonneurs (?Noverre), Vienna, 1770, *Wn*
Agamemnon (Der Tod Agamemnons) (Noverre), Vienna, 1771, arr. pf (Mainz, n.d.)
Atlante, Vienna, 1771, *D-Rtt*
Les cinque soltanes, Vienna, 1771, *A-Wn, CS-K, Pnm*
Roger et Bradamante (Noverre), Vienna, 1771, *A-Wn, CS-K, Pnm*, passepied ed. W. Fischer and K. Geiringer (Vienna, 1925)
Adèle de Ponthieu (Noverre), Vienna, 1773, *K*
Il Cid (Angiolini), Vienna, 1774, *K*
Le ninfe (?Angiolini), Vienna, 1774, *K*

Les Horaces et les Curiaces (Noverre), Vienna, 1774, *K, F-Po*
Les moissonneurs (Angiolini), Vienna, 1775, *CS-K*
Montezuma (Angiolini), Vienna, 1775
Teseo in Creta (Angiolini), Vienna, 1775, *K*

Undated, *K*, ?perf. Vienna: La bianca e la rossa; La toilette de Venus (Noverre); Le gelosie del serraglio; Nation; Venere e Adone
Doubtful: L'amore medico, St Petersburg; Les aventures champêtres, Strasbourg, formerly *D-DS*, lost; Le chevalier boiteux (Hilverding), St Petersburg, 1766; Die Fischer (?Angiolini), Vienna, 1774; Die Handlung [? *recte* Landung] der Spanier auf den amerikanischen Küsten, *D-Rtt*; Le matin/Le midi/Le soir/La nuit, Laxenburg, 1755; Parodie de Medée; Les muses, ?identical with Le muse protette (Angiolini); music by Angiolini; I pastori di tempi; Le roi et le fermier (Noverre), Vienna, 1774; L'école enchantée (L. Paradis), collab. Paradis, mentioned in Mooser (1945), p.49 [but cf Mooser (1948–51), ii, 46, 53, 302]

OTHER WORKS

Vocal: La passione di Gesù Christo (Metastasio), oratorio, Vienna, 1778, *A-Wn*; Die drei Pächter (Singspiel), Vienna, *Wn*; Die Wildschützen (Singspiel), doubtful; Handel arrs.: Judas Maccabaeus, Vienna, 1779, *Wn*, St Cecilia Ode, Tr. cat. (1804, no.205) with wind parts by Starzer, ?identical with Mozart's arr. (κ592)
Orch: Vn Conc., *Wgm*, ed. in Diletto musicale, lxxxii (Vienna, 1964); 7 syms., *CS-Pnm*; 6 menuetti, *A-Wn*; Menuetto e contradanze, *CS-Pnm*; Conc., 2 orch, perf. Vienna, 23 March 1779, lost; Conc. (?symphonie concertante), 2 cl, 2 hn, bn, perf. Vienna, 14 March 1780, lost; Sym., D, Br. cat. (1776–7); Die Belagerung Wiens, ov., Tr. cat. (1799, no.28); 5 syms., *I-Gi(l)*, spurious
Chamber, str: 2 str qts, *A-Wn*, ed. in DTÖ, xxxi, Jg.xv/2 (1908); 7 str qts, *CS-Pnm*, inc.; 15 str qts, partly arr. from ballets, *Pnm*; 2 sonatas, str qt, inc., *Pnm*; 3 str trios, incl. 2 for 2 vn, vc, 1 for vn, va, vc, *Pnm*
Chamber, wind: Musica da camera (5 pieces), 2 chalumeaux/fl, 3 C-clarinos, 2 D-clarinos, timp (St Petersburg, before 1768), copy by L. Mozart (κ187/Anh.C.17.12), *A-GÖ*; Cassatio, Tr. cat. (1799, no.159); 2 Parthien, 12 pieces, Tr. cat. (1804, p.52 [*recte* 25]); Le matin et le soir, octet, 2 ob, 2 eng hn/cl, 2 hn, 2 bn, *A-Wgm, CS-K*; Duette, 2 hn, Tr. cat. (1799, no.292)

BIBLIOGRAPHY

C. F. Pohl: *Denkschrift aus Anlass des hundertjährigen Bestehens der Tonkünstler-Sozietät* (Vienna, 1871)
H. Abert: 'J. G. Noverre und sein Einfluss auf die dramatische Balletkomposition', JbMP 1907, 29
K. Riedel: 'Josef Starzer', *Wiener Instrumentalmusik vor und um 1750 I*, DTÖ, xxxi, Jg.xix/2 (1908)
L. Braun: 'Die Ballettkomposition von Joseph Starzer', SMw, xiii (1926), 38
R. Haas: 'Der Wiener Bühnentanz von 1740–67', JbMP 1936, 77
E. F. Schmid: 'Gluck-Starzer-Mozart', ZfM, civ (1937), 1198
R. A. Mooser: *Opéras, intermezzos, ballets, cantates, oratorios joués en Russie durant le 18e siècle* (Geneva, 1945, 2/1955)
——: *Annales de la musique et des musiciens en Russie* (Geneva, 1948–51)
W. Senn: 'Mozarts Skizze der Ballettmusik zu Le gelosie del serraglio KV Anh. 109/135a', AcM, xxxii (1961), 169
G. Zechmeister: *Die Wiener Theater nächst der Burg und nächst dem Kärntnerthor von 1747 bis 1776* (Vienna, 1971)
L. Finscher: *Studien zur Geschichte des Streichquartetts*, i (Kassel, 1974)
G. Croll: 'Bemerkungen zum "Ballo primo" (KV Anh. 109/135a) in Mozarts Mailänder "Lucio Silla" ', SM (in preparation)
J. Sonnleithner: material on Viennese theatres (MS, *A-Wgm*)
M. von Portheim: material on Starzer's life and family (MS, *Wst*)

GERHARD CROLL

Stasimon (Gk. from *sta-*: 'stand'). One of the three or more choral performances between the scenes (*epeisodia*) of an ancient Greek tragedy; they occurred when the chorus was in position (*stasis*) in the *orchēstra*, rather than while entering or leaving (*see* PARODOS and EXODOS). They were not so called because the chorus stood still: the metrical structure of a *stasimon*, in which an exactly corresponding strophe and antistrophe are followed by an epode, suggests that they danced as well as sang, repeating the music and steps of the strophe exactly in the antistrophe. The term may have implied that such aspects of the performance as rhythm and tempo were restrained and moderate (see Kranz, p.114). Normally the chorus sang and danced as a whole, with aulos accompaniment, but it was sometimes divided into two semichoruses; the third *stasimon* of Euripides' *Hippolytus* is thought by some to have been divided antiphonally between a main chorus of women and an extra chorus (*parachorēgēma*) of men. Originally the *stasima* were the essence of the whole performance. From the late 5th century BC, however, Agathon, and others imitating him, made the *stasima* choral interludes unconnected with the plot (*see* EMBOLIMON) and characterized by the style known to modern scholars as the 'new music', with its novel rhythmic and modal variety (*see* EURIPIDES; MELANIPPIDES; PHERECRATES; TIMOTHEUS).

BIBLIOGRAPHY

W. Kranz: *Stasimon: Untersuchungen zu Form und Gehalt der griechischen Tragödie* (Berlin, 1933)
A. Pickard-Cambridge: *The Dramatic Festivals of Athens* (Oxford, rev. 2/1968)

HECTOR THOMSON

Stasis. One of the subdivisions of a Byzantine KATHISMA, containing from one to five psalms.

Stasov, Vladimir Vasil'yevich (*b* St Petersburg, 14 Jan 1824; *d* St Petersburg, 23 Oct 1906). Russian critic of art and music. Son of one of the greatest architects of the day. Stasov was early taught foreign languages, drawing and music, the last by Antoni Gerke privately and by Adolf Henselt at the so-called Law School for civil servants, where he studied from 1836 to 1843. There he appeared as a solo pianist with the school orchestra and formed an intimate friendship with A. N. Serov, later famous as a music critic and composer, though differences in tastes were later to change the friendship to bitter enmity. After leaving the Law School, Stasov served in various government departments, and in 1847 began reviewing books and music for the *Otechestvenniye zapiski* ('National notes'). From summer 1851 until early 1854 he was in Italy, mostly in Florence, as Russian secretary to Prince A. N. Demidov; having discovered the Abbé Santini's collection of old music, he had some 400 works from it (mostly from the 16th, 17th and 18th centuries) copied and sent home. He published at his own expense a study entitled *L'Abbé Santini et sa collection musicale à Rome*, and in 1870 presented all the MS copies to the St Petersburg Public Library.

It was in this library that he spent the rest of his life, first cataloguing the vast section of 'Rossica', and then from 1856 working as personal assistant to the director. In the same year he met the 20-year-old Balakirev, and before long became the belligerent champion of the circle of composers Balakirev gathered about him; later, in 1867, he inadvertently coined a nickname which stuck to them, the *moguchaya kuchka* ('Mighty Handful'). In 1872 he became head of the department of art in the library, and on two occasions later he was offered the directorship of the library, which he declined; as he told his brother in 1899, acceptance of the directorship would have put an end to his 'bold light-hearted, jolly polemics'.

Stasov was a man of vast learning in many fields and of overpowering personality. As a critic, the basis of his aesthetic was that inseparability of art from humanity first preached by Belinsky, adopted by all the progressive Russian thinkers of the 1850s and 1860s, and preserved in modern times in the Soviet doctrine of socialist realism. As a historian, he was a passionate lover of everything Russian – legend, literature and the heroic past; he was also indefatigable in pressing themes from these fields on his artistic and musical friends, including Repin, Antokol'sky and Kramskoy as well as Balakirev, Borodin and Musorgsky. Nor was he content merely to point out subjects; he wrote 'programmes' and scenarios, and unearthed historical material. He played a leading role in the inception of Rimsky-Korsakov's *Sadko* (both the early orchestral piece and the later opera), of Musorgsky's *Khovanshchina* and *Songs and Dances of Death*, and of Borodin's *Prince Igor*. Nor was he a narrow nationalist, for he published many writings on foreign art, literature and music and, when Balakirev was working on his *King Lear* music, sought out English tunes from William Chappell's collection. He provided Tchaikovsky with the programme for his symphonic fantasia *The Tempest*, and in 1868, in the wake of enthusiasm for Byron after the Russian performance of Berlioz's *Harold in Italy*, he suggested Manfred to Balakirev as a subject for an orchestral piece. Balakirev disliked the idea and submitted it to Berlioz, but it was not until 1885 that Tchaikovsky eventually took it up for his *Manfred Symphony*.

Of Stasov's writings on music, far fewer than those on art, the most substantial are his biography of Musorgsky (1881), an extended essay 'Nasha muzïka za posledniye 25 let' ('Our music during the last 25 years', 1883), a biography of Borodin (1889), published anonymously, and an article on Liszt, Schumann and Berlioz (1889). In the last his gusto and first-hand knowledge more than atone for factual inaccuracies and violent partisanship.

WRITINGS
(only those on music)

L'Abbé Santini et sa collection musicale à Rome (Florence, 1854)
'Modest Petrovich Musorgsky: biograficheskiy ocherk' [Biographical essay], *Vestnik Evropï* (1881), no.5, pp.285–316; no.6, pp.506–45
'Nasha muzïka za posledniye 25 let' [Our music during the last 25 years], *Vestnik Evropï* (1883), no.10, pp.561–623
Alexander Porfir'yevich Borodin: evo zhizn', perepiska i muzïkal'nïye stat'i [Life, correspondence and articles on music] (St Petersburg, 1889)
'List, Shuman i Berlioz v Rossii', *Severnïy vestnik* (1889), no.7, pt.1, pp.115–57; no.8, pt.1, pp.73–110
Sobraniye sochineniy 1847–1906 [Collected works 1847–1906] (St Petersburg, 1894–1906) [writings on music in vols. iii and iv]
ed. A. V. Ossovsky and A. N. Dmitriyev: *V. Stasov: izbrannïye stat'i o muzïke* [Selected articles on music] (Leningrad, 1949)
ed. A. S. Ogolovets: *V. Stasov: izbrannïye stat'i o M. P. Musorgskom* [Selected articles on Musorgsky] (Moscow, 1952)
ed. E. D. Stasova and others: *V. Stasov: izbrannïye sochineniya: zhivopis' skul'ptura, muzïka* [Selected works on art, sculpture and music] (Moscow, 1952)
ed. V. A. Kiselyov: *V. Stasov: stat'i o Rimskom-Korsakove* [Articles on Rimsky-Korsakov] (Moscow, 1953)
ed. T. N. Livanova and V. L. Protopopov: *V. Stasov: izbrannïye stat'i o M. I. Glinke* [Selected articles on Glinka] (Moscow, 1955)
trans. F. Jonas: *Vladimir Vasilevich Stasov: Selected Essays on Music* (London, 1968)

BIBLIOGRAPHY

N. F. Findeyzen: 'V. V. Stasov: ocherk evo zhizni i deyatel'nosti kak muzïkal'novo pisatelya' [Essay on his life and career as a writer on music], *RMG* (1895), 513, 604
N. F. Findeyzen: 'Stasov i evo muzïkal'naya deyatel'nost': biograficheskiye otrïvki' [Stasov and his musical activities: biographical fragments], *RMG* (1907), 431, 477, 509, 541, 573, 685, 725, 797, 989, 1043, 1077, 1101, 1149
V. Karenin, ed.: 'V. V. Stasov i P. I. Chaykovsky: neizdannïye pis'ma' [Stasov and Tchaikovsky: unpublished letters], *Russkaya mïsl'* (1909), no.3, pp.93–149
E. E. Lineva: 'Mïsli V. V. Stasova o narodnosti v muzïke' [Stasov's thoughts on nationalism in music], *Nezabvennomu Vladimiru Vasil'yevichu Stasovu* (St Petersburg, 1910), 52ff
V. V. Yakovlev: 'Vladimir Stasov 1824–1906', *Muzïka i revolyutsiya* (1926), no.10, p.3

A. N. Rimsky-Korsakov, ed.: *M. P. Musorgsky: pis'ma i dokumentï* [Letters and documents] (Moscow and Leningrad, 1932)

V. Karenin, ed.: *Perepiska M. A. Balakireva s V. V. Stasovïm* [Correspondence between Balakirev and Stasov], i (Moscow, 1935)

A. N. Rimsky-Korsakov: 'Stasov i muzïka' [Stasov and music], *Vladimir Vasil'yevich Stasov 1824–1906* (Moscow and Leningrad, 1949), 66ff

Yu. A. Kremlyov: *Russkaya mïsl' o muzïke: ocherki istorii russkoy muzïkal'noy kritiki i estetiki v XIX veke* [Russian thoughts on music: essays on the history of Russian music criticism and aesthetics in the 19th century], i (Leningrad, 1954)

S. A. Dianin: *Borodin: zhizneopisaniye, materialï i dokumentï* [Biography, materials and documents] (Moscow, 1955)

M. O. Yankovsky, ed.: *Ts. A. Kyui: izbrannïye pis'ma* [Cui: selected letters] (Leningrad, 1955)

A. S. Ogolovets: *V. V. Stasov: k pyatidesyatiletiyu so dnya smerti* [On the 50th anniversary of Stasov's death] (Moscow, 1956)

E. N. Viner and others, eds.: *Vladimir Vasil'yevich Stasov: materialï k bibliografii, opisaniye rukopisey* [Materials for a bibliography, list of manuscripts] (Moscow, 1956) [contains complete list of writings]

N. D. Chernikov, ed.: *V. V. Stasov: pis'ma k deyatel'yam russkoy kul'turï* [Letters to those active in Russian culture], i (Moscow, 1962)

A. S. Lyapunova, ed.: *N. Rimsky-Korsakov: literaturnïye proizvedeniya i perepiska* [Literary works and correspondence], v (Moscow, 1963), 321–456

G. Abraham: 'V. V. Stasov: Man and Critic', *Vladimir Vasilevich Stasov: Selected Essays on Music*, trans. F. Jonas (London, 1968), 1ff

GERALD ABRAHAM

Šťastný [Stiasny, Stiastny]. Czech family of musicians.

(1) Jan Šťastný (i) (*b* Klatovy, Bohemia; *d* Prague, *c*1779). Oboist, member of the Prague theatre orchestra. According to Burney (1773) he was an excellent performer on the oboe. Among his pupils was the renowned player Joseph Fiala.

(2) Bernard (Václav) Šťastný (*b* Prague, *c*1760; *d* Prague, *c*1835). Composer, cellist and pedagogue, son of (1) Jan Šťastný. He studied music with his father and later music theory with J. F. N. Seger. As early as 1789 his and his younger brother's names were entered in the *Schematismus für das Königreich Böheim* among the public performers on the cello. In 1800 he was referred to by the *Allgemeine musikalische Zeitung* (ii, 506) as Prague's foremost cellist. He was a member of the Prague theatre orchestra from about 1778, played in various Prague churches and taught the cello at the Prague Conservatory from its foundation (1811) to 1822. His works reveal a predilection for contrapuntal procedures. Both he and (3) Jan Šťastný were outstanding cellists and pedagogues. Their compositions are for the most part instructive and were highly appreciated for their pedagogical value combined with musicality.

WORKS

Il maestro ed il scolare, 8 imitazioni e 6 pezzi con fughe, 2 vc (Bonn, *c*1814)

6 sonates progressives et instructives, 2 vc (Prague, n.d.)

Violoncell-Schule (Mainz, n.d.)

Sonata, vc, b, *D-Bds* [autograph]

(3) (František) Jan Šťastný (ii) (*b* Prague, *c*1764; *d* after 1826). Composer and cellist, son and pupil of (1) Jan Šťastný. Like his elder brother, he was a member of the Prague theatre orchestra; later he was active as a cellist at Mainz (1789–97) and Frankfurt am Main (in the second decade of the 19th century), then as music director at Nuremberg, leaving there for Mannheim in 1826. He probably also visited Paris and London. The edition of his op.3 (from the time of his appointment at Frankfurt am Main) is dedicated to the students at the Paris Conservatoire; and the prints of opp.7, 8, 10 and 13 have English dedicatees.

WORKS

op.

— ? Sammlung einiger Lieder für die Jugend bei Industrialarbeiten

(Prague, 1789)

1 Six duos, 2 vc (Offenbach, n.d.)
2 Deux sonates, vc solo, vc (Bonn, *c*1806–7)
3 Divertimento, vc solo, va, b (Mainz, n.d.)
4 XII pièces faciles et progressives, vc, b (Bonn, *c*1814)
5 Six pièces faciles, vc, b (Bonn, *c*1815)
6 Trois duos, 2 vc (Bonn, *c*1816–17)
7 Concertino, vc solo, fl, 2 va, vc, db (Bonn, *c*1817–18)
8 Trois duos, 2 vc (Bonn, *c*1819–20)
9 Six pièces faciles, vc, b (Leipzig, *c*1821)
10 Andante with variations, vc solo, fl, 2 vn, va, vc (Bonn, n.d.)
11 Six solos, vc, b (Mainz, *c*1821), possibly by B. V. Šťastný
12 Rondo et variations, vc solo, 2 vn, va, vc (Leipzig, *c*1821)
13 Grand trio, vc solo, va, vc (London, n.d.)

BIBLIOGRAPHY

EitnerQ; *FétisB*; *GerberNL*

C. Burney: *The Present State of Music in Germany, the Netherlands and the United Provinces* (London, 1773, 2/1775); ed. P. Scholes as *Dr. Burney's Musical Tours* (London, 1959)

AMZ, ii–xxviii (1800–26)

G. J. Dlabacž: *Allgemeines historisches Künstler-Lexikon*, iii (Prague, 1815), 193f

O. Teuber: *Geschichte des Prager Theaters*, i (Prague, 1883), 342

J. Branberger: *Das Konservatorium für Musik in Prag* (Prague, 1911), 28, 48, 249

G. Herbert: 'Stiastný', *Grove 5*

P. Nettl: 'Prager Lieder aus der Mozart-Zeit', *MJb 1953*, 116

A. Gottron: 'Čeští hudebníci 18. století ve středním Porýní' [Czech musicians of the 18th century in the mid-Rhineland], *Zprávy Bertramky* (Prague, 1967), no.52, p.4

MILAN POŠTOLKA

Statham, Heathcote D(icken) (*b* London, 7 Dec 1889; *d* Norwich, 29 Oct 1973). English organist, conductor and composer. The son of Henry Heathcote Statham (1839–1924), an architect who wrote *The Organ and its Position in Musical Art* (London, 1909), he was a chorister of St Michael's College, Tenbury, and studied at Cambridge and under Parratt at the RCM. He returned to St Michael's as organist from 1920 to 1925, took the Cambridge MusD degree in 1923, and was subsequently organist of St Mary's, Southampton (1926–8), and Norwich Cathedral (1928–66). He shared in the conducting of the Norwich Triennial Festivals, 1936–61, and between 1943 and 1946 conducted a number of London Symphony Orchestra concerts. He edited a series entitled 'Fourteen Full Anthems by John Blow' (London, 1925). Of his own compositions the most important are Rhapsody on a Ground and Rhapsody in C, both for organ, and his church music includes a *Te Deum* for the centenary of St Michael's College and an Evening Service in E minor. He received the CBE in 1967.

WATKINS SHAW

Statkowski, Roman (*b* Szczypiórno, nr. Kalisz, 24 Dec 1859; *d* Warsaw, 12 Nov 1925). Polish composer and teacher. After law studies at Warsaw University he studied under Żeleński at the Warsaw Music Institute and under Soloviov and Rubinstein at the St Petersburg Conservatory, where he graduated in 1890. For some time he taught in Kiev, then in 1903 he won first prize in the London International Opera Competition with his *Filenis*. In 1904 he returned to Warsaw as professor at the conservatory, proving an outstanding teacher. He was a founder-editor in 1911 of the *Kwartalnik muzyczny*. Statkowski was influenced by Russian music, particularly that of Musorgsky, and by contemporary German music: Strauss's symphonic poems and Pfitzner's operas. Lyrical and richly melodic, his work represents a link between the post-Moniuszko composers and the generation of Szymanowski.

WORKS
(selective list)

Operas: Filenis (2, Statkowski, after H. Erler), 1897; Maria (3, Statkowski, after Malczewski), 1903–4

Orch: Polonais, op.20, 1900; Sym. Fantasy, op.25, 1900

Chamber: 5 str qts incl. no.1, F, op.10, 1896, no.4, E♭, op.38 (1948), no.5, E, op.40 (1929); Alla cracovienne, D, op.7, vn, pf, n.d.; 3 mazurkas, op.8, vn, pf, n.d.; 3 pièces, op.17, vn, pf, n.d.; 2 feuilles d'album, op.32, vn, pf, n.d.

Pf: 3 mazurkas, op.2, n.d.; 2 valses, op.5, n.d.; 3 piècettes polonaises, op.9, n.d.; 3 mélodies, op.12, n.d.; Chansons libres, op.15, n.d.; 6 pièces, op.16 (1894); 4 idylles, op.18 (1894); Immortelles, op.19 (1896); Polonica: 4 oberki, 5 krakowiaków, 4 mazurki, opp.22–4, n.d.; Pièces caractéristiques, op.27, n.d.; Toccata, A, op.33 (1928); 6 préludes, op.37 (1928)

BIBLIOGRAPHY

SMP

J. W. Reiss: *Statkowski–Melcer–Mlynarski–Stojowski* (Warsaw, 1949), 4ff

TERESA CHYLIŃSKA

Staubinger, Mathias. *See* STABINGER, MATHIAS.

Staudigl, Joseph (i) (*b* Wöllersdorf, 14 April 1807; *d* Michaelbeueangrund, nr. Vienna, 28 March 1861). Austrian bass. In 1816 he entered the Wiener Neustadt Gymnasium, where he was noted as a boy soprano. From 1823 he attended the Krems philosophical college and in 1825 entered the Melk monastery to begin his novitiate. Moving to Vienna in September 1827 as a medical student, he ran short of money and joined the chorus of the Kärntnertortheater. From this position he advanced and gradually took over solo roles. Although his career was based in Viennese opera houses he regularly sang abroad. He was equally in demand in opera, oratorio and church music, and became particularly associated with the Vienna Tonkünstler-Sozietät, singing in 80 of their concerts. In England Staudigl appeared at both Covent Garden and Her Majesty's Theatre (1842 and 1847) and created the part of Elijah in Mendelssohn's oratorio (1846). His performances of Schubert's songs were especially admired.

DAVID CHARLTON

Staudigl, Joseph (ii) (*b* Vienna, 18 March 1850; *d* Karlsruhe, April 1916). Austrian baritone, youngest son of Joseph Staudigl (i). He studied under Rokitansky at the Vienna Conservatory. During 1875–83 he often sang at the Karlsruhe court theatre and also at court. From 1884 to 1886 he was principal baritone at the Metropolitan Opera House, and he later performed oratorio in Germany and Switzerland. He was married in 1885 to the contralto Gisela Koppmayer (*d* 1929).

DAVID CHARLTON

Staudt, Johann Bernhard (*b* Wiener Neustadt, 23 Oct 1654; *d* Vienna, 6 or 7 Nov 1712). Austrian composer and teacher. From 1666 to 1670 he was a boarder at the Jesuit college in Vienna, and during the academic year 1667–8 he also attended lectures at the university. Nothing is known of him between 1670 and 1684, since the college archives were destroyed after the dissolution of the order in 1773. From 1684 until his death he was *regens chori* at the Jesuit monastic house in Vienna. He was much respected, as is indicated by his being made a freeman of the city. He was responsible for the musical education of the pupils at the college. In accordance with the educational ideal of the Jesuit order, the ceremonial organization of grand occasions was central to this work. For them he had to compose both secular and sacred music and was responsible for its rehearsal.

These occasions traditionally centred on dramatic performances and were the chief social events of the city, usually attended by the emperor and empress.

Staudt composed music for 39 plays performed between 1684 and 1707, most of which were by the Jesuit Johann Baptist Adolph (1657–1708), who spent most of his life in Vienna and whose plays are often considered the culmination of Jesuit dramatic art as a Baroque display of pomp and power. All show the main features of school theatre about 1700: a moral as all-embracing as possible, the demonstration of the achievements of both the pupils and the Society of Jesus as a whole, and last but not least the strengthening and confirmation of faith. This was usually connected with homage to the sovereign, as, for example, the epilogue to *Ferdinandus quintus* (1684) shows; it is an encomium of the Habsburgs and the Emperor Leopold I, whom personifications of the crown lands come forward to praise impressively as conqueror of the Turks and defender of the West and the Catholic Church. Other than in this piece, where the music played a much larger role than usual, Staudt is, in Kramer's words, 'the technically well-trained writer, prolific but deadened by routine', though one ought not to forget that these works were written primarily for didactic purposes. The choruses and the usually short ritornellos (which Wellesz misleadingly described as 'stylized dance forms' – see Kramer) are simply constructed. Roulades are frequently found in the arias, however, and strophic songs and pieces in a single section are built up into da capo forms with ritornellos. Kramer is justified in his criticism of the structure of the recitative. The instrumentation is clearly modelled on that of Kerll's Jesuit play *Pia et fortis mulier in S. Natalia* (1677).

In addition to his music for school plays, Staudt was required to compose liturgical works, but only a few survive and have so far not been examined.

WORKS

MUSIC FOR SCHOOL PLAYS
(sacred)

Patientis Christi memoria, 1685; Reconciliatio Naturae, 1686; Orbis Eucharisticus, 1690; Eucharistia dissidentium, 1697; Tractatus pacis, 1697; Eucharistia thema laudis specialis, 1698; Hospitalitas divinae Sapientiae, 1700; Sponsus animae, 1701; Eucharistia iter ad gloriam, 1702; Eucharistia Amoris nexus, 1704: *A-Wn*

(secular)

Ferdinandus quintus, 1684, ed. in DTÖ (in preparation); Gloriosus de tyrannide, 1685; Humilis Patientia, 1692; Carnevale, 1696; Alvilda, 1697; Guarinus poenitens, 1697; Mulier fortis, 1698; Metamorphosis vinculorum, 1699; Occupationes Honoris et Virtutis, 1699; Osculum Justitiae et Pacis, 1699; Animi humani cura medica, 1700; Carnis privium, 1700, ed. in DTÖ (in preparation); Fatum inevitabile, 1700; Amor patriae, 1701; Triumphus veri Amoris, 1701

Alexandri magni victoria, 1702; Coecus in via, 1702; Judaei Machabaei, 1702; Mens regnum bona possidet, 1702; Fides aulica, 1703; Nemo malus felix, 1703; Virtus non postulat annos, 1703; Pietas in peregrinos, 1704; Virtutis de tempore triumphus, 1704; Tyrannis humiliata, 1705; Hercules, 1706; Parturiunt montes, 1707, ed. in DTÖ (in preparation); Philemon et Apollonius, 1707; Sancta Caecilia, 1707

SACRED VOCAL
Vesper psalms, Magnificat, Regina caeli, *CS-KRa*

LOST WORKS
Victricis Innocentiae de calumnia triumphus, Linz, 1698
Catholicorum Christianorum dogma, 1699

BIBLIOGRAPHY

E. Wellesz: 'Die Opern und Oratorien in Wien von 1660–1708', *SMw*, vi (1919), 5–138

O. Wessely: 'Unbekannte Linzer Drucke des siebzehnten Jahrhunderts', *Oberösterreichische Heimatblätter*, vi (1952), 218

W. Kramer: *Die Musik im Wiener Jesuitendrama von 1677–1711*

(diss., U. of Vienna, 1961), 21ff, 310, 322
W. Pass: Introduction to DTÖ (in preparation)

WALTER PASS

Staurotheotokion. A Byzantine TROPARION in which the presence of the mother of God at the foot of the cross is mentioned.

Stave. See STAFF.

Staynov, Petko (*b* Kazanlak, 1 Dec 1896; *d* Sofia, 25 June 1977). Bulgarian composer. Having lost his sight when he was five, Staynov took up a musical career rather than follow the family traditions in commerce. He studied at the Sofia Institute for the Blind and was then active for five years as a pianist in his native town. From 1920 to 1924 he studied composition with Wolf and the piano with E. Münch in Brunswick and Berlin. On his return to Bulgaria he became very active in Bulgarian cultural life from 1927; he was a piano teacher at the Institute for the Blind until 1941, president of the Bulgarian Choral Union and of the Contemporary Music Union and director of the Sofia National Opera (1941–4). In 1941 he was made a member of the Bulgarian Academy of Sciences. After the revolution of 1944 he held important positions as the first music adviser to the Ministry of Culture, and as director of the Institute for Music (founded in 1948) of the Bulgarian Academy of Sciences. Staynov's compositions are almost exclusively orchestral and choral. Of the Bulgarian composers of his generation, he stands closest to such predecessors as Khristov in his technique, form and folk music colouring. His works are monumental in conception, richly and densely orchestrated and readily comprehensible through their clear construction; Staynov's music often shows affinities with Bulgarian verse, as with Bulgarian peasant music.

WORKS
(selective list)

Orch: Trakiiski tantsi [Thracian dances], 1926; Legenda, sym. poem, 1927; Prikaska [Tales], 1930; Balkan, ov., 1936; Trakiya, sym. poem, 1937; Sym. Scherzo, 1938; 2 syms., 1945, 1949; Mladezhka kontsertna uvertyura [Youth ov.], 1953

Many unacc. choruses, choral ballads

Principal publisher: Nauka i Izkustvo (Sofia)

LADA BRASHOVANOVA

Stebbins, George Coles (*b* Orleans County, NY, 26 Feb 1846; *d* Catskill, NY, 6 Oct 1945). American evangelistic song leader, composer and compiler of gospel hymns. See GOSPEL MUSIC, §I. He wrote *Reminiscences and Gospel Hymn Stories* (New York, 1924).

Steber, Eleanor (*b* Wheeling, West Virgina, 17 July 1916). American soprano. After attending the New England Conservatory, Boston, and studying privately with Paul Althouse and William Whitney, she won the 1940 Metropolitan Opera radio auditions. This led to her début, on 7 December, as Sophie. She remained a leading soprano with the Metropolitan until 1963, bringing distinction to a broad variety of French, Italian and German roles. As her voice matured, its silvery sheen gave way to greater warmth and breadth, and she began to undertake heavier roles such as the Marschallin, Elsa and Donna Anna. She was particularly noted for the suavity and poise of her Mozart heroines – the Countess, Fiordiligi, Pamina, Donna Elvira and Constanze, which she sang at the Metropolitan première of *Die Entführung aus dem Serail* in 1946. She also created the title role in Barber's *Vanessa* (1958), sang the title role in the American première (Metropolitan, 1955) of *Arabella*, and was Marie in the first Metropolitan *Wozzeck* (1959). She appeared at the Edinburgh Festival (1947), Bayreuth (as Elsa, 1953), Vienna (1953) and Florence (1954), as well as with numerous American companies; she was Miss Wingrave in the American première of Britten's opera (Santa Fe, 1973). An admired concert singer and recitalist she commissioned and gave the first performance of Barber's *Knoxville: Summer of 1915* (1948); in 1964 she gave three recitals at the Wigmore Hall, London. In later years she appeared in musical comedy, and divided her time between concerts (sometimes in duet with Blanche Thebom) and teaching.

MARTIN BERNHEIMER

Stecker, Karel (*b* Kosmonosy, nr. Mladá Boleslav, 22 Jan 1861; *d* Mladá Boleslav, 13 March 1918). Czech theorist, composer and teacher. Having studied law and aesthetics at Prague University, and at the Organ School, he turned at first to music criticism. In 1885 he was appointed teacher at the Organ School, and after the school was joined to the conservatory in 1890 he became professor of composition, organ, theory and history of music. Stecker was a very intelligent musician with scientific aspirations, but conservative in his views and lacking a modern academic scientific method. He published many articles and books, among them the first Czech textbook on musical forms and their history. He tended in his compositions mostly to church music, in strict ecclesiastical style, which also attracted his interest as a theorist.

WRITINGS

Kritické příspěvky k některým sporným otázkám vědy hudební [Critical contributions to some controversial questions of musicology] (Prague, 1889; Ger. trans., *VMw*, vi, 1890, 437)
Všeobecný dějepis hudby [History of music] (Mladá Boleslav, 1892–1903)
Formy hudební [Musical form] (Mladá Boleslav, 1905)
'Kantáta a hudba církevní' [Cantatas and church music], *Antonín Dvořák, sborník o jeho životě a díle* (Prague, 1912)

WORKS
(selective list; many MSS in CS-Pk)

6 masses, incl. Missa solemnis, op.3, solo vv, 4vv, org, orch, 1884 (Prague, 1890)
26 motets in 3 bks, opp.6, 8, 10, S, A (T, B, ad lib), orch (Prague, 1890–c1910)
31 other sacred vocal works
1 secular cantata, 1 chorus, 10 songs
1 sonata, org, 1884 (Leipzig, n.d.)
Andante scherzino, str qt, op.4, 1882 (Prague, n.d.)
3 romances, vn, pf, op.7, 1892 (Prague, n.d.), 10 others

BIBLIOGRAPHY

B. Vomáčka: 'Karel Stecker, život a dílo' [life and work], *Tempo*, xvii (1937–8), 105
O. Ším: 'Karel Stecker teoretik', *Tempo*, xvii (1937–8), 104
C. Sychra: *Karel Stecker* (Prague, 1946) [incl. complete list of works and bibliography]

MIROSLAV ČERNÝ

Steckler, Anne-Marie. Maiden name of Anne-Marie Krumpholtz, German harpist and wife of Jean-Baptiste Krumpholtz; *see* KRUMPHOLTZ family.

Štědroň. Czech family of composers and musicologists.

(1) Vladimír Štědroň (*b* Vyškov, 30 March 1900). Composer. His father, a choirmaster, music teacher and bandmaster, was the leader of local musical life. After studying at the town Gymnasium in 1919 the young Štědroň left for Prague, where he studied law at the university and composition under Foerster at the conservatory. He was then a master-class pupil of Novák, and of Suk, under whom he completed his composition studies with the *Variační fantasie na lidovou píseň* ('Variation fantasy on a folksong') for string quartet (1923). Starting on a legal career, he went to Brno, where he attended Helfert's musicology lectures and took part in musical life as a conductor and organizer. He was later transferred to smaller towns and only in 1950 did he return to Prague. Between 1951 and 1960 he taught at the academy of music, the university and the conservatory. His music took its origin from that of Suk, whose subjective expression he greatly admired. But he never lost contact with his Moravian background, the source of his music's modality and volubility (which sometimes disturbed the classical formal structure of his work). He composed irregularly, sometimes with breaks of several years, and his output is not large; but, particularly in the compositions of the 1920s and 1930s, he showed unusual talent, inventiveness and technical command.

WORKS
(selective list)

Str Qt no.1, 1921; Svitání [Dawn] (Majkov, Theer, Sova), 1v, pf, 1921; Variační fantasie na lidovou píseň [Variation fantasy on a folksong], op.1, str qt, 1923; Preludy, sym. poem, 1935–6; Malá domácí suita [Little domestic suite], 2 vn, va, 1937; Str Qt no.2, 1945; Moment musical, orch, 1954; Alla marcia, sym. prelude, 1954; Lidové taneční fantasie [Folkdance fantasy], orch, 1952–5; Pf Sonatina, 1957; Brněnské moře [Brno sea], concert waltz, orch, 1964; Furiantova předehra [Furiant prelude], orch, 1966
Choral works, folksong arrs., occasional pieces

BIBLIOGRAPHY
V. Helfert: *Česká moderní hudba* [Modern Czech music] (Olomouc, 1936), 138f
J. Racek: *Leoš Janáček a současní moravští skladatelé* [Janáček and contemporary Moravian composers] (Brno, 1940), 32ff
J. Smolka: *Česká hudba našeho století* [Czech music of our century] (Prague, 1961), 99
J. Fukač: 'Moravská skladatelská škola po Janáčkovi', *HV*, iv (1967), 257

(2) **Bohumir Štědroň** (*b* Vyškov, 30 Oct 1905). Musicologist, brother of (1) Vladimír Štědroň. His early musical training in a large family of musicians was supplemented by theory lessons with Josef Blatný (1925–8) and piano lessons from Vilém Kurz (1926–8). Later he appeared as a pianist in chamber music with his brothers and ensembles such as the Moravian Quartet; he also conducted a number of choirs. While studying history and geography at the University of Brno (1925–9; graduation 1929) he attended Helfert's lectures in musicology and later became Helfert's unpaid assistant (1932–8), concurrently teaching music education at a teacher-training college (1931–9). After a study trip to Italy in 1931 he obtained the doctorate in Brno in 1934 with a dissertation on Bassani's sacred cantatas. He taught music history at Brno Conservatory (1939–45, 1950–52) and in 1945 joined the arts faculty of Brno University, becoming assistant lecturer (1950), lecturer (1955) and professor (1963); he also taught as professor and director of the music education department in the education faculty (1946–51).

Štědroň joined Helfert and Černušák briefly as editor in 1939–40 of *Pazdírkův hudební slovník* ('Pazdírek's music dictionary') before publication was stopped by the Nazis, and this experience led to his editorship, with Černušák and Zdenko Nováček, of the *Československý hudební slovník osob a institucí* ('Czechoslovak music dictionary of places and institutions', 1963–5), for which he wrote many articles himself. His publications include several studies of various composers' connections with Moravia, but he is known chiefly for his research on Janáček. His collection of reminiscences and letters, *Leoš Janáček ve vzpomínkách a dopisech* (1945), achieved wide popularity in its German and English translations (1955) as almost the only book on the composer available in those languages at the time. He was responsible for the introductions to several editions of Janáček's music and for a number of detailed historical and source studies, many of them concentrating on Janáček's speech-melody theory, his opera *Jenůfa* and related works. Much of this material was assembled in his book (1968) on the genesis of *Jenůfa*, for which he was awarded the DSc (1969). His 1976 book on the composer, though designed for the general reader, fastidiously incorporates much new research by other scholars and his own earlier studies. Štědroň's standard catalogue of Janáček's compositions (1959) has been published in several languages.

WRITINGS
'Leoš Janáček na mužském učitelském ústavu v Brně' [Janáček at the men's teaching institute in Brno], *Tempo*, xiii (1933–4), 315; repr. in *Rytmus*, xi (1947–8), 140
Sólové chrámové kantáty G. B. Bassaniho [Bassani's solo church cantatas] (diss., U. of Brno, 1934)
'Lidová píseň v díle Josefa Suka' [Folksong in Suk's works], *Josef Suk: život a dílo*, ed. J. M. Květ (Prague, 1935), 412
Vyškovsko v hudbě a zpěvu [The Vyškov district in music and song] (Vyškov, 1935)
Leoš Janáček a Luhačovice [Janáček and Luhačovice] (Luhačovice, 1939)
Dr. Vladimír Helfert: přehled práce českého učence [Helfert: survey of the work of a Czech scholar] (Prague, 1940)
Smetanův Pražský karneval [Smetana's *Prague Carnival*] (Prague, 1940)
Ferdinand Vach (Prague, 1941)
Chrámová hudba v Brně v XVIII. století [Church music in Brno in the 18th century] (Habilitationsschrift, U. of Brno, 1945; extracts in *Věstník České akademie věd a umění*, lii/1 (1943), 1–29)
Leoš Janáček ve vzpomínkách a dopisech (Prague, 1945; rev. Ger. trans., 1955; rev. Eng. trans., 1955, as *Leoš Janáček: Letters and Reminiscences*)
'Pavel Křížkovský na Starém Brně' [Křížkovský in Old Brno], *Slezský sborník*, xliv (1946), 1
'Janáček – učitel zpěvu' [Janáček as a singing teacher], *Ročenka pedagogické fakulty Masarykovy university v Brně* (1947), 223
'Janáček-upravovatel Lisztovy mše' [Janáček's arrangement of Liszt's Mass], *Cyril*, lxxii (1947), 90; Ger. trans., *SM*, v (1963), 295, and *Sborník prací filosofické fakulty brněnské university*, F7 (1963), 139
Josef Bohuslav Foerster a Morava [Foerster and Moravia] (Brno, 1947)
'Česká hudba za nesvobody' [Czech music during the occupation], *Musikologie*, ii (1949), 106–46
'Antonín Dvořák a Leoš Janáček', *Vlastivědný věstník moravský*, vi (1951), 139, 172; enlarged version in *Musikologie*, v (1958), 105, 324–59
'K dějinám dělnické písně' [The history of workers' songs], *Časopis Matice moravské*, lxx (1951), 204, 485
'Seznam Janáčkových skladeb a úprav' [A list of Janáček's compositions and arrangements], *Slezský sborník*, l (1952), suppl.2, pp.1–48; rev. as *Dílo Leoše Janáčka: bibliografie a diskografie* (Prague, 1959; Ger. trans., *BMw*, ii/3–4 (1960), 120–53; iii/1 (1961), 34–77; Russ. trans., 1959; Eng. trans., 1959)
'Zdeněk Fibich a Morava' [Fibich and Moravia], *Zdeněk Fibich: sborník dokumentů a studií*, ii, ed. A. Rektorys (Prague, 1952), 269–318
'Zemští trubači a tympanisté v Brně' [Provincial trumpets and drummers in Brno], *Vlastivědný věstník moravský*, vii (1952), 122, 167
'Husitské náměty v české a světové hudbě' [Hussite themes in Czech and world music], *Časopis Národního musea: vědy společenské*, cxxii (1953), 62–92
'Janáček a Čajkovskij' [Janáček and Tchaikovsky], *Sborník prací filosofické fakulty brněnské university*, ii (1953), 201
'Janáček a Polsko' [Janáček and Poland], *Sborník prací filosofické fakulty brněnské university*, C1 (1954); Ger. trans. in *Chopin Congress: Warszawa 1960*, 618
with I. Stolařík: 'K dějinám hudby v Ostravském kraji' [The history of music in the Ostrava region], *Slezský sborník*, liii (1955), 195–229
'Mozart a Morava' [Mozart and Moravia], *Kongressbericht: Wien*

Mozartjahr 1956, 603

'K Janáčkovým národním tancům na Moravě' [Janáček's national dances from Moravia], *Sborník prací filosofické fakulty brněnské university*, F2 (1958), 44

'K Janáčkově opeře Osud' [Janáček's opera *Fate*], *Živá hudba*, i (1959), 159

'Beiträge zur Kontroverse um die tschechische Herkunft und die Nationalität von Jan Václav Stamic', *Sborník prací filosofické fakulty brněnské university*, F6 (1962), 123; repr. in *BMw*, vi (1964), 16, as 'Zur Nationalität von J. V. Stamic'; Cz. trans., *HRo*, xvi (1963), 666

'Ke korespondenci a vztahu Leoše Janáčka a Karla Kovařovice' [The correspondence and relations between Janáček and Kovařovic], *Sborník prací filosofické fakulty brněnské university*, F9 (1962), 31–69

ed., with G. Černušák and Z. Nováček: *Československý hudební slovník osob a institucí* [Czechoslovak music dictionary of places and institutions] (Prague, 1963–5)

'K Janáčkovým nápěvkům mluvy: zárodky jeho operního slohu' [Janáček's speech-melodies: the origins of his operatic style], *Sborník pedagogické fakulty university karlovy k šedesátým narozeninám Prof. Dr. Josefa Plavce* (Prague, 1966), 197–235

Vítězslav Novák v obrazech [Novák in pictures] (Prague, 1967)

'Die Landschafts-Trompeter und -Tympanisten im alten Brünn: zur Entwicklungsgeschichte einer unbekannten Musikgesellschaft im 17. und 18. Jahrhundert', *Mf*, xxi (1968), 438

ed.: *Hudba Vyškovska* [Music in Vyškov] (Vyškov, 1968)

Zur Genesis von Leoš Janáčeks Oper Jenůfa (Brno, 1968, rev. 2/1971) [incl. several articles on *Jenůfa* and related topics orig. pubd in Cz.; two chaps. pubd in Eng. in *Sborník prací filosofické fakulty brněnské university*, H3 (1968), 42–74; H5 (1970), 91]

'Leoš Janáček kritikem brněnské opery v letech 1890–1892' [Janáček as a critic of the Brno Opera 1890–92], *Otázky divadla a filmu*, i (Brno, 1970), 207–48; Ger. trans., *Leoš Janáček-Gesellschaft: Mitteilungsblatt* (Zurich, 1971), nos.3–4

'Die Inspirationsquellen von Janáčeks Concertino', *Musica cameralis: Brno VI 1971*, 423

'Janáčkova korespondence s Universal Edition v letech 1916–18 týkajíci se Její pastorkyně' [Janáček's correspondence with Universal Edition in 1916–18 concerning *Jenůfa*], *Otázky divadla a filmu*, ii (Brno, 1971), 249–312

'Ein Chorinventar aus dem Jahr 1768 in Deutsch Brod (Havlíčkův Brod) in tschechischer Sprache', *Sborník prací filosofické fakulty brněnské university*, H7 (1972), 31

'Leoš Janáček a Ruský kroužek v Brně' [Janáček and the Russian circle in Brno], *Program: divadelni list Státního divadla v Brně*, xliv (1972–3); xlv (1973–4)

Leoš Janáček: k jeho lidskému a uměleckému profilu [Janáček's personal and artistic profile] (Prague, 1976)

Further articles in *Operní dílo Leoše Janáčka: Brno 1965*, *GfMKB Leipzig 1966*, *IMSCR*, x *Ljubljana 1967*, *Internationaler Beethoven-Kongress: Berlin 1970*

EDITIONS

with J. Štědroň: *Češti klasikové* [Czech classics], MAB, xi (1953, 2/1965)

——: *J. H. Voříšek: Sonata op.5*, MAB, xxx (1956)

——: *J. L. Dussek: Sonata op.69*, MAB, xli (1959)

——: *F. Benda: 4 Sonatas*, MAB, lvii (1962)

BIBLIOGRAPHY

J. Vysloužil: 'Bohumír Štědroň', *HV*, iii (1966), 25

Sborník prací filosofické fakulty brněnské university, H2 (1967) [dedicated to B. Štědroň on his 60th birthday; incl. list of writings and edns. to 1966 compiled by M. Štědroň]

(3) Miloš Štědroň (*b* Brno, 9 Feb 1942). Composer and musicologist, nephew of (1) Vladimír Štědroň and (2) Bohumír Štědroň. He studied musicology and Czech at Brno University (1959–64), where his teachers included Racek, Vysloužil and his uncle Bohumír. From 1965 to 1970 he studied composition and music theory under Piňos, Ištvan and Kohoutek at the Brno Academy; he received the doctorate in 1967 from Brno University. Between 1963 and 1972 he worked at the music department of the Moravian Museum in Brno, conducting research into Janáček's music and organizing concerts. In 1972 he was appointed lecturer in music theory at Brno University. His theoretical work has been concerned with Janáček's relationship with western European practice and analysis, and with the problems of employing new musical ideas and of using modality in contemporary music. His own music makes use of modality together with collage forms. Štědroň's

diverse compositional interests have included music for tape, collaboration with jazz bands and pop groups (he has written some successful songs) and work for the theatre, television and cinema. With Parsch, Piňos and Růžička he has engaged in collective composition, and he has also been concerned with the authentic realization of Baroque and Classical works.

WORKS
(selective list)

Stage: Apparat (opera, after Kafka), 1967–9; Justina, ballet; Mann ist Mann (musical, after Brecht)

Elec: Utis, 1966; Panychida, 1967; O Sancta Caecilia, 1968; Bis, 1969; Kuře krákoře [Chicken clucking], 1970, collab. Parsch; Viva Che, 1972, collab. Parsch

Other works: 5 cantatas; Sym.; Conc., db, str; Str Qt

WRITINGS

'Leoš Janáček und die 2. Wiener Schule', *Operní dilo Leoše Janáčka: Brno 1965*, 55

'Zur Frage der "Adaptation" der Oper Griechische Passion von Bohuslav Martinů', *The Stage Works of Bohuslav Martinů: Brno I 1966*, 183

Janáček a hudba 20. stoleti [Janáček and the music of the 20th century] (diss., U. of Brno, 1967)

'Participación del racionalismo e irracionalismo en la nueva musica checa', *Sonda*, i (Madrid, 1967)

'Die Versionen der Violinsonate in A dur von František Benda', *Musica antiqua: Brno II 1967*, 142

'Několik poznámek k Janáčkově tektonice' [Some remarks on Janáček's construction], *Časopis Moravského musea*, lii (1967), 271; Eng. trans., rev. and abridged, in *Leoš Janáček et musica europaea: Brno III 1968*, 119, as 'The Tectonic Montage of Janáček'

'Leoš Janáček in avantgarda dvajsetih let', *MZ*, iv (1968), 88

'Janáček und der Expressionismus', *Sborník prací filosofické fakulty brněnské university*, H5 (1970), 105

'Janáček: verismus a impresionismus', *Časopis Moravského musea*, liii–liv (1968–9), 125–54; Ger. trans. in *Leoš Janáček-Gesellschaft: Mitteilungsblatt* (Zurich, 1970), no.1, as 'Janáček und die Veristen'

'Das Zunehmen musikfremder Elemente in den Kammerkompositionen der neuen Musik der 60. Jahre', *Musica cameralis: Brno VI 1971*, 497

'K podstatě tzv. sociálního a slovanského expresionismu u Leoše Janáčka' [The essence of the so-called social and Slavonic expressionism in Janáček], *Česká hudba světu: svět české hudbě*, ed. J. Bajer (Prague, 1974), 119

'K analýze vokální melodiky Janáčkovy Věci Makropulos s využitim samočinného počítače' [The analysis of the voice part of Janáček's *The Makropulos Affair* using a computer], *HV*, xii (1975), 46 [with Ger. summary]

BIBLIOGRAPHY

J. Bártová: 'Autoři team-worku' [The authors of team-work], *HRo*, xxii (1969), 419

JOSEF BEK (1), JOHN TYRRELL (2), JIŘÍ FUKAČ (3)

Steel, (Charles) Christopher (*b* London, 15 Jan 1939). English composer and teacher. He studied composition at the RAM with John Gardner (1957–61) and in Munich with Harald Genzmer (1961–2). Since 1968 he has been director of music at Bradfield College, Reading. He is a fluent and resourceful composer, who had already written three symphonies by the time he was 26 and who readily provides occasional works for amateurs and children. By 20th-century standards, Steel's music is not difficult to approach; he has said himself that he hopes 'it will always have recognizable melody, harmony and rhythm'. It is, however, generally closely organized, harmonically and thematically. In the *Shakespeare Symphony* (no.3) for soloists, chorus and orchestra Steel makes use of a 12-note series, harmonically organized, as a source of thematic material; in general his music embodies a technique of 'extended tonality' possibly deriving from Hindemith (Genzmer's teacher). His works include a mass, two cantatas, a choral symphony and three other symphonies, five concertos, chamber music and two sonatinas for piano. His principal publisher is Novello.

HUGO COLE

Steel band [tinpanny]. An ensemble of tuned percussion instruments made from oildrums, with a few rhythm instruments. First developed in Trinidad, British West Indies, in the 1930s and 1940s as bands for masked processions and parades during Carnival, they supplanted tamboo–bamboo bands which had existed during the previous 70 years. These, in turn, had replaced African and East Indian drums whose use in religious ceremonial and street processions had been forbidden since 1884.

There are five steps in making a pan: sinking (pounding the head into a concave shape), grooving (marking the position of each note with a steel punch), burning (tempering the metal), cutting the drum-barrel to the required length, and tuning (making the final adjustments for each pitch with a small hammer). The note layout is not consecutive; each unit gives off to some degree the pitch of its neighbours, and therefore contiguous units are tuned, when possible, to octaves, 5ths and 4ths. Pan sticks are rubber-headed. Pans can be slung from the player's neck, mounted on racks or wheels for Carnival or on stands for stationary concert performances. Pitch, tuning, note layout and nomenclature are not standardized; using current (1979) Trinidad terminology, there are three basic categories: tenor pans (formerly ping-pongs), which are tune-playing pans, may cover two octaves upwards from c' or one and a half octaves upwards from f, partly or completely chromatically; rhythm pans (including double second pans, double guitar pans, treble guitar pans and cello pans) may contain a diatonic octave upwards from c; and bass pans (formerly tuned-booms) may have three to five notes in the octave upwards from C.

Steel bands are no longer restricted to Carnival and other public festivities in their function and repertory.

Members of the London All Stars Steel Band playing tenor pans at the Notting Hill Carnival, 1976; see also TRINIDAD AND TOBAGO, *fig.2*

At the 1961 Trinidad Carnival, for instance, both 'instrumental' and steel bands chose Francisco Slinger's *Royal Jail* as their road march. By 1950, Winston Spree Simon, generally believed to have been the first to play a tune on a pan, was including waltzes, foxtrots and even a selection from Tchaikovsky's First Piano Concerto in concert performances. The Trinidad All Stars Percussion Orchestra, specially formed to play in England during the 1951 Festival of Britain, used chromatically tuned pans and had both Caribbean and arranged European items in its repertory; these were taught by means of a number tablature devised by the orchestra's director. A US Navy Steel Band, founded in Puerto Rico in 1959, was taught initially by Ellie Manete, a Trinidad panman.

In urban Trinidad, steel band performances are often extremely polished, whether for inhabitants or tourists. In some of the smaller Caribbean islands and in Surinam local steel bands play for community festivities and for family celebrations such as weddings; the repertory may be largely local in origin. Bands that play for international cabarets and clubs tend to have a pan-American repertory, including the Trinidad CALYPSO and limbo, and Latin American and North American items. A sizable recording industry produces discs of several kinds of steel band music.

European works using steel drums, such as the *Vermutungen über ein dunkles Haus* from the opera *Amerika* by Haubenstock-Ramati, have little in common with the Caribbean music for the instruments; they are presumably always played from full notation by orchestral percussionists. A considerable number of amateur and semi-professional steel bands exist in Great Britain and steel bands have been used in music education since the 1970s in urban districts where a sizable part of the population is of West Indian origin.

BIBLIOGRAPHY
P. Seeger: 'The Steel Drum', *Journal of American Folklore*, lxxi (1958), 52
E. Hill: *The Trinidad Carnival* (Austin, Texas, 1972), 45ff
JOAN RIMMER

Steel drum (Fr. *tambour d'acier*; Ger. *Trinidad-Gongtrommel*; It. *tambour d'acciaio*). A tuned idiophone usually made from an oil drum, which is played in a STEEL BAND. The steel drum developed in Trinidad in the 1930s and 1940s; *see also* TRINIDAD AND TOBAGO.

Steele, (Hubert) John (*b* Wellington, 13 April 1929). New Zealand musicologist. After taking his BA at Victoria University College, Wellington, and his MA at the University of Otago (1953), he was awarded the first New Zealand government bursary in musicology and became a research student under Thurston Dart at Jesus College, Cambridge, where he took his PhD in 1959. He was appointed lecturer in music at the University of Sydney in 1959. In 1962 he became lecturer in music at the University of Otago, where he has been associate professor since 1969. He has specialized in early English keyboard music, the motets and madrigals of Peter Philips and Marenzio, and in Italian Baroque church music (his special interests being Monteverdi and A. Scarlatti).

WRITINGS
English Organs and Organ Music, 1500–1650 (diss., U. of Cambridge, 1959)
'The Later Madrigals of Luca Marenzio', *SMA*, iii (1969), 17

'Dixit Dominus: Alessandro Scarlatti and Handel', *SMA*, vii (1973), 19

EDITIONS
J. Bull: Keyboard Music I, MB, xiv (1960)
A. Scarlatti: St Cecilia Mass (London, 1968)
P. Philips: Select Italian Madrigals, MB, xxix (1970)
L. Marenzio: Il settimo libro de madrigali a 5 voci (New York, 1975)
A. Scarlatti: Dixit Dominus (London, 1975)

J. M. THOMSON

Steele, Joshua (*b* Ireland, 1700; *d* Barbados, 1791). British inventor and writer on many subjects. He lived for many years in London where in 1775 he invented a notation for writing down speech. He devised his system after reading the portion on music of an anonymous tract, *Of the Origin and Progress of Language* (Edinburgh, 1773–92), by James Burnett, Lord Monboddo. Monboddo's understanding of music arose from his interpretation of Greek and Latin writings. He divided music into two domains, pitch and time, and assigned to time the following properties: quantities of notes, varieties of loud and soft, pauses and divisions into bars.

Steele's interpretation of music arose from his readings in physics. He divided music into three domains, pitch, time and force, and made a clear distinction between the concepts of 'metre' and 'rhythm'. The essence of rhythm was 'the instinctive sense and idea of dividing the duration of all sounds and motions, by an equal periodical pulsation, like the oscillations or swings of a pendulum'. Bar-lines were the graphic representations of these pulsations and were analogous to the concept 'cadence' in language. The separation of quantity and force from the material of rhythm helped to pave the way in Britain for the development of theories of rhythm.

Steele's invention consisted of a staff with clef and various symbols for signifying the several modifications of pitch, time and force in speech. The types for the symbols were made by Joseph Jackson. Use of the types continued after Steele's death, for his invention became the basis of elocutionary systems taught by John Thelwall, James Chapman and Richard Roe. The two last named published treatises on the subject of prosody in which they dealt also with metrical and rhythmical facets of music.

WRITINGS
(*only those related to music*)
An Essay towards establishing the Melody and Measure of Speech to be expressed and perpetuated by Peculiar Symbols (London, 1775, 2/1779) [includes correspondence between Steele and Lord Monboddo]
'Of a Musical Instrument . . . from the Isle of Amsterdam in the South Seas', *Philosophical Transactions of the Royal Society*, lxv (1775), 67
'Remarks on a Larger System of Reed Pipes from the Isle of Amsterdam, with Some Observations on the Nose Flute of Otaheite', *Philosophical Transactions of the Royal Society*, lxv (1775), 72

BIBLIOGRAPHY
W. Bewley: Review of *An Essay towards establishing the Melody and Measure of Speech*, *Monthly Review*, lv (1776), 1
W. Mitford: *An Inquiry into the Principles of Harmony in Language, and of the Mechanism of Verse, Modern and Ancient* (London, 2/1804)
J. Thelwall: Letter to the editor, *Monthly Magazine*, xxiii (1807), 28
J. Chapman: *The Music, or Melody and Rhythmus of Language* (Edinburgh, 1818)
R. Roe: *The Principles of Rhythm, both in Speech and Music; especially as exhibited in the Mechanism of English Verse* (Dublin, 1823)
P. Fussell jr: *Theory of Prosody in 18th-century England* (New London, Conn., 1954/R1966)
M. Demmery: 'The Hybrid Critic', *ML*, xxxvii (1956), 128
JAMIE CROY KASSLER

Steenwick, Gisbert (van) (*b* early 17th century; *d* Kampen, 1679). Dutch composer, organist and carillonneur. He became a member of the collegium musicum 'Caecilia' at Arnhem in 1663 and was appointed organist of St Eusebius there in 1665. In 1675 he left to become organist and carillonneur at Kampen. He is known today only by some keyboard pieces in a volume that he compiled before 1675 for Anna Maria van Eyl, the daughter of a patrician in Arnhem, who was probably his pupil (MS at *NL-At*; edn. in MMN, ii, 1959). The MS contains 33 keyboard pieces all based on folksongs and displaying sophisticated variation techniques. Nine pieces are signed by Steenwick, but others may be attributed to him on stylistic grounds.

RANDALL H. TOLLEFSEN

Steere [Steer], John Wesley (*b* Southwick, Mass., 10 April 1824; *d* Springfield, Mass., 11 Dec 1900). American organ builder. He was apprenticed to William A. Johnson, eventually becoming a voicer. In 1867 he began his own business in Westfield, Massachusetts, with another former Johnson man, George W. Turner (1829–1908). Turner left in 1892 and Steere's sons John S. Steere (1847–98) and Frank J. Steere entered the firm, which then moved its factory to Springfield. At this time the firm rose to prominence through its pioneering of tubular pneumatic action. After Steere's death the firm was reorganized, and continued until 1920, when it was bought by Ernest Skinner. The firm's most important installations include those in Christ Church (1885) and the Municipal Auditorium (1915), both in Springfield.

BARBARA OWEN

Stefan [Stefan-Grünfeldt], Paul (*b* Brno, 25 Nov 1879; *d* New York, 12 Nov 1943). Austrian writer on music. From 1898 he lived in Vienna, where he studied law, philosophy and art history, taking a doctorate in law in 1904, and concurrently studying music theory with Hermann Grädener and Schoenberg. He became a critic and freelance writer on music in Vienna, and as a staunch champion of modern music played a leading part in the Ansorge-Verein, founded in 1903 for the propagation of new music. From 1921 to 1938 he was editor of and a major contributor to *Musikblätter des Anbruch*. In 1938 he emigrated by way of Switzerland, France and Portugal to the USA; for many years he wrote for daily newspapers (e.g. *Neue Zürcher Zeitung*) and periodicals (e.g. *Musical America*). He was a founder-member (1922) of the ISCM. His many biographical books are compiled from secondary sources but contain his own aesthetic assessments; many ran to several editions. They include one on Max Reinhardt and another on Hugo von Hofmannsthal, and his editorial activities likewise extended to non-musical subjects.

WRITINGS
Gustav Mahler (Munich, 1910, 4/1920; Eng. trans., enlarged, 1913)
Das Grab in Wien: eine Chronik 1903–11 (Berlin, 1913)
Das neue Haus: ein Halbjahrhundert Wiener Opernspiel (Vienna, 1919)
Die Feindschaft gegen Wagner (Regensburg, 1919)
Neue Musik und Wien (Leipzig, 1921)
Anna Bahr-Mildenburg (Vienna, 1922)
Franz Schubert (Berlin, 1928)
ed. and trans. with F. Werfel: *Giuseppe Verdi: Briefe* (Vienna, 1926; Eng. trans., enlarged, 1942, as *Verdi: the Man in his Letters*)
Die Wiener Oper (Vienna, 1932)
Arturo Toscanini (Vienna, 1935; Eng. trans. 1936)
Dvořák, Leben und Werk (Vienna, Leipzig and Prague, 1935) [abridged trans. of O. Šourek: *Život a dílo Antonína Dvořáka* (Prague, 1916–33)]

Bruno Walter (Vienna, 1936)
Georges Bizet (Zurich, 1952)

BIBLIOGRAPHY
Foreword to *Georges Bizet* (Zurich, 1952)

RUDOLF KLEIN

Stefani, Agostino. *See* STEFFANI, AGOSTINO.

Stefani, Andrea (*fl* Florence, *c*1400). Italian composer, poet and singer. He is known not only as the composer of two ballate and one madrigal in *I-La* 184 (nos.61, 72, 73), but also as the poet and composer of three-voice *laude* of which the music has not survived. In 1399 he served as leader and singer in the processions of the Bianchi Gesuati in Florence. Stylistically Stefani made use of both the Florentine technique of writing for two voices and the French manner of three-voice writing with contratenor. The first three lines of the text of his madrigal are taken from Petrarch's *Amor, se vou' chi'i' torni.*

WORKS
Editions: *The Music of Fourteenth-Century Italy*, ed. N. Pirrotta, CMM, viii/5 (1964) [P]
  Italian Secular Music, ed. W. T. Marrocco, PMFC, x (Monaco, 1974)

BALLATE
Con tucta gentileçça, 3vv, P 38
I' senti' matutino, 2vv, P 38 (all 3 stanzas after the ripresa sung to second section of music)

MADRIGAL
Morte m'à sciolt', Amor, 2vv, P 36

BIBLIOGRAPHY
E. Li Gotti: 'Per la biografia di due minori musicisti italiani dell' "Ars Nova"', *Restauri trecenteschi* (Palermo, 1947), 98
A. Bonaccorsi: 'A. Stefani: musicista dell'ars nova', *RMI*, xxi (1948), 103
F. Ghisi: 'Strambotti e laude nel travestimento spirituale della poesia musicale del Quattrocento', *Collectanea historiae musicae*, i (1948), 48
K. von Fischer: *Studien zur italienischen Musik des Trecentos und frühen Quattrocentos* (Berne, 1956), 24, 46, 56, 85
N. Pirrotta: Preface to CMM, viii/5 (1964), iii
U. Günther: 'Die "anonymen" Kompositionen des Manuskripts Paris, B.N., fonds it. 568 (Pit)', *AMw*, xxiii (1966), 90

KURT VON FISCHER

Stefani, Giovanni (*fl* 1618–26). Italian music editor, ?organist and ?composer. According to Fétis he was organist of the Gnadenkirche, Vienna. This information may have derived from his lost fourth book of canzonettas, but it seems unlikely that he was able to assemble from Vienna the contents of his books of canzonettas, which, more obviously than most publications of the time, were intended to cater for the new demand in Italy for books of simple strophic songs. The title-pages of the extant books cite no appointment for him and announce him as the collector of the pieces; it is possible that he wrote a few himself, though in a preface to the second book he explained that his 'feeble talent' allowed him only to collect the songs of others. Only one of the composers has been identified. There survive 87 Italian songs, and in the first two books there are altogether four Sicilian and six Spanish songs too. Nearly all the songs are simple strophic pieces, easy to sing, often with pleasing tunes and lively rhythms; some are influenced by dances, others by folk music. The first book in particular was extremely popular; five editions appeared in a period of eight years.

WORKS
Affetti amorosi: canzonette, 1v, bc (Venice, 1618, 5/1626); ed. (except for 3 songs) in Biblioteca di rarità musicali, iii (Milan, 1886)
Scherzi amorosi: canzonette, 1v, bc (Venice, 1619 [lost], 3/1622) [1 by Peri]

Concerti amorosi: terza parte delle canzonette in musica (Venice, ?1623, 2/1623)
Ariette amorose (Venice, 1626), lost; according to *FétisB* (the 1649 catalogue of the Venetian publisher Vincenti lists a Quarto libro, presumably identical with the volume mentioned by *FétisB*)

BIBLIOGRAPHY
A. W. Ambros: *Geschichte der Musik*, iv (Leipzig, rev. 3/1909 by H. Leichtentritt), 884ff
B. Szabolcsi: *A melódia története* (Budapest, 1950; Eng. trans., 1966, as *A History of Melody*), chap.5
N. Fortune: *Italian Secular Song from 1600 to 1635: the Origins and Development of Accompanied Monody* (diss., U. of Cambridge, 1954)
J. Racek: *Stilprobleme der italienischen Monodie* (Prague, 1965), 13, 70, 73, 102, 146, 221
N. Fortune: 'Solo Song and Cantata', *NOHM*, iv (1968), 165, 175f
R. Hudson: 'The Folia Melodies', *AcM*, xlv (1973), 107

NIGEL FORTUNE

Stefani, Jan (*b* Prague, 1746; *d* Warsaw, 24 Feb 1829). Polish composer, conductor and violinist of Bohemian origin. His elementary education was at the Benedictine school in Prague; later he went to Italy, and about 1765 became a violinist in the orchestra of Count G. Kiński in Vienna. In February 1779 he settled in Warsaw and was violinist and conductor of the court orchestra of King Stanisław August Poniatowski; at about the same time he was appointed Kapellmeister at the cathedral. After 1795 Stefani sporadically conducted the orchestra of the Teatr Narodowy (National Theatre) in Warsaw and the choirs of various Warsaw churches; from 1799 to 1811 he was merely a violinist at the Teatr Narodowy.

In the history of Polish music Stefani is outstanding as a composer of opera. His best-known work is *Cud mniemany* ('The supposed miracle'), still reckoned the peak of Polish opera during the Enlightenment. A notable feature of his music is the use of the polonaise which gave rise to the sentimental style and character of Polish music in the period before Chopin. Stefani wrote about 100 polonaises for orchestra.

Several of Stefani's children were musicians, including Kazimierz (1791–1811) and Jan (1797–1826), violinists in the opera orchestra, Karolina (1784–1803) and Eleonora (1802–31), opera singers, and JÓZEF STEFANI.

WORKS
(*all stage works produced in Warsaw*)
Miłość każdemu wiekowi przystoi [Love becomes every age], ballet, 4 Nov 1785
Król w kraju rozkoszy [The king of Cockaigne] (3, F. Zabłocki, after M.-A. Legrand), 3 Feb 1787, lib, *PL-Kz*
Cud mniemany czyli Krakowiacy i Górale [The supposed miracle or Krakovians and Highlanders] (2, W. Bogusławski), 1 March 1794, Warsaw Music Society Library
Wdięczni poddani czyli Wesele wiejskie [Thankful serfs or The country wedding] (3, J. Drozdowski), 24 July 1796; also performed as Przyjazd pana czyli Szczęśliwi wieśniacy [The arrival of the lord or Happy country folk]
Drzewo zaczarowane [The magic tree] (Zabłocki, after P.-L. Moline), 1796
Frozyna czyli Siedem razy jedna [Frozine or Seven times dressed up] (1, J. Adamczewski, after J.-B. Radet), 21 Feb 1806, lib (Warsaw, 1806)
Rotmistrz Górecki czyli Oswobodzenie [Captain Górecki or The liberation] (3, W. Pękalski), 3 April 1807
Polka czyli Oblężenie Trembowli [The Polish woman or The siege of Trembowla] (3, J. Wybicki), 22 May 1807
Stary myśliwy [The old huntsman] (3, trans. W. Pękalski), 31 Jan 1808
Papirus czyli Ciekawość dawnych kobiet [Papyrus or The curiosity of women in ancient times] (1, trans. J. Adamczewski, after P.-A. Vieillard), 15 May 1808, lib (Warsaw, 1810)
Niechaj wiekom wiek podawa [May this age survive in history], cantata, 25 Nov 1791, Warsaw Music Society Library, edn. in *Kultura muzyczna Warszawy XVIII wieku* [Music in Warsaw in the 18th century], appx (Kraków, 1955)
Kantata na uroczystość instalacji arcybiskupa Kajetana Kickiego [for

the installation of Archbishop Kajetan Kicki], Lwów, 12 March 1798, lost
Some masses and offertories, lost
7 polonaises, orch, Łowicz Regional Museum, fragment
3 songs, 1v, pf; 1 polonaise, pf: in Wybór pięknych dzieł muzycznych i pieśni polskich [Collection of the finest musical works and Polish songs], i–viii (Warsaw, 1803–5)
1 song in Muzyka do pieśni wolnomularskich [Music to freemason songs] (Warsaw, 1811); 1 freemason song, Kz

ALINA NOWAK-ROMANOWICZ

Stefani, Józef (b Warsaw, 16 April 1800; d Warsaw, 19 March 1876). Polish composer, conductor, violinist and teacher, son of JAN STEFANI. He studied first with his father and later under Elsner at the Warsaw Conservatory of Music (1821–4). From 1813 he sang and played the violin in the chorus and orchestra of the Warsaw Opera, and later was conductor of the ballet. From 1827 he taught singing, and was director of music to several Warsaw churches. In 1861 he was appointed inspector at the Music Institute in Warsaw. A prolific composer, he was successful both in ballet and in religious music. He also wrote three elementary instruction manuals for vocal and keyboard students.

WORKS

All MSS in Warsaw Music Society Library; all stage works first produced in Warsaw.
About 15 ballets, incl. Mimili czyli Styryjczycy [Mimili, or The Styrians], 2 Feb 1837, PL-Kj; Stach i Zośka, 17 Oct 1839, lost
12 comic operas and melodramas, incl. Lekcja botaniki [Botany lesson] (2, trans. F. Szymański), 15 March 1829, lost; Figle panien [Girls' frolics] (1, F. Skarbek), 6 Aug 1832, Wn; Żyd wieczny tułacz [The wandering Jew] (melodrama, 5, after E. Sue), 1 Jan 1850, lost
c20 masses; Requiem, male vv, brass band; Te Deum, 4vv, orch; Stabat mater, 4vv, orch; many cantatas, hymns, sacred songs
Concertino, tpt, orch; many orchestral dances and marches
c40 songs, 1v, pf, some with vn/vc acc.

THEORETICAL WORKS
(all MSS in Warsaw Music Society Library)
Początkowa szkoła na fortepian [Primary school for the piano]
Wszechstronne ćwiczenia głosowe . . . dla początkujących [Universal exercises for beginners], S, T, pf acc.
Osiem dwuśpiewów dla poczynających naukę śpiewu [8 songs for beginners], 2vv, 1859

ALINA NOWAK-ROMANOWICZ

Stefanini, Giovanni Battista (b Modena, baptized 8 July 1574; d Rome, 1630). Italian composer. He was a singer at Modena Cathedral from 1593 until 1602 under Orazio Vecchi and wrote several mascheratas (which have not survived) for the Modenese court between 1599 and 1602. He was maestro di cappella at Turin Cathedral from 1602 to at least 1604, at S Maria della Scala, Milan, in 1606 and 1608 and at the Madonna della Consolazione, Rome, in 1614. From 7 January 1615 he was back in Modena as maestro at the cathedral, although he maintained contacts with Rome to the extent of outstaying leave from Modena in 1619, for which he was suspended until an apology was forthcoming. He finally returned to Rome in 1625. His output is of sacred music, mainly motets, showing a preference for the fuller textures of the conventional polyphonic or double-choir styles rather than for the new concertato idiom. In this he was typical of Roman composers, with whom he seems to have identified himself, and he designated his 1618 collection 'all'uso di Roma'.

WORKS

Motetti, liber I, 6, 7vv (Venice, 1604)
Motetti, libro I, 2, 3vv (Milan, 1606)
Il secondo libro de motetti, 5–8vv, et le lettanie della beata vergine . . . bc (org) (Venice, 1608)

Concerti ecclesiastici, 8vv, cioè motetti, messa, salmi, Magnificat, con le letanie della beata vergine, libro III, bc (org) (Rome, 1614)
Motetti concertati all'uso di Roma, 8, 9vv, con le letanie della beata vergine, libro IV, bc (org), op.6 (Venice, 1618)
Motetti concertati, 2–5vv, bc (org), libro I, op.7 (Rome, 1626)
11 motets in 1607⁷, 1611¹, 1612³, 1613², 1621²; 1 work in 1610¹

BIBLIOGRAPHY
G. Roncaglia: La cappella musicale del duomo di Modena (Florence, 1957), 87ff

JEROME ROCHE

Stefanis, Gaetano de (b Chieti; d after 1710). Italian composer. Information about him derives from his surviving works. He was a minorite and was maestro di cappella of the cathedral at Split, Dalmatia, in 1700 and of Forlì Cathedral in 1710. He published Messe a quattro voci op.1 (Venice, 1700) and Salmi pieni per tutto l'anno a otto voci con violini ad lib. brevi e facili, con litanie della B. V. op.3 (Bologna, 1710); there is no trace of his op.2. There are four masses in op.1. The 18 psalms in op.3 are for two four-part choruses, with two optional violin parts and continuo, and are rather conservative in style.

BIBLIOGRAPHY
D. Sparacio: 'Musicisti minori conventuali', Miscellanea francescana, xxv (1925), 105

BOJAN BUJIĆ

Stefano, Giuseppe di. See DI STEFANO, GIUSEPPE.

Stefano di Cino. Italian poet and merchant of the 14th century. Two madrigals, Non dispregiar virtù and Sommo felicità, with musical settings by Niccolò da Perugia and Francesco Landini respectively, are extant.

BIBLIOGRAPHY
N. Sapegno, ed.: Poeti minori del trecento (Milan and Naples, 1952)

W. THOMAS MARROCCO

Stefanov, Vassil (b Shumen, 6 May 1913). Bulgarian conductor and violinist. He studied the violin from childhood and, after graduating from the Sofia State Academy of Music in 1933, he was for many years leader of the Royal SO (the Sofia State Philharmonia from 1946). He was also a member of the Academic Quartet and began to appear as a conductor. After further study under Talich in Prague (1947–8), he became deputy conductor of the Sofia State Philharmonia from 1948, and soon afterwards was appointed chief conductor of the State Radio SO. He taught the violin at the Sofia Academy, 1951–3, took part in the forming of the Shumen SO in 1954, and from 1961 also conducted the Gusla male choir; he toured abroad with the choir and with the State Radio SO. He gave the first performances of many Bulgarian works, and made several records. His conducting is marked by a strong sense of rhythm and conscientious attention to the composer's requirements throughout a comprehensive repertory.

LADA BRASHOVANOVA

Stefanović, Dimitrije (b Pančevo, 25 Nov 1929). Yugoslav musicologist. He studied English literature at the University of Belgrade and musicology at the Academy of Music in Belgrade. Having developed an interest in the study of Byzantine notation, he went in 1958 to Lincoln College, Oxford, to study with Egon Wellesz and in 1960 obtained the BLitt. He then worked at the Musicological Institute of the Serbian Academy of Arts and Sciences in Belgrade until 1964, when he returned to Oxford and completed a DPhil thesis in 1967. Since then he has again been an associate of the Musicological Institute in Belgrade. In the year 1970–71 he was a research Fellow at Lincoln College. He was elected a corresponding member of the Serbian Academy of Arts and Sciences in 1976.

Although leading Byzantine scholars, especially Egon Wellesz, have long stressed the importance of the Serbian medieval liturgical chant, it had been studied by Yugoslav scholars only sporadically and often superficially. Stefanović was the first to study it in detail and throw light on its relationship to the main body of Byzantine chant. He has often performed Serbian chant with the Belgrade Madrigal Choir in Yugoslavia and abroad and made several gramophone recordings.

WRITINGS

'Einige Probleme zur Erforschung der slavischen Kirchenmusik', *KJb*, xliii (1959), 1

'Izgoreli neumski rukopis br. 93 Beogradske narodne biblioteke' [The burnt neumatic MS 93 of the National Library in Belgrade], *Bibliotekar*, xiii (1961), 379

'The Serbian Chant from the 15th to the 18th Centuries', *Musica antiqua Europae orientalis I: Bydgoszcz 1966*, 71

'The Influence of the Byzantine Chant on the Music of the Slavonic Countries', *XIIIth International Congress of Byzantine Studies: Oxford 1966*, 141

The Tradition of the Sticheraria Manuscripts (diss., U. of Oxford, 1967)

'Crkvena muzika od XV do XVIII veka' [Church music from the 15th century to the 18th], *Srpska pravoslavna crkva 1219–1969: spomenica o 750-godišnjici autokefalnosti* [The Serbian Orthodox Church from 1219 to 1969] (Belgrade, 1969), 209

'Muzika u srednjovekovnoj Srbiji' [Music in medieval Serbia], ibid, 117

'Some Aspects of the Form and Expression of Serbian Mediaeval Chant', *Musica antiqua Europae orientalis II: Bydgoszcz 1969*, 61

'Neumske zapise iz hilandarskih rukopisa XVIII veka u note preneo D. S.' [Neumatic notation from 18th-century Hilandar sources transcribed by D. S.], *O Srbljaku* (Belgrade, 1970), 479

'Pojanje stare srpske duhovne poezije' [Chanting of the old Serbian poetry], ibid, 129

'Stihire Srbima svetiteljima' [Stichera to Serbian saints], ibid, 459

'Crkvenoslovenski prevod priručnika vizantijske neumske notacije u rukopisu 311 manastira Hilandara' [A church Slavonic translation of a Byzantine manual of neumatic notation in MS 311 at Hilandar Monastery], *Hilandarski zbornik*, ii (1971), 113

'Les sources de la recherche sur la vieille musique sacrée serbe', *La musique serbe à travers les siècles*, ed. S. Đurić-Klajn (Belgrade, 1973), 142

'The Eastern Church', *Music from the Middle Ages to the Renaissance*, A History of Western Music, i, ed. F. W. Sternfeld (London, 1973), 83

'Services for Slavonic Saints in Early Russian Music Manuscripts', *Musica antiqua Europae orientalis IV: Bydgoszcz 1975*, 211

BOJAN BUJIĆ

Stefánsson, Fjölnir (*b* Reykjavík, 9 Oct 1930). Icelandic composer and teacher. He studied composition with Jón Thórarinsson at the Reykjavík College of Music, graduating in 1954, and with Seiber in England (1954–8). After a period of teaching at the Reykjavík College of Music (1958–68) he was appointed principal of the Kópavogur Music School. He was appointed to the board of the Iceland Music Information Centre (1968) and the Union for Copywriters (1974). In general his works are conservative – some are written in a Palestrinian style – and yet he has composed instrumental pieces in a quasi-serial manner.

WORKS
(selective list)

Vocal: 3 Songs (Icelandic Gradual), chorus, 1958; 3 Songs (S. Steinarr), S, pf, 1958, orchd 1967; Songs, children's chorus, 1960; 5 Songs, S, pf, 1963–5; 7 Folksongs, S, pf, 1974

Inst: Trio, fl, cl, bn, 1951; Sonata, vn, pf, 1954; 5 Sketches, pf (1969); Duo, ob, cl, 1974

BIBLIOGRAPHY
A. Burt: *Iceland's Twentieth-century Composers and a Listing of their Works* (Fairfax, Virginia, in preparation)
AMANDA M. BURT

Stefan the Serb (*fl ?c*1450). Serbian composer and DOMESTIKOS. He composed three chants for the Byzantine liturgy. The first is a setting, in the 2nd mode (plagal), of the CHEROUBIKON for the Liturgy of the Presanctified, 'Now the powers of heaven invisibly worship with us', with both Slavonic and Greek texts; the second is a setting, in the 1st mode, of the corresponding communion chant, 'O taste and see', also in both languages. The two appeared in *YU-Bn* 93, a mid-15th-century manuscript which was destroyed during World War II, and the Greek communion chant alone is to be found in the bilingual MS anthology *GR-Ae* 928. In the Belgrade version, the bilingual communion chant contains yet a third Greek text, 'Praise the Lord in the heavens', which is the normal Sunday communion hymn.

There are no surviving Serbian manuscripts from earlier than the middle of the 15th century, and thus it is impossible to be certain about the period in which Stefan lived; nevertheless, a Sunday communion chant by him in the 3rd plagal mode appears in 16th-century Moldavian manuscripts, and this is evidence that his work was popular even outside Serbia.

DIMITRI CONOMOS

Steffan, Josef Antonín. *See* ŠTĚPÁN, JOSEF ANTONÍN.

Steffani [Staffani, Steffano, Stefani, Stephani], **Agostino** (*b* Castelfranco, nr. Venice, 25 July 1654; *d* Frankfurt am Main, 12 Feb 1728). Italian composer, churchman and diplomat. He exerted a considerable influence on the rise of opera in northern Germany, where he spent most of his life, and his celebrated chamber duets for two voices and continuo represent an important stage in the development of Italian secular vocal music between Carissimi and Handel.

1. LIFE. The Steffani family can be traced back to mid-16th-century Venice, but Agostino's immediate ancestors originated in Padua and moved to Castelfranco in about 1570. He was the fifth of seven children. His only brother to survive infancy was the librettist Ventura Terzago (*b* 2 Jan 1648), who took his name from the maternal uncle who adopted him. Steffani probably attended a municipal school in Padua. There are signs that he learnt to sing as a boy; he sang on various occasions later in life including, apparently, at one of Cardinal Ottoboni's concerts in Rome in winter 1708–9.

In July 1667 Steffani was taken to Munich by the Elector Ferdinand Maria of Bavaria. He remained there for 21 years. For the first year he was placed in the care of Count von Tattenbach. An entry in the court accounts for 1668 suggests that he sang in *Le pretensioni del sole* (November 1667) by the Kapellmeister, J. K. Kerll. By a decree of July 1668 Kerll was given custody of the 'Camer: und Hof *Musico Augustino Steffani*' and instructed to give him organ lessons. After three years with him, Steffani spent a year (from October 1671) with the *valet de chambre* and treasury official Augustin Sayler. In October 1672 he went to Rome, where he studied composition with Ercole Bernabei, *maestro di cappella* at St Peter's. After little more than a year he published a collection of vesper psalms, *Psalmodia vespertina*. Other pieces composed between 1673 and 1674, but not published, survive in what is thought to be an autograph manuscript (in *GB-Cfm*). It is not known whether he composed any of his secular music in Rome, but it seems likely that he became acquainted there with cantatas by such composers as Carissimi, Cesti and Stradella. He returned to Munich in July 1674, with Bernabei, who had been appointed Kapellmeister after Kerll's departure the previous year.

Some time after his return Steffani was appointed court organist. The earliest reference to the 'Hof und Camer *Organisten Augustino Steffani'* is in a decree of 4 July 1678, but the appointment may have taken effect immediately, for on 1 March 1675 he was granted an increase in salary backdated to the previous July. No accounts of his organ playing survive, but impressions presumably of his harpsichord playing are found in the dispatches of the Bavarian resident at Turin, J. B. Schalck. Between 1678 and 1679 Steffani visited Paris and Turin. In Paris he played before the king and probably heard the first performance of Lully's opera *Bellérophon*. In Turin his '*habileté* unnd *addresse*' and 'zierliches unnd *delicates* spillen' were much admired.

While he was away, Ferdinand Maria died in Munich. With the accession of the young Elector Maximilian II Emanuel in 1680, Steffani's career developed rapidly. On 1 January 1681 he was appointed director of chamber music, a post created specially for him, and later that month his first opera, *Marco Aurelio*, received its first performance. The libretto was by his brother, Ventura Terzago, who had moved to Munich in 1677. The question of the elector's marriage provided Steffani with his first significant experience of secret diplomacy. He was asked to explore the possibility of a match with Princess Sophie Charlotte of Hanover. His negotiations (1682–4) brought him into contact with Ortensio Mauro, his future librettist, and with the courts of Düsseldorf and Vienna.

Steffani composed four more operas for Munich (1685–8; no new operas were performed there between 1682 and 1684). Two of the librettos were by Terzago

and the other two by a new court poet, Luigi Orlandi. *Servio Tullio* (Terzago, 1686) was written to celebrate the marriage of the elector to Maria Antonia, Archduchess of Austria. His other Munich works include a serenata 'alla maniera d'Italia' (1682; words and music lost) for the marriage of Countess M. A. T. von Preysing; a tourney, *Audacia e rispetto* (Terzago, 1685; music lost); a collection of motets, *Sacer Ianus quadrifons*; and chamber duets and cantatas.

In summer 1688 Steffani entered the service of Duke Ernst August of Hanover. His main reason for leaving Munich seems to have been that he had no immediate prospect of becoming Kapellmeister there; Ercole Bernabei was succeeded in January 1688 by his son, Giuseppe Antonio (vice-Kapellmeister since 1677), and by May Steffani had made arrangements to leave. He spent 15 years at Hanover (1688–1703). The first half of this period was devoted mainly to musical activities, the second mainly to diplomatic. His arrival coincided with the establishment of the first permanent Italian opera company there. Ernst August built a magnificent new theatre, imported leading Italian singers and appointed Steffani as Kapellmeister; the orchestra was led by J.-B. Farinel. The opera lasted eight years (1689–97; the duke died in 1698). Of the ten works performed in that period Steffani probably composed eight, all to librettos by Ortensio Mauro. *Briseide*, given in Carnival 1696, may well be by Pietro Torri, who was engaged as Kapellmeister for the occasion, and *La costanza nelle selve* (1697) is by Luigi Mancia.

In the 1690s Steffani became increasingly involved in diplomatic affairs. He was sent to Vienna in 1691 to help negotiate the elevation of Hanover to the ninth electorate. In 1693 he was appointed Hanoverian envoy extraordinary to the Bavarian court at Brussels (the Elector Maximilian was made Imperial Lieutenant of the Spanish Netherlands in 1691 and moved to Brussels the following year); his mission was to secure recognition of Hanover's electoral status. He spent most of 1695 in Brussels and lived there from 1696. He also played an active part in the manoeuvres preceding the War of the

1. *Autograph of the opening of Steffani's chamber duet 'E perchè non m'uccidete' (GB-Lbm R.M.23.k.14, f.43v)*

Spanish Succession. His main concern was to persuade the Elector Maximilian to support the emperor rather than Louis XIV; he failed, and returned to Hanover in July 1702, exhausted and dejected. He sought consolation in music: that autumn he began to revise and prepare a new complete manuscript collection of his chamber duets (now in *GB-Lbm*). He appears to have broken off work by spring 1703, however, and the copying was completed by two scribes.

In March 1703 Steffani entered the service of the Elector Palatine, Johann Wilhelm, at Düsseldorf. At the same time he virtually gave up music; from 1709, at the very latest, his works circulated under the name of one of his copyists, Gregorio Piva. Of the three operas performed at Düsseldorf and normally attributed to Steffani, only one, *Il Tassilone* (1709), is certainly a new composition. *Arminio* (1707) is a pasticcio assembled from some of his earlier operas; it is not certain that he had any hand in it. *Amor vien dal destino* (1709) appears to have been composed at Hanover; it may have been intended for performance in 1694, but no new opera was produced there that year, perhaps on account of the Königsmark affair. Apart from a few chamber duets, Steffani composed little else until his very last years.

Steffani's duties at Düsseldorf, where he remained for six years (1703–9), were mainly political. He was appointed initially as privy councillor and president of the Spiritual Council for the Palatinate and the duchies of Jülich and Berg. Late in 1703 he was made general president of the Palatine Government, and from 1703 to 1705 he was first *rector magnificus* and then a curator of Heidelberg University. At Düsseldorf he also reached the climax of his career as a churchman. This career had begun many years earlier at Munich: he was ordained a priest in 1680, and in 1683 he was appointed Abbot of Lepsingen, a sinecure in the Protestant earldom of Oettingen-Wallerstein, halfway between Augsburg and Nuremberg. By 1695 he was an apostolic prothonotary (the date of this appointment is not known; the information appears in the sub-title of his short dissertation on the nature and origins of music, *Quanta certezza*). In September 1706 he was elected Bishop of Spiga *in partibus infidelium* (Asia Minor). He was in Rome from November 1708 to April 1709 to mediate in the war between the pope and the emperor; the pope showed his gratitude for the success of his negotiations by making him a Domestic Prelate and Assistant to the Throne.

Steffani's most important ecclesiastical appointment, Apostolic Vicar in northern Germany, came in April 1709. Like earlier vicars, Steffani chose Hanover as his base. He returned there in November 1709 and apart from a short period in Italy remained there for the rest of his life. He continued to act as minister and Grand Almoner to the Elector Johann Wilhelm, however, a title he had held since 1706. The post of Apostolic Vicar was extremely taxing. Steffani was responsible for founding and maintaining missions and churches in Brunswick, the Palatinate and Prussia. He was constantly frustrated by lack of money. Apart from Lepsingen, he had three sources of income – a stipend from the Sacra Congregatio de Propaganda Fide in Rome, the abbacy of S Stefano in Carrara, near Padua, and a provostship in the Rhenish town of Seltz. The stipend was small, his agent in Padua was a swindler,

2. Agostino Steffani: lithograph (1816) by Heinrich E. von Winter

and most of the revenue from Seltz was seized by French Jesuits at Strasbourg. His difficulties were aggravated between 1714 and 1718 by the loss of several people who had given him material and psychological support: Duke Anton Ulrich of Brunswick-Wolfenbüttel (*d* 1714), the Elector Georg Ludwig of Hanover (moved to England 1714), the Elector Johann Wilhelm (*d* 1716), the philosopher Gottfried Leibniz, a friend since at least 1688 (*d* 1716), and Franz Arnold von Metternich, Prince-Bishop of Münster and Paderborn (*d* 1718). In summer 1722 he retired to Padua, but in summer 1725 he yielded to pressure from Rome and returned to Hanover that October.

Steffani's last years were brightened by his election on 1 June 1727 as president of the Academy of Vocal Music in London (later known as the Academy of Ancient Music). His contact in London was the Modenese resident Giuseppe Riva. In addition to sending the academy copies of his earlier works, he composed at least three new pieces for them – the madrigal *Gettano i rè dal soglio* (by 31 December 1726), the motet *Qui diligit Mariam* (by 7 July 1727) and the *Stabat mater* (after 16 September 1727) – and possibly two others, *Al rigor d'un bel sembiante* and *Se già t'amai crudele*. But his fortunes did not improve, and during winter 1727–8 his health deteriorated. On his way back to Italy he stopped in Frankfurt to sell some books and *objets d'art*. He died there of apoplexy on 12 February 1728 and was buried two days later in the church of St Bartholomäus. Two chests of papers concerning his diplomatic and ecclesiastical activities found their way into the archives of the Sacra Congregatio de Propaganda Fide (Fondo Spiga), but a third containing musical documents went to his next of kin and is lost. The papers he left in Hanover are now in the Niedersächsisches Staatsarchiv (Registratur des Bischofs von Spiga).

2. WORKS. The cornerstone of Steffani's output is his chamber duets. They cover most of his creative career, and their supple melody, elegant counterpoint and perfect formal balance epitomize his style, which may be compared (not unfavourably) with that of Stradella, Corelli, Alessandro Stradella and the young Handel. Steffani composed most of his duets by late 1702, when he began to revise them, but at least two are later. Four were written for Princess Sophie Charlotte, one to a text of her own (*Crudo Amor, morir mi sento*); other poets include Bartolomeo d'Ariberti, Anastasio Guidi, 'Abbate Paglia', Francesco Palmieri and, most important, Ortensio Mauro. The texts are concerned principally with unrequited love and seem typical of the Arcadian verse of the Italian solo cantata of the time.

The duets are for various pairs of voices, of which the commonest are SA, ST and SB, with continuo. They may have up to six movements, solos as well as duets. Over half of the works are in closed forms (e.g. da capo, rondo and strophic-rondo) typical of the mid-17th-century cantata; the remainder are in open forms (e.g. *AB*, *ABC*, *ABCD* etc) that seem closer to the Renaissance madrigal. Paradoxically, these are generally later in date – a growing preference for open forms is evident in the revisions. The most obvious type of revision affecting form is the omission of movements and sections, especially repeats and solos. The omissions allowed Steffani to expand the remaining duet movements, and this he did by exploring more thoroughly the contrapuntal potential of the material (often modifying it for the purpose). The forms of the revised versions are a direct result of his use of double counterpoint, stretto and other fugal procedures, of which he demonstrates an effortless mastery.

This mastery is evident also in his sacred music, a category that includes his earliest datable compositions. Although *Psalmodia vespertina* (1674) is scored for antiphonal choirs and is mainly homophonic in texture, the contemporary pieces in the Fitzwilliam manuscript are more varied: *Sperate in Deo* (SSATB and organ) includes duets for two sopranos and recitatives for tenor and bass and ends with a five-part fugue. The motets of 1685 are for various trios of voices (SSB, SAT, SAB, STB, ATB) with continuo but may also be performed as duets, any voice being omitted. Since they are predominantly imitative in texture, this represents a considerable tour de force.

The operas indicate that Steffani also assimilated features of the French style. Arias in dance rhythms such as the minuet and gavotte are common. Most of the Munich operas had ballets as entr'actes (by Melchior d'Ardespin and François Rodier), and the overtures to the Hanover operas are in the French style. The basic orchestral requirements are four- or five-part strings, two flutes, two oboes, bassoon and continuo, with the frequent addition of trumpets and drums. *Alarico il Baltha* requires two piffari and *Niobe* four viols; *Amor vien dal destino* includes an ensemble for four chalumeaux, two bassoons and two theorbos and an obbligato for lute. The arias are predominantly in da capo form. About half are accompanied by instruments, the remainder by continuo only; some scenes have strings (one has trumpets and drums) without continuo. Both types of aria exhibit Steffani's predilection for duet

textures: in continuo arias the bass often imitates the voice, and in orchestral arias obbligatos are often for pairs of instruments. His full-length Hanover operas also include an exceptionally high proportion of vocal duets, apart from sextets (*La superbia d'Alessandro*) and a quartet (*Le rivali concordi*). These six works provided an important stimulus for the development of opera in northern Germany. They were translated into German by Gottlieb Fiedler and staged in Hamburg between 1695 and 1699; performances elsewhere followed, and extracts appeared in print. It seems fitting that two of Steffani's operas (*Alarico* and *Henrico Leone*) should be based not on standard classical or mythological subjects but on episodes from German history.

Despite the influence of his operas, Steffani's reputation rests largely on his chamber duets. These were imitated by Handel (who owned a book of them in 1706), used as *solfeggi*, and praised by such figures as Kuhnau, Mattheson, Hawkins, Burney, Padre Martini and E. T. A. Hoffmann.

WORKS

Edition: *A. Steffani: Ausgewählte Werke*, ed. A. Einstein, A. Sandberger and H. Riemann, DTB, xi, Jg.vi/2 (1905/R); xxi, Jg.xi/2 (1911/R); xxiii, Jg.xii/2 (1912/R) [DTB]

DRAMATIC
(all 3-act operas unless otherwise stated)

Revivals (under original title, unless otherwise stated below) listed in Croll (1960): bibliography of MSS and prints, compiled H. Riemann, in DTB xxi.

Marco Aurelio (V. Terzago), Munich, 1681, *GB-Lbm*; sinfonia, 3 arias ed. in DTB xxiii

Serenata for the wedding of Countess von Preysing, Munich, 1682 music and text lost

Solone (Terzago), Munich, 1685, music lost

Audacia e rispetto (tourney, Terzago), Munich, 1685, music lost

Servio Tullio (Terzago), Munich, 1686, *A-Wn*; sinfonia, 6 arias with recits, 1 acc. recit ed. in DTB xxiii

Alarico il Baltha, cioè L'audace rè de' gothi (L. Orlandi), Munich, 1687, *Wn*; ed. in DTB xxi

Niobe, regina di Tebe (Orlandi), Munich, 1688, *Wn*; 1 aria ed. H. Riemann, *Musikgeschichte in Beispielen* (Leipzig, 1912), 221; sinfonia, 8 arias with recits, 1 acc. recit ed. in DTB xxiii

Henrico Leone (O. Mauro), Hanover, 1689, *GB-Lbm*; ov., dance music in Sonate da camera (Amsterdam, c1705); ov. ed. in NM, cxli (1938); 1 aria in HAM, ii, 122f; ov., 4 arias with recits ed. in DTB xxiii; Ger. version arr. G. C. Schürmann, Brunswick, 1716, ed. T. W. Werner, *Musikalische Denkwürdigkeiten*, i (Hanover, 1926)

La lotta d'Hercole con Acheloo (divertimento drammatico, 1, Mauro), Hanover, 1689, *Lbm*; ov., 1 aria with recit, 1 recit, 1 inst movt ed. in DTB xxiii

La superbia d'Alessandro (Mauro), Hanover, 1690, *Lbm*; revived as Il zelo di Leonato, Hanover, 1691; ov., dance music in Sonate da camera (Amsterdam, c1705); ov., 3 arias with recits ed. in DTB xxiii

Orlando generoso (Mauro), Hanover, 1691, *Lbm*; arias (Lübeck, 1699) and in Les air à joüer (Amsterdam, c1704–5); ov., dance music in Sonate da camera (Amsterdam, c1705); ov., 2 arias with recits, 1 duet ed. in DTB xxiii; ov. ed. A. Einstein, *Beispielsammlung zur Musikgeschichte* (Leipzig and Berlin, 4/1930), 66

Le rivali concordi (Mauro), Hanover, 1692, *Lbm*, facs. (New York, 1978); ov., dance music in Sonate da camera (Amsterdam, c1705); duet in Meslanges de musique latine, française et italienne (Paris, 1725); ov., 3 arias with recits ed. in DTB xxiii

La libertà contenta (Mauro), Hanover, 1693, *Lbm*; ov., dance music in Sonate da camera (Amsterdam, c1705); duet in Meslanges de musique latine, française et italienne (Paris, 1725); ov., 2 arias with recits, 1 duet ed. in DTB xxiii

Baccanali (favola pastorale, 1, Mauro), Hanover, 1695, *Lbm*

I trionfi del fato [Le glorie d'Enea] (Mauro), Hanover, 1695, *Lbm*; ov., dance music in Sonate da camera (Amsterdam, c1705); ov., 2 arias ed. in DTB xxiii

Arminio (pasticcio, 5, S. B. Pallavicino), Düsseldorf, 1707, score *Lbm*, score and parts *D-WD*

Amor vien dal destino (?Mauro), Düsseldorf, 1709, *Lbm*, ?composed for Hanover, 1694, as Il Turno; introduction, 5 arias with recits ed. in DTB xxiii

Il Tassilone (5, Pallavicino), Düsseldorf, 1709, score *E-Mn*, parts *GB-Lbm*; ed. in Denkmäler rheinischer Musik, viii (1958); 5 arias ed. in DTB xxiii

SACRED VOCAL

Psalmodia vespertina, 8vv, org (Rome, 1674): 13 vesper psalms, 1 Magnificat

Sacer Ianus quadrifons, 3vv, bc (Munich, 1685): 12 motets; 2 ed. in DTB xi

Sperate in Deo, 5vv, org, 1674; Triduanas a Domino, 8vv, 20 Nov 1673; Beatus vir, 3vv, 2 vn, bc; Laudate Dominum, 8 S, 30 Dec 1673; Laudate pueri, 9vv, Nov 1673: *GB-Cfm*

Beatus vir, 8vv, bc, 16 Sept 1676, *I-Ac*

Motetto per ogni tempo, 4vv, orch, *Fc*

Qui diligit Mariam [Filium/Dominum/Christum], 5vv, bc, by 7 July 1727, principal sources *GB-Lbm, Lcm, Ob*

Stabat mater, 6vv, str, bc, after 16 Sept 1727, principal source *Lbm*; ed. C. K. Scott (London, 1938) and H. Sievers (Wolfenbüttel, 1956)

CHAMBER DUETS

(all for 2vv, bc; principal sources D-Mbs, GB-Lbm, I-Fc)

* – also exists in rev. version of 1702–3 (only rev. version pubd); thematic index in DTB xi; catalogue and transcr. in Timms (1976)

*Ah! che l'hò sempre detto; *Aure, voi che volate; *Begl'occhi, oh Dio, non più; *Cangia pensier, mio cor; Che sarà di quel pensiero; Che volete, o crude pene (F. Palmieri), by 1699, ed. in DTB xi; [Crede ogn'un, cited in *MGG* as lost duet = 2nd verse of S solo in Oh che voi direste bene]; Cruda Lilla, che ti fece questo cor; Crudo Amor, morir mi sento (Sophie Charlotte of Brandenburg), by 1698; Dimmi, Cupido, e quando mai; Dir che giovi al dio d'amore, ?*c*1688; Dolce è per voi soffrire, by 1711, ed. in DTB xi; Dolce labbro, amabil bocca, 1712–13, ed. in DTB xi

E così mi compatite; *E perchè non m'uccidete; E. spento l'ardore; Forma un mare il pianto mio, in *HawkinsH*, iv, 291; *Fredde ceneri gradite, rev. as Saldi marmi che coprite; Fulminate, saettate; *Gelosia, che vuoi da me, nel mio sen; Gelosia, che vuoi da me? Folte schiere (B. d'Ariberti), ed. in DTB xi; Già tu parti, io che farò, ed. in DTB xi; Hò scherzato in verità; Il mio seno è un mar di pene; In amor chi vuol godere; Inquieto mio cor (?Carlo Conti), by 1699, ed. in DTB xi; Io mi parto, o cara ('Abbate Paglia'), by 1700; Io mi rido de' tuoi dardi; Io voglio provar

La fortuna su la ruota; Labri belli, dite un pò; Libertà l'infelice umanità, in Duetti del Sig.r Agost.o Stefani (London, 1787), ed. in La Fage; Libertà! non posso soffrir; Lilla mia, non vuoi ch'io pianga; Luci belle, non tanta fretta, ed. in Reissmann; Lungi dall'idol mio, 1702–3 rev. of doubtful work, ed. in DTB xi; M'hai da piangere, 1702–3 rev. of doubtful work, ed. in DTB xi; Mi voglio far intendere; Mia speranza illanguidita; M'ingannasti, fanciullo bendato, as 'Prithee leave me' in Songs in the New Opera call'd Thomyris (London, [1707]), Songs in the New Opera of Thomiris (London, [1707]), Apollonian Harmony (London, [*c*1790]), Social Harmony (London, [1817])

Navicella che t'en vai; Nel tempo ch'amai, in C. Ballard, Recueil d'airs serieux et a boire (Paris, 1707) and Recueil des meilleurs airs italiens (Paris, 1708); No, no, no, mai nol dirò, ed. J. A. Fuller Maitland, *Duetti da camera*, ii (London, 1904); No, no, no, non voglio se devo amare, ?*c*1680, ed. Fuller Maitland, *Duetti da camera*, i (London, 1904); Non sò chi mi piagò ('Abbate Averara'); Non te lo dissi, o core, in Ballard, Recueil d'airs serieux et a boire (Paris, 1707) and Recueil des meilleurs airs italiens (Paris, 1708); Non ve ne state a ridere; *Occhi belli, non più; *Occhi, perchè piangete, in A. Bailleux, Nouveaux solfeges d'Italie (Paris, *c*1784), ed. in *Auswahl vorzüglicher Musik-Werke*, ii/1 (Berlin, 1842), DTB xi, GMB and R. Jakoby, *Die Kantate*, Mw, xxxii (1968), 47; Oh che voi direste bene, by 1688

Parlo e rido; Più non amo e non vaneggio; Placidissime catene, by 1699, in Bailleux, Nouveaux solfeges d'Italie (Paris, *c*1784), and Duetti del Sig.r Agost.o Stefani (London, 1787), ed. in A. E. Choron, *Principes de composition des écoles d'Italie*, iii (Paris, 1808), and Pietro l'alma incenerita; *Pria ch'io faccia, ed. in DTB xi; Quando mai verrà quel dì (Anastasio Guidi); Quando ti stringo, o cara, ?1712–13; *Quanto care al cor; Quest'è l'ultima per me; Questo fior che involo al prato (Guidi); Ravvediti, mio core; *Ribellatevi, o pensieri; *Rio destin, ed. in DTB xi

Saldi marmi che coprite, rev. version of Fredde ceneri gradite, last movt in Bailleux, Nouveaux solfeges d'Italie (Paris, *c*1784), ed. in DTB xi; Sia maledetto Amor; Siete il più bizzarro umore; Sol negl'occhi del mio bene; Su, ferisci, alato arciero, ed. Fuller Maitland, *Duetti da camera*, i (London, 1904); *Tengo per infallibile, ed. in DTB xi; Tien m'il cor la gelosia; *Torna a dar vita al core, rev. ?1702–3; *Troppo cruda è la mia sorte, ed. in DTB xi, and ed. Riemann, *Musikgeschichte in Beispielen* (Leipzig, 1912); Tu m'aspettasti al mare; Turbini tempestosi spinsero Enea; Vestite bruno, lost [?identical with Occhi belli, non più]; Vo dicendo al mio pensiero; Voi ve ne pentirete; *Vorrei dire un non sò che

Chamber duets with lost, unspecified inst parts: Corri all'armi; D'un faggio all'ombra assiso; Fuggi da questo seno; Senti, Filli spietata; S'intimi guerra a la beltà; Stille degl'occhi amare

OTHER SECULAR VOCAL

6 scherzi, 1v, insts, bc, *I-MOe*; 2 ed. in DTB xi

*c*80 arias and cantatas attrib. Steffani, most for S, insts, bc; principal sources *A-Wn*, *D-Mbs*, *GB-Lbm*, *Lgc*; perhaps not all authentic; 1 recit and 5 arias ed. in SCMA, xi (1951); Occhi miei, lo miraste, cantata, ed. A. Einstein, *ZMw*, i (1918–19), 457

3 madrigals, principal sources *GB-Cfm*, *DRc*, *Lam*, *Lbm*; Al rigor d'un bel sembiante, 3vv, bc; Se gia t'amai crudele, 4vv, bc; Gettano i rè dal soglio, 5vv, bc, ed. C. Timms, *MT*, cxix (1978), Feb suppl.

INSTRUMENTAL

Les ouvertures, chacconnes et les autres airs à joüer (Amsterdam, *c*1705), lost; probably identical with Sonate da camera

Sonate da camera, 2 vn, va, bc (Amsterdam, *c*1705)

THEORETICAL

Quanta certezza habbia da suoi principii la musica (Amsterdam, 1695) [Ger. trans., 1699–1700, as *Musikalisches Send-Schreiben*, rev., enlarged 2/1760 as *Sendschreiben*]

DOUBTFUL WORKS

Briseide (opera, 3, F. Palmieri), Hanover, carn. 1696, ?by P. Torri, *D-Mbs*; 3 arias ed. in SCMA, xi (1951); ov., 5 arias with recits, 1 acc. recit ed. in DTB xxiii

Confitebor tibi Domine, 3vv, bc, *GB-Lbm*; Dixit Dominus, Estote fortes in bello, both cited in *EitnerQ*; 6 motets, *GB-DRc* E.22, *Ob* Mus.d.100

Chamber duets: Dite la verità, principal sources *B-Bc*, *GB-Cfm*, *Lbm*, *Ob*; Lontananza crudel, tu mi tormenti, *D-BNms*, *I-Bc*, *Nc*, *Pca*, in Bailleux, Nouveaux solfeges d'Italie (Paris, *c*1784), ed. in DTB xi; Lungi dall'idol mio, later rev. Steffani, *B-Bc* F.15371, *GB-Lbm* RM 23.f.10, *I-Bc* DD.43; M'hai da piangere, later rev. Steffani, *GB-Lam*, *I-Bc* DD.43; Non voglio, non voglio, no, no, *F-Pn*; Porto ne' lumi un mare, *GB-Lbm*, *I-Fc*; Son tutto contento, *D-BNms*; Trionfate, o mie pupille, *D-BNms*

Sonata, vn, bc, *WD*

SPURIOUS WORKS

Chamber duets: Bel tempo addio, *D-BNms*, ascribed G. A. B[ernabei]; Cangia pensier, mio cor, *D-Dlb* 2110/L/2, *GB-Lbm* Add.31492, attrib. B. Marcello; Lilla mia non vuoi ch'io pianga, Pria ch'io faccia, both *D-Dlb* 2110/L/2; Duetti da camera (Munich, 1683) cited in *FétisB*; at least 24 others, see Timms (1976)

Trio sonatas: Sonate da camera (Munich, 1679), cited in *FétisB*; trio sonatas ed. in NM, v (1927) and xii (1928) are by A. Caldara: see E. Schenk, *ZMw*, xii (1929–30), 247

BIBLIOGRAPHY

SOURCE MATERIAL

BurneyH; *HawkinsH*; *WaltherML*

J. Mattheson: *Der vollkommene Capellmeister* (Hamburg, 1739/*R*1954)

[J. Hawkins]: *Memoirs of the Life of Agostino Steffani* (London, *c*1749–52); repr. in *The Gentleman's Magazine*, xxxi (1761), 489

G. Riccati: 'Notizie di Monsig. Agostino Steffani', *Nuova raccolta d'opuscoli scientifici e filologici*, xxxiii (Venice, 1779)

F. W. Woker: *Aus den Papieren des kurpfälzischen Ministers Agostino Steffani, Bischofs von Spiga, spätern apostolischen Vicars von Norddeutschland . . . 1703–1709: erste Vereinsschrift der Görresgesellschaft* (Cologne, 1885)

——: *Agostino Steffani, Bischof von Spiga i.p.i., apostolischer Vikar von Norddeutschland 1709–28: dritte Vereinsschrift der Görresgesellschaft* (Cologne, 1886)

E. Bodemann, ed.: *Der Briefwechsel des Gottfried Wilhelm Leibniz in der königlichen öffentlichen Bibliothek zu Hannover* (Hanover, 1889)

J. J. Maier: 'Archivalische Excerpte über die herzoglich bayerische Hofkapelle', *KJb*, vi (1891), 69

A. Einstein: 'Kritischer Kommentar, A: Quellen in alphabetischer Reihenfolge der Fundorte; B: Thematisches Verzeichnis der Kammerduette und Scherzi des Agostino Steffani', DTB, xi, Jg.vi/2 (1905/*R*)

A. Ebert: 'Briefe Agostino Steffanis an die Königin Sophie Charlotte von Preussen', *Die Musik*, vi (1906–7), 158

A. Einstein: 'Die Briefe der Königin Sophie Charlotte und der Kurfürstin Sophie an Agostino Steffani', *ZIMG*, viii (1906–7), 85

——: 'Notiz über den Nachlass Agostino Steffani's im Propaganda-Archiv zu Rom', *ZIMG*, ix (1908–9), 172

P. Hiltebrandt: *Preussen und die römische Kurie . . . nach den römischen Akten bearbeitet* (Berlin, 1910)

H. Riemann: 'Bibliographie der in Handschriften und Drucken nachweisbaren 18 Bühnenwerke von Agostino Steffani', DTB, xxi, Jg.xi/2 (1911/*R*)

T. W. Werner and A. Einstein: 'Die Musikhandschriften des Kestnerschen Nachlasses im Stadtarchiv zu Hannover', *ZMw*, i (1918–19), 441

A. Einstein: 'Ein unbekanntes Duett von Agostino Steffani?', *ZMw*, xv (1932–3), 170

J. Schelder: 'Aus Düsseldorfs italienischer Zeit: römische Quellen zu Agostino Steffanis Leben', *Beiträge zur rheinischen Musikgeschichte*, i (1952), 17–53

A. della Corte: 'Qualche lettera e qualche melodramma di Agostino

Steffani', *RaM*, xxxii (1962), 25
P. Keppler: 'Agostino Steffani's Hannover Operas and a Rediscovered Catalogue', *Studies in Music History: Essays for Oliver Strunk* (Princeton, 1968), 341

LIFE AND WORKS

A. de La Fage: *Essais de diphthérographie musicale* (Paris, 1864)
A. Reissmann: *Allgemeine Geschichte der Musik*, iii (Leipzig, 1864)
W. G. Cusins: 'Steffani, Agostino', *Grove 1*
F. W. Woker: 'Der Tondichter Agostino Steffani', *Der Katholik*, lxvii (1887), 312, 421
——: *Geschichte der katholischen Kirche und Gemeinde in Hannover und Celle* (Paderborn, 1889)
L. Pastor: *The History of the Popes from the Close of the Middle Ages*, trans. Antrobus and others (London, 1891–1953), vol.xxxiii
F. W. Woker: 'Der apostolische Vikar des deutschen Nordens Agostino Steffani, Bischof von Spiga, und die Abtei Selz', *Der katholische Seelsorger*, xi (1899), 425, 468, 514
A. Neisser: *Servio Tullio: eine Oper aus dem Jahre 1685 von Agostino Steffani* (Leipzig, 1902)
A. Ebert: *Attilio Ariosti in Berlin (1697–1703)* (Leipzig, 1905)
H. Botstiber: 'Ein Beitrag zu. J. K. Kerll's Biographie', *SIMG*, vii (1905–6), 634
A. Untersteiner: 'Agostino Steffani', *RMI*, xiv (1907), 509
A. Einstein: 'Agostino Steffani, i: Münchener Zeit. 1654–1688', *KJb*, xxiii (1910), 1–36
H. Riemann: 'Basso ostinato und Basso quasi ostinato', *Festschrift ... Rochus Freiherrn von Liliencron* (Leipzig, 1910), 193
——: 'Wann machte Händel die Bekanntnis Steffanis?', *Der Merker*, ii (1911), 1001
——: 'Agostino Steffani als Opernkomponist', DTB xxiii, Jg.xii/2 (1912/R)
J. Metzler: *Die apostolischen Vikariate des Nordens* (Paderborn, 1919)
T. W. Werner: 'Agostino Steffanis Operntheater in Hannover', *AMf*, iii (1938), 65
A. Yorke-Long: *Music at Court: Four Eighteenth-century Studies* (London, 1954)
A. Einstein: *Essays on Music* (London, 1956, rev. 2/1958)
W. H. Baxter jr: *Agostino Steffani: a Study of the Man and his Work* (diss., Eastman School of Music, Rochester, 1957)
G. Croll: Preface to *A. Steffani: Tassilone*, Denkmäler rheinischer Musik, viii (1958) [review by P. H. Lang, *MQ*, xlv (1959), 412]
——: *Agostino Steffani (1654–1728): Studien zur Biographie, Bibliographie der Opern und Turnierspiele* (diss., U. of Münster, 1960)
——: 'Zur Chronologie der "Düsseldorfer" Opern Agostino Steffanis', *Festschrift K. G. Fellerer zum 60. Geburtstag* (Regensburg, 1962), 82
C. Timms: 'Revisions in Steffani's Chamber Duets', *PRMA*, xcvi (1969–70), 119
——: 'Handel and Steffani: a New Handel Signature', *MT*, cxiv (1973), 374
——: *The Chamber Duets of Agostino Steffani (1654–1728): with Transcriptions and Catalogue* (diss., U. of London, 1976)
——: 'Steffani and the Academy of Ancient Music', *MT*, cxix (1978), 127
——: 'Gregorio Piva and Steffani's Principal Copyist', *Source Materials and the Interpretation of Music: a Memorial Volume to Thurston Dart* (in preparation)

COLIN TIMMS

Steffani, Josef Antonín. See ŠTĚPÁN, JOSEF ANTONÍN.

Steffen, Wolfgang (*b* Neuhaldensleben, 28 April 1923). German composer. He studied composition with Tiessen and conducting with Ahlendorf at the Municipal Conservatory and the Staatliche Hochschule für Musik in Berlin. At the same time he attended seminars in musicology and drama at the Free University of Berlin. From 1947 to 1959 he worked as a choirmaster and conductor, and in 1974 he was appointed to teach music theory at the Staatliche Hochschule für Musik, Berlin. He is also active in that city as chairman of the German Composers' League, head of the Studio for New Music and panel member of the Council of Culture.

WORKS
(selective list)

Stage: Aus dem Lebensbuch eines Tänzers, op.13a, 1955, also orch suite
Orch: Serenade im alten Stil, op.4, fl, str, 1948; Sinfonietta, op.5, str, 1949; Intrada seria, op.10, 1953; Pf Conc., op.16,1956; Vn Conc., op.32, 1966; Polychromie, op.38, pf, 10 insts, 1970, arr. pf, orch,

1971; Klangsegmente, op.41, cimb, hpd, harp, orch, 1973; Sinfonia da camera, op.46, 1976
Choral: Nachtwachen, op.15, 1955; Hermann Hesse Zyklus, op.19, 1956; Altspanischer Zyklus, 1958; Vertrauen auf Gott, op.28a, 1964; Griechische Kantate, chorus, 9 insts, 1967; Fünf Länder Kantate, male vv, fl, cl, tpt, trbn, perc, 1973; Erfahrungen, op.40 (I. Drewitz), 6 speakers, chorus, vn, pf, perc, org on tape, 1973; Botschaft, op.45 (Drewitz), 2 speakers, chorus, children's vv, org, orch, 1976
Numerous chamber works and *c*35 songs

ALFRED GRANT GOODMAN

Steffens [Stephani], Johann [Johannes] (*b* Itzehoe, Holstein, *c*1560; *d* Lüneburg, *c* summer 1616). German composer and organist. His father, a member of Itzehoe town council, early encouraged his musical gifts and (according to a letter of recommendation dated 1589) had him trained by, among others, an organ builder, who may have been Hans Scherer (i). In 1592 he was engaged as assistant to Jost Funcke, the aged organist of the Johanniskirche, Lüneburg. When Funcke died in 1593, Steffens was appointed to succeed him, at first provisionally, and then officially from Easter 1595, after which he held the post for 20 years. His reputation seems to have grown quickly beyond Lüneburg: in 1596 he took part in the famous organ trial at Gröningen, near Halberstadt, where as one of 53 organ experts he played and assessed the new instrument. At Lüneburg he gave organ lessons and temporarily looked after the organ at St Spiritus. His close collaboration with the town musician Johann Sommer led to his contributing instrumental pieces to *RISM* 1609[30]. The collection of his madrigals and dance-songs that his son Heinrich published posthumously in 1619 shows the unmistakable influence of Hans Leo Hassler.

WORKS

Newe teutsche Gesäng nach Art der Madrigalien, 4–8vv (Nuremberg, 1599); lost, cited in G. Draudius: *Bibliotheca ... classica* (Frankfurt am Main, 1611), ed. K. Ameln, in *Verzeichnisse deutscher musikalischer Bücher 1611 und 1625* (Bonn, 1957); 1 repr. in 1609[28]
Newe teutsche weltliche Madrigalia und Balletten, 5vv (Hamburg, 1619); ed. in EDM, 1st ser., xxix (1958)
10 works, a 5, 1609[30]; ed. in Engelke
4 motets, 8vv, 1593, *D-Hs*; 1 ed. in Engelke
4 Christmas motets, 9vv, 1604–6, inc., *Lr*
4 works, org: 2 in Celler Orgeltabulatur (1601), extracts ed. in Ritter, ii, no.73; G. Frotscher, *Geschichte des Orgel-Spiels und der Orgel-Komposition* (Berlin, 1935–6, enlarged 3/1966), Beispielband, 22f; Apel, 339f; 1 in Zellerfelder Orgeltabulatur, 1 in *Mbs*

BIBLIOGRAPHY

EitnerQ; GerberNL
A. Werckmeister: *Organum gruningense redivivum* (Quedlinburg, 1705, repr. 1932)
A. G. Ritter: *Zur Geschichte des Orgelspiels* (Leipzig, 1884), i, 108f
B. Engelke: *Musik und Musiker am Gottorfer Hofe*, i (Breslau, 1930), 14ff, 139ff
F. Welter: *Katalog der Musikalien der Ratsbücherei Lüneburg* (Lippstadt, 1950), 305
G. Fock: Introduction to EDM, 1st ser., xxix (1958)
W. Apel: *Geschichte der Orgel- und Klaviermusik bis 1700* (Kassel, 1967), 339ff; (Eng. trans., rev. 1972), 347
H. Walter: *Musikgeschichte der Stadt Lüneburg vom Ende des 16. bis zum Anfang des 18. Jahrhunderts* (Tutzing, 1967), 48ff

HORST WALTER

Steffens, Walter (*b* Aachen, 31 Oct 1934). German composer. He studied musicology at Hamburg University (1958–64) and until 1967 attended the Musikhochschule there, where his teachers were Klussmann and Jarnach (composition), Maler (theory) and Henry (piano). In 1962 he was appointed lecturer in theory and composition at the Hamburg Conservatory, and from 1969 he took a composition class at the Nordwestdeutsche Musikakademie in Detmold, becoming professor there in 1971. By his own account he was at first stimulated by literary works, but after 1970 was increasingly influenced by constructivist painting and kinetic sculpture. The two operas are distinctly eclectic.

WORKS
(selective list)

Stage: Botschaften an den Prinzen Jussuf [on theme of Schubert] (ballet, after F. Marc), str, perc; Eli (opera, 3, after N. Sachs), Dortmund, 1967; Pintura del mundo (ballet, after Bosch), 1969; Unter dem Milchwald (opera, 3, after Thomas), Hamburg, 1973

Orch: Pintura del mundo, conc. for orch (from ballet), 1969; Triade, fl, str orch, 1971; Tarec: Versuch eines Abschieds, orch, 1972

Vocal: Epitaph auf Rimbaud, A, chamber orch, 1964; Neue Gleichnisse (T. Rózewicz), S, fl, cl, va, 1966; Johannes-Passion, solo vv, chorus, org, orch, 1972–3

Chamber and inst: Hommage à Béla Bartók, cl, pf, 1964; Str Qt no.1 'Ekstase', 1964; Str Qt no.2 'Quartetto lirico', 1965; Pluie de feu (Feuerregen), pf, 1970; Lumière rouge en cage, fl, bn, hpd, 1973; Sfumato, 2 ens, 1973–4; Luna, variable ens, 1974

Principal publisher: Breitkopf & Härtel

HANSPETER KRELLMANN

Steffkin [Steffkins, Stefkins, Steiffkin, Stephkins], **Theodore** [Stoeffken, Ditrich] (*b* early 17th century; *d* Cologne, ?Dec 1673). German viol player and composer. He was already resident in England by February 1634, when he played in *The Triumph of Peace*; in the receipts for payment for the masque he signed himself 'Ditrich Stoeffken', though he was generally known as 'Mr Steffkin' or 'Steffkins'. In January 1636 he was admitted as a 'musician for the consort in ordinary' to Charles I. During the Commonwealth he was in Hamburg, where in February 1653 Robert Bargrave, and in June 1654 Cromwell's ambassador Bulstrode Whitelocke heard him play. At the Restoration he resumed his place in 'his Majesty's private musick' and in 1661, 1663 and 1671 was entrusted with the purchase of viols 'for his Majesty's service'; he is also listed among those 'Musitians that doe service in the Chappell Royall'. Pepys heard him on 17 July 1663 and found him a 'temperate sober man'. His death abroad ('apud Coloniam Agrippinae') is recorded in a probate administration of February 1674.

Steffkin was one of the most admired viol players of his day, and his compositions reflect the brilliance of solo playing at its zenith. During his earlier sojourn in England his skill possibly inspired some of William Lawes's demanding parts for lyra or division viol. In later years, North related, 'a particular friendship' was cultivated between him and Jenkins, who had played with him in 1634 and who when nearly 80 sent him in London 'kind tokens, which were peices of fresh musick'.

His sons Frederick William and Christian also became 'eminent violists' and were active until early in the 18th century.

WORKS
2 sets of divisions on a ground, b viol, bc, *GB-DRc, Ob*
Airs for b viol, *US-NYp*
Airs for vn, allemande for 2 b viols, *GB-Ob*
Pieces for lyra viol, *EIRE-Dm*

BIBLIOGRAPHY
T. Salmon: *A Proposal to Perform Musick, in Perfect & Mathematical Proportions* (London, 1688)
——: 'The Theory of Musick Reduced to Arithmetical and Geometrical Proportions', *Philosophical Transactions of the Royal Society*, xxiv (1705), 2094
B. Whitelocke: *A Journal of the Swedish Ambassy in the years 1653 and 1654* (London, 1772)
H. C. de Lafontaine: *The King's Musick* (London, 1909/R1973)
J. A. Westrup: 'Foreign Musicians in Stuart England', *MQ*, xxvii (1941), 70
J. Wilson, ed.: *Roger North on Music* (London, 1959)
J. M. Richards: *A Study of Music for Bass Viol written in England in the 17th Century* (diss., U. of Oxford, 1961)
M. Tilmouth: 'A Calendar of References to Music in Newspapers published in London and the Provinces (1660–1719)', *RMARC*, i (1961/R)
M. Lefkowitz: 'The Longleat Papers of Bulstrode Whitelocke', *JAMS*, xviii (1965), 42
F. B. Zimmerman: *Henry Purcell (1659–1695): his Life and Times* (London, 1967)
M. Tilmouth: 'Music on the Travels of an English Merchant: Robert Bargrave (1628–61)', *ML*, liii (1972), 143

CHRISTOPHER D. S. FIELD

Steg (Ger.). BRIDGE.

Steger, Werner (*b* Emmendingen, 24 Jan 1932). German musicologist and composer. He studied musicology at Heidelberg University under T. G. Georgiades (1952–8), and composition with W. Fortner at the Heidelberg Institute of Church Music, with Hans Vogt at the Hochschule für Musik und Theater at Mannheim, and privately with Karl Marx (1959–60). He took the doctorate at Heidelberg in 1962 with a dissertation on G. H. Stölzel's treatise on recitative. From 1961 to 1964 he was an assistant lecturer in the musicology department at Heidelberg, and from 1964 to 1972 he was a lecturer in musicology at the Karlsruhe Hochschule für Musik. From 1957 he was also a music critic.

WRITINGS
G. H. Stölzels 'Abhandlung vom Recitativ' (diss., U. of Heidelberg, 1962)
'Musik und Musikschaffen – gestern und heute', *Das grosse Nordbaden-Buch*, ed. O. Bischoff and others (Neustadt an der Weinstrasse, 1967), 103
'Rhythmische Kernformeln in Mozarts letzten Sinfonien', *Mf*, xxiii (1970), 41

WORKS
(selective list)

Str Trio, 1954; Sextet, fl, ob, cl, va, vc, db, 1956; Präludium und Fuge, str orch, 1956; Suite, orch, 1958; Suite nach alten Volksliedern, str orch, 1960; 2 serenades, str orch, 1961, 1965; Str Qt, 1970–71; Musik für Orgel, 1976

Songs, choral works, pf and org pieces

Principal publisher: Mannheimer Musik-Verlag

HANS HEINRICH EGGEBRECHT

Stegereif (Ger.). A TRIANGLE resembling a medieval stirrup.

Steglich, Rudolf (*b* Rats-Damnitz, Pomerania, 18 Feb 1886; *d* Scheinfeld, nr. Nuremberg, 8 July 1976). German musicologist. He studied in Dresden under Liszt's pupil Bertrand Roth (1900–06), to whom he later felt greatly indebted. After studying musicology for one term at Munich University under Sandberger and for one term at Berlin University under Wolf (to whom he owed the subject of his dissertation), Steglich found his true teacher in Hugo Riemann at Leipzig University. He obtained his doctorate in Leipzig in 1911 with a study of the *Quaestiones in musica* and its possible author, Rudolf of St Trond (1070–1138). Between 1919 and 1929 he was music correspondent for the *Hannoverscher Anzeiger* and from 1925 he taught at the Hanover Conservatory. In 1930 he completed his *Habilitation* in musicology at Erlangen University with a dissertation on musical rhythm. He then taught there as head of the musicology department; he was appointed *ausserplanmässiger Professor* in 1934 and retired in 1956. From 1935 to 1944 he was also a lecturer at the Nuremberg Conservatory and at the Nuremberg Wirtschaftshochschule. He was editor of the *Händel-Jahrbuch* (1928–33), *Archiv für Musikforschung* (1936–40) and, with M. Schneider, of the Hallische

Händel-Ausgabe (from 1955). Steglich specialized in the music of the 18th and 19th centuries, laying particular emphasis on Bach and his sons, Handel, Mozart, Beethoven and Schumann. His remarkable research into musical rhythm and its standardization, and the bearing this has on the natural ebb and flow of the pulse, tempo and dynamics, and into the acoustic properties of historical instruments, went hand in hand with his passionate insistence that music should be properly performed and properly listened to – any mere paper analysis was anathema to him. His view of the importance of scientific study in helping people to understand music was a comprehensive one, and his numerous articles, discussions of operatic productions and book reviews for periodicals (particularly in the *Zeitschrift für Musik* from 1922 and in *Musica* from 1948) exerted a considerable influence on musical scholarship.

WRITINGS

Die Quaestiones in Musica und ihr mutmasslicher Verfasser Rudolf von St. Trond (1070–1138) (diss., U. of Leipzig, 1911; Leipzig, 1911/R1970)
'K.Ph.Em. Bach und der Dresdner Kreuzkantor G.A.Homilius im Musikleben ihrer Zeit', *BJb*, xii (1915), 39–145
'H. Riemann als Wiedererwecker älterer Musik', *ZMw*, i (1918–19), 603
'Das c-moll-Präludium aus dem ersten Teil des Wohltemperierten Klaviers J. S. Bachs: ein Beitrag zu einer musikalischen Disziplin des Formhörens', *BJb*, xx (1923), 1
'Händels Opern', *Handbuch der Musikgeschichte*, ed. G. Adler (Frankfurt am Main, 1924, 2/1929), 663
Die elementare Dynamik des musikalischen Rhythmus (Habilitationsschrift, U. of Erlangen, 1930; Leipzig, 1930)
J. S. Bach (Potsdam, 1935)
Mozarts Flügel klingt wieder (Nuremberg and Salzburg, 1937)
'Über die Wesensgemeinschaft von Musik und Bildkunst', *Musik und Bild: Festschrift Max Seiffert* (Kassel, 1938), 23
Robert Schumanns Kinderszenen (Kassel, 1949)
Wege zu Bach (Regensburg, 1949)
'Das melodische Hauptmotiv in Beethovens "Fidelio"', *AMw*, ix (1952), 51
'Ein Lehrstück spätmittelalterlichen Liedvortrags', *AMw*, x (1953), 280
Über die "kantable Art" der Musik J. S. Bachs (Zurich, 1958)
'Zwei Titelzeichnungen zu Robert Schumanns Jugendalbum als Interpretationsdokumente', *DJbM*, iv (1959), 38
Georg Friedrich Händel (Wilhelmshaven, 1960)
Tanzrhythmus in der Musik J. S. Bachs (Wolfenbüttel and Zurich, 1962)
'Über einige Merkwürdigkeiten in J. S. Bachs Werken', *DJbM*, ix (1964), 28
Articles in *HJb* (from 1930) and *Neues Mozart-Jb* (from 1941); in congress reports from Leipzig, 1925, Vienna, 1927, and Salzburg, 1931; *IMSCR*, iv *Basle 1949*, *GfMKB*, *Lüneburg 1950* and *IMSCR*, vii *Cologne 1958*; and in Festschriften for Max Schneider (1955), Fischer (1956), Schmidt-Görg (1957), Orel (1960), Besseler (1961), Schenk (1962), Deutsch (1963) and Engel (1964)

EDITIONS

C. P. E. Bach: Die preussischen Sonaten (1714–88) für Klavier, NM, vi, xv (1927–8)
C. P. E. Bach: Die württembergischen Sonaten (1714–88) für Klavier, NM, xxi, xxii (1928)
Alte deutsche Weihnachtsmusik für Klavier oder Orgel, NM, xcv (1932, 2/1952)
J. M. Pfeiffer: Konzert für Cembalo und 2 Violinen, NM, lxxix (1932)
22 altdeutsche Tänze, NM, lxxx (1932, 2/1951)
G. F. Handel: Weihnachtsarie: Und Siehe Der Engel des Herrn kam über sie, NM, civ (1933)
V. Rathgeber: Musikalischer Zeitvertreib auf dem Klavier, NM, cv (1933, 2/1960)
G. F. Handel: Zwölf Märsche für Streichorchester mit Bläsern nach Belieben, NM, cviii (1934)
J. C. Bach: Sechs Quintette, op.11, EDM, 1st ser., iii (1935); nos.4 and 6 printed separately in NM, cxxiv, cxxvii (1935)
C. P. E. Bach: Vier Orchester-Sinfonien mit zwölf obligaten Stimmen, EDM, 1st ser., xviii (1942)
G. F. Handel: Klaviermusik I: Die acht grossen Suiten, Hallische Händel-Ausgabe, iv/1 (Kassel, 1955); *Xerxes*, ibid, ii/39 (Kassel, 1959)

BIBLIOGRAPHY

F. Krautwurst: 'Rudolf Steglich 70 Jahre', *Musica*, x (1956), 157
W. Siedel: *Über Rhythmustheorien der Neuzeit* (Berne and Munich, 1975)

Obituary, *Mf*, xxix (1976), 382
F. Krautwurst: 'Zum Tode Rudolf Steglichs', *Musica*, xxx (1976), 428

HANS HEINRICH EGGEBRECHT

Stegmann, Carl David (*b* Staucha, nr. Meissen, 1751; *d* Bonn, 27 May 1826). German tenor, harpsichordist, conductor and composer. He received his initial musical training from the local organist at Staucha, then studied in Dresden with J. F. Zillich (from 1760), at the Kreuzschule (1766–70) and later under Homilius and the violinist H. F. Weisse. Thereafter he rose rapidly as singer, actor and harpsichordist; he went to Breslau in 1772 (with the Wäser theatre company), Königsberg in 1773, Heilsberg in 1774 (as court harpsichordist to the Bishop of Ermeland), Danzig in 1775, Königsberg again in 1776 (with the Schuch company) and later appeared in Gotha (at the court theatre). From 1778 to 1783 he made the first of two extended visits to Hamburg, winning particular renown as a harpsichordist. By that time six of his operas and Singspiels, first produced earlier in Königsberg and Danzig, were attracting performances elsewhere in northern Germany. In 1783 he left Hamburg to join the Grossmann company in Bonn. He then became attached to the court theatre at Mainz in association with which he made highly acclaimed guest appearances in Frankfurt. He sang in the first German-language *Don Giovanni* (Mainz, 13 March 1789), produced or conducted other operas by Mozart, Salieri, Gluck and Gassmann, composed incidental music (e.g. to Bürger's version of *Macbeth*, 30 August 1785) and acted in dramas by Lessing and Schiller.

The summit of Stegmann's activities in Frankfurt was the production of his allegorical Singspiel *Heinrich der Löwe* (15 July 1792) to commemorate the coronation of Emperor Franz II. By the time of his return to Hamburg in November 1792, he was esteemed as a leading operatic producer and adapter, which compensated for the declining vocal prowess that forced him to restrict his appearances to comic roles (*AMZ*, i, 1798–9, col.713). In 1798 he joined the directorate of the Hamburg theatre, remaining there until 1811; thereafter he attracted attention mainly as a composer of incidental music and a series of instrumental works (*AMZ*, iv, 1801–2, col.261), including keyboard and multiple concertos. His earlier close acquaintance with the operas of Gluck and Mozart, and his later keyboard arrangements (published by his friend Simrock) of Haydn's symphonies, Mozart's string quintets and Beethoven's Trios op.9, enabled him to produce instrumental music notable for contrapuntal and textural ingenuity, combined with an imaginative, if sometimes overladen, instrumentation.

As a composer for the theatre, Stegmann has attracted attention for his harmonic and tonal organization and for using antecedent forms of the leitmotif, showing an early interest in dramatic and psychological continuity.

WORKS

DRAMATIC

Der Kaufmann von Smirna (comic opera, 1, C. F. Schwan, after Champfort), Königsberg, 1773, *B-Bc*; vocal score (Leipzig and Königsberg, 1773)
Der Deserteur (operetta, 3), Danzig, 1775; vocal score (Leipzig and Königsberg, 1775)
Die Rekruten auf dem Lande (comic opera, 3), Danzig and Königsberg, 1775, *D-Dlb* (autograph)
Das redende Gemählde (comic opera, 2, J. Anseaume), Königsberg, 1775; vocal score (Mitau and Hasenboh, 1775)
Sultan Wampum oder Die Wünsche (opera, 3, after A. von Kotzebue), Mainz, National, 7 March 1791
Heinrich der Löwe (Singspiel, 2, H. G. Schmieder), Frankfurt am Main,

National, 15 July 1792, ov. (Vienna, 1792)
Der Triumph der Liebe oder Das kühne Abentheuer (Singspiel, 4, E. F. Jester), Hamburg, Gänsemarkt, 27 Feb 1796, *B*; vocal score, arr. Stegmann (Königsberg, 1796)
Die Roseninsel (opera, 3, K. L. Costenoble), Hamburg, 24 Nov 1806, *Dlb* [listed in Gerber as Der umgearbeitete obige Triumph]

Other stage works: Apollo unter den Hirten (prelude with songs), Königsberg, 1776 (Königsberg and Leipzig, 1776); Erwin und Elmire (play with songs, Goethe), Königsberg, 1776 (Königsberg and Leipzig, 1776); Furcht und Hoffnung (prelude with songs), Hamburg, 1798; Moses (ov., choruses etc), Hamburg, 1807 (Bonn, *c*1812); incidental music to: Macbeth (Bürger, after Shakespeare), 1784, Die Jungfrau von Orleans (Schiller), Maria Stuart (Schiller); Die herrschaftliche Küche (ballet), Danzig, 1775, Philemon und Baucis (Singspiel), Gotha, 1777, both cited in Gerber, lost; adaptations of other operas, including P. Wranitzky: Oberon, N.-M. Dalayrac: Raoul, sire de Créqui, Mozart: Così fan tutte (in Ger.); single vocal pieces from stage works (Hamburg, n.d.); further stage works cited in Gerber

OTHER WORKS

(*all printed works published in Bonn unless otherwise stated*)

Inst: Conc., pf, ob, bn, orch, *B-Bc*; Conc., 2 pf, vn, str, *Bc*; 2 concs., 2 pf, 3 pf, *Bc*; Concerto à 11 stromenti, Concerto doppio, 2 kbd, Sinfonia à 8: *D-SWl*; Ouverture caractéristique: Das Siegesfest (n.d.); other concs., pf works and chamber music cited in Gerber
Lieder: Die Liebe und das L'hombre-Spiel, pf acc. (*c*1812); Kriegslied der Teutschen (n.p., n.d.); Neue Melodien zu Freimaurerliedern, i, 1–4vv, pf (1816); further lieder in contemporary anthologies (1783) (Copenhagen, 1785–7); further pubd works cited in Gerber
Pf arrs.: Paer: Achilles (opera) (*c*1783); Gluck: Alceste (opera) (n.d.); Haydn: syms. (*c*1813). 6 qts, 4 hands (Bonn and Cologne, 1819); Mozart: qnt, 4 hands (Bonn and Cologne, 1820–22); Beethoven: 3 Trios, op.9, 4 hands (Bonn and Cologne, n.d.) [for Haydn, Mozart and Beethoven arrs., see *AMZ*, xvii (1815), col.676, xx (1818). col.411, xxv (1823), col.308, xxvi (1824), col.196]

BIBLIOGRAPHY

GerberNL
A. Peiba: *Gallerie von Teutschen Schauspielern und Schauspielerinnen* (Vienna, 1783); repr. in *Schriften der Gesellschaft für Theatergeschichte*, xiii (Berlin, 1910)
J. F. Schütze: *Hamburgische Theatergeschichte* (Hamburg, 1794)
E. Metzel: 'Karl David Stegmann: aus dem Leben eines Bühnenkünstlers des 18. Jahrhunderts', *Archiv für Theatergeschichte*, i (Berlin, 1904), 129
A. Gottron: *Mainzer Musikgeschichte von 1500 bis 1800* (Mainz, 1959)
A. McCredie: 'Symphonic Music in the Haydn–Mozart Era: the North German Manuscripts: an Interim Survey', *MMA*, ii (1967), 75–158
ANDREW D. McCREDIE

Stegmayer, Matthäus (*b* Vienna, 29 April 1771; *d* Vienna, 10 May 1820). Austrian composer, poet and singer. As a boy he was a powerful treble in the Dominican church choir in Vienna, and toured the provinces with itinerant theatre troupes after completing his secondary education. He returned to Vienna in 1792 or 1793, joining the Theater in der Josefstadt; he took leading parts and composed Singspiels and occasional music. In the summer of 1796 he moved to Schikaneder's Freihaus-Theater, appearing as composer for the first time there with a score for Gieseke's *Die zwölf schlafenden Jungfrauen* on 4 June. Before the year was out he had also written two plays for the company. During the next two and a half decades he provided the Viennese theatres with a large number of original plays and adaptations, as well as complete or part-scores for other poets. The need for haste in composing theatre music frequently led to his sharing the task with Seyfried, Henneberg and others (e.g. for Perinet's *Liebe macht kurzen Prozess*, 1798, and his own *Holga die Göttin des Kristallengebirges*, 1800). He gradually gave up composition (his works also include some church compositions) but continued to turn out plays with great regularity. Although he is reported to have left Schikaneder for the court theatre in 1800, there is no pause in the series of works he wrote for the former. He

was also chorus director and producer at the court theatre, ran the Hoftheater-Musikverlag and started a music copying and hire business. In 1804 he joined the Theater an der Wien as actor and chorus master, and continued to provide many plays and librettos, including the popular *Idas und Marpissa* (10 October 1807), with music by Seyfried. His greatest success was achieved with the quodlibet *Rochus Pumpernickel*, a local adaptation of Molière's *Monsieur de Pourceaugnac*; with a score by Haibel and Seyfried, this work proved one of the most popular products of the Viennese theatre – it was given innumerable performances all over German-speaking lands and ran to several editions (book and vocal score) and at least three sequels.

Matthäus's son Ferdinand Stegmayer (*b* Vienna, 25 Aug 1803; *d* Vienna, 6 May 1863) was a pianist, conductor and composer who at 22 was appointed music director at the Königstädtisches Theater, Berlin, and later founded the Academy of Singing in Vienna (1858).

BIBLIOGRAPHY
M. Stegmayer: Autobiographical sketch (*A-Wgm*)
C. von Wurzbach: *Biographisches Lexikon des Kaiserthums Oesterreich*, xxxvii (Vienna, 1878), 327
A. Reissmann, ed.: *Musikalisches Conversations-Lexikon*, ix (Berlin, 1878), 413
F. Blitzenetz: *Matthäus Stegmayer* (diss., U. of Vienna, 1929)
O. E. Deutsch: *Das Freihaus-Theater auf der Wieden* (Vienna, 1937)
A. Bauer: *150 Jahre Theater an der Wien* (Zurich, 1952)
——: *Opern und Operetten in Wien* (Graz and Cologne, 1955)
PETER BRANSCOMBE

Stehman, Jacques (*b* Brussels, 8 July 1912; *d* Brussels, 20 May 1975). Belgian composer and critic. He studied the piano and theory at the Brussels Conservatory, where Absil was his most important teacher. Then he played an important part in Brussels musical life as music reporter for Radio Télévision Belge and critic of the daily paper *Le soir*. He returned to the conservatory as professor of practical harmony (1954) and of music history (1968), also teaching at the Chapelle Musicale Reine Elisabeth. A fluent composer, he could express deep tragedy, as in the *Chant funèbre*, but more frequently his music is designed to divert. The piano pieces (e.g. *Matins*, 1938) and songs (e.g. *Rimes enfantines*, 1949) are within the French tradition; more developed works employ impressionist detail within conventional forms – for example, the Suite for strings takes the form (and also recaptures the spirit) of an 18th-century suite. The *Symphonie de poche* (1950) is also built on Classical lines, although on reduced proportions, with oppositions between soloists and groups in place of tuttis. Some of Stehman's works, such as the *Trois rythmes* (1955), display the rhythmic influence of jazz. He published an introduction to music, *Histoire de la musique européenne* (Verviers, 1964). His music is published by CeBeDeM, which holds his MSS, and Vriamont.

BIBLIOGRAPHY
R. Wangermée: *La musique belge contemporaine* (Brussels, 1959)
Music in Belgium (Brussels, 1964) [CeBeDeM publication]
HENRI VANHULST

Steibelt, Daniel (*b* Berlin, 22 Oct 1765; *d* St Petersburg, 20 Sept 1823). German composer and pianist. His father was a maker of harpsichords and pianos. At an early age he attracted the attention of the crown prince (later Friedrich Wilhelm II of Prussia), who sent him to study with Kirnberger. Steibelt's first published composition, a song of eight bars, appeared in a song collection in 1782. He joined the Prussian army some time before 1784, for in that year he deserted and fled the country. His movements during the next three years are imperfectly documented; he may have spent at least part of the time in Vienna. In 1788 he was in Munich, where the three sonatas of his op.1 were published; in 1789 he gave concerts in Saxony and Hanover; and in 1790 he took up permanent residence in Paris, which he probably visited in the years immediately before, as his reputation was already well established there. His contest at court with David Hermann (1764–1852) indicates that he had been in Paris before the Revolution. Each contributed a movement to the sonata *La coquette*: Hermann the first and Steibelt the rondo, and the fashionable Steibelt was adjudged the winner. In 1792 he set a libretto by his patron, the Vicomte de Ségur, based on Shakespeare's *Romeo and Juliet*. The work was intended for the Paris Opéra. On its rejection it was recast with spoken dialogue in place of the recitatives and very successfully produced at the Théâtre Feydeau on 10 September 1793. Fraudulent dealings with Boyer, his publisher, brought Steibelt into bad repute, and he left Paris towards the end of 1796, making his way to London by way of Holland.

An appearance at Salomon's benefit concert on 1 May 1797 may have been his first in London. Two weeks later he played one of his own concertos at an opera concert, and it was probably at Salomon's concert on 19 March 1798 that he first played his celebrated Third Concerto, the finale of which, a rondo pastoral 'in which is introduced an imitation of a storm', achieved enormous popularity and was still in print as recently as 1933. On 11 December 1798 *Albert and Adelaide, or The Victim of Constancy*, 'a new grand Heroic Romance', was produced at Covent Garden. This opera was a pasticcio both verbally and musically well adapted to the English taste. Steibelt was the nominal composer, but there were numerous borrowings (e.g. from Cherubini's *Lodoïska*) and some of the 'original' music was composed by Attwood (see the *Morning Chronicle*, 22 January 1799). While in London Steibelt conceived a predilection for English pianos and he married a young Englishwoman who was a skilled performer not only on the piano but also on the tambourine, a fact that occasioned him to add tambourine parts to many of his later compositions.

Steibelt was in Hamburg on 9 October 1799, and in the same month was officially pardoned for his desertion from the army of 15 years before. He gave a concert at Dresden on 4 February 1800 and also visited Prague, Berlin and Vienna, where, at the home of Count Fries, he entered into the contest with Beethoven described by Ries in his *Biographische Notizen über L. v. Beethoven* (Koblenz, 1838), in which Steibelt was decisively worsted and his success in Vienna impaired. He was back in Paris in August 1800; he had brought with him a score of Haydn's *The Creation* which he performed in Napoleon's presence at the Opéra on 24 December, in a translation by Ségur and with musical alterations and additions of his own that caused much offence. His ballet, *Le retour de Zéphire*, was given successfully at the Opéra on 3 March 1802, and he left for London 19 days later.

The next six years were divided more or less equally between London and Paris. Two ballets, *Le jugement de berger Paris* and *La belle laitière* were produced at the King's Theatre, Haymarket, and an intermezzo, *La fête*

de Mars, composed to celebrate the Austerlitz campaign, at the Paris Opéra. A three-act opera, *La princesse de Babylone*, was in active preparation at the Opéra in the autumn of 1808, when Steibelt suddenly fled from his importunate creditors. During these six years he composed much of his piano music, including the Fourth and Fifth Concertos, the *Méthode* (Paris, 1805), in which he claimed to have invented the signs for the pedals adopted by Clementi, Cramer and Dussek, and his longest-lived work, the *Etude* op.78.

Steibelt gave concerts at Frankfurt (2 November 1808), Leipzig, Breslau and Warsaw on his way to St Petersburg, where he was to take up an appointment as director of the French Opera. When Boieldieu left St Petersburg at the end of 1810, Steibelt was appointed *maître de chapelle* to the emperor in his stead. He spent the rest of his life there, managing and composing for the French Opera, teaching, and composing for the piano; and there he met John Field, who became one of his few real friends, being loyal and generous to him. In St Petersburg he produced the operas *Cendrillon* (26 October 1810), *Sargines*, *La princesse de Babylone* and a revised version of *Roméo et Juliette*, as well as the ballets *La fête de l'Empereur* and *Der blöde Ritter*. When Napoleon entered Moscow in 1812, Steibelt composed a piano fantasy, *L'incendie de Moscou*. On 16 March 1820 he broke a six years' silence as a pianist to give the first performance of his Eighth Concerto, a work in which he anticipated Busoni by writing a choral finale. His last illness was painful and protracted, and he died on 20 September 1823. He was given a semi-public funeral. The military governor of St Petersburg, Count Milardovich, organized a concert for the benefit of Steibelt's family who, despite his fabulous earnings, had been left in comparative poverty.

Title-page of Steibelt's 'Six Sonates' op.27 (Paris: Imbault)

Steibelt appears to have been extraordinarily vain, arrogant, discourteous, recklessly extravagant and even dishonest. He fobbed off old works as new, disguising them with minor alterations and the addition of unnecessary ad lib parts. Meissner in his *Rococo-Bilder* (pp.209f) recorded that

Steibelt sold to the music publisher Nadermann three piano sonatas for 500 francs to be paid on the spot. Steibelt had played them and Nadermann admired them as very beautiful. When Nadermann's son came home he played the sonatas which Steibelt had left and found that they were not the sonatas which the composer had played (from memory) but three quite insignificant ones.

As a musician Steibelt has often been dismissed as a charlatan, to some degree unjustly. His powers as a pianist must have been considerable, even though he was reputed to have laboured under the disadvantage of a poor left-hand technique and to have been unable to produce singing tone in slow, sustained music, which he consequently seldom attempted. Like much of his music, his playing probably had a superficial brilliance that captivated his first audiences.

Full scores of his major works have almost all disappeared. On the evidence of the published score of *Roméo et Juliette* he was a capable enough operatic composer. The long concerted finales to Acts 2 and 3 are in their way admirable and the arias are well fashioned. The rather full scoring of some of the accompaniments possibly prompted the astonishing verdict in the *Moniteur* of 23 September 1793, where the music was described as 'learned, but laboured and ugly'. Steibelt's scoring could indeed be a model of delicacy. A passage near the beginning of the overture is remarkable for varied and sensitive doubling of woodwind instruments and the use of solo horn to conjure up romantic atmosphere. Steibelt's concertos have expansive first movements in the classical Mozartian form, slow movements eked out with much decorative writing for the solo instrument, and final rondos in a popular vein. The sonatas, some of which have obbligato violin or flute parts and many ad lib parts variously for violin, cello, flute, etc, range from small sonatina-like pieces to quite expansive works. Many are in two movements only (Allegro and Rondo). Slow movements, when they appear, are generally perfunctory and often based on popular national airs, as are many of the rondos. Most of Steibelt's music now seems doomed to oblivion, especially the innumerable potboilers in the shape of waltzes, variations, bacchanals, potpourris and descriptive pieces, though an abridgement of one of the latter, *La journée d'Ulm*, as well as one of the bacchanals, was recorded by Valda Aveling in 1968 on a 'giraffe' piano of *c*1810. The three quintets for piano and strings op.28 are more substantial, as are the 50 studies of the *Etude* op.78, some of which anticipate the style of Mendelssohn and all of which are admirably designed for their purpose.

WORKS

A selected list from the 110 op. nos. and countless unnumbered works. All works published unless otherwise indicated, mostly in Paris, but also in Leipzig, London, Offenbach, St Petersburg and Vienna. See detailed list in Mee.

STAGE

Roméo et Juliette (3-act opera, J. A. P. de Ségur, after Shakespeare), Paris, Feydeau, 10 Sept 1793, full score pubd
Albert and Adelaide, or The Victim of Constancy (3-act pasticcio opera, after Schoerer, and others), London, Covent Garden, 11 Dec 1798, pf score of ov. pubd; incl. music by Cherubini and Attwood
Le retour de Zéphire (1-act ballet), Paris, Opéra, 3 March 1802, *F-Po*, vocal score pubd, also called La valée de Tempé; incl. music by T. Winter

Le jugement de berger Paris (3-act ballet), London, King's, 24 May 1804, vocal score pubd
La belle laitière, ou Blanche, Reine de Castille (ballet), London, King's, 26 Jan 1805, vocal score pubd
La fête de Mars (intermezzo, d'Esmenard), Paris, Opéra, 4 March 1806, *F-Po*
La princesse de Babylone (3-act opera), St Petersburg, *c*1812, not pubd; originally composed *c*1808 for Paris Opéra
La fête de l'Empereur (ballet), St Petersburg, 1809, not pubd
Der blöde Ritter (ballet), St Petersburg, *c*1810, not pubd
Sargines (3-act opera), St Petersburg, *c*1810, not pubd
Les folies amoureuses (pasticcio opera), St Petersburg, *c*1810, full score pubd
Cendrillon (3-act opera, C. G. Etienne), St Petersburg, 26 Oct 1810, not pubd
Le jugement de Midas (opera), *c*1823, not pubd; unfinished but apparently performed at St Petersburg

ORCHESTRAL AND CHAMBER

Overture en symphonie (1796); several waltzes, orch, tambourine, triangle, not pubd
8 pf concertos: no.1, C (1796); no.2, e, vn/orch acc. (*c*1796); no.3, E, 'L'orage', op.33 (1799); no.4, E♭ (*c*1800); no.5, E♭, 'A la chasse', op.64 (1802); no.6, g, 'Le voyage au Mont St Bernard' (*c*1816); no.7, e, 'Grand Military Concerto, dans le genre des Grecs', with 2 orchs (*c*1816); no.8, E♭, with Bacchanalian Rondo, acc. chorus, 1820, not pubd
6 string quartets (1790s)
1 trio; 1 qt; 3 qnts, op.28: all pf, str (1790s)
Harp concerto (1807)

PIANO AND HARP

All numbers are approximate, as Steibelt published identical works under different op. nos. and different works under identical op. nos. Many works were also published both with and without obbligato or ad lib accompaniments.

*c*160 sonatas and sonatinas, pf; *c*180 sonatas, pf, inst acc.
16 sonatas, pf 4 hands; 7 sonatas, 2 pf; 5 duos, pf, harp
1 sonata, harp; 9 sonatas, harp, inst acc.
20 potpourris, pf, incl. 1 also arr. for pf, orch acc.
36 waltzes, 36 bacchanals, 12 divertissements, pf, tambourine and triangle ad lib
6 waltzes, pf 3 hands
Numerous divertissements, variations, preludes, caprices, rondos, fantasias, serenades, marches and descriptive pieces, pf, and pf, inst acc.
Etude, pf, op.78 (1805)
Méthode de pianoforte (1805)

SONGS

Mélanges d'airs et chansons en forme de scène [30 songs], op.10 (1794)
6 romances (1798)
[5] Airs d'Estelle (1798)
Several songs in contemporary anthologies, 1782–4

BIBLIOGRAPHY

P. Smith: 'Steibelt à Rouen', *Revue et gazette musicale de Paris*, xiii (23 Aug 1846)
A. Meissner: *Rococo-Bilder, nach Aufzeichnungen meines Grossvaters* (Gumbinnen, 1871)
M. Dietz: *Geschichte des Musikdramas in Frankreich während der Revolution* (Vienna, 1885, 2/1893), 301ff, 449ff
J. H. Mee: 'Steibelt, Daniel', *Grove 1*
E. Prout: 'Some Forgotten Operas, III: Steibelt's *Roméo et Juliette*', *MMR*, xxxiv/9–11 (1904)
G. Müller: *Daniel Steibelt: sein Leben und seine Klavierwerke* (Leipzig and Zurich, 1933/*R*1973)
N. Slonimsky: 'Musical Oddities', *Etude*, lxxii (1954), 5
H. C. Schonberg: *The Great Pianists* (London, 1964), 67ff
K. A. Hagberg: *Daniel Steibelt's Cendrillon: a Critical Edition with Notes on Steibelt's Life and Works* (diss., Eastman School of Music, 1975)

FRANK DAWES

Steier, Sylvester (*fl* 1583). German composer. He is known by a single collection, *Hymnorum oeconomicorum, in octonas heptadum classes distributorum libri duo ... Christliche Hausshymni, in zwei Bücher, und jedes in acht sibenfache Classes underschieden* (Nuremberg, 1583; two melodies in Zahn, i, no.405, and iii, no.4497*b* respectively, one ed. K. Ameln and others, *Handbuch der deutschen evangelischen Kirchenmusik*, iii/2, Göttingen, 1935–6, p.388, and one ed. K. Ameln and W. Thomas, Kassel, 1930). He subjoined to his name the word 'Leovallae', which Ameln interpreted as indicating that he came from Liebenthal, Silesia. He is more likely, however, to have worked in Upper Franconia, the Upper Palatinate or in Bohemia, since the people named in his book lived in these areas. The dedication suggests that he was a monk, a supposition borne out by the fact that the contents were intended 'for the canonical hours'. The hymns for the various times of day – morning, evening, mealtimes and so on – are in a simple homophonic style; the texts (hymns and biblical sayings) are underlaid throughout in Latin and German. The 'seven classes' mentioned in the title were probably intended to match the days of the week; there are eight songs in each class.

BIBLIOGRAPHY

J. Zahn: *Die Melodien der deutschen evangelischen Kirchenlieder* (Gütersloh, 1889–93/*R*1963)
K. Ameln: 'Steier, Sylvester', *MGG*
U. Siegele: *Die Musiksammlung der Stadt Heilbronn* (Heilbronn, 1967)
WALTER BLANKENBURG

Steiffkin, Theodore. *See* STEFFKIN, THEODORE.

Steigleder. German family of organists and composers.

(1) **Utz Steigleder** (*d* Stuttgart, 7 or 8 Oct 1581). He is first traceable in 1534 in the service of Duke Ulrich of Württemberg in Stuttgart, where he was court and abbey organist. From 1568, when Duke Ludwig became ruler, the court chapel reached its heyday; from 1572, when Steigleder went into semi-retirement, he was assisted by Simon Lohet. His only surviving work is a six-part *Veni Sancte Spiritus* (edn., Die Motette, no.457, Stuttgart, 1963), which has affinities with procedures in Hans Buchner's *Fundamentum*.

(2) **Adam Steigleder** (*b* Stuttgart, 19 Feb 1561; *d* Stuttgart, 8 Nov 1633). Son of (1) Utz Steigleder. He studied under Simon Lohet between 1575 and 1578 and at Duke Ludwig of Württemberg's expense in Rome with unknown teachers from 1580 to 1583. He was successively organist at the abbey church, Stuttgart (from 1583), the Michaeliskirche, Schwäbisch Hall (from October 1592), and Ulm Minster (from 1595). He retired to Stuttgart in 1625. His sole surviving works, the fruits of an Italian training seen through German eyes, are a *Passa è mezo* (a *passamezzo antico* with three variations, the last a galliard; see M. Schuler, *Mf*, xxi, 1968, p.42) and a *Toccata primi toni* based on *Veni, Redemptor gentium* (the latter in *EMDC*, II/vii, 1926, pp.1224ff, and in *ZMw*, viii, 1925–6, p.633). A *Fuga colorata* assigned to him in J. Woltz: *Nova musices organicae tabulatura* (Basle, 1617) is ascribed to Giovanni Gabrieli in other sources (*A-Wm*, *D-B*, *I-Tn* Foà 3; it is anon. in *D-Mbs* Mus.4480, but is attrib. Steigleder in *EMDC*, II/vii, 1224ff).

(3) **Johann Ulrich Steigleder** (*b* Schwäbisch Hall, 22 March 1593; *d* Stuttgart, 10 Oct 1635). Son of (2) Adam Steigleder, who was his only teacher. Though lame he became organist of the Stephanskirche, Lindau, on Lake Constance, in 1613. He was organist of the abbey church, Stuttgart, from 1617 and also ducal organist from 1627; though nominated as organist of Heilbronn Cathedral, he was never appointed. He died of plague during the Thirty Years War.

His known works comprise four isolated vocal and instrumental pieces and his two published collections (edn., CEKM, xiii/1, 1968); in addition, 15 anonymous liturgical works for organ (in *GB-Lbm*) have been attributed to him by Hirtler. The year 1624 represented a landmark in German keyboard music, for it was then that Scheidt and Steigleder, in their *Tabulatura nova* and *Ricercar tabulatura* (published at Stuttgart) respectively, adopted five-line musical notation in place of lettering. Furthermore Steigleder introduced keyboard scoring and employed engraved copper plates (crudely cut by himself) for the first time in Germany. He also took the initiative in replacing modal nomenclature (*primi toni* etc) by that of key. The first six ricercares are accordingly in D minor, E minor, F, G, A minor and C (though with modal implications), this cyclic sequence repeating itself in the second six.

Contrasted with the vocally orientated ricercares of his older contemporaries Hassler and Erbach, Steigleder's are definitely instrumental in character, with English virginal style a major influence – not surprisingly considering the strong contingent of English musicians with whom he worked at the Stuttgart court. Elements of this style apparent in the ricercares include echo effects (no.11), faburden (no.6), off-beat figuration (no.10), imitative figuration (no.2), cross-rhythms (no.10) and hocket (no.6). Another influence, shared with Froberger (whose father was Kapellmeister at Stuttgart), was the lute playing of the Englishmen John and David Morell and Andrew Borell, strikingly illustrated in Ricercare no.1 (bars 143ff). The ricercares show great diversity, befitting works avowedly written 'to please students'. Nos.3 and 9, both outstanding pieces, demonstrate an imaginative treatment of the cuckoo's call and a subtle use of diminution respectively.

Steigleder's second collection is the *Tabulatur Buch* (Strasbourg, 1627). The practical use of this didactic anthology comprising 40 variations on the chorale *Vater unser* is stressed: players finding the first fantasia overlong may substitute the shorter second and third, while voices or instruments of appropriate pitch may reinforce the chorale in the cantus firmus pieces in discant, tenor and bass, which predominate. The three-part settings have ornamental accompanying figures, the four-part ones a more polyphonic texture; nos.17 and 15, which are worthy precursors of Bach's *Orgel-Büchlein*, are good examples of the two types. The chorale undergoes a wide variety of structural treatment: it is divided phrase by phrase between discant and tenor, the remaining two parts being imitative (no.35), in strict canon between bass and discant with a middle part in ostinato style (no.29), in double counterpoint (no.12), in canon at the 4th using hocket and resembling Tallis's *Lesson: Two Parts in One* (no.24) and treated as a fugal bicinium foreshadowing Bach's chorale-partita writing (no.22). The concluding tripartite toccata, again stylistically influenced by lute and virginal textures, shows Steigleder at his most inventive.

BIBLIOGRAPHY

W. Tappert: 'Johann Ulrich Steigleders "Tabulaturbuch" ', *MMg*, xix (1887), 13
J. Sittard: *Zur Geschichte der Musik und des Theaters am Württembergischen Hofe* (Stuttgart, 1890–91)
E. Emsheimer: *Johann Ulrich Steigleder: sein Leben und seine Werke* (Kassel, 1928)
F. Hirtler: 'Neuaufgefundene Orgelstücke von J. U. Steigleder und J. Benn', *AMf*, ii (1937), 92
L. Schierning: *Die Überlieferung der deutschen Orgel- und Klaviermusik aus der ersten Hälfte des 17. Jahrhunderts* (Kassel, 1961), 11ff
W. Apel: *Geschichte der Orgel- und Klaviermusik bis 1700* (Kassel, 1967; Eng. trans., rev. 1972)
——: 'Solo Instrumental Music: the South German Organists', *NOHM*, iv (1968), 659

R. Kopff: 'Les compositeurs de musique instrumentale en Alsace au XVIIe siècle', *La musique en Alsace hier et aujourd'hui* (Paris, 1970), 83

G. B. SHARP

Stein, Erwin (*b* Vienna, 7 Nov 1885; *d* London, 17 July 1958). Austrian writer on music and editor. He studied with Schoenberg from 1906 to 1910 and became a close friend of Berg and Webern. During World War I he was répétiteur and conductor at various German opera houses. From 1920 to 1923 he was director of performances in Schoenberg's Verein für musikalische Privataufführungen. He edited the periodical *Pult und Taktstock* from 1924 to 1930, and was until 1938 artistic adviser to Universal Edition in Vienna, making, among other things, a vocal score of the unfinished third act of Berg's *Lulu*. In 1938 he emigrated to England where his association with Universal Edition secured him a post with its English agents, Boosey & Hawkes.

Stein was an ardent champion of Schoenberg and the 12-note school in general and wrote many articles analysing and explaining the technical aspects of this music. In England he also became interested in the work of Benjamin Britten.

WRITINGS
Orpheus in New Guises (London, 1953) [collection of articles]
ed.: *Arnold Schoenberg: ausgewählte Briefe* (Mainz, 1958; Eng. trans., 1964)
Form and Performance (London and New York, 1962; Ger. trans., 1964)

BIBLIOGRAPHY
A. Gishford: Obituary, *Opera*, ix (1958), 600
Earl of Harewood: 'Erwin Stein', *Tempo*, no.49 (1958), 35

MOSCO CARNER

Stein, Fritz (Friedrich Wilhelm) (*b* Gerlachsheim, 17 Dec 1879; *d* Berlin, 14 Nov 1961). German musicologist, organist and conductor. He studied theology in Heidelberg but from 1902, encouraged by the church musician Philipp Wolfrum, he devoted himself entirely to music. After his studies in Leipzig under Krehl and Nikisch as well as Straube and Riemann, he became university music director and municipal organist of Jena in 1906. There he took up the cause of Reger, who was awarded an honorary doctorate by the University of Jena in 1908. Stein received his own doctorate at Heidelberg University in 1912 with a dissertation on the history of music in Heidelberg, but was unable to succeed Reger as conductor in Meiningen as had been planned because of the outbreak of war in 1914. From 1918 to 1923 he was organist in Kiel; in 1920 he became reader in musicology at the university there, and in 1928 he was appointed professor. As conductor of the municipal symphony concerts and of the oratorio society, which he founded, he was awarded the title of *Generalmusikdirektor* in 1925 and was responsible for organizing music festivals devoted to Bach, Handel and contemporary composers. In 1933, on the recommendation of Furtwängler, he took over the directorship of the Staatliche Hochschule für Musik in Berlin and held this post until 1945. He was able to keep Hindemith at this institution until 1935 while obtaining an honourable discharge for other teaching personnel unacceptable to the Nazi regime.

Stein's musical and scholarly gifts were equal and he published early vocal and instrumental works in practical new editions: these included cantatas by Nikolaus Bruhns, J. C. Bach symphonies and G. J. Werner's *Musikalischer Instrumentalkalender*. He always regarded the Jena Symphony, which he had discovered, as an early work by Beethoven; it is now generally ascribed to F. Witt. The life and works of his friend Reger are central to Stein's research and he published the standard monograph (1939) and a thematic catalogue (1953). As a conductor Stein promoted Scandinavian composers (Nielsen, Sibelius, K. Atterberg, L. L. Emborg, N. O. Raasted) as well as such German composers as Hindemith, J. N. David, A. Huth, H. Kaminski, G. Raphael and K. Thomas.

WRITINGS
'Max Reger', *Max Hesses deutscher Musikkalender* (1908), 168, 176
'Ernst Raumann', *ZIMG*, xii (1910–11), 158
'Eine unbekannte Jugendsymphonie Beethovens?', *SIMG*, xiii (1911–12), 127–72
Zur Geschichte der Musik in Heidelberg (diss., U. of Heidelberg, 1912; enlarged Heidelberg, 1921 as *Geschichte des Musikwesens in Heidelberg bis zum Ende des 18. Jahrhunderts*)
'Max Regers letzte Werke', *Neue Musikzeitung*, xxxvii (1916), 281
'Ein vergessenes Zeugnis Bachschen Familienhumors', *Die Musikwelt*, i (1921)
'Zu Gerhard von Keusslers Oratorien', *Der Auftakt*, v (1925), 285
'Zur Entstehungsgeschichte des 100.Psalms von Max Reger', *Mitteilungen des Max-Reger-Gesellschaft*, v (1926), 1
'Heinrich Kaminskis Magnificat', *Pult und Taktstock*, iii (1926)
Staat und Chorgesang, Organisationsfragen des Chorgesangswesens (Leipzig, 1929)
'Philipp Wolfrum', *AMz*, lvi (1929), 1231
'Kaminskis Chorwerke', *Die Musikpflege*, i (1930), 439; viii (1936), 144
'Ein unbekanntes Symphonie-Fragment Max Regers', *Die Musik*, xxiii (1930–31), 254
'Erinnerungen an Max Reger', *ZfM*, Jg.100 (1933), 207
'Die erzieherischen Aufgaben der Musikhochschule', *Völkische Musikerziehung*, i (1934), 17
'Ein unbekannter Evangelienjahrgang von Augustin Pfleger', *Max Schneider zum 60. Geburtstag* (Halle and Eisleben, 1935), 126
Max Reger (Potsdam, 1939)
Max Reger: sein Leben in Bildern (Leipzig, 1941, 2/1956)
Thematisches Verzeichnis der im Druck erschienenen Werke von Max Reger (Leipzig, 1953)
'Eine komische Schulmeisterkantate von G. Ph. Telemann und J. A. Hasse', *Festschrift Max Schneider* (Leipzig, 1955), 183
'Künstlers Erdenwallen', *ÖMz*, xi (1956), 365
'Gregor Joseph Werners musikalischer Instrumentalkalender', *Musica*, xi (1957), 390
'Zum Problem der "Jenaer Symphonie"', *IMSCR, vii Cologne 1958*, 259
Pantalon: ein unveröffentlichter Ballettsatz Max Regers zur Uraufführung beim Dortmunder Reger-Fest 1960 (Dortmund, 1960)

EDITIONS
L. van Beethoven: *Jenaer Symphonie* (Leipzig, 1911) [not by Beethoven, probably by F. Witt]
N. Bruhns: *Kirchenkantaten I–III*, EDM, 2nd ser., *Schleswig-Holstein und Hansestädte*, i (Brunswick, 1937); *Kirchenkantaten VIII–XII*, EDM, 2nd ser., *Schleswig-Holstein und Hansestädte*, ii (Brunswick, 1939)
A. Pfleger: *Passionsmusik*, Cw, lii (Wolfenbüttel, 1939)
J. C. Bach: *5 Symphonien*, EDM, 1st ser., xxx (Wiesbaden, 1956)
G. J. Werner: *Musikalischer Instrumentalkalender*, EDM, 1st ser., xxxi (Kassel, 1956)

BIBLIOGRAPHY
H. Hoffmann and F. Rühlmann, eds.: *Festschrift Fritz Stein* (Brunswick, 1939) [incl. list of writings and editions]
O. Söhngen: 'Fritz Stein zum 75. Geburtstage', *Der Kirchenmusiker*, v (1954), 173
'Festgabe für Fritz Stein', *Mitteilungen des Max-Reger-Instituts*, x (1959), 1–35
H. Wirth: 'Fritz Stein zum Gedächtnis', *Mf*, xv (1962), 153
O. Söhngen: 'Fritz Stein zum Gedächtnis', *Mitteilungen des Max-Reger-Instituts*, xiii (1962), 3

HELMUT WIRTH

Stein, Horst (*b* Elberfeld, 2 May 1928). German conductor. After studies at the Musikhochschule in Cologne and a first engagement at the municipal theatre in Wuppertal, he was appointed Kapellmeister at the Hamburg Staatsoper in 1951. He was state Kapellmeister at the Berlin Staatsoper (1955–61), and opera director and general music director in Mannheim (1963–70); in 1970 he was appointed principal conductor at the Vienna Staatsoper, and in 1972 became general music director at the Hamburg Staatsoper. A conductor of wide experience, always intent on achieving a satisfactory balance between singer and orchestra, he has been most successful with Wagner's works: he conducted *Tristan und Isolde* at the Teatro Colón in Buenos Aires, where he also directed the South American première of Schoenberg's *Gurrelieder* in 1964; he has conducted *Der fliegende Holländer* at the Sofia State Opera, *Parsifal* at the Paris Opéra, and the *Ring* at the Bayreuth Festival and the Hamburg Staatsoper. Stein also has a special affection for Mozart's operas and Bruckner's symphonies.

HANS CHRISTOPH WORBS

Stein, Johann (Georg) Andreas (*b* Heidelsheim, 6 May 1728; *d* Augsburg, 29 Feb 1792). German keyboard instrument maker. He was probably trained by his father, Johann Georg Stein, an organ builder in Heidelsheim. Before embarking on his itinerant apprenticeship, Johann Andreas purchased a leather-bound notebook in which for many years he jotted down observations about instruments, persons and places he visited. His arrival in Strasbourg is dated there as 4 August 1748, and J. A. Silbermann's records confirm that he was hired that day to work under Johann Daniel Silbermann, another member of the renowned family of organ builders. Leaving Strasbourg on 9 June 1749 Stein continued his travels throughout Germany, studying and occasionally repairing organs. From October 1749 to January 1750 he remained in Regensburg to work for F. J. Späth. In the summer of 1750 he reached Augsburg, where an excellent opportunity for employment had arisen following the death in 1749 of the city's sole organ builder, J. C. Leo. After assisting his father in Gochsheim for several months, he returned to settle in Augsburg.

From 1755 to 1757 Stein was occupied with his greatest masterpiece, the organ of the Barfüsserkirche in Augsburg; on 19 August 1757 he was appointed organist there. (His last large organ-building project, in the Holy Cross Church, was completed in 1766.) In 1758 he spent a few months in Paris with his friend, the pianist and painter J. G. Eckard, visiting the Silbermann workshop in Strasbourg both en route (19 October 1758) and again while returning (6 January 1759). In 1760 he married Maria Regina Burkhardt of Augsburg. When the Mozart family visited Augsburg on a concert tour in 1763, they purchased a portable practice keyboard instrument from Stein.

Like other 18th-century instrument makers Stein experimented with various inventions, generally action and register combinations. His first solution to the problem of creating a keyboard instrument capable of expression was the 'Poli-Toni-Clavichordium' (*Augsburger Intelligenzblatt*, 5 October 1769), a harpsichord and piano combined in a rectangular case with keyboards at each end that could be coupled. In 1772 he described another instrument on which he had been working for 15 years. This was the 'Melodika', a set of pipes with a compass of three and a half octaves, and a type of swell built into the keys that provided a cantabile upper voice to the accompaniment of the keyboard instrument on which it was placed. As there was little local response to these endeavours, he visited Paris again in 1773. There he

succeeded in astounding both the court and the musical élite, and sold both instruments before returning to Augsburg.

The 'vis-à-vis Flügel' that Stein took to Vienna in 1777 may be the one now located in the Museo Civico, Verona (it has a disposition rather like the 'Poli-Toni-Clavichordium'). Shortly after his return to Augsburg he was visited by Mozart, who praised the escapement and damper mechanisms of his instruments. At an exhibition in Augsburg in 1783 he displayed a new 'vis-à-vis Flügel' (possibly the one dated 1783, now in the Naples Conservatory), and a 'clavecin organisé' commissioned by a Swedish customer; the latter, a combination of organ and piano, is now in the Historiska Museum, Göteborg. Stein's fourth type of combination instrument, the 'Saitenharmonika', was delivered to a customer in Mannheim in 1789. It had a spinet register (i.e. a third set of strings that could be played alone or together with the piano, or left unengaged).

A distinctive feature of Stein's instruments was the ingenious innovation (whether or not he invented it) of replacing the stationary rail (*Prelleiste*) of the simple German action with individually hinged and spring-loaded escapement levers to keep the hammers from jamming against the strings (*see* PIANOFORTE, fig.5). The arc of gyration of the *Kapsel* (point of pivot) and the hammer shank work together so that when the key is depressed slowly the hammer rises and the beak (the opposite end of the hammer shank) escapes from the notch in which it rests just before the hammer touches the string. Then the hammer falls back to its rest post. When the key is lifted, the beak slides down the face of the escapement lever into its notch. Rapid repetition is possible by depressing a key only slightly, thereby not allowing the beak to escape at all.

Stein used both round, hollow hammers similar to those of the Silbermanns, and short, solid hammers tapered on all sides towards the bottom. Also characteristic of the Stein action are wooden *Kapseln* and posts with a flexible material on top to absorb the shock of the returning hammer, supporting it in a resting position above the level of the keys. (For a detailed description, with illustrations, of a Stein piano, *see* PIANOFORTE, §I, 3.)

The typical Stein instrument case has a double bent-side with the inside liner sawn from solid wood. The inner frame is braced by two or three frame members perpendicular to the spine and several diagonal supports. The grain of the bottom is parallel to the straight part of the bentside. Stein's damper mechanism is raised by knee levers (there is no evidence to suggest these were of his own invention).

Stein's most famous pupils were his own children, Nannette [Anna Maria, Maria Anna] Stein (*b* Augsburg, 2 Jan 1769; *d* Vienna, 16 Jan 1833) and Matthäus Andreas Stein (*b* Augsburg, 12 Dec 1776; *d* Vienna, 6 May 1842). Both were trained as performers as well as instrument makers. Nannette in particular was known as a child prodigy and often played her father's instruments in public. During Stein's last years and for two years after his death, his children maintained the business in Augsburg. Soon after Nannette's marriage to the pianist J. A. Streicher in 1794 the workshop was moved to Vienna, where she and her brother remained partners until 1802. Matthäus Andreas then established his own firm, André Stein. His son Carl Andreas (*b* Vienna, 4 Sept 1797; *d* Vienna, 28 Aug 1863), a pianist and composer, expanded the business further after his father's death.

BIBLIOGRAPHY

K. A. Fischer: 'J. A. Stein, der Augsburger Orgel- und Klavierbauer', *Zeitschrift des historichen Vereins für Schwaben und Neuburg*, 1 (1932), 149

E. Hertz: *Johann Andreas Stein (1728–1792): ein Beitrag zur Geschichte des Klavierbaues* (Berlin, 1937)

F. J. Hirt: *Meisterwerke des Klavierbaues* (Olten, 1955), 457ff

F. Göthel: 'Stein', *MGG*

MARIBEL MEISEL, PHILIP R. BELT

Stein, Julius. See STYNE, JULIUS.

Stein, Leon (*b* Chicago, 18 Sept 1910). American composer and writer on music. He studied at DePaul University (MM 1935, PhD 1949), where he taught in various capacities, 1931–76. He was also director of the Institute of Music of the College of Jewish Studies, Chicago (1952–7). From 1955 he was conductor of the Chicago Sinfonietta, with which he toured the USA and Canada. He published *Structure and Style: the Study and Analysis of Musical Forms* (Evanston, 1962, 2/1965) and a companion volume, *Anthology of Musical Forms*. Among his large-scale compositions are two operas (*The Fisherman's Wife*, 1954; *Deirdre*, 1956), four symphonies (1940, 1942, 1950–51, 1974), and several other orchestral works; he also wrote much chamber and instrumental music, including five string quartets.

Stein, Leonard (*b* Los Angeles, 1 Dec 1916). American musicologist. He studied at the University of Southern California (1935–6) and at the University of California at Los Angeles (BA 1939, MM 1941); he was Schoenberg's teaching assistant at the latter (1939–42) and in 1965 received the DMA from the former with the dissertation *The Performance of Twelve-tone and Serial Music for the Piano*. From 1946 he taught at institutions in California, and was adjunct professor at the School of Music at the University of Southern California in 1975. That year he was elected director of the Arnold Schoenberg Institute of Southern California and editor of its journal. Besides writing articles on Schoenberg and the Second Viennese School, he has edited many of Schoenberg's collections of essays, notably *Fundamentals of Musical Composition* (London, 1967), *Structural Functions of Harmony* (London, rev. 2/1969) and *Style and Idea* (London, 1975), as well as several compositions for the complete edition. He has toured the USA and Europe as a pianist and conductor.

Stein, Nikolaus (*b* Steinau an der Strasse; *d* Frankfurt am Main, *c*20 Jan 1629). German music dealer and music publisher. In 1602 he and the printer Wolfgang Richter founded a printing and publishing association in Frankfurt am Main which existed until 1615 under the name of Typographia Musica; it was one of the leading German music publishing firms before the Thirty Years War, and concentrated on Catholic church music, also publishing numerous collections of dances and lieder.

BIBLIOGRAPHY

E. L. Berz: *Die Notendrucker und ihre Verleger in Frankfurt am Main von den Anfängen bis etwa 1630* (Kassel, 1970), 80ff

THEODOR WOHNHAAS

Stein, Richard Heinrich (*b* Halle, 28 Feb 1882; *d* Santa Brigida, Canary Islands, 11 Aug 1942). German music theorist and composer. He graduated from the University of Erlangen in 1911 with the dissertation *Die psychologischen Grundlagen der Wundtschen Ethik*. After a period in Spain (1914–19) he went to Berlin, where he was musical director of Berlin radio and gave lessons in composition and the piano until 1933. He wrote many piano pieces and songs as well as a few orchestral pieces. His *Zwei Konzertstücke* op.26 (1906) for cello and piano are reputed to be the first published quarter-tone music; he also devised a quarter-tone clarinet (1914) but withdrew it as it conflicted with his musical intentions.

Steinbach, Emil (*b* Lengenrieden, 14 Nov 1849; *d* Mainz, 6 Dec 1919). German conductor, brother of Fritz Steinbach. After studying at the Leipzig Conservatory (1867–9), he was appointed Kapellmeister in Mannheim (1871–4), Hamburg, Darmstadt (Hofkapellmeister, 1874–7) and Mainz (1877–1909). A great champion and well-known interpreter of Wagner's music, he gave the first public performance of *Siegfried Idyll* in 1877; he also conducted *Tristan und Isolde* and *Siegfried* at Covent Garden in 1893, when he was found competent but uninspiring. He composed orchestral and chamber music and songs.

JOHN WARRACK

Steinbach, Fritz (*b* Grünsfeld, 17 June 1855; *d* Munich, 13 Aug 1916). German conductor and composer, brother of Emil Steinbach. He was taught music by his brother before entering the Leipzig Conservatory in 1873. He also studied with Vincenz Lachner in Karlsruhe and Gustav Nottebohm in Vienna. From 1880 to 1886 he was second Kapellmeister in Mainz and he then moved to Meiningen, first as Hofkapellmeister and later as Generalmusikdirektor. Under his direction the orchestra enjoyed much success, both at home and abroad. He took it to London in 1902, making a great impression with his cycle of Brahms's symphonies; he later returned to conduct the LSO. He became Kapellmeister and director of the Cologne Conservatory in 1903, continuing to tour widely, to Russia, the USA and elsewhere. As a conductor, he was in Bülow's tradition of keen discipline, flexible tempos and clear phrasing. A friend of Brahms and a well-known interpreter of his music, he conducted the first Brahms festival at Munich in 1909. On his first London visit he was praised for the 'life and impulse' of his conducting in Brahms, but on his return it was said that his conducting was 'decidedly strenuous, but at least the virtue of this fault enabled him to develop superb climaxes' (*MT*, xlvi, 1905, 41). He composed some chamber music, including a popular septet op.7, piano music and songs.

BIBLIOGRAPHY

MT, xlv (1904), 445

B. Eldering: *Gedächtnisworte gelegentlich der Trauerfeier für Fritz Steinbach im Konservatorium der Musik zu Cöln am 1. 10. 1916* (Cologne, 1916)

W. Blume: *Brahms in der Meininger Tradition: seine Sinfonien und Haydn-Variationen in der Bezeichnung von Fritz Steinbach* (Stuttgart, 1933)

W. Braunfels: *Festschrift zur Feier der Gründung des Kölner Konservatoriums im Jahre 1850* (Cologne, 1950), 16

I. Fellinger: 'Fritz Steinbach', *Rheinische Musiker*, iv, ed. K. G. Fellerer (Cologne, 1966), 158

——: 'Steinbach', *MGG*

JOHN WARRACK

Steinbacher, Johann Michael (*fl* 1727–40). Austrian composer. He was an organist in Graz from at least 1727, and in 1740 became parish organist, a post he held only briefly. Manuscripts of his six harpsichord concertos and eight harpsichord partitas, from the collection of the Attems family in Styria around the middle of the 18th century, are in the Studijska knjižnica, Ptuj. The oldest examples of their genre in Austria, the harpsichord concertos must have dated from earlier than those of M. G. Monn, J. A. Scheibl, J. A. Sgatberoni, G. C. Wagenseil and J. G. Zechner, and are evidently modelled on the form of the Italian solo concerto, while the partitas, both in their character and in the designation of their movements, show an affinity with the older suite (two each are in MAM, xxxv and xliii–xliv).

BIBLIOGRAPHY
J. Höfler and I. Klemenčič: *Glasbeni rokopisi in tiski na slovenskem do leta 1800: katalog* [Music manuscripts and printed music in Slovenia before 1800: catalogue] (Ljubljana, 1967)
H. Federhofer and G. M. Schmeiser: 'Grazer Stadtmusikanten als Komponisten vorklassischer Klavierkonzerte', *Historisches Jb der Stadt Graz*, iv (1971), 73
HELLMUT FEDERHOFER

Steinberg, Maximilian Oseyevich. *See* SHTEYNBERG, MAXIMILIAN OSEYEVICH.

Steinberg, (Carl) Michael (Alfred) (*b* Breslau [now Wrocław, Poland], 4 Oct 1928). American music critic. He was educated at Princeton University (AB 1949), and then studied musicology with Strunk and theory and analysis with Cone and Babbitt. He was head of the music history department at the Manhattan School of Music in New York (1954–5, 1957–64) and then became critic of the *Boston Globe*, while also teaching at various colleges and universities, including Hunter, Smith, Brandeis and the New England Conservatory. In 1976 he became director of publications with the Boston SO; three years later he became artistic adviser and publications director to the San Francisco SO.

Steinberg is one of the most knowledgeable music critics working in the USA and probably the daily critic most highly regarded by musicologists, although by the nature of his position his writings are seen mainly in the New England area. His chief concern is contemporary music, and he has been notably sympathetic to amateur and semi-professional performances. He constantly emphasizes the value of scholarship in performance. Since 1970 he has also been active in the training of music critics, giving seminars in connection with the Music Critics Association.

PATRICK J. SMITH

Steinberg, William [Wilhelm] **(Hans)** (*b* Cologne, 1 Aug 1899; *d* New York, 16 May 1978). American conductor of German birth. As a boy he composed and conducted (at 13 directing his own setting for chorus and orchestra of passages from Ovid's *Metamorphoses*) as well as playing the piano and the violin. He studied conducting with Abendroth at the Cologne Conservatory. After appointments at the Cologne Opera (as Klemperer's assistant, then first conductor from 1924) and Prague (1925) he moved in 1929 to Frankfurt as musical director; while there he conducted the premières of Schoenberg's *Von heute auf morgen* and Antheil's *Transatlantic* and an early performance of Weill's *Mahagonny*. He also conducted regularly at the Berlin Staatsoper. After Hitler came to power, Steinberg's activities were restricted to concerts for the Jewish Culture League in Frankfurt and Berlin. He emigrated in 1936 and was co-founder with Huberman of the Palestine Orchestra (later Israel PO) and, after the inaugural concert, conducted by Toscanini, became its first conductor. At Toscanini's invitation he went to the

USA in 1938 as associate conductor of the NBC SO, also appearing as a guest with many orchestras and the San Francisco Opera. In 1945 he became music director of the Buffalo PO, and in 1952 of the Pittsburgh SO. He held several posts concurrently with Pittsburgh, being musical director of the LPO (1958–60), senior guest conductor of the New York PO (1966–8) and musical director of the Boston SO (1969–72). After his success as a guest in Boston in 1960 it was expected that he would succeed Münch there: but in response to the urgings of RCA, for which the Boston SO then recorded, he was passed over for the younger Erich Leinsdorf. When Steinberg went to Boston as Leinsdorf's successor, he was reduced in health and strength. In his 70s he restricted his activities, and his always economical gestures became minimal.

A cultivated man and an exceedingly private personality, Steinberg embodied the probity and selflessness of Toscanini and Klemperer, the two conductors so influential in his career. In his best years his stick technique was unsurpassed in cleanness and clarity. Until the late 1960s, he disfigured with cuts some of the music – Bruckner, Mahler, Elgar – for which he had the deepest sympathy: it was characteristic that relatively late in his career he would so thoroughly reconsider such a question. When young he was sympathetic to new music; later his performances of modern works rarely went beyond dutiful note-reading. He was a strong and straight conductor particularly of Beethoven (for earlier music his touch was rather heavy), Wagner, Bruckner, Elgar and, when not in too fiercely antineurotic a mood, Mahler. In Strauss, of whose music his performances were elegantly understated, he was unsurpassed; and his Boston performances of Verdi's Requiem on the 100th anniversary of Manzoni's death, while not fiery, were among the most honest and the most moving since Toscanini's.

MICHAEL STEINBERG

Steinberg, Zeev (Wolfgang) (*b* Düsseldorf, 27 Nov 1918). Israeli composer and violist. He began to play the violin and to compose at an early age; during the years 1932–5 he wrote several works indebted to Reger, an influence which remained perceptible. In 1933 he studied under Eldering at the Cologne Academy, and in 1934 he settled in Palestine, where his studies were completed under Partos (1940–42). Steinberg joined the Palestine SO (later the Israel PO) as a violist in 1942; he has also appeared as a soloist and frequently as a chamber musician (he was a founder of the New Israel Quartet in 1957). From 1969 to 1972 he lectured on chamber music at the Tel-Aviv Academy. The Viola Sonata (1949) showed a first interest in Schoenbergian 12-note serialism, which came to dominate his work.

WORKS
Va Sonata, 1949; Sonata, 2 va, 1956; Canonic Pieces, str qt, 1959; 6 Miniatures, vc, pf, 1961; Conc. da camera, va, str, 1962; Conc. da camera, vn, 8 insts, 1966; Ma'aseh b'Rachav [The story of Rahab and the spies], vv, insts, 1969; 2 Songs without Words, va, str qt, strs, 1970; Little Suite for a Big Flute, b fl, 1972; pieces for org, hpd, recs, etc; arrs., incl. Bach: Art of Fugue, str qt, 1970

Principal publisher: Israel Music Institute

BIBLIOGRAPHY
Y. W. Cohen: *Werden und Entwicklung der Musik in Israel* (Kassel, 1976) [pt.ii of rev. edn. of M. Brod: *Die Musik Israels*]
W. Y. Elias: *The Music of Israel* (in preparation) [bibliography]
WILLIAM Y. ELIAS

Steinberger, Gábor. *See* DARVAS, GÁBOR.

Steinecke, Wolfgang (*b* Essen, 22 April 1910; *d* Darmstadt, 23 Dec 1961). German music critic and administrator. He studied music at the Hochschulen in Essen and Cologne, and musicology at the universities of Cologne and Kiel, taking his doctorate at Kiel in 1934 with a dissertation on parody in music. From 1934 to 1961 he was a music critic for various daily newspapers: *Rheinisch-Westfälische Zeitung* (Essen), *Deutsche allgemeine Zeitung* (Berlin) and *Der Mittag* (Düsseldorf). From 1945 he was for three years cultural adviser to the town of Darmstadt, where in 1946 he started the Internationale Ferienkurse für Neue Musik and the International Music Institute, in which he played a major part in stimulating the development of avant-garde music and which he continued to run until his death.

WRITINGS

Das Parodieverfahren in der Musik (diss., U. of Kiel, 1934; Wolfenbüttel, 1934/*R*1970 as *Die Parodie in der Musik*)
Sieben Jahre internationale Ferienkurse für neue Musik (Darmstadt, 1952)
ed.: *Darmstädter Beiträge zur neuen Musik*, i–iii (Mainz, 1958–60)
ed.: *Neue Musik in der BRD*, i (Frankfurt, 1958); ii (Mainz, 1959); iii (Berlin, 1960); iv (Kassel, 1961)
'Kranichstein: Geschichte, Idee, Ergebnisse', *Darmstädter Beiträge zur neuen Musik*, iv (Mainz, 1961), 112

BIBLIOGRAPHY

T. W. Adorno: 'Gedenkrede auf Wolfgang Steinecke', *Neue Musik in der BRD*, v–vi, ed. E. Thomas (Darmstadt, 1961–3), 7
E. Thomas: 'Wolfgang Steinecke gestorben', *Das Orchester*, x (1962), 78
'In memoriam Wolfgang Steinecke', *Melos*, xxix (1962), 54 [Tributes by Boulez, Fortner, Maderna, Nono and Stockhausen]
K. Stockhausen: 'Steineckes Tod', *Texte*, ii (Cologne, 1964), 243
HANSPETER KRELLMANN

Steiner, Johann Ludwig (*b* Zurich, 1 July 1688; *d* Zurich, 27 March 1761). Swiss composer. He was a member of the Paruel family, who had moved to Zurich from Stein am Rhein by 1620, and who for several generations provided one of the three city trumpeters on St Peter's Tower. Under his father's guidance, Steiner became proficient on various instruments and in thoroughbass playing. For a year he was a pupil of the organist L. Kellersberger in Baden (Aargau). He succeeded his father as town trumpeter in 1705 and held the post for the rest of his life; at the same time he joined the company known as 'Ab dem Musik-Saal', with which he remained until old age, becoming roommaster, librarian and accountant. As a sideline, he engaged in clock-making, and was active as an inventor and maker of mechanical toys. From 1746 he was a member of the Physical Society, where he gained respect through his 'good natural understanding, and wide experience in various arts'; this membership suggests that he was able to throw off the shackles of his modest professional origins and to gain a respected position among his fellow citizens.

Steiner is known as a composer of pietistic sacred music and especially as author of the *Neues Gesangbuch*, the earliest printed song collection in Switzerland by a single composer; it did not, however, have the public success of the later collections by Bachofen and Schmidlin. The collection *Musicalisch-Italienischer Arien Crantz* (Zurich, 1724), which was edited by Steiner, shows his familiarity with Italian musical practice. With his use of thoroughbass and the Italian style of solo singing, Steiner did much to counter Switzerland's isolation in composition and performance; this development has led to his being called 'the Swiss Caccini' (Nef). Steiner expounded his pedagogical ideas in the prefaces to many of his collections, and particularly in his theoretical publication, *Kurz-leicht-und grundtliches Noten-Büchlein* (Zurich, 1728).

WORKS

(*all printed works published in Zurich unless otherwise stated*)

Auf die Dedicass das Neüwerbauhten Musicsahles, ob, tpt, fl, 2 vn, vc, SSATB, bc, 1717, *CH-Zz*
Neues Gesang-Buch auserlesener, geistreicher Liedern, 2–3vv, bc, i (1723); ii (1735)
Monatlich-Musicalische Miscellanea, 2vv, bc (1724)
Bassus generalis Davidica, 4vv, bc (1734); bc and vocal arr. of Lobwasser Psalter
Gott-Geheiligte Fest- und Zeit-Gedancken, 2vv, bc (1739)
Musicalische Gemüths-Ergötzung, 2vv, bc (1753)
At least 20 New Year cantatas for the Zurich Musiksaalgesellschaft, pubd singly (1717–39)
Lost works: 3 sonate, vn, bc (*c*1717); 6 sonate da camera, vc, bc (Nuremberg, 1731); [6] Monatische Oden (n.d.); some 1000 concertos, arias, cantatas and large-scale sacred works, 2–4vv, some with insts; see Cherbuliez

BIBLIOGRAPHY

A. Nef: *Das Lied in der deutschen Schweiz* (Zurich, 1909)
M. Fehr: *Spielleute im alten Zürich* (Zurich, 1916)
T. Goldschmid: *Schweizerische Gesangbücher früherer Zeiten* (Zurich, 1917)
——: *Geistliche Sologesänge und Duette* (Zurich, 1917–42)
A. Geering: 'Von der Reformation bis zur Romantik', *Schweizer Musikbuch*, ed. H. Ehinger, E. Refardt and W. Schuh (Zurich, 1939), i, 54–130
A.-E. Cherbuliez: *Johann Ludwig Steiner Stadttrompeter von Zürich* (Zurich, 1964)
PETER ROSS

Steiner, Max(imilian Raoul Walter) (*b* Vienna, 10 May 1888; *d* Hollywood, 28 Dec 1971). American composer of Austrian birth. Born into a prominent Viennese musical family (his godfather was Richard Strauss) Steiner showed talent as a child; he studied at the Imperial Academy for a year and at 14 composed and conducted an operetta which ran at the Orpheum theatre for a year. From 1905 to 1911 he conducted musical comedy in London, then in Paris, Berlin, Moscow and Johannesburg. In 1914 he worked on Broadway as arranger and conductor and in 1929 moved to Hollywood. Hollywood film music really began with his music for *Cimarron* and *Symphony of Six Million* and during the 1930s he inaugurated underscoring techniques that soon became standard practice. He worked for RKO Radio Pictures, Selznick International and Warner Brothers and completed over 300 scores.

Steiner had a warm and spontaneous melodic facility which made him an ideal composer for films on homespun and unsophisticated subjects, such as *Come Next Spring*, *The Adventures of Mark Twain* and *Spencer's Mountain*. Musically, he never outgrew Vienna and could produce a waltz for a love theme as deftly as Lehár or Strauss. His dramatic music often lacked substance and fell back too readily on clichés. Nevertheless many films were well served by his taut thematic characterization. His best scores were for *The Adventures of Mark Twain*, *The Informer*, *The Life of Emile Zola*, *The Letter*, *The Big Sleep*, *The Fountainhead* and *This is Cinerama*.

See also FILM MUSIC.

WORKS

FILM MUSIC
(*selective list*)

Cimarron, 1931; Symphony of Six Million, 1931; King Kong, 1933; The Lost Patrol, 1934; The Informer, 1935; The Charge of the Light Brigade, 1936; The Life of Emile Zola, 1937; Jezebel, 1938; Gone with the Wind, 1939
The Letter, 1940; Now Voyager, 1942; The Adventures of Mark Twain, 1944; Passage to Marseilles, 1944; Since You Went Away, 1944; Mildred Pierce, 1945; The Big Sleep, 1946; Johnny Belinda, 1948; The Fountainhead, 1949
Operation Pacific, 1951; This is Cinerama, 1953; Come Next Spring,

1956; Death of a Scoundrel, 1956; John Paul Jones, 1959; A Summer Place, 1959; Spencer's Mountain, 1963

WRITINGS

'Scoring the Film', *We Make the Movies*, ed. N. Naumberg (London, 1938), 216

CHRISTOPHER PALMER

Steiner [née Piette], **Ruth** (*b* Oak Park, Ill., 2 Feb 1931). American musicologist. She studied with Jan LaRue and Hubert Lamb at Wellesley College, receiving the BA in 1952. After working with Reese at the Manhattan School of Music from 1952 to 1953, she began graduate work at the University of California at Berkeley, receiving the MA in 1957. She took the PhD at the Catholic University of America in 1963 and has been on the staff there since 1962. Her main area of study has been medieval liturgical music. Her articles in scholarly journals have dealt primarily with groups of chants in the Sarum and Gregorian rites, the MS sources for these compositions, and problems of style analysis and dating.

WRITINGS

'Some Questions about the Gregorian Offertories and their Verses', *JAMS*, xix (1966), 162

'The Prosulae of the MS Paris, Bibliothèque Nationale, f. lat. 1118', *JAMS*, xxii (1969), 367

'The Responsories and Prosa for St. Stephen's Day at Salisbury', *MQ*, lvi (1970), 162

'Some Melismas for Office Responsories', *JAMS*, xxvi (1973), 108

'Cursus', 'Hymn', §II, 'Invitatory', 'Liturgy and liturgical books', §§I–II, 'Trope (i)', *Grove 6*

PAULA MORGAN

Steiner, Sigmund Anton. Austrian music publisher, active in the firm of HASLINGER.

Steinert, Moritz [Morris] (*b* Scheinfeld, Bavaria, 9 March 1831; *d* New Haven, Conn., 21 Jan 1912). American music dealer and collector of instruments. He moved to New Haven in 1854, and in 1856 moved to Savannah, Georgia. Shortly after the Civil War broke out he returned to New Haven, and his name appeared in the New Haven City Directory in 1862; by 1866 he was listed as a piano and music dealer. He formed the Mathushek Pianoforte Co. and later the M. Steinert & Sons Co., which sold pianos in Boston, Providence, New Haven and other cities. He was active in the musical life of New Haven where he was organist at St Thomas's Church, taught music and formed a quartet in which he played cello. He later formed an orchestra which was to become the nucleus around which he founded the New Haven SO in 1894. This orchestra is the fourth oldest in the USA with a continuous existence. He became interested in antique musical instruments and the problems involved in playing them, and assembled a collection of considerable importance which was exhibited in Vienna in 1892 at the International Exhibition of Music and the Drama, and in 1893 at the World's Columbian Exposition. In 1893 he published *The Catalogue of the M. Steinert Collection of Keyed and Stringed Instruments*, dedicated to his friend A. J. Hipkins. In 1900 he published his *Reminiscences*. In the same year he donated his collection to Yale University, forming the basis for what has become one of the world's important collections of musical instruments.

RICHARD REPHANN

Steingaden [Staingaden], **Constantin** (*b* Wangen, Bavaria, *c*1618; *d* Konstanz, 6 March 1675). German composer resident in Switzerland. In 1631 he entered the Jesuit College at Lucerne. By 1644 he was a Franciscan monk and was living at Engelberg, where he was recognized as an authority on organs. Later he was Kapellmeister of the Franciscan monastery at Konstanz and at the cathedral there. He probably held these positions until his death; certainly at the time of his surviving publications in 1666 he was Kapellmeister of the cathedral. These publications are *Flores hyemnales prompti ex horto a 3. 4. vocibus, cum 2 violinis, motettis, missis, sonatis et vesteris* op.4 (Konstanz, 1666), and *Messe concertate* for four and five voices, with instruments (Innsbruck, 1666); in MSS at *S-Uu* there are two masses and three motets by him for four to six voices, most of them with strings. His mass settings are unpretentious and always well conceived for their liturgical purpose. The text is never cut. Themes with a wide range and a moderate use of melismas ensure that the text can be clearly heard. The masses make modest use of instruments: some require only two violins as accompanying instruments. Stylistically they present a mixture of old and new elements. On the one hand expressive melodic lines are given broad scope, and there are many solo passages. In concertate sections Steingaden avoided over-frequent interchange between groups of performers: in those movements with long texts the disposition of the forces generally remains the same within each verse. On the other hand there are frequent traces of the old church modes.

BIBLIOGRAPHY

K. Eubel: *Geschichte der oberdeutschen (Strassburger) Minoriten-Provinz* (Würzburg, 1886)

W. Vogt: *Die Messe in der Schweiz im 17. Jahrhundert* (Schwarzenburg, 1940)

LUISE MARRETTA-SCHÄR

Steingräber. German firm of piano makers. One of the oldest and most notable Bavarian piano manufacturers, it was founded by Eduard Steingräber (*b* Rudolstadt, 20 Aug 1823; *d* Bayreuth, 14 Dec 1906), who from 1840 to 1844 trained as a piano maker under his father Christian Heinrich Steingräber and his uncle Gottlieb Steingräber in Rudolstadt. After three years of travels, when he also met Streicher in Vienna, he returned to his father's workshops in 1848. In 1852 he founded his own piano workshops in Bayreuth, where his sons Georg Steingräber (*b* 1858) and Burkhard Steingräber (1866–1945) became partners in 1892. Georg moved to Berlin in 1906 and became a leading maker of modern harpsichords. Burkhard's son-in-law Heinrich Hermann became head of the firm Steingräber & Sons in 1920. From 1951 Heinrich Schmidt, Hermann's nephew, directed the firm.

BIBLIOGRAPHY

Zum 75jährigen Bestehen der Hofpianoforte- und Flügelfabrik Steingräber & Söhne, Bayreuth (Bayreuth, 1927)

F. J. Hirt: *Meisterwerke des Klavierbaues* (Olten, 1955; Eng. trans., 1968)

THEODOR WOHNHAAS

Steingräber, Theodor Leberecht (*b* Neustadt an der Orla, 25 Jan 1830; *d* Leipzig, 5 April 1904). German music publisher. He acquired a reputation as a music teacher and under the pseudonym Gustav Damm published a world-famous piano tutor (1868); subsequently he founded the Steingräber publishing house in Hanover (1878), moving it to Leipzig in 1890. The central feature of the publishing programme was a series of editions of classical works (Edition Steingräber) prepared by Hans Bischoff, Hermann Keller, Franz

Kullak, Henri Marteau and others. The arrangers and editors of school and teaching material included M. A. Frey, Julius Klengel and Richard Kleinmichel. A son-in-law of Steingräber, Walter Friedel, managed the firm from 1903 to 1916 and it has remained in the family's possession. After suffering severe damage in World War II it moved to Frankfurt in 1953, and to Offenbach am Main in 1956.

HANS-MARTIN PLESSKE

Steinhardt, Milton (*b* Miami, Oklahoma, 13 Nov 1909). American musicologist. He attended the University of Kansas for two years, then studied the violin in New York, Munich, Paris and Berlin. He returned to America to take the BMus at the Eastman School of Music (1936); the following year he received the MMus from Eastman. In 1937 and 1938 he worked with Kinkeldey as a graduate student at Cornell University, then began studies at New York University, where his professors included Sachs and Reese; he was awarded the PhD by New York University in 1950. He taught at Central Washington College (1938–1942) and was on the faculty of Michigan State College (1948–50) and at Ohio University (1950–51). In 1951 he was appointed chairman of the department of music history at the University of Kansas; he retired in 1975.

Steinhardt's research has centred on the sacred music of the 16th-century composers at the Habsburg court, particularly Jacobus Vaet. His monograph on the composer (1951) includes a biographical study, a stylistic analysis of the motets which constitute the bulk of Vaet's output, and an evaluation of Vaet's position and influence among his contemporaries. The book was later supplemented by a seven-volume edition of Vaet's music.

WRITINGS
Jacobus Vaet and his Motets (diss., New York U., 1950; East Lansing, Mich., 1951)
'The Hymns of Jacobus Vaet', *JAMS*, ix (1956), 245
'Addenda to the Biography of Jacobus Vaet', *The Commonwealth of Music, in Honor of Curt Sachs* (New York, 1965), 229
'The *Missa Si me tenes*: a Problem of Authorship', *Aspects of Medieval and Renaissance Music: a Birthday Offering to Gustave Reese* (New York, 1966), 756
Review of C. MacClintock: *Giaches de Wert (1535–1596): Life and Works* (Rome, 1966), *MQ*, liii (1967), 585
'The "Notes de Pinchart" and the Flemish Chapel of Charles V', *Renaissance-muziek 1400–1600: donum natalicium René Bernard Lenaerts* (Louvain, 1969), 285

EDITIONS
J. Vaet: Sämtliche Werke, DTÖ, xcviii, c, ciii–civ, cviii–cix, cxiii–cxiv, cxvi, cxviii (Vienna, 1961–8)
A. du Gaucquier: Sämtliche Werke, DTÖ, cxxiii (Vienna, 1971)
P. de Monte: New Complete Edition (Louvain, 1975–)

PAULA MORGAN

Steinitz, (Charles) Paul (Joseph) (*b* Chichester, 25 Aug 1909). British organist, conductor and teacher. After study at the RAM and privately with George Oldroyd, he became parish church organist at Ashford, Kent (1933–42). In 1947 he founded a chorus, the South London (later simply London) Bach Society, and from 1949 to 1961 was organist and choirmaster at St Bartholomew-the-Great, London. His performances of the *St Matthew Passion* there, from 1952, were the first in Britain to give the work complete, in German, and with small forces – a pioneering emancipation of Bach from the traditional English adaptation. He was probably the first conductor in Britain to revive the use of the old clarino trumpet in Bach (City of London Festival, 1962). Under his direction the London Bach

Society has toured in Germany, the Low Countries, Israel, Italy and the USA, sometimes with his own Steinitz Bach Players (founded 1969). In 1953 the society gave the first performance of Rubbra's *Song of the Soul* and in 1963 the first performance in Britain of Dallapiccola's *Canti di prigionia*. Steinitz has conducted orchestras in New Zealand (1970) and Australia (1971) and has recorded choral music by Bach, Handel and Schütz. He was appointed a professor at the RAM in 1945, and was on the teaching staff of Goldsmiths' College, University of London, from 1948 to 1976. The discipline he cultivated as a teacher and writer was reinforced in his conducting by strong personal qualities: the London Bach Society's performance (1967) of Schoenberg's *Friede auf Erden*, given with the rarely heard supporting orchestral parts, was praised for its urgency and commitment. He has published several books directed towards the study of harmony and counterpoint based on the example of great composers.

WRITINGS
'German Church Music', *Opera and Church Music 1630–1750*, NOHM, v (1975), 557–776
Bach's Passions (London and New York, 1979)

ARTHUR JACOBS

Steinkopf, Otto (*b* Stolberg, 28 June 1904; *d* Celle, 17 Feb 1980). German woodwind instrument maker. As a boy he learnt to play many wind instruments, and after graduating from high school in Magdeburg he studied music in Berlin, and later musicology with Curt Sachs. He attended the Stern Conservatory, and thereafter was employed by the Leipzig Gewandhaus Orchestra, the Berlin PO and the Berlin RSO. From 1950 to 1953, he worked at the Berlin Instrument Collection of the Institut für Musikforschung as a restorer of woodwind instruments, and began to copy old instruments. In 1953 he performed at the Schütz Festival in Hereford; the concerts included a quartet of crumhorns made by himself. In 1954 he became a performing member of and instrument maker for the Cappella Coloniensis. From 1955 Steinkopf was most active as a maker of historical woodwind instruments, and from 1964 he worked in collaboration with the firm of Hermann Moeck in Celle.

Steinkopf was the first maker in the 20th century to reproduce many Renaissance and Baroque woodwind instruments. He renewed traditions of design and craftsmanship lost many generations ago. He performed on many of his instruments and made several gramophone records. His work is outstanding in the making of crumhorns, kortholts, rackets, dulcians, shawms, cornetts and Baroque bassoons and oboes. Seldom content to copy old instruments exactly, he frequently added keys to increase the instruments' range, or altered their design to suit his standards of intonation, pitch and tone quality.

FRIEDRICH VON HUENE

Steinmetz. *See* STAMITZ family.

Steinmetz, Johann Erhard (*fl c*1750). Oboist, probably of German extraction. He appears in the Dresden court calendars of 1747 and 1750 as a wind player in the court hunting-band. Several subsequent references identify him as a composer, possibly owing to the erroneous use of the name Steinmetz on many works actually by Johann Stamitz. Breitkopf's *Verzeichniss musicalischer*

Werke (i, 1761, p.51) lists without incipits 'VI. partite à 6 voci' by 'Steinmetz, musico in Dresda'; these are probably identical in part with the 'V. partite del Sigr. Steinmetz, a 6 e 4 voci' given in the Breitkopf catalogue of 1765 (p.11). The catalogue of 1762 lists 'VI. sinfonie del Steinmetz, musico in Dresda' (p.26); however, at least five of these symphonies are of doubtful authenticity, a fact that calls Breitkopf's reliability on the entire matter into question: two (nos.5–6) are definitely by Stamitz, and three others (nos.1–2, 4) exist in one or more manuscripts with conflicting attributions. A further reference to Steinmetz as a composer occurs in Hiller's *Wöchentliche Nachrichten*, though this information could have been taken directly from Breitkopf's listings, which Hiller would surely have known. Gerber's article on Steinmetz (1792), which maintains that about 1758 he was 'known and loved for his various instrumental works in manuscript such as symphonies, partitas, and works for harp', is apparently indebted to both Hiller and Breitkopf, and has little value as independent evidence. It appears that most of the works attributed to Steinmetz in 18th-century manuscripts – insofar as they are correctly attributed at all – are by Stamitz.

A second musician referred to as Steinmetz was a horn player in various orchestras in Paris in the years 1754–7. A horn player whose name is given as both Stamitz and Stamich in Parisian listings for 1757 and 1759 is probably identical with him.

See also STAMITZ family, (1) Johann.

BIBLIOGRAPHY

GerberL

J. A. Hiller, ed.: *Wöchentliche Nachrichten*, ii (1767–8/*R*1970), 92n

F. Noack: 'Die Steinmetz-Manuskripte der Landes- und Hochschulbibliothek Darmstadt', *Mf*, xiii (1960), 314

P. Gradenwitz: 'Die Steinmetz-Manuskripte der Landes- und Hochschulbibliothek Darmstadt', *Mf*, xiv (1961), 214

J. LaRue and J. B. Holland: 'Steinmetz, Johann Erhard', *MGG*

B. S. Brook, ed.: *The Breitkopf Thematic Catalogue, 1762–1787* (New York, 1966)

E. K. Wolf: *The Symphonies of Johann Stamitz: Authenticity, Chronology, and Style* (diss., New York U., 1972)

EUGENE K. WOLF

Steinmeyer, G. F. German firm of organ builders. It was founded by Georg Friedrich Steinmeyer (*b* Walxheim, Württemberg, 21 Oct 1819; *d* Oettingen, 22 Feb 1901) who, after a period of study with A. Thoma of Oettingen, became an assistant of E. F. Walker of Ludwigsburg, set up on his own in Oettingen in 1847 and produced his first organ in 1848 at Frankenhofen. Under his management over 700 organs were built, including the cathedral organs of Bamberg, Munich and Speyer. His son Friedrich Johannes Steinmeyer (*b* Oettingen, 27 June 1857; *d* Oettingen, 22 July 1928) became a partner in 1884, and owner in 1901. He was responsible for the preservation of the Trinity organ built by K. J. Riepp at the Benedictine abbey of Ottobeuren (restored despite the abbey's plans for its reconstruction). In 1928 he built for Passau Cathedral the largest church organ in the world (at that time), with five manuals and 208 stops. His son Hans Steinmeyer (*b* Oettingen, 6 Aug 1889; *d* Oettingen, 3 Jan 1970) worked in the USA as an organ builder from 1913 to 1920 before returning to Oettingen, where he became a partner in the firm in 1924 and owner in 1928. The knowledge and skill which he had gained in the USA were applied successfully to his instruments, which included those in the Friedenskirche, Nuremberg (1929, four manuals, 67 stops); Trondheim Cathedral (1929,

four manuals, 139 stops); the university church at Erlangen (1935, four manuals, 70 stops); St Lorenz, Nuremberg (1937, five manuals, 157 stops); St Mary's organ at Ottobeuren (five manuals, 82 stops); St Michaelis, Hamburg (1960, five manuals, 90 stops); the Hercules Hall at Munich (1962, four manuals, 75 stops) and the Meistersingerhalle at Nuremberg (1963, four manuals, 86 stops). From 1967 the firm has been managed by Hans Steinmeyer's son, Fritz (*b* Oettingen, 8 Dec 1918), who has built organs at the Christuskirche, Düren (1967, four manuals, 65 stops); the church of the Holy Spirit, Schweinfurt (1967, three manuals, 45 stops); the town church of Pforzheim, four manuals, 61 stops); St Mark's Church, Stuttgart (1969, three manuals, 62 stops); the Lutheran church at Remscheid (1971, three manuals, 38 stops); the Hall of Congress, Augsburg (1972, four manuals, 65 stops); the Herz-Jesu-Kirche, Nuremberg (1973, three manuals, 38 stops); SS Vitus and Deokar, Herrieden (1974, three manuals, 35 stops), and St Stephen's, Lindau (1975, three manuals, 48 stops).

Until 1890 Steinmeyer & Co. built nearly all their organs with cone valve chests and mechanical actions; subsequently pouch chests controlled by tubular pneumatic action came into use, but after 1945 these were superseded by slider chests with tracker action. The firm, which has clients in Austria, Norway, Argentina and the USA, carried out important restoration work at Ottobeuren in 1914 and 1922 (on a 1757 organ with four manuals, 48 stops; and a 1766 organ with two manuals, 27 stops) and at Weingarten in 1954 (on a large organ of 1737–50). The instrument built under the direction of Max Reger for the Shooting Gallery Hall in Meiningen (1913, three manuals, 45 stops) is now a memorial organ in Berlin.

BIBLIOGRAPHY

E. Rupp: *Die Entwicklungsgeschichte der Orgelbaukunst* (Einsiedeln, 1929)

O. Dietz and J. G. Mehl: *Lorenzer Orgelbüchlein* (Kassel, 1937)

H. Meyer: *Karl Joseph Riepp, der Orgelbauer von Ottobeuren* (Kassel, 1938)

J. Wörsching: *Der Orgelbauer Karl Riepp* (Mainz, 1940)

F. Högner: *Hundert Jahre G. F. Steinmeyer & Co.* (Oettingen, 1947)

J. G. Mehl: 'Nürnberg – "die deutsche Orgelstadt" ', *Gottesdienst und Kirchenmusik*, iii (1953), 79

Marienorgel Ottobeuren (Augsburg, 1957)

H. Fischer: '125 Jahre Orgelbau Steinmeyer', *Ars organi*, xx (1972), 1782

H. Fischer and T. Wohnhaas: *Orgelbau Steinmeyer seit 1847* (Oettingen, 1972)

R. Quoika: *Steinmeyer Orgeln seit 1847* (Oettingen, 1972)

HANS KLOTZ

Steinmez. *See* STAMITZ family.

Steinpress, Boris Solomonovich. *See* SHTEYNPRESS, BORIS SOLOMONOVICH.

Steinspiel (Ger.). LITHOPHONE.

Steinway. American firm of piano makers. Heinrich Engelhard Steinway (Steinweg) (*b* Wolfshagen, 15 Feb 1797; *d* New York, 7 Feb 1871) built his first piano in 1836, and exhibited two squares and a grand at the Brunswick state fair in 1839. Emigrating to New York in 1850 he established his firm there in 1853 and took a prize at the 1855 American Institute fair with an overstrung iron-framed square which was widely acclaimed in the USA where square pianos were still popular. The application of similar techniques to a grand in 1859, and to an upright in 1863 was, however, of far greater consequence. Within its first decade Steinway was already producing 2000 instruments a year, but the death of Heinrich Steinway's sons, Henry (1831–65), who was responsible for the first seven patents, and Charles (1829–65), precipitated a crisis. It was met by C. F. Theodor Steinweg (1825–89, who in the USA took the name Theodore Steinway), the eldest of Heinrich Engelhard's sons, who sold his German business (later GROTRIAN-STEINWEG) and joined the family in New York. A gifted scientist and superb craftsman, Theodore consolidated a technological revolution that fundamentally changed conceptions of piano design and tone throughout the world. Massive iron frames were overstrung in a fan-like design (see PIANOFORTE, figs.28 and 29), with heavy strings at high tensions. Bridges were placed at the centre of the soundboard, and large, machine-covered hammers with thick felts were used. Actions were adapted to give the player complete control over a tone of unprecedented volume and richness. 41 patents were registered by Theodore during his 20 years in the USA, including the duplex scale, cupola metal frame, middle sustaining pedal (which retains the dampers of notes already held down) and capo d'astro agraffe. Steinway instruments of the late 1880s were essentially modern pianos, a generation ahead of their competitors.

It was fortunate that Theodore's skills should be complemented by the entrepreneurial flair of his brother William Steinway (1836–96), a resourceful business man who could play the piano and was interested in music – a rare combination of qualities in the annals of the industry. His techniques of promotion and marketing were essentially the same as those adopted by the great piano makers of the past: the cultivation of an image of excellence by association with eminent musicians and aristocratic patronage. But he operated on an international scale, with an extraordinary grasp of the potentialities of new markets and communications. Railways enabled him to transform a tour by a virtuoso into the marathons undertaken by Anton Rubinstein (215 concerts during the 1872–3 American season) and later by Rosenthal and Paderewski. Costly appearances at the great exhibitions, a unique feature of this period, were rewarded by highly publicized prizes and the rapid acquisition of an international reputation. A London success in 1862 was merely a preliminary to victory at the magnificent Paris Exhibition of 1867. There followed an acrimonious dispute with Chickering, Steinway's only serious, and longer established, rival in the USA, as to which firm had gained the higher award. The verdict (probably in Steinway's favour) was less significant than the fact that both names were firmly imprinted on people's minds. In view of later confusion about their respective contribution to the new technology, however, it should be noted that the Chickering grand and upright pianos exhibited in 1867 had parallel strings – only their squares were overstrung. It was the 'Steinway system', freely acknowledged as such, which was adopted by German manufacturers with resounding acclaim at the 1873 Vienna Exhibition, and by virtually every successful maker thereafter. Patronage was led by the courts of Europe and the Rothschilds; musicians' endorsements included those of Berlioz, Wagner, Liszt and Saint-Saëns.

A Hamburg branch was opened in 1880 and annual production was about 2500 pianos, shared between the two factories. By the 20th century their supremacy was challenged in Europe (outside France) only by Bechstein and, perhaps, Blüthner, and in the USA by Baldwin,

Knabe, and Mason & Hamlin. During the 1930s output was substantially reduced, but the firm survived, and the general standard of materials and workmanship was arguably higher than at any time before or since. Several refinements were patented during this period, including the 'accelerated action' perfected for the pianist Josef Hoffman.

Since World War II Steinway pianos have continued to dominate concert platforms, although Bösendorfer in Europe and Baldwin in the USA are formidable rivals. The association with leading pianists continues to lend a prestige to Steinway's pianos, enabling some of them, including uprights, to command prices higher than equivalent instruments by other makers. But in the mid-1960s Steinway withdrew their finest upright model (model K) and in 1972 the firm was sold to CBS.

BIBLIOGRAPHY

A. J. Hipkins: *A Description and History of the Pianoforte* (London, 1896, rev. 3/1929/R1975)
A. Dolge: *Pianos and their Makers* (Covina, Calif., 1911/R1972)
T. E. Steinway: *People and Pianos* (New York, 1953, 2/1961)
A. Loesser: *Men, Women and Pianos: a Social History* (New York, 1954)
C. Ehrlich: *The Piano: a History* (London, 1976)

CYRIL EHRLICH

Steinway Hall. (1) New York concert hall, open 1866–90, where STEINWAY promoted concerts.

(2) London concert hall, built next to the Steinway & Sons premises in 1878; see LONDON, §VI, 5(iii).

Steinweg, C(arl) F(riedrich) Theodor [Steinway, Theodore] (*b* Seesen, nr. Goslar, 6 Nov 1825; *d* Brunswick, 26 March 1889). German piano manufacturer, who worked first for the German firm that was later known as GROTRIAN-STEINWEG and later in his father's New York firm STEINWAY.

Steinweg, Heinrich Engelhard (*b* Wolfshagen, 15 Feb 1797; *d* New York, 7 Feb 1871). German instrument maker, founder of the American piano-making firm of STEINWAY.

Stella, Alfred. Pseudonym of ROBERT ROY PATERSON.

Stella, Scipione [Don Pietro Paolo] (*b* ?Naples, ?1559; *d* Naples, between 1610 and 1630). Italian organist and composer. He was recommended in 1579 by his teacher G. D. Nola, *maestro di cappella* of the Annunziata in Naples, for the job of organist at that church. He held the post from October 1583 until some time in 1593, possibly May. On 7 February 1590 the governors of the Annunziata contracted F. Scoppa and C. Scala to build a second organ there to Stella's satisfaction, and Giovanni Macque became the second organist. Sebastián Raval mentioned in May 1593 that Stella had performed Raval's madrigals with Scipione Dentice, Marenzio and others in Cardinal Montalto's palace in Rome. By 1594 Stella was in the service of Gesualdo and accompanied him to Ferrara for his wedding to Leonora d'Este. While he was there Stella prepared for publication Gesualdo's first two books of madrigals in 1594 and his own book of five-part motets in 1595, which he dedicated to Duke Alfonso II. In 1601 Cerreto mentioned Stella as an excellent organist and composer. Some time between 1601 and 1603 he entered the Theatine monastery of S Paolo Maggiore in Naples, titling himself Don Pietro Paolo Stella; in 1603 he supervised the construction of an organ for the monastery. On 29 July 1610 Stella's nephew Francesco dedicated to Cardinal Montalto a book of five-part hymns which Stella had composed for the devotions in the monastery. In 1618, Fabio Colonna mentioned that his friend 'Padre Stella' had built an enharmonic harpsichord with eight sets of strings and had composed music for it. Both Capaccio and De Pietri in 1634 referred to Stella's death.

Stella's motets only rarely paraphrase chant; they are thoroughly imitative, show little rhythmic contrast or chromaticism and have few strong cadences. The hymns, however, which use chromatic chords in strong rhythms, are akin to the frottolas which later became popular in Naples. They are to be performed *alternatim* with the appropriate chant. Stella's extant madrigals are similar to those of Scipione Dentice and Nenna, showing none of the extremes characteristic of Gesualdo's music.

WORKS

SACRED

[20] Motectorum liber primus, 5vv (Ferrara, ?1595)
[20] Hymnorum ecclesiasticorum liber primus, 5vv (Naples, 1610)
Pange lingua gloriosa, 3vv; O quam suavis, 3vv: *I-Nc*
Masses, Vespers: lost, cited by C. Tutini (MS, *Nn*)

SECULAR

Primo libro de madrigali, 5vv (Naples, 1609); lost, cited in Wolffheim catalogue
Madrigals, 1587[12], 1615[14]
3 further books of madrigals; lost, cited in Müller von Asow

INSTRUMENTAL

Variation, 1609[34] [on a piece by A. Ferrabosco]
4 canzonas, a 4, *Nc* 4.6.3
3 keyboard works, *GB-Lbm* Add.30491

BIBLIOGRAPHY

F. Colonna: *La sambuca lincea* (Naples, 1618), 6, 69
G. C. Capaccio: *Il forastiero* (Naples, 1634), 7
F. De Pietri: *Dell'historia napoletana* (Naples, 1634), 70
C. D'Addosio: *Origine vicende storiche e progressi della Real S. Casa dell'Annunziata di Napoli Ospizio dei Trovatelli* (Naples, 1883)
U. Prota-Giurleo: 'La musica a Napoli nel Seicento', *Samnium*, i (1928), 69f
Versteigerung der Musikbibliothek des Herrn Dr. Werner Wolffheim, ii (1929), 373
E. H. Müller von Asow, ed.: *Heinrich Schütz: Gesammelte Briefe und Schriften* (Regensburg, 1931), 117f
G. Pannain: *L'oratorio dei Filippini e la scuola musicale di Napoli*, IMi, v (1934), xix–xx, xlviii–liii

KEITH A. LARSON

Stelle, Officium (Lat.: 'Ceremony of the star'). The title sometimes given in medieval manuscripts and adopted by modern scholars to denote a group of medieval Latin church plays, or dramatic ceremonies, of the 11th to 13th centuries, dealing with the visit of the Magi to the infant Christ. Their Latin title reflects the prominence given to the guiding star, which in the performances was drawn along a cord. To judge from the surviving texts (listed in Young, Lipphardt and Donovan), the development did not follow an orderly chronological plan from simple to complex, nor did such a development lag behind that of the Easter plays. Compared with the number of *Visitatio sepulchri* texts, the Christmas plays are few, but they are varied and complex. Some 14 or 15 texts with music survive, including elaborate versions from Fleury (*F-O* 201) and Rouen (*F-R(m)* 384). In its most characteristic form the *Officium stelle* opens with a threefold chant, based on an antiphon of Lauds, *Stella ista*; the musical amplifications include antiphons, responsories, hymns and processional chants, as well as newly composed melodies. Liturgically, some of the plays may have originated as dramatized offertories (in the Mass) at which the Magi brought gifts. But the liturgical placing of the plays is very variable. The two

most noteworthy dramatic additions to the simple *oblatio* (offering) are an un-scriptural encounter between the Magi and the shepherds, and the introduction of Herod in a court setting.

For further information and bibliography *see* MEDIEVAL DRAMA, §II, 2, esp. Young (1933), Donovan (1958) and Lipphardt (1963).

JOHN STEVENS

Stellfeld, Jean-Auguste (*b* Antwerp, 17 Feb 1881; *d* Antwerp, 14 Sept 1952). Belgian jurist and musicologist. After studies in law at the University of Louvain he established himself as a lawyer in Antwerp, becoming a judge and eventually vice-president of the local court. In his youth, he spent his spare time building up an important collection of old instruments, music MSS and rare prints, the Bibliotheca Stellfeldiana, which grew into one of the richest private music collections in the world, and his house became a meeting place for Belgian and foreign musicologists. After his death the collection was acquired by the University of Michigan and is now part of the music library at Ann Arbor. Among its 20,000 volumes are works of principal composers of the 16th to 18th centuries, in particular the Bach sons, 18th-century French operas and 16th-century Flemish songs.

Stellfeld was keenly involved in the cultural life of his native town. He was a whole-hearted supporter of the Concerten voor Gewijde Muziek (1903–14), and he became secretary of the Supervisory Commission of the Koninklijk Vlaams Conservatorium (1913–52). He was founder and first president of the Vereniging voor Muziekgeschiedenis (1931–52), the first president of the Conservatorium Concerten (1934–52) and vice-president of the Société Belge de Musicologie (1946–52). His musicological research was almost exclusively historical; he concentrated particularly on the Golden Age of Antwerp.

WRITINGS

'Het muziekhistorisch belang der catalogi en inventarissen van het Plantijnsch archief', *Vlaams jaarboek voor muziekgeschiedenis*, ii–iii (1940–41), 5–50
Bronnen tot de geschiedenis der Antwerpsche clavecimbel- en orgelbouwers in de XVI en XVII eeuwen (Antwerp, 1942)
Andries Pevernage: zijn leven – zijne werken (Louvain, 1943)
Bibliographie des éditions musicales plantiniennes (Brussels, 1949)

BIBLIOGRAPHY

L. E. Cuyler, G. A. Sutherland and H. T. David: 'The University of Michigan's Purchase of the Stellfeld Music Library: a Summary of the Collection', *Notes*, xii (1954–5), 41
A. Corbet: 'In memoriam Jean-Auguste Stellfeld', *Jaarboek van de Vereniging voor muziekgeschiedenis te Antwerpen*, v (Antwerp, 1959), 14

JACQUES VAN DEUN

Stellovsky, Fyodor Timofeyevich (*b* 1826; *d* 1875). Russian music publisher. He built up his firm on the basis of Klever's publishing house, which he acquired in about 1850. He also took over the smaller business of Gurskalin, who had been publishing music in St Petersburg from 1838 and who owned Denotkin's printing press, established in 1844. Stellovsky was particularly known as the publisher of Glinka's music; in fact it was his editions that first introduced Rimsky-Korsakov to Glinka's two operas. He also published the works of Balakirev (who, in his early, impecunious years, helped Stellovsky to prepare other composers' scores for publication), Serov and Dargomïzhsky. After Stellovsky's death the business was carried on by his widow and then by his sister; in 1886 it was taken over by Gutheil.

BIBLIOGRAPHY

B. P. Yurgenson: *Ocherk istorii notopechataniya* [An outline of the history of music printing] (Moscow, 1928)

A. S. Lyapunova: 'Kratkiy obzor istorii izdaniya proizvedeniy M. I. Glinki' [A short account of the history of the publication of Glinka's works], *M. A. Balakirev: perepiska s notoizdatel'stvom P. Yurgensona*, ed. V. A. Kiselyov and A. S. Lyapunova (Moscow, 1958), 369

E. Garden: *Balakirev: a Critical Study of his Life and Music* (London, 1967)

B. L. Vol'man: *Russkiye notnïye izdaniya XIX – nachala XX veka* [Russian music publishing in the 19th and early 20th centuries] (Leningrad, 1970)

GEOFFREY NORRIS

Stellwagen. German family of organ builders. Friedrich Stellwagen (*b* Halle; *d* Stralsund, 1659) went to Hamburg as a journeyman with Gottfried Fritzsche, whose daughter he subsequently married. In 1635 he moved to Lübeck to set up on his own, and carried out extensive work on the cathedral organ (1635–6) and on the organs of the Jakobikirche (1636–7), St Mary's (1637–41, 1653–5), St Peter's (1643–6) and St Egidius' (1648). He also undertook work in Lüneburg, at the churches of St Mary (1650), St John (1651–2) and St Lambert (1652; this work was in fact not carried out until 1661–5 by his son-in-law, Michael Berigel). In Hamburg Stellwagen worked at the church of St Katharine (1664–7) and in Mölln at St Nicolas's (1637–41), where he criticized Jakob Scherer's pipework. His most significant instrument was at the church of St Mary in Stralsund (1653–9), with 51 stops on three manuals and a pedal keyboard (restored by H. J. and K. Schuke, 1946–59).

Stellwagen built his organs in the north-German Baroque style, developed by Hans Scherer the elder and Gottfried Fritzsche; in addition to complete choruses of diapason scaled pipes, reed stops and wide-scaled pipes, the organs had a number of other stops such as Blockflöte, Querflöte, Quintadena and Tierce Zimbel. Stops such as the Feldpfeife (a stop blown at the octave) and the Trichterregal (a reed stop with funnel-shaped resonators, probably invented by Stellwagen) seem to have been special features of his instruments.

Stellwagen's son Gottfried (*fl* ?1660–65) worked as an organist and organ builder in Güstrow about 1661, and subsequently moved to Heide, Holstein, by about 1664.

BIBLIOGRAPHY

W. Stahl: *Geschichte der Kirchenmusik in Lübeck* (Kassel, 1931)

H. Distler and E. Thienhaus: *Die beiden Orgeln in St. Jakobi zu Lübeck* (Lübeck, 1935)

D. W. Prost: 'Die Stellwagen-Orgel in der Marienkirche zu Stralsund: Beschreibung und Geschichte', *Greifswald-Stralsunder Jb*, vi (1966). 225; vii (1967), 267; viii (1969), 197

HANS KLOTZ

Stemmelius [Stemmele], **Gregor** (*d* Irsee, nr. Kaufbeuren, Swabia, 16 May 1619). German composer. About 1600, together with Johann Seytz and Carolus Andreae, he composed liturgical music for the Benedictine abbey at Irsee, of which he was a member. His surviving works show that he handled competently the techniques of vocal polyphony.

WORKS

(in D-Rp unless otherwise stated)

Missa super 'Si ignoras te', 6vv

2 antiphons, responsories, 6 hymns, falsobordoni, 4–6vv

2 motets, 4, 5vv, *As*

Motet, 8vv, *Mbs* (org tablature)

BIBLIOGRAPHY

U. Kornmüller: *Die Pflege der Musik im Benedictiner-Orden* (Würzburg and Vienna, 1881), ii, 231

AUGUST SCHARNAGL

Stenborg, Carl (*b* Stockholm, 25 Sept 1752; *d* Stockholm, 1 Aug 1813). Swedish tenor, impresario and composer. He was the son of Petter Stenborg, a theatre manager. From the age of 14 he sang at concerts in Stockholm and studied vocal and instrumental music with the court Kapellmeister F. Zellbell. From 1767 he pursued government office work and theatre work concurrently, before studying for a time at the University of Uppsala. Encouraged by the king to make his opera début he sang Peleus in F. A. B. Uttini's *Thetis och Pelée* for the inaugural performance of the Royal Swedish Opera (1773). In 1782 he was appointed singer to the court and elected a member of the Academy of Music.

Stenborg composed and conducted incidental music for plays performed at his father's theatre, and in 1780 undertook its management. With the librettist Carl Envallsson he adapted Singspiels and *opéras comiques* for performance in the theatre. He engaged the conductors Haeffner and Zander successively, introducing works by Dezède, Duni, Grétry, Monsigny, Pergolesi, Philidor, Piccinni and Sacchini. After Zander's death in 1796 the theatre declined in popularity and closed in 1799. Stenborg managed another theatre after his retirement from the Royal Opera in 1806.

Stenborg's known works include music for two plays, *Casper och Dorothea* (1775) and *Konung Gustaf Adolfs jagt* (1777), as well as *Petis och Thelée* (C. I. Hallman), a parody of Uttini's opera produced in Stockholm on 27 September 1779. His most important composition is the Singspiel *Gustaf Ericsson i Dalarna* (Envallsson), performed in 1784. Several of his arias and songs were published in Stockholm journals and anthologies between 1789 and 1798.

BIBLIOGRAPHY

J. Flodmark: *Stenborgska skådebanorna* (Stockholm, 1893)

——: *Elisabeth Olin och Carl Stenborg* (Stockholm, 1903)

N. Personne: *Svenska teatern*, i–iii (Stockholm, 1913–15)

S. Lindström: 'Vårt första nationella sångspel', *STMf*, xxiv (1942), 68

KATHLEEN DALE/C.-G. S. MÖRNER

Stendhal [Beyle, Henri] (*b* Grenoble, 23 Jan 1783; *d* Paris, 22 March 1842). French writer. His passionate love of Italy and the Italians derived from his fascination with Italian opera, and explains the epitaph on his tombstone: 'Arrigo Beyle, cittadino Milanese'. He regretted that he had not devoted his life to music, being certain that he was a born composer. When in Milan he would study the libretto of the opera he was to attend and instinctively add his own music to the words; during the performance he found he often preferred his own melodies to those of Cimarosa.

Stendhal's musical education was scanty, being limited to a few singing, violin and clarinet lessons. He attached himself to Angelina Bereyter, *seconda diva* of the Odéon, of whose performances in *Il matrimonio segreto* he claimed to have attended 60 to 100 between 1811 and 1813, sometimes three a week. Cimarosa was the composer he most admired, followed by Mozart and Rossini, and, as distant emulators, Paisiello, Pergolesi and Simon Mayr. In later years, however, he found Cimarosa trifling and Rossini flighty. With the exception of Mozart, whose works he appreciated at a time when they were little known, Stendhal never really liked instrumental music. His remarks on Haydn were all plagiarized from Giuseppe Carpani's *Le Haydine, ovvero Lettere sulla vita e le opere del celebre maestro Giuseppe Haydn* (1812); he even appropriated

Carpani's private reminiscences of Haydn and Vienna, in *Lettres . . . sur le célèbre compositeur Haydn* published under the pseudonym of César Bombet (1814).

The only other work dealing directly with music is his *Vie de Rossini*, witty and urbane, erroneous in detail yet stimulating as a work of art. Rossini himself never read it. At the time of its publication (1824), Rossini was universally idolized and Stendhal practically unknown. The assumption that Stendhal tried to use this vehicle as a means to instant fame is confirmed by his account of his supposed meeting with Rossini in Terracina in 1812 (see the entry in his *Rome, Naples et Florence en 1817* for the date *7 février*; significantly, this page was deleted in the 1826 edition). Many years later, a mutual acquaintance, an Italian in Rossini's entourage, noticed Stendhal at a reception in a Paris salon and offered to introduce him to the composer, saying to Rossini 'C'est celui qui se vante partout de vous connaître', adding that Stendhal had published Rossini's biography, claimed to have made his acquaintance in Italy and bragged of having been in his intimacy for a long time. Rossini considered Stendhal for a moment, then declined the invitation, saying that he did not wish to encourage liars and braggarts.

WRITINGS
Lettres . . . sur le célèbre compositeur Haydn, suivies d'une vie de Mozart, et de considérations sur Métastase (Paris, 1814, rev. 2/1817 as *Vies de Haydn, de Mozart et de Métastase*; Eng. trans., 1972)
Vie de Rossini (Paris, 1824, rev. 2/1922 by H. Prunières; Eng. trans., 1956, rev. 2/1970)

BIBLIOGRAPHY
A. Arnoux: 'Le goût de la musique chez Stendhal', *BSIM*, iv (1908), 397
R. Rolland: 'Stendhal et la musique', *Revue de Paris*, cv (1913), 462
J. Tiersot: *La chanson populaire et les écrivains romantiques* (1931), 291ff
J. W. Klein: 'Stendhal as Music Critic', *MQ*, xxix (1943), 18
H. H. H. Remak: 'Goethe on Stendhal', *Goethe Bicentennial Studies* (1950), 207
L. Guichard: *La musique et les lettres au temps du romantisme* (1955), 258–96
V. del Litto: Preface to *Vie de Rossini*, les oeuvres de Stendhal, ed. V. del Litto and E. Abravanel, iii (Lausanne, 1960), 9
A. RICHARD OLIVER

Stenger, Nicolaus [Nikolaus] (*b* Erfurt, 31 Aug 1609; *d* Erfurt, 5 April 1680). German theologian, teacher, hymnologist, writer on music and organist. He spent his whole life at Erfurt. He first attended the St Michael Lateinschule, where he received special encouragement from the Kantor, Bartholomäus Löneissen, a noted scholar. In 1621 he transferred to the Protestant Ratsgymnasium, which was at that time noted for its fostering of music and where one of his teachers was Liborius Capsius, director of the collegium musicum and an important Erfurt University professor. He matriculated at the university in 1626; he took his bachelor's degree in 1628 and became a Master of Philosophy in 1629. He then became organist at the Protestant church of St Thomas and at the Catholic church of the Neuwerk monastery. From 1632 to 1635 he was Kantor and teacher at the Protestant school of preaching and also studied theology. In 1635 he was ordained and became deacon (in 1638 pastor) of the Kaufmannskirche in succession to Joseph Bötticher, who had won a good reputation as a musician. In 1654 he moved to Erfurt University as professor of philosophy and in 1661 became professor of theology. In 1657 and 1664 he was elected the university's Rector Magnificus, and as pro-chancellor in 1666 and 1667 he was entrusted with administration of the chancellor's

office by the electorate of Mainz, which from 1664 exercised absolute power over Erfurt. From 1661, as head of the Protestant ministry, he was in charge of the clergy of the city and district of Erfurt. He was held in the highest regard at Erfurt as organist, Kantor, preacher and university teacher of theology and oriental languages, as well as a church and school inspector.

Besides many theological publications Stenger produced two significant musical works. The first was a textbook for use in schools, *Manuductio ad musicam theoreticam, das ist: Kurtze Anleitung zur Singekunst* (Erfurt, 1635, enlarged 2/1659, 4/1666). In this book, written in German and widely used, he provided in dialogue form a short practical introduction to figural music, followed by an anthology of fugues by various composers, most of them with words. He is specially important for his editing of the Erfurt hymnbook, *Christlich-neuvermehrt und gebessertes Gesangbuch* (Erfurt, 1663). In his 11-page preface he pointed to the frequently observed arbitrary alteration of well-known hymn tunes and expressed his desire to provide churches, schools and families with a hymnbook with correct melodies. Most of the 300 or so melodies (three of which are for two voices), for over 400 hymns, date from the first half of the 16th century; the others are from 17th-century songbooks or by Thuringian composers. A number were printed for the first time in this book, making it an important source of melodies. It was in use at Erfurt until the mid-18th century.

BIBLIOGRAPHY
EitnerQ; FétisB; GerberL; WaltherML
J. C. Motschmann: *Erfordia literata, oder Gelehrtes Erffurth*, iv (Erfurt, 1731), 568ff
J. Adlung: *Anleitung zu der musikalischen Gelahrtheit* (Erfurt, 1758/R1953), 114f, 177, 664, 672; (2/1783)
C. von Winterfeld: *Der evangelische Kirchengesang*, ii (Leipzig, 1845/R1966), 566ff
J. Zahn: *Die Melodien der deutschen evangelischen Kirchenlieder*, vi (Gütersloh, 1893/R1963), 220
S. Kümmerle: *Encyclopädie der evangelischen Kirchenmusik*, iii (Gütersloh, 1894/R1967), 516f
F. Wiegand: 'Übersicht über die Rektoren der ehemaligen Universität Erfurt von 1637 bis 1816', *Beiträge zur Geschichte der Universität Erfurt (1392–1816)*, viii (1961), 85
——: *Erfurt: eine Monographie* (Rudolstadt, 1964), 75ff, 86, 90, 180f
H. Engel: *Musik in Thüringen* (Cologne and Graz, 1966), 90
S. Orth: 'Zur Geschichte der Musikpflege an der ehemaligen Universität Erfurt', *Beiträge zur Geschichte der Universität Erfurt (1392–1816)*, xiii (1967), 130
KARL-ERNST BERGUNDER

Stenhammar, (Karl) Wilhelm (Eugen) (*b* Stockholm, 7 Feb 1871; *d* Stockholm, 20 Nov 1927). Swedish composer, pianist and conductor. He grew up in a home where the arts were strongly encouraged: his father Per Ulrik Stenhammar (1828–75) was an architect and composer (a pupil of Lindblad, he wrote sacred choral works and songs in a Mendelssohnian style) and his mother a fine draughtswoman; his uncle and aunt, Oskar Fredrik and Fredrika Stenhammar, were both singers, and their daughter Elsa (Elfrida Marguerite) became a choral conductor (she published an edition of her mother's letters, Stockholm, 1958). The Stenhammar children and their friends formed a vocal group which was highly esteemed in the upper-class circles where they entertained. Wilhelm began to compose and to play the piano as a child, without much formal training. Indeed, he never went to a conservatory but passed the organists' examination privately in 1890, after two years with Heintze and Lagergren. He did, however, attend the music school run by the eminent piano teacher Richard Andersson; and he had theory lessons from Joseph Dente in 1888–9 ('terribly boring', according to his diary sketch of 1891) and later from Emil Sjögren and Andreas Hallén. Nevertheless, in composition and conducting he must be regarded as self-taught. Several of his early compositional efforts, such as the *Tre körvisor* (c1890) and some songs, have continued to hold a place in the repertory.

Stenhammar may have considered his lack of formal instruction a handicap, for as late as 1909 he started a nine-year course of exercises, eventually covering 500 pages, based on Heinrich Bellermann's *Der Contrapunkt*. It is likely that his uncertainty and self-questioning were exacerbated by his high ambitions and by his feeling that he was seeking his own way, a way not quite in accord with what his contemporaries Peterson-Berger and Alfvén were doing. He completed his piano studies with Heinrich Barth in Berlin (1892–3) and in spring 1902 made a remarkable triple début: he performed Brahms's First Piano Concerto with the *hovkapell*; he played with the Aulin Quartet; and he had his *I rosengård* for solo voices, chorus and orchestra (1888–9) presented. Following this he appeared frequently as a soloist and gave some 1000 concerts with Aulin and his quartet all over Sweden.

Stenhammar's début as a conductor had come earlier, in 1897, when he directed the first performance of his concert overture *Excelsior!*. He held appointments as artistic director of the Stockholm Philharmonic Society (1897–1900), of the Royal Opera for one season, of the New Philharmonic Society (1904–6) and of the newly formed Göteborgs Orkesterförening (1906–22). In this last post he made the city a musical rival to Stockholm: he invited Nielsen to conduct, and he organized grand choral festivals involving large numbers of composers (notably his friend Sibelius), performers and listeners. When in 1924–5 he returned to the Royal Opera, he was already sick and physically broken.

As a composer Stenhammar began in the late Romanticism typical of Scandinavia, imbued with influences from such composers as Wagner, Liszt and Brahms. Later his work came to be dominated by a classicism of his own, based principally on a profound study of Beethoven but also on Haydn and Mozart (a fruit of his prodigious activity as a chamber musician), and on Renaissance polyphony. In his greatest compositions these traits are always tinged with a specifically Nordic colour relating to Swedish folk music, though he did not quote genuine themes to the extent that Peterson-Berger and Alfvén did. His two early music dramas, *Gildet på Solhaug* and *Tirfing*, were not successful, and though he loved the theatre and wrote a great deal of excellent incidental music, he never returned to opera. *Tirfing* (1897–8) provoked a crisis, causing him seriously to question Romantic aesthetics – and above all Wagner – but not entirely to reject them.

Stenhammar's 'second period' found him striving for more concentrated motivic work and a deeper manner. The magnificent cantata *Ett folk* (1904–5) shows these tendencies in an emotive outburst of eager national feeling; the unaccompanied hymn 'Sverige' included in the work has become one of Stenhammar's most appreciated choral pieces, though here the patriotic feeling is noble and intimate. A new stylistic advance came with the much played Second Piano Concerto, whose Beethovenian dialogue between soloists and orchestra, with the tonalities of D♯ and C♯ in contest, has a finely

improvised form. The First Symphony, however, was discarded by the composer, since the work was too obviously dependent on Beethoven, Bruckner and Wagner.

Stenhammar's third and final period may be dated from the Fifth String Quartet (1910), the first work composed after his studies in strict counterpoint. This piece lives up to its sub-title 'Serenade' in its vitality and humour, and comes to terms with folklorism in a masterly series of variations on the nursery rhyme *Riddaren Finn Komfusenfej*. Other works of the last period include two orchestral compositions which stand among the greatest in the Swedish repertory, the Serenade and the Second Symphony. The former shows Stenhammar's ripe, deep knowledge of orchestration and has a tinge of impressionist lightness combined with a quite Scandinavian nature poetry (there are hints of Strauss and Sibelius); it is at once the most aristocratic and most lighthearted of his larger works. The symphony, on the other hand, aims at objectivity, even asceticism, as may be exemplified by the Dorian feeling of its G minor tonality and the expert handling of fugato in the finale. At the same time it is full of allusions to Swedish folk music and, in the first and scherzo-like third movements, folkdance rhythms: it brings together all the best qualities he had so far displayed.

Outstanding among Stenhammar's later compositions is the cantata *Sången*, written for the 150th anniversary of the Swedish Royal Academy of Music. It consists of two main parts, the first seemingly recalling youthful *Sturm und Drang*, the second austere and slightly Handelian; these are linked by an interlude, 'Mellanspel', which is often performed separately. His other important vocal works include the early ballad *Florez och Blanzeflor*, with its brilliant orchestral accompaniment, and a large number of very finely wrought songs to poems chosen with discriminating taste. Several of these are among the most prized art songs of Sweden; the collection *Visor och stämningar* provides some exquisite examples, full of ingenious formal ideas. Finally, his series of six quartets was unique in Sweden at the time; they range from rather subservient Beethoven copies to an increasingly personal and assured style in the last three.

Stenhammar's son Claes Göran Stenhammar (1897–1968) was cantor at the Storkyrkan in Stockholm and later a teacher at the conservatory. Stenhammar himself had few pupils, though Rosenberg received certain decisive influences from him and may be said to have passed these on to younger generations.

WORKS
(selective list)

STAGE

Operas: Gildet på Solhaug op.6 (3, after Ibsen), 1892–3; Tirfing, op.15 (mystical saga-poem, prol, 2, epilogue, A. Boberg), 1897–8
Incidental music: Ett drömspel (Strindberg), concert version arr. Rosenberg, unpubd; Lodolezzi sjunger (H. Bergman), also suite, unpubd; Chitra (Tagore), suite arr. Rosenberg; Romeo och Julia (Shakespeare), also suite, unpubd

ORCHESTRAL AND VOCAL ORCHESTRAL

Orch: Pf Conc. no.1, b♭, 1893; Excelsior!, op.13, sym. ov., 1896, unpubd; Sym. no.1, F, 1902–3, unpubd; Pf Conc. no.2, d, op.23, 1904–7; 2 sentimentala romanser, f, A, op.28, vn, orch, 1910; Serenade, F, op.31, 1911–13, rev. 1919; Sym. no.2, g, op.34, 1911–15
Choral orch: I rosengård (K. A. Melin), solo vv, vv, orch, 1888–9, unpubd; Norrland (D. Fallström), male vv, orch, full score lost, arr. male vv, military band by I. Widner; Snöfrid, op.5 (V. Rydberg), solo vv, vv, orch, 1891; Ett folk, op.22 (V. von Heidenstam), Bar, vv, orch, 1904–5; Midvinter, op.24, vv, orch, 1907; Folket i Nifelhem,

Vårnatt, op.30 (O. Levertin), 1911–12, unpubd; Sången, op.44 (T. Rangström), solo vv, vv, orch, 1921
Solo vocal orch: Florez och Blanzeflor, op.3 (Levertin), Bar, orch, 1891; Ur idyll och epigram av J. L. Runeberg, op.4a, Mez, orch, 1893; Ithaka, op.21 (Levertin), Bar, orch; 4 Stockholmsdikter, op.38 (B. Bergman)

SONGS
(all 1v, pf)
Sånger och visor, c1888: I skogen (A. T. Gellerstedt), Ballad (K. A. Melin), När sol går ned (Melin)
2 visor ur En glad gut av Björnsterne Björnson, c1888: Lokkeleg, Aftenstemning
Ur Idyll och epigram av J. L. Runeberg, op.4b, 1893: Flickan kom från sin älsklings möte, Flickan knyter i Johannenatten
7 dikter ur Ensamhetens tankar av Verner von Heidenstam, op.7, 1893–5: Där innerst i min ande bor en gnista, I enslighet försvinna mina år, Min stamfar hade en stor pokal, Kom, vänner låt oss sätta oss ned, I Rom, i Rom, dit ung jag kom, Du sökte ryktbarhet, Du hade mig kär
5 visor ur Idyll och epigram av J. L. Runeberg, op.8, 1895–6: Lutad mot gärdet, Dottern sade till sin gamla moder, Den tidiga sorgen, Till en ros, Behagen
2 Minnelieder, op.9 (Walter von der Vogelweide), 1895–6: Ein Kuss vom rothen Munde, Heil sei der Stunde
2 digte af J. P. Jacobsen, op.10: Du blomst i dug, 1895, Irmelin rose, 1888–9
4 svenska sånger, op.16, 1893–7: Låt oss dö unga (Heidenstam), Guld och gröna skogar (T. Hedberg), Ingalill (Fröding), Fylgia (Fröding)
3 Lieder von Heinrich Heine, op.17, c1890: Ich liebe eine Blume, Ein Fichtenbaum steht einsam, Sie liebten sich beide
5 sånger av Bo Bergman, op.20, 1903–4: Stjärnöga, Vid fönstret, Gammal nederländare, Månsken, Adagio
Visor och stämningar, op.26, 1906–9: Vandraren (Ekelund), Nattyxne (Karlfeldt), Stjärnan (Bergman), Jungfru Blond och Jungfru Brunett (Bergman), Det far ett skepp (Bergman), När genom rummet fönsterkorsets skugga glider (Heidenstam), Varför till ro så brått? (Heidenstam), Lycklandsresan (Fröding), En strandvisa (Fröding), Prins Aladin av lampan (Fröding)
Kejsar Karls visa, op.32 (Levertin), 1910
4 dikter av Verner von Heidenstam, op.37, 1918: Jutta kommer till Folkungarna, I lönnens skymning, Månljuset, Vore jag ett litet barn
4 Stockholmsdikter, op.38 (Bergman), 1917–18: Kväll i Klara, I en skogsbacke, Mellan broarna, En positivvisa
Efterskörd: Var välsignad, milda ömsinthet (Fröding), 1904; Tröst (Fröding), 1904; Klockan (Bergman), 1923; Människors ögon (Bergman), 1923; Hjärtat (Bergman), 1917
5 posthuma sånger, 1917–24: Melodi (Bergman), Under vintergatan (Bergman), Amiens' sång: Blås, blås du vintervind (Shakespeare), Minnessång (Karlfeldt), Orfeus med sin lutas klang (Shakespeare)

OTHER WORKS
Unacc. choral: 3 körvisor till dikter av J. P. Jacobsen, c1890; Norrland [from cantata Norrland]; Sverige [from cantata Ett folk]
Chamber: Str Qt no.1, C, op.2, 1894; Str Qt no.2, c, op.14, 1896; Str Qt no.3, F, op.18, 1897–1900; Sonata, a, op.19, vn, pf, 1899–1900; Str Qt no.4, a, op.25, 1904–9; Str Qt no.5 (Serenade), C, op.29, 1910; Str Qt no.6, d, op.35, 1916
Pf: Sonata. g, 1890; 3 fantasier, op.11, 1895; Sonata, A♭, op.12, 1895; Sensommarnätter, op.33, 5 pieces, 1914

Principal publishers: Erik, Gehrman, Nordiska Musikförlaget

BIBLIOGRAPHY
W. Stenhammar: 'Självbiografisk skiss', Musikmänniskor, ed. M. Pergament (Uppsala, 1943)
H. Rosenberg: 'Wilhelm Stenhammar', Musikmänniskor, ed. M. Pergament (Uppsala, 1943)
B. Wallner: 'Wilhelm Stenhammar och kammarmusiken', STMf, xxxiv (1952), 28; xxxv (1953), 5; xliii (1961), 355
J. Rabe: 'En musikalisk dagbok av Wilhelm Stenhammar', STMf, xl (1958), 191
——: Dikt och ton (Stockholm, 1959)
Musikrevy, xxvi/6 (1971) [special issue]
H. Connor: 'Wilhelm Stenhammar', in A. Aulin and H. Connor: Svensk musik (Stockholm, 1974), 405–50
B. Wallner: Wilhelm Stenhammar: tonsättaren, pianisten, dirigenten (in preparation)
BO WALLNER, HANS ÅSTRAND

Stenhouse, William (b Roxburghshire, 1773; d Edinburgh, 10 Nov 1827). Scottish antiquarian. He was an Edinburgh accountant and folksong enthusiast who was commissioned c1815 by the publisher John Blackwood to write a scholarly work Illustrations of the Lyric Poetry and Music of Scotland; this was a series of short notes, one on each of the 600 songs in The Scots Musical Museum (1787–1803), and was intended to accompany a reprint of that collection. A letter describing the progress of Stenhouse's Illustrations appeared in Blackwood's Magazine in July 1817; in 1820 it was completed and the type was set up, but for various reasons the publication was delayed until 1839, after Stenhouse's death.

Stenhouse's 600 short articles contain essential information on Scottish folk music in the late 18th century. Described by Laing in 1839 as 'a mass of curious matter regarding the poetry and music of the last century', they include reminiscences by and about Robert Burns, James Johnson, Stephen Clarke, George Thomson and others involved in Scottish folksong research c1790, as well as Stenhouse's own recollections of music in Roxburghshire in his childhood. Stenhouse tended to copy inaccurate facts from earlier studies, and to be over-dogmatic in supplying dates and nationalistic origins to individual tunes; for these reasons his work was attacked by William Chappell (1859) and John Glen (1900).

BIBLIOGRAPHY
D. Laing: Preface to The Scots Musical Museum (Edinburgh, 1839)
DAVID JOHNSON

Stenings, Henry. See STONING, HENRY.

Stentando (It.). See STENTATO.

Stentato (It.: 'with difficulty'; past participle of stentare, to be in difficulty). An expression mark often used by Verdi in vocal lines at moments of extreme anguish. But its history goes back much further; Brossard wrote in his Dictionaire de musique (1703):

It is put in to show not only that one should work or 'se donner de la peine' in singing a piece, but also that one should push the voice with all possible strength and sing as though one were suffering much, or in a manner which might make one feel or which expresses the sadness that has penetrated one.

The gerund stentando ('having difficulty') is also found.

For bibliography see TEMPO AND EXPRESSION MARKS.
DAVID FALLOWS

Stenton, Paul. Pseudonym of SEPTIMUS WINNER.

Stentorphone. An ORGAN STOP.

Stentzsch, Rosine. Singer and actress; see LEBRUN family, (4).

Stenzl, Jürg (Thomas) (b Berne, 23 Aug 1942). Swiss musicologist. He received a classical education at Berne, studying at the same time at the conservatory, where he learnt the recorder and violin (from 1949) and the oboe with W. Huwiler (from 1961). He studied musicology with Geering and Dickenmann at Berne University (1963–5; 1966–8), spending a year in 1965 at the University of Paris, where he worked under Chailley. He took the doctorate at Berne University in 1968 with a thesis on the 40 clausulas of F-Pn lat.15139. He then began teaching at the University of Fribourg, where he completed his Habilitation in 1974. In 1971 he became a member of the central committee of the Société Suisse de Musicologie (appointed secretary in 1972) and in 1975 editor of the Schweizerische Musikzeitung.

Stenzl is known as a medievalist, specializing in the Notre Dame school, though his interests also include Swiss music history and contemporary music. Together with Darbellay he is working on a new edition of

Refardt's *Historisch-biographisches Musiker-Lexikon der Schweiz*.

WRITINGS

'Das Dreikönigsfest in der Genfer Kathedrale Saint-Pierre', *AMw*, xxv (1968), 118

'Die Sittener Osterfeier', *KJb*, lii (1968), 37

Die vierzig Clausulae der Handschrift Paris, Bibliothèque Nationale, latin 15139 (Saint Victor-Clausulae) (diss., U. of Berne, 1968; Berne, 1970)

'Eine unbekannte Sanctus-Motette vom Ende des 13. Jahrhunderts', *AcM*, xlii (1970), 128

'Osterfeiern aus den Diözesen Basel und Lausanne', *KJb*, lv (1971), 1

'Un fragment de Dufay au Grand-Saint-Bernard', *Revue musicale de Suisse romande*, xxiv (1971), 5

'Karlheinz Stockhausens Kreuzspiel (1951)', *Zeitschrift für Musiktheorie*, iii (1972), 35

'Zur Kirchenmusik im Berner Münster vor der Reformation', *Festschrift Arnold Geering* (Berne, 1972), 89

Repertorium der liturgischen Musikhandschriften der Diözesen Sitten, Lausanne und Genf, i: *Diözese Sitten* (Fribourg, 1972)

'Der liturgische Gesang der römischen Kirche im Mittelalter', 'Antiphonen und Responsorien', *Geschichte der katholischen Kirchenmusik*, ed. K. G. Fellerer, i (Kassel, 1972), 172, 277

'Un'intavolatura tedesca sconosciuta della prima metà del cinquecento', *L'organo*, x (1972), 51

'Eine unbekannte Notre Dame-Quelle: die Solothurner Fragmente', *Mf*, xxvi (1973), 311

'Ueber den Grossaufbau und die Bedeutung von Händels "Messiah" ', *NZM*, Jg.135 (1974), 732

'Bewahrende und verändernde musikalische Überlieferung', *AMw*, xxxii (1975), 117

ed.: *Luigi Nono: Texte – Studien zu seiner Musik* (Zurich, 1975)

'Zur Überlieferung des Sittener Hymnars um 1300', *KJb*, lix (1975), 1

'Monteverdi 1976', *SMz*, cxvi (1976), 291

Articles in *Grove 6, MGG, NDB*

ETIENNE DARBELLAY

Step (Ger. *Schritt, Tonschritt*). The melodic interval of a major or minor 2nd (i.e. a tone or a semitone), in contrast to a skip or leap. Melodic movement by tones and semitones is called 'stepwise' or 'conjunct' motion.

Štěpán [Steffan, Steffani, Stephan, Stephani etc], **Josef Antonín** [Joseph Anton; Giuseppe Antonio] (*b* Kopidlno, Bohemia, baptized 14 March 1726; *d* Vienna, 12 April 1797). Czech composer, keyboard teacher and virtuoso active in Vienna. His musical gifts were probably first nurtured by his father, who was organist and schoolmaster in Kopidlno. When the Prussian army invaded Bohemia in 1741 the boy fled to Vienna, where he sought the patronage of the lord of the Kopidlno estate, Count František Jindřich Šlik [Schlick]. He studied the violin with the count's Kapellmeister, Hammel (whom he later succeeded), and became a favourite harpsichord and composition pupil of the court composer G. C. Wagenseil, for whom he may have deputized. Štěpán distinguished himself as a gifted composer and as one of the most brilliant harpsichordists in Vienna. He enjoyed a considerable reputation as a teacher, and throughout his career composed short didactic pieces. On 14 July 1766 he was appointed *Klaviermeister* to the young princesses Maria Carolina and Maria Antonia (later Queen of France), but by August 1775 he had ceased his court duties. Partly because of a temporary loss of sight he was allowed to retain his annual income of 500 florins as a pension. But he was soon able to continue private teaching, and was a frequent guest in fashionable salons. He also continued composing until his very last years. He died in obscurity, the obituary notice in the *Wiener Zeitung* of 19 April 1797 merely recording his sudden death from a stroke. In his will, dated 5 August 1795, he left the greater part of his considerable estate in trust for

the school in Kopidlno. His pupil, the novelist Caroline Pichler, described him in her memoirs as 'a humorous man of a distinctive personality, who combined the oddities common to all artists, especially musicians, with some peculiarities of his own. But he knew his art thoroughly and had an inexhaustible fund of good humour.'

Štěpán's role as a herald of the Classical style and the intrinsic value of his music still await full recognition. He is acknowledged for the historical importance of his collections of lieder, the first of their kind to be published in Vienna, but his real significance lies in the keyboard music, which spans the whole of his creative life. The suite-like divertimentos and sonatas of the early period, before about 1755, already show a mastery of the new Italian manner and a gift for attractive ideas creatively worked out in some distinctly forward-looking pieces. The slow minor-key introduction to a sonata dating from before 1757 became the prototype for later examples in sonatas and concertos. During the next decade Štěpán firmly established a colourful individual style, and in the publications of the 1770s, all substantial four-movement works, produced some of the most interesting of Viennese sonatas. His keyboard idiom is characterized by a full texture animated by complex part-writing, intricate thematic configurations and an impressive rhythmic vitality and impetus.

The mature keyboard works, from the late 1770s, are conceived for the piano, with appropriate stylization and an idiosyncratic use of dynamics. Štěpán's style in all genres shows a successful transformation into a Classical manner that is close to Mozart in its cantabile themes and melodic chromaticism, and to Haydn in keyboard style and structural ingenuity, with many stylistic parallels in addition. Štěpán's individuality is evident in the continuing incorporation of fantasia effects (capriccios, concerto cadenzas) and programmatic elements (sonatas, and the subjective *Duello* and *Spirito incostante*). The trend towards thematic integration and his liking for formal experiments resulted in the creation of hybrid forms on sonata, variation and rondo principles for single-movement capriccios, *Variazioni combinate* and sonatas. Other late sonatas are in two or three extended movements, sometimes with an introduction, but always without a minuet. His expressive range extends from introspective gravity and temperamental outbursts to witty exuberance. Some late keyboard and chamber music pieces show self-borrowing and an exaggerated use of favourite motifs and other devices.

Štěpán's keyboard concertos are unique in the regular use of expressive minor-key slow introductions, with the soloist taking part. In his first movements proper he transformed the traditional ritornello pattern to produce a variety of formal schemes, finally favouring movements based, unconventionally, on sonata form principles. The slow movements were the last to develop in individuality, but eventually he dispensed with the customary prolific solo figuration and they became vehicles for melodic and dramatic interest. The character of the finales was changed, as in the sonatas, by the adoption of folksong-like themes as a means to further progress. The finales of the late concertos are large-scale movements in various types of sonata form, and are as weighty as first movements. Štěpán maintained an independent course which led him to anticipate the 'accompanied sonata' concept of the concerto, in which the soloist dominates almost completely. He was one of the most advanced concerto composers in Vienna before Mozart, but after his death his music soon fell into neglect.

WORKS

(printed works published in Vienna unless otherwise stated)
Br. cat. – *listed in Breitkopf catalogues*
(complete thematic catalogue in Picton)

SACRED

Stabat mater, 1v, pf (Prague and Vienna, 1782)
2 masses, 1 Laudate pueri, 1 Beatus vir, *D-SWl*
2 Christmas pastorellas: C, 1762, collab. J. G. Zechner, *A-GÖ*; D, M
7 hymns in Lieder zur öffentlichen und häuslichen Andacht (Prague, 1783); hymns in Leitmeritzer Choralbuch (Leitmeritz, 1846)
Lost: Requiem, formerly attrib. Dittersdorf; Der unschuldig angeklagte . . . Weltheiland, oratorio, perf. Prague, 1757, mentioned in Dlabač (1815); De martyre; De sancto; Litaniae Lauretanae

SECULAR VOCAL

Edition: *Das Wiener Lied von 1778 bis Mozarts Tod*, ed. M. Ansion and I. Schlaffenberg, DTÖ, liv, Jg.xxvii/2 (1920/*R*1960)

Sammlung [24] deutscher Lieder, i (1778), *A-Wn* [incl. 2 unpubd songs]; 3 repr. in Sammlung verschiedener Lieder von guten Dichtern und Tonkünstlern (Nuremberg, 1780)
Sammlung [25] deutscher Lieder, ii (1779)
Gesang bei dem Beschlusse der . . . Prüfung der 31 Unteroffiziere und Gemeinen (1780)
Sammlung [24] deutscher Lieder, iv (1782)
1 song in Wienerischer Musenalmanach (1781)

Der Doktor Daunderlaun (Singspiel, 2), *A-Wgm*, *CS-Pnm*

KEYBOARD

6 divertimenti [op.1] (1756), ed. in MAB, lxiv (1964)
6 sonate, op.2 (?1759–60), 1 movt ed. in MVH, xv (1966)
40 preludi per diversi tuoni (1762)
Parte 1a del op.3 continente 3 sonate, before 1757 (1763); Parte 2a . . . continente 3 sonate (1771); Parte 3a, lost; pts.1–2 ed. in MAB, lxiv (1964); 7 minuets from opp.1–3 ed. in MVH, ix (1962)
Sonata I (1771), II (?1771), III (1776); all ed. in MAB, lxiv (1964)
6 sonates choisies, hpd/pf, par . . . Steffann et Rutini (Paris, 1773–4) [from opp.1–3]
Parte 2a continente 90 cadenze, fermade, e capricci, hpd/pf (1783)
25 variationi, pf (Vienna, 1785–92)

21 divertimentos and sonatas, incl. 6 soli [no.4 lost], Br. cat. 1768, *B-Bc*, *CS-KRa*, *D-B*, *H-Bn*, *I-Vc*; 8 sonatas ed. in MAB, lxx (1968)
5 capriccios, *A-Wgm*, *CS-KRa*, *Pnm*, *D-B*, ed. A. Weinmann (Munich and Duisburg, 1971)
5 sets of variations, *CS-KRa*, *D-B*, *H-Bn*
3 programmatic pieces, 10 contradanze, *CS-KRa*
23 minuets, *CS-Pnm*, 13 minuets, *CS-Pk*, *D-B*, 12 minuets, *D-Dlb*, *I-Vc*
8 deutsche Galanterie Stücke, *A-Wn*, *D-B*
11 single sonata movts, 3 alternative versions of sonata movts, 4 sinfonia arrs., 6 spurious pieces, *A-Wgm*, *Wn*, *B-Bc*, *CS-KRa*, *Pnm*, *D-B*, *Bds*, *ROu*, *H-Bn*, *I-Vc*; cadenza for kbd conc. by Vanhal, *A-Wgm*
Fantasia, Br. cat. 1769, lost

OTHER INSTRUMENTAL

Orch: 6 sinfonie, incl. 2 in Br. cat. 1766, *A-Gd*, *CS-Pnm*, *D-SWl*, *H-Gc*; 4 sinfonie, Br. cat. 1766, lost; Parthie, 1760, lost
Concs.: 6 concs., hpd/harp, op.3 (Paris, *c*1773), nos.3–6 lost; 36 concs., hpd/pf, incl. 12 in Br. cat. 1763, 1766, 1767, *A-Wn*, *Wgm*, *B-Bc*, *CS-Bm*, *KRa*, *Pk*, *Pnm*, *TC*, *D-B*, *Dlb*, *Rtt*, *H-Bn*, *I-Vc*, 2 ed. H. Picton (Oxford, 1976; Madison, Wisc., in preparation); 1 conc., hpd/pf, 1771, lost; 2 concs., 2 hpd, *D-B* (incl. 1 arr. and pubd as Haydn's HXVIII: G2)
Chamber: Concertino, hpd, fl, vn, vc, Br. cat. 1769, *D-B*; Concertino, hpd, fl, vn, b, 2 hn, Br. cat. 1769, *CS-KRa*, *D-B*, *SWl*, ed. in MAB, xxxix (1959); 7 trios, vn, vc, hpd/pf, incl. 1 in Br. cat. 1766, 1 in 1767, *A-Wn*, *B-Bc*, *CS-KRa*, 1 also arr. 2 hpd, ed. in DČHP; Sonata, vn, pf, *D-B*; Variations, vn, pf, *A-Wgm*, *CS-KRa*, *D-B*
Wind insts: 2 Harmonie, *D-SWl*; Serenata, *CS-Pnm*; 6 partitas, Br. cat. 1785–7, lost

BIBLIOGRAPHY

EitnerQ; *FétisB*; *GerberL*; *GerberNL*; *RiemannL* 12
F. W. Marpurg: *Kritische Briefe über die Tonkunst*, ii/2 (Berlin, 1761)
J. A. Hiller, ed.: *Wöchentliche Nachrichten und Anmerkungen die Musik betreffend*, i (Leipzig, 1766/*R*1970), 100
I. N. Forkel: *Musikalischer Almanach 1783* (Leipzig, 1782/*R*1974)
C. F. Cramer, ed.: *Magazin der Musik*, i (Hamburg, 1783/*R*1971)
Jb der Tonkunst von Wien und Prag (Vienna and Prague, 1796)
G. J. Dlabacž: *Allgemeines historisches Künstler-Lexikon* (Prague, 1815/*R*1973)

F. A. Vacek: 'Jozef Štiepán z Kopidlna', in J. G. Ziegler: *Přitel mlàdeže* [Friend of youth], iii (Prague, 1827), 32
C. von Wurzbach: *Biographisches Lexikon des Kaiserthums Oesterreich* (Vienna, 1878)
M. Friedlaender: *Das deutsche Lied im 18. Jahrhundert* (Stuttgart and Berlin, 1902)
A. Schering: *Geschichte des Instrumentalkonzerts bis auf die Gegenwart* (Leipzig, 1905, 2/1927/*R*1965)
K. Hůlka: 'Josef Antonín Štěpán', *HR*, vii (1913–14), 13, 67, 124
C. Pichler: *Denkwürdigkeiten aus Altösterreich*, v (Munich, 1914)
I. Pollak-Schlaffenberg: 'Die Wiener Liedmusik von 1778–89', *SMw*, v (1918), 97–139
J. Bušek: 'Za naší hudební minulostí: XII. Josef Antonín Štěpán' [Our musical past: XII. Josef Antonín Štěpán], *Hudební výchova*, xiii/1 (1932), 7
H. Gericke: *Der Wiener Musikalienhandel von 1700 bis 1778* (Graz and Cologne, 1960)
T. Straková: 'Josef Antonín Štěpán a Haydnovo Divertimento Es dur/ Josef Antonín Štěpán and Haydns Divertimento in Es dur', *Časopis Moravského musea*, xlvi (1961), 127
C. Schoenbaum: 'Die böhmischen Musiker in der Musikgeschichte Wiens vom Barock zur Romantik', *SMw*, xxv (1962), 475
W. S. Newman: *The Sonata in the Classic Era* (Chapel Hill, 1963, rev. 2/1972)
D. Šetková: *Klavírní dílo Josefa Antonína Štěpána* [The keyboard works of Josef Antonín Štěpán] (Prague, 1965)
——: 'Štěpán, Josef Antonín', *MGG*
E. Wellesz and F. W. Sternfeld: 'The Concerto', *NOHM*, vii (1973)
H. J. Picton: *The Life and Works of Joseph Anton Steffan (1726–1797)* (diss., U. of Hull, 1976) [incl. thematic catalogue]
HOWARD PICTON

Štěpán, Pavel (*b* Brno, 28 May 1925). Czech pianist, grandson of Vilém Kurz. His parents were well-known pianists. His grandfather taught him the piano, and he gave his first public performance at the age of 16, playing Bach and Debussy. In 1943, with the Czech PO under Rafael Kubelík, he played Mozart's Concerto in C minor, and the following year he gave a solo recital. Štěpán's repertory centres on Mozart's piano concertos, but embraces works by Bach, Beethoven, Schubert, Brahms, Debussy and Prokofiev, in which his refined technique and poetic expressiveness are also revealed; he often includes Czech and contemporary works in his programmes. Occasionally he plays quintets by Schumann and Dvořák with the Smetana Quartet, and he often performs piano duets or duos with Ilja Hurník. In 1961 Štěpán began teaching at the Prague Academy of Music and at interpretation seminars abroad. He has given successful concerts in many European countries, and his recordings have been highly praised. He has written for the daily press and publishes occasional reviews in *Hudební rozhledy*. He was named Artist of Merit in 1975.

BIBLIOGRAPHY

I. Jirko: 'Návrat Pavla Štěpána' [The return of Pavel Štěpán], *HRo*, xi (1958), 35
M. Kulijevyčová: 'S Pavlem Štěpánem o interpretaci' [Pavel Štěpán on interpretation], *HRo*, xvi (1963), 151
ALENA NĚMCOVÁ

Štěpán, Václav (*b* Pečky, nr. Kolín, Bohemia, 12 Dec 1889; *d* Prague, 24 Nov 1944). Czech pianist, writer and composer, father of Pavel Štěpán. He studied musicology under Nejedlý at Prague University, graduating in 1913, and continued his studies both at the German University in Prague and in Berlin. He appeared as a pianist from the age of 18, giving Novák premières (*Pan*, *Exotikon*) by the time he was 22. His piano studies, begun with Josef Čermák in Prague (1895–1908), continued with James Kwast in Berlin and, after the war, with Blanche Selva in Paris. The Paris influence was especially important and led to a number of concert tours of Paris and the French provinces (1919, 1920, 1922) and other engagements in London (1919), Berlin and Yugoslavia (1924). In Prague he taught aesthetics and later piano at the conservatory and appeared frequently both as soloist and chamber player with the Ševčík and the Czech Quartets. Although he specialized in new Czech music, introducing works by Suk, Novák, Axman, Křička, Vomáčka, etc, he also gave the first complete performance of Smetana's Czech Dances and Polkas (1913–14). He was active as editor, critic and writer (an authority on Suk and Novák) and wrote the Czechoslovak entries in A. E. Hull's *Dictionary of Modern Music and Musicians* (1924). A pupil of Novák, he composed piano, chamber and vocal works, many of which were published in Paris and Vienna. After the age of 30, however, he abandoned composition in favour of his other activities.

WRITINGS

Symbolika z příbuzné zjevy v programní hudbě [Symbolism and related phenomena in programme music] (Prague, 1915)
'Její pastorkyně' [Jenůfa], *HR*, x (1917), 28
'Estetický problém současné hudby' [The problems of aesthetics in contemporary music], *Tempo*, vii (1928), 227
'Dramatický význam Smetanovy polyfonie' [The dramatic significance of Smetana's polyphony], *Tempo*, xi (1932), 6
Novák a Suk (Prague, 1945) [Collection of Štěpán's major articles on Novák and Suk]

BIBLIOGRAPHY

ČSHS [incl. list of compositions]
B. Vomáčka: 'Václav Štěpán', *Listy Hudební matice*, v (1926), 166
F. Bartoš: 'In memoriam dra Václava Štěpána', *Smetana*, xxxvii (1944), 150
B. Vomáčka: 'Václav Štěpán', *HRo*, vii (1954), 801
——: 'Vzpomínáme Václava Štěpána', *HRo*, xii (1959), 932
JOHN TYRRELL

Step'annos Siunetsi. Armenian 8th-century theorist and possibly a notational innovator; *see* ARMENIAN RITE, MUSIC OF THE.

Stepanova, Elena Andreyevna (*b* Moscow, 17 May 1891). Russian soprano. She studied singing with M. Polli. From 1908 she sang in the chorus of the Bol'shoy Opera, until after a successful début as Antonida (Glinka's *Ivan Susanin*) she became a soloist of the company in 1912. Stanislavsky, who had great influence on her development as a singer and actress, prepared her in the Bol'shoy opera studio for the roles of Gilda (1919) and Tatyana (1921); she was also influenced by such noted company members as the conductors Václav Suk, Cooper and Golovanov, the director Lossky and the singers Shalyapin, Sobinov and Nezhdanova. Her singing was distinguished by rare clarity, crystalline lightness in coloratura and artistic sensitivity. Her portrayals in Rimsky-Korsakov operas were fascinating: Marfa (*The Tsar's Bride*), the Snow Maiden, Pannochka (*May Night*) and the Queen of Shemakhan (*The Golden Cockerel*), among others. Her repertory also included Glinka's Lyudmila, Violetta, Elsa, Meyerbeer's Marguerite de Valois, and Lakmé, performed throughout the USSR. She left the opera stage in 1944, appearing in concerts until 1950. In 1937 she was made a People's Artist of the USSR.

BIBLIOGRAPHY

A. Shaverdian: *Bol'shoy Teatr SSSR* (Moscow, 1952), 37, 112f
E. A. Stepanova (Moscow, 1953)
K. Konstantinov: 'E. A. Stepanova: 70-letiyu so dnya rozhdeniya' [E. A. Stepanova: for her 70th birthday], *Muzïkal'naya zhizn'* (1961), no.10, p.11
I. M. YAMPOL'SKY

Step'anyan, Haro Levoni (*b* Elizavetpol [now Kirovobad], Azerbaijan, 25 April 1897; *d* Erevan, 9 Jan 1966). Armenian composer. He studied composition under Gnesin at the Moscow music college (1923–7) and under Shcherbachev and K'ushnaryan at the Leningrad Conservatory (1926–30). Thereafter he settled in Erevan, teaching at the conservatory and holding the presidency of the Armenian Composers' Union (1938–48). His operatic, orchestral and chamber music played an important part in the development of Armenian music in the 1930s and 1940s; though he followed the Armenian tradition, and in particular the work of Komitas, he drew into it certain features from Prokofiev and Shostakovich. Folk music remained an essential source of thematic material. Step'anyan's operas cover a wide range, from the improbable, satiric *K'adj Nazar* ('Brave Nazar') to the epic *Sasuntsi Davit*, from the revolutionary *Lusabatsin* ('At dawn') to the historical, romantic *Nune*. The use of the chorus is a major feature, whether in the static, oratorical writing of *Sasuntsi Davit'* or the dynamic material of *At Dawn*. In *Sasuntsi Davit'* the archaic setting is evoked through the use of *sharakan* melodies, hymns, heavy rhythms and strict polyphony; these are also found in the First Symphony, an epic piece of harmonic richness and contrapuntal mastery, after the model of Komitas's choruses. Step'anyan was also a master of the lyrical miniature: his song accompaniments are of great refinement, and some piano pieces (the preludes and the sonata) show traces of impressionism.

WORKS
(*selective list*)

Operas: K'adj Nazar [Brave Nazar] (D. Demirdjyan), 1934; Sasuntsi Davit' (Demirdjyan, after trad. epic), 1936; Lusabatsin [At dawn] (T. Akhumyan), 1937; Nune (A. Adamyan, V. Vagharshyan), 1947; Geroinya (Adamyan), 1950
Orch: Lur-da-lur, sym. poem, 1944; 3 syms., 1944, 1945, 1953; Pf Conc., 1959
Vocal: Kolkhoznaya kantata [Cantata of the collective farm] (Sarmen), 1949; Anīreli zangagatun [The incessant bell-tower] (oratorio, P. Sevak), 1964; *c*160 songs to Armenian texts
Inst: 4 str qts, 1940, 1941, 1957, 1958; Sonata, vc, pf, 1943; 2 sonatas, vn, pf, 1943, 1947; Pf Preludes, 1948, 1956; Pf Sonata, 1949; several other pieces

BIBLIOGRAPHY

G. Tigranov: *Armyanskiy muzïkal'nïy teatr* [The Armenian music theatre], ii (Erevan, 1960), 71–125
M. Katsakhyan: *Haro Step'anyan* (Erevan, 1962)
G. Tigranov: *Aro Stepanyan* (Moscow, 1967)
SVETLANA SARKISIAN

Stephan, Clemens. See STEPHANI, CLEMENS.

Stephan, Josef Antonín. See ŠTĚPÁN, JOSEF ANTONÍN.

Stephan, Rudi (*b* Worms, 29 July 1887; *d* nr. Tarnopol, Galicia, 29 Sept 1915). German composer. He studied with Sekles at the Hoch Conservatory in Frankfurt (1905) and with Louis for composition and Schwartz for the piano in Munich (1906–8), where he also studied philosophy at the university. His instrumental compositions of 1911–13, all simply called *Musik für . . .*, attracted attention for their avoidance of established forms and of programmes. Stephan was in contact with Reger during this period, and his works were seen as belonging to a new classical movement for pure, absolute music. Their tonality is highly chromatic and the counterpoint is marked, though colour and instrumentation suggest impressionist influence. In his vocal music Stephan was less iconoclastic: his fine songs follow Wolf and his opera looks back to Beethoven and

Gluck. A promising career was cut short by his death in action.

WORKS

Die ersten Menschen (opera, O. Borngräber), 1914; Frankfurt, 1920
Musik für sieben Saiteninstrumente, pf, harp, str qt, db, 1911; Musik für Orchester, 1912; Musik für Geige und Orchester, 1913; Liebeszauber (Hebbel), Bar, orch, 1913; 16 songs, 1913–14

Principal publisher: Schott

BIBLIOGRAPHY

K. Holl: *Rudi Stephan: Studie zur Entwicklungsgeschichte der Musik am Anfang des 20. Jahrhunderts* (Saarbrücken, 1920, 2/1922)
——: 'Das lyrische Schaffen Rudi Stephans', *Melos*, ii (1921), 157
——: 'Rudi Stephan', *Melos*, vii (1928), 121
A. Machner: *Rudi Stephans Werk* (diss., U. of Breslau, 1943)
——: 'Zwischen gestern und heute: ein Wort für Rudi Stephan', *Musica*, viii (1954), 9
A. D. McCredie: 'The Munich School and Rudi Stephan (1887–1915): some Forgotten Sources and Byways of Musical Jugendstil and Expressionism', *MR*, xxix (1968), 197

Stephan, (Gustav-Adolf Carl) Rudolf (*b* Bochum, 3 April 1925). German musicologist. Until 1947 he was educated in Heidelberg, studying the violin at the conservatory and music theory under W. Fortner at the Institute of Protestant Church Music; at the university he studied musicology (with H. Besseler), philosophy (with K. Jaspers and E. Hofmann) and art history. He then continued at the University of Göttingen, studying musicology under R. Gerber and philosophy under N. Hartmann. He took his doctorate there in 1950 with a dissertation on early motets. In 1963 he completed his *Habilitation* in musicology at Göttingen with a study of the antiphon and subsequently became a lecturer there. In 1967 he was appointed professor of musicology at the Free University of Berlin. Since 1968 he has been editor in charge of the Schoenberg Gesamtausgabe and, since 1960, president of the Institut für Neue Musik und Musikerziehung, Darmstadt, some of whose publications he has also edited.

Stephan's main areas of research are medieval music and music after 1700; he has concentrated particularly on Bach, Mahler and Schoenberg. He is primarily interested in drawing on important new sources, in combining the theoretical with the technical aspect of composition and in establishing criteria for musical quality and so for historical placing, a concern which also governs his interest in questions relating to present-day music. His dictionary, *Musik* (1957), and his book *Neue Musik* (1958) are expressed admirably in a style that is both scholarly and universally accessible.

WRITINGS

Die Tenores der Motetten ältesten Stils (diss., U. of Göttingen, 1950)
'Die Wandlung der Konzertform bei Bach', *Mf*, vi (1953), 127
'Hindemith's Marienleben', *MR*, xv (1954), 275
'Über das Ende der Generalbasspraxis', *BJb*, xli (1954), 80
with C. Dahlhaus: 'Eine "dritte Epoche" der Musik?', *Deutsche Universitätszeitung*, xi (1956)
'Prinzipielles zu den Leopoldsoffizien', *Mf*, ix (1956), 64
'Aus der alten Abtei Reichenau', *AMw*, xiii (1956), 61
'Lied, Tropus und Tanz im Mittelalter', *Zeitschrift für deutsches Altertum und deutsche Literatur*, lxxxvii (1956), 147
with A. Bertau: 'Zum sanglichen Vortrag mittelhochdeutscher strophischer Epen', *Zeitschrift für deutsches Altertum und deutsche Literatur*, lxxxvii (1956), 153–270
Musik (Frankfurt am Main, 1957)
Neue Musik (Göttingen, 1958, 2/1973)
'Über J. M. Hauer', *AMw*, xviii (1961), 265
Antiphonar-Studien (Habilitationsschrift, U. of Göttingen, 1963)
Gustav Mahler: 4. Symphonie g-Dur (Munich, 1966)
ed.: *Neue Wege der musikalischen Analyse* (Berlin, 1967)
'Sichtbare Musik', *Der Berliner Germanistentag 1968*, ed. K. H. Borck and E. Henss (Heidelberg, 1970), 90
'Zu Beethovens letzten Quartetten', *Mf*, xxiii (1970), 245
'Schönbergs Entwurf über "das Komponieren mit selbständigen Stimmen"', *AMw*, xxix (1972), 239
'Weberns Werke auf deutschen Tonkünstlerfesten', *ÖMz*, xxvii (1972), 121
ed.: *Die Musik der sechziger Jahre* (Mainz, 1972)
ed.: *A. Schoenberg: Modelle für Anfänger im Kompositionsunterricht* (Vienna, 1972)
'J. S. Bach und das Problem des musikalischen Zyklus', *BJb*, lix (1973), 39
ed.: *Zwischen Tradition und Fortschritt* (Mainz, 1973)
'Schönberg als Symphoniker', *ÖMz*, xxix (1974), 267
Alexander Zemlinsky (Kiel and Vienna, 1978)
Articles on medieval topics in *GfMKB, Lüneburg 1950* and *GfMKB, Hamburg 1956* and on Webern in *Musik und Kirche*, xxiv (1954) and *Deutsche Universitätszeitung*, xi (1956)

HANS HEINRICH EGGEBRECHT

Stephănescu, George (*b* Bucharest, 13 Dec 1843; *d* Bucharest, 25 April 1925). Romanian composer, conductor and teacher. He studied harmony and the piano with Wachmann at the Bucharest Conservatory (1864–7); at the Paris Conservatoire (1867–71) he was a pupil of Réber (harmony), Auber and Thomas (composition), Delle (singing) and Marmontel (piano). Returning to Romania, he taught singing and opera from 1872 until 1904 at the Bucharest Conservatory, where his pupils included Teodorini, Darclée, Nuovina and many others who were to make international reputations as opera singers. Stephănescu himself was never a professional singer, but he was an outstanding teacher, and he summarized his method in *Despre mecanismul vocal* ('On the vocal mechanism') (Bucharest, 1896). He conducted at the Bucharest National Theatre from the foundation of the Romanian Opera in 1877, and he also helped to further opera in the city by training the house singers and by financially supporting productions by private companies. To assist in the establishment of a national repertory he composed many stage works, some of them in a patriotic vein (e.g. *Peste Dunăre* and *Petra*). Stephănescu was also the composer of the first Romanian symphony (1869) and of many songs, often drawing on folk music. Other works that present folk-like melodies in bold relief include the *Uvertura naţională* and, above all, the short symphonic poems suggested by the landscape of the Căpăţîneni village where he spent summer holidays. Stephănescu did not use authentic peasant tunes, but rather original themes in folk style, harmonizing them within the major-minor system. It is in the songs that his powers as a melodist are most finely displayed, particularly in *Kamadeva, Somnoroase păsărele* ('Sleepy little birds') and *Şi dacă ramuri bat în geam* ('And when the branches knock against windows'). In addition to his other activities, Stephănescu reformed the curricula of the Bucharest Conservatory, wrote music criticism for the Romanian press and translated several opera librettos. He was perhaps the greatest Romanian musician before Enescu.

WORKS
(selective list)

VOCAL

Stage: Peste Dunăre [Across the Danube] (operetta, G. Ventura), 1880; Sînziana şi Pepelea (musical fairy tale, V. Alecsandri), 1880; Scaiul bărbaţilor[Men'sburf](operetta, G. Bengescu-Dabija), 1885; Cometa (operetta, Th. Sperania), 1900; Petra (opera, E. Aslan), 1902
Cîntările Sf Liturghii a lui Ioan Gură de Aur [Liturgical songs of St John Chrysostom], 1894; Lieduri (Eminescu), 1887–95; Visul Sclavului [The slave's dream] (V. Conta), 1v, pf, 1902

INSTRUMENTAL

Orch: Sym., A, 1869; Uvertura naţională, 1876; In munţi [In the mountains], sym. poem, 1888; In crîng [In the meadow], sym. poem, ?1889; Intre flori, sym. poem, ?1890; In alte timpuri [In old times], sym. poem, 1895; Idilă, sym. poem, 1902
Chamber: Pf sonata, A, 1863; Vc sonata, 1863; Octet, G, 1866; Septet, G, ?1870; Str Qt, F, ?1870

Principal publisher: Gebauer (Bucharest)

BIBLIOGRAPHY

M. G. Posluşnicu: *Istoria musicei la români* (Bucharest, 1928), 291ff
V. Cosma: 'Un mare luptător pentru formarea unei culturi naţionale' [A great fighter for the growth of a national culture], *Viaţa militară*, xii (1953), 87
V. Tomescu: 'Un înaintaş al muzicii noastre' [A forefather of our music], *Muzica*, i (Bucharest, 1954), 1
G. Stephănescu: *George Stephănescu: viaţa în imagini* [Stephănescu: life in pictures] (Bucharest, 1962)
V. Tomescu: 'Stephănescu, George', *MGG*
Z. Vancea: *Creaţia muzicală românească: sec. XIX–XX* (Bucharest, 1968), 106ff
V. Cosma: *Muzicieni români* (Bucharest, 1970), 406ff

VIOREL COSMA

Stephani, Agostino. *See* STEFFANI, AGOSTINO.

Stephani [Stephan, Stephanus], **Clemens** (*b* Buchau [now Bochov], nr. Carlsbad [now Karlovy Vary, Czechoslovakia], probably *c*1530; *d* Eger [now Cheb, Czechoslovakia], mid-Feb 1592). Bohemian music editor, poet, printer, bookseller and ?composer. He may have attended the Lateinschule at Eger or the one at Joachimsthal (now Jáchymov). In 1554, according to his own testimony, he was a student at Leipzig. From April 1558 for about a year he was Kantor at the Lateinschule at Eger. In 1561 he applied again for this post but was refused. Between 1559 and 1567 he seems to have travelled about a good deal – he is known to have visited Budweis (now Ceské Budějovice), whose choir he praised highly, Ossegg, Prague and Nuremberg – and he also had several private pupils. Title-pages of his prints indicate that from at least 1567 until 1569 he was again living at Eger. In 1569–70 he probably stayed for some time at Nuremberg. From 1571 to 1574 he worked as a bookseller at Schlaggenwald, Bohemia, and from 1574 until his death he lived at Eger, where he was permitted to engage in bookselling only at public markets and where he also for some time owned a printing press. He was a difficult, quarrelsome man, who was unable to obtain a settled professional position and even spent some time in prison. J. Goldammer, Rektor at Eger, wrote in 1584 of his 'poisonous, blasphemous tongue', and the Eger town council forbade performances of his play *Alexander* because it contained libellous verses about Goldammer. He knew well Johann Hagius and Jobst vom Brandt. He died completely penniless and left many debts.

Stephani was once known chiefly as a dramatic poet in the Hans Sachs tradition, but his numerous other activities, especially as a humanist scholar and music editor, deserve recognition. In his various literary and scholarly publications he strove for the improvement of national education and the moral uplift of his fellow men on the basis of his Protestant faith. He may well have had much to do with the cultural flowering at Eger between about 1565 and 1585 and may have been responsible for the appointment in 1570 of Hagius – another contentious figure – as town preacher. The bulk of his publications appeared between 1567 and 1572–3, several of them in a single year, 1568. In his music anthologies, international composers rub shoulders with little-known men of mainly local interest, such as Melchior Bischoff, Christophorus Cervius, Wolfgang Ottho Egranus, Valentin Rabe, Josephus Schlegel and Andreas Schwartz (Francus). Despite the obviously conservative view of music found in his remarkable preface to Brandt's *Geistliche Psalmen* (1572–3), he by no means published only the works of long-dead composers such as Isaac, Josquin, La Rue and Stoltzer or of somewhat more recent composers, of the generation of Crecquillon, Ducis, Gombert, Heugel, Morales, Senfl, Vaet, Johann Walter (i) and Willaert, but also – especially in the highly original, somewhat enigmatic *Beati omnes* collection (1569) – the works of younger composers, Joachim a Burck, David Köler, Lassus, Jacob Meiland and Nicolaus Selnecker. Except for a single motet, Brandt's sacred music is known entirely from Stephani's edition of it of 1572–3. His rapturous praise of Brandt is no less remarkable than the fact that he published Walter's *St Matthew Passion* as his own work. Whether he himself was also a composer, as Quoika and Frank – unlike Eitner and Riess – tended to assume, cannot yet be decided, but the music in *Eine geistliche Action* in particular may be by him.

WORKS

(published in Nuremberg unless otherwise stated)

EDITIONS

Suavissimae et incundissimae harmoniae, 4, 5, 8vv (1567[1])
Cantiones triginta selectissimae, 5–8, 12, 24, 36vv (1568[7])
Liber secundus suavissimarum et iucundissimarum harmoniarum, 4, 5vv (1568[8])
Schöner ausserlessner deutscher Psalm, und anderer künstlicher Moteten und geistlichen Lieder XX, 4vv (1568[11])
Beati omnes: psalmus CXXVIII Davidis, modis septendecim concinnatus, 4–6vv (1569[1])
J. Hagius: Kurze ausserlesene Symbola Maximiliani secundi romischen Keysers, 4vv (1569)
J. Walter (i): Passio secundum Matthaeum, 4vv (1570)
J. vom Brandt: Der erste Theil geistlicher Psalmen und teutscher Kyrchengeseng, 4–9vv, insts (incl. trbns) (Eger, 1572–3)

WRITINGS

Eine geistliche Action auss Ludovici Bero[aldi] Dialogo (prologue and 5 acts) (1568) [incl. canon, 4vv, 1 other vocal work, 3vv]

BIBLIOGRAPHY

EitnerQ; WaltherML

A. Hauffen: 'Klemens Stephani', *Sudetendeutsche Lebensbilder*, ed. E. Gierach, i (Reichenberg, 1926), 106
K. Riess: *Musikgeschichte der Stadt Eger im 16. Jahrhundert* (Brno, 1935)
H. Albrecht: 'Die deutschen Psalmen und Kirchengesänge des Jobst vom Brandt', *AMf*, vii (1942), 218
E. Frank: *Clemens Stephani* (Brno, 1944)
R. Quoika: *Die Musik der Deutschen in Böhmen und Mähren* (Berlin, 1956), 46
H. Haase: *Jobst vom Brandt (1517–1570): ein Beitrag zur Musikgeschichte Deutschlands im 2. Drittel des 16. Jahrhunderts* (Kassel, 1967)

based on *MGG* (xii, 1264–5) by permission of Bärenreiter

HANS HAASE

Stephani, Hermann (*b* Grimma, Saxony, 23 June 1877; *d* Marburg, 3 Dec 1960). German musicologist, conductor and composer. He attended the Leipzig Conservatory and took the doctorate at Munich University in 1902 with a dissertation on the sublime in music. After holding posts as a choral conductor in Sonderburg (1903–4), Flensburg (1905) and Eisleben (1906–21), he was appointed music director and lecturer at Göttingen University (1921). He moved that year to Marburg University, where he completed his *Habilitationsschrift* (1921) with a work on the character of different keys; he became reader in 1927 and retired in 1946. Stephani introduced the so-called 'unified score' (*Einheitspartitur*) in which he advocated that an orchestral score be notated exclusively in the treble clef; another preoccupation of his writings is acoustical psychology. As a composer he wrote some orchestral works (Festival Overture, a ten-movement 'Festspiel' *Hl. Elisabeth* and incidental music for *William Tell*), choral works, many songs and vocal canons.

WRITINGS

'Partituren', *ZIMG*, ii (1900–01), 313

Das Erhabene, insonderheit in der Tonkunst (diss., U. of Leipzig, 1902; Leipzig, 1903, 2/1907)

'Der Stimmungscharakter der Tonarten', *Die Musik*, iv/3 (1904–5), 20

'Tonmathematik-Tondeutung', *Melos*, i (1920), 38

Der Charakter der Tonarten (Habilitationsschrift, U. of Marburg, 1921; Regensburg, 1923)

'Das Vierteltonproblem', *Die Musik*, xv (1922–3), 738

'Das Verhältnis von reiner und pythagoreischer Stimmung als psychologisches Problem', *Kongressbericht: Leipzig 1925*, 417

Grundfragen des Musikhörens (Leipzig, 1926)

'Enharmonik ("Polare Harmonik") bei Beethoven', *Beethoven-Zentenarfeier: Wien 1927*, 83

'Der letzte Schubert', *Die Musik*, xxi (1928–9), 37

'Veranschaulichung der Tonhöhenverhältnisse in Laut und Bewegungssymbolen', *Musikpädagogische Gegenwartsfragen*, ed. L. Kestenberg (Leipzig, 1928)

'Felix Draeseke', *ZMw*, xvii (1935), 426

Das Problem des Orgelstils (Essen, 1942)

'Ursprung oder Zielweiser unserer Tonvorstellung? Betrachtung über die Kernfrage', *ZfM*, Jg.116 (1955), 194

Rationales und Überrationales im ethnischen und ästhetischen Werturteil (Marburg, 1958)

BIBLIOGRAPHY

H. Heussner: 'Hermann Stephani zum Gedächtnis', *Mf*, xvi (1961), 138

ALFRED GRANT GOODMAN

Stephani, Johann. See STEFFENS, JOHANN.

Stephani, Josef Antonín. See ŠTĚPÁN, JOSEF ANTONÍN.

Stephanie, (Johann) Gottlieb (*b* Breslau, 19 Feb 1741; *d* Vienna, 23 Jan 1800). Austrian dramatist and actor, sometimes referred to as 'the younger', half-brother of (Christian) Gottlob Stephanie ('the elder'). He enrolled as a law student at Halle but enlisted as a Prussian hussar in the Seven Years War, was captured by the Austrians in 1760 and became an Austrian soldier in 1761. He left the army in 1765 and in 1768 was encouraged towards a stage career by the Mozarts' friend Anton Mesmer. Stephanie joined the National-Schaubühne company in 1769, and in 1779 he succeeded J. H. F. Müller as director of the National-Singspiel. Apart from several once-popular plays (especially *Der Deserteur aus Kindesliebe* (*kindlicher Liebe*), 1773) he adapted Farquhar's *The Recruiting Officer* (1769) and Shakespeare's *Macbeth* (1772) for the Viennese stage. He is, however, chiefly remembered as a librettist. He provided or adapted nearly 20 librettos for the National-Singspiel venture between 1778 and 1786, including those for Umlauf's *Die schöne Schusterin, oder Die pücefarbenen Schuhe* (1779), *Das Irrlicht* (1782) and *Die glücklichen Jäger* (1786), for Mozart's *Die Entführung aus dem Serail* (1782) and *Der Schauspieldirektor* (1786), for Dittersdorf's *Der Apotheker und der Doktor* (1786) and *Die Liebe im Narrenhause* (1787), and for operas by Mederitsch, Gassmann, F. Teyber, Süssmayr and others; he also translated operas by numerous French and Italian composers, including Grétry, Sacchini, Anfossi, Paisiello, Piccinni and Sarti. Although early in his career he was a supporter of the old popular tradition, and as an actor favoured broadly comic roles, he later turned towards his brother's more 'enlightened' attitudes.

WRITINGS

Stephanie des Jüngeren sämmtliche Lustspiele (Vienna, 1771)

Stephanie des Jüngeren sämmtliche Schauspiele (Vienna, 1775–86)

Sechs Operetten (Vienna, 1783)

Sämmtliche Singspiele (Liegnitz, 1792)

BIBLIOGRAPHY

C. von Wurzbach: 'Stephanie, Gottlieb', *Biographisches Lexikon des Kaiserthums Oesterreich*, xxxviii (Vienna, 1879), 222ff

K. Goedeke: *Grundriss zur Geschichte der deutschen Dichtung*, iv/1 (Dresden, 1891), 76

O. Walzel: 'Stephanie, Gottlob "der Jüngere"' [sic], *ADB*

O. Teuber and A. von Weilen: *Die Theater Wiens*, ii/1–2 (Vienna, 1896–1903)

H. Bussmann: *Die Schauspielkunst Gottlieb Stephanies d.J.* (diss., U. of Jena, 1923)

A. Bauer: *Opern und Operetten in Wien* (Graz and Cologne, 1955)

S. Hochstöger: 'Gottlieb Stephanie der Jüngere', *Jb der Gesellschaft für Wiener Theaterforschung*, xii (1960), 3–82

PETER BRANSCOMBE

Stephanus, Clemens. See STEPHANI, CLEMENS.

Stephen [Stephens; Jones]**, Edward** [Tanymarian] (*b* Maentwrog, Merionethshire, baptized 15 Dec 1822; *d* Llanllechid, 10 May 1885). Welsh minister and composer. Edward Jones was apprenticed to a tailor, and started preaching at the age of 18; in 1843 he gave up his trade and went to read for the ministry at Bala. There, to avoid being confused with another student, he called himself Edward Stephen Jones, adding his father's Christian name, but the surname was frequently omitted and he became known as Edward Stephen(s). In 1847 he was ordained and became minister of the Welsh Independent Church at Dwygyfylchi, North Wales, where he remained until 1856 when he accepted the ministry of two churches in Llanllechid. He married his predecessor's widow and adopted as his bardic name 'Tanymarian', after the small mansion which was their home. A popular, original and witty preacher, he was much concerned with the place of music in Welsh nonconformist worship. His compositions were well known and included besides anthems and hymn tunes ('Tanymarian' is a fine example) *Ystorm Tiberias*, the first Welsh oratorio (1855, rev. 1887) and a Requiem in memory of the powerful Welsh preacher John Jones, Talysarn (1858). He also had a part in editing *Cerddor y Cysegr* (1859) and *Llyfr Tonau ac Emynau* (1868), to the latter of which he added a supplement in 1879. His articles, which are distinguished by their lively style, appeared in *Cronicl y Cerddor*, *Y Cerddor Cymreig*, *Y Cerddor* and *Y Dysgedydd*. Although not in complete agreement with John Roberts over the most effective way to include congregational singing in nonconformist services, he supported him in establishing the *gymanfa ganu* (singing festival) during the 1859 religious revival, and edited (1861–3) *Greal y Corau*, the journal of the Choral Association of Wales. He travelled widely conducting such singing festivals and adjudicating at competitive eisteddfods. He was also a prolific poet and a good singer.

BIBLIOGRAPHY

R. D. Griffith: *Hanes canu cynulleidfaol Cymru* (Cardiff, 1948)

——: 'Stephen, Edward (Jones)', *Dictionary of Welsh Biography* (London, 1959)

OWAIN EDWARDS

Stephen of Liège. Late 10th-century Bishop of Liège and composer of the Gregorian Office of the Trinity; *see* HERIGERUS.

Stephens, Catherine (*b* London, 18 Sept 1794; *d* London, 22 Feb 1882). English soprano and actress, daughter of Edward Stephens, carver and gilder, of Grosvenor Square. In 1807 she began to study singing with Gesualdo Lanza. Under his care she appeared in various provincial towns, and in 1822 took small parts with an Italian opera company at the Pantheon in London. Later that year she studied with Thomas Welsh. On 23 September 1813 she made a successful début at Covent Garden as Mandane in Arne's *Artaxerxes*, following it with appearances as Polly in *The Beggar's Opera*, as Rosetta in *Love in a Village* and as Clara in *The Duenna*. She remained at Covent Garden until 1822, when she went to Drury Lane, returning to Covent Garden in 1828.

Catherine Stephens never mastered Italian. It was as an exponent of 'English style on Italian rudiments' that she made her name as one of the most popular artists of the day, in concerts and oratorio as well as in the theatre, in provincial cities as well as in London. She appeared in ballad operas, in new operas and dramatic entertainments by Bishop and others, and in adaptations and arrangements of operas from abroad which, by 20th-century standards, are extraordinary. She sang Susanna in the first performance in English of *Le nozze di Figaro* (Covent Garden, 1819), and had previously sung Zerlina in *The Libertine*, an afterpiece based on Shadwell's play, with Mozart's music, which is counted as the first performance in English of *Don Giovanni* (Covent Garden, 1817). On the same evening she played Ophelia in *Hamlet* on the occasion of John Philip Kemble's last appearance in the role (in 1814 she had been hissed for introducing Purcell's *Mad Bess* into this play). Stephens was one of three sopranos who sang Agnes (Agathe) in Hawes's English adaptation of *Der Freischütz* (English Opera House, 1824). When he was in London in 1826, Weber wrote for her the song *From Chindara's warbling fount I come*, his last composition. She retired in 1835 and on 19 April 1838 she married the recently-widowed Earl of Essex in his London house in Belgrave Square. He died the next year at the age of 81. She lived in the same house until her death.

Contemporary writers agreed on the sweetness of her voice, which was rich if not outstandingly brilliant. Hazlitt, who placed her with Kean as one of 'the only theatrical favourites I ever had', compared her 'simple, artless manner' with Braham's elaborate artifice. Leigh Hunt praised her 'exquisite vein of gentle pathos'. Her acting may have been no more than charm of personality, yet her colleague Macready, not an easy man to please, described her in his *Reminiscences* as 'the favourite of all', and commented on the 'correctness of judgment that never deserted her'.

RONALD CRICHTON

Stephens, Edward. *See* STEPHEN, EDWARD.

Stephens, John (*b* Gloucester, *c*1720; *d* Salisbury, 15 Dec 1780). English cathedral musician. He was appointed organist of Salisbury Cathedral in 1746, having previously been organist of St James's, Bristol. He took the Cambridge degree of MusD in 1763 and conducted the Gloucester Music Meeting of 1766. He is the composer of one of the chimes of Gloucester Cathedral, and a volume of his cathedral music was published in 1805.

WATKINS SHAW

Stephenson, Edward (*b* 1759; *d* Farley Hill, Berks., 15 Sept 1833). English music collector. He studied at Oxford, was a member of a banking firm, and in 1794 was appointed sheriff of Berkshire. A friendship with the musician Karl Friedrich Horn (Stephenson and J. P. Salomon were godfathers to Horn's son Charles Edward) may have led to his activities in the cause of J. S. Bach, which ranged from his gathering Bach enthusiasts to celebrate Bach's birthday at his London home in 1810 to his preparation in about 1808 of an

English translation of J. N. Forkel's biography. This translation, which Horn and Samuel Wesley planned to publish, is not known to be extant; its relationship to the first published translation (London, 1820) is unknown. W. T. Parke called Stephenson's collection of Cremona violins (which included Stradivari's 1704 'Glennie' violin and 1731 'Paganini' viola) 'perhaps the best and most valuable . . . of any private gentleman in England'. Stephenson's manuscript collection included J. C. Smith's copy of Handel's opera *Radamisto* (now in *GB-Lbm*). His eldest son, Rowland (*c*1790–1843), assumed the surname Standish in 1834 in respect of an inheritance, and published as Orlando Standish the primer *Elementi di contrappunto* (Florence, 1836); his Florence home contained a theatre where musical performances were given. He should not be confused with his brother-in-law Rowland Stephenson (1782–1856), MP for Leominster 1827–9, who has been mistaken for the Stephenson involved in the English Bach revival.

BIBLIOGRAPHY
C. E. Horn: MS Journal, *J-Tn*
W. T. Parke: *Musical Memoirs* (London, 1830), i, 301f
Obituary of Rowland Standish, *AMZ*, xlv (1843), columns 668, 915
J. T. Lightwood: *Samuel Wesley, Musician* (London, 1937)
E. N. Doring: *How Many Strads?* (Chicago, 1945)
MICHAEL KASSLER

Stephenson, Kurt (*b* Hamburg, 30 Aug 1899). German musicologist. From 1919 he studied musicology at the universities of Hamburg under Anschütz, Frankfurt am Main under Bauer, Freiburg under Gurlitt and (from 1921) Halle under Schering, taking his doctorate at Halle in 1924 with a dissertation on Johann Schop. Subsequently he was active in Hamburg as a music critic, as an assistant at the State and University Library and as a teacher at the conservatory. He completed his *Habilitation* in musicology at Freiburg in 1937 with a work on Andreas Romberg. He was appointed lecturer (1939) and (1948, after six years of military service) *ausserplanmässiger Professor* in musicology at Bonn; he retired in 1964. Stephenson has concentrated on music history since the 17th century, especially on the music history of Hamburg and the history of the student song. From 1961 to 1971, while making scholarly contributions to the history of the lied, he was director of the editorial board of *Darstellungen und Quellen der deutschen Einheitsbewegung im 19. und 20. Jahrhundert*. He was the co-founder and president of the Hamburg Brahms-Gesellschaft (1969–73), and he was awarded the Brahms Medal of the City of Hamburg (1973).

WRITINGS
Johann Schop (diss., U. of Halle, 1924)
Hundert Jahre Philharmonische Gesellschaft in Hamburg (Hamburg, 1928)
Andreas Romberg (Habilitationsschrift, U. of Freiburg, 1937; Hamburg, 1938)
Hamburgische Oper zwischen Barock und Romantik (Hamburg, 1948)
Ludwig van Beethoven: sein Vermächtnis in unserer Zeit (Hamburg, 1948)
Die musikalische Klassik, Mw, vi (1953; Eng. trans., 1962)
'Musikalisches Biedermeier in Hamburg', *Beiträge zur Hamburgischen Musikgeschichte*, ed. H. Husmann (Hamburg, 1956), 7
Johannes Brahms und Fritz Simrock: Weg einer Freundschaft: Briefe des Verlegers an den Komponisten (Hamburg, 1961)
Romantik in der Tonkunst, Mw, xxi (1961; Eng. trans., 1961)
'Der junge Brahms und Remenyis ungarische Lieder', *SMw*, xxv (1962), 520
'Johannes Brahms und Georg Dietrich Otten', *Festschrift Karl Gustav Fellerer* (Regensburg, 1962), 503
ed. with A. Scharff: *Darstellungen und Quellen zur Geschichte der deutschen Einheitsbewegung*, v (Heidelberg, 1965) [incl. 'Das Lied der studentischen Erneuerungsbewegung 1814–1819', 9–126]
'Charakterköpfe der Studentenmusik', *Darstellungen und Quellen zur*

Geschichte der deutschen Einheitsbewegung, vi (Heidelberg, 1965), 12–64

Clara Schumann (Bonn, 1969)

ed.: *Johannes Brahms in seiner Familie: der Briefwechsel* (Hamburg, 1973)

'Der Komponist Brahms im eigenen Urteil', *Brahms-Studien*, i (1974), 7

Articles in *MGG* and other dictionaries

EDITIONS

J. Brahms: Klavierwerke (Frankfurt am Main, 1973–6)

BIBLIOGRAPHY

K. Stephenson: 'Stephenson, Kurt', *Rheinische Musiker*, iv, ed. K. G. Fellerer (Cologne, 1967), 160 [lists writings to 1967]

HANS HEINRICH EGGEBRECHT

Stephkins, Theodore. *See* STEFFKIN, THEODORE.

Sterbini, Cesare (*b* Rome, 1784; *d* Rome, 19 Jan 1831). Italian librettist. A Roman civil servant with a knowledge of classics and a familiarity with French and German literature, he was a librettist by vocation, not profession. In 1813 he made his first attempt at dramatic poetry with a cantata, *Paolo e Virginia*, set to music by Migliorucci for the Mombelli sisters. His meeting with Rossini brought him to opera. First he wrote for him a *semiserio* libretto on an argument of tragic character worked out in a Romantic scenario, *Torvaldo e Dorliska* (Rome, 1815), which shows a mastery of dramatic form and expression that was immediately confirmed in *Almaviva, ossia L'inutile precauzione* (Rome, 1816). He infused Beaumarchais' comedy *Le barbier de Séville* (already used by Petrosellini for Paisiello) with a new spirit – a well-defined social perspective, sharpened by means of an obvious interplay of existing formulae and types, which nonetheless become entangled in unexpected ways, and an inventive and agile language, chastened with irony and based on neat articulation and rapid declamation to match Rossini's music. In his few later librettos Sterbini displayed a gift for choosing Romantic themes or deftly modernized ones, and masterful restraint in his treatment of irony and the affections. By virtue of his broad education he was able to reveal existing forms and structures in a new light and to invest them with new purpose.

BIBLIOGRAPHY

J. Ferretti: 'Cesare Sterbini', *Museo drammatico italiano e straniero*, v (Rome, 1831)

——: *Una conferenza inedita di Jacopo Ferretti sulla storia della poesia melodrammatica romana*, ed. A. Cametti (Pesaro, 1896)

A. Cametti: *La musica teatrale a Roma cento anni fa: 'La Cenerentola'* (Rome, 1917)

R. Bacchelli: *Gioacchino Rossini* (Turin, 1941)

FRANCA CELLA

Sterkel, Johann Franz Xaver (*b* Würzburg, 3 Dec 1750; *d* Würzburg, 12 Oct 1817). German composer, pianist and organist.

1. LIFE. His musical gift was evident at a young age; he had rigorous musical training from the court organist A. Kette and from Weismandel in Würzburg, where he entered the university in 1764. In 1768 he was tonsured and became organist in the collegiate chapter of Neumünster, later rising to sub-deacon (1772), deacon (1773) and finally priest (1774). His lifelong service to the church provided a subsistence without noticeably affecting his musical activities.

As a result of a performance at the Würzburg court, Sterkel was invited to perform for the court at Mainz, noted for its orchestra and its active musical life. His trip included a visit to Mannheim, where Mozart heard him perform and condemned his excessive tempos (letter of 26 November 1777). Early in 1778 Sterkel was called to Mainz to fill a position in the Liebfrauen chapter and was named court chaplain as well. Late in 1779 Elector Friedrich Karl Joseph von Erthal sent Sterkel and his younger half-brother, the violinist F. Lehritter, on an extended tour of Italy. Sterkel, who had already published several sets of chamber sonatas, seems nevertheless to have gained much in his mature style from his extended exposure to Italian taste. He visited all the major cities of Italy, frequently performing as a pianist. For the Naples court he played duo sonatas and concertos with Lady Catherine Hamilton; the queen commissioned his only opera, *Il Farnace*, performed in an elaborate production with ballets at the S Carlo on 12 January 1782. Travelling north again in May, he spent several weeks with Padre Martini in Bologna, then was recalled to Mainz to fill a canonry of his chapter, visiting Stein's piano workshop in Augsburg en route. In Mainz before the end of the year, he plunged into a period of intense music-making and composition.

Sterkel's well-known meeting with Beethoven, as reported by Simrock and Wegeler (see Schiedermair), occurred early in 1791. Sterkel played one of his own sonatas, accompanied by Andreas Romberg on the violin. Beethoven was reluctant to perform in turn, and was challenged to play his own demanding Righini variations, which had recently been published; he played those that he remembered and improvised additional ones, successfully imitating throughout the distinctive light, graceful performing style just displayed by Sterkel.

When the Mainz court was disrupted by the French invasion in October 1792, the director, Sterkel's brother-in-law Vincenzo Righini, was called to Berlin. On the regaining of Mainz, Sterkel was named Kapellmeister (1793) and charged with rebuilding the court music, but the war caused further difficulties and the royal chapel was disbanded in 1797. Except for a visit to Righini in Berlin, Sterkel spent the next years in Würzburg. The court there fostered mainly sacred performances, and he composed much church music, including several festival masses generally similar to those of Haydn from the same period. From about 1802 Sterkel was in Regensburg, where his unceasing efforts on behalf of the musical life brought accolades (*AMZ*, ix, 1806–7, col.502); he established a choir school to provide good vocalists and wrote most of his partsongs at that time. After his Regensburg patron, Karl Theodor von Dalberg, was made Grand Duke of Frankfurt, Sterkel followed him to Aschaffenburg in April 1810 and was named his music director. Among other duties he was responsible for theatrical productions, including performances of Mozart's *Die Zauberflöte* and *Die Entführung aus dem Serail*. When Aschaffenburg was annexed to Bavaria in 1814 the court was dissolved. In 1815 Sterkel visited Munich, then returned to Würzburg. Beethoven is said once to have called Sterkel the 'royal composer' (*Reichskomponist*), as his published dedications form a roster of the highest members of the nobility. Sterkel was also an effective teacher, whose pupils included the pianists C. P. Hoffmann, G. C. Zulehner, Catherina Bauer and T. Horgniés, and the singers E. Eck, L. Barensfeld, N. Häckel, J. C. Grünbaum and G. Weichselbaum.

2. WORKS. Sterkel was famed in his time as both a pianist and a composer. His output was voluminous, and

the editions published in the Rhine valley (Mainz, Frankfurt am Main etc), especially of chamber music, were quickly reprinted in Paris, London and elsewhere. Notable among the works for unaccompanied piano are those for four hands and the collections of short pieces. The latter were regarded as among the best of the type (*AMZ*, iv, 1801–2, col.672). Sterkel's many sonatas are mostly for piano accompanied by violin or violin and cello. His handling of the duo relationship is flexible but after the first publications the violin is never dispensable; as with his contemporaries, the cello only gradually gained in importance. Generally the piano parts are fluent and only moderately difficult. Several writers find the few chamber works of larger proportions – the string quintet and the piano quartet, a kind of chamber concerto – to be the most attractive for modern performance. Far fewer in number than the chamber works, but of some interest, are the concertos, symphonies and overtures (see Gottron).

Sterkel has been regarded as one of the important composers in translating characteristics of the Mannheim style into keyboard chamber music, despite his tenuous connections with that school. Some contemporaries found the lyricism of his works more noteworthy: Burney (*Rees's Cyclopaedia*) remarked that 'he has not only collected all the vocal flowers of the greatest opera singers of the present times, but scattered them liberally through his works'. The lyricism and curiously prolix, loose-knit structure of many of his sonatas point towards Schubert and others.

Sterkel's vocal works include Italian arias with orchestra, Italian songs and ensembles, and a series of lied collections. In some of the later lieder he succeeded in enriching the expressive contribution of the accompaniment.

Sterkel's prominence in the 18th century is suggested by two works: a compilation of lessons (sonatas) for piano published by John Relfe (London, 1786) including works by Haydn, Sterkel, Schobert, Kozeluch, Vanhal, Edelmann and the compiler; and Clementi's *Musical Characteristics* op.19 (1787) comprising 'Preludes' and 'Cadences' composed in the style of eminent keyboard composers – Sterkel, Haydn, Kozeluch, Mozart, Vanhal and Clementi himself. Along with his success, Sterkel also came under frequent critical attack. His playing was described as effeminate (*damenartig*), his sonatas suitable only for ladies' diversion, and he was accused of being able to play only his own works. The criticisms were not wholly unwarranted, considering the marked discrepancy of style between Sterkel and the more impassioned north German school of C. P. E. Bach. Nevertheless Sterkel, through the example of his unique performing style, his impact on students and the widespread diffusion of his works, was significant in the early development of a pianistic style.

WORKS

INSTRUMENTAL
(*thematic index of chamber music in DTB, xxviii, Jg.xvi, 1915*)
Orch: 4 syms., op.7 (Paris, 1782), 3 also as op.1 (Berlin, 1783); 4 syms., op.11 (Paris, 1786); 2 sinfonies périodiques, op.35 (Mainz, 1792); Sinfonia, B♭ (Mainz, 1792–4; Leipzig, *c*1809); 11 further syms., *CH-Bu*, *D-Rtt*; 6 pf conc.: 1 as op.20 (Mainz, 1785) [also as op.18], 3 as op.24 (Vienna), lost, 3 as op.26 (Mainz, 1788) [no.1 = op.20], 1 as op.31 (Mainz, 1789) [also as op.24], 1 as op.40 (Offenbach, 1792) [8 listed in Boyer catalogue (Paris, 1787)]; 4 ovs.: nos.1–3 (Leipzig, n.d.), no.3 lost, copy of no.4 owned by Gottron
Pf/hpd trios: 3 as op.1 (Frankfurt am Main, 1774); 3 as op.2 (Frankfurt am Main, 1774); 3 as op.3 (Frankfurt am Main, *c*1776; Amsterdam, 1791); 3 as op.5 (Frankfurt am Main, 1776; Amsterdam, 1791) [also

as op.4]; 3 as op.6 (Frankfurt am Main, *c*1777) [also as op.5]; 3 as op.7 (Frankfurt am Main, 1777); 3 as op.9 (Mannheim, 1782); 3 as op.12 (Paris, *c*1782); 6 as op.17 (Mainz, 1784); 3 as op.30 (Vienna, 1789) [also as op.23]; 3 as op.32 (Vienna, 1790); 3 as op.34 (Offenbach, 1793); op.45 (Berlin, 1805); op.46 (Leipzig, 1808); 2 grand trios, op.47 (Leipzig, *c*1810), op.48 (Berlin, *c*1810); 2 grand trios, op. posth. (Bonn, *c*1818)
Sonatas, pf/hpd, vn: 3 as op.4 (Frankfurt am Main, *c*1776); 3 as op.15 (Mainz, *c*1784) [also as op.19]; 3 as op.16 (Mainz, *c*1784) [also as opp.20, 22]; 3 as op.18 (Mainz, *c*1785) [also as op.23], 1 ed. in DTB, xxviii, (1915); op.25 (Mainz, *c*1786); op.27 (Offenbach, 1787); 6 as op.33 (Mainz, 1793) [3 also as op.34]; op.41 (Offenbach, 1804); Grande sonate, op.44 (Vienna, 1805)
Other chamber: Grand quintette, 2 vn, 2 va, vc (Vienna, *c*1790), ed. A. Gottron (Heidelberg, 1961); Pf Qt (Leipzig, 1804); 6 duos, vn, va, op.8 (Paris, *c*1779)
Solo pf: 30 pièces, 12 as op.10 (Vienna, *c*1780), 18 as opp.22, 24 (Mainz, 1784); Ariettes variées (Berlin, 1797), ?as op.35 (Offenbach, n.d.); 3 sonatas, op.34 (Mainz, 1798); Grande sonate, op.36 (Offenbach, 1798); Fantaisie en rondo, op.37 (Offenbach, *c*1798); 3 grandes sonates, op.39 (Offenbach, n.d.); Divertissement, op.48 (Leipzig, n.d.); 20 petites pièces (Bonn, Offenbach, Mainz, n.d.); Air and variations, op.35 (Offenbach, n.d.); Variations on Das Geheimnis (Leipzig, *c*1808); 6 sonatas, 4 hands: op.21 [also as op.15], op.24, 4 as op.28 (Mainz, by 1787); collections of single works, 4 hands (Mainz, Offenbach, from 1809); others in 18th-century anthologies

VOCAL
Dramatic: Il Farnace (dramma per musica, 3), Naples, S Carlo, 12 Jan 1782, *I-Nc*, ov. arr. pf, vn (Frankfurt am Main, *c*1785)
Sacred: 4 festival masses, 4vv, chorus, orch, *D-Bds* (autograph), *Dlb*, *Mbs*; 2 Te Deum, 4vv, chorus, orch, 1 in *Mbs*, 1 composed 1793, lost; further single works with insts, *Bds*, *OB*, Stifthaus, Würzburg
Secular: 8 arias (scenas, rondos), S, str/orch: Ah parlate, oh Dio!, Se tutti i mali miei (Leipzig, n.d.), Caro mio ben (Mainz, n.d.), Passeremo il ciglio amato, Fedele mio diletto, *Rp*, Vaghe amabili pupille, *Rp*, La mia morte, *DO*; Sammlung [125] neuer Lieder, acc. kbd, 16 vols. (Mainz, from *c*1788) [some vols. pubd elsewhere]; 15 collections of Italian songs, 1–3vv, pf, further single songs and lieder, vocal works in anthologies [see Scharnagl for details]

BIBLIOGRAPHY
FitnerQ; *FétisB*; *GerberL*; *GerberNL*
J. B. von Siebold: Biographical sketch, *Fränkische Chronik* (Würzburg, 1807)
A. Schmitz: *Beethovens 'Zwei Prinzipe'* (Berlin and Bonn, 1923)
O. Kaul: *Geschichte der Würzburger Hofmusik im 18. Jahrhundert* (Würzburg, 1924)
L. Schiedermair: *Der junge Beethoven* (Leipzig, 1925/*R*1972, 4/1970)
K. Schweikert: *Die Musikpflege am Hofe der Kurfürsten von Mainz im 17. und 18. Jahrhundert* (Mainz, 1937)
A. Scharnagl: *Johann Franz Xaver Sterkel* (Würzburg, 1943)
A. B. Gottron: *Mainzer Musikgeschichte von 1500 bis 1800* (Mainz, 1959)
R. Fuhrmann: *Mannheimer Klavier-Kammermusik* (Marburg, 1963)
W. S. Newman: *The Sonata in the Classic Era* (Chapel Hill, 1963, rev. 2/1972)

RONALD R. KIDD

Sterling, Antoinette (*b* Sterlingville, NY, 23 Jan 1850; *d* London, 9 Jan 1904). American contralto. Her first important teacher was Abella, in New York (1867); the next year she went to England, then to Cologne for study with Mathilde Marchesi, and to Baden for study with Pauline Viardot-García. She also had lessons with Manuel García in London. In 1871 she returned to the USA and was soloist in Henry Ward Beecher's church in Brooklyn. A concert at Irving Hall, Boston, on 13 May 1873 proved to be her farewell to the USA: soon afterwards she moved permanently to London (except for a tour with the Theodore Thomas Orchestra in 1875). Sterling's London début was at a Covent Garden Promenade Concert (5 November 1873); she continued to be a popular singer, mainly of lighter works, for many years. She introduced Arthur Sullivan's *The Lost Chord* (31 January 1877) and other songs – some written especially for her – destined for great popularity. Her voice was one of great richness and volume; its range was e♭ to f″. Her daughter, Jean Sterling MacKinlay, was also a singer; her son compiled a biography *Antoinette Sterling and Other Celebrities* (London, 1906).

H. WILEY HITCHCOCK

Stern. German family of printers and publishers. The bookbinder Johann Stern (*d* 1614) set up a printing and publishing business in Lüneburg, where it is still active. His sons Johann (*d* 1656) and Heinrich (1592–1665) established a branch at Wolfenbüttel which became one of the most important publishing concerns of the Thirty Years War; they received royal privileges and were ennobled in recognition of their achievements. The founder's grandson Johann (1633–1712) published particularly interesting imprints of H. Rist and his circle, including works by J. W. Franck, F. Funcke, F. E. and J. Praetorius, T. Selle and J. J. Weiland.

BIBLIOGRAPHY
H. Dumrese and F. C. Schilling: *Lüneburg und die Offizin der Sterne* (Lüneburg, 1956)
H. Walter: *Beiträge zur Musikgeschichte der Stadt Lüneburg im 17. Jahrhundert und beginnenden 18. Jahrhundert* (diss., U. of Cologne, 1962), 32, 160ff, 187ff
J. Benzing: *Die Buchdrucker des 16. und 17. Jahrhunderts im deutschen Sprachgebiet* (Wiesbaden, 1963)
H. Walter: *Musikgeschichte der Stadt Lüneburg: vom Ende des 16. bis zum Anfang des 18. Jahrhunderts* (Tutzing, 1967)

THEODOR WOHNHAAS

Stern, Isaac (*b* Kremenets, 21 July 1920). American violinist of Russian birth. When he was a year old he was taken to San Francisco. He studied at the San Francisco Conservatory (1928–31), then with Louis Persinger; from 1932 to 1937 he studied with Naoum Blinder, a violinist of the Russian school, and his principal teacher. He made his début in 1935 in recital and with the San Francisco SO under Monteux in 1936. In the same year he played with the Los Angeles PO under Klemperer. He made his New York début on 11 October 1937 but returned to San Francisco for further study. After his second New York recital on 18 February 1939 he quickly joined the front rank of American violinists. In 1943–4 he played for Allied troops in Greenland, Iceland and the South Pacific.

Stern made his European début in 1948 at the Lucerne Festival under Münch and after that toured Europe regularly. He first played at the Casals Festival, Prades, in 1950 and at the Edinburgh Festival in 1953; he toured the USSR in 1956. He has also played in Australia, Japan, South America and Israel. In 1960, with Eugene Istomin and Leonard Rose, he formed a trio which has received wide acclaim. For the Beethoven bicentenary the trio gave notable Beethoven programmes in London, Paris, New York and other centres. Stern has played the great concertos from Bach to Bartók, the complete trios of Beethoven and Brahms as well as a chamber music series with Casals, and sonatas with his piano partner Alexander Zakin. He has also given the premières of concertos by William Schuman and Leonard Bernstein and has recorded soundtracks for films, such as *Humoresque* (1946), *Tonight we Sing*, in which he impersonated Ysaÿe (1953), and *Fiddler on the Roof* (1971). As a soloist and with the trio, Stern has performed at the White House on several occasions.

Stern is recognized as one of the world's foremost violinists. His distinctive style reflects his vibrant personality, total involvement in music and intense communication with his listeners. His interpretations are vital and exuberant, his tone warm and expressive. His feeling for style is impeccable; invariably he finds the right inflection to bring the music alive. His technique is subordinate to his musical concept. 'To use the violin to make music, never to use music just to play the violin' is his principle. Stern's favourite violins are two by Guarneri 'del Gesù', the so-called 'Vicomte de Panette' of 1737 and the one formerly played by Eugène Ysaÿe, made in 1740.

In 1960 Stern organized a group to save Carnegie Hall, and became president of the Carnegie Hall Corporation, responsible for the cultural programmes. In 1964 he helped to establish the National Endowment for the Arts, sponsored by the US Government, and was appointed a member of the advisory board by President Johnson. As chairman of the board of the America–Israel Cultural Foundation, he is playing a vital role in aiding the careers of many young musicians.

BIBLIOGRAPHY
I. Whyntie: 'Isaac Stern', *Audio Record Review*, ii/11 (1963), 16 [with discography by F. F. Clough and G. J. Cuming]

BORIS SCHWARZ

Stern, Julius (*b* Breslau, 8 Aug 1820; *d* Berlin, 27 Feb 1883). German conductor. He received his early musical training under Maurer, Ganz and Rungenhagen in Berlin. In 1843 he went to Dresden to study singing and then to Paris, where he was conductor of the German Gesangverein; among the works he performed there was Mendelssohn's *Antigone*, which drew from the composer a characteristic letter (27 May 1844). He returned to Berlin in 1846 and the next year founded the Sternscher Gesangverein, which he conducted until 1874. In 1850, with Kullak and Marx, he founded the Berlin Conservatory (from 1857 the Stern Conservatory); notwithstanding the defection of his two colleagues, the conservatory flourished to become one of the finest in Europe. Stern was also conductor of the Berlin Sinfonie-Kapelle (1869–71) and was responsible for the two seasons of the Reichshall concerts (1873–5). He published many vocal pieces and arrangements; his editions of singing exercises by Vaccai, Crescentini and others were widely used.

GEORGE GROVE/R

Stern, Leo(pold Lawrence) (*b* Brighton, 5 April 1862; *d* London, 10 Sept 1904). English cellist. His father was a violinist of German origin, his mother an English pianist. As a child, he played the drum in the Brighton Symphony Society, conducted by his father. In 1877 he went to London to study chemistry, but also started cello lessons with Hugo Daubert. In 1883 he entered the Royal Academy of Music, London, studying first with Pezze, then Piatti; in 1885 he visited Leipzig to have lessons with Klengel and Davïdov. On his return in 1886 he played in London and the provinces and in 1888 made a tour with Adelina Patti; subsequently he made concert appearances with Sauret, Paderewski and Albani, and with Godard and Massenet in Paris. He received Queen Victoria's patronage and a diamond pin, and became teacher to her youngest son-in-law, Prince Henry of Battenberg.

In 1895 Stern played in Prague, where he met Dvořák. Although the composer had promised the première of the concerto to its dedicatee, Hanuš Wihan, the latter was not available for the date arranged by the London Philharmonic Society, which therefore engaged Stern. Dvořák eventually agreed to this arrangement and conducted the performance on 19 March 1896; at Dvořák's request, Stern subsequently played it in Leipzig, Prague and Berlin. After this he spent much time in the USA and Canada, but his health, always delicate, could no longer stand the strain of public appearances; he was forced to abandon an American tour and return to London, where he died after a protracted illness.

Stern was presented with the 'General Kyd', a large Stradivari of 1684, and towards the end of his life played on the 1726 'Baudiot' Stradivari later owned by Piatigorsky.

BIBLIOGRAPHY

E. van der Straeten: *The History of the Violoncello* (London, 1915/*R*1971)

J. Clapham: *Antonín Dvořák: Musician and Craftsman* (London, 1966)

W. W. COBBETT/LYNDA LLOYD REES

Sternberg, Erich Walter (*b* Berlin, 31 May 1891; *d* Tel-Aviv, 15 Dec 1974). Israeli composer. After graduating in law from Kiel University he decided in 1918 to make his career in music, and he then studied composition with Hugo Leichtentritt and the piano with H. Praetorius. Several of his works from the next 14 years were introduced by leading musicians: *David and Goliath* was first performed by the Berlin PO (1927), the Amar Quartet gave the première of the Second Quartet at the 1928 Schwerin Festival, and in 1931 Scherchen conducted the first performance of *Halochem ha'amitz* ('The gallant soldier'). It was in the next year that Sternberg settled in Palestine, which he had been visiting regularly since 1925. He taught at the Tel-Aviv Conservatory, collaborated with Huberman in forming the Palestine SO (later the Israel PO) and was chairman of the Israeli branch of the ISCM (1938–54). Twice he received the Engel Prize: in 1946 for the choral cycle *Yishtabach* ('Praise ye') and in 1961 for *Ha'orev* ('The raven') for baritone and orchestra. Sternberg's great interest in the Bible, and in poetry in general, is expressed in a largely vocal output. Biblical or other Jewish subjects have scarcely affected his European late-Romantic style, notwithstanding some folk ideas introduced after his move to Israel.

WORKS

(selective list)

Stage: Dr Doolittle (children's opera, 3), 1937, orch suite, 1941; Pacificia (opera, 3, R. Hunter), 1974

Orch: Ov. to a Comedy, 1932; Quodlibet, 1935; Amcha [Thy people], 1936; Joseph and his Brethren, 1937; The Twelve Tribes of Israel, 1942; Shema Israel [Hear, O Israel], 1947; Noah's Ark, 1960

Vocal orch: David and Goliath (M. Claudius), Bar, orch, 1927; Kol nidrei, Bar, orch, 1930; Halochem ha'amitz [The gallant soldier] (Heine), Bar, orch, 1930; Ami [My people] (E. Lasker-Schüler), S, orch, 1945; Shirim mukdamim [Early songs] (Rilke, Morgenstern), S, orch, 1946; Ha'orev [The raven] (Poe), Bar, orch, 1949; Sichot haruach [Dialogues with the wind] (Elisheva), A, orch, 1955; Songs of Hafis, 1v, orch, 1959; Shirei nezirūt [Songs of resignation] (George), Bar, orch, 1958

Other vocal: Inferno (Claudius, Shi-king), chorus 6–8vv, perc, 1930; Hachalil bamerchakim [The distant flute] (Klabund, after Li Tai Po), A, fl, 1958; Love Songs (Sternberg), chorus, orch, 1969; *c*100 solo songs (Sternberg and others)

Inst: Str Qt no.1, with A solo, 1924; Str Qt no.2, 1928; Sonata, vn, pf, 1956; Pf Trio, Wind Qnt, pf pieces

Principal publishers: Israel Music Institute, Israeli Music Publications, Education and Culture Centre of the General Federation of Labour Histadrut

BIBLIOGRAPHY

Y. W. Cohen: *Werden und Entwicklung der Musik in Israel* (Kassel, 1976) [pt.ii of rev. edn. of M. Brod: *Die Musik Israels*]

W. Y. Elias: *The Music of Israel* (in preparation) [bibliography]

WILLIAM Y. ELIAS

Sternefeld, Daniel (*b* Antwerp, 27 Nov 1905). Belgian conductor and composer. He studied the flute and theory at the Antwerp Conservatory (1918–24), later taking lessons in composition with Gilson and in conducting with F. van der Stucken (1928). In 1931–2 he pursued his conducting studies with Paumgartner, Krauss and Karajan in Salzburg. He joined the orchestra of the Royal Flemish Opera, Antwerp, as a flautist in 1929, and became second conductor in 1938 and principal conductor in 1944. In 1948 he left Antwerp to become conductor of the Belgian RSO, in which post he remained until his retirement in 1971. He has appeared as a guest conductor in several European countries, in Israel and in the Americas. *Mathis der Maler* and *Peter Grimes* are among the many works whose Belgian premières he directed. The pressure of his conducting work forced him to give second place to composition. He has given conducting courses at the Antwerp Conservatory.

WORKS

Dramatic: Mater dolorosa, opera, 1936; Pierlala, ballet, 1937; Salve Antverpia (ballet, J. Brabants), 1975; incidental music for plays by Shakespeare, Sophocles, Vondel, Buckner and others; music for son et lumière at St Baaf Abbey, Ghent, 1957

Orch: Sym. Variations, 1928; Elégie, 1929; Vlaamse en waalse volksliedern, suite, 1934; Sym., C, 1944; Variations, brass, 1954

CORNEEL MERTENS

Sternfeld, F(rederick) W(illiam) (*b* Vienna, 25 Sept 1914). British musicologist of Austrian birth. At the University of Vienna from 1933 he was a pupil of Lach and Wellesz, but he also spent extended periods in England, studying with Dent at Cambridge. In 1938 he emigrated to the USA and completed the doctorate under Schrade at Yale University in 1943. He taught at Wesleyan University, Middletown (Conn.), 1940–46, and Dartmouth College, Hanover, New Hampshire, 1946–56; in 1954 he held a Guggenheim Fellowship and the following year was a member of the Institute for Advanced Studies at Princeton. In 1956 he moved to a lectureship at Oxford University and subsequently took British citizenship. He was made reader in the history of music at Oxford in 1972.

Sternfeld's writings have ranged from the Renaissance to the 20th century, and his unpublished studies, lectures and editorial work have also embraced the Middle Ages and antiquity. However, his concern for music in relation to the other arts and its place in cultural and intellectual history in general has been especially characteristic. His doctoral dissertation was on Goethe and music, and he has written on James Joyce and on film music. A long series of Shakespeare studies is headed by the classic *Music in Shakespearean Tragedy* (1963, 2/1967); and his interest in English drama and poetry has also produced work on the lutesong and 17th-century masque and the revision (with David Greer) of Fellowes's *English Madrigal Verse* (1967). A more recent preoccupation has been the role of music in the *intermedio* and the early development of opera. He was a founder-editor of *Renaissance News*, editor (1957–62) of the *Proceedings of the Royal Musical Association* (of which association he became a vice-president in 1971), and his other editorial work includes the seventh volume of *The New Oxford History of Music* (with Egon Wellesz) and two volumes of a history of Western music. His breadth of interests has also made him especially influential as a teacher.

WRITINGS

'Guidonian Hand', *Grove 4*, suppl.

Goethe and Music (diss., Yale U., 1943)

'Some Russian Folksongs in Stravinsky's *Petrouchka*', *Notes*, ii (1944–5), 95; repr. in *Stravinsky: Petrushka*, ed. C. Hamm (New York, 1967), 203 [Norton Critical Score]

'Renaissance Music in Goethe', *Germanic Review*, xx (1945), 241

'Music in the Schools of the Reformation', *MD*, ii (1948), 99

'Copland as a Film Composer', *MQ*, xxxvii (1951), 161

Goethe and Music: a List of Parodies and Goethe's Relationship to Music: a List of References (New York, 1954/*R*1979)

'*Troilus and Cressida*: Music for the Play', *English Institute Essays 1952* (New York, 1954), 107–38

'The Melodic Sources of Mozart's most Popular Lied', *MQ*, xlii (1956), 213

'A Song from Campion's *Lord's Masque*', *Journal of the Warburg and Courtauld Institutes*, xx (1957), 373

'Poetry and Music: Joyce's *Ulysses*', *English Institute Essays 1956* (New York, 1957), 16–54

'Vautrollier's Printing of Lasso's *Recueil de Mellange*', *AnnM*, v (1957), 199

'Lasso's Music for Shakespeare's *Samingo*', *Shakespeare Quarterly*, ix (1958), 105

'Song in Jonson's Comedy: a Gloss on Volpone', *Studies in the English Renaissance Drama in Memory of Karl Julius Holzknecht* (New York, 1959), 310

'Music and the Cinema', *Twentieth Century Music*, ed. R. H. Myers (London, 1960), 95

'La musique dans les tragédies élisabéthaines inspirées de Sénèque', *Les tragédies de Sénèque et le théâtre de la Renaissance: CNRS Royaumont 1962*, 139

Music in Shakespearean Tragedy (London, 1963, 2/1967)

'Ophelia's Version of the Walsingham Song', *ML*, xlv (1964), 177

Songs from Shakespeare's Tragedies (London, 1964)

Articles on music in *New Cambridge Modern History*, viii (1965); ix (1965); vi (1970)

'Expression and Revision in Gluck's Orfeo and Alceste', *Essays Presented to Egon Wellesz* (Oxford, 1966), 114

rev. with D. Greer: E. H. Fellowes: *English Madrigal Verse 1588–1632* (Oxford and New York, 3/1967)

rev. and enlarged: E. Dent: 'Music and Drama', *NOHM*, iv (1968), 784

with M. Joiner: 'Come live with me and be my love', *Comparative Literature*, xxii (1970), 173

'Goethe and Beethoven', *GfMKB, Bonn 1970*, 587

'Les intermèdes de Florence et la genèse de l'opéra', *Journées internationales d'étude du Baroque IV: Montauban 1970*, 25

'Shakespeare and Music', *A New Companion to Shakespeare Studies*, ed. K. Muir and S. Schoenbaum (Cambridge, 1971), 157

'La technique du finale: des intermèdes de l'opéra', *Les fêtes de la Renaissance III: CNRS Tours 1972*, 267

ed.: *A History of Western Music* (London, 1973) [i, v only]

ed. with E. Wellesz: *The Age of Enlightenment 1745–1790*, NOHM, vii (1973) [incl. 'The Early Symphony', 366–433, 'The Concerto', 434–502 [both with E. Wellesz]; 'Instrumental Masterworks and Aspects of Formal Design', 611]

'Aspects of Italian Intermedi and Early Operas', *Convivium musicorum: Festschrift Wolfgang Boetticher* (Berlin, 1974), 359

ed. with others: *Essays on Opera and English Music in Honour of Sir Jack Westrup* (Oxford, 1975)

'The Birth of Opera: Ovid, Poliziano, and the *lieto fine*', *AnMc*, no.19 (1979), 30

EDWARD OLLESON

Stesichorus (*b* ?Mataurus [now Marro], *c*610 BC; *d* ?Catana [now Catania], Sicily, *c*535 BC). Greek lyric poet. Uncertainty surrounds the traditional accounts of Stesichorus; his very name, 'marshal of the chorus', may have been a sobriquet. It seems clear that he came from the Greek cities at the southern tip of Italy, where the active musical life of Locri (Mataurus was founded by Locrians) probably influenced him. Both the Athenians and the Spartans performed his compositions. These works were transitional: Quintilian described him as 'sustaining the weightiness of epic poetry with the lyre' (*Institutes*, x, chap.1, §62). The content was epic, the form lyric. He employed a variety of dactylic rhythms, longer or more complex than the epic hexameter; this fact is mentioned by Glaucus of Rhegium and by (?)Aristoxenus in the Pseudo-Plutarchian *De musica* (chap.7, §1133*f*; 12, §1135*c*; cf 3, §1132*c*). Glaucus declared that Stesichorus imitated Olympus rather than

Orpheus or Terpander and used the 'chariot nome'. This associates him doubly with the aulos; nor does any connection with the kithara appear in the fragments. Fragments nos.47–8 (ed. Edmonds), which contain a direct reference to the lyre, must be assigned to the later poet of the same name, victorious at Athens in 370 or 369 BC (*Parian Chronicle*, §73). The likelihood of such a connection is nevertheless strong on a number of grounds. Stesichorus apparently held Apollo in special regard, and he would have been free to choose either the aulos or the kithara for purposes of accompaniment.

The fragments include several lines from a version of the Orestes myth (nos.37–8, ed. Edmonds). They are cited by the scholiast on Aristophanes' *Peace*, ll.797ff – these lines are themselves taken in part from Stesichorus. The latter spoke of 'devising a Phrygian tune' (*melos*) for gentle spring songs in celebration of the Graces. Like Plato, he ignored current views concerning the ethos of the Phrygian mode. The evidence of papyri now indicates that several of his poems were epic in length. This weakens the usual assumption that he was simply a choral poet; it supports the thesis (see West) that he composed and sang long monodies with kithara accompaniment. Possibly, as a transitional figure, he practised both types of composition.

The 10th-century Byzantine *Suda* lexicon contains a statement that the whole of Stesichorus's poetry displayed a triadic structure of strophe, antistrophe and epode. This claim, still repeated, has no basis either in the metrical schemes of the fragments or in early critical sources. There can be little doubt that the poems on erotic or romantic themes were the work of a later writer.

BIBLIOGRAPHY

H. W. Smyth: *Greek Melic Poets* (London and New York, 1900/*R*1963), 187f, 255ff

J. Vürtheim: *Stesichoros' Fragmente und Biographie* (Leiden, 1919)

J. M. Edmonds, ed. and trans.: *Lyra graeca* (London and Cambridge, Mass., 1922–7, 2/1928–40), ii, 14–77

P. Maas: 'Stesichoros 1), 2)', *Paulys Realencyclopädie der classischen Altertumswissenschaft*, 2nd ser., iii (Stuttgart, 1929), 2458

C. M. Bowra: *Greek Lyric Poetry* (Oxford, 1936, 2/1961), 74–129

D. L. Page, ed.: *Poetae melici graeci* (Oxford, 1962), 94–141

D. A. Campbell, ed.: *Greek Lyric Poetry* (London and New York, 1967), 38f, 253ff

M. Treu: 'Stesichoros', *Paulys Realencyclopädie*, suppl.xi (Stuttgart, 1968), 1253

M. L. West: 'Stesichorus', *Classical Quarterly*, xxi (1971), 302

W. Kraus: 'Stesichoros 1), 2)', *Der kleine Pauly*, v (Stuttgart, 1974), 367

WARREN ANDERSON

Stęszewski, Jan (*b* Koźmin, nr. Poznań, 20 April 1929). Polish musicologist. He studied the piano with Z. Lisicki and theory with W. Rogal at the Poznań College of Music, then history and theory of music under Chybiński and ethnomusicology under Sobieski at Poznań University (1948–52). In 1965 he took the doctorate with a thesis on songs from the Kurpie district. From 1952 he was a research worker of the Institute of Polish Art at the Polish Academy of Sciences, first at Poznań and from 1954 in Warsaw. He lectured in ethnomusicology at the universities of Warsaw (1967–71) and Kraków (1969–); in 1975 he was appointed chairman of the musicology department of Poznań University. He was chairman of the musicological section of the Union of Polish Composers from 1969 to 1973, when he became the union's president. His chief interest is in ethnomusicology, particularly Polish folklore, methodological problems and the history of Polish music.

WRITINGS

'Morfologia rytmów mazurkowych na Mazowszu Polnym: studium analityczne' [The morphology of mazurka rhythms in Mazowsze Polne: an analytical study], *Muzyka*, iv/4 (1959), 147; v/2 (1960), 29

with Z. Stęszewska: 'Zur Genese und Chronologie des Mazurka-rhythmus in Polen', *Chopin Congress: Warszawa 1960*, 624

'Pieśni kurpiowskie w twórczości Karola Szymanowskiego' [Songs from the Kurpie district in Szymanowski's works], *Karol Szymanowski: księga sesji naukowej* (Warsaw, 1964), 274

'Chmiel: szkic problematyki etnomuzycznej wątku' [*Chmiel*: a sketch of its ethnomusicological problems], *Muzyka*, x/1 (1965), 3–33

'Polish Folk Music', *Polish Music*, ed. S. Jarociński (Warsaw, 1965), 200

Problematyka historyczna pieśni kurpiowskich [Historical problems in songs from the Kurpie district] (diss., U. of Poznań, 1965)

with L. Bielawski: 'Zur Klassifikation der polnischen Volkslieder', *Methoden der Klassifikation von Volksliedweisen: Symposia II: Bratislava 1965*, 47

'Die Apokope, eine Eigentümlichkeit im Volksliedervortrag', *Festschrift für Walter Wiora* (Kassel, 1967), 641

'Marcina Mielczewskiego Canzon prima a 2 na tle rękopisu Biblioteki Jagiellońskiej sygn.127/56' [Mielczewski's Canzon prima *a* 2 in the light of MS 127/56 in the Jagellonian Library], *Muzyka*, xii/1 (1967), 27

'Rola Bartóka w etnomuzykologii' [Bartók's role in ethnomusicology], *Zeszyty naukowe PWSM w Warszawie* (Warsaw, 1967), no.2, p.115

'The Problem of Historicity in European Folksong', *IMSCR, x Ljubljana 1967*, 329

'Z zagadnień wariabilności muzyki ludowej' [Some problems in variability of folk music], *Studia Hieronymo Feicht septuagenario dedicata* (Kraków, 1967), 55

'Z zagadnień teorii i metod polskich badań folkloru muzycznego' [Some problems of theory and methods in Polish folk music research], *Muzyka*, xv/2 (1970), 11; Eng. trans., *Polish Musicological Studies*, i (1977)

'Sachen, Bewusstsein und Benennungen in ethnomusikologischen Untersuchungen (am Beispiel der polnischen Folklore)', *Jb für Volksliedforschung*, xvii (1972), 131–70

'Polish Research on Musical Folklore after 1945', *9th International Congress of Anthropological and Ethnological Sciences: Chicago 1973*, 109

'Remarques concernant les recherches sur la tradition vivante des chants religieux polonais', *Etat des recherches sur la musique religieuse dans la culture polonaise* (Warsaw, 1973), 123

'Uwagi o etnomuzycznej regionalizacji Polski' [Notes on the ethnomusicological regionalization of Poland], *Dyskurs o tradycji* (Wrocław, 1974), 323

'Geige und Geigenspiel in der polnischen Volksüberlieferung', *Die Geige in der europäischen Volksmusik*, ed. W. Deutsch (Vienna, 1975), 16

EDITIONS

M. Fedorowski: *Lud białoruski* [The Belorussian people], v–viii (Warsaw, 1958–69)

with Z. Stęszewska: *Tańce polskie z Vietoris-Kodex* [Polish dances from the Vietoris MS] (Kraków, 1960)

S. Mierczyński: *Muzyka Huculszczyzny* [Music from East Carpathia] (Kraków, 1965)

with J. Gołos: *Muzyczne silva rerum z XVII wieku: rękopis 127/56 Biblioteki Jagiellońskiej* [The musical 'silva rerum' from the 17th century: MS 127/56 from the Jagellonian Library] (Kraków, 1970)

ZYGMUNT M. SZWEYKOWSKI

Stettin (Ger.). SZCZECIN.

Steuccius [Steucke], **Heinrich** (*b* Weissenfels, 12 Dec 1579; *d* Naumburg, 14 Sept 1645). German composer and lawyer. He came from an old-established Weissenfels family, and his father was both Kantor and town councillor there. Although primarily a student of philosophy and law at the universities of Leipzig and Wittenberg (in 1602 he stated that he had been studying for nearly eight years), he began composing early and by the age of 17 had dedicated a mass to the Weissenfels council. By the time his only collection of music appeared in 1602, he had already written 'all kinds of sacred pieces and motets, as well as secular songs'. However, only two motets are known to have been composed after this date. By 1613 he was in Naumburg as legal adviser to the cathedral foundation, and he continued to live there until his death. His *Amorum ac*

leporum contains 97 pieces, 15 of them dances, the remainder songs. It continues the line of similar publications by Harnisch, Mancinus and others. Although its contents cannot be said to reach the heights of, for example, Hassler's contributions to the tradition, they are not without importance. Occasionally, when inspired by a suitable text, he shed the foursquareness characteristic of the north German style and set the words with real effect. He sometimes showed a strong sense of form too. He was also conscious of key relationships and devised carefully worked-out modulatory schemes. The music is predominantly syllabic, but passages of closely imitative texture alternate with simple homophony without the essential simplicity of the genre being lost. The motets of 1618–21 are for two choirs, though neither choir is treated as a separate entity; forceful homophonic writing contrasts with passages of flowing counterpoint.

WORKS

Amorum ac leporum, 4–6vv (Wittenberg, 1602–3); 5 songs in Vetter, ii

Motet, 8vv, bc, in 1618[1]

Motet, 8vv, bc, in 1621[2]

BIBLIOGRAPHY

GerberNL; *WaltherML*

W. Vetter: *Das frühdeutsche Lied*, i (Münster, 1928), 52

H. J. Moser: *Heinrich Schütz: sein Leben und Werk* (Kassel, 1936, rev. 2/1954; Eng. trans., 1959), 26, 558

G. Saupe: 'Heinrich Steuccius: ein Weissenfelser Zeitgenosse von Heinrich Schütz', *Jb Sachsen und Anhalt*, xvi (1940), 205

A. Schmiedecke: 'Heinrich Steucke 1579–1645', *Mf*, xvii (1964), 40

A. LINDSEY KIRWAN

Steude, Wolfram (*b* Plauen, 20 Sept 1931). German musicologist. He studied at the Dresden Kirchenmusikschule (1950–52), the Leipzig Musikhochschule (1952–5) and at Leipzig University (1955–8), where he studied art history and musicology with Besseler, Serauky, Wolff and Eller; he took the doctorate at Rostock in 1973 with a dissertation on 16th-century music manuscripts from central Germany. In 1955 he began serving as a teacher and church musician in Leipzig and Dresden, and from 1962 as a freelance musicological assistant at the Sächsische Landesbibliothek, Dresden; in 1972 he became director of the Dresden Cappella Sagittariana, a group specializing in early Dresden music and using historic instruments. His chief area of research is musical life in central Germany from the 16th century to the 18th, concentrating particularly on the 16th century, Schütz and 17th-century music in Dresden, as well as the early career of Telemann. He has also been responsible for several performing editions, mainly of cantatas by Telemann, Schütz, Biber, Walther and J. G. Reichard.

WRITINGS

'Neue Schütz-Ermittlungen', *DJbM*, xii (1968), 40–74

'Wegweiser in die Zukunft? – Heinrich Schütz', *Credo musicale … Festgabe zum 80. Geburtstag … Rudolf Mauersberger* (Kassel, 1969), 21

'Die Markuspassion in der Leipziger Passionen-Handschrift des Johann Zacharias Grundig', *DJbM*, xiv (1970), 96

Untersuchungen zu Herkunft, Verbreitung und spezifischem Inhalt mitteldeutscher Musikhandschriften des 16. Jahrhunderts (diss., U. of Rostock, 1973; Leipzig, in preparation, rev. as *Untersuchungen zur mitteldeutschen Musiküberlieferung und Musikpflege im 16. Jahrhundert*)

Die Musiksammelhandschriften des 16. und 17. Jahrhunderts in der Sächsischen Landesbibliothek zu Dresden (Leipzig and Wilhelmshaven, 1974) [catalogue]

Articles in *Grove 6*, incl. 'Dresden', §1

Steuerlein [Steurlein, Steurlin], **Johann** [Johannes] (*b* Schmalkalden, Thuringia, 5 July 1546; *d* Meiningen, 5

May 1613). German composer, organist, poet and administrator. From 1559 he attended the grammar school at Magdeburg, where the Kantor, Gallus Dressler, had recently inherited the flourishing musical tradition built up by Martin Agricola. In 1562 he entered the University of Wittenberg, at the same time earning his living as a chancery clerk at Burgbreitungen, not far from Schmalkalden. He may well have continued his studies on a part-time basis at Jena. From 1569 to 1589 he was town clerk, Kantor and organist at Wasungen, near Meiningen, where he wrote most of his works and where Melchior Vulpius was one of his pupils. From 1589 until his death he was chancellory secretary to the Elector of Saxony at Meiningen and as such was in 1604 also promoted public notary and mayor of the town. In his old age he was crowned poet laureate. He ranks with the many lesser central German composers of the late 16th century who through their use of a cantus firmus in the highest voice gave a popular yet still sophisticated flavour to German-language motets and polyphonic songs; in this he had much in common with the somewhat older Leonhard Schroeter and with his exact contemporary Joachim a Burck. The works of all three were widely disseminated in their day, not least in anthologies.

Steuerlein's six-part song *Das alte Jahr vergangen ist*, which is still widely known, was printed only post-humously; probably only some of the verses are by him, and the melody now in use is an arrangement by W. C. Briegel printed in the Darmstadt hymnbook of 1687. His *St John Passion* is closely connected histor-ically with Burck's *St John Passion* (*Die deutsche Passion*), the second edition of which had been pub-lished by the same printer three years earlier.

WORKS

Intereunt iusti, funeral motets for Count Poppo of Henneberg, 5vv (n.p., 1574)
Das deutsche Benedicite und Gratias vor und nach Tische, 5vv (Erfurt, 1575)
Weltliche Gesänge, 4, 5vv (Erfurt, 1575); some ed. G. Kraft (Wolfenbüttel, 1930)
21 geistliche Lieder . . . zugerichtet durch L. Helmbold, 4vv (Erfurt, 1575)
Die deutsche Passion . . . nach . . . S. Johanne, in Figural Gesang, 4vv (Erfurt, 1576), inc.
Das alte Jahr vergangen ist, ein christlicher Gesangk, New Year motet, 5vv (Erfurt, 1577)
[24] Cantiones sacrae, 4–6vv (n.p., 1578)
[20] Epithalamia, 4–6vv (Erfurt, 1587)
27 newe geistliche Gesenge . . . der lieben jugendt zu gut, 4vv (Erfurt, 1588); 2 ed. in C. von Winterfeld, *Der evangelische Kirchengesang*, ii (Leipzig, 1843/R1966), 1 ed. in *Handbuch der deutschen evangelischen Kirchenmusik*, ii/1 (Göttingen, 1935)
Psalm cl, Missa ad imitationem praecedentis cantilenae, 4vv (Erfurt, 1588); MS copy in *GB-Lbm*, together with anon. frag. of antiphonal Passion probably by Steuerlein
8 cantiones sacrae, 4vv (Erfurt, 1589)
Erhalt uns Herr bei deinem Wort, 5vv (n.p., 1593)
2 christliche Muteten, 6vv (n.p., 1596)
20 fugae ex solmizandi exercitio (n.p., n.d.); repr. from C. Schneegass: Isagoges musicae libri duo (2/1596)
3 motets, 4vv, 1597[8]
Eteostichon rhythmicum: Auspice Christo, 6vv (n.p., 1597)
Prosphonesis consolatoria: Non sis chare parens, 6vv (n.p., 1598)
Der 67. Psalm, 4vv (Erfurt, 1599)
Psalm cxvii auff dreyerley Weise, 4vv (Erfurt, 1599)
2 christliche Grabgesenge, 4vv (Schleusingen, 1611)
Das alte Jahr vergangen ist, 6vv, *D-Rp*
Declinatio vini: Vinum quae pars, 5vv (n.p., n.d.)
Vexilla regis, ? formerly *D-Rp*; ed. J. Seiler, *Laudate Dominum*, ii (Paderborn, 1871)
O crux ave, ? formerly *Rp*; ed. J. Seiler, *Laudate Dominum*, ii (Paderborn, 1871)
12 deutsche und lateinische Gesänge, 4, 5vv (Wittenberg, 1571), inc., probably by Steuerlein
Other inc. and lost works, see Kraft (1940)

BIBLIOGRAPHY

O. Kade: *Die ältere Passionskomposition bis zum Jahre 1631* (Gütersloh, 1893)
G. Kraft: 'Johann Steuerlein (1546–1613)', *ZMw*, xiii (1930–31), 425
——: *Die thüringische Musikkultur um 1600*, ii: *Johann Steuerlein (1546–1613): Leben und Werke* (Würzburg, 1940)
WALTER BLANKENBURG

Steuermann, Edward [Eduard] (*b* Sambor, 18 June 1892; *d* New York, 11 Nov 1964). American pianist and composer of Polish birth. His education as a pianist was with Vilém Kurz (Lwów) and Busoni (Berlin). He was to have studied composition with Humperdinck, but was so shocked when asked whether he wanted to compose in the Brahmsian or the Wagnerian manner that he never went back. Busoni, therefore, sent him to Schoenberg. In 1912 he took part in the first performance of *Pierrot lunaire* and, with the exception of the Songs op.48, played at the première of every subsequent Schoenberg work with a piano part. He was also the first to play Berg's Sonata and Chamber Concerto as well as most of Webern's chamber music with piano. He was the pianist for the Society for Private Musical Performances, founded in 1918 by Schoenberg, and introduced works by Skryabin and much new French music to Vienna. During his Viennese years (he emigrated to the USA in 1938) he was often the pianist for Karl Kraus's readings and recitations. In 1952 the ISCM gave him its highest award, the Schoenberg medal.

He was an illuminating interpreter of the standard repertory, and his Beethoven recitals in New York in the early 1950s were, with their structural clarity and pianistic beauty, among the most remarkable events of that time. His distinguished teaching career began in Poland in 1918 and continued there, in Vienna, Prague, in the USA (he taught at the Juilliard School from 1952 until his death), Israel, Darmstadt, the Salzburg Mozarteum and Dartington Hall. His pupils included Theodor W. Adorno, Alfred Brendel, Jakob Gimpel, Natalie Hinderas, Lorin Hollander, Joseph Kalichstein, Lili Kraus, Moura Lympany and Russell Sherman.

Steuermann composed songs and choruses, music for solo piano, chamber works including Seven Waltzes for String Quartet (1946), a piano trio (1954), a string quartet, *Diary* (1961), and pieces for orchestra, among them a set of Variations (1958) and a Suite for Chamber Orchestra (1964). Some freely atonal, some serial, they are of economical, fastidious workmanship, imbued always with a keen feeling for instrumental style and sonority, bearing, in their sensuousness, traces of his involvement with Debussy and Skryabin. Pianistic fantasy is evident also in his bravura transcription for solo piano of Schoenberg's Chamber Symphony op.9 and in his version for three pianos of Schubert's *Wohin?*

BIBLIOGRAPHY

G. Schuller: 'A Conversation with Steuermann', *PNM*, iii/1 (1964), 22
M. Stubenrauch: 'In Memoriam: Eduard Steuermann', *ÖMz*, xx (1965), 126
MICHAEL STEINBERG

Stevens, Bernard (George) (*b* London, 2 March 1916). English composer. He studied composition with Dent and Rootham at Cambridge (1934–7; MusD 1968) and with Morris and Jacob at the RCM (1937–40). The first of his works to attract public attention was *A Symphony of Liberation*, played by the LPO under Sargent (London, 1946) and awarded first prize in the *Daily Express* Victory Competition. In 1948 Stevens was appointed professor of composition at the RCM. His compositional outlook has been decisively influenced by Marxist convictions, though he is in no sense a dogmatist: he finds no party holding a monopoly of Marxist theory, and he rejects Belinsky's idea that art should concern itself primarily with the portrayal of reality. Rather he sees art as a 'part of reality itself'. Nevertheless, precise views on the function of music in society have led him to strive for formal simplicity and accessibility, and it is perhaps his greatest achievement to have followed this approach in the Classical genres without loss of serious intent. *A Symphony of Liberation* impresses by its emotional impact and its competent craftsmanship, as does the Dance Suite, whose subtle rhythms relate equally to modern dance and to the Elizabethan madrigal. There has been a steady refinement of technique in Stevens's work, but little stylistic change. Often a whole work is shaped from a very small number of basic melodic or harmonic motifs, developed with inventive simplicity.

WORKS
(*selective list*)

Orch: Vn Conc., op.4, 1943; Ricercar, op.6, str, 1944; A Sym. of Liberation, op.7, 1945; Sinfonietta, op.10, str, 1948; Vc Conc., op.18, 1952; Dance Suite, op.28, 1957; Variations, op.36, 1964; Choriamb, op.41, 1968; Introduction, Variations and Fugue on a Theme of Giles Farnaby, op.47, 1972

Vocal: The Pilgrims of Hope, op.27, cantata, S, Bar, SATB, ens, 1956; 2 Poetical Sketches, op.32, female chorus, str orch, 1961; Et resurrexit, op.43, cantata, A, T, SATB, orch, 1969

Inst: Theme and Variations, op.11, str qt, 1949; Sonata in 1 Movt, op.25, pf, 1954; Lyric Suite, op.30, str trio, 1958; Trio, op.38, hn, vn, pf, 1966; Suite, op.40, 6 insts, 1967

Principal publishers: Lengnick, Novello, Universal

MSS in *GB-Lmic*

WRITINGS

'An Open Letter to Shostakovich', *New Reasoner* (1957), no.1, p.25
'Music in the Soviet Union', *European Music in the Twentieth Century*, ed. H. Hartog (London, 1957)
'Rutland Boughton', *New Reasoner* (1959), no.8, p.74

BIBLIOGRAPHY

R. Stevenson: 'Bernard Stevens', *MT*, cix (1968), 525

RICHARD COOKE

Stevens, Denis (William) (*b* High Wycombe, 2 March 1922). English musicologist. He studied music at Jesus College, Oxford, with R. O. Morris, Wellesz and Hugh Allen (1940–42, 1946–9, MA 1947). After war service in India and Burma he was a violinist and violist in the Philharmonia Orchestra and in chamber music groups (1946–9). On joining the BBC Music Department as a programme planner and producer (1949–54) he worked principally on early music and mounted programmes on Machaut, Dufay, Dunstable, Tallis and Monteverdi and important radio opera productions such as Monteverdi's *Orfeo* and Charpentier's *Médée*. Latterly he provided appropriate music for drama productions at the BBC and elsewhere (e.g. the York Mystery Plays, 1954, 1957). During the Dunstable quincentenary (1955) he toured Italy as a British Council lecturer; subsequently he was visiting professor of music at Cornell University (1955) and Columbia University (1956). After some years teaching at the RAM, London (1956–61), during which time he took over on Eric Blom's death the editing of the supplement to *Grove 5*, he returned to the USA as visiting professor at the University of California at Berkeley (1962) and Pennsylvania State University (1963–4) and was appointed professor of musicology at Columbia University (1965); he was visiting professor at the University of California at Santa Barbara (1974) and was appointed to the Brechemin Distinguished Chair of Music History at the University of Washington at Seattle (1976–7). He

is a co-founder of the Ambrosian Singers and president and artistic director of the Accademia Monteverdiana, chamber ensembles specializing in early as well as contemporary music. He has toured throughout Europe and the USA and made (by 1975) about 55 records. His major critical works are his book *Tudor Church Music*, his monograph on Thomas Tomkins and *A History of Song*; his many critical editions include works by Machaut and Monteverdi and two important collections, *The Mulliner Book* and *Early Tudor Organ Music*. He is a fellow of the Society of Antiquaries (1957), a past secretary of the Plainsong and Mediaeval Music Society, an honorary member of the RAM (1961) and a member of the Worshipful Company of Musicians (1961), and he has received an honorary degree from Fairfield University, Connecticut (1967).

A professionally trained violinist, he has always insisted on a close connection between research, editorial activity and performance. As a historian he has dealt with a wide range of music in a thoroughly scholarly yet accessible manner.

WRITINGS

'A Unique Tudor Organ Mass', *MD*, vi (1952), 167
'Franz Liszt (1811–1883)'; 'Ferruccio Busoni (1866–1924)', *The Concerto*, ed. A. Robertson (Harmondsworth, 1952), 179; 282
'Purcell's Art of Fantasia', *ML*, xxxiii (1952), 341
'The Keyboard Music of Thomas Tallis', *MT*, xciii (1952), 303
The Mulliner Book: a Commentary (London, 1952)
'La chanson anglaise avant l'école madrigaliste', *Musique et poésie au XVIe siècle: CNRS Paris 1953*, 121
'La musique d'orgue en Angleterre', *RdM*, xxxii (1953), 151
'Les sources de l'"in nomine"', *La musique instrumentale de la Renaissance: CNRS Paris 1954*, 85
'Seventeenth-century Italian Instrumental Music in the Bodleian Library', *AcM*, xxvi (1954), 67
'The Background of the "In nomine"', *MMR*, lxxxiv (1954), 199
'A Recently Discovered English Source of the Fourteenth Century', *MQ*, xli (1955), 26
'Pièces de théâtre et "pageants" Tudor', *Les fêtes de la Renaissance I: CNRS Abbaye de Royaumont 1955*, 259
'Processional Psalms in Faburden', *MD*, ix (1955), 105
Tudor Church Music (New York, 1955/*R*1973, rev., enlarged 2/1961, 3/1966)
'Further Light on "Fulgens praeclara"', *JAMS*, ix (1956), 1
'A Musical Admonition for Tudor Schoolboys', *ML*, xxxviii (1957), 49
'Duet Sonatas without Wind Instruments (from 1700)', *Chamber Music*, ed. A. Robertson (Harmondsworth, 1957), 253–87
'L'interprétation de la musique de Claudio Monteverdi', *Le Baroque musical: Wégimont IV 1957*, 241
Thomas Tomkins 1572–1656 (London, 1957, rev. 2/1967)
'Ornamentation in Monteverdi's Shorter Dramatic Works', *IMSCR, vii Cologne 1958*, 284
'The Second Fountains Fragment: a Postscript', *ML*, xxxix (1958), 149
'Thomas Preston's Organ Mass', *ML*, xxxix (1958), 29
'The Manuscript Edinburgh Adv.Lib.5.1.15', *MD*, xiii (1959), 155
ed.: *A History of Song* (London, 1960, rev. 2/1970) [incl. 'The Renaissance', 67–116]
'Music in Honour of Queen Elizabeth I', *MT*, ci (1960), 698
ed., with A. Robertson: *The Pelican History of Music* (Harmondsworth, 1960–68) [incl. 'Ars antiqua', i (1960), 211–58; 'Baroque Instrumental Music', ii (1963), 297]
'German Lute-songs of the Early 16th Century', *Festschrift Heinrich Besseler* (Leipzig, 1961), 253
'Problems of Editing and Publishing Old Music', *IMSCR, viii New York 1961*, 150
ed., with E. Blom: *Grove 5*, suppl.
'Where are the Vespers of Yesteryear?', *MQ*, xlvii (1961), 315
Plainsong Hymns and Sequences (London, 1965)
'Polyphonic Tropers in 14th-century England', *Aspects of Medieval and Renaissance Music: a Birthday Offering to Gustave Reese* (New York, 1966, rev. 2/1978)
'"Madrigali guerrieri, et amorosi": a Re-appraisal for the Quatercentenary', *MQ*, liii (1967), 161; repr. in *The Monteverdi Companion*, ed. D. Arnold and N. Fortune (London, 1968), 227
'Claudio Monteverdi: Selva morale e spirituale', *Congresso internazionale sul tema Claudio Monteverdi e il suo tempo: Venezia, Mantova e Cremona 1968*, 423
with S. Stevens: *Music and Art in Society* (University Park, Penn., 1968) [trans. of F. Lesure: *Musica e società*, Milan, 1966]
'John Taverner', *Essays in Musicology in Honor of Dragan Plamenac* (Pittsburgh, 1969), 331

'Monteverdi's Double-choir Magnificat', *MT*, cx (1969), 587
'Music in Honor of St Thomas of Canterbury', *MQ*, lvi (1970), 311–48; repr. in *Scritti in onore di Luigi Ronga* (Milan and Naples, 1973), 613–49
'Monteverdi's Necklace', *Quadrivium*, xii/2 (1971), 33; repr. in *MQ*, lix (1973), 370
'Über das Vibrato: ästhetische, stilistische, geschichtliche Betrachtungen', *Musica*, xxv (1971), 462
'Lower Music and Higher Education in the 1970s', *College Music Symposium*, xii (1972), 41
'Some Observations on Performance Practice', *CMc* (1972), no.14, p.159
'Petrarch's Greeting to Italy', *MT*, cxv (1974), 834
'The Worcester Fragments', *MT*, cxvi (1975), 784
'The Violin – a Short History'; 'Bach's Sonatas and Partitas', in Y. Menuhin and W. Primrose: *Violin and Viola* (London, 1975)
Claudio Monteverdi: Sacred, Secular and Occasional Music (New York, 1977)
'Ceremonial Music in Medieval Venice', *MT*, cxix (1978), 321
'Monteverdi, Petratti, and the Duke of Bracciano', *MQ*, lxiv (1978), 275
ed. and trans.: *The Letters of Claudio Monteverdi* (London 1980)

EDITIONS

The Mulliner Book, MB, i (1951, rev. 2/1954, 3/1962)
T. Tallis: Complete Keyboard Works (London, 1953)
In Nomine: altenglische Kammermusik, HM, cxxxiv (1956)
R. Carver: The Two Extant Motets: O bone Jesu; Gaude flore virginali, Collected Works, i, CMM, xvi/1 (1959)
C. Monteverdi: Vespers of 1610 (London, 1961); *Combattimento di Tancredi e Clorinda* (London, 1962); *L'Orfeo: favola in musica* (London, 1967); *Magnificat* (London, 1969) [with J. Steele]
Penn State Music Series (University Park, Penn., 1963–)
The Treasury of English Church Music, i: *1100–1545* (London, 1965)
R. Fayrfax: Missa 'Tecum principium', Cw, xcvii (1966)
Early Tudor Organ Music, ii: *The Mass*, EECM, x (1969)
Music in Honour of St Thomas of Canterbury (London, 1970)
Venetian Ceremonial Motets (London, 1978)

Stevens, George (*b* Norway, Maine, 22 April 1803; *d* East Cambridge, Mass., 15 Aug 1894). American organ builder. He went to the Boston area as a young man, and worked first as a carpenter, then as a journeyman with WILLIAM MARCELLUS GOODRICH, whom he succeeded in 1833. His brother William Stevens (1808–96) worked with him for a time, but later went into business for himself (though never on as large a scale as George). Stevens broke little new ground, but produced over his long career a great number of small- and medium-sized sturdy organs with a good tone. These he sold for moderate prices, and many still survive in rural New England. One of his largest organs was built in 1852 for a church in Charlestown, Massachusetts. A good businessman, he was also active in banking and local politics.

BARBARA OWEN

Stevens, Halsey (*b* Scott, NY, 3 Dec 1908). American composer, musicologist and teacher. Stevens studied composition with William Berwald at Syracuse University and with Bloch at the University of California, Berkeley. He taught at Syracuse University (1935–7), Dakota Wesleyan University (1937–44), the College of Music of Bradley Polytechnic Institute (1941–6) and the University of Redlands, California (1946–7). Since 1948, he has taught at the University of Southern California, Los Angeles, where he is chairman of the composition faculty and of the Council of Graduate Studies in Music. He has been a visiting professor at Yale University (1960–61) and at Williams College (1970), and has lectured at many universities on the problems of modern music. A Guggenheim Fellow in 1964–5 and 1971–2, he has received many awards and commissions for his music. In 1967, he was awarded an honorary LittD by Syracuse University. Stevens is a noted authority on the music of Béla

Bartók, on whom he has written the standard biography in English. He has published many articles and reviews on Bartók's music and related subjects, and has contributed to a number of publications and symposia.

A prolific composer, with over 80 published compositions, Stevens has written for a great variety of instrumental and vocal combinations. In his music, he uses vigorous rhythms, firm control of tonal centres and brilliant instrumental and vocal writing. In *Symphonic Dances* (1962), chromatically coloured neoclassical tonality and complex thematic transformations are firmly deployed within a large musical structure. The Clarinet Concerto (1969) uses similar compositional means in a highly personal and expressive manner. His many chamber works exhibit a fine command of texture and proportion.

WORKS

(*selective list*)

ORCHESTRAL

Pf Concertino, 1936; Sym. no.1, 1945; Sym. no.3, 1946; A Green Mountain Ov., 1948–54; Triskelion, 1954; Ballad of William Sycamore (Benet), chorus, orch, 1955; Sinfonia breve, 1957
Symphonic Dances, 1962; Vc Conc., 1964; Threnos, 1968; Cl Conc., 1969

CHAMBER

Str Qt no.1, 1931; Str Sextet, 1936; Pf Trio no.1, 1937; Sonatina no.1, vn, pf, 1937
Fl Sonatina, 1943; Str Qt no.2, 1944; Sonatina no.2, vn, pf, 1944; Suite, cl, pf, 1945; Pf Qnt, 1946
Str Qt no.3, 1952; Suite, va, 1952; Pf Trio no.3, 1954; Suite, vn, 1954; Septet, wind, str, 1957; Sonata, vc, 1958
Suite, va, pf, 1960; Sonatina, bn, pf, 1961; Vc Sonata, 1965; Partita, va, pf, 1966; Sonata, vc, 1967; 8 Yugoslavian Folksongs, 1970

VOCAL

When I am Dead, My Dearest (C. Rossetti), chorus, 1938
Go, Lovely Rose (Waller), chorus, 1942
Cuatro canciones, S, pf, 1962; Siete canciones, Bar, pf, 1963

Principal publishers: Peters, Boosey & Hawkes, Composers Facsimile Edition (ACA)

WRITINGS

The Life and Music of Béla Bartók (New York, 1953, rev. 2/1964)
'Some "Unknown" Works of Bartók', *MQ*, lii (1966), 37
'Stravinsky: a Critical Decade', *IMSCR, x Ljubljana 1967*
'The Choral Music of Zoltán Kodály', *MQ*, liii (1967), 147
'The Sources of Bartók's Rhapsody for Violoncello and Piano', *International Musicological Conference in Commemoration of Béla Bartók: Budapest 1971*, 65

BIBLIOGRAPHY

P. Pisk: 'The Music of Halsey Stevens', *American Composers Alliance Bulletin*, iv/2 (1954), 2

RICHARD SWIFT

Stevens, Horace (Ernest) (*b* Melbourne, 26 Oct 1876; *d* Melbourne, 18 Nov 1950). Australian bass-baritone. He was educated at St Kilda, Melbourne, and sang as a lay clerk in St Paul's Cathedral in Melbourne until World War I, in which he served with distinction. Afterwards he devoted himself wholly to singing and made his London début at a concert conducted by Sir Henry Wood at Queen's Hall in September 1919. He soon became a familiar figure at all the great English festivals, and was especially renowned for his forceful and dramatic reading of the part of Elijah. American audiences frequently heard him in this and other oratorios. He also appeared successfully with the British National Opera Company and other English companies, notably as Wotan and in other Wagnerian parts.

DESMOND SHAWE-TAYLOR

Stevens, John (Edgar) (*b* London, 8 Oct 1921). English musicologist. He studied at Christ's Hospital and won a classics scholarship to Magdalene College, Cambridge, where he read classics (1940–41) and English (1946–8; BA 1948). His research began in 1948 under the supervision of Thurston Dart (PhD 1953); in 1950 he was elected into a bye-fellowship, and later to a research fellowship, at Magdalene. He was appointed a university lecturer in English in 1952, was elected into an official fellowship at Magdalene in 1958, and in 1974 was appointed university reader in English and music history. He became professor of medieval and Renaissance English in 1978. In 1980 he was appointed CBE.

Stevens's main musicological preoccupations are a direct outgrowth of his doctoral work on early Tudor song, which provided the basis for his distinguished book *Music and Poetry in the Early Tudor Court*, the pioneering and standard discussion of the subject. For Musica Britannica he has also produced critical editions of the three principal manuscript sources of the Tudor song repertory. Although his work has broadened in scope during recent years, it continues to be primarily concerned with the relationships between words and music in medieval and Renaissance song.

WRITINGS

'Carols and Court Songs of the Early Tudor Period', *PRMA*, lxxvii (1950–51), 51
'Rounds and Canons from an Early Tudor Songbook', *ML*, xxxii (1951), 29
Early Tudor Song Books (diss., U. of Cambridge, 1953)
'Music in Medieval Drama', *PRMA*, lxxxiv (1957–8), 81
'The Elizabethan Madrigal: Perfect Marriage or Uneasy Flirtation?', *Essays and Studies*, ed. B. Willey (London, 1958), 17
'Gerard Manley Hopkins as Musician', *The Notebooks and Papers of Gerard Manley Hopkins*, ed. H. Howse and G. Storey (London, 2/1959), i, 458–97 [with transcrs. of all Hopkins's songs]
Music and Poetry in the Early Tudor Court (London, 1961, rev. 2/1979)
'Shakespeare and the Music of the Elizabethan Stage', *Shakespeare in Music*, ed. P. Hartnoll (London, 1964), 3–48
'The *Granz Biens* of Marie de France', *Patterns of Love and Courtesy: Essays in Memory of C. S. Lewis* (London, 1966), 1
'Dante and Music', *Italian Studies*, xxxiii (1968), 1
'Music in some Early Medieval Plays', *Studies in the Arts*, ed. F. Warner (Oxford, 1968), 21
Medieval Romance (London, 1973)
' "La grande chanson courtoise": the Songs of Adam de la Halle', *PRMA*, ci (1974–5), 11
'Carol', §§1, 2, 'Medieval drama', *Grove 6*
'The Manuscript Presentation and Notation of Adam de la Halle's Courtly Chansons', *Source Materials and the Interpretation of Music: a Memorial Volume to Thurston Dart* (in preparation)

EDITIONS

Mediaeval Carols, MB, iv (1952, rev. 2/1958)
Music at the Court of Henry VIII, MB, xviii (1962, rev. 2/1969)
with R. Axton: *Medieval French Plays* (Oxford, 1971)
Early Tudor Songs and Carols, MB, xxxvi (1975)

DAVID SCOTT, IAIN FENLON

Stevens, Richard John Samuel (*b* London, 27 March 1757; *d* London, 23 Sept 1837). English composer. His father, John Stevens, was in the textile trade. By 1764 he was a chorister at St Paul's Cathedral, and on 15 December 1768 he was apprenticed for seven years to William Savage, Master of the Children at St Paul's. After several years as a freelance glee singer, organist, school teacher and composer, he was in 1781 elected organist of St Michael, Cornhill, at a salary of £40. This was followed by appointments as organist of the Temple Church (1786) and of the Charterhouse (1796), in each case with some assistance from the Lord Chancellor, Lord Thurlow, who had become his friend and patron. Another supporter was Samuel Birch, alderman and later Lord Mayor of London, by whose influence Stevens in 1801 was appointed Gresham Professor of Music. In this office he gave lectures on music at the Royal Exchange for many years. In 1808 he received yet another appointment, as music master at Christ's Hospital.

In 1810 Stevens married Anna Jeffery, after a long courtship: they had one son, Richard George, born in 1811. At his wife's request he gave up his pluralistic appointments, retaining only the Gresham professorship and the Charterhouse position. He gradually assembled a considerable collection of old music, with an emphasis on Italian music of the 17th and 18th centuries; much of it is now in the Royal Academy of Music. His three-volume edition, *Sacred Music . . . from the Works of the Most Esteemed Composers, Italian and English*, was published from about 1798 to 1802. He was one of the judges of the Gresham Prize for sacred music from its inception in 1831.

Stevens's chief claim to attention is as a composer of glees. He was not prolific, considering the length of his life; the bulk of his composing was done between 1780 and 1800. His glees are among the most polished of their time, at their best rising to the level of Webbe and Callcott. They are not in the 'pure' style of the older glee, but begin to show the influence of instrumental music, especially that of Haydn, whom he admired more than any other composer of his time. The result often approached the later partsong in style, with the melody in the uppermost voice, straightforward harmony, little counterpoint, and a structure that was often close to sonata form. Stevens was more careful than many contemporaries in his choice of texts, and devoted special attention to Shakespeare. Of his 15 Shakespearean glees, composed between 1782 and 1807, five are among his best-known pieces: *Ye spotted snakes* (1782, rev. 1791), *Sigh no more, ladies* (1787), *Crabbed age and youth* (1790), *Blow, blow, thou winter wind* (1792) and *The cloud-cap't towers* (1795). As Cudworth has pointed out, the word-setting in these pieces is 'very apt for the period, for Stevens came from a family which loved good literature and particularly good poetry'. The music is relatively restrained in its emotional response to the text.

Among Stevens's compositions that did not outlive him were some anthems, including several for Christ's Hospital; three keyboard sonatas; and a few songs and hymn tunes. He kept a journal for much of his life, and also wrote recollections (now in *GB-Cpl*; extracts reproduced by Trend and Cudworth); they contain illuminating anecdotes and commentaries on the musical life of the time.

WORKS

(all printed works published in London)

Emma (opera), *GB-Cfm*
The Captivity (oratorio), *Cfm*
Glees: 8 Glees, 4–5vv, op.3 (*c*1792); 8 Glees expressly composed for the Ladies, op.4 (*c*1795); 10 Glees, 3–6vv, op.5 (*c*1798); 7 Glees with a Witches' song and chorus, op.6 (*c*1808); 16 pubd separately (*c*1783–*c*1811); others, *Cfm*
Songs: 10 Songs, 1v, 2 vn, pf, op.2 (*c*1788); 6 pubd separately; others, *Cfm*
Church music: The Collect for the First Sunday in Advent (*c*1808); Easter Anthems for Christ's Hospital (*c*1808–10); hymn tunes, anthems, *Cfm*
Kbd: 3 Sonatas, hpd/pf, vn, op.1 (*c*1786); sonatinas, marches, etc, *Cfm*

BIBLIOGRAPHY

D. Baptie: *Sketches of the English Glee Composers* (London, 1896), 41f
J. B. Trend: 'Jonathan Battishill', *ML*, xiii (1932), 264
——: 'R. J. S. Stevens and his Contemporaries', *ML*, xiv (1933), 128
C. L. Cudworth: 'R. J. S. Stevens 1757–1837', *MT*, ciii (1962), 754, 834
A. H. King: *Some British Collectors of Music* (Cambridge, 1963), 58
C. L. Cudworth: 'Two Georgian Classics – Arne and Stevens', *ML*, xlv (1964), 146

——: 'An 18th-century Musical Apprenticeship', *MT*, cviii (1967), 602
NICHOLAS TEMPERLEY

Stevens, Risë (*b* New York, 11 June 1913). American mezzo-soprano of Norwegian origin. A pupil of Anna Shoen-René at the Juilliard School of Music, she effected a modest début with the Little Theatre Opera Company in 1931. Approached by the Metropolitan Opera, she turned a deaf ear and sailed for Europe to study with Marie Gutheil-Schoder. She sang in Prague and in Vienna. Her New York Metropolitan début was on 17 December 1938 as Mignon. She remained there to sing, among other roles, Carmen, Octavian and Cherubino through several seasons, also appearing with other companies, in films and in concerts. In 1939 she sang at Glyndebourne. She retired in 1964 and became active in various undertakings connected with opera. She had a warm lyric mezzo of specialized repertory, unsuited to Wagner and the heavy Verdi roles.

MAX DE SCHAUENSEE

Stevenson, Sir John (Andrew) (*b* Dublin, Nov 1761; *d* Kells, Co. Meath, 14 Sept 1833). Irish composer. His father was John Stevenson, a violinist in the State Band in Dublin. In 1771 he was admitted a chorister of Christ Church Cathedral, Dublin, and from 1775 to 1780 he was in the choir of St Patrick's Cathedral. He became a vicar-choral of St Patrick's in 1783 and of Christ Church in 1800. He obtained an honorary MusD at Dublin in 1791, and his knighthood from the Lord Lieutenant (Lord Hardwicke) in 1803. In 1814 he was appointed the first organist and musical director at the Castle Chapel. Stevenson composed music for several theatrical productions in Dublin and London, and contributed songs to several more. He also wrote some church music, and innumerable separate songs, duets, glees and catches. But he is best known for his 'symphonies and accompaniments' to Thomas Moore's collection of Irish melodies, in which he showed himself a follower of Haydn. Although his arrangements seem today much too elaborate for the tunes they were intended to enhance, they remained extremely popular in the second half of the 19th century.

WORKS

STAGE

All printed music (vocal scores) published in London; unless otherwise indicated, all first performed in Dublin.

The Contrast (comic opera, R. Houlton), Smock Alley, 14 May 1782, lib pubd; rev. as The Double Stratagem, Capel Street, 19 May 1784; collab. P. Cogan
Love in a Blaze (comic opera, J. Atkinson), Crow Street, 29 May 1799, lib pubd; collab. Cogan
The Bedouins, or The Arabs of the Desert (comic opera, 3, E. Irwin), Crow Street, 1 May 1801 (*c*1801), lib pubd
The Patriot, or The Hermit of Saxellen (H. B. Code), Hibernian, 1811 (*c*1811), lib pubd
Border Feuds, or The Lady of Bucchleuch (musical play, 3, after Scott: The Lay of the Last Minstrel), 1811 (*c*1811), lib pubd
The Spanish Patriots, or A Thousand Years Ago (opera, Code), London, Lyceum, 22 Sept 1812 (*c*1812), lib pubd
The Russian Sacrifice, or The Burning of Moscow (play, Code), 1813 (*c*1813), lib pubd
Edwin and Angelina (after Goldsmith), 1815, collab. J. Clifton
The Cavern, or The Outlaws (comic opera, S. Isdell), Hawkins Street, 22 April 1825

Additional songs for 3 operatic farces by J. O'Keeffe: The Son-in-Law, 1781, The Dead Alive, 1781, The Agreeable Surprise, 1782; *see* ARNOLD, SAMUEL
Additional songs for ?Shadwell's Psyche; for J. Kenney's False Alarms, London, Drury Lane, 1807, *see* ADDISON, JOHN (i); for Kenney's Benyowsky, Drury Lane, 1826, *see* COOKE, THOMAS SIMPSON

VOCAL

12 Canzonets, 1v, pf/hpd/harp acc., op.4 (Dublin, *c*1780)

12 Glees, 3–5vv (Dublin, *c*1785)
Morning, Noon, Evening & Night, 4 Ballads, 1v, hpd/pf acc., op.4 (London, *c*1793)
8 Songs & 4 Duetts, pf/hpd acc. (Dublin, *c*1794)
A Second Sett of 12 Glees, 3–5vv, op.5 (London, *c*1795)
Morning and Evening Services and Anthems (London, 1825)
Parodies on Popular Songs (London, 1826)
Thanksgiving (oratorio), Dublin Musical Festival, 1831
31 single ballads, songs, canzonets, duets, catches, glees, see *BUCEM*
173 glees and quartets, see Baptie; some pubd in contemporary collections, incl. J. Bland's The Ladies Collection of Catches and Glees (London, *c*1787–96)

EDITIONS

First Selection of French and English Songs, gui acc. (London, 1797)
A Selection of Irish Melodies (T. Moore), 1–4vv, pf 4 hands (Dublin, 1807–21/*R*1963)
A Series of Sacred Songs [selected from Mozart and others] (Moore) (London, 1816–24)
A Selection of Popular National Airs (London, 1818–22)

BIBLIOGRAPHY

J. S. Bumpus: *Sir John Stevenson: a Biographical Sketch* (London, 1893)
D. Baptie: *Sketches of the English Glee Composers* (London, 1896), 52ff
J. C. Haddon: 'Stevenson, Sir John Andrew', *DNB*
W. H. HUSK/W. H. GRATTAN FLOOD/BRUCE CARR

Stevenson, Robert (*fl* Chester, *c*1570–1600). English organist and composer. From Michaelmas to Christmas 1571 he received six months' salary as choirmaster of Chester Cathedral, presumably in immediate succession to Robert White. Between 1571 and 1596 he was paid unusually large sums for his work as copyist, which suggests that he was at work building up a new repertory for the choir. The cathedral records for 1597 to 1600 are lacking and in those for 1601 Stevenson's name is replaced by that of Thomas Bateson. In 1583 he supplicated for the degree of MusB at Cambridge. The Grace Book records the award of the degree in 1587, Stevenson having then been a 'student of music' for 33 years. He took the doctorate from Cambridge in 1596. His extant compositions include an instrumental *Miserere* (*GB-Lbm* Add.18936–9), a Whole Service and two anthems, *Behold how good and joyful* and *When the Lord turned again* (*GB-Cp*, *DRc*, *Lbm*, *Y*), the second of which is an early example of the provincial verse anthem.

BIBLIOGRAPHY

J. C. Bridge: 'The Organists of Chester Cathedral', *Journal of the Architectural, Archaeological, and Historic Society for the County and City of Chester and North Wales*, xix/2 (1913), 63–124
R. T. Daniel and P. le Huray: *The Sources of English Church Music, 1549–1600*, EECM, suppl.i (1972)
PETER LE HURAY

Stevenson, Robert M(urrell) (*b* Melrose, New Mexico, 3 July 1916). American musicologist. He studied music at the University of Texas at El Paso (BA 1936), the Juilliard School of Music (graduated 1939), Yale University (MM) and the University of Rochester (PhD in composition 1942); further study took him to Harvard University (STB 1943), Princeton Theological Seminary (ThM 1949) and Oxford University (BLitt 1954). His teachers included Schrade and Westrup (musicology), Hutcheson and Schnabel (piano), and Hanson and Stravinsky (composition). After working as an instructor and assistant professor at the University of Texas (1941–3, 1946) and as a staff member of Westminster Choir College, Princeton, New Jersey (1946–9), he was appointed professor of musicology at the University of California at Los Angeles (1949). He has received several awards.

Stevenson's chief interest has been Latin American colonial music, in which his work has been outstanding;

through archival research in Mexico, Guatemala, Colombia, Ecuador, Peru, Bolivia and Chile, he was the first to discover essential documents for the reconstruction of cathedral music history, and to make known many colonial music manuscripts. He has also contributed substantially to the history of Spanish music and of American church music. His extensive publications reveal an impressive command of bibliographical tools and of the literature. *The Music of Peru* (1960), *Renaissance and Baroque Musical Sources in the Americas* (1970) and *Foundations of New World Opera* (1973) provide new information and understanding for a wealth of Latin American colonial music; *Spanish Music in the Age of Columbus* (1960) and *Spanish Cathedral Music in the Golden Age* (1961) give valuable accounts of a much neglected aspect of Renaissance music. In 1978 he became editor of the newly founded *Inter-American Music Review*.

WRITINGS

'Music in the Cathedral of Mexico in the 16th Century', *Hispanic American Historical Review*, xxvi (1946), 293
Music in Mexico: a Historical Survey (New York, 1952/R1971)
'The First Dated Mention of a Sarabande', *JAMS*, v (1952), 29
Patterns of Protestant Church Music (Durham, NC, 1953)
'Sixteenth and Seventeenth Century Resources in Mexico', *FAM*, i (1954), 69; ii (1955), 10
Music before the Classic Era (London, 1955/R1973 with musical appx)
'The "Distinguished maestro" of New Spain: Juan Gutiérrez de Padilla', *Hispanic American Historical Review*, xxxv (1955), 363
'Ancient Peruvian Instruments', *GSJ*, xii (1959), 17
J. S. Bach, su ambiente y su obra (Lima, 1959)
'Opera Beginnings in the New World', *MQ*, xlv (1959), 8
'Early Peruvian Folk Music', *Journal of American Folklore*, lxxiii (1960), 112
Juan Bermudo (The Hague, 1960)
'Music Instruction in Inca Land', *JRME*, viii (1960), 110
Spanish Music in the Age of Columbus (The Hague, 1960, rev. 2/1964)
The Music of Peru: Aboriginal and Viceroyal Epochs (Washington, DC, 1960)
Spanish Cathedral Music in the Golden Age (Berkeley, 1961)
'Colonial Music in Colombia', *The Americas*, xix/2 (1962)
'La música colonial en Colombia', *Revista musical chilena*, nos.81–2 (1962), 153
'Música en Quito', *Revista musical chilena*, nos.81–2 (1962), 172
'The Bogotá Music Archive', *JAMS*, xv (1962), 292
'The Sarabande, a Dance of American Descent', *Inter-American Music Bulletin*, no.36 (1962), 1
'Music in Quito, Four Centuries', *Hispanic American Historical Review*, xliii (1963), 247
'Mexico City Cathedral Music: 1600–1750', *The Americas*, xxi (1964), 111
'European Music in 16th Century Guatemala', *MQ*, l (1964), 341
'La música en la catedral de México: 1600–1750', *Revista musical chilena*, no.92 (1965), 11
'Estudio biográfico y estilístico de T. L. de Victoria', *Revista musical chilena*, no.95 (1966), 9
Protestant Church Music in America: a Short Survey of Men and Movements from 1564 to the Present (New York, 1966)
'Francisco Correa de Arauxo, New Light on his Career', *Revista musical chilena*, no.103 (1968), 7–42
'La música chilena en la época de Santa Cruz', *Boletin interamericano de música*, no.67 (1968), 3; Eng. orig. in *Inter-American Music Bulletin*, no.67 (1968), 1
'Les musiques incas et aztèques, et leurs survivances', *Encyclopédie des musiques sacrées*, ed. J. Porte, i (Paris, 1968), 105
Music in Aztec and Inca Territory (Berkeley, 1968)
'Some Portuguese Sources for Early Brazilian Music History', *Yearbook, Inter-American Institute for Musical Research*, iv (1968), 1–43
'The Afro-American Legacy (to 1800)', *MQ*, liv (1968), 475
Philosophies of American Music History (Washington, DC, 1970)
Renaissance and Baroque Musical Sources in the Americas (Washington, DC, 1970)
'The First New World Composers: Fresh Data from Peninsular Archives', *JAMS*, xxiii (1970), 95
'Josquin in the Music of Spain and Portugal', *Josquin des Prez: New York 1971*, 217–46
'Tribute to José Bernardo Alcedo, 1788–1878', *Inter-American Music Bulletin*, no.80 (1971), 1
'America's First Black Music Historian', *JAMS*, xxvi (1973), 383

'English Sources for Indian Music until 1882', *EM*, xvii (1973), 399–442
Foundations of New World Opera (Lima, 1973)
'The South American Lyric Stage (to 1800)', *Inter-American Music Bulletin*, no.87 (1973), 1
'The Toledo Manuscript Polyphonic Choirbooks and some other Lost or Little Known Flemish Sources', *FAM*, xx (1973), 87
'Written Sources for Indian Music until 1882', *EM*, xvii (1973), 1–40
'Protestant Music in America', in F. Blume: *Protestant Church Music: a History* (London, 1974), 637–90 [enlarged Eng. trans. of F. Blume: *Die evangelische Kirchenmusik* (1931)]
A Guide to Caribbean Music History (Washington, DC, 1975)
Music in Aztec and Inca Territory (Berkeley and Los Angeles, 1977)
'American Musical Scholarship: Parker to Thayer', *19th Century Music*, i (1977–8), 190
'Sixteenth- through Eighteenth-century Resources in Mexico', *FAM*, xxv (1978)
'Music in the San Juan, Puerto Rico Cathedral to 1900', *Inter-American Music Review*, i (1978–9), 73
'South American National Library Publications', *Notes*, xxxv (1978–9), 31
'Liszt at Madrid and Lisbon: 1844–45', *MQ*, lxv (1979), 493
Numerous articles in *MGG*, *Grove 5*, *Grove 6*, *Ricordi-Rizzoli*, *RicordiE*, *McGraw Hill Biographical Encyclopedia*, *New Catholic Encyclopedia*, *AnM*

EDITIONS

Christmas Music from Baroque Mexico (Berkeley, 1974)
Seventeenth-century Villancicos from a Puebla Convent Archive (Lima, 1974) [transcr. with optional added parts from ministriles]
Latin American Colonial Music Anthology (Washington, DC, 1975) [with transcrs.]
T. de Torrejón y Velasco: La púrpura de la rosa (Lima, 1976) [with introductory essay]
Vilancicos portugueses (Lisbon, 1976)

BIBLIOGRAPHY

S. Claro: 'Veinticinco años de labor iberoamericana del doctor Robert Stevenson', *Revista musical chilena*, nos.139–40 (1977), 122

GERARD BÉHAGUE

Stevenson, Ronald (*b* Blackburn, 6 March 1928). Scottish composer, pianist and writer on music. He studied at the Royal Manchester College of Music and at the Accademia di S Cecilia, Rome. In 1952 he took up residence in Scotland, and after a brief spell as senior lecturer in composition at the University of Cape Town (1963–5) he returned to the Scottish border country, devoting himself to composition and to freelance work as a pianist. He has performed widely in Europe and given numerous recitals and broadcasts in the United Kingdom. In December 1968 he was guest speaker at the Fourth Congress of Soviet Composers.

Stevenson's prolific creative work embodies some colourful contrasts. Although he was born into a working-class background whose origins were both Scottish and Welsh, his approach to composition is that of the intellectual aristocrat. His virtuosity is balanced by the scholarliness of his researches; he is both folklorist and contrapuntist, Scottish nationalist and advocate of 'world music'. This idea of the acculturation of the music of all continents is expressed in his two most extended works: the *Passacaglia on DSCH* (an 80-minute single movement for piano, based on the four-note motif derived from the initials of Shostakovich, the dedicatee) and the Second Piano Concerto, subtitled 'The Continents'. In each of these pieces Stevenson incorporates elements drawn from the musical cultures of Asia, Africa and America, as well as from Europe and in particular from Scotland. He has composed folk-song suites based on the national musics of lands as diverse as South Uist, China and Ghana. He has also written music for children and has arranged pieces by Grainger and Delius for small hands.

He has made a close study of Scottish pibroch, which he frequently develops symphonically. Much of his music employs variation form or fugue. Stevenson's reputation rests largely on his piano music, arguably the most considerable body of work for the instrument by any living British composer. There are also several fine song cycles, among them *Border Boyhood*, commissioned by Pears for the 1971 Aldeburgh Festival. Stevenson is a pianist in the grand manner. His playing is distinguished by intellectual breadth, a wide range of dynamics and an eloquent cantabile; his free rubato has more in common with the style of the great pianists of the turn of the century than with that of most of his contemporaries. He also has an unusually catholic repertory. As a writer he has published a popular brief history of Western music, and he has contributed often provocative articles to numerous periodicals. His researches have concentrated on Busoni in preparation for a large-scale biographical study. For his BBC Busoni centenary radio programme he was awarded a Harriet Cohen International Music Award.

WORKS
(selective list)

INSTRUMENTAL

Orch: Berceuse symphonique, 1951; Waltzes, 1953; Pavan after John Bull, 1955; Pf Conc. no.1 'Faust Triptych', 1960; Jamboree for Grainger, 1961; 3 Scottish Folk Music Settings, str, 1961–5; Keening Sang for a Makar, 1963; Simple Variations on Purcell's 'Scotch' Tune, cl, str, 1964; Scots Dance Toccata, 1965; Pf Conc. no.2 'The Continents', 1972; Choral Sym. 'Ben Dorain', 1973–; Vn Conc. 'The Gypsy', 1973–

Pf: 3 sonatinas, 1945–8; A 20th Century Music Diary, 1956–9; 6 pensées sur des préludes de Chopin, 1959; Prelude, Fugue and Fantasy on Themes from Busoni's Faust, 1949–59; Passacaglia on DSCH, 1960–62; A Wheen Tunes for Bairns tae Spiel, 1963; 4 folksong suites, 1965; A Modern Scottish Triptych, 1967; 3 Scots Fairytales, 1970; Peter Grimes Fantasy on themes from Britten, 1971; short pieces, transcrs.

Other pieces: Prelude and Fugue on a Theme of Liszt, org, 1961; Variations, vn, 1961–2; Meditations, str qt, 1964; Anger Dance, gui, 1965; Nocturne 'Homage to John Field', cl, pf, 1965; 2 Cambrian Cantos, harp, 1966; Sonata, hpd, 1968; Duo Sonata, harp, pf, 1970

VOCAL

Sapphic Fragments, S, female chorus, harp, 1963; A Medieval Scottish Triptych, SATB, 1966; Vietnamese Miniatures (Ho), T, harp, 1966; No Coward Soul is mine (E. Brontë), SSAA, harp/pf, 1966; Anns an Airde as an Doimhe (Maclean), SATB, 1968; Vocalise Variations on 2 Themes from 'The Trojans', Mez, orch, 1969; Border Boyhood (MacDiarmid), T, pf, 1970; The Infernal City (MacDiarmid, Maclean), T, pf, 1970–71; 9 Haiku, S/T, pf/harp, 1971; Ballattis of Luve, 1v, lute, 1972; over 200 other songs

Principal publishers: Boosey & Hawkes, Novello, Oxford University Press, Schott

MSS in *GB-Gsma*

WRITINGS

'The Emergence of Scottish Music', *Memoirs of a Modern Scotland* (London, 1970)

Western Music (London, 1971)

'MacDiarmid, Joyce and Busoni', *MacDiarmid Festchrift* (Edinburgh, 1972)

Articles in the *Listener*, *MT*, *Music and Musicians*, *MR*, *Score*, etc

BIBLIOGRAPHY

C. Scott-Sutherland: 'The Music of Ronald Stevenson', *MR*, xxvi (1965), 118

A. Orga: 'Ronald Stevenson', *Music and Musicians*, xvii/2 (1968), 26

——: 'The Piano Music of Ronald Stevenson', *MO*, xcii (1969), 292

'Composers Anthology 3: Ronald Stevenson', *Recorded Sound* (1971), no.42–3, p.747

F. Rimmer: *A History of Scottish Music* (London, 1973), 80f

COLIN SCOTT-SUTHERLAND

Stewart, James (*b* ?Scotland, late 18th century; *d* ?London, ? after 1860). British piano manufacturer. He trained as an organ builder in London, and went to Baltimore, Maryland, in 1812 to join the piano manufacturing business of his brother Adam Stewart (who had learnt his trade with the London Clementi firm). When this partnership ended in March 1813 James continued to build both pianos and organs in Baltimore until June 1819, when the Philadelphia newspapers announced the establishment of the piano rooms of 'James Stewart from London, late of Baltimore'. The Philadelphia city directories list James in business there from 1820 until 1822, along with a Thomas Stewart. Although some sources place James in the Boston piano shop of John Osborne as early as 1820, little mention is made of him there until November 1822, when the periodical *The Euterpeiad* praised a piano 'at the manufactory of Messrs. Osborn and Stewart' which had an improved, detached soundboard invented by Stewart ('recently arrived in this City from Philadelphia') and patented by him on 14 November 1822. In 1823 Stewart joined with one of Osborne's apprentices, Jonas Chickering, to form the firm of Stewart & Chickering, a partnership that was dissolved when Stewart returned to London in 1826.

Taking with him several pianos made by Stewart & Chickering, Stewart joined the London firm of Collard & Collard, where he is said by Spillane to have served as foreman for more than 35 years. In England he was granted seven patents dealing with piano improvements, the most influential being no.5475 (17 September 1827), which formed the basis of modern stringing by replacing two unison strings (each secured with a loop to its own hitch-pin) with one continuous wire of double length passed around a single hitch-pin.

Most of Stewart's pianos have a range of F' to c'''' and most have wooden frames. A Stewart & Chickering instrument at the Smithsonian Institution has a metal plate on the right to which the hitch-pins are secured; the soundboard extends across the entire length of the keyboard, while on most instruments it extends over only the top octave. Stewart's instruments are of fine workmanship and were praised in their day as 'unrivalled in tone, touch, and action'.

BIBLIOGRAPHY

D. Spillane: *History of the American Pianoforte* (New York, 1890/R1969), 30, 42, 57, 127, 142, 157

R. E. M. Harding: *The Piano-forte: its History Traced to the Great Exhibition of 1851* (Cambridge, 1933, rev. 2/1978)

CYNTHIA ADAMS HOOVER

Stewart, Sir Robert (Prescott) (*b* Dublin, 16 Dec 1825; *d* Dublin, 24 March 1894). Irish organist, conductor, composer and teacher. He was educated as a chorister at Christ Church Cathedral, Dublin, and became organist there and at Trinity College, Dublin, in 1844. In 1846 he became conductor of the University Choral Society. He graduated MusB and MusD in 1851 and the following year became organist also of St Patrick's Cathedral. In 1861 he became professor of music in the university, and ten years later a professor in the Irish Academy of Music. He composed a choral fantasia for the Boston Peace Festival of 1872, though he did not attend; in this year he was knighted by Earl Spencer. In 1873 he was appointed conductor of the Dublin PO, and in 1877 conductor of the Belfast Harmonic Society.

Stewart wrote odes and cantatas (including an ode for the Cork Exhibition of 1852 and one for the Tercentenary Festival of TCD, 1892), anthems and services, glees (Baptie mentioned 25) and songs, and orchestral and instrumental music. He edited the *Irish Church Hymnal* (Dublin, 1876).

BIBLIOGRAPHY

O. J. Vignoles: 'Reminiscences of Sir Robert Prescott Stewart', *MT*, xxxv (1894), 318

D. Baptie: *Sketches of the English Glee Composers* (London, 1896), 177f
R. H. Legge: 'Stewart, Sir Robert Prescott', *DNB*
O. J. Vignoles: 'Brief Sketch of the Career of Sir Robert P. Stewart', *PMA*, xxiv (1897–8), 95
——: *Memoir of Sir Robert P. Stewart* (London, 2/1899)
J. C. Culwick: *The Works of Sir Robert Stewart* (Dublin, 1902)

W. H. HUSK/R. J. PASCALL

Stewart, S(amuel) S(wain) (*b* Philadelphia, 8 Jan 1855; *d* Philadelphia, 6 April 1898). American maker of banjos and music publisher. After instruction on the violin and other instruments he studied the banjo with George C. Dobson; in 1878 he opened a banjo school and shortly thereafter began to make banjos. By 1880 he was in business at 221–3 Church Street, Philadelphia, and on 18 January 1882 began the publication of *Stewart's Banjo and Guitar Journal* from the same address. This journal (published under various titles until April 1901) contained news and photographs of banjoists and banjo clubs, fulminations against competing manufacturers, testimonials from satisfied customers and music arranged for the banjo. Through this and over 15 other publications, Stewart was highly influential in promoting the popular enthusiasm for fretted instrument clubs and orchestras which lasted into the 1930s.

His banjos, lighter than the 'Electric' model of his competitor, A. C. Fairbanks, were very well made in a wide variety of styles, from the cheap 'Student' and 'Amateur' models to the highly decorated 'Thorough-bred' and 'Presentation' models. Stewart's only important patent (no.355,896) was taken out in 1887 on an improved neck brace for his own invention, the ban-jeaurine, a small banjo pitched a 4th above the standard banjo and used as a lead instrument in banjo ensembles. On 1 January 1898 Stewart merged his business with George Bauer, maker and importer of mandolins and guitars. The factory and sales rooms were moved to 1410–12 North 6th Street and the publishing business moved to 1016 Chestnut Street, both branches doing business as Stewart & Bauer. After Stewart's death his interest in the business was continued by his sons, Fred and Lemuel, who ended the partnership with Bauer in 1901 and moved to New York. Banjos bearing Stewart's name were sold by them until about 1904, by Bauer until about 1910, and were made by the Vega Co., Boston, between 1903 and 1914. The Stewart trade name was subsequently applied to a line of fretted instruments sold by the New York firm of Buegeleisen & Jacobson. Stewart banjos are in the Smithsonian Institution, Washington, DC, and the Vleeshuis Museum, Antwerp.

WRITINGS
S. S. Stewart: *Sketches of Noted Banjo Players* (Philadelphia, 1881)
——: *Complete American Banjo School* (Philadelphia, 1883)
——: *The Banjo: a Dissertation* (Philadelphia, 1888)

JAY SCOTT ODELL

Stewart, Thomas (James) (*b* San Saba, Texas, 29 Aug 1928). American baritone. He studied at the Juilliard School, New York, and made his début there while still a student as La Roche in the first North American performance of *Capriccio* in 1954; this was followed by his début at the New York City Opera as Mozart's Commendatore, and appearances in Chicago. Not a true bass, he had little success, but in 1956 he and his wife, the soprano Evelyn Lear, were awarded Fulbright fellowships for further study in Europe. In 1958 Carl Ebert engaged him as a baritone for the Berlin Städtische Oper, where he made his début as Escamillo; he sang the role at Covent Garden in 1960, returning for Gunther (1963 and 1964), Don Giovanni (1964) and the Flying Dutchman (1972). In 1960 he sang Donner, Gunther and Amfortas at Bayreuth, where he sang regularly until 1975, adding the Dutchman, Wotan and Wolfram to his repertory; he also sang Wotan in the Salzburg Easter Festival under Karajan. He gave his first Hans Sachs at Nuremberg and his first Kurwenal in New York, both in 1971. Stewart's Metropolitan Opera début had been as Ford in 1966, and he has returned there regularly. In 1971 he appeared in San Francisco as Onegin with his wife as Tatyana – their first appearance together in opera in the USA. Stewart also sings in concert and oratorio. His voice, more lyrical than dramatic, is nevertheless incisive and of sufficient volume to encompass the heroic Wagner roles.

HAROLD ROSENTHAL

Šteyer, Matěj Václav (*b* Prague, 16 Feb 1630; *d* Prague, 7 Sept 1692). Czech hymnologist. A Jesuit, Šteyer studied philosophy and theology at Prague and Olomouc, taught (Jindřichuv Hradec, 1656), preached, and helped translate the St Wenceslas Bible. His *Český kancionál* (Prague, 1683) contains 851 hymn texts and 680 unharmonized hymn tunes, half of which are either modal or tonally indeterminate. The greatly esteemed second edition (1687; 923 texts, 911 melodies) is considerably larger than the Catholic hymn collections of Hlohovský, Michna, Holan Rovenský and Božan.

BIBLIOGRAPHY
J. Bužga: *Český kancionál Matěja Václava Šteyera, I. a II. vydání* (diss., U. of Prague, 1953); abstract, *MMC*, no.2 (1957), 27
——: 'Holan-Rovenský: představitel měšť'anské hudební kultury koncem 17. století' [Holan Rovenský: a representative of the bourgeois music culture towards the end of the 17th century], *HV*, iv (1967), 420

JOHN CLAPHAM

Sthoken, Johannes de. *See* STOKEM, JOHANNES DE.

Stiasny [Stiastny]. *See* ŠŤASTNÝ family.

Stibilj, Milan (*b* Ljubljana, 2 Nov 1929). Yugoslav composer. He studied psychology at Ljubljana University and composition at the academy of music with K. Pahor. Later he was a composition pupil of Kelemen at the Zagreb Academy of Music (1963–4) and studied electronic techniques in Utrecht (1966–7). In 1967–8 he worked in West Berlin as the guest of the Berliner Künstlerprogramm. After playing the violin in various Ljubljana orchestras he lived as a freelance composer. He was secretary of the Slovene Jeunesses Musicales (1971–3). Freeing himself from impressionist tendencies in his early music, Stibilj went through various phases in achieving a successful synthesis of the newest compositional ideas.

WORKS
(selective list)

Sym. 'The Nightingale and the Rose', 1961; Congruences, pf, orch, 1963; Impressions, fl, harp, str, 1963; Epervier de ta faiblesse, domine, speaker, perc, 1964; Verse, orch, 1964; Mondo, vn, cl, db, perc, 1965; Assimilation, vn, 1965; Contemplation, ob, str, 1966; Apokatastasis, Slovene requiem, T, chorus, orch, 1967; Condensation, trbn, 2 pf, perc, 1967; Ekthesis, orch, 1968; Rainbow, tape, 1968; Zoom, cl, bongos, 1970; Séance, pf trio, 1971; Kathai, rec, spinet, 1972; Chirologie, fl, pf, 1973; Indijansko poletje, fl, vn, cl, db, perc, 1974

Principal publisher: Bärenreiter

ANDREJ RIJAVEC

Sticcado-Pastrole. A small glass dulcimer or xylophone manufactured by George Smart in London in the second half of the 18th century. To play it, tuned bars were beaten with sticks furnished with knobs of ivory and wood. For further details see *Grove 5*.

Stich, Johann Wenzel. *See* PUNTO, GIOVANNI.

Sticherarion (Gk., from *stichos*: 'line of writing', 'verse'). A manuscript containing stichēra (*see* STICHĒRON), hymns which follow the order of the evening and morning services of the Orthodox Church. The term occurred first in Greek in a manuscript of AD *c*1050 (*GR-ATSvatopedi* 1488, f.1*r*), where it referred only to the 40 days of Lent; it is found in the form 'stikhierar', a phonetic transliteration, in 12th-century Russian manuscripts with notation.

1. Structure. 2. History.

1. STRUCTURE. A complete sticherarion contains three extensive collections of hymns: first, stichēra of the mēnaia; second, a collection consisting of two sections (stichēra of the triōdion and stichēra of the pentekostarion); and third, stichēra of the oktōēchos and the eōthina anastasima. The stichēra of the mēnaia contain *stichēra idiomela* for the immovable feasts of the liturgical year in a sequence from 1 September to 31 August; the second collection contains *stichēra idiomela* for the movable feasts, in a sequence beginning before Lent and extending to All Saints. Within this second collection, the stichēra of the triōdion contain stichēra for the Sundays of the Publican and the Pharisee, of the Prodigal Son, of the Apokreos (meat-fast), for the week of the Tyrophagos (cheese-fast), and for the six weeks of Lent, including Holy Week. The stichēra of the pentekostarion include stichēra for Easter, for the Sundays of St Thomas, of the Myrrh-bearing Women, the Paralytic, the Samaritan, the Blind Man, the Holy Fathers, and for Pentecost and All Saints, as well as for two midweek services for Wednesday of the mesopentekostēs and Thursday of the Ascension. The third main section of a sticherarion contains stichēra for the eight Sunday Offices, which include the anastasima (hymns of the Resurrection), and 11 eōthina anastasima (morning hymns of the Resurrection).

Some manuscripts also contain prosomoia for Lent (*see* PROSOMOION) and theotokia (*see* THEOTOKION), dogmatika and staurotheotokia; some manuscripts have appendixes with pieces not usually included or for local use only, e.g. Ohrid, National Museum, 53 (39), an 11th-century manuscript.

Stichēra for a particular feast are arranged in some manuscripts according to their order in the service, in others according to their modality. Within this arrangement hymns may be found with initials making an acrostic, either incorporating the author's name (e.g. in the theotokia of the stichēra alphabētika) or following the order of the alphabet (e.g. in the 24 alphabētika).

2. HISTORY. Approximately 650 sticheraria survive from before AD 1500. Of these, the earliest do not contain all the collections found in later sticheraria: these originally appeared in separate volumes and were combined only later. Internal evidence, including that of palaeography and notation, shows that the earliest surviving manuscripts (shown in the following list) date from the late 10th and 11th centuries:

GR-LA gamma 12 (10th or 11th century): stichēra of the triōdion, inc.; stichēra of the pentekostarion, without notation: reproduced in Strunk (1966), pl.5*b*

GR-LA gamma 67 (late 10th or 11th century): stichēra of the triōdion, inc.; stichēra of the pentekostarion and oktōēchos: reproduced in Strunk (1966), pls.6–12

GR-LA gamma 72 (*c*1025): stichēra of the triodion, inc.; stichēra of the pentekostarion: reproduced in Strunk (1966), pl.13

GR-LA gamma 74 (*c*1025): stichēra of the mēnaia, only from 25 Nov to 31 Aug; Christmas Office reproduced in Strunk (1966), pls.14–22

IL/ET-S 1219 (early 11th century): stichēra of the mēnaia, only from 24 Sept to 22 Aug; Christmas Office reproduced in Strunk (1966), pls.142–52

GR-ATSvatopedi 1488 (*c*1050): stichēra of the triōdion, pentekostarion, and oktōēchos; reproduced in Follieri and Strunk (1975).

In the first half of the 11th century there was a thorough revision of the sticherarion: a number of saints' days were eliminated from the calendar, and the repertory of the remaining feasts was fixed. This revised version was adopted universally, except in a few later manuscripts which preserved some of the older hymns, the so-called 'apokrypha' (concerning the term 'apokryphon', see Strunk (1960), i, 20 and n.44). It contained about 1400 hymns and is found in manuscripts with Coislin and Middle Byzantine notation; its calendar, melodies and notation remained in use from the late 11th century until the end of the 15th century or later.

EDITIONS

C. Høeg and others, eds.: *Codex Vindobonensis theol. graec. 181*, MMB, main ser., i (1935)

E. Wellesz, ed.: *Die Hymnen des Sticherarium für September*, MMB, *Transcripta*, i (1936)

H. J. W. Tillyard, ed.: *The Hymns of the Sticherarium for November*, MMB, *Transcripta*, ii (1938)

——: *The Hymns of the Octoechus*, i, MMB, *Transcripta*, iii (1940); ii, MMB, *Transcripta*, v (1949)

R. Jakobson, ed.: *Fragmenta Chiliandarica palaeoslavica*, MMB, main ser., v (1957) [reproduction of *GR-ATSch* 307, with stichēra of the triōdion and of the pentekostarion, both inc.]

E. Wellesz, ed.: *Die Musik der byzantinischen Kirche* (Cologne, 1959), 28ff

H. J. W. Tillyard, ed.: *The Hymns of the Pentecostarium*, MMB, *Transcripta*, vii (1960)

O. Strunk, ed.: *Specimina notationum antiquiorum*, MMB, main ser., vii (1966) [187 selected plates from 45 MSS from mid-10th century to 13th]

E. Follieri and O. Strunk, eds.: *Triodium Athoum*, MMB, main ser., ix (1975)

BIBLIOGRAPHY

O. Strunk: 'The Notation of the Chartres Fragment', *AnnM*, iii (1955), 7

——: 'The Antiphons of the Oktoechos', *JAMS*, xiii (1960), 50

E. Wellesz: *A History of Byzantine Music and Hymnography* (Oxford, 2/1961), 142f, 243ff, 385ff

D. Stefanović: 'Codex Peribleptos', *Recueil des travaux de l'Institut d'études byzantines*, viii (1964), 393

S. V. Lazarević: 'Stichērarion – an early Byzantine Hymn Collection with Music', *Byzantinoslavica*, xxix (1968), 290

C. Floros: *Universale Neumenkunde*, i, iii (Kassel, 1970)

DIMITRIJE STEFANOVIĆ

Stichēron (Gk.: 'verse'). In Orthodox churches, a hymn sung after psalm verses (stichoi), comparable with the antiphons of the Latin Church. At first stichēra were called troparia, a term still used for those attributed to Sophronios, who was Patriarch of Jerusalem from 634 to 638, for the great vigils of Christmas, Epiphany and Good Friday. The term 'stichēron' was in due course transliterated into Slavonic characters; it first appeared in a Church Slavonic manuscript in the *Euchologium Sinaiticum* (*IL/ET-S* f.83*v*) written in Glagolitic characters in the 11th century. With the growth of hymnography, stichēra were composed in rhythmical prose in honour of feasts or saints. Verses from the scriptures were often quoted. Those in early manuscripts were for Vespers, after the concluding verses of the set psalm (Psalms cxl, cxli, cxxix and cxvi); for Matins (the 'ainoi'), after the concluding verses of Psalms cxlviii–cl; for the end of Vespers and Matins, after the stichoi (the 'aposticha'); and after the lesser doxology which follows each of the above groups. For lesser feasts only hymns of the latter group, the so-called doxastika, were prescribed. For greater feasts there were more hymns, the additional ones being described as 'alla' or 'hetera'. Stichēra might also be designated 'of the feast' or 'after the feast'. Most early Greek manuscripts indicated at which point in the service the stichēra were to be interpolated. They were designated as processional in Greek manuscripts only from the 14th century.

Other rubrics concerned the musical structure of the stichēra; most of them were idiomela, some were automela and some prosomoia. The idiomela were not composed upon existing models, but had their own metrical and melodic structure. The automela served as models for the prosomoia. Although generally following the melodic pattern of the automela, prosomoia did not repeat their melodies literally (as did, for example, the troparia and heirmoi of the early kanons) because the number of syllables of a prosomoion is not always that of its model hymn. With regard to their musical settings, stichēra stand between the simple forms of the heirmologion and the melismatic kontakion; in content, style and prosody they resemble troparia. They are described according to their theme by such terms as anastasima (hymns of the Resurrection), dogmatika, theotokia, staurotheotokia and others.

BIBLIOGRAPHY

C. Høeg and others, eds.: *Codex Vindobonensis theol. graec. 181*, MMB, main ser., i (1935), 13f

E. Wellesz: *A History of Byzantine Music and Hymnography* (Oxford, 2/1961), 243ff

H. Husmann: 'Modulation und Transposition in den bi- und trimodalen Stichera', *AMw*, xxvii (1970), 1

For further bibliography *see* STICHĒRARION.

DIMITRIJE STEFANOVIĆ

Stichos. Byzantine equivalent of versicle; a verse from Scripture which follows the PROKEIMENON in Orthodox services.

Stich-Randall, Teresa (*b* West Hartford, Conn., 24 Dec 1927). American soprano. She studied at the Hartford School of Music and Columbia University, New York. While at Columbia she created the role of Gertrude Stein in Virgil Thomson's *The Mother of us All* (1947) and the title role of Otto Luening's *Evangeline* (1948). In 1949 she was the Priestess in Toscanini's broadcast and recording of *Aida*, and in 1950 Nannetta in his *Falstaff*. She won the 1951 Lausanne Singing Competition, making her European début at Florence that summer as the Mermaid in *Oberon*. After a season at Basle she scored a success at the 1952 Salzburg Festival singing Mozart concert arias under Paumgartner; this led to her engagement by the Vienna Staatsoper – in 1962 she became the first American to be made an Austrian Kammersängerin. From 1953 to 1971 she appeared at the Aix-en-Provence Festival as Fiordiligi, Countess Almaviva, Constanze, Donna Anna and Pamina. She played Gilda in Chicago in 1955 and made her Metropolitan Opera début as Fiordiligi in 1961. In addition to appearances in Italy, in Mozart and as Strauss's Ariadne, she has sung with distinction in recital and concert, being particularly admired in Bach and Handel. Her pure and sweet voice has sometimes been used in an excessively mannered way; but at its best her cultivated and gracious style has won wide praise.

BIBLIOGRAPHY

G. Gualerzi: 'Stich-Randall, Teresa', *Le grandi voci* (Rome, 1964) [with opera discography]

HAROLD ROSENTHAL

Sticker. A rigid rod, usually of wood, exerting a pushing action in organ and piano mechanisms. The principle of the sticker is applied to several parts of the organ: (a) chiefly, as a shorter or longer rod pushed down or up when a key is depressed and so transmitting that motion directly or indirectly to the appropriate wind-chest pallet; (b) as a short rod opening such valves as the pipe-pallets of each stop in a spring-chest, the sprung valve of a tremulant, etc. The term has an uncertain history, being used by builders long before theorists; J. Talbot (MS treatise, *c*1695) made somewhat ambiguous use of it, and in 18th-century England it was sometimes replaced by 'strikers' (W. Tans'ur, 1772).

PETER WILLIAMS

Stickl, Franz (*b* Diessen am Ammersee, nr. Munich; *fl* 1727–41). German composer. He studied at Salzburg University, and between 1727 and 1741, when his various publications appeared, he held the post of organist at a church in Ingolstadt.

His church music is unusual in that he wrote optional parts for three violas as well as for the usual two violins and organ; also, in his masses (Augsburg, 1727), he subdivided the longer sections more than was customary at the time, though the individual movements are very short. He published two sets of vespers (Augsburg, 1728, 1741). His music is typical of the church music written by many competent composers at that time, and his style most interesting for its varied choral textures and unusually purposeful bass lines.

ELIZABETH ROCHE

Stiebler, Ernstalbrecht (*b* Berlin, 29 March 1934). German composer and radio producer. He studied composition with Klussmann and music education at the Hamburg Musikhochschule (1953–9), where in 1964 he received the diploma in theory for his dissertation on Schoenberg's quartets. In 1969 he was appointed to produce contemporary music programmes for Hesse Radio, Frankfurt. His compositions are predominantly in chamber genres, and are characterized by introversion and restrained dynamics. He received significant influences from the Darmstadt summer courses, notably from Stockhausen's classes.

WORKS
(selective list)

Studien I–II, pf, 1958–60; Klangmomente, 2 pf, 1961; Labile Aktion, pf, 1962; Extension, str trio, 1963; Stadien, 3 cl, 1964; Attaques, org, 1965; Fragment, female chorus, insts, 1966; Betonungen, org, 1968; Zeilen, pf, 1970; Extension II, cl, trbn, vc, pf, 1972; Modell, chamber orch, 1973; Intonation I, chorus, org, 1973; Continuo, ens, 1974; Swing, synth, 1975; Intonation II, chorus, org, 1976

RUDOLF LÜCK

Stiedry, Fritz (*b* Vienna, 11 Oct 1883; *d* Zurich, 8 Aug 1968). American conductor of Austrian birth. After studying at the Vienna Academy of Music, he was engaged on Mahler's recommendation as assistant to Ernst von Schuch at Dresden, 1907–8. He held appointments at Teplice, Poznań, Prague, Nuremberg and Kassel, and in 1914 became principal conductor at the Berlin Staatsoper, where he remained until 1923; he then succeeded Weingartner as director of the Vienna Volksoper (1924–5). From 1928 to 1933 he was again in Berlin, as principal conductor at the Städtische Oper where he collaborated with Carl Ebert on productions of *Macbeth* and *Simon Boccanegra*, operas then seldom performed, and conducted the first performance of Weill's *Die Bürgschaft* (1932). In March 1933 he was forced to leave his post by the Nazi regime. He went to Russia and conducted concerts and opera in Leningrad and Moscow until 1937 when he was appointed director of the newly founded New Friends of Music orchestra in New York. He conducted at the Chicago Civic Opera, 1945–6, and regularly at the Metropolitan Opera, 1946–58, specializing in Verdi and Wagner. In 1947 he conducted Gluck's *Orfeo ed Euridice* at Glyndebourne, in a renewed collaboration with Ebert; Kathleen Ferrier sang Orpheus and the performance was recorded. He first appeared at Covent Garden in 1953–4 to conduct a new production of the *Ring* and a revival of *Fidelio*. His performances then were criticized as musically unpolished, but in general he was a direct, unfussy conductor in the best tradition of Austrian-trained musicians.

ALAN BLYTH

Stieff. American firm of piano manufacturers. It was established by Charles Maximilian Stieff (*b* Württemberg, 19 July 1805; *d* Baltimore, 1 Jan 1862), who had been educated in Stuttgart in science and the classics. In 1831 he emigrated to Lebanon County, Pennsylvania, moving soon after with his wife Charlotte to Baltimore, Maryland, where for ten years he taught music and ancient and modern languages at the Haespert School. In the early 1840s he began to import European pianos, including those of Rosenkrantz, Keine and Miller. After a trip to Europe (1852) to study methods among various piano manufacturers he set up his own piano factory at 7–9 Liberty Street, Baltimore, where his brother-in-law Jacob Gross joined him as superintendent in 1856.

After Stieff's death his widow headed the business for five years assisted by their sons, who themselves carried on after 1867: John L. Stieff (1831–1901), who left the firm in 1876; George Waters Stieff, who was with the firm from about 1878 until 1891; Charles Stieff (*d* 1917), who retired in 1911, and Frederick Philip Stieff (1845–1918). Under Charles and Frederick the firm expanded its manufacture and retail branch stores to establish the Stieff piano as one of the most popular in the bordering states of Maryland and Pennsylvania and also, in particular, the southern states. The firm bought the Shaw Piano Company of Erie, Pennsylvania, moving it to Baltimore in 1900, and in 1904 bought the factory and stock of the Bennett-Bretz Piano Company of Harrisburg, Pennsylvania.

In 1920, two years after the death of Frederick Philip Stieff, his sons George Waters and Frederick Philip jr moved the offices to 315 North Howard Street, where they remained until the firm went out of business in 1952. The six-storey building was faced with marble columns and decorated with panelled walls, mirrors and murals depicting the manufacture of pianos; on display inside were medals won by the firm at such expositions as the Philadelphia 1876 Centennial, the Paris 1878 Exposition and the Chicago Columbian Exposition of 1893. Many musical events were heard in the 300-seat concert hall which became a favourite for recitals in Baltimore.

BIBLIOGRAPHY
The Biographical Cyclopedia of Representative Men of Maryland and District of Columbia (Baltimore, 1879), 686f
A. Dolge: *Pianos and their Makers* (Covina, Calif., 1911/*R*1972), 291f
Purchasers' Guide to the Music Industries (New York, 1922), 187ff
CYNTHIA ADAMS HOOVER

Stiehl, Carl [Karl] **(Johann Christian)** (*b* Lübeck, 12 July 1826; *d* Lübeck, 1 Dec 1911). German writer on music and conductor, brother of Heinrich Stiehl. His father Johann Diedrich Stiehl (*b* Lübeck, 9 July 1800; *d* Lübeck, 27 June 1872) studied the organ with M. A. Bauck, whom he succeeded as organist of the Jakobikirche, Lübeck, on 10 July 1835. Carl studied in Weimar with J. C. Lobe and at the Leipzig Conservatory. He taught the organ and singing in Jever (1848–58) and Eutin (1858–77), where he was also music director to the Grand Duke of Oldenburg (from 1860). On his return to Leipzig in 1877 he taught singing and conducted the Singakademie until 1901. He also directed the concerts of the Musikverein and founded the Philharmonic Concerts (1886–96) which succeeded them. He was an important figure in the musical life of Lübeck, both for his writings on the city's history in such books as *Musikgeschichte der Stadt Lübeck* (Lübeck, 1891) and *Geschichte des Theaters zu Lübeck* (Lübeck, 1901) and for his bibliographical work for the Lübeck library. He discovered and edited works by Buxtehude.

BIBLIOGRAPHY
C. Stiehl: *Lübeckisches Tonkünstlerlexikon* (Leipzig, 1887)
J. Hennings: 'Unsere Künstler – Karl Stiehl', *Neue Musik-Zeitung*, xxvii (1906), 464
W. Stahl: 'Carl Stiehl', *Vaterstädtische Blätter* (Lübeck, 1911), 197
J. Hennings and W. Stahl: *Musikgeschichte Lübecks* (Kassel, 1951)
GAYNOR G. JONES

Stiehl, Heinrich (Franz Daniel) (*b* Lübeck, 5 Aug 1829; *d* Reval [now Tallinn], 1 May 1886). German organist and composer, brother of Carl. He studied with Lobe in Weimar, then at the Leipzig Conservatory with Gade, Hauptmann and Moscheles. After a position in St Petersburg as organist at St Peter's he went on concert tours as an organist, living in Vienna, Paris, Gotha and Lüneburg. He conducted the Philharmonic and Cecilia Societies in Belfast from 1874, and then taught the piano in Hastings until he took a post as organist at St Olai's church in Reval, Russia. His numerous compositions include the Singspiels *Jery und Bätely* and *Der Schatzgräber*, choral and orchestral works as well as chamber and instrumental music; his piano pieces show the influence of Mendelssohn in their melodic writing. He conducted the first Russian performance of Bach's *St Matthew Passion* on 17 March 1883.

BIBLIOGRAPHY
C. Stiehl: *Lübeckisches Tonkünstlerlexikon* (Leipzig, 1887)
W. Niemann: 'Meister der Klaviermusik: Heinrich Stiehl', *Neue Musik-Zeitung*, xxxiii (1912), 336
W. Stahl: 'Heinrich Stiehl', *Lübeckisches Jb der Vaterstädtlichen Blätter 1929–30* (Lübeck, 1930)
J. Hennings and W. Stahl: *Musikgeschichte Lübecks* (Kassel, 1951)
GAYNOR G. JONES

Stieler, Caspar von (*b* Erfurt, 1 March 1632; *d* Erfurt, 24 June 1707). German poet and playwright. He studied theology and medicine in Leipzig, Erfurt and Giessen between 1648 and 1650, when he went to Königsberg for further study in philosophy and theology. He was a secretary to a Prussian cavalry regiment from 1654 to 1657 and saw action in the Polish–Swedish war. He then began a four-year period travelling, first in north Germany and then in Holland, France, Spain, Italy and Switzerland. In 1662, a year after he returned to Germany, he studied law in Jena. In 1663 he was chamber secretary in Schwarzburg-Rudolstadt, and from 1666 to 1676 he was in Eisenach as secretary to the Duke of Saxe-Weimar; at this period he was enrolled as 'Der Späte' in the society known as the Fruchtbringende Gesellschaft. For the last 30 years of his life he held various appointments in Jena, Weimar, Holstein, Hamburg and finally Erfurt, where he worked as writer, lawyer and private tutor.

Stieler's importance for music lies primarily in his *Die geharnschte Venus, oder Liebes-Lieder im Kriege gedichtet* (Hamburg, 1660; facs. and edn., Munich, 1968), which until recently was wrongly ascribed to Schwieger. This collection of 70 strophic songs contains solo lieder with basso continuo by six composers indicated by initials only which may be interpreted thus: J.K. (Jakob Kortkamp or Johann Kruss), C.B. (Christoph Bernhard), J.S. (Johann Schop), M.C. (Martin Köler [Coler] and possibly a second composer too), J.M.R. (Johann Martin Rubert) and C.S. (Stieler himself). Five other pieces are taken from French ballets and four more from other French works; one lied is a madrigal. Stieler also figures in the history of German dramatic music before the opening of the Hamburg Opera; he included music during his plays and between the acts, but it has been lost.

BIBLIOGRAPHY
H. Kretzschmar: *Geschichte des neuen deutschen Liedes* (Leipzig, 1911/R1966)
K. Meyer: *Die Musik der Geharnschten Venus* (Munich, 1925)
W. Vetter: *Das frühdeutsche Lied* (Münster, 1928)
J. H. Baron: *Foreign Influences on the German Secular Solo Continuo Lied of the Mid-seventeenth Century* (diss., Brandeis U., Waltham, Mass., 1967)
M. Bircher: 'Ein neu aufgefundenes Frühwerk von Kaspar Stieler', *Frontiers of American Culture*, ed. R. B. Browne (Lafayette, Ind., 1968), 283
JOHN H. BARON

Stierhorn (Ger.: 'bull horn', 'cow horn'). The war horn or great bugle horn of antiquity and the early Middle Ages. A straight conical brass instrument of this name is called for in Wagner's *Ring*. See COW HORN.

Stierlein [Stierlin], Johann Christoph (*b* Nuremberg; *d* Nuremberg, July 1693). German organist, theorist and composer. He is first heard of in 1677 at the Stuttgart court, where he was court organist, and in 1690 he was appointed vice-Kapellmeister. He is most notable for his brief, carefully written introduction to the study of music, *Trifolium musicale consistens in musica theoretica, practica, & poetica* (Stuttgart, 1691). In the first of his 'three folios' he offered rudiments of musical notation, explanations of transposition and common musical terminology and eight interesting examples of frequently used vocal ornaments or 'figures'. The second and most significant part of the manual is a succinct and, for that date in Germany, rather uncommon introduction to the art of organ continuo playing, including details for realizing thoroughbass figures. In the third part Stierlein put forward a curious suggestion for composing four-part music without using the usual musical notation. Instead, each staff line and space of the bass, tenor, alto and soprano clefs is given a number, beginning with 1 on the F below the bass staff. The examples of vocal music that Stierlein provided are in effect set out in a pseudo-tablature notation of no practicality. His only known music is *Musicalische geistliche Zeit- und Ewigkeit-Betrachtung bestehend in 25 Arien* (Stuttgart, 1688), for solo voice and continuo.

Three other musicians called Stierlein, presumably belonging to the same family, worked, mainly as organists and directors of music, at Stuttgart during the 18th century. Of these, Philipp David Stierlein (*b* 1711; *d* 31 March 1801) is known to have written an Arioso for two violins, bass and harpsichord, which is now lost.

BIBLIOGRAPHY
J. Sittard: *Zur Geschichte der Musik und des Theaters am Württembergischen Hofe* (Stuttgart, 1890–91/R1970)
GEORGE J. BUELOW

Stierlein, Philipp David. German 18th-century musician, probably related to JOHANN CHRISTOPH STIERLEIN.

Stierlin, Johann Christoph. *See* STIERLEIN, JOHANN CHRISTOPH.

Stiévenard, Alexandre (*b* Cambrai, 18 Aug 1769 or 1767; *d* Ludwigslust, 24 Sept 1855). French violinist, guitarist and composer. The son of a wealthy merchant, he began his musical education at an early age. In 1789 he fled from the Revolution to Belgium and the Netherlands, where he gave concerts and worked first as a violinist and then as director of music in an Ostend theatre. When the French invaded Belgium he fled again, to Bremen and to Hamburg, becoming first violinist of the new Schauspielhaus. In 1796 he became elocution teacher to the children of Duke Rantzau at Ludwigslust and from 1801 was also active as a violinist there. In 1837 he retired and settled at the Schwerin court. A cultured and versatile figure, Stiévenard was an outstanding amateur musician, and his eight-volume *Biographie ou Mémoires* (*D-SWl*) provides a critical view of the musical life of his time. Most of his compositions, including violin concertos, quintets, quartets, arias and songs, are lost; the *Recueil d'airs aisez avec accompagnement de guitare* (*SWl*) is stylistically firmly based in the Rococo.

BIBLIOGRAPHY
O. Kade: *Die Musikalien-Sammlung des Grossherzoglichen Mecklenburg-Schweriner Fürstenhauses aus den letzten zwei Jahrhunderten*, ii (Schwerin, 1893)
C. Meyer: *Geschichte der Mecklenburg-Schweriner Hofkapelle* (Schwerin, 1913)
based on *MGG* (xii, 1801–2) by permission of Bärenreiter
URTE HÄRTWIG

Stignani, Ebe (*b* Naples, 10 July 1904; *d* Imola, 5 Oct 1974). Italian mezzo-soprano. She studied at the Naples Conservatory with Agostino Roche and made her début at the San Carlo in 1925 as Amneris. In 1926 Toscanini engaged her for La Scala, where she first appeared as Eboli in *Don Carlos*. In successive seasons at the Scala she added to her repertory all the leading mezzo-soprano parts in Italian opera and a large number of other roles including Delilah, Ortrud, Brangäne, Gluck's Orpheus and a few surprising trifles such as Aennchen in *Der Freischütz* and Hänsel; she also appeared as the capricious heroine of Rossini's *L'italiana in Algeri*. But it was in the tragic characters of Verdi, above all Azucena in *Il trovatore*, that she found the greatest scope and won her greatest successes. At Covent Garden she sang Amneris (1937, 1939, 1955), Azucena (1939, 1952), and Adalgisa to the Norma of Maria Callas (1952 and 1957). She had a voice of rich quality and ample range, extending from *f* to *c'''*, and on the concert platform she occasionally attempted soprano music, such as the vengeance aria from *Don Giovanni*. Judged by former standards, neither her vocalization nor her phrasing was impeccable, yet her singing was always grandiose and authoritative and she brought to the fierce mezzo parts of Verdi – as to the mezzo part in his Requiem – an intensity and a dramatic fire that made her for many years the leading exponent of such music. Her last appearance was as Azucena in London in 1958.

Ebe Stignani as Amneris in Verdi's 'Aida'

BIBLIOGRAPHY
H. Rosenthal: 'Ebe Stignani', *Opera*, vi (1952), 334
R. Celletti: 'Stignani, Ebe', *Le grandi voci* (Rome, 1964) [with opera discography by R. Vegeto]
E. Davidson: 'All about Ebe', *Opera News*, xxxv/21 (1971), 28
    DESMOND SHAWE-TAYLOR/HAROLD ROSENTHAL

Stile (It.). STYLE.

Stile antico (It.: 'old style'). A term most frequently used to describe church music written after 1600 in an archaic style that imitated Palestrina. It was one of the hallmarks of the Baroque period that a self-conscious antithesis between *antico* and *moderno* should spring up within church music itself; initially the terms *prima prattica* and *seconda prattica* were used by Monteverdi (preface to the fifth book of madrigals, 1605) to distinguish between the older Netherlands Renaissance style where the music was master of the words and the progressive madrigal idiom from Rore onwards where

the reverse prevailed. These terms and (in church music) others like 'da capella' and 'da concerto' seemed to mean the same as *antico* and *moderno*, and several composers, starting with Monteverdi in 1610, published volumes of church music with works in both old and new styles. In northern Italy the old style was often reserved for masses and vesper psalms – the unchanging, mostly neutral parts of the liturgy – while the more modern appeared in motets, where more text expression was possible and greater freedom of choice of texts prevailed. Thus nearly all Monteverdi's surviving mass music is marked 'da capella' and written in the *stile antico*, although none of it exactly conforms to a particular Renaissance idiom.

The true inheritors of Palestrina's style and the founders of the *stile antico* tradition were his Roman pupils and admirers, Soriano, the Anerios, the Naninos and Gregorio Allegri. Their music conformed to his, though even they began to rearrange his music for fewer voices and added continuo. As Palestrina became idolized, the details of his polyphonic art were gradually lost. Although the term 'stile alla Palestrina' continued to be used, the contrapuntal rules of Bontempi (1660) clearly infected the strict style with subtle licences. The ability to write in *stile antico* for certain church music spread widely – Alessandro Scarlatti, Francesco Durante, Leo, Gasparini, Pergolesi and Lotti all turned to it, while with the propagation of the Italian manner north of the Alps, Kerll, Biber, Caldara, Georg Muffat and Fux all wrote in it at some time. Fux's *Gradus ad Parnassum* (1725) was the contrapuntal treatise that set the seal on the abstract conception of strict counterpoint, but by that time Palestrina's art seemed quite unnatural and Fux could only reinterpret it subjectively: some of Fux's *stile antico* music was harmonically anachronistic and rhythmically foursquare.

The *stile antico* was equally important in Protestant Germany after the propagation of late Renaissance Italian music in about 1600 through the anthologies of Schadaeus and Bodenschatz. Music from these collections appeared up to Bach's time – Bach had a copy of a Palestrina mass with orchestral doubling, a characteristic addition. Schütz upheld the study of Palestrina to would-be composers in the preface to the *Geistliche Chor-Musik* (1648), whose contents reflect less a confrontation between old and new than a fusion of the elements that persisted in the German motet tradition. His pupil Christoph Bernhard coined the term 'stylus gravis' for the old style.

Although the *stile antico* was a concept of the style-conscious Baroque period, its currency outlived that period and it influenced Classical and even Romantic composers of church music, as seen, for example, in the incursion of solid *alla breve* counterpoint as a contrast to 'modern' writing, or in some unaccompanied choral passages by Rossini and Verdi written after the start of the Palestrina revival. Since the days of Fux, *stile antico* has been connected with the idea of strict counterpoint as an academic discipline. Though associated with church music, it was never assumed by composers to be a proper style for all church music, and it has always coexisted with the styles of the day.

BIBLIOGRAPHY
O. Ursprung: *Restauration und Palestrina-Renaissance in der katholischen Kirchenmusik der letzten zwei Jahrhunderte* (Augsburg, 1924)
K. G. Fellerer: 'Der stile antico in der katholischen Kirchenmusik des 18. Jahrhunderts', *Beethoven-Zentenarfeier: Wien 1927*, 244
——: *Der Palestrinastil und seine Bedeutung in der vokalen Kirchen-*

musik des achtzehnten Jahrhunderts (Augsburg, 1929/*R*1972)
M. F. Bukofzer: *Music in the Baroque Era* (London, 1948)
F. W. Riedel: 'Fux und die Römische Palestrina-Tradition', *Mf*, xiv (1961), 14
J. Roche: 'Monteverdi and the Prima Prattica', *The Monteverdi Companion*, ed. D. Arnold and N. Fortune (London, 1968), 167
C. Wolff: *Der Stile Antico in der Musik Johann Sebastian Bachs* (Wiesbaden, 1968)

JEROME ROCHE

Stile concitato (It.: 'agitated style'). A term used by Monteverdi to denote a particular style of composition. Monteverdi, following Greek philosophers, believed that music should express three main emotional states of mankind, 'anger, moderation, and humility or supplication'. Music must therefore have three equivalent styles or manners: 'agitated' (*concitato*), 'soft' (*molle*) and 'moderate' (*temperato*). He equated the first of these with Plato's description of music which 'would fittingly imitate the utterances and the accents of a brave man who is engaged in warfare' (translation by O. Strunk, *Source Readings in Music History*, 1950, p.413). The Greek philosophers describe the pyrrhic measure as useful for warlike dances, the spondaic for calm dances, and Monteverdi's solution to the problem of finding the equivalent in modern music was to make a single semibreve correspond to one spondaic beat and to divide this into 16 semiquavers for the 'agitated' style. These semiquavers are repeated on a single note, thus resembling superficially the modern tremolo; but they must be strictly measured, and it is quite wrong to reduce them to an unmeasured tremolando, as has frequently been done in 20th-century performances of Monteverdi's music.

Monteverdi worked out the concept in some detail in *Il combattimento di Tancredi e Clorinda* (1624), and later in numerous works published in his *Madrigali guerrieri ed amorosi* (1638), the preface to which discusses his intentions. There are also frequent passages in his late operas where suitable words are set in the *concitato* manner. Later composers to use the technique included Alessandro Grandi (i) and Schütz, while a passage in Handel's *Dixit Dominus*, setting the phrase 'conquassabit capita', is so close in style to that used by Grandi in composing the same psalm that it seems possible that the *stile concitato* was still known in the early 18th century.

DENIS ARNOLD

Stile moderno (It.). A term most frequently used, in antithesis to STILE ANTICO, to refer to church music written after 1600 in an up-to-date style.

Stile rappresentativo (It.: 'theatrical style'). The term used in a generic sense denotes the solo vocal style employed in the earliest theatrical pieces set completely to music. It was first used publicly by Giulio Caccini in the title and dedication (signed on 20 December 1600) of his *Euridice* to describe its music. A broader concept than recitative, it includes a variety of styles. G. B. Doni (*Annotazioni sopra il Compendio de' generi, e de' modi della musica* (Rome, 1640), 60ff), distinguished three types of musical setting in the early pastorals: the narrative style, as in Daphne's report of the death of the heroine in Peri's *Euridice* (Florence, 6 October 1600), using many repeated notes and fast speech-like rhythm over rather static harmony; the expressive style, such as in Ariadne's lament in Monteverdi's *Arianna* (Mantua, 1608), which has a more marked melodic profile, free dissonances and more frequent changes of harmony; and the recitation style (*speciale recitativo*), as in the prologue of Peri's score, patterned after the *aria da cantar rime* once used to chant heroic poems, with melodic formulae of narrow compass strophically repeated or varied and coordinated rhythmically with the bass, and broad cadences at the ends of lines. This last type, properly called 'strophic aria', sometimes offered a vehicle for virtuoso improvisation, as in 'Possente spirto' in Monteverdi's *Orfeo* (Mantua, 1607). In addition, dance-songs or canzonettas, sometimes with choral refrains or instrumental ritornellos, also figured in the early pastorals and sacred plays.

The earliest surviving music in this style is some fragments by Peri from *Dafne* (Florence, 1598) and the *Rappresentatione di Anima et di Corpo* by Cavalieri (Rome, February 1600). It was Peri who realized a style of recitative that was to become the model for other composers, such as Marco da Gagliano and Monteverdi. He liberated the voice from the chordal accompaniment by giving it a fluid declamatory rhythm, allowing it – particularly on unstressed syllables and words – to pass through notes that escape from the harmony of the chords. He acknowledged that he sought a style midway between song and speech such as scholars then believed was used in the ancient Greek theatre. The accompaniment was improvised over a figured bass on a group of chordal instruments, which might include harpsichords, a portative organ, chitarroni, theorbos, lyres and lutes.

BIBLIOGRAPHY
A. Solerti: *Le origini del melodramma* (Turin, 1903/*R*1969)
W. V. Porter: 'Peri and Corsi's *Dafne*: Some New Discoveries and Observations', *JAMS*, xviii (1965), 170
B. R. Hanning: *The Influence of Humanist Thought and Italian Renaissance Poetry on the Formation of Opera* (diss, Yale U., 1968)
C. V. Palisca: *Baroque Music* (Englewood Cliffs, NJ, 1968), chap.3
N. Pirrotta: 'Early Opera and Aria', *New Looks at Italian Opera: Essays in Honor of Donald J. Grout* (Ithaca, NY, 1968), 39–107
H. M. Brown: 'How Opera Began: an Introduction to Jacopo Peri's *Euridice* (1600)', in E. Cochrane: *The Late Renaissance* (New York, 1970), 401–43

CLAUDE V. PALISCA

Still, Robert (*b* London, 10 June 1910; *d* Bucklebury, Berks., 13 Jan 1971). English composer. He was educated at Eton, at Trinity College, Oxford (1929–32), and at the Royal College of Music, London (1932–4). Only after World War II did he begin to compose in earnest. In 1963 he was given the Oxford DMus for his Third Symphony, a work typically firm in its commitment to tonality. Psychology interested him deeply: he founded the Imago Group with Adrian Stokes in 1953, published 'Gustav Mahler and Psychoanalysis' in the *American Imago* (xvii/3, 1960), and based his Fourth Symphony on a published case history of persecution complex.

WORKS
(*selective list*)

Opera: Oedipus (3, Stokes, after Sophocles), 1954–6
Orch: Sym. no.1, 1954; Ballad of the Bladebone Inn, ov., 1956; Sym. no.2, 1956; Sym. no.3, 1960; Conc., str, 1964; Sym. no.4, 1964; Vn Conc., 1969; Pf Conc., 1970
Choral: Elegie (M. Arnold), Bar, vv, small orch, 1963, rev. 1965
Chamber and inst: Cl Qnt; 5 str qts; Ob Qt, Trio, fl, ob, pf; Trio, cl, vn, pf; 3 pf sonatas; Other People, pf suite
Other works: *c*25 songs, partsongs

GRAHAM HATTON

Still, William Grant (*b* Woodville, Mississippi, 11 May 1895; *d* Los Angeles, 3 Dec 1978). Black American composer. After his father, the town bandmaster, died the family moved to Little Rock, Arkansas. There Still began studying the violin. He matriculated at Wilberforce College intending to study medicine but became involved in musical activities; during this period he was influenced by Coleridge-Taylor. Still left Wilberforce College without graduating and then worked with various music ensembles, including that of W. C. Handy in 1916. He then enrolled at Oberlin Conservatory where his teachers encouraged him to compose. His studies there were interrupted by navy service in World War I; shortly after his return to Oberlin he left for New York in search of work. He joined Handy's publishing company, played the oboe in theatre orchestras and studied on a scholarship with Varèse. In 1923 Still was offered a scholarship by Chadwick who urged him to write specifically American music. He began to write large-scale works in the early 1920s and in 1931 the Rochester PO performed his *Afro-American Symphony* – the first symphony by a black American to be played by a leading orchestra. Still was also the first black American to conduct a major orchestra, the first to have an opera performed by an important company and one of the first to write for radio, films and television. His many honours include Rosenwald and Guggenheim fellowships; the Harmon Award (1927); honorary doctorates from Howard University (1941), Oberlin (1947), Bates College (1954) and the University of Arkansas (1971); and prizes from CBS, the New York World's Fair (1939), the League of Composers and leading orchestras. Still became best known for his nationalist works, employing negro and other American folk idioms. After a period of avant-garde experiment he turned in a neoromantic direction, with graceful melodies supported by conventional harmonies, rhythms and timbres; his music has a freshness and individuality that have brought enthusiastic response.

WORKS
(for fuller list see Haas)

ORCHESTRAL
6 sym. poems: Darker America, 1924; Dismal Swamp, 1933; Kaintuck, 1935; A Song at Dusk, 1936; Old California, 1941; Poem, 1944
6 suites: From the Black Belt, 1926; Bells, 1944; Archaic Ritual, 1946; Wood Notes, 1947; The American Scene, 1957; Patterns, 1960
5 syms.: no.1 'Afro-American', 1930; no.2, 1937; no.5 'Western World' [originally no.3], 1945; no.4 'Autochthonous', 1947; no.3, 1958
In memoriam: The Colored Soldiers who died for Democracy, 1943; Festive Ov., 1944; Serenade, 1957; Threnody in memory of Jan Sibelius, 1965; Miniature Ov., 1965; Choreographic Prelude, 1970
Pieces for young people incl. The Little Red School-house, 1957

VOCAL
Operas: A Bayou Legend (3, V. Arvey), 1941; Troubled Island (3, L. Hughes, Arvey), 1941; Costaso (3, Arvey), 1950; Mota (3, Arvey), 1951; The Pillar (3, Arvey), 1956; Minette Fontaine (3, Arvey), 1958; Highway no.1, USA (2, Arvey), 1962
Ballets: La guiablesse, 1927; Sahdji, 1930; Lenox Avenue, 1937; Miss Sally's Party, 1940
Other vocal: Rising Tide (A. Stillman), 1v, pf, 1939; arr. as Victory Tide, chorus, pf, 1939; arr. as Song of a City, chorus, orch, 1939; And they Lynched him on a Tree (K. G. Chapin), solo vv, chorus, orch, 1940; Plain Chant for America (Chapin), chorus, orch, 1941; Those who wait (Arvey), chorus, orch, 1942; Wailing Women (Arvey), chorus, orch, 1946; Songs of Separation (A. Bontemps, P.-T. Marcelin, P. L. Dunbar, C. Cullen, Hughes), S, pf qnt, 1949; Rhapsody (Arvey), S, orch, 1955; From the Hearts of Women (Arvey), S, fl, ob, str, pf, 1961; other solo/choral works, spiritual arrs.

INSTRUMENTAL
Summerland, pf, 1936; 3 Visions, pf, 1936; 7 Traceries, pf, 1939; Suite, vn, pf, 1943; Bells, pf, 1944; From the Delta, band, 1945; Incantation and Dance, ob, pf, 1945; Pastorela, vn, pf, 1946; Danzas de Panama, suite, str, 1948; To you, America, band, 1951; Ennanga, harp, pf, str, 1956; Folk Suite, band, 1963; Ring Play, pf, 1964; other

inst pieces, incidental music for the theatre, cinema, broadcasting
Principal publishers: Ditson, Fischer, Presser, Robbins, G. Schirmer, Southern

BIBLIOGRAPHY
E. Southern: *The Music of Black Americans: a History* (New York, 1971)
——, ed.: *Readings in Black American Music* (New York, 1972)
R. Haas, ed.: *William Grant Still and the Fusion of Cultures in American Music* (Los Angeles, 1972)
'A Birthday Offering to William Grant Still', *Black Perspective in Music*, iii/2 (1975), 129

EILEEN SOUTHERN

Stillingfleet, Benjamin (*b* Norfolk, 1702; *d* London, 15 Dec 1771). English naturalist and amateur musician. He was educated at Norwich and Cambridge, and in 1724 became tutor to William Windham in Felbrig, Norfolk. In 1737 he and his pupil embarked on a tour of the Continent. In Rome Stillingfleet met Robert Price, and in 1738 Price, Windham, Stillingfleet and others formed a common room in Geneva for the purpose of reading and acting plays and pantomimes. Stillingfleet was director of scenes and machinery; he also composed some airs. After his return to England he studied Greek music theory, performed on the cello and collaborated in the composition of oratorios with J. C. Smith. Influenced by Price's explication of Rameau, Stillingfleet undertook to write a commentary and partial translation of Giuseppe Tartini's *Trattato di musica* (Padua, 1754). The book also contains miscellaneous observations on ancient music and on the effects of music.

WRITINGS
(only those on music)
Moses and Zipporah; Joseph; David and Bathsheba; Medea (London, 1760) [printed but not pubd]
Paradise Lost (London, 1760) [set by J. C. Smith and first performed at Covent Garden, 29 Feb 1760]
Principles and Power of Harmony (London, 1771) [pubd anonymously]
Autograph letter to Elizabeth Montagu, 24 Oct 1771, *US-PRu*

BIBLIOGRAPHY
[W. Bewley]: Review of *Principles and Power of Harmony*, *Monthly Review*, xlv (1771), 369, 477
A Catalogue of the Library of Benjamin Stillingfleet, Esq; lately deceased; ... to be sold by Auction ... on Monday, February the 3d, 1772 (London, 1772)
[W. Coxe]: *Anecdotes of George Frederick Handel, and John Christopher Smith* (London, 1799), 63
W. Coxe, ed.: *Literary Life and Select Works of Benjamin Stillingfleet* (London, 1811)
[A. Chalmers]: Review of W. Coxe, ed.: *Literary Life and Select Works of Benjamin Stillingfleet*, *Gentleman's Magazine*, lxxxi (1811), Jan, 41

JAMIE CROY KASSLER

Stilwell, Richard (*b* St Louis, Missouri, 6 May 1942). American baritone. Trained by Frank St Leger at Indiana University, and later by Daniel Ferro in New York, he began his career as a soloist with the US Army Chorus. He made his operatic début in April 1970 with the New York City Opera as Pelléas – a role that was to bring him worldwide prominence. His evenly modulated light baritone, his dramatic intensity and youthful ardour made him a virtually ideal interpreter of Debussy's princely hero. In February 1974 he created Constantine in Thomas Pasatieri's *The Seagull* with the Houston Opera; a month earlier he had sung the title role in the stage première in the USA of Monteverdi's *Il ritorno d'Ulisse in patria* at the Kennedy Center, the role which had introduced him to Glyndebourne in 1973. His Covent Garden début, as Pelléas, was in December 1974. Stilwell's elegantly delineated performances have also been applauded at La Scala, the Metropolitan Opera (Guglielmo in *Così fan tutte*),

Chicago, San Francisco, the Holland Festival, Vienna, Paris, Hamburg, Venice, Aix-en-Provence, Buenos Aires and Santa Fe. His roles include Mozart's Count and Papageno, Billy Budd, Olivier in *Capriccio*, Gluck's Orpheus, Rossini's Dandini, Otho in *L'incoronazione di Poppea* and Eugene Onegin. In 1976 he created the leading male role in Pasatieri's *Inez di Castro* in Baltimore, and opened the Glyndebourne season as Ford in *Falstaff*.

MARTIN BERNHEIMER

Stimmbogen (Ger.). CROOK.

Stimmbücher (Ger.). PARTBOOKS.

Stimme (Ger.: 'voice', 'part'). A voice (e.g. *Sopranstimme*: 'soprano voice'; *Altstimme*: 'alto voice'); a vocal or instrumental part (e.g. *Flötenstimme*: 'flute part'). 'Stimme' is also used to mean an organ stop and the soundpost of a string instrument.

Stimmer (Ger.). DRONE (i).

Stimmführung (Ger.). PART-WRITING.

Stimmgabel (Ger.). TUNING-FORK.

Stimmgabelwerk (Ger.). *See* SOSTENENTE PIANO, §1.

Stimmkreuzung (Ger.). PART-CROSSING.

Stimmstock (Ger.). (1) WREST PLANK.
  (2) SOUNDPOST.

Stimmtausch (Ger.). VOICE-EXCHANGE.

Stimmung (Ger.). (1) Mood. A word encountered in many musical contexts. *Stimmungsmusik* is 'background music' or 'mood music'.
  (2) Tuning.

Stimmwirbeln (Ger.). WREST PINS.

Stimmzug (Ger.). TUNING-SLIDE.

Stinfalico, Eterio. Pseudonym of ALESSANDRO MARCELLO.

Sting. A term used in 17th-century England for a normal, single-finger vibrato in lute playing. *See* ORNAMENTS, §III, 2, and VIBRATO, §1(i).

Stiva. Synonym for NEUMA.

Stivori, Francesco (*b* Venice, *c*1550; *d* probably at Graz, 1605). Italian composer and organist. He is traditionally said to have studied with Claudio Merulo and Giovanni Gabrieli. It is, however, unlikely that the latter taught him, for Stivori was, if not somewhat older, at least the same age as Gabrieli, who described him in a document of 16 October 1604 as 'mio cordialissimo amico'. The title-pages of printed collections show that from 1579 to 1601 he was town organist at Montagna, near Padua. He went to Graz, apparently in 1602, to serve as organist at the court of Archduke Ferdinand of Inner Austria. He held this post, with the exceptionally high salary of 45 guilders a month, until his death. Costanzo Antegnati praised him in his *Arte organica*

(Brescia, 1608). Though Stivori was a prolific and influential representative of the Venetian school, his works have not yet been studied as they deserve. Through his MS collection of eight-part hymns (in *YU-Lu*) and his *Musica austriaca* (1605), the publication of which was made possible by a subsidy of 100 guilders from Archduke Ferdinand, he played an important part in introducing into Austria music for multiple choirs. On the other hand he did not go so far as to write monodies.

WORKS
(*all printed works published in Venice unless otherwise indicated*)

SACRED

Sacrarum cantionum liber secundus, 5vv (1579)
Sacrarum cantionum liber tertius, 5–7vv (1593)
Sacrae cantiones, 4 equal vv (Verona, 1595)
Sacrarum cantionum liber quartus, 6–8vv (1596)
In Sanctissimae Virginis Mariae canticum modulationes ... liber quintus (1598, 2/1608)
Sacrarum cantionum liber sextus, 8vv (1601)
Missa 'Audite me', 16vv, *A-Wn*; 3 Magnificat, 12, 15, 16vv, *Wn*; 1 Magnificat, 8vv, *YU-Lu*; 1 Magnificat, 8vv, *A-Gu*

SECULAR

Il primo libro de madrigali, 4vv (1583)
Il primo libro de madrigali, 5vv (1585)
Ricercari. a 4 (1589)
Madrigali ... libro primo, 3vv (1590[22])
Il secondo libro de ricercari, a 4 (1594, ?lost)
Madrigali e dialoghi, 8vv (1598)
Ricercari, capricci et canzoni, libro terzo, 4vv (1599)
Concenti musicali, libro secondo, 8, 12, 16vv (1601)
Madrigali e canzoni, libro terzo, a 8 (1603)
Musica austriaca, 8, 12, 16vv (1605)
1 madrigal, 3vv, in 1587[6]; 1, 3vv, in 1588[20]; 6, 4vv, in 1595[5]; 3, 5vv, in 1595[7]; 2, 4vv, in 1597[15]

BIBLIOGRAPHY

H. Federhofer: *Musikpflege und Musiker am Grazer Habsburgerhof der Erzherzöge Karl und Ferdinand von Innerösterreich (1564–1619)* (Mainz, 1967)

HELLMUT FEDERHOFER

Stobaeus [Stobäus, Stobeus, Stoboeus], **Johann** [Johannes] (*b* Graudenz [now Grudziadz], 6 July 1580; *d* Königsberg [now Kaliningrad], 11 Sept 1646). German composer. He first attended school at Graudenz and then, from 1595, went to the Schola parochialis at Königsberg. In 1600 he entered Königsberg University. He studied music with Johannes Eccard from 1599; in the preface to the 1634 volume of chorales by Eccard and himself he described the Königsberg ecclesiastical ministry as 'true disciples of the late honourable, respected and artistic Johannes Eccard, just as he was a true disciple of the celebrated, world-famous Orlandi [Lassus]'. In 1602 Stobaeus entered the Königsberg Kapelle as a bass; this was the Kapelle of Margrave Georg Friedrich of Brandenburg-Ansbach in his former capacity as administrator of Prussia, and Eccard was in charge of it. In 1603 Stobaeus became Kantor at the cathedral church and school at Kneiphof, Königsberg. At this time his first printed composition appeared, a wedding song for the Kneiphof town councillor Albert Rackau. He held his post as Kantor until the end of 1626, when the then administrator of Prussia, the Elector Georg Wilhelm, appointed him Kapellmeister to the Königsberg court. Eccard wrote a wedding song for the second of his three marriages (1607), and Sweelinck wrote one for the third (1617).

During his long years at Königsberg, Stobaeus formed a close association with many members, both old and young, of the Königsberg circle of poets, including Peter Hagen, Georg Reimann, Valentin Thilo,

Georg Weissel, Simon Dach (who learnt singing from him at Königsberg cathedral school), Robert Roberthin, Christoph Kaldenbach and Georg Mylius. Under the name Delphis he seems actually to have been a member of the younger group of poets. Heinrich Albert, a pupil of Stobaeus for many years, belonged to the group around Dach. In spite of the esteem in which he was held, Stobaeus lived in very depressing outward circumstances, and although his situation improved slightly in his last years he died in debt. His last work was a *Canon a tre in unisono post tempus*, which he wrote on 29 May 1646 in the album (now lost) of the son of his Elbing friend Christoph Alt, with the text *Fide, sed cui, vide*. After his death his pupil Georg Colb and Dach expressed in the five-part motet *Wer wird in der Engel Chor* their 'grateful thanks and memorial'. Thilo wrote *Memoria Stobaeana* (Königsberg, 1646), which he sent to Marco Scacchi, another friend of Stobaeus, who published a volume of music in his memory in 1647.

Stobaeus was not inferior as a composer to his teacher Eccard and his pupil Albert, and he was a leading representative of the Königsberg school. Like Eccard he had his stylistic roots in the techniques of the second half of the 16th century and took no notice of Italian innovations such as chromaticism, monody and the basso continuo. He developed Eccard's advancement of north German chorale-based music: they both made chorales more accessible to congregations by renewing and increasing the stock of hymns and by harmonizing and arranging already familiar melodies. More than 20 hymns became popular in Stobaeus's masterly settings. His *Cantiones sacrae* (1624) bears comparison with the finest collections of the time. As well as motets for four to ten voices the collection includes four five- and six-part settings of the *Magnificat*, in which he used in the tenor both his own melodies and others by Lassus and Eccard. Besides these exacting works, he wrote far more easily performable Protestant hymns, chorales and festal songs, which he included in his three editions of works by Eccard. His edition (1634) of Eccard's 1597 volume was widely welcomed. The chorale arrangements in it, both Eccard's and his own, are generally homophonic or pseudo-polyphonic in style, and the chorale appears in the highest voice, following the lead given by Lucas Osiander in 1586. But according to Blume the 1642 and 1644 volumes take a middle path between simply harmonized chorales and elaborate motets. In those pieces here with newly written texts – many by members of the Königsberg poets' circle – the upper part, occasionally carrying the melody, is songlike in character, while the remaining parts are treated independently and expressively, as in motets. The notable flowering of occasional composition in East Prussia in the first half of the 17th century was due not least to Stobaeus, who as court Kapellmeister at the height of his career was frequently commissioned by his friends and admirers as well as by the authorities to write funeral music, and festive music for weddings, celebrations of peace and academic occasions.

WORKS

Editions: *J. Eccard und J. Stobaeus: Preussische Festlieder, 5–8vv*, ed. G. W. Teschner (Leipzig, 1858) [34 works from 1542 and 1544 vols.]

Schatz des liturgischen Chor- und Gemeindegesangs, ed. L. Schoeberlein, i–iii (Göttingen, 1865–72) [12 works]

Preussische Festlieder, ed. J. Müller-Blattau, EDM, 2nd ser., *Ostpreussen und Danzig*, i (1939) [5 works from 1542 and 1544 vols.]

Die teutsche Litaney neben etlichen geistlichen Liedern, deren meiste bei christliche Leichenbegängnissen können ... gesungen werden, 5vv (Königsberg, 1610), lost, cited in *EitnerQ*

Cantiones sacrae harmoniae, 4–10vv, item aliquot Magnificat, 5–6vv (Frankfurt am Main, 1624)

Geistliche Lieder auff gewöhnliche preussische Kirchen Melodeyen, 5vv (Danzig, 1634³) [45 by Stobaeus, 57 by J. Eccard]

Erster Theil der preussischen Fest-Lieder vom Advent an bis Ostern, 5–8vv (Elbing, 1642) [13 by Stobaeus, also incl. works by Eccard]

Ander Theil der preussischen Fest-Lieder von Ostern an bis Advent, 5–8vv (Königsberg, 1644) [21 by Stobaeus, also incl. works by Eccard]

280 occasional works; 6 sacred works, 5vv; 2 motets; 2 chorales, 5vv: *USSR-KA*

Other works listed in *EitnerQ*

BIBLIOGRAPHY

EitnerQ; *FétisB*; *GerberL*; *GerberNL*; *WaltherML*

C. von Winterfeld: *Der evangelische Kirchengesang*, ii (Leipzig, 1845/R1966)

G. Döring: *Zur Geschichte der Musik in Preussen* (Elbing, 1852)

J. Müller: *Die musikalischen Schätze der Universitäts- und Stadtsbibliothek zu Königsberg, Preussen* (Bonn, 1870)

R. Eitner: 'Stobaeus oder Stoboeus', *MMg*, iii (1871), 130

L. H. Fischer: 'Biographisches über Johann Stobaeus', *MMg*, xv (1883), 67

——: 'Johann Stobaeus ein Mitglied des Königsberger Dichterkreises', *MMg*, xvi (1884), 89

A. Mayer-Reinach: 'Zur Geschichte der Königsberger Hofkapelle in den Jahren 1578–1720', *SIMG*, vi (1904–5), 32

A. Fischer and W. Tümpel: *Das deutsche evangelische Kirchenlied des 17. Jahrhunderts*, iii (Gütersloh, 1906/R1964)

H. Leichtentritt: *Geschichte der Motette* (Leipzig, 1908)

L. Kamieński: *Johann Stobaeus* (Poznań, 1928)

F. Blume: *Die evangelische Kirchenmusik*, HMw, x (1931, rev. 2/1965 as *Geschichte der evangelischen Kirchenmusik*; Eng. trans., enlarged, 1974 as *Protestant Church Music: a History*)

J. Müller-Blattau: *Geschichte der Musik in Ost- und Westpreussen* (Königsberg, 1931)

H. Haase: 'Eine wichtige Quelle für Johannes Stobaeus Grudentinus: 6 Sammelbände aus Königsberger Beständen in Göttingen', *Festschrift Friedrich Blume* (Kassel, 1963), 176

based on *MGG* (xii, 1362–5) by permission of Bärenreiter

DIETER HÄRTWIG

Stobaeus Lutebook (*GB-Lbm* Sloane 1021). *See* SOURCES OF LUTE MUSIC, §3.

Stoccken, Johannes de. *See* STOKEM, JOHANNES DE.

Stochastic. A term used in music on the basis of its use in probability theory, where it applies to a system producing 'a sequence of symbols (which may ... be letters or musical notes, say, rather than words) according to certain probabilities' (Weaver, p.267). The term (from Gk. *stochos*: 'goal') means in modern parlance 'random'. A stochastic process operates on a family of random variables which is indexed by another set of variables with compatible probability of distribution. A stochastic process particularly appropriate to music is the Markov process. In this the probabilities at any one point depend on the occurrences of events so far; the process thus contains a high degree of uncertainty in its initial stages, an increasing certainty as events unfold, and a high degree of determinacy in its closing stages.

The principal user of stochastic processes in musical composition has been IANNIS XENAKIS, who uses them to determine such elements as durations, speeds and 'intervals of intensity, pitch, etc.' (p.13), particularly when he is composing with 'clouds' or 'galaxies' of sounds in which very large numbers of events are present. The idea of the stochastic process also appears in the musical application of INFORMATION THEORY, and forms an important part of the aesthetic theory of Leonard B. Meyer, who sees music as a Markov process or chain.

See also PSYCHOLOGY OF MUSIC, §I, 5(i).

BIBLIOGRAPHY

W. Weaver: 'Recent Contributions to the Mathematical Theory of Communication', *Etc.: a Review of General Semantics*, x (1953), 261

F. Attneave: 'Stochastic Composition Processes', *Journal of Aesthetics*, xvii (1959), 503

I. Xenakis: *Musiques formelles* (Paris, 1963; Eng. trans., 1971)

L. B. Meyer: *Music, the Arts, and Ideas: Patterns and Predictions in Twentieth-century Culture* (Chicago, 1967)

Stochem, Johannes de. *See* STOKEM, JOHANNES DE.

Stöchs, Georg. *See* STUCHS, GEORG.

Stöchs, Johann (*d* ?Nuremberg, after 1546). German printer, son of GEORG STUCHS.

Stock, Frederick [Friedrich August] (*b* Jülich, 11 Nov 1872; *d* Chicago, 20 Oct 1942). American conductor of German birth. He attended the Cologne Conservatory as a student of the violin and composition; Humperdinck and Franz Wüllner were among his teachers there. In 1895, after four years as a violinist in Cologne, he joined the Chicago SO, became assistant conductor in 1899, and took charge of all concerts outside Chicago from 1903. When Theodore Thomas died in 1905, Stock was appointed conductor of the Chicago SO, a post he held for the rest of his life. In his early years there he was forward-looking, quick to introduce new compositions of Debussy, Ravel, Mahler, Skryabin and Schoenberg, and in the 1920s he was a vigorous promoter of Hindemith and Prokofiev (whose Third Piano Concerto had its première in Chicago with the composer as soloist).

Stock is also remembered for consolidating and advancing the tradition of excellence and virtuosity established by Thomas; for campaigning for benefits for orchestra members; for instituting children's concerts, which he conducted himself; and for establishing the Chicago Civic Orchestra as a training orchestra of professional quality under Chicago SO sponsorship and using Chicago SO players as teachers and coaches. He composed two symphonies and other orchestral works, a Violin Concerto (introduced in 1915 by Zimbalist) and chamber music. The few recordings he made do not justify the esteem in which he was held as an interpreter.

BIBLIOGRAPHY

W. A. Holmes: 'Frederick Stock', *Grand baton*, vi/2 (1969), 3 [with articles and discography by W. A. Holmes and J. L. Hurka]

MICHAEL STEINBERG

Stock-and-horn. An obsolete type of 18th-century pastoral reedpipe, resembling the melody pipe of a bagpipe but with a single reed (like the PIBGORN). It appears to have been played in the southern half of Scotland. The reed was inserted into the upper end of the tube, or 'stock'; the mouthpiece, when present, consisted of an elongated wooden capsule fitted to this end. At its lower end the stock terminated in a bell of natural horn. A distinction must be made between the stock-and-horn and the stockhorn: from Sir John Skene's description of the stockhorn as used in 1597 it is clear that it was a crude type of forester's horn, such as he had seen blown in Switzerland in 1568, and not the reed instrument later known as stock-and-horn. The poets Allan Ramsay and Robert Burns were familiar with the stock-and-horn. In *The Gentle Shepherd* (1725) Ramsay wrote:

> When I begin to tune my Stock-and-Horn
> Wi a' her face she shaws a cauldrife scorn.
> Last night I play'd – ye never heard sic spite!

Stock-and-horn: detail of watercolour 'A Domestic Scene' (c1785) by David Allan, in Glasgow Art Gallery and Museum

> O'er Bogie was the spring and her delyte; –
> Yet tauntingly she at her cousin speer'd
> 'Gif she could tell what tune I play'd?' and sneer'd.
> Flocks wander where ye like, I dinna care,
> I'll break my reed and never whistle mair.

There are several other literary references to the stock-and-horn and depictions of it in art (see illustration), but only two original specimens are known to survive: one at the Royal College of Music, London, and the other (a double pipe) at the Scottish National Museum of Antiquities, Edinburgh (a facsimile of this instrument is in the Museum of Fine Arts, Boston). F. W. Galpin remarked that the object of the double bore in the Edinburgh instrument appears to have been to produce a strong beating tone from mistuned consonances (as in the Egyptian *zummāra*).

BIBLIOGRAPHY

H. Balfour: 'The Old British "Pibcorn" or "Hornpipe" and its Affinities', *Journal of the Anthropological Institute of Great Britain and Ireland*, xx (1891), 142

N. Bessaraboff: *Catalogue of the Museum of Fine Arts* (Boston, 1941)

L. G. Langwill: 'Stock-and-horn', *Grove 5* [with iconography]

LYNDESAY G. LANGWILL/R

Stockem, Johannes de. *See* STOKEM, JOHANNES DE.

Stocker, Caspar. *See* STOQUERUS, GASPAR.

Stockhausen. German–Alsatian family of musicians.

(1) **Franz (Anton Adam) Stockhausen** (*b* Cologne, 1 Sept 1789; *d* Colmar, 10 Sept 1868). German harpist, teacher and composer. From about 1812 he was a harp teacher in Paris. He accompanied his wife Margarethe in concert tours of Europe from the mid-1820s; after 1840 they lived in Alsace. His compositions include harp arrangements, a mass for four voices accompanied by two harps and other instruments (performed at Notre Dame, 20 May 1817; published Paris, 1822), a *Vidimus stellam* for soprano solo, chorus, harp and organ of 1835 (manuscript in *CH-Bu*) and an Introduction and Variations on a Swiss air for harp (published in London).

(2) **Margarethe Stockhausen** [née Schmuck] (*b* Gebweiler [now Guebwiller], 29 March 1803; *d* Colmar, 6 Oct 1877). Alsatian soprano, wife of (1) Franz Stockhausen. She studied singing with Gioseffo

Catrufo in Paris, and in 1825 gave concerts with her husband in Switzerland and then in Paris; she became an honorary member of the French royal chapel in 1827. From 1827 to 1840 she appeared frequently in London and the provinces with great success; her first German tour was in 1833. Her repertory included oratorios and operatic excerpts.

(3) Julius (Christian) Stockhausen (b Paris, 22 July 1826; d Frankfurt am Main, 22 Sept 1906). German baritone, conductor and teacher of Alsatian descent, son of (1) Franz Stockhausen and (2) Margarethe Stockhausen. He showed his musical gifts early and during his school years learnt singing and musical rudiments from his parents and the piano from Karl Kienzl, also having lessons on the organ, violin and, later, the cello. In 1843 he visited Paris, where he was a pupil of Cramer for a short while. From 1844 he made Paris the centre of his musical education, spending some time at the Conservatoire (from 1845) but learning harmony from Matthäus Nagiller and singing from Manuel García outside the institution.

Stockhausen's early concert successes were in Switzerland and England, beginning in 1848 with a performance of Elijah at Basle. In 1849 he followed García to London, and while in England he appeared before Queen Victoria. He sang again in Switzerland in the first half of 1850 (including a performance of Hérold's Zampa in Lucerne); he returned to England in the summer, and in 1851 performed in Beethoven's Ninth Symphony and Haydn's Creation. During the next decade his activities and reputation expanded to include most of the important musical centres of Europe. He was at Mannheim in 1852–3 as second baritone at the court theatre under Lachner, though his stage career led to strained relations with his parents, who were devout Roman Catholics. He gave the first public performance of Die schöne Müllerin as part of a series of Vienna concerts in May 1856; his first German tour, in the same year, included appearances in Elijah, Alexander's Feast and the Ninth Symphony at the Lower Rhine Music Festival in Düsseldorf, where he met Brahms and the poet Klaus Groth, both of whom became close friends. From 1856 to 1859 he was engaged by the Paris Opéra-Comique, where his roles included the seneschal in Boieldieu's Jean de Paris. He founded a choral society that specialized in Bach cantatas in 1858 and during the next five years made further tours of Germany and England, while holding the unexacting post of Kammersänger to the Hanoverian court.

Stockhausen's musical association with Brahms began with a concert in Cologne soon after their first meeting. In 1861 they gave recitals in Hamburg, which included the singer's first public performance of Dichterliebe; shortly afterwards Brahms began composing the Magelone Lieder for him. In 1863 Stockhausen was chosen in preference to Brahms for the conductorship of the Hamburg Philharmonische Konzertgesellschaft and the Singakademie; his first concert with the society included an uncut performance of Schubert's C major Symphony, and his first Singakademie concert (12 January 1864) consisted of Bach's cantata 'Wachet auf', Beethoven's Choral Fantasia (with Clara Schumann as soloist) and the third part of Schumann's Faust, in which Stockhausen sang. After resigning his positions in 1867 to resume travelling, he spent part of the next year touring Germany and Denmark with Brahms. He sang the baritone solo in the first performance of the German Requiem, conducted by the composer at Bremen Cathedral (Good Friday, 10 April 1868), but press reports indicate that he did not sing well and was apparently ruffled by the experience.

After a year (1869–70) as Kammersänger to Karl I of Württemberg and four years (1874–8) in Berlin as director of the Sternscher Gesangverein, Stockhausen settled in Frankfurt am Main, where he remained for the rest of his life. Until his falling out with two successive directors, Raff and Bernhard Scholz, he taught at the Hoch Conservatory, from its opening in 1878 to 1880, and in 1883–4. Mostly, however, he taught at his own school of singing, founded in 1880; among his pupils were Hermine Spiess, Antonia Kufferath, Anton van Rooy and Max Friedlaender. He was also active as a concert organizer, and published a number of works on singing, including the Gesangsmethode (Leipzig, 1884).

Although Stockhausen made important contributions as a conductor and teacher, and was a distinguished singer of opera and oratorio, it is probably as an interpreter of lieder that he left the strongest impression. He did much to stimulate popularity of the songs of Schubert and Schumann, and he was an inspiration and formative influence for Brahms. His art, for which he acknowledged a debt to García, Viardot and Jenny Lind, was acclaimed by many contemporary commentators, including Sir George Grove (Grove 1):

Stockhausen's singing in his best days must have been wonderful. Even to those, who, like the writer, only heard him after he had passed his zenith, it is a thing never to be forgotten . . . His delivery of opera and oratorio music . . . was superb in taste, feeling and execution; but it was the lieder of Schubert and Schumann that most peculiarly suited him, and these he delivered in a truly remarkable way. The rich beauty of the voice, the nobility of the style, the perfect phrasing, the intimate sympathy, and, not least, the intelligible way in which the words were given – in itself one of his greatest claims to distinction – all combined to make his singing of songs a wonderful event . . . But perhaps his highest achievement was the part of Dr Marianus in the third part of Schumann's Faust, in which his delivery of the scene beginning 'Hier ist die Aussicht frei', with just as much of acting as the concert room will admit – and no more – was one of the most touching and remarkable things ever witnessed.

(4) Franz Stockhausen (b Gebweiler [now Guebwiller], 30 Jan 1839; d Strasbourg, 4 Jan 1926). Alsatian pianist, conductor and teacher, brother of (3) Julius Stockhausen. He was first taught music by his parents, then studied the piano with Alkan in Paris, and from 1860 to 1862 was a pupil of Moscheles, Hauptmann and Davïdov at the Leipzig Conservatory. From 1863 to 1866 he was director of music at Thann, Alsace, and in 1868 moved to Strasbourg, where he was conductor of the Société de Chant Sacré (1868–79), music director at the cathedral (from 1868) and director of the conservatory and municipal concerts (1871–1908).

BIBLIOGRAPHY

E. R. H. Friebel: 'Der Sänger Julius Stockhausen', NZM, xliv (1856), 189, 197

K. Kienzl: Musikalische Geschichte der Stadt Gebweiler (Mühlhausen, 1868)

L. Spach: Moderne Culturzustände im Elsass (Strasbourg, 1873)

J. Sittard: Geschichte des Musik- und Concertwesens in Hamburg (Altona and Leipzig, 1890)

H. Hanau: Dr Hoch's Conservatorium zu Frankfurt am Main (Frankfurt am Main, 1903)

Obituary, The Spectator (27 Oct 1906) [Julius Stockhausen]

I. Knorr: Festschrift zur Feier des 100jährigen Bestehens der Frankfurter Museumsgesellschaft 1808 bis 1908 (Frankfurt am Main, 1908)

A. Weissmann: Berlin als Musikstadt: Geschichte der Oper und des Konzerts von 1740 bis 1911 (Berlin and Leipzig, 1911)

J. Wirth: *Julius Stockhausen: der Sänger des deutschen Liedes* (Frankfurt am Main, 1927) [incl. further bibliography]

A. H. Fox Strangways: 'Julius Stockhausen', *MMR*, lxxix (1949), 69

E. Anderson, ed.: *The Letters of Beethoven* (London, 1961)

K. Blum: *Hundert Jahre Ein deutsches Requiem von Johannes Brahms* (Tutzing, 1971)

R. J. PASCALL

Stockhausen, Karlheinz (*b* Burg Mödrath, nr. Cologne, 22 Aug 1928). German composer and theorist. He has pioneered electronic music, new uses of physical space in music, open forms, live-electronic performance, 'intuitive music' and many other important developments in music after 1950. In his music and in his writings, he has evolved a uniquely coherent system of generalizations from the premises of total serialism, paying attention to aesthetic and philosophical consequences as well as to matters of technique and music theory. Each of his discoveries is compellingly demonstrated in his music. He has also been widely active as a teacher, and has taken part – as either conductor or performer – in many performances of his own music, forming his own performing group in 1964.

1. Early career. 2. After 'Momente'. 3. Theory.

1. EARLY CAREER. Orphaned during the war years, Stockhausen pursued his higher education under conditions in which he had to struggle to sustain his material life. Between 1944 and 1947 – the year in which he took his school-leaving examination in Cologne – he worked as a stretcher-bearer at a military hospital, a farmhand, a dancing instructor's pianist, and a répétiteur and conductor of operettas. Although he had also played the violin and the oboe, the piano had been his first instrument at school, and during the years he now spent at the Cologne Hochschule für Musik he made his living as a pianist in jazz and light music. At the Hochschule he studied the piano with Hans Otto Schmidt-Neuhaus (from 1947), musical form with Hermann Schroeder (1948) and composition with Martin (1950); he specialized in school music and piano teaching. Concurrently he enrolled at Cologne University as a student of musicology, philology and philosophy. Up to this time, he might have seemed to be preparing for a career in music education. (His father had been a teacher in a primary school.) The compositions for chorus he had written up to 1950 were simply stylistic exercises. Nevertheless, he had been avidly studying the work of contemporary composers (notably Schoenberg, Stravinsky and Bartók), and this music left its mark on the student works – *Drei Lieder* for contralto and chamber orchestra, and a Sonatine for violin and piano – that he composed under Martin. But it was not until he became acquainted with music by Webern and by the new generation of serialist composers at Darmstadt during the summer of 1951 that he found his own path as a composer.

His visit to Darmstadt followed a suggestion by Eimert, with whom Stockhausen had become friendly in Cologne and at whose instigation he also began to give a number of broadcast talks on contemporary music. A composer and writer on music, Eimert played an important role in Stockhausen's career both at this time and later, when the two men worked together at the Cologne electronic music studio. At Darmstadt Stockhausen was deeply impressed by the new music he heard, particularly Messiaen's *Quatre études de rythme* and Goeyvaerts's Sonata for Two Pianos. It is from this time, with the composition shortly afterwards of *Kreuzspiel* for oboe, bass clarinet, piano and percussion, that Stockhausen dates the start of his real career as a composer. In *Kreuzspiel*, with its series of pitch, duration and intensity, timbre stands outside the scope of serial organization, and is used to articulate the work's internal structure as well as its 'point' (i.e. isolated event) sound world.

In January 1952 Stockhausen moved to Paris in order to study with Messiaen. He also made contact with Boulez at the time when the latter was working on total serialization in his *Structures I*. Stockhausen's studies in analysis were complemented by a thorough investigation of the physical nature of sounds. At the suggestion of Goeyvaerts, he decided to study at the *musique concrète* studio of French radio; there he could analyse, with the help of tape, the acoustical constituents of sounds of various timbres. The Etude he composed at the studio is of small importance compared with the theoretical fruits of his work there, which were to be of momentous consequence when he applied himself to electronic music on his return to Cologne.

During his 14 months as a student in Paris, Stockhausen worked on a number of compositions in which the isolated points of *Kreuzspiel* gradually gave way to the development of more solid and varied structural entities which he called 'groups': homogeneous agglomerations of points, the totality characterized by markedly individual features. The technical transition was paralleled by an aesthetic broadening, in that the terse intensity of *Kreuzspiel* made room for a more florid, even garrulous manner. *Spiel* for orchestra (1952) was performed at the 1952 Donaueschingen Festival before the composer withdrew the score. A *Schlagquartett*, likewise to be withdrawn, exploited the meeting of dualistic polarities in a confrontation between solo piano and six timpani. *Punkte* for orchestra (1952) remained unperformed until it was considerably revised by the composer in 1962. On the other hand, *Kontra-Punkte* (1952–3) was performed at the 1953 Cologne Festival of New Music and became Stockhausen's first published work. Like *Kreuzspiel* and the *Schlagquartett*, it grew from a simple dramatic idea: the gradual elimination of the various extreme contrasts (in timbre, dynamics and duration) thrown up by point-type serialism. *Kontra-Punkte* and the first of the *Klavierstücke* are the first pieces in which Stockhausen deployed the concept of the 'group'.

Shortly after his return to Cologne, Stockhausen began work at the newly founded studio for electronic music which West German radio had set up under the direction of Eimert. There he composed two short pieces, *Studie I* and *Studie II*, in which he systematically explored the potential of the new medium. In the first piece (1953) he constructed the entire composition from sine-wave sounds: indeed, it is the first work to have been thus composed. At the same time, the organization obeys strict mathematical principles derived from total serialism. *Studie II* (1954) proceeds in a different way: here Stockhausen begins with 'white noise', and subtracts from this (using filters) in order to arrive at the work's structures – a technique whose application to an instrumental composition can be seen in the 1962 version of *Punkte*. *Studie II* was later published as a score – again, the first of its kind.

Between 1953 and 1956 Stockhausen studied communications theory and phonetics with Werner Meyer-Eppler at Bonn University. This led him to pay closer attention than hitherto to the human element in performing and listening to music. In his *Klavierstücke I–IV* he had reached an extreme point in the demands he made on the performer, both in the simultaneous performance of precisely graded dynamic levels and in the realization of intricate temporal subdivisions. He now embarked on a second set (*Klavierstücke V–X*, 1954–5) in which, more realistically, the performer was called on to judge relative values for himself instead of having to strain after an accurate rendering of notated absolute values. The new simplicity and flexibility of style are in some part due to Stockhausen's discussions with the pianist David Tudor, to whom the pieces are dedicated. The last two pieces in the set made their appearance only in 1961 and are in many respects to be considered as separate works.

With these piano pieces Stockhausen had formed certain clear ideas on what constituted the essential difference, from the composer's point of view, between electronic and instrumental music. During 1956 he proceeded to produce his first major works in both fields. *Zeitmasze* for woodwind quintet uses a relative scale of tempos based on the shortest and the longest durations that a performer can comfortably execute. Interplay between the instruments is cunningly judged to heighten the effect of improvisatory flexibility. In *Gesang der Jünglinge* electronic music reached an unprecedented degree of sophistication. Stockhausen introduced transformations of a recording of a boy's voice mingled with purely electronic sounds; the text embedded in the work is that of the *Benedicite*, recalling that the work was originally planned to be performed in Cologne Cathedral. Again, this piece features an important innovation: composed for five loudspeaker groups, the music issues from spatially separated sources, and its movement between these sources is an integral part of the work. For the first time physical space was annexed as a component of serial music.

Concurrently Stockhausen employed the same idea in instrumental terms in *Gruppen* for three orchestras (1955–7), a work in which the instrumental forces surround the audience on three sides (*see* ORCHESTRA, fig.7). This arrangement enabled Stockhausen to use simultaneous combinations of independent tempos, as he had done in *Zeitmasze*; at the same time, the dramatic consequences of this technique inescapably impinge on the listener with a new kind of physical impact. During 1956 Stockhausen also wrote *Klavierstück XI*, a piece which takes the performer's freedom into a new sphere: that of determining the form of the work in any given performance. 19 'groups' are laid out on a single sheet of paper, and the pianist, starting with any one of them, is to play them spontaneously in a random order. Chance therefore plays a large part in controlling the course of the music – less being left to the free and conscious decision of the interpreter than in Boulez's Third Piano Sonata (1957).

1957 was the year in which Stockhausen was first invited to teach composition at the Darmstadt summer courses, where he had been giving lectures since 1953. In the course of a few years he developed highly individual teaching methods which resulted in an unusual degree of collective work within the groups of composers who came to him. His renown as a teacher soon began to rival that of his own teacher Messiaen. In 1963 he founded the Cologne Courses for New Music, later to become the Cologne Institute for New Music,

which offered an alternative to the strictly seasonal specialized instruction available at Darmstadt. And at the end of 1958 Stockhausen embarked on the first of his concert and lecture tours of the USA, described in 'Eindrücke einer Amerikareise' (1959; reprinted in *Texte*, ii, 1964).

As part of his work for Darmstadt, Stockhausen composed a test piece for percussion players in 1959. This was *Zyklus*, a work planned as a physical and musical circle: the soloist is surrounded by a large array of instruments on all sides, and in the course of the piece he completes a circuit round them; the score itself is printed on a number of spiral-bound pages, any of which may form the beginning of the work, with the rest following in cyclical sequence. A still more unusual score is that of *Refrain* for three players (1959), in which there is a movable strip of transparent plastic bearing the recurrent features of the 'refrain'; the position of the strip in relation to the score is variable and must be chosen afresh for each performance. Various phonetic sounds are included in the score so that the instrumentalists also participate vocally.

Phonetic sounds, this time interspersed with a few personal names, also form the 'text' of *Carré* for four orchestras and choruses (1959–60). The score was not completed by Stockhausen himself, but was left to an assistant (Cornelius Cardew) working under the composer's supervision. Though the work is laid out much as is *Gruppen*, with the performers surrounding the audience, *Carré* unfolds at a much more leisurely pace; the interdependent 'groups' of the earlier work are here well on their way to becoming autonomous 'moments'.

In the concept of the 'moment' Stockhausen sought a resolution of listeners' difficulties in experiencing form in serial music. Each individually characterized passage in a work is regarded as an experiential unit, a 'moment', which can potentially engage the listener's full attention and can do so in exactly the same measure as its neighbours. No single 'moment' claims priority, even as a beginning or ending; hence the nature of such a work is essentially 'unending' (and, indeed, 'unbeginning'). Significantly, each 'moment' is, in Stockhausen's view, equally dispensable, rather than equally indispensable, to the listener: his unending forms are the outcome not only of his pursuit of equality among all constituents of a work, but also of his leanings towards indeterminacy, which he accurately enough attributes to the durations and intensities of his listeners' attentiveness. The listener's unpredictable ecstatic involvement with the 'now' of one 'moment' can be bought only at the risk of an equally unpredictable withdrawal from some other. Such 'moments', grouped in succession to make up a 'moment form', formed the structural constituents of *Kontakte* (1959–60), a work which appeared both as a purely electronic composition and as '*Kontakte* for electronic sounds, piano and percussion'. Another example of 'music in space', with four loudspeaker groups placed around the auditorium, *Kontakte* presents an encounter between electronic music and instrumental music with the emphasis on shared characteristics of timbre.

The music of *Kontakte* was incorporated into *Originale* (1961), an exercise in music-theatre which ran for 12 nights in Cologne. The actions of the numerous participants were meticulously timed and coordinated in a specially composed score; this was subsequently published in Stockhausen's *Texte* (ii, 1964), and the performances have been described by Wörner. 1961 was also the year in which Stockhausen put the finishing touches to his *Klavierstücke IX* and *X*. The former is a study in periodic and aperiodic divisions of time, beginning with a passage of regular reiterations of a single chord; the latter piece similarly presents varying degrees of order and disorder, bringing into play note clusters and glissando writing which demands considerable virtuosity of the performer.

His major work using open form, on which he began work in 1961, is *Momente* for soprano solo, four choral groups and 13 instrumentalists. The work is designed as a sequence of 'moments', some of which may be omitted as occasion demands. The general structure is such that additional moments have been inserted freely in subsequent versions without necessitating any alteration to the existing music. In this work, Stockhausen's imaginative range in combining words with music reaches perhaps its fullest expression; the texts are taken from many sources (the Song of Songs, Malinowski's *The Sexual Life of Savages*, passages from letters and personal names, onomatopoeic words and samples of audience reaction), but the role of the chorus is not restricted to singing – it also makes clicking, stamping and clapping noises and performs on small percussion instruments. A further version of *Momente*, in which Stockhausen composed additional music-theatre as a realization of Oskar Schlemmer's *Triadische Ballett*, was prepared in 1962.

2. AFTER 'MOMENTE'. Stockhausen's involvement in other art forms is something of a Wagnerian trait, and he firmly believes in the translatability of particular forms of organization from one art to another. This belief stimulated a lively exchange of ideas with the painter Mary Bauermeister (who was to become Stockhausen's second wife, and of whom *Momente* is said to be a 'portrait'). The work *Plus–Minus* (1963)

was born of this exchange. It is not a score for direct performance, but a scheme for realization containing seven pages of symbols representing compositional gambits which can be translated into a musical score with the aid of a further seven pages which furnish the notes themselves. Thus without actually completing a score, Stockhausen has here composed a process which will readily translate into a piece of music. It is the first of a series of works in which he has preferred to give directions for the making of music rather than to draw up a symbolic model (i.e. musical score) of the finished product, though such earlier scores as *Klavierstück XI* and *Zyklus* had already tended in this direction.

In much contemporary notation for percussion (and in *Zyklus*), the wealth of graphic signs seems as much a description of the performer's actions as of sounds. This may have suggested to Stockhausen the idea of *Mikrophonie I*, which he composed in 1964 after conducting a number of experiments with a large tam-tam; he and his assistant (Jaap Spek) found that with the aid of microphones and electrical filters the instrument could be made to yield an enormous variety of sounds, simply by performing a number of different actions upon it. In the course of the same year he formed his own group of performers to play live-electronic music, and *Mikrophonie I* had its first performance in Brussels in December 1964. Stockhausen's small ensemble has survived some changes of personnel and has remained much in demand. At first the group was inevitably most closely associated with *Mikrophonie I*, but Stockhausen has since written a number of other works for it. Another new venture of 1964 into the field of live-electronic music was *Mixtur* for orchestra, sine-wave generators and ring modulators (version with chamber orchestra, 1967). Mixed with the orchestral sounds in this work are sounds generated electronically; this 'mixture' is carried out electronically by means of ring modulators, and it dramatically modifies the sounds

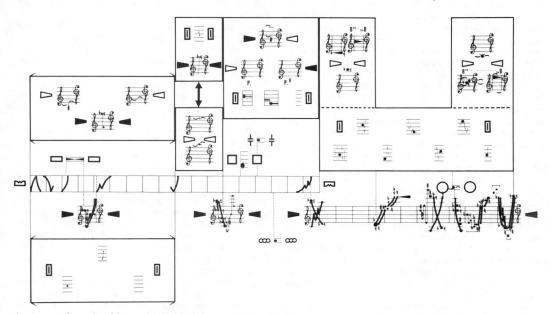

1. A page from Stockhausen's 'Zyklus' for percussion (1959) in which graphic signs represent instruments as well as performance directions

originally made by the instruments. Moreover, these 'raw' sounds are heard simultaneously with the modulated sounds in a further mixture. A similar use of ring modulators occurs in *Mikrophonie II* (1965), though in this work there are no sounds of purely electronic origin; it is scored for chorus, Hammond organ and four ring modulators. In each of these three works, the introduction of electronic modifications prohibits the drawing-up of a conventionally readable score: once more, what the score presents is in some part actions, comparable to his later 'processes'.

His next use of live-electronic means was to include a superimposed tape recording of a performance while the latter was still in progress; he presented this technique in *Solo* for melody instrument and tape recorder (1965–6), which he took with him to Japan in 1966 for its first performances. This visit produced a further electronic work, *Telemusik*, which he realized in the studio for electronic music of Japanese Radio between January and April 1966. It is a relatively conventional work, in which the composer used sophisticated techniques of collage, drawing into the sphere of purely electronic sounds a diversity of recorded human music-making from folk and traditional sources. In this respect *Telemusik* recalls the earlier *Gesang der Jünglinge*, but it is clear that what Stockhausen was aiming at was a fusion between the techniques of electronic music and those of *musique concrète*. His subsequent *Hymnen* (1967) represents a synthesis of the two on a vast scale. In this work, which lasts for about two hours, the musical 'found objects' include an assortment of national anthems – as symbolic as had been the folk music in *Telemusik* of the 'music of the whole world' which Stockhausen was seeking to compose. A version of *Hymnen* with soloists (Stockhausen's ensemble) also exists (1967), and there is an abbreviated version with orchestra (1969).

One of the most typical works in which Stockhausen's role was that of 'process planner' is *Prozession* (1967), which he wrote for his own group of performers. No new musical material was composed for this work – the players have to perform variants of passages from Stockhausen's earlier works: *Klavierstücke I–XI, Gesang der Jünglinge, Kontakte, Momente, Mikrophonie I, Telemusik* and *Solo*. The score merely provides a sequence of procedures for the performers to apply to this raw material; the material is played from memory, and in interpreting the composer's instructions the instrumentalists are allowed considerable latitude for improvisation. Shortly after writing this work Stockhausen applied the same principle to his teaching of composition at a course in Darmstadt. 12 students took part in an exercise in collective composition, each writing a part for one instrument and tape or short-wave receiver; the students worked according to a plan that had been devised by Stockhausen, and he then gathered together their individual contributions into a collective whole, in which only a few relatively short passages could be identified as the work of any one individual. The piece was given the title *Ensemble* and was performed during August 1967 at Darmstadt. A similar procedure was adopted with the more elaborate *Musik für ein Haus*, performed at Darmstadt in September 1968.

The use of short-wave receivers in *Ensemble* demonstrates yet another way in which Stockhausen has imagined the 'music of the whole world'. By this use of radio, he found he could bring together at any moment sounds issuing simultaneously from countries all over the globe. Such sounds had already appeared in *Hymnen*, and they were to become the basic musical material of *Kurzwellen*, which he composed for his own ensemble in 1968. The score is again no more than a sequence of procedural instructions to the six performers. The four instrumentalists imitate and vary sounds they have picked up on short-wave receivers; there is in addition a microphonist, who works with the tam-tam player as in *Mikrophonie I*, and a player for the electronic filters and potentiometers which modify and transform the sounds of the instruments. Stockhausen also wrote a work for one soloist with short-wave receiver (*Spiral*, 1969), and in 1969 his group gave a performance of *Kurzwellen mit Beethoven*, in which short-wave sounds are replaced as raw material by recordings of the works of Beethoven. This version of the work, devised for the Beethoven bicentenary and sub-titled 'Stockhoven–Beethausen Opus 1970', quickly became available in a commercial recording, and it provides the listener with easy access to the manner of process which Stockhausen had planned in *Kurzwellen*.

The universalization of Stockhausen's musical material took a different direction in *Stimmung* for six vocalists (1968), where the performers have to pitch their voices as closely as they can to a single series of natural harmonics throughout the 75-minute course of the piece. The text of the work is short poems composed by Stockhausen himself and a collection of 'magic names' which, together with the fact that the singers sit cross-legged in a small circle, create an atmosphere of ritual. The musical process at the base of the work concentrates on the integration and assimilation of foreign elements (principally the magic names) into the music's prevailing harmony. New techniques of vocal articulation are required, and the work's numerous performances have so far been largely the preserve of its original performers, the specially trained Collegium Vocale Köln.

After the notation of actions in *Zyklus, Mikrophonie I* and the music-theatre pieces, and the notation of compositional processes in *Plus–Minus, Prozession* and *Kurzwellen*, the logical next step – the notation of ideas for improvisatory realization – followed in the work *Aus den sieben Tagen* (May 1968), which in fact comprises 15 compositions. The scores of these, as of the later 17 texts of *Für kommende Zeiten* (1969–70), are of a purely verbal nature, and were written with the composer's own performing ensemble in mind. In order to ensure the freedom of the performers' musical intuitions, Stockhausen has sedulously avoided notated music in these scores: the directions are poetically expressed indications of a mental outlook; translated into music (a step which can only be accomplished by the intuition) they provide a general direction for performance, but nothing more. Sympathetically treated the music can yield a meditative, even yogic quality, highly characteristic of the composer's work after *Stimmung*.

In 1970 Stockhausen's music was featured in the German Pavilion at the Osaka World Fair, where it was performed every day for six months. It was after the composer himself had visited Osaka that he composed *Mantra* for two pianists (1970). As its name suggests, the work links up with the oriental thinking that is at the root of the meditative, intuitive works. As in *Stimmung*, an element of ritual (specifically associated with the noh

2. Karlheinz Stockhausen performing in 'Aus den sieben Tagen' at the Darmstadt summer courses in 1969

drama of Japan) comes to the fore. Still more strikingly, however, the score is fully written out in the conventional manner. The whole work is based on a single melodic formula (or 'mantra'), subjected to much repetition and much modification, notably by ring modulation, yet retaining the freshness of its identity as an object of creative contemplation. This is a lengthy and impressive work, and Stockhausen's imagination was evidently fired by his return to the strict working-out of compositional detail. But in his next major work Stockhausen was to revert to meditation and intuition. *Sternklang* (1971) is a large work for open-air performance in which the music, played by several groups distributed around a park, is to be 'read off' the night constellations, whose names are periodically called out in ritual manner. Here, Stockhausen achieved for himself a music which could truly correspond to what he said in 1951 of Messiaen's *Mode de valeurs et d'intensités*: *Sternklang* too is a 'fantastic music of the stars'.

3. THEORY. Critics have seen in Stockhausen's music and in his attitudes more than an echo of Romanticism and of Wagnerian megalomania, and it is true that his latest music shows symptoms of gigantism, few of his works since *Hymnen* lasting less than an hour and some of them lasting appreciably longer. Their 'breath', if not their style, also recalls Bruckner, and if one bears in mind the important influence of Indian religion on

Stockhausen's thinking, it could be argued that the music is one of this century's supreme examples of religious expression. In his essays Stockhausen has constantly related his music to abstract conceptual propositions of a philosophical or religious nature, and conversely, his music has frequently been a concrete or symbolic representation of such propositions. But the philosophy of Stockhausen's music remains an unscaled peak: no scholar or critic has yet gained the perspective from which a comprehensive exegesis would be feasible, and consequently, discussion of his ideas and his system of reference necessarily remains somewhat piecemeal.

It is clear, though, that the foundation of all Stockhausen's musical thinking has been the serial principle, which constitutes in his mind a sort of general theory of musical relativity. In his earliest works he abode rigorously by the procedures of total serialization whereby pitch, duration, dynamics and timbre are all subject to the same laws. If these early works are remarkably free from outside influences, it is because Stockhausen was determined to rethink the craft of musical composition down to its smallest detail: it was 'as if my whole musical education had proved totally useless' ('Von Webern zu Debussy: Bemerkungen zur statistischen Form', 1954, reprinted in *Texte*, i, 1963). To begin with he worked only with the most basic of available musical components, 'points' or single sounds. And when, by the use of electronic apparatus, the fun-

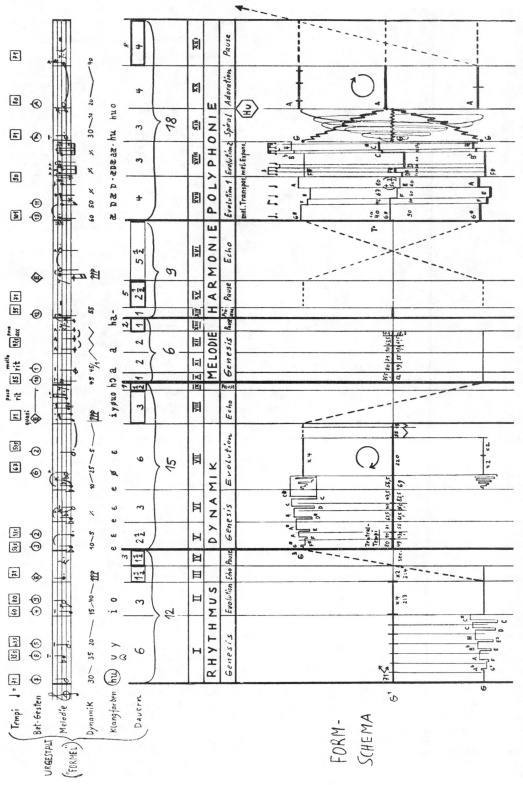

3. *Autograph score of Stockhausen's form-scheme for 'Inori', composed 1973–4*

damental elements of sound, sine waves, also became available, he turned to these as well.

Very quickly, however, he realized that the serial principle in itself had sufficient flexibility to govern broader structures than the chains of single notes to which its application had traditionally been restricted, and that – once the magic number 12 had been deposed from its sovereignty over serial thought – serialism offered a coherent means of organizing the greatest diversity of material and ideas. He coined the concept of the 'group', a number of interrelated single notes seen as a larger unit; and he introduced the notion of the statistical block whose general properties (density, pitch range, pace, dynamics and timbres) could be organized on serial lines. By 1955 his studies in communications theory had led him to see the rate of musical transformation in any given passage as the crucial factor in experiential time, and this dimension, too, fell under the rule of the series. Finally, physical space was incorporated into the organization of music and means were found of 'serializing' the spoken word (as in *Gesang der Jünglinge*).

A much more startling development in Stockhausen's thought came with the discovery that all these different dimensions, or 'parameters', could be regarded as part of one and the same continuum. In '. . . wie die Zeit vergeht . . .' (1956, reprinted in *Texte*, i, 1963) Stockhausen demonstrated that the phenomena of duration, pitch and timbre are all reducible to a single common factor – the acoustical impulse. The number of impulses in any sound will determine its duration; their frequency will determine its pitch; and their rhythmic organization will determine its timbre. Here, then, was a new approach to the basic constituents of music and their organization; it was the ultimate answer to those critics who had found total serialization arbitrary in its attempt to bring all the different parameters into line. The basic components of music were seen in terms of 'microtime', and their further organization into structures and forms was a direct extension of this into 'macrotime'.

Stockhausen's approach to the question of open form provides interesting comparisons with that of Boulez. Where the latter is always careful to leave his personal imprint on the shaping of an open form by restricting the number of possible alternatives from which the performer may choose (see, for example, his Third Piano Sonata, 1957), Stockhausen is willing to leave much more to the performer's inspiration of the moment. He contrasts this valuable human element in the interpretation of instrumental music with the absolute pre-ordained rigour with which magnetic tape fixes an electronic composition. It was in reaction to his earliest electronic works that he began to include relative, empirical values in his piano pieces of 1954–5. (It should be noted, however, that his first gesture in this direction had been the 'as fast as possible' directive of the earlier piano pieces.) The trust Stockhausen has continued to place in the interpreter has undoubtedly been nurtured by his close and continuing association with performers of the highest stamp (including Tudor, Caskel and Kontarsky, and, among conductors, Boulez, Maderna and Gielen), and latterly by the mutual understanding he has established among his own performing ensemble.

The 'dramatic' effect of much of Stockhausen's music has already been mentioned, and could be regarded as a hallmark of his musical style. His handling of resources, both electronic and instrumental, is masterly, combining fullness of sound with quite remarkable clarity; but this is equally true of his handling of the entire musical material, of which the chosen medium is in fact simply one more integral parameter. The essence of Stockhausen's style remains intact even when he reduces the determinacy of his composition (as in 'variable' and 'polyvalent' forms, and even more interestingly in the passages of 'statistical' notation in *Mixtur*, where only general characteristics – of register, rhythm, density and so forth – may be prescribed). Examination of his ideas and methods can leave only one conclusion about Stockhausen's style: that he has gathered together in a great synthesis all the means available to the composer of the 20th century, not excluding his heritage from the past, and that he has drawn from serial thought the techniques – indeed, the new language – which can present them in a fashion at once ordered and elemental. It is this elementality which explains the 'drama' of Stockhausen's music; and in the breadth of the synthesis it achieves lies all the justification for its grandeur.

WORKS

(*the numbering is Stockhausen's*)

no.

$\frac{1}{11}$ Chöre für Doris (Verlaine), 3 pieces, 1950; ORTF Chamber Chorus, cond. Couraud, Paris, 21 Oct 1971

$\frac{1}{10}$ Drei Lieder: Der Rebell (Baudelaire), Frei (anon.), Der Saitenmann (anon.), A, fl, 2 cl, tpt, trbn, perc, xyl, pf, hpd, str, 1950; B. Fassbänder, Ensemble Musique Vivante, cond. Stockhausen, Paris, 21 Oct 1971

$\frac{1}{9}$ Choral, SATB, 1950

$\frac{1}{8}$ Sonatine, vn, pf, 1951; Marschner, Stockhausen, Cologne, 1951

$\frac{1}{7}$ Kreuzspiel, ob, b cl, pf, 3 perc, 1951; Cologne, Dec 1951

$\frac{1}{6}$ Formel, 29 insts, 1951; Ensemble Musique Vivante, cond. Stockhausen, Paris, 22 Oct 1971

$\frac{1}{5}$ Etude, 1-track tape (Paris), 1952, unpubd

$\frac{1}{4}$ Spiel, orch, 1952; South-west German RSO, cond. Rosbaud, Donaueschingen, 11 Oct 1952; rev. 1973

$\frac{1}{3}$ Schlagquartett, pf, 6 timp (3 players), 1952; Hamburg, 12 March 1953; rev. 1974 as Schlagtrio, pf, 6 timp (2 players)

$\frac{1}{2}$ Punkte, orch, 1952, rev. 1962; South-west German RSO, cond. Boulez, Donaueschingen, 20 Oct 1963; rev. 1964, 1966

1 Kontra-Punkte, fl, cl, b cl, bn, tpt, trbn, pf, harp, vn, vc, 1952, rev. 1953; Cologne RSO, cond. Scherchen, Cologne, 26 May 1953

2 Klavierstücke I–IV, 1952–3; Mercenier, Darmstadt, 21 Aug 1954

3 Elektronische Studien, 1-track tape (Cologne): I, 1953, unpubd; II, 1954

4 Klavierstücke V–X, 1954–5, IX–X rev. 1961; V–VIII, Mercenier, Darmstadt, 1 June 1955; IX, Kontarsky, Cologne, 21 May 1962; X, Rzewski, Palermo, 10 Oct 1962

5 Zeitmasze, fl, ob, eng hn, cl, bn, 1955–6; Domaine Musical, cond. Boulez, Paris, 15 Dec 1956

6 Gruppen, 3 orchs, 1955–7; Cologne RSO, cond. Maderna, Boulez, Stockhausen, Cologne, 24 March 1958

7 Klavierstück XI, 1956; Jacobs, Darmstadt, 28 July 1957

8 Gesang der Jünglinge (Daniel), 5 1-track tapes (Cologne), 1955–6; Cologne, 30 May 1956; rev. 4-track tape

9 Zyklus, perc, 1959; Caskel, Darmstadt, 25 Aug 1959

10 Carré, 4 choruses, 4 orchs, 1959–60, partly realized Cardew; North German Radio Chorus and SO, cond. Gielen, Kagel, Markowski, Stockhausen, Hamburg, 28 Oct 1960

11 Refrain, pf + woodblocks, cel + crotales, vib + cowbells + glock, 1959; Tudor, Cardew, Rockstroh, Berlin, 2 Oct 1959

12 Kontakte, 4-track tape (Cologne), 1959–60; used as music for theatre piece Originale, 1961; Cologne, 26 Oct 1961

12½ Kontakte, pf, perc, 4-track tape (= no.12), 1959–60; Tudor, Caskel, Cologne, 11 June 1960

13 Momente (Song of Songs, Bauermeister, Stockhausen etc), S, 4 choruses, 4 tpt, 4 trbn, 2 elec org, 3 perc, 1961–4; Arroyo, Cologne Radio Chorus and SO, cond. Stockhausen, Cologne, 21 May 1962

13½ Momente, enlarged 1964; Arroyo, Cologne Radio Chorus and SO, cond. Stockhausen, Donaueschingen, 16 Oct 1965

13⅔ Momente, enlarged 1972; Davy, Cologne Radio Chorus, Ensemble Musique Vivante, cond. Stockhausen, Bonn, 8 Dec 1972

14 Plus–Minus, 2 × 7 pages for elaboration, unspecified forces, 1963; Cardew, Rzewski, Rome, 14 June 1964

15 Mikrophonie I, tam-tam (2 players), 2 mic, 2 filters and potentiometers, 1964

15½ Mikrophonie I, Brussels version, 1964; Stockhausen Ens, Brussels, 9 Dec 1964
16 Mixtur, 5 orch groups, sine-wave generators, 4 ring mod, 1964; North German RSO, cond. Gielen, Stockhausen Ens, Hamburg, 9 Nov 1965
16½ Mixtur, 5 small orch groups, elec as for no.16, 1967; Hudba Dneska Ens, cond. L. Kupkovič, Stockhausen Ens, Frankfurt, 23 Aug 1967
17 Mikrophonie II (H. Heisenbüttel: Einfache grammatische Meditationen), 6 S, 6 B, Hammond org, 4 ring mod, 4-track tape, 1965; Cologne Radio Chorus, Studio Chorus for New Music, Kontarsky, Stockhausen Ens, Cologne, 11 June 1965
18 Stop, 6 small orch groups, 1965
18½ Stop, Paris version, 18 insts, 1969; Ensemble Musique Vivante, cond. Masson, Paris, 2 June 1969
18⅔ Stop, London version, 19 insts, 1973; London Sinfonietta, cond. Stockhausen, London, 9 March 1973
19 Solo, melody inst, tape rec, 1965–6; Hirata (trbn), Noguchi (fl), Tokyo, 25 April 1966
20 Telemusik, 4-track tape (Tokyo), 1966; Tokyo, 25 April 1966
21 Adieu, fl, ob, cl, bn, hn, 1966; Cologne RSO Wind Qnt, Calcutta, 30 Jan 1967
22 Hymnen, 4-track tape (Cologne), 1966–7; Cologne, 30 Nov 1967
22½ Hymnen, insts, 4-track tape (=no.22), 1966–7; Stockhausen Ens, Cologne, 30 Nov 1967
22⅔ Dritte Region der Hymnen mit Orchester, orch, 4-track tape (= part of no.22), 1969; New York PO, cond. Stockhausen, New York, 25 Feb 1971
23 Prozession, 4 insts, mics, filters, potentiometers, 1967; Stockhausen Ens, Helsinki, 21 May 1967
24 Stimmung (Stockhausen etc), 2 S, Mez, T, Bar, B, 6 mic, 1968; Collegium Vocale Köln, Paris, 9 Dec 1968
25 Kurzwellen, 4 insts, mics, filters, potentiometers, 4 short-wave receivers, 1968; Stockhausen Ens, Bremen, 5 May 1968; realized, with music by Beethoven, as Kurzwellen mit Beethoven (Stockhoven–Beethausen Opus 1970), 1969); Stockhausen Ens, Düsseldorf, 17 Dec 1969
26 Aus den sieben Tagen, 15 text pieces, May 1968: Richtige Dauern, *c*4 players; Unbegrenzt, ens; Verbindung, ens; Treffpunkt, ens; Nachtmusik, ens; Abwärts, ens; Aufwärts, ens; Oben und unten, theatre piece; Intensität, ens; Setz die Segel zur Sonne, ens; Kommunion, ens; Litanei, to the player; Es, ens; Goldstaub, small ens; Ankunft, any number of musicians
27 Spiral, soloist, short-wave receiver, 1969; Holliger, Zagreb, May 1969
28 Für Dr K., fl, cl, pf, vib + tubular bells, vn, vc, 1969
29 Fresco, wall sounds for meditation, 4 orch groups, 1969; Beethovenhalle Orch, cond. Wangenheim, Fritsche, B. Kontarsky, Földes, Bonn, 15 Nov 1969
30 Pole für zwei, 2 players, 2 short-wave receivers, 1969–70; Vetter, Fritsch, Osaka, 20 March 1970
31 Expo für drei, 3 players, 3 short-wave receivers, 1969–70; Boje, Eötvös, Gehlhaar, Osaka, 21 March 1970
32 Mantra, 2 pf + woodblock + crotales, 2 ring mod, 1969–70; Kontarskys, Donaueschingen, 28 Oct 1970
33 Für kommende Zeiten, 17 text pieces: Kommunikation, Über die Grenze, Übereinstimmung, Verkürzung, Verlängerung, all Aug 1968; Intervall, Sept 1969; Anhalt, Ausserhalb, Innerhalb, all Feb 1970; Schwingung, Spektren, Wellen, Japan, Vorahnung, Zugvogel, Ceylon, Wach, all July 1970
34 Sternklang, park music for 5 groups, 1971; Collegium Vocale Köln, Intermodulation, Gentle Fire, Stockhausen Ens, dir. Stockhausen, Berlin, June 1971
35 Trans, orch, tape, 1971; South-west German RSO, cond. Bour, Donaueschingen, 16 Oct 1971
36 Alphabet für Liège, 13 musical scenes for soloists and duos, 1972; Liège, Sept 1972
36½ Am Himmel wandre ich . . . (Indianerlieder) [from Alphabet] (American Indian chants), S, Bar, 1972
37 Ylem, 19 players/singers, 1972; London Sinfonietta, London, 9 March 1973
38 Inori [Adorations], 1/2 soloists, orch, 1973–4; E. Clarke (mime), South-west German RSO, cond. Stockhausen, Donaueschingen, 20 Oct 1974
38½ Vortrag über HU, introductory lecture to Inori, 1v, 1974; Davy, Donaueschingen, 20 Oct 1974
39 Atmen gibt das Leben, chorus, 1974; North German Radio Chorus, cond. Stockhausen, Hamburg, 16 May 1975; rev. as 'choral opera', chorus, orch/tape, 1977
40 Herbstmusik, 4 players, 1974; Stockhausen Ens, Bremen, 4 May 1974
40½ Laub und Regen [closing duet from Herbstmusik], cl, va, 1974
41 Musik im Bauch, 6 perc, 1975
41½ Tierkreis, 12 melodies, melody inst and/or harmony inst, 1975
41⅔ Tierkreis, high S/high T, harmony inst, 1976
41¾ Tierkreis, S/very high T, harmony inst, 1976
41⅘ Tierkreis, Mez/A/low T, harmony inst, 1976
41⅚ Tierkreis, Bar, harmony inst, 1976
41 6/7 Tierkreis, B, harmony inst, 1976
41⅞ Tierkreis, chamber orch, 1977
42 Harlekin, cl, 1975
42½ Der kleine Harlekin, cl, 1975
43 Sirius, S, B, tpt, b cl, elec, 1975–7
44 Amour, 5 pieces, cl, 1976
45 Jubiläum, orch, 1977
46 In Freundschaft, fl/cl/ob/tpt/vn/va, 1977
47 Der Jahreslauf [scene from Licht: Dienstag], dancers, orch, 1977
48 Michaels Reise um die Erde [scene from Licht: Donnerstag, pt.ii], tpt, orch, 1978
49 Michaels Jugend [3 scenes from Licht: Donnerstag, pt.i], S, T, B, tpt, basset hn, trbn, modulated pf, 3 dancers, tape, 1978–9
50 Michaels Heimkehr [scene from Licht: Donnerstag, pt.iii], S, T, B, tpt, basset hn, trbn, 3 dancers, chorus, orch, 1979

(*unnumbered works and projects*)

Study on one sound, tape, Paris, 1952; discarded, but sketches survive
Klavierstücke 5½ and 6½ [related to V and VI], 1954, unpubd; Kontarsky, Cologne, Musikhochschule, 18 Jan 1974
Monophonie, orch, 1960–, inc.
Ensemble, 12 insts, elec, Darmstadt, 1967
Projektion, 9 orch groups, film, 1967–, inc.
Musik für ein Haus, 14 insts, elec, Darmstadt, 1968
Hinab-hinauf
Tunnel-Spiral
Vision, 2 pf, 1969–, inc.
Singreadfeel (Aurobindo), singer with special insts, 1970

Principal publishers: Universal, Stockhausen-Verlag

WRITINGS

BOOKS

Texte zur elektronischen und instrumentalen Musik, i (Cologne, 1963)
Texte/zu eigenen Werken/zur Kunst anderer/Aktuelles, ii (Cologne, 1964)
Ein Schlüssel für Momente (Kassel, 1971)
Texte zur Musik 1963–1970, iii (Cologne, 1971)
with others: *Weltmusik*, ed. E. Pütz and H. W. Schmidt (Cologne, 1974)

ARTICLES

Most collected in *Texte*, 1963–71; only translations and uncollected items listed here
'Actualia', *Die Reihe* (1958), no.1, p.45 [Eng.]
'. . . how time passes. . .', *Die Reihe* (1959), no.3, pp.10–41
'Electronic and Instrumental Music', *Die Reihe* (1961), no.5, p.59
'Music in Space', *Die Reihe* (1961), no.5, p.67
'The Concept of Unity of Electronic Music', *PNM*, i/1 (1962), 39
'Music and Speech', *Die Reihe* (1964), no.6, p.40
'Stockhausen Miscellany', *Music and Musicians*, xxi/2 (1972), 28
'Musique et graphique', *Musique en jeu* (1973), no.13, p.94
'Musique universelle', *Musique en jeu* (1974), no.15, p.30
'Proposals for the Future of the Orchestra', *The Listener*, xci (1974), 478
Also notes on works pubd in trans. in the Eng. edn. of Wörner (1973)

BIBLIOGRAPHY

MONOGRAPHS

K. H. Wörner: *Karlheinz Stockhausen: Werk und Wollen* (Rodenkirchen, 1963; Eng. trans., enlarged, 1973)
J. Cott, ed.: *Stockhausen: Conversations with the Composer* (New York, 1973)
J. Harvey: *The Music of Stockhausen: an Introduction* (London, 1975)
R. Maconie: *The Works of Karlheinz Stockhausen* (London, 1976)

ARTICLES

D. Schnebel: 'Karlheinz Stockhausen', *Die Reihe* (1958), no.4, p.119; Eng. trans. in *Die Reihe* (1960), no.4, p.121
C. Cardew: 'Report on Stockhausen's Carré', *MT*, cii (1961), 619
G. M. Koenig: 'Kommentar zur Stockhausens . . . wie die Zeit vergeht . . .', *Die Reihe* (1962), no.8, p.73; Eng. trans. in *Die Reihe* (1968), no.8, p.80
E. Karkoschka: 'Stockhausens Theorien', *Melos*, xxxii (1965), 5
B. McElheran: 'Preparing Stockhausen's Momente', *PNM*, iv/1 (1965), 33
K. Boehmer: *Zur Theorie der offenen Form in der neuen Musik* (Darmstadt, 1967)
J.-Y. Bosseur: 'Chronique musicale: aspect de l'innovation musicale au XXe siècle: "Momente" de Stockhausen', *Pensée* (1967), no.134, p.118
R. Smalley: 'Stockhausen's Gruppen', *MT*, cviii (1967), 794
R. Gehlhaar: 'Zur Komposition Ensemble', *Darmstädter Beiträge zur neuen Musik* (1968), no.11
J. Harvey: 'Stockhausen: Theory and Music', *MR*, xxix (1968), 130
G. Marcus: 'Stockhausen's Zeitmasse', *MR*, xxix (1968), 142
T. Zieliński: 'Karlheinz Stockhausen', *Ruch muzyczny* (1968), no.6, p.6; no.7, p.16
K. Boehmer: 'Werk-Form-Prozess', *Musik auf Flucht vor sich selbst*, ed.

U. Dibelius (Munich, 1969), 52

R. Smalley: 'Stockhausen's Piano Pieces: some Notes for the Listener', *MT*, cx (1969), 30

R. Maconie: 'Stockhausen's Setz die Segel zur Sonne', *Tempo* (1970), no.92, p.30

F. Ritzel: 'Musik für ein Haus', *Darmstädter Beiträge zur neuen Musik* (1970), no.12

R. Smalley: 'Stockhausen and Development', *MT*, cxi (1970), 379

'Karlheinz Stockhausen', *VH 101* (1970–71), no.4, p.110 [interview]

P. Heyworth: 'Spiritual Dimensions', *Music and Musicians*, xix/9 (1971), 32 [interview]

W. Krüger: 'Karlheinz Stockhausen: Allmacht und Ohnmacht in der neuesten Musik', *Forschungsbeiträge zur Musikwissenschaft*, xiii (1971)

U. Stürzbecher: *Werkstattgespräche mit Komponisten* (Cologne, 1971)

M. E. Keller: 'Gehörte und komponierte Struktur in Stockhausens Kreuzspiel', *Melos*, xxxix (1972), 10

R. Maconie: 'Stockhausen's Mikrophonie I', *PNM*, x/2 (1972), 92

K. Boehmer: 'Karlheinz Stockhausen oder Der Imperialismus als höchstes Stadium des Kapitalistischen Avantgardismus', *Musik und Gesellschaft*, xxii (1973)

J. Purce: 'The Spiral in the Music of Stockhausen', *Main Currents in Modern Thought* (New Rochelle, NY, 1973), Sept–Oct; Fr. trans. in *Musique en jeu* (1974), no.15, p.7

R. Smalley: 'Momente: Material for the Listener and Composer–1', *MT*, cxv (1974), 23

——: 'Momente: Material for the Listener and Performer – 2', *MT*, cxv (1974), 289

J. Harvey: 'Stockhausen's "Hymnen"', *MT*, cxvi (1975), 705

R. P. Morgan: 'Stockhausen's Writings on Music', *MQ*, lxi (1975), 1

R. Toop: 'Stockhausen's Konkrete Etüde', *MR*, xxxvi (1976), 295

G. W. HOPKINS

Stockholm. Capital city of Sweden, founded in 1255 as a small island fortress between Lake Mälar and the Baltic. It soon grew into an important trade centre, with a large proportion of German inhabitants. It was in the German Church in the 16th century that polyphony became an important part of the service. Wolfgang Burchardt was Kantor in the German Church and rector of the German school in Stockholm from 1579 to 1599, and appears to have imported a large proportion of the 103 polyphonic works by German, Dutch and Italian composers forming the 'German collection' of the Swedish Royal Academy of Music; it was probably because of his influence that the Swedish churches adopted polyphony. Further impetus was given to the city's musical life when the king took up permanent residence there in about 1600. King Gustavus II enlarged his *kapell* in 1620 to include several types of string and wind instruments in addition to singers. In the same year the first composer of any importance in Sweden, Andreas Düben, arrived from Amsterdam, where he had studied with Sweelinck. He and his descendants dominated the musical life of Stockholm in the 17th century, holding positions as leaders of the *hovkapell* and as organists.

There are records of town musicians in the 17th century, and evidence of music in the Latin schools, which were intended mainly for priests and officials. These schools performed plays, sometimes of a rustic and humorous character, in which songs and instrumental pieces were included. The German school was the most active – one of its teachers, Petrus Pachius, wrote a Christmas play in 1635, and three years later *Perseus* by Johann Rist was performed. The pupils also sang at funerals and other ceremonies, providing the schools with a considerable income. Songs and instrumental pieces were also performed in Stockholm by German

1. Interior of the theatre at the palace of Drottningholm

2. Interior of the Stockholm opera house: engraving from 'Illustrerad tidning av Gellersted-Malmström' (2 February 1869)

wandering players. Ballets were given by the Dutch Fornenbergh troupe in the 1660s.

The king's musicians were also important as church organists and as performers in concerts and balls held in the wealthier homes. From 1731 they gave public concerts in the Riddarhuset ('Palace of nobility'). These concerts became more numerous after 1758, when F. A. Uttini conducted them. He performed music by Handel, Pergolesi, Hasse and Graun, in addition to his own arias and symphonies. From 1766 to 1786 the literary and musical society Utile Dulci was active; music played an important part in the meetings of the society. Receptions and presentations were graced with specially composed music, and some public concerts were given. Uttini gave some assistance to the society, but most of the musicians and singers were aristocratic amateurs. G. J. Vogler was active in Stockholm between 1786 and 1799, and, although his organ concerts were composed largely of such picturesque and pictorial works as *Venetianisches Schifferlied* and *Himmel und Hölle*, his influence resulted in a general improvement of performance standards among Stockholm's organists. Vogler also started a music school and published music instruction books.

At the royal palace of Drottningholm, about 10 km from the centre of Stockholm, a theatre was built in 1754. It burnt down in 1762, but was replaced by a larger theatre which was opened in 1766, built on a symmetrical plan, with a very deep stage (19 metres) and a capacity of 400 (see fig.1). Queen Lovisa Ulrika built the theatre, and it was inherited by her son Gustavus III, who was himself an outstanding playwright; he wrote the plots for several Swedish operas, which were put into verse by J. H. Kellgren. Gustavus's enthusiasm for medieval chivalry led him to arrange several festivals about 1780, including tournaments and carousels; he planned to make Drottningholm a rival of Versailles. However, the theatre fell into disuse after 1800, until it was restored in the 1920s. It has survived largely intact, complete with costumes, scenery and machinery, and has been a valuable source of information on 18th-century theatrical practice. Since the 1940s about 50 performances have been given there every summer. In addition to works by Alessandro Scarlatti, Handel, Haydn, Grétry, Gluck, Rossini and others, Swedish operas of the period have been revived, including Vogler's *Gustav Adolf och Ebba Brahe*, and excerpts from Uttini's *Il re pastore* (1755), which was written for the original theatre, and J. M. Kraus's *Proserpin* have been played.

With the patronage of Gustavus III the first opera in

Swedish was performed in 1773, Uttini's *Thetis och Pelée*. Other productions of that year included the heroic ballet *Acis och Galatea*, with music adapted from Handel and others, and Gluck's *Orfeo*. These operatic productions, given in the Bollhuset (a games room) until 1782, attracted musicians from Germany, including C. F. G. Berwald, violinist in the *hovkapell*, 1773–1806.

From 1782 Stockholm had its own opera house, which opened with a performance of *Cora och Alonzo* by J. G. Naumann. It was also used for concerts and for masked balls, the most famous of which was the one in March 1792, at which Gustavus III was shot (this incident later provided the plot for operas by Auber, Verdi and Werle). In the early 19th century plays and comic operas were given in the Arsenal near the opera house, until it burnt down in 1823. Smaller theatres with small orchestras included the Nya Svenska Teater ('New Swedish theatre'), directed by Carl Stenborg (1784–1801), which had a large repertory of comic operas; and the Mindre Teater ('Smaller theatre', 1846–63), directed by Edvard Stjernström and others. The Oscarsteater (1906) specialized in operetta and, later, musical comedy; it opened with a production of *Les brigands* (given in Swedish as 'Frihetsbröderna') by Offenbach.

During the 19th century the opera was the centre of musical life, and the best musicians and singers were employed there. Of the many fine singers Jenny Lind became the most famous; after acting a number of speaking roles she made her singing début in 1835 in A. F. Lindblad's *Frondörerna* and subsequently sang in many other operas until she left Stockholm in 1844. Johan Fredrik Berwald was the chief conductor of the opera from 1823 to 1849; he also gave many chamber concerts and conducted the oratorio performances of the Harmoniska Sällskap choral society in the 1820s and 1830s. Haydn's *The Creation*, first heard in Stockholm in 1801, was performed several times. Johan Mazer, a merchant, organized many concerts in his home, and since his death in 1847 a chamber music society organized in his memory, the Mazerska Kvartettsällskap, has been active. Mazer bequeathed a large collection of music to the academy, consisting of several thousand items.

Oratorio concerts, which diminished in number during the 1850s, were revived in 1860 by the foundation of the Nya Harmoniska Sällskap conducted by Ludvig Norman. The society was reorganized as the Musikföreningen in 1880, and continued in cooperation with the opera orchestra. Many choral works by Liszt, Brahms and Rubinstein were performed, as well as works by Beethoven, Handel and Bach (including the first Swedish performance of the Mass in B minor in 1896), and works by Vilhelm Svedbom, founder of the Musikförening, and other Swedish composers.

A special feature of Stockholm's musical life in the 19th century was the growing interest in Nordic folk music. Folktunes were introduced into rustic plays, such as *En majdag i Värend* ('A May day in Värend'), with music arranged by Berwald (1843). Concerts of folk music were organized from 1844 by Richard Dybeck and from 1845 by J. N. Ahlström. The folklorist Artur Hazelius was interested in music, and when in 1891 he realized his project for an open-air museum, the Skansen, he incorporated fiddlers and folksingers to give an authentic atmosphere.

In the 19th century symphony concerts were sometimes given by the opera orchestra, but virtuosos from Europe were not attracted to Stockholm until the 1880s when Bülow visited the city. The biggest restaurants maintained orchestras from about 1870; August Meissner's orchestra at Bern's restaurant was outstanding, and sometimes gave symphony concerts. Military bands were popular during the summer, and from the 1890s variety shows and music halls became prominent. Important figures in the concert life of late 19th-century Stockholm were Andreas Hallén, who conducted the Filharmoniska Sällskap during the decade 1885–95 and performed mainly choral works, and Tor Aulin, who gave many chamber music concerts from 1887 and in 1902 founded the Konsertförening, which in 1914 instituted its own symphony orchestra. The third symphony orchestra in Stockholm, the Swedish Radio SO, was founded in 1937.

The old opera house (see fig.2) was demolished in 1891 and a new building was opened in 1898. Here the 150th anniversary (1923) of the first Swedish opera was commemorated with a cantata by Wilhelm Peterson-Berger, who later tried to convey something of the atmosphere of Stockholm in his Fourth Symphony, 'Holmia' (1929). The 200th anniversary was commemorated by a specially commissioned opera, *Tintomara*, by L. J. Werle (1973). The new opera house was the scene for the débuts of Jussi Björling, Set Svanholm, Birgit Nilsson and other renowned singers.

In 1926 the two halls of the Konserthus were opened; it was the first building in Stockholm designed for concerts. The building is owned by the Konsertförening and the resident orchestra is the Filharmonin; among its outstanding conductors have been Schnéevoigt (1915–23), Talich (1926–36), Fritz Busch (1937–41) and Dorati (1966–73). The two halls are also used for other types of concerts. A chamber music organization, Fylkingen, was founded in 1933 with the aim of promoting contemporary music; it subsequently became the Swedish section of the International Society for Contemporary Music (1952) and, in the 1960s, a forum for electronic music, cooperating with the electronic music studio built in 1964 by Swedish Radio under the supervision of Knut Wiggen.

Other institutions in Stockholm include a museum of musical history, founded in 1899, which has large collections of instruments and of Swedish folktunes, and presents historical concerts; the Svenskt Visarkiv ('Archive of Swedish folksong'), founded in 1952; and the Svenskt Musikhistoriskt Arkiv ('Archive of Swedish musical history'), founded in 1965. The Par Bricole Society has been active since its foundation in 1779 by Olof Kexel and Carl Michael Bellman. Music has always been prominent at its meetings, particularly in the form of cheerful songs reflecting all aspects of Stockholm life. Bellman was the supreme master of this genre and his songs have remained very popular in Sweden.

Higher musical education was one of the main objects of the Royal Swedish Academy of Music after its foundation in 1771; however, its means were too small for this aim to succeed until the 1850s when regular classes for church musicians and soloists were introduced. Since then this institution has grown in importance, and in 1971 it was separated from the academy and became a separate musical high school. Other important music schools are the Adolf Fredrik Lindblads Musikskola (1827–72), the Richard Anderssons Musikskola (founded 1886), the Borgarskolans Musiklinje ('Music class of the civic school', 1943) and the Stockholms Musikpedagogiska Institut (1960).

BIBLIOGRAPHY

P. Vretblad: *Konsertlivet i Stockholm under 1700-talet* [Concert life in Stockholm in the 18th century] (Stockholm, 1918)

R. Engländer: *Johann Gottlieb Naumann als Opernkomponist (1741–1801), mit neuen Beiträgen zur Musikgeschichte Dresdens und Stockholms* (Leipzig, 1922/R1970)

T. Norlind and E. Trobäck: *Kunglig hovkapellets historia 1526–1926* [History of the royal court chapel] (Stockholm, 1926)

A. Beijer: *Slottsteatrarna på Drottningholm och Gripsholm* [Palace theatres of Drottningholm and Gripsholm] (Stockholm, 1937)

M. Tegen: *Musiklivet i Stockholm 1890–1910* [Musical life in Stockholm, 1890–1910] (Stockholm, 1955)

G. Hilleström: *Drottningholmsteatern förr och nu* [The Drottningholm Theatre past and present] (Stockholm, 1956) [in Swed. and Eng.]

M. Tegen: 'Stockholm', *MGG*

Svenska musikperspektiv: Minneskrift vid Kungl. Musikaliska Akademiens 200-årsjubileum [Swedish music perspectives: commemorative volume for the 200th anniversary of the Swedish Academy of Music] (Stockholm, 1971)

MARTIN TEGEN

Stockmann, (Christine) Doris (*b* Dresden, 3 Nov 1929). German ethnomusicologist. She studied the piano, opera production and music theory at the Dresden Hochschule für Musik (1947–9) and musicology (with Dräger, Meyer and Vetter), theatre history and art history at the Humboldt University, Berlin. She also studied ethnography, folklore and linguistics with Steinitz (1953–8), taking the doctorate at Berlin in 1958 with a dissertation on Altmark songs. She has made study visits to many European countries; in 1953 she was appointed scientific assistant for ethnomusicology and folk music research at the Institute for German Folklore of the Academy of Sciences, Berlin. She was a lecturer at the Humboldt University, Berlin (1967–8), and visiting lecturer at the universities of Uppsala (1965) and Göteborg (1969). Her main areas of research are German and European folk music, in particular, early forms of partsong, medieval musical practices, processes of change in the 19th and 20th centuries and transcription methods; she has also taken part in International Folk Music Council study groups on the classification and investigation of early sources.

WRITINGS

Der Volksgesang in der Altmark (diss., Humboldt U. of Berlin, 1958; Berlin, 1962, as *Der Volksgesang in der Altmark: von der Mitte des 19. Jahrhunderts bis zur Mitte des 20. Jahrhunderts*)

with E. Stockmann: 'Die vokale Bordun-Mehrstimmigkeit in Südalbanien', *Ethnomusicologie III: Wégimont V 1960*, 85–135

'Zur Vokalmusik der südalbanischen Çamen', *JIFMC*, xv (1963), 38

'Wandlungen des deutschen Volksgesanges vom 19. Jahrhundert bis zur Gegenwart', *VII Mezhdunarodïy kongress antropologicheskikh i etnograficheskikh nauk: Moskva 1964*, vii, 238; also in *Musa–mens-musici: im Gedenken an Walther Vetter* (Leipzig, 1969), 357

'Zur musikalischen Struktur einiger mehrstimmiger Gesänge der südalbanischen Laben', *Deutsches Jb für Volkskunde*, xi (1965), 173

'Das Problem der Transkription in der musikethnologischen Forschung', *Deutsches Jb für Volkskunde*, xii (1966), 207–42

ed., with J. Stęszewski: *Analyse und Klassifikation von Volksmelodien: 3. Arbeitstagung der Study Group of Folk Music Systematization des IFMC: Radziejowice 1967* [incl. 'Zur Arbeit der Study Group of Folk Music Systematization des IFMC', 9]

'Hörbild and Schallbild als Mittel musikethnologischer Dokumentation', *Festschrift für Walter Wiora* (Kassel, 1967), 503

'Elektronische Datenverarbeitung in der Ethnologie und den ihr nahestehenden Wissenschaften', *Deutsches Jb für Volkskunde*, xv (1969), 134

'Musik als kommunikatives System: Informations- und zeichentheoretische Aspekte insbesondere bei der Erforschung mündlich tradierter Musik', *DJbM*, xiv (1969), 76

'Zur öffentlich-rechtlichen Signalpraxis im deutschen Bauernkrieg', *4. Arbeitstagung der Studiengruppe zur Erforschung und Edition älterer Volksmusikquellen des IFMC: Kraków 1971*

'Deutsche Rechtsdenkmäler des Mittelalters als volksmusikalische Quelle', *SM*, xv (1973), 267–302

'Entwicklungsstufen der musikethnologischen Transkription', *4. Seminarium Ethnomusikologicum der Slowakischen Akademie der Wissenschaften: Bratislava 1973*

'Der Kampf um die Glocken im deutschen Bauernkrieg: ein Beitrag zur öffentlich-rechtlichen Signalwesen des Spätmittelalters', *BMw*, xvi (1974), 163–93

'Transkription', *MGG*

'Die Erforschung vokaler und instrumentaler Praktiken im mittelalterlichen Rechtsleben', *DJbM*, xix (1974)

'Die Glocke im Profangebrauch des Spätmittelalters', *Festschrift to Ernst Emsheimer* (Stockholm, 1974), 224

'Die Problematik der Erarbeitung leistungsfähiger Computer-Programme und die Rolle der notenschriftlichen Aufzeichnung im musikfolkloristischen Analyseprozess', *1. Erevanisches Seminar der Armenischen Akademie der Wissenschaften 1975 über 'Maschinelle Aspekte der algorithmischen Analyse musikalischer Texte': Erevan 1975* [in Russ.]

'Musik und Sprache unter klassifikatorischen Aspekten', *JbMP 1975–6*

'Zur Analyse schriftlosüberlieferter Musik', *BMw*, xviii (1976), 235

'Aspects of Musical Perception', *YIFMC*, ix (1977)

'Musik–Sprache–Tierkommunikation', *IRASM*, x (1979), 5–45

with E. Stockmann: *Einführung in die Musikfolklore* (Leipzig, in preparation)

FOLKSONG EDITIONS

with E. Stockmann and W. Fiedler: *Albanische Volksmusik*, i: *Gesänge der Çamen*, Veröffentlichungen des Instituts für deutsche Volkskunde, xxxvi (Berlin, 1965)

HORST SEEGER

Stockmann, Erich (*b* Stendal, 10 March 1926). German ethnomusicologist. He studied musicology and German at Greifswald University (1946–9) and with Dräger, Meyer and Vetter at Humboldt University, Berlin (1950–52), where he took the doctorate in 1953 with a dissertation on electrical musical instruments. He then began working as an ethnomusicologist at the Institute for German Folklore of the Academy of Sciences, Berlin, and in 1957 was appointed lecturer in ethnomusicology and organology at the musicological institute of the Humboldt University. He has been largely responsible for the development of an ethnomusicological research centre at the Berlin Academy of Sciences, leading the first ethnomusicological expedition to collect folk music in Albania (1957). In his study of German and European folk music he has done much to promote research into folk instruments, editing, with Ernst Emsheimer, a documentary monograph series (Handbuch der europäischen Volksmusikinstrumente, Leipzig, 1967–) and encouraging international cooperation. He became a member of the executive board of the International Folk Music Council in 1964 and vice-president in 1975. In 1962 he founded the IFMC study group on folk instruments, serving as its director and editing its serial publication, *Studia instrumentorum musicae popularis* (Stockholm, 1969–), whose contents include the proceedings of several international meetings that he has organized. He is also editor, with Oskár Elschek and Ivan Mačák, of the *Annual Bibliography of European Ethnomusicology* (Bratislava, 1967–).

WRITINGS

Der musikalische Sinn der elektro-akustischen Musikinstrumente (diss., Humboldt U. of Berlin, 1953)

Des Knaben Wunderhorn in den Weisen seiner Zeit (Berlin, 1958)

with E. Stockmann: 'Die vokale Bordun-Mehrstimmigkeit in Südalbanien', *Ethnomusicologie III: Wégimont V 1960*, 85–135

'Klarinettentypen in Albanien', *JIFMC*, xii (1960), 17

'Vorbemerkungen zu einem "Handbuch der europäischen Volksmusikinstrumente"', *AcM*, xxxii (1960), 47

'Zur Sammlung und Untersuchung albanischer Volksmusik', *AcM*, xxxii (1960), 102

'Zum Terminus Volksmusikinstrument', *Forschungen und Fortschritte*, xxxv (Berlin, 1961), 337

'Die europäischen Volksmusikinstrumente', *Deutsches Jb für Volkskunde*, x (1964), 238

'Towards a History of European Folk Music Instruments', *JIFMC*, xvii

1965), 155

'Volksmusikinstrumente und Arbeit', *Arbeit und Volksleben: deutscher Volkskundekongress: Marburg 1965*, 331; also in *Deutsches Jb für Volkskunde*, xi (1965), 245

'Volksmusikinstrumente', *MGG*

'Aufgaben der Volksmusikinstrumentenforschung', *Jb des österreichischen Volksliedwerkes*, xvi (1967), 73

'Neue Beiträge zur Erforschung der europäischen Volksmusikinstrumente', *Festschrift für Walter Wiora* (Kassel, 1967), 512

with H. Strobach and others: *Sowjetische Volkslied- und Volksmusikforschung: ausgewählte Studien* (Berlin, 1967)

with O. Elschek: 'Zur Typologie der Volksmusikinstrumente', *Deutsches Jb für Volkskunde*, xiv (1968), 225; also in *Studia instrumentorum musicae popularis*, i (1969), 11

'The Diffusion of Musical Instruments as an Inter-ethnic Process of Communication', *YIFMC*, iii (1971), 4

'Das Musikinstrument als Gegenstand anthropologischer und historischer Forschung', *IMSCR*, xi *Copenhagen 1972*, 131

'Internationale und interdisziplinäre Zusammenarbeit in der Volksmusikinstrumentenforschung', *Studia instrumentorum musicae popularis*, ii (1972), 11

'Die Darstellung der Arbeit in der instrumentalen Hirtenmusik', *Festschrift to Ernst Emsheimer* (Stockholm, 1974), 233

'The Study Group on Folk Musical Instruments: its Achievements in Fifteen Years', *YIFMC*, viii (1976)

'Albania', *Grove 6*

FOLKSONG EDITIONS

I. Weber-Kellermann, L. Parisius und seine altmärkischen Volkslieder, Veröffentlichungen des Instituts für deutsche Volkskunde, x (Berlin, 1957)

with D. Stockmann and W. Fiedler: *Albanische Volksmusik*, i: *Gesänge der Çamen*, Veröffentlichungen des Instituts für deutsche Volkskunde, xxxvi (Berlin, 1965)

HORST SEEGER

Stodart. English firm of piano makers. It was founded by Robert Stodart (*fl c*1770–96) in 1775 when he set up his own harpsichord- and piano-making business in Wardour Street. He had been apprenticed to John Broadwood before 1772 and had assisted Broadwood and Americus Backers in inventing the English grand action; in 1777 he patented a piano-harpsichord, which included the earliest patent for this action. Some of his grand pianos survive including one from 1781 at Heaton Hall, Manchester, which is five octaves in compass with an undivided, single-pinned, harpsichord-type bridge and three metal gap spacers to strengthen the gap between the soundboard and the wrest plank. One square piano by him survives with a five-octave compass and the English single action.

Robert's son, William Stodart, was a partner in the firm from the early 1790s. In 1795 William patented 'an upright grand pianoforte in the form of a bookcase'. It was simply a vertical grand enclosed in a rectangular cupboard, placed on a stand with four legs, the action being behind the soundboard and striking through from behind. By about 1816 William was manufacturing on his own, his output of squares having reached 4000.

In 1820 two of Stodart's workmen, James Thom and William Allen, invented a 'compensation frame' (*see* PIANOFORTE, §I, 4) to prevent fluctuations in pitch arising from temperature changes. It is doubtful that it achieved the stability of pitch that was hoped for but its tubular braces proved stronger than other forms of metal bracing then in use, resisting string tensions excellently. This was a vital beginning in the development of bracing in pianos and enabled heavier strings to be used to obtain a richer tone; surviving instruments have a beautifully resonant sound. Few makers adopted the compensation frame; however, the Stodart firm used it until the 1850s, exhibiting a grand with the frame at the Great Exhibition of 1851. Stodart also experimented with baize hammer coverings in the bass about 1820.

The firm became William Stodart & Son (*c*1825) when William's son, Malcolm Stodart, joined the firm; it ceased manufacture in 1861.

BIBLIOGRAPHY

W. Pole: *Musical Instruments in the Great Exhibition of 1851* (London, 1851)

R. E. M. Harding: *The Piano-forte: its History Traced to the Great Exhibition of 1851* (Cambridge, 1933, rev. 2/1978)

A. Loesser: *Men, Women and Pianos: a Social History* (New York, 1954)

D. H. Boalch: *Makers of the Harpsichord and Clavichord 1440–1840* (London, 1956, rev. 2/1974)

MARGARET CRANMER

Stoeckl, Boniface [Johann Evangelist] (*b* Pilling, 27 Nov 1745; *d* Amberg, 27 Sept 1784). German composer. He came from a rural family, received his musical instruction in Geiselhörung and, according to Lipowsky, was also a pupil of Leopold Mozart. He completed his studies in the arts and philosophy at the Benedictine lyceum at Freising. Many of his compositions originated there, some of which are possibly among the seven masses and two litanies mentioned in the thematic catalogue of the Dommusikalien of Freising (Munich Staatsarchiv HL III F.41 ex.Nr.41). After completing his studies Stoeckl entered the Benedictine abbey at Mallersdorf and took his vows on 27 October 1771. On 18 July 1773 he was ordained priest, and in the following year took over the office of music prefect in the abbey. From the autumn of 1781 he worked as professor of humanities at the Gymnasium in Amberg. His compositions for the school theatre are lost, but several sacred works are in Bavarian churches (*D-BB*, *Mbm*, *SBj*, *TEI*, *WEY*, *WS*). Stoeckl was an ardent composer who mastered both the contrapuntal and concertante styles.

BIBLIOGRAPHY

F. J. Lipowsky: *Baierisches Musik-Lexicon* (Munich, 1811/R1971)

R. Münster: 'Stoeckl, Boniface', *MGG* [with list of works]

ROBERT MÜNSTER

Stoeffken, Ditrich. *See* STEFFKIN, THEODORE.

Stoelzel, Heinrich. *See* STÖLZEL, HEINRICH.

Stoessel, Albert (*b* St Louis, Missouri, 11 Oct 1894; *d* New York, 12 May 1943). American violinist, conductor and composer. After early musical training in his native city, he studied the violin, composition and conducting at the Hochschule für Musik in Berlin, where he made his début as a violinist. After a European tour he returned to the USA, appearing as soloist with the St Louis Orchestra. During World War I he was a lieutenant in the US Army (1917–19), obtaining, as a military bandmaster, his first conducting experience and eventually directing the school for bandmasters of the American Expeditionary Force in France. In 1920 he appeared as a violin soloist with the Boston SO and in 1921 toured with Caruso.

In 1922 Stoessel succeeded Walter Damrosch as conductor of the Oratorio Society of New York, became director of music of the Chautauqua Institution in the same year and conductor of the Worcester (Mass.) Music Festival in 1925. He appeared as a guest conductor of the symphony orchestras of Boston, Cleveland, St Louis, etc. In 1923 he was appointed head of the music department of New York University, from which he received the honorary MA. He resigned in 1930 to accept the directorship of the opera and orchestra departments of the Juilliard Graduate School, where he did valuable work by giving the first New York performances of Malipiero's *Il finto Arlecchino*, Strauss's *Ariadne auf Naxos*, etc, the world premières of several American operas (including his own *Garrick*), and revivals of works by Cimarosa, Pergolesi and others. He also gave gifted young American singers the sort of practical experience their European colleagues received in secondary opera houses on the Continent. He died while conducting.

Stoessel's orchestral compositions have been widely played throughout the USA. His works, besides choral compositions, and pieces for violin and piano (e.g. the interesting *Flitting Bats*, which, to facilitate the playing of glissandos in diminished 5ths, uses scordatura, the first string being tuned to e♭″ and the fourth to a♭), include pedagogical works on violin playing.

WORKS
(selective list)

Vn Sonata, G (Boston, 1921)
Hispania, suite, orch, 1921; version for pf (New York, 1922)
Suite antique, 2 vn, chamber orch, 1922 (New York, 1925)
Cyrano de Bergerac, sym. portrait after Rostand, orch, 1922 (Boston, 1931)
Early Americana, suite, orch, 1935 (Boston, 1936)
Concerto grosso, orch (New York, 1935)
Garrick (opera), 1936; New York, Juilliard Graduate School, 1937; Suite, orch (New York, 1938)

GUSTAVE REESE

Stöhr, Richard (*b* Vienna, 11 June 1874; *d* Montpelier, Vermont, 11 Dec 1967). Austrian writer on music and composer. After graduating in medicine (1898) he studied at the Vienna Conservatory, where he returned as a lecturer (1903–38). On emigrating to the USA, he was appointed to teach at the Curtis Institute, Philadelphia (1939–42), and at St Michael's College, Winooski, Vermont (1943–50). He published several theoretical books, notably *Praktischer Leitfaden der Harmonielehre* (Vienna, 1909, 21/1963) and *Musikalische Formenlehre* (Leipzig, 1911, rev. 1933 as *Formenlehre der Musik*). His compositions (listed in H. Sittner: *Richard Stöhr: Mensch, Musiker, Lehrer*, Vienna, 1965) include operas, symphonies and concertos as well as much chamber and instrumental music.

Stoin, Elena (*b* Samokov, 12 April 1915). Bulgarian folklorist, daughter of Vassil Stoin. She graduated from the State Academy of Music in Sofia in 1938 and was a music teacher in various schools until 1945. In 1946 she was appointed research assistant in the Ethnographical Museum in Sofia and from 1950 to 1970 she worked as junior research fellow of the folk music department in the Music Institute of the Bulgarian Academy of Sciences, becoming senior research fellow in 1970. She has delivered numerous papers at folk music conferences outside Bulgaria: in Czechoslovakia, the USSR, Belgium and on several occasions in Yugoslavia.

WRITINGS

'Savremennata balgarska narodna pesen' [Contemporary Bulgarian folksong], *IIM*, i (1952), 125
'Lazaruvane v selo Negoshevo' [Use in folk music of 'Lazaruvane' in the village of Negoshevo], *IIM*, ii–iii (1956), 189
'Narodnite pesni na Strandzhanskiya kray' [Folksongs from the region of the Strandzha mountains], *Strandzhanska ekspeditsiya 1955* (Sofia, 1958), 425
'Dneshnoto sastoyanie na narodnata muzika v severozapadna Balgariya' [The present state of folk music in north-west Bulgaria], *Kompleksna nauchna ekspeditsiya v severozapadna Balgariya 1956* [The complete scientific expedition in north-west Bulgaria], ed. Balgarska Akademiya na Naukite (Sofia, 1958), 365
Angel Bukureshtliev (Sofia, 1961)

'Narodnata pesen v Transko i Kyustendilsko' [Folksong in the Tran and Kjustendil regions], *Kompleksni nauchni ekspeditsii v zapadna Balgariya: Transko, Bresnishko, Kyustendilsko 1957/58* [The complete scientific expeditions in west Bulgaria: the Tran, Bresnik and Kyustendil regions, 1957–8], ed. Balgarska Akademiya na Naukite (Sofia, 1961), 447–82
'Narodnite pesni v Srednogorieto' [Folksongs in Sredna Gora], *IIM*, x (1964), 97–164
'Napevat v haydushkite pesni' [Melody types in Haiduk songs], *Balgarska muzika* (1968), no.9, p.19
'Narodni pesni ot Samokov, zapisani ot Vassil Stoin' [Folksongs from Samokov notated by Vassil Stoin], *IIM*, xiii (1969), 365
'Musikalno-folklorni dialekti v Balgariya' [Folk music dialects in Bulgaria], *Balgarska muzika* (1969), no.5, p.49
'Narodnata pesen v sredna zapadna Balgariya' [Folk music in central west Bulgaria], *IIM*, xv (1970), 97–186
'Melodichno izgrazhdane na balgarskiya yunashki epos' [Melodic construction in Bulgarian heroic epics], *Sbornik za narodni umotvoreniya i narodopis*, liii (1971), 104
'Rayna Katsarova', *IIM*, xviii (1974), 5–46

EDITIONS

with I. Kachulev: *Balgarski savremenni narodni pesni* [Bulgarian contemporary folksongs] (Sofia, 1958)
with R. Katsarova and I. Kachulev: *Balgarski narodni pesni ot severo-iztochna Balgariya* [Bulgarian folksongs from north-west Bulgaria] (Sofia, 1963)
with V. Stoin: *Sbornik narodni pesni ot Samokov i Samokovsko* [Collection of folksongs from Samokov and the Samokov region] (Sofia, 1975)

LADA BRASHOVANOVA

Stoin, Vassil (*b* Samokov, 5 Dec 1880; *d* Sofia, 5 Dec 1938). Bulgarian folklorist. He taught himself the violin at the age of ten. After graduating from the ecclesiastic seminary in Samokov in 1897, he taught in neighbouring villages until 1907 and was able to take down many of the folksongs from the area. He then studied at the Brussels Conservatory (1907–10) and from 1911 to 1922 taught music in Sofia, Turnovo, Plovdiv and Samokov, organizing and conducting choirs and school orchestras. In 1922 he began teaching at a primary school in Sofia, in 1924 he lectured for a year at a teachers' training college and in 1925 he taught singing at a secondary school. At the same time he began lecturing in folk music at the State Academy of Music, where in 1927 he became a professor and, for a few months in 1931, director. He also held the post of president of the Union of Bulgarian Musicians and in 1926 founded a folk-music department in the National Ethnographical Museum. Together with Rayna Katsarova and other musicians Stoin established the tradition of collecting and publishing texts and melodies of thousands of Bulgarian folksongs. In addition to four theoretical studies and a number of articles Stoin collected 9000 songs from the whole of Bulgaria, often under difficult conditions and with scarcely any technical equipment. This activity laid the foundations for Bulgarian folklore studies.

WRITINGS

'Kam balgarskite narodni napevi' [On Bulgarian folktunes], *Bulletin du Musée national d'ethnographie de Sofia*, iv/3–4 (1924), 71
Hypothèse sur l'origine bulgare de la diaphome (Sofia, 1925)
Balgarskata narodna muzika, metrika i ritmika [Bulgarian folk music, metre and rhythm] (Sofia, 1927)
'Balgarski narodni instrumenti: svirka dvoyanka' [Bulgarian national instruments], *Bulletin du Musée national d'ethnographie de Sofia*, xii/1 (1936), 86
Balgarska narodna muzika [Bulgarian folk music] (Sofia, 1956) [collected edn. of folk music studies]

EDITIONS

Narodni pesni ot Timok do Vita [Folksongs from the Timok to the Vita] (Sofia, 1929) [4076 songs]
Narodna pesnopoika [Popular songbook] (Sofia, 1930) [245 songs]
Narodni pesni ot sredna severna Balgariya [Folksongs from central north Bulgaria] (Sofia, 1931) [2718 songs]
with A. Bukureshtliev and R. Katsarova: *Rodopski pesni* [Songs from the Rhodope mountains] (Sofia, 1933) [700 songs]

Sbornik za narodni umotvoreniya i narodopis [A collection of Bulgarian folklore and folk stories] (Sofia, 1934) [1252 songs]
Balgarski narodni pesni ot istochna i zapadna Trakia [Bulgarian folksongs from east and west Thrace] (Sofia, 1939) [1684 songs]

BIBLIOGRAPHY
S. Brashovanov: 'Vassil Stoin', *IIM*, ii–iii (1956), 351
LADA BRASHOVANOVA

Stojanović, Petar (*b* Budapest, 6 Sept 1877; *d* Belgrade, 11 Sept 1957). Yugoslav composer and violinist. He graduated from the Budapest Conservatory as a violin pupil of Hubay in 1896; thereafter he studied with Grün (violin) and with Fuchs and Heuberger (composition) at the Vienna Conservatory, graduating in 1904. Early in the century he gained a reputation in Vienna as a composer and as a performer in solo and ensemble recitals. His renown was increased when the Budapest Opera staged his comic piece *Der Tiger* in 1905, and confirmed with the première of the Violin Concerto no.2, performed by Jan Kubelík in Prague in 1916. In 1925 he moved to Belgrade to become professor of violin (until 1937) and director (until 1928) of the Stanković Music School. He was then professor of violin at the academy (1937–45). A prolific composer, he was at his best in concertante and, to a lesser extent, chamber pieces. The style is late-Romantic, except in some late works, such as the Piano and Violin Concerto (1950), where more modern harmonies and jazz-like rhythms are introduced. He published *Osnovna škola za violinu* (Belgrade, 4/1956) and other teaching works.

WORKS
Stage: Der Tiger, comic opera, 1, 1905; Liebchen am Dach, operetta, 1917; Der Herzog von Reichstadt, operetta, 1921; Blaženka zakletva [Blaženka's oath], music drama, 1934; Mirjana, ballet, 1942; Devet svećnjaka [9 candlesticks], ballet, 1944
Orch: Smrt junaka [The hero's death], sym. poem, 1918; Sava, sym. poem, 1935; 7 vn concs., 2 va concs., 2 vc concs., concs. for fl, pf, hn, a sax; Sinfonia concertante, vn, va, orch; Conc., vn, pf, orch, 1950
Chamber: Pf Qnt, c, op.9; Pf Qt, D, op.15; Pf Trio, C, op.16; other pieces

Principal publishers: Doblinger, Posveta, Udruženje Kompozitora Srbije

BIBLIOGRAPHY
D. Gostuški: 'P. Stojanović: in memoriam', *Zvuk* (1957), no.13–14
STANA ĐURIĆ-KLAJN

Stojowski, Zygmunt (Denis Antoni) (*b* Strzelce, 14 May 1870; *d* New York, 6 Nov 1946). Polish composer, pianist and teacher. He studied composition with Żeleński in Kraków and was then a pupil of Diémer (piano) and Delibes (composition) in Paris; for a short time he had lessons with Paderewski, Saint-Saëns and Massenet. He gave successful concerts in Paris, London, Brussels and Berlin before moving in 1906 to the USA, where he was head of the piano department at the New York Institute of Musical Art until 1912. Thereafter he taught privately and each year organized concerts and master classes throughout the Americas; he wrote extensively on piano teaching. In 1938 he took American citizenship. His technically accomplished music drew on Wagner, Saint-Saëns and Franck, although in later works there was a development of harmony and structure under the influence of French impressionism. Stojowski's vivid melodic invention was always strongly connected with national colour. His greatest achievement was in his virtuoso piano and orchestral music.

WORKS
(selective list)
Orch: Pf Conc. no.1, f♯, op.3 (1893); Romanza, op.20, vn, orch (1901); Sym. no.1, d, op.21, 1899; Vn Conc., G, op.22, 1900; Rapsodie symphonique, op.23, pf, orch (1904); Vc Conc., op.31 (1922); Pf Conc. no.2, A♭, op.32, 1910
Pf: 2 orientales, op.10 (1894); Danses humoresques, op.12 (1893–4); Polish Idylls, op.24 (1901); Auf Sturm und Stille, op.29, n.d.; Etudes de concert, op.35, n.d.; Aspirations, op.39 (1914)
Choral: Le printemps, op.7, chorus, orch (1895); Modlitwa za Polskę [Prayer for Poland], op.49 (Z. Krasiński), S, Bar, chorus, orch (1915)
Chamber: Pf Qnt; 2 sonatas, vn, pf; 2 sonatas, vc, pf

BIBLIOGRAPHY
SMP
J. W. Reiss: *Statkowski-Melcer-Młynarski-Stojowski* (Warsaw, 1949), 20ff
TERESA CHYLIŃSKA

Stokem [Stockem, Stokhem, Stochem, Stoken, Stoccken, Sthoken; Prato], **Johannes de** (*b* c1445; *d* after 1501). Netherlands composer. He began his career at St Lambert, Liège, as a *duodenus* in 1455. Because of gaps in the account books there is no trace of him between 1464 and 1471. In September 1471 he was still in Liège as second intoner and was referred to as rector of the altar of Ste Aldegonde, one of the 12 benefices that the cathedral chapter reserved for musicians. He disappears from the records in 1474; his successor, Regnault Pelletier, was first mentioned in 1477. On 4 November 1478 Stokem gave up his benefice from the altar of St Georges and Ste Aldegonde to become canon of the Petite-Table, replacing the late *duodenus* Henricus de Prato, who was probably related to him. Stokem is mentioned in the account books there until 14 July 1481, when Johannes Lathomi received the canonry of the Petite-Table resigned by him. Stokem was then appointed Kapellmeister to Mathias Corvin, King of Hungary; soon after, in 1483, the chapel's music was highly praised by the papal nuncio, Bartholomeius de Mandii. On 28 January 1484 Tinctoris sent Stokem a part of his treatise, *De inventione et usu musicae*. It is probable that Stokem knew Tinctoris at Liège, and that the latter's influence on his erstwhile pupil, Beatrice of Aragon, helped Stokem to gain his post with her husband, the king. About 1487–9 Stokem was a member of the pontifical chapel; he was still alive in 1501. However, it is not certain that he was the Johannes de Prato who was a cantor in Maximilian I's chapel in 1503, or the Johannes de Prato whom the chapter of St Donatian in Bruges tried in vain to engage as succentor in 1508.

The melodic charm of Stokem's chansons hides the contrapuntal skill of their composer. Both *Je suis d'Alemagne* and *Brunette* have a lyrical melody in one voice, surrounded in the former by rapidly-moving counterpoint, and in the latter by a double canon of great skill. *Ha! traitre amours*, although written in a style of pervading imitation, is nonetheless highly expressive. *Ave maris stella*, discovered by Seay in a collection of treatises, is a tour de force of technical skill in the use of proportions and coloration to provide complex rhythmic groupings.

WORKS
Edition: *O. Petrucci: Harmonice musices odhecaton A*, ed. H. Hewitt (Cambridge, Mass., 1942) [H]

Brunette, 4vv, H; Ha! traitre amours, 3vv, H (intabulated for lute/kbd in 1536¹³); Helas ce n'est pas, 4vv, H; J'ay pris mon bourdon, 4vv, 1504³; Je suis d'Alemagne, 4vv, ed. H. M. Brown, *Theatrical Chansons of the Fifteenth and Early Sixteenth Centuries* (Cambridge, Mass., 1962); Pourquoy je ne puis dire/Vray dieu d'amour, 4vv, 1503², H; Serviteur soye, 4vv, 1504³
Gloria, 4vv, 1505¹
Ave maris stella, 2vv, ed. in Seay

BIBLIOGRAPHY
E. Haraszti: 'Les musiciens de Mathias Corvin et de Béatrice d'Aragon', *La musique instrumentale de la renaissance: CNRS Paris 1954*, 35

J. Quitin: 'Les maîtres de chant de la cathédrale Saint-Lambert à Liège du 15e au 18e siècle', *RBM*, viii (1954), 5

A. Seay: 'An "Ave Maris Stella" by Johannes Stockem', *RBM*, xi (1957), 93

JOSÉ QUITIN

Stoke-on-Trent. English city, formed in 1925 by the federation of Tunstall, Burslem, Hanley, Stoke-upon-Trent, Fenton and Longton. It is the centre of an industrial region dominated by the coalmining and pottery industries (hence 'The Potteries'). Of all the larger English cities it has most extensively developed a distinctive culture from the aspirations and capabilities of its working class.

The choral societies of the area, with roots in the Methodist movement, have become justly famous. The establishment of Sunday school choirs led to the publication of *Salem's Lyre* (Burslem, 1830), a collection of hymns suitable for children. However, it was not until the introduction of Tonic Sol-fa that notable progress in choral singing was made. J. W. Powell, town clerk of Burslem, transcribed Mendelssohn's *Elijah* in sol-fa, and he proved the value of the system with the Burslem Tonic Solfa Choir, which he founded. In June 1884 the choir was awarded the first prize of £35 in a Tonic Solfa Festival held in the Crystal Palace, said to have been 'a striking testimony to the spread of music amongst the humbler members of the community' (*Musical World*). In 1891 the jubilee of the Solfa Association was celebrated with a festival in London, and the contingent from the Potteries taking part in the massed choir numbered 1000. Also active at this time were the Hanley Glee and Madrigal Society (founded 1882), conducted by James Garner, a working potter, and James Docksey's Burslem Choir.

The North Staffordshire District Choral Society was founded in 1901 by a disabled miner, James Whewall. The members of the chorus were experienced singers drawn from the many church and chapel choirs of the neighbourhood and from such bodies as the Hanley Male Voice Choir and the Longton Glee Union. The *Dream of Gerontius* was given its first London performance by the society in 1903, and six years later Beecham chose the choir to give the London première of Delius's *Sea Drift*. The monopoly enjoyed by the society (renamed the City of Stoke-on-Trent Choral Society after World War II) was challenged in the 1930s by Bertrand Rhead, a potter's merchant turned impresario, who founded a Ceramic City Choir, sometimes conducted by Sargent. During the Depression the Etruscan Singers (named after Etruria where the Wedgwood works were situated) was formed from unemployed pottery workers and miners by Harry Vincent (*d* 1957), a shoemaker and entirely self-taught musician; he also turned a disused mission hall in Etruria into a concert hall.

The first music festival in the area was given in the parish church in Stoke on 12 November 1833. The programme of the festival consisted largely of movements from Handel's oratorios and excerpts from works by Beethoven, Haydn, Paisiello, Grétry, Boyce, Kent and Callcott. But it was not until the Victoria Hall, Hanley, was opened in 1888 that adequate accommodation for large-scale musical performances was available. The first North Staffordshire Festival was held there in that year, conducted by Charles Swinnerton Heap, a Leipzig-trained musician. Its festival choir was a coalition of nine choirs and formed the basis for subsequent

festivals. In 1896 and 1899 respectively, first performances of *King Olaf* by Elgar, who had played in the 1888 festival orchestra, and Coleridge-Taylor's 'The Death of Minnehaha' (part of the *Hiawatha* trilogy) were conducted by their composers at the festival; in 1908 Delius was invited to conduct the second English performance of *Appalachia* in Hanley. In 1975 a Stoke-on-Trent competitive festival was re-established.

During the latter part of the 19th century the pottery firm of J. & G. Meakin supported music in many ways, most notably through the Meakin Concerts in the Victoria Hall; Paderewski gave a piano recital in 1895. Meakins also provided wind instruments for its workers to form a band. On 1 November 1905 the first concert of the amateur North Staffordshire Symphony Orchestra was given, conducted by John Cope, a local man who had studied in Munich with Rheinberger. Cope was one of the first to appreciate and to perform the instrumental works of Havergal Brian, born in the Potteries town of Dresden, whose career may be regarded as symbolic of the musical life of the region.

The Victoria Hall, Hanley, designed by a local surveyor, has fine acoustics particularly suited to the performance of large-scale works. The organ, built by Willis after the specification of S. H. Weale, the first city organist, was inaugurated on 4 May 1922.

At the end of the 19th century when nonconformist reservations about the use of the organ had been overcome, organ builders – notably Steele and Keay, Binns, Kirkland, and Jardine – were extremely active in the district. A basic musical education was available in almost every church and chapel. However, from the second half of the century the general musical interest of the people of the Potteries was reflected in the curriculum of the elementary schools. Stoke-on-Trent was one of the first cities to appoint a superintendent of music to be responsible for musical education in all its branches. A school of music was founded after World War II by John Harvey. The music department of Keele University, near Stoke-on-Trent (the first of the postwar universities), was the first in England to have a seminar in American musical studies.

BIBLIOGRAPHY

Stoke-upon-Trent Musical Festival Programme 1833 (Stoke, 1833)

Musical World, lxii (1884), 389

Musical Herald, 1 (1895), 13, 46, 78, 109, 143, 206, 239, 302, 333, 366

R. W. Ship: *History of the Hanley Glee and Madrigal Society* (Hanley, 1901)

——: *History of the North Staffordshire District Choral Society* (Hanley, 1910)

R. Nettel: *Music in the Five Towns* (London, 1944)

G. Thompson: 'Music in the Five Towns: a Postscript', *MT*, c (1959), 383

PERCY M. YOUNG

Stoker, Richard (*b* Castleford, Yorks., 8 Nov 1938). English composer. His early studies in composition were with Winifred Smith at the Huddersfield Music School. In 1958, on the advice of Benjamin, he went to the Royal Academy of Music to study with Berkeley. There he won the first Royal Amateur Orchestral Society Award with his overture *Antic Hay*, the first Eric Coates Memorial Prize for the *Petite suite*, and the Dove Prize. In 1962 he left the RAM as a Mendelssohn scholar and went to study with Nadia Boulanger in Paris. She was a key influence on his musical development and his dramatic cantata *Ecce homo*, written shortly before he returned to England, is dedicated to her. In 1963 he was appointed professor of composition at the RAM and since 1969 has been editor of *Composer*. Stoker's preference is for a serially orientated style maintaining a strict tonal centre. Besides composing he paints, and he has published a collection of poems.

WORKS
(selective list)

Johnson Preserv'd, op.30, opera, 1967; Thérèse Raquin, opera, 1975
Petite suite, op.1, orch, 1962; Antic Hay, ov., op.2, 1962; Little Symphony, op.23, 1969; Feast of Fools, ov., 1969
3 str qts: op.4, 1960; op.9, 1966; op.36, 1969; Wind Qnt, op.6, 1963; Sextet, op.16, cl, bn, hn, str trio, 1965; Ob Qt, op.40, 1970
Many other chamber pieces, choral works, educational music

Principal publishers: Ashdown, Boosey & Hawkes, Breitkopf & Härtel, Chappell, Leeds, Peters

BIBLIOGRAPHY

E. Brophy: 'Richard Stoker's Dr Johnson Opera', *Opera*, xviii (1967), 543
R. Townend: 'Richard Stoker', *MT*, cx (1968), 424
J. Knight: 'Richard Stoker's Modern Music for Dance', *Dancing Times*, lx (1970), 431
C. Norris: 'Richard Stoker', *Music and Musicians*, xxiv/1 (1975), 16
B. Schlotel: 'Richard Stoker's Music for Young People', *Music Teacher*, liv/2 (1975), 9

RICHARD TOWNEND

Stokhem, Johannes de. *See* STOKEM, JOHANNES DE.

Stokowski, Leopold (Anthony) [Antoni Stanisław Bolesławowich] (*b* London, 18 April 1882; *d* Nether Wallop, Hants., 13 Sept 1977). American conductor of British birth, and Polish and Irish parentage. He began learning the violin, piano and organ from early childhood and at 13 became the youngest student by then admitted to the RCM, where he studied with Parry, Stanford and Walford Davies, and gained the FRCO diploma in 1900. In 1902 he was appointed organist and choirmaster at St James's, Piccadilly, and the next year took the BMus at Queen's College, Oxford. He went to the USA in 1905 as organist of St Bartholomew's, New York, but returned to continue summer studies in Berlin, Munich and Paris. He made his conducting début at Paris in 1908 when another conductor fell ill, and his London début in 1909 (with the New SO).

Representatives of the Cincinnati SO, which needed a new conductor, chanced to hear Stokowski's Paris concert and recommended him. His initial success at Cincinnati from 1909 led in 1912 to the start of a 25-year appointment at Philadelphia that brought him and its orchestra international fame, and revolutionized the American musical scene. Stokowski took American citizenship in 1915, and achieved unprecedented popularity for himself and the music he conducted through the force of his personality and the elegance of his image. Abandoning the use of a baton from 1929, he improved the technical standards and tonal qualities of performance, the 'Philadelphia sound' being the sobriquet applied to his concern for a wider dynamic range and different perspectives of ensemble; and he continually extended the boundaries of his audience's experience by his enthusiasm for contemporary music. It was calculated in 1971 that Stokowski had by then conducted over 2000 first performances in about 7000 concerts. Most of the new works were by American composers, major and minor. The premières included three of Rakhmaninov's works (Symphony no.3, Piano Concerto no.4, *Rhapsody on a Theme of Paganini*), several by Varèse, Ives's Fourth Symphony, and the introduction to the USA of Stravinsky's *The Rite of*

Leopold Stokowski

Spring (both in concert and ballet form), Mahler's Eighth Symphony, Berg's *Wozzeck*, and the orchestral music of Schoenberg (including his *Gurrelieder*). Stokowski took early advantage of radio and gramophone, making his first record with the Philadelphians in 1917 and going on to create one of the century's richest legacies of recorded music. He also involved himself in several films, notably a collaboration with Walt Disney in *Fantasia* (1941), an experiment in sound and vision unique in its time, artistically flawed, but which remains a favourite with children.

After two seasons (1936–8) of joint conductorship at Philadelphia with his successor, Eugene Ormandy, Stokowski left to continue an independent career. He formed other orchestras: the All-American Youth Orchestra (1940; he had pioneered youth concerts at Philadelphia from 1933); the New York SO (1944); the Hollywood Bowl SO (1945) and, after five seasons as principal conductor of the Houston SO (1955–60), the American SO (1961). In 1951 he began a new series of European guest tours that included his first London concerts since 1912, and in 1972, at the age of 90, he twice repeated the identical programme he had conducted with the LSO 60 years earlier (thereby providing the basis for one more record album). He continued concert appearances until July 1975 (Vence Festival, France) and recording work until 1977. His last London concert was at the Albert Hall on 14 May 1974.

Stokowski became a controversial figure through his orchestral transcriptions of works by Bach and others, and his persistently revised instrumentations of established classics from Beethoven and Brahms to Wagner and Puccini (whose *Turandot* was the only opera he conducted at the Metropolitan). Such editorial activities earned him the antagonism of many scholars, but although he was apt to prefer his own spirit to the composer's letter, that spirit often became a force to be reckoned with on its own terms. He constantly sought improved tonal quality through unconventional orchestral platform arrangement (*see* ORCHESTRA, fig.11), and his research into acoustics and electronics, in the USA, Germany and the Netherlands, has been used to improve techniques of recording and radio transmission. His interests extended at various times to Asian musical languages, medical research and farming; his musical achievement, both live and recorded, was often wilfully unorthodox, sometimes astonishing, and never less than stimulating.

Stokowski married the pianist and critic Olga Samaroff in 1911, Evangeline Brewster Johnson in 1926 and Gloria Vanderbilt di Cicco in 1945.

WRITINGS
Music for All of Us (New York, 1943)

BIBLIOGRAPHY
H. C. Schonberg: *The Great Conductors* (New York, 1967)

H. Kupferberg: *Those Fabulous Philadelphians* (New York, 1969)

D. Wooldridge: *Conductor's World* (London, 1970)

E. Johnson: 'Stokowski Looks Back', *Music and Musicians*, xix/11 (1971), 22

E. Johnson, ed.: *Stokowski: Essays in Analysis of his Art* (London, 1973) [with discography by I. Lund and lists of works and arrangements]

A. Hodgson: 'The Stokowski Sound', *Records and Recording*, xx/8 (1977), 16

A. Chasins: *Leopold Stokowski: a Profile* (New York, 1979)

NOËL GOODWIN

Štolcer [Štolcer-Slavenski], **Josip.** *See* SLAVENSKI, JOSIP.

Stolczer, Thomas. *See* STOLTZER, THOMAS.

Stolle, der junge. German poet; *see* SPERVOGEL, (3).

Stolle, Johann (*b* Calbe an der Saale, *c*1566; *d* Weimar, 25 Oct 1614). German composer, music copyist and poet. It was apparently because of the early loss of his parents that he attended the grammar school at Zwickau, where he was a pupil of Cornelius Freundt. Although he did not complete his university studies he was appointed Kantor at nearby Reichenbach in 1590 and succeeded Freundt at Zwickau in 1591. From 1604 until his death he was Kapellmeister to the Weimar court, in succession to Johannes Herold and as the predecessor of Schein. His output as a composer, which is not extensive, consists most notably of occasional sacred works and also of liturgical music – a Latin mass, Latin motets and German hymns. He had a penchant for chord sonorities: several of his more important works are scored for double choir, totalling eight parts, while his motet *Laetare cum uxore*, composed for the marriage of the Elector Johann Georg of Saxony and Magdalena Sibylle of Brandenburg in 1607, is in 18 parts and three independent choral groups and is his most ambitious work. He is most important, however, for three manuscript collections (in *D-Z*) that he compiled at Zwickau, mostly in his own hand; they contain a valuable and interesting repertory of liturgical music drawn from the period of Lassus, Jacob Handl and Hans Leo Hassler. Several poetic works by Stolle have also survived.

WORKS
(MSS in D-Z unless otherwise stated)

Surge propera, wedding song for Christoph Seling, double choir 8vv (Leipzig, 1596)

Von Gott ist mir, wedding song for Elector Johann Georg of Saxony, double choir 8vv (Leipzig, 1596)

Miserere mei, Domine, 4vv; Herr Jesu Christ, mein Herr und Gott, double choir 8vv; Buss wirk in mir, 4vv: funeral songs for Johann of Saxony (Jena, 1606)

Lux mea beata, wedding song for Jeremias Röller, 6vv (Jena, 1606)

Si mihi quae debes, wedding song for Paul Wolf, double choir 8vv (Jena, 1608)

In aller meiner Angst und Not, funeral song for Countess Johanna of Saxony, 5vv (Jena, 1609)

Ego dormio, wedding song for Eusebius Bohemus, 6vv (Jena, 1614)

Christus ist erstanden von des Todes Banden, hymn (Dresden, 1632)

Missa 'Vespere autem Sabbati', 6vv (on Ruffo's motet)

Laetare cum uxore, wedding song for Elector Johann Georg of Saxony, triple choir 18vv, 1607, *D-Dlb*

Cantate Domino, double choir 8vv, *D-Kl*; Da Christus geboren war, 4vv; Deus meus in adjutorium meum, 6vv; Deus patrum meorum, double choir 8vv; Heut ist unser Heiland, 3vv, ed. in *Handbuch der deutschen evangelischen Kirchenmusik*, i (Göttingen, 1935), 212; Jesus flevit super Jerusalem, 5vv; O regem coeli, 6vv; Scriptum est in lege, 5vv; Von einer Jungfrau auserkorn, 4vv; Zion die werte Gottesstadt, 5vv

For full list, incl. inc. and lost works, see Müsel

BIBLIOGRAPHY
A. Aber: *Die Pflege der Musik unter den Wettinern und wettinischen Ernestinern: von den Anfängen bis zur Auflösung der Weimarer Hofkapelle 1662* (Leipzig, 1921)

W. Reich: *Threnodiae sacrae: Katalog der gedruckten Kompositionen des 16.–18. Jahrhunderts in Leichenpredigtsammlungen innerhalb der Deutschen Demokratischen Republik* (Dresden, 1966)

A. Müsel: *Kantor Johann Stolle (um 1566 bis 1614): Leben und Schaffen* (Cologne and Vienna, 1970)

WALTER BLANKENBURG

Stolle, Philipp (*b* Radeburg, Saxony, 1614; *d* Halle, 4 Oct 1675). German composer. In 1631 he was at the Dresden court as a discant singer and theorbo player; he had studied the theorbo under Kaspar Kittel. Ten years later Schütz supported him in these positions and also as a violinist, player of other string instruments and teacher of the choirboys. Meanwhile, in 1634 he was in Denmark in the service of Prince Christian; he probably had accompanied Schütz there, and he certainly did so for a further period of service in 1642. In 1650 he sang in Schütz's ballet *Paris und Helena* and moved to the court chapel in Halle, where four years later he succeeded Scheidt as director. Duke August had made Halle a centre of opera, to which Stolle was immediately drawn. He wrote a number of operas, all but one now lost; in 1660 he gave up his position as Kapellmeister to devote himself entirely to opera but remained, next to the new director David Pohle, the highest-paid musician at court.

Stolle's importance lies in his contributions to early German opera and in his songs. The one surviving opera definitely attributable to him, *Charimunda*, is a Singspiel with strophic songs and choruses. His songs appear in a collection by David Schirmer: that the most important poet in Dresden at the time chose Stolle to set 68 strophic lieder for soprano and basso continuo is a measure of the great esteem in which he held him. The songs are similar to Adam Krieger's rather than to those of the Hamburg school by composers such as Rist in that the music treats the text fairly freely; their popularity is attested in Schoch's *Comoedia vom Studenten-Leben* (Dresden, 1657).

WORKS
David Schirmers Singende Rosen oder Liebes- und Tugendlieder, S, bc (theorbo/va da gamba) (Dresden, 1654)

Neu-anmuthiges Schau-Spiel, genahmt Charimunda oder Beneideter Liebes-Sieg (Halle, 1658)

BIBLIOGRAPHY
H. Kretzschmar: *Geschichte des neuen deutschen Liedes* (Leipzig, 1911/R1966)

F. Bose: 'Stolle, Philipp', *MGG*

JOHN H. BARON

Stoll Theatre. London theatre built in 1911 and known as the London Opera House until 1916; *see* LONDON, §IV, 3.

Stolpe, Antoni (*b* Puławy, nr. Lublin, 23 May 1851; *d* Merano, 7 Sept 1872). Polish composer and pianist. He first studied the piano with his father, Edward Stolpe (1812–72), then composition with Freyer and Moniuszko at the Warsaw Music Institute, where he graduated in 1867 with first prize. After three concerts of his own compositions (1868–9) he went to Berlin, where he studied composition with Kiel and the piano with Kullak. He then taught the piano at the Stern Conservatory in Berlin. Ill-health forced him to resign his teaching post, and he lived for a short time in Salzbrunn and Merano. Highly talented, both as a pianist and as a composer, he died at the age of 21, leaving a fair number of compositions in manuscript.

WORKS
(selective list; MSS in PL-Kj)

Orch: Sym., a, 1867; Sym. Ov., 1868; Concert Ov., 1869; Pf Conc., 1869

Inst: 2 str qts, 1866, 1869; Pf Sextet, 1867; Pf Sonata, a, 1867; Str Qnt, 1868; Caprice-étude de concert, pf, 1869; Pf Trio, 1869; Pf Sonata, d, 1870; Variations, d, pf, 1870; Sonata, vn, pf, 1872; Variations, str qt, 1872

Vocal: Credo, mixed vv, org, str qnt, 1867; songs with pf acc.

BIBLIOGRAPHY
S. Golachowski: 'Antoni Stolpe: szkic biograficzny' [A biographical sketch of Stolpe], *Muzyka polska* (1935), no.7

T. Bronowicz: *Twórczość fortepianowa Antoniego Stolpego* [The piano works of Stolpe] (MS, *PL-Kj*, 1953)

BOGUSŁAW SCHÄFFER

Stoltz, Rosine [Noël, Victoire] (*b* Paris, 13 Feb 1815; *d* Paris, 28 July 1903). French mezzo-soprano. After appearances as a concert singer under the name of Rose Niva, in 1832 she made her stage début, as Victoire Ternaux, at the Théâtre de la Monnaie, Brussels, singing small parts and in the chorus. She then sang at Spa, Antwerp, Amsterdam and Lille, before returning to Brussels, now calling herself Heloise Stoltz. At La Monnaie she sang Alice in *Robert le diable* (1835) and Rachel in *La juive* (1836). She married the theatre's director, Alphonse Lescuyer, in 1837, and as Rosine Stoltz she made her début that year at the Paris Opéra in *La juive*. During the ten years that she was engaged at the Opéra she sang in the first performances of four works by Halévy: *Guido et Ginevra* (1838), *La reine de Chypre* (1841), *Charles VI* (1843) and *Le lazzarone* (1844). She created Ascanio in Berlioz's *Benvenuto Cellini* (3 September 1838), Marguerite in Auber's *Le lac des fées* (1 April 1839), Léonore in Donizetti's *La favorite* (2 December 1840) and Zaida in the same composer's *Dom Sébastien* (13 November 1843). Her other roles included Donna Anna, Valentine in *Les Huguenots*, Desdemona in Rossini's *Otello* and Isolier in *Le comte Ory*.

On 30 December 1846, while Stoltz was singing in Niedermayer's Rossini pasticcio, *Robert Bruce*, there were hostile demonstrations against her; she was already unpopular because of the influence she wielded as the mistress of Léon Pillet, director of the Opéra, and in 1847 both she and Pillet were forced to resign. During the next few years she toured the French provinces and sang in Lisbon, Vienna and Turin. She also made several artistically and financially successful tours of Brazil at the Emperor's invitation. She eventually returned to the Paris Opéra in 1854 and 1855, and sang Léonore again, as well as Fidès in *Le prophète*. Her last stage appearances were at Lyons in 1860, though she continued to sing in concert for several years. In 1865 her current protector, Ernst II of Württemberg, made her Baroness Stoltzenau and Countess of Ketschendorf. A few years later she became the Duchess of Lesignana, and in 1878 she married a Spanish prince, Manuel Godoi Bassano de la Paix.

Despite the flamboyance of her private life, Stoltz was

Rosine Stoltz as Léonore in Donizetti's 'La favorite': engraving by Charles Geoffroy

a serious and genuinely talented interpretative artist, with a fine voice and a magnificent stage presence. Berlioz praised her performance in *Benvenuto Cellini* and also admired her in *La favorite*. Even in his version of *Der Freischütz*, where he had to transpose much of Agathe's music down for her, he commended the energy and excitement of her singing.

BIBLIOGRAPHY
H. Berlioz: *Mémoires* (Paris, 1870; Eng. trans., 1969)

G. Bord: *Rosina Stoltz de l'Académie royale de musique* (Paris, 1909)

J.-G. Prod'homme: *L'Opéra (1669–1925)* (Paris, 1925)

H. Weinstock: *Donizetti and the World of Opera in Italy, Paris and Vienna in the First Half of the 19th Century* (New York, 1963)

ELIZABETH FORBES

Stöltzel, Gottfried Heinrich. *See* STÖLZEL, GOTTFRIED HEINRICH.

Stoltzenberg [Stolzenberg, Stolzenberger], **Christoph** (*b* Wertheim, 21 Feb 1690; *d* Regensburg, 11 June 1764). German composer. His parents died soon after he was born and he grew up among friends, brothers and sisters. He began his musical training with singing lessons under the Kantors of Wertheim. He was a pupil at the Heiliggeistschule in Nuremberg, 1701–3, then moved to Worms, and, in 1706–8, lived in Frankfurt am Main, where he attended the Gymnasium. After returning to Nuremberg in 1708 he travelled extensively through Bohemia and Saxony to Hamburg and Harburg, where he spent a year; from there he went through Lüneburg to Lower Lusatia, through Dresden to Bohemia and Moravia, and finally through Bavaria to Salzburg. He was unsuccessful in his attempt to complete his musical studies in Italy. After some time in Regensburg and Altdorf (where he toyed with the idea of studying theology), he returned to Nuremberg, where he received instruction in composition from the Kantor of the Heiliggeistkirche, Nikolaus Deinl, and played in the collegia musica (keyboard, flute, horn and string instruments). In 1711 he became Kantor in Sulzbach near Amberg and in 1714 he was appointed temporary tutor and Kantor at the Gymnasium Poeticum in Regensburg. After 50 years in office he was presented with a Festschrift and a cantata in his honour, set to music by his son, Ehrenreich Carl (1721–85).

Stoltzenberg's works (according to his autobiography, published by Mattheson) include a complete cycle of cantatas for the church year, written during his time in Sulzbach; each work in this cycle 'begins with a biblical text (usually in fugue), continues with several arias, and concludes with a chorale'. He later composed other annual cycles, in which recitatives were used. Stoltzenberg was also noted as a composer of occasional pieces.

WORKS

Sacred cantata cycles and occasional pieces, texts only extant (all pubd in Regensburg), see Scharnagl
20 sacred cantatas, *D-B, Bds, Rp*, incl. Kommt her zu mir alle, ed. E. Kraus (Regensburg, 1973)
113 chorales, pubd according to Mettenleiter, lost
Numerous other Latin and German sacred works, other occasional pieces incl. music for school dramas, concertos with tpts, timp, some with hns: all lost

BIBLIOGRAPHY

EitnerQ
J. Mattheson: *Grundlage einer Ehren-Pforte* (Hamburg, 1740); ed. M. Schneider (Berlin, 1910/R1969), 51, 348ff, appx, 37ff
D. Mettenleiter: *Musikgeschichte der Stadt Regensburg* (Regensburg, 1866), 206ff, 217, 224ff, 251
——: *Musikgeschichte der Oberpfalz* (Amberg, 1867), 100, 195
R. Wagner: 'Beiträge zur Lebensgeschichte Johann Philipp Kriegers und seines Schülers Nikolaus Deinl', *ZMw*, viii (1925–6), 159
A. Scharnagl: 'Stoltzenberg, Christoph', *MGG*
H. Kümmerling: *Katalog der Sammlung Bokemeyer* (Kassel, 1970), 128, 259

GÜNTER THOMAS

Stoltzer [Stolczer, Scholczer], **Thomas** (*b* Schweidnitz, Silesia, *c*1480–85; *d* nr. Znaim, Moravia, early 1526). German composer. After Heinrich Finck and Paul Hofhaimer he was the most important German composer of the early 16th century. He probably belonged to the same family as Clemens Stoltzer, a town clerk of Schweidnitz. He may have been Heinrich Finck's pupil; certainly he studied Finck's works, as his frequent musical quotations show. From 1519 he was a priest in Breslau holding a benefice at St Elisabeth's, and was *vicarius discontinuus* at the cathedral. Although his later works show that he supported the Reformation he did not do so openly for fear of his livelihood (contemporary letters show him to have been timid and easily influenced).

On 8 May 1522 Ludwig II appointed him *magister capellae* at the Hungarian royal court in Ofen on the recommendation of his wife Mary, daughter of Philip the Fair. His motet, *Beati omnes*, had probably been performed at their wedding on 13 January 1522 in Buda. At her request he set Luther's translations of the four great psalms (Psalms xii, xiii, xxxvii and lxxxvi) between 1524 and 1526. With the Hungarian court chapel at his disposal he was able to produce more demanding works; his late compositions show how he exploited these resources. In the only extant personal document of Stoltzer's, a letter (now in *D-Ga*) dated

23 February 1526 to Duke Albrecht of Prussia in Königsberg, he described his recently completed *Erzürne dich nicht über die Bösen* (Psalm xxxvii) which, he said, he 'composed in a particular way like a motet'. He also hinted that he would like to enter the service of Albrecht, whom he knew personally from the duke's visits to the Hungarian court. An observation dated March 1526 on the original letter refers to 'the late Thomas'. Earlier speculation that Stoltzer died with Ludwig in the battle of Mohács, 29 August 1526, is incorrect, for an elegy by his former colleague at the court chapel, Lang, on the death of Casparus Velius, states that Stoltzer was drowned in the Taja.

There are some 150 works by Stoltzer in 30 publications and 60 manuscripts. Since all of them date from after 1530 he presumably did not begin composing before about 1510. His works were most popular in what is now Saxony, at the centre of the Reformation. The Wittenberg music publisher Georg Rhau printed no fewer than 70 of his compositions. His works were known, however, throughout central Europe, at least wherever German was spoken. Many were still being passed on more than 40 years after his death, since his German psalm motets were almost unsurpassable models for German motets based on biblical texts. The circulation of his manuscripts continued until the end of the 16th century. By that time cantus firmus compositions like Stoltzer's were old-fashioned and the new Italian style was gradually penetrating into Germany.

Stoltzer composed in all the forms of the day: mass, motet, hymn and partsong, although he did not give all genres the same attention, concentrating principally on the motet. In Breslau he composed mainly liturgical works, such as motets for the Proper of the Mass, responsories, antiphons and hymns. Works of his later period at the Hungarian court tend to be more in the form of Latin and German psalm motets or sacred songs. There are also a few secular pieces composed specifically for the court. Most works can be dated only approximately. His group of *Octo tonorum melodiae*, eight five-part instrumental fantasias arranged according to the ecclesiastical modes and connected by common motifs, is almost certainly the first cycle of motet-style compositions intended for instruments, and is probably one of his late works.

The four masses (without Credos) are composed on a chorale and some sections are intended for *alternatim* performance, common in Germany at that time. The chorale melody is lightly embellished and often moves from voice to voice, but always fits in smoothly with the flow of the composition. The existence of 14 introits for the Christmas to Easter period suggests that he may have intended to write a complete cycle for the ecclesiastical year.

Two distinct styles can be seen in his motet compositions. His earlier pieces show Finck's influence and are old-fashioned in their use of cantus firmus and mensural proportions; *Inter natos mulierum* contains extremely complicated proportion changes which could have been familiar to few 16th-century performers. A Kyrie printed in 1522 by Gregor Faber in his *Musices practicae erotematum* is similarly constructed. In his later works on the other hand characteristics of the late Netherlands school are to be found, such as imitation and the use of contrasted choirs. The antiphon *Anima mea liquefacta est* obviously belongs to this period together with *O admirabile commercium*, which thanks to its sensitive treatment of text was so popular that it exists in 11 sources.

39 hymns by Stoltzer were printed in Rhau's *Sacrorum hymnorum liber primus* (1542). Two more processional hymns, *Gloria, laus et honor* and *Salve festa dies*, are in manuscript. This genre reveals various techniques and ranges from archaic pieces with a tenor cantus firmus in long notes to flexible imitative motet-like settings. His four sacred songs to German texts, no doubt intended as an expression of his Lutheran sympathies, are through-composed. The ten lieder are cantus firmus pieces predominantly based on love lyrics and court songs. *König, ein Herr ob alle Reich* with its acrostic 'König Ludwig' and 'Maria' is dedicated to the Hungarian royal couple.

Stoltzer's greatest compositions were his 14 Latin and four German psalm motets. He liked setting psalms, preferring those written in the first person. Their expression of personal involvement together with a wealth of imagery and ideas could not but have inspired the composer of the Renaissance. The cantus firmus plays a subordinate role and the music for the most part depicts and interprets the text. His mastery is most clearly revealed in the four German motets with five to seven parts, based on Luther's translation of the psalter: *Hilf, Herr, die Heiligen haben abgenommen, Herr, wie lang, Erzürne dich nicht über die Bösen* and *Herr, neige deine Ohren*. They are among the first large-scale religious compositions in the vernacular, successfully uniting traditional German features with the late Netherlands style of Josquin Desprez.

WORKS
(principal sources only)

Editions: *Newe deudsche geistliche Gesenge (1544)*, ed. J. Wolf, DDT, xxxiv (Leipzig, 1908/*R*) [W]

Das deutsche Gesellschaftslied in Österreich von 1480–1550, ed. L. Nowak, DTÖ, lxxii, Jg.xxxvii/2 (1930/*R*) [N]

T. Stoltzer: Sämtliche lateinische Hymnen und Psalmen, ed. H. Albrecht and O. Gombosi, DDT, lxv (1931/*R*) [G]

T. Stoltzer: Ausgewählte Werke, I–II, ed. H. Albrecht and L. Hoffmann-Erbrecht, EDM, xxii (1942/*R*), lxvi (1969) [A i–ii]

G. Forster: Frische teutsche Liedlein (1539–1556), I, ed. K. Gudewill, EDM, xx (1942/*R*) [Gu]

G. Rhau: Sacrorum hymnorum liber primus, I–II, ed. R. Gerber, EDM, xxi, xxv (1942–3/*R*) [Ge]

G. Rhau: Vesperarum precum officia, ed. H. J. Moser, Musikdrucke aus den Jahren 1538 bis 1545 in praktischer Neuausgabe, iv (Kassel, 1960) [M]

MASSES AND MAGNIFICAT SETTINGS
Missa duplex per totum annum (Ky, Gl, San, Ag), 4vv, A i, 1; Missa 'Kyrie angelicum' (Ky, Gl), 4vv, A i, 17; Missa 'Kyrie summum' (Ky, Gl, San, Ag), 4vv, A i, 9; Missa paschalis (Ky, Gl, San), 4vv, ed. in Cw, lxxiv (1958)

Magnificat [2nd or 8th tone], 4vv, *H-BA* 23 (bass only); Magnificat [4th tone], 4vv, *BA* 23 (bass only); Magnificat [6th tone], 4vv, *BA* 23 (bass only); Magnificat [6th tone], 5vv, *D-LEu* Thomaskirche 49/50; Magnificat [6th tone], 5vv, *H-BA* 22 (tenor only)

INTROITS, SEQUENCES, RESPONSORIES, ETC
Accessit ad pedes Jesu peccatrix, 4vv, A i, 31; Agnus redemit oves, 5vv, *BA* 23 (bass only); Benedicamus patrem, 5vv, A i, 43; Circumdederunt me gemitus mortis, 4vv, 1549[16], *D-LEu* Thomaskirche 49/50; Dies est laetitiae, 4vv, *H-BA* 23 (bass only); Discubuit Jesus, 4vv, *D-Z* 81,2, inc.; Domine ne longe facias auxilium, 4vv, *LEu* Thomaskirche 49/50; Ecce advenit dominator, 4vv, 1545[5]; Ecce concipies et paries, 4vv, *Z* 100,4 (tenor only); Ecclesiam vestris doctrinis, 4vv, *H-BA* 22 (tenor only); Esto mihi in Deum protectorem, 4vv, *LEu* Thomaskirche 49/50; Euge Dei porta, 4vv, *Z* 81,2, inc.; Exsurge quare abdormis, 4vv, *LEu* Thomaskirche 49/50

Gaude Maria, 4vv, A i, 34; Homo quidam fecit, ?4vv, *Z* 81,2, inc.; Illius nomen omnis haereticus, 4vv, *H-BA* 22 (tenor only); Ingressus Pilatus, 4vv, A i, 26; Inter natos mulierum, 4vv, *D-LEu* Thomaskirche 49/50; Invocavit me, 4vv, 1545[6], *LEu* Thomaskirche 49/50; Jube Domine benedicere, 4vv, *Z* 81,2, inc.; Judica me Deus, 4vv, 1549[16], *LEu* Thomaskirche 49/50; Laetare Hierusalem et con-

ventum, 4vv, *LEu* Thomaskirche 49/50; Laudemus et super exaltemus, 4vv, M 30; Liber Generationis ex contrapuncto, 4vv, Legnica, Bibliotheca Rudolphina 4901–8 (olim 18), lost

Mihi autem nimis, 5vv, *H-BA* 22, inc.; Misereris omnium, Domine, 4vv, 1545[6], *D-LEu* Thomaskirche 49/50; Non est bonum hominem, 4vv, *H-BA* 23 (bass only); Oculi mei semper ad Dominum, 4vv, 1549[16], *D-LEu* Thomaskirche 49/50; Puer natus est nobis, 4vv, 1545[5]; Reminiscere miserationum, inc., 4vv, *Dlb* Chorbuch Pirna VI; Requiem aeternam, 4vv, *LEu* Thomaskirche 49/50; Resurrexi . . . Domine probasti me, 4vv, *LEu* Thomaskirche 49/50; Resurrexi . . . Domine tu cognovisti, 4vv, 1539[14]; Rorate coeli, 4vv, *Dlb* Chorbuch Pirna VI; Scio cui credidi, 4vv, *LEu* Thomaskirche 49/50; Stabat mater dolorosa, 4vv, *H-BA* 22 (tenor only); Super salutem et omnem pulchritudinem, 5vv, A i, 48; Te namque profitemur, 4vv, *BA* 22 (tenor only); Verbum caro factum est, 5vv, A i, 54; Viri Galilei, 4vv, 1539[14]

ANTIPHONS
Angelus autem Domini, 4vv, *D-Z* 81,2, inc.; Anima mea liquefacta est, 4vv, A i, 22; Assumpta est Maria, 4vv, *Z* 81,2, inc.; Christi virgo dilectissima, 5vv, *Z* 73; Dum complerentur dies, 4vv, *Z* 81,2, inc.; Ecce completa sunt omnia, 5vv, *H-BA* 23 (bass only); Judea et Hierusalem nolite, 4vv, *D-Z* 81,2, inc.; O admirabile commercium, 5vv, A i, 63; O beata infantia, 4vv, *Z* 81,2, inc.; O beatum virum cuius anima, 5vv, *H-BA* 22, inc.; O praeclara stella Maria, 4vv, *D-Z* 81,2, inc.; Pater manifestavi, 4vv, *Dlb* Mus.1/D/2 (olim B 1272); Sacerdos in aeternum Christus Dominus, 4vv, *Z* 81,2, inc.; Tecum principium in die, 4vv, *Z* 81,2, inc.; Vespere autem sabbati, 4vv, *H-BA* Imp.VI

HYMNS
Alvus tumescit virgines, 5vv, G 3, Ge no.5; Anna regum progenies, 4vv, G 28, Ge no.86; Ave maris stella, 4vv, G 8, Ge no.25; Beata quoque agmina, 4vv, G 35, Ge no.102; Beata quoque agmina, 5vv, G 37, Ge no.103; Beatus auctor saeculi, 4vv, G 4, Ge no.7; Christe qui lux es, 4vv, G 7, Ge no.17; Clamat anus, 4vv, G 25, Ge no.81; Conditor alme siderum, 4vv, G 1, Ge no.1; Confestim montes adiit, 4vv, G 26, Ge no.82; Conscendit iubilans, 4vv, G 11, Ge no.49; Cui luna sol et omnia, 4vv, G 33, Ge no.93; Foeno iacere pertulit, 4vv, G 5, Ge no.8

Genus superni luminis, 4vv, G 9, Ge no.27; Gloria, laus et honor, 5vv, G 52; Gloria, laus et honor, 4vv, *H-BA* 22 (tenor only); Haec Deum coeli, 4vv, G 6, Ge no.13; Hoc in templo, 4vv, G 49, Ge no.130; In cuius nunc praeconia, 5vv, G 42, Ge no.108; In supremae nocte caenae, 4vv, G 18, Ge no.64; Janitor coeli, 4vv, G 23, Ge no.80; Jesus Christus nostra salus, 4vv, G 22, Ge no.71; Nobis natus, nobis datus, 4vv, G 16, Ge no.63; Nobis natus, nobis datus, 5vv, G 20, Ge no.69; Non ex virili semine, 4vv, G 2, Ge no.4

Oramus Domine, 4vv, G 12, Ge no.50; Primum virtutes igneae, 4vv, G 39, Ge no.104; Quae virgo peperit, 4vv, G 34, Ge no.97; Quarta et sexta feria, 4vv, G 45, Ge no.112; Quem terra pontus, 4vv, G 32, Ge no.92; Qui pace Christi, 4vv, G 40, Ge no.106; Qui paracletus diceris, 4vv, G 13, Ge no.53; Qui pius prudens, 4vv, G 47, Ge no.124; Qui vagitus infantiae, 4vv, G 44, Ge no.111; Quo Christus invictus leo, 4vv, G 10, Ge no.44; Quo Christus invictus leo, *BA* 23 (bass only); Quocunque pergis, 4vv, G 48, Ge no.127

Salve festa dies, *D-Dlb* Chorbuch Pirna VI; Sprevit hic mundi, 4vv, G 29, Ge no.89; Te mane laudum carmine, 4vv, G 15, Ge no.59, M 29; Trinitas sancta, 4vv, G 51, Ge no.134; Tu cum virgineo, 5vv, G 30, Ge no.91; Vos saecli iusti iudices, 4vv, G 46, Ge no.115

PSALMS
Fauxbourdon: Beatus vir qui timet Dominum, 4vv, M 53; Confitemini Domino, 4vv, M 142; Dilexi quoniam exaudies, 4vv, M 89; In exitu Israel, 4vv, M 58; Levavi oculos meos, 4vv, M 98

Psalm motets: Beati omnes, qui timent Dominum, 5vv, A ii, 97, G 119; Beatus vir, qui non abiit, 4vv, A ii, 6, G 64; Benedicam Dominum in omni tempore, 5vv, A ii, 26, G 78; Cum invocarem, 4vv, A ii, 14, G 70; Deus misereatur nostri, 5vv, A ii, 50, G 95; In convertendo Dominus, 5vv, A ii, 82, G 108; In Domino confido, 3vv, A ii, 22, G 75; Laetatus sum, 4vv, A ii, 77, G 104; Laudate Dominum, 4vv, A ii, 57, G 101; Laudate Dominum, 4vv, A ii, 61, G 130; Levavi oculos meos, 5vv, A ii, 68; Nisi tu Domine, 5vv, A ii, 90, G 114; Omnes gentes plaudite, 5vv, A ii, 40, G 88; Saepe expugnaverunt me, 5vv, A ii, 104, G 125

Erzürne dich nicht, 6vv, A ii, 128; Herr, neige deine Ohren, 6vv, A ii, 156; Herr, wie lang willst du mein so gar vergessen, 5vv, A ii, 121, W 110; Hilf, Herr, die Heiligen haben abgenommen, 6vv, A ii, 110

LIEDER
Sacred: In Gottes Namen fahren wir, 4vv, W 140; König, ein Herr ob alle Reich, 4vv, ed. R. Eitner: *Ein hundert fünfzehn weltliche und einige geistliche Lieder, II*, PÄMw, ii (1875), 178; O Gott, Vater, du hast Gewalt, 4vv, W 152; Unser grosse Sünde und schwere Missetat, 4vv, W 14

Secular: Die Welt, die hat ein tummen Mut, 5vv, N 66; Entlaubet ist der Walde, 4vv, N 67, Gu 85; Erst wird erfreut mein traurigs Herz, 4vv, N 68, Gu 102; Es dringt doher, 4vv, N 68, Gu 9; Es müht viel Leut, 4vv, N 69, Gu 109; Heimlich bin ich in Treuen dein, 4vv, N 70; Ich klag den Tag, 4vv, N 71, Gu 46; Ich stund an einem Morgen, 2vv, N 71; Ich wünsch alln Frauen ehr, 4vv, N 72; Ihrsgleichen lebt auf Erden nicht, 4vv, N 73, Gu 90

INSTRUMENTAL

Octo tonorum melodiae, a 5, A i, 67

DOUBTFUL WORKS

Beatus vir, qui non abiit, 4vv, A ii, 1, G 60
Deus pacis reduxit a mortuis, 4vv, ed. A. Smijers: *Josquin Desprez: Motetten*, Werken, iii/14, fasc.xxxviii (Amsterdam, 1954), 116 (Josquin), attrib. Stoltzer in *D-Z* 81,2, anon. in *H-BA* Imp.VI
En deitatis Sabulon, 4vv, A i, 65
Kyrie eleison, 3vv, in G. Faber: Musices praticae eromatum libri secundi (Basle, 1553)
Nesciens mater, ?7vv, *DK-Kk* Gl.k.saml.1872 Nr.122
[Textless composition], 3vv, in G. Faber: Musices praticae eromatum libri secundi (Basle, 1553)
Christ ist erstanden, 4vv, W 26 (Stoltzer), HAM i, 122 (Stoltzer), attrib. Isaac in *A-Wn* Mus.18810, *CH-Bu* F.X.1–4
Heut triumphiret Gottes Sohn, 6vv, attrib. 'T.S.' in Legnica, Bibliotheca Rudolphina 5006–10 (olim 49), ?lost
Man sieht nun wohl, wie stet du bist, 4vv, N 73 (Stoltzer), Gu 96 (Stoltzer), *L. Senfl: Sämtliche Werke*, v, ed. A. Geering and W. Altwegg (Wolfenbüttel, 1949), 17 (Senfl)
So wünsch ich ihm/ihr ein gute Nacht, 4vv, N 74 (Stoltzer), Gu 183 (M. Wolff)

BIBLIOGRAPHY

R. Eitner: 'Briefe von Thomas Stoltzer, Adrian Rauch und Sylvester Raid', *MMg*, viii (1876), 65
O. Kade: 'Thomas Stoltzers Psalm: Noli aemulari, 6 vocum', *MMg*, viii (1876), 133
J. Fogel: *II. Lajos udvartartása* [The court of Ludwig II] (Budapest, 1917)
H. J. Moser: 'Thomas Stoltzers Psalm Noli aemulari', *ZMw*, xiv (1931–2), 241
——: 'Lutheran Composers in the Habsburg Empire (1525–1732)', *MD*, iii (1949), 3
G. Reese: *Music in the Renaissance* (New York, 1954, rev. 2/1959), 723ff
L. Hoffmann-Erbrecht: 'Thomas Stoltzers Octo tonorum melodiae', *AMw*, xvi (1957), 16
——: 'Neue Dokumente zum Leben Thomas Stoltzers', *IMSCR, vi Cologne 1958*, 139
——: Datierungsprobleme bei Kompositionen in deutschen Musik-Handschriften des 16. Jahrhunderts', *Festschrift Helmuth Osthoff* (Tutzing, 1961), 47
L. Finscher: 'Zur Cantus firmus-Behandlung in der Psalmmotette der Josquin-Zeit', *Hans Albrecht in memoriam* (Kassel, 1962), 55
K. L. Hampe: 'Über zwei deutsche Psalmen Thomas Stoltzers', *Musik des Ostens*, i (Kassel, 1962), 146
L. Hoffmann-Erbrecht: *Thomas Stoltzer: Leben und Schaffen* (Kassel, 1964)
O. Wessely: 'Beiträge zur Geschichte der Hofkapelle Lajos' II. Jagello, Königs von Böhmen und Ungarn', *Festschrift Bruno Stäblein* (Kassel, 1967), 293
L. Hoffmann-Erbrecht: 'Stoltzer, Thomas', *MGG* [incl. facsimile of Stoltzer's letter]
——: 'Die Bedeutung Thomas Stoltzers für die deutsche und europäische Musikkultur', *Musik in Schlesien* (Dülmen, 1970), 7
W. Dehnhard: *Die deutsche Psalmmotette in der Reformationszeit* (Wiesbaden, 1971)
W. Steude: *Untersuchungen zu Herkunft, Verbreitung und spezifischem Inhalt mitteldeutscher Musikhandschriften des 16. Jahrhunderts* (diss., U. of Rostock, 1973)
L. Hoffmann-Erbrecht: 'Stoltzeriana', *Mf*, xxvii (1974), 18

LOTHAR HOFFMANN-ERBRECHT

Stolyarsky, Pyotr Solomonovich (*b* Lipovets, Ukraine, 30 Nov 1871; *d* Sverdlovsk, 24 April 1944). Ukrainian violinist and teacher. He studied the violin with his father, and later had lessons at the Warsaw Conservatory with Stanislaw Barcewicz and at the Odessa Music School with Emil Młynarski and Y. Karbulko, from whose class he graduated in 1898. From 1898 to 1914 he played in the orchestra of the Odessa Opera and taught in his own music school. He showed exceptional ability as a teacher, and taught at the Odessa Conservatory, joining the staff in 1920, and becoming a professor in 1923. In 1933 he founded the first Soviet special music school for gifted children, which is named after him. Stolyarsky was one of the founders of the Russian school of violin playing. His teaching method was based on his belief that a child should be taught from the start about the whole range of professional and artistic skills that he would need as a performer. The child learnt to play not so much 'on' as 'with' the violin. Stolyarsky's immense ability as a teacher and organizer, and his exceptional determination, enabled him to achieve striking results: among his pupils were David Oistrakh, Milstein, Elizabeta Gilels, Fikhtengol'ts and Zatulovsky. He was made a People's Artist of the USSR.

BIBLIOGRAPHY

I. Yampol'sky: *David Oystrakh* (Moscow, 1964, 2/1968), 8
M. Grinberg and V. Pronin: 'V klasse P. S. Stolyarskovo', *Muzïkal'noye ispolnitel'stvo*, vi (Moscow, 1970), 162

I. M. YAMPOL'SKY

Stolz, Robert (Elisabeth) (*b* Graz, 25 Aug 1880; *d* Berlin, 27 June 1975). Austrian composer and conductor. He was a son of Jacob Stolz, a conductor and music teacher, and Ida Bondy, a concert pianist. From them he received his initial musical training; he gave his first public piano recital at the age of seven with Brahms, a family friend, in the audience. Later he studied under Fuchs at the Vienna Conservatory and with Humperdinck in Berlin. In 1897 he was appointed répétiteur in Graz, in 1898 second conductor at Marburg an der Drau, in 1902 first conductor in Salzburg, and in 1903 conductor at the German Theatre in Brno. A meeting with Johann Strauss in 1899 had turned Stolz's thoughts to the composition of light music, and his first operetta *Studentenulke* (Marburg, 1899) had been followed by further efforts. In 1907 he became conductor at the Theater an der Wien, where he conducted the initial runs of *Die lustige Witwe* (from about the 420th performance) and other leading Viennese operettas of the time, but his own first lasting success came with a song, *Servus, du!* (1911), which was followed by several other popular Viennese songs. He first enjoyed international popularity with the song *Hallo, du süsse Klingelfee* (1919), sung by Jean Gabin at the Casino de Paris, and with the operetta *Der Tanz ins Glück* (1920), produced in England as *Whirled into Happiness* and in the USA as *Sky High*. In 1924 he took a job in cabaret in Berlin and his period of greatest success began with scores for early Berlin film musicals. He went to the USA in 1940 where he composed music for Hollywood films and conducted concerts of Viennese music. In 1946 he returned to Vienna and from 1952 to 1971 he wrote the music for the ice revues. He also continued to conduct on concert tours and for records. His honours include decorations from many countries, film Oscars, the title 'professor' (1947), honorary citizenship of Vienna (1970) and a statue in his native city (1972).

WORKS
(selective list)

OPERETTAS

c65 operettas and musicals (many pubd in vocal score or individual numbers in Vienna or Berlin) incl. Der Favorit (2, F. Grünbaum, W. Sterk), Berlin, Komische Oper, Oct 1916; Das Sperrsechserl (2, R. Blum, Grünwald), Vienna, Colosseum, 1 April 1920; Der Tanz ins Glück (3, R. Bodanzky, B. Hardt-Warden), Vienna, Colosseum, 18 Oct 1921; Mädi (3, Grünwald, L. Stein), Berlin, Berliner Theater, 1 April 1923; Wenn die kleinen Veilchen blühen (2, Hardt-Warden), The Hague, Princess, 1 April 1932
Venus im Seide (3, Grünwald, L. Herzer), Zurich, Stadttheater, 10 Dec 1932; Der verlorene Walzer [after Zwei Herzen im Dreivierteltakt] (3, P. Knepler, J. M. Welleminsky, R. Gilbert, after W. Reisch, F. Schulz), Zurich, Stadttheater, 30 Sept 1933; Grüzi (Himmelblaue Träume) (R. Gilbert), Zurich, Stadttheater, 1934; Frühling im Prater (2, E. Marischka), Vienna, Stadttheater, 22 Dec 1949; Trauminsel

(Gilbert, P. Schwenzen), Bregenz, Lake Stage, 21 July 1962; Frühjahrsparade [after film] (2, Marischka, H. Wiener), Vienna, Volksoper, 25 March 1964

OTHER WORKS

c100 film scores incl. Der Millionenonkel, 1913; Zwei Herzen im Dreivierteltakt, 1930; Das Lied ist aus, 1930; Ein Tango für dich, 1930; Liebeskommando, 1931; Mein Herz ruft immer nur nach dir, 1933; Frühjahrsparade, 1934; Ich liebe alle Frauen, 1935; Herbstmanöver, 1935; Ungeküsst sollst du nicht schlafen geh'n, 1936; Confetti, 1936; Zauber der Boheme, 1937; Spring Parade, 1941; It Happened Tomorrow, 1943; Une nuit à Tabarin, 1947; Rendezvous im Salzkammergut, 1948; Deutschmeister, 1955; A Breath of Scandal, 1959; Yesterday, Today and Tomorrow, 1959; Der Kongress amüsiert sich, 1966

Hundreds of individual songs incl. Servus, du!, op.102 (B. Vigny), 1911; Wien wird bei Nacht erst schön, op.216 (Sterk), 1915; Im Prater blüh'n wieder die Bäume, op.247 (K. Robitschek), 1916; In Wien gibt's manch' winziges Gasserl, op.249 (Robitschek), 1916; Hallo, du süsse Klingelfee, op.341 (A. Rebner), 1919; Salome, op.355 (Rebner), 1919; 20 Blumenlieder, op.500 (Hardt-Warden), 1927; Vor meinem Vaterhaus, op.614 (Hardt-Warden), 1933

Waltzes, marches, other orch works, pf pieces

BIBLIOGRAPHY

G. Holm: Im Dreivierteltakt durch die Welt (Linz, 1948)

W.-D. Brümmel and F. van Booth: Robert Stolz: Melodie eines Lebens (Stuttgart, 1967)

O. Herbrich: Robert Stolz, König der Melodie (Vienna and Munich, 1975)

ANDREW LAMB

Stolz [Stolzová], **Teresa** [Teresina, Terezie] (b Elbekosteletz [Kostelec nad Labem], 5 June 1834; d Milan, 23 Aug 1902). Bohemian soprano. She was one of a large musical family. Her twin sisters Francesca (Fanny, Františka, b 1826) and Ludmila (Lidia, 1826–c1910), both sopranos, became the youthful mistresses (and Ludmila later the wife) of the composer Luigi Ricci, who wrote operas for and fathered a child on each of them. Teresa was trained at the Prague Conservatory; in 1856 she joined Ricci and the twins in Trieste, had

Teresa Stolz as Aida in the first Italian performance of Verdi's opera

further lessons from Ricci and in 1857 made her operatic début in Tbilisi. For some five years she sang in Odessa, Constantinople, and often Tbilisi. Her earliest Italian appearances to have been traced were in Turin, autumn 1863. Her successes in Nice (Il trovatore, December 1863) and then Granada (Ernani, April 1864) led to a Trovatore in Spoleto (September 1864), and then Ernani and Guillaume Tell in Bologna. The Bologna performances were conducted by Angelo Mariani, to whom she later became engaged. In 1867 she was chosen for the Italian première of Don Carlos, in Bologna, and two years later for the revised La forza del destino, at La Scala, Milan; Verdi himself supervised the latter production. In 1872, again at La Scala, Stolz was the first Italian Aida, and in 1874 (and subsequently, during the tour of the work to Paris, London and Vienna) the first soprano of the Verdi Requiem. Verdi's operas had from the start been prominent in her repertory and, both in Italy and abroad, she became a leading and frequent interpreter of his later heroines, from Amelia in Un ballo in maschera to Aida. Her last operatic engagement was in St Petersburg (1876–7) and her last public appearance in a performance of the Requiem at La Scala (1879), conducted by Verdi for the benefit of flood victims.

After 1872, her only non-Verdian roles were Alice in Robert le diable and Rachel in La juive. She was the Verdian dramatic soprano par excellence, powerful, passionate in utterance but dignified and disciplined in manner, with a voice that extended securely from g to $c\sharp'''$. After hearing the Requiem in Paris, Blanche Roosevelt wrote of her thus (Chicago Times, June 1875):

Mme Stolz's voice is a pure soprano, with an immense compass and of the most perfectly beautiful quality one ever listened to, from the lowest note to the highest. Her phrasing is the most superb I ever heard and her intonation something faultless. She takes a tone and sustains it until it seems that her respiration is quite exhausted, and then she has only commenced to hold it. The tones are as fine and clearly cut as diamond, and sweet as a silver bell; but the power she gives a high C is something amazing ... She opens her mouth slightly when she takes a note, without any perceptible effort, and the tone swells out bigger and fuller, always retaining that exquisite purity of intonation, and the air seems actually heavy with great passionate waves of melody.

Much has been written about the troubled personal relationships between Stolz, Mariani, Verdi and his wife. That Stolz became Verdi's mistress has been both asserted and denied, but there is no doubt that the attentions he paid her between 1872 and 1876 caused pain to Giuseppina Verdi. The fullest and fairest account of the matter – and (except for the unfortunate Mariani) its happy conclusion – is Frank Walker's.

BIBLIOGRAPHY

G. Cenzato: 'Verdi e la Stolz', Corriere della sera (30 Oct 1932); repr. in Itinerari verdiani (Parma, 1949), 148ff; (Milan, 2/1955), 127ff

A. Luzio, ed.: 'Il carteggio di Verdi con la Stolz e la Waldmann', Carteggi verdiani, ii (Rome, 1935), 222–91; other Stolz letters, Carteggi verdiani, iv (Rome, 1947), 189ff

J. Šolín: T. Stolzová: první a nejslavější Aida [Stolz: the first and most celebrated Aida] (Mělník, 1944, 2/1946)

U. Zoppi: Mariani, Verdi e la Stolz (Milan, 1947)

F. Walker: The Man Verdi (London, 1962), 283–446

ANDREW PORTER

Stolze, Gerhard (b Dessau, 1 Oct 1926; d Garmisch-Partenkirchen, 11 March 1979). German tenor. He studied in Dresden with Willy Bader and Rudolf Dittrich, and in Berlin with Hermann Weiszenborn. He joined a drama ensemble in 1946, then in 1949 Keilberth engaged him for the Dresden Staatsoper where he made his début as Augustin Moser in Die Meistersinger von

Nürnberg. From 1953 to 1961 he was a member of the Berlin Staatsoper. At Bayreuth he took minor roles in 1951, then in 1956 sang David and in 1957 Mime, a role he continued to sing there until 1969, and in which he made his Covent Garden début in 1960. In 1959 he created the part of the Forstmeister in Erbse's *Julietta* at Salzburg and the next year Satan in Martin's *Le mystère de la Nativité*. His musical intelligence and dramatic gifts specially suited him to such character roles as Herod, the Captain in *Wozzeck*, and Oberon in Britten's *A Midsummer Night's Dream.*

HAROLD ROSENTHAL

Stölzel [Stöltzel, Stözl], **Gottfried Heinrich** (*b* Grünstädtel, nr. Schwarzenberg, Erzgebirge, 13 Jan 1690; *d* Gotha, 27 Nov 1749). German composer and theorist. He received his first music instruction from his father, a pupil of the Halle court organist Moritz Edelmann. When he was 13 he went to the grammar school in Schneeberg, where he studied under the Kantor Christian Umlaufft, a pupil of Johann Kuhnau; he then attended the Gymnasium in Gera, where he was encouraged to compose by Emanuel Kegel, director of the Kapelle. After a few years he played in public and aroused the interest of the court. In 1707 he went to Leipzig University, but felt himself drawn more towards the opera, recently reopened there, and to the collegium musicum (founded by Telemann and at that time directed by Melchior Hofmann). He proved to be a helpful copyist to Hofmann, who soon recognized his gifts as a composer. Stölzel's first works were performed under his teacher's name; they appeared only later under his own.

In 1710 Stölzel went to Breslau, where he taught singing and keyboard in aristocratic circles. He also composed for the collegium musicum and produced his first dramatic work. A teacher of Italian with whom he was friendly recommended that he go to Italy to improve his composition; but he went next to Halle, wrote a pastorale for the court at Gera, and (through the negotiations of Johann Friedrich Fasch and Johann Theile) received a commission from the Zeitz court for which he composed three operas for the fair at Naumburg. Afterwards he received from both Gera and Zeitz offers of the post of court Kapellmeister, which he refused. At the end of 1713, with additional travel funds from the Duchess of Zeitz, he went to Italy, passing through Bayreuth, Nuremberg and Augsburg, where he played on the occasion of the sitting of the Reichstag.

In Venice, with the help of Johann David Heinichen (also studying there), Stölzel met Francesco Gasparini, Alessandro Marcello, Carlo Francesco Pollarolo, Antonio Vivaldi and other composers. In Florence, where he was a guest of the court, he wrote numerous cantatas and a duet as his contribution to a gala concert. He is said to have refused offers to remain there for religious reasons. After a short stay in Rome, where he met Antonio Bononcini and Domenico Scarlatti, he returned to Florence, undertook trips to Pisa and Livorno (paid for by the court) and finally travelled home by way of Bologna, Venice and Trieste. In 1715 he went to Prague, where he remained for three years: he took a lively part in the musical activities there, and composed dramatic works, oratorios, masses and instrumental music. He declined an offer of a position at the Dresden court, which would have included a study

trip to France, and in 1717 he returned to Bayreuth, where he was commissioned to compose church music for the 200th anniversary celebration of the Reformation and other pieces to mark the duke's birthday.

By the beginning of 1718 Stölzel was Kapellmeister at the court at Gera. On 25 May 1719 he married Christiane Dorothea Knauer. An application to the court at Sondershausen was unsuccessful but from 24 November 1719 Stölzel received a fixed salary from the court at Saxe-Gotha, which was followed by an official appointment as Kapellmeister there on 24 February 1720. For 30 years he held this appointment, which obliged him to fulfil various duties as a composer for the church, the opera and other court festivities. He also executed commissions for the courts at Sondershausen and Gera. About this time he allowed some of his works to be copied, including sets of cantatas for the church year, and his reputation grew with the dissemination of his music. From the evidence of various applications to his patrons, it seems that Stölzel was the author of the texts of his own vocal works. He acquired a wide reputation as a teacher and theorist, took pupils, and was applied to for references. In 1739 he was elected a member of Lorenz Christoph Mizler's Societät der Musikalischen Wissenschaften. In his late 40s, his mental powers seem to have declined as a result of overwork.

The extent of Stölzel's reputation is reflected in the fact that Mizler placed him above J. S. Bach in his list of leading German composers. Bach himself valued Stölzel's music, and included his Partia in G minor (with his own trio added to the minuet) in *Das Clavier-Büchlein vor Wilhelm Friedemann Bach*. From the existence of transcriptions in the Leipzig Thomasbibliothek, now lost, it appears that Bach may have performed Stölzel's vocal music. Like that of many of his contemporaries (including Bach), Stölzel's music was increasingly forgotten during the later 18th century and an extensive collection of his manuscripts in Gotha was lost during the time of his successor, Georg Benda. Interest in Stölzel was reawakened in the 20th century with Arnold Schering's edition of the Concerto Grosso in D for quadruple orchestra, which soon found a place in the repertory; further new editions were largely confined to instrumental music. Not until 1965 was it possible for a chronological catalogue of the cantatas based on morphological, palaeographical and stylistic criteria; it documents, among other things, 12 annual cantata cycles (including some double cycles).

Stölzel's only work printed in his lifetime is a treatise on canon. His other works on music theory are merely compilations, except for his *Abhandlung vom Recitativ*, the first major specialized treatise on recitative, which reflects Stölzel's unrivalled superiority in this field, acknowledged by his contemporaries. Stölzel had a special preference for recitative with a number of voices which both alternated and combined. His work in general is marked, as is typical of the transitional period to which he belonged, by a contradiction between the traditional architectonic design and the new principles of form evolving within it. The traditional da capo aria, which he favoured, serves to provide development, imagery and contrast. Where the contradiction is absent, as in some of the polyphonic choral movements, he favoured schematic designs. Because Stölzel was so prolific over a short period there are inevitably superficialities in his work; but his best music shows not only skill in composition and richness of idea but also the nucleus of the material with which the coming generation would build.

WORKS

STAGE
(music lost; lost librettos may also be by composer)

Narcissus (musical drama, Stölzel), Breslau, 1711/12; ?rev. Gotha, 1734–5
Valeria (opera, Stölzel), Naumburg, 1712
Rosen und Dornen der Liebe (pastorale), Gera, 1713
Artemisia (opera/Singspiel, Stölzel), Naumburg, 1713
Orion (opera, Stölzel), Naumburg, 1713
Venus and Adonis (musical drama, Stölzel), Prague, 1715–17; rev. Altenburg, 1728–30; also known as Adonis
Acis und Galathea (musical drama, Stölzel), Prague, 1715–17, lib in *D-Bds*; ?rev. Gotha, 1729; also known as Die triumphirende Liebe
Das durch Liebe besiegte Glück (Stölzel), Prague, 1715–17
Diomedes (opera), Bayreuth, 1718
Der Musenberg ([musical] drama, Stölzel), Gotha, 1723
Die beglückte Tugend (pastorale), Gotha, 1723
Hercules Prodicius oder die triumphirende Tugend ([musical] drama, Stölzel), Gotha, 1725, lib in *D-Bds*, *ALa*
Die Ernte der Freuden (pastorale), Gotha, 1727; rev. Altenburg, 1727 as Die Freuden-Ernde, lib in *Ju*
Thersander und Demonassa oder die glückliche Liebe (pastorale), Gotha, 1733
L'amore vince l'inganno (drama pastorale), Gotha, 1736, lib in *US-Wc*
Endymion (musical Schäfer-Spiel, ?Stölzel), Gotha, 1740, lib in *D-Gs*
Die gekrönte Weisheit (Singspiel), Gotha, 1742
Die mit Leben und Vergnügen belohnte Tugend (Singspiel), Gotha, 1744, lib in *HAu*

SACRED VOCAL
(music lost unless otherwise stated)

Jesus patiens (oratorio), Prague, 1715/16
Die büssende und versöhnte Magdalena (oratorio), Prague, 1716
Caino, overo Il primo figlio mavaggio (oratorio), Prague, 1715–17
Die leidende und am Creutze sterbende Liebe Jesu (Passion oratorio), Gotha, 1720
Sechs Andachten aus der . . . Historie des bitteren Leidens und Sterbens unsers allertheuresten Erlösers Jesu Christi (Passion oratorio), Gotha, 1723
Fall und Trost des menschlichen Geschlechts (oratorio), Gotha, 1724
Der für die Sünde der Welt gemarterte und sterbende Christus (Passion oratorio, B. H. Brockes), Gotha, 1725, *D-SHs*
Jesus, als der für das verlorene Schäflein leidend- und sterbende gute Hirte (Passion oratorio, G. H. Stölzel), Gotha, 1727, *B*
O Welt! sieh hier dein Leben (Passion oratorio), Gotha, 1729
Ein Lämmlein geht und trägt die Schuld (Passion oratorio), ?Gotha, 1731, *B*, *SHs*
Die mit Busse und Glauben ihren leidenden Jesus bis zum Grabe begleitende Seele (Passion oratorio), Gotha, 1737
Numerous masses (mostly Missae breves), incl. Missa canonica, ed. G. Poelchau (Vienna, 1820); Deutsches Te Deum; Magnificat; 2 Miserere; other works: principal sources *A-Wgm*, *Wn*, *D-B*, *Bds*, *DL*, *GOl*, *LEm*, *Mbs*, *SHs*
442 cantatas, 10 fragmentary, extant; 342 cantatas, text extant, music lost; 39 cantatas, title only extant, text and music lost; see catalogue in Hennenberg; incl. Liebster Jesu deine Liebe, A, vn, va, bc, ed. J. Bachmair (Leipzig, 1926); Aus der Tiefe rufe ich, Herr, zu dir, B, str, bc, ed. A. Adrio (Berlin, 1948, 2/1957); Kündlich gross ist das gottselige Geheimnis, chorus, SA, ob, str, bc, ed. in Organum, i/28 (Lippstadt, 1953); Lob und Danck, chorus, T, ob d'amore, str, bc, ed. in Organum, i/29 (Lippstadt, 1954)

SECULAR VOCAL
82 cantatas incl. 65 dramatic cantatas for soloists, chorus, orch, written for courts at Gotha and Sondershausen, music for only 12 extant, *D-Bds*, *SHs*: incl. Das durch himmlisches Schicksahl über allen Unbestand triumphirende Fürsten-Wohl, 1732, parodied as Glücklicher Zustand anmuthiges Leben; Fontinalia Schwarzburgica, 1732; Irene and Apollo, 1733 [?rev. of Die beschütze Irene, Altenburg, 1722, lost], parodied twice, 2nd as Sonne spiel in reinsten Lichte; Die Liebe als die Quelle aller fürstliche Ruhmwürdigkeiten, 1734; Alles was sonst lieblich heisset [?rev. of Die Harmonie der Tugende, Gotha, 1725, lost]; Alles in einem, 1737; Was herrlich fürtrefflich und prächtig erscheinet, 1737; Aussnehmender Vortheil vortrefliche Krafft, 1737; Das mir angenehmster Sorge erfüllte Fürsten-Hertz, 1738
17 solo cantatas, all in *D-SHs*: 1 for B, str, bc; 16 for S, bc, incl. Die Rose bleibt der Blumen Königen, ed. R. Eitner, *MMg*, xvi (1884); see catalogue in Hennenberg

INSTRUMENTAL
Orch: Concerto grosso a 4 chori, *D-GOl*, ed. in DDT, xxix–xxx (1907/*R*); Concerto grosso, e, *Dlb*; Concerto grosso, b, *S-Uu*; Concerto grosso, F, *D-B*, *Dlb*, ed. H. Winschermann (Wolfenbüttel

and Zurich, 1963); Concerto, ob, g, *D-SWl*; Concerto, ob, D, *Dlb*, ed. H. Töttcher (Hamburg, 1954); Concerto, fl, e, *RH*, *S-Uu*; Concerto, fl, G, *D-RH*; Concerto, 2 ob d'amore, D, *RH*
Chamber music: 3 qt, *D-Bds*; c23 trio sonatas in B, *Bds*, *Dl*, *S-Uu*, incl. e, ed. in Collegium musicum, lxxii (Leipzig, 1943); C, ed. G. Frotscher (Cologne, 1937); D, ed. G. Frotscher (Hamburg, 1957); G, ed. G. Frotscher (Hamburg, 1958); F, ob, hn, vn, bc, ed. in Collegium musicum, lxxix (Leipzig, 1952); G, ed. G. Hausswald (Heidelberg, 1955); c, ob, vn, bc, ed. in Collegium musicum, lxxvi (Leipzig, 1950); B♭, ed. in Collegium musicum, lxxxii (Leipzig, 1956); D, ed. in Collegium musicum, lxxxi (Leipzig, 1955); f, ed. in NM, cxxxiii (1937, 2/1959)
Enharmonische Sonata, F, hpd, in *Musikalisches Allerley von verschiedenen Tonkünstlern*, ii (Berlin, 1761–3), ed. E. W. Böhme (Kassel, 1936)
Partia, g, hpd, ed. in *J. S. Bach: Klavierbüchlein für Wilhelm Friedemann Bach*, Neue Ausgabe sämtlicher Werke, v/5 (Kassel, 1962)

WRITINGS
Practischer Beweis, wie aus einem . . . Canone perpetui in hypodiapente quatuor vocum, viel und mancherley . . . Canones perpetui à 4 zu machen seyn (1725)
Abhandlung vom Recitativ (MS, *A-Wgm*), ed. in Steger
Other theoretical writings in *D-Bds*, *A-Wgm* or lost

BIBLIOGRAPHY
EitnerQ; *GerberL*; *GerberNL*; *WaltherML*

J. Mattheson: *Grundlage einer Ehren-Pforte* (Hamburg, 1740); ed. M. Schneider (Berlin, 1910/*R*1969)
L. C. Mizler: *Neu eröffnete Musikalische Bibliothek*, iv (Leipzig, 1754/*R*1966)
F. W. Marpurg: *Historisch-kritische Beyträge zur Aufnahme der Musik*, i (Berlin, 1754–5/*R*)
J. A. Hiller: *Lebensbeschreibungen berühmter Musikgelehrten und Tonkünstler*, i (Leipzig, 1784)
G. J. Dlabacž: *Allgemeines historisches Künstler-Lexikon*, iii (Prague, 1815/*R*)
G. Lutze: *Aus Sondershausens Vergangenheit*, ii (Sondershausen, 1909)
P. Brausch: *Die Kantate* (diss., U. of Heidelberg, 1921)
W. Lott: 'Zur Geschichte der Passionkomposition von 1650–1800', *AMw*, iii (1921), 285–320
E. W. Böhme: 'Gottfried Heinrich Stölzel in Gera', *ZMw*, xiii (1930–31), 333
——: *Die frühdeutsche Oper in Thüringen* (Eisenberg and Stadtroda, 1931)
F. Treiber: 'Die thüringisch-sachsische Kirchenkantate zur Zeit des jungen Johann Sebastian Bach etwa 1700–1723', *AMf*, ii (1937), 128–59
W. Schmidt-Weiss: *Gottfried Heinrich Stölzel als Instrumentalkomponist* (diss., U. of Munich, 1938)
F. W. Beinroth: *Musikgeschichte der Stadt Sondershausen* (diss., U. of Innsbruck, 1943)
A. Fett: *Musikgeschichte der Stadt Gotha* (diss., U. of Freiburg, 1952)
F. H. Neumann: 'Gottfried Heinrich Stölzels musiktheoretische Schriften', *Sammlung musikwissenschaftlicher Abhandlungen: Festschrift für Rudolf Gerber* (MS, Göttingen, 1952)
——: *Die Theorie des Rezitativs im 17. und 18. Jahrhundert* (diss., U. of Göttingen, 1955)
W. Steger: *Gottfried Heinrich Stölzels 'Abhandlung vom Recitativ'* (diss., U. of Heidelberg, 1962)
W. Blankenburg: 'Die Aufführungen von Passionen und Passionskantaten im Schlosskirche auf dem Friedenstein zu Gotha zwischen 1699 und 1770', *Festschrift Friedrich Blume zum 70. Geburtstag* (Kassel and Basle, 1963)
F. Hennenberg: *Das Kantatenschaffen von Gottfried Heinrich Stölzel* (diss., U. of Leipzig, 1965; rev., abridged, Leipzig, 1976)

FRITZ HENNENBERG

Stölzel [Stoelzel], **Heinrich** (*b* Scheibenberg, Saxony, 1772; *d* Berlin, 1844). German instrument maker and horn player. His name is best known for its association with the earliest satisfactory piston valves for brass instruments. Stölzel's playing was, by all accounts, of no more than average distinction. He was a member of the Prince of Pless's private band and from 1817 of the Royal Opera orchestra in Berlin, from which post he retired with a pension in 1829. Stölzel had by then begun the manufacture of brass wind instruments. His name appears in a price list in A. Sunderlin's *Die Instrumentierung für das Orchester* (1828). In it Stölzel referred to his registered trade mark, and described himself as chamber musician and instrument mechanic (repairer) to the King of Prussia. According to

Wieprecht (as quoted by Kastner) Stölzel died in poverty, leaving a widow and children.

BIBLIOGRAPHY
G. Kastner: *Manuel général de musique militaire* (Paris, 1848), 192
R. Morley-Pegge: *The French Horn* (London, 1960)

PHILIP BATE

Stolzenberg [Stolzenberger], **Christoph.** *See* STOLTZEN-BERG, CHRISTOPH.

Stolzer, Josip. *See* SLAVENSKI, JOSIP.

Stolzová, Teresa. *See* STOLZ, TERESA.

Stomius [Mulinus, Muling], **Johannes** (*b* Perlesreut, nr. Passau, 1502; *d* Salzburg, 14 Jan 1562). German music theorist and composer. He had music lessons from an early age and was friendly with Hofhaimer. In 1530 he founded a private school in Salzburg, attended mainly by children of the aristocracy; in spite of his Protestant sympathies he remained its director for 32 years. His music treatise, *Prima ad musicen instructio* (Augsburg, 1537), intended for use in schools, takes as its chief subjects solmization, modes and mensural theory. He used in it a number of striking erudite terms: for example, he described the fugue as 'mimesis', a term which was not used again until the 17th century. A short final chapter sums up advice for the singer: as well as the usual rules of vocal performance, Stomius recommended that the singer determine the range of a piece in order to start at the right pitch, sing a few melodic phrases to establish the mode, and occasionally make a diminution for artistic effect on longer note values. As an example of the combination of different mensurations he printed a textless four-part piece by Isaac and as an example of a fugue Senfl's four-voice canon *Manet alta mente repositum*. Eight motets by Stomius survive (in *D-Rp*). Like most of the examples in the treatise they are limited to three-part settings and were clearly intended for the school choir. Some of them are reworkings of Lutheran hymn tunes.

BIBLIOGRAPHY
K. Weinmann: 'Johannes Mulichius (ca.1590–1641) und Johannes Stomius v. Mulinus (1502–1562)', *KJb*, xxi (1908), 62
H.-J. Moser: *Paul Hofhaimer* (Stuttgart and Berlin, 1929/*R*1966)
——: *Die Musik im frühevangelischen Österreich* (Kassel, 1954)
P. Mohr: *Die Handschrift B 211–215 der Proske-Bibliothek zu Regensburg* (Kassel, 1955)

MARTIN RUHNKE

Stonard [Stoner, Stonerd, Stonnard], **William** (*b* ?Oxfordshire, ?c1550–75; *d* Oxford, 1630). English organist and composer. According to Wood he was probably descended from the Storey or Strover family of Watlington in Oxfordshire. On 1 January 1609 he graduated BMus at Oxford, for which he wrote an eight-part hymn. In the same year he became organist of Christ Church, Oxford; he held the post until his death. Stonard's extant church music comprises seven verse anthems (of which three are incomplete) and two full Evening Services (the score of one, in *GB-Lbm* Harl.7337–42, is wrongly dated 1558). The words of three more anthems, now lost, were printed by Clifford in *The Divine Services and Anthems* (London, 1663, 2/1664). His two catches *Ding dong bell* (for four voices) and *Cuckoo* (for three) were first published in Hilton's *Catch that Catch Can* (London, 1652). An In Nomine setting in *GB-Ob* attributed to 'William Stannar' may be by Stonard.

BIBLIOGRAPHY
A. Wood: *Notes on the Lives of Musicians* (MS, *Gb-Ob* Wood D.19[4])
P. le Huray: *Music and the Reformation in England, 1549–1660* (London, 1967), 321

NORMAN JOSEPHS

Stone [Stane, Stoue] (*fl c*1440–70). Composer, presumably English. He is known from three antiphon settings, two complete, and a third fragmentary. The presence of this last piece in the Archivio di Stato, Lucca, strongly suggests that its composer was the 'Stane' mentioned by John Hothby in a list of excellent composers, 'many of whom are still alive' (CSM, x, p.95: written in Lucca in the late 1470s). Stone's music is all in duple metre, and its edgy rhythms and often awkward gait suggest that he was a younger contemporary of Walter Frye. He might conceivably have been John Stone, the well-known chronicler of Christchurch, Canterbury (*d* 1480), whose writings show some interest in music. The most likely identification, though, is with the John Stone who joined the Chapel Royal of Edward IV in 1465 or 1466 and was still there in 1468. The tenor of *Ibo mihi* has its chant almost unornamented, yet in fast-moving rhythms indistinguishable from the freely composed voices – a unique experiment.

WORKS
Deo gratias agamus, ?3vv, *I-La* 238 (frag.)
Ibo mihi ad montem myrrhe, 3vv, *MOe* α.X.1, 11 (Sarum ant chant in iii)
Tota pulchra es, 3vv, *MOe* α.X.1, 11 (ant chant not used)

BIBLIOGRAPHY
A. Seay: 'The Dialogus Johannis Ottobi Anglici in arte musica', *JAMS*, viii (1955), 95
F. Ll. Harrison: *Music in Medieval Britain* (London, 1958, 2/1963), 42f, 173, 189f [John Stone of Canterbury]
B. L. Trowell: *Music under the later Plantagenets* (diss., U. of Cambridge, 1960), i, 65ff; ii, 193, 314
R. Strohm: 'Ein unbekanntes Chorbuch des 15. Jahrhunderts', *Mf*, xxi (1968), 40ff

BRIAN TROWELL

Stone, John. English chronicler, who may be identifiable with the composer STONE.

Stone, Kurt (*b* Hamburg, 14 Nov 1911). American musicologist of German birth. He studied at Hamburg University and, from 1933, at the Royal Danish Conservatory in Copenhagen, where he graduated in 1937; he moved to New York in 1938. He taught in Hamburg, Copenhagen and New York, including at the Dalcroze School of Music. From 1942 he worked in music publishing, with various firms, notably Associated Music Publishers, G. Schirmer, Alexander Broude and Joseph Boonin. He has been particularly concerned with the publication of modern American music, but has also been involved in publishing earlier music and has prepared a number of editions, including some of works from the Renaissance and Baroque periods. In 1971 he established the Index of New Musical Notation at New York Public Library, and he has been much engaged in matters concerning notational methods in contemporary music. His writings include articles on publishing, notation and contemporary music in *Musical Quarterly*, *Notes*, *Perspectives of New Music* and other journals. He collaborated with his wife, Else, in editing *The Writings of Elliott Carter* (Bloomington, Ind., 1977).

Stone, Lew (*b* London, 28 May 1898; *d* London, 13 Feb 1969). English band-leader, arranger and pianist. He wrote scores for Bert Ralton's band and rapidly became known as one of the most inventive arrangers of his time, blending elements of jazz, symphonic and commercial music within single arrangements. From 1927 he provided several outstanding arrangements for Ambrose's band, introducing a rhythm string section. He first led a band in 1932, at the Monseigneur Restaurant, and later formed his own band there with exceptionally good players and the singer Al Bowlly. Stone was musical director for British and Dominion Films (1931–5) and the British National Film Company (1936–9), appearing with his band in several films; he also played in clubs, theatres, restaurants etc, made recordings and broadcast, latterly with a sextet (1959–67). He directed such musicals as *On your Toes* (Rodgers and Hart, 1937) and *Annie Get your Gun* (Irving Berlin, 1947–9). During his last years he ran an agency. He wrote *Harmony and Orchestration for the Modern Dance Band* (1935, rev. 2/1944).

BIBLIOGRAPHY
A. McCarthy: *The Dance Band Era* (London, 1971)
K. Trodd: *Lew Stone: a Career in Music* (London, 1971) [with discography]

Stone, Robert (*b* Alphington, Devon, 1516; *d* London, 2 July 1613). English composer. Rimbault referred to his early education at Exeter Cathedral and stated that he was drafted into the choir of the Chapel Royal. Stone was not among those who sang at the coronation of Edward VI, but his name appears in a list of Gentlemen of the chapel which is believed to date from *c*1550. He was still an active member of the chapel at the turn of the century. He was fourth in order of seniority (senior to Byrd) at the coronation of James I, and he regularly attended business meetings of the chapel choir at this time. The Cheque Book of the Chapel Royal records his death in 1613 'at the age of iiijxx xvij' (fourscore years and 17). His popular setting of the Lord's Prayer dates from about 1550, and was published by John Day in his *Certaine Notes* (1565). It is notable for its freely rhythmic structure, suggestive of the late 16th-century French technique of *vers mesuré*.

BIBLIOGRAPHY
E. F. Rimbault: *The Old Cheque-Book or Book of Remembrance of the Chapel Royal*, Camden Society, iii (London, 1872/*R*1966)
PETER LE HURAY

Stone, William Henry (*b* London, 8 July 1830; *d* London, 8 July 1891). English physician and amateur musician. The son of a rector of Spitalfields, he read classics at Oxford, then medicine in London and Paris. After a brief period of work in Trinidad he returned to London, where he had a distinguished medical career mostly spent at St Thomas's Hospital, where he was physician and lecturer, and at the Brompton. He was a brilliant scholar, and his interests extended to physics and music; he was also an enthusiastic amateur performer on instruments of the clarinet and bassoon families. He lectured on acoustics at Trinity College of Music in London, and his publications ranged from papers on medical subjects (including the Harveian Oration of 1887) and electricity to textbooks on acoustics and contributions to *Grove 1*. These articles on wind instruments are rather conservative in tone and have since been shown to contain factual errors. He wrongly identified the oboe da caccia as a small bassoon or tenoroon, examples of which he had in his collection and on which he performed Bach parts written for the former instrument. He also claimed credit for the develop-

ment of the wide bore version of the double bassoon first invented in 1847 by Haseneier of Koblenz as the 'contrabassophon'. He introduced one into England, playing it at the Handel Festival of 1871; subsequently Morton based his version of the instrument on it. Stone's collection of instruments is in the Bate Collection at Oxford.

WRITINGS
Sound as Music (London, 1876)
The Scientific Basis of Music (London, 1878)
Elementary Lessons on Sound (London, 1879)
BIBLIOGRAPHY
Obituary, *MT*, xxxii (1891), 485
WILLIAM WATERHOUSE

Stoner [Stonerd], **William.** *See* STONARD, WILLIAM.

Stoning [Stonninge, Stoninges, Stenings], **Henry** (*fl* *c*1600). English composer. He was described by Anthony Wood as 'a noted musician living in [the] reign of Queen Elizabeth [and] king James I'. Three five-part works for consort are in *GB-Lbm* Add.31390 – a *Miserere*, a *Browning* and an In Nomine (which is also in *Ob* Mus.Sch.D.212–16, as is a simpler, four-part In Nomine; all ed. in MB, xliv, 1979). There is a four-part Latin *Magnificat* in *Lbm* Add.17802–5.

BIBLIOGRAPHY
D. R. Key: *Two Instrumental MSS from the Elizabethan Period* (diss., U. of Rochester, 1960)
NORMAN JOSEPHS

Stonnard, William. *See* STONARD, WILLIAM.

Stop. (1) A rare term, now obsolete, for the holes of a wind instrument or the key used to block them.

(2) The registers of an organ or harpsichord, i.e. the single or multiple ranks of pipes or jacks controlled by one lever (*see* ORGAN STOP and HARPSICHORD).

(3) The stop-knob itself.

In a general sense, a 'stop' was by 1525 a strip of wood, etc, checking the motion of a moving part; in a musical sense, the LECKINGFIELD PROVERBS (*c*1520) use 'stoppes' to refer both to the holes of a recorder and, it seems, to the register-levers of an organ, as do other references of 1513, 1521 ('stoppys of iron' at St Andrew, Canterbury) and 1526. There are two possible explanations for the term, which itself suggests a blocking of organ sound, not an opening: (*a*) that it refers to the SLIDER whose protruding end was often worked directly by the organist and which, when extracted, is seen as a strip of wood pierced regularly with holes, and (*b*) that it refers to the mechanisms (sliders or otherwise) that cut off or stop certain ranks from the BLOCKWERK Mixture. Thus the 'fewe stops as may be convenient' dividing the *Blockwerk* at All Hallows, London, in 1519 may refer not to stop-knobs, etc, or even to sliders, but to Dutch-style spring chests and double chests that allowed some ranks to be stopped off by means of a secondary valve. This would correspond with the German term *Sperrventil*, i.e. 'stopping' valve. By 1540 terminology was stabilized and Henry VIII's inventories refer even to 'halfe stoppes' and 'one [w]hole stoppe' in a modern way. Other languages use clearer terms: *tirant* (15th-century Spain: small organs with 'drawing' sliders), *registre* (Fougères, 1474), *registri* (Cattaro, 1488), *Registern* (A. Schlick, 1511), *regestres sive tirans* (Avignon, 1539).

PETER WILLIAMS

Stopped flute ensemble. A term used to designate an

ensemble based on sets of end-blown flutes stopped at their distal ends by natural nodes or by movable tuning plugs. They are mostly single-note flutes, each blown by one man while dancing, accompanied by drumming and singing. Scholars of African music have frequently used the terms 'reed-pipe' or 'reed-flute' for such instruments, but the flutes can be made of material other than reeds, and the term 'reed-pipe' is best restricted to pipes fitted with a vibrating reed or reeds at one end. Ensembles of panpipes such as those played in the Solomon Islands and parts of Africa (e.g. the *nyanga* ensembles of Mozambique) could also be included in this term since each panpipe is essentially a raft or bundle of stopped flutes. Cone-flute ensembles, such as those used in the court music of several of the former kingdoms of the inter-lacustrine area of east-central Africa, though obviously related in musical style as well as organologically, often include instruments with one or more finger-holes and a small vent (also fingered) at the bottom end.

The music of the true stopped flute ensemble has fascinated observers in Africa since Vasco da Gama reported them during his exploratory voyage around the tip of southern Africa in 1497. Kirby (1933) documented this and other accounts and mapped the distribution of such ensembles in southern Africa. Further north, in eastern parts of Zaïre, the occasional use of these ensembles by Mbuti pygmies and Tetela children has been reported. They are also found in Mozambique, Zambia (if panpipe ensembles are included), along the line of the western rift valley into Uganda and the Sudan, as far north as Ethiopia (where they are played in the central highlands and by Cushitic-speaking peoples in the south) and in Cameroon, where an isolated occurrence has been recorded by Nikiprowetzky. However, they are not nearly as widespread as the trumpet ensembles that are played in a similar manner. Outside Africa stopped flutes are used in Lithuania (see UNION OF SOVIET SOCIALIST REPUBLICS, §VII, 2 (vi)), Burma and some of the Pacific Islands.

Many aspects of the African ensembles are apparently common to them all. Since each flute usually can play only one pitch, the ensembles generally perform in hocket style, like many African trumpet ensembles. This performing technique results in pieces that can hardly be considered simply as representations of single melodies. The use of 'harmonic equivalents' (see Blacking) and a considerable amount of apparent improvisation within the constraints of a basic pattern produce descending series of chord progressions (the Ethiopian ensembles appear to be exceptions in this last respect). Only men and boys may play; where women participate in the dancing they usually make their own circle around that of the males. The dances are central to the musical and social life of the peoples who perform them: for example, the *tshikona* flute dance of the Venda of the Transvaal is considered their 'national' dance (see VENDA MUSIC); the *eluma* dance of the Amba of western Uganda brings together all the men and youths of an extended family and serves to strengthen kinship bonds; and the *embilta* (notched flute) dances of Ethiopia are focal points of weddings, funerals and other family gatherings.

BIBLIOGRAPHY

P. Kirby: 'The Reed Flute Ensembles of S. Africa', *Journal of the Royal Anthropological Institute*, cxiii (1933), 313–88

——: *The Musical Instruments of the Native Races of South Africa* (London, 1934, 2/1965)

J. M. Shaffer: 'Bamboo Pipes of the Batetela Children', *Journal of the African Music Society*, i (1954), 74

J. N. Maquet: 'Les instruments à vent du Congo belge', *Journal mensuel de la Fédération Nationale des Jeunesses musicales de Belgique* (1956)

C. Ballantine: 'The Polyrhythmic Foundation of Tswana Pipe Melody', *African Music*, iii/4 (1965), 52

T. Nikiprowetzky: *Musiques du Cameroun*, Ocora OCR25 (1966) [disc notes]

J. Blacking: *Venda Children's Songs* (Witwatersrand, 1967), 168

A. Tracey: 'The Nyanga Panpipe Dance', *African Music*, v/1 (1971), 73

PETER COOKE

Stopped notes. (1) On string instruments, notes sounded with the string pressed hard to the finger-board as opposed to those produced by the full length of the string (except for fretted instruments, where the string is pressed against the fret).

(2) On the HORN, some notes outside the harmonic series proper to any given length of tube can be obtained by closing the bell to a greater or lesser degree with the bunched fingers of the right hand. This lowers the harmonics concerned but with marked difference in tone quality between the open and closed notes even though the right hand always remains in the bell to support the instrument. Before the introduction of valves this procedure enabled a skilled player to sound chromatic intervals fairly evenly over about an octave and a half, from the 4th harmonic upwards. A second type of stopped note is obtained by completely occluding the bell and attacking the note sharply. In this case a rise of pitch occurs in proportion to the tube length in use. On the horn in F it is almost exactly a semitone. Stopped notes are now sometimes demanded for the sake of their tone-colour, but stopping should not be confused with muting (see MUTE). Hand stopping may have been used with specially coiled trumpets in the 17th and 18th centuries.

PHILIP BATE

Stopped pipe. In the terminology of organ building, a flue pipe in which the end remote from the mouth is closed by a movable stopper or airtight cap. This provides a means of tuning.

In general, a stopped pipe is any tube that communicates freely with the ambient air at one end and is completely closed at the other. The AIR COLUMN in such a tube will vibrate with an antinode at the open end and a node at the closure. The fundamental is approximately an octave lower than that given by a pipe of equal dimensions open at both ends, and its wavelength is four times that of the tube itself. The harmonic series of a stopped pipe lacks the even-numbered partials; OVERBLOWING begins a 12th above the fundamental. Because it shows this characteristic the clarinet is sometimes loosely termed a stopped pipe. Among folk instruments the stopped pipe is represented by many end-blown flutes of varying degrees of sophistication.

PHILIP BATE

Stoppelaer, Michael (*b* c1710; *d* London, 1777). Irish tenor and actor. He was a singer in booths at the London fairs in 1729 and 1730 and from 1731 he sang young leads, mainly in ballad opera afterpieces, on the London stage. He had small parts in Handel's *Ariodante* (1735) and *Saul* (1739). After 1737 the principal tenor roles were sung by Beard at Drury Lane and Salway at Covent Garden, so 'Mich.' Stoppelaer became primarily a small-part character actor at Covent Garden. He sang occasionally, sometimes comic Irish songs. He had benefits until May 1777; his will was proved on 4 July of the same year.

OLIVE BALDWIN, THELMA WILSON

Stopping. (1) A technique used in playing the HORN. (2) *See* MULTIPLE STOPPING.

Stop time. A jazz device in which the rhythm section stops playing, either for an entire 12- or 32-bar 'chorus' or periodically during one, while a soloist (or originally a tap dancer) improvises. It is also known as 'stop chorus'. The rhythm section might play only the first beat of every other bar, or strike only every second and fourth beat. Outstanding examples of 'stop time' occur in Louis Armstrong's *Potato Head Blues* (1927), Lester Young's *Lester Leaps In* (1939) and Bill Evans's solo in George Russell's *All about Rosie* (1957).

GUNTHER SCHULLER

Stoquerus, Gaspar (*fl c*1570). German theorist resident in Italy and Spain; originally his name was probably Caspar Stocker. He resided in Italy (chiefly, it would seem, in Venice) before going to Spain. There he attended lectures by Francisco de Salinas at the University of Salamanca (Salinas first lectured there in 1567), and he referred to him as his teacher. He is the author of a treatise of 40 folios on text underlay – *De musica verbali libri duo* (*c*1570), unique in music theory in being, as far as is known, the only work devoted exclusively to this topic – and of one of nine folios on solmization appended to it; both survive in a single manuscript copy (*E-Mn* Cod.6486). For his discussion of text underlay Stoquerus drew, and expanded, on the ten rules laid down by Zarlino (*Le istitutioni harmoniche*, 1558, book 4, chap.33); to these he added the concept of obligatory rules (so indispensable as to demand attention by all) and optional ones (followed by those intent on a more meticulous coordination of pitches and syllables) and he distinguished between the practices of 'ancients' (the Josquin generation) and moderns (Willaert and his school). He established 15 rules, five obligatory, five optional for earlier composers and five optional for moderns, some of these being additions, others exceptions, to the Zarlino canon. He provided a rational explanation of them as conforming to nature and to the dictates of logic and as applicable to all forms of music, sacred and secular. They exist before the act of composition; hence the *a priori* necessity of complying with them. Stoquerus detected a gradually increasing readiness to observe them from one generation to the next, so that by Willaert's time the exceptions to the rules seemed to have disappeared and the practice had become standardized to correspond to the demands of the 'natural judgment' of the ear. The same treatise also provides valuable information for determining the origins of Willaert's *Musica nova*.

BIBLIOGRAPHY

E. E. Lowinsky: 'A Treatise on Text Underlay by a German Disciple of Francisco de Salinas', *Festschrift Heinrich Besseler* (Leipzig, 1961), 231

D. Harrán: 'New Light on the Question of Text Underlay prior to Zarlino', *AcM*, xlv (1973), 24–56

DON HARRÁN

Storace. Italian-English family of musicians.

(1) Stephen [Stephano] **Storace (i)** (*b* Torre Annunziata, *c*1725; *d c*1781). Italian double-bass player. By 1748 he was working in Dublin and already using the angli-

cized form of his name; there is no real evidence that it was originally Sorace, as has been alleged. Thomas Sheridan engaged him when he enlarged the Smock Alley Theatre band in 1748, and in the following year Storace was running the music in Dublin's New Gardens and a little later the music at Johnson's Music Hall in partnership with Niccolò Pasquali. He soon had good English, as is shown by a letter he wrote from Dublin in 1753 to the editor of the *Gentleman's Magazine*, about the relationship between the tarantella and the tarantula (partly reprinted by Scholes). By 1758 he was in London. In that year he translated Pergolesi's *La serva padrona* for performance in Marylebone Gardens (where he directed the music), adding a scene and a character in the middle; there were nearly 70 performances that season and many revivals later. In the following year Storace translated two more intermezzos, *La strattaggemma* (allegedly by Pergolesi) and Galuppi's *La cicisbea alla moda*, which he called *The Coquette*; when the latter was revived in 1771, Storace's translation was published. In 1761 he married the daughter of the proprietor of Marylebone Gardens, Elizabeth Trusler, who bore him two children, Stephen in 1762 and Nancy in 1765, both of whom became famous. As well as playing in the band at the King's Theatre, Storace was rather strangely billed as a double-bass player at every Three Choirs Festival from 1759 to 1770; he also engaged the singers. He kept up his friendship with the Sheridans. When Richard Brinsley Sheridan married Elizabeth Linley in 1773, they stayed with the Storaces at 72 Marylebone High Street while looking for a home nearby. In 1778 Storace took his family to Italy; he presumably died there two or three years later.

BIBLIOGRAPHY

P. A. Scholes: 'Tarantella', *Oxford Junior Companion to Music* (London, 1954)

E. K. Sheldon: *Thomas Sheridan of Smock Alley* (Princeton, 1967)

(2) Stephen (John Seymour) Storace (ii) (*b* London, 4 April 1762; *d* London, 19 March 1796). English composer, son of (1) Stephen Storace (i). He showed early promise as a violinist, and about 1776 he was sent to study at the S Onofrio Conservatory in Naples; he lived there with his uncle, who was a bishop. According to the artist Thomas Jones, he did not take music very seriously, and was more interested in painting. He also found time to climb Vesuvius and make expeditions down the coast. Late in 1778 his parents and sister came out to Naples, partly to see if Stephen was wasting his time. They did in fact remove him from S Onofrio.

By 1782 Stephen was back in London on his own. He published a set of songs, said to be the first in England to have a fully written-out keyboard accompaniment, but his progress as a composer was so slow that at one time he seriously thought of setting up in Bath as an artist; Kelly, our informant, did not date this temporary change of heart. However, the three chamber works he published in 1784 restored his confidence. The Piano Quintet in B♭ is especially notable, with its five movements and its unusual thematic links. The relationship between the Minuet and its Trio in the D major Piano Quintet can be paralleled elsewhere, but in the B♭ Quintet it is the main themes of the Scherzo and of the Minuet that are related, as also are those of their respective trios. The central slow movement is based on the allegedly 'Scotch' song, *De'il tak' the Wars*. Some years later Storace adapted the last two movements of the D

1. Title-page of the vocal score of 'The Pirates' (London: J. Dale, 1792) by Stephen Storace

major Quintet for his overture *The Pirates*.

No doubt he sent a copy of these chamber works to his sister in Vienna, and it was probably because he showed it to the emperor that Stephen was commissioned to compose a comic opera, *Gli sposi malcontenti*. It was well received, as was *Gli equivoci*, which had an amusing libretto by Da Ponte based on a French translation of Shakespeare's *The Comedy of Errors*. Storace came to Vienna for both productions, and though it might have paid him to claim Italian blood, he had himself billed as 'Ein Engländer'. His sister and Michael Kelly sang leads in both operas; and the works were later produced in Leipzig, Dresden and elsewhere. *Gli equivoci* is competently written and well orchestrated; the influence of *Le nozze di Figaro* is especially apparent in the long and animated finales.

Though there seems to be no positive evidence, it is likely that Storace had lessons from Mozart, who may even have helped him with the scoring of the two operas. The Storaces and the Mozarts were certainly close friends. Kelly mentioned a quartet evening at the Storaces' house at which the violins were played by Haydn and Dittersdorf, the viola by Mozart and the cello by Vanhal; Paisiello was among the guests.

In March 1787 the Storaces and Kelly returned to London. In Paris they heard some French operas, and when Stephen came to compose an *opera buffa* for London, *La cameriera astuta*, he wrote a cod French aria for Nancy, 'Beaux yeux', and published it in full score; the plot required Nancy to disguise herself as a French maid. But Stephen was not much encouraged at the King's Theatre. As he wrote to the English ambassador in Vienna in his only surviving letter (*GB-Lbm*), even Nancy 'has had great opposition from the Italians,

who consider it an infringement on their rights that any person should be able to sing that was not born in Italy'. Nevertheless Nancy sang at the King's Theatre until it was burnt down in 1789, whereas Stephen was not asked for another opera. *La cameriera astuta* had been found too much 'in the German style of Gluck, leaded with harsh and terrifying music of trumpeting and drumming'; it lacked sufficient 'soft and melodious Italian music'. Storace's overture looks Mozartian, which no doubt was what the critic disliked.

Storace brought back from Vienna music which formed the basis of his 'Collection of Original Harpsichord Music' (but really for piano), a lavish anthology of concertos, quartets, trios, sonatas, etc, which he published in instalments between 1787 and 1789. As well as the keyboard part there were separate parts for all the other instruments. Kozeluch was a favourite composer, but Storace also published an early edition of Mozart's Piano Quartet in E♭ (K493) only three months after Artaria's had appeared and from a different source, and the first edition anywhere of Mozart's Piano Trio in G (K564). As this had not been written when the Storaces left Vienna, Mozart must have sent Storace the MS by post. Also in the collection were three Mozartian piano trios by Storace himself; they merit revival.

On 23 August 1788 Storace married Mary, daughter of John Hall, the engraver (there are decorations by him in the 'Harpsichord Collection'). They had one son, Brinsley John, who died in February 1807 – aged 19, according to the *Gentleman's Magazine*; if so, he was born before his parents were married. His names suggest that Sheridan was his godfather, which makes it the more strange that Sheridan at first turned down *No*

Song, No Supper, though it should be added that he saw only the words. However, when Nancy joined the Drury Lane Company in the summer of 1789 he accepted Stephen's The Haunted Tower, and it proved, after The Duenna, the most successful full-length English opera of the century. From the first it was realized both that this success was due entirely to the music, and that Storace was trying to write opera of a kind new to the play-houses. As is even more apparent in his later operas, his ensembles and finales were not sung as in Shield's operas with the singers facing the audience in line; Nancy and Michael Kelly demonstrated that such music was much more interesting if the singers went on acting as they sang, and Stephen went out of his way to encourage this. The new approach meant that the composer had to dominate the author, and, according to the Thespian Dictionary, Storace was known to have declared 'that it was impossible for any author to produce a good opera without previously consulting his intended composer; for the songs must be introduced as he [the composer] pleases, and the words (which are a secondary consideration) be written agreeable to his directions'. For England this was a revolutionary theory, but it certainly contributed to the success of Stephen's English masterpiece, The Pirates (1792). The exciting plot is set on the Italian coast south of Naples, which Storace knew and Cobb did not, and the scenery and title-page of the vocal score were based on sketches Storace had made on the spot (see fig.1). As in all his operas, he borrowed a small proportion of the music from elsewhere – on this occasion mainly from himself; the long and spirited finale to Act 2 is mainly taken from the Act 1 finale of Gli equivoci, which he despaired of staging in London.

In June 1791 Drury Lane was pulled down to make way for a much larger theatre, and until this was opened in March 1794 the company made do with the King's Theatre when it was not being used for Italian operas, and with the Little Theatre over the road when it was. For one of these seasons, 1792–3, Storace was in charge of the Italian operas as well as of those given by the Drury Lane company. For the Italian season he created with Noverre a 'heroic pantomime ballet', Venus and Adonis, but the music looks undistinguished. He also risked an all-sung English opera, Dido, Queen of Carthage, but the playhouse audience was bored by the long stretches of recitative demanded by Metastasio's original. It failed, and the music is lost.

Storace exerted himself much more in his full-length operas than in his afterpieces. Of the latter only No Song, No Supper has any musical substance, and even that was written in imitation of Shield's rather naive style. But The Cherokee, the first English opera about the Wild West, is full of interest, though let down by its fustian words. The Red Indians' C minor chorus has something of the energy and drive of Beethoven, and Mrs Bland sang a charming song, 'A shepherd once had lost his love', in the character of a Welsh maid. This was later mistaken for a Welsh folksong, though quite unlike one, and twice set as a folksong by Beethoven (e.g. as his op.105 no.1 where, however, the theme is called Scottish).

Early in 1796 Storace was struggling to finish two major works at once. The Iron Chest was a version by George Colman of Godwin's novel, Caleb Williams, but Colman was so dilatory about delivering the text that nothing was properly rehearsed; the result was a fiasco.

When Colman later staged the work at his own theatre, it was a success. Storace's overture, the best he ever wrote, well conveys the gloom of the plot. Partly through overwork, he died just after the first night, and Mahmoud had to be completed by his sister and Kelly with music from other operas (possibly including Dido). The two works were published together for the benefit of Storace's widow and son. Except in the case of No Song, No Supper, the full scores and orchestral parts of all his operas were destroyed in theatre fires early in the following century; it was not wholly his fault that he is so little known.

WORKS

(all printed works published in London)

BT – Burgtheater, Vienna KT – King's Theatre in the Haymarket
DL – Drury Lane LT – Little Theatre in the Haymarket

OPERAS

Gli sposi malcontenti (Brunati), BT, 1 June 1785, not pubd; A-Wgm, D-Dlb

Gli equivoci (Da Ponte, after Shakespeare: The Comedy of Errors), BT, 27 Dec 1786, not pubd; A-Wgm, D-Dlb, etc; lib pubd, no copy in Britain

La cameriera astuta, KT, 4 March 1788; ov. pubd in pf arr., 2 arias and quartet pubd in full score, remainder lost; lib pubd, no copy in Britain

Dido, Queen of Carthage (Hoare, after Metastasio), KT, 23 May 1792; music not pubd

DIALOGUE OPERAS

(vocal score and lib published unless otherwise stated)

(long – full-length opera; short – afterpiece opera)

The Doctor and the Apothecary (short, Cobb, after Stephanie), DL, 25 Oct 1788; half by Storace, remainder from Dittersdorf's Doktor und Apotheker

The Haunted Tower (long, Cobb), DL, 24 Nov 1789

No Song, No Supper (short, Hare), DL, 16 April 1790; GB-Lcm; ed. R. Fiske, MB, xvi (London, 1959)

The Siege of Belgrade (long, Cobb, after Da Ponte), DL, 1 Jan 1791; half by Storace, remainder from Martín y Soler's Una cosa rara

The Cave of Trophonius (short, Hoare), DL, 3 May 1791; only song texts pubd; not a version of Salieri's La grotta di Trofonio

Poor old Drury!!! (short, Cobb), KT, 22 Sept 1791; music, lib not pubd

The Pirates (long, Cobb), KT, 21 Nov 1792

The Prize (short, Hoare), LT, 11 March 1793

My Grandmother (short, Hoare), LT, 16 Dec 1793

Lodoiska (long, J. P. Kemble), DL, 9 June 1794; music from operas of same name by Cherubini, Kreutzer, with new music by Storace

The Glorious First of June (short pastiche, Cobb etc), DL, 2 July 1794

The Cherokee (long, Cobb), DL, 20 Dec 1794

The Three and the Deuce (short, Hoare), LT, 2 Sept 1795

The Iron Chest (long, Colman, after Godwin), DL, 12 March 1796

Mahmoud (long, Hoare), DL, 30 April 1796; completed by M. Kelly and others; lib not pubd

OTHER VOCAL WORKS

8 Canzonetts, 1v, pf/harp acc. (c1782)

Ah! Delia, see the fatal hour (after Metastasio), ariette (c1785)

Care donne che bramate (Badini), aria for Paisiello's Il re Teodoro in Venezia, KT, 8 Dec 1787; full score pubd, autograph US-Wc

? Io non era, aria for Sarti's Le nozze di Dorina, KT, 26 Feb 1793; full score pubd

Captivity, a Ballad supposed to be sung by the unfortunate Marie Antoinette during her Imprisonment (J. Dibden), 1v, ?str (1793)

Lamentation of Marie Antoinette on the Morning of her Execution, 1v, str, bn (1793)

INSTRUMENTAL WORKS

2 quintets, str, pf/hpd, op.2 (1784); incl. Sextet, fl, str, pf/hpd

3 trios, D, C, E♭, vn, vc, pf, in Storace's Collection of Original Harpsichord Music (1788–9); also pubd separately

6 sonatinas, pf/hpd, for the improvement of juvenile performers (1790)

Venus and Adonis (ballet, Noverre), KT, 26 Feb 1793; pf arr. (1793)

BIBLIOGRAPHY

The Thespian Dictionary (London, 1805)

M. Kelly: Reminiscences (London, 1826, 2/1826/R1968)

T. Jones: Memoirs (London, 1951)

R. Fiske: Preface to No Song, No Supper, MB, xvi (London, 1959)

——: 'The Operas of Stephen Storace', PRMA, lxxxvi (1959–60), 29

——: English Theatre Music in the Eighteenth Century (London, 1973)

K. and I. Geiringer: 'Stephen and Nancy Storace in Vienna', Essays on Bach and Other Matters: a Tribute to Gerhard Herz (in preparation)

(3) Nancy [Ann Selina; Anna] **Storace** (*b* London, 27 Oct 1765; *d* London, 24 Aug 1817). English soprano, daughter of (1) Stephen Storace. She was known professionally as Anna and commonly as Nancy. The date of her birth has only recently come to light; her father seems to have falsified her age and that of her brother in the hope of furthering their careers as child prodigies. Nancy had singing lessons in London from Sacchini and, more pleasurably, from Rauzzini, and sang in public as a child at the Hereford Three Choirs Festival of 1777 and elsewhere earlier still. Late in 1778 her parents took her to Italy where her brother had been studying for some time, and one of their objects was to launch Nancy on her career as an opera singer. She sang leading roles in Florence at 15, in Parma at 16, and in Milan at 17. About this time her father seems to have died, but her mother continued to chaperone her during her four years as prima donna in Vienna (1783–7). Soon after she arrived in Vienna, she married an English composer more than twice her age, John Abraham Fisher; late in 1783 Mozart was writing for 'Signora Fischer' the part of Emilia in his unfinished comic opera, *Lo sposo deluso*. The marriage was a disaster from the start, and the Emperor Joseph II, as keenly interested in his opera singers as in his operas, took the extraordinary step of ordering Fisher to leave Vienna, ostensibly because he had ill-treated his wife, but partly at least because the emperor wanted Nancy as his mistress. He was so eager to please her that he commissioned a comic opera from her brother, although Stephen had had no theatre experience. In the middle of the first night of *Gli sposi malcontenti* Nancy lost her voice and the performance had to be abandoned. Her popularity was such that her recovery was celebrated by a cantata composed jointly by Mozart, Salieri and Cornetti; no copy seems to survive.

Nancy's short, plumpish figure made her ineffectual in serious opera, but she was inimitable in the comic ones that constituted most of the Vienna repertory. She sang Rosina in Paisiello's *Il barbiere di Siviglia*, and when Mozart set its sequel, *Le nozze di Figaro*, she was at first to have taken the same part, but Rosina married is a mainly serious character and Nancy was switched to the servant girl, Susanna. She was so successful that later in London she played a succession of similarly charming servants. Jahn suggested that Mozart was in love with her, and that he symbolized this love in his concert aria for soprano, piano and orchestra, *Ch'io mi scordi di te* (K505); 'für Mselle Storace und mich' he wrote in his thematic catalogue. But there is no positive evidence that they felt for each other any stronger emotion than friendliness. When the Storace family returned to London early in 1787 they expected that with their wide experience they would be welcome at the King's Theatre, the home of Italian opera, and they hoped to be able to invite Mozart to compose for the following season. In fact their welcome was grudging, and though Nancy sang at the King's until it burnt down in 1789, Mozart never came.

In autumn 1789 Nancy joined the Drury Lane company; she sang in almost all her brother's English operas, a little handicapped in the spoken dialogue by the Italian accent she affected. She and Michael Kelly raised vocal standards to a level unprecedented at the playhouses. Nancy also sang in Handel oratorios, and was back at the King's for a season in 1793. In 1796 Stephen suddenly died. The loss for Nancy was both

2. Nancy Storace as Euphrosyne in 'Comus' by Thomas Arne: engraving from the 'Attic Miscellany', 1792

personal and artistic; Drury Lane no longer had a musical director she could respect. That summer she left the company and in 1797 she began a successful tour on the Continent with the tenor John Braham; though nine years her junior, he became her lover. They could not marry because Fisher was still alive. In 1802 they had a son, Spencer. By this time Nancy was singing again at the playhouses; she retired in 1808.

In 1816 Nancy and Braham quarrelled; the split is poignantly recorded in numerous letters now at the Sir John Soane Museum in London, and they vividly reveal the personalities of all concerned, especially of Spencer who was by now a very unhappy schoolboy at Winchester. (He later changed his name to Meadows, and became a minor canon at Canterbury Cathedral.) Nancy emerged from the dispute with some dignity and a broken heart; she died in Dulwich the following year, being survived by her mother. Thereafter she was underpraised by reminiscing writers from a wish not to offend Braham, who was by then the leading tenor of the day and a respectable family man. Nancy had received endless acclaim abroad, but was less appreciated in London. Burney thought her 'a lively and intelligent actress', but found 'a certain crack and roughness' in her voice. Lord Mount-Edgcumbe wrote that she was 'totally unfitted for serious opera' but sounded magnificent in Westminster Abbey, 'for in that space the harsh part of her voice was lost, while its power and clearness filled the whole of it'.

BIBLIOGRAPHY

BurneyH
Earl of Mount-Edgcumbe: *Musical Reminiscences* (London, 1823)
M. Kelly: *Reminiscences* (London, 1826, 2/1826/R1968)
B. Matthews: 'The Childhood of Nancy Storace', *MT*, cl (1969), 733
K. and I. Geiringer: 'Stephen and Nancy Storace in Vienna', *Essays on Bach and Other Matters: a Tribute to Gerhard Herz* (in preparation)
ROGER FISKE

Storace, Bernardo (*fl* late 17th century). Italian composer. All that is known of Storace's life derives from the title-page of his sole collection of music: in 1664 he was *vicemaestro di cappella* to the senate of Messina, Sicily. Since the music was published in Venice and seems more akin to that of northern Italy than to that of the Neapolitan–Roman school, it may be inferred that he originated in the north. It is not known whether he was an antecedent of the STORACE family active in England at the end of the 18th century.

Storace's surviving music is all contained in his *Selva di varie compositioni d'intavolatura per cimbalo ed organo* (Venice, 1664; ed. in CEKM, vii, 1965). It is an important link between that of Frescobaldi and Pasquini. He concentrated on larger structures in the form of variations on bass patterns. One group of nine, including variations on passamezzos, romanesca, *spagnoletta*, *monica* and Ruggiero, features longer patterns of up to 24 bars, while the other group, comprising four passacaglias and a ciaccona, involves brief four-bar patterns repeated many times. In the former some variations (*parti*) are marked 'gagliarda' and 'corrente'. The passacaglias are divided into *partite*, each consisting of a number of statements of the bass distinguished in metre or mood or, most notably, by tonality, with sequences of keys such as D–A–E–b and f–b♭–E♭. These sequences are connected by brief modulating passages marked 'passa ad altro tono' pointing up Storace's grasp of tonality. Significantly the pieces are the first to be designated as being on *Alamire*, *Csolfaut*, etc, rather than on the traditional ecclesiastical tones still used by Frescobaldi. Altogether Storace wrote some 320 four-bar phrases on some form of descending tetrachord.

Storace's two toccatas, each followed by a canzona, are less dynamic and passionate than those of his Neapolitan and Roman predecessors. They are much briefer, smoother and more consonant and dwell only on tonic, dominant and subdominant harmonies. The two ricercares are more striking, especially the first, which has three sections, each on a separate theme, followed by a fourth section in which the three themes are combined; the first is that used by Frescobaldi as the opening theme of his *Ricercare con l'obbligo di cantare la quinta parte senza tocarla* in his *Fiori musicali* (Venice, 1635). The volume also includes four dances, and the final piece is a very long Pastorale with the most ingeniously contrived repeated patterns and variations in texture and mood, all over a D pedal.

BIBLIOGRAPHY

G. Pannain: *Le origini e lo sviluppo dell'arte pianistica in Italia dal 1500 fino al 1730 circa* (Naples, 1917)
W. Apel: 'Die süditalienische Clavierschule des 17. Jahrhunderts', *AcM*, xxxiv (1962), 128ff
——: *Geschichte der Orgel- und Klaviermusik bis 1700* (Kassel, 1967; Eng. trans., rev., 1972)
R. A. Hudson: *The Development of Italian Keyboard Variations on the Passacaglio and Ciaccona from Guitar Music in the Seventeenth Century* (diss., U. of California, Los Angeles, 1967)

BARTON HUDSON

Storaket. A sign marking a secondary pause in Armenian EKPHONETIC NOTATION.

Storchio, Rosina (*b* Venice, 19 May 1876; *d* Milan, 24 July 1945). Italian soprano. A pupil at the Milan Conservatory, she made her début there in 1892 at the Teatro dal Verme as Micaëla in *Carmen*. She sang for several seasons in the provinces, then appeared at La Scala in 1895 as Sophie in *Werther*; at Venice in 1897

she took part in the first performance of Leoncavallo's *La bohème*. The best years of her career began when she sang the title role in the première of *Zazà*, also by Leoncavallo (Teatro Lirico, Milan, 1900), and continued with the successes she obtained at La Scala as Donizetti's Linda (1902), Stefana in the first performance of Giordano's *Siberia* (1903), Novina (1905) and Violetta (1906). She also created the title role of *Madama Butterfly* (1904) at La Scala, and returned there occasionally until 1918. She was very popular in Spain, singing frequently at Barcelona between 1898 and 1923, and in Buenos Aires (1904–14). In 1921 she appeared at the Manhattan Opera House, New York, and in Chicago. Among her notable parts were Mimì, Massenet's Manon, and the title role in Mascagni's *Lodoletta*, which she sang at the first performance (Rome, 1917). Her voice was not large, but flexible, pure and sweet; at the height of the popularity for *verismo* opera she personified the lyrical, refined, gentle and sensitive school of singing. Her plaintive and fragile Cio-Cio-San was typical of this approach, in contrast to the more lively and dramatic style of Krusceniski and Destinn. But in other roles, such as Violetta or Manon, her acute sensitivity led her to depict the characters with passionate and touching impulsiveness.

BIBLIOGRAPHY

G. Monaldi: *Cantanti celebri* (Rome, 1929), 246f
R. Celletti: 'Rosina Storchio', *Musica e dischi* (1954), no.91, p.4
G. Lauri-Volpi: *Voci parallele* (Milan, 1955), 41f
T. Hutchinson: 'Rosina Storchio', *Record Collector*, xii (1958), 53 [with discography]
E. Gara: *Carteggi pucciniani* (Milan, 1958)
R. Celletti: 'Rosina Storchio', *Record News*, iv (1960), 429 [with discography by K. Hardwick]
W. Ashbrook: *The Operas of Puccini* (New York, 1968)

RODOLFO CELLETTI

Storck, Karl G(ustav) L(udwig) (*b* Dürmenach, Alsace, 23 April 1873; *d* Olsberg, Westphalia, 9 May 1920). German writer on music. He studied musicology, literature and art history at the universities of Strasbourg and Berlin, where his teachers included Erich Schmidt. He took the doctorate in Berlin in 1895 with a dissertation on Brentano's fairy tales, for which he was awarded the Grimm prize. For many years he was the chairman of the Deutscher Schriftstellerverband and art editor of the magazine *Der Türmer*. He coined the term 'Musikpolitik' to describe the awakening of public interest and participation in music that he fostered. He worked for the reform of school music education, the revival of domestic music and the establishment of folk-music libraries; his ideas on contemporary church and folk music, and for establishing a pension scheme for performing musicians, were realized only 30 years after his death. In addition to his works on music he wrote a standard history of German literature.

WRITINGS

Der Tanz (Bielefeld, 1903)
Geschichte der Musik (Stuttgart, 1904, 6/1926)
Das Opernbuch (Stuttgart, 1905) [many reprints]
Die kulturelle Bedeutung der Musik (Stuttgart, 1906)
ed.: *Mozarts Briefe in Auswahl* (Stuttgart, 1906, 2/1912 as *Mozarts Briefe*, 3/1927)
ed.: *Schumanns Briefe in Auswahl* (Stuttgart, 1906; Eng. trans., 1907)
Mozart: sein Leben und Schaffen (Stuttgart, 1908)
ed.: *Beethovens Briefe in Auswahl* (Stuttgart, 1910, 3/1934)
Musik und Musiker in Karikatur und Satire (Oldenburg, 1910, 2/1913)
Musik-Politik (Stuttgart, 1911)
Emile Jaques-Dalcroze: seine Stellung und Aufgabe in unserer Zeit (Stuttgart, 1912)

ALFRED GRANT GOODMAN

Storioni, Lorenzo (*b* ?Cremona, 1751; *d* ?Cremona, *c*1800). Italian violin maker. Although Cremona's greatest years, which ended with the deaths of Stradivari, Guarneri 'del Gesù' and Carlo Bergonzi, were over before he was born, Storioni had among his contemporaries J. B. Guadagnini (Parma and Turin), Balestrieri (Mantua), and the comparatively inactive Nicolo Bergonzi (Cremona). Storioni complemented each of these, a productive maker drawing something from the traditions of his predecessors, adding to them his own strongly individual character, and keeping Cremonese violin making alive and healthy.

Storioni's work is rough by Cremonese standards, though well proportioned. The roughness, together with a rather ordinary choice of locally grown wood, is a feature common to many lesser late 18th-century Italian violin makers, whose instruments sometimes now bear Storioni labels in place of their own. This sometimes obscures Storioni's real merit: genuine Storioni instruments are rarely less than very good on all important counts. Curiously there is very little to be seen of the influence of Stradivari or Amati; on the whole, there is more of the flavour of Guarneri 'del Gesù'. The outline of his instruments is characterized by a feeling of extra width in the lower part of the centre bouts, a certain straightness coming towards the corner block that is matched by the stiff, slanting soundholes. The scrolls are often heavy and not at all deeply cut, in contrast to a rather shallow pegbox. The varnish varies, the best being of a pleasing orange-red colour, though usually brittle in consistency.

In addition to his many violins, Storioni made some cellos and a number of small violas, a little over 39·5 cm in body length; larger violas are very rare. Storioni's work after about 1790 sometimes has unexpectedly delicate features, evidence of the hand of his pupil J. B. Ceruti. His instruments are highly regarded by players for their breadth of tone, a bright, open, powerful sound suitable for soloists.

BIBLIOGRAPHY

W. L. Lütgendorff: *Die Geigen- und Lautenmacher vom Mittelalter bis zur Gegenwart* (Frankfurt am Main, 1904, rev. 6/1922/*R*1968)

R. Vannes: *Essai d'un dictionnaire universel des luthiers* (Paris, 1932, 2/ 1951/*R*1972 as *Dictionnaire universel des luthiers*, suppl. 1959)

CHARLES BEARE

Störl, Johann Georg Christian (*b* Kirchberg an der Jagst, 14 Aug 1675; *d* Stuttgart, 26 July 1719). German composer and organist. He grew up in Gaildorf, near Backnang, and, according to Mattheson, was a chorister at the Stuttgart court at the age of 12; but he is recorded there only after 16 April 1690 (he remained a chorister until 22 January 1695). He received his basic training in music at the hands of the Hofkapellmeister Theodor Schwartzkopff, who later boasted that he had taught Störl many good things for seven years and had 'brought him so far in the field in instrumental achievement, especially on the keyboard' that even as a junior member of the Kapelle Störl was capable of 'playing the organ for ordinary occasions at court'. At the beginning of 1697 Duke Eberhard Ludwig sent him to Pachelbel in Nuremberg, where Störl received instruction in composition and keyboard. He returned to Stuttgart and in 1699 became court organist. In 1701 the duke granted him permission to spend time studying under F. T. Richter in Vienna; while there he played before the emperor. In February 1702 he travelled to Maastricht, then by sea to Venice,

and then on to Ferrara, Bologna and Rome, where he arrived on 8 March and remained until 11 January 1703. While in Rome he came into contact with Francesco Grassi, Bernardo Pasquini and Arcangelo Corelli. The return journey took him through Florence, Bologna, Ferrara and Venice, where he stayed from 23 January until 24 March (here he met C. F. Pollarolo), and on through Maastricht, Augsburg and Ulm. He reached Stuttgart again on 5 May, having been appointed Hofkapellmeister there on St George's Day (23 April). He worked in this post alongside his former teacher, Schwartzkopff, under the senior Kapellmeister; until 1704 that position was held by J. S. Kusser, and from 1706 by J. C. Pez. Disagreements with Pez and the poor remuneration in this post were the reasons behind Störl's application for the post of organist at the Stiftskirche at the beginning of 1707; he was appointed on 19 February and took up office on St George's Day, but apparently remained Hochfürstlich Württembergischer Kapellmeister. In his new capacity he did much to reorganize the music of the chapter. His hymnbook for the organ (his melodies are typical of the taste of the period) contains some original settings, some of which continued in use until fairly recent times. Schubart, writing of Störl's ecclesiastical cantatas, considered the 'tuttis and the final choruses to be particularly masterly'. Störl's dignified, two-movement sonatas for cornett and three trombones were presumably intended as tower music for the Stiftskirche.

WORKS

Neubezogenes Davidisches Harpfen- und Psalter-Spiel, oder: Neuaufgesetztes Würtembergisch-vollständiges . . . Schlag-, Gesang- und Noten-Buch, 1v, bc (Stuttgart, 1710–11)

Die in Christo Jesu erschiedene Freundlichkeit und Leutseeligkeit Gottes durch dessen Menschwerdung und Geburt in einer Cantata vorgestellet (W. F. Walliser), S, 2 vn, 2 fl, hpd (Stuttgart, n.d.) [5 arias arr. Q. G. van Blankenburg in Airs allemans de Mr. Störl, 1714, ?*D-ROu*]

4 cantatas, 16 arias in F. C. Hiller, Denck-Mahl der Erkentniss, Liebe und Lob Gottes, S, bc (Stuttgart, 1711)

6 sonatas, cornett, 3 trbn, ed. in EDM, 1st ser., xiv (1941)

Complete yearly cycle of cantatas and other liturgical pieces, according to Mattheson; Te Deum, 1713, according to Schubart; pieces for kbd, according to Eitner; other works cited in music catalogue of Rudolstadt Hofkapelle, March 1711 [according to Stiefel in *D-ROu*, for 2 ob, 2 hn, bn]

BIBLIOGRAPHY

EitnerQ; *GerberL*

J. Mattheson: *Grundlage einer Ehren-Pforte* (Hamburg, 1740), 52, 351f; ed. M. Schneider (Berlin, 1910/*R*1969)

C. F. D. Schubart: *Ideen zu einer Ästhetik der Tonkunst* (Vienna, 1806), 148f

J. F. Lobstein: *Beiträge zur Geschichte der Musik im Elsass und besonders in Strassburg, von der ältesten bis auf die neueste Zeit* (Strasbourg, 1840), 69

C. F. Becker: *Die Choralsammlungen der verschiedenen christlichen Kirchen* (Leipzig, 1845), 107, 110f, 116, 121

C. von Winterfeld: *Der evangelische Kirchengesang und sein Verhältniss zur Kunst des Tonsatzes*, iii (Leipzig, 1847/*R*1966), 495ff

J. Sittard: *Zur Geschichte der Musik und des Theaters am Württembergischen Hofe*, i (Stuttgart, 1890), 71, 83ff, 90, 313f, 324ff

R. Eitner: 'Störl, Johann Georg Christian', *ADB*

J. Zahn: *Die Melodien der deutschen evangelischen Kirchenlieder*, vi (Gütersloh, 1893/*R*1963), 288ff, 331f, 355f

E. Praetorius: 'Beiträge zur Quirijn van Blanckenburg's Leben und Werken', *TVNM*, viii/1 (1905), 32

A. Bopp: 'Beiträge zur Geschichte der Stuttgarter Stiftsmusik', *Württembergische Jb für Statistik und Landeskunde 1910* (Stuttgart, 1911), 230

F. Jehle: 'Christian Störl 1675–1719', *Monatschrift für Gottesdienst und kirchliche Kunst*, xxiv (Göttingen, 1919), 261

M. Blindow: *Die Choralbegleitung des 18. Jahrhunderts in der evangelischen Kirche Deutschlands* (Regensburg, 1957)

W. Pfeilsticker: *Neues Württembergisches Dienerbuch*, i (Stuttgart, 1957), §§885, 948, 959

B. Baselt: 'Die Musikaliensammlung der Schwarzburg-Rudolstädtischen Hofkapelle unter Philipp Heinrich Erlebach (1657–1714)', *Traditionen und Aufgaben der Hallischen Musikwissenschaft* (Halle, 1963), 124, 126

F. Krummacher: *Die Überlieferung der Choralbearbeitungen in der frühen evangelischen Kantate* (Berlin, 1965)

E. Stiefel: 'Störl, Johann Georg Christian', *MGG*

GÜNTER THOMAS

Storto (It.). CRUMHORN.

Stothart, Herbert (*b* Milwaukee, Wisc., 11 Sept 1885; *d* Los Angeles, 1 Feb 1949). American composer. Stothart was educated at the University of Wisconsin and in Europe. After some years as a teacher he became active on Broadway as composer and conductor, and in 1929 moved to Hollywood where he was appointed general musical director of MGM. He composed scores for over 100 feature films and conducted many film musicals (*see* FILM MUSIC). Despite a liking for thematic material borrowed from (and generally credited to) other composers, such as Delius (*The Yearling*) and Tchaikovsky (*The Three Musketeers*), Stothart produced some well-made and dramatic scores, notably those for *The Good Earth*, *A Tale of Two Cities*, *David Copperfield* and *The Picture of Dorian Gray*.

CHRISTOPHER PALMER

Stotijn, (Jacob) Haakon (*b* The Hague, 11 Feb 1915; *d* Amsterdam, 3 Nov 1964). Dutch oboist, son of Jaap Stotijn. He studied with his father. For some time he worked at Berne, and in 1940 was appointed first oboe with the Concertgebouw Orchestra. As a soloist he made tours through the Netherlands and abroad and was regarded as one of the best oboists in Europe. Besides the usual works his repertory included modern compositions, such as those of Ibert, Dresden, Van Hemel and Voormolen. He also enjoyed a reputation as a chamber musician, and took part in the instrumental sextet Alma Musica, and other groups. With his father he gave countless performances of Alexander Voormolen's Concerto for two oboes, composed for them. He taught at the Amsterdam Muzieklyceum and at the Amsterdam Conservatory (Edo de Waart was among his pupils).

TRUUS DE LEUR

Stotijn, Jaap (*b* The Hague, 22 Sept 1891; *d* The Hague, 5 April 1970). Dutch oboist and pianist, father of Haakon Stotijn. He studied at The Hague Conservatory, winning the Fock Medal. Having played in various orchestras he became first oboe with The Hague PO, 1919–46, and taught at The Hague Conservatory. He enjoyed a great reputation as a soloist admired for his powerful but refined tone, as a chamber musician, and as a teacher. Dresden, Cor de Groot and Voormolen composed concertos for him. For a long time he played in a trio with the flautist Johannes Feltkamp and the pianist and composer Piet Ketting, and he also conducted various amateur orchestras. As a pianist he frequently accompanied other instrumentalists. Among his pupils were his son, Haakon, and Han de Vries. He devised a new style of reed scrape, a subject on which he has written.

BIBLIOGRAPHY

W. Paap: 'Jaap Stotijn 75 jaar', *Mens en melodie*, xxi (1966)

TRUUS DE LEUR

Stoudios [Stoudion, Stoudiou, Studios]. Greek Orthodox monastery founded in 463 between the Golden Gates in Constantinople. It was an influential centre of Byzantine hymnography and liturgical activity between the 9th century and 12th and probably the most important such centre in Constantinople. The monastery (dedicated to St John the Baptist) was founded by Studius (or Stoudios), a former consul. It may originally have been populated by *akoimētēs*, 'sleepless' monks who in turn incessantly chanted the 'praise of the Lord'. Fleeing before the Arabs, monks of this type from the monastery of Sakkoudion in Bithynia, near Brussa, settled in Stoudios in 798 under Theodore (759–826), who was an important defender of the veneration of icons in the iconoclastic controversy and was repeatedly exiled. Theodore reputedly drew up a monastic rule which included provision for manuscript copying (rather unusual in eastern monasteries); the Stoudios scriptorium still existed in 1350. The Studite rule (typikon) was, in the 10th century, adopted on Mount Athos; during the patriarchate of Alexios the Studite (1025–43) it was transmitted to Russia and survived there even after the introduction of the Jerusalem typikon in the 14th century. (The Stoudios typikon provided for simpler services; that of Jerusalem provided for more festive services.) The monastery was ravaged by the crusaders in 1204; the last period of its significance started with its renovation in 1294 and ended with the Turkish conquest of Constantinople in 1453. Part of the monastery served as a mosque until the earthquake in 1894 and the fire of 1920 left it in ruins.

Between the 9th century and the 12th many monks there composed hymns and wrote treatises. Theodore the Studite and his brother Joseph (the metropolitan of Thessaloniki) are believed to have brought the triōdion into its present form; both contributed hymns to it.

BIBLIOGRAPHY

E. Wellesz: *A History of Byzantine Music and Hymnography* (Oxford, 1949, 3/1963)

H. G. Beck: *Kirche und theologische Literatur im byzantinischen Reich* (Munich, 1959), 127, 213, 491ff

E. Spuler: 'Studiten', *Die Religion in Geschichte und Gegenwart*, vi (Tübingen, 3/1962), 430

R. Janin: 'Studios', *Thriskeftiki ke ithiki enkyklopedia*, xi (Athens, 1967), 492

MILOŠ VELIMIROVIĆ

Stoue. See STONE.

Stourton. See STURTON.

Stout, Alan (*b* Baltimore, Maryland, 26 Nov 1932). American composer and teacher. He received his musical training jointly at the Peabody Conservatory of Music and Johns Hopkins University (1950–54) and completed his formal study in composition and Swedish at the University of Washington (MA, 1959). A year at the University of Copenhagen in 1954–5 instilled a deep interest in the music and literature of Scandinavia, whose culture has continued to exert a strong influence on his music. His principal teachers were Henry Cowell, Wallingford Riegger, Vagn Holmboe and John Verrall. The recipient of numerous important musical commissions, Stout has been on the faculty of Northwestern University since 1963, active as a scholar, pianist and conductor in the Chicago area.

Stout's humanitarian concern is reflected in his choice of texts and his large body of sacred works. His eclectic musical style displays a personal mixture of both experimental and traditional elements. An early innovatory feature (first appearing in the germinal Second Symphony of 1951–66) is the use of large chromatic tone clusters, whose constant movement contributes to the overall form. A relaxed application of the 12-note system results in dissonant writing employing many 2nds and sounding closer to such American pioneers as Ruggles, Varèse and Cowell than to the Viennese masters. Many of the composer's works since 1960 have a continuous rubato in which performers are free to mould micro-rhythms within strict metres. Stout has been especially active on behalf of fellow composers, editing and translating works of Scandinavian composers and promoting performances of neglected 20th-century American masters and young European composers.

WORKS
(*selective list*)

VOCAL

2 Hymns (Bible), T, orch, 1952; The Great Day of the Lord (Bible), chorus, org, 1956; Die Engel (Rilke), S, brass, perc, pf, 1957; Ariel Songs (Shakespeare), S, ens, 1957; Laudi (from Finnish proverb, Keats, St John of the Cross), S, Bar, orch, 1961; Canticum canticorum, S, ens, 1962; Christmas Poem (Cummings), S, ens, 1962; George Lieder, Bar, orch, 1962; 5 Songs from Aftonland (Lagerkvist), S, pf, 1967; Solo (E. Coleman), S, orch, 1968; Nocturnes (from Ekelöf, Boye), A, speaker, orch, 1970; Dialogo per la Pascua (Bible), solo vv, chorus, harp, str septet, 1970; Passion, solo vv, chorus orch, 1973; O altitudo, S, fl, female chorus, orch, 1974

INSTRUMENTAL

3 Hymns: Lux perpetua, Sonata da chiesa, Epilogue, orch, 1953–4; Intermezzo, eng hn, orch, 1954; Sym. no.1, 1959; Movements, vn, orch, 1962; Sym. no.2, 1951–66; Sym. no.4, small chorus, orch, 1970 Str Qt no.1, 1953; Solemn Prelude, trbn, orch, 1953; Str Qt no.7, 1960; Str Qt no.10, 1962; Suite, fl, perc, 1962; Music, ob, pf, 1965; Music, fl, hpd, 1965; Toccata, a sax, perc, 1965; Sonata, vc, pf, 1966; Capriccio, Recitative and Aria, ob, harp, perc, 1967; Movements, cl, str qt, 1969; Pulsar, brass, timp, 1972; Suite, sax, org, 1973 Ricercare and Aria, org, 1952; Music for Good Friday, pf, 1955; 8 Org Chorales, 1960; Fantasy, pf, 1962; Elegy, pf, 1965; Study in Densities and Durations, org, 1967; 3 Org Chorales, 1967; 2 Studies, pf, 1967; Sonata, 2 pf, 1975; Waltz, pf, 1977

Principal publishers: Peters, Augsburg Publishing House

WRITINGS

'Den Internationale Musikfest', *Nordisk musikkultur*, iv (1955), Feb, 78
'Solo', *Beyond the Square: a Tribute to Elliott Coleman*, ed. R. K. Rosenburg (Baltimore, 1972), 37
'Webern in Chicago', *Music and Musicians*, xx/12 (1972), 8
'The Music of Fartein Valen', *Numus West*, iii (1973), 14

BIBLIOGRAPHY

A. Parsons: Chicago SO programme notes, 80th season/27th subscription week (1971), 9
'A Conversation between Bengt Hambraeus and Alan Stout', *Church Music*, i (1972), 40

DON C. GILLESPIE

Stoutz, Edmond de (*b* Zurich, 18 Dec 1920). Swiss conductor and instrumentalist. He studied law at Zurich University, then the piano, cello, oboe, percussion and composition at the Zurich Musikhochschule, and later in Salzburg and Vienna. From 1952 until 1954 he was a cellist and percussionist with the Zurich Tonhalle Orchestra. In 1954 he founded a string ensemble, the Zurich Chamber Orchestra, which he has continued to direct and with which he has made many tours in Switzerland and abroad. He also directs the Zurich Konzertchor, which he founded in 1962. Stoutz is a notable champion of contemporary music.

RUDOLF LÜCK

Stöwe, Charlotte Wilhelmine Caroline. *See* BACHMANN, CHARLOTTE WILHELMINE CAROLINE.

Stoyanov(-Ivanov), Stoyan (*b* Sofia, 3 Sept 1912). Bulgarian musicologist. He learnt the violin as a child and

in 1921 had lessons with Nikola Abadzhiev, with whom he continued his studies while a student in the theory department of the State Academy of Music in Sofia. There he studied music history, education and aesthetics with Stoyan Brashovanov. He graduated in 1935 and earned his living as a violinist and, from 1948 to 1952, as conductor to Sofia Radio. From 1956 to 1964 he was editor-in-chief of the periodical *Balgarska muzika*, then director of the Sofia State Philharmonic (1958–61) and a secretary of the Bulgarian Composers' Union (1962–5). In 1964 he became senior research fellow at the department of theory and aesthetics in the Music Institute of the Bulgarian Academy of Sciences. In addition to his other writings he has been active as a music critic.

WRITINGS

ed., with S. Petrov: *15 godini balgarska muzikalna kultura* [15 years of Bulgarian musical culture] (Sofia, 1959) [incl. 'Nyakoi otlichitelni cherti na novata balgarska sinfonichna muzika', p.58]
Savremenni muzikalni problemi [Contemporary music problems] (Sofia, 1959)
Philipp Kutev (Sofia, 1962; enlarged Russ. trans., 1965)
'Balgarskoto istorichesko muzikoznanie na nauchni pozitsii' [Bulgarian historical research on scientific positions], *IIM*, xii (1967), 289
'Vliyanie na savetskata muzika varchu balgarskata muzika' [The influence of Soviet music on Bulgarian music], *IIM*, xiv (1969), 5–45
Sreshti s muzikata [Encounters with music] (Sofia, 1973)
Intonatsiya i muzikalen obraz [Intonation and the musical image] (in preparation)

LADA BRASHOVANOVA

Stoyanov, Vesselin (*b* Shumen, 20 April 1902; *d* Sofia, 29 June 1969). Bulgarian composer. A son of one of the first Bulgarian music teachers, he received his early music education at home, together with his brother Andrei who was for many years a piano professor. In 1926 Stoyanov completed his studies at the Sofia State Academy of Music, and then studied at the Vienna Hochschule für Musik with Franz Schmidt (composition) and Ebenstein and de Cone (piano). Back in Bulgaria he worked as a concert pianist for a short time. In 1937 he was appointed to the staff of the Sofia Academy, where he was made professor extraordinary in 1943 and professor of form and composition in 1945; Stoyanov directed the institution during the years 1943–4 and 1956–62. He was director of the National Opera in 1953–4. Stoyanov was a reflective composer whose works are distinguished by classical formal logic, monumental scale, expressiveness, rich orchestration and, not infrequently, a certain sensuousness. In his early works he tried to incorporate folk elements into a conventional western European tonal style, but his last pieces, with their optimistic melodies and masterly instrumentation, show an attempt at a closer relationship with Bulgarian peasant music. Stoyanov often drew on Bulgarian humorous folk mythology, as in his works on the heroes Bai Ganju and Hitar Peter.

Stoyanov's son Pancho (*b* Sofia, 9 Feb 1931), also a composer, studied in Sofia and Moscow; he has written four symphonies (1958–75) as well as other orchestral and chamber music.

WORKS
(*selective list*)

Dramatic: Jensko zarstwo [Women's realm], opera, perf. 1935; Salambo (opera, after Flaubert), perf. 1940; Hitar Peter [Cunning Peter], opera, perf. 1958; Papessa Joánna, ballet, perf. 1969; film scores
Orch: Bai Ganju, 1941; 3 pf concs., 1942, 1953, 1966; Karwawa péssen [Bloody song], 1947; Vn Conc., 1948; Mladejko concertino [Youth concertino], vn, orch, 1950; Rhapsodie, 1956; Prasnitshna uwertjura [Festival ov.], 1959; Vc Conc., 1960; Sym. no.1, 1962; 2

suites from *Papessa Joánna*, 1967, 1969; Sym. no.2 'Welikii Preslaw' [The great Preslaw], 1969
Inst: Suite, pf, 1931; Sonata, vn, pf, 1933; 3 str qts, 1933–5
Vocal: Da bade den [The day is dawning], Bar, chorus, orch, 1952; songs, choruses
Principal publishers: Muzgiz, Nauka i iskustvo (Sofia), Peters, Universal

LADA BRASHOVANOVA

Stözl, Gottfried Heinrich. *See* STÖLZEL, GOTTFRIED HEINRICH.

Stracciari, Riccardo (*b* Casalecchio di Reno, 26 June 1875; *d* Rome, 10 Oct 1955). Italian baritone. After singing in the chorus in operetta (1894), he studied with Ulisse Masetti at Bologna, where he made his début in 1898 in Lorenzo Perosi's oratorio *La resurrezione di Cristo*. In 1901 he appeared at Lisbon, then at La Scala (1904–5), Covent Garden (1905), the Metropolitan (1906–7), the Paris Opéra (1909), the Real, Madrid (1909–10), and other leading theatres. He then sang mostly in Italy, Spain and Argentina, though from 1917 to 1919 he was a member of the Chicago Opera Company. His vocal decline can be dated from 1928, but though he devoted himself to teaching, first in Naples (1926), then later in Rome, he did not leave the stage until 1942 and in 1944 appeared again in *La traviata* at the Teatro Lirico, Milan. His mellow, velvety voice, coloured and resonant over its whole range, with an extended and penetrating upper register, made him, between 1905 and 1915, the rival of Titta Ruffo and Pasquale Amato. His repertory included all the great baritone roles and among the dramatic parts he preferred those in *Il trovatore*, *Rigoletto* and *Aida*. But, thanks to a technique characteristic of the best traditions of the 19th century, he excelled in works which allowed him to display his courtly enunciation, smooth singing, elegant phrasing and musical delicacy: *La favorite*, *Ernani* and above all *La traviata*, in which he played the heavy father with exceptional, gripping effect. He was also a noted Figaro in *Il barbiere di Siviglia*.

BIBLIOGRAPHY

J. Subirá: *Historia y anecdotario del Teatro Real* (Madrid, 1949)
M. de Schauensee: 'A Visit with Riccardo Stracciari', *Opera News* (20 Dec 1954)
R. Celletti: 'Riccardo Stracciari', *Musica e dischi* (1955), no.106, p.18 [with discography by R. Vegeto]
G. Lauri-Volpi: *Voci parallele* (Milan, 1955), 177f
R. Celletti: 'Riccardo Stracciari', *Record News*, iii (1958), 75 [with commentary by K. Hardwick and discography by F. Armstrong]

RODOLFO CELLETTI

Strada, Giovanni Battista. *See* STRATA, GIOVANNI BATTISTA.

Strada del Pò, Anna Maria (*fl* 1720–40). Italian soprano. She was a native of Bergamo, and in 1720–21 in the service of Count Colloredo, governor of Milan. In that season she sang in four operas at Venice, the first of them Vivaldi's *La verità in cimento*. In 1724–6 she appeared at the S Bartolomeo theatre, Naples, in Vinci's *Eraclea* and *Astianatte*, Porpora's *Semiramide*, Leo's *Zenobia in Palmira* and two operas by Giovanni Porta. While in Naples she married Aurelio del Pò, who for a time managed the theatre and signed the dedication of a number of librettos in 1721–5. He is said to have married Strada because he owed her 2000 ducats and could find no other means of satisfying her. Handel presumably heard her in Italy early in 1729, and engaged her for London at a salary of £600 – signifi-

cantly less than the £800 he offered the contralto Merighi.

From 1729, when she made her début as Adelaide in *Lotario* on 2 December, until June 1737 Strada was Handel's leading soprano in all his operas and oratorios, and never missed a performance except through occasional indisposition (the only production in which she may not have appeared was the revival of *Floridante* in March 1733, when she was ill). She sang more major Handel parts than any other singer, appearing in at least 24 operas, the serenatas *Acis and Galatea* (June 1732) and *Il Parnasso in festa* (March 1734), the opera-ballet *Terpsicore* (November 1734), the ode *Alexander's Feast* (February 1736) and the oratorios *Esther* (May 1732), *Deborah* (March 1733), *Athalia* (July 1733 in Oxford, 1735 in London) and *Il trionfo del tempo* (March 1737). She repeated most of these parts in later seasons. In oratorio she sang in English or Italian as required. She was the only member of Handel's company who did not go over to the Opera of the Nobility in the summer of 1733 (earlier, in June 1732, she had refused to sing in a serenata by Bononcini, 'for Reasons best known to the said Aurelio del Pò and his Wife'). The list of Handel roles composed for Strada is long: Adelaide in *Lotario* (1729), Partenope (1730), Cleofide in *Poro* (1731), Fulvia in *Ezio* (1732), Elmira in *Sosarme* (1732), Angelica in *Orlando* (1733), Deborah (1733), Josabeth in *Athalia* (1733), Arianna (1734), Erato in *Terpsicore* (1734), Ginevra in *Ariodante* (1735), Alcina (1735), the soprano part in *Alexander's Feast* (1736), Atalanta (1736), Tusnelda in *Arminio* (1737), Arianna in *Giustino* (1737) and Berenice (1737). She was the first singer of Clio in *Il Parnasso in festa*, though the part consisted wholly of old music. Handel added much new material for her as Galatea, as Esther and as Bellezza in *Il trionfo del tempo*. Between 1730 and 1734 she sang in revivals of 11 other Handel operas, taking eight parts composed for Cuzzoni and one for Faustina. Nearly all were modified, occasionally by new music but more often by the insertion of arias from other operas or even from other characters in the same opera. Handel composed two new arias for Strada's benefit in *Giulio Cesare* on 21 March 1730. She appeared in a number of pasticcios under Handel and in his revival of Ariosti's *Coriolano* in March 1732 as well as at occasional concerts. In a letter of 7 April 1734 Mrs Pendarves described a party in her house at which Strada sang to Handel's accompaniment. Burney said that in 1737, the year of Handel's stroke, del Pò sued the composer for arrears of salary due to Strada. There is no confirmation of this, but it may be significant that she never sang under Handel after June 1737, although she remained in England for another year. On 17 June 1738 she left for Breda at the command of the Princess of Orange (a daughter of George II and pupil of Handel), 'from whence she intends to go to Italy'. A press statement denied allegations that she was responsible for the miscarriage of Heidegger's operatic plans for the following season, asserting on the contrary that she had reached an agreement with him. But she never returned to England. She was singing (for a low fee) with Senesino at Naples in 1739–40, and then retired to Bergamo.

Burney attributed Strada's success largely to Handel. She 'was a singer formed by himself, and modelled on his own melodies. She came hither a coarse and aukward singer with improvable talents, and he at last polished her into reputation and favour'. And again:

This singer had many prejudices to combat on her first arrival in this country . . . and Strada's personal charms did not assist her much in conciliating parties, or disposing the eye to augment the pleasures of the ear; for she had so little of a Venus in her appearance, that she was usually called the *Pig*. However, by degrees she subdued all their prejudices, and sung herself into favour, particularly with the friends of Handel, who used to say that by the care he took in composing for her, and his instructions, from a coarse singer made a fine voice, he rendered her equal at least to the finest performer in Europe.

The prejudices, in the minds of admirers of Faustina and especially Cuzzoni, are attested by Rolli's letters to Riva, and Strada's lack of personal allure by those of Mrs Pendarves ('her person *very bad*, and she makes *frightful mouths*'); but she was clearly no negligible artist when she arrived. Rolli, a hostile witness, wrote before her London début that she was 'simply a copy of Faustina with a better voice and better intonation, but without her charm and brio', and he agreed with Mrs Pendarves and others about her success with the London public. In December 1729 he quoted Handel as saying that:

she sings better than the two who have left us, because one of them [Faustina] never pleased him at all and he would like to forget the other [Cuzzoni]. The truth is that she has a penetrating thread of a soprano voice which delights the ear, but oh how far removed from Cuzzoni! Bononcini, who was with me at the opera, agrees with me as to this.

She was famous for her shake; as Burney noted, her first aria on the London stage, 'Qual cor che mi donasti' in *Lotario*, seems chiefly calculated to display it, and her whole part in this opera is of great brilliance. She seems to have combined something of Faustina's dramatic flair with the seductive warbling for which Cuzzoni was renowned; the former is apparent in *Alcina*, the latter in *Poro*, *Ezio*, *Sosarme* and *Ariodante*. Her parts point to a wide range in emotional and expressive power as well as in compass. In the earlier operas this extended for two octaves (c' to c'''), though the top C occurs only in *Partenope*. Later it was slightly restricted (d' to bb'' in the operas of 1737), but there is no evidence of any marked decline. Mrs Pendarves wrote in November 1736 that Strada 'sings better than ever she did', and this may well have been true.

WINTON DEAN

Stradella, Alessandro (*b* Rome, 1 Oct 1644; *d* Genoa, 25 Feb 1682). Italian composer. He was one of the leading composers in Italy in his day and one of the most versatile.

1. LIFE. Apart from occasional trips to the north of Italy Stradella's interests and activities were centred on Rome until 1677. His education and musical training can only be surmised; according to Francesco Maria Veracini he was a pupil of Ercole Bernabei. Stradella's earliest recorded musical activity is as a singer of 'musica cantata di Quaresima' in 1655 at S Marcello del Crocifisso. In the same year his father died and in 1656 his mother. Who then cared for the boy is not known. In 1658 he was recommended as a singer to Queen Christina of Sweden; he was also said to be able to play the lute and violin and to write Latin verses. In 1663 Christina commissioned him to compose a motet for the anniversary of Filippo Neri, and for this he wrote the words and music of *Chare Jesu suavissime*, his first known composition. In December 1664 the queen commissioned a cantata for the feast of the Immaculate Conception with a text by Nicolò Minato. Stradella was appointed Christina's *servitore di*

camera and also entered the service of Lorenzo Onofrio Colonna and his wife Maria Mancini; during this period he wrote music for various confraternities and churches in Rome. His first semi-dramatic work, *Accademia d'amore*, was given at the Colonna palace in Carnival 1665. (Pirrotta suggested that a second surviving version of this work, with completely new music, might more properly be entitled *Torneo d'amore*.) Motets commissioned by Christina were also performed at S Marcello in 1665. In the same year Stradella went with the Colonna family to Venice, where they stayed for Carnival 1666. Passing through Florence on the return journey, he probably met Filippo Acciaiuoli, who, together with the queen's adviser Count d'Alibert, later opened the first public opera house in Rome.

An unnamed oratorio (now lost), most likely in Latin, was commissioned from Stradella by the Arciconfraternità del Ss Crocifisso and presented at S Marcello on 11 February 1667. The following year several prologues and an intermezzo by him, largely to operas by other composers, were given at the Colonna palace and elsewhere. In May his operetta *La Circe*, for Olimpia Aldobrandini, commissioned to honour the new Medici cardinal, Leopoldo, who had recently arrived in Rome, was performed at the Villa Aldobrandini at Frascati.

Stradella may have been a *gentiluomo*. His friends Acciaiuoli and the Cavaliere Monesio were certainly of this social rank. He seems not to have been dependent on any church, theatre or patron; even his compositions for the queen and the Colonna family were apparently written on commission. He enjoyed the role of the carefree nobleman, spending his time as he pleased; throughout his life he had many adventures with women (including the singers Pia Antinori and Giorgina Cesi and the nun-widow Lisabetta Marmorani), and friendships with people of the lower classes. In 1669 he joined with the abbot Antonio Sforza and the violinist Carlo Ambrogio Lonati in a plot to embezzle money from the Roman Catholic Church. The theft was soon discovered, Sforza imprisoned and Stradella urged to leave the city until the scandal quietened down. He returned in time for the opening of the new public theatre, the Tordinona; the first two seasons saw the presentation of his prologues, intermezzos and other music in connection with the revival of *Scipione africano* and *Giasone* (with the title *Il novello Giasone*) by Cavalli, and *Dori* and *Tito* by Cesti. All these operas had enjoyed success in Venice, and some had been performed during Stradella's visit there. From the same period dates *Il Biante*, an *azione drammatica* produced by the Colonnas in honour of Pope Clement X. The cantata *L'avviso al Tebro giunto* was written in the autumn of 1671 to celebrate the marriage of Anna Teresa Pamphili Aldobrandini and Prince Giovanni Andrea Doria of Genoa.

In 1673 Acciaiuoli left the Tordinona and the attention formerly given to Stradella was transferred to other composers; Stradella began to compose on private commission, producing the oratorio *Ester*, a semi-dramatic work, *Lo schiavo liberato*, and the serenata *Vola, vola in altri petti*. As the theatres were closed for Holy Year 1675, his attention turned to sacred music; the oratorio *S Giovanni Battista* was given at S Giovanni dei Fiorentini on 31 March with the young Corelli among the instrumental performers.

Although not precisely datable, several works are shown by their texts to have been written during

Stradella's years in Rome: *Ecco amore che altero risplende*, *Che speranza aver si può*, *Fra quest'ombre*, *Qui dove fa soggiorno*, *Il mar gira ne' fiumi* and *Pugna certamen*. The oratorios *S Pelagia* and *S Giovanni Crisostomo* probably date from this period, like the serenatas *Qual prodigio* and *Il Damone*, which follow the Roman practice of concerto grosso instrumentation.

In 1677 Stradella incurred the anger of Cardinal Alderan Cibo and once again was forced to leave Rome, never to return. He apparently went first to Venice, where Alvise Contarini, a member of a powerful Venetian family, hired him to teach music to his mistress. After a brief stay Stradella left Venice with the young lady, much to the anger of the Contarinis. The couple went to Turin, probably invited by d'Alibert, who was trying to establish the new Teatro Regio there. With the aid of Marquis San Tommaso, the minister of affairs, Stradella was introduced to court and found favour with the regent, Maria Giovanna of Nemours. Soon after, a committee of about 40 men arrived, headed by Alvise Contarini himself, intent on taking the girl away and killing Stradella. However, the regent discovered the plot and managed to protect the couple. Contarini left Turin, but sent two of his *bravi* with orders to kill the composer, which they unsuccessfully attempted to do on 10 October 1677. There are conflicting versions of the outcome of the incident, but in any case Stradella left Turin alone and arrived in Genoa at the beginning of 1678. If he had intended to compose for the Teatro Regio, he was not given the opportunity to do so. His only works that seem to have been written for Turin are the cantatas *Se del pianeta ardenta* and *Sciogliete in dolci nodi*; both texts refer to Maria Giovanna. They are unique among his works in their use of a four-part division of the string orchestra, probably a reflection of musical practices at court.

Apparently even before his encounter with the Venetian bandits, Stradella had been in contact with Genoa. He may have been arranging the presentation of his comic opera *Il Trespolo tutore*, which was given there around this time (not in Rome, as formerly thought). In 1678 his opera *La forza dell'amor paterno* was performed and in 1679 *Le gare dell'amor eroico* (also known as *L'Oratio*), both at the Teatro Falcone. The sacred cantata *Esule dalle sfere* is dated 1680, as is the 'cantata morale' *Alle selve, agli studii* to a text by Cardinal Benedetto Pamphili. Most likely from this same period is another cantata, *Crudo mar di fiamme*. Stradella probably spent the rest of his life in Genoa; the only performance of his music outside the city at this time was that of the oratorio *Susanna* at Modena in 1681. In that year he composed the wedding serenata *Il barcheggio*; on the title-page of the Modena score is written 'l'ultima della sue sinfonie'. Another intrigue with a woman, this time involving the powerful Lomellini family of Genoa, ended in his death at the hands of a soldier from Alessandria at the Piazza Bianchi, Genoa.

For more than a decade after his death Stradella's music continued to be performed in Modena: in 1684 *S Editta*; in 1686 *Il Trespolo tutore*; in 1687 *Susanna*; in 1688 *S Giovanni Battista* and *S Pelagia*; in 1692 *S Editta* and *Susanna*; and in 1693 *S Giovanni Battista*. Such sustained interest may indicate a personal connection between the composer and the court or may have come about simply because after Stradella's death his brother offered much of the music for sale to the duke. There were posthumous performances of Stradella's music in Rome as well: in 1690 several works were sung at the palace of Cardinal Pietro Ottoboni, and in 1695 the opera *Il moro per amore* (also known as *Floridoro* and *Rodrigo*) was given at the Teatro Capranica. Interest in Stradella's music seems to have survived longest in England, to judge by the many 18th-century copies of his compositions there.

2. WORKS. Although he was only 37 when he died, Stradella left a significant mark on composition. His output includes works in all major categories, both instrumental and vocal. His surviving instrumental music comprises 27 works: 12 for one violin and continuo, nine for two violins and continuo, two for violin, violone (or cello) and continuo, one for keyboard and three for larger ensembles designated 'sinfonia' or 'sonata' (some of the individual movements are headed 'canzona' or 'aria'). With exception of no.12 (a set of 25 variations over a bass) all the pieces are *sonate da chiesa* and have three to six sections. The largest of the sectional works is 333 bars in length. The commonest key is D; 17 of the 26 string pieces have all movements in the same key. About a fifth of the movements are in binary form, though the style is based more on motivic play than on the grouping of phrases. Imitation is a dominant technique; coupled with a strong rhythmic drive it gives insistence and unity to the music. None of Stradella's movements bears a dance title, but several have the characteristic rhythms of typical Baroque dances. Most of this music is clearly tonal; in many works the main keys are tonic, dominant and subdominant. Major and minor 5-3 chords are the most frequent, and secondary dominants are plentiful.

Stradella's string writing makes idiomatic use of scales, arpeggios and characteristic figuration but does not exploit the technical possibilities of the instruments. Two of the instrumental compositions reflect his experience with sacred vocal music. The four-part sonata no.24 is written for two 'cori', the first consisting of two violins and continuo, the second of two cornetts and continuo. They are handled in all three movements as independent groups in the manner of vocal *cori spezzati*, and the two timbres are never mixed. The four-movement *Sonata a otto viole con una tromba* (no.26), in which two groups of four strings alternate, shows a similar treatment, but with the addition of an obbligato trumpet part.

Stradella's greatest contribution to the development of instrumental music is his use of concerto grosso instrumentation, employed first as an accompaniment to vocal music, then in opening sinfonias to vocal works and finally for an independent instrumental composition. In the *Sonata di viole* (no.25) a concertino of two violins and lute alternates with a 'concerto gross di viole'. Although the concertino is not given more difficult music than the concerto grosso, a distinction in volume is maintained, since the groups rarely join together (they do so only in the third movement). There is some imitation within each group. This earliest known concerto grosso would seem to have been the model for Corelli's op.6, the first published concerti grossi – a plausible supposition, since the two composers were apparently acquainted.

Stradella made a clear differentiation between aria and recitative in his vocal music, but in general their succession is still fluid and unordered. Notes of quaver

Opening of Stradella's cantata 'Ah! troppo è ver' (I-MOe Mus.F.1145)

and semiquaver value are employed in free fashion in the recitatives to simulate the rhythms of speech. Formal melody is not attempted there, but the lines have clear contours and proceed largely in conjunct movement. The full cadence is used only at major points of verbal punctuation; otherwise the flow is maintained by a denial of cadence. Occasionally the bass is static for long phrases, encouraging the creation of a dramatic mood. Cadences with the last syllable placed on the penultimate note, widely used in the earlier 17th century, are still common in Stradella's music. He used arioso to heighten the emotional content of recitative without disturbing the flow of the drama, to relieve the monotony of an extended recitative and to organize recitative by its repetition as a refrain. In some works, such as *Corispero*, the arioso also serves as a formal bridge between recitative and aria, appearing consistently at the end of recitative sections which precede arias.

Stradella used several aria forms without any marked preference; common types include the popular *ABB¹* and *AB* forms, as well as the *ABA* aria with or without clear sectional contrasts of key and metre. Many of these arias, whose dimensions vary considerably, have two strophes. A number of arias are built on ostinatos, which usually migrate to other pitch levels in the course of a piece and may be varied as well. A feature related to the ostinato principle is Stradella's employment of a single rhythmic motif throughout a section, imparting insistence and drive to the music. In all his vocal music the preferred texture is a contrapuntal one: instruments and voices generally proceed in imitation, creating a full

concertato texture. Where an orchestra is used it may play only ritornellos, alternate phrases with the voice or serve as a continuous accompaniment. The vocal music is clearly tonal in its chord progressions, modulation and a preference for opening motifs that outline the tonic chord.

The texts of Stradella's oratorios show considerable variety. *S Editta*, with its arguments between the abstract characters Nobility, Beauty, Humility, Greatness and the Senses (each of whom tries to claim the saint as his own), recalls Cavalieri's *La rappresentatione di Anima et di Corpo*. Also in the realm of allegory is *S Pelagia* with characters such as Religion and the World; however, the inclusion of Pelagia's grandfather indicates an attempt to humanize the story. *Susanna*, on the other hand, has a *testo* who relates a biblical tale with the aid of a chorus of commentators in addition to the principal characters, very much in the manner of Carissimi's oratorios. *S Giovanni Crisostomo* and *Ester* belong to the same tradition. The latter even uses two voices as *testo* (bass in the first part, soprano in the second), a treatment typical of Carissimi. Although *Ester* and *Susanna* both present historical figures in a most human manner, the oratorio which best achieves this is *S Giovanni Battista*, which has no allegorical figures and no *testo* and is a drama of real passions straightforwardly presented.

The oratorios are musically diverse as well. Accompaniments range from continuo alone (*S Giovanni Crisostomo*), through two violins and continuo (*Susanna* and probably *S Editta* and *Ester*, which lack the indicated orchestral parts) and two violins, viola and continuo (*S Pelagia*) to a concertino of two violins and continuo with a concerto grosso of violin, two violas and continuo (*S Giovanni Battista*). The polyphonic ensembles of *S Editta* reveal Stradella's training in *stile antico* counterpoint. *S Pelagia* resembles a cantata in its able lyrical writing. *Susanna* (probably not an early work, as Giazotto claimed) exhibits an interest in rhythm, instrumental motifs and the free use of ostinatos characteristic of Stradella's mature years. The concerto grosso principle is used in *S Giovanni Battista* with variety and skill. It occurs in seven other vocal compositions and one instrumental work but in no other oratorio. Ostinatos appear only in the arias with continuo accompaniment and are used in a free manner. Some arias have two strophes; the da capo form is rare, but does occur. The recitatives are close to those of the cantatas in their lyricism and frequent use of arioso.

All of Stradella's operas have serious main plots, with the exception of *Il Trespolo tutore*, an early *opera buffa* and one of the first to have a comic bass in the leading role. The rapid recitative is of the patter type, filled with repeated notes. Trespolo's arias are in a light, quick vein and make use of running quavers or square, folklike melodies. Occasional use of falsetto also heightens his *buffo* aspect. More serious scenes, such as those in which the eight arias with orchestral accompaniment appear, serve as a relief to the comedy; however, the melodic style is entirely devoid of coloratura.

Stradella's opera orchestra consists of two violin parts and continuo; it plays the sinfonias which introduce the acts, the ritornellos of continuo arias and accompaniments to some of the other arias. The later operas (*La forza dell'amor paterno*, *Il moro per amore*) use the orchestra for more continuous accompaniment of the voice, as well as for exchanges with the voice, but arias with only continuo accompaniment are also plentiful. Although *Le gare dell'amor erioco* was performed in 1679, its emphasis on the ensemble, its related interest in *stile antico* writing and its lack of organization of musical means towards a dramatic end suggest that it is an earlier work. *Il Corispero* reveals Stradella's awakening interest in rhythm through a melodic style which is more motivic and instrumental. Occasionally a rhythmic figure is used so frequently in all parts that it becomes the single characteristic motif of the aria.

La forza dell'amor paterno contains a strong element of vocal virtuosity. Coloratura passages abound in all but the comic roles; the voice is consistently exploited in concertato fashion, either sustained over several bars of instrumental activity or in rapid exchanges of short phrases with the instruments. The same contrapuntal texture predominates in *Il moro per amore*. In both these works, probably Stradella's most mature operas, da capo arias are in the majority, but arias in all forms are numerous and often extended.

Many of Stradella's sacred vocal compositions are called 'mottetto' in the sources: such works may consist of a series of arias (*Sinite lacrimari*), a regular alternation of recitative and aria (*Plaudite vocibus*), a single duet (*Ave regina caelorum*) or an irregular mixture of recitative and aria (*Locutus est Dominus*). Some are accompanied by orchestra, others by continuo alone. All have Latin texts and a predominantly contrapuntal texture and treat the voice in a lyrical manner.

The cantatas also show a variety of construction. In some cases the music, rather than creating a form,

simply follows that of the text and changes in response to it. At other times a clear musical organization is obvious, such as in *Fra quest'ombre*: the opening phrase for soprano returns several times in the course of the cantata as a ritornello and the third aria presents the second strophe of the first. Often there is no dramatic progression: two people are in love, and the intent of the cantata is simply to communicate this fact. Other cantatas are less static, as when, for example, a reconciliation is effected during the work. The cantatas range in scope from a sequence of two arias with their recitatives for soprano and continuo (*Il mar gira ne' fiumi*) to an irregular series of arias and recitatives with a polyphonic madrigal for six voices, the whole accompanied by concertino and concerto grosso (the Christmas cantata *Ah! troppo è ver*). They include both simple syllabic settings and works filled with *fioriture* of a rhythmic and motivic nature. All aspects of Stradella's writing noted in his operas and oratorios are also found in the cantatas.

See also SERENATA.

WORKS

OPERAS

Il Trespolo tutore (G. Villifranchi), Genoa, *c*1677, *I-MOe*; extracts ed. in Hess

La forza dell'amor paterno, Genoa, Teatro Falcone, 1678, *Tn* [revision of N. Minato's Seleuco]

Le gare dell'amor eroico, Genoa, Teatro Falcone, 1679, *MOe*, *GB-Lbm* [revision of Minato's Mutio Scevola; also known as L'Oratio]

La rosaura, Rome, Teatro Pamphili, 1688; lost, probably by A. Scarlatti

Il moro per amore (F. Orsini), Rome, Teatro Capranica, 1695, *A-Wn*, *F-Pc*, *I-MOe*, *Tn* [also known as Floridoro or Rodrigo]; extracts ed. in Hess; 1 scena ed. in Alte Meister des Bel Canto, ii (Leipzig, 1912)

Il Corispero, *MOe*; 1 aria, HAM, ii

Doriclea, formerly *RI*, removed by M. Tiberti

OTHER STAGE WORKS

Accademia d'amore (G. P. Monesio), 8vv, insts, Rome, Palazzo Colonna, 1665, *MOe*, *Tn*

Aita, numi, aita (F. Acciaiuoli), prologue, 4vv, 2 vn, tpt, 5 str, bc, Rome, Teatro Tordinona, 1672, *MOe*, *Tn*

Amanti, che credete (?G. F. Apollonio), intermezzo, 1v, chorus, bc, Rome, Teatro Tordinona, 1671, *MOe*, *Rvat*, *Tn*

Che fai, Dorilla mia, intermezzo, 2vv, 2 vn, bc, *MOe*, *Tn*

Che nuove, o ragionevoli, prologue, 3vv, 2 vn, bc, ?Aix-la-Chapelle, ?1668, *MOe*, *Tn*

Chi me l'havesse detto, intermezzo, 4vv, bc, Rome, *c*1668, *Tn*

Chi mi conoscerà (?Apollonio), intermezzo, 3vv, bc, Rome, Teatro Tordinona, 1671, *MOe*, *Tn*

Con meste luci (F. M. Sereni), prologue, 1v, bc, ?Rome, ?1668, *MOe*, *Tn*

Dal luminoso impero, prologue, 1v, bc, ?Modena, ?1681, *MOe*, *Tn*

Dormi, Titone, addio (Apollonio), prologue, 3vv, 2 vn, bc, Rome, Teatro Tordinona, 1671, *B-Bc*, *I-MOe*, *Tn*

È dovrò dunque in solitaria stanza, prologue, 1v, 2 vn, bc, ?1668, *MOe*, *Tn*

Fermate, homai (Apollonio), prologue, 3vv, 2 vn, bc, Rome, Teatro Tordinona, 1671, *MOe*, *Tn*

Il barcheggio, 3vv, tpt, 2 vn, bc, Genoa, 1681, *MOe*, *Tn*

Il Biante, azione drammatica, 4, 7vv, 2 vn, bc, Rome, Palazzo Colonna, *c*1670–72, *MOe*, *Tn* [also known as La Laurinda; 1 canzonetta ed. in Alte Meister des Bel Canto, ii (Leipzig, 1912)]

Il Damone, serenade, 2vv, chorus, insts, Rome, 1677, *MOe*, *Tn* [2 versions]

La Circe (Apollonio), operetta, 3vv, 2 vn, bc, Frascati, 1668, *MOe* [2 versions]

La ruina del mondo, intermezzo, 2vv, bc, ?Genoa, ?1679, *Tn*

Lasciai di Cipro il soglio, prologue, 1v, chorus, 2 vn, bc, ?Rome, ?1668, *Tn*

Lo schiavo liberato (S. Baldini), 4vv, insts, *MOe*, *Tn*

O di Cocito oscure deità (Acciaiuoli), prologue, 4vv, 2 vn, bc, Rome, Palazzo Colonna, 1668, *MOe*, *Rvat*, *Tn*

O ve', che figurace (Acciaiuoli), intermezzo, 2vv, bc, Rome, Teatro Tordinona, 1672, *MOe*, *Tn*

Questo è il giorno prefisso (Apollonio), prologue, 5vv, 2 vn, bc, Rome, Teatro Tordinona, 1671, *MOe*, *Tn*

Reggetemi, non posso più (F. Orsini), prologue, 3vv, 2 vn, bc, ?Rome,

?1666, *MOe*, *Tn*
Soccorso, aita, ohimè (?Acciaiuoli), intermezzo, 2vv, 2 vn, bc, ?Rome, Palazzo Colonna, ?1668, *MOe*, *Tn*
Sù, miei fiati canori, intermezzo, 1v, bc, ?Modena, ?1675, *Tn*
Sù, sù, si stampino (?Apollonio), intermezzo, 2vv, chorus, 2 vn, bc, Rome, Teatro Tordinona, 1671, *MOe*, *Rvat*, *Tn*

ORATORIOS

Ester, liberatrice del populo ebreo, 5vv, ?2 vn, bc, inc., *MOe*
S Giovanni Battista (Abbate Ansaldi), 5vv, insts, Rome, S Giovanni dei Fiorentini, 1675, *D-B*, *F-Pc*, *GB-Cfm*, *Lbm*, *T*, *I-Bc*, *Fc*, *MOe*
S Giovanni Crisostomo, 5vv, bc, *DK-Kk*, *I-MOe*
S Editta, vergine e monaca, regina d'Inghilterra (L. Orsini), 5vv, ?2 vn, ?bc, inc., ?Rome, S Marcello, *MOe*
S Pelagia, 4vv, 2 vn, va, bc, *MOe*
Susanna (G. B. Giardini), 5vv, 2 vn, bc, Modena, 1681, *MOe*; 1 aria ed. in GMB (1931), no.230
1 other oratorio (G. Lotti), Rome, S Marcello, Arciconfraternità del Ss Crocifisso, 1667; lost, title unknown

MASS, MOTETS

Missa 'Ad te clamamus', 16vv, bc, *Rvat*
Ave regina caelorum, 2vv, bc, *MOe*; Benedictus dominus Deus, 2vv, bc, *GB-Cfm*, *Lbm*, *Ob*, *Och*, *US-Wc*; Chare Jesu suavissime, 3vv, 2 vn, bc, *I-MOe*; Convocamini, congregamini, 6vv, 2 vn, bc, *MOe*; Dixit angelis suis iratus Deus, 1v, bc, *MOe*; Et egressus est a filia Sion, 1v, bc, *MOe*; Exultate in Deo fideles, 1v, 2 vn, bc, *MOe*; In tribulationibus, in angustiis, 5vv, 2 vn, bc, *MOe*; Laudate Dominum (Ps cxvi), 6vv, bc, *A-Wn*, *D-MÜs*, *F-Pc*; Locutus est Dominus de nube ignis, 1v, 2 vn, bc, *I-MOe*; Lux perpetua, 6vv, bc, *A-Wn*, *D-B*, *D-MÜs*, *F-Pc*, *US-CA*
Nascere virgo potens, 3vv, bc, *I-MOe*; O majestas aeterna, 2vv, bc, *MOe*; O vos omnes qui transitis, 1v, 2 vn, bc, *MOe*; Pereat humanitas, 5vv, 2 vn, bc, *MOe*; Plaudite vocibus, 1v, bc, *MOe*; Pugna certamen, 4vv, insts, *MOe*; Sinite lacrimari, 3vv, 2 vn, bc, *MOe*; Sistite sidera, coeli motus otiamini, 1v, bc, *D-B*, *I-MOe*; Surge cor meum, 1v, bc, *MOe*; Tantum ergo sacramentum, 2vv, bc, *MOe*

CANTATAS

Includes works called 'serenata' or 'madrigale' in source; full source list of works for 1–3vv in Jander (1969)
Edition: *Selected Solo Cantatas by Alessandro Stradella*, ed. O. Jander, WE, vii (in preparation)
A che vale il sospirar, 1v, bc; A difender le mura dell'antica Sionne, 1v, bc; A dispetto della sorte, 2vv, bc; Adorata liberta dal mio core non partir, 1v, bc; Agli assalti del cieco volante, 1v, bc; Ahi che posar non puote, 2vv, bc; Ah! troppo è ver, 6vv, chorus, str, lute, harp, *I-MOe*; All'apparir del sole, 5vv, *US-NYp*; Alle selve, agli studii, 4vv, bc, 1680, *MOe*; Amor, io son contento, 1v, bc; Amoroso mie catene, non vi chiedo libertà, 1v, bc; A pie' d'annoso pino, 1v, bc; Apre l'uomo infelice, 1v, bc; A quel candido foglio, 1v, bc
Ardo, sospiro, e piango, 2vv, bc; Arrest'il pie' fugace, 1v, bc; Arsi già d'una fiamma, 3vv, 2 vn, bc; Aure fresche, aure volanti, 2vv, bc; Aure, voi che spirate, 1v, bc; Avete torto, occhi miei cari, 1v, bc; Avrò pur d'aspettar più, 1v, bc; Baldanzosa una bellezza, 2vv, bc; Begl'occhi, il vostro piangere, 1v, bc; Bella bocca, taci, 1v, bc; Bel tempo, addio, son fatto amante, 1v, bc; Ben è vile quel core, 1v, bc
Cara e dolce libertà, 1v, bc; Care labbra che d'amore, 2vv, bc; Che vuoi speri, mio cor, 1v, bc; Che speranza aver si può, 3vv, bc; Che vuoi più da me, 1v, bc; Chi avesse visto un core, 1v, bc; Chi dà fede a la speranza, 1v, bc; Chi dirà che nel veleno, 2vv, bc; Chi non sa che la Bellezza, 1v, bc; Chi non sa che la costanza, 1v, bc; Ch'io nasconda il mio foco, 1v, bc; Ch'io non ami, o questo no, 1v, bc; Clori languendo spira, 5vv, *D-B*; Clori son fido amante, 5vv, bc ad lib, *GB-Cfm*, *Lbm*, *T*, *F-Pc*, *I-MOe*; Colpo de' bei vostr'occhi, 1v, bc; Come vive il cor mio, 5vv, *A-Wn*, *D-B*, *F-Pc*; Congiurati a fiera guerra, 1v, bc; Con mesto ciglio e dolorosi accenti, 2vv, bc; Con un cor tutto pianti, 1v, bc
Costanza, mio core, 1v, bc; Crudi ferri, empii marmi, 1v, bc; Crudo mar di fiamme orribili, 1v, 2 vn, bc; Da cuspide ferrate, 1v, 2 vn, bc; Da Filinda aver chi può, 1v, bc; Dai legami amorosi, 1v, bc; Dal grondo lusinghiero, 1v, bc; Dalla Tessala sponda scese d'Argo la prora, 1v, bc; Dalle sponde del Tebro, 1v, bc; Da mille pene e mille stanco afflitto, 1v, bc; Da una beltà superba, 1v, bc; Deggio penar così, 1v, bc; Deh, frenate i furori, 1v, bc; Dell'ardore ch'il core distempra, 1v, bc; Dietro l'orme del desio, 2vv, bc; Difendetemi pensieri, 1v, bc; Disperata rimembranza, 1v, bc; Di tal tempra è la ferita, 3vv, bc
Dopo incessante corso di lagrimoso umore, 1v, bc; Dove aggiri mia vita, 1v, bc; Dove gite, o pensier', 1v, bc; Dove il Tebro famoso, 1v, bc; Dove l'ali spiegate, 1v, bc; Ecco amore che altero risplende, 3vv, 2 vn, bc; Ecco che già nell'aria, 1v, bc; Eccomi accinto, o bella sponde, 1v, bc; Ecco ritorno ai pianti, 3vv, bc; Empio Amor, tiranno arciero, 1v, bc; È pur giunta mia vita, 3vv, bc; E pur sempre a miei desiri, 1v, bc; Esule dalle sfere, 2vv, chorus, 2 vn, bc, 1680; Fedeltà sin che spirto in petto avrò, 1v, bc; Feritevi, ferite, viperette mordaci, 3vv, bc
Ferma, ferma il corso, 1v, bc; Fermatevi, o bei lumi, 1v, bc; Figli, amici,

Agrippina, 1v, bc; Figli del mio cordoglio, 1v, bc; Foresennato pensier, 1v, bc; Fra quest'ombre, 2vv, bc; Fulmini quanto sa quel sembiante lusinghiero, 2vv, bc; Fuor della Stigia sponda, 1v, bc; Genuflesso a tue piante, 1v, bc; Già languiva la notte, 1v, bc; Già le spade nemiche, 1v, bc; Giunto vivo alla tomba, 1v, bc; Il destin vuol ch'io pianga, 1v, bc; Il mar gira ne' fiumi, 1v, bc; Il mio cor ch'è infelicissimo, 1v, bc; Il penare per te bella, 1v, bc; Il più misero amante, 1v, bc; Il più tenero affetto, 1v, bc
Infinite son le pene, 3vv, 2 vn, bc; In grembo all'oblio, 2vv, bc; In quel sol che in grembo al Tago, 1v, bc; In si lontano lido, 1v, bc; Io che lasciato fui più, 1v, bc; Io non vo' più star così, 1v, bc; Io rimango stordito, 2vv, bc; Io vi miro, luci belle, 1v, bc; La bellissima speranza, 2vv, bc; La dolcissima speranza, 2vv, bc; L'anima incenerita ai rai, 1v, bc; La speranza del mio core, 1v, bc; L'avete fatta a me, 1v, bc; L'avviso al Tebro giunto, 3vv, bc, 1671; Leggiadra pastorella, 5vv, bc, *GB-Lbm*; Le luci vezzose volgetemi, 1v, bc; Lilla mia, su queste sponde, 3vv, bc; Lontananza e gelosia son tormenti, 1v, bc
Me ne farete tanto che più, 2vv, bc; Mentre d'auree facelle, 1v, bc; M'è venuto a fastidio lo sperare, 1v, bc; Mio cor, che si fa, 1v, bc; Misero amante, a che mi vale, 2vv, bc; Mortali, che sarà, 1v, bc; Noiosi pensieri, 1v, bc; Non avea il sole ancora, 1v, bc; Non ci pensate mai, 1v, bc; Non disserrate ancora avea le porte, 1v, bc; Non me ne fate tante, 1v, bc; Non mi curo di fedeltà, 1v, bc; Non più piaghe al mio cor, 1v, bc; Non sei contento ancora, 1v, bc; Non sia mai, ah no, 1v, bc; Non si creda alla fortuna, 1v, bc; Non si muove onda in fiume erbetta, 2vv, bc; Non sperar beltà lusinghiera, 1v, bc
Occhi belli, e che sara del mio duol, 2vv, bc; Ombre, voi che celate, 1v, bc; O mio cor quanto t'inganni, 1v, bc; Or che alla dea notturna, 2vv, 2 vn, bc; Or che siam soli, Amore, 1v, bc; Patienza finirà l'influenza, 2vv, bc; Per molti anni è stato occulto, 1v, bc; Per pietà, qualche pietà, 1v, bc; Per tua vaga beltade, 2vv, 2 vn, bc; Piangete, occhi dolenti, 2vv, bc; Piangete, occhi dolenti, 5vv, bc ad lib, *GB-Cfm*, *Lbm*, *F-Pc*, *I-MOe*; Piangete, occhi, piangete, 1v, bc; Pietà di Belisario, 1v, bc; Presso un rivo ch'avea d'argentato cristal, 1v, bc; Pria di punir crudele, 1v, bc; Pria di scior quel dolce nodo, 1v, bc; Privo delle sue luci, 1v, bc; Pupillette amorose, 5vv, *B-Bc*, *D-B*, *GB-Cfm*, *Lbm*, *F-Pc*, *I-MOe*
Qual di cieca passione, 1v, bc; Qual prodigio è ch'io miri, 3vv, insts, ed. in *Georg Friedrich Händels Werke*, suppl.3 (Leipzig, 1889); Quandro mai vi stanchereto, 1v, bc; Quando sembra che nuoti quest' alma, 1v, bc; Quando stanco dal corso in grembo, 1v, bc; Quanto è bella la mia stella, 1v, bc; Quel tuo petto di diamante, 2vv, bc; Qui dove fa soggiorno, 2vv, bc; Sarà ver ch'io mai disciolga, 2vv, bc; Sciogliete in dolci nodi, 2vv, 4 str, 1677; Sciogliete pur, sciogliete i vostri accenti, 1v, bc; Scorrea lassù negli stellati campi, 1v, bc; Se amor m'annoda il piede, 1v, bc
Se del pianeta ardente, 1v, 4 str, 1677; Se di gioie m'alletta il sereno, 1v, bc; Se Nerone lo vuole, 1v, bc; Se non parti, o gelosia, 1v, bc; Se t'ama Filli, o cor, 1v, bc; Si apra al riso agni labbro, 3vv, 2 vn, bc; Si ch'io temo e non disamo, 1v, bc; Si giocoso mi fanno, 5vv, bc, *GB-Lbm*; Si salvi chi può, 1v, bc; Soccorso, olà, Cupido, 1v, bc; Soffro misero e taccio, 1v, bc; Solca il mar da rie tempeste, 1v, bc; Solcava incauto legno, 1v, bc; Solitudine amata della pace, 2vv, 2 vn, bc; Son gradito e pur m'affanno, 1v, bc; Sono in dubbio d'amar, 1v, bc; Son principe, son re, 1v, bc; Son pur dolci le ferite che m'aperse, 2vv, bc; Sopra candido foglio, 1v, bc; Sopra tutte l'altre belle, 1v, bc; Sopra un'eccelsa torre (Il Nerone), 1v, bc
Sotto l'aura d'una speme lusinghiera, 1v, bc; Sotto vedovo cielo, privo de rai, 1v, bc; Sperai nella partita, 3vv, bc; Spiran l'ultimo fiato, 5vv, bc, *A-Wn*, *D-B*, *F-Pc*; Spuntava il di quando la rosa, 3vv, bc; Sprezzata mi credei, 1v, bc; Stanco della speranza di sognante pensier, 1v, bc; Stelle, non mi tradite, 1v, bc; Tante perle non versa l'aurora, 1v, vc, bc; Tiranno di mia fè, 1v, bc; Tirsi un giorno piangea, 5vv, *D-B*, *F-Pc*, *GB-Cfm*, *Lbm*, *I-MOe*, *Rli*; Tradito mio core, non pianger, 1v, bc; Trionfate, invitti colli, 2vv, 2 vn, bc; Troppo oppressa dal sonno, 1v, bc; Tu partisti, crudel, 1v, bc
Udite, amanti, un prodigio novello, 1v, bc; Un'editto l'altro dì in Parnaso, 1v, bc; Un mongibello ardente, 1v, bc; Vaganti pensieri il volo arrestate, 1v, bc; Vaghe calme, io non vi credo, 1v, bc; Vincesti, o Ciel, 1v, bc; Voi che avaro desio nel sen nudrite, 1v, bc; Voi siete sventurate, 1v, bc; Voi volete, il mio cor, 1v, bc; Vola, vola in altri petti, 4vv, insts, *D-MÜs*, *F-Pc*, *GB-Cfm*, *Lbm*, *I-Tn*, ed. in Jander, 1962

ARIAS, CANZONETTAS

Edition: *La flora*, i, ed. K. Jeppesen (Copenhagen, 1949) [incl. 3 arias]
Al rigor di due tiranni, 1v, bc, *I-Vnm*; Che mi giovan le Vittorie, 1v, 2 vn, bc, 1671, *MOe*; Chi mi disse ch'amor dà tormento, 1v, bc, *Bc*, *MOe*; Chi vuol libero il suo piè, 1v, bc, *Vnm*; Deh, vola o desio, 1v, bc, *MOe*, *Tn*; Delizie contenti, 1v, 2 vn, bc, 1671, *MOe*; Destatevi o sensi, 1v, 2 vn, bc, 1671, *Bc*, *MOe*; Dovunque il piè rivolgo, 2vv, vn, bc, 1671, *MOe*; È pazzia d'innamorarsi, 1v, bc, *Vnm*; L'amor mi dà contento, 1v, bc, *D-MÜs*; Parti, fuggi dal mio seno, 1v, bc, *I-Vnm*; Perchè ritorni a me, 1v, bc, *Vnm*; Senz'il vostro ristoro, 2vv, bc, *GB-Lbm*; Speranze smarrite, 1v, 2 vn, bc, *I-Vnm*; Tì lascierò, 1v, *GB-Lbm*; Torna amor, dammi il mio bene, 1v, bc, *MOe*
4 canzonettas, 1679[6]

INSTRUMENTAL
(nos. refer to those in McCrickard, 1971)

12 sinfonias/sonatas, vn, bc, I–XII
9 sinfonias/sonatas, 2 vn, bc, XIII–XXI [XIII = Sinfonia for Susanna; XIV = Sinfonia for Esule dalle sfere]
2 sinfonias/sonatas, vn, vle/vc, bc, XXII, XXIII
1 sonata, 2 vn, bc/2 cornetts, bc, XXIV
1 sonata, 2 vn, lute, str, XXV
1 sonata, tpt, 8 str, bc, XXVI
Toccata, kbd, *I-Rsc*

WRITINGS
Libro de' primi elementi (MS, *I-Bc*)

BIBLIOGRAPHY
BurneyH

G. O. Pitoni: *Notitia de contrapuntisti e de compositori di musica* (MS, *I-Rvat*, C.G., I/1–2, c1725)
A. Catelani: *Delle opere di Alessandro Stradella esistenti nell'archivio musicale della R. Biblioteca Palatina di Modena* (Modena, 1866)
F. Filippi: 'Alessandro Stradella e l'archivio musicale dei Contarini alla Biblioteca di S. Marco in Venezia', *Il politecnico*, parte letterario-scientifica, 4th ser., ii/4 (1866), 433
P. Richard: 'Stradella et les Contarinis', *Le ménestrel*, xxxii/51–2 (1865); xxxiii/1–5 (1866), 12
A. Gandini: *Cronistoria dei teatri di Modena dal 1539 al 1871* (Modena, 1873)
A. Ademollo: *I teatri di Roma nel secolo decimosettimo* (Rome, 1888/R1969)
G. Baccini: 'Lettere di Matteo del Teglia', *Giornale di erudizione*, iii (1890–91), 277
H. Hess: *Die Opern Alessandro Stradella's* (Leipzig, 1906)
S. Taylor: *The Indebtedness of Handel to Works by Other Composers* (Cambridge, 1906)
A. Einstein: 'Ein Bericht über den Turiner Mordanfall auf Alessandro Stradella', *Festschrift zum 50. Geburtstag Adolf Sandberger* (Munich, 1918), 135
A. Gentili: 'Un'opera di Alessandro Stradella ritrovata recentemente', *Il pianoforte*, viii (1927), 210
E. Dufflocq: 'Alessandro Stradella', *Bollettino bibliografico musicale*, iv (1929), 1
A. della Corte: '*La forza d'amor paterno* di Alessandro Stradella', *Musica d'oggi*, xiii (1931), 389
R. Casimiri: 'Oratorii del Masini, Bernabei, Melani, Di Pio, Pasquini e Stradella, in Roma nell'anno santo 1675', *NA*, xiii (1936), 157
A. Cametti: *Il Teatro Tordinona, poi di Apollo* (Tivoli, 1938)
M. Tiberti: 'Un importante rinvenimento musicale, la *Doriclea*, opera di Alessandro Stradella', *Musica d'oggi*, xx (1938), 85
G. Roncaglia: 'La cantata per il SS. Natale di Alessandro Stradella', *Rivista nazionale di musica*, xviii (1940), 4395
——: 'Le composizioni strumentali di Alessandro Stradella esistenti presso la R. Biblioteca Estense di Modena', *RMI*, xliv (1940), 81, 337; xlv (1941), 1
——: *Il genio novatore di Alessandro Stradella* (Modena, 1941)
J. A. Westrup: 'Stradella's *La forza d'amor paterno*', *MMR*, lxxi (1941), 52
G. Roncaglia: 'Le composizioni vocali di Alessandro Stradella', *RMI*, xlv (1941), 133; xlvi (1942), 1
R. Giazotto: *La musica a Genova* (Genoa, 1951)
E. Allam: 'Alessandro Stradella', *PRMA*, lxxx (1953–4), 29
G. Roncaglia: 'Il *Trespolo tutore* di Alessandro Stradella: "la prima opera buffa"', *RMI*, lvi (1954), 326
L. Montalto: *Un Mecenate in Roma barocca* (Florence, 1955)
R. Allorto: 'A. Stradella e la cantata a 3 per il SS. Natale', *Musicisti della scuola emiliana*, Chigiana, xiii (1956), 91
E. Krohn: 'Some Solo Cantatas of Alessandro Stradella', *Manuscripta*, ii (1958), 3
O. Jander: *A Catalogue of the Manuscripts of Compositions by Alessandro Stradella found in European and American Libraries* (Wellesley, Mass., 1960, rev. 2/1962)
R. Giazotto: *Vita di Alessandro Stradella* (Milan, 1962)
O. Jander: *Alessandro Stradella and his Minor Dramatic Works* (diss., Harvard U., 1962)
N. Pirrotta: 'Stradella, Alessandro', *ES*
——: 'Alessandro Stradella', *LaMusicaE*
O. Jander: 'Concerto Grosso Instrumentation in Rome in the 1660s and 1670s', *JAMS*, xxi (1968), 168
L. Bianchi: *Carissimi, Stradella, Scarlatti e l'oratorio musicale* (Rome, 1969)
O. Jander: *Alessandro Stradella*, WECIS, iv (1969) [thematic index of cantatas]
——: 'The Prologues and Intermezzos of Alessandro Stradella', *AnMc*, no.7 (1969), 87
H. Dietz: 'Muzikalische Struktur und Architektur im Werke Alessandro Stradellas', *AnMc*, no.9 (1970), 28
C. Gianturco: *The Operas of Alessandro Stradella (1644–1682)* (diss., U. of Oxford, 1970)
E. McCrickard: *Alessandro Stradella's Instrumental Music* (diss., U. of North Carolina, 1971)
C. Gianturco: 'Caratteri stilistici delle opere teatrali di Stradella', *RIM*, vi (1972), 211–45
——: 'The Revisions of Alessandro Stradella's *Forza dell'amor paterno*', *JAMS*, xxv (1972), 407
——: 'A Possible Date for Stradella's "Il Trespolo tutore"', *ML*, liv (1973), 25
——: 'Corelli e Alessandro Stradella', *Studi corelliani: 2° congresso internazionale: Fusignano 1974*
——: 'Sources for Stradella's *Moro per amore*', *Quadrivium*, xii/2 (1975 [dated 1971]), 129
K. Chaikin: *The Solo Soprano Cantatas of Alessandro Stradella* (diss., Stanford U., 1975)
C. Gianturco: 'Evidence for a Late Roman School of Opera', *ML*, lvi (1975), 4
——: 'Stradella e Pasquini: due approcci al libretto comico del Trespolo tutore', *L'opera comica nei sei-settecenti a Venezia e in Italia: Venezia 1975*
——: 'The Oratorios of Alessandro Stradella', *PRMA*, ci (1974–5), 45
——: '*Invenzione per un Barcheggio* (1681) di A. Stradella', *Ottavo incontro con la musica polacca e italiana: Bologna 1976*
H. E. Smither: *A History of the Oratorio*, i (Chapel Hill, 1977)
E. F. McCrickard: 'Temporal and Tonal Aspects of Alessandro Stradella's Instrumental Music', *AnMc*, no.19 (1979), 186–243

CAROLYN M. GIANTURCO

Stradivari, Antonio (*b* ? Cremona, 1644; *d* ?Cremona, 18 Dec 1737). Italian maker of violins and other instruments. Since the end of the 18th century he has been universally regarded as the greatest of all violin makers. In point of tonal excellence, design, beauty to the eye and accuracy of workmanship his instruments have never been surpassed. From his teacher, Nicolo AMATI, Stradivari inherited more than 100 years of Cremonese violin-making tradition, and upon this firmest of foundations he built his own unique career. At the peak of a working life spanning almost 70 years he brought his art to a perfection which has not been

1. Violin by Antonio Stradivari, Cremona, 1688 (private collection)

equalled. Later two of his sons worked with him, but they seem to have had no independent careers. In all, some 650 of his instruments survive, many of them used by the world's leading string players.

No record has been found of the exact date and place of Stradivari's birth, but his name is an old Cremonese one, and his parents, Alessandro and Anna, are known to have lived in Cremona until at least 1628–30, when first a famine and then a plague caused many of the inhabitants to leave the city. Antonio's birth-year is deduced from the labels of certain violins dating from the end of his life, upon which, no doubt with pride, he recorded his age. It is thought that as a young man he may at first have been apprenticed as a woodcarver, but he must have become connected with Nicolo Amati in some capacity in the early 1660s, for on his first known violin label (dated 1666) he claimed to be Amati's pupil. A violin from that year shows a hand already adept in the use of woodcarving tools, though inexperienced in certain of the finer points of violin construction. In July 1667 he married Francesca Feraboschi, a young widow who bore him six children, including Francesco (b 1 Feb 1671; d 11 May 1743) and Omobono (b 14 Nov 1679; d 8 June 1742), both of whom became violin makers.

The rarity of surviving violins by Stradivari from 1666 to 1680 is surprising, unless only a part of his time was devoted to their manufacture. It has been suggested that he also worked for other makers, including Amati. It seems probable, however, that during this period he also occupied himself with a large variety of other musical instruments, principally plucked ones. Stradivari's original designs for harps, lutes, mandolins, guitars and a tromba marina (see TRUMPET MARINE) are now in the Civic Museum in Cremona (the Dalla Valle Collection), together with many patterns and moulds for instruments of the viol and violin families, and certain of his tools. Of all the plucked instruments that he must have made, only two guitars and the neck of a third are known to survive. (For an illustration of one of these, in the Ashmolean Museum, Oxford, see GUITAR, fig.8.) Of violins from this early period there are fewer than 20, and one viola; all are thoroughly Cremonese in character, and beautifully made, though perhaps not stamped with the mark of genius: these are the instruments to which the term 'Amatisé' is correctly applied. Two works deserve special mention for their originality, each a landmark of its kind. One is the contralto (i.e. smaller-sized) viola of 1672, of original design and a fairly rare size for the period, its body measuring just over 41 cm (now in the collection of Rolf Habisreutinger, St Gall, Switzerland). The other is the first of ten known 'inlaid' instruments, the 'Lever du soleil' violin of 1677 (sold in 1971–2 to a private collector). In this the traditional

2. Violin (the 'Messiah') by Antonio Stradivari, Cremona, 1716 (Ashmolean Museum, Oxford)

purfling is replaced by a strip of dark paste, flanked by purfling at each side, into which are set alternate ivory or bone diamonds and circles. The sides and scroll are also ornamented, with painted or inlaid designs. Such embellishment was not entirely new to violins, and was perfectly normal for fine guitars; Stradivari, however, carried it out with a delicacy and charm unequalled by others (see VIOLIN, fig.13).

In 1680 Stradivari moved with his family to the Piazza S Domenico, where he lived and worked for the rest of his life. With the move came a change of emphasis in Stradivari's work, and from 1680 he made many more violins and quite a number of cellos. With the death of Amati in 1684, Stradivari was recognizably superior to all his competitors, and his fame began to spread beyond Cremona. From 1680 to 1690 his work moved away from Amati's and his instruments became more robust in certain features, particularly the corners. The varnish, however, is still often the soft, honey-coloured Amati covering, with an occasional warm orange tint. Tonally these violins are more powerful than those of the Amati family.

After 1690 there was a surge of individuality, the beginning of a new era of violin making. The heavy corners of the previous decade were now matched by wider purfling, bolder soundholes, stronger arching in the tables, varnish of deeper colour which often crumbled readily away from the wood, forming spontaneously the splendid patterns of wear which so excite the eye. Stradivari was also active with a change in design, the introduction of the 'Long Strad', whose outlines preoccupied him all through the 1690s. With this increased length he doubtless sought to introduce some of the tonal qualities of the old Brescian makers, whose violins offered a darker sound than those of the Cremonese, combined with extra strength of response. These elegant violins, representing a huge improvement on everything that had gone before, are not always as well appreciated for their tone as perhaps they should be.

In 1698 Stradivari's first wife died, and in the following year he married Antonia Maria Zambelli, who bore him five more children, including Paolo (b 26 Jan 1708; d 14 Oct 1775). By this time Francesco and Omobono were presumably fully occupied in the workshop, though it is rare at any period but the very last to find an instrument made without their father's participation. It is hard to escape the impression that both sons were completely dominated by Antonio, that they carried out the rough work and were only occasionally allowed to complete a cheaper order, using inferior-looking maple or beechwood.

The period from about 1700 to 1720 (the 'golden' period to most writers) shows the ultimate development of Stradivari's powers, with the highest pinnacle being reached in about 1715. The gradual adoption of a broader, squarer-looking centre bout saw out the last noticeable sign of Amati's influence, and the varnish took on the ultimate, now well-known orange brown colour. These developments were complemented by magnificently flamed maple backs, in one and two pieces, so that the appearance of the whole leaves nothing to be desired. So it is too with the tone, for in these instruments there is incredible richness and ease of response, with an ample reserve of power. Outstanding examples are far too numerous to list comprehensively, though no account of Stradivari could fail to note the 'Betts' (1704), the 'Alard' (1715) and the 'Messiah'

(1716), and that most of the world's finest artists have preferred these violins for two centuries. The 'Betts', one of Stradivari's greatest achievements, was purchased by the dealer of that name for only £1; in excellent condition, it is now in the Library of Congress, Washington, DC. The 'Alard' is regarded by Hill and others as marginally the finest Stradivari in existence. The 'Messiah' remained in Stradivari's family for a long time after his death, and was passed in perfect condition to the collector–dealer Tarisio by Count Cozio di Salabue. Its next purchaser, Vuillaume, unfortunately modernized the violin, replacing the original bass bar and fingerboard and lengthening the neck. It is still the most perfectly preserved Stradivari, looking almost new. It is now in the Ashmolean Museum in Oxford (see fig.2).

At the turn of the century Stradivari began to direct his inventive mind towards the problems of the cellist. Previously his cellos had been exclusively large: all but one out of 35 or so have now had their dimensions reduced. Maggini had made some smaller cellos, and the last quarter of the 17th century saw Cremonese and other Italian makers doing likewise, facilitating the emergence of a new breed of virtuoso cellist. Stradivari's first concessions to this trend came in 1699–1700, but between about 1707 and 1710 he designed and made smaller cellos, which have served as a model for almost every maker since the beginning of the 19th century. His achievement with this numerically small series of instruments (only about 20 survive) is no less than that with the violins. They have an extraordinary quality of sound that carries through a hall even when played pianissimo, and have an immediate response and swelling power. The sound projects forward from the instrument in such a way that the player is at first not aware how much volume he can produce. In the last ten years of his life Stradivari narrowed his outline to produce a cello with similar proportions to those of the 'Long Strad' violins. Another model retained the width but shortened the length. Though excellent instruments, these last creations are not really as satisfactory as the 'Duport' (owned by Rostropovich) and its sisters.

Stradivari's achievement with violas is rather less significant, since fewer than a dozen complete examples are now known. It is curious that he should have made so few, for no-one doubts the greatness of those that are still heard.

After 1720, Stradivari seems to have been less easily able to obtain the most handsome maple. Wood of local origin predominates from this date to 1730. Signs of old age are few and far between in the workmanship, and players are at least as well served by these later violins. Nor can there have been any slowing down of production. After 1730 there are signs of Stradivari's old age, though almost to the end his craftsmanship was superb. He was still making violins in his last year, at the age of 92, and his sons survived him by only a few years.

Stradivari's work was copied from the first, but towards the end of the 18th century players and makers alike realized his superiority over the models of Amati and Stainer. To follow his pattern was one thing, but in the 19th century the art of imitation was developed, particularly in France and England. Today hundreds of thousands of inferior factory-made instruments bear copies of Stradivari's label. Most of them were made at the end of the 19th century for sale through music shops, with no intent to deceive. These turn up in attics all over the world, providing for their owners a brief period of ecstatic anticipation, but their similarity to the real thing is minimal to a trained eye.

Much has been written of Stradivari's varnish and the loss of its recipe. The influence of varnish on the quality and carrying power of violin tone is considerable. A varnish which, when completely dry, has a hard consistency generally causes an instrument to produce a hard, glassy sound with a limited range of tone-colour. A thick, heavy, oily coating inhibits the wood's vibrations in a different way and is equally unsatisfactory. Somewhere between the two is a varnish that dries to the point of forming a light, delicate, elastic skin but no further. This is the characteristic of most old Italian varnish, and that used by Stradivari and certain of his contemporaries seems to represent the ideal. Many varnishes used by modern makers pass through a phase during the drying process when their consistency resembles that of the varnish on old Italian instruments. This may be after a day, a month, or a year or two, but the long-term quality of an instrument cannot be judged until the varnish has settled to its final consistency. This is the rock on which the extravagant claims of so many violin makers and players have eventually foundered.

The varnish, which has defied so many attempts at analysis and rediscovery, is only a part of the 'secret' of Stradivari. He succeeded in all branches of the violin maker's art, given the best initial training, as fine a hand and eye as it is possible to have, a comprehending and inventive mind, and a long working life in a superior artistic environment. His understanding of design and structure was probably unique, at least until the emergence of Guarneri 'del Gesù', and the remarkable appearance and effect of his best varnish is but one more triumph of his genius.

For further illustrations of instruments by Stradivari, *see* VIOLIN, fig.1.

BIBLIOGRAPHY
F. J. Fétis: *Notice d'Antoine Stradivari* (Brussels, 1856; Eng. trans., 1864)
G. Hart: *The Violin: its Famous Makers and their Imitators* (London, 1875)
L. A. Vidal: *Les instruments à archet* (Paris, 1876–8/*R*1961)
W. E. Hill & Sons: *The Salabue Stradivari* (London, 1891)
——: *The Tuscan Stradivari* (London, 1891)
W. H., A. F. and A. E. Hill: *Antonio Stradivari: his Life and Work* (London, 1902, 2/1909/*R*1963; Fr. trans., 1907)
E. N. Doring: *How Many Strads?* (Chicago, 1945)
A. Baruzzi: *La scala nuziale* (London, 1962)
D. D. Boyden: *Catalogue of the Hill Collection of Musical Instruments in the Ashmolean Museum, Oxford* (London, 1969)
S. F. Sacconi: *I 'segreti' di Stradivari* (Cremona, 1972)
H. K. Goodkind: *Violin Iconography of Antonio Stradivari 1644–1737* (Larchmont, NY, 1973) [lists 700 known instruments with past and present owners]

CHARLES BEARE

Straesser, Joep (*b* Amsterdam, 11 March 1934). Dutch composer. He studied musicology at Amsterdam University (1952–5), the organ with Van der Horst (1956–9) and theory with Felderhof (1959–61) at the Amsterdam Conservatory, and composition with De Leeuw (1960–65). After several years as an organist, he was appointed lecturer in theory at the Utrecht Conservatory (1962), where he has directed groups in improvisation.

WORKS
(*selective list*)

Vocal: Psalm cxlviii, 1958; 22 Pages, 3 male vv, wind orch, perc, 1965; Herfst der muziek, chorus, 1966; Musique pour l'homme (UN Declaration of Human Rights), S, A, T, B, orch, 1968; Rainsongs, male vv, 1971; Eichenstadt und Abendstern, S, pf, 1972; 3 Psalms,

chorus, 1976; Intervals (on Haiku poems), chorus, fl, harp, vc, 1976
Orch: Summer Conc., ob, chamber orch, 1969; Enclosures, wind, perc, 1970; Intersections II, 100 + insts, 1970; Chorai Revisited, 1974–5
Chamber and inst: Emergency Case, fl + pic + a fl, 1970; Sight-seeing V, str qt, 1971; Intersections III, pf, 1971; Intersections IV, ob qt, 1972; Encounters, b cl, 6 perc, 1973–5; Intersections V, sax qt, 1974; Intersections V-2, b cl, pf, 1975; Splendid Isolation, passacaglia, org, 1976–7

Principal publisher: Donemus

BIBLIOGRAPHY
E. Vermeulen: '22 Pages by Joep Straesser', *Sonorum speculum* (1967), no.31, p.15
J. Vriend: 'The Autumn of Music by Joep Straesser', *Sonorum speculum* (1967), no.31, p.11
G. Werker: 'Musique pour l'homme van Joep Straesser', *Mens en melodie*, xxiii (1968), 363
E. Vermeulen: 'Musique pour l'homme by Joep Straesser', *Sonorum speculum* (1969), no.38, p.15
D. Manneke: 'Intersections III', *Sonorum speculum* (1973), no.53, p.24

ROGIER STARREVELD

Straeten, Edmond vander [Vanderstraeten, Edmond] (*b* Oudenaarde, 3 Dec 1826; *d* Oudenaarde, 25 Nov 1895). Belgian musicologist, critic and librarian. After studying classics in Aalst and philosophy at the University of Ghent, he returned to Oudenaarde, where he directed several opera performances and began his research into local archives. In 1857 he went to Brussels, where he studied harmony with Bosselet and counterpoint and palaeography with Fétis, becoming his private secretary. On Fétis's recommendation he was appointed music critic for *Le nord* and in 1859 joined the catalogue department of the Bibliothèque Royale. He also wrote reviews for *L'écho du parlement*, *L'étoile belge* and other publications. Subsequently he did research at the Algemeen Rijksarchief in Brussels (1862–75) and in Italy, France and Spain. He represented the Belgian government on several missions; at Weimar in 1870 he attended performances of Wagner's operas and supported them enthusiastically in his report, *Muzikale feesten van Weimar*. In 1884 he returned to Oudenaarde and devoted himself to publishing the results of his research.

Vander Straeten's chief contribution to musicology is *La musique aux Pays-Bas avant le XIXe siècle*. Although he has frequently been criticized for his unsympathetic approach, unsubstantiated opinions, mistakes in reading and interpretation of archival notices, inconsistency in the citation of composers' names and other faults in method, it is an invaluable collection of documents on Netherlands music, musical institutions and musicians active in the Low Countries, Italy, Spain, France and elsewhere.

WRITINGS
Coup d'oeil sur la musique actuelle à Audenarde (Oudenaarde, 1851)
Notice sur Charles-Félix de Hollandre, compositeur de musique sacrée (Ghent, 1854)
Notice sur les carillons d'Audenarde (Ghent, 1855)
Recherches sur la musique à Audenarde avant le XIXe siècle (Antwerp, 1856)
Examen des chants populaires des Flamands de France, publiés par E. de Coussemaker (Ghent, 1858)
Jacques de Gouÿ, chanoine d'Embrun: recherches sur la vie et les oeuvres de ce musicien du XVIIe siècle (Antwerp, 1863)
Jean-François-Joseph Janssens (Brussels, 1866)
Aldenardiana en Flandriana (Oudenaarde, 1867–76)
La musique aux Pays-Bas avant le XIXe siècle (Brussels, 1867–88/*R*1969) [reviewed by R. Eitner, *MMg*, v (1873), 10; viii (1876), 56; x (1878), 152; xii (1880), 112; xv (1883), 39]
with D. van de Casteele: *Maîtres de chant et organistes de Saint-Donatien et de Saint-Sauveur à Bruges* (Bruges, 1870)
Muzikale feesten van Weimar: Wagner, verslag aan den heer minister van binnenlandsche zaken (Brussels, 1871)

Le théâtre villageois en Flandre: histoire, littérature, musique, religion, politique, moeurs (Brussels, 1874–80, 2/1881)
Voltaire musicien: concerts intermèdes (Mozart à Ferney); Lullisme, Ramisme. Gluckisme; prophétie pour 1886: l'opéra, l'opéra-comique; organographie, acoustique; biographies; locutions, anecdotes (Brussels, 1876, 2/1878/R1977)
Les ménestrels aux Pays-Bas du XIIIᵉ au XVIIᵉ siècle: leurs gildes, leurs statuts, leurs écoles, leurs fonctions, leurs instruments, leur répertoire, leurs moeurs, etc. (Brussels, 1878/R1972)
La mélodie populaire dans l'opéra 'Guillaume Tell' de Rossini (Paris, 1879)
Lohengrin: instrumentation et philosophie (Paris, 1879)
Turin musical, pages détachées: chansons populaires, concerts, théâtres lyriques, critique musicale, wagnérisme (Oudenaarde, 1880)
Jacques de Saint-Luc, luthiste athois du XVIIᵉ siècle (Brussels, 1887)
La musique congratulatoire en 1454 de Dijon à Ratisbonne (Brussels, 1889)
ed.: *Cinq lettres intimes de Roland de Lassus* (Ghent, 1891)
Notes sur quelques instruments de musique (Ghent, 1891)
Les ballets des rois en Flandre: xylographie, musique, coutumes (Ghent, 1892)
Charles-Quint musicien (Ghent, 1894)
with C. C. Snoeck: *Etude biographique et organographique sur les Willems, luthiers gantois du XVIIᵉ siècle* (Ghent, 1896)
Notes on the music chapel of Ghent Cathedral etc, *B-Bc* 17.233 and 27.381 [material for an unwritten vol. ix of *La musique aux Pays-Bas*]

BIBLIOGRAPHY
FétisB; FétisBS
E. E. Lowinsky: Introduction to E. vander Straeten: *La musique aux Pays-Bas avant le XIXᵉ siècle* (New York, R1969)
                                        M. E. C. BARTLET

Straeten, Edmund S(ebastian) J(oseph) van der (*b* Düsseldorf, 29 April 1855; *d* London, 17 Sept 1934). German cellist, writer on music and composer. He studied the cello with Johannes Hoecke and Ludwig Ebert in Cologne, making his début in 1875. Later he was a pupil of Gustav Libotton at the Guildhall School of Music, London, and Louis Hegyesi in Cologne. He also studied composition with Humperdinck. In 1888 he returned to London and was appointed cello teacher at the North-East London Institute. Here with Prout he began a chamber music society which sponsored performances of little-known Classical and Baroque works, as well as modern compositions (for example, they gave the London première of d'Indy's Clarinet Trio). In 1900 he and Emil Sauret founded the Tonal Art Club, St John's Wood, which later became the London Musicians' Club. Van der Straeten was important for his participation in the revival of viol playing: he wrote numerous articles for *The Strad* about basic techniques, instruments and repertory and traced the viol's development in his *History of the Violoncello* (1915); he also formed a trio with his son Ludwig and his pupil Norman Greiffenhagen, which performed music by Marais, Simpson and Jenkins. He composed several chamber works and made arrangements for viola da gamba and piano of works by Abel, Hammer and Kühnel.

WRITINGS
The Technics of Violoncello Playing (London, 1898, 4/1923)
'The Revival of the Viols', *The Strad*, xix–xxiii (1908–12)
The Romance of the Fiddle: the Origin of the Modern Virtuoso and the Adventures of his Ancestors (London, 1911)
History of the Violoncello, the Viol da Gamba, their Precursors and Collateral Instruments with Biographies of All the Most Eminent Players of Every Country (London, 1915/R1971)
A Handbook of Musical Form for Instrumental Players and Vocalists (London, 1919)
The Art of Violoncello Playing (London, 1922–6)
Notable Violin Solos, how to Play Them with Understanding, Expression and Effect (London, 1922–7)
Well-known Violoncello Solos, how to Play Them with Understanding, Expression and Effect (London, 1922–7)
'The Literature for the Viols', *The Strad*, xlii (1931–2), 20, 212, 300
The History of the Violin, its Ancestors and Collateral Instruments from Earliest Times to the Present Day (London, 1933)

Articles for *Cobbett's Cyclopedic Survey of Chamber Music* (London, 1930), *Grove 3*, *MMR*

BIBLIOGRAPHY
G. R. H.: Obituary, *MT*, lxxv (1934), 1040
Obituary, *The Strad*, xlv (1934–5), 248
                                        M. E. C. BARTLET

Straková [née Švehlíková], **Theodora** (*b* Vienna, 21 Dec 1915). Czech music historian. She studied German and French at Brno University (1935–9) and at the same time attended Helfert's musicology lectures. After World War II she continued her studies in musicology with Jan Racek (1945–9) and in 1953 obtained her doctorate with a dissertation on an anonymous Moravian organ tablature. In 1942 she married the music historian and critic Vincenc Straka. She had begun working in the music collection of the Moravian Regional Museum in Brno (today the music history institute of the Moravian Museum) in 1937; in 1948 she succeeded Racek as director. She enlarged the institute's scope and initiated the large-scale cataloguing of its music source materials and Janáček archives. In addition to her administrative work she lectured on music archival method at Brno University from 1952 to 1972. In 1968 she obtained her CSc degree with a dissertation on court music in Brtnice. Her published work deals mainly with 17th- and 18th-century Moravian court and church music and with Janáček.

WRITINGS
'O neznámém skladateli předklasického období (Amandus Ivanschitz)' [An unknown composer of the pre-classical era], *Časopis Moravského musea*, xxxiv (1949), 218
Anonymní varhanní tabulatura moravského původu [An anonymous organ tablature of Moravian origin] (diss., U. of Brno, 1953; extracts in 'Starobrněnská varhanní tabulatura', *Musikologie*, v (1958), 11–48)
'K vasický hudební inventář z roku 1757' [A musical catalogue from Kvasice, 1757], *Časopis Moravského musea*, xxxviii (1953), 105–49
'Pastorely Jakuba Jana Ryby', *Časopis Moravského musea*, xxxix (1954), 135–81
'Janáčkovy hudebně dramatické náměty a torsa' [Janáček's projected and fragmentary stage works], *Musikologie*, iii (1955), 417–49
'Tomáškovy písně na Goethovy texty' [Tomášek's songs on Goethe's texts], *Časopis Moravského musea*, xl (1955), 214–52
'Janáčkova opera Osud', *Časopis Moravského musea*, xli (1956), 209–60; xlii (1957), 133–64
'Setkání Leoše Janáčka s Gabrielou Preissovou' [Janáček's meeting with Gabriela Preissová], *Časopis Moravského musea*, xlii (1958), 145
'Neznámé nástrojové skladby Leoše Janáčka' [Janáček's unknown instrumental compositions], *Časopis Moravského musea*, xliv (1959), 163
'Václav Tomášek a jeho klavírní eklogy', *Časopis Moravského musea, vědy společenské*, xlv (1960), 175
'Josef Antonín Štěpán a Haydnova Divertimento v Es-dur', *Časopis Moravského musea, vědy společenské*, xlvi (1961), 127
'Vladimír Helfert a F. X. Šalda', *Časopis Moravského musea, vědy společenské*, xlvi (1961), 209
'Václav Pichl a jeho vztah k Giov. Batt. Martinimu' [Pichl and his relation to Martini], *Časopis Moravského musea, vědy společenské*, xlvii (1962), 163
'Brtnický hudební inventář' [A music catalogue from Brtnice], *Časopis Moravského musea, vědy společenské*, xlviii (1963), 199–234
'Hudba na brtnickém zámku v 17. století' [Music at the Brtnice castle in the 17th century], *Časopis Moravského musea, vědy společenské*, l (1965), 183
'Hudebníci na collattovském panství v 18. století' [Musicians on the Collalto estate in the 18th century], *Časopis Moravského musea, vědy společenské*, li (1966), 231–68
'Das Problem der adeligen Hofkapellen und die Instrumentalmusik in böhmischen Ländern der Barockzeit', *IMSCR, x Ljubljana 1967*, 326
'Janáček und der Verismus', *Leoš Janáček et musica europaea: Brno III 1968*, 67
'K hudební minulosti Dubu u Olomouce' [The musical past of Dub, near Olomouc], *Časopis Moravského musea, vědy společenské*, liii–liv (1968–9), 5
'Manierismus und die tschechische Renaissancemusik', *Musica bohemica et europaea: Brno V 1970*, 159
with J. Sehnal and S. Přibáňová: *Průvodce po archivních fondech ústavu*

dějin hudby Moravského musea [A guide to the archives of the music history institute of the Moravian Museum] (Brno, 1971)
'Rajhradský hudební inventář z roku 1725' [A music catalogue from Rajhrad, 1725], *Časopis Moravského musea, vědy společenské*, lviii (1973), 217–46
'Die tschechische Musikwissenschaft in dem Jahren 1945–1975', *AcM*, xlix (1977), 103 [see also p.280]
'Jaroměřice a jejich význam v hudební historii Moravy' [Jaroměřice and its importance in the music history of Moravia] (in preparation)
JIŘÍ SEHNAL

Strambotto (It.: 'rustic song'). A stanzaic form of Italian poetry set by composers of the frottola and 16th-century madrigal, also known as *ottava rima* and *rispetto*. Each stanza consists of eight lines of 11 syllables. Three types of strambotto exist, distinguished by their rhyme scheme: the *strambotto toscano*, with a rhyme scheme of *abababcc*, was the more common form set to music in the 15th and 16th centuries; the *strambotto siciliano*, with a rhyme scheme of *abababab*, seems to have been the poetic form common to early 17th-century monodies known as *arie siciliane* (*see* SICILIANA); and the *strambotto romagnuolo*, with a rhyme scheme of *ababccdd*, the least commonly set kind of strambotto. *See* FROTTOLA, §2.

DON HARRÁN

Strand Theatre. London theatre built in 1905; *see* LONDON, §IV, 3.

Strang, Gerald (*b* Claresholm, Alberta, 13 Feb 1908). American composer. His principal teachers were Koechlin, Toch and Schoenberg; he also served as Schoenberg's teaching assistant and later edited his *Fundamentals of Composition* (with L. Stein, 1967). He took the doctorate at the University of Southern California, and has taught at Long Beach City and State Colleges, San Fernando Valley State College and the University of California at Los Angeles. Strang is probably best known through his association with the New Music Edition, of which he was managing editor during the years 1936–40. His more recent activities have been chiefly in electronic and computer music and as an acoustician and building design consultant; he has published several articles in these areas.

WORKS
(*selective list*)

Perc Music, 3 perc, 1935; 2 syms., 1942, 1951; 3 Excerpts from Walt Whitman, chorus, 1950; Conc., vc, pf, wind, 1951; Conc. grosso, orch, 1951; Divertimento and Variations, 4 ww, str, 1948, 1956; Compuisitions, computer-synthesized tape pieces, 1963–72; Synthions, synthesized tape pieces, 1969–72; pf pieces

Principal publisher: New Music Edition
MSS in American Composers' Alliance, New York
STEVEN E. GILBERT

Strange, Le. *See* L'ESTRANGE family.

Strangways, A. H. Fox. *See* FOX STRANGWAYS, A. H.

Stransky, Josef (*b* Humpolec, Bohemia, 9 Sept 1872; *d* New York, 6 March 1936). Czech conductor. He studied medicine in Prague and Leipzig, getting his degree in Prague in 1896, but simultaneously worked in music, his teachers including Jadassohn, Fibich, Fuchs, Bruckner and Dvořák. He conducted a student orchestra in Prague, and in 1898 had his first professional engagement at the German Theatre there. In 1903 he moved to the Hamburg Opera as principal conductor, and in 1910 became associated with the Blüthner Orchestra in Berlin.

The peak of Stransky's career was his appointment in 1911 as Mahler's successor at the New York PO (to the distress of Strauss, who thought Stransky would give German conducting a bad name abroad). In Germany he was thought a fiery Bohemian and in New York a somewhat staid German; on the whole, he pleased his New York audience with his uncontroversial but not altogether unspiced programmes. He resigned in 1923 but stayed in New York to conduct the newly formed State SO for a year. He conducted the première (7 December 1922) at the Philharmonic of Schoenberg's Bach chorale-prelude transcriptions, and received a sulphurous letter from Schoenberg (9 September 1922).

Stransky gave up music in 1924 and became an art dealer. He composed songs (some introduced by Schumann-Heink), orchestral and other instrumental music, and an operetta, *Der General*. His editions include an adaptation of Berlioz's *Béatrice et Bénédict*, which he felt wanted reorchestrating for modern taste.

MICHAEL STEINBERG

Strappato (It., from *strappare*: 'to tear off', 'to wrench'). A term, used by Vivaldi, which probably indicates that the notes in question are to be played sharply accented.

Strasbourg (Ger. Strassburg). French city on the Rhine in Alsace. It was a free imperial city from the 13th century until 1681, when it was reunited with France. From 1871 to 1919 it was part of Prussia.

1. To 1600. 2. 17th century. 3. 18th century. 4. 19th century. 5. After 1900.

1. TO 1600. By the early 6th century Alsace was Christian. Monks composed hymns in Latin and in the vernacular, and in the 8th century, Heddo, Bishop of Strasbourg, introduced Gregorian chant. In 775 Charlemagne founded the choir school of Strasbourg Cathedral, which is rich in sculptures showing many musical instruments. Towards the end of the 12th century mystery plays began to be performed at St Etienne and at the cathedral. Jacob Twinger von Königshoven, Kantor of the cathedral school, director of the choir of St Thomas and librarian of the chapter, was the author of a famous German chronicle and of a tonary written in about 1415 (*CS-Pu* Strasbourg C XI E9). The Flagellants (*Geissler*), who appeared in Alsace at that time, encouraged popular sacred song and influenced the works of Heinrich Laufenberg, who lived in Strasbourg until 1460.

Secular music was cultivated by jongleurs or minstrels and Minnesinger. The jongleurs were wandering musicians, scorned by the church and beyond the faith and the law. The guilds eventually forbade them to perform in Strasbourg, and the bishops drove them from churches and processions, where their buffoonery was a joy to the faithful. The Minnesinger, who formed themselves into a guild in the 13th century, gave more refined musical performances, close to Gregorian monody. They included Gotfrid von Strassburg (*c*1210), author of 20,000 verses of *Tristan et Yseut*, Hesso de Strasbourg (*c*1230) and Nicolas de Strasbourg (14th century).

Towards the end of the Middle Ages musical instruments were permitted in church, and a small organ was donated to the cathedral in 1260. The first large organ (1292) was burnt in 1298. Claus Karlen constructed a new one (1324–7) that had between 16 and 24 manual ranks and a 12-key pedal-board; it was destroyed by fire in 1384 and replaced the following year. St Thomas's had an organ as early as 1333.

In the 16th century Strasbourg was at the height of its fortunes, theological and cultural as well as political and economic. Musical life in the city was supported less by the activity of individuals of genius than by broad participation at a popular level; printing played an essential role. In 1500 there were already more than 20 printing firms, most of which later served the cause of the Reformation, which was preached at the cathedral from about 1518. In 1524 Wolfgang Köpphel printed *Teutsch Kirchenampt mit Lobgesengen und göttlichen Psalmen*, the first Protestant collection of canticles, with the melody on a five-line staff. In 1539 Calvin, exiled from Geneva, organized the printing of *Aulcuns pseaumes et cantiques mys en chant*, including five psalms adapted by Calvin himself to fit melodies from the *Teutsch Kirchenampt*. Bernhard Jobin printed his own lute tablatures (1572) and those of Neusidler (1574), Sixt Kargel (1574) and Bernhard Schmid (i) in 1577 and the *Thesaurus motettarum* by Jakob Paix (1589).

Secular music also benefited from printing, and enjoyed the protection of the bishops of Strasbourg; for example Sebastian Virdung dedicated his *Musica getutscht* (1511) to Bishop Guillaume de Honstein. A group of renowned humanist musicians gathered around Johann Rudolphinger, including Symphorianus Pollio, Thomas Sporer and Sixt Dietrich; all composed polyphonic songs, some of which appeared in 1536 in *Fünff und sechzig teütscher Lieder*. In 1515 Othmar Luscinius, organist at St Thomas's, had his *Musicae institutiones*, lectures on music given in Vienna, published in Strasbourg.

The melodies of the Protestant psalms that came into use after the Reformation were often borrowed from Gregorian chant. Polyphony and the use of the organ were thought to be largely responsible for the decadence of religion; the Strasbourg Reformation excluded them both from worship and allowed only the unison chorale. In 1563 a work (*Bellum musicale*) by the Metz organist Claudius Sebastiani appeared in Strasbourg; in it the author lamented the conflict between polyphony and plainchant in the church. Protestant Kantors who composed secular polyphonic songs and psalm melodies included Wolfgang Dachstein, organist at St Thomas's and at the cathedral, and Matthias Greiter, who became a teacher at the Gymnasium and wrote a treatise on music education, *Elementale musicum juventuti accommodum* (1544).

The history of the organ in 16th-century Strasbourg reflects the religious upheavals of the period. In 1529, 1531 and 1541 the magistrate of Strasbourg ruled that the cathedral organ (built in 1489 and probably neglected) could be used. After a long period of inactivity other organs in the city were repaired (that of St Thomas's in 1560 and that of St Pierre-le-Jeune in 1591) and a new organ was donated to St Pierre-le-Vieux in 1590. An ordinance of 1598 governed church music strictly, defining the role of the organ. A new tolerance of polyphony is indicated by the publications of Bernhard Schmid (i) and (ii): nevertheless, the basis of Protestant church music continued to be unison singing by the congregation. Towards the end of this troubled century the city considered granting official status to *maîtres chanteurs* and subsidizing them. The Counter-Reformation attempted to introduce hymn singing in the vernacular.

2. 17TH CENTURY. At the beginning of the 17th century music in Strasbourg was dominated by C. T. Walliser, *maître de chapelle* at St Nicolas in 1598 and *musicus ordinarius* of the Gymnasium in 1600. In 1605 he inaugurated a weekly *publicum exercitium musicum*, at which his own works were performed. For theatrical productions at the Gymnasium he composed songs in Latin and Greek. He combined polyphony and the chorale, using both the organ and instruments to accompany the congregation in the rich polyphony of his chorale arrangements, collected in his *Ecclesiodae* (1614–25). He also composed music for *Moïse*, a play presented on the occasion of the Gymnasium's transformation into the university (1621).

The Thirty Years War (1618–48) did not extinguish all musical life: sacred works continued to be performed in private homes and in some parish churches, and the *maîtres chanteurs* and minstrels were active. The minstrels' guild was powerful, and any musician caught without his guild card had his instruments confiscated. Several outstanding composers of instrumental music were active during this period and published works in Strasbourg: Matthias Mercker (organist at St Nicolas, c1620); Elias Mertel (*Hortus musicalis*, 1615); J. U. Steigleder, who published an organ tablature in 1627; Vincenz Jelić (*Parnassia militia*, 1622); P. F. Böddecker (*Sacra partitura*, 1651); Valentin Strobel (ii); and J. E. Rieck (organist at St Thomas's, 1639–77). Georg Muffat, one of the leading exponents of the French style outside France, grew up in Strasbourg, and about 1669 became organist of the cathedral. In the preface to his *Florilegium primum* (1695) he wrote: 'I was perhaps the first to bring any idea of these things to musicians of good taste in Alsace'.

In 1681 Strasbourg was unified with France by Louis XIV, and the cathedral reverted to Catholicism. The focus of musical life moved to the Temple Neuf, a Dominican church given to the Protestants by way of compensation. In 1685 the Council of XIII decided that one of the duties attached to the position of organist was to enrich the repertory of 'figured' religious music, sacred songs and psalms. Among Catholic musicians J. S. Kusser was in the service of Bishop Guillaume IV Egon de Fürstenberg in Strasbourg, where in 1682 he published his *Composition de musique*, containing instrumental suites with French overtures. Sébastien de Brossard's work in Strasbourg consolidated French influence there; *maître* of the cathedral choir from 1689, he founded a society for the presentation of French operas, the Académie de Musique. J. G. Rauch (i) succeeded Brossard in 1698, and was also cathedral organist (1687–1710); in 1697 he published his *Cithara Orphei*, a collection of 12 trio sonatas.

3. 18TH CENTURY. Organ building flourished in Strasbourg during the 18th century; in 1702 Andreas Silbermann settled there and built organs in St Nicolas (1707), St Pierre-le-Vieux (1708–9), the cathedral (1713–16), Ste Aurélie (1718) and St Guillaume (1728). His son Johann Andreas built about 50 organs in Alsace and Baden from 1736 to 1783, including those of St Thomas (1737–40), Temple Neuf (1749) and St Pierre-le-Jeune (1780) in Strasbourg. One of

Silbermann's workmen, Konrad Sauer, also founded a dynasty of organ builders in Strasbourg. It was on the Silbermann organs of St Thomas and Temple Neuf that Mozart gave three concerts in 1778.

Throughout the first half of the 18th century J. C. Frauenholtz had a marked influence on the city's musical life. He held, as was the custom, the two posts of *maître de chapelle* at Temple Neuf and director of municipal concerts (1727–54). During this period municipal concerts were organized by the Académie de Musique de Strasbourg, founded in 1730, and grew in number to 30 each year.

F. X. Richter arrived in Strasbourg from Mannheim in 1769, and the musical life of Strasbourg reached a new peak. Richter was appointed *maître de chapelle* at the cathedral, where at that time the orchestra and choir were second in France only to those at Versailles (in 1782 it comprised 17 singers and 28 instruments); he also conducted the municipal concerts in the Salle au Miroir during the visit of Marie Antoinette (1770) and the centenary of Strasbourg's reunification with France (1781). Ignace Pleyel succeeded Richter from 1783 to 1793 and wrote his best works in Strasbourg. With J. P. Schönfeld (*maître de chapelle* at Temple Neuf, 1777–90, and director of the municipal concerts from 1781), he organized the 'Pleyel–Schönfeld' concerts, which enjoyed great success.

The Revolution dealt a blow to Strasbourg's musical life, attacking the institutions of the *ancien régime*; most musicians chose exile. In 1792 the *Marseillaise*, battlesong of the Rhine Army, was composed in Strasbourg. The minstrels' guild dissolved in 1791 after 600 years of existence; among the few compositions tolerated at this time were hymns glorifying the Revolution. After the Terror sacred music came to be tolerated at the cathedral, although mostly in the form of plainchant and fauxbourdon. The *grand motet* was authorized for major feasts.

4. 19TH CENTURY. Kreutzer played a part in the revival of musical life in Strasbourg after the upheavals of the Revolution, and Stanislaus Spindler succeeded Pleyel as *maître de chapelle*. However, the recovery was largely due to the people. Choral societies, and music societies such as the Union Alsacienne de Musique (1830), grew up. In 1827 the Académie de Chant was founded, and in 1830 the first Alsace music festival took place. The Strasbourg Ecole Normale included music in its curriculum. Many vocal works were written in the Alsace dialect; the German language dominated the repertory. About 1840 greater interest was taken in the music played in Paris; however, the first choral festival (1856) was again dominated by the German language. At the 1863 festival Berlioz conducted his *L'enfance du Christ*. In 1854, attempting to remedy the decline of the municipal orchestra, the town founded the Strasbourg Conservatory, directed by Théodore Hasselmans, who, as conductor of the Théâtre Municipal (1825), introduced the works of Wagner. The younger Franz Stockhausen raised the standard of the conservatory to international level; from 1868 to 1879 he also directed the Société de Chant Sacrée at the cathedral.

In 1871 Strasbourg was seized by Prussia, and subsequently profited from Wilhelm II's desire to provide an artistic showcase on the Rhine. Musical life flourished with new vigour although French music was virtually banned for more than 30 years. In 1872 the Männergesangverein was founded, and in 1903 the Sängerhaus (later the Palais des Fêtes) was constructed for the society; Widor gave the inaugural organ performance there in 1909. The Polish pianist and composer Ignacy Paderewski taught at the conservatory from 1885 to 1886. Some Strasbourg composers became well known, such as Waldteufel, Nessler, and Georges Merckling, who edited the *Elsasslothringische Gesang- und Musikzeitung* and wrote biographies of local musicians. From 1872 Gustav Jacobsthal taught at the university, where a chair of musicology was created for him in 1875.

Among the leading figures in Strasbourg's musical life during this period were Ernest Münch (1859–1928), organist at St Guillaume in 1882, who founded the choir of St Guillaume in 1885 to perform the music of Bach; and F. X. Mathias, organist at Strasbourg Cathedral from 1898 to 1908, who reorganized Gregorian chant and reformed organ building in collaboration with Emile Rupp (organist at St Paul, 1896–1939); and also Albert Schweitzer. All three joined in editing the *Internationales Regulativ für Orgelbau* (Vienna and Leipzig, 1909), which initiated a 'return to Silbermann'.

5. AFTER 1900. In 1905 Friedrich Ludwig succeeded Jacobsthal in the chair of musicology at the German University of Strasbourg; he was succeeded by Théodore Gérold (1919), Yvonne Rokseth (1937), Fritz Münch (1949) and Marc Honegger (1958). Pfitzner replaced Stockhausen as head of the conservatory in 1907, also conducting the municipal concerts and the opera; he completed his opera *Palestrina* there. Generally the German neo-Romantic aesthetic was still dominant, but, at the Alsace-Lorraine Festival (1905, 1907, 1910 and 1913) works by French composers were also performed. In 1913 Mathias founded the Institut de Musique Sacrée St Léon IX and the review *Caecilia*.

Joseph Guy Ropartz, a pupil of Franck, was appointed head of the conservatory in 1919; he introduced the contemporary French school of composition to Strasbourg, created the Société des Amis du Conservatoire and conducted subscription concerts. Alphonse Hoch, a priest at the cathedral in 1925, reorganized music there; under his direction the cathedral choir improved its *a cappella* singing and made numerous tours. Under Ernest Münch and, later, his son Fritz (1924–61), the St Guillaume choir expanded its repertory, and Schweitzer played the organ for the choir's concerts. The choir of the Eglise Réformée, conducted by Edouard Niesberger (1897–1927), Charles Muller (1929–61) and Marc Münch (from 1961), performs a Bach cantata every month, following a tradition dating from 1890. In 1929 Fritz Münch took over the direction of the conservatory and of the municipal orchestra.

In 1932 the Congrès International d'Organologie was organized in Strasbourg, and the Strasbourg Music Festival was established. The festival was financed by the Société des Amis de la Musique de Strasbourg, founded in 1932, and was the first organized festival in France. From the outset it was an enormous success, presenting such artists as the Cortot–Thibaud–Casals Trio (1933), the Busch Quartet (1934), and Schnabel and Klemperer (1936), and it continues to attract international performers. World premières given at the festivals have included Florent Schmitt's String Quartet

(1948) and Symphony (1958), and Poulenc's *Stabat mater* (1951) and Flute Sonata (1963). In August 1933 the Session d'Etudes Musicales de Strasbourg took place, organized by Fritz Münch and Hermann Scherchen: in ten days 64 contemporary works were performed and seven lectures were given, and among the participants were Bartók and Roussel. In 1958 the Journées Annuelles de la Société Internationale pour la Musique Contemporaine took place in Strasbourg simultaneously with the festival. Since then the festival has maintained its high standards, presenting many outstanding performers, including the renowned Les Percussions de Strasbourg, established in 1961.

In the 1960s, under Louis Martin's direction, the conservatory became one of the foremost in France, particularly for the study of the organ. It was endowed with a large Schwenkedel organ (three manuals, 45 stops) in 1964, and has spread to many local annexes, including the Villa Greiner in 1966. In 1969 it became the national conservatory of the region. From 1960 the Institute of Musicology (founded in 1919) was responsible for organizing an annual university festival, the Journées de Chant Choral. There are four important music collections in Strasbourg, at the National and University library, the Institute of Musicology, the Great Seminary and the Protestant Seminary.

There are many musical associations in the city. In 1960 the Amis des Jeunes Artistes Musiciens was founded with the aim of discovering talented young musicians. Until 1974 the city had two important symphony orchestras: that of Radio Strasbourg and the Municipal Orchestra, which became the Philharmonic Orchestra in 1971. The association Musique de Notre Temps organized lectures and recitals with commentary. The Municipal Theatre is the home of the Opéra du Rhin, which is centred on Strasbourg, Colmar and Mulhouse. Instrument making has benefited from the renewal of interest in early music; in addition to the important Strasbourg organ builders (Roethinger, Schwenkedel, Kern, Muhleisen and the Manufacture Alsacienne d'Orgues), several young organ and harpsichord makers have settled in the Strasbourg area.

BIBLIOGRAPHY
C. M. Berg: *Aperçu historique sur l'état de la musique à Strasbourg pendant les 50 dernières années* (Strasbourg, 1840)
J. F. Lobstein: *Beiträge zur Geschichte der Musik im Elsass und besonders in Strassburg* (Strasbourg, 1840)
F. Streinz: 'Zur Geschichte des Meistergesangs in Strasbourg', *Jb für Geschichte, Sprache und Literatur Elsass-Lothringens*, ix (1893), 76
F. Hubert: *Die Strassburger liturgischen Ordnungen im Zeitalter der Reformation* (Göttingen, 1900)
M. Vogeleis: *Quellen und Bausteine zu einer Geschichte der Musik und des Theaters im Elsass, 500–1800* (Strasbourg, 1911)
A. Oberdoerffer: *Nouvel aperçu historique sur l'état de la musique en Alsace. . .et à Strasbourg. . .de 1840 à 1913* (Strasbourg, 1914)
A. Goehlinger: *La musique à la cathédrale de Strasbourg* (Strasbourg, 1920)
T. Gérold: 'Les premiers recueils de mélodies religieuses protestantes à Strasbourg', *RdM*, ix (1925), 49
T. Gérold and E. Wagner: *Les plus anciennes mélodies de l'église protestante de Strasbourg et leurs auteurs* (Paris, 1928)
G. Skopnik: *Das Strassburger Schultheater* (Gelnhausen, 1934)
E. Jung: *Le choeur de St. Guillaume de Strasbourg* (Strasbourg, 1947)
F. Raugel: *Les orgues et les organistes de la cathédrale de Strasbourg* (Colmar, 1948)
J. Müller-Blattau: 'Elsass', *MGG*
Y. Rokseth: 'Les premiers chants de l'église calviniste', *RdM*, xxxvi (1954), 7
F. Krummacher: *Die Überlieferung der Choralbearbeitungen in der frühen evangelischen Kantate* (Berlin, 1965)
M. Lang: 'Bibliographie de l'histoire de la musique en Alsace', *La musique en Alsace hier et aujourd'hui* (Strasbourg, 1970), 373–459
C. M. Roper: *The Strasbourg French Psalter 1539–1553* (diss, U. of Southern California, 1972)
H. Reinhardt: 'Petit historique des orgues de la cathédrale, 1260–1714', *Bulletin de la Société des amis de la cathédrale de Strasbourg*, xi (1974), 57
E. Weber: *Musique et théâtre dans les pays rhénans au XVIème siècle* (Paris, 1974)

JEAN HAPPEL

Strasbourg Manuscript (destroyed in 1870). *See* SOURCES, MS, §VII, 3.

Strascinando (It., from *strascinare*: 'to drag'). A direction to perform a passage in a heavily slurred manner. The form *strascicante* (from the verb *strascicare*) is practically synonymous.

Strassburg. *See* STRASBOURG.

Strata [Strada], **Giovanni Battista** (*fl* 1609–51). Italian organist and composer. He was second organist and priest at Genoa Cathedral about 1610. He later seems to have worked at S Maria delle Vigne, Genoa, before resuming his post at the cathedral on 21 July 1648. He was succeeded there on 13 March 1651, perhaps because he had died. His music is simple and unpretentious and was probably all intended for performance in the churches and religious houses of Genoa.

WORKS
Messa, motetti, Magnificat, 5vv, bc (Venice, 1609)
Arie di musica, . . . 1–4vv, sopra le lodi spirituali . . . letanie della madonna e quelle de' santi, 8vv, . . . et il salmo Miserere mei Deus in falsobordone, 4, 8vv/insts, bc (Genoa, 1610) [the litanies and psalm also pubd separately in 1610]
Missa primi toni 'D'un si bel foco', 5vv, bc (org), in 1618²; 5 motets, 5vv, bc, in 1609⁶, 1612³, 1613², 1617¹
51 works, 1–4vv, bc, Genoa Cathedral Library; Biblioteca Brera, Milan

BIBLIOGRAPHY
R. Giazotto: *La musica a Genova nella vita pubblicae privata dal XIII al XVIII secolo* (Genoa, 1951)

SERGIO MARTINOTTI

Stratas, Teresa [Strataki, Anastasia] (*b* Toronto, 26 May 1938). Canadian soprano of Greek descent. As a child she sang in her parents' restaurant and appeared on radio. She later studied at the Toronto Conservatory under Irene Jessner and made her début in Toronto with Canadian Opera in 1959 as Mimì. Having won the 1959 Metropolitan Opera Auditions of the Air, she made her début at the Metropolitan Opera that October, as Poussette (*Manon*). Her regular appearances in New York have included those as Sardula (Menotti's *Le dernier sauvage*), Lisa (*The Queen of Spades*), Liù, Nedda, Micaela, Zerlina, Cherubino, Despina and Hansel. In 1960 she created the title role in Peggy Glanville-Hicks's *Nausicaa* at the Athens Festival, and in 1962 Queen Isabella in Falla's *Atlántida* at La Scala. She made her Covent Garden début as Mimì in 1961 and has been heard as Susanna there and at Salzburg (1972–3); she makes regular guest appearances in Munich, Hamburg and Paris, and has also performed at the Bol'shoy Opera. Her repertory includes Verdi's Joan of Arc, Violetta, Tatyana and Mélisande. Stratas has a lyric-dramatic voice of individuality and a keen sense of the stage. Deep involvement in her roles distinguishes all her appearances.

Strategier, Herman (*b* Arnhem, 10 Aug 1912). Dutch composer and organist. He studied with Dusch (piano), Winnubst (theory) and Andriessen (organ and composition) at the Roman Catholic School of Church

Music, Utrecht, later continuing studies with Andriessen (the greatest influence on his work) for several years. In addition to teaching at the conservatories of Utrecht and Rotterdam and at Utrecht University, he was until 1973 conductor of the Dutch Madrigal Choir of Leiden.

WORKS
(selective list)

Orch: Introduzione e passacaglia, 1940; Pf Conc., 1948; Sym. no.1, 1949; Praeludium en fuga, 1951; Partita in modi antichi, 1954; Triptiek, cl, wind orch, 1960; Accordion Conc., 1969; Musica festiva, 1969; Concertante speelmuziek, fl, bn, orch, 1971; Intrada festiva, 1976

Vocal: Koning Swentibold, oratorio, 1948; Don Ramiro, chorus, orch, 1943; Arnhemsce psalm, oratorio, 1955; Rembrandt cantate, 1956; Requiem, 1961; 3 motetten, 1963; Te Deum, 1967; Cantica pro tempore natali, 1969; Colloquia familiara, S, chorus, str orch, 1969; Psalm ciii, S, chorus, orch, 1971; Mors responsura, 4vv, orch, 1972; Ligeia or The Shadow out of Time, chorus ad lib, fl, 6 perc, org, harp, elec, 1973; masses and other liturgical music

Chamber and org pieces

Principal publisher: Donemus

BIBLIOGRAPHY

W. Paap: 'Nederlandsche componisten van onzen tijd, VI: Herman Strategier', *Mens en melodie*, i (1946), 261

L. Hanekroot: 'Het oratorium Koning Swentibold van Herman Strategier', *Mens en melodie*, iii (1948), 278

ROGIER STARREVELD

Stratford, William (*fl* c15th–16th centuries). English composer. He is described in the Eton Choirbook (*GB-WRec* 178) as 'monachus Stratfordiae', i.e. a monk of the Cistercian abbey of Stratford-atte-Bowe in Essex. He may be identifiable with the 'Parker monke of Stratforde' a single part of whose song *O my lady dure* survives in *GB-Lbm* Roy.App.58. He is represented in the Eton Choirbook by one of its few surviving complete settings of the *Magnificat* (in four parts; printed in MB, xii, no.48). It is a competent piece of counterpoint for men's voices in the florid style of the late 15th century.

JOHN CALDWELL

Strathspey. A Scottish dance, a REEL of slower tempo, allowing the use of more elaborate steps both in the setting step and in the travelling figure. It usually leads into another reel without a break, or vice versa. It is written in common time, crotchet 160 to 168, or slower. Musically, the strathspey is characterized by its dotted quaver-semiquaver rhythm and the inversion of this, the 'Scotch snap' (see ex.1).

The strathspey made its appearance in about the mid-18th century. Two tunes, each labelled 'A New Strathspey Reel', appeared in Oswald's *Caledonian Pocket Companion* (c1742). Robert Bremner's *A Collection of Scots Reels* (c1757) contains about ten tunes marked as strathspeys, of which the first bears the note, 'The Strathspey Reels are play'd much slower than the others'. Thomas Newte in 1785 ascribed the composition of early strathspey tunes to the Strathspey families of fiddlers, the Browns and Cummings. The strathspey was essentially music conceived for the fiddle, and as such exploited the peculiar bowing technique of the Scots fiddler.

The slow strathspey was purely an exhibition recital piece for the fiddler, and did not normally accompany the dancing of the strathspey. Its performance on the fiddle was highly stylized, its chief characteristic being the substitution of a rest for the duration of the dot of the dotted quaver, giving a detached, staccato effect; considerable rubato was also used. However, a dance for two dancers known as the 'strathspey minuet' was sometimes performed to the slow strathspey.

For bibliography *see* REEL.

FRANCIS COLLINSON

Stratico, Michele (*b* ?Zara [now Zadar, Yugoslavia], c1721; *d* c1782). Italian amateur violinist and composer. He came from an aristocratic provincial Venetian family of some intellectual distinction; his relative Simone (1733–1824) was a prominent physician, educator and scientist known to Goldoni and Voltaire. He studied law at the University of Padua, and later practised in Venice. Tartini was his teacher and friend.

To judge from the quality of his music Stratico was a dilettante. He composed a large quantity of instrumental music for strings, including violin duos and sonatas, trio sonatas, three- and four-part sinfonias, and concertos for one and two violins. Stratico's best works appear among his violin concertos, where his style is barely distinguishable from that of his master Tartini. On the whole his work has greater historical interest than intrinsic worth, for, undistorted by the idiosyncrasies of a very original mind, it reflects with great clarity the fashions in form, style and technique of north Italian chamber music in the 1750s and 1760s. Of special note here are violin solo ornamentation studies (some exercises survive in Stratico's hand); the firm appearance in Italy at this time of early Classical melodic and harmonic styles, with near-crystallization of sonata allegro form; and the clear distinction Stratico makes between an orchestral style in the sinfonias, and a chamber or soloistic style in the sonatas.

WORKS

6 sonate, vn, vc/hpd, op.1 (London, c1763)

273 instrumental works in MS catalogued by Duckles and Elmer; all in *US-BE*; a few duplicates and other Stratico works in *D-B, I-Pca, Vlevi, Vnm, US-Wc*; 3 ed. M. Roeder (Bryn Mawr, Penn., 1976)

BIBLIOGRAPHY

V. Duckles and M. Elmer: *Thematic Catalogue of a Manuscript Collection of 18th-century Italian Instrumental Music in the University of California, Berkeley, Music Library* (Berkeley, Calif., 1963)

M. Elmer: 'Stratico, Michele', *MGG*

JAMES L. JACKMAN

Strattner, Georg Christoph (*b* Gols, nr. Pressburg, c1644; *d* Weimar, buried 11 April 1704). German composer of Hungarian birth. He went to Pressburg about 1651 as a chorister and schoolboy to stay with SAMUEL FRIEDRICH CAPRICORNUS, director of music

Ex.1 *Highland Whisky*

there, who was his cousin and whom he followed to Stuttgart in 1657. After Capricornus's death (in November 1665) he was Kapellmeister at the court of Baden-Durlach, from 1666 until 1682. Because of the destruction of Durlach in 1689, very few of his numerous compositions from this period have survived. In 1675 he was already performing his own works at Frankfurt am Main, and in 1682 he was appointed Kapellmeister at the Barfüsserkirche there. This post also entailed the supervision of performances in the other Frankfurt churches, as well as teaching music at the Gymnasium. In addition to his own works, he regularly performed those of other composers of his day, including W. C. Briegel and J. P. Krieger. At the 'instigation of high and distinguished persons and valued friends' he published at Frankfurt, with his own melodies, a new edition of the influential hymn collection of 1680 of JOACHIM NEANDER. Strattner's activities at Frankfurt ended abruptly in 1692, when he was found guilty of adultery and banished. He remained without a new post until 1694, when he became a tenor and chancery clerk at Weimar. In 1695 he was appointed vice-Kapellmeister there in order to relieve J. S. Drese, director of the Hofkapelle, who was in poor health; he held this post until his death. Like Bach later, he was required to write a new church composition every fourth Sunday, and he was responsible for the chamber music too. He was also appointed director of the Weimar opera house when it opened in 1697, though it is not certain whether he himself wrote works for it.

Comparatively little of Strattner's large, mainly sacred output has survived. It is therefore difficult to undertake a definitive appraisal, particularly as most of the surviving works date from his Frankfurt period, when, in the wake of Pietist influence, church music tended to be rather simple. The individual features of his music may also be in part the product of Pietist devotion. He usually set biblical texts in his cantatas, which are close to the form of the dialogue cantata. He generally favoured an all-embracing form, with fine rhythmic and melodic differentiations and frequent modulations to intensify the meaning of the text. His Passion cantata, *Sehet doch, ihr Menschenkinder*, marks an important stage in the development towards the Passion oratorio.

WORKS

SACRED VOCAL

(in D-F unless otherwise stated)

Ach, mein Vater, ich habe gesündigt, 4vv, 2 vn, 3 va, vle, org, 1689
Aus der Tiefe, 5vv, 2 vn, 3 va, bc, 1685
Barmherzig treuer Gott, 4vv, 2 vn, 3 va, vle, org, c1687
Beatus vir (anon., probably by Strattner)
Die Welt, das ungestüme Meer, 4vv, 2 vn, 2 va, bn, org, 1690 or earlier
Drei sind, die da zeugen, 3vv, 2 vn, vle, org, 1680 or earlier
Du Hirt Israel, 4vv, 2 vn, 3 va, va di basso/bn, org, c1686
Erstanden ist des Todes Tod, 4vv, 2 vn, 2 fl/cornett, 2 va, 3 trbn, va di basso/bn, c1682
Getreuer Schöpfer, der du mich, 4vv, 2 vn, 4 va, org, before 1686
Gott sei mir gnädig (anon., probably by Strattner)
Herr, der du uns hast anvertraut, 4vv, 2 vn, 3 va, bc, c1682
Herr, wie lange wilstu mein so gar vergessen, 1v, 4 vn, bc, before 1670, *D-Bds*
Himmel und Erde werden vergehen, 4vv, 2 vn, 3 va, bc, 1687, *Bds*
Ich komm, o höchster Gott, zu dir (anon., probably by Strattner)
Ich stelle mich bei meinem Leben, 5vv, 2 vn, 4 va, bc, 1676
Ich will den Herrn loben, 5vv, 2 vn, 2 va, bn, vle, org, 1690
Ihr Himmelsfeste, 7vv, 2 vn, 3 va, org, 1693
In corde dixit fatuus, 3vv, 2 vn, bc (org), 1675
Levavi oculos, 1v, vn, bc, before 1670, *Bds*
O Gott, du Ursprung aller Liebe, wedding cantata, 4vv, 2 ob, 2 va, vle, bc, after 1682

Sehet doch, ihr Menschenkinder, Passion cantata, 6vv, 2 vn, 4 va, org, 1692

For lost cantatas see Schaal, Noack (1921), Seiffert

HYMNS

4 novissima (A. Gryphius), 1v, 2 vn, bc (Frankfurt am Main, 1685), lost
64 hymns in J. Neander: Vermehrte Glaub- und Liebesübung . . . Bundeslieder und Danck-Psalmen (Frankfurt, 5/1691)
Others in several hymnbooks

39 ed. in Zahn; 3 ed. in Winterfeld; 14 ed. F. Noack, *Die Kirchenmusik*, i (Langensalza, 1920); 6 ed. K. Isenberg, *Geistliche Sololieder des Barock*, i (Kassel, n.d.)

SECULAR VOCAL

3 songs, 1v, bc, *D-Ka*
Tafelstücke, lost, see Schaal

STAGE

Glück und Tugend, Tanzspiel, Aug 1666; Der Liebestriumph, Singballett, 1670; Musen-Preiss-Ballett, 1670; Atlas, oder Die vier Theil der Welt, Singballett, 1681: lost, see Schaal in Ansbach inventory, 1686, see Schaal; see also Noack (1921) and Brockpähler

(doubtful, all performed during Strattner's Weimar period)

Von der denen lasterhaften Begierden entgegengesetzten tugendlichen Liebe, 19 Oct 1696; Die erhöhte Dienstbarkeit, 19 Oct 1697; Die von zweyen Schäfern geliebte . . . Delicanda, Kromsdorf, Lusthaus, 16 Nov 1698; Die siegende Flora, Oct 1699; Lustspiel von einer Bauern-Tochter Marein, 1699; Operettgen, perhaps, Die verliebte Eigensinnigkeit, Kromsdorf, 1699; Tancredo und Constantia, Wilhelmsburg, 1699

INSTRUMENTAL

Balletto di cavallo, c1667, *D-KL*

BIBLIOGRAPHY

EitnerQ; GerberL; WaltherML
C. von Winterfeld: *Der evangelische Kirchengesang*, ii (Leipzig, 1845/R1966)
J. Zahn: *Die Melodien der deutschen evangelischen Kirchenlieder* (Gütersloh, 1889–93/R1963)
C. Valentin: *Geschichte der Musik in Frankfurt am Main vom Anfange des XIV. bis zum Anfange des XVIII. Jahrhunderts* (Frankfurt am Main, 1906/R1972)
M. Seiffert: 'Die Chorbibliothek der St. Michaelisschule in Lüneburg zu Seb. Bach's Zeit', *SIMG*, ix (1907–8), 593
E. Noack: *Georg Christoph Strattner: sein Leben und seine Werke* (diss., U. of Berlin, 1921; extract in *AMw*, iii (1921), 447–83)
——: *Wolfgang Carl Briegel* (Berlin, 1963)
R. Brockpähler: *Handbuch zur Geschichte der Barockoper* (Emsdetten, 1964)
W. Blankenburg: 'Die Kirchenmusik in den reformierten Gebieten des europäischen Kontinents', in F. Blume: *Geschichte der evangelischen Kirchenmusik* (Kassel, 2/1965; Eng. trans., enlarged, 1974 as *Protestant Church Music: a History*)
F. Krummacher: *Die Überlieferung der Choralbearbeitungen in der frühen evangelischen Kantate* (Berlin, 1965)
H. Engel: *Musik in Thüringen* (Cologne, 1966)
R. Schaal: *Die Musikhandschriften des Ansbacher Inventars von 1686* (Wilhelmshaven, 1966)
H. Kümmerling: *Katalog der Sammlung Bokemeyer* (Kassel, 1970)
SUSETTE CLAUSING

Stratton, George (Robert) (*b* London, 18 July 1897; *d* London, 4 Sept 1954). English violinist. He studied the violin and composition at the Guildhall School of Music, London. He led the LSO from 1933 to 1952, the orchestra at Glyndebourne from its foundation in 1934, and from 1936 he was leader and manager of the Queen's Hall Orchestra, which was revived for recording. He became violin professor at the RCM in 1942, and conductor in 1944. He was associate conductor of the LSO during the last few years of his life. He was a founder-member in 1927 of the Stratton String Quartet (later renamed the Aeolian String Quartet) and this quartet was chosen by Elgar to record his Quartet and Quintet in 1933. Stratton was also a founder-member of the Reginald Paul Piano Quartet (1932–42). He was a most distinguished all-round musician. He wrote, with Alan Frank, *The Playing of Chamber Music* (London, 1935, reissued 1951).

WATSON FORBES

Stratton, John F(ranklin) (*b* West Swanzey, New Hampshire, 14 Sept 1832; *d* Brooklyn, NY, 23 Oct 1912). American manufacturer and importer of musical instruments. He established large factories in Germany to supply his own New York store and his brother's in Boston. Both Stratton and George William, his brother, older by two years, were precocious young musicians. For three years beginning in 1839 the boys and their father travelled about New England giving concerts. Both boys studied music avidly, George learning the clarinet and the violin and John the trombone, E♭ key bugle and cornet.

John began his career as a bandleader in Worcester, Massachusetts. He then went to Hartford, Connecticut, where he directed the Hartford Cornet Band and opened his first music store. He moved to New York in 1857 and established a brass instrument factory while leading Stratton's Palace Garden Orchestra. The business prospered during the Civil War years and as soon as the war was over Stratton began establishing factories to produce his instruments in Germany. After brass instrument factories at Markneukirchen in 1866 and in Leipzig in 1868, in 1869 Stratton built a very large factory making 50 to 100 violins a day at Gohlis bei Leipzig. These factories were sold in 1883 and Stratton returned to New York, continuing his business there until 1912. Instruments by John F. Stratton are found in most American collections, notably the instrument collection at the University of Illinois and the Greenleaf collection at the National Music Camp, Interlochen, Michigan.

BIBLIOGRAPHY

E. L. and L. Bill: *General History of the Music Trades of America* (New York, 1891), 81

B. Read: *History of Swanzey* (Salem, Mass., 1892), 558ff

ROBERT E. ELIASON

Stratus (Lat.: 'stretched'). An adjective used to describe a neume whose final element is the ORISCUS. For instance, a VIRGA (single note of relatively higher pitch) with added *oriscus* forms a *virga strata* (also known as the FRANCULUS or *gutturalis*). As with all neumes that include the *oriscus*, there is doubt as to the exact significance of the *stratus* type. A peculiarity of execution or an ambiguity of pitch may be involved (for illustration *see* NEUMATIC NOTATIONS, Table 1).

BIBLIOGRAPHY

P. Ferretti: 'Etude sur le pes stratus', *Le codex 903 de la Bibliothèque nationale de Paris*, PalMus, 1st ser., xiii (1925), 186

L. Charpentier: 'Etude sur la virga strata', *Revue grégorienne*, xii (1927), 1, 64, 154; xiii (1928), 1

M. Huglo: 'Les noms des neumes et leur origine', *Etudes grégoriennes*, i (1954), 53

Straube, Karl (Montgomery Rufus Siegfried) (*b* Berlin, 6 Jan 1873; *d* Leipzig, 27 April 1950). German organist, teacher and choral conductor. The son of an organist and instrument maker, he received his early training from his father and other Berlin organists, but he never had a formal music education. His knowledge derived from practical experience (in 1895 he became deputy organist at the Kaiser-Wilhelm-Gedächtniskirche in Berlin) and from the thriving musical and intellectual life of Berlin. He took Hans von Bülow as his model for interpretation and in 1897 formed a lifelong friendship with Reger, whose music he championed. That year he became cathedral organist at Wesel, in the Lower Rhine valley; his success there led to his appointments at the

Thomaskirche, Leipzig, as organist (1902) and Kantor (1918). Straube began teaching the organ in Leipzig in 1907 and was known as 'der Organistmacher', training and guiding numerous church musicians and organists. Up to 1913 he favoured the 'orchestral organ' style of registration and performance, in the manner of Liszt and Wagner, but he later changed his style to reflect the characteristic tone-qualities of Praetorius, Schnitger and Silbermann organs. This was exemplified in his weekly performances of Bach's motets at the Thomaskirche and at six Bach festivals he directed between 1904 and 1923. In 1919 he founded the Kirchenmusikalische Institut der Evangelisch-Lutherischen Landeskirche Sachsen at the Leipzig Conservatory. He merged the Leipzig Bach and Gewandhaus Choirs in 1920 and conducted them until 1932, and from 1931 to 1937 he conducted regular performances by the Thomanerchor and Gewandhaus Orchestra of all Bach's cantatas. Straube made several European tours with the Thomanerchor, and promoted choral works by Honegger, Kodály, Arnold Mendelssohn and Raphael among others. He received an honorary doctorate of arts and divinity from Leipzig University.

BIBLIOGRAPHY

G. Robert-Thornow: *Max Reger und Karl Straube* (Göttingen, 1907)

J. Wolgast: *Karl Straube* (Leipzig, 1928)

Karl Straube zu seinem 70. Geburtstag (Leipzig, 1943)

U. Fischer: 'Straubes neue Ausgabe der Bachsen Orgelwerke', *Musik und Kirche*, xxii (1952), 163

K. Voppel: 'Karl Straube und das Wesen des deutschen Orgelspiels', *Musik und Kirche*, xxv (1955), 90

H. Böhm: 'Der elfte Nachfolger Bachs, Gedenkblatt für Karl Straube zum 100. Geburtstag', *Musica*, xxvii (1973), 51

Straube, Rudolf (*b* Trebnitz, 1717; *d* London, *c*1780). German lutenist and composer. He sang in the choir of the Leipzig Thomasschule under J. S. Bach in the early 1730s, and entered the university at Leipzig on 27 February 1740. Early in 1754 he visited Erfurt and presented various compositions to J. Adlung, who described him as a good lutenist, a well-trained keyboard student of J. S. Bach, and one who at that time was interested only in travel. His travels evidently took him to London: C. F. Pohl included Straube among a list of musicians active there in 1759.

Straube's keyboard works reflect most of the prevailing elements of the Baroque style, usually enhanced by a pronounced rhythmic vitality. His compositions for lute and guitar are thoroughly idiomatic, often accompanied by a violin or keyboard. A dialogue between Straube and Thomas Gainsborough on the latter's manner of purchasing a lute and lute music, and a diagram of a fingerboard and tuning system by Straube, are in *GB-Lbm* Add.31698.

WORKS

2 lute sonatas (Leipzig, 1746)

5 sonatas, gui, 3 with kbd, vc, 2 with vn (London, 1768)

The Mecklenburg Gavotte with variations, hpd/pf (London, 1768)

2 kbd sonatas, *D-Mbs*; 3 pieces, theorbo lute, *GB-Lbm*, attrib. Straube

BIBLIOGRAPHY

J. Adlung: *Anleitung zur musikalischen Gelahrtheit* (Leipzig, 1758/*R*1953, 2/1783)

G. Schilling: *Encyklopädie der gesammten musikalischen Wissenschaften oder Universal-Lexikon der Tonkunst* (Stuttgart, 1835–8)

P. Spitta: *Johann Sebastian Bach* (Leipzig, 1873–80, 5/1962; Eng. trans., 1884–99/*R*1951)

DOUGLAS A. LEE

Straus, Oscar (*b* Vienna, 6 March 1870; *d* Bad Ischl, 11

Jan 1954). Austrian composer and conductor. On the recommendation of Brahms he studied with Hermann Grädener and in 1891 went to Berlin as a pupil of Bruch. Advised by the younger Johann Strauss to gain practical theatrical experience in the provinces, he conducted between 1893 and 1899 in Bratislava, Brno, Teplitz, Mainz and Hamburg. During the same period he was active as a composer of stage works and a good deal of salon music. He was conducting in Berlin when, in 1900, he was engaged as pianist and composer in the newly founded Überbrettl cabaret, and he enjoyed his first popular successes with songs such as *Die Musik kommt* and *Der lustige Ehemann*. Having returned to Vienna he began a series of operettas of which *Ein Walzertraum* rivalled *Die lustige Witwe* in popularity and first brought Straus international success. Its successor, *Der tapfere Soldat* (1908), gained particular success in the USA as *The Chocolate Soldier*. Subsequent operettas failed to add to his success until *Der letzte Walzer* (1920), in which the lead was played by Fritzi Massary around whom several of Straus's later works were written. *Eine Frau die weiss was sie will* (1932) was produced in London as *Mother of Pearl*, and *Drei Walzer* (1935), which used the music of Johann Strauss I and II in the first two acts and that of Straus himself in the third, achieved its greatest success with Yvonne Printemps in Paris. In 1939 he left Vienna and lived in France (where he was awarded the Légion d'honneur), New York and Hollywood, returning to settle in Bad Ischl in 1948. He continued to conduct his music on concert tours and for gramophone records, and his compositions included the operetta *Die Musik kommt* (1948), which used some of the tunes from his Überbrettl days, and music for the film *La ronde* (1950) with which he enjoyed a new world-wide success. Straus's final stage work was *Božena*, on which he had worked since 1936, although he subsequently revised the scores of *Ein Walzertraum*, *Drei Walzer* and *Eine Frau die weiss was sie will*. His son Erwin was a pianist and composer.

WORKS
(selective list)

OPERETTAS

Over 40 works (most pubd in vocal score in Vienna or Berlin) incl. Die lustigen Nibelungen (3, Rideamus [F. Oliven]), Carltheater, 12 Nov 1904; Hugdietrichs Brautfahrt (3, Rideamus), Carltheater, 10 March 1906; Ein Walzertraum (3, F. Dörmann, L. Jacobson, after H. Müller: Das Buch der Abenteuer), Carltheater, 2 March 1907; Der tapfere Soldat (3, R. Bernauer, Jacobson, after Shaw: Arms and the Man), Theater an der Wien, 14 Nov 1908; Rund um die Liebe (3, R. Bodanzky, F. Thelen), Johann Strauss, 9 Nov 1914
Der letzte Walzer (3, J. Brammer, A. Grünwald), Berlin, Berliner Theater, 12 Feb 1920; Mariette, ou comment on écrit l'histoire (3, Guitry), Paris, Edouard VII, 1 Oct 1928; Eine Frau, die weiss was sie will (3, Grünwald, after L. Verneuil), Berlin, Metropol, 1 Sept 1932; Drei Walzer (3, P. Knepler, A. Robinson), Zurich, Stadttheater, 1935; Die Musik kommt (3; Knepler, Robinson), Zurich, Stadttheater, 1948; rev. as Ihr erster Walzer, Munich, Gärtnerplatz, 1950; Božena (3, Brammer, Grünwald), Munich, Gärtnerplatz, 16 May 1952

OTHER WORKS

Ballets: Colombine, Berlin, 1904; Die Prinzessin von Tragant (Regel), Vienna, Hofoper, 13 Nov 1912
Film scores: Jenny Lind, 1930; The Smiling Lieutenant, 1932; The Southerner, 1932; One hour with you, 1932; Die Herren von Maxim, 1933; Frühlingsstimmen, 1934; Land without Music, 1935; Make a wish, 1935; La ronde, 1950; Madame de . . ., 1952
*c*500 cabaret songs, chamber music, orch works, pf pieces, choruses

BIBLIOGRAPHY
B. Grun: *Prince of Vienna: the Life, Times and Melodies of Oscar Straus* (London, 1955)

ANDREW LAMB

Strauss. Austrian family of dance musicians and composers. They raised popular music to a new expressive level, and by a melodic charm and a rhythmic verve, allied to a vivid sense of occasion, they gave the Viennese waltz in particular its classic expression.

(1) Johann (Baptist) Strauss (i) (*b* Vienna, 14 March 1804; *d* Vienna, 25 Sept 1849). Composer, conductor and violinist. He was of humble origin, his father Franz (*b* 1764; *d* 1816) being the innkeeper of the little tavern 'Zum heiligen Florian' in the house ('Zum guten Hirten') at Flossgasse 7. The Strauss family lived in the Leopoldstadt, the Vienna suburb between the Danube and the Danube Canal, which had long been the settling place for the Jews who came in growing numbers from the eastern provinces to the imperial capital. Johann Strauss, popularly known as 'black Schani', did everything he could to keep his Jewish origins secret and made no attempt to contradict the legend that he was a natural son of Count Musin-Pushkin, who had spent part of his time in Vienna and who was a grandson of Peter the Great's 'favourite moor' and the grandfather of Pushkin. However, the documented fact that Johann was descended from a Hungarian grandfather, Wolf Strauss, never interfered with his artistic activities or worldwide fame, although the German Reichs-Kulturkammer, already having sacrificed many operetta composers, in 1939 resorted to falsifying the parish register of St Stephen's, Vienna, in order to rescue the Strauss family from the Nazi pillory.

Intended for the bookbinding trade, Strauss turned to music very early. He learnt to play the violin with Polischansky and later studied theory with Ignaz von Seyfried, Kapellmeister of the Theater an der Wien. While still in his teens he played the viola in the popular dance orchestra of Michael Pamer (1782–1827), a noted composer of dance music (*Linzer Tänze*) and the immediate precursor of Strauss and Josef Lanner in the Viennese waltz. There he made friends with Lanner, a violinist in the Pamer orchestra, and in 1819 joined Lanner's small band. In 1824 when Lanner divided the orchestra, meanwhile grown to full Classical size, Strauss became his second conductor, but the partnership lasted only until September of the following year.

On 11 July 1825 Strauss married Maria Anna Streim, the daughter of the innkeeper of 'Zum roten Hahn' in Lichtenthal; after the birth in October of their first son, Johann, Strauss left Lanner, formed his own orchestra and thereafter worked independently at his music. He soon won the favour of audiences at several Viennese inns, and by 1829 was performing his first important compositions, the *Täuberln-Walzer* op.1, the *Döblinger Reunion-Walzer* op.2, the two sets of *Kettenbrücken-Walzer* opp.4 and 19, the *Krapfen-Waldel-Walzer* op.12 and the *Josefstädter Tänze* op.23, the titles indicating, as was the fashion, the place where each piece was first performed. But his real rise to fame began with an engagement at the Sperl ('Zum Sperl'), a fashionable Leopoldstadt establishment of which Pamer was the music director and for which Strauss composed his *Sperls Fest-Walzer* op.30 in 1829. To the Sperl, with its large beer-garden and dance hall, came many foreign visitors, among them the young Chopin ('Strauss and his waltzes obscure everything else'), the 19-year-old Wagner ('Strauss, the magic fiddler, the genius of Vienna's innate musical spirit') and Hans Christian Andersen, who described a Strauss evening in

1. Johann Strauss (i): lithograph (1835) by Josef Kriehuber

his autobiography:

In Hietzing I saw Strauss and heard him play. He stood there in the middle of his orchestra, the heart of the whole waltz scene. It was as if the melodies were streaming out of him. His eyes were shining. He was both the life of this place and its leader, that was plain to see.

Although dances occupied the largest part of these open-air concerts, it was also customary to include orchestral fantasies and paraphrases on the symphonic and operatic music of the day; there are even characteristics of the opera overture style in Strauss's (and Lanner's) waltz introductions. This practice of musical borrowing was used by Lanner in his *Aufforderung zum Tanze*, a version of Weber's rondo for piano (1819) which he arranged for his small orchestra in about 1828, long before Berlioz's orchestration. Strauss continued in the same vein, basing a number of his dances on airs and motifs from operas and instrumental music: *Walzer à la Paganini* op.11, *Tell-Galopp* op.29b, cotillons from *La muette de Portici* op.32, *Zampa-Walzer* op.57, *Cäcilien-Walzer* op.120, with motifs from the Kreutzer Sonata, and many other examples. By combining the classics with dance-tunes, Strauss presented to a wider public the serious music which had previously been the property mainly of court audiences.

In 1833 Strauss, spurred on by an entrepreneurial talent, began taking his orchestra of 28 players on tours abroad; over the years they travelled to all the principal towns of Austria, Bohemia, Germany, France and England, everywhere creating a sensation. In Paris, despite rivalries involving Musard and Dufresne, the leading French light musicians of the period, Strauss achieved an unprecedented success with even the great names of French music. Berlioz, in an enthusiastic article in the *Journal des débats*, wrote of 'the fire, the intelligence and poignant rhythmic coquetry' of Strauss's music and conducting. During his first Paris visit Strauss became acquainted with the quadrille, which he later introduced to Vienna. In fashionable circles it had been the custom to dance in facing rows for over 100 years; not until Fasching (Carnival) 1840 did the 'quadrille française' revolutionize Vienna's public balls. A host of Viennese composers now followed the innovation which Strauss had brought back from his encounters with Musard, Tolbecque, Dufresne and Jullien.

Strauss and his orchestra paid their first visit to England from mid-April until the end of November 1838. After the first concert on 17 April in the Hanover Square Rooms, the London *Morning Post* proclaimed their virtuosity:

So perfect a band was never before heard on this side of the Channel! The perfection of such an ensemble our orchestras have never yet reached. The accuracy, the sharpness, the exquisite precision with which every passage is performed, can be the result only of the most careful and persevering practice . . . We must notice the superior element of Strauss himself on the violin; he performs with peculiar energy, and imparts much of his own spirit to the band, the combined effect of which more resembles the unity of one single, powerful instrument than any orchestra that has yet been heard in this country.

Strauss participated in the coronation celebrations of Queen Victoria in Buckingham Palace, where on 10 May the first performance of his homage to Victoria, the waltz op.103, was given, as well as in many court balls and concerts, and in aristocratic and other wealthy homes in most of the larger towns of England and Scotland. The *Edinburgh Advertiser* wrote on 9 November:

His compositions had made us familiar with his style, long before he came amongst us, but they by no means prepared us for the wonderful display of every musical excellence to which we were witnesses . . . What most astonished the audience, no doubt, was the accuracy with which the performers took up their parts . . . Pianissimos and fortissimos were really what these terms signify, and every degree of loudness of sound then was marked with the exactness of a nicely graduated scale. . . .

Strauss later became Kapellmeister of a Vienna citizen's regiment and also wrote dance music for the court balls; the title *k.k. Hofballmusikdirektor* (imperial-royal director of music for balls) was created specially for him and bestowed upon him on 24 January 1846. His wife Anna bore him six children: (2) Johann, (3) Josef, Anna (Netty, 1829–1903), Theresia (1831–1915), Ferdinand (who died at the age of two) and (4) Eduard. In 1842 he left his family to live with a pretty young seamstress named Emilie Trampusch, with whom he had seven more children. He was only 45 when, after playing at the Sperl on 19 September 1849 while already infected with the scarlet fever he had caught from one of his children, he died on 25 September.

Like Lanner, Strauss had his musical roots in a century-old tradition of Viennese light music (Schmelzer, Fux, etc), culminating in the orchestral dances of Haydn, Mozart and Beethoven and in Schubert's piano waltzes and ländler. The tradition became marked by a local Austrian colour as it absorbed elements from the folksongs and dances of the south German Alps. This folk flavour, still strongly felt in the early waltzes and ländler of Strauss and Lanner, gradually assumed a more sophisticated character, which with Strauss is particularly evident in the refinement and piquancy of his rhythmic idiom, with its frequent cross-rhythms, syncopations, dotted figures and an ingenious use of pauses and rests. These features give his style its cachet and were responsible for its galvanizing effect on dancers and listeners alike.

As with Lanner and his eldest son Johann, Strauss's melodic style was largely determined by the peculiarities of the violin, which was to the 19th-century Viennese dance conductor what the cimbalom is to the gypsy musician. Yet, in contrast with his rhythmic ingenuity, Strauss was less than inspired in his melodic and harmonic invention. His melodies are often shortwinded and patched together from neat little figures, thus lacking the sweep of Lanner's and his son's, and in his harmony he was sometimes conventional, stereotyped, dry to the point of being academic, and without Lanner's feeling for romantic modulations. Strauss's fame rested mainly on two factors: the verve, fire and finesse of his conducting and the novelty of the Viennese waltz in the early 19th century. His importance is chiefly historical, and although some of his best waltzes are still played, he is more often remembered as the composer of the racy Radetzky-Marsch op.228, which at once became the symbol of the military might of the old Habsburg monarchy, as 19 years later his son's *An der schönen, blauen Donau* became that of imperial Vienna.

WORKS

Unless otherwise stated, all works were published in Vienna for pf 2 hands; most also appeared simultaneously in arrangements for pf 4 hands and for vn and pf; for unpublished works, other arrangements and complete MS and publication details, see Schönherr and Reinöhl (1954) and Weinmann (1956); principal MS sources are *A-Wgm*, *Wn*, *Ws* and *Wweinmann*.

Editions: *J. Strauss (i)*: Werke, ed. J. Strauss (ii) (Leipzig, 1889) [pf 2 hands; S]

J. *Strauss (i): 8 Walzer*, ed. H. Gál, DTÖ, lxviii, Jg.xxxv/2 (1928) [orch; G]

WALTZES AND COTILLONS

Täuberln-Walzer, op.1, 1826 (1829), S i, G; Döblinger Reunion-Walzer, op.2 (1827), S i; Wiener Carneval-Walzer, op.3 (1828), S i, G; Kettenbrücken-Walzer [i], op.4 (1828), S i; Gesellschafts-Walzer, op.5 (1827), S i; Wiener Launen-Walzer, op.6 (1828), S i; Walzer à la Paganini, op.11 (1828), S i; Krapfen-Waldel-Walzer, op.12 (1828), S i; Die beliebten Trompetenwalzer, op.13 (1829), S i; Champagner-Walzer, op.14 (1828), S i

Die so sehr beliebten Erinnerungs-Ländler, op.15 (1829), S i; Fort nacheinander, op.16 (1828), S i; Lustlager-Walzer, op.18 (1829), S i; Kettenbrücken-Walzer, ii, op.19 (1829), S i; Es ist nur ein Wien, op.22 (1829), S i; Josefstädter Tänze, op.23 (1829), S i; Hietzinger Reunion-Walzer oder Weissgärber-Kirchweih-Tänze, op.24 (1829), S i; Frohsinn im Gebirge, op.26 (1829), S i; Sperls Fest-Walzer, op.30 (1829), S i; Des Verfassers beste Laune: Charmant-Walzer, op.31 (1829), S i; Schwarzsche Ball-Tänze, cotillons on themes from Auber's La muette de Portici, op.32 (1830), S i; Benefice-Walzer, op.33 (1830), S i

Gute Meinung für die Tanzlust, op.34 (1830), S i; Souvenir de Baden: Helenen-Walzer, op.38 (1830), S i; Tivoli-Rutsch-Walzer, op.39 (1830), S i; Wiener Damen-Toilette-Walzer, op.40 (1830), S i; Fra Diavolo, cotillons, op.41 (1830), S i; Tivoli Freudenfest-Tänze, op.45 (1831), S i; Vive la danse, op.47 (1831), S i; Heiter auch in ernster Zeit, op.48 (1831), S i; Das Leben ein Tanz oder Der Tanz ein Leben, op.49 (1831), S i; Cotillons, on themes from Bellini's La straniera, op.50 (1832), S i; Hofball-Tänze, op.51 (1832), S i; Bajaderen-Walzer, op.53 (1832), S i; Alexandra-Walzer, op.56 (1832), S i; Zampa-Walzer, op.57 (1832), S i; Mein schönster Tag in Baden, op.58 (1832), S i

Die vier Temperamente, op.59 (1832), S ii; Carnevals-Spende, op.60 (1833), S ii; Tausendsapperment-Walzer, op.61 (1833), S ii; Der Frohsinn, mein Ziel, op.63 (1833), S ii; Robert-Tänze, op.64 (1833), S ii; Mittel gegen den Schlaf, op.65 (1833), S ii; Emlék Pestre (Erinnerungen an Pesth), op.66 (1834), S ii; Gabrielen-Walzer, op.68 (1834), S ii; Pfennig-Walzer, op.70 (1834), S ii; Elisabethen-Walzer, op.71 (1834), S ii, G; Cotillons, on favourite themes from Hérold's Le pré aux clercs, op.72 (1834), S ii; Iris-Walzer, op.75 (1834), S ii; Rosa-Walzer, op.76 (1835), S ii

Erinnerung an Berlin, op.78 (1835), S ii; Gedankenstriche, op.79 (1835), S ii; Huldigungs-Walzer, op.80 (1835), S ii; Grazien-Tänze, op.81 (1835), S ii; Philomelen-Walzer, op.82 (1835), S ii, G; Merkurs-Flügel, op.83 (1836), S ii; Heimat-Klänge, op.84 (1836), S ii; Erinnerung an Deutschland, op.87 (1836), S ii; Die Nachtwandler, op.88 (1836), S ii; Eisenbahn-Lust-Walzer, op.89 (1836), S ii; Krönungs-Walzer, op.91 (1837), S ii; Cotillons, on themes from Meyerbeer's Les Huguenots, op.92 (1837), S ii; Künstler-Ball-Tänze, op.94 (1837), S ii; Brüssler Spitzen, op.95 (1837), S ii

Ball-Racketen, op.96 (1837), S ii; Pilger am Rhein, op.98 (1837), S iii; Bankett-Tänze, op.99 (1837), S iii; Paris, op.101 (1838), S iii;

Hommage à la reine de la Grande Bretagne, orig. op.102 (London, 1838), as Huldigung der Königin Victoria von Grossbritannien, op.103 (1838), S iii; Freuden-Grüsse, op.105 (1839), S iii; Exotische Pflanzen, op.109 (1839), S iii; Taglioni-Walzer, op.110 (1839), S iii; Londoner-saison-Walzer, op.112 (1839), S iii; Die Berggeister, op.113 (1839), S iii; Rosen-Blätter, op.115 (1840), S iii; Wiener-Gemüts-Walzer, op.116 (1840), S iii; Myrten, op.118 (1840), S iii, G; Tanz-Rezepte, op.119 (1840), S iii

Cäcilien-Walzer mit dem beliebten Tremolo, op.120 (1840), S iii; Palm-Zweige, op.122 (1840), S iii; Amors-Pfeile, op.123 (1841), S iii; Elektrische Funken, op.125 (1841), S iii; Deutsche Lust oder Donaulieder ohne Text, op.127 (1841), S iii; Apollo-Walzer, op.128 (1841), S iii; Adelaiden-Walzer, op.129 (1841), S iii; Die Wettrenner, op.131 (1842), S iii; Die Debütanten, op.132 (1842), S iii; Egerien-Tänze, op.134 (1842), S iii; Die Tanzmeister, op.135 (1842), S iii; Stadt- und Landleben, op.136 (1842), S iii

Die Fantasten, op.139 (1842), S iii; Musik-Verein-Tänze, op.140 (1842), S iii; Minnesänger, op.141 (1843), S iv; Latonen-Walzer, op.143 (1843), S iv; Minos-Klänge, op.145 (1843), S iv; Die Lustwandler, op.146 (1843), S iv; Walhalla-Toaste, op.147 (1843), S iv; Die Dämonen, op.149 (1843), S iv; Künstler-Ball-Tänze, op.150 (1843), S iv; Tanz-Capricen, op.152 (1844), S iv; Loreley-Rhein-Klänge, op.154 (1844), S iv; Brüder Lustig, op.155 (1844), S iv; Asträa-Tänze, op.156 (1844), S iv; Nur Leben, op.159 (1844), S iv

Waldfräuleins Hochzeits-Tänze, op.160 (1844), S iv; Frohsinns-Salven, op.163 (1844), S iv; Aurora-Festklänge, op.164 (1844), S iv; Rosen ohne Dornen, op.166 (1844), S iv; Wiener Früchteln, op.167 (1845), S iv; Willkommen-Rufe, op.168 (1845), S iv; Maskenlieder, op.170 (1845), S iv, G; Eunomien-Tänze, op.171 (1845), S iv; Odeon-Tänze, op.172 (1845), S iv; Faschings-Possen, op.175 (1845), S iv; Geheimnisse aus der Wiener Tanzwelt, op.176 (1845), S iv; Österreichische Jubelklänge, op.179 (1845), S iv; Sommernachts-Träume, op.180 (1845), S iv

Heitere Lebensbilder, op.181 (1846), S iv; Die Landjunker, op.182 (1846), S v; Concordia-Tänze, op.184 (1846), S v; Sofien-Tänze, op.185 (1846), S v; Moldau-Klänge, op.186 (1846), S v; Die Vortänzer, op.189 (1846), S v; Epionen-Tänze, op.190 (1846), S v; Festlieder, op.193 (1846), S v; Die Unbedeutenden, op.195 (1846), S v; Bouquets, op.197 (1847), S v; Ländlich, sittlich, op.198 (1847), S v; Themis-Klänge, op.201 (1847), S v; Herz-Töne, op.203 (1847), S v; Helenen-Walzer, op.204 (1847), S v; Schwedische Lieder, op.207 (1847), S v; Die Schwalben, op.208 (1847), S v

Marien-Walzer, op.212 (1847), S v; Feldbleameln, op.213 (1848), S v; Die Adepten, op.216 (1848), S v, G; Tanz-Signale, op.218 (1848), S v; Aeaciden, op.222 (1848), S v; Amphion-Klänge: Techniker-Ball-Tänze, op.224 (1848), S v; Äther-Träume: Mediziner-Ball-Tänze, op.225 (1848), S v; Sorgenbrecher, op.230 (1848), S v, G; Landesfarben, op.232 (1849), S v; Des Wanderers Lebewohl, op.237 (1849), S v; Die Friedensboten, op.241 (1849), S v; Soldaten-Lieder, op.242 (1850), S v; Deutsche Jubellaute, op.247 (1850), S v

Without op. no.: Walzer mit Coda in F (1818); Walzer für den Carneval 1820 (1819–20); 7 Walzer in F (1825)

GALOPS

(all in S vi)

Alpenkönig-Galopp, op.7 (1828); Champagner-Galopp, op.8 (1828); Seufzer-Galopp, op.9 (1828); Gesellschafts-Galopp, op.17 (1827); Chineser-Galopp, op.20 (1828); Carolinen-Galopp, op.21[a] (1827); Kettenbrücke-Galopp, op.21[b] (1828); Erinnerungs-Galopp [op.27] (1829); Hirten-Galopp [op.28] (1829); Wettrennen-Galopp, op.29[a] (1829); Wilhelm Tell-Galopp, op.29[b] (1829); Einzugs-Galopp, op.35 (1830); Ungarischer Galopp [no.1], op.36 (1831)

2ter ungarischer Galopp (1831); 3ter ungarischer Galopp (1831); Sperl-Galopp, op.42 (1831); Bajaderen-Galopp, op.52 (1832); Zampa-Galopp, op.62[a] (1832); Montecchi-Galopp, op.62[b] (1833); Fortuna-Galopp, op.69 (1834); Venetianer-Galopp, op.74 (1834); Reise-Galopp, op.85 (1836); Ballnacht-Galopp, op.86 (1836); Jugendfeuer, op.90 (1836); Galopp, on themes from Meyerbeer's Les Huguenots, op.93 (1837); Cachucha-Galopp, op.97 (1837); Der Carneval in Paris, op.100 (1838); Boulogner-Galopp, after Auber's L'ambassadrice, op.104 (1839)

Versailler-Galopp, op.107 (1839); Gitana-Galopp, op.108 (1839); Indianer-Galopp, op.111 (1839); Furioso-Galopp, on themes by Liszt, op.114 (1840); Gibellinen-Galopp, op.117 (1840)

QUADRILLES

(all in S vii)

Contredanses, op.44 (1831); Kontratänze, op.54 (1832); Wiener Carnevals-Quadrille, op.124 (1841); Jubel-Quadrille, op.130 (1841); Mode-Quadrille, op.138 (1842); Haute-volée-Quadrille, op.142 (1843); Saison-Quadrille, op.148 (1843); Kaiser Ferdinand-Quadrille, op.151 (1843); Kaiserin Anna-Quadrille, op.153 (1844); Volksgarten-Quadrille, op.157 (1844); Redoute-Quadrille, op.158 (1844); Orpheus-Quadrille, op.162 (1844); Fest-Quadrille, op.165 (1845); Quadrille, on favourite themes from Balfe's Les 4 fils Aymon, op.169 (1845); Musen-Quadrille, op.174 (1845); Flora-Quadrille, op.177 (1845)

Stradella-Quadrille, op.178 (1845); Amoretten-Quadrille, op.183 (1846); Concert-Souvenir-Quadrille, op.187 (1846); Zigeunerin-Quadrille, op.191 (1846); Eldorado-Quadrille, op.194 (1846); Charivari-Quadrille, op.196 (1846); Souvenir de Carneval 1847, op.200 (1847); Triumph-Quadrille, op.205 (1847); Najaden-Quadrille, op.206 (1847); Beliebte Quadrille, on themes from Auber's La part du diable, op.211 (1847); Nádor Kör (Palatinal-Tanz), op.214 (1847); Martha-Quadrille, op.215 (1847); Schäfer-Quadrille, op.217 (1848)

Quadrille im militärischen Style, op.229 (1848); Huldigungs-Quadrille, op.233 (1849); Louisen-Quadrille, op.234 (1849); Almack's Quadrille (London, 1849), as op.243 (1850); Quadrille ohne Titel, op.248 (1850)

MARCHES
(all in S vi)

[6] Wiener Bürger-Märsche: Original-Parade-Marsch (1832), Marsch, after Zampa (1832), Marsch, after Robert le diable, Original-Parade-Marsch, op.73 (1834), Original-Parade-Marsch, op.102 (1838). Esmeralda-Marsch, op.192 (1846); Parade-Marsch, op.144 (1843); Österreichischer Fest-Marsch, op.188 (1846); Österreichischer Defilier-Marsch, op. 209 (1847); Österreichischer National-Garde-Marsch, op.221 (1848); Marsch der Studenten-Legion, op.223 (1848)

Freiheits-Marsch, op.226 (1848); Marsch des einigen Deutschlands, op.227 (1848); Radetzky-Marsch, op.228 (1848); Brünner National-Garde-Marsch, op.231 (1848); 2 Märsche der königlichen spanischen Nobel-Garde: Triumph-Marsch, Manövrir-Marsch, op.240 (1849); Jellačić-Marsch, op.244 (1850); Wiener Jubel-Marsch, op.245 (1850); March of the Royal Horse Guards (London, 1849), slightly altered as Wiener Stadt-Garde-Marsch, op.246 (1850)

Letzter Gedanke von Johann Strauss (1849) [inc. sketch for Radetzky-Bankett-Marsch]

OTHER WORKS
(unless otherwise stated, all in S vi)

Polkas: Beliebte Sperl-Polka, op.133 (1842); Beliebte Annen-Polka, op.137 (1842); Salon-Polka, op.161 (1844); Marianka-Polka, op.173 (1845); Neujahrs-Polka, op.199 (1846); Eisele- und Beisele-Sprünge, op.202 (1847); Beliebte Kathinka-Polka, op.210 (1847); Fortuna-Polka, op.219 (1848); Wiener Kreuzer-Polka, op.220 (1848); Piefke-und Pufke-Polka, op.235 (1849); Damen-Souvenir-Polka, op.236 (1849); Alice Polka (London, 1849); as op.238 (1849); Frederika Polka (London, 1849), as op.239 (1849); Exeter-Polka, op.249 (1851)

Potpourris: Der unzusammenhängende Zusammenhang, op.25 (1829); Wiener Tagsbelustigung, op.37 (1830); Musikalisches Ragout, op.46 (1831); Ein Strauss von Strauss: aus Tonblumen, op.55 (1832); 1te Walzer-Girlande, op.67 (1834), S ii; 2te Walzer-Girlande, op.77 (1835), S iii; Le télégraphe musicale, op.103 (London, 1839), as Musikalischer Telegraph, op.106 (1839); 3te Walzer-Girlande, op.121 (1840), S ii; Fliegende Blätter, op.250 (1851)

Fantasies: Erinnerung an Ernst oder Der Carneval in Venedig, op.126 (1841); Melodische Tändeleien, op.251 (1851)

Other works: Tempête, Polstertanz und Galoppade, op.10 (1828), S vii; Favorit-Boleros, from Auber's La muette de Portici, in Wiener Tivoli-Musik, i (1830) [collection also incl. parts of opp.32, 34 and 35 and Grosser Fest-Marsch, attrib. Strauss]; Der Raub der Sabinerinnen: charakteristisches Tongemälde, op.43 (1831), S i

(2) Johann (Baptist) Strauss (ii) (*b* Vienna, 25 Oct 1825; *d* Vienna, 3 June 1899). Composer, conductor and violinist, eldest son of (1) Johann Strauss (i) and the most eminent member of the family. He was only six when he wrote his first 36 bars of waltz music, later published as *Erster Gedanke*. Although a musical atmosphere surrounded the home at Rofranogasse 76 (from 1862, Lerchenfelderstrasse 15), the elder Strauss was against his son's taking up a musical career, and after attending the Schottengymnasium for four years and the commercial department of the Polytechnikum for one, the young Johann was intended for banking. While still a boy and with his mother's encouragement, he had taken violin lessons in secret from Franz Amon, the leader of his father's band, and after the elder Strauss left his family in 1842, Johann underwent proper musical training. He continued on the violin with Anton Kohlmann, co-répétiteur for ballet in the opera (at that time this post was still held by a violinist) and until 1844 studied theory with Joseph Drechsler, choirmaster of St Stephen's Cathedral as well as Kapellmeister and

house composer at the Leopoldstadt Theatre, the home of Viennese comic opera; a gradual, *Tu qui regis totum orbem*, for chorus, winds, brass and timpani dates from this time. Although he was still a minor, the young Strauss was granted a *Musiklicenz* (official permit to give public concerts) and, in September 1844, after signing an agreement with 24 musicians, he made his début at Dommayer's Casino at Hietzing on 15 October with a programme that included six of his own compositions and his father's new waltzes, *Loreley-Rhein-Klänge* op.154. The *soirée dansante* was by all accounts so successful (the waltzes *Sinngedichte* op.1 were encored at least 19 times) that it established him as his father's most serious rival, and after (1) Johann's death in 1849 the two Strauss orchestras were merged into one, under his direction.

After overcoming certain difficulties (some of his topically named compositions caused Strauss to be regarded as an 1848 revolutionary), he was appointed in 1863 to the post of *k.k. Hofballmusikdirektor*, and from that time his activity each year reached fever-point during Fasching (Carnival), the Viennese ball season. The international reputation of his father meant that trips abroad were also expected of the younger Strauss; between 1856 and 1886 he toured most of Europe with his orchestra, including Russia, where, at Pavlovsk in 1865, he conducted the first performance of a set of Tchaikovsky's *Characteristic Dances*. He was acclaimed everywhere as Austria's most successful ambassador and the 'king of the waltz'. In 1867 he paid his only visit to England, conducting interludes daily, usually only two sets of waltzes and a polka, in enormous 'music for all' concerts, arranged and directed by other illustrious musicians, including the bass player Giovanni Bottesini. Despite the many collaborators, it was Strauss who attracted public attention. *The Times* wrote on 16 August:

Each of the three pieces . . . was received with genuine enthusiasm. This gentleman who strongly resembles his father in manner, seems also to possess a large share of those qualities which led to his father's renown. He conducts the orchestra, like his father, fiddle in hand, and joins in the passages of most importance.

Because of a chronic ailment, Strauss requested and was granted a release from his position as *k.k. Hofballmusikdirektor* in January 1871. In 1872 he accepted an invitation from the American musician and manager Patrick S. Gilmore to go to Boston for an 'International Peace Jubilee' confirming the idea of world peace after the end of the Franco-Prussian War. 20,000 singers from many countries, 10,000 orchestral musicians and other artists from Europe were assembled for this event in the grand style. Again he conducted only a couple of waltz sets with added chorus (*An der schönen, blauen Donau* op.314 and *Wein, Weib und Gesang* op.333) and one polka, though in extraordinary circumstances, with about 100 sub-conductors, and he must have been happy simply to have survived this nightmare, for which he was compensated with enormous jubilation, worldwide popularity and three concerts in the New York Academy of Music. The customary 'new' compositions eagerly awaited by press and public on this festive occasion were merely pastiches on melodies already composed and published in Vienna. However, from Vienna, in July 1876 Strauss dedicated the newly composed *Centennial Waltzes* to the citizens of the USA on the 100th anniversary of the Declaration of Independence. Far more significant music resulted from the Russian

2. Johann Strauss conducting his orchestra at a Viennese ball: lithograph after a watercolour (c1853) by Theo Zasche

visits (including the waltzes opp.184, 195, 210 and 227; the polkas opp.196, 211, 258, 260, 269, 336 and the *Pizzicato-Polka*, composed with (3) Josef Strauss; the polka mazurkas opp.197 and 425; and the marches opp.183, 212, 289, 335 and 426), but the most famous waltz masterpieces, which originated from Viennese soil and were composed for a world public, date from the 1860s and early 1870s (opp.234, 279, 307, 314, 316, 325, 333, 340 and 354).

The quickly growing popularity of the Offenbach *opéras bouffes* in Vienna, stimulated by guest performances by the original members of the Bouffes Parisiens, kept Viennese theatre directors, librettists and, especially, Franz von Suppé busy, producing Viennese operettas. Suppé's stage works were immediate hits (*Das Pensionat*, 1860, *Zehn Mädchen und kein Mann*, 1862, *Flotte Bursche*, 1863), and the directing committee of the Theater an der Wien persuaded Strauss as well to

3. Title-page of Strauss's 'Taglioni-Walzer' op.110 (Vienna: Haslinger, 1839)

compose for the stage. Although he produced with great facility a vast number of dance-tunes which have survived a century, he found it cumbersome and restricting to compose to prescribed texts. However he was able to piece together a finale whose exact words he did not yet know, and a host of eager librettists were turning out texts and verses for his use, which were unworthy of Strauss's genius for melodies. If *Die Fledermaus* and *Der Zigeunerbaron* have deservedly claimed a central place in the standard operetta repertory, much of the credit is due to the exceptional talents of the *Fledermaus* librettist, Richard Genée (also a composer, Kapellmeister and arranger), to the *Zigeunerbaron* librettist Ignaz Schnitzer and to the producer and designer Franz Jauner.

Meanwhile Strauss's brothers (3) Josef and (4) Eduard had successfully entered on the dance music scene, not only as first violinists but also as composers, and the three representatives of the waltz family now held complete control of music for the balls, concerts and private festivities of Vienna's aristocratic and non-aristocratic houses and of the numerous social societies in the city and its suburbs. After Josef's death, Johann left the family orchestra completely to the direction of Eduard and accepted invitations to conduct in Budapest, Paris, London and Italy. And almost annually, in countless German towns, as the highlight of the programme and assuming the famous Strauss pose with fiddle in hand, he conducted performances of his best-known compositions (especially *An der schönen, blauen Donau*) and invariably found himself acclaimed by swarms of admirers.

Strauss was married three times, first to the singer Henriette (Jetty) Treffz, after her death to the young actress Angelika Dittrich, whom he divorced after nine years, and finally to Adele Strauss, the young widow of the banker Anton Strauss (no relation to Johann's family). The separation from Angelika brought with it considerable difficulties, for Strauss had to become a Protestant, and, after having as recently as October 1884 sworn the Viennese citizens' oath of loyalty, was also obliged to give up his Austrian citizenship in 1885 and take on that of the Duchy of Saxe-Coburg-Gotha (1886), which he retained until his death.

Strauss lived in and represented what was on the surface one of the most brilliant and prosperous periods of the Habsburg monarchy. Subversive tongues used to say that the Emperor Franz Joseph I reigned only until Strauss's death. The charm, elegance, vivacity and sophistication of his music mirrored the glitter and *joie de vivre* of 19th-century imperial Vienna. It is music that no longer breathes the air of country inns, common city taverns and beer-gardens, as his father's and Lanner's still did to a certain extent, but reflects a society in which Vienna's hedonistic spirit found its most articulate expression. Technically his chief merit lies in having developed the Viennese waltz to its classic perfection. His early waltzes differed little from his father's, having the same rhythmic verve and piquancy, and the same shortwinded tunes, but his mature sets (from *Accellerationen* op.234, 1860) show an individual fusion of his father's rhythmic style with Lanner's lyrical vein. His own particular genius is evident in an inspired melodic invention, a gift of writing wide, sweeping melodies and a trained ear for harmonic and orchestral details. Through his great variety of melodic–rhythmic patterns, or rather the ingenious combination of such patterns, he succeeded in softening and even covering up the tyrannical monotony of the regular 3/4 accompaniments. He once said that his waltzes were merely a feeble attempt to extend the form handed down to him by his father and Lanner. But although in actual form his are almost identical with the later sets of his two predecessors – slow introduction, (usually) five waltzes and coda – the individual sections are considerably enlarged, and at the same time are more organic in themselves and in relation to one another. Many introductions are in the nature of mood pictures (e.g. opp.234, 292, 314, 325, 364, 390, 437, 438, 443 and 444) and some (opp.74, 141, 193, 227 and 390) show quasi-symphonic features such as developmental passages, a more elaborate texture than is found in the actual waltz numbers and picturesque, imaginative orchestration. In addition to having had a more or less systematic training, unlike his predecessors, Strauss was for a time under the influence of Liszt and Wagner, and at his concerts he did yeoman service for Wagner by conducting his music when Vienna was still antagonistic to the composer of *Tannhäuser* and *Lohengrin*. In the 1850s he imitated these two masters' style in his waltzes, to such an extent (*Wellen und Wogen* op.141, *Schneeglöckchen* op.143, *Schallwellen* op.148, etc) that Hanslick accused him of flirting with the 'muses of Weimar' and spoke of waltz requiems because of their heavy orchestral armour. Short though this phase was, it helped him in some ways to develop the form of the Viennese waltz *qua* music, to give it a more individual stamp in a technical sense and thus to make it as suitable for the concert hall as for the ballroom. Through this enrichment of both form and content Strauss contrived to do in his waltzes what the Classical composers did in their dances, to write light music inspired by genius.

He had fewer triumphs as a composer for the stage. In *Die Fledermaus* he transformed Gallic (Offenbachian) wit and parody into Viennese humour and mock-sentimentality, producing a score that in its sparkling brilliance, tunefulness and rhythmic piquancy represents one of the few masterpieces of Viennese operetta. In *Der Zigeunerbaron* he achieved a most successful amalgam of comic opera and operetta, where the mixture of romantic Hungarian and Viennese atmosphere is attractively mirrored in the music, with its gypsy songs and choruses, exotic harmony and orchestration and lighthearted waltzes. With the second finale of *Der Zigeunerbaron* and its music written with an eye to opera, a new type of operetta, diametrically opposed to Offenbach's, was born, one which was successfully taken up by Lehár and others, but which was stigmatized in the next century to the point of defamation by critics including Karl Kraus and Theodor W. Adorno. The rest of Strauss's stage works, which include the more serious *Ritter Pázmán* and a posthumous ballet, *Aschenbrödel* (Cinderella), failed to establish themselves. Strauss was no judge of librettos, and being fundamentally an instrumental composer,

with neither an eye for the dramatic demands of the stage nor a sure feeling for dramatic vocal writing, his usual method was to look chiefly at the mood and the verbal rhythm of a given text, often writing a whole act with only a scenario before him. For this reason it is not entirely surprising (nor without justification in certain instances) that attempts to modernize the librettos, to change them completely or to construct new operettas around popular Strauss melodies, have never ceased. By helping and advising Kapellmeister Adolf Müller when he created the pastiche operetta *Wiener Blut*, Strauss himself initiated a long series of such enterprises and thereby gave his consent to it.

WORKS

Printed works were published in Vienna unless otherwise stated; the dances and marches first appeared for pf 2 hands, and most were also published in versions for vn and pf and for orch; authors' names are given with works which also appeared in vocal or male-chorus arrangements; opus number 445 was used twice and 451 was not used; for complete arrangement, MS and publication details, see Weinmann (1956); principal MS sources are *A-Wgm, Wn, Wph, Wst, Wweinmann,* Wiener Konzerthausgesellschaft.

PF – *polka française*; PM – *polka mazurka*; PS – *polka schnell*

Editions: *J. Strauss (ii): Gesamtausgabe*, ed. F. Racek (Vienna, 1967–) [orch; R]
  J. Strauss (ii): 3 Walzer, ed. H. Gál, DTÖ, cxiii, Jg.xxxii/2 (1925) [orch; G]

STAGE

Unless otherwise stated, all are 3-act operettas, first performed at the Theater an der Wien, Vienna, and published in vocal scores; pieces extracted and published separately follow each operetta.

Indigo und die vierzig Räuber (3, M. Steiner), 10 Feb 1871 (1871); Shawl-Polka, op.343 (1871), Indigo-Quadrille, op.344 (1871), Auf freiem Fusse, PF, op.345 (1871), Tausend und eine Nacht, waltz, op.346 (1871), Aus der Heimat, PM, op.347 (1871), Im Sturmschritt, PS, op.348 (1871), Indigo-Marsch, op.349 (1871), Lustger Rat, PF, op.350 (1871), Die Bajadere, PS, op.351 (1871)

Der Carneval in Rom (3, J. Braun, C. Lindau, after Sardou), 1 March 1873 (1875); Vom Donaustrande, PS, op.356 (1873), Carnevalsbilder, waltz, op.357 (1873), Nimm sie hin, PF, op.358 (1873), Gruss aus Österreich, PM, op.359 (1873), Rotunde-Quadrille, op.360 (1873); full score, ed. H. Swarowsky (London, 1968)

Die Fledermaus (3, C. Haffner, R. Genée, after Meilhac and Halévy), 5 April 1874 (1874); Fledermaus-Polka, op.362 (1873); Fledermaus-Quadrille, op.363 (1874); Tik-Tak, PS, op.365 (1874), An der Moldau, PF, op.366 (1874), Du und Du, waltz, op.367 (1874), Glücklich ist, wer vergisst, PM, op.368 (1874), ballet music (1874)

Cagliostro in Wien (3, F. Zell, Genée), 27 Feb 1875 (1876); Cagliostro-Quadrille, op.369 (1875), Cagliostro-Walzer, op.370 (1875), Hoch Österreich (Genée), march, op.371 (1875), Bitte schön, PF, op.372 (1875), Auf der Jagd, PS, op.373 (1875), Licht und Schatten, PM, op.374 (1875)

Prinz Methusalem (3, C. Treumann, after Delacour and Wildér), Vienna, Carltheater, 3 Jan 1877 (1878); O schöner Mai waltz, op.375 (1877), Methusalem-Quadrille, op.376 (1877), I Tipferl, PF, op.377 (1877), Banditen-Galopp, op.378 (1877), Kriegers Liebchen, PM, op.379 (1878), Ballsträusschen, PS, op.380 (1878)

Blindekuh (3, R. Kneisel), 18 Dec 1878 (Hamburg, 1880); Kennst du mich?, waltz, op.381 (1879), Pariser Polka, PF, op.382 (1879), Nur fort, PS, op.383 (1879), Opern-Maskenball-Quadrille, op.384 (1879), Waldine, PM, op.385 (1879)

Das Spitzentuch der Königin (3, H. Bohrmann-Riegen, Genée, after Cervantess), 1 Oct 1880 (1881); Rosen aus dem Süden, waltz, op.388 (Hamburg, 1880), Gavotte der Königin, op.391 (1881), Spitzentuch-Quadrille, op.392 (1881), Stürmisch in Lieb und Tanz, PS, op.393 (1881), Liebchen, schwing dich, PM, op.394 (1881)

Der lustige Krieg (3, Zell, Genée), 25 Nov 1881 (Hamburg, 1882); Der lustige Krieg, march, op.397 (Hamburg, 1882), Frisch ins Feld, march, op.398 (Hamburg, 1882), Was sich liebt, neckt sich, PF, op.399 (Hamburg, 1882), Kuss-Walzer, op.400 (Hamburg, 1882), Der Klügere gibt nach, PM, op.401 (Hamburg, 1882), Entweder – oder, PS, op.403 (Hamburg, 1882), Violetta, PF, op.404 (Hamburg, 1882), Nord und Süd, PM, op.405 (Hamburg, 1882), Italienische Walzer, op.407 (1882)

Eine Nacht in Venedig (3, Zell, Genée), Berlin, Friedrich Wilhelms-städtisches Theater, 3 Oct 1883 (Hamburg, 1884), R ii/9; Lagunen-Walzer, op.411 (Hamburg, 1883), Papacoda, PF, op.412 (Hamburg, 1884), So ängstlich sind wir nicht, PS, op.413 (Hamburg, 1884), Die Tauben von San Marco, PF, op.414 (Hamburg, 1884), Annina,

PM, op.415 (Hamburg, 1884), Quadrille, op.416 (Hamburg, 1884)
Der Zigeunerbaron (3, I. Schnitzer, after M. Jókai), 24 Oct 1885 (Hamburg, 1886); Brautschau, PF, op.417 (Hamburg, 1886), Schatz-Walzer, op.418 (Hamburg, 1886), Kriegsabenteuer, PS, op.419 (Hamburg, 1886), Die Wahrsagerin, PM, op.420 (Hamburg, 1886), Husaren-Polka, op.421 (Hamburg, 1886), Zigeunerbaron-Quadrille, op.422 (Hamburg, 1886)
Simplicius (3, V. Léon), 17 Dec 1887 (Hamburg, 1889); Donauweibchen, waltz, op.427 (Hamburg, 1888), Reitermarsch, op.428 (Hamburg, 1888), Quadrille aus Simplicius, op.429 (Hamburg, 1888), Soldatenspiel, PF, op.430 (Hamburg, 1888), Lagerlust, PM, op.431 (Hamburg), 1888, Mutig voran, PS, op.432 (Hamburg, 1888)
Ritter Pázmán (comic opera, 3, L. Dóczi, after J. Arany), [op.441], Vienna, Court Opera, 1 Jan 1892 (Berlin, 1892); ballet music (Berlin, 1891–2); Pázmán-Walzer, Pázmán-Polka, Csárdás, Eva-Walzer, Pázmán-Quadrille
Fürstin Ninetta (3, H. Wittmann, J. Bauer), 10 Jan 1893 (Hamburg, 1893); Ninetta-Walzer, op.445 (Hamburg, 1893), Ninetta-Quadrille, op.446 (Hamburg, 1893), Ninetta-Marsch, op.447 (Hamburg, 1893), Diplomaten-Polka, op.448 (Hamburg, 1893), Neue Pizzicato-Polka, op.449 (Hamburg, 1893), Ninetta-Galopp, op.450 (Hamburg, 1893)
Jabuka (Das Apfelfest) (3, M. Kalbeck, G. Davis), 12 Oct 1894 (1894); Ich bin dir gut, waltz, op.455 (1894), Živio, march, op.456 (1894), Das Komitat geht in die Höh, PS, op.457 (1894), Tanze mit dem Besenstiel, PF, op.458 (1894), Sonnenblume, PM, op.459 (1894), Jabuka-Quadrille, op.460 (1894)
Waldmeister (3, Davis), 4 Dec 1895 (Berlin, 1896); Trau, schau, wem, waltz, op.463 (Berlin, 1896), Herrjemineh, PF, op.464 (Berlin, 1896), Liebe und Ehe, PM, op.465 (Berlin, 1896), Klipp-Klapp, galop, op.466 (Berlin, 1896), Es war so wunderschön, waltz, op.467 (Berlin, 1896), Waldmeister-Quadrille, op.468 (Berlin, 1896)
Die Göttin der Vernunft (3, A. M. Willner, B. Buchbinder), 13 March 1897, vocal score (1897): Heut' ist heut', waltz, op.471 (1897); Nur nicht mucken, PF, op.472 (1897); Wo unsre Fahne weht, march, op.473 (1897)
Wiener Blut (3, Léon, L. Stein), Vienna, Carltheater, 25 Oct 1899 (Hamburg, 1899) [arr. and ed. A. Müller jr]
Aschenbrödel (ballet, 3, H. Regel, after A. Kollmann), Berlin, Royal Opera, 3 May 1901 (1900) [adapted and arr. J. Bayer]

WALTZES

Sinngedichte, op.1 (1845); Gunstwerber, op.4 (1845); Serailtänze, op.5 (1845); Die jungen Wiener, op.7 (1845); Faschings-Lieder, op.11 (1846); Jugend-Träume, op.12 (1846); Sträusschen, op.15 (1846); Berglieder, op.18 (1846); Lind-Gesänge, op.21 (1846); Die Österreicher, op.22 (1846); Zeitgeister, op.25 (1846); Die Sanguiniker, op.27 (1846); Die Zillerthaler, op.30 (1847); Irenen-Walzer, op.32 (1847); Die Jovialen, op.34 (1847); Architekten-Ball-Tänze, op.36 (1847); Sängerfahrten, op.41 (1847); Wilde Rosen, op.42 (1847); Ernte-Tänze, op.45 (1847)
Dorfgeschichten, op.47 (1848); Klänge aus der Walachei, op.50 (1848); Freiheits-Lieder, op.52 (1848); Burschen-Lieder, op.55 (1848); Einheits-Klänge, op.62 (1849); Fantasiebilder, op.64 (1849); D'Woaldbuama [Die Waldbuben], op.66 (1849); Äols-Töne, op.68 (1850); Die Gemütlichen, op.70 (1850); Frohsinns-Spenden, op.73 (1850); Lava-Ströme, op.74 (1850); Maxing-Tänze, op.79 (1850); Luisen-Sympathie-Klänge, op.81 (1850); Johannis-Käferln, op.82 (1850); Heimats-Kinder, op.85 (1851); Aurora-Ball-Tänze, op.87 (1851)
Hirten-Spiele, op.89 (1851); Orakel-Sprüche, op.90 (1851); Rhadamantus-Klänge, op.94 (1851); Idyllen, op.95 (1851); Fraunkäferln, op.99 (1851); Mephistos Höllenrufe, op.101 (1852); Windsor-Klänge, op.104 (1852); 5 Paragraphe aus dem Walzer-Codex, op.105 (1852); Die Unzertrennlichen, op.108 (1852); Liebeslieder, op.114 (1852); Lockvögel, op.118 (1852); Volkssänger, op.119 (1853); Phönix-Schwingen, op.125 (1853); Solon-Sprüche, op.128 (1853); Wiener Punsch-Lieder, op.131 (1853); Vermählungs-Toaste, op.136 (1853); Knallkügerln, op.140 (1854)
Wellen und Wogen, op.141 (1854); Schneeglöckchen, op.143 (1854); Novellen, op.146 (1854); Schallwellen, op.148 (1854); Ballg'schichten, op.150 (1854); Myrten-Kränze, op.154 (1854); Nachtfalter, op.157 (1855); Panacea-Klänge, op.161 (1855); Glossen, op.163 (1855); Sirenen, op.164 (1855); Man lebt nur einmal, op.167 (1855); Freuden-Salven, op.171 (1855); Gedanken auf den Alpen, op.172 (1856); Erhöhte Pulse, op.175 (1856); Juristenball-Tänze, op.177 (1856); Abschieds-Rufe, op.179 (1856); Libellen-Walzer, op.180 (1856); Grossfürstin Alexandra, op.181 (1857)
Krönungslieder, op.184 (1857); Paroxysmen, op.189 (1857); Kontroversen, op.191 (1857); Wien, mein Sinn, op.192 (1857); Phänomene, op.193 (1857); Telegraphische Depeschen, op.195 (1857); Souvenir de Nizza, op.200 (1858); Vibrationen, op.204 (1858); Die Extravaganten, op.205 (1858); Cycloiden, op.207 (1858); Jux-Brüder, op.208 (1858); Spiralen, op.209 (1858);

Abschied von St Petersburg, op.210 (1859); Gedankenflug, op.215 (1859); Hell und voll, op.216 (1859); Irrlichter, op.218 (1859) [? by Josef Strauss]: 'Deutsche', op.220 (1859); Promotionen, op.221 (1859); Schwungräder, op.223 (1859)
Reiseabenteuer, op.227 (1860); Lebenswecker, op.232 (1860); Sentenzen, op.233 (1860); Accellerationen, op.234 (1860); Immer heiterer, op.235 (1860); Thermen, op.245 (1861); Grillenbanner, op.247 (1861); Wahlstimmen, op.250 (1861); Klangfiguren, op.251 (1861); Dividenden-Walzer, op.252 (1861); Schwärmereien, op.253 (1861); Die ersten Kuren, op.261 (1862); Colonnen-Walzer, op.262 (1862); Patronessen, op.264 (1862); Motoren, op.265 (1862); Konkurrenzen, op.267 (1862); Wiener Chronik, op.268 (1862); Carnevals-Botschafter, op.270 (1863); Leitartikel, op.273 (1863)
Morgenblätter, op.279 (1864), G; Studentenlust, op.285 (1864); Aus den Bergen, op.292 (1865), R i/18; Feuilleton, op.293 (1865), R i/18; Bürgersinn, op.295 (1865), R i/18; Hofball-Tänze, op.298 (1866), R i/18; Flugschriften, op.300 (1866), R i/18; Bürgerweisen, op.306 (1866), R i/19; Wiener Bonbons, op.307 (1866), R i/19; Feenmärchen, op.312 (1867), R i/19; An der schönen, blauen Donau (J. Weyl, 1867; F. von Gernerth, 1890), op.314 (1867), G, R i/19; Künstlerleben, op.316 (1867), R i/19; Telegramme, op.318 (1867), R i/20; Die Publizisten, op.321 (1868), R i/20; Geschichten aus dem Wienerwald, op.325 (1868), R i/20
Festival Waltz (London, 1867), as Erinnerung an Covent-Garden, op.329 (1868), R i/20; Illustrationen, op.331 (1869); Wein, Weib und Gesang (Weyl), op.333 (1869); Königslieder, op.334 (1870); Freut euch des Lebens, op.340 (1870); Neu-Wien (Weyl), op.342 (1870), G; Wiener Blut, op.354 (1873); Bei uns z'Haus (A. Langer), op.361 (1874); Wo die Zitronen blühn, op.364 (1874); Ins Zentrum, op.387 (1880); Nordseebilder, op.390 (1880); Myrtenblüten (A. Seuffert), op.395 (1882); Italienischer Walzer, on themes from Der lustige Krieg, op.407 (Hamburg, 1882)
Frühlingsstimmen (Genée), op.410 (Hamburg, 1883); Wiener Frauen, op.423 (Hamburg, 1887); Adelen-Walzer, op.424 (Hamburg, 1886); Kaiser-Jubiläum, op.434 (Hamburg, 1889); Sinnen und Minnen, op.435 (Hamburg, 1889); Kaiser-Walzer, op.437 (Berlin, 1889); Rathausball-Tänze, op.438 (Berlin, 1890); Gross-Wien (Gernerth), op.440 (Berlin, 1891); Seid umschlungen, Millionen, op.443 (Berlin, 1892); Märchen aus dem Orient, op.444 (Berlin, 1892); Hochzeitsreigen, op.453 (1894); Gartenlaube-Walzer, op.461 (Berlin, 1895); Klug Gretelein (A. M. Willner), op.462 (1895); An der Elbe, op.477 (Dresden, 1897)
Without op.no.: Erster Gedanke, 1831 (1881); Autograph Waltzes (Boston, 1872); Engagement Waltzes (Boston, 1872); Jubilee Waltz (Springfield, Mass., 1872); Manhattan Waltzes (?New York, 1872); Walzer-Bouquet no.1 (1873); Centennial Waltzes (Boston, 1876); The Herald Waltz, New York Herald (14 Oct 1894); Abschieds-Walzer, ed. (Leipzig, 1900); Ischler Walzer, ed. (Leipzig, 1900); Odeon-Walzer, ed. (1907)
Unpubd: Wer bei den Flöten; Blumenflur

POLKAS

Herzenslust, op.3 (1845); Amazonen-Polka, op.9 (1845); Czechen-Polka, op.13 (1846); Jux-Polka, op.17 (1846); Fidelen-Polka, op.26 (1846); Hopser-Polka, op.28 (1847); Bachus-Polka, op.38 (1847); Explosions-Polka, op.43 (1847); Ligourianer Seufzer, Scherz-Polka, op.57 (1849); Geisselhiebe, op.60 (1849); Scherz-Polka, op.72 (1850); Heiligenstädter Rendezvous-Polka, op.78 (1850); Heski-Holki-Polka, op.80 (1850); Warschauer Polka, op.84 (1851); Herrmann-Polka, op.91 (1851); Vöslauer Polka, op.100 (1851); Albion-Polka, op.102 (1851); Harmonie-Polka, op.106 (1852)
Elektro-magnetische Polka, op.110 (1852); Blumenfest-Polka, op.111 (1852); Annen-Polka, op.117 (1852); Zehner-Polka, op.121 (1853); Satanella-Polka, op.124 (1853); Freudengruss-Polka, op.127 (1853); Äskulap-Polka, op.130 (1853); Veilchen-Polka, op.132 (1853); Tanzi-Bäri-Polka, op.134 (1853); Neuhauser-Polka, op.137 (1853); Pepita-Polka, op.138 (1853); Wiedersehen-Polka, op.142 (1854); Bürgerball-Polka, op.145 (1854); Musen-Polka, op.147 (1854); Elisen-Polka, PF, op.151 (1854); Haute-volée-Polka, op.155 (1854); Schnellpost-Polka, op.159 (1855); Ella-Polka, op.160 (1855)
Souvenir-Polka, op.162 (1855); Aurora-Polka, op.165 (1855); Leopoldstädter Polka, op.168 (1855); Marie Taglioni-Polka, op.173 (1856); Armenball-Polka, op.176 (1856); Sans-souci-Polka, op.178 (1856); L'inconnue, PF, op.182 (1857); Demi-fortune, PF, op.186 (1857); Herzel-Polka, op.188 (1857); Etwas Kleines, PF, op.190 (1857); Olga-Polka, op.196 (1857); Alexandrinen-Polka, PF, op.198 (1858); L'enfantillage, PF, op.202 (1858); Helenen-Polka, op.203 (1858); Champagner-Polka, op.211 (1858)
Bonbon-Polka, PF, op.213 (1859); Tritsch-Tratsch-Polka, op.214 (1858); La favorite, PF, op.217 (1859); Auroraball-Polka, PF, op.219 (1859); Nachtigall-Polka, op.222 (1859); Gruss an Wien, PF, op.225 (1860); Niko-Polka, op.228 (1860); Jäger-Polka, PF, op.229 (1860); Kammerball-Polka, op.230 (1860); Drollerie-Polka, op.231 (1860); Taubenpost, PF, op.237 (1860); Die Pariserin, PF, op.238 (1861); Maskenzug-Polka, PF, op.240 (1861); Bijoux-Polka, PF, op.242 (1861)

Diabolin-Polka, op.244 (1861); Rokonhangok (Sympathieklänge), op.246 (1861); Camilien-Polka, op.248 (1861); Hesperus-Polka, op.249 (1861); Sekunden-Polka, PF, op.258 (1862); Furioso-Polka quasi Galopp, op.260 (1862); Studenten-Polka, op.263 (1862); Luzifer-Polka, op.266 (1862); Demolirer-Polka, op.269 (1863); Bluette-Polka, PF, op.271 (1862); Patrioten-Polka, op.274 (1863); Bauern-Polka, PF, op.276 (1864); Neues Leben, PF, op.278 (1864); Juristenball-Polka, PS, op.280 (1864); Vergnügungszug, PS, op.281 (1864)

Gut bürgerlich, PF, op.282 (1864); Patronessen, PF, op.286 (1864); Newa-Polka, PF, op.288 (1865); 's gibt nur a Kaiserstadt, 's gibt nur ein Wien, PS, op.291 (1865); Prozess-Polka, PS, op.294 (1865), R i/18; Episode, PF, op.296 (1865), R i/18; Electrophor-Polka, PS, op.297 (1865), R i/18; Kreuzfidel, PF, op.301 (1866), R i/18; Die Zeitlose, PF, op.302 (1866), R i/18; Kinderspiele, PF, op.304 (1866), R i/19

Damenspende, PF, op.305 (1866), R i/19; Par force, PS, op.308 (1866), R i/19; Sylphen-Polka, PF, op.309 (1866), R i/19; Express-Polka, PS, op.311 (1867), R i/19; Wildfeuer, PF, op.313 (1867), R i/19; Postillon d'amour, PF, op.317 (1867), R i/20; Leichtes Blut, PS, op.319 (1867), R i/20; Figaro-Polka, PF, op.320 (1868), R i/20; Unter Donner und Blitz, PS, op.324 (1868), R i/20; Freikugeln, PS, op.326 (1869), R i/20; Sängerslust (Weyl), PF, op.328 (1869), R i/20

Eljen a Magyar, PS, op.332 (1869); Im Krapfenwaldl, PF, op.336 (1870); Von der Börse, PF, op.337 (1870); Louischen-Polka, PF, op.339 (1871); Frisch heran, PS, op.386 (1880); Burschen-Wanderung (Seuffert), PF, op.389 (1881); Rasch in der Tat, PS, op.409 (Hamburg, 1883); Auf zum Tanze, PS, op.436 (Hamburg, 1889); Durchs Telephon, op.439 (Berlin, 1890); Herzenskönigin, PF, op.445 (Berlin, 1893)

Polka mazurkas: La viennoise, op.144 (1854); Nachtveilchen, op.170 (1855); Le papillon, op.174 (1856); Une bagatelle, op.187 (1857); Spleen, op.197 (1857); Concordia, op.206 (1858); Der Kobold, op.226 (1860); Polka mazurka champêtre, op.239 (1861); Fantasieblümchen, op.241 (1861); Invitation à la Polka Mazur, op.277 (1864); Tändelei, op.310 (1867), R i/19; Lob der Frauen, op.315 (1867), R i/19; Stadt und Land, op.322 (1868), R i/20; Ein Herz, ein Sinn, op.323 (1868), R i/20; Fata Morgana, op.330 (1869); An der Wolga, op.425 (Hamburg, 1886); Unparteiische Kritiken, op.442 (Berlin, 1892)

QUADRILLES

Debut-Quadrille, op.2 (1845); Cytheren-Quadrille, op.6 (1845); Quadrille, on themes from Balfe's Les puits d'amour, op.10 (1845); Serben-Quadrille, op.14 (1846); Elfen-Quadrille, op.16 (1846); Dämonen-Quadrille, op.19 (1846); Zigeunerin-Quadrille, on themes from Balfe's The Bohemian Girl, op.24 (1846); Odeon-Quadrille, op.29 (1847); Quadrille, on themes from Balfe's The Siege of Rochelle, op.31 (1847); Alexander-Quadrille, op.33 (1847); Industrie-Quadrille, op.35 (1847); Wilhelminen-Quadrille, op.37 (1847)

Quadrille, on themes from Boisselot's Ne touchez pas à la reine, op.40 (1847); Fest-Quadrille, op.44 (1847); Martha-Quadrille, on themes from Flotow's opera, op.46 (1848); Seladon-Quadrille, op.48 (1848); Marien-Quadrille, op.51 (1848); Annika-Quadrille, op.53 (1848); Quadrille, on themes from Halévy's L'éclair, op.59 (1848); Sanssouci Quadrille, op.63 (1849); Nikolai-Quadrille, op.65 (1849); Künstler-Quadrille, op.71 (1850); Sofien-Quadrille, op.75 (1850); Attaque-Quadrille, op.76 (1850); Bonvivant-Quadrille, op.86 (1851); Slaven-Ball Quadrille, op.88 (1851)

Maskenfest-Quadrille, op.92 (1851); Promenade-Quadrille, op.98 (1851); Vivat, op.103 (1852); Tête-à-tête-Quadrille, op.109 (1852); Melodien-Quadrille, on themes by Verdi, op.112 (1852); Hofball-Quadrille, op.116 (1852); Nocturne-Quadrille, op.120 (1853); Indra-Quadrille, op.122 (1853); Satanella-Quadrille, op.123 (1853); Motor-Quadrille, op.129 (1853); Bouquet-Quadrille, op.135 (1853); Carnevals-Spektakel-Quadrille, op.152 (1854); Nordstern-Quadrille, on themes by Meyerbeer, op.153 (1854); Handels-Elite-Quadrille, op.166 (1855); Bijouterie-Quadrille, op.169 (1855)

Strelna-Terrassen-Quadrille, op.185 (1857); La berceuse, op.194 (1857); Le beau monde, op.199 (1858); Künstler-Quadrille, op.201 (1858); Dinorah-Quadrille, on themes from Meyerbeer's opera, op.224 (1860); Orpheus-Quadrille, op.236 (1860); Neue Melodien-Quadrille, on themes from It. operas, op.254 (1861); St Petersburg, op.255 (1861); Chansonette-Quadrille, op.259 (1862); 'Un ballo in maschera', on themes from Verdi's opera, op.272 (1863); Lieder-Quadrille, op.275 (1863); Saison-Quadrille, op.283 (1864); Quadrille sur des airs français, op.290 (1865)

L'africaine, on themes from Meyerbeer's opera, op.299 (1865), R i/18; Bal champêtre, op.303 (1866), R i/18; Le premier jour de bonheur, on themes from Auber's opera, op.327 (1869), R i/20; Slovanka-Quadrille, on Russian themes, op.338 (1871); Promenade Quadrille (London, 1867), as Festival-Quadrille, op.341 (1871)

Without op. no.: Quadrille, on themes from Auber's La part du diable (1847)

MARCHES

Patrioten-Marsch, op.8 (1845); Austria-Marsch, op.20 (1846); Fest-Marsch, op.49 (1848); Revolutions-Marsch, op.54 (1848); Studenten-Marsch, op.56 (1849); Brünner-Nationalgarde-Marsch, op.58 (1848); Kaiser Franz Joseph Marsch, op.67 (1849); Triumph-Marsch, op.69 (1850); Wiener-Garnison Marsch, op.77 (1850); Ottinger Reitermarsch, op.83 (1850); Kaiser-Jäger-Marsch, op.93 (1851); Viribus unitis, op.96 (1851); Grossfürsten-Marsch, op.107 (1852); Sachsen-Kürassier-Marsch, op.113 (1852); Wiener Jubel-Gruss-Marsch, op.115 (1852)

Kaiser Franz Joseph I: Rettungs-Jubel-Marsch, op.126 (1853); Caroussel-Marsch, op.133 (1853); Kron-Marsch, op.139 (1854); Erzherzog Wilhelm Genesungs-Marsch, op.149 (1854); Napoleon-Marsch, op.156 (1854); Alliance-Marsch, op.158 (1855); Krönungs-Marsch, op.183 (1857); Fürst Bariatinsky-Marsch, op.212 (1859); Deutscher Kriegermarsch, op.284 (1864); Verbrüderungs-Marsch, op.287 (1865); Persischer Marsch, op.289 (1865); Egyptischer Marsch, op.335 (1870); Jubelfest-Marsch (Genée), op.396 (1881)

Matador-Marsch, on themes from Das Spitzentuch der Königin, op.406 (Hamburg, 1883); Habsburg Hoch, op.408 (Hamburg, 1883); Russischer Marsch, op.426 (Hamburg, 1886); Spanischer Marsch, op.433 (Hamburg, 1888); Fest-Marsch, op.452 (1894); Deutschmeister-Jubiläumsmarsch, op.470 (n.p., 1896); Aufs Korn (V. Chiavacci), op.478 (1898)

Without op. no.: Serbischer Marsch (1847); Kaiser Alexander Huldigungs-Marsch (1864); Aufzugs-Marsch (1883) [from Eine Nacht in Venedig]; Freiwillige vor (1887); Einzugs-Marsch (1895) [from Der Zigeunerbaron]

Unpubd: Fanny Marsch (1847), c1870

OTHER WORKS

Pesther Csárdás, op.23 (1846); Slaven-Potpourri, op.39 (1847); Neue steirische Tänze, op.61 (1849); Romanze, d, op.243 (1861); Romanze, g, op.255 (1861); Veilchen, mazurka on Russian themes, op.256 (1862); Perpetuum mobile: musikalischer Scherz, op.257 (1862); Fest-Polonaise, op.352 (1872); Russische Marsch-Fantasie, op.353 (1872); Im russischen Dorfe, fantasy, op.355 (1873); Auf dem Tanzboden, musical illustration to Defregger's painting, op.454 (1894); Hochzeits-Präludium, vn, org/harmonium, harp, op.469 (Berlin, 1896); Klänge aus der Raimundzeit, op.479 (1898)

Without op. no.: Hommage au public russe, potpourri (St Petersburg, 1856); Sängergruss, male vv (Cologne, 1882); D'Hauptsach (L. Anzengruber), Allgemeine Kunstchronik, xi (1887), 9; Bauersleut im Künstlerhaus (Anzengruber), Allgemeine Kunstchronik, xiii (1889), 9; Ein Gstanzl vom Tanzl (Auf der Alm) (Dóczi) (1894); Traumbilder (1889)

Unpubd: Tu qui regis totum orbem, grad, 4vv, 2 ob, 2 cl, 2 bn, 2 hn, 3 trb, timp, 1844; Josefinen-Tänze; Dolci pianti, romance, vc, orch; Albumblatt für Nikolaus Dumba

COLLABORATIONS

Johann (ii), Josef: Hinter den Coulissen, quadrille (1859); Vaterländischer Marsch (1859); Monstre-Quadrille (1860); Pizzicato-Polka (1870)

Johann (ii), Josef, Eduard: Trifolien, waltzes (1865); Schützen-Quadrille (1868)

(3) Josef [Joseph] Strauss (b Vienna, 20 Aug 1827; d Vienna, 22 July 1870). Composer and conductor, son of (1) Johann Strauss (i). He studied theory with Franz Dolleschal, who ran a music school, and the violin with Franz Amon, (2) Johann's old teacher. From his earliest years Josef was afflicted with a disease of the brain and the spinal cord and occasionally suffered intense headaches and fainting fits. After refusing his father's wish that he should become a professional soldier, he first turned to architecture and engineering, and invented, among other things, a street-cleaning machine for the Vienna municipality. Although the doctors advised him to take plenty of exercise in the fresh air and to lead a quieter life, he spent his nights in dance halls overheated by gas lights and, driven by an inborn industriousness, devoted the rest of his free time to composing. His début as composer and conductor was on 23 July 1853, when he conducted his first set of waltzes, which bear the significant title of Die Ersten und Letzten. Not until the publication of his waltzes Die Vorgeiger op.16 in 1856, and after long persuasion by his ambitious brother, did he decide to take up a musical career in earnest.

5. Josef Strauss

Until their younger brother (4) Eduard's début in the spring of 1862, Josef and Johann shared the direction of the Strauss orchestra; from 1862 the leadership of the orchestra was divided between the three brothers until the following year when Johann was appointed *k.k. Hofballmusikdirektor* and withdrew from regular work with the family orchestra. Josef accepted a number of guest conducting engagements later in his career, and in 1864 he travelled to Breslau with a poorly assembled orchestra of his own. In 1869 he conducted with Johann in Pavlovsk, where he had deputized for his elder brother in 1862; this time Johann introduced him personally and intended eventually to leave the field to Josef, but nothing came of the plan. In 1870 Josef travelled to Warsaw, where, in poor health, he was unable to cope with the problems and excitement of touring. He was already a dying man; after his last Viennese appearance on 17 April 1870, the Warsaw tour, in the course of which he had an argument with an orchestra member during a concert, led to his complete collapse. He was rushed home to Vienna and died there soon after.

Unlike his elder brother, Josef Strauss was a melancholy introvert, to whom the Viennese used to refer as 'the romantic-looking, chaotically pale Josef'. As a composer he lacked his brother's spontaneity and light touch, though he was a profounder and more cultivated musician. In addition to his superior craftsmanship, shown in the more balanced and concentrated form of his waltzes, and a generally greater ingenuity in both harmonic and melodic invention, there is true poetry and a pessimistic, romantic touch about his music. The influence of Schubert and Chopin, and especially that of

Berlioz, Liszt and Wagner, can be traced in the waltzes and their introductions and even in certain mazurkas. If Josef had not been obliged to submit his best musical ideas to the yoke of dance rhythms and had he lived longer, his development might have been different. Some of his compositions have greater intrinsic musical value than many of those by his brother Johann (e.g. opp.39, 71, 172, 173, 174, 184, 207, 212, 235, 275, 277, 279 and 280), but he also succeeded in writing genuine popular waltzes (opp.44, 61, 164, 249, 258 and 263).

A seductive Wagnerian undercurrent is detectable in some of his elder brother's waltzes, and it is intriguing that Josef should have composed a waltz set *Irrlichter* ('Will o' the wisps') in June 1858, which disappeared from the opus number series, and that waltzes bearing the same name by Johann appearing in January 1859 (op.218) should have been criticized for missing the *gemütlich* sounds of Viennese dance music and instead providing *Tannhäuser* reminiscences. It will probably never be known how far Josef's generosity towards his brother extended or into whose hands his controversial lost manuscripts passed. Other original works which he performed, including the waltzes *Stimmen der Zeit* (May 1859), *Lieb und Leben* (October 1859), a piece called *Ideale* (June 1858) and the tone poem *Ode an die Nacht* for chorus and orchestra (October 1858), which received a highly favourable critical reception, have disappeared.

WORKS

Selective list; all works were published in Vienna for pf 2 hands and in various chamber and orchestral arrangements; for complete catalogue see Weinmann (1967).

PF – *polka française*; PS – *polka schnell*

Editions: *Josef Strauss: 3 Walzer*, ed. H. Botstiber, DTÖ, lxxiv, Jg.xxxviii/2 (1931) [orch; B]

WALTZES

Die Ersten und Letzten, op.1 (1856); Die Vorgeiger, op.16 (1856); Die guten, alten Zeiten, op.26 (1856); Mai-Rosen, op.34 (1857); Perlen der Liebe, op.39 (1857); 5 Kleeblad'ln, op.44 (1857); Wiener Kinder, op.61 (1858); Flattergeister, op.62 (1859); Schwert und Leier, op.71 (1860); Helden-Gedichte, op.87 (1860); Wiener Bonsmots, op.108 (1862); Hesperus-Ball-Tänze, op.116 (1862); Freudengrüsse, op.128 (1863); Fantasiebilder, op.151 (1864)
Dorfschwalben aus Österreich, op.164 (1865), B; Herztöne, op.172 (1865); Geheime Anziehungskräfte (Dynamiden), op.173 (1865); Aktionen, op.174 (1865); Gedenkblätter, op.178 (1865); Transaktionen, op.184 (1865); Heilmethoden, op.189 (1866); Helenen-Walzer, op.197 (1867); Friedenspalmen, op.207 (1867); Delirien, op.212 (1867); Marien-Klänge, op.214 (1867); Herbstrosen, op.232 (1868); Sphären-Klänge, op.235 (1868), B; Wiener Stimmen, op.239 (1868); Wiener Fresken, op.249 (1868); Aquarellen, op.258 (1869); Mein Lebenslauf ist Lieb und Lust, op.263 (1869), B
Nilfluten, op.275 (1870); Frauenwürde, op.277 (1871); Hesperusbahnen, op.279 (1871); Tanz-Prioritäten, op.280 (1871); Rudolfs-Klänge, op.283 (1871)

POLKAS

Lustlager-Polka, op.19 (1856); Jucker-Polka, op.27 (1856); Sylphide, PF, op.28 (1857); La simplicité, PF, op.40 (1857); Steeplechase, op.43 (1857); Matrosen-Polka, op.52 (1858); Moulinet, PF, op.57 (1858); Laxenburger-Polka, op.60 (1858); Saus und Braus, PS, op.69 (1859); Gruss an München, PF, op.90 (1860); Tag und Nacht, PS, op.93 (1861); Amaranth, PF, op.119 (1862); Auf Ferienreisen, PS, op.133 (1863); Sturmlauf, PS, op.136 (1863)
Rudolfsheimer-Polka, op.152 (1864); Pêle-mêle, PS, op.161 (1865); Springinsfeld, PS, op.181 (1865); Mailust, PF, op.182 (1865); Verliebte Augen, PF, op.185 (1865); For ever, PS, op.193 (1866); Carrière, PS, op.200 (1867); Schwalbenpost, PS, op.203 (1867); Farewell, PS, op.211 (1867); Jocus-Polka, PS, op.216 (1867); Allerlei, PS, op.219 (1867); Die Windsbraut, PS, op.221 (1867); Victoria, PF, op.228 (1868); Im Fluge, PS, op.230 (1868); Lock-Polka, op.233 (1868); Gallopin-Polka, PS, op.237 (1868); Eingesendet, PS, op.240 (1868)
Plappermäulchen: musikalischer Scherz, PS, op.245 (1868); Buchstaben-Polka, op.252 (1869); Vélocipède, PS, op.259 (1869);

Ohne Sorgen, PS, op.271 (1870); En passant, PF, op.273 (1870); Künstler-Gruss, PF, op.274 (1870); Jokey-Polka, PS, op.278 (1871); Heiterer Mut, PF, op.281 (1871)

Polka mazurkas: Sehnsucht, op.22 (1856); Une pensée, op.35 (1857); Minerva, op.67 (1859); Sympathie, op.73 (1860); Bellona, op.94 (1861); Die Lachtaube, op.117 (1862); Lieb und Wein, op.122 (1862); Brennende Liebe, op.129 (1863); Die Schwätzerin, op.144 (1863); Frauenherz, op.166 (1865), B; Pauline, op.190 (1866); Thalia, op.195 (1866); Die Libelle, op.204 (1867); Arm in Arm, op.215 (1867); Nachtschatten, op.229 (1868); Dithyrambe (J. Weyl), op.236 (1868); Die Galante, op.251 (1869); Aus der Ferne, op.270 (1869); Die Emanzipierte, op.282 (1871)

OTHER WORKS

Quadrilles: Policinello-Quadrille, op.21 (1856); Musen-Quadrille, op.46 (1858); Lanciers-Quadrille, op.64 (1859); Stegreif-Quadrille, op.80 (1860); Folichon-Quadrille, op.115 (1862); Sofien-Quadrille, op.137 (1863); Herold-Quadrille, op.157 (1864); Tournier-Quadrille, op.169 (1864); Colosseum-Quadrille, op.175 (1865); Pariser-Quadrille, op.209 (1867); Theater-Quadrille, op.213 (1867)

Marches: Avantgarde-Marsch, op.14 (1856); Wallonen-Marsch, op.41 (1857); Österreichischer Kronprinzen-Marsch, op.59 (1858); Deutscher Union-Marsch, op.146 (1863); Prinz Eugen-Marsch, op.186 (1866); Schwarzenberg-Monument-Marsch, op.210 (1867); Ungarischer Krönungs-Marsch, op.225 (1867); Schützen-Marsch, op.250 (1868)

Other works: Schottischer Tanz, op.20 (1856); Waldblumen, ländler, op.79 (1860); Ständchen (1861); Die Nasswalderin, ländler, op.267 (1869); Das musikalische Österreich, potpourri (1864)

For collaborations see (2) Johann Strauss (ii).

(4) Eduard Strauss (i) (*b* Vienna, 15 March 1835; *d* Vienna, 28 Dec 1916). Composer and conductor, youngest son of (1) Johann Strauss (i). He was originally intended for the Austrian consular service and was educated in classical languages. As with (3) Josef, it was (2) Johann who induced him to turn to music, the increasing demand for waltzes and orchestral tours necessitating the youngest brother's collaboration. Eduard had a thorough musical training; he studied theory and composition with Gottfried Preyer and Simon Sechter, the violin with Amon and the harp with

6. Eduard Strauss: silhouettes by Otto Böhler

Parish-Alvars and Zamara. After acquiring experience as a harpist in Johann's orchestra he made his début both as a composer and as a conductor at the Wintergarten of the Dianabad-Saal on 6 April 1862. The theatrical paper *Der Zwischenakt* wrote on 7 April:

Eduard Strauss, who in his whole manner involuntarily recalls the elder Strauss, was received with thunderous applause when he appeared at the side of his brother Johann. With rare agility and confidence he conducted all the new waltzes composed this season by Johann Strauss. His performance revealed him as a conductor worthy to be ranked with his brother.

Until Josef's death in 1870 he directed the famous Strauss orchestra jointly with him. In February 1872 Eduard was appointed *k.k. Hofballmusikdirektor*; he remained with his orchestra until April 1878, when the players, most of whom were musicians only in their spare time, chose C. M. Ziehrer to succeed him as their Kapellmeister. Thereafter Eduard made annual summer concert tours throughout Europe, conducting local orchestras. He went to London for the first time in 1885, on the occasion of the International Inventions Exhibition (for which he composed a polka, op.239), and returned to England in 1895 and 1897. In July 1897 the *Musical Times* wrote:

The man is the very incarnation of the lilt and swing of the waltz. He conducts with his whole body, his hands, his feet, and even his eyebrows. There are some excellent players in the band, but the quality of tone is nothing out of the common; what lends attractiveness to their performance are the unanimity with which they follow the indications of their leader and the spirit and abandon of their playing.

In 1890 Eduard took his orchestra to the USA for the first time. In 1894 he went to St Petersburg, and in October 1900 he returned to the USA for a tour of 106 concerts in 81 towns. When family matters prevented him from continuing his musical activities, he requested in March 1901 to be relieved of his duties as *k.k. Hofballmusikdirektor* and returned to private life.

Although he was never more than a competent violinist, through his continuous rehearsing and performing of the Wagner overtures and preludes in addition to the dances of Lanner and the Strauss family, Eduard's conducting skill developed considerably and, according to contemporary reports, he became the best conductor among the Strauss brothers. Gradually he took on interpretative mannerisms, of which traces can still be heard in Strauss interpretations by some modern conductors. In particular the expressive use of rubato for which Wagner, Liszt and Bülow were much admired served Eduard as a model, but Johann, in his letters, admonished Eduard to play his waltzes more strictly in time. Eduard's compositions show sound craftsmanship, but are otherwise merely a pale reflection of his elder brothers' style. The opus numbers reach 300 and, as in Josef's case, old programmes contain the titles of works which either have vanished or cannot be identified. He published his memoirs in 1906.

WORKS

Selective list; all listed works were published in Vienna for pf 2 hands and in various chamber and orchestral arrangements; for complete catalogue see Weinmann (1967).

PF – *polka française*; PS – *polka schnell*

Waltzes: Deutsche Herzen, op.65 (1871); Akademische Bürger, op.68 (1871); Fesche Geister, op.75 (1872); Doktrinen, op.79 (1872); Myrten-Sträusschen, op.87 (1872); Manuskripte, op.90 (1872); Expositionen, op.103 (1873); Verdikte, op.137 (1876); Konsequenzen, op.143 (1876); Das Leben ist doch schön, op.150 (1877); Ball-Chronik, op.167 (1878); Lustfahrten, op.177 (1879); Glockensignale, op.198 (1881); Schleier und Krone, op.200 (1881); Lebende Blumen, op.205 (1882); Wiener Dialekt, op.237 (1885); Für lustige Leut, op.255 (1887)

Polkas: Bahn frei, PS, op.45 (1869); Mit Dampf, PS, op.70 (1872); Bruder Studio, PF, op.78 (1872); Aus Lieb zu ihr (J. Kowy), PF, op.135 (1876); Ausser Rand und Band, PS, op.168 (1878); Pfeilschnell, PS, op.179 (1879); Original-Bericht, PF, op.189 (1880); Mit Chic, PS, op.221 (1884); Organ für Tanzlustige, PF, op.225 (1884); Mit Vergnügen, PS, op.228 (1884); Im Flug mit ihr, PS, op.231 (1884); Ohne Bremse, PS, op.238 (1885); Old England for ever Polka, op.239 (1886); Carnevals-Bulletin, PF, op.253 (1887)

Polka mazurkas: Mit der Feder, op.69(1872); Liebesbotschaft, op.160 (1878)

Galops: Pest-Ofener Eissport-Galopp, op.96 (1873); Um die Wette, op.241 (1886)

For collaborations see (2) Johann Strauss (ii).

(5) Johann (Maria Eduard) Strauss (iii) (*b* Vienna, 16 Feb 1866; *d* Berlin, 9 Jan 1939). Composer and conductor, son of (4) Eduard Strauss (i). He studied commerce and became an accountant in the ministry of education. After the success of his only operetta, *Katze und Maus* (Theater an der Wien, December 1898; libretto by F. Gross and V. Léon, based on Scribe), was envied by even his old uncle Johann, he left his job to follow in the family tradition; in 1900 he took up the baton and made a seven-month conducting tour. Like his father, he was not a particularly accomplished violinist and was more concerned with striking the celebrated 'Strauss pose'. From 1901 to 1905 he directed the music for balls at the imperial-royal court, but he had to forfeit the coveted title of *k.k. Hofballmusikdirektor* upon accruing heavy debts and incurring a conviction in a court of law. He moved to Berlin (some historic gramophone recordings survive from this period), only returning to Vienna for two years during World War I. His collaboration with the Austrian poet Josef Weinheber is of some note; Weinheber wrote verses to Johann's waltz composition *Lob der Heimat*, the only text written to a Strauss melody by a real poet.

(6) Eduard (Leopold Maria) Strauss (ii) (*b* Vienna, 24 March 1910; *d* Vienna, 6 April 1969). Conductor, nephew of (5) Johann Strauss (iii). After directing the operetta class of the New Vienna Conservatory, he first conducted a public concert in 1949, under the auspices of the Vienna Johann Strauss Society. His early appearances were with the Vienna Stadtorchester; later he also conducted the Vienna SO in recordings which immediately won him a devoted public at home and abroad. On concert tours with the Vienna Johann Strauss Orchestra or as a guest conductor of other orchestras he became a celebrated bearer of the family tradition, although, not being a violinist, he used the baton to conduct.

BIBLIOGRAPHY

L. Scheyrer: *Johann Strauss's musikalische Wanderung durch das Leben* (Vienna, 1851) [with list of works]

A. W. Ambros: *Culturhistorische Bilder aus dem Musikleben der Gegenwart* (Leipzig, 1860), chap. 'Die Tanzmusik seit 100 Jahren'

E. M. Oettinger: *Meister Johann Strauss und seine Zeitgenossen* (Berlin, 1862) [novel, with list of works]

E. Hanslick: *Aus dem Concertsaal* (Vienna, 1870), chap. 'Tanzmusik und die Söhne von Strauss und Lanner'

R. Schumann: *Gesammelte Schriften über Musik und Musiker*, ed. H. Simon (Leipzig, 1888)

L. Eisenberg: *Johann Strauss: ein Lebensbild* (Vienna, 1894)

G. Adler: 'Johann Strauss', *Biographisches Jb und Deutscher Nekrolog*, ed. A. Bettelheim (Berlin, 1897–1900), iv, 27

C. Flamme: *Verzeichnis der sämtlichen im Druck erschienenen Kompositionen von Johann Strauss (Vater), Johann Strauss (Sohn), Josef Strauss und Eduard Strauss* (Leipzig, 1898)

E. Hanslick: 'Johann Strauss als Operncomponist', *Die moderne Oper*, ix (Berlin, 1900), 305f

R. von Procházka: *Johann Strauss* (Berlin, 1900, 2/1903)

R. Heuberger: *Im Foyer* (Leipzig, 1901)

F. Lange: *Joseph Lanner und Johann Strauss: ihre Zeit, ihr Leben und ihre Werke* (Vienna, 1904, 2/1919)

E. Strauss: *Erinnerungen* (Vienna, 1906)

R. Specht: *Johann Strauss* (Berlin, 1909, 2/1922)

F. Lange: *Johann Strauss* (Leipzig, 1912)

E. Neumann: *Die Operetten von Johann Strauss: ihre Formen und das Verhältnis von Text und Musik* (diss., U. of Vienna, 1919)

H. Weisse: *Der instrumentale Kunstwalzer* (diss., U. of Vienna, 1919)

E. Rieger: *Offenbach und seine Wiener Schule* (Vienna, 1920)

F. Scherber: 'Die Entwicklung der Walzerform bei Johann Strauss', *Der Merker* (1920), June

J. Schnitzer: *Meister Johann: bunte Geschichten aus der Johann Strauss-Zeit* (Vienna, 1920)

E. Decsey: *Johann Strauss* (Stuttgart, 1922, rev. 2/1948 by E. Rieger)

K. Kobald: *Johann Strauss* (Vienna, 1925)

F. Lange: *Johann Strauss: der Walzerkönig* (Berlin, 1925) [novel, with newly published letters]

S. Loewy: *Rund um Johann Strauss: Momentbilder aus einem Künstlerleben* (Vienna, 1925)

I. Mendelssohn: 'Zur Entwicklung des Walzers', *SMw*, xiii (1926), 57

A. Strauss, ed.: *Johann Strauss schreibt Briefe* (Berlin, 1926)

K. Huschke: 'Johannes Brahms, Johann Strauss und Hans von Bülow', *Unsere Tonmeister unter einander*, v (Pritzwalk, 1928), 68

F. Lange: *Katalog der Johann Strauss Ausstellung* (Vienna, 1932)

H. E. Jacob: *Johann Strauss und das neunzehnte Jahrhundert: die Geschichte einer musikalischen Weltherrschaft* (Amsterdam, 1937, rev. 3/1962)

H. Sündermann: *Johann Strauss: ein Vollender* (Brixlegg, 1937, 3/1949)

W. Jaspert: *Johann Strauss: sein Leben, sein Werk, seine Zeit* (Vienna, 1939, 2/1949)

M. Kronberg: *Johann Strauss* (Paris, 1939)

A. B. Teetgen: *The Waltz Kings of Old Vienna* (London, 1939)

A. Witeschnik: *Die Dynastie Strauss* (Vienna and Leipzig, 1939, 3/1958)

E. Schenk: *Johann Strauss* (Potsdam, 1940)

D. Ewen: *Tales from the Vienna Woods: the Story of Johann Strauss* (New York, 1944)

F. Hadamowsky and H. Otte: *Die Wiener Operette* (Vienna, 1947)

M. Carner: *The Waltz* (London, 1948)

P. Ruff: *Johann-Strauss-Festschrift: Juni–September 1949* (Vienna, 1949)

J. Andriessen: *Johann Strauss de koning van de vals* (Amsterdam, 1950)

W. Reich, ed.: *Johann Strauss-Brevier: aus Briefen und Erinnerungen* (Zurich, 1950)

J. Pastene: *Three-quarter Time: the Life and Music of the Strauss Family of Vienna* (New York, 1951)

P. Kuringer: *Johann Strauss* (Haarlem, 1952)

H. E. Jacob: *Johann Strauss Vater und Sohn* (Hamburg, 1953)

E. Nick: *Vom Wiener Walzer zur Wiener Operette* (Hamburg, 1954)

M. Schönherr and K. Reinöhl: *Johann Strauss Vater: ein Werkverzeichnis, Das Jahrhundert des Walzers, i* (Vienna, 1954)

A. Weinmann: *Verzeichnis sämtlicher Werke von Johann Strauss Vater und Sohn* (Vienna, 1956)

E. Krenek: *Zur Sprache gebracht* (Munich, 1958; Eng. trans., 1966), chap. 'Ein paar Worte über Johann Strauss'

K. Pfannhauser: 'Eine menschlich-künstlerische Strauss-Memoire', *Festschrift Alfred Orel* (Vienna and Wiesbaden, 1960), 139

B. Grun: *Kulturgeschichte der Operette* (Munich, 1961)

H. Markl: *Berühmte Ruhestätten auf Wiener Friedhöfen* (Vienna, 1961)

E. Meylikh: *Johann Strauss* (Leningrad, 1962, 2/1964)

M. Schönherr: 'Der "Gasteiner Walzer" von Johann Strauss', *ÖMz*, xix (1964), 12

——: 'Beiträge zu einer Bibliographie der Dynastie Strauss', *ÖMz*, xix (1964), 33

F. Grasberger: *Die Walzer-Dynastie Strauss: eine Ausstellung zum Neujahrskonzert der Wiener Philharmoniker* (Vienna, 1965–6)

H. Jäger-Sustenau: *Johann Strauss: der Walzerkönig und seine Dynastie, Familiengeschichte, Urkunden* (Vienna, 1965)

F. Feldkirchner: 'Johann Strauss und sein Palais auf der Wieden', *ÖMz*, xxii (1967), 23

M. Schönherr: 'An der schönen blauen Donau: Marginalien zur 100. Wiederkehr des Tages der Uraufführung', *ÖMz*, xxii (1967), 3

H. Schöny: 'Von den Bildnissen des Walzerkönigs', *ÖMz*, xxii (1967), 16

A. Weinmann: *Verzeichnis sämtlicher Werke von Josef und Eduard Strauss* (Vienna, 1967)

A. Lamb: 'Nights in Venice: a Note on Revisions of Strauss's Operetta', *Tritsch-Tratsch*, vii (1968), 8

M. Schönherr: 'An der schönen blauen Donau in London', *ÖMz*, xxiii (1968), 3, 82

E. Werba: 'In memoriam Eduard Strauss', *ÖMz*, xxiv (1969), 332

L. Licherfeld: 'Genie wider Willen: zum 100. Todestag des Kapellmeisters und Kompositeurs Joseph Strauss', *NZM*, Jg.131 (1970), 382

H. Fantel: *Johann Strauss, Father and Son, and their Era* (Newton Abbot, 1971)
A. Lamb: 'The Composition of "A Night in Venice"', *Tritsch-Tratsch*, xvii (1971), 8; xviii (1972), 7
O. Schneidereit: *Johann Strauss und die Stadt an der schönen blauen Donau* (Berlin, 1972)
D. Stoverock: *Die Fledermaus*, Die Oper: Schriftenreihe über musikalische Bühnenwerke (Berlin-Lichterfelde, 1973)
J. Wechsberg: *The Waltz Emperors* (London, 1973)
H.-U. Barth: 'Das Original ist immer besser Erfahrungen bei "Eine Nacht in Venedig"', *Flugschriften: Deutsche Johann Strauss Gesellschaft, Mitteilungsblatt*, i (1975), 21
F. Endler: *Das Walzer-Buch: Johann Strauss: Die Aufforderung zum Tanz* (Vienna, 1975)
F. Feldkirchner: 'Johann Strauss – Gedenkstätten in Wien', *ÖMz*, xxx (1975), 287
F. Mailer: *Das kleine Johann Strauss Buch* (Salzburg, 1975)
M. Prawy: *Johann Strauss: Weltgeschichte im Walzertakt* (Vienna, 1975)
F. Racek: *Johann Strauss zum 150. Geburtstag: Ausstellung der Wiener Stadtbibliothek 22. Mai bis 31. Oktober 1975* (Vienna, 1975)
——: 'Zur Entstehung und Aufführungsgeschichte der "Fledermaus"', *ÖMz*, xxx (1975), 264
G. and L. Reimers: *Wienervalsen och familjen Strauss* (Stockholm, 1975)
M. Schönherr: 'Modelle der Walzerkomposition: Grundlagen zu einer Theorie des Walzers', *ÖMz*, xxx (1975), 273
E. Strauss: 'Die Leopoldstädter Zeit der Familie Strauss', *Flugschriften: Deutsche Johann Strauss Gesellschaft, Mitteilungsblatt*, i (1975), 15
J. Viedebantt: 'Fünf Paragraphen aus dem Walzer-Codex (zur Gründung einer Deutschen Johann Strauss-Gesellschaft)', ibid, 3
——: ' "In Strauss und Bogen" ', ibid, 25
A. Weinmann: 'Die Johann Strauss-Literatur: Versuch einer Zusammenfassung', *ÖMz*, xxx (1975), 298
J. Whitten: 'Johann Strauss und der Wiener Männergesang-Verein', *ÖMz*, xxx (1975), 516
F. Mailer: 'Man tut mir zuviel Ehre an: Gedanken zum Persönlichkeitsbild von Johann Strauss', *ÖMz*, xxxi (1975), 257
M. Schönherr: 'Ästhetik des Walzers', *ÖMz*, xxxi (1976), 57–120
F. Mailer: *Joseph Strauss: Genie wider Willen* (Vienna and Munich, 1977)

MOSCO CARNER/MAX SCHÖNHERR

Strauss, Christoph (*b* ?Vienna, *c*1575–80; *d* Vienna, mid-June 1631). Austrian composer and organist. He came from a musical family with a long record of continuous service to the imperial house of Habsburg. He himself entered its service in 1594 and by 1601 was organist of the court church of St Michael. His remuneration did not prove sufficient for his needs, since he had a growing family to support, and in 1614 he was given the better-paid task of administering the estate of Kattenburg, an imperial property on the site of modern Schönbrunn. In May 1617 he became director of the court music but did not remain so for long: his patron and constant supporter, the Emperor Matthias I, died in 1619, and the new emperor, Ferdinand II, who had earlier opposed his appointment to Kattenburg, now replaced him as Kapellmeister by Giovanni Priuli, and he had difficulty in obtaining the salary due to him. From at least 1626 until his death he was in charge of the music at St Stephen's Cathedral, Vienna.

Of Strauss's two volumes of sacred music that of 1613 contains 36 motets in five to ten parts, including the essential use of instruments but without continuo. They are very much a product of the transitional period at the turn of the century, with contrasts between traditional polyphony and block homophony, madrigalian word-setting and closely worked imitation, and refrain forms and the use of plainsong tones; there are also Gabrielian effects in the use of *cori spezzati* and the disposition of instruments. Strauss's fondness for employing instruments in families (e.g. groups of trombones, viols, etc) is a typically German feature; the pieces requiring instrumental participation are de-

scribed in the index as concertos, in the Gabrielian sense of the term. Constant variety of texture, tessitura and instrumentation and the dramatic presentation of the words combine to make this a collection full of interest.

Strauss's other volume, the *Missae* (prepared for publication before his death and published by his son Matthias), contains 16 masses, including two requiems, for eight to 20 vocal and instrumental parts and shows him to be a composer of considerable invention, sensitivity and contrapuntal skill. Most of the works are parody masses, in which the basic melodic units appear in many different guises throughout and lend unity to the whole. Four of the masses, on the other hand, are marked 'concertata', and it is in them that the most progressive tendencies occur. The concerto element includes not only the contrast between vocal, instrumental and mixed groups but also the juxtaposition of powerful tuttis and sections for one, two or three voices, sometimes accompanied by instruments: the great masses of the 18th century can trace their ancestry back to works such as these. Various dynamic markings, literal word-painting and precise instrumentation indicate a truly Baroque approach to the text. The influence of the Venetian school can again be seen, especially in the rhythms and style of the vocal writing and in the treatment of the polychoral medium.

Strauss was without doubt one of the finest Austrian composers of his day: his music is not only of considerable intrinsic worth but is also historically important.

WORKS

Nova ac diversimoda sacrarum cantionum compositio seu [36] motettae, 5–10vv, insts (Vienna, 1613); O sacrum convivium, ed. in SEM, xii (1977)
Missae, 8–20vv, insts, bc (org) (Vienna, 1631); Missa pro defunctis, ed. G. Adler, DTÖ, lix, Jg. xxx/1 (1923/R); Missa 'O sacrum convivium', ed. in SEM, xii (1977)
Motet, 3vv, bc, in 1629[1]

BIBLIOGRAPHY
G. Adler: 'Zur Geschichte der Wiener Messkomposition in der zweiten Hälfte des 17. Jahrhunderts', *SMw*, iv (1916), 5–45
A. Smijers: 'Die kaiserliche Hofmusik-Kapelle von 1543–1619', *SMw*, ix (1922), 72
K. Geiringer: 'Christoph Strauss: ein Wiener Künstlerdasein am Beginn des 17. Jahrhunderts', *ZMw*, xiii (1930–31), 50

A. LINDSEY KIRWAN

Strauss, Isaac (*b* Strasbourg, 2 June 1806; *d* Paris, 9 Aug 1888). French conductor, composer and violinist. He was already an accomplished violinist in 1826 when he entered the Paris Conservatoire. In 1828 he was a co-founder of the Société des Concerts du Conservatoire and shortly thereafter began a 15-year engagement as violinist at the Théâtre-Italien. He became known as a composer of dance music and conductor of instrumental ensembles at court and noble functions, and in 1852 he replaced Musard as music director of the court balls; he held this post until 1870 and then became director of the opera balls until 1872. He also conducted the spa orchestra in Vichy (1843–63), where his luxurious villa was used as a residence by the emperor and empress in the summers of 1861 and 1862. In his later years he was a generous benefactor to old and needy musicians. His large art and archaeological collection is in the Salle Strauss of the Cluny Museum, Paris.

Strauss's vast output of waltzes, polkas, galops and quadrilles achieved considerable popularity in his day. Some of the works bear titles identical with pieces by

Johann Strauss (i), and the omission of Isaac's first name from the title-pages of piano editions caused some of his works, such as the set of waltzes *Le diamant*, to be falsely attributed to the Viennese Strauss.

BIBLIOGRAPHY
A. Lamb: 'The Parisian Strauss', *Tritsch-Tratsch* (1972), no.20, p.7
MAX SCHÖNHERR

Strauss, Richard (Georg) (*b* Munich, 11 June 1864; *d* Garmisch-Partenkirchen, Bavaria, 8 Sept 1949). German composer and conductor. Unlike his contemporaries Debussy and Mahler he early received high estimation: before the age of 21 he had been hailed as the successor to Brahms and Wagner, and the tone poems written in his 20s and early 30s immediately entered the international repertory. After 1900 his interests were centred on opera: with *Salome* and *Elektra* (1903–8) he seemed to be in the forefront of musical advance; but *Der Rosenkavalier* (1909–10), if representing a 'retreat', has remained his most popular opera. In his last works he brought to a fine culmination and balance those features which, to varying extents, had always been present in his music: Wagnerian fullness, Mozartian grace and a personal warmth of feeling.

1. Boyhood and youth, 1864–85. 2. The conductor and tone-poem composer, 1885–98. 3. The acclaimed opera composer, 1898–1918. 4. After World War I, 1919–49. 5. Works: introduction. 6. Early works. 7. Tone poems and other orchestral works. 8. Operas. 9. Choral music and lieder.

1. BOYHOOD AND YOUTH, 1864–85. Strauss was the first child of Franz Joseph Strauss (1822–1905), principal horn player in the Munich Court Orchestra for 49 years, and Josephine Pschorr (1837–1910), his second wife. Fräulein Pschorr was a member of the family of brewers, which enabled her husband to enjoy financial independence and meant that Strauss and his sister had a happy, carefree childhood. Strauss showed musical promise from his earliest years: at the age of four he had piano lessons from his father's orchestral colleague August Tombo, and four years later he was taught the violin by his father's cousin Benno Walter, leader of the court orchestra. Franz Strauss was intensely conservative in his musical tastes – though he played Wagner magnificently he detested both the music and the man – and did not allow his son to hear anything but the classics until he was in his early teens. A powerful influence on the boy was his freedom to attend rehearsals of the Munich Court Orchestra under Hermann Levi. From the age of 11 he received instruction in theory, harmony and instrumentation from one of Levi's assistant conductors, Friedrich Wilhelm Meyer. His first compositions were written when he was six, and from then until the last days of his life he composed regularly and copiously.

After elementary schooling Strauss entered the Ludwigsgymnasium, Munich, in 1874, remaining there until he matriculated at the age of 18. (He never went to an academy of music, going from school to Munich University for the winter and spring terms of 1882–3 to read philosophy, aesthetics and the history of art.) His first encounter with the operas of Wagner came during and after 1874, when he saw performances of *Tannhäuser*, *Siegfried* and *Lohengrin* and found them beyond his power of appreciation. 'It was not until, against my father's orders, I studied the score of *Tristan*, that I entered into this magic work, and later

into *Der Ring des Nibelungen*, and I can well remember how, at the age of seventeen, I positively wolfed the score of *Tristan* as if in a trance', he wrote many years later in his reminiscences (1949). Some years earlier Franz Strauss had formed a semi-professional orchestra known as 'Wilde Gung'l'. From the age of 13 Strauss was allowed to play at a back desk of the violins and he gradually moved up to the front desks. A particularly significant month was March 1881, when he was 16. On the 14th his String Quartet in A was performed in Munich by Benno Walter's quartet; on the 26th the Wilde Gung'l performed his *Festmarsch* in E♭ and on the 30th Levi conducted the court orchestra in the Symphony in D minor. That year he composed the Piano Sonata in B minor op.5 and the Five Piano Pieces op.3. All these juvenilia were published and are extant, with the exception of the symphony, which survives in manuscript.

Strauss's career as a composer began in earnest when performances of his works were given outside his native Munich where he enjoyed a favoured position. On 5 December 1882 his Violin Concerto was performed in Vienna by Benno Walter with Strauss as pianist. But of more importance to his future was the performance a week earlier by the Dresden Court Orchestra under Franz Wüllner of the Serenade in E♭ for 13 wind instruments. In winter 1883–4, by which time he had left university in order to concentrate on music, Strauss visited Berlin for the first time. During his stay he heard operas, met the city's artistic circle, developed his lifelong addiction to card playing and wrote another symphony. He also met Hans von Bülow, at this time conductor of the Meiningen Court Orchestra, which he had made into the most disciplined ensemble in Europe. Strauss's first publisher, Eugen Spitzweg, knew Bülow and had sent him the score of Strauss's Serenade. Bülow was impressed enough not only to put the work into his orchestra's repertory but to describe Strauss as 'by far the most striking personality since Brahms'. The Serenade was performed in Berlin, in Strauss's presence, by the Meiningen Orchestra, after which Bülow invited the 19-year-old composer to write a similar piece for Meiningen, the result being the Suite in B♭. Bülow arranged for the first performance to be given in Munich when the Meiningen Orchestra played there on 18 November 1884 and invited Strauss to conduct his piece.

The years 1881–5 were highly productive: Strauss composed the Horn Concerto no.1, the Cello Sonata, the *Stimmungsbilder* for piano, the Piano Quartet, the Goethe setting *Wandrers Sturmlied* for six-part chorus and orchestra, the Symphony no.2 in F minor and nine settings of poems by Gilm for voice and piano which include *Zueignung*, *Die Nacht* and *Allerseelen* (still among the most admired of Strauss lieder). The symphony had its first performance in New York, conducted by the enterprising Theodore Thomas, who when visiting Europe had been shown the manuscript by Franz Strauss. Early in 1885 Wüllner conducted this symphony in Cologne; and at Meiningen on 4 March Bülow conducted the first performance of the Horn Concerto no.1. Before his 21st birthday, therefore, Strauss had heard his music interpreted by the outstanding German conductors of the day, one of whom, Bülow, had dubbed him 'Richard the Third', a jest because he meant that after 'Richard the First' (Wagner) there could be no

Richard the Second. It certainly could not have meant that Bülow regarded Strauss as a revolutionary innovator, because what he admired in the young composer's music was its adherence to traditional practices. Nevertheless it was an astonishing compliment, and indicative of Strauss's rapid rise to fame.

2. THE CONDUCTOR AND TONE-POEM COMPOSER, 1885–98.

In summer 1885, when the post of assistant conductor to Bülow at Meiningen became vacant, Bülow offered it to Strauss who, in spite of his inexperience with the baton, accepted. He attended all Bülow's rehearsals, learning by watching and by answering Bülow's searching questions about scores. On 15 October, after only a fortnight, Strauss made his public début as solo pianist in Mozart's C minor Concerto K491, for which he composed cadenzas, and conducted his own F minor Symphony. Brahms was in Meiningen for rehearsals of his new Symphony no.4, which was to have its first performance ten days later, and he listened to the young man's work, remarking that it was 'quite attractive' but 'too full of thematic irrelevances' (see Strauss's memoirs). A few days later Bülow resigned his post and Strauss was appointed his successor by the Duke of Saxe-Meiningen. But without the kudos of Bülow as his conductor, the duke began to reduce the orchestra and Strauss, despite misgivings, accepted a three-year contract as third conductor at the Munich Court Opera. He left Meiningen in April 1886 having gained invaluable experience on the rostrum. He had also been an assiduous attender of performances by the famous Meiningen Court Theatre, where his deep knowledge of dramatic and theatrical effectiveness developed.

Another profound personal influence on Strauss at Meiningen had been his friendship with one of the orchestral violinists, Alexander Ritter, a devout follower of Wagner and Liszt who had married Wagner's niece. Ritter had found the young conductor–composer fertile ground for conversion to the faith of 'Zukunftsmusik' (music of the future). He had interested him in Wagner's essays and in Schopenhauer and had persuaded him that 'new ideas must search for new forms – this basic principle of Liszt's symphonic works, in which the poetic idea was really the formative element, became henceforward the guiding principle for my own symphonic work' (Strauss's memoirs). The immediate musical result of this conversion was the symphonic fantasy *Aus Italien*, a halfway stage between the Mendelssohnian conventionality of his early works and the Lisztian models to follow. It recorded the impressions of his first visit to Italy in summer 1886, before he took up his Munich post. He remained in Munich for three years, somewhat fretfully because, as third conductor, he was denied the chance to direct the important works. But among the lesser operas that came his way were Mozart's *Così fan tutte* and Verdi's *Un ballo in maschera*, a classification indicative of public taste at the time. *Aus Italien* was first performed in Munich in March 1887 and divided the audience into applauders and booers, thereby giving this eminently uncontroversial work a *cachet de scandale* which assisted its progress. In 1887, while guest conducting in Leipzig, Strauss met Mahler, whom he immediately admired and liked; and on his summer holiday he fell in love with a soprano, Pauline de Ahna, daughter of a Wagner-loving general. The principal work on which he was engaged was a symphonic poem – or tone poem, to use the term he preferred – based on Shakespeare's *Macbeth*, and when it was completed in 1888 he at once began another, *Don Juan*. His mentor was still Bülow, who suggested revisions in *Macbeth* and also recommended him to the Weimar Opera as assistant conductor.

Strauss left Munich in 1889; during that summer he worked as répétiteur at Bayreuth, where he found favour with Cosima Wagner. He took with him to Weimar the completed score of *Don Juan* and the two tasks on which he was working, his libretto for an opera, *Guntram*, and a rough sketch of a tone poem, *Tod und Verklärung*. His employers at Weimar were deeply impressed by *Don Juan* when he played it to them on the piano, and they insisted that its first performance should be at a Weimar concert. Although he was doubtful of the orchestra's ability to cope with the work's unprecedented technical difficulties, Strauss conducted it on 11 November 1889. It was his biggest triumph to date and thenceforward he was generally regarded as the most significant and progressive German composer since Wagner. Seven months later, at an Eisenach concert, he conducted the first performances of his *Burleske* for piano and orchestra and *Tod und Verklärung*. The following October he conducted the revised *Macbeth* at Weimar. Meanwhile Pauline de Ahna had joined the Weimar company and sang Isolde in *Tristan* when Strauss conducted it, uncut, after advice from Cosima, in January 1892. With *Così fan tutte* it remained Strauss's favourite opera throughout his life.

1. Richard Strauss, c1890

In June 1892 Strauss was seriously ill and spent the winter in Egypt. He completed the music of *Guntram* in Cairo and conducted the first performance in Weimar in May 1894 with Pauline as the heroine Freihild. An indication of Strauss's reputation at this date is that, after Bülow's death in 1894, the Berlin PO invited him to take over Bülow's concerts, but the venture was not a success, Strauss admitting that he was not yet ready for such a post. He had, however, been asked back to Munich as associate to the ailing Levi and had accepted, though with reluctance, on Cosima Wagner's advice. He was to begin his duties there on 1 October 1894; in the preceding August he conducted for the first time at Bayreuth (*Tannhäuser*) and on 10 September he married Pauline. His wedding present to her was the four superb songs of his op.27, *Morgen, Cäcilie, Ruhe, meine Seele* and *Heimliche Aufforderung*.

With Levi frequently ill, Strauss had the satisfaction in Munich of conducting *Tristan* and *Die Meistersinger* and a Mozart festival of *Die Entführung, Così fan tutte* and *Don Giovanni*. In his second season *Guntram* was staged for one disastrous performance. Two of the leading singers refused to take part and the orchestra petitioned the Intendant to spare them from 'this scourge of God'. Strauss was embittered by this attitude in his native city and eventually had his revenge. The years 1894–9 were exceptionally prolific in compositions. In addition to many lieder he wrote, one after the other, four of his best orchestral works, *Till Eulenspiegels lustige Streiche* (1894–5), *Also sprach Zarathustra* (1895–6), *Don Quixote* (1896–7) and *Ein Heldenleben* (1897–8). All were well received and consolidated his position as the outstanding composer of his day, regarded as the arch-fiend of modernism and cacophony because of the huge instrumental forces, the innovatory design and the naturalistic effects employed in these masterpieces.

But it is easy to overlook Strauss's ability and reputation as a conductor, which he regarded as his principal role at this time. The musical life of Germany and Austria in the 1890s and 1900s was dominated by three conductors who were known also as composers, Mahler, Strauss and Weingartner. Strauss was in constant demand as guest conductor of his own works and he visited Holland, Spain, France and England in 1897, the year in which his son was born. By now he was chief conductor of the Munich Opera, Levi having retired in 1896, but he had no hesitation in 1898 in accepting the post of chief conductor of the Royal Court Opera in Berlin. This was no sinecure: in his first eight-month season he conducted 71 performances of 25 operas, including two first performances and a *Ring* cycle. In the ensuing years he made many conducting tours and also conducted concerts of the Berlin Tonkünstler Orchestra and later the Berlin PO. He was ever ready to champion the unfamiliar and new. At Weimar he had revived several Liszt works (such as the *Faust Symphony*) and these remained in his repertory. In Berlin he conducted the music of Reger, Mahler, Schillings, Sibelius and Elgar. Another important feature of Strauss's life at this period was the beginning in 1898 of his seven-year campaign for a revision of German copyright law and the establishment of a performing-right society. He was always alive to the value of money, and many are the gibes about his constant talk of royalties. But he saw no reason why a composer

should not be well remunerated for his work and persistently championed his colleagues' rights in this respect as well as his own.

3. THE ACCLAIMED OPERA COMPOSER, 1898–1918. In 1898 Strauss met the poet and satirist Ernst von Wolzogen (1855–1934) to whom he confided his wish to 'wreak some vengeance' on Munich for the way it had treated him over *Guntram* by composing an opera lampooning the city's philistinism. Strauss found a suitable subject in a Flemish medieval legend. Wolzogen transferred the action to medieval Munich and introduced puns and allusions into the text about the sorcerer, Richard Wagner, and his apprentice Strauss, thus providing Strauss with an equal opportunity for musical jokes and quotations. The one-act opera was called *Feuersnot* and was completed in 1901. Its première was in Dresden, under Ernst von Schuch, thereby inaugurating a long association between Strauss and the Dresden Opera. *Feuersnot* was an instant success, being a considerable advance on the pseudo-Wagnerian *Guntram*, and it was introduced to Vienna by Mahler and to London (in 1910) by Beecham. In 1903 Strauss completed another large-scale orchestral work, the *Symphonia domestica*, which described events in his home life. He conducted the first performance on 21 March 1904 in New York on his first visit to the USA. The content of the work caused a furore, but this was nothing compared with the sensational reaction to his next opera, *Salome*, a setting of a German translation of Oscar Wilde's play. It was produced at Dresden on 9 December 1905. Almost everywhere *Salome* ran into censorship trouble and was regarded as the ultimate in salacious and blasphemous art. But this merely provided profitable publicity for the opera, which was a great success with the public, who like to be shocked, and was performed by 50 opera houses within two years. With the royalties Strauss built the villa at Garmisch in which Pauline and he lived from 1908 until the ends of their lives. Strauss followed *Salome* with *Elektra*, another one-act opera about an obsessed woman, his first collaboration with the Austrian poet and dramatist Hugo von Hofmannsthal. Strauss had seen Max Reinhardt's stage production of Hofmannsthal's version of Sophocles and had asked the poet if he would adapt it as a libretto. From the first Strauss recognized the possibilities in a permanent association with Hofmannsthal, poles apart though they were in character and outlook. 'We were born for one another and are certain to do fine things together', he wrote. *Elektra* was produced at Dresden under Schuch on 25 January 1909. It failed to make as great an impression as *Salome* had, but opera houses were eager to stage it and it enjoyed notoriety as the height (or depth) of cacophonous modernity, even Ernest Newman referring to the music as 'abominably ugly'.

The next Strauss–Hofmannsthal collaboration was a three-act 'comedy for music', *Der Rosenkavalier*, set in the 18th-century Vienna of the Empress Maria Theresia and making glorious anachronistic use of the waltz. It was composed between spring 1909 and September 1910. Schuch again conducted the first performance, lavishly produced under Reinhardt's supervision and with settings by Alfred Roller, at Dresden on 26 January 1911. By now Strauss's operas were awaited with the highest expectations and attended by intensive

2. Design by Alfred Roller for Act 3 of 'Der Rosenkavalier', first performed at the Dresden Court Opera on 26 January 1911; see ROLLER, ALFRED *for one of his designs for 'Elektra'*

advance publicity. Special *Rosenkavalier* trains ran from Berlin to Dresden, and several other opera houses produced the work within days of the Dresden première. The opera won an immediate public acclaim which has never abated; indeed it has intensified. *Der Rosenkavalier* was followed in 1912 by the unusual experiment of the first version of *Ariadne auf Naxos*, in which the first part was a performance of Molière's *Le bourgeois gentilhomme* with incidental music by Strauss, and the second a one-act opera *Ariadne auf Naxos*, in which characters from the *commedia dell'arte* intermingled with the mythological figures. It was not a success and had little prospect of a future because such a hybrid depended on the extreme difficulty of obtaining first-rate companies of actors and singers simultaneously. In 1916 Strauss and Hofmannsthal, who had come near to a split over this work, revised it by scrapping the Molière play and substituting a sung prologue which proved to be one of Strauss's most effective and novel stage pieces. In this form the work was produced in Vienna on 4 October 1916, with Lotte Lehmann singing the travesty role of the Composer in the prologue, Maria Jeritza as Ariadne and Selma Kurz as Zerbinetta. Notwithstanding this vocal galaxy, it was still not a success and made its way comparatively slowly towards its present relative popularity. In fact, after *Der Rosenkavalier*, Strauss never again enjoyed unalloyed success with any of his works. Those who expected him to continue to provide the sensational frissons of *Salome* and *Elektra* were convinced that with *Rosenkavalier* he had 'gone soft', changed direction and retreated into comfortable note-spinning.

Strauss's first non-operatic collaboration with Hofmannsthal was in 1912–14 on a ballet for Dyagilev, *Josephs-Legende*, for which Hofmannsthal and Count Harry Kessler devised the scenario. Produced on an excessively lavish scale in Paris on 14 May 1914, it was also staged in London at Drury Lane on 23 June conducted by Beecham, who had introduced all Strauss's existing operas except *Guntram* to London between 1910 and 1913. While in England Strauss received the honorary degree of DMus from Oxford University to mark his 50th birthday. He was already at work on another opera, *Die Frau ohne Schatten*, a symbolic fairy tale that Hofmannsthal described as 'related to

Zauberflöte as *Rosenkavalier* is to *Figaro*'. Progress was interrupted by the outbreak of war in August 1914 (one consequence of which was the sequestration of a large part of his savings, which he had banked in England with the German-born financier Sir Edgar Speyer). Strauss therefore completed scoring the last of his important orchestral tone poems, *Eine Alpensinfonie*, on which he had been working intermittently since 1911, and conducted the first performance on 28 October 1915 in Berlin. In 1917 he then added more incidental music for a further Hofmannsthal adaptation of *Le bourgeois gentilhomme*. Strauss told Hofmannsthal in 1916 that he wanted to compose 'an entirely modern, absolutely realistic domestic and character comedy', but the poet responded with distaste and recommended Hermann Bahr as a possible librettist. Strauss outlined his ideas for an opera based on a marital misunderstanding between Pauline and himself some years earlier. Bahr sketched out a libretto; Strauss replied with some of his own suggestions which Bahr enjoyed so much that he withdrew, insisting that in this case the composer should be his own librettist: in July 1917 Strauss completed the libretto of *Intermezzo*, but he did not complete the music until 1923.

4. AFTER WORLD WAR I, 1919–49. Since 1910 Strauss had been a regular guest conductor of the Berlin Opera but this association ended in 1918. He thereupon signed a five-year contract with the Vienna Staatsoper, to run from 1919, as joint director with Franz Schalk. Just before this association began Schalk conducted the first performance of *Die Frau ohne Schatten* on 10 October 1919. The work's difficulties in the matter of staging proved a severe handicap to its success, despite a brilliant cast. Strauss and Schalk had at their command the services of such singers as Jeritza, Lehmann, Kurz, Elisabeth Schumann, Maria Olczewska, Leo Slezak, Alfred Piccaver, Richard Tauber, Karl Aagard-Oestvig, Alfred Jerger and Richard Mayr. Strauss not only conducted but in effect produced the great classical repertory in a memorable manner. He was incontestably a great conductor. The demonstrative gestures of his youth had given way to a laconic almost motionless style, but its effectiveness was undeniable. Erich Kleiber has described how Strauss, like Nikisch, could produce

3. Strauss at work on 'Die schweigsame Frau'

tremendous crescendos in the final pages of *Tristan* simply by slowly raising his left hand. In spite of these artistic successes, however, there was continual tension between Schalk and Strauss; moreover, the Austrian civil servants who now ran the Staatsoper considered that Strauss was financially extravagant (his reply was: 'I am here to lose money'). The inevitable result was his engineered resignation in 1924, although to mark his 60th birthday the city of Vienna had presented him with a plot of land in the Belvedere on which he built a splendid house. He therefore remained an influential figure in the city and two years later returned to the Staatsoper as a guest conductor.

Strauss's creative output slackened during his Vienna conductorship, which accounted for his slow progress with *Intermezzo*. His ballet *Schlagobers* (completed 1922, performed 1924) was a flop, and in 1924 he wrote the *Parergon zur Symphonia domestica* for piano and orchestra for the one-armed pianist Paul Wittgenstein. *Intermezzo* was produced at Dresden on 4 November 1924, conducted by Fritz Busch. The partnership with Hofmannsthal was resumed in 1923 with the two-act opera *Die ägyptische Helena*, which Busch also conducted at its Dresden première on 6 June 1928. It was a failure there and in Vienna and New York; it strengthened the general contemporary critical view that Strauss the composer was an extinct volcano, out of touch with the postwar world and having not only nothing new but nothing at all to say. Since 1922 Strauss had persistently asked Hofmannsthal for 'another *Rosenkavalier*, without its mistakes and longueurs'. Hof-

mannsthal believed in 1928 that he had found the answer in *Arabella*, which was also set in Vienna but otherwise bore little resemblance to the earlier work. He and Strauss were still revising the completed libretto when on 15 July 1929 Hofmannsthal died from a stroke. Strauss began to compose the music as a tribute, but after rapidly completing the first act he faltered and did not finish the rest until 1932.

In the meantime, in 1931, Strauss had found a new librettist, the Jewish novelist and biographer Stefan Zweig, who offered him an adaptation of Ben Jonson's *Epicene, or The Silent Woman*. Strauss was delighted with it and in 1933 began to compose *Die schweigsame Frau*. But this was the year the National Socialists, with Hitler as chancellor, came to full power in Germany. Strauss had spent his life until he was over 50 as a court composer, accustomed to ignoring politics while he carried out his musical duties. He was totally obsessed by music, which was in every sense his life. He was contemptuous of most politicians: they came and went while he went his chosen way. Yet he was a German patriot too. Also, he was nearing 70, late in life to abandon one's home and country as other German musicians were doing. The Nazis realized that Strauss's eminence was valuable to them as propaganda. He played into their hands at the 1933 Bayreuth Festival when he conducted *Parsifal* in place of Toscanini, who had withdrawn in protest against the Nazis' attitude to the Jews. Strauss acted to save the festival and because of his veneration of Wagner, but his gesture was misunderstood by the opponents of Hitler and he was branded as a supporter of the dictator. Goebbels, minister of propaganda, capitalized on this in November 1933, when he established a state music bureau, the Reichsmusikkammer, and proclaimed Strauss as president without even consulting him.

The realities of the situation began to dawn on Strauss when German theatres were forbidden to produce works by Jews and he was denounced on the radio for working with Zweig. Wisely, Zweig went to Zurich and realized that he could no longer collaborate with Strauss. But Strauss could not accept this and suggested a secret arrangement. All that Zweig would agree to do was to suggest subjects and to supervise their compilation by others. Strauss replied to Zweig in an indiscreet letter posted in Dresden, where *Die schweigsame Frau* was in rehearsal, and which was intercepted by the Gestapo. He discovered that Zweig's name had been omitted from the posters and programmes and demanded its restoration. This was done, but Hitler and Goebbels, who had promised to attend the première, stayed away, and after four performances the opera was banned throughout Germany. At the same time Strauss was ordered to resign his presidency of the Reichsmusikkammer on the grounds of ill-health. Strauss then wrote an obsequious letter to Hitler, but he was now desperate to protect not himself but his daughter-in-law Alice, who was Jewish, and her children.

Zweig recommended the Viennese theatrical archivist Josef Gregor as librettist for the next opera subject that Strauss and he had selected, an episode in the Thirty Years War. Strauss did not much like Gregor or his work and treated him contemptuously. The opera was to be entitled *Friedenstag*, and Zweig revised the sections of libretto with which Strauss was dissatisfied. *Friedenstag* is a hymn to peace and it is extraordinary that it was accepted in Nazi Germany when it had its first performance in Munich in July 1938; indeed, it achieved 100 performances in two years. It is in one act and was intended as half of a double bill with *Daphne*, completed in 1937, though they are usually performed separately. Strauss's third opera with Gregor, *Die Liebe der Danae*, was a reworking of a scenario Hofmannsthal had sent to Strauss in 1920. As in *Daphne*, certain problems in the libretto were solved by the conductor Clemens Krauss, who had been a favourite Strauss interpreter since the 1920s, and it was Krauss who became librettist of what proved to be Strauss's last opera, the 'conversation piece' *Capriccio*, composed in 1940–41 and first performed in Munich in October 1942.

After the outbreak of war in 1939 the 75-year-old Strauss was of little interest to the Nazi authorities, but in Garmisch his refusal to allow evacuees into his home resulted in ostracism for Alice Strauss and her children. In 1941 the Strauss family were permitted to reoccupy their Vienna home. Strauss was content anywhere, provided he could work, and in Vienna he wrote the Horn Concerto no.2 and the first of two sonatinas for wind instruments, almost, it would seem, in deliberate reversion to the type of music he wrote as a youth. As one might have expected, the enormities of what Nazi Germany had brought upon the world and itself only began to affect him when related to music. The destruction of the Munich Nationaltheater in 1943, followed by the destruction of the opera houses of Dresden, Weimar and Vienna, finally brought home to him the tragedy of his country. He had also fallen foul of Hitler's second-in-command, Martin Bormann, and was protected only by the favour of Baldur von Schirach, governor of Vienna. Although celebrations of Strauss's 80th birthday in June 1944 were officially discouraged, both Schirach and Krauss ensured that it was substantially marked. Strauss had adamantly refused to allow a production of *Die Liebe der Danae* until after the war, but he yielded to Krauss's persuasion and the première was arranged for the 1944 Salzburg Festival. After the bomb plot against Hitler in July 1944, the festival was cancelled and the *Danae* première became a dress rehearsal on 16 August. Strauss's creative response to the ghastly shambles around him was to compose *Metamorphosen* in spring 1945. This 'study for 23 solo strings' is an elegy for the German musical life of which Strauss had been a leader for half a century. After the surrender of Germany in May 1945 Strauss began the Oboe Concerto, which reflects nothing of the time in which it was written. In October that year he and Pauline went into voluntary exile in Switzerland. Because he had held official office under the Nazi regime Strauss was an automatic candidate for a 'denazification' tribunal. In Zurich and Montreux he was unmolested and heard the first performances of his Oboe Concerto, *Metamorphosen*, the Wind Sonatina no.2 and the Duett-Concertino for clarinet, bassoon and strings. These are all mellow in spirit and wonderfully refined in technique, and are generally known as the works of Strauss's 'Indian summer', a convenient name for his final period, which may be said to have begun with *Capriccio*.

The hand of reconciliation was extended to Strauss by Britain in 1947, when Beecham instigated a Strauss festival in London and invited him to attend. He spent 4–31 October in London, his first visit since 1936 when he had received the gold medal of the Royal Philharmonic Society, and conducted several of his compositions. On his return to Switzerland his health began to fail. In June 1948 he heard that his name had been cleared by the denazification board and he was free to return to Garmisch. First, however, he had a severe operation, and did not go home until May 1949, taking with him four wonderful songs with orchestra, composed during 1948, which were to be his last work and were published posthumously as *Vier letzte Lieder*. He took part in the Munich celebrations of his 85th birthday, but his heart began to fail in August and he died peacefully on 8 September 1949. One of his last remarks, utterly characteristic, was made to his daughter-in-law: 'Dying is just as I composed it in *Tod und Verklärung*'.

5. WORKS: INTRODUCTION. During his lifetime and afterwards Strauss was the centre of controversy, and he remains one of those composers who arouse extremes of sympathy or antipathy. There are inevitable variations in the quality of his work, some of it not much more than musical journalism of the kind most court composers turned out as part of their obligations. But the distance between the peak and the base in a graph of Strauss's output is not as wide as it was once believed, and the former critical ordinance that he declined into a state of unimaginative self-repetition after about 1918 is untenable when his achievement is judged in perspective. It is easy to understand how such a view of him became widespread outside Germany, and even inside it.

The years from roughly 1890 to 1910 were a brilliant noonday for Strauss, as they were for Elgar in England, when he bestrode the musical world and audiences hung on his every note. He dazzled, he shocked, he amazed. After such a sustained *fortissimo* there was bound to be a diminuendo, and in Strauss's case it was all the steeper because, with the cataclysm of World War I followed by his absorption into the world of the Vienna Staatsoper, he effectively 'disappeared' for a decade. Within that time the face of music changed. Strauss's audacities became the norm; worse, they became outdated clichés in the postwar reaction against Romanticism. A new modernism sprang up. Many strident voices competed for a hearing, Bartók, Stravinsky, Hindemith, Berg, Schoenberg, Satie and Prokofiev among them. It was not that Strauss had nothing left to say within his idiom; people no longer listened to him. His new works rarely penetrated beyond Germany and Austria; opera houses and orchestras contented themselves with the pre-1914 successes. It was as if he were dead.

Strauss saw no reason to change his style to accord with what his friend Romain Rolland called the 'new frenzy' in music. But he was still much concerned with extending his range within the confines of his style and creative personality. This involved a certain amount of experiment, tame by prevailing standards, and not all appreciated at the time. No retrogression was involved, for instance, in the opera *Intermezzo*, which adopted a cinematic stage technique paralleled by mastery of conversational recitative. The *Parergon zur Symphonia domestica* was one pianist's property, but the music had a harmonic toughness and melodic inventiveness which contradicted the self-indulgent confectionery of *Schlagobers*. Each of the operas *Arabella*, *Die schweigsame Frau* and *Daphne* marked a new stage in Strauss's treatment of words and music. Each was in a style appropriate to its content, showing a continual process of refinement which culminated in *Capriccio* and the other masterpieces of his last decade. The clues to Strauss's aesthetic are in two of his pronouncements: 'New ideas must search for new forms' – each of his 15 operas fulfils this precept – and 'Work is a constant and never tiring source of enjoyment to which I have dedicated myself'. This dedication to the 'holy art of music' (*Ariadne auf Naxos*) dominated Strauss's life as conductor and composer. He was a disciplined worker, planning months ahead and keeping to his schedule, goaded by his extraordinary wife. This is not a virtue in itself, nor does it guarantee good results, but because of Strauss's objective, self-denigrating attitude to his work, about which there are many anecdotes, the impression is sometimes given of a casual dilettante. Nothing could be further from the truth. He was completely professional.

Strauss's seemingly relaxed attitude to life, whether he was composing, conducting or playing skat, was a primary source of inspiration. 'Everything I have done casually, with my left hand, has turned out particularly well', he remarked. The elegant *Bourgeois gentilhomme* music was, he said, done with his 'left hand'. Like Elgar, he claimed to think in terms of music at all hours. His sketchbook never left his side; he composed an important theme of *Rosenkavalier* while playing skat. He was unusually and interestingly frank about his methods:

I often write down a motif or a melody, then put it away for a year. When I return to it I find that quite unconsciously something in me – the imagination – has been at work on it. . . . Before I note down even the slightest sketch for an opera I allow the text to permeate my mind for at least six months and take root within me, so that I am wholly familiar with the situations and characters. Only then do I allow musical ideas to enter my head. The preliminary sketches become more elaborate sketches which are written down, worked on, put into shape as a piano score and worked on again, often up to four times. This is the difficult part of the work. I finally write the score in my study, straight through and without effort, working up to twelve hours a day.

Karl Böhm has related how in 1936, when Strauss showed him the libretto of *Daphne*, he noticed that on the margins Strauss had jotted down notes concerning rhythms, tonality and precise indications of the musical form concerning several characters. 'And he had needed', Böhm said, 'scarcely any more time than it took to read through the text.' Strauss was a master of melody: he thought of himself as able to invent only short themes, and many of his wide-spaced operatic melodies are derived from fragmentary phrases. 'I work on melodies for a very long time', he told Max Marschalk, 'what matters is not the beginning of the melody but its continuation, its development into a perfect melodic shape.' Strauss here seems to be supporting the epigram that inspiration means perspiration, yet his ability, which never deserted him, to invent an immediately memorable phrase to depict a character or situation was perhaps his greatest asset as a composer. Examples that come readily to mind are the eruption at the start of *Don Juan* (once described as 'like champagne corks popping'), the *Till Eulenspiegel* motif on the horn, the first bars of *Der Rosenkavalier*, the clarinet arpeggio in C♯ minor that opens *Salome*, the *Don Quixote* theme, the Falcon's cry in *Die Frau ohne Schatten*, and the Child's theme in the *Symphonia domestica*. He was also a thematic kleptomaniac. He made quotation and self-quotation into an art, and many of his motifs are modelled on those of other composers (he

4. Richard Strauss, 1947

would have echoed Vaughan Williams's 'Why should music be original?'). His credo was expressive beauty of sound, vocal and instrumental. He remained true to it, and if there are times when he settled too easily for a cloying sweetness in place of a changing harmonic texture that is an entry on the debit side of an account overwhelmingly in credit.

6. EARLY WORKS. The music Strauss wrote as a youth amply confirms his statement that his father refused to let him study anything but the classics. The prevalent influences are Beethoven and Mendelssohn. There is no doubt about the melodic fertility and facility, but the disciplines of sonata form were obviously irksome and unwelcome. The A major String Quartet is a student's exercise, accomplished but unremarkable. It is significant that the first glimpses of the mature Strauss occur in the piano pieces *Stimmungsbilder* of 1882–4, where formal restrictions were abandoned in favour of atmospheric tone-painting. Strauss's struggle for self-expression while fettered by classical procedures is eloquently evident in the Cello Sonata, a splendid work in spite of its formal deficiencies. Joachim congratulated Strauss on the lyrical opening outburst, with good reason, for the work, though heavily overlaid with sequential repetitions, has a vitality that has ensured its survival. The slightly earlier Violin Concerto is less ambitious but melodically attractive; it has no cadenza.

Much the best of the works composed in 1881–3, however, are the one-movement Serenade for 13 wind instruments (normal double woodwind, four horns and contrabassoon or optional bass tuba) and the Horn Concerto no.1. Although Strauss himself later dismissed the Serenade as 'no more than the respectable work of a music student', it is easy to hear how its mellifluous grace must have attracted Bülow. Although the work is in sonata form, Strauss avoided his weak point, the development, by substituting an independent central episode in B minor linking exposition and recapitulation. Unity is maintained in this section by pervasive use of a six-note figure derived from the work's second subject. But the outstanding feature is the assured blending and contrasting of instrumental sonorities. The Suite in B♭ for the same combination is in four movements and exposes formal deficiencies, but it is prophetic of Strauss's skill in manipulating short themes and has instrumental felicities, such as the oboe solos, which are pointers to his maturity. It is in the Horn Concerto no.1 that Strauss first fully overcame structural difficulties. Three short movements are played without a break. The solo horn's opening fanfare is metamorphosed into the rondo finale's principal subject, while another horn figure is worked into the texture of each movement. There are other thematic links throughout. An odd feature of the concerto is that while the solo part is written for the valved F horn, the orchestral horn parts are for the valveless E♭ crook. Compared with this delightful and still fresh-sounding concerto, the Symphony in F minor of 1883–4 is a reversion. On a large scale and in cyclic form, it displays Strauss's orchestral mastery in the Scherzo and Andante cantabile; but the contrived recapitulation in the finale of themes from the preceding movements makes a lame conclusion to a work that won high praise at its early performances but was soon to be overtaken by Strauss's progress in new directions. It was in any case overtaken

by the contemporaneous Piano Quartet in C minor, also on a large scale but more successful in its formal procedures. The melodic content is heavily indebted to Brahms, but at last Strauss's first-movement development section is logical and sounds spontaneous, and he was in full control of his grandiose design. Therefore the quartet represented a significant advance, consolidated four years later, in 1887, in Strauss's last chamber work and his last 'classical' piece, the Violin Sonata. It is true that this excellent work tends to break the bonds of its format – the violin part has an operatic grandeur and the piano writing suggests orchestration – but it is exciting and rewarding to perform, as Heifetz's lifelong affection for it testifies, and it contains many surprises in the shape of references to Schubert's *Erlkönig* and Beethoven's 'Pathétique' Sonata and in the chromatic modulations in the coda to the finale.

The Violin Sonata was composed later than the two works that marked the true end of the period of apprenticeship, the *Burleske* for piano and orchestra and the symphonic fantasy *Aus Italien*. They are especially significant as signposts to the later Strauss. The *Burleske* began as a Scherzo which Strauss wrote in 1885 for Bülow, who from a sight of the score declared it unplayable while Strauss himself wrote it off as 'nonsense' after a run-through with the Meiningen Orchestra. Not until he showed it in 1890 to Eugen d'Albert, who was enthusiastic, did he give it its present title. It is in extended sonata form, a weakness because it is just a few minutes too long, and there are still Brahmsian echoes, but here for the first time is the witty, sparkling Strauss, playboy of the orchestra, teeming with ideas. Here, too, is the first intrusion of waltz rhythm into a Strauss work. Like Mahler with the march and the ländler, Strauss was happy to draw elements of popular music into his scheme, and the waltz fulfilled this purpose admirably until it became a mannerism. *Aus Italien* was composed in 1886, and Strauss called it 'the connecting link between the old and new methods'. It is not yet a tone poem, nor, in spite of its four movements, is it a symphony, at least no more than is Berlioz's *Harold en Italie*, the genre to which it belongs. But certainly 'the poetic idea was really the formative element' of this picturesque evocation of the sights, sounds and atmosphere of Strauss's first visit to Italy. The Lisztian first movement, 'Auf der Campagna', is structurally the best and most advanced, but the divided strings of the second movement and the vivid depiction of sunlight on sea in the third by means of 'cascades' for violins and flutes are outstanding pointers to the brilliance of the later tone poems. This third movement is noteworthy in three other respects: as in the wind Serenade an independent episode takes the place of a development; Strauss imitated Liszt's example in following his poetic instinct by juxtaposing the various sections of the movement, eliminating the 'rules' of classical procedure; and in the final bars he first used his favourite device of a harmonic side-slip (i.e. writing as if he was to modulate into a distant key and suddenly sidling into the tonic).

7. TONE POEMS AND OTHER ORCHESTRAL WORKS. Between 1888 and 1898 Strauss composed the tone poems on which his fame and popularity in the concert hall chiefly rest. The first, *Macbeth*, is experimental and still not mature Strauss. There is no attempt to follow the detailed action of Shakespeare's play, though certain

5. *The opening of 'Ein Heldenleben', from the autograph fair copy, begun 2 August 1898*

incidents are used. Instead the work is a psychological study. It is in one movement of extended sonata form, in which the lengthy development incorporates two self-contained episodes. *Macbeth* is a striking work, but not as striking as its successors, hence its relative neglect. Its opus number, 23, is later than that of *Don Juan* (op.20), because it was heavily revised and was not performed and published until 1890, a year after *Don Juan*. Like *Macbeth*, *Don Juan* is a sonata movement with self-contained episodes, but the difference is remarkable. Under the impact of his love for Pauline de Ahna, Strauss turned to Lenau's fragmentary poem about Don Juan as the basis for a controlled masterpiece into which the fiery ardour of youth was injected with a passion that has never faded. From it dates the appearance of the real Strauss. Its magnificent opening, a theme comprising all the principal elements of the structure, is presented with an orchestral virtuosity that is the strongest evidence of what Strauss had already learnt as a conductor. What he had learnt as a composer is evident in every bar, but nowhere more impressively than in the love scenes, which besides being extremely ardent are distinguished by the broad sweeping cantilena that he was to exploit so tellingly in his operas. Not only had he learnt unprecedented pyrotechnics, at the same time he had mastered the secret of musical continuity.

For *Tod und Verklärung* (1888–9) Strauss provided a detailed synopsis which the music exactly illustrates: an artist, on his deathbed suffering physical agonies, recalls his youth and his unfulfilled idealism; he dies, and his soul achieves transfiguration. The poem by Alexander Ritter printed in the score was written after the music had been composed. The design of this tone poem can still be distantly related to sonata form, divided into slow introduction, symphonic *allegro* and epilogue, the principal themes recurring cyclically. Harmonic dissonances, no longer remarkable, caused a stir in 1890 and contributed to Strauss's growing notoriety as an *enfant terrible*. Although the concluding 'transfiguration' section in C major falls some way short of its sublime target, the harmonic modulations, most imaginatively deployed, are of great beauty if sensitively played.

Five years passed before the appearance of the next tone poem, *Till Eulenspiegels lustige Streiche* (1894–5), described as a rondo (the work's full title in English is 'Till Eulenspiegel's merry pranks, after the old rogue's tale, set for large orchestra in rondo form'). Strauss had contemplated a one-act opera on this subject, but the failure of *Guntram* in 1894 discouraged him. His change of mind was fortunate, though, for in the tone poem the witty and pawky side of Strauss appears fully clad in his new-found virtuosity. *Till* is a masterpiece on every level, as a programmatic description of the rogue's pranks in detail, as a generalized portrait of a scamp, or as an example of musical humour. It is in some respects, too, a self-portrait of Strauss delighting in his affront to the bourgeois philistines of Munich who thought his music so outrageous; he exploited this vein of waspish humour five years later in the opera *Feuersnot*. The thematic transformations in *Till* are ingenious and spontaneous, the scoring deft, picturesque and always apt; and the expansion in the coda-epilogue of the 'once upon a time' introduction is one of those inspired finishing touches, like the end of *Der Rosenkavalier*, in which Strauss specialized. *Till* requires quadruple woodwind, including the D clarinet. The horns were increased to six in *Also sprach Zarathustra* (1895–6), a musical commentary on Nietzsche's poem rather than its programmatic musical equivalent. If Strauss's strong sense of publicity governed his choice of a subject involving the controversial doctrine of the 'superman', it was surely his Bavarian sense of humour that presented the 'Dance of the Superman' as a luscious Viennese waltz. *Zarathustra* marks an advance in Strauss's use of one-movement form, the work being a free fantasia unified by the C–G–C nature motif heard at the outset. The orchestral mastery may be taken for granted, but

Strauss's full maturity can be gauged from his confident exploitation of the contrasts between the tonalities of C and B, unresolved even in the final chords. If the use of the 12 notes of the chromatic scale in the slow fugue theme denoting science seems contrived, the still astonishing polytonal effects elsewhere in the work and its beautiful final nocturne have ensured it a secure place in the repertory of great orchestras.

In 1896–7 Strauss composed the most poetic, if not the finest of his orchestral works, *Don Quixote*, 'fantastic variations on a theme of knightly character'. It was an inspiration to use variation form for the Don's adventures; inspired, too, to cast the work as a kind of sinfonia concertante, with solo cello and viola representing (though not exclusively) Don Quixote and Sancho Panza. Strauss's command of musical pictorialism becomes almost arrogantly realistic in *Don Quixote*: windmills, sheep (woodwind and muted brass playing minor 2nds in flutter-tonguing) and the flying horse are as vividly illustrated as by any graphic artist, and it is this aspect of the work which has too often been emphasized at the expense of the extremely subtle psychological portrayal of Don Quixote's unhinged mental state by means of discordant and 'clouded' harmony, resolved only when the Don rides home over a throbbing pedal point.

Strauss regarded his next tone poem, *Ein Heldenleben* (1897–8), as a companion-piece to *Don Quixote*. They were companions in misunderstanding by some commentators. Because it coincided with the superman ethos of Kaiser Wilhelm II's Germany, with the growth of Prussian militarism and the architectural bombast of pre-1914 Berlin, *Ein Heldenleben* was ascribed to Strauss's 'megalomaniac' tendencies – here was a composer writing musical autobiography in terms of superhuman grandiosity, demanding eight horns, five trumpets and quadruple woodwind. But this was the age of the huge orchestra and Strauss, like Mahler, gloried in it. *Ein Heldenleben* is essentially another product of Strauss's Bavarian capacity for self-parody. His hero is no Nietzschean superman but a composer, a Kapellmeister, whose adversaries are the music critics, who is soothed and cajoled by his capricious wife (represented by the solo violin), whose battle against the critics is halted by his 'works of peace' – his own compositions – and who seeks peace, like Don Quixote, by retiring to the country (with a view of the Alps, as at Garmisch). That is the programme, divided into six sections, and illustrated by music of such inventiveness, humour and homogeneity that it is completely convincing as an abstract composition. Its only rival as musical autobiography on a scale as bizarre as it is undeniably effective is Berlioz's *Symphonie fantastique*.

Autobiography of a more intimate kind is the background of the *Symphonia domestica* (1902–3). Although Strauss removed details of the programme because, like Mahler, he wanted his music to be judged purely as music, the 'domestic symphony' is what its title implies: a picture of Strauss and Pauline at home, quarrelling, bathing the baby, working, loving, dreaming, waking. It is a one-movement symphony in four sections, and valid if regarded as nothing more. Again a vast orchestra is used, including four saxophones, but the scoring is often of chamber music delicacy. The invention is of high quality and the work has generally been underrated. In spite of the complex orchestral

6. Autograph sketch for Electra's monologue

apparatus used, there is some simplification of the harmonic style and this is carried further in *Eine Alpensinfonie* (1911–15), in which Strauss described a day in the mountains he could see from his study window in Garmisch. This work is the apotheosis of the Straussian orchestra (over 150 players), a gigantic piece of nature-painting in 22 sections which has a pantheistic exaltation, often expressed in naive diatonic terms, related to that of Mahler's Third Symphony. Of all his great orchestral works it relies least on any knowledge of the programme, and Strauss could claim with justice that he had fully learnt how to merge pictorialism and 'absolute' music into a seamless unified structure. *Eine Alpensinfonie* lacks the pungency of the earlier tone poems and the frenzied orchestral manner of the operas *Salome* and *Elektra*, but its superb contrapuntal texture and the sheer splendour of its sound contradict any suggestion of a creative decline simultaneous with the composition of *Der Rosenkavalier*. The fact that Strauss admitted that he enjoyed composing and said it came easily to him has perhaps engendered a too puritanical resistance by some listeners to such a sumptuous work as *Eine Alpensinfonie*.

Of Strauss's ballet scores, *Josephs-Legende* (1912–14) is the best because it comes nearest to being another tone poem. Strauss confessed difficulty in working up interest in 'good boy Joseph', and his invention became banal when called on to emulate innocence and purity. He could find the music for these qualities in Sophie in *Der Rosenkavalier*, but if they were associated with religion they had no appeal for his muse. *Schlagobers*

(1921–2) has little to commend it beyond a glib orchestral expertise decked out garishly. Strauss's arrangements of Couperin were originally made for the ballet stage in 1921 and 1941, but are better known as concert suites; they are among the several works for small orchestra that he wrote in the second half of his life, the first and finest of them being the suite of items salvaged from the incidental music to *Le bourgeois gentilhomme* (1920). The twin influences on Strauss's work were Wagner and Mozart, and his output could almost be divided into Wagner works and Mozart works, with some mixtures (*Der Rosenkavalier*, for example). The *Gentilhomme* music is a Mozart work, though it pays lip-service to Lully. It is no 17th-century pastiche; rather the age of Molière is re-created by a 20th-century artist with incomparable wit and grace. The spirit of Mozart is more explicitly acknowledged in the 'Indian summer' works of 1942–8. The two late wind sonatinas outstay their welcome because Strauss, who admitted he had 'a complicated brain', seems to have been enjoying solving ingenious contrapuntal problems for their own sake. The Oboe Concerto, however, is almost perfect in form and execution, a late swallow of particular charm. But the greatest of the last orchestral works is *Metamorphosen*, a symphonic *adagio* of Mahlerian intensity in which Strauss's inveterate skill in weaving elaborate string textures is no mere 'wrist exercise' but a profound expression of his agony of mind over the destruction of the German culture that had nurtured him. The music's poignancy is heightened by the thematic allusions to Wagner and Beethoven.

8. OPERAS. Strauss's operas cover the development of his style from 1892, when he began to compose *Guntram*, to 1941, when he wrote the magical ending of *Capriccio*. They are his most important contribution to music. A leitmotif of his operatic career was his preoccupation with the clarity of the words, culminating in his using the relative importance of words and music in opera as the theme of his last stage work. His harmonic and tonal procedures deserve close study throughout, especially his predilection for associating certain keys with individuals or situations (e.g. in *Elektra*, B♭ for Agamemnon and E♭ for Chrysothemis). He had worked out his eloquent and agile harmonic idiom in the tone poems, and it stood him in good dramatic stead in the operas. At the start of *Don Juan*, there is an abrupt switch from C major into E major, and at the close of the *Heldenleben* love-music the modulation from G minor to D minor is above a sustained G♭ major chord. The polytonal 'excesses' of *Elektra*, with A major and E♭ minor combined, shocked Debussy because of their 'cold-blooded' audacity. The rich and sustained harmonic texture of the operas from *Rosenkavalier* derives from a technique involving frequent use of multiple suspensions, passing notes and anticipations, and the combination of major and minor elements. The superb arching love-songs are usually in keys with many flats or sharps, D♭ major especially and F♯ major.

Strauss's first opera *Guntram* (1892–3) has never held the stage, even in its heavily cut revision of 1940, when Strauss ruefully acknowledged that 'the whole of *Guntram* is a prelude'. He inherited from Wagner the principle of a continuous, seamless texture and a leitmotif system with the orchestra in a dominating role. But only in *Guntram* did he use opera as a propaganda vehicle for a doctrine. It was a work he had to get out of his system, though there is delight to be found in its anticipations of later and greater works, as well as amusement at the plagiarisms from *Tristan* and other Wagner operas. Nor can there be any denial of the mastery of orchestral and vocal techniques; coming after *Don Juan* and *Tod und Verklärung* it can scarcely be called immature. But veneration for Wagner all too often in *Guntram* snuffed out the original Strauss who composed those masterpieces. How well Strauss had learnt his lesson seven years later is apparent in *Feuersnot* (1900–01), which, whatever its faults and difficulties, is a brilliantly effective satire on philistinism executed in Strauss's lighter manner. The seeds of *Der Rosenkavalier* (and its waltzes) can be found throughout *Feuersnot*. The plot was considered shocking in its day and contributed to the impression of Strauss as a scandalizer, which received vast reinforcement with the production of *Salome* (1903–5).

Like *Feuersnot*, *Salome* is in one act and, with slight exaggeration, can be called a tone poem with vocal interludes. All the atmospheric power and thematic dexterity of the tone poems are used in this story of a 16-year-old virgin's perverse obsessions. Naturally the word 'decadence' was much applied to this opera, a tribute to Strauss's skill, perhaps with one eye on the success of *Tosca*, in purveying the flavour of Wilde's *fin-de-siècle* Romanticism even in German translation. The instrumental inventiveness of the score is breathtaking, but its sultry beauty, the evocation of the Palestinian night, the vivid delineation of Herod's character and Salome's final 'Liebestod' after her controversial dance

are its lasting assets. It is a virtuoso display of the creation of atmospheric colour by instrumental means.

However, its successor, *Elektra* (1906–8), on what is in several respects a similar subject, owes its power to its musical structure, to architecture rather than to painting. In his excitement with his first Hofmannsthal libretto, Strauss matched the gruesome subject of Electra's obsession with revenge with his most advanced music, outdoing anything in *Salome* in dissonance and harmonic waywardness. The harmony derives from a single germinal chord whose flavour pervades the score. The dissonant polytonal episodes, sometimes crossing the border into atonality, are offset by passages of simple diatonicism, which usually arise from Strauss's contrapuntal textures but occasionally are used for a shock effect. A larger orchestra is used than in *Salome*, the wind including eight clarinets of various sorts, a heckelphone and Wagner tubas. Yet this array is controlled and balanced with an extraordinary precision which explains Strauss's *bon mot* that *Salome* and *Elektra* should be conducted 'as if they were fairy music by Mendelssohn'. Controversy continues, not over the dissonances of *Elektra*, which are now familiar enough, but over whether Strauss deliberately retreated into a cosier world from the expressionist anarchy that he had opened up, whether Hofmannsthal failed to provide challenging librettos or whether Strauss himself recognized that he could not repeat *Elektra*. The last seems the most tenable of these suppositions. He remained anxious to discover 'new forms' but they lay along more realistic lines, as in *Intermezzo*.

Not the least of Strauss's achievements in *Salome* and *Elektra* was the magnificent understanding he displayed in exploiting the female voice, something he learnt, presumably, from his wife Pauline, whom he described as the finest interpreter of his lieder. Both operas contain dramatic female roles, Salome and Herodias in the former and Electra, Chrysothemis and Clytemnestra in the latter. Clytemnestra's aria, rewritten three times before Strauss was satisfied, is the first 20th-century musical portrayal of corruption of body and soul, the forerunner of many. In Strauss's next opera, the comedy *Der Rosenkavalier* (1909–10), three very different soprano roles were created that have become touchstones by which operatic reputations are assessed. A legion of great singers since 1911 has revelled in the rewarding challenges of Sophie, Oktavian and the Marschallin, some having sung all three, progressing from the first to the last as their voices have developed. *Der Rosenkavalier* remains the most successful and popular of Strauss's operas. Its superior libretto, its 18th-century Vienna setting, its mingling of romance, farce, wit, sentimentality and tenderness, its human characterizations, its feast of melody dominated by waltz rhythms – all these positive virtues outweigh the occasional longueurs, the excessive, even fussy orchestral detail and the distastefulness of Baron Ochs's humiliation. The work is easily vulgarized, but the key to a successful interpretation can, as always, be found among Strauss's own writings: 'Light, flowing tempi, without compelling the singers to rattle off the text. In a word: Mozart, not Lehár'. Strauss rarely excelled the vocal opulence of the Act 3 trio for the three sopranos (Oktavian, a breeches role, is usually sung by a mezzo, but the score designates a soprano), and it is typical of Strauss that he fashioned its soaring melody from a comic phrase sung

7. *Hugo von Hofmannsthal and Strauss, c1915*

earlier in the act by Oktavian disguised as a maid-servant.

Strauss and Hofmannsthal remained in the 18th century in *Ariadne auf Naxos* (1911–12, 1916). The first version, with the Molière play performed before the *Ariadne* opera, is rarely heard; the more familiar 1916 version with the felicitous prologue contains some of Strauss's best music and also the character of the Composer (sung by an Oktavian soprano). Although it is comparatively short, this role has attracted leading singers from Lotte Lehmann onwards because it is so satisfying to perform. Hofmannsthal's happy conception of a mingling of *commedia dell'arte* characters with the tragedians of *Ariadne* appealed to Strauss, after initial hesitations, and gave him free rein for a combination of the Mozart and Wagner sides of his personality (or the *Eulenspiegel* and *Heldenleben* sides). The prologue, as full of action as the levée in *Rosenkavalier* and juxtaposing sentiment and force in a manner highly agreeable to Strauss, rarely fails in performance; but whether the total conception succeeds is more doubtful, since Hofmannsthal's highminded symbolism in the *Ariadne* section worried Strauss from the outset and there is a fatal dichotomy between the librettist's subtleties and the composer's attempts to clarify them for the audience. Only great singing can save the final duet in *Ariadne* from bathos. The use of a small orchestra (37 instruments) is one of the work's happiest features, revealing Strauss as a master of small-scale sonorities yet never sounding thin or etiolated. The second 'Grecian' opera by Strauss and Hofmannsthal, *Die ägyptische Helena* (1923–7), was marred by a comparable but more damaging divergence of aim between composer and librettist. As early as 1916, in the middle of the war, Strauss had told Hofmannstahl that 'my tragic vein is more or less exhausted . . . I feel downright called upon to become the Offenbach of the 20th century. . . . Sentimentality and parody are the sensations to which my talent responds most forcefully and productively'. He added, engagingly: 'After all, I'm the only composer nowadays with some real humour and a sense of fun and a marked gift for parody'. So when the collaborators decided to write an opera about Helen of Troy, the project started out lightheartedly, with Strauss composing the first act as fluently as he had *Rosenkavalier*. But in Act 2 Hofmannsthal began to philosophize and to complicate, with the inevitable result that the work can seem broken-backed and has flaws. Strauss's music, composed for a legendary group of Vienna singers, is in his equivalent of a bel canto style, and the refined yet luscious orchestration is extraordinarily persuasive.

Between *Ariadne* and *Helena*, Strauss had composed two of his most important operas, *Die Frau ohne Schatten* (1914–18) with Hofmannsthal, and the 'bourgeois comedy' *Intermezzo* (1918–23) to his own libretto. The interruptions of war prolonged the genesis of *Die Frau* to a point where Strauss called it his 'child of sorrow'. The libretto is Hofmannsthal's most symbolic and intellectual creation, a mixture of fairy tale, magic and Freudian psychology. Strauss, as devil's advocate on behalf of the audience, steered his librettist away from some of his more oblique ideas, and once confessed himself unable to find 'red corpuscles' in the characters. Yet he recognized that it was Hofmannsthal's finest achievement and some think that it is also Strauss's. There are good reasons to hold this opinion. No work of his, not even *Don Quixote*, is more memorably scored, a large orchestra being used with a Mahlerian virtuosity in contrasts of opulent exoticism and chamber music intimacy (the influence of *Das Lied von der Erde* is detectable). The roles of the Empress, the Dyer's Wife and the evil Nurse again challenged Strauss to produce outstanding music for female voices, but he was unexpectedly successful with the tenor role of the Emperor and even more with the delightfully human and warm bass-baritone part of Barak the Dyer (one of several roles from which it is possible to deduce a musical self-portrait). As a contrast from the high-flown Romanticism of this masterpiece Strauss enjoyed the relaxation of creating *Intermezzo*, which marks a radical change in his style (at a time when he was supposed to be extinct). The musical aspects of *Intermezzo* were obscured in its first years by the publicity surrounding its plot, a blatant slice of the Strausses' real life when Pauline falsely accused Richard of adultery. Domestic quarrels, rows with the cook, skiing, a lullaby for the child, a skat game, reconciliation, all are vividly re-created in a taut structure comprising a succession of short scenes linked by orchestral interludes (the parallel with *Wozzeck* is apparent and coincidental). The novel use of *secco* recitative was dictated by Strauss's preoccupation with the audibility of the text. In *Intermezzo*, he warned conductors, 'all passages of pure dialogue – in so far as they do not change for short periods of time into lyrical outpourings – in other words, all passages resembling *recitativo secco*, should be presented *mezza voce* throughout'. In its insistence on a naturalistic style of operatic performance, *Intermezzo*, this 'harmless comedy' as Strauss called it, was ahead of its day. It is a more serious piece than it seems – as the sensitive Hofmannsthal realized when he saw it – and it occupies a crucial place in Strauss's development of conversational operatic dialogue between the *Ariadne* prologue and the near-perfection he attained in *Capriccio*; and no doubt he would have been the first to acknowledge his debt to the Sachs–Eva scene in *Die Meistersinger*. Yet the piece was not taken seriously until 50 years after it was written. Compared with the realism of *Wozzeck*, the 'opera domestica' of Strauss was altogether too bourgeois a comedy for its day.

The last of the Hofmannsthal operas, *Arabella* (1930–32), is a strange, flawed work. This attempt at a 'second *Rosenkavalier*', an opera it in no way resembles except in its Vienna setting of a century later, is handicapped because the libretto of the second and third acts was left unrevised as a memorial tribute to Hofmannsthal, whereas the number of alterations to Act 1 made at Strauss's behest is a pointer to the need for later improvements. (Many of the best dramatic effects in their operas were Strauss's ideas.) As if to disguise the obvious weaknesses of plot, Strauss wrote an especially euphonious score, with orchestration of particular delicacy and variety of colour. Paradoxically he transformed his librettist's effort to provide him with the operetta he craved into a full-scale operatic portrait of the heroine. Her love-duet with Mandryka, her Croatian suitor, is among Strauss's most deeply felt creations in this genre. The lighter aspects of the opera benefit from the dialogue style of *Intermezzo*, but the rather obvious emulation of *Die Fledermaus* in Act 2 can wear thin in all but a supreme production. Yet the undeniable charm of the work, its mixture of sympathetic and bizarre characters, appeals to the public, is theatrically effective and makes *Arabella* a pleasing entertainment. It pleases more than its successor *Die schweigsame Frau* (1933–4). This was Strauss's first opera with Zweig, and he said that its composition came more easily than any of his previous operas. It was also the libretto that he altered least. It is his only 'Italian opera', a *buffa* work paying homage to Rossini and to the Verdi of *Falstaff*,

the character of Sir Morosus being modelled on that of the Shakespeare–Verdi knight. Ben Jonson's London is updated to 1780 in order that an opera company can be introduced, providing Strauss with the opportunity he so enjoyed for working quotations into the score. There is a music-lesson scene (based on a Monteverdi theme) and several elaborate ensembles. The vocal writing for the soprano Aminta and the high tenor Henry is of extreme difficulty but very effective. The clever score is full of 'gems', sparkling and genuine, but the total effect fails fully to embody the composer's gleeful enjoyment, principally because the melodic invention is not of prime Straussian cut.

For his next two operas, with librettos by Gregor supervised by Zweig, Strauss reverted to the one-act form of his pre-war successes. *Friedenstag* (1935–6), set in a beleaguered fortress during the Thirty Years War, is the most austere of his operas and the finest of those that are little known and underrated. Never loath to acknowledge his dependence on models – *Meistersinger*, *Figaro*, *Zauberflöte* and *Il barbiere di Siviglia* among them – Strauss here ventured into the contrasts of darkness and light, war and freedom, that characterize *Fidelio*. It was a brave work to write in 1936 in Nazi Germany but, politics apart, its harmonic strength, ambitious use of the chorus, reliance on mainly male voices and Mahlerian juxtaposition of the popular and the esoteric overcome defects in Gregor's libretto and compel ungrudging admiration for a septuagenarian's elasticity of approach to operatic form. Its companion-piece, *Daphne* (1936–7), is in total contrast filled with pastoral lyricism, autumnal tints and an impression of warm sunlight captured, it seems, from the Italian surroundings in which most of it was composed. It was

8. Playbill for the first performance of the one-act version of 'Ariadne auf Naxos', Stuttgart, 1912

9. Final page of the autograph score of 'Capriccio', dated 3 August 1941

unusual for Strauss to write for two tenors, and the roles of Apollo and Leukippos are skilfully and sympathetically drawn; but the singer of Daphne is blessed with one of Strauss's most appealing female roles, demanding a sustained, light, lyrical line combined with occasional dramatic weight. Monotony is avoided by the Dionysian dances and by a command of orchestration by now so magisterial that it was mistaken for habit. Yet no mere habit could have produced the F♯ major iridescence of the final transformation scene nor of the 'shower of gold' episode in the next and last Gregor opera *Die Liebe der*

Danae (1938–40). This was Strauss's last excursion into the opulence of *Die Frau ohne Schatten*, a 'cheerful mythology' in three acts which began as a lighthearted idea by Hofmannsthal in 1920 and was expanded by Gregor, at Strauss's insistence, becoming weightier in the process. Yet for all the sneers at Gregor because of the undoubted obscurity of some points in the libretto, the fact remains that Strauss set it and considered that some of the music was as fine as he had ever written, as indeed it is. The score requires a producer and conductor who can bring its extraordinary luminosity to full life in a manner to match the old composer's touchingly noble and festive celebration of all that the Greek classical tradition had meant to him. The solo parts for Jupiter (bass-baritone) and Danae (soprano) are melodically and harmonically as rich as any Strauss created, while the quartet for Jupiter's four ex-mistresses and the structural strength of other ensembles deserve the adjective 'Olympian'. His reluctance to allow this, the last of his big-scale works, to be performed because of his experiences with *Die Frau ohne Schatten*, is an eloquent admission that he knew how much it depended for full success on an imaginative and extravagant production in tune with its multi-faceted mood.

The last opera was *Capriccio* (1940–41), to a libretto by Clemens Krauss which owed much to assistance from Hans Swarowsky, Strauss himself, Zweig and even Hofmannsthal. It is described as a 'conversation piece', the term Strauss had applied to *Intermezzo* in his preface to that opera in 1924. *Capriccio* might so easily have been an old man's indulgence, an opera with, as its basic idea, an unresolved discussion on Strauss's favourite topic of the relative importance in opera of words and music – a long way, this intellectual subject, from the solar-plexus realities of *Elektra*. Yet by setting the scene in a pre-Revolution French château, the house of a beautiful young widowed Countess and her brother, by symbolizing the problem through the rivalry for the Countess's love of a poet and a musician, by introducing the character of a theatre director with elements of Reinhardt in his make-up and by the crowning inspiration (by the Count) that poet and musician should compose an opera about the events they are enacting, Krauss provided Strauss, through this marvellous one-act libretto, with what he had for so long craved, 'a second *Rosenkavalier*, without the longueurs'. Without the coarse humour, too, and without the waltzes, yet with the chances for parody (there is even another Italian aria), with the equivalent of another levée scene, and, best of all, with a central female character who embodies features of the Marschallin, Arabella, Danae and Daphne and is more admirable than any of them. Strauss took the bait. None of his opera scores is more refined, more translucent, more elegant, more varied and none ends so magically, with a long soliloquy for the Countess in which Strauss's melodic vein and consummate stagecraft show no diminution in their capacity to enslave an audience. If *Capriccio* perhaps lacks the dramatic weight of earlier works, it excels them in the sheer art of economical composition. In this respect, and in its place at the end of a long line of theatrical explorations, it can compare with Verdi's *Falstaff*.

9. CHORAL MUSIC AND LIEDER. If only a comparatively small percentage of Strauss's 200 and more songs is well known, the plight of his choral works is worse. Yet the vocal equivalent of the orchestral wizardry of his tone poems is to be found in the 16-part complexities of the *Deutsche Motette* (1913, Rückert) and of the *Zwei Gesänge* op.34 (1897), *Der Abend* (Schiller) and *Hymne* (Rückert). Of particular interest, from the end of his career (1943), is *An den Baum Daphne*, a difficult but magnificent setting of Gregor's original choral finale to the opera *Daphne*, which Strauss discarded in favour of the orchestral transformation scene. Incidentally, the principal motif of *Daphne* is derived from the first theme of the 1935 setting for double chorus of

Rückert's *Die Göttin im Putzzimmer*.

The bulk of Strauss's output of lieder was composed between 1885 and 1906. Throughout this time his wife, Pauline de Ahna, was professionally active and many of the songs were written for her to sing, with Strauss as her accompanist. Others were written with particular favourite performers in mind, for example Elisabeth Schumann and Paul Knüpfer. Strauss's outstanding contribution to the development of the lied was his continuation of the Berlioz–Wagner–Mahler style of song with orchestra. He orchestrated many of his songs and sanctioned orchestrations by others, and in some cases the accompaniment was originally composed for orchestra. He was as unselective as Schubert in his choice of texts, provided they generated the impulse for music in him. He described his methods candidly:

Musical ideas have prepared themselves in me – God knows why – and when, as it were, the barrel is full, a song appears in the twinkling of an eye as soon as I come across a poem more or less corresponding to the subject of the imaginary song. . . . If I find no poem corresponding to the subject which exists in my sub-conscious mind, then the creative urge has to be re-channelled to the setting of some other poem which I think lends itself to music. It goes slowly, though. . . . I resort to artifice.

The melodic lyricism of Strauss's style, so evident in his operas, is no less marked in his songs and burst forth in 1885, when he was 21, in his Gilm settings op.10. These include the ornate setting of *Allerseelen* and the masterly *Die Nacht*, which has hardly ever excelled for creation of atmosphere by tonal ambiguity. It is possibly an even finer song than the justly celebrated *Morgen!* op.27 no.4 of 1894, an example of that simplicity which the 'complicated brain' of Strauss could always produce when he was in the mood. *Morgen!* was one of the first of his songs to be orchestrated (1897), and he preserved its mood of rapture by delicate scoring for three horns, harp and strings, including solo violin. *Cäcilie*, a passionate love-song from the same set, was also orchestrated in 1897, when Strauss transposed the E major piano accompaniment to a heroic E♭. Curiously, the first song of this group, *Ruhe, meine Seele*, was not orchestrated until 1948, when Strauss conjured a transparent sound from huge forces but, perhaps deliberately, changed the mood of the song from rapt stillness to pessimistic gloom. As one would expect from his operas, Strauss was at ease with the 'character' song, especially when a bantering or mocking tone was required. Good examples of this are *Wozu noch, Mädchen* op.19 no.1, a Schack setting, *All' mein Gedanken* op.21 no.1, to words by Dahn, and *Muttertändelei* op.43 no.2 (Bürger). The superb cantilena that is a Straussian hallmark is to be heard in *Morgen!*, of course in *Freundliche Vision* op.48 no.1 (Bierbaum), a revolutionary song in its day (1900) because the voice part appeared to have no connection with the piano accompaniment, and in *Traum durch die Dämmerung* op.29 no.1 (Bierbaum), a song in which Strauss uncharacteristically altered the key signature from F♯ major to B♭ when the poem switches from a description of twilight to a description of love. Among the greatest of his songs are the six Brentano settings of op.68 (1918), wide-ranging in mood, challenging in technical difficulty and completely apposite in word-setting. From 1918, too, comes a curiosity, the *Krämerspiegel* op.66, 12 settings of satirical verses by Alfred Kerr which make scurrilous references by means of puns to various publishers. The hiatus between 1906 and 1918 in composition of lieder was only partly caused by opera composition; it is also attributable to a lengthy wrangle over copyright of songs which came to a head when Bote & Bock threatened Strauss with an action for breach of contract. Strauss took his revenge in these songs and offered them to Bote & Bock (who refused them). They are far from negligible, but the cycle's importance is in the melody of the piano introduction to no.8, which Strauss 'borrowed' over 20 years later as the most romantic and evocative melody in *Capriccio*. If that was a case of recovery of buried treasure, there are other treasures to be found among Strauss's songs, notably in the 'radical' settings of Dehmel, such as *Der Arbeitsmann* op.39 no.3, and the Rückert songs of op.46.

Fittingly, and with all the flair for bringing down the curtain at the right moment which distinguished his sense of theatre, learnt all those years ago at Meiningen, Strauss ended his composing career with the *Vier letzte Lieder* with orchestra which have become, deservedly, loved by the public and admired by the connoisseur. These 1948 settings of three poems by Hesse and one by Eichendorff are not only extremely beautiful; they continue the vein of introspection that had been opened in *Metamorphosen*, or even earlier in the 1935 Rückert song for bass voice, *Im Sonnenschein*. Gloriously written for the soprano voice, the cantilena as cunningly spread as ever, the harmonies as ensnaring, the melody as richly suggestive of the halcyon days of German song, the orchestration as gorgeous as in *Arabella* yet as discreet as in *Capriccio*, these songs have a solemn profundity that makes them an appositely contrived ending to the career of a composer who compensated for what he lacked in spirituality by his astonishing insight into the human heart. The poems ask 'Is this perhaps death?' (and Strauss quoted from *Tod und Verklärung*) and speak of summer closing its weary eyes. No better end could be imagined to the 50 years of musical autobiography by this entertainer of the public who never made the mistake of either exaggerating or underestimating his flawed but generous capabilities. On his last visit to London in 1947 he remarked: 'I may not be a first-rate composer, but I *am* a first-class second-rate composer', perhaps consciously echoing Verdi's remark about himself – that he may not have been a great composer but he was a very experienced one. Strauss was making the same modest claim, but he can no more be denied the greatness than can Verdi.

WORKS

Works without op.no are given the no. assigned them in E. H. Mueller von Asow: *Richard Strauss: thematisches Verzeichnis* (Vienna, 1959–74), iii [AV]

op.

OPERAS

25 Guntram (3, Strauss), 1892–3; Weimar, Court Theatre, 10 May 1894; rev. 1934–9, Weimar, Deutsches Nationaltheater, 29 Oct 1940
50 Feuersnot (1, E. von Wolzogen), 1900–01; Dresden, Court Opera, 21 Nov 1901
54 Salome (1, Wilde, trans. H. Lachmann), 1903–5; Dresden, Court Opera, 9 Dec 1905
58 Elektra (1, Hofmannsthal), 1906–8; Dresden, Court Opera, 25 Jan 1909
59 Der Rosenkavalier (3, Hofmannsthal), 1909–10; Dresden, Court Opera, 26 Jan 1911
60 Ariadne auf Naxos (1, Hofmannsthal), 1911–12; Stuttgart, Court Theatre, 25 Oct 1912; 2nd version 1916, Vienna, Court Opera, 4 Oct 1916
65 Die Frau ohne Schatten (3, Hofmannsthal), 1914–18; Vienna, Staatsoper, 10 Oct 1919
72 Intermezzo (2, Strauss), 1918–23; Dresden, Staatsoper, 4 Nov 1924

75 Die ägyptische Helena (2, Hofmannsthal), 1923–7; Dresden, Staatsoper, 6 June 1928; Act 2, rev. (L. Wallerstein), 1932–3, Salzburg, Festspielhaus, 14 Aug 1933
79 Arabella (3, Hofmannsthal), 1929–32; Dresden, Staatsoper, 1 July 1933
80 Die schweigsame Frau (3, Zweig, after Jonson), 1933–4; Dresden, Staatsoper, 24 June 1935
81 Friedenstag (1, Gregor), 1935–6; Munich, Staatsoper, 24 July 1938
82 Daphne (1, Gregor), 1936–7; Dresden, Staatsoper, 15 Oct 1938
83 Die Liebe der Danae (3, Gregor, after Hofmannsthal), 1938–40; Salzburg, Festspielhaus, 16 Aug 1944 (dress rehearsal for cancelled première); Salzburg, Festspielhaus, 14 Aug 1952
85 Capriccio (1, Krauss), 1940–41; Munich, Staatsoper, 28 Oct 1942

OTHER STAGE WORKS

— Romeo und Julia (incidental music, Shakespeare), AV86; Munich, 23 Oct 1887
60 Der Bürger als Edelmann (incidental music, Hofmannsthal, after Molière) [incl. frags. from Lully], 1912; Stuttgart, Hoftheater, 25 Oct 1912; rev. 1917; Berlin, Deutsches Theater, 9 April 1918
63 Josephs-Legende (ballet, 1, H. G. Kessler, Hofmannsthal), 1912–14; Paris, Opéra, 14 May 1914
70 Schlagobers (ballet, 2, Strauss), 1921–2; Vienna, Staatsoper, 9 May 1924
— Verklungene Feste (ballet, P. and P. Mlakar), AV128, 1940 [Tanzsuite, AV107, orch, 1923, with 6 new nos. later incl. in Divertimento, op.86], 1941; Munich, Bayerische Staatsoper, 5 April 1941

ORCHESTRAL

— Overture for Singspiel Hochlands Treue, AV15, 1872–3
— Concert Overture, b, AV30, 1876
1 Festmarsch, Eb, 1876
— Serenade, G, AV32, 1877
— Overture, E, AV51, 1878
— Romanze, Eb, AV61, cl, orch, 1879
— Overture, a, AV62, 1879
— Symphony, d, AV69, 1880
4 Suite, Bb, 13 wind, 1884
7 Serenade, Eb, 13 wind, 1881
8 Violin Concerto, d, 1880–82
11 Horn Concerto no.1, Eb, 1882–3
— Romanze, F, AV75, vc, orch, 1883
— Lied ohne Worte, Eb, AV79, 1883
— Concert Overture, c, AV80, 1883
12 Symphony, f, 1883–4
— Der Zweikampf, Bb, AV82, polonaise, fl, bn, orch, ?1884
— Festmarsch, D, AV84, 1884–5, rev. 1888
— Burleske, d, AV85, pf, orch, 1885–6
16 Aus Italien, sym. fantasy, 1886
— Festmarsch, C, AV87, 1889
20 Don Juan, tone poem after Lenau, 1888–9
23 Macbeth, tone poem after Shakespeare, 1886–8, rev. 1889–90, 1891
24 Tod und Verklärung, tone poem, 1888–9
— Fanfare for A. W. Iffland's play Der Jäger, AV88A, 1891
— Music for tableaux vivants at the celebrations of the golden wedding of the Grand Duke and Grand Duchess of Weimar, AV89, 1892; no.1 rev as Kampf und Sieg, 1931
28 Till Eulenspiegels lustige Streiche, nach alter Schelmenweise – in Rondeauform, 1894–5
30 Also sprach Zarathustra, tone poem after Nietzsche, 1895–6
35 Don Quixote, fantastische Variationen über ein Thema ritterlichen Charakters, vc, orch, 1896–7
40 Ein Heldenleben, tone poem, 1897–8
53 Symphonia domestica, 1902–3
57 Zwei Militärmärsche, 1906
— Feierlicher Einzug der Ritter des Johanniter-Ordens, AV103, brass, timp, 1909
60 Suite from Der Bürger als Edelmann, 1918
61 Festliches Präludium, 1913
64 Eine Alpensinfonie, 1911–15
— Tanzsuite aus Klavierstücken von François Couperin, AV107, 1923
— Vier sinfonische Zwischenspiele aus Intermezzo
— Wiener Philharmoniker Fanfare, AV109, brass, timp, 1924
— Fanfare zur Eröffnung der Musikwoche der Stadt Wien im September 1924, AV110, brass, timp, 1924
— Music for the film Der Rosenkavalier [arrs. of various pieces and new march], AV112, 1925
73 Parergon zur Symphonia domestica, pf left hand, orch, 1924
74 Panathenäenzug, symphonische Etüden in Form einer Passacaglia, pf left hand, orch, 1927
— Interludio, for Mozart's Idomeneo, c, AV117, 1930 (see 'Arrangements, etc')
— Suite from Schlagobers, 1932
— Waltz Sequence [no.2] from Der Rosenkavalier, Act 3, 1934

— München, ein Gelegenheitswalzer, AV125, 1939; rev. AV140, 1945
84 Festmusik zur Feier des 2600jährigen Bestehens des Kaiserreichs Japan, 1940
86 Divertimento [after Couperin], small orch, 1940–41
— Horn Concerto no.2, E♭, AV132, 1942
— Festmusik der Stadt Wien, AV133, brass, timp, 1943
— Fanfare der Stadt Wien, AV134, brass, timp, 1943
— Sonatina no.1 'Aus der Werkstatt eines Invaliden', F, AV135, 16 wind, 1943
— Waltz Sequence [no.1] from Der Rosenkavalier, Acts 1–2, AV 139, 1944
— Metamorphosen, AV142, study, 23 str, 1945
— Sonatina no.2 (Symphony) 'Fröhliche Werkstatt', E♭, AV143, 16 wind, 1944–5
— Oboe Concerto, AV144, 1945 (finale rev. 1948)
— Sinfonische Fantasie aus Die Frau ohne Schatten, 1946
— Symphonic Fragment from Josephs-Legende, 1947
— Duett-Concertino, AV147, cl, bn, str, harp, 1947

CHORAL
(with orchestra)
— Chorus from Elektra (Sophocles), AV74, male vv, small orch, ?1881
14 Wandrers Sturmlied (Goethe), 6vv, orch, 1884
— Bardengesang (Kleist), male vv, orch, 1885, lost
— Licht, du ewiglich Eines, AV91, female 4vv, brass band, orch, 1897
52 Taillefer (Uhland), S, T, Bar, 8vv, orch, 1903
55 Bardengesang (Klopstock), 12 male vv, orch, 1905
76 Die Tageszeiten (Eichendorff), TTBB, orch, 1928
78 Austria (A. Wildgans), male vv, orch, 1929
— Olympische Hymne (R. Lubahn), AV119, SATB, orch, 1934

(unaccompanied)
— Zwei Lieder (Eichendorff), AV25, SATB, 1876: Morgengesang, Frühlingsnacht
— Kyrie, Sanctus, Benedictus, Agnus Dei, AV31, SATB, 1877
— Sieben Lieder, AV67, SATB/S, A, T, B, 1880: Winterlied (Eichendorff), Spielmannsweise (Gensichen), Pfingsten (Böttger), Käferlied (Reinick), Waldessang (Böttger), Schneeglöcklein (Böttger), Trüb blinken nur die Sterne (Böttger)
— Schwäbische Erbschaft (Löwe), AV83, TTBB, 1884
34 Zwei Gesänge, 16vv, 1897: Der Abend (Schiller), Hymne (Rückert)
— Soldatenlied (A. Kopisch), AV93, 4 male vv, 1899
42 Zwei Männerchöre (Herder: Stimmen der Völker in Liedern), TTBB, 1899: Liebe, Altdeutsches Schlachtlied
45 Drei Männerchöre (Herder: Stimmen der Völker in Liedern), TTBB, 1899: Schlachtgesang, Lied der Freundschaft, Der Brauttanz
— Sechs Volksliedbearbeitungen, AV101, male vv, 1905–6: Geistliche Maien, Misslungene Liebesjagd, Tummler, Hüt' du dich, Wächterlied, Kuckuck
62 Deutsche Motette (Rückert), S, A, T, B, 16vv, 1913
— Cantate (Hofmannsthal), AV104, male 4vv, 1914
— Die Göttin im Putzzimmer (Rückert), AV120, 8vv, 1935
— Drei Männerchöre (Rückert), AV 123, 1935: Vor den Türen, TTBB, Traumlicht, TTBBB, Fröhlich im Maien, TTBB
— Durch Einsamkeiten (Wildgans), AV124, male 4vv, 1938
— An den Baum Daphne (Gregor), AV137, epilogue to Daphne, 9vv, 1943

SONGS
— Weihnachtslied (C. F. D. Schubart), AV2, 1870
— Einkehr (Uhland), AV3, 1871
— Winterreise (Uhland), AV4, 1871
— Waldkonzert (J. N. Vogel), AV5, ?1871
— Der böhmische Musikant (O. Pletzsch), AV7, ?1871
— Herz, mein Herz (E. Geibel), AV8, 1871
— Der müde Wanderer (A. H. Hoffmann von Fallersleben), AV13, ?1873
— Husarenlied (Hoffmann von Fallersleben), AV14, ?1873
— Der Fischer (Goethe), AV33, 1877
— Die Drossel (Uhland), AV34, 1877
— Lass ruhn die Toten (A. von Chamisso), AV35, 1877
— Lust und Qual (Goethe), AV36, 1877
— Spielmann und Zither (T. Körner), AV40, 1878
— Wiegenlied (Hoffmann von Fallersleben), AV41, 1878
— Abend- und Morgenrot (Hoffmann von Fallersleben), AV42, 1878
— Im Walde (Geibel), AV43, 1878
— Der Spielmann und sein Kind (Hoffmann von Fallersleben), AV46, 1v, orch, 1878, also pf version
— Nebel (Lenau), AV47, ?1878
— Soldatenlied (Hoffmann von Fallersleben), AV48, ?1878
— Ein Röslein zog ich mir im Garten (Hoffmann von Fallersleben), AV49, ?1878
— Waldesgesang (Geibel), AV55, 1879

— In Vaters Garten heimlich steht ein Blümchen (Heine), AV64, 1879
— Die erwachte Rose (F. von Sallet), AV66, 1880
— Begegnung (O. E. Gruppe), AV72, 1880
— John Anderson, mein Lieb (Burns, trans. F. Freiligrath), AV73, 1880
— Rote Rosen (K. Stieler), AV76, 1883
10 Acht Lieder aus Letzte Blätter (H. von Gilm), 1885: Zueignung, Nichts, Die Nacht, Die Georgine, Die Verschwiegenen, Die Zeitlose, Allerseelen; no.1 orchd 1940
— Wer hat's gethan? (Gilm), AV84a, 1885
15 Fünf Lieder, 1884–6: Madrigal (Michelangelo), Winternacht (A. F. von Schack), Lob des Leidens (Schack), Aus den Liedern der Trauer (Dem Herzen ähnlich) (Schack), Heimkehr (von Schack)
17 Sechs Lieder (Schack), 1885–7: Seitdem dein Aug' im meines schaute, Ständchen, Das Geheimnis, Aus den Liedern der Trauer (Von dunklem Schleier umsponnen), Nur Muth!, Barkarole
19 Sechs Lieder aus Lotusblättern (Schack), 1885–8: Wozu noch, Mädchen, soll es Frommen; Breit über mein Haupt dein schwarzes Haar; Schön sind, doch kalt die Himmelssterne; Wie sollten wir geheim sie halten; Hoffen und wieder verzagen; Mein Herz ist stumm, mein Herz ist kalt
21 Schlichte Weisen (F. Dahn), 1887–8: All' mein Gedanken, mein Herz und mein Sinn; Du meines Herzens Krönelein; Ach Lieb, ich muss nun scheiden; Ach weh, mir unglückhaften Mann; Die Frauen sind oft fromm und still
22 Mädchenblumen (Dahn): Kornblumen, 1888; Mohnblumen, 1888; Efeu, 1886–8; Wasserrose, 1886–8
26 Zwei Lieder (Lenau), 1891: Frühlingsgedränge, O wärst du mein
27 Vier Lieder, 1894: Ruhe, meine Seele (K. Henckell); Cäcilie (Hart); Heimliche Aufforderung (J. H. Mackay); Morgen (Mackay); no.1 orchd 1948, nos.2 and 4 orchd 1897
29 Drei Lieder (Bierbaum), 1895: Traum durch die Dämmerung, Schlagende Herzen, Nachtgang
— Wir beide wollen springen (Bierbaum), AV90, 1896
31 Drei Lieder: Blauer Sommer (Busse), 1896; Wenn (Busse), 1895; Weisser Jasmin (Busse), 1895; Stiller Gang (Dehmel) [added no.], with va, 1895
32 Fünf Lieder, 1896: Ich trage meine Minne (Henckell), Sehnsucht (Liliencron), Liebeshymnus (Henckell), O süsser Mai (Henckell), Himmelsboten (Des Knaben Wunderhorn): no.3 orchd 1897
33 Vier Gesänge, 1v, orch: Verführung (Mackay), 1896; Gesang der Apollopriesterin (E. von und zu Bodman), 1896; Hymnus, 1896; Pilgers Morgenlied (Goethe), 1897
36 Vier Lieder: Das Rosenband (Klopstock), 1897; Für funfzehn Pfennige (Des Knaben Wunderhorn), 1897; Hat gesagt – bleibt's nicht dabei (Des Knaben Wunderhorn), 1898; Anbetung (Rückert), 1898; no.1 orchd 1897
37 Sechs Lieder: Glückes genug (Liliencron), 1898; Ich liebe dich (Liliencron), 1898; Meinem Kinde (Falke), 1897; Mein Auge (Dehmel), 1898; Herr Lenz (Bodman), 1896; Hochzeitlich Lied (A. Lindner), 1898; no.2 orchd 1943; no.3 orchd 1897; no.4 orchd 1933
39 Fünf Lieder, 1898: Leises Lied (Dehmel), Junghexenlied (Bierbaum), Der Arbeitsmann (Dehmel), Befreit (Dehmel), Lied an meinen Sohn (Dehmel); no.4 orchd 1933
41 Fünf Lieder, 1899: Wiegenlied (Dehmel), In der Campagna (Mackay), Am Ufer (Dehmel), Bruder Liederlich (Liliencron), Leise Lieder (Morgenstern); no.1 orchd ?1916
43 Drei Lieder, 1899: An Sie (Klopstock), Muttertändelei (G. A. Bürger), Die Ulme zu Hirsau (Uhland); no.2 orchd 1900
44 Zwei grössere Gesänge, A/B, orch, 1899: Notturno (Dehmel), Nächtlicher Gang (Rückert)
— Weihnachtsgefühl (Greif), AV94, 1899
46 Fünf Lieder (Rückert): Ein Obdach gegen Sturm und Regen, 1900; Gestern war ich Atlas, 1899; Die sieben Siegel, 1899; Morgenrot, 1900; Ich sehe wie in einem Spiegel, 1900
47 Fünf Lieder (Uhland), 1900: Auf ein Kind, Des Dichters Abendgang, Rückleben, Einkehr, Von den sieben Zechbrüdern; no.2 orchd 1918
48 Fünf Lieder, 1900: Freundliche Vision (Bierbaum), Ich schwebe (Henckell), Kling! (Henckell), Winterweihe (Henckell), Winterliebe (Henckell); nos.1, 4 and 5 orchd 1918
49 Acht Lieder: Waldseligkeit (Dehmel), 1901; In goldener Fülle (P. Remer), 1901; Wiegenliedchen (Dehmel), 1901; Das Lied des Steinklopfers (Henckell), 1901; Sie wissen's nicht (O. Panizza), 1901; Junggesellenschwur (Des Knaben Wunderhorn), 1900; Wer lieben will (C. Mündel: Elsässische Volkslieder), 1901; Ach, was Kummer, Qual und Schmerzen (Mündel: Elsässische Volkslieder), 1901; no.1 orchd 1918
51 Zwei Gesänge, B, orch: Das Thal (Uhland), 1902; Der Einsame (Heine), 1906; no.2 also in pf version
56 Sechs Lieder: Gefunden (Goethe), 1903; Blindenklage (Henckell), 1903–6; Im Spätboot (Meyer), 1903–6; Mit deinen blauen Augen (Heine), 1903–6; Frühlingsfeier (Heine), 1903–6; Die heiligen drei Könige aus Morgenland (Heine), 1903–6; no.5

orchd 1933, no.6 orchd 1906
— Der Graf von Rom (textless), AV102, 2 versions, 1906
66 Krämerspiegel (A. Kerr), 1918: Es war einmal ein Bock; Einst kam der Bock als Bote; Es liebte einst ein Hase; Drei Masken sah ich am Himmel stehn; Hast du ein Tongedicht vollbracht; O lieber Künstler sei ermahnt; Unser Feind ist, grosser Gott; Von Händlern wird die Kunst bedroht; Es war mal eine Wanze; Die Künstler sind die Schöpfer; Die Händler und die Macher; O Schöpferschwarm, o Händlerkreis
67 Sechs Lieder, 1918: I Lieder der Ophelia (Shakespeare, trans. K. Simrock): Wie erkenn ich mein Treulieb vor andern nun?; Guten Morgen, 's ist Sankt Valentinstag; Sie trugen ihn auf der Bahre bloss; II Aus den Büchern des Unmuts der Rendsch Nameh (Goethe): Wer wird von der Welt verlangen; Hab' ich euch denn je geraten; Wanderers Gemütsruhe
68 Sechs Lieder (Brentano), 1918: An die Nacht; Ich wollt' ein Sträusslein binden; Säusle, liebe Myrthe; Als mir dein Lied erklang; Amor; Lied der Frauen; nos.1–5 orchd 1940, no.6 orchd 1933
69 Fünf kleine Lieder, 1918: Der Stern (A. von Arnim), Der Pokal (Arnim), Einerlei (Arnim), Waldesfahrt (Heine), Schlechtes Wetter (Heine)
— Sinnspruch (Goethe), AV105, 1919
71 Drei Hymnen von Friedrich Hölderlin, S/T, orch, 1921: Hymne an die Liebe, Rückkehr in die Heimat, Die Liebe
— Durch allen Schall und Klang (Goethe), AV111, 1925
77 Gesänge des Orients (trans. Bethge), 1928: Ihre Augen (Hafiz), Schwung (Hafiz), Liebesgeschenke (Die chinesische Flöte), Die Allmächtige (Hafiz), Huldigung (Hafiz)
— Wie etwas sei leicht (Goethe), AV116, 1930
87 Vom künftigen Alter (Rückert), B, AV115, 1929; Erschaffen und Beleben (Goethe), AV106, 1922; Und dann nicht mehr (Rückert), AV114, 1929; Im Sonnenschein (Rückert), AV121, 1935
— Zugemessne Rhythmen (Goethe), AV122, 1935
88 Das Bächlein, AV118, 1933; Blick vom oberen Belvedere (J. Weinheber), AV130, 1942; Sankt Michael (Weinheber), AV129, 1942; no.1 orchd 1935
— Xenion (Goethe), AV131, 1942
— [Vier letzte Lieder], AV150, S/T, orch, 1948: Frühling (Hesse), September (Hesse), Beim Schlafengehen (Hesse), Im Abendrot (Eichendorff)

OTHER VOCAL WORKS

— Der weisse Hirsch (Uhland), AV6, A, T, B, pf, ?1871
— Four scenes for a Singspiel (? Strauss), AV28, vv, pf, 1876: Gnomenchor, Lied Mariechens, Ensemble mit Arie und Rezitativ des Wurzel, Arie des Wurzel und Szenenmusik
— Alphorn (J. Kerner), AV29, 1v, hn, pf, 1876
— Arie der Almaide (Sei nicht beklommen) (Goethe: Lila), AV44, S, orch, ?1878
— Utan svafvel och fosfor [From a Swedish matchbox]; AV88, T, T, B, B, 1889
38 Enoch Arden (Tennyson, trans. A. Strodtmann), melodrama, speaker, pf, 1897
— Das Schloss am Meere (Uhland), AV92, melodrama, speaker, pf, 1899
— Hans Huber in Vitznau sei schönstens bedanket (Strauss), AV95, 4-part canon, 1899
— Scatcanon (Strauss), AV95A, 4vv, 1904
— Zwei Lieder aus Der Richter von Zalamea (Calderón), AV96, 1904: Liebesliedchen, T, gui, harp; Lied der Chispa, Mez, unison male vv, gui, 2 harps
— Hymne auf das Haus Kohorn (Strauss), AV113, T, T, B, B, 1925
— Hab Dank, du güt'ger Weisheitspender (Strauss), AV126, B, 1939
— Notschrei aus den Gefilden Lapplands (Strauss), AV127, S/T, 1940
— Wer tritt herein (Strauss), AV136, S/T, 1943

CHAMBER AND INSTRUMENTAL

— Zwei Etüden, no.1 for E♭-hn, no.2 for E-hn, AV12, ?1873
— Piano Trio no.1, A, AV37, 1877
— Introduction, Theme and Variations, E♭, AV52, hn, pf, 1878
— Piano Trio no.2, D, AV53, 1878
— Introduction, Theme and Variations, G, AV56, fl, pf, 1879
— Five-part Fugue, AV65/3, vn, pf, 1880
2 String Quartet, A, 1880
6 Sonata, F, vc, pf, 1880–83
13 Piano Quartet, c, 1883–4
18 Sonata, E♭, vn, pf, 1887
— Andante from an inc. sonata, AV86A, hn, pf, 1888
— Hochzeitspräludium, AV108, 2 harmonium, 1924
— Harpsichord Suite [from Capriccio], ?1944
— Daphne-Etüde, G, AV141, vn, 1945
— Allegretto, E, AV149, vn, pf, 1948

PIANO

— Schneider-Polka, AV1, 1870
— Moderato, C, AV9, ?1871
— Panzenburg-Polka, AV10, 1872
— Slow movement, g, AV11, ?1872
— Five Little Pieces, AV16, ?1873
— Three sonatinas, C, AV17, F, AV18, B♭, AV19, 1874
— Untitled composition, c, AV20, ?1874
— Fantasy, C, AV21, ?1874
— Two Little Pieces, AV22, ?1875
— Sonata no.1, E, AV38, 1877
— Twelve Variations, D, AV50, 1878
— Aus alter Zeit: eine kleine Gavotte, AV57, 1879
— Andante, c, AV58, 1879
— Skizzen, AV59, 5 pieces, 1879
— Sonata no.2 (Grosse Sonate), c, AV60, 1879
— Scherzo, b, AV63, ?1879
— Four-part Fugue, C, AV65/1, 1879; Double Fugue, B♭, AV65/2, 1880
— Two Little Pieces, AV68, 1879–80
— Scherzando, G, AV70, 1880
— Fugue on Four Themes, C, AV71, 1880
3 Five Pieces, 1880–81: Andante, Allegro vivace scherzando, Largo, Allegro molto, Allegro marcatissimo
5 Sonata, b, 1880–81
— Largo, a, AV77, ?1883
— Stiller Waldespfad, AV78, 1883
9 Stimmungsbilder, 1882–4: Auf stillen Waldespfad, An einsamer Quelle, Intermezzo, Träumerei, Heidebild
— Improvisation and Fuge über ein Originalthema, AV81, 1884 [only fugue survives]
— Parade-Marsch des Regiments Königs-Jäger zu Pferde no.1, AV97, 1905
— Parade-Marsch Cavallerie no.2, AV98, 1905
— De brandenburgsche Mars, AV99, 1905–6
— Königsmarsch, AV100, 1906

ARRANGEMENTS, ETC

C. W. Gluck: *Iphigénie en Tauride*, 1899; Weimar, Hoftheater, 9 June 1900
L. van Beethoven: *Die Ruinen von Athen* (text rev. Hofmannsthal), 1924; Vienna, Staatsoper, 20 Sept 1924
W. A. Mozart: *Idomeneo* (text rev. L. Wallerstein), 1930; Vienna, Staatsoper, 16 April 1931
Cadenza for Mozart's Pf Conc. K491, 1885

Principal publishers: Boosey & Hawkes, Fürstner, Universal

WRITINGS

W. Schuh, ed.: *Richard Strauss: Betrachtungen und Erinnerungen* (Zurich, 1949, enlarged 2/1957; Eng. trans., 1953) [collected essays]

*– ed. in Schuh
(*Asow nos. given in parentheses*)

Aus Italien [analysis] (307), 1889; *Tannhäuser*-Nachklänge (308), 1892; Tagebuch der Griechenland- und Ägyptenreise (309), 1892; Über mein Schaffen (310), 1893; Rundschreiben über die *Parsifal*-Schutzfrage (311), 1894; Handschreiben zur Reform des Urheberrechtsgesetzes von 1870 (312), 1898; Autobiographische Skizze (313), 1898; *Einleitung zu *Die Musik*: Sammlung illustrierter Einzeldarstellungen (314), 1903; *ed. and enlarged: Instrumentationslehre von Hector Berlioz (316–17), 1904–5; Zum Tonkünstlerfeste: Begrüssung anlässlich des Tonkünstlerfestes des Allgemeinen Deutschen Musikvereins (318), 1905; Bemerkungen über amerikanische Musikpflege (319), 1907; *Gibt es für die Musik eine Fortschrittspartei? (320), 1907; Salomes Tanz der sieben Schleier (320A), ?1908; Zum *Salome*-Verbot in Amerika (320B), 1908; Rechtfertigung der Aufführung der *Symphonia domestica* im Warenhaus Wannemaker (320C), 1908; *Elektra*: Interview für den Berliner Lokalanzeiger (320D), 1908
*Geleitwort zu Leopold Schmidt *Aus dem Musikleben der Gegenwart* (321), 1908; Die hohen Bach-Trompeten (322), 1909; *Persönliche Erinnerungen an Hans von Bülow (328), 1909; Dementi zu falschen Pressenotizen über die neue Oper *Ochs von Lerchenau* (*Der Rosenkavalier*) (327), 1909 or 1910; *Gustav Mahler (328), 1910; Die Grenzen der Komponierbaren (329), 1910; *Der Rosenkavalier* (330), 1910; *Mozarts *Così fan tutte* (331), 1910; Erwiderung auf Angriffe gegen den 'Programm-Musiker' (331A), 1911; Antwort auf die Rundfrage 'Worin erblicken Sie die entscheidende Bedeutung Franz Liszts für die Entwicklung des deutschen Musiklebens?' (331B), 1911; *Zur Frage des *Parsifal*-Schutzes: Antwort auf eine Rundfrage (332), 1912; *Offener Brief an einen Oberbürgermeister (333), 1913; *Städtebund-Theater: eine Anregung (334), 1914; Eine Kundgebung Richard Strauss' (335), 1919; Begrüssungsansprache

des neuen Wiener Operndirektors Richard Strauss (336), 1919; *The Composer Speaks (in D. Ewen: *The Book of Modern Composers*, 1945, p.54) (336A), 1921; *Novitäten und Stars: Spielplanerwägungen eines modernen Operndirektors (337), 1922; Einleitung zu *Schlagobers* (338), 1924; *Vorwort zu *Intermezzo* (2 versions) (339–40), 1924; *Über Johann Strauss (341), 1925; *Gedächtnisrede auf Friedrich Rösch (342), 1925
*Die 10 goldenen Lebensregeln des hochfürstlichen bayerischen Kammerkappelarius Hans Knappertsbuch, Monachia (343), 1927; Der Dresdner Staatsoper zum Jubiläum (344), 1928; *Interview über *Die ägyptische Helena* (345), 1928; *Die Münchener Oper (346), 1928; Über Schubert: ein Entwurf (347), ?1928; *Über Komponieren und Dirigieren (348), 1929; Die schöpferische Kraft des Komponisten (349), 1929; *Vorwort zu Hans Diestel: *Ein Orchestermusiker über das Dirigieren* (350), 1931; *Die ägyptische Helena* (351), 1931; Über den musikalischen Schaffensprozess (352), 1931; Gedenkworte für Alfred Roller (353), 1933; Über Richard Wagner (354), 1933; An die Schriftleitung *Musik im Zeitbewusstsein* (355), 1933; *Zeitgemässe Glossen für Erziehung zur Musik, für einen befreundeten Pädagogen (356), 1933; Ansprache des Präsidenten der Reichsmusikkammer Dr. Richard Strauss anlässlich der Eröffnung der ersten Arbeitstagung der Reichsmusikkammer (357), 1934; Appell zum 'Schutz der ideelen Interessen am Kunstwerk' (358), 1933 or 1934; Ansprache bei der öffentlichen Musikversammlung am 17. Februar in der Berliner Philharmonie (359), 1934; Ansprache am ersten Komponistentag in Berlin (359A), 1934; Zur Urheberrechtsreform (359B), 1934; Musik und Kultur (360), 1934; *Dirigentenerfahrungen mit klassischen Meisterwerken (361), 1934; Anmerkungen zur Aufführungen von Beethoven Symphonien (362), ?1934
Über die Besetzung der Kurorchester (363), 1934; Brief anstelle eines Vorwortes zu Joseph Gregor, *Richard Strauss*[: *Der Meister der Oper*] (363A), 1935; Geschichte der *Schweigsamen Frau* (364), 1935; *Arabella* (365), 1937; *Bemerkungen zu Richard Wagners Gesamtkunstwerk und zum Bayreuther Festspielhaus (366), 1940; Bemerkungen zu Wagners *Oper und Drama* (367), ?1940; *Erinnerungen an meinen Vater (325), c1940; *Aus meinen Jugend- und Lehrjahren (326), c1940; *Vom melodischen Einfall (368), c1940; Omaggio a Giuseppe Verdi (368A), 1941; Anstelle eines Vorwortes zu Anton Berger: *Richard Strauss als geistige Macht* (369), 1941; *Zur Josephslegende (370), 1941; *Meine Werke in guter Zusammenstellung (371), 1941; Mozart, der Dramatiker (373), 1941; Glückwunsch für die Wiener Philharmoniker (374), 1942; *Geleitwort zu *Capriccio* (375), 1942; *Erinnerungen an die ersten Aufführungen meiner Opern von *Guntram* bis *Intermezzo* (376), 1942; Vorwort zu *Divertimento* (377), 1942; Über Wesen und Bedeutung der Oper (*rev. version) (378, 385), 1943, 1945; Geleitwort zu Willi Schuh: *Das Bühnenwerk von Richard Strauss* (379), 1944; *Über Mozart (380), 1944; Zum Kapitel Mozart (381), 1944; Über die Generalprobe der Oper *Die Liebe der Danae* (382), 1944; Gedanken über die *Weltgeschichte des Theaters* und Entwurf eines Briefes an Josef Gregor, den Verfasser (383), 1945; *Brief über das humanistische Gymnasium an Professor Reisinger (384), 1945: Geschichte der Oper *Die Liebe der Danae* (386), 1946; Pauline Strauss-de Ahna (387), 1947; *Glückwunsch für die sächsische Staatskapelle (388), 1948; Garmische Rede am 85. Geburtstag (389), 1949; Letzte Aufzeichnung (390), 1949

BIBLIOGRAPHY

CORRESPONDENCE

F. Strauss, ed.: *Richard Strauss: Briefwechsel mit Hugo von Hofmannsthal* (Berlin, 1925; Eng. trans., 1928)
Richard Strauss et Romain Rolland: correspondance, fragments de journal (Paris, 1951; Eng. trans., 1968)
F. von Schuch: *Richard Strauss, Ernst von Schuch und Dresdens Oper* (Leipzig, 1952, 2/1953)
W. Schuh, ed.: *Richard Strauss und Hugo von Hofmannsthal: Briefwechsel: Gesamtausgabe* (Zurich, 1952, enlarged 2/1955; Eng. trans., 1961)
W. Schuh and F. Trenner, eds.: 'Hans von Bülow/Richard Strauss: Briefwechsel', *Richard Strauss Jb 1954*, 7–88; separate Eng. trans. (1955)
W. Schuh, ed.: *Richard Strauss: Briefe an die Eltern 1882–1906* (Zurich, 1954)
R. Tenschert, ed.: *Richard Strauss und Joseph Gregor: Briefwechsel 1934–1949* (Salzburg, 1955)
F. Zagiba: 'Bella als Vorkämpfer des jungen Richard Strauss: Strauss' Künstlerisches Credo in sienen Briefen an Bella', *Johann Leopold Bella (1843–1936) und das Weiner Musikleben* (Vienna, 1955), 46
W. Schuh, ed.: *Richard Strauss, Stefan Zweig: Briefwechsel* (Frankfurt am Main, 1957; Eng. trans., 1977)
E. Krause, ed.: 'Richard Strauss: ein Brief an Dora Wihan-Weis', *Richard Strauss Jb 1959–60*, 55

W. Schuh, ed.: 'Richard Strauss und Anton Kippenberg: Briefwechsel', *Richard Strauss Jb 1959–60*, 114–46
'Erlebnis und Bekenntnis des jungen Richard Strauss', *Internationale Mitteilungen: Richard-Strauss-Gesellschaft* (1961), no.30, p.1 [letter to Cosima Wagner]
W. Schmieder: '57 unveröffentlichte Briefe und Karten von Richard Strauss in der Stadt- und Universitätsbibliothek Frankfurt/Main', *Festschrift Helmuth Osthoff* (Tutzing, 1961), 163
D. Kämper, ed.: *Richard Strauss und Franz Wüllner im Briefwechsel* (Cologne, 1963)
G. K. Kende and W. Schuh, eds.: *Richard Strauss, Clemens Krauss: Briefwechsel* (Munich, 1963, 2/1964)
G. K. Kende: 'Aus dem Briefwechsel Richard Strauss/Clemens Krauss: 12 unveröffentlichte Briefe', *SMz*, cvi (1966), 2
F. Grasberger, ed.: *Der Strom der Töne trug mich fort: die Welt um Richard Strauss in Briefen* (Tutzing, 1967)
A. Ott: 'Richard Strauss und sein Verlegerfreund Eugen Spitzweg', *Musik und Verlag: Karl Vötterle zum 65. Geburtstag* (Kassel, 1968), 466
——, ed.: *Richard Strauss und Ludwig Thuille: Briefe der Freundschaft 1877–1907* (Munich, 1969)
W. Schuh, ed.: *Richard Strauss: Briefwechsel mit Willi Schuh* (Zurich, 1969)
K. W. Birkin: 'Strauss, Zweig and Gregor: Unpublished Letters', *ML*, lvi (1975), 180

CATALOGUES, DOCUMENTARY MATERIAL, MEMOIRS, ICONOGRAPHY

R. Specht: *Richard Strauss: vollständiges Verzeichnis der im Druck erschienenen Werke* (Vienna, 1910)
T. Schäfer: *Also sprach Richard Strauss zu mir: aus dem Tagebuch eines Musikers und Schriftstellers* (Dortmund, 1924)
E. Wachten: *Richard Strauss, geboren 1864: sein Leben in Bildern* (Leipzig, 1940)
S. Zweig: *Die Welt von gestern: Erinnerungen eines Europäers* [1942] (Stockholm, 1944; Eng. trans., 1943)
R. Tenschert: *Anekdoten um Richard Strauss* (Vienna, 1945)
F. Busch: *Aus dem Leben eines Musikers* (Zurich, 1949)
E. Roth, ed. *Richard Strauss: Bühnenwerke* (London, 1954) [text in Ger., Eng., Fr.]
W. Schuh: *Das Bühnenwerk von Richard Strauss in den unter Mitwirkung des Komponisten geschaffenen letzten Münchner Inszenierungen* (Zurich, 1954)
F. Trenner: *Richard Strauss: Dokumente seines Lebens und Schaffens* (Munich, 1954)
L. Kusche: *Heimliche Aufforderung zu Richard Strauss mit 15 zeitgenössischen Karikaturen* (Munich, 1959)
R. Petzoldt: *Richard Strauss: sein Leben in Bildern* (Leipzig, 1962)
H. Zurlinden, ed.: *Erinnerungen an Richard Strauss: Carl Spitteler, Albert Schweitzer, Max Huber, Cuno Amiet, Artur Honegger* (St Gall, 1962)
A. Jefferson: *The Operas of Richard Strauss in Britain 1910–1963* (London, 1963)
B. Domin: *Richard Strauss in Würdigung seines 100. Geburtstages am 11. Juni 1964: eine Auswahl aus den Beständen der Stadtbibliothek Koblenz, Musikbücherei* (Koblenz, 1964)
F. E. Dostal, ed.: *Karl Böhm: Begegnung mit Richard Strauss* (Vienna, 1964)
F. Grasberger and F. Hadamowsky, eds.: *Richard-Strauss-Ausstellung zum 100. Geburtstag* (Vienna, 1964)
L. Kusche: *Richard Strauss im Kulturkarussell der Zeit 1864–1964* (Munich, 1964)
O. Ortner: *Richard-Strauss-Bibliographie, Teil 1: 1882–1944* (Vienna, 1964)
A. Ott, ed.: *Richard Strauss-Festjahr München 1964 zum 100. Geburtstag von Richard Strauss* (Munich, 1964)
W. Schuh: *Ein paar Erinnerungen an Richard Strauss* (Zurich, 1964)
W. Schuh and E. Roth, eds.: *Richard Strauss: Complete Catalogue* (London, 1964)
S. von Scanzoni, ed.: *Katalog der Ausstellung Richard Strauss und seine Zeit* (Munich, 1964)
W. Thomas: *Richard Strauss und seine Zeitgenossen* (Munich, 1964)
F. Grasberger: *Richard Strauss: hohe Kunst, erfülltes Leben* (Vienna, 1965)
K. Böhm: *Ich erinnere mich ganz genau* (Zurich, 1968)
W. Deppisch: *Richard Strauss in Selbstzeugnissen und Bilddokumenten* (Reinbek, nr. Hamburg, 1968)
G. Brosche, ed.: *Richard-Strauss-Bibliographie, Teil 2: 1944–1964* (Vienna, 1973)
A. Jefferson: *Richard Strauss* (London, 1975)
A. Ott: 'Die Briefe von Richard Strauss in der Stadtbibliothek München', *Beiträge zur Musikdokumentation: Franz Grasberger zum 60. Geburtstag* (Tutzing, 1975), 341
F. Trenner: *Die Skizzenbücher von Richard Strauss aus dem Richard-Strauss-Archiv in Garmisch* (Tutzing, 1977)

LIFE, WORKS

G. Brecher: *Richard Strauss: eine monographische Skizze* (Leipzig, 1900)

R. Batka: *Richard Strauss* (Charlottenburg, 1908)

M. Steinitzer: *Richard Strauss* (Berlin, 1911, final enlarged edn. 1927)

H. T. Finck: *Richard Strauss: the Man and his Work* (Boston, 1917)

S. Kallenberg: *Richard Strauss: Leben und Werk* (Leipzig, 1926)

J. F. Cooke: *Richard Strauss: a Short Biography* (Philadelphia, 1929)

E. Gehring, ed.: *Richard Strauss und seine Vaterstadt: zum 70. Geburtstag am 11. Juni 1934* (Munich, 1934)

F. Gysi: *Richard Strauss* (Potsdam, 1934)

J. Kapp: *Richard Strauss und die Berliner Oper* (Berlin, 1934–9)

W. Brandl: *Richard Strauss: Leben und Werk* (Wiesbaden, 1949)

E. Bücken: *Richard Strauss* (Kevelaer, 1949)

K. Pfister: *Richard Strauss: Weg, Gestalt, Denkmal* (Vienna, 1949)

C. Rostand: *Richard Strauss* (Paris, 1949, 2/1965)

R. Tenschert: *Richard Strauss und Wien: eine Wahlverwandtschaft* (Vienna, 1949)

O. Erhardt: *Richard Strauss: Leben, Wirken, Schaffen* (Olten, 1953)

E. Krause: *Richard Strauss: Gestalt und Werk* (Leipzig, 1955, rev. 3/1963; Eng. trans., 1964)

N. Del Mar: *Richard Strauss: a Critical Commentary on his Life and Works* (London, 1962–72/R with corrections 1978)

H. Kralik: *Richard Strauss: Weltbürger der Musik* (Vienna, 1963)

F. Hadamowsky: *Richard Strauss und Salzburg* (Salzburg, 1964)

W. Panofsky: *Richard Strauss: Partitur eines Lebens* (Munich, 1965)

F. Grasberger: *Richard Strauss und die Wiener Oper* (Tutzing, 1969)

A. Jefferson: *The Life of Richard Strauss* (Newton Abbot, 1973)

M. Kennedy: *Richard Strauss* (London, 1976)

W. Schuh: *Richard Strauss: Jugend und Meisterjahre: Lebenschronik 1864–98* (Zurich, 1976)

CRITICAL AND ANALYTICAL STUDIES

G. Brecher: 'Richard Strauss als Symphoniker', *Leipziger Kunst*, i (1899), 400, 417

G. Jourissenne: *Richard Strauss: essai critique et biographique* (Brussels, 1899)

H. Merian: *Richard Strauss' Tondichtung 'Also sprach Zarathustra': eine Studie über die moderne Programmsymphonie* (Leipzig, 1899)

E. Urban: *Richard Strauss* (Berlin, 1901)

——: *Strauss contra Wagner* (Berlin, 1902)

A. Guttmann: 'Richard Strauss als Lyriker', *Die Musik*, iv (1904–5), 93

O. Bie: *Die moderne Musik und Richard Strauss* (Berlin, 1906)

L. Gilman: *Strauss' Salome: a Guide to the Opera* (New York, 1906)

P. Marsop: 'Italien und der ''Fall Salome'', nebst Glossen zur Kritik und Ästhetik', *Die Musik*, vi (1906–7), 139

J. C. Mannifarges: *Richard Strauss als Dirigent* (Amsterdam, 1907)

E. Schmitz: *Richard Strauss als Musikdramatiker: eine aesthetisch-kritische Studie* (Munich, 1907)

E. von Ziegler: *Richard Strauss und seine dramatischen Dichtungen* (Munich, 1907)

E. Newman: *Richard Strauss* (London, 1908/R1970)

H. Walden, ed.: *Richard Strauss: Symphonien und Tondichtungen erläutert von G. Brecher, A. Hahn, W. Klatte, W. Mauke, A. Schattmann, H. Treibler, H. Walden, mit einer Einleitung: Richard Strauss' Leben und Schaffen* (Berlin, 1908)

P. Bekker: *Das Musikdrama der Gegenwart* (Stuttgart, 1909)

——: 'Elektra: Studie', *Neue Musik-Zeitung*, xxx (1909), 293, 330, 387

E. Fischer-Plasser: *Einführung in die Musik von Richard Strauss und Elektra* (Leipzig, 1909)

G. Gräner: *Richard Strauss: Musikdramen* (Berlin, 1909)

C. Mennicke: 'Richard Strauss: Elektra', *Riemann-Festschrift* (Leipzig, 1909), 503

F. Santoliquido: *Il dopo-Wagner: Claude Debussy e Richard Strauss* (Rome, 1909)

O. R. Hübner: *Richard Strauss und das Musikdrama: Betrachtungen über den Wert oder Unwert gewisser Opernmusiken* (Leipzig, 1910)

E. Hutcheson: *Elektra by Richard Strauss: a Guide to the Opera with Musical Examples from the Score* (New York, 1910)

W. Klein: 'Die Harmonisation in Elektra von Richard Strauss: ein Beitrag zur modernen Harmonisationslehre', *Der Merker*, ii (1911), 512, 540, 590

C. Paglia: *Strauss, Debussy e compagnia bella: saggio di critica semplicista e spregiudicata per il gran pubblico* (Bologna, 1911)

A. Seidl: *Straussiana: Aufsätze zur Richard Strauss-Frage aus drei Jahrzehnten* (Regensburg, 1913)

F. Dubitzky: 'Richard Strauss' Kammermusik', *Die Musik*, xiii (1913–14), 283

E. Thilo: 'Richard Strauss als Chorkomponist', *Die Musik*, xiii (1913–14), 504

M. Steinitzer: *Richard Strauss in seiner Zeit, mit einem Abdruck der auf der Strausswoche zu Stuttgart im Kgl. Hoftheater gehaltenen Rede und einem Bildnis* (Leipzig, 1914)

O. Bie: *Die neuere Musik bis Richard Strauss* (Leipzig, 1916)

B. Diebold: 'Die ironische *Ariadne* und der *Bürger als Edelmann*', *Deutsche Bühne*, i (1918), 219

L. Gilman: 'Richard Strauss and his Alpine Symphony', *North American Review*, xxiv (1919), 920

H. Scherchen: 'Tonalitätsprinzip und die Alpen-Symphonie von Richard Strauss', *Melos*, i (1920), 198, 244

P. Bekker: *Kritische Zeitbilder* (Stuttgart, 1921)

R. Specht: *Richard Strauss und sein Werk* (Leipzig, 1921)

H. W. von Waltershausen: *Richard Strauss: ein Versuch* (Munich, 1921)

E. Bloch: 'Mahler, Strauss, Bruckner', *Die Musik*, xv (1922–3), 664

A. Rosenzweig: *Zur Entwicklungsgeschichte des Strauss'schen Musikdramas* (diss., U. of Vienna, 1923)

R. Specht: 'Vom *Guntram* zur *Frau ohne Schatten*', *Almanach der Deutschen Musikbücherei auf das Jahr 1923* (Regensburg, 1923), 150

W. Klatte: 'Aus Richard Strauss' Werkstatt', *Die Musik*, xvi (1923–4), 636

M. Steinitzer: 'Der unbekannte Strauss', *Die Musik*, xvi (1923–4), 653

H. Windt: 'Richard Strauss und die Atonalität', *Die Musik*, xvi (1923–4), 642

W. Schrenk: *Richard Strauss und die neue Musik* (Berlin, 1924)

A. Lorenz: 'Der formale Schwung in Richard Strauss' *Till Eulenspiegel*', *Die Musik*, xvii (1924–5), 658

R. Tenschert: 'Die Kadenzbehandlung bei Richard Strauss: ein Beitrag zur neueren Harmonik', *ZMw*, viii (1925), 161

A. Seidl: *Neuzeitliche Tondichter und zeitgenössische Tonkünstler: gesammelte Aufsätze, Studien und Skizzen* (Regensburg, 1926)

E. Stein: 'Mahler, Reger, Strauss und Schönberg: kompositionstechnische Betrachtungen', *25 Jahre neue Musik: Jb 1926 der Universal-Edition* (Vienna, 1926), 63

K. Westphal: 'Das musikdramatische Prinzip bei Richard Strauss', *Die Musik*, xix (1926–7), 859

T. Armstrong: *Strauss' Tone Poems* (London, 1931)

G. Röttger: *Die Harmonik in Richard Strauss' Der Rosenkavalier: ein Beitrag zur Entwicklung der romantischen Harmonik nach Richard Wagner* (diss., U. of Munich, 1931)

M. Steinitzer: 'Richard Strauss' Werke für Klavier', *Die Musik*, xxiv (1931–2), 105

E. Wachten: *Das psychotechnische Formproblem in den Sinfonischen Dichtungen von Richard Strauss (mit besonderer Berücksichtigung seiner Bühnenwerke)* (diss., U. of Berlin, 1932; abridged, Berlin, 1933)

P. Bekker: 'Brief an Richard Strauss', *Die Musik*, xxv (1932–3), 81

R. Tenschert: 'Die Tonsymbolik bei Richard Strauss', *Die Musik*, xxvi (1933–4), 646

——: 'Wandlungen einer Kadenz: Absonderlichkeiten der Harmonik im *Don Quixote* von Richard Strauss', *Die Musik*, xxvi (1933–4), 663

W. Reich: 'Bemerkungen zum Strauss'schen Opernschaffen, anlässlich des 70. Geburtstages', *Der Auftakt*, xiv (1934), 101

K. H. Ruppel: 'Richard Strauss und das Theater', *Melos*, xiii (1934), 175

R. Tenschert: 'Verhältnis von Wort und Ton: eine Untersuchung an dem Strauss'schen Lied ''Ich trage meine Minne'' ', *ZfM*, Jg.101 (1934), 591

——: 'Versuch einer Typologie der Richard Strauss'schen Melodik', *ZMw*, xvi (1934), 274

K.-J. Krüger: *Hugo von Hofmannsthal und Richard Strauss: Versuch einer Deutung des künstlerischen Weges Hugo von Hofmannsthals, mit einem Anhang: erstmalige Veröffentlichung der bisher ungedruckten einzigen Vertonung eines Hofmannsthalschen Gedichtes durch Richard Strauss* (Berlin, 1935)

H. Röttger: *Das Formproblem bei Richard Strauss gezeigt an der Oper Die Frau ohne Schatten, mit Einschluss von Guntram und Intermezzo* (diss., U. of Munich, 1935; abridged, Berlin, 1937)

A. Lorenz: 'Neue Formerkenntnisse, angewandt auf Richard Straussens *Don Juan*', *AMf*, i (1936), 452

J. Gregor: *Richard Strauss: der Meister der Oper* (Munich, 1939, 2/1942)

——: 'Zur Entstehung von Richard Strauss' *Daphne*', *Almanach zum 35. Jahr des Verlags R. Piper & Co., München* (Munich, 1939), 104

R. Tenschert: 'Autobiographisches im Schaffen von Richard Strauss', *ZfM*, Jg.106 (1939), 582

——: 'Hosenrollen in den Bühnenwerken von Richard Strauss', *ZfM*, Jg.106 (1939), 586

R. Hartmann: *Capriccio: ein Konversationsstück für Musik in 1 Aufzug von Clemens Krauss und Richard Strauss, op.85: Regieangaben nach Erfahrungen der Uraufführung, Staatsoper München, 28. Oktober 1942* (Berlin, 1943)

G. Becker: *Das Problem der Oper an Hand von Richard Strauss' Capriccio* (diss., U. of Jena, 1944)

C. Blessing: *Das instrumentale Schaffen von Richard Strauss im Spiegelbild der Presse und der zeitgenössischen Kritik* (diss., U. of Munich, 1944)

A. Mathis: 'Stefan Zweig as Librettist and Richard Strauss', *ML*, xxv (1944), 163, 226

W. Schuh: 'Eine nicht komponierte Szene zur *Arabella*', *SMz*, lxxxiv (1944), 231

R. Tenschert: *Dreimal sieben Variationen über das Thema Richard Strauss* (Vienna, 1944, 2/1945)

O. Gatscha: *Librettist und Komponist: dargestellt an den Opern Richard Strauss'* (diss., U. of Vienna, 1947)

A. Pryce-Jones: *Richard Strauss: Der Rosenkavalier* (London, 1947)

W. Schuh: *Über Opern von Richard Strauss* (Zurich, 1947)

R. Raffalt: *Über die Problematik der Programmusik: ein Versuch ihres Aufweises an der Pastoral-Symphonie von Beethoven, der Berg-Symphonie von Liszt und der Alpensinfonie von Strauss* (diss., U. of Tübingen, 1949)

F. Trenner: *Die Zusammenarbeit von Hugo von Hofmannsthal und Richard Strauss* (diss., U. of Munich, 1949)

D. Lindner: *Richard Strauss/Joseph Gregor: Die Liebe der Danae: Herkunft, Inhalt und Gestaltung eines Opernwerkes* (Vienna, 1952)

R. Schopenhauer: *Die antiken Frauengestalten bei Richard Strauss* (diss., U. of Vienna, 1952)

W. Schuh, ed.: *Hugo von Hofmannsthal: Danae oder die Vernunftheirat: Szenarium und Notizen* (Frankfurt, 1952)

G. Hausswald: *Richard Strauss: ein Beitrag zur Dresdener Operngeschichte seit 1945* (Dresden, 1953)

W. Wendhausen: *Das stilistische Verhältnis von Dichtung und Musik in der Entwicklung der musikdramatischen Werke Richard Strauss'* (diss., U. of Hamburg, 1954)

G. K. Kende: *Richard Strauss und Clemens Krauss: eine Künstlerfreundschaft und ihre Zusammenarbeit an Capriccio (op.85): Konversationsstück für Musik* (Munich, 1960)

S. von Scanzoni: *Richard Strauss und seine Sänger: eine Plauderei über das Musiktheater in den Wind gesprochen* (Munich, 1961)

G. Baum: *'Hab' mir's gelobt, ihn lieb zu haben . . .': Richard Strauss und Hugo von Hofmannsthal nach ihrem Briefwechsel dargestellt* (Berlin, 1962)

A. Natan: *Richard Strauss: die Opern* (Basle, 1963)

E. Newman: *Testament of Music* (London, 1963)

A. Berger: *Richard Strauss als geistige Macht: Versuch eines philosophischen Verständnisses* (Gisch, 1964)

L. Lehmann: *Five Operas and Richard Strauss* (New York, 1964; as *Singing with Richard Strauss*, London, 1964)

W. Mann: *Richard Strauss: a Critical Study of the Operas* (London, 1964)

K. Pörnbacher: *Hugo von Hofmannsthal/Richard Strauss: Der Rosenkavalier* (Munich, 1964)

W. Schuh: *Hugo von Hofmannsthal und Richard Strauss: Legende und Wirklichkeit* (Munich, 1964)

A. Goléa: *Richard Strauss* (Paris, 1965)

R. Gerlach: *Tonalität und tonale Konfiguration im Oeuvre von Richard Strauss: Analysen und Interpretationen als Beiträge zum Verständnis von tonalen Problemen und Formen in sinfonischen Werken und in der 'Einleitung' und ersten Szene des Rosenkavalier* (diss., U. of Zurich, 1966; Berne, 1966, as *Don Juan und Rosenkavalier*)

Festschrift Dr. Franz Strauss (Tutzing, 1967)

R. H. Schäfer: *Hugo von Hofmannsthals Arabella* (Berne, 1967)

H. Federhofer: 'Die musikalische Gestaltung des *Krämerspiegels* von Richard Strauss', *Musik und Verlag: Karl Vötterle zum 65. Geburtstag* (Kassel, 1968), 260

W. Gruhn: *Die Instrumentation in den Orchesterwerken von Richard Strauss* (diss., U. of Mainz, 1968)

H. Schnoor: *Die Stunde des Rosenkavalier: 300 Jahre Dresdner Oper* (Munich, 1968)

W. Schuh: *Der Rosenkavalier: 4 Studien* (Olten, 1968)

——: 'Richard Strauss und seine Libretti', *GfMKB, Bonn 1970*, 169

J. Knaus: *Hugo von Hofmannsthal und sein Weg zur Oper Die Frau ohne Schatten* (Berlin, 1971)

W. Schuh, ed.: *Hugo von Hofmannsthal, Richard Strauss: Der Rosenkavalier: Fassungen, Filmszenarium, Briefe* (Frankfurt am Main, 1971)

A. A. Abert: *Richard Strauss: die Opern: Einführung und Analyse* (Hanover, 1972)

G. I. Ascher: *Die Zauberflöte und die Frau ohne Schatten: ein Vergleich zwischen zwei Operndichtungen der Humanität* (Berne, 1972)

A. Jefferson: *The Lieder of Richard Strauss* (London, 1972)

A. A. Abert: 'Richard Strauss' Anteil an seinen Operntexten', *Musicae scientiae collectanea: Festschrift Karl Gustav Fellerer* (Cologne, 1973), 1

——: 'Richard Strauss und das Erbe Wagners', *Mf*, xxvii (1974), 165

W. W. Colson: *Four Last Songs by Richard Strauss* (diss., U. of Illinois, 1974)

D. G. Daviau and G. J. Buelow: *The 'Ariadne auf Naxos' of Hugo von Hofmannsthal and Richard Strauss* (Chapel Hill, 1975)

A. Forchert: 'Zur Auflösung traditioneller Formkategorien in der Musik um 1900: Probleme formaler Organisation bei Mahler und Strauss', *AMw*, xxxii (1975), 85

W. Schuh: 'Metamorphosen einer Ariette von Richard Strauss',

Opernstudien: Anna Amalie Abert zum 65. Geburtstag (Tutzing, 1975), 197

B. A. Petersen: *Ton und Wort: the Lieder of Richard Strauss* (Ann Arbor, 1979)

MICHAEL KENNEDY (text),
ROBERT BAILEY (work-list, bibliography)

Stravaganza (It.: 'extravagance', 'fantastic eccentricity'). A term for a piece in no specific form involving melodic, harmonic, rhythmic or other features of an extraordinary kind. It appears adjectivally by the end of the 16th century in works such as Giovanni de Macque's *Consonanze stravaganti* for organ (HAM, no.174) which exhibit harmonic mannerisms, similar to those employed by Gesualdo, that became part of the *stylus phantasticus* of the Baroque period. The word occasionally appears as a title in 17th- and 18th-century violin music: Karlo Farina's *Capriccio stravagante* (1627), a taxing virtuoso piece for violin and strings including the imitation of birds and animals, was extremely influential; and a *Stravagance* by the elder Matteis from the late 17th century is characterized by wide leaps across the strings. On the other hand, Vivaldi's set of concertos called *La stravaganza* (op.4) is more remarkable for its musical originality than for extravagant features of technique or musical style. Carlo Tessarini probably adopted the title from Vivaldi for his own op.4 of 1736–7. A cantata by Benedetto Marcello, *Stravaganze d'amore* (excerpt in C. Parrish, ed.: *A Treasury of Early Music* (New York, 1958), no.49), is a musical and textual satire on the genre as amusing as the same composer's *Teatro alla moda*. North was highly critical of many features adopted in the genre. Although it must be admitted that in pursuing novelty composers sometimes achieved effects that were merely awkwardly unconvincing, the value of these experiments in discovering new expressive resources was not altogether negligible.

BIBLIOGRAPHY
J. Wilson, ed.: *Roger North on Music* (London, 1959), 129ff
MICHAEL TILMOUTH

Stravinsky, Fyodor Ignat'yevich (*b* Noviy Dvor, Minsk govt., 20 June 1843; *d* St Petersburg, 4 Dec 1902). Russian bass of Polish descent, father of Igor Stravinsky. He attended the Lyceum at Nezhin, and then studied law. While a student, he sang with great success in public concerts and eventually decided to make a career as a singer. He entered the St Petersburg Conservatory in 1869, where, from September 1871, he studied with Camillo Everardi. In 1873, the year in which he graduated, his performance as Don Basilio in a student production of *Il barbiere di Siviglia* attracted the attention of the critics. He was engaged to sing at the opera theatre in Kiev and made his public début as Count Rodolpho in *La sonnambula* on 3 September 1873. He remained in Kiev until 1876, when he became one of the principal basses at the Mariinsky Theatre in St Petersburg, appearing there regularly until the year of his death. Stravinsky possessed a many-sided dramatic talent, and played both serious and comic roles with great mastery. He made a total of 1235 appearances in 64 different roles. He was particularly successful in Russian opera, being noted for his portrayals of Holofernes in Serov's *Judith*, the miller in Dargomïzhsky's *Rusalka*, Rangoni and Varlaam in *Boris Godunov* (Rimsky-Korsakov wrote the drinking scene in *Sadko* especially for Stravinsky after seeing him as Varlaam), Golova in Rimsky-Korsakov's *May Night* and Panas in his *Christmas Eve*, and Andrey Dubrovsky in Nápravník's *Dubrovsky*. Stasov considered that in the role of Farlaf (in Glinka's *Ruslan and Lyudmila*) Stravinsky was the 'worthy successor to Osip Petrov'. Tchaikovsky was a great admirer of Stravinsky, and asked that he should play the comparatively small part of Orlik in his opera *Mazepa*, since this part in particular required a 'good artist'. Stravinsky sang in the first performance of several of Tchaikovsky's operas.

An intelligent and hardworking performer, Stravinsky scorned the purely routine and superficial approach to his art and made a thorough psychological study of each character he portrayed, jotting down ideas for his interpretation in a notebook which he always carried. He took an interest in every aspect of stagecraft, and was an authority on make-up and costume design. Although his voice was not intrinsically beautiful, it was powerful and of a wide range (over two octaves). He strove to achieve evenness of tone, flexibility and variety of colour, so that he could use his voice to both musical and dramatic ends with equal success. He was an excellent concert singer; ballads such as Glinka's *Nochnoy smotr* ('The night review') and Musorgsky's *Polkovodets* ('The field marshal') were ideally suited to his histrionic gifts. Stravinsky was a bibliophile whose library numbered over 7000 volumes, and a collector of pictures. His son records that he had an uncontrollable temper, and was a somewhat distant and unpredictable parent. For most of his last year he was semi-paralysed, and he died from cancer of the spine.

BIBLIOGRAPHY

E. A. Stark: 'Fyodor Ignat'yevich Stravinsky', *EIT 1903–4*, suppl. to xiv, pp.116–73

I. Stravinsky: *Chronicle of my Life* (London, 1936)

E. A. Stark: *Peterburgskaya opera i eyo mastera 1899–1910* [The St Petersburg opera and its masters] (Leningrad, 1940)

V. Bogdanov-Berezovsky: *Fyodor Stravinsky* (Moscow and Leningrad, 1951)

M. Montagu-Nathan: 'Shaliapin's Precursors', *ML*, xxxiii (1952), 232

V. V. Stasov: *Izbrannïye sochineniya* [Selected works], iii (Moscow, 1952)

I. Stravinsky and R. Craft: *Expositions and Developments* (London, 1959)

——: *Memories and Commentaries* (London, 1959)

A. Gozenpud, ed.: *F. Stravinsky: stat'i, pis'ma, vospominaniya* [Articles, letters, reminiscences] (Leningrad, 1972)

JENNIFER SPENCER

Stravinsky, Igor (Fyodorovich) (*b* Oranienbaum [now Lomonosov], 17 June 1882; *d* New York, 6 April 1971). Russian composer, later of French (1934) and American (1945) nationality. His life was a varied one, and his music too went through several changes, often startling at the time but revealing an inner consistency when viewed with hindsight. His early years, from 1882 to 1910, found Stravinsky in Russia, absorbing influences from his elder compatriots and others. The years 1910–14 saw the beginning of his international career, with Dyagilev's Ballets Russes in Paris, and the premières of *The Firebird*, *Petrushka* and *The Rite of Spring*. Then, between 1914 and 1920, he made his home in Switzerland, his exile becoming permanent after the Russian Revolution, though the connection with his homeland continued in his works. The period from 1920 to 1939, which he spent in France, was that of the great neo-classical compositions, reactivating the

modes and manners of the 18th century. This stylistic inclination persisted in the earlier part of his American residence (1939–52), gradually giving way to a highly individual use of serial techniques in his last years.

1. Up to 1910. 2. 1910–14. 3. 1914–20. 4. 1920–39. 5. 1939–52. 6. 1953–71.

1. UP TO 1910.

(i) *Life*. Stravinsky's father, Fyodor Ignat'yevich Stravinsky, had a fine bass voice and was engaged as an opera singer first at Kiev, where he met Anna Kholodovsky, who became his wife, and then at the imperial opera house, the Mariinsky, St Petersburg. Igor was the third of four children, all of them boys. He was fond of his youngest brother Gury, who became a promising singer and was killed on the Romanian front in 1917; but he does not seem to have got on particularly well with the other members of his family. His youth was divided between winters in St Petersburg, where his parents had an apartment on the Krukov Canal, and summers in the country, where the family visited various estates belonging mainly to his mother's sisters and their husbands. There was Pavlovka in the government of Samara, where the Ielachich family lived; Pechisky near Proskurov and Yarmolintsi, which belonged to aunt Katerina; and an estate at Ustilug in Volin which had been bought in the 1890s by Gabriel Nossenko and his wife Maria.

Stravinsky attended the St Petersburg School no.27 from the age of 11 until he was 15, and went on to the Gurevich School. He then spent eight terms at St Petersburg University reading law; but by his own account he was a bad student at both school and university. It was a different matter with music. At home he frequently heard his father practising his operatic roles; and from an early age he was encouraged to attend ballet and opera performances at the Mariinsky. In later life one of his treasured memories was of seeing Tchaikovsky during the interval of a gala performance to celebrate the 50th anniversary of Glinka's *Ruslan and Lyudmila* a few weeks before that composer's sudden death in 1893.

At the age of nine Stravinsky began to take piano lessons from a Mlle A. P. Snetkova, and she was succeeded a few years later by Mlle L. A. Kashperova, a pupil of Anton Rubinstein. His parents seem to have hoped that in the course of time he might become a professional pianist. He received harmony lessons from Fyodor Akimenko and, later on, instruction in both harmony and counterpoint from Vassily Kalafaty. In his teens he found much enjoyment in improvisation, and his interest began to turn to composition. One of his student friends was Vladimir Rimsky-Korsakov, the youngest son of the composer; and when in the summer of 1902 Stravinsky accompanied his parents to Bad Wildungen and discovered that the Rimsky-Korsakov family was in the neighbourhood, he accepted an invitation to visit them, and in the course of this visit found an opportunity to consult Rimsky-Korsakov about his future career. At first he was disappointed by Rimsky-Korsakov's lack of enthusiasm for the little piano pieces he had brought with him; but the older man's counsel was sound. He advised Stravinsky not to enter the conservatory, but to continue his private studies in harmony and counterpoint. He thought his work of composition should be systematically supervised and added

1. Stravinsky (extreme left) and his wife Katerina (extreme right) at the home of Rimsky-Korsakov (seated next to Stravinsky) in 1908; also in the picture are Rimsky-Korsakov's daughter Nadezhda, and her fiancé Maximilian Shteynberg

that he personally would be prepared to offer advice if consulted. Shortly after this meeting, Stravinsky's father died, on 3 December 1902, and during the next six years Rimsky-Korsakov was to become something of a father figure to the young composer as well as his intimate musical adviser.

Stravinsky's circle of friends and his musical interests now began to widen. He became a regular attendant at the weekly musical gatherings at the Rimsky-Korsakov house. Some of his friends established the 'evenings of contemporary music', where music by contemporary German and French composers was performed as well as works by young Russians. Here his early Piano Sonata in F♯ minor (see fig.2) received its first public performance. This sonata had caused him some trouble when he started it in 1903; and following Rimsky-Korsakov's advice, he went to consult him in his summer retreat at Lzy. There followed a period of nearly three years during which he received regular instruction from Rimsky-Korsakov, mainly in instrumentation.

In 1905 Stravinsky's university career came to an end, and that autumn his engagement to his cousin Katerina Nossenko was announced. As they were first cousins and there was an imperial statute forbidding such marriages, the wedding had to be a quiet one. It took place in the village of Novaya Derevnya near St Petersburg on 23 January 1906. After a honeymoon at Imatra, the newly married couple settled down in the Stravinsky family apartment on the Krukov Canal for about a year before moving to an apartment of their own

on the English Prospekt. The summers continued to be spent in Ustilug, which Stravinsky found congenial to composition; and he now built his own house there on a site provided by his father-in-law. A son, Fyodor, was born to the couple in 1907 and a daughter, Ludmila, in 1908.

After his marriage Stravinsky continued to see Rimsky-Korsakov regularly, showing him his compositions in draft and discussing them with him movement by movement. His first work with an opus number, the Symphony in E♭, was dedicated to Rimsky-Korsakov, who arranged for a private performance to be given by the court orchestra under Wahrlich on 9 May 1907. Later that year Stravinsky showed him his *Scherzo fantastique* for orchestra and the sketches for the first act of his projected opera *Solovey* ('The Nightingale'), the libretto of which he had written in collaboration with his friend Stepan Mitusov. The following winter Rimsky-Korsakov's health began to fail. In spring 1908 Stravinsky told him of his intention to compose an orchestral fantasy, *Feu d'artifice* ('Fireworks'), to celebrate the forthcoming wedding of Rimsky-Korsakov's daughter Nadezhda to Maximilian Shteynberg. This was written at Ustilug; but by the time it was finished Rimsky-Korsakov had died at Lzy. After the funeral Stravinsky returned to Ustilug and composed a funeral dirge in his master's memory. Unfortunately this work, performed that autumn at a Belyayev concert at St Petersburg, was not published, and the musical material disappeared some years later; but Stravinsky remem-

2. Autograph MS of the beginning of Stravinsky's Piano Sonata in F♯ minor, composed 1903–4 (USSR-Mcm)

bered it with affection as the best of his compositions before *Zhar'-ptitsa* ('The Firebird').

When the *Scherzo fantastique* and *Fireworks* were performed in St Petersburg they made a deep impression on some members of the audience, including particularly the impresario Sergey Dyagilev, who had been closely associated with special manifestations of Russian art in Paris. For 1909 he was planning a mixed season of opera and ballet; and among his advisers were the dancer and choreographer Mikhail Fokin and two artists of distinction, Leon Bakst and Alexandre Benois, but as yet no musician. After hearing a concert performance of these two works Dyagilev realized that Stravinsky was almost certainly the composer he needed to complete his advisory group. For his 1909 season in Paris he asked Stravinsky to orchestrate Grieg's *Kobold* for a ballet, *Le festin*, and two Chopin piano pieces for *Les sylphides*. For his 1910 season he invited him to write the music for a ballet to be based on the Russian fairy tale of the Firebird. This was Stravinsky's first large-scale commission. He began the score when staying at the Rimsky-Korsakov country house at Lzy in the autumn of 1909 and finished it in St Petersburg early the following spring. The first performance of *The Firebird* with choreography by Fokin was given by the Ballets Russes at the Paris Opéra on 25 June 1910.

(ii) Works. The Firebird is the earliest of Stravinsky's scores to have won and held a place in the repertory; and yet he was in his 28th year by the time he composed

it. It cannot be regarded as a fully mature work, although it is a better and more original one than he himself was later to rate it. This gives some indication of the difficulty that Stravinsky had from the first in finding and forming his individual voice. Style was to be at once a problem and a creative stimulus to him at various periods throughout his long career – and not only because of the vicissitudes of his outward life, with its two exiles, unsettling though these undoubtedly were. For Stravinsky, as for many Russian composers before and since, history posed certain choices of outlook and allegiance, and in his case these were compounded rather than solved by a restlessly inquiring mind and an insatiable appetite for the sonorous raw materials of his art.

The music Stravinsky composed before *The Firebird* is mainly of interest for the way in which it reveals, as clearly as fossils in a succession of geological strata, the influences that came the way of a young man in a cultivated bourgeois home in St Petersburg in the first decade of the 20th century, and the way in which this particular one assimilated them. Of the two posthumously published early piano works the little Scherzo of 1902 is a very modest genre piece, some way after Tchaikovsky, whose only pointer towards things to come is the displaced chordal accent in its third bar; but the Sonata of 1903–4, the first fruits of his studies with Rimsky-Korsakov, is altogether more ambitious. Here again Tchaikovsky is the clearest influence – most obviously in the scherzo, but also in the more weighty first and last movements; in these Tchaikovsky's own father figure, Schumann, can be detected both in the textures and in the characteristic dotted rhythms. This is the work of a would-be cosmopolitan Petersburg composer for whom 'sonata' inevitably implied an adherence to German tradition, though there is little or nothing of the Beethoven influence that Stravinsky himself, in much later years, thought he remembered. Clearly he had already, in his early 20s, acquired a sound if conventional grasp of 'piano style'; what is weak in the sonata is not so much the disparity between its various ingredients as the clumsiness of the transitions between them.

This is a weakness, of course, only in a composer who accepts certain traditional formal assumptions, and Stravinsky was to discover himself precisely by jettisoning these. But not at once. For the present he was still bent on conforming to them, and the Symphony in E♭ op.1, composed under Rimsky-Korsakov's close supervision, shows a clear gain in professionalism of this conventional kind. Along with the increased technical assurance there goes a new (compared with the sonata) emphasis on folk-influenced melodic material, and this gives the music much more rhythmic variety and vitality. Tchaikovsky reappears in the scherzo (though the trio melody seems more like a domesticated relation of the *Petrushka* nursemaids), but the strongest influence apart from that of Rimsky-Korsakov now seems to be that of Borodin, and no doubt there is some debt to Glazunov too, though Stravinsky's personal dislike of the man may later have led him to play this down. The young composer shows his individuality in his occasional tentative forays into Wagnerian orchestral effect (e.g. the tremolandos at fig.24 of the first movement) and chromatic harmony. The stylistic inconsistency which this produces was later to be turned to valid dramatic use in *The Firebird*, and the end of the rather Franckian slow movement again foreshadows that score (the transition from the 'Berceuse' to the final scene) – but such indications of the future are, perhaps naturally, more pronounced in the smaller-scale, less 'symphonic' works of the period.

In *Favn' i pastushka* ('Faun and Shepherdess'), a setting for mezzo-soprano and small orchestra of words by Pushkin composed in 1906, the appearance of the Faun at the beginning of the second song is accompanied by an orchestral gesture that immediately recalls the appearance of the Firebird herself, and the very end of the song cycle clearly prefigures that of the ballet, even as regards key. Tchaikovsky is still present at times, particularly in the yearning phrases of the first song, but with a stronger admixture of Wagner; Rimsky-Korsakov was worried by a tincture of Debussian modernism that was more conspicuous to him than it is to a modern listener. The vocal writing is rhythmically rather unadventurous, and scarcely less so in the two Gorodetzky songs for mezzo and piano composed during the two following summers – but in this Stravinsky may already have been reflecting the syllabic character of Russian folksong. What is more interesting is the curiously empirical chromaticism of the harmony; progressions are not marked by any strongly marked sense of a controlling bass, but rather edge from one chord to another, as if worked out at the piano. This is also a characteristic of the Four Studies for piano, composed in the summer of 1908, but in them it is exploited more systematically – and the first two, at

least, are also systematic in their exploitation of opposed rhythms in the two hands (3 or 2 against 5; 6 against 4 or 5), which give the music a peculiarly Skryabinesque fluidity. In the third study Stravinsky is for once closer to Rakhmaninov, but in the last, and best, he is already clearly himself; the sense of harmonic drive in this *moto perpetuo* is unmistakably original.

The distance Stravinsky had already travelled in the four or five years since the sonata is remarkable, but no doubt the Studies seemed less important at the time, to him and his audiences, than the two short pieces for large orchestra of 1907–8, the *Scherzo fantastique* and the fantasy *Fireworks*. Both of these show, far more clearly than the songs or the piano music, the impact (so much deplored by Rimsky-Korsakov) of the new French music. Dukas' *L'apprenti sorcier* makes an almost literal appearance in the middle section of *Fireworks*, but the most pervasive influence is that of Debussy's *Nocturnes*, which Stravinsky had heard at one of Siloti's concerts in St Petersburg; he himself would later describe it as 'among the major events of my early years'. But the most major event was unquestionably his being commissioned by Dyagilev, on the strength of these two scores, to compose a ballet for his company's 1910 season in Paris. Here for the first time Stravinsky was faced with the challenge of composing an orchestral work nearly an hour in length, and of telling a dramatic story through it with no irksome formal constrictions. For the first time, too, he was stimulated to explore what turned out to be one of his most characteristic gifts, the ability to express physical gestures and movements (and the psychological states that prompt them) in purely musical terms – a gift in which he has had no rival since Wagner.

In retrospect Stravinsky claimed to have been already out of sympathy with the aesthetic premises of the folk-tale scenario, above all with its traditional division into set dances and mimed action, reflecting the arias and recitatives of opera, but if this was so he concealed the fact with remarkable success: the dialogue between Ivan and Kashchey, for instance, which he criticized for its over-literalness, is incomparably vivid and assured. It is hard not to feel that Stravinsky may have read back into his attitude at this time the strongly anti-'realist' stance he was to take up later (for an account of this specifically Russian aesthetic controversy see R. Taruskin: 'Realism as Preached and Practised: the Russian *opéra dialogué*', *MQ*, lvi (1970), 431). In later years he was concerned mainly to praise the score's technical novelties of orchestration – notably the ingenious natural-harmonic arpeggios at bar 14 – and it is true that it was clearly designed to outdo Rimsky-Korsakov in sheer picturesqueness. But Stravinsky also borrowed from his late master the device (used in *The Golden Cockerel*) of using chromaticism and a melodic and harmonic vocabulary based on the augmented 4th for the supernatural characters, good and evil, and a modal-diatonic style for the human protagonist, Ivan, and the enchanted princesses whom he rescues. This does much to pull together the music's centrifugal repertory of styles. In addition to the influences already mentioned, the Firebird's dance of supplication is pure Balakirev, and Ravel's *Rapsodie espagnole* is laid under contribution in her 'Berceuse'; but although it can be (and has been) objected that *The Firebird* is a thesaurus of current styles, this in no way weakens its impact in the theatre,

3. *Stravinsky* (*immediately behind seated lady*) *with members of the Ballets Russes at Monte Carlo, 1911: among those present are Dyagilev, Benois, Nizhinsky and Karsavina*

where every section seems apt to its own place in the action. Stravinsky himself later expressed some doubts about the 'Mendelssohnian–Tchaikovskian' idiom of the Princesses' scherzo, yet in context this seems as completely in keeping as the fantastic music invented for the demon Kashchey and his grotesque retinue. Whatever reservations the sophisticated young composer may have felt about the piece as he was composing it, the musical vitality which has kept the concert suites, at least, in the repertory is some indication that he was genuinely stimulated by the project as a whole.

2. 1910–14.

(*i*) *Life*. The success of *The Firebird* altered the course of Stravinsky's life. At that time Paris was the international centre of the world of art; the Ballets Russes one of its prime sensations; and Stravinsky's most important original score in the ballet repertory. This meant that overnight he became known as the most gifted of the younger generation of Russian composers, and during the next few years his music became better known and appreciated in western Europe than in his native Russia. Before the end of the Ballets Russes season in Paris that summer, he brought his wife and family over from Ustilug to share his triumph with him. It was clear that his musical future would be closely bound up with the fortunes of the Ballets Russes, and as the company looked on Paris as its base, he would have to be prepared to spend a good part of his time in western Europe.

Fortunately there was no dearth of ideas for new works. Already in April or May 1910, when finishing the full score of *The Firebird* in St Petersburg, he had had a dream which gave him the idea of writing a symphonic work based on a pagan ritual sacrifice. In Paris that summer he mentioned this to Dyagilev, who encouraged him to proceed; but when Dyagilev visited Stravinsky later that summer in Lausanne, where Katerina was expecting the birth of her third child (Svyatoslav Sulima), he found to his surprise that the composer had started to write a completely different work, a kind of Konzertstück for piano and orchestra. As Stravinsky had had in mind a 'picture of a puppet, suddenly endowed with life, exasperating the patience of the orchestra with diabolical cascades of arpeggios', he had provisionally entitled the piece *Petrushka*. Dyagilev immediately saw the dramatic possibilities of the subject and managed to persuade the composer to alter the course of the work and turn it into a ballet score. Benois was chosen to be his collaborator; and *Petrushka* was composed that autumn and winter in Lausanne, Clarens and Beaulieu, with a break in the composition at Christmas when Stravinsky returned to St Petersburg for a few days to attend conferences with Dyagilev, Fokin, Nizhinsky and Benois about the progress of the ballet.

Petrushka was first performed at the Théâtre du Châtelet, Paris, on 13 June 1911 and proved just as successful with the public and critics as *The Firebird* had been; but it was undoubtedly a more original work.

In the first place, Stravinsky had been able to play a leading part in the construction of the scenario, which had not been the case with *The Firebird*. Secondly, whereas the music of *The Firebird* showed that the pupil had learnt all that his master had had to teach him, in *Petrushka* for the first time the authentic voice of the new master is heard.

After the Ballets Russes Paris season that summer, Stravinsky retired to Ustilug where he remained working on *Vesna svyashchennaya* ('The Rite of Spring'), as the 'great sacrifice' project was now called, until the autumn, when he and his family moved to Clarens, Switzerland. By the New Year the first half of the score was virtually complete; but now it became apparent to Dyagilev that he would be unable to mount *The Rite of Spring* in the summer of 1912 as originally planned. So its production was postponed a year; and this meant Stravinsky could work more slowly on the remainder of the score. It also enabled him to complete *Zvezdolikiy* ('The King of the Stars'), a short cantata for male choir and large orchestra setting a transcendental poem by Bal'mont, before leaving Ustilug to attend the Ballets Russes seasons in Paris and London that summer (1912). By this time he was a well-known figure in Parisian musical circles and on friendly terms with Debussy, Ravel and numerous other musicians and celebrities. After his visit to London (his first) he returned to Ustilug for the remainder of the summer – a stay that was interrupted by an invitation from Dyagilev to join him in Bayreuth for a performance of *Parsifal* – and in the autumn the Stravinsky family moved back to Clarens. By then the score of *The Rite of Spring* was virtually complete, and Stravinsky had started to set three Japanese lyrics for soprano and piano (or small chamber orchestra). This left him free to visit Berlin, Budapest, Vienna and London during an extended Ballets Russes tour between November 1912 and February 1913. It was in the course of this Berlin visit that he met Schoenberg for the first time and heard a performance of his *Pierrot lunaire*, which impressed him deeply. After London he returned to Clarens, where Ravel joined him, and they collaborated on an adaptation of Musorgsky's *Khovanshchina* for production by the Ballets Russes in Paris that summer.

The first night of *The Rite of Spring* (Théâtre des Champs-Elysées, Paris, 29 May 1913) gave rise to one of the great theatrical scandals of all time. Even during the orchestral introduction mild protests against the music could be heard. When the curtain rose the audience became exacerbated by Nizhinsky's choreography as well as Stravinsky's music, and protests and counter-protests multiplied. At times the hubbub was so loud that the dancers could not hear the music they were supposed to be dancing to. Audiences at subsequent performances in Paris and London that summer behaved with normal decorum; but to those present on the first night the riot in the theatre was a traumatic experience. As for Stravinsky, a few days after the first night he fell ill with typhoid fever and had to spend several weeks in a nursing-home at Neuilly. When he recovered, he returned to Ustilug for the rest of the summer and was back in Clarens with his family in the early autumn. He had recently received a commission from the newly founded Free Theatre of Moscow to complete his opera *The Nightingale* for production there in 1914. Act 1 had been written at Ustilug in 1908–9. Acts 2 and 3 were now added at Clarens and Leysin

where the family moved early in 1914, because Katerina Stravinsky, who was expecting her fourth child (a daughter, Milena), had fallen ill with tuberculosis and needed hospital treatment. In the event the Moscow Free Theatre project collapsed; and Dyagilev offered to assume responsibility for the production of *The Nightingale* by the Ballets Russes during its seasons in Paris and London that summer – an offer that was accepted.

The Stravinsky family did not return to Ustilug that summer but remained in Switzerland, moving from Leysin to Salvan, where Stravinsky composed three pieces for string quartet. He was now contemplating the idea of a cantata celebrating Russian village wedding customs. Realizing that his library in Russia contained some useful works dealing with Russian popular verse and song that he would need for this cantata (subsequently entitled *Svadebka*, 'The Wedding'), he made a hurried trip to Ustilug and Kiev in mid-July; shortly after his return to Switzerland war broke out.

(ii) Works. It may be some indication of the primary importance that Stravinsky was coming to attach to formal coherence that he should originally have conceived that most dramatic of ballets, *Petrushka*, as a concert piece for piano and orchestra. The 'advanced' idiom characteristic of Petrushka's own music (in the ballet's second scene) is thus the heart of the work; the 'normal', extrovert music of the carnival scenes, with their post-Rimskian exuberance of rhythm and colour, and their strongly folk-influenced melodic vocabulary (see F. W. Sternfeld: 'Some Russian Folksongs in Stravinsky's *Petrouchka*', *Notes*, ii (1944–5), 95) thus represents the relatively conventional shell from which the chicken of Stravinsky's own style was beginning to emerge. These crowd scenes are characterized by the

4. Stravinsky in his study at Ustilug, 1912

5. First page of Stravinsky's sketches for 'The Rite of Spring', 1911–13 (F-Pmeyer)

use of largely diatonic harmony, often with extended ostinatos (notably the accordion-like alternation of 5ths and 3rds) and internal pedals. A basic regularity of rhythmic pulse is cunningly varied by episodes of calculated asymmetry and syncopation. The 'Russian Dance' which forms the last part of the first tableau, with its hammered parallel triads and diatonic added-note ostinatos, clearly has much in common with this idiom, but the other section deriving from the original concert-piece kernel of the work, 'Petrushka's Cry' as it was originally called, is very different. Here the diatonic language alternates with, and is sometimes combined with, a far more dissonant harmonic idiom based essentially on bitonal combinations, of which the famous

Petrushka chord (C major and F♯ major superimposed) is the most important. Yet it should be noted that even in these sections, for all their elaboration of harmony, instrumental colour and rhythm, the melodic language itself is still essentially diatonic.

This essential dichotomy between melody and harmony is still to some extent a feature of the third of Stravinsky's famous pre-war ballet scores, *The Rite of Spring*, but here burlesque and parodistic elements have been shed completely, and the result is a far greater degree of homogeneity than in *Petrushka*. This is already foreshadowed in the two pairs of songs composed in 1910 and 1911. The Verlaine settings, in keeping with their texts, are very French in their musical language too: whole-tone phrases and an occasional chord of the 13th suggest Debussy and Ravel respectively. But a passage of stepwise descending minor chords against a rising sequence of 7ths in the bass (on the word 'apaisement') points unmistakably to the prelude to the second part of *The Rite of Spring*; likewise in the second of the much barer and more linear Bal'mont songs Stravinsky experimented briefly with an ostinato of superimposed duple and triple rhythms which he was later to take up in more extended fashion in the introduction to the whole ballet. As chordally conceived as the Bal'mont songs are linear is the short cantata on a text by the same poet, for male-voice choir and huge orchestra, *The King of the Stars*. Dedicated to Debussy, this was Stravinsky's most single-minded exploration to date of advanced harmony. Its bitonality frequently results in characteristic simultaneous major–minor formations, such as had already appeared momentarily in *Petrushka* and were soon to be used much more frequently in *The Rite of Spring*. Probably because of the mystical nature of the text, however, Stravinsky here affected a quasi-liturgical uniformity of rhythm, and the music makes a somewhat stagnant impression when compared with, for example, the 'Mysterious Circles' section of the latter ballet.

A connection between the Bal'mont songs and *The Rite of Spring* has already been pointed out; it is a curious but convincing indication of the organic nature of Stravinsky's development that one work is often foreshadowed in a brief passage in one of its predecessors. In the same way, towards the end of the gestation of one section of a work, his imagination would often throw up a forerunner of the following one, as the published sketches of *The Rite of Spring* demonstrate remarkably clearly (see fig.5). They also show that Stravinsky's initial ideas, however abstractly he might later choose to develop them, were at this stage almost always generated by specific visual images, and that they fall essentially into two categories, melodic and harmonic. The harmonic 'germ' of *The Rite of Spring* is again a bitonal combination of two adjacent chords – this time of E♭ major (with added minor 7th) and F♭ major; it is presented both as a running semiquaver *moto perpetuo* and congealed into a repeated chord. Melodic ideas, on the other hand, are often surprisingly straightforward in their initial form, but are then subjected to radical transformations, above all of note order, tempo and rhythm. Rhythm, in fact, the most strikingly original aspect of the score, is not a purely spontaneous manifestation, but is the product of quite as much intense creative effort as the harmony. Yet it would be wrong to regard the rhythmic element as being in any sense arbitrary or unrelated to the rest: on the contrary, the convulsive asymmetry of

The Rite's rhythms should rather be seen as a direct function of its harmonic tensions. This score, whose subject matter concerning the ambiguous triumph and cruelty of spring and the process of natural renewal evidently stirred Stravinsky to his creative depths, marks both a high level of inspiration and an extreme point along one line of technical development. Stravinsky had found not only a voice, but an utterly individual vocabulary, yet it was a vocabulary that could essentially be used once. The quest for a style, conceived not as a response to particular expressive needs but as a language for civilized everyday discourse, had to continue.

On this quest *The Nightingale* represents something of a side-road. The first act, having been composed even before *The Firebird*, is stylistically still very much indebted to Debussy (it starts with an almost literal quotation from the *Nocturnes*, this time 'Nuages'); both the vocal lines and the harmony are closely related to those of the Verlaine songs. But by the time Stravinsky took the score up again in the autumn of 1913 he had lived through four years of the most rapid development that any composer has ever experienced, a coming-of-age all the more intense for being belated; it was impossible for him to return to the initial style. Fortunately, however, the story's own in-built contrast between rustic innocence and the corruption of the imperial court provides at least a superficial justification for the marked change in style. Stravinsky evidently enjoyed concocting the harmonically and instrumentally sophisticated chinoiserie of the court scenes, though their artificiality inevitably seems a little contrived after the blazing urgency of *The Rite of Spring*. The most original music is probably that of the third act; here, as in the slightly earlier *Tri stikhotvoreniya iz yaponskoy liriki* ('Three Japanese lyrics'), the violence and imaginative abundance of the ballet has been distilled into music of the most extreme refinement.

3. 1914–20.

(i) Life. The war inevitably dislocated the pattern of Stravinsky's life. Whereas during the past four years the family visits to Switzerland had been occasional trips undertaken partly for health reasons and partly so that he could be within easy reach of Paris, now Switzerland became a permanent haven of refuge. Wartime conditions made it impossible for the Ballets Russes to function on normal lines in western Europe; Stravinsky's music publishers were mostly in enemy territory (Germany); and he could no longer depend on the income from his Russian estate. He began to find himself in financial straits; it was only as the result of a generous gift of money from Thomas Beecham that he was able to finance his mother's return to St Petersburg at the outbreak of war.

The composition of *The Wedding* occupied a considerable amount of his time, though he no longer had a deadline to work to. First he constructed the libretto, a selection of words, phrases, sentences from Kireevsky's collection of folksongs. Then he set the words for four-part chorus and four soloists. There were numerous interruptions to the work; but the short score was completed on 11 October 1917. It was dedicated to Dyagilev, who had been moved to tears when he first heard Stravinsky play the sketches for scenes i and ii. However, it took Stravinsky another six years before he found the right instrumental formula for the accompan-

6. Front cover by Picasso for the first edition (1919) of Stravinsky's piano arrangement of his 'Rag-time'

iment to the voices. The instrumentation was eventually finished on 6 April 1923 at Monaco; and the Ballets Russes gave the first performance at the Théâtre de la Gaîté Lyrique, Paris, on 13 June 1923.

Stravinsky's intensive researches into Russian folk material at the time he was working on *The Wedding* produced a number of by-products – the text for a farmyard burlesque, *Bayka* ('Reynard'), and various groups of Russian songs, particularly the *Pribaoutki* and the *Berceuses du chat* ('Cat's Cradle Songs').

Shortly after the outbreak of war the Stravinsky family rented a house in Clarens belonging to the young Swiss conductor Ernest Ansermet for part of the winter; and in 1915 they moved to Morges, where they stayed until 1920. As Switzerland was neutral Stravinsky was able to undertake a few trips abroad. He spent a fortnight with Dyagilev in Florence in autumn 1914. The following February he visited Dyagilev in Rome, where they both attended the first Italian concert performance of *Petrushka* (conducted by Casella). On this occasion he met Gerald Tyrwhitt, later Lord Berners, and Prokofiev, newly arrived from Russia. The following month Dyagilev visited Switzerland, staying at Ouchy, where he assembled a small group of artists in view of the forthcoming visit by the Ballets Russes to the Metropolitan Opera House, New York. Ansermet was to be in charge of the orchestra, and before leaving for the USA he effected two introductions that were to prove of importance to Stravinsky during this period.

First he introduced him to C. F. Ramuz, a well-known author in French-speaking Switzerland. The acquaintance with Ramuz blossomed into friendship; and the Swiss writer supplied Stravinsky with French versions of the texts of *The Wedding*, *Reynard* and various groups of songs, although he knew no Russian and had to rely on Stravinsky's literal translations for his basic material. In 1918 the two collaborated over the text of *Histoire du soldat* ('The Soldier's Tale'), which

(on Stravinsky's suggestion) was based on one of the stories in Alexander Afanas'yev's collection. Later, in 1929, Ramuz published an account of their friendship, *Souvenirs sur Igor Strawinsky*, which, though warm in tone and perceptively written, did not please the composer, who felt his privacy had been unjustifiably invaded. Ansermet's second introduction was to Aladar Racz, a Hungarian cimbalom player, whose virtuoso performance at Maxim's, Geneva, inspired Stravinsky to make himself proficient in playing the instrument and to write cimbalom parts in several of his works, including *Reynard* and *Rag-time* (1918).

Just before the Ballets Russes left for the USA Dyagilev arranged two charity matinées for the Red Cross, one at Geneva (20 December 1915) and one in Paris nine days later. Stravinsky was engaged to conduct *The Firebird* in both programmes, the concert suite at Geneva and the ballet in Paris; and these were his first public appearances as a conductor, though at Ansermet's suggestion he had taken the Montreux Kursaal Orchestra through his Symphony in E♭ at a concert rehearsal in April 1914.

After the company set sail for New York, Stravinsky called on his friend the Princess Edmond de Polignac in Paris, and she offered to commission a small chamber work from him. He had already made some preliminary sketches for *Reynard*; and it was now agreed he should finish this, although there was no immediate likelihood of its production.

The Ballets Russes's American visit finished at the end of April 1916, and the company then returned to Spain. Stravinsky joined Dyagilev in Madrid for a few weeks in May, and to this visit may be attributed various Spanish elements in some of his works of this period, such as the Study for pianola, the 'Española' (one of the Easy Pieces for piano four hands), and the 'Royal March' in *The Soldier's Tale*. When the Ballets Russes returned to the USA later in the year, Dyagilev remained behind and, in the course of discussing future plans with Stravinsky, suggested *The Nightingale* might be presented in ballet form. Stravinsky countered with the proposal that the homogeneous music of Acts 2 and 3 should be turned into a symphonic poem (without voices). This was done, the resulting work being *Chant du rossignol* ('The Song of the Nightingale'); later it was used as a ballet score.

In spring 1917 Dyagilev went to Rome, where he arranged four performances at the Teatro Costanzi, the first of which was a gala in aid of the Italian Red Cross. The programme included *The Firebird* and *Fireworks*, both of them conducted by the composer, and the latter with special lighting effects by the Italian futurist painter Giacomo Balla. The news of the Russian Revolution of February 1917 had recently come through: so it seemed inappropriate to begin the performance with 'God Save the Tsar', and Stravinsky arranged the *Song of the Volga Boatmen* at short notice for wind and percussion as a substitute.

At first the revolutionary news from Russia seemed encouraging to a liberal like Stravinsky. On 24 May 1917 he telegraphed his mother, who was still living in the Stravinsky family apartment in Petrograd: 'All our thoughts are with you in these unforgettable days of joy for our beloved Russia freed at last'. But by October the position had radically changed; gradually he realized that the Bolshevik Revolution had made it impossible for him to return to his native land, and he and his family would probably have to live their lives in permanent exile.

The beginning of 1918 was a particularly dark moment in the conduct of the war, and this affected Stravinsky and several of his friends. One day he and Ramuz had an idea. Why not write something quite simple, for two or three characters and a handful of instrumentalists, something that could be played in modest conditions, in village halls and the like? Out of this was born the idea of *The Soldier's Tale*, a piece 'to be read, played and danced'. A backer was found (Werner Reinhart of Winterthur); the Lausanne Theatre hired; and on 28 September 1918 the new work had its first performance with Ansermet conducting. This was a great success; but unfortunately a severe outbreak of influenza forced the organizers to cancel the tour that had been planned to follow the Lausanne performance.

When the war ended it was no longer necessary for Stravinsky to continue to live in Switzerland. At first he thought of settling in Rome, but ultimately decided in favour of France. He did not leave Switzerland until summer 1920; and the latter part of 1919 and the early months of 1920 were spent in writing a new ballet score for Dyagilev, who had suggested he might adapt some music by Pergolesi for a ballet with a *commedia dell'arte* theme. The choreography was by Massin; the décor and costumes by Picasso. Stravinsky obviously fell in love with the Pergolesi pieces that had been put at his disposition; and the resultant ballet *Pulcinella* was a great success when produced at the Paris Opéra (15 May 1920).

(*ii*) *Works*. The true and logical successor to *The Rite of Spring* in Stravinsky's output is not *The Nightingale* but *The Wedding*. The first idea of this work occurred to him while he was engaged on *The Rite*, but it was not until 1914 that he was able to think about it seriously, not until 1917 that the music was essentially complete, and not until 1923 that it received its definitive instrumental form. *The Wedding* is thus the central work of this entire period. As profoundly concerned with the cycle of regeneration as *The Rite of Spring*, it represents a kind of Orthodox counterpart to the imaginary pagan ritual of that work and, whether consciously or not, a civilized 'social' answer to its explosive individualism. Such a function demanded a very different style, and it is not surprising to find, among the compositions of the early war years, several which can be regarded as studies for the main work in hand.

First in point of time, and most seminal in content, are the Three Pieces for string quartet (1914). In these Stravinsky seems to have isolated, as in a process of self-analysis, three of the basic musical components of his creative personality. The first, a stylized Russian dance, explores the effects of repetition and permutation of a brief melodic cell against a constant but irregularly grouped pulse; the second, apparently suggested by the antics of the English clown Little Tich, substitutes spastic rhythms and extreme contrasts of theme and texture; the third is a frozen litany, whose harmonic tensions have reached a point of almost complete stasis – the forerunner of many of Stravinsky's later codas. The ideas which these pieces encapsulate were too basic to find their fulfilment immediately, and the first of the works in which Stravinsky explored more specifically the possibilities of a Russian folk melos wedded to an uncompromisingly individual harmonic style is

Pribaoutki, settings of nonsense-songs in which a tight-knit melodic line is set against an accompaniment containing a harmonic tension that places it in a new and piquant light – as in the first song, where the accompaniment to an E♭ melody concerns itself principally with the notes F♯, G and A♭, or the last, in which a melody with A as a tonal centre is set over a G♯ drone. The traditional tonal hierarchy of dissonance and resolution is being exploited negatively, in the setting-up of tensions which are deliberately not resolved. The result is a certain stiffness of harmonic language, analogous to aspects of cubist painting; tonal centres, ambiguous or not, are established by repetition, and replaced not by modulation but by simple shift. These, in fact, are only technical procedures of *The Rite of Spring* applied on a smaller scale; what is new is the affectionate exploration of a melodic idiom dictated by Russian popular verse. None of these works (unlike *Petrushka*, for instance) uses genuine folk melodies, but all are impregnated with their style, and Stravinsky seized with particular delight on one feature of the original melodies, their metrical independence of the word-stress. This was to become a feature of his own setting of texts in whatever language, French, Latin, English or Hebrew. The *Cat's Cradle Songs* of 1915–16 are even shorter and simpler, with *Pribaoutki*'s accompaniment of mixed wind and strings replaced by the homogeneous timbre of three clarinets (of various sizes), suggested by the 'cat-like' character of the poems.

7. *Choreography by Nathalia Gontcharova for four women in Stravinsky's 'The Wedding', first performed at the Théâtre Gaîté Lyrique on 13 June 1923: pen and ink drawing heightened with white ink (Victoria and Albert Museum, London)*

8. Design (1921) by Mikhail Larionov for Stravinsky's 'Reynard', first performed at the Paris Opéra on 18 May 1922: watercolour (Museum of Modern Art, New York)

Animals are much in evidence in these Russian-style works of the early war years – partly, no doubt, because they occur frequently as characters in the popular texts with which Stravinsky was preoccupied, but also because circumstances had cooped him up in Switzerland with a family of four small children; the nursery world of farmyard tales attracted him as a valid stylization, a mask through which human characteristics could be portrayed without the invitation to identification which had come to seem banal. The world of folk poetry also provided a much needed temporary escape from the hothouse sophistication of the Dyagilev–Paris ambience, even if Stravinsky did, in the event, carry his new-found interest back there with him. *Reynard*, at any rate, the most extended essay in this stylized farmyard vein, was designed for a princess's Paris drawing-room. Its larger format entails an increase in forces: only five solo strings (used for the most part percussively), but seven wind and a group of percussion instruments headed by Stravinsky's new discovery, the cimbalom, whose nasal timbre dictates much of the score's character. It is also notable that the four male voices in no way represent the individual characters in the narrative: the action is danced and mimed, while the voices, placed in the orchestra, singly or collectively utter the characters' words at any given moment. Stravinsky's 'anti-realism' at this stage led him to reject completely the implied mimesis of traditional opera, though he would later come to terms with it on occasion.

The Wedding (conceived earlier, though completed later) shares this characteristic with *Reynard*, but in other ways is rather different. Where *Reynard* is a large-scale small work, consisting of a number of contrasting episodes linked primarily by their instrumentation and by a very few literal recurrences (hence the need for the framing march that brings the players on and escorts them off at the end), *The Wedding* is, in the widest but the truest sense, symphonic. Melodically it is unified by a close cellular kinship between the various themes that emerge from its texture for development and transfor-mation; rhythmically it is perhaps the most closely knit of all Stravinsky's works. Recognizing that tonal relationships were, for him, as for Debussy, no longer capable of sustaining a lengthy symphonic argument, and perhaps recognizing too that the profound instinc-tive unity of *The Rite of Spring* could not always be relied on, Stravinsky had looked for other methods of ensuring continuity and devised a form of large-scale rhythmic development more pervasive than anything in his earlier music. Every new tempo in the work is proportionally geared to its predecessor, and so ultimately to a basic pulse that can be felt, if not con-sciously heard, to run through the entire work; this contains its extreme (and steadily increasing) contrasts of mood, which find their ultimate resolution in the ritual greeting of the newly wedded bride by her hus-band, and the almost liturgical bellstrokes that consum-mate their union. It is a procedure common to many, perhaps most, of Stravinsky's succeeding works, but nowhere is it more essential to the music's inner life than in this, the one for and through which it was evolved. No doubt it was in order to emphasize the immensely important role of rhythm in the score that Stravinsky, after experimenting with other, more highly coloured possibilities, eventually decided on a 'black and white' instrumentation, using only pianos and percussion. This has probably militated against *The Wedding*'s popular-ity, but unlike *The Rite of Spring* it cannot be vulgarized into an orchestral tour de force, and retains, both in and out of the theatre, its unique impact.

By the end of the war years Stravinsky was already beginning to react against his own intense preoccupation with Russian folk material. *The Soldier's Tale*, though based on that material, deliberately aims at transcending national limitations. A Russian accent may still be detected in some of the music, but it is subordinated to such new influences as the Spanish pasodoble band (in the 'Royal March'), tango and ragtime – not to mention the chorales which mark the work's dramatic climax. In this sense, just as *Reynard* sums up the Russian studies,

The Soldier's Tale sums up the parodistic vein which goes back as far as *Petrushka* and which had been explored more recently in the two sets of pieces for piano duet and in the Study for pianola (1917), based on impressions of Madrid night music. The impact of jazz (or rather ragtime; Stravinsky's knowledge of the idiom was so far limited to printed music brought to him from the USA by Ansermet) can also be heard in two further works of the period: *Rag-time*, for a group of 11 instruments, including *Reynard*'s cimbalom but closer in composition to that of *The Soldier's Tale*, and the *Piano-rag-music* written for Artur Rubinstein; both pieces aim rather at a cubist impression of the style than at direct parody in the manner of Les Six. Stravinsky had already passed beyond the stage when he could derive much from jazz apart from a passing frisson, and he would not return to it until the *Ebony Concerto* written for Woody Herman in 1945.

Far more important for Stravinsky's future development was the fortuitous involvement with 18th-century music brought about by Dyagilev's invitation to arrange a ballet score from music by (or attributed to) Pergolesi. Although all that Dyagilev had in mind was an arrangement comparable to Tommasini's of Scarlatti in *The Good-humoured Ladies*, Stravinsky's imagination was more deeply stirred than either of them could have foreseen. The act of composing against the background of a harmonic and rhythmic system as regular and familiar as that of Pergolesi, and with a similarly restricted orchestral palette, made Stravinsky aware how powerful an effect could be achieved, within such a context, by quite small and subtle dislocations. For much of its length *Pulcinella* stays too close to the original to be quite fully Stravinsky, though there is scarcely a bar that does not reveal his presence by some felicity of phrasing, harmony or sonority; but the experience of composing it did undoubtedly point him towards the consistent stylistic persona for which he had been consciously or unconsciously searching – one that would, in the event, serve him for some 30 productive years.

4. 1920–39.

(*i*) *Life*. Stravinsky brought his family from Switzerland to Brittany in the summer of 1920; and in September Gabrielle Chanel placed her home in the Paris suburb of Garches at his disposal. The following year the family moved, first to a house at Anglet near Biarritz, and later to a villa in the centre of Biarritz. Although he continued to compose at home, his musical activities in Paris led to his making fairly regular use of a studio which the Pleyel company put at his disposal in their pianola warehouse. At that moment he was particularly interested in the recording of his works for player piano, just as later on he was to spend much time supervising the recording of his works for gramophone.

The first major work to be finished after Stravinsky left Switzerland was the Symphonies of Wind Instruments. He had contributed a short instrumental chorale to a special musical supplement that the *Revue musicale* issued in memory of Debussy and this became the final section of the Symphonies, the last major work to be written in what had become his characteristic Russian idiom. In 1921 he joined the Ballets Russes while it was on tour. He went to Spain in April when the company was playing in Madrid, and spent Easter with Dyagilev in Seville. In the summer the company visited

London and Stravinsky attended the first concert performance in England of *The Rite of Spring*, conducted by Eugene Goossens (Queen's Hall, 7 June). Sergey Koussevitzky, who happened to be in London at the same time, decided at short notice to include the Symphonies of Wind Instruments in a concert he was giving at the Queen's Hall. The work seems to have been under-rehearsed and badly presented (10 June). But, apart from that fiasco, Stravinsky's London visit appears to have been an enjoyable one; and it gave him the chance to hold a number of important talks with Dyagilev. In the first place, Dyagilev told him about his plan to revive *The Sleeping Beauty* at the Alhambra, London, for a run; and Stravinsky agreed to help with the arrangement of the score. Then Stravinsky told Dyagilev of his intention to compose an *opera buffa* on a story by Pushkin (*Mavra*). Boris Kochno, whom the theatrical designer Serge Soudeikine had recently introduced to Dyagilev, and whom Dyagilev had engaged as his personal secretary, was chosen as librettist.

Earlier that year Stravinsky had met Soudeikine's wife, Vera (née de Bosset), who was to appear in the non-dancing role of the Queen in the revival of *The Sleeping Beauty*. He fell deeply in love with her, and she with him. During the next 18 years they saw as much of each other as possible – mainly in Paris, but sometimes also when she was able to accompany him on concert tours. One of the first results of this liaison was that his next composition after *Mavra*, the Octet for wind instruments (1922–3), was dedicated to her, though the dedication did not appear in the published edition of the work.

Shortly after the Russian Revolution Stravinsky had written to Arthur Lourié, then commissar of music in Petrograd, asking him to help his mother obtain a visa to leave Russia for France. Permission for her to emigrate was held up for some years; and by the time it came through Lourié himself was in Paris, where he was introduced to Stravinsky by Vera Soudeikine and became his musical assistant for several years. Ultimately, Stravinsky's mother was allowed to travel by boat through the Baltic to Stettin, where she was met by her son in the summer of 1922. She joined the family in Biarritz and accompanied them on their later moves, to Nice in 1924, to Voreppe near Grenoble in 1930 and to Paris in 1934.

A considerable number of people were now financially dependent on Stravinsky; and remembering his wartime difficulties, when he had been unable to rely on a regular income as a composer, he decided he must diversify his working life. This meant devoting time to carrying out engagements as a pianist and conductor at the expense of composing. The first noticeable effect of this decision was the appearance of a number of new works for piano. At Anglet in 1921 he had made a virtuoso piano transcription of three movements from *Petrushka* for Artur Rubinstein. Now he saw to it that his new piano works fitted his own limited executive capacity. He wrote the Concerto for piano and wind instruments (1923–4) and the Capriccio for piano and orchestra (1928–9) with this requirement in mind, retaining in each case the exclusive rights of performance for a period of five years. Later, when his younger son Sulima became a professional pianist, he wrote a Concerto for two solo pianos (1931–5) which was widely performed by father and son. He also wrote two solo pieces, the Sonata (1924), which he played at the ISCM Festival in Venice in summer 1925, and the Serenade in A. His 1924 concert tours took him to over a dozen European towns; and in 1925 he undertook his first American tour, scoring an undoubted success in his dual role of conductor and pianist. This visit led to his being commissioned by a gramophone company to write a piano work in four movements, each of which would fill one side of a ten-inch record, and the result was the Serenade, which he dedicated to his wife.

Stravinsky now had less time to devote to the Ballets Russes. It was true that Dyagilev revived Stravinsky's pre-war ballets and in 1923 gave the long delayed first performance of *The Wedding*. He also mounted productions of *Reynard* and *Mavra* (though not *The Soldier's Tale*). But after *Pulcinella* Stravinsky accepted no more commissions from the Ballets Russes. Instead he planned a special tribute to commemorate the 20th anniversary (in 1927) of the launching of Dyagilev's great theatrical enterprise in Paris and western Europe. This was the composition of *Oedipus rex*, which he cast in the form of an opera–oratorio, using as text the Latin translation of a libretto by Jean Cocteau. Because of production difficulties both Stravinsky and Dyagilev had to be content with a concert performance of *Oedipus rex* mounted in the same programme as a stage

9. Stravinsky at the Café Gaillac, Paris, 1923

performance of *The Firebird*. Dyagilev was reserved in his attitude to *Oedipus rex* – 'un cadeau très macabre' he called it – and the majority of the audience did not like it. It needed a good stage production before its great qualities could be appreciated. In 1928 Stravinsky allowed Dyagilev to acquire the European rights of *Apollon musagète* (later renamed *Apollo*), which had been commissioned by Elizabeth Sprague Coolidge for production at the Library of Congress, Washington, DC. But shortly afterwards, to show that he no longer felt exclusively bound to Dyagilev and the Ballets Russes, even in Europe, he accepted a commission from Ida Rubinstein, who was forming a new ballet company of her own; and *Le baiser de la fée* ('The Fairy's Kiss', 1928), based by Stravinsky on songs and piano pieces by Tchaikovsky, was produced at the Paris Opéra (27 November 1928). Dyagilev was scathing about what he considered to be Stravinsky's defection from his fold; but there was not sufficient time for the breach to be healed, for on 19 August 1929 Dyagilev died in Venice and was buried on the island of S Michele. His death was followed by the immediate disbandment of his company.

In the mid-1920s Stravinsky experienced a spiritual crisis. He had been born and baptized into the Russian Orthodox Church, but at the age of 18 had abandoned the practice of his faith. In 1926 he rejoined the Orthodox Church, becoming a communicant once more; and the same year he had a profoundly moving religious experience when attending the 700th anniversary celebrations of St Anthony in Padua. This spiritual change affected some of his compositions. Between 1926 and 1934 he wrote three Slavonic sacred choruses, *Otche nash'* ('Our Father'), *Simvol' verï* ('Symbol of Faith', i.e. *Credo*) and *Bogoroditse devo* ('Blessed Virgin', i.e. *Ave Maria*); and when Koussevitzky asked him to write a major symphonic work to celebrate the Boston SO's 50th anniversary in 1930, he decided to compose a Symphony of Psalms to Latin texts selected from the Vulgate.

In 1931 he was introduced to the violinist Samuel Dushkin by Willy Strecker of Schott, Mainz. Out of this meeting came the idea of a close cooperation between the two musicians. First, Stravinsky wrote the Violin Concerto in D (1931), which Dushkin played in many countries with Stravinsky conducting. They then decided to become recitalists, and Stravinsky wrote the *Duo concertante* (1931–2) for violin and piano. This became the major work in their recital programmes, which also included a number of special transcriptions of some of Stravinsky's shorter pieces.

In the mid-1930s it seemed that the French phase in Stravinsky's life was approaching a climax. He had never shown himself much addicted to the language – so far his only setting of a French text had been the Verlaine songs of 1910 – but now a further ballet commission from Ida Rubinstein led to a collaboration with Gide. The proposal was that Stravinsky should make a musical setting of an early poem of Gide's, based on the Homeric hymn to Demeter. Stravinsky accepted; and his *Perséphone*, cast in the form of a musical melodrama, was produced at the Paris Opéra (30 April 1934). Gide seems to have been considerably upset by Stravinsky's 'syllabic' treatment of his text, which did not fit in with his strongly held views on the nature of French prosody; and the work had a rather muted reception, despite the express approval of at least one important critic, Valéry. On 10 June 1934 Stravinsky's naturalization papers came through, and he became a French citizen. The following year, reacting to the promptings of various friends (including Valéry), he sought election to the seat in the Institut de France left vacant by Dukas' death; but he was beaten in the poll by Florent Schmitt. This was the moment he chose to publish an autobiographical work in French, *Chroniques de ma vie* (1935). His first authorized publication had been an article on his Octet published in the periodical *The Arts* (January 1924); and thereafter he had issued a number of manifestos heralding each of his major new compositions. But *Chroniques de ma vie* was his first book as such; and in writing it he enjoyed the assistance of Walter Nouvel.

While failing to consolidate his position as a French artist in France, Stravinsky found an increasing demand for his music in the USA. In 1935 he carried out a second American tour, conducting many of the American orchestras and appearing with Dushkin at a number of violin and piano recitals. The following year he and his son Sulima played the Concerto for two solo pianos on a tour through South America. He then received an invitation from Lincoln Kirstein and Edward Warburg to write a ballet score to be choreographed by Balanchin for the recently formed American Ballet. The outcome was *Jeu de cartes* ('The Card Party'), composed in 1936 and first performed at the Metropolitan Opera House, New York (27 April 1937), with the composer conducting. Other American commissions followed. For Mr and Mrs Robert Woods Bliss he wrote a concerto for chamber orchestra (1937–8) which became familiarly known as the 'Dumbarton Oaks' Concerto after the name of their property in Washington, DC. Mrs Bliss was also largely responsible for obtaining for him a commission for a symphony to celebrate the 50th concert season of the Chicago SO in 1940–41. About the same time an invitation reached him from Harvard University, offering him the chair of poetry for the academic year 1939–40.

These commissions and invitations came at a crucial moment. By now it was clear that Europe was poised on the brink of another world war; and at the same time ill-health (mainly tuberculosis) struck down several members of Stravinsky's family. His elder daughter, Ludmila, died in 1938 aged 30; his wife died in March 1939 aged 57; his mother three months later aged 85. He himself spent some time in the sanatorium where his wife and daughter had been; but by September 1939, shortly after the outbreak of war, he was sufficiently recovered to embark for New York on his fourth and what was to prove his longest visit to North America.

(*ii*) *Works*. Although *Pulcinella* had pointed the way forward to a more universal musical style, Stravinsky's first major works after the end of the war constituted rather a final sublimation of his national idiom. Both the Concertino for string quartet (so called because of the prominence of the first violin part) and the Symphonies of Wind Instruments contain climactic sections in the 'Russian dance' style that goes back through the first of the Three Pieces for string quartet to *Petrushka*; the Symphonies, moreover, make use of the two other cardinal elements isolated in the string quartet pieces, developing them and bringing them into a new and completely original synthesis by means of metrically geared juxtaposition; the final chorale which crowns the

work (the original memorial to Debussy) is the first fully developed example of the Stravinskian codas already referred to. Undervalued for many years, the Symphonies of Wind Instruments have eventually been recognized as a landmark in Stravinsky's output and have exercised a seminal influence on composers since World War II – notably on Stockhausen, of whose 'moment form' it has been proclaimed (however implausibly) a precursor.

The primacy of the 18th century (interpreted as including the last years of its predecessor) or Baroque music (interpreted as including Haydn and Mozart) as a stylistic persona for Stravinsky during his 'neo-classical period' should not blind one to the fact that he occasionally felt drawn to other idioms, among them those which formed part of his personal Russian heritage – not the atavistic heritage of folk melos which he had so fruitfully explored already, but that of Russian 19th-century art music. The little comic opera *Mavra*, scarcely more than an extended single scene with contrasting episodes, is dedicated to Pushkin (from whom the story is taken), Glinka and Tchaikovsky. The musical idiom makes more reference to Glinka, with his characteristic mixture of Italian and Russian turns of phrase, than to Tchaikovsky, who was to receive his own individual tribute in *The Fairy's Kiss* six and a half years later. Both the harmonic and the rhythmic aspects of *Mavra* show a new lucidity, and this is reflected in the instrumentation for a sizable wind ensemble (cf the Symphonies) with only a small complement of strings. This reversal of the traditional orchestral balance is carried through into the internal balance of the string section (the score calls for two violins, one viola, three cellos and three basses), and it reflects Stravinsky's total rejection at this period of the expressive excesses, as he and many of his generation felt them to be, of the symphonic composers of the German Romantic tradition. That this rejection has a great deal to do with the traumatic experience of World War I is obvious, though more purely musical reasons can also be found for it. At any rate the clarity of timbre and attack characteristic of the wind band predominates in other Stravinsky scores of the early 1920s, notably the Octet and the Piano Concerto. It represents a slight enrichment of the black and white palette of *The Wedding*, but only with the opera–oratorio *Oedipus rex* (1926–7) did Stravinsky work his way back to full acceptance of the symphony orchestra and the traditional role of the strings in it – an acceptance which was then celebrated in *Apollo*, for strings only. In this ballet, a hymn to the concepts of reason and enlightenment as the foundation of beauty, Stravinsky rejoices in the sonority of strings, augmented in this instance by a divided cello section, as completely as he had once rejected it. But it must be emphasized that he remained throughout his career an empiricist in the matter of instrumentation. While accepting the general outline of the symphony orchestra until the end of his neo-classical period, he varied it in numbers and in detailed composition. Each work was seen as a fresh problem in finding the appropriate, elegant and economical sound either for the external circumstances (as in the *Ebony Concerto*) or more often for the inherent needs of the musical idea.

There is an element of affectionate parody in Stravinsky's use of Russian materials in *Mavra* and *The Fairy's Kiss*, but his use of 'classical' styles evidently reflected a still deeper need, since it contained no admixture of irony, at least at first. For Stravinsky the period of music, and more generally of culture, bounded by Lully and Mozart represented an ideal of civilization, which attracted him both as a Russian, and thus as an alien to the charmed circle of nations for whom it was a part of their heritage, and also as a refugee from an at least theoretically egalitarian political system. The style of his middle years is thus quite literally and consciously reactionary, and has been rejected as such by those whose allegiance is to a Romantic and often doctrinaire notion of artistic progress. What Stravinsky's style is not, however, is conservative, and indeed his willingness, at this period, to retain the manner of a traditionalist while totally rejecting the matter, has proved a stumbling-block to genuine conservatives in their turn. The justification of this 'neo-classical' idiom lies, in any case, in the works which embody it. Stravinsky's adoption of some mannerisms of 18th-century music, together with his maintenance of the notion of related centres of tonal gravity even while rejecting the traditional means of establishing them, provided him with a language capable of many very different kinds of utterance, which he exploited fully in the interwar years. The lyrical beauty of the Octet, the Piano Sonata and Serenade, and above all the *Duo concertante*, apart from works already mentioned, would have been impossible without what Eric Walter White has called, in a memorable phrase, Stravinsky's 'sacrifice to Apollo'. At the same time his acceptance of neo-Baroque formal disciplines also made it possible for him to compose masterpieces with the specific gravity of *Oedipus rex*, the Symphony of Psalms, and the balletic retelling of the regeneration-mystery, *Persephone*.

All three of these great works are, in their distinct ways, eclectic in style but highly original in form and tone. In *Oedipus rex* and *Persephone* Stravinsky makes prominent use of the spoken voice in conjunction with music, though to quite different effect. In the former the use of a narrator, speaking the audience's language, to introduce the scenes of a drama composed in the liturgical 'dead' language, Latin, strengthens their sense of monumentality. In *Persephone*, however, the performer of the title role, intended for Ida Rubinstein, declaims Gide's flowery text over the music, where the other characters sing it; this introduces a weakening shift of dramatic focus, as well as making the composed (most unusually in Stravinsky) serve as a background to the uncomposed. Both works – the one a tragedy, the other a mystery – convey an almost ritual weight of utterance, but this is most consistently felt in the Symphony of Psalms. The text is drawn from verses of the Vulgate version, arranged (as in Stravinsky's later religious works) to form a highly characteristic sequence of repentance, faith and praise. Characteristic too is the deliberate avoidance of self expression (the reverse of Beethoven's or Bruckner's religious music) and the cultivation of an impersonal, objective liturgical persona. The work is a symphony only in the loosest of senses, and may have been so called only because the Boston SO had commissioned a symphonic work. Not for another decade would Stravinsky come to terms with the traditional symphony, as represented by Haydn and Beethoven, in the Symphony in C. Insofar as the Symphony of Psalms refers to the past at all, it is to the choral works of the Baroque period, in which chorus and orchestra are used on an equal footing for contrapuntal development. The composition of the orchestra also reflects Stravinsky's desire for an archaic monumentality: not only are violins and violas absent, but also those 'modern' instruments, the clarinets. The wind section is large, however, and two pianos are prominent among the percussion.

After *Persephone* it must be admitted that some flagging of creative impulse can be felt in Stravinsky's works of the later 1930s. The Concerto for two solo pianos, in which he again tackled the challenge of abstract composition without the stimulus either of stage action or of instrumental colour, is a tough, impressive, but not entirely convincing work; *The Card Party* (1936) is a brilliant and inventive ballet score, but without the powerful resonance of *Apollo* and its predecessors, and the 'Dumbarton Oaks' Concerto, though witty and resourceful in its evocation of Bach's Brandenburg manner, remains a minor work. Family tragedies, political anxieties, his own ill-health and, perhaps more important, a feeling that his music was insufficiently recognized in his adopted country, probably all took their toll of Stravinsky's vitality at this time. Thus his second emigration, to the USA, though it was undoubtedly disturbing and unsettling, may well have helped to bring about the eventual renewal of his creative activity.

5. 1939–52.

(i) *Life*. Stravinsky landed in New York on 30 September 1939 and went straight to Cambridge, Massachusetts. His six Charles Eliot Norton lectures on the poetics of music had been written in French with the aid of Roland-Manuel before he left Paris, and were delivered them (also in French) to large audiences in Harvard's New Lecture Hall. In 1942 the original text was published by the Harvard University Press as *Poétique musicale*.

In December 1939 Stravinsky conducted concerts in San Francisco and Los Angeles, returning to New York in time to meet Vera de Bosset when she arrived (on 13 January 1940) by sea from Genoa. On 9 March they were married in Bedford, Massachusetts, and in May they went to Galveston and Houston on an ill-planned honeymoon trip. Because he had found the Californian climate suited him, they decided to settle in Hollywood. In July that summer they applied for visas and went to Mexico to establish quota qualifications and, re-entering the USA as Russian non-preference quota immigrants, they filed declarations of intent to become American citizens.

When Stravinsky had reached America only the first two movements of the symphony intended for the Chicago SO were complete. The third was written during the period of his Harvard lectures, the fourth in Hollywood in summer 1940; the first performance of the Symphony in C was given that autumn in Chicago with the composer conducting.

Once he had settled in Hollywood Stravinsky was inevitably approached with suggestions that he should write music for films. Some of these projects were so fatuous they were dismissed at once; but others engaged his interest, and in a few cases he had begun to compose music before they were abandoned. Fortunately he was able to salvage a considerable part of this abortive film music and use it again in such works as *Four Norwegian Moods* (1942), the *Ode* (1943), the *Scherzo à la russe* (1944) and the Symphony in Three Movements (1942–5).

Shortage of cash may have played some part in leading Stravinsky for the first and only time in his life to accept a private composition pupil: Ernest Anderson went to him in March 1941 and received approximately 215 lessons during the next two years. The same factor may also help to explain the alacrity with which he accepted some slightly offbeat commissions – particularly the *Circus Polka* (1942) to be danced by young elephants in the Barnum and Bailey Circus, and *Babel* (1944) which formed part of a composite biblical cycle called *Genesis*, commissioned by Nathaniel Shilkret, in which seven different composers (including Shilkret himself) were involved. Other wartime commissions included *Danses concertantes* (1941–2), a concert score written for the Werner Janssen Orchestra of Los Angeles, though later it was used for ballet purposes, and *Scènes de ballet* (1944) written for a ballet that was incorporated in Billy Rose's Broadway revue *The Seven Lively Arts*.

The most important work of this period was the result of a commission from the New York Philharmonic Symphony Society, which arrived when Stravinsky was contemplating the possibility of writing another piano concerto. In the event, much of the music sketched out for this concerto was incorporated in the first movement of the Symphony in Three Movements, while some of his abortive film music was used in the second movement. The Symphony in Three Movements made a powerful impression when it was first performed by the New York PO on 24 January 1946.

Stravinsky and his wife were now American citizens, their naturalization papers having gone through on 28 December 1945. This gave him a chance to review his work to date and see what he could do to safeguard his earlier copyrights. His early music was not protected in the USA, as at the time it was written Russia and the USA had not ratified the Berne copyright convention. Later he had tried to safeguard the copyrights of his new compositions by the subterfuge of appointing an American editor; but when he became a French citizen in 1934 he found that all his works from 1931 onwards became automatically protected in the USA. At the end of 1945 he signed an agreement with Ralph Hawkes of Boosey & Hawkes giving that firm exclusive publication rights for all his future compositions; and at the same time they took over those earlier works of his, ranging from *Petrushka* to *Persephone*, that had formerly been published by the Editions Russes de Musique. (This did not affect works of his published by other firms, such as Chester and Schott.) Now it became possible for him to make new versions of his earlier Editions Russes scores, to revise his music where necessary, to correct the numerous errors that marred some of the early editions, and to make sure that the copyright of these revised versions was properly protected. Some of his revisions were extensive. He rescored *Petrushka* for smaller orchestra (1946); and the make-up of the orchestra was changed in the new version of the Symphonies of Wind Instruments (1947). Less radical changes were made in the revised versions of *Apollo* (1947), the *Pulcinella* suite (1947), *Oedipus rex* (1948), the Symphony of Psalms (1948), the concert suite from *The Fairy's Kiss* entitled 'Divertimento' (1949), the Capriccio (1949), *Persephone* (1949), the Concerto for piano and wind instruments (1950), *The Fairy's Kiss* (1950), the Octet (1952) and *The Nightingale* (1962).

The end of the war brought Stravinsky a commission from Europe, the first for over ten years. This was for the Concerto in D for string orchestra, which he wrote in 1946 at the behest of Paul Sacher for the Basle Chamber Orchestra. It was followed by *Orpheus*, a new ballet score, commissioned by Lincoln Kirstein for the Ballet Society, which produced it in 1948 with choreography by Balanchin in New York.

Since *Oedipus rex* it had become exceedingly rare for Stravinsky to write a non-commissioned work. In 1942, however, he decided for personal reasons that he wanted to write a mass, a 'real' mass, and by that he meant a Roman Catholic mass that could be used liturgically. The initial impetus came from his discovery of some Mozart masses in a second-hand music store in Los Angeles; and he planned his mass for mixed chorus and double wind quintet. The Kyrie and Gloria were written in 1944; the Credo, Sanctus and Agnus Dei followed in 1947 and 1948. The first performance was given at La Scala, Milan, on 27 October 1948 with Ansermet conducting. Performances of the Mass as part of a church service have been comparatively rare.

Stravinsky now made an important decision – that he would compose a full-length opera in English. Although the work had not been commissioned by any specific person or institution, his relations with Boosey & Hawkes were so satisfactory that he felt justified in deciding to devote three years of his composing life to this opera. This would also be his first full-length work for the stage, for hitherto none of his operas or ballets had played for more than an hour. In the course of a visit to the Chicago Art Institute in 1947 he had been greatly impressed by a set of Hogarth's engravings depicting *The Rake's Progress*. Here Stravinsky thought was material for an opera libretto, and on the advice of his friend and neighbour Aldous Huxley he approached Auden and invited him to visit him in Hollywood. The meeting was successful; and, with the collaboration of Chester Kallman, Auden was able to hand over the completed libretto in Washington, DC, on 31 March 1948. Each of the three acts took roughly a year to write, and the completed opera was ready by April 1951. The first performance was given in Venice on 11 September 1951 at La Fenice during the 14th International Festival of Contemporary Music. La Scala supplied the chorus and orchestra, while the principal roles were cast from the best singers available; the composer himself conducted.

The Rake's Progress was an undoubted success and firmly re-established Stravinsky's reputation in postwar Europe. What was not realized at the time, however, was that in perspective it would be seen not only as the climax of his neo-classical period, but also as its peroration. Shortly afterwards Auden offered him another libretto to set, this time a masque entitled *Delia*; but by temperament Stravinsky was never inclined to run the risk of repeating himself. Instead, on returning to the USA, he chose four early English anonymous lyrics from an anthology edited by Auden and Norman Holmes Pearson and set them for soprano, tenor, chorus and small instrumental ensemble as the Cantata (1951–2). This work received its first performance by the Los Angeles Symphony Society in autumn 1952.

(ii) Works. Stravinsky's removal to the USA did not bring about any immediate change in his style, but this is hardly surprising when one considers that his professional activities there had been increasing since the mid-

10. Igor Stravinsky in London, 1958

works, such as the *Circus Polka* and the *Scherzo à la russe*; others contain uncomfortable variations of tone which perhaps reflect his unsettled state and his emotional involvement in the war. If the final apotheosis of *Scènes de ballet* seems suddenly to be charged with an intensity quite out of scale with what has gone before, or with its function in a Broadway revue, this is no doubt due to the fact that Stravinsky received the news of the liberation of Paris while he was at work on it, as he noted in the score. Similar considerations may account for the startlingly Dionysian quality of parts of the Symphony in Three Movements, composed only five years after the Symphony in C, but utterly different from it in mood and even in technique. Where the earlier work seems to have been conceived from the first as a lucid and clearsighted essay in the mode of the classical symphony, the later one is rather a concatenation of various ideas. Some of them were suggested (according to Stravinsky) by images in wartime newsreels; the middle movement, however, was originally composed to accompany the apparition of the Virgin in the film of Franz Werfel's *Song of Bernadette*, and its connection with the other two is purely one of contrast. The work's coherence comes less from Stravinsky's highly accomplished compositional craft than from the inherent vitality of its constituent ideas; it is this that transcends the work's abrupt transitions and the inconsistency of its textures, and makes of it a more popular, though perhaps less perfect, score than the Symphony in C.

As if in reaction to this Dionysian upsurge, a new austerity made itself heard in two immediately postwar works, though both also suggest that Stravinsky was beginning to cast his net wider in terms of historical reference. In the Mass liturgical function imposes a certain simplicity of style, but within that the voices (which are kept in the forefront throughout) borrow gestures from 14th-century Ars Nova and 16th-century polyphony as well as from the syllabic chant characteristic of Stravinsky's Orthodox church music. In the ballet *Orpheus* the concertante use of the harp may have been suggested by a similar feature in the central aria of Monteverdi's operatic treatment of the same myth. Otherwise its stylistic links are mostly within Stravinsky's own music: the second act of *Persephone* (with which it is connected by its subject matter) and, in the dance in which the Bacchantes tear Orpheus to pieces, the violent sections of the Symphony in Three Movements. Certain sections, notably the two thematically related fugal interludes and the final apotheosis, with its free canonic writing for two horns, betray a new interest in counterpoint that looks forward to Stravinsky's last creative period.

Before that, though, there came the amazing achievement, utterly unpredictable in its youthful exuberance, of *The Rake's Progress* – at about two and a half hours Stravinsky's longest work, though it was completed in his 69th year. The fluency with which the work was composed owed much to the mutual respect and sympathy between Stravinsky and Auden (though he was assisted by Chester Kallman, Auden's was clearly the dominant poetic character). The subject itself suggested an 18th-century frame of musical reference, and this found an immediate response in Auden's own, more amateur, enthusiasm for the older opera (unlike Stravinsky he was also a keen Wagnerian). The artistic development of both men had led them to a willing, if

1930s. Although the first two movements of the Symphony in C were composed in Europe it is hard to agree with Stravinsky's own assertion that there is a marked stylistic difference between them and the last two. It was at this time that he gave, in the Harvard lectures, the definitive account of his aesthetic stance; whether the stimulus was external, from the change of scene, or internal, from a new consciousness of the challenge of symphonic form, the Symphony in C represents an intensification of his neo-classicism. The work places great emphasis on motivic relationships, but it also makes deliberate and effective use of delayed or contradicted expectation – not only on the foreground level of rhythmic and harmonic detail, but on the larger formal level as well. This is not the wit of a Haydn or a Beethoven, playing with conventions they essentially accept; Stravinsky's attitude towards tonality, his means of establishing and relating tonal centres, are quite different from those of the Baroque and Classical composers whose manners and mannerisms he occasionally saw fit to borrow. The controlled dislocation he cultivated here, beneath an urbane exterior, reveals a sensibility that rejects the banal without placing any reliance on spontaneous expression.

That a subtly ambiguous form of expression can nevertheless be achieved by these means is proved above all by the opera *The Rake's Progress*, the summa of Stravinsky's neo-classical period, in which he was fortunate enough to be abetted by a librettist whose sensibility was completely in tune with this aspect of his own; there, at last, the irony latent in the style is for the first time exploited. But although these two works, the Symphony in C and the opera, mark the beginning and end of the first period of Stravinsky's life in the USA, they are far from exhausting its musical character. From the first years after his settlement in Hollywood, when money was a problem and commissions a permanent temptation, there date a number of frankly lightweight individual, acceptance of convention as a defence against chaos and formlessness; they shared, too, a need to screen the unconscious springs of their inspiration behind a scrupulous preoccupation with craftsmanship. Thus *The Rake's Progress*, in spite of its use of arias and recitatives (dry and accompanied), of ensembles and choruses, not to mention the 18th-century turns of expression in both music and text, is far from being a mere pastiche. Indeed the very strictness of the conventional framework seems to have liberated an unusual directness of emotional expression in Stravinsky. Like all his major theatrical works, *The Rake's Progress* is as much fable as story; it demands both empathy with the characters and an awareness of their meaning. The story, though loosely based on Hogarth, combines at least two of Stravinsky's main dramatic preoccupations: the conflict of good and evil in the human soul (as in *The Soldier's Tale*) and the cyclical regeneration of nature seen as a metaphor for that of mankind (the seasonal framework which he had suggested for *Persephone* is here made explicit). The vaudeville epilogue, for all its apparent flippancy, is much more than an antiquarian nod to *Don Giovanni*. 'For idle hands/ And hearts and minds/The Devil finds/A work to do . . .'; it is a succinct and witty statement of the philosophical viewpoint that underlies both Stravinsky's and Auden's sustained creative activity.

6. 1953–71.
(*i*) *Life*. In summer 1947 Robert Craft, then a young man of 23, wrote to Stravinsky from New York asking if he might borrow a copy of the score of the Symphonies of Wind Instruments (then unobtainable) for a concert of the Chamber Art Society, New York, which he was to conduct. The correspondence led to a generous offer by Stravinsky – that he was ready himself to take part in the concert by conducting the Symphonies and *Danses concertantes* without fee, leaving Craft to conduct the Capriccio and the Symphony in C. At the end of March 1948 Craft travelled to Washington, DC, to arrange details and was introduced to Stravinsky and his wife by Auden, who happened to be delivering the final text of the libretto of *The Rake's Progress* at the same time. The meeting was a success, and later Craft was invited to stay with the Stravinskys in Hollywood, where he helped the composer by cataloguing a substantial batch of his music manuscripts that had just arrived from Paris and answering various queries that arose from his setting of Auden's libretto. The friendship prospered; and Craft's position as musical aide and assistant was confirmed when it was realized that there were many ways in which he could be of continuing help to the composer, now in his 70s.

Craft, who had always been interested in the music of the Viennese serialists as well as that of Stravinsky, was at first surprised to find that in Hollywood Stravinsky and Schoenberg, who lived within a few miles of each other, kept strictly to themselves. After Schoenberg's death (13 July 1951) he encouraged Stravinsky to listen to recordings of a wide range of serial music, and the composer found himself growing receptive to the music of Webern. His own approach to serialism as a composer was a cautious one. In May 1952, when visiting Paris, he still maintained in replying to a journalist's question that the serialists were prisoners of the number 12, while he felt greater freedom with seven. Never-

theless, this was the moment when he began to experiment with some of the processes used by the serialists.

The world-wide success of *The Rake's Progress* meant that sooner or later Stravinsky was bound to be asked to write another opera; and in 1953 Boston University offered him such a commission. The Stravinskys had been favourably impressed when they heard Dylan Thomas give one of his poetry readings at Urbana in 1950; now he was invited to cooperate with Stravinsky as librettist. The two men met in Boston in May 1953 and liked each other on sight; it was agreed that Thomas should visit the Stravinskys in Hollywood that autumn in order to draft a suitable scenario. Unfortunately this visit never took place, for Thomas died in New York on 9 November. The opera project lapsed; instead Stravinsky composed an elegy, *In memoriam Dylan Thomas* (1954), in which a setting of Thomas's poem 'Do not go gentle into that good night' for tenor and string quartet is framed by dirge canons for a quartet of trombones.

The organizers of the Venice Biennale now commissioned a new work from Stravinsky for 1956. Wishing to make this work particularly Venice's own, he decided to inscribe it to Venice's patron, St Mark, and design it for performance in St Mark's Cathedral. The *Canticum sacrum*, for tenor and baritone, chorus and orchestra, was a setting of various passages from the Vulgate arranged in a cycle of five movements. As the work lasted for only 17 minutes – one of the characteristics of Stravinsky's new serial idiom being its increasing compression – he originally intended the programme should include a recomposed work by Gesualdo as well; but the Venetians refused to admit the music of a Neapolitan in St Mark's, so he offered an instrumental arrangement of Bach's canonic variations on *Vom Himmel hoch, da komm' ich her* instead. The première of the *Canticum sacrum* was given in Venice on 13 September 1956 with the composer conducting.

1957 saw the completion of a new ballet score, *Agon*, which had been commissioned by Lincoln Kirstein and Balanchin as the result of a grant made to the New York City Ballet by the Rockefeller Foundation. Stravinsky found a prototype for some of his dance movements in Lauze's *Apologie de la danse* (1623) and Mersenne's music examples. The composition of this score started as early as December 1953, but was interrupted by the need to complete *In memoriam Dylan Thomas* and the *Canticum sacrum*. When Stravinsky returned to *Agon* in 1956 he found he had to recast some of the early numbers to link them more sympathetically to his serial music, the technique of which was now fully developed. The first concert performance of the new score was given on 17 June 1957, when it was conducted by Craft as part of a special Los Angeles festival programme to commemorate Stravinsky's 75th birthday. The first stage production was given by the New York City Ballet on 1 December 1957.

In connection with Stravinsky's 75th birthday Craft had the idea that it might be helpful publicity (and save the composer the fatigue of being interviewed by too many reporters) if he himself interviewed Stravinsky and published the resultant text with the composer's approval. He did so; and 'Answers to 35 Questions' duly appeared in numerous periodicals. As this particular formula appeared to work satisfactorily, the two authors became more ambitious. Other questions were asked; other answers given; opportunities were found to include some of the correspondence Stravinsky had received from friends at various stages of his life; and *Conversations with Igor Stravinsky* was published in 1959.

Other volumes compiled by the two collaborators followed, *Memories and Commentaries* (1960), *Expositions and Developments* (1962), *Dialogues and a Diary* (1963), *Themes and Episodes* (1966) and *Retrospectives and Conclusions* (1969). As this collaboration progressed the formula for compiling the books started to change. In the first place, the last three volumes contained substantial extracts from Craft's diaries, which were later reprinted in his book *Stravinsky: Chronicle of a Friendship 1948–1971* (1972). Then it appeared that the two authors were beginning to sink their individual identities in a new character which was distinguished by some of the salient characteristics of both. Yet the authentic voice of the composer remained until the end, as is confirmed by Stravinsky's foreword to the English edition of his contributions to the last two volumes (retitled *Themes and Conclusions*, 1972) written only five weeks before his death.

A further commission for Venice was received in 1957. This time it came from North German Radio, whose orchestra and chorus gave the first performance of the cantata *Threni* in the Sala della Scuola Grande di S Rocco on 23 September 1958 as part of the Venice Biennale programme. *Threni* was followed by Movements for piano and orchestra (1958–9), written for Margrit Weber; and a further commission from Paul Sacher resulted in *A Sermon, a Narrative and a Prayer* (1960–61).

During the war Stravinsky had accepted a number of conducting engagements, mainly in the USA. His return to Europe in 1951 at the time of the first performance of *The Rake's Progress* had led to a renewal of invitations to conduct overseas, mainly in Italy, Germany and Switzerland, and occasionally in Paris and London. He now discovered that Craft could be of great help to him by preparing and rehearsing the orchestra before he took over, and sometimes also by sharing the burden of conducting. The fact that Craft was able and willing to accompany Stravinsky and his wife made these trips more agreeable and less onerous. From 1958 for a period of about ten years the number of these tours increased enormously; and, instead of being confined to North America and Europe, they now spread all over the world – to South America, the Far East, Australasia and Africa. In the 1950s Stravinsky also entered into a contract with Columbia under which all his works were to be recorded with the composer as conductor. Here too Craft was invaluable in helping rehearse the orchestra before Stravinsky took over for the final run-through and recording.

Plans to celebrate Stravinsky's 80th birthday in 1962 proceeded on a much more extensive scale than those for his 75th. On 16 January he received the State Department's medal, and two days later he and his wife were guests of the President and Mrs Kennedy at a dinner party in the White House. The following month a new anthem to words by Eliot, 'The dove descending breaks the air', was given at one of the Los Angeles Monday Evening Concerts; the same month *A Sermon, a Narrative and a Prayer* had its première in Basle; and the television broadcast of *The Flood* by CBS, who commissioned the work, took place on 14 June. Stravinsky celebrated his 80th birthday in Hamburg, where a special programme consisting of *Orpheus*, *Agon* and *Apollo*, all with choreography by Balanchin, was mounted by the New York City Ballet.

Undoubtedly the most important event of 1962, however, was Stravinsky's return to Russia after an absence of nearly half a century. The previous year a deputation of Soviet musicians had transmitted to him in Hollywood an official invitation to visit the USSR and conduct a concert of his own music on the occasion of his 80th birthday. A number of his friends and acquaintances thought that for political and other reasons he should refuse; but in the end saner counsels prevailed, and he agreed to give a series of concerts in Moscow and Leningrad. The Russian visit came at the end of an extensive tour embracing Toronto, Paris, Brazzaville, Johannesburg, Pretoria, Cape Town, Rome, Hamburg and Israel. The Stravinskys, together with Craft, arrived in Moscow on 21 September. Three concerts were given there, and two in Leningrad; and the intervening days were passed in a whirl of sight-seeing and lavish entertainment. On their last day in Moscow (11 October) they were received by Khrushchev in the Kremlin. The visit was undoubtedly a great success. It marked the beginning of a more liberal attitude to Stravinsky's music in the USSR; and, for the composer himself, Craft perceptively noted in his diary, 'To be recognised and acclaimed as a Russian in Russia, and to be performed there, has meant more to him than anything else in the years I have known him'.

Stravinsky's next composition was a work commissioned by the Israel Festival Committee, the sacred ballad for baritone and small orchestra *Abraham and Isaac* (1962–3). He set the text in the original Hebrew; which brought the number of languages he had set to seven, the others being Russian, French, Italian, Church Slavonic, Latin and English. The first performance of *Abraham and Isaac* took place in Jerusalem on 23 August 1964.

As Stravinsky's life lengthened many of his friends and acquaintances died, and occasionally he felt prompted to write some kind of musical epitaph. *In memoriam Dylan Thomas* belongs to this category; so too do two miniature serial works, both composed in 1959, both lasting only just over a minute, and both creating an effect of classical summation – the *Epitaphium* for flute, clarinet and harp 'für das Grabmal des Prinzen Max Egon zu Fürstenberg' and the Double Canon for string quartet 'Raoul Dufy in memoriam'. The assassination of President Kennedy on 22 November 1963 led Stravinsky to write a miniature *Elegy for J.F.K.* for baritone and three clarinets (1964) to four stanzas specially written by Auden, each a 'free' haiku. On the day of Kennedy's assassination Aldous Huxley also died, and Stravinsky decided to dedicate to his memory a work he had already started to compose, the Variations for orchestra.

It is probable that towards the end of 1964 Stravinsky had in mind the idea that he might compose a Requiem mass; but the death of his friend Eliot in London on 4 January 1965 precipitated the composition of a single movement, *Introitus*, which was completed six weeks later. A commission from Princeton enabled him to give more attention to the requiem idea. It was a condition of the commission that the work should be dedicated to the memory of Helen Buchanan

Seeger; but in reality the *Requiem Canticles* (1965–6) were written with his own approaching death in mind. This proved to be Stravinsky's last major composition. Shortly after its first performance at Princeton University (8 October 1966) he completed a lightweight setting of Lear's *The Owl and the Pussy-cat* for soprano and piano, which he dedicated to his wife. Early in 1968 he started to compose an extra instrumental prelude to the *Requiem Canticles* for a special performance of the work in memory of Martin Luther King; but he was unable to complete this in time. He also drafted some sketches for a piano sonata; but these were ultimately abandoned. An instrumental transcription of two sacred songs from Wolf's *Spanisches Liederbuch* was made in San Francisco in May 1968 and performed in Los Angeles later that year; but instrumental transcriptions of two preludes and fugues from Bach's '48' were withdrawn by Craft from a concert in Berlin in October 1969.

By 1967 Stravinsky's health was beginning to fail. In January he made his last recording (of the 1945 suite from *The Firebird*); and in May he conducted his last public performance (of the *Pulcinella* suite, in Toronto). After that he was occasionally 'in attendance' at concerts of his works conducted by Craft. He was tended devotedly by his wife and various nurses; after his composing faculty had started to fail Craft was successful in getting him to spend more time listening to the recorded music of other composers – particularly Beethoven – which gave him much pleasure. In 1969 the Stravinskys decided to move from Hollywood to New York; the following year they flew to Europe in the summer and spent three months at Evian on Lake Geneva. On 6 April 1971 Stravinsky died at his home in New York. At his widow's suggestion he was buried in Venice on the island of S Michele, not far from Dyagilev's grave.

(ii) Works. Various circumstances combined to produce, in the years immediately following *The Rake's Progress*, the most profound change in Stravinsky's musical vocabulary that it had undergone for more than 30 years. One was the adoption into his family circle of Craft, whose enthusiasm for the music of the Second Viennese School certainly helped to focus Stravinsky's attention on it. Another was his return to Europe for the première of *The Rake* in 1951, and the contacts that this brought with a new generation of European composers, many of them strongly influenced by the postwar rediscovery of Schoenbergian serialism. And perhaps most important of all there was the death, earlier in 1951, of Schoenberg himself, for many years Stravinsky's fellow exile and neighbour (virtually unacknowledged) in Hollywood. The post-Romantic characteristics of Schoenberg's music and the doctrinaire cast of his thought, not to mention the prickliness of his personality, had prevented Stravinsky from coming to terms with him while he lived, and the two men had been cast by their respective followers as opponents in a quasi-ideological battle of style comparable to that of Wagner and Brahms two generations earlier. As Stravinsky now gradually began to come to terms (his own, it must be said) with some aspects of serial practice, and moved further away from the tonal waters in which his music had hitherto sailed under a flag of convenience, many of his own most embattled followers undoubtedly felt a sense of betrayal. Yet in fact Stravinsky's 'conversion', unlike that of some other composers at about this time,

was very far from being a capitulation. It was much more like an annexation of the enemy's resources to his own perennial purposes, and it was carried out with immense caution, each stylistic step being tested by the only criteria he had ever admitted, his instinct and his ear.

There were already precedents in Stravinsky's own music for treating a melody as a series (i.e. as a sequence of pitches with no inherent rhythmic or harmonic implications); examples occur in the variations of the Octet (1923), the last two movements of the Concerto for two pianos (1935) and the interludes in *Orpheus* (1947), in all of which the resulting series is, significantly enough, sooner or later treated fugally. Stravinsky now began to explore the spatial, purely intervallic implications of this practice by applying to such series the basic serial transformational procedures of retrograde, inversion and retrograde inversion. Thus in the middle movement of the Cantata on early English texts, a setting for tenor and instrumental quintet of the rhymed life of Christ 'Tomorrow shall be my dancing day', the solo line, with the exception of its punctuating refrain, is strictly derived from an initial sequence of 12 notes (as are some of the counterpoints to it). This is not an orthodox Schoenbergian series, since it involves only the seven pitches contained within an augmented 4th, and the serial procedures themselves do not penetrate all voices of the movement or all sections of the work, but it does involve a new emphasis on purely melodic aspects of development and integration. In the Septet (1953) for the Schoenbergian combination of three wind, three strings and piano, composed in E♭, like the 'Dumbarton Oaks' Concerto (1938), these procedures are taken further. Although the first movement is not far in style from its neo-Bachian predecessor, the second is a passacaglia on a 16-note theme, which provides, by serial and canonic manipulation, most of the contrapuntal texture around it, and the final gigue takes up the eight different pitches which the passacaglia theme contains and treats them as a transposable scale from which to derive a succession of fugue subjects; these too appear in retrograde and inverted form. The contrapuntal action in the Septet is increasingly dense and the harmonic movement increasingly rapid and dissonant. The Three Shakespeare Songs for mezzo-soprano, flute, clarinet and viola, and *In memoriam Dylan Thomas* for tenor and string quartet, with the addition of four funereal trombones (cf Schütz's *Fili mi Absalon* and Beethoven's *Equali*) in the canonic prelude and postlude, are further explorations of this essentially linear serialism, whose anti-tonal consequences are mitigated by the use of smaller pitch collections than the full spectrum of 12 and by a free use of transposition.

Just as the short vocal and instrumental works of 1914–16 have tended to be obscured by the larger works (*Reynard*, *The Wedding*) for which they were in some sense studies, so these short works of 1952–4 have inevitably been overshadowed by the larger and more confident works that followed them; yet in spite of their rather cramped melodic style they are highly individual works in their own right. But with the *Canticum sacrum* a new breadth is immediately audible. Apart from the Ars Nova-like epigraph with which it begins, the work is strictly symmetrical, its groundplan apparently based on that of St Mark's. The Byzantine architecture may also have suggested the style of the choral first and fifth movements (the latter a palindrome

11. *Autograph MS of p.6 from Stravinsky's* Variations for Orchestra (*in memory of Aldous Huxley*), *1963–4 (US-Wc)*

of the former); they seem like a throwback to the Russian Stravinsky of *The Wedding* and the Symphonies of Wind Instruments. But the three middle movements – a lightly accompanied lyrical tenor solo, a solemn celebration of the three cardinal virtues of faith, hope and charity by the work's full forces, and an intensely dramatic setting for baritone and chorus of a prayer for faith drawn from St Mark's gospel – all these make use, with whatever concessions to Stravinsky's desire for tonal anchorages, of full 12-note series. That such a variety of textures and techniques is juxtaposed

with no sense of incongruity is sufficient indication of the extent to which he had already succeeded in making over serial procedures to his own long-established musical purposes, but in *Agon* he achieved a more remarkable feat still: moving from diatonicism, through polytonality and partial serialism to a complete 12-note serialism (in the climactic pas de deux and the concerted dances that follow it), he then succeeded in returning without incongruity to the diatonic music with which the work began.

Threni, however, a setting of carefully selected portions of the Lamentations of Jeremiah for six solo voices, chorus and a rather large orchestra (including flügelhorn and sarrusophone but no trumpets or bassoons), is Stravinsky's first completely serial score. In the lightly scored *Agon* Stravinsky had come closest to Webern, whose pointillist, intervallic version of serial technique was far more congenial to him than Schoenberg's more harmonically orientated style. *Threni*, in keeping with its sombre text, is altogether more weighty in sound, and reveals very clearly the incompatibility of Stravinsky's harmonic sense with that of orthodox serialism. In the fuller sections repeated notes and phrases are constantly allowed to set up fields of tonal attraction, and although the more contrapuntal sections for smaller forces (notably the extraordinary set of unaccompanied canons for solo male voices in the 'Querimonia') avoid this almost completely, the music is finally brought, by cunning transposition of the various forms of the series, to a quasi-tonal cadence that sounds almost like A minor. Stravinsky's sense of the dramatic connotations of his text clearly demands a resolution of this kind, however contrary it may be to the theoretical principles that are supposed to underlie, and indeed justify, serial practice.

If the series remains, in *Threni*, an essentially linear entity, *Movements*, a brief but densely composed concert piece for piano and orchestra, achieves a new freedom by refracting the series into its constituent smaller motifs and recombining them in various ways – a form of serial punning. Rhythmically, too, *Movements* is far more flexible than *Threni*, or indeed any previous music by Stravinsky, but the work is given a firm framework by reserving a separate group of instruments to each section and by using the last few bars of each of its five brief movements (except the last) to introduce the tempo of the following one. *A Sermon, a Narrative and a Prayer* is to some extent a New Testament counterpart to *Threni*, but its texts take up the central burden of the *Canticum sacrum*, that of the three cardinal virtues: St Stephen, praying for his murderers in the moment of his martyrdom, is taken as the archetype of Christian love proceeding from faith and hope. Technically the work brings into Stravinsky's sacred music, especially in the central narrative of the martyrdom, some of the freedoms newly won in *Movements*, such as the flexibility of rhythm and the fragmentation of the orchestra's sonorities; this is extended to the voices, as when speaking and singing voices are ingeniously mingled, and when alto and tenor are dovetailed to form a composite solo voice of preternatural range. Only in the final section (almost the last, and certainly one of the greatest, of the long series of epitaphs with which Stravinsky had, throughout his life, commemorated the death of his friends) does the novel use of three tam-tams of different sizes to suggest the tolling of bells indicate a link with a much earlier Stravinsky.

In *A Sermon* Stravinsky's shaping genius is at its surest, placing and balancing the diverse textures and tempos with an unerring hand. In *The Flood*, a treatment of the Chester miracle play with additional material from the York cycle and elsewhere, commissioned by and designed for television, this large-scale architectural sense seems for once to have deserted him. The two danced sections – the building of the ark and the flood itself – show all his newly expanded mastery, but the remainder seems to contain music of too much diversity and not enough density to balance the lengthy spoken narration, in spite of such vivid and typical touches as the use of two basses in homophony to represent the impersonal voice of God (cf the bridegroom's request for a blessing in *The Wedding*), the insinuating high tenor for Satan (cf *Reynard*), the brass chords that accompany God's curse, and the woodwind and harp that depict the rainbow. Stravinsky's apparent attraction to themes already treated by Britten (a not altogether friendly emulation, one suspects) is carried a stage further by his setting of the story of *Abraham and Isaac*, where the sounds of the Hebrew text, as interpreted to Stravinsky by his friend Sir Isaiah Berlin, were the starting-point for the composition. The narrative given to the baritone soloist is kept in the forefront of the texture throughout, and the chamber orchestra (which surprisingly contains two trumpets, two trombones and tuba) is used with extreme economy; only at the climactic prophesy, in fact, that 'in thy seed shall all nations of the earth be blessed' are the above-mentioned brass used together, and then only *piano*. Although the language of the text is likely to limit the work's full appreciation, it is beautifully composed, and its density repays detailed study.

This density is likewise a feature of the orchestral Variations dedicated to the memory of Aldous Huxley, even though the first variation, after the opening cadences, is a monody shared between different groups of instruments – a very Stravinskian interpretation of Schoenberg's *Klangfarbenmelodie*. Here, as in all Stravinsky's later music, timbre and texture play a crucial role in articulating the form; the score contains his most extreme example of sustained polyrhythm – three sections for 12 rhythmically distinct instruments (cf the middle section of Messiaen's *Chronochromie*), first violins, then violas with two double basses, and lastly wind. The complexity of these sections is the most difficult feature of the score to grasp; Stravinsky himself claimed that with repeated hearings they would appear to change perspective, like mobiles, but it is unfortunate that most hearings so far have been of the same (recorded) performance.

The last two in the series of sacred choral works that bulks so large in Stravinsky's final period, the *Introitus* and the *Requiem Canticles*, are far less hermetic in style. The former picks up and briefly reworks ideas from the Voice of God sequences in *The Flood*, with its two-part texture of muffled drumming (the pitches clarified by string doublings) and its solemn, unmistakably Stravinskian cadences. The *Requiem Canticles* are more complex and varied, but the textures are still relatively speaking simple, though the sonorities are used with unfailing imagination. The text, like that of the *Introitus*, is taken from the mass for the dead: part of the opening gradual, parts of the sequence 'Dies irae', and most of the final responsory 'Libera me'. They are prefaced by a prelude for strings alone (whose constantly repeated semiquavers provide a harmonic underpinning to the cumulatively polyrhythmic refrain above), separated by a woodwind interlude which Stravinsky himself referred to as 'the formal lament', and rounded off by a litany in which still chords for high wind, piano, harp and horn punctuate quicker moving chords on celesta, bells and vibraphone. Unlike *Abraham and Isaac* the *Requiem Canticles* do not eschew illustration of the text: the 'Dies irae' in particular is as vivid in its own rarefied context as Verdi's is in its. This 'pocket Requiem', as Stravinsky referred to it, is a distillation both of the liturgical text and of his own musical means of setting it, evolved and refined through a career of more than 60 years.

WORKS

Publication: Publishers are indicated by means of abbreviations as follows: Associated [A], Belyayev [Bel], Bessell [Bes], Boosey & Hawkes [B], Breitkopf & Härtel [Br], Chappell [Chap], Charling [Char], Chester [C], Faber [F], Hansen [H], Henn [He], Jurgenson [J], Leeds [L], Mercury [M], Edition Russe de Musique [R], Schott [S], Sirène [Si].

DRAMATIC

Zhar'-ptitsa (L'oiseau de feu) [The firebird] (fairy story ballet, 2 scenes, Fokin), orch, 1909–10; Paris, Opéra, 25 June 1910; (J 1910, S)

Petrushka (Pétrouchka) (burlesque, 4 scenes, Benois), orch, 1910–11; Paris, Châtelet, 13 June 1911; (R 1912), rev. 1946 (B 1947)

Vesna svyashchennaya (Le sacre du printemps) [The rite of spring (literally 'Sacred spring')] (scenes of pagan Russia, 2 pts., N. Roerich), orch, 1911–13; Paris, Champs-Elysées, 29 May 1913; (R 1913 [for pf 4 hands], R 1921 [full score]), rev. (B 1947), Sacrificial Dance separately in substantial rev., 1943 (A 1945); facs. sketches (B 1969)

Solovey (Le rossignol) [The nightingale] (musical fairy tale, 3, Stravinsky, S. Mitusov after Andersen), solo vv, chorus, orch, Act 1 1908–9, Acts 2–3 1913–14; Paris, Opéra, 26 May 1914; (R 1923, B 1947), rev. (B 1962)

Bayka (Renard) [Reynard] (burlesque in song and dance, Stravinsky after Russ. trad.), 2 T, 2 B, small orch, 1915–16; Paris, Opéra, 18 May 1922; (He 1917, C)

Pesnya solov'ya (Chant du rossignol) [The song of the nightingale] (sym. poem/ballet, Stravinsky after Andersen) [arr. from The nightingale], orch, 1917; concert perf., Geneva, 6 Dec 1919; staged, Paris, Opéra, 2 Feb 1920; (R 1921, B)

Histoire du soldat (The Soldier's Tale) (to be read, played and danced, 2 pts., C. F. Ramuz), 3 actors, female dancer, cl, bn, cornet, trbn, perc, vn, db, 1918; Lausanne, Municipal, 28 Sept 1918; (C 1924)

Pulcinella (ballet with song, 1) [after Pergolesi and others], S, T, B, chamber orch, 1919–20; Paris, Opéra, 15 May 1920; (C 1920 [vocal score], R [full score], B

Mavra (opera buffa, 1, B. Kochno after Pushkin: The Little House in Kolomna), S, Mez, A, T, orch, 1921–2; Paris, Opéra, 3 June 1922; (R 1925, B 1947)

Svadebka (Les noces) [The wedding] (Russian choreographic scenes, 4 scenes, Stravinsky after Russ. trad.), short score 1914–17, scored for S, Mez, T, B, SATB, 4 pf, perc ens, 1921–3; Paris, Gaîté Lyrique, 13 June 1923; (C 1922 [vocal score], C c1923 [full score]); also 2 frags. in abandoned earlier instrumentations: opening section, solo vv, chorus, orch; scenes i–ii, solo vv, chorus, pianola, harmonium, 2 cimb, perc ens

Oedipus rex (opera-oratorio, 2, Cocteau, Lat. trans. J. Daniélou), narrator, solo vv, male chorus, orch, 1926–7; concert perf., Paris, Sarah Bernhardt, 30 May 1927; staged, Vienna, 23 Feb 1928; (R 1927), rev. 1948 (B 1949)

Apollon musagète (ballet, 2 scenes), str orch, 1927–8; Washington, Library of Congress, 27 April 1928; (R 1928), rev. as Apollo, 1947 (B 1949)

Le baiser de la fée (The Fairy's Kiss) (allegorical ballet, 4 scenes, Stravinsky after Andersen) [after songs and pf pieces by Tchaikovsky], orch, 1928; Paris, Opéra, 27 Nov 1928; (R 1928), rev. 1950 (B 1952)

Perséphone (Persephone) (melodrama, 3 scenes, Gide), speaker, T, SATB, TrA, orch, 1933–4; Paris, Opéra, 30 April 1934; (R 1934), rev. 1949 (B 1950)

Jeu de cartes (The Card Party) (ballet in 3 deals, Stravinsky, M. Melaïeff), orch, 1936; New York, Metropolitan, 27 April 1937; (S 1937)

Circus Polka (for a young elephant), 1942, scored for band by D. Reksin; New York, Madison Square Gardens, spr. 1942; unpubd in this version

Scènes de ballet (for revue The Seven Lively Arts), orch, 1944; Philadelphia, 1944; (Chap 1945)

Orpheus (ballet, 3 scenes), orch, 1947; New York, City Center, 28 April 1948; (B 1948)

The Rake's Progress (opera, 3, Auden, Kallman), solo vv, chorus, orch, 1948–51; Venice, La Fenice, 11 Sept 1951; (B 1951)

Agon (ballet), orch, 1953–4, 1956–7; concert perf., Los Angeles, 17 June 1957; staged, New York, 1 Dec 1957; (B 1957)

The Flood (musical play, Craft after York and Chester mystery plays, Genesis), solo vv, actors, orch, 1961–2; CBS television, broadcast 14 June 1962; staged, Hamburg, Staatsoper, 30 April 1963; (B 1963)

ORCHESTRAL

Symphony no.1, E♭, op.1, 1905–7 (J 1914)

Scherzo fantastique, op.3, 1907–8 (J, S)

Feu d'artifice (Fireworks), op.4, 1908 (S 1910)

Chant funèbre, op.5, wind, 1908, unpubd, lost

Suite from 'The Firebird', 1911 (J 1912); 2nd suite, reduced orch, 1919

(C); 3rd suite, reduced orch, 1945 (L 1946–7)

March [arr. of 3 Easy Pieces, pf 4 hands: no.1], 12 insts, 1915, unpubd

Rag-time, fl, cl, hn, cornet, trbn, perc, cimb, 2 vn, va, db, 1918 (Si 1919, C 1920)

Symphonies of Wind Instruments, 23 insts, 1920 (R 1926 [pf reduction]); rev. 1945–7 (B 1947)

Suite no.2 [arr. of 3 Easy Pieces, pf 4 hands, and 5 Easy Pieces, pf 4 hands: no.5], small orch, 1921 (C)

Suite from 'Pulcinella', chamber orch, c1922 (R 1924); rev. 1947 (B 1949)

Concerto, pf, wind, timp, dbs, 1923–4 (R 1924 [2 pf reduction], R 1936 [full score]); rev. 1950 (B 1950)

Suite no.1 [arr. of 5 Easy Pieces, pf 4 hands: nos.1–4], small orch, 1917–25 (C)

Four Studies [arr. of 3 Pieces, str qt, and Study, pianola], nos.1–3 1914–18, no.4 1928 (R, B)

Capriccio, pf, orch, 1928–9 (R 1930); rev. 1949 (B 1952)

Violin Concerto, D, 1931 (S 1931)

Divertimento [arr. from The Fairy's Kiss], 1934 (R 1938); rev. 1949 (B 1950)

Preludium, jazz band, 1936–7, unpubd; reorchd 1953 (B 1968)

Concerto 'Dumbarton Oaks', E♭, chamber orch, 1937–8 (S 1938)

Symphony, C, 1939–40 (S 1948)

Danses concertantes, chamber orch, 1941–2 (A 1942)

Circus Polka, 1942 (A 1944)

Four Norwegian Moods, 1942 (A 1944)

Ode, elegiacal chant in 3 parts, 1943 (S 1947)

Scherzo à la russe, jazz band, 1944, unpubd; orch version, 1943–4 (Chap 1945)

Symphony in Three Movements, 1942–5 (A 1946)

Ebony Concerto, cl, jazz band, 1945 (Char 1946)

Concerto, D, str, 1946 (B 1947)

Concertino [arr. of str qt work], vn, vc, fl, ob, eng hn, A-cl, 2 tpt, trbn, b trbn, 1952 (H 1953)

Tango [arr. of pf work], 19 insts, 1953 (M 1954)

Greeting Prelude [after C. F. Summy: Happy Birthday to you], 1955 (B 1956)

Movements, pf, orch, 1958–9 (B 1960)

Eight Instrumental Miniatures [arr. of Les cinq doigts, pf], 15 insts, 1962 (C 1963)

Variations, 1963–4 (B 1965)

Canon on a Russian Popular Tune [theme from finale of The Firebird], 1965 (B 1966)

CHORAL

cantata, chorus, pf, 1904, lost

Zvezdolikiy (Le roi des étoiles) [The king of the stars (literally 'Starfaced')] (Bal'mont), TTBB, orch, 1911–12 (J 1913)

Podblyudnïya [Saucers] (Four Russian Peasant Songs), female vv, 1914–17 (S c1930, C 1932); rev. for equal vv, 4 hn, 1954 (C 1958):
1 U spasa v' Chigisakh' [On saints' days in Chigisakh], 4vv, 1916
2 Ovsen' [Ovsen], 2vv, 1917
3 Shchuka [The pike], 3 solo vv, 4vv, 1914
4 Puzishche [Master Portly], solo v, 4vv, 1915

Otche nash' [Our Father] (Slavonic text), SATB, 1926 (R 1932); rev. as Pater noster (Lat. text), 1949 (B)

Symphony of Psalms (Pss xxxviii.13–14, xxxix.2–4, cl), TrATB, 1930 (R 1930 [vocal score], R 1932 [full score]); rev. 1948 (B 1948)

Simvol' verï [Symbol of faith] (Slavonic text), SATB, 1932 (R 1933); rev. as Credo (Lat. text), 1949 (B); rev. (Slavonic text), 1964

Bogoroditse devo [Blessed Virgin] (Slavonic text), SATB, 1934 (R 1934); rev. as Ave Maria (Lat. text), 1949 (B)

Babel (Genesis xi.1–9), cantata, male narrator, male vv, orch, 144 (S 1953)

Mass (Lat. text), TrATB, 2 ob, eng hn, 2 bn, 2 tpt, 3 trbn, 1944–8 (B 1948)

Cantata (late medieval Eng. verse), S, T, female vv, 2 fl, ob, ob + eng hn, vc, 1951–2 (B 1952)

Canticum sacrum ad honorem Sancti Marci nominis (Bible), T, Bar, chorus, orch, 1955 (B 1956)

Threni: id est Lamentationes Jeremiae prophetae, S, A, 2 T, 2 B, chorus, orch, 1957–8 (B 1958)

A Sermon, a Narrative and a Prayer (St Paul, Acts, Dekker), cantata, A, T, speaker, chorus, orch, 1960–61 (B 1961)

Anthem 'The dove descending breaks the air' (Eliot: Little Gidding, pt.IV), SATB, 1962 (appendix to Eng. edn. of Expositions and Developments, 1962, B)

Introitus (Requiem aeternam), male vv, pf, harp, 2 timp, 2 tam-tams, va, dbs, 1965 (B 1965)

Requiem Canticles, A, B, chorus, orch, 1965–6 (B 1967)

SOLO VOCAL

Storm Cloud (Pushkin), romance, 1v, pf, 1902, unpubd

The Mushrooms Going to War, song, B, pf, 1904, unpubd

Favn' i pastushka (Faune et bergère) [Faun and shepherdess], op.2, song suite, Mez, orch, 1906 (Bel 1908, B):
1 Pastushka, 2 Favn', 3 Reka [Torrent]

Pastorale (textless), S, pf, 1907 (J 1910, C, S); arr. S, ob, eng hn, cl, bn, 1923 (S)

Deux mélodies, op.6 (Gorodetsky), Mez, pf, 1908 (J ?1912, B 1968):
1 Vesna (Monastïrskaya) [Spring (The cloister)]
2 Rosyanka (Khlïstorskaya) [A song of the dew (Mystic song of the ancient Russian flagellants)]

Deux poèmes de Paul Verlaine, op.9, Bar, pf, 1910 (J 1911, B 1954); arr. Bar, chamber orch, 1951 (B 1953):
1 Un grand sommeil noir, 2 La lune blanche

Two Poems of Konstantin Bal'mont, S/T, pf, 1911 (R 1912, B); arr. S/T, 2 fl, 2 cl, pf, str qt, 1954 (B):
1 Nezabudoochka–tsvetochek' [The flower], 2 Golub' [The dove]

Tri stikhotvoreniya iz yaponskoy liriki (Trois poésies de la lyrique japonaise) [Three Japanese lyrics] (trans. A. Brandta), S, pf/(2 fl, 2 cl, pf, str qt), 1912–13 (R 1913, B):
1 Akahito, 1912, 2 Mazatsumi, 1912, Tsaraiuki, 1913

Tri pesenki 'Iz' vospominaniy yunosheskikh' godov" [Three little songs 'Recollections of my childhood'] (Russ. trad.), 1v, pf, c1906, rev. 1913 (R 1914, B); arr. 1v, small orch, 1929–30 (R 1934, B):
1 Sorochen'ka [The magpie], 2 Vorona [The rook], 3 Chicher' yacher' [The jackdaw]

Pribaoutki (Russ. trad.), male v, fl, ob + eng hn, cl, bn, vn, va, vc, db, 1914 (He 1917, C):
1 Kornilo [Kornillo], 2 Natashka, 3 Polkovnik' [The colonel], 4 Starets' i zayats' [The old man and the hare]

Berceuses du chat (Cat's Cradle Songs) (Russ. trad.), A, Eb-cl + cl, cl + A-cl, A-cl + b cl, 1915–16 (He 1917, C):
1 Spi kot' [The tom-cat], 2 Kot' na pechi [The tom-cat on the stove], 3 Bay-bay [Bye-bye], 4 U kota kota [O tom-cat, tom-cat]

Trois histoires pour enfants (Russ. trad.), 1v, pf, 1915–17 (C 1920); no.1 arr. 1v, orch, 1923 (S):
1 Tilim'-bom' [Tilimbom], 1917, 2 Gusi, lebedi [Geese, swans], 1917, 3 Pesenka medvedya [The bear's little song], 1915

Berceuse (Stravinsky), 1v, pf, 1917 (in Eng. edn. of Expositions and Developments, 1962)

Four Russian Songs (Russ. trad.), 1v, pf, 1918–19 (C 1920):
1 Selezen (Khorovodnaya) [The drake (Round)], 1918
2 Zapevnaya [Counting-song], 1919
3 Podblyudnaya [Table-mat song], 1919
4 Sektantskaya [Dissident song], 1919

Chanson de Paracha [from Mavra], S, orch, 1922–3 (R ?1933)

Petit Ramusianum harmonique (Stravinsky), 1v/unison vv, 1937 (in Hommage à C.-F. Ramuz, Lausanne, 1938)

Petit canon pour la fête de Nadia Boulanger (J. de Meung), 2T, 1947, unpubd

Three Songs from William Shakespeare, Mez, fl, cl, va, 1953 (B 1954):
1 Musick to Heare, 2 Full Fathom Five, 3 When Dasies Pied

Four Songs (Stravinsky) [arrs. of 4 Russian Songs: nos.1 and 4, and 3 histoires pour enfants: nos.2 and 1], 1v, fl, harp, gui, 1953–4 (C 1955):
1 The Drake, 1953, 2 A Russian Spiritual, 1954, 3 Geese and Swans, 1954, 4 Tilimbom, 1954

In memoriam Dylan Thomas (Thomas: Do not go gentle), dirge canons and song, T, str qt, 4 trbn, 1954 (B 1954)

Abraham and Isaac (Genesis xxii, in Heb.), sacred ballad, Bar, chamber orch, 1962–3 (B 1965)

Elegy for J. F. K. (Auden), Bar, 3 cl, 1964 (B 1964); rev. Mez, 3 cl, 1964 (B 1964)

The Owl and the Pussy-cat (Lear), 1v, pf, 1966 (B 1967)

CHAMBER AND INSTRUMENTAL

Three Pieces, str qt, 1914 (R 1922, B 1947)

Polka [arr. of 3 Easy Pieces, pf 4 hands: no.3], cimb, 1915, unpubd

Canons, 2 hn, 1917, unpubd

Study, pianola, 1917, roll 1967 B (Aeolian Co.), unpubd in score

Duet, 2 bn, 1918, unpubd

Suite from 'The Soldier's Tale', cl, bn, cornet, trbn, perc, vn, db, 1918 (C 1922); 5 movts arr. vn, cl, pf, 1919 (C 1920)

Three Pieces, cl + A-cl, 1919 (C 1920)

Concertino, str qt, 1920 (H 1923)

Octet, fl, cl, 2 bn, C-tpt, A-tpt, trbn, b trbn, 1922–3 (R 1924), rev. 1952 (B 1952)

Suite d'après thèmes, fragments et pièces de Giambattista Pergolesi [arr. from Pulcinella], vn, pf, 1925 (R 1926, B)

Prélude et Ronde des princesses [arr. from The Firebird], vn, pf, 1929 (S); Ronde rev. as Scherzo, 1933, collab. Dushkin (S)

Berceuse [arr. from The Firebird], vn, pf, 1929 (S); rev. 1933, collab. Dushkin (S)

Duo concertante, vn, pf, 1931–2 (R 1933, B)

Chants du rossignol et Marche chinoise [arr. from The Nightingale], vn, pf, 1932, collab. Dushkin (R, B)

Suite italienne [arr. from Pulcinella], vc, pf, 1932, collab. Piatigorsky (R 1934, B)

Suite italienne [arr. from Pulcinella], vn, pf, 1932, collab. Dushkin (R 1934, B)

Divertimento [arr. of orch work], vn, pf, 1932, collab. Dushkin (R, B)

Pastorale [arr. of vocalise], vn, pf, 1933, collab. Dushkin (S 1934); arr. vn, ob, eng hn, cl, bn, 1933 (S 1934)

Chanson russe [arr. from Mavra], vn, pf, 1937, collab. Dushkin (R 1938, B); arr. vc, pf, collab. D. Markevich (R, B)

Elégie, va, 1944 (Chap 1945)

Ballad [arr. from The Fairy's Kiss], vn, pf, 1947, collab. J. Gautier (B 1951)

Septet, cl, bn, hn, pf, vn, va, vc, 1952–3 (B 1953)

Epitaphium, fl, cl, harp, 1959 (B 1959)

Double Canon, str qt, 1959 (B 1960)

Lullaby [arr. from The Rake's Progress, tr rec, a rec (B 1960)

Fanfare for a New Theatre, 2 tpt, 1964 (B 1968)

PIANO

Tarantella, 1898, unpubd

Scherzo, 1902 (F 1975)

Sonata, f#, 1903–4 (F 1975)

Four Studies, op.7, 1908 (J 1910)

Valse des fleurs, 2 pf, 1914, unpubd, lost

Three Easy Pieces, 4 hands, 1914–15 (He 1917, C):
1 March, 2 Waltz, 3 Polka

Souvenir d'une marche boche, 1915 (in E. Wharton, ed.: The Book of the Homeless, London, 1916)

Five Easy Pieces, 4 hands, 1916–17 (He 1917, C):
1 Andante, 2 Española, 3 Balalaika, 4 Napolitana, 5 Galop

Valse pour les enfants, c1917 (in Le figaro, 21 May 1922)

Piano-rag-music, 1919 (C 1920)

Les cinq doigts, 8 easy pieces, 1921 (C 1922)

Three Movements from 'Petrushka', 1921 (R 1922, B)

Sonata, 1924 (R 1925, B)

Serenade, A, 1925 (R 1926, B)

Concerto, 2 pf, 1931-5 (S 1936)

Tango, 1940 (M 1941)

Sonata, 2 pf, 1943–4 (Chap 1945)

REDUCTIONS OF OWN WORKS

Arrangements intended as independent works are listed above; the following reductions were made only for rehearsal or amateur use.

Vocal scores: Faun and Shepherdess, The King of the Stars, The Nightingale, Pribaoutki, Cat's Cradle Songs, Reynard, Pulcinella, Mavra, The Wedding, Oedipus rex, Babel, Cantata, Three Songs from William Shakespeare, In memoriam Dylan Thomas, Canticum sacrum

Pf solo: The Firebird, The Song of the Nightingale, The Soldier's Tale, Rag-time, Apollon musagète, The Fairy's Kiss, The Card Party, Preludium, Circus Polka

Pf 4 hands: Petrushka, The Rite of Spring, Concertino

2 pf: Concerto for pf and wind, Capriccio, Concerto 'Dumbarton Oaks', Septet, Agon, Movements

Vn, pf: Violin Concerto

ARRANGEMENTS

E. Grieg: Kobold, orch (for ballet Le festin), 1909, unpubd

F. Chopin: Nocturne, Ab; Valse brillante, Eb, orch, 1909 (for ballet)

Two Songs of the Flea (Goethe) [arrs. of Beethoven: op.75 no.3 and Musorgsky], B, orch, 1910 (Bes, B)

M. Musorgsky: Khovanshchina, 1913, collab. Ravel; unpubd except for vocal score of Stravinsky's final chorus, based on theme by Musorgsky (Bes 1914)

Song of the Volga Boatmen, orch, 1917 (C 1920)

M. Musorgsky: Boris Godunov: Prologue, pf, 1918, unpubd

R. de Lisle: La marseillaise, vn, 1919, unpubd

P. Tchaikovsky: The Sleeping Beauty: Variation d'Aurore; Entr'acte symphonique, orch, 1921, unpubd; Bluebird Pas-de-deux, small orch, 1941 (S 1953)

The Star-spangled Banner, orch, 1941 (M)

J. S. Bach: Choral-Variationen über das Weihnachtslied 'Vom Himmel hoch da komm' ich her', chorus, orch, 1955–6 (B 1956)

C. Gesualdo di Venosa: Tres sacrae cantiones, sextus and bassus parts supplied, 1957–9 (B 1957 [no.3], B 1960 [complete]): 1 Da pacem Domine, 1959, 2 Assumpta est Maria, 1959, 3 Illumina nos, 1957

Monumentum pro Gesualdo di Venosa ad CD annum [arrs. of madrigals Asciugate i begli occhi, Ma tu, cagion di quella and Belta poi che t'assenti], orch, 1960 (B 1960)

J. Sibelius: Canzonetta, op.62a, 2 cl, 4 hn, harp, db, 1963 (Br 1964)

H. Wolf: Two Sacred Songs [from the Spanisches Liederbuch], Mez, 9 insts, 1968 (B)

J. S. Bach: Two Preludes and Fugues [from the '48'], str, ww, c1969

WRITINGS

with W. Nouvel: Chroniques de ma vie (Paris, 1935–6, 2/1962; Eng. trans., 1936; Eng. trans. as An Autobiography, 1936/R1975; Sp. trans., 1936–7; Ger. trans., 1937; Russ. trans., 1964; Bulg. trans., 1966; Hung. trans., 1969)

Poétique musicale (Cambridge, Mass., 1942; Eng. trans., 1947; Ger. trans., 1949, 3/1966; It. trans., 1954; Dan. trans., 1961; Rom. trans., 1967; Eng.-Fr. edn., 1970)

Leben und Werk (Zurich and Mainz, 1957) [reprints of Ger. trans. of *Chroniques de ma vie* and *Poétique musicale* with 'Answers to 35 Questions', incl. one question omitted in *Conversations*]

with R. Craft: *Conversations with Igor Stravinsky* (London and New York, 1959; Russ. trans., 1971)

——: *Memories and Commentaries* (London and New York, 1960; Russ. trans., 1971)

——: *Stravinsky in Conversation with Robert Craft* (Harmondsworth, 1962; Ger. trans., 1961) [= *Conversations* and *Memories*]

——: *Expositions and Developments* (London and New York, 1962; Russ. trans., 1971)

——: *Dialogues and a Diary* (New York, 1963, enlarged London, 1968; Russ. trans., 1971)

——: *Themes and Episodes* (New York, 1966, 2/1967)

——: *Retrospectives and Conclusions* (New York, 1969)

——: *Themes and Conclusions* (London, 1972; Ger. trans., 1972) [*Themes and Episodes* and *Retrospectives and Conclusions*]

ed. L. Kutateladse: *Statī, pisma, vospominaniya* [Articles, letters, memoirs] (Leningrad, 1972)

ed. L. S. Dyachkova: *Statī i materiali* [Articles and materials] (Moscow, 1973) [incl. 60 letters]

BIBLIOGRAPHY

CATALOGUES

Stravinsky and the Dance: a Survey of Ballet Productions 1910–1962 (New York, 1962)

Stravinsky and the Theatre: a Catalogue of Decor and Costume Designs for Stage Productions of his Works (New York, 1963)

D. Hamilton: 'Igor Stravinsky: a Discography of the Composer's Performances', *Perspectives on Schoenberg and Stravinsky*, ed. B. Boretz and E. T. Cone (Princeton, NJ, 1968, 2/1972)

D.-R. de Lerma, ed.: *Igor Fedorovitch Stravinsky: a Practical Guide to Publications of his Music* (Kent, Ohio, 1974)

MONOGRAPHS

A. Casella: *Igor Strawinski* (Rome, 1926, enlarged, 2/1947, 3/1961)

Y. Vainkop: *Stravinsky* (Leningrad, 1927)

B. de Schloezer: *Igor Stravinsky* (Paris, 1929)

I. Glebov: *Kniga o Stravinskom* [Book on Stravinsky] (Leningrad, 1929)

P. Collaer: *Strawinsky* (Brussels, 1930)

E. W. White: *Stravinsky's Sacrifice to Apollo* (London, 1930)

D. de'Paoli: *L'opera di Strawinsky* (Milan, 1931)

H. Fleischer: *Strawinsky* (Berlin, 1931)

A. Schaeffner: *Strawinsky* (Paris, 1931)

D. de'Paoli: *Igor Strawinsky: da 'L'oiseau de feu' a 'Persefone'* (Turin, 1934)

G. F. Malipiero: *Strawinsky* (Venice, 1945)

E. W. White: *Stravinsky: a Critical Survey* (London, 1947; Ger. trans., 1950)

F. Onnen: *Stravinsky* (Stockholm and London, 1948)

T. Strawinsky: *Le message d'Igor Strawinsky* (Lausanne, 1948; Ger. trans., 1952; Eng. trans., 1953)

A. Tansman: *Igor Strawinsky* (Paris, 1948; Eng. trans., 1949; Sp. trans., 1949)

J. E. Cirlot: *Igor Strawinsky: su tiempo, su significación, su obra* (Barcelona, 1949)

R. H. Myers: *Introduction to the Music of Stravinsky* (London, 1950)

L. Oleggini: *Connaissance de Stravinsky* (Lausanne, 1952)

J. van Ackere: *Igor Strawinsky* (Antwerp, 1954)

H. Strobel: *Stravinsky: Classic Humanist* (New York, 1955; Ger. orig., 1956)

F. Sopeña: *Strawinsky: vida, obra y estilo* (Madrid, 1956)

H. H. Stuckenschmidt: *Strawinsky und sein Jahrhundert* (Berlin–Dahlem, 1957)

H. Kirchmeyer: *Igor Strawinsky: Zeitgeschichte im Persönlichkeitsbild* (Regensburg, 1958)

M. Monnikendam: *Strawinsky* (Haarlem, 1958)

R. Vlad: *Strawinsky* (Rome, 1958; Eng. trans., 1960, rev., enlarged 3/1979; Rom. trans., 1967)

R. Siohan: *Stravinsky* (Paris, 1959, 2/1971; Ger. trans., 1960; Eng. trans., 1966)

F. Herzfeld: *Igor Stravinsky* (Berlin, 1961)

L. Fábián: *Igor Sztravinszkij* (Budapest, 1963)

B. Yarutovsky: *Igor Stravinsky* (Moscow, 1963, 2/1969; Ger. trans., 1966)

N. Nabokov: *Igor Strawinsky* (Berlin, 1964)

G. Tintori: *Strawinsky* (Milan, 1964; Fr. trans., 1966)

G. Berger: *Igor Strawinsky* (Wolfenbüttel, 1965)

P. Faltin: *Igor Strawinsky* (Bratislava, 1965)

M. Philippot: *Igor Stravinsky* (Paris, 1965)

E. W. White: *Stravinsky: the Composer and his Works* (London, 1966, rev., enlarged 2/1979)

O. Nordvall: *Stravinsky: ett porträtt med citat* (Stockholm, 1967)

P. M. Young: *Stravinsky* (New York and London, 1969)

A. Dobrin: *Igor Stravinsky* (New York, 1970)

V. V. Smirnov: *Tvorcheskoye formirovaniye Igor Fyodorovich Stravinskovo* [Stravinsky's creative progress] (Leningrad, 1970)

M. Druskin: *Igor' Stravinsky: lichnost', tvorchestvo, vzglyadï* [Personality, works, views] (Leningrad, 1974, rev., enlarged 2/1979; Ger. trans., 1976)

F. Routh: *Stravinsky* (London, 1975/R1977)

V. Stravinsky and R. Craft: *Stravinsky in Pictures and Documents* (London and New York, 1978)

SPECIALIZED BOOKS AND COLLECTIONS OF ESSAYS

ReM, v/2 (1923) [special no.]

V. Belaiev: *Igor Stravinsky's 'Les noces': an Outline* (London, 1928)

C. F. Ramuz: *Souvenirs sur Igor Strawinsky* (Lausanne, 1929, 3/1952; Ger. trans., c1956)

Contemporaneos, v/15 (Mexico City, 1929) [special no.]

Cahiers de Belgique, iii/10 (1930) [special no.]

E. Evans: *Stravinsky: 'The Fire-bird' and 'Petrushka'* (London, 1933)

Neujahreblatt der Allgemeinen Musikgesellschaft in Zürich, no.121 (1933) [special no.]

M. Armitage, ed.: *Igor Stravinsky* (New York, 1936)

ReM, no.191 (1939) [special no.]

M. D. Fardel: *Strawinsky et les Ballets russes* (Nice, 1943)

Dance Index, vi/10–12 (1945) [special nos.]

Tempo, no.8 (1948) [special no.]

E. Corle, ed.: *Igor Stravinsky* (New York, 1949)

M. Lederman, ed.: *Stravinsky in the Theatre* (London and New York, 1949/R1975)

Musik der Zeit, ix (1952) [special no.]

R. Craft, A. Piovesan and R. Vlad: *Le musiche religiose di Igor Strawinsky* (Venice, 1956)

H. Lindlar: *Igor Strawinskys sakraler Gesang* (Regensburg, 1957)

The Score, no.20 (1957) [special no.]

P. Meylan: *Une amitié célèbre: C. F. Ramuz/Igor Stravinsky* (Lausanne, 1961)

M. Cosman and H. Keller: *Stravinsky at Rehearsal* (London, 1962; Ger. trans., 1962)

L. Erhardt: *Balety Igor Stravinskego* (Kraków, 1962)

Feuilles musicales, xv/2–3 (1962) [special no.]

MQ, xlviii/3 (1962) [special no.]; repr. as *Stravinsky: a New Appraisal of his Work*, ed. P. H. Lang (New York, 1963)

Tempo, no.61–2 (1962) [special no.]

I. Ya. Vershinina: *Ranniye baleti Stravinskovo* [Stravinsky's early ballets] (Moscow, 1967)

Tempo, no.81 (1967) [special no.]

B. Boretz and E. T. Cone, ed.: *Perspectives on Schoenberg and Stravinsky* (Princeton, NJ, 1968, 2/1972)

H. Ettl: *Petruschka* (Stuttgart, 1968)

D. Révész, ed.: *In memoriam Igor Stravinsky* (Budapest, ?1971)

Melos, xxxviii/9 (1971) [special no.]

PNM, ix/2–x/1 (1971) [special no.]

Tempo, no.97 (1971) [special no.]

Les cahiers canadiens de musique, no.4 (1972) [special no.]

R. Craft: *Stravinsky: Chronicle of a Friendship 1948–1971* (London and New York, 1972)

P. Horgan: *Encounters with Stravinsky: a Personal Record* (London and New York, 1972)

L. Libman: *And Music at the Close: Stravinsky's Last Years: a Personal Memoir* (New York, 1972)

G. Pestelli: *Il giovane Stravinsky (1906–13)* (Turin, 1973)

N. Goldner: *The Stravinsky Festival of the New York City Ballet* (New York, 1974)

H. Kirchmeyer: *Stravinskys russische Ballette* (Stuttgart, 1974)

OTHER LITERATURE

Most of the valuable literature on Stravinsky is contained in the books and symposia listed above. The following is a selection, from many hundreds of essays and articles, of the more important additional material. Fuller bibliographies may be found in many of the monographs and in K. Thompson: *A Dictionary of Twentieth-century Composers 1911–1971* (London, 1973).

J. Rivière: 'Le sacre du printemps', *Nouvelle revue française* (1 Nov 1913)

T. W. Adorno: *Philosophie der neuen Musik* (Tübingen, 1949, 3/1969; Fr. trans., 1962; Hung. trans., 1970; Eng. trans., 1973)

P. Boulez: 'Stravinsky demeure', *Musique russe*, i (Paris, 1953); repr. in *Relevés d'apprenti* (Paris, 1966) [analysis of *The Rite*]

H. Lindlar: 'Christ-kultische Elemente in Strawinskys Bauernhochzeit', *Melos*, xxv (1958), 63

D. C. Johns: 'An Early Serial Idea of Stravinsky', *MR*, xxiii (1962), 305

R. Stephan: 'Vom alten und vom neuen Petruschka: Igor Stravinsky 1910 und 1946', *NZM*, Jg.123 (1962), 5

T. W. Adorno: 'Stravinsky: ein dialektisches Bild', *Quasi una fantasia* (Frankfurt, 1963)

R. Birkan: 'O poeticheskom tekste "Svadebki" Stravinskovo', *Russkaya muzïka na rubezhe XX veka*, ed. M. K. Mikhailov and E. M. Orlova (Moscow, 1966)

V. N. Kholopova: 'O ritmicheskoy tekhnike i dinamiicheskikh svoystvakh ritma Stravinskovo', *Muzïka i sovremennost*, iv (1966)

G. Mokreyeva: 'Ob evolyutsii garmonii rannevo Stravinskovo' [On the evolution of harmony in early Stravinsky], *Teoricheskiye problemï muzïki XX veka*, i, ed. Yu. N. Tyulin (Moscow, 1967)

A. Shnitke: 'Osobennosti orkhestrovovo golosovedeniya rannikh proizvedeniy Stravinskovo' [Characteristics of the orchestral part-writing in Stravinsky's early works], *Muzïka i sovremennost*, v (1967), 209

V. Smirnov: 'O predposïlkakh evolyutsii Stravinskovo k neoklasitsismu' [On the grounds for Stravinsky's evolution towards neo-classicism], *Voprosi teorii i estetiki muzïki*, v (1967)

V. Smirnov: 'U istokov kompozitorskovo puti Igor Stravinskovo' [On the beginning of Stravinsky's path as a composer], *Voprosi teorii i estetiki muzïki*, viii (1968)

G. Grigor'yeva: 'Russkiy folklor v sochineniyakh Stravinskovo' [Russian folklore in Stravinsky's works], *Muzïka i sovremennost*, vi (1969)

T. Clifton: 'Types of Symmetrical Relations in Stravinsky's "A Sermon, a Narrative and a Prayer" ', *PNM*, ix/1 (1970), 96

R. Birkan: 'O tematizme "Svadebki" Stravinskovo', *Iz istorii muzïki XX veka*, ed. R. S. Druzkin (Moscow, 1971)

H. Pousseur: 'Stravinsky selon Webern selon Stravinsky', *Musique en jeu*, no.4 (1971), 21; no.5 (1971), 107; Eng. trans. in *PNM*, x/2 (1972), 13–51; xi/1 (1972), 112–45

D. Bancroft: 'Stravinsky and the "NRF" ', *ML*, liii (1972), 274; lv (1974), 261

J. Hunkemöller: 'Igor Strawinskys Jazz-Porträt', *AMw*, xxix (1972), 45

R. Maconie: 'Stravinsky's Final Cadence', *Tempo*, no.103 (1972), 18

L. Somfai: 'Symphonies of Wind Instruments (1920): Observations on Stravinsky's Organic Construction', *SM*, xiv (1972), 355

A. Forte: *The Structure of Atonal Music* (New Haven and London, 1973)

D. Gutknecht: 'Strawinskys zwei Fassungen des "Apollon Musagète"', *Musicae scientiae collectanea: Festschrift Karl Gustav Fellerer* (Cologne, 1973), 199

R. Middleton: 'Stravinsky's Development: a Jungian Approach', *ML*, liv (1973), 289

B. M. Williams: 'Time and the Structure of Stravinsky's Symphony in C', *MQ*, lix (1973), 355

D. Bancroft: 'Stravinsky and the "NRF" (1920–29)', *MR*, lv (1974), 261

V. Cholopova: 'Russische Quellen der Rhythmik Strawinskys', *Mf*, xxvii (1974), 435

R. Craft: 'Stravinsky's Svadebka', *Prejudices and Disguises* (New York, 1974)

L. Somfai: 'Sprache, Wort und Phonem im vokalen Spätwerk Stravinskys', *Veröffentlichungen der Institut für neue Musik und Musikerziehung Darmstadt*, xiv (1974)

R. Craft: ' "Le sacre du printemps": the Revisions', *Tempo* (1977), no.112, p.2

ERIC WALTER WHITE (life, bibliography),
JEREMY NOBLE (works)

Strayhorn, Billy [William] (*b* Dayton, Ohio, 29 Nov 1915; *d* New York, 31 May 1967). Black American jazz composer, arranger and pianist. He received an extensive musical training in his youth in Hillsboro, North Carolina, and in Pittsburgh. In December 1938 he submitted his composition *Lush Life* to Duke Ellington, who recorded Strayhorn's *Something to Live for* three months later. Strayhorn worked briefly as a pianist in Mercer Ellington's orchestra, and joined the Duke Ellington band in autumn 1939 as associate arranger and second pianist; he remained with Duke Ellington until his death. Their relationship was described by Ellington himself (*Music is my Mistress*, 1973, p.156): 'He was my listener, my most dependable appraiser, and as a critic he would be the most clinical, but his background – both classical and modern – was an accessory to his own good taste and understanding, so what came back to me was in perfect balance'. Strayhorn wrote or collaborated in more than 200 contributions to Ellington's repertory including the band's theme song *Take the A Train*, and many other tunes considered Ellington 'classics' such as *Chelsea Bridge*, *Passion Flower*, *Midriff*, *Johnny Come Lately*, *Raincheck* and *UMMG*.

JOSÉ HOSIASSON

Straziante (It.: 'heartrending'; present participle of *straziare*: 'to torture', 'lacerate'). Azucena has this direction at the words 'il figlio mio' in her Act 2 *racconto* in Verdi's *Il trovatore*.

Streatfeild, Richard Alexander (*b* Edenbridge, 22 June 1866; *d* London, 6 Feb 1919). English music critic and musicologist. Educated at Oundle and Pembroke College, Cambridge, he entered the Department of Printed Books in the British Museum in 1889, and served there until his death. Although he never worked in the Music Room, he was encouraged in his research by Barclay Squire. A gifted amateur tenor, he acted as music critic of the *Daily Graphic* from 1898 to 1902 and contributed regularly to English and foreign journals. Though he was keenly interested in the new music of his time, he was also an ardent Handelian, an enthusiasm partly inspired by his friendship with Samuel Butler, whose literary executor he was, editing the posthumous novel *The Way of all Flesh* (1903) and several of his other books. Streatfeild's book on Handel, though old-fashioned in some respects, is a balanced and penetrating study which is still valuable.

WRITINGS

Masters of Italian Music (London, 1895)

The Case of the Handel Festival (London, 1897)

The Opera (London, 1897, rev., enlarged 2/1902, rev. 5/1925 by E. J. Dent)

Modern Music and Musicians (London, 1906, 2/1907; Fr. trans., 1910)

Handel (London, 1909, rev. 2/1910/R1964)

Handel Autographs at the British Museum (London, 1912)

Musiciens anglais contemporains (Paris, 1913)

Handel, Canons and the Duke of Chandos (London, 1916)

ALEC HYATT KING

Street cries. Calls of vendors in streets and open markets, often involving short melodic motifs. The custom of hawking wares led at a very early date to stereotyped phrases, which became a distinctive part of each hawker's formula as a kind of musical trademark. Modern commercial communication has helped to make this colourful practice all but obsolete, but street cries may still occasionally be heard in large cities, for example in London (ex.1).

Ex.1

A - ny old i - ron?

Historically, the chief repository of street cries has been the QUODLIBET. From the Middle Ages to the 18th century veritable 'catalogues' of vendors' calls frequently appear among its borrowed materials, thus preserving a kind of music that would otherwise have passed into oblivion. The earliest known examples come from 13th-century motets intended for sophisticated private amusement. One such work in the Montpellier Codex. *On parole/A Paris/Frèse nouvele* (HAM, no.33*b*), underscores two poems in praise of Paris with an ostinato tenor consisting of a Parisian vendor's cry, 'Frèse nouvele! Muere france!' ('Fresh strawberries! Wild blackberries!'). The same cry also appears along with many others in a 14th-century motet, *Je commence ma chanson/Et je seray/Soules vieux (I–IV)*.

Street cries became especially popular in the art music and theatre of the 15th and 16th centuries. In the *Farce de bien mondaine* Virtue enters hawking a basket of honey cakes with a cry ('Obly, obly, obly') that also appears in the chanson *Vous qui parle/E Molinet (I-PAVu* Ald.362), and in the *Farce des cris de Paris* the Fool interrupts two gentlemen's conversation on love with the cry 'Eschaudez, tous chautz eschaudez' ('Cakes, really hot cakes'). Another well-known street cry, 'Beurre frais', became the basis for a basse danse (Attaingnant, 1530). Both Janequin (*Les cris de Paris*, 1550) and Jean Servin (*Fricassée des cris de Paris*, 1578) composed pieces made up entirely of street cries, the authenticity of which is proved by their appearance in other quodlibets (*see* FRICASSÉE). One of these cries, 'Rammonez vo cheminées, jeunes femmes, rammonez' ('Sweep your chimneys, young ladies') appears with obscene connotations in the *Farce du rammoneur de cheminées*.

Street cries in Italian music, like the Italian quodlibet in general (*see* INCATENATURA), still need detailed research. A caccia by Nicola Zacharia, *Cacciando per gustar*, quotes a virtuoso series of market cries advertising oil, mustard, vinegar, etc, and such cries were also quoted occasionally in 15th-century *canti carnascialeschi*, as in Lorenzo de' Medici's *Canto di uomini che vendono bericuocoli e confortini*. Isaac's music for this 'Song of the Sweetmeat Sellers' is lost, but a fragment survives in *Donna tu pure invecchi*, an *incatenatura* which has a section composed of market cries.

The German quodlibet of the 16th and early 17th centuries made considerable use of street cries. Matthias le Maistre's *Venite ir lieben Gesellin* (1566) includes 'Brüe heiss, kauff', and Nicolas Zangius's *Ich will zu land ausreiten* (1597) quotes a fishmonger's cry. Two early 17th-century quodlibets by Melchior Franck, *Nun fanget an* and *Kessel, Multer binden*, quote cries such as 'Kauft gute Milch, ihr Weiben', 'Schöne Schmalz, gute Buttermilch' and 'Kauft gute Schleppehäs', and similar calls appear in quodlibets by Paul Rivander (1615), Andreas Rauch (1627) and Jakob Banwart (1652). German quodlibets also include a number of works devoted entirely to market scenes. Franziscus de Rivulo, for example, musically depicted the Danzig market (1558), Zangius the Cologne market (*Ich ging einmal spazieren*, 1603), and Daniel Friderici the market at Rostock (1622). J. E. Kindermann's *Nürnbergische Quodlibet* appeared in 1655, J. C. Horn's description of the Leipzig market in 1680 and G. J. Werner's *Der wiennerische Tandlmarkt* in 1750.

Thomas Ravenscroft included many street cries arranged as rounds in his *Pammelia* (1609) and *Melismata* (1611), but the most famous English quodlibets are undoubtedly three fantasias for voices and instruments by Thomas Weelkes, Orlando Gibbons and Richard Dering (*c*1600) that incorporate no less than 150 London street cries (Dering also composed a *Country Cries* in the same vein). The cries of the London hawkers were the subject of several sets of engravings, notably those issued by Pierce Tempest in 1711 (see illustration) and the well-known set by Francis Wheatley at the end of the 18th century. Some cries were also used by Handel in his opera *Serse* (Act 2 scene i) which may be authentic, at least in part.

BIBLIOGRAPHY

J. F. Bridge: *Old Cryes of London* (London, 1921)

P. A. Scholes: 'Street Music', *The Oxford Companion to Music* (London, 1938, rev. 10/1970 by J. O. Ward)

For further bibliography *see* QUODLIBET.

MARIA RIKA MANIATES

Street organ. *See* BARREL ORGAN.

Strehler, Giorgio (*b* Barcola, Trieste, 14 Aug 1921).

A vendor of knives, combs and inkhorns: engraving by Pierce Tempest after Marcellus Laroon from 'The Cryes of the City of London' (1711)

Italian producer. He was born into a musical family and studied in Milan at the Accademia dei Filodrammatici. He began his career as an actor in 1940 and made his début as a producer the following year. In 1947 he co-founded the Piccolo Teatro in Milan, and that same year saw his first opera production, *La traviata*, at La Scala. At the Piccolo Teatro his company soon became Italy's foremost art theatre, providing him with a workshop for his farsighted ideas, many of which he has carried into the opera house. Brecht praised him as an interpreter of his plays, and Strehler remains famous for his productions of Brecht, Shakespeare and Goldoni. Brecht's influence is evident in his work, both in its often epic scale and its political commitment.

Strehler has produced for the Paris Opéra and the Salzburg Festival, but most of his work in opera has been at La Scala and the Piccolo Scala, the experimental opera studio which he was instrumental in founding in 1955. His La Scala production of Verdi's *Simon Boccanegra* (seen in London in 1976) displayed his social and political sensibilities, stressing class struggle and political intrigue; this interpretation gives the piece great power and topicality and, by eliminating lengthy scene changes and reducing the intervals to one, Strehler increased the pace and tension of the work. His *Die Entführung aus dem Serail*, seen at La Scala and Salzburg (1965), was noted for the influence of the *commedia dell'arte* on the rhythm and movement and for the original use of silhouette. More controversial was his 1974 *Die Zauberflöte* at Salzburg with settings by Luciano Damiani, a neo-classical and not at all fanciful production, set in a barren space; the visual emphasis was on illusion, with settings appearing and disappearing as if by magic, and supporting Strehler's interpretation: that only wisdom is not an illusion. His productions of Brecht and Weill's *Die Dreigroschenoper* both at the Piccolo Teatro, 1956 and 1973, remain among the finest: Strehler was the first to react against the spirit of divertissement in the piece and to stress its sordid social aspects rather than produce it as an aggressively inoffensive, colourful picture of the proletarian underworld.

BIBLIOGRAPHY

Piccolo Teatro, 1947–58 (Milan, 1958)

E. Gaipa: *Giorgio Strehler* (Bologna, 1959)

G. Guazzotti: *L'Opera da tre soldi di Bertolt Brecht e Kurt Weill* (Bologna, 1961) [analysis of Strehler's production]

E. Fechner: *Giorgio Strehler inszeniert* (Velbert, 1963)

E. Gaipa: *Giorgio Strehler* (Berlin, 1963)

Piccolo Teatro di Milano, 1947–1967 (Milan, 1967)

PAUL SHEREN

Streich (Ger.: 'stroke', 'blow'). In compound words, *Streich*- may mean 'string-' as in Streichquartett or Streichensemble. *Streicher* may mean 'the [musical] strings', but the usual term for the string of an instrument is *Saite*.

Streich normally means 'bow' only in such contexts as 'stroked with a bow' (the usual term for 'bow' being *Bogen*): thus, 'die Geige mit dem Bogen streichen' ('to stroke the violin with the bow'). The word for 'types of bowing' (or 'bowstrokes') is *Stricharten*. One may say also: 'das Streichen über dem Griffbrett' ('bowing over the fingerboard').

DAVID D. BOYDEN

Streich, Rita (*b* Barnaul, 18 Dec 1920). German soprano of Soviet and German parentage. She studied with Willi Domgraf-Fassbänder, Maria Ivogün and Erna Berger, and made her début at Aussig in 1943 as Zerbinetta. From 1946 to 1951 she sang at the Berlin Staatsoper, making a name for herself in such roles as Zerlina, Blonde, Gilda, Sophie and Olympia. In 1951 she joined the Berlin Städtische Oper, extending her repertory to include Zerbinetta, the Queen of Night and Constanze. She joined the Vienna Staatsoper in 1953 and made her London début with that company at the Festival Hall in 1954 as Zerlina and Susanna. She made her American début in San Francisco in 1957 as Sophie, and was Zerbinetta in the first performance there of *Ariadne auf Naxos*. Her Glyndebourne début was in the latter role in 1958; she also appeared at Salzburg, Aix-en-Provence and Bayreuth, where she sang the Woodbird in 1952. She was at her best in medium-sized auditoria, for her exquisite art and voice were lost in larger theatres. In the 1960s and 1970s she won renown as a recitalist, and in 1974 she was appointed a professor of singing at Essen.

HAROLD ROSENTHAL

Streichbogen (Ger.). BOW.

Streicher. Austrian firm of piano makers. It was founded in 1802 when the daughter of JOHANN ANDREAS STEIN, Nannette (Maria Anna) Stein Streicher (*b* Augsburg, 2 Jan 1769; *d* Vienna, 16 Jan 1833), began building pianos independently from her brother Matthäus Andreas Stein. Stein's children had carried on their father's firm after his death and moved the firm from Augsburg to Vienna after Nannette's marriage to the pianist, composer and teacher Johann Andreas Streicher

(*b* Stuttgart, 13 Dec 1761; *d* Vienna, 25 May 1833) in 1794. Nannette, also a fine pianist, had learnt piano making from her father, and her business – 'Nannette Streicher née Stein' – flourished; her husband, a professor of music at Vienna, gave up his job to join her. Weber (1813) was far more impressed by the pianos of Streicher and Brodmann than by those of Schanz, Walter, Wachtl and others, and Streicher became the most eminent firm in Vienna. Beethoven was friendly with the couple and apparently advised on some aspects of manufacture. Surviving grands are beautifully veneered and usually have four pedals: una corda, bassoon (a yellow silk-padded rail pressed against the strings), pianissimo (a felt inserted between the hammers and strings) and a damper pedal. In 1823 the firm became 'Nannette Streicher geb. Stein und Sohn' when Johann Baptist Streicher (*b* Vienna, 3 Jan 1796; *d* Vienna, 28 March 1871) became a partner. The Viennese action was perfected by the firm, although it built Anglo-German and English actions in increasing numbers as the popularity of the Viennese action waned after the mid-century. In 1825 the firm made a successful down-striking piano action for Hummel, in which the hammer is returned by a spring. J. B. Streicher assumed complete control of the firm after his parents' death, and his son Emil Streicher (1836–1916) became a partner in 1857 and managed the business for a while after his father's death. When he retired the firm ceased. The composer THEODOR STREICHER (1874–1940) was a great-grandson of Johann Andreas Streicher.

See also PIANOFORTE, §I, 5.

BIBLIOGRAPHY

R. E. M. Harding: *The Piano-forte: its History Traced to the Great Exhibition of 1851* (Cambridge, 1933, rev. 2/1978)

F. J. Hirt: *Meisterwerke des Klavierbaues* (Olten, 1955; Eng. trans., 1968)

Katalog der Sammlung alter Musikinstrumente, i: *Saitenklaviere* (Vienna, 1966)

Katalog zu den Sammlungen des Händel-Hauses in Halle, v: *Tasteninstrumente* (Halle, 1966)

MARGARET CRANMER

Streicher, Theodor (*b* Vienna, 7 June 1874; *d* Wetzelsdorf, nr. Graz, 28 May 1940). Austrian composer, son of Emil STREICHER. He studied from 1895 to 1900 with Ferdinand Gregori for elocution, Heinrich Schulz-Beuthen for counterpoint and composition, Ferdinand Jäger for singing and Löwe for the piano and instrumentation. His first published works attracted little attention, but his *30 Lieder aus Des Knaben Wunderhorn* (1903) created a sensation in the German-speaking world: Streicher was acclaimed the successor to Wolf and the saviour of German song. However, he remained in the forefront of Austrian composers for only a few years, and after about 1920 his music was seldom performed. His second wife was Edith Thorndike, some of whose poems he set.

WORKS
(*selective list*)

Choral: Mignons Exequien (Goethe), chorus, children's chorus, orch (1907); Wandrers Nachtlied (Goethe), male chorus (1908); Szenen und Bilder aus Goethes Faust (1911)

Songs: 30 Lieder aus Des Knaben Wunderhorn (1903); 20 Lieder, 4 Sprüche und Gedichte von Richard Dehmel (1903), pubd together as 24 Lieder (1909); 6 Lieder aus Des Knaben Wunderhorn (1904); 4 Kriegs- und Soldatenlieder (1904); Hafis-Lieder (trans. G. F. Daumer), i–vi (1907–8); Lieder nach Gedichten von Edith Thorndike (1916–19); 12 Lieder (Michelangelo), i–iii (1922); Schaukal-Lieder, i–iii (1929–31); c100 others unpubd

Chamber: Str Sextet (1912)

Principal publisher: Breitkopf & Härtel

BIBLIOGRAPHY

P. Klanert: *Theodor Streicher in seinen Liedern* (Leipzig, 1911)

E. Newman: 'Theodor Streicher', *MT*, liii (1912), 303

T. Bolte: *Die Musikerfamilien Stein und Streicher* (Vienna, 1917)

V. Junk: 'Theodor Streicher', *ZfM*, Jg.104 (1937), 491

R. B. Wursten: 'The Vocal Music of Theodor Streicher', *NATS Bulletin*, xxxiii/2 (1976); xxxiii/3 (1977)

——: *Theodor Streicher: his Life and Music* (diss., U. of Wisconsin, 1977)

RICHARD B. WURSTEN

Streichharmonium (Ger.). *See* SOSTENENTE PIANO, §1.

Streichquartett (Ger.). STRING QUARTET.

Streit (Ger.: 'contest'). A term used in Konrad von Würzburg's second *Leich* to describe its form; *see* LAI, §1(i).

Strene. A square black note with a descending (occasionally ascending) tail on either side. The name and description occur in the 14th-century *Chorister's Lament* (see F. Utley in *Speculum*, xvi, 1946, p.194) and in the preface to Merbecke's *The Booke of Common Praier Noted* (London, 1550). A strene has twice the value of a black breve (i.e. the same note shape without tails). Polyphony notated in only black breves and strenes is found in late 15th- and early 16th-century English sources (e.g. *GB-Lbm* 5665, 17001, 17802–5, Roy.App.58).

BIBLIOGRAPHY

M. Bent: 'New and Little-known Fragments of English Medieval Polyphony', *JAMS*, xxi (1968), 149 [with edn. of 1 piece]

Strenger Satz (Ger.). STRICT COUNTERPOINT.

Strengthfeild, Thomas (*fl* 1657). English composer. Virtually nothing is known about Strengthfeild, whose only surviving music is a group of harpsichord suites dated 27 February 1656/7 found in the Elizabeth Rogers Virginal Book (*GB-Lbm* Add.10337). This probably indicates that he was a harpsichord teacher during the Commonwealth, and that Elizabeth Rogers may have been one of his pupils. The style of his short dance movements, one of which has varied repeats, is typical of much of the keyboard music written in England at the time.

B. A. R. COOPER

Strepitoso (It.: 'noisy', 'loud'). A direction to perform forcefully, found particularly as a qualification to a tempo mark, and somehow including the idea of 'tumbling down'. Liszt's *Tasso* opens *allegro strepitoso*; Elgar often used it as an expression mark; and the word appears on bravura passages in the virtuoso piano repertory as well as on joyful or confused headlong orchestral tutti passages in the later 19th century. It also appears earlier: the overture to Lemoyne's opera *Les prétendus* (1789) is marked *allegro con molto strepito*.

See also TEMPO AND EXPRESSION MARKS.

DAVID FALLOWS

Strepponi, Giuseppina [Clelia Maria Josepha] (*b* Lodi, 8 Sept 1815; *d* Sant'Agata, nr. Busseto, 14 Nov 1897). Italian soprano, second wife of Verdi. She was the eldest daughter of Feliciano Strepponi (1797–1832), organist of Monza Cathedral and composer of several operas, of which *Ullà di Bassora* enjoyed some success at La Scala in 1831. She was admitted to the Milan Conservatory as a paying pupil at 15 (a year over the age limit). There she studied the piano and singing to such good effect

Giuseppina Strepponi holding a score of Verdi's 'Nabucco': anonymous portrait (c1850) in the Museo Teatrale alla Scala, Milan

that on her father's death she was awarded a scholarship to complete her training. In 1834 she left the conservatory, having won the first prize for bel canto. Her stage début may have been at Adria in December 1834; her first triumph was in Rossini's *Matilda di Shabran* in Trieste in the spring of 1835. In the same year she appeared in Vienna as Adalgisa in *Norma* and as the heroine of *La sonnambula*, which became one of her most famous roles. With the impresario Alessandro Lanari as manager, she often appeared with the tenor Napoleone Moriani and the baritone Giorgio Ronconi. She was now the breadwinner of her family: hence her unremitting activity, which, combined with a liaison with Moriani, by whom she had at least two illegitimate children, considerably shortened her career. During the late 1830s, however, she aroused fanatical enthusiasm. Donizetti wrote his *Adelia* (Rome, 1841) for her, and only the fact that the impresario had sold more seats than the theatre held prevented the première from being a success.

Strepponi made her début at La Scala in 1839. Verdi's first opera, *Oberto* (1839), was accepted for production there largely because she and Ronconi recommended it; their approval of *Nabucco* in December 1841 (when she first met Verdi) was also decisive for its production. She created the role of Abigaille but by this time her powers were in decline. Apart from a disastrous season in Palermo in 1845, she thereafter appeared only sporadically (mostly in operas by Verdi) until her retirement in February 1846. In October 1846, armed with a letter of introduction from Verdi to the Escudier brothers, his French publishers, she arrived in Paris; she gave some concerts under their auspices and set up as a singing teacher. In July 1847 Verdi joined her on his return from London; from then on her history is that of his life-partner, though they were not legally married until 1859.

As a singer Strepponi was described as having a 'limpid, penetrating, smooth voice, seemly action, a lovely figure; and to Nature's liberal endowments she adds an excellent technique'. She was also praised for her 'deep inner feeling'. She interpreted Donizetti's Lucia, Bianca in Mercadante's *Il giuramento* and most of Bellini's heroines especially well. She was equally at home in comedy – as Adina in *L'elisir d'amore* and Sandrina in Luigi Ricci's *Un'avventura di Scaramuccia*. Yet the most famous of all the roles she created, Verdi's Abigaille, was probably the one least suited to her vocal means. Although she was highly talented, she never sang outside Italy after 1835. As Verdi's second wife she retained little of the prima donna beyond the traditional passion for domestic animals. Her copious correspondence (much of it on behalf of Verdi) reveals an endearing personality; intelligent and cultivated, she was a good linguist, was gifted with tact and a sense of humour and remained unfailingly generous in heart and mind.

BIBLIOGRAPHY

E. de Amicis: 'Giuseppina Verdi-Strepponi', *Nuovi ritratti letterari ed artistici* (Milan, 1902); repr. in *Verdi: bollettino quadrimestrale dell'Istituto di studi verdiani*, i/2 (1960), 779
A. Luzio: 'La "Traviata" e il dramma intimo di Verdi', *Nuova antologia* (1937), no.390, p.270; repr. in *Carteggi verdiani*, iv (Rome, 1947), 250
M. Mundula: *La moglie di Verdi: Giuseppina Strepponi* (Milan, 1938)
E. Gara: 'La misteriosa giovinezza di Giuseppina Strepponi', *Corriere della sera* (27 Jan 1951)
F. Walker: *The Man Verdi* (London, 1962)
'Ebbe una figlia a Trieste la moglie di Giuseppe Verdi', *Corriere della sera* (6 March 1965)
M. Medici: '"Quel prete" che sposò Verdi', *Verdi: bollettino dell' Istituto di studi verdiani*, i/2 (1970), 657
C. Sartori: 'La Strepponi e Verdi a Parigi nella morsa quarantottesca', *NRMI*, viii (1974), 239

JULIAN BUDDEN

Stretta. *See* STRETTO (2).

Stretto (It.: 'narrow', 'tight'; past participle of *stringere*). (1) In FUGUE, the introduction of two or more subject entries in close canon. To qualify as stretto the entries must be noticeably closer than in the exposition (ex.1). The German word *Engführung* is the

Ex.1 Bach: '48', i, 1

(a) fugal exposition

(b) stretto

equivalent for this meaning. Stretto was used at a very early stage in the history of fugue, and is common particularly in the RICERCARE and FANTASIA of the early 17th century. The effect of intensification it produced was first recognized by G. M. Bononcini (i) (*Il musico prattico*, 1673) and Angelo Berardi (*Documenti armonici*, 1681). Stretto became a requisite in academic fugue, where, in theory, the strettos were supposed to become gradually closer in time so as to produce a climax, an effect found only sporadically in practice. A 'stretto maestrale' involves all the voices in a fugue (Bach, *Das wohltemperirte Clavier*, i, no.22, bars 67–71). 'False stretto' occurs when the voices concerned all begin the subject, but at least one does not complete it – a matter usually of little concern to the listener, who, after hearing the opening, tends to supply the rest of the subject mentally (*Das wohltemperirte Clavier*, ii, no.5, bars 27–9; alto incomplete). A 'stretto exposition' is one in which the entries are already very close (Bach Cantata no.29, first chorus, adapted as 'Gratias agimus' and 'Dona nobis pacem' in the Mass in B minor).

(2) The term is sometimes used, alternatively with *stretta*, to indicate a faster tempo at the climactic concluding section of a piece; such sections are often headed 'stretto' or 'stretta'. Frescobaldi used the term 'stretto' in the preface to his 1615 volume of toccatas and partitas, and in the same year G. M. Trabaci marked a piece in his *Secondo libro de ricercate* 'verso secundo in battuta stretta'. Brossard (*Dictionaire de musique*, 1703) wrote: '*Stretto* means *serré*, tight, and is very often placed to indicate that one should make the beats tight or short and consequently very fast. So it is the opposite of or contrary to *largo*'. He also implied (article 'Tripla') that *stretto* was equivalent to *presto*. The use of *stretto* (in this context the form *stretta* is usually preferred) is common in Italian opera: examples are the closing section of the Act 2 finale to Mozart's *Le nozze di Figaro* and Violetta's Act 1 aria in Verdi's *La traviata*. The faster closing section of the finale of Beethoven's Fifth Symphony has been referred to as a *stretto*. Sometimes *stretto* seems, by an extension of meaning, simply to indicate a climactic effect, as in the finale of Bartók's Fifth String Quartet, where the tempo of the *stretto* at bar 781, minim = 150, is actually slower than that of the preceding section, minim = 168. *See also* STRINGENDO.

ROGER BULLIVANT

Stretton, Thomas (*fl* 1530–?1552). English musician. He instructed the children who took part in the Drapers' midsummer pageants of 1541, and may be the 'Streton' who was a clerk at All Hallows, Lombard Street, London, in 1552. A quodlibet by him, *Behold and see how byrds dothe fly*, has been added in MS in the British Museum copy of the bassus partbook of *XX Songes*, 1530.

BIBLIOGRAPHY

H. Baillie: 'Some Biographical Notes on English Church Musicians, chiefly working in London (1485–1560)', *RMARC*, ii (1962), 53

DAVID GREER

Stricciate (It., ? from *strecciate*: 'divide', 'untwist'). Used in Vivaldi's music in connection with unslurred repeated demisemiquavers in *allegro* (see *Le opere di Antonio Vivaldi*, ix, Rome, 1951), where Vivaldi wanted 'divided' notes, rapidly played in a measured tremolo, probably with the bow on the string.

Striccius, Wolfgang (*b* Wunstorf, nr. Hanover, *c*1555–60; *d* ?Pattensen, nr. Hanover, *c*1615). German composer, schoolmaster and public official. The first mention of him in an official position is as Kantor at the district school at Laibach (now Ljubljana) in 1591 or 1592. He had earlier worked as a private tutor to various Austrian professional families, for example at Krems and Emmersdorf. In 1593 at least, he revisited his native Lower Saxony: he had one of his works printed at Uelzen in that year and in the dedication to it, signed from there, he described himself as a notary. He finally returned to Lower Saxony probably in 1596, as a consequence of the Counter-Reformation, which was then becoming more firmly established in Slovenia. He became town clerk and notary at Pattensen and seems also to have worked as a schoolmaster. He had evidently had a good education and must at least have attended a grammar school, for only this could explain his versatility in working as Kantor, schoolmaster, tutor, notary and composer. He may have been a pupil of Andreas Crappius at Hanover, since he dedicated his publication of 1593 to, among others, Crappius and the other teachers at the grammar school at Hanover. Like many lesser composers about 1600 he seems to have confined himself almost entirely to the composition of polyphonic songs for small forces. He published three collections: *Neue teutsche Lieder mit 4 Stimmen, mehrer thails ad pares voces* (Nuremberg, 1588); *Das erste Theil newer teutscher Gesenge zu 5 und 4 Stimmen* (Uelzen, 1593); and *Neue teutsche Gesenge zu 3 Stimmen* (Helmstedt, 1600; lost). The designation 'ad pares' in the title of the 1588 book indicates that he wrote some at least of his music for educational purposes. He also produced sociable and humorous songs (some excerpts given as examples in Moser). There is a six-part motet by him in manuscript (in *A-Wgm*).

BIBLIOGRAPHY

H. J. Moser: *Die Musik im frühevangelischen Österreich* (Kassel, 1954)
D. Cvetko: *Zgodovina glasbene umetnosti na Slovenskem* [The history of music in Slovenia] (Ljubljana, 1958), 122f, 129
A. Rijavec: *Glasbeno delo v obdobju protestantizma na Slovenskem* [Music in Protestant times in Slovenia] (diss., U. of Ljubljana, 1964)
WALTER BLANKENBURG

Strich (Ger.: 'stroke', 'line'). In bowing, *Aufstrich* is upbow, *Niederstrich* downbow. But a *Taktstrich* is a bar-line. The *Mensurstrich*, a line drawn between and not through the staves, has been used in many modern editions of medieval and Renaissance music, beginning with those made by Heinrich Besseler in the 1920s; it was invented to minimize interruptions to the rhythmic flow and to avoid ties for syncopated notes. Medieval MSS written in modal notation sometimes include vertical strokes to call the singer's attention to a change of syllable in the text; these are called *Silbenstriche*. (See F. Ludwig: *Repertorium organorum recentioris et motetorum vetustissimi stili*, i (Halle, 1910), p.49.)

HOWARD MAYER BROWN

Stricker, Augustin Reinhard (*d* after 1720). German composer. He joined the royal orchestra in Berlin as a tenor and violinist in 1702. From 1712 to 1717 he was Kapellmeister at Cöthen, where he was J. S. Bach's predecessor. In autumn 1717 he went to Neuburg an der Donau in the service of the Elector Palatine Carl Philipp. He probably died before 1723. Stricker wrote two German operas for the Berlin court, *Sieg der Schönheit über die Helden* (with Volumier and Finger; December 1706) and *Alexanders und Roxanens Heirat* (28 November 1708). For the Neuburg court he set parts of two Italian operas, *Crudeltà consuma amore* (overture by Finger, Acts 1 and 3 by Greber, Act 2 by Stricker; 1717) and *L'amicizia in terzo, overo Il Dionigio* (overture and ballet music by Finger, Act 1 by an amateur, 'Cavaliere Messa', Act 2 by Stricker, Act 3 by J. D. Heinichen; 1718). None of his operatic music survives. Stricker published six Italian solo cantatas at Cöthen in 1715 (op.1); two flute sonatas and a flute trio are extant in MS in Rostock and Dresden. One oratorio is lost. He was a dedicatee of Mattheson's *Das beschützte Orchestre* (1717).

ALFRED LOEWENBERG/ELISABETH NOACK

Strict counterpoint (Fr. *contrepoint sévère*; Ger. *strenger Satz*; It. *contrappunto rigoroso*). Contrasted with free counterpoint, a discipline that demands the rigorous application of the principles of consonance and dissonance, as well as of part-writing in general, in the fitting of a polyphonic part or parts to a given melodic line. The given line is called a cantus firmus, and the parts fitted to it are usually referred to as the 'solution'. Among the various branches of this discipline, INVERTIBLE COUNTERPOINT (which involves the interchange of melodic and bass functions between parts) and SPECIES COUNTERPOINT (which teaches the art of counterpoint as a progression from making simple note-against-note settings to composing florid melodic lines to the cantus firmus) have been particularly important in the study of composition.
See COUNTERPOINT.

Stride. A solo jazz piano style that arose after 1910, and especially in the 1920s, in Harlem, New York, and hence sometimes takes the name 'Harlem school' (*see* JAZZ, §5). It is largely derived from ragtime, adapting ragtime's left-hand patterns to form the distinctive 'stride bass' (ex.1). Such patterns were often varied,

Ex.1

however, and in the best performances led to spontaneous and inventive cross-rhythms, polymetres and surprising harmonic effects. The bass represents only one of the increased virtuoso demands of the stride style, which in general called for fast tempos, full use of the piano's range and a wide array of pianistic devices, some from the classical repertory in which many of the Harlem pianists (notably James P. Johnson and Fats Waller) were trained. The style was practised most widely at social gatherings, particularly at Harlem's informal 'rent parties'. Johnson, Waller and Willie 'The Lion' Smith were much recorded, though other leading stride pianists like Luckey Roberts are less well represented on disc, and the apparently influential Abba Labba (Richard McLean) made no recordings. The style exercised great influence on subsequent jazz pianism, Duke Ellington, Art Tatum and Thelonious Monk freely expressing their debt to it.

BIBLIOGRAPHY

R. Blesh and H. Janis: *They All Played Ragtime* (New York, 1950, 4/1971)
G. Schuller: 'Harlem Pianists', *Early Jazz* (New York, 1968)
BRADFORD ROBINSON

Striegler, Kurt (*b* Dresden, 7 Jan 1886; *d* Wildthurn, nr. Landau, 4 Aug 1958). German conductor and composer. He attended the Kapellknabeninstitut of the Catholic Hofkirche (1896–1900) and the Dresden Conservatory (1900–05), where he studied composition with Draeseke, conducting with Kutzschbach and the organ with Fährmann. In 1905 he was engaged as répétiteur at the Dresden Staatsoper, with which he remained associated for 50 years, from 1913 as conductor, and later as state Kapellmeister for Saxony. He also taught at the Dresden Conservatory (1905–45), where he was artistic director between 1933 and 1936. In 1950 he moved to Munich, but he continued to conduct at the Dresden Staatsoper and for Bavarian radio. His music is rooted in the Romantic tradition; many of his pieces have a religious basis, and the Requiem is his greatest achievement.

WORKS
(selective list)

Choral: Requiem, 4 solo vv, chorus, orch, 1956; Kleine Passion, Bar, chorus, 1958; many other works

Orch: Vn Conc., 1905; Rondo concertante, db, orch, 1958; many other works

BIBLIOGRAPHY

H. Böhm: 'Kurt Striegler 70 Jahre', *Musica*, xi (1956), 160
——: 'In memoriam Kurt Striegler', *Musica*, xiii (1958), 624

Striggio [Strigi, Strigia], **Alessandro (i)** (*b* Mantua, *c*1540; *d* Mantua, 29 Feb 1592). Italian composer and instrumentalist. He was one of the leading composers of madrigals and stage music in the second half of the 16th century.

1. LIFE. The title-pages of his publications refer to him as 'gentilhuomo mantovano', and he evidently enjoyed a social position of some importance since, in 1567, Cosimo I de' Medici, Duke of Florence, sent him as a political emissary to the English court for 15 days. Later he was created a marquis and was described at his death as 'gran cancelliere' ('head chancellor') of the Gonzaga court at Mantua. He married Virginia Vagnoli of Siena, who was admired by contemporaries as a singer and lutenist; they had several children including Alessandro Striggio (ii). The setting of *Amor l'arco* ascribed to 'Sandrino' (an italianized form of Sandrin) in the 1557 edition of Rore's *Il quarto libro de madrigali a cinque voci* is probably by Striggio; if so, it was his earliest published work.

In the 1560s Striggio established himself as the principal composer at the Medici court in Florence, effectively ousting Francesco Corteccia as the musician primarily responsible for impressive state occasions, an integral part of court life during Cosimo's later years. The celebrations for the marriage on 25 December 1565 of Joanna of Austria and Cosimo's heir Francesco de' Medici included a performance of d'Ambra's comedy *La cofanaria* with *intermedi* by G. B. Cini; Striggio composed the music for the first, second and fifth *intermedi*, the other three being set by Corteccia. When the first child of this marriage was baptized in S Giovanni in 1568, Striggio provided music for the subsequent celebration; he collaborated with Corteccia and Stefano Rossetto on the *Mascherata di cacciatori*, and composed all six *intermedi* for the performance of L. del Mazzo's comedy *I Fabii*. When the Archduke Karl of Austria visited Florence in 1569, Striggio composed music for the traditional *Mascherata delle bufole* given on 5 May, and for the five *intermedi* presented with G.

B. Cini's *La vedova*. Meanwhile, his reputation had evidently travelled beyond the Alps, since his 40-part motet *Ecce beatam lucem* was sung at, and presumably commissioned for, the marriage of Duke Albrecht IV of Bavaria in 1568.

Little is known of Striggio's activities during the 1570s; the cultivation of music at the Medici court declined during Cosimo's last years and under the new Grand Duke Francesco until his marriage to Bianca Cappello in 1579. Letters from the Bavarian court suggest that Striggio's contacts with Munich became closer. It was probably during this period that he became acquainted with Vincenzo Galilei who settled at Florence in 1572; the only source for Striggio's *Fuggi speme mia*, performed during one of the *intermedi* for *La cofanaria* in 1565, is the second edition of Galilei's treatise *Il Fronimo* (1584). For the Grand Duke's wedding in 1579 Striggio composed music for the elaborate entertainment presented in the courtyard of the Palazzo Pitti, and for the anthology *Trionfo di musica di diversi* (*RISM* 1579³), edited by Massaino and produced in honour of the bride. In the same year he is recorded as *cavaliere*, together with Giulio Caccini and Antonio Pace (i) who were also employed at the Medici court.

In July 1584 Striggio was invited by Alfonso II d'Este to stay at Ferrara for 15 days. According to one of Striggio's letters, the purpose of the visit was to hear the duke's *concerto di donne* (the famous 'Ladies of Ferrara'), but it is also clear from his correspondence with the Grand Duke Francesco de' Medici at Florence that the latter had commissioned Striggio to set some madrigals in the Ferrarese style – a piece of artistic piracy presumably unknown to Alfonso. None of the works mentioned in the correspondence survives. Striggio was certainly a frequent visitor to the Este court; both Giustiniani and Tasso mentioned him in connection with Ferrara. Some time in 1584 he returned to Mantua where he remained until his death, and about 1586 he was, according to Canal, employed at the Gonzaga court there as a supernumerary musician without salary. He did not, however, sever his ties with the Medici, and in 1586 he composed the first, second and fifth *intermedi* of the six performed with Count Bardi di Vernio's comedy *L'amico fido* during the celebrations for the marriage of Cesare d'Este and Virginia de' Medici in Florence. This seems to have been his last work for a state occasion; he composed no music for the marriage of Christine of Lorraine and Grand Duke Ferdinand I in 1589, although he took part in the celebrations as a performer, as did 'Striggino', probably his son. After Striggio's death three books of his madrigals were collected and published by Alessandro Striggio (ii), though some had already appeared in anthologies.

Striggio's contemporary reputation as a performer seems to have been considerable. Bartoli praised him for his skill on the 'viola' which 'he plays . . . in four voices at one time with such elegance and fullness of tone that he amazes the listeners'. The 'viola' was probably the *lirone* or *lira da gamba*, first described only two years earlier in the 1565 *intermedi*, where Striggio himself may have played it. A detailed description of the *lirone*, which was evidently difficult to play, is given in a letter of 3 August 1574 from Duke Wilhelm V of Bavaria to his father Albrecht V (see Einstein, 1949, p.762). In the 1589 *intermedi* Striggio played not only the *lirone* but also the 'sopranino di viola', probably the descant viol.

Title-page of Striggio's 'Il cicalamento delle donne al bucato' (Venice: Scotto, 1567)

2. WORKS. Criticism of Striggio's secular music has concentrated on its conservative aspects, although, as Pirrotta remarked, evaluations based on his comparatively sparse use of dissonance and chromaticism ignore the expressive qualities of his rich melodic and contrapuntal invention. In the music for *intermedi* the careful fusion of homophony and counterpoint and an adroit handling of textures and spatially separated choirs show his surprisingly flexible approach to an often perfunctory genre. The pieces for larger forces have open textures, frequent antiphonal effects and changes in timbre, while the more modest pieces make greater use of short imitative motifs and other contrapuntal devices. Rhythms are usually incisive and lively and there is often a foretaste of the declamatory style, an important element in Wert's later works. Striggio's music for *intermedi* seems to have been influenced by Rore's early five-voice madrigals, particularly by their use of counterpoint and rhythm.

After the theatre music, *Il cicalamento delle donne al bucato* has received the most critical attention, notably because of the widely held 19th-century opinion that it was a forerunner of opera. Apart from the historical *non sequitur* involved, this judgment overemphasizes the novelty of the work, which is clearly related to Ruffo's canzoni and Janequin's chansons but nevertheless influenced the madrigalesque entertainments of Vecchi and Banchieri. Of the last three books of madrigals only *Il quarto libro* survives complete; these pieces show that Striggio flirted with more modern techniques in his later madrigals. Contemporary commentators associated him with progressive circles at Ferrara rather than Florence, and his own letters (in *I-Fas*; some in Gandolfi) contain

references to pieces in the Ferrarese virtuoso style, probably for two or three voices and basso continuo in the manner of Luzzaschi's *Madrigali . . . a uno, e doi, e tre soprani* (1601). There is even evidence that he toyed with monody, since the index to the manuscript collection *I-Fn* Magl.XIX.66, generally thought to have been written after 1590, ascribes to him *Se più del pianto mio l'orribil fiato* for solo voice and basso continuo; however, this is one of the pieces missing from the collection. Einstein's suggestion (*VogelB*, suppl., 703) that the anonymous four-voice *Villotte mantovane* (Venice, 1583) is by Striggio remains unsupported and is incompatible with the composer's interest in progressive styles at that time.

Striggio seems to have composed little sacred music. The 40-part motet *Ecce beatam lucem*, for four choirs (of eight, ten, sixteen and six voices) and organ continuo is known to have been performed in 1568 although the only surviving manuscript copies are dated 1587. The voices were accompanied on that occasion by eight trombones, eight violas, eight flutes, harpsichord and bass lute. In its alternation of soloists and chorus and in its spatially separated choirs this work resembles his large dialogue finales written in the 1560s for the Florentine *intermedi*, particularly the fifth *intermedio* for *La vedova* (1569). The *Missa in dominicis diebus*, for *alternatim* performance, is one of a number based on the same 'purified' chant of the S Barbara liturgy written by composers employed in, or closely associated with, the ducal chapel of S Barbara at Mantua, including Gastoldi, Rovigo, Wert and Palestrina. It survives in two manuscript sources dating from between 1580 and 1585 and was later published in *Missae dominicales quinis vocibus diversorum auctorum* (*RISM* 1592[1]). The motets ascribed to Striggio in the second and third volumes of Michael Herrer's *Hortus musicalis* (*RISM* 1609[14], 1609[15]) are contrafacta.

While Striggio was much admired by his contemporaries as a performer, his compositions seem to have brought him more widespread fame and popularity. Secular pieces by him are included in a large number of foreign manuscripts, including the Olkuz manuscript (compiled about 1579, see Perz) and the Lerma Codex. In England his music seems to have been widely appreciated; one of his madrigals was included in Watson's *The First Sett, of Italian Madrigals Englished* (*RISM* 1590[29]), he was much admired by Morley and his music is quoted in works by Weelkes and Farmer. Monte's *Missa 'Nasce la pena mia'* is based on one of his most popular pieces, Lodovico Agostini's *Il nuovo echo* (1583) includes pieces composed 'ad imitatione del S. Aless. Striggio' and Ludovico Balbi parodied *Se da vostri begli occhi* in his *Musicale essercitio* (1589). Monteverdi described him (letter, 28 November 1601) as 'famoso' and he was cited by Giulio Cesare Monteverdi in the Artusi controversy.

WORKS

Editions: *Composizioni sacre e profane a più voci secoli XIV, XV e XVI*, ed. L. Torchi, AMI, i (1897/*R*1968) [AMI]
R. Tadlock: *The Early Madrigals of Alessandro Striggio* (diss., U. of Rochester, 1958) [T]

SECULAR VOCAL
(all published in Venice)

Il primo libro de madrigali, 5vv (1558, lost, 2/1560) [1558]
Il primo libro de madrigali, 6vv (1560[22]) [1560]
Il cicalamento delle donne al bucato et la caccia . . . con un lamento di Didone ad Enea per la sua partenza di Cipriano Rore, 4–7vv (1567[23]) [1567]

Il cicalamento delle donne al bucato et la caccia . . . con il Gioco di primiera, 5vv (1569) [1569]
Il secondo libro de madrigali, 5vv (1570) [1570]; T
Il secondo libro de madrigali, 6vv (1571) [1571]; T
Il terzo libro de madrigali, 5vv (1596) [1596a]
Il quarto libro de madrigali, 5vv (1596) [1596b]
Il quinto libro de madrigali, 5vv (1597) [1597]

Works in 1557[23], 1559[16], 1561[15], 1565[16], 1566[3], 1566[23], 1567[13], 1568[12], 1570[15], 1575[12], 1576[5], 1577[7], 1579[2], 1579[3], 1582[5], 1583[15], 1584[4], 1584[15], 1586[7], 1586[10], 1588[14], 1588[17], 1588[18], 1588[21], 1590[15], 1591[23], 1592[11], 1592[15], 1594[6]

Ahi com'à un (Guarini), 5vv, 1596b; Ahi dispietato Amor (B. Tasso), 1571, T; Alba cruda, 5vv, 1575[12]; All'hor che lieta, 5vv, 1592[15]; All'acqua sagra, 6vv, 1571, T; Alla mia dolce e vaga donna, 6vv, 1571, T; All'apparir della leggiadra figlia, 8vv, 1584[4]; Alma che da celeste, 6vv, 1571, T; Alma città, 5vv, *I-VEaf*; Al mio signor, 5vv, 1596b; Altr'io che queste spighe, 12vv, 1584[4]; Al vago e incerto, 5vv, 1569; A me che fatta, 8vv, 1584[4], ed. in Osthoff; Amor io fallo (Petrarch), 6vv, 1560; Amor l'arco, 5vv, 1557[23] [doubtful, ? by P. Sandrin]; Amor m'impenna l'ale (Tansillo), 6vv, 1566[23]; Ancor ch'io possa dire, 6vv, 1560, extract ed. in *BrownI*; A pie d'un, 5vv, 1596b; Apri apri homai, 6vv, 1560; Ardendo e grido, 5vv, 1558; Ardo e non me'l, 5vv, 1596a; Arse cosi per voi, 5vv, 1558; Aura gentil, 5vv, 1596a; Aura gentil, 5vv, 1597

Ben sperai col partire da voi, 5vv, 1570, T; Caro dolce ben mio, 5vv, 1558; Che crederia d'amore il miracol altero, 5vv, 1570, T; Che deggio far, 5vv, 1558; Che fai, che pensi (Petrarch), 6vv, 1560; Che nova luce, 5vv, 1596b; Che scorger non saprei, 5vv, 1570, T; Chi brama al maggior calde, 5vv, 1558; Chi fara fed'al ciel, 5vv, 1566[3]; Chi puo fuggir amor, 5vv, 1570, T; Come l'effetto al nome, 6vv, 1571, T; Con l'aura di sospir, 5vv, 1582[5]; Con pieta vi rimiro, 5vv, 1583[15]; Contra i disegni, 5vv, 1596a; Cresci germe real, 6vv, 1571, T

Dall'angelico viso, 5vv, 1597; Dalle gelate braccia, 4–7vv, 1567; Da queste altere soglie, 6vv, 1571, T; Deh foss'il ver, 6vv, 1571, T; Di questa bionda e vaga treccia, 5vv, 1567[13], AMI; Ditemi o donna mia, 5vv, 1558; D'ogni gratia e d'amor, 6vv, 1571, T; Dolce mio ben amor, 6vv, 1571, T; Dolce ritorn' amor, 6vv, 1567[13]; Doloroso martir (Tansillo), 5vv, 1577[7]; Donna felice e bella, 5vv, 1558; Donna se nel, 5vv, 1597; D'un si bel foco, 10vv, 1588[21]; Ecco che fa, 8vv, 1584[4]; Ecco lo strale, 5vv, 1596a; Ecco ò dolce (R. Arlotti), 5vv, 1596b; Ecco scesa fra noi, 5vv, 1570, T; E mentre più affligea, 5vv, 1570, T; Entr'un gran nuvol d'or, 5vv, 1568[12]; Era un bia virtu, 5vv, 1558; Era'l bel viso suo, 5vv, 1558; Eran le ninfe e pastori (M. Manfredi), 6vv, 1592[11], AMI; Eransi sol a far perpetua guerra, 5vv, 1570, T; Et chi vede'l gran, 5vv, 1558

Felice l'alma che per voi, 5vv, 1558; Fortuna alata il pie, 6vv, 1560; Fra i vaghi e bei crin d'oro, 5vv, 1591[23]; Fuggi, speme mia, 5vv, lost, intabulated lute, 1584[15], ed. in Brown (1972); Gia ninfa hor, 8vv, 1588[21]; Giovane illustre, 5vv, 1558; Giovani che'l gran, 5vv, 1596b; Gravi pene, 4vv, 1561[15]; Herbosi prati e liete valli amene, 5vv, 1570, T; Hor che le stelle, 5vv, 1588[14]; Hor che lucent'e chiara, 5vv, 1558; Hor che sia che vendetta, 5vv, 1570, T; Hor ch'un grave dolor, 4vv, 1571,T; Hor se mi mostra (Ariosto), 6vv, 1571, T; I dolci colli, ov'io lasciai (Petrarch), 6vv, 1560; Illustre alma gentile, 5vv, 1558; In questi verdi, 5vv, 1596a; Intesi venni, 5vv, 1575[12]; Invidioso amor, 5vv, 1559[16]; Invita alma, 5vv, 1597; Io t'amo, 5vv, 1596a; Ite guerrier, 5vv, 1597; I vaghi fiori, 5vv, 1596a

La dea d'amor, 5vv, 1597; L'alma mia fiamma, 6vv, 1560; L'amorosa Ero, 5vv, 1588[17], ed. H. B. Lincoln: *L'amorosa Ero* (New York, 1968); La natura v'armo (Tasso), 5vv, 1596b; La pastorella con la verga in mane (Tasso), 5vv, 1567[13]; L'aria s'oscura, 5vv, 1560; Lascia deh Tirsi mio, 5vv, 1570, T; Lasciat'hai morte (Petrarch), 6vv, 1560; La ver aurora (Petrarch), 6vv, 1560; Le vag'herbette e l'amorose fronde, 5vv, 1576[5], AMI; Longi da voi mia vita, 5vv, 1570, T; L'un mi raccend'al cor l'alto desio, 5vv, 1570, T; Madonna in voi, 5vv, 1597; Madonna poi ch'occider, 6vv, 1560; Madonn'il vostro petto, 5vv, 1558; Ma non giov'al mio mal, 5vv, 1558; Ma tu per darm'al cor maggior tormento, 5vv, 1560; Mentre la donna, 5vv, 1558; Mentre la greggia sua, 6vv, 1579[2]; Mentre nel più felice e lieto stato, 5vv, 1576[5]; Mentre l'un Polo, 8vv, 1579[3], ed. in Cw, lxxx (1960); Mentr'io fugiva l'amoroso fuoco, 5vv, 1570, T; Mi dispiet' amor, 6vv, 1571, T; Miglior Ruberto, 5vv, 1571, T; Misero ohime, 5vv, 1558; Misero più d'ogn'huom, 5vv, 1558; Movend'apparo con mill'il corso, 5vv, 1565[16]

Nasce la pena mia, 6vv, 1560, ed. J. van Nuffel, *P. de Monte: Missa Nasce la pena mia* (Düsseldorf, n.d.); Nella vaga stagion, 4–7vv, 1567, ed. B. Somma, *Capolavori polifonici del secolo XVI*, iv (Rome, 1947); Ne perch'il mio desio, 6vv, 1571, T; Ninfe che dal superb'Adriatico seno, 1590[15]; Ninfe leggiadre, 5vv, 1575[12], AMI; Noi qui nove sorelle, 6vv, *B-Bc*; Non è pena maggior, 5vv, 1571, T; Non fiammeggiar'ancor, 5vv, 1558; Non men gioioso, 5vv, 1596b; Non più ingegno, 5vv, 1558; Non rumor di tamburi (Ariosto), 6vv, 1571, T; Non visse la mia vita, 5vv, 1586[10], AMI; Notte felice, 5vv, 1558; Notti felic'e care, 5vv, 1570, T; O ben felice, 5vv, 1596b; O che

strano scompiglio, 4–8vv, *Bc*; O della bella Etruria, 5vv, 1558; O fer'aspro dolore, 9vv, 1584[4]; O giovenil ardire, 10vv, 1584[4]; Oime ch'io spasmo, 6vv, 1560; Ombre del oscuro abisso, 4–6vv, *Bc*; O messagi del cor sospiri, 6vv, 1560; Ondeggiava il crin d'or, 1568[12]; O passi sparsi (Petrarch), 11vv, 1584[4]; O passi sparsi (Petrarch), 12vv, 1584[4]

Paghi dunque il mio, 5vv, 1558; Partirò dunque, 6vv, 1566[23]; Pansai lasso fra, 5vv, 1558; Per questo vivo, 5vv, 1597; Per un'alma gentil, 6vv, 1571, T; Poi che mort'è colei, 5vv, 1558; Poi che spiegat'ho l'ale, 6vv, 1560; Pour mes loygner e changer, 5vv, 1570, T; Qual bianchezza, 5vv, 1596b; Qual più si trova, 5vv, 1570[15]; Qual tu ti sia qui vieni, 6vv, 1571, T; Quando privo di te, 5vv, 1558; Quando vede'l pastor, 6vv, 1560; Quanto m'apparv'amor, 5vv, 1570, T; Quanto più m'allontano dal mio cor, 5vv, 1570, T; Quest'amor piu improvisa, 6vv, 1560; Questa ch'appar, 5vv, 1596a; Quest'a par dell'antichita e casta e bella, 5vv, 1570, T; Questi ch'indicio fan (Ariosto), 6vv, 1567[13]; Qui cadd'un bel, 5vv, 1597; Rallegratevi homai, 7vv, 1584[4]; Ridon liete le rive, 5vv, 1558; Rosa eterna, 6vv, 1560; Rosata l'alba, 5vv, 1596a

Scorte dal chiaro, 5vv, 1597; Se ben di sette stelle, 6vv, 1560; Se da l'ardent' humore, 6vv, 1571, T; Se d'altr' amante, 5vv, 1570, T; Se da vostri begli occhi, 4vv, 1588[18]; Se più fiera durezza, 5vv, 1570, T; Si dolc'e d'amar voi, 5vv, 1558; Si dolcemente, 5vv, 1575[12]; S'io moro haime hor del mio error, 5vv, 1570, T; S'io t'ho ferito, 5vv, 1570, T; Siringa al bel Narciso, 1594[6]; S'ogni mio ben havete, 6vv, 1571, T; Sparget'Arabi odori, 6vv, 1586[7]; Sù rapidissim'onda, 6vv, 1566[23]; Tolse Barbara, 5vv, 1596a; Torbido il mincio corre, 5vv, 1558; Tronchisi homai, 5vv, 1596b; Una celeste nube, 5vv, 1558; Voglia mi sprona Amor, 6vv, 1560; Voi Federico, 5vv, 1558; Voi se col raggio, 5vv, 1558; Voi sete la mia, 5vv, 1596b; Vous qui voiez, 5vv, 1597

SACRED VOCAL

Missa in dominicis diebus, 5vv, *I-Mc* (2 copies)
Ecce beatam lucem, motet, 40vv, *D-Z*

LOST WORKS

All intermedi settings; first lines taken from contemporary descriptions unless otherwise stated.

Alle spose novelle l'addolatura Damigella Dalmatia; Cor mio mentr'io vi miro (mentioned in Gandolfi); D'ogni altra furia e poste; Ecco dal ciel le nove sorelle; Fuor del lucido fresco; Hor che vedove e sole; Il nubiloso velo; Odi quel che destina; O giovanile ardire; Oh altero miraculo novello; Oh di quanta ira, e sdegno; Perchè giovine a te perigli, oltraggio; Per voi, lasso, conviene (mentioned in Gandolfi); Se più del pianto mio (Rinuccini), 1v, bc (cited in index to *I-Fn* Magl.XIX.66); Tratte dal tristo abisso; Verso la fresca lama

BIBLIOGRAPHY

C. Bartoli: *Ragionamenti accademici sopra alcuni luoghi difficili di Dante* (Venice, 1567)
M. Troiano: *Dialoghi* (Venice, 1569)
T. Morley: *A Plaine and Easie Introduction to Practicall Musicke* (London, 1597/*R*1971); ed. R. A. Harman (London, 1952), 58, 60f
G. C. Monteverdi: Preface to *C. Monteverdi: Il quinto libro de' madrigali a cinque voci* (Venice, 1605); facs. in *C. Monteverdi: Opera omnia*, ed G. F. Malipiero (1926–42), x, 69ff; Eng. trans. O. Strunk, in *Source Readings in Music History* (New York, 1950), 412
G. Rovetta: Preface to *Salmi concertati* (Venice, 1626)
V. Giustiniani: *Discorso sopra la musica* (MS, *I-La*, 1628); ed. and Eng. trans. C. MacClintock, MSD, ix (1962)
P. Canal: *Della musica in Mantova* (Venice, 1881)
A. Bertolotti: *Musici alla corte dei Gonzaga in Mantova dal secolo XV al XVIII* (Milan, 1890/*R*1969), 59, 76, 78, 86, 92
U. Angeli: *Notizie per la storia del teatro a Firenze nel secolo XVI, specialmente circa gli intermezzi* (Modena, 1891), 13ff
A. Solerti: *Musica, ballo e drammatica alla corte medicea dal 1600 al 1637* (Florence, 1905/*R*1968)
O. G. Sonneck: 'A Description of Alessandro Striggio and Francesco Corteccia's Intermedi "Psyche and Amor" 1565', *MA*, iii (1911), 40; repr. in *Miscellaneous Studies in the History of Music* (New York, 1921), 269
R. Gandolfi: 'Lettere inedite, scritte musicisti e letterati, appartenanti alla seconda metà del secolo XVI', *RMI*, xx (1913), 527
M. Schneider: *Die Anfänge des Basso Continuo und seiner Bezifferung* (Leipzig, 1918), 67
A. Saviotti: 'Un'artista del cinquecento: Virginia Vagnoli da Siena', *Bolletino senese di storia patria*, xxvi (1919), 105
A. Einstein: 'Firenze prima della monodia', *RaM*, vii (1934), 263
F. Ghisi: *Alle fonti della monodia* (Milan, 1940)
A. Einstein: *The Italian Madrigal* (Princeton, 1949/*R*1971)
F. Fortune: 'A Florentine Manuscript and its Place in Italian Song', *AcM*, xxiii (1951), 124
L. Schrade: 'Les fêtes du mariage de Francesco dei Medici et de Bianca Cappello', *Les fêtes de la Renaissance I: CNRS Abbaye de Royaumont 1955*, 107
R. Tadlock: 'Alessandro Striggio, Madrigalist', *JAMS*, xi (1958), 29

E. Raimondo, ed.: *T. Tasso: Dialoghi* (Florence, 1958), ii/2, 649f

R. Tadlock: *The Early Madrigals of Alessandro Striggio* (diss., U. of Rochester, 1958)

J. Kerman: *The Elizabethan Madrigal: a Comparative Study* (New York, 1962), 57, 59, 177, 201, 231, 243, 251

A. M. Nagler: *Theatre Festivals of the Medici 1539–1637* (New Haven, 1964), 1, 18ff, 36, 40f, 53, 58

E. Kenton: 'A Faded Laurel Wreath', *Aspects of Medieval and Renaissance Music: a Birthday Offering to Gustave Reese* (New York, 1966), 500

W. Elders: 'The Lerma Codex: a Newly-discovered Choirbook from Seventeenth-century Spain', *TVNM*, xx/4 (1967), 187

A. Newcomb: *The Musica Secreta of Ferrara in the 1580's* (diss., Princeton U., 1969)

W. Osthoff: *Theatergesang und darstellende Musik in der italienischen Renaissance* (Tutzing, 1969), i, 343ff, 348, 354; ii, 122ff

M. Perz: 'Rekopiśmienne partesy olkuskie' [The Olkuz manuscripts], *Muzyka*, xiv/2 (1969), 18

N. Pirrotta and E. Povoledo: *Li due Orfei: da Poliziano a Monteverdi* (Turin, 1969, enlarged 2/1975)

H. M. Brown: 'Psyche's Lament: some Music for the Medici Wedding in 1565', *Words and Music; the Scholar's View . . . in Honor of A. Tillman Merritt* (Cambridge, Mass., 1972), 1

D. de Paoli: *Claudio Monteverdi: Lettere, dediche e prefazione* (Rome, 1973), 17f; Eng. trans. in *The Monteverdi Companion*, ed. D. Arnold and N. Fortune (London, 1968), 22f

H. M. Brown: *Sixteenth-century Instrumentation: the Music for the Florentine Intermedii*, MSD, xxx (1973), 46

J. Haar: 'Madrigals from Three Generations: the MS Brussels, Bibl. du Conservatoire Royal, 27.731', *RIM*, x (1975), 252

I. Fenlon: *Patterns of Style and Patronage: Music at the Mantuan Court c 1565–1600* (diss., U. of Cambridge, 1977)

D. S. Butchart: *The Madrigal in Florence, 1560–1630* (diss., U. of Oxford, 1979)

IAIN FENLON

Striggio, Alessandro [Alessandrino] **(ii)** (*b* Mantua, ?1573; *d* Venice, ?15 June 1630). Italian nobleman, diplomat, librettist and musician, son of Alessandro Striggio (i). He appears as a viol player in the list of musicians who took part in the famous Florentine festivities celebrating the wedding of Grand Duke Ferdinando I in 1589. He subsequently studied law at Mantua in preparation for a diplomatic career in the service of the Gonzaga family (although in 1596–7 he undertook to publish posthumously his father's last three books of five-part madrigals). In June 1611 he became secretary to Duke Vincenzo I and for some years served as ambassador to Milan. Having been made a count, then a marquis, he was elevated to the rank of chancellor in January 1628. During the war over the succession to Vincenzo II he attempted to obtain military and political aid for Mantua in Madrid and in Venice, where he died of the plague.

Striggio's most important link with the musical world was through his collaboration with Monteverdi, for whom he wrote the librettos of *Orfeo* (Mantua, 1607; repr. in A. Solerti: *Gli albori del melodramma*, Milan, 1904/R1969, iii, pp.241–74) and probably of *Tirsi e Clori* (1615); in Solerti: op cit, pp.285ff) as well as the lost *Lamento d'Apollo*. After Monteverdi's removal to Venice in 1613 Striggio's position as his patron and closest ally at the Mantuan court is eloquently documented by their correspondence, for the majority of Monteverdi's extant letters are addressed to him. Several of his own letters survive (in *I-MAc*). *Orfeo* is in five acts, each having a masterly dramatic structure which centres upon a climax. His model in many respects was *Euridice* by Ottavio Rinuccini, who altered the Ovidian fable to effect a happy ending. Striggio's libretto, however, adheres to the original tragic version of the myth, whereas in Monteverdi's setting Orpheus is rescued by a *deus ex machina*. This discrepancy may have been necessitated by the circumstances of the earliest performances, for neither the rooms of the Accademia degli Invaghiti, who promoted the opera, nor those at court allowed for the use of machinery.

Striggio also wrote *Il trionfo d'onore* and *Il sacrificio d'Ifigenia* (the latter in Solerti: op cit, pp.275ff), both set by Marco da Gagliano and performed in Mantua in June 1608. He was a member, known as 'Il Ritenuto' ('the reserved one'), of the Accademia degli Invaghiti.

BIBLIOGRAPHY

L. C. Volta: *Compendio cronologico-critico*, iv (Mantua, 1833)

C. d'Arco, ed.: 'Due cronache di Mantova dal 1628 al 1631', in G. Muller: *Raccolta di cronisti e documenti storici lombardi inediti*, ii (Milan, 1857)

A. A. Abert: *Claudio Monteverdi und das musikalische Drama* (Lippstadt, 1954)

L. Mazzoldi, R. Giusti and R. Salvadori: *Mantova: la storia*, iii (Mantua, 1963)

N. Pirrotta: 'Teatro, scene, e musica nelle opere di Monteverdi', *Claudio Monteverdi e il suo tempo*, ed. R. Monterosso (Venice, 1968), 45ff

—: 'Scelte poetiche di Monteverdi', *NRMI*, ii (1968), 10

B. R. Hanning: *The Influence of Humanist Thought and Italian Renaissance Poetry on the Formation of Opera* (diss., Yale U., 1968), chaps.3–4

N. Pirrotta: 'Monteverdi e i problemi dell'opera', *Studi sul teatro veneto fra rinascimento ed età barocca*, ed. M. T. Muraro (Florence, 1971), 321ff

B. RUSSANO HANNING

Strinasacchi [Strina Sacchi], **Regina** (*b* Ostiglia, nr. Mantua, 1764; *d* Dresden, 11 June 1839). Italian violinist. She was educated at the Conservatorio della Pietà in Venice and probably later studied in Paris. From 1780 to 1783 she travelled through Italy and was admired for her appearance and manners as well as for her playing. In 1784 she scored a great success in Vienna with two concerts. Mozart performed with her at the second of these and composed for the occasion one of his finest sonatas (in Bb, K454). He praised her to his father as 'a very good violinist' who 'has a great deal of taste and feeling in her playing'. Leopold agreed when he heard her in Salzburg late in 1785 and wrote to his daughter (8 December 1785):

She plays no note without feeling, so even in the symphonies, she always played with expression. No-one can play an adagio with more feeling and more touchingly than she. Her whole heart and soul are in the melody she is playing, and her tone is both beautiful and powerful.

In chamber music also she established a fine reputation, achieving special distinction in Haydn quartets.

In 1785 Strinasacchi married Johann Conrad Schlick, a distinguished cellist of the ducal court in Gotha. She joined her husband in the orchestra there, and for the next 25 years the couple made occasional concert tours together. Gerber reported that he visited her in 1801 and found her artistry and charm undiminished. At Gotha she became known also as an expert guitarist. She retired from concert life in 1810; after the death of her husband in 1825, she lived with her son in Dresden.

Although Eitner listed a cello concerto by Strinasacchi in Traeg's catalogue (1799), it is probably not by Regina; there is no other reference to her composing.

BIBLIOGRAPHY

EitnerQ; GerberL; GerberNL

L. Spohr: *Selbstbiographie* (Kassel, 1860–61; Eng. trans., 1865/R1969)

W. A. Bauer and O. E. Deutsch, eds.: *Mozart: Briefe und Aufzeichnungen*, iii (Kassel, 1963), 311, 467

CHAPPELL WHITE

String (Fr. *corde*; Ger. *Saite*, *Streich*-; It. *corda*). A string for a musical instrument may be made of any material that can produce a musical sound when the string is held stretched and then plucked, bowed, struck or otherwise excited. Gut, silk and wire, and more recently plastic, are the most common, but many other materials have been used.

The frequency at which a given string of negligible stiffness will vibrate is inversely proportional to its length, proportional to the square root of its tension and inversely proportional to the square root of its mass. In free vibration (i.e. vibration unhampered by any resistance in the string or in adjacent bodies) a string will produce harmonic overtones, i.e. overtones with frequencies that are multiples of the frequency of the lowest note of which the string is capable (the fundamental). These are perceived subliminally by most people, although tuners distinguish them consciously. Several factors may cause the strings of musical instruments to depart from the harmonic series.

First, the stiffness of the string resists its natural tendency to subdivide indefinitely into shorter and shorter vibrating lengths. Thus the upper harmonics become successively weaker and are of limited number. Second, the method of excitation affects the quality of sound radiated by a string. Bowing, striking and plucking each produce characteristic effects which differ significantly from each other (see ACOUSTICS). Third, the free vibration of solid bodies other than strings does not produce a series of harmonics whose frequencies are multiples of the fundamental. Hence their tone is clangy or metallic (see INHARMONICITY). To the extent that a plucked or struck string reacts like a bar of metal, dissonant and non-continuous elements (transients) are introduced into its tone. This inharmonicity is manifested in the bell-like timbre of bass notes on a piano, and also, perhaps, in the silvery buzz that seems to envelop the sound of a harpsichord. Fourth, strings of musical instruments are not in free vibration but are coupled to structures whose resonant characteristics impose themselves upon the signal radiated by the instrument, damping vibrations at certain frequencies and reinforcing those at others. Lastly, any particular inequality of thickness, stiffness or straightness will displace the nodes of a vibrating string, causing the frequencies of certain partials to diverge peculiarly from multiples of the fundamental; beats within the timbre can then often be heard.

Thus when the sound produced by a string instrument is analysed by measuring the relative energy present at each frequency in the spectrum emitted by a single tone, it is found that the frequencies present do not conform to the predictable pattern of the harmonic series but that certain clusters of frequencies are powerful and others weak. These clusters of strong frequencies, called formants, help determine the characteristic timbre of the instrument.

In pursuing their artistic ends, musical instrument makers manipulate this distortion of the harmonic series. It is remarkable, for example, that even in instruments such as the piano and the harpsichord where the strings (except in the bass) are doubled in length for each octave of descent, the string diameters are steadily increased from treble to tenor. This enlargement increases the capacity of the lower strings to absorb and radiate energy. In pianos the mass of the hammers is also increased as the scale is traversed downwards, and in harpsichords the plectra are left thicker in the tenor than in the treble: thus more energy is transmitted to the strings tuned to the lower frequencies than to those at the upper end of the instrument. Strings in the tenor region which are not thickened sound false and weak. This falseness is probably the result of the attempt to impart too much energy to the string. At the ends of the string the natural resistance of the wire to bending tends to make the effective acoustic length somewhat shorter than the measured length. If the string is set in vibration with a very large amplitude the nodes at the ends of the string move outward, flattening the pitch. As the sound attenuates the nodes return to their original positions and the pitch consequently rises, producing an effect of falseness.

At the lower end of the tenor range, where the strings are no longer doubled in length for each octave of descent, the stiffness of a string massive enough to absorb sufficient energy becomes excessive and the tone colour harsh and unpleasant. In the harpsichord and several other instruments the usual solution is to change the material of the string to a metal (usually brass) that is less stiff than steel and somewhat more massive. Pianos and another group of instruments including harps and clavichords resort to overspun strings for the bass register.

In the West the manufacture of strings has chiefly involved the techniques of the metal worker (for wire drawing) and of the gut string maker. Although there is evidence of drawn gold wire as early as the 5th or 6th century BC in Persia, it seems that the draw plate was not used in medieval Europe until the 10th century, from which time drawn iron wire was available for musical instruments. By the 14th century it was being drawn in considerable quantity by water power. In the 18th century Liège, Cologne, Hamburg, Switzerland and Sweden were particularly esteemed as sources of ferrous wire.

Iron (or steel) wire depends chiefly on its carbon content for its tensile strength and stiffness. The method of making ferrous wire, from the Middle Ages until the Industrial Revolution, involved smelting the ore and casting the iron, as it ran from the furnace, into large blooms, very high in carbon. These masses of cast iron were forged either by hand or water-powered hammer into rods capable of being drawn into wire. The many reheatings necessary, especially when the blooms were forged by hand, burned out most of the carbon, leaving nearly pure iron or very low-carbon steel. As larger and larger tilt hammers came into use, fewer heatings were necessary and it became possible to produce rods fairly high in carbon. Thus there seems to have been a gradual increase in the tensile strength and stiffness of the wire available to musical instrument makers. This was reflected in a steady lengthening of the scaling (and a corresponding increase in tension) of the strings in their instruments. A. J. Hipkins (*Grove 5*) made some interesting remarks on the history of steel wire in the 19th century; it is significant that he equated quality with high tensile strength.

The procedure in the manufacture of gut strings is well described in the article 'Corde' in Diderot's *Encyclopédie* (1751–65). After cleansing and pickling in alkaline solutions of gradually increasing strength, the guts of seven- or eight-month old lambs are twisted together under tension and polished with hair pads. It is the number of guts employed which determines the final diameter of the string. This varies from two for the smallest mandoline string to 120 for a double bass. In early times the best gut strings came from Italy; by the 18th century manufacture was spreading elsewhere.

According to Jean Rousseau (*Traité de la viole*, 1687), Sainte-Colombe first suggested overspinning gut strings in about 1675. By the early 18th century the lowest string of the violin, and occasionally the D string as well, were overspun. Plain gut A and E strings held their own until the 20th century when covered A strings and steel E strings became common. E strings of steel covered with a flat ribbon of aluminium are occasionally found. Aluminium-covered A and D strings are normal, as are silver or even gold-covered G strings. Instead of a gut core, plastic is sometimes used.

FRANK HUBBARD

Stringari, Antonio [Patavinus, Antonius Stringarius] (*fl* 1505–14). Italian composer. He probably came from Padua, for some of his works are ascribed to 'Ant. String. Patavinus'. He was a versatile frottolist whose music has survived exclusively in Petrucci's frottola books. His earlier contributions are accomplished settings of *barzellette*, *ode*, etc., including a frottola using the popular tune *Scaramella* as a refrain; the substantial group of his pieces in Petrucci's 11th book, which includes settings of Petrarch and Tebaldeo, places him among the forward-looking composers concerned with the new move towards higher verse forms and literary values. The frottola *Don don al foco al foco* has a *ripresa* in the form of a dialogue.

WORKS
(for titles see Jeppesen, i)

12 frottolas, 1505⁶ [anon., attrib. Stringari elsewhere], 1507⁴, 1514²; 1 ed. B. Disertori, *Le frottole per canto e liuto intabulate da Franciscus Bossinensis* (Milan, 1964); 1 ed. in Jeppesen, ii

BIBLIOGRAPHY

A. Einstein: 'Das elfte Buch der Frottole', *ZMw*, x (1927–8), 613
F. Torrefranca: *Il segreto del quattrocento* (Bologna, 1939), 176
K. Jeppesen: *La frottola* (Århus and Copenhagen, 1968–70)

JOAN WESS

String drum [lion's roar]. (Fr. *tambour à cordes*; Ger. *Löwengebrüll*; It. *rugghio di leone*). A membranophone in the form of a friction drum, consisting of a cylindrical or bucket-shaped vessel with one end open and the other closed with a membrane. A length of cord or a gut string passing through a hole in the membrane is resined and rubbed with coarse fabric or a glove, or alternatively the end of the string is loosely secured to a wooden handle to form a whirled friction drum.

The first described string drum was originally known in England as the 'jackdaw'. An instrument of this type is still used in Hungarian folk music. In southern Turkey a string drum is used to scare away wild animals. In Germany a whirled friction drum in the form of a child's toy is known as the *Waldteufel*. Similar instruments are known in China and India.

Composers have made occasional use of the string drum. Varèse included it as *tambour à corde* in *Hyperprism* (1924) and *Ionisation* (1934). Alexander Goehr specifies 'lion's roar' in his *Romanza* for cello and orchestra (1968). Carl Orff wrote for a whirled friction drum in his score for *A Midsummer Night's Dream* (1934–52). The variable bass drum in Britten's *Children's Crusade* (1969) can be classified as a string drum: variable pressure on a stretched cord which passes through the drumhead controls the pitch of the instrument which, in addition to being struck with drumsticks, is further vibrated by means of 'bowing' the stretched string.

The TAMBOURIN DE BÉARN of southern France is generally designated a 'string drum'.

See also the entry 'String drum' in Appendix A.

JAMES BLADES

Stringendo (It.: 'drawing tight', 'squeezing'; gerund of *stringere*). A direction to perform with more tension and therefore specifically faster. It is sometimes abbreviated *string*. As a tempo modification it appears frequently in scores of the later 19th century, especially in Liszt, to indicate the development towards some climax. The past participle of the same word is STRETTO.

For bibliography *see* TEMPO AND EXPRESSION MARKS.

DAVID FALLOWS

Stringfield, Lamar E(dwin) (*b* nr. Raleigh, North Carolina, 10 Oct 1897; *d* Asheville, North Carolina, 21 Jan 1959). American composer, flautist and conductor. He studied the flute, conducting and composition at the New York Institute of Musical Art. In 1932 he organized the institute of folk music at the University of North Carolina, and later he established the North Carolina State SO. He also made flutes, engraved music and invented various writing devices. His music, dominated by folktunes and folklike material, is based in traditional harmony but overlaid with unconventional chord progressions, major–minor ambiguity and free dissonance. *From the Southern Mountains* won him a Pulitzer Prize in 1928.

WORKS
(selective list)

Stage: The Mountain Song, opera, 3 scenes, 1929; Carolina Charcoal (musical folk comedy, 2), 1955; 9 incidental scores
Orch: Mountain Suite, band, 1922; From the Southern Mountains, suite, 1927; The Seventh Queue, sym. ballet, 1928; The Legend of John Henry, sym. ballad, 1932; From the Blue Ridge, suite, 1936; Georgia Buck, band, 1949
Chamber: Mountain Echoes, suite, vn, pf, 1920; Indian Sketches, suite, fl, str qt, 1922; Mountain Sketches, suite, fl, vc, pf, 1923; Introduction and Scherzo, wind qnt, tpt, timp, str qt, 1926; Impromptu, fl, vc, 1927; Wind Qnt, 1932; Moods of a Moonshiner, str qt, 1933; Mountain Dawn, fl, str, 1945; My Lonely Flute, 1950
Vocal: Peace (cantata, M. Sims), SATB, orch, 1949; many songs

Principal publishers: M. Baron (Oyster Bay, NY), Fischer, J. Fischer (Glen Rock, NJ), Musicus

BIBLIOGRAPHY

S. Spaeth, ed.: *Music and Dance in the Southeastern States* (New York, 1952)
D. R. Nelson: *The Life and Works of Lamar Stringfield (1897–1959)* (diss., U. of North Carolina, 1971) [incl. Stringfield's *Guide for Young Flutists*, c1945]

DOUGLAS R. NELSON

String quartet (Fr. *quatuor à cordes*; Ger. *Streichquartett*; It. *quartetto di cordi*, *quartetto d'archi*). A composition for four solo string instruments, usually two violins, viola and cello. The term 'string quartet' (and its equivalents in other languages) was scarcely used until the 19th century. The genre to which it is now normally applied was not firmly established until Haydn's op.9 (1769–70), though its points of origin may be located in various kinds of late Baroque music.

1. Early developments. 2. Haydn, Mozart and their contemporaries. 3. 19th century. 4. 20th century.

1. EARLY DEVELOPMENTS. Four-part writing for strings occurs in pieces designated *sonata a quattro* or *concerto a quattro*, in the Italian *sinfonia*, the French *sonate en quatuor* and *ouverture à quatre*, and very frequently in such Classical and pre-Classical forms as the divertimento, cassation, notturno and serenade. But in many of these forms, including sometimes even the sonata,

orchestral performance was possible or actually required, while a keyboard instrument realizing the functions of a continuo part may on occasion still have been used even when such a part was not specified by the composer.

In the early 18th-century Italian sinfonia, three- and four-movement works deriving their structures from the opera overture and *sonata da chiesa* respectively are found in compositions for two violins, viola and continuo by G. B. Sammartini, Tartini and others. These works are written in an orchestral rather than a chamber style, however, with viola and bass frequently doubling in octaves and a predominance of interest in the first violin part. Earlier, works like A. Scarlatti's *Sonate a quattro per due violini, violetta e violoncello senza cembalo* (c1715–25), though a somewhat isolated phenomenon, had achieved a more genuine balance of interest between the parts though conceptually their style remains that of the late Baroque except in the forward-looking dance movements, mostly minuets, with which each sonata ends (see ex.1). But the removal of the

Ex.1 A. Scarlatti: *Sonata a quattro* no.2, Minuet

continuo and the adoption of the cello for the bass line was a gradual and uneven process, though Galuppi followed Scarlatti in this respect in 1740.

Sammartini's quartets have some importance in the history of the form. As in his symphonies the first violin dominates the texture but the melodic line is elegantly shaped in a style in which Classical features are replacing those of the Baroque. These three- or four-movement works, generally with a minuet finale, were to influence the young Mozart in his so-called 'Milanese' quartets as well as Boccherini whose quartets were never to absorb fully the Classical motivic style but remained in essence a development of Sammartini's manner.

In 18th-century France four-part writing for strings is found in the *sonates en quatuor*, usually for three violins and *basse continue*, as well as in many arrangements of fashionable airs, opera tunes and overtures

under such titles as *ouverture réduite en quatuor*. The appearance of a genuine string quartet literature had to await the arrival in Paris of works by émigré composers such as Boccherini and Cambini. In central and north Germany, too, Baroque forms and styles resisted new developments in instrumental music with Telemann, J. G. Graun, Fasch and others contributing to a literature of *sonate a quattro* but scarcely venturing on anything resembling a genuine string quartet.

The real source of the development of the Classical string quartet is to be found in south Germany, Austria and Bohemia, in the quartet–symphonies of the Mannheim school dating from about 1745 onwards (J. W. A. Stamitz, F. X. Richter, Holzbauer, Filtz, C. Cannabich and Eichner), and in the divertimentos of a more popular character by composers such as Asplmayr, Camerloher, Starzer, Gassmann and J. Haydn. Six 'quartets' by the Viennese composer M. G. Monn (DTÖ, xxxix, Jg.xix/2) show the close relationship of the incipient quartet style of the period to that of the symphony. In one source they appear as two-movement works, the fourth quartet for example being a transcription of the first and second movements of a Monn *sinfonia da chiesa*, while the sixth is similarly derived from a symphony. The variety of scoring found in different sources of certain works at this time suggests that there was as yet little general interest in the particular way in which four solo strings could create a fully realized texture. The fifth 'quartet' of Haydn's op.1 as published is in fact a symphony with the wind parts omitted; of his op.2, nos.3 and 5 also exist as sextets with wind instruments, a reflection of the flexible performing practices of the time. Some publishers issued these early quartets with figured bass parts, and for the most part no great harm is done to their musical content by performance with multiple strings and the addition of a keyboard continuo. Nevertheless, a comparison of op.1 no.5 with the remainder of that set shows that Haydn, even in these early pieces, differentiated between the style of writing appropriate in a symphony and that suited to a quartet. Moreover, the five-movement structure with two minuets of the real quartets reflects their origins in the divertimento or in serenades for solo instruments unsupported by a continuo which, in outdoor serenades at any rate, would have been impracticable. In whatever manner they were presented by publishers and performers of his day, there is no doubt that Haydn intended most of these pieces to be played by an instrumental group corresponding to the string quartet as the term is now understood.

Reflecting the various origins of the string quartet, structures in the 1750s and 1760s show great variety: F. X. Richter's six quartets op.5 (c1765–7) are three-movement works, and nos.3 and 4 have minuet finales. The viola and cello parts have considerable prominence in a texture which is frequently rather conservatively contrapuntal: polyphony, once thought to have been resurrected by Haydn only in his op.20, in fact remained a fairly regular feature in chamber music of this period of transition between the Baroque and Classical eras. Works by other Mannheim composers (DTB, xxvii–xxviii, Jg.xv–xvi) such as Holzbauer, Wendling, Giuseppe Toeschi, Carl Stamitz and Christian Cannabich vary between two, three and four movements. Four-movement divertimentos are found, for instance, in the work of the Viennese composer and violinist Starzer (DTÖ, xxi, Jg.xv/2) in which a genuine interplay between the instruments is becoming evident.

There is no figured bass in Starzer's quartets, and the disappearance of the continuo part is a feature of other works of the 1750s and 1760s apart from those of Haydn and Starzer (Boccherini op.1, Sacchini op.2, Vanhal op.3). The lowest part generally continues to be designated 'Basso' until the 1770s, but this does not necessarily imply that in performance the cello was doubled or replaced by a double bass. In music of the Viennese orbit in particular the term 'Basso' was often used in pieces described as divertimentos, though it must be remembered that in this area 'divertimento' was a term applied to much solo chamber or keyboard music, not necessarily with the extended structure of five or more movements that came to be characteristic of the Classical divertimento. Haydn, who called his early piano sonatas 'divertimento', continued to describe his four-movement quartets up to op.20 as 'divertimenti a quattro'; other composers used similar terminology (including the term 'quadro') for works close to the Classical string quartet.

2. HAYDN, MOZART AND THEIR CONTEMPORARIES. As was the case with the symphony, the early Viennese string quartet often retained stylistic features of Baroque forms such as the trio sonata. With his op.9 (1769–70), which Haydn later came to regard as marking the beginning of his series of true string quartets, a four-movement scheme was adopted with a generally well-distributed four-part texture for a self-sufficient group of solo strings embodying that give and take of theme and motif which is the essence of the true quartet style. Though sharing in some of these developments composers like Richter and Starzer, F. X. Dušek in his quartets of the 1760s, or Holzbauer in his F minor Quartet (EDM, 1st ser., xxiv – which nevertheless still

clings to the old title of *sonata da camera*), cannot affect Haydn's pre-eminence, displayed most powerfully in a work like the D minor Quartet op.9 no.4.

Concertante elements remained prominent in the quartets of the 1760s and 1770s, particularly in the rich cantilenas of slow movements conceived in the vein of arias, sometimes even with cadenzas. At the opposite pole was the use of contrapuntal devices, including fugue, which inevitably secured near equality of part-writing. In Monn's quartets the fugues are very much a survival of the polyphonic second movement of the *sonata da chiesa*. In the works of Kraus, Albrechtsberger (*Six quatuors en fugue*, DTÖ, xxxiii, Jg.xvi/2), Michael Haydn, Wagenseil and others the fugal movements are variously placed. The first of Leopold Gassmann's *Quartetti* has a fugal third movement. Each of Ordonez's six quartets op.2, published in the 1770s, has a fugal second movement, except one, where the finale is a sonata-form movement incorporating fugal treatment, a scheme found also in Michael Haydn and later in Mozart's K387. The fugues on two, three and four subjects that constitute the finales of Haydn's op.20 nos.5, 6 and 2 respectively may seem somewhat selfconscious, but their function in Haydn's development was crucial: they helped to reorientate his thinking towards matters vital to the string quartet – the melodic and contrapuntal freedom of the bass line and the removal of any suggestion that the quartet, emerging as it did during the *galant* period, should be tied in texture to a concept deriving solely from *galant* homophony.

After the experimentalism of opp.9, 17 and 20 Haydn achieved in his op.33 quartets, written as he declared 'in a new and special way', a clarity of structure and balance of texture of which he rarely lost sight in later works. The opening of the development section of the

String quartet: silhouette, c1750

first movement of op.33 no.2 is a model of lucid thinking in four parts of a kind perhaps only to be realized after the fugal experiments of op.20 (see ex.2). In op.33 the scherzo is introduced, though not until op.77 did Haydn write scherzos of the cast primarily associated, through Beethoven, with the form. Haydn's later quartets remain essentially true chamber music though, as in the symphonies, concertante elements were never wholly suppressed: the quartets of opp.54, 55 and 64 allowed opportunities for Tost's brilliant manner of performing, and in opp.71 and 74 the use of arresting introductions and a more extrovert and forceful style of writing has been related to the possibility of the works' being conceived for public performance in London. In op.76 a new experimentalism appears, with features anticipating Beethoven: the fragmentation between the four instruments of what is really a single-line texture at the *più allegro* in the finale of op.76 no.4 or before the recapitulation in the Menuetto of op.76 no.6 foreshadow divided passages in Beethoven's op.59 no.2 and near the close of the Alla Tedesca in his op.130. The Allegretto that opens Haydn's op.76 no.5 is an entirely original structure which, with the variations and fugue and fantasia of op.76 no.6, shows how far Haydn was prepared to move from traditional patterns in a four-movement scheme.

Although no contemporary other than Mozart reached the level achieved and sustained by Haydn in the medium, their quartets are simply the high points in an intensive cultivation of the string quartet in Vienna in the last quarter of the 18th century, which made it a major preoccupation of composers, publishers and performers alike. Contributing to this were Wagenseil, Ordonez, Vanhal, Haydn's pupil Pleyel, Gyrowetz and Dittersdorf, among whom the prolific Vanhal (over 100 quartets) and Ordonez (over 30) produced work by no means negligible in quality.

Mozart's quartets found their roots initially in the other main point of origin of the string quartet, in the Milanese style established by Sammartini whose quartets of the 1760s, with their 'singing allegros' dominated by the first violin, influenced Mozart's work for some time, especially in K155–60. Mozart's quartets of 1773 (K168–73), however, are Viennese rather than Milanese, though it is arguable that Ordonez and such lesser figures exerted as powerful an influence in their shaping as did Haydn. It was not until the set of quartets dedicated to Haydn was written that Mozart fully assimilated the influence of Haydn's op.33, and in so doing he produced a group of works greater than their model, key works in Mozart's output and in the literature of the string quartet as a whole. In their turn they undoubtedly helped to shape some features of Haydn's later quartet style such as the more chromatic idiom found in op.55 no.3.

Elsewhere in Europe there were fewer developments of real importance in the string quartet literature of the 18th century. In the second half of the century London proved a receptive centre for repertories imported from Mannheim and Paris and for the activities of émigré composers such as J. C. Bach, C. F. Abel, Kammel and Giardini. Although Giardini composed a considerable number of string quartets (they constitute his opp.21, 22, 23, 25 and 29) a publication such as the *Six Quartettos for a German Flute, Violin, Tenor, and Bass, or Two Violins, a Tenor and Bass, by Messrs. Bach, Abel, & Giardini* (1777) is more typical, with its preference for a mixed ensemble including a woodwind instrument, a tendency that had previously been noticeable in the chamber music of the Mannheim school.

Following the example of Italian singers, who sold their talents in every quarter of Europe, many of the leading Italian instrumentalists too found it worth their while to travel north. In Italy the string quartet scarcely advanced at all in the century after Sammartini, since composers such as Giardini, Cirri, Cambini and Boccherini preferred to live and work in cities like Vienna, Paris, London and Madrid, and those who did not actually emigrate often spent prolonged periods abroad (e.g. Sacchini and Pugnani). All these composers adopted a style of quartet writing which, like that of Sammartini, placed emphasis on the first violin part.

Ex.2 Haydn: op.33 no.2, 1st movt

This species of composition was to develop into the *quatuor brillant*, which was scarcely more than an accompanied solo throughout with passages of a purely mechanical brilliance and opportunities for cadenzas exactly as might appear in a concerto. Cambini wrote many works of this type, which was taken up by other composers in France (Dalayrac, Davaux, Fodor, Gossec, Viotti) and, transplanted by Pierre Rode and others to Germany, was adopted by Romberg, Spohr, Kreutzer and others, flourishing well into the 19th century. The rudimentary interest of the lower parts typical of such works is illustrated in ex.3, from the first movement of Spohr's *Quatuor brillant* in E op.43. In a chapter 'Vom Vortrage des Quartetts' in his *Violinschule*, Spohr drew a clear distinction between the *quatuor brillant* and the 'regular' quartet, a distinction carefully made in his own published quartets. He acknowledged that a true performance of any of the parts in a 'regular' quartet (i.e. the motivically elaborated kind developed by Haydn and Mozart) required the most refined taste and knowledge, and would have its exponents study the theory of composition to develop that.

Distinct from the *quatuor brillant* (which sometimes took the form of the *quatuor d'airs connus* or the *quatuor d'airs variés*) was the QUATUOR CONCERTANT, developed largely in Paris in the 1770s possibly as a result of the powerful influence of the *symphonie concertante* at that time. In the *quatuor concertant* the instruments are treated in turn in a solo fashion, the others meanwhile being relegated to the function of accompaniment, though passages in dialogue are not ruled out. Clearly, if the accompaniment figurations are motivically elaborated this type of quartet approximates to the genuine rapport between the four parts which was Haydn's ideal; some of Haydn's own quartets were in fact published in Paris as *quatuors concertants*. Against this historical background Mozart's so-called 'Prussian' quartets (K575, 589 and 590), with their prominent cello parts, can be seen as a fusion of the *concertant* and *brillant* concepts.

The prolific Cambini subscribed to the genre of the *quatuor concertant* too, but the most significant of the Italians in the Parisian musical world towards the end of the century was Luigi Boccherini, for although he was resident there only briefly, much of his chamber music was published in Paris. His op.2 quartets (G159–64, 1761) are *galant* in style and movement structure, deriving much from his fellow countrymen Sammartini and Pugnani. His structures vary from the two-movement 'quartettini' of op.26 (G195–200, 1778), through the three-movement cycles finishing with minuets (op.2 and op.8, G165–70), to the four-movement quartets that appear in the sets op.9 (G171–6, 1770) and op.32 (G201–6, 1780), the latter with finales in sonata or rondo form and opportunities for cadenzas in the shape of 'capricci' for the first violin. In the *Quartetti concertanti* op.24 (G189–94) of 1777, in particular, the cello part is treated in a brilliant style.

Boccherini's idiom is typically Italian in its suavity of melody. He remained virtually oblivious of, or unconcerned by, Haydn's development of the quartet. Boccherini's quartets of op.58 (G242–7, 1799) do not differ significantly in outlook from those of 1761: during the selfsame period in which Haydn had dynamically revolutionized the form Boccherini was content with a virtually static art, albeit one of abundant charm and grace.

3. 19TH CENTURY. Viennese musical life had brought the string quartet to fruition in the later years of the 18th century; in the first quarter of the 19th Vienna remained a most productive centre and nourished the most important developments in the medium. Meeting at the house of E. A. Förster, himself a prolific composer of chamber music (see DTÖ, lxvii, Jg.xxxv/1), the musicians who were to form the Schuppanzigh Quartet played the works of one guest, Haydn, and gave another, the young Beethoven, the experience of fine perform-

Ex.3 Spohr: *Quatuor brillant* in E op.43, 1st movt

ances of the Viennese repertory. Although in op.18 Beethoven worked largely within the framework of an established convention, the first of the set, in F, already hints at the expansion of scale which marks the Razumovsky Quartets, op.59, as belonging to the post-*Eroica* period, while the fourth, in C minor, indulges in batteries of chords in the first movement which, like some features of Haydn's opp.71 and 74, seem to move the string quartet from the chamber towards the public hall with its demands for a broader rhetoric and more emphatic gestures.

In the string quartet, as in other forms, it was Beethoven's middle-period works which marked the point of departure for many later composers of the 19th century. Their expanded scale may be seen in such features as the imposing slow introductions of op.59 no.3 and op.74 or the scherzos with a five- rather than a three-part structure of op.59 no.2, op.74 and op.95, characteristics shared with Beethoven's other instrumental music of the period. Counterpoint assumes a new dramatic purpose in the quartet, lending a fierce driving quality to the finale of op.59 no.3 far removed from the formality of Haydn's fugal finales in op.20 or the humorous alternation of homophony and polyphony in Mozart's K387. But Beethoven's preoccupation with such extrovert qualities did not lead him to ignore fine detail: the slow movements of the middle-period quartets, perhaps that of op.74 especially, are scored with an ear for richly sonorous and elaborated textures.

The late quartets show no decline in the keenness of Beethoven's imagination for sonorities, indeed rather the reverse, for they bring together textures at one moment lean and spare, suggesting rather than stating, at the next a profusion of lavishly wrought detail in which new effects may be achieved by the displacement of instruments from their normal tessitura, as in the finale of op.132 (ex.4). Perhaps it is significant that variation movements play an increasingly important part in the formal concepts of these quartets for variations elicit from a composer the maximum textural contrasts.

Beethoven's textures are affected too by his predilection for a more polyphonic musical thought that is a characteristic of all his late works but perhaps finds its most natural outlet in the late quartets. It is evident not only in movements of an overtly fugal character (opp.131, 133), but in many passages in other types of movement such as the opening Allegro of op.127, where Beethoven's thought becomes an indivisible entity of four parts.

The formal concepts of these late quartets were the product of the same fresh thinking that moulded the piano sonatas of the third period. Rather than merely continue the expansion of individual movements in a four-movement scheme after op.127, Beethoven adopted five-, six- and then seven-movement schemes for opp.132, 130 and 131 successively, returning to four movements only for the comparatively short op.135. The sonata form movement is displaced to the end of the cycle in op.131, the finale thus acquiring a greater weight; if op.130 is played with the original *Grosse Fuge* finale a similar shift in structural emphasis is even more apparent in that work. The larger issue of whether opp.132, 130 and 131 (and some would include also opp.127 and 135) constitute a cycle has been much debated, but it is doubtful whether Beethoven viewed them as such.

The range of Beethoven's thought in the late quartets

Ex.4 Beethoven: op. 132, Finale
Allegro appassionato

is immense, outdistancing that of his contemporaries in every respect. Even within individual quartets Beethoven encompasses both deep seriousness and lighthearted gaiety without incongruity. The Alla Tedesca stands beside the Cavatina in the B♭ quartet, and the complex musical ratiocination of its first movement is followed by a terse and abrupt little scherzo, over in a few moments. In op.135 Beethoven's most crabbed scherzo and wildly grotesque trio are prelude to a movement of grave spirituality and tender beauty. The galloping storm clouds of the finale of op.131 suddenly break to reveal a beatific vision. Mahler's view of the symphony was of an all-embracing world of sound; Beethoven's late quartets, with their violent contrasts, their mixture of the earthy and the sublime, the serious and the comical, their searching exploration of every mood, had already gone far towards creating such a universe in their own genre.

Almost inevitably, the achievement of the Romantics in the string quartet was less, both quantitatively and qualitatively. In conceptual terms the 19th century had little to add to Beethoven's forward-looking late quartets, and in many respects other than that of musical idiom it retreated to the stance of his middle period. Even Mendelssohn's borrowings in his opp.12 and 13 capture the letter rather than the elusive spirit of Beethoven's late quartets. Schubert and Mendelssohn both started with the advantage of being good string players themselves and their earlier works were written to answer the needs of their own domestic musical circles. Mendelssohn's juvenilia include nine fugues and five sinfonias for string quartet; the sinfonias together with Schubert's early quartets are often orchestral in style and show that even at this date the distinction that Haydn had begun to draw in his opp.1 and 2 was still not always very carefully observed.

In his later and much more idiomatic quartets Schubert adhered to the traditional four-movement design, contributing his own individuality in such matters as the exploitation of a more lyrical style derived partly from the incorporation of material from songs and partly from the use of patterns of accompaniment (such as that at the beginning of the A minor Quartet D804) that would seem perfectly natural in a lied.

Schubert could have been influenced by Beethoven's late quartets only in his G major Quartet D887, but its almost virtuoso richness and elaboration of texture, with the cello in its high register in the trio and at the opening of the Andante, are more likely to reflect his own searching Romantic spirit than to be the result of any direct Beethovenian influence. The outburst in the slow movement (ex.5), suggestive of an orchestra with trombones and trumpets, is similarly a typically Romantic treatment of the medium in its attempt to capture or suggest another sound world through that of the string quartet.

This deliberate mimesis is quite different in character from the orchestral traits of Schubert's early works which resulted rather from a confusion of idioms. But in some Romantic quartets orchestral qualities of writing are pursued to a fault. The tremolos so prominent at the opening of Mendelssohn's D major Quartet op.44 no.1 and in his F minor Quartet op.80 aim at intensity but capture only a sense of spurious industry. In movements such as the Intermezzo of his op.13 quartet, however, and in the fleet and delicate scherzos of several other works Mendelssohn added an element as important to the string quartet as to other genres. Perhaps it was inevitable in view of the Romantic preoccupation with the piano that pianistic forms and idioms should be assimilated to other media. The slow movement of Mendelssohn's E minor Quartet op.44 no.2 is to all intents and purposes a Song without Words in conception. Pianistic figurations play an even larger part in Schumann's quartets: the scoring of the opening of the slow movement of his op.41 no.1 looks almost like a transcription of a piano piece. On the other hand, Schumann's liking for ties from weak to strong beats becomes an effect less rhythmically confusing on strings than on the piano since string players can stress the tied strong beat in a way that a pianist cannot. In the first movement of op.41 no.3 Schumann added a typical offbeat figuration to devices of quartet accompaniment (ex.6) – another example of a successful transfer of a pianistic idiom.

Ex.5 Schubert: Quartet in G D887, 2nd movt

Ex.6 Schumann: op. 41 no.3, 1st movt

Thematic integration in cyclic works is less frequent in the string quartet of the first half of the 19th century than in the symphony, though Boccherini had used certain cyclic devices in his quartets. Mendelssohn followed some of Beethoven's leads in this direction in a work like the Eb Quartet op.12. Berwald's Eb Quartet (1849) is interesting for its arch form in which a slow movement is inserted before the recapitulation of a sonata-form movement, and that slow movement itself is divided to contain a scherzo. Although Liszt's Piano Sonata in B minor similarly adopts a radically new approach to sonata structure, Berwald's experiments have few parallels in chamber music until the quartet of César Franck.

It was a feature of Romanticism that composers continued to cultivate, often in a rather selfconscious manner, Classical forms like the sonata and string quartet. But genuine creative interest in them lessened and there was a falling away from the peak of production of string quartets achieved in Vienna in the late 18th century. Many lesser composers in Germany tended to follow the example of Spohr, writing variations on popular airs, potpourris, and *quatuors brillants*. In Italy composers like Paisiello, Capuzzi and Rolla, who had remained in their home country rather than follow so many of their fellow countrymen abroad, pursued the style of Boccherini and Cambini. Among Donizetti's early works are some quartets in the manner of Haydn but after that the 19th century in Italy is almost a blank but for Verdi's E minor Quartet of 1873.

In France few composers escaped the continuing tyranny of the *quatuor brillant*; among those who attempted to do so Reicha and Onslow rivalled the productivity of the 18th century with 20 and 35 quartets each respectively. The quartets of M. A. Guénin and Cherubini too rise above the average, the latter's particularly in their scherzos. Schumann admired that of Cherubini's E♭ Quartet, a movement whose nimbleness could well have influenced and helped to shape what has always been regarded as a uniquely Mendelssohnian contribution to instrumental music. The presence in Paris of Arriaga, the only Spanish composer of the period to make any significant contribution to chamber music, reminds one (taken with names like Reicha, Onslow and Cherubini) of the extent to which Paris remained in so many ways a centre of musical internationalism.

To composers of the second half of the 19th century preoccupied with the more grandiose conceptions of symphony and symphonic poem the intimate forms of chamber music and of the string quartet in particular seemed to present few possibilities. So abstract a medium offered limited resources for programme music: Raff, whose symphonies are mostly programmatic works, provides a rare instance of such a quartet in his 'Die schöne Müllerin' op.192 no.2, based (like Schubert's song cycle) on Müller's poems. But Smetana's E minor Quartet, 'From my Life' (1876), and its successor of 1882 remain the only significant examples – though it is worth remembering that Wagner's *Siegfried Idyll* started life as a string quartet. Wolf's *Italian Serenade* (1887), one of a mere handful of short or single-movement pieces for quartet, uses the medium most felicitously in a work far removed from the usual sonata-form concept though the excellence of the result perhaps seems less surprising when the quartet-like texture of the accompaniments to some of the songs is remembered.

Inevitably, the quartet found stronger adherents in Germany among composers such as Brahms and Reger who resisted the 'music of the future' and hoped to continue the Classical tradition. But the demand of the period for rich and opulent textures was more easily satisfied in ensembles larger than the string quartet. His intermezzo-like movements, akin in character to some of his late piano pieces, are Brahms's most individual contribution to the quartet concept, though the B♭ Quartet op.67 is notable for the way in which in the

third movement Brahms did for the viola what Mozart had done for the cello in his 'Prussian' quartets.

As in the case of the symphony, the late 19th century was not prodigal with ideas for the development of the quartet as a genre. Apart from an increasing tendency to treat the form cyclically the most obvious shift in emphasis resulted from the introduction of nationalist elements. The dumka, furiant, *sousedská*, polka, *skočná* and other dances provided some of the strongest elements in the quartets of Smetana and Dvořák. From the beginning of the 19th century chamber music in Russia by composers like Alyabyev and Glinka had subscribed to the rather trivial *brillant* tradition, the result of its performance primarily at soirées where musical culture was largely of the imported variety and the music little more than a sparkling decoration for a social event. The ten string quartets of Anton Rubinstein are fluent works in a Germanic style but at least show that the composition of serious chamber music was becoming possible. In spite of Balakirev's view that no Russian composer would achieve anything worthwhile in such an outworn medium several members of The Five, Cui, Rimsky-Korsakov and Borodin, turned to it and brought specifically Russian qualities to their quartets as to a lesser extent did Tchaikovsky, Taneyev and Glazunov.

Both Borodin and Tchaikovsky introduced Russian folktunes into their quartets as well as on occasions that exoticism which in musical terms represents the Russian view of the East. The search for brilliance of style in many late 19th-century nationalist works often led to an exaggeratedly orchestral manner of writing and occasionally to novel attempts to exploit colouristic effects such as the use of natural harmonics in the trio of Borodin's Quartet no.1 (ex.7).

Ex.7 Borodin: Quartet no.1, Trio

The revival of chamber music in France owed a good deal to César Franck, whose D major Quartet (1889), the last of his chamber compositions, was completed after much revision aimed at perfecting a concept of cyclic form which Franck had been steadily approaching in earlier works in common with other 19th-century composers. Franck's motto theme articulates the sonata form of the first movement though it is scarcely apparent in the scherzo and slow movement; in the finale, after a Beethoven-like review of the material of the earlier movements, it assumes a dominating role. To Vincent d'Indy this was one of the great masterworks of the 19th century, a seminal influence on his own music and, through his teaching at the Schola Cantorum, on many French and other composers of the late 19th century and the early 20th in their chamber compositions and other works too.

4. 20TH CENTURY. The shift of emphasis away from the string quartet in the 19th century has not been reversed in the 20th, but the medium has nevertheless continued to attract composers who have responded to the severity of its challenge with a production of modest proportions but often of high quality. The very absence of the colouristic possibilities of a mixed ensemble or orchestra has stimulated rather than suppressed invention, and the existence of many professional quartets of great excellence has encouraged composers to write works demanding to both players and listeners if in the process domestic music for the amateur has been largely ignored.

Interest in the string quartet has been more evenly distributed than at earlier periods. Since Debussy and Ravel, French composers have not been successful in writing string quartets that have achieved a similar currency to theirs outside their own country but Milhaud, Fauré, Roussel, Honegger, Ibert and Françaix added significantly to the repertory until members of the group La Jeune France headed by Messiaen turned primarily to mixed combinations in their chamber music, as did Boulez before starting his *Livre pour quatuor*. Janáček and Bartók continued the process of emancipation from Classical forms and their works taken together represent an eastern European contribution to the development of the quartet which is one of the most important in the 20th century. Bartók's six quartets were written between 1908 and 1939. In their continuous exploration of musical form they can be compared with Beethoven's late quartets with which indeed they share other features such as the combination of serious and popular elements, excursions into the grotesque, a virtuoso handling of textures and a strong emphasis on contrapuntal thinking.

In Russia several composers have been prolific in their output of string quartets though generally in idioms less advanced than that of Bartók. Myaskovsky's 13 quartets, like his symphonies, have made little impact outside the USSR; nor indeed has the chamber music of better-known figures such as Kabalevsky and Khachaturian. But Prokofiev has fared better and the 15 quartets of Shostakovich, if less important than those of Bartók, represent one of the most important contributions to the form of the 20th century.

In Germany Hindemith brought the changing styles of the first half century to the quartet, culminating in that particular brand of neo-classicism which marks his own work and that of many followers. More far-reaching in their influence was the work of Schoenberg and other members of the Second Viennese School, particularly in their serial works. Schoenberg's influence continued to be felt in Austria in the quartets of H. E. Apostel but pupils such as Krenek, Toch, Pisk and Wellesz carried it abroad though none of their quartets seems destined to enter the repertory as Schoenberg's and Berg's have done.

In northern Europe composers had clung to largely traditional procedures or inflected them with an individuality that was perhaps not radical. In England Stanford, Parry, Mackenzie and others of the 19th century had trodden a basically conventional path in their

chamber music; the Cobbett prizes elicited some interesting experiments in form but little of musical value. They did, however, help to make the public more aware of chamber music and by the 1930s English composers were turning increasingly to the string quartet. A high level was achieved by Walton, Bliss, Rubbra, Rawsthorne and Berkeley but the most individual works likely to be longest remembered are those of Britten and Tippett. Many of that generation, including Lutyens, Rainier and émigrés like Seiber and Gerhard, turned to serial techniques but symptomatic of the subsequent reaction against this are works such as Maxwell Davies's quartet of 1961, which contains aleatory elements within a firmly controlled framework.

The course of events elsewhere has been similar. At the turn of the century Scandinavian composers such as Nielsen and Sibelius made small but characteristic contributions to the repertory; subsequently Valen and Vagn Holmboe turned to serial writing in their quartets but many of the younger generation are now adopting other techniques in which collage and parody play a considerable part. In Italy there was a somewhat artificial revival of interest in the quartet largely due to the patronage of Elizabeth Sprague Coolidge rather than to the development of a flourishing amateur or professional chamber music life. Quartets by Petrassi and Malipiero were a product of this, those of the latter often bearing titles (such as *Rispetti e strambotti*) derived from poetic forms. Berio's String Quartet of 1955, however, adopts a post-Webernian manner with a strong emphasis on texture and colour.

In the USA such quartets as were written in the 19th century were usually by European émigrés or by Americans who deliberately adopted a similar, primarily German-orientated tradition. Few attempted to follow the path of Ives in his desire to create a more genuinely national music, and after the emigration of figures like Stravinsky, Schoenberg, Bartók, Hindemith, Bloch and others composers were inclined to follow neo-classical, atonalist or nationalist tendencies and group themselves about the appropriate figurehead. Prominent among quartet composers of the 20th century are Harris, William Schumann, Piston and Barber, who already had an independent stance. Among the neo-classicists may be grouped Ross Lee Finney, Persichetti, Porter and Benjamin Lees (the last of whom also wrote a concerto in 1964 with a string quartet as concertino group, following in the isolated steps of Spohr's op.131 and Elgar's Introduction and Allegro). Subsequently many composers adopted serial methods either wholeheartedly or in the more limited sense of giving a serial basis to their thematic material.

With the rapidly changing idioms of the 20th century the formal concept of the string quartet, as with other media, has often shifted away from the basically four-movement structure that was the legacy of the 19th century. Where multi-movement structures have been retained these have often been drawn together by cyclical methods deriving from 19th-century techniques of thematic metamorphosis or the example of Franck, or resulting necessarily from the application of serial techniques. The quartet of Debussy, though written in 1893, seems to usher in the 20th-century string quartet. Like Ravel's quartet it lies firmly within the concept of form deriving from Franck as indeed does Bartók's Quartet no.1 and many other early 20th-century works.

Programmatic intentions have not been much more

evident in the 20th-century quartet than they were in that of the 19th century though clearly Janáček's two quartets carry on the Czech tradition of Smetana in this respect, while Ives's Quartet no.2, with its movements entitled 'Discussions', 'Arguments' and 'The Call of the Mountains', attempts to create a new American one. By and large, however, the quartet has remained staunchly a vehicle for abstract musical thought though this has been expressed in forms of great diversity. Each of Bartók's six quartets follows a different plan: no.1 is in

any length and none of the Bagatelles exceeds ten bars in duration. To Webern the expansive canvas of Classical sonata form was largely irrelevant. His one string quartet on a larger scale, op.28, is cast in three movements each of which is concerned with canonic developments of a note row based on the B–A–C–H motif. Webern's pointillist idiom, so different from the neo-romantic lines of Schoenberg, led to a radically different texture of which the opening of the last movement of op.28 is typical (ex.8).

Ex.8 Webern: op.28, last movt

three motto-linked movements in successively faster tempos, no.2 makes a centrepiece of its scherzo and ends with a bleak slow movement, nos.3–5 have their movements in arch forms, and no.6 uses a variably scored motto to introduce a Vivace, a March and a Burlesque. Shostakovich's forms too are remarkably free. No.2 consists of an Overture, Recitative and Romance, Waltz and Theme and Variations. Nos.9 and 11 have respectively five and seven linked movements, while the last, no.15, consists of a succession of six elegiac slow movements. The character of individual movements is widely varied too: there are impressive passacaglias in nos.6 and 10, and no.11 includes an Etude and a Humoresque.

Single-movement structures remain rare in string quartets. Perhaps following up his own *Verklärte Nacht* sextet, Schoenberg achieved this in his op.7 quartet by expanding a sonata scheme so as to absorb the elements of scherzo, slow movement and rondo finale (cf Berwald), but he did not return to that plan. Genuinely single-movement works like Blacher's *Epitaph* op.4 ('Zum Gedächtnis von Franz Kafka') and Penderecki's quartets are exceptional.

Also comparatively rare are groups of short movements forming a suite-like structure. Significant examples are the Three Pieces for string quartet of Stravinsky and Webern's Five Pieces op.5 and Six Bagatelles op.9. Webern's microstructure in these pieces is so intensely wrought that few expand to movements of

Berg's musical idiom, however, led him to develop his works on a much more expansive time scale. Although his op.3 quartet consists of only two movements, in the *Lyrische Suite* he adopted a scheme of six movements, alternately quick and slow but planned in such a way that in the course of the work the quick movements get quicker and the slow movements get slower, thus continuously increasing the tension: 1 – Allegretto gioviale; 2 – Andante amoroso; 3 – Allegro misterioso; 4 – Adagio appassionato; 5 – Presto delirando; 6 – Largo desolato.

Side by side with this diversification of form in the string quartet the 20th century has seen a considerable expansion in the range of effects and textures demanded by composers. Even in Debussy's Quartet (1893) it is the kaleidoscopic changes of texture and the textures themselves rather than its cyclical form that make it important for 20th-century developments. Ravel's, particularly in the slow movement, goes much further in its pursuit of expressiveness: thematically and motivically the movement is tightly controlled but the experience to the listener is a purely sensory one, like the fragrances of a garden, some unique and some recalling those of another place, but all blended into an exquisite and heady perfume.

Both Janáček and Bartók, significantly, continued to widen the range of expressive effects. The former's style of development, with its piling up of short phrases and creation of textures by the almost manic repetition of tiny motifs, is very characteristic, and undermined the

Classical process of development in its own way as much as Debussy's methods did. Bartók enlarged the colouristic possibilities of the string quartet considerably, calling for great virtuosity from the players, for the use of harmonics, col legno, and a wide range of pizzicato effects, and occasionally the use of quarter-tones as in the Burletta of no.6.

In some respects the weight of Classical tradition and certain apparent limitations in the technical possibilities of string instruments have meant that the string quartet has resisted radical change and escaped experimentation to a greater extent than most other media in the 20th century. But as early as 1922, in Hindemith's Quartet no.2, the second violin is required to reiterate a figure without regard to the tempo in the other parts, a technique tentatively foreshadowing the development of aleatory devices such as began to appear in works like Gunther Schuller's Quartet no.1 (1957) with its improvisation on groups of notes from the series in the last movement.

Occasionally the voice has been added to the string quartet just as it was added earlier in the symphony (e.g. Schoenberg's op.10 and Milhaud's Quartet no.3 – a two-movement work in memory of the poet Léo Latil, whose verses are sung by a soprano). Whether the resulting ensemble should still be considered as a string quartet is another matter. Equally fundamental is the shift away from the Classical concept of a balanced and unified ensemble of four instruments. Elliott Carter's Quartet no.2 (1959) is concerned with the superposition of distinctive types of expression in the four instruments – bravura in the first violin, espressivo in the viola, and so on. The sections of the work are linked by cadenzas for the first violin, the viola and the cello, and the players are spatially separated to clarify the different characteristics of the music allotted to each. Carter's Quartet no.3 (1971) is similarly concerned with the interaction between contrasted material, though in this instance the parts are grouped as two duos, first violin and cello on the one hand, and second violin and viola on the other.

Some of the most radical rethinking of string quartet composition has, however, come from Poland, where, in common with other European countries a period of flirtation with 12-note techniques has been followed by a reaction against them. In his two quartets (1960, 1968) Penderecki attempted to develop the vocabulary of unusual sounds that can be produced from the instruments using, for example, quarter-tones and indeterminate pitches, notes produced between the bridge and tailpiece, bowing on the string-holder itself, and the drumming effects of the open hand, the finger-nails, or the frog of the bow either on the strings or on the belly of the instrument. Glissando effects are employed too, and a controlled vibrato ranging from a rapid pulsation to a very slow one with a quarter-tone oscillation. Special notational symbols are used to represent these requirements (ex.9). The effects used previously in a limited way by Bartók and Shostakovich have thus been magnified and enlarged in scope to

Ex.9 Penderecki: String Quartet no.2

*) mit der Fingerkuppe auf den Steg schlagen
tap with finger-tip on the bridge

become the basic terms of Penderecki's musical language (though pitched notes are still used). Form in such music is largely concerned with the effective juxtaposition of textures achieved by these means, their recall and their dynamic manipulation.

From tentative beginnings the string quartet has evolved for just over 200 years. During that period it has been the chosen medium for some of the most profound and personal musical thought at several points in history. To many the Classical Viennese repertory represents the highest peak achieved in chamber music, when composers wholly in tune with its ideals arguably entrusted their finest thoughts to the string quartet. Its future is uncertain. The support now given to quartets of a high professional standing, for example by universities in the USA and in Britain, might suggest that it is assured. But the attempts to alter radically its expressive potential could prove to be its undermining. In 1924 Dyson wrote of the second of Stravinsky's Three Pieces that 'If this type of passage has any proper place in the art of the string quartet, then the end is near'. Yet equally if it fails to develop such new potential the end of the string quartet is quite certain: it will join the trio-sonata and other forms with a similarly glorious repertory as part of musical history.

BIBLIOGRAPHY

CATALOGUES
W. Altmann: *Handbuch für Streichquartettspieler* (Berlin, 1927–31)
——: *Kleiner Führer durch die Streichquartette für Haus und Schule* (Berlin, 1950)

GENERAL LITERATURE
E. Sauzay: *Haydn, Mozart, Beethoven: étude sur le quatuor* (Paris, 1861)
A. Ehrlich: *Das Streichquartett in Wort und Bild* (Leipzig, 1898)
E. J. Dent: 'The Earliest String Quartet', *MMR*, xxxiii (1903), 202
E. Goossens: 'The String Quartet since Brahms', *ML*, iii (1922), 335
R. Clarke: 'The History of the Viola in Quartet Writing', *ML*, iv (1923), 6
J. Brown: 'The Amateur String Quartet', *MT*, lxviii (1927), 508, 600, 714, 798, 907, 1078
A. E. Hull: 'The Earliest Known String Quartet', *MQ*, xv (1929), 72
M. Pincherle: 'On the Origins of the String Quartet', *MQ*, xv (1929), 77
H. Mersmann: *Kammermusik* (Leipzig, 1930–33)
H. Rothweiler: *Zur Entwicklung des Streichquartetts im Rahmen der Kammermusik des 18. Jahrhunderts* (Tübingen, 1934)
U. Lehmann: *Deutsches und italienisches Wesen in der Vorgeschichte des klassischen Streichquartetts* (Würzburg, 1939)
P. Schlüter: *Die Anfänge des modernen Streichquartetts* (Bleicherode, 1939)
M. Pincherle: *Les instruments du quatuor* (Paris, 1948)
J. Kramarz: *Das Streichquartett* (Wolfenbüttel, 1961)
L. Finscher: 'Zur Sozialgeschichte des klassischen Streichquartetts', *GfMKB, Kassel 1962*, 37
D. Klein: *Le quatuor à cordes français en 18e siècle* (diss., U. of Paris, 1970)
J. Levy: *The 'Quatuor concertant' in Paris in the Latter Half of the 18th Century* (diss., Stanford U., 1971)
C. Rosen: *The Classical Style: Haydn, Mozart, Beethoven* (London, 1971, 2/1972), 111ff
J. Webster: *The Bass Part in Joseph Haydn's String Quartets and in Austrian Chamber Music 1750–1780* (diss., Princeton U., 1973)
K. Geiringer: 'The Rise of Chamber Music', *NOHM*, vii (1973), 552
L. Finscher: *Studien zur Geschichte des Streichquartetts, i: Die Entstehung des klassischen Streichquartetts: von den Vorformen zur Grundlegung durch Joseph Haydn* (Kassel, 1974)

ON PERFORMANCE
L. Spohr: 'Vom Vortrage des Quartetts', *Violinschule* (Kassel, 1831), 246
E. Kornstein: 'How to Practise a String Quartet', *ML*, iii (1922), 329
A. Betti: 'Quartet Playing', *ML*, iv (1923), 1
A. Pochon: *A Progressive Method of String-quartet Playing* (New York, 1924)
M. D. Herter Norton: *String Quartet Playing* (New York, 1925, 2/1966)
J. Léner: *The Technique of String Quartet Playing* (London, 1935)
B. Aulich and E. Heimeran: *Das stillvergnügte Streichquartett* (Munich, 1936, 16/1964; Eng. trans., 2/1964)
L. Tertis: 'The String Quartet', *ML*, xxxi (1950), 148
A. Gertler: 'Advice to Young Quartet Players', *Score* (1951), no.5, p.19
A. Page: *Playing String Quartets* (London, 1964)
See also CHAMBER MUSIC and bibliographies on individual composers.

MICHAEL TILMOUTH

String quintet. A composition for five string instruments. The term is usually applied to works written since the mid-18th century rather than to consort music of the 16th and 17th centuries. The string quintet's early history runs parallel to that of the string quartet; there are certain works (e.g. by Mysliveček; see MAB, xxxi) in which a true chamber style, as distinct from an orchestral one, is not yet apparent.

The instrumental combination most often used consists of two violins, two violas and cello, a grouping that enables the viola to figure more prominently as a melody instrument, without its accompaniment being impoverished, than is possible in a string quartet. Before Mozart there was a tendency to treat the medium as an accompanied duet for first violin and first viola, and Mozart himself relied a good deal on this device in his early B♭ Quintet K174; it is by no means forgotten in the slow movement of K515, although in general Mozart's later string quintets realize much more fully the textural variety of which the combination is capable, such as antiphonal effects between upper and lower groupings of instruments, rich octave doublings of 3rds and 6ths, and real five-part polyphony, as well as the sort of fragmentation of texture found in the slow movement of K516. A quintet by Michael Haydn seems to have initiated Mozart's interest in the genre, and Mozart may also have encountered examples by Boccherini; but more important was his evident desire to bring to the string quintet the new techniques he had observed in Haydn's op.20 quartets. After the peak reached by Mozart, the quintets of Beethoven and Mendelssohn are disappointing, as in neither case do the composer's works in this medium represent a highpoint in his instrumental music. Bruckner, Niels Gade and Stanford wrote string quintets, but in the 19th century only Brahms's two are on a high level. Martinů and Milhaud are among the few 20th-century composers to have written for the medium.

The quintet for two violins, one viola and two cellos, with different textural symmetries and richer sonorities, has also been extensively cultivated. Its chief exponent in the 18th century was Boccherini, himself a cellist and (more significantly) employed by cello-playing patrons. His use of this combination enabled him to write brilliantly for the first cello without losing a real bass line. Quintets with two cellos were also written by Onslow, whose *Quintette de la balle* is a programmatic work recalling the hunting accident which led to his partial deafness. It is as likely to have been Onslow's quintets as Boccherini's that inspired the one towering masterpiece for this ensemble, Schubert's Quintet in C D956. The few examples composed since include one by Glazunov. Brahms's Piano Quintet in F minor was originally scored as a cello quintet, an origin that occasionally shows through in the final version.

A few string quintets are scored for two violins, viola, cello and double bass. Onslow, who apparently was convinced of the medium's effectiveness after hearing one of his own cello quintets with the second cello part played by the double bass virtuoso Dragonetti, again provides examples. The best-known quintet for this unusual group is undoubtedly Dvořák's op.77; there is also an early suite by Janáček for the combination.

BIBLIOGRAPHY

W. Altmann: *Handbuch für Streichquartettspieler*, iii (Berlin, 1928)
C. Rosen: *The Classical Style: Haydn, Mozart, Beethoven* (London, 1971, 2/1972), 264ff

MICHAEL TILMOUTH

String trio. A composition for three string instruments. The term is generally used to refer to works from the Classical period to the present, scored either for two violins and cello or for violin, viola and cello; many Renaissance consort pieces and Baroque sonatas, however, were also written for three string instruments, either viols or violins, with or without continuo (*see* SONATA, §II).

The trio for two violins and cello was an outgrowth of the Baroque trio sonata, and many such works in the mid-18th century bore the title 'sonata', including trios by J. G. Schwanenberger, J. F. Reichardt and C. A. Campioni (*Six Sonatas or Trio's*, c1764). There was a tendency at this time, as in much pre-Classical music, towards a texture in which the two violins were treated on more or less equal terms while the bass was used to provide harmonic support and a pulsating rhythm. In some cases (Campioni's sonatas and Pugnani's op.1, 1754) the bass part was still figured for keyboard continuo. In Schwanenberger's sonatas and in trios by Filtz, Haydn, J. C. and C. P. E. Bach, Boccherini and Dittersdorf, it is impossible to be certain whether or not a continuo instrument was still envisaged by the composer, although in the later examples by Boccherini this is most unlikely.

Johann Stamitz's op.1 and Christian Cannabich's op.3 (1766) were to be played 'ou à trois ou avec toutes l'orchestre', and are typical of many works published predominantly in Paris in the 1760s and 1770s. With Myslivecek's *Six Orchestra Trios* (London, 1768) and sets like Koczwara's op.5 and Vanhal's op.12 (both with optional horn parts), they are characteristic of a genre precariously balanced between orchestral and true chamber music, in which orchestral performance was either permissible or actually called for. (A similar flexibility in the medium of performance is found in the early history of the string quartet.)

During the 1770s and 1780s both the use of continuo and the possibility of orchestral performance were gradually dropped. Although the trio for two violins and cello was not wholly abandoned even during the 19th century, that for violin, viola and cello began to take precedence. Haydn seems to have been the first to use this combination, soon followed by Simon Le Duc (op.1, 1768), Boccherini (op.14, 1772) and Giardini (opp.17 and 20). The 1770s also saw the development, stemming largely from Paris, of the *trio concertant* (*see* QUATUOR CONCERTANT), a genre which persisted to the close of the century, in which the three instruments were treated with equality in an obbligato fashion in a comparatively rich and elaborate texture. Cambini's opp.1 and 2 are typical, although the former retains the somewhat old-fashioned instrumentation of two violins and cello.

The earlier Classical trio often adopted a three-movement plan with an extended minuet as finale; subsequently a four-movement scheme became usual, although a five- or six-movement divertimento structure was also commonly employed. The highpoint of the string trio repertory is Mozart's Divertimento for violin, viola and cello K563, a *trio concertant* in six movements. Beethoven's early string trios exemplify both types: op.3 is closely modelled on Mozart's Divertimento, while the three trios of op.9 belong to the four-movement category. Mozart's fine introductions to his arrangements of fugues by J. S. and W. F. Bach and the two trios by Schubert complete the most valuable part of the Viennese repertory.

The term 'Grand Trio' was used at the beginning of the 19th century to distinguish full-scale and technically advanced compositions from those of slighter proportions often intended for amateurs or students. The *trio brillant* (e.g. Rodolphe Kreutzer's op.16, c1800) represents another category in which one instrument is treated in a soloistic fashion with brilliant passage-work, double stops and sometimes cadenzas, while the others provide little more than an accompaniment. Such trios often consisted of or incorporated variations on fashionable operatic airs. The violin was not invariably the concertante instrument: B. H. Romberg's op.38 is for concertante cello with a viola and a second cello.

The slender nature of the medium seems to have been unattractive to late 19th-century composers. There are trios by Reger and Brahms's friend Heinrich von Herzogenberg; but the most rewarding is Dvořák's Terzetto for two violins and viola, a rather unusual combination which, however, had been used previously in the *Six trio* (1764) of J. C. Bach and later by Cambini, and was revived later by Martinů and Henk Badings.

In the 20th century trios for the conventional combination have been written by Dohnányi (a serenade, op.10), Hindemith, Roussel and Milhaud. The formation of professional groups such as the Pasquier, Vienna and Carter Trios led to a considerable number of works being written for them, for example those of Jean Françaix, E. J. Moeran, Florent Schmitt and Egon Wellesz. Trios by Lennox Berkeley and Douglas Lilburn represent a conservative treatment of the medium; Webern's op.20 (1927) and Schoenberg's op.46 (1945) use 12-note techniques as do those by Benjamin Frankel and Hanns Jelinek.

BIBLIOGRAPHY

C. Engel: 'Beethoven's Opus 3 – An "Envoi de Vienne"?', *MQ*, xiii (1927), 261
W. Altmann: *Handbuch für Streichquartettspieler*, iii, iv (Berlin, 1928–31)
E. Stein: 'Weberns Trio op.20', *Neue Musikzeitung*, xlix (1928), 517
A. Einstein: 'Mozart's Four String Trio Preludes to Fugues of Bach', *MT*, lxxvii (1936), 209
W. Hymanson: 'Schoenberg's String Trio (1946)', *MR*, xi (1950), 184
O. W. Neighbour: 'Dodecaphony in Schoenberg's String Trio', *Music Survey*, iv (1952), 489
W. Kirkendale: 'More Slow Introductions by Mozart to Fugues of Bach?' *JAMS*, xvii (1964), 43
E. Platen: 'Beethoven's Streichtrio D-Dur, opus 9 nr.2: zum Problem der thematischen Einheit mehrsätziger Formen', *Colloquium amicorum: Joseph Schmidt-Görg zum 70. Geburtstag* (Bonn, 1967), 260
H. Unverricht: *Geschichte des Streichtrios* (Tutzing, 1969) [incl. bibliography]

MICHAEL TILMOUTH

Strisciando (It.). GLISSANDO.

Strobel, Heinrich (*b* Regensburg, 31 May 1898; *d* Baden-Baden, 18 Aug 1970). German music critic and administrator. He was a répétiteur for a year (1918) at the Regensburg Staatstheater before studying musicology under Sandberger and Kroyer and theory under H.

K. Schmidt at Munich University, where he took the doctorate in 1922 with a dissertation on Johann Wilhelm Hässler's life and works. He was music critic successively of the *Thüringer Allgemeine Zeitung* in Erfurt (from 1921), of the *Berliner Börsenkurier* (1927–33) and of the *Berliner Tageblatt* (1934–8). In 1933–4 he was editor of *Melos* and then, when *Melos* was suppressed, of the *Neue Musikblatt* (1934–9). He moved to France in 1939, and resumed the editorship of *Melos* when it was revived in 1946. In the same year he was appointed director of the music division of Southwest German Radio, Baden-Baden, and in 1956 he became chairman of the ISCM. He worked constantly and energetically to promote contemporary music and young artists; he was an early supporter of Hindemith and helped many young musicians by initiating annual festivals such as Donaueschingen, concert series and regular broadcasts of contemporary music. In the 1950s he wrote a number of opera librettos for Rolf Liebermann. He received many honours, including the Schoenberg medal (1952) and an honorary doctorate from Basle University (1961).

WRITINGS

Johann Wilhelm Hässlers Leben und Werke (diss., U. of Munich, 1922)
'Die Opern von E. R. Méhul', *ZMw*, vi (1923–4), 362
Paul Hindemith (Mainz, 1928, enlarged 3/1948)
Claude Debussy (Paris and Zurich, 1943, 5/1961; Fr. trans., 1952)
'Lebendiger Kompositionsunterricht!', *6° congresso internazionale di musica: Firenze 1949*, 67
Musikalische Poetik (Mainz, 1949, 3/1966) [trans. of I. Stravinsky: *Poétique musicale*, Cambridge, Mass., 1942]
'La musique nouvelle en Allemagne', *ReM* (1952), no.212, p.23
'Neue Musik und Humanitas', *SMz*, xciii (1953), 485
'Ein deutscher Weltbürger: Richard Strauss', *Richard Strauss Jb 1954*, 128
Stravinsky, Classic Humanist (New York, 1955)
Igor Strawinsky (Zurich and Freiburg, 1956)
'Bedeutung und Aufgabe des IGNM', *Melos*, xxv (1968), 147
Introduction to *Paul Hindemith: Zeugnis in Bildern* (Mainz, 1961)
'Deutsche Musik zwischen den Weltkriegen', *Melos*, xxx (1963), 273
'Deutschland seit 1945', *Melos*, xxx (1963), 404
'Vier Jahrzehnte deutsches Musiktheater', *Melos*, xxx (1963), 326
'So ich sehe Webern', *Melos*, xxxii (1965), 285
'Reflexionen über Debussy', *Melos*, xxxiii (1966), 349

BIBLIOGRAPHY

H. Lindlar: 'Heinrich Strobel 60 Jahre', *Musica*, xii (1958), 300
'Heinrich Strobel 70 Jahre alt', *Melos*, xxxv (1968), 177 [incl. tributes by L. Strecker, E. Larff, W. Egk, H. H. Stuckenschmidt, M. Hürlimann, W. Fortner, C. Chávez, H. Oesch, C. Rostand, R. Liebermann]
G. W. Baruch and others: 'In memoriam Heinrich Strobel', *Melos*, xxxvii (1970), 381

ALFRED GRANT GOODMAN

Strobel, Otto (*b* Munich, 20 Aug 1895; *d* Bayreuth, 23 Feb 1953). German musicologist. He studied musicology at Munich University, where he received a doctorate in 1924 for his dissertation on Wagner's view of his works. During the emergence of national socialist Germany and the enthusiasm for Wagner that went with it, Strobel turned his attention to sifting and evaluating the vast number of autograph manuscripts owned by the Wagner family. From 1932 he was archivist of the Wahnfried Archives, Bayreuth, and from 1938 director of the short-lived Richard Wagner Forschungsstätte. He wrote extensively on Wagner's sketches and working methods, mostly in short articles for the *Bayreuther Festspielführer* and local German periodicals, and edited the first publication of some important documents, including the manuscript texts of the *Ring* and the correspondence between Wagner and Ludwig II. Although his exclusive and largely uncritical devotion to Wagner limited the intellectual perspective of his writings, his work is regarded as an important foundation-stone in Wagner scholarship.

WRITINGS

Richard Wagner über sein Schaffen: ein Beitrag zur 'Künstlerästhetik' (diss., U. of Munich; Munich, 1924)
'Richard Wagner als Arbeitsgenie', *AMz*, lvi (1929), 523, 543, 563
Richard Wagner: Skizzen und Entwürfe zur Ring-Dichtung (Munich, 1930)
'Aus Wagners Musikerwerkstatt', *AMz*, lviii (1931), 463, 479, 495
Genie am Werk: Richard Wagners Schaffen und Wirken im Spiegel eigenhandschriftlicher Urkunden: Führer durch die einmalige Ausstellung einer umfassenden Auswahl von Schätzen aus dem Archiv des Hauses Wahnfried (Bayreuth, 1933, rev. 2/1934)
König Ludwig II und Richard Wagner: Briefwechsel (Karlsruhe, 1936)
Richard Wagner: Leben und Schaffen: eine Zeittafel (Bayreuth, 1952)

JOHN DEATHRIDGE

Strobel, Valentin [Valten, Walten] (i) (*b* Thuringia, *c*1575–80; *d* Weimar, buried 16 Oct 1640). German lutenist and composer, father of Valentin Strobel (ii). He was employed in the Hofkapelle of the Ernestine court by 1602, the year in which the court moved from Altenburg to Weimar. From at least 1611 he served in the Hofkapelle at Halle and was on friendly terms with Scheidt, who was there from 1609. He left before the Thirty Years War spread to the Halle area in 1625 and moved back to Weimar, where he is still recorded as a member of the Kapelle in 1638 and 1640. As a composer he is known by seven pieces in G. L. Fuhrmann, ed.: *Testudo Gallo-Germanica* (Nuremberg, 1615²⁴) and a praeludium in H. D. Bruger, ed.: *Schule des Lautenspiels*, ii (Wolfenbüttel, 1925). Among his works are arrangements of pieces by John Dowland. His pieces are of some artistic worth, with independent partwriting, imitative passages and sequences.

BIBLIOGRAPHY

A. Aber: *Die Pflege der Musik unter den Wettinern und wettinischen Ernestinern* (Bückeburg and Leipzig, 1921), 126, 131, 162
W. Serauky: *Musikgeschichte der Stadt Halle*, ii/l (Halle and Berlin, 1939), 25f, 196

HANS RADKE

Strobel, Valentin (ii) (*b* Halle, baptized 18 Oct 1611; *d* Strasbourg, after 1669). German composer and lutenist, son of Valentin Strobel (i). From 1629 he worked as a lutenist and theorbo player in the Hofkapelle at Darmstadt. After a temporary stay at the Stuttgart court, where he obtained 30 florins as severance pay on 1 June 1634, he entered the service of Margrave Friedrich V of Baden-Durlach. The margrave was forced to leave his territories after the battle at Nördlingen on 6 September 1634, and he moved with his court to near Strasbourg. Together with other musicians, Strobel was dismissed after 1638, but he remained in Strasbourg. He married there on 28 July 1640, and on 15 August of the same year he acquired rights of citizenship.

Chappuzeau reported that 'Messieurs Gumprecht & Strobel touchent le lut avec une délicatesse merveilleuse. L'un & l'autre est parfaitement honeste homme, & en grande estime dans Strasbourg'. Strobel was also an admirable composer of lute music. He adopted the new French arpeggiated manner of playing – the *style brisé* – but combined it in many pieces with a cantabile style. The bass is often melodically independent. Most of the pieces require an 11-course lute, and a few a 12-course lute, in the new French D minor tuning. Some pieces require scordatura: those in G minor and B♭, $C–D–E♭–F–G–B♭–d–f–b♭–d'–f''$; those in D, $C♯–D–E–F♯–G–A–d–f♯–a–d'–f♯'$; and those in A, $C♯–D–E–F♯–$

$G\sharp-A-d-f\sharp-a-c\sharp'-e'$. Strobel's *Melodien* are dance-songs, which include ritornellos for two violins.

Strobel had a son, Johann Valentin (*b* Strasbourg, baptized 16 November 1643; *d* Darmstadt, buried 30 August 1688), who matriculated at the University of Strasbourg on 12 April 1664 and was employed on 12 June 1668 at the Darmstadt court as a valet and lutenist.

WORKS
VOCAL
Melodien, Erster Theil: uber teutsche wältliche Lieder, 1v, 2 vn, b inst (Strasbourg, 1652)
Lieb kämpfendes Hirten Gespräch des Koridons und der Fillis (n.p., n.d., *c*1652)
Melodien, Ander Theil, 1v, 2 vn, b inst (Strasbourg, 1654)

INSTRUMENTAL
Concerts, 3–4 lutes, mandora, s and b insts (Strasbourg, 1648), lost
Concerts, 3–4 lutes, mandora, s and b insts (Strasbourg, 1651), lost
Symphonies, 3–4 lutes, mandora, s and b insts (Strasbourg, 1654), lost
Concerts, 2 angelicas, theorbo, s and b insts (Strasbourg, 1668), lost
4 dances, insts, bc, in 1658[4]
Lute: Gigue, *F-B* 279.152, *S-L* Lit.G 34, *CS-Pu* II.Kk.84; 4 pieces, *D-DS* Mus. 1655; 8 pieces, *ROu* XVII.18.54; 14 pieces, formerly in Vienna library of J. Pölzer
Angelica: 12 pieces, *F-Pc* Rés.169; 4 pieces, *D-SWl* Mus.640
Organ: Gigue, *S-Sk* Cod.holm.S.228; Gigue, *Sk* Cod.holm.S.176; Sarabande, *D-DS* Mus.17; 1 piece, formerly in *Bds* Mus.40147

BIBLIOGRAPHY
S. Chappuzeau: *Suite de l'Europe vivante contenant la relation d'un voyage fait en Allemagne . . . 1669* (Geneva, 1671), 555
W. Nagel: 'Zur Geschichte der Musik am Hofe von Darmstadt', *MMg*, xxxii (1900), 22, 25, 44, 48
A. Göhler: *Verzeichnis der in den Frankfurter und Leipziger Messkatalogen der Jahre 1564–1759 angezeigten Musikalien* (Leipzig, 1902/*R*1965)
H. Kretzschmar: *Geschichte des neuen deutschen Liedes*, i (Leipzig, 1911), 107
F. Noack: 'Die Tabulaturen der Hessischen Landesbibliothek zu Darmstadt', *Kongressbericht: Basel 1924*, 278
R. Kopff: 'Les compositeurs de musique instrumentale en Alsace au XVIIᵉ siècle', *La musique en Alsace hier et aujourd'hui*, Publications de la Société savante d'Alsace et des régions de l'Est, x (Strasbourg, 1970), 87

HANS RADKE

Strobl, Rudolf (*b* Opawa [now Opava], Silesia, 15 April 1831; *d* Warsaw, 14 May 1915). Polish pianist and teacher, probably of German descent. He studied under Joseph Fischhof and Friedrich Volkmann at the Vienna Conservatory, then taught music in Zhitomir. In 1855 he moved to Warsaw, where he quickly won a high reputation as a teacher. From 1866 to 1896 he taught the piano at the Warsaw Institute of Music, of which he was administrative chairman from 1888. Strobl taught a whole generation of distinguished pianists, including Paderewski, Śliwiński, Lewita, Aleksander Różycki and Melcer. He prepared teaching editions of music and a new edition of the collected works of Chopin, *Fryderyk Chopin: Dzieła fortepianowe* (Warsaw, 1902–3), based on Kleczyński's revisions.

BIBLIOGRAPHY
SMP
Echo muzyczne, teatralne i artystyczne, v (1888), 403
Tygodnik ilustrowany, xxi (1915), 332

ZOFIA CHECHLIŃSKA

Stroe, Aurel (*b* Bucharest, 5 May 1932). Romanian composer. At the Bucharest Conservatory (1951–6) he studied harmony with M. Negrea, composition with M. Andricu and orchestration with T. Rogalski; in addition he received instruction from Kagel, Ligeti and Stockhausen at the 1966–9 Darmstadt summer courses. In 1962 he returned to the Bucharest Conservatory as reader in composition. One of Stroe's aims is the creation of a complex work of art uniting the various forms of visual art and music and dependent on the contribution of technology; a first materialization of this concept was the cycle of eight orchestral pieces *Démarche musicale* (1962–71). Using all manner of contemporary techniques, Stroe carefully controls a range from powerful explosions of sound to the most delicate nuances; he has employed the mathematics of probability, deployed with the aid of computers, and timbre is of central importance in his music. Works have been commissioned by the Kassel Opera and by the Royan Festival (*Canto II*, 1971).

WORKS
(*selective list*)
Operas: Oedipe la Colonos, 1963; Ça n'aura pas le prix Nobel, 1969; La paix, 1974
Orch: Démarche musicale: Arcades 1962; Armonica, 1963; Muzică de concert, pf, 4 perc, 12 brass, 1964; Laudes I, str, 1966; Canto I, 1967; Laudes II, 1968; Canto II, 1971
Vocal: 5 cîntece, S, pf, 1949; Cantata da cameră, Mez, chorus, chamber orch, 1959; Monumentum, male chorus, orch, 1961; Only through time, rime is conquered (Eliot), Bar, org, 4 trbn, 4 gong players, 1965; Il giardino delle strutture + Rime di Michelangelo, Bar, trbn, str trio, hpd, tape, 1975
Wind Trio, 1953; Pf Sonata, 1955; Midi le juste, tape, 1970; Rêver c'est désengrener les temps superposés, 2 pf, fl, perc, 1970

Principal publishers: Ars Viva (Mainz), Editura Muzicală (Bucharest), Salabert

BIBLIOGRAPHY
D. D. Gezzo: 'Direcţii moderne ale actualului creator muzical', *Tomis*, v (1966), 11
E. Manu: 'Cu Aurel Stroe despre muzică, matematică şi poezie' [With Stroe on music, mathematics and poetry], *Astra*, vii (1966), 17
C. Nemescu: 'Cu Aurel Stroe despre muzică, matematică şi despre multe altele', *România literară*, ix (1968), 29
V. Cosma: *Muzicieni români* (Bucharest, 1970), 411ff
G. R. Koch: 'Der Nobelpreis wird nicht verliehen', *Frankfurter Allgemeine Zeitung* (30 Nov 1971)

VIOREL COSMA

Strogers [Strowger, Strowgers], **Nicholas** (*fl* 1560–75). English composer, possibly related to E. Strowger. The name was common in East Anglia in the 15th and 16th centuries. He was a parish clerk at St Dunstan in the West, London, from Christmas 1564 to 1575, and was in charge of music there and probably played the organ. As the position of parish clerk was usually offered to aged and distinguished church musicians, it is unlikely that Strogers lived long after he left St Dunstan. Hawkins's statement that he was an organist during the reign of James I may thus be erroneous; it was probably based on the inclusion of Strogers's Short Service in Benjamin Cosyn's collection, where it is described as one of 'the six Services for the kings Royall chappell' (*GB-Lbm* R.M.23.1.4). The service was printed by Barnard in 1641, but its style and certain archaic elements in the text suggest that it was composed before 1580. The same service occurs in the Chirk Partbooks (*US-NYp*) as 'Short Service for meanes' attributed to 'Strogers of Heareford'. Thomas Whythorne noted a 'mr Strgrs' as one of the most famous musicians of his time in his list of doctors and bachelors of music. Since Strogers's music is often found with that of Byrd and Parsons he may have been associated with them during the 1560s.

Although Strogers was not a composer of the first rank he nevertheless had a pleasing melodic gift. His musical style is redolent of that of the 1560s and 1570s. The Short Service was the most widely copied of all his works, a fact which has misled some writers into believing that more than one such service by Strogers exists. The shortness refers to the style rather than to the number of movements, for this setting includes all the movements normally set to music in Elizabethan times. with a different setting of the Kyrie in some sources and a *Deus misereatur* as an alternative to the *Nunc dimittis*. An interesting technical feature is the opening common to, or at least similar in, each movement (except the alternative Kyrie). His only other Anglican works are a five-voice setting of the Collect for the ninth Sunday after Trinity (*Graunt unto us O Lord*) and an incomplete consort anthem. Of his Latin church music, the two *Magnificat* verses are merely exercises in counterpoint.

The consort songs best show Strogers's melodic gift. Particularly appealing is *A doleful deadly pang*, with its D major coda to the repeated 'I die' of the text. Some In Nomines for strings survive complete, but the remaining instrumental ensemble music is too fragmentary to be evaluated. The keyboard works are ascribed simply to 'Mr Strowger' or 'Mr Strowgers', but there can hardly be any doubt that Nicholas Strogers is the composer rather than E. Strowger. These non-liturgical pieces are analogous to the string In Nomines rather than to E. Strowger's liturgical *Miserere*, which must date from before 1549. The cantus firmus of the 'Ut re my fa soul la' must be played by a second person in notes which are 'two [semibreves] long', possibly at the same keyboard.

WORKS

SACRED

Short service (Ven, TeD, Bs, Ky I and II, Cr, Mag, Nunc, DeM), 4vv, *GB-Cp, DRc, Lbm, Llp, Och, Ojc, US-NYp*, 1641⁵/*R*1973
Magnificat verses: Esurientes, 3vv; Sicut locutus, 2vv; *GB-Och*
Domine non est exaltatum, 5vv, inc., *Cp* (Ct missing)
Non me vincat, 5vv, *Och*
Graunt unto us, 5vv, *T, US-NYp*
O heavenly God, 1v, 4 insts, ed. in MB, xxii (1967)

SECULAR

A doleful deadly pang, 1v, 4 insts, ed. in MB, xxii (1967)
By croked ways, inc., *GB-Lbm* (lute part only)
Mistrust not truth, 1v, 4 insts, ed. in MB, xxii (1967)
The world is a world, inc., *T* (A only)
When stormes of care, inc., *Lbm* (lute part only)
Yf thee my deere, inc., *Lbm* (lute part only)

CONSORT MUSIC

A solis ortus cardine, a 5, inc., *T*
'Crotchet' pavan and 2 galliards, fl, b viol, cittern, inc., *Cu* (galliard I, flute and b viol only; galliard II, b viol only)
In Nomine, a 5, *CF* D/DPZ6/1; *Lbm* Add.31390; *Ob* Mus.Sch.D.212–16; *Och* 984–8; *T* 389
In Nomine, a 5, *Lbm* Add.29246, 31390, 32377; *Ob* Mus.Sch.D.212–16; *Och* 984–8
In Nomine, a 5, *Lbm* Eg.3665; *Ob* Mus.Sch.D.212–16; *Och* 984–8
In Nomine, a 5, inc., *Lbm* Add.32377
In Nomine, a 5, inc., *CF* D/DPZ6/1
'In Nomine' pavan and galliard, tr viol, fl, b viol, cittern, pandora, lute, inc., *EIRE-Dtc, GB-Lbm* (lute part lost; galliard lacks tr viol) [probably = In Nomine and In Nomine galliard, lute, Berkshire County Record Office, Reading, Trumbull MS]; pavan only in Morley (1599, enlarged 2/1611²¹); ed. S. Beck, *T. Morley: First Book of Consort Lessons* (New York, 1959)
Pavan, a 5, inc., *Lbm*

KEYBOARD

Fantasia, *Cfm*, ed. J. A. Fuller Maitland and W. B. Squire (London, 1899/*R*1963)
3 In Nomines, *Och* 371 (1 inc. and anon.); 1 ed. D. Stevens, *Altenglische Orgelmusik* (Kassel, 1953)
[Duet] Upon ut re my fa soul la ij longe, *Och* 371

BIBLIOGRAPHY

E. Meyer: *English Chamber Music* (London, 1946, 2/1951/*R*1971)
P. le Huray: 'Towards a Definitive Study of pre-Restoration Anglican Service Music', *MD*, xiv (1960), 167
J. M. Osborn, ed.: *The Autobiography of Thomas Whythorne* (Oxford, 1961), 302
J. C. Pistor: *Nicholas Strogers, Tudor Composer, and his Circle* (diss., U. of Oxford, 1971) [includes a virtually complete transcription of Strogers's extant works]
R. T. Daniel and P. le Huray: *The Sources of English Church Music 1549–1660*, EECM, suppl. i (1972)

JOHN CALDWELL, SUSI JEANS

Strohfiedel. A simple, early type of European XYLOPHONE.

Strohm, Reinhard (*b* Munich, 4 Aug 1942). German musicologist. He studied musicology at the University of Munich with Thrasybulos Georgiades and Wolfgang Osthoff, as well as Latin and Italian literature, then at the Technische Universität, Berlin, with Carl Dahlhaus, obtaining the PhD in 1971. During this time he spent several periods of study in Italy. From 1964 to 1970 he collaborated with the Deutsche Arbeitsgruppe of *RISM*, and since 1970 he has been an editor of the Richard-Wagner-Gesamtausgabe. In 1975 he was appointed lecturer in music at King's College, London. He was awarded the Dent medal of the Royal Musical Association in 1977. Strohm's field of research ranges from early polyphony to 19th-century opera. He has made fundamental contributions to the social history of music in the 15th century, to the documentation of the life and works of Handel and to the editing of Wagner's operas.

WRITINGS

'Ein englischer Ordinariumssatz des 14. Jahrhunderts in Italien', *Mf*, xviii (1965), 178
'Neue Quellen zur liturgischen Mehrstimmigkeit des Mittelalters in Italien', *RIM*, i (1966), 77
'Zum Verhältnis von Textstruktur und musikalischer Struktur in Verdis Arien', *I° congresso internazionale di studi verdiani: Venezia 1966*, 247
'Ein Zeugnis früher Mehrstimmigkeit in Italien', *Festschrift Bruno Stäblein* (Kassel, 1967), 239
'Osservazioni su "Tempro la cetra"', *RIM*, ii (1967), 357
'Ein unbekanntes Chorbuch des 15. Jahrhunderts', *Mf*, xxi (1968), 40
'Zu Vivaldis Opernschaffen', *Venezia e il melodramma del settecento: Venezia 1973*, 237
'Taddeo Wiel und die Venezianische Opernbibliographie', *DJbM*, xviii (1973–7), 101
'Händel in Italia: nuovi contributi', *RIM*, ix (1974), 152
'Händels Pasticci', *AnMc*, no.14 (1974), 208–69
'Alessandro Scarlatti und das Settecento', *Colloquium Alessandro Scarlatti: Würzburg 1975*, 153
'Hasse, Scarlatti, Rolli', *AnMc*, no.15 (1975), 220–57
'Händel und seine italienischen Operntexte', *HJb 1975–6*, 99–157
'Italienische Opernarien des frühen Settecento (1720–1730)' *AnMc*, no.16 (1976) [whole vol.]
'"Rienzi" and Authenticity', *MT*, cxvii (1976), 725
'Handel, Metastasio, Racine: the Case of "Ezio"', *MT*, cxviii (1977), 901
'Dramatic Time and Operatic Form in Wagner's "Tannhäuser"', *PRMA*, civ (1977–8), 1
'Ein Opernautograph von Francesco Gasparini?', *Hamburger Jb für Musikwissenschaft*, iii (1978), 205
'Merkmale italienischer Versvertonung in Mozarts Klavierkonzerten', *AnMc*, no.18 (1978), 219
Die italienische Oper im 18. Jahrhundert (Wilhelmshaven, 1979)
'Die Missa super "Nos amis" von Johannes Tinctoris', *Mf*, xxxi (1979), 34

EDITIONS

R. Wagner: Rienzi, der Letzte der Tribunen, Richard-Wagner-Gesamtausgabe (Mainz, 1972–) [with E. Voss; incl. *Dokumentenband*, 1976]; *Tannhäuser* (Dresdner Fassung), ibid (in preparation)

Stroke. A sign used in English virginal music and elsewhere to indicate an ornament of some kind. See ORNAMENTS, §VI.

Stromentato (It., now *strumentato*: 'scored for instruments'). Short for *recitativo stromentato*, i.e. recitative accompanied by the orchestra. It is sometimes held that the term implies a recitative in which the orchestra plays an independent part, in the form of dramatic interpolations, as opposed to accompagnato, where it merely accompanies. It is not possible, however, to draw any clear distinction between the two.

JACK WESTRUP

Strong, George Templeton (*b* New York, 26 May 1856; *d* Geneva, 27 June 1948). American composer. His father, also George Templeton Strong, was a lawyer and musical amateur, founder of the New York Church Music Association and president of the New York Philharmonic Society (1870–74). As a youth Strong studied the oboe and, thanks to his parents, was able to become familiar with a great deal of music through concerts and rehearsals. He stated that he had not studied harmony before going to Leipzig in 1879, but he had begun to compose. In Leipzig he studied privately with Jadassohn (counterpoint), Hofmann (orchestration) and Gumpert (horn). Then in around 1881 he spent some time in Frankfurt and there became acquainted with Raff, who encouraged him to return to Leipzig for further study. During the years 1881–6 he visited Weimar, where he associated with Sauer, Siloti, Friedheim and other pupils of Liszt. To Liszt, who took an interest in him, he dedicated the symphonic poem *Undine*.

In 1886 Strong settled in Wiesbaden, where began a lasting friendship with MacDowell. After returning to the USA in 1888, MacDowell brought Strong's music to the attention of the American public, and he urged Strong to return, helping to obtain for him a position as theory teacher at the New England Conservatory (1891–2). Strong then went back to Europe, and, apart from occasional visits to the USA, he spent the remainder of his life in Switzerland. For a few years after his return he gave up composition for watercolour painting, discouraged by the failure of American composers to achieve recognition in their native land; he founded the Société Vaudoise des Aquarellistes.

Of a kindly and sympathetic nature, Strong attracted a wide circle of friends, from Raff, Liszt and MacDowell to Ansermet and Szigeti. As an act of homage he orchestrated the second movement of Raff's Seventh Quartet, and his early works were influenced by Raff, Liszt and, to some extent, Tchaikovsky. Later compositions employ chromatic, tritone harmonies. Strong had a deep love of literature, and many of his pieces have literary subjects or inscriptions; many also refer to dark woods, to ghosts, elves, witches and other supernatural beings. A number of unpublished manuscripts, including the first two movements of the First Symphony, were stored in Vevey but lost.

WORKS

ORCHESTRAL

Ein Totentanz, op.11, sym. poem, 1878, unpubd; Finsterniss, sym. poem, 1879, unpubd; Ein Märchen: Gestrebt, Gewonnen, Gescheitert, op.12, *c*1880; Undine, op.14, sym. poem, after De la Motte Fouqué, 1882–3; unpubd; Sym. no.1 'In den Bergen', 1882–6, movts 1–2 lost; Sintram (Sym. no.2), op.50, after de la Motte Fouqué, 1887–8; An der See, sym. poem (Sym. no.3), unpubd, ?lost; Americana, 2 little poems, vn, orch, 1904; Die Nacht, 4 little sym. poems, 1913; Le roi Arthur, sym. poem, 1891–1916
Elégie, vc, orch, 1917; Une vie d'artiste, sym. poem, vn, orch, 1917; Berceuse, str trio, orch, 1923; Suite, vc, orch, 1923; Hallali, hn, orch (1923); Chorale on a Theme by Leo Hassler, 1929; Pollainiana, vc, orch, 1930–31; Perpetuo mobile, vn, orch (*c*1935); Une voix dans la forêt, bn, orch (*c*1935); D'un cahier d'images I–III (*c*1945); Ondine [?rev. Undine], sym. poem (*c*1945)

CHORAL

Asmund (dramatic cantata, Strong), solo vv, male chorus, orch, unpubd; The Knights and the Naiads, unpubd, ?lost; Wie fahrender Hornist sich ein Land erblies, op.26 (M. von Strachwitz), solo vv, male chorus, orch (*c*1885); Die verlassene Mühle, op.30 (A. Schnezler), T, male chorus, orch (1887); Now is the Month of Maying, Sister Awake (1891); The Trumpeter, ballad, T, Bar, chorus, orch (1897); 4 Noëls, op.48, female vv, org/harmonium (1903)
Male vv: L'armailli, A l'hirondelle (Ronsard), La dernière feuille

(Gautier), D'un vanneur de blé aux vents (du Bellay), L'apaisement (C. Fuster), Le forgeron (A. Paychère), Chant de bataille (Paychère), Je plante en ta faveur (Ronsard), Voulant o ma douce moitié (Ronsard), Au matin (Richepin), all (1929)
Female vv: Du printemps (J. A. du Baif), La lune (L. Delarue-Mardrus), Lauda Sion, Sancta Maria, all (1930)

CHAMBER

Tonstück, eng hn, org, *c*1885, unpubd, ?lost; Romanze, G, op.23, vn, pf (*c*1885); Trio (Der Dorfmusikdirektor), G, 2 vn, va, 1904, rev. 1915; Légende, F, 4 hn, 1913; Petite rêverie et scherzo, e, 3 vc, db, 1916; Sonata, G, va, vc, 1916; 4 nocturnes, vn, va, pf (1929); Sérénade, vc, harp (1929); Str Qt, c, 1930, unpubd; 5 aquarelles, fl, ob, cl, bn, 1933; 2 pièces, org/harmonium (*c*1935); Hommage à Genève, org/harmonium (*c*1935); Str Qt (*c*1935)

SONGS

Annabel Lee (Poe), 1879; 3 Gesänge, op.32: Spinnerlied (Bürger), Geisternähe (H. Kieskamp), Friedel (F. Greiner) (1887); Treu bis zum Tod, op.35 (J. C. Glücklich) (1888); 3 Songs, op.38: Shall a Smile or Guileful Glance (W. Corkine), Come, ah Come, my Life's Delight (Campion), Philon (Byrd) (1892); 5 Songs, op.43 (M. Merington): How Fair the Night, By Chance, Misunderstanding, To one who Offered Pansies, If (1893)
Foreboding (Shakespeare), 1899; Parce domine (Strong, after A. Theuriet), 1907; 2 Lieder (Heine): Asche, Du liebst mich nicht, 1907; Songs of an American Peddler (Strong): The Bull at the Picnic, The Violet, The Brook, The Crow, The Churchyard, 1922; An Indian Chief's Reply (Strong), 1926; 3 chants; Les cloches du soir (M. Desbordes-Valmore), Il passa (H. Vacaresco), C'était en avril (E. Pailleron), 1929
3 chants: Fumée (Gautier), Le gué (Pailleron), Le voyage (Florian), 1929; 3 aquarelles: Le chante-matin (H. Pourrat), Il pleure . . . (Verlaine), Le chant de l'eau (Verhaeren), 1931; 5 mélodies: Feuilles mortes (M. Vaucaire), La bergère (Florian), Marche des cornemuseaux (Berry), A la claire fontaine, Le menuisier des trépassés (Moréas), 1931; Our Lord's Prayer, 1940

PIANO

5 Charakterstücke, op.6 (*c*1885); In Tirol, op.7 (*c*1885); Suite, op.8 (*c*1885); Sounds from the Harz Mountains, op.17, duet (*c*1885); 3 Bagatelles, op.21, duet (*c*1885); Ballade no.1, g, op.22 (*c*1885); 3 Charakterstücke, op.24 (*c*1885); 3 sinfonische Idyllen, op.29, 2 pf (1887); Erzählungen, op.31 (1887); Ballade no.2, g, op.34 (1888); Esquisses (1890); Miniaturen, op.41 (1891); 5 Character Pieces, op.42 (1891); 2 marches, op.39, duet (1892); 4 Poems, op.36 (1896); In the Twilight, op.44 (1896)
Petite suite, 1917; Au pays des peaux-rouges, 1918; Au pays de Pan, 1918; 3 morceaux, 2 pf (1924); 3 pièces, duet (1926); 25 préludes, 1929; 11 miniatures (1929); 12 petites esquisses (1929); Pro juventute (1930); 3 Village Scenes, 2 pf (*c*1935); 3 idylles, 2 pf (*c*1935)

Principal publishers: Breitkopf & Härtel, Foetisch, Henn, F. Jost, Jost & Sander, Kistner, Schmidt, Editions du Siècle Musical
MSS in *US-Wc*

WRITINGS

'Edward MacDowell as I knew him', *Music Student*, vii/12, viii/1–10 (1915–16)
'George Templeton Strong Makes a Correction', *Musical Courier*, lxxxvi/5 (1923), 59
Unpubd correspondence and papers in *US-Wc*

BIBLIOGRAPHY

C. H. Wise: ' "Sintram": a Remarkable Symphony by a Too Little-known Composer', *Music Student*, v (1913), 299
P. A. Scholes: 'An American Composer: George Templeton Strong', *Music Student*, vii (1915), 238
R. Godet: Introduction to score of *Le roi Arthur* (Geneva, 1922)
J. Szigeti: *With Strings Attached* (New York, 1947, 2/1967), chap.13
W. Tappolet: 'George Templeton Strong', *SMz*, lxxxviii (1948), 365
A. Nevins and M. H. Thomas: *The Diary of George Templeton Strong* [sr]: *Post-war Years 1865–1875* (New York, 1952)
J. L. Matthey: *Inventaire du fonds musical George Templeton Strong* (Lausanne, 1973)

JAMES R. SMART

Strophic. Term applied to songs in which all stanzas of the text are sung to the same music, in contrast to those that are THROUGH-COMPOSED and have new music for each stanza. The vast majority of folksongs and folk ballads are strophic, as are many 18th-century art songs which attempt to capture their spirit (*volkstümliches Lied*). Schubert used the form in setting simple lyrics and some narrative poems (*Heidenröslein, Der Fischer*) but frequently modified the basic structure by slightly changing the vocal line from stanza to stanza or by varying the figuration of the accompaniment (*Im Frühling*). One or more stanzas may also be set to different music or with a change of tonality (Schubert's *Die Forelle*; Brahms's *Wie bist du, meine Königin*). In fact every shade of modification is possible between the purely strophic and the through-composed song.

MICHAEL TILMOUTH

Strophicus. In Western chant notations, the name sometimes given to the APOSTROPHE, and to groups of two or more *apostrophes* (DISTROPHA, TRISTROPHA etc); it is also used as an adjective to describe neumes including the *apostrophe*. The *strophicus* was distinguished from the VIRGA or PUNCTUM (or groups of these) probably by the manner of its performance, although it is not certain what this may have entailed. Aurelian of Réôme spoke of a staccato delivery (*GS*, i, 57), an interpretation favoured by most modern writers. Wagner believed that intervals of less than a semitone might have been involved (for illustration *see* NEUMATIC NOTATIONS, Table 1, 'Apostrophe').

Strophic variations. A form of Italian vocal chamber music of the first half of the 17th century in which the vocal melody of the first strophe is varied in subsequent strophes while the bass is repeated unchanged or with only slight modifications, generally of rhythm; the term itself is modern and was not used by composers or theorists of the period. The sectional nature of works in this form, which are normally secular solo songs or duets, distinguishes them from those built on a ground bass or ostinato over which the music unfolds continuously. Strophic variations undoubtedly originated in variation techniques used in the 16th century in instrumental as well as in vocal music. It is significant that popular melodies dating from that period, such as the romanesca or Ruggiero, were used in the early 17th century as the bass in many strophic-variation settings of ottavas, a schematic type of verse with which they had often been associated. There are several such settings by Antonio Cifra in particular, Sigismondo d'India and other composers of monodies and duets; the most celebrated is Monteverdi's duet *Ohimè, dov'è il mio ben* (seventh book of madrigals, 1619).

Whether a bass was traditional or the composer's own it was common in strophic variations for each pair of lines of an ottava to be set over one statement of it. The equally schematic form of the sonnet was sometimes subjected to a comparable division into four strophes, nearly always over the composer's own bass. Having served as the foundation of the four-line strophes of the octave, an original bass could be adapted to fit the three-line strophes of the sestet more conveniently than could a borrowed bass; Stefano Landi's *Altri amor fugge* (*Arie*, 1620), for solo voice and continuo, is a good example of a sonnet set as strophic variations in four sections. Larger and, very rarely, smaller divisions of a poem are also found. It was common for the last phrase of the bass in any section (but especially the final one) to be repeated with new music over it. The texts in each section are not of course genuine strophes but arbitrary, though regular, sections of a complete strophe or poem. Composers sometimes suggested that their music for such a text might be used for other texts identical in structure.

The principle of strophic variation was sometimes applied to settings of genuinely strophic poems, which, however, in early 17th-century Italy (as in other countries and periods) were normally set simply as strophic songs, with the same music for each verse. In some settings of such poems not only does the vocal line change from verse to verse but the bass too changes so much that the songs cannot still be called strophic variations. Conversely, in songs such as Caccini's *Ard'il mio petto misero* (*Le nuove musiche*, 1601/2) the changes from verse to verse are so slight that the pieces are virtually written-out strophic songs. Caccini called that song an aria, but most sets of strophic variations are similar in style to solo madrigals (i.e. in common time and with relatively slow-moving basses). Orpheus's great song 'Possente spirto' in Act 3 of Monteverdi's *Orfeo* (1607) is essentially a set of strophic variations, in which, in the dramatic context, the form is treated with notable imagination and psychological acumen. The ritornellos between its strophes are an element found in some other songs in this form. In the songbooks of the period the first genuine strophic variations on composed basses appeared as late as 1616: examples occur in the collections of songs and duets published in that year by the Florentines Domenico Belli and Domenico Visconti. Rome became the most important centre of them: Landi and G. D. Puliaschi were prominent composers of them, and there are several examples as late as the sonnets of Domenico Mazzocchi's *Dialoghi, e sonetti* (1638).

By the 1630s, however, the technique of strophic variation was dying out in all parts of Italy, though there are later instances of it, for example, Roman cantatas of the mid-17th century and certain arias in the operas of Cavalli. In Venice (where Cavalli worked) such composers as Alessandro Grandi (i) and G. P. Berti had begun to apply it from at least 1620 to sectional songs whose repeated basses move more actively, predominantly in crotchets. They called such pieces cantatas, and it is customary to refer to them now as strophic-bass cantatas: *see* CANTATA, §I, 1. Grandi also adopted this technique in motets.

The term 'strophic variations' is occasionally used too of music of other periods, for example isorhythmic motets of the 14th century, constructed according to principles similar to those outlined above.

BIBLIOGRAPHY
A. Einstein: '*Orlando furioso* and *La Gerusalemme liberata* as Set to Music during the 16th and 17th Centuries', *Notes*, viii (1950–51), 623
N. Fortune: *Italian Secular Song from 1600 to 1635: the Origins and Development of Accompanied Monody* (diss., U. of Cambridge, 1954), chap.9
——: 'Solo Song and Cantata', *NOHM*, iv (1968), 169ff, 181
NIGEL FORTUNE

Strouse, Charles (Louis) (*b* New York, 7 June 1928). American songwriter. He studied at the Eastman School of Music (BM 1947), and was a composition pupil of David Diamond, Arthur Berger, Nadia Boulanger, Aaron Copland and Israel Citkowitz. He has written numerous songs for revues (e.g. *Shoestring Revue*, 1955; *Shoestring '57*), musical plays dealing with aspects of contemporary American society (e.g. *Bye Bye Birdie*, 1960; *All American*, 1962; *Golden Boy*, 1964; *Annie*, 1976) and films.

Strowger, E. (*fl* 1540). English composer, possibly related to Nicholas Strogers. His sole surviving composition is a short canonic *Miserere* for organ (*GB-Lbm* Add.29996; in EECM, vi, no.22).

JOHN CALDWELL

Strowger [Strowgers], **Nicholas**. *See* STROGERS, NICHOLAS.

Strozzi, Barbara (*b* Venice, 6 Aug 1619; *d* ?Venice, 1664 or later). Italian composer and singer, adopted daughter of GIULIO STROZZI. She was the daughter of Isabella Griega, but by 1628 she was Strozzi's heiress and a member of his household. She was a pupil of Cavalli. Nicolò Fontei stated in the dedication of his first set of *Bizzarrie poetiche* (1635) that its contents, all settings of poems by Giulio Strozzi, were commissioned by her. So too were the songs in the second set (1636), and in its dedication he lavished praise on her as a singer. She was clearly the leading singer – and apparently a seductive attraction in other respects – at the Accademia degli Unisoni, which met at Giulio Strozzi's house. The published papers of the academy (the *Veglie*) were dedicated to her; she is mentioned in them several times, and she was asked to select the subject for discussion at one of the *veglie*. Her deportment at the academy brought her some notoriety, and she was viciously satirized in the *Satire, e altre raccolte per l'Accademia de gli Unisoni*. She was commended in the section devoted to Giulio Strozzi in *Le glorie de gli Incogniti*, a collection of eulogies of the members of the Accademia degli Incogniti.

Barbara Strozzi was undoubtedly an able composer. Like Fontei's book of 1635, her own first publication (1644) consists entirely of settings of words by her adoptive father. Here and in her later volumes her style owes something to that of her teacher Cavalli. At their best her short and quite simple ariettas are as notable for their attractive melodies and piquant rhythms as are her extended cantatas for their sure handling of form and for their numerous imaginative touches. Even in some of her shorter pieces there are frequent changes of metre and, by implication, tempo; an excellent example is *Cara Filli, quella tu sei*, a solo song from op.3, in which a 12-bar section mainly in 3/4 time (*A*) acts as a rondo refrain in an *ABACA* form where *B* and *C* are contrasting sections in 4/4 and 6/4 respectively. The lament *Udite, amanti, la cagione* (in op.2), which includes very varied treatment of the solo vocal line over a stock ground bass, is a fine example of a more extended piece. Finer still is the cantata *Lagrime mie* from op.7, a notably imaginative work, which, like several of her cantatas, is on a very large scale and contains a wide range of writing, from impassioned recitative to a tripping arietta. In her melodies she often stated a motto, repeated it sequentially and expanded it, showing imaginative development of short motifs that are impelled onwards by her inventive rhythmic and harmonic vocabulary. Her bass lines are active and frequently playful and as a rule dovetail effectively with the vocal parts. She was sensitive to the rhythms and emotional content of the texts that she set, and her expert personal knowledge of the human voice clearly stood her in good stead.

WORKS

(all printed works published in Venice)

Edition: *Ariette di Francesca Caccini e Barbara Strozzi*, ed. A. Bonaventura (Rome, 1930)

Il primo libro de madrigali, 2–5vv, bc (1644)

Cantate, ariette e duetti, 1–2vv, bc, op.2 (1651); 2 ariettas ed. K. Jeppesen, *La flora*, ii (Copenhagen, 1949)

Cantate e ariette, 1–3vv, bc, op.3 (1654)

Sacri musicali affetti, libro I, op.5 (1655)

Ariette a voce sola, op.6 (1657) [incl. 1 for 2vv]

Diporti di Euterpe, overo Cantate e ariette a voce sola, op.7 (1659); 1 cantata, Lagrime mie, pr. in Racek, 251ff, and ed. C. MacClintock, *The Solo Song, 1580–1730: a Norton Music Anthology* (New York, 1973), 81ff

Diporti di Euterpe, overo Madrigali a due voci, op.8 (1660)

Arie a voce sola, op.9 (1664); 1 ed. F. Vatielli, *Antiche cantate d'amore* (Bologna, 1907–20)

2 arias, 1656[4]; 4 songs (according to *EitnerQ*), *D-Kl*, *GB-Lbm* (?from opp.2 or 3), *I-MOe* (from op.9)

BIBLIOGRAPHY

Veglie de' Signori Unisoni (Venice, 1638)
Satire, e altre raccolte per l'Accademia de gli Unisoni in casa di Giulio Strozzi (*I-Vnm* Cl.X, Cod.CXV = 7193)
Le glorie de gli Incogniti (Venice, 1647), 280ff
A. Bonaventura: 'Un'arietta di Barbara Strozzi', *Nuova musica*, x (1905), 61
E. Schmitz: *Geschichte der weltlichen Solokantate* (Leipzig, 1914, rev. 2/1955), 81f
A. Bonaventura: 'Le donne italiane e la musica', *RMI*, xxxii (1925), 522
M. Maylender: *Storia delle accademie d'Italia*, v (Bologna, 1930), 396f
J. Racek: *Stilprobleme der italienischen Monodie* (Prague, 1965), 14, 64, 170, 192, 227, 251ff, 296
E. Rosand: 'Barbara Strozzi, *virtuosissima cantatrice*: the Composer's Voice', *JAMS*, xxxi (1978), 241–81

CAROLYN RANEY

Strozzi, Giulio [Zorzisto, Luigi] (*b* Venice, 1583; *d* Venice, 31 March 1652). Italian librettist, poet and dramatist; BARBARA STROZZI was his adopted daughter. He was the illegitimate (later legitimized) son of Roberto Strozzi, a Venetian banker and member of a prominent Florentine family, of which PIERO STROZZI was an earlier member. He was educated in Venice and at the University of Pisa, where he graduated in law. He then moved to Rome, where he attained the rank of apostolic prothonotary and was instrumental in founding about 1608 the Accademia degli Ordinati. This literary circle, which met at the house of Cardinal Giovanni Battista Deti, was formed in opposition to the influential Accademia degli Umoristi. Strozzi later resigned from the position of prothonotary and left Rome, where he seems to have become a controversial figure. He worked for a time at Padua, where he wrote the tragedy *Erotilla* (Venice, 1615), and at Urbino, where he served the duke as 'prefect of the bedchamber'. He finally returned to Venice, probably in the early 1620s, and spent most of the rest of his life there.

Strozzi was active in Venice in both literary and musical circles. He was a member of the Accademia degli Incogniti and himself founded two academies. The first of these met at the house of Marquis Martinenghi Malpaga. The second – the Accademia degli Unisoni, founded in 1637 – met at Strozzi's house and was devoted not only to the reading of academic discourses but also to musical performances in which Barbara Strozzi played a major role; the published papers of the academy – *Veglie de' Signori Unisoni* (Venice, 1638) – are dedicated to her. Strozzi and his academy seem to have achieved some notoriety: both were attacked in an anonymous and strongly worded series of satires which partly parody the *Veglie*.

Strozzi's literary output includes orations, plays, poetry and descriptions of Venetian ceremonial, several of which contain useful information on Venetian musical life. His published description of the memorial service for Cosimo II, Grand Duke of Tuscany, held in Venice on 25 May 1621, contains references to a requiem mass composed for the occasion by Monteverdi (the music is lost); in the 12th canto of his heroic poem *La Venetia edificata* (Venice, rev. 2/1626) he praised several Venetian musicians, among them Monteverdi and Alessandro Grandi (i); and his *Le glorie della Signora Anna Renzi romana* (Venice, 1644) contains biographical information about, and a critical appreciation of, the famous soprano (*see* RENZI, ANNA).

Strozzi is best known, however, for his operatic librettos, which were set to music from the mid-1620s onwards. Little survives of the musical settings. His two earliest operatic collaborations were with Monteverdi. *La finta pazza Licori* (1627), written for Mantua, is known only from Monteverdi's letters. These detail the various stages in the preparation of libretto and score and reveal Monteverdi's evident pleasure in working with Strozzi. Their second collaboration, *Proserpina rapita*, was first performed at the Palazzo Mocenigo, Venice, in 1630. The libretto is extant, and a setting for three voices and continuo of a section of the text, 'Come dolce hoggi l'auretta', survives in a posthumous collection of Monteverdi's *Madrigali e canzonette* (Venice, 1651). (*Proserpina rapita* was not, as has previously been asserted, reset by Francesco Sacrati in 1644.)

Strozzi was one of the small group of librettists involved in the creation of Venetian opera. Badoaro and Busenello were his friends. The latter contributed a laudatory ode for the publication of *La Venetia edificata* and also dedicated several poems to Strozzi. Another librettist, Paolo Vendramin, was a member of the Accademia degli Unisoni. Several of Strozzi's librettos (all extant) were set for performance at the new public opera houses: he must thus be accounted an important and influential figure in the literary history of early Venetian opera. *La Delia, o sia La Sera sposa del Sole*, with music by Francesco Manelli (music lost), was performed at the opening of the Teatro SS Giovanni e Paolo in 1639 and was considered by Osthoff (1964) 'the prototype of Venetian opera'. Even more important was *La finta pazza* (which has no connection with *La finta pazza Licori*); it was first performed with music by Sacrati (which is lost) for the opening of the Teatro Novissimo in 1641. Among several revivals of it outside Venice the most notable was in Paris in 1645, with stage designs by Giacomo Torelli and choreography by G. B. Balbi; for this, one of the earliest performances of Italian opera in Paris, some of the recitatives were replaced by spoken dialogue. Of the music for *La finta savia* (Venice, Teatro Novissimo, 1643; music by Filiberto Laurenzi, Tarquinio Merula, Arcangelo Crivelli, Alessandro Leardini, Benedetto Ferrari and Vincenzo Tozzi), only the arias contributed by Laurenzi survive. The setting of *Il Romolo e 'l Remo* (Venice, Teatro SS Giovanni e Paolo, 1645), attributed on uncertain grounds to Cavalli, is lost, but Cavalli's score for Strozzi's last libretto, *Veremonda* (performed Naples, 1652; Venice, probably 1653), survives. On the title-page of the libretto, which was a reworking of G. A. Cicognini's *Celio* (Florence, 1646), Strozzi's name appeared anagrammatically as Luigi Zorzisto.

A number of Strozzi's smaller-scale texts were also set by Venetian composers. Here again Monteverdi was first in the field. His setting (now lost) of the sonnets *I cinque fratelli* was written in 1628 for performance at a banquet given by the Venetian Republic to honour a visit by Grand Duke Ferdinando of Tuscany and his brother Carlo de' Medici. The earliest of Strozzi's texts to survive with music, however, is the large-scale pas-

Giulio Strozzi: portrait attributed to Simon Vouet in the Ashmolean Museum, Oxford

toral dialogue *La Gelosia placata*, of which Giovanni Rovetta included a setting in his first book of madrigals (Venice, 1629). The text, adapted from Act 3 scene i of Strozzi's comedy *Il natal di Amore: anacronismo* (Venice, rev. 4/1629), is cleverly constructed and is distinguished by its unusually energetic language; the musical setting foreshadows stylistic features of early Venetian opera and employs the *stile concitato*. Continuing his association with composers working in Venice, Strozzi contributed the texts for Nicolò Fontei's first book of *Bizzarrie poetiche poste in musica* (Venice, 1635) and the majority of those for the second book (Venice, 1636). The text of Laurenzi's serenata *Guerra non porta* (in his *Concerti et arie*, Venice, 1641) is by Strozzi, and he also wrote the texts for Barbara Strozzi's first book of madrigals (Venice, 1644). In her later volume, *Cantate, ariette e duetti* (Venice, 1651), she included her own settings of texts from the operas, *La finta pazza* and *Il Romolo e 'l Remo*.

BIBLIOGRAPHY

Satire, e altre raccolte per l'Accademia de gli Unisoni in casa di Giulio Strozzi (I-Vnm Cl.X, Cod.CXV = 7193)

Sentimenti giocosi havuti in Parnaso per l'Accademia degli Unisoni (I-Vmc Cod.Cic.2999/18)

Sonetto portato da Parnaso ai Sig.ri Accademici Destici, venuti qui in Parnaso à spiare come sia trattato ... Giulio Strozzi (I-Vmc Cod.Cic.1798), f.264v

G. F. Loredano and M. Dandolo: 'La contesa del canto, e delle lagrime' [papers read at the Accademia degli Unisoni], in G. F. Loredano: *Bizzarrie academiche* (Venice, 1638), 182ff; Eng. trans. as *Academical Discourses* (London, 1664), 99ff

G. F. Busenello: *Poesie (I-Vmc* Cod.Cic.1082, pp.1041ff; Cod.Cic.1054, ff.177f)

Feste theatrali per La finta pazza, dramma del Sig.r Giulio Strozzi ... e da Giacomo Torelli da Fano inventore (Paris, 1645)

G. B. Balbi: *Balletti d'invenzione nella finta pazza* (n.p., n.d.)

Le glorie de gli Incogniti (Venice, 1647), 280ff

I. N. Erythraei [pseud. of G. V. Rossi]: *Pinacotheca imaginum illustrium doctrinae vel ingenii laude, virorum qui, auctore superstite, diem suum obierunt*, iii (Amsterdam, 1648), 193ff

L. Crasso: *Elogii de gli huomini letterati* (Venice, 1666)

P. Litta: *Celebri famiglie italiane* (Milan, 1839–), ix: Strozzi family, table xix

A. S. Barbi: *Un accademico mecenate e poeta, G. B. Strozzi il giovane* (Florence, 1900), 55, 57

H. Prunières: *L'opéra italien en France avant Lulli* (Paris, 1913), 73ff

A. Livingston: *La vita veneziana nelle opere di Gian Francesco Busenello* (Venice, 1913)

M. Maylender: *Storia delle accademie d'Italia* (Bologna, 1926–30), iv 140f; v, 396f

G. F. Malipiero: *Claudio Monteverdi* (Milan, 1929), 249ff, 273

L. Schrade: *Monteverdi: Creator of Modern Music* (New York, 1950, repr. 1964), 275, 309ff, 313, 320, 347

G. Spini: *Ricerca del libertini* (Rome, 1950)

A. A. Abert: *Claudio Monteverdi und das musikalische Drama* (Lippstadt, 1954), 130ff, 149

A. della Corte: *Drammi per musica dal Rinuccini allo Zeno* (Turin, 1958), i, 333ff

W. Osthoff: *Das dramatische Spätwerk Claudio Monteverdis* (Tutzing, 1960), 60, 119

N. Pirrotta: 'Strozzi', §(i), *ES*

D. Arnold: *Monteverdi* (London, 1963), 35, 40, 43, 118

W. Osthoff: 'Masque und Musik', *Castrum Peregrini*, lxv (1964); It. trans., *NRMI*, i (1967), 16

M. F. Robinson: *Opera before Mozart* (London, 1966), 76

H. MacAndrew: 'Vouet's Portrait of Giulio Strozzi and its Pendant by Tinelli of Nicolò Crasso', *Burlington Magazine*, cix (1967), 266

P. Petrobelli: 'Francesco Manelli: documenti e osservazioni', *Chigiana*, xxiv (1967), 43

T. Antonicek: 'Zum 300. Todestag von Francesco Manelli', *ÖMz*, xxiii (1968), 617

D. Arnold and N. Fortune, eds.: *The Monteverdi Companion* (London, 1968), 62f, 65ff, 70ff

C. Sartori: 'La prima diva della lirica Italiana: Anna Renzi', *NRMI*, ii (1968), 430

——: 'Un fantomatico compositore per un'opera che forse non era un'opera', *NRMI*, v (1971), 788

W. Osthoff: 'Filiberto Laurenzis Musik zu "La finta savia" in Zusammenhang der frühvenezianischen Oper', *Venezia e il melodramma nel Seicento: Venezia 1972*, 173

T. Walker: 'Gli errori di "Minerva al tavolino": osservazioni sulla cronologia delle prime opere veneziane', *Venezia e il melodrama nel Seicento: Venezia 1972*, 7

L. Bianconi and T. Walker: 'Dalla *Finta pazza* alla *Veremonda*: storie di Febiarmonci', *RIM*, x (1975), 379–425

B. and C. L. Brancaforte: *La primera traducción del 'Lazarillo de Tormes' por Giulio Strozzi* (Ravenna, 1977)

JOHN WHENHAM

Strozzi, Gregorio (*b* S Severino, southern Italy, *c*1615; *d* probably Naples, after 1687). Italian composer and organist. He was a pupil of Giovanni Maria Sabino in Naples. He became second organist at Ss Annunziata, Naples, in 1634 and was still in that position in 1643 despite a promise of promotion. In 1645 he became chaplain at the principal church in Amalfi, and he held a benefice there. Some time after 1655 he became a doctor of both canon and civil law at the University of Naples and also an apostolic notary.

Strozzi's output includes a collection of choral works for Holy Week and a set of two-part textless pieces for instructional purposes, *Elementorum musicae praxis*, but the *Capricci da sonare* is his most important volume. Intended for performance on harpsichord or organ (apparently in that order of preference), its 29 pieces cover almost every form found in keyboard music at the time: learned contrapuntal works (capriccios, ricercares, sonatas), virtuoso toccatas, dance pieces (gagliardas, correntes, ballettos), variations (on the romanesca and *eufonia*, and a *toccata de passagagli*) and an intabulated madrigal (based on Arcadelt's *Ancidetemi pur*). They are in the Neapolitan-Roman tradition of keyboard music typified by Macque, Mayone, Trabaci, Frescobaldi and Salvatore, and their style suggests that despite the late date of their publication they are early works. There are certain archaic features: it is one of the last Italian keyboard sources to be presented in open score; ecclesiastical tones are indicated; the opening capriccio, a long set of nine contrapuntal variations on the hexachord, may well be the last composition on this material; and similarly the romanesca variations may be the last Baroque work of its kind.

The ricercares are complex works in which two, three or four themes are treated simultaneously in the fashion of Salvatore's ricercares and Frescobaldi's fantasias. Several pieces, notably the toccatas, are in an elaborate fantasia style reminiscent of that of Macque and Frescobaldi but more exaggerated: it involves chromaticism, abrupt harmonic progressions and sharp dissonances, in the manner of the *consonanze stravaganti* and the *durezze e ligature* that Macque and Frescobaldi respectively used elsewhere. Figurations passing through the entire texture, and erratic, pointed rhythms, often of the Lombard variety, are two specially striking features which sometimes become so affected and passionate that supplementary performance directions are needed: *arpeggiando*, *accentando*, *gruppeggiando* (very pointed Lombardic rhythm), *largo*, *stretto*, *a battuta*, *piano*, *forte*. The music is also profusely ornamented.

The first of the three sonatas bears the remark 'inappropriately called by others Canzona francese'. This points up very clearly the well-known relationship between the sonata and the older variation canzona of Frescobaldi. Strozzi's pieces have three or four contrasted movements, a few of them employing related material, and are the earliest known keyboard pieces called 'sonata' to be in more than one movement. The dance pieces seem to have been influenced by Trabaci's, though Strozzi's are more tonal. Only the outer parts of the last five correntes and the two ballettos are given; the harmonic filling is to be supplied from figures, which are unique in denoting intervals below the soprano as well as above the bass.

WORKS

Responsoria, lamentationes, improperia, psalmi, hymni, motecta et evangelia passionis (quoad turbam), quae ad musicam in Hebdomada Sancta spectant, 4vv, bc, op.1 (Rome, 1655)

Officio del Sancto Natale, op.2 (lost; known from an allusion in op.4)

Elementorum musicae praxis, utilis non tantum, incipientibus, sed proficientibus, et perfectis, op.3 (Naples, 1683)

Capricci da sonare cembali, et organi, op.4 (Naples, 1687); ed. B. Hudson, CEKM, xi (1967)

BIBLIOGRAPHY

U. Prota-Giurleo: 'La musica a Napoli nel seicento (dal Gesualdo allo Scarlatti)', *Samnium*, i (1928), 67

W. S. Newman: *The Sonata in the Baroque Era* (Chapel Hill, North Carolina, 1959, 2/1966)

W. Apel: 'Die süditalienische Clavierschule des 17. Jahrhunderts', *AcM*, xxxiv (1962), 128

U. Prota-Giurleo: 'Due campioni della scuola musicale napoletana del XVII secolo', *L'organo*, iii (1962), 118

M. Reimann: 'Randbemerkungen zu W. Apel's "Die süditalienische Clavierschule des 17. Jahrhunderts" ', *AcM*, xxxv (1963), 154

W. Apel: *Geschichte der Orgel- und Klaviermusik bis 1700* (Kassel, 1967; Eng. trans., rev., 1972)

B. Hudson: 'Notes on Gregorio Strozzi and his *Capricci*', *JAMS*, xx (1967), 209

BARTON HUDSON

Strozzi, Piero (*b* Florence, *c*1550; *d* Florence, after 1 Sept 1609). Italian amateur composer. He was a nobleman, who played an important intellectual role in fostering the 'new music' in Florence during the late 16th century. GIULIO STROZZI was a younger member of his family. He was a member of the Camerata of Count Giovanni de' Bardi and a chief participant in its discussions on the reform of music. In apparent acknowledgment of his significance in the group, Vincenzo Galilei made him one of the two interlocutors (the other was

Bardi) in his *Dialogo della musica antica e della moderna* (1581). He was also a member of the Camerata of Jacopo Corsi and was one of those before whom Peri (as he reported in the preface to *Euridice*) first demonstrated the new manner of singing, which Corsi's group encouraged. Later he was a principal member of Marco da Gagliano's Accademia degli Elevati, which flourished in Florence from 1607 to 1609. In 1579 he composed music for the *Carro della Notte* (text by Palla Rucellai) and the *Carro di Venere* (the younger G. B. Strozzi), both of which were presented in Florence on the occasion of the marriage of Grand Duke Francesco I de' Medici and Bianca Cappello. In 1596 his music was used in the *Mascherata degli accecati* (Rinuccini), and in 1600 he composed a chorus, the 'Coro di Amori', for Caccini's *Il rapimento di Cefalo* (Chiabrera), which was presented to mark the marriage of Henri IV of France and Maria de' Medici in Florence. All this music is lost. Only three compositions by him are extant: *Fuor dell'humido nido* (in *I-Fn*; transcr. in Ghisi, 1940, and Fortune), which Caccini sang 'over his own and many other viols' in the *Carro della Notte*, and two five-part madrigals, *Vago augelletto che cantando vai*, in Luca Bati's second book of five-part madrigals (*RISM* 1598¹¹), and *Portate, aure del ciel*, in memory of Corsi, in Gagliano's second book of five-part madrigals (*RISM* 1604¹⁷).

BIBLIOGRAPHY

E. Vogel: 'Marco da Gagliano: zur Geschichte des Florentiner Musiklebens von 1570–1650', *VMw*, v (1889), 550
A. Solerti: *Musica, ballo e drammatica alla corte medicea dal 1600 al 1637* (Florence, 1905/R1968, 1969), 9f
F. Ghisi: *Feste musicali della Firenze medicea, 1480–1589* (Florence, 1939/R1969), pp.xxxv ff, 89
——: *Alle fonti della monodia* (Milan, 1940), 13, 18, 46
O. Strunk: *Source Readings in Music History* (New York, 1950), 305ff, 375
N. Pirrotta: 'Temperaments and Tendencies in the Florentine Camerata', *MQ*, xl (1954), 172, 181
L. Schrade: 'Les fêtes du mariage de Francesco dei Medici et de Bianca Cappello', *Les fêtes de la Renaissance I: CNRS Abbaye de Royaumont 1955*, 113f, 120ff, 130, pl.9
A. M. Nagler: *Theatre Festivals of the Medici, 1539–1637* (New Haven, Conn., 1964), 54f, plates.31f
N. Fortune: 'Solo Song and Cantata', *NOHM*, iv (1968), 149f, 154
N. Pirrotta and E. Povoledo: *Li due Orfei: da Poliziano a Monteverdi* (Turin, 1969, rev. 2/1975), 253f
C. V. Palisca: 'The "Camerata Fiorentina": a Reappraisal', *Studi musicali*, i (1972), 208, 212, 231, facing 218
E. Strainchamps: 'New Light on the Accademia degli Elevati of Florence', *MQ*, lxii (1976), 507

EDMOND STRAINCHAMPS

Strube, Gustav (*b* Ballenstedt, 3 March 1867; *d* Baltimore, 2 Feb 1953). American composer, conductor and violinist of German birth. He studied the violin under Brodsky at the Leipzig Conservatory and played in the Gewandhaus Orchestra until 1891. On emigrating to the USA, he became a violinist in the Boston SO (1891–1913) and was then appointed lecturer at the Peabody Conservatory, Baltimore, later becoming its director (1916–46) and conductor of the Baltimore SO (1916–30). His compositions include two operas (*Ramona*, 1916, and *The Captive*, 1938), the 'Lanier' Symphony, two violin concertos and other orchestral works; he also wrote much chamber music, including a wind quintet (1930), two string quartets (1923, 1936) and sonatas for string instruments.

Struck, Paul (Friedrich) (*b* Stralsund, 6 Dec 1776; *d* Pressburg [now Bratislava], 14 May 1820). Swedish-German composer. After studying with Albrechtsberger in 1795 and with Haydn from 1796 to 1799 in Vienna, he travelled by way of Prague, Dresden, Berlin and Stralsund to Stockholm, on the recommendation of his friend Fredrik Samuel Silverstolpe, a Swedish diplomat residing in Vienna. During his stay in Stockholm (1800–01) he became a member of the Swedish Royal Academy of Music and took part in the first Swedish performance of Haydn's *The Creation* (3 April 1801), though he failed to obtain a post as a conductor of the royal orchestra. Among the compositions written in Stockholm were a symphony in D (performed in February and March 1801) and a cantata dedicated to Queen Fredrika. In the autumn of 1801 Struck left Stockholm and went to Florence, returning to Vienna the following year, where he settled as a piano teacher. In 1809 he married, and he settled in Pressburg with his wife and children eight years later.

Struck's music hardly rises above the conventional. In a letter of 12 May 1801, Silverstolpe described him as unquestionably a genius, but vain, lacking and despising culture, and satisfied with studying only the technical aspects of composition. His Fourth Symphony was severely criticized in the *Allgemeine musikalische Zeitung* (1809, 1811), but his chamber music found more favour there (1807, 1819).

WORKS

VOCAL

Die Geburts-Feyer einer Mutter, cantata, S, T, pf (Vienna, 1798)
Cantate für Ihre Königliche Majestät die Königin (C.G. af Leopold), S, orch, 1801
Trauer-Cantate beym Tode seines Kindes, op.16 (Vienna, 1817)
Songs: 1v, pf; 3vv; 4vv, pf

INSTRUMENTAL

4 syms.: no.1, C, lost; no.2, E♭, lost; no.3, D, lost; no.4, E♭, op.10 (Offenbach, 1810)
Pf conc.
Str qt, op.2 (Offenbach, 1797); qt, pf, fl, 2 hn, op.5 (Vienna, c1800) [arr. for pf qt as op.12]; sonata, pf, cl, hn 1/vn, hn 2/vc, op.17 (Leipzig, c1815)
3 sonatas, hpd/pf, vn, b, op.1, ded. Haydn (Offenbach, 1797); Grand trio, pf, vn, b, op.3 (Offenbach, 1798); 3 sonatas, pf, fl/vn, b, op.4 (Offenbach, 1798)
Grand duo, cl/vn, pf, op.7 (Vienna, 1804); sonata, vn, pf
Short pieces, pf solo and pf 4 hands

BIBLIOGRAPHY

AMZ, ix (1807), 288; xi (1809), 654f; xiii (1811), 741; xxi (1819), 625f
C. F. Hennerberg: *Paul Struck, ein Wienerkomponist aus Haydns und Beethovens Tagen* (Stralsund, 1931) [with introduction by J. L. Struck]
C.-G. Stellan Mörner: *Johan Wikmanson und die Brüder Silverstolpe* (Stockholm, 1952)
I. Leux-Henschen: 'Till 150-årsdagen av uppförandet av Haydns "Skapelsen" 1802 i Bergen på Rügen', *STMf*, xxxiv (1952), 111
——: 'Strucks Stockholmsvistelse 1800–01', *STMf*, xxxv (1953), 85
C.-G. Stellan Mörner: 'Haydniana aus Schweden um 1800', *Haydn-Studien*, ii/1 (1969), 1

ANDERS LÖNN

Structuralism and music. Structuralism is the method of study, characteristic of much 20th-century thinking, which sees human social phenomena of all sorts (for example, customs, myths, kinship and marriage, language) as 'wholes' (or 'structures') rather than as constituent elements. It seeks to uncover the laws governing the relationships between those elements. A 'structure' is a closed network of such relationships; that is, each element of the whole has an individual relationship with every other element, so that a modification to any one alters all parts of the structure. Music lends itself to structuralist analysis because it is so manifestly concerned with interrelationships between musical ideas rather than with 'meanings', and because simultaneity and restatement bring musical ideas into direct juxtaposition (*see* ANALYSIS, §III, 7). The main branch of this structuralist analysis is termed the SEMIOLOGY of music. The chief exponents of structuralism are the Belgian anthropologist Claude Lévi-Strauss, the Swiss psychologist Jean Piaget, the French literary critic Roland Barthes and the American linguistics scholar Noam Chomsky.

BIBLIOGRAPHY
C. Lévi-Strauss: *Anthropologie structurale* (Paris, 1958; Eng. trans., 1963)
J. Piaget: *Le structuralisme* (Paris, 1968; Eng. trans., 1971)
M. Lane, ed.: *Structuralism: a Reader* (London, 1970)
For further bibliography, *see* ANALYSIS.
IAN D. BENT

Strumentato. *See* STROMENTATO.

Strumentini (It.). WOODWIND INSTRUMENTS.

Strumento (It.). Instrument. *Strumenti a corde* are string instruments; *strumenti d'arco*, bowed instruments; *strumenti di legno*, woodwind instruments; *strumenti d'ottone* or *di metallo*, brass instruments; *strumenti di penna*, quilled keyboard instruments; *strumenti a percossa*, percussion instruments; *strumenti a fiato* or *di vento*, wind instruments; *strumenti da tasto*, keyboard instruments; and so on.

The *strumento d'acciaio* ('steel instrument') required by Mozart in *Die Zauberflöte* was probably not a BELL-LYRA but a keyboard instrument such as a CELESTA.

Strungk [**Strunck**], **Delphin** (*b* 1600 or 1601; *d* Brunswick, 1694, buried 12 Oct). German composer and organist. He was organist at the principal church in Wolfenbüttel from 1630, then at the court in Celle (1632–7), and finally he moved to Brunswick, where he was organist of the Marienkirche from May 1637 and where he remained until his death. He later also became organist of other churches in Brunswick. In his *Kurtzer, doch ausführlicher Bericht von den Modis musicis* (Königsberg, 1652), Conrad Matthaei reported that Strungk was 'much admired' as an organist.

Very little of Strungk's music survives. An autograph MS of June 1671 (in *D-W*) contains a work for five voices, nine instruments and continuo entitled *Musikalischer glückwünschender Zuruff . . .*, the text beginning 'Kommet und sehet die Wercke des Herren'; and there are another five pieces of church music for voices and instruments (in *D-Bds*). A group of six chorale preludes and fantasias in an organ tablature (in *D-Lr*) show that he was by no means a negligible composer (examples in, among other edns., Die Orgel, xi–xii, Lippstadt, 1960; K. Straube, ed., *Alte Meister des Orgelspiels*, Leipzig, 1904, and C. H. Trevor, ed.: *Seasonal Chorale Preludes with Pedals*, i, London, 1963).

BIBLIOGRAPHY
Walther ML
M. Seiffert: 'Zur Biographie Delphin Strunck's', *AMw*, ii (1919–20), 79
GWILYM BEECHEY

Strungk [**Strunck**], **Nicolaus Adam** (*b* Brunswick, baptized 15 Nov 1640; *d* Dresden, 23 Sept 1700). German composer, violinist and organist, son of DELPHIN STRUNGK. He studied keyboard instruments with his father, and at the age of 12 became his assistant organist at St Magnus's Church, Brunswick. Later, while studying at Helmstedt University, he took violin lessons with

Nathaniel Schnittelbach at Lübeck. His first appointment was as a first violinist at the Wolfenbüttel court chapel in 1660; soon he moved to the court at Celle, where his salary was 200 thaler. In 1661 he paid his first visit to Vienna, played the violin at court before Emperor Leopold I and stayed until 1665. On returning to Celle he found that the court orchestra had been dissolved after Duke Christian Ludwig's death, so he moved to the court chapel of the Elector Johann Friedrich at Hanover. The extent of his activities there is not entirely clear, but his reputation in the late 1660s and 1670s must have increased, and clearly he became more widely recognized. In 1678 he was appointed director of music to the cathedral and city of Hamburg; during his four years there his gifts as a composer matured rapidly and found a wider outlet.

From 1682 to 1686 Strungk was in Hanover as court composer and organist with a salary of 460 thaler. He paid a visit to Italy in 1685 and according to Hawkins met Corelli in Rome. In July 1686 he was again in Vienna. On 26 January 1688 he was appointed vice-Kapellmeister and chamber organist at Dresden with a salary of 500 thaler. He succeeded Carlo Pallavicino, who at his death left unfinished his opera *L'Antiope*, which Strungk was invited to complete. He worked in collaboration with Christoph Bernhard, whom he succeeded as Kapellmeister on the latter's death in November 1692 with a salary of 1000 thaler. In the same year he obtained permission to found an opera house in Leipzig, and it was opened on 18 May 1693 with his *Alceste*. He settled in Leipzig permanently in 1696 and wrote several operas for the theatre there, which, however, was not a financial success, and on his death his family was left heavily in debt. He had retained his Dresden post until 1697, when he was pensioned off with 300 thaler.

Esther (typically German in being based on a biblical subject) and *Semiramis* seem to have been the most successful of his Hamburg operas. Like Bernhard's his career at Dresden was affected by the wrangling factions of German and Italian musicians, and many of the latter (whose forebears had come to Germany at Bernhard's instigation in 1655) resented Strungk's music and his management of the opera. He was essentially a serious-minded composer. His counterpoint is rather stiff and uncompromising, and his melodic inspiration, which shows Italian influence, is often a little disappointing. As an operatic composer he lacked the flair and facility of Keiser and other composers from whom the young Handel received his earliest operatic experiences in Halle and Hamburg: his sturdy, dogged style commends itself more readily in his instrumental music.

WORKS

OPERAS

Der glücklich-steigende Sejanus (C. Richter, after N. Minato), Hamburg, 1678
Der unglücklich-fallende Sejanus (Richter, after Minato), Hamburg, 1678
Alceste (J. P. Förtsch, after Quinault), Hamburg, 1680
Die Liebreiche, durch Tugend und Schönheit erhöhete Esther (Singspiel, J. M. Köler), Hamburg, 1680; recit. and various arias, ed. H. C. Wolff, ii (1957)
Die drei Töchter Cecrops (A. von Königsmarck), Hamburg, 1680
Doris, oder Der königliche Sklave (Förtsch, after Ital. orig.), Hamburg, 1680
Semiramis (W. Franck or Köler), Hamburg, 1681
Theseus (L. von Bostel, after Quinault), Hamburg, 1683
Floretto (after C. Weise: Die triumphirende Keuschheit), Hamburg, 1683
L'Antiope (S. B. Pallavicino), Dresden, 1689; acts 1 and 2 by C. Pallavicino; *D-Dlb*

Alceste (P. Thymach, after A. Aureli: L'Antigona delusa d'Alceste), Leipzig, 1693
Nero (Thymach, after G. C. Corradi), Leipzig, 1693
Syrinx, Leipzig, 1694
Phocas (C. L. Boxberg), Leipzig, 1696
Ixion (Boxberg, after Perisetti: L'Isione), Leipzig, 1697
Scipio und Hannibal (Boxberg), Leipzig, 1698
Agrippina (Boxberg), Leipzig, 1699
Erechtheus (Boxberg), Leipzig, 1700

Possibly by Strungk, all first performed in Leipzig, between 1694 and 1699: Julius Caesar, Die Schäfferinne Cloris, Atalanta, Rosalinda (A. Marchi), Jupiter und Alkmene, Pyrrhus und Demetrius, Zenobia. Der geliebte Adonis (Postel), Berenice, Alexander Magnus, Circe

100 auserlesene Arien zweyer Hamburgischen Operen, Semiramis und Esther (Hamburg, 1684)
100 auserlesene Arien . . . darinnen erbauliche Moralia (Hamburg, 1685)

SECULAR VOCAL
Leucoleons Galamelite, oder Allerhand keusche Lust- und Liebeslieder, 1v, bc (Frankfurt am Main, c1670)
19 duetti da camera cited in *EitnerQ*, lost

SACRED
Die Auferstehung Jesu (oratorio, after Fürstenau), Dresden, 1688; formerly *D-Bds*, now lost
Latin and German motets, 1 or more vv, insts, bc, *D-Bds*, *Dlb*, *LUC*, *W* Dixit Dominus, lost

INSTRUMENTAL
Musikalische Übung, vn, va da gamba . . . in etlichen Sonaten über die Festgesänge, ingleichen etlichen Ciaconen, 2 vn (Dresden, 1691), lost
9 keyboard pieces in *US-NH*; 2 ed. M. Seiffert, Organum, iv/18 (Leipzig, 1938); 1 wrongly attrib. G. Reutter in *Viennese Clavier and Organ Compositions*, ed. H. Botstiber, DTÖ, xxvii, Jg.xiii/2 (1906), 74
Sonata in A minor, a 6, bc; ed. F. Stein, HM, ciii (1952)
Sonata in D minor, a 3, bc (org); ed. M. Seiffert, Organum, iii/18 (Leipzig, 1929)
Les [10] airs avec les flauts douces, c1692–7, Dresden, *D-W*; partly transcr. D. Degen, *Suiten und Airs* (Leipzig, 1942)
Other works in *A-Wn*, *D-Bds*, *Dl*, *S-Uu*

BIBLIOGRAPHY
EitnerQ; *HawkinsH*; *WaltherML*
M. Fürstenau: *Zur Geschichte der Musik und des Theaters am Hofe zu Dresden* (Dresden, 1861–2/R1971)
A. G. Ritter: *Zur Geschichte des Orgel-Spiels im 14.–18. Jahrhundert* (Leipzig, 1884)
J. Sittard: *Geschichte des Musik- und Concertwesens in Hamburg* (Altona, 1890)
F. Zelle: *Drei Beiträge zur Geschichte der ältesten deutschen Oper*, ii (Berlin, 1891)
H. Kretzschmar: 'Das erste Jahrhundert des deutschen Oper', *SIMG*, iii (1901–2), 270
G. Fischer: *Musik in Hannover* (Hanover, 1903)
F. Berend: *Nicolaus Adam Strungk, 1640–1700: sein Leben und seine Werke. Mit Beiträgen zur Geschichte der Musik und des Theaters in Celle, Hannover und Leipzig* (Freiburg, 1915)
G. F. Schmidt: 'Zur Geschichte, Dramaturgie und Statistik der frühdeutschen Oper, 1627–1750', *ZMw*, v (1922–3), 582, 642; vi (1923–4), 129, 496–530
F. Reuter: *Geschichte der deutschen Oper in Leipzig, 1693–1720* (diss., U. of Leipzig, 1922)
L. Krüger: *Die Hamburgische Musikorganisation im 17. Jahrhundert* (Leipzig, 1933)
I. Schreiber: *Dichtung und Musik der deutschen Opernarien, 1680–1700* (diss., U. of Berlin, 1934)
W. Schulze: *Die Quellen der Hamburger Oper, 1678–1738* (Hamburg and Oldenburg, 1938)
A. Loewenberg: *Annals of Opera: 1597–1940* (Cambridge, 1943, 2/1955)
O. E. Deutsch: *Handel: a Documentary Biography* (London, 1955)
H. C. Wolff: *Die Barockoper in Hamburg (1678–1738)* (Wolffenbüttel, 1957)

GWILYM BEECHEY

Strunk, (William) Oliver (*b* Ithaca, NY, 22 March 1901; *d* Grottaferrata, 24 Feb 1980). American musicologist. As a boy he visited Germany, where he studied the piano and theory with Mannstädt. He attended Cornell University (1917–19), where his father was a professor of English, and after private studies in composition with Royce returned there as a musicology student of Kinkeldey (1926–7). After a year (1927–8)

at Berlin University studying under Wolf, Blume, Sachs and Schering, he joined the staff of the Library of Congress (1928) and later succeeded Carl Engel as head of its music department (1934–7), concurrently lecturing at the Catholic University of America, Washington. In the years immediately preceding World War II he took a leading part in welcoming eminent refugee music scholars and finding places for them in the USA. From 1937 he taught at Princeton University, where he was appointed professor (1950); on his retirement (1966) he moved to Grottaferrata, near Rome.

Strunk was an original member of the American Musicological Society, the first editor of its journal (1948) and its president (1959–60); he also served on the editorial board of Monumenta Musicae Byzantinae (from 1958) and succeeded Carsten Høeg as director (1961–71). His honorary awards included membership of the Royal Musical Association, the Danish Academy and the British Academy (corresponding fellow), and doctorates from the universities of Rochester (1936) and Chicago (1970); in 1961 he received the American Council of Learned Societies prize for distinguished scholarship in the humanities.

Strunk was one of the founders of American musicology and one of its most influential and versatile practitioners. His published papers cover an exceptionally wide range of subjects, including the Italian Ars Nova, 15th-century English polyphony, the 16th-century motet, Palestrina's masses, the style and chronology of Haydn's works and the output of Verdi. His unpublished work includes substantial studies on aspects of the Ars Antiqua through Venetian opera and on to Beethoven and Wagner. His best-known work is *Source Readings in Music History*, a critical anthology of translated writings on music from the Greeks to Wagner. His own preferred subject, to which he contributed massively though often in little-known journals, was the liturgical chant of the Eastern and Western churches. He was responsible for establishing a sound theoretical basis for the transcription of the Byzantine round notation of the 12th and 13th centuries, and developed methods for transcribing the previously impenetrable paleo-Byzantine and paleo-Slavonic notations. He also uncovered important repertories of Byzantine and Slavonic melismatic chants that were previously ignored or poorly understood.

The breadth and solidity of Strunk's achievement reflect not only a vigorous intellect but also his felicitous encounter (in his twenties) with German musicological scholarship at its most impressive. Forbearing to ally himself with any particular system of analysis or historical interpretation, or to create general theories, he combined intellectual scepticism with a knowledge of the cultural context and an ingenuity in evolving and exploiting various methods of inquiry; he liked to take apparently self-contained problems and develop far-reaching conclusions based on irrefutable facts. His teaching, like his writing, was influential beyond its immediate scope and was marked by an exceptional generosity with ideas and information. His pupils include Robert Bailey, Charles Hamm, Joseph Kerman, Lewis Lockwood, Harold S. Powers, Don Randel, Charles Rosen and Leo Treitler.

WRITINGS
'Vergil in Music', *MQ*, xvi (1930), 482
'Haydn's Divertimenti for Baryton, Viola, and Bass', *MQ*, xviii (1932), 216–51

State and Resources of Musicology in the United States (Washington, DC, 1932)

'Haydn', *From Bach to Stravinsky: the History of Music*, ed. D. Ewen (New York, 1933), 77; repr. in *The World of Great Composers*, ed D. Ewen (Englewood Cliffs, 1962), 91

'Sources and Problems for Graduate Study in Musicology', *Proceedings of the Music Teachers National Association*, xxviii (1933), 105

'Notes on a Haydn Autograph', *MQ*, xx (1934), 192

'The Historical Aspect of Musicology', *Proceedings of the Music Teachers National Association*, xxxi (1936), 14; also in *PAMS 1936*, 14

'Origins of the "L'homme armé" Mass', *BAMS*, ii (1937), 25

'Some Motet-types of the 16th Century', *PAMS 1939*, 155

'The Tonal System of Byzantine Music', *MQ*, xxviii (1942), 190

'Intonations and Signatures of the Byzantine Modes', *MQ*, xxxi (1945), 339

'Guglielmo Gonzaga and Palestrina's *Missa Dominicalis*', *MQ*, xxxiii (1947), 228

'The Music of the Old Hall Manuscript – a Postscript', *MQ*, xxxv (1949), 244; repr. with adds in M. Bukofzer: *Studies in Medieval and Renaissance Music* (New York, 1950), 80

'Intorno a Marchetto da Padova', *RaM*, xx (1950), 312

Source Readings in Music History (New York, 1950/R1965)

'The Classification and Development of the Early Byzantine Notations', *1° congresso internazionale di musica sacra: Roma 1950*, 111

'St. Gregory Nazianzus and the Proper Hymns for Easter', *Late Classical and Medieval Studies in Honor of Albert Mathias Friend, Jr.* (Princeton, 1955), 82

'The Notation of the Chartres Fragment', *AnnM*, iii (1955), 7–37

'The Byzantine Office at Hagia Sophia', *Dumbarton Oaks Papers*, nos. 9–10 (1956), 75

'Influsso del canto liturgico orientale su quello della chiesa occidentale', *L'enciclica 'Musicae sacrae disciplina' di Sua Santità Pio XII: testo e commento, a cura dell'Associazone italiana S. Cecilia* (Rome, 1957), 343

'The Antiphons of the Oktoechos', *JAMS*, xiii (1960), 50

'A Further Note on the Proper Hymns for Easter', *Classica et mediaevalia*, xxii (1961), 176

'Melody Construction in Byzantine Chant', *XIIᵉ congrès international d'études byzantines: Ochride 1961*, i, 365

'A Cypriote in Venice', *Natalica musicologica Knud Jeppesen* (Copenhagen, 1962), 101

'The Latin Antiphons for the Octave of the Epiphany', *Recueil de travaux de l'Institut d'études byzantines*, viii/2 (Belgrade, 1963–4), 417

'Zwei Chilandari Chorbücher', *Anfänge der slavischen Musik: Symposia I: Bratislava 1964*, 65

'Byzantine Music in the Light of Recent Research and Publication', *XIIIth International Congress of Byzantine Studies: Oxford 1966*, 245

ed.: *Specimina notationum antiquiorum*, MMB, main ser., vii (1966)

'Verdiana alla Library of Congress', *1° congresso internazionale di studi verdiani: Venezia 1966*, 452

'Padre Lorenzo Tardo ed il suo Ottoeco nei mss. melurgici: alcune osservazioni sugli Stichera Dogmatika', *Bollettino della Badia greca di Grottaferrata*, new. ser., xxi (1967), 21

'Church Polyphony Apropos a New Fragment at Grottaferrata', *L'ars nova italiana del trecento II: Certaldo 1969*, 305

'Tropus und Troparion', *Speculum musicae artis: Festgabe für Heinrich Husmann* (Munich, 1971), 305

'Die Gesänge der byzantinischen-griechischen Liturgie', *Geschichte der katholischen Kirchenmusik*, i, ed. K. G. Fellerer (Kassel, 1972), 128

'A Little Known Sticheron for the Translation of St. Nicholas', *La chiesa greca in Italia dall' VIII al XVI secolo*, Italia Sacra, nos.20–22 (Padua, 1973), 1261

'The Menaia from Carbone at the Biblioteca Vallicelliana', *Bollettino della Badia greca di Grottaferrata*, new ser., xxviii (1973), 3

Essays on Music in the Western World (New York, 1974) [collected articles]

with E. Follieri: *Triodium Athoum*, MMB, main ser., ix (1975)

Essays on Music in the Byzantine World (New York, 1977) [collected articles]

BIBLIOGRAPHY

H. S. Powers, ed.: *Studies in Music History: Essays for Oliver Strunk* (Princeton, 1968) [incl. 'Scholar and Teacher', p.3; list of writings to 1967, p.511]

L. Lockwood: Foreword to O. Strunk: *Essays on Music in the Western World* (New York, 1974)

C. Rosen: 'A Master Musicologist', *New York Review of Books*, xxii/1 (6 Feb 1975), 32 [review of *Essays on Music in the Western World*]

K. Levy: Foreword to O. Strunk: *Essays on Music in the Byzantine World* (New York, 1977)

KENNETH LEVY

Strutt, John William. *See* RAYLEIGH, JOHN WILLIAM STRUTT.

Strutz [Strutius], Thomas (*b* Stargard, nr. Neubrandenburg, *c*1621; *d* Danzig, buried 5 Oct 1678). German composer and organist. There were several organists with the name Strutz in 17th-century Germany, including another called Thomas who also died in 1678. The subject of this article became organist of Holy Trinity, Danzig, in 1642 and five years later a citizen of that city. In 1668 he succeeded Paul Siefert as organist of St Mary's, Danzig. His duties at Holy Trinity and at the adjoining Gymnasium brought him into contact with J. Maukisch, an educationist who sought simple, direct means as the basis of instruction in school and church: he envisaged a thorough reform of the liturgy whereby folklike chorales, with vernacular texts and in settings immediately accessible to the congregation, replaced both the old traditional polyphonic motet and the new Italianate concerto. For two decades Strutz and he wrote a number of works that furthered the cause of religious education. Whereas his Danzig colleagues, Crato Bütner and Balthasar Erben excelled in the concerto calling for large forces, Strutz wrote smaller works of a more intimate nature – sacred songs, dialogues, small concertos and oratorio Passions – most of them to texts by Maukisch.

Lobsingende Hertzens-Andacht (1656) is typical of Strutz's sacred music. It contains 76 four- and five-part songs for all Sundays and church festivals in place of the usual motets, concertos and cantatas. They are very short, averaging 12–16 bars, and are either homophonic or freely imitative; the short points of imitation are drawn from the chorale-like melodies, composed by Strutz himself, which appear in the highest part. The songs were so popular that they were used at Holy Trinity until the first half of the 18th century. *Geistliche Singe- und Bet-Stunden* (1657) consists of 34 solo songs with continuo for use at home or school; they are good examples of the methods of Maukisch and Strutz. *Vierfache musicalische Dienstwilligkeit* (1655) contains similarly simple solo songs with singable melodies for use in the Gymnasium; all are strophic, even the dialogues, in which the verses are divided between the two singers.

The dramatic element of the dialogues is also seen in *Zweyfache Christliche Auffmunterung* (1664), an oratorio Passion resembling Schütz's *Die sieben Worte . . . Jesu Christi*. Instead of the usual forms of chorale Passion and motet Passion, the biblical text is replaced by a lyrical paraphrase sung by the various characters and choir and interspersed with familiar chorales sung by the congregation. Three works whose texts alone survive were in a similar form: a *St Matthew Passion* in which the sung material is divided among soloists chorus and congregation, a Christmas dialogue in which lyrical sacred verses and chorale texts generally replace the biblical text, and a dialogue on the subject of Dives and Lazarus in which the text is divided between the two characters. Such treatments of scripture point to the influence of Martin Opitz and his circle and run parallel to developments in German sacred songs.

WORKS

(all printed works published in Danzig)

Musicalisches Freuden Gedichte auff des . . . A. Rosenbergs . . . Hochzeit (1655)

Vierfache musicalische Dienstwilligkeit . . . in 4 unterschiedlichen Melodien, 1, 2vv, bc (1655)

Lobsingende Hertzens-Andachts über die Evangelia, 4, 5vv (1656); 8 ed. in Zahn

Geistliche Singe- und Bet-Stunden, 1v, bc (1657)

Zweyfache Christliche Auffmunterung . . . in einem Dialogo oder musicalischem Gespräch (1664)
Psalmus C and other sacred works; see Günther
Sonata a 8, bc (1658; repr. in appx of 1659³)
Several sacred works, 1–3vv, insts, *D-Bds, Dlb,* Marienbibliothek, Elbing [now Elblag], *Lm* (lost, cited in library catalogue), formerly *PL-GD, S-Uu*; see Günther

LOST WORKS
(*known only from texts*)
Abriss der musicalischen Passions-Andacht, 5vv (1664)
Christlich wolmeynende Weynachts Gedanken . . . in einem musicalischen Gespräch (1664)
Einfältige Abbildung des ewigen himmlischen Freuden Lebens . . . der Lehrreichen Geschicht von Lazaro und dem Reiche Manne (n.d.)

BIBLIOGRAPHY
C. von Winterfeld: *Der evangelische Kirchengesang,* ii (Leipzig, 1845/R1966), 152
G. Döring: *Zur Geschichte der Musik in Preussen* (Elbing, 1852)
J. Zahn: *Die Melodien der deutschen evangelischen Kirchenlieder* (Gütersloh, 1889–93/R1963)
A. Fischer and W. Tümpel: *Das deutsche evangelische Kirchenlied des 17. Jahrhunderts,* iii (Gütersloh, 1906/R1964)
O. Günther: 'Musikgeschichtliches aus Danzigs Vergangenheit', *Mitteilungen des Westpreussischen Geschichtsvereins,* x (1911)
JERROLD C. BAAB

Strzeskowsky Lutebook. *See* SOURCES OF LUTE MUSIC, §3.

Stuart. British royal family, important patrons of music in the 17th century; *see* LONDON, §II.

Stuart, Leslie [Barrett, Thomas Augustine] (*b* Southport, 15 March 1864; *d* Richmond, Surrey, 27 March 1928). English composer. At the age of 15 he was made organist at Salford Cathedral, and he held this post for seven years. Afterwards he was organist for a further seven years at the Church of the Holy Name, Manchester, supplementing his salary by teaching and composing church music. He also promoted and conducted popular orchestral concerts in the city. In 1895 he moved to London, his ballad *The Bandolero* having been successfully promoted by Signor Foli and a song *Lousiana Lou* having been accepted by George Edwardes for *The Shop Girl*. His song *Soldiers of the Queen* gained wide popularity, and he followed it with 'coon' songs including *Little Dolly Daydream* (1897) and *Lily of Laguna* (1898), which were written for Eugene Stratton and which have remained among the best known of music-hall songs. In 1899 a musical comedy *Florodora* was also a considerable success, not only in Britain but also in the USA and Europe, owing particularly to the double sextet 'Tell me, pretty maiden'. Stuart's range, however, was limited, and rhythmic mannerisms tended to recur, so that later stage works were less successful. In 1915 he appeared on the variety stage, accompanying his daughter May Leslie-Stuart in his own songs, and he later went to the USA. He returned to England in 1921 and again appeared on the variety stage playing his own compositions, most notably in a revue at the Palladium shortly before his death, at which time he had just signed a contract for the production of a new stage work, *Nina.*

WORKS
(*selective list*)
Musical comedies: Florodora (2, O. Hall, E. Boyd-Jones, P. Rubens), 1899; The Silver Slipper (2, Hall, W. H. Risque), 1901; The School Girl (2, H. Hamilton, P. Potter), 1903; The Belles of Mayfair (2, C. H. E. Brookfield, C. Hamilton), 1906; Havana (3, G. Grossmith, G. Hill, A. Ross, G. Arthurs), 1908; Captain Kidd (2, S. Hicks, Ross), 1910; The Slim Princess (2, H. Blossom), 1910; Peggy (2, Grossmith, C. H. Bovill), 1911; Midnight Frolic, 1917
Probably more than 100 songs incl. numbers for musical comedies from The Shop Girl (1895) to The Lady of the Rose (1922); ballads incl.

The Bandolero (1895), Rip Van Winkle (1896); music-hall songs incl. Soldiers of the Queen (1895), Little Dolly Daydream (1897), Lily of Laguna (1898), The Little Octoroon (1899), The Banshee (1900), I may be Crazy (1902)

BIBLIOGRAPHY
T. Roberts: 'Stories of some Successful Songs', *Royal Magazine,* iii (1900), 422
ANDREW LAMB

Stubbs, Simon (*fl c*1620). English composer. He contributed a setting of the tune 'Martyrs' to Thomas Ravenscroft's *The Whole Booke of Psalmes* (1621). An Evening Service (*Magnificat, Nunc dimittis*) is in *GB-T,* together with a verse anthem, *The Lord is my shepherd*; the verse anthem *Have mercy upon me, O God,* is in *GB-Lbm* (Myriell's *Tristitiae remedium*) as is a full anthem, *Father of love* (also in *GB-Och*).

BIBLIOGRAPHY
R. T. Daniel and P. le Huray: *The Sources of English Church Music, 1549–1660,* EECM, suppl.i (1972)
PETER LE HURAY

Stuber [Stuberus, Stueber], **Conrad** (*b* Schwendi, nr. Laupheim, Swabia, *c*1550; *d c*1605). German composer and theorist. He attended the University of Freiburg, probably from 1572, and in 1574 he was awarded his master's degree; in 1577–8 he was registered in the medical faculty. In 1587 he was a priest and choirman in the Kantorei at the court of Count Eitelfriedrich IV von Hohenzollern-Hechingen at Hechingen, Swabia. At the beginning of 1591 he was recommended for a benefice by Christoph Truchsess von Waldburg of Riedlingen an der Donau. At Freiburg he had studied with J. T. Freigius, a pupil of Glarean, who must have thought highly of him since he used Stuber's *De musica* (now lost) as the basis of the dialogue forming the fifth part, 'De musicae elementis primus', of his *Paedagogus* (Basle, 1582). Count Eitelfriedrich was an ardent advocate of the Counter-Reformation, the spirit of which is evident in the texts, entirely sacred, set by Stuber in his few surviving compositions. Rubsamen (in *MGG*) singled out *Veni, Sancte Spiritus* as an example of his mastery of imitative counterpoint, which nevertheless manages to convey meticulously the sense of the words, with, for example, syncopation at 'Qui per diversitatem linguarum' and a canonic duet at 'in unitate'.

WORKS
Litany, 6vv, 1596²
Maria werd, so mein Seel kert, 5vv, 1604⁷
Fecit potentiam, 3vv, 1605¹
Laudate pueri, 3vv, 1605¹

Missa ad imitationem cantionis Maria Magdalena, 6vv, *D-Nla*
Christi favente gratis, hymn (de S Benedicto Abbate), 6vv, *Mbs*
Christi fons omnis boni, hymn (de S Chrysogono), 6vv, *Mbs*
Veni Sancte Spiritus, 5vv, *Nla*

THEORETICAL WORKS
De musica, lost

BIBLIOGRAPHY
W. Rubsamen: 'The International "Catholic" Repertoire of a Lutheran Church in Nürnberg (1574–1597)', *AnnM,* v (1957), 229–327
E. F. Schmid: *Musik an der schwäbischen Zollernhöfen der Renaissance* (Kassel, 1962)
W. Rubsamen: 'Stuber, Conrad', *MGG*
ANTHONY F. CARVER

Stuchs [Stüchs, Stöchs], **Georg** (*b* ?Sulzbach, Upper Palatine; *d* Nuremberg, 1520). German printer. Although Stuchs himself gave Sulzbach as his place of birth in his publications, he may have been the son of the Nuremberg organ builder Friedrich Stuchs. He became a citizen of Nuremberg in 1484 and began printing in the same year. His last publication is dated

1517; after this he was active only as a bookseller, leaving the printing business in the hands of his son, Johann, under whose name publications had been issued as early as 1509.

The elder Stuchs, whose known publications number 132, was famous above all as a printer of liturgical books, particularly missals. He served a large circle of clients from all parts of Europe, including, for example, the bishoprics of Regensburg, Salzburg, Prague, Kraków, Magdeburg and Linköping. In 1491 he introduced musical notes into his liturgical books, using the double-impression technique derived from Petrucci. Stuchs was known for the superior quality of his type forms, which he frequently sold to other printers, and for the woodcuts, often by prominent artists, with which he decorated his volumes. The younger Stuchs devoted himself in later years to the cause of the Reformation, printing many of the writings of Luther and his followers. His sole contribution to music consists of a reprint of Johannes Cochlaeus's treatise *Tetrachordum musices* in 1512.

BIBLIOGRAPHY

P. Molitor: *Deutsche Choral-Wiegendrucke* (Regensburg, 1904)
W. Baumann: 'Die Druckerei Stuchs zu Nürnberg (1484–1537)', *Gutenberg-Jb* (1954), 122 [with list of publications]
J. Benzing: 'Die Stuchsdruckerei zu Nürnberg im Dienst der Reformation', *Archiv für Geschichte des Buchwesens*, iv (1961–3), 1585
K. Meyer-Baer: *Liturgical Music Incunabula: a Descriptive Catalogue* (London, 1962)
T. Wohnhaas: 'Stuchs, Georg', *MGG*

MARIE LOUISE GÖLLNER

Stuchs [Stüchs], **Johann** (*d* ?Nuremberg, after 1546). German printer, son of GEORG STUCHS.

Stück (Ger.). Piece. In Bach's day, *Stück* could also mean the principal concerted piece in a church service, that is, the cantata.

Stuck [Stück], **Jean-Baptiste** [Baptistin, Batistin] (*b* 1680; *d* Paris, 8 Dec 1755). Italian composer and cellist of German descent. He called himself 'Florentin', although Lesure gave Livorno as his birthplace. In the libretto of *Rodrigo in Algeri* (Naples, 1702), a reworking of Albinoni's *L'inganno innocente*, he was called 'virtuoso della Contessa di Lemos'. His appearance in Paris was marked by the publication of an aria in Ballard's *Recueil d'airs sérieux* of 1705. A virtuoso cellist, he played there under the patronage of the Prince of Carignan, who died in 1740. On the title-pages of his four books of cantatas (1706–14) he was called 'Ordinaire de la musique de ... Monseigneur le Duc d'Orléans'. *La prise de Lérida*, from book 2, celebrates a military victory that may also have been the motivation for his *Te Deum*, commissioned by the Duchess of Chartres and performed at the Palais Royal on 27 November 1707. In 1708 he wrote an aria for a revival of Collasse's *Thétis et Pélée*. His first two French operas, *Méléagre* and *Manto la fée*, were performed in 1709 and 1711 with little success.

According to Loewenberg, Stuck left France and spent some time in the service of Elector Max Emanuel of Bavaria (*c*1714). His opera *Il Cid* was performed at Livorno at Carnival 1715, and in the same year he married Bonne-Françoise Berain, daughter of Louis XIV's court painter. He was given a pension of 500 livres as *ordinaire de la musique du Roy* on 18 December 1718. His third French opera, *Polidore*, was presented in 1720 and revived in 1739, and his duet cantata *Démocrite et Héraclite* was performed at the Opéra in November 1722. The death of the librettist La Font in 1725 prevented his completing the opera *Orion*, but an arietta appeared in the *Mercure*. He was active at the Concert Spirituel: an aria, four cantatas and the divertissement *L'union de la musique italienne et françoise* were given 18 performances in 1727–9; Stuck, Guignon and Blavet played a trio on 24 and 25 December 1728; and a motet was performed on 13 April 1738. He became a French citizen in June 1733.

Although Stuck was not, as La Borde stated, the first to play the cello at the Opéra, the success of his performances as a solo cellist hastened the decline in the gamba's popularity. Ancelet and Maisonelle agreed that he was the first cellist to be admired in France, and Corrette wrote that the rise to prominence of the cello began with the arrival in Paris of Stuck and L'Abbé, both virtuosos. His operas are of little importance, but his French cantatas, published shortly after those of J. B. Morin, are models of the genre. In book 1 the melodies are strongly Italianate, but in the later books he succeeded in his attempt to fuse Italian and French musical styles: the recitatives become ariosos and the fluent violin lines gradually lose their complexity. Of particular interest is *Démocrite et Héraclite*, which shows two allegorical figures, Optimism and Pessimism; the music changes character for their solos, and their sentiments are juxtaposed in the duet. D'Aquin de Château-Lyon wrote that in the realm of the cantata Stuck is 'the rival of Clérambault'.

WORKS
(printed works published in Paris unless otherwise stated)

DRAMATIC
(operas unless otherwise stated)

Arias in Rodrigo in Algeri, Naples, S Bartolomeo, ?10 Dec 1702, music lost [rev. of T. Albinoni: L'inganno innocente (F. Silvani), Venice, 1701]
Air for rev. of P. Collasse: Thétis et Pélée (B. Fontenelle), Paris, Opéra, 16 April 1708, collab. A. Campra (1708)
Méléagre (F. A. Jolly), Paris, Opéra, 24 May 1709 (1709); prol as L'union de la musique italienne et françoise (divertissement), Paris, Opéra, Nov 1722, lost
Manto la fée (Mennesson), Paris, Opéra, 29 Jan 1711 (1711)
Il [gran] Cid (G. G. Alborghetti [L. Mereo]), Livorno, S Sebastiano, carn. 1715 (Massa, 1715)
Polidore (J.-L.-I. de la Serre), Paris, Opéra, 15 Feb 1720 (1720, 2/1739)
Orion (La Font), 1725, inc., 1 air pubd in Mercure de France (Feb 1725)

OTHER WORKS
Cantatas: [6] Cantates françoises, S, 2 vn, bc, some with insts, bk 1 (1706); [6] Cantates françoises, S, B, bc, some with insts, bk 2 (1708); [2] Cantates françoises, S, 2 vn, bc, and S, B, 2 vn, bc, bk 3 (1711); [6] Cantates françoises, S, bc, some with insts, bk 4 (1714); 5 Italian cantatas, F-Pn; Les troubles de l'amour, music lost, text in J. Bachelier: Recueil de cantates (1728)
Te Deum, perf. Paris, Chapelle du Palais royal, 27 Nov 1707, lost; motet, perf. Paris, Concert Spirituel, 13 April 1738; several airs, etc, pubd in 18th-century anthologies

BIBLIOGRAPHY

M. Corrette: *Méthode théorique et pratique* (Paris, 1741/R1972)
Ancelet: *Observations sur la musique, les musiciens et les instrumens* (Amsterdam, 1757)
Maisonelle: *Réponse aux observations sur la musique, les musiciens et les instrumens* (Avignon, 1758)
J.-B. de La Borde: *Essai sur la musique ancienne et moderne*, iii (Paris, 1780/R1972)
A. Loewenberg: 'Stuck, Jean-Baptiste', *Grove 5*
M. Barthélemy: 'Les cantates de Jean-Baptiste Stuck', *RMFC*, ii (1962), 125
S. Milliot: 'Réflexions et recherches sur la viole de gamba et le violoncelle en France', *RMFC*, iv (1964), 179
F. Lesure: 'Stuck, Jean-Baptiste', *MGG*
S. Milliot: 'Jean-Baptiste Stück', *RMFC*, ix (1969), 91
J. R. Anthony: *French Baroque Music from Beaujoyeulx to Rameau* (London, 1973, rev. 2/1978)

D. Tunley: *The Eighteenth-century French Cantata* (London, 1974)
C. Pierre: *Histoire du Concert spirituel 1725–1790* (Paris, 1975)
BARRY KERNFELD

Stucken, Frank (Valentine) van der (*b* Fredericksburg, Texas, 15 Oct 1858; *d* Hamburg, Germany, 16 Aug 1929). American conductor and composer. In 1865 his family moved to Antwerp, where he became a student of Peter Benoit. In 1876, after a visit to the Bayreuth Festival, he settled in Leipzig for two years' study with Reinecke, Langer and Grieg. His first professional engagement was at the municipal theatre, Breslau, in 1881; he composed incidental music for Shakespeare's *The Tempest* as part of his duties. In 1883 with the sponsorship of Liszt and the participation of, among others, Ziloti, he gave a successful concert of his own works at Weimar. The next year he returned to the USA, where he became conductor of the Arion Society, a male chorus in New York; he conducted the first American performances of Brahms's Symphony no.3, Chabrier's *España*, Berlioz's *Les troyens* (concert performance) and a series of programmes of recent American music. He introduced much American music to Europe, his all-American concert at which MacDowell played his own D minor Piano Concerto at the Paris Exposition of 1889 being an especially notable event.

In 1895 van der Stucken became a central part of Cincinnati's musical life, as the first conductor of the Cincinnati SO (until 1907), as director of the college of music and later (1906–12, 1923–7) as director of the May Festival. From 1908 until 1917 he lived in Hanover and in the last two decades of his life he was generally more active in Europe than in the USA. His compositions include orchestral and choral works as well as many songs.

MICHAEL STEINBERG

Stuckenschmidt, Hans Heinz (*b* Strasbourg, 1 Nov 1901). German music critic and musicologist. After attending secondary schools in Berlin, Ulm and Magdeburg, he studied the violin, piano and composition under private teachers and was self-taught in music theory and music history. From 1920 he made a living as a freelance composer and writer on music in Bremen, Hamburg, Vienna, Paris and Berlin. In 1923–4, with J. Rufer, he organized the Hamburg Neue Musik concerts, and in 1927–8 he directed the concerts of the Berlin November-Gruppe; at the same time he worked for various periodicals (e.g. *Aufbruch*, *Auftakt*, *Melos* and *Modern Music*) and newspapers. In Prague (1928–9) he was chief music critic of the *Bohemia* and he then succeeded A. Weissmann (1929) as music critic of the *Berliner Zeitung am Mittag*. He attended Schoenberg's course on musical analysis as an observer (1931–3). Because of his support for modern music and for Jewish musicians he was forbidden in 1934 to participate in any journalistic activity in Germany. From 1937 he was in Prague again, initially on the *Prager Tageblatt* and (from 1939) on the *Neuer Tag* until he was forbidden to publish there as well. In 1942 he was conscripted into the armed forces as an interpreter. After his return from American captivity in 1946, he was given the directorship of the department of new music at RIAS, Berlin, was appointed music critic of the *Neue Zeitung* (1947) and with J. Rufer edited the periodical *Stimmen* (1947–9). Subsequently he became lecturer (1948), reader (1949) and professor (1953) in music history at the

Technische Universität in Berlin where he remained until his retirement (1967). He has also been Berlin music correspondent for the *Neue Zürcher Zeitung* (1946–57) and music critic for the *Frankfurter allgemeine Zeitung* (1957–). He is married to the soprano Margot Hinnenberg-Lefèbre, well known as an interpreter of Schoenberg. In 1974 he was made a member of the Akademie der Künste, Berlin.

As a music critic Stuckenschmidt has been a sound judge and indefatigable supporter of contemporary music. He gave early recognition to the historical significance of Schoenberg and Stravinsky in particular. With the public recognition of new music, Stuckenschmidt emerged as a critic of international importance. Schoenberg has occupied the central position in his many books and essays on 20th-century music; his comprehensive biography of the composer is based on about 4000 source documents.

WRITINGS

Arnold Schönberg (Zurich and Freiburg, 1951, 2/1957; Eng. trans., 1960)
Neue Musik zwischen den beiden Kriegen (Berlin and Frankfurt am Main, 1951)
ed.: *F. Busoni, Entwurf einer neuen Ästhetik der Tonkunst* (Wiesbaden, 1954)
Glanz und Elend der Musikkritik (Berlin, 1957)
Strawinsky und sein Jahrhundert (Berlin, 1957)
Schöpfer der Neuen Musik (Frankfurt am Main, 1958)
Boris Blacher (Berlin, 1963)
Oper in dieser Zeit (Velber, 1964) [collected reviews]
Johann Nepomuk David (Wiesbaden, 1965)
Maurice Ravel (Frankfurt am Main, 1966; Eng. trans., 1968)
Ferruccio Busoni (Zurich, 1968; Eng. trans., 1970)
Twentieth Century Music (London, 1968; Ger. orig., 1969)
'Gedanken zur Vernichtung des Kunsturteils durch Soziologie', *Studien zur Wertforschung*, ii (Graz, 1969), 26
'Kriterien und Grenzen der Neuheit', *Das musikalische Neue und die Neue Musik*, ed. H. P. Reinecke (Mainz, 1969), 7
Twentieth Century Composers (London, 1970; Ger. orig., 1971)
Schönberg: Leben, Umwelt, Werk (Zurich, 1974; Eng. trans., 1978)
Die Musik eines halben Jahrhunderts: 1925–1975 (Munich, 1976)

BIBLIOGRAPHY

W. Burde, ed.: *Aspekte der neuen Musik: Professor Hans Heinz Stuckenschmidt zum 65. Geburtstag* (Kassel, 1968)
W. Schwinger: 'Mitschöpfer der neuen Musik: H. H. Stuckenschmidt siebzig Jahre', *Musica*, xxv (1971), 609

HANS HEINRICH EGGEBRECHT

Stucki, Hans [Johannes]. *See* TUGI, HANS.

Studer, Hans (*b* Muri, nr. Berne, 20 April 1911). Swiss composer. After attending the Muristalden Evangelical Teachers' Training College, where Burkhard was his piano teacher, he worked as a country primary schoolteacher for several years. He studied under Graf, Balmer and Hirt at the university and conservatory in Berne (1934–8), and then worked as a training college music teacher in Berne, also directing several leading local choral societies. In composition he had no formal training. His first works are entirely late Romantic in character: the decisive encounter with contemporary music came at a choral festival in Thun in 1931. Besides Bartók, Hindemith and Stravinsky, the strongest influence on him has been that of Burkhard, in whose music he discovered an inner sympathy in the tendency towards lyricism and intimacy, the strict and economical counterpoint (frequently leading to a pronounced austerity) and a certain restraint and objectivity, expressed characteristically in a neo-Baroque idiom. This alignment is also reflected in Studer's predilection for church music. His compositions are grounded in tonality, often with modal traits but often, too, pushed to its limits by the employment of impressionist and highly dissonant harmonies. Studer received the Music Prize of the City of Berne in 1968.

WORKS
(selective list)

Vocal: Die Leiden Hiobs, oratorio, A, Bar, chorus, orch, 1944–6; 5 geistliche Konzerte, 1v, insts, 1943, 1950, 1957, 1960, 1967; Pan kai Aphrodite, cantata, A, female chorus, orch, 1950; In Dich hab ich gehoffet, Herr, cantata, B, chorus, org, 1951; Das Totenhemdchen, cantata, A, female chorus, str qt, cel, str orch, 1953; Der Lobgesang, cantata, S, chorus, 8 insts, 1954; 5 other cantatas, 1957, 1958, 1961, 1962, 1963; other choral and solo pieces

Inst: Concertino, fl, ob, str orch, 1943; Chamber Conc., pf, small orch, 1948; Little Conc., pf duet, fl, str orch, 1952; Conc., org, wind, perc, 1952; Cassation, small orch, 1958; Sinfonia, str, 1959; Fantasie, str, 1961; Choralfantasie, org, 1963; Disegno su distese, fl, 3 str qts, 2 db, 1970; Epitaph, orch, 1970; 3 Stücke, school orch, 1972; many other chamber and org pieces

Principal publishers: Bärenreiter, Eulenburg, Hug, Krompholz

BIBLIOGRAPHY

H. Studer: 'Vorstellung der Jungen/Présentation des jeunes', SMz, lxxxiii (1943), 319

E. Nievergelt: 'Die Leiden Hiobs, ein Oratorium von Hans Studer', Reformierte Schweiz, iv (1947)

P. Mieg: 'Hans Studer', 40 schweizer Komponisten der Gegenwart (Amriswil, 1956), 190

T. Käser: 'Hans Studer, Gestalt und Werk: der evangelische Kirchenchor', Musik und Gottesdienst, xx (1966), 64

W. Tappolet: 'Eine Weihnachtsvesper von Hans Studer', Musik und Gottesdienst, xxiii (1969), 15

FRITZ MUGGLER

Studio der frühen Musik [Early Music Quartet]. Ensemble, founded at Munich in 1960, directed by Thomas Binkley. Binkley, primarily a lutenist, and Sterling Jones, primarily a string player, had studied musicology at the University of Illinois in Urbana, where they had taken part in George Hunter's collegium musicum and performed on his important Machaut record. In Munich they were joined by the Estonian singer Andrea von Ramm. The fourth member of the group was the tenor Nigel Rogers (1960–64), who was succeeded by Willard Cobb (1964–70) and then Richard Levitt. In 1972 the ensemble joined the staff of the Schola Cantorum at Basle. In 1977 it disbanded, though without excluding the possibility of further activity. The Studio der frühen Musik toured throughout the world, first under the auspices of the Goethe-Institut, then independently; it has made over 30 records.

Although the group's recordings include music by Machaut, Landini, Ciconia, Dufay and Dowland, their most important records are perhaps those that explore the earlier monophonic repertories. Beginning with records of songs from the Carmina burana (1964, 1967) and Minnesang (1966), they developed a performing style partly based on Andalusian music and employing a freedom of expression possible only with musicians who are performing regularly as an ensemble; their style became increasingly independent of folk origins and moved towards an appraisal of the characteristics of each of the different repertories concerned. The ensemble always performed from memory, with results that gained correspondingly in fluidity and freedom of expression as well as more direct communication.

DAVID FALLOWS

Studios. See STOUDIOS.

Studley Royal Fragments. See SOURCES, MS, §VI, 3.

Study (Fr. étude; Ger. Etüde, Studie; It. studio). An instrumental piece, usually of some difficulty and most often for a stringed keyboard instrument, designed primarily to exploit and perfect a chosen facet of performing technique, but the better for having some musical interest. Though a study was at one time the same as an exercise (Fr. exercice; Ger. Übung; It. essercizio), the latter term now usually implies a short figure or passage to be repeated ad lib, whether unaltered, on different degrees of the scale or in various keys. The distinction is illustrated by Schumann's Studien op.3 (1832), which are preceded by short Übungen based on technical difficulties found in the studies themselves.

Before the 19th century both terms were used more loosely. Thus the 'studies' in Francesco Durante's Sonate per cembalo divise in studii e divertimenti (c1732) are contrapuntal movements unassociated with specific problems of keyboard technique, while Domenico Scarlatti's 30 Essercizi per gravicembalo (1738) are no different in scope and significance from his remaining 525 sonatas. The four parts of J. S. Bach's Clavier-Übung (1731–42) contain not only a wide variety of masterpieces for harpsichord (such as the Italian Concerto, French Overture, six Partitas and the monumental Goldberg Variations) but also a number of large-scale works for organ.

Although the title 'study' rarely occurs in early keyboard music, much of the repertory was avowedly didactic in aim. Thus the many variously named pieces in instrumental treatises and instruction manuals may be considered studies, including the toccatas in Diruta's Il transilvano (1593), the lessons (i.e. dances and airs) in Locke's Melothesia (1673), the preludes in François Couperin's L'art de toucher le clavecin (1716), the Probestücke in C. P. E. Bach's Versuch über die wahre Art das Clavier zu spielen (1753) and the Handstücke in Türk's Clavierschule (1789). Other pieces intended at least partly for pedagogic use might be included, even if not necessarily aimed at the development of technical facility. For example, Frescobaldi's Il primo libro di capricci, canzon francese e recercari (1626) opens with a preface addressed to 'gli studiosi dell'opera' (the students of the work), while 11 of the preludes of J. S. Bach's Das wohltemperirte Clavier, as well as all his Two- and Three-part Inventions, were originally included in the Clavier-Büchlein vor Wilhelm Friedemann Bach (1720), a manuscript compiled expressly for the instruction of his ten-year-old son.

From the early years of the 19th century the rapidly growing popularity of the piano brought a flood of teaching material aimed at the amateur and the budding professional, including innumerable volumes of graded studies whose technical usefulness generally outweighed their musical value. Typical of such publications are the studies published by J. B. Cramer between 1804 and 1810, the earlier parts of Clementi's Gradus ad Parnassum (1817, 1819, 1825–6), Moscheles's Studien op.70 (1826) and the many collections by Czerny. The later studies in the Gradus are of greater musical interest, some illustrating particular styles as well as technical problems (e.g. 'le style élégant' and 'le style sévère), and Moscheles's Characteristischen Studien op.95 (1837) are clearly intended as much for performance as for instruction. The latter are, in fact, undemanding examples of a newly developed genre, the concert study.

The origins of the concert study can be traced to Liszt's youthful Etude en 12 exercices (c1827). Although scarcely more advanced in technique than

Clementi's *Gradus*, these 'exercises' were later enormously expanded to become the *Grandes études* (1839), probably the most difficult concert studies ever written. In 1852 Liszt revised the latter texturally and reissued them as the slightly less taxing though still formidable *Etudes d'éxécution transcendante* (dedicated to Czerny). Meanwhile the poetic possibilities of the study had been revealed by Chopin. His 12 *Grandes études* op.10 (1833, dedicated to Liszt), 12 *Etudes* op.25 (1837) and *Trois nouvelles études* (1840) are the crowning glory of the genre and have never been equalled for their combination of technical brilliance, textural beauty and range of emotion. Schumann's *Etudes symphoniques* op.13 (1834) and Brahms's virtuoso Variations on a Theme of Paganini op.35 (1866) showed how perfectly the idea of the concert study could be adapted to variation form. Transcriptions, too, were easily transformed into concert studies, as can be seen not only from the keyboard versions of Paganini's violin studies (called caprices) made by Liszt (1838–51) and Schumann (op.3, 1832; op.10, 1833) but also from Brahms's more unusual five piano studies (1869–79). The latter, presumably not intended for concert use, include an arrangement for the left hand alone of the chaconne from Bach's Partita in D minor for solo violin (BWV1004) and versions of pieces by Bach, Weber and Chopin in which the originals are subjected to a variety of contrapuntal contortions. Among other notable collections are Alkan's vast *12 études dans les tons majeurs* op.35 (1848) and *12 études dans les tons mineurs* op.39 (1857), the 26 studies of Skryabin (1887–1908), Rakhmaninov's two sets of *Etudes-tableaux* op.33 (1911) and op.39 (1916–17), Debussy's magnificent 12 studies (1915) dedicated to Chopin's memory, Bartók's *Three Etudes* op.18 (1918) and Messiaen's *Quatre études de rythme* (1949–50).

Studies for many other instruments have been written since the beginning of the 19th century. By far the greater number are more concerned with technical problems than with musical values, as can be seen from the collections for violin by Fiorillo, Rodolphe Kreutzer, Rode, Baillot and Bériot, and for cello by Dotzauer and Grützmacher. Altogether outstanding are Paganini's *24 Capricci* op.1 (published in 1820) for solo violin; besides these concert studies of unmatched brilliance, they had sufficient musical interest to evoke the piano transcriptions of Liszt and Schumann referred to above, and the theme of one, no.24 in A minor, is so concisely striking that it has inspired sets of variations from Brahms (op.35), Rakhmaninov (for piano and orchestra, 1934), Lutosławski (for two pianos, 1941), Boris Blacher (for orchestra, 1947) and others.

The French word 'étude' (as well as the English 'study') has been used as the title of a number of 20th-century orchestral works, some requiring unusually facile technique from individual members of the ensemble or exploiting particular aspects of the composer's craftsmanship. Examples include Stravinsky's *Quatre études pour orchestre* (1929), Henze's *Symphonische Etuden* (1955) and Frank Martin's *Etudes pour orchestre à cordes* (1956) as well as Rawsthorne's *Symphonic Studies* (1939).

BIBLIOGRAPHY

E. Gurk: *Die Klavieretüde von Mozart bis Liszt unter besonderer Berücksichtigung der Methode des Klavierunterrichts* (diss., U. of Vienna, 1930)
W. Georgii: *Klaviermusik* (Zurich, 1941, 2/1950)
W. Kahl: 'Etüde', *MGG*
P. F. Ganz: *The Development of the Etude for Pianoforte* (diss., Northwestern U., 1960)

HOWARD FERGUSON

The opening of Paganini's 'Capricci' op.1 no.24 (Milan: Ricordi, 1820)

Studziński. Polish family of musicians.

(1) **Wincenty Studziński** (*b* Kraków, 30 March 1815; *d* Kraków, 15 or 14 July 1854). Violinist and composer. He was the son of Marcin Studziński, a member of a Jesuit band and a military orchestra in Kraków at the beginning of the 19th century. From 1831 to 1833 he was a drummer in a military orchestra in Kraków, and from 1836 to 1848 a violinist and conductor of the theatre orchestra. At the same time he taught the violin in the music school of the Kraków Technical Institute. Most of his compositions remained unpublished, and include a string quartet in E op.28 (MS in *PL-Kj*), three other string quartets, mazurkas for piano (published in 1853, 1854 and in Warsaw, 1860), ten krakowiaks for voice (Leipzig, n.d.), a choral piece *Taniec i śpiew szkieletów* ('Dance and song of the skeletons', published in 1884), other songs and instrumental and orchestral pieces.

(2) **Wiktoria Studzińska-Marczewska** (*b* Kraków, 1818; *d* Kraków, 1881). Operatic soprano, sister of (1) Wincenty Studziński. She performed in the opera houses of Warsaw, Kraków and Lwów.

(3) **Piotr Studziński** (*b* Kraków, 16 Oct 1826; *d* Kraków, 20 or 19 April 1869). Organist, horn player and composer, brother of (1) Wincenty Studziński. He was educated in the music school of Kraków Technical Institute, where he studied the organ with Gorączkiewicz. From 1831 he played the horn in military and theatre orchestras in Kraków, and later

taught wind instruments at his former school. From 1851 to 1853 he was a band conductor in Kraków and Tarnów. On the death of Gorączkiewicz (1858) he became organist and conductor at the Wawel chapel, Kraków Cathedral. He composed four one-act vaude-villes, including *Łobzowianie*, to a libretto by W. L. Anczyc (Kraków, 31 December 1854); he also com-posed sacred and secular songs, krakowiaks and vocal mazurkas.

(4) **Karol Studziński** (*b* Kraków, 24 Jan 1828; *d* Warsaw, 15 or 16 March 1883). Violinist, viola player and composer, brother of (1) Wincenty Studziński. He was a pupil of Gorączkiewicz. In 1843 he became a member of the theatre orchestra in Kraków, playing also in Kalisz and Radom. From about 1853 until his death he lived in Warsaw, where he played for many years in the Wielki Theatre orchestra and in Kątski's string quartet. In 1856 he founded and then directed a male-voice double quartet, which flourished until 1862. He was professor of music theory and solfeggio at the Music Institute (1863–4); from 1865 he was deputy to Moniuszko in the choral singing department, and in about 1870 he succeeded Moniuszko as professor, a post he held until 1882. He composed masses (two of which were performed in Warsaw in 1858 and 1859), sacred and secular vocal music and children's songs. He also wrote educational books, including *Zasady muzyki* ('The principles of music', Warsaw, 1869) and *Początki śpiewu* ('The basics of singing', Warsaw, 1871).

(5) **Kajetan Studziński** (*b* Kraków, 1832; *d* Warsaw. 1855), brother of (1) Wincenty Studziński. He was a member of the Wielki Theatre orchestra in Warsaw, and composed songs and dances.

BIBLIOGRAPHY
FétisB
S. Orgelbrand: *Encyklopedia powszechna* (Warsaw, 1859–68)
A. Sowiński: *Słownik muzyków polskich* (Paris, 1874)
A. P[ług]: 'Karol Studziński', *Kłosy* (1883)
J. W. Reiss: *Almanach muzyczny Krakowa 1780–1914* (Kraków, 1939), 36, 45, 65
                    BARBARA CHMARA-ŻACZKIEWICZ

Stueber, Conrad. *See* STUBER, CONRAD.

Stufe (Ger.). DEGREE.

Štuhec, Igor (*b* Zg-Ščavnica, Maribor, Slovenia, 15 Dec 1932). Yugoslav composer. At the Academy of Music, Ljubljana, he studied composition under Lucijan Marija Škerjanc and Matija Bravničar. His studies were con-tinued at the Vienna Academy of Music and Dramatic Art under Jelinek, and also at Darmstadt. After some early neo-classical orchestral works that show his mas-tery of traditional techniques, Štuhec gradually moved towards the adoption of new techniques in the early 1960s. Although in 1955 he had produced a *musique concrète* composition in *Biological Transformation*, the radical change came with the chamber pieces *Situacija* (1963) and *Silhuete* (1964) and the orchestral *Differentiations* (1964), all of which exhibit his assimila-tion of 12-note and aleatory procedures. Štuhec is at his best in such miniatures as the *Minikoncert*, where his writing is at its most delicate and the textures are almost always crystal clear.

WORKS
(*selective list*)
VOCAL AND ORCHESTRAL
Županova Micka (opera, A. T. Linhart), 1948, rev. 1955, 1971; Suite, 1948; Sinfonietta, 1950; Serenada, str, 1954; Concertino, pf, orch, 1953–8; 2 fatalni pesmi, S, fl, harp, 1959; Sym. no.1, 1959–60; Fantasia concertante, hn, str, 1962; Sym. no.2, 1962–3; Differentiations, 1964; Platero y yo (J. R. Jiminez), S, T, chamber orch, 1966; Minikoncert, pf, chamber orch, 1967; Concertino, vn, orch, 1967; Fl Conc., 1969; Tpt Conc., 1967–70; Moon Dawn (opera, S. J. Smith Miller), 1970–73; Va Conc., 1971; Poesies, T, orch, 1971–2; In memoriam, 1972; Vn Conc., 1973; Entuziazmi, 1974

CHAMBER, INSTRUMENTAL AND TAPE
Sonata, pf, 1954; 12 Pieces, pf, 1948–55; 10 pieces, pf, 1949–55; Str Qt, 1955; Biological Transformation, tape, 1955; 7 Anecdotes, cl, pf, 1955–8; 12 Pieces, pf duet, 1957–8; Divertimento, fl, cl, bn, 1958; 4 pieces, hn, pf, 1959–60; Tema con variazioni, vn, hn, pf, 1962; Prelude and Chaconne, pf, 1962; Situacija, vn, pf, 1963; Silhuete I–IV, ens, 1964, rev. 1966; A Study, tape, 1966; Participation, ens, 1967; Sonata à 3, cl, bn, pf, 1968; Variazioni, vn, ens, 1970; Consolation, pf trio, 1971; Sonata, vn, pf, 1972; Ction, ens, 1974
Principal publisher: Društvo slovenskih skladateljev (Ljubljana)
                    NIALL O'LOUGHLIN

Stumm. German family of organ builders. They came from Rhaunen-Sulzbach in the Hunsrück district of the Rhineland-Palatinate, and were active for six gen-erations in the Mannheim–Saarbrücken–Koblenz–Frankfurt am Main region. The most important mem-bers of the family are its founder, Johann Michael (*b* Sulzbach, 10 April 1683; *d* Sulzbach, 22 April 1747), and his sons, Johann Philipp (*b* Sulzbach, 24 Aug 1705; *d* Sulzbach, 27 June 1776) and Johann Heinrich (*d* Sulzbach, 23 Aug 1788). Johann Michael was originally a 'very famous goldsmith' (his brother Nikolaus founded a well-known Saarland dynasty of smelters); he built organs for the Pfarrkirche at Münstermaifeld (1721; two manuals, 22 stops), the Stiftskirche at Karden (1728; three manuals, 37 stops; extant), the Pfarrkirche at Leutesdorf (*c*1735; three manuals, 28 stops; extant), the Hofkirche at Mühlheim, Eis (*c*1735; two manuals, 23 stops), and elsewhere. The organ in the Grosse Kirche at Kirchheimbolanden (three manuals, 36 stops; extant) is attributable to him, to his sons, or to both. Johann Philipp and Johann Heinrich, the 'Gebrüder Stumm', built organs for St Stephani, Simmern (Hunsrück) (two manuals, 27 stops; extant), the Liebfrauenkirche, Koblenz (1751; three manuals, 43 stops), the Ludwigskirche, Saarbrücken (1762; three manuals; 38 stops), and the Schlosskirche, Meisenheim (1764; two manuals, 30 stops; extant). Both brothers signed the contract in 1774 for the organ in the abbey church at Amorbach, completed in 1782 (three man-uals, 46 stops; the case and parts of the pipework sur-vive). Johann Heinrich was the only signatory for an instrument for the Katharinenkirche in Frankfurt am Main (1778–89; three manuals, 40 stops); his sons Franz and Michael built one for the Dreikönigskirche in Frankfurt (1781–3; two manuals, 29 stops).

The typical Stumm organ was developed during Johann Michael's career and was not substantially modified by his descendants. The *Positiv* was originally laid out as a *Rückpositiv*; when it later became an *Unterpositiv*, the console of the organ was placed to one side. The full Stumm Principal choruses on *Hauptwerk*, *Positiv*, Echo and Pedal consist of 8′ 4′ 2⅔′ 2′ 1⅓′ Mixtur IV 1′ (with repetitions on *g* and *g*′); 8′ 4′ 2′ 1⅓′ Mixtur III 1′ (with repetitions on *c*′ and *c*′′); 2′ 1⅓′ (from *c*′ 2⅔′); 16′ 8′ 5⅓′ 4′ Mixtur. The Gedeckt group comprises 16′ 8′ 4′; 8′ 4′; 8′ 4′; 16′. The group of narrow-scale flues is represented by Viola da gamba 8′ Quintaden 8′ Salizett

4′; Flauto traverso 8′ treble Salizional 2′ (from *c′* 4′); Flauto traverso 8′ treble Salizional 2′ (from *c′* 4′); Violone 16′. The reed group consists of Trompete 8′ Clarine 4′ bass Vox angelica 2′ Bass; Krummhorn 8′ Vox humana 8′; Krummhorn 8′ bass Trompete 8′ treble Vox humana 8′; Posaune 16′ Trompete 8′ Clarine 4′ Kornett 2′. There is also a Kornett V on the *Hauptwerk*. The type clearly involves a synthesis of influences from Lorraine and Luxembourg on the one hand and from southern Germany and Austria on the other. The most prominent difference between a Stumm instrument and one by Johann Andreas Silbermann, for example, is the narrow-scaled stops of the Stumm. Other differences are that the Nasard, Tierce and Larigot are not wide in scale but like Principals, that there are two Principal ranks in the Echo instead of a Kornett, and that in the Pedal the Posaune 16′ is preferred to the Trompete 8′. The superior technical and tonal qualities of the Stumm organ have contributed to the survival of some 140 examples, out of some 370 documented original instruments.

BIBLIOGRAPHY

E. F. Schmid: 'Die Orgeln der Abtei Amorbach, ihr Bau und ihre Stellung in der Musikgeschichte des Odenwaldklosters', *Zwischen Neckar und Main, Heimatblätter des Bezirksmuseums Buchen eingetragener Verein*, xvii (1938), 42
O. Conrad: 'Die Geschichte der Orgelbauerfamilie Stumm aus Rhaunen-Sulzbach und ihrer Werke', *Mitteilungen des Vereins für Heimatkunde Birkenfeld*, xix (1955); xx (1956)
T. Peine: *Der Orgelbau in Frankfurt am Main und Umgebung von den Anfängen bis zur Gegenwart* (diss., U. of Frankfurt am Main, 1956)
H. Klotz: 'Vom rheinischen Orgelbau im 18. Jahrhundert', *Beiträge zur rheinischen Musikgeschichte*, xix (1957), 29
F. Bösken: 'Die Orgelbauerfamilie Stumm aus Rhaunen-Sulzbach und ihr Werk: ein Beitrag zur Geschichte des Orgelbaus am Mittelrhein', *Mittelrheinisches Jb für Archäologie, Kunst und Geschichte*, 1v (1960), 1–108
——: 'Stumm', *MGG*

HANS KLOTZ

Stump. An English instrument of the early 17th-century. It is known only by name and by one surviving piece of music (*GB-Och* Mus.532), headed 'Alman R. Johnson to the stump by F.P.' (ed. A. Sundermann, *Robert Johnson: Complete Works for Solo Lute*, London, 1972). This is written in six-line French tablature and shows that the stump had seven fingered string courses tuned like a Renaissance lute, with eight extra bass diapasons. The left-hand stretches indicate a maximum string length of not more than 60 cm, so it cannot have been a bass instrument like the PENORCON, as has sometimes been suggested. Assuming a top string at *a′*, the tuning would be $F'-G'-A'-B\flat'-C-D-E-F/G-A-d-g-b-e'-a'$; the piece would then be in G minor. As with the POLIPHANT, the invention of the stump was attributed by John Playford to Daniel Farrant. Talbot (see Gill), though he did not mention the stump by name, remarked that some orpharions 'like the English Theorbo carrie 5 double 8ve ranks on 5 Nutts on long Head beside those (7) on the Plate [fingerboard]'. Two more diapasons or 'double 8ve ranks' would make this an exact description of the stump required for the one and only piece.

BIBLIOGRAPHY

D. Gill: 'James Talbot's Manuscript: the Wire-strung Fretted Instruments and the Guitar', *GSJ*, xv (1962), 60

IAN HARWOOD

Stumpf, (Friedrich) Carl (*b* Wiesentheid, Lower Franconia, 21 April 1848; *d* Berlin, 25 Dec 1936). German psychologist, acoustician and musicologist. Both his parents were musical, and at his various schools he learnt to play six instruments, teaching himself harmony and counterpoint. From 1865 he studied philosophy (with Brentano) and theology at Würzburg University, and philosophy and natural sciences at Göttingen University, where he took the doctorate and in 1870 completed his *Habilitation* in philosophy. He was professor of philosophy at the universities of Würzburg (1873), Prague (1879), Halle (1884), Munich (1889) and Berlin (1893–1928), where he founded (1893) and directed the Institute of Psychology and, with his pupils Hornbostel and Abraham, founded the Berlin Phonogrammarchiv (1900). He directed *Beiträge zur Akustik und Musikwissenschaft* (Leipzig, 1898–1924) and, with Hornbostel, *Sammelbände für vergleichende Musikwissenschaft* (1922–3). In 1928 he received the Order of Merit, and he was a member of the Berlin Academy of Sciences.

Stumpf formulated the concept of 'Tonpsychologie' in 1883 and was the first to treat the subject systematically. In his main work, *Tonpsychologie*, he continued Helmholtz's research in physics and physiology from a psychological standpoint, shifting the emphasis from the organ of hearing to the sensory experience of sound and its function. He regarded the experienced fusion of tones as the basic factor of consonance: influenced by Riemann's argument that the concept of fusion is inadequate to explain triads and chords of more than three notes, in 1911 Stumpf adopted the terms 'concordance' or 'concord' for all major and minor triads, including their inversions, and 'discordance' or 'discord' for all other chords. In this respect, as with his basic concept founded on a psychological elementalism, his position has proved untenable against that of Krueger or his own pupils, especially Hornbostel. Through his ethnological research and recordings and particularly through *Die Anfänge der Musik* (1909) Stumpf became the true founder of comparative musicology. He continued Helmholtz's investigations, employing the methods of physics, and in his late work *Die Sprachlaute* (1926), which he substituted for the planned third volume of *Tonpsychologie*, he analysed and reconstructed vocal and instrumental notes according to interference procedure. He harnessed physics, physiology, psychology, ethnology, philosophy and (especially) aesthetics in the service of systematic musicology, and secured its recognition as an independent discipline at Berlin University's philosophy department. In his writings he combined a profound understanding of music with scientific, historical and philosophical knowledge and reflection, concentrating finally on philosophy: his last (posthumous) work was a theory of knowledge, *Erkenntnislehre* (Leipzig, 1939–40).

WRITINGS

ed., with E. M. von Hornbostel: *Sammelbände für vergleichende Musikwissenschaft* (Munich, 1922–3) [S]
ed.: *Beiträge zur Akustik und Musikwissenschaft* (Leipzig, 1898–1924) [B]

Tonpsychologie (Leipzig, 1883–90/*R*1965); see also *VMw*, i (1885), 127; vii (1891), 429
'Musikpsychologie in England', *VMw*, i (1885), 261–349
'Lieder der Bellakula-Indianer', *VMw*, ii (1886), 405; also in S, i (1922)
'Mongolische Gesänge', *VMw*, iii (1887), 297; also in S, i (1922)
'Über Vergleichung von Tondistanzen', *Zeitschrift für Psychologie und Physiologie der Sinnesorgane*, no.1 (1890), 419–62; see also 'Wundts Antikritik', no.2 (1891), 266 and 'Meine Schlusswort gegen Wundt', no.2 (1891), 438
'Phonographierte Indianermelodien', *VMw*, viii (1892), 127; also in S, i (1922)
'Hermann von Helmholtz und die neuere Psychologie', *Archiv für Geschichte der Philosophie*, viii (1895), 303

'Die pseudo-aristotelischen Probleme über Musik', *Abhandlungen der Preussischen Akademie der Wissenschaften: philosophisch-historische Klasse*, iii (1896), 1–85

'Ueber Ermittlung von Obertönen', *Annalen der Physik und Chemie*, new ser., no.57 (1896), 660

'Geschichte der Konsonanzbegriffes, i', *Abhandlungen der Bayerischen Akademie der Wissenschaften: philosophisch-philologische Klasse*, xxi (1897), 1–78; pubd separately (Munich, 1901)

'Neueres über Tonverschmelzung', *Zeitschrift für Psychologie und Physiologie der Sinnesorgane*, no.15 (1897), 280; also in B, no.2 (1898), 1

with M. Meyer: 'Schwingungszahlbestimmung bei sehr hohen Tönen', *Annalen der Physik und Chemie*, new ser., no.61 (1897), 760; see also 'Erwiderung', no.65 (1898), 641

'Die Unmusikalischen und die Tonverschmelzung', *Zeitschrift für Psychologie und Physiologie der Sinnesorgane*, no.17 (1898), 422; see also 'Erwiderung', no.18 (1898), 294

'Konsonanz und Dissonanz', B, no.2 (1898), 1–108

with M. Meyer: 'Massbestimmung über die Reinheit consonanter Intervalle', *Zeitschrift für Psychologie und Physiologie der Sinnesorgane*, no.18 (1898), 321–404; also in B, no.2 (1898), 84–167

'Beobachtungen über subjektive Töne und über-Doppelthören', *Zeitschrift für Psychologie und Physiologie der Sinnesorgane*, no.21 (1899), 100; also in B, no.3 (1901), 30

'Ueber den Begriff der Gemüthsbewegung', *Zeitschrift für Psychologie und Physiologie der Sinnesorgane*, no.21 (1899), 47–99

'Ueber die Bestimmung hoher Schwingungszahlen durch Differenztöne', *Annalen der Physik und Chemie*, new ser., no.68 (1899), 105

'Tonsystem und Musik der Siamesen', B, no.3 (1901), 69–138; pubd separately (Leipzig, 1901); also in S, i (1922)

'Über das Erkennen von Intervallen und Akkorden bei sehr kurzer Dauer', *Zeitschrift für Psychologie und Physiologie der Sinnesorgane*, no.27 (1902), 148–86; also in B, no.4 (1909), 1–39

'Differenztöne und Konsonanz', *Zeitschrift für Psychologie und Physiologie der Sinnesorgane*, no.39 (1905), 269; no.59 (1911), 161; also in B, no.4 (1909), 90; no.6 (1911), 151

with K. L. and M. Schaefer: 'Über zusammengesetzte Wellenformen', *Zeitschrift für Psychologie und Physiologie der Sinnesorgane*, no.39 (1905), 241; also in B, no.4 (1909), 62

'Das Berliner Phonogrammarchiv', *Internationale Wochenschrift*, ii (Munich, 1908)

'Die Anfänge der Musik', *Internationale Wochenschrift*, iii (1909); pubd separately (Leipzig, 1911)

'Beobachtungen über Kombinationstöne', *Zeitschrift für Psychologie und Physiologie der Sinnesorgane*, no.55 (1910), 1–142; also in B, no.5 (1910), 1–142

with E. M. von Hornbostel: 'Über die Bedeutung ethnologischer Untersuchungen für die Psychologie und Ästhetik der Tonkunst', *4. Kongress für experimentelle Psychologie: Innsbruck 1910*, 256; also in B, no.6 (1911), 102

'Konsonanz und Konkordanz', *Zeitschrift für Psychologie und Physiologie der Sinnesorgane*, no.58 (1911), 326; also in B, no.6 (1911), 116–50; abridged in *Festschrift . . . Rochus Freiherrn von Liliencron* (Leipzig, 1910/R1970), 329

'Über neuere Untersuchungen zur Tonlehre', *6. Kongress für experimentelle Psychologie: Göttingen 1914*, 305; also in B, no.8 (1915), 17–56

suppl. to S. Baley: 'Versuche über die Lokalisation beim dichotischen Hören', *Zeitschrift für Psychologie und Physiologie der Sinnesorgane*, no.70 (1914), 347; also in B, no.8 (1915), 102

'Apologie der Gefühlsempfindungen', *Zeitschrift für Psychologie und Physiologie der Sinnesorgane*, no.75 (1916), 1–38

'Binaurale Tonmischung, Mehrheitsschwelle und Mitteltonbildung', *Zeitschrift für Psychologie und Physiologie der Sinnesorgane*, no.75 (1916), 330; also in B, no.9 (1924), 17

'Verlust der Gefühlsempfindungen im Tongebiete', *Zeitschrift für Psychologie und Physiologie der Sinnesorgane*, no.75 (1916), 39; also in B, no.9 (1924), 1

'Trompete und Flöte', *Festschrift Hermann Kretzschmar* (Leipzig, 1918/R1973), 155

'Singen und Sprechen', *Zeitschrift für Psychologie und Physiologie der Sinnesorgane*, no.94 (1923), 1–37; also in B, no.9 (1924), 38–74

Die Sprachlaute: experimentell-phonetische Untersuchungen nebst einem Anhang über Instrumentalklänge (Berlin, 1926)

BIBLIOGRAPHY

T. Lipps: 'Der Begriff der Verschmelzung und damit Zusammenhängendes in C. Stumpfs Tonpsychologie II', *Philosophische Monatshefte*, xxviii (Berlin, 1892), 547–91

R. Münnich: 'Von der Entwicklung der Riemannschen Harmonielehre und ihrer Verhältnis zu Oettingen und Stumpf', *Riemann-Festschrift* (Leipzig, 1909), 60

Festschrift für Carl Stumpf (Berlin, 1919)

'Carl Stumpf zum 75. Geburtstag', *Psychologische Forschung*, iv (Berlin, 1923); pubd separately (Berlin, 1923)

E. Schumann: 'Die Förderung der Musikwissenschaft durch die akustische-psychologische Forschung Carl Stumpfs', *AMw*, v (1923), 172

E. M. von Hornbostel: *Geschichte des Phonogrammarchiv der Staatlichen Hochschule für Musik in Berlin* (Berlin, 1925)

C. Sachs: 'Zu Carl Stumpfs achtzigstem Geburtstag', *ZMw*, x (1927–8), 385

E. M. von Hornbostel: 'Carl Stumpf und die vergleichende Musikwissenschaft'; 'Das Berliner Phonogrammarchiv', *Zeitschrift für vergleichende Musikwissenschaft*, i (1933), 25; 40

N. Hartmann: 'Gedächtnisrede auf Carl Stumpf', *Sitzungsberichte der Preussischen Akademie der Wissenschaften* (Berlin, 1 July 1937); also pubd separately

G. Schünemann: 'Carl Stumpf†', *AMf*, ii (1937), 1

J. Handschin: *Der Toncharakter* (Zurich, 1948)

H. Husmann: 'Verschmelzung und Konsonanz (den Manen Carl Stumpfs)', *DJbM*, i (1956), 66

H. Besseler: 'Das musikalische Hören der Neuzeit', *Bericht über die Verhandlungen der Sächsischen Akademie der Wissenschaften zu Leipzig*, civ/6 (1958)

A. Wellek: *Musikpsychologie und Musikästhetik* (Frankfurt am Main, 1963), 30, 43, 64

F. Benestad: 'Teorier om musikkens opprinnelse', *Norsk musikktidsskrift*, viii (1971), 1

based on *MGG* (xii, 1640–43) by permission of Bärenreiter
    ALBERT WELLEK, BERTHOLD FREUDENBERGER

Stumpf, Johann Christian (*b c*1740; *d* ?Frankfurt am Main, ?1801). German composer. The birth and death dates commonly given for him may actually be those of another musician with the same surname. Historians have referred to the death entry of 11 April 1801 in the Frankfurt Catholic parish records ('D. Ludovicus Stumpf Mogonus, Musicus Exercitu Reipublicae Gallicae, aetatis 38 annorum'), yet works by Johann Christian appear in catalogues of Parisian publishers as early as 1762, and none of his works bear the name 'Ludovicus' or its cognates. In a concert of 17 May 1778 at the Frankfurt Comic Theatre, a 'Mr. Stumpf' played the bassoon in the same programme as the violinist Benda. Stumpf lived in Paris around 1785. After playing the bassoon with the Altona Orchestra in Germany until 1798, he worked under Cannabich as choral coach at the Frankfurt Opera.

A review of Stumpf's 12 divertissements for two flutes in the *Allgemeine musikalische Zeitung* (14 November 1806) describes him as 'understanding the instrument and the *galant* style' and writing music that is 'flowing, melodious'. As examples of his most significant area of work, Stumpf's symphonies op.2 for strings, horns and oboes or flutes are all written in four movements, with a minuet and trio as third movement. Characteristic of many symphonies written after about 1765, these works show symmetrical phrase repetitions, slow harmonic rhythm and clear differentiation between primary and secondary themes.

WORKS

(all published in Paris unless otherwise stated)

Ballet music: Die Geburt des Harlequin (ballet, 3), arr. kbd, *D–B*; 4 vols. of entr'actes, orch (Offenbach, n.d.); entr'acte with variations by P. Winter and Stumpf, orch (n.d.)

Orch: 6 syms., op.2 (1767); Syms. à 6, op.11 (1768); Syms., op.9 (?1772); 6 syms. à 8, op.3 (1779); Bn Conc. (1780); 2 syms. concertantes (1781); Fl Conc., op.15 (Augsburg, n.d.); 4 bn concs. (Bonn, n.d.); Fl Conc., op.6 [cf *AMZ*, x (1807–8), Intelligenz-Blatt]

Chamber: Qt, op.10 (1772); Qt, bn, vn, va, vc (Bonn, n.d.); 2 Quartetto concertante, str qt, *D–Bds*; 6 Trios, fl, vn, b, op.1 (1762); 6 Trios à 3 ou grand orchestre, op.2 (n.d.); Trios, vns, op.4 (?1772); 6 trio d'airs connus et dialogués (1786); Vn Duos, op.2 (1765); Vn Duo (?1772); 6 Vc Duos, op.6 (?1776–7); 6 Va Duos, ?op.15 (1782); Vc Duos, opp.16–17 (n.d.); Cl Duos, op.18 (1788); 12 duos amusants, 2 fl (Mainz, n.d.); 12 divertissements, 2 fl (Hamburg, n.d.)

Numerous arrs. of opera excerpts

BIBLIOGRAPHY

EitnerQ; FétisB; GerberNL

AMZ, viii (1806–7), col.128

C. Israel, ed.: *Frankfurter Concert-Chronik von 1713–80* (Frankfurt am Main, 1876)

H. Mendel and A. Reissmann: *Musikalisches Conversations-Lexikon* (Berlin, 1870–79, 3/1890–91/R1969)

C. Johansson: *French Music Publishers' Catalogues of the Second Half of the Eighteenth Century* (Uppsala, 1955)

H. O. Hiekel: 'Stumpf, Johann Christian', *MGG*

W. Matthäus: *Musikverlag Johann André* (Tutzing, 1973)

S. FORSBERG

Stumpff, Carolus (*fl* early 18th century). German composer. He wrote church music for the court of Baden, performed when it was visiting its secondary residence at Schlakenwerth (now Ostrov, near Karlovy Vary), as it did for varying periods between 1690 and 1721. Stumpff is not mentioned in the list of musicians appointed to serve at Rastatt (near Karlsruhe) when the court re-established itself there in 1713 after the War of the Spanish Succession.

Stumpff's church music, all for four voices and orchestra, is typical of the less difficult church music written by Viennese composers in the early 18th century. Though his masses are cantata-like, each section being divided into many movements, he wrote few elaborate arias, and made much use of mixed ensemble of solo and tutti voices, in which the tutti is the more important part and vocal coloratura is used sparingly. His violin writing is unusually simple, often doubling the upper voices or maintaining an accompaniment figure. Only in *Opus musicum* did he write in a more elaborate and Italianate style, which makes considerable technical demands on solo singers and instrumentalists.

WORKS

(all 4vv, orch, D-KA)

Missa S Georgii, Missa S Ludovici, Missa pastoritia

2 litanies, Te Deum

2 Alma redemptoris mater, 2 Salve regina, 2 Ave regina, 2 Regina coeli

Opus musicum pro sacro sepulcro

Quatuor versiculi pro fugas deducti pro festo Corporis Christi

Pastoral cantatas

ELIZABETH ROCHE

Stuntz, Joseph Hartmann (*b* Arlesheim, nr. Basle, probably 23 July 1793; *d* Munich, 18 June 1859). Swiss composer of German origin. The son of a painter, he first studied with Peter von Winter in Munich (1808–12), then with Salieri in Vienna (1813–16) and then became conductor of the Italian Opera in Munich. His first opera, *La rappresaglia*, written during his first stay in Italy (1818–20), was received with warm applause on both sides of the Alps; it was produced successively in Munich, Vienna, Stuttgart and Berlin in a German translation as *Das Schloss Lowinsky*. This success, however, was not achieved by his next operas, and Stuntz decided to settle at Munich, where in 1825 he was appointed Winter's successor as first conductor of the Royal Opera. Owing to his methods as a conductor (he tended to slow tempos, and preferred the new way of leading the orchestra from the piano rather than as first violinist) he was replaced by Franz Lachner, but retained the post as a conductor of the court orchestra until his death.

While his Italian operas are written in the neo-Neapolitan style, both his two German dramatic works written for Munich, the Singspiel *Heinrich IV zu Givry* (1820, libretto adapted from Voltaire's *Charlot*) and the tragic opera *Maria Rosa*, fail as attempts at 'deutsche Oper'. *Garibaldi der Agilolfinger* (1824), arranged for King Maximilian's 25th jubilee, is a rather odd adaptation of Mozart's *La clemenza di Tito*; only the

introduction and the second finale are original, the rest being taken over from Mozart's music. Stuntz also wrote a large number of ballets, cantatas, masses and other works for official occasions. He was the founder of the male choir tradition in Munich, and his songs and choruses became popular in southern Germany.

BIBLIOGRAPHY

K. Gross: *Joseph Hartmann Stuntz als Opernkomponist* (diss., U. of Munich, 1934; part pubd., Würzburg, 1936)

F. R. BOSONNET

Stupan von Ehrenstein, Johann Jakob (*b* 1664; *d* Vienna, 17 Jan 1739). Austrian composer and court official. He is first heard of on 31 July 1709, when the Jesuit drama *Martis exilium, e pacis reditus* was performed with his music in Vienna before the emperor and empress. He worked for the imperial court in Vienna from 1710, when he was appointed high steward; in the same year he also became secretary in Vienna to Prince Maximilian Wilhelm of Brunswick-Lüneburg, who was the empress's cousin. His final appointment was as councillor to the Dowager Empress Amalie. All his known music dates from the years 1702–11, before his busy years as a successful courtier. He wrote three Jesuit dramas, the above-mentioned *Martis exilium* (1709) and *Radimirus ex reo rex* (1710), both of which are lost, and *Nundinae deorum* (1711; MS in *A-Wn*), which according to Kramer played an important role in the development of Jesuit drama and suggests that he was a gifted composer. With its 'bravura arias firmly in the Neapolitan style and accompanied by various instrumental combinations ... brief, unassuming secco recitatives [and] extended, well-wrought arias', it shows that the genre had shed the features that characterized it up to about 1700. Stupan is otherwise known as a composer of instrumental music: two collections of three-part music – *Rosetum musicum in 6 divisum arcolas, vulgo partittas* (Ulm, 1702) and *Armonica compendiosa* (Ulm, 1703) – survive; a collection for solo violin – *Horae p[r]omeridianae harmonicae, seu Symphoniae XII* (Ulm, 1710) – is lost.

BIBLIOGRAPHY

E. H. Meyer: *Die mehrstimmige Spielmusik des 17. Jahrhunderts in Nord- und Mitteleuropa* (Kassel, 1934), 251

W. Kramer: *Die Musik im Wiener Jesuitendrama von 1677–1711* (diss., U. of Vienna, 1961), 264ff, 310, 312, 314, 320f, 323f, 328

WALTER PASS

Sturgeon, N(?icholas) (*d* between 31 May and 8 June 1454). English composer. On election as a scholar of Winchester College in 1399 he was described as coming from Devon (probably from Ashburton). The external facts of his career are exceptionally well documented, and many details are given in A. B. Emden: *A Biographical Register of the University of Oxford to A.D. 1500* (Oxford, 1957). Numerous references appear in the Close, Patent and Norman rolls of the period. At various times he held canonries at Exeter, Wells, St Stephen's Westminster, Hastings and Kirkby Castles, Windsor (from 1442) and St Paul's Cathedral (from 1432, precentor from 1442). In 1442 the Privy Council commissioned him to select six English singers for the imperial chapel of Frederick III. Sturgeon was a member of the Royal Household Chapel (recorded at various dates from 1413 to 1452, including the expedition to Harfleur in 1415 and a designation as sub-dean in 1428). The earlier part of this period was contemporaneous with the royal chaplaincies of Damett, Burell and Cooke, though neither his canonries at Windsor nor those at St Paul's coincide with the dates of Damett's tenure of prebends at these institutions. Detailed payments to Sturgeon are recorded in the Windsor archives between 1441 and 1451, during which period he held office variously as treasurer and steward. His name appears as a founder member of the Gild of Parish Clerks in 1449, whose Bede roll (*GB-Lgc* 4889/Pc) records him as a deceased member in 1455, varying his designation between *Dominus* and *Magister*. His will, written in English, is dated 31 May 1454, when he was alive, and was proved on 8 June of the same year, by which time he was presumably dead. It is printed in Furnivall: *The Fifty Earliest English Wills* (London, 1882), pp.131ff, and supplies several names of relatives, none of whom (where identifiable) advances our knowledge of Sturgeon himself. Although it refers extensively to other benefices and allegiances, there is no reference to music.

His seven surviving compositions are known exclusively from the second layer of the Old Hall MS, and may possibly be autograph. No personal features of style emerge sufficiently strongly to permit the ascription of further, anonymous, works to him. No use of plainsong has been traced except for the tenor of his only motet, which continues the chant used by Damett for his motet. This compositional relationship can only be deliberate, and it has been suggested that both motets marked the triumphal return to London of Henry V after the Agincourt victory. Bukofzer has proposed that both motets can be seen as elaborately troped settings of the Sanctus, a view supported by their position in the MS, the opening syllable of both of Sturgeon's texts and one of Damett's, as well as the use of a Sanctus plainsong. *Salve mater* is a felicitous and very English work which wears the ingenious sophistries of its isorhythm unobtrusively.

All of Sturgeon's compositions make considerable use of coloration, often with slight syncopation. All except nos.2 and 5 have at least one change of mensuration. The pieces written in score (nos.1, 4, 6) are not sharply distinct in style from those in separate parts, though the latter tend to have relatively more movement in the topmost part. Nos.6, 2 and 3 have extensive duet writing, and in nos.3 and 6 the contratenor crosses above the discantus as well as below the tenor. The melodic style is smooth and shapely; harmonic and rhythmic roughnesses are minimal.

WORKS

Edition: *The Old Hall Manuscript*, ed. A. Hughes and M. Bent, CMM, xlvi (1969–72) [OH]

1 Gloria, 3vv, OH no.9 (in score)
2 Gloria, 3vv, OH no.15
3 Gloria, 3vv, OH no.40
4 Credo, 3vv, OH no.64 (in score)
5 Credo, ?3vv, OH no.69 (only discantus survives)
6 Sanctus, 3vv, OH no.114 (in score)
7 Salve mater Domini/Salve templum gratie/-it in nomine Domini, 3vv, OH no.113 (Sarum Sanctus 3 in T continuing the T of Damett's motet, OH no.111, but untransposed)

For bibliography *see* OLD HALL MS.

MARGARET BENT

Sturges. *See* TURGES, EDMUND.

Sturm, Kaspar (*b* Schneeberg; *d* after 10 Dec 1599). German organ builder. He became a citizen of Regensburg on 31 December 1564 and organist of the Neupfarrkirche there in 1565. In 1568 he entered the court chapel in Munich, directed at that time by Lassus. He became a citizen of Ulm on 15 January 1580, made a journey to Italy in 1586, and renewed his citizenship of Regensburg on 7 January 1594. Sturm built two organs for the Munich court (1568 and 1574) and organs for the monasteries at Indersdorf, Blaubeuren and Scheyern in or before 1575. He built the large organ in Ulm Minster in 1576–8 (tried out by Bernhard Schmid, among others), as well as other instruments for Vienna, Regensburg, Linz, Graz, Abensberg and, in 1591, for the Neupfarrkirche in Regensburg.

Like Jörg Ebert, Balthazar Mygel of Altenmygelburg, Eusebius Amerbach and Martin Ruck, the south German conservatives of the period, Sturm set greatest store by the Principal chorus: the *Hauptwerk* of his instrument, for example, had 8′ 4′ $2\frac{2}{3}'$ 2′ Mixtur V–VIII (4′) Zimbel II, Gedeckt 16′ 8′; the *Rückpositiv* had 4′ 2′ $1\frac{1}{3}'$ Mixtur V–VII (2′), Gedeckt 8′; the *Brustwerk* had 2′ Zimbel II, Gedeckt 4′, Posaune 8′ and Regal 4′; and the Pedal had 16′ Mixtur VI–VII (8′), Posaune 8′. Sturm was also one of the few masters known to have equipped their manual mixtures with a relatively large number of octave ranks, but with very few ranks of 5ths (and those very high). This had been recommended by Arnolt Schlick in 1511; Praetorius gave an example of it in 1619, and it is found in the instrument of 1585 in St Vaast, Arras, by Jean Barbaise and Pieter Isoore. The Mixtur on the *Hauptwerk* of Sturm's Ulm instrument was as follows: from *C*, 4′ 2′ 1′ $\frac{1}{2}'$ $\frac{1}{3}'$; from *c*, 4′ 2′ $\frac{2}{3}'$ $\frac{1}{2}'$ $\frac{1}{2}'$; from *c*′, 4′ 4′ 2′ 2′ $1\frac{1}{3}'$ 1′ 1′; and from *c*″ 4′ 4′ 4′ $2\frac{2}{3}'$ $2\frac{2}{3}'$ 2′ 2′ 2′. The *Rückpositiv* Mixtur was equipped with: 2′ 1′ $\frac{1}{2}'$ $\frac{1}{4}'$ $\frac{1}{6}'$; 2′ 1′ $\frac{1}{2}'$ $\frac{1}{2}'$ $\frac{1}{3}'$; 2′ 2′ 1′ 1′ $\frac{2}{3}'$ $\frac{2}{3}'$; and 2′ 2′ 2′ 2′ $1\frac{1}{3}'$ $1\frac{1}{3}'$ $1\frac{1}{3}'$.

BIBLIOGRAPHY

E. Emsheimer: 'Lucas Osiander als Orgelbauer', *Musik und Kirche*, iii (1931), 180, 236
H. Klotz: *Über die Orgelkunst der Gotik, der Renaissance und des Barock* (Kassel, 1934, 2/1975), 207ff, 240ff
R. Quoika: *Die altösterreichische Orgel der späten Gotik, der Renaissance und des Barock* (Kassel, 1953)
O. Eberstaller: *Orgeln und Orgelbauer in Österreich* (Graz and Cologne, 1955)
A. Layer: 'Sturm', *MGG*
R. W. Sterl: 'Der Orgelbauer Kaspar Sturm in Ulm', *Ulm und Oberschwaben*, xxxviii (1967), 109
——: 'Die Orgelbauer Eusebius Amerbach und Kaspar Sturm', *Mf*, xxii (1969), 42

HANS KLOTZ

Stürmer, Bruno (*b* Freiburg, 9 Sept 1892; *d* Bad Homburg, 19 May 1958). German composer, conductor and teacher. He studied at Heidelberg University (under Philipp Wolfrum) and at Munich University (musicology under Sandberger and Kroyer, fine arts under Wölfflin, and German literature under Muncker). During the 1920s he worked as an opera conductor in Heidelberg, Remscheid and Essen, and in 1925 he became a choral conductor in Duisburg; he also founded a school of music in Homberg, on the lower Rhine. In the 1930s he moved to Kassel to devote more time to composition. From 1945 he worked as a composer, critic and teacher in the Frankfurt area; he was also director of the Darmstadt Orchestral School for a time. Stürmer's very extensive output ranges from short choruses to full-scale symphonic pieces, written in an objective style employing quartal and quintal harmony. His best-known pieces are those for male chorus.

WORKS

More than 100 choral works incl. Wanderers Nachtlied (Goethe), male chorus, 1918, Die Messe des Maschinenmenschen, Bar, male chorus, orch, 1931, Das Ludwigsburger Tedeum, boys' chorus, male chorus, brass band, 1954; also orchestral works

Principal publishers: Schott (Mainz), Tonger
WRITINGS
Frisch fröhlich woll'n wir singen (Cologne, 1956)
BIBLIOGRAPHY
Bruno-Stürmer-Konzert (Schwanden, 1958)

RUDOLF LÜCK

Sturmmarsch (Ger.). Double-quick march; *see* MARCH, §1.

Sturm und Drang (Ger.: 'storm and stress'). A movement in German letters, reflected in the other arts, that reached its highpoint in the 1770s. It is most easily defined by its artistic aims: to frighten, to stun, to overcome with emotion. In line with these aims was an extreme emphasis on an anti-rational, subjective approach to all art. The young Goethe was the leading figure, with his play *Götz von Berlichingen* (1773) on a medieval German subject.

The movement had been prepared by various creative spirits of the mid-century, who were still half part of the fashionable appeal to sentimentality of the time, so-called 'Empfindsamkeit'. On an international level it is necessary to give credit to Edward Young's *Night Thoughts* (1742; Ger. trans., 1751). Also prefiguring the movement was Rousseau's rediscovery of nature at its most awesome, from Alpine peaks to ocean depths. A special kinship may also be established with Diderot because of his frequent and influential calls for sombre, savage and grandiose qualities in painting, poetry and music. Mercier worked these precepts into a treatise on drama that found a wide response among German writers, partly because of its social aspects, with emphasis on class struggle. No less important was the widespread revival of Shakespeare's tragedies, which had the effect of liberating dramatists from subservience to the style and the rules of classicistic drama and giving them a sense of historicism. The expression 'Sturm und Drang' comes from a play about the American Revolution, written in 1776 by Maximilian Klinger. With Schiller's play *Die Räuber* (1780–81) the movement is generally accounted to have reached its zenith, after which both Schiller and Goethe gradually returned to more universal standards.

There were parallel movements in the other arts. The fashion for storms and shipwrecks in painting, associated particularly with Joseph Vernet and Philippe de Loutherbourg, capitalized on the delight in conveying fear and terror. Painters who specialized in nightmarish visions fall into the same category. Goethe wrote to a friend in 1779: 'I have got hold of some paintings and sketches by Fuseli, which will give you all a good fright'. Blake proved a worthy disciple of Fuseli. The vogue of Piranesi's *Carceri* from mid-century on bespeaks another aspect of the revelling in gloom and tortured feelings, as well as the appeal of a remote and more romantic past. Gothic dungeons à la Piranesi afforded some of the strongest statements in visual terms upon the operatic stages of the time. A related phenomenon was the strongly anti-rational appeal of 'Gothic novels', which began with Horace Walpole's *Castle of Otranto* (1764). At the same time James MacPherson published his primitivistic *Ballads of Ossian*, passing them off as translations from the Gaelic (1762–3).

A musical parallel is best approached in the theatre, where all the arts meet. Stimulating strong emotional responses was a prime aim of the operatic reform about 1760. What was experienced at the time as a most potent weapon for passionate, unbridled expression was obbligato (or orchestrally accompanied) recitative. In the hands of Italian masters like Jommelli and Traetta, this language of orchestral commentary was pushed to unheard-of lengths of tone-painting. A related territory, by virtue of its freedom of action and fluid, transitional techniques, was the dramatic ballet, where music painted various pantomimic gestures. The choreographers Noverre (*Lettres sur la danse*, 1760) and Angiolini were both significant in advancing towards the pantomime ballet; the latter devised the stage action in Gluck's *Don Juan* (1761) and wrote a programme note that clearly proclaimed 'Sturm unnd Drang' ideals: '[Gluck] a saisi parfaitement le terrible de l'Action. Il a taché d'exprimer les passions qui y jouent, et l'épouvante qui règne dans la catastrophe'. The ferocious intensity of the D minor finale was indeed well calculated to evoke terror – Mozart's *Don Giovanni*, 25 years later, was still beholden to it. From here it was but a step to the scene with the furies in Gluck's *Orfeo ed Euridice* (1762), also choreographed by Angiolini. The resources of obbligato recitative and the dramatic ballet gave composers a ready-made arsenal with which to fashion the continuous web of pictorial music necessary to accompany *mélodrame* (spoken drama supported by orchestral mood music). Rousseau pioneered this genre with his *Pygmalion* (1770). It was quickly taken up by Goethe and other literary figures. Georg Benda's music for *Ariadne* and *Medea* (1774–5) achieved the greatest successes for the genre. Mozart first came into contact with them in 1777–8 at Mannheim, where one of the German companies specializing in Shakespeare put on *Medea*. His pleasantly astonished reaction led to experiments with the technique in *Zaide* (1779) and in his revisions of the stage music for *König Thamos*. He also planned to write a fully-fledged *mélodrame*, on the subject of Semiramide, on which Gluck had written the most radically innovatory of his dramatic ballets (1765). Obbligato recitative was pushed to its utmost expressive consequences in *Idomeneo* (1780–81), a product of his Mannheim and Paris experiences. His utterances about this opera betray a typical 'Sturm und Drang' attitude towards dramatic realism ('Man muss glauben es sey wircklich so!', written in connection with the oracular pronouncement accompanied by trombones in Act 3), and with regard to evoking fear and terror from the audience (e.g. the storm scenes in C minor and F minor, the D minor flight chorus, described in the libretto as a pantomime of 'Angst und Schrecken'). Mozart's power in expressing the macabre and the terrible also sometimes came to the fore in his earlier stage works, notably in the tomb scene of *Lucio Silla* (1772) and in parts of *La finta giardiniera* (1774).

Other composers have been linked with the 'Sturm und Drang' movement with more or less appropriateness. In north Germany, Rolle went far beyond the merely sentimental in works such as his *Tod Abels* (published 1771), *Abraham* (1776), *Lazarus* (1778) and *Thirza* (1781), which may be compared with Benda's *mélodrames* in terms of tragic grandeur, dramatic fluidity, use of unifying motifs, and large-scale tonal planning. The second Berlin school of lied composers, although they went beyond the first school's insistence upon being pleasing at all times, never produced such stark and uncompromising music as did Rolle at his best. Bücken assessed the operas of Schweitzer on texts of Wieland (*Alceste*, 1773; *Rosemunde*, 1777) as falling between 'Sturm und Drang' and 'galant Empfindsamkeit', with the composer leaning towards the former and the poet towards the latter. In south Germany the main centres were Stuttgart (with Jommelli pupils like Zumsteeg) and Mannheim (Schobert and Eckhard have been singled out as pioneers of a robust piano style that imitated the famed orchestral fireworks of the Mannheim band). Even Mozart admired the fiery music in Holzbauer's *Günther von Schwarzburg* (1778 – another medieval German subject). Among the Mannheim composers, Vogler was the foremost 'Stürmer' with his frankly sensational programme overtures (*Hamlet*, 1778), his ballets and other stage works. Of the storm in his *mélodrame*, *Lampedo* (1778), he wrote: 'the orchestra cannot be distinguished from the thunder ram above the timber-work of the theatre, the rain machine, and the lightning that pierces the darkness on stage; all work together to contribute to the dramatic realism by which a horrible tempest is conjured up for the eyes and ears'. Gradations of lighting in the theatre accompanied these storms and other incidences of nature in upheaval, an important visual counterpart to the dramatic fluidity sought through music (Loutherbourg was a pioneer here). Vogler's significance in establishing a new, more 'romantic' approach to the lyric stage emerges from his *Betrachtungen der Mannheimer Tonschule* (1778–80) no less than from his music. As the respected teacher of a younger generation including Winter, Weber and Meyerbeer, he may be considered one of the seminal figures linking the 'Sturm und Drang' variety of 'romanticism' with that of the early 19th century.

A persuasive case has been made (Brook, 1970) for considering Haydn's phase of passionate works in the minor mode, characteristic of the years round 1770, along with similar works of other Austrian symphonists, as a 'Sturm und Drang' phenomenon; Brook compared Haydn's turn towards more Olympian ideals in the following decades with the turn of events in German letters, and with Goethe in particular. Although parallel movements to the musical 'Sturm und Drang' can be discerned in other countries, it seems unwise to apply this term, because of its very nature, beyond the German-speaking lands. C. P. E. Bach has been held up as an archetypal representative in music of the 'Sturm und Drang' movement. While such a case can be made, his age and his reluctance to participate directly in musical theatre make it more appropriate to view him as a particularly powerful creator within the preceding and related aesthetic sphere of Empfindsamkeit.

See also CLASSICAL; EMPFINDSAMKEIT; ENLIGHTENMENT; GALANT; ROCOCO.

BIBLIOGRAPHY

E. Bücken: *Die Musik des Rokokos und der Klassik* (Potsdam, 1927)
R. Pascal: *The German Sturm und Drang* (Manchester, 1953)
R. Mortier: *Diderot en Allemagne* (Paris, 1954)
H. H. Eggebrecht: 'Das Ausdruckprinzip in Musikalische Sturm und Drang', *Deutsche Vierteljahrsschrift für Literatur- und Geistesgeschichte*, xxix (1955), 323
H. C. R. Landon: 'La crise romantique dans la musique autrichienne vers 1770: quelques précurseurs inconnus de la Symphonie en sol mineur (KV 183) de Mozart', *Les influences étrangères dans l'oeuvre de Mozart: CNRS Paris 1956*, 27
L. Hoffmann-Erbrecht: 'Sturm und Drang in der deutschen Klaviermusik von 1753–1763', *Mf*, x (1957), 466
J. and B. Massin: 'Mozart et le "Sturm und Drang" (à propos des oeuvres de l'hiver 1772–73)', *Essais sur la musique*, xiii (1959), 29
H. Majewski: 'L. S. Mercier: a Pre-Romantic View of Paris', *Studies in Romanticism*, v (1965), 16
W. Heckscher: 'Sturm und Drang: Conjectures on the Origins of a Phrase', *Simiolus*, i (1966–7), 94
B. S. Brook: 'Sturm und Drang and the Romantic Period in Music', *Studies in Romanticism*, ix (1970), 269
D. Heartz: 'Sturm und Drang im Musikdrama', *GfMKB, Bonn 1970*, 432
P. F. Marks: 'The Rhetorical Element in Musical Sturm und Drang: Christian Gottfried Krause's "Von der musikalischen Poesie" ', *IRASM*, ii (1971), 49
E. Loewenthal, ed.: *Sturm und Drang: kritische Schriften* (Heidelberg, 1972)
K. Clark: *The Romantic Rebellion* (London, 1973) [chaps. on Piranesi, Fuseli and Blake]
G. Gruber: 'Glucks Tanzdramen und ihre Musikalische Dramatik', *ÖMz*, xxix (1974), 17
M. Mann: *Sturm und Drang Drama: Studien und Vorstudien zu Schillers 'Räubern'* (Berne, 1974)

DANIEL HEARTZ

Sturt, John (*fl* 1612–25). English lutenist and composer. In 1612 he was among those who received an allowance for mourning livery for the funeral of Prince Henry. He is listed among the lutenists who received £2 each for playing in Chapman's *Masque of the Middle Temple and Lincoln's Inn* in February 1613. From August 1613 until 1625 he was one of the city waits.

He compiled a collection of lute pieces, and its contents suggest that this work was done between about 1612 and 1616. Many of the compositions are for a ten-course lute. The manuscript (now *GB-Lbm* Add.38539) is of special interest for the number and variety of ornament signs used, and for the care with which the left-hand fingering is marked. Sturt's own compositions are represented in his book: concordances are in the British Museum and Cambridge University Library. He wrote two almains, two voltas, one prelude and a coranto.

DIANA POULTON

Sturton [Stourton] (*fl* early 16th century). English composer. He was perhaps the William Sturton, Gentleman of the Chapel Royal in 1503 and 1509–10, but it must be noted that in the Eton Choirbook the christian name 'Edmundus' has been added in a later hand. His six-voice *Gaude virgo mater Christi* in this MS (ed. in MB, x, 2/1967, no.8) contains an unusual progression to a D♭ chord in bar 168, the only use of this accidental in the choirbook. *Ave Maria, ancilla Trinitatis*, also for six voices, on the cantus firmus *Gloria tibi Trinitas* (in *GB-Llp*) has frequent false relations.

BIBLIOGRAPHY
F. Ll. Harrison: *Music in Medieval Britain* (London, 1958, 2/1963)

Sturzenegger, Richard (*b* Zurich, 18 Dec 1905; *d* Berne, 24 Oct 1976). Swiss cellist and composer. After matriculation he entered the Zurich Conservatory, where he studied the cello under Reitz, and then went to Paris to study with Alexanian, Casals and Nadia Boulanger. He became first cellist at the Dresden State Opera and pursued his studies under Emanuel Feuermann and Ernst Toch. In 1935 he settled in Berne as first cellist in the Musikgesellschaft Orchestra and a teacher at the conservatory. For many years he was cellist of the Berne String Quartet, which disbanded in 1949. He succeeded Alphonse Brun as director of the Berne Conservatory in 1963. His compositional activity was at first intermittent, but in the 1940s he began to produce more music in an individual tonal style, his works after that period displaying depth of feeling, thoughtfulness and refined sensitivity.

WORKS
(selective list)

Choral: Cantata on Old German Words, S, 7 old insts, 1934; Chorale Fantasy, A, tpt, drums, str orch, 1941; Gesangs-Szene (Grillparzer), A, chamber orch, 1942; Liebeslied (Rilke), A, T, harp, 1944; 8 Texte Michelangelos (trans. Rilke), Bar, str qt, 1944; Cantico di San Francesco, solo vv, chorus, harp, str, 1945; Omaggio (Tasso), S, fl, str qnt, 1945–8; Uelisbrunner Liturgie, chorus, 1952; Atalante, opera, 1968; 3 geistliche Lieder (K. Marti), chorus, 1969; 3 Sprüche, 3 female vv, 1970

Inst: 4 vc concs., 1933, 1937, 1946–7, 1972; Str Trio, 1937; Str Qt, 1940; Elegie, vc, ob, harp, va, vc, db, 1950; Triptychon, orch, 1951; Invention: hommage à Paul Sacher, pf, 1952; 8 Little Piano Pieces, 1957; Conc. (3 Gesänge Davids), vn, str, 1963; Pf Trio, 1964; Fresco, str orch, 1965; Kalender, 2 vc, 1969; Passion nach dem Evangelisten Lukas und Johannes, 5vv, 1975

Principal publishers: Reinhardt, Schott (Mainz)

BIBLIOGRAPHY

P. Mieg: 'Richard Sturzenegger', *40 Schweizer Komponisten der Gegenwart* (Amriswil, 1956), 196

E. Hochuli, ed.: *Variationen: Festgabe für Richard Sturzenegger zum siebzigsten Geburtstag* (Berne, 1975) [with list of works and bibliography]

A. Rubeli: 'Richard Sturzenegger: Passion nach dem Evangelisten Lukas und Johannes', *SMz*, cxvi (1976), 306

KURT VON FISCHER/JÜRG STENZL

Stutschewsky, Joachim [Yehoyachin] (*b* Romny, Ukraine, 7 Feb 1891). Israeli cellist, teacher, composer and ethnomusicologist. Born into a family of musicians, he gained proficiency as a cellist at an early age and then studied under Klengel, Paul and Sitt at the Leipzig Conservatory (1909–12). In 1912 he joined Alexander Schaichet in the Jena String Quartet, and it was in Jena that he established relations with Reger and first appeared as an orchestral soloist. Thereafter he was active as a soloist, chamber musician, composer, teacher and editor in Zurich (1914–24), where he began his internationally recognized treatise *Die Kunst des Cellospiels*, and Vienna (1924–38). He was a member of the Kolisch Quartet, which gave many early performances of works by Schoenberg, Berg and Webern, and in 1928 he founded in Vienna the Society for the Development of Jewish Music under the patronage of the Masada Lodge of Bnei Brith. At the same period he organized concerts of Jewish works in many European cities and wrote on Jewish music for the Viennese Zionist newspapers *Die Stimme* and *Selbstwehr*.

Stutschewsky moved in 1938 to Palestine, where he continued his many-sided musical activities and became a greatly respected figure. In the same year he established the avant-garde forum in Beit Brenner, Tel-Aviv, and travelled throughout the country, lecturing on Jewish music and encouraging composers to develop a nationalist style by drawing on Jewish folk traditions. He himself was one of the first to adopt this programme, and he followed Idelsohn in pursuing research into Jewish folk music. Among the awards he has received are three Engel Prizes (1958, 1959 and 1966), the Artists' Club of Israel Prize (1958), the Piatigorsky Prize of the New York Cello Society (1963) and the Israel PO prize (1973) for the symphonic suite *Israel*.

WORKS
(selective list)

Orch: Concertino, cl, str, 1958; Fantasia, ob, harp, str, 1959; Tsfat (Safed), sym. poem, 1960; Concertante, fl, str, 1963; Israel, sym. suite, 1964; Music for Str Orch, 1965; Little Suite, str, 1967

Cantatas: Shirei ha'etsev hakoren [Songs of radiant sadness], narrator, Mez, B, chorus, orch, 1958; Yemama bashimsha [From dawn to dawn], narrator, S, T, ens, 1960

Chamber: Duo, vc, 1941; Old Hassidic Tune, vn, pf, 1944; 5 Pieces, str qt, 1959; Str Trio, 1960; Sextet, wind qnt, hn, 1960; Three for Three, 3 vc, 1967; Dialogues variés, 2 tpt, 1970; Imaginations, fl, pf trio, 1971; Mini-duets, vn, pf, 1975; unacc. ww pieces

Vc, pf: Danse orientale, 1923; 3 Hebrew Pieces, 1936; Jewish Song, 1939; Ballade, 1940; Israeli Suite, 1942; Andante religioso, 1942; Hassidic Suite, 1946; Legend (Wilnaer balabessel), 1952; Sabbath, 1953; T'hina [Supplication], 1953; Kaddish, 1957; The Little Cellist, 1958

Pf: 4 Jewish Dances, 1929; Rikud [Dance], 1930; Bagatelles, 1932; Hora, 1937; 3 Pieces, 1941; Jewish Dance, 1944; Hassidic Dance, 1945; Miniatures for Children, 3 vols., 1946; Shivivim [Splinters], 1975

Many other vc works, incl. edns. and arrs. of music by Beethoven, Boccherini, Dvořák, Haydn, Mendelssohn, Mozart, Offenbach, Schubert, Schumann and Weber; *c*100 songs, 1v, pf; songs with various inst accs., children's songs, choral songs

Principal publishers: Culture and Education Centre of the Histadrut, Hug, Israel Music Institute, Israeli Music Publications, Or-Tav, Peters, Schott, See-saw, Universal

For fuller list see *Seventieth Anniversary Catalogue: Works of Joachim Stutschewsky 1891* (Tel-Aviv, 1961)

WRITINGS

Die Kunst des Cellospiels, i–ii (Mainz, 1929), iii–iv (Vienna, 1938)

Mein Weg zur Jüdischen Musik (Vienna, 1935)

Musika yehudit [Jewish music] (Tel-Aviv, 1946)

The Cello and its Masters: History of Cello Playing, 1950, unpubd

Klezmerim (Tel-Aviv, 1959) [On Jewish folk musicians]

Musical Folklore of Eastern Jewry (Tel-Aviv, 1959)

BIBLIOGRAPHY

J. Stutschewsky: *Korot hayav shel musikai yehudi* [The life of a Jewish musician] (Tel-Aviv, 1975)

Y. W. Cohen: *Werden und Entwicklung der Musik in Israel* (Kassel, 1976) [pt.ii of rev. edn. of M. Brod: *Die Musik Israels*]

W. Y. Elias: *The Music of Israel* (in preparation) [bibliography]

WILLIAM Y. ELIAS

Stuttgart. City in the Federal Republic of Germany, the capital of Baden-Württemberg. It is one of south-west Germany's most important cultural centres, and has a rich musical history.

1. To 1600. 2. 17th and 18th centuries. 3. After 1800.

1. TO 1600. The Stuttgart Hofkapelle and a boys' choir at the Chorherrenstift of the collegiate church had been founded by the 15th century, but Stuttgart's musical life reached its first peak under Duke Ulrich (1503–50), who keenly supported music. The Hofkapelle acquired the services of such outstanding musicians as Heinrich Finck, Virdung, Brack and Siess and won widespread recognition as a centre of vocal and instrumental music. Apart from sacred music, the cantus firmus lied was the most important genre cultivated at Ulrich's court. From 1510 to 1514 Finck was Hofkapellmeister; his *Missa in summis* was probably performed at the marriage of Duke Ulrich and Sabina of Bavaria in 1511. In 1519 the duke was overthrown by the Swabian Alliance, and the Hofkapelle was disbanded, but following his victorious return in 1534 it was restored to its former brilliance, particularly through the arrival of Hans Hickas, Utz Steigleder and Hemmel, all outstanding composers.

Duke Ulrich acknowledged the Reformation, and the Hofkapelle became an important centre of Protestant sacred music. It retained its ecclesiastical functions during the reign of Duke Christoph (1550–68), who occasionally transferred the chapel to his other residence in Tübingen. Christoph was closely associated with Johann Walter (ii) and Lassus, both of whom dedicated works to him. The spiritual and intellectual life of Württemberg was greatly enhanced by Christoph's completion of the grandly conceived consistory, the Lutheran Theological Foundation, founded by Duke Ulrich in 1536; Hegel, Mörike and Hölderlin were later to belong to this institution. From its inception the consistory attached special importance to the cultivation of music, particularly choral singing and instrumental music.

1. Part of a pageant held at Stuttgart on 6 November 1609 to celebrate the marriage the previous day of Johann Friedrich, Duke of Württemberg to Barbara Sophia, daughter of the Elector of Brandenburg: watercolour in the Victoria and Albert Museum, London

The Stuttgart Hofkapelle flourished once more under dukes Ludwig (1568–93) and Friedrich (1593–1608). Outstanding Hofkapellmeisters were the composers Ludwig Daser (1572–89) and Balduin Hoyoul (1589–94), a pupil of Lassus. By the end of the 16th century the Hofkapelle had grown to over 50 members, and increasingly performed secular as well as sacred music; instrumental music generally began to replace vocal music. Leonhard Lechner became a member of the Hofkapelle in 1585, and from 1594 to 1606 was a highly respected Hofkapellmeister. The larger part of his works were composed in Stuttgart, including the 15-part motet *Laudate dominum, quia bonus est*, composed for the marriage of Württemberg's Princess Sibylle Elisabeth in Dresden. Among the more distinguished organists at the court and the consistory were Johann Ulrich and Adam Steigleder and Simon Lohet, all of whose works display the characteristics of the south German organ style. Lucas Osiander, composer of the *Fünfftzig geistlichen Lieder und Psalmen* in four-voice cantional settings (1586), which laid the foundations for Lutheran congregational song, was minister at the court and the consistory.

2. 17TH AND 18TH CENTURIES. A separate body of chamber musicians was added to the ducal Hofkapelle by the end of the 16th century. Between 1609 and 1628 it included an *engelländische compagnia*, including the cornettist John Price and lutenists George Vichet, David and John Morrell and John Dixon. Basilius Froberger directed the Hofkapelle through the many reversals of the Thirty Years War (1618–48) until his death in 1637; his son, Johann Jacob Froberger, may have received his formative musical impressions during his youth in Stuttgart. He probably studied with Johann Ulrich Steigleder and possibly met Scheidt during the latter's visit to Stuttgart in 1627.

Polyphonic music at the consistory church was the responsibility of the preceptors and Pädagogium students. In 1618 a Stiftsmusik consisting of a master and five apprentices was founded to support polyphonic and congregational singing. Its first director was Joachim Böddecker, father of the important composer and consistory organist Philipp Friedrich Böddecker. A later organist and Kantor at the consistory, J. G. C. Störl, was a student of Pachelbel; he published a hymn book in Stuttgart in 1710. From 1690 to 1692 Pachelbel was organist to Duchess Magdalena Sibylla in Stuttgart.

After the defeat of Nördlingen in 1634 the Hofkapelle was disbanded, and only reorganized in 1657 through the efforts of Samuel Capricornus, Hofkapellmeister until 1665. The Lusthaus, which had been the main centre of theatrical performances in Stuttgart, proved unable to meet the city's demands for theatre, and in 1674 the new Komödienhaus was opened in the court pleasure garden. The Stuttgart Opera began its greatest period with the appointment of J. S. Kusser as Hofkapellmeister in 1700. Kusser brought high standards to the Hofkapelle and performed, besides his own works, operas by such composers as Steffani and, probably, Lully. He was succeeded by J. C. Pez and, from 1716 to 1755, by G. A. Brescianello.

Under Duke Eberhard Ludwig the castle of Ludwigsburg was constructed 15 km north of Stuttgart as the new ducal residence; the entire Hofkapelle was transferred there in 1728. In 1744 the young Duke Carl Eugen, who had grown up at the court of Frederick the Great in Potsdam and received tuition from C. P. E. Bach, began his reign, and Stuttgart became one of the most important centres of European music and opera. The duke devoted himself to raising his opera, orchestra and ballet to the highest artistic level and used every means to attain that goal. He assured for Stuttgart an international reputation in opera and concerts with the appointment of Jommelli and in ballet with that of Noverre. A successful opera composer and producer, Jommelli engaged such leading musicians as Nardini and Lotti and such outstanding singers as the soprano Cuzzoni. Complementing Jommelli's newly instituted opera, Noverre was able to bring his ideal of *ballet en action* to full realization. The Konzertmeister F. J. Deller and the horn virtuoso J. J. Rudolph, among others, composed music for the ballets, which were used as intermezzos in Jommelli's operas. Leopold Mozart stayed in Ludwigsburg with both his children from 9 to 12 July 1763. The family was not received by the duke, but was introduced to Jommelli, on whom young Wolfgang made a lasting impression.

Opposition by the provinces forced the duke in 1767 to limit his expenditure. As a result Noverre was dismissed, Jommelli retired, and the orchestra, opera and ballet were drastically reduced. From 1780 Duke Carl Eugen turned his attention entirely to the Hohe Carls-Schule, which he himself had founded. The music department of this school became, under the duke's supervision, the place of instruction for young prospective musicians for the opera and orchestra. Among the graduates of the school were Schiller, Schubart and, most important, J. R. Zumsteeg. Zumsteeg directed court music from 1793 to 1804; his ballads, the most significant of his time, served as models for Schubert. During this period Dittersdorf's *Doctor und Apotheker* (1788) and Mozart's *Le nozze di Figaro* (1790), *Die Zauberflöte* (1795) and *Don Giovanni* (1796) were performed for the first time in Stuttgart.

3. AFTER 1800. With the death of Duke Carl Eugen the court theatre found itself in severe financial straits. The resulting artistic poverty in opera and drama was described by Goethe, who visited Stuttgart in 1797. Zumsteeg was succeeded as Hofkapellmeister by J. F. Kranz of Weimar and Franz Danzi, previously Kapellmeister to the Munich court. Weber lived in Stuttgart and Ludwigsburg from 1807 to 1810 as secretary to Duke Ludwig, during which time he composed *Silvana*, the music for *Turandot*, some piano and chamber works and the opera *Abu Hassan* (to a libretto by the court councillor Franz Karl Hiemer), which was performed in 1811 under the direction of Danzi. Two new directors brought renewed importance to the Stuttgart Opera: Conradin Kreutzer, composer of the opera *Ein Nachtlager in Granada* and of numerous lieder inspired by his contact with Ludwig Uhland and the Swabian *Dichterkreis*; and Hummel, who produced Beethoven's *Fidelio* in Stuttgart as early as 1817. Both, however, left Stuttgart after a few years. From 1819 to 1856 Lindpainter, a conductor praised by Mendelssohn and Berlioz, once again brought considerable esteem to the Opera by engaging outstanding vocalists, leading painstaking rehearsals and constantly widening the Opera's repertory. He also directed regular subscription concerts, with performances by such virtuosos as Liszt, Paganini and Henry Vieuxtemps, in addition to local musicians. Meyerbeer conducted his *L'étoile du Nord* (1854) and *Dinorah* (1859) with great success, and *Tannhäuser* (1859) was the first of Wagner's operas to be performed there. The Hofkapellmeister J. J. Abert brought high standards to the symphony concerts and directed numerous choral works, including a performance of Brahms's *German Requiem* in 1871 in the presence of the composer. F. P. Lachner, Carl Reinecke, Bruch (who conducted *Fritjof* in 1872) and Saint-Saëns were among Stuttgart's guest conductors. Clara Schumann gave frequent concerts in Stuttgart from 1834, and in 1881 Brahms conducted a concert of his own works.

With the appointment of Max von Schillings in 1908 the Stuttgart Opera was again among the most important centres of German stage production. The court

2. The court pleasure gardens, showing the building (right) later used as the Komödienhaus: engraving (c1620) by Matthäus Merian after Pierre Aubry

theatre was destroyed by fire in 1902, and in 1912 the new Grosses und Kleines Haus was opened. In the same year Richard Strauss conducted the première of *Ariadne auf Naxos* there, with Max Reinhardt supervising the production, and Schillings produced his own opera *Mona Lisa* in 1915. In 1918 Fritz Busch took charge of the Opera and symphony concerts, and under his direction contemporary works, including Schreker's *Der Schatzgräber* and several short operas by Hindemith, received world premières. Carl Leonhardt, general music director from 1922 to 1937, performed the complete operas of Weber in 1926, the centenary of the composer's death, and the complete works of Wagner on the 50th anniversary of his death (1933). He was succeeded by Herbert Albert and Philipp Wüst.

Stuttgart's musical life resumed after World War II with the first performance in German of Hindemith's *Mathis der Maler* in 1946 under Bertil Wetzelsberger, who also conducted the première of Orff's *Die Bernauerin* in 1947. In this year Ferdinand Leitner was appointed director of the Württemberg Staatstheater, and under his direction Stuttgart gave the first German performance of Stravinsky's *The Rake's Progress* in 1951. In 1954 he directed a production of *Fidelio*, influenced by the renewal of music drama in Bayreuth; Wieland Wagner was in charge of the production. Leitner gave the premières of Orff's *Comoedia de Christi resurrectione* (1957), *Oedipus der Tyrann* (1959), *Ludus de nato Infante mirificus* (1960) and *Prometheus* (1968). In 1969 Václav Neumann became general music director and was succeeded by Silvio Varviso in 1972. On Varviso's appointment to the Paris Opéra the Stuttgart position was taken by Dennis Russell Davies (from 1980). The Stuttgart Opera Ballet achieved a high standard under the direction (1961–73) of John Cranko.

The Stuttgart Musikschule was founded in 1857; in 1865 it became the Konservatorium für Musik and in 1921 was renamed the Württembergische Hochschule für Musik. Its directors since 1907 have included Max Pauer, Kempff, Erpf, Hermann Keller and Hermann Reutter. A Staatliche Hochschule für Musik und Darstellende Kunst has been directed by Wolfgang Gönnenwein since 1973.

Stuttgart's outstanding choral societies are the Stuttgarter Liederkranz (1824), the Stuttgarter Oratorienchor (1847), the Philharmonische Chor, the Gächinger Kantorei, the Schwäbische Singkreis, the Hymnus-Knaben-Chor, the Süddeutsche Madrigal-Chor, the chorus of the Süddeutscher Rundfunk in Stuttgart and the Schola Cantorum.

In addition to the Württembergisch Staatsorchester, regular symphonic concerts are presented by the symphony orchestra of the Süddeutscher Rundfunk (directed by Hans Müller-Kray, 1948–9, and since then by guest conductors including Michael Gielen and Sergiu Celibidache), and the Stuttgart Philharmonic, mostly in the Konzerthaus Stuttgarter Liederhalle (1956; three halls, capacity 2000, 750 and 355). The Stuttgart Chamber Orchestra, founded in 1945 under Karl Münchinger, has won worldwide acclaim.

Stuttgart's instrument builders have achieved recognition through the work of several violin builders and the piano factories of Schiedmayer und Söhne, Schiedmayer, Carl Matthaes and Carl Pfeiffer. The music division of the Stuttgart Landesbibliothek possesses a valuable collection of music manuscripts and first editions.

BIBLIOGRAPHY

J. Sittard: *Zur Geschichte der Musik und des Theaters am Württembergischen Hofe* (Stuttgart, 1890/*R*1970)
G. Bossert: articles on the Hofkantorei and Hofkapelle in *Württembergische Vierteljahrsheft für Landesgeschichte*, new ser., vii–xxv (1898–1916)
H. Abert: 'Die dramatische musik', *Herzog Karl Eugen von Württemberg und seine Zeit* (Esslingen, 1905)
R. Krauss: *Das Stuttgarter Hoftheater* (Stuttgart, 1908)
H. Abert: 'Zur Geschichte der Oper in Württemberg', *IMusSCR, iii Vienna 1909*, 186
A. Bopp: 'Beiträge zur Geschichte der Stuttgarter Stiftsmusik', *Württembergische Jb für Statistik und Landeskunde 1910* (Stuttgart, 1911), 211–50
K. Haering: *Fünf schwäbische Liederkomponisten des 18. Jahrhunderts* (diss., U. of Tübingen, 1925)
O. zur Nedden: 'Zur Frühgeschichte der protestantischen Kirchenmusik in Württemberg', *ZMw*, xiii (1930–31), 24
F. Blume: *Die evangelische Kirchenmusik*, HMw, x (1931, rev. 2/1965 as *Geschichte der evangelischen Kirchenmusik*; Eng. trans., enlarged 1974, as *Protestant Church Music: a History*)
O. zur Nedden: 'Zur Geschichte der Musik am Hofe Kaiser Maximilians', *ZMw*, xv (1932–3), 309
E. F. Schmid: *Ein schwäbisches Mozartbuch* (Stuttgart, 1948)
A. Yorke-Long: 'Charles Eugene of Württemberg', *Music at Court: Four Eighteenth-century Studies* (London, 1954), 43
U. Seelmann-Eggebrecht: 'Theaterstadt Stuttgart 1912–1962', *Festschrift der Württembergischen Staatstheater* (Stuttgart, 1962)
H. Erpf: 'Musikleben in Württemberg', *Baden-Württemberg, Staat, Wirtschaft, Kultur* (Stuttgart, 1963)
E. Stiefel: 'Stuttgart'; 'Württemberg', *MGG*
W. Supper: 'Die Orgellandschaft Württemberg', *Acta organologica*, i (1967), 127

EBERHARD STIEFEL

Style. A term denoting manner of discourse, mode of expression; more particularly the manner in which a work of art is executed. In the discussion of music, which is orientated towards relationships rather than meanings, the term raises special difficulties; it may be used to denote music characteristic of an individual composer, of a period, of a geographical area or centre, or of a society or social function.

1. Definition. 2. Import of style. 3. Phenomena of style. 4. Conditioners and dynamics of stylistic differences. 5. Stylistic awareness.

1. DEFINITION. Style is manner, mode of expression, type of presentation. For the aesthetician style concerns surface or appearance, though in music appearance and essence are ultimately inseparable. For the historian a style is a distinguishing and ordering concept, both consistent of and denoting generalities; he groups examples of music according to similarities between them. A style may be seen as a synthesis of other styles; obvious cases are J. S. Bach's keyboard style or Mozart's operatic style (both comprise distinctive textural styles, distinctive harmonic styles, distinctive melodic styles etc, and both are fusions of various stylistic traditions). A style also represents a range or series of possibilities defined by a group of particular examples, as in such notions as 'homophonic style' and 'chromatic style'.

Style, a style or styles (or all three) may be seen in any conceptual unit in the realm of music, from the largest to the smallest; music itself is a style of art, and a single note may have stylistic implications according to its instrumentation, pitch and duration. Style, a style or styles may be seen as present in a chord, phrase, section, movement, work, group of works, genre, life's work, period (of any size) and culture. Style manifests itself in characteristic usages of form, texture, harmony, melody, rhythm and ethos; and it is presented by creative personalities, conditioned by historical, social and geographical factors, performing resources and conventions.

2. IMPORT OF STYLE. 'Style' derives from the word for a Greek and Roman writing implement (Lat. *stilus*), a tool of communication, the shaper and conditioner of the outward form of a message. While the antithesis of appearance and essence, or style and import, is clear in this original graphical usage, the relationship is more complex than simple antithesis where art is concerned. It is widely accepted (e.g. by Sachs and Lippman) that in speaking of the style of an epoch or culture one is treating of import, a substantive communication from a society, which is a significant embodiment of the aspirations and inner life of its people. The same is true of smaller units of artistic endeavour; genres speak of the men who created them and the people who readily received them, and a personal style speaks of the artist's view of life. But in the individual art work other, more intentional messages are also present.

These are not of course messages in the verbal sense. But by the act of creative will a composer asserts something; he makes a statement of some kind. He inherits a usable past and acts by intuitive vision. The product of his vision builds on a stylistic heritage, has a style and import of its own and bequeaths an altered heritage. The stylistic heritage may be seen as general procedures which condition the composer's intuitive choice and invention, the general which limits the particular, the relevant available resource, the essential context of creation. Such notions are embodied in Schoenberg's opposition of style and idea, though this is an opposition which, sadly, Schoenberg took on trust in his book, as in the essay from which its title derives.

The idea works through style. Thus the opening of the *thema regium* in Bach's *Musicalisches Opfer* is a stately, measured, disjunct, minor, monophonic melody suitable for fugal treatment, rather than simply five minims C, E♭, G, A♭, B♮. An important part of the significance of this theme is the concatenation of qualities enumerated above, and to some extent the particular idea acts as the medium of style and the play of successive and coincident styles as the substance of the music. But the particular articulation of the stylistic concatenation is also part of the significance; five minims C, E♭, F, G, B♭ would fit this albeit crude stylistic analysis, but Bach's (or Frederick the Great's) creation is specifically not that. In music the particular and the general embodied therein and articulated thereby together form meaning or significance. They do so because music is stylized. There is no consistent natural meaning in music by relation to natural events, and there is no specific arbitrary meaning as in language. The meaning in music comes from arbitrary order evolved in inherited logic and developed dynamically. A good listener hears both style and utterance, and savours meaning through history. Style is thus the general which surrounds the particular and gives it significance.

3. PHENOMENA OF STYLE. Brossard, Apel, Bukofzer and Lippman regard style and form as opposed. Style in this sense may be used to describe the shape of details, and form the shape of the whole. The whole, however, is made up of its parts and their relationships, and form may be regarded as a phenomenon of style. Each piece has its own unique form, which controls, relates and comprehends all its details. This form belongs to a class of forms, and classes of forms by characteristic procedures which concentrate on particular parts of musical technique generate and carry distinctive stylistic details. Fugal style and sonata style are familiar terms; variation style and ternary style are also meaningful and important, though not often used as concepts. Forms may also be viewed as taking their beginnings from stylistic details; it was certain features in the details of musical language around 1750 that promoted the evolution and prominence of sonata form. Forms suggest, incorporate, belong to and grow out of specific styles.

In different periods characteristic forms have depended on different elements of musical material in different emphases. Thus in the Ars Nova, for instance, texture was an important formal determinant, whereas in the Classical and Romantic periods forms largely depended on long-range thematic and harmonic thinking. Whatever parameter is used as the chief presenter of form, two general formal principles may be postulated. Forms can be based on continuity or on discontinuity (evolution or contrast, flow or disjunction). The two principles never exist in isolation, and specific forms have characteristic mixtures of them. A basically continuous form like a Bach fugue shows points of articulation and changes of material, but the overriding impulse is customarily one of evolution and growth rather than contrast and comparison. Discontinuous forms, such as the sectional *formes fixes* of 14th- and 15th-century secular polyphony, have continuity within sections, and no form can avoid temporal sequence. In the 19th century continuous forms, among which sonata form was prime, were complicated by greater contrast elements, and disjunctive forms such as the multimovement structure of sonata, quartet and symphony, and such as ternary and rondo forms, were complicated by incorporating thematic similarities to bridge the points of articulation. This bridging of articulations in contrast forms had happened before (e.g. in the 15th-century cyclic mass). Repetition is a type of contrast, and varied repetition is, perhaps paradoxically, formally more evolutionary; this may be understood by comparing strophic and variation forms.

Texture is the disposition of the elements of musical argument on the chosen forces; it is sonority, and is conditioned by tone-colour, idiom and compositional technique. The term applies both to simultaneous and consecutive sounds. As with form, texture is a means of presenting style, and indeed textural features have given rise to stylistic names: monodic style, homophonic style, polyphonic style (stratified or imitative), keyboard style etc. A good composer will use textural possibilities to shape and enhance his musical statement, and textures will both generate and be generated by the musical material. Texture is sometimes of formal significance, as in the motet (of any period) or the fugue.

The opposing principles of texture are homogeneity and heterogeneity. This begins with the selection of musical forces, which may be, in the terms of the late Renaissance, either a 'whole consort' or a 'broken consort'. A whole consort is a selection of instruments or resources of the same family but different pitches, and a broken consort is a mixture of different instruments or resources. Voices alone are thus a whole consort, but they readily mix with instruments even from earliest polyphonic times to form a broken consort. The texture of a composition may likewise depend on similar constituents (voices or parts which do similar things) or stratified constituents. Stratified texture is a feature of the Franconian motet, whereas homogeneous texture occurs in the 16th-century motet. The opposite principles, as with those of form, are not mutually exclusive: heterogeneous textures blend in the ear and homogeneous textures consist of different parts. Idiomatic usages will link broken consorts and heterogeneous texture, and whole consorts are apt for homogeneous texture.

Harmony as a vehicle for style is mostly an indicator of historical position; it is part of idiom, and its procedures must be regarded in the light of changing conventions. It may be modal, diatonic, chromatic or atonal. Some composers however have stretched and enriched the harmonic resource of their times for expressive purposes (Gesualdo, Wagner and Debussy), and opera composers have often deliberately juxtaposed different harmonic styles for such reasons (*Parsifal* is merely a great example among many that use chromaticism as a symbol for evil, magic or sensuality and diatonicism for goodness, naturalness and innocence). Besides being rhetorical or expressive, or both, harmony also has opposite principles related to these – principles resulting from part-writing or resulting from sonorous imagination. Harmony resulting primarily from part-writing is a characteristic of successive composition, such as occurred in pre- and early Renaissance times, and can well be seen in Machaut's Mass; harmony resulting from sonorous imagination may be seen in some Wagner and impressionist styles. Again the two principles never exist in isolation. Successively composed parts were written with some awareness of how they would fit; Wagner's harmonic expression is often through chord juxtapositions, and *Tristan* shows harmonic sensuousness expressed through counterpoint.

Melody is of great importance as a musical feature; it is possible to regard it as the essential condition of music, which is guided by form, supported by harmony and articulated by texture and rhythm. While that is somewhat metaphysical there is no doubt that the ethos of the generative themes for a tonal piece represents a very large part of the musical statement and impact, or that the characteristic convolutions of an early Renaissance line are a beguiling, immediate and forceful experience. Melody should not be underrated as an element of form; it is not a by-product or necessary evil which the musical accept as a means to higher kinds of statement, nor is it something to be separated from the total form as something better than that. Melody is a prime connective feature in the continuum of audible time, and as such is an important and form-carrying stylistic phenomenon. It consists of a single line of related pitches, but arpeggio-based melodies (especially of the Baroque period) can imply more than one line (or at least strongly suggest their own harmony), contrapuntal forms combine melodies simultaneously, and modern music can exist as a textural sequence (as in Penderecki's *Polymorphia*); in such cases the horizontal expands into and blends with the vertical. Melodic styles may be regular or irregular, flowing or spasmodic, motivic or additive, presentational or developmental, conjunct or disjunct, vocal or instrumental, ornamental or structural, decorated or simple.

Rhythm is the very life-blood of music; it is the term for ordered change, however complex. It is an integral part of formal, textural, harmonic and melodic considerations. Musical rhythm may be viewed as a combination of objective temporal segments (pulse) and emotional sequence (the ebb and flow created by, for instance, discord and resolution, cadence, differentiated melodic and harmonic note values, melodic shape, agogic accents, syncopation). Such a felt experience of time gains significance from its enforced comparison with pulse. Pulses may be more or less strongly grouped in metres, each with its own stylistic suggestions, and the ebb and flow of feeling more or less strongly organized in phrases, periods or sections. Irregularity of metre or phrase structure has a natural tendency to contrast with regularity. Rhythmic styles may favour an even progression, as in much pre-Renaissance and dance music, or the excitement of growth to and recession from points of climax or animation, as in much 19th-century music. On the small scale undifferentiated or disjunct rhythmic styles offer much scope for distinctive utterance. In the rhythmic aspect of style the art forms of music and dance are closest, and the influence of dance on music is an important area of criticism.

These aspects of musical language which present style are united in unique blends by unique expressive purposes. The addition of factors does not explain their relationship, and the factors assume new significance in new relationships and contexts. The expressive purpose may be related to social function, or to a more or less detailed programme (as in the symphonic poem, and any setting of words), or may be more abstract – an expressive purpose to be seen and savoured in purely musical terms. Expressive purposes may also have style names, both general (sacred style, secular style) or more specific (heroic style, reflective style, everyday style, pastoral style); and character descriptions like 'sad', 'desolate', 'happy', 'ebullient', carry stylistic implications.

4. CONDITIONERS AND DYNAMICS OF STYLISTIC DIFFERENCES. Personal style is one of the commonest units for discussion in modern music criticism. As a differentiating factor in style it is of variable importance, partly because of the differing attitudes of societies and composers. It is not an important feature in many non-Western musical cultures, in plainsong or in Western folk musics; such repertories may depend for their formation on individuals and their idiosyncratic performing styles, but in this formation the individual is subordinate to a communal artistic purpose. Personal style may be more important to objective analysis than to the society in which the artist worked, as in German Baroque music, or personal differences may be encouraged by social attitudes so that personal styles become more distinctive, as in the 19th century. The relative importance of personal style is a significant and to some extent distinguishing feature of the Western tradition, and it may be seen with notation as part of the process of comparatively fast development of musical idiom in the West.

Stylistic change is inherent in meaningful creation, at least within the Western tradition, and the personal styles of great composers are hardly ever static; such a composer learns from himself and is constantly adding to his usable past. The amount of change over a lifetime varies according to its length, according to personality and intellectual development, and according to outward cultural and economic circumstances. Normal processes of apprenticeship, maturity and refinement may be largely undisturbed (Palestrina and Brahms), or have imposed on them more dramatic changes affecting style and deriving from a change of ideals (Liszt, Wagner) or changes in external requirements (Bach and Handel).

Styles of composers working at the same time may be compared, like those of Haydn and Mozart or Bruckner and Mahler, and when similarities are drawn questions of epochal style may arise. Such a concept denotes a general range of resource and usage available at any one time; like personal style, epochal style is therefore in a constant state of flux. It is possible however to use the concept stretched over large periods of time because this flux shows differing types of change; some changes have been much more radical or dramatic, or both, than others. Historians from Adler onwards have divided Western musical style at about 1000 and 1600. The change from the monophonic era to the polyphonic was gradual, with polyphony improvised at least as early as the 9th century and plainsong composed even after the 14th. But the development of monophony into polyphony by way of parallelism (a differentiation of texture) to melodic and rhythmic independence of parts, and the evolution of polyphony from an improvised semi-automatic elaboration into a written and composed phenomenon form a fundamental change in the means of expression – a change that justifies grouping in major style areas the music before and after it. Similarly the developments of modality into tonality and of linear into harmonic thought which reached a crux around 1600 are also both gradual and fundamental changes in technique. A further change of this type and magnitude, away from tonality, may be seen around 1900.

In more recent historiography, writers (e.g. Reese, Bukofzer, Blume) have further divided music since 1000 and the epochal styles of Ars Antiqua, Ars Nova, Renaissance, Baroque, Classic and Romantic have become familiar concepts. Blume has convincingly argued the inner coherence of Classic and Romantic as one stylistic period, and these epochs then depend on significant and radical stylistic change at intervals of about 150 years (though a detailed chronology of stylistic developments in the 12th century is a matter for conjecture). New styles grow out of suggestions inherent in the old, and any example of a style will have relics of its predecessors and premonitions of its successors.

The changes in the 12th century and in about 1300, 1450, 1600, 1750 and 1900 show consistently new treatments of rhythm; in most cases formal, textural, harmonic and melodic characteristics change too, but rhythmic change is a strong and dramatic initial factor in the formation of these epochal styles. The 12th century saw the adoption of modal rhythm as a central feature; the beginning of the Ars Nova depends on increased importance of duple rhythm and syncopation, and that of the Renaissance on the homogenization of the rhythmic constituents of polyphonic texture and an awareness of the rhythm of growth. The Baroque begins with the new affective rhythm of monody, the continuo madrigal and Frescobaldi's toccatas; the Classical period begins with a new interest in phrase structure and a greater diversity of note values within melodies; and the modern period begins with the rhythmic revitalizations of Bartók and Stravinsky.

The epochal styles are however not always best characterized in rhythmic terms; the Baroque for instance is primarily the age of the continuo, the Classic and Romantic period the age of tonality as a large-scale structural force, the modern era the age of alternatives

to tonality and triadic harmony. The aphoristic characterization of each period however is always problematic, for periods themselves include much change; styles begin, grow and die. Initially, new techniques of expression are explored and adjusted to by composers learning, like children, the possibilities. These techniques are incorporated into suitable forms which become established in a phase of consolidation, which may be seen in terms of a balance between controlled development of style and newness of import. Consolidation leads to refinement and complication and the styles of composers at the end of epochs, such as Bach, Brahms and Wagner are nothing if not complex; sometimes this phase includes what are after regarded as overripe modes of expression, like the elaborations of Petrus da Cruce, Gesualdo and Reger.

Style is greatly conditioned by the expectations and requirements of an audience or other patrons of composers, especially in matters of genre and ethos. The genres of mass, opera and chamber music become popular with composers partly because of popular demand, and they carry their own stylistic characteristics. Associated ethos, such as the expression of religious emotions in church, of theatrical emotions in opera and of refinement in the chamber are also the result of social expectations and taste. Sometimes more than acceptability and expectation is involved; there is a functional role and demand for military music, and the requirements of Soviet realism have a quasi-legal force. Stylistic cross-overs, such as Mahler's use of military music in a symphony or Strauss's use of chamber music in an opera (*Capriccio*), have denotive value.

Geographical location is a strong conditioner of style, and can involve particular social pressures which exist only in certain places: examples are the birth of opera in Italy, the requirements of the 17th-century French court, and Russian realism of both the 19th and 20th centuries. Geographical differences are important in cultural development because of difficulties of communication, and local styles may grow up in a city (such as Mannheim or Vienna), a region (as with the various German organ schools of the middle Baroque), a country or a continent. The folk culture of a country often has strong influences on style (especially in the 19th century), and these influences may be consciously enhanced by composers as a means of national assertion. Language also has a decisive effect on national styles, as Abraham has shown in his fascinating comparison of Italian and Czech styles (1974, chap.4). A preference of southern races for melody and of northern races for the greater technical intricacies of counterpoint has been remarked, and is attributed to interactions of climate, religion, personality and language. Sometimes styles become international, as with late Renaissance Netherlands style, Baroque Italian opera, or early 19th-century Germanic style. The interaction of styles born in distinct localities is an absorbing study. The mutual influence of Dufay and Dunstable and the ways in which Dunstable differs from English composers working in England show some of the intricacy of the issues. Historical accidents of communication can have far-reaching consequences for the evolution of musical style; Agincourt, spreading the English style on the Continent at a time when Renaissance style was in embryo, and the marriage of Philip II of Spain, bringing the Iberian keyboard variation to England in time for the English virginalists to develop, have artistic as well as political significance.

The resources of performance are important formative influences on style, and Parry (1911) used the relationship between resources and utterance as the starting-point for and main feature of a definition of style. Characteristic sounds are a direct element of style, while the techniques of performing on specific resources, with attendant idiomatic proclivities and possibilities, influence melody, rhythm and texture. Conventions in the grouping of resources and in performing practice underlie various distinctive personal, epochal, social and geographic styles. Each resource has its own especially suitable forms of expression. Voices are good at sustained, conjunct music, while instruments are suited to agility and disjunction. The violin has a capacity for wide-ranging melody, as Corelli exploited, and very high tessitura, as Romantic composers found; the organ pedals particularly require figures involving the use of alternate feet, giving rise to patterns that became a feature of late Baroque German organ music. Instruments come, develop and go, and the techniques of playing them develop (usually in the direction of greater facility and complication, but not always, as may be seen from horn and trumpet technique in the 18th century); such changes are integral in determining style. Idioms from one instrument pass into other usages, as did the vocal ornaments of the late Renaissance into the violin repertory and the lute style of the early Baroque into keyboard resource.

For further discussion of the factors governing epochal styles, *see* ARS ANTIQUA; ARS NOVA; ARS SUBTILIOR; MEDIEVAL; RENAISSANCE; BAROQUE; ROCOCO; GALANT; EMPFINDSAMKEIT; CLASSICAL; BIEDERMEIER; ROMANTIC; *see also* HISTORIOGRAPHY; MUSICOLOGY, §II, 1. Geographical and instrumental styles are discussed in entries of the countries and instruments concerned.

5. STYLISTIC AWARENESS. Composers have always been aware of stylistic differences, as may easily be seen from any cursory examination of Western music and its supporting body of theoretical literature. That is why plainsong composers produced Alleluia melodies different from settings of the Agnus Dei, why Dufay wrote chansons in treble-dominated style and discant-tenor style, and why Liszt wrote differently for the piano and for the orchestra. Theorists and critics too have been aware of stylistic distinctions. Musical style in Greece was a subject for philosophers because of the ethic and educative powers of different styles; Johannes de Garlandia (13th century) distinguished between discant, copula and organum, and Johannes de Grocheo (c1300) between *musica vulgaris, musica composita* or *mensurata* and *musica ecclesiastica*. It was however in the late Renaissance and early Baroque that theoretical discussion of style became an important area of literary production; indeed the word 'style' enters the vocabulary of music commentary at this time.

Monteverdi (like Philippe de Vitry before him and C. P. E. Bach after him) was one of the great composers who was also an important theorist. He drew distinctions between *prima prattica* (really late Renaissance styles) and *seconda prattica* (the new affective styles of the early Baroque), and between *stile concitato, molle* and *temperato* (in the preface to the eighth book of madrigals, 1638); he divided secular music into *teatrale, da camera* and *da ballo*. The distinction between the two practices continued in Doni (*Discorso*, 1635), who spoke of *stile antico* and *stile moderno*, and in

Christoph Bernhard (*Tractatus compositionis augmentatus*, c1660), who spoke of *contrapunctus gravis* or *stylus antiquus* and *contrapunctus luxurians* or *stylus modernus*. Bernhard also introduced the concepts of 'Figurenlehre' and 'Affektenlehre', which combine stylistic details and expressive purposes and which are so important for the high Baroque aesthetic. Kircher (*Musurgia*, 1650) synthesized a stylistic system that found much popularity and acceptance, based on differences of musical purpose, genre, personality, location and mood. Style dependent on personality and temperament Kircher called *stylus impressus*, style dependent on technique and 'Affekt' *stylus expressus*; further he distinguished *stylus ecclesiasticus, canonicus, motecticus, phantasticus, madrigalescus, melismaticus, choriacus sive theatralis* and *symphoniacus*. Brossard (1703) and J. G. Walther (1732) followed him. The important basic stylistic classification of the late Baroque period however was *stylus ecclesiasticus, stylus cubicularis* and *stylus scenicus*. This appeared first in Marco Scacchi (*Breve discorso sopra la musica moderna*, 1649) and was continued by Berardi (*Ragionamenti musicali*, 1681) and Mattheson (*Das neu-eröffnete Orchestre*, ii, 1717; *Der vollkommene Capellmeister*, 1739; *Grundlage einer Ehren-Pforte*, 1740). Mattheson also spoke of national styles ('welschen und frantzösischen') to which Scheibe (*Critischer musicus*, 1745) added performing practice as a stylistic phenomenon; they followed Bach, Telemann, Rameau and others who composed music in specific, and specified, national or local styles. The differences between and the relative merits of the French and Italian styles of composition and performance, in particular, were an important part of 18th-century musical consciousness.

In the Classical and Romantic periods the fashion for stylistic theory abated, but by the end of the 19th century the fundamental concerns of modern musicology as a discipline of cultural history were well established. Adler (1855–1940) described music history as the history of style, and the theory of style as an epochal concept was subsequently treated of by Bücken, Mies, Riemann, Handschin, Gurlitt and Schering. Epochal names were taken from art history and from literature. Major modern achievements in epochal historiography are the *Oxford History of Music* and the Norton series including work by Reese, Bukofzer and Einstein. Studies of personal styles, beginning with work by Baini and Winterfeld in the early 19th century have been continued in the 20th by such as Jeppesen's study of Palestrina (1922) and Rosen's of Haydn, Mozart and Beethoven (1971). The study of folk cultures was an important aspect of 19th-century musicology and has been expanded in this century by the discipline of ethnomusicology. Analysis of the style of examples of music is basic to all these branches of musicology; such analysis has become more justified in its own right since the work of Schenker and Tovey. (For a discussion of style analysis, *see* ANALYSIS, §II.) Stylistic criticism is the means of both cultural history and the human response to an art work. It distinguishes the blend and origin of styles as they are presented in the individual art work, which is a fixing or crisis of tradition. A work cannot properly be appreciated or studied in isolation; neither can stylistic evolution and trends be distinguished without a thorough understanding of individual examples. By the application of stylistic questions one may arrive at a deeper view of musical utterance, an intellectual interpretation of music which enriches the response to it.

BIBLIOGRAPHY

S. de Brossard: *Dictionaire de musique* (Paris, 1701, 2/1703/R1964)
H. Riemann: *Kleines Handbuch der Musikgeschichte mit Periodisierung nach Stilprinzipien und Formen* (Leipzig, 1908)
G. Adler: *Der Stil in der Musik* (Leipzig, 1911)
C. H. H. Parry: *Style in Musical Art* (London, 1911)
H. Wölfflin: *Kunstgeschichtliche Grundbegriffe* (Munich, 1915)
G. Adler: *Methode der Musikgeschichte* (Leipzig, 1919)
W. Nagel: 'Eine musikalische Stillehre', *Neue Musikzeitung*, xli (1919–20), 364, 382
H. von Waltershausen: *Musikalische Stillehre in Einzeldarstellungen* (Munich, 1920)
J. Middleton Murry: *The Problem of Style* (London, 1922)
E. Bücken and P. Mies: 'Grundlagen, Methoden und Aufgaben der musikalischen Stilkunde', *ZMw*, v (1922–3), 219
K. Meyer: 'Zum Stilproblem in der Musik', *ZMw*, v (1922–3), 316
P. Mies: 'Werdegang und Eigenschaften der Definition in der musikalischen Stilkunde), *Kongressbericht: Leipzig 1925*, 120
W. Harburger: *Form und Ausdrucksmittel in der Musik* (Stuttgart, 1926)
E. Katz: *Die musikalischen Stilbegriffe des 17. Jahrhunderts* (diss., U. of Freiburg, 1926)
A. Schering: 'Historische und nationale Klangstile', *JbMP 1927*, 31
A. O. Lorenz: 'Periodizität in der Musikgeschichte', *Die Musik*, xxi (1928–9), 644
W. Danckert: 'Stil als Gesinnung', *Bärenreiter Jb*, v (1929), 24
E. Bücken: *Geist und Form im musikalischen Kunstwerk*, HMw, vii (1929–32)
E. Closson: 'Du style', *AcM*, iii (1931), 99
O. Ursprung: 'Stilvollendung', *Theodor Kroyer: Festschrift zum sechzigsten Geburtstage* (Regensburg, 1933)
G. Adler: 'Style-Criticism', *MQ*, xx (1934), 172
H. Rosenberg: 'On the Analysis of Style', *AcM*, ix (1937), 5
W. Apel, ed.: 'Style', *Harvard Dictionary of Music* (Cambridge, Mass., 1944, rev. 2/1969)
C. Sachs: *The Commonwealth of Art* (New York, 1946)
M. Bukofzer: *Music in the Baroque Era* (New York, 1947)
R. H. Rowen: 'Some 18th Century Classifications of Musical Style', *MQ*, xxxiii (1947), 90
A. Schoenberg: *Style and Idea* (New York, 1950, enlarged 2/1975)
F. Blume: 'Barock', *MGG* [Eng. trans. in *Renaissance and Baroque Music: a Comprehensive Survey* (New York, 1967)]
H. Raynor: 'Form and Style', *The Chesterian*, xxviii (1953–4), 42, 73
H. L. Clarke: 'Toward a Musical Periodization of Music', *JAMS*, ix (1956), 25
L. B. Meyer: *Emotion and Meaning in Music* (Chicago, 1956)
A. L. Kroeber: *Style and Civilizations* (Ithaca, 1957)
W. Weisbach: *Stilbegriffe und Stilphänomene: vier Aufsätze* (Vienna, 1957)
F. Blume: 'Klassik', *MGG* [Eng. trans. in *Classical and Romantic Music: a Comprehensive Survey* (New York, 1970)]
L. Hibberd: 'A Note on Musical Styles', *MR*, xix (1958), 201
H. Truscott: 'Style in Music', *MR*, xix (1958), 211
J. E. Youngblood: 'Style as Information', *JMT*, ii (1958), 24
J. S. Ackerman: 'A Theory of Style', *Journal of Aesthetics*, xx (1962), 227 [repr. in *Aesthetic Inquiry* (Belmont, 1967), 54]
W. D. Allen: *Philosophies of Music History: a Study of General Histories of Music 1600–1960* (New York, 1962)
J. LaRue: 'On Style Analysis', *JMT*, vi (1962), 91
F. Blume: 'Renaissance', *MGG* [Eng. trans. in *Renaissance and Baroque Music: a Comprehensive Survey* (New York, 1967)]
——: 'Romantik', *MGG* [Eng. trans. in *Classical and Romantic Music: a Comprehensive Survey* (New York, 1970)]
Z. Lissa: 'Über die nationalen Stile', *BMw*, vi (1964), 187
E. A. Lippman: 'Stil', *MGG*
R. L. Crocker: *A History of Musical Style* (New York, 1966)
L. B. Meyer: *Music, the Arts, and Ideas* (Chicago, 1967)
E. Shaper: 'The Concept of Style: the Sociologists' Key to Art?', *British Journal of Aesthetics*, ix (1969), 246
J. LaRue: *Guidelines for Style Analysis* (New York, 1970)
G. Abraham: *The Tradition of Western Music* (London, 1974)

R. J. PASCALL

Style brisé (Fr.: 'broken style'). A term used to denote the use of a broken, arpeggiated texture in keyboard music. It has been used in a special sense to characterize the transference to the harpsichord of figurations idiomatic to the lute; this is particularly marked in French music of the mid-17th century (for example in the harpsichord music of Louis Couperin, Chambonnières and d'Anglebert). The unmeasured preludes of French harpsichordists of this period provide telling examples of the wholesale adoption of such lute techniques to the keyboard. At the beginning of the 18th century François Couperin referred to the 'style luthé' (see e.g. *Les charmes* from his ninth *ordre*) to characterize the consistent application of the arpeggiated lute style to the harpsichord. (The term 'luthé', based on historical usage, has much to recommend it.) The broken style also led to one of the most expressive ornaments of the French harpsichord school – the *suspension* (a term coined by François Couperin in his first book of harpsichord pieces, 1713), where the melody note is momentarily delayed. Bach adopted the *style brisé* of the French harpsichordists in his keyboard music. The C major prelude of the first book of *Das wohltemperirte Clavier* is a notable example, but more subtly the broken style is used to give rhythmic diversity to a style that has its own contrapuntal life (e.g. in the Allemande of the French Suite in C minor). Arpeggiated textures were of course as effective on the harpsichord as on the lute, and their adoption by keyboard composers must not be seen as a servile act of dependence on figurations established first by lutenists.

The *style brisé* did not fall into disuse with the emergence of the Classical school. The opening bars of Mozart's Fantasia in D minor K397/385g reveal its currency in the second half of the 18th century, and the first movement of Beethoven's Piano Sonata op.27 no.2 in C♯ minor ('Moonlight') is also, though indirectly, indebted to the *style brisé* of the earlier French harpsichordists.

BIBLIOGRAPHY

A. Souris: 'Apport du répertoire du luth à l'étude des problèmes d'interprétation', *L'interprétation de la musique française aux XVIIe et XVIIIe siècles: CNRS Paris 1969*, 107

EDWARD HIGGINBOTTOM

Style galant. See GALANT.

Style luthé (Fr.). A term used by François Couperin to characterize the consistent application of the arpeggiated lute style to the harpsichord; see STYLE BRISÉ.

Styne [Stein], **Jule** [Julius] **(Kerwin)** (*b* London, 31 Dec 1905). American songwriter and pianist of English birth. At the age of eight he moved to Chicago and performed as a soloist with the Detroit and Chicago Symphony Orchestras; from 1914 he studied at the Chicago College of Music and from 1927 at Northwestern University. After working with a jazz ensemble and as a vocal coach in Hollywood, he became known as an arranger and (from 1941) composer for films, mostly to lyrics by Sammy Cahn (including *Three Coins in the Fountain*, 1954). In 1947 they wrote *High Button Shoes*, the first of his over 20 stage musicals; among the most successful were *Gentlemen Prefer Blondes* (1949), *Gypsy* (1959) and *Funny Girl* (1964). Styne's best songs have reflective, sometimes romantic lyrics, with slow melodies based on repetition of short, distinctive phrases.

BIBLIOGRAPHY

D. Ewen: *Popular American Composers* (New York, 1962, suppl. 1972)
R. D. Kinkle: *The Complete Encyclopedia of Popular Music and Jazz 1900–1950* (New Rochelle, NY, 1974)

DEANE L. ROOT

Suabe Flöte (Ger.). An ORGAN STOP (*Suavial*).

Suard, Jean Baptiste Antoine (*b* Besançon, 15 Jan 1735; *d* Paris, 20 July 1817). French man of letters. Suard went to Paris in 1750 after a turbulent youth and was introduced into literary circles by Marmontel. In his multifarious activity in philosophy, literature and politics, he was a dramatic censor from 1777 and an administrator of the Opéra from 1781; elected to the Académie française in 1772, he became its secretary in 1803. He collaborated with La Harpe on the *Journal de politique et de littérature* (1778–81) and with Arnaud in various journals and the miscellany *Variétés littéraires*. Suard had an especial interest in English literature and philosophy; among his friends were Hume and Walpole, and he translated Richardson's *Clarissa*. He began editing the musical part of the *Encyclopédie méthodique*, published by his brother-in-law Pancoucke; pressure of other interests forced him to relinquish the work to N. E. Framery.

An eager controversialist, Suard is said to have taken music lessons the better to defend Gluck, who appealed to him for support; thus equipped he refuted La Harpe's criticisms ably and in detail in a series of letters to the *Journal de Paris* and *Mercure de France*. He also made the most effective reply to Coquéau's *Entretiens sur l'état actuel de l'Opéra*. A friend of Gluck's opponents, Suard disguised himself by a pseudonym, 'L'anonyme de Vaugirard'. Some of these letters were reproduced in Leblond's *Mémoires pour servir à l'histoire de la révolution opérée dans la musique par M. Le Chevalier Gluck* (1781), and in Suard's own five-volume *Mélanges de littérature* (Paris, 1803–4). Other writings on music and translations appear in the *Variétés littéraires* (1768–9), the supplement to La Borde's *Essai sur la musique*, the *Encyclopédie méthodique* and the *Nouveau choix de pièces tirées des anciens Mercures et des autres journeaux* (1758–65).

BIBLIOGRAPHY

D. J. Garat: *Mémoires historiques sur le XVIII siècle, sur les principaux personnages de la Révolution française, ainsi que sur la vie et les écrits de M. Suard, secrétaire de l'Académie* (Paris, 1820)
A. Suard: *Essais de mémoires sur M. Suard* (Paris, 1820)
A. Hunter: *J.-B.-A. Suard, un introducteur de la littérature anglaise en France* (Paris, 1925)

JULIAN RUSHTON

Suárez Rebelo, João. *See* REBELO, JOÃO SOARES.

Suavial. An ORGAN STOP.

Suba'a. Short Office replacing Compline in the Assyrian Church; *see* SYRIAN CHURCH MUSIC.

Sub-Bass (Ger.). An ORGAN STOP.

Subbulakshmi, Madurai Shanmukhavadivu (*b* Madurai, Tamil Nadu, 16 Sept 1916). Indian singer. She is the daughter of the celebrated *vīṇā* player Madurai Shanmukhavadivu, who was her first teacher. Brought up in a musical home, she showed her gifts at an early age; before she was ten she performed with her mother at recitals, and she soon became known as a soloist. Her reputation became a national one in 1944 when she appeared before a distinguished audience at the All India Music and Dance Conference in Bombay; her reputation was also much enhanced by her film *Meera* where she took the role of a 16th-century princess of that name and was much admired for her singing of devotional songs attributed to Meera. She has travelled extensively abroad, appearing at the Edinburgh Festival in 1963 and at the United Nations in 1966. She has received numerous awards and titles of honour as well as several honorary doctorates.

NARAYANA MENON

Subdominant. The fourth step or DEGREE of the major or minor scale, so called because it lies as much below the tonic as the dominant lies above the tonic, namely a 5th – not, as it is sometimes believed, because it lies one step below the dominant.

Subdupla (Lat.). In the system of PROPORTIONS of the late Middle Ages and Renaissance, the *proportio subdupla* (1/2) augmented the relative value of each note shape in the ratio 1:2. It was most frequently used to cancel the effect of a previous diminution of note values.

Subfinal (Lat. *subfinalis*). In Gregorian chant theory, the degree below the FINAL, or concluding scale degree, of an AUTHENTIC MODE. In the Dorian, Phrygian and Mixolydian modes the subfinal, which lies a tone below the final, is the same as the SUBTONIUM and came to be the theoretical lower limit for the mode. The Lydian mode, however, whose lower limit was the final F itself, had no subfinal.

HAROLD S. POWERS

Subirá (Puig), José (*b* Barcelona, 20 Aug 1882). Spanish musicologist. He occasionally used the pseudonym Jesús A. Ribó. He studied the piano and composition at the Madrid Conservatory, where he won prizes for the piano (1900), harmony (1901) and composition (1904). His failure to win the 1905 Prix de Rome with his lyrical legend *Rayo de luna* made him give up composition completely, even though the composer Tomás Bretón, director of the conservatory and president of the jury, encouraged him to continue; he dedicated himself instead to musicography.

Subirá's immense musicological output is particularly remarkable in that, unlike any other Spanish musicologist, he never held any remunerative musical post. After failing to acquire the professorship in music history at the Madrid Conservatory (1921) he never again applied for an appointment in music, but lived with rigorous economy as an employee of the Madrid City Council and similar organizations. His musicological work was prompted solely by his passionate enthusiasm, and was carried out in his spare time. From 1896 he lived in Madrid, except during a few absences caused by his administrative career (for instance as secretary to the Argentinian consulate in Amberes, 1908–10). He is a member of numerous academies and societies in Spain and abroad; in 1952 he was elected a member of the Real Academia de Bellas Artes de San Fernando in Madrid, and from 1950 until his retirement he was head of the Madrid section of the Spanish Musicological Institute.

Along with Anglès, Subirá is the finest 20th-century Spanish musicologist. His work is distinguished by its remarkable diversity and by the originality that he brings to every subject he treats. This is particularly evident in his articles, which probably represent his best work, being moreover astonishingly erudite and well documented, with new information drawn from primary sources and arranged concisely. They are written in the fluid, elegant and attractive style which characterizes all his work and was often the result of spontaneity: he never made rough drafts of articles, but typed the final text directly. His chief interest has been theatrical music in Spain, especially Madrid. His books can be divided into two groups: those involving research (e.g. *La tonadilla escénica, La música en la Casa de Alba, El compositor Iriarte, Historia y anecdotario del Teatro Real*), which are based on solid documentary evidence and present some new and sometimes extremely important information; and the 'histories', translations, adaptations and biographies in which Subirá simply synthesized the research of others, though with his customary erudition and elegance.

WRITINGS

Los grandos músicos: Bach, Beethoven, Wagner (Madrid, 1907, 2/1925)

Músicos románticos: Schubert, Schumann, Mendelssohn (Madrid, 1925)

La música en la Casa de Alba (Madrid, 1927)

La tonadilla escénica (Madrid, 1928–30)

La música: sus evoluciones y estado actual (Madrid, 1930)

Tonadillas teatrales inéditas: libretos y partituras (Madrid, 1932)

'*Celos aun del aire matan': opera del siglo XVII, texto de Calderón y música de Juan Hidalgo* (Barcelona, 1933) [with edn. of Act 1]

La tonadilla escénica: sus obras y sus autores (Barcelona, 1933)

Historia de la música teatral en España (Barcelona, 1945)

Historia universal de la música (Madrid, 1945, 2/1953)

with H. Anglés: *Catálogo musical de la Biblioteca nacional de Madrid* (Barcelona, 1946–51)

ed.: *Compendio de armonía* (Barcelona, rev. 4/1946) [trans., R. Gerhard, of H. Scholz: *Harmonielehre*, Berlin and Leipzig, 1920]

La ópera en los teatros de Barcelona (Barcelona, 1946/R1978)

Historia de la música Salvat (Barcelona, 1947, enlarged 3/1958)

Historia y anecdotario del Teatro Real (Madrid, 1949)

El compositor Iriarte (1750–1791) y el cultivo español del melólogo (melodrama) (Barcelona, 1949–50)

La música: etapas y aspectos (Barcelona, 1949)

El teatro del Real palacio (1849–1851), con un bosquejo preliminar sobre la música palatina desde Felipe V hasta Isabel II (Madrid, 1950)

with H. Anglés: *Historia de la música* (Barcelona, 1950, rev. 2/1965) [trans. of A. Della Corte and G. Pannain: *Storia della musica*, Turin, 1936]

'La Sección de música de nuestra Academia', *Academia: anales y boletín de la Real academia de bellas artes de San Fernando*, ii (1953), 143; iv (1954), 335; xvii (1963), 19; xxix (1969), 33–71

Compendio de historia de la música (Madrid, 1954, 2/1966)

'El archivo epistolar de don Jesús de Monasterio', *Academia: anales y boletín de la Real academia de bellas artes de San Fernando*, v (1955–7), 81–146; xiii (1961), 41; xxxiv (1972), 39

with J. Casanovas: *Breve historia de la música* (Barcelona, 1956, 2/1964)

Musikgeschichte von Spanien, Portugal, Lateinamerika (Zurich, 1957)

ed.: *Tú y la música: una introducción para los aficionados al arte musical* (Barcelona, 1957, rev. 2/1961) [trans., F. M. Biosa, of F. Herzfeld: *Du und die Musik*, Berlin, 1950]

Historia de la música española e hispanoamericana (Barcelona, 1958)

ed.: *Historia de la música* (Barcelona, rev., enlarged 4/1958) [trans. of J. Wolf: *Geschichte der Musik*, Leipzig, 1925–9, incl. critical study of Spanish music history by H. Anglés]

ed.: *La magia de la batuta: el mundo de los grandes directores, los grandes conciertos y las grandes orquestas* (Barcelona, 1958) [trans., J. Bedmar, of F. Herzfeld: *Magie des Taktstocks*, Berlin, 1953]

'Dos músicos del Rey Felipe IV, B: Jovenardi y E. Butler', *AnM*, xix (1964), 185

ed.: *La música del siglo XX* (Barcelona, 1964) [trans., M. F. de Petit, of F. Herzfeld: *Musica nova*, Berlin, 1954]

'Calderón de la Barca, libretista de ópera', *AnM*, xx (1965), 59

Catálogo musical de la Biblioteca municipal de Madrid (Madrid, 1965–73)

'Pretéritos músicos hispánicos', *Academia: anales y boletín de la Real academia de bellas artes de San Fernando*, xx (1965), 9–43; xxi (1965), 15–56

'El Teatro real y los teatros palatinos: páginas históricas', *Academia: anales y boletín de la Real academia de bellas artes de San Fernando*, xxiii (1966), 35–66

'Músicos madrileños y músicos madrileñizados', *Anales del Instituto de estudios madrileños*, i (1966), 209

'Relaciones musicales hispano-italianas en el siglo XVIII: panoramas y esclarecimientos', *Revista de ideas estéticas*, xxiv (1966), 199

Cien óperas: autores, personajes, argumentos (Madrid, 1967)

'Dos madrileñizados músicos del siglo XVIII: Luigi Cherubini y Gaetano Brunetti', *Anales del Instituto de estudios madrileños*, ii

(1967), 323

'Músicos al servicio de Calderón y de Comella', *AnM*, xxii (1967), 197

'Nuestro pretérito Teatro real', *Academia: anales y boletín de la Real academia de bellas artes de San Fernando*, xxiv (1967), 33

'Dos grandes músicos "desmadrileñizados": Manuel García (padre e hijo)', *Anales del Instituto de estudios madrileños*, iii (1968), 229

'Música madrileña en la época del "vapor" ', *Revista de ideas estéticas*, xxvi (1968), 117

'Lo histórico y lo estético en la "zarzuela" ', *Revista de ideas estéticas*, xxvii (1969), 103

'Necrología de Monseñor Higinio Anglés', *Academia: anales y boletín de la Real academia de bellas artes de San Fernando*, xxix (1969), 5

'Una arpista madrileñizada: Teresa Roaldes', *Anales del Instituto de estudios madrileños*, iv (1969), 365

'Un insospechado inventario musical del siglo XVIII', *AnM*, xxiv (1969), 227

'Dos directores musicales madrileños: Ricardo Villa y Emilio Vega', *Anales del Instituto de estudios madrileños*, vi (1970), 465

'Un panorama histórico de lexicografía musical', *AnM*, xxv (1970), 125

'Nuevas ojeadas históricas sobre la tonadilla escénica', *AnM*, xxvi (1971), 119

Temas musicales madrileños (Madrid, 1971)

'Don Jesús de Monasterio: novísimos apuntes biográficos', *Academia: anales y boletín de la Real academia de bellas artes de San Fernando*, xxxv (1972), 11–43

'Felipe Pedrell y el teatro musical español', *AnM*, xxvii (1972), 61

'La estética ante Amadeo Vives', *Revista de ideas estéticas*, xxx (1972), 3

'Loas escénicas desde mediados del siglo XVIII', *Segismundo* (Madrid, 1973), nos.7–8, p.73

'Recordando a Casals', *Academia: anales y boletín de la Real academia de bellas artes de San Fernando*, xxxvii (1973), 5

'Un insígne folklorista español: Manuel García Matos', *Revista de ideas estéticas*, xxxii (1974), 137

EDITIONS

Four Tonadillas for Voices and Small Orchestra (New York, 1968)

La tonadilla escénica: transcripciones y armonizaciones (Madrid, 1970–73)

BIBLIOGRAPHY

J. M. Llorens: 'El. Excmo. Sr. D. José Subirá Puig', *AnM*, xviii (1963), 3 [with list of publications to 1963]

'Homenaje a la tonadilla escénica y al Académico D. José Subirá', *Academia: anales y boletín de la Real academia de bellas artes de San Fernando*, xxx (1970), 29–70 [with list of publications to 1970]

F. J. León Tello: 'Don José Subirá cumple 90 años', *Revista de ideas estéticas*, xxxi (1973), 47

L. Romero Tobar: 'Conversación con Subirá', *Anales del Instituto de estudios madrileños*, ix (1973), 631

JOSÉ LÓPEZ-CALO

Subito (It.: 'suddenly', 'immediately'). A word found in musical scores in such contexts as *subito piano* ('suddenly quiet'), *volti subito* ('turn [the page] quickly').

Subject. A theme (or group of themes) on which a composition is based. The term has been in use since the 16th century, both in theoretical writings and in printed volumes of practical music, one of the earliest references being the printing of borrowed tunes marked 'subiectum' above several of the basse danses in Attaingnant's *Dixhuit basses danses* (1530). In modern English usage the term has two main uses, in fugue and in sonata form.

In discussions of fugue, it is used in two ways: it may refer to the main theme of a fugue in general; or it may refer only to the initial entry of that theme and to those subsequent entries in the fugue's exposition that follow the same scale position (*see* FUGUE, §1). It is thus distinct from ANSWER, which denotes those exposition entries of the theme which are at a different position, usually at the 4th or 5th from the subject. (German terminology is clearer than English, using *Thema* for the first of these two senses and *Führer* for the second.) When the main theme of the fugue is accompanied in its initial entry by subsidiary themes, the subsidiary themes may also be called subjects, though they are perhaps better regarded as counter-subjects, the term 'subject' being reserved for subsidiary themes given their own exposition later in the fugue. Fugues on multiple subjects are known as double (triple etc) fugues.

In sonata form, the term 'subject' is often used for each of the two principal thematic ideas that in the theoretical model are the principal features of the exposition. In practice each 'subject' may be a group of themes (hence the term 'subject group' or simply 'group') or the material may be non-thematic (*see* SONATA FORM, §3).

Subject group. A term, coined by Tovey, often used for each of the two sections that make up the exposition of a movement in SONATA FORM. It may be preferred to simply 'subject' (or 'theme') in that it implies that the section may be made up of a multiplicity of themes or other material, defined rather by their function (and, usually, their tonality) than by their nature as themes.

Submediant. In the major–minor tonal system the sixth scale-step or DEGREE, reckoned upwards from the keynote (e.g. A in the key of C). It is so named because it lies as much below the tonic (i.e. a 3rd) as the mediant lies above the tonic. The submediant of any major scale is brought into prominence chiefly as the tonic of its relative minor.

Subotnick, Morton (*b* Los Angeles, 14 April 1933). American composer and teacher. He attended the University of Denver (BA 1958) and Mills College (MA 1960), where he studied composition with Darius Milhaud and Leon Kirchner. He was in the US Army from 1955 to 1957. In 1959 and 1960 he was a Fellow of the Institute for Advanced Musical Studies, Princeton University. He has taught at Mills College (1959–66), New York University (1966–9) and, since 1969, at the California Institute of the Arts. He was founder and director of the San Francisco Tape Music Center (1961–6), and has performed extensively as clarinettist and conductor.

Sound Blocks (1959) was his first composition to explore relations among musical, visual and verbal elements. In subsequent compositions, he has used instruments, films, lighting effects and taped electronic sounds. Pitch structures (both instrumental and electronic) are frequently derived from serial operations. Some compositions incorporate quasi-improvisational sections, while in recent works events may be derived from aspects of game theory. *Silver Apples of the Moon* (1966) was the first electronic composition commissioned by a recording company. The electronic sounds in Subotnick's compositions are realized on Buchla synthesizers.

WORKS
(*selective list*)

Orch: Play! no.2, orch, tape, 1964; Lamination I, orch, tape, 1965; Before the Butterfly, 7 amp insts, orch, 1975; Two Butterflies, amp orch, 1975

Ens and inst: Prelude no.3, pf, tape, 1964; Prelude no.4, pf, tape, 1966; Ten, fl, ob, tpt, trbn, 3 perc, pf, va, db, 1964, rev. 1976

Vocal: Two Life Histories, Bar, cl, elec, 1976

Tape: Silver Apples of the Moon, 2-track, 1966; The Wild Bull, 2-track, 1967; Reality I, 2-track, 1967; Reality II, 2-track, 1967; Touch, 4-track, 1969; Sidewinder, 4-track, 2-track, 1970; Until Spring, 4-track, 2-track, 1974–5; Cloudless Sulphur, part I, 4-track

Mixed media: Mandolin, va, tape, film, 1962; Play! no.1, wind qnt, pf, tape, film, 1964; Play! no.3, pf, tape, film, 1965; Play! no.4, S, pf, vib, vc, tape, 6 actors, 2 films, 1965; Four Butterflies, 4-track tape, 3 films, 1973

Incidental music: The Caucasian Chalk Circle (Brecht), narrator, 1v, chorus 3vv, perc, mand, accordion, 1965; 4 tape scores

Principal publisher: MCA

WRITINGS
'Pauline Oliveros: *Trio*', *PNM*, ii/1 (1963), 77

BIBLIOGRAPHY
J. M. Perkins: 'Morton Subotnick, Serenade No. 1', *PNM*, ii/2 (1964), 100
R. Norton: 'The Vision of Morton Subotnick', *Music Journal*, xxviii/1 (1970), 35, 48
RICHARD SWIFT

Subsemitonium (modi) (Lat.). The note that lies a semitone below the final of an authentic mode (*e* below *f* in the Lydian, *B* below *c* in the Ionian), or that rises by a semitone to establish a linear cadence at the interval of an octave or unison. In late medieval and Renaissance theory, if one of the parts in this cadence falls by a tone, the other must rise by a semitone. In ex.1 the sub-

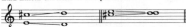

Ex.1 Linear cadences in two parts on D

semitonium, *c♯′*, is produced by chromatic alteration of the seventh degree of the Dorian mode. *See also* MUSICA FICTA.

Subsesquialtera (Lat.). In the system of PROPORTIONS of the late Middle Ages and Renaissance, the *proportio subsesquialtera* augmented the relative value of each note shape in the ratio 2:3, as did *proportio subsesquitertia* in the ratio 3:4. They were used to cancel the effect of a previous diminution of values.

Subsesquitertia (Lat.). In early music theory, the ratio 3:4; *see* SUBSESQUIALTERA.

Substitute chord. A chord that can take the place of a given chord without changing its harmonic function. Often the common interval of a 3rd is sufficient for one chord to substitute for another; for instance, the chord of the supertonic (II) can be used in place of a subdominant (IV). Substitute chords are an important feature of jazz since they enable the improviser to make subtle changes in the harmony from one chorus to the next without altering the harmonic design of the original theme.

Subtonic. The seventh scale DEGREE in a harmonic context; in a melodic context this degree is usually called the LEADING NOTE. 'Subtonic' is sometimes used as an English equivalent for SUBTONIUM, the note below the final of the Dorian, Phrygian or Mixolydian mode.

Subtonium (Lat.). The note that lies a tone below the octave range by which a church mode is identified. The subtonium of the Dorian mode is *c*, of the Hypodorian *G*, of the Phrygian *d* and so on. Neither the Lydian nor the Hypolydian mode has a subtonium since the note below the characteristic octave of each mode lies a semitone, not a tone, below the lowest note in that octave. The subtonium of an AUTHENTIC MODE is also called its SUBFINAL.

Subtripla (Lat.). In the system of PROPORTIONS of the late Middle Ages and Renaissance, the *proportio subtripla* (1/3) augmented the relative value of each note shape in the ratio 1:3. It was most frequently used to cancel the effect of a previous diminution of note values.

Succentor. A member of the Anglican Church clergy; *see* CATHEDRAL MUSIC AND MUSICIANS, ANGLICAN.

Sucher, Josef (*b* Döbör, Hungary, 23 Nov 1843; *d* Berlin, 4 April 1908). Austrian conductor and composer. As a boy he sang in the choir of the Vienna court chapel. He studied with Sechter and became a répétiteur at the Vienna Court Opera in 1870 and assistant conductor in 1873. The following year he was appointed conductor at the Komische Oper and from 1876 to 1878 he conducted in Leipzig. Travelling through north Germany in search of singers, at Danzig he discovered the soprano Rosa Hasselbeck whom he engaged for the Leipzig company, and whom he married the following year. He conducted the first complete *Ring* cycle at Leipzig (1878), then moved to Hamburg, where he conducted the first local performance of *Tristan und Isolde* (November 1882). From 1888 to 1899 he was chief conductor at the Berlin Court Opera and was responsible for many fine performances of Wagner operas, including a complete cycle of the works from *Rienzi* to *Götterdämmerung* given in June 1889. He composed a number of vocal works.

BIBLIOGRAPHY

A. Neumann: *Erinnerungen an Richard Wagner* (Leipzig, 1907; Eng. trans., 1909)
J. Kapp: *Geschichte der Staatsoper Berlin* (Berlin, 1937)
H. Fetting: *Die Geschichte der Deutschen Staatsoper* (Berlin, 1955)
ELIZABETH FORBES

Sucher [née Hasselbeck], Rosa (*b* Velburg, 23 Feb 1849; *d* Eschweiler, 16 April 1927). German soprano. At the age of 14 she sang solos in the church at Velburg where her father was choirmaster. In 1871 she was engaged at the Court Opera, Munich, for small roles such as Waltraute in *Die Walküre*. After singing in Trier and Königsberg, in 1875 she appeared as Agathe in *Der Freischütz* at the Kroll Opera, Berlin. The following year she sang at Danzig and in 1877 at Leipzig, where she married the conductor, Josef Sucher. She sang Sieglinde in the first complete *Ring* cycle at Leipzig in 1878, and later that year she and her husband were engaged by the Hamburg Opera. She made her London début in May 1882 as Elsa in *Lohengrin* at Drury Lane; during that season she also sang Senta in *Der fliegende Holländer*, Elisabeth in *Tannhäuser*, Eva in the first London *Die Meistersinger* (30 May) and Isolde in the first London *Tristan und Isolde* (20 June). She also sang Isolde at Hamburg (1882), Bayreuth (1886) and Munich (1893). Her other roles at Bayreuth were Kundry (1886), Eva (1888), Venus (1891) and Sieglinde (1896). Her Wagner performances, particularly of Elsa, Sieglinde and Isolde, were marked by a warmth and intensity seldom matched by any other soprano, and she was also, in a statuesque and dignified manner, a compelling actress. She made guest appearances in Vienna, singing in *Der Freischütz*, *Euryanthe* and *Oberon* during 1886, the Weber centenary year. From 1888 to 1898 she was engaged at the Court Opera, Berlin, where she sang Leonore at the performance of *Fidelio* that marked the retirement of the tenor Albert Niemann (20 September 1888), and Brünnhilde in *Götterdämmerung* (27 September 1888). In 1892 she appeared at Covent Garden, singing Brünnhilde in *Siegfried* (8 June) and Isolde (15 June). She made her New York début as Isolde with the Damrosch Opera Company at the Metropolitan on 25 February 1895. She retired in 1903 after a final performance of Sieglinde in Berlin. On her husband's death in 1908 she moved to Vienna, where she taught singing. Her autobiography was published in 1914.

BIBLIOGRAPHY

A. Ehrlich: *Berühmte Sängerinnen der Vergangenheit und Gegenwart* (Leipzig, 1895)
H. Klein: *Thirty Years of Musical Life in London* (London, 1903)
R. Sucher: *Aus meinem Leben* (Leipzig, 1914)
J. Kapp: *Geschichte der Staatsoper Berlin* (Berlin, 1937)
H. Fetting: *Die Geschichte der Deutschen Staatsoper* (Berlin, 1955)
H. Rosenthal: *Two Centuries of Opera at Covent Garden* (London, 1958)
H.-L. de La Grange: *Mahler* (New York, 1973–)
ELIZABETH FORBES

Suchoň, Eugen (*b* Pezinok, west Slovakia, 25 Sept 1908). Slovak composer. A son of a teacher and choirmaster, he became familiar with art music from childhood. He studied the piano and composition at the Bratislava Academy of Music from 1927; Kafenda, his composition teacher, had a decisive influence in shaping his technique. From 1931 to 1933 he took part in Novák's master classes at the Prague Conservatory. Appointments followed as professor of theory at the Bratislava Academy (1933), professor of music education at the Bratislava High School for Education (1950) and professor of music theory at Bratislava University (1959–74), where he retired with the title of professor emeritus. He has also served as permanent president of SOZA, the Slovak performing right society, vice-president of CISAC (1966–8), president of the Slovak Composers' Union (from 1972) and president of the Czechoslovak Composers' Organization (from 1973). Among the awards he has received are the Bratislava Civic Prize (1936), the Slovak Regional Prize (1937), the State Prize (1941, 1951, 1953, 1973), the Order of Work (1968) and an honorary doctorate of Bratislava University (1969).

Suchoň's youthful works are homophonic and draw on the Classical and Romantic music he knew at home. The period of study with Kafenda saw a transition to linear thought, and his first contacts with folk modality brought a national colour to his music. While with Novák he abandoned certain formalist tendencies for a more spontaneous expression; this period, in which he oscillated between modality and chromaticism, ended with the *Burleska* for violin and orchestra (1933). A new phase was to last from the male choral cycle *O horách* ('About the mountains', 1934–42) to *Metamorfózy* (1953), a suite of symphonic variations on original themes. During these years he established a new Slovak national style on the basis of extended tonality (e.g. chords including 11ths and 13ths) with markedly folk-based themes and social-critical positions. His large-scale treatment of folk music reached its culmination in the national opera *Krútňava* ('The whirlpool', 1949), where new psychological elements are apparent. Most of Suchoň's folksong arrangements date from this nationalist period. A new direction, characterized by modally inflected 12-note series, began with the opera *Svätopluk* (1959). Suchoň's serial writing leads to a polymodality in which horizontal and vertical dimensions are structurally linked, and in which the harmonies emphasize 2nds, 4ths and 7ths. There is also an advanced handling of timbre, which marks a new period lasting from the song cycle *Ad astra* (1961) to the *Symfonická fantázia na BACH* (1971). Suchoň has theoretically developed a system of chords ranging from what he terms the 'diatonic total' to the '12-note total'.

WORKS
(selective list)

STAGE

Angelika, ballet, 1927; On a jeho sestra [He and his sister], incidental music, 1927; Král' Svätopluk, op.10, prelude to play, 1934; Krútňava [The whirlpool] (opera, 6 scenes, Suchoň, S. Hoza, after M. Urban), 1949; Svätopluk (music drama, 3, I. Stodola, J. Krčméry, Suchoň), 1959

CHORAL

Vel'ký pôst [The great fast] (A. Sládkovič), 1927; Slovenské l'udové piesne [Slovak folksongs], T, chorus, small orch, 1930; O horách [About the mountains], op.8, cycle, male vv, 1934–42; Žalm zeme Podkarpatskej [Psalm of the sub-Carpathian land], op.12, T, chorus, orch, 1938; Spievanky [Folksongs], 1v, chorus, small orch, 1950; Terchovské spevy [Terchová songs], 1v, chorus, small orch, 1950; O človeku [On man] (J. Smrek), cycle, 1962; Slovenská pieseň (Smrek), male vv, 1973

ORCHESTRAL

Noc čarodejnic [Night of witches], sym. poem cycle, 1927; Burleska, op.7, vn, orch, 1933, rev. as Fantázia a burleska, 1948; Baladická suita, op.9, orch/pf, 1934; Sonatina, op.11, vn, orch, 1937; Metamorfózy, orch/pf, 1953; 6 skladieb [6 compositions], str, 1963; Rapsodická suita, pf, orch, 1965; Kaleidoskop, pf, org, str, perc, 1968; Symfonická fantázia na BACH, org, str, perc, 1971; Cl Conc., 1975; Prielom Sym., 1976

OTHER WORKS

Solo vocal: Bačovské piesne [Shepherd songs], Bar, pf, 1929; Nox et solitudo, op.4, 5 songs, Mez, small orch/pf, 1932; Ad astra (S. Žáry), 5 songs, S, small orch/pf, 1961; Kontemplácie, reciter, pf, 1964
Inst: Malá suita s passacagliou [Little suite with passacaglia], op.3, pf, 1930, orchd 1967; Sonata, op.1, vn, pf, 1930; Str Qt, op.2, 1931; Serenáda, op.5, wind qnt, 1932, arr. str orch, 1933; Pf Qt, op.6, 1933; Obrázky zo Slovenska [Pictures from Slovakia], pf, 1957; Poème macabre, vn, pf, 1963; 2 pezzi concertanti, cl, pf, 1973; Toccata, pf, 1973
Folksong arrs.

Principal publishers: Matica Slovenská, Opus, Slovenské Hudobné Vydavatel'stvo, Slovenský Hudobný Fond, Supraphon, Universal

BIBLIOGRAPHY
E. Zavarský: *Eugen Suchoň* (Bratislava, 1955)
V. Donovalová: 'Charakteristika postáv v Suchoňovej opere Krútňava' [Characteristic forms in Suchoň's opera Krútňava], *Hudobnovedné štúdie*, v (1961), 5–91
J. Kresánek: *Národný umelec Eugen Suchoň* [National artist Suchoň] (Bratislava, 1961)
V. Donovalová: 'K hudobnej dramaturgii Suchoňovho Svätopluka', *Hudobnovedné štúdie*, vi (1963), 5–55
L. Burlas: 'Einheit und Entwicklung im Werke von Eugen Suchoň', *SH*, xi (1967), 359
I. Vajda: 'Suchoňova kantáta Žalm zeme Podkarpatskej', *Musicologica slovaca*, i/1 (1969), 43–89

LADISLAV BURLAS

Suchý, František (i) ['pražský'] (*b* Březové Hory u Příbrami, central Bohemia, 21 April 1891; *d* Prague, 13 June 1973). Czech composer and writer. He studied at the teaching institute in Příbram from 1906 to 1910, and took up a teaching career. Subsequently he studied with Horník and Stecker at the Prague Conservatory (1913–14) and attended Nikisch's conducting classes in Leipzig (1914–16). While teaching in Slovakia he founded and directed several amateur groups, including the Turiec PO and the Komárno Orchestral Association and Choir. Between 1946 and 1948 he directed the Prague Teachers' Orchestral Association. His music is direct and simple, influenced principally by folk music and by the environment of his native region, the mining area of Příbram. Besides working as a composer, conductor and performer he contributed to specialist educational journals (*Komenský* and *Hudba a škola*). His other writings include *História a topografia Komárna* (Komárno, 1932), the volume of fiction *Hudební povídky* ('Musical tales', Prague, 1931) and many articles on puppetry in the magazine *Loutkář*.

WORKS
(selective list)

Operas: Lásky div [The wonder of love] (J. Zeyer), 1923, Ostrava,

1925; Havéři [The miners] (Suchý, after V. Mejstřík, J. Palivec), 1947–57
Ballet: Porcelánové království [The porcelain kingdom], 1922, Turčiansky svätý Martin, 1924
Orch: Rokoková suita [Rococo suite], small orch, 1931; Stříbrné město [The silver town], sym., 1935
Vocal: Missa festiva Pascha nostrum, 1939; Havéři [The miners] (16th-century mining books), 3 songs, 1941; Praha – píseň Čech [Prague – song of Bohemia], chorus, 1941; Havéři, cycle, 3 male choruses, 1944; Píseň země horníků [Song of the miners' country], 1950
Kbd: 2 Nocturnes, pf, 1918; Preludium and Postludium, org, 1945
Edns: *Dymokurské písně* [Songs of Dymokury] (Prague, 1915); *Slovenské vojenské* [Slovak military] (Prague, 1923); *Hornické písně* [Mining songs] (Prague, 1950), with K. Fiala; *Lidové písně a tance z Polabí na Králové-Městecku* (Prague, 1955)

Principal publishers: Barvitius; Hudební Matice; Orbis; Státní Nakladatelství Krásné Literatury, Hudby a Umění; Mojmír Urbánek

BIBLIOGRAPHY
J. Janík: 'František Suchý', *Nový svet*, xii/19 (1937), 12
J. Němeček: *Hudební Příbramsko* [Music in Příbram] (Příbram, 1940), 53ff
F. Suchý: 'Autoportrét', *Rytmus*, x/9–10 (1946), 27
M. Kuna: 'Lidové písně z Polabí', *HRo*, ix (1956), 58

OLDŘICH PUKL

Suchý, František (ii) (*b* Libina u Šumperka, 9 April 1902; *d* Brno, 12 July 1977). Czech composer, oboist and teacher. He studied the oboe with Wagner and composition with Kvapil at the Brno Conservatory, graduating in 1927; his studies were continued in Novák's master classes at the Prague Conservatory until 1937. From 1927 to 1947 he was first oboist in the Brno Radio Orchestra, and then became professor of oboe at the Brno Conservatory and professor of oboe and theory at the academy. This work gained him the title Teacher of Merit. In addition he appeared as a soloist and chamber musician, notably in the Moravian Wind Quintet, of which he was a founder-member in 1928. As a composer he consistently followed the neo-classical style of the 1920s, though he developed greater expansiveness of form. Suchý also published theoretical works and edited old Czech music: in 1946 he prepared a reconstruction of F. A. Míča's Symphony in D.

WORKS
(selective list)

Orch: Variační suita, 1932; Fl Conc., 1939; Barokní koncert, vn, orch, 1944; 4 syms., 1946, 1950, 1957, 1962; Ob Conc., 1948; Vysočina [Uplands], sym. suite, 1957
Vocal: V Gethsemaně, oratorio, 1933; Léto [Summer], song cycle, 1v, chamber orch, 1935; Svobodní [Free], cantata, 1947; Maryla (opera, after A. Jirásek), 1956; Otčina [Homeland], cantata, 1959
Inst: Sonatina, ob, pf, 1927; Wind Qnt, 1928; Sonatas for vn, va, cl, hn; 2 nonets, 1943, 1958; Koncertantní kvintet, wind, 1947; Wind Qnt, 1958; Wind Sextet, 1960

JAN TROJAN

S Uciredor. *See* RODERICUS.

Suck, Charles J. (*fl* 1780). English oboist and composer, perhaps of central European descent. Pohl listed him as an oboe virtuoso playing in London in 1781 and said that he was a pupil of J. C. Fischer in London. Otherwise he is known only as the composer of six trios (London, 1784), two each for oboe, flute and violin, with violin and cello. The list of subscribers included the Prince of Wales, Fischer and Mr Papendick (sic). The music is competent, melodious and well suited to the chosen instruments.

BIBLIOGRAPHY
EitnerQ
C. F. Pohl: *Mozart und Haydn in London* (Vienna, 1867/*R*1970), ii, 372

PETER PLATT

Sudan. Although the Sudan covers a large area (2·5 million sq km) its population is relatively small since the Sahara spreads across most of the northern, north-western and north-eastern part of the country. In spite of this it includes many different ethnic groups that still maintain their cultural independence and their own way of life. The greatest unifying factor among these different groups is the Arabic language, which is spoken or understood by much of the population. Islam is the chief religion and it has tended to reduce some of the cultural differences, though less in the case of music than of other aspects of culture. Some musical practices that can be traced back to pagan rites are still found among Muslim communities. The close relationship between music and language has tended to preserve regional differences in rhythm, melody and even timbre among peoples who still retain their own languages, such as the Nubians, the Nilotes, the Funge, the Nuba of the western Sudan and the Mahas.

1. Secular music. 2. Religious and ritual music. 3. Instruments.

1. SECULAR MUSIC. Although people marry in accordance with Islamic law in the northern, central, eastern and western Sudan, the wedding customs are traditional. The celebrations last from three to seven days and include a great deal of music and dance. Songs are usually performed during the procession of the groom and his relatives and friends to the bride's home. In all areas, except among the Galien, these processional songs, known as *sayra*, are performed by women and are in responsorial form in 6/8 metre. They are accompanied by the *daluka* drum (fig.1) and two smaller drums known as *shatam*. A special dance, the 'neck dance', is performed by unmarried girls. While henna is being applied to the groom's hands and feet, a song for his well-being and happiness is sung in free time by an elderly woman, usually the groom's mother or aunt, with the other women repeating the refrain. The bride performs a special dance for women visitors, especially for her husband's relatives who have come to admire her beauty. In the towns men and women dance separately, but in rural areas dances are almost always mixed – for instance in the western Sudan the *nugara*, *mardoom*, *hassis* and other dances are always performed by men and women together.

Dobeit and *gardagi* are well-known types of song. *Dobeit* is a solo song in a free style, common among nomads. They sing it at night when travelling alone on camels, and believe that the camel likes the melody and travels better when the rider sings it. The texts of *dobeit* often refer to camels, either in direct praise of the animal or using it as a symbol of bravery, a common practice in Arabic classical and folk poetry. There used to be two or three melodies to which a *dobeit* might be sung, but now there is a single universal melody, or rather a single characteristic tonal structure. *Dobeit* probably derives from a Persian word meaning 'two verses'. Besides being a type of song, it is also a form of oral poetry chiefly found in the eastern Sudan. El Hardallo, a Shukriya poet of the latter half of the 19th century, wrote long poems in *dobeit* form. *Dobeit* is sung only by men, and the themes of its texts are limited to praise and love.

Among the Baggara nomads of the western Sudan is the *gardagi*, which was introduced there by the Guhaina

Arabs. It may be either a praise song or a song of censure, and is sung by both men and women in a free style, sometimes to the accompaniment of a single-string fiddle. The singer usually begins with known verses of an older song and then improvises new ones for the occasion. His words and the sharpness of his wit are the main points of interest.

The southern part of Sudan is populated mostly by various Nilotic peoples. Of these groups the Dinka are noted for their rich repertory of songs. Whereas in most other parts of the Sudan a soloist sings the main verses of the song, and the chorus repeats the refrain (usually the first verse or part of it), among the Dinka the solo singer sometimes repeats the refrain while the chorus introduces new verses. This technique is also found in the songs of other Nilotic peoples, such as the Shilluk and the Nuer. Among the Ingassana in the south-eastern Sudan the soloist first vocalizes to the syllables *ammmma* or *ayyyya* using an interval of a 4th, then the chorus and the soloist sing the verse together to the accompaniment of the large *shangar* lyre.

2. RELIGIOUS AND RITUAL MUSIC. Among Muslim communities religious songs were introduced under the Funge, who established the first Islamic states in the Sudan between the 16th and 19th centuries. During this period the Koran schools were founded, upon which formal education in the country was based, and the Sudanese Sufi movement developed. The Sufi introduced their own songs to accompany the *ziker* dance. *Ziker*

1. Daluka (goblet drum)

(Arabic: 'remembrance') is a communal process through which the individual forgets earthly pleasures and concentrates on the remembrance of God, saints and their good deeds, and life after death. Each Sufi sect has its own repertory of songs and distinct set rhythms. Ex.1 shows a typical *ziker* pattern. The instruments introduced by the Sufi to accompany *ziker* are drums, cymbals, triangles and tambourines, and occasionally a rattle attached to the top of a flag.

Ex.1 *Ziker* dance pattern; transcr. M. Ismail

Large drum

Small hand drum

Cymbals

Another form of religious song, *madieh* ('praise'), appeared at this time. It is sung in houses or in village squares. The performers, or *madahien*, used to travel, usually on donkeys, from village to village singing and bringing news. *Madieh* is a religious substitute for secular song, from which nearly all its melodies are borrowed. Its rhythms are those of the *daluka* wedding dance, and when an occasional dance is performed to *madieh* songs its main elements are those of the *arda*, the men's wedding dance. *Madieh* is performed by a soloist with three or four chorus singers: the soloist sings the verses and plays a large single-headed drum, while the chorus repeats the refrain and plays smaller drums.

The *moshembe da* is an exorcism dance of the southeastern Sudan, performed to free a sick person or a house from evil spirits. The ritual begins with the participants dancing in pairs, one couple at a time. The dancers face each other without touching, their hands on their waists to emphasize their hip movements. The healer then performs a solo dance which culminates in his inhaling the smoke from burning spices and coffee beans to induce the evil spirits to enter his own body, from which he finally expels them outside the house. The dance is accompanied by a group of five musical instruments: a *bangia* lyre and four *penah* gourd trumpets.

Waza is the ritual music of the Berta in the southeastern Sudan, and is played either at agricultural ceremonies, to ensure a good rainfall during the rainy season or as a thanksgiving at harvest time, or upon the death of an important person. At other times the sound of *waza* is a bad omen and for this reason the instruments on which the music is performed (a set of ten, sometimes eleven, composite gourd trumpets also called *waza*) are usually kept in a special hut in the house of the chief or a religious leader.

Kambala forms part of an initiation rite among the Nuba Miere in the Nuba hills of the western Sudan, during which a ritual dance is performed by the young men. The dancers wear a special costume which includes ankle rattles made of dried palm leaves woven to form pouches which contain small stones; they provide a percussive accompaniment to the dance. Besides the rattles the dancers carry a ring of jingles in the right hand and a hair fan in the left. The *kambala* is strictly a dance for men, and women participate only by singing and clapping, though a woman may sometimes approach one of the dancers and hold the horn he wears on his head, dancing a few steps with him as a sign of admiration or love. The dancers move mainly in a single line but occasionally form a circle.

3. INSTRUMENTS. The three most important idiophones used in the Sudan are the *rongo* xylophone, the *kundi* lamellaphone, and the *gugu*, a slit-drum.

The *rongo* (fig.2) is played by the Ndogo in the southern Sudan. It has ten ebony keys mounted on a wooden frame with ten matched gourd resonators attached below. A small hole in the bottom of each resonator is covered with a mirliton made from the membrane of a spider's silk. The semicircular wooden frame holds the instrument away from the player's body and attached to the ends of this frame is a leather strap which enables the player to hang the instrument from his neck. The ten keys are pentatonically tuned and paired in octaves; when playing the *rongo* the musician uses a pair of rubber-headed beaters in each hand so that he can strike a key and its lower octave simultaneously.

The *kundi* is a box-resonated LAMELLAPHONE with nine or ten metal lamellae, used by the Azande in the southern Sudan. The lamellae are arranged so that four fall under the player's left thumb and five under his right, with the longest in the centre and the shortest on the outside. Small rings are attached to ends of the lamellae furthest from the player, producing a characteristic buzzing effect. The instrument is about 15 cm long, 10 to 13 cm wide, and 6 to 8 cm deep. There is a small round hole in the bottom of the resonator which is stopped by the player to alter the timbre. The *kundi* is played by young men, especially when journeying on foot.

The *gugu* drum is another Azande instrument. It is made from a hollowed-out tree trunk and is normally about 105 cm long and about 45 cm high. It is usually carved in the shape of a bull or a wild boar, and has a single slit in the top. The two long edges of the slit are of unequal thickness so that the instrument can produce two different pitches. The player sits sideways on top of the instrument with his right leg over the slit. He uses two short drumsticks in each hand to strike each side of the slit, opening or closing the slit with his leg as he plays to modify the sound.

Drums of different kinds are used in nearly all areas of the Sudan. One of the most important is the *nihass*, derived from the Arabic word for copper. The *nihass* (fig.3) is a large copper kettledrum with a skin made of cowhide. It is used in the northern, central and western Sudan, and is played in time of war, or to announce a great calamity or the death of a chief. In tribal wars in the past the victors immediately took possession of the opponents' *nihass*. These drums are now owned only by ruling families, and some of them date back hundreds of years.

The Sudan is very rich in wind instruments; whistles, flutes and trumpets of all kinds are used. The *baal* is a set of ten to thirteen bamboo flutes used in the southeastern Sudan for ritual dances. The *zumbara* (fig.4) is a flute used by nomads, with two finger-holes and a perforated metal disc that partly closes the open end. It is about 90 cm long and was originally made from a dried root of a tree hollowed out with a thin piece of hot iron. The *penah* (fig.5) is a set of lip-vibrated gourds of varying sizes, apparently a type of spherical trumpet. The largest is about 75 cm in diameter and is called 'the mother'; the next is about 60 cm in diameter ('the father');

2. *Rongo* (*xylophones*) *of the Ndogo*

3. *Nihass* (*kettledrum*)

4. *Zumbara* (*flute*)

5. *Penah* (*gourd trumpets*) *and bangia* (*lyre*) *for the dance moshembe da*

6. Waza (gourd trumpets) of the Berta

and the two smallest instruments are each about 45 cm in diameter ('the children'). Each gourd has a hole opposite the mouth-hole so that it can be muted with one hand. The *penah* provides a drum-like rhythmic accompaniment to the *bangia* lyre for the *moshembe da* dance.

Horns are popular for the hunt and for dancing in the southern Sudan; young men of the Madi tribe use horns to signal their presence in ritual dances. The *manzisi* trumpet of the Bongo people is made from a tree trunk, hollowed out and carved on the outside into the shape of a limbless man. The player produces low staccato sounds by blowing into a square mouth-hole. The *waza* (fig.6) is a set of ten, sometimes eleven, large end-blown trumpets used by the Berta in the south-eastern Sudan. Each is made from sections of gourd joined together with beeswax and held in place by thin strips of bamboo

lashed to the tubes; the mouthpiece of each instrument is also made of gourd. The largest instrument is 200 to 210 cm long, the diameter of the bell being 18 to 20 cm, and that of the mouthpiece about 5 cm. Each instrument produces only one note and the set is played in hocket fashion. Each player carries a hooked piece of ebony on his right shoulder and beats out a rhythm with a short stick while blowing the trumpet.

The lyre is the most widely used chordophone in the Sudan. In the northern Sudan it is played by the Nubians, Mahas and Shaikia and is known as *tambour* (fig.7). In the west among the Nuba it is called *brimbiri*, while in the south-east it is known as *bangia* by the Berta and *shangar* by the Ingassana. The Bija in the eastern Sudan call it *rababa*. Despite its many different names there is little difference in form or tuning except

7. Tambour (lyre)

in the case of the *shangar*, which has a slightly different shape, and gut instead of steel strings. The *bangia* is typical of the others: it has a wooden bowl-resonator, a sound-table of hide, into which two soundholes are cut, and a small wooden bridge. The five strings, formerly made of gut, are of steel. Each string is fastened to a strip of cloth wound around the yoke and can be tuned by twisting the cloth. The *bangia* is strummed across all five strings with a small leather plectrum held in the right hand, while the fingers of the left hand damp all but one string at a time. The damped strings produce a dry percussive rhythm accompanying the melody.

The *umkiki* is a single-string fiddle played by the Baggara in the western Sudan to accompany *gardagi* songs. The instrument was introduced by immigrant Arabs and is a type of RABĀB. The *kurbi* is a harp used in the far west of the Sudan. It was originally used by the Nubians in the north, but is no longer known in that area. The *kurbi* has five strings which the player plucks with the fingers of both hands. At the same time he uses his right hand to drum a rhythmic accompaniment on the leather cover of the resonator.

BIBLIOGRAPHY

G. A. Schweinfurth: *Artes africanae* (Leipzig, 1875)
H. Zöllner: 'Einiges über sudanesische Musik', *Musikalisches Wochenblatt*, xvi (1885), 446
'La musique chez les nègres', *Congo illustré*, ii/9 (1893), 66
P. Karsten: 'Tambura der Krieger des Mahdi (Sudanneger)', *Neue musikalische Rundschau*, i (1908)
W. Heinitz: 'Transkription zweier Lieder aus Nil-Nubien', *ZMw*, ii (1919–20), 733
H. Baumann: 'Die materielle Kultur der Azande und Mangbetu', *Baessler Archiv*, xi (1927), 3–129
A. N. Tucker: 'Music in South Sudan', *Man*, xxxii (1932), 18
——: 'Children's Games and Songs in the Southern Sudan', *Journal of the Royal Anthropological Institute*, lxiii (1933), 165
——: *Tribal Music and Dancing in South Sudan at Social Ceremonial Gatherings* (London, 1933)
F. Giorgetti: *Musica d'Africa* (Strenna, 1940)
A. Mischlich: *Über die Kulturen im mittel-Sudan* (Berlin, 1942)
F. Giorgetti: 'Musica e tamburi fra gli Azande', *Nigrizia*, lxx (1951), 15
——: *Note de musica Zande: con trascrizioni musicali di uccelli, tamburi, xilofoni e canti Zande* (Verona, 1951)
——: 'African Music (with Special Reference to the Zande Tribe)', *Sudan Notes and Records*, xxxiii/2 (1952), 216
——: 'Musica e tamburi fra gli Azande: hanno la musica nel sangue', *Africana*, ii (1955), 12
R. C. Carlisle: 'Women Singers in Darfur, Sudan Republic', *Anthropos*, lxviii (1973), 785
G. A. Plumley: *El Tanbur: the Sudanese Lyre or Nubian Kissar* (Cambridge, 1976)

MAHI ISMAIL

Sudrophone. A group of valved brass instruments, soprano to contrabass, invented by the Parisian maker François Sudre and patented in 1892. Although the principal length of tubing was folded back on itself as in the OPHICLEIDE, and the valve assemblies bracketed out at one side, the proportions of the air column and acoustic characteristics were similar to those of the SAXHORN.

The unique feature of sudrophones was a device which permitted the player to modify the tone at will, and it was even claimed that reed or string timbre could be simulated. A brass cylinder attached to the bell communicated with both the air column and the external air through two opposed slots. An inner cylinder carried an adjustable stretched membrane of silk. By turning the inner cylinder to the left or right, the slot in the bell was either closed off or occupied by the membrane, whose vibrations modified the tone after the principle of the EUNUCH-FLUTE. (*See also* MIRLITON.)

PHILIP BATE

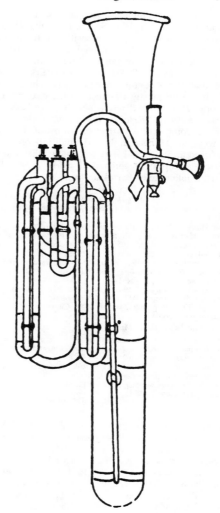

Sudrophone by François Sudre, Paris, after the maker's catalogue of 1905

Südwestdeutsche Philharmonie. Orchestra founded in KONSTANZ in 1932.

Suevus, Felician. *See* SCHWAB, FELICIAN.

Suffrages. In the Anglican rite, a series of intercessionary prayers spoken or sung in the form of versicles and responses; *see* VERSICLE.

Sufi music. *See* ISLAMIC RELIGIOUS MUSIC.

Suga, Michio. *See* MIYAGI, MICHIO.

Sugár, Rezső (*b* Budapest, 9 Oct 1919). Hungarian composer. He studied composition with Kodály at the Budapest Academy of Music (1937–42) and concurrently attended courses in philosophy at the university.

After teaching at a Budapest secondary school (1943–6) and at the Municipal High School for Music (1946–9), he was appointed to teach composition at the Budapest Conservatory, where he remained until 1968 when he was made professor of composition at the Budapest Academy of Music. Sugár received the Erkel Prize in 1953 and the Kossuth Prize in 1954. Until around 1950 he wrote mostly chamber music; next came the oratorio *Hősi ének* ('Heroic song') and the cantata *Kőmíves Kelemen* ('Kelemen the mason'), works which may be compared with the oratorios of Honegger. Drawing on Hungarian history and folklore, Sugár developed an individual style with nationalist and neoclassical affinities; the orchestral works of the 1960s show the influence of Bartókian form.

WORKS
(selective list)

Stage: A tenger lánya táncjáték [The daughter of the sea], dance-play, 1961

Vocal: Hunyadi: hősi ének [Hunyadi: heroic song] (oratorio, J. Romhányi), chorus, orch, 1951; 6 Songs, 1v, pf, 1954; Kínai dalok [Chinese songs], 1v, pf, 1954; Kőmíves Kelemen [Kelemen the mason], ballad, S, Bar, chorus, orch, 1958

Orch: Divertimento, str, 1948; Szvit, 1954; Conc. in memoriam Béla Bartók, 1962; Metamorfosi, 1966; Partita, str, 1967; Sinfonia a variazione, 1970; Epilógus, 1973

Inst: Barokk szonatina, pf, 1943–6; Szerenád, 2 vn, va, 1943; Sonata, vn, pf, 1946; 3 str qts, 1947, 1950, 1969; Frammenti musicali, wind qnt, pf, 1958; Rapszódia, vc, pf, 1959; Capriccio, vc, pf, 1961; Kammersymphonie, 1973

Principal publisher: Editio Musica

BIBLIOGRAPHY
J. S. Weismann: 'Guide to Contemporary Hungarian Composers', *Tempo* (1957–8), no.47, p.25
I. Fábián: 'Ungarische Musik nach Bartók', *ÖMz*, xxi (1966), 620
Contemporary Hungarian Composers (Budapest, 1970)
G. Kroó: *A magyar zeneszerzés 25 éve* [25 years of Hungarian composition] (Budapest, 1971)

MELINDA BERLÁSZ KÁROLYI

Suggia, Guilhermina (*b* Oporto, 27 June 1888; *d* Oporto, 31 July 1950). Portuguese cellist. After lessons with her father, she was playing publicly at the age of seven, leading the cellos in the Orpheon Portuense at 12. A royal scholarship took her to Leipzig in 1904 for study with Julius Klengel; in 1905 she joined the Gewandhaus Orchestra and appeared as a soloist under Nikisch. She worked and lived with Casals, 1906–12, and was billed on some programmes as 'Mme P. Casals-Suggia', but they were never married. She later moved to England, where her performances were highly admired for many years. In 1923 her portrait (*see* VIOLONCELLO, fig.5) was painted by Augustus John, who gave dramatic expression to her grace, style and magnetism as a performer. She came out of retirement in Portugal to appear at the 1949 Edinburgh Festival, and she left her Stradivari to the RAM, London.

ROBERT ANDERSON

Sughithā. A category of chant in SYRIAN CHURCH MUSIC.

Suhl, Johann Matthias (*fl* mid-18th century). German harpsichordist and composer. He was a keyboard player in the Duke of Mecklenburg-Schwerin's court orchestra around the middle of the 18th century; the date of his arrival at the Schwerin court has not been traced, but in 1752 he was succeeded by E. G. Müthel. His name appears as Sühl on his manuscripts in the Schwerin Landesbibliothek, which include seven sonatas for violin and continuo and a concerto for solo violin and string

orchestra. The anonymous violin solo with continuo in Schwerin (Mus. MS 508) is probably also by him, while a violin concerto in C which was formerly there has been lost; his symphonies and oboe and bassoon concertos mentioned in Breitkopf catalogues have not been traced either.

Suhl's works in the Schwerin manuscripts show an autonomous musical personality influenced by the stylistic changes of his century. They follow the Baroque motivic principles but approach the early *Sturm und Drang* style of C. P. E. Bach in emotionally charged melodic figures and leaps.

BIBLIOGRAPHY
Gerber L
O. Kade: *Die Musikalien-Sammlung des grossherzoglich Mecklenburg-Schweriner Fürstenhauses aus den letzten zwei Jahrhunderten*, i–ii (Schwerin, 1893)
B. S. Brook, ed.: *The Breitkopf Thematic Catalogue, 1762–1787* (New York, 1966)

DIETER HÄRTWIG

Suisse (i) (Fr.). SWITZERLAND.

Suisse (ii). Probably the common form from which the names of four Renaissance organ builders, who may have been related to each other, originally derived. Liebing (also Lieven, Levinus) Sweys (also Zwits), sometimes given the cognomen 'von Köln', was active in Oppenheim around 1438, became a citizen of Frankfurt am Main in 1439–40 and subsequently worked in Frankfurt, Cologne, Koblenz, Brussels, Cleve, Delft, Utrecht and Antwerp, the latest recorded date being 1469; thus he clearly enjoyed a more than local reputation. Sebastian Zwysen, also known as 'Sebastian van Diest alias Moukens', was working as an organ builder in Hasselt and Diest from 1523 to 1527; Joos Swijssen worked at St Joris in Antwerp in 1510.

The name of Hans Suys (*d* Amsterdam, between 1542 and 1544), occurs in a number of variants, including Suest, Suess, Zuess and also 'Hans Blangz' – the last evidently a translation of the form 'Hans Zwits', but based on a misinterpretation of the surname as 'White'. He is also sometimes given the cognomens 'von Nürnberg' (1498 and 1509) or 'von Köln' (1500, 1506–7 and 1511 onwards). He worked in the Cathedral of Frankfurt am Main in 1498, in St Michel, Liège, in 1500 and 1513, in Strasbourg Cathedral in 1506–7, 1511–12 and 1516, in the Cathedral of Our Lady, Antwerp, in 1509–14, in St Nikolai, Kalkar, in 1515–16, in Xanten Cathedral in 1518, in the Oude Kerk in Amsterdam from 1539 onwards (with Heinrich Niehoff, then his partner) on an organ with three manuals and 25 stops, and elsewhere at various times. Hans Suys was one of the greatest masters in the history of organ building, certainly one of the most sought-after of his day. He was a leader both in his preservation of tradition (his Principal choruses continued to be praised long after his death and probably provided the model for Niehoff's equally acclaimed Principal choruses) and in his adoption of innovations, notably the families of stops that first appeared in organs in the decades around 1500 in south-west Germany, having reeds with full-length resonators, Horn mixtures including tierce ranks, and narrow-scale flues. No other instrument of the period has so great a number of any of these features as Hans von Köln's Antwerp instrument of 1509–14; this organ was a fascinating prototype that sparked off the brilliant development of organ building in the Low Countries.

His Amsterdam organ, which – owing to the contributions of Johann Kovelens and Heinrich Niehoff – also manifested the best qualities of the art of organ building in the Rhineland below Cologne, was later played by Sweelinck, and remained the standard model for the north Brabantine school for the next century.

It remains an open question whether Hans Suys is to be identified with Jan van Zwanenbroeck (in Delft, 1501), Jannes Zwaneberch van Cölen (Diest, 1502) and Magister Hans (Besançon, 1512 and 1517). Jasper Johannsen, Heinrich Niehoff's partner after Hans Suys's death, was a son of Johann (Brouckmann) of Münster, not of Hans Suys.

BIBLIOGRAPHY

J.-A. Stellfeld: 'Bronnen tot de geschiedenis der Antwerpse clavecymbelen orgelbouwers in de XVIe en XVIIe eeuwen', *Vlaams Jb voor muziekgeschiedenis*, iv (1942), 3–110

M. A. Vente: *Die brabanter Orgel* (Amsterdam, 1958, enlarged 2/1963)

G. Pietzsch: 'Süss', *MGG*

H. Klotz: 'Svijs', *Rheinische Musiker*, iv, ed. K. G. Fellerer (Cologne, 1966), 172

HANS KLOTZ

Suisse Romande, Orchestre de la. Orchestra founded in GENEVA in 1918 by Ernest Ansermet.

Suite. In a general sense, any ordered set of instrumental pieces meant to be performed at a single sitting; during the Baroque period, an instrumental genre consisting of several movements in the same key, some or all of which were based on the forms and styles of dance music; then and later, a group of pieces extracted from a larger work, especially an opera or ballet, such as *Carmen Suite* or *Nutcracker Suite*. The term (from the French, meaning 'those that follow' or 'succession') did not come into common use until the last quarter of the 17th century, but the kinds of set to which it was eventually applied had a long history, and pairing of dances may be found as early as the 14th century. The suite served not only as a form for newly composed pieces, but also as a convenient way to arrange existing pieces in groups for publication and especially performance. After about 1750 the 'classical' form of the Baroque suite, which included allemande, courante, sarabande and gigue, became obsolete along with the term. The idea of the suite, however, taken in its more general sense, continued to flourish under various guises, and the term itself has since been revived.

1. Terminology. 2. Theories about the suite. 3. Early history to about 1600. 4. Early 17th century. 5. The classical suite before the addition of the gigue. 6. The classical suite after the addition of the gigue: (i) Germany (ii) England (iii) France (iv) Low Countries. 7. Non-classical suites of the high Baroque. 8. Couperin and the 18th-century French suite. 9. Handel and the English suite. 10. Bach and the Germans. 11. 1750–1900. 12. 20th century.

1. TERMINOLOGY. 'Suite' entered the terminology of music in 1557 as a designation for a group of branles (see §3 below), and continued with that meaning until such groups ceased to be danced. A rare clue to what must have been common early 17th-century usage is provided by a contract for music lessons in 1631: the *valet de chambre* of the Marquise de Maulny was to be taught to play 'les Branles de Belleville et suittes d'iceux, avecq les diminutions, les ballets de Monsieur avecq touttes leurs suittes' on his violin. The broadening application of the term and the uncertainty whether it meant 'group' or 'succeeding pieces' are also apparent in a letter written by Constantijn Huygens to Du Mont in 1655: 'ie vous ay faict copier toute la suite de ceste mesme Alemande'. It seems to have been Thomas Mace,

however, and not a Frenchman, who first used suite (or 'suit') to refer to a particular composite form consisting of prelude, allemande, ayre, courante, sarabande, toy 'or what you please' (*Musick's Monument*, 1676, p.120); according to Mace the pieces should be linked by a common tonic and 'some kind of Resemblance in their Conceits, Natures, or Humours'. Two years before, Dietrich Becker had brought out *Erster Theil zweystimmiger Sonaten und Suiten*, the first publication to use 'suite' in the title. Here, however, since each sonata (resembling a *sonata da chiesa*) is followed by a group of dances, Becker may have used *Suiten* in the earlier sense of 'sonatas with their suites' (i.e. with their attached dances), a sense which finds its echo as late as Walther's *Lexicon* (1732), where the allemande is likened to a rhetorical 'Proposition, woraus die übrigen Suiten, als die Courante, Sarabande, und Gique, als Partes fliessen'.

'Sett' was used by Mace as a synonym for suite, and it has been so used from time to time right up to the present (e.g. Henry Symonds, 1733; Henry Cowell, 1957). In *The Musicall Grammarian* (1728) Roger North also spoke of 'setts of musick w[hi]ch were called fancys', in which a fantasia is followed by dance movements (see FANTASIA-SUITE). But 'set' more often meant a number of works of the same type, and except for sets of variations, it does not normally imply performance at a single sitting. During the 1750s, when the English keyboard suite was being replaced by the sonata, the meanings of 'set', 'sonata' and 'lesson' became confusingly tangled. Barnabas Gunn (1750) used 'Six Setts of Lessons' as the title of a print consisting of six multi-movement works headed 'lesson', not 'sett'. J. C. Gillier (1757) did the same, while William Felton (1752 and 1757) and J. C. Smith (1755) put 'suits of lessons' in their titles and used 'lesson' to head what are in effect sonatas. Finally, both 'set' and 'suit' were dropped from Gillier's *Eight Sonatas or Lessons* (1759). Another careless use of 'suite' is to be found in Roseingrave's edition of 42 Scarlatti sonatas, which are, of course, single pieces: *XLII suites de pièces* (1739), translated later as *Forty-two Suits of Lessons* (1754–6).

Both 'sonata' and 'sinfonia' have from time to time been applied to suites, even when the contents seem entirely removed from the influence of the Italian SONATA DA CAMERA, as in Silvius Weiss's *Sechs Sonaten* for lute (in manuscript). The interrelations of suite and *sonata da camera* are intricate, especially when the latter designation was used by non-Italians. Johann Rosenmüller seems to have been the first German to call a collection of suites *Sonate da camera* (1667, reprinted three years later), but he had been living in Venice for at least seven years, and the term 'sonata' had in any case been thoroughly naturalized in Germany long before. Rosenmüller's *sonate da camera* are ensemble suites of the type he had been composing since 1645 with added introductory sinfonias. A wavering between sonata and suite may be seen in violin music at the beginning of the 18th century, particularly as the influence of Corelli was felt. François Duval (1704) used 'sonata' and 'suite' interchangeably to designate sonatas, while J. C. Pez entitled a collection *Sonate da camera or Chamber-musick consisting of Several Suites of Overtures and Aires* (London, 1710).

Other terms that were used occasionally in the sense of suite include PARTITA (*Parthie*, *Partia* etc), OVERTURE and ORDRE. The Germans, in particular, had a great affection for titles that indicated the social attitudes and intentions underlying their vast production. They may be roughly classified as 'pleasure' (J. C. Pezel, *Delitiae musicales*; Esaias Reusner (ii), *Gesellschafts-Ergetzung*; Andreas Werckmeister, *Privat-Lust*), 'garden' (J. A. Reincken, *Hortus musicus*; J. C. F. Fischer, *Blumen-Büschlein*), 'table' (Schein, *Banchetto musicale*; Biber, *Mensa sonora*; and a variety of *Früchte*) and 'deprecatory' (David Kellner, *Handvol kurzweiliger Zeitvertreib*; Matthias Kelz, *Joco-seria harmonia sacro-profana*). These titles were usually followed by a listing of each type of piece in the collection; the division into suites, at least in collections before about 1675, can only be deduced from an examination of the contents.

France was the last country in the 18th century to abandon 'suite' as a musical term. In 1767 C. F. Clément finally dropped it as a designation for the groups of arrangements from favourite operas in his *Journal de clavecin*; at the same time (without introducing the term 'sonata') he put the middle 'movements' of his groups in contrasting keys. N. J. Hüllmandel's *Six divertissements ou IIe suite de petits airs* (c1780), Joseph Pouteau's *Potpourri, ou Suite d'airs* (1782), or *Deux suites* in Michel Corrette's hurdy-gurdy method (1783) show in what surroundings the suite fell into disuse. For the next half-century and more, the suite was memorialized in music dictionaries as an obsolete genre and term. Schumann, in his review of William Sterndale Bennett's *Suite de pièces* op.24 (1841) – one of the first serious examples of the form in the 19th century – called it a 'good old word'. Gradually, 'suite' worked its way back into the normal terminology and practice of music and by the latter part of the century it was again used by composers and arrangers. In dictionaries, however, it continued to be treated as a historical term whose meaning had crystallized roughly along the lines of Bach's 'English Suites'.

2. THEORIES ABOUT THE SUITE. Underlying nearly all serious writing about the suite has been the Darwinian notion of an organic form, the issue of a single act of composition, evolving from the *Tanz–Nachtanz* pair via the sturdy craftsmanship of Peuerl, Schein and Froberger to the supreme artistry of Bach, through a process of continual annexation of foreign elements and integration into an ever higher governing plan. This conception can be found expressed a century ago in arrogantly chauvinistic terms by Spitta (Eng. trans., ii, 84ff) and more mildly in a more recent study of the subject (Beck, Mw, Eng. trans., 1966, p.52). It was inevitable that Bach's suites should have tempted scholars to discover in them a constructive principle which, once identified, could be taken as the essence of the suite idea and traced back through this evolution, serving as a basis for comparative analysis. By shutting out the period of the Thirty Years War in Germany and most French and English instrumental music of the first 60 years of the 17th century, it is just possible to discern a continuous historical process (painted in *trompe l'oeil*) wherein a suite principle might be concealed. Some of the principles that have been proposed are decreasing stylization (Besseler, Pearl), the alternation of stepping and leaping dances (Norlind, Seiffert, Riemann, Nef, etc), the alternation of company and couple dances (Klenz, in connection with the *sonata da camera*), and the alternation or pairing of tempos and degrees of tension (Reimann and others). From such principles it is

also possible to proceed to theories of 'open' and 'closed' forms (Reimann) and to systems of classification, like *Kunstsuite* versus *Gebrauchssuite* (Blume).

In all this theorizing and in similar unitary views of the suite there is the palpable implication of an analogy between suite and sonata. Marpurg was one of the first to imply it when he said that 'a series of three or more keyboard pieces that are related to one another and so made that they cannot be separated but must remain together and be played one after the other ... is sometimes called a suite ... and sometimes a sonata' (*Clavierstücke*, i, 1762, 5). A remarkable amount of the speculation about principles of ordering is based on fixed ideas of the character of the dances, which in fact changed greatly during the course of the 17th century. The sarabande, for example, was sometimes fast and sometimes slow, and it is by no means always possible to tell from appearances what the speed is supposed to be. The gigue, especially, existed in radically varying guises, and one cannot be sure of the correct way of playing the many examples in 2/2 or 4/4 time. Far more important is the fact that the majority of suites, taken over the whole history of the genre, are simply too diverse to support a unified theory. Furthermore, for a large number of them, including some very influential ones like those from Lully and Handel's 'Eight Great' harpsichord suites, the composition of the pieces and their arrangement in order were two separate acts, sometimes carried out by two different people. Often it cannot be known how a suite came to be in its existing form. Finally, one cannot even be sure that many series of pieces (especially French ones) were meant to be played one after another at a single sitting. In practice, the pieces were more often than not played out of context, especially at home and in informal settings.

If the search for a principle of the suite is futile, there may be, nevertheless, one characteristic that always distinguishes suites from other multi-movement works. The quality of an aggregate – the character of a pastiche – seems never to be wholly absent. Unlike a sonata, a suite normally consists of individual pieces whose identity derives partly from the outside, even when one piece is generated from another by rhythmic transformation, as in a variation suite. Usually the pieces are based on the pre-existing forms and styles of dances, but they may also have programmatic associations indicated by titles, or they may actually have been assembled from some pre-existing work like a ballet. The suite character of Berg's *Lyric Suite*, to choose an example apparently far removed from a pastiche, is suggested by the tempo markings: Allegretto gioviale, Andante amoroso, Largo desolato, etc; each piece is devoted to an explicit affection. Usually the references to the outside are less subtle.

In the late Baroque period, when the interaction of sonata and suite was complex, tonality became a useful test of whether a piece should be called one or the other, and it was so recognized by 18th-century writers. The principle that all the pieces of a suite are in the same key became a part of dictionary definitions up to the present (a principle abandoned after 1800 by composers, needless to say). A rationale for key unity was invented; it was said that suites do not change key because of the difficulty of retuning one's lute – as if all lute repertory for a given tuning were in the same key, or as if the lute's imaginary limitations should determine the tonal plan of suites for all media, but not of sonatas. Given the nature of the suite as a gathering-together of pieces, it was only natural that one of the oldest classification systems of Western music should govern the grouping: that of mode or key. Until tonality was explicitly recognized as a structural resource it would not have occurred to musicians to juxtapose whole pieces in different keys for tonal contrast (the odd exception by Marini or Jenkins notwithstanding). The tonal variety in the sonata was a result of its ancestry in single, multisectional pieces like the canzona, in which cadences in various keys succeeded one another. When composers finally recognized the suite as a genre in its own right, the tradition of key unity was already strong enough to have acquired the momentum to carry it well into the 18th century. This tradition did not prevent composers from contrasting the major and minor modes, however, a practice which was especially common in paired, alternating dances from the last quarter of the 17th century.

The unification of the suite by other than tonal means has been an intermittent concern of composers throughout its history. The true variation suite is the most obvious manifestation of this concern, but much more common is a linking of two or three (rarely all) pieces by thematic similarities that are sometimes unequivocal but perhaps more often vague enough to make it difficult to decide whether they are intentional, the result of chance, or the workings of the subconscious mind. In Handel's suite no.6 from the 1733 collection, for example, the courante is hardly more than a triple-metre version of the allemande (ex.1). A courante by Hardel

Ex.2

(*F-Pn* Vm⁷Rés.674, f.35*v*), a pupil of Chambonnières, is also unmistakably based on the allemande (f.34*r*), but it is freer in its details (ex.2). In J. S. Bach's first cello suite, however, the thematic relationship is much more subtle, and only the emphasis on the *b*–*c'*–*b* at the top of the figuration suggests that it was not unintentional (ex.3).

The English fantasia-suites of the 17th century were often terminated with 'conclusions', outside the tempo and form of the final piece, which must be interpreted as a way of rounding off the whole work, and thus conferring a sort of unity on it. The same device was also used by Hieronymus Gradenthaler (1676), Pezel (1678) and Biber (1680). Preludes or introductions can produce the same effect; the longer they are, the more the following dances are felt as appendages, thereby seeming to depend upon the opening movement and to form a whole with it. Large-scale symmetries or balance within suites suggest the effort to construct a composite whole (see below in connection with J.-H. d'Anglebert and Christophe Moyreau). Finally, the movements may be

Ex.1

connected by half-cadences or they may be continuous with one another, as often happens in the 19th and 20th centuries (in Tchaikovsky's *Nutcracker Suite*, for example). In later suites, tonal contrast of the inner movements produces the unity of an arch form.

3. EARLY HISTORY TO ABOUT 1600. The earliest instrumental dances to have survived come from the early and late 14th century in two manuscripts of French and Italian provenance respectively (*F-Pn* f.fr.844 and *GB-Lbm* Add.29987). Each contains eight *estampies*, numbered from one to eight in the earlier source and provided with titles in the later. In neither case is it a question of sequential performance, however, and hence of a 'suite'; the length and complexity of the individual pieces, as well as the fact that they are in different keys, make this unlikely. But two other much shorter pieces in the Italian source, entitled *Lamento di Tristano* and *La Manfredina*, are each paired with a faster-moving piece using the same thematic material condensed and speeded up, called 'La Rotta'. Here, for the first time, there is contact with a dance tradition extending back indefinitely into unwritten history and carrying forward to form one of the many evolutionary threads of Renaissance and Baroque suite composition: the *Tanz* and *Nachtanz*, low and high, gliding and leaping pairs, whose most familiar English manifestation is the pavan and galliard.

The surviving dance music of the 15th century is contained chiefly in dance manuals and collections of basse danse tenors. The dance manuals, notably those of Domenico da Piacenza (or Da Ferrara; 1416), Antonio Cornazano (1455), Guglielmo Ebreo da Pesaro (c1453), and Giovanni Ambrosio, supply evidence that confirms and illuminates what is adumbrated in *La Manfredina* and *Lamento di Tristano*, namely a practice widespread in Italy and extending to Germany of creating pairs and sometimes larger groups of dances out of the same material. In the case of the archetypal bassadanza–saltarello pair, the material was a *tenore* (cantus firmus) which served as the basis for improvised polyphony. It could be danced in four mensurations, corresponding to four dance types: the grave bassadanza, the moderate *quadernaria*, the livelier saltarello and the quick piva. Three and even four of these were used in the pantomimic balli, though the norm for ordinary dancing was the pair (*see* BASSE DANSE).

The French equivalent of the bassadanza–saltarello, known principally through the dance treatise of Michel Toulouze (1480s) and the magnificent manuscript *B-Br* 9085, was the basse danse and *pas de Brabant*, though the evidence for coupling the latter to the former is indirect. The combination was called *basse danse majeure*, and the freer ballo, *basse danse mineure*. An internationally popular example of the latter, *Rôti bouilli joyeux*, in the version in the Brussels manuscript (facs. in J. L. Jackman, ed.: *Fifteenth-century Basse Dances*, Wellesley, Mass., 1964) shows certain features linking it to the suite idea (see Heartz, 'A 15th-century Ballo', 1966). Three dance tenors in three different kinds of rhythm succeed one another: 'Roti boully ioyeulx en pas de breban'; 'Lomme et la famme ensemble doibvent faire cecy deux fois. Et puis sensuit la basse danse'; and the basse danse itself with choreographic directions. Evidently the order of basse danse–*pas de Brabant* was reversed for the *basse danse mineure*. The order was determined by choreographic rather than musical considerations, but to the ear the result would have been a

set of three rhythmically contrasting pieces unified by the melodic similarity of the tenors of the first and last and enlivened by the improvised accompaniments of the other instruments.

Although no written part-music clearly intended for dancing has survived from the 15th century, an idea of the probable character of these accompaniments can be formed from a four-voice dance pair discovered and published by Heartz ('Hoftanz', 1966); a 16th-century source (*D-Bds* 1516) also offers evidence of the penetration of the basse danse into Germany under the name of 'Hoftanz', albeit with rhythmic modifications. In this case, the afterdance, called 'Tripl' (another term, 'Hoppertanz', suggests saltarello), is based on a different tenor from that of its companion, whose tune, *Le petit Rouen*, appears in basse danse sources of the preceding century.

Some time in the later 15th century, a new kind of basse danse appeared, called 'commune' (the older type being then called 'incommune'). The first polyphonic examples now known, those in Attaingnant's lute and ensemble collections of 1530, were based not on the old tenors but mainly on the newly fashionable *chansons musicales*, adapted to fit the two sections of 20 and 12 steps into which the variable 15th-century choreography had crystallized. The second section, called by Attaingnant *recoupe*, by Arbeau *retour*, and more generally *moitié*, was often followed by a third piece, of independent lineage, called *tourdion*; and the three, unified by key, though not necessarily by musical material or even mode, were recognized as a typical set as late as 1589 by Arbeau (Heartz, 1964).

Another grouping of three dances, descended from the second, third and fourth mensural transformations of the bassadanza, made its appearance in the fourth book of Petrucci's *Intabulatura de lauto* (1508). Here the arranger, J. A. Dalza, called attention to what he must have felt was an important feature of his collection: 'Nota che tutte le pauane hanno el suo saltarello e piua'. In 1546, Dalza's grouping of pieces was used (rhythmically, if not in the choice of terms for the dances) in a tablature by Andrea Rotta, and, with the second and third pieces reversed, in another by Domenico Bianchini of the same year. This new order, in Bianchini's terminology, *Pass'e mezzo, La sua padoana, Il suo saltarello*, was taken up in the four collections of 1561–79 by Giacomo Gorzanis and in Matthäus Waissel's tablature of 1573. The Italians continued in general to base all the dances of a group on the same thematic material, using techniques involving variation on a ground, parody and paraphrase. P. P. Borrono (1536, 1546 and 1548) was an exception with his sets, which consisted of a pavan followed by three saltarellos, of which only the first was derived from the pavan. The second of these collections contains a remark indicative, like Dalza's, of a concern for the overall form of his groups in performance: where the last two saltarellos are missing, one should borrow them from other groups. Here an Italian was recommending explicitly what others had tacitly practised, namely the occasional compilation of suites from independent sources.

The first known groups of pieces bearing the name of 'suite' were the *suyttes de bransles* in Estienne du Tertre's *Septième livre de danceries* of 1557 (facs. of table of contents in *MGG*, xii, col.1709). Arbeau (*Orchésographie*) described many sequences of branles, a common one being *branle double, branle simple* (these

1. Title-page of Estienne du Tertre's 'Septième livre de danceries' (Paris: Attaingant, 1557)

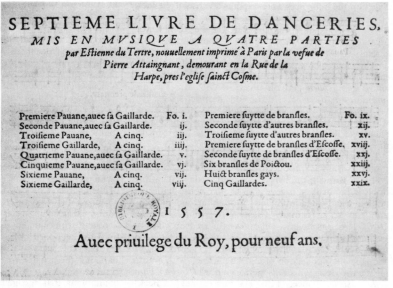

SEPTIEME LIVRE DE DANCERIES, MIS EN MVSIQVE A QVATRE PARTIES par Estienne du Tertre, nouuellement imprimé à Paris par la vefue de Pierre Attaingnant, demourant en la Rue de la Harpe, pres l'eglife fainct Cofme.

		Fo.			Fo.
Premiere Pauane, auec fa Gaillarde.		i.	Premiere fuytte de branfles.		ix.
Seconde Pauane, auec fa Gaillarde.		ij.	Seconde fuytte d'autres branfles.		xij.
Troifieme Pauane,	A cinq.	iij.	Troifieme fuytte d'autres branfles.		xv.
Troifieme Gaillarde,	A cinq.	iiij.	Premiere fuytte de branfles d'Efcoffe.		xviij.
Quatrieme Pauane, auec fa Gaillarde.		v.	Seconde fuytte de branfles d'Efcoffe.		xxj.
Cinquieme Pauane, auec fa Gaillarde.		vj.	Six branfles de Poictou.		xxiij.
Sixieme Pauane,	A cinq.	vij.	Huict branfles gays.		xxvj.
Sixieme Gaillarde,	A cinq.	viij.	Cinq Gaillardes.		xxix.

1 5 5 7.

Auec priuilege du Roy, pour neuf ans,

two sedate ones for the elderly at a ball), *branle gay* (for the young marrieds), and *branles de Champagne* or *de Bourgogne* (for the youngest and most agile). For Arbeau, the gavotte was a 'miscellany of double branles, selected by musicians and arranged in a sequence' (Eng. trans., p.175); here and elsewhere (pp.129,137) he made it clear that it was normally the musicians at a dance who assembled the branles into suites, drawing on their memory or on tablatures in which the branles were classified by type, if at all, and ordering them according to the demands of the dancers or current fashion. Thus, with rare exceptions, the printed 'suites' of branles constituted the raw material for practical use, and not the finished products themselves; for the groups as played, there could be no question of musical unification beyond similarity of key.

The vast majority of dance groups from the 1540s to the end of the century are pairs; and of this majority, the overwhelming majority again are pairs of which the first dance is either a pavan or a passamezzo and the second either a galliard or a saltarello. Since the two dances in each position are rhythmically and historically related, the actual variety of pairs drawn from these four dances is smaller than the names might suggest. Normally, the dances of a pair are based on the same material – one of the passamezzo progressions, perhaps with a tune as well, a vocal piece, an earlier version of one of the dances etc.

Here, not less than in larger dance groups (branles excepted), the tangential relation to variation sets is obvious, and with the expansion of the individual dances of a group into subsets of variations, written or improvised, to meet the requirements of the ballroom or to amuse the amateur player, the interrelations of variation and suite become reticulate. Two ambitious complexes by Giorgio Mainerio (first printed in *Il primo libro de balli*, 1578) are essentially expanded passamezzo–saltarello pairs in which both dances are followed by a *ripresa* (which carries on with the rhythm and certain motifs of the parent dance but abandon its phraseology and passamezzo progression). The first three of the resulting four sections are presented in three to five 'modi', or variations. Each complex has a total of 13

strains, all more or less related thematically. Such complexes became very common in German lute music.

In Italy, France and England towards the end of the century the development of entertainments involving both theatrical and social dancing (mascheratas, balli, *ballets de cour* and masques) brought further initiatives with consequences for the suite. Successions beginning with an entrée or intrada and continuing with varied dances were either chosen from among current social types or specially composed to accompany mimed action. On the evidence of the music that has survived from these early, quasi-theatrical festivities – most of it known in early 17th-century arrangements for lute (Ballard, 1611 and 1614) or ensemble (Praetorius, 1612) or through the schematic renderings of André Philidor (1680–1700), or through dance manuals (Fabritio Caroso, 1581, Cesare Negri, 1602) – groups of pieces were unified by key and sometimes by subtle thematic connections, though not usually by variation procedures. Contrast was achieved through rhythm, shifts of mode, occasional harmonic surprises (Ballard, ballets *Des esclaves* and *Des chevaux*), and, if Ballard's versions reflect anything of the originals, sharply distinctive textures.

4. EARLY 17TH CENTURY. The two decades preceding the Thirty Years War saw an extraordinary burst of creativity in European instrumental music, accompanied by and perhaps partly resulting from a lively exchange of musicians among all countries and a growing consciousness of national styles. The English presence throughout northern Europe was especially prominent during this period owing to the travels of the musicians themselves and to extensive German publication of their works. Italy continued to be a magnet and a training-ground, and the traffic between England and France was intense because of royal connections. France exported dancing-masters and lutenists, and German anthologists made a special place for Polish dances in their collections. The Low Countries were a crossroads and haven for exiles; the Italians took up the Spanish guitar and its music with enthusiasm. All this mobility left its mark on the suite, though it is not always possible to tell in what

direction the influences were moving because of the lack of dates to establish precedence.

The usual groupings of dances of the late Renaissance persisted until after 1600, though the popularity of the ensemble canzona in Italy apparently diverted further development of the large passamezzo complexes from ensemble to keyboard (e.g. a 30-page *Pass'e mezzo antico di sei parti* and *Saltarello* in Giovanni Picchi's *Intavolatura di balli*, 1621, for harpsichord). The favourite dance in Italy was the galliard without pavan, which was rare in Italy at this period (G. F. Anerio and Salamone Rossi, 1607; also G. M. Trabaci, 1615, with nine galliards in a row).

It was mainly in the field of practical dance music that the Italians produced suites during this period. Antonio Brunelli published a 'balletto' 'danced by the noble ladies of Pisa' in a version for five voices with text and an ornamented intabulation for chitarrone 'per sonare solo senza cantare' (*Scherzi ... lib.III*, Venice, 1616). It consisted of a *ballo grave*, a *seconda parte in gagliarda*, and a *terza parte in corrente* all related thematically (Nettl). Two years later, Lorenzo Allegri brought out a collection of eight balli, each with a note giving the occasion of its performance (*Il primo libro delle musiche*, Venice, 1618). The first (printed in Beck) has the same scheme as Brunelli's. Others have four or more pieces, including two *brandi*, a *canario* and a *gavotta*. In both Brunelli and Allegri, the dances are derived from the first of the group by rhythmic transformation. In Monteverdi's *Scherzi* of 1607, there is an *entrata* followed by seven texted dances in contrasting rhythms. The dances have but one strain and several are connected by half-cadences (the composer may be Monteverdi's brother, Giulio Cesare).

One of the liveliest figures in Germany at the turn of the century was Valentin Haussmann, who gathered Polish and East Prussian dances for his collections and also included English pavans and galliards in a publication of 1604. Like Brunelli's balletto, Haussmann's many dance pairs show the overlap between vocal and instrumental music at the time. His *Neue liebliche Melodien* (five editions, 1598–1606) have German texts but are 'mehrern Theils zum Tantze zu gebrauchen', and some of his *Neue artige und liebliche Täntze* (six editions between the same years) are texted, some not. In the preface to *Venusgarten* (1602), Haussmann confirmed what common sense suggests: that after-dances could be improvised where needed; at the same time, he made a puzzling distinction: as an alternative to extemporization, the players might follow 'Polish usage' (unexplained). Other composers or anthologists of ensemble dance music in the first decade of the century were Coler, J. C. Demantius, Melchior Franck, Balthasar Fritsch, Johann Groh, H. L. Hassler, Georg Hasz, Mathias Mercker, S. T. Staden and Johann Staricius. Zacharias Füllsack and Johann Hildebrand of Hamburg brought out two important collections containing much English music in 1606 and 1609. The younger Balthasar Schmid's keyboard tablature of 1607 ends with 12 galliards. A few passamezzo complexes for lute are in the Gresse manuscript and the tablature of J. Arpinus. In general, groupings in all this production are confined to *Tanz–Nachtanz* pairs, with other dances distributed at random in the sources or else (especially in the case of galliards) arranged by type.

With the exception of the lute tablatures of Anthoine Francisque (*Trésor d'Orphée*, 1600) and the expatriate J. B. Besard (*Thesaurus*, 1603), and an anonymous collection of *Airs nouveaux et chansons à dancer ... bransles, voltes, courantes, ballets & autres* (1608), there is a remarkable lack of dated sources for French dance music from these years. But the evidence of what remains and of slightly later sources like Robert Ballard's lute tablature of 1611 makes it clear that the typical suites were sets of airs from ballets or the traditional sets of branles. Other dances were classified by type – Besard devoted whole volumes to a single type. Within these volumes, pieces with the same tonic (but sometimes with different tunings of the bass strings) were grouped together. The French were not interested in dance pairs of the German type, though the varied repeats in Ballard's pieces exhibit a richly developed technique based perhaps on English models but with less of the character of 'divisions'.

Across the Channel, the pavan–galliard complexes continued, reaching their limit of expansion perhaps in Scotland with William Kinloch's 'lang' pavan and galliard for keyboard from Duncan Burnett's music book (*c*1610). This set, which runs to no fewer than 243 long bars, has the usual varied repeats in the pavan, and the resulting complex is again varied. But what is not so common is that the galliard is entirely based on the pavan and duplicates its pattern of variations (Caldwell).

The impulse towards new suite-like groupings seems to have emanated from England, the chief agents being William Brade and Giovanni Coprario. But there is no evidence to prove that the former did not find the stimulus for his ideas in Germany, or the latter for his in Italy; nor is it possible to say anything more precise about Coprario's fantasia-suites than that they must have been written before his death in 1626. Nothing is known of Brade before his appearance as an established musician on the Continent in 1594; his suites *a 5*, consisting of paduana, galliard and either 'allmand' or 'coranta', cannot be completely explained by reference either to English or German practice, though his coupling in certain instances of a canzona (i.e. a free contrapuntal piece) with dance movements suggests a possible link with Coprario. In any case, the first publication anywhere to consist of suite-like groupings as a series of uniformly constituted composite works was Peuerl's *Newe Padouan, Intrada, Däntz und Galliarda* of 1611. The individual dances were simply numbered consecutively, as was to be the practice for the next 75 years, but the tenfold recurrence of four dances in the order indicated by the title, the key unity, and above all the similarity of thematic material make clear the composer's intention to compose integrated 'suites'.

The climax of this brief evolution, Schein's *Banchetto musicale* (1617), contains 20 sequences of paduana, *gagliarda*, *courente*, *allmande* and tripla. Here, the principle of decreasing stylization cited above (§2) can be seen at its clearest: the richly polyphonic five-part pavanes in the English manner resolve gradually to the less complicated textures of the popular allemande (the German *Tantz*) and tripla, the simplicity of these last two reflected in the reduction of the number of parts from five to four. The dances of each suite were so ordered 'dass sie beydes in *Tono* und *inventione* einander fein *respondiren*' (composer's preface); and indeed the thematic correspondence among the more stylized dances is varied, elaborate and often subtle. The tripla, on the other hand, is merely the allemande (itself a kind of reduction of the preceding dances to thematic essentials) transformed metrically, in the manner of an extemporized *Nachtanz*.

A year later, Isaac Posch (like Peuerl, an Austrian) published his *Musicalische Ehrnfreudt*, with some *Balletten* and 15 sets of three thematically related dances of which the second, a *Tantz*, corresponds to Schein's *allmande* and is similarly followed by its tripla. The first dance is either a galliard or a courante. Posch's title and foreword supply precious information about the way this music was used. As one might imagine, it was played at dinner, banquets, weddings and 'andern erlichen Conviviis' in distinguished households; but the composer wrote that the *Balletten* were most suitable for the table, while the suites could be used either at table or afterwards for dancing. On the extemporizing of *Nachtänze* (he used the term 'Proportion'), he complained that the practice by 'most composers' of omitting the *Nachtanz* allows each musician to play it as he likes, leading to great disorder. A correct *Proportion*, such as the 'most distinguished present-day dancers' are accustomed to, is therefore provided for each *Tantz*.

The variation suite of three or more dances occupies but a tiny corner of published German dance music of the first 20 years of the 17th century – four collections out of more than 50, all appearing between 1609 and 1618. Its importance was a matter of high musical quality rather than of representative or seminal force. Brade, Peuerl and Posch all went on to publish later collections, but none continued with the suite idea, reverting to the more usual pairs and miscellanies. The vitality went out of the variation suite, and although suites of thematically related dances continued to be written throughout the 17th century, they never again constituted a systematic collection like the *Banchetto musicale*.

The *Terpsichore* of Michael Praetorius (1612) was altogether exceptional, and belongs rather to the history of French dance music than to German. Praetorius said in his preface that most of the more than 400 tunes were given him by Antoine Emeraud, dancing-master to the Duke of Brunswick; those, Praetorius himself harmonized. Others had been composed by P. F. Caroubel, and of still others Praetorius had the treble and bass and supplied the inner parts. The melodies, if not all the settings, may safely be taken as representative of the repertory of the French court violinists under Henri IV. Somewhat less than half the collection is taken up with ballets and suites of branles. To what extent the former are complete or the latter were assembled by Praetorius himself is not clear. Neither the suites of branles nor the ballets always stay in the same key. The second set of branles, called 'Branle simple de Novelle', has its first six tunes (the same as the first six in the *Ballet des cornemuses*, R. Ballard, 1614) transposed from D to C because players might find the key of D 'sehr schwehr und gar zu frembd'! There follow four tunes in D minor or D major and two more in C, after which one is to finish the suite with nine tunes from the preceding set, which is in G major and minor. Nothing is said about transposing to bring all these dances into the same key, though a general remark giving licence to transpose occurs in the preface. Transposition is not indicated for the ballets, however, which sometimes drift through several keys (*Ballet de Monseigneur le prince de Brunsweig*; *Ballet de Monsieur de Vendosme faict a Fontainebleau*). The dances of the ballets are not thematically related. Some of the branle groups, however, are subtly unified through a similarity of the melodic curve (II) or of motifs (XIV).

5. THE CLASSICAL SUITE BEFORE THE ADDITION OF THE GIGUE. The 'classical' suite (the inverted commas are a reminder that the meaning is not 'the suite of the Classical period') is a historical fact but not a taxonomic necessity, and it need not be defined narrowly. It is understood to be a group in one key containing allemande, courante, sarabande and gigue in that order (hereafter identified as A–C–S–G). The question whether the gigue must be the final piece or whether additional pieces may come after it is important for those interested in theories of 'open' and 'closed' form as applied to the suite, but it is of little historical moment. Reduplication of the dances, especially courantes, the addition of *doubles* (variations), the interpolation of pieces among the basic four dances, and the presence of introductory movements do not affect the 'classical' status so long as the basic condition is met that the suite should be of reasonable length for playing in a single sitting.

The development of the classical suite took place in two stages, marked off by the introduction of the gigue in the years around 1650. The gigue was never very firmly attached, however, and suites with an A–C–S core continued to be written in great numbers. Suites lacking one or two of these dances may be said at least to bow in the direction of 'classicism' if the remaining ones come at the beginning or just after the introduction. The beginning of this development can be located quite accurately in the decade 1620–30 and on the London–Paris axis; but at what point on the axis it occurred, or on the initiative of which composers, is not yet known.

Allemandes and courantes are found in considerable numbers in Netherlands publications beginning around 1570, and when the two dances are listed in titles, the allemandes are usually mentioned before the courantes. This conventional order (with or without interpolated dances) persists in titles and is reflected in collections throughout the history of the two dances. It is so ubiquitous, in fact, that one must remind oneself that A–C pairs are extremely rare and can in no sense be considered an ancestor of the classical suite. The two dances are first found in regular juxtaposition only in connection with the sarabande, whose introduction seems to have had a catalytic effect on the formation of the suite. The first musical examples of the sarabande do not predate 1595, and the French type, the one incorporated into the classical suite, is much later (Devoto). The initiative for the A–C–S group must have lain in one of three places: with the Parisian lutenists, with the dancing-masters of the French court, or with composers of English consort music, especially William Lawes. Lefkowitz claimed for Lawes a version of his *Royall Consort* dating back to the 1620s, which would put him among the first to combine A–C–S in one suite. Yet the first such groups that can be firmly dated occur in the *Tablature de mandore de la composition du Sieur Chancy* (Paris, 1629). This little-known publication, perhaps the most important single milestone in the history of the suite, contains six 'pre-classical' suites and a suite of branles whose contents deserve to be listed in full: *Recherche* (a kind of unmeasured prelude) A–3C–S–*passemaise*–chanson–*volte* (*Ie veux mourir au cabaret*); recherche–A–2C–S; recherche–A–2C–S;

recherche–A–3C–S; 7 branles; *recherche*–A–2C–S– *Les Rocantins*; *recherche*–A–2C–*volte pour Dardon*–S. It is not likely that a completely new kind of suite was invented for such a modest instrument as the mandora; furthermore, there is nothing tentative about the arrangement of these suites: the A–C–S core is unvarying.

The appearance of A–C–S groups coincides with two other developments that tend to support the hypothesis that it was the French lutenists who were responsible: the introduction of new tunings for the lute and a thoroughgoing transformation of the style of the allemande from the square-phrased, popular Renaissance type to the stylized, quasi-contrapuntal, irregularly phrased type of the 17th century. In 1623 Robert Ballard had issued a collection entitled *Tablature de luth de differents auteurs sur l'accord ordinaire et extraordinaire*, in which some of the pieces evidently required modifications of the traditional Renaissance tuning (the *vieil ton*: G–D–F–A–D–G); unfortunately nothing remains but the title-page. In 1631 the same publisher put out a collection in which the *vieil ton* was abandoned altogether in favour of two new ones: G–C–F–A♭–C– E♭ and G–C–F–A–C–E. Here, for the first time, tunings may be observed influencing suite groupings. In Ballard's anthology, a dozen pieces by François de Chancy are divided into two groups of entrée (another term for an unmeasured prelude)–A–3C–S, the first in A♭ using tuning no.1 and the second in C using the other tuning. Later in the same collection, two A–2C–S groups by Chevalier are similarly differentiated, though the suite in tuning no.2 is in D minor instead of C. A looser and perhaps more typical group is that by Dufaut, all in one key and one tuning, and consisting of P–4A–5C–2S.

In 1625 Charles I married Henrietta Maria, sister of Louis XIII, and with the new queen came a new wave of French musical influence, which was felt especially as it impinged on the court masque. The sarabande, rare in masques before 1632, appeared suddenly after that date in 'hundreds' of examples at the end of A/Ayre–C– S suites (Lefkowitz, *Trois masques*, 1970, p.19). At the same time, manuscript copies of Lawes's *Royall Consort* began to proliferate in which the number and order of the particular pieces is never the same, but the scheme A/Ayre+–C+–S (+ means one or more), sometimes introduced by a pavan or a fantasia, frequently recurs in key groups as simple as A–C–A–C–S or as extended as Ayre–A–C–Echo–C–S–Pavan–3Ayres–C– 2S–2Ayres–2C–A–C–S. His 'Harpe Consorts' are much more uniform; but in neither series are the suite groups marked with any headings.

There can be no doubt that the initiative for A–C–S formations lay elsewhere than in keyboard music. There is but one keyboard source containing allemandes, courantes and sarabandes even part of which can be dated with any certainty in the 1620s; this is a German keyboard tablature originating possibly in Rostock and bearing against one piece in the first section the date 1626 (*DK-Kk* kgl.samml.376). The allemandes, courantes, and sarabandes in this part cannot possibly be connected in groups, however (as has been claimed); the only plausible groups in the manuscript are much later and are in any case under the heavy influence of French lute music. The compilation of an important Sweelinck source (*D-Lü* Lynar A 1), though it may have begun as early as 1615 (Breig, Gustafson), extended over decades. There is but one A–C–S group and it comes at the very end. With a fantasia that precedes it, it is set off by peculiarities which, while reinforcing the impression that a suite is intended, suggest that it was added well after the rest of the manuscript was complete. Not far back are eight courantes, most or all arranged from French lute pieces, showing that the compiler could not have written down his suite in ignorance of the Parisian repertory.

There is no evidence in French sources for a keyboard equivalent of the first lute suites; indeed, before 1650 there are no French keyboard sources of any kind that contain the classical suite dances, much less suites. Evidently French harpsichordists improvised diminutions on fashionable *airs* during this period, as Mersenne illustrated with Pierre de La Barre (iii)'s fragmentary variations on *O beau soleil* (1636), but the sudden appearance of all the suite dances and a few suites in numbers of keyboard manuscripts immediately after 1650 provides circumstantial evidence of a development of the genre extending back several years.

The situation with French orchestral music is similar to that of keyboard music: the first source after *Terpsichore* is the Kassel manuscript, written between approximately 1650 and 1668. Here, along with sets of branles, are half a dozen A–C+–S sequences, incorporated in larger groups. The background to these groupings can only be surmised: the music is French, but the setting was German, and by the time the manuscript was begun the Germans had already begun publishing ensemble suites using allemande, courante and sarabande.

Italy's contribution to the classical suite can be briefly summarized. In ensemble music, the Italians kept the old Renaissance classification of dances by genre until well after the mid-century. The various groupings characteristic of the mature *sonata da camera* became general usage only in the 1660s and 1670s (Klenz). Torelli's *Concerti da camera* (1686), 12 three-movement suites for two violins and bass, begins with a single A–C–S; all the other groups are different. Harpsichord music was also conservative in its arrangement; not until late in the century with Pasquini are suite groups found in any quantity, and these are based not on the classical model but on the *sonata da camera* (Apel). In 1650, Bernardo Gianoncelli ('Il Bernardello') published a theorbo tablature containing original little groups of 'tasteggiata', 'gagliarda' and 'spezzata' – the first being a prelude and the last a *double* of the second. Only the guitarists seemed to care for the A–C–S arrangement (A. M. Bartolotti, 1640; Francesco Corbetta, 1643; G. B. Granata, 1651).

The first appearance of A–C–S groups in Germany occurred in keyboard music, as mentioned above, apparently under French influence. The keyboard tablature of Regina Clara Imhoff of Nuremberg, compiled probably between about 1630 and 1645 for home use, has allemandes, courantes and sarabandes, but they are not grouped as suites. Not until J. E. Kindermann and Froberger (i.e. nearly 1650) was there a firm acceptance of A–C–S. Ensemble music lagged as well. The title of Andreas Hammerschmidt's *Erster Fleiss* (1636) seems to acknowledge both the classical grouping and its origin: *Paduanen, Galliarden, Balletten, Mascheraden, Françoischen Arien, Courentten, und Sarabanden*; but the contents are a patternless succession of dances and keys. Kindermann's *Deliciae studiosorum* (1640–43) is nearly as loose in its organization, though there is an occasional sarabande at the end of a key group. Sarabandes are also included in Nicolaus Bleyer's *Erster Theil newer Paduanen* (1642), but it was not until the late 1640s that the typically German conception of the suite as a composite whole, a conception so brilliantly realized by Schein a generation before and soon after abandoned by German composers, began to regain its hold. Rosenmüller (1645, 1654, 1667). Johann Neubauer (1649), Nikolaus Hasse and Werner Fabricius (1656), J. H. Beck (1666), C. H. Abel (1674) and also perhaps others known only through the titles of their publications, contributed to the stream of ensemble suites built on the A–C–S core. Most included a ballo either after the allemande or the sarabande, and with the notable exceptions of Froberger and Hasse, began with an introductory piece or two (after a *Paduan*).

6. THE CLASSICAL SUITE AFTER THE ADDITION OF THE GIGUE.

(i) *Germany*. The addition of the gigue to suite formations occurred in the decade surrounding 1650, apparently everywhere at once: in Vienna with Froberger (1649), in France with Denis Gaultier (1650s), with Germain Pinel in Schwerin, in England with Playford (1655) and in Sweden (*S-Uu* 409; see Riedel). As with the first step in the 1620s, there is some reason to think that the Parisian lutenists were again responsible, if not for the original idea, which may have come from England with musicians fleeing the Commonwealth, at least for its dissemination. The Kassel manuscript of French orchestral music (c1650–68) contains one A–C–G–S group, hardly enough to allow the innovation to be imputed to the 24 Violons. Until thorough studies of the manuscript sources of this time are undertaken, the details of precedence are a matter for surmise. The gigue enjoyed only scattered acceptance at first and rarely assumed its classical position at the end; indeed, it took twice as long for A–C–S–G to supersede A–C–S, even partly (it never did completely), as it did for A–C–S to come into normal usage in the first place.

Froberger left only one A–C–S–G suite of unchallengeable authenticity. It was accompanied by five A–C–S suites in a magnificent presentation manuscript of 1649. The French influence on Froberger at this time is manifest in his music and proved by documentation; he is known to have requested pieces by Chambonnières before the 1649 manuscript was written. Between this date and that of a second manuscript containing six suites, Froberger spent three years in Brussels, with visits to Paris and London. His acquaintance with the art of the French lutenists and *clavecinistes* broadened through personal contacts; his decision to make the gigue a regular part of his suites (five out of six in the new collection) and to move it from last to second place, just after the allemande, had some slight precedent in French music, and his binary gigue notation is often found in Denis Gaultier. Still, his music is of a complexity and expressive intensity quite beyond anything French that he could have known, and his cultivation of the suite as a compact, closed unit, often knit more tightly by thematic links among the pieces, was characteristically German, not French.

The A–G–C–S order was remarked on by his contemporary, Matthias Weckmann: 'NB . . . Undt so Setzt er Nun fast alle seine Sachen in Solcher Ordnung. NB' (*US-NH* Ma.21.H.59; after Riedel, p.97). It was found unacceptable and changed to A–C–S–G by Froberger's first publishers, Mortier and Roger, in 1697–8 and by Guido Adler 200 years later (in DTÖ). Such revisions of the music of a great composer by editors in two different ages are striking proof of the stubborn hold of the classical suite on musical thinking. They serve also as a warning always to view with scepticism the arrangement of suites in sources known to have been prepared outside the control of the composer.

It was as if other composers were waiting until Froberger's death (1667) to challenge him on his own ground. Weckmann wrote two keyboard suites in the A–G–C–S order and two with the gigue at the end, but of their dates one can say only that they were composed before his own death in 1674. The titles of ensemble collections by J. H. Beck (1654 and 1666) and K. F. Rieck (1658) indicate an A–G–C–S core with interpolations and additions. But during Froberger's lifetime there was little German suite writing of any kind for keyboard, and what there was (e.g. Kindermann's) was on the A–C–S model. The rich production of ensemble suites was either based on Rosenmüller or lay outside the classical canon altogether. Then, quite suddenly, in the year of Froberger's death, the classical suite came into its own and remained in force to the end. The first A–C–S–G suites to be published in Germany were for neither ensemble nor keyboard, but for lute: Esaias Reusner (ii)'s *Delitiae testudinis* (1667). From then until the end of the century almost every year saw at least one publication of suites built on the classical core for lute, keyboard, ensemble, gamba or violin (not to mention the many manuscripts of uncertain date). The first classical ensemble suites were included in Dietrich Becker's *Musicalische Frühlings-Früchte* (1668); they consist of three sequences of sonata–A–C–S–G. Unless the A–C–S–G suites of Alessandro Poglietti, J. A. Reincken or others known only in late sources have precedence, the first examples for keyboard and the first keyboard suites of any kind to be printed in Germany were the eight in Benedict Schultheiss's *Muht- und Geist-ermuntrender Clavier-Lust* (1679–80). 'Firsts' of which only the titles are known are J. P. von Westhoff's collection of A–S–C–G (the middle dances reversed) for solo violin without bass (1679) and prelude–A–C–S–G suites for gamba by Peter Zachau (1683).

The ensemble suite based on the A–C–S–G core had a rather circumscribed life beginning with Dietrich Becker in 1668 and ending with the introduction of the overture-suite into Germany by J. S. Kusser in 1682. The tradition established before 1650 of including a ballo, usually between the courante and the sarabande, was occasionally observed as late as Jakob Scheiffelhut (1684–5); an equally common piece for insertion was the 'aria'. The majority of ensemble suites began with an Italianate 'sonata', sometimes called 'sonatina' or 'sinfonia'. The first suites to proclaim themselves as such in the title were Dietrich Becker's ensemble suites of 1674 (not 1679); in 1687 C. H. Abel combined the new French overture with A–C–S–G (lost). It should be pointed out again that in the realm of the ensemble suite, the old A–C–S core persisted almost as late as A–C–S–G.

The history of the German classical keyboard suite, so vital to an understanding of Bach, is beset with problems of dating and authenticity. Almost all of Pachelbel's suites have now been relegated to anonymity (Riedel); two by Buxtehude are really Lebègue's; those of Weckmann, Kerll, Buxtehude, Reincken and Böhm resist dating. Almost the only important milestone after Schultheiss that can be precisely dated is Kuhnau's *Neue Clavier-Übung*, 14 *Partien* that appeared in 1689 and 1692, whose planning and style must have deeply influenced Bach. J. P. Krieger's *Sechs musicalische Partien* (1697) were 'practically unknown to his contemporaries' (Riedel). J. C. F. Fischer's *Pièces de clavessin* (1696) were outside the classical canon, having been inspired by the new Lullian orchestral suites. From the points of view of quantity and consistency of design, the suites of Kuhnau, Buxtehude and Böhm, along with the first publications of Froberger 'en meilleur ordre', may be said to have set the classical norm. The departures from the strict sequence of A–C–S–G may be quickly dealt with. Kuhnau's all begin with a prelude or other introduction and some of them close with a substitute for the gigue. In one case the sarabande is replaced by an aria, in one a gavotte is inserted before the gigue, and in several cases dances are provided with *doubles*. In the case of Buxtehude, three missing gigues and a missing sarabande may be copyist's omissions. The provision of an extra sarabande in four of the suites is unusual. Böhm has but one prelude; there is a gigue missing from one suite and replaced in another. (One of Böhm's suites is in the manner of Fischer.) The total number of almost strictly classical suites by these three composers is about 40, to which the ten engraved ones by Froberger should be added. One may assume that Bach knew most of them. In possibly over half of these suites (it is difficult to be sure in many cases) there is some degree of thematic similarity among the pieces, most often between the allemande and courante, but sometimes extending to the others. It is no wonder that these coherent, disciplined works have lured generations of musicologists into misleading theories about the nature of the suite. The German lutenists after Reusner, J. B. Peyer (*c*1672), Jacques Bittner (1682), Silvius Weiss (contemporary with Bach) and possibly others (e.g. J. G. Gumprecht) all adhered to the classical suite, as did Konrad Höffler, in 12 suites for gamba and bass (1695).

(*ii*) *England*. England was the first country to print full classical suites with gigues. Playford's *Court-ayres* (1655) contains among its 245 pieces eight A–C–S–G groups by William Lawes (apparently), Sandley, John Cobb, George Hudson, John Carwarden, William Gregory and (?Valentin) Oldis. One is preceded by a praeludium, one by a pavan–almaine, and one only is incorporated in a larger series; otherwise, all are set off by a change of key or composer, so that they are clearly recognizable as suites. Yet there is evidence that the jigs (gigues) themselves were not considered a regular part of the suite: the ones attached to the two suites by Lawes were put there by the publisher; moreover, Playford's *Masquing Ayres* (1662) seems to repudiate the innovation. Of the 100 pieces from 1655, to which 200 new ones were added, there are but four A–C–S–G suites. Five of the above composers and their suites were omitted, and the jig was dropped from one of Lawes's suites and transferred from the other to a different group.

At this same period, the suite entered English keyboard music in the form of A–C–S groups by Locke (*US-NYp* Drexel 5611, *c*1650) and Thomas Strengthfeild (*GB-Lbm* Add.10337, 1656/7: see Caldwell, 153f), and of A–C–S–G groups by Benjamin Rogers (*GB-Och* 1236) and Sandley (*Musick's Handmaid*, 1663; the same one that was dropped from *Court-ayres*). The allemande by Locke ostentatiously mimics the French *style brisé*, in spite of Locke's recorded contempt for everything French except the occasional courante. Locke's anthology, *Melothesia* (1673), has a Prelude–A–C–S–G by Locke himself and another with a 'rant' in place of the gigue; there is also an A–C–S–G set by Moss. There are other A–C–S–G suites in English sources of the later 17th century by Albert Bryne (Cooper), Blow, Francis Forcer and Purcell. Not only was the classical suite with gigue the exception rather than the rule, however, but those that did exist were no more immune from loss or substitution of members than the compilations in *Court-ayres* (see especially Caldwell, 183ff). Babell's collection (*GB-Lbm* Add.39569) consists entirely of suites compiled from the most diverse authors – English, French, South Netherlands, German. The lute suites in Mace's *Musick's Monument* (1676) end with a 'Tattle de Moy' instead of a gigue; otherwise they are more or less classical. In general, A–C–S, not A–C–S–G, continued to be the most common starting-point for the English suite, but a perusal of the tables of contents of several 17th-and early 18th-century keyboard collections (Caldwell, 182ff, 212ff) suggests that suite writing was a distinctly secondary concern of English musicians in the late Baroque period.

(*iii*) *France*. Contemporary with mid-17th-century developments in England, the first French harpsichord manuscripts since the 16th century began to appear, finally shedding light on the art that Chambonnières, the La Barres, the Richards and perhaps Henry Du Mont had been shaping since the 1630s. The earliest manuscript of importance, completed before 1661 (since it finished with a large collection of autograph organ music by Louis Couperin, who died in that year), is in private hands and inaccessible (Oldham); three more were written probably in the 1660s (*F-Pn* Vm⁷ Rés.674–5, the 'Bauyn Manuscript', the principal source for Louis Couperin's harpsichord music and a major one for most other composers; *F-Pc* Rés.89*ter*, now known to have been written by D'Anglebert; and *F-Psg* 2348). Finally, in 1670, the first engraved collections appeared, the two books by Chambonnières.

In all these sources there is only one example of a fully classical suite in the German sense, that is, with the gigue at the end; it is by Hardel and has A–3C–S–G. Resemblances between the allemande and one of the courantes are discussed and illustrated in §2 above. There are, however, two disguised A–C+–S–G suites in Chambonnières' engraved collections (entirely compiled from existing pieces). The suite in D minor in the first book ends with a gigue misnamed 'courante' in the Bauyn Manuscript and carrying only the title *Les Baricades* in the print; and in the suite in C major in the second book the galliard occupying the place of a sarabande is in fact called a sarabande elsewhere. That the classical suite was 'in the air' is shown by A–C+–S–G sequences (usually followed by other dances in the same key) made up of pieces by different composers (in the Bauyn Manuscript and Rés.89*ter*, later in *US-BE* Parville); such arrangements could hardly have been accidental. *F-Pc* Rés.89*ter*, for example, opens with such a suite in C major: Prelude–A (D'Anglebert)–2C (Chambonnières)–S (Pinel; a transcription)–G (Cham-

2. The opening of the prelude to the third suite from D'Anglebert's 'Pièces de clavecin', i (Paris: Author, 1689)

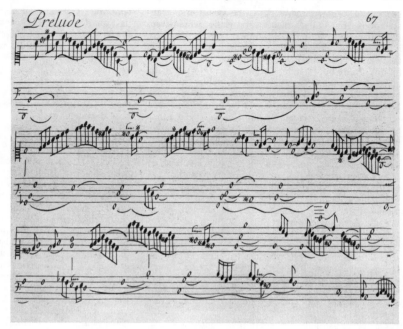

bonnières). All the pieces except the first two have *doubles* (probably by D'Anglebert) and there are a number of other C major pieces after the gigue.

During the half-century preceding the publication of François Couperin's first book of harpsichord pieces (1713), the French suite for all media (along with European instrumental music in general) enjoyed its period of greatest stability; it is perhaps no accident that this period is precisely that of the effective reign of Louis XIV. There was, to be sure, a differentiation corresponding to the different instruments. The lute school, long past its prime, was unconcerned, even at its most systematic, with the classical suite or any other particular arrangement. Denis Gaultier (or his compiler) did produce suites clearly meant to be such in the *Rhétorique des dieux* (c1655), but they, like those in his *Pièces de luth* (1669) and in Charles Mouton's collection of 1698–9, were highly variable in the choice and order of pieces. The large groups organized by key (16–20 pieces) of Jacques Gallot (ii) (1673–5) and Perrine (1680) can hardly be called suites, any more than the frequently cited sequence of 28 C major pieces by Chambonnières in the Bauyn Manuscript. The newly burgeoning school of solo viol music, on the other hand, was remarkable for its adherence to the classical suite. Four viol suites by Du Buisson (first name unknown; in *US-Wc*, 1666) are the first dated prelude–A–C–S–G groups after Playford's for any medium. The violist Machy continued with eight suites of prelude–A–C–S–G–gavotte–menuet (1685; the fourth prelude is a chaconne) which were the first printed pieces for the seven-string gamba. After him were Louis Heudelinne with three prelude–A–C–S–G–gavotte (1701) and Morel with four prelude–A–C–S–G groups, three of them followed by other pieces (1709). All this repertory, previously ignored in writings on the suite, was surveyed by Schwendowius (1970).

The norm for harpsichord music of the same period

was similar to that of the viol suites (not to viol music in general, since the most prolific composer for the instrument by far, Marin Marais, greatly padded and distorted the classical grouping after his first book of 1686). Lebègue's suites (1677 and 1687), which were probably the most influential of all French keyboard music in Germany before Couperin, adumbrate without embracing this norm. There is some reason to think that the order of the engraving is jumbled in places, but one may cautiously infer that the composer had a rather firm idea of a suite beginning with an unmeasured prelude (supplied only in the first book but doubtless expected everywhere in performance), continuing with A–C+–S with occasional *doubles* (these also perhaps to be played even where not supplied), and closing with a group made up of a gigue, a gavotte, a minuet or a pair of them, a bourrée, a canary, or a chaconne. The order of pieces in the closing group may well have been determined by the page-layout of the engraving, but in performance it was quite possibly gigue, gavotte, minuet and one of the remaining. This closing group, usually ending with the minuet, can be descerned in the great majority of the three dozen or so French harpsichord suites by composers between Lebègue and Couperin (D'Anglebert, J. N. Geoffroy, J. F. Dandrieu, Louis Marchand and E. C. Jacquet de la Guerre). Dieupart was the only French harpsichord composer to end each of a whole set of suites with a gigue (and the first to begin with an *ouverture*).

D'Anglebert's suites deserve special mention for a number of reasons not the least of which is their position at the very pinnacle of French harpsichord classicism. Four were published in 1689; more were promised, but only fragments survive. The first three suites are vast structures beginning with unmeasured preludes and covering more than 30 pages each. The full classical core including gigue is there, followed by a closing group with gavotte and minuet. But the most striking feature of these works is the inclusion of transcriptions from Lully, which at first glance would seem to destroy whatever unity they might possess. Yet there is a remarkable consistency of plan in all three. Each falls into three large sections: (prelude)–A–C–S–G, modified only by the reduplication of C, S or G, or the addition of a *double* to one of the courantes; an intermediate section on the lines of a 'closing group' which begins with a galliard, includes a gavotte and a minuet, and in two cases a chaconne or a *passacaille*; and a final section formed on the model of the orchestral suites compiled from Lully's operas and ballets, beginning with an overture and closing with a chaconne (first suite), a *passacaille* (second suite), or an interminable set of variations on the *Folies d'Espagne* (third suite). The first suite (the conclusion is irresistible that these are the actual 'programmes' of the kind that a professional player might use for a concert) has the following order: Prelude–A–C (with *double*)–2C–S–2G; Galliard, *Chaconne en rondeau*, Gavotte, Minuet; Overture (*Cadmus*), *Ritournelle des jées* (*Roland*), Minuet (*Trios pour le coucher du roi*), Chaconne (*Phaëton*). The expansive architecture of D'Anglebert's suites has its one real counterpart in the *Livres de clavecin* of Christophe Moyreau (1753; see §9 below), but it may also have provided a precedent for the long *ordres* in Couperin's first book (1713).

On the basis of the foregoing, two conclusions may be drawn regarding the French harpsichord suite. First, during the third quarter of the 17th century, the suite was above all a way of arranging pieces that had already been composed; in other words, it was a performing order. Pieces in the same key, but not necessarily even by the same composer, were arranged in order to form a little concert programme. In this, French and English attitudes seem to have coincided. Courantes and other dances were sometimes generated out of the material of allemandes, just as one composer borrowed material from another (Du Mont from Constantijn Huygens, Louis Couperin from Froberger, Lebègue from Louis Couperin, Froberger from Chambonnières etc), but this practice did not seem to entail any obligation to respect the integrity of the resulting suite. The same pieces repeatedly appear in different sources, but never the same suites.

The second conclusion is that the French normally put their additional dances after, not before, the gigue; the most usual choices were a gavotte and a minuet (Lebègue seems to have set the fashion for introducing these dances in pairs). What is most frustrating to the logical German point of view (Reimann, *Untersuchungen*, 44f) is the seeming indifference of the French to finishing off their suites with a rousing finale (i.e. a gigue), thus leaving their forms 'open'. This point of view fails, of course, to take note of the fact that many gigues of Louis Couperin, Lebègue and d'Anglebert are anything but rousing, being richly textured, moderately paced and sometimes even sombre. The French suite is also distinguished from the English and German by its common provision of more than one courante.

(iv) Low Countries. The development of the suite in the Low Countries was not unlike that in the surrounding countries, so far as may be seen from the very slim repertory. The ensemble publications of Paulus Matthysz in the 1640s may have inspired Playford's slightly later ones; their contents were similar to contemporary German collections. The Gresse manuscript (last quarter of the 17th century) has Sandley's A–C–S–G from *Musick's Hand-maid* and an anonymous Prelude–A–C–S–G whose pieces are related by head motifs. Bustijn's nine suites (between 1710 and 1716) are more German classical than French, though they do not always end with the gigue. The most significant activity with respect to the suite in the Netherlands was that of the Amsterdam presses, which made possible the wide dissemination of an international repertory for all instruments.

7. NON-CLASSICAL SUITES OF THE HIGH BAROQUE. Except for French-influenced court dancing and entertainments, the classical suite was primarily a vehicle for solo or chamber music (in the modern sense) during a period of about 125 years beginning in the 1620s. The limitless repertory of suites lying outside the classical canon and fading off to merge with other categories can, paradoxically, be dealt with much more summarily, because the categories and types are a function of application, and their history and morphology a matter of externals. The formation and disappearance of suite types responded to practical, dramatic and musical needs that were (and are) a part of other histories than that of the suite: dancing, ballet and theatre; court and civil entertainment; concert programmes; neo-classicism; and so forth. There can be no question of 'development' of the suite across these boundaries, only of bodily transfer, obvious to the observer. It is a curious fact that with the exception of the classical suite and the suite of branles, no conventional order of pieces ever emerged, even within a single category, so that one can hardly speak even of sub-developments of the suite as such.

The alternative to an interminable list of particulars is some kind of classification, but this should be regarded as a mere convenience and not as an exhaustive taxonomy. Standing on a middle ground between classical and non-classical suites are those like Denis Gaultier's (*c*1655–72), which are made of preludes, allemandes, courantes, sarabandes, gigues and other pieces, but in arbitrary and ever-changing sequence. Most of the rest of the middle Baroque suite repertory is derived in one way or another from ballet. There is a very large category, divisible along national lines, consisting of the instrumental music from actual ballets and related entertainments.

This survives almost entirely in manuscript, and very little of it has appeared in modern editions. The Philidor collections for France and those of the Schmelzers in Vienna (*A-Wn* 16583 and 16588) are two of the largest groups of such sources. The Schmelzers, who supplied ballet music for Italian opera in Vienna and for the famous equestrian ballets, often began with an intrada and closed with a retirada, but the dances between varied. Another category (all these are closely related) is made up of collections of instrumental pieces from diverse sources, but especially the operas and ballets of Lully, arranged in arbitrary suites whose pieces were drawn from different works. When such suites begin with an overture, one may speak of a third category; and when new suites were composed expressly in imitation of these, there is another very important category, the 'overture-suite', a speciality of the Germans from J. S. Kusser to Telemann. All of this could be and was used as *Tafelmusik*, but throughout the Baroque period ensemble collections were expressly designated as music for dining, especially by the Germans, and such collections constitute still another category. Any of these ensemble types could be transferred to the keyboard, either directly, as transcriptions, or indirectly, as new compositions in the same manner. Finally, key groups of pieces with titles and no clear identity as dances could form suites, especially for solo instruments. Often such suites began with an allemande, or even an allemande and a courante, as a kind of gesture to tradition, but continued with character-pieces inspired by the moment.

These classifications are far from mutually exclusive. Biber's *Harmonia artificiosa-ariosa* (posth.) and *Mensa sonora* (1680), both collections for entertainment or the table, contain suites whose variety may serve to exemplify many in the latter part of the 17th century. They range from a near-classical arrangement of Sonata–A–C–S–Gavotte–G–Sonatina (a seven-bar 'conclusion'), and a Viennese ballet type with Intrada–Balletto–Trezza–G–Gavotte–G–Retirada, to a French-inspired Prelude–A–Amener (i.e. *branle à mener*)–Balletto–G–Ciacona.

Behind much of the kaleidoscopic non-classical suite production of the middle and late Baroque stood the giant figure of Lully. Though Lully himself wrote almost no suites as such, pieces from his stage works were used almost everywhere for the making of suites. It was for Louis XIV himself that the greatest number of these pastiches were assembled, and their remains are in such manuscripts as *Suite des symphonies des vieux ballets de M. de Lully . . . qui se joüent ordinairement entre les actes des comédies chez le roy* (1703; *GB-T* 255–8), containing 22 sets, each beginning with an overture (in spite of the singular form of 'suite'), and *Suite des symphonies et trio de M. de Lully . . . pour les petits concerts qui se font les soirs devant sa majesté* (1713; *F-Pc* Rés.F 670), containing 66 suites, the titles of which indicate two of the uses to which such suites were put. The works of other composers were used for similar collections (as in *F-V* Mus.1134–8, which contains no fewer than 835 pieces in 83 suites drawn from André Philidor, one of the Marchands, Lalande, Campra and Charpentier). Lalande's *Symphonies pour les soupers du roi* (*F-Pc* Rés.581) were on the same model; a note to the table of contents explains that all the *airs* were taken from Lalande's ballets and divertissements. There are 12 'suites', so called, each of which consists of at least two key groups. The fifth, for example, has Overture–2 *airs*–Chaconne in B♭; 3 *airs*–2S–*Grande pièce ou Caprice* in G; and *Grand air*–Loure–*Trio de haubois*–*Dernier air* in D.

The first original suites along these lines seem to have come out of Germany, with J. C. Horn's five grand ballets 'nach der lustigen Französischen Manier' (1664), Georg Bleyer's *Lustmusik* (1670), again 'nach jetziger Französischer Manier', and most important, the *Composition de musique suivant la méthode françoise contenant six ouvertures de théâtre accompagnées de plusieurs airs* (1682) by J. S. Kusser, who had lived for six years 'in intimate friendship' with Lully. One of the most bizarre figures in the history of the suite requires mention in this context: Gerhard Diessener, who, in works that must have been written between about 1660 and 1673, embodies English, French, German and Italian characteristics in motley profusion. He worked at Kassel during the period when the French musical establishment flourished and the Kassel manuscript was written. An undated English print contains ten suites by him, many beginning with overtures, along with pieces labelled *I beg your pardon, Love me little and love me long*, or *Horrid Music* (complete contents in *MGG*). It is not impossible that further research will reveal Diessener to have been a major carrier of national peculiarities in instrumental music.

Both Frenchmen and Germans followed these initiatives, including Marais (from 1692), Montéclair and J. C. Gillier (1697), Joseph Marchand (1707), L. A. Dornel (1709) and J. D. Mayer (1687 and 1692), P. H. Erlebach (1693), J. C. F. Fischer and B. A. Aufschnaiter (1695), J. A. Schmierer (1698), Georg Muffat (1695–8), Kusser again (1700), Johann Fischer (1702–6), Jakob Scheiffelhut (1707). By 1718 Telemann claimed to have composed no fewer than 200 orchestral suites (autobiography), and he had a good deal to say about the origin of these works: he was stimulated by his youthful acquaintance with Handel; he studied the works of Lully and Campra in Sorau, Polish music in Pless, and more of the French style with Pantaleon Hebenstreit in Eisenach. All these ingredients went into the suites, for which his princely employers seem to have had an insatiable appetite.

8. COUPERIN AND THE 18TH-CENTURY FRENCH SUITE. The ensemble suites of François Couperin may be divided into three categories: *Les nations*, which are *ordres* in Couperin's terminology, combine Italian *sonate da chiesa* with classical suites *à la française*, that is, with (in three cases) pieces after the gigue; 12 of the 14 *Concerts royaux* begin with a prelude, but otherwise vary from classical to quite free (as in no.10, with Prelude–*Air tendre*–*Plainte*–*La tromba*); the remaining two *Concerts*, nos.8 and 9, and the *Apothéoses* are theatrical or programme suites. If Couperin had not revealed the history of *Les nations* (three of the sonatas were written early in his career and the suites added much later), one would suspect a connection with the many German examples of the combination by Rosenmüller, Pezel and others; in fact, they were another exercise in the reconciliation of Italian and French styles.

The ensemble suites were clearly meant to be performed at a single sitting: the *Nations* at 'académies de musique' and 'concerts particuliers', with the sonatas serving as 'introductions' to the suites, and at least some of the *Concerts* at chamber concerts for the king during the years 1713–15. The programmes of the two *Apothéoses* would also have demanded their performance in full. The evidence with regard to the harpsichord music is conflicting, however. On the one hand there is Couperin's statement in the preface to the first book that 'different occasions' supplied the ideas for the various pieces, as reflected in the titles. He spoke of 'pieces' in his preface, never 'suites' or *ordres*. All the pieces in the first book and probably many in the second had been written long before 1713 (the publication date of the first book); six from the first, second and fifth *ordres* had already been published in an anthology in 1707. In the second book, the ninth *ordre* begins with an allemande for two harpsichords and continues with nine pieces for a single player, which would seem rather uneconomical planning. All of this implies an element of pastiche in the formation of these *ordres*, and it suggests that some were never meant to be played from beginning to end.

On the other hand, Couperin referred in the preface to the fourth book to 'My original plan, in beginning the 25th *ordre*', which means that at least this one *ordre* was conceived as a unit. There is further confirmation of a concern for the *ordre* as a form in a change of plan that occurred to the composer after he had written the first piece, in C minor. He decided to put the second in E♭, then return to the tonic. This experiment went awry when the two C minor pieces were lost, so that the *ordre* as engraved begins out of the main key.

There are but five more or less classical suites in the 27 *ordres* (in nos.1, 2, 3, 5 and 8, consisting of five to ten pieces each). They are set off from the rest of the *ordre* by terminology; the dividing line is the end of the dance group and the beginning of the titled pieces. The first *ordre*, for example, has A–2C–S–Gavotte–G– Minuet and 11 titled pieces. The fact that the sarabande and gigue bear supplementary titles does not alter the case. Another nine *ordres* begin with allemandes (sometimes so labelled, sometimes not; some are a special type, invented by Couperin, which begin on the half-bar rather than on the first beat). For at least the first two books, one must assume a prelude as well, chosen from *L'art de toucher le clavecin* (1716). It is a curiosity of these works that except for the token initial alle-mandes, there is no middle ground between the *ordres* with classical suites and those without; no gradual peel-ing away of the courante, sarabande and gigue. An original feature of four of the free *ordres* is the program-matic set-within-a-suite: *Les petits âges* (7), *Les fastes de la grande et anciénne Mxnxstrxndxsx* (11), *Les folies françoises* (13), and a group of bird pieces (14). In addition, there are several programmatically linked pairs or groups of three. An exhaustive analysis of the *ordres* as suites was undertaken by Reimann (*Untersuchungen*), who, in effect, gave up. The free *ordres* are original, personal, and inexplicable: the savour is there, but the recipes have been thrown away.

During the 20 years between Couperin's first book and his death, only four Frenchmen published harpsi-chord collections, but this number was increased to 30 during the following 20 years. The four were Nicolas Siret (1716 and 1719), a conservative; Dandrieu (1724 and 1728) and L. A. Dornel (1731), both imitators of Couperin's free *ordres*; and Rameau (1724 and *c*1728). Couperin's impact on the traditional suite is nowhere more clearly shown than in Dandrieu's repudiation of his first three books of *c*1705–10; the 1724 collection is called 'book 1', and for his last book (1734) he bor-rowed pieces from the early ones, updating the style and substituting modish titles for the dance labels. Rameau's two collections contain four suites in all. Each book begins with a traditional group: A–C–G (actually a pair of rondeaux) and A–C–S respectively; these suites con-tinue with four or five pieces, the second ending with a brilliant set of variations on a gavotte. The ending groups of each book are free sequences showing little sign of planning. The impact of Rameau's collections was as great as that of Couperin's, but his influence was felt in matters of style rather than suite formations.

The history of French harpsichord music after 1730 is usually presented as one of decline, but inventiveness in suite design went on longer in this repertory than in any other, and it was here that the last collection of Baroque suites was published, apparently in 1772, by Dufour (first name unknown). The idea of Couperin's sets-within-suites was expanded by Dandrieu to include divertissements inspired by the theatre; these became very fashionable. Pierre Février (1734) began two of his suites with fugues, the first and last French-man to do so. Demars (1735) began some of his with sweeping preludes in a quite un-Gallic manner; in both cases, a Handelian influence may have operated. In 1753, Christophe Moyreau published six vast suites, two in one book, the last four with a book to themselves, suggesting the same architectural approach seen in D'Anglebert. Each suite opens with an overture and two to five of the traditional dances, followed by up to 14 character-pieces, sometimes including a divertissement. Each suite then continues with a second overture, fol-lowed by a complete sonata, a concerto, or both. The sonatas are modelled after the Corellian *sonata da chiesa* and the concertos after late Baroque Italian examples. Key unity is again challenged by Simon Simon (1761): 'Instead of issuing solo harpsichord suites in the usual way in a single key (which would have caused me to fall into a kind of uniformity and dryness which is better avoided), I thought I ought to compose some with violin accompaniment'. This curious sentence shows that tonal contrast was associated with the ac-companied sonata (dating back to Mondonville in 1734), but it does not prepare the reader to find solo suites with key changes, especially a choice such as E♭ minor–G minor–E♭ major. The preference for three-movement groups in this collection, even when the pieces are labelled as dances, is also reminiscent of the accompanied sonata.

The last harpsichord suites, Dufour's, would seem from their contents to be 50 years behind the times: a prelude, a courante, and two each of A–S–G, though not in that order, and the usual character-pieces interspersed with minuets. The suites have three to seven pieces, all with the same tonic; and only a pair of 'concertos' (which do not change key) at the end seem at all up to date. What is extraordinary, however, is the style – one of the sarabandes, for instance, seems totally devoid of metrical pulse. The French, who probably invented this kind of suite, kept their originality to the end.

9. HANDEL AND THE ENGLISH SUITE. Except for the Water Music and Music for the Royal Fireworks, and such multi-movement overtures as the one to *Rodrigo*, Handel's suite writing seems to have been confined to the keyboard. There are about 22 surviving keyboard suites, the exact number depending on the admission of borderline cases. For example, one would be inclined to exclude the second of the 'Eight Great', as it is a sonata in everything but name. Another five may have existed at one time in a Swiss collection. Handel has acquired the reputation of a 'free thinker' in suite composition. The 'great' suites of 1720, all of which are different, only one being classical (no.4), are seen as an inspired synthesis of Italian and German elements in ever-varying balance. Their perfection is said to lie at polar distance from that of Bach (Beck, p.64). This view needs revision, though there is space here only for conclusions (for evidence, see the writings of Abraham, Dale, W. Smith and Best).

In fact, Handel seems to have taken little interest in the suite as a form. Basically, his conception was con-ventional throughout his life. The two suites he wrote for Princess Louise (*c*1736, Smith; or *c*1739, Best) are purely classical (A–C–S–G), though their styles are sharply differentiated: he evidently wanted to provide the girl with examples of Italian style versus a second style that he may have thought of as German, French or English. A–C–S–G suites are in a majority among his works, and most of the non-classical ones are pastiches explainable in a variety of ways, but rarely, if ever, as an attempt to manipulate form. It is not paradoxical but logical that Handel should be the great composer whose suites are most often unified by thematic means: his technique verges on laziness, and Dale (p.240) was right to point out the risks of monotony he ran in taking the materials of his allemandes into his courantes in so obvious a manner.

The only suite composed almost entirely for the 1720 collection is no.3 in D minor, and it is one of Handel's best. The allemande and courante are related, and masterfully, the most inspired touch being the courante's forthright correction of the 'soft' C♮ in the first bar of the allemande. The air is second-hand, but the new finale was based on its first bar, giving two thematically related pairs. In general, the 1720 collection seems to have been put together from the best pieces, not suites, which already existed; the new additions (with the exception of no.3) were all introductory movements 'to make the Work more useful', that is, to give weight and scale to small groups.

The direct influence of Handel's suites on English keyboard music was slight, though it can be traced in Thomas Chilcot's suites of 1734 (Caldwell) and those of J. C. Smith. There were other foreign influences as well: one of Dieupart's suites, without its overture, was published by Walsh in 1705; the others were probably also known through the composer's teaching activities in England. G. B. Draghi's *Six Select Sutes* (sic) appeared in 1707, a suite by Alexander Maasmann, about 1715, and about the same time a set of six by J. B. Loeillet which perhaps reflected Dieupart's influence, since all have A–C–S–aria/gavotte–minuet–G. Henry Symonds was more varied but equally systematic in his *Six Sets of Lessons* (1733), which contained four A–C–S–gavotte–minuet–G, two with preludes, and two 'sonatas'. The influence of the Italian *sonata da camera* was felt more and more strongly in English harpsichord music beginning, perhaps, with Robert Jones (ii) (1732) and continuing with James Nares, Barnabas Gunn and John Jones. (The final victory of the sonata in England is described briefly in §1 above.)

10. BACH AND THE GERMANS. Bach wrote about 45 suites, setting in them such a standard as to compel all others to be measured against it. They may be surveyed quickly in order of diminishing 'classicism'. At the top are the six cello suites, prelude–A–C–S–X–G, where X is a pair of minuets in the first two, a pair of bourrées in the second two and a pair of gavottes in the last two. Unification among the pieces, obvious in no.3, moves from subtlety to concealment (or non-existence) in no.5, whose allemande and gigue, however, quote the F♯ minor Suite of Gaspard Le Roux, one of the French composers whose music Bach possessed. The next set in the hierarchy, the English suites, begins with another, more extensive quotation from Le Roux, this time the gigue from his A major suite. Dannreuther (*Musical Ornamentation*) discovered a resemblance between Bach's prelude and a Dieupart gigue, but the resemblance to Le Roux is even closer, suggesting that Le Roux (1705) took it from Dieupart (1701) and passed it on. Again the scheme is prelude–A–C–S–X–G, but the

variations are slightly less mechanical: Suite no.1 has a second courante with two *doubles*, nos.2, 3 and 6 have *doubles* for the sarabandes, and although the X's are still all pairs, the repertory is enlarged to include the passepied. The opening bars of A, C, S and G of no.5 in E minor are characterized by a descending scale motif; whether there was a conscious intent to relate the pieces is impossible to say. Except for this, unification is not a feature of the set.

The French suites have no preludes and a varying number of pieces between the sarabande and gigue (one in no.1 and four in no.6). There are no obvious thematic links between the pieces, though Beck (p.59) showed motivic resemblances in no.1, and Pearl (p.265) in no.3. For as long as discussion of Bach's suites goes on, there will be new proposals to explain why these two sets are called 'English' and 'French'. It is possible that whoever attached the labels (it was not Bach) had something definite in mind, but it is certainly not evident in the styles or forms of either collection, unless it is the borrowing from Le Roux, which would make the English suites French. Forkel said the English suites were written for an Englishman; J. C. Bach's copy had 'fait pour les anglois' at the head of Suite no.1. Possibly the other set was called French simply to distinguish it from the English suites.

The climax of Bach's mastery of the suite was reached in the six harpsichord partitas. The forms introduce modest liberties by comparison with the French suites: the fourth and sixth have an aria and an air respectively before the sarabande: the second ends with a capriccio instead of a gigue; and the repertory of inserted pieces further expands to include a burlesca, a scherzo and a rondeau. The sarabande of the Sixth Partita recalls the opening toccata, but in general, thematic connections among the pieces are far from obvious. Pearl claimed intricate but very subtle interrelationships within the partitas in C minor and G major, but such connections are much stronger among the pieces of the solo violin partitas in B minor and D minor. There they are a matter of similar harmonic progressions, similar melodic contours (when stripped of ornament), and similar emphasized scale degrees, all in the first few bars of each piece, where the effect of recall is the most powerful. Each of the three partitas is intentionally different: the first has a bourrée instead of a gigue and brilliant *doubles* to each dance; in the second, the A–C–S–G are hardly more than a composite prelude to the gigantic chaconne; and the last is a piece of *Tafelmusik* (Preludio–Loure–*Gavotte en rondeau*–a pair of minuets–Bourrée–Gigue).

The qualities that set Bach's suites apart from all others have nothing to do, strictly speaking, with the history of the suite. The choices of pieces, their order and any techniques of unification all have their precedents and counterparts. What is unique is Bach's use of the suite as a building-block in a larger structure, not the same thing as De Machy's or Dieupart's stringing together six nearly identical suites. It is a matter of arranging each suite to do something different – or the same thing in a different way – so that the set as a whole becomes a kind of thesaurus of the suite for that particular medium. This encyclopedic approach is clearest in the varied introductions to the keyboard partitas and is essentially didactic. Another quality is Bach's tendency to mask the identity of a genre with writing that is texturally complex and technically demanding.

The sarabande of the Partita in E minor, for example, challenges the player's ability to project the underlying melody and pulse. A third is the tendency to make exercises out of pieces. Thus one suspects, though there is no real evidence, that at least the last three pieces of the Sixth Partita are exercises in notational problems: sheer complexity in the sarabande; the assimilation of duple notation to triple movement in the gavotte; and the proper rhythmic interpretation of a gigue in binary rhythm.

The four orchestral suites do not appear to have been conceived as a set and were written more for public entertainment. Indeed, during the second quarter of the 18th century, the orchestral suite was widely cultivated in Germany as entertainment music; a manuscript in the library of the Thomasschule, Leipzig, contains two dozen overture suites by J. F. Fasch, C. H. Förster, Schneider, Hasse, J. G. Wiedner, J. N. Tischer and Fuchs (?Fux). Other composers in this generation are J. Ludwig Bach, J. Bernhard Bach, probably Pantaleon Hebenstreit (though the authenticity of a collection of suites attributed to him has been questioned), Heinichen, Kuntzen, Johann Pfeiffer and J. D. Zelenka. The most prolific were Graupner, with 87 surviving orchestral suites, and again Telemann, whose total output in this form is put at something approaching 1000 by Büttner; 135 have survived (Hoffmann). This extraordinary fecundity in a foreign form was, of course, a perfect example of the effect of the fragmentation of the Empire on art: the ordinary demands of court music were multiplied by tens and hundreds.

Classical suites were written by the keyboard composers J. M. Leffloth and Vincent Lübeck (1728), Gottlieb Muffat and J. P. Kellner (1739), Krebs (1745), and especially Graupner, whose 57 *Partien* span the years from 1718 to about 1740. Freer keyboard suites, influenced by the orchestra suite or (occasionally) the *sonata da camera*, and sometimes called *Galanterien-Partien*, came from F. A. Maichelbeck (1736), J. C. F. Fischer and F. A. Hugl (1738), J. N. Tischer, Isfrid Kayser and Trippenbach (1746) and J. P. Kellner (1752).

The German lutenists were among the last to relinquish the suite, Silvius Weiss, J. M. Conradi, David Kellner, Adam Falckenhagen and others continuing to write them until mid-century. One of the last uses of the suite in Germany, as in France (see §1 above), was in anthologies, as a convenience in arranging the contents, and probably as a suggestion to the player how to make little programmes. Marpurg's *Raccolta delle più nuove compositioni* (1756) was the first of a projected yearly anthology whose purpose was 'to please everyone', and to this end mingled French, Italian and German pieces in all forms, both vocal and instrumental. The contents of each volume were divided into 12 suites, called *Partita*. For example, no.7 of 1756 had a gavotte in A major (Seyfarth), a pair of minuets in A minor and a rondeau in A minor (C. P. E. Bach).

11. 1750–1900. The disappearance of the suite in the second half of the 18th century was a matter of several quite independent processes. It was the sonata, symphony and concerto that ultimately filled the functions vacated by the suite; and where composers had been writing both suites and the newer types, making a clear distinction, they simply stopped writing suites and went on with the others. More commonly, however, the suite

itself began to undergo modifications and experiments. If the number of pieces was reduced to three, say, A–S–G, and the first two provided with Italian tempo marks instead of the dance titles, the resemblance to a sonata was close – still closer if the sarabande was in a contrasting key. This happened in certain cases – for example, the music of Simon, and it may be seen in the three-movement layout associated with the accompanied sonatas in Jacques Duphly's third harpsichord book (1758), where accompanied 'sonatas' (unlabelled) form part of larger suites. Under the influence of the *sonata da camera*, abstract movements began to appear in suites in positions other than that of the first piece; another way of putting it would be to say that *sonate da camera* began to appear masquerading as suites, as in Handel's second 'great' suite. In orchestral music, the overture, sinfonia and suite overlapped in internal arrangement and terminology, producing an anarchic situation from which the symphony emerged the victor. In England the process was curiously incomplete: the music changed, but the old term, 'overture', persisted.

In Vienna the transition from suite to sonata took place behind the screen of the term 'divertimento' (Webster). The term itself, which was the preferred one for any non-orchestral ensemble piece, light or serious, between 1750 and 1780, overlapped with 'partita', which was a similarly general designation up to about 1760. Both could be used for keyboard music as well; 'divertimento' carried no implication regarding the number or order of movements or the key-scheme. In the earlier part of the century the usual influences had been felt in the *Parthien*: those of the French lutenists in the *Lauthenkonzert* (Jacques de Saint-Luc, J. B. Weichenberger, Hinterleithner and others); of Lully, in the Muffats; of German pedantry in Fux. But the suite was never a favourite vehicle in Austria, and the quantity necessary for statistical observations seems not to have been produced.

The Viennese were much more interested in a genre which has been arbitrarily excluded from consideration here: the sets of ballroom dances which Haydn, Mozart, Beethoven, Schubert, Dittersdorf, Hummel and many others wrote for the annual fancy-dress balls to benefit the Pensionsgesellschaft Bildender Künstler, and for other occasions. Many of these sets of six or 12 dances were organized on symmetrical key-schemes and some had codas. A remote connection with the suite was suggested by Schindler, who referred to Beethoven's *Mödlinger Tänze* as 'einige Partien Walzer'. The Strauss waltz cycles are the offspring of these sets.

Although the suite survived after 1800 in ballet, incidental music, periodical anthologies, potpourris and military music, the word itself had acquired strong classical (A–C–S–G) associations, so that in dictionaries and ordinary musical thinking of the period the entire concept was regarded as something that belonged to the past. This did not prevent the proliferation of sets of pieces meant to be performed at a sitting; it simply released them from a generic term and from the conventions associated with it. To write a 'suite' then became an exercise in an archaic form, as it was with Mozart's K399/385i, inspired by the Bach and Handel concerts at Baron van Swieten's home in 1782. The introduction, which is a prelude and fugue adumbrating the great fantasia for automatic organ K608, runs into the allemande without a break. The work remained a torso, and the experiment seems not to have been repeated for half a century.

Freed from *a priori* conceptions of what the form ought to be, at least one composer, Schumann, appears to have seized the idea of the suite as a way of combining a number of small romantic gestures into a larger whole, with no inherited restrictions inhibiting their more subjective interrelations. To a greater degree than in any other composite form, the resulting structures were determined and generated by the materials themselves, and the suites made out of them differed utterly from one another. Possibly such a set as Beethoven's op.126 *Bagatelles* served Schumann as a model, but more likely is the example of the song cycle, in which the ultimate unifying force is the poetic idea, and the freedom to invent musical interrelations is absolute. *Papillons*, *Kreisleriana*, *Carnaval*, *Faschingsschwank aus Wien* and the others (not all the Schumann piano sets are units, however) are too varied and too few to furnish the basis for any classification system. None of them is called a suite, but one can perhaps guess at Schumann's reaction to being told they were suites from his remark in the review of William Sterndale Bennett's *Suite de pièces* op.24 (1841) quoted above. Sterndale Bennett's work (the English seem to have been pioneers of the suite in the 19th century as well as the 17th) is in six movements with Italian tempo headings (pr. in MB, xxxvii, 38).

A curious link between the suite and the song cycle is afforded by Joachim Raff's *Die schöne Müllerin*, a work for string quartet in six movements whose four-hand piano arrangement is called 'suite'. The same work provides a link with a third genre through its sub-title, *Cyklische Tondichtung*; in fact, the historical continuum between the orchestral programme suite and the programme symphony, via the symphonic poem in several titled movements, admits no division into separate genres except on the basis of the composers' terminology. The first and only systematic attempts to revive the suite as an alternative to the sonata and symphony were made between about 1857 and 1880, by Franz Lachner and Raff. If Raff's *Italian Suite* in E minor was written 'during his time at Weimar', that is, before 1856 (Riemann, *Geschichte der Musik seit Beethoven*, p.429), this would make it among the earliest. Raff's suites, which number over a dozen, were written for a wide variety of media: piano, orchestra, piano and orchestra, violin and piano, violin and orchestra, and quartet; at least nine of these were also arranged for piano duet. They have four to seven titled movements in a variety of key-schemes, and all the usual Baroque types appear interspersed with more up-to-date pieces such as *moto perpetuo*, *Rhapsodie* and *Romanze*. Occasionally a suite is nothing but a sonata under another name (e.g. op.162 for piano, 1870–71, whose movements are Elegie in Sonatenform, Volkslied mit Variationen, Ländler, Märchen).

Close to the time when Raff wrote his first suite Woldemar Bargiel brought out his Piano Suite op.7, as well as a number of sets of character-pieces undesignated as suites. Another group were the eight orchestral suites by Lachner (1861–74). Here also, the movements were titled and each suite had its sarabande, gigue, minuet and so on; but the distinction between suite and symphony was sometimes arbitrary. Suite no.1 op.113 (1861), for example, has Praeludium, Menuet, Variationen und Marsch (there are 23 variations) and

Introduction und Fuge, which is suite-like enough until one realizes that the first movement is in full sonata form with a repeated exposition. Another Praeludium is a sonata-form piece in French overture style. Among the few suites by J. G. Rheinberger (1880–1900) is one for the unusual combination of organ, violin, cello and orchestra (Con moto, Thema mit Veränderungen, Saraband-trio, Finale).

Saint-Saëns seems to have been one of the first to follow Sterndale Bennett with a suite (1866), so designated, which was free from dances or other echoes of the 18th century. It is a big virtuoso work for cello and piano, consisting of a perpetual-motion prelude (D minor), serenade (G minor), scherzo (E♭ major), romance (E major) and finale (D major). Op.49 (1877) for orchestra and op.90 (1892) for piano both introduce two or three of the old dances, while op.60 (1881), the *Suite algérienne*, is a programme suite with Prélude, Rhapsodie mauresque, Rêverie du soir and Marche militaire française. By 1880 the suite was no longer a curiosity in France, and Massenet had begun his series of nine orchestral suites, most of them programmatic and the last two with singers and a speaker. During the last decades of the century, composers of peripheral countries (especially northern ones) found the suite a congenial form for music of an exotic or nationalistic flavour (Grieg, Asger Hamerik, N. V. Gade, Sibelius, Nielsen, Tchaikovsky, Rimsky-Korsakov, Glazunov and MacDowell).

The suite of extracts had since the 17th century always been a major ingredient of the concert repertory; it continued thus throughout the 19th century (e.g. Schumann's *Manfred, poème dramatique: fragments disposés en suite d'orchestre*) and remains so in the 20th. Such suites are extracted by the composer himself or by anyone who can secure the right to do so. The pieces, if suitable (as may happen with a ballet), can simply be selected and reproduced without alteration. If there are voice parts these can be removed or worked into the instrumental texture. The keys may be changed, the medium changed (as with a piano reduction, for example), the pieces shortened, run together or provided with bridges between them, introductions and conclusions added – in effect the whole thing may be rewritten. An extreme example is Stravinsky's *Pulcinella*, in which a subtle stylistic transformation takes place in addition to the other liberties.

12. 20TH CENTURY. The factors which led to the re-emergence of the suite as a major form in the 20th century had all appeared by the end of the 19th: the historicism, the nationalism, the urge to experiment, the academic associations of sonata and symphony, and, in the case of extract suites, the expediency. But after the turn of the century, every one of these factors intensified. Musicology began to bring to light some of the vast forgotten suite literature of the Baroque period, and the winds of neo-classicism (which more often meant neo-Baroque style) began to blow away the Wagnerian mists. The breakdown of the tonal system in certain circles discouraged sonata writing, and the search for new styles and forms became ever more conscious and systematic. Finally, the 'market' for music increased exponentially for well-known reasons.

For a time the suite *à l'antique* enjoyed a considerable vogue among composers, including Hindemith (after Gervaise), Strauss (after Couperin), Egk (after

Rameau), Stravinsky (after pseudo-Pergolesi), Schoenberg, Debussy and Respighi, to name only a few. At the other end of the stylistic spectrum were the 'characteristic' suites, which continued the late 19th-century tradition of nationalistic and 'geographical' suites. These programme suites are most often for orchestra and range in tone from serious (e.g. Holst's *The Planets*) to the frankly popular (e.g. Grofé's *Grand Canyon Suite*). They have a function analogous to that of extract suites, and one type merges into the other.

But it was neither the antique suite, the characteristic suite, nor the extract suite which became the vehicle for the most advanced and original contributions of the 20th century. These three types were recognizable as suites and were often even entitled suites. As such they had associations unattractive to a composer determined (as many in the 20th century have been) not to be derivative. It was the suite idea, unrecognized (or differently named) and consequently free, that underlay the originality of, for example, Lawes, Couperin and Schumann and that has served and continues to serve composers whose ideas result in sets of pieces meant to be performed at a sitting. As Beck remarked in the case of Schumann: 'What are these if they are not suites?'. One of the first in the 20th century to make the set of pieces his own was Satie; *Chapitres tournés en tous sens* (1913) will have to serve as one example for many. But throughout the first 75 years of the 20th century the suite has served composers in many ways and for many reasons: Schoenberg's Five Orchestral Pieces (1909) at one end of the period and Stockhausen's *Momente* at the other frame a multitude of works in which the relationship of the parts to the whole is newly worked out in each. Ample scope remains for the investigation of this repertory from the standpoint of the history of musical sets.

BIBLIOGRAPHY

Brown I
T. Arbeau: *Orchésographie* (Langres, 1588; Eng. trans., 1948)
P. Spitta: *Johann Sebastian Bach* (Leipzig, 1873–80, 5/1962; Eng. trans., 1884–99/R1951)
M. Seiffert: *Geschichte der Klaviermusik* (Leipzig, 1899/R1966)
K. Nef: *Zur Geschichte der deutschen Instrumentalmusik in der zweiten Hälfte des 17. Jahrhunderts* (Leipzig, 1902/R1973)
H. Riemann: 'Zur Geschichte der deutschen Suite', *SIMG*, vi (1904–5), 501
S. Condamin: *La suite instrumentale* (Paris, 1905)
T. Norlind: 'Zur Geschichte der Suite', *SIMG*, vii (1905–6), 172–203
J. Ecorcheville: *Vingt suites d'orchestre* (Paris and Berlin, 1906/R1970)
A. Arnheim: 'Englische Suitenkompositionen des xvii. Jahrhunderts und ihre in Deutschland erschienenen Sammlungen', *IMusSCR*, iv *London 1911*, 93
H. Quittard: 'Les origines de la suite de clavecin', *Courrier musical*, xiv (1911), 675, 740
E. Wellesz: *Die Ballett-Suiten von Johann Heinrich und Anton Andreas Schmelzer* (Vienna, 1914)
L. Brav: *Die Entwicklung der Tanzfolgen für Orchester bis zur Mitte des 30-jährigen Krieges* (Berlin, 1921)
K. Nef: *Geschichte der Sinfonie und Suite* (Leipzig, 1921/R1970)
P. Nettl: 'Die Wiener Tanzkomposition in der zweiten Hälfte des 17. Jahrhunderts', *SMw*, viii (1921), 64
F. Blume: *Studien zur Vorgeschichte der Orchestersuite im 15. und 16. Jahrhundert* (diss., U. of Leipzig, 1921; Leipzig, 1925/R1973)
H. Besseler: *Beiträge zur Stilgeschichte der deutschen Suite im 17. Jahrhundert* (diss., U. of Freiburg, 1923)
W. Fischer: *Zur Chronologie der Klaviersuiten J. S. Bachs* (Leipzig, 1925)
F. Kahle: *Georg Friedrich Händels Cembalosuiten* (diss., U. of Berlin, 1929; Eisenach, n.d.)
G. Oberst: *Die englische Orchestersuiten um 1600* (Wolfenbüttel, 1929)
J. Dieckmann: *Die in deutscher Lautentabulatur überlieferten Tänze des 16. Jahrhunderts* (Kassel, 1931)
E. Meyer: *Die mehrstimmige Spielmusik des 17. Jahrhunderts in Nord- und Mitteleuropa* (Kassel, 1934)
R. Münnich: *Die Suite: musikalische Formen in historischen Reihen* (Berlin, 1934/R1957)
G. Abraham: 'Handel's Clavier Music', *ML*, xvi (1935), 278
H. Büttner: *Das Konzert in den Orchestersuiten Georg Philipp Telemanns* (Wolfenbüttel, 1935)
E. Epstein: *Der französische Einfluss auf die deutsche Klaviersuite im 17. Jahrhundert* (Würzburg, 1940)
M. Reimann: *Untersuchungen zur Formgeschichte der französischen Klaviersuite* (Regensburg, 1940/R1969)
G. Walter: 'Unbekannte Klavierkompositionen von G. F. Händel', *SMz*, lxxxii (1942), 141
K. von Fischer: 'Zur Satztechnik von Bachs Klaviersuiten', *GfMKB, Lüneburg 1950*, 124
F. Lesure: 'Die Terpsichore von Michael Praetorius und die französische Instrumentalmusik unter Heinrich IV', *Mf*, v (1952), 7
M. Reimann: 'Zur Entwicklungsgeschichte des Double', *Mf*, v (1952), 317; vi (1953), 97
K. Dale: 'The Keyboard Music', *Handel: a Symposium*, ed. G. Abraham (London, 1954/R1969), 233
W. Smith: 'Catalogue of Works', *Handel: a Symposium*, ed. G. Abraham (London, 1954/R1969), 275
L. Moe: *Dance Music in Printed Italian Lute Tablatures from 1507 to 1611* (diss., Harvard U., 1956)
M. Pearl: *The Suite in Relation to Baroque Style* (diss., New York U., 1957)
M. Lefkowitz: *William Lawes* (London, 1960)
G. Oldham: 'A New Source of French Keyboard Music of the Mid-17th Century', *RMFC*, i (1960), 51
F. Riedel: *Quellenkundliche Beiträge zur Geschichte der Musik für Tasteninstrumente* (Kassel, 1960)
L. Schierning: *Die Überlieferung der deutschen Orgel- und Klaviermusik* (Kassel, 1961)
W. Klenz: *Giovanni Maria Bononcini of Modena* (Durham, North Carolina, 1962)
H. Beck: *Die Suite*, Mw, xxvi (1964; Eng. trans., 1966)
D. Heartz: *Preludes, Chansons, and Dances for Lute* (Neuilly-sur-Seine, 1964)
D. Starke: *Frobergers Suitensätze* (diss., U. of Munich, 1964)
D. Devoto: 'De la zarabanda à la sarabande', *RMFC*, vi (1966), 27
D. Heartz: 'A 15th-century Ballo: *Rôti bouilli joyeux*', *Aspects of Medieval and Renaissance Music: a Birthday Offering to Gustave Reese* (New York, 1966), 359
——: 'Hoftanz and Basse Dance', *JAMS*, xix (1966), 13
W. Apel: *Geschichte der Orgel- und Klaviermusik bis 1700* (Kassel, 1967; Eng. trans., rev., 1972)
W. Breig: *Die Orgelwerke von Heinrich Scheidemann* (Wiesbaden, 1967)
L. Schrade: *Die handschriftliche Überlieferung der ältesten Instrumentalmusik* (Tutzing, 1968)
A. Ashbee: 'John Jenkins's Fantasia-suites', *Chelys*, i (1969), 3
M. Ellis: 'Inventory of the Dances of Jean-Baptiste Lully', *RMFC*, ix (1969), 21–55
A. Hoffmann: *Die Orchestersuiten Georg Philipp Telemanns* (Zurich, 1969)
C. Field: 'Matthew Locke and the Consort Suite', *ML*, li (1970), 15
M. Lefkowitz, ed.: *Trois masques à la cour de Charles Ier d'Angleterre* (Paris, 1970)
B. Schwendowius: *Die solistische Gambenmusik in Frankreich von 1650 bis 1740* (Regensburg, 1970)
T. Best: 'Handel's Keyboard Music', *MT*, cxii (1971), 845
J. Johnson: *The English Fantasia-suite ca. 1620–1660* (diss., U. of California, Berkeley, 1971)
H. Upper: *A Study of Selected Twentieth-century Keyboard Suites* (diss., Indiana U., 1971)
B. Cooper: 'Albertus Bryne's Keyboard Music', *MT*, cxiii (1972), 142
——: 'The Keyboard Suite in England before the Restoration', *ML*, liii (1972), 309
J. Caldwell: *English Keyboard Music before the Nineteenth Century* (Oxford, 1973)
A. Ashbee: 'Towards a Chronology and Grouping of some Airs by John Jenkins', *ML*, lv (1974), 30
J. Webster: 'Towards a History of Viennese Chamber Music in the Early Classical Period', *JAMS*, xxvii (1974), 222
B. Gustafson: *The Sources of Seventeenth-century French Harpsichord Music* (diss., U. of Michigan, 1976; Ann Arbor, 1979)
M. Parker: 'Some Speculations on the French Keyboard Suites of the Seventeenth and Early Eighteenth Centuries', *IRASM*, vii (1976), 203

DAVID FULLER

Suitner, Otmar (*b* Innsbruck, 16 May 1922). Austrian conductor. He studied the piano under Weidlich at the Innsbruck Conservatory, and under Ledwinka at the Salzburg Mozarteum, 1940–42, as well as conducting under Clemens Krauss, whom he acknowledges as his model. After performing chiefly as a pianist and occasional conductor for some years, he became musical director of the Pfalz orchestra at Ludwigshafen in 1957, and then secured more frequent guest engagements at Berlin, Hamburg, Munich, Vienna and elsewhere. The turning-point of his career was in 1960 when he was appointed chief conductor of the Dresden Staatsoper and Staatskapelle, with which he toured in east Europe and the USSR. In 1964 he was appointed general music director of the Deutsche Staatsoper. He conducted the premières there of Dessau's *Puntila* (1966) and *Einstein* (1974), and toured with the Berlin company to Cairo, Lausanne, Paris and Warsaw. His Berlin performances of Mozart, Wagner and Strauss are much praised, and he is also widely admired in the Italian repertory (his mother was Italian). His interpretations are marked by freshness of expression and wide dynamic range, consistent with the score but fashioned from an Apollonian intellect with a fine sense of form. He has undertaken guest engagements in various European countries, in the USA (San Francisco Opera, regularly from 1969) and in Japan, where he was made honorary conductor of the Tokyo NHK SO in 1973. The German Democratic Republic has awarded him its Nationalpreis.

Suivez (Fr.: 'follow'; imperative of *suivre*). A direction in musical scores that has two different meanings. It can indicate that the next movement or section is to follow immediately, like the Italian word 'attacca'. Or it can direct that the accompanying parts are to follow a voice or solo instrument which happens for the moment to move independently of the prescribed rhythm or tempo, as in the Italian *colla voce* or *colla parte*.

Suk, Josef (i) (*b* Křečovice, 4 Jan 1874; *d* Benešov, nr. Prague, 29 May 1935). Czech composer and violinist.

1. Life. 2. Works. 3. Style.

1. LIFE. He learnt the piano, the violin and the organ from his father, Josef Suk (1827–1913), schoolmaster and choirmaster in the Bohemian village of Křečovice. In 1885 he entered the Prague Conservatory, where he studied the violin with Bennewitz, theory with Foerster, Knittl and Stecker, and from 1888 chamber music with Wihan. He began composing seriously in his third year at the conservatory and in 1891 graduated with his Piano Quartet op.1. He remained an extra year at the conservatory for special tuition in chamber music with Wihan and composition with Dvořák, who had joined the teaching staff in January 1891. Under Wihan, Suk played second violin in the group which in 1892 became known as the Czech Quartet; its first concert in Vienna (1893) won the approval of Brahms and Hanslick and inaugurated a distinguished international career during which it gave more than 4000 concerts until Suk's retirement in 1933. Under Dvořák, Suk graduated from the conservatory in 1892 with his *Dramatická ouvertura* op.4. He was Dvořák's favourite pupil and in 1898 married his daughter Otilie (Otylka). Simrock had published his Serenade for strings op.6 (1892) in 1896 on Brahms's recommendation and by the turn of the century Suk was regarded, with Novák, as the leading composer of the modern Czech school. In 1922 he was appointed professor of composition for the advanced classes of the Prague Conservatory, where he trained 35 composers, including Bořkovec, Ježek, Hlobil, Martinů, Reiner, Vačkář and several Yugoslavs. During his four

terms as rector (1924–6, 1933–5) he worked energetically to raise the standards of the conservatory. He was an extraordinary (1901) and ordinary (1913) member of the Czech Academy of Sciences and in 1933 was awarded an honorary doctorate by Brno University.

2. WORKS. Suk won early success as a composer, writing some of his best-known pieces (the Serenade for strings and the *Píseň lásky*, 'Song of love', from his op.7 piano pieces, 1891–3) before he was 20, and was soon regarded as Dvořák's natural successor. Despite opportunities through his constant travels as a performer to hear the latest European novelties he was subject to no other strong musical influences; his virtuoso orchestral technique and subtle control of sound show his awareness of Strauss and the French impressionists, but he followed his own path in a steady, organic development from lyrical Romanticism towards a complex polytonal musical language.

Like his teacher Dvořák he was most at home with instrumental music. His early mass, the *Křečovická mše* (1888–9), was his only venture into liturgical music; he wrote almost no songs; and the three choral sets of 1900, opp.15, 18 and 19, though well made and effective, are essentially explorations of a genre to which he returned only once more with his male-voice choruses op.32 (1911–12). He wrote no operas but the second of the two plays for which he supplied incidental music, *Pod jabloní* ('Beneath the apple tree'; op.20, 1900–01), includes sustained choral scenes which give the suite (1912) arranged from it an almost oratorio-like character. As in the earlier score *Radúz a Mahulena* ('Radúz and Mahulena', 1897–8), there are, in addition to the instrumental pieces, a few short songs and some melodrama passages for important scenes.

It is surprising that as a professional quartet player Suk wrote so little chamber music. Much of it originated from his student days as he tried out various combinations (the String Quartet in D minor, 1888; Piano Trio op.2, Piano Quartet op.1 and Piano Quintet op.8, 1889–93). The most successful chamber work from this period is the String Quartet op.11 (1896), which has all the freshness and melodic charm of Suk's early music and, in its slow movement, a foretaste of the more serious and personal style of *Asrael*. He wrote only one more quartet (op.31, 1911). Although his only important works for the solo violin are the well-known Four Pieces op.17 (1900) and a one-movement concerto, the Fantasy op.24 (1902–3), the sound of the solo violin combining with the orchestra is one that permeates much of Suk's music, from the famous *Radúz* solo onwards. Suk was also a fine pianist, performing frequently to his friends and occasionally in public, and he wrote rather more piano music. The earlier compositions were generally published in small groups of characteristic pieces (opp.7, 10 and 12, 1891–6) whose full-blooded, well-placed chords suggest Brahms, but whose undemanding forms, rich if meretricious harmony, melodic clichés and fluent passage-work more often suggest the salon. The Suite op.21 (1900, originally planned as a sonatina) attempts a more balanced design, continued in the programmatic suites *Jaro* ('Spring') op.22a and *Letní dojmy* ('Summer moods') op.22b, both written in 1902 after the birth of his son. They illustrate Suk's subjective Romantic piano style at its ripest, the last piece of op.22a, *V roztoužení* ('In love'), achieving a popularity similar to that of the *Song of Love* from op.7.

But op.22a also contains *Vánek* ('The breeze'), a delicate, impressionistic piece, revealing a more imaginative approach to figuration, and a type of harmony that was turning from heavy chromaticism to a more modal idiom. These qualities, and the intimate nature of *O*

Josef Suk

matince ('About mother'; op.28, 1907), written after the death of his wife, are developed in Suk's greatest work for the piano, the suite of ten short pieces *Životem a snem* ('Things lived and dreamt'; op.30, 1909). All have detailed descriptions of their character, some have additional programmes (no.5 'on the recovery of my son') and all inhabit a very personal world; in their economical evocation of mood, their exploration of new musical means and their assured piano technique they foreshadow Debussy's *Préludes*.

Suk's central achievement was in orchestral music. The high point of his early orchestral writing is the Serenade for strings op.6 (1892) and the op.16 suite, *Pohádka* ('Fairy tale', 1899–1900), arranged from the *Radúz* music. The more ambitious works that followed, the Violin Fantasy op.24 (1902–3) and the Straussian tone poem *Praga* op.26 (1904), have a slightly portentous quality that seems out of keeping with Suk's limited emotional range up to then. The deaths of Dvořák (1904) and his daughter (1905), Suk's young wife, within the space of 14 months shattered the composer's life and attitudes and set into motion the vast *Asrael* symphony op.27 (1905–6). It is arguably his greatest work, and one of the finest and most eloquent pieces of orchestral music of its time, comparable with Mahler in its structural mastery and emotional impact, but without Mahler's neuroticism. Together with his next three orchestral works, *Pohádka léta* ('A summer's tale'; op.29, 1907–9), *Zrání* ('The ripening'; op.34, 1912–17) and *Epilog* op.37 (1920–29, revised up to 1933), it makes up a huge symphonic cycle, united by Suk's moving and

pure-hearted striving to come to terms with himself, with nature around him and with his ultimate fate. *A Summer's Tale* is the lightest of these, a suite more than a symphony, showing a serene acceptance of life whose equanimity is only briefly disturbed by the poignancy of the 'Blind Musicians' movement or the Mahlerian imagery of the fourth movement, 'In the Power of Phantoms'. *The Ripening* (the harvest of nature and of man) is a massive, superbly sustained symphonic poem whose complexity of language and structure was developed in the *Epilog*, with soloists and chorus singing biblical passages to express more concretely a meditation on the last things of man.

3. STYLE. Unlike most of his Czech contemporaries, Janáček, Vycpálek and Novák, Suk derived almost no stimulus from folk music and very little from literary sources. Julius Zeyer's was the only important literary influence on him: his *Radúz and Mahulena*, with its legendary Slavonic world, its message of true, courageous love and clearcut moral values articulated much of the young Suk's outlook on life. Its dreamy, slightly sad, introspective mood is one that runs through much of Suk's early music, at first no more perhaps than as a fin-de-siècle pessimism, but soon acquiring a specifically Slavonic direction characterized by his dumka music. Suk wrote dumkas in opp.7 and 21 (the *poco triste* movement of op.17 was also originally entitled 'Dumka') but there are dumka-like movements (such as the *Legenda* of op.10) in all his early music. The funeral march is another *Radúz* feature, anticipated in Suk's early orchestral funeral march (1888, dedicated to himself), apotheosized in the second movement of *Asrael* and becoming terrifyingly grim in the march section of *The Ripening* (based on the seventh piece, marked 'forthright, later with an expression of overpowering force', of *Things Lived and Dreamt*). In the polka music for the 'game of the swan and the peacocks' in *Radúz* (later worked into the second movement of the suite) Suk wrote in a popular style, clearly Czech but independent of Czech folksong. There are other such pieces among the piano music (notably the minuet from op.21) and even during the years of *The Ripening* and *Epilog* Suk wrote light, appealing music such as the *Ella Polka* (1909) or the marches *V nový život* ('Towards a new life'; op.35c, 1919–20), which won him an award at the 1932 Olympics at Los Angeles, and *Pod Blaníkem* ('Beneath Blaník', 1932). His last composition was a Czech dance, a *Sousedská* (1935) for small chamber ensemble.

Radúz is central to Suk's development. He identified the young couple Radúz and Mahulena with himself and his wife at the happiest time of their lives; it drew from him his most radiant, tender, earnest and abundantly melodic music. He remodelled some of it in his next work, the women's choruses op.15. It also became a point of reference for future works, its death motif of two augmented 4ths recurring prominently from *Asrael* onwards. There are other examples in Suk's later music (notably in his most private work, *Things Lived and Dreamt*) of self-quotation and other personal symbols, understandable in a composer thrown so much on to himself and his inner life. One facet of his music which cannot be traced back to *Radúz* is that found in the series of 'fantastic dances'. Early examples are the 'Bacchanale' in *Beneath the Apple Tree* (1900–01) and the *Fantastické scherzo* op.25 (1903), a *danse macabre* with banal waltz rhythms, quirky chromatic tunes and highly imaginative orchestration. Later metamorphoses in the scherzo movements of *Asrael* and *A Summer's Tale* suppress the dance element and heighten the malevolence of the fantasy.

Suk's late orchestral music had become very complicated. His harmony was originally sensuously Romantic, with a fondness for augmented chords, chromatic alteration, Neapolitan relations and the tonal ambiguity produced by frequent pedals (e.g. in pedal movements such as the lullaby from *About Mother* and the second movement of *Asrael*); he now began to exploit polytonality more explicitly and systematically, achieving a pungency and dense harmonic texture in *The Ripening* and *Epilog* that borders on atonality. Suk's type of melody changed less: he continued to employ weak-beat openings, two-note slurrings, melodies with characteristic leaps of 3rds and 6ths, and well-defined tunes permeated by the same intense lyricism; but these features became less prominent once regular periodicity was loosened and when obscured in the complex polyphonic web of orchestral sound. Suk was able to make these last scores comprehensible only by his precise aural imagination and his superb craftsmanship as an orchestrator, a skill on which he placed great emphasis as a teacher.

Suk's later formal control grew from unpretentious beginnings. Most of his piano pieces have simple repetitive structures; he successfully employed (e.g. in the violin *Balada*, 1890) the fashionable monothematicism of the time but his early attempts at sonata form, even in the last movement of the Serenade for strings, are uneven, lacking a sense of the dramatic opposition of key centres (so striking in *Asrael*) and tending towards an uncharacteristic long-windedness. The seams of the one-movement Violin Fantasy are carelessly concealed, but the later single-movement string quartet is much more subtle and adept. It cost Suk much effort, even at the height of his powers, and prepared the way for the impressive single span of *The Ripening*. *The Ripening* and *Epilog* showed Suk's musical language at its utmost sophistication. They also showed him dangerously far from his roots as a simple 'muzikant' of the Czech *kantor* tradition. From about 1912 his rate of composition noticeably slackened. His tiring life as a performer meant that composition was a spare-time occupation; his duties at the Prague Conservatory, which he took very seriously, made further demands, but as the premières of his works became more spaced out it became clear that neither these commitments nor the increasing effort that the later scores must have cost fully explained the gaps. Suk seems to have had misgivings about his increasingly complicated musical speech, alien to many of his listeners; indeed, he derived a childlike pleasure from the enthusiasm that his popular pieces (like the *New Life* march) aroused. In view of his sudden death it is not clear whether the *Epilog* was to have marked the end of his creative life or merely the end of one line of its musical development.

WORKS

op.

ORCHESTRAL AND VOCAL ORCHESTRAL

— Planned works: Ve stínu lípy [In the shade of the lime tree], sym. cycle after S. Čech, 1896; cycle of sym. poems from Czech history, 1915–17
— Early compositions, str: Fantasy, d, 1888; Smuteční pochod [Funeral march], c, 1889, rev. 1934
4 Dramatická ouvertura, a, 1891–2
6 Serenade, E♭, str, 1892
9 Pohádka zimního večera [Tale of a winter's evening], ov. after Shakespeare, 1894, rev. 1926
14 Symphony, E, 1897–9
16 Pohádka [Fairy tale], suite from Radúz a Mahulena, 1899–1900
24 Fantasy, vn, orch, 1902–3
25 Fantastické scherzo, 1903
26 Praga, sym. poem, 1904
27 Asrael, sym., 1905–6
29 Pohádka léta [A summer's tale], sym. poem, 1907–9
— Pod jabloní [Beneath the apple tree], 5 tableaux from op.20, A, SATB, orch, 1911–12
34 Zrání [The ripening], sym. poem, 1912–17
35a Meditace na staročeský chorál 'Svatý Václave' [Meditation on an old Czech hymn 'St Wenceslas'], str/str qt, 1914
35b Legenda o mrtvých vítězích [Legend of the dead victors], commemorative piece, 1919–20
35c V nový život [Towards a new life], march, 1919–20; pf duet version, 1919
37 Epilog, sym. piece (Pss, Moses, Zeyer, arr. Vycpálek), S, Bar, B, SATB (small), SATB (large), orch, 1920–29, rev. up to 1933
— Pod Blaníkem [Beneath Blaník], march, 1932, orchd J. Kalaš

PIANO

— Early compositions: Sonata, C, 1883, unpubd; Ov., 1884–5, unpubd; Polonaise, ?1886–7; Untitled piece, B♭, ?1886–7; Untitled piece, G, 1886–7; Jindřichohradecký cyklus [Jindřichův Hradec suite], 1886–7; Fugue, c, 1888, unpubd; Fugue, c, 1890, also arr. str qt, 1890, both unpubd
— Tři písně beze slov [Three songs without words], 1891
5 Fantaisie-polonaise, 1892
7 [6] Piano Pieces, 1891–3
— Capriccietto, G, 1893
— Humoreska, 1894
— Lístek do památníku [Albumleaf], 1895
10 Nálady [Moods], 5 pieces, 1895
12 [8] Piano Pieces, 1895–6
13 Sonatina, g, 1897, rev. as op.21
— Vesnická serenáda [Village serenade], 1897
— Bagatelle arr. of original third movt of Sym., op.14, 1898
21 Suite, 1900
22a Jaro [Spring], 5 pieces, 1902
22b Letní dojmy [Summer moods], 3 pieces, 1902
28 O matince [About mother], 5 pieces, 1907
— Psina španělská [Spanish joke], 1909
30 Životem a snem [Things lived and dreamt], 10 pieces, 1909
33 Ukolébavky [Lullabies], 6 pieces, 1910–12
36 O přátelství [Friendship], 1920
— Episody [Episodes]: slow movt of Sonatina op.13, 1897; Ella Polka, 1909; Lístek do památníku [Albumleaf], 1919 or 1920; O štědrém dni [About Christmas Day] [orig. 2-part song with vn], 1924

CHAMBER

— Early compositions: Polka, G, vn, 1882; Str Qt, d, 1888; Fantasy, d, str qt, pf ad lib, 1888
1 Piano Quartet, a, 1891
2 Piano Trio, c, 1889, rev. 1890–91
— Balada, d, str qt, 1890
3/1 Balada, d, vc, pf, 1890
3/2 Serenade, A, vc, pf, ?1898
— Balada, d, vn, pf, 1890
— Melodie, 2 vn, 1893
8 Piano Quintet, g, 1893
11 String Quartet, B♭, 1896; last movt rev. 1915 but left as independent piece
17 Four Pieces, vn, pf, 1900
23 Elegie (Pod dojmem Zeyerova Vyšehradu) [Under the impression of Zeyer's Vyšehrad], vn, vc, str qt, harmonium, harp, 1902, unpubd; arr. for pf trio, 1902
31 String Quartet, 1 movt, 1911
35a Meditace na staročeský chorál 'Svatý Václave' [Meditation on an old Czech hymn 'St Wenceslas'], str qt/str orch, 1914
— Quartet movt [rev. last movt of op.11], 1915, unpubd
— Bagatelle (S kyticí v ruce) [Carrying a bouquet], fl, vn, pf, 1917
— Sousedská, 5 vn, db, cymbals, triangle, large and small drums, 1935

CHORAL AND SONGS

— Křečovická mše [Křečovice mass], B♭, SATB, str, org, 1888–9, rev. before 1932
— Songs: Hory, doly, samý květ [In full bloom over hill and dale] (J. V. Sládek), 1890, lost; Ukolébavka [Lullaby] (B. Mühlsteinová), child's v, pf, 1891; Noc byla krásná [The night was beautiful] (V. Hálek), 1891; Ach wärst du mein (Lenau), ?1892, inc.; Mé ženě [To my wife] (Sládek), 1902
— Nechte cizí, mluvte vlastní řečí [Speak your own and not a foreign

tongue] (J. Kollár), TTBB, 1896
15 Ten Songs (Slavonic trad.), SSA, pf 4 hands, 1899
18 Four Songs (Serbian trad.), TTBB, 1900
19 Three Songs (Cz. trad., Slovak trad., F. J. Čelakovský), SATB, pf ad lib, 1900
32 Male Choruses (Slavonic trad.), TTBB, 1911–12
—   O štědrém dni [About Christmas Day], 2 vv, vn, 1924

INCIDENTAL MUSIC

13 Radúz a Mahulena [Radúz and Mahulena] (J. Zeyer), A, T, reciters, SATB, orch, 1897–8, rev. 1912
20 Pod jabloní [Beneath the apple tree] (Zeyer), A, reciters, SATB, orch, 1900–01, rev. 1911, 1915 (vocal score only)

Principal publishers: Breitkopf & Härtel, Český Hudební Fond, Hudební Matice, Státní Nakladatelství Krásné Literatury, Hudby a Umění, Simrock, Státní Hudební Vydavatelství, Universal, F. A. Urbánek, M. Urbánek

BIBLIOGRAPHY

ČSHS [incl. detailed list of works and bibliography]
K. Hoffmeister: *Asrael, Pohádka léta, II. smyčcový kvartet* [Asrael, A Summer's Tale, Second String Quartet] (Prague, 1912)
Zrání [The Ripening] (Prague, 1919) [incl. Talich's analysis]
'Na počest 60. narozenin Josefa Suka' [In honour of Suk's 60th birthday], *Tempo/Listy Hudební matice*, xiii (1933–4), no.5 [incl. Suk's view on his development as a composer, Květ's study of Suk and Zeyer, and other documents and reminiscences]
J. M. Květ, ed.: *Josef Suk: život a dílo: studie a vzpomínky* [Life and works: studies and reminiscences] (Prague, 1935) [incl. articles by Květ, K. Hoffmeister, V. Štěpán, O. Šourek, B. Vomáčka, O. Šín, B. Štědroň, K. Reiner, A. Hába, F. Pícha, M. Bezděk, H. Boettinger, and a list of Suk's published works]
J. M. Květ: *Josef Suk* (Prague, 1936) [obituary for the Czech Academy of Sciences]
J. M. Květ, ed.: *Z pamětí Českého kvarteta* [From the reminiscences of the Czech Quartet] (Prague, 1936)
J. Šach, ed.: *Josef Suk: vzpomínková mozaika* [A mosaic of reminiscences] (Prague, 1941)
R. Newmarch: *The Music of Czechoslovakia* (London, 1942/R1969), 201ff
V. Štěpán: *Novák a Suk* (Prague, 1945) [repr. of 3 substantial essays on Suk]
J. M. Květ, ed.: *Živá slova Josefa Suka* [In Suk's own words] (Prague, 1946)
O. Filipovský: *Klavírní tvorba Josefa Suka* [Suk's piano works] (Plzeň, 1947)
J. M. Květ: *Josef Suk* (Prague, 1947)
J. Berkovec: *Josef Suk (1874–1935): život a dílo* [Life and works] (Prague, 1956, 2/1962, rev. and abridged 1968 as *Josef Suk*; Eng., Ger., Fr. and Russ. trans., 1968) [all versions contain full list of works and extensive bibliography]
M. Skalická: 'Význam thematické práce v prvním kompozičním období Josefa Suka', [The importance of thematic work in Suk's first creative period], *MMC*, ii (1957), 115
J. Zich: 'Instrumentace smyčcové serenády Josefa Suka' [The instrumentation of Suk's Serenade for strings], *Živá hudba*, ii (1962), 165 [incl. Ger. summary]
J. M. Květ: *Josef Suk v obrazech* [Suk in pictures] (Prague, 1964)
V. Lébl: 'Vítězslav Novák o Josefu Sukovi' [Novák on Suk], *Vítězslav Novák: život a dílo* (Prague, 1964), 366
R. Budiš, ed.: *Josef Suk: výběrová bibliografie* [select bibliography] (Prague, 1965) [incl. chronological and alphabetical catalogues of works, annotated bibliography, and discography]
Z. Sádecký: *Lyrismus v tvorbě Josefa Suka* [Lyricism in Suk's works] (Prague, 1966) [incl. bibliography, commentary on sources, list of Suk's articles, speeches and letters]
M. Kuna: 'Josef Suk Václavu Talichovi: korespondence z Talichovy pozůstalosti' [Suk to Talich: correspondence from Talich's estate], *HV*, vii (1970), 356–89
A. Payne: 'Case of Neglect II: . . . Suk's *Zrání*', *Music and Musicians*, xix/8 (1970–71), 22
Z. Sádecký and V. Lébl: 'Josef Suk', *Dějiny české hudební kultury 1890–1945*, i (Prague, 1972), 153
V. Štědroň: 'Josef Suk a jeho žák' [Suk and his pupil], *OM*, iv (1972), 14
E. Hlobil: 'O Josefu Sukovi' [On Suk], *HRo*, xxvii (1974), 34
S. Jareš and E. Illingová: 'Josef Suk a České kvarteto' [Suk and the Czech Quartet], *HV*, xi (1974), 386 [iconography]
J. Rozanovová: 'Klavírní kvintet Josefa Suka ve srovnání s Klavírním kvintetem Sergeje Tanějeva' [Suk's Piano Quintet compared to Taneyev's]; J. Doubravová: 'Secesní rysy díla Josefa Suka' [*Jugendstil* traits in Suk's works]; L. Ginsburg: 'České kvarteto v Rusku' [The Czech Quartet in Russia], *Česká hudba světu: svět české hudbě*, ed. J. Bajer (Prague, 1974), 132; 138; 151

JOHN TYRRELL

Suk, Josef (ii) (*b* Prague, 8 Aug 1929). Czech violinist, grandson of Josef Suk (i) and great-grandson of Dvořák. He was taught from childhood by Jaroslav Kocian, whose pupil he remained until Kocian's death in 1950; he also studied at the Prague Conservatory until 1951, and then with M. Hlouňová and Alexander Plocek at the Prague Academy (1951–3). He first appeared in public in 1940. In 1948 he was chosen to take part in exchange concerts in Paris and Brussels, but it was a Prague recital in 1954 that confirmed his maturity as an artist. At this time he was leading the orchestra for drama productions at the Prague National Theatre, where he was engaged from 1953 to 1955. A continuing interest in chamber music from his student days brought about his leadership of the Prague Quartet (1951–2) and his formation in 1952 of the Suk Trio, with Josef Chuchro (cello) and Jan Panenka (piano). He occasionally appears with the Smetana Quartet as the first viola in Dvořák's String Quintet in E♭, op.97.

Suk's reputation as a violinist flourished more widely from 1959, when he appeared as soloist with the Czech PO on a tour of three continents; he has also made a number of world tours with the Suk Trio. He was named soloist of the Czech Philharmonic from 1961, and made his British début at the 1964 Promenade concerts in concertos by Mozart and Dvořák, when he was highly praised for his silken tone, expressive fervour and immense technical skill. His playing reveals his clear perception of style and content, expressed with a rich fund of lyric feeling that avoids excessive display. He plays violins by Antonio Stradivari (the 'Libon' dated 1729), Guarneri del Gesù ('Prince of Orange', 1744) and Giovanni Guadagnini ('Ex Vieuxtemps', 1758), and his many gramophone records, which include an outstanding album of unaccompanied Bach, have won several international awards. He retains a particular interest in sonata playing and formed a duo with Zuzana Růžičková in 1963 and a trio with Janos Starker and Julius Katchen for two years before Katchen's death in 1969, as well as recording with Panenka and appearing with Stephen Bishop-Kovacevich and other pianists. Suk received a Czech State Prize in 1964, was named Artist of Merit in 1970 and National Artist in 1977.

BIBLIOGRAPHY

ČSHS
J. Kozák: *Československtí koncertní umělci a komorní soubory* [Czechoslovak concert artists and chamber ensembles] (Prague, 1964), 143ff
R. Budiš: *Slavní čeští houslisté* [Famous Czech violinists] (Prague, 1966), 173f
J. K.: 'V tradici houslové slávy' [In the tradition of violin glory], *HRo*, xxi (1968), 64
J. Bártová: 'Permanentně přerušovaný interview s Josefem Sukem' [Permanently interrupted interview with Josef Suk], *OM*, iii (1971), no.4
J. Creighton: *Discopaedia of the Violin 1889–1971* (Toronto, 1974), 739ff

ALENA NĚMCOVÁ

Suk, Václav [Váša, Vyacheslav Ivanovich] (*b* Kladno, 16 Nov 1861; *d* Moscow, 12 Jan 1933). Russian conductor and composer of Czech birth. After studying the violin at the Prague Conservatory and composition privately with Fibich, he spent his career in Russia from 1880 and is regarded there as among the most distinguished Soviet conductors: he was created People's Artist in 1925. He became leader of an opera orchestra in Kiev, 1880–82, and then from 1882 to 1887 was a violinist in the orchestra of the Bol'shoy Theatre. From 1885 he became known as a conductor in various

Russian cities and in 1906 was appointed a conductor at the Bol'shoy, remaining until 1932. From 1927 he was also principal conductor of the Stanislavsky Opera Theatre in Moscow. He was much esteemed for his thoroughness in operatic preparation, and Gozenpud called him one of the best interpreters of Rimsky-Korsakov's works. He also appeared as a concert conductor. A memorial concert at the Bol'shoy on 12 March 1933 included Suk's symphonic poem, *Jan Hus*. Among his other works is an opera with Czech text by J. V. Frič, *Lesův pán* ('Lord of the forests') based on K. H. Mácha's verse classic, *Maj* ('May'): it was first produced in Russian translation at Kharkov in 1900, and in Czech at Prague in 1903.

BIBLIOGRAPHY

I. Remezov: *Vyacheslav Ivanovich Suk* (Moscow and Leningrad, 1933)
——: *V. I. Suk* (Moscow and Leningrad, 1951)
A. Gozenpud: *Russkiy sovetskiy opernĭ teatr* (Leningrad, 1963)

ARTHUR JACOBS

Šulek, Stjepan (*b* Zagreb, 5 Aug 1914). Yugoslav composer, conductor and violinist. He completed his studies in the violin under Huml at the Zagreb Academy of Music, where in 1945 he was appointed professor of composition. Although he has played the violin as a soloist and in chamber music, he is better known as a conductor, since it was under his direction that the Zagreb Radio Chamber Orchestra grew into a fully professional body, giving successful concerts in many European cities. Šulek has evolved an individual style from a union of Baroque polyphony with Romantic expressiveness, a combination of structural clarity and great intensity of feeling expressed in the broadly designed movements of his orchestral pieces. A typical example is the Symphony no.2 'Eroica', an expression of Šulek's conviction that truth and justice must overcome the destructiveness of war. His opera *Koriolan* is symphonically built from leitmotifs; his 'classical concertos' take the Baroque concerto grosso as a model, colouring the counterpoint with brilliant instrumentation. Among the solo concertante works the Violin Concerto is outstanding for the beauty of its slow movement.

WORKS
(selective list)

Operas: Koriolan (Šulek, after Shakespeare), Zagreb, 12 Oct 1958; Oluja [The tempest] (Šulek, after Shakespeare), Zagreb, 28 Nov 1969
Orch: 6 syms., 1944, 1946, 1948, 1954, 1963, 1966; 3 classical concs., 1944, 1952, 1957; concs. for pf, 1949, 1951, 1970; vc, 1950; vn, 1952; bn, 1958; va, 1959; cl, 1967; hn, 1972; org, 1974; Epitaph, 1971
Other works: The Last Adam (cantata, after S. S. Kranjčević), 1964; Pjesma mrtvog pjesnika [The song of a dead poet] (song cycle, D. Cesarič), 1971; pf pieces

Principal publisher: Jugoslavenska akademija znanosti i umjetnosti

BIBLIOGRAPHY

K. Šipuš: *Stjepan Šulek* (Zagreb, 1961)
K. Kovačević: *Hrvatski kompozitori i njihova djela* [Croatian composers and their works] (Zagreb, 1966), 465ff
——: *Muzičko stvaralaštvo u Hrvatskoj 1945–1965* [Musical creation in Croatia 1945–65] (Zagreb, 1966)
'Estetika Stjepana Šuleka: sintetični pregled osnovnih koncepcij' [The aesthetics of Stjepan Šulek: a synthetic survey of his basic conceptions], *MZ*, v (1969), 101

KREŠIMIR KOVAČEVIĆ

Suling. The Indonesian term for any vertically played bamboo ring flute. The upper end is closed by a node which has a flat rattan band or ring wound around it. The node itself is chipped off at one point of the edge so that the air from the player's lips passes through the opening and over the soundhole cut in the back of the pipe just below the rattan ring. The instrument has four

to six finger-holes. It is an essential part of the Sundanese *kacapi* ensemble that accompanies the singing of classical poetry, the Sundanese *gamĕlan dĕgung*, the central Javanese gamelan, and the Balinese *gambuh* ensemble with its gigantic flutes (*see* INDONESIA, fig.8). Another Balinese ensemble, the *gong suling*, consists principally of from 15 to 25 flutes.

See INDONESIA, §§III, 1(iii), IV, 1(iii).

ERNST HEINS

Sulla tastiera [sul tasto] (It; Fr. *sur la touche*; Ger. *am Griffbrett*). In string playing, to bow near or over the fingerboard, resulting in a flute-like tone. *See* FLAUTANDO.

Sullivan, Sir **Arthur (Seymour)** (*b* Lambeth, London, 13 May 1842; *d* London, 22 Nov 1900). English composer and conductor. Although he was considered the leading British composer during his lifetime, his serious works have failed to establish a lasting popularity. His comic operas, however, particularly those written to librettos by W. S. Gilbert, represent a peculiarly English style of operetta which achieved an exceptional and lasting renown and made Sullivan one of the most widely popular of all British composers.

1. Early career. 2. Maturity. 3. Posthumous reputation. 4. The comic operas.

1. EARLY CAREER. His mother, Mary Clementina Coghlan, was of Italian extraction and his father, Thomas Sullivan, was an Irishman who became bandmaster at the Royal Military College, Sandhurst, and later professor of brass instruments at the Royal Military School of Music, Kneller Hall. From his father he early gained a keen musical appreciation and in April 1854 he entered the Chapel Royal as a chorister, on the recommendation of Sir George Smart. He remained there until 1858, receiving instruction from the Rev. Thomas Helmore; his sacred song *O Israel* was published by Novello in 1855. In July 1856 he became the first holder of the Mendelssohn Scholarship at the Royal Academy of Music where he became a pupil of Sterndale Bennett, Arthur O'Leary and John Goss. As an extension of the scholarship he then went to the Leipzig Conservatory (1858–61), studying counterpoint and fugue with Moritz Hauptmann, composition with Julius Rietz, conducting with Ferdinand David and the piano with Ignaz Moscheles and Louis Plaidy. His contemporaries there included Grieg and Carl Rosa.

Late in 1860 Sullivan began work on incidental music to *The Tempest*, and this was performed at Leipzig in April 1861 and in revised and extended form at the Crystal Palace in April 1862. Its success at the Crystal Palace was such that it was repeated the following week, and in January 1863 was played at a Hallé concert. Sullivan was thus marked out as a composer of considerable promise, and during the 1860s he had several concert works performed, notably a symphony, a cello concerto and some overtures. In 1869 his oratorio *The Prodigal Son* was performed at the Worcester Festival with Tietjens, Trebelli, Sims Reeves and Santley as soloists. On his return from Leipzig he had become organist at St Michael's, Chester Square, and from 1867 to 1872 he held a similar position at St Peter's, Cranley Gardens. He also did some teaching and composed many drawing-room songs.

Sullivan's early success gave him many valuable contacts in the musical and artistic world. With Henry F.

1. *Arthur Sullivan: portrait (1888) by John Everett Millais in the National Portrait Gallery, London*

Chorley and Charles Dickens he was in Paris in December 1862 and there met Rossini. He collaborated with Chorley on a masque *Kenilworth* and an opera *The Sapphire Necklace*, but the latter remained unperformed apart from some excerpts. He was also organist under Costa at Covent Garden, the theatre for which he wrote the ballet *L'île enchantée*. Another early contact was John Everett Millais, who later painted a famous portrait of Sullivan (see fig.1), and a special friend was George Grove, whom he accompanied to Paris for the Exhibition of 1867 and later that year to Vienna where they discovered Schubert's lost *Rosamunde* music. Through Grove he met Tennyson, with whom he collaborated on a song cycle, *The Window*, which was originally intended to have illustrations by Millais. He also made the acquaintance of the royal family, with whom he remained on unusually close terms, particularly with the Duke of Edinburgh.

It was also through his social contacts that Sullivan first embarked on the type of composition in which he came to excel. In 1866, to produce a successor to Offenbach's *Les deux aveugles* for performance at some private all-male smoking parties, he and F. C. Burnand of *Punch* adapted Maddison Morton's popular comedy *Box and Cox*. The resulting operetta *Cox and Box* was first given with improvised piano accompaniment, but when a performance was arranged for charity in May 1867 Sullivan orchestrated the piece and for a further charity performance in July 1867 added an overture. By this sequence of chances Sullivan came to discover his talent for comic opera, and later that year he collaborated again with Burnand on *The Contrabandista* for the newly initiated St George's Hall venture of Thomas German Reed. Neither the work, which was hurriedly

written, nor the theatre was successful. It was at German Reed's Royal Gallery of Illustration, during the run of the first professional production of *Cox and Box* in 1869, that Sullivan was introduced by his friend Frederic Clay to the author W. S. Gilbert; and in 1871 they were invited by John Hollingshead of the Gaiety Theatre to collaborate on a Christmas piece, *Thespis*. It was moderately successful, but was never revived and the score was subsequently lost.

At the time these were only sidelines to Sullivan's career. He continued to compose substantial serious works, and his commissions also included writing and arranging hymn tunes for various collections and arranging vocal scores of operas for Boosey & Co. In 1871 he conducted Balfe's *The Rose of Castile* for the short-lived Royal National Opera project at the St James's Theatre, and later he was conductor at the Royal Aquarium, Westminster (1874–6), of the Glasgow Choral Union (1875–7) and of the Promenade Concerts at Covent Garden in 1878 and 1879. From 1876 to 1881 he was principal of the National Training School at South Kensington; pupils during his term of office included Eugene d'Albert, Landon Ronald and Arthur Goring Thomas. He received doctorates of music at Cambridge in 1876 and Oxford in 1879, and in 1878 he was made an Officer of the Légion d'honneur after acting as British Commissioner for Music at the Paris International Exhibition of that year.

2. MATURITY. Sullivan's increasing conducting and teaching commitments gradually brought a dwindling in his output of serious works, and the balance was further shifted by his increasing success with comic opera. In 1875 he was commissioned to set a one-act libretto by Gilbert as an afterpiece to Offenbach's *La Périchole* at the Royalty Theatre; the result was *Trial by Jury*, in which Sullivan's elder brother Frederic played the Judge. *The Zoo* (written with B. C. Stephenson in the same year) was less successful, but the popularity of *Trial by Jury* was such that the impresario Richard D'Oyly Carte took the lease of the Opéra Comique Theatre and formed a company expressly for the purpose of performing works by Gilbert and Sullivan. *The Sorcerer* (1877) was followed by *HMS Pinafore* (1878), which really established 'Gilbert and Sullivan' as an institution after Sullivan had performed a selection at the Covent Garden Proms. *HMS Pinafore*'s vogue was no less spectacular in the USA, where it was so extensively pirated that Carte decided not only to take the original production to New York but also to give there the première of a new work, *The Pirates of Penzance* (a single prior performance was given for copyright purposes in Paignton, where a D'Oyly Carte company was on tour).

In 1881, during the London run of the next work *Patience*, the company transferred to the newly built Savoy Theatre, where subsequent 'Savoy Operas' were performed, the most successful of which were *The Mikado* (1885) and *The Gondoliers* (1889), which ran for 672 and 554 consecutive performances respectively. In 1883 Sullivan was knighted. During this period his chief serious works were the cantatas *The Martyr of Antioch* and *The Golden Legend*, both written for the Leeds Triennial Festival of which he had become conductor in 1880 in succession to Costa. He was also conductor of the Philharmonic Society concerts from 1885 to 1887. Never very prolific, he found time for little other composing, particularly in view of his love of racing, gambling and society functions, and by reason of the kidney disease from which he suffered for many years. He frequently travelled abroad, and regularly spent his winters in Monte Carlo. He never married, but for the last 20 years of his life Mrs Mary Frances Ronalds, an American, was a regular and faithful companion; and in 1883 Sullivan took into his household his nephew Herbert, the son of his brother Frederic who had died in 1877 aged 39.

The small amount of Sullivan's serious output caused much comment that he was squandering his talents on ephemeral work, and he became increasingly frustrated by the restrictions of his collaboration with Gilbert. In 1888 Carte evolved a scheme for more ambitious Gilbert and Sullivan works in a new, larger theatre, which he built as the Royal English Opera House. But Gilbert declined to branch away from comic opera, and for the 'romantic opera' *Ivanhoe* which opened the new theatre in 1891 Sullivan's librettist was Julian Sturgis. The work had been planned to play in a continuous run, and as such achieved over 150 performances. But the expense of the project proved prohibitive, and in 1892 the theatre closed and became the Palace Music Hall (now the Palace Theatre).

The relationship between Sullivan and Gilbert, two very different personalities, had always been professional rather than social, and it often became strained. In 1890, during the composition of *Ivanhoe*, trouble arose between Gilbert and Carte over the production expenses for *The Gondoliers*, and the matter went to court with Sullivan reluctantly drawn in as a party to a three-way agreement. Though the dispute was quickly resolved, much bitterness remained, and Gilbert had by then withdrawn his works from the Savoy. Sullivan collaborated with Sidney Grundy on *Haddon Hall* before the partnership with Gilbert was resumed in *Utopia Limited* (1893) and finally *The Grand Duke* (1896) – both of which were only limited successes. Further comic operas with various collaborators followed, of which *The Rose of Persia* (1899, libretto by Basil Hood) was the most successful; *The Emerald Isle* (libretto by Hood), left unfinished at Sullivan's death, was completed by Edward German.

The relative failure of Sullivan's last works, whether with Gilbert or others, was due to a combination of declining powers and changing fashion. Sullivan revised *Ivanhoe* for a production by the Carl Rosa Opera Company in 1895, but he made no progress with a project to compose an opera on King Arthur, a subject for which he had already written some incidental music. The ill-health that dogged him throughout these years eventually forced him to resign the conductorship at Leeds after the 1898 festival. After developing bronchitis in October 1900, Sullivan died at his home at 58 Victoria Street, Westminster, on 22 November. His funeral brought out a vast crowd for the procession to St Paul's Cathedral, where he was buried.

3. POSTHUMOUS REPUTATION. In his lifetime Sullivan's music was often performed and published outside the English-speaking world. Among his serious works, the

2. Interior of the Savoy Theatre during the opening run of 'Patience' (1881) showing the revolutionary use of electric lighting: engraving

3. Programme for the opening run of 'Patience' (1881)

overture *In memoriam* was performed in Leipzig in 1867 and Paris in 1878, while Berlin heard *The Golden Legend* and *Ivanhoe* in 1887 and 1895 respectively. But none of these achieved any lasting success abroad, and even in Britain the serious orchestral works never really gained a firm hold in the concert repertory; after his death the oratorios, songs and partsongs also gradually fell out of favour. *Ivanhoe* was revived by Beecham at Covent Garden in 1910, but thereafter it remained unstaged for over 60 years. Thus, apart from the comic operas, only the sparkling *Overture di ballo*, the hymn tune for *Onward, Christian soldiers* ('St Gertrude', 1871) and, to a lesser extent, the ballad *The Lost Chord* (1877) were still well known by the late 1960s, when some of the other works began to reappear as a result of the increasing interest in forgotten 19th-century music. Since then many of the concert works have been revived and recorded, though the unpublished cello concerto, broadcast in 1953, is believed to have been destroyed along with other Sullivan material in a fire at Chappell & Co. in 1964.

Unless there is a revival of sympathetic interest in the whole Victorian musical climate in England, Sullivan's serious works are unlikely to find a completely fair assessment. However, it is clear that, whatever was believed in his lifetime, his real genius lay elsewhere. Lacking emotional depth and a grasp of large-scale structures, his eclectic style too easily led him beyond the limits of his inspiration. In two large late works, *The Golden Legend* and *Ivanhoe*, the music tends to be episodic, forming no convincing dramatic whole; and these

problems are epitomized by the overture *In memoriam*. Written on his father's death, it is full of appealing tunes and delightful instrumental writing, but culminates in a banal finale and altogether fails to match up to the pretensions of its title. The Symphony in E ('Irish') on the other hand, begun when he was only 21, is delightfully fresh and unpretentious, while the *Overture di ballo* is even more successful, thanks to its uninhibited light-heartedness and melodic ebullience, combined with the masterly handling of instrumental colour that was one of Sullivan's most consistent strengths. His talents as a miniaturist may be seen in Shakespeare settings such as *Orpheus with his Lute* and in the Tennyson cycle *The Window*. But many of his songs were sentimental ballads written for a ready market, and when Sullivan no longer depended on them for income their appearance promptly ceased.

In the comic operas, particularly those written with Gilbert, Sullivan most consistently found the stimulus to bring out his special talents. As early as *Cox and Box*, particularly in Box's account of his 'suicide', he had shown how a humorous situation appealed to his boyish sense of fun. Not only did Gilbert's satirical subjects and witty verses continue to provide Sullivan with such stimuli, but his well-made librettos provided the structure that Sullivan the composer seemed unable to provide for himself, and the appropriate vehicle for his music, which could seem shallow or banal in a serious context. Several of the comic operas enjoyed a vogue in various continental countries during the 1880s and 1890s, but only *The Mikado* has found a place in the European operetta repertory. By contrast, in English-speaking countries the Gilbert and Sullivan comic works achieved a unique popularity that has never declined. For a century the D'Oyly Carte Opera Company has presented them in London and on tour in Britain and abroad, and since 1903 the company has been able to devote itself exclusively to these dozen or so pieces, with the single addition of *Cox and Box* in a shortened version in 1921. Until copyright on the joint works expired in 1961, the D'Oyly Carte company jealously guarded the production rights, maintaining a style of presentation set out by Gilbert himself. Even though some textual changes were introduced, the D'Oyly Carte productions remained the model for countless amateur productions.

Fears of a spate of unorthodox productions led to a petition by some devotees to have copyright extended by Act of Parliament. In fact the expiry proved salutary, leading to productions by the Sadler's Wells Opera Company and others and to an all-round improvement in standards and a reawakening of imaginative interest. And as none of the comic operas had been readily accessible in full score, interest was also stimulated during the 1960s by the reappearance of many of Sullivan's manuscripts. These had passed to his nephew Herbert Sullivan and then to the latter's widow before being sold at auction at Sotheby's in June 1966. Though dispersed, some found their way to the extensive collection of Sullivan scores, papers and memorabilia amassed by Reginald Allen and now in the Pierpont Morgan Library, New York. The expiry of copyright in Sullivan's music in 1950 had already led to the opulently orchestrated ballet score *Pineapple Poll* (1951), arranged by Charles Mackerras entirely from music in the Gilbert and Sullivan comic operas and using a scenario based on one of Gilbert's *Bab Ballads*; and after the expiry of Gilbert's copyright some of Sullivan's less familiar music was adapted to the surviving text for *Thespis* and to a comic opera version of *Engaged*, a play by Gilbert.

4. THE COMIC OPERAS. Sullivan's role in setting Gilbert's lyrics was essentially a subservient one – a fact that increasingly rankled with him. Yet it was in furthering the effect of Gilbert's verses that he produced his best work, and the fact that he accepted the situation for so long is at once illustrative of his easy-going nature and indicative that he himself recognized his true métier. Gilbert's dominance helps to explain the comic operas' relative lack of success on the Continent, where audiences accustomed to operetta librettos as pegs for flowing melodies in popular dance rhythms must have found it difficult to accept the individual style of both libretto and music. During his formative years Sullivan had absorbed a wide variety of musical styles, and in his comic operas he drew on elements from such diverse sources as opera, ballads, choral and church music and composers ranging from Purcell and Handel to Schubert, Mendelssohn and Bizet. He inherited no native comic opera tradition, and his distillation of the various elements of Victorian music-making was doubtless an important factor in establishing the works' success in Britain.

Gilbert's verses are distinguished by their verbal inventiveness and metrical ingenuity; but in setting them Sullivan generally ignored the natural metre and concentrated on the sense and accentuation of the words, experimenting with rhythmic schemes until he found a

suitable one and then shaping a melody to fit the selected rhythmic scheme. Considering this laborious evolution it is remarkable that the tunes sound so natural. 'The sun whose rays' (*The Mikado*) is a well-known case where Sullivan fitted Gilbert's verses into a quite unexpected rhythm, extending the note values in the second part of the melody to delicious effect. Although here the same melody serves for both verses, Sullivan was not usually content with such straightforward repetition. A change of key and slight modification of the vocal line in the third verse increase the musical tension in 'Our great Mikado, virtuous man' (*The Mikado*); and where successive verses are taken by different singers, as in 'Expressive glances' (*Princess Ida*), Sullivan also used the technique for characterization. Perhaps nowhere is his skill better shown than in the passage beginning 'Now Marco, dear' in the Act 1 finale of *The Gondoliers*. Ex.1 shows the settings of corresponding parts of the two verses, illustrating the variations of key, rhythm and vocal line and the opening out of the melody at key words for emotional effect.

Ex.1 *The Gondoliers*

The emphasis Sullivan placed on word-setting generally prevents his solos from being memorable vocal display pieces. But lively and rewarding choruses are a feature of all the comic operas and have contributed much to the lasting popularity of the works with amateur societies. The male and female choruses each have their particular characteristics. From the start Sullivan gave the female entrance numbers some of his brightest and liveliest tunes, and his male choruses have correspondingly manly characteristics – jauntily nautical in *HMS Pinafore*, swaggering and military in *Patience*, dignified and aristocratic in *Iolanthe*. It is often such contrasted male and female melodies that feature in Sullivan's most individual trick of 'tune combination', of which one of the best examples is in *The Pirates of Penzance*, where the ladies chatter away about the weather in 2/4 time while the hero and heroine pour out their hearts to each other in waltz time. A different but no less fine example of his contrapuntal skill is the combination of three baritone tunes (previously heard separately) in 'I am so proud' (*The Mikado*). Best of all, perhaps, is the quartet 'In a contemplative fashion' (*The Gondoliers*), where three

4. Autograph MS from Act 2 of Sullivan's 'The Yeomen of the Guard', first produced at the Savoy Theatre on 3 October 1888 (GB-Lcm FS, f.186r)

characters continue the initial tranquil melody while each of the four in turn steps forward with a different vocal line and the two ladies increasingly lose their tempers.

In his accompaniments Sullivan often relied on a simple tonic pedal – a valuable device in patter songs and elsewhere where clarity of diction is essential ('The sun whose rays' is a happy example), but which leads to dullness where words and melody alone fail to hold the attention. Another weakness was his recourse to

Ex.2 *The Yeomen of the Guard*

Is this Phoe-be?   What,   lit-tle

Phoe - be?   etc

mawkish harmonic progressions to introduce a touch of cheap pathos into the cadences of numbers. His harmonic language was generally unadventurous, though within his limits resourceful enough, as in the 'Nightmare Song' (*Iolanthe*), where a particularly effective transition depicts the coming of dawn. His accompaniments as a whole are highly inventive in their colouring, echoing, decorating and extending of the vocal line, sometimes adding an extra voice as in ex.2 from *The Yeomen of the Guard*, where the accompaniment brilliantly points up the absurdity of a situation where the hero fails to recognize his supposed sister.

Particularly in the earlier works Sullivan complemented Gilbert's comic situations with some musical fun, as with the parodies of Handelian and Bellinian ensemble in 'He'll tell us how he came to be a judge' and 'A nice dilemma' (both from *Trial by Jury*), of patriotic songs in 'He is an Englishman' (*HMS Pinafore*) and of the dramatic absurdities of opera in the policemen's reluctance to leave the stage in *The Pirates of Penzance*. More subtle is the setting of ridiculous words with tongue in cheek, as in 'Silvered is the raven hair' (*Patience*), which, with words suitably altered, achieved a separate existence as a drawing-room ballad. More than once a humorous effect is achieved through solemn Handelian recitative. Yet it should not too readily be assumed that all such apparent references to other composers are necessarily parody. Sullivan was essentially an eclectic, and apparent incongruities of style are to be found also in his more serious works.

In his later comic operas Sullivan's humour tended to be less broad, and he made increasing use of instrumental means to point up textual references. The woodwind chuckling in 'Three little maids from school' (*The Mikado*) and the clarinet and bassoon quotation of Bach's organ Fugue in G minor at the words 'Bach interwoven with Spohr and Beethoven' in the Mikado's song are two examples. In the same work flutes and oboe add a touch of tenderness at the words 'fluttering heart' in the opening number of Act 2 (ex.3). He was at his happiest when writing for the wind instruments he had learnt to play as a child, and one of his most original instrumental effects is the off-beat clarinet adding a splash of colour in the quintet 'If Saphir I choose to marry' (*Patience*). A feature of his string writing is a fondness for pizzicato, often depicting feminine tenderness as in 'Kind sir, you cannot have the heart' (*The Gondoliers*). The ponderous double bass passage introducing the policemen in *The Pirates of Penzance* is another example of characterization by instrumental means; his portly baritones are frequently accompanied by bassoon figures, while his groups of young ladies are consistently introduced by tripping upper strings and flutes.

Orchestration seemed to come naturally to Sullivan, and he could – and often did – complete the scoring of an opera after rehearsals had begun, working at high speed late into the night. Whereas in his serious orchestral and choral works he often wrote for large instrumental forces (and in *Ivanhoe* for an orchestra of 60), in the comic operas he was restricted to some 30 players – strings, two flutes, oboe, two clarinets, bassoon (two from *The Yeomen of the Guard* onwards), two horns, two cornets, two trombones and one percussionist. Though his orchestration is distinguished by the delicacy and restraint with which he used these forces he could nevertheless produce a remarkably full sound when required, as in the sonorous tower music in *The Yeomen of the Guard* or for the Venetian warmth of *The Gondoliers*.

In the short mood-setting introductions to individual acts Sullivan was often inspired to effective and picturesque orchestral writing, as in Act 2 of *The Mikado*. By contrast the overtures are an oddly assorted lot. Only exceptionally was a formal overture part of his plan, and if convention demanded that one be provided he happily left the job to an assistant. Of the Gilbert works, only *Patience*, *Iolanthe*, *Princess Ida*, *The Yeomen of the Guard*, *The Gondoliers* and *The Grand Duke* have overtures or preludes accepted as Sullivan's own, and only those to *Iolanthe* and *The Yeomen of the Guard* are fully worthy independent pieces. This last was required for dramatic reasons, but in providing a formal overture for

Ex.3 *The Mikado*

his fairy opera Sullivan might have been inspired by the precedents of Weber and Mendelssohn. Certainly the opening of the *Iolanthe* overture bears a striking resemblance to that of *Oberon*.

Whatever the various musical influences on Sullivan, however, it was Gilbert's texts that consistently drew them together, providing an immediate stimulus to his inspiration and giving him just sufficient scope for his limited yet original talents. When Gilbert supplied the opportunity for extended stretches of word-setting, as in *Trial by Jury* (which contains no spoken dialogue) and in the long opening number of *The Gondoliers*, Sullivan produced some of his gayest and most tuneful music. When Gilbert furnished the impetus for descriptive writing, Sullivan responded with some first-rate miniature tone poems: 'When the night wind howls' (*Ruddigore*) is perhaps his finest piece of sustained descriptive writing; but hardly less effective in a different way is the spinning song 'When maiden loves' (*The Yeomen of the Guard*). Apart from the simple enjoyment that his music has given to countless millions throughout the English-speaking world, moments such as these have won Sullivan a unique place in the field of comic opera – in Eric Blom's words – 'as an inexhaustible melodic inventor, an incomparably graceful and accomplished craftsman, and a comic artist of endless wit and versatility'.

WORKS

(printed works published in London unless otherwise stated: where no source indication given for unpublished works MS not traced)

STAGE

Edition: *W. S. Gilbert, A. Sullivan: The Operas: a Critical Edition*, ed. S. Ledbetter and P. Young (New York, in preparation)

(unless otherwise stated, all comic operas first performed in London and published in vocal score)

OC – *Opéra Comique Theatre*;   ST – *Savoy Theatre*;   * – *autograph full score*

CR – *T. Rees collection, London*;   CW – *J. Wolfson collection, New York*

Title and genre	Text	First production	Publication and MSS; Remarks
The Tempest, incidental music, op.1	Shakespeare	Leipzig, Gewandhaus, 6 April 1861; rev. version, Crystal Palace, 5 April 1862	full score (1891)
The Sapphire Necklace (later The False Heiress)	H. F. Chorley	Crystal Palace, 13 April 1867 (excerpts)	ov. military band, *US-NYpm*, 1 song, 1 madrigal (1885–98), *lost; composed 1863–4, ?re-used

Title and genre	Text	First production	Publication and MSS; Remarks
L'ile enchantée, ballet	—	Covent Garden Theatre, 14 May 1864	*NYpm; partly re-used
Cox and Box, or The Long-lost Brothers	1, F. C. Burnand, after J. M. Morton: Box and Cox	private perf. (pf acc.), May 1866; Adelphi Theatre, 13 May 1867 (orch version)	(1869), ov. full score, ed. N. Richardson (1966), *NYpm
The Contrabandista, or The Law of the Ladrones	2, Burnand	St George's Hall, 18 Dec 1867	(c1870), *CR; rev. 1894 as The Chieftain
The Merchant of Venice, incidental music	Shakespeare	Manchester, Prince's Theatre, 19 Sept 1871	full score (Leipzig, 1898)
Thespis, or The Gods Grown Old	2, W. S. Gilbert	Gaiety Theatre, 26 Dec 1871	1 song (1872), *lost; partly re-used
The Merry Wives of Windsor, incidental music	Shakespeare	Gaiety Theatre, 19 Dec 1874	1 song (1875), *CW
Trial by Jury	1, Gilbert	Royalty Theatre, 25 March 1875	(1875), NYpm
The Zoo	1, B. Rowe [pseud. of B. C. Stephenson]	St James's Theatre, 5 June 1875	ed. G. Morton (1969), ed. R. Spencer (1975)
Henry VIII, incidental music	Shakespeare	Manchester, Theatre Royal, 29 Aug 1877	full score (1878), *CW
The Sorcerer	2, Gilbert	OC, 17 Nov 1877; rev. version, ST, 11 Oct 1884	(1877), rev. version (1884), *CW
HMS Pinafore, or The Lass that Loved a Sailor	2, Gilbert	OC, 25 May 1878	full score (Brunswick, 1882), *A. A. Houghton jr collection, New York
The Pirates of Penzance, or The Slave of Duty	2, Gilbert	Paignton, Royal Bijou Theatre, 30 Dec 1879, New York, Fifth Avenue Theatre, 31 Dec 1879	(1880), *NYpm
Patience, or Bunthorne's Bride	2, Gilbert	OC, 23 April 1881	(1881), *GB-Lbm
Iolanthe, or The Peer and the Peri	2, Gilbert	ST, 25 Nov 1882	(1883), * Bridget D'Oyly Carte, London
Princess Ida, or Castle Adamant	3, Gilbert, after Tennyson: The Princess	ST, 5 Jan 1884	(1884), *Ob
The Mikado, or The Town of Titipu	2, Gilbert	ST, 14 March 1885	full score (Leipzig, 1898), *Lam, facs., ed. G. Jacob (Farnborough, 1968)
Ruddigore, or The Witch's Curse	2, Gilbert	ST, 22 Jan 1887	(1887), *ST
The Yeomen of the Guard, or The Merryman and his Maid	2, Gilbert	ST, 3 Oct 1888	(1888), *Lcm
Macbeth, incidental music	Shakespeare	Lyceum Theatre, 29 Dec 1888	ov. full score (1893), *anon. New York collection
The Gondoliers, or The King of Barataria	2, Gilbert	ST, 7 Dec 1889	(1890), *Lbm
Ivanhoe, romantic opera	3, J. Sturgis, after Scott	Royal English Opera House, 31 Jan 1891; rev. version, Liverpool, Court Theatre, 14 Feb 1895	full score (1891), *CW
The Foresters, incidental music	Tennyson	New York, Daly's Theatre, 17 March 1892	(1892), *CR
Haddon Hall	2, S. Grundy	ST, 24 Sept 1892	(1892), *CR
Utopia Limited, or The Flowers of Progress	2, Gilbert	ST, 7 Oct 1893	(1893)
The Chieftain	2, Burnand	ST, 12 Dec 1894	(1894), *CR; rev. from The Contrabandista, 1867
King Arthur, incidental music	J. Comyns Carr	Lyceum Theatre, 12 Jan 1895	(1904), ed. W. Bendall, *US-NYpm
The Grand Duke, or The Statutory Duel	2, Gilbert	ST, 7 March 1896	(1896), *CW
Victoria and Merrie England, ballet	C. Coppi	Alhambra Theatre, 25 May 1897	arr. pf (1897)
The Beauty Stone	2, A. W. Pinero, Carr	ST, 28 May 1898	(1892)
The Rose of Persia, or The Story-teller and the Slave	2, B. Hood	ST, 29 Nov 1899	(1900), ?full score (Leipzig, 1901)
The Emerald Isle, or The Caves of Carig-Cleena	2, Hood	ST, 27 April 1901	(1901); completed by E. German

CHORAL WITH ORCHESTRA

(all printed works published in vocal score unless otherwise stated)

Cum sancto spiritu, fugue, ?1857

Psalm (Ger.), ?1858

Kenilworth (H. F. Chorley), masque, op.4, Birmingham Festival, 8 Sept 1864 (1865)

The Prodigal Son (Sullivan), oratorio, Worcester Festival, 8 Sept 1869 (1869), *CR

On Shore and Sea (T. Taylor), cantata, London, Albert Hall, 1 May 1871 (1871), orch parts (1900–02), *CR

Te Deum and Domine salvam fac reginam, London, Crystal Palace, 1 May 1872, full score (1872)

The Light of the World (Sullivan), oratorio, Birmingham Festival, 27 Aug 1873 (1873), rev. version (1890), *GB-Ouf

The Martyr of Antioch (H. H. Milman), sacred music drama, Leeds Festival, 15 Oct 1880, rev. as opera, Edinburgh, 15 Feb 1898, full score (1899), *Lam

Ode for opening of Colonial and Indian Exhibition (Tennyson), London, Albert Hall, 4 May 1886 (1886), *US-NYpm

The Golden Legend (J. Bennett, after Longfellow), cantata, Leeds Festival, 16 Oct 1886, full score (1886), *GB-Lcm

Ode for laying of Imperial Institute foundation stone (L. Morris), 4 July 1887 (1887)

Te Deum, 1900, St Paul's Cathedral, 8 June 1902, full score (1902)

ORCHESTRAL

Timon of Athens, ov. after Shakespeare, c, ?1857, *lost

Overture, d, London, RAM, 13 July 1858, *lost

Rosenfest, ov. after Moore: Lalla Rookh, Leipzig, Gewandhaus, 25 May 1860, *lost

Princess of Wales's March (Marche danoise), arr. pf (1863)

Procession March (The Royal Wedding: Grand March), London, Crystal Palace, 10 March 1863, arr. pf (1863)

'Irish' Symphony, E, London, Crystal Palace, 10 March 1866, full score (1915), *Novello & Co, London

In memoriam, ov., C, Norwich Festival, 30 Oct 1866, full score (1885), *Lbm

Cello Concerto, D, London, Crystal Palace, 24 Nov 1866, *lost, vc part only, US-NYpm

Marmion, ov. after Scott, London, St James's Hall, 3 June 1867

Overture di ballo, E, Birmingham Festival, 31 Aug 1870, full score (1889), *CR

Imperial March, London, Imperial Institute, 10 May 1893, arr. pf (1893), *anon. New York collection

CHAMBER

Scherzo, pf, 1857

Capriccio no.2, pf, 1857

Piano Sonata, ?1857, *lost

String Quartet, d, perf. Leipzig, May 1859, *lost

Romance, g, str qt, Sept 1859, ed. (1964)

Thoughts, pf, op.2 (1862): Allegretto con grazia, Allegro grazioso [later pubd as Reverie, A, Melody, D, vn, pf]

An Idyll, vc, pf 1865 (1899), *US-STu

Allegro risoluto, bb, pf, 8 May 1866, ed. J. Parry (1976), *Lbm

[6] Day Dreams, pf, op.14 (1867): Andante religioso, Allegretto grazioso, Andante, Tempo di valse, Andante con molto tenerezza, A l'hongroise, Allegretto

Duo concertante, vc, pf, op.2 (1868)

Twilight, pf, op.12 (1868)

SERVICES AND ANTHEMS

Te Deum, D (1866); Jubilate, Kyrie, D (1872)

Anthems: By the Waters of Babylon, c1850; Sing unto the Lord, 1855; Ps ciii, 1856; We have heard with our ears, ?1860 (1865); O Love the Lord (1864); O God, Thou art worthy, 1867 (1871); O taste and see (1867); Rejoice in the Lord (1868); Sing, O heavens (1869); I will worship towards thy holy temple (1871); I will mention thy loving-kindness (1875); I will sing of thy power (1877); Hearken unto me (1877); Turn thy face (1878); Who is like unto Thee? (1883); I will lay me down in peace, c1900 (1910); There is none like unto the God of Jeshurun (1882) [composed by J. Goss, completed by Sullivan]

HYMN TUNES

(collected edition, 1902; index of first lines in Grove 5)

Angel voices (M. B. Whiting: 'Stars of evening') (1872); Audite audientes me (H. Bonar: 'I heard the voice') (1874); Bishopsgarth (Bishop of Wakefield: 'O King of kings') (1897); Bolwell (G. Thring: 'Thou, to whom the sick') (1902); Carrow (A. A. Procter: 'My God, I thank thee') (1875); Chapel Royal (G. Matheson: 'O love that wilt not let me go') (1902); Christus (J. Condor: 'Show me not only Jesus dying') (1874); Coena Domini (trans. J. M. Neale: 'Draw nigh and take') (1874); Constance (trans. B. H. Kennedy: 'Who trusts in God') (1874); Coronae (M. Bridges: 'Crown him with many crowns') (1874); Courage, brother (N. Macleod) (1872)

Dominion Hymn ('God bless our wide Dominion') (1880); Dulce sonans (Whiting: 'At thine altar, Lord') (1874); Ecclesia (J. Montgomery: 'O where shall rest') (1874); Evelyn (R. Herrick: 'In the hour of my distress') (1874); Ever faithful (Milton: 'Let us with a gladsome mind') (1874); Falfield, see Formosa; Fatherland, see St Edmund; Formosa, or Falfield (C. Wesley: 'Love divine') (1867); Fortunatus, see Welcome, happy morning; Gennesareth, or Heber (R. Heber: 'When through the torn sail') (1869); Gentle Shepherd, or The long home (trans. C. Winkworth: 'Tender Shepherd') (1872); Golden sheaves (W. C. Dix: 'To thee, o Lord') (1874)

Hanford (C. Elliott: 'Jesu, my Saviour') (1874); Heber, see Gennesareth; Holy City (trans. J. Ellerton: 'Sing alleluia forth') (1874); Hushed was the evening hymn (J. D. Burns) (1874); Hymn of the Homeland (H. R. Haweis) (1867); Lacrymae (I. Williams: 'Lord in this') (1872); Litany no.1 (T. B. Pollock: 'Jesu, we are far away') (1875); Litany no.2 (Pollock: 'Jesu, life of those who die') (1875); Lux eoi (trans. E. Caswall: 'Hark a thrilling voice') (1874); Lux in tenebris (J. H. Newman: 'Lead, kindly light') (1874); Lux mundi (W. W. How: 'O Jesu, thou art standing') (1872)

Mount Zion (A. M. Toplady: 'Rock of ages') (1867); Of thy love, or St Lucian (T. Kelly) (1868); Paradise (F. W. Faber: 'O paradise!') (1874); Pilgrimage (T. Kelly: 'From Egypt's bondage') (1874); Promissio Patris (H. Auber: 'Our blest Redeemer') (1874); Propior Deo (S. F. Adams: 'Nearer, my God, to thee') (1872); Rest, see Venite; Resurrexit (A. T. Gurney: 'Christ is risen!') (1874); Safe home (trans. Neale) (1872); St Edmund, or Fatherland (T. R. Taylor: 'We are but strangers here') (1872); St Francis (trans. Winkworth: 'Father of heaven') (1874); St Gertrude (S. Baring-Gould: 'Onward, Christian soldiers') (1871)

St Kevin (Neale: 'Come, ye faithful') (1872); St Lucian, see Of thy love; St Luke, or St Nathaniel (W. Cowper: 'God moves in a mysterious way') (1867); St Mary Magdalene, see Saviour, when in dust to thee; St Millicent (trans. R. F. Littledale: 'Let no tears') (1874); St Nathaniel, see St Luke; St Patrick (A. P. Stanley: 'He is gone') (1874); Saints of God (Maclagen: 'The saints of God') (1874); St Theresa (T. J. Potter: 'Brightly gleams our banner') (1874); Saviour, when in dust to thee, or St Mary Magdalene (R. Grant) (1872)

The long home, see Gentle Shepherd; The roseate hues (C. F. Alexander) (1902); The strain upraise (trans. Neale) (1868); Thou God of love (J. E. Brown) (1868); Ultor Omnipotens (H. F. Chorley, Ellerton: 'God the all-terrible') (1874); Valete (Faber: 'Sweet Saviour!') (1874); Veni Creator (trans. J. Cosin: 'Come, Holy Ghost') (1874); Venite, or Rest (trans. Neale: 'Art thou weary') (1872); Victoria (M. B. Whiting: 'To mourn our dead') (1902); Welcome, happy morning, or Fortunatus (trans. Ellerton) (1872)

12 arrs. also in collected edn. (1902) [listed in *Grove 5*]

PARTSONGS
(for SATB unless otherwise stated)

Madrigal, 1857, ?lost; It was a lover and his lass (Shakespeare), 2 S, chorus, London, RAM, 14 July 1857; Seaside Thoughts, male vv, 1857 (1904); The last night of the year (H. F. Chorley) (1863); O hush thee, my babie (Scott) (1867); The rainy day (Longfellow) (1867)

7 Partsongs (1868): Evening (Houghton, after Goethe); Joy to the victors (Scott); Parting Gleams (A. de Vere); Echoes (T. Moore); I sing the birth (B. Jonson); The long day closes (Chorley), 4 male vv; The Beleaguered (Chorley), 4 male vv

All this night (old carol) (1870)

5 Sacred Partsongs (1871): It came upon the midnight clear; Lead, kindly light (J. H. Newman); Through sorrow's path (H. Kirke White); Watchman, what of the night?; The way is long and drear (A. A. Procter)

Upon the snow-clad earth (carol) (1876); Hark! what mean those holy voices? (carol) (1883); Wreaths for our graves (L. F. Massey), 1897 (1898); Fair daffodils (Herrick) (1903)

2 choruses adapted from the Russ. (1874): Turn Thee again, Mercy and truth

SONGS, DUETS AND TRIOS
(for 1v, pf, unless otherwise stated; see Poladian, 1961)

O Israel, sacred song (1855); Ich möchte hinaus es jauchzen (A. Corrodi), 1859, facs. in Baily (1952); Lied mit thränen halbgeschrieben (Eichendorff), 1861, *US-NYpm*; Bride from the north (Chorley) (1863); I heard the nightingale (C. H. Townsend) (1863); Sweet day, so cool (G. Herbert) (1864); The roads should blossom, 1864, *NYpm*; Thou art lost to me (1865); Will he come? (A. A. Procter) (1865); Arabian Love Song (Shelley) (1866); 5 Shakespeare Songs, 1863–4 (1866): Orpheus with his Lute, O mistress mine, Sigh no more ladies, The Willow Song, Rosalind (From east to western Ind); If doughty deeds (R. Graham) (1866); She is not fair to outward view (H. Coleridge) (1866); A weary lot is thine, fair maid (Scott), 1866

County Guy (Scott) (1867); Give (Procter) (1867); In the summers long ago (1867) [later pubd as My love beyond the sea] (J. P. Douglas); The Maiden's Story (E. Embury) (1867); What does little birdie say? (Tennyson) (1867); I wish to tune my quiv'ring lyre (Byron, after Anacreon) (1868); The moon in silent brightness (R. Heber) (1868); The Mother's Dream (W. Barnes) (1868); O fair dove, o fond dove (J. Ingelow) (1868); O sweet and fair (A.F.C.K.) (1868); The snow lies white (Ingelow) (1868)

Dove Song (W. Brough), 1v, orch, *US-NYpm*, acc. pf (1869); Sad Memories (C. J. Rowe) (1869); The Troubadour (Scott) (1869); A life that lives for you (L. H. Lewin) (1870); Looking Back (L. Gray) (1870); The Village Chimes (Rowe) (1870); The Window, or the Songs of the Wrens (Tennyson), cycle (1871): On the Hill, At the Window, Gone!, Winter, Spring, The Letter, No Answer ('The mist and the rain'), No Answer ('Winds are loud and you are dumb'), The Answer, Ay! [poem not set], When?, Marriage Morning

Golden Days (Lewin) (1872); Evermore (Lewin) (1872); None but I can say (Lewin) (1872); Oh! ma charmante (Hugo) (1872) [as Oh! bella mia (F. Rizzelli) (1873), as Sweet Dreamer (H. B. Farnie) (1874)]; Once again (Lewin) (1872); The Sailor's Grave (H. F. Lyte) (1872); The White Plume (J. P. Douglas) (1872); Coming home (R. Reece), S, Mez (1873); Looking Forward (Gray) (1873); There sits a bird in yonder tree (G. H. Barham: Ingoldsby Legends) (1873); 2 songs from The Miller and his Man (F. C. Burnand) (1873): The Marquis de Mincepie, Care is all fiddle-de-dee

The Young Mother, 3 simple songs (1873): The days are cold (Cradle Song) (anon.), Ay de mi, my bird (G. Eliot), The First Departure (E. Monro) [nos.1 and 2 later pubd as Little Darling, Sleep Again and The Chorister (F. E. Weatherley)]; The Distant Shore (W. S. Gilbert) (1874); Living Poems (Longfellow) (1874); Mary Morison (Burns) (1874); My dear and only love (Marquis of Montrose) (1874); Sleep, my love (R. Whyte Melville) (1874); Tender and true (1874); Thou art weary (Procter) (1874); Christmas Bells at Sea (C. L. Kenney) (1875); Let me dream again (B. C. Stephenson) (1875); The love that loves me not (Gilbert) (1875)

The River (anon.), in *The Sunlight of Song* (1875); Sweethearts (Gilbert) (1875) [also pubd as duet]; Thou'rt passing hence (F. Hemans: The Highland Message) (1875); We've ploughed our land (anon.), in *The Sunlight of Song* (1875); My dearest heart (anon.) (1876); The Lost Chord (Procter) (1877); Sometimes (Lady Lindsay of Balcarres) (1877); When thou art near (W. J. Stewart) (1877); I would I were a king (A. Cockburn, after Hugo) (1878); Morn, happy morn (W. G. Wills), 3vv, for play Olivia, London, Court Theatre, 30 March 1878 (1878); Old Love Letters (S. K. Cowan) (1879); St Agnes' Eve (Tennyson) (1879); Edward Gray (Tennyson) (1880); The Sisters (Tennyson), 2 female vv (1881)

A Shadow (Procter) (1886); Ever (Mrs B. Moore) (1887); You sleep (G. Mazzucato: E tu nol sai, trans. Stephenson), perf. in Pinero's The Profligate, London, Garrick Theatre, 24 April 1889 (1889); Bid me at least good-bye (S. Grundy), for play An Old Jew, London, Garrick Theatre, 6 Jan 1894 (1894); The Absent-minded

Beggar (Kipling) (1899); O swallow, swallow and Tears, idle tears (Tennyson: The Princess) (Cincinnati, 1900); My child and I (F. E. Weatherley) (1901); To one in Paradise (Poe) (1904); Longing for home (Ingelow) (1904); My heart is like a silent lute (B. Disraeli: Henrietta Temple) (1904)

Re-texted songs: Birds in the night (1869) [from Cox and Box]; In the twilight of our love (1881) [from Patience]

BIBLIOGRAPHY

BIOGRAPHY

'Arthur Sullivan', University Magazine, iv (London, 1879), 483
L. Engel: From Handel to Hallé (London, 1890), 95
C. Willeby: Masters of English Music (London, 1893)
M. A. von Zedlitz: 'Sir Arthur Sullivan', Strand Musical Magazine, i (London, 1895), 169
A. H. Lawrence: 'Sir Arthur Seymour Sullivan', Strand Magazine, xiv (London, 1897), 649
——: Sir Arthur Sullivan: Life Story, Letters and Reminiscences (London, 1899)
A. S. Sullivan: 'Days of My Youth', M.A.P. (London, 1899), Feb
W. J. Wells: Souvenir of Sir Arthur Sullivan, Mus. Doc., M.V.O. (London, 1901)
H. S. Wyndham: Arthur Sullivan (London, 1903)
B. W. Findon: Sir Arthur Sullivan: his Life and Music (London, 1904/R, rev. 2/1908 as Sir Arthur Sullivan and his Operas)
H. S. Wyndham: Arthur Seymour Sullivan (London, 1926)
H. Sullivan and N. Flower: Sir Arthur Sullivan: his Life, Letters and Diaries (London, 1927, 2/1950)
H. Pearson: Gilbert and Sullivan (London, 1935)
L. Baily: The Gilbert and Sullivan Book (London, 1952, 3/1966)
——: Gilbert & Sullivan and their World (London, 1973)
R. Allen and G. R. D'Luhy: Sir Arthur Sullivan: Composer & Personage (New York, 1975)
C. Brahms: Gilbert and Sullivan: Lost Chords and Discords (London, 1975)
A. Jacobs: 'The Secret Diaries of Sir Arthur Sullivan', High Fidelity, xxvii (1977), 46
J. Wolfson: Sir Arthur Sullivan (New York, 1976)

PERSONAL REMINISCENCES AND PERIOD STUDIES

G. Grossmith: A Society Clown: Reminiscences (Bristol, 1888)
E. Swayne: 'Sullivan as a Boy', Music, Chicago, xviii (1900), 219
V. Blackburn and J. C. Carr: 'Arthur Sullivan', Fortnightly Review, lxix (1901), 81
G. Grossmith: 'Sir Arthur Sullivan: A Personal Reminiscence', Pall Mall Magazine, xxiii (1901), 250
'Sir Arthur Sullivan as an Old Friend Knew him', Argosy, lxxiii (1901), 161
C. L. Graves: The Life and Letters of Sir George Grove, C.B. (London, 1903)
H. Klein: Thirty Years of Musical Life in London, 1870–1900 (London, 1903)
F. C. Burnand: Records and Reminiscences (London, 1904)
E. Dicey: 'Recollections of Arthur Sullivan', Fortnightly Review, lxxvii (1905), 74
J. F. Barnett: Musical Reminiscences and Impressions (London, 1906)
J. Bennett: Forty Years of Music 1865–1905 (London, 1908)
J. C. Carr: Some Eminent Victorians (London, 1908)
R. C. Lehmann: Memories of Half a Century (London, 1908)
C. V. Stanford: Studies and Memories (London, 1908)
C. K. Rogers: Memories of a Musical Career (Chicago, 1919)
E. Smyth: Impressions that Remained (London, 1919)

ANALYTICAL AND HISTORICAL

P. H. Fitzgerald: The Savoy Operas and the Savoyards (London, 1894, 2/1899)
J. A. Fuller Maitland: 'Sir Arthur Sullivan', Cornhill Magazine, x (1901), 300
A. C. Mackenzie: 'The Life-work of Arthur Sullivan', SIMG, iii (1901–2), 539
C. Maclean: 'Sullivan as National Style-builder', PMA, xxviii (1901–2), 89
F. Cellier and C. Bridgeman: Gilbert, Sullivan and D'Oyly Carte (London, 1914, 2/1927)
H. M. Walbrook: Gilbert and Sullivan Opera (London, 1922)
S. Dark and R. Grey: W. S. Gilbert: his Life and Letters (London, 1923, 2/1924)
S. J. A. Fitz-Gerald: The Story of the Savoy Opera (London, 1924)
A. H. Godwin: Gilbert and Sullivan (London, 1926)
T. F. Dunhill: Sullivan's Comic Operas: a Critical Appreciation (London, 1928)
I. Goldberg: The Story of Gilbert and Sullivan (London, 1929)
I. Parrott: 'Arthur Sullivan (1842–1900)', ML, xxiii (1942), 202
W. A. Darlington: The World of Gilbert and Sullivan (New York, 1950)
A. Jacobs: 'Sullivan, Gilbert and the Victorians', MR, xii (1951), 122
——: Gilbert and Sullivan (London, 1951)
A. Williamson: Gilbert and Sullivan Opera: a New Assessment (New

York, 1953)
H. S. Wyndham and E. Blom: 'Sullivan, (Sir) Arthur (Seymour)', Grove 5
R. Allen: The First Night Gilbert and Sullivan (New York, 1958, rev. 2/1975)
H. Raynor: 'Sullivan Reconsidered', MMR, lxxxix (1959), 163
G. Hughes: The Music of Arthur Sullivan (London, 1960)
——: 'Sullivan 1962', Opera, xiii (1962), 8
R. Mander and J. Mitchenson: A Picture History of Gilbert and Sullivan (London, 1962)
C. Rollins and R. J. Witts: The D'Oyly Carte Opera Company in Gilbert and Sullivan (London, 1962)
T. Rees: Thespis: a Gilbert and Sullivan Enigma (London, 1964)
M. Cooper: 'The Fickle Philistine', Opera News (20 April 1968), no.32, p.8
H. and G. Jellinek: 'The One World of Gilbert and Sullivan', Saturday Review (26 Oct 1968), no.51, p.69
P. M. Young: Sir Arthur Sullivan (London, 1971)
L. Ayre: The Gilbert & Sullivan Companion (London, 1972)
M. Hardwick: The Osprey Guide to Gilbert and Sullivan (Reading, 1972)
J. Wolfson: Final Curtain: the Last Gilbert and Sullivan Operas (London, 1977)

MISCELLANEOUS

F. R. Spark and J. Bennett: A Full History of the Leeds Musical Festivals, 1858–89 (Leeds and London, 1892)
W. S. Gilbert: Original Plays (London, 1902)
H. A. Simcoe: Sullivan v. Critic; a Study in Press Phenomenon (London, 1906)
H. S. Wyndham: August Manns and the Saturday Concerts (London, 1909)
M. B. Foster: History of the Philharmonic Society, 1813–1912 (London, 1912)
The Gilbert and Sullivan Journal (London, 1926–)
S. Poladian: Sir Arthur Sullivan: an Index to the Texts of his Vocal Works (Detroit, 1961)
B. S. Abeshouse: A Medical History of Sir Arthur Sullivan (New York, 1966)
J. Helyar, ed.: Gilbert and Sullivan International Conference: Kansas 1970
T. Joseph: 'Towards a "G. & S." Bibliography', Library Review (1971)
B. Matthews: 'Onward Christian Soldiers: a Centenary Note', MT, cxiii (1972), 1232
A. Lamb: 'A Note on Sullivan's Instrumental Works', MT, cxvi (1975), 234
S. Meares: Performing Sullivan's Ivanhoe (Chesham Bois, 1975) [private circulation]

ANDREW LAMB

Sullivan, Daniel (d Dublin, 13 Oct 1764). Irish countertenor. He is said to have begun his career as a boy singer in Dublin in 1737. He appeared at Chester with the Lampes in 1741 and made his London début at Drury Lane on 2 February 1743 as Moore in *The Dragon of Wantley*. In that season and the next he sang in several other stage pieces by Lampe, at Drury Lane and the New Haymarket, as well as in songs between acts and at Ranelagh. Handel engaged him for his Covent Garden oratorios in spring 1744; he created the parts of Athamas in *Semele* and the title role in *Joseph and his Brethren*, and sang Micah in *Samson* and David in *Saul*. According to Mrs Delany he was 'a block with a very fine voice', which put Handel 'mightily out of humour'. His voice was a low alto, with a compass of g or a to c''; Handel seems to have transposed the part of Joseph down for him before performance, and he may have been able to sing tenor roles such as Acis at pitch.

Sullivan returned to Dublin in winter 1745–6 (Garrick described him as looking 'gay and sensible as usual'), rejoined the Drury Lane company for the 1746–8 seasons, and was engaged by Thomas Sheridan for Dublin (Smock Alley) in winter 1748. Most of his later career was spent there and at Bath, where he was associated with Chilcot, Linley and Passerini in Handel's oratorios and similar works, especially *Acis and Galatea*, between 1755 and 1759 (he had sung God save the King there on George II's birthday in 1745). In Dublin he appeared in stage works by Purcell, Boyce and Carey at Smock Alley, and in a concert with Guadagni at Crow Street Music Hall in March 1752. With Marella, the elder Storace and the music seller Samuel Lee he had leased the building in July 1751; but the syndicate quarrelled two years later, and it was used for an exhibition of anatomical waxworks.

WINTON DEAN

Sul ponticello (It.: 'On the bridge'; Fr. *au chevalet*; Ger. *am Steg*). In string playing, a bowing performed close to (or even on) the bridge of the instrument, resulting in a thin, nasal, glassy sound.

Sultzberger, Johann Ulrich (*b* Schaffhausen, baptized 17 Dec 1638; *d* Berne, Jan 1701). Swiss trumpeter, cornettist, teacher and composer. He grew up in Winterthur, where his father was a civic trumpeter from 1639, and he too learnt the trumpet. In 1657 his family moved to St Gallen. In 1661 after he had become self-supporting, he went to Berne as a cornettist, where he soon rose to prominence as a civic trumpeter and became the leading light in the city both in instrumental and vocal music. In 1672 he founded Berne's first collegium musicum and in 1675 was made the city's first musical director. The Reformation had banished music from the churches of Berne, much to the detriment of the city's musical life. After 150 years of inactivity a musical revival then took place, thanks to Sultzberger, not only in the churches but also in the schools and in the home. Adverse circumstances, however, clouded the last years of his life, and much of his good work was undone. He was most important for his educational work: as founder and director of the collegium musicum he exercised a decisive influence on the musical education of the students. His work as a composer is less significant. The original songs in the two publications of 1674 failed to establish themselves, although the psalm settings in his *Transponiertes Psalmenbuch* were sung in the churches of Berne until the 19th century.

WORKS

Salomons des Ebreischen Königes geistliche Wohl-Lust oder hohes Lied ... mit beygefügten Newen, vom fürtrefflichen Johann Schoppen gesetzten Sangweisen ... fürgestellt durch Filip von Zesen, jetzunder aber ... vermehrt durch Johann Ulrich Sultzberger (Berne, 1674)

Dreygestimmter Zesischer Salomon ... mit vielen Melodeyen vermehret, sampt beygefügter geistlichen Seelen-Lust und noch einem Appendice in Truck verfertiget von Johann Ulrich Sultzberger (Berne, 1674)

Transponiertes Psalmenbuch, das ist, D. Ambr. Lobwassers Psalmen Davids, worinn die Hoch-Clavierten Psalmen transponiert und samt den gewohnlichen Fest-Gesängen in ein gleichen Schlüssel gesetzt (Berne, 1675)

BIBLIOGRAPHY

G. Becker: *La musique en Suisse* (Geneva, 1874)
F. Brönnimann: *Der Zinkenist und Musikdirektor Johann Ulrich Sultzberger* (diss., U. of Berne, 1920)
A. Fluri: *Bibliographie der bernischen Kirchengesangbücher* (Berne, 1920–22)
E. Refardt: *Historisch-biographisches Musikerlexikon der Schweiz* (Leipzig and Zurich, 1928)
M. Zulauf: *Die Musikunterricht in der Geschichte des bernischen Schulwesens* (Berne, 1934)
A.-E. Cherbuliez: *Geschichte der Musikpädagogik in der Schweiz* (Zurich, 1944)
E. Nievergelt: *Die Tonsätze der deutschschweizerischen reformierten Kirchengesangbücher im XVII. Jahrhundert* (diss., U. of Zurich, 1944)

MAX ZULAUF

Sulzer, Johann Anton (*b* Rheinfelden, 18 Sept 1752; *d* Konstanz, 8 March 1828). Swiss writer and composer. He attended the Jesuit Gymnasium in Solothurn from 1763 and studied Catholic theology at Fribourg from 1772 until 1774; he then took a doctorate in law at the University of Freiburg im Breisgau (1783) and became a high magistrate at the Swiss monastery of Kreuzlingen (1785). In 1798 he obtained a post as librarian and professor of ecclesiastical law at the lyceum in Konstanz and taught history and practical philosophy there from 1807. He repeatedly applied without success for a chair in philosophy or law at the University of Freiburg.

Though he never received instruction in composition, Sulzer composed more than 80 songs and various pieces for the piano and violin (piano sonatas op.1, *Sammlung von Clavierstüken ... mit beständiger Begleitung einer Violine*, 1789 and violin sonatas op.3). He set poems by his friends Johann Caspar Lavater and Ignaz von Wessenberg (administrator for the bishopric of Konstanz), and contributed melodies to the Konstanz *Christkatholisches Gesang- und Andachtsbuch* (1812), which became the model for numerous other German diocesan hymnals. In his own time his compositions enjoyed considerable popularity, despite their now apparent dilettantish weaknesses.

BIBLIOGRAPHY

K. Nef: *Das Lied in der deutschen Schweiz Ende des 18. und Anfang des 19. Jahrhunderts* (Zurich, 1909), 77, 89, 115
E. Refardt: *Historisch-biographisches Musikerlexikon der Schweiz* (Leipzig and Zurich, 1928), 308
G. Boner: *Biographisches Lexikon des Aargaus 1803–1957* (Aarau, 1958), 757ff

MANFRED SCHULER

Sulzer, Johann Georg (*b* Winterthur, 16 Oct 1720; *d* Berlin, 27 Feb 1779). Swiss aesthetician and lexicographer. Following theological studies in Zurich he held posts as a vicar in a nearby town and as a tutor in Magdeburg. These positions provided opportunities for studies in the sciences and mathematics and enabled him to assimilate the poetic and aesthetic theories of Johann Bodmer and Jacob Breitinger. In 1747 Sulzer became professor of mathematics at the Joachimsthal Gymnasium in Berlin and three years later was elected to the Royal Academy of Sciences. During this period he wrote articles on philosophy and aesthetics and embarked on his most important work, the *Allgemeine Theorie der schönen Künste*. The work is an encyclopedia containing articles on both general and specific topics in the arts. Sulzer's approach was eclectic, incorporating ideas assimilated from such authors as Dubos, Batteux, Lord Kames, J. A. Schlegel and A. G. Baumgarten. By the time the *Allgemeine Theorie* appeared, many of its ideas were out of date, a situation reflected in unfavourable criticism from Herder and Goethe. Nonetheless the work influenced later writers such as Koch.

Having little or no training in music, Sulzer relied on Johann Philipp Kirnberger and J. A. P. Schulz for the articles on music. Kirnberger and Sulzer jointly wrote the musical articles as far as 'Modulation', but Sulzer's failing health made it impossible for him to continue. Kirnberger and Schulz wrote the articles from 'Preludiren' up to the letter S, and from that point the work was entirely by Schulz except for the article 'System', which had been written earlier by Sulzer and Kirnberger.

See also ANALYSIS, §II, 2 and THEORY, THEORISTS, §12.

WRITINGS

Allgemeine Theorie der schönen Künste in einzeln, nach alphabetischer Ordnung der Kunstwörter auf einander folgenen Artikeln abgehandelt

(Leipzig, 1771–4, rev. 2/1778–9, 3/1786–7 ed. F. von Blankenburg; 4/1792–9/*R*1967)
'Ueber eine neu erfundene Notenschreibmaschine', *Jb der Königlichen Akademie der Wissenschaften zu Berlin* (1771)
Vermischte philosophische Schriften aus den Jahrbüchern der Akademie der Wissenschaften zu Berlin gesammelt (Leipzig, 1773–81, 2/1782–1800, 3/1800)
Lebensbeschreibung von ihm selbst aufgesetzt (Berlin and Stettin, 1809)

BIBLIOGRAPHY

'Eloge de Mr. Sulzer', *Mémoires de l'Académie des sciences de Berlin* (1779)
K. J. Gross: *Sulzers Allgemeine Theorie der schönen Künste* (Berlin, 1905)
J. Leo: *Johann Georg Sulzer und die Entstehung seiner Allgemeine Theorie der schönen Künste* (Berlin, 1907)
A. Tumarkin: *Der Ästhetiker Johann Georg Sulzer* (Leipzig, 1933)
H. Wili: *Johann Georg Sulzer: Persönlichkeit und Kunstphilosophie* (diss., U. of Fribourg, 1954)
W. Seidel: *Über Rhythmustheorien der Neuzeit* (Berne and Munich, 1975)

HOWARD SERWER

Sulzer, Salomon (*b* Hohenems, 30 March 1804; *d* Vienna, 17 Jan 1890). Austrian Jewish cantor and composer. He was the first musician since Salamone Rossi to raise the standards of composition and performance in the synagogue. Three outstanding qualities made him legendary among Jews of the western world. First, his baritone-tenor voice drew admiration not only from the Viennese community whom he served as Obercantor from 1826 until 1881, but also from scholars, musicians (including Meyerbeer, Schubert, Schumann and Liszt), and even the aristocracy; in 1868 he became Knight of the Order of Franz Joseph. Second, his fiery temperament created a vogue among contemporary cantors, who tried to imitate both his singing style and his everyday deportment. Third, and most significant in the development of Jewish music, his compositions became the models upon which almost every newly emancipated congregation based its synagogue ritual covering the entire year. *Schir Zion* (music for the synagogue service), published in two separate volumes (1838–40 and 1865–6), constitutes the earliest complete and thoroughly organized repertory in Hebrew to be set for cantor and four-part male choir. Sulzer's aim, as stated in the preface to volume i, was 'to consider, as far as possible, the traditional tunes bequeathed to us, to cleanse the ancient and dignified type of the later accretions of tasteless embellishments, to bring them back to the original purity, and to reconstruct them in accordance with the text and with the rules of harmony'.

BIBLIOGRAPHY

S. Sulzer: *Denkschrift an die hochgeehrte Wiener israelitische Cultus-Gemeinde zum fünfzigjährigen Jubiläum des alten Bethauses* (Vienna, 1876)
A. Z. Idelsohn: *Jewish Music in its Historical Development* (New York, 1929), 246ff
A. Sendrey: *Bibliography of Jewish Music* (New York, 1951)
E. Mandell, 'Salomon Sulzer, 1804–1890', *Journal of Synagogue Music*, i (1968), no.4, p.3

ALEXANDER KNAPP

Sumatra. *See* INDONESIA, §VII.

Sumaya, Manuel de. *See* ZUMAYA, MANUEL DE.

Sumeria. *See* MESOPOTAMIA.

Sumer is icumen in. A singularly elaborate specimen of the ROTA, composed *c*1250, probably in Reading (and therefore often referred to as the Reading Rota). It is also known as the Summer Canon. The piece is related to the motet, because the round is supported by a texted *pes* (*see* PES (i)), the two halves of which are combined with each other by means of voice-exchange. The secondary Latin poem (*Perspice christicola*) may have been added in order to make the composition fit for inclusion in the manuscript (now *GB-Lbm* Harl.978, f.11*v*; see illustration). It seems to have been an afterthought, since the *pes* has only an English text, which is related to the English words of the rota. (It has been contended that the piece was conceived as a special kind of Latin motet, since the five notes of one of the *pedes* happen to represent the beginning of a Gregorian cantus firmus that might be considered seasonally relevant to the Latin text of the rota. A good many factors, however, argue against this suggestion.)

The proper mode of performance is explained in the source (*Hanc rotam . . .*):

This round can be sung by four fellows, but must not be performed by fewer than three, or at least two, apart from those performing the *pes*. It is sung as follows: While the others remain silent, one begins together with those who have the *pes*, and when he shall have come to the first note after the cross, another begins, and so on with the rest. But each shall pause at the written rests, and not elsewhere, for the duration of one long note. One singer repeats this [the first *pes*] as often as necessary, observing the rest at the end. Another sings this [the second *pes*] with a rest in the middle but not at the end, at which point he at once repeats the beginning.

No ending is specified for the piece, which may be conveniently concluded when the leading voice has sung its part twice. No other composition specifically written for as many as six voices is known before the late 15th century. (Actually, the tune is so constructed that it could be sung as a rondellus for three, four, six, eight or twelve voices.)

Facets characteristic of most 13th-century polyphony preserved in English sources are quintessentially embodied in the Summer Canon: major mode, stress on the chords of tonic and supertonic, *pes*, frequency of triads, predilection for regular periodicity, and the easy rhythmic swing best represented by 6/8 metre in modern transcription. (Both the date and the rhythm of *Sumer is icumen in* suggested by Bukofzer in 1944 are erroneous.) The Summer Canon is the earliest extant secular composition that must be called a tonal organism, both harmonically and melodically. Owing to freakish luck it has been preserved through the centuries and indicates the prior existence of a highly developed musical culture that evidently exerted a vital influence on the specifically English evolution of the conductus and the motet in 13th-century England as well as on the second generation of Notre Dame composers.

See also WYCOMBE, W. DE.

BIBLIOGRAPHY

C. Brown and R. H. Robbins: *The Index of Middle English Verse* (New York, 1943; suppl. 1965 by R. H. Robbins and J. L. Cutler), no.3223
M. F. Bukofzer: ' "Sumer is icumen in": a Revision', *University of California Publications in Music*, ii/2 (1944), 79
B. Schofield: 'The Provenance and Date of "Sumer is icumen in" ', *MR*, ix (1948), 81
N. Pirrotta: 'On the Problems of "Sumer is icumen in" ', *MD*, ii (1948), 205
J. Handschin: 'The Summer Canon and its Background', *MD*, iii (1949), 55–94; *MD*, v (1951), 65–113
W. Wiora: 'Der mittelalterliche Liedkanon', *GfMKB, Lüneburg 1950*, 71
G. Abraham, ed.: *The History of Music in Sound*, ii (1953), frontispiece, 42f
F. Ll. Harrison: *Music in Medieval Britain* (London, 1958, 2/1963), 141ff
E. H. Sanders: 'Duple Rhythm and Alternate Third Mode in the 13th Century', *JAMS*, xv (1962), 263
——: 'Tonal Aspects of 13th-century English Polyphony', *AcM*, xxxvii (1965), 19

The rota 'Sumer is icumen in', composed c1250 (GB-Lbm Harl.978, f.11v)

E. Reiss: *The Art Of the Middle English Lyric* (Athens, Georgia, 1972), 8ff

For further bibliography *see* ENGLAND: BIBLIOGRAPHY OF MUSIC TO 1600.

ERNEST H. SANDERS

Summonte, Antonio (*b* Naples; *d* Naples, 10 Dec 1637). Italian composer. In his last years he was prior of the Carmine Maggiore monastery at Naples. He published *Il primo libro di madrigali a quinque voci* (Naples, 1618). The texts of most of the 20 madrigals in it are drawn from Pomponio Nenna's popular seventh book (1608) and G. B. Nanino's third book (1612) of five-part madrigals. Of the two surviving parts, the cantus includes short, syllabic phrases in inflexible rhythms and with unimaginative melodic contours. There is apparently little chromaticism. In a note to singers Summonte explained that he had included *passaggi* on the vowel 'u' in the madrigal *Filli mi rid'e fugge* to confound those who forbade them on this vowel. He may also have published in 1618 a book of motets for three to five voices.

BIBLIOGRAPHY
G. Gaspari: *Miscellanea musicale* (MS, *I-Bc* UU.12), ii, 929
L. Bianconi: 'Weitere Ergänzungen zu Emil Vogels "Bibliothek der gedruckten weltlichen Vocalmusik Italiens aus den Jahren 1500–1700" aus italienischen Bibliotheken', *AnMc*, no.9 (1970), 186f

KEITH A. LARSON

Summy-Birchard. American music publishing firm in Evanston, Illinois. In 1931 John F. Sengstack acquired the Clayton Summy Company, founded in Chicago in 1888. In 1957 it merged with the C. C. Birchard Company of Boston (founded 1901), which had a particular interest in American music; Birchard commissioned American composers to write for his pioneering school and community songbooks and was an early publisher of Bloch, Copland, Hanson, Ives and Varèse. Summy-Birchard subsequently issued the Birchard Music Series. The company specializes in instructional materials and the Suzuki method, for which it is the exclusive North American publication agent. David K. Sengstack succeeded his father as president of the firm in 1958.

W. THOMAS MARROCCO, MARK JACOBS

Sumner, William Leslie (*b* Airmyn, Yorks., 24 April 1904; *d* Nottingham, 5 Aug 1973). English physicist, educationist and authority on the organ. He gained a first-class honours degree in physics at King's College, London (1925), where he also studied theology. He taught at Southampton University and King Edward VII School, Sheffield, before becoming successively lecturer, senior lecturer and reader (1955) in the department of education at Nottingham University; he retired in 1969. He wrote several standard works on science in education.

His career as a specialist on the design, construction, history and repertory of the organ began with studies in Paris; at King's College he served as chapel organist. During the 1920s he travelled widely in Europe and explored the Baroque organs of Arp Schnitger and the Silbermanns long before the neo-classical movement in England; one product of his research, *The Organ*, was received as the most comprehensive work on the subject this century. He was frequently consulted on organ design, notably at Southwell Minster and Ely Cathedral. He was awarded a PhD by Nottingham University in 1953 and made a Fellow of the Royal School of Church Music in 1969.

WRITINGS
A History and Account of the Organs of St. Paul's Cathedral (London, 1931)
The Organ (London, 1952, 4/1973)
The Organ of Bach and Gottfried Silbermann, Organ Builder (London, 1956)
Henry Willis, Organ Builder and his Successors (London, 1957)
Bach's Organ Registration (London and New York, 1961)
The Parish Church Organ (London, 1961)
The Pianoforte (London, 1966, 3/1970)
Numerous articles for *Grove 5, The Organ, MO* from 1930

BIBLIOGRAPHY
L. Elvin: 'William Leslie Sumner: 1904–1973', *The Organ*, lii (1973), 85

STANLEY WEBB

Sumponya. A musical term occurring in the book of *Daniel*; *see* JEWISH MUSIC, §I, 4(iv).

Sumsion, Herbert (Whitton) (*b* Gloucester, 14 Jan 1899). English organist. His career centred on the Three Choirs Festival. He became a boy chorister at Gloucester Cathedral at a time when more new English music was being heard than at any time since Purcell, and the triennial music meetings had acquired a new momentum under G. R. Sinclair at Hereford, Ivor Atkins at Worcester and Herbert Brewer at Gloucester. Sumsion was Brewer's pupil and assistant, and succeeded him as organist in 1928. He held the post for 39 years, during which his open-minded approach to new music helped the festivals to adjust to changing taste. His association with Kodály, Elgar, Vaughan Williams and Holst was close; his *Dream of Gerontius* sounded as if Elgar himself were conducting; in later years he negotiated the first performance of Herbert Howells's *Hymnus Paradisi* and new works by Gerald Finzi, both close friends. Sumsion composed mostly for voices and organ and his *Festival Benedicite* in D was given a first performance at the 1971 Gloucester festival, when the rebuilt organ was inaugurated. As well as being a skilled conductor and organist, Sumsion is an able accompanist and chamber music player. He was awarded a Lambeth DMus in 1947 and made CBE in 1961.

STANLEY WEBB

Sunday school hymnody. Hymns composed and collected as a result of the rapid growth in the American Sunday school movement in the 19th century; *see* GOSPEL MUSIC, §I, 1(ii).

Sundberg, Johan Emil Fredrik (*b* Stockholm, 25 March 1936). Swedish musicologist. After qualifying as an organist and cantor (Uppsala, 1957) he studied musicology, aesthetics, philosophy and mathematics at Uppsala University (BA 1961, MA 1963), where he took the doctorate with a dissertation on the scaling of open-flue organ pipes (1966). From 1964 he worked at the Royal Institute of Technology, Stockholm, and in 1967 was appointed part-time lecturer in musicology at Uppsala University. His chief areas of research are acoustics and the perception of music (particularly singing), music theory (with special reference to intervals and the scale) and phonetics. He was treasurer of the Swedish Acoustical Society (1972–6), of which he became president in 1976.

WRITINGS
Mensurens betydelse i öppna labialpipor (diss., U. of Uppsala, 1966)
'The "Scale" of Musical Instruments', *STMf*, xlix (1967), 119
'Some Differences between Formants in Speech and Singing', *14e congrès international de logopédie et de phoniatrie: Paris 1968*
with B. Lindblom: 'A Quantitative Theory of Cardinal Vowels and

the Teaching of Pronunciation', *Applications of Linguistics: 2nd International Congress of Applied Linguistics: Cambridge 1969*, 319
'Formant Structure and Articulation of Spoken and Sung Vowels', *Folia phoniatrica*, xxii (1970), 28
with B. Lindblom: 'Towards a Generative Theory of Music', *STMf*, lii (1970), 71
with B. Lindblom: 'Acoustical Consequences of Lip, Tongue, Jaw, and Larynx Movement', *Journal of the Acoustical Society of America*, 1 (1971), 1166
'Voice Source Properties of Bass Singers', 'Real-time Notation of Performed Melodies by Means of a Computer' [with P. Tjernlund], 'Perception of the Octave Interval' [with J. Lindqvist], *7th International Congress on Acoustics: Budapest 1971*
'Production and Function of the "Singing Formant"', *IMSCR*, xi *Copenhagen 1972*, 679
with P. Tjernlund and F. Fransson: 'Grundfrequenzmessungen an schwedischen Kernspaltflöten: die Aussagen der Messergebnisse', *Studia instrumentorum musicae popularis*, ii (Stockholm, 1972), 77
with E. Jansson: 'Long-time-average-spectra applied to Analysis of Music', *Speech Transmission Laboratory*, iv (1972), 40; Ger. trans., *Acustica*, xxxiv (1975–6), 15, 269, 275
'Naturvetenskaplig metodik i musikforskning', *STMf*, liv (1972), 103
with J. Lindqvist: 'Musical Octaves and Pitch', *Journal of the Acoustical Society of America*, liv (1973), 922
Musikens Ijudlära (Lund, 1973)
'The Source Spectrum in Professional Singing', *Folia phoniatrica*, xxv (1973), 71
'Articulatory Interpretation of the "Singing Formant"', *Journal of the Acoustical Society of America*, lv (1974), 838
with B. Fritzell and O. Hallén: 'Evaluation of Teflon Injection Procedures for Paralytic Dysphonia', *Folia phoniatrica*, xxvi (1974), 414
with F. Fransson and P. Tjernlund: 'The Scale in Played Music', *STMf*, lvi (1974), 49
'Formant Technique in a Professional Female Singer', *Acustica*, xxxii (1975), 89
'Effects of the Vibrato and the "Singing Formant" on Pitch', *Memory Book in Honor of the Late Miroslav Filip* (Bratislava, 1976)
'Generative Theories in Language and Music Descriptions', *Cognition*, iv (1976), 99
c30 articles in the *Speech Transmission Laboratory Quarterly Progress and Status Report*, Royal Institute of Technology, Stockholm (1964–)
'Acoustics', §5, *Grove 6*

Suneburg [Sunnenburg], **Friedrich von.** *See* FRIEDRICH VON SUNNENBURG.

Suñol (y Baulenas), Gregorio Maria (*b* Barcelona, 7 Sept 1879; *d* Rome, 26 Oct 1946). Spanish priest and teacher of plainsong. He took his vows as a Benedictine monk at Montserrat Abbey on 14 September 1895, was ordained priest on 20 September 1902 and in 1943 appointed abbot of Ste Cecilia of Montserrat. He was impressed by Mocquereau on his first visit to the Solesmes monks (then refugees on the Isle of Wight); he remained a faithful, intelligent disciple of the Solesmes school. From 1907 to 1928 he directed the choir at Montserrat. He spread this teaching enthusiastically throughout Spain, setting up a number of schools for its propagation. His *Método completo de canto gregoriano según la escuela de Solesmes* was an enormous success (eight editions from 1905 to 1943) and was translated into French (Tournai, 1906, 7/1932), into German, English, Italian and Portuguese. But his most important work was the *Introducció a la paleografía musical gregoriana* (Montserrat, 1925), completed, revised and translated into French with help from René Renaudin (Tournai, 1935; bibliography by H. Anglès). In 1931 Suñol was summoned to Milan by Cardinal Schuster, who made him the director of the Pontifical School of Ambrosian Chant and asked him to prepare a new practical edition of Ambrosian chant. This latter was an immense labour, but was undertaken and completed with astonishing rapidity: *Praeconium paschale* (Milan, 1934), *Cantus missalis* (Milan, 1935), *Antiphonale missarum* (Rome, 1935), *Officium et missa pro Defunctis*

(Rome, 1936), *Ordinarium Missae et cantus varii* (Rome, 1936), *Liber vesperalis* (Rome, 1939). In 1930 he succeeded Ferretti as director of the Istituto Pontifico di Musica Sacra in Rome.

BIBLIOGRAPHY
H. Anglès: 'Il canto gregoriano e l'opera dell'abate Don G. M. Suñol', *Revue grégorienne*, xxvii (1948), 161

EUGÈNE CARDINE

Sun Ra [Bourke, Sonny; Le Sony'r Ra] (*b* May *c*1928). Black American jazz composer and band-leader. He played the piano in Fletcher Henderson's orchestra in 1946–7, and first attracted attention as an arranger. Later he led his own band at the Grand Terrace in Chicago. During the mid-1950s his band, the Myth-Science (or Solar) Arkestra, became significant in Chicago's avant-garde jazz movement, and began to issue records. He moved to New York in 1960, by which time he had begun to develop a unique and highly inventive ensemble style that was to attract a considerable following, particularly among European jazz enthusiasts. In the 1970s Sun Ra and the Arkestra toured and lectured at American colleges and universities, also playing in the film documentary *The Cry of Jazz*, for which Sun Ra composed the score.

Along with Cecil Taylor and Ornette Coleman, Sun Ra significantly influenced the new jazz styles of the 1960s. His earlier work derived from the popular and commercial jazz of the time; *Reflections in Blue* (1957) is in a conventional bop style, also incorporating blues patterns and common formal designs. Within ten years, however, pieces such as *Cosmic Chaos* were to show a radical, complex, often frenetic idiom, and an obsession with percussion instruments. He employed freely improvised solos in busy combinations with microtonal melodies and electronic effects, often juxtaposing standard jazz tunes with aleatory solo work on such instruments as the piccolo, violin and Moog synthesizer in addition to saxophones and trumpets. These musical innovations were combined with novel mixed-media

Sun Ra

techniques loosely based on astronomical and ancient Egyptian imagery; his performances commonly included modern dance, slide and light shows.

BIBLIOGRAPHY

M. Harrison: 'Sun Ra', *Jazz on Record*, ed. A. McCarthy (London, 1968), 275
R. Townley: 'Sun Ra', *Down Beat* (20 Dec 1973), 18
E. Jost: 'Sun Ra', *Free Jazz* (Graz, 1974), 180
J. Cooke: 'Sun Ra', *Modern Jazz: the Essential Records*, ed. M. Harrison (London, 1975)

ROBERT DICKOW

Suono di bottiglia (It.). BOUTEILLOPHONE.

Superius (Lat.: 'top', 'uppermost'). A term used particularly in the 16th century to denote the highest voice of a polyphonic composition. In sources of 14th- and 15th-century music lower voices are usually identified as tenor, contratenor, contratenor bassus etc, but upper voices are normally not specified at all. The term 'superius' came into common use with the advent of music publishing, when it became necessary for each partbook to carry some identification (*see* PARTBOOKS).

OWEN JANDER

Superoctave. As the name of an organ stop, Superoctave (*Superoktave*) denotes the Principal-scaled rank an octave above the so-called Octave (*Oktave*). The latter was itself an octave above the basic Principal rank of the department concerned. Thus if the *Prinzipal* is 16′ and the *Oktave* 8′, the *Superoktave* is 4′; or respectively 8′, 4′ and 2′. Not until German influences became strong in the mid-19th century was the term ever used on English organs in preference to 'Fifteenth'. In Germany itself, *Superoktave* as a rank in large organs emerged out of the Mixture only from *c*1550, previous 2′ ranks being scaled as flutes of various types. As the name of an organ coupler, Superoctave is normally a misnomer, the coupler concerned being an Octave coupler playing notes an octave above, not an octave above the octave.

PETER WILLIAMS

Superposition. *See* ÜBERGREIFEN.

Supertonic. The second step or DEGREE of the major or minor scale, so called because it lies one step above the tonic.

Supervia, Conchita (*b* Barcelona, 9 Dec 1895; *d* London, 30 March 1936). Spanish mezzo-soprano; a magnetic personality as well as an outstanding artist. Educated at the Colegio de las Damas Negras in Barcelona, Supervia can have had little specifically musical training when, at 14, she made her operatic début in minor roles with a visiting Spanish company at the Teatro Colón, Buenos Aires (1 October 1910 in Stiattesi's *Blanca de Beaulieu*). In November 1911, before she was 16, she had already been chosen as the Octavian of the Rome première of *Der Rosenkavalier*; in the 1915–16 season she appeared in Chicago in leading French roles (Charlotte, Mignon, Carmen), and during the 1920s sang widely in Spain, at La Scala (Octavian, Cherubino, Humperdinck's Hänsel and Ravel's Concepcion) and elsewhere in Italy. Her international fame began with her assumption of the brilliant mezzo roles in Rossini's then neglected *L'italiana in Algeri* and *La Cenerentola*, and her appearances in the original mezzo version of *Il barbiere*; these roles, together with that of Carmen (in which she was greatly admired in Paris), formed the staple of her stage repertory during the last decade of her life, and brought her to Covent Garden in 1934 and 1935. By then she had married an Englishman, Ben Rubenstein, and settled in London, where she became also very popular on the concert platform, especially as an interpreter of Spanish song. She died after childbirth when her career was at its height.

Conchita Supervia in the title role of Bizet's 'Carmen'

Supervia possessed exceptional vocal gifts, together with a temperament and musicianship that could turn them to the finest account. Her rich and vibrant mezzo, extending from *g* to *b″*, was developed to a high degree of flexibility, although a certain vehemence of emission affected the evenness of her scale. Few singers conveyed so keen a pleasure in the sheer act of singing, or such a power of establishing immediate contact with the listener. Her phrasing was precise and shapely, and her enunciation uncommonly vivid, whether in her native Spanish, in almost flawless French and Italian, or in the amusingly personal English of her later years. These virtues, allied with a mischievous sense of humour and a delightful stage and platform personality, made her a superb interpreter of Rossini and Bizet, as of Falla, Granados and Spanish folksong. Her numerous gramophone records, though sometimes adding an untruthfully strident quality to her louder tones, convey very well the vivacity, charm and intimacy of her singing.

BIBLIOGRAPHY

H. M. Barnes and V. Girard: 'Conchita Supervia', *Record Collector*, vi (1951), 54 [with discography]
D. Shawe-Taylor: 'Conchita Supervia (1895–1936)', *Opera*, xi (1960), 16
H. M. Barnes, D. Cattana, V. Girard and others: discography in *Recorded Sound* (1973), no.52, p.212
I. Newton: 'Conchita Supervia', *Recorded Sound* (1973), no.52, p.205

DESMOND SHAWE-TAYLOR

Supičić, Ivo (*b* Zagreb, 18 July 1928). Yugoslav musicologist. He studied the piano at the Academy of Music in Zagreb, graduating in 1953. Between 1960 and 1963 he was attached to the CNRS in Paris, and in 1962 completed the doctorate in musicology at the Sorbonne. In 1964 he began to teach at the department of musicology of the Zagreb Academy of Music. In 1967–8 he was a visiting Fellow at Harvard University. He is a member of the editorial board of *Acta musicologica* and *Arti musices* and editor of the *International Review of the Aesthetics and Sociology of Music*. In his numerous publications he has discussed the sociological aspects of music, especially of the 20th century, and the aesthetic outlook of several contemporary Croatian composers within a broader context of contemporary philosophy of music.

WRITINGS

La musique expressive (Paris, 1957)
Elementi sociologije muzike (diss., U. of Paris, Sorbonne, 1962; Zagreb, 1964; Pol. trans., 1969; Fr. trans., enlarged, 1971, as *Musique et société: perspectives pour une sociologie de la musique*)
'Problèmes de la sociologie musicale', *Cahiers internationaux de sociologie*, xxxvii (1964), 119
'Note sur la tradition', *SMz*, cv (1965), 22
'Pour une sociologie de la musique', *Revue d'esthétique*, xix (1966), 66
'L'essenza della musica e l'estetica contemporanea', *Rivista di estetica*, xiii (1968), 332
'Estetika Stjepana Šuleka: sintetični pregled osnovnih koncepcij' [The aesthetics of Stjepan Šulek: a synthetic survey of his basic conceptions], *MZ*, v (1969), 101
'Science on Music and Values in Music', *Journal of Aesthetics and Art Criticism*, xxviii (1969), 71
'Aesthetic Views in Contemporary Croatian Music', *Arti musices*, special issue (1970), 107
'Matter and Form in Music', *IRASM*, i (1970), 149
'Expression and Meaning in Music', *IRASM*, ii (1971), 193
'Sens et non-sens en musique', *IRASM*, iii (1972), 187
'Zvok kot gradivo ali znak in smisel glasbe' [Sound as material or the symbol and meaning of music], *MZ*, ix (1973), 108
'Problem značenja u glazbi' [The problem of meaning in music], *Arti musices*, v (1974), 39
'Contemporary Aesthetics of Music and Musicology', *AcM*, xlvii (1975), 193
'Suvremena estetika i umjetnička glazba' [Contemporary aesthetics and art music], *Arti musices*, vi (1975), 39–70

BOJAN BUJIĆ

Suppan, Jakob. *See* ZUPAN, JAKOB.

Suppan, Wolfgang (*b* Irdning, 5 Aug 1933). Austrian musicologist. At Graz he studied the clarinet, violin, piano and music theory at the conservatory, and musicology with Federhofer and Marx at the university (1954–9), where he took his doctorate in 1959 with a dissertation on H. E. J. von Lannoy. After working in Freiburg as an assistant at the East German Folklore Institute (1961–3) and director of the music department at the Folksong Archive (1963–71), he completed his *Habilitation* in 1971 at the University of Mainz with a study of German song in the second half of the 16th century, and became reader there. In 1974 he was appointed professor and director of the Ethnomusicological Institute at the Graz Musikhochschule. His research has been in ethnomusicology, particularly European (in 1967 he became co-chairman of the IFMC commission for research on and editions of historic folk music sources), wind music, music education outside schools and the music of Styria.

WRITINGS

Heinrich Eduard Joseph von Lannoy (1787–1853): Leben und Werke (diss., U. of Graz, 1959; Graz, 1960)
Hanns Holenia: eine Würdigung seines Lebens (Graz, 1960)
'Bi- bis tetrachordische Tonreihen im Volkslied deutscher Sprachinseln Süd- und Osteuropas', *SM*, iii (1962), 329
Steirisches Musiklexikon (Graz, 1962–6)

'Über die Totenklage im deutschen Sprachraum', *JIFMC*, xv (1963), 18
'Die Beachtung von "Original" und "Singmanier" im deutschsprachigen Volkslied', *Jb für Volksliedforschung*, ix (1964), 12
'Melodiestrukturen im deutschsprachigen Brauchtumslied', *Deutsches Jb für Volkskunde*, x (1964), 254
'Moses Mendelssohn und die Musikästhetik des 18. Jahrhunderts', *Mf*, xvii (1964), 22
'Schubert-Autographe im Nachlass Weis-Ostborn, Graz', *SM*, vi (1964), 131
'Die Lage der Volksmusikforschung in den deutschsprachigen Ländern', *AcM*, xxxvii (1965), 1 [with F. Hoerburger]
'Die Liederhandschrift I/17 des Kärntner Landesarchivs', *Carinthia*, 1st ser., no.155 (1965), 519
'Die Liederhandschrift Y 56 der Thurgauischen Kantonsbibliothek zu Frauenfeld', *Schweizerische Archiv für Volkskunde*, lxi (1965), 117–201
'Die Musiksammlung des Freiherrn von Lannoy', *FAM*, xii (1965), 9
Otto Siegl: eine Studie (Vienna, 1966)
Volkslied: seine Sammlung und Erforschung (Stuttgart, 1966, 2/1974)
'Die seit 1945 erschienene deutschsprachige Literatur zum Jazz', *Jb für Volksliedforschung*, xii (1967), 182
' "In der wyss, Wer ich ein edler Falcke" ', *Festschrift für Walter Wiora* (Kassel, 1967), 651
'The Problem of Historicity in European Folksong', *IMSCR, x Ljubljana 1967*, 329–58
'Volksmusik im Berzirk Weiz', *Weizerische Geschichte und Landschaft in Einzeldarstellungen*, viii (Weiz, 1967), 19–59
'Nikolaus Beuttners Gesangbuch, Graz 1602, und die mündliche Überlieferung', *Joannea*, iii (Graz, 1968), 261–95
'Zur Musik der Erlauer Spiele', *SM*, xi (1969), 409
'Lieder einer steirischen Gewerkensgattin aus dem 18. Jahrhundert', *Beiträge zur Erforschung steirischer Geschichtsquellen*, xlix (Graz, 1970), 1–43
Die Schichtung des deutschen Liedgutes in der 2. Hälfte des 16. Jahrhunderts (Habilitationsschrift, U. of Mainz, 1971; Tutzing, 1973)
Lexikon des Blasmusikwesens (Freiburg, 1971, 2/1976)
'Der Beitrag der Europäischen Musikethnologie zur Jazzforschung', *Jazzforschung*, iii–iv (1971–2), 35
'Der Ritter aus der Steiermark', *Kretzenbacher Festschrift* (Munich, 1973), 261
'Folklore im Grazer Konzertleben des Biedermeier', *Historisches Jb der Stadt Graz*, v–vi (1973), 119–46
'Das melismatische Singen der Wolga-Deutschen in seinem historischen und geographischen Kontext', *Festschrift to Ernst Emsheimer* (Stockholm, 1974), 237
'Melodram und melodramatische Gestaltung', *Festschrift zum zehnjährigen Bestand der Hochschule für Musik und darstellende Kunst in Graz* (Vienna, 1974), 243
'Germany', §II, *Grove 6*

EDITIONS

with H. Federhofer and L. Ergens: *J. J. Fux: Pulcheria, K.303, Sämtliche Werke*, v/2 (Graz, 1967)

FOLKSONG EDITIONS

with A. Michl and K. Stekl: *Musik aus der Steiermark* (Vienna, 1959–)
with R. W. Brednich and W. Heiske: *Deutsche Volkslieder mit ihren Melodien* (Freiburg, 1965)
with R. W. Brednich: *Gottscheer Volkslieder* (Mainz, 1969–72)
——: *Die Ebermannstädter Liederhandschrift* (Kulmbach, 1972)
Alta musica (Tutzing, 1976–)
with W. Stief: *Melodietypen des deutschen Volkesgesangs* (Tutzing, 1976–)

Suppé [Suppè], Franz (von) [Francesco Ezechiele Ermenegildo Cavaliere Suppé Demelli] (*b* Spalato, Dalmatia [now Split, Yugoslavia] 18 April 1819; *d* Vienna, 21 May 1895). Austrian composer and conductor of Belgian descent. His father and grandfather were Austrian civil servants working in Dalmatia, and his mother was Viennese by birth. Despite paternal opposition Suppé showed his musical talent at an early age, encouraged by the bandmaster Ferrari and the cathedral choirmaster Cigalla; a *Missa dalmatica*, written when Suppé was 13, was considered worthy of being revised and published 40 years later. He was sent to study law at Padua, but he nevertheless heard and made much music, undertaking visits to Milan and meeting, as well as hearing the operas of, Rossini, Donizetti and Verdi.

After his father's death in 1835, he and his mother went to Vienna. Having considered studying medicine, he took up music in earnest, taught and encouraged by Seyfried and Sechter; although the former's testimonial of 14 March 1840 (reproduced in Keller's monograph, 1905) emphasizes Suppé's abilities in serious composition, he helped secure him an initially unpaid post as third Kapellmeister at the Theater in der Josefstadt in the autumn of 1840. There his first score was very successfully given on 5 March 1841; under the title of *Jung lustig, im Alter traurig, oder Die Folgen der Erziehung* it received a favourable review in the *Theaterzeitung*, being praised for qualities associated with his later masterpieces:

Melodious, rich in tender ideas [and] fine nuances, clearly and effectively orchestrated and containing such surprising modulations and transitions, that the overture and most of the songs and choruses had to be encored . . . The whole composition has traces of the Italian style but now and then goes in for thoroughly vernacular, simply handled themes.

Suppé himself is reported to have said later that much of the success was due to his having unconsciously (owing to his very limited knowledge of German) treated a *Jodler* in the style of a sentimental Donizettian farewell, through misunderstanding the text. Donizetti, a distant relative, encouraged Suppé during one of his visits to Vienna (? the early 1840s) when the young man showed him the score of an opera, *Gertrude della valle*, that he was then writing, and Donizetti was probably instrumental in bringing about Suppé's later visits to Italy.

Until 1845 Suppé wrote well over 20 scores for the Theater in der Josefstadt (and for the director Pokorny's other theatres in Baden, Ödenburg (Sopron) and Pressburg, in which he was mainly employed in and around 1843); among them were *Marie, die Tochter des Regiments, Ein Morgen, ein Mittag und ein Abend in Wien* (both 1844), and a score for *A Midsummer Night's Dream*; he also appeared with success as a singer on the provincial stages, making his début in that capacity as Dulcamara (in Donizetti's *L'elisir d'amore*) at Ödenburg on 2 May 1842.

In 1845 Suppé moved to Pokorný's newly acquired Theater an der Wien, where for the next 17 years he was Kapellmeister, sharing the duties with Lortzing in 1846–8, and with Adolf Müller from 1848. Apart from a string of more or less successful theatre scores, he conducted many important operatic performances – for instance the productions of Meyerbeer's *Die Gibellinen in Pisa* (*Les Huguenots*) in May 1846 with Jenny Lind and Tichatschek, and the same composer's *Vielka* (*Ein Feldlager in Schlesien*) with Jenny Lind and Staudigl in February 1847.

In 1860 Suppé's *Das Pensionat* was the first successful attempt at a genuine Viennese operetta in answer to the French product, which since October 1858 (the Carltheater's production of Offenbach's *Le mariage à la lanterne*) had been gaining a firm hold on the repertory of Vienna's theatres. In 1862 Suppé moved to the Kaitheater and in 1865 to the Carltheater (formerly known as the Theater in der Leopoldstadt). Year after year he turned out a series of theatre scores, ranging from overtures and incidental music to operettas, opera parodies and even the occasional opera. Among his greatest successes were *Gervinus, Flotte Bursche* and *Fatinitza*, all of which received 100 or more performances in a few years; and, above all, *Boccaccio*, which he referred to as 'the greatest success of my life'. In the late 1870s he purchased an estate in the Lower Austrian countryside, and his increasing fame was reflected in

invitations to visit the first Bayreuth festival in 1876, and Paris, Brussels, Germany and Italy (1879). In 1881 he was given the freedom of the City of Vienna. In 1882 he retired from his post as Kapellmeister to the Carltheater, though he continued to compose until the end of his life, enjoying successes in Germany in 1883 when he conducted his latest operetta, *Die Afrikareise*. Although he was working on another operetta, *Das Modell*, at the time of his death, his last works were mainly sacred. His last years were clouded by neuralgia and finally cancer.

Suppé is the earliest Viennese composer of musical farces whose works still survive as viable stage scores (and popular overtures), and later in his career he became the first master of the classical Viennese operetta in the train of the acclimatized scores of Offenbach. His light, fluent style includes the ability to vary a phrase length or melodic and rhythmic figure in a personal and immediately effective way. Though now remembered mainly as the composer of overtures such as *Poet and Peasant*, *Light Cavalry* and *Morning, Noon and Night in Vienna*, his ambitions extended to the composition of large-scale church compositions and operas. He is at his best and most characteristic in the series of famous operettas from *Die schöne Galathea* (1865) to *Boccaccio* (1879). Numbers like 'Hab ich nur deine Liebe', 'Mia bella Fiorentina' and 'Holde Schöne' from *Boccaccio* have an irresistible elegance and élan, and his scoring is worthy of the finest orchestras rather than the bands that so often seize upon the overtures in particular. The song 'O du [Das ist] mein Österreich' of 1849 has become virtually Austria's second national song.

WORKS

Overtures, potpourris, marches and songs from many of the stage works were published – usually with no date, but presumably soon after the premières; chief sources of MSS and printed music are *A-Wgm* (including many autograph scores), *Wn, Wst*; all performances and printings cited below were in Vienna unless otherwise stated.

TJ – Theater in der Josefstadt
CT – Carltheater
TW – Theater an der Wien
KT – Kaitheater

Virginia (opera, L. Holt), 1837, not perf.
Gertrude della valle (opera, G. Brazzanovich), 1841, not perf.
Jung lustig, im Alter traurig, oder Die Folgen der Erziehung (comedy with songs, 3, C. Wallis), TJ, 5 March 1841
Die Hammerschmiedin aus Steyermark, oder Folgen einer Landpartie (local farce with songs, 2, J. Schickh), TJ, 14 Oct 1842
Ein Morgen, ein Mittag und ein Abend in Wien (local play with songs, 2), TJ, 26 Feb 1844
Marie, die Tochter des Regiments (vaudeville, 2, F. Blum, after J. H. St Georges and J. F. A. Bayard), TJ, 13 June 1844
Der Krämer und sein Kommis (farce with songs, 2, F. Kaiser), TJ, 5 Sept 1844
Die Müllerin von Burgos (vaudeville, 2, J. Kupelwieser), TJ, 8 March 1845
Sie ist verheiratet (comedy with songs, 3, Kaiser), TW, 7 Nov 1845
Dichter und Bauer (comedy with songs, 3, K. Elmar), TW, 24 Aug 1846, full score (1900)
Das Mädchen vom Lande (opera, 3, Elmar), TW, 7 Aug 1847
Martl, oder Der Portiunculatag in Schnabelhausen (farce with music, parody of Flotow: Martha, 3, A. Berla), TW, 16 Dec 1848
Des Teufels Brautfahrt, oder Böser Feind und guter Freund (magic farce with songs, 3, Elmar), TW, 30 Jan 1849
Gervinus, der Narr von Untersberg, oder Ein patriotischer Wunsch (farce with songs, 3, Berla), Braunhirschen-Arena [and TW], 1 July 1849
Unterthänig und unabhängig, oder Vor und nach einem Jahre (comedy with songs, 3, Elmar), TW, 13 Oct 1849
s'Alraunl (romantic tale with songs, 3, A. von Klesheim), TW, 13 Nov 1849
Der Dumme hat's Glück (farce with songs, 3, Berla), TW, 29 June 1850
Dame Valentine, oder Frauenräuber und Wanderbursche (Singspiel, 3, Elmar), TW, 9 Jan 1851
Der Tannenhäuser (dramatic poem with music, H. von Levitschnigg),

TW, 27 Feb 1852

Wo steckt der Teufel? (farce with songs, 3, ?Grün), TW, 28 June 1854

Paragraph 3 (opera, 3, M. A. Grandjean), Hofoper, 8 Jan 1858

Das Pensionat (operetta, 1, C. K.), TW, 24 Nov 1860, vocal score (n.d.)

Die Kartenschlägerin (Pique-Dame) (operetta, 1), KT, 26 April 1862

Zehn [later as many as 25] Mädchen und kein Mann (operetta, 1, W. Friedrich), KT, 25 Oct 1862, vocal score (n.d.)

Die flotten Burschen (Flotte Bursche) (operetta, 1, J. Braun), KT, 18 April 1863, vocal score (n.d.)

Das Corps der Rache (operetta, 1, J. L. Harisch), CT, 5 March 1864

Franz Schubert (Liederspiel, 1, H. Max), CT, 10 Sept 1864

Dinorah, oder Die Turnerfahrt nach Hütteldorf (parody opera, of Meyerbeer, 3, F. Hopp), CT, 4 May 1865

Die schöne Galatea (Galathée) (comic-mythological operetta, 1, P. Henrion), Berlin, Meysels-Theater, 30 June 1865, vocal score (n.d.)

Die leichte Kavallerie (operetta, 2, C. Costa), CT, 21 or ?24 March 1866, vocal score (n.d.)

Die Tochter der Puszta (operetta, 1), CT, 24 March 1866

Die Freigeister (operetta, 2, Costa), CT, 23 Oct 1866

[Die] Banditenstreiche (operetta, 1, B. Boutonnier), CT, 27 April 1867

Die Frau Meisterin (magic operetta, 3, Costa), CT, 20 Jan 1868, vocal score (Leipzig, n.d.)

Isabella (operetta, J. Weyl), CT, 5 Nov 1869

Tantalusqualen (operetta), CT, 3 Oct 1868

Lohengelb, oder Die Jungfrau von Dragant (parody operetta, of Wagner: Lohengrin, 3 Costa, Grandjean), CT, 30 Nov 1870

Canebas (operetta, 1, J. Doppler), CT, 2 Nov 1872

Fatinitza (operetta, 3, F. Zell, R. Genée), CT, 5 Jan 1876, full score (n.d.)

Der Teufel auf Erden (fantastic operetta, 3, J. Hopp), CT, 5 Jan 1878, vocal score (London, n.d.)

Boccaccio (operetta, 3, Zell, Genée), CT, 1 Feb 1879, full score (Hamburg, n.d.)

Donna Juanita (operetta, 3, Zell, Genée), CT, 21 Feb 1880, full score (Brussels, n.d.); arr. K. Pauspertl as Die grosse Unbekannte, 1925

Der Gascogner (operetta, 3, Zell, Genée), CT, 21 or ?22 March 1881, vocal score (Hamburg, n.d.)

Das Herzblättchen (operetta, 3, C. Tetzlaff), CT, 4 Feb 1882

Die Afrikareise (operetta, 3, M. West, Genée, O. F. Berg), TW, 17 March 1883, full score (Hamburg, n.d.)

Des Matrosen Heimkehr (romantic opera, 2, A. Langner), Hamburg, 4 May 1885, vocal score (Hamburg, 1885)

Bellman (comic opera, 3, West, L. Held), TW, 26 or ?24 Feb 1887

Joseph Haydn (musical portrait with melodies by Haydn, F. von Radler), TJ, 30 April 1887

Die Jagd nach dem Glücke (operetta, 3, Genée, B. Zappert), CT, 27 Oct 1888, full score (Hamburg, n.d.)

Das Modell (operetta, 3, V. Léon, Held), CT, 4 Oct 1895, full score (Leipzig, n.d.) [completed by J. Stern and A. Zamara]

Die Pariserin, oder Das heimliche Bild (operetta, 3, Léon, Held), CT, 26 Jan 1898 [arr. of Die Frau Meisterin, 1868]

c200 other stage works

Other works: Requiem, 1855 [for F. Pokorný]; 3 masses and other church music; secular choral works; songs; syms.; ovs., incl. 1 based on Dalmatian folksongs; dances; str qts

BIBLIOGRAPHY

C. von Wurzbach: Biographisches Lexikon des Kaiserthums Oesterreich, xl (Vienna, 1880), 337 [with lists of stage works and publications]

G. Sabalich: Franz Suppé e l'operetta (Zara, 1888)

O. Keller: Franz von Suppé: der Schöpfer der deutschen Operette (Leipzig, 1905)

E. Rieger: Offenbach und seine Wiener Schule (Vienna, 1920)

O. Keller: Die Operette in ihrer geschichtlichen Entwicklung (Leipzig, 1926)

A. Würz, ed.: Reclams Operettenführer (Stuttgart, 1938, 11/1962), 9ff

F. Hadamowsky and H. Otte: Die Wiener Operette (Vienna, 1947)

A. Bauer: 150 Jahre Theater an der Wien (Zurich, 1952)

——: Opern und Operetten in Wien (Graz, 1955)

——: Das Theater in der Josefstadt zu Wien (Vienna, 1957)

B. Grun: Kulturgeschichte der Operette (Munich, 1961)

G. Hughes: Composers of Operetta (London, 1962)

PETER BRANSCOMBE

Supposition. The concept, proposed by Rameau (Traité de l'harmonie, 1722), that chords of the 9th and 11th, among others, arise from a 7th chord by placing a 'supposed' bass one or two 3rds below the FUNDAMENTAL BASS. For instance, in the chord f–a–c'–e'–g'–b' the fundamental bass is c', while the 'supposed' bass is f. The doctrine of chords by supposition was adopted and modified by Roussier, Marpurg and others; A. F. C. Kollmann claimed to confute it by averring that it was theoretically simpler to treat Rameau's 'supposed' bass as the fundamental and to regard the 9th and 11th, following Kirnberger, as structurally inessential transient notes.

Rameau, in calling his concept 'supposition', extended a sense in which the word had been used to describe notes of a melody that do not belong to the concurrent harmony; see, for instance, the definition of 'supposition' in J. G. Walther's Musicalisches Lexicon (1732).

MICHAEL KASSLER

Supraphon. Czechoslovak firm of publishers of gramophone records, music and books on music. It arose out of the change of name, on 20 February 1967, of the Státní Hudební Vydavatelství (State Music Publishers); before the foundation of that firm on 1 January 1961 records were made by the Gramofonové Závody (Gramophone Works, nationalized 1946), while the production of music and books on music (after the nationalization of the publishing firms in 1949) was conducted first by the firms Orbis and HUDEBNÍ MATICE and then (1953–60) by Státní Nakladatelství Krásné Literatury, Hudby a Umění (State Publishers of Literature, Music and Art).

The production of gramophone records in the early 1970s had reached an annual total of about 2000 titles, including most genres of classical and popular music, jazz and all types of folk music. In addition Supraphon produces anthologies of music from the Czech and Moravian archives, and early Czech organ music. It also exchanges recordings for publication with well-known foreign firms. The firm publishes annually about 275 scores and 20 books on music. A wide range of music is covered, including editions of Smetana, Dvořák, Fibich and Janáček. Early music is published in the series Musica Antiqua Bohemica, Musica Viva Historica, Documenta Historica Musicae and Medailon, and the firm also publishes works by contemporary composers. The publicity department issues the magazine G-Gramorevue, and is responsible for cultural societies in Prague and Ostrava as well as an exhibition hall in Prague. In 1971, when state music-publishing activities were decentralized, an independent publishing firm, Opus, was founded in Bratislava, and this took over Supraphon's activities in Slovakia.

ZDENĚK CULKA

Supries, Joseph (b Cotignac, Var, 19 Nov 1761; d Aix-en-Provence, 27 July 1822). French composer and organist. On 14 June 1781 he was admitted to an ecclesiastical position in Aix-en-Provence; later he obtained the office of deacon. He was a pupil of Padre Santo-Vito at the maîtrise of St Sauveur Cathedral, Aix-en-Provence, and on 21 February 1787 he became the cathedral organist. He held this position until his death, apart from an interruption caused by the Revolution, when he went to Rome, returning only in 1807 after the reinstatement of the cathedral chapter. Supries and Balthazare Michel (1749–1825), the maître de chapelle of the cathedral, were early teachers of Félicien David.

According to Abbé Arnaud, Supries was a 'talented accompanist, fertile improviser and faultless harmonist' (see Marbot). His melodies are often attractive but suffer from excessive vocal ornamentation. His harmony is colourful, and his treatment of modulation rich and original; instrumentation is carefully handled.

WORKS
(all are MSS in F-AIXmc)

3 masses: 1 in E♭, 4 male vv, orch, 1807; 1 in D, 4vv, orch; 1 in D, 3vv, 2 bn, org

Te Deum, 4vv, orch, 1814

Psalms: Laudate pueri, 4vv, orch, 1804; Beatus vir, 3vv, orch, 1806; Confitebor tibi, 4vv, orch

Motets: Tantum ergo, 4vv, org, 1822; Domine salvum fac, 4vv, orch; Ecce sacerdos magnus, 4vv, orch; O salutaris hostia, 3vv, org

BIBLIOGRAPHY
E. Marbot: *Les musiciens de Saint-Sauveur* (Aix-en-Provence, 1906)

H.-A. Durand: 'Sur une prétendue messe des morts de Gilles et Campra', *RdM*, xlv (1960), 86

based on *MGG* (xii, 1758) by permission of Bärenreiter

HENRI-ANDRÉ DURAND

Supuerta [Sopuerta], **Miguel de** (*fl* late 17th century). Spanish composer. It is known only that he took holy orders. There exist two organ tientos of modest quality in *P-Pm* 1577, Loc.B, 5 (*Libro de cyfra*); they are transcribed in B. Hudson: *A Portuguese Source of Seventeenth-century Iberian Organ Music: MS 1577, Loc.B, 5, Municipal Library, Oporto, Portugal* (diss., Indiana U., 1961).

BARTON HUDSON

Suriani [Suriano, Surianus], **Francesco**. *See* SORIANO, FRANCESCO.

Surinach, Carlos (*b* Barcelona, 4 March 1915). American composer of Spanish origin. He studied with Morera at the Barcelona Conservatory and then moved to Germany, where he studied in the Oberklasse for piano at the Düsseldorf Conservatory, attended conducting classes given by Pabst at the Cologne Hochschule, studied composition with Trapp at the Prussian Academy in Berlin and attended lecture-seminars under Strauss. In 1944 he was made conductor of the Barcelona PO and the Liceo, and in 1947 he moved to Paris. He made guest appearances as a conductor in several European countries before settling in the USA in 1951 (he took American citizenship in 1959). There he quickly established himself as a composer and conductor. In 1954 he visited in Barcelona the heirs of Albéniz, who persuaded him to complete the orchestration of seven pieces from *Iberia*. He was visiting professor of composition at Carnegie-Mellon University in 1966–7 and his honours include the Bax Society Medal for Non-Commonwealth Composers (1966) and the title Knight Commander of the Order of Isabella I of Castile (1972).

Surinach has won particular eminence as a composer for the dance. In 1963, for instance, the Joffrey Company took his *Feast of Ashes* on its Russian tour (the ballet has been performed more than 500 times in Europe and the USA) and Graham included *Acrobats of God* and *Embattled Garden* in her Edinburgh Festival programmes. In this field his Catalan background provided him with a sense of naturalistic realism, to which his education in Germany added a grasp of formal techniques which has matured with the years. Also, his practical activity in music-making on both sides of the Atlantic has given his work a note of international chic, while an innate feeling for melody and rhythm stamps his scores with a pronounced individuality. The clichés that abound in Spanish music he has treated with the skill of a professional, though he can also write

music which is quite un-Spanish (e.g. the Passacaglia-Symphony and the *Doppio concertino*). His orchestrations of older Spanish music (18th-century stage pieces and late 19th-century dance music) are as deft and stylish as his original works.

WORKS
(selective list)

STAGE
Opera: El mozo que caso con mujer brava, Barcelona, 1948

Ballets: Montecarlo (P. Goube), Barcelona, 1945; Ritmo jondo (D. Humphrey), New York, 1953; Embattled Garden (Graham), New York, 1958; Acrobats of God (Graham), New York, 1960; David and Bathsheba (J. Butler), CBS Television, 1960; Apasionada (P. Lang), New York, 1962; Los renegados (J. Anduze), San Juan, Puerto Rico, 1965; Venta quemada (G. Skibine), Cannes, 1966; Agathe's Tale (P. Taylor), New London, 1967; Suite española (J. de Udaeta), Barcelona, 1970

Ballets to other scores incl. Feast of Ashes [Doppio concertino and Ritmo jondo] (Ailey), Leningrad, 1963

ORCHESTRAL
Passacaglia-Sym., 1945; Danza andaluza, chamber orch, 1946; Sym. no.2, 1950; Sinfonietta flamenca, 1953; Doppio concertino, vn, pf, 9 insts, 1954; Fandango, 1954; Hollywood Carnival, chamber orch, 1954; Concertino, pf, str, cymbals, 1956; Feria mágica, ov., 1956; Madrid 1890, chamber orch, 1956; Sinfonia chica, 1957; Conc. for Orch, 1959; Sym. Variations, 1962; Drama jondo, ov., 1965; Melorhythmic Dramas, 1966; Pf Conc., 1973; The Trumpets of the Seraphim, ov., 1973

VOCAL
Choral: Cantata de S Juan, SATB, perc, 1963; Songs of the Soul, SATB, 1964; The Missions of S Antonio, male vv, orch, 1969; Via crucis, vv, gui, 1972

Solo vocal: 3 Songs of Spain, S, pf/chamber orch, 1945; Romance, oracion y saeta, S, pf/orch, 1958; 3 cantares, S, pf/orch, 1958; Flamenco Meditations, 1v, pf, 1965; Prayers, 1v, gui, 1973

OTHER WORKS
Chamber: Pf Qt, 1944; 3 cantos berberes, fl, ob, cl, va, vc, harp, 1952; Tientos, harp/hpd/pf, eng hn, timp, 1953; Flamenco cyclothymia, vn, pf, 1967

Pieces for accordion, gui, pf, band; arrs. of earlier Spanish music

Principal publishers: Associated, Peer, Peters, Ricordi

JAMES G. ROY JR

Surinam. Surinam (formerly Dutch Guiana) is situated between French Guiana and Guyana on the north-east coast of South America. Bounded to the south by Brazil and to the north by the Atlantic Ocean, it has an area of 163,820 sq km. Surinam is notable for its heterogeneous population: ethnic groups among its 385,000 inhabitants include East Indians ('Hindustanis', 37%), creoles (31%), Indonesians (15%), bush negroes (descendants of escaped slaves, 10%), Chinese (2%), Europeans (1%), and other minorities such as Lebanese. The indigenous inhabitants were the Carib, Arawak and Warrow Indians, and American Indians comprise 3% of the present population, retaining their own languages and aspects of their religious and musical traditions. There is no state religion; most creoles are either Protestant or Roman Catholic, the majority of the East Indians are Hindu although some are Muslim, most of the Indonesians are Muslim, and the bush negroes maintain African religious beliefs.

In 1651 the English founded the first European settlement in the territory and in 1667 Surinam was ceded to the Dutch. From the mid-17th century slaves from west Africa were brought to work on the sugar-cane plantations, and after the abolition of slavery in 1863, Chinese, Javanese and East Indian indentured workers were introduced to meet the severe labour shortage that followed emancipation.

The official language of Surinam is Dutch, but English is spoken by many; *Taki-taki* (which combines Dutch, English, French, Spanish and Hebrew) is a widespread creole, serving as lingua franca among the different groups.

1. American Indians. 2. Bush negroes. 3. Rural and urban creoles and blacks. 4. East Indians. 5. Javanese.

1. AMERICAN INDIANS. American Indian tribes of upper Surinam are the Wayana, the Trio and the Akurio. The Akurio are nomads; the Wayana and the Trio are semi-nomadic cultivators. Although there has been little musicological research, it is known that the Wayana have a variety of instruments and a diversified musical tradition including shaman songs, used to communicate with spirits during healing ceremonies, and *maraké* (adolescent initiation ritual) music and dance (such as the *kanawa*, the *maipuli* and the *kalau*). The *kalau*, sung in a secret language, tells the principal myth of the Wayana tradition. Bamboo side-blown flutes accompany the songs and most dances are accompanied by stamping sticks and seed rattles tied around the ankle.

The Indians of lower Surinam – the Kribisi (Carib) and Arawak – are settled cultivators and have had extensive contact with the urban and rural creoles. Unacculturated Indian songs, flute music and dances are remembered only by old people, while the young Arawak use the *kawna* music of the rural blacks (see §3) at feasts. The Carib, by contrast, have maintained their traditional music and use it extensively at shaman ceremonies, *kasiri* (a fermented beverage) feasts and initiation and funeral rites. The most important *oremi* ('songs') are the *peai oremi* or shaman songs, *karwasi oremi*, women's songs accompanied by *karwasi* rattles (small closed baskets without a handle, containing dry seeds), and *sambura oremi*, usually sung by men. *Sambura oremi* are accompanied on the *sambura*, a double-headed cylindrical drum with a diameter greater than its height; it is generally played in sets of two or three, hung from a horizontal bar and struck with a padded stick.

2. BUSH NEGROES. To escape slavery, groups of blacks fled inland to the forests and jungle, establishing small settlements along the main rivers. Bush negro groups of the 20th century include the Ndjuka, the Aluku or Boni, the Paramaka, the Saramaka, the Matuay and the Kwinti. Each has different religious practices with a secret language, ritual songs and ceremonial drum music. The Ndjuka songs and dances used at ancestral cults and funeral wakes are the *awasa*, the *songé* and the *susa*. The most popular, the *awasa*, can be performed without rhythmical accompaniment, by a male or female singer and a chorus of women who sing the responses. When they are performed as a dance, however, *awasa* are accompanied by the *apinti*, a single-headed conical drum of Ashanti origin, played with bare hands.

The most important cults of the Saramaka are the *ampuku* (for the gods of the jungle) and the *kromanti* (for the violent bush spirits). These cults are accompanied on the *asankembu* (a large single-headed conical drum, played with a stick). Non-religious forms used during the village feasts are the *seketi*, the *adonké* and the *seketikofutu*. The Matuay do not practise their traditional religious forms extensively and most of the ceremonies are unknown to the younger generation. Non-religious forms such as the *adonké* and the *fositenseketi* are known only by the older people. The only Matuay form regularly used at feasts is the *banya*: the songs and dances are accompanied by two or three *apinti* and a *kwakwa* (a little wooden bench, beaten with two sticks).

Matuay feasts are now also varied by the *kawna* music of rural blacks. Drum languages are common among the bush negroes; these serve both for signalling and to transmit mythology.

3. RURAL AND URBAN CREOLES AND BLACKS. Ceremonies for the *winti* or *komfo* (spirits or deities) are essential to the religious life of both rural and urban blacks since it is believed that the *masa gran gado* (supreme deity) cannot be worshipped directly. The classification and the characteristics of *winti* vary according to different regions and 'schools': spirits include earth, water and sky *winti*, snake *winti* (the *vodu* and the *dagwé*), the *ampuku* (little inhabitants of the bush) and the *kromanti* (strong African *winti*). The *winti* are addressed in their own songs and drum rhythms. Each song presents in a short text a complex of ideas about the nature of the *winti*; during ritual observance participants possessed by *winti* perform dances in their honour. Drums used for these ceremonies are the *apinti*, the *agida*, *pudya*, *langadron* and *mandron* (single-headed cylindrical drums of different sizes) and the *kwakwa* bench.

The *kawna* or *kawina*, a popular musical form of rural blacks, consists of songs in leader-chorus form accompanied by the *kawna* band, which comprises the *apinti*, the *kawnadron* (small double-headed cylindrical drums), the *cuatro* (small four-string guitar) and a pair of rattles made of tins. The *kaseko* bands that play the genre called *skratjipoku* are typical urban ensembles; they consist of wind instruments (clarinets and saxophones), a banjo, a pair of gourd rattles and a military drum set, and are used to accompany the *setdansi* (a type of square dance) and for various festive occasions in Paramaribo.

Other forms include the *anansi* stories (tales of the spider-trickster Anansi), which often have songs; and

1. *Saramaka bush negro drum ensemble with (left to right) dei dei, tumao and apinti at Guyaba, Brokopondo district*

2. Javanese jaran kepang (ritual dance of horse spirits) accompanied by a gamelan ensemble of kĕndang (barrel drum), gambang (xylophone) and kĕnong (gong)

the *banya*, *laka* and *susa*, various dance ceremonies, less popular in the 20th century than formerly, but still organized during festivities commemorating emancipation.

Although little European music is performed in Surinam, creole music often combines European melodies and metres with creole texts; harmonized Protestant psalm singing is sometimes heard, even in the performance of the *winti* melodies. European musical influence has been exerted by Roman Catholic and Moravian missionaries, especially on the American Indians and on the blacks.

4. EAST INDIANS. The Hindus and Muslims who came from India to work on the sugar plantations as indentured labourers constitute an important segment of the population and have influenced 20th-century Surinam culture and society. The musical activities of the Hindus are integrated with their religious observances; of these the most important are *Holi* or *Phagwa* (a springtime celebration), ceremonies of the wedding cycle, the *bhagavad* (service to fulfil religious obligations) and the weekly *puja* (worship service). During most of the ceremonies mantras (sacred Sanskrit texts) are recited by a pandit (Hindu priest) with characteristic three-pitch inflections, interspersed with passages played on the *śaṅkha* (conch shell) and the *ghanti* (bronze gong). During and after the temple ceremonies religious songs are performed by the congregation and the musicians of a small instrumental ensemble. In the wedding cycle and at *bhagavad* observances such song genres include the *bhajan*, *ṭhumrī*, *malar* and *chowtal*. Often these events are varied by a 'duel' between two singers, improvising what is known as *kandan*. Music for various religious and social events is performed by the *samadj* ('band'), the commonest combination being a harmonium (Indian hand organ), *ḍholak* (north Indian double-headed barrel drum, played with the hands), *dandtal* (iron rod struck with a curved piece of iron) and various small bronze bells, cymbals and tambourines. A male chorus is frequently accompanied by the *naqqārā* (pair of kettle-drums played with sticks); wedding feasts often include the popular performance of a male dancer dressed as a

woman, accompanied by a singer, two *sāraṅgī* (three-string fiddle), *ḍholak* and a *dandtal*. Most bands also perform Muslim *qawwālī* (sometimes also performed by Hindus). Since the 1940s Indian film music has had a strong influence, especially on the younger generation (see TRINIDAD AND TOBAGO).

5. JAVANESE. Most Surinam Javanese are Muslim, speak Javanese, and have retained many Indonesian traditions. Their most important events are the celebration of Indonesian independence, wedding feasts, circumcision ceremonies and the *jaran kepang* (a dance in which participants in a state of trance mime horses; see fig.2). At feasts a *wayang kulit* (shadow-puppet play) or a *tayop* is usually performed; the *tayop* includes songs and dances of the *ledeh* (female singer-dancer) who is accompanied by a gamelan orchestra. The *wayang kulit* is based on the Hindu epic drama, the *Rāmāyana*. The *ḍalang*, who handles the puppets and sings the texts, is a versatile artist who knows the ancient languages for the plays and partly directs the orchestra. The *ludruk*, a mixture of folk theatre, music and dance, is also very popular. The gamelan music of Surinam is based exclusively on the *slendro* tuning system. Usually the gamelan consists of a *kĕndang* (double-headed barrel drum whose player leads the gamelan), *gambang* (xylophone), *dĕmung* (metallophone) and various gongs including *kĕnong* and imitations of the Javanese bronze gongs. The number of instruments varies from five to eight; some gamelan also include the *suling* (end-blown bamboo flute). An authentic classical Javanese gamelan with instruments of both *slendro* and *pelog* tunings is housed in the Indonesian Embassy; Surinam musicians use only the *slendro* section of the set.

BIBLIOGRAPHY

W. Ahlbrinck: *Encyclopaedie der Karaïben* (Amsterdam, 1931)

M. J. and F. S. Herskovits: *Suriname Folklore* (New York, 1936)

Nederlandse stichting voor culturele samenwerking met Suriname en de Nederlandse Antillen [Netherlands institution for cultural cooperation between Surinam and the Dutch Antilles] (Amsterdam, 1961) [bibliography]

A. de Waal Malefijt: *The Javanese of Surinam: a Segment of a Plural Society* (Assen, 1963)

U. Arya: *Ritual Songs and Folksongs of the Hindus of Surinam*

(Leiden, 1968) [song texts in original Hindi and Bihari dialects, and English]
D. G. A. Findlay: *Trio and Wayana Indianen in Suriname* (Paramaribo, 1970)

T. AGERKOP

Surman, John (Douglas) (*b* Tavistock, 30 Aug 1944). English jazz saxophonist and clarinettist. At the Plymouth Arts Centre he first met the band-leader Mike Westbrook, with whom he was later associated after they both moved to London. He studied at the London College of Music (1962–5) and London University (1965–6). From 1969 to 1972 he toured internationally with his trio, which included Barre Phillips and Stu Martin. After returning to England he worked with Mike Osborne and Alan Skidmore, and was later involved in ballet music with the Grandes Recherches du Théâtre de l'Opéra de Paris. He is remarkable for having transferred John Coltrane's characteristic phrasing to the baritone saxophone, a feat requiring considerable technical powers. The album *Extrapolation* (1969) represents his range and fluency, but already he was turning to more personal methods of expression, and his solos in the collection *Westering Home* (1972) explored folk-related themes on a variety of instruments in addition to the saxophone and clarinet, at the same time making effective use of multiple recording techniques.

MICHAEL JAMES

Surnāy. Sassanid reed pipe; *see* PERSIA, §3(ii) and Appendix A.

Surrey Chapel. London proprietary chapel, musically the most important of the 18th century; *see* LONDON, §I, 5.

Surzyński. Polish family of musicians of whom three brothers were particularly active. Their father Franciszek Surzyński (1826–78) was an organist, teacher and conductor, and their brother Piotr Surzyński (1859–1935) was an organist.

(1) **Józef Surzyński** (*b* Śrem, 15 March 1851; *d* Kościan, 5 March 1919). Theologian, reformer of church music, composer, conductor and musicologist. From 1872 until 1874 he studied mathematics and music theory (with Oscar Paul) in Leipzig, where he also attended the conservatory and played the viola in the Thomaskirche. He studied theology in Rome (1874–9), obtaining his doctorate in 1880, and worked as a chaplain in Paris (1879–80). After returning briefly to Poland he moved to Regensburg, where at the school of church music he absorbed the principles of the Caecilian movement. In Poznań he worked as cathedral organist (1881–7), conductor of the cathedral choir, teacher, organizer and official of the St Wojciech Society (1883–94). From 1894 to 1919 he was curate at Kościan, where he continued to involve himself in a wide range of activities as performer, organizer and teacher. He also founded societies of church music and arranged concerts in Kraków, Lwów, Przemyśl, Tarnów, Warsaw and other Polish towns, in which he conducted or lectured.

Surzyński did much towards the reform of church music on Caecilian lines in Poland, and he was rewarded by the pope with the order of Pro Ecclesia et Pontifice. His critical and editorial work on old Polish music was of particular importance, and his archival researches enabled him to publish a four-volume collec-

tion of source material, *Monumenta musices sacrae in Polonia*, which contains examples of Polish music from the 16th century to the 18th. He published music in the supplements to the periodical *Muzyka kościelna* ('Church music'), to which he also contributed many articles and of which he was editor from 1884 to 1902. His compositions include mass settings, small liturgical pieces, religious songs and organ miniatures, and show the influence of the Regensburg school of church music.

WRITINGS
Directorium chori (Poznań, 1885)
Monumenta musices sacrae in Polonia (Poznań, 1885–96)
Śpiewnik kościelny dla użytku parafii rzymsko-katolickich [Church songbook for use in Roman Catholic churches] (Poznań, 1886)
'Krótki pogląd na historyę muzyki kościelnej w Polsce' [A short survey of the history of church music in Poland], *Muzyka kościelna*, viii/3 (1888), 17
'Kilka uwag o pieśni Bogurodzica' [Some notes on the song Bogurodzica], *Muzyka kościelna*, ix/8 (1889), 49, 57
Muzyka figuralna w kościołach polskich od XV do XVIII wieku [Figural music in Polish churches from the 15th century to the 18th] (Poznań, 1889)
'Rys historyczny śpiewu chóralnego' [A historical sketch of choral singing], *Muzyka kościelna*, ix/5 (1889), 34; xix/5–6 (1899), 33; xix/7 (1899), 45
Cantionale ecclesiasticum (Poznań, 1891)
Polskie pieśni kościoła katolickiego od najdawniejszych czasów do końca XVI stulecia [Polish Catholic church songs from earliest times to the end of the 16th century] (Poznań, 1891)
'Szkoła Palestryny' [The Palestrina school], *Muzyka kościelna*, xx/10–11 (1900), 47
'Główne okresy historyi muzyki' [The principal periods of music history], *Muzyka kościelna*, xx/3 (1901), 13
Matka Boska w muzyce polskiej [The mother of God in Polish music] (Kraków, 1905)
'Najnowsze prace w dziedzinie historyi muzyki w Polsce' [Latest research on the heritage of music in Poland], *Obchód setnej rocznicy urodzin Fryderyka Chopina i pierwszy zjazd muzyków polskich: Lwów 1910*, 117

BIBLIOGRAPHY
L. T. Błaszczyk: *Dyrygenci polscy i obcy w Polsce działający w XIX i XX wieku* [Polish and foreign conductors working in Poland in the 19th and 20th centuries] (Kraków, 1864)
K. Winowicz: *Józef Surzyński* (diss., U. of Poznań, 1964)

(2) **Stefan Surzyński** (*b* Środa, 31 Aug 1855; *d* Lwów, 6 April 1919). Organist, teacher, conductor and composer, brother of (1) Józef Surzyński. He studied at the Regensburg school of church music, and was employed as organist at Poznań Cathedral, and as choral conductor in Poznań and Brzeżany. From 1888 to 1913 he was organist and director of church music at Tarnów Cathedral, and from 1913 to 1919 he was organist and conductor at Lwów Cathedral.

(3) **Mieczysław Surzyński** (*b* Środa, 22 Dec 1866; *d* Warsaw, 11 Sept 1924). Organist, teacher, conductor and composer, brother of (1) Józef Surzyński. He studied in Leipzig, Berlin and at the Regensburg school of church music, and then worked as an organist and teacher in Poznań, Libawa, St Petersburg, Saratov and Kiev. From 1904 he was a choral conductor in Warsaw, from 1906 taught at the Warsaw Conservatory and from 1909 was organist at St John's Cathedral. He composed some vocal and organ pieces.

BIBLIOGRAPHY
E. Wrocki: *Mieczysław Surzyński: życie i działalność* [Life and works] (Warsaw, 1924)
H. Majkowski: 'Dzieła kompozytorskie Mieczysława Surzyńskiego', *Muzyka kościelna*, xiv/3 (1939), 59
L. T. Błaszczyk: *Dyrygenci polscy i obcy w Polsce działający w XIX i XX wieku* [Polish and foreign conductors working in Poland in the 19th and 20th centuries] (Kraków, 1964)

KATARZYNA MORAWSKA

Susato, Johannes de. *See* SOEST, JOHANNES VON.

Susato, Tylman (*b* ?c1500; *d* ?Antwerp, 1561–4). Composer and music publisher in Antwerp. Because of the name Susato (= De Soest) it is generally thought that he came from Soest in Westphalia. Soest lay within the bishopric of Cologne, which perhaps explains why he occasionally styled himself Tylman Susato Agrippinensis (or Agrippinus), from the old name, Colonia Agrippina. On the other hand, he may have been born in Antwerp, into a family from Soest: for in 1377 a citizen of Antwerp, 'Tielmano de susato Coloniensis', is mentioned in the cathedral archives, and in the preface to the first *Musyck boexken* (1551), a book of Flemish songs, Susato referred to 'our Flemish mother tongue'.

In 1529 and 1530 Tylman worked as a calligrapher at Antwerp Cathedral and in 1531 also as a trumpeter there. The following year 'Tielman van Colen' appears in the Antwerp archives as a town player who owned several instruments: 9 flutes in a case, 3 trumpets and a tenor pipe. He continued as a town player until 1549, but from 1543 until 1561 worked mainly as a music publisher, establishing the first important music press in the Low Countries. In 1541 he formed a partnership with two other Antwerp printers, Henry ter Bruggen, an engraver and publisher of maps, who received a privilege to print music dated 22 December 1541, and Willem van Vissenaecken; however, this partnership

did not flourish. Susato formed another on 12 September 1542 with van Vissenaecken and the same year a volume of motets, *Quatuor vocum musicae modulationes, numero XXVI*, was published by van Vissenaecken alone; on 9 April 1543 this second contract was dissolved. Susato acquired his own privilege on 20 July 1543 and that year established his press in the Twaalfmaandenstraat. He stayed there until 1551 when he moved to a new house, called the 'Cromhorn', where he may have combined his printing activities with a musical instrument business. During his 18 years as a publisher, Susato issued 25 books of chansons (mostly in two series); 3 books of masses; 19 books of motets (in two series); and 11 *Musyck boexken*, the first two being collections of Flemish songs, the third a book of dances arranged by Susato, based on popular tunes, and the remaining eight books of *Souterliedekens* (psalter songs).

In his printing he used two founts of single-impression music type: the first (which may have been cut by Henry ter Bruggen) until 1551 and the second (which may be of German provenance) from 1551 onwards. When Susato died, he was succeeded by his son Jacques, who published Lassus's *Premier livre de chansons* in 1564. Jacques died on 19 November 1564. His widow sold all the printing materials to CHRISTOPHER PLANTIN, and a fragmentary set of

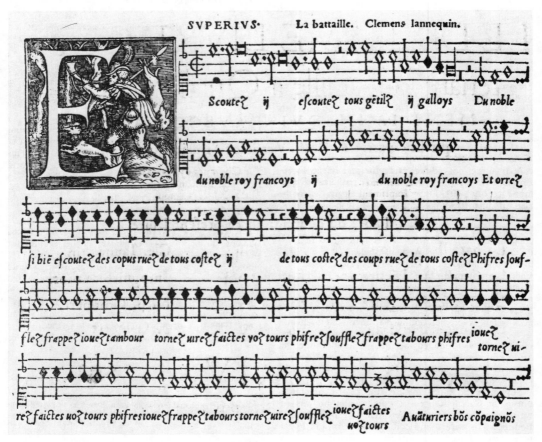

Opening of the superius voice of the chanson 'La bataille' from 'Le dixiesme livre contenant la Bataille a quatre de Clement Jannequin . . .', printed by type from single impression by Susato (Antwerp, 1545)

matrices for the second music type is in the Museum Plantin–Moretus, Antwerp.

Susato, who was himself a practical musician, composer and calligrapher, was well qualified for the profession of music printing – an art which, according to the dedication of his first publication, he had long sought to master. Many of his volumes are dedicated to persons of high standing, including prominent citizens of Antwerp, some of whom appear to have been his friends. In 1546 three citizens of Antwerp testified to Susato's good character, perhaps in connection with the renewal of his printing privilege. Most of his chanson and motet publications were anthologies, although he occasionally published a book devoted to one composer, for example Manchicourt and Crecquillon. He often printed music by Flemish composers, such as Crecquillon, Clemens non Papa, Canis, Gombert, Baston, Appenzeller, Guyot, Handl and Lupi. His seventh book of chansons (1545) was a retrospective publication, containing pieces by Josquin Desprez and three epitaphs on his death. Susato also published Janequin's popular chanson La bataille (see illustration) in a volume of programme chansons (1545). On the other hand, a forward-looking approach is seen in his publication of Lassus's chansons in 1555 (he was one of Lassus's first publishers); in 1560 Susato also published a volume of his motets. He showed enterprise in his Musyck boexken series; in the preface to the first book he asked Flemish composers to send him songs 'suitable for publication' so that he could prove that Flemish songs were as agreeable and artistic as those with French, Latin or Italian words. However, very few were published during the century: two of Susato's 1551 books, one by Baethen (1554) and one by Phalèse (1572) are the only dated volumes containing only Flemish songs. In the publication of Souterliedekens in polyphonic arrangements by Clemens non Papa and his pupil G. Mes, Susato undoubtedly met public demand. These metrical Dutch psalm settings, intended for domestic rather than for church use, were very popular during the 16th century in the Netherlands.

As a composer, Susato is particularly important as the author of two books of cantus firmus chansons composed 'à 2 ou à 3 parties' (i.e. with an optional bass part). He wrote in the preface that his purpose was to teach and encourage young singers who were unaccustomed to singing with larger groups. The 50 cantus firmus chansons contained in these two volumes are the largest number extant by any composer, and may have been the model for those composed by Claude Gervaise. Susato's motets are written in an imitative polyphonic style, while a more homophonic and simpler texture is shown in the dances (allemandes, branles, galliards, basses danses etc) arranged by Susato and based on popular tunes of the time.

PUBLICATIONS
(selective list; all published in Antwerp)

Masses: Liber I[–III] missarum (1545[1]–6[4])

Motets: Liber primus [–IV] sacrarum cantionum (1546[6]–7[6]); Liber primus [–XIV] ecclesiasticarum cantionum (1553[8]–7[3]) [Liber XV contains only compositions by O. de Lassus; liber XIII, 1557, lost]

Musyck boexken: Het ierste musyck boexken ... nieuwe amoreuse liedekens, 4vv (1551[18]), ed. in UVNM, xxix (1908); Het tvueetste musyck boexken, 4vv (1551[19]); T. Susato: Het derde musyck boexken ... alderhande danserye (1551); Clemens non Papa: Souterliedekens I[–IV]: Het vierde [–VII] musyck boexken, 4vv (1556–7); G. Mes: Souterliedekens V–VII ... musieckboucken no.VII–XI, 4vv (1561)

Chansons: Vingt et six chansons, 5vv (1543[15]); Le premier [–14] livre des chansons (1543[16]–55[19]); T. Susato: Premier livre des chansons, 2/3vv (1544); T. Susato: Tiers livre des chansons, 2/3vv (?1552)

[livre III, lost]; La fleur des chansons ... livre I[–VI] (1552[7]) [livre III, lost]

Doubtful publications: Clemens non Papa: Motecta, 5vv (1546), listed in Goovaerts; Madrigali e canzoni francesi, 5vv, mentioned in Fétis, but perhaps pubd by Laet, 1558; Evangelia dominicorum, attrib. Susato in Goovaerts, pubd by Berg & Neuber, 1554[10]–6[9]

WORKS
(all published in Antwerp)

Sacred: Missa 'In illo tempore', 5vv, 1546[3]; Domine da nobis, 4vv, 1545[2]; Fili quid fecisti, 4vv, 1527[7]; In illo tempore, 5vv, 1545[3]; Musica domum Dei optime, 6vv, 1540[7]; Nihil homini firmum, 2vv, 1549[16]; Peccata mea Domine, 5vv, 1554[9]; Salve quae roseo decora serto, 5vv, 1546[6]; 10 souterliedekens in Het IV–VII musyck boexken (1556–7)

Secular: Premier livre des [31] chansons, 2/3vv (1544); Tiers livre des [30] chansons, 2/3vv (?1552); also 30 chansons in 1543[15], 1543[16], 1544[10], 1544[12], 1545[14], 1549[29], 1552[7], 1552[8]; 6 Flemish songs in Het I–II Musyck boexken (1551[18–19])

Instrumental: Het derde musyck boexken ... alderhande danserye (1551), ed. F. J. Giesbert: Danserye zeer lustich ... om spelen op alle musicale instrumenten (1551), 2 vols. (Mainz, 1936)

BIBLIOGRAPHY
FétisB

A. Goovaerts: *Histoire et bibliographie de la typographie musicale dans les Pays-Bas* (Antwerp and Brussels, 1880/R1963)

U. Meissner: *Der Antwerpener Notendrucker Tylman Susato* (Berlin, 1967)

H. D. L. Vervliet: *Sixteenth Century Printing Types of the Low Countries* (Amsterdam, 1968)

L. Bernstein: 'The Cantus Firmus Chansons of Tylman Susato', *JAMS*, xxii (1969), 197–241

S. Bain: *Music Printing in the Low Countries in the Sixteenth Century* (diss., U. of Cambridge, 1974)

SUSAN BAIN

Susay [Suzoy], **Jo(hannes)** (*fl c*1380). French composer. He was perhaps the son of the Pierre de Susay who in 1332 was a clergyman in the French royal chapel. The anonymous *Règles de la seconde rhétorique* mention Iehan de Susay as being still alive. The extremely complicated style of the three-voice ballades indicates that they were composed in the 1380s. The four-voice work, still close to Machaut in its style, could have been composed earlier.

WORKS
Edition: *French Secular Compositions of the Fourteenth Century*, ed. W. Apel, CMM, liii/1 (1970) [A]

MASS MOVEMENT
Gloria, 3vv; ed. in CMM, xxix (1962)

BALLADES
A l'arbre sec, 4vv; A
Pictagoras, Jabol et Orpheus, 3vv; A
Prophilias, un des nobles, 3vv; A

BIBLIOGRAPHY
E. Langlois, ed.: *Recueil d'arts de seconde rhétorique* (Paris, 1903)

A. Pirro: *La musique à Paris sous le règne de Charles VI* (Strasbourg, 1930)

G. Reaney: 'The Manuscript Chantilly, Musée Condé 1047', *MD*, viii (1954), 77

U. Günther: 'Die Anwendung der Diminution in der Handschrift Chantilly 1047', *AMw*, xvii (1960), 17

——: 'Der Gebrauch des tempus perfectum diminutum in der Handschrift Chantilly 1047', *AMw*, xvii (1960), 291

H. Stäblein-Harder: *Fourteenth-century Mass Music in France*, MSD, vii (1962), 48

G. Reaney: 'New Sources of Ars Nova Music', *MD*, xix (1965), 63

URSULA GÜNTHER

Sušil, František (*b* Rousínov, nr. Slavkov, 14 June 1804; *d* Bystřice pod Hostýnem, 31 May 1868). Moravian priest, literary scholar and folksong collector. He was educated at the grammar school at Kroměříž, a centre of Baroque music in Moravia, and took orders in Brno in 1827. Contact with the folklore of his birthplace and other parts of Moravia and Silesia determined his Czech national consciousness and Slavonic cultural interests. By 1832 he had prepared for publication the first folksong collection in Moravia; the result of Sušil's systematic, and in his time unique, collecting activity, *Moravské národní písně* ('Moravian folksongs'), grew into one of the most remarkable monuments of Czech culture of the first half of the 19th century, containing 2091 tunes and 2361 texts. It includes every basic kind of folksong, traditional ballads, ceremonial songs, shepherds' tunes and typical dance-songs from the whole of Moravia and the southern part of Silesia. *Moravian Folksongs* did not claim the status of a scientific work, but as documented evidence of the contemporary Moravian folksong repertory the collection has been valuable both as a source for musicologists and for its relatively accurate notation. Sušil carefully recorded the use of dialect in the texts and respected and preserved such characteristic features of the melodies as their non-diatonic inflections. However, his musical education was influenced by Baroque and Classical music theory, and his use of conventional key signatures in the transcriptions shows that he regarded the songs as being basically either in major or minor tonality. He organized the rhythm in regular bars, mostly 2/4, 3/4 and 4/4, and only occasionally used compound metres. His views on the character of the Slavonic and Czech folk music in Moravia, expressed in the preface to the collection, had a direct influence on the growth of modern Czech music, particularly upon Křížovský, who first harmonized and later artistically reshaped and incorporated a number of melodies and texts from the *Moravian Folksongs* in his unaccompanied male choruses. Other composers who used Sušil's texts and melodies in their works include Dvořák, Janáček, Novák and Martinů.

EDITIONS

Moravské národní písně [Moravian folksongs] (Brno, 1835, rev., enlarged 2/1840)
Moravské národní písně nápěvy do textu vřaděnými [Moravian folksongs with the tunes fitted to the texts], i–iv (Brno, 1853), v (1856), vi (1857), vii (1859), viii (1860) [incl. songs from *Moravské národní písně*]; i–viii (1860); ed. R. Smetana and B. Václavek (Prague, 1941/R1952)

BIBLIOGRAPHY

P. Vychodil: *František Sušil: životopisný nástin* [Sušil: biographical outline] (Brno, 1898, 2/1904)
——: *Z doby Sušilovy* [From Sušil's times] (Brno, n.d.) [letters]
J. Vysloužil and J. Racek, eds.: *L. Janáček: O lidové písni a lidové hudbě* [Janáček: on folksong and folk music] (Prague, 1955)
J. Trojan: 'František Sušil a jeho harmonizátoři' [Sušil and his harmonizers], *HV*, v (1968), 351 [with Eng. summary]
——: 'František Sušil – hudebník' [Sušil – musician], *Český lid*, lv (1968), 321 [with Ger. summary]
H. Laudová: 'Nevyužité rukopisné sběřatelské záznamy Františka Sušila' [The neglected handwritten material of the collector Sušil], *Český lid*, lv (1968), 325 [with Ger. summary]
J. Vysloužil: 'Sušils Sammlung mährischer Volkslieder "Moravské národní písně" aus metrorhythmischer Sicht: Beitrag zur Kritik der Notationsweise des Volksliedes', *Sborník prací filosofické fakulty brněnské university*, H5 (1970), 41

JIŘÍ VYSLOUŽIL

Suspension (Fr. *suspension*; Ger. *Vorhalt*; It. *sospensione*). In part-writing, a dissonance configuration in which the dissonant or NON-HARMONIC NOTE is tied over from the previous chord (where it occurs in the same part) and resolves by step, usually downwards; a suspension whose non-harmonic note resolves upwards is sometimes called a 'retardation' (from Lat. *retardatio*, a term used in the 17th and 18th centuries).

Susskind, (Jan) Walter (*b* Prague, 1 May 1918; *d* Berkeley, 25 March 1980). British conductor of Czech birth. He studied composition with Josef Suk and Hába and the piano with Karel Hoffmeister at the Prague State

Conservatory, and conducting with Szell at the German Academy of Music. On graduating in 1934 he became Szell's assistant at the German Opera, Prague, making his conducting début with *La traviata*; he had already been heard as a pianist and composer at the Prague Mozarteum in 1931. On the closure of the German Opera in 1938 he went to England, where he performed as pianist of the Czech Trio until he resumed his conducting career in 1941. He was music director of the Carl Rosa Opera Company, 1943–5, and made his orchestral début with the Liverpool PO in 1945. From 1946 to 1952 he was music director of the Scottish Orchestra, which became the Scottish National Orchestra. For the next two years he directed the Victoria SO in Melbourne, using Australia as a base for many Far Eastern and American tours. In 1956 he became musical director of the Toronto SO, and founded the National Youth Orchestra of Canada two years later. During his nine years at Toronto he explored the orchestral repertory widely, and gave the first Canadian performances of symphonies by Bruckner and Mahler. He directed the Aspen Festival, 1962–8, and was music director of the St Louis SO, 1968–75, where he continued his policy of exploratory programme-building. He continued to make guest appearances and resumed composition: his works include a song cycle for tenor and chamber orchestra based on poems by Ogden Nash, and a Passacaglia for timpani and wind orchestra.

RICHARD BERNAS

Süssmayr [Süssmayer], **Franz Xaver** [Dolcevillico, Francesco Saverio] (*b* Schwanenstadt, Upper Austria, 1766; *d* Vienna, 17 Sept 1803). Austrian composer. He received his earliest instruction in singing and in playing the violin and organ from his father Franz Karl Siessmayr (1743–1805), a teacher and choirmaster in Schwanenstadt. From November 1779 he attended the monastery school at Kremsmünster as a boarder and from 1784 to 1787 he studied philosophy and law at the Ritterakademie there. At the same time he received training in composition from Maximilian Piessinger (1753–1826), Georg von Pasterwiz, and possibly from Bonifaz Schwaigert (1734–94). He joined in the musical performances in the monastery, initially as an alto and organist, and from 1781 as a tenor, violinist and organist. From 1785 some of his compositions were performed there. He left Kremsmünster in the autumn of 1787 and settled in Vienna in July 1788 as a private music teacher. He became acquainted with Mozart, perhaps in 1790 or 1791, and received training in composition from him. He was also employed by Mozart as a composer and occasionally as a collaborator. After Mozart's death Süssmayr took instruction in the composition of vocal music from Salieri. From 1792 Süssmayr was employed as a harpsichordist and acting Kapellmeister at the National Theatre in Vienna. At this time he also began to attract public attention in Vienna and Prague as a highly successful composer of operas. He was Kapellmeister of the German opera at the National Theatre from 1794 until his death, though he remained unsuccessful in his attempts to succeed Pierre Duttilou as composer for the court theatre.

In his own lifetime Süssmayr gained fame as the composer of the Singspiel *Der Spiegel von Arkadien* (1794), one of the works written in the tradition of *Die Zauberflöte*, and of the ballet *Il noce di Benevento*

(1802), which was given in German and Italian theatres up to about 1835. The popularity of Süssmayr's works is also attested by Beethoven's piano variations (WoO76, 1799) on the terzetto 'Tändeln und scherzen' from *Soliman der Zweite*, and by Paganini's *Le streghe* op.8, which borrows a theme from one of his ballets. Süssmayr's stage works show familiarity not only with Viennese musical comedy but also with late Neapolitan *opera buffa* and French *tragédie lyrique*. His church music, which, as regards thematic invention and treatment and polyphonic mastery, belongs to the declining tradition of the south German and Austrian Baroque, survived in the repertory until the mid-19th century.

Süssmayr is now remembered primarily for his completion of Mozart's Requiem K626. There has been some dispute about the extent of his work: Constanze Mozart alleged that her husband had composed or drafted sections that Süssmayr claimed as his own. He completed Mozart's draft score from the Dies irae to the Hostias by adding instrumental parts to the vocal parts and continuo of the original; probably he also composed anew the Sanctus, the Benedictus and the Agnus Dei, following instructions which Mozart himself had given and possibly using Mozart's sketches. In these sections Süssmayr adopted the principle of thematic links between movements which had been used by Mozart himself in the other movements, thereby showing an essentially deeper penetration into the inner structure of the work than has previously been assumed. The relationship of the two composers' contributions might be clarified further by a detailed stylistic comparison between their works. Süssmayr also probably wrote the secco recitative in his *La clemenza di Tito* (K621), and may have had some share (along with Johann Anton André and Johann Friedrich Eck) in the work known as Mozart's Violin Concerto in E♭ (K268/Anh.C14.04), whose authenticity has long been questioned.

His brother Joseph Süssmayr (*b* Schwanenstadt, 1776; *d* Schwanenstadt, 21 Sept 1830) was a schoolmaster in his native town; he was also municipal and church Kapellmeister there and in 1822 he founded a society for church music.

WORKS
(* – autograph)

STAGE
(*first performed in Vienna unless otherwise stated*)

Die Liebe für den König oder Karl Stuart (5, G. Stephanie, B. Planck), Kremsmünster, Stift, 25 April 1785, *A-KR*
Die Drillinge (R. Bonin, Planck), Kremsmünster, Stift, 19 Feb 1786
Der Bürgermeister (Brühl, Planck), Kremsmünster, Stift, 6 Aug 1786, *KR*
Die gar zu strenge Kinderzucht (F. X. Jann, Planck), Kremsmünster, Stift, 4 Feb 1787
Nicht mehr also sechs Schüsseln (Singspiel, B. Wallner, after F. W. Grossmann), Kremsmünster, Stift, 10 June 1788
Die väterliche Rache (Jann, Planck), Kremsmünster, Stift, 1 July 1789
Die Liebe auf dem Lande (Singspiel, 3, C. F. Weisse), *c*1785–9, unperf.
Der rauschige Hans (Singspiel, M. Lindemayr), 1791, unperf.
Moses oder Der Auszug aus Ägypten (2), auf der Wieden, 4 May 1792, *D-DS*
Der Vogelsteller (ballet, A. Muzzarelli), National, 8 Aug 1792
L'incanto superato [Der besiegte Zauber] (2, G. Bertati), National, 8 July 1793, Prague, 1793, *H-Bn*
Piramo e Tisbe (2, M. Coltellini), *c*1793, inc., *Bn* (partly*)
Meister Schnaps oder Er führt ihm's Mädchen selbst zu (farce, 1), ?1793, inc., *Bn*
Il turco in Italia (Il musulmano in Napoli) (opera buffa, 2, C. Mazzolà), Prague, Landesständisches, 12 Feb 1794, *Bn*
Der Spiegel von Arkadien (comic opera, 2, E. Schikaneder), auf der Wieden, 14 Nov 1794; as Die neuen Arkadier, Weimar, Hof, 2 Feb 1796, *D-Bds*
Idris und Zenide (comic opera, 2, C. L. Giesecke, after C. M. Wieland), auf der Wieden, 11 May 1795

Die edle Rache (comic opera, 2, F. X. Huber), Kärntnertor, 27 Aug 1795, *Bds*, *H-Bn**
Die Freiwilligen (1, Stephanie), Kärntnertor, 27 Sept 1796
Der Wildfang (comic opera, 2, Huber, after von Kotzebue), Kärntnertor, 4 Oct 1797, *D-Bds*, *H-Bn**
Liebe macht kurzen Prozess oder Heirat auf gewisse Art (pasticcio, 2, J. Perinet, after J. Rautenstrauch), auf der Wieden, 26 March 1798, collab. J. Wölfl, J. Henneberg, M. Stegmayr, F. A. Hofmeister, J. Ritter von Seyfried, J. J. Haibel, J. Triebensee; *D-Bds*, *Mbs*
Der Marktschreyer (Singspiel, 1, K. F. Lippert), Kärntnertor, 6 July 1799, *DS*, *H-Bn**; ov. (Offenbach, n.d.)
Soliman der Zweite oder Die drei Sultaninnen (Singspiel, 2, Huber, after C.-S. Favart), Kärntnertor, 1 Oct 1799, *D-Bds*, *Dlb*, *DS*, *H-Bn**
Gülnare oder Die persische Sklavin (Singspiel, 1, Lippert, after B. J. Marsollier), Kärntnertor, 5 July 1800, *Bn**
Phasma oder Die Erscheinung im Tempel der Verschwiegenheit (2), Kärntnertor, 25 July 1801, *D-DS*
Das Hausgesinde (farce, 1), 1802, unperf., *H-Bn**
Il noce di Benevento . . . oder Die Zauberschwestern (ballet, S. Viganò), Kärntnertor, 14 Jan 1802, *I-Mc*
List und Zufall (comic opera, 2, Stegmayr), 11 Jan 1806
L'imbarazzo degli amanti (farce, 1), unperf.
Gl'uccellatori (dramma giocoso, after ?C. Goldoni), inc., *A-Wgm*, *H-Bn*
Alcidoro e Dalisa o sia Gli amanti in Tempe, *Bn* (1 scene only)

Sections of unidentified operas, items for insertion into operas by other composers, *H-Bn* (some autograph); for details see Kecskeméti

VOCAL
Masses: Missa solemnis, 4vv, orch (Vienna, ?1810); 4 masses, *A-KR*, *D-LEt*; 2 German requiems, incl. 1 dated 1 Feb 1786
Other sacred, some in *A-KR*: 1 vesper; Te Deum, vv, orch, 1792; Ave verum, 1792, *H-Bn**; 3 grads; 6 offs; Tantum ergo; 2 Predigtlieder; Alleluia, *Bn*; other works, *Bn**
Cantatas: Feyer Lied zum Geburtstag . . . Franz II, 12 Feb 1794, Prague, Teynkirche, *Bn**; Cantata per la nascita della . . . archiduchessa Carolina (G. Arrivabene), Vienna, 13 Dec 1795, *A-KR*, *H-Bn* (partly*), as O ihr glücklichen Ufer der Krems, Kremsmünster, 24 June 1796; Der Retter in Gefahr (J. L. Rautenstrauch), Vienna, 19 Sept 1796, *A-Wn*, *H-Bn**; Kantate für die Ankunft des Erzherzogs Karl, 1796; Böhmens Erretter, 1796; Das Namensfest (J. B. Bergopzoomer), 23 Nov 1799, *Bn**, ed. I. Kecskeméti (Budapest, 1965); Der Kampf für den Frieden (Rautenstrauch), Vienna, 23 Dec 1800, *Bn**; Lob des Ofnerweines (Süssmayr), B solo, str qt, Vienna, 20 Oct 1802, *A-KR**; Cantata (Huber), 3vv, chorus, *H-Bn**; Zeila, 2vv, chorus, *Bn* (frag.), doubtful; 14 single works, ? from cantatas, *Bn**
Other secular: Lieb und Freundschaft geben uns ein grosses Gut, 4vv, *A-Wn*; Die Freundschaft und die Liebe, canon 3vv; Ger. and Fr. lieder, *GB-Lbm**

INSTRUMENTAL
Orch: 2 syms., *A-Wgm*, *H-Bn*; Synfonia turchesa, *A-KR*, *H-Bn*; Pf Conc., *Bn* (1 movt only); 2 cl concs.; Ov., *Bn**, ed. I. Kecskeméti (Budapest, 1965); divertimentos, 4 in *A-KR*; cassations; *c*30 dances, *Wn*, *H-Bn**; march, *D-Bds*, *H-Bn*
Chamber: Qnt, fl, ob, vn, va, vc, *A-KR*, *Wgm*; Qnt, ob, eng hn, vn, vc, gui; 4 str trios; Serenade, 1797, fl, va, hn; March, 2 fl

BIBLIOGRAPHY
G. L. P. Sievers: *Mozart und Süssmayr* (Mainz, 1829)
H. Conrat: 'Mozarts Requiem und Süssmayr', *AMz*, xxxiv (1907), 355, 373, 389, 405, 421, 437
G. von Keussler: 'Mozarts Requiem ohne Süssmayr', *Deutsches Musik-Jb*, i (1923), 210
W. Lehner: *Franz Xaver Süssmayr als Opernkomponist* (diss., U. of Vienna, 1927); extracts in *SMw*, xviii (1931), 66
C. Preiss: 'Franz Xaver Süssmayr', *Heimatgaue*, xvii (1937), 21
J. Winterberger: *Franz Xaver Süssmayr: Leben, Umwelt und Gestalt* (diss., U. of Innsbruck, 1946)
W. Wlcek: *Franz Xaver Süssmayr als Kirchenkomponist* (diss., U. of Vienna, 1953; Tutzing, 1978)
E. Hess: 'Zur Ergänzung des Requiems von Mozart durch F. X. Süssmayr', *MJb 1959*, 99
K. M. Pisarowitz: 'Süssmayrs Ahnenheimat', *Mitteilungen der Internationalen Stiftung Mozarteum*, viii (1959), 9
F. Blume: 'Requiem but no Peace', *MQ*, xlvii (1961), 147
I. Kecskeméti: 'Süssmayr-Handschriften in der Nationalbibliothek Széchényi, Budapest', *SM*, ii (1962), 283–320; viii (1966), 297–377 [incl. thematic catalogue]
K. Marguerre: 'Mozart und Süssmayr', *MJb 1962–3*, 172
H. H. Hausner: *Franz Xaver Süssmayr* (Vienna, 1964) [review by O. E. Deutsch, *ÖMz*, xx (1965), 235]
——: 'Süssmayrs kirchenmusikalisches Werk', *Mitteilungen der Internationalen Stiftung Mozarteum*, xii/3–4 (1964), 13
W. Jerger: 'Mozarts Schüler und Mitarbeiter: zu Franz Xaver Süssmayrs 200. Geburtsjahr', *Acta mozartiana*, xiii (1966), 91
F. Giegling: 'Zu den Rezitativen von Mozarts Oper "Titus" ', *MJb 1967*, 121

F. Beyer: 'Mozarts Komposition zum Requiem: zur Frage der Ergänzung', *Acta Mozartiana*, xviii (1971), 27
G. Duda: 'Neues aus der Mozartforschung', *Acta Mozartiana*, xviii (1971), 32
R. Angermüller: 'Süssmayr: ein Schüler und Freund Salieris', *Mitteilungen der Internationalen Stiftung Mozarteum*, xxi/1–2 (1973), 19

OTHMAR WESSELY

Sust, Johannes von. *See* SOEST, JOHANNES VON.

Sustaining pedal [damper pedal, loud pedal]. A name often used for the right pedal of the piano, which when depressed raises the dampers from all the strings, allowing them to vibrate freely in sympathy with any notes being played. In earlier pianos, this effect was sometimes achieved by the use of knee-levers or hand-stops. It was frequently possible to raise the treble and bass dampers separately, as on those instruments provided with a divided pedal or the less common ones with two damper pedals.

EDWIN M. RIPIN

Sutāra. Office of the Syrian Churches corresponding to Compline; *see* SYRIAN CHURCH MUSIC.

Suter, Hermann (*b* Kaiserstuhl, canton of Aargau, 28 April 1870; *d* Basle, 22 June 1926). Swiss conductor and composer. He studied with his father, an organist and precentor, at Laufenburg, by correspondence with Gustav Weber in Zurich, and then during his high school and university years in Basle with Hans Huber and Alfred Glaus. At the Stuttgart Conservatory he was a pupil of Faisst, and subsequently he studied with Reinecke and Homeyer at the Leipzig Conservatory. In 1892 he returned to Switzerland, settled in Zurich and became conductor of the Uster male choir. He also took over the conductorships of the Schaffhausen (1893) and Wiedikon (1894) male choirs, and in 1894 he was appointed organist of the Enge-Zurich church. Two years later he became a professor at the Zurich Conservatory. In 1897 he was made conductor of the Winterthur City Choral Society, and in 1901 of the Zurich Mixed Choir, a large oratorio chorus which held an important place in the musical life of the city. He moved to Basle in 1902 to take the conductorships of the Basler Gesangverein, the Basler Liedertafel and the Allgemeine Musikgesellschaft symphony concerts. The following year he came to international renown as principal conductor of the Allgemeine Deutsche Musikgesellschaft festival in Basle. He received an honorary doctorate from Basle University in 1913, and from 1918 to 1921 directed the Basle Music School and Conservatory. In 1925 illness compelled him to relinquish his posts as a choral conductor, but he continued to conduct the symphony concerts until his death, also serving on the management committee of the Schweizerischer Tonkünstlerverein.

Suter's compositional output is small but of enduring value. Although deeply rooted in the late Romantic tradition as represented by the new German school, he incorporated into his style certain typically Swiss elements: melodic and harmonic turns of phrase, and also, more generally, a characteristic distanced quality, exemplified, for instance, in his handling of classical large-scale forms. As a result of this his music is not always easy to approach, but it is filled with true feeling and a biting strength. The oratorio *Le laudi di S Francesco d'Assisi* (1925) was the work that brought him world-wide recognition, though his chamber and orchestral works (particularly the Violin Concerto, dedicated to Adolf Busch) were already known outside Switzerland.

WORKS
(*selective list*)

Choral orch: Schmiede im Walde, op.4 (M. R. von Stern), male vv, orch, 1905; Die erste Walpurgisnacht, op.5 (Goethe), solo vv, vv, orch, 1910; Riehener Festspiel, op.24 (A. Oeri), solo vv, vv, boys' vv, orch, 1923; Le laudi di S Francesco d'Assisi, op.25, solo vv, vv, boys' vv, org, orch, 1925
Unacc. choral: 4 Settings of Old Poems, op.3; 4 Patriotic Songs, op.6, male vv; 2 Songs, op.7, male vv; Vigilien, op.9 (Goethe), male vv; 3 romantische Lieder, op.11, male vv; 3 Festival Songs, op.14 (G. Keller), male vv; 3 Settings of Old Poems, op.16; Heimatlieder für die Jugend, op.19, children's/female vv; 2 Songs, op.21, male vv; Dem Sonnengott, op.27 (Hölderlin), male vv
Incidental music: St Jakob an der Birs, op.13 (C. A. Bernoulli), 1912
Orch: Sym., d, op.17; Vn Conc., A, op.23, 1924
Chamber: 3 str qts, D, op.1, 1901, c, op.10, 1910, C, op.20, 1921; Sextet, C, op.18, str qt, vc, db, 1921
Songs: 5 Songs, op.2, 1v, pf; 2 Songs, op.8, B, vn, vc, org; 3 Songs, op.12, T, pf; 4 Duets, op.15, A, B, pf; 4 Songs, op.22, 1v, pf
Pf and org music, arrs.

Principal publisher: Hug

BIBLIOGRAPHY
Hermann Suter: ein Lebensbild als Beitrag zur schweizerischen Musikgeschichte (Basle, 1936)
W. Merian: *Hermann Suter: der Dirigent und der Komponist* (Basle, 1936)

HANS EHINGER/FRITZ MUGGLER

Suter, Robert (*b* St Gall, 30 Jan 1919). Swiss composer. After attending school in his native town, he entered the Basle Conservatory in 1937. He began his studies with piano as his main subject and, after a long interruption caused by the war, he graduated with a diploma in the teaching of theory. His composition teacher was Walther Geiser, a pupil of Busoni. From 1945 to 1950 Suter taught at the Berne Conservatory, and then he returned to Basle to teach counterpoint, harmony, improvisation and composition at the Academy of Music; in 1968 he was appointed to the staff of Basle radio.

One of his first works was the important *Musikalisches Tagebuch* (1946), a cycle for voice and seven instruments which displays essential traits that permeate Suter's music. The texts are from the neo-Romantic symbolist Hofmannsthal and the cryptic expressionist Trakl: Suter's penchant for nocturnal, sometimes brooding imagery is constantly in evidence in the chamber pieces which dominate his oeuvre – even when they are without words. The *Musikalisches Tagebuch* comprises 11 sections: Adagio, Danza I, 'Vorfrühling' (Hofmannsthal), Danza II, 'An Mauern hin' (Trakl), Lento, 'Wintergang' (Trakl), Danza III, 'Glückliches Haus' (Hofmannsthal), Danza IV, Adagio. The suite is a favourite form of Suter's, but this sequence is pinned together by motivic relationships between palindromically placed sections, most notably in the final Adagio, a free reprise of the initial section. In the centre stands a Lento dolcissimo, so that the whole arch form rests on three slow, lyrical movements. The opening two bars of the Lento show a melodic and harmonic procedure bearing the imprint of the pre-serial music of the Second Viennese School. An upward-moving broken triad of A minor in the melody is immediately followed by the chromatically complementary cell E♭–A♭–C♭, this technique leading to the presentation of the total chromatic within an extremely short period. Not only the sporadic use of Sprechgesang but also the densely woven motivicism recalls Schoenberg, whose *Pierrot lunaire* has had a lasting influence on Suter. In the *Musikalisches Tagebuch*, the draughtsman-like linear writing and delicate balance of rhythm and melody are remarkable.

During the 1950s, Suter's attendance at the Darmstadt summer courses and his composition studies with Wladimir Vogel gave him an increasingly assured control over the compositional process. The chamber cantata *Heilige Leier* (1960) shows rigorous discipline in its scoring for soprano, flute and guitar, and constructional elements become more prominent. The instrumental bars which open the Prologue are ordered strictly palindromically and form a continuously woven invention on the note E. Similarly, the opening motif of 'Invention II' appears in retrograde at the close of the section. Moreover, this motif is reminiscent of the xylophone rhythm in the third movement of Bartók's Music for Strings, Percussion and Celesta, and it is possible that the many mirrored motifs of Suter's counterpoint were suggested by Bartók.

According to his own account, Suter endeavours to achieve unity in his music through a special differentiation of structural and expressive details. His intervallic structures indicate an intense preoccupation with Schoenberg's serial thought, but without their being completely serial. He has repeatedly written for large orchestral forces in more expansive forms, a particular landmark being the Brecht cantata *Die Ballade von des Cortez Leuten* (1960), in whose introductory bars Wildberger identified a significant feature of Suter's style: 'The conflict between an arresting temperament and the abrupt and unsuspected appearance of doubt; a tense restraint which has nothing to do with contemplative restfulness'.

After this work Suter's style began to change: the linear writing became flexible, the instrumentation brilliant and colourful, and the influence of contemporary compositional developments became noticeable. Thus in his *Trois nocturnes* (1968–9, commissioned by Sacher) for viola and an orchestra including a large percussion section, and in the *Pastorale d'hiver* (1972) Suter employed sections in which the performers have a limited choice from a set of notes. These occur as careful stylistic contrasts which are integrated into the more conventional language that Suter has evolved.

WORKS
(selective list)
VOCAL

Musikalisches Tagebuch I (Hofmannsthal, Trakl), S, fl, ob, bn, vn, va, vc, db, 1946, rev. 1960; Musikalisches Tagebuch II (Rückert, Jacobsen, Hofmannsthal), Bar, fl, cl, b cl, hn, vn, va, vc, 1950; Heilige Leier, sprich, sei meine Stimme (ancient Gk., trans. E. Peterich), S, fl, gui, 1960; Die Ballade von des Cortez Leuten (Brecht), speaker, chorus, speaking chorus, chamber orch, 1960; Die sollen loben den Namen des Herrn (Ps cxlviii), motet, unacc. chorus, 1971; . . . aber auch lobet den Himmel (after Brecht), vv, insts, 1976

INSTRUMENTAL

Lyric Suite, chamber orch, 1959; Fantasia, cl, harp, 16 str, 1964–5; Sonata, orch, 1967; Epitaffio, brass, str, perc, 1968; Trois nocturnes, va, orch, 1968–9; Musik, orch, 1975–6

Str Qt no.1, 1952; 4 Movements, str trio, 1961; 4 Studies, wind qnt, 1962; Serenata, fl, ob, cl, harp, vn, va, vc, 1963–4; Sonata, pf, 1966–7; Pastorale d'hiver, hn, vn, va, vc, perc, 1972; Airs et ritournelles, perc, inst groups, 1973; Sonata, pf trio, 1977

Music for theatre and radio, pieces for jazz ensemble

Principal publishers: Bärenreiter, Heinrichshofen, Modern

WRITINGS

'Vom Avantgardisten zum Musiker', *SMz*, cvii (1968), 157

BIBLIOGRAPHY

D. Larese and J. Wildberger: *Robert Suter* (St Gall, 1967)

J. Wildberger: 'Robert Suter – Schweizer Komponist', *SMz*, cvii (1967), 320

RUDOLF HÄUSLER

Sutermeister, Heinrich (*b* Feuerthalen, canton of

Schaffhausen, 12 Aug 1910). Swiss composer. After studying philology in Basle and Paris he turned to music in 1931, and from 1932 to 1934 studied at the Munich Hochschule für Musik as a pupil of Courvoisier, Röhr and Orff. He was for a short time opera coach at the Berne Municipal Theatre before settling at Vaux-sur-Morges, on Lake Geneva, as a freelance composer. In 1958 he was made president of the Mechanlizenz, the Swiss association for mechanical copyrights, and from 1963 to 1975 he was in charge of a composition class at the Hanover Hochschule für Musik.

During the 1940s Sutermeister achieved international renown as an opera composer. The most significant event in this development was a performance of one of his works at La Scala. Sutermeister regarded a close sympathy between audience and singers as one of the fundamental principles of opera, and he looked for models to Italian opera, in particular to the work of Verdi and Boito, whose *Otello* and *Falstaff* he found the peaks of the opera repertory. Another important influence, however, was the instruction received from Orff. Sutermeister's aims were realized in a style emphasizing sweeping melodic lines, diatonic tunefulness and, generally, ease of comprehensibility. The more important among the early works, such as the ballet *Das Dorf unter dem Gletscher* and the radio opera *Die Schwarze Spinne*, still draw directly on Orff, but in the magnificent *Andreas Gryphius* and the Divertimento Sutermeister's striving after rhythmic and harmonic simplicity is strikingly evident. A leaning towards the Baroque also became conspicuous at this time (cf *Barocklieder* and *Andreas Gryphius*).

Sutermeister's first success beyond Switzerland was with the opera *Romeo und Julia* (1939), a work that displays highly skilled handling of the theatre in its dramatically arresting moments and its effective melody. The next opera, *Die Zauberinsel*, has rather less musical substance, relying almost exclusively on effect. And in *Niobe* and *Raskolnikoff* even more is made of superficial artifice: ostinatos, cries, accents and sonorous coagulations. Here music is a background, and any thematic working is deliberately avoided. Immediately after the war *Romeo und Julia* was often performed, but it subsequently disappeared from the stage. *Raskolnikoff* and *Titus Feuerfuchs*, however, retained their popularity, while *Madame Bovary* received a mixed reception at its first performance. In the 1960s Sutermeister was more successful with his work for the cinema, radio and television. His music – still structurally straightforward, pleasing and effective – made ready contact with a broad public. The choral works have been extremely popular with amateur groups.

WORKS
(selective list)
STAGE

Das Dorf unter dem Gletscher, ballet, A. Rösler, 1937; Romeo und Julia (opera, Sutermeister, after Shakespeare), perf. 1940; Die Zauberinsel (opera, Sutermeister, after Shakespeare: The Tempest), perf. 1942; Niobe (opera, P. Sutermeister), perf. 1946; Raskolnikoff (opera, P. Sutermeister, after Dostoyevsky), perf. 1948; Der rote Stiefel (opera, Sutermeister, after W. Hauff), perf. 1951; Titus Feuerfuchs (opera, Sutermeister, after Nestroy: Der Talisman), 1956–8

Das Einsiedler grosse Welttheater (opera, Eichendorff, after Calderón), 1960; Seraphine (Die stumme Apothekerin) (opera, Sutermeister, after Rabelais), 1961; Madame Bovary (opera, Sutermeister, after Flaubert), 1967

CINEMA, RADIO AND TELEVISION

Die schwarze Spinne (radio opera, Rösler, after J. Gotthelf), 1936, rev. for stage 1948; Die Füsse im Feuer (radio ballad, after C. F. Meyer), rev. for stage, 1950; Fingerhütchen (radio ballad, after Meyer), rev. for stage, 1950; Wozzeck (radio, Büchner), 4 solo vv, orch, 1953; Das Gespenst von Canterville (television opera, Sutermeister, after Wilde), 1966; La croisade des enfants (fresques audio-visuelles, Schwob), 1968–9; Der Flaschenteufel (television opera, R. K. Weibel, after R. L. Stevenson), 1969–70

VOCAL

6 Barocklieder, T, female chorus, 3 insts, 1934; Jorinde und Joringel (chamber oratorio, after Grimm), 1936; 7 Liebesbriefe, T, str, 1937; Andreas Gryphius, cantata, chorus, 1938; Kantate 1944, chorus; Missa in E♭, chorus, 1949; Max und Moritz (W. Busch), S, A, T, B, pf duet, 1951; Missa da requiem, 2 solo vv, chorus, orch, 1952; Cantata no.3 'Dem Allgegenwärtigen', 2 solo vv, chorus, orch, 1957–8

Cantata no.4 'Das Hohelied', chorus, orch, 1961; Cantata no.5 'Der Papagei aus Kuba', chorus, orch, 1961; Cantata no.6 'Erkennen und Schaffen', solo vv, chorus, orch, 1963; Cantata no.7 'Sonnenhymne', male chorus, 2 hn, 3 tpt, 2 trbn, 1965; Cantata no.8 'Omnia ad unum', 1v, chorus, orch, 1965–6; Ecclesia (P.-A. Tâche), S, B, chorus, orch, 1974; Te Deum 1975, S, chorus, orch, 1975

INSTRUMENTAL

Orch: 3 pf concs., 1943, 1954, 1961; Orazione per Giuseppe Verdi, 1949; Marche fantasque, 1/2 pf, orch, 1950; 2 vc concs., 1955–6, 1971; Divertimento no.2, 1959–60; Cl Conc., 1975; Quadrifoglio, 4 wind insts, orch, 1977

Chamber: Divertimento no.1, str, 1936; Serenade no.1, 4 wind, 1949; Serenade no.2, 6 wind, 1961; Poème funèbre en mémoire de Paul Hindemith, 13 str, 1965; Sérénade pour Montreux, 2 ob, 2 hn, str, 1970; Modeste Mignon (after waltz by Balzac), 10 wind insts, 1974

Pf: Bergsommer, 1941; Sonatine, E♭, 1948; Hommage pour Arthur Honegger, 1956

Principal publishers: Hug, Schott

WRITINGS

'Essentials of Opera', *Music* (1953), no.4

'Selbstporträt', *Musik der Zeit* (1955), no.4, p.44

'Brief an einen jungen angehenden Komponisten', *SMz*, xcviii (1958), 336

'Zeitgenössische Oper "unzeitgemäss"', *Musik der Zeit* (1960), no.9, p.31

BIBLIOGRAPHY

P. Mieg: 'Heinrich Sutermeister', *40 Schweizer Komponisten der Gegenwart* (Amriswil, 1956)

D. Larese: *Heinrich Sutermeister* (Amriswil, 1972)

KURT VON FISCHER/FRITZ MUGGLER

Suthaus, (Heinrich) Ludwig (*b* Cologne, 12 Dec 1906; *d* Berlin, 7 Sept 1971). German tenor. He studied in Cologne and made his début at Aachen in 1928 as Walther von Stolzing. Engagements followed at Essen (1931–3), Stuttgart (1933–41), the Berlin Staatsoper (1941–8) and the Berlin Städtische Oper (1948–65). He first sang at Bayreuth in 1943 as Walther, returning in 1944 in the same role, and in 1956–7 as Loge and Siegmund. His London début was at the Albert Hall in 1948 in Act 1 of *Die Walküre*, and he sang Tristan at Covent Garden in the 1952–3 season. His American début (1953) was as Aegisthus (*Elektra*) at San Francisco, where he also sang Tristan and Siegmund; he returned in 1956 as Erik and Siegmund. At Vienna, where he appeared from 1948 until shortly before his death, his roles included Florestan, Othello and Herman (*The Queen of Spades*). In 1949 he sang the Emperor in *Die Frau ohne Schatten* at the Teatro Colón, Buenos Aires, and the next year sang Števa in the first South American production of *Jenůfa*. His large repertory also included Rienzi, Bacchus, Pedro (*Tiefland*), Samson, the title role in *Sadko*, which he took at the German première in Berlin (1947), and the Drum Major (*Wozzeck*). Furtwängler considered Suthaus the finest *Heldentenor* of his day and engaged him to sing in his recordings of *Tristan und Isolde* and *Die Walküre*, and in his famous performances of the *Ring* for Italian radio (1953). Suthaus appeared at La Scala as Siegfried (*Götterdämmerung*) in 1954, and Siegmund (*Die Walküre*) in 1958. His voice was similar to Melchior's

in size and sound, and of a kind that had become unfamiliar by the late 1970s.

HAROLD ROSENTHAL

Sutherland, Dame **Joan** (*b* Sydney, 7 Nov 1926). Australian soprano. She was taught piano and singing by her mother until she was 19, when she won the first of several singing competitions; she then began to receive professional tuition in Sydney from John and Aida Dickens. They developed her hitherto neglected soprano register, and she sang her first operatic role as Dido in Purcell's *Dido and Aeneas* in a concert performance at the Lyceum Club, Sydney, in 1947. Further competition successes in 1949–50 brought her sufficient monetary capital to venture a musical future in London, but before leaving Australia she made her operatic stage début in June 1951 at Sydney Conservatorium in the title role of *Judith* by Sir Eugene Goossens, the Conservatorium director.

In London Sutherland studied at the RCM with Clive Carey and at the Opera School, eventually gaining a Covent Garden contract in 1952, after three auditions, and making her début with the company that year as First Lady in *Die Zauberflöte*. Her regular accompanist at singing lessons in London was a fellow-Australian, Richard Bonynge, whom she married in 1954, and who increasingly became her preferred conductor during her international successes in the 1960s. At the time they married he had begun to encourage and coach her vocal technique in florid music, with special concern for the Italian bel canto repertory (for which he later wrote much *fioritura* in period style for her to sing). Sutherland progressed through a variety of roles with the Covent Garden company, including a single Aida

Joan Sutherland in the title role of Donizetti's 'Lucia di Lammermoor'

(Manchester, 1954), creating Jenifer in Tippett's *The Midsummer Marriage* (1955), and gaining particular success as Gilda in *Rigoletto* (1957) and in the title role of *Alcina* (for the Handel Opera Society) the same year. Her performance in Zeffirelli's production of *Lucia di Lammermoor* at Covent Garden on 17 February 1959 won immediate acclaim and set her on the threshold of her subsequent international career as a dramatic coloratura soprano specializing in Italian and French opera of the 19th century.

Her singing customarily combines ease and brilliance of tone and ornamentation, clarity above the staff, and intense emotional commitment in phrasing, sometimes, when consonants are insufficiently articulated, at the expense of verbal intelligibility. A disinclination to tolerate what she considers to be unsympathetic or ill-judged conducting has provoked occasional displays of protest from an otherwise generous and loyal personality. In 1960 she settled in Switzerland.

Sutherland first sang in North America at Vancouver (Donna Anna, 1958), in the USA at Dallas, Texas (Alcina, 1960), followed by the Metropolitan, New York (Lucia, 1961). She sang Donna Anna at the Vienna Staatsoper in 1959, made her Italian début at Venice (Alcina, 1960), followed by La Scala, Milan, in 1961 (Lucia, then Bellini's Beatrice di Tenda the same season). A return to Australia in the 1965–6 season with her own touring company, under Bonynge as artistic director, brought her recognition as the greatest Australian singer since Melba. Other roles closely associated with her are Norma (Bellini), Cleopatra (in Handel's *Giulio Cesare*) and all three sopranos in *Les contes d'Hoffmann* (Offenbach). Her gramophone repertory ranges from opera to an album of Noël Coward songs, and includes 'The Art of the Prima Donna', two discs on which her vocal challenge to 16 great sopranos of history and their most famous roles is triumphantly vindicated. She was made DBE in 1979.

BIBLIOGRAPHY
R. Braddon: *Joan Sutherland* (London, 1962)
E. Greenfield: *Joan Sutherland* (London, 1972) [with discography]
J. B. Steane: *The Grand Tradition* (London, 1975), 383ff
NOËL GOODWIN

Sutherland, Margaret (Ada) (*b* Adelaide, 20 Nov 1897). Australian composer and pianist. Her father was a writer and amateur pianist, and her other relatives included musicians, artists, scientists and academics. Her musical education included studies in the piano with Edward Goll and in composition with Fritz Hart at the Marshall Hall (now Melba) Conservatorium and later at the Melbourne University Conservatorium. At the age of 19 she was invited by the director of the New South Wales State Conservatorium of Music, Henri Verbrugghen, to appear as soloist with the NSW State Orchestra in public concerts under his direction. She gave recitals and taught theory and piano during the years of World War I and up to 1923, and the latter aspect of her work is reflected in a number of short teaching pieces she has written for the instrument. Resident in Melbourne since 1901, she left Australia in 1923 for further study in composition (as well as in orchestration and conducting) in London and Vienna. In London she was for a time a pupil of Bax; during this period she produced her first published works, including the Violin Sonata, which received especially warm praise from Bax. She returned to Melbourne in 1925.

The period between 1925 and 1935 was fallow, but

since then she has been active as a composer, performer (principally of chamber music) and teacher, contributing greatly to the musical and cultural development of Australia, and as a vigorous champion of the music of other Australian composers. For many years, her own works gained comparatively little recognition. During the 1960s, however, the rapid growth of performances, recordings, publication and commissioning of Australian compositions made reparation. Her considerable services to Australian music received official recognition in 1969 when she was awarded an honorary DMus from the University of Melbourne, and again in 1970 when she was made an OBE.

Sutherland has become recognized as one of the first 20th-century Australian composers to write in an idiom comparable with that of her generation in Europe. Her music has also been influenced by that of her teacher, Bax, and by the English pastoral idiom; the richer, more sensuous elements of this style are most noticeable in some early songs, keyboard and chamber music. Unlike many Australian composers of the first half of the 20th century, however, she soon integrated these influences in a personal idiom, absorbing a wide range of stylistic sources, contemporary continental as well as English. The influence of Bartók and Hindemith is particularly evident, and also the neo-classicism found in Ravel, Milhaud or Poulenc.

Her music at times betrays romantic warmth and often displays considerable strength of utterance and rhythmic vitality, although restraint, conciseness of expression and a strong taste for contrapuntal development must be considered basic qualities. This last element is especially prominent in many of her chamber works and is aptly reflected in the title of one of the best of these, *Discussion* for string quartet. Her chamber music also shows a typically 20th-century interest in varied, often unusual instrumental combinations. Romantic elements are perhaps most marked in orchestral works such as the Violin Concerto and the tone poem *Haunted Hills* (a musical evocation of the Dandenong Ranges near Melbourne and one of her few works with programmatic intentions). One of the finest and most characteristic of her larger works is the Concerto grosso, in which two fast movements, characterized by an effective use of dissonant counterpoint as well as by rhythmic drive and rhetorical strength, enclose a lyrical slow movement of brooding melancholy. Lyrical qualities are also to be found in her many songs; the settings of poems by Judith Wright contain some fine examples. Her single stage work, the one-act chamber opera *The Young Kabbarli*, was given its première at the Festival of Contemporary Opera and Music in Hobart in 1965.

WORKS
(*selective list*)
STAGE AND ORCHESTRAL
Opera: The Young Kabbarli (1, Casey), Hobart, 1965
Ballets: Dithyramb, pf, 1937, orchd ?1941; The Selfish Giant
Incidental music: A Midsummer Night's Dream
Orch: Pavan, 1938; Prelude and Jig, str, 1939; Suite on a Theme of Purcell, 1939; Pf Concertino, 1940; Conc., str, 1945; Rondel, 1945; Adagio, 2 vn, orch, 1946; Threesome, 1947; Ballad Ov., 1948; 4 Sym. Concepts (Studies), 1949; Bush Ballad, ?1950; Haunted Hills, 1950; Open Air Piece, 1953; Vn Conc., 1954; Conc. grosso, 1955; Outdoor Ov., 1958; 3 Temperaments, 1958; Movt, 1959; Concertante, ob, str, perc, 1961; Fantasy, vn, orch, 1962

VOCAL
Choral: The Passing, SATB, orch, ?1939; A Company of Carols, SATB, pf, 1966; miscellaneous short pieces
Solo vocal: Songs for Children (Martyr), 1v, pf, ?1929; 3 Songs

(Thompson), 1v, vn, pf, 1930; 5 Songs (Shaw Neilson), 1v, pf, 1936; The Gentle Water Bird (Shaw Neilson), 1v, vn/ob, pf; The Orange Tree (Shaw Neilson), 1v, cl, pf, ?1938; 4 Blake Songs, 1v, pf, ?1950; The World and the Child (Wright), Mez, pf/str qt, 1960; Sequence of Verses into Music (Casey), speaker, fl, bn, va, 1964; 6 Australian Songs (Wright), 1v, pf, 1967; other settings, folksong arrs.

CHAMBER AND INSTRUMENTAL

For 3–4 insts: Trio, cl, va, pf, 1934; House Qt, cl/vn, va, hn/vc, pf, 1936; Str Qt no.1, ?1939; Adagio and Allegro giocoso, 2 vn, pf, ?1945; Trio, ob, 2 vn, 1951; Disucssion (Str Qt no.2), 1954; Qt, eng hn, str, 1955; Divertimento, str trio, 1958; Little Suite, wind trio, ?1960; Str Qt no.3, 1967; Qt, cl, str, 1967

For 2 insts: Sonata, vn, pf, 1925; Fantasy Sonatina, sax, pf, ?1935; Rhapsody, vn, pf, 1938; Sonata, vc/sax, pf, 1942; Ballad and Nocturne, vn, pf, 1944; Sonata, cl/va, pf, 1949; Contrasts, 2 vn, 1953; 6 Bagatelles, vn, va, 1956; Sonatina, ob/vn, pf, ?1957; Fantasy, vn, pf, ?1960

For kbd: Burlesque, 2 pf, ?1927; 2 Chorale Preludes on Bach's Chorales, pf (1935); 2 suites, pf (1937); Miniature Ballet Suite, pf (1937); Miniature Sonata, pf, ?1939; 6 Profiles, pf, ?1946; Pf Sonatina (1956); Pavan, 2 pf (1957); Canonical Piece, 2 pf (1957); Pf Sonata (1966); Extension, pf, 1967; Chiaroscuro I–II, pf, 1968; Voices I–II, pf, 1968; 3 Pieces, hpd

Educational: str pieces (1967), pf pieces

Principal publisher: Albert (Sydney)

BIBLIOGRAPHY

I. Moresby: *Australia Makes Music* (London, 1948), 127
J. Garretty: *Three Australian Composers* (diss., U. of Melbourne, 1963), 49–102
R. Covell: *Australia's Music: Themes of a New Society* (Melbourne, 1967), 152ff, 261
A. McCredie: *Musical Composition in Australia* (Canberra, 1969)
——: *A Catalogue of 46 Australian Composers and Selected Works* (Canberra, 1969), 18
F. Callaway and D. Tunley, eds.: *Australian Composition in the Twentieth Century* (London, 1979)

DAVID SYMONS

Sutton, John (*fl* late 15th century). English composer. A John Sutton was MA and Fellow of Magdalen College, Oxford, in 1476, resigning his fellowship in 1477 on election to a fellowship at Eton College. After 1479 his name disappears from the Eton records. A 'Sutton' graduated MusB at Cambridge in 1489. The Eton Choirbook (*GB-WRec* 178; edited in MB, x–xii, London, 1956–61) contains Sutton's only known composition: a fine *Salve regina* in seven parts, which has as its cantus firmus *Libera nos*, the antiphon which members of Eton College had to recite daily.

BIBLIOGRAPHY

F. Ll. Harrison: *Music in Medieval Britain* (London, 1958, 2/1963)
NICHOLAS SANDON

Suvini Zerboni. Italian firm of music publishers. It was founded in 1930, and owes its development to Paolo Giordani who was its head from 1932 until his death in 1948. He aimed to build up a collection of Italian compositions and make them internationally known, but his efforts were interrupted by World War II. He was joined after the war by the Hungarian Ladislao Sugar, who became head of the firm. Sugar brought Hungarian composers into the firm's catalogue, so that it now includes many compositions by Sándor Veress, Dorati, Seiber and others. He also negotiated an agency agreement with Editio Musica of Budapest and important reciprocal agency agreements with Schott and other firms. Suvini Zerboni publishes works by contemporary Japanese composers as well as editions of Italian classical music (including the series Orpheus Italicus). By far the greater part of its catalogue (which numbered about 4000 items in 1975) is contemporary Italian music, including many of the works of Berio, Castiglioni, Aldo Clementi, Dallapiccola, Donatoni,

Ghedini, Maderna, Gianfrancesco and Riccardo Malipiero, and Pizzetti.

ALAN POPE

Suyāke. A category of chant in SYRIAN CHURCH MUSIC.

Suys, Hans. Organ builder; *see* SUISSE (ii).

Suzoy, Johannes. *See* SUSAY, JO.

Suzuki, Shin'ichi (*b* Nagoya, 18 Oct 1898). Japanese educationist and violin teacher, founder of the Suzuki method. His father Masakichi Suzuki (1859–1944) was first a maker of *shamisen* (Japanese string instruments), but he later began to manufacture violins, successfully mechanizing production in 1900 and founding the Suzuki Violin Seizō Co. in 1930. The company became the largest violin-making firm in Japan, while Masakichi himself went on making instruments by hand. Shin'ichi went to the Nagoya Commercial School (graduating in 1915), and concurrently studied the violin under Kō Andō (1878–1963), a pupil of Joachim; he went to Berlin (1921–8), where he became a pupil of Karl Klingler, another of Joachim's pupils. On his return he established the Suzuki Quartet with three of his brothers. In 1930 he became president of the Teikoku Music School; a few years later he founded the Tokyo String Orchestra and as its conductor introduced Baroque music to Japanese audiences.

Suzuki's educational method is not a mere process of music education, but his philosophy and its application. In 1933 he realized that children of any nationality could freely speak their mother tongue regardless of their intelligence, remembering 4000 words by the age of five. He also noticed that young children accept high-level stimuli with hardly any pain, form voluntary desires and acquire excellent abilities, while learning their mother tongue as naturally as they develop their characters. He believed that good environments and conditions are conducive to the development of ability, as in learning speech, and decided to apply this principle to his violin teaching. Although not ruling out hereditary factors, he believed that any child could develop a high standard of ability by adapting external stimuli. The repetition of stimuli, and the period, the frequency and the time of stimuli given to the child are important conditions; his theory is related to the physiology of cerebra. His first pupil taught by this new method was Toshiya Etō, then a small child.

Towards the end of World War II Suzuki moved to Matsumoto, Nagano prefecture, where he organized the Yōji Kyōiku Dōshikai (Group for Child Education). In 1948 he won the cooperation of the master of Hongo Primary School, Matsumoto, where he organized an experimental class of 40 students. Pupils in any subject were given only a few exercises, easy enough to enable the whole class to answer perfectly; the next day the same exercises were reviewed before proceeding. In this way it was possible for everyone to reach the same high standard. Suzuki went on to found the Sainō Kyōiku Yōji, Gakuen, where a class of 60 children aged three to five is taught Japanese pronunciation, Chinese letters, expression, calligraphy, drawing, English conversation and gymnastics, following his method.

In the Sainō Kyōiku Kenkyū-kai, Matsumoto (founded in 1950), Suzuki taught violin playing according to his method. As his main purpose was the develop-

Shin'ichi Suzuki teaching a class of children in Japan

ment of character through musical education, or more specifically through violin playing, he avoided using the words 'music' or 'violin' in the name of his institute. 196 pupils graduated in 1952; in 1972 the graduates included 2321 violinists. At the annual meeting of the institute at the Budō-kan, Tokyo, there is usually a performance of such pieces as a Bach gavotte or a Boccherini minuet by 3000 children or of a Mozart violin concerto by a small group of older students. The Sainō Kyōiku Kenkyū-kai has 83 local chapters throughout Japan, with 280 classes, 160 teachers and 6000 students. The Suzuki method has also been applied to the cello, flute, piano and other instruments. From 1964 Suzuki frequently toured the USA with his students, giving lectures and demonstrations; violin lessons according to his method are given at several American universities and conservatories, including Oberlin Conservatory of Music. In 1973 he visited England, Switzerland and the USA with nine violin pupils. Among internationally known violinists those who were taught by the Suzuki method are Toshiya Etō, Kōji Toyota, Takeji Kobayashi, Kenji Kobayashi, Shūtarō Suzuki, Senya Urakawa, Yuriko Kuronuma, Tomiko Shida and Yōko Satō.

BIBLIOGRAPHY

T. R. Brunson: *An Adaptation of the Suzuki–Kendall Violin Method for Heterogeneous Stringed Instrument Classes* (diss., U. of Arizona, 1969)

C. A. Cook: *Suzuki Education in Action* (New York, 1970)

J. Sperti: *Adaptation of Certain Aspects of the Suzuki Method to the Teaching of the Clarinet* (diss., New York U., 1970)

S. Suzuki: *Saino kaihatsu no jissai* [The practice of developing talent] (Tokyo, 1971)

R. K. Keraus: *An Achievement Study of Private and Class Suzuki Instruction* (diss., U. of Rochester, 1973)

E. Mills and T. C. Murthy, eds.: *The Suzuki Conception: an Introduction to a Successful Method for Early Music Education* (Berkeley, Calif., 1973)

MINAO SHIBATA

Svanholm, Set (Karl Viktor) (*b* Västerås, 2 Sept 1904; *d* Saltsjö-Duvnäs, nr. Stockholm, 4 Oct 1964). Swedish tenor. He was organist at Tillberga from 1922, and at Säby from 1924, then studied at the Royal Conservatory, Stockholm, 1927–9. Appointed precentor of St James's church in 1929, he became interested in opera singing and for a year was a pupil of John Forsell at the Conservatory Opera School. In 1930 he made his début with the Swedish Royal Opera in the baritone roles of Silvio and Rossini's Figaro, and in 1937 he was permanently engaged by the company. In 1936 he made his tenor début as Radamès, and subsequently took on such heavy tenor parts as Othello, Siegmund, Parsifal and Tristan. He sang at Salzburg and Vienna (1938), Berlin, Budapest and Milan (1941–2) and Bayreuth (1942). In 1946 he visited North and South America, singing Tristan in Rio de Janeiro, Lohengrin in San Francisco and Siegfried at the Metropolitan Opera. At Covent Garden he sang regularly from 1948 to 1957. He was always reliable, and though his voice had neither the warmth nor the splendour to match that of Flagstad (with whom he often sang), his performances were admired for intelligence and musicianship, and he had the stamina and the power to sustain his exacting roles. In 1946 he was appointed Singer to the Royal Swedish Court. He was director of the Swedish Royal Opera from 1956 to 1963, and introduced several contemporary operas (among them Britten's *The Rape of Lucretia* and *The Turn of the Screw*, *Mathis der Maler* and *The Rake's Progress*), as well as reviving Handel's *Alcina*, and *Les troyens*. He also taught singing in Stockholm.

Set Svanholm as Tristan in Wagner's 'Tristan und Isolde'

BIBLIOGRAPHY

H. Rosenthal: 'Set Svanholm', *Opera*, vi (1955), 357
B. Hagman: 'Porträtt av operachef', *Musikrevy*, xii (1957), 253
H. Rosenthal: *Great Singers of Today* (London, 1966)

CARL L. BRUUN

Švara, Danilo (*b* Ricmanje, nr. Trieste, 2 April 1902). Yugoslav composer and conductor. While at the Handelshochschule, Vienna, he studied the piano privately with Trost (1920–22). He completed studies in politics and law at Frankfurt University (1922–5), at the same time studying the piano with Malata and conducting with Scherchen. After a period as répétiteur and conductor at the Ljubljana Opera (1925–7) he attended the Hoch Conservatory, Frankfurt (1927–30), as a pupil of Szekles (composition), von Schmiedel and Rottenberg (conducting) and Wallenstein (stage direction). Švara was then active as a conductor (he was director of the Ljubljana Opera from 1957 to 1959), music critic and teacher of conducting at the Ljubljana Music Academy. A follower of radical compositional trends in the 1930s, he later employed a more moderate style, returning to expressionist atonality and 12-note technique in the 1960s. His strength lies in his stage and orchestral music.

WORKS
(selective list)

Stage: Kleopatra, opera, 1937; Veronika Deseniška, opera, 1943; Slovo od mladosti [Farewell to youth], opera, 1952; Nina, ballet, 1962; Ocean, opera, 1963
Orch: 3 syms., 1933, 1935, 1947; Valse interrompue, 1948; Sinfonia da camera in modo istriano, 1954; Conc. grosso dodecafono, 1961; 2 suites, 1962
Dodekafoniai: I, Duo concertante, fl, hpd, 1967; II, Vn Conc., 1966; III, Ob Conc., 1966; IV, Symposium, ob, va, harp, 1968; V, Cl Conc., 1969
Vizija, cantata, 1931; chamber, pf, choral and film music, songs

Principal publisher: Edicije DSS

ANDREJ RIJAVEC

Svéd, Sándor [Sved, Alexander] (*b* Budapest, 28 May 1904). Hungarian baritone. He studied in Budapest and later in Italy with, among others, Sammarco and Stracciari, making his Budapest début in 1930 as di Luna. In 1936 he first appeared at the Vienna Staatsoper and (less successfully) at Covent Garden, and in December 1938 at La Scala as Macbeth – the first of several Milan roles that included the elder Germont, Fanuél (in Boito's *Nerone*), Prince Igor, a much-praised William Tell and Amfortas. After his Metropolitan début in 1940 as Renato, he sang there regularly (as Alexander Sved) until his return to Hungary in 1950, when he again became a member of the Budapest Opera. After 1956 he taught singing in Stuttgart. A somewhat stiff actor, Svéd owed the length and distinction of his career to the Italianate beauty, and the fine technique, of his powerful yet velvet-toned voice, best suited to the Italian lyric repertory but capable of other, more dramatic roles like Rigoletto, Michele in *Il tabarro* and Telramund. His records include excerpts from *Il trovatore*, *Guillaume Tell* and *Un ballo in maschera*.

BIBLIOGRAPHY

L. Riemens: 'Sved, Sándor von', *Le grandi voci* (Rome, 1964) [with opera discography by R. Vegeto]

PÉTER P. VÁRNAI

Svedbom, (Per Jonas Fredrik) Vilhelm (*b* Stockholm, 8 March 1843; *d* Stockholm, 25 Dec 1904). Swedish composer and teacher. He first devoted himself to studies in the humanities at Uppsala University. He took his doctor's degree in 1872 and became university lecturer in the history of literature. From 1873 to 1876 he travelled in England and on the Continent for the purpose of further study, becoming a pupil of Friedrich Kiel in Berlin. He was elected a member of the Musikaliska Akademien in Stockholm in 1876, and was its secretary until 1901. He then became director of the conservatory of the academy where he had been teacher of the history of music since 1877. Svedbom also held other important musical posts. He was secretary of the Musikaliska Konstföreningen, an association for the publication of unprinted Swedish music, from 1878; and in 1880 he and Ludvig Norman founded the Musikföreningen i Stockholm for the performance of choral works with the assistance of the royal chapel. He was the president of this society.

Most of his own compositions are vocal music. He wrote a few cantatas (e.g. *I rosengården*). Of his choral songs his arrangement of the folksong *Hej dunkom* for male voices is still performed. His most famous solo song is the ballad *Sten Sture*.

BIBLIOGRAPHY

M. Galschiöt: *Skandinaver i Rom for halvhundred aar siden* (Copenhagen, 1923), 139ff
M. Tegen: 'Tre svenska vikingaoperor', *STMf*, xli (1960), 12–75
A. Helmer: *Svensk solosång 1850–1890* (diss., U. of Uppsala, 1972)

FOLKE BOHLIN

Sveinbjörnsson, Sveinbjörn (*b* nr. Reykjavík, 28 June 1847; *d* Copenhagen, 23 Feb 1927). Icelandic composer and pianist. He took a degree in theology before deciding (probably on the encouragement of the Norwegian composer Johan Svendsen, who visited Iceland in 1867) to embark on a musical career. Sveinbjörnsson went to Copenhagen in 1868, where he studied privately with V. C. Ravn. In 1870 he went to Edinburgh and taught the piano there to finance further studies with Carl Reinecke in Leipzig (for eight months, 1872–3), after which he returned to Edinburgh, where he lived as a piano teacher until 1919. He was a founder of the Edinburgh Society of Musicians (1887) and an active performer, undertaking two extensive concert and lecture tours of the USA and Canada (1911–13 and 1919–22). His remaining years were divided between Iceland and Denmark. He died in Copenhagen, but was buried in Reykjavík.

Sveinbjörnsson was a refined and lyrical composer, sometimes bordering on the sentimental, sometimes attaining an expression of heroic dignity. The influence of Danish songs (chiefly by Berggreen and Gade) during his youth in Iceland was intensified by his studies in Copenhagen; later, he came into direct contact with the Mendelssohn tradition in Leipzig. His English contemporaries detected in him a 'Nordic strain' and he was commissioned to compose the incidental music to the Icelandic scenes in Hall Caine's *The Prodigal Son* (Drury Lane, 1905); Icelanders, however, found him cosmopolitan or English. Sveinbjörnsson himself became increasingly aware of his heritage of Icelandic folksong, and always regarded himself as an Icelandic composer.

His works consist chiefly of songs with piano accompaniment, mostly through-composed, the piano often subtly illustrating the text. About three-quarters of them are settings of English texts, as are some of his 30 choral pieces. Some of his songs (e.g. *King Sverre*) appeared in more than one edition during his lifetime. His *Royal Cantata* (1907, composed for the visit of King Frederik VIII of Denmark to Iceland) was for a long time the most ambitious musical composition by an Icelander, and earned him the highest royal honour. The hymn which he composed for the 1000th anniversary (1874) of the Norse settlement in Iceland became the Icelandic national anthem. His piano pieces include many paraphrases of Icelandic folksongs, such as the *Idyl* and *Vikivaki* (Icelandic dance); some were composed primarily for teaching purposes (*Descriptive Pieces for the Young* and a Duet in A for four hands, based on Scottish dances). His most important chamber works are the Sonata in F for violin and piano and two trios (for voice, cello and piano) in E minor and A minor. Two *Icelandic Rhapsodies*, mostly paraphrases of Icelandic folksongs, are his principal orchestral compositions.

In 1954 his widow Eleanor Sveinbjörnsson (née Christie) presented his MSS to the Icelandic people (the collection is now in *IS-Rn*).

BIBLIOGRAPHY
J. Thórarinsson: *Sveinbjörn Sveinbjörnsson* (Reykjavik, 1969)
THORKELL SIGURBJÖRNSSON

Sveinsson, Atli Heimir (*b* Reykjavík, 21 Sept 1938). Icelandic composer and teacher. He studied the piano with Sigurjónsson at the Reykjavík College of Music, took composition, conducting and piano under Raphael, Petzold and Zimmermann at the Staatliche Hochschule für Musik, Cologne (1959–62), and attended the Darmstadt (1959–61) and Cologne courses given by Stockhausen, Pousseur and others. In 1964 he took a course in electronic music under Koenig in Bilthoven. He teaches at the Reykjavík Grammar School and has worked as a freelance producer for Icelandic broadcasting. A member of Musica Nova, he was appointed president of the Icelandic Composers' Society in 1972 and of the Nordic Composers' Council in 1975. His compositional style varies from piece to piece, exhibiting influences from all current avant-garde mainstreams.

The impression of serial technique is evident in his early works, but in later scores there is a new romanticism influenced by oriental music.

WORKS
(*selective list*)
Orch: Könnun, va, orch, 1971; Tengsl, 1972; Fl Conc., 1973; Flower Shower, orch, tape, 1974
Vocal: I Call it, A, pf, 2 perc, vc, 1974
Inst: Klif, fl, cl, bn, 1970; Spectacles, perc, tape, 1970; Bizzarreries, 3 insts, 1973; Iter mediae noctis, org, 1974; Night in the Cathedral, org, tape, 1975; Xanties, fl, pf, 1976

BIBLIOGRAPHY
A. Burt: *Iceland's Twentieth-century Composers and a Listing of their Works* (Fairfax, Virginia, in preparation)
AMANDA M. BURT

Sveinsson, Gunnar Reynir (*b* Reykjavík, 28 June 1933). Icelandic composer. He studied with Jón Thórarinsson at the Reykjavík College of Music, graduating in 1961. At this time he was also working as a professional jazz and dance-band musician (1950–63) and as first percussionist with the Iceland SO (1956–64). He continued his studies with De Leeuw and Orthel at the Amsterdam Conservatory (1964–7) and with Koenig and Kaegi at the Institute for Sonology, Utrecht (1973–4). His earliest works are in a Hindemithian style, which gave way to various atonal excursions; the most successful of his compositions (the vocal pieces) are traditional in form, with considerable use of parallel chords.

WORKS
(*selective list*)
Choral: Mass, S, T, B, chorus, 1961; 7 Songs (Eng. medieval), 1963; Althyduvisur um ástina [Common songs of love], 1972; The Songs of the Valley Children, children's vv, 1972; Ur söngbok Gardars Holm, 1972; Crucifixus, 1973; Ég vakti í nótt, 1974; Thegar Tregar dýran dag, male vv, 1975; many other songs
Inst: Sveiflur, fl, vc, perc, 1966; Samstaedur, jazz ens, 1970

Principal publishers: Iceland Music Information Centre, Sveinsson

BIBLIOGRAPHY
A. Burt: *Iceland's Twentieth-century Composers and a Listing of their Works* (Fairfax, Virginia, in preparation)
AMANDA M. BURT

Svendsen, Johan (Severin) (*b* Christiania [now Oslo], 30 Sept 1840; *d* Copenhagen, 14 June 1911). Norwegian violinist, composer and conductor.

1. LIFE. His father was a military musician who gave him instruction in a variety of instruments. At the age of nine he began to play in local dance orchestras and at 11 to compose dances and marches, two of which were later published. He joined the army and soon transferred to the regimental band, where he became solo clarinettist. The violin was his principal instrument, however; he took lessons from F. Ursin and played in the orchestra of the Norwegian Theatre, of which Ibsen was director. His first experience of the symphonic repertory was as a first violinist in the series of subscription concerts arranged by H. Kjerulf and J. G. Conradi in 1857–9, when Beethoven's music made a deep impression on him. He then became a pupil of Carl Arnold, whose instruction he always valued highly, though it seems to have consisted mainly of a thorough study of Beethoven's and Mozart's violin sonatas. In 1859 he met Ole Bull and in 1860 conducted a concert in Bergen. He also organized a little orchestra of his own, the Norwegian Music Society. In 1862 he travelled through Sweden and Denmark to north Germany, hoping to make his way by playing the violin, but in Lübeck, in the middle of winter, having reached the end of his resources, he appealed for a loan to the Norwegian–Swedish consul, who, impressed by his

playing, obtained a stipend for him from the king to study in Leipzig. In Lübeck Svendsen composed a Caprice for orchestra with solo violin, which he sent with his application to Leipzig. Offered a place in an advanced class, he thought his education so deficient that he asked to start at the beginning.

Svendsen began at the conservatory in autumn 1863, studying with Moritz Hauptmann, Ferdinand David, E. F. Richter and Reinecke. Intended to prepare for a career as a violin virtuoso, by the end of 1864 he had shifted his interest to composition. In 1865 a nervous complaint in the fingers of his left hand compelled him to stop playing for a time. As compensation he was allowed to substitute for David as conductor of the conservatory orchestra. His performance was greeted with approval, as was his String Quartet op.1. At the end of 1865 he was at work on his String Octet op.3 and the Symphony no.1 in D op.4. When the Octet was performed at the conservatory in 1866, it was received with such enthusiasm that Breitkopf & Härtel asked to publish it and Svendsen was awarded the conservatory's first prize. When he left the conservatory in May 1867 he had completed the symphony and the String Quintet op.5.

Svendsen spent summer 1867 accompanying the German publisher Brockhaus on a North Atlantic tour that took them to Copenhagen (where he met Gade), Scotland, the Faroe Islands and Iceland. In August he returned to Norway after an absence of five years and in October conducted a concert of his orchestral music, including his First Symphony, the Caprice, the Andante of his Quintet and his orchestrations of Liszt's Second Hungarian Rhapsody and of a minuet by the peasant fiddler Johan Steenberg. An enthusiastic (anonymous) review by Grieg recognized Svendsen's freshness and originality as a composer and his complete command of the orchestra, both as a brilliant orchestrator and authoritative conductor. However, the lack of public response to his concert confirmed Svendsen's misgivings about musical conditions in Christiania, and he left Norway to spend the winter on a state stipend in Leipzig. In spring 1868 he went to Paris, where he heard a great deal of music and had the String Quartet and Quintet performed at musical soirées. He was accompanied by Saint-Saëns in an early performance of Grieg's Second Violin Sonata, dedicated to him. In May he attended the music festival in Weimar, where a group of Germany's best virtuosos played his Octet, and where he met Liszt, who impressed him as being unbearably vain. The Franco-Prussian war prevented his return to Paris, and his expected engagement in Leipzig was postponed. Once he reached Leipzig, however, he completed the Violin Concerto op.6, begun in Paris, and a one-movement Cello Concerto op.7; during the Gewandhaus season (1870–71) he scored a great success conducting his First Symphony. At about the same time he announced his engagement to Sara Levett, an American whom he had met in Paris, and in summer 1871 they were married in New York. Back in Leipzig at the end of September, Svendsen became leader and second conductor of the Euterpe concerts, where his Symphonic Introduction to Sigurd Slembe (a drama by Bjørnstjerne Bjørnson) was performed that year. In spring 1872 Svendsen was one of the musicians invited to play in the large orchestra assembled to perform Beethoven's Ninth Symphony under Wagner's direction for the laying of the foundation stone of the Festival Theatre in Bayreuth. Svendsen was a great admirer of Wagner's music, and in Bayreuth the two soon became close friends. When Svendsen's Jewish wife decided to receive Christian baptism, Wagner and Cosima stood as godparents to her.

In autumn 1872 Svendsen returned to Christiania as joint conductor with Grieg – from 1874 sole conductor – of the Music Society concerts. For Grieg this was 'the richest season I have experienced in Norway, thanks to my brilliant colleague Johan Svendsen' – as it was also for Svendsen, both as composer and conductor. His compositions during this period include some of his most interesting works, such as the orchestral legend Zorahayda op.11 and the orchestral fantasy Romeo og Julie op.18, the Festival Polonaise op.12, the Norsk kunstnerkarneval op.14, the Symphony no.2 in B♭ op.15 and the first three Norwegian Rhapsodies opp.17, 19 and 21, as well as a number of arrangements of folk melodies for string orchestra. This, the most productive period of his creative life, was no doubt encouraged by the congeniality of his native environment and by the government's award to him of an annual composer's salary in 1874.

In 1877 Svendsen obtained a leave of absence from the Music Society and in the autumn conducted his Second Symphony in Leipzig. He spent the winter in Rome, where he completed his Fourth Norwegian Rhapsody op.22. Although he enjoyed the company of Sgambati, he found musical life in Rome uninteresting and in spring 1878 went to London. There he met Sarasate, who assisted in the performance of all his chamber music and generously put at his disposal his Paris residence when Svendsen moved there in the autumn. In Paris Svendsen found the musical environment he had been missing. He heard a great deal of new music, renewed old acquaintances and made new ones, including Mme Viardot. Pasdeloups included one of his Norwegian Rhapsodies in his concerts and Svendsen conducted a concert in Angers which was so successful that he was offered a post there. But two sets of songs, nine in all, was the apparent total of his creative achievement during these two years. In 1880 he returned to Christiania, where in the succeeding three years he also produced very little. However, one work from this period, the Romance for violin and orchestra op.26, deservedly became internationally popular, although the high quality of the piece was often obscured by the innumerable arrangements to which it was subjected. This was virtually the end of Svendsen's career as a composer, with the exception of a few relatively unimportant works commissioned for specific occasions.

Svendsen's importance as a conductor, the greatest in Scandinavia, continued to grow. During the 1881–2 season he gave two performances, the first in Norway, of Beethoven's Ninth Symphony, which raised musical standards in Christiania to a level that impressed Bülow on his visit there in May 1882. In October, after conducting in Stockholm, he conducted two concerts of his own works in Copenhagen, as a result of which the administration of the Royal Opera invited him to go to Copenhagen to succeed the aging Paulli as conductor there. He was appointed in 1883. That the highest musical post in Denmark should go to an outsider aroused resentment, and Svendsen's efforts to introduce changes and improvements were criticized. However his genius and personal charm won him the confidence of the theatre administration, the respect of his colleagues outstanding was Carl Nielsen, who played under him from 1889 to 1905 and was always warm in his expressions of gratitude and admiration.

2. WORKS. It is inevitable that Svendsen's name should be coupled with Grieg's, as these two constitute the culmination of national Romanticism in Norway. Yet, though they present an attractive picture of mutual admiration, respect and affection, lasting throughout their lives, they were complementary rather than similar. As Grieg himself observed in a letter in 1882, '[Svendsen] has precisely all that which I don't have' – that is, a natural mastery of the orchestra and of the large classical forms. In his review of Svendsen's Christiania concert in 1867 Grieg found Svendsen's Caprice rather formless, but Svendsen pointed out that it had been composed before he had studied form in Leipzig, though he also argued that 'one cannot always maintain the old forms when one wants to present new ideas'. Svendsen's student works show the ease with which he used the old forms. He found little need to experiment with these, although the Quintet is in only three movements, of which the second is a theme and variations (as is his arrangement for string orchestra of *I fjoll gjaett'e gjeitinn*), and the Cello Concerto is in one movement, with a slow section inserted between the development and the recapitulation.

At the same time Grieg expressed (in a letter) his admiration for Svendsen's orchestration, tentatively daring to see the influence of Berlioz. This suggestion would seem to gain support from the Berliozian subjects of some of the works composed after his first stay in Paris: *Karneval i Paris*, *Zorahayda*, *Norsk kunstnerkarneval* and *Romeo og Julie*, in which, as perhaps also in the Symphonic Introduction to *Sigurd Slembe*, he seemed to forsake classical ideals in favour of descriptive music using freer forms designated 'An Episode', 'A Legend' or 'A Fantasy'. Only *Zorahayda* has a literary programme, drawn from Washington Irving's *Legend of the Rose of the Alhambra*, which is inserted in the score as a guide to the piece's six sections. Here Svendsen also used motivic transformation, and the Spanish–Moorish subject allowed him to create an exotic orchestral atmosphere. In *Norsk kunstnerkarneval*, which depicts a Norwegian artists' carnival in Rome, the city is represented by an Italian folksong and the artists by a Norwegian one. This was the first occasion on which Svendsen used folk material. In 1867 Grieg had written of 'the boldest national tone' of the First Symphony and thought the Scherzo to be 'national through and through', but in 1881 he 'searched for the Scandinavian' in the Introduction to *Sigurd Slembe*. Svendsen was unquestionably a patriot with strong feelings for his homeland; after his move to Copenhagen he wrote to his father of his longing for Norway and confessed 'sometimes it is as if I will not be able to endure it down here for any length of time'. He loved the folk melodies of his people and made sensitive and attractive arrangements of a number of them, as well as treating them superbly in his four Rhapsodies, which are much more than folksong arrangements. Characteristic traces of these national melodies are also found in his own melodies and motifs – in the scherzo movements of both symphonies, for example. But despite his Romanticism Svendsen was too 'classical', too objective a personality to submerge himself and his art in patriotic fervour as had Ole Bull or Grieg.

Johan Svendsen: portrait by Georg Achen (1860–1912) in the Royal Theatre, Copenhagen

and the affection of the public, and his years in Copenhagen are remembered as a peak in the city's musical life. Svendsen also gave an annual series of orchestral concerts and raised the royal chapel orchestra to the level of the best in Europe. He also visited Vienna, Moscow, London, Brussels, Helsinki and elsewhere as a guest conductor.

Obliged to retire in 1908 because of ill-health, Svendsen continued to live in Copenhagen, where, after the dissolution of his first marriage in 1901, he had married the ballerina Juliette Vilhelmine Haase. As he had, for patriotic reasons, retained his Norwegian citizenship, he was not entitled to a Danish pension, but the state awarded him an honorary one. The Norwegian government also reinstated the composer's salary that had been suspended when he left Norway in 1883, though his work as a composer after that time is of relatively minor importance (in 1892 he had been given leave of absence from conducting to compose three works for the golden wedding anniversary of King Christian IX and Queen Louise; of these, the ballet *Foraaret kommer* ('Spring is coming') op.33 is the last work to which he gave an opus number).

On the podium Svendsen was a majestic figure of commanding, almost military, authority, completely in control and with the confidence born of careful intelligent preparation and a perfect musical memory. Those who played under him said that he had an ideal beat, discrete, precise, easy to follow, and a hypnotic glance. Off the podium he was modest and congenial, generous and helpful. Of the young musicians who benefited from his teaching, advice and encouragement, the most

The Violin Concerto was the first by a Norwegian, apart from the two virtuoso works by Ole Bull, and the Cello Concerto was presumably the first of its kind in Norway. Both are very attractive and well written, but it is perhaps their weakness that the beauty and elegance of the solo parts do not sufficiently compensate the soloist for the lack of virtuoso display. While they cannot be expected to rival the lovely Romance in popularity, they deserve a more frequent hearing than they have had. The two symphonies are not the first by a Norwegian, but they are the earliest to have won an audience in Norway and to have remained in the repertory. They are among Svendsen's finest and most representative works; the return to classical principles evident in the Second effectively contradicts the impression that Svendsen had been converted to the more radical Romanticism of Berlioz and Wagner in the years following the composition of the First. He was a born symphonist: Grieg observed 'the perfect balance between the ideas and the technical means' in his First Symphony; and in the Second the wealth of ideas and the greater expressivity of the mature artist perhaps make this his masterpiece. It was certainly to be expected that his future development as a composer would be as a symphonist, when his move to Copenhagen virtually put an end to his creative work. The blame for this sterility has been attributed to the demands made on him as a conductor, but there is reason to suppose that personal problems also raised great obstacles to his inspiration and concentration. It is known that in 1887 he was at work on a third symphony, which it has been supposed was never finished. However, from an unfinished volume of memoirs by John Paulsen, *Aftnerne i Arbinsgade*, it appears that this work suffered a fate worse than incompletion. He had completed the symphony, he told Paulsen, but one day his wife Sara took the manuscript in a rage and cast it into the fire. This tragic incident came to Ibsen's knowledge and provided the basis for the famous scene in *Hedda Gabler* (1890) in which Hedda casts Eilert Løvborg's manuscript into the fireplace.

Svendsen's style was very much his own, although attempts have been made to relate it to that of Beethoven, Schumann, Mendelssohn and Gade on the one hand, and Berlioz, Liszt and Wagner on the other. He stands somewhere between the two camps, a cosmopolitan rather than an eclectic. His melodic style is normally firmly tonal and diatonic; sometimes a descending root-position triad, often at the end of a phrase and perhaps with repetitions which waver between major and minor modes, suggests the influence of Norwegian folk music. Chromatic passages usually occur in slow tempos and express a mood of Romantic longing, as in *Zorahayda* and in the openings of the Romance for violin and of the last movements of both symphonies. His harmony is normally quite traditional and functional, not nearly so daring in the use of dissonance as Grieg's (though Svendsen shared with his progressive countryman a trick of harmonizing melodies with descending chromatic chords). His rhythm is straightforward and uncomplicated, rarely indulging in cross-rhythms and with a fondness for dotted rhythms in quick passages. Yet the rhythmic element, clean, well-marked and elastic, was an essential feature of Svendsen's work both as composer and conductor. Carl Nielsen called his treatment of rhythm his greatest gift to Danish music.

WORKS

ORCHESTRAL

Caprice, vn, orch, 1863; Sym. no.1, D, op.4, c1865–6 (Leipzig, 1868); Vn Conc., A, op.6, 1869–70 (Leipzig, n.d.); Vc Conc., d, op.7, 1870 (Leipzig, n.d.); Sym. Introduction to Bjørnson's Sigurd Slembe, op.8 (Leipzig, 1872); Karneval i Paris, episode, op.9, 1872 (Leipzig, 1877); Funeral March for King Carl XV, op.10, 1872; Zorahayda, legend, op.11, 1873 (Christiania, 1879); Festival Polonaise, op.12, 1873 (Christiania, 1886); Coronation March for Oscar II, op.13, 1873 (Leipzig, n.d.)

Norsk kunstnerkarneval, op.14, c1874 (Leipzig, n.d.); Sym. no.2, B♭, op.15 (Leipzig, 1877); 4 Norwegian Rhapsodies: no.1, op.17, no.2, op.19, no.3, op.21, all c1876 (Christiania, 1877), no.4, op.22 (Christiania, 1878); Romeo og Julie, fantasy, op.18, 1876 (Christiania, n.d.); Romance, vn, orch, op.26, 1881 (Christiania, 1881); Polonaise no.2, D, op.28 (Christiania, 1881); Foraaret kommer [Spring is coming], ballet, op.33, for golden wedding of Christian IX, 1892, excerpt, arr. pf (Copenhagen, n.d.); Andante funèbre, 1894 (Copenhagen and Leipzig, n.d.); Festival Prelude, 1898; Prelude, arr. pf (Copenhagen, 1911)

OTHER WORKS

Chamber: Str Qt, a, op.1, 1865 (Leipzig, n.d.); Str Octet, A, op.3, 1865–6 (Leipzig, n.d.); Str Qnt, C, op.5, 1867 (Leipzig, n.d.); Paraphrase sur des chansons populaires du nord, arr. G. Tronchi, humorous march, vn, vc, pf, op.16 (Copenhagen, 1916)

Vocal: 2 partsongs, male vv, op.2, 1865 (Leipzig, n.d.): Till Sverige [To Sweden], Aftnrøster [Evening voices]; 5 Songs (Fr. and Ger.), 1v, pf, op.23, 1879 (Paris, n.d.); 4 Songs (Fr. and Ger.), 1v, pf, op.24, 1879 (Paris, n.d.); 2 Songs, 1879 (Christiania, 1880): Violen [The violet] (B. Svendsen), Frühlingsjubel; Cantata, op.25, for unveiling of the Wergeland monument, 1881; Cantata, op.29, for U. of Christiania, celebration of wedding of Crown Prince Gustav, 1881; Cantata, op.30, for the Holberg Jubilaeum, 1884; Hymn and Festival cantata, op.31–2, for golden wedding of Christian IX, 1892

Pf: Anna, polka, 1854 (Christiania, n.d.); Til saeters [To the mountain pasture], waltz, 1856 (Christiania, n.d.)

Arrs., str orch: 2 Icelandic Melodies (Leipzig, 1877); O. Bull's Saeterjentens Søndag [The girl's Sunday on the mountain pasture], 1872 (Christiania, 1878); Norwegian Folk-melody, 1874 (Leipzig, n.d.); 2 Swedish Folk-melodies, op.27, 1876 (Christiania, 1878); Schumann's Abendlied (Christiania, 1887)

BIBLIOGRAPHY

H. von Bülow: 'Skandinavische Concertreiseskizzen, April und Mai 1882', *Allgemeine deutsche Musik-Zeitung*, ix (1882)

C. Nielsen: 'Johan Svendsen', *Politiken* (Copenhagen, 30 Sept 1900)

J. Paulsen: *Erindringer*, vi (Copenhagen, 1903), 63

C. Nielsen: 'Tale til Johan Svendsen, 12. november 1907', *Tilskueren*, xxv (1908), 42

G. Hauch, ed.: 'Breve fra Johan Svendsen', *Samtiden*, xxiv (1913), 481–512

O. M. Sandvik and G. Schjelderup, eds.: *Norges musikhistorie*, ii (Christiania, 1921), 107

O. Gurvin: 'Litt or Johan Svendsens dagbok frå Islandsferda 1867', *Norsk musikkgransknings årbok 1937*, 51

——: *Johan Svendsen: 30 september, 1840 – 30 september, 1940* (Oslo, 1940)

N. Schiørring: 'Svendsen, Johan Severin', *DBL*

J. Paulsen: 'Aftnerne i Arbinsgade' [Evenings in Arbinsgade], ed. H. Beyer, *Edda*, xliii (1943), 42

O. E. Ravn: 'Johan Svendsen', *Levende musik*, iii (Copenhagen, 1944), 57, 93

N. Friis: *Det kongelige kapel* (Copenhagen, 1948), 170ff

V. Gandrup: *Fem taktstokkens mestre* [5 masters of the baton] (Copenhagen, 1957), 15

Ø. Gaukstad, ed.: *E. Grieg: artikler og taler* (Oslo, 1957)

F. Benestad: 'Johan Svendsens Violinkonsert', *Norsk musikkgransknings årbok 1956–8*, 209–65

N. Grinde: 'Svendsen, Johan Severin', *Norsk biografisk leksikon*, xv (Oslo, 1966), 351

Ø. Eckhoff: 'Noen saerdrag ved Johan Svendsens instrumentalstil', *Festskrift til Olav Gurvin* (Drammen and Oslo, 1968), 56

N. Grinde: *Norsk musikkhistorie* (Oslo, 1971), 182

JOHN BERGSAGEL

Svendsen, Oluf (*b* Christiania [now Oslo], 19 April 1832; *d* London, 15 May 1888). Norwegian flautist. Trained initially by his father, Svendsen was at 14 first flute at the Christiania Theatre. Five years later he became a pupil of Niels Petersen, and in 1853 entered the Brussels Conservatory. He was engaged by Jullien for his London concerts of 1855 and the following year joined the Crystal Palace orchestra, where he remained until 1858. In 1861 Svendsen was appointed both to the Philharmonic Society's orchestra and first flute in the Queen's Private Band. He was a member of the regular orchestra at Her Majesty's Theatre, London, for ten years; as a teacher at the RAM from 1867, he exerted great influence in English orchestral circles.

PHILIP BATE

Svenska Samfundet för Musikforskning (Swedish Society for Musicology). A society founded in 1919 by members of the Swedish section of the Internationale Musikgesellschaft, to promote musicology, especially research into Swedish music. At the time of its foundation musicology was not an established discipline in Sweden so that from its first volume the *Svensk tidskrift för musikforskning* was of seminal importance. The society has published early Swedish music, in the series Äldre Svensk Musik (1930s), and on a more ambitious scale in the Monumenta Musicae Svecicae (1958–), and the complete works of Berwald. Studies, bibliographies and documents are published in the series Musik i Sverige (1969–). Outstanding presidents of the society have been Tobias Norlind (1919–26 and 1943–4), Einar Sundström (1939–42), C.-A. Moberg (1945–61) and Ingmar Bengtsson (1961–); in 1975 it had about 500 members.

BIBLIOGRAPHY
I. Bengtsson: 'Svenska Samfundet för Musikforskning 50 år (1919–1968)', *STMf*, li (1969), 7–48
E. Kjellberg: 'Svenska Samfundet för Musikforskning', *AcM*, xlvii (1975), 290

Sverige (Swed.). SWEDEN.

Sveshnikov, Alexander Vasil'yevich (*b* Kolomna, 11 Sept 1890). Soviet choral conductor and teacher. He studied singing under Stepan Vlasov and theory under Boleslav Yavorsky at the Moscow Conservatory (1908–9), then composition with Arseny Koreshchenko and the double bass with A. Shmuklovsky at the Moscow Philharmonic School (1909–11). He conducted workers' choirs and taught singing in schools, and for some years lived in Poltava, where he formed and directed a Ukrainian choral ensemble, and was one of the founders of the Poltava Opera, working as conductor and chief choirmaster there until he returned to Moscow in 1923. He directed the vocal section of the Moscow Arts Theatre's first studio, and in 1928 formed the All-Union Radio Choir, which he directed until 1936. From 1937 to 1941 he was artistic director of the Glinka Academic Choir in Leningrad, and from 1941 was director of the State Academic Choir of Russian Song. As well as founding the Moscow Choral School in 1944, he became a professor at the Moscow Conservatory in 1946 and its director, 1948–74. A master of the interpretation and performance of Russian folksong, Sveshnikov brought the State Academic Choir to a high standard; they had a range of tone from soft but sonorous to powerful but not forced, firm breath control and clarity of diction as well as expressive verbal inflection. He supplemented their repertory of Russian folksong and choral works of the Russian and western European repertory with many masterly choral arrangements and transcriptions of his own, and after 1945 toured widely with the choir in the USSR, in Hungary, Romania, Italy and Scandinavia. He was made People's Artist of the USSR in 1946 and a Hero of Socialist Labour.

WRITINGS
Khorovoye peniye: iskusstvo istinno narodnoe [Choral singing: a true people's art] (Moscow, 1962)
Sbornik statey [Collected articles] (Moscow, 1970)

BIBLIOGRAPHY
K. Ptitsa: 'Bol'shoy russkiy talant' [A great Russian talent], *SovM* (1965), no.10

I. M. YAMPOL'SKY

Svetlanov, Evgeny (Fyodorovich) (*b* Moscow, 6 Sept 1928). Soviet conductor, composer and pianist. He graduated from the Gnesin Institute (1951), where he studied composition with Mikhail Gnesin and the piano with Mariya Gurvich (a pupil of Metner). In 1955 he also graduated from Shaporin's composition class and Gauk's conducting class at the Moscow Conservatory. He began his conducting career with All-Union Radio in 1953 (while still a student at the conservatory), and from 1955 was an assistant and then a conductor at the Bol'shoy Theatre; later he was principal conductor (1962–4). The theatre and opera were in his blood from childhood: his father had been a soloist at the Bol'shoy and his mother an artist in a mime ensemble. He conducted many of Rimsky-Korsakov's operas, Dargomïzhsky's *Rusalka*, Borodin's *Prince Igor* and Tchaikovsky's *The Queen of Spades*; his interpretations of these works, especially the monumental choral scenes, sounded fresh and colourful. He also conducted Soviet works, including Shchedrin's *Not Love Alone* (1962), Karayev's ballet *By a Path of Thunder* (1959) and Balanchivadze's ballet *Pages of Life* (1961), as well as many new foreign works including Bartók's *Bluebeard's Castle*. In 1964 he conducted the Bol'shoy company's productions at La Scala.

While conducting at the Bol'shoy, Svetlanov did not abandon his concert work. In 1965 he became principal conductor of the USSR State SO, and it was from this time that he became noted as a symphonic conductor (his recordings of all Tchaikovsky's symphonies have won international acclaim). Svetlanov is one of the most versatile Soviet musicians: a gifted composer of large-scale symphonic works, instrumental chamber music and vocal pieces, and a fine pianist. His conducting style is characterized by sensitive attention to detail, allied to

Evgeny Svetlanov

an ability to grasp and mould the overall structure; his interpretations reveal power of emotional feeling, free of any superficiality or showmanship. His programmes include works by Myaskovsky (he has devoted much attention to popularizing Myaskovsky's symphonic music), Shostakovich, Prokofiev, Khachaturian, Shebalin, Knipper, Shchedrin and Eshpay. He performs these in Moscow and during his numerous foreign tours (to Italy, Britain, the USA, the Netherlands, Czechoslovakia, Japan, West Germany and elsewhere). His life and work have been the subject of a film *Dirizhor* ('The conductor'). He was made People's Artist of the USSR in 1968, and was awarded the Lenin Prize in 1972 and the Glinka Prize in 1975.

BIBLIOGRAPHY
E. Ratser: 'Evgeny Svetlanov', *SovM* (1963), no.2, p.65
L. Grigoroyev and Ya. Platek: 'Evgeny Svetlanov', *Muzikal'nïy zhizn'* (1968), no.16, p.6
A. Blyth: 'Yevgeny Svetlanov Talks', *Gramophone*, xlvii (1970), 1423
V. Tol'ba: '*Dirizhor* glazami dirizhora' [*The Conductor* seen through the eyes of a conductor], *SovM* (1973), no.11, p.54
I. M. YAMPOL'SKY

Sviridov, Georgy Vasilevich (*b* Fatezh, Kursk region, 16 Dec 1915). Russian composer and pianist. After preliminary education at the music school in Kursk (1929–32), he studied composition under M. A. Yudin at the Central Music College in Leningrad (1932–6). His next teacher was Shostakovich, with whom he studied composition and orchestration at the Leningrad Conservatory, graduating in 1941. Four years later he began his career as a concert pianist. He became a member of the USSR Union of Composers in 1936, a People's Artist of the RSFSR in 1963 and a People's Artist of the USSR in 1970. In 1962 he was appointed secretary of the USSR Union of Composers and in 1968 he became first secretary of the RSFSR Union of Composers.

Sviridov has always been attracted to setting texts: his first essay was the set of Six Romances to words by Pushkin (1935). While he makes a point of projecting the national and patriotic qualities in the words he uses, he has not restricted himself to Russian poets, as witnessed by the Burns songs of 1955. Identification with the homeland is very evident in *Land of My Fathers* (1950), but the feeling reached its culmination in the *Poem to the Memory of Sergey Yesenin* (1955–6). This work was originally planned as a cycle for solo voice and piano, but the kaleidoscopic nature of the conception caused Sviridov to write the piece for a tenor soloist, chorus and orchestra. Oratorio elements, dealing with heroic popular movements, are combined with the evocation of nature in cantata-like sections, and a more intimate song style in passages dealing with the poet himself. The several short numbers are linked by leitmotif-like musical and textual associations.

Such a formal plan was used again in the *Pathetic Oratorio* (1959) and the Kursk songs (1964). The former uses seven poems by Mayakovsky, agit-prop pieces which invoke the memory of Lenin in crude and vulgar, larger than life terms. Sviridov's music mirrors these qualities, and the work won him the Lenin Prize in 1960. The later piece also uses seven texts, this time from a collection of Kursk folksongs made by A. V. Rudneva, the head of the department of folk culture at the Moscow Conservatory. This cycle develops the theme of the fate of women in an old Russian village, and Sviridov's approach is analogous to Lyadov's in the

Eight Russian Folksongs op.58 (1906). The original material is treated with great respect: the charming strophic form is retained, and the harmony and scoring use the material of the songs without any alien additions. As a result, the work is a splendidly effective combination of Sviridov's style and the ethnic origins. Similar principles run through the whole of Sviridov's oeuvre. His major achievement is in the thorough fusion of words and music in a manner directly appealing to Russian audiences, although his work is less convincing to listeners lacking the required linguistic and ideological background.

WORKS
(selective list)

Poema pamyati Sergeya Yesenina [Poem to the memory of Sergey Yesenin] (Yesenin), T, chorus, orch, 1955–6; Pateticheskaya oratoriya [Pathetic oratorio] (Mayakovsky), B, chorus, orch, 1959; Kurskiye pesni [Kursk songs] (trad.), chorus, orch, 1964; Wooden Russia (Yesenin), T, chorus, orch, 1964; other oratorios and cantatas

Land of My Fathers (A. Isaakian), T, B, pf, 1950; Burns Songs (trans. S. Marshak), B, pf, 1955; Peterburgskiye pesni [Petersburg songs], S, Mez, Bar, B, pf, vn, vc, 1961–3; other songs

Piano Trio, 1945; Music for Chamber Orchestra, 1964; Small Triptych, orch, 1964; Time, forward!, orch, 1967; other instrumental works

Principal publishers: Muzgiz, Sovetskiy kompozitor, Muzïka (Moscow)

BIBLIOGRAPHY
M. R. Hofmann: *La musique russe des origines à nos jours* (Paris, 1968), 258ff
L. Polyakova: *Vokal'nïye tsiklï G. Sviridova* [Sviridov's song cycles] (Moscow, 1970)
——: '*Kurskiye pesni*' *G. Sviridova* [Sviridov's 'Kursk Songs'] (Moscow, 1970)
S. D. Krebs: *Soviet Composers and the Development of Soviet Music* (London, 1970), chap. 'Georgii Sviridov'
C. L. O'Riordan: *Aspects of the Inter-relationship between Russian Folk and Composed Music* (diss., U. of Cambridge, 1970), chap. 'The Approach to "Narodnost" by Sviridov in his Song Cycle "Kursk Songs"'
D. Frishman, ed.: *Georgy Sviridov* (Moscow, 1971)
M. Elik: '*Poema pamyati Sergeya Yesenina*' *G. Sviridova* (Moscow, 1971)
A. Sokhor: *Georgy Sviridov* (Moscow, 1972)
D. Frishman: '*Peterburgskiye pesni*' *G. Sviridova* [Sviridov's 'Petersburg songs'] (Moscow, 1972)
B. Schwarz: *Music and Musical Life in Soviet Russia 1917–1970* (London, 1972), 293f, 326f
COLIN L. O'RIORDAN

Svoboda, Josef (*b* Časlav, 10 May 1920). Czech stage designer. He was the son of a cabinet maker, and was at first apprenticed in his father's profession before studying (1941–3) to be an interior architect; it was through his hobby, painting, that he became interested in stage design. His first work was for an amateur theatre group in Časlav (1942), after which he did designs for the Novy Soubor ('New Group'), of which he was a founder member, in Prague (1943–4). After World War II he studied architecture at Prague Art College (1945–50), and at the same time (1945) took over the direction of design at the 'Grand Opera of 5 May', which became the Smetana Theatre in 1948. He was appointed chief designer and technical director of the National Theatre in 1951 and has exercised a decisive influence on the development of Czech music-theatre. His work outside Czechoslovakia since the late 1950s has also considerably affected the international opera scene.

Influenced by the architectonically plastic quality of Czech stage design in the 1930s and 1940s (e.g. František Tröster) and by the ideas of Adolphe Appia and Gordon Craig, Svoboda developed the concept of a 'psychoplastic stage' whose basic elements of space, time, rhythm and light combine to form a dynamic continuum, allowing for the development of the music drama as a homogenous kinetic process. The emancipatory experiences of Cubo-Futurism, Constructivism and the Bauhaus are assimilated but largely reinterpreted in a symbolist way, concentrating on the 'inner' (or 'immanent') meaning of the work and the psychology of action (e.g. the dualism of the towers in Verdi's *Il trovatore*, Berlin, 1966). Svoboda's revival of the Constructivist concept of the unity of art and technique campaigning 'for a theatre that truly reflects its age and its scientific spirit' has opened new formal horizons to contemporary stage art: the dynamics of the visual processes are not left to stage machinery but are based on a mechanics of transformation, specially designed, and in particular the use of modern lighting techniques. Svoboda makes inspired use of such effects as low-voltage light walls, dividing up the stage area (*Les vêpres siciliennes*, Hamburg, 1969) or laser beams and holograms (*Die Zauberflöte*, Munich, 1970). In particular, he has developed a superb projection technique, involving a complex system of colour projections which sometimes combine to animate a mobile plastic framework (*Oberon*, Munich, 1968, directed by Rudolf Hartmann) or with a transparent cyclorama, hangings, mirrors and lenses (the *Ring*, Covent Garden, 1976), which themselves form the variable stage area (*Pelléas et Mélisande*, London, 1969). From the combination of slide and film projections based on collage, new forms were devised which have been used in such operas as Nono's *Intolleranza* (Venice, 1961, *see* OPERA, fig.54; with a third medium, television, Boston, 1965) and Zimmermann's *Die Soldaten* (Munich, 1969). There are formal similarities, especially in the montage technique, to the epic, distancing theatre of Piscator and Brecht. But in opposition to this, Svoboda's 'psycho-plastic' stage art is a suggestive and subjective one that seeks to lead on the spectator's imagination vivifying 'the theatre's traditionally evocative, inherently metaphoric power' (Burian).

See also OPERA, §VIII, 7.

WRITINGS
(selection)
'Nouveaux éléments en scénographie', *Le théâtre en Tchechoslovaquie: scénographie*, ed. V. Jindra (Prague, 1962), 58
'Designing for the Stage', *Opera*, xviii (1967), 631
'Szenographie als Teil der Aufführung', *Bühnentechnische Rundschau*, lxii/6 (1968), 11

BIBLIOGRAPHY
J. Grossman: 'Josef Svoboda', *Le théâtre en Tchechoslovaquie: scénographie*, ed. V. Jindra (Prague, 1962), 45ff
V. Jindra: *Who is Josef Svoboda?* (Prague, 1968)
Josef Svoboda: Bühnenbilder und Szenographien: eine Ausstellung des Theaterinstitutes in Prag und der Akademie der Künste vom 6. September bis 12 Oktober 1969 (Berlin, 1969) [exhibition catalogue; incl. list of productions]
D. Bablet: *La scena e l'immagine: saggio su Josef Svoboda* (Turin, 1970)
——: *Josef Svoboda* (Prague, 1970) [in Eng.]
J. M. Burian: 'Josef Svoboda: Theatre Artist in an Age of Science', *Educational Theatre Journal*, xxii (1970), 123
——: *The Scenography of Josef Svoboda* (Middleton, Conn., 1971) [incl. list of productions]
MANFRED BOETZKES

Svoboda, Tomáš (*b* Paris, 6 Dec 1939). American composer of Czech origin. He studied at the Prague Conservatory (1954–62) and Prague Academy (1962–4). He left Czechoslovakia in 1964, settling in the USA, where he continued his studies at the University of Southern California, Los Angeles (1966–9), and became professor of composition and conducting at Portland State Uni-

versity, Oregon (1970). His compositions include four symphonies (1957, 1962, 1965, 1974), a Piano Concerto (1974) and several other orchestral works; he has also written a Double Octet for eight flutes and eight cellos (1971), two string quartets (1960, 1967) and much other chamber and instrumental music.

Svošovský z Lorbenthalu, Jan Petr (*fl* 1st half of the 17th century). Czech hymnologist. Svošovský was provost of Roudnice nad Labem. His Roman Catholic hymnal, *Katolické staročeské psničky a některé litanye* (Litoměřice, 1624), contains 27 texts and 16 melodies of old Czech songs, including *Hospodine, pomiluj ny* ('Lord, have mercy') and *St Wenceslas* in versions with basso continuo.

BIBLIOGRAPHY
V. Blažek: 'Pisně k sv. Václavu v kancionále Svošovského' [Songs to St Wenceslas in Svošovský's hymnal], *Cyril*, liv (1928), 7
JOHN CLAPHAM

Swaen, Willem [Guilielmus] **de** (*b* Gouda, *c*1610; *d* Gouda, 12 July 1674). Dutch clergyman and poet. He was a Catholic and was active in Gouda from about 1640. He is best known for his songbook *Den singenden swaen* (Antwerp, 1655, enlarged 2/1664, repr. 1728); the title – 'The singing swan' – includes a pun on his name. It consists of his own texts fitted to folksongs and dance tunes. The songs cover a wide variety of subjects and include many about saints: they are ordered according to the ecclesiastical year, beginning with 1 January. The book is very reliable as a source for melodies.

BIBLIOGRAPHY
C. Janssens-Aerts: 'De twee uitgaven van Willem de Swaen's geestelijke liederbundel (1655 en 1664)', *Ons geestelijke erf*, xxxvi (1962), 194
RUDI A. RASCH

Swale, (John) David (*b* York, 21 Feb 1928). Australian musicologist. He was a chorister and organ student at York Minster under E. C. Bairstow, and went to Gonville and Caius College, Cambridge, as organ scholar in 1949, studying under Hadley, Dart, Guest and Ord (BA 1952, MusB 1955). He taught at Christ's Hospital and then (1961–5) at St Peter's College, Adelaide, succeeding J. V. Peters in 1963 as organist and Master of the Choristers at St Peter's Cathedral. In 1965 he was appointed lecturer in music at the University of Adelaide, and became chairman of the department of music in 1976. He has also lectured at the University of Western Australia (1968) and at the NSW State Conservatorium of Music, Sydney (1972). Swale's scholarly activities have included the preparation of performing editions of Netherlands liturgical music and operas, motets and instrumental works by 17th-century Venetian composers; his publications include an article on Alessandro Scarlatti's oratorios (*MMA*, ix, 1977, p.145). He has also been active as conductor and keyboard player especially in Baroque and pre-Classical repertories but also in 20th-century music, including works by Australian composers. He contributed a section on Nigel Butterley to *A Symposium on Australian Composers* (Sydney, 1977).
ANDREW D. McCREDIE

Swan, Alfred J(ulius) (*b* St Petersburg, 9 Oct 1890; *d* Haverford, Penn., 2 Oct 1970). American musicologist and composer of English descent. He studied law at Oxford University (BA 1911, MA 1934), devoting much time to musical activities, and then studied music at the St Petersburg Conservatory under V. P. Kalafaty and A. A. Winkler (1911–13). After doing relief work with refugee children's colonies in Siberia (1918–19) he went to the USA, where he taught at the University of Virginia and Sweetbriar College (1921–3) and at the Seymour School, New York (1923–6), before being appointed head of the music departments at Swarthmore and Haverford colleges, Pennsylvania (1926). After retiring (1958) he continued to teach and lecture, at Haverford College, Temple University, the University of Aix-Marseille, and in Russia, Germany and England. Swan specialized in Russian music and his particular interest in music for the Eastern Orthodox liturgy is reflected in many of his own compositions. He was critical of 18th-century chants with chromatic Western harmonizations, preferring music based on earlier Russian sources, harmonized in modal style, with a judicious use of dissonance and Western imitative procedures.

His nephew Donald (Ibrahim) Swann (b 1923) is known in England as an entertainer and a composer of light music and choral pieces.

WORKS
(selective list)
Sacred: Glorification of St Nicholas, chorus, 2 pf, 1942; 10 Liturgical Canticles (1956–9); 3 Christmas Carols (1957); Liturgy of St John Chrysostom, large chorus, 1960; Pieces from the Liturgy (1960–71); Vespers and Matins, 1961; Song of Glorification and Thanksgiving (1964); Canticles of the Eastern Church (1976)
Orch: Introduction and Allegro, str, 1965
Chamber: Trio, fl, cl, pf (1936); Sonata, vn, pf, 1948; Epiphany, fl, ob, pf, 1965; Str Qts nos.1–6, no.2 for fl, str (1965–8); Trio Sonata, 2 vn, pf, 1966; Sonata no.3, vn, pf (1970)
Pf: Sonata no.1 (1937); Kinder-rondeau (1937); 2 sonatas, 1945, 1947; Into a Child's Album, 1949; Sonata K566 [after Scarlatti] (1958); Album of Pieces (1964)
Folksong arrs.: Songs from Many Lands (1923); 8 Negro Songs from Bedford County, Va. (1924); 6 Russian Folksongs from Gorodishtshe, Pechorsky district, Estonia, 1936; Recueil de chansons russes (1939)
Principal publishers: Albert House (London), Belyayev, Enoch, Orthodox (Berkeley), Paxton

WRITINGS
'The Three Styles of Moussorgsky', The Chesterian (1922), no.27, p.77 [incl. 10 Musorgsky letters translated by Swan]
Scriabin (London, 1923/R1969)
'Moussorgsky and Modern Music', MQ, xi (1925), 271
Music 1900–1930 (New York, 1929)
'The Znamenny Chant of the Russian Church', MQ, xxvi (1940), 232, 365, 529
The Music-director's Guide to Musical Literature (New York, 1941)
'The Nature of the Russian Folk-song', MQ, xxix (1943), 498
'Rachmaninoff: Personal Reminiscences', MQ, xxx (1944), l, 174
'Harmonizations of the Old Russian Chants', JAMS, ii (1949), 83
The Muse and the Fashion (Haverford, Penn., 1951) [trans. of N. Metner: Muza i moda, Paris, 1935]
Russian Music from the Beginning of the Nineteenth Century (Ann Arbor, 1953) [trans. of B. V. Asaf'yev: Russkaya muzïka ot nachala xix stoletiya, Moscow and Leningrad, 1930]
'Russian Chant', Early Medieval Music up to 1300, NOHM, ii (1954), 52
'Russian Church Music', 'Znamenny', Grove 5
'Russian Liturgical Music and its Relation to Twentieth-century Ideals', ML, xxxix (1958), 265
'Die russische Musik im 17. Jahrhundert', Jb für Geschichte Osteuropas, new ser., xii (1964), 161
'Das Leben Nikolai Medtners (1880–1951)', Musik des Ostens, iv (1967), 65–116; Russ. trans., rev., as 'Iz vospominaniy o N. K. Metnere' [Reminiscences of Metner], SovM (1972), no.7, p.117
with J. Swan: 'The Survival of Russian Music in the Eighteenth Century', The Eighteenth Century in Russia, ed. J. G. Garrard (Oxford, 1973), 300
Russian Music and its Sources in Chant and Folk Song (London, 1973)

BIBLIOGRAPHY
J. B. Swan and W. Kirchner: 'An Episode in the Great Russian Revolution: the Children's Colonies in Siberia', Delaware Notes, xxii (1949), 1

RAMONA H. MATTHEWS

Swan, Marcus Lafayette (b ?c1837; d Bellefonte, Alabama, 1869). American teacher and tune book compiler (see SHAPE-NOTE HYMNODY, §3). With his uncle W. H. Swan he published Harp of Columbia (Knoxville, 1848, 7/1855) in seven-shape notation, and under his own name the New Harp of Columbia ([Bellefonte, Alabama] Nashville, 1867, 3/1921), which is still used by the 'old harp' singers of eastern Tennessee.

HARRY ESKEW

Swan, Timothy (b Worcester, Mass., 23 July 1758; d Northfield, Mass., 23 July 1842). American composer; see PSALMODY (ii), §II.

Swan, W. H. (fl Knoxville, Tenn., 1849). American composer; see SHAPE-NOTE HYMNODY, §3.

Swan Concerts. London concert series in the 18th century; see LONDON, §VI, 1.

Swansea. After Cardiff the largest town and most important centre for music in south Wales. Swansea owes its present importance largely to developments which have taken place there since World War II.

The Swansea Festival of Music and the Arts was inaugurated in 1948, and has been held annually in October ever since. Though occasionally including concerts in which a local choir takes part, the festival exists mainly to bring orchestras, singers and instrumentalists to the town from Britain and abroad, following the pattern established at Edinburgh, though on a more modest scale. Several works have been commissioned by the festival from Welsh composers, notably Alun Hoddinott, Daniel Jones, William Mathias and Grace Williams.

The long and still flourishing traditions of choral singing in Swansea are best represented today by the Swansea Philharmonic Choir, founded in 1960 by its conductor, Haydn James, and also by the Swansea Bach Society, founded in 1965 by John Hugh Thomas under the auspices of the extra-mural department of the university. As a corollary to the Bach Society's activities a residential Bach Week is held annually at the university, with specialist lectures and recitals concentrating upon the music of Bach and his contemporaries. Other concerts and recitals are promoted throughout the year by the Swansea Music Society (founded 1947) and by the Welsh Arts Council, and the town is regularly visited by the Welsh National Opera.

MALCOLM BOYD

Swanson, Howard (b Atlanta, Georgia, 18 Aug 1907; d New York, 12 Nov 1978). Black American composer. His family moved from Atlanta to Cleveland where he studied the piano from the age of nine. In 1937 he graduated from the Cleveland Institute of Music, and studied in France with Nadia Boulanger in 1938. He settled permanently in New York in 1941. Although his compositions were performed as early as 1946, he first attracted national attention when Marian Anderson sang his The Negro Speaks of Rivers (Langston Hughes) at a New York recital in 1949. She later sang other works by him on concert tours. His Short Symphony, given its première by Mitropoulos in 1950, received the New York Music Critics' Circle Award in 1952. Other honours included Rosenwald and Guggenheim Fellowships, a National Academy of Arts and Letters grant, and the William and Nona Copley Award. His compositions have been frequently played in special series such as the Composers' Forum Series at Columbia University, the American Music Festival, the American International Cultural Relations concerts in Europe, the Edinburgh Festival and other international music festivals.

Swanson wrote graceful, appealing melodies and used individual harmonic colouring in a basically neo-classical style that allows for free use of dissonance. Critics have labelled his music as elegant, intense and spare, while noting at the same time the ever-present, although subtle, influence of Negro folk music idioms.

WORKS
(selective list)

ORCHESTRAL

Symphony no.1, 1945; Short Symphony, 1948; Night Music, chamber orch, 1950; Concerto for Orchestra, 1954; Fantasy Pieces, sax, str orch, 1969; Symphony no.3, 1970

CHAMBER AND INSTRUMENTAL

2 pf sonatas, 1946, 1970; Suite, vc, pf, 1948; Sound Piece, brass qnt, 1951; Vista no.2, str octet, 1969; Trio, fl, ob, pf, 1976

MISCELLANEOUS

30 songs, incl. The Valley, Joy, Still Life, Pierrot, A Death Song; pieces for solo pf, vn, chamber groups, pf with orch

Principal publishers: Leeds, Weintraub

EILEEN SOUTHERN

Swarbutt, Thomas. See SCHWARBROOK, THOMAS.

Swarenote. See SQUARE.

Swarowsky, Hans (b Budapest, 16 Sept 1899; d Salzburg, 10 Sept 1975). Austrian conductor. He studied theory with Schoenberg (from 1920) and Webern (until 1927), and conducting with Weingartner and Richard Strauss. He held appointments at the opera houses of Stuttgart, Hamburg and Berlin, but was not allowed to conduct in Germany between 1936 and 1944, and so turned to opera management (Munich, Salzburg Festival), and sometimes worked abroad (Zurich Opera, 1937–40). For a short time in 1944 he was conductor of the Polish PO in Kraków. After the war, invitations to conduct in international opera houses and concert halls became frequent. He was director of the opera house in Graz from 1948 to 1950; in 1957 Karajan, who had recently become director of the Vienna Staatsoper, appointed him permanent conductor and he also succeeded Karl Rankl as musical director and principal conductor of the Scottish National Orchestra, 1957–9. Swarowsky's interpretations, particularly in Classical works, always followed the score faithfully, an approach that he advocated in his teaching (he became director of the conducting class at the Vienna Academy of Music in 1946) and in his articles. Abbado and Mehta were his students. His interpretations of the symphonies of Mahler and Bruckner were particularly commended, and he was a strong advocate of the works of Schoenberg, Berg and Webern. He had close links with Richard Strauss, who called him his 'secret associate' on the libretto of *Capriccio*, and he made German translations of operas by Monteverdi, Gluck, Haydn, Verdi and Puccini.

WRITINGS

'Persönliches von Richard Strauss', *ÖMz*, xii (1957), 137, 186
'Operndeutsch', *ÖMz*, xiv (1959), 417
'Giuseppe Verdi – eine geistige Macht', *ÖMz*, xviii (1963), 453
'Randbemerkungen um den Dirigenten', *ÖMz*, xxii (1967), 706
'Marginalien zu Fragen des Stils und der Interpretation', *ÖMz*, xxiv (1969), 681; xxv (1970), 745

'Bemerkungen zur Interpretation der Schubert-Symphonien', *ÖMz*, xxvii (1972), 186
'Johann Strauss – Inkarnation der Wiener Musik', *ÖMz*, xxx (1975), 242
Wahrung der Gestalt, ed. M. Huss (Vienna, 1979) [collected writings]

RUDOLF KLEIN

Swarsbrick, Thomas. See SCHWARBROOK, THOMAS.

Swart, Peter Janszoon de (b ?Montfoort, 1536; d Utrecht, March 1597). Dutch organ builder. He used the family name de Swart only towards the end of his life; his son and successor, Dirk Peterszoon de Swart (d Utrecht, 20 Nov 1626), used the family name regularly. Peter signed all documents 'Peter Jans'.

Although de Swart was probably born in Montfoort, he was living in Utrecht by 1560. He began his career as a partner of the Utrecht organ builder Cornelis Gerritszoon (d 1559), whose father (Gerrit Peterszoon, d Haarlem, 1527) and grandfather (Peter Gerritszoon, d Utrecht, 1480) both built important organs in and around the city of Utrecht. After the death of Cornelis Gerritszoon, de Swart finished the organ in the Hofkapel of The Hague (1560). Some years later, de Swart associated himself with Jan Jacobszoon du Lin (van Lyn) (i); Dirk Peterszoon de Swart worked with Jacob Janszoon du Lin (d before 29 Jan 1623), who in turn was succeeded by Jan Jacobszoon du Lin (ii) (d c1632). Dirk Peterszoon de Swart stopped building organs in c1620, when he became a city bailiff.

Before 1560, the organs in Utrecht were built not only by these local organ builders, but also by such exceptionally important masters as Jan van Covelens from Amsterdam (d 1532) and Hendrik Niehoff from 's-Hertogenbosch (d 1560). Peter Janszoon de Swart must be seen as the perpetuator of the old Utrecht traditions, but also as an artist who assimilated the radical improvements of the Brabant organ school. He was more conservative than Niehoff, for in his large new organs (like that for Utrecht Cathedral, 1569–71) he still built a 'blokwerk', a principal chorus not divided into separate registers.

De Swart's output is impressive. He was responsible not only for the repair of all organs in the city and province of Utrecht, but also worked in almost all the cities in western Holland and in a number of cities in Gelderland. Although the Reformation affected the liturgical function of the organ, the importance of the instrument in public musical life increased considerably. This explains why de Swart had so much work even after the Reformation (1573 in western Holland, 1579–80 in Utrecht).

Although none of de Swart's organs survives in its original form, fragments of his work do exist. The present organs in Utrecht Cathedral and in the Hooglandse Kerk (St Pancras) of Leiden still contain numerous stops which clearly demonstrate his mastery.

Through this work, de Swart had regular contact with the greatest musicians of the country, including Sweelinck (restoration and repairs to the organs in the Oude Kerk, Amsterdam), Cornelis Boskoop in Delft, Floris and Cornelis Schuyt in Leiden, Philips Janszoon van Velsen in Haarlem and Peter Wyborgh in Utrecht.

BIBLIOGRAPHY

M. A. Vente: *Bouwstoffen tot de geschiedenis van het Nederlandse orgel in de 16e eeuw* (Amsterdam, 1942)
——: *Proeve van een repertorium van de archivalia over het Nederlandse orgel en zijn makers tot omstreeks 1625* (Brussels, 1956)

——: *Die Brabanter Orgel* (Amsterdam, 1958, 2/1963)

F. Peeters and M. A. Vente: *The Organ and its Music in the Netherlands* (Antwerp, 1971)

MAARTEN ALBERT VENTE

Swarthout, Gladys (*b* Deepwater, Missouri, 25 Dec 1904; *d* Florence, 7 July 1969). American contralto. She studied singing in Chicago, making her operatic début there in 1924, and progressing slowly to leading roles. Her début role at the Metropolitan was La Cieca (*La Gioconda*, 15 November 1929); she performed there regularly until 1945, as Siebel, Preziosilla, Adalgisa and – her most famous roles – Mignon and Carmen. She also made successful films. After 1954 she retired to Florence. Swarthout had a fine, well-placed voice which was admirably but not very imaginatively used. On stage, her presence was beautiful yet often placid, hampered by a lack of genuine temperament.

BIBLIOGRAPHY

G. Swarthout: *Come Soon, Tomorrow* (New York, 1945) [autobiography]

MAX DE SCHAUENSEE

Sweden (Swed. Sverige). Scandinavian kingdom. Southern Sweden was united under one king in the 12th century, and by the Union of Kalmar (1379) Sweden, Norway and Denmark were united under Danish rule. With the accession of Gustav Vasa (1523) the country became independent and subsequently rose to a peak of imperial power in the 17th century, when its provinces included Finland (which had long been under Swedish rule), Livonia, Pomerania and Bremen; most of these were lost under the Peace of Nystad (1721).

I. Art music. II. Folk music.

I. Art music

1. To 1600. 2. The 17th century. 3. 1718–1809. 4. 1809–90. 5. From 1890.

1. TO 1600. Archaeological finds in Sweden include pre-Christian musical instruments, the most famous of which are the bronze trumpets of about 1200–800 BC. Among other discoveries are flutes, animal horns, rattles and a few bridges from string instruments, some of which were probably imported. Stone carvings showing instruments have been interpreted as depicting religious ceremonies; little is known about other functions that music may have had. In the 11th century Christian missionaries introduced a new musical culture. Liturgical chant, at first following English models, soon became dominated by continental influences. As the ecclesiastical organization developed, the needs of church music were also taken into account, and detailed regulations for cathedral music are known from several dioceses. Monasteries were also important musical centres, parts of the monastic liturgical traditions being taken over by the lay churches; the Dominicans were especially influential, above all in Finland, the eastern part of the kingdom. Similarly, an originally Swedish tradition was taken to other countries, including England, by the Ordo Sanctissimi Salvatoris, founded in the 14th century by St Birgitta. All convents of the order used a special Office in honour of the Virgin, the *cantus sororum*, consisting of seven *hystoriae*, one for each day of the week. Compiled by Petrus Olavi, the Office was set mainly to well-known Gregorian chants, as was Swedish liturgical poetry in general. Gregorian chant of medieval Sweden survives in several complete manuscripts and in thousands of fragments. A gradual printed in Germany, probably in 1493, for the diocese of Västerås, has been reprinted in facsimile as *Graduale arosiense impressum* (1959–65).

The Reformation did not destroy the Gregorian tradition, even though much of it was abandoned because of the introduction of non-biblical texts. Although parts of the liturgy, such as the Ordinary of the Mass, were translated into Swedish, singing in Latin continued, at least in cities with schools; while the State deprived the Church of its economic means and cathedral music could not be maintained, sacred music remained an important subject in schools. In order to revive the Latin school song repertory in Sweden the young Finnish student Theodoricus Petri Nylandensis edited his famous collection *Piae cantiones* (Greifswald, 1582).

Parisian Ars Antiqua polyphony seems to have been performed in Uppsala Cathedral in the 13th century, for the choir statutes of 1298 record occasions on which organum was sung. There are remains of several organs from about 1400, but they seem not to have been used for polyphonic music; a more modern type is represented by an organ in Malmö Museum, built about 1500 for the Church of St Petri in Malmö. A report of a church festivity in 1489 at St Birgitta's, Vadstena, mentions polyphonic music (*discantus in nova mensura*), although Birgitta herself had forbidden polyphony; it was performed by schoolboys and by the *cantores* of Sten Sture the Elder, who then governed the country.

Court music did not become firmly established until Gustav Vasa freed Sweden from the union with Denmark in the early 16th century. Gustav and other members of his dynasty were very interested in music; his son Erik XIV was a composer, and a fragment of a Latin motet by him survives. As Duke of Finland Erik's brother Johan kept his own court musicians in Åbo (Turku), and as King of Sweden he later tried in various ways to enrich the new Swedish liturgy and its music, although without lasting results.

2. THE 17TH CENTURY. In the many cities founded after 1600 musical life was regulated by the guild system, the church organist being the leading musician. Singing, especially at funerals, was still an important source of income for the schools, although school music became predominantly instrumental. At Uppsala University some of the printed dissertations were on musical subjects. In the last quarter of the 17th century collegia musica were organized by the professors Olaus Rudbeck and Harald Vallerius, who were also responsible for the musical editing of the new official hymnbook (1697), which had a figured bass for most of the melodies; it was the first Swedish hymnbook with all the melodies printed, although, since 1530, there had been many hymnbooks containing only texts; a 1586 edition contains the earliest Swedish music printing. Congregational hymn singing became more widespread during the 17th century. The Thirty Years War (1618–48) had a great effect on musical life of the country, partly through instruments and music taken as war booty. Many German organists, organ builders, composers and other musicians went to Sweden. Most important of the German court musicians who went to Stockholm about 1620 was the composer Andreas Düben, a pupil of Sweelinck and the first of a dynasty of *hovkapellmästare*.

In 1647 Queen Christina engaged six French

musicians for her court ballets, and it was they who introduced the violin to Sweden. They were replaced in 1652 by an Italian opera company under the direction of Vincenzo Albrici, whose 'Fadher wår' (the Lord's Prayer) was the first choral work with a Swedish text. The queen also heard English consort music played by Ambassador Whitelocke's musicians; after her abdication in 1654 she lived in Rome, where Alessandro Scarlatti was among those in her service.

Gustaf Düben (i) succeeded his father as *hovkapell-mästare* and as organist of the German Church in Stockholm in 1662. Among his works the *Odae sveticae* (1674) was the first song collection with Swedish texts. In five volumes of *Motteti et concerti* Düben transcribed over 250 pieces of sacred music, mostly Italian, into organ tabulature; he also collected hundreds of works by contemporary German composers such as Buxtehude, Pfleger, Capricornus and Geist. His collection (in *S-Uu* since 1732) is now regarded as one of the main sources of 17th-century music.

3. 1718–1809. The political changes in Sweden after 1718 had important consequences for the country's musical life. Although the court and the nobility kept their leading positions, the middle class became increasingly influential. In Stockholm, Sweden's leading musical city throughout the 18th century, the first public concerts were given in 1731 by the *hovkapell*; later the 'Musical Areopague' of the Utile Dulci Society (active 1766–86) arranged some 'Cavalier Concerts' (1769–70). Music education was largely restricted to the cathedral schools in various cities. Church music consisted mainly of performances of Passions and oratorios by Pergolesi, Graun and others; the hymnal of 1697 remained the official one for services until 1820–21. During the 18th century writings on musical subjects appeared, culminating in the first book in music on music history, A. A. Hülphers's *Historisk afhandling om musik* (1773), containing an extensive inventory of Swedish organs.

Opera at first occupied a somewhat secondary position and was in general restricted to court festivities, although many plays with music were performed at smaller theatres. For a long time most of the works were of foreign origin and most of the artists were engaged from abroad. An Italian opera company arrived in 1755 but soon dispersed; however, its leader, the composer F. A. Uttini, settled in Stockholm and in 1767 became leader of the *hovkapell*. During the reign of Gustav III (1771–92) many projects initiated during the previous decades were realized: the Swedish Royal Academy of Music was founded in 1771, the Royal Opera at Stockholm was inaugurated in 1773, and an operatic style based on the ideas of Gluck was developed under the king's patronage.

Many of the composers living in Sweden were of foreign origin, including H. P. Johnsen, who wrote stage works, instrumental pieces and vocal odes; during the 1770s and 1780s the German-born composers J. M. Kraus, J. G. Naumann and G. J. Vogler wrote operas and instrumental works, making that period outstanding in Swedish music history, especially for opera. The most important native composer was J. H. Roman, who in his extensive instrumental production absorbed influences from Handel and from contemporary Italian music; in his Mass he 'showed the fitness of the Swedish language for church music'. Composers of instrumental music

were J. J. Agrell, who lived in Germany from the 1720s, Ferdinand Zellbell (i), A. N. von Höpken and Johan Wikmanson, who wrote fine string quartets and other chamber music (Zellbell and von Höpken also wrote operas). Parody songs became popular, culminating in the works of C. M. Bellman, whose collections were published by Olof Åhlström, the first Swedish music printer and editor of the periodical *Musikaliskt tidsfördrif* (1789–1834) as well as a composer.

4. 1809–90. Sweden's political and cultural history reached a low ebb during the decades after the assassination of Gustav III (1792). After 1809 (the year of the new constitution) musical life gradually revived in a new form. The initiative was largely taken over by the middle classes, which, despite many idealistically inspired efforts to promote musical activity, led to the domination of narrow-minded dilettantism. Many new music societies were founded, not only in Stockholm (1800), but also in Göteborg (1809), Visby (1815) and Jönköping (1817). After the mid-century, as communications improved, cities and audiences grew and the demand for higher musical standards became more widespread, professional orchestras and music institutions came into being. With the reorganization of the Stockholm Conservatory in 1866 music education became more firmly established. The cancellation of Åhlström's royal privilege in 1823 opened the way for a number of music printing firms, but many of them were short-lived. Later the music publishing trade was dominated by a few firms, all in Stockholm: A. Hirsch (from 1842), A. Lundquist (1856) and Elkan & Schildknecht (1859).

During the first half of the 19th century the stylistic trends of Swedish composers were determined by a deep veneration for the Viennese Classicists, as well as certain Romantic orientations and a growing interest in folk music that was furthered by the collection *Svenska folkvisor* (1814–17, edited by E. G. Geijer, A. A. Afzelius and J. C. F. Haeffner) and by many later musicians, among them J. N. Ahlström and Richard Dybeck. At first the amount of instrumental music composed was small; among the most important composers were B. H. Crusell (sinfonie concertanti, chamber music), Geijer (chamber music with piano) and A. F. Lindblad (two symphonies and four string quartets). Only one Swedish opera was completed and staged, Lindblad's *Frondörerna* (1835); stage music consisted mainly of folklike Singspiels such as Andreas Randel's ever popular *Värmlänningarne* (1846). Most of the music composed in Sweden consisted of smaller vocal works, for example lieder by Crusell, Geijer, Lindblad, J. E. Nordblom, Isidor Dannström, J. A. Josephson and Gunnar Wennerberg, and choral music and vocal quartets by Geijer, A. F. Lindblad, O. J. Lindblad and Prince Gustaf. The author C. J. L. Almqvist wrote *songes* ('dreams'), strange and expressive melodies without accompaniment. The works of Franz Berwald, one of the greatest Swedish composers, found no real sympathy among contemporary musicians and listeners because of their individual and personal style; a deeper understanding was apparent only at the end of the century.

In the 1840s and 1850s a number of young Swedish musicians studied abroad, especially at the Leipzig Conservatory, thus introducing influences from new German music, which along with the vital interchanges with Danish and Norwegian music determined stylistic developments during the following decades. Symphonic works were produced in greater number (by Ludvig Norman, J. A. Hägg, O. F. B. Byström and Andreas Hallén), as were chamber works (string quartets by Norman, violin sonatas by Emil Sjögren). A tenacious classicism and the influence of the German Romantics form the background to the expansive, sometimes symphonically conceived works of Fritz Arlberg and Sjögren. On the stage operettas and vaudevilles came into favour, while at the Royal Opera, Stockholm, Wagner's works were performed, beginning with *Rienzi* in 1865, stimulating great interest and lively debate; Wagnerian influence is especially prominent in the works of Hallén. The operatic works of I. C. Hallström are more in the style of French opera, and his *Den bergtagna* (1874) was one of many attempts to create a national opera. The outstanding late 19th-century Swedish composer, J. A. Söderman, was notable for his stage music, his intensely expressive ballads, and above all his choral works and lieder.

5. FROM 1890. Towards the end of the 19th century the gradual creation of modern concert life provided a platform for the development of a wider range of musical creativity. Hallén, although belonging to the earlier generation, started this movement in the three main cities with the reconstruction of the Musikförening in his native Göteborg (1872), the Filharmoniska Sällskapet in Stockholm (1885) and the Sydsvenska Filharmoniska Förening in Malmö (1902). His isolated activities were followed by the creation of the first symphony orchestras, eventually to replace the operatic *hovkapell*, which gave only infrequent orchestral concerts: the Stockholms Konsertförening (1902), the Göteborgs Orkesterförening (1905) and the much smaller orchestras in Gävle, Helsingborg and Norrköping (1911–12); there were many 'popular' concerts. In Stockholm platforms for this expanding concert life were, first, the concert hall of the Swedish Royal Academy of Music (1878), followed in 1925 by the present Konserthus; Göteborg's Konserthus (1935) replaced the wooden hall of 1905.

Against this background, three important composers of contrasting individuality appeared around 1890, revitalizing the somewhat dormant creative life and re-establishing links with European traditions: Wilhelm Peterson-Berger, a fervent Wagnerian but also a symphonist and miniaturist; Hugo Alfvén, who introduced a Straussian brilliance with his symphonies and nationalistic symphonic poems; and the great pianist and conductor Wilhelm Stenhammar, who gradually moved away from nationalism and found inspiration in Beethoven, Brahms, Berwald, Sibelius and Nielsen.

The years before World War I saw a new group of composers moving towards a more cosmopolitan language: Natanael Berg, who wrote several operas (notably *Engelbrekt*, 1929) and colourful symphonies; Oskar Lindberg, well known as a teacher and church musician; and Kurt Atterberg, who wrote an impressive series of nine symphonies as well as operatic works. Ture Rangström's songs are among the finest Swedish vocal music, while Edvin Kallstenius is noted for his 12-note works. These composers, especially Berg, Atterberg and Lindberg, were responsible for the organization of a composers' society, the Förening Svenska Tonsättare (1918) and of the complementary STIM (Swedish Performing Rights Society, 1923), both of which have played an important part in supporting Swedish composers.

Stronger influence from European movements was introduced by three members of a new generation: Hilding Rosenberg, a symphonist and oratorio composer who linked expressionism to a Nordic idiom largely independent of nationalism and who became the teacher of a considerable number of younger composers (Blomdahl, Bäck, Lidholm etc); Gösta Nystroem, who brought impressionism to Sweden, thereby strengthening the influence of French music; and Moses Pergament, a cosmopolitan of Finnish birth, Russian training and with a Jewish musical background. In the 1930s neo-classicism and French influence became prominent in the works of Dag Wirén and Gunnar de Frumerie, whereas Lars-Erik Larsson turned more to Sibelius and Nielsen. The 1940s saw the breakthrough of modernism with the varied activities of the 'Monday Group' (Karl-Birger Blomdahl, Sven-Erik Bäck and Ingvar Lidholm), whose members revitalized Fylkingen (the Society for Contemporary Music, from 1950 part of the ISCM, with a well-equipped special hall for 'intermedia' performances, including a small electronic music studio) and created the important radio series 'Nutida Musik' and the Electronic Music Studio (EMS, one of the leading computerized studios).

During the 1950s there was a reaction to modernism among a group of Larsson's pupils who promoted a nationalist Romantic revival, influenced by Prokofiev and Shostakovich. Jan Carlstedt founded the concert society Samtida Musik (1960), which reacted against the avant-garde tendencies of Fylkingen and 'Nutida Musik'; the music of Hans Eklund, Maurice Karkoff and Bo Linde is also retrospective, whereas Gunnar Bucht is a more independent symphonist. Bengt Hambraeus was the first Swedish composer to visit Darmstadt and continental electronic music studios and introduced new styles and ideas to Sweden; Bo Nilsson followed similar paths. Within these groups many individual composers and styles form the complex reality. Among the older generation are Hilding Hallnäs, with Nystroem one of the leading composers in Göteborg; Sven-Eric Johanson, formerly a member of the Monday Group; Erland von Koch, who has pursued Dalecarlia folk traditions; Allan Pettersson, who has written long, Mahlerian symphonies; Åke Hermanson, known for moderately progressive orchestral works; Torsten Nilsson, who has written church music using modern techniques; and Hans Holewa, who brought Schoenbergian dodecaphony to Sweden. Younger composers include Arne Mellnäs; the organ and 'happening' virtuoso K.-E. Welin; J. W. Morthenson, noted for his 'meta-music'; Siegfried Naumann, who renounced his earlier works and started afresh in radical idioms; and the opera composer L.-J. Werle. There is also an active group of electronic music composers, including Knut Wiggen, pioneering as studio leader of the EMS, Ralph Lundsten with his private 'Andromeda' studio, and Leo Nilson. Sten Hanson and B. E. Johnson are known as 'text-sound' composers, while S.-D. Sandström has written brilliant instrumental works.

Swedish radio administers a music department, including a symphony orchestra and choirs (under Eric Ericson) that have become internationally known. The Rikskonserter (Institute for National Concerts), founded in 1963, stresses the widening support of the authorities, as does the Kulturråd (Arts Council, 1974), and great efforts are made to support 'alternative' music activities. There are 22 regional (formerly military) music corps in Sweden. New opera companies have been established in Göteborg and Malmö, where in 1971 the private conservatories became national music academies. Smaller music-theatre groups in Umeå and Karlstad exemplify the decentralization of musical life, as do Levande Musik in Göteborg and Ars Nova in Malmö.

See also GÖTEBORG; MALMÖ; STOCKHOLM; UPPSALA.

BIBLIOGRAPHY
H. von Bülow: *Skandinavische Conzertreiseskizzen* (Berlin, 1882)
T. Norlind: 'Die Musikgeschichte Schwedens in den Jahren 1630–1730', *SIMG*, i (1899–1900), 165–212
W. Niemann: *Die Musik Skandinaviens* (Leipzig, 1906)
C.-A. Moberg: *Über die schwedischen Sequenzen* (Uppsala, 1927)
——: 'Musik und Musikwissenschaft an den schwedischen Universitäten', *Mitteilungen der Internationalen Gesellschaft für Musikwissenschaft*, i (1929), 54; ii (1930), 10, 34
——: 'Der gregorianische Gesang in Schweden während der Reformationszeit', *KJb*, xxvii (1932), 84
B. Wester: 'Orgelbaukunst in Schweden von 1600 bis 1800', *Musik und Kirche*, iv (1932), 74
S. Walin: *Beiträge zur Geschichte der schwedischen Sinfonik: Studien aus dem Musikleben des 18. und des beginnenden 19. Jahrhunderts* (Uppsala, 1941)
C.-A. Moberg: *Från kyrko- och hovmusik till offentlig konsert* (Uppsala, 1942/R1970)
——: *Die liturgischen Hymnen in Schweden*, i (Uppsala, 1947)
Å. Davidsson: *Bibliografi över svensk musiklitteratur 1800–1945* (Uppsala, 1948)
B. Wallner: *La musique en Suède* (Stockholm, 1951)
I. Bengtsson: 'Schwedische Musik des 20. Jahrhunderts', *Melos*, xxiii (1956), 338
E. Erici: 'Eine kurze schwedische Orgelgeschichte im Lichte des heutigen Bestandes', *Musik und Kirche*, xxvi (1956), 97, 176
C.-A. Moberg: 'Das Musikleben in Schweden', *GfMKB, Hamburg 1956*, 33
Å. Davidsson: *Studier rörande svenskt musiktryck före år 1750* (Uppsala, 1957)
B. Wallner: 'Modern Music in Scandinavia', *European Music in the Twentieth Century*, ed. H. Hartog (London, 1957, 2/1961), 131
B. Wallner: 'ISCM-konserterna i Stockholm 1923–31', *STMf*, xxxix (1957), 157
R. Engländer: 'Die Gustavianische Oper', *AMw*, xvi (1959), 314
——: 'Händel in der Musik Schwedens', *HJb 1959*, 161
G. Larsson, ed.: *Fylkingen 1933–1959* (Stockholm, 1959)
J. Horton: *Scandinavian Music* (London, 1963)
R. Gustafson, ed.: *Musik i Skåne* (Malmö, 1971)
G. Hilleström, ed.: *Svenska musikperspektiv* (Stockholm, 1971)
B. Wallner: *40-tal: en klippbok om Måndagsgruppen och det svenska musiklivet* (Stockholm, 1971)
G. Bergendal: *33 svenska komponister* (Stockholm, 1972)
A.Helmer: *Solosången i Sverige 1820–90* (Uppsala, 1972)
H. Sjögren, ed.: *Music for Sweden* (Stockholm, 1972)
Ord och ton, STIM under 50 år 1923–1973 (Stockholm, 1973)
C. M. Cnattingius: *Contemporary Swedish Music* (Stockholm, 1973)
K. Ralf, ed.: *Operan 200 år: jubelboken* (Stockholm, 1973)
A. Aulin and H. Connor: *Svensk musik*, i: *Från Vallåt till Arnljot* (Stockholm, 1974)
Å. Holmquist: *Från signalgivning till regionmusik* (Stockholm, 1974)
K. Ralf, ed.: *Kungliga Teatern i Stockholm, repertoar 1773–1973* (Stockholm, 1974)
J. H. Yoell: *The Nordic Sound* (Boston, 1974)
Vi tycker om musik: en debattbok kring musiken i Sverige (Stockholm, 1975)
S. Jacobsson: *Musiken i Sverige: skivlyssnarens handbok i svensk musik från aldsta tid till 1970-talet* (Västerås, 1975)
F. K. Prieberg: *Musik und Musikpolitik in Schweden* (Herrenburg, 1976)
H. Connor: *Svensk musik*, ii: *Från Midsommarvaka till Aniara* (Stockholm, 1977)

II. Folk music. The Swedish folk music tradition remained fairly stable until the late 19th century, when industrialization began to affect the conditions necessary for the music of this essentially rural population. Some musical genres were brought into Sweden from other countries. The medieval ballad was probably introduced in this way during the late Middle Ages, possibly by Swedish students who had studied in Paris. During the 16th and 17th centuries many songs were introduced from Germany, and there was considerable contact with central Europe during the Thirty Years War. The interest of the upper classes in French culture after the middle of the 17th century, and particularly during the 18th century, gradually affected popular dance music. Some French dances were assimilated, and many local variants evolved. Certain parts of the country were quick to adopt innovations, particularly the coastal districts in southern Sweden and the area around Stockholm. Other districts, such as the province of Dalarna, were much more conservative. Swedish folk music must also be viewed in a Scandinavian context, the songs in particular being largely common to the whole region. They were formerly performed solo and unaccompanied. *Fäbodmusik*, a peculiarly functional vocal genre associated with herding in the summer mountain pastures, is of particular interest. The instrumental repertory consists largely of dance music.

1. Sources and collections. 2. Herding music. 3. Folksongs and ballads. 4. Instrumental music.

1. SOURCES AND COLLECTIONS. Historical research is hampered by the lack of early sources. Though some song texts survive in manuscripts dating from the end of the 16th century, the major work of collection did not begin until it was prompted by antiquarian interest in the 17th century. The 19th-century spirit of romantic nationalism inspired the work of collecting and notating melodies. Some of this work was published in Geijer and Afzelius's *Svenska folkvisor* ('Swedish folksongs') in the years 1814–17. But this interest was almost entirely confined to the medieval ballad; other kinds of folksong were largely ignored until the mid-19th century, when L. C. Wiede began collecting in Östergötland and R. Dybeck became the first to record *fäbodmusik*.

At the end of the 19th century A. Bondeson was collecting songs in western Sweden and published many of them in his *Visbok* ('Songbook'). This period saw the formation of societies interested in the preservation and study of local dialects, and large collections of material were received by such institutions. Many thousands of song texts were printed in broadsheets of which more than 30,000 survive. They include both songs from oral tradition, and new texts specially written for broadsheets.

The early source material for instrumental music consists of a number of 18th- and 19th-century *spelmansböcker* (fiddlers' tune books), but it is not clear to what extent these represent an authentic folk repertory. The collection of instrumental folk music began only in the late 19th century, in particular with the work of A. Fredin in Gotland. Foremost among other collectors were Nils and Olof Andersson, who collected some 15,000 tunes from all but the northernmost parts of Sweden. About half of these were printed in *Svenska låtar* ('Swedish melodies'). Swedish radio and the Svenskt Visarkiv (Swedish Centre for Folk Song and Folk Music Research) began recording all types of folk music in the 1950s. Original material is kept in a number of institutions including the Royal Library, the Nordiska Museet, Musikhistoriska Museet, Dialekt- och Folkminnesarkivet in Uppsala, and the Svenskt Visarkiv. The last-named also receives copies of material from other institutions. Recent research has moved away from the question of origins and is more concerned with social function and with the evolution of melodic variants. In assessing material more consideration is now given to the singers themselves or to the collectors; Jan Ling's study (1965) of L. C. Wiede's collecting work in the 1840s is an example of the latter.

2. HERDING MUSIC. In Sweden, as in Norway, much music is associated with herding. Traditional methods of intensive cattle breeding once practised in large areas of northern and central Sweden have survived until modern times in some isolated areas. Every farm also had a *fäbod* (mountain dairy or shieling) around which the animals grazed freely during the summer months, watched over by dairy maids. A particular type of functional music evolved. For instance, if a woman wanted to call the cows home from the wood, or to contact another maid a long way off, she blew a signal on a *lur* (long trumpet) or an oxhorn. The *barklur* was made of bark and was a half to 1 metre long, and the *länglur* or *näverlur* (long or birchbark *lur*) was made of wood bound together with birchbark and was up to 2 metres in length. The horn, from a cow or a goat, was boiled, cleaned out and given a number of finger-holes.

But it was perhaps more usual to use a *lockrop* (herding call; see ex.1), sung in a kind of falsetto at a very

Ex.1 *Lockrop* (herding call), Transtrand, Dalarna

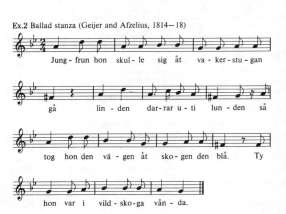

Recorded in 1954 by Swedish Radio.

high pitch, by stretching the throat muscles taut. The *lockrop* has long been used both as a call to animals, and to communicate with other people, particularly to give them warning signals, since it can be heard over a distance of 4 or 5 km. It may consist of either short phrases or long ornamented melodies, varying according to function and occasion as well as from one district to another. The technique itself is thought to be ancient and it is also found in such other European mountain regions as the Alps, Pyrenees and the Balkan mountains of Bulgaria.

Knowledge of Swedish *fäbod* music is based partly on literary sources and collections made since the 1840s (particularly that of R. Dybeck), and partly on surviving examples of the tradition. Research into herding tunes

and *lockrop* began only in the 1930s when Tobias Norlind examined the evolutionary aspects of the material and concluded that the simple call was the original form, and the longer, melismatic call more recent. Carl-Allan Moberg has made a special study of herding music and presented his findings in two long articles in 1955 and 1959. In the first he dealt with the musical organization of the *fäbod* and with *lockrop* technique, and in the second analysed the tune structures. Moberg believed *fäbod* music parallels the alpine *Kuhreigen* with its division into three sections, the middle one consisting of the names of the cows. He also showed that the often long and ornamental *lockrop* is built on a melodic framework, often coloured by contemporary material, and is thus a product of its time.

Important new research into this music has been carried out in the 1970s at Uppsala University where Anna Johnson has studied herding calls with the aid of melograms (*see* MELOGRAPH). She concluded that the calls are not formulated to a fixed pattern, but their length and form are determined by their function and by the singer's instinct and ability to vary the phrases in her repertory.

3. FOLKSONGS AND BALLADS. Swedish folksongs can be classified according to various criteria, namely textual content, typological history, musical structure and function. While research is concerned mainly with folksong proper, it also considers songs which are known to have a particular literary origin but which have since passed into oral tradition and have become subject to variation. Traditionally there were no professional folksingers.

The true folksongs include the medieval Scandinavian ballads, made up of two- or four-line stanzas and a refrain. These have a typically formal and objective narrative style and treat of the lives of the medieval nobility, medieval Christianity and popular beliefs, and often record events. Many of their themes have parallels outside Scandinavia, particularly in the 'Child' ballads of the British Isles and North America. The ballads, which have roots in medieval French poetry, were probably introduced into Sweden during the 13th century. Gradually they became a wholly orally transmitted rural art. Originally they were connected with dancing, a singer singing the verses and a dancing chorus joining in the refrains; but this connection disappeared early. The ballad melodies which have survived represented many different stages of style, and have been influenced by various local musical traditions and by church

Ex.2 Ballad stanza (Geijer and Afzelius, 1814—18)

Jung-frun hon skul-le sig åt va-ker-stu-gan
gå   lin-den dar-rar u-ti lun-den så
tog hon den vä-gen åt sko-gen den blå.   Ty
hon var i vild-sko-ga vån-da.

music, as have other kinds of folksong to a greater or lesser extent. The ballads, however, have kept more of the older features than have other types of folksong, as for example in their more formally constructed melodies (ex.2). The number of singers who have sung ballads is smaller than for other categories of folksong. Nevertheless, some 250 different text types are known, a few still surviving in oral tradition.

Melodies related to those of the ballads are found in various old collections of humorous songs and singing-games, many of which have refrains. A few examples from both these genres have survived in oral tradition. Some singing-games owe their survival to their association with modern Christmas festivities and are generally sung as children's games for dancing round the tree.

Popular nursery rhymes and lullabies, known as *småvisor* ('small songs'), are still well represented in oral tradition; but only a very few melody types are used for them. The commonest of these is that best known with the words 'Ro, ro till fiskeskär' ('Row, row to the fishing rocks'). Ex.3 gives one of the many variants of this tune,

Ex.3 *Småvisa*, children's song, Dalarna (Andersson, 1922–40)

which also has parallels outside Scandinavia. It is almost identical with that of the anonymous trouvère song *A pris ai qu'en chantant plour*.

A few of the lyrical songs introduced by 16th- and 17th-century songbooks survived in later tradition, though love-songs appear not to have reached the public in large number until the 18th and 19th centuries. These were almost all sung in the minor key, and their texts were often disseminated in broadsheets (ex.4).

Work songs with rhythms matching the labourers' movements are either short and sung – or almost shouted – by a single singer, or very rhythmic and generally sung by a group of workers. The first, together with herding music, are the only forms of non-strophic folksong in Sweden.

Some seasonal songs are found, though not so many as in most countries. These are chiefly associated with the festivities of Boxing Day, Twelfth Night, Walpurgis Night and May Day, when young people went around singing for money. May Day singing was almost entirely confined to the former Danish territory in southern Sweden. In some regions during the 18th century there evolved a special tradition of performing

Ex.4 Lyrical song, Östergötland; rec. L. Wiede

Protestant hymns in a way peculiar to each locality. These popular variants lived on, developing alongside the authorized settings in the hymnals. They are marked by their melismatic style, in contrast to the syllabic style given in the hymnbooks.

Among the literary songs in oral tradition are a number by known authors which were also chiefly introduced by means of broadsheets. Of these the song *O tysta ensamhet* by Olof von Dalin, an 18th-century writer, is still current in the tradition. Some songs by the popular poet C. M. Bellman from the end of the 18th century gained a wide circulation: his *Gustafs skål* originated as a Swedish royal anthem but survives in tradition as a singing-game. In the 18th century E. Tegnér's cycle of poems *Fritiofs saga* was set to music by B. Crusell and became popular.

The directions printed on the broadsheets give valuable information about the melodies used for these songs and show which ones were most popular. *Folie d'Espagne* seems to have held a unique position; it was used in a great number of popular songs from the 17th century onwards and is still alive in oral tradition and also as an instrumental tune. The hymnal of 1697 also had great influence on popular song, for during the 17th and 18th centuries hymn tunes were cited as the melodies of about half of the songs printed on broadsheets.

The melodies of the songs are not generally linked to one specific song or genre, but interchange from text to text. A single set of words was sung to several different melodies, and a single melody used for several quite unrelated texts. Different chronological layers can be recognized in the melodies, the oldest being found chiefly with folksong proper, while currently popular tunes usually of more recent origin were chosen for the broadsheet songs. For older songs a minor scale with no sixth degree was common, the melody revolving around the tonic. As early as 1810 J. C. F. Haeffner argued that there was a minor scale type with a variable seventh degree, and this has since been largely confirmed. During the 19th century a more harmonic conception of music prevailed, probably because of the trend towards self-accompaniment on the guitar, zither or psalmodikon. This last instrument, a type of bowed zither with one melody string and several drone strings, was devised in the 1820s. From the middle of the 19th century the guitar and plucked zither developed as instruments to accompany the songs of the religious revival, the melodies of which were also widely used with secular words.

1. Hommel (zither) player from Blekinge

4. INSTRUMENTAL MUSIC. This is based on a string instrument tradition in its broader Scandinavian context. The oldest instrument still in use is the NYCKELHARPA (keyed fiddle). Though it is bowed like a violin, the strings are shortened by keys instead of by the fingers (see fig.2). The *nyckelharpa* has a flat bridge and several drone strings which give the instrument its characteristic sound. It was depicted in medieval church paintings and may date from the 14th or 15th century. Nowadays the *nyckelharpa* tradition is found only in the province of Uppland in central Sweden.

The violin is the instrument most associated with Swedish folk music. It was probably in general use among the rural population throughout Sweden by the middle of the 18th century. It remained the most widely used instrument for dancing and ceremonial music until the end of the 19th century, when for various reasons it declined in popularity and its repertory began to die out. The whole social structure was changed by the 19th-century industrial revolution, and peasant society, where this *spelmansmusik* (fiddlers' music) functioned and flourished, gradually disintegrated. The wave of religious revivalism which spread throughout Sweden towards the end of the 19th century also did much harm to the old music. Preachers denounced the violin as the instrument of the devil, and many fiddlers laid their fiddles aside for good, or even smashed or burnt them. Those fiddlers still active at the turn of the century had to compete with the accordion, which gradually succeeded the violin as the most popular instrument for dance music.

The fiddler's function had been the same throughout Sweden. He was first and foremost a dance musician, and his repertory consisted of the tunes of whatever dances were in fashion (e.g. the *polska*, waltz, schottische and *polkett* in the 19th century). The function and structure of the tunes are generally the same throughout Sweden but the melodies and the way they evolved, as well as playing styles, varied greatly from place to place. This was partly because tunes were transmitted orally, since very few players were taught to read music or had any classical violin training. Most of the music was in the keys of A, D and G which could be played using only 1st position. In many areas double stopping and chordings were used, and sometimes the violin was tuned differently to make this easier. Certain tunes, such as the *stenbockslåtar* (steinbock tunes), were played in the special tuning $a-e'-a'-c\sharp''$ (ex.5). Great players,

Ex.5 *Stenbockens polska* Halland (Andersson, 1922–40)

such as Lapp Nils (1804–70) of Jämtland in north-west Sweden, could set their stamp on tunes in a wide area over a long period of time: his particular style was

2. Nyckelharpa (keyed fiddle) player from Uppland

marked by its virtuosity, use of harmonics and fast triplets (ex.6). Fiddlers often regarded their playing as a

Ex.6 *Lapp-Nils-polska*, Jämtland
tuning

hobby or a sideline to their ordinary peasant or artisan occupations. In Skåne, the most southerly province of Sweden, there was some organized professionalism during the 18th and 19th centuries. Special musicians were appointed by the district authorities and they alone had the right to play for reward at dances or weddings within their district.

In some parts of Sweden, particularly the eastern provinces, popular instrumental music was influenced by that played by professional musicians and orchestras which performed at manor houses and mills. Similarly, trained church organists helped to introduce the techniques of 'classical' music into folk styles. The *polska* from Gotland (ex.7) is a conscious imitation of

Ex.7 *Romins polska* (Fredin, 1909–33)

Baroque style with its triadic semiquaver figuration. Popular wedding marches borrowed melodies from military music, and in the process the clarinet became a popular instrument, performing the same function with the same repertory of dance and ceremonial music as the violin.

The *polska* (Polish dance) is a type of tune favoured by Swedish players. Though there are many theories as to its origin and its development in Sweden, no basic research has been done. It is derived from the European polonaise, a dance in 3/4 time and popular throughout Sweden from the beginning of the 18th century until the end of the 19th. In Sweden its musical development was rich, in both rhythm and melody, and it superseded and fused with older Swedish melodic material, as can be seen from the types of scale used in many *polska* melodies. Probably because of its musical qualities the *polska* repertory has outlived the dance itself. In both

rhythm and melody it is considerably more complicated than the waltz or the polka and has always been highly esteemed by musicians. The *polska* also occurs as a song type, often with a single verse of nonsense words (ex.8).

Ex.8 *Vispolska*, sung *polska*, Gagnef (Forsslund: *Med Dalälven från källorna till havet*)

Stor Sti - na   sa - de des - sa or - den: Om ja ha - de min

Pel - le gift!   Ja,   Pel - le   han vor' bra   å

nit - ti till att ha,   ba - rä su - pen han villa'nt ta!

During the 20th century instrumental music has developed in various directions. During the period 1910–30 the accordion became the most popular instrument, either solo or in a band with fiddle and guitar. The repertory was no longer restricted regionally, the gramophone and radio having increased standardization throughout the country. The Spelmansrörelse ('fiddlers' movement') which grew up in the early years of the 20th century has helped to maintain the fiddle tradition by establishing competitions and meetings. Fiddlers have organized themselves into a fiddlers' association, one result being the growth of fiddle bands which have appeared in public with great success.

BIBLIOGRAPHY
COLLECTIONS

A. A. Afzelius and O. Åhlström: *Traditioner af svenska folkdansar* [Swedish folkdance traditions] (Stockholm, 1814–15/R1972)

E. G. Geijer and A. A. Afzelius: *Svenska folkvisor* [Swedish folksongs] (Stockholm, 1814–17, 3/1957–60)

A. I. Arwidsson: *Svenska fornsånger* [Early Swedish songs] (Stockholm, 1834–42)

R. Dybeck: *Svenska vallvisor och hornlåtar* [Swedish herding songs and horn melodies] (Stockholm, 1846/R1974)

A. G. Rosenberg: *420 svenska danspolskor* [420 Swedish *polskas*] (Stockholm, 1876–82/R1969)

J. Nordlander: *Svenska barnvisor och barnrim* [Swedish children's songs and rhymes] (Stockholm, 1886/R1971)

N. Andersson: *Skånska melodier* [Melodies from Skåne] (Stockholm, 1895–1916)

K. P. Leffler: *Folkmusik från norra Södermanland* [Folk music from north Södermanland] (Stockholm, 1899–1900)

A. Bondeson: *Visbok* [Songbook] (Stockholm, 1902–3, 2/1940)

A. Fredin: *Gotlandstoner* [Melodies from Gotland] (Stockholm, 1909–33)

K. P. Leffler: *Folkmusiken i Norrland* [Folk music in Norrland] (Härnösand, 1921–4)

N. Andersson: *Svenska låtar* [Swedish tunes] (Stockholm, 1922–40/R1974)

C. H. Tillhagen and N. Dencker: *Svenska folklekar och danser* [Swedish folk games and dances] (Stockholm, 1949–59)

P. A. Säve: *Gotländska visor* [Folksongs from Gotland] (Uppsala, 1949–55)

J. Dicander: *Folkliga koraler från Dalarna* [Folk hymns from Dalarna] (Falun, 1975)

STUDIES

K. P. Leffler: *Om nyckelharpospelet på Skansen* [Keyed-fiddle playing in Skansen] (Stockholm, 1899)

T. Norlind: *Svensk folkmusik och folkdans* [Swedish folk music and folkdance] (Stockholm, 1930)

K. Liestøl, ed.: *Folkevisor* [Folksongs], Nordisk kultur, ix/A (Stockholm, Oslo and Copenhagen, 1931)

O. Andersson, ed.: *Musik och musikinstrument* [Music and musical instruments], Nordisk kultur, xxv (Stockholm, Oslo and Copenhagen, 1934)

S. Walin: *Die schwedische Hummel* (Stockholm, 1952)

C.-A. Moberg: 'Om vallåtar: en studie i de svenska fäbodarnas musikaliska organisation' [Of herdmen's songs: a study of the musical organization of the Swedish *fäbodar*], *STMf*, xxxvii (1955), 7–95

O. Andersson: *Spel opp i spelemänner: Nils Andersson och den svenska spelmansrörelsen* [Play up, fiddlers! Nils Andersson and the Swedish fiddlers' movement] (Stockholm, 1958)

C.-A. Moberg: 'Om vallåtar II: musikaliska strukturproblem', *STMf*, xli (1959), 10–57

Om visor och låtar: studier tillägnade Sven Salén (Stockholm, 1960)

B. R. Jonsson: 'Volkslied', *Schwedische Volkskunde: Quellen, Forschung, Ergebnisse: Festschrift für Sigfrid Svensson* (Stockholm, 1961), 491

M. Arnberg: *Den medeltida balladen: én orientering och kommentar till Sveriges radios inspelningar* [The medieval ballad: introduction and commentary on Swedish radio recordings] (Stockholm, 1962) [with Eng. summary]

J. Ling: *Svensk folkmusik: bondens musik i helg och söcken* [Swedish folk music: peasant music for holy days and weekdays] (Stockholm, 1964)

J. Ling: *Levin Christian Wiedes vissamling: én studie i 1800-talets folkliga vissång* [Levin Christian Wiede's song collection: a study of 19th-century folksong] (Uppsala, 1965) [with Eng. summary]

B. R. Jonsson: *Balladkällor och balladtyper* [Ballad sources and types] (Stockholm, 1967) [with Eng. summary]

J. Ling: *Nyckelharpan: studier i ett folkligt musikinstrument* [The keyed fiddle: studies on a folk instrument] (Stockholm, 1967) [with Eng. summary]

C.-A. Moberg: *Studien zur schwedischen Volksmusik* (Uppsala, 1971)

M. Jersild: *Skillingtryck: studie i svensk folklig vissång före 1800* [Broadsheets: studies on the Swedish popular ballads before 1800] (Stockholm, 1975) [with Eng. summary]

FOLKE BOHLIN (I,1), AXEL HELMER (I,2),
HANS ÅSTRAND (I,3),
MARGARETA JERSILD, MÄRTA RAMSTEN (II)

Swedish Society for Musicology. *See* SVENSKA SAMFUNDET FÖR MUSIKFORSKNING.

Sweelinck, Dirck Janszoon (*b* Amsterdam, baptized 26 May 1591; *d* Amsterdam, 16 Sept 1652). Netherlands organist, composer and music editor, son of Jan Pieterszoon Sweelinck. He was a pupil of his father, never married, and was organist of the Oude Kerk, Amsterdam, from his father's death in 1621 until his own (though not before the post had been offered to, and rejected by, the blind Pieter Alewijnszoon de Vois, another Sweelinck pupil). His successor was Jacob van Noordt. He was known for his improvisation. In January 1645 he was severely reprimanded by the church authorities for holding an old-fashioned Christmas celebration at the Oude Kerk to which many 'papists' had been invited – thus the question again arises whether any of the Sweelincks became Protestants (*see* SWEELINCK, JAN PIETERSZOON, §4). He belonged to the Muiderkring, a cultural circle of intellectuals under the leadership of the poet P. C. Hooft; other musicians in this company included Joan Albert Ban and the organist Cornelis Helmbreecker. In 1645 Sweelinck inspected the new organ in the Laurenskerk at Alkmaar. He edited in 1644 a collection of songs of a popular nature (*RISM* 1644³) of which there is a later, undated edition (Amsterdam, *c*1657, inc.). It contains the only pieces certainly by him, four songs to Dutch texts for two to five voices, of which the most important are the *Cecilia Liedt* and the three-voice canon *Oculus non vidit* (these and one other piece ed. B. van den Sigtenhorst Meyer, Amsterdam, n.d.). A set of keyboard variations on *Hoe schoon lichtet de morghen ster* (in *D-Bds*) has been attributed to him by Noske (in *J. P. Sweelinck: Opera omnia*, i/3).

BIBLIOGRAPHY

J. Koning: *Geschiedenis van het slot te Muiden* (Amsterdam, 1827), 128f

B. van den Sigtenhorst Meyer: *Jan P. Sweelinck en zijn instrumentale muziek* (The Hague, 1934, enlarged 2/1946)

——: 'De familie Sweelinck', *TVNM*, xiv/2 (1934), 111; xv/4 (1939), 234

——: 'Een volledig exemplaar van het "Livre septieme" ', *TVNM*, xv/4 (1939), 252

A. Curtis: *Sweelinck's Keyboard Music: a Study of English Elements in Seventeenth-century Dutch Composition* (Leiden and London, 1969, rev. 2/1972)

RANDALL H. TOLLEFSEN

1. Jan Pieterszoon Sweelinck: engraving (1624) by J. Müller

Sweelinck [Swelinck, Zwelinck, Sweeling, Sweelingh, Sweling, Swelingh], **Jan Pieterszoon** (*b* Deventer, ?May 1562; *d* Amsterdam, 16 Oct 1621). Netherlands composer, organist and teacher. He was not only a famous organist and one of the most influential and sought-after teachers of his time but also one of the leading composers, of vocal as well as of keyboard music.

1. Life. 2. Sweelinck as teacher. 3. Works: introduction. 4. Vocal works. 5. Keyboard works.

1. LIFE. Sweelinck was the elder son of Peter Swybbertszoon and his wife Elske Sweeling. Swybbertszoon, Sweelinck and Sweelinck's son Dirck were successively organists of the Oude Kerk, Amsterdam, almost uninterruptedly from about 1564 to 1652, and Sweelinck's paternal grandfather and uncle were also organists. For as yet unknown reasons Sweelinck adopted the family name of his mother, first using it on the title-page of his *Chansons* of 1594. From his early youth until his death he lived at Amsterdam. He never left the Low Countries and was never away from Amsterdam for longer than a few days at a time (except perhaps for a stay in Haarlem for study); the oft-repeated tale of his study in Venice with Zarlino, first related by Mattheson in 1740, is without foundation. His early general education was in the hands of Jacob Buyck, pastor at the Oude Kerk, and came to an end with the Reformation of Amsterdam in 1578. Besides his father, who probably gave him his first music lessons

but who died when he was 11, his only known music teacher was Jan Willemszoon Lossy, a countertenor and shawm player at Haarlem, of whom little is known. Lossy was not an organist but may have taught Sweelinck composition. Cornelis Boskoop, briefly his father's successor at the Oude Kerk in 1573, may have been among his organ teachers, and if Sweelinck indeed studied at Haarlem he would certainly have heard, and may have studied with, the organists Claas Albrechtszoon van Wieringen (active 1529–75) or the well-known Floris van Adrichem (organist 1575–8), both of whom improvised daily in the Bavokerk there.

Cornelis Plemp, a pupil and friend of Sweelinck, stated that his master was an organist for a period of 44 years. If this is true he would have started in 1577 at the age of 15. His tenure of the position at the Oude Kerk, Amsterdam, can, however, be traced only from 1580, although it may have begun earlier, as the church records from 1577 to 1580 are lacking. His initial salary of 100 florins was doubled in 1586 (the year after his widowed mother died, when he took upon himself the care of his younger brother and sister). In 1590 his salary was raised to 300 florins, with the provision that, should he marry, it would be raised by another 100 or he could live rent-free; later that year he married and chose the latter. His last rise, to 360 florins, came in 1607; he still lived rent-free. Contrary to tradition, he was not engaged as both organist and carillonneur (the latter post was entrusted to the organ builder Artus Gheerdinck). Nor did his duties include the supplying of music for the regular ceremonial and social occasions of the city magistrate, as was the case in many other cities at that time, although he did provide this music on a few special occasions. This seemingly conscious restriction of his duties has been seen as an attempt by him to keep enough free time for his extensive work as a teacher, for which he became celebrated (see §2 below). But one must not underestimate the demands of his post. Since the Calvinists saw the organ as a worldly instrument and forbade its use during services, Sweelinck was actually a civil servant employed by the city of Amsterdam (which in any case owned the organs). His contract does not survive, but, on the evidence of various second-hand reports and contracts of organists in other important Dutch cities of the period, it is generally assumed that his duties were to provide music twice daily in the church – an hour in the morning and in the evening. When there was a service this musical hour came before and/or after it. Sweelinck was known for his organ and harpsichord improvisations: more than once the proud city authorities brought important visitors to the church to hear the 'Orpheus of Amsterdam'. The instruments at his disposal in the Oude Kerk were a large organ with three manuals and pedal built originally by Hans van Coelen and Hendrik Niehoff in 1538–42, and a small one with two manuals and pedal built in 1544–5 by Niehoff and Jasper Johanszoon (they are described by C. H. Edskes in Curtis, 1969).

Sweelinck led an uneventful, well-regulated life. His few documented absences from Amsterdam (except for his marriage) were entirely in conjunction with his professional activities. He inspected new organs at Haarlem (1594, with Philip Janszoon van Velsen and Willem Aertszoon), Middelburg (1603), Nijmegen (1605, with Van Velsen) and Dordrecht (1614, with H. J. Speuy) and the restored or repaired organs at Harderwijk

(1608) – where he also wrote a canon for the mayor – and Deventer (1616), his birthplace, which he had also visited in 1595, perhaps to give advice about the forthcoming restoration of the organ. In 1610 he was at Rotterdam to act as adviser for planned improvements to the organ in the Laurenskerk, and he played the organ at Rhenen in 1616 during an informal visit with the organ builder Kiespennink, who had restored the instrument five years earlier. His longest journey was in 1604 to Antwerp, where he purchased a harpsichord (possibly by Ruckers) for the city of Amsterdam.

Sweelinck was buried in the Oude Kerk. He was survived by his wife and five of his six children, of whom only the eldest, DIRCK JANSZOON SWEELINCK, was a musician. John Bull, who was probably a personal friend, wrote a fantasia on one of his themes shortly after his death (see MB, xiv, 1960, rev. 2/1971, p.12). There are two portraits of him. One, a painting of 1606 (in NL-DHgm), is attributed to his brother Gerrit, a talented painter and the teacher of Pieter Lastman, who in turn taught Rembrandt. The other is an engraving made in 1624 (see fig.1); its model is lost.

2. SWEELINCK AS TEACHER. Sweelinck's gifts as a teacher, for which he was famous throughout northern Europe, are an essential part of his importance for music history, for the founders of the so-called north German organ school of the 17th century (culminating in Bach) were among his pupils. His local pupils included talented dilettantes as well as a number of young professional musicians. The most important of the latter were Cornelis Janszoon Helmbreecker and his own son Dirck; others were Pieter Alewijnszoon de Vois, Jan Pieterszoon van Reynsburch, Willem Janszoon Lossy (son of his Haarlem teacher) and Claude Bernard. After the turn of the century his reputation attracted pupils from Germany. These included Andreas Düben, Peter Hasse, Samuel and Gottfried Scheidt and Paul Siefert, as well as Ulrich Cernitz, Jacob Praetorius (ii) and Heinrich Scheidemann, who later held the three principal organists' posts at Hamburg – hence the description of Sweelinck as 'hamburgischen Organistenmacher' (see Mattheson). The pupils of 'Master Jan Pieterszoon of Amsterdam' were seen as musicians against whom other organists were measured, and it was for this reason that talented young men were sent to study with him at the expense of their city councils. The costs included room and board at his house, as well as instruction, and may have totalled 200 florins a year per student. None of the manuscript composition rules ascribed to Sweelinck and based on the third part of Zarlino's Le istitutioni harmoniche is in his hand; they can be considered as nothing more than detailed notebooks (or copies thereof) written by pupils during their study with him.

3. WORKS: INTRODUCTION. As well as being one of the most famous organists and teachers of his time, Sweelinck was the last and most important composer of the musically rich golden era of the Netherlanders. Recent research into this period as a whole has brought his music and influence into better focus. He is no longer seen as the lone north European giant of his time but rather as a gifted craftsman and musician who was the equal of his European contemporaries. His influence, however, cannot be said to have extended beyond about

2. Title-page of Sweelinck's 'Cinquante pseaumes de David' (Amsterdam: 1604)

1650, whereas that of Frescobaldi, for instance, lasted until the end of the century. His keyboard music is now seen to be less the work of an innovator than of one who perfected forms derived from, among others, the English virginalists and transmitted them through his pupils to north Germany. His immediate influence can be seen in the music of Samuel Scheidt and Anthoni van Noordt. His surviving output amounts to 254 vocal works, including 33 chansons, 19 madrigals, 39 motets and 153 psalms (three existing in two versions), as well as about 70 keyboard works, principally in the form of fantasias, echo fantasias, toccatas and variations. Only four pieces, all canons, are known in autograph sources. All his vocal works were printed, and one can assume that he himself corrected most of the proofs. On the other hand, none of his instrumental music was published during his lifetime; since the manuscript copies (or copies of copies) in which it survives vary in their reliability, reconstruction of 'authentic' versions of it is an all but impossible task.

4. VOCAL WORKS. In none of Sweelinck's vocal works, which predominate in his output, is there a setting of a text in his native language – they are for the most part in French – and none of those on sacred texts was written for performance during public worship services. Most are for five voices. Although the performance of one or more vocal parts by instruments is suggested only on the title-page of the *Chansons*, this is not to say that the rest of his vocal music is to be sung *a cappella*: one or more voices of the *Rimes*, for instance, lend themselves well to instrumental performance.

Sweelinck's first publications were of chansons: the collection of 1594 (the year 1584 after the dedication is a typographical error) contains 18 five-part chansons, to which were added four by Cornelis Verdonck. There may have been two further collections (1592–3). Sweelinck published 12 chansons and 15 madrigals in *Rimes françoises et italiennes* (1612). They have an elegance and transparency – inherent in two- and three-part writing – not found in the earlier chansons, and they often include long canonic sections. At least five of the madrigals are modelled on works by Ferrabosco, Andrea Gabrieli, Macque and Marenzio.

Sweelinck's polyphonic setting of the Psalter has been justifiably called a monument of Netherlands music unequalled in the sphere of sacred polyphony. From the outset he intended to set the entire Psalter, and the publication of his music for it spanned the whole of his creative life: his first two psalm settings appeared anonymously in a collection of 1597, his first book of psalms was published in 1604, and the fourth and final book appeared shortly after his death. The texts are from the French metrical Psalter of Marot and De Bèze, not the Dutch version of Datheen (1566) used in most Dutch churches until 1773. This was probably because the psalms were not intended for use in public Calvinist services but rather within a circle of well-to-do musical amateurs among whom French was the preferred language. This supposition is strengthened by the dedications of the first and second books respectively to the burgomasters and aldermen of Amsterdam and to a number of Calvinist merchants of the city, the latter probably being members of the 'compagnie des nourissons, disciples, fauteurs et amateurs de la douce et saincte musique' of which Sweelinck was the leader. In style and technique the psalms follow in the tradition of Clemens non Papa, Goudimel and their Venetian contemporaries. Homophony appears alongside strict counterpoint, with imitation in all voices; both the strict motet and madrigal style and the lighter chanson and villanella style can be found. Although Sweelinck explored all harmonic possibilities, chromaticism appears only sporadically. The cantus firmi – the melodies of the Genevan Psalter – provide the unifying element in each psalm. Most of the settings fall into one of three general categories: the cantus firmus psalm, where each line of the melody (in superius and/or tenor), separated by related interludes, is accompanied by a rhythmically altered form of the melody in the other voices; the 'lied psalm', where the uninterrupted melody appears in the superius; and the 'echo psalm', where the full cantus firmus is found in two separate voices, often in canon.

Sweelinck's other important vocal collection, the *Cantiones sacrae* (1619), is the musical and religious antithesis of the psalms. It comprises 37 motets on texts from the Catholic liturgy and is dedicated to his young Catholic friend and pupil Cornelis Plemp; it thus raises the question as to whether Sweelinck remained a Catholic in the service of the ruling Calvinist minority.

These motets show that in his compositional technique he kept abreast of the music of his time. The lack of a cantus firmus tends to make them more compact, but at the same time they have lost the transparency and vitality of the psalms. Several modern techniques are used; for example, there is more chromaticism, and the counterpoint is more harmonic and ornamental; but the basso continuo is more accurately termed a *basso seguente* (this is the only time that Sweelinck called for a separate instrumental part in a vocal collection). 14 of the motets have codas on the word 'Alleluia', some of them quite extended.

5. KEYBOARD WORKS.
Apart from a few undistinguished pieces for lute, Sweelinck's instrumental music is entirely for keyboard instruments and reveals a thorough knowledge of English music of the time. Although it was never printed it enjoyed wide circulation through the numerous copies made by his pupils. Many works have probably been lost, but those that survive clearly demonstrate his genius.

Sweelinck's works in the free forms – fantasias and toccatas – were developed from similar works by Italians (Andrea Gabrieli, Merulo), Spaniards (Cabezón, Milán), Portuguese (Coelho) and Englishmen (Bull, Philips). The passage-work is perhaps less brilliant than the Italians' but has a more structural purpose, and there are no traces of colourist ornamentation. The various technical difficulties – above all the manner in which they are incorporated into the toccatas – point to a pedagogical purpose. Most of the toccatas have a homophonic or imitative introduction followed by a section of extended passage-work, and a few close with a short fugato section. Sweelinck brought a balanced construction, sharper and more concise in its musical conception, to this form, which in lesser hands could become wayward and diffuse. For him there was no longer a distinction between fantasia and ricercare. His fantasias are built on a single theme and are usually fugal in character, presenting the theme in augmentation and diminution and introducing a number of secondary themes developed either independently in fugato or used as counterpoints to the main theme. They are in several sections, interspersed with free interludes and imitative sections on important secondary themes, and they have a toccata-like close. They are notable for their monumental construction and strict composition. From a historical point of view they have a special place among Sweelinck's works, for they led the way to the later development of the monothematic fugue. The echo fantasias form a separate genre. They are actually free fantasias without a basic theme; they contain homophonic sections in which there is extensive use of echo effects achieved by alteration of register (octave transposition) or colour (use of different manuals). An earlier, more conservative use of echo can be found in works by Bull and Philips.

Sweelinck was also attracted to variation form, in which the style of his music points clearly to the English virginalists, some of whom, notably Bull and Philips, were among his acquaintances. His variation cycles tend to form ordered units and are not a random selection of individual variations. The settings of secular melodies are characterized by the development in each variation of a new musical idea derived from the theme, which thereby often undergoes major alterations or is subjected to ornamentation. The chorale variations are built on another principle, which clearly shows the influence of William Blitheman (see Lowinsky). This involves using a different number of voices in each variation, placing the unchanged or slightly embellished cantus firmus each time in a different voice and providing variation through the change in contrapuntal treatment.

At least two further prints are lost: a *Chyterboeck* (1602 or 1608) with which Sweelinck was in some way connected – whether as composer (perhaps of only the first piece), arranger or collector, or as the composer whose works were arranged by another – and a collection of fantasias (c1630) edited by his pupil Samuel Scheidt; both are known only through auction or book fair catalogues.

WORKS

Editions: *J. P. Sweelinck: Werken*, ed. M. Seiffert (The Hague and Leipzig, 1894–1901/R1968) [S]
    J. P. Sweelinck: Werken voor orgel en clavecimbel, ed. M. Seiffert (Amsterdam, 1943, enlarged edn. of S i) [K]
    J. P. Sweelinck: Werken, ed. A. Annegarn (Amsterdam, 1958, suppl. to K) [A]
    J. P. Sweelinck: Opera omnia, editio altera, ed. R. Lagas and others, UVNM (Amsterdam, 1957–) [O]

PSALMS, CANTICLES

50 pseaumes de David, mis en musique (C. Marot, T. De Bèze), 4–7vv (Amsterdam, 1604, 2/1624 as Premier livre des pseaumes de David, mis en musique . . . seconde edition) [1604]

Rimes françoises et italiennes . . . 2, 3vv, avec une chanson, 4vv (Leiden, 1612) [1612]

Livre second des pseaumes de David, nouvellement mis en musique (Marot, De Bèze), 4–8vv (Amsterdam, 1613) [1613]

Livre troisieme des pseaumes de David, nouvellement mis en musique (Marot, De Bèze), 4–8vv (Amsterdam, 1614) [1614]

Sechs-stimmige Psalmen, auss dem ersten und andern Theil seiner aussgangenen französischen Psalmen (A. Lobwasser), 6vv, ed. M. Martinius (Berlin, 1616)

Vierstimmige Psalmen, auss dem ersten, andern und dritten Theil seiner aussgangenen französischen Psalmen (Lobwasser), 4vv, ed. M. Martinius (Berlin, 1618)

Livre quatriesme et conclusionnal des pseaumes de David, nouvellement mis en musique (Marot, De Bèze), 4–8vv (Haarlem, 1621) [1621]

2 works in 1597[6]

A Dieu ma voix j'ay haussee, 5vv, 1613; S iii, 11; O iii, 11
Ainsi qu'on oit le cerf bruire, 8vv, 1614; S iv, 27
Alors qu'affliction me presse, 4vv, 1614; S iv, 4
Alors que de captivité, 5vv, 1614; S iv, 6
Après avoir constamment attendu, 6vv, 1604; S ii, 38; O ii, 38
A toy, mon Dieu, mon coeur monte, 5vv, 1613; S iii, 12; O iii, 12
A Toy, ô Dieu qui es là haut aux cieux, 5vv, 1604; S ii, 25; O ii, 25
Aux parolles que je veux dire, 5vv, 1621; S v, 12
Avec les tiens, Seigneur, tu as fait paix, 5vv, 1621; S v, 19
Ayes pitié, ayes pitié de moy, 5vv, 1621; S v, 16
Bienheureuse est la personne qui vit, 6vv, 1614; S iv, 19
Bienheureux est quiconques, 3–4vv, 1613; S iii, 5; O iii, 5
Cantique de Siméon (see Or laisses, Createur)
C'est en Judee proprement, 8vv, 1621; S v, 43
C'est en sa tres-saincte Cité, 8vv, 1621; S v, 42
Chantez à Dieu chanson nouvelle, chantez, ô terre, 4vv, 1621; S v, 1
Chantez à Dieu chanson nouvelle, et sa louange, 4vv, 1621; S v, 2
Chantez à Dieu nouveau cantique, 5vv, 1613; S iii, 8; O iii, 8
Chantez de Dieu le renom, 6vv, 1613; S iii, 21; O iii, 21
Chantez gayement, 6vv, 1621; S v, 38
Deba contre mes debatteurs, 6vv, 1614; S iv, 18
Dès ma jeunesse ils m'ont fait mille assauts, 6vv, 1604; S ii, 18; O ii, 18
Des qu'adversité nous offense, 6vv, 1621; S v, 36
De tout mon coeur t'exalteray, 4vv, 1604; S ii, 3; O ii, 3
Dieu est assis en l'assemblee, 8vv, 1614; S iv, 29
Dieu est regnant de grandeur tout vestu, 4vv, 1621; S v, 8
Dieu nous soit doux et favorable, 6vv, 1613; S iii, 17; O iii, 17
Dieu pour fonder son tresseur habitacle, 5vv, 1621; S v, 26
Di moy malheureux, qui te fies, 5vv, 1604; S ii, 22; O ii, 22
Donne secours, Seigneur, il en est haute, 5vv, 1613; S iii, 15; O iii, 15
Donnez au Seigneur gloire, 5vv, 1621; S v, 15
D'ou vient cela, Seigneur je te suppli' (i), 5vv, 1597[6] (anon.); S ix, 3
D'ou vient cela, Seigneur, je te suppli' (ii), 5vv, 1621 (reworking of 1597[6] work); S v, 14
D'ou vient, Seigneur, que tu nous as espars, 4vv, 1614; S iv, 2
Du fonds de ma pensée, 5vv, 1613; S iii, 9; O iii, 9
Du malin le meschant vouloir, 5vv, 1613; S iii, 9; O iii, 9
Du Seigneur Dieu en tous endroits, 8vv, 1621; S v, 41

Du Seigneur les bontés sans fin je chanteray, 6vv, 1614; S iv, 17
Enfans, qui le Seigneur servez, 8vv (2 choirs), 1614; S iv, 24
Enten à ce que je veux dire, 6vv, 1613; S iii, 22; O iii, 22
Enten pourquoy je m'escrie, 8vv, 1613; S iii, 29; O iii, 29
Entre vous conseilliers qui estes, 5vv, 1621; S v, 29
Estans assis aux rives aquatiques, 6vv, 1604; S ii, 13; O ii, 13
Exauce, ô mon Dieu, ma prière, 4vv, 1621; S v, 7
Helas, Seigneur, je te pri' sauve moy, 5vv, 1604; S ii, 21; O ii, 21
Il faut que de tous mes esprits, 4vv, 1604; S ii, 6; O ii, 6
Incontinent que j'eu ouï, 4vv, 1604; S ii, 7; O ii, 7
Jamais ne cesseray, 6vv, 1614; S iv, 16
J'ay de ma voix à Dieu crié, 6vv, 1604; S ii, 42; O ii, 42
J'ay dit en moy, de pres je viseray, 5vv, 1621; S v, 25
J'ayme mon Dieu, car lors que j'ay crié, 5vv, 1621; S v, 18
J'ay mis en toy mon esperance, 6vv, 1621; S v, 34
J'ay mis en toy mon esperance, 7vv, 1621; S v, 39
Je t'aymeray en toute obeissance, 6vv, 1621; S v, 33
Jusques à quand as establi, 6vv, 1604; S ii, 36; O ii, 36
Las en ta fureur aigue, 5vv, 1621; S v, 21
La terre au Seigneur appartient, 3–4vv, 1604; S ii, 2; O ii, 2
Le Dieu, le fort, l'Eternel parlera, 6vv, 1604; S ii, 34; O ii, 34
Le fol malin en son coeur dit et croid, 6vv, 1604; S ii, 37; O ii, 37
Le fol malin en son coeur dit et croit, 4–7vv, 1621; S v, 40
Les cieux en chacun lieu, 5vv, 1614; S iv, 9
Le Seigneur est la clarté qui m'addresse (i), 5vv, 1604; S ii, 32; O ii, 32
Le Seigneur est la clarté qui m'addresse (ii), 3–5vv, 1613; S iii, 7; O iii, 7
Le Seigneur ta priere entende, 4vv, 1604; S ii, 1; O ii, 1
Les gens entrez sont en ton heritage, 5vv, 1621; S v, 20
L'Eternel est regnant, 6vv, 1604; S ii, 44; O ii, 44
Le Toutpuissant à mon Seigneur et maistre, 6vv, 1614; S iv, 15
Loué soit Dieu, ma force en tous alarmes, 6vv, 1604; S ii, 41; O ii, 41
Louez Dieu, car c'est chose bonne, 5vv, 1621; S v, 23
Louez Dieu, car il est benin, 6vv, 1604; S ii, 40; O ii, 40
Louez Dieu tout hautement, 5vv, 1604; S ii, 31; O ii, 31
Misericorde à moy, povre affligé, 5vv, 1604; S ii, 26; O ii, 26
Misericorde au povre vicieux, 6vv, 1604; S ii, 39; O ii, 39
Mon ame en Dieu tant seulement, 7vv, 1614; S iv, 21
Mon coeur est dispos, ô mon Dieu, 6vv, 1604; S ii, 48; O ii, 48
Mon Dieu, j'ay en toy esperance, 6vv, 1614; S iv, 20
Mon Dieu, l'ennemy m'environne, 5vv, 1621; S v, 13
Mon Dieu me paist sous sa puissance haute, 4–6vv, 1604; S ii, 10; O ii, 10
Mon Dieu, mon Dieu, pourquoy m'as tu laissé, 4vv, 1621; S v, 4
Mon Dieu, mon Roy, haut je t'esleveray, 5vv, 1621; S v, 17
Ne sois fasché, durant ceste vie, 5vv, 1614; S iv, 10
Ne vueilles pas, ô Sire, 4vv, 1621; S v, 3
Non point à nous, non point à nous, Seigneur, 6–7vv, 1613; S iii, 24; O iii, 24
O bienheureuse la personne, 5vv, 1621; S v, 10
O bienheureux celuy dont les commises, 5vv, 1604; S ii, 23; O ii, 23
O bienheureux, qui juge sagement, 8vv, 1614; S iv, 29
O combien est plaisant et souhaittable, 5–6vv, 1614; S iv, 8
O Dieu des armees, combien, 5vv, 1613; S iii, 14; O iii, 14
O Dieu, donne moy delivrance, 6vv, 1604; S ii, 28; O ii, 28
O Dieu Eternel, mon Sauveur, 5vv, 1621; S v, 11
O Dieu, je n'ay Dieu fors que toy, 6vv, 1613; S iii, 19; O iii, 19
O Dieu, la gloire, qui t'est deuë, 6vv, 1613; S iii, 27; O iii, 27
O Dieu, mon honneur et ma gloire, 6vv, 1621; S v, 35
O Dieu, ne sois plus à recoy, 5vv, 1621; S v, 24
O Dieu où mon espoir j'ay mis, 5vv, 1614; S iv, 12
O Dieu, qui es ma forteresse, 3–5vv, 1613; S iii, 10; O iii, 10
O Dieu qui nous as deboutés, 5vv, 1604; S ii, 29; O ii, 29
O Dieu tout puissant, sauve moy, 5vv, 1604; S ii, 27; O ii, 27
O Dieu, tu cognois qui je suis, 4–5vv, 1621; S v, 28
O Eternel, Dieu des vengeances, 5vv, 1621; S v, 1
On a beau sa maison bastir, 3–4vv, 1613; S iii, 4; O iii, 4
O nostre Dieu et Seigneur amiable, 5vv, 1604; S ii, 16; O ii, 16
O Pasteur d'Israël, escoute, 5vv, 1604; S ii, 15; O ii, 15
O que c'est chose belle, 6vv, 1604; S ii, 35; O ii, 35
Oraison Dominicale (see Pere de nous)
Or avons nous de nos oreilles, 4vv, 1613; S iii, 3; O iii, 3
Or est maintenant, 6vv, 1621; S v, 32
Or laisses, Createur (Cantique de Siméon) [Nunc dimittis], 5–6vv, 1604; S ii, 51; O ii, 51
Or peut bien dire Israël maintenant, 3–6vv, 1621; S v, 31
Or soit loué l'Eternel, 8vv, 1614; S iv, 30
Or sus, louez Dieu tout le monde, 5vv, 1604; S ii, 30; O ii, 30
[Or sus, serviteurs du Seigneur (i)] (not pubd; indexed in 1597[10] but replaced by a chanson by Verdonck)
Or sus, serviteurs du Seigneur (ii), 6vv, 1604; S ii, 49; O ii, 49
Or sus, serviteurs du Seigneur (iii), 4vv, 1614; S iv, 5
Or sus tous humains, 5vv, 1613; S iii, 13; O iii, 13
O Seigneur, à toy je m'escrie, 5vv, 1613; S iii, 16; O iii, 16

O Seigneur, loué sera, 4vv, 1613; S iii, 6; O iii, 6
O Seigneur, que de gents (i), 6vv, 1597[6] (anon.); S ix, 4
O Seigneur, que de gents (ii), 6vv, 1604 (reworking of 1597[6] work); S ii, 43; O ii, 43
O Seigneur, que de gents (iii), 4vv, 1614; S iv, 3
Pere de nous, qui es là haut és cieux (Oraison Dominicale) [Lord's Prayer], 3vv, 1612, 1614; S iv, 31
Peuples oyez et l'oreille prestez, 6vv, 1604; S ii, 46; O ii, 46
Pourquoy font bruit et s'assemblent les gents?, 5vv, 1604; S ii, 11; O ii, 11
Propos exquis faut que de mon coeur sorte, 5vv, 1604; S ii, 12; O ii, 12
Quand Israël hors d'Egypte sortit, 4vv, 1613; S iii, 2; O iii, 2
Quand je t'invoque, helas escoute, 6vv, 1614; S iv, 14
Que Dieu se monstre seulement, 6vv, 1621; S v, 37
Qui au conseil des malins n'a esté, 4vv, 1614; S iv, 1
Qui en la garde du haut Dieu, 6vv, 1613; S iii, 25; O iii, 25
Qui est-ce qui conversera, 3–4vv, 1604; S ii, 8; O ii, 8
Rendez à Dieu louange et gloire, 6vv, 1604; S ii, 47; O ii, 47
Resveillez vous chacun fidele, 8vv, 1613; S iii, 30; O iii, 30
Revenge moy, pren la querelle, 8vv, 1614; S iv, 23
Seigneur Dieu, oy l'oraison mienne, 6vv, 1613; S iii, 20; O iii, 20
Seigneur, enten à mon bon droit, 4vv, 1621; S v, 6
Seigneur, enten ma requeste, 4vv, 1604; S ii, 5; O ii, 5
Seigneur, garde mon droit, 4vv, 1604; S ii, 4; O ii, 4
Seigneur, je n'ay point le coeur fier, 8vv, 1614; S iv, 23
Seigneur, le Roy s'esjouïra, 4vv, 1621; S v, 5
Seigneur, pui que m'as retiré, 5vv, 1621; S v, 27
Si est-ce que Dieu est tres-doux, 5vv, 1621; S v, 30
Sois ententif, mon peuple, à ma doctrine, 5vv, 1604; S ii, 14; O ii, 14
Sois moy, Seigneur, ma garde et mon appuy, 3–6vv, 1614; S iv, 7
Sus, essgayons nous au Seigneur, 6vv, 1604; S ii, 33; O ii, 33
Sus, louez Dieu, mon ame, en toute chose, 3–6vv, 1614; S iv, 13
Sus mon ame, qu'on benie, 6–7vv, 1613; S iii, 28; O iii, 28
Sus, sus, mon ame, il te faut dire bien, 5vv, 1621; S v, 9
Sus, qu'un chascun de nous sans cesse, 7vv, 1604; S ii, 50; O ii, 50
Tes jugements, Dieu veritable, 5vv, 1604 [version Ehre sei Gott, 5vv, bc, 1641[2]]; S ii, 19; O ii, 19
Toutes gents, louez le Seigneur, 6vv, 1604; S ii, 45; O ii, 45
Tout homme qui son esperance, 6vv, 1613; S iii, 18; O iii, 18
Tu as esté, Seigneur, nostre retraicte, 4vv, 1613; S iii, 1; O iii, 1
Vers les monts j'ay levé mes yeux, 4vv, 1604; S ii, 9; O ii, 9
Veuilles, Seigneur, estre recors, 5vv, 1604; S ii, 20; O ii, 20
Veu que du tout en Dieu mon coeur s'appuye, 6vv, 1613; S iii, 23; O iii, 23
Vouloir m'est pris de mettre en escriture, 8vv, 1614; S iv, 25
Vous tous les habitans des cieux, 7vv, 1614; S iv, 22
Vous tous, Princes et Seigneurs, 5vv, 1604; S ii, 24; O ii, 24
Vous tous qui la terre habitez, 3–5vv, 1614; S iv, 11

MOTETS

Canticum in honorem nuptiarum . . . Iohannis Stoboei . . . et . . . Reginae . . . Davidis Mölleri . . . relicta vidua, 8vv (Königsberg, 1617) [1617]
Cantiones sacrae, 5vv, bc (Antwerp, 1619) [1619]
Melos fausto quondam thalamo . . . conjugum Paris dicatum . . . studio et cura Iohannis Stobaei, 5vv (Danzig, 1638) [1638]

Ab Oriente venerunt Magi, 5vv, bc, 1619; S vi, 3; O vi, 3
Angelus ad pastores ait, 5vv, bc, 1619; S vi, 35; O vi, 35
Beati omnes qui timent Dominum, 5vv, bc, 1619; S vi, 28; O vi, 28
Beati pauperes spiritu, 5vv, bc, 1619; S vi, 6; O vi, 6
Cantate Domino canticum novum, 5vv, bc, 1619; S vi, 8; O vi, 8
De profundis clamavi ad te Domine, 5vv, bc, 1619; S vi, 20; O vi, 20
Diligam te Domine, fortitudo mea, wedding motet, 8vv, 1617; S ix, 7
Diligam te Domine, fortitudo mea, 5vv, bc, 1619; S vi, 5; O vi, 5
Domine Deus meus in te speravi [original: sperabo], 5vv, bc, 1619; S vi, 25; O vi, 25
Ecce nunc benedicite Dominum, 5vv, bc, 1619; S vi, 7; O vi, 7
Ecce prandium meum paravi, 5vv, bc, 1619; S vi, 2; O vi, 2
Ecce virgo concipiet et pariet filium, 5vv, bc, 1619; S vi, 31; O vi, 31
Euge serve bone et fidelis, 5vv, bc, 1619; S vi, 16; O vi, 16
Felix auspiciis dies secondus, 5vv, 1638 [sacred contrafactum by ? J. Stobaeus of lost wedding motet]; S ix, 6
Gaude et laetare, Jerusalem, 5vv, bc, 1619; S vi, 18; O vi, 18
Gaudete omnes et laetamini, 5vv, bc, 1619; S vi, 32; O vi, 32
Hodie beata virgo Maria puerum Jesum praesentavit, 5vv, bc, 1619; S vi, 30; O vi, 30
Hodie Christus natus est, 5vv, bc, 1619; S vi, 13; O vi, 13
In illo tempore postquam consummati sunt, 5vv, bc, 1619; S vi, 22; O vi, 22
In te Domine speravi, 5vv, bc, 1619; S vi, 4; O vi, 4
Iusti autem in perpetuum vivent, 5vv, bc, 1619; S vi, 12; O vi, 12
Laudate Dominum omnes gentes, 5vv, bc, 1619; S vi, 11; O vi, 11
Magnificat anima mea Dominum, 5vv, bc, 1619; S vi, 34; O vi, 34
Non omnis qui dicit mihi Domine, 5vv, bc, 1619; S vi, 1; O vi, 1
O Domine Jesu Christe, pastor bone, 5vv, bc, 1619; S vi, 10; O vi, 10
O quam beata lancea, 5vv, bc, 1619; S vi, 21; O vi, 21
O sacrum convivium, 5vv, bc, 1619; S vi, 14; O vi, 14

Paracletus autem Spiritus sanctus, 5vv, bc, 1619; S vi, 23; O vi, 23
Petite et accipietis, 5vv, bc, 1619; S vi, 15; O vi, 15
Qui vult venire post me, 5vv, bc, 1619; S vi, 19; O vi, 19
Regina coeli laetare, 3–5vv, bc, 1619; S vi, 33; O vi, 33
Tanto tempore vobiscum sum, 5vv, bc, 1619; S vi, 36; O vi, 36
Te Deum laudamus, 5vv, bc, 1619; S vi, 37; O vi, 37
Timor Domini principium sapientiae, 5vv, bc, 1619; S vi, 29; O vi, 29
Ubi duo vel tres congregati fuerint in nomine meo, 5vv, bc, 1619; S vi, 27; O vi, 27
Venite exultemus Domino, 5vv, bc, 1619; S vi, 9; O vi, 9
Vide homo, quae pro te patior, 5vv, bc, 1619; S vi, 17; O vi, 17
Videte manus meas et pedes meos, 5vv, bc, 1619; S vi, 24; O vi, 24
Viri Galilaei, quid statis aspicientes in coelum, 5vv, bc, 1619; S vi, 26; O vi, 26

CHANSONS

Chansons . . . de M. Iean Pierre Svvelingh organiste, et Cornille Verdonq nouvellement composées . . . accommodées tant aux instruments, comme à la voix, 5vv (Antwerp, 1594⁵ [1594⁵]
Rimes françoises et italiennes . . . 2, 3vv, avec une chanson, 4vv (Leiden, 1612) [1612]
Works in 1597¹⁰, 1608¹¹

Au mois de May que l'on saignoit la belle, 5vv, 1594⁵; S vii, 17
Beaux yeux, par qui l'Amour entretient sa puissance, 2vv, 1612; S viii, 4
Bouche de Coral precieux, 5vv, 1594⁵ [arr. 2vv, lute, 1601¹⁸]; S vii, 7
De Jan, Jan (see Tu as tout seul)
Depuis le jour que je vous vei, maistresse, 5vv, 1594⁵; S vii, 12
Elle est à vous, douce maistresse, 5vv, 1594⁵; S vii, 3
Face donques qui voudra amour un petit ange, 5vv, 1594⁵; S vii, 16
Jamais n'avoir, et tousjours desirer, 5vv, 1594⁵; S vii, 25
Jan, Jan (see Tu as tout seul)
Je ne fay rien que requerir, 4vv, 1608¹¹ (inc.); S ix, 10
Je pars, non point de vous, mais de moy seulement, 2vv, 1612; S viii, 2
Je sens en moy une flamme nouvelle, 5vv, 1594⁵; S vii, 18
Je sens l'ardeur d'amour nouvelle, 5vv, 1594⁵; S vii, 1
Jeune beauté, bon esprit, bonne grace, 5vv, 1594⁵; S vii, 9
Je voy mille clairtez et mille choses belles, 3vv, 1612; S viii, 12
La belle que je sers, 5vv, 1594⁵; S vii, 15
Las que me sert, quand la douleur me blesse, 2vv, 1612; S viii, 1
L'Aubespin chasse tout malheur, 5vv, 1594⁵; S vii, 4
Lors que le trait par vos yeux decoché rompit, 2vv, 1612; S viii, 3
Marchans qui traversez tout le rivage More, 2vv, 1612; S viii, 6
Mon Dieu, que j'ayme ma Deesse, 5vv, 1612; S viii, 15
Plus tu cognois que je brusle pour toy, 5vv, 1594⁵; S vii, 10
Pourquoy tournez vous voz yeux gratieus de moy, 5vv, 1594⁵; S vii, 14
Quand je voy ma maistresse, 5vv, 1594⁵; S vii, 2
Regret, soucy et peine m'ont fait de mauvais tours, 5vv, 1594⁵; S vii, 11
Rozette, pour un peu d'absence vostre coeur vous avez changé, 4vv, 1612; S viii, 28
Si j'ayme ou non, je n'en dis rien, 5vv, 1594⁵; S vii, 13
Susanne un jour d'amour sollicitée, 5vv, 1594⁵; S vii, 8
Sus, je vous prie que l'on me donne dedans ce cristal, 5vv, 1594⁵; S vii, 6
Tes beaux yeux causent mon amour, 4vv, 1597¹⁰; S ix, 8
Tu as tout seul, Jan [De Jan, Jan], 5vv, 1597¹⁰; S ix, 9
Un jour l'aveugle Amour, 3vv, 1612; S viii, 14
Voicy du gay Printemps l'heureux advenement, 2vv, 1612; S viii, 5
Vostre amour est vagabonde, 5vv, 1594⁵; S vii, 5
Yeux, qui guidez mon ame en l'amoureux voyage, 3vv, 1612; S viii, 13

MADRIGALS

Rimes françoises et italiennes . . . 2, 3vv, avec une chanson, 4vv (Leiden, 1612) [1612]
Works in 1601⁵, 1605⁹, 1608¹¹, 1610¹⁴

Amor, io sent' un respirar si dolce, 3vv, 1612 (on Macque, 1583¹⁴); S viii, 23
Che giova posseder cittadi e regni, 2vv, 1612; S viii, 10
Chi vuol veder quantunque può natura, 6vv, 1601⁵ (inc.); S ix, 13
Dolci labri amorosi portieri, 3vv, 1612; S viii, 21
Dolcissimo ben mio, speme di questo core, 3vv, 1612 (on A. Gabrieli, 1583¹⁴); S viii, 24
Facciam, cara mia File, un concento, una musica gentile, 3vv, 1612; S viii, 17
Garrula rondinella, che nel spuntar del die, 2vv, 1612; S viii, 11
Hor che suave l'auri'n ogni canto, 4vv, 1608¹¹ (inc.)
Io mi son giovinetta, e volentieri, 2vv, 1612 (on D. Ferrabosco, 1542¹⁷); S viii, 18
Lascia Filli mia cara, 3vv, 1612; S viii, 16
Liquide perle Amor da gl'occhi sparse, 2vv, 1612 (on Marenzio); S viii, 19
Madonna con quest' occhi, 6vv, 1601⁵, 1605⁹; S ix, 12
Morir non puo'l mio core, 2vv, 1612; S viii, 9
Per te rosa gentile, 3vv, 1612; S viii, 18
Poi che voi non volete ch'io vi baci, 5vv, 1610¹⁴; S ix, 11
Qual vive Salamandra in fiamma ardente, 3vv, 1612 (on Marenzio, 1583¹⁴); S viii, 22

Ricco amante son'io, per voi tesore mio, 3vv, 1612; S viii, 26
Un sol bacio to dono, ingrata, e ti lamenti, 3vv, 1612; S viii, 19
Vaga gioia amorosa, bocca bella, e pregiata, 3vv, 1612; S viii, 20

LATIN OCCASIONAL

Canticum nuptiale: in honorem . . . Iacobi Praetorii et . . . Margaritae a Campis [Sponse musarum genus et sacerdos], 5vv (Hamburg, 1608) (inc.); S ix, 5
Wedding motet, lost (pubd as sacred contrafactum, see 'Motets': Felix auspiciis dies)

CANONS

[Ave maris stella], 3vv, D-Hs 5396 (autograph, 12 Nov 1614); S ix, no. 14, p.77 (facs.)
Beatus qui soli Deo confidit, 4vv, 1644³, 2/c1657; 1657⁴; S ix, 19
Miserere mei, Domine, 'in unisono', 4vv, LÜh 61b (autograph, 3 Dec 1618); S ix, no.16, p.79 (facs.)
O Mensch, bewein' dein Sünde gross, 3vv, lost, formerly Hs (incl. in Composition Regeln) [doubtful, attrib. Sweelinck by Gehrmann, S x, p.7f]
Sine cerere et Baccho friget Venus (i), 4vv, Hs 5396 (autograph); S ix, no.17, p.81 (facs.)
Sine cerere et Baccho friget Venus (ii), 4vv, 1644³, 1657⁴; facs. in TVNM, xv (1939), facing p.256
Vanitas vanitatum, et omnia vanitas (i), 4vv, autograph, 24 May 1608, in Album amicorum of E. Brinck, Mayor of Harderwijk; S ix, no.15, p.81 (facs.)
Vanitas vanitatum, et omnia vanitas (ii), 4vv, 1644³, 1657⁴; S ix, 18

KEYBOARD
(free forms)

Echo fantasia (Dorian), A-Wm, B-Lu; S i, 9; K 14; O i/1, 11
Echo fantasia (Aeolian), D-Bgk; S i, 11; K 16; O i/1, 12
Echo fantasia (Ionian), Bds, Bgk, I-Pu, Tn; S i, 12; K 17; O i/1, 13
Echo fantasia (Ionian), A-Wm, D-Bds; S i, 13; K 18; O i/1, 14
Fantasia (Dorian), Bds; S i, 2; K 2; O i/1, 2
Fantasia (g-Dorian), GB-Cfm; S i, 3; K 3; O i/1, 3
Fantasia (a-Phrygian), D-Bds, I-Pu, Tn; S i, 4; K 5; O i/1, 4
Fantasia (Mixolydian), D-Bds; S i, 6; K 8; O i/1, 6
Fantasia (g-Dorian), Bds; K 4; O i/1, 8
Fantasia (Mixolydian), Bds; S i, 7; K 9; O i/1, 9
Fantasia (g-Dorian), USSR-Lit; O i/1, 10
Fantasia chromatica (Dorian), A-Wm, Wn, D-Bds, Bgk; S i, 1; K 1; O i/1, 1, 1a
Hexachord fantasia (F-Ionian), GB-Cfm, Och, I-Pu, Tn; S i, 5; K 6; O i/1, 5
Praeludium (F-Ionian), D-Bds, I-Tn; K 33, 73; O i/1, 27, 27a
Ricercar (Aeolian), Pu, Tn; S i, 4; K 10; O i/1, 7
Toccata (Dorian), D-Bds, I-Pu, Tn; S i, 14; K 20; O i/1, 15
Toccata (Aeolian), B-Lu, D-Bds, Lr, GB-Cfm, I-Pu, Tn; S i, 15; K 21; O i/1, 16
Toccata (Aeolian), D-Bds, I-Pu, Tn; S i, 16; K 22; O i/1, 17
Toccata (Mixolydian), D-Bds, Bgk, I-Tn; S i, 21; K 28; O i/1, 18, 18a
Toccata (Ionian), A-Wm, B-Lu, D-Bds; S i, 23; K 30; O i/1, 19, 19a
Toccata (Ionian), Bgk, I-Tn; S i, 24; K 31; O i/1, 20
Toccata (g-Dorian), D-Bds; S i, 18; K 24; O i/1, 21
Toccata (g-Dorian), Bgk; S i, 19; K 25; O i/1, 22
Toccata (Mixolydian), Bgk, I-Tn; S i, 20; K 27; O i/1, 23
Toccata (Aeolian), D-Bgk, GB-Lbm, I-Tn; S i, 22; K 29; O i/1, 24, 24a
Toccata (Ionian), A-Wm; K 32; O i/1, 25
Toccata (Mixolydian), USSR-Lit; O i/1, 26
Toccata (g-Dorian), D-Bds (inc.); K 72; O i/1, 28

(sacred)

Allein Gott in der Höh sei Ehr (4 variations by Sweelinck), Bds [collab. other composers]; K 35; O i/2, 1
Allein zu dir, Herr Jesu Christ, CZ; O i/2, 2
Christe qui lux es et dies, A-Wm, D-Bds, I-Tn; K 37; O i/2, 3
Da pacem Domine in diebus nostris, D-Bds; S i, 25; K 38; O i/2, 4
Des boosdoenders wille seer quaet [Ps.xxxvi: Du malin le mechant vouloir], I-Tn; O i/2, 10
Erbarm dich mein, o Herre Gott, D-Bds, CZ, I-Tn; K 41; O i/2, 5
Ich ruf zu dir, Herr Jesu Christ, D-Bds, H-BA; K 40; O i/2, 6
Ik heb den Heer lief [Ps.cxvi: J'aime mon Dieu], D-Bds; K 51; O i/2, 11
Nun freut euch, lieben Christen gemein, A-Wm, D-Bds; K 48; O i/2, 7
O mijn Godt, wilt mij nu bevrijden [Ps.cxl: O Dieu, donne-moy delivrance], Bds, GB-Cfm; S i, 26; K 52; O i/2, 12
Onse Vader in hemelrijck [Vater unser im Himmelreich], D-CZ, H-BA (incl. 3 variations probably not by Sweelinck, see 'Doubtful Keyboard: sacred'); K 54; O i/2, 9
Ons is gheboren een kindekijn [Puer nobis nascitur], Bds; K 53; S i/2, 8
Wir glauben all an einem Gott, A-Wm, D-Bds, I-Tn; K 56; O i/2, 13

(secular)

Ballo del granduca, H-BA; K 65; O i/3, 1
Engelsche fortuyn [Von der Fortuna werd ich getrieben], D-Bgk, I-Tn; S i, 35; K 64; O i/3, 2
Est-ce Mars, A-Wm, D-Bds; S i, 31; K 58; O i/3, 3

Ick voer al over Rhijn [Ich fuhr mich uber Rheine], *Bds*; S i, 30; K 59; O i/3, 4

Malle Sijmen, pavan, *USSR-Lit*; O i/3, 5

Mein junges Leben hat ein End', *D-Bds*; S i, 27; K 60; O i/3, 6

Onder een linde groen [Unter der Linden grüne], *Bds*, *Bgk*; S i, 28; K 63; O i/3, 8

Pavana hispanica, *Bgk*, *S-Uu* (both incl. 4 variations by Scheidt); S i, 36; S ix, 2; K 68; O i/3, 9

Pavana Lachrimae, *H-BA*; K 66; O i/3, 10

Pavana Philippi, *D-Bds*; S i, 29; K 69; O i/3, 11

Poolsche dans [Soll es sein], *Bds*, *H-BA*; S i, 32; K 62; O i/3, 12

(anon. attrib. Sweelinck)

Fantasia (Aeolian), *D-Bds* (attrib. Sweelinck, by Leonhardt, O i/1); K 11; O i/1, 32

Heer, die ons hebt verstooten al [Ps lx O Dieu, qui nous as deboutez], *Bds* (attrib. Sweelinck, see Breig and Curtis, 1963); O i/2, 16

Mein Hütter undt mein Hirtt [Ps xxiii], *Bds* (attrib. Sweelinck or one of his pupils, see Curtis, 1969); ed. in Curtis (1963)

Hoe schoon lichtet de morghen ster [Wie schön leucht uns der Morgenstern], *Bds* (attrib. Sweelinck or Dirck Sweelinck, see Breig and Curtis (1969); attrib. D. Sweelinck by Noske, O i/3); ed. in Curtis (1963)

More Palatino, *A-Wm* (attrib. Sweelinck by Seiffert and Noske, see K and O i/3); K 61; O i/3, 7

DOUBTFUL KEYBOARD

(free forms)

Capriccio (Aeolian), *D-Bds* (corrupt version of a work possibly by Sweelinck, see O i/1); S i, 33; K 70; O i/1, 29

Echo fantasia (Dorian), *B-Lu*, *D-Bds* (doubtful, see O i/1); S i, 10; K 15; O i/1, 34, 34a

Echo fantasia (Ionian), *Bds* (probably not by Sweelinck, see Curtis, 1969, and O i/1); K 19

Fantasia (Ionian), *Lr* (probably not by Sweelinck, see O i/1; last 8 bars = those of Fantasia ut sol fa mi, and may be by Sweelinck); S i, 8; K 13

Fantasia (Ionian), *I-Tn* (attrib. 'J.P.S.', see O i/1); A 1; O i/1, 36

Fantasia (Dorian), *Tn* (attrib. 'J.P.S.', see O i/1); A 2; O i/1, 37

Fantasia (Mixolydian), *Tn* (attrib. 'J.P.S.', see O i/1); A 3; O i/1, 38

Fantasia (Dorian), *Tn* (attrib. 'G.P.S.', see O i/1); A 5; O i/1, 40

Fantasia (F-Ionian), *D-Bds* (probably not by Sweelinck, see O i/1); K 7

Fantasia ut sol fa mi (Ionian), *Bds* (also attrib. Bull, see Dart, 1959; last 8 bars = those of Fantasia in S i, 8, and may be by Sweelinck, see O i/1); K 12; O i/1, 33

Ricercar (Dorian), *I-Tn* (attrib. J. Peterle; probably not by Sweelinck, see O i/1); O i/1, 35

Ricercar (Dorian), *Tn* (attrib. 'J.P.S.', see O i/1); A 4; O i/1, 39

Toccata (g-Dorian), *A-Wm*, *I-Tn* (attrib. J. Hassler, see O i/1); K 26; O i/1, 30

Toccata (Dorian), *D-Bgk*, *I-Tn* (attrib. H. L. Hassler, see O i/1); S i, 17; K23; O i/1, 31

(sacred)

Ach Gott vom Himmel sieh darein, *D-Bds* (anon., probably not by Sweelinck, see Breig and O i/2); K 34

Allein zu dir, Herr Jesu Christ, *Bds* (anon., probably not by Sweelinck, see Breig and O i/2); K 36

Dies sind die heil'gen zehn Gebot, *A-Wm* (anon.; probably not by Sweelinck, ? by Scheidemann, see Breig and O i/2); K 39

Durch Adams Fall ist ganz verderbt, *Wm* (anon.; probably not by Sweelinck, ? by Scheidemann, see Breig and O i/2); K 40

Es ist das Heil uns kommen her, *Wm* (anon.; probably not by Sweelinck, ? by Scheidemann, see Breig and O i/2); K 42

Es spricht der unweisen Mund wohl, *H-BA* (anon.; probably not by Sweelinck, see Breig and O i/2); K 43

Herr Christ der einig Gottes Sohn, *A-Wm* (anon.; probably not by Sweelinck, ? by Scheidemann, see Breig and O i/2); K 44

Herzlich lieb hab ich dich, O Herr, *H-BA* (corrupt version, see Breig, Curtis, 1963 and O i/2); K 45; O i/2, 14

Nun freut euch, lieben Christen gemein, *BA* (anon.; probably not by Sweelinck, see Breig and O i/2); K 47

Nun komm der Heiden Heiland, *A-Wm* (anon.; probably not by Sweelinck, see Breig and O i/2); K 49

O lux beata Trinitas, *Wm*, *D-CZ* (formerly attrib. Sweelinck, actually by Scheidemann); K 50

Onse Vader in hemelrijck [Vater unser im Himmelreich], *H-BA* [3 of the 4 variations probably not by Sweelinck, see Breig, Curtis 1963 and O i/2; see also 'Keyboard: sacred']); K 54; O i/2, 15

Wie nach einem Wasserquelle [Ps xlii], *BA* (formerly attrib. Sweelinck, actually by H. Speuy, 1610); K 55

Wo Gott der Herr nicht bei uns hält, *D-Bds*, *H-BA* (anon.; probably not by Sweelinck, see Breig and O i/2); K 57

(secular)

Allemande de Chapelle, Bomann Museum, Celle (on theme by J. Champion (ii); see O i/3, 2 variations probably not by Sweelinck); ed. in EMN, ii (1965)

Bergamasca, Bomann Museum, Celle (theme and 8 variations probably not by Sweelinck; see O i/3); ed. in EMN, ii (1965)

Passamezzo moderno, *H-BA* (? by a pupil, see O i/3); K 67; O i/3, 13

Windeken daer het bosch af drift, *A-Wm*, *D-Bds*, *W* (3 variations attrib. Sweelinck, actually by Scheidt, see Curtis, 1963)

LUTE

Psalm v, *NL-Lt* (inc.); O i/3, 14

Psalm xxiii, *Lt* (inc.); O i/3, 15

(arr. from vocal works, all NL-Lt)

Bienheureux est quiconques; De tout mon coeur t'exalteray; La terre au Seigneur appartient; Le Seigneur ta priere entende; Mon Dieu me paist sous sa puissance haute; Ne vueilles pas, ô Sire; Pourquoy font bruit et s'assemblent les gents?: see 'Psalms, Canticles'

(anon. attrib. Sweelinck)

Psalm xxiii, *Lt*; O i/3, 16

Courante, *GB-Cfm* (attrib. 'Pietreson', possibly by Sweelinck, see O i/3); O i/3, 17

Volte (i), *Cfm* (attrib. 'Pietreson', possibly by Sweelinck, see O i/3); O i/3, 18

Volte (ii), *Cfm* (attrib. 'Pietreson', possibly by Sweelinck, see O i/3); O i/3, 19

Volte (iii), *Cfm* (attrib. 'Pietreson', possibly by Sweelinck, see O i/3); O i/3, 20

LOST WORKS

Chansons, 4, 5vv (Antwerp, 1592) (mentioned in Draudius: *Bibliotheca exotica*, Frankfurt, 1625, but possibly = 1594[5])

Chansons, 5vv (Antwerp, 1593) (mentioned in Draudius: *Bibliotheca exotica*, Frankfurt, 1610, but possibly = 1594[5])

Nieuw Chyterboeck, genaemt Den corten wegwijser die 't hert verheugt (Amsterdam, 1602/1608) (mentioned in Draudius: *Bibliotheca exotica*, Frankfurt, 1610, 1625, and in catalogues of 1647 and 1759; see Tollefsen, 98, 109)

Tabulatura: Fantasien mit 3 Stimmen der alle 8 Tonos, von J. P. Sweelinck Organisten zu Amsterdam komponiert, und von Samuele Scheid Hallense kolligirt (Halle, *c*1630) (see A. Göhler: *Verzeichnis der in den Frankfurter und Leipziger Messkatalogen der Jahre 1564 bis 1759 angezeigten Musikalien*, i, Leipzig, 1902, 915)

Tablature containing preludes, fugues, chorales by Sweelinck and others, dated 1673, formerly Bibliothèque Royale, Strasbourg

Fugue, model for Bull's Fantasia op de fugue van M. Jan Pietersz.; S i, 34; K 71; MB xiv, 4

MSS containing works by Sweelinck, formerly *D-Bds* (microfilm copies *US-CA* and Deutsches Musikgeschichtliches Archiv, Kassel), *D-Hs*

THEORETICAL WORK

Compos[i]tion Regeln, *A-Wm*, *D-Bds*, formerly *Hs* (2 copies, both lost) (formerly attrib. Sweelinck but not by him); S x

BIBLIOGRAPHY

G. Baudartius: *Memoryen ofte cort verhael*, ii (Arnhem, 1625), 163

J. Mattheson: *Grundlage einer Ehren-Pforte* (Hamburg, 1740); ed. M. Schneider (Berlin, 1910/R1969), 69, 328, 330ff

J. J. Dodt van Flensburg: 'Jan Pietersz. Zwelinck', *Algemeene Konst- en Letterbode voor het jaar 1840*, i/25 (1840), 396

F. C. Kist: 'J. P. Swelinck', *Nederlandsch Muzikaal Tijdschrift*, iv (1842), 181, 191

H. Tiedeman: 'Jan Pieterszoon Sweelinck: een biographische schets', *UVNM*, i (1869); enlarged in *UVNM*, vi (1876)

R. Eitner: 'Jan Pieters (oder Pieterszoon) Sweelinck', *MMg*, ii (1870), 76

——: 'Ueber die acht, respektive zwölf Tonarten und über den Gebrauch der Versetzungszeichen im XVI. und XVII. Jahrhunderte nach Joh. Peter Sweelinck', *MMg*, iii (1871), 133

P. Scheltema: 'Dr Cornelis Gijsbertszoon Plemp en zijne beschrijving van Amsterdam', *Aemstels Oudheid*, vi (1872), 1

——: 'Jan Pieterszoon Swelingh', *Aemstels Oudheid*, vi (1872), 177

A. Goovaerts: *Histoire et bibliographie de la typographie musicale dans les Pays-Bas* (Antwerp, 1880/R1963)

C. M. Dozy: 'Jan Pietersz. Sweelinck en andere organisten der 16e eeuw', *Oud-Holland*, iii (1885), 277

M. Seiffert: 'J. P. Sweelinck und seine direkten deutschen Schüler', *VMw*, vii (1891), 145–260; summary in *TVNM*, iv/1 (1892), 1

——: *Geschichte der Klaviermusik*, i (Leipzig, 1899)

——: 'Matthias Weckmann und das Collegium Musicum in Hamburg', *SIMG*, ii (1900–01), 76–132

C. van den Borren: *Les origines de la musique de clavier en Angleterre* (Brussels, 1912; Eng. trans., 1913)

——: *Les origines de la musique de clavier dans les Pays-Bas (Nord et Sud) jusque vers 1630* (Brussels, 1914)

——: 'Quelques notes sur les chansons françaises et les madrigaux italiens de J. P. Sweelinck', *Gedenkboek aangeboden aan Dr. D. F. Scheurleer* (The Hague, 1925), 73

L. Schrade: 'Ein Beitrag zur Geschichte der Tokkata', *ZMw*, viii (1925–6), 610

O. Gombosi: 'Ein neuer Sweelinck-Fund', *TVNM*, xiv/1 (1932), 1
E. Lowinsky: 'English Organ Music of the Renaissance', *MQ*, xxxix (1933), 373, 528
B. van den Sigtenhorst Meyer: *Jan P. Sweelinck en zijn instrumentale muziek* (The Hague, 1934, enlarged 2/1946)
——: 'De familie Sweelinck', *TVNM*, xiv/2 (1934), 111; xv/4 (1939), 234
——: 'Jan Willemszoon Lossy, Sweelinck's leermeester, 1545–1629', *TVNM*, xiv/4 (1935), 237
G. Frotscher: *Geschichte des Orgel-Spiels und der Orgel-Komposition* (Berlin, 1935–6, enlarged 3/1966)
J. Legène: 'Jan Pieter Sweelinck', *Musik und Kirche*, viii (1936), 65
B. van den Sigtenhorst Meyer: 'Een volledig exemplaar van het "Livre septieme" ', *TVNM*, xv/4 (1939), 252
——: *Jan P. Sweelinck* (Amsterdam, [1941])
——: *De vocale muziek van Jan P. Sweelinck* (The Hague, 1948)
T. Dart: 'English Music and Musicians in 17th-century Holland', *IMSCR*, v *Utrecht 1952*, 139
M. Reimann: 'Zur Deutung des Begriffs Fantasia', *AMw*, x (1953), 253
B. Bijtelaar: 'De orgels van Sweelinck', *Het Orgel*, xlix (1953), 137ff, 151ff, 165ff; 1 (1954), 1ff, 21ff; see also Vente, 1954
M. A. Vente: 'Nogmaals: de orgels van Sweelinck', *Het Orgel*, 1 (1954), 73, 85
H. A. Bruinsma: 'The Organ Controversy in the Netherlands Reformation to 1640', *JAMS*, vii (1954), 205
D. Hellmann: 'Betrachtungen zur Darstellung der Sweelinckschen Werke für Tasteninstrumente', *Musik und Kirche*, xxv (1955), 287
M. Reimann: 'Pasticcios und Parodien in norddeutschen Klaviertabulaturen', *Mf*, viii (1955), 265
A. Voigt: *Die Toccaten Jan Pieterszoon Sweelincks: ein Beitrag zur frühen Instrumentalmusik* (diss., U. of Münster, 1955)
T. Fedtke: 'Der niederländische Orgelbau im 16. Jahrhundert und seine Bedeutung für Sweelincks Instrumentalmusik', *Musik und Kirche*, xxvi (1956), 60
G. Gerdes: *Die Choralvariationen J. P. Sweelincks und seiner Schüler* (diss., U. of Freiburg, 1956)
T. Dart: 'Lord Herbert of Cherbury's Lute-book', *ML*, xxxviii (1957), 136
A. C. F. Koch: 'Sweelinck's afkomst', *Verslagen en mededelingen van de Vereeniging tot beoefening van Overijsselsch regt en geschiedenis*, vii/2 (1957), 77
F. Noske: 'Luitcomposities van Jan Pieterszoon Sweelinck', *Orgaan van de Koninklijke Nederlandsche Toonkunstenaars-Vereeniging*, xii (1957), 46
——: 'Remarques sur les luthistes des Pays-Bas (1580–1620)', *Le luth et sa musique: CNRS Neuilly-sur-Seine 1957*, 179
R. L. Tusler: *The Organ Music of Jan Pieterszoon Sweelinck* (Bilthoven, 1958)
M. A. Vente: *Die Brabanter Orgel* (Amsterdam, 1958, enlarged 2/1963)
T. Dart: 'Sweelinck's "Fantazia on a theme used by John Bull" ', *TVNM*, xviii/4 (1959), 167
R. L. Tusler: 'Style Differences in the Organ and Clavicembalo Works of Jan Pieterszoon Sweelinck', *TVNM*, xviii/4 (1959), 149; see also J. H. van der Meer, xix/1–2 (1960), 67; F. Noske, ibid, 80; and A. van Gool, xix/3–4 (1962–3), 203
W. Breig: 'Der Umfang des choralgebundenen Orgelwerkes von Jan Pieterszon Sweelinck', *AMw*, xvii (1960), 258
F. W. Riedel: *Quellenkundliche Beiträge zur Geschichte der Musik für Tasteninstrumente in der 2. Hälfte des 17. Jahrhunderts (vornehmlich in Deutschland)* (Kassel, 1960)
B. Dubbe: 'Bijdrage tot de geschiedenis van het muziekleven te Deventer tot het eind van de 18de eeuw', *Verslagen en mededelingen van de Vereeniging tot beoefening van Overijsselsch regt en geschiedenis*, lxxvi (1961), 111–55
L. Schierning: *Die Überlieferung der deutschen Orgel- und Klaviermusik aus der ersten Hälfte des 17. Jahrhunderts* (Kassel, 1961)
M. A. Vente: 'Bijdragen tot de geschiedenis van het vroegere grote orgel in de St. Bavo en zijn bespelers tot 1650', in *Nederlandse orgelpracht* (Haarlem, 1961), 1–34
F. Noske: 'Nederlandse klaviermuziek uit de 16de en 17de eeuw', *Mens en Melodie*, xvii (1962), 3
D. Philips: 'Banden tussen de familie Sweelinck en Venendaalse geslachten', *Maandblad van Oud Utrecht*, xxxv (1962), 101
F. Noske: 'Sweelinck na vier eeuwen', *TVNM*, xix/3–4 (1962–3), 125
M. A. Vente: 'Sweelinckiana', *TVNM*, xix/3–4 (1962–3), 186
A. Curtis: *Sweelinck's Keyboard Works: a Study of English Elements in Dutch Secular Music of the 'Gouden Eeuw'* (diss., U. of Illinois, 1963)
O. Mischiati: 'L'intavolatura d'organo tedesca della Biblioteca Nazionale di Torino', *L'organo*, iv (1963), 1–154
M. Reimann: 'Die Autoren der Fuge Nr. 23 in Lüneburg KN-208[1] und der Fantasia Ut sol fa mi in Lübbenau, Ms. Lynar A[1]', *Mf*, xvi (1963), 166
J. H. Schmidt: 'Eine unbekannte Quelle zur Klaviermusik des 17. Jahrhunderts, das Celler Klavierbuch 1662', *AMw*, xxii (1965), 1
A. Curtis: *Sweelinck's Keyboard Music: a Study of English Elements in Seventeenth-Century Dutch Composition* (Leiden and London, 1969, 2/1972)
R. H. Tollefsen: 'Jan Pietersz. Sweelinck: a Bio-Bibliography, 1604–1842', *TVNM*, xxii/2 (1971), 87–125 [quotes from or summarizes, and evaluates many early items not included in this bibliography]
M. A. Vente: 'Sweelincks Orgelreisen', *TVNM*, xxii/2 (1971), 126
M. C. Bradshaw: 'The Toccatas of Jan Pieterszoon Sweelinck', *TVNM*, xxv/2 (1975), 38

For further studies see *JVNM*, i–iii (1872–81) and *TVNM*, i (1882–5), iv–vi (1892–1900), ix–xx (1914–65), xxii (1971)

RANDALL H. TOLLEFSEN

Sweitzl (*fl c*1420). German or Swiss composer. His name is found in the index of *D-Mbs* 3232*a* as the composer of a Sanctus of which only two voices are extant there. The piece appears with an added contra-tenor in *PL-Wn* 8054 and as a fragment in the Aosta MS (*I-AO*). The tenor is derived from a variant of the Sanctus of Mass XVII. The trope *Gustasti necis pocula* is used.

BIBLIOGRAPHY
G. de Van: 'A Recently Discovered Source of Fifteenth Century Polyphonic Music, the Aosta Manuscript', *MD*, ii (1948), 5

TOM R. WARD

Swelinck [Sweling, Swelingh], **Jan Pieterszoon**. *See* SWEELINCK, JAN PIETERSZOON.

Swell. A device for the gradation of volume in keyboard instruments.

1. The organ. 2. The harpsichord and piano.

1. THE ORGAN. The Swell organ is that manual department of an organ whose chest and/or pipes are enclosed on all sides by a box, one side of which incorporates a device (lid, flap, shutters, sashed panel, etc) that can be opened and closed by connection with a foot-lever or pedal. A stop or half-stop may be thus enclosed, or several departments (Choir organ, Solo organ) or even the whole organ (examples by S. Green, *c*1780). The connection from foot-lever to swelling device can be mechanical, pneumatic, electrical, etc, and may be so made that fine gradations in the degree of closure are possible.

Some examples of the small BRUSTWERK of the 16th century may have had doors that could be opened; most authenticated examples before *c*1700, however, have semi-fixed fretwork doors. The idea of foot-operated movable doors or, in chamber organs, flaps, occurred occasionally to builders (T. Mace, 1676) but the first Swells of significance are the enclosed Echo boxes of Spanish and later English organs provided with liftable lids or, also later, sliding front panels like sash windows. In Spain (Alcalá, *c*1680) the Swell box was often put round a stop or two on the main manual chest; only later did it enclose a whole department, usually either on the floor of the organ or tucked away at the top. Single stops were always those for treble solos of an expressive nature (Corneta, Trompeta, Flute); they were so in England until *c*1780. French and English organs had their Echo stops on their own treble keyboard, the chest placed in the breast of the organ. Abraham Jordan's advertisement in the *Spectator* (8 February 1712) for his new Swell in St Magnus, London Bridge ('never . . . in any organ before'), refers to an organ with four sets of keys; thus the Swell was probably an extra Echo department. By 1740 (though not earlier) a Swell organ was regarded as indispensable; it took a larger chest, was moved into a position above the great chest and by *c*1800 had ousted the Choir organ as the chief second manual.

Despite Burney's failure to find them, Swell organs were not uncommon in Europe: large departments low in the organ case, with vertical or horizontal shutters (Venice, c1770), little Echo boxes with a solo stop or two (Berlin, 1727; Rostock, 1770), the whole organ in a box (Abbé Vogler, 1784), perhaps with a 'balanced' Swell pedal-lever (Frankfurt, 1827) not requiring to be notched into place like the 'nag's head swell'. Swelling the sound could also be obtained by double or triple touch and by playing free reeds on a higher wind pressure (J. Wilke, 1823). Even in the 1850s, English and French builders like Hill and Cavaillé-Coll made noticeably more discreet Swell organs in their ecclesiastical than in their secular organs. Refinement in the making of Swell organs has since concerned the size and variety of chests, their positioning, the accuracy of the pedal and the characteristic flue-and-reed battery that inspired most organ composers from 1840 to 1940. The device has since been recognized as essentially irrelevant to the nature of the true organ and thus without a place in the modern classical designs despite attempts in Germany and elsewhere to compromise by enclosing traditional *Oberwerk* and *Brustwerk* chests.

2. THE HARPSICHORD AND PIANO. Two kinds of device for producing crescendo effects were applied to English harpsichords (and much more rarely to square pianos as well) in the third quarter of the 18th century. In the earlier of these, the 'lid swell' or 'nag's head swell', depressing a pedal gradually raised a hinged section at the right side of the harpsichord's lid. With the second type, the 'Venetian swell', the entire area of the soundboard was covered by an inner lid fitted with pivoted louvres like those of a Venetian blind, which could be opened by depressing a pedal. The lid swell is first mentioned in the patent specification of Roger Plenius's Lyrachord (1755) and seems to have begun to be applied to harpsichords in the early 1760s. The Venetian swell was patented by Burkat Shudi in 1769 and appears to have been an improvement only to the extent that the operation of its louvres is visually less obtrusive than the flapping of a large section of the instrument's lid.

Both types of swell have two important disadvantages. When they are closed in order to reduce the harpsichord's volume, they severely muffle its tone as well, and even when they are entirely open, they rob the instrument of some of its volume and brilliance. In addition, most of the crescendo that is produced occurs with the first opening of the swell, which is also accompanied by an abrupt brightening of the instrument's tone. Despite these disadvantages, the swells do increase the range of crescendo effects beyond those available with only a 'machine' stop. By providing a lower level of *pianissimo* when closed, they increase the instrument's overall dynamic range, and they also permit the player to achieve crescendos and decrescendos when only one or two registers are in use.

Although the swell certainly helped the harpsichord to survive after the piano's rise to prominence in the 1770s, it is not correct to state that the swell was developed in order to enable the harpsichord to compete with the newer instrument. The piano was, in fact, only little known when the swell was first applied to the harpsichord and had not achieved any great popularity at that early date.

For bibliography *see* HARPSICHORD and ORGAN.

PETER WILLIAMS (1), EDWIN M. RIPIN (2)

Sweney, John R. (*b* West Chester, Penn., 31 Dec 1837; *d* Chester, Penn., 10 April 1899). American evangelistic song leader and composer of gospel hymns. *See* GOSPEL MUSIC, §I.

Swert, Isidore de. Belgian cellist, brother of JULES DE SWERT.

Swert, Jules de (*b* Louvain, 15 Aug 1843; *d* Ostend, 24 Feb 1891). Belgian cellist. He was first taught by his father, choirmaster of the Louvain Cathedral, and began playing in public at about the age of ten; later, Servais heard him and induced him to become his pupil at the Brussels Conservatory. Graduating with *premier prix* in 1858 he visited Paris (where Rossini expressed great admiration for his playing) and toured for some years. In 1865 he settled as Konzertmeister in Düsseldorf, where he gave notable trio performances with Clara Schumann and Auer. In 1868 he moved to Weimar as soloist of the Hofkapelle, but was called to Berlin the following year as royal Konzertmeister and became one of the first teachers at the Hochschule für Musik. He resigned from this post in 1873 and spent the next three years near Wiesbaden, composing and occasionally touring. His London début in 1875 was an immediate success, and the next year Wagner entrusted him with the formation of the orchestra at Bayreuth. In 1878 de Swert's first opera, *Die Albigenser*, was successfully produced at Wiesbaden; three years later he moved to Leipzig. *Graf Hammerstein*, his second opera, was produced at Mainz in 1884, and a cello concerto was well received in Berlin in 1886. De Swert moved to Ostend in 1888 as director of the music school and professor at the conservatories in Ghent and Bruges. He was a significant figure in the Brussels school of cellists, and an excellent musician; he had a fine technique, and his tone was powerful yet sweet.

His elder brother, Isidore (Jean Gaspar) de Swert (*b* Louvain, 6 Jan 1830; *d* Brussels, Sept 1896), studied with François de Munck at the Brussels Conservatory, graduating with *premier prix* in 1846. He became a teacher at the Bruges music school in 1850, and was solo cellist of the theatre orchestra before moving to Brussels to become solo cellist at the Théâtre de la Monnaie in 1856. He was appointed to the Louvain Conservatory in 1866 and succeeded Servais at the Brussels Conservatory the same year.

LYNDA LLOYD REES

Sweys, Liebing. Organ builder; *see* SUISSE (ii).

Swieten, Gottfried (Bernhard) Baron **van** (*b* Leiden, 29 Oct 1733; *d* Vienna, 29 March 1803). Musical patron of Dutch birth. He was the son of the distinguished doctor Gerhard van Swieten, and the family moved to Vienna in 1745 when his father was appointed personal physician to Empress Maria Theresia. After completing his education at the 'Theresianum', Vienna's exclusive Jesuit school, Gottfried briefly held a post in the Austrian civil service before embarking on an extended period of diplomatic training. Between 1755 and 1777 much of his time was spent abroad, with lengthy stays in Brussels (1755–7) and Paris (1760–63) and a visit to England in 1769. He had a short-lived term with ministerial rank in Warsaw (1763–4), but his one major diplomatic posting was as ambassador to Berlin (1770–77), where he was responsible for Austria's interests in the negotiations with Frederick the Great over the first partition of Poland. He returned to

Vienna as Prefect of the Imperial Library, a post he held until his death. During the 1780s as President of the Court Commission on Education and Censorship he was one of the main instruments of Joseph II's liberal policies, but he was relieved of his office by Leopold II on 5 December 1791 (the day of Mozart's death).

As a young man in Vienna, Brussels and Paris, van Swieten was active in amateur music. Two *opéras comiques* of his own survive, *Les talents à la mode* and *Colas, toujours Colas* (MSS in *D-Rtt*), and performances are recorded of a third, *La chercheuse d'esprit*, now lost. Together with Monsigny and Philidor he contributed to the pasticcio *La rosière de Salency*, which was performed before the French court and later publicly in 1769. Of his output of at least ten symphonies seven are known (MSS in *Rtt*), three of which appeared in print under Haydn's name (see Landon, 1955), and there was a performance of one of them as late as 1782 in a Vienna Augarten concert that also featured Mozart. The unpretentious little operas have a certain naive charm and colour, but the chief characteristics of the conservative, three-movement symphonies are tautology and paucity of invention.

As a composer van Swieten is insignificant; his importance lies in his activities as a patron. During his years in Berlin, presumably through Kirnberger and the circle around Princess Anna Amalia, he developed a taste for old music, especially J. S. Bach and Handel. From C. P. E. Bach, Princess Amalia's titular Kapellmeister though now resident in Hamburg, he commissioned the six symphonies for strings, w182 (1773). On his return to Vienna he was an active champion of these three composers, and in particular of Handel. The performance (in an arrangement by Starzer) of *Judas Maccabaeus* by the Tonkünstler-Sozietät in 1779 was surely due to his influence. In 1781 C. P. E. Bach dedicated to him his third set of *Sonaten für Kenner und Liebhaber* w57, evidently as a mark of thanks for van Swieten's promotion of his music in Vienna. At the regular informal meetings on Sundays in van Swieten's rooooms at the library, Mozart excitedly made the acquaintance of the music of J. S. Bach and Handel in 1782–3.

Probably in the second half of the 1780s, van Swieten organized a group of aristocratic patrons known as the 'Associierte' to sponsor private performances of oratorios, and it was for these concerts that Mozart made his arrangements of Handel's *Acis and Galatea* (1788), *Messiah* (1789) and the *Ode for St Cecilia's Day* and *Alexander's Feast* (1790). This sponsorship continued throughout the 1790s and reached its peak in the promotion of Haydn's *Seven last Words* (choral version, 1796), *The Creation* (1798) and *The Seasons* (1801). In each instance the 'Associierte' paid Haydn a handsome honorarium and bore the costs of the performance (in the town house of Prince Schwarzenberg, one of the sponsors), and van Swieten was responsible for the text. In the case of the *Seven last Words* this amounted to little more than minor revisions to the earlier choral arrangement by Friebert (see Sandberger), but *The Creation* was a more substantial adaptation and translation from an English libretto (reputedly intended in the first place for Handel) brought back by Haydn from London, while *The Seasons*, though based on James Thomson's poem, is to a large extent van Swieten's own work. The suggestions he made (probably at Haydn's request) as to the colourful depiction of the words also had some effect on the music. During van Swieten's final years Haydn relied heavily on his advice in dealings with publishers.

Beethoven was also taken up by van Swieten in his early years in Vienna and dedicated his First Symphony to him. Another dedication, recognizing van Swieten's role as an early representative of the Bach revival, was that of Forkel's biography of J. S. Bach (1802).

BIBLIOGRAPHY
'Aus einem Briefe des Herrn Geheimen Raths, Freyherrn van Swieten', *AMZ*, i (1798–9), 252
C. F. Pohl and H. Botstiber: *Joseph Haydn* (Leipzig and Berlin, 1878–1927)
A. Sandberger: 'Zur Entstehungsgeschichte von Haydns "Sieben Worte des Erlösers am Kreuze"', *JbMP 1903*, 45
M. Friedlaender: 'Van Swieten und das Textbuch zu Haydns Jahreszeiten', *JbMP 1909*, 47
H. Abert: *W. A. Mozart* (Leipzig, 1919–21, 3/1965–6)
R. Bernhardt: 'Aus der Umwelt der Wiener Klassiker, Freiherr Gottfried van Swieten', *Der Bär: Jb von Breitkopf & Härtel 1929–30*, 74–166
P. Baumgärtner: *Gottfried van Swieten als Textdichter von Haydns Oratorien* (diss., U. of Vienna, 1930)
E. F. Schmid: 'Beethovens Bachkenntnis', *NBJb*, v (1933), 64
E. Anderson, ed.: *The Letters of Mozart and his Family* (London, 1938, rev. 2/1966)
E. F. Schmid: 'Gottfried van Swieten als Komponist', *MJb 1953*, 15
H. C. R. Landon: *The Symphonies of Joseph Haydn* (London, 1955)
——: *The Collected Correspondence and London Notebooks of Joseph Haydn* (London, 1959)
H. Seeger: 'Zur musikhistorischen Bedeutung der Haydn-Biographie von Albert Dies (1810)', *BMw*, i/3 (1959), 24
D. Bartha: 'A "Sieben Worte" változatainak keletkezése az Esterházy-gyüjte-mény kéziratainak tükrében' [The origin of the 'Seven last Words' as revealed by the Haydn collection in Budapest], *Zenetudományi tanulmányok*, viii (1960), 107–86 [with Ger. summary]
A. Holschneider: 'Die "Judas-Maccabäus"-Bearbeitung der österreichischen Nationalbibliothek', *MJb 1960–61*, 173
——: 'Die musikalische Bibliothek Gottfried van Swietens', *GfMKB*, *Kassel 1962*, 174
E. Olleson: 'Gottfried van Swieten, Patron of Haydn and Mozart', *PRMA*, lxxxix (1962–3), 63
W. Kirkendale: 'More Slow Introductions by Mozart to Fugues of J. S. Bach?', *JAMS*, xvii (1964), 43
E. Olleson: 'Georg August Griesinger's Correspondence with Breitkopf & Härtel', *Haydn Yearbook*, iii (1965), 5–53
M. Stern: 'Haydns "Schöpfung": Geist und Herkunft des van Swietenschen Librettos', *Haydn-Studien*, i (1966), 121–98
D. E. Olleson: *Gottfried, Baron van Swieten and his Influence on Haydn and Mozart* (diss., U. of Oxford, 1967)
H. Walter: 'Gottfried van Swietens handschriftliche Textbücher zu "Schöpfung" und "Jahreszeiten"', *Haydn-Studien*, i (1967), 241–77
E. Olleson: 'The Origin and Libretto of Haydn's "Creation"', *Haydn Yearbook*, iv (1968), 148
G. Croll: 'Mitteilungen über die "Schöpfung" und die "Jahreszeiten" aus dem Schwarzenberg-Archiv', *Haydn-Studien*, iii (1974), 85
EDWARD OLLESON

Swift, Richard (*b* Middleport, Ohio, 24 Sept 1927). American composer. After private studies in the 1940s, he was a pupil of Leland Smith, Grosvenor Cooper and Leonard Meyer at the University of Chicago (MA 1956). He then taught at the University of California at Davis; he has received numerous awards. Swift has been active in the San Francisco Composers' Forum and the New Music Ensemble; the influence of the latter is reflected in improvisatory elements in his works of the 1960s. Most of his music is serial, and in large part 12-note.

WORKS
(selective list)
Fl Sonata, 1951; A Coronal, orch, 1954; 4 str qts, 1955, 1958, 1964, 1973; Serenade Concertante, pf, wind qnt, 1956; 8 Stravaganzas, inst/ens, 1956–74; Sonata, cl, pf, 1957; Vn Sonata, 1957; Trio, cl, pf, 1957; Conc., pf, ens, 1961; Extravaganza, orch, 1962; Domains: I, Bar, ens, II, perc, III, ens, all 1963; The Trial of Tender O'Shea, opera, 1, 1964; Music for a While, I, II, 3 insts, 1965, 1969; Carmina Archilochi, S, ens, 1965; Summer Notes, pf, 1965;

Thrones, a fl, db, 1966; Tristia, orch, 1967; Vn Conc., 1968; Sym., 1970; Thanatopsis, Mez, chorus, ens, 1971; Specimen Days, S, ens, 1972; many incidental scores

Principal publishers: Presser, University of California Press

BIBLIOGRAPHY
K. Kohn: 'Richard Swift: Concerto', PNM, ii/1 (1963), 90
BRIAN FENNELLY

Swijssen, Joos. Organ builder; see SUISSE (ii).

Swing. (1) The name given to a jazz style (see JAZZ, §§8–10) and to a related phase of American popular music (see POPULAR MUSIC, §III, 2) both of which arose in the 1930s and were characterized in particular by the use of 'big bands'.

(2) A quality attributed to jazz performance. Being basic to the perception and performance of jazz, swing has resisted concise definition or description. Most attempts at such refer to it as primarily a rhythmic phenomenon, resulting from the conflict between a fixed pulse and the wide variety of accent and rubato that a jazz performer plays against it. However such a conflict alone does not necessarily produce swing, and a rhythm section may even play a simple fixed pulse with varied amounts or types of swing. Clearly other properties are also involved, of which one is probably the forward propulsion imparted to each note by a jazz player through manipulation of timbre, attack, vibrato, intonation or other means; this combines with the proper rhythmic placement of each note to produce swing in a great variety of ways.

BIBLIOGRAPHY
A. Hodeir: Hommes et problèmes du jazz (Paris, 1954; Eng. trans., 1956/R1975 as Jazz: its Evolution and Essence), chap.12
G. Schuller: Early Jazz (New York, 1968), 6ff
BRADFORD ROBINSON

Swingle Singers. French pop vocal group. The eight academically trained singers were brought together in Paris in 1962 by Ward Lemar Swingle (b 1927) and Christiane Legrande (b 1930) to improve their sight-singing and musicianship. They developed a distinctive style with scat-singing arrangements of Baroque and Classical instrumental music, adding a jazz bass and percussion as accompaniment, embellishing rhythmic sections and improvising solos. They toured Europe and the USA, and made several successful recordings. In summer 1973 the group disbanded and Swingle formed a new English group, Swingle II. Using less scat-singing, they performed a wider repertory including madrigals, early jazz and pop songs, and introduced new music by such composers as Luciano Berio.

RAYMONDE S. KRAMLICH

Switzerland (Fr. Suisse; Ger. Schweiz; It. Svizzera). An inland republic in western Europe, consisting of a confederation of 22 cantons. Its musical culture owes as much to the church as to secular influences.

I. Art music. II. Folk music.

I. Art music. Swiss musical history must be seen against the background of regional differences and of the circumstances which governed the formation of the country. Four languages are spoken, German, French, Italian and Romansh, and there are two religions, Catholic and Protestant. The German-speaking Swiss are the descendants of a Germanic tribe, the Alemanni, and the French-speaking Swiss of the Burgundii.

Founded in 1291, Switzerland was the first group of German-speaking cantons to break away from the domination of the Holy Roman and Habsburg empires. After the Roman era most of French-speaking western Switzerland came under the rule of Savoy and, from 1536 to 1798, of Berne. Switzerland did not take on its modern geographical form until 1848.

Under Roman domination the main centres held by the legions, such as Avenches and Vindonissa, practised whatever music was current in Rome. The abbeys of St Maurice (founded in 515) and Romainmôtier (5th century), the Cloister of Disentis (5th century), the monasteries Engelberg and Einsiedeln, and the bishops' palaces at Sion, Geneva, Lausanne and Basle were important cultural centres. The Benedictine monastery of St Gall (founded in 720) was the most important musical centre. In the 9th century Notker composed sequences there which were sung in Cluny and in England, Spain and Italy, and in the 10th century Notker Labeo wrote there the earliest known musical treatise in German; in the 11th century Ekkehard IV introduced Gregorian chant to the monastery. From the 13th century the cathedrals played a significant part in the development of ecclesiastical chant; organs were built in Basle and Einsiedeln (14th century), Sion (c1400), Fribourg, Lausanne, Zurich and other towns. Landmarks in this development included the appearance of polyphony in the liturgy (in Zurich in the late 13th century and in Geneva c1500) and the performance of Passion plays in the 13th and 14th centuries in Basle, Einsiedeln, Engelberg and Selzach.

During approximately the same period, troubadours and trouvères toured the country and songs by Swiss Minnesinger are found in German collections. From the 14th and 15th centuries onwards instrumental music was performed in the main cities, which maintained fife and drum bands for public holidays and official ceremonies; nevertheless, vocal music predominated.

With the Reformation the development of music virtually ceased. Zwingli in Zurich and Calvin in Geneva forbade the use of organs and other instruments during services, claiming that they distracted the faithful. They allowed only the singing of psalms, which were taught at school. Basle was less affected by these restrictions; its university taught music from its foundation (1460). Church music developed more there than elsewhere, particularly under French and Flemish influences. Instrumental music continued to be performed in the main centres, but Ludwig Senfl and Heinrich Glarean, who both lived mainly abroad, were the only composers who became widely known.

After the austerity of the Reformation, organs reappeared in churches in the 17th and 18th centuries, while monasteries remained important for church music and musical studies. By the 19th century music was practised at all levels of society. German influence began to be felt and from 1808 the Société de Musique Helvétique gave annual concerts with a large number of performers; in 1842 Mendelssohn's *Lobgesang* was performed in Lausanne in the composer's presence with 182 instrumentalists and 533 singers, and in 1860 more than 500 people took part in a performance in Basle of Handel's *Jephtha* and of Beethoven's Ninth Symphony. Inspired by Nägeli, Hegar and Zwyssig, unaccompanied male-voice choirs grew up in German-speaking Switzerland, heavily dependent on the German repertory.

In French-speaking Switzerland French solo songs

and folksongs were preferred, though German or Swiss–German conductors soon introduced their native chorales. Whether in the secular or in the religious spheres, the public preferred works for large choral and instrumental bodies and favoured events such as the Fête des Vignerons (held every 25 years at Vevey) and the Einsiedeln Passion Plays. The time spent by Wagner in Zurich and Lucerne, by Brahms in Zurich, Winterthur and Thun, and by Tchaikovsky in Montreux, all influenced the activities of Swiss orchestras, many of which were founded at this time. Switzerland became fully aware of its musical potentialities from the late 19th century. In German-speaking areas such composers as Hermann Suter and Hans Huber were distinguished from their great German contemporaries by their uniquely Swiss characteristics: a more cautious lyricism and a deep religious feeling. In French Switzerland such musicians as Gustave Doret (who was also a writer on music) and Jaques-Dalcroze, originator of eurhythmics, gradually directed the music of French Switzerland away from Germany and towards France; this resulted in particularly imaginative orchestration in the work of some composers.

Every large town has its own symphony or chamber orchestra, the most famous being the Orchestre de la Suisse Romande. Swiss conductors have included Ansermet, Sacher (conductor of the Basler Kammerorchester and the Collegium Musicum Zürich), Scherchen, Denzler and Desarzens. Such composers as Schoeck, Burkhard, Honegger and Martin are internationally known and have sought a kind of synthesis between German and French influences. Stravinsky, who lived in Montreux and Morges (1914–20), collaborated with C. F. Ramuz, whose scenarios he used in *Renard*, *The Wedding* and *The Soldier's Tale*. Librettos by René Morax were used by Doret for *La servante d'Evolène* and by Honegger for *Le roi David* and *Judith*; Morax founded the Théâtre du Jorat in Mézières (near Lausanne), which opened in 1908 with Doret's *Henriette* and represented a new type of lyric theatre. Ansermet and Sacher have conducted works by their contemporaries, including the first performances of works dedicated to them by Bartók, Stravinsky, Martinů and Malipiero. There are opera houses in Zurich, Basle, Geneva and Berne. The Association des Musiciens Suisses organizes annual concerts of Swiss music with Swiss performers. In large towns the proportion of concert-goers is one of the highest in western Europe, particularly for subscription concerts.

An active avant garde, of which the leading members are Klaus Huber, Holliger, Guyonnet, Wildberger and Kelterborn, has grown up and includes pupils of Boulez, who taught at Basle. The operas of Heinrich Sutermeister have been produced all over Europe.

Journals such as the *Schweizerische Musikzeitung* (*Revue musicale suisse*; Zurich, founded 1862) and the *Revue musicale de la Suisse romande* (Morges-Yverdon, founded 1948) reflect Swiss musical life. There are important festivals in Lucerne, Zurich, Montreux, Lausanne, Gstaad and other towns. The Eidgenössicher Musikverein, a confederation founded in 1862 to promote wind music in Switzerland, has over 1800 member societies with a total of almost 69,000 members, all amateur musicians. In some cantons nearly every village has a choir or a brass band: the large number of choirs is characteristic of Switzerland, and the Société Fédérale de Chant has 200 male-voice choirs with a total of 15,000 members. These large numbers of musicians make amateur performances of the great oratorios possible. There are also small professional choirs, maintained by broadcasting authorities; Swiss radio plays an important role in the development of new music by broadcasting and commissioning new works. In the absence of private patrons of the arts the government, through the Fondation Pro Helvetia, promotes and encourages music in Switzerland.

Because there are four national languages, education is the responsibility of individual cantons and thus varies considerably. School music is not as important as in Germany or eastern Europe, though Jeunesses Musicales (with about 4000 Swiss members) cultivates an interest in music by organizing concerts, competitions and summer camps. There are conservatories at Geneva (founded in 1835), where Liszt taught, Zurich (the largest), Basle and other large towns. The library at Einsiedeln Abbey contains manuscripts dating from 1530, including works by Praetorius, G. B. Sammartini, J. C. Bach, Haydn and Mozart; concerts of religious works are given there in the autumn. Every July a Semaine Romande de Musique Sacrée is held at the abbey of St Maurice.

See also BASLE; BERNE; GENEVA; LAUSANNE; LUCERNE; MONTREUX; WINTERTHUR; ZURICH.

BIBLIOGRAPHY
FasquelleE
A. Niggli: *Die Schweizer Musikgeschichte* (Zurich and Leipzig, 1886)
A. Soubies: *Histoire de la musique suisse* (Paris, 1899)
G. Becker: *La musique en Suisse depuis les temps les plus reculés jusqu'à la fin du 18ème siècle* (Geneva, 1923)
E. Refardt: *Historisch-biographisches Musikerlexikon der Schweiz* (Zurich, 1928)
A. E. Cherbuliez: *Die Schweiz in der deutschen Musikgeschichte* (Frauenfeld, 1932)
E. Isler: '25 Jahre schweizerischer Musik (1914–39)', *SMz*, lxxix (1939), 323
F. Martin: 'La musique en Suisse romande', *ReM* (1940), no.96, p.161
E. Refardt: *Musik in der Schweiz* (Berne, 1952)
40 compositeurs suisses contemporains (Amriswil, 1956)
W. Tappolet: 'De quoi vit le compositeur suisse?', *SMz*, ci (1961), 246
W. Schuh and others, eds.: *Dictionnaire des musiciens suisses* (Zurich, 1964)

II. Folk music. By its mode of transmission and cultural setting, Swiss folk music can be classed either as *Musikfolklore* (folk music proper) or as *Musikfolklorismus* (folkloristic music). *Musikfolklore* embraces all those musical phenomena that belong to traditional culture and are still subject to the vagaries of oral transmission; such music includes the *Betruf* or *Alpsegen* (Alpine prayer or blessing), *Juchzer* ('shout of joy'), yodelling, *Löckler* (cattle calls), cradle songs, children's songs etc, which are all functionally related to traditional rituals, customs and work. By contrast, *Musikfolklorismus* refers to those phenomena that, by being notated, become stereotyped, or are literary compositions: in both cases they are transmitted by means of notation and include yodelling songs, national songs, popular compositions, songs for festivals, folksong arrangements and songs composed in a folklike style. They are mostly designed for public performances, chiefly by societies and associations.

Because of her linguistic and cultural diversity, Switzerland has maintained a lively reciprocal relationship with the musical repertory of neighbouring countries for centuries. This applies equally to the historical folksongs of the 16th century to the 18th (many of which circulated among Swiss mercenaries in foreign armies) and to the more recent song-tunes and instrumental pieces of the late 18th and early 19th centuries. 'We come to the conclusion that, in Switzerland as a whole, there is hardly anything in our treasury of traditional folksong that is characteristic of all Switzerland' (R. Weiss). Just as the Franco-Swiss folksong repertory is shared with that of Alsace, so German-Swiss music has much in common with that of Baden-Württemberg, Swabia and the Tyrol, and Rhaeto-Romanic and Ticinese music with that of Piedmont and Lombardy, because Switzerland's political boundaries straddle several different language groups.

1. The history of interest in folk music. 2. General characteristics. 3. Folkloristic music.

1. THE HISTORY OF INTEREST IN FOLK MUSIC. Although there was a sporadic interest in folk customs during the Renaissance, it was not focussed directly on folksongs or instrumental music. However, the following references give some pointers to the nature and distribution of folk music at that time: the *Kühreihen* or ranz des vaches (herdsman's song) from Appenzell in Georg Rhaw's *Bicinia* (Wittenberg, 1545); the Swiss dance *Der Sibentaler genandt* (1556) by Urban Weiss, in W. Heckel's *Lautten-Buch* (Strasbourg, 1562); and scattered references to *Alpsegen*, dancing, singing at Easter and New Year, *Sternsingen* (Epiphany songs) and nightwatchmen's songs in Cyssat's *Collectanea chronica und denkwürdige Sachen* (1565; ed. J. Schmid, Lucerne, 1969–72). There are other brief references to folk music in contemporary sources, such as those by Thomas Platter the Elder (*Ein Lebensbild aus dem Jahrhundert der Reformation*, ed. H. Kohl, Leipzig, 1921) and Felix Platter (*Tagebuchblätter ... des 16. Jahrhunderts*, ed. H. Kohl, Leipzig, 1913); the first detailed account of the alphorn and its use (Conrad Gesner: *De raris et admirandis herbis*, 1555); the general interest shown in historical battle songs by the 15th- and 16th-century chroniclers following the rise of the Confederation. However, these and other lesser sources tell little about the music itself. Johannes Hofer's medical dissertation, printed in 1688, refers to the homesickness experienced by exiled shepherds when they heard the 'Cantilena Helvetica'. This was the first of a long series of references to the effect of alphorn music or of the ranz des vaches on Swiss expatriates, particularly those engaged in foreign military service. During the 18th century, with the growth of Helvetian patriotism and Rousseau's advocacy of a 'return to Nature', the ranz-des-vaches, whether sung or played (on alphorn or bagpipe) was increasingly regarded as the essence of Swiss *Nationalmelodie*. Since the 17th century secular song had been shunned by the upper classes and censured by the authorities as 'frivolous', to be replaced by compulsorily introduced psalm singing. They aimed, in the words of M. P. Planta, 'to suppress vexatious and corrupting songs and introduce beneficial ones in their place' and were supported by men like J. J. Bodmer (1698–1783), Lavater and their followers. They were offended by the real folksongs of the period: such genres as the *Kiltlieder* (wooing songs), cowherd's sayings and teasing verses were considered unworthy of attention. Later, in the second edition of the *Sammlung von Schweizer-Kühreihen ... Volksliedern* (1812), there appears the regretful, ironic and self-accusing statement, 'Our old national songs are in part lost or extinct, in part spoiled and misrepresented'.

With the advent of true feeling for the Alps, which was inspired above all by Haller's poem *Die Alpen* (1729), independent interest in folksong was aroused for the first time in Switzerland, and was sustained by the collecting activity of G. S. Studer, begun before 1778: he was inspired by his enthusiasm for Ossian and Haller and by the 'Kreise der Berner Bergfreunde', groups of Bernese mountain-lovers. Foreign visitors in the late 18th century such as von Stolberg and J. G. Ebel, and the letters of Küttner, evince lively interest in individual folksongs and customs. The influx of travellers from other countries and the beginnings of an interest in and awareness of a national folk identity, together with the pastoral festival at Unspunnen near Interlaken in August 1805, resulted in the first edition of genuine folksongs, the *Acht Schweizer-Kühreihen mit Musik und Text* (1805). This was the foundation of Swiss folksong research and by the fourth edition it included 76 songs with guitar or piano accompaniment. A few art songs by G. J. Kuhn and Ferdinand Huber were also inserted, for the aim was to offer the people new and better folksongs as well as old ones. It was hoped to satisfy the 'townsman's longing for the idyllic' by reviving extinct customs and songs, and to inspire visiting tourists with an interest in Swiss folk-life. There was also a political aspect to the Unspunnen festival, for it marked the reinstatement of Berne as the 'directing canton' for that year, following Napoleon's Act of Mediation in 1803. By means of public exercises in alphorn playing, by singing and by Alpine contests, country folk were prepared for later self-glorification in the ranz des vaches and cowherd songs (Küher- und Sennenlieder) composed in popular style during the 19th and 20th centuries. Thus *Musikfolklorismus*, the use of traditional folklore to create and rationalize history, was established by the early 19th century.

Folksong collection and study first began in educated circles, among the followers of J. R. Wyss, S. Wagner, G. J. Kuhn and F. Huber in Berne, and those of M. Usteri, D. H. Hess and J. U. Hegner in Zurich. Isolated songs and airs soon appeared in calendars, weekly journals and almanacs, and individual collections also appeared, such as the *Allgemeines Schweizer-Liederbuch* (1825) and the *Schweizerisches Taschen-Liederbuch 'Alpenröschen'* (1849). The attentions of the German Romantic literary movement introduced a philological approach. In addition to the object lessons provided by Herder, Brentano, Liliencron, Erk and Böhme, the work of a long succession of immigrants and scholars from Germany (Stolberg, Meisner, Szadrowsky, Rochholz, J. Meier etc) first stimulated and later paved the way for systematic collecting. Interests were still predominantly philological until the foundation of the Schweizerisches Archiv für Volkskunde, but conditions improved from 1906 with the founding, under the inspiration of J. Meier, of the Volksliedarchiv (Basle), firstly for collections of German-Swiss folktunes, then (from 1907) of French, and soon afterwards of Rhaeto-Romanic and Italian. Since then the research findings of A. Tobler, H. In der Gand, O. von Greyerz, A. Rossat, G. Züricher, S. Grolimund, A. L. Gassmann, M. Maissen and many others have been published regularly in the *Schriften der Schweizerischen Gesellschaft für Volkskunde*. Although folksong research is affiliated to this society, scientific work has gradually ceased owing to the recession of the folksong movement after World War II. In the 1970s Switzerland still has no folksong institute and research is a matter for individuals, so that current publications are devoted chiefly to regional and local interests. However, occasional lectures are given and classes held at the universities of Basle, Berne, Fribourg and Zurich. An inventory of folk music instruments is being prepared as part of a project to compile a comprehensive survey of European folk music instruments.

2. GENERAL CHARACTERISTICS. Most traditional singing is for solo voice, except in western Switzerland where some songs have choral refrains. Songs connected with Christmas, New Year, Epiphany, mid-Lent, St Nicholas and other church festivals are similar to soldiers' songs, professional and vocational songs, in that they are sung in parallel 3rds and 6ths or, less often, in an improvised polyphonic style derived from the practice of schools and choirs. Partsinging of a pre-19th-century origin can be found in the area of the Ticino canton; according to Geering (1951, p.62) this 'is not just a degenerate form of art music' but the last 'offshoot of the practice of partsinging . . . which predates written music'.

In the Appenzell canton there is another type of partsinging which is neither transmitted in writing nor deliberately rehearsed. Here a solo yodel or yodel-song is supported by an improvised vocal harmony based on the root position primary triads: thus the solo yodeller, often followed by a second singer, is given supporting resonance from sustained block harmony (see ex.1).

Ex.1 *Gradhäba*, rec. and transcr. M. Baumann (Baumann, 1976)

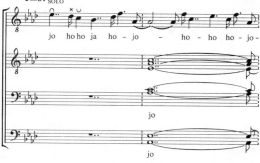

jo ho ho ja ho – jo – – ho – ho ho – jo –

jo

jo

– jo ho ho ho ho jo – – – etc

jo o jo jo jo o etc

etc

jo jo etc

This kind of singing, known as *Gradhäba* ('that which sustains the notes evenly'), must have evolved from a 17th- and 18th-century homophonic psalm-singing style. This yodel is often accompanied by idiophonic timbres such as *Schellenschütteln* (the shaking of large cowbells, see fig.1) and *Talerschwingen* (in which a coin is swished around in an earthenware basin; see fig.2). Similar multi-part *Naturjodel* are also found in Toggenburg, in central and upper Berne, in Emmental

1. *Yodellers accompanied by Schellenschütteln (shaking of large cowbells)*

and also around Gruyères. Yodel duets and trios with independent part-movement are known principally in central Switzerland, especially in the Muotathal and Weggis regions. Yodels in the Schwyz region and in Appenzell, and the ranz des vaches and *Betruf*,

2. *Yodellers accompanied by Talerschwingen (the swishing of coins round earthenware basins)*

frequently incorporate the so-called 'alphorn-fa', that is, a sharpened 4th degree derived from the natural 11th harmonic of the alphorn. The *Naturjodel* proper, which is confined to the northern side of the Alps, can be classified into individual yodel dialects and yodel regions according to its use of free rhythm; its slow or swift and dance-like tempos; its use of the 'alphorn-fa' mode; and the various different conventions of extemporization. However, these characteristics still await basic study and classification.

A form comprising alternate solo yodelling and singing, known as *Jodellied* or *Gsätzli*, appeared with increasing frequency towards the end of the 19th century. Its development is most closely associated with the work of J. H. Tobler, F. Huber and F. W. Kücken, who accentuated the particularly Swiss element in their choral songs. F. Huber, A. Glutz of Solothurn and J. Lüthy concluded their songs with a yodel-like coda: such songs could be regarded as 'the forerunners of the yodelling songs much-beloved of contemporary folkloristic circles' (Zulauf). Because of the close association of the *Jodellied* with the 'stylised yodel' defined by A. Tobler (a yodelling melody whose vocables are replaced by words), and with the analogous type of ranz des vaches whose melody has also been given words, it is difficult to distinguish these song types in performance.

Under the influence of the Federal Yodel Union, which introduced 'structural rules' (*Rahmengesetze*) and standardized vocalization, the primarily extemporized form of the yodelling song became a kind of male-voice partsong for quartet, quintet or sextet. This kind of song, the 'new yodelling song', is classed as folkloristic music.

3. *The Alpsegen: woodcut by Joseph Balmer from 'Schweizerisches Kunst-Album' (1862)*

The more monotonic ranz des vaches or *Kühreihen* (see ex.2) is usually distinct from yodelling. The earliest recorded use of the German term 'einem den kuoreien pyfen' ('to pipe the *Kühreihen* to one') was in 1531. It is described variously as 'driving-in song', *Chuedreckeler* (milking-song), or *Lockgesang* (calling or coaxing song). It generally uses no falsetto and is further distinguished from the wordless yodel by its pastoral text which expresses affection for the cows. Some instrumental performances of *Kühreihen* have also been noted, played on the alphorn, the bagpipe and even the violin or *Schweizerpfeife* (Swiss fife). It is no longer performed by the peasantry: A. Tobler (*fl c*1903), who described himself as the last singer of the traditional ranz des vaches, suggested that either the texts no longer appeal or the musical demands are too great.

Like the *Viehlöckler* (cattle call) and the ranz des vaches, the *Betruf* (prayer call), also known as *Alpsegen* (Alpine blessing), was once associated with the magical cults of shepherds and cattle drovers (see fig.3). Like the *Juchzer*, the ordinary yodel and the *Lockruf* (call-tune), the *Betruf* has no definite structure, being a type of Sprechgesang whose form depends on the verbal content. The psalm-like prayer requests the protection of the Virgin Mary and the individual patron saints of the stock farmers. To whatever distance the sound carries through the *Folle* (wooden or tin megaphone) the pastures are placed under the care of St Anthony, St George, St Gallus and St Wendelin, and evil is exorcised. The *Betruf* has a wide distribution in Catholic areas and during summer pasturing it is still, to some extent, called every evening in the Obwalden and Uri cantons, in the St Gall highlands, in Goms (Valais) and in Entlebuch.

The songs which still live in oral tradition are mostly associated with customs or religion. In addition to sacred and narrative songs the following, with few exceptions, are of 19th-century origin: Epiphany and Christmas hymns, May songs, songs sung in the spinning-room, children's songs, joking songs, patriotic songs and love-songs. Alongside this folk heritage proper, songs in folk style or composed 'for the folk', known as *Schweizerlieder*, have a wide distribution. Hundreds of them came into circulation with the growth of national and patriotic consciousness after the French Revolution and through the activity of rifle clubs, gymnastic clubs and students' unions (e.g. the Zofinger songbooks). Historical sources suggest that only a few extant melodies predate the 18th century: they include those of a few *Juchzer*, yodels, alpine blessings, incantations, nightwatchmen's songs, children's and cradle songs, religious and historical songs, mercenaries' songs and ballads (such as the *Tannhäuser* ballad).

Instrumental music includes fife and drum marches of the 'old Switzers', French marches and *Landesgemeindemärsche* (in the Graubünden, Obwalden and Valais cantons) and other fife and drum tunes for public processions and ceremonies in the Val d'Anniviers. They nearly all date from the 18th century and are frequently of German, French or English origin. Noise-making customs known as *Lärmbräuche* include *Geisselknallen* (whip-cracking) during the feast of St Nicholas and *Rumpelmetten*, the noisy call to Mass which replaces bell-ringing during Lent. For the latter custom, rattles, including *Schnarren* (large cog rattles), *Klapperbretter* (clap-boards) and *Chlefeli* (a type of castanet) are used. The *Hackbrett* (dulcimer) and the zither are played in

Ex.2 *Ranz des vaches*, transcr. M. Baumann (Baumann, 1976)

Valais, Appenzell, Emmental and Toggenburg. The *Concerti* sounded in churches in the Italian-speaking Ticino canton and carillon playing in French-speaking Valais are two distinctive forms of church bell music.

From the end of the 19th century the mass media and the growing tourist traffic increased the influx of non-Swiss music. To some extent the adoption and adaptation of songs in non-Swiss dialects paralleled the intrusion of dialects from the Lower Rhine, Baden-Württemberg, Alsace and Swabia into the development of the spoken language. After World War II, a reactionary trend towards purism set in and, within the more extreme nationalistic folkloristic circles, support is increasingly voiced for the *Echt-Schweizerische* ('genuine Swiss spirit').

3. FOLKLORISTIC MUSIC. The publication of the *Acht Schweizer-Kühreihen* and the occasion of the Unspunnen festival in 1805 marked the first steps in the development of folkloristic music: such music was conceived as the transformation of the 'primitive' into the aesthetically pleasing, and traditional music was seen as taking on 'a new existence' with this change in its function. The alphorn, previously used for calling or calming cattle, or as a signal of threatening danger and sickness, came to be played as a spectacle for tourists. The Alpine blessing and certain folkdances were given similar treatment. At the Unspunnen festival the victors in the alphorn playing contest were decorated with a 'Spanish ewe and lamb' and given a 'medal with a silken cockade'. Folkloristic performances became more and more commercialized, although socio-economic problems were often the background to such activity, which included,

for instance, horn blowing by beggars. Even so, folk-song and folkdance arrangements, produced for domestic music-making in the alien surroundings of towns, supplanted traditional pastoral music, and the yodel and the ranz des vaches, performed by coloratura sopranos, resounded in concert-halls. It was only a small step from the process of arranging folksong to that of imitating 'original' folklore. F. Huber and G. J. Kuhn had already imitated the ranz des vaches and the yodel in their own folklike compositions. In contrast to the early *Schweizerlieder* with words by Lavater and melodies by Egli (1770), some of these folklike songs promptly became popular. These imitative products were originally supposed to lead the peasantry itself back to making its own local songs (*Dialektlieder*), but the movement took a new direction leading to the growth of musical societies in towns. At the end of the 19th century *Jodlerverbände* evolved from the gymnastic clubs (e.g. the Alte Sektion Zurich) and their singing, for all its urban surroundings, was chiefly in praise of the cowherd and his Alpine dairying life.

In 1912 a Swiss yodel association was officially founded, comprising a number of yodel groups; in 1924 it became the Schweizerischer Jodlerverband and, in 1932, the Eidgenössischer Jodlerverband; in 1975 there were over 15,000 affiliated members and over 600 branches. The repertory promoted by the Schweizerische Gesellschaft volkstümlicher Autoren, Komponisten und Verleger (an association of authors, composers and publishers, founded in 1922) consists of folkloristic compositions whose texts glorify the peasantry in an idealistic and nationalistic manner. Yodel songs such as *Der Chüejerstand*, *Buurebluet*, *D'r Geissbueb*, *Alpaufzug* and many others proclaim as 'echoes of the homeland', in self-glorifying manner, the existence of an alien and completely different type of society in which employees and workers strive after a vanished rural way of life. Efforts are now being made, by extending the subject matter of the texts, to counteract the impression that townspeople sing the praises of a pastoral way of life that they know only from hearsay.

The Schweizerische Trachtenvereinigung (Swiss Folk-costume Society) is the leading society concerned with folk-costume and folkdances. Because they are organized and presented as theatrical spectacles, traditional dances are changing more and more. They include the *Allamanda* (or *Alewander*) from Engadine and Obwalden; the widely distributed polkas, ländler, écossaises and mazurkas; the ritual *Klausjagen* (at the Rigi); certain carnival and masked dances such as the *Röllibutze*, *Nüsslet* and *Vogel Gryff*; and, most commonly, couple-dances (known in central Switzerland as *Gäuerle* and in Appenzell as *Hierig*). Traditional couple-dances have to some extent survived independently of folkloristic activities. Although published collections of Swiss folkdances mostly include more recent dances, older dances such as circle-dances (ribbon dances and wedding dances), *Coraules* (sung dances), the pantomimic dances known as *Picoulet* and *Vögelschottisch* and the couple-dances known as *Matelote* and *La Champérolaine* feature prominently in folk-costume festivals, known as *Trachtenfeste*.

Dance music is provided by small ensembles comprising various combinations of the following: fiddles, clarinets, *Schwäfelpfeiffen* (a type of fipple flute), trumpets and *Schwyzer Orgeli* (accordions); a string bass usually accompanies these instruments. The *Hackbrett* (dulcimer) is still used in the ländler bands in Appenzell, Valais and the highlands of Berne. Less traditional bands include the piano and even the saxophone.

There are numerous organizations, including workers' singing associations and societies for wind music, concerned in different ways with maintaining the tradition of folkloristic music; among the more important ones not already mentioned are the Schweizerische Vereinigung für Volkslied und Hausmusik, the Jodler-Dirigenten-Vereinigung and the Vereinigung Schweizerischer Volkmusikfreunde.

BIBLIOGRAPHY

FasquelleE

GENERAL

K. Geiser: 'Der Knabe der das Alphorn blies', *Berner Taschenbuch*, xlii–xliii (1893–4), 113

K. Nef: *Schriften über Musik und Volksgesang* (Berne, 1908)

P. Geiger: *Volksliedinteresse und Volksliedforschung in der Schweiz vom Anfang des 18. Jahrhunderts bis zum Jahre 1830* (Berne, 1912)

W. Merian: 'Das schweizerische Volkslied in musikalischer Beziehung', *Die Garbe*, ii (1918), no.4, p.116; no.5, p.149; no.6, p.176

O. von Greyerz: *Das Volkslied der deutschen Schweiz* (Frauenfeld and Leipzig, 1927)

P. Budry, ed.: *Die Schweiz, die singt: illustrierte Geschichte des Volksliedes, des Chorgesanges und der Festspiele in der Schweiz* (Erlenbach and Zurich, 1932)

R. Weiss: 'Musik und Gesang', *Volkskunde der Schweiz* (Erlenbach, 1946), 223ff

W. Wiora: *Zur Frühgeschichte der Musik in den Alpenländern* (Basle, 1949)

A. Geering: 'Schweiz', §E, *MGG*

M. Zulauf: *Das Volkslied in der Schweiz im 19. Jahrhundert* (Berne, 1972)

COLLECTIONS

Acht Schweizer-Kühreihen (Berne, 1805, rev. and enlarged, 2/1812 as *Sammlung von Schweizer-Kühreihen und alten Volksliedern*, 4/1826)

S. Wagner: *Sammlung aller Lieder, Gedichte und andern Schriften auf das schweizerische Alphirten-Fest zu Unspunnen im Kanton Bern* (Berne, 1805)

E. L. Rochholz, ed.: *Eidgenössische Lieder-Chronik: Sammlung der ältesten und werthvollsten Schlacht-, Bundes- und Parteilieder* (Berne, 1835, 2/1842)

——: *Alemannisches Kinderlied und Kinderspiel aus der Schweiz* (Leipzig, 1857)

F. J. Schild: *Der Grossätti aus dem Leberberg* (Solothurn, 1863–73)

A. von Flugi: *Die Volkslieder des Engadin* (Strasbourg, 1873)

L. Tobler: *Schweizerische Volkslieder* (Frauenfeld, 1882–4/R1975)

A. Tobler: *Kühreihen oder Kühreigen, Jodel und Jodellied in Appenzell* (Leipzig, 1890)

P. J. Derin: 'Chanzuns popularas engiadinaisas', *Annalas della Societad Rhaeto-Romanscha*, vi (1891), 34–75; vii (1892), 45

A. Rossat: 'Chants patois jurassiens', *Schweizerisches Archiv für Volkskunde*, iii (1899), 257–90; iv (1900), 133–66; v (1901), 81–112, 201; vi (1902), 161, 257; vii (1903), 81, 241

C. Decurtins, ed.: *Rätoromanische Chrestomathie*, ii (Erlangen, 1901), 180–625, 680ff; iii (1902); iv (1911), 264–337, 416ff, 1014ff; ix (1908); x (1916), 1104ff

M. E. Marriage and J. Meier: 'Volkslieder aus dem Kanton Bern', *Schweizerisches Archiv für Volkskunde*, v (1901), 1–47

A. L. Gassmann: *Das Volkslied im Luzerner Wiggertal und Hinterland* (Basle, 1906)

V. Pellandini: 'Canti popolari ticinesi', *Schweizerisches Archiv für Volkskunde*, xii (1908), 36, 268

O. von Greyerz: *Im Röseligarte: schweizerische Volkslieder* (Berne, 1908–25)

S. Grolimund: *Volkslieder aus dem Kanton Solothurn* (Basle, 1910)

——: *Volkslieder aus dem Kanton Aargau* (Basle, 1911)

A. L. Gassmann: *'s Alphorn: 100 echte Volkslieder, Jodel und G'sätzli* (Zurich and Leipzig, 1913)

——: *Juhui! Volksliedbüchlein für die Schweizer Jugend: 60 echte Volkslieder, Jodel und Gsätzli für eine Vor- und Nachstimme* (*Naturbegleitung*) (Zurich, 1914)

K. Aeschbacher: *50 Appenzeller Volkstänze* (Trogen, 1915, 6/1944)

H. In der Gand: *Das Schwyzerfähnli: ernste und heitere Kriegs-, Soldaten- und Volkslieder der Schweiz aus dem 16., 17., 18. und 19. Jahrhundert* (Biel, 1915–17)

A. Rossat: *Les chansons populaires recueillies dans la Suisse romande* (Basle, 1917–31)

A. L. Gassmann: *D'Ländlermusik: 100 Ländler und Buuretänz aus dem Hügelland und den Schweizer Bergen* (Zurich, 1920)

A. Stoecklin: *Weihnachts- und Neujahrslieder aus der Schweiz* (Basle, 1921)

G. Züricher: *Kinderlieder der deutschen Schweiz* (Basle, 1926)

E. Fisch: *22 canti popolari ticinesi* (Zurich, 1927–31)

F. R. Berger: *Das Basler Trommeln: nebst vollständigem Lehrgang und einer Sammlung aller Basler Trommelmärsche* (Basle, 1928)

T. Dolf: 'Las melodias dellas canzuns popularas de Schons', *Annalas de la Società retoromantscha*, xliii (1929), 131

A. Maissen, A. Schorta and W. Wehrli, eds.: *Die Lieder der Consolaziun dell'olma devoziusa*, Rätoromanische Volkslieder, i (Basle, 1945)

G. G. Cloetta: *Chanzunettas popularas rumauntschas* (Basle, 1958)

A. L. Gassmann: *Was unsere Väter sangen: Volkslieder und Volksmusik vom Vierwaldstättersee, aus der Urschweiz und dem Entlebuch* (Basle, 1961)

M. Vernet: *Les carillons du Valais* (Basle, 1965)

Schweizer Liedermacher, i: *Ernst Born, Martin Hauzenberger, Jürg Jegge, Walter Lietha, Fritz Widmer: Portraits und Materialen* (Berne, 1976)

STUDIES

G. Tarenne: *Recherches sur les ranz des vaches, ou sur les chansons pastorales des bergers de la Suisse* (Paris, 1813)

H. Sczadrowsky: 'Nationaler Gesang bei den Alpenbewohnern', *Jb des Schweizer Alpenclub*, i (1864), 504

——: 'Die Musik und die tonerzeugenden Instrumente der Alpenbewohner', *Jb des Schweizer Alpenclub*, iv (1867–8), 275–352

L. Gauchat: *Etude sur le ranz des vaches fribourgeois* (Zurich, 1899)

A. Tobler: *Das Volkslied im Appenzellerlande* (Zurich, 1903)

——: 'Der Volkstanz im Appenzellerlande', *Schweizerisches Archiv für Volkskunde*, viii (1905), 1, 100, 178

A. Rossat: *La chanson populaire dans la Suisse romande* (Basle, 1917)

M. Bukofzer: 'Magie und Technik in der Alpenmusik', *Schweizer Annalen* (1936), 205

H. in der Gand: 'Volkstümliche Musikinstrumente der Schweiz', *Schweizerisches Archiv für Volkskunde*, xxxvi (1937), 73–120

W. Sichardt: *Der alpenländische Jodler und der Ursprung des Jodelns* (Berlin, 1939)

V. Alford: 'Music and Dance of the Swiss Folk', *MQ*, xxvii (1941), 500

H. Spreng: *Die Alphirtenfeste zu Unspunnen 1805 und 1808* (Interlaken, 1946)

L. Witzig: *Dances of Switzerland* (London, 1949)

A. Geering: 'Von der Tessiner Volksmesse', *Schweizerisches Archiv für Volkskunde*, xlvii (1951), 55

J. Burdet: *La danse populaire dans le pays de Vaud sous le régime bernois* (Basle, 1958)

W. Senn: 'Jodeln: ein Beitrag zur Entstehung und Verbreitung des Wortes', *Jb des Österreichischen Volksliedwerkes*, xi (1962), 150

K. Klenk: 'Der Volkstanz in der Schweiz', *Jb herausgegeben von den Sekundarlehrerkonferenzen der Ostschweiz* (1963), 54

M. Vernet: *Cloches et musique* (Neuchâtel, 1963)

G. Duthaler: 'Die Melodien der alten Schweizermärsche', *Schweizerisches Archiv für Volkskunde*, lx (1964), 18

J. Burdet: 'Chansons populaires', *La musique dans le canton de Vaud au XIXe siècle* (Lausanne, 1971), 330–406 [with disc]

M. P. Baumann: *Aus Tradition und Gegenwart der Volksmusik im Oberwallis* (Brig, 1972)

W. Meyer and H. Oesch: 'Maultrommelfunde in der Schweiz', *Festschrift Arnold Geering* (Berne, 1972), 211

A. Schmid and B. Geiser: *Chlefeli: Instrumente zur Fastenzeit* (Schwyz, 1973)

M. P. Baumann: 'Zur Lage der Volksmusikforschung in der Schweiz', *SMz*, xv (1975), 249

H. van der Meer, B. Geiser and K. H. Schickhaus: *Das Hackbrett, ein alpenländisches Musikinstrument* (Herisau and Trogen, 1975)

M. P. Baumann: *Musikfolklore und Musikfolklorismus: eine ethno-musikologische Untersuchung zum Funktionswandel des Jodels* (Winterthur, 1976)

B. Geiser: *Das Alphorn in der Schweiz* (Berne, 1976) [with Fr. and Eng. summary]

M.-J. Glanzmann: *My nächschte Lied: 20 Jahre Schweizer Chanson* (Zurich and Cologne, 1976)

PIERRE MEYLAN (I), MAX PETER BAUMANN (II)

Swybbertszoon, Peter. Netherlands organist, father of JAN PIETERSZOON SWEELINCK.

Swynford (*fl c*1400). English composer. Nothing is known of his life, though the coincidence of names with Catherine Swynford (stepmother to Henry IV and third wife of John of Gaunt) tempts conjecture. His sole surviving composition is a four-part Credo in the Old

Hall MS (no.86), which is one of the more old-fashioned pieces in the MS. The text is telescoped between the top two and the third upper parts, and the tenor is freely isorhythmic. The musical style shows some signs of Italian influence.

For bibliography see OLD HALL MS.

MARGARET BENT

Syberg, Franz (Adolf) (*b* Kerteminde, 5 July 1904; *d* Kerteminde, 11 Dec 1955). Danish composer. He was the son of the painter Fritz Syberg. After studying in Leipzig (1923–8) with Karg-Elert and others, he returned to Copenhagen, studied the organ with Peter Thomsen and took the organists' examination in 1932. The following year he was appointed organist in Kerteminde, where he worked until his death. His sparse output – he ceased composing in the early 1940s – is influenced by Nielsen and the neo-classical trends of the 1930s. Among the orchestral works his Symphony is an exciting and original attempt to continue the symphonic tradition of Nielsen in an orchestral structure tending towards colouristic chamber music.

WORKS
(*selective list*)

Stage: Uffe hin Spage (incidental music to marionette play, S. Clausen), 1929; Leonce og Lena (incidental music, Büchner), 1931; Ett drömspel (prelude, Strindberg), 1941
Orch: Concertino, ob, str, 1932; Sinfonietta, 1934; Adagio, str, 1938; Sym., 1939
Chamber: Str Qt, 1930–31; Qnt, fl, cl, str trio, 1931; Str Trio, 1933; Wind Qnt, 1940
Org music
MSS in *Dk-Kk*

NIELS MARTIN JENSEN

Sychra, Andrey Osipovich. See SIKHRA, ANDREY OSIPOVICH.

Sychra, Antonín (*b* Boskovice, 9 June 1918; *d* Prague, 21 Oct 1969). Czech musicologist and aesthetician. His musicology studies under Helfert at Brno University were interrupted by the closing of the universities under the Nazi occupation, during which he became a member of the underground resistance led by the Communist party. After the liberation he completed his musicology studies in Prague, where he was attracted by Jan Mukařovský's structuralist aesthetics, an analytical method he used in his doctoral dissertation at Prague (1946) on music and word in folksong. Before completing his doctorate he had begun working in the art department of the Education Research Institute in Prague and lecturing at the education faculty. In 1948 he was appointed lecturer at the Prague Academy (AMU), where he later became dean (1950) and professor (1951). He completed his *Habilitation* at Prague University in 1952 with a work on the semiotics of music, becoming lecturer in the aesthetics and history of music. In 1959 he completed his DSc dissertation with a work on the aesthetics of Dvořák's symphonic works; from 1959 to his death he was director of the aesthetics department at Prague University. From 1945 he was one of the most enterprising organizers of Czech musical and musicological life, playing an essential part in its restructuring in accordance with the socialist cultural pattern. His influence was most evident in the Czechoslovak Composers' Union, where he held a number of important posts. He represented Czech musicology and aesthetics at many international organ-izations (e.g. as an IMS committee member, 1961–9).

Sychra's work was marked by his determined efforts at creating a positive Marxist musicology and aesthetics capable of shedding light on basic theoretical questions. His initial apologist stance, in response to the political and cultural demands of the time, alternated with more systematic work, in which he mastered and profitably exploited Soviet work, in particular Asaf'yev's intonation theory, several ideas from Czech structuralism, information theory, cybernetics etc. At the same time he never abandoned his Marxist approach and attempted to keep Marxist aesthetics, and in particular its musicology, an open system, capable of responding creatively to current theoretical and practical trends. He achieved fruitful results particularly in the field of musical semantics, which he elaborated in collaboration with the physiologist Karel Sedláček into a solid basis for experimental research.

WRITINGS

Hudba a slovo v lidové písni [Music and word in folksong] (diss., U. of Prague, 1946; Prague, 1948)
'Realismus Bedřicha Smetany' [Smetana's realism], *HRo*, i (1948), 165
'O novou hudební vědu' [The new musicology], *Musikologie*, ii (Brno, 1949), 72–105
Stranická hudební kritika: spolutvůrce nové hudby [Party music criticism: a co-creator of new music] (Prague, 1951; Ger. trans., 1953)
'Novátorství a tradice' [Avant garde and tradition], *HRo*, v/10 (1952), 7
O hudbu zítřka [The music of tomorrow] (Prague, 1952) [selected essays]
Semiotika hudby [Semiotics of music] (Habilitationsschrift, U. of Prague, 1952)
Estetika Zdeňka Nejedlého [Zdeněk Nejedlý's aesthetic conception] (Prague, 1956)
Leoš Janáček, velký představitel kritického realismu v české hudbě [Janáček, the great representative of critical realism in Czech music] (Prague, 1956)
with O. Chlup: *O estetické výchově* [Aesthetic education] (Prague, 1956)
'W. A. Mozart et la musique populaire tchèque', *Les influences étrangères dans l'oeuvre de Mozart: CNRS Paris 1956*, 189
'Smetanovo pojetí symfonické básně' [Smetana's conception of the symphonic poem], *HRo*, x (1957), 402, 444
'Die Einheit von "absoluter" Musik und Programmusik', *BMw*, i/3 (1959), 2
Estetika Dvořákovy symfonické tvorby [The aesthetics of Dvořák's symphonic works] (diss., U. of Prague, 1959; Prague, 1959; Ger. trans., 1973)
'Leos Janacek: instruction à une analyse de style', *Essais sur la musique à la lumière du marxisme* (Paris, 1959), 58
'Über die Bedeutung von Beethovens Skizzen zur IX. Symphonie', *Internationale Konferenz zum Andenken Joseph Haydns: Budapest 1959*, 147
'Vladimír Helfert a smysl české hudby' [Helfert and the essence of Czech music], *HRo*, xiv (1961), 184
'Melodie jako faktor emocionálního výrazu' [Melody: a factor of emotional expression], *HV 1962*, 55
with K. Sedláček: *Hudba a slovo z experimentálního hlediska* [Music and word – an experimental approach] (Prague, 1962)
'Hudba a kybernetika' [Music and cybernetics], *Nové cesty hudby* (Prague, 1964), 234–68
'Janáčkův spisovatelský sloh – klíč k sémantice jeho hudby' [Janáček's literary style – the key to the semantics of his music], *Estetika*, i (1964), 109
'Musikwissenschaft und neue Methode der wissenschaftlichen Analyse', *Intonation und Gestalt in der Musik*, ed. B. M. Yarustovsky (Moscow, 1965), 10
'Möglichkeiten der Anwendung der Kybernetik und der Informationstheorie in der marxistischen Musikwissenschaft', *BMw*, vii (1965), 402
'Objektivní a subjektivní momenty v hudební analýze' [Objective and subjective moments in musical analysis], *Sborník prací filosofické fakulty brněnské university*, F9 (1965), 309
'Forma e contenuto dal punto di vista della semantica integrata', *Linguaggio e ideologia nel film*, ed. F. Cafieri (Rome, 1968), 171
'Obsah a forma z hlediska integrujících sémantických tendencí' [Message and form seen from the point of semantic integration tendencies], *Estetika*, v (1968), 215
'Specifický problém estetiky ve světle experimentálního výzkumu'

[Specific problems of aesthetics in experimental research], *Estetika*, vi (1969), 2

with K. Sedláček: 'The Method of Psychoacoustic Transformation Applied to the Investigation of Expression in Speech and Music', *Kybernetika*, v (Prague, 1969), 1

'Die Anwendung der Kybernetik und der Informationstheorie in der marxistischen Ästhetik', *BMw*, xii (1970), 83

'K sémantice fugy a polyfonního slohu' [Semantics of the fugue and polyphonic style], *Estetika*, vii (1970), 67

BIBLIOGRAPHY

Obituaries: J. Volek, *Estetika*, vi (1969), 242; J. Jiránek, *HV*, vii (1970), 4; M. Jůzl, *SH*, xiv (1970), 29; K. Knepler, *BMw*, xii (1970), 133

JOSEF BEK

Sychra, Josef Cyril (*b* Ústí nad Orlicí, east Bohemia, 12 March 1859; *d* Stará Boleslav, central Bohemia, 21 Aug 1935). Czech composer, choirmaster and *regens chori*. The son of Václav Sychra, a singer, instrumentalist and *regens chori*, he studied under František Zdeněk Skuherský at the Prague Organ School (1875–8) and at the same time was organist at the monastery of Na Slovanech, also known as Emauzy. Subsequently he worked in Stará Boleslav (1879–89) as organist and later choirmaster, also directing the Václav choir of Stará Boleslav and the Bojan choir of Brandýs nad Labem. He was then *regens chori* in Mladá Boleslav (1889–1923), where he directed the Boleslav choir and founded his own music school. His sons Cyril and Method Lumír were also musicians, the former a writer on music, the latter an organist.

Sychra composed about 450 works, most of which remain unpublished. They consist mainly of church music, but he also wrote songs and choruses for secular performance, these being practically designed for amateur groups. Some of his liturgical music, which was identified with the 'Cyril' movement, was printed by foreign and ecclesiastical publishers. His style was basically eclectic, synthesizing Classical and Romantic features, and yet capturing well the vocal traditions of Czech music before Smetana.

WORKS
(*selective list*)

Masses: Missa in honorem S Josephi (1880); Missa in honorem SS Cyrilli et Methodii (1882); Mše ke cti svatého Václava [Mass in honour of St Václav] (1883); Missa iuventutis studiosae (1899); Missa solemnis (1906); Missa brevissima (1906–7); Missa in honorem S Ludmilae (1911); První česká mše [First Czech mass] (1920)

Other sacred choral works: Na Golgotě, cantata (1912); Svatováclavská kantáta (1929); Requiem, motets, psalms, hymns, etc

Secular choral: Modlitba za vlast [Prayer for the country] ii (1905), iii (1929); Bůd pozdraven [Be welcome] (1919); 2 Double Choruses (1927)

Songs: 5 Songs, A/B, pf (1900); 5 Songs, S/T, pf (1907)

Org: 125 krátkých a snadných předeher [125 short and simple preludes] (1918); Fantasie na husitskou hymnu (1932); contributions to J. Diebold: *Orgelstücke moderner Meister* (Leipzig, 1906–7), O. Gauss: *Orgelkompositionen aus alter und neuer Zeit* (Regensburg, 1910), A. J. Monar: *Laudete eum in chordis et organo* (Paderborn, n.d.) and F. W. Trautner: *Präludienbuch* (Leipzig and Regensburg, n.d.)

Principal publishers: Barvitius, Česká hudba [journal], Coppenrath, Cyril [journal], O. Junne, Mikuláš Knapp (Karlín), V. Kotrba (Prague), L. R. Pazdírek (Olomouc), L. Schwann, F. Urbánek

BIBLIOGRAPHY

-el: 'Josef Cyril Sychra', *Věstník pěvecký a hudební*, xxx (1926), 97

J. Fähnrich: 'K sedmdesátinám J. C. Sychry' [On Sychra's 70th birthday], *Cyril*, lv (1929), 13, 26

——: 'Soupis tvorby J. C. Sychry' [Catalogue of Sychra's works], *Cyril*, lv (1929), 80

J. N. Boháč: 'Mistr Sychra ve svých vzpomínkách' [Master Sychra from his own reminiscences], *Cyril*, lxi (1935), 78, 113

C. Sychra: 'Světské skladby' [Secular works], *Věstník pěvecký a hudební*, xli (1937), 159 [catalogue]

A. Weissenbäck: *Sacra musica* (Klosterneuburg, 1937)

'J. C. Sychra: sbormistr a dirigent' [Sychra: choirmaster and conductor], *Věstník pěvecký a hudební*, lii (1948), 134

'J. C. Sychrova hudba světská' [Sychra's secular music], *Věstník pěvecký a hudební*, lii (1948), 78

OLDŘICH PUKL

Sydeman, William (Jay) (*b* New York, 8 May 1928). American composer. He studied with Travis and Salzer at Mannes College (1946–51, 1953–5, BS 1955), with Franchetti at Hartt College (1956–8, MM 1958) and with Sessions and Petrassi at Tanglewood (1955, 1956); in addition, he was a private pupil of Sessions in 1954–5. From 1958 to 1970 he taught at Mannes College. He has received an award from the National Institute of Arts and Letters as well as other honours and commissions. His compositions are linear, motivic and intricately structured, employing complicated and free rhythms. Most of his music is freely atonal, but he has used tonal and serial techniques, and also aleatory episodes. After 1970 for a while he emphasized theatrical aspects, with his own texts or compilations and such accessories as slides, film, tape, lights and props, but his works after 1974 are more compact and strictly musical.

WORKS
(*selective list*)

Orch: Conc. da camera, va, orch, 1958; Orchestral Abstractions, 1958; Conc. da camera, vn, orch, 1959; Conc. da camera no.2, vn, orch, 1961; Study for Orch no.2, 1963; Oecumenicus, conc. for orch, 1964; Conc. da camera no.3, vn, orch, 1965; Music for Va, Winds and Perc, 1965; Study for Orch no.3, 1965; In memoriam: J. F. Kennedy, narrator, orch, 1966; Conc., pf 4 hands, orch, 1967; Texture Studies, 1969; 5 Movts, wind, 1973

Vocal: Songs, S/T, fl, vc, 1959; Lament of Elektra (Sophocles), A, chorus, chamber orch, 1964; Malediction, T, str qt, tape, 1970; Full Circle, 3 solo vv, cl, trbn, perc, org, vc, 1971

Chamber: 7 Movts, 7 insts, 1958; Wind Qnt no.2, 1959–61; Pf Sonata, 1961; Music for Fl, Va, Gui and Perc, 1962; Homage to 'L'histoire du soldat', cl, bn, tpt, trbn, perc, vn, db, 1962; Qt, fl, cl, pf, vn, 1963; Duo, va, hpd, 1963; Duo, vn, pf, 1963; Fantasy Piece, hpd, 1965; Duo, tpt, perc, 1965; Texture Studies, wind qnt, 1966; Projections no.1, amp vn, tape, slides, 1968; Trio, b cl, bn, pf, 1969; Piece, cl, tape, 1970; Duo, hn, pf, 1971; Duo, perc, 1971; Duo, vn, db, 1972; Trio montagnana, cl, pf, vc, 1972; Duo, 2 cl, 1975; Fugue, str qt/ens, S ad lib, 1975; Music for Solo Xylophone, 1975; Duo, 2 hn, 1976; 18 duos, 2 vn, 1976; The Last Orpheus, b fl/a fl, 1976; Duo, cl, t sax, 1977; Duo, xyl, vib, 1977

Principal publishers: Associated, Ione, Peters, Seesaw

BIBLIOGRAPHY

K. Stone: 'Review of Records', *MQ*, l (1964), 546 [on *Music*, 1962]

N. B. Reich, ed.: *A Catalog of the Works of William Sydeman* (New York, 1968)

NANCY B. REICH

Sydney. Capital of New South Wales, Australia. The first European settlement in Australia was at Sydney Cove in 1788 and the earliest European music to be heard in Australia came from regimental bands which supplied music for battalion marches, church services and balls. The white inhabitants listened in amazement to the music of aboriginal corroborees, but this music was not studied systematically until the 20th century. The early settlers, isolated from their homeland by 19,000 km, turned to their own folksongs, plays and ballad operas as an emotional reminder of their culture. The tradition of looking to western Europe as the main source of musical inspiration persists, although links with Asia have been established. By the 1840s there were choirs in Sydney as well as concert and opera performances, but during the second half of the 19th century musicians were attracted to Melbourne. After a period of comparative inactivity Sydney's musical life revived with the opening of the Conservatorium of

Music (1916) and the establishment of the Australian Broadcasting Commission (ABC, 1932).

In 1916 the State Conservatorium Orchestra was formed and conducted by Henri Verbrugghen (the first concert was in April 1916). In 1918 it was given a government subsidy and entitled the New South Wales State Orchestra (or Symphony Orchestra); the subsidy continued until the end of 1922, when the orchestra was disbanded. For more than a decade Sydney's orchestral life depended on the students' orchestra of the NSW Conservatorium, where such musicians as Alfred Hill, Arundel Orchard and Edgar Bainton maintained the orchestral tradition despite appalling difficulties. This was the situation until 1934 when the existing instrumental ensemble of the ABC was expanded to orchestral proportions. After further expansion in 1936 the title ABC Sydney Orchestra was used for broadcasting purposes and Sydney Symphony Orchestra for subscription and schools concerts. The latter name became permanent only in 1946. Subscription concerts, introduced in 1936, remain the chief means of concert promotion. Sir Eugene Goossens, resident conductor for ten years, gave the orchestra international status. Resident conductors have included Joseph Post, Nikolay Malko, Dean Dixon, Moshe Atzmon and Willem van Otterloo. The orchestra has an annual schedule of over 160 concerts in Sydney and country areas and a subscription list of about 20,000, including subscribers to three series of youth concerts. Musica Viva Australia, founded by Richard Goldner in 1945, is based in Sydney and is the largest chamber music society in the world. It promotes tours to city and country areas by leading Australian and foreign groups and presents regular subscription concerts.

Older institutions, such as the City of Sydney Eisteddfod, suburban musical societies and choirs, exist alongside newer interests, such as the Renaissance Players (director Winsome Evans). The training orchestra run by the ABC (conductor Robert Miller) gives basic orchestral training to young instrumentalists. Organ music is currently receiving increased attention, with a revival in classical organ building both for school chapels and churches and the construction of organs for Sydney University, the Conservatorium and the opera house. The many chamber groups include the Austral Quartet (formed in 1958 by leading members of the Sydney SO), which promoted the performance of Australian chamber music, the Australian Chamber Orchestra and the Sydney String Quartet. The Sydney branch of the ISCM, founded by Professor Donald Peart in 1956, also presents concerts.

Australian Opera, a national touring company formed in 1956 by the Elizabethan Theatre Trust, spends part of the year in Sydney. The permanent company is Australian, with guest artists each season from abroad. Before 1967 it and the Australian Ballet relied on the permanent ABC orchestras, but the difficulties of schedule arising from this arrangement led to the formation of the Elizabethan Trust Sydney Orchestra (1967) and the Elizabethan Trust Melbourne Orchestra (1969).

Until the 1970s many Australian singers have pursued opportunities abroad, but the rapidly increasing interest in opera in Australia may ameliorate this. Singers born in Sydney include Yvonne Minton, Joan Sutherland (trained at the New South Wales Conservatorium) and Marilyn Richardson.

The Sydney Opera House, completed in 1973, juts into the waters of Sydney Harbour (see fig.1). It contains a concert hall (capacity 2700; fig.2), the opera theatre (capacity 1500), a drama theatre (capacity 550), a chamber-music–cinema room (capacity 420) and several rehearsal rooms. The building is used mainly by the two national touring companies, Australian Opera and Australian Ballet, the Musica Viva Australia chamber music society and the Australian National Film Theatre; the ABC uses it for subscription concerts,

1. The Sydney Opera House

2. Interior of the Sydney Opera House concert hall

youth concerts and recital series. A five-manual organ with 10,000 pipes and 128 stops was planned.

Small-scale opera productions are given in Sydney by several groups, including the Sydney Opera Company, the Conservatorium Opera School and the music departments of Sydney University and the University of New South Wales.

The founding of the New South Wales State Conservatorium of Music in 1915 gave new impetus to Sydney's musical development. Successive directors did much for music in the community as well as for musical education: Henri Verbrugghen (1916–22) organized orchestral, chamber and choral music, and Sir Eugene Goossens (1947–56) instigated the concept of the Sydney Opera House. Alfred Hill was an influential professor of harmony and composition from 1916 to 1934. Other directors have included Sir Bernard Heinze, Joseph Post and Rex Hobcroft. The Conservatorium's diploma course concentrates mainly on performance, while the department of music at Sydney University, founded in 1948 with Donald Peart as professor (succeeded by Peter Platt in 1975), provides degree courses and places more emphasis on research and composition. Peter Sculthorpe instigated studies in Asian music. A music department was established at the University of New South Wales in 1966 under Roger Covell.

The Music Board (established in 1973) of the Australia Council (formerly the Australian Council for the Arts, formed in 1967–8 with H. C. Coombs as chairman) assists opera, music groups and special pro-jects. The Arts Council of Australia, formed as a private body in Sydney in 1944 by Dorothy Helmrich and now with branches in all states, receives government grants and is concerned with all aspects of the performing arts and in particular promotes music in country districts. The Australian Elizabethan Theatre Trust, founded in 1954, was responsible for the formation of the Australian Opera, Australian Ballet, Australian Ballet School and several theatre companies; it organizes tours of opera, dance and drama companies throughout the country. The Australasian Performing Right Association is based in Sydney. The Australia Music Centre (national director James Murdoch), established in 1974, opened in 1976 as a music information centre and national resource centre for the promotion of Australian music.

BIBLIOGRAPHY

J. Fowles: *Sydney in 1848* (Sydney, 1848)
C. Bertie: *The Story of the Royal Hotel and the Theatre Royal* (Sydney, 1927)
A. Orchard: *The Distant View* (Sydney, 1943) [mainly about the founding of the Sydney Conservatorium of Music]
I. Brodsky: *Sydney Takes the Stage* (Sydney, 1963)

For further bibliography *see* AUSTRALIA, §I.

ANN CARR-BOYD

Sydney Wind Soloists. Australian chamber ensemble. The members are Donald Westlake and Kevin Murphy (clarinets), John Cran and John Noble (bassoons) and Clarence Mellor and Antony Buddle (horns); Neville Amadio (flute) and Guy Henderson and Graham

Powning (oboes) frequently appear with them. Formed in the mid-1970s, the Sydney Wind Soloists developed from the New Sydney Woodwind Quintet (formed in 1965) whose members were Amadio, Henderson, Westlake, Crann and Mellor, all leading players of the Sydney SO; they established a reputation as an ensemble of superlative standard through recordings and many tours. In 1969 they represented Australia at the opening of the Cultural Centre in Manila, and further tours in 1971 and 1973 included the Philippines, South Korea, Japan, Thailand and India. The quintet recorded music by Poulenc, Nielsen, Dreyfus, Sculthorpe, Butterley and English. The Sydney Wind Soloists specialize in 18th-century music, much of it previously unknown.

ANN CARR-BOYD

Syfert, Paul. *See* SIEFERT, PAUL.

Sygar, John (*fl c*1500–14). English composer. A four-part setting of the *Magnificat* attributed simply to 'Sygar' survives incomplete in the Eton Choirbook (incipit in MB, xii, no.64); another setting, listed in the index to the choirbook, is lost. A probable identification is with John Sygar, chaplain of the choir of King's College, Cambridge, from 1499 to 1501 and again from 1508 to 1514, who was frequently employed in copying polyphonic music for use in the college chapel.

ROGER BOWERS

Sygietyński, Antoni (*b* Gosławice, 5 March 1850; *d* Warsaw, 14 June 1923). Polish writer and critic of literature, art and music. In 1874 he completed his studies at the Warsaw Institute of Music, where he learnt the piano with R. Strobel, harmony with Moniuszko and counterpoint with Żeleński; he continued his studies at the Leipzig Conservatory with Jadassohn and Reinecke. In Paris from 1878 to 1882 he attended lectures by Hippolyte Taine on aesthetics, and by Charles Blanc on art history. He won fame for his study of the contemporary French novel (*Ateneum*, 1881–3), and for a series of articles on literature and the arts (*Wędrowiec*, 1884–7). He also devoted himself to teaching music, conducting a piano class at the Warsaw Institute of Music (1882–1910). From 1896 to 1909 he contributed regular music criticism to the *Kurier Warszawski*, *Gazeta Polska*, *Goniec Wieczorny* and other journals. Sygietyński's son, Tadeusz (1896–1955), was a composer and the founder of the well-known folk-singing and -dancing choir Mazowsze.

BIBLIOGRAPHY
S. Jarociński: *Antologia polskiej krytyki muzycznej* (Kraków, 1955), 238–90

STEFAN JAROCIŃSKI

Syllabic style. In plainsong, the setting of text mainly with one note per syllable, whether as a recitation tone or a fully developed melody (e.g. of the Credo of the Mass). It is contrasted with neumatic or group style (mainly two to four notes per syllable) and melismatic style (characterized by florid groups of notes, each sung to one syllable).

Sylva, Andreas de. *See* DE SILVA, ANDREAS.

Sylva, Tristam de. *See* SILVA, TRISTÃO DA.

Sylvestris, Floridus de. *See* SILVESTRI, FLORIDO DE.

Symeon of Thessaloniki (*fl* early 15th century). Archbishop of Thessaloniki and author of a treatise describing the contemporary Office of HESPERINOS.

Symon. *See* SIMON.

Symon [Simon], P. (*fl* 1546–51). French composer. He might have been Pellegryne Symon whose name appears in the records of the English Chapel Royal as a trombone player in 1526, 1538 and 1547. This is only a slight possibility, however, for Symon's first printed chansons came out in Paris as late as 1546.

25 chansons attributed to Symon survive in chansonniers printed by Attaingnant and Du Chemin between 1549 and 1551. Of these, more than half are settings of texts especially popular in the middle of the 16th century, having also been set around that time by Certon, Du Tertre, Gervaise, Goudimel and Janequin, among others. Symon's settings are not as a rule related musically to these other settings, but in most instances his was the first in print. So his chansons may have been well known, during the short period when they flourished since they seem to have provided texts for composers of far greater reputation than Symon himself.

Symon's chansons are short homophonic pieces that demonstrate good part-writing and a clear sense of harmonic consciousness. His melodies rely heavily on the clichés of the Parisian chanson, and reflect the da capo form, internal repetition, ternary interpolations and frequent cadences: all characteristic of that genre.

WORKS

25 chansons: 2 in 1546[14], 1 in 1547[8], 1 in 1547[10], 2 in 1547[12], 1 in 1548[4], 2 in 1549[19], 1 in 1549[20], 1 in 1549[21], 3 in 1549[22], 4 in 1549[23], 1 in 1549[24], 4 in 1550[5], 1 in 1550[11], 1 in 1551[9]; 1 ed. in PÄMw, xxiii (1899), 114

BIBLIOGRAPHY
W. Nagel, ed.: 'Annalen der englischen Hofmusik von der Zeit Heinrichs VIII. bis zum Tode Karls I. (1509–1649)', suppl. to *MMg*, xxvi (1894)

LAWRENCE F. BERNSTEIN

Symon Britonis. *See* SIMON, §(2).

Symon de Insula. *See* SIMON, §(3).

Symon de Sacaglia, Magister (*fl* early or mid-13th century). Composer or scribe, working probably in Paris between the time of Robertus de Sabilone and that of Franco. He is mentioned only by the theorist Anonymous IV (ed. Reckow, 1967, i, 50) writing about 1275.

See ORGANUM AND DISCANT: BIBLIOGRAPHY.

IAN D. BENT

Symon le Breton. *See* SIMON, §(1).

Sympathetic strings (Fr. *cordes sympathiques*; Ger. *Resonanzsaiten*; It. *corde di resonanza*). In string instruments, strings that are not played (i.e. not bowed or plucked) but nevertheless sound 'in sympathy' with the same note (or one of its partials) emanating from another sounding string, generally one activated by bowing. Consequently, sympathetic strings are generally, although not always, tuned in unison with the bowed strings, and they are used in varying numbers on such instruments as the viola d'amore, baryton, Hardanger fiddle and trumpet marine. A typically strung, large 18th-century viola d'amore, for instance, has six or seven bowed strings and, in addition, six or more (up to

14) 'sympathetic' wire or brass strings, strung from the tuning-pegs and thence underneath the fingerboard and running through holes in the middle of the bridge to pins securing the strings at the tailpiece. These last-mentioned strings are not bowed but vibrate sympathetically in unison with the fundamental or partial of the bowed strings, creating a silvery resonance. Sympathetic strings are sometimes added to the highest register of the piano, and are called 'ALIQUOT strings'. Introduced originally (1873) into the upper registers of Blüthner pianos, they give an added resonance.

DAVID D. BOYDEN

Symphonia. (1) In late Greek and medieval theory, consonance, as opposed to *diaphonia* or dissonance; see G. Reese: *Music in the Middle Ages* (New York, 1940), p.250. The word *symphonos* also sometimes meant a unison as distinct from *antiphonos*, an octave, and *paraphonos*, a 4th or 5th; see O. Kinkeldey: 'The Term "Paraphonista" and Its Meaning', *JAMS*, iii (1950), p.158.

(2) In the Middle Ages and later, the word was used to describe various instruments, and especially those capable of playing more than one note simultaneously. 'Symphonia' in the Book of Daniel is sometimes translated as bagpipe; and one Italian word for bagpipe, *zampogna*, does in fact seem to be a corruption of *symphonia*. To ISIDORE OF SEVILLE (*d* 636) it was a drum. In France from the 12th century onwards, *symphonia* (or *symphonie*, *sinfonie*, *chifonie* and so on) meant organistrum or HURDY-GURDY. And Praetorius (1619) called all string keyboard instruments 'symphony' (for example, spinet, virginal and harpsichord or *clavicymbel*).

(3) A word used in the 17th century (along with the more common SINFONIA) to denote an orchestral piece, usually an introduction to an opera, a suite or a cantata. For further information *see* SYMPHONY.

BIBLIOGRAPHY
H. J. Marx: 'Zur Bedeutung des Begriffs "Symphonia" im Mittelalter', *IMSCR*, xi *Copenhagen 1972*, 541

HOWARD MAYER BROWN

Symphonic jazz. A term coined in the 1920s primarily to promote Paul Whiteman's attempts to fuse the jazz idiom with simplified classical forms. The idea seems to have originated with George Gershwin's one-act opera *Blue Monday* (1922), but it was Gershwin's next extended work, *Rhapsody in Blue*, commissioned and given its première by Whiteman in 1924, that remains the most famous example of the trend. Whiteman's later efforts include a number of extended pieces such as Ferde Grofé's influential *Metropolis* (1928), which in England stimulated Spike Hughes's two-movement *Harlem Symphony* (1932), Federico Elizalde's four-part *Heart of a Nigger* (1933), Reginald Forsythe's *Southern Holiday* (1935) and other extended works for large jazz ensemble. Though excessively praised at the time, Whiteman's ambitious efforts at symphonic jazz did at least help to establish jazz as music for listening to as well as dancing to, and he even extended jazz orchestral techniques; Whiteman's *Sweet Sue* (1928), for example, obviously influenced Ellington's *Mystery Song* (1931). Symphonic jazz prompted similar large-scale ventures by Ellington, such as the four-part *Reminiscing in Tempo* (1935) and the unrecorded *Blue Belles of Harlem* (1942, commissioned by Whiteman) which placed a similar emphasis on written composition rather than improvisation.

BIBLIOGRAPHY
P. Whiteman and M. McBride: *Jazz* (New York, 1926)
P. Tanner: 'Federico Elizalde', *Jazz Monthly*, xvi (1971), Jan, 26
——: 'Spike Hughes', *Jazz Monthly*, xvii (1971), June–July, 8; July–Aug, 13
M. Harrison: *A Jazz Retrospect* (Newton Abbot, 1976), 234ff

MAX HARRISON

Symphonic poem (Ger. *Symphonische Dichtung*; Fr. *Poème symphonique*). An orchestral form in which a poem or programme provides a narrative or illustrative basis.

1. Introduction. 2. Origins. 3. Liszt. 4. The Czech lands. 5. Russia. 6. France. 7. Germany. 8. Other countries. 9. Conclusion.

1. INTRODUCTION. The form flourished in the second half of the 19th century and in the early part of the 20th and was generally in one movement; 'poematic symphony' is a name sometimes given to the kindred form in more than one movement. Although some piano and chamber works are effectively symphonic poems, the form is almost exclusively orchestral. Though related to opera and sung music in its aesthetic outlook, it is distinct from them in its exclusion of a sung text. In many ways it represents the most sophisticated development of instrumental programme music in the history of music. Like a number of other ephemeral forms, such as the madrigal and the concerto grosso, it had a relatively short life, lasting from its origins in the late 1840s until its rapid decline in the 1920s: it enjoyed the extreme favour of fashion and suffered consequent severe eclipse. It is thus typical of its period in a way that opera and symphony, for example, cannot claim to be, and it satisfied three of the principal aspirations of the 19th century: to relate music to the world outside, to integrate multi-movement forms (often by welding them into a single movement) and to elevate instrumental programme music to a level higher than that of opera, the genre previously regarded as the highest mode of musical expression. By fulfilling such needs it played a major role in the advanced music of its time, and was a vehicle for some of the most important works of the period.

2. ORIGINS. Programme music in the 19th century took a decisive step forward with such works as Beethoven's Pastoral Symphony and Berlioz's *Symphonie fantastique*, and most subsequent 'poematic' symphonies derive to some extent from these two works. The origins of the symphonic poem, however, can be seen more clearly in Beethoven's overtures, which display a concentration and expressive power characteristic of many later single-movement works. The *Egmont* and *Coriolan* overtures, for example, and the third *Leonore* overture, with its explicit enactment of dramatic events, show an independence of their theatrical origins which was to lead within a few years to the designation OVERTURE for purely concert works such as Beethoven's own *Namensfeier* (1814–15) and *Die Weihe des Hauses* (1822) and for more dramatic pieces such as Berlioz's *Waverley*, *Rob Roy* and *Roi Lear* overtures (1827–31). Though none of these three portrays an explicit sequence of action, all are related to their literary sources. Mendelssohn's *A Midsummer Night's Dream* overture (1826) is more strictly programmatic, with clear references to characters and incidents in the play, and his overtures *Die schöne Melusine*, *Meeresstille und*

glückliche Fahrt and *Hebrides*, of a few years later, are direct prototypes of the Lisztian symphonic poem; indeed in 1884 Hans von Bülow described them as attaining the perfect ideal of the symphonic poem. Schumann's overture to *Manfred* (1848–9) and his three concert overtures of 1851, *Julius Cäsar, Die Braut von Messina* and *Hermann und Dorothea*, may also be seen as encapsulating a literary source within a single orchestral movement on lines followed shortly afterwards in innumerable symphonic poems. The closest Berlioz came to the narrative symphonic poem was in the 'Chasse royale et orage' in Act 4 of *Les troyens* (1857), even though it calls for stage representation and has a part for chorus. Wagner's *Eine Faust Ouvertüre* (1840, revised 1855) had an important formative influence on Liszt and indicates how closely Wagner's imaginative world might have approached the symphonic poem had he not devoted himself so single-mindedly to music drama.

3. LISZT. Liszt foreshadowed his own adoption of the symphonic poem in a number of piano works, especially in the *Album d'un voyageur* (1835–6), later published as *Années de pèlerinage*. *Chapelle de Guillaume Tell*, for example, is a portrait of the Swiss national hero, and both *Au Lac de Wallenstadt* and *Vallée d'Obermann* bear literary quotations in the manner of the later orchestral pieces. *Après une lecture de Dante*, in the second book, is an extended paraphrase of a poem by Victor Hugo. Liszt's preference for one-movement form was already evident by the time he made his first ventures into orchestral music along similar lines, and his invention of the term 'symphonische Dichtung' indicates his desire for the form to display the traditional logic of symphonic thought, even in one movement. Although his period at Weimar from 1848 to 1861 saw the composition of the *Faust* and *Dante* symphonies (1854–7), the B minor Piano Sonata (1852–3) and many other works, it is the series of 12 symphonic poems that most clearly represents his style and outlook in this period and most vividly illustrates his far-reaching ambitions as a composer.

Liszt had an idealized view of the symphonic poem to which few of his followers aspired. He refrained on the whole from narrative and literal description, and though the meaning of individual passages is usually plain his imagination was more poetic than visual. He only rarely achieved in his symphonic poems the directness and subtle timing that narrative requires. *Mazeppa* (1851), one of the most descriptive of them even though it is an expanded version of one of the *Etudes d'exécution transcendante* (1838), illustrates Hugo's poem about the wild horse that carries the banished Mazeppa tied to its mane, until he is rescued by the Ukrainians and enthroned as their chieftain. *Les préludes* (1848) was not given its title, after Lamartine's poem, until after it had been composed. The first and longest, *Ce qu'on entend sur la montagne* (1848–9), named after a poem by Hugo, takes as its basic idea the contrast between the voice of Nature and that of Man and describes at the beginning the immense, confused sound out of which the voice of Nature is born. *Die Ideale* (1857) is based on Schiller's poem of that name, from which quotations are printed in the score at appropriate moments. *Hunnenschlacht* (1857) is vividly descriptive of the battle between Huns and Christians in 451, the victory of the Christians being symbolized by the appearance of the hymn *Crux*

fidelis. This work, like the later *Von der Wiege bis zum Grabe* (1881–2), was inspired by a painting. *Héroïde funèbre* (1849–50) and *Festklänge* (1853) are occasional pieces, the one mournful, the other festive, neither with programmes. *Hamlet* (1858), one of the best of the series, includes a passage descriptive of Ophelia but is otherwise a general evocation of Hamlet's character. *Prometheus* (1850) and *Orpheus* (1853–4), which are also among the best of these works, are musical elaborations of poetic themes. In *Orpheus* the theme is the uplifting power of art, in *Prometheus* the suffering of creative genius. Both of these works, and *Tasso* (1849) too, can be seen as reflections of Liszt's own problems as an artist and his search for expressive truth.

Liszt's *Faust Symphony* and *Dante Symphony* adopt the same aesthetic stance as his symphonic poems, even though they are divided into separate movements and call upon a chorus. *Two Episodes from Lenau's Faust* of about 1860 should also be considered with the symphonic poems. The first, 'Der nächtliche Zug', is closely descriptive of Faust as he watches a passing procession of pilgrims by night, and the second, 'Der Tanz in der Dorfschenke' (also known as the 'First Mephisto Waltz'), tells of Mephistopheles seizing a violin at a village dance. Narrative pieces such as these dictated their own forms, but the problem of organizing longer and more allusive pieces was considerable. Liszt relied on a loose episodic form in which sections follow one another without overriding musical logic, and he used motifs and their transformations in a manner akin to that of Wagner. Many of his dramatic gestures in the symphonic poems – for example the short drooping phrase with isolated chords that stress the angularity and expressiveness of the melodic line – are to be found both in Wagner and in the large corpus of music prompted by the example of Liszt himself. A forceful theme stated in the bass instruments unaccompanied is also a common mannerism, looking back to Berlioz's *Roi Lear* and beyond that to the opening of the finale of Beethoven's Ninth Symphony. Unequal in scope and achievement though Liszt's symphonic poems are, they looked forward at times to more modern developments and sowed the seeds of a rich crop of music in the two succeeding generations.

4. THE CZECH LANDS. Liszt's successors in the cultivation of the symphonic poem were more conspicuous outside Germany – in Bohemia and Russia on the one hand and in France on the other – than in Germany itself. These were the nations that took the symphonic poem most assiduously to heart, with the added potential, in the former case, of using it as a vehicle for the nationalist ideas that were then beginning to burgeon. Smetana visited Weimar in 1857, was befriended by Liszt and immediately embarked on a group of symphonic poems on literary subjects, *Richard III* (1857–8), *Wallensteins Lager* (1858–9) and *Hakon Jarl* (1860–61), after Shakespeare, Schiller and Öhlenschläger respectively. They clearly illustrate both his admiration for Liszt's music and a straightforward approach to musical description. A piano work of the same period, *Macbeth a čarodějnice* ('Macbeth and the witches', 1859), is similar in scope and bolder in style. Smetana's greatest achievement in this genre is his set of six symphonic poems under the general title *Má vlast* ('My Country'), composed between 1872 and 1879; in thus

expanding the form he created one of the monuments of Czech music. The cycle presents selected episodes and ideas from Czech history and embodies his personal belief in the greatness of the nation, which he also expressed in his opera *Libuše*. Two recurrent themes are used to unify the cycle, one representative of Vyšehrad, the fortress overlooking the River Vltava (whose course provides the material of the second work in the cycle), the other an ancient Czech hymn, *Kdož jste Boží bojovníci* ('Ye who are God's warriors'), which unites the last two of the cycle's poems, *Tábor* and *Blaník*. *Šárka*, relating a bloodthirsty episode from Czech legend, is the most narrative, *Z českých luhů a hájů* ('From Bohemia's Woods and Fields') the most lyrical. The whole cycle is a masterly application of new forms to new purposes and was succeeded by a profusion of symphonic poems from his younger compatriots in the Czech lands and Slovakia: Dvořák, Fibich, Janáček, Foerster, Novák, Suk and Ostrčil.

Dvořák's principal symphonic poems, dating from the 1890s, fall into two groups, the first of which forms a cycle after Smetana's example, with a single theme running through the three constituent pieces. Originally conceived as a trilogy, entitled *Příroda, Život a Láska* ('Nature, Life and Love'), they finally appeared as three separate overtures, *V Přírodě* ('In Nature's Realm'), *Carnaval* and *Othello*. The last has notes in the score to indicate incidents in the play, but the sequence and characters are scarcely Shakespeare's. Of the five works comprising the second group, four – *Vodník* ('The Water Goblin'), *Polednice* ('The Noon Witch'), *Zlatý kolovrat* ('The Golden Spinning Wheel') and *Holoubek* ('The Wild Dove') – are based on poems by K. J. Erben's *Bouquet of Folk Tales*. Dvořák intended incidents and characters to be clearly represented; indeed he arrived at some of the themes by setting actual lines of the poetry to music. By symphonic standards these works may seem diffuse, but their literary sources define the sequence of events and the course of the musical action. *Píseň bohatýrská* ('Heroic Song') is the only one of the group not to have a detailed programme.

Zdeněk Fibich and Vitězslav Novák were prolific composers of programme works of many kinds. Both, for example, wrote symphonic poems on the Czech tale *Toman a lesní panna* ('Toman and the Wood Nymph'), and Fibich's *Othello* preceded Dvořák's by 20 years. Suk's *Prague* (1905) opened a series of works by him of increasing abstraction and personal significance. *Asrael* and *Pohádka léta* ('Summer Tale') are descriptive symphonies in separate movements; *Zrání*, completed in 1919, is an elaborate picture of the harvest as a projection of human life, written in a complex, advanced idiom, and *Epilogue*, although entitled 'symphonic poem', is a choral work, once again of great personal significance. Janáček's symphonic poems belong to his late creative flowering. His subject matter is more traditional than that of Suk, but the musical style is more individual. In *Šumařovo dítě* ('The Fiddler's Child', 1912) he used individual instruments, violin and oboe, to depict the fiddler and his child in straightforward narrative, in *Taras Bulba* (1915–18) he turned Gogol's poem into an expression of Czech heroism in full orchestral dress, and in *Balada blanická* ('The Ballad of Blaník', 1920) he returned to one of Smetana's subjects; he planned *Dunaj* ('The Danube') in four parts but did not complete it. Despite his attachment to the

form it is hard not to see these works as overshadowed by the Sinfonietta and the operas of the same period.

5. RUSSIA. The cultivation of the symphonic poem in Russia reflected that country's admiration for Liszt and a devotion to national subjects very similar to that found among Czech composers. 'Virtually all Russian symphonic music is programmatic', wrote V. V. Stasov, and the Russians' great love of story-telling found wide expression in the symphonic poem. They regarded Glinka's *Kamarinskaya* (1848) as a prototype of descriptive orchestral music, despite his denial that it bore a programme; his *Taras Bulba*, had he completed it, would have been nearer to the spirit of the descriptive symphony and the symphonic poem, both of which Stasov and Balakirev embraced with ardour. Of Balakirev's three symphonic poems the most successful is undoubtedly *Tamara* (1867–82), closely based on a poem by Lermontov; it is full of atmosphere, well-paced and richly evocative of the fairy-tale orient. *In Bohemia* ('Overture on Czech themes', 1867, 1905) and *Russia* ('Second overture on Russian themes', 1884 version) are looser gatherings of national melodies without narrative content. Musorgsky's *St John's Night on the Bare Mountain* (1867) and Borodin's *In the Steppes of Central Asia* (1880) are powerful orchestral pictures, each unique in its composer's output. Rimsky-Korsakov, perhaps surprisingly, wrote only two works that can be classed as symphonic poems, *Sadko* (1867–92, later reworked into the opera of the same name) and *Skazka* ('Legend', 1879–80), originally entitled *Baba-Yaga*; *Antar* and *Sheherazade* are both entitled 'symphonic suite' and are akin to these two works in conception. Baba-Yaga, the witch of Russian folklore, also provided material for symphonic poems by Dargomïzhsky and Lyadov. The latter's *Kikimora* and *The Enchanted Lake* again show a deep feeling for national subjects, as does Glazunov's *Stenka Razin*.

Tchaikovsky, as in much else, stands a little apart from his compatriots. None of his symphonic poems has a Russian subject (*The Voyevoda* is on a Polish original). *Romeo and Juliet* (1869; rev. 1880) is entitled 'overture-fantasy' and *Francesca da Rimini* (1876) 'fantasia', but both are in fact highly developed symphonic poems in which the exigencies of musical form and of literary material are held in masterly balance. These are deservedly pillars of the orchestral repertory, and *Hamlet* (1888), though less well known, is scarcely less powerful. Tchaikovsky's attitude to programmes was equivocal, but at least in these symphonic poems he had no doubts about the propriety of clothing literary material with music. In treating Byron's *Manfred* (1885) in four movements as a symphony he looked back more to Berlioz than to Liszt.

Of later Russian symphonic poems it must suffice to indicate Rakhmaninov's evident debt to Tchaikovsky in *The Rock* and the masterly independence of *The Isle of the Dead* (1909), inspired by Böcklin's famous painting. Stravinsky's debt is rather to his teacher Rimsky-Korsakov in his symphonic poem *The Song of the Nightingale*, which he deftly extracted from his opera *The Nightingale*. Skryabin's *Poem of Ecstasy* (1905–8) and *Prometheus* (1908–10) are the twin peaks of his orchestral output, remarkable in detail, in their advanced harmonic idiom and in their projection of an egocentric theosophic world unparalleled elsewhere in the symphonic poem. Since realism is applauded in

Soviet aesthetics, programme music has survived in favour there longer than in the West, as Shostakovich's symphonic poem *October* (1967) shows.

6. FRANCE. A tradition of illustrative music existed in France, especially in the music of Berlioz and Félicien David, before Liszt's ideas were taken up there, and César Franck had written an orchestral piece on Hugo's poem *Ce qu'on entend sur la montagne* before Liszt himself used it for his own first symphonic poem in 1848–9. The symphonic poem came to life in the 1870s, supported by the newly founded Société Nationale and its promotion of younger French composers. In the year after its foundation, 1872, Saint-Saëns composed his *Le rouet d'Omphale*, which he soon followed up with three other symphonic poems, the best known of which is the *Danse macabre* (1874) and the most ambitious – and the closest to Liszt in style – *La jeunesse d'Hercule* (1877). Niecks justly called Saint-Saëns' symphonic poems 'illustrations, not translations', for they attempt no deep penetration of their subjects. Saint-Saëns was followed by d'Indy, whose trilogy *Wallenstein* (1873, 1879–81), called 'three symphonic overtures', may be compared with Smetana's *Má vlast*. Significantly he began it in the year, 1873, in which he visited Liszt. Duparc's remarkable *Lénore* (1875) introduced the warmth of Wagnerian harmony into French music, and it is here allied to a bold musical imagination. Franck returned to the symphonic poem in 1876 with the delicately evocative *Les Eolides*, and he followed it in 1882 with the step-by-step narrative of *Le chasseur maudit*, based like *Lénore* on a ballad by G. A. Bürger peculiarly well suited to musical illustration. His *Les Djinns* (1884), on a poem by Hugo, uses a piano soloist in a manner similar to that found in Liszt's *Totentanz* and *Malédiction*, and the second part of *Psyché* (1887–8) includes a three-part chorus; he also applied the term 'symphonic poem' to his choral work *Rédemption*. The lesser composers of Franck's circle found the symphonic poem much to their liking, and they often displayed a penchant for mythological subject matter in deference to Wagner. Chausson's *Viviane* (1882) is a good example, and among the others are the numerous symphonic poems of Augusta Holmès, several of which, for example *Irlande* (1882) and *Pologne* (1883), have national themes.

Three works hold a special place in French music in this genre. Debussy originally intended his *Prélude à l'après-midi d'un faune* (1892–4), drawn from Mallarmé's poem, as a triptych. In his own words the music is 'a very free illustration . . . a succession of settings through which the Faun's desires and dreams move in the afternoon heat'. It is explicitly decorative, not narrative, and the originality of its idiom, its tonal ambiguity and the delicate, fragmented orchestral style look forward to a new world of musical expression. By contrast Dukas' *L'apprenti-sorcier* (1897) is a brilliantly executed example of the narrative type of symphonic poem, with distinctive musical material and an assured orchestral style. Third, Ravel's ballet *La valse* (1921) is parody of the highest order, a portrait of Vienna in an idiom no Viennese would recognize as his own.

Two French composers carried the symphonic poem well into the 20th century. Roussel's first major orchestral work was a symphonic poem on Tolstoy's novel *Resurrection* (1903), and he soon followed it with *Le poème de la forêt* (1904–6), which is in four cyclically related movements. *Pour une fête de printemps* (1920), originally conceived as the scherzo of his Second Symphony, is an unusually reflective celebration of spring. Koechlin wrote several symphonic poems, extending in time from *En mer, la nuit* in 1899 to as late as the 1940s. *La cité nouvelle* (1938) is called a 'dream of the future'; *Le buisson ardent* (1945) is related to Romain Rolland's novel *Jean-Christophe*. There is a group of three symphonic poems, *Le livre de la jungle*, after Kipling; the third of them, *Les bandar-log* (1939), is a satirical sketch of musical styles in the present century and is probably Koechlin's most familiar work.

7. GERMANY. Although Liszt, working in Germany, and Strauss represent respectively the inception and the culmination of the symphonic poem, the form was cultivated less enthusiastically in Germany than in other countries. The reason for this lies in the domination of German music at this period by Wagner and Brahms, neither of whom – though for opposite reasons – wrote symphonic poems. Single-minded devotion to music drama on the one hand and to symphonic thought on the other led them away from Liszt's brilliant compound of the two. Bruckner and Mahler also ignored the form. Thus apart from the work of Strauss and numerous programme overtures by lesser men, there are only isolated examples by German and Austrian composers, among which should be mentioned Bülow's *Nirwana* (1866), Wolf's *Penthesilea* (1883–5) and Schoenberg's *Pelleas und Melisande* (1902–3). Schoenberg's *Verklärte Nacht* (1899), in which there is a clear structural relationship between poem and music, is a symphonic poem for string sextet and thus a rare nonorchestral example of the form.

Strauss's symphonic poems brought orchestral technique to a new level of complexity and treated subjects that had previously been considered ill-suited to musical illustration. He extended the boundaries of programme music, taking realism to unprecedented lengths as well as widening the imprecisely expressive functions of music. In the years before World War I these works were held to be in the vanguard of modernism, an indication of how rapidly the symphonic poem had taken hold of public imagination within half a century.

Strauss began to write programme music under the direct influence of Alexander Ritter – who himself composed six symphonic poems of Lisztian mould – and arrived at the form of the symphonic poem through a descriptive symphony, *Aus Italien* (1886–8). His first essay, *Macbeth* (1888), is a bold, characterful work with little more than a hint of sonata form, yet it is overshadowed by the series of masterpieces that followed: *Don Juan* (1888–9), *Tod und Verklärung* (1888–9), *Till Eulenspiegel* (1894–5), *Also sprach Zarathustra* (1895–6), *Don Quixote* (1896–7), *Ein Heldenleben* (1897–8) and *Sinfonia domestica* (1902–3). The range of subject matter is wide and embraces literature, legend, philosophy and autobiography. The seriousness of *Tod und Verklärung* contrasts sharply with the high spirits of *Till Eulenspiegel*, while *Don Quixote* cleverly captures Cervantes's worldly vision behind the ridiculous exploits of his knight. *Also sprach Zarathustra* attempts to give musical expression to eight selected passages from Nietzsche's philosophical poem rather than to the poem as a whole. Strauss said of the work: 'I meant to convey in music an idea of the evolution of the human race from its origin, through the various phases of development, religious as well as scientific, up to Nietzsche's idea of the *Übermensch*'. This ambitious idea may seem to have been tempered when he turned to himself as subject, yet in *Ein Heldenleben* he attempted to give his own existence a higher significance, portraying himself as the archetypal hero-artist in conflict with his enemies. But it has too an unmistakably personal element in the character of the wife and in its mellow contemplation (at the age of 34) of the hero's past achievements. For all its musical interest and expertise the *Sinfonia domestica* has been bedevilled by its unashamed treatment of the trivial in domestic life, though Strauss believed that the very universality of family life makes such scenes of interest to everyone. In the portrayal of character, however, it is with the legendary figures, Don Juan and Don Quixote, rather than in the projection of himself, that Strauss succeeds best.

In his handling of form Strauss called upon his abundant skill both in the transformation of themes and in interweaving one with another in elaborate orchestral counterpoint. The variation form of *Don Quixote* is specially felicitous; *Till Eulenspiegel*, though described on the title-page as in rondo form, is in fact as episodic as the story it depicts, with a single, compressed recapitulation, the whole neatly enclosed in a prologue and epilogue of touching simplicity. *Tod und Verklärung* resembles Liszt's *Tasso* in presenting glorification as an ecstatic musical goal. Strauss liked to use a simple but descriptive theme – for instance the three-note motif at the opening of *Also sprach Zarathustra*, or striding, vigorous arpeggios to represent the manly qualities of his heroes. His love themes are honeyed and chromatic and generally richly scored, and he is fond of the warmth and serenity of diatonic harmony as balm after torrential chromatic textures, notably at the end of *Don Quixote*, where the solo cello has a surpassingly beautiful D major transformation of the main theme.

The vividness and descriptive power of these works is directly due to the virtuosity of the orchestration. In the first place Strauss usually requires a large orchestra, with extra instruments such as the quartet of saxophones in the *Sinfonia domestica* or the offstage brass of *Ein Heldenleben*. Second, he used instruments for sharp characterization, best exemplified by Don Quixote's cello and Sancho Panza's tenor tuba or by the shrill woodwind of the critics in *Ein Heldenleben*. The portrayal of sheep with *cuivré* brass in *Don Quixote* is deservedly famous for its uncanny skill. Strauss had the confidence, the effrontery even, of a composer whose mastery of technical means was complete, and he succeeded best in those works, such as *Till Eulenspiegel* and *Don Quixote*, where his pretensions were less exalted and where wit and imagination were of more value than profundity.

Strauss wrote one more programmatic work, the *Alpensymphonie* (1911–15) – actually a symphonic poem. The orchestral requirements are immense, the scoring brilliantly imaginative and the picture of alpine scenery magnificently captured. In form it over-extends itself, and many fine passages are spoilt by Strauss's reluctance to bring them to an end. But by now he had outgrown the symphonic poem, having contributed a unique body of great works to its repertory.

8. OTHER COUNTRIES. The symphonic poem did not enjoy as clear a sense of national identity in other countries as in the Czech lands, Russia and France, even though innumerable works of the kind were written elsewhere, for example by William Wallace, Bantock, MacCunn, Mackenzie and Bax in Great Britain, Loeffler, MacDowell and Howard Hanson in America, and Pizzetti, Respighi and Malipiero in Italy. Elgar's *Falstaff* (1913) is an exceptionally fine orchestral portrait, and was preceded by three programme overtures, of which *Cockaigne* (1901) is the most distinctive. As a portrait of London it makes an interesting comparison with, say, Suk's *Prague*, Ravel's *La valse* and Delius's *Paris* (1899). Delius later wrote a number of descriptive orchestral pieces closely allied to the symphonic poem and to the impressionist style of Debussy. Frank Bridge was similarly drawn to nature painting, as in his symphonic poems *Summer* (1914) and *Enter Spring* (1927).

Sibelius, with well over a dozen symphonic poems and a number of similar, shorter orchestral pieces, showed exceptional dedication to the form. These works span his whole career, from *En saga* (1892) to *Tapiola* (1926), and express more clearly than anything else his identification with Finland and its mythology. The *Kalevala* provided ideal episodes and texts for musical setting, and his natural feeling for symphonic concentration is clearly demonstrated by the taut, organic structure of many of these works, *Tapiola* especially. *Pohjola's Daughter* (1906) – called 'symphonic fantasy' – is the most closely dependent on its programme but has at the same time a sureness of outline that was rare in other composers. Yet it is surpassed by the powerful landscape of *Tapiola*, composed at a time when Sibelius's own creative life was coming to an end and when the symphonic poem as a form was rapidly disappearing from view.

9. CONCLUSION. The decline of the symphonic poem in the 20th century may be attributed to the rejection of Romantic ideas and their replacement by notions of the abstraction and independence of music. The expressive function of music came under widespread attack, and the assumptions that had made the symphonic poem such a satisfactory vehicle for musical expression were swiftly supplanted. It should be said too that the problem of matching music and literature was, in the end, insoluble and that both had made severe sacrifices in attempting the compromise of fusion. For the natural architecture of music is not that of poetry; music's instinctive need to recapitulate and balance itself with repetition has no equivalent in narrative, with its inescapable forward movement. Even lyric poetry is rarely parallel to music in form. Sonata form, for example, is a conception with no real application outside music, and yet symphonic poems constantly attempted to reconcile classical formal principles with external literary concepts. Perhaps the nearest the symphonic poem came to finding a satisfactory form to match narrative was the long and gradual growth of an idea in pace and intensity, leading to a climax or solution, perhaps in triumph, perhaps in despair. Dukas' *L'apprenti-sorcier* is a good example of this continuously developing form. The apt use of variation in *Don Quixote* has already been mentioned. The element of contrast implicit in sonata form was sometimes usefully adapted, as for example in Liszt's *Hamlet*, where masculine and feminine elements are clearly placed in opposition. An even clearer case is d'Indy's *Max et Thécla* (1874, part of the Wallenstein trilogy) whose virile first theme portrays Max and the

contrastingly supple second theme represents Thécla. But in general, rather than embracing balance and repetition, symphonic ideas were confined to the development of musical material, with a predilection for short malleable thematic elements. Indeed Strauss firmly called his symphonic poems 'Tondichtungen' to avoid any symphonic implication, and 'tone poem' enjoyed considerable currency as the English term at the beginning of the 20th century.

From the point of view of its subject matter the symphonic poem was as successful in depicting imprecise ideas, such as heroism, lamentation, creativity and so forth, as in narrative, for too detailed a programme may burden or distract the listener. In general the dramatic poetry of Goethe, Bürger, Lenau and Hugo provided excellent material, and no source was as frequently drawn upon as Shakespeare's plays. Legends, historical events, cities, countries, seasons, philosophical concepts and much else besides were subjected to musical illustration, and the wide acceptance of some kind of linguistic equivalence between music and ideas resolved the aesthetic problem of how such pieces should be interpreted. The elaborate conventions of programme music, developed to a high point in the late 19th century, supplied the composer with working material and the listener with an immediate point of reference. Once the validity of these conventions had been called in question, the symphonic poem was bound to lose its vitality and popularity. Yet its flowering was spectacular and its fruit includes some of the finest and most enduring works in the orchestral repertory.

BIBLIOGRAPHY

R. Wagner: 'Über Franz Liszts symphonische Dichtungen', *Gesammelte Schriften*, v (Leipzig, 1872), 237
E. Newman: 'Programme Music', *Musical Studies* (London, 1905), 103
F. Niecks: *Programme Music* (London, 1907)
O. Klauwell: *Geschichte der Programmusik* (Leipzig, 1910)
H. Antcliffe: 'Musical Form and the Symphonic Poem', *IMusSCR*, iv London 1911, 206
R. W. S. Mendl: 'The Art of the Symphonic Poem', *MQ*, xviii (1932), 443
K. Schubert: *Die Programmusik* (Wolfenbüttel, 1933, 2/1961)
D. F. Tovey: *Essays in Musical Analysis*, iv: *Illustrative Music* (London, 1937/R1972)
E. Tanzberger: *Die symphonische Dichtungen von Jean Sibelius* (Würzburg, 1943)
J. Chantavoine: *Le poème symphonique* (Paris, 1950)
R. Fiske: 'Shakespeare in the Concert Hall', in *Shakespeare in Music*, ed. P. Hartnoll (London, 1964, 2/1967), 177–241
H. Wirth: 'Symphonische Dichtung', *MGG*
R. Kloiber: *Handbuch der symphonischen Dichtung* (Wiesbaden, 1967)
J. Clapham: 'Dvořák's Unknown Letters on his Symphonic Poems', *ML*, lvi (1975), 277
L. Orrey: *Programme Music* (London, 1975)

For further bibliography *see also* PROGRAMME MUSIC and articles on individual composers.

HUGH MACDONALD

Symphonie. (1) (Fr.) SYMPHONY.
(2) (Lat.) HURDY-GURDY.

Symphonie concertante (Fr.; It. *sinfonia concertante*). A concert genre of the late 18th and early 19th centuries for solo instruments – usually two, three or four, but on occasion as many as seven or even nine – with orchestra. The term implies 'symphony with important and extended solo parts', but the form is closer to concerto than symphony.

1. Definition and description. 2. Terminology. 3. Early history. 4. Flowering. 5. Social basis. 6. Later developments.

1. DEFINITION AND DESCRIPTION. The form flourished from about 1770 to 1830, during the high Classical and early Romantic eras. Symphonies concertantes were primarily intended for performance in public concert halls by virtuoso soloists. Solo instrumentation varied: during the early years of the genre's popularity, two principal violins was the most frequent, then other pairs (wind or mixed strings) and, finally, three or four instruments became common, with steadily increasing wind participation. Unusual combinations abound, for example keyboard, four hands (Theodor von Schacht); harpsichord, violin and piano (J.-F. Tapray); piano, mandolin, trumpet and bass (Leopold Kozeluch); harp, basset horn and cello (J. G. H. Backofen); violin, solo voices, choruses and large orchestra (C. Wagner); flute, oboe, clarinet, two bassoons, horn and cello (J. C. M. Widerkehr); two violins, two violas, two oboes, two horns and cello (J. C. Bach).

The symphonie concertante is a genre of the Classical period in style and structure, but has a character of its own. It has often been likened to the Baroque concerto grosso, but the resemblance is only superficial; each calls for a solo instrumental group and an orchestra, but there the similarity ends. The symphonie concertante resembles the concerto grosso no more than the Classical solo concerto resembles its Baroque antecedent. Unlike the concerto grosso, in which solo and ripieno are arrayed as sonorous adversaries in an equal contest, the symphonie concertante places the solo group in the forefront, assigning to it most of the important thematic material, and often extended cadenzas, while usually relegating the orchestra to a primarily accompanying function (except during the first exposition). The number and variety of solo instruments is often greater in the symphonie concertante than in the concerto grosso and the number of tutti–solo alternations fewer; and the solo instruments are assigned more themes unrelated to the orchestral material. There is furthermore a 100 to 1 difference in the frequency of the minor mode: about 50% of concerti grossi are in the minor as against 0·5% of symphonies concertantes (there are only two or three known symphonies concertantes in minor keys). This extreme difference exceeds considerably the fundamental Baroque–Classical ratio; about 2·5% of Classical symphonies, for example, are in the minor. The almost total absence of minor-key symphonies concertantes is a reflection of their special mood and function.

The symphonie concertante resembles the Classical divertimento forms in its lighthearted character. Melodic variety is its hallmark. Although a symphonie concertante may include a poignant Andante, the prevailing mood is usually relaxed, gracious and happy, rarely dramatic, never sombre or intense. Although similar in length and form to the symphony, which it often replaced on concert programmes, the symphonie concertante did not develop into a vehicle for the expression of intense or profound emotion. There are occasional traces in the earlier works (Holzbauer, J. C. Bach) of the Baroque ritornello form, but the structure of the first movement is generally similar to that of the Classical concerto with its orchestral statement followed by an exposition for soloists and orchestra, though there tends to be less motivic development or bold modulation in the symphonie concertante. About half the works are in two movements; virtually all the rest have three, and there are almost never four or five. The two-movement works lack slow movements. Even the three-movement works contain nothing slower than an Andante; an

Adagio is virtually unknown. The last movement in both two- and three-movement works is most often a rondo, or occasionally a theme and variations (these two forms provide maximum opportunity for solo display) or a minuet and trio.

In the period from about 1767 to 1830, some 570 works specifically entitled 'symphonie concertante', 'sinfonia concertante' or simply 'concertante' were written by about 210 composers. About 70 French composers (including a few foreigners settled in France) wrote about half of these; the remainder were produced by about 140 composers from the rest of Europe. The French emphasis is even greater than the figures indicate. Some of the most prolific non-French composers of symphonies concertantes wrote their works in the 1770s and 1780s while in Paris. Thus in the first two decades of its existence the genre was primarily a French and specifically a Parisian one, though significantly influenced by second-generation Mannheim composers. Its popularity spread fairly quickly to other large cities in western Europe, more gradually to German towns and courts. The French preferred two- rather than three-movement form by more than two to one; in other centres the three-movement form was favoured.

The significance of the term 'symphonie concertante' as the name for a specific genre is demonstrated by the fact that it was used about three times more frequently than titles like 'Concerto for two [three, four etc] instruments' during the period cited. As is suggested below (§5), the new name became established because the genre it represented was fulfilling a specific function in a specific locale and thus needed to be differentiated from the old-fashioned concerto terminology. In 1771 Nicolas Framéry urged that the 'insipid sonata' and the 'overlong concerto' should be replaced by the 'innovation of the symphonies concertantes', a genre ideal for the Concert Spirituel which had the most gifted virtuosos available (*Journal de musique*, March 1771).

2. TERMINOLOGY. The French name 'symphonie concertante' was used with sufficient frequency and consistency in the late 18th and early 19th centuries to warrant its being accepted as a genre in its own right rather than as a hybrid form. Attempts to replace the name with terms that were never or rarely used at the time can only create confusion. To be avoided are: 'Koncert-Sinfonie', used by Scheibe in *Critischer Musicus* (1745, p.629), meaning a symphony with obbligato rather than 'filler' wind); 'sinfonia concertata' used by Koch and Schilling in their 19th-century lexicons (but hardly ever found elsewhere); 'concerted symphony' or 'ensemble concerto' used by a few writers seeking to anglicize the term; teutonizations such as 'Gruppenkonzert' (Blume, *Syntagma musicologicum*, 1973, p.694), 'Concertantes' or 'Konzertierendes Quartett' (the work attributed to Mozart, K Anh.9/Anh.C.14.01, Breitkopf & Härtel edition), or even the legitimate 18th-century term 'Concertierende Sinfonien für verschiedene Instrumente' (used by André in Offenbach in his edition of the A major work of J. C. Bach first published by Sieber in Paris as *Simphonie concertante à plusieurs instruments*). 'Symphonie concertante' is historically as valid as the terms concerto grosso or divertimento, about which some terminological confusion also exists; on the other hand, it would be adding anachronism to misnomer to

apply the name either to Baroque works which originally bore the title 'concerto grosso' or 'concerto a più stromenti' (as has been done with compositions by Handel, G. B. Sammartini and others) or to later works for a single solo instrument and orchestra (as has been done by various 20th-century composers), or which have no fully-fledged soloists at all.

As to whether the Italian or French form of the name should be used, the latter is clearly favoured by both contemporary usage and historical considerations. The French name was used all over Europe (sometimes with different French spellings, such as 'simphonie concertante', or 'sinfonie concertante', a standard French form although 'sinfonie' is also a German spelling), infinitely more often than the Italian version. Mozart, writing from Paris, preferred the French spelling, a fact obscured by current practice (e.g. Emily Anderson's translation of his letters). He used the common French form 'sinfonie concertante' in five of six separate references in his letters to the work for four wind instruments (flute, oboe, bassoon and horn, K297*B*) written in Paris in 1778, and Leopold's response also uses a French form, 'synfonie concertante' (the sixth edition of Köchel's catalogue retains the Italian spelling for the lost autograph). There are no references in the letters to the violin and viola work, K364/320*d*, of which the autograph is also missing. The autograph of the fragment Anh.104/320*e*, written in the Italianate atmosphere of Salzburg in 1779, was entitled 'Sinfonia concertante a tre stromenti violino, viola e violoncello'.

Related terms of the time include 'concertino' and 'concertone', meaning, roughly, small and large concerto respectively. The first was quite common, being applied to the most diverse kinds of piece; the second is very rare and closely approximates to the symphonie concertante. Composers who have used 'concertone' include Sarti, Gherardeschi and Mozart. Other terms used by composers and publishers include: Duet concertino (P. J. Lindpaintner), Duetto concerto (Anton Stamitz), Trio concertante (G. S. Mayr), Fantasie concertante (C. H. Meyer), Divertimento concertante (Adalbert Gyrowetz), Quartet Concerto (Spohr), Concerto concertant (H.-J. Rigel), and Konzertant Konzert and Grand Concerto Concertant (Beethoven, Triple Concerto: autograph of the piano part and first edition of the instrumental parts respectively). All of these special titles taken together represent a very small percentage of the works for soloists and orchestra, especially before about 1810.

Attempts at explicating the term 'symphonie concertante' have foundered on two counts: first, on the confusion between the adjective 'concertante', loosely employed in the 18th century, and the noun-complex 'symphonie concertante', which refers to a specific genre; and second, on the difference between works called 'symphonie concertante' and those, also with more than one solo instrument, called 'concerto for two [three, four] instruments'.

As a substitute for the two-word grouping, the word 'concertante' has been used as a noun, especially in England and Germany. After 1790, Pleyel's *Sinfonie concertante à neuf instruments* (Paris, 1788) was published by Preston in London as *A Favorite Concertante in E flat*. The Arnold edition of Handel's works of 1787–93 used 'Concertante' as the title of the C major Concerto Grosso (Händel-Gesellschaft, xxi, p.63). Haydn called the work he wrote in London for solo violin, cello, oboe, bassoon and orchestra 'Concertante' (HI: 103). A German example is Simrock's publication (Bonn, *c*1795) of Josef Reicha's *Concertante pour violon et violoncelle avec toutes les parties d'orchestre*, op.1. As an adjective applied to an instrument, the word 'concertante' cannot easily be distinguished from the related and overlapping terms, such as 'solo', 'obbligato', 'récitant' and 'principale'.

There seems to be little or no difference between a symphonie concertante and a concerto for two or more instruments; indeed, the terms were often interchanged. Most multiple concertos, whatever title they may have been given by their composers or publishers, were almost inevitably called 'symphonie concertante' by the French, even well into the 19th century (Fétis did so consistently). In Germany and England, the terms 'concertante' or 'concerto' (for two or more instruments) became increasingly prevalent. 166 works from 1767 to 1830 have been identified with titles like 'Concerto for two instruments'; almost all were written outside France. An analytical and historical comparison between this corpus of 'multiple concertos' and the 570 known 'symphonies concertantes' would be necessary to clarify any stylistic and national differences. Mendel and Reissmann (*Conversations-Lexikon*, 1870–79, vols.ii and ix) attempted to define both terms but without shedding much light on the distinctions between them (see McCredie, 1976). Mozart, however, made a distinction when he called the two works of this type that he completed in Paris in 1778 by different names: the one for four visiting Mannheim wind virtuosos, designed for public performance at the Concert Spirituel, was called 'sinfonie Concertante', the salon piece for the Count of Guines and his daughter, both amateurs, and intended for private performance, was referred to as a concerto for flute and harp (K299/297c). The distinction did not take hold, but it has intriguing sociological implications.

3. EARLY HISTORY. The concertato principle – the opposition of contrasting and not too unequal forces – had been observed throughout the Baroque period, back to the time of its greatest practitioner, Giovanni Gabrieli. By 1750 its main vehicle, the concerto grosso, had become outmoded, and the developing Classical symphony with its different stylistic objectives could not provide the proper context for the concept; more appropriate were the lighter orchestral forms (serenade, cassation), the multiple concerto and, around 1770, the symphonie concertante.

The use of the adjectives 'concertante' and 'concertata' is common throughout this period; the specific term 'symphonie concertante' is not met until the late 1760s, though there is a French periodical reference to an otherwise unidentified 'Symphonie-concert del Signor Wagenseil' performed at the Concert Spirituel in February 1759. Haydn anticipated the symphonie concertante in his triptych 'Le matin', 'Le midi' and 'Le soir', Symphonies nos.6, 7 and 8 (1761), which abound in extended and difficult solo passages that detach themselves from the orchestral fabric. 'Le soir' is sub-titled 'a più stromenti concertanti'. But these are symphonies with solo parts, in which the relationship of solos to tutti is flexible and unformalized, unlike that of the later true symphonie concertante. Several recent descriptions of the genre, like Blume's – 'the new form of the three-movement orchestral symphony that projected occasional solo sec-

tions from within itself and thus produced a cross between the symphony and the solo concerto' (in D. Mitchell and H. C. R. Landon, eds.: *A Mozart Companion*, 1956, p.209) – apply in some contexts, for example to these Haydn works and to certain of the early Mannheim symphonies concertantes, for example by Holzbauer and Cannabich (see Winzenburger, 1967); such definitions are inadequate for the great majority of symphonies concertantes.

Two earlier works, published in France, the music of which is lost, may indicate a significant intermediary phase between concerto grosso and symphonie concertante. The first is a set of pieces by Louis-Gabriel Guillemain (1705–70) advertised in the *Annonces, affiches et avis divers* of 17 January 1753 as *Simphonies d'un goût nouveau en forme de concerto, pour les musettes, vielles, flûtes ou hautbois avec accompagnement de deux violons et basse* op.16. The second, announced in the *Mercure de France* of March 1757, p.182, by Papavoine (*c*1720–?1793), is entitled *Grandes symphonies en concerto pour deux violons, alto et violoncelle obligés et deux autres violons et basse, que l'on peut supprimer*. Known contemporary works by Guillemain (e.g. 6 Concertinos op.7, 1740) and Papavoine (e.g. 6 Symphonies op.1, 1752) are conventional three-movement symphonic pieces for orchestra in early Classical style. G. B. Sammartini provided an example of an intermediary phase in his Concerto in E♭ (London, 1756): it called for 'two violins & two hautboys obbligato' with two horns and strings. The lineage of this work may be traced back to Tartini (Blume: *Syntagma musicologicum*, 1973, p.694) but it is more Classically orientated.

In Vienna, Wagenseil and Dittersdorf (see the Breitkopf Catalogue, 1766, p.34) were among the earliest composers of pieces, called concertos, which resembled the symphonie concertante in character while not using the term itself. The two-word complex may first have been used in print in May 1767 for works published in Paris by Venier: *Sei sinfonie concertanti o sia quintetti per due violini, due viole, e basso dell Sig. Misliwecek detto il Boemo*, op.2. These are quintets rather than symphonies concertantes since they have no orchestral accompaniment. Similarly titled sets of works by Cannabich (op.7), announced by Venier in November 1768, and by Schiesser, published by La Chevardière in 1772, demonstrate a terminological vagueness which was soon clarified. Appearing in December 1767 and listed in the Venier catalogue as no.37 in the category *Sinfonies periodiques* is a 'Sinf concertante' by Ricci. No copy is known, but if it is the same as one of the works in Ricci's *Trois simphonies concertantes* op.9 published by Van Laack (The Hague, *c*1773), it may be the first published symphonie concertante in both name and fact.

4. FLOWERING. Around 1770 the symphonie concertante began, with extraordinary rapidity, to enjoy enormous popularity. Its success reflected profound social changes: the advent of bourgeois audiences, the public concert halls, the larger orchestras. Musically, it embodied the tastes of these audiences: an increasing fascination with virtuoso display, a fondness for big sonorities, and particularly an all-pervading enthusiasm for the pleasing melodic line. Not only were large numbers of symphonies concertantes written, performed and

published, some in many editions and in arrangements from other genres or popular airs, but in Paris at least this output soon exceeded that of the solo concerto and of the conventional symphony.

With a few exceptions, like J. C. Bach, F. P. Ricci and Gaetano Brunetti, the earliest composers were Mannheimers and Parisians, and the first symphonie concertante publishers were almost all French. A perusal of French publishers' catalogues provides striking proof of its rapid rise: the new rubric appeared suddenly and the number of listings under it increased steadily (see Johansson, 1955, facsimiles 104–17). (Waldkirch's claims for Mannheim composers' primacy do not stand up to examination: his cited Cannabich works are the quintets mentioned above and others by Cannabich and Toeschi are undated or later, while many of the Mannheim works he referred to were composed in Paris.)

Significant French symphonie concertante composers include François Devienne (7), F. J. Gossec (7), I. J. Pleyel (8), J. B. Bréval (10), the Chevalier de Saint-Georges (11), J. C. M. Widerkehr (12), J.-B. Davaux (13) and G. M. Cambini (80). Other composers of smaller output but of equal or greater talent include Isidore Bertheaume, N.-J. Chartrain and Simon Leduc. To judge by the number of performances recorded in the contemporary press and by their favourable critical reception, Davaux, though second to Cambini in output, was easily first in popularity; his fame persisted well into the 19th century, and J. N. Bouilly in 1837 called him 'le créateur de la symphonie concertante'. Davaux was essentially a talented amateur with a penchant for facile melody. Of greater intrinsic merit are the works of Bréval (important in the history of the cello) and of the Chevalier de Saint-Georges, whose symphonies concertantes are among the most charming in the repertory. Cambini was an Italian who spent half a century in Paris. A shrewd judge of popular taste, he established a monthly subscription for the sale of his assembly-line production of symphonies concertantes. Mozart suspected that Cambini was responsible for the suppression of his own symphonie concertante at the Concert Spirituel.

The most important Mannheim composers of symphonies concertantes are Cannabich (12, including the six 'o sia quintetti'), Holzbauer (3), Franz Danzi (4, including one for flute, oboe, clarinet and bassoon in E♭ with interesting resemblances to the work for the same combination ascribed to Mozart (see Stoltie)), Anton Stamitz (4) and Carl Stamitz (over 30, second numerically only to Cambini). Carl Stamitz's works were written in the French manner and were issued regularly in the 1770s by French publishers; they are pleasant pieces, mainly in two movements. His third symphonie concertante, in D minor, is unusual in being in a minor key. His solo group is generally made up of two string instruments (violin and cello, violin and viola or two violins).

In London the scene is dominated by J. C. Bach. His 15 concerted symphonies (not 31, as listed by Terry), written for his own Bach–Abel concerts and for the Concert Spirituel in Paris, are among the finest works in the genre. Ten are in three movements, five in two. The solo group is usually made up of three or more instruments, varied in composition: e.g. oboe, violin, cello and piano (B♭), flute, oboe, violin and cello (C), and a unique grouping of nine instruments: two violins,

two violas, two oboes, two horns and cello (in E♭, with orchestra made up of two violins and bass). This solo group approaches the size of an orchestra, suggesting a possible relationship between Bach's symphonies for double orchestra (op.18) and the symphonie concertante. In the Hummel edition of the *Concert ou symphonie à deux violons obligés* (Amsterdam, *c*1775) the curious title is doubtless the publisher's; the work was first issued by Sieber (Paris, 1773) as *Simphonie concertante no. 2 à plusieurs instruments*.

The Italian contribution to the genre was very limited. The number of works actually written or published in Italy is extremely small, and few manuscripts are to be found in Italian libraries; Italian composers using the form mostly worked outside their homeland. The leading ones (excluding Cambini, considered with the French group) are F. P. Ricci (3), Ignazio Fiorillo (5), Prospero Cauciello (3), G. B. Viotti (2) and especially Boccherini and Brunetti (5 each). All but one of Brunetti's, dated between 1769 and 1794, were for two 'violons principaux'; they remained unpublished in his lifetime. Boccherini's works were published for the most part in Paris and Lyons in the 1770s and 1780s under such headings as: *Simphonie concertante à 8 instruments obligés*, *Serenade*, *Concertino a più stromenti concertanti* and *Grande symphonie*.

Composers in Habsburg lands who produced a modest number of variously titled but significant works included the Bohemians Mysliveček, Kozeluch, Wranitzky and Gyrowetz. The Viennese composer G. C. Wagenseil wrote seven concertos for two keyboards and small orchestra; some date from the 1760s and are among the first examples of early Classical multiple concertos. Other Austrians include Vanhal, Dittersdorf, Pichl and Hoffmeister with three or four works each.

Title-page of Carl Stamitz's 'Deux simphonies concertantes' op.18 (Paris: Bailleux, c1776)

Haydn's role in the development of the concertante principle in Classical music can hardly be overestimated; his originality is everywhere apparent, for example in his *Sei divertimenti concertanti* op.31 (Vienna, 1781) and in more than a third of his symphonies. He wrote only a single fully-fledged symphonie concertante, his op.84 in Bb for violin, cello, oboe and bassoon, written in 1792 for the Salomon concerts in London. As Landon (1955, p.556) has indicated, it shows the influence of the London concert hall and the presence of talented local virtuosos.

Mozart's first concertante piece was written in 1773 and called *Concertone*, K190/186E. It is a scintillating *galant* work in C with solos for two violins, oboe and cello. Both Leopold Mozart and the flautist Wendling referred to it as 'just the thing for Paris'. During his 1778 stay in Paris and in the year immediately following, Mozart was spurred to attempt no fewer than six symphonies concertantes. In addition to the one for four wind instruments he wrote two others in Eb: the masterwork for violin and viola, K364/320d, and another for two pianos, K365, as well as the Concerto for flute and harp in C. Two other works of magnificent promise remain only as fragments: one in D for piano and violin, K Anh.56/315f and one in A for violin, viola and cello, K Anh.104/320e.

Germany, aside from Mannheim, presents no unified picture. Composers were dispersed in many different cities (Berlin, Dresden, Hamburg, Leipzig, Munich, Darmstadt) and courts (Ludwigslust, Württemberg, Regensburg, Donaueschingen, Harburg), each a separate unit. Few wrote more than one or two works, and these usually bear the name 'concerto' rather than 'symphonie concertante' or 'concertante', terms which were not used until the late 1780s and 1790s. The numerous concertos for two keyboards (W. F. Bach, C. P. E. Bach, C. H. Graun) or two flutes (J. J. Quantz, J. F. Kleinknecht etc) seem designed for the private salon rather than the public concert hall. In Beethoven's generation and later, the situation changed considerably. Many large-scale virtuoso concertante pieces were written, e.g. by J. B. Moralt, G. A. Schneider, C. H. Meyer, J. J. B. Martinn, F. Westenholz, P. J. Lindpaintner, H. A. Hoffmann, Franz Weiss etc (see McCredie). Isolated examples of the concertante genre may be found elsewhere in Europe, for example in Sweden by Bernard Crusell and in Denmark by Schall.

5. SOCIAL BASIS. The symphonie concertante came into being in response to external social forces rather than to internal musical imperatives. It is only from a sociological vantage point that one can answer questions as to why, for example, the symphonie concertante came into fashion so precipitously around 1770, why it flourished so brilliantly and why it virtually burnt itself out in a few decades; the answers relate to the genre's function in the musical life of the time, to the changing social status of the musician, and to the changing natures of concert life, concert audiences and means of music dissemination.

At the onset of the high Classical era, around 1770, the rate of change in musical style increased perceptibly. There was an unusual expansion of public concert and opera activities and a marked increase in the dissemination of manuscript and especially printed music. Concomitantly there was a heightened awareness of the musician's role in society and his potential for social improvement; the composer was coming to see his position in a new light. It was less that he was liberating himself 'from the shackles of aristocratic patronage' in order to become a 'free spirit' than that he was reaching out to become part of the bourgeoisie – by expressing its malaise in *Sturm und Drang* symphonies, by catering for its tastes with such forms as the symphonie concertante, and by exercising increasingly a variety of commercial functions in a growing music industry that could help make him independent of courtly or ecclesiastical patronage. The symphonie concertante provided a vehicle for the instrumental composer and performer to display his wares and profit from his talent.

It was no accident that the focal point for the development of the genre was Paris, which provided a hospitable climate for the composer–performer of instrumental works pleasing to the large concert-going public. The symphonie concertante was designed for this milieu. Musicians were able to improve their status and augment their income by performing their own and each other's works, dazzling the public with melodious, scintillating and instrumentally varied pieces. These men were not for the most part peregrinating virtuosos but first-rate local musicians, some of whom had no aspirations towards a soloist's career. Their participation as symphonie concertante principals, however, sufficed to place their names before the public, helping them to secure additional pupils, wider sales of their printed works and better contracts with publishers. Composers who were motivated to build their careers in the commercial world found that the new appeal of the symphonie concertante helped them. Similarly, extra-musical factors in the early 19th century help explain the decline of the genre. The symphonie concertante no longer had a valid function in concert life, especially after the Napoleonic wars when the cult of the individual became a guiding consideration. The glamour of the travelling virtuoso replaced the concept of 'concerted' action by local composers and performers working together.

6. LATER DEVELOPMENTS. The popularity of 'symphonie concertante' as the name of a piece declined considerably in the second and third decades of the 19th century. The word 'concertante' used as a noun persisted, as did the title 'concerto for two [three etc] instruments'. But the symphonie concertante as a genre virtually disappeared. Multiple concertos came to be called fantasy, rondo, potpourri, variation or Konzertstück as well as concerto, concertino and concertante. Such works were extremely varied in character and appeared sporadically, often as *pièces d'occasion* or for specific soloists. Among the most important works for several soloists and orchestra written after Beethoven's Triple Concerto are Mendelssohn's two youthful concertos for two pianos, Spohr's five concertantes and one quartet concerto, Schumann's Konzertstück for four horns, Brahms's Double Concerto and Bruch's Concerto for two pianos.

20th-century composers have occasionally used the term 'symphonie concertante' or its cognates; usually more as an exotic title or for works of a symphonic rather than concerto-like character with a single solo instrumental, rather than as a reincarnation of the 18th-century genre. Examples include Szymanowski's Symphonie concertante for piano and orchestra (1932), Jongen's Symphonie concertante for organ and orchestra (1926), Enescu's Symphonie concertante for cello and orchestra (1901), Rubbra's Sinfonia concertante for piano and orchestra (1934) and Prokofiev's Symphony-Concerto op.125 for cello and orchestra (1950–52). A more legitimate use of the title was made by Hilding Rosenberg who wrote a Symphonie concertante for violin, viola, oboe, bassoon and orchestra (1935) and by Frank Martin with his Petite symphonie concertante for piano, harpsichord, harp and strings (1945).

BIBLIOGRAPHY

EitnerQ; *FétisB*

B. Count of Lacépède: *La poétique de la musique*, ii (Paris, 1785)

A. de Momigny: 'Symphonie concertante', *Encyclopédie méthodique*, ii (Paris, 1818), 416

M. Brenet: *Les concerts en France sous l'ancien régime* (Paris, 1900/*R*1969)

A. Schering: *Geschichte des Instrumentalkonzerts bis auf die Gegenwart* (Leipzig, 1905, 2/1927)

F. Torrefranca: 'Le origini della sinfonia', *RMI*, xx (1913), 291–346; xxi (1914), 97, 278–312; xxii (1915), 431

L. de La Laurencie: *L'école française de violon de Lully à Viotti* (Paris, 1922–4/*R*1972)

F. Tutenberg: *Die Sinfonik Johann Christian Bachs* (Wolfenbüttel, 1928)

C. S. Terry: *John Christian Bach* (London, 1929, rev. 2/1967)

F. Waldkirch: *Die Konzertanten Sinfonien der Mannheimer im 18. Jahrhundert* (Ludwigshafen, 1931)

G. de Saint-Foix: *Les symphonies de Mozart* (Paris, 1932)

H. Boese: *Die Klarinette als Soloinstrument in der Musik der Mannheimer Schule* (diss., U. of Dresden, 1940)

H. Engel: 'Concerto Grosso', *MGG*

A. Sorel-Nitzberg: 'Davaux', *MGG*

C. Johansson: *French Music Publishers' Catalogues of the Second Half of the Eighteenth Century* (Stockholm, 1955)

H. C. R. Landon: *The Symphonies of Joseph Haydn* (London, 1955; suppl., 1961)

F. Blume and H. C. R. Landon: 'The Concertos', *The Mozart Companion*, ed. H. C. R. Landon and D. Mitchell (London, 1956, 2/1965), 200–82

E. J. Simon: 'The Double Exposition in the Classic Concerto', *JAMS*, x (1957), 111

J. A. White jr: *The Concerted Symphonies of John Christian Bach* (diss., U. of Michigan, 1957)

E. J. Simon: 'A Royal Manuscript: Ensemble Concertos of J. C. Bach', *JAMS*, xii (1959), 161

B. S. Brook: 'The Symphonie Concertante: an Interim Report', *MQ*, xlvii (1961), 493; xlviii (1962), 148

A. J. B. Hutchings: *The Baroque Concerto* (London, 1961, rev. 3/1973)

M. Rasmussen: 'A Bibliography of *Symphonies concertantes, Concerti grossi*, etc. Including Solo Parts for the Horn as Compiled from Twenty Selected Sources', *Brass Quarterly*, v/2 (1961), 62

B. S. Brook: *La symphonie française dans la seconde moitié du XVIIIe siècle* (Paris, 1962)

J. M. Stoltie: *A Symphonie Concertante Type: the Concerto for Mixed Woodwind Ensemble in the Classic Period* (diss., U. of Iowa, 1962)

B. Churgin: *The Symphonies of G. B. Sammartini* (diss., Harvard U., 1963)

J. B. Winzenburger: *The Symphonie Concertante: Mannheim and Paris* (diss., Eastman School of Music, U. of Rochester, 1967)

B. S. Brook: 'The Symphonie Concertante: its Musical and Sociological Bases', *International Review of the Aesthetics and Sociology of Music*, vi (1975), 9

A. D. McCredie: 'Symphonie Concertante and Multiple Concerto in Germany (1780–1850): some Problems and Perspectives for a Source-Repertory Study', *MMA*, viii (1976), 115

BARRY S. BROOK

Symphonische Dichtung (Ger.: 'symphonic poem'). A term first coined by Liszt to describe 12 works he composed between 1848 and 1858 – the first of them *Ce qu'on entend sur la montagne*, the last *Hamlet* – and generally adopted in Germany for orchestral works in this form. Richard Strauss, however, preferred the term 'Tondichtung'.

See SYMPHONIC POEM.

Symphony (Fr. *simphonie, symphonie*; Ger. *Sinfonie*; It. *sinfonia*). A term now normally taken to signify an extended work for orchestra. The symphony became the chief vehicle of orchestral music in the late 18th century, and from the time of Beethoven came to be regarded as its highest and most exalted form. The adjective 'symphonic' applied to a work implies that it is extended and thoroughly developed.

The word 'symphony' derives from the Greek *syn* ('together') and *phōnē* ('sounding'), through the Latin SYMPHONIA, a term used during the Middle Ages and the Renaissance. It is essentially in this derivation that the term was used by Giovanni Gabrieli (*Sacrae symphoniae*, 1597), Schütz (*Symphoniae sacrae*, 1629) and others for concerted motets, usually for voices and instruments. In the 17th century the term 'symphony' or (more commonly) 'sinfonia' was applied to introductory movements to operas, oratorios and cantatas (*see* OVERTURE, §2), to the instrumental introductions and ritornellos of arias and ensembles (*see* RITORNELLO), and to ensemble works that could be classified as sonatas or concertos. The common factor in this variety of usage was that sinfonias or symphonies were usually part of a larger framework, such as another composition, an 'academy' or a church service. (For a fuller discussion *see* SINFONIA.)

The immediate antecedent of the modern symphony is commonly considered to be the opera sinfonia, which by the early 18th century had a standard structure of three sections or movements: fast, slow, and fast dance-like movement. That form was extensively used by Alessandro Scarlatti and his contemporaries and was widely adopted outside Italy, particularly in Germany and England (less in France, where the FRENCH OVERTURE held sway). The terms 'overture' and 'symphony' or 'sinfonia' were widely regarded as interchangeable for much of the 18th century.

I. 18th century. II. 19th century. III. 20th century.

I. 18th century

1. Introduction. 2. Sources. 3. Form. 4. Italy. 5. North Germany. 6. Vienna. 7. Mannheim. 8. Paris. 9. London, other local centres. 10. Haydn and Mozart.

1. INTRODUCTION. To understand Classicism there is no better exercise than to follow the long evolution of the 18th-century symphony. While other media may occasionally carry specific aspects of Classicism to notable heights, the symphony remains, for a number of reasons, the basic standard of achievement and comparison. First, the sheer volume of surviving sources staggers the imagination. By 1975 the Union Thematic Catalogue of 18th-century Symphonies of *c*1720 to *c*1810 (see LaRue, 1959) contained entries for more than 12,350 works, many of solid competence. In German-speaking Europe there is hardly a market town that does not possess 18th-century symphonies (more often manuscripts than prints) in its local town or castle library. Valuable collections have been discovered from Finland to Sicily and from Kiev to Salem, North Carolina. The leading area in symphonic activity was probably Vienna, followed by Mannheim, Italy, France, north Germany, south Germany and England, with smaller but significant activity in Czechoslovakia, Scandinavia, Poland and Russia.

A second important aspect is the uninterrupted continuity of the symphony's development, beginning in the late 17th century with the skeletal necessities of instrumentation and tempo contrast, leading gradually by experimentation to a balanced array of procedures that ultimately define the Classical style. Third, and equally important, both in its experimental and its mature phases the symphony dominated a broad spectrum of 18th-century musical life, providing brilliant openings and finales to countless concerts (and banquets), heavily in demand as a genre over many decades, as can be seen from publishers' catalogues: in 1770 Breitkopf offered 65 symphonies but only 48 concertos and 42 string quartets, although the latter genres required less engraving.

The external features of the Classical symphony – title, tempo plan, and instrumentation – may be traced to the Italian overture in the last two decades of the 17th century. In *Tutto il mal', non vien per nuocere* (1681), Alessandro Scarlatti had turned away from the typically Baroque plan of the church sonata (slow–fast–slow–fast) to a briefer, more dramatic scheme (fast–slow–fast) that set the pattern for both the 18th-century overture and its offshoot, the concert symphony. At about the same time the orchestral grouping changed from the Corelli–Vivaldi tradition of tutti–solo string masses to a more varied ensemble including pairs of brass and woodwind. By about 1730 the instrumentation of strings, two oboes and two horns became increasingly frequent, and this combination should be regarded as the standard orchestra of early Classicism, continuing as a norm until nearly the end of the century. Small establishments, of course, continued to perform symphonies with modest groups, sometimes merely a trio or quartet with harpsichord. Reflecting such practices, a number of provincial composers (for example Camerloher) wrote symphonies almost exclusively for strings as late as 1770. The expansion of the orchestra to full Classical size (strings with two each of flutes, oboes, clarinets, bassoons, trumpets, horns and timpani, with harpsichord often assumed even with this large group) was erratic rather than consistent, and the whole development is closely linked to local possibilities. Symphonies for petty courts with a considerable military programme could call for a full complement of trumpets, horns and drums (when not busy on the parade ground).

2. SOURCES. The enormous number of symphonies obviously results in even more enormous numbers of sources. A popular symphony by Pleyel, for example, may be found in as many as 50 libraries; such works persisted strongly even in remote locations. For example, the records of the Philharmonic Society at Breslau (now Wrocław) show performances of Pleyel's op.30 extending from about 1805 to 1833; copies of symphonies by Gossec and Pierre van Maldere are in provincial church archives in lower Slovakia; many Italian overtures found their way into Russian libraries; and at least one Russian symphony–overture, by Berezovsky, is in the Doria-Pamphili Collection in Rome.

To identify symphonies according to a 'semantic principle' (such as that adopted by W. S. Newman in his books on the sonata, i.e. to include only works with the literal title 'sinfonia') would be a great loss, since true symphonies, not mere aberrant copies, occur under various titles, such as sonata, trio, quadro, quintetto, parthia, divertimento, cassatione, serenata, pastorale, concerto, concertino, introduzione, intrada, prelude and overture. A more serious question of 'when is a

work a symphony?' arises with regard to the use of operatic overtures as concert symphonies, a usage that reached its peak at about 1760 and then tapered to a small number, as the distinction between the two styles became more clear. For the present survey, multi-movement overtures that served concert purposes will be treated as concert symphonies.

A final and most elusive problem with symphony sources concerns misattributions. Haydn frauds receive ample publicity, but similar problems affect many less important composers and may lead to similar misunderstandings of their styles. Such mistakes can take place under the best of auspices, as the publication in a collected edition (DTÖ, xxxi, Jg.xv/2) of a mature Classical symphony under the name of the early Viennese composer M. G. Monn shows. This symphony has troubled three generations of writers attempting to explain the Viennese school; stylistically it does not fit with the modest instrumentation and short phrase structure of Monn. The locator file of the Union Thematic Catalogue shows that it was written by Franz Pokorny in Regensburg; the attribution had been erased and changed to Monn. Misattributions of this sort affect about 7% of Classical symphonies. Although the Union Catalogue locator files can bring these conflicts to the surface, the task of determining the correct composer may still be almost insoluble: there is one symphony that has been attributed to no fewer than five composers.

3. FORM. Internally the Scarlatti type of fast–slow–fast overture furnished few precedents for the Classical symphony, unless one takes into account the dance-like (often 3/8) finales. The three brief movements (21, 18 and 27 bars) of Scarlatti's *Eraclea* overture (1700) still depend on Baroque procedures such as the sequential treatment of motivic ideas, beat-marking rhythm with little variety in values, and ritornello forms with solo–tutti exchanges and migrant tonality.

Three particular variants of textbook sonata form are met with in the symphony literature. One is a type of binary, common in the works of Mannheim composers, where the first idea returns in the tonic after, not before, the second group. Another is 'exposition–recapitulation form', consisting simply of exposition and recapitulation, without development; this appears frequently in opera overtures, where a further variant with a slow movement taking the place of a development also occurs (see §4 below). A third variant is the movement with a recapitulation where the primary material returns in a key other than the tonic, such as the subdominant or submediant; this, familiar in isolated movements by Mozart and Schubert, was often used by Gassmann. (For a fuller discussion *see* SONATA FORM, §3.)

A familiar question arises over the introduction of the minuet into the symphony, for which priority has been claimed on behalf of both the Mannheim and Vienna schools. The question is in fact unnecessary: dance-like finales in 3/8 and 3/4 occur in Italian overtures from the very beginning. A more useful question, 'Who changed the character of the finale?', will be discussed below (especially in §4).

Although textbook sonata form is an abstraction, rare in actual music, it need not be avoided in discussion of the symphony, particularly as symphony designs show a distinct evolution towards its procedures. It should however be understood as having many variants, and as being less a form than a collection of essential techniques, including: balanced phrases; enlargement of structural units to $4 + 4$ and $8 + 8$ bar groupings; tensional contrast and directional modulation between tonic and dominant areas; slowing of harmonic rhythm to stabilize thematic areas; thematic differentiation; development involving progressive changes in material; full recapitulation; and orchestration that selectively enhances these procedures.

Many characteristic features of Classicism occur in isolated contexts long before 1730, a date that serves well to mark the change towards its predominance. No mere collection of traits, however, can generate the full character of Classicism, which results not from individual processes but rather from a higher control, or concinnity, a skilful and elegant arrangement and adjustment of the various elements. Once this central technique became current, composers could perfect various other characteristics that distinguish a Classical symphony, notably a hierarchy of punctuation necessary to clarify more complicated phrase, sentence and paragraph structures; and a differentiation and later specialization of sections (primary, transitional, secondary and closing). There are apparently similar procedures in the Baroque period, for many dance forms differentiate closing and even secondary material; yet the homogeneity of material tends to mask these changes. The Classical style signals the contrast between primary and secondary groups not merely from changes in melody but also from changes in dynamics, texture, rhythm (both chord and surface) and phrase unit. The symphonies that do not reach such full control obviously provide some of the most instructive clues to this whole evolution. The sinfonia to *Lucio Papirio* (1737; by either Leo or Feo), for example, firmly establishes a four-bar unit by repeating every two-bar idea (see §4 below). More important, the composer makes a recognizable differentiation between primary, transitional, secondary and closing material; yet having achieved so much, he then merely recapitulates using the exposition–recapitulation form so common in the Italian overture.

Apart from converted overtures, the number of symphonies that can be reliably dated to the 1730–40 period is extremely small. The composers who made the largest contribution during these years seem to have been Johann Stamitz, Sammartini, Brioschi, Solnitz and the little-known J. G. Harrer (1703–55), Bach's follower at the Thomaskirche, Leipzig – a composer who during the 1730s wrote symphonic first movements with well-differentiated expositions as well as respectable developments and full recapitulations.

4. ITALY. Through the first two decades of the century, most of the steps in the evolution of the symphony were taken in the Italian operatic overture. Eventually most composers followed the fast–slow–fast pattern and began to create a style distinct from that of chamber music by increasing the size of thematic units, at first by mere repetition. The more substantial character of these new thematic areas not only produced larger movements, but also served to underline tonic–dominant polarization inherited from binary suite forms. Slow movements developed more gradually, often merely carrying a dignified rhythmic pattern through a few bars of modulatory transition to a speedy fanfare- or dance-like finale. The works of these early 18th-century composers such as L. A. Predieri (1688–1767), Leonardo Vinci (c1690–1730), Leonardo Leo (1694–1744) and G. B. Pergolesi (1710–36) mix Baroque and Classical

features with an insouciance suitable to confound the historian. Predieri, one of the earliest to write miniature but effective sonata forms in a number of his overtures (including those for oratorios), carried his advances to Vienna, where he became Kapellmeister in 1746, an important connection in the symphonic network. In Pergolesi and Leo the transition can be followed between Baroque and Classical by comparing the phrase rhythms in first-movement themes. Pergolesi opened with a typical Baroque motivic cell one beat in length, using adjacent rhythms (semiquaver, quaver, crotchet) arranged in a one-bar unit. Leo multiplied by two, grouping one-bar motifs in a two-bar unit. Apart from this type of enlargement and differentiation, however, the first Italian generation made comparatively small advances in defining the character of symphony movements.

Baldassare Galuppi (1706–85) typifies a second generation of operatic composers whose overtures commonly occur in the sources as concert symphonies without further identification. Though he was based in Venice, his travels produced premières in more than a dozen cities, including not only the Italian centres but also London, Madrid and St Petersburg. He was less concerned than Leo and Vinci with church music and *opera seria*, putting his main emphasis (like many of his contemporaries) on the new fashion of *opera buffa*. Probably as a parallel to the comic librettos he invented catchy melodies with turn figures, snap rhythms and brisk auxiliary-note elaborations of the familiar triad patterns. This fluency of thematic production did not necessarily lead to consistent solutions; though *Il filosofo di campagna* (1754) shows the mid-century overture at its best, balanced in thematic structure and also in the exposition–development–recapitulation sequence, *Antigono* (1746) gives evidence of experimentation and incomplete control. Yet in differentiation of thematic areas Galuppi made great strides; larger

1. Opening of the first violin part of Jommelli's 'Sinfonia a più stromenti obligati' (Paris: Cousineau)

melodic structures (phrase and sub-phrase) have begun to assume settled patterns, such as statement and response.

At this time many slow movements followed the *ABA* shape influenced by the operatic aria, often in the tonic minor rather than subdominant or dominant. Like older composers, Galuppi tended to establish small, active rhythmic patterns that work against cantabile feeling. Finales reflect not only his talent for brisk tempos but also his breadth of choice, including both fast and slow minuets, gigue rhythms, and even a quick 2/4, rare in this genre.

Nicolò Jommelli (1714–74) exceeds Galuppi in importance partly because of his greater musical versatility; he was equally distinguished in theatre and church. He perfected a number of procedures already partly assimilated (second group in the minor, motifs from the primary group recurring in the transition and closing sections: see *Ciro riconosciuto*, 1744), and he showed how they could be connected to form a strong framework. One of his favourite and enduring devices, signalling the transition by shifting part of the primary material to the bass line, persisted in comic opera late into the 19th century. The large Stuttgart orchestra gave Jommelli an opportunity to develop dynamic and timbre effects that enhanced the effect of his symphonies; he had used the orchestral crescendo as early as *Merope* (1741). Less productive and far less known, Rinaldo di Capua (*c*1705–80) deserves careful study for his thematic ideas, first for the coordination of line with rhythmic and harmonic activity, and, even more important, for a higher degree of contrast between primary and secondary material.

The mid-century decades generated a number of experiments, including Jommelli's unique Allegro–Chaconne design (in a work published by Venier in an anthology) and his complex version of the da capo overture: Allegro exposition up to the modulation to the dominant; short Andante in the tonic minor; Allegro da capo, again only up to the transition; and a Presto 3/8 finale (*I-Gi(l)*). The idea of substituting a slow movement for the development section makes an excellent effect, and numerous composers followed the scheme in various ways, continuing even in later concert symphonies such as those of the Florentine violinist G. F. Mosel (1754–*c*1812). Notice that both these solutions represent a shortening of the overture. This trend towards compactness – it led to the one-movement Allegro overture – diverged sharply from the tendency towards elaboration of the concert symphony, which now developed independently except for occasional operatic echoes such as triadic themes, snap rhythms or bustling tremolo in transitions. Nevertheless, the overture continued in favour for concert purposes, as the survival of compositions from late in the century (for example by Paisiello) in hundreds of libraries, typically listed only as 'sinfonia', testifies.

The independent Italian concert symphony presents a different evolutionary picture from the overture. Beginning somewhat later, G. B. Sammartini produced the earliest datable concert symphony in fully recognizable sonata form, originally the overture to *Memet* (1732, *A-HE*). He established a large-scale plan for the expanding symphony, separating it from the *galant* style of the chamber genres and showing how various traits of the Baroque could be redirected for Classical purposes. The powerful beat-marking rhythms moved to the bass, so that the upper voices could articulate larger units; counterpoint submitted to coordinated cadences lest it obscured the main thematic line; the superb Baroque motivic development survived and flourished, particularly in Sammartini's intensive developments; and the deft elisions and overlappings so common in the high Baroque now functioned as links to prevent loss of momentum between heavily punctuated phrases. Innovations in the Classical style were even more influential. Sammartini consistently differentiated between the four sections in sonata-form expositions, not only by familiar contrasts of key and texture but also by equally perceptible but less obvious means such as changes in chord rhythm. In slow movements he used *galant* ornamentation and highly expressive (sometimes almost eccentric) chromaticism both in harmony and in affective intervals such as augmented 4ths and diminished 7ths. Writing mainly three-movement symphonies, Sammartini was among the first to grasp the change in psychology in the finale of the concert symphony. Whereas the overture finale is an exciting upbeat to a larger event, the concert symphony finale stands alone; it must make an impressive ending to a substantial instrumental work. Towards this end Sammartini contributed many well-crafted 3/4 minuets (rather than the breezy 3/8 type of the overtures), and, more important, he developed compact sonata forms that require the listener's full attention.

Sammartini's pre-eminence helped to identify Milan as the centre of north Italian instrumental music, and several capable composers in the area confirm the Milanese contribution to the new symphony; these include Count Giorgio Giulini (1717–80), Antonio Brioschi (*fl* 1730–50), Ferdinando Galimberti (*fl* 1730–50), G. B. Lampugnani (1706–*c*1786) and Melchiorre Chiesa (*fl* 1758–99). The symphonies of two great contemporaries, Padre Martini and Giuseppe Tartini, though significant in musical quality, belong mainly to the Baroque motivic tradition.

The next generation included one of the finest Classical composers, Luigi Boccherini (1743–1805). The attractions of Boccherini's melodies have led many writers to overlook his profound control of other musical opportunities: his handling of rhythmic details as well as phrasing gives a sophisticated impression of both vigour and wit. In complex thematic hierarchies his orchestral imagination unfailingly provided matching levels of contrast. The themes may reflect familiar Italianate lyricism, but he often reached a new intensity by use of a large-scale line that embraced several four- or eight-bar phrases. In his concern for inner parts he seems to have inherited Sammartini's understanding of coordinated polyphony as a way of enhancing texture without losing thematic control. Gaetano Pugnani (1731–98), for a time nearly as popular as Boccherini, especially in England, compares favourably with him in lyricism, giving special flavour to his symphonies by using cantabile ideas even for primary sections. He lacked Boccherini's long line and soundly woven textures, but avoided stereotypes by his somewhat experimental attitude, sometimes regressive in tendency (tempo schemes such as Andante–Allegro–Minuet, a throwback to chamber style), sometimes strikingly pre-Romantic (impulsive line and dynamics in slow movements, descriptive attempts in his 'Werther' symphony, *c*1795).

Quite different in emphasis from these sometimes blandly lyric composers, Gaetano Brunetti (1744–98) wrote a number of stormy works with an unusually high proportion of minor tonalities matched by abrupt rhythms and jagged lines. Brunetti, who worked in Spain, is one of the most original of the *Kleinmeister*; his music is effective in performance and appealing for its Haydnesque rhythmic verve and taut continuity. In one small but important respect he made a unique contribution: to avoid the stereotyped minuet–trio–minuet sequence, he reversed the plan, beginning with a 'quintetto' of woodwind, followed by full orchestra and then a return of the quintetto. This scheme revitalizes the minuet, perhaps a bit whimsically, and lends the first tutti of the finale an additional impact. Other *Kleinmeister* whose names should be noted are Fortunato Chelleri (*c*1690–1757), Gaudenzio Comi (*fl* 1785), P. M. Crispi (*c*1737–1797), Gaetano Latilla (1711–88), F. P. Ricci (1732–1817), Gregorio Sciroli (1722–*c*1781), Giuseppe Scolari (?1720–*c*1774) and Tommaso Traetta (1727–79).

Most Italian composers failed to realize the potential that Sammartini had so clearly initiated, perhaps because of a disinclination towards the 'serious style' implicit in the evolution of the symphony. Yet in the supreme works of Mozart and Haydn there is never a movement that does not by some touch of cantabile line or rhythmic spark pay tribute to the Italian background.

5. NORTH GERMANY. Although north Germany produced and imported a number of excellent composers during the second half of the 18th century, the north German school made a surprisingly slight contribution to the history of the symphony. Among the influences that tended to deflect creative energies in other directions were, first, the strength of Lutheran traditions, with resulting emphases on vocal composition and organ music (the latter carrying over to the keyboard concerto rather than to the symphony); second, the French cultural presence, to be seen in elegant ornamentation and binary suite forms, both of which worked against the evolution of broader units and recapitulatory designs; and third (perhaps most important), a preoccupation with Italian opera. The senior figure of the north German group, J. A. Hasse (1699–1783), apparently wrote no symphonies, though his overtures appear in virtually every 18th-century concert repertory, often not identified with the opera to which they belonged. While his celebrated arias show the voice in both its suave and brilliant aspects, the overtures fall into repetitious, motivic rhythms, particularly unfortunate at this time of stylistic change. In the high Baroque style, even the most note-repetitive themes would have gained relief from rapid chord changes and sequential modulations; in the emerging Classical style, however, the stabilized harmony and balanced sub-phrases turn Hasse's potentially vigorous ideas into arid repetitions. The cross-currents of transition also produced expositions with Classical thematic contrast alongside rigid ritornello forms and a tiny Grave in Scarlattian style long after the development of slow movements in expansive binary design. Where the phrase problem did not intervene, Hasse showed great originality, for example in finding new sounds (two english horns in *Il trionfo di Clelia*, 1762) and new forms (the minuet-rondo finale of *Asteria*, 1737).

Of the brothers Graun, who worked at the court of Frederick the Great, Carl Heinrich (1703/4–59) became the Kapellmeister, composing operas in the Italian style with three-movement overtures that rivalled Hasse for tick-tock rhythm. Graun never fully absorbed Italian vocal grace, but compensated with north German virtues: his motivic treatment in development sections and his stronger weaving of inner parts furnished a useful model for younger composers. J. G. Graun (1702/3–71), leader of the court orchestra, wrote numerous and better symphonies than his more famous brother, though also relying on Italian formal precedents. Somewhat addicted to drumming rhythms, like Hasse, he showed a much firmer sense of Classical balance, whether in phrases or in the well-planned climaxes of his development sections.

J. W. Hertel (1727–89), almost a generation younger, has not received appropriate credit for his well-constructed symphonies, perhaps because they still include old-fashioned characteristics such as rhythmic stereotypes. But on the other hand there are themes with well-developed rhythmic and melodic outlines. Equally up to date in orchestration, Hertel moved away from the string orchestra, adding flutes and bassoons to the by now familiar horns; bassoons can usually be assumed, even if not indicated, and Hertel wrote specific bassoon solos in slow movements.

C. P. E. Bach occupies an enigmatic position in the history of the symphony. Only a few of his works achieved wide distribution and, since most composers seemed unable either to adopt or adapt his style, his influence though intense was selective. The fundamental enigma of his style results from an almost bewildering combination of Baroque, Classical and pre-Romantic traits. The shifts from one style to another, though sometimes shockingly abrupt, nevertheless, by the skill of his treatment, produce unforgettable moments. The influence of J. S. Bach can be felt in the frequent polyphonic textures, whether ingenious, casual imitation or serious fugato. Equally Baroque are his passages in undifferentiated rhythm or adjacent note values such as a quaver and two semiquavers. The motivic treatment, however, has evolved beyond mere linear continuation to a process of significant change and growth that is fully Classical in character. C. P. E. Bach's mastery of the developmental process, including development by fragmentation or permutation, contrapuntal explorations and new harmonic or orchestral coloration, leads beyond his contemporaries to Haydn and Beethoven. Parallel with this redefinition of motivic play, Bach also deepened the function of ornaments, turning them from charming appliqués into affective vehicles of the *Empfindsamer Stil*, capable of reflecting every nuance of feeling, yet fully integrated into the melodic line. Similarly affective, his chromatic or dissonant ornaments and sudden dynamic shifts concentrate one's responses on brief crises of violent feeling and there almost seems to be an effort to shock the listener. Neither these Romantic moments nor the Baroque details of rhythm and ornamentation require a large musical unit, and thus even Bach's long movements do not necessarily achieve a fully Classical breadth.

In symphonic style, original and colourful details may interrupt the flow or disrupt the balance of the larger design. C. P. E. Bach's attitude may be understood by a comparison between his use of surprise and Haydn's. For Bach, surprise was important in itself, for its emotional impact; for Haydn too it created emotional excitement, but the excitement is structural, and enhances the awareness of a total, unfolding design. This difference in Bach's emphasis implies no lack of understanding of Classical continuity or articulation, and his acute sensitivity to harmonic tension and excursion went far beyond the conventional tonal patterns, including the use of remote keys for slow movements and as developmental goals. Among his numerous originalities are the skilful connection of movements by devices such as deceptive cadences; the use of unusual ranges and textural distributions; the exploitation of new chord types and new dissonant combinations; and a command of dynamics that influenced the next century more than his own.

Two members of the Benda family excelled in the north German development. Franz Benda (1709–86), a chamber musician of Frederick the Great, learnt the rhythmically stiff style of the Grauns and remained more conservative in his symphonies than in his concertos. Georg Benda (1722–95), known more for his pioneering melodramas than for his symphonies, moved beyond contemporary motivic material to a broader thematic style with stronger potentialities for contrast. During this same period a Swede, J. J. Agrell (1701–65), held the post of Kapellmeister in Kassel, as well as others in Nuremberg. He followed the Hasse–Graun style of symphony, but developed ways to make the motivic units interesting by recombination into larger units: motifs one or two beats long may be part of sub-phrases, then pleasingly extended to varying lengths.

6. VIENNA. The traditional position of Vienna as a crossroads in European civilization stimulated many special achievements. In the 18th century the web of cultural influence spread unusually wide, owing to the extent of the Austro-Hungarian Empire, and the confluence of talent brought an incomparable richness of ideas and creative activity to bear on the evolution of the symphony. Paris may have exceeded Vienna in brilliance of musical performance, but the imperial capital early in the century drew together an impressive number of musician–composers, supported by a unique proliferation of patronage: hundreds of the Austrian nobility supported musical establishments. In such a climate of opportunity every talent flourished, and all musical genres bloomed. The spread and disparate character of the Viennese evolution of the symphony contrasts with the more unified developments in north Italy and Mannheim. There are symphonies with full sonata form but Baroque material of chamber music proportions, and others with detailed thematic differentiation but slight development or aborted recapitulation. The scattered pieces began to fall into place about 1750.

The influence of Italian opera persisted in Vienna throughout the 18th century; the characteristic Viennese feeling for recapitulation may owe a good deal to this long exposure to operatic ritornello and da capo. Equally important, the operatic aria had made important advances towards Classical phrase units. These local developments apparently contributed to the advancement of Italian composers in Vienna, whereas Italian symphonists in Italy, such as Sammartini, were somewhat inhibited (especially in phrase growth) by the strong Torelli–Vivaldi tradition, with its exciting yet conservative concentration on motivic rhythm.

The first important Viennese symphonic composers were the Italians F. B. Conti (1681–1732) and L. A.

Predieri, both of whom worked in Vienna in their mature years. Conti's overture to *Pallade trionfante* (1722) has often been cited (see Botstiber, 1913) as a pivotal work, because its first movement contains a skeletal sonata form with clear thematic contrast and a full recapitulation. These advanced procedures do not produce a Classical work, however, largely because the thematic material is motivic, and its unfolding by sequence, imitation and ritornello-like recurrences in foreign keys inevitably recalls Baroque style. Predieri had written small overtures with recapitulations in oratorios for Bologna as early as 1723; he then brought this experience to bear on early opera overtures for Vienna (e.g. *Il sogno di Scipione*, 1735) which rival Conti in their convincing sense of recapitulation, though still small in size and less effective in differentiating thematic material.

No less important than opera to the Viennese development was the active cultivation of chamber music in the musical establishments of a myriad of lesser nobility and larger merchants. There was a gradual rise in the syntactic level of the musical material from the motivic particles of the Baroque to the larger structures of Classical phrase, an expansion that prepared in turn for works of true symphonic dimensions. For example, in the partitas of Matthaeus Schlöger (1722–66) there are not only full recapitulatory forms but also significant advances in phrase enlargement, such as the clear connection of sub-phrases in the relationships of statement and response (doubled units, 2 from $1 + 1$), as opposed to the unconnected sub-phrases of *Fortspinnung* or simple contrast (single units, 1, 1, 1 . . .).

About 1735 the Viennese symphony, drawing on these two significant stylistic sources (opera overture and chamber music) began to establish an independent course, notably in the works of M. G. Monn (1717–50) and G. C. Wagenseil (1715–77). A symphony by Monn including a minuet and dated 1740 has been treated as a turning-point by scholars supporting Austrian primacy. In fact, apart from the order of its four tiny movements, the work is conspicuously regressive in character: all movements are in the same key; the thematic material is motivic; and, most significant, there is no recognizable sonata form. Accompanied by such conservatism, the innovatory four-movement format had little impact; and Monn himself wrote almost exclusively three-movement works. These later symphonies, though equally conservative, reflect great sensitivity to line and a remarkable feeling for harmony, both in his choice of unusual tonalities and his sharply expressive use of dissonance. His works mark a transition between chamber music and symphony.

Wagenseil, a prolific composer more in touch with the full spectrum of Viennese musical life, began his career by composing Italian operas for the Viennese court. Their overtures and his independent concert symphonies were published both in France and England; these were mostly trio symphonies, typically Viennese in their firm grasp of the principle of recapitulation but still small in dimension and texture. His works after about 1765 contain more four-movement cycles. Rhythmic vigour and a strong sense of continuity give an immediate appeal to many of his symphonies, but he rarely escaped the emphases characteristic of small-scale works: his snap rhythms, syncopation, sweeping upbeats and quick turns enliven the individual beat, but the grouping of beats into larger units – sub-phrases and phrases – lacks profile and may involve merely a chain of repeated beats without differentiation. The combination of motivic material and strong rhythmic continuity tends to work against thematic contrast, and many of Wagenseil's expositions, though clear in tonal–textural outlines, lack a parallel thematic clarity because of constantly recurring motifs.

Florian Gassmann (1729–74) made his reputation as an opera composer in Italy, and later served as Kapellmeister to the Viennese court. In Gassmann's symphonies, as compared with Wagenseil's, much more of the operatic lyricism carries over, even affecting vigorous fast movements. He experimented constantly with first-movement form, using shapes ranging from ritornello structures to sophisticated thematic plans in which the transitional, secondary and closing material are each variants of the primary yet at the same time serve their characteristic functions. Most unusual are a number of works with recapitulations beginning in a key other than the tonic. In other details of style Gassmann's most striking talent is his control of rhythmic outline both as a means of creating a smooth rise and fall of activity in the phrase and as a way of building excitement towards a major climax. His management of texture, especially in careful deployment of partial tuttis and mixed groups with the cello or even the viola serving as bass, reflects a constant awareness of the broad objectives of each movement. Carlo d'Ordonez (1734–86), who composed more than 70 symphonies, mainly three-movement works in the Monn–Wagenseil tradition, left one work opening with a slow movement connected to a following Allegro, dated 1756; this seems to be not a perpetuation of the slow–fast opening of the trio sonata, but a prototype of the slow symphonic introduction. Like Monn, with his four-movement symphony, Ordonez did not exploit his innovatory slow introduction, but the precedent may have been known to Hofmann and Haydn, who turned it to good use in the following decade.

Apart from Haydn and Mozart, the highest achievements in the Viennese Classical symphony were those of a quartet of prolific, gifted composers who were nearly exact contemporaries: Leopold Hofmann, Dittersdorf, J. B. Vanhal and Michael Haydn. The sources of the symphonies of Leopold Hofmann (1738–93) are second in number only to Haydn and Pleyel in European archives – a significant measure of contemporary popularity. It was he, not Haydn, who was the first to adopt a four-movement form with slow introduction as well as minuet and trio (copies as early as 1761, *A-GÖ*; Breitkopf catalogue, 1762). Though only slightly younger than Gassmann and Ordonez, he matured at the right time to exploit the new internal coordination and the larger unit of the Classical style; as a result, his sonata structures and thematic types leave an impression of both clarity and differentiation. Much of his music has a pre-Mozartian smoothness extending even to lyrical Allegro themes. In view of his convincing style and the wide distribution of his music, there is no doubt that Hofmann's four-movement symphonies exercised a strong influence on the evolution of the final symphonic form.

Dittersdorf (1739–99) was the most prolific Classical symphonist (J. M. Molter composed more but smaller works in post-Baroque style); he wrote at least 130. Although one expects (and finds) many recurrent formulae, there is much genuine invention and instinctively good structure. The large-scale movement of his line is convincing, and he was equally skilful in a brisk Allegro or in a sophisticated cantabile with smoothly balanced phrases. There are many small niceties of thematic relationship and development, using techniques such as imitation (never long pursued), diminution, augmentation and recombination of motifs. On occasion, like Haydn, he could simulate (or perhaps remember) a catchy peasant tune to fit a rustic mood. Also like Haydn, Dittersdorf introduced many touches of the specialized musical humour that results from phrase extensions or truncations, displaced accents or other bar-line manoeuvres. But there is a lack of rhythmic variety in lower parts, and the harmony from bar to bar lacks interest. Possibly because of his success in dramatic music, Dittersdorf began very early to give descriptive titles to symphonies, including a seven-movement work describing the humours of mankind, a series based on Ovid's *Metamorphoses*, and a *Sinfonia nel gusto di cinque nazioni* (1767) with movements that supposedly reflect German, Italian, English, French and Turkish taste. Though these are the remote ancestors of the 19th-century programmatic symphony, Dittersdorf's descriptive symphonies contain scarcely more actual description than the touches that gave Haydn's Paris symphonies their nicknames: for example, the croaking of the farmers changed into frogs and Actaeon, transformed into a stag, jumping in a 6/8 *tempo di caccia*. Except for the polyglot symphony, these are among Dittersdorf's least interesting works.

His contemporary Vanhal (1739–1813), with symphonies published in London in Bremner's *Periodical Overture* series, others issued by Breitkopf and Hummel, as well as a large corpus of manuscript sources, was unusually popular in northern Europe. Although they are soundly constructed, with attractive, well-contrasted themes and skilful formal techniques, the true reason for his popularity may be a quality of pathos, reflected in the unusual number of minor tonalities in his work, and more specifically in a remarkable spectrum of tragic expression, ranging from melancholy introspection to fiery tragedy. Vanhal made few experiments and no contributions to the evolving symphonic convention; but, more than Hofmann or Dittersdorf, he seems to parallel Haydn in the ability to make his music move in a tight process of continuation, with each phrase containing the genetic code for its successor. There is also a kinship to Mozart in the use of gentle, retrospective closing themes that interpolate a moment of quiet before the final trumpets. Vanhal seems to have been the first to use four and five horns in a symphony.

The oldest of the quartet of Viennese-orientated *Kleinmeister* was Michael Haydn (1737–1806); he spent most of his life in Salzburg, but his style belongs more to the Viennese school than elsewhere. Yet curiously, as with Leopold Mozart, there are qualities that set him apart. In the first place there is an almost Baroque rhythmic continuity with many similar note values – bar after bar of quavers, for example; in similarly continuous and undifferentiated passages, Joseph Haydn found ways of punctuating and regulating the flow by harmony or texture. Another somewhat old-fashioned characteristic in Michael's music is both welcome and more successful in the Classical context: the use of contrapuntal textures and devices, which lend unusual interest to many of his movements. His music is specially impressive for its harmonic inventiveness, which contributes not only highly unusual modulations and the dramatic placement of remote chords, but also sinuously chromatic lines much like passages of Mozart; it is impossible to be sure who influenced whom.

7. MANNHEIM. While Vienna presents a truly imperial diversity of symphonic activity, Mannheim stands at the opposite pole in its concentration of talent and energy in a single electoral court, a single orchestra and a single Kapellmeister, J. W. A. Stamitz (1717–57), a man of exceptional drive and innovatory talent who gathered an orchestra of virtuosos and trained them to a pitch of discipline that astounded all listeners. The Mannheim orchestral effects, such as the famous crescendo and *sforzando–piano*, were actually more Italian than Palatinate innovations. But the expert ensemble of the Mannheim group, particularly when playing Mannheim symphonies specifically composed to exploit these effects, created an overwhelming impression that Mannheim was the centre of a new and distinctive style.

The sheer volume of symphonies produced by the composers there played a part in Mannheim's prominence. The virtuosos that Stamitz collected were nearly all active composers, and his tireless activity gave them both motivation and a successful model. About 1740, partly capitalizing on advances by Italians such as Jommelli (see Wolf, 1968), Stamitz worked out several basic Classical procedures that left Monn and Wagenseil temporarily far behind. As a first problem,

larger dimensions required broader contrasts, which in turn required clearer stabilization of the main tonal areas as foundation for those contrasts. In earlier works neither melodic nor rhythmic contrasts could take full effect against the hyperactive Baroque harmony and bass line. Secondly, stabilization in small dimensions – the slowing down of chord rhythm at the phrase level – is a further prerequisite for Classical contrast. Finally, as if sensing the dangers of too much stability, Stamitz typically constructed musical ideas with rhythms that created momentum, or with connective features such as thematic upbeats and matching activity in other parts, so that each phrase seems impatient to launch into the next. This quality of general rhythmic élan and the homogeneity of this type of material obviously implies a considerable degree of interchangeability; and Stamitz often developed ideas, not only in the development itself, as much by permutation of phrases and sub-phrases as by variation. Using these principles as a foundation, Stamitz's colleagues and pupils were able for a time (*c*1740–60) to produce an unusually high proportion of effective symphonies.

The Stamitz model, despite its confident movement and exciting orchestration, contained a fatal ambiguity in its uncertainty of recapitulation. His characteristic first-movement design was not a fully recapitulatory sonata form but an expanded binary, with a well-differentiated exposition followed by a statement of the primary material in the dominant and extensive developmental exploration after the double-bar (or after the dominant plateau, if there is no double-bar). At this point, Stamitz apparently felt no need to return to the primary material in the tonic. Structurally, the secondary and closing sections by themselves cannot stabilize the tonic sufficiently to balance the forceful Mannheim exposition and development. A recapitulation of only the secondary and closing material may produce too abrupt a conclusion. Concern on this point can be seen in the music itself: in numerous Mannheim works weight is added towards the end of the movement, for example with a final quasi-ritornello based on the primary material or interjections of it in the secondary or closing sections.

The first generation of Mannheim composers included men both older and younger than Stamitz. The oldest, F. X. Richter (1709–89), looked backward in his motivic rhythms, imitative textures, compact miniature forms and conservative orchestration (often without wind). As in the music of Monn, however, this generally regressive orientation did not exclude imaginative details in harmony or interesting tonal plans. Richter's occasional attempts to adopt Stamitz's new slower chord rhythms and clearly punctuated themes are particularly instructive: for example, about 16 bars of a Symphony in A (op.4 no.5; DTB, iv, Jg.iii/1, 118) sounds like a mature work of Stamitz or of a second-generation Mannheimer; thereafter it returns to undifferentiated rhythm and motivic sequence techniques far from the Classical spirit. The most individual trait of Richter's music is its frequent use of surprise, most commonly in the form of pauses and unexpected rhythmic twists.

Ignaz Holzbauer (1711–83), born in Vienna, went to Mannheim in 1753 after a long career mainly as a composer of Italian opera. In early life Holzbauer had written small, rather dull trio symphonies much like

2. Title-page of Michael Haydn's 'Tre Sinfonie a Grand Orchestra' (Vienna: Artaria, c1785)

those of Wagenseil. His style developed considerably, perhaps as a result of his travels: he retained a firm grip on the Viennese habit of full recapitulation while writing a fairly advanced type of statement–response theme that sounds more typical of Mannheim. In general Holzbauer fell behind Stamitz in both thematic contrast and orchestral craft. But his more consistent use of full recapitulation may have influenced the trend of younger Mannheimers.

Younger than Stamitz by half a generation, Anton Filtz (1733–60) had fewer Baroque remnants to overcome and a more instinctive feeling for Classical syntax. His natural, sure-footed movement, easy melodic style and uncomplicated textures led to early popularity. The immediate appeal of his music hides an extremely subtle phrase structure, arranged to produce an under-the-surface excitement all the more interesting because concealed. For example, his Symphony in A opens with a long crescendo underlined by accelerating surface rhythm, rising line and expanding texture. Less immediately noticeable, but extremely powerful, is his parallel acceleration and deceleration in phrase rhythm: for example $2 + 2$, 2; $2 + 2$, $2 + 1$, 1, 1, 1, $2 + 2$. As if to balance this fine art Filtz drew on the folk idiom not only for minuets but also for main movements.

The second generation of Mannheim composers included a larger group of resident composers and many more who show unmistakable influence of Stamitz's effective phrase design and orchestral style. The most important figures were C. J. Toeschi, Cannabich, Carl Stamitz, Ernst Eichner and F. I. Beck. Born within the Classical period itself, these composers show little Baroque influence except for obviously retrospective procedures such as fugato or sequence, usually in their development sections. Many Mannheim composers made annual or more frequent visits to Paris, and this French influence may account for a sharp rise in the number of three-movement symphonies in the work of the second generation. Though some ambiguity still affects the recapitulations, the example of Haydn and other successful Viennese undoubtedly furnished an important new model. At the same time the main achievements of the elder Stamitz in structure and orchestration carried over with continuing vitality. In these two areas Mozart evidently learnt a good deal from Mannheim.

The modern editions of symphonies of Toeschi (1731–88) include a cautionary example of slanting of evidence: Riemann, concerned to prove that Mannheim originated the four-movement symphony, selected possibly the only such work of Toeschi; about 50 others of his symphonies take the three-movement form (see Münster, 1956). This symphony is exceptional in other ways: motivic thematic material, frequent imitative textures and lack of sectional contrast. Elsewhere he wrote in an uncomplicated style with simple textures, clearly punctuated themes and effective orchestration noted for its difficult violin parts. The smoothly lyrical quality that distinguishes Toeschi's themes may relate to his Italian background. He liked his own ideas; the frequent repetition approaches a deadly predictability. Neither this habit nor his frequent return to Stamitz's ambiguous binary form seemed to trouble Toeschi's public.

Christian Cannabich (1731–98), after writing dozens of rather pedestrian symphonies, produced late in life (after the electoral court moved to Munich) a few larger, more complicated works of striking quality, notably a symphony in B♭ (DTB, xv, Jg.viii/2) that in melodic appeal, instrumental colour and developmental ingenuity ranks with the best of the century. The early works lack melodic invention, but Cannabich at times recaptured in them the electric quality of Stamitz's rhythmic drive, and made more use of the four-movement plan than any other second-generation composer (including a work with slow introduction, 1763, nearly as early as Hofmann and Haydn).

Ernst Eichner (1740–77) well illustrates the concentration of talent in Mannheim, since he established a triple reputation as violinist, bassoonist and composer. Writing symphonies only in his last eight years, he could base his work on a style already well evolved, and his symphonies (mainly in three movements) are among the most clearly articulated, formally the best balanced, and most sensitively orchestrated of those of the second generation. He attained a particularly advanced thematic differentiation that not only contrasted secondary sections but also individualized the material of transitions and closing sections; at the same time he was able to embed these ideas in sentences and paragraphs with strong directional flow. In approaching a climax, the nicety of balance achieved between harmonic tension, melodic line and rhythmic activity goes far beyond most of the other Mannheimers.

F. I. Beck (1734–1809), one of Stamitz's most original pupils, found difficulty in controlling his vivid imagination within the balanced rationality of Classicism, as can be heard in moments of exaggerated dynamic contrast, abrupt rhythm, excessively poignant dissonance or dramatically impulsive pauses. Yet elsewhere he used the normal Classical language with skill and individuality, writing in minor mode and in four-movement cycles more than most of his second-generation colleagues. He was at his best in the treatment of detail, making convincing use of Stamitz's techniques of permutation and motivic compression. Apparently less concerned with larger dimensions, he did not apply his mastery of instant contrast to the clarification of the dominant area of his expositions, which are often less well differentiated than those of Toeschi or Eichner.

Johann Stamitz lived just long enough to be aware of the precocious talent of his elder son, Carl Stamitz (1745–1801), a worthy successor and even more prolific symphonist. Born nearly at mid-century and hence inheriting a fully developed Classical syntax, Carl represents the height of Mannheim formal achievements in his use of characteristic types of theme for all the exposition sections. Within these thematic phrases there is a combination of soundly balanced line and rhythm with a less easily described melodic charm that influenced dozens of other composers, including Mozart. Probably owing to the large number of compositions and the rapid circumstances of production, Stamitz occasionally fell victim to his own versions of Mannheim clichés, such as the ubiquitous 'sigh', yet even the presence of clichés does not spoil the polished succession of phrases and sentence structures. Apart from thematic specialization, Stamitz's finest expression is in slow movements, where he managed to introduce a surprising amount of counterpoint without distracting attention from his long, singing upper line.

8. PARIS. In the second half of the 18th century Paris was the greatest centre of musical performance and industry, but not of symphony composition. The domin-

ation of French music by the opera gave little encouragement to French symphonists, and the surprising total of more than 1000 works compiled by Brook (1962) must be seen in the light of his inclusion of works in the SYMPHONIE CONCERTANTE form.

The 1740 publication of *VI symphonies dans le goût italien en trio* op.6 of L. G. Guillemain (1705–70) places the beginnings of the Parisian symphony in a chronology closely parallel to that of Vienna and Mannheim. The 'Italian taste' mentioned in this title (and repeated in Guillemain's op.14, 1748) probably refers to the insistent quality of beat-marking quaver and semiquaver rhythms in a quasi-contrapuntal, three-part texture that recalls the Corelli–Vivaldi tradition. Also, while the consistent one- and two-bar units give a less motivic feeling than early works of Monn and Wagenseil, the exact repetition of many bars evokes the tutti–solo echos of the Baroque concerto. These retrospective details, however, do not outweigh a basically Classical impression caused by clear differentiation of primary, secondary and closing material, with matching punctuation not only by rests but also by slower chord and surface rhythm; by the fresh treatment of derived material in developments occasionally longer than their respective expositions; and by the full, literal recapitulations. The confluence of characteristic traits of Classicism clearly identifies Guillemain as the pioneer of the Parisian symphony.

A decade later François Martin (ii) (1727–57) published a title as significant as that of Guillemain, *Simphonies et ouvertures* op.4 (1751). Here the overtures have slow introductions followed by fugal allegros; the symphonies do not. This in turn raises doubt as to whether (as Landon and others have suggested) the slow introduction of the Classical symphony derives from the opening Grave of the French overture. As Martin's segregation shows, there is a clear separation between genres and little chronological continuity between the height of the French overture and the maturity of the symphonic introduction. The few introductions in early symphonies of Gossec sound quite unlike French overtures.

The long productive life of François-Joseph Gossec (1734–1829), the ablest composer of the Parisian group, did much to establish and maintain the strength of the French symphony. In his first six works, op.3 (1756), Italian influence is evident in snap rhythms and obvious triadic themes; and at first Gossec did not differentiate ideas as well as Guillemain. Even in his early work, however, there is strong rhythmic control. By op.4 (c1758) Gossec had assimilated most features of the mature Classical symphony, and in using well-planned sonata form in many slow movements and finales he kept the Parisian model up to date. Here and in op.5 he paralleled Viennese developments in clarity of divisions, thematic contrast and full recapitulation, though fewer of the French symphonies have slow introductions. With the broad sweep of his melodic lines and the telling use of warm harmonic touches, particularly diminished 7ths, Gossec created a personal style recognizable even among the hundreds of contemporary works. His frequently asymmetrical treatment of phrasing brought charges from the critics that he imitated Haydn, and in other respects Gossec's symphonies maintained a high level and serious tone, noticeable in the large proportion of works in the minor and in the frequency of well-worked textures with clean-lined

counterpoint. In these points he stood out against the characteristically facile tone of many later Parisian symphonies. The works of his own middle period move away from the four-movement plan and include unusual instrumental combinations and unconventional designs, ideas that provided more food for thought than convincing listening.

It was impossible for the French symphony to maintain any national identity after 1750 in the bustling cosmopolitanism of Paris. First came the invasion from Mannheim, whose virtuosos brought the brilliantly effective new style to Paris on their visits. Second, the growing Paris publishing industry found that the most marketable composer was Joseph Haydn. Finally, as the capital of the performing world, Paris attracted countless foreign musician–composers, many of them respectable symphonists. Though in the last quarter of the century a separate French style cannot often be recognized, the excellent models available to Parisian composers and the stiff competition from foreign talent made the last phase of the Parisian symphony surprisingly strong.

The Italian influence noted in early Parisian symphonies received further impetus from the arrival of the Roman flautist–composer, Filippo Ruge (c1725–after 1767), who brought numerous Italian works with him. He wrote symphonies with early examples of programmatic titles (op.1 no.4, *La tempesta*, 1756). A more important immigrant composer was H. J. Rigel (1741–99), who wrote 20 symphonies of notable thematic inspiration and strong harmonic pathos in slow movements. Born in Germany and influenced by the Mannheim group, he wrote three-movement symphonies that typify the Parisian style about 1770. Opening with appealing cantabile or neatly articulated melodies, the movements unfold smoothly because of the composer's mastery of phrase formation and connection. The range of thematic types in each work adds a vitality of impression that easily explains his popularity at the time. Other significant figures among the immigrant composers were G. M. Cambini (1746–1825) and Valentin Roeser (*fl* 1760–89).

Simon Leduc *l'aîné* (c1745–1777), after Gossec the most forceful native composer, lived too short a time to develop his early promise. Like Gossec he commands attention first by rhythmic force, but he goes beyond the older composer in his more highly developed ability to support rhythmic fluctuations with appropriate orchestration and chord rhythm. He raised rhythmic control beyond surface rhythm to the level of phrases, maintaining a variety in these phrase rhythms that recalls Haydn's imaginative treatments. Again like Gossec, his slow movements in no way fall behind the driving allegros, though their power derives less from rhythm than through the accumulation of harmonic interest from the tension of exceptionally long lines.

In the decades after 1760 the pace of French publishing became almost feverish, a trend reflected in the invention of a new sales device, the 'Symphonie périodique' (i.e. new symphonies issued at stated intervals), a concept imported to London by Robert Bremner as the 'Periodical Overture'. About 1770 the Parisian composers, possibly in response to public preference for lively, colourful works, developed a new type of two-movement concerto (Allegro, Rondeau), which they misleadingly called the 'Symphonie concertante'. Many of the better composers, such as Cambini, J.-B. Davaux, M.-A. Guénin, L.-C. Ragué and J. B. Saint

Georges, wrote almost exclusively in the new genre, no doubt in part because of the overwhelming success of Haydn's symphonies. A Haydn pupil, I. J. Pleyel (1757–1831), became the outstanding composer of the last phase of the Parisian symphony. He brought back the four-movement style, often with slow introductions (which also returned in the late works of Gossec). Pleyel made several valuable innovations, such as the insertion of a quick episode in a slow movement or the addition of a short bridge between trio and returning minuet (cf Haydn's no.104). Exceedingly facile in generating thematic variants, he sometimes expanded a development to as many as three episodes. His orchestration invariably fits the musical material aptly, and he approached strings, woodwind and brass not merely as blocks of sound but as flexible combinations, for example using single woodwind with strings, or viola as bass for a thematic woodwind passage. Contemporaneous with Pleyel's are symphonies of a quite different type, such as *La bataille de Gemmapp* (1794) of Devienne and *La tempête et le calme* (1794) of Massonneau: the intent of these works is obviously romantic, and they are mentioned here only to indicate the point of transition.

9. LONDON, OTHER LOCAL CENTRES. Like the Italian symphony, the origin of the English symphony lies in the operatic overture. As early as *The Fairy Queen* (1692) Purcell wrote a substantial multi-movement fourth act tune. Cudworth's research has shown that by the time of Handel's arrival the fashion was changing from French to Italian, and English composers such as Croft (*The Twinn Rivalls*, 1703) and Barrett (*Tunbridge Walks*, 1703) as well as Italian visitors such as Francesco Mancini (*Hydaspe fedele*, 1710) used the fast–slow–fast pattern of the sinfonia. An idea of the growth in size and complexity of the English overture can be gained by a study of Pepusch's masque *Apollo and Daphne* (1716), Greene's opera *Florimel* (1734) and Arne's *Eight Overtures* (1751), two of them in sinfonia form. Still Baroque in character are Boyce's *Eight Symphonys in Eight Parts* op.2 (1760), compiled from overtures as early as his *Solomon* (1743). Several of Arne's later overtures (*Artaxerxes*, 1762; *The Guardian Outwitted*, 1764) show Classical tendencies, but even at this late date the English symphony had not established a Classical pattern. Through many centuries London had offered hospitality to continental musicians, most recently to Handel, Pepusch and countless Italian performer–composers. Again two foreign composers of central importance brought full Classicism to Britain in the decade in which Paris also experienced a wave of foreign influence. C. F. Abel (1723–87) and J. C. Bach (1735–82) arrived in London in 1759 and 1762 respectively, joining forces to produce the Bach–Abel concerts, a series decisive for the development of the Classical style in England. Abel, best known as a viola da gamba virtuoso, published six sets of extremely popular symphonies, all in three movements, some with minuet finales of the mid-century Italian type. More careful as a craftsman than many Italians, he wrote symphonies with energetic movement, clearly punctuated form and strongly woven texture. His advanced thematic construction, with well-balanced statement-response phrases, led to better differentiation and logical development. Abel's symphonies in general sound more competent than inspired, but in slow movements there are some exceptionally beautiful long lines and graceful

chromatic appoggiaturas later called 'Mozartian'.

Scrupulously educated by his elder brother, Carl Philipp Emanuel, and Padre Martini, J. C. Bach also reflects a wealth of his own operatic experience in the exquisite lyricism of his andantes. No-one before Mozart understood as well as Bach how to underline the curve of a superb melody with a suitable ebb and flow of harmony and surface rhythm; at the same time many skilful small imitations in the bass or inner parts give added charm to the texture, again recalling Mozart's effortless devices. Even more important, Bach used this control to make small connections between sub-phrases, phrases and sentences, developing the musical equivalents of commas, semicolons and full stops. His combination of imagination and technical mastery made possible a wide variety and subtle gradation of thematic ideas, which he then distinguished according to expositional functions: even out of context his themes sound like primary, transitional, secondary or closing material.

Several other resident or touring Germans contributed to the English symphony. Friedrich Schwindl (1737–86) visited England in 1765 and later arranged for the publication of three symphonies in Mannheim style that were reprinted many times. Antonín Kammel (1730–c1787) published a set of 'overtures' (op.10, 1775) which because of their repetitiveness give a poor impression by comparison with his attractive chamber music. The younger generation of British composers started out well with *Six Symphonies* op.1 by Thomas Erskine, Earl of Kelly (1732–81), a pupil of Johann Stamitz who had obviously learnt something of Stamitz's rhythmic drive, dynamic orchestral treatment and thematic contrast. John Collett's op.2 contains the only English four-movement symphony of the time, but before the minuet a note is printed, 'Either or both of the following movements to be played', an excellent summary of the status of the four-movement style. The small works of William Smethergell (*fl* 1780) sound at times like the beginnings of the second Mannheim generation, but his forms are too brief to take advantage of the Mannheim achievements. The ablest of the younger British composers was J. A. Fisher (1744–1806), whose symphonies (c1775), again extremely short, show sensitive and knowledgeable orchestral writing, including bassoon solos and a very early use, for printed music, of triple *piano*. John Marsh (1752–1828) moved away from the miniature proportions used by his contemporaries, later writing several four-movement symphonies and considerably enlarging the individual movements; his inventive *Conversation Sinfonie* (1784) exploits the idea of a dialogue between two small orchestras, doubtless in imitation of the three double-orchestra symphonies of J. C. Bach's op.18.

There seems little doubt that English admiration for Handel and the continuing stress on his music in performance and publication exercised a strongly inhibiting influence on the development of an English Classical style. As a result, the major achievement of the time was not the London symphony but the London audience of connoisseurs whose appreciation drew forth the greatest works of J. C. Bach and Haydn.

As the symphony reached maturity, local centres could claim progressively less individuality, since all shared in a more-or-less international style. Among many fine composers not prominently identified with a particular school the following are outstanding: P. C. von Camerloher (1718–82), Kapellmeister to the

Bishop of Freising, who created intricate rhythmic permutations with simple materials; Pierre van Maldere (1729–68), violinist–composer to Charles of Lorraine, who wrote symphonies good enough to be confused with those of Haydn; F. X. Pokorny (1729–94), Kapellmeister at Regensburg, who wrote some of the most difficult horn parts ever seen; Václav Pichl (1741–1805), Kapellmeister to the Archduke Ferdinand in Milan, who invented a confusing type of exposition that repeated the secondary and closing material for no good reason; J. M. Kraus (1756–92), who emigrated from Germany to become a greatly admired Kapellmeister to the King of Sweden; and F. A. Rosetti or Rössler (c1750–1792), who composed for the courts at Maihingen and Schwerin in a style very close to Mozart's, especially in its well-balanced treatment of phrase structure.

10. HAYDN AND MOZART. Because of the long span of years that Haydn and Mozart each devoted to symphony composition, as well as the number and size of their works, the symphonic style may certainly be taken as one of the most important and representative aspects of each composer. Their achievements place them far above any of the local groupings suggested above, but for curiously opposite reasons. Mozart assimilated procedures from many sources besides Austrian ones, most notably from Italy and Mannheim, elevating and enriching as well as enlarging the original idea and scheme. Haydn, though he spoke of playing other music to stimulate his own ideas, in fact intensified his own procedures more than he refined or expanded processes from others.

(i) *Haydn*. With more than 40 years of composing symphonies, Haydn exceeds all other composers in seniority. It is however difficult to arrange his prodigious output in periods, because the similarities between any chronologically adjacent symphonies are less important than their differences and individualities. His works often reflect the circumstances of their composition. In early life he worked for small establishments with chamber music as the main activity, and the earliest symphonies reflect this, though his approach to the symphony can be felt even in no.1. During the next few years Haydn wrote in more different symphonic types and styles than in any other period, including works with concertante movements, suggestions of the church sonata in tempo arrangement or cantus firmus techniques, and a preponderance of fast–slow–fast patterns that should not be wholly credited to the Italian overture background since, like other Austrians, Haydn early gave the symphony finale more weight and interest than operatic high spirits would permit. These different styles, however, should be regarded not merely as experiments but as responses to changing professional circumstances. In later years, too, Haydn responded to the challenge of special requirements with unusually imaginative solutions, for example no.31, the 'Horn-signal', a brilliant example of concertante treatment. Haydn wrote a full four-movement cycle (Allegro–Andante–Minuet–Presto) as early as no.3 (by 1762), and as early as no.15 (before 1764) he added a slow introduction before the opening Presto, thus completing, though not yet establishing, the basic outlines of an infinitely variable and durable plan.

Haydn later produced many variants from this basic plan in the number, character and order of movements: opening slow movements (nos.5, 11, 15, 21), minuet as

second movement (nos.25, 44), occasional reversions to the three-movement pattern after no.15 (some Paris publishers removed the minuets from Haydn symphonies, apparently to satisfy French preferences), occasional works with more than four movements (no.60) and symphonies with programmatic intent (nos.6–8). Important for later composers are various internal refinements such as thematic relationships between slow introduction and following fast movement (no.103), unification of minuet and trio with a connecting transition after the trio (no.104), and an effective new combination of major–minor variations with rondo form for slow movements (no.93).

Haydn's appointment at the Esterházy court in 1761 required a steady production of symphonies for immediate performance, providing a unique opportunity for creation and self-criticism. Within the general form just described Haydn now began an internal expansion, enlarging his thematic ideas, working out new means of development, evolving more remote tonal excursions, and extracting the most effective and varied sounds from a group that often numbered less than 20.

These opportunities resulted in a large number of fine symphonies showing characteristic procedures, for example whole expositions built on a single thematic idea, producing an extremely tight continuity as well as the new situation of thematic development before the development proper (no.17, first movement); Haydn's capacity for exploiting the unexpected, unpredictable because the source of surprise changes in each work; or the idea of creating a zone of climax to lend profile and character to the development section, often built up on an unresolved dominant of the submediant that may then turn deceptively towards the tonic and the recapitulation. Most important are two seemingly opposed processes that contribute to Haydn's sense of movement: extension (ABB^1B^2 . . . so that four bars may become seven or eleven), and compression (by means of phrase elision, which causes the new phrase to arrive one bar earlier than expected; no.104, though later, provides an unusually clear example at the end of the Allegro theme). These opposite processes, extension and compression, both induce a state of organic tension as the rhythmic uncertainty produces a sense of urgency and suspense.

Several biographers have identified a period of 'Sturm und Drang' in Haydn's life during the late 1760s and early 1770s. Storm and stress can certainly be recognized in powerful minor-mode works such as nos.39 and 49. This colourful interpretation, however, may encourage two misconceptions: that dramatic works in the minor are necessarily the best ones (no.48 in C should be noted), and that stress is confined to a particular period (e.g. no.95 in C minor). Works in the minor occur steadily, if less frequently, later; and it would be hard to find more stress than in the development section of a late major-mode symphony, no.102.

Beginning in 1776, probably because of his heavy new operatic responsibilities, Haydn's activity in the symphony seems to have reached a temporary plateau: first, the rate of production declined (in 1771–5 he wrote 16, in 1776–80 only ten); second, a number of these works seem curiously neutral, lacking characteristic or innovatory features despite their mastery of the symphonic idiom. At this time there are several direct connections with stage or opera: no.60 is the overture to a comedy, *Il distratto*, and nos.63 and 73 include movements from Haydn's opera overtures. His supreme achievements in the symphony as a whole began about 1785. A Paris commission of 1785 resulted in six new symphonies for the Concert de la Loge Olympique, works (nos.82–7) in which Haydn reached new heights of ingenuity, humour and unpretentious intellectuality, the last chiefly in matters of development and thematic relationship. Five years later the London invitations yielded 12 symphonies (nos.93–104) that equal the Paris group in all those qualities and exceed them in breadth of conception, melodic appeal, and magisterial but never pompous dignity.

Haydn was an innovator in all directions. Nearly every line contains ideas of a variety that defies categorization. Two recurrent but constantly changing procedures give some insight into his methods: by treating the phrase less as a goal in itself than as a part of higher rhythmic groupings (sentence, paragraph), he generated an unusually broad rhythmic control, to which the monothematic expositions and elision techniques also contribute; and by using development techniques in the exposition and recapitulation (as in no.98) he demonstrated revolutionary potentialities in sonata form. These ideas exercised a strong influence on Beethoven.

The range of Haydn's imagination can only be hinted at by reference to a few representative examples. He used many fresh sounds, including a drum-roll opening (no.103), the replacement of oboes by english horns (no.22), violin scordatura (finale of no.60) and four concertante horns (nos.13, 31, 51, 72). His famous dynamic surprises (e.g. the drum-stroke in no.94, the 'Surprise' Symphony, or the characteristic 'thunderclap' repetitions of primary themes) go beyond mere effect to delineate structure and vitalize rhythmic flow, purposes also noticeable even in details such as the use of accents to emphasize cross-rhythm patterns, another technique appropriated by Beethoven.

Haydn's range of symphonic tonalities is the broadest of any 18th-century composer; in contradiction to the myth of 'cheerful' Haydn, he actually wrote a larger proportion of works in the minor than most 18th-century symphonists (exceptions are Vanhal, Beck and Gossec). No.45 is the only symphony of the 18th century in F♯ minor – ending in A, a unique turn of events. Tonal relationships between movements are less adventurous than in his chamber music, though the G major second movement of no.99 in E♭ must have been surprising in its time. Within movements, however, modulations explore daringly remote tonalities by new pathways, such as indirect 3rd relationships (i.e. in a G major movement, modulating via an E♭ chord, borrowed from G minor, to A♭; see no.88, first movement, development). Here Haydn clearly anticipated Beethoven and Schubert.

Haydn's concern for structure may account for his apparently lesser emphasis on melody in itself; despite occasional themes of great appeal, he impresses more with motivic evolutions than with original material. Many of his themes contain this motivic accretion and development even in the initial statement. The folklike quality of some Haydn themes (few actual folksongs are quoted) may result less from folk influence than from this developmental intent, which requires thematic material that is simple in both melody and rhythm, to leave room for later manoeuvres.

Haydn was one of the first to differentiate the bass line, using the cello alone as bass for a light texture and relying on the bassoon alone to support the woodwind section. Even more remarkable, however, are passages calling for double bass alone (nos.6–8, trios; nos.31 and 72, finales). The many concertante treatments of solo strings and wind were considered exemplary by critics in the epicentre of the *symphonie concertante*, Paris itself.

(*ii*) *Mozart*. Mozart began writing symphonies in London, more than a quarter of a century before Haydn's visits. With this very early start, at the age of eight or nine, Mozart's composition of symphonies spans nearly 25 years; but his activity was sporadic, resulting from the needs of particular circumstances rather than the fulfilment of the requirements of a permanent appointment. This led to a somewhat heterogeneous instrumentation and style, which do not necessarily reflect his preferences or stylistic development. The friendly contact with Abel and J. C. Bach furnished Mozart with an enduringly significant model: a warmly Italianate style of compelling lyricism and graceful rhythmic movement, to which the Austro-German background added harmonic depth, textural interest, subtlety of phrasing and orchestral virtuosity. He blended the Italian influence smoothly with Austro-German traits from his solid early training and travel experiences, an intricate process in which he could emulate his London mentors.

Mozart's own natural gifts, especially his feeling for colour and balance, set the pattern for a number of specific differences from Haydn. His sensitivity to colour produced more assignments for the wind instruments and a more idiomatic style of writing. His feeling for instrumental sound means that his counterpoint may be heard for its textural colour as much as for its linear combinations. It was this colour sense, too, that called forth his rich chord vocabulary and ingenious modulations (though they rarely go as far afield as Haydn's; that might have threatened good balance). Colour even affects the province of rhythm: if it is taken to connote variety, Mozart's variegated rhythms may be seen as yet another aspect of it. He commanded a remarkable rhythmic vocabulary, which may also be a by-product of a larger colour contrast, as part of Mozart's strong characterization of structural areas by the creation of special thematic types; one can usually recognize the precise expositional function of a Mozart theme even when it is taken out of its context.

This concern for colour obviously affected Mozart's handling of development sections. The reliance on modulation, often without significant thematic alteration, has caused some writers to consider Mozartian developments less substantial than Haydn's. Yet the character of Mozart's expositions to some extent demanded his own particular solution: after a number of highly characteristic ideas that establish a strong movement to the dominant, elaborate motivic development might confuse the thematic personalities carefully distinguished in the exposition. Mozart maintained interest by refreshing one or more of these established thematic types with a trip through unfamiliar orchestral and harmonic country, so that the tonic reprise can be recognized as their proper home.

The word 'symmetry', sometimes too casually applied to Mozart's music, usually expresses qualities of coordination and balance. In any single phrase the activity of all the musical elements is coordinated to an unusual degree. This is best seen at cadence points, where melodic action and surface rhythm move towards longer values; with a decelerating chord frequency underneath, these elements fashion an elegant cadential stability. Furthermore, when applied above the single-phrase level, this control makes possible similarly exquisite balances in activity between elements: at the opening of the 'Jupiter' Symphony K551, the strong rhythmic activity of the first two bars (but lesser melodic and harmonic action) leads to a balancing pair of bars with activity centring on melody and harmony while rhythm is relatively quiescent. These shifting priorities, also beautifully adjusted between the larger sections of a piece, explain much of the convincing flow of Mozart's music, a motion very different from Haydn's driving motivic development and broad tensions.

Though Mozart's earliest symphonies are often described as Italian in style, it requires only four bars of no.1 to feel the stylistic blending mentioned earlier. It opens with three bars of a bustling operatic triad announcement, but in bar 4 there are held chords in all parts except the bass, which moves in an off-beat crotchet figure, so that the effect resembles a Fux counterpoint exercise. Though presumably composed under the Bach–Abel influence, the first movement is a differentiated binary of a sort common in Vienna but rare in the Italian overture. The brief three-movement form and 3/8 finale, however, as well as the scurrying turns and tremolos, again derive from the opera house. The second London symphony (K19) opens with a statement-and-response cliché remarkably like the Abel symphony Mozart had copied. Apart from omitting the double-bar, however, Mozart did not follow the well-crafted Abel work, for after contrasted secondary and closing themes, an *fp subito* briefly develops both secondary and closing material and then prepares a return on the dominant – to the secondary and closing ideas, as if in a regular reprise. This unbalanced and incomplete design contains a number of sophisticated touches, yet despite these impressive signs of Mozart's advance (in many respects he was already beyond Leopold's help) the piece sounds foursquare, owing to abrupt rhythms and a general lack of linear direction. This lack is immediately remedied in the tiny Andante, however, where leisurely Italianate lines stretch to unexpected lengths. No more than a year later, K22 in B♭ reflects new experiences. The first movement contains two recognizable Mannheim features, an extended orchestral crescendo and a recurrence of tutti primary material at the middle and end of the movement. The slow movement, a three-part Andante in G minor, contains more counterpoint than most such movements in 1765, and Mozart could already make a momentary inflection to the remote key of E♭ minor through its own dominant diminished 7th, a passage that foreshadows the characteristic touches of harmonic pathos in later works.

With the little symphonies of 1767–8 Mozart made a seemingly sharp turn towards the four-movement Vienna style. More important than the number of movements, the blend of German and Italian continues. Almost every transition brings in the familiar Italian tremolos; trill, snap and turn figures activate many themes; and there are cantabile Andantes and 3/8, 6/8 and 12/8 finales. But there are also rather squarely phrased slow movements (K48), plodding divertimento-style triplet lines (K45, minuet), and themes like remnants of counterpoint exercises (opening of K45). One of the best of this group is K48, whose 'affinity with such works as Haydn's Symphonies Nos.3 and 13 is quite obvious' (Larsen, *Mozart Companion*, 1956) and can be recognized in the strong rhythmic drive, the dynamic contrasts and the surprise cadence in the closing section. The presence of these Haydn traits, however, draws attention to Mozart's development: though using highly rhythmic material, Mozart maintained his identity by characteristically orderly punctuation between phrases and theme groups, Italianate lines and chromaticism in the slow movement, and the incredible exuberance of the minuet, which after four sober opening bars explodes in violin semiquaver scales that rush up two octaves in two bars. The first-movement forms show a continuing diversity: among these supposedly Vienna-orientated works, K43 and 45 approximate to the developed binary design favoured by many Mannheim composers, and although Mozart must have heard many fully evolved sonata forms by Viennese composers such as Hofmann and Dittersdorf (probably less of Haydn at this time) only K48 has a convincing reprise of primary material, and even here one secondary idea of the exposition never returns.

The 1769–71 period includes two trips to Italy, separated by a short period in Salzburg. The five symphonies from the first journey strongly reflect familiar Italian usages, such as a prevailing choice of three-movement form, linking of the first and second movements (K74), and exposition–recapitulation forms (sometimes connected by short transitions over dominant pedals; K84/73q, 74). By contrast a symphony in G (K110/75b), written in Salzburg in 1771, illustrates the growing fusion of styles: the German background entails four movements, with developed sonata form in the first movement, a vigorous minuet that contains a free canon between violins and bass, and a rousing finale (also with a hint of violin–bass imitation at the beginning) with a well-developed episode in the relative minor. In the slow movement, however, a leisurely Italianate melody betrays thoughts far from rainy Salzburg, though here again the well-schooled Germanic texture includes a clever dialogue between violins and other attractive inner lines and brief imitations. Back again in Milan, K112 in F falls much less under the Italian spell than the symphonies of the first journey. In the secondary section a charming dialogue between oboes and violins immediately evokes an *opera buffa* argument scene by its snap rhythms, and the 3/8 finale begins like a typical curtain-raiser; but now there is more stress on the balanced unfolding of ideas, an attitude already noticed in the development of the first movement and the meticulous slow movement. These works show the beginnings of Mozart's exploitation of the contrast of German and Italian styles, inexhaustible sources of colour and balance that were to become the main underlying characteristics of his personal style. By this time Mozart was progressing towards an effectively integrated style, and many phrases contain evidence of originality, charm and strength; but an unavoidable segmentation tends to interrupt the basic movement, and prevents a broader continuity.

The highly productive 1772–3 period yielded more than a dozen symphonies. There are still stylistic mixtures not yet fully assimilated: Mannheim binary with ritornello crescendo at the beginning and end (K133), and Italian exposition–recapitulation designs (κ181/162b) and connected movements (κ184/161a, 181/162b). As representatives of his most evolved style at this time, two particularly well-balanced works, κ132 in Eb and κ134 in A, deserve more frequent revival: κ132 shows how the Italian high spirits can be applied in a fully developed sonata form, and κ134, which contrasts a highly continuous 3/4 Allegro (Haydnesque except in beginning the recapitulation with secondary material) with a spacious early version of the Andante cantabile mood found in 'Porgi amor' (from Le nozze di Figaro).

Summer 1773 marks the beginning of Mozart's maturity as a symphonist. When he returned to Salzburg at the end of September from a ten-week stay in Vienna he began writing works in a more fully realized style that resolved earlier conflicts and imbalances, at the same time increasing the size and expressive range. The design of first movements follows the full sonata pattern, emphasized by sharper punctuation between sections and higher thematic contrast, both melodically and orchestrally. Now there are no static lines, no dead spots, no loose ends. From then dates his first complete minor-mode symphony (κ183/173dB, in G minor), a work of precocious feeling, with an opening in syncopated octaves that recalls Haydn's 'Lamentatione' (no.26 in D minor, written almost a decade earlier). Balancing this darker part of the spectrum, the following symphony in A (κ201/186a) contains two of the most hilarious passages anywhere in Mozart: at the end of the minuet, where the oboes and horns add two bars of dotted musical parody, and in the finale where (similarly located at the end of the exposition) a rising whirlwind scale appears out of nowhere in the violins – left up in the air here, and also in the development and recapitulation, the whirlwind is brought down to earth only at the last possible moment by the closing chords of a tiny coda. Mozart had already assimilated the strategy of Haydn's structural question-marks.

Mozart's mature symphonies show increasing complexity and enlargement of scale, as well as the occasional predominance of other models (Parisian in no.31, Mannheim style and Italian form in no.32, etc). Two points not so far emphasized may be worth noting. First, some aspects of Mozart's rhythmic control, though less noticeable on the surface than Haydn's motivic drive, contribute significantly to the fundamental movement. For example, the progress of the harmonic rhythm, especially as reflected in the speed of chord change, can effect a compelling climax. In the first bars of no.40 in G minor the chord rhythm accelerates in an almost geometric progression: one four-bar chord, two two-bar chords, seven one-bar chords, six half-bar chords, and four crotchet chords, pausing finally on a two-bar dominant. A second point, also generally overlooked, concerns Mozart's unique invention of an ending that included both serenity and brilliance, which leads in mature works to an expanded closing section. Between the usual cadential themes he introduced a piano penultimo: a quiet, reflective theme that enhances the brilliance of the final cadential trumpeting. This heightened contrast in the closing area lends a special conviction and definitive repose to Mozartian conclusions, noticeable in embryo as early as κ134. In perfecting other parts of the movement he had attained a superb balance of phrases, thematic areas and main divisions. Now, for the end of a movement, with equal inspiration he discovered a totally satisfying finality that left his contemporaries far behind.

BIBLIOGRAPHY

[G. J. Vogler]: Betrachtungen der Mannheimer Tonschule (Mannheim, 1778–81)
K. Bitter: Carl Philipp Emanuel und Wilhelm Friedemann Bach und deren Brüder (Berlin, 1868)
M. Brenet: Histoire de la symphonie à orchestre depuis ses origines jusqu'à Beethoven inclusivement (Paris, 1882)
J. Sittard: Zur Geschichte der Musik und des Theaters am Württembergischen Hofe (Stuttgart, 1890–91/R1970)
F. Walter: Geschichte des Theaters und der Musik am kurpfälzischen Hofe (Leipzig, 1898)
C. Pierre: Musique des fêtes et cérémonies de la révolution française (Paris, 1899)
M. Brenet: Les concerts en France sous l'ancien régime (Paris, 1900/R1969)
H. Riemann: 'Die Mannheimer Schule', DTB, iv, Jg.iii/1 (1902), ix
A. Heuss: 'Die Venetianischen Opern-Sinfonien', SIMG, iv (1902–3), 404–77
C. Mennicke: Hasse und die Brüder Graun als Symphoniker: nebst Biographien und thematischen Katalogen (Leipzig, 1906)
H. Riemann: 'Der Stil und die Manieren der Mannheimer', DTB, xiii, Jg.vii/2 (1906), xv
——: 'Einleitung [Mannheimer Symphoniker]', DTB, xv, Jg.viii/2 (1907), vii
M. Flueler: Die norddeutsche Sinfonie zur Zeit Friedrichs des Grossen und besonders die Werke Ph. Em. Bachs (diss. U. of Berlin, 1908)
L. Kamieński: 'Mannheim und Italien', SIMG, x (1908–9), 307
L. de La Laurencie and G. de Saint-Foix: 'Contribution à l'histoire de la symphonie française vers 1750', Année musicale, i (1911), 1–123
H. Botstiber: Geschichte der Ouvertüre und der freien Orchesterformen (Leipzig, 1913)
G. Cucuel: Etude sur un orchestre au XVIIIe siècle: l'instrumentation chez les symphonistes de La Pouplinière: oeuvres musicales de Gossec, Schencker et Gaspard Procksch (Paris, 1913)
F. Torrefranca: 'Le origini della sinfonia', RMI, xx (1913), 291–346; xxi (1914), 97–121, 278–312; xxii (1915), 431
W. Fischer: 'Zur Entwicklungsgeschichte des Wiener klassischen Stils', SMw, iii (1915), 24–84
K. Nef: Geschichte der Sinfonie und Suite (Leipzig, 1921/R1970)
R. Sondheimer: 'Die formale Entwicklung der vorklassischen Sinfonie', AMw, iv (1922), 85, 123
——: Die Theorie der Sinfonie und die Beurteilung einzelner Sinfoniekomponisten bei den Musikschriftstellern des 18. Jahrhunderts (Leipzig, 1925) [index in AcM, xxxvii (1965), 79]
H. P. Schökel: Johann Christian Bach und die Instrumentalmusik seiner Zeit (Wolfenbüttel, 1926)
F. Tutenberg: 'Die Durchführungsfrage in der vorneuklassischen Sinfonie', ZMw, ix (1926–7), 90
——: 'Die Opera buffa-Sinfonie und ihre Beziehungen zur klassischen Sinfonie', AMw, viii (1926–7), 452
E. Bücken: Die Musik des Rokokos und der Klassik (Potsdam, 1928)
F. Tutenberg: Die Sinfonik Johann Christian Bachs; ein Beitrag zur Entwicklungsgeschichte der Sinfonie von 1750–80 (Wolfenbüttel, 1928)
C. S. Terry: John Christian Bach (London, 1929, rev. 2/1967)
W. Fischer: 'Instrumental Musik von 1750–1828', Handbuch der Musikgeschichte, ed. G. Adler (Berlin, rev. 2/1930/R1961), 795–833
G. de Saint-Foix: 'Sonate et symphonie', EMDC, II/v (1930), 3130
F. Noack: Sinfonie und Suite von Gabrieli bis Schumann (Leipzig, 7/1932)
H. Opieński: 'La symphonie polonaise au XVIIIe siècle', RdM, xv (1934), 193
B. Rywosch: Beiträge zur Entwicklung in Joseph Haydns Symphonik 1759 bis 1780 (Turbenthal, 1934)
R. von Tobel: Die Formenwelt der klassischen Instrumentalmusik (Berne, 1935)
A. Carse: 'Early Classical Symphonies', PMA, lxii (1935–6), 39
K. M. Komma: Johann Zach und die tschechischen Musiker im deutschen Umbruch des 18. Jahrhunderts (Kassel, 1938)
W. H. Reese: Grundsätze und Entwicklung der Instrumentation in der vorklassischen und klassischen Sinfonie (diss., U. of Berlin, 1939)
E. Blom: 'The Minuet-Trio', ML, xxii (1941), 162
S. Walin: Beiträge zur Geschichte der schwedischen Sinfonik: Studien aus dem Musikleben des 18. und des beginnenden 19. Jahrhunderts (Stockholm, 1941)
H. Werner: Die Sinfonien von Ignaz Holzbauer (diss., U. of Munich, 1942)
E. Leuchter: La sinfonia, su evolucion y su estructura (Rosario, 1943)
A. E. F. Dickinson: 'The Founders of the Symphony', MMR, lxxvii (1947), 227; lxxviii (1948), 4, 42, 92
F. Mahling: Die deutsche vorklassische Sinfonie (Berlin, 1948)
R. S. Tangeman: The Transition Passage in Sonata-form Movements of

the *Viennese Classical Period* (*with Special Reference to the Works of Haydn, Mozart, and Beethoven*) (diss., Harvard U., 1948)

[? R. T. Dart]: 'An Eighteenth-century Directory of London Musicians', *GSJ*, ii (1949), 27

L. G. Langwill: 'Two Rare Eighteenth-century London Directories', *ML*, xxx (1949), 37

L. G. Ratner: 'Harmonic Aspects of Classic Form', *JAMS*, ii (1949), 159

A. Weinmann: *Beiträge zur Geschichte des Alt-Wiener Musikverlages* (Vienna, 1948–72)

A. Carse: *18th Century Symphonies: a Short History* (London, 1951)

H. Vogg: *Franz Tuma als Instrumentalkomponist* (diss., U. of Vienna, 1951)

C. L. Cudworth: 'The English Symphonies of the Eighteenth Century', *PRMA*, lxxviii (1951–2), 31

H. S. Livingston: *The Italian Overture from A. Scarlatti to Mozart* (diss., U. of North Carolina, 1952)

W. P. Stedman: *Form and Orchestration in the Pre-classical Symphony* (diss., U. of Rochester, 1953)

B. Brook: 'Fakaerti – Incognito Symphonist, or Cutting Down the Anhang', *FAM*, ii (1955), 166

F. von Glasenapp: 'Eine Gruppe von Sinfonien und Ouvertüren für Blasinstrumente von 1793–1795 in Frankreich', *Festschrift Max Schneider* (Leipzig, 1955), 197

H. C. R. Landon: *The Symphonies of Joseph Haydn* (London, 1955; suppl., 1961)

[J. Marsh]: 'An Essay by John Marsh; Introduced by C. L. Cudworth', *ML*, xxxvi (1955), 155

P. Bryan: *The Symphonies of Johann Vaňhal* (diss., Michigan U., 1956)

R. Engländer: *Die Dresdener Instrumentalmusik in der Zeit der Wiener Klassik* (Uppsala, 1956)

R. Münster: *Die Sinfonien Toeschis: ein Beitrag zur Geschichte der Mannheimer Sinfonie* (diss., U. of Munich, 1956)

L. G. Ratner: 'Eighteenth-century Theories of Musical Period Structure', *MQ*, xlii (1956), 439

J. W. Hertel: *Autobiographie*, ed. E. Schenk (Graz and Cologne, 1957)

V. Kreiner: *Leopold Hofmann als Sinfoniker* (diss., U. of Vienna, 1958)

S. Sadie: 'Concert Life in Eighteenth Century England', *PRMA*, lxxxv (1958–9), 17

J. LaRue: 'A Union Thematic Catalogue of 18th Century Symphonies', *FAM*, vi (1959), 18

H. Gericke: *Der Wiener Musikalienhandel von 1700 bis 1778* (Graz and Cologne, 1960)

E. E. Helm: *Music at the Court of Frederick the Great* (Norman, 1960)

J. LaRue: 'Major and Minor Mysteries of Identification in the 18th-century Symphony', *JAMS*, xiii (1960), 181

H. Engel: 'Die Quellen des klassischen Stils', *IMSCR*, viii *New York 1961*, i, 285 [see also ii, 135]

G. Feder: 'Bemerkungen über die Ausbildung der klassischen Tonsprache in der Instrumentalmusik Haydns', *IMSCR*, viii *New York 1961*, i, 305

J. LaRue: 'Significant and Coincidental Resemblance between Classical Themes', *JAMS*, xiv (1961), 224

B. Brook: *La symphonie française dans la seconde moitié du XVIIIe siècle* (Paris, 1962)

J. P. Larsen: 'Zur Bedeutung der "Mannheimer Schule" ', *Festschrift Karl Gustav Fellerer* (Regensburg, 1962), 303

H. Brofsky: *The Instrumental Music of Padre Martini* (diss., New York U., 1963)

B. Churgin: *The Symphonies of G. B. Sammartini* (diss., Harvard U., 1963)

J. P. Larsen: 'Sonatenform-Probleme', *Festschrift Friedrich Blume* (Kassel, 1963), 221

P. Mechlenburg: *Die Sinfonie der Mannheimer Schule* (diss., U. of Munich, 1963)

W. Salmen: *Johann Friedrich Reichardt: Komponist, Schriftsteller, Kapellmeister und Verwaltungsbeamter der Goethezeit* (Freiburg and Zurich, 1963)

J. Vinton: 'The Development Section in Early Viennese Symphonies: a Re-valuation', *MR*, xxiv (1963), 13

R. G. Pauly: *Music in the Classic Period* (Englewood Cliffs, 1965)

G. Wolf and J. LaRue, eds.: 'A Bibliographical Index to Robert Sondheimer's *Die Theorie der Sinfonie*', *AcM*, xxxvii (1965), 79

G. B. de Stwolinski: *The Mannheim Symphonists: their Contribution to the Technique of Thematic Development* (diss., U. of Rochester, 1966)

J. Węcowski: 'La musique symphonique polonaise du XVIIIe siècle', *Musica antiqua Europae orientalis I: Bydgoszcz 1966*, 334

L. Hoffmann-Erbrecht: *Die Sinfonie*, Mw, xxix (Cologne, 1967; Eng. trans., 1967)

A. D. McCredie: 'Investigations into the Symphony of the Haydn–Mozart Era. The North German Manuscripts: an Interim Survey', *MMA*, ii (1967), 75–154

A. Mayeda: 'Die Sinfoniën von Nicola Antonio Porpora', *Annuario di Istituto giapponese di cultura*, v (1967–8), 27–82

B. Churgin: 'Francesco Galeazzi's Description (1796) of Sonata Form', *JAMS*, xxi (1968), 181

F. Lippmann: 'Die Sinfonien–Manuskripte der Bibliothek Doria-Pamphilij in Rom', *AnMc*, no.5 (1968), 201–47

R. Macdonald: *François-Joseph Gossec and French Instrumental Music* (diss., Michigan U., 1968)

E. Suchalla: *Die Orchestersinfonien C. P. E. Bachs* (Augsburg, 1968)

J. K. Wolf: *The Orchestral Works of Christian Cannabich: a Documentary Study* (diss., New York U., 1968)

G. Abraham: 'Some Eighteenth-century Polish Symphonies', *Studies in Eighteenth-century Music: a Tribute to Karl Geiringer* (New York and London, 1970), 13

G. R. Hill: *A Preliminary Checklist of Research on the Classic Symphony and Concerto to the Time of Beethoven* (*excluding Haydn and Mozart*) (Hackensack, NJ, 1970)

M. Reissinger: *Die Sinfonien Ernst Eichners* (Wiesbaden, 1970)

R. D. Sjoerdsma: *The Instrumental Music of Franz Christoph Neubauer* (diss., Ohio State U., 1970)

R. Würtz: *Ignaz Fränzl: ein Beitrag zur Musikgeschichte der Stadt Mannheim* (Mainz, 1970)

A. Downs: *The Symphonies of Fredrich Schwindl* (diss., New York U., 1971)

H. Hell: *Die Neapolitanische Opernsinfonie in der ersten Hälfte des 18. Jahrhunderts: N. Porpora–L. Vinci–G. B. Pergolesi–L. Leo–N. Jommelli* (Tutzing, 1971)

E. Apfel: *Zur Vor- und Frühgeschichte der Symphonie* (Baden-Baden, 1972)

F. H. Bawel: *A Study of Developmental Techniques in Selected Haydn Symphonies* (diss., Ohio State U., 1972)

W. Lebermann: 'Zu Franz Xaver Richters Sinfonien', *Mf*, xxv (1972), 471

D. A. Sheldon: 'Johann Friedrich Fasch: Problems in Style Classification', *MQ*, lviii (1972), 92

M. E. Soutar: *Christian Cannabich: an Evaluation of his Instrumental Works* (diss., U. of Aberdeen, 1972)

E. K. Wolf: *The Symphonies of Johann Stamitz* (diss., New York U., 1972)

G. P. Jones: *Heinrich Christoph Koch's Description of the Symphony and a Comparison with Selected Symphonies of C. P. E. Bach and Haydn* (diss., U. of California, Los Angeles, 1973)

J. Schwartz: *Phrase Morphology in the Early Classic Symphony* (diss., New York U., 1973)

G. Hill: *The Symphonies of F. L. Gassmann* (diss., New York U., 1975)

E. K. Wolf: 'Authenticity and Stylistic Evidence in the Early Symphony', *A Musical Offering: Essays in Honor of Martin Bernstein* (New York, 1977)

II. 19th century

1. Beethoven and his time. 2. Conservative Romantics: Schubert, Mendelssohn, Schumann, Brahms, Tchaikovsky, minor composers. 3. Radical Romantics: Berlioz, Liszt, d'Indy, Franck. 4. Nationalists: Balakirev, Borodin, Dvořák. 5. Bruckner and his time.

1. BEETHOVEN AND HIS TIME. Beethoven's First Symphony (1801) hailed the new century with sounds that now seem to speak for their epoch. The early 19th-century symphony is nowadays typified by Beethoven. But to the audiences of the early 1800s the symphony was an idea, compounded of certain strong reminiscences and expectations, in which Beethoven played but a small part. It will be as well to reconstruct this idea before considering Beethoven's impact upon it.

The symphony of 1800, though designed more for the public concert hall than for the court, retained much of the regal stature of earlier times. It was by no means an 'orchestral sonata', as it has been called. Perceptible differences between the two forms remained to betray their different origins. Four movements were normal (at any rate north of the Alps) in the symphony, three in the sonata; and the movements in the symphony were more strictly conventional in plan, whereas the sonata might include variations or fantasia-like movements and could begin or even end with a complete slow movement. Symphonies frequently included portentous slow introductions. Perhaps more important was the air of princely festivity that the symphony retained. The loud fanfares of Mozart's no.41 or Haydn's no.97 remained a normal and expected feature. Played by trumpets and drums, long the trappings of royalty, they imparted a glamour to the symphony, even when it was played to a middle-class audience under the auspices of a revolutionary government. They made the music sound important, and commanded a degree of respectful attention that would hardly be paid to a concerto, divertimento or quartet. The almost invariable presence of the stately minuet, no longer fashionable in the ballroom, was another reminder of the symphony's royal ancestry.

Symphonies at this date were generally performed as part of a miscellaneous concert that also included overtures, concertos, chamber music and operatic excerpts. The orchestra was the standard one assembled for such concerts: strings, double woodwind, horns, trumpets and drums, with a piano as a nominal survival of the continuo but with no independent part to play in a symphony. The principal performers in such concerts were generally the soloists who sang arias or played concertos; but the symphony, which might at one time have been treated as little more than an introduction to 'play the audience in', was beginning to be the most important part of the programme. There was little domestic or amateur cultivation of the symphony. Some of Haydn's had been published in keyboard arrangements in London, and a few in arrangements for piano quintet or sextet, but the normal method of printing symphonies was in orchestral parts only. Scores were unknown until the editions of Breitkopf & Härtel, Leipzig (1807–9) and Cianchettini & Sperati, London (1809).

The new importance and stature of the symphony did not derive from its formal and regal associations themselves, but, on the contrary, from the new significance with which these qualities were infused. The composer's status had changed from servant and hired entertainer to independent creative artist. Haydn moved from the privileged serfdom of Eszterhaza to the stimulating freedom of London, and Mozart freed himself from the restraints of court employment; in doing so they changed not so much the outward forms of their music as its content and symbolic meaning. The grandeur and brilliance of the older symphonies were still there: but where they had been tributes to the rank and power of monarchs they now expressed the triumph of the composer himself, as the spokesman of a new spirit of enlightenment and liberation. The expressive melody of *galanterie*, formerly a mere polite recognition of the amorous dalliances of princes and courtiers, could now be made a vehicle of the composer's own feeling. The resulting music was vastly more arresting, complex and difficult than that of the previous generation. For many in the early 19th century the discovery and comprehension of the greater works of Haydn and (particularly) Mozart was achieved only with intense intellectual and emotional effort. Having accomplished it, they had reached a musical ideal to which Beethoven's mature art seemed an intrusive irrelevance. This was so for C. F. Zelter, for Jean-Paul Richter, Schumann's mentor, and for such as Weber, Spohr and Rossini, all composers of symphonies. In the first 20 years of the 19th century many symphonies were composed in direct continuation of Mozart's work, almost as if Beethoven did not exist. Weber's two symphonies of 1807, and Rossini's two of 1808, are in this category. So are the many symphonies of such as Gyrowetz, Ries, Andrea Romberg and Peter Winter, some of which were played more frequently than Beethoven's. For posterity, however, no symphonies are more obscure than those of Beethoven's contemporaries, Schubert alone excepted. Once Beethoven's masterpieces were appreciated they effectively eliminated all competitors.

The first full appreciation of Beethoven's genius was perhaps E. T. A. Hoffmann's essay of 1813, and Romantic poets and philosophers were soon claiming him as one of their own. Despite his chronological position at the height of the Romantic movement, musical historians have with good reason preferred to regard him as the culmination of the Classical era. From first to last he kept in mind the Classical ideal of the symphony, and Haydn was his chief model. He never abandoned the sonata forms; all his first movements are in strict sonata-allegro form, however much it may be expanded. Other movements also use the traditional structures – minuet and trio, rondo and varied rondo, sonata rondo, simple ternary; only in the Third and Ninth Symphonies did he experiment with untried structures. In the First, Second, Fourth and Seventh he successively extended Haydn's slow introductions, while never forgetting their purpose in building expectation for the onset of the Allegro. Within the larger movements, more especially the first movements, Beethoven developed Haydn's methods to a point of unparalleled intensity and scope. For the themes of his principal movements he used such inimitable gestures as the famous 'hammer of fate' in the Fifth, or the violently descending blows of the Ninth, or a quietly unobtrusive phrase such as that of the Sixth. In every case, even when the first theme was an extended 'tune' as in the Seventh, it was used as a source for Beethoven's endlessly inventive thematic development, which always goes on throughout exposition, recapitulation and coda as well as in the actual 'development section'. He often, like Mozart, introduced a series of new and even contrasting tunes in the course of an exposition – or even, as in the Third Symphony, in the development; but they are rarely closed in structure, nor do they dissipate the momentum previously built up. Of course, Beethoven enormously expanded each section of the sonata-form movement, especially the coda, which sometimes equalled one of the other sections in length and importance. His expansion of the orchestra was slight, though he brought in instruments such as trombones, piccolo and double bassoon which had hitherto been found mainly in opera orchestras. His orchestral advance lay in his treatment of individual instruments – he gave the bassoons, timpani and double basses an independence they had never known – and in his expansion of the orchestra's range of power and expression.

Like no-one before, Beethoven seized the listener's attention and compelled him to follow the intense emotional conflicts in his music through to their resolution. His symphonies, particularly the Third, Fifth and Ninth, have always conveyed a sense of actual struggle, though critics have differed as to what the struggle is about. Some have depicted it as the heroic struggle of man against fate; others have tried to see an expression of Beethoven's personal circumstances (his deafness, his unhappy sexual and family relationships); Lang found a 'struggle to maintain this disciplined command in the face of the changing artistic world about him'. Whether one sees the struggle on a symbolic, a personal or a technical level, it is impossible to avoid being caught up in it, so imperious and intense is Beethoven's manner. It was through his personal force of character and technical control that the methods of the Classical symphony were able to remain intact, as a living and developing process, for another generation after Haydn and Mozart had brought them to a height that others accepted as the summit of possible achievement. This was a period of great change in society and in ideas, and of great technical change in music; in piano music, for example, a new aesthetic was being evolved that allowed an escape from life's struggles into a dream world of easily satisfied feelings. Beethoven chose instead to confront the personal, social and ethical problems of his time in his music. At a technical level this meant accepting forms which had been evolved for polite entertainment, and stretching them to contain and embody his intensity of feeling and to involve his audiences in that feeling. Few of his contemporaries or successors attempted anything of the kind.

The first two symphonies showed an evolutionary development from Haydn's, but the Third was a departure, far beyond any music that had been composed before. In his prefatory note in the first edition of the score he gave notice that this was no ordinary symphony. By his dedication of it to Napoleon, later erased when Napoleon had crowned himself emperor, and by the subsequent title 'to the memory of a hero', he showed that the grandeur and power of his music celebrated personal courage and the unconquerable human spirit, not the trappings of monarchy, which still threatened to deprive mankind of the fruits of its endeavour. In the symphony itself heroism is celebrated in the funeral march, and heroism is actually carried out in the other movements through the symbolic triumph over technical difficulties. In the last movement the very elements of the craft of music are laid bare – melody, bass, counterpoint, rhythm and harmony, in confrontation – and after they have been forged into a new synthesis in the section that follows, the victory is celebrated by a repetition of blazing tonic chords, far exceeding the normal key confirmation that ends a Haydn symphony. It seems justified by the knowledge that its splendour has been won by moral effort, not by accident of birth or circumstance. Beethoven himself is the real hero.

The later symphonies each work out in fresh terms the same type of struggle as the Third, and all end in triumph. After the Fifth, the veteran of so many musical battles began to rest on his laurels, and the next three symphonies show a marked increase in those lyrical, contemplative scenes that had always been present, if only as a respite from the heat of the struggle. The Eighth (1812) even shows a regression to a point closer to the original Haydn model. Then Beethoven abandoned the symphony, as he had earlier abandoned the opera and the concerto; he moved for a time into a less heroic world where symphonies had no place.

The Choral Symphony (composed 1817–23, performed 1824) can only be treated as a solitary masterpiece, with no immediate predecessor or successor; in this it resembles the symphonies of the radical Romantics, treated below, and the immense influence it had was on the late 19th-century composers, not on those of its own time. For Beethoven it was the outcome of decades of musical and emotional preparation: thematic ideas for it are found in his sketchbooks from as early as the 1790s, and there is a clear relationship to the Choral Fantasia op.80 (1808). It brought together two projects that had long been in the composer's mind, a gigantic symphony in D minor (he had gone far in the planning of an instrumental finale) and a choral setting of Schiller's 'Ode to Joy'. The manner in which the two elements were fused has been the subject of unending controversy and speculation. The first three movements, however awe-inspiring, are clearly perceived as expansions of traditional form; the last is unique, not in its introduction of voices (Winter, for example, had anticipated Beethoven in this) but in its extraordinary formal structure. The chaotic opening is followed by an orchestral recitative, later provided with words of Beethoven's own choosing, which unmistakably 'rejects' the openings of all three preceding movements. It can hardly be imagined that Beethoven by this gesture meant to deny the value of these movements, the summit of his instrumental art; nor can one believe with Wagner that he meant to imply that instrumental music itself was dead. The rejection must be taken in a more general sense: a condemnation of all those petty and unedifying human weaknesses which, despite revolutions, Beethoven found still dominant in the world around him. In the setting of Schiller's poem that followed, Beethoven defiantly reasserted the ideals of universal love which, it seemed to him in his loneliness, the world was more and more forgetting.

2. CONSERVATIVE ROMANTICS: SCHUBERT, MENDELSSOHN, SCHUMANN, BRAHMS, TCHAIKOVSKY, MINOR COMPOSERS. Felix Weingartner, looking back over the 19th century, concluded that it was futile to try to write a symphony after Beethoven; and others have thought that Romantic composers were inhibited in writing symphonies by the greatness of Beethoven's models. There is truth in this only insofar as a symphony is regarded as necessarily following Beethoven's lead. Few ventured to rival Beethoven in his own sphere, though it could be argued that Brahms or Bruckner succeeded in doing so. Beethoven had continued through sheer force of personality to maintain the Classical symphonic ideals when these no longer embodied the musical inclinations of the time; and at the same time other composers were capturing popular taste with less demanding symphonies.

Mozart, in his E♭ and G minor symphonies, nos.39 and 40, had left examples which, however tightly constructed, still made their chief effect by an almost continuous outpouring of spontaneous melody, enriched by inventive touches of harmony and orchestration. As the public accustomed itself to the complexities of Mozart's idiom, its rich lyricism, rather than its architectural strength, appealed most strongly to a Romantic generation; and it was this that was imitated and extended, sometimes to the detriment of structural factors.

Spohr was a leading composer who took Mozart as the model for his symphonies (the first dating from 1811), developing especially the more chromatic style of Mozartian melody and harmony. His art was fundamentally antagonistic to Beethoven's. To him Beethoven was 'wanting in aesthetical feeling and in a sense of the beautiful', whereas Beethoven said of Spohr: 'He is too rich in dissonances: pleasure in his music is marred by chromatic melody'. In his time, Spohr's symphonies made a substantial impact. After Beethoven's death he made some interesting experiments in symphonic form. His Fourth Symphony (1832), which he called 'The Consecration of Sounds: Characteristic Tone-Painting in the form of a Symphony, after a Poem by Carl Pfeiffer', departed much more radically than any

Beethoven symphony from the traditional forms. Later experiments include a 'Historical Symphony' (1839), with four movements supposedly in the styles of 1720, 1780, 1810 and 1840 (but all, as Schumann pointed out, sounding like pure Spohr); a symphony for double orchestra entitled 'Earthly and Divine in Human Life' (1841); and a 'Seasons' Symphony (1850).

Schubert's symphonies were a failure in his own time, and only in recent generations has their full stature been recognized. It has often been said that he lived too much in Beethoven's shadow to be a great symphonist, but that is misleading. The symphony was admittedly not his most natural form of expression, yet he produced nine examples, including two masterpieces, before dying at an age by which Beethoven had produced only his First. If Schubert was timid, it was not Beethoven who intimidated him, but the world of power and fashion, so remote from the intimate warmth of the musical gatherings of friends in which his art was most at home. In the grandest form of all, opera, he failed altogether; in the next grandest, the symphony, he won no public success, and was slow to find self-confidence. So far as Beethoven's symphonies influenced him, the influence was entirely positive. The Seventh had a specially profound effect on him, and was obviously ringing in his ears when he wrote many works of various kinds, including his 'Great' C major Symphony.

But his concept of the symphony was quite different from Beethoven's. It was closer in many ways to the mainstream of musical development, deriving primarily from Mozart. Schubert, like Spohr, often dwelt on the lovely details of a tune and its harmony. Where Haydn's second subject was often barely distinguishable in the continuing momentum of the exposition, Mozart tended to provide at least one melody of some distinction in the dominant or relative key. Schubert went beyond that, often introducing one or two melodies in a foreign key before modulating to the dominant and following up with several more. He played freely with chromatic modulations, largely for their delightful effect, and with little regard for the tonal duality and its resolution which had made the Classical symphony a logically satisfying experience. It is true that in his last two symphonies, the 'Unfinished' (1822) and especially the 'Great' C major (1828), Schubert showed himself perfectly capable of symphonic development on a large scale. And yet it is the melodies, with their wonderful adornments of chord, counterpoint and colour, that stand out in these works, and are eagerly expected by the listener. The prime popular symbol of Beethoven's symphonies is the great four-note motif of the Fifth, a wholly 'symphonic' theme that pervades the movement, if not the whole work. With Schubert it is the second subject of the first movement of the 'Unfinished' that is recalled before all else. In a sense this too pervades the movement, for one is constantly awaiting its recurrence, or, at the end, lamenting its last departure.

It is this ill-concealed preference for melody, this lavishing of invention and decoration on the lyrical portions of the symphony sanctioned as such by Mozart, that tends to make the intervening sections of development and dramatic contrast seem cold and perfunctory. There was no reason in principle why the symphony should not have been adapted to suit the leanings of Romantic musicians towards 'endless melody', of the kind that was achieved in Chopin's ballades, Liszt's symphonic poems or Wagner's music

dramas. But these were new forms invented to satisfy precisely this need. The symphony was different: it was a well-established entity, almost a monument. Certain things were expected of a symphony, and the more conservative Romantics provided them, both out of deference for the public which was now their master, and out of respect and love for the work of the great Viennese symphonists. The result was sometimes an uncomfortable compromise – especially in first movements, where the pressure to discipline the lyrical urge was felt most strongly. Even the most skilful technician was hard put to it to conceal his lack of genuine interest in the 'symphonic' aspect of his work. That is the chief source of weakness in the symphonies of Mendelssohn, Schumann and Tchaikovsky, not to mention a host of lesser composers whose works were once in the public eye.

Mendelssohn composed 12 symphonies (all recorded) before he published one, written at the age of 15 in 1824. Of the four mature symphonies that survive, two, the *Reformation* (1830) and *Lobgesang* (1840), have specific religious associations; the other two have vaguely programmatic titles, *Italian* (1833) and *Scottish* (1842). Only the finales of the first two depart from the Classical formal conventions, and the composition and treatment of the orchestra in all of them are clearly modelled on Mozart. None has a really strong first movement. The *Italian* has one of the most brilliant openings in all music, but its lustre already begins to fade after ten bars. Mendelssohn conscientiously went through all the proper procedures for an opening Allegro, with a new tune contrapuntally treated in the development section. The music has a high polish and is technically almost infallible. But predictability is too great, tension does not accumulate as it does in Mozart; and the melodies are much less appealing than Schubert's. In the other three movements, however, Mendelssohn is perfectly at home: in the charming processional Andante and in the Minuet and Trio he gave free rein to his lyrical impulses, and in the final Saltarello he recaptured the elfin poetry of his overture to *A Midsummer Night's Dream* – which, however, together with the *Hebrides* Overture, had reached a far higher level of consistent inspiration than any of his symphonies were to achieve. These concert overtures represented a new genre which was to prove, on the whole, more congenial to Romantic spirits than the symphony, and they are direct forebears of the symphonic poem.

Schumann's principal symphonies all date from later life, when, partly under the influence of Mendelssohn, he turned with varying success to traditional forms and styles. The four symphonies are in the same lyrical tradition as Mendelssohn's, and have none of the radical innovatory force of his early piano music. Schumann treated sonata-allegro form with greater freedom than Mendelssohn in his first movements, and did not feel obliged to produce his themes in the right order or the right keys; but he had little interest in forging new structural methods to replace the old. Instead there is a spontaneous following up of new ideas as they occur to him, which, at best, can be delightful. Schumann went somewhat further than Mendelssohn in altering the movement structure of the symphony, usually following Beethoven's precedents. He frequently brought back fragments of earlier movements, like Beethoven in the Fifth and Ninth; he introduced an extra movement in the Third (*Rhenish*) (1850), as in Beethoven's Sixth; he provided two trios to the scherzo in the First (1841), which was a common practice with Mozart (though not in symphonies) and also recalls the playing of the same trio twice in Beethoven's Fourth and Seventh. His orchestra was of modest Classical dimensions, but he used it far less happily than Mendelssohn, frequently producing a thick and colourless timbre through unfortunate doublings.

There was a tendency among the conservative Romantics to make the symphony continuous. Beethoven had, in the Fifth, let the scherzo run straight into the finale, and similarly in the Sixth (with the intervention of the Storm). In Mendelssohn's *Scottish* (1842) the movements are played without a break: Schumann followed suit for the revised version (1851) of his Fourth. In a time when audiences tended to burst into applause at any point where an impression of finality was given, this trend was obviously aimed at holding the hearer's attention unbroken throughout a complete work of art. Some composers sought further means to 'unify' their works, following Beethoven's example of introducing recognizable resemblances and connections between the various movements. Mendelssohn had little interest in that, though he did bring back a snatch of the slow introduction in the Scottish. Schumann not only recapitulated actual sections of previous movements, but in many cases based several themes on a single melodic germ: again the Fourth provides a clear example. The process falls short of actual thematic transformation, for the stress patterns of the motif are never distorted (even in inversion) and it is readily recognizable by the ear at each appearance. In Schumann's symphonies these motifs act simply as a starting-point for the exercise of his melodic imagination. He had already, in *Carnaval* and other piano pieces, shown almost unlimited resource in the invention of different and contrasting melodies originating in the same motif.

The 'programmatic' tendency of the conservative Romantics had little to do with the trend of Berlioz and Liszt towards the dramatic and the narrative. It took the form of vaguely evocative titles such as 'Italian', 'Scottish' or 'Rhenish', and of the suggestion of tableaux, as in the processional slow movement of the *Italian* or the movement evoking Cologne Cathedral in the *Rhenish*. This was mood painting, bringing music closer to the visual than to the dramatic arts. It had also a connection with poetry, and it has often been said that many a Romantic melody may have been suggested by poetic lines. This tendency in the symphony can be traced through Schubert back to Mozart: the melody of the closing section in the first movement of the 'Jupiter' has associations with *opera buffa*, and many others (like the main themes of nos.39 and 40) exactly fit standard poetic metres. The Mendelssohn *Lieder ohne Worte* type of melody finds many parallels in his symphonies, particularly in second subjects, and so it is with Schumann, Brahms and Tchaikovsky: Abraham has pointed out how large a number of Brahms's instrumental melodies have demonstrable connections with a poetic text. The result of this prosodic genesis of melody was a closed type of tune, generally somewhat square in phrase structure, that in its very nature discouraged the type of symphonic treatment developed by Haydn and Beethoven. Mozart, and Beethoven himself (the E minor melody in the 'Eroica'), could encompass such tunes without neglecting the growth and impetus of their sym-

phonic plan. Of their successors, only Brahms acquired the expertise to do so consistently and successfully. The others managed it only in an occasional tour de force: generally their symphonic art relied to a great degree on the attractiveness of these tunes themselves, and on their decoration and elongation.

With programmatic titles, and the musical clues suggesting landscapes or other pictorial images, a composer invited the listener to focus his imagination on a specific scene: the phrase structure of the melodies, and their often pianistic accompaniment texture, suggested the lied or ballad. By both these means the hearer was invited to escape from the conflicts of urban society into a pastoral or cloistered world of satisfied longing, as easily as he could by contemplating a watercolour landscape or reading a Wordsworth poem. It has often been pointed out how rarely the subjects of Romantic painting and poetry dealt realistically with the lives of the artists or of their public. The same is true of the 'subjects' of Romantic symphonies: even the symbolic grappling with difficulties that was the heritage of Haydn and Beethoven is replaced by an escape into a world of pleasant dreams.

With Brahms, however, forces deep in his nature impelled him to a sterner self-discipline. Though his 'position as the heir of Mendelssohn and Schumann is too obvious to be disputed' (Abraham), he chose to take Beethoven, Bach and Palestrina as his masters. In somewhat the same way as Beethoven himself, he tamed and channelled the lyrical and romantic impulses that pervaded the musical world in which he grew up and lived, and forced them into the methods of another era – 'symphonic' methods, which were barely compatible with the style of mid-19th-century German music. The resulting conflict, which at his best Brahms resolved by strength of personality, makes him in a sense the only true symphonic heir of Beethoven.

In externals Brahms showed his principles by rejecting not only the radical innovations of Berlioz, Liszt and Wagner, but even the more modest advances of Mendelssohn and Schumann. He returned to the old plan of four completely separate movements, using strict sonata form in his first movements and in some of the others as well; he rejected programmes and titles; he used only the modest orchestra of Beethoven's time, disdaining even to take advantage of the full chromatic compass of valved horns and trumpets. He frequently resorted to the nearly obsolete technical devices of fugue and strict canon, or even, in the last movement of the Fourth, to the venerable passacaglia. But however deeply he studied the music of the remoter past, his spontaneous musical style was in the literary, lyrical, warmly emotional and escapist tradition of Schubert, Mendelssohn and Schumann. His impulse was to write stanza-like melodies, richly harmonized and gorgeously decorated with details of accompaniment, as in his songs and partsongs. His long period of apprenticeship before he produced his First Symphony (1876) was to a great extent taken up with efforts to change this style, and to evolve an appropriate mode of orchestration. His efforts at Classical forms are seen in the early piano sonatas and chamber works: the sonata op.5 goes further than he did in the symphonies in the direction of 'integration' of movements by thematic relationships. He developed his characteristic orchestral style, often criticized as 'thick' and 'grey' but precisely appropriate for his purpose, in the two serenades (1859), the D minor Piano

Concerto (1859), the *German Requiem* (1868) and the St Anthony Variations (1873). Most of these works, like much of the symphonies, were composed at the piano; the D minor Concerto had been conceived as a two-piano sonata, then as a symphony, and the heroic grandeur of its opening movement is obviously visualized in terms of Beethoven's Ninth Symphony, which Brahms had first heard in 1853.

When Brahms's First Symphony appeared, Hanslick hailed it as the only true successor to Beethoven's Ninth, and Wolf said the same thing in a less flattering way: 'Brahms writes symphonies as if nothing had happened since Beethoven'. Its debt to Beethoven is obvious, in the rejection of subsequent musical 'progress', in the modes of thematic development, above all in the grand tune of the finale, which is reminiscent of the 'Ode to Joy'. But although Brahms succeeded in mastering much of Beethoven's method, the best points in the symphony remain those in which he indulged his voluptuous lyrical gifts. The long passage of transitional and second-subject material in the first movement (bars 99–156) is a good example: just as in Schubert's 'Unfinished', it is there to be enjoyed, but it is so long that it dissipates the momentum generated earlier. Similar passages can be found in the first movements of all the symphonies. After the First, indeed, when Brahms was no longer quite so much on his mettle to prove himself the heir of Beethoven, he gave way more readily to lyricism.

Brahms's chief innovation in the external form was his substitution (in the first three symphonies) of a gentle Allegretto grazioso for the Beethovenian scherzo. In these, and in the slow movements, there is little to stand in the way of sensuous enjoyment. But Shaw, who rightly perceived this as the true Brahms, was wrong in thinking him 'too ... addle-headed to make anything great out of the delicious musical luxuries he wallows in'. In these soft, melancholy movements, where Brahms was most himself, he showed an exceptional subtlety in the extension, variation, combination and instrumentation of melodies; the result is certainly great, even if not heroic. His supreme skill was always in the manipulation of melodies. Like Schumann he could create numberless tunes from one small motif. He revived abstruse crafts of canon, inversion and fugue, but contrived to make them sound effortless and natural; and he was perhaps the greatest master of melodic variation. In his piano music it is the variation sets that rise highest in cumulative effect, and he turned to a variation form to achieve the consummation of his greatest symphony, the Fourth (1885). Working with the strict passacaglia form, he skilfully transformed the long series of eight-bar sections into an endlessly changing, slowly growing procession, leading to the heights in one of the most satisfying of all symphonic conclusions.

German composers, from Haydn to Brahms, dominated the symphonic scene to such an extent that it was hard for composers of other countries to find an independent voice. Symphonies had played little or no part in Russian musical life, and when the Russian Music Society was founded by the Rubinstein brothers in 1859 its goal was rather to bring European music to Russia than to foster any nationalistic school. Anton Rubinstein's six symphonies, which won great popularity throughout Europe, are ponderous imitations of Mendelssohn. Tchaikovsky gained a more lasting fame for his, founded on their expressive melodies, brilliant orchestration and piquant harmony. So firmly was the Classical ideal of the symphony fixed in his mind that he used the forms quite rigidly – for example in the Fourth (1878) and Fifth (1888) – without any apparent effort to mould them to suit his melodic materials. His second-subject material is so completely unconnected with its surroundings that a slowing-down is often called for, with dangerously sentimental effect. There is no better example of a Romantic composer treating the Classical forms as textbook models, mere skeletons on which any kind of music could be hung; as Tchaikovsky himself admitted, 'the seams show' and 'there is no organic union between the separate episodes'. His efforts at thematic transformation and cyclic recall of earlier movements are of little avail. He despised Brahms as an uninspired pedant, but his larger works would have gained enormously from some of Brahms's skill at concealing seams and giving the impression of continuous cumulative development.

Like the other conservative Romantics, Tchaikovsky composed passages of great beauty. His style is highly individual; indeed most of the symphonies follow 'programmes' describing the artist's emotions, but these programmes did not serve the same purpose as Mendelssohn's (let alone Berlioz's) for they were revealed only privately to friends, or, in the case of the Sixth ('Pathetic', 1893), kept secret. Tchaikovsky used Russian folk melodies at several points in his symphonies, but he cannot be called a nationalist composer because he made little effort to adapt his style to accommodate the folk idiom. Like other Romantics, he was most at ease in the simpler middle movements, especially those in dance forms: the polonaise of the Third, the sparkling scherzo of the Fourth, the waltzes of the Third and Fifth, and the march of the Sixth are among his most completely satisfying movements. The finales are often the weakest sections: that of the Fourth oscillating frenetically between triumph and despair, that of the Fifth blaring and vulgar. The finale of the Sixth represents Tchaikovsky's only significant innovation in symphonic form, for it is a slow movement, closing in a mood of deepest gloom. In Dent's words, 'Tchaikovsky has here painted us the portrait of a soul in torment with a lurid intensity which no other composer has ever equalled'.

Other Russians of the conservative school were Rimsky-Korsakov (with three symphonies) and Glazunov (with eight). The Scandinavian symphonists were even more obviously an offshoot of the German. Niels Gade composed eight symphonies along Mendelssohnian lines, at least one of which earned extravagant praise from Schumann. Franz Berwald's four symphonies are in the same category.

In England, Cipriani Potter maintained almost single-handed a Mozartian symphonic tradition in the 1820s. His pupils G. A. Macfarren and Sterndale Bennett continued on conservative-Romantic lines. Nothing remotely resembling a 'nationalist' symphony appeared until Stanford's 'Irish' (1887). The first American symphony is believed to be George Bristow's in E♭ (1845); he composed three more, the last entitled 'Arcadian' (1874). Speaking for the European-trained group of American symphonists of the 1880s and 1890s, D. G. Mason wrote: 'The truth is, our whole view of music was based on the style of classic and romantic symphonists, beginning with Haydn and Mozart and ending with Mendelssohn and Schumann'. A large number of minor German composers continued the conservative tradition. In France, German influence was slow to take hold. In Saint-Saëns' first two symphonies (1853, 1859), Bizet's (1855, recovered only in 1933), and Gounod's three, one finds the influence of Mozart, Auber and Rossini, but little of Mendelssohn and Schumann, and none of Berlioz or Liszt. The later work of French symphonists is considered below.

3. RADICAL ROMANTICS: BERLIOZ, LISZT, D'INDY, FRANCK. A second group of composers in the 19th century, also regarded as Romantics but often in conflict with the Mendelssohn–Schumann–Brahms tradition, was less inclined to provide 'escape' from the realities of the age. Confronted with the Philistinism of popular musical taste, they did not retreat to a defence of 'pure' values and the ideals of the past; neither did they cater completely to the public. Instead, they tried to develop musical forms that would sweep the public onwards and upwards to larger and higher ideals. They played to a wide audience, catching its attention with spectacular gestures and sensational effects, but sought ways to forge newly productive musical forms which that audience would comprehend.

The symphony, with its weight of tradition and convention, did not naturally suggest itself as a suitable medium for such a goal. Wagner, the foremost of the group, never completed a symphony after an early work in C (1832) which he acknowledged to be in imitation of Mozart. His music dramas are 'symphonic' in a broader sense. Liszt, as he turned to the composition of symphonies, began at about the same time to develop the symphonic poem (he first used the term in 1854). For many it provided a solution to the problem of the Romantic symphony; it was imitated by composers as diverse as Tchaikovsky, Smetana, Franck, Saint-Saëns, Strauss and Elgar (see SYMPHONIC POEM). The adjective 'symphonic' now comprehended only those aspects of the symphony that the later Romantics found spontaneous and congenial: the massive orchestra, the seriousness of purpose, the literary or pictorial setting, the development and transformation of themes with stated or implied labels. Other 'symphonic' genres emerged: symphonic pictures (Rimsky-Korsakov, *Sadko*, 1867); symphonic variations (Dvořák, op.78, 1877; Franck, 1885); symphonic rhapsodies (Chabrier, *España*, 1883); symphonic dances (Grieg, op.64, 1898); symphonic suites (Bridge, *The Sea*, 1910). In all these the word seems to claim the importance and scale of the symphony while denying its structure.

But, to some of the more advanced Romantics, the presence of the symphony as an idea was a challenge that they could not ignore. With their near-sighted view of Beethoven as a giant who had taken on and conquered the forces of musical tradition, they could not but aspire to equal or surpass his feat. They saw the composition of a symphony as a tremendous psychological drama, in which the artist's emotions must fire his musical invention to white heat, to cast the old metals in a new shape. It is not surprising that their symphonies are few in number, each one standing as an individual monument to its composer's creativity, having neither predecessor nor successor; and it is notable that none of these few symphonies to be classified as 'radical Romantic' was by a German. The German composers were too much aware of the symphony as an evolving element in their own culture to be willing to overthrow its conventions for any short-term gain.

To Berlioz the symphonies of Beethoven had come with the force of a revelation, on top of his discovery of Shakespeare during the short feverish burst of French xenophile Romanticism just before 1830. Not only Beethoven's symphonies, but Mozart's and Haydn's as well, had been virtually unknown to Paris until Habeneck's Conservatoire concerts opened in 1828. Few French musicians had either the will or the ability to absorb this exotic new influence. The symphony did not occupy an important place in French musical life: French composers aspired to the opera, where at this time Rossini was at the height of his fame.

Alone among composers of his generation in any country, Berlioz accepted Beethoven's symphonies, not as incredible demonstrations of musical power which none could equal, but as models for immediate imitation and further development. He set to work at once to build a symphony that would stand on the shoulders of Beethoven's. Beethoven had expanded the scale of the symphony; Berlioz expanded it again, to a five-movement form lasting an hour. Beethoven had stretched the technique of orchestral instruments; Berlioz stretched them further, and added instruments and devices unknown to the concert hall. Beethoven in his Sixth Symphony had written a programme; Berlioz wrote a more explicit one, embodying the wildest and most sensational Romantic ideas of the day, as well as much of his personal emotional experience.

The programme of the *Symphonie fantastique* (1830) is in fact different in kind from that of the 'Pastoral' Symphony, and from the vaguely evocative titles used by Mendelssohn and Schumann: it is an effort to force the listener to go through the composer's specific emotional experiences, in a way that music alone cannot possibly do. Many writers have tried to explain it away on the grounds that the music stands alone without need of the programme – or, if it does not, so much the worse for the music. But in fact this work deviates so far from the expected course of a symphony (only the exposition of the first movement resembles the Classical form) that the design is unintelligible without it. Berlioz knew this well, and therefore required the distribution of the programme to the audience when the symphony was performed. The famous *idée fixe*, a long, lyrical and intensely emotional melody, is not well suited to symphonic development. So Berlioz brought it back complete at various points in the symphony, transformed in mood and detail but not in melodic shape. At the end of the 'Marche au supplice' the melody begins and is then decapitated. The shameless vulgarity of this device shows how he meant to carry the public with him; so does the sentimental waltz that forms the second movement. But nobody could possibly guess the 'meaning' of these features without reading the programme.

In the second symphony, *Harold en Italie* (1834), the solo viola part (written for Paganini) is supposed to represent Harold, but there is no discernible 'programme' connecting the music with the text of Byron's *Childe Harold*, and the movement titles are mere tableau indications, defining a general scene depicted in the music, as with the conservative Romantics. The four movements, including the final Orgy, are closer to Classical symphonic form than those of the *Symphonie fantastique*. In his third symphony, however (*Roméo et Juliette*, 1839), Berlioz brought to remarkable fruition his idea of the dramatization of instrumental music. The dramatic programme is actually sung in a special kind of unison chant, a possibility Berlioz had foreshadowed in a footnote to an 1836 version of the *Symphonie fantastique* programme. Soloists and chorus also play a considerable part in the work, but most of the larger movements are exclusively instrumental, including the love music that forms the slow movement of the symphony and is one of the composer's finest inspirations. Other works of Berlioz, *Lélio* and *La damnation de Faust*, are still farther along the line between symphony and drama; neither was called a symphony by its composer, yet they clearly have symphonic elements. The *Symphonie funèbre et triomphale* (1840), on the other hand, is hardly to be treated as a symphony at all, for it is not primarily concert music though it is a good example of his ideal of art for the masses.

Berlioz's greatest contribution to symphonic writing lay in his instrumentation. In a century of great orchestrators he outclassed all in the brilliance and daring of his orchestral effects. For the first time orchestration itself became an element in symphonic design, contributing significantly to the pattern of drive, climax, expectation, disappointment and fulfilment. His style was radical (and, to many contemporaries, unintelligible) because it paid so little deference to the element of predictability that makes for easy comprehension and, hence, for stable form. Almost every phrase takes an unexpected turn, almost every expected cadence is delayed, altered, or even denied altogether. But in the *Symphonie fantastique* and *Roméo et Juliette* he succeeded in creating a new model, in which a dramatic text was an essential and guiding element in the structure, but did not stop the work from being recognizably a symphony.

The model attracted few imitators. Félicien David's 'ode-symphonies', such as *Le désert* (1844) and *Christophe Colomb* (1847), are no longer played. The most important sequel was the two symphonies of Liszt. There is no doubt of the Berlioz succession in the case of the *Faust Symphony* (1854): it was Berlioz who had introduced Liszt to Goethe's *Faust*, and had shown in his *La damnation de Faust* how well suited the subject was to musical treatment; and it was to Berlioz that Liszt dedicated his symphony. He called it 'A Faust Symphony in three character sketches, after Goethe'. The programme is not explicit, but refers back to Goethe's work, with which the audience is presumed to be familiar; and the music depicts character traits and their conflict rather than specific scenes or events. The exception is an interlude in the second movement where Gretchen plucks the petals of a flower, saying 'He loves me . . . he loves me not'. The three movements are in general character those of a symphony without a scherzo, and represent respectively Faust, Gretchen and Mephistopheles; the choral coda was added in 1857. In the Mephistopheles movement Liszt brilliantly transformed all the Faust themes into grotesque caricatures of themselves. As in Berlioz's *Symphonie fantastique*, this procedure is justified by the debasement of personality that forms part of the programme. Musically effective though it is, it could hardly have become part of the symphonic stock-in-trade; and so, like the other symphonies of the radical Romantics, this work remains an isolated tour de force, though Strauss adopted some of its processes into his symphonic poems.

Liszt's other symphony, *Dante* (1857), likewise the result of decades of thought about the subject, was at first planned to accompany a lantern-slide show on the new 'bioscope'. It too is in three movements; originally these were to correspond with the three parts of Dante's *Divina commedia*, the Inferno, Purgatorio and Paradiso, but Liszt, persuaded by Wagner that the joys of paradise were beyond human portrayal, wrote a choral *Magnificat* for the finale. The first movement begins with a trombone passage representing the terrible inscription over the gates of hell, the words of which are actually written under the notes in the score: the last line, 'Lasciate ogni speranza voi ch'entrate', is an important theme in the movement that follows. The two instrumental movements are both in a loosely constructed ternary form, with scant resemblance to the Classical symphony. There is little use of thematic transformation. The final *Magnificat*, for women's voices only, is conspicuously diatonic and archaic in its harmonies. The great diversity of style, as well as medium, is hardly symphonic, and it is the programme that provides the chief logical connection between the movements.

Liszt's pupil Vincent d'Indy produced another isolated novelty, the *Symphonie sur un chant montagnard français* (1886). It can be seen as remotely derived from Berlioz's *Symphonie fantastique*, for it employs a tune, not a theme, as the basis of all three movements. The song is first announced in plain form; it is transformed into the main theme of each of the movements, and also returns in original form here and there. The style is permeated with Wagnerian harmony and texture.

Lalo's Symphony (1887) and Saint-Saëns' Third (with parts for piano duet and organ, 1889) also show the influence of Liszt and Wagner in their style and in their use of thematic transformation. César Franck's Symphony in D minor (1889) goes further in the same direction, though (as Abraham has pointed out) Franck had anticipated Liszt in this technique in his Piano Trio in F♯ minor (1841). The Symphony is entirely abstract (it was d'Indy, not Franck, who nicknamed one of its themes the 'motif of faith') and its three-movement form bears only a superficial resemblance to the traditional symphony. It is, however, a real 'symphony' in being a single conception, owing its unity to the pervasive development of themes, the skilful use of expanded harmony and tonality (the tonal polarity between D and F in the first movement is balanced by a polarity between D and B in the last), and a pattern of broad climaxes of a Wagnerian kind.

4. NATIONALISTS: BALAKIREV, BORODIN, DVOŘÁK. The most radical composer of the Russian nationalist group, Musorgsky, never wrote a symphony; his ideals and methods could not be bent to the traditions of symphonic form. The style based on Russian folksongs was at its best in miniature forms, or in forms such as opera, ballet or variations in which small units could be joined together with little total musical integration. It fell to Balakirev and Borodin to discover how to weld such units into a symphony, a form practically non-existent in the Russian musical tradition. In his First Symphony (begun 1864, finished 1897) Balakirev abandoned all pretence of sonata form in his first movement. The slow introduction states a striking and pregnant theme which is the basis of all the melodies in the Allegro; they are spun out by means of repetition, variation and extension into a movement that owes much of its success to harmonic freshness and instrumental colour. The other

three movements have even less 'development' and rely largely on the alternation of attractive melodies. Borodin completed his First Symphony (1867) after studying for several years with Balakirev, who touched up the score after the composer's death and then passed it on to Rimsky-Korsakov for re-orchestration. It too has a monothematic first movement, based on a theme stated in the slow introduction, but it is recognizably in sonata form. The Second (1869–76) is also largely monothematic. In both cases the composer's exuberant vitality and the colourful use of folk idioms and pictorial suggestions carry the listener through the work with little help from Germanic techniques of symphonic development.

The Czech nationalist school was closer to the mainstream of west European music, owing to centuries of cultural domination by Germany and Austria. Prague, unlike Moscow, had a strong symphonic tradition, by no means a mere provincial offshoot of the German. A line of Czech composers can be traced back to the origins of the symphony. But until the time of Smetana and Dvořák there was little to distinguish their style from that of contemporary German composers. Smetana, like Musorgsky, never attempted to cast his ideas into the form of a symphony. Dvořák remained close enough to the Germanic tradition to feel comfortable as a symphonist. Beneath the rather superficial local colour of some of his melodies he belongs clearly to the conservative-Romantic tradition. His earlier symphonies are those of a predominantly lyrical composer whose technique was sufficient to place his melodies in the framework of traditional forms. He had little interest in formal innovation, and his music reminds the listener from time to time of Schubert, Mendelssohn or Brahms. In the Eighth (1889) and Ninth, 'From the New World' (1893), Dvořák applied his command of a more typically nationalist approach to composition, allowing his melodic gifts a freer rein and relying on variation, alternation and colour more than thematic development or cumulative tension for his effects.

5. BRUCKNER AND HIS TIME. By the end of the 19th century the symphony had become a bastion of the orthodox world of music. Concert programmes throughout Europe and the USA were far more heavily dominated by German music than they had been at the beginning of the century, and it was now beyond serious dispute that the symphony was preponderantly a German form. By far the most popular symphonies were Beethoven's; the only earlier ones regularly performed were Haydn's last 12 and Mozart's last six. Of later symphonies it was the conservative-Romantic, predominantly German school that maintained a regular place in concert programmes. Many new symphonies were composed – some commissioned by concert societies or for royal or national occasions – but it often happened that their first performance was also their last. Musical knowledge was now widespread in middle-class circles: all the standard symphonies had been published in miniature score, for private study, and in piano and piano duet arrangements for home performance. With some 30 to 50 symphonies now established and familiar to most of the concert-going public, there was little real demand for new ones. Since 1900 few symphonies have successfully challenged the popularity of their predecessors.

The opulent orchestra of the time included triple woodwind, the third players doubling with additional woodwind instruments; as many as 15 or even 20 brass instruments; a battery of percussion; harps; and at least 60 string instruments. Berlioz, Wagner and Tchaikovsky had shown how to use these immense forces as a sensitive instrument of vast range and expressive power: its sound was thought of as 'symphonic', as in such forms as the symphonic poem, and in the USA the word 'symphony' came to be used for the orchestra itself. But the symphony as a form seemed to have become a prisoner of the past. The majority of symphonies played were old ones; the majority of those composed followed old designs that did not really suit their content. To evolve a genuinely new, genuinely symphonic form apparently required a prodigious creative effort which few were prepared to make; where this succeeded, it produced only an isolated masterpiece, satisfactory in its own terms but not susceptible to imitation.

One composer alone succeeded in creating a new school of symphony writing – Anton Bruckner. The source of his art was in Vienna, the centre of the conservative symphonic tradition, and it was rooted in the agrarian culture that had long supported Vienna's imperial hegemony. So Germanic was his musical personality that he has been fully appreciated only in the German-speaking countries, where he is commonly ranked second only to Beethoven as a symphonist. A deeply religious man, who could dedicate his Ninth Symphony 'to my dear God', he lacked the selfconsciousness that affected most of his contemporaries in their dealings with the symphony. They trimmed their spontaneous gifts in deference to symphonic conventions, or strove mightily to create new ones. Bruckner did neither, but with enviable naturalness and serenity composed one symphony after another in forms that renewed the old.

Some have classed him as a conservative, some as a radical. Really he was neither, or alternatively was the culminating fusion of both. The Wagnerian party sought to adopt him as its symphonic representative in the running battle against the Brahms–Hanslick forces. He deeply admired Wagner, and accepted this position, but was never comfortable in it: his music, though often Wagnerian in its orchestration and in its huge rising and falling periods, patently has its roots in older styles. Bruckner took Beethoven's Ninth Symphony as his starting-point. Like other works of Beethoven's last period, the Ninth had merely bewildered his immediate successors, but in the later 19th century it was beginning to have a profound influence: Brahms and Franck, for instance, were obviously in its debt. For Bruckner it was the model not just of one symphony but of all his symphonies. Conceived as a unique solution to a personal artistic problem, it became, 60 years later, the model for a whole world of symphonies, for Bruckner and later for Mahler. The very scale of Bruckner's symphonies, bloated by ordinary standards, is normal beside it. The introduction to the first movement, beginning mysteriously and climbing slowly with fragments of the first theme to the gigantic full statement of that theme, was taken over by Bruckner; so was the awe-inspiring coda of the first movement. The scherzo and slow movement, with their alternation of melodies, are models for Bruckner's spacious middle movements, while the finale with a grand culminating hymn is a feature of almost every Bruckner symphony.

Bruckner is the first composer since Schubert about whom it is possible to make such generalizations. His symphonies deliberately followed a pattern, each one building on the achievements of its predecessors. His orchestra gradually grew in size, from the modest dimensions of the First to the full Wagnerian scope of the Eighth; the time-scale, large from the beginning, also increased. His melodic and harmonic style changed little, and it had as much of Schubert in it as of Wagner. He was entirely conservative in retaining the conventional four movements, and in the clear Classical basis for the internal structure of these movements; moreover, he used no programmes (or at least did not reveal them) and only once a title, 'Romantic' for the Fourth. In orchestration he learnt much from Wagner, but was so unsure of his skill that he allowed well-meaning friends to re-orchestrate and even rewrite some of his music: the original versions are generally agreed to be superior. His technique in the development and transformation of themes, learnt from Beethoven, Liszt and Wagner, was unsurpassed, and he was almost the equal of Brahms in the art of melodic variation. Non-Germanic audiences are apt to be bored by the great length and slow pace of his works, by their lack of sufficient internal contrast, and by their similarity one with another. It is indeed true that Bruckner recognized only one mood and purpose for the symphony: an aspiration to the sublime.

BIBLIOGRAPHY

E. T. A. Hoffmann: 'Beethovens Instrumental-Musik', *Zeitung für die Elegante Welt* (Leipzig, 1813)
H. Berlioz: *A travers chants* (Paris, 1862; Eng. trans., 1913–18); ed. L. Guichard (Paris, 1971)
F. Weingartner: *Die Symphonie nach Beethoven* (Leipzig, 1897; Eng. trans., 1904)
G. B. Shaw: *Music in London 1890–1894* (London, 1932), i, 18f
D. F. Tovey: *Essays in Musical Analysis*, i–ii (London, 1935)
G. Abraham: *A Hundred Years of Music* (London, 1938, 4/1974)
A. Carse: *The Orchestra from Beethoven to Berlioz* (Cambridge, 1948)
K. Blaukopf, ed.: *Lexikon der Symphonie* (Teufen-St Gallen, 1952)
F. Blume: 'Romantik', *MGG* (Eng. trans. in *Classic and Romantic Music*, New York, 1970)
H. Pleasants, ed. and trans.: *E. Hanslick: Music Criticisms 1846–99* (New York, rev. 2/1963)
R. Simpson, ed.: *The Symphony*, i: *Haydn to Dvořák* (Harmondsworth, 1966)
K. Pahlen: *Symphonie der Welt* (Zurich, 1967)
R. Simpson: *The Essence of Bruckner* (London, 1967)
J. Horton: *Brahms Orchestral Music* (London, 1969)
P. H. Lang: 'The Symphony in the Nineteenth Century', *The Symphony 1800–1900* (New York, 1969)
H. Macdonald: *Berlioz Orchestral Music* (London, 1969)
J. Warrack: *Tchaikovsky Symphonies and Concertos* (London, 1969)
M. J. E. Brown: *Schubert Symphonies* (London, 1970)
R. Simpson: *Beethoven Symphonies* (London, 1970)
A. Salop: 'Intensity and the Romantic Sonata Allegro', *Studies in the History of Musical Style* (Detroit, 1971), 251–92
U. von Rauchhaupt, ed.: *Die Welt der Symphonie* (Hamburg, 1972; Eng. trans., 1973)
L. Cuyler: *The Symphony* (New York, 1973)
R. Kloiber: *Handbuch der klassischen und romantischen Symphonie* (Wiesbaden, rev.2/1976)

III. 20th century

Just as the first decade of the 19th century had seen the crystallization, in Beethoven's middle period, of a new type of symphony, so the first decade of the 20th brought that type to its fullest maturity and also effectively to its end. Not until then did the purely formal attempt to cast a Romantic symphony in a Classical mould give way once more to symphonic forms arising directly from the nature of their materials. Though the recovery was, for historical reasons, short-lived, it was to have important consequences.

1. 1901–18: Mahler, Sibelius, Nielsen. 2. France and Germany after 1918. 3. Stravinsky; France after 1930. 4. Hindemith. 5. The USA. 6. Britain. 7. Scandinavia after Nielsen. 8. The USSR: Shostakovich. 9. Poland, Hungary, Czechoslovakia. 10. Germany after World War II.

1. 1901–18: MAHLER, SIBELIUS, NIELSEN. The most important symphonists before World War I are Mahler, Sibelius, Elgar and (though his greatest symphonies came later) Nielsen: to these may be added Skryabin, and Schoenberg if the decided chamber character of his First Chamber Symphony (1906) is allowed to be outweighed by its masterly deployment of heterogeneous instrumental and musical means within a single, extended and closely argued movement. Its four-movement-in-one design is already prophetic of a vital tendency towards complete fusion of contrasting elements in the modern symphony, whereas the one-movement form of Skryabin's later symphonies (*Poem of Ecstasy*, 1907; *Prometheus*, 1909) springs rather from something static in the music's harmony, notwithstanding its heady rhythmic and contrapuntal activity. These works are symphonic poems, as are Strauss's enormous *Symphonia domestica* (1902–3) and the picturesque *Alpensymphonie* (1915), neither of them distinguished either by compression or rigour of thought. One of the most beautiful works in this genre is the third of Szymanowski's four symphonies, a vocal-orchestral work subtitled 'Song of the Night' (1916). Its ecstatic tone reveals the influence of both Skryabin and Debussy.

By the turn of the century Mahler had completed his first four symphonies. They form a group related to the early song cycle, *Lieder eines fahrenden Gesellen*, and to the *Des Knaben Wunderhorn* songs, examples of which appear as independent movements. Remarkable though these symphonies are at the imaginative level, they hardly achieve a true symphonic fusion of their diverse ingredients. When Mahler told Sibelius in 1907 that 'the symphony must be like the world; it must be all-embracing', he was merely echoing the instinctive Romantic feeling that all products of the one imagination enjoyed *ipso facto* a sufficient unity, the test being only one of quality. However, his own last five completed symphonies (nos.5–9, of which all but the last were completed before the meeting with Sibelius) retreat significantly from this position. The Fifth (1902), Sixth (1904) and Seventh (1905) form a second group, distinguished from the first not only because they are purely orchestral but because of a new discipline in the thematic and formal craftsmanship. No doubt the two points are related. But Mahler's orchestral music after 1900 still alludes to contemporary vocal works (for instance, the various references to the *Kindertotenlieder* and Rückert songs in the Fifth Symphony) and moreover he still evidently saw the symphony in narrative theatrical terms. All three begin with marches of a funereal or tragic character, and the hero either overcomes his troubles (in the exuberant rondo finales of nos.5 and 7, both of which end in keys other than that in which the work began) or confronts them in a stern spirit of acceptance (no.6). On the other hand, these symphonies are designedly more Classical in method than their predecessors. The four-movement plan of the Sixth appears to be a conscious attempt to reassert the autonomous musical form of the Classical symphony. Its stringent motivic procedures are in the greatest possible contrast with the loose assemblage of picturesque themes in the vast first movement of no.3. Similarly in the Fifth, though the form appears more random, its operation is precise, direct and economical. The adumbration of the rondo's jubilant climax at the end of the otherwise anguished first part is a master stroke that enables the finale to clinch the whole design in a way both musically and psychologically apt.

But Mahler's attempts to restore the conventional quadripartite form of the Classical symphony had to contend with a critical problem of late Romantic music: namely, that if musical ideas were to be the direct arbiter of form, the separation of the slow movement from the mainstream of symphonic argument could no longer serve a useful purpose. Large-scale Adagio movements in fact do not occur in Mahler's middle symphonies. When they reappear, in *Das Lied von der Erde* (1908) and the Ninth Symphony (1909), they are on a massive scale as finales. The first movement of the otherwise fragmentary Tenth is likewise an immense Adagio, while the first movement of the Ninth is also predominantly slow. There are signs here of a tendency to fuse the traditional ingredients of the symphony. But Mahler, still perhaps in the grip of his Romantic theory of universality, did not live to follow this tendency to its logical conclusion.

That his Scandinavian contemporaries Sibelius and Nielsen did, however, follow it up was not simply because they lived longer. Something decidedly anti-Romantic in their temperaments, a certain objectivity of stance, prompted them to refine and compress to the point where the fusion of contrasting elements assumed much greater importance than the insistence on their individual or picturesque nature. In the light of what happened after World War I this was a prophetic attitude. In the Third (1907) and Fourth (1911) Symphonies of Sibelius the anti-rhetorical streak in his nature already brought a new economy of gesture and form which only helped increase the force, energy and ultimately even the epic stature of what was said. Their prophetic character can be seen if they are compared with other symphonies of the decade before the war, not only those of Mahler and Skryabin, but Suk's massive *Asrael Symphony* (1906), Rakhmaninov's sumptuous but very indulgent Second (1907), and the two symphonies of Elgar (1908 and 1910). Elgar was at the height of his powers when he wrote these works, and they are rightly admired for their uninhibited Romantic invention, their subtle ambivalence of tone, and their brilliant orchestration. But symphonically they are weakened by rhapsodic elements which stretch them out to an extravagant length not justified by a consistent musical impulse. The peremptory grandeur of Sibelius's Fourth might be a direct rebuttal of everything that Elgar's Second stands for. Yet linguistically Sibelius is hardly in advance of Elgar. The change is primarily one of attitude. The artist's time-honoured *amour propre* is subjected to ruthless scrutiny, and everything spurious, pretentious or solipsistic is thrown out: not, perhaps, before time.

After the war Sibelius continued to develop his technique until, in his Seventh and final symphony (1924), he arrived at the point where large musical conflicts could truly be resolved in a single-movement symphony of 20 minutes' duration. The Seventh is a masterpiece as compact as it is varied and inspired. Its exact status as a symphony can moreover be tested against another one-movement masterpiece Sibelius wrote soon afterwards, the tone poem *Tapiola*. Though in one sense more unified than the symphony, since all its material comes directly from the initial theme, *Tapiola* precisely for that reason lacks the dialectical and dynamic force of the symphony. As a descriptive and imaginative work *Tapiola* is a considerable achievement. But it can hardly be denied that the symphony, in satisfactorily resolving more complicated issues within the same time-span, is musically and intellectually the more self-sufficient work.

Nielsen, like Sibelius, started by writing four-movement symphonies along fairly traditional lines. On his first three works in the genre the influence of Dvořák and Brahms is apparent. But already in no.1 (1892) a new direction is taken. Though the work is 'in' G minor, it ends in C, and the composer acknowledged this ambiguity by opening the symphony with a chord of C major; what follows is, conceptually speaking, a struggle to affirm an initially doubtful proposition. But what is most significant is the exuberance and energy Nielsen brings to that struggle. Here at last is a composer whose ability to develop his musical ideas is not crippled by introspection or a gratuitous emotionalism. But it was some years before Nielsen realized all the implications of this early work. His Second Symphony (1902) keeps the four traditional movements, while admitting that the arrangement has become a purely external matter by naming them after the four temperaments of medieval physiology. As late as the Fourth Symphony (1916) Nielsen was still paying formal court to a quadripartite sequence, though the work is continuous, with a powerful thrust towards a clinching tonality which is other than the starting key. A sub-title, 'The Inextinguishable', alludes to what the composer called 'the elemental Will of Life'. This life force eventually triumphs graphically in the Fifth Symphony (1922), which represents the forces of destruction in a famous side-drum cadenza improvised against the main second theme, and the triumph of will in two masterly fugues in which order is finally and conclusively imposed on the material.

That Nielsen's and Sibelius's culminating symphonies were both written after the war is of some importance, since it emphasizes that their affirmations were, so to speak, properly informed. It would have been better still if they had been able to go on in the same spirit. But Nielsen's last symphony, no.6 (1925), is a distraught, embittered work, and Sibelius wrote nothing of significance after *Tapiola*.

2. FRANCE AND GERMANY AFTER 1918. As it is, the shock effect of the war is as well illustrated in the symphony as in any other artistic medium. Indeed, in the subversive and unstable atmosphere of the 1920s it was the symphony that seemed to stand most for pre-war individualism and moral certainty, values which the New Art set itself to undermine. Avant-garde composers either did not write symphonies, or they wrote symphonies in which received standards were deliberately outraged. Milhaud's six symphonies for small orchestra, written between 1917 and 1923, are as tiny, emotionally neutral and formally inconsequential as Mahler's had been vast, romantic and complex. In 1920 Stravinsky composed his *Symphonies of Wind Instruments*, using the plural form to disarm the inevitable criticism that the work was not a symphony at all but an experimental arrangement of dissociated sound-blocks. And in 1924 Prokofiev, whose Symphony no.1 (the so-called 'Classical' of 1917) had charmingly aped

the courtesies of Baroque dance music, snapped back at his Parisian audience with a dissonant and fearsomely contrapuntal Second Symphony, piquantly modelled on Beethoven's C minor Piano Sonata op.111. In Germany, the former home of the symphony, the genre went through its dimmest phase. Almost the only notable symphonies composed there in the 1920s were Pfitzner's First (1925), the earlier of Weill's two interesting and well-wrought symphonies (1921) and, in Austria, the Third Symphony (1928) of the romantically inclined Franz Schmidt and Webern's exquisite 12-note Symphony for nine instruments (1928), which must, for the purposes of this article, be regarded as a chamber work. This list speaks for itself. It contains not a single name of importance in the history of the symphony. The Weill piece, an eclectic one-movement work influenced by Busoni and the two principal modernists of the day, Stravinsky and Schoenberg, almost inevitably substitutes academic solidness for compelling structural energy (Weill's Second Symphony, however, composed in 1933, is a more assured neo-classical work which shows the loss incurred by serious music when he later defected to Broadway). Schmidt's late symphonies illustrate in a different way the dilemma of German music in the postwar years. His long, tragic, hauntingly beautiful Fourth (1933) yearns nostalgically for the age of Mahler, Reger and the young Strauss. The year of its composition is thus as significant as the year of Schmidt's death, 1939.

In due course many leading avant-garde figures of the 1920s in France and Germany made their peace with the symphony, but the truce was never more than partial and always apparently contingent on some compromise of their modernity. If the symphony went with stability (or a quest for stability), it also apparently went to some extent with traditionalism. The reason is not hard to find. Since World War I the avant garde has been preoccupied with two initially opposed but eventually related aesthetics: on the one hand the extreme arithmetical cerebration arising out of serialism, on the other the anti-cerebral transcendentalism of chance music. Ultimately both these movements stand against such ideas as change or progress, which had always been central to the symphony (this distinction, though purely historical and to a large extent arbitrary, has normally been respected in practice by both avant-garde and traditional composers). After World War II the avant garde expressed its search for new means in titles that emphasized both the novelty and the particularity of the means themselves, and conventional generic titles, when they appear at all, either take a specifically non-classical form (as in Maxwell Davies's *Sinfonia* of 1962 on material from Monteverdi's Vespers), or have some critical or ironic sense (as in Penderecki's Symphony of 1973, where the clash between title and style seems studiedly provocative), or both, as in Berio's *Sinfonia* (1968), where collage is brilliantly used to satirize the listening habits of those who attend repertory symphony concerts. Of the important exceptions (especially Lutosławski, Henze, Gerhard and Panufnik) more will be said later.

3. STRAVINSKY; FRANCE AFTER 1930. In France the reconciliation started soon in the 1930s. Stravinsky's *Symphony of Psalms* (1930), though fully choral and in no way formally indebted to the symphonic tradition, has nevertheless the force of a symphony in its combination of a strong formal thrust with a deep unity of material. What it lacks, in terms of the traditional symphony, is any idea of conflict or resolution. The substance of things hoped for is already, for Stravinsky as for St Paul, faith; and it is the music's neo-Baroque religious symbolism, its fugues and spiralling ostinatos, which supply both the impetus and, ultimately, the stability. The work is a masterpiece *sui generis*, as is a later and more massive symphony of a quasi-religious character, Messiaen's *Turangalîla* (1948), one of whose musical ancestors is Stravinsky's *Symphonies of Wind Instruments*. *Turangalîla* is a difficult work to place in the history of the symphony, being devoid of the dialectical properties one instinctively associates with the genre, though by no means without development, thematic extension, or indeed drama. Its later companions, *Et exspecto resurrectionem mortuorum* and *La Transfiguration*, no longer carry the generic designation. Stravinsky's own later orchestral symphonies, in C (1940) and in Three Movements (1945), are a clear attempt to revive the symmetries and contrasts of the high Classical symphony. Their technical and imaginative brilliance tends to conceal the fact that their specifically symphonic procedures (such as the sonata form of the Symphony in C first movement) are as much fancy dress as the Baroque trappings of *Dumbarton Oaks*. So far from the procedures arising from the nature of the material, the reverse is true, and hence comes that curious and disheartening feature of all neo-classicism (or indeed neo-anything): the feeling that the supposed genre has no necessary connection with the real impulse behind the music.

Among Stravinsky's French or French-based contemporaries, Milhaud and Honegger both turned to symphonic writing in the 1930s. Like so much of his music, Milhaud's 12 symphonies display the essentially conversational character of his talent, and where they aspire to conventional symphonic 'stature' they clearly overstep the plausible limits of their content. In any case, Milhaud's style remained static, picturesque, anecdotal, perhaps modestly hieratic.

Arthur Honegger wrote five symphonies between 1930 and his death in 1955. As a group they show how irrelevant this serious-minded German–Swiss composer's association with the subversive Parisian Six had been. His symphonies are tensely argued, harmonically crabbed essays, at first still dependent on the chugging rhythms of orthodox neo-classicism, later adopting a more polyphonic style propelled with a certain diabolic energy. As music they are more determined than inspired, and certainly lack the combination of variety and finesse which still brings the Third and Fourth Symphonies of Roussel (1930 and 1934) the occasional performance. Roussel's Third was composed for the same occasion – the 50th anniversary of the Boston Symphony Orchestra – as Honegger's First, with which it has superficial points in common. But Roussel's eclecticism was broader, more urbane and productive than Honegger's, incorporating something of that burlesque humour which had always been so alien to Honegger, along with more orthodox ingredients of the traditional symphony. At its best Roussel's symphonic writing is lucid and exhilarating, though it can seem artificial and melodically insipid. Roussel is probably best seen as a modern descendant of that classic French

19th-century type, the academic symphonist, for his mastery of procedure generally outstripped his imaginative flair.

4. HINDEMITH. While the symphony in France thus struggled back to life, in Germany and Austria it must have seemed quite dead; here more than anywhere one can see how the erosion of secure social values had undercut the received forms of art. Thus Schmidt's Fourth Symphony, weary in style and content, was a fitting epitaph to an old order. Strauss and Pfitzner, Germany's two most distinguished composers, were symphonically spent. Of the younger figures, Hartmann and Blacher were delayed by Nazism, while Krenek, having produced three noisy and dissonant symphonies in Berlin in the early 1920s, retired to his native Vienna on the proceeds of the opera, *Jonny spielt auf*, and came under the influence of Schoenberg.

The one shining light in the darkness was Hindemith, and it is apt that the darkness comprehended him not. Hindemith's avant-gardism in the 1920s had mainly been of an academic rather than ideological cast, and by the early 1930s he was at work on an opera, *Mathis der Maler*, which specifically argued that the artist should concern himself above all with art and not interfere in politics. For reasons not directly connected with its subject, this opera was obstructed by the Nazis. However, in 1934 Furtwängler conducted a three-movement symphony excerpted from it, and this was to be the first of a line of symphonic masterpieces in which Hindemith re-established his place in the classic line of German instrumental composers. Like Stravinsky, Hindemith drew heavily on Baroque phraseology, but his symphonies (eight in number if the *Symphonic Metamorphoses* and the *Sinfonietta* are included) are traditional in that they basically follow Classical and 19th-century formal procedures, and modern in that they are entirely true to Hindemith's personal manner of expression, from which they derive their great vitality. Of the later symphonies the most notable are the Symphony in Eb (1940) and the symphony from the opera *Die Harmonie der Welt* (1951). Hindemith's symphonies are tonal, with an admixture of 4th-based harmony, and indeed are energetically so. In the *Mathis der Maler* symphony (1934), for instance, the first movement derives much fuel from the tension between G major and its relative Lydian C on the one hand, and Db–F♯ on the other, Db being the key both of the introductory chorale and of the final apotheosis, while the second subject of the first movement is in F♯. Hindemith's writing is rhythmically sometimes stereotyped, but he handled counterpoint like a master, in which respect his ancestry can be traced directly from the last great classical Germany symphony, Brahms's Fourth.

5. THE USA. Like many contemporary composers, Hindemith spent World War II in the USA. This exodus, while culturally damaging for Europe, was undoubtedly of immense benefit to America. There the absence of a truly indigenous musical tradition had the initial effect of encouraging, not the invention of new formal prototypes, but on the contrary the adoption of established European types. Thus for example Henry Cowell, whose outrageous cluster technique influenced Bartók and through him a whole younger generation of European composers, wrote some 21 symphonies, though their naive, primitive exoticism is far from the European idea of symphonic style. That the academic tradition of the symphony was, from the 1930s, embodied substantially in American music is beyond question.

Cowell himself was influenced by Ives, whose biographer he is. But it has to be remembered that, in the main, Ives's music was not known before the late 1920s, and not widely known until long after that. His tumultuous Fourth Symphony, one of the earliest examples of pluralism and collage in music, was completed in 1916 but not heard in full until 1965. After World War I the main impulse towards a new American music came, paradoxically, from Paris, where Copland, Harris and Piston all studied with Nadia Boulanger. Copland remained the most cosmopolitan, and that is perhaps precisely why he has written the fewest symphonies. The Third (1946) is an imposing work of epic-romantic proportions, but the so-called 'Short' Symphony (no.2, 1931–3) is by a long way the more interesting: a rather anti-heroic work that draws attention to small symphonic processes and eschews rhetoric.

Copland would certainly have been the last composer, on this form, to use the symphony to embody the 'American Dream'. That was left instead to Roy Harris, whose seven orchestral symphonies seem to express the pioneer's religious faith in his mission, its honest purpose and sure outcome. His one-movement Third (1937) is famous and outstandingly the best. It remains the locus classicus of that muscular prairie romanticism which subsequent American symphonists took over with such effortless self-confidence. The strength of this manner is best shown in the tremendous diatonic thrust of the Harris piece, and in Piston's more sophisticated and technically correct symphonies. Its limitations loom balefully in Harris's own later symphonies, especially the Fifth (1942), whose primitivism is forced and therefore pointless, and in the nine symphonies of his pupil, William Schuman, where the muscle-flexing has moved into the boardroom and been transformed into a glib and polished oratory somewhat out of touch with the plain morality that once justified it. Schuman never cured a tendency to bully the ear. But his symphonies are expertly assembled and still show the benefit of that formal compression which Harris and Copland took with them from Europe.

The above are, broadly, the tonal school of American symphonists. To them one must add Barber, whose brilliant if slightly bombastic First Symphony (1943) in one movement shares the unbroken momentum of Harris's Third; the younger Bernstein, Mennin and Persichetti; the gifted Mexican Carlos Chávez, whose *Sinfonía India* (1936), also in one movement, is one of the best adaptations of exotic folk materials to a symphonic form; and finally the Czech-born, Paris-trained Martinů, whose six symphonies were all composed in the USA after his emigration there in 1941. In Paris Martinů picked up a liking for brisk motor rhythms. But the essentials of his style are Czech: the eloquent string cantilenas, the chattering ostinato motivic fabric, and the drifting cross-rhythms, which are both Martinů's trademark and, at times of failing inspiration, his mannerism. Like Dvořák he wrote nostalgically about his native Bohemia from distant New York, and like Dvořák he owed much to Brahms (see for instance his use of orchestral antiphony in the Fourth and Fifth

Symphonies) as well as something to his adopted American compatriots.

About the American tonal symphonists in general there is perhaps a certain excess heartiness. It may be that in the last resort the most interesting American symphonist is the subtle and introspective Roger Sessions. Sessions's First Symphony, written in Europe in 1927, is neo-classical with some flavour of jazz. But thereafter his symphonies are increasingly chromatic, atonal and (from 1953) dodecaphonic. Unlike Riegger, whose Fourth Symphony (1957) tries to crystallize a tonal sense from 12-note ingredients, Sessions has always accepted the consequences of his style, though it rapidly took him into areas where the traditional idea of symphonic writing – so basic for Harris, Piston and Schuman – could hardly function. Since the Second (1946), all Sessions's symphonies have had an inward-going as well as onward-going character, and sometimes their density of texture and equivocal sense of direction may call to mind the later music of Elliott Carter. But with Sessions line and pulse, though shifting, are always clear, and shape is never obscured by detail. The fact that the shape itself does not culminate in the traditional way is a modern but not necessarily unsymphonic quality; in the Eighth Symphony, for example, the concluding reprise of the opening music has the effect, not of invalidating the intervening discourse, but of setting it in a new dimension – one familiar from opera, where an aria may hold up the action in order to detail a character's feelings without endangering the general sense of continuity.

6. BRITAIN. Britain has also had atonal symphonists, but they have not in the main evolved forms that arise properly from the special character of the materials and procedures. Searle's five symphonies suffer from stereotyped gestures that belong to a Romantic idiom; Bennett and McCabe, among younger composers, have written symphonies of much surface brilliance but little urgency of content. In the symphonies of Fricker, Goehr, Hoddinott and Frankel there is more solid and coherent invention. But perhaps the most impressive figure in this category is the underrated William Alwyn, whose dark but forthright neo-Romanticism gives his symphonies something of the sweep of the American tonal school, though the basis of his style is strictly speaking atonal. Alwyn certainly has little in common with Sessions (more perhaps with Piston), whereas a Schoenberg pupil, Roberto Gerhard, who was born in Spain but lived in England after the Civil War, is like Sessions at least in having evolved an autonomous and self-contained symphonic style out of dodecaphony, though the glittering surface of his Third (1960) and Fourth (1967) Symphonies, with their skilful, extrovert arrangement of block textures and collage, and their coruscating instrumentation, may conceal little of a more searching nature.

By contrast the tonal symphonic tradition has a secure base in the music of Elgar and of Vaughan Williams, whose nine symphonies astonishingly span the years 1910 to 1957. Vaughan Williams's popularity, and his quasi-paternal status, have tended to obscure the unevenness of his output. But the central block of four symphonies, from the Pastoral Symphony (no.3, 1921) to no.6 (1944–7), are sufficient witness to his originality and visionary power. It was once fashionable to praise the bellicose Fourth (1931–4) and Sixth at the expense of the other two, partly no doubt because it was felt that they stood a better chance of establishing Vaughan Williams internationally. Indeed they are fine achievements, and the desolate epilogue to the Sixth particularly exemplifies that ambivalent, enigmatic strain which grew, perhaps, out of Vaughan Williams's friendship with Holst, and which has proved the least imitable aspect of both (compare, for example, the tortuous reflectiveness of another 'post-Tudor' symphonist, Rubbra; and, on the other side of the coin, the blatant tub-thumping in the finale of Walton's First (1935), an otherwise compelling and individual score influenced in sound rather than method by Sibelius). But the Third and Fifth (1943) are surely bolder and more remarkable. The Pastoral Symphony, while still distantly indebted to the composer's one-time teacher Ravel, achieved at a stroke a private, mystical rural vision which could well support the music's superficial monotony of harmony and movement. In the Fifth Vaughan Williams placed this achievement on a specifically spiritual plane by allusion to Bunyan's Pilgrim's Progress (there are superscriptions from Bunyan in the score, and some of the music later reappeared in Vaughan Williams's opera on the subject; here again static harmonies and flowing, unvarying rhythms serve an essentially contemplative end.

That such qualities are not to be mistaken for dullness may be seen by comparing these two symphonies with the once-admired seven by Bax. Bax also strove for a mystical union with nature, but through a language of a distinctly neurotic character, in which unsettled harmonies lead the music, not towards any clearly envisaged destination, but into rambling byways from which Bax was often apparently powerless to extricate himself or his listeners. A more interesting symphonist of that generation is Havergal Brian, who lived to the age of 96 and completed 32 symphonies, all but 11 of them after his 80th birthday. Brian's idiom is more compact and functional than Bax's, though his earlier symphonies are on a large scale. Its rhetorical gestures have definite force, without concealing that Brian's creative technique is defective in various respects: for instance, his development of ideas is often shortwinded, and certain types of music seem beyond his grasp (a 'gritty' Allegro and a menacing or elegiac tone prevail). At his best, however, in for instance the Sixth Symphony (1948), he merits close attention, if not the ludicrous panegyrics he has attracted.

One of his admirers, Robert Simpson, is himself the author of several fine symphonies, influenced at first by Nielsen, later by a more direct wish to restore the formal, harmonic and above all spiritual values of Beethoven. Curiously, the same preoccupation underlies Tippett's Third Symphony (1972), though masked by an irony absent from its two very different predecessors (1945 and 1957). Tippett's Second, formidably difficult to play, is one of the most brilliantly affirmative of postwar symphonies. From the first Tippett was a pathfinding genius, whereas the ambitions of his contemporaries Rawsthorne and Berkeley, each the author of three finely crafted symphonies, were always more modest. Even Britten, however, generally fought shy of the symphony, though his two unequivocal essays in the genre, the Sinfonia da requiem (1940) and the Cello Symphony (1963), both show mastery of the difficult art of manipulating symphonic materials over a large canvas and in purely abstract terms. Of a younger generation only the Australian-born Williamson has shown, in his highly original modal–serial Second Symphony (1969), any serious desire to reconcile modern non-directional procedures (influenced by Messiaen) with traditional symphonic form.

7. SCANDINAVIA AFTER NIELSEN. In Scandinavia, likewise, the main tendency since the 1920s has been to support the traditional status of the symphony rather than to transplant it to a wholly new aesthetic. This is in keeping with the achievements of Sibelius and Nielsen themselves, and it evidently incurs the risk of epigonism, which only the strongest personalities have survived. In Finland Sibelius has dominated the prevailing style to such an extent that among local symphonists only Kokkonen has produced much of distinctive character (his Third Symphony of 1967 has a Sibelian economy but is gesturally original). In Sweden and Denmark, on the other hand, Sibelius has had a more helpful impact, while Nielsen has been relatively less copied. This is chiefly for methodological reasons. Sibelius's austere motivic devices could be adapted, in theory at least, to any musical idiom, whereas Nielsen's more expansive formal procedures could be sustained only by a style as rhetorical as his own, which seems to have been generally thought inappropriate and was certainly hard to copy without plagiarism. In Denmark the outstanding symphonist is a Sibelian, Vagn Holmboe, whose symphonies brilliantly invest the master's rigorous thematic methods with a pulsating energy that obviously springs from neoclassicism and yet sounds quite fresh and personal. Vagn Holmboe's Eighth Symphony (1952) exemplifies his muscular and for the most part sparing way of developing short themes which often act, though never purely mechanically, as ostinatos.

Of the Swedish symphonists the most notable are Hilding Rosenberg and K.-B. Blomdahl. Both are eclectics, as is their lesser (but better-known) compatriot, Wirén. Rosenberg was influenced for a time by Schoenberg, and his style is both denser and more lyrical than Holmboe's, though still often recalling both Sibelius and Nielsen. His six symphonies vary enormously in scale. Blomdahl flirted with more up-to-date influences, but not always so discriminatingly. His last symphony (no.3, 'Facets', 1948) is a reasonably compact piece with arresting moments rather than compelling momentum.

8. THE USSR: SHOSTAKOVICH. While the poverty of symphonic writing in France and Germany between the wars reflected the general social instability as much as a confusion over aesthetic values, the rise of the symphony in the USA and Scandinavia has a mainly artistic background. Where music was shallow-rooted it needed careful and traditional husbandry. In the USSR, by contrast, the symphony, though associated with a discarded past, nevertheless survived but under new colours – those of the ideological programme symphony, a genre that skirts the disputed borderlands of the cantata, the symphonic poem and the 'pure' symphony. That a totalitarian regime should be suspicious of abstract music is to be expected; but the Russian preference would in any case be for a documentary type of symphony, and the really damaging aspect of Soviet interference in music was its insistence on popularistic styles and unremitting optimism of content.

The baleful history of this 'socialist realism' is redeemed almost solely by the genius of Shostakovich and the honesty of Myaskovsky. They appear to be the only Soviet symphonists who struggled to reconcile a personal expressive impulse with the declared needs of a society to which they acknowledged allegiance. To them must be added Prokofiev, whose last three symphonies (nos.5–7) were composed after his return to the USSR in 1933. But Prokofiev, a lyrical melodist of Tchaikovskian stamp and a brilliantly original orchestrator, had no difficulty in reverting to an accessible idiom (he probably did so with relief), while his international fame allowed him comparative freedom of genre until the Zhdanov purges of 1948, from which no composer of talent was exempt.

Myaskovsky, though not a composer of the first rank, is an interesting eclectic figure whose 27 symphonies do not all deserve neglect. A pupil of Glier, he was influenced also by Liszt, Skryabin and Mahler, and his early symphonies productively, if too remorselessly, counterpoint an excitable sensibility with a rhetorical revolutionary optimism, which in the 1920s must have seemed a highly satisfactory channelling of creative energy. But Myaskovsky was troubled by a pessimistic cast of mind, which comes out in the perfunctory (but Tchaikovsky-like) Symphony no.21 (1940) and its Lisztian companion, the so-called Symphonic Ballad (no.22, 1941), whose triumphant ending has a decidedly spurious air. From such dilemmas Myaskovsky retreated into a folksy academicism, though even that was not colourless enough for Zhdanov.

Shostakovich, by contrast, kept up to the end the struggle between his personal introspection and pessimism and the official cultural dogma of clarity, simplicity and optimism. His 15 symphonies come from both sides; yet not one of them is without interest and there is never any abject sacrifice of quality, though the output is inevitably unequal and sometimes contains misjudgments. The purely documentary symphonies are nos.2 and 3 (1927 and 1929) which belong to the early revolutionary period, before the denunciation of the opera, *Lady Macbeth of Mtsensk*, are still vaguely modernistic; no.7 (1941), the so-called 'Leningrad', which Bartók parodied in a famous passage of his Concerto for Orchestra; and nos.11 and 12 (1956 and 1961), which describe respectively the revolutions of 1905 and 1917. That Shostakovich was genuinely moved by these subjects is repeatedly shown by the quality of the music (for instance in the wonderfully atmospheric first movement of no.11). His most personal symphonies, however, are no.1 (1925), a brilliant student work influenced by Hindemith, Prokofiev and perhaps Bartók; no.4 (withdrawn in 1936 but released for performance in the early 1960s); nos.6 and 10 (1939 and 1953); and the vocal-orchestral symphonies nos.13 and 14 (1962 and 1969). The other scores (including the popular Fifth of 1937)–'a Soviet composer's answer to just criticism' after his withdrawal of no.4– come somewhere in between, in that they are abstract works that nevertheless show certain effects of state ideology. Technically it might even be said that nos.5 and 8 (1943) are (with no.10) Shostakovich's best works. But they do not exactly define his position as a modern symphonist.

It was once tempting to see Shostakovich as the

natural successor to the great post-Romantic intellectual symphonists, Sibelius, Nielsen and Mahler. But this is borne out neither by the technique nor the philosophy of his most original music. The influence of Mahler has been much remarked in his large symphonies, but a movement like the first of no.10, perhaps his most completely successful, is closer to Nielsen in its slow but inexorable linear build-up to a powerful dramatic climax. There is a comparable effect in the first movement of no.6. But Shostakovich was often unsuccessful in achieving such sustained tension by purely contrapuntal means, and when he did so one is left with a feeling of exhaustion quite different from the exhilaration and transcendence of Nielsen's best work. Moreover, such movements are slow-moving in Shostakovich. For him, quick music usually fulfilled either a cathartic or satirical function, or followed the purely conventional Prokofiev 'motor' scherzo. This raises the important question of his musical philosophy. Where Nielsen was, broadly, an epic composer, and Sibelius was more or less neutral over such questions, Shostakovich was unquestionably, in himself, antiheroic, sceptical and pessimistic. The parodistic tone of the First Symphony, the strangely whimsical finale of the Sixth, the witty, classical Ninth coming at a time when a 'Victory' symphony was expected (1945), the enigmatic, quicksilver finale of no.10, and the barely relieved sardonic pessimism of the Babi-Yar Symphony, no.13: all these fascinating works show that for Shostakovich there were no clear solutions or final triumphs, only tragedy and irony and moral uncertainty, and, in the song cycle no.14, death.

9. POLAND, HUNGARY, CZECHOSLOVAKIA. That Shostakovich never lost his sense of artistic truth under the most trying personal circumstances stands to his credit. His achievement is all the greater in the light of the almost complete failure of other gifted composers to survive the final ideological battering administered through Zhdanov by Stalin. Outside Russia, in the satellite countries, music went through its bleakest phase after World War II. The specific stylistic données of socialist realism, coupled with the loss of contact with new music in western Europe, stifled original creative work, and continued to do so for some years after the general liberalization in the middle and late 1950s. The point may be illustrated by comparing the Polish composer Lutosławski's First Symphony, which had its first performance in 1948, with its epoch-making successor. Though the earlier work is skilful and effective, it lacks the exploratory power, brilliance and intellectual conviction of the Second, completed in 1967 – a score that dazzlingly combines aleatory procedures (admittedly of a comparatively controlled type) with clear and forthright dialectical thinking. Panufnik's entertaining if eccentric *Sinfonia rustica* (1948) is an exception to this general rule. But Panufnik fled from Poland to Britain before the 1956 risings, and his precisely chiselled, geometric later symphonies – notably the *Sinfonia sacra* (1963) and *Sinfonia di sfere* (1976) – benefit eclectically from a wider range of musical stimulus, including some of a ritualistic and exotic character.

In the other east European countries there have been many symphonists but few of note. The Hungarian Kadosa has composed eight symphonies of which the last four, written in the 1960s in a quasi-serial idiom, are more impressive than their predecessors. Kodály's solitary late Symphony in C (1961) is by comparison a feeble essay in an evidently uncongenial form and neoclassical style. The three symphonies of the Czech composer Krejčí, especially the witty Second (1958), are much more successful and likable. Kabeláč has written symphonies of a relatively ambitious cast, but lacking subtlety or true originality.

10. GERMANY AFTER WORLD WAR II. That composers in the communist bloc should have begun to take in advanced technical and stylistic influences without completely slipping their traditionalist anchors is heartening, but perhaps less so than the modest postwar revival of the symphony in the countries where it once seemed completely moribund, above all Germany (but also France, where Dutilleux has produced two fine, somewhat balletic symphonies). In Germany the renascence was initiated, significantly, in 1940 by Karl Amadeus Hartmann, in a vocal-orchestral symphony, *Versuch eines Requiem*, to poems by Whitman. Hartmann seems to have opposed the Nazis with some courage, and his style, even during the war, shows openness to influences regarded as anathema by the cultural authorities, notably Mahler and Berg. After the war Hartmann wrote seven more symphonies, always in a complex but translucent atonal style animated now and then by the influence of Stravinsky and Bartók, and later that of Henze's Italian period, with its saturated counterpoint. Henze's own first five symphonies are no less eclectic, though the fusion of serial and neo-classical ingredients which they share with Hartmann is in the end quite personal (it shows, however, the influence of Henze's teacher Fortner, whose own Symphony (1947) made a big impact in West Germany after the war). But Henze lacks the intellectual rigour of the born symphonist, and the best of these earlier works, the Fourth Symphony (1955, but largely taken from the opera *König Hirsch*), is successful because its music is intoxicatingly beautiful rather than because its single half-hour movement has a really strong formal impulse. Soon after his conversion to communism (in about 1966) Henze wrote one further symphony, his Sixth (1969), also in a single movement and with a large orchestra deployed as two distinct chamber orchestras; again the work depends as much on imaginative exuberance as on any real binding together of its heterogeneous materials, which include Cuban popular dance. But Henze's willingness still to compose works called 'symphonies' is in itself important, for the traditionalism it suggests is not at all the cultural rigor mortis of which the 20th century has seen too much, but a feeling for history as a living and continuing process.

The symphonies of Henze, together with those of Lutosławski, Tippett and Sessions, and a few others, should thus give pause to those who try to imprison music within critical definitions drawn from history. Since Haydn the symphony has developed as an intellectual discipline, not of this or that kind, but in essence. It is the artist, not the critic, who must refute Coleridge's allegation that 'the light which experience gives is a lantern on the stern, which shines only on the waves behind us'.

BIBLIOGRAPHY
D. F. Tovey: *Essays in Musical Analysis*, ii (London, 1935)
N. Slonimsky: *Music since 1900* (New York, 1937, 4/1971)
G. Abraham: *A Hundred Years of Music* (London, 1938, 4/1974)
A. Salazar: *La musica moderna* (Buenos Aires, 1944; Eng. trans., as *Music in our Time*, 1948)
W. Mellers: *Studies in Contemporary Music* (London, 1947)

R. Hill, ed.: *The Symphony* (London, 1949)

B. Shore: *Sixteen Symphonies* (London, 1949)

K. Blaukopf, ed.: *Lexikon der Symphonie* (Teufen-St Gallen, 1952)

D. Ewen: *Complete Book of Twentieth-century Music* (Englewood Cliffs, 1952)

H. Hartog, ed.: *European Music in the Twentieth Century* (London, 1957, rev. 2/1961)

W. Mellers: *Romanticism and the Twentieth Century* (London, 1957)

H. Renner: *Reclams Konzertführer* (Stuttgart, 1959)

R. Myers, ed.: *Twentieth Century Music* (London, 1960, rev. 2/1968)

W. Mellers: *Music in a New Found Land* (London, 1964)

P. H. Lang and N. Broder, eds.: 'Contemporary Music in Europe', *MQ*, li/1 (1965); also pubd separately (New York, 1965)

W. W. Austin: *Music in the Twentieth Century* (New York, 1966)

F. Howes: *The English Musical Renaissance* (London, 1966)

E. Salzman: *Twentieth-century Music: an Introduction* (Englewood Cliffs, 1967, 2/1974)

R. Simpson, ed.: *The Symphony, ii: Elgar to the Present Day* (Harmondsworth, 1967)

J. Häusler: *Musik im 20. Jahrhundert* (Bremen, 1969)

N. Rossi and R. A. Choate: *Music of our Time* (Boston, Mass., 1969)

H. H. Stuckenschmidt: *Twentieth Century Music* (London, 1969)

S. D. Krebs: *Soviet Composers and the Development of Soviet Music* (London, 1970)

L. Davies: *Paths to Modern Music* (London, 1971)

N. Nabokov, ed.: *Twentieth Century Composers* (London, 1972)

F. Routh: *Contemporary British Music* (London, 1972)

B. Schwarz: *Music and Musical Life in Soviet Russia* (London, 1972)

L. Cuyler: *The Symphony* (New York, 1973)

M. Cooper, ed.: *The Modern Age, 1890–1960*, NOHM, x (1974)

JAN LaRUE (I), NICHOLAS TEMPERLEY (II), STEPHEN WALSH (III)

Symphony Society. New York orchestral society founded in 1878 and merged with the Philharmonic Society in 1928; see NEW YORK, §5.

Symphosius Amalarius. See AMALAR.

Symposium [comissatio, symposion]. In ancient Greece and Rome, a drinking party, often with musical entertainments, after the *deipnon* or evening meal; weddings, birthdays, victors' feasts and the arrival and departure of friends were typical occasions on which a *symposium* would have been held. The order of events generally followed a prescribed plan; they included libations (drink-offerings), and a paean sung to the accompaniment of the aulos each time a fresh *kratēr* of mingled wine and water was brought. There were numerous entertainments: the guests might sing *skolia* (see SKOLION) or solo drinking-songs, female aulos players were generally in attendance (although women of good character and children were most often excluded), and dancers, either professionals or individual guests, could perform individually or in groups. Other entertainments included games and puzzles. Later, when the popularity of the *symposium* increased, the mime and the pantomime were an important part of the entertainment. The occasion might end as a KŌMOS, from which the *symposium* was not always sharply distinguished, or alternatively and more informally as a brawl.

Music was inseparably associated with the *symposium*: even when some writers attacked the usual pastimes of the *symposium* as frivolous, suggesting that wiser people might entertain themselves with serious conversation, the topic thus discussed seems often to have been music (as it was by Aristoxenus, according to Athenaeus, xiv, §632*a–b*).

BIBLIOGRAPHY

A. Mau: 'Comissatio', *Paulys Real-Encyclopädie der classischen Altertumswissenschaft*, iv (Stuttgart, 1901), 610

A. Hug: 'Symposion', *Paulys Real-Encyclopädie der classischen Altertumswissenschaft*, 2nd ser., iv (Stuttgart, 1932), 1266

GEOFFREY CHEW

Sympson, Christopher. *See* SIMPSON, CHRISTOPHER.

Synaxarion (Gk.). A liturgical book containing the lives of the saints of the Eastern Church. A portion of this book is read during ORTHROS after the sixth ode of the KANŌN. *See also* MARTYROLOGY.

Syncopation. The regular shifting of each beat in a measured pattern by the same amount ahead of or behind its normal position in that pattern; in polyphonic textures this may occur in all or some of the parts. Syncopation, as it is most widely understood, is restricted to situations in which the strong beats receive no articulation. This means either that they are silent, as in ex.1 (in this connection, *see also* OFF-BEAT), or that

Ex.1 Beethoven: Sonata in Ab op.110, 3rd movt

each note is articulated on a weak beat (or between two beats) and tied over to the next beat, as in ex.2. Because any syncopated musical line can be perceived as contrary to the pulse established by the organization of the

Ex.2 Bach: Two-Part Invention no.6

music into bars, syncopation is related to, and sometimes used as a term for, CROSS-ACCENT, AGOGIC accent and CROSS-RHYTHM; the term has also been applied, though mistakenly, to the superposition of polyphonic parts in conflicting metres (*see* POLYRHYTHM).

Phrasing or articulation may be called 'syncopated' if regularly shifted ahead of or behind the beat to create tension against the established pulse.

See also RHYTHM.

Synemba kai teleia. Pair of signs used in Greek EKPHONETIC NOTATION.

Synket. An electronic sound synthesizer designed and constructed in 1964 by Paul Ketoff, an Italian engineer. The Synket generates and modulates frequency, timbral spectrum, amplitude and duration. It has a console that permits pre-setting of sound combinations, and three keyboards that may be used for live performance. The composers John Eaton, Jerome Rosen and William O. Smith have written music using the Synket as a solo instrument. *See also* ELECTRONIC INSTRUMENTS, SYNTHESIZER.

BIBLIOGRAPHY

F. L. McCarty: 'Electronic Music Systems: Structure, Control, Product', *PNM*, xiii/2 (1975), 98

RICHARD SWIFT

Synnet. See SENNET.

Synodikon (Gk.). In the Byzantine rite, a book containing the acts of church synods and councils; for its liturgical use, *see* LITURGY AND LITURGICAL BOOKS, §III, 3.

Synoditai [synodeitai]. *See* TECHNITAI.

Syntagma musicum. Dutch early music ensemble, named after the Praetorius treatise (1614–18). Directed by KEES OTTEN, who founded it in 1963, the group comprises six or so performers and specializes in medieval and Renaissance music. It is based in Amsterdam but has made several world tours; a number of recordings, several of which have won awards, have established the group's reputation. Its style of presentation is greatly influenced by Otten's buoyant personality.

J. M. THOMSON

Synthesizer. A machine which generates and modifies sounds electronically. Electronic music synthesizers evolved in the 'classical' electronic music studios, where many of their components were developed independently. For a general discussion of synthesizers *see* ELECTRONIC MUSIC.

1. Basic concepts. 2. Audio signal generating and processing equipment. 3. Control equipment.

1. BASIC CONCEPTS. Each synthesizer consists of an assemblage of individual components, each concerned with a specific function. Sometimes the components are supplied in a 'standard' configuration; sometimes the user has to assemble a 'modular' machine. Synthesizer components may generally be classified as generators or as processors of a signal, though some combine aspects of both functions. The interconnection of components is termed 'patching', and it is most commonly accomplished by means of a wire, or 'patch cord', from the output of one device to the input of another; pin matrices and sliding switches are also used for these connections in some systems.

The signals generated or processed within a synthesizer have different and sometimes multiple functions. Obviously there are sounds, or 'audio signals'. Other signals, 'control voltages', are used to determine the operating characteristics of synthesizer devices. In the case of an oscillator, for example, a higher control voltage will produce a higher pitch, unless the oscillator has a processing control to modify the control voltage so that its effect is changed (the oscillator is then an example of a component combining functions of generation and processing). A control voltage may or may not have the same electrical properties as an audio signal, depending on the synthesizer design. A third type of signal is the 'trigger' or 'timing pulse', which is used to initiate sounds and to control rhythm in various ways.

By these means a sound is generated by one device and processed by others until it has all of the characteristics required by the user. Many or all of the synthesizer components may be deployed in the production of a single sound.

2. AUDIO SIGNAL GENERATING AND PROCESSING EQUIPMENT.
(*a*) *Oscillators.* An oscillator generates a sound, usually of a single variable pitch. Many types of oscillator are able to produce different waveforms, and some can vary the waveform. Common waveforms are the sine wave (no harmonics), the sawtooth wave (all harmonics in

amplitudes related as $1/n$, where n is the harmonic number) and the square wave (all odd-numbered harmonics in the same amplitude relationship as in the sawtooth wave). The pitch of a sound generated by a voltage-controlled oscillator may be governed by a control voltage, thus facilitating rapid pitch changes.

(*b*) *Noise generators.* Noise (sound containing all audio frequencies) is often used for percussive effects.

(*c*) *Amplifiers.* A voltage-controlled amplifier is used to control the dynamic characteristics of a sound.

(*d*) *Mixers.* A mixer combines two or more sounds; the device usually contains volume controls for the inputs and sometimes also for the outputs.

(*e*) *Filters.* A filter affects the frequency content of a sound by resonating (increasing) or attenuating (decreasing) the amplitudes of frequencies of a given range. A 'high pass' (or treble) filter passes high frequencies and attenuates low ones; a 'low pass' (or bass) filter has the reverse operation. The 'cutoff frequency' is the value at which attenuation begins. A 'band pass' filter passes frequencies within a particular band (or range) by resonating those frequencies; a 'band reject' filter passes everything except a particular band. In these types the 'centre frequency' is the value at the centre of the affected band. Filters of all varieties are used to modify the timbres of sounds; some of the filter characteristics may be altered by control voltages.

(*f*) *Envelope generators.* The 'envelope' of a sound denotes its growth and decay characteristics. An envelope generator controls these by producing an attack and a decay, and sometimes other variations. Such a device allows control of the time over which attack or decay occurs, and often of the duration of the sound. The output of an envelope generator is usually employed to control an amplifier and so modify the amplitude of a sound, but it may alternatively be connected to other devices.

(*g*) *Spatial locators.* A spatial locator permits the illusion of a sound moving through space, an effect produced by varying the amplitudes of the same sound heard from two or more loudspeakers.

(*h*) *Reverberators.* A reverberator produces artificial reverberation or echo.

(*i*) *Ring modulators.* A ring modulator combines two input signals so that the output consists of the sum and difference frequencies of the inputs. *See also* MODULATION (ii) and RING MODULATOR.

(*j*) *Frequency shifters.* A frequency shifter differs from a ring modulator in that there is a separate output for the sum frequencies and another for the difference frequencies.

(*k*) *Combination devices.* These combine several audio signal generating and processing components together with control processing elements. An example is the combination oscillator-filter-amplifier with processing controls on the control voltage inputs.

3. CONTROL EQUIPMENT.
(*a*) *Voltage control.* Control devices produce control voltages which govern the audio signal generating and processing equipment. They may themselves be generators or processors.

(*b*) *Keyboards.* Keyboards are the most important manual control devices within synthesizers. Although they are often modelled on the black-and-white semitonal keyboards of conventional instruments, many other designs are in use; black and white keys do not

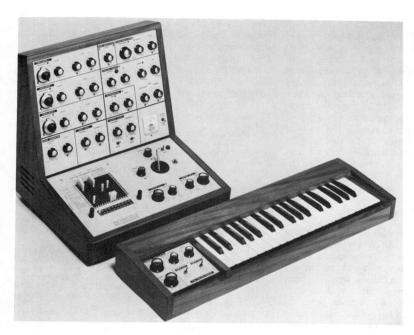

*1. A small performance
synthesizer, the VCS3,
with its keyboard acces-
sory, the DK2 (Electronic
Music Studios, London)*

*2. A large studio-type synthesizer, the Synthi 100; the basic programming is set in a pin matrix of 3600 holes, and to the
operator's right are a two-manual keyboard, a tape recorder and a mixing console (Electronic Music Studios, London)*

always indicate semitonal tuning, though the pitches are normally separated by equal intervals. A keyboard produces two simultaneous outputs: a control voltage to govern the pitch of an oscillator, and a timing pulse, which usually initiates the attack and which is sustained as long as the key is depressed. The outputs may be used in other ways through a changed patching, but their nature suggests the limitation of the keyboard as a performing device. Most keyboards are monophonic, and those that are not have complications in the ways in which separate sounds are controlled. Synthesizer keyboards have a number of special features: the keys may be pressure-sensitive, allowing a new means for the control of some property of the sound; there may be a portamento facility; tuning is generally variable; and there may be buttons or switches to transpose the keyboard. Many other features are provided in different individual systems.

(c) *Touch-sensitive devices*. Synthesizers may include 'linear' or 'ribbon' controllers and 'touch-sensitive keyboards'. A device of the former type consists of a length of ribbon or plate which produces a voltage varying directly with the position at which it is touched. Such devices are useful for producing continuous changes. A touch-sensitive keyboard contains a series of positions activated simply by being touched, not depressed; these positions may also be pressure-sensitive. All touch-sensitive devices produce control voltages, and so may be used to control any sound property.

(d) *Sequencers*. A sequencer permits the automatic control of a limited number of musical events; it returns to the beginning after reproducing a series of events, so giving a repeated pattern. Like a keyboard, a sequencer produces control voltages and timing pulses, the former to govern pitches and other characteristics, the latter to determine rhythms. The controls must be preset and then the sequencer activated; since only a few controls may be varied during the production of the music, the sequencer is of limited use as a performance device. A more powerful function is in the automatic generation of portions of a composition, but here the sequencer's memory is a limitation.

(e) *Sample-and-hold devices*. Such devices allow a value of a changing voltage to be selected and retained until a new value is desired. In this manner a continuously changing event may be divided into a number of discrete steps. Sample-and-hold devices are usually incorporated into other components but are sometimes available separately.

(f) *Random voltage sources*. These produce control voltages randomly within a given range, and so their uses range from the synthesis of 'random' music to the addition of aperiodic timbral nuances. Connection to a sample-and-hold device causes the random voltage to be sustained until a new voltage is desired, making possible a sequence of 'random' events; random voltage sources may also be made to produce an output fluctuating constantly between controllable extremes.

(g) *Envelope followers*. An envelope follower tracks an audio signal input and produces a control voltage output proportional to its amplitude, thus 'following' the envelope of the sound. This allows the envelope of one sound to be used to characterize another; other applications are possible, particularly when the device is used in conjunction with others, such as sample-and-hold devices. A very useful application is for the storage of control voltages as audio amplitudes on tape, since the

tape may be played through an envelope follower to convert the amplitudes back into control voltages for the determination of an entire passage of music.

(h) *Frequency followers*. A frequency follower differs from an envelope follower in following frequency instead of amplitude. Its functions are similar to those of the envelope follower.

BIBLIOGRAPHY

J. Chadabe: 'New Approaches to Analog-Studio Design', *PNM*, vi/1 (1967), 107
R. A. Moog and others: 'Symposium: Programmed Control', *Electronic Music Review* (1967), no.1, p.23
——: 'Symposium: Mixers and Level Controls', *Electronic Music Review* (1967), no.4, p.10
——: 'Symposium: Tape Recording', *Electronic Music Review* (1968), no.6, p.12
J. Seawright: 'What Goes into an Electronic Music Studio', *Music Educators Journal*, 1v/3 (1968)
'Synthesizers', *Synthesis* (1971), no.2 [detailed descriptions of equipment made by ARP, Buchla, CBS, Electronic Music Laboratories, Moog, MuSonics, Putney]
H. S. Howe jr: 'Compositional Limitations of Electronic Music Synthesizers', *PNM*, x/2 (1972), 120
A. Strange: *Electronic Music: Systems, Techniques and Controls* (Dubuque, Iowa, 1972)
P. Earls, E. Hafner and R. Pellegrino: 'Colloquium: New Developments in Synthesizers and Live Synthesizer Performance', *Proceedings of the American Society of University Composers* (1972–3), nos.7–8, p.44
H. U. Humpert: 'Was ist und wie funktioniert ein Synthesizer?', *Melos*, xl (1973), 207
G. Trythall: *Principles and Practice of Electronic Music* (New York, 1974)
H. S. Howe jr: *Electronic Music Synthesis* (New York, 1975)
                                                HUBERT S. HOWE JR

Synthétistes. A group of Belgian composers formed in 1925 to synthesize the elements of contemporary music; *see* LOW COUNTRIES, §I, 5.

Syrbē. *See* TYRBASIA.

Syria. *See* ARAB MUSIC and SYRIAN CHURCH MUSIC.

Syrian church music. The ecclesiastical music of the various ancient Christian churches ultimately springing from the patriarchate of Antioch, and related rites: the Syrian Orthodox (Jacobite, West Syrian), Assyrian (Nestorian, East Syrian), Syro-Antiochene, Chaldean and Maronite Churches, the St Thomas (Mar Thoma) Church of south India, the Malabar, Malankar and Melkite (Melchite) Churches. This article refers to the chant of all such churches, whether now uniate (i.e. in union with the Roman Catholic Church) or not: they possess a basic unity of musical tradition despite differences of detail.

1. History. 2. Liturgy and liturgical books: (i) General (ii) Syrian Orthodox Divine Office (iii) Assyrian Divine Office (iv) Eucharist. 3. Modal system: (i) Syrian Orthodox (ii) Assyrian (iii) Maronite. 4. Musical forms and styles: (i) Liturgical recitatives (ii) Antiphonal psalmody (iii) Polyphony (iv) Interpolated hymns (v) Independent hymns (vi) The mimra. 5. Notation.

1. HISTORY. In modern times the importance of the history of the ancient non-Greek Christian Churches of the East has been recognized increasingly: previously, they were generally dismissed in Europe as antiquated or schismatic. The four great patriarchates of early Christianity were Alexandria, Antioch, Byzantium and Rome; the non-Greek Churches sprang from the first two, and the Byzantine (whether Greek, Slavonic or other) and Latin Churches from the last two. The patriarchate of Alexandria is traditionally held to have been founded by St Mark the Evangelist; from it sprang the Coptic and Ethiopian Churches (*see* COPTIC RITE, MUSIC OF THE; ETHIOPIAN RITE, MUSIC OF THE), and the

Churches (now defunct) in Nubia and Cyrenaica. (Only isolated literary evidence survives concerning the music of the defunct churches.) Another defunct African church, based at Carthage, was influenced by Rome rather than Alexandria and had St Augustine as a member.

The Syrian, or Antiochene, Churches all derive ultimately from the patriarchate of Antioch, the city at which 'the disciples were for the first time called Christians' (*Acts* xi.26). The Antiochene Churches claim greater antiquity and continuity with the apostolic tradition than any other; according to the tradition of Eusebius, the see was founded by St Peter.

The separation of all these churches from the Greek and Latin Churches, and from each other, dates particularly from the Christological controversies of the 5th century. Diophysitism, or the doctrine that Christ possesses two separate natures and persons, human and divine, was condemned at the Council of Ephesus (431). Its ostensible advocate, Archbishop Nestorius of Constantinople, was deposed on questionable grounds, and died in exile (*c*451). Part of the Antiochene Church espoused diophysitism (colloquially termed 'Nestorianism') in defiance of the Council; this church today terms itself the Church of the East, or unofficially 'Assyrian' (the term used in this article), since its members claim descent from the ancient Assyrians. This church was able to maintain its independence owing to its geographical position in Persia (i.e. in an area similar to modern Turkey, Iraq and Iran); subsequently, in a remarkable missionary endeavour, it expanded to Turkestan, India and Tibet, and it had reached China by the early Middle Ages. (The St Thomas Church of south India probably originated during this expansion of the Assyrian Church, although the two are now separate.) It has been suggested that the ritual of Tibetan lamaism was subject to Nestorian influence (Atiya, 1968, pp.263f). This wide influence of the Assyrian Church, now confined to the Middle East and very limited, was curtailed after the rise of Islam and of the Mongols.

The party supporting the emperor, and hence Greek orthodoxy, at the Council of Ephesus was termed 'Melkite' (or 'Melchite', i.e. 'royalist', from Syriac *malkōyē*). This term is generally used today, however, to refer to Syrian churches in communion with Rome, and is so used in this article.

At the Council of Chalcedon (451) the opposite doctrine to diophysitism – that Christ has one nature and one person, a combination of the human and the divine – was condemned as diophysitism had been. The Greek and Latin Churches, together with the Georgian Church (henceforth in the Greek orbit: *see* GEORGIAN RITE, MUSIC OF THE), subsequently opted for the Chalcedonian doctrine of two natures within a single person. The opposite view, later termed monophysitism, was espoused by the Alexandrine (Coptic and Ethiopian) Churches and by the Antiochene 'Syrian Orthodox' Church of the Middle East and India. The latter church is colloquially termed 'Jacobite', after its reformer, Bishop James (Jacob) Baradeus (Ya'qūb al-Barda'i, *c*500–78). Monophysitism was espoused also by the Church of Armenia, which had even earlier rejected all claims to control by any of the four ancient patriarchates (*see* ARMENIAN RITE, MUSIC OF THE).

After the Middle Ages, groups within the ancient Eastern churches were persuaded to submit to the Roman Catholic Church while largely retaining their local customs and rites, including the chant. Thus virtually every rite derived from the patriarchates of Antioch and Alexandria has a parallel 'uniate' rite. An offshoot of the Assyrian Church, uniate since the 16th century, is termed 'Chaldean' ('Chaldaic') in Mesopotamia and 'Malabar' in India. The analogous offshoot of the Syrian Orthodox Church, uniate since the 17th century, is termed 'Syro-Antiochene'; another in India, uniate only since 1930, is termed 'Malankar' or 'Syro-Malankar'. A further uniate rite in the Lebanon, the Maronite rite, differs in practice from the Syrian Orthodox tradition more than the other uniate rites, since it came into existence as early as the Crusades.

2. LITURGY AND LITURGICAL BOOKS.

(*i*) *General.* The principal Offices of the Syrian Churches are *Lelyā*, *Ṣaprā* and *Ramshā*, corresponding to Matins, Lauds and Vespers respectively; *Ramshā* is also termed *Nāgah* in the Syrian Orthodox Church, which possesses also the Offices of *Tlāth shā'in*, *Sheth shā'in*, *Tsha' shā'in* and *Sutārā*, corresponding to Terce, Sext, None and Compline respectively. (Sext is known also as *Pelgāh d-yawmā*, 'midday'.)

The texts of the Offices are divided among various liturgical books, which are still largely manuscript in Orthodox churches but often printed in India and in uniate churches (to a certain extent, however, Orthodox and uniate books are regarded as interchangeable). The Syrian Orthodox *shḥimtā* ('simple', 'ferial') contains the weekday Offices, and the *bayth gazā* ('treasury') the texts of the model stanzas of the chants for Sundays and festivals; Proper texts for these are arranged in books according to the church year, for Sundays and saints' days. The Assyrian *kitāba* (*bayt*) *daqdhām wadbāthar* ('book (house) before and after': see below, §2, iii) corresponds to the *shḥimtā* but contains Sunday and other Offices as well; the Assyrian Proper Office texts are distributed among the *gazā* ('treasure') for the immovable feasts, the *hūdhrā* ('cycle') for Sundays and for Easter, and the *kashkul* for weekdays.

The Syrian Divine Office, like that of the Latin Church, centres on the recitation of psalms, except for the Little Hours of the Syrian Orthodox Church, corresponding to Terce, Sext and None, whose texts are free poetry. The Psalter is read in its entirety in a period varying between a day (in Maronite and Syrian Orthodox monasteries) and a fortnight. Beside psalms, *qāle* ('melodies', sing. *qālā*) dominate the Syrian Orthodox Office and are important also in the Assyrian Office (see below, §4, iv). In the Offices a *qālā* is followed by a *bā'uthā* ('petition', also termed *tbārtā*). Other categories include the *madrāshā*, which plays a part in the night Office (see below, §4, v) and is answered by an *'unithā*, or choral refrain; the *sughithā*, related to the *madrāshā* and used particularly in the Maronite Divine Office (see below, §4, v); the *prumion* (derived from Gk., *prooimion*), which precedes the *qālā* and is itself preceded by the *sedrā*; and the *kārūzuthā*, a litany with choral refrains which characterizes the Assyrian rite.

The Maronite liturgy in general resembles that of the Syrian Orthodox Church, and the same categories of hymn are found in both; but in some ways it is simpler and more regular than the Syrian Orthodox liturgy. (For details of the differences, see Husmann, 'Die Gesänge der syrischen Liturgie', 1972, pp.84ff.)

(*ii*) *Syrian Orthodox Divine Office.* Of the Offices of the Syrian Orthodox tradition the three Little Hours are the simplest in structure: they comprise the three basic elements of those Offices, *sedrā* and *prumion*, *qālā*, and *bā'uthā*, without any additions. The form of the *bā'uthā* used at Terce (with 12-syllable verses) is known as the *bā'uthā d-Yā'qub* (i.e. ascribed to Yā'qub of Serugh, *c*500), and that (with five-syllable verses) used at Sext and None is known as the *bā'uthā d-Balai* (i.e. ascribed to St Balai, *c*400). Those with seven-syllable verses are ascribed to St EPHREM SYRUS. Introductory prayers such as the Lord's Prayer, doxology, Trisagion and Kyrie eleison precede all the Offices as they do in the Latin rite.

The Syrian Orthodox *Lelyā*, like its equivalent, Matins, comprises an introductory section followed by three nocturns (*qawme*, sing. *qawmā*), with a fourth *qawmā* added on Fridays. The introductory section contains an initial prayer followed by troped psalms (Psalms cxxxiv, cxix, §T, and cxvii – in the Syrian numbering, cxxxiii, cxviii and cxvi). The tropes are termed *mā'irāne* ('vigil songs') although such tropes elsewhere in Syrian church music are usually termed *'eny-āne* ('answers', 'responds'): each psalm verse is answered by a trope verse.

A prayer opens the series of *qawme*. Each nocturn contains a *madrāshā*, a *sedrā* and *prumion*, a *qālā* and a *bā'uthā* (the last is 'of Yā'qub' in the first *qawmā*, 'of Aphrem' (i.e. Ephrem Syrus) in the second, and 'of Balai' in the third). The third *qawmā* contains an extensive closing section subdivided into two groups: the first forms the climax of the whole Office and contains a *sedrā* with *prumion*, the *Magnificat* with an *'enyānā*, Psalm cxxxiii (Syrian cxxxii) with *'enyānā*, Psalms cxlviii–cl and cxvii (Syrian cxvi) (untroped), a *ququlion* and *'eqbā* (trope); the second of these groups is shorter, containing a *sedrā* with *prumion*, *qālā* and *bā'uthā d-Yā'qub*, and concluding with the prayer of St Athanasius and the blessing.

The Office of *Ṣaprā* begins with Psalm 1, Psalm lxiii with an *'enyānā*, and Psalms cxiii and cxlviii–cl (untroped). A second section contains *sedrā* and *prumion*, first *qālā* with *ququlion* and *'eqbā*, *sedrā* and *prumion*, second *qālā* and *bā'uthā d-Yā'qub*. Prayers for the censing (*'etra*) and the blessing conclude the Office.

The Syrian Orthodox *Ramshā* comprises an 'introductory prayer' and the Office proper; the former consists of Psalms cxli, cxlii, cxix, §N, and cxvii (Syrian cxl, cxli, cxviii and cxvi respectively), with the Gloria and *'eqbā*. The Office itself comprises three sections. The first contains a *sedrā* with *prumion* and first *qālā*; the second an incense prayer (*'etrā*) and second *qālā*, *ququlion*, Gloria and *'eqbā*; and the third a *sedrā* with *prumion*, third *qālā*, *bā'uthā d-Yā'qub*, concluding prayer and blessing. On Saturday evenings the third group also contains an alleluia and Gospel reading.

The Office of *Sutārā*, like its equivalents Compline and Apodeipnon in the Latin and Greek rites respectively, begins with Psalm iv concluding with the lesser doxology. An *'eqbā* is added in the Syrian Orthodox rite, however. The main substance of the Office follows, comprising a *sedrā* and *prumion*, *qālā* and *bā'uthā d-Aphrem*. This is followed (as in the Latin rite) by a section whose subject matter is nightfall: here it comprises Psalms xci and cxxi (Syrian xci and cxx respectively), with an alleluia interpolated between each half-verse of the psalms. A prayer of praise, the Creed and the blessing follow.

Differences from the patterns outlined above may occur: in the normal secular rite, for example, these Offices are considerably extended on feast days, notably in the singing of texts from Greek kanones (the so-called *qanūne yawnāye*: see below, §4, iv).

A number of medieval Syriac manuscripts, including a 13th-century *shḥimtā* (*GB-Lbm* Add.17241, from a Syrian desert monastery in north Egypt), probably reflect an early type of monastic liturgy which also differs in a number of respects from the secular rite. It is characterized, for example, by the use of the *ma'niāthā* of SEVERUS OF ANTIOCH (*d* 538) and of other hymns by John bar-Aphthonius of Qeneshre and others. In *Ramshā*, Psalm lxxxvi is sung at the beginning, and the *'eqbā* after the psalms is omitted. *Lelyā* has only two nocturns, termed *teshmeshtā*. (For further details, see Husmann, 'Die Gesänge der syrischen Liturgie', 1972, esp. pp.86ff.)

(*iii*) *Assyrian Divine Office.* The Offices of the Assyrian and related rites resemble those of the Syrian Orthodox tradition in their basic structure, though differing in individual detail. Subsections of the Offices are often preceded and followed by the same liturgical genres, in a characteristic symmetrical structure; the books containing these forms are in consequence termed 'before and after' (see above, §2, i). All the chants are introduced by prayers the names of which derive from the chants they precede. Many chants have two forms, used in alternate weeks.

Besides the reading of Ordinary psalms at Matins, Lauds and Vespers, the Psalter is read once a fortnight continuously in the Assyrian Offices, with the two halves of the choir alternating week by week with the intonations. For this purpose the Psalter, termed *dawīdhā* ('David'), is divided into 20 *hullāle* analogous to the Greek kathismata with a 21st *hullālā* of Old Testament canticles. Each *hullālā* contains between three and 11 psalms, and is further subdivided into two or three *marmyāthā* (sing. *marmithā*, analogous to Greek *staseis*) each containing between one and four psalms.

The number of nocturns in the Assyrian Office of *Lelyā* varies between one for ordinary weekdays and three on feast days. Introductory prayers immediately precede the first nocturn, containing from one to seven *hullāle*; the *qālthā*, comprising more psalms, follows on Sundays. The next section is termed the *māwtbā* (meaning 'seat', like the Greek kathisma), and comprises an *'unithā*, a *qālā*, a *kānonā* ('refrain'), a *teshbohtā* ('song of praise', roughly analogous to the *Te Deum*), a *kārū-zuthā* (litany with choral refrains) and a *madrāshā*. If there are several nocturns, the last is termed *qāle d-shahre* ('songs of vigil') and is similarly constructed from a *hullālā*, an *'unithā*, a *shubāhā* ('song of praise'), *kānonā*, a *teshbohtā* and a *kārūzuthā*.

The Assyrian *Ṣaprā* commences with introductory prayers and a characteristic group of morning psalms (Psalms c, xci, civ, cxiii, xciii, cxlviii–cl, cxvii; Syrian numbering identical with Hebrew except for the last, cxvi). This is followed on weekdays by an *'unithā* or the *lākhumārā* ('Thee, O Lord', a canticle similar to the Trisagion). The Office ends with the Trisagion, the Lord's Prayer (to which is added on weekdays the *qāle d-sāhde*, 'songs of the martyrs') and the blessing.

The Assyrian Office of *Ramshā* comprises introductory prayers, Gloria in excelsis, the Lord's Prayer, Sanctus and 'evening prayer', followed by one *marmithā* from the Psalter (or two on weekdays). After the 'incense prayer' and the 'prayer of the *lākhumārā*' there follows the *lākhumārā*. A central group of evening psalms follows, which occurs also in the Syrian Orthodox rite (Psalms cxli, cxlii, cxix, §N, cxvii; Syrian numbering: cxl, cxli, cxviii, cxvi); it is preceded by a *shurāyā* 'before' and an *'unithā* 'before', and followed by a *shurāyā* 'after' and an *'unithā* 'after' (with introductory prayer). (The *shurāyā* ('beginning') contains the initial verses of psalms, but the number of psalm verses in its text varies, normally between three and eight.) The Office concludes with a twofold *kārūzuthā*, the Trisagion, a *vāsāliqe* ('royal prayer'), an *'unithā* and the closing prayer; a closing psalm (*suyāke*) and Gospel reading may be added. After the Office proper, a short section termed *Suba'a* replaces Compline.

(*iv*) *Eucharist.* The Eucharist or Divine Liturgy in the Eastern churches corresponds in basic structure to the Latin Mass (*see* MASS, §I, 4), with a preliminary Liturgy of the Word, or synaxis, intended for both catechumens and the faithful, and a second section including the consecration and Communion which is intended for the faithful only. This basic twofold structure is preceded by an enarxis, or introductory section including prayers at the vesting of the priest and the preparation of the altar and the oblations. The lessons at the Eucharist include not only Epistle and Gospel, as in the traditional Roman Mass, but often additional Old Testament lessons (mostly from the Prophets) at the beginning. (*See* EPISTLE, §1.)

Some of the musical forms used in the Eucharist are the same as those of the Divine Office. The Syrian Orthodox Eucharist, for example, prescribes a *sedrā* and *prumion*, Trisagion, and alleluia with verse before the Gospel; the Assyrian rite prescribes the *lākhumārā*, *shurāyā* and *kārūzuthā*. Some, on the other hand, correspond to items of the Latin Mass: psalms, Creed, Lord's Prayer, Sanctus and the sections allotted to the celebrant in the central part of the Mass of the Faithful, such as the Preface and words of institution, except that in the consecration prayer the epiclesis (invocation of the Holy Spirit) is almost entirely confined to the Eastern and Byzantine churches.

3. MODAL SYSTEM. Of the churches under consideration here, the Syrian Orthodox Church, and the parallel uniate Syro-Antiochene Church, are the only ones now possessing a system of eight ecclesiastical modes analogous to the oktōēchos of the Byzantine Church and the eight-mode Gregorian system. The Assyrian Church must formerly have possessed a modal system, as all oriental music did; this may have been the Byzantine system, or an older Persian system (*see* PERSIA, §4, iii). Modern Assyrian, uniate Chaldean and Maronite musicians refer to their scales by the names of Arabic *maqāmāt*, and identify them with these *maqāmāt*; the Maronites formerly possessed, but no longer use, the Syrian Orthodox modal system.

(*i*) *Syrian Orthodox.* The eight modes of the Syrian Orthodox system are usually numbered consecutively from 1 to 8; some manuscripts, however (probably under Melkite influence), use Greek terminology, beginning with *protos* and concluding with *plagis tetartos*. The 5th–8th modes are plagal modes, corresponding to the authentic modes represented by

the 1st–4th modes respectively. The modes may be listed from 1 to 8 in order (i.e. first the four authentic modes, then the four plagal), in a manner similar to that of Byzantine chant; alternatively, they appear in some early manuscripts such as the *ma'niāthā* (sometimes wrongly termed OKTŌĒCHOS) of Severus of Antioch in the order 1–5–2–6–3–7–4–8, in a manner similar to that of Gregorian chant, with each pair of modes (authentic and plagal) sharing a common final grouped together (see Husmann, 'Hymnus und Troparion', 1971, esp. pp.46–58). Indeed, the Gregorian eight-mode system is directly related to the Syrian Orthodox system, even when the latter uses Greek terminology.

In modern practice this system shows Arab and Turkish influence: Syrian church musicians freely admit this, claiming to be Christian Arabs. In order to discover whether the original Syrian system was identical with the Greek oktōēchos, or an indigenous system to which Greek terminology was only superficially applied, it is necessary to attempt to distinguish the elements originally present in the repertory from those that derive from Arab and Turkish origins.

In the Syrian rites, as in the Greek, the chants are organized in an eight-weekly modal cycle: all the chants of a week are in a single mode, and the modes are taken in order. In the Greek rite the texts also vary, and thus any particular text is sung, to a single melody, once every eight weeks. In the Syrian rites, however, the texts remain the same from week to week, but are sung to different melodies depending on the mode of the week. In the Syrian rites, moreover, the authentic or plagal mode corresponding to the mode of the week is used on Monday, Wednesday and Friday, with the main mode of the week on the remaining days.

Ex.1 shows the first two lines of a *madrāshā* in each mode as it is sung in successive weeks by Archbishop Kyrillos Yakobos, Syrian Orthodox Metropolitan of Damascus (from Husmann, *Die Melodien der jakobitischen Kirche*, i, 1969, pp.15f). In the example, the 1st mode (with D as final) corresponds to the 1st Byzantine and Gregorian mode. The 2nd mode, also on D, is the first plagal mode (i.e. Byzantine 5th mode, Gregorian 2nd mode) and thus corresponds with the peculiarly Syrian order of some ancient manuscripts. The 3rd mode, however, is on F and thus corresponds to the Byzantine 3rd mode; the 4th mode similarly corresponds to the Byzantine 4th mode (here, as in modern Greek church music, based on C rather than on F as in the medieval Byzantine system); this may be the result of Arab influence, since *rāst*, the corresponding Arab *maqām*, is based on C. The 5th mode, on F, can only be a repetition (with the same melody) of the 3rd Byzantine mode or the 5th Gregorian mode: it thus represents another example of correspondence with the Gregorian order, and with that of some of the Syriac manuscripts (the 5th Byzantine mode, or *plagalis protos*, had already been allocated the second place). The use of the same mode and melody for the 3rd and 5th modes is a peculiarity of the individual singer here recorded. The 6th mode concludes on E, but all the sections of the melody except the last conclude on A, which seems to represent the final; the construction is, in this case, inverted, with the lower note used as a dominant and the note a 5th above as the final. This type of construction is unknown in the medieval Byzantine and Gregorian systems, but occurs in the Arab *maqām 'ajam*. The 7th mode can be regarded as the medieval 7th *barys* mode of

Ex.1

Mode I

Btul - ta .gra - tani d'i - mar shar - bah kad ta - har' na

Mode II

Mode III

Mode IV

Mode V

Mode VI

Mode VII

Mode VIII

Byzantine chant, transposed on to C, but the intervals used (e.g. three-quarters of a tone between C and D and between E and F) are modified under Arab influence. The 8th mode similarly contains C–D♭–E–F in its structure: this does not occur in modern or medieval Greek chant, but corresponds to the Arab maqāmāt ḥijāz and ḥijāz-kar (the same scale pattern is part of the so-called 'gypsy' scale). It will be seen, therefore, that the eight modes as represented in the example show anomalies due, on the one hand, to nomenclature derived partly from the Byzantine system and partly from the Old Syrian system (which resembles the Gregorian), and, on the other hand, to Arab influence.

A broader view of Syrian modality, based on analyses of large quantities of material, shows that a single modal name (e.g. 1st mode) may serve at different times and places for a number of different modes; these may be indigenous Syrian or Arab modes, and may exchange places. It shows too that the Syrian modes, like those of Gregorian and Byzantine chant, have notes with special functions, comparable to the finals and dominants of medieval chant. Within a mode, the final and dominant can exchange places (see Husmann, 'Eine Konkordanztabelle', 1974): for example, in the 1st mode, D can be the final and F or G the dominant at one time, and F can be the final and D the dominant at another. This exchange of functions occurs also in the modern Greek ecclesiastical modal system; in both cases it can be explained as the result of Arab influence (see above, where an example of this exchange of functions was explained as the result of the influence of the Arab maqām 'ajam).

Another variable factor in the modal system is that of ambitus. A single modal number may refer to scales with different ranges (e.g. mainly above, or mainly

below, the final) even when the final remains the same. Thus in Syrian chant the 'authentic' and 'plagal' varieties of a mode may often be grouped as subdivisions of a single mode, rather than as two separate modes.

The following list (based chiefly on an analysis of the qāle: see Husmann, Die Melodien der jakobitischen Kirche, ii, 1971) gives details of the modes as they are used in practice; indications are given in parentheses of correspondences with Gregorian and Byzantine modes. It will be seen that almost all the Gregorian and Byzantine modes are represented, although the numbering is different, owing partly to a confusion between the original Byzantine and Gregorian numberings and partly to the replacement of some old modes by Arabic maqāmāt.

1st mode: D final; occasionally F final (1st authentic and 1st plagal modes)

2nd mode: D and G finals, analogous to the Arabic maqāmāt bayātī and nawā; F is often tuned a quarter-tone sharp in the Arabic manner (Arabic scale)

3rd mode: E final, with ambitus above or below E; F often tuned a quarter-tone sharp (2nd authentic and 2nd plagal modes, i.e. Gregorian 3rd and 4th modes, Byzantine 2nd and 6th) (The 3rd mode in ex.1 is an exception to this rule, and may represent an error on the part of the singer)

4th mode: C final, or occasionally D; leading note below C may be B or B♭; E tuned a quarter-tone sharp (4th authentic mode, i.e. Gregorian 7th mode, Byzantine 4th mode)

5th mode: E and F finals (G final as a variant) even in the same melody and with the same singer (with F as final, 3rd plagal mode, i.e. Gregorian 6th mode, Byzantine 7th mode)

6th mode: E and D finals; characteristic motif C–E, drawn from the Arabic maqām 'ajam (Arabic scale)

7th mode: E (or E a quarter-tone flat) and F finals; D and E both often tuned a quarter-tone flat (Arabic scale)

8th mode: C and E finals, corresponding to medieval Byzantine custom, or D final, with a scale including B♭ and C♯, in the Arabic manner; F tuned a quarter-tone sharp (partly 4th authentic mode, i.e. Gregorian 7th mode, Byzantine 4th mode; partly Arabic ḥijāz and ḥijāz-kar maqāmāt).

(ii) *Assyrian.* The modes of the Assyrian and Chaldean chant are given names of Arabic *maqāmāt*; it may be assumed that the church singers thoroughly understand the Arabic musical system. The great Chaldean singer E. Bédé (see Husmann, 'Die Tonarten der chaldäischen Breviergesänge', 1969, and 'Arabische Maqamen in ostsyrischer Kirchenmusik', 1970) has claimed that Chaldean chant uses the *maqāmāt rāst, nihawand, urfalī* or *diwānī, sah-gāh, ḥijāz (ḥijāz-kar), ṣabā, ṭūrānī, araibūnī* and *bayātī.* Of these, *urfalī* ('from Urfa', i.e. 'from Edessa'), *ṭūrānī* ('mountain *maqām*') and *araibūnī* are peculiar to north Iraq and the rest well known in the whole Arab world, although oriental musicians claim that *araibūnī* is simply a variant of *bayātī* (*Congrès de musique arabe: Caire 1932*, p.150).

The *rāst maqām* corresponds to the C major scale; the tuning in Iraq (as with E. Bédé) is diatonic, but in Arabia includes the intervallic progression of a whole tone followed by two steps each of three-quarters of a tone. *Bayātī* is the minor scale on D mentioned as the 2nd mode of the Syrian Orthodox system. *Nawā* and *nihawand* represent the D minor scale with D, F and G as finals; again the tuning is diatonic in Iraq and includes intervals of three-quarters of a tone in Arabia. *Ḥijāz* and *ḥijāz-kar* are constructed from tetrachords comprising an interval of one and a half tones with a semitone either side of it: this tetrachord is used for both halves of *ḥijāz-kar*, whereas *ḥijāz* has a diatonic upper tetrachord.

Sah-gāh and *ṣabā* are Arabic scales, including intervals of three-quarters of a tone. *Sah-gāh* includes E and B each tuned a quarter-tone flat and has E, tuned a quarter-tone flat, as final; these notes are altered to diatonic tuning (E and B) in Turkey and northern Iraq, but with D♯ as a leading note. *Ṣabā* has D as final; its scale is C–D–E(quarter-tone flat)–F–G♯–A–B♭–C–D♯. As performed by E. Bédé, *urfalī* and *ṭūrānī* are also minor scales. Since 'Urfa' (derived from Syriac 'Urha') is pronounced 'Ruha' in Arabic, and 'from Ruha' becomes 'ruhawī' in Arabic, it seems likely that *urfalī* is simply a Turkish translation of the Arabic *maqām* name *rahāwī.* The latter exists, moreover, in a variant on D which may correspond with the *urfalī* (for which, see *maqām* 31 in D'Erlanger, vol.v, and, transposed on to C, as ex.109 in D'Erlanger, vol.vi).

In the Assyrian system there are, therefore, major and minor diatonic modes besides Arabic scales; these diatonic modes, like those in the Syrian Orthodox modal system, may represent survivals of the ancient Syrian modal system.

(iii) *Maronite.* According to the great Maronite singer M. Murad, the most usual *maqāmāt* in Maronite chant are the *'ajam, nawā, nihawand, rāst, jaharka* (the Pythagorean major scale on F), *ṣabā* and *sah-gāh.* These are all widely known Arabic scales; the particular frequency of the *'ajam* is noteworthy.

4. MUSICAL FORMS AND STYLES.

(i) *Liturgical recitatives.* Much of the Syrian Divine Office is chanted to a recitative, as is almost the whole of the Eucharist (the latter in a manner without parallel in the West, as a dialogue between the celebrating priest and a deacon or deacons). The particular details of the recitative are freely improvised, whether the singer uses normal speech, heightened speech or (as in the readings at the Eucharist from the Old Testament and the Epistles) a fixed reciting-note with simple cadential for-

mulae such as the fall of a tone or semitone. Even in this free improvisation, however, the singers defer to tradition, since they invariably use familiar formulae learnt from their teachers. (*See* CENTONIZATION.)

(ii) *Antiphonal psalmody.* In the Syrian Divine Office, the psalms are spoken, rather than sung, by the two halves of the choir in alternation (i.e. in the manner known in the West as antiphonal). Sung hymns are interpolated between the verses of the psalms, and these are also antiphonal, with the alternation occurring strophe by strophe as in Ambrosian hymns; the strophes are marked with the letters A and B in the margins of the manuscripts, to indicate which half of the choir is to sing them (see Husmann, 'Die antiphonale Chorpraxis', 1972). According to Western medieval tradition, antiphonal psalmody was of Eastern origin and was introduced to the West at Milan by St Ambrose: this view is not contradicted by present Syrian practice (but *see also* AMBROSE).

(iii) *Polyphony.* Both in the spoken antiphonal psalms and in the sung antiphonal hymns, primitive improvised polyphony often occurs in the various Syrian churches: the chant is reinforced in various ways with parallel intervals. The crudest examples of this polyphony use parallel 2nds, 3rds and 4ths together; the most sophisticated practice comprises only parallel 4ths (or, rarely, 5ths) (see Husmann, 1966). Western polyphony, like Western antiphonal psalmody, may therefore derive ultimately from Eastern practice.

(iv) *Interpolated hymns.* Most of the Syrian hymns are sung in alternating strophes interpolated between the verses of the psalms and canticles and are thus analogous to the Byzantine *stichēra* and *troparia.* The Byzantine distinction between the latter categories is, however, not drawn in Syrian hymnody: all these interpolations are given the name *'enyānā,* which is derived from the root *'nā* ('answer') and which thus corresponds etymologically with the Latin *responsorium* ('respond', 'responsory') and the Greek *antiphōna* ('antiphon').

A special category of hymn, the *qālā,* occurs extensively in the Syrian Offices (see above, §2). The strophes of a *qālā,* in most current Syrian practice, are sung between psalm verses of diverse origin; but the original pattern, in which the strophes of the *qālā* are interpolated into single continuous psalms or canticles, survives in Maronite chant. *Qāle* are found in manuscripts as early as the 9th century; the simpler Assyrian *qāle* may, however, date from as early as the 4th century. Most of those in the Syrian Orthodox rite are attributed to Simeon the Potter (*Quqāyā, c*500) and are cast in a developed *AABBCC...* structure including an alleluia and resembling that of the later Western sequence. One of the most widely known *qāle, 'm kulhun qadishaik,* found in the Syrian Orthodox, Maronite and Old Syrian rites, is unique in being a translation of a Greek kontakion, *Meta tōn hagiōn.*

The melody of the psalm verse that precedes a *qālā* may be taken from the beginning of the strophe of the *qālā* itself (ex.2). In some *qāle,* the melodic variants are slight when the versions of different singers are compared; in others, there are considerable divergences. (Even within the Syrian Orthodox rite the melodies of the older Indian tradition are sometimes more elaborate than those of the other branches of the tradition.) Indeed, the melodies may differ from one rite to another so widely that it is impossible to reconstruct their original form: the differences must result from the long separation of the traditions, but there is usually no way of discovering at what period melodies were adopted in particular rites, nor in which rite they originated.

Ex.2 Qālā 'Al 'eṭrā dbesme

Psalm verse: Sha-baḥo za - di - ge lmar-iā. Qālā: 'al 'e - ṭrā dbesme . . .

Some Syrian Orthodox qāle, sung on ordinary weekdays, however, have an extra 'ferial' melody besides the eight melodies, one for each mode, with which they are sung at festivals (the qāle for vigils have only the eight modal melodies). The ninth melody is generally simpler than the others, and is normally identical in the Syrian Orthodox, Maronite and Assyrian rites. It is probably, therefore, the original melody, and the other eight were probably composed after the introduction of the system of eight modes into Syrian Orthodox chant. It is possible that one of the eight modal melodies of the qāle for vigils was the original melody (being already suitable for use in one of the modes) and that the others were added: these qāle, and presumably their melodies, are not recent compositions since they occur in the oldest surviving manuscripts.

The normal structure of the qālā Quqāyā, like that of the sequence it resembles, may be subject to extension, abbreviation or interpolation. The alleluia may be omitted; the strophes of qāle may be preceded by short verses (pethgāme) summarizing the content of the strophe, though the last strophe is always preceded by the lesser doxology. In the Syrian Orthodox rite these latter are spoken, but in the Assyrian rite sung. The Assyrian qāle are simpler in style than those of the Syrian Orthodox rite, but exist also in variants (shuchlāfe) whose melodies are quite unrelated to those of the qāle. Both qāle and shuchlāfe may have as many as 30 to 50 strophes.

Another special category of Syrian hymn is represented by the qanūne yawnāye ('Ionian [i.e. Greek] kanones'), which are translations of Greek kanones associated with the nine biblical canticles. Their melodies permit a particularly interesting comparison between modern Syrian and medieval Byzantine melodies (ex.3), where it can be seen – despite differences – that the melodic tradition has remained essentially the same. These qanūne yawnāye appear in Syrian manuscripts from the 10th and 11th centuries (e.g. in GB-Lbm Add.14507; see Wright, i, 1870, pp.283ff).

Another species of hymn, the ma'nithā (like 'enyānā, 'unāyā and 'unithā, from 'na: 'answer'; pl. ma'niāthā), occurs more rarely, except in manuscripts reflecting a Syrian Orthodox monastic rite. A large collection of ma'niāthā, often wrongly termed oktōēchos, for the church year was made by Severus of Antioch; the original Greek version is lost, but a later Syriac revision survives. (The original Greek term represented by ma'nithā may be 'hypēchēsis', although it is usually translated back into Greek as 'antiphona'.) Each ma'nithā has a single strophe in most manuscripts, preceded by a psalm verse, but in practice the strophe may have been followed (as in Greek troparia) by the lesser doxology and then repeated or replaced by a theotokion in honour of the Virgin Mary. In monastic Syrian Orthodox manuscripts, the ma'niāthā are grouped in fours, with the first half of the lesser doxology prescribed before the psalm verse of the third ma'nithā and the second half of the doxology before the psalm verse of the fourth ma'nithā.

Manuscripts of the ma'niāthā had an appendix of other chants, including a Syriac version of the ancient Greek troparion Hypo tēn sēn eusplanchnian (i.e. the Latin Sub tuum praesidium; see CHRISTIAN CHURCH, MUSIC OF THE EARLY, §3).

(v) Independent hymns. The madrāshā is a category of independent strophic hymn whose invention is attributed to St Ephrem Syrus. Each strophe is followed by a short refrain, whose melody is generally that of the first half of the strophe. Although the madrāshā is commonly regarded as the ancestor of the Byzantine kontakion, there are structural differences between the two categories: the strophes of the kontakion end only at the conclusion of the refrain (the last verse of the prooimion, termed the koukoulion), which differs in metre from the strophe.

Several of the madrāshe are sung in both the Syrian Orthodox and Assyrian traditions (including the parallel uniate rites in each case): it is thus possible to compare the melodic traditions. Variations occur in the optional embellishments and in the tuning of the scales used; they also occur particularly at the beginnings of melodies where (as in folksong and other comparable traditions) the singer is 'searching' for the melody (ex.4). These variations are not essential, however, and the rites may well share a common melodic tradition in the madrāshe.

At the beginning of a madrāshā, the incipit of the original text sung to the melody of the madrāshā is given. Thus madrāshe are in effect contrafacta. The incipits are not always consistent, however: a single

Ex.3

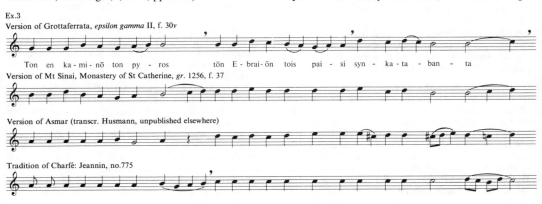

Version of Grottaferrata, epsilon gamma II, f. 30v

Ton en ka-mi-nō ton py - ros   tōn E-brai-ōn tois pai-si syn-ka-ta-ban- ta

Version of Mt Sinai, Monastery of St Catherine, gr. 1256, f. 37

Version of Asmar (transcr. Husmann, unpublished elsewhere)

Tradition of Charfé: Jeannin, no.775

melody may appear with several different titles, which may therefore represent the incipits of contrafacta rather than the original title. In his edition of Ephrem's hymns, Beck has investigated this nomenclature, and has shown that in most of the cases where nomenclature varies, one of the titles used is also attested as the incipit of a *madrāshā* by Ephrem. It seems, therefore, that all these melodies may originally have been composed by Ephrem, and subsequently used by him for constructing contrafacta; this fact may discredit the medieval tradition that early Christian hymnographers used secular or pagan melodies in order to win the hearts of the people.

Ex.4 The melody of the *madrāshā Tao nettoe harka* in three versions
(a) As sung by the Assyrian priest A. Debaz in Chicago

(b) As sung by the Chaldaic cantor E. Bédé at Cairo

[variants G or G♭ on first note]

(c) As sung by the Syrian Orthodox Archdeacon Asmar at Beirut

[variant of first two notes: E♭ – F]

Syrian musicians believe that all the *madrāshe* originally had eight melodies, although in current practice all except the 'great' four have only one. At the time of Ephrem (*d* 373), however, the church year was not divided into eight-weekly cycles according to the modal system, and the hymns of Severus of Antioch (*d* 538) were not originally categorized according to mode (*see* OKTŌĒCHOS); there would therefore have been no reason for each *madrāshā* to have eight melodies. Accordingly, the melodies of the great *madrāshe* (perhaps all eight of each, or seven if the original melody was retained) must have been composed after the introduction of the eight-weekly cycle.

The *sughithā* (pl. *sughiāthā*) resembles the *madrāshā* in form, but includes alphabetical acrostics in its text. Its text often features dialogue in direct speech, and it may thus be regarded as a prototype of liturgical drama. There are two *sughiāthā* in a fragment, now bound into a Sinai manuscript (*IL-S* Monastery of St Catherine, *syr*.233), to which Paleo-Byzantine notation was later added (see Husmann, 'Eine alte orientalische christliche Liturgie', 1976).

Smaller hymn forms include the *bā'uthā* (*tbārtā*), which is divided into three categories according to metre (see above, §2, ii). Each text has eight melodies, whose musical style is simple; the *bā'uthā* like the *qālā* (see above, §4, iv) may have *shuchlāfe*. The melodies,

like those of some of the other categories, are used according to the eight-weekly modal cycle.

(*vi*) *The mimra*. The *mimra*, a particularly popular genre, is a sermon in prose or verse; there are some among the works of St Ephrem Syrus. Those in verse are analogous to the rhymed sermons of the West in the Middle Ages. All of them are only spoken in current practice; but the *mimre* in verse must originally have been sung, and the Sinai fragment cited above (*syr*.233) contains *mimre* with musical indications. These include details of the mode and terms such as 'low' and 'he declares' (? 'spoken'). It is remarkable that only short sections of the *mimra* remain in the same mode: there is constant modulation.

5. NOTATION. Most Syrian liturgical books lack musical notation, except in the Melkite rite. Paleo-Byzantine notation, supplemented with some Middle Byzantine signs to clarify the size of the melodic intervals, occurs in a Melkite manuscript (*IL-S*, Monastery of St Catherine, *syr*.261 (see fig.1); facs. ed. Husmann, 1975–6; see also Husmann, 'Ein syrisches Sticherarion', 1975). This notation is used also in the *sughiāthā* of Sinai *syr*.233 (see above, §4, v). A more primitive version of Paleo-Byzantine notation – using only a limited number of its signs – occurs in Syrian manuscripts, especially for marking melismas; it occurs also in Greek manuscripts, where (on account of its lavish use of the Greek letter *thēta*) it has been termed a 'theta notation' by

1. Page with heōthina (morning hymns) notated in Paleo-Byzantine neumes, supplemented by Middle Byzantine signs, in a Melkite sticherarion copied (c1233–4) at the Monastery of St Catherine, Sinai (syr.261, f.195v)

2. Old Melkite notation in an undated MS fragment (Bibliothèque du Seminaire de Charfe, Lebanon)

J. Raasted (1962). Another Syrian Orthodox notation, discovered by Husmann in a musical notebook, uses mainly *oxeiai*.

A distinctive Old Melkite notation occurs in Syrian Melkite manuscripts: though this is more highly developed than the notations described above using *thēta* signs and *oxeiai*, it is still less developed than Byzantine or Latin chant notation. It was first discovered in 1898 by Parisot, and published in facsimile by Thibaut (1907; see fig.2). This notation appears also in manuscripts from Sinai (of which *syr*.80 is particularly rich in neumes), and there are good examples of it in *I-Rvat syr*.331–3.

A similar notation is used in some Syrian Orthodox manuscripts, especially those at Berlin, where there are also Assyrian and Chaldean manuscripts with neumes constructed with dots. Such neumes also occur in Chaldean manuscripts in Iraq (according to a private communication from E. Bédé).

See also EKPHONETIC NOTATION, §1.

For further information *see* PERSIA.

BIBLIOGRAPHY

G. P. Badger: *The Nestorians and their Rituals* (London, 1852)
W. Wright: *Catalogue of Syriac Manuscripts in the British Museum* (London, 1870–72)
W. R. Stevenson: 'Syriac Hymnody', *A Dictionary of Hymnology*, ed. J. Julian (London, 1892, 5/1925)
A. J. Maclean: *East Syrian Daily Offices* (London, 1894)
F. E. Brightman: *Liturgies Eastern and Western*, i (Oxford, 1896)
J. Parisot: 'Essai sur le chant liturgique des églises orientales', *Revue de l'orient chrétien*, iii (1898), 221
——: 'Rapport sur une mission scientifique en Turquie d'Asie', *Nouvelles archives des missions scientifiques et littéraires*, ix (1899), 265–511
P. G. Jazzini: *Messe maronite et psaumes* (Beirut, 1901)
J. Parisot: 'Les huit modes du chant syrien', *Tribune de Saint-Gervais*, vii (1901), 258
H. Abert: *Die Musikanschauungen des Mittelalters und ihre Grundlagen* (Halle, 1905)
A. Gastoué: *Les origines du chant romain* (Paris, 1907)
J.-B. Thibaut: *Origine byzantine de la notation neumatique de l'église latine* (Paris, 1907)
E. W. Brooks, ed.: *James of Edessa: the Hymns of Severus of Antioch and Others*, Patrologiae orientalis, vi (Paris, 1909), 1–179; vii (Paris, 1911), 595–802; xiv (Paris, 1920), 292ff

A. Baumstark: *Festbrevier und Kirchenjahr der syrischen Jakobiten, Studien zur Geschichte und Kultur des Altertums*, iii/3–5 (Paderborn, 1910)
——: *Die christlichen Literaturen des Orients* (Leipzig, 1911)
J. C. Jeannin: 'Le chant liturgique syrien', *Journal asiatique*, x/20 (1912), 295; xi/2 (1913), 65, 389
S. Euringer: 'Die neun Töpferlieder des Simeon von Gêsîr', *Oriens christianus*, new ser., iii (1913), 22
J. C. Jeannin and J. Puyade: 'L'octoëchos syrien: étude historique, étude musicale', *Oriens christianus*, new ser., iii (1913), 82, 277
A. Rücker: 'Die liturgische Poesie der Ostsyrer', *Vereinsschrift der Görresgesellschaft*, iii (1914), 54
L. Bonvin: 'On Syrian Liturgical Chant', *MQ*, iv (1918), 593
A. Rücker: 'Über einige nestorianische Liederhandschriften, vornehmlich der griechischen Patriarchatsbibliothek in Jerusalem', *Oriens christianus*, new ser., ix (1920), 107
A. Gastoué: 'La musique byzantine et le chant des églises d'orient', *EMDC*, I/i (1921), 541
A. Rücker: 'Die wechselnden Gesangstücke der ostsyrischen Messe', *Jb für Liturgiewissenschaft*, i (1921), 61
A. Baumstark: *Geschichte der syrischen Literatur mit Ausschluss der christlich-palästinensischen Texte* (Bonn, 1922)
A. Z. Idelsohn: 'Der Kirchengesang der Jakobiten', *AMw*, iv (1922), 364
E. Wellesz: *Aufgaben und Probleme auf dem Gebiete der byzantinischen und orientalischen Kirchenmusik* (Münster, 1923)
J. C. Jeannin, J. Puyade and A. Chibas-Lassalle: *Mélodies syriennes, Mélodies liturgiques syriennes et chaldéennes*, i (Paris, 1924–8) [the 2nd section containing Chaldean chants not pubd, MS at the seminary at Mosul]
P. P. Ashkar: *Cantiques arabes* (Beirut, 1928)
O. Heiming: 'Die 'Eniänehirmen der Berliner Handschrift Sachau 349', *Oriens christianus*, 3rd ser., v (1930), 19–55
R. d'Erlanger: *La musique arabe* (Paris, 1930–59)
T. Gérold: *Les pères de l'église et la musique* (Paris, 1931)
H. Besseler: *Die Musik des Mittelalters und der Renaissance* (Potsdam, 1931–4)
O. Heiming: *Syrische 'Eniäne und griechische Kanones* (Munich, 1932)
Congrès de musique arabe: Caire 1932
T. Weiss: *Zur ostsyrischen Laut- und Akzentlehre*, Bonner orientalische Studien, v (Stuttgart, 1933)
C. Høeg: *La notation ekphonetique*, MMB, *Subsidia*, i/2 (1935), esp. 142ff
J. C. Jeannin: 'Octoëchos syrien', *Dictionnaire d'archéologie chrétienne et de liturgie*, xii/2 (1935), 1888
K. Wachsmann: *Untersuchungen zum vorgregorianischen Gesang* (Regensburg, 1935)
Breviarum iuxta ritum Syrorum orientalium id est Chaldaeorum (Rome, 1938)
P. P. Ashkar: *Mélodies liturgiques syro-maronites* (Jounieh, Lebanon, 1939)
G. Reese: *Music in the Middle Ages* (New York, 1940), 67ff
G. Dix: *The Shape of the Liturgy* (London, 1944, 3/1947), 173–207
A. Raes: *Introductio in liturgiam orientalem* (Rome, 1947, 2/1962)
H. Husmann: 'Akzentschriften', §2, *MGG*
P. P. Ashkar: *Messe maronite et psaumes* (Beirut, 1952)
M. Vadakel and P. Aurelius, ed.: *Liturgical Melodies of the Chaldaic Syrian Rite* (Alwaye, India, 1954) [edn. of the Indian melodies of the Chaldean rite; texts in Malayalam, music in European notation]
E. Wellesz: 'Early Christian Music', *NOHM*, ii (London, 1954), 1
E. Beck, ed.: *Ephraem Syri: Hymni*, Corpus scriptorum christianorum orientalium, cliv, clv, clxix, clxx, clxxiv, clxxv, clxxxvi, clxxxvii, cxcviii, cxcix, ccxii, ccxiii, ccxviii, ccxix, ccxxii, ccxxiv, ccxl, ccxli, ccxlvi, ccxlvii, ccxlviii, ccxlix, ccv, ccvi, ccci, ccxx, cccxxi, cccxxii, cccxxiii, cccxxxiv, cccxxxv (Louvain, 1955–73)
R. Dempe: *Die syrischen Hymnen von Ephrem* (diss., U. of Jena, 1958)
G. Lerchundi: 'Notation musicale syrienne', *L'orient syrien*, iv (1959), 114
J. Mateos: *Lelya – Ṣapra: essai d'interprétation des matines chaldéennes*, Orientalia christiana analecta, clvi (Rome, 1959)
J. Molitor, ed.: *Chaldäisches Brevier: Ordinarium des ostsyrischen Stundengebets* (Düsseldorf, 1961)
P. Youssef, ed.: *Cantus missae SS apostolorum iuxta ritum ecclesiae Chaldaeorum* (Rome, 1961) [traditional Chaldean chants of the Divine Liturgy according to the practice of Mosul]
P. Dib: *Histoire de l'église maronite* (Beirut, 1962)
J. Raasted: 'A Primitive Palaeobyzantine Musical Notation', *Classica et mediaevalia*, xxiii (1962), 301
J. M. Sauget: *Bibliographie des liturgies orientales 1900–1960* (Rome, 1962)
L. Hage: 'Réforme du chant maronite', *Cahiers de philosophie et de théologie*, ii (1963), 7
P. E. Gemayel: *Avant-messe maronite*, Orientalia christiana analecta, clxxiv (Rome, 1964)

——: 'La structure des Vêpres maronites', *L'orient syrien*, ix (1964), 105

H. Husmann: 'The Practice of Organum in the Liturgical Singing of the Syrian Churches of the Near and Middle East', *Aspects of Medieval and Renaissance Music: a Birthday Offering to Gustave Reese* (New York, 1966), 435

L. Hage: 'Les mélodies-types dans le chant maronite', *Melto*, iii/1–2 (1967), 325–409

H. Husmann, ed.: *Die Melodien des chaldäischen Breviers-Commune nach den Traditionen Vorderasiens und der Malabarküste*, Orientalia christiana analecta, clxxviii (Rome, 1967); review by J. Kuckertz, *Mf*, xxiii (1970), 371

A. S. Atiya: *A History of Eastern Christianity* (London, 1968)

L. Hage: 'Le chant maronite', *Encyclopédie des musiques sacrées*, ed. J. Porte, ii (Paris, 1969), 218

T. Hannick: 'Syriens occidentaux et syriens orientaux', *Encyclopédie des musiques sacrées*, ed. J. Porte, ii (Paris, 1969), 214

H. Husmann, ed.: *Die Melodien der jakobitischen Kirche*, i: *Die Melodien des Wochenbreviers (Shimta)*, Sitzungsberichte der Österreichische Akademie der Wissenschaften, Philosophisch-historische Klasse, cclxii/1 (Vienna, 1969); review by J. Kuckertz, *Mf*, xxiii (1970), 371

——: 'Die Tonarten der chaldäischen Breviergesänge', *Orientalia christiana periodica*, xxxv (1969), 215–48

J. Kuckertz: 'Die Melodietypen der westsyrischen liturgischen Gesänge', *KJb*, liii (1969), 61

H. Husmann: 'Arabische Maqamen in ostsyrischer Kirchenmusik', *Musik als Gestalt und Erlebnis: Festschrift Walter Graf* (Vienna, 1970), 102

I.-H. Dalmais: 'Die nichtbyzantinischen orientalischen Liturgien', *Handbuch der Ostkirchenkunde*, ed. E. von Ivánka and others (Düsseldorf, 1971), 386

L. Hage: 'Music of the Maronite Church', *Parole de l'orient*, ii/1 (1971), 197

H. Husmann, ed.: *Die Melodien der jakobitischen Kirche*, ii: *Die Qâle gaoānāie des Beit gazā*, Sitzungsberichte der Österreichische Akademie der Wissenschaften, Philosophisch-historische Klasse, cclxxiii/4 (Vienna, 1971)

H. Husmann: 'Hymnus und Troparion', *Jb des Staatlichen Instituts für Musikforschung Preussischer Kulturbesitz Berlin 1971*, 7–86

I. Totzke: 'Die Musik in den nichtchalkedonischen Kirchen', *Handbuch der Ostkirchenkunde*, ed. E. von Ivánka and others (Düsseldorf, 1971), 444

L. Hage: *Le chant de l'Eglise maronite* (Beirut, 1972)

H. Husmann: 'Die antiphonale Chorpraxis der syrischen Hymnen nach den Berliner und Pariser Handschriften', *Ostkirchliche Studien*, xxi (1972), 281

——: 'Die ostkirchlichen Liturgien und ihre Kultmusik', 'Die Gesänge der syrischen Liturgie', 'Die Gesänge der melkitischen Liturgie', *Geschichte der katholischen Kirchenmusik*, i, ed. K. G. Fellerer (Kassel, 1972), 57, 69, 160

——: 'Eine Konkordanztabelle syrischer Kirchentöne und arabischer Maqamen in einem syrischen Musiknotizbuch', *Symposium syriacum 1972*, Orientalia christiana analecta, cxcvii (Rome, 1974), 373

——: 'Ein syrisches Sticherarion mit paläobyzantinischer Notation (Sinai syr.261)', *Hamburger Jb für Musikwissenschaft*, i (1975), 9–57

——, ed.: *Die melkitische Handschrift Sinai Syr.261*, Göttinger Orientforschungen, ix/1–2 (Wiesbaden, 1975–6)

H. Husmann: 'Eine alte orientalische christliche Liturgie: altsyrisch-melkitisch', *Orientalia christiana periodica*, xlii/1 (1976), 156–96

——: 'Madraše und Seblata – Repertoireuntersuchungen zu den Hymnen Ephraems des Syrers', *AcM*, xlviii (1976), 113–50

——: 'Die tonale Struktur des maronitischen Kirchengesanges', *Orientalia christiana periodica* (in preparation)

HEINRICH HUSMANN

Syrinx. Greek term for the type of instrument generally referred to as PANPIPES, that is, a row of hollow pipes sounded by blowing across their tops. Originally it was made from cane pipes of equal length, joined together to produce a rectangular raft-like shape. Changes in pitch were achieved by filling part of the pipe with material such as wax (a process described in Aristotle's *Problemata physica*). The Romans and Etruscans cut the pipes to their proper lengths, thus producing a wing-like shape. The cane pipes came to be replaced by wood, clay or bronze, and sometimes the instrument was made from one piece in which the holes were bored. Greek

and Roman iconography shows the syrinx with from five to 13 pipes, approximately eight being the norm.

In mythology the instrument is the attribute of PAN, the half-goat, half-man god of shepherds. His father, Hermes, had been pictured with it in the archaic period, but by the classical period it had become exclusively his. The central myth is related in Ovid's *Metamorphoses*: Pan was pursuing the nymph Syrinx, who fled to a river and begged the nymphs there for help. She was allowed to conceal herself by taking the form of a reed-bed, from which Pan subsequently picked the reeds to fashion his pipes.

In keeping with its mythology the syrinx has always had a strongly pastoral connotation. Plato, for example, excluded it from his *Republic* while deeming it appropriate for shepherds in the field. The Romans retained this association but broadened the usage of the instrument so that it came to have a secondary importance in the pantomime.

BIBLIOGRAPHY

C. Sachs: *The History of Musical Instruments* (New York, 1940)

M. Wegner: *Griechenland*, Musikgeschichte in Bildern, ii/4 (Leipzig, 1963)

G. Fleischhauer: *Etrurien und Rom*, Musikgeschichte in Bildern, ii/5 (Leipzig, 1964)

H. Becker: 'Syrinx bei Aristoxenos', *Musa–mens–musici: im Gedenken an Walther Vetter* (Leipzig, 1969), 23

JAMES W. McKINNON

Syrmatikē kai teleia. Pair of signs used in Greek EKPHONETIC NOTATION.

Syrmen, Maddalena Laura. See SIRMEN, MADDALENA LAURA.

System (i) (Ger. *Akkolade*; It. *accollatura*). Two or more staves, usually joined together by a brace at the left-hand end and often with barlines drawn continuously through them, which together present the whole of the musical texture for any one line of music on the page. In scores, successive systems on a page are often separated by two parallel diagonal strokes between them at the left-hand side. (*See* NOTATION and SCORE.)

In German the word is used as an abbreviation of *Liniensystem*, meaning 'staff' or 'stave'.

System (ii). A term introduced in the 1960s to describe a variety of new compositional practices, the common feature being an emphasis on repetition. Systematic, or 'minimal', music may consist of extended reiterations of a motif or group of motifs, as in much of the work of Riley. Alternatively, the element of repetition may be governed by a system: the progressive lengthening of the repeated material (Glass), changing discrepancies from simultaneity (Reich), or large-scale rhythmic schemes based on integers (Hobbs, White). Among others who have been closely associated with repetitive music are Young (probably first in the field), Cardew and many younger American and English musicians. In most cases the rhythmic repetition is coupled with an unwavering tonality. The origins of systematic music may be traced to some of Satie's pieces and the early works of Cage, but more particularly to the music of Bali, black Africa and India.

BIBLIOGRAPHY

B. Dennis: 'Repetitive and Systematic Music', *MT*, cxv (1974), 1036

M. Nyman: *Experimental Music: Cage and Beyond* (London, 1974)

PAUL GRIFFITHS

Systema participato (It.). MEAN-TONE.

Szabados, Béla Antal (*b* Pest, 3 June 1867; *d* Budapest, 15 Sept 1936). Hungarian composer. He first studied composition and the piano with Erkel, later with Volkmann, Koessler and Sándor Nikolits. In 1888 he joined the staff of the Academy of Music and Dramatic Art as accompanist and coach, and in 1893 was appointed piano teacher and coach at the reorganized Academy of Music. His First String Quartet was awarded the Milleniumi Király-dij (Millennial King's Prize) in 1896. He was appointed professor of singing at the academy in 1920 and two years later he became head of the newly established department for training professors of singing. In 1927 he was appointed principal of the National Conservatory, in which position he remained until his death.

Szabados's music, at once poetic and restrained, is essentially conservative in character; his language never advanced beyond that of the late Romantics. He was principally known as a composer for the theatre and also as a singing teacher: his pedagogical works were in official use by the academy.

Szabados's brother Károly (*b* Pest, 28 Jan 1860; *d* Budapest, 25 Jan 1892) was also a pianist and composer and studied with Liszt, Erkel and Volkmann. In 1880 he was conductor at the National Theatre of Kolozsvár; later he became assistant conductor at the Royal Hungarian Opera House. His three-act ballet *Vióra* (1891) enjoyed considerable success.

BIBLIOGRAPHY
V. Papp: *Arcképek a magyar zenevilágból* [Portraits of Hungarian musical life] (Budapest, 1925)
B. A. Szabados: 'Visszaemlékezések' [Reminiscences], *A zene*, vii (1925)
E. Major: 'Szabados Béla', *A Nemzeti Zenede évkönyve az 1936–37 évröl* [Annual report of the National Conservatory] (Budapest, 1937), 3

JOHN S. WEISSMANN/PÉTER P. VÁRNAI

Szabelski, Bolesław (*b* Radoryż, nr. Łuków, 3 Dec 1896; *d* Katowice, 27 Aug 1979). Polish composer, teacher and organist. He studied with Łysakowski at the Polish Musical Society School, in Kiev (1915) and at the Warsaw Conservatory with Surzyński for organ and with Szymanowski and Statkowski for composition. Thereafter he embarked on a career as a composer, virtuoso organist and teacher. He was professor of the organ and composition at the Katowice Conservatory (1929–39 and 1954–67), where his pupils included Górecki. Among the many honours he received are the Katowice Municipal Prize (1948), the State Prize Second Class (1953 for the Third Symphony), the prize of the Polish Composers' Union (1960), the State Prize (1962 for the orchestral *Sonety*) and the Gold Medal of Merit of the Katowice region (1963).

Szabelski had a most important part in the development of 20th-century Polish music through his use of pre-Classical forms in a manner that has been termed, not entirely accurately, 'neo-Baroque'. This interest, which began early, was undoubtedly linked with his work as an organist and exponent of old music. It is also significant that he was one of the few to study with Szymanowski, with whom he shared a tendency to concertato writing and massive, mixed-timbre orchestration. But, in contrast with Szymanowski, Szabelski explored with great determination and thoroughness a limited area of style and language, choosing these limitations freely. The orchestral Toccata (1938) is a fully characteristic piece, showing considerable technical command, particularly in polyphony and instrumentation. The language is already developed and individual, though not so precisely defined as in such post-1950 works as the Third and Fourth Symphonies, the Concerto grosso and the Piano Concertino no.2, all of which indicate a development undertaken with unusual awareness. Those features of the Toccata which were to remain typical include the orchestration – not at all neo-Baroque, but using a range of individualized colours – and the harmony, which demonstrates Szabelski's extensively developed technique of modal stratification.

His output is not large (many inter-war compositions have been lost, and after the war he wrote no more than one work each year) and it is concentrated in the orchestral field. This concentration enabled Szabelski to develop his particular interests intensively, though there were some lapses in evolution and craftsmanship. He long preferred Baroque forms, and even his sonatas show him endeavouring to use Classical structural ideas to counter a Baroque foundation. The coherence of his forms – sometimes monumental, as in the 45-minute Third Symphony – results not so much from a unity of conception as from the skilful development of concertante elements, virtuoso orchestration, discrete dynamic degrees and complex polymodal counterpoint. Passacaglia, toccata and fugue are all employed as structural bases, often replacing motivic working; forward motion is supplied by motor rhythms or ostinatos, these borrowed from contemporary neo-classical conventions without any attempts to make them more dynamic or more organic in their development. Fundamentally Szabelski's music during this long first period (1926–58) was based on a simple, natural approach, not transformed by the suggestions of folk music in the Third Symphony and other pieces.

A fundamental turning-point took place in 1958 with the composition of the orchestral *Sonety*, a work of firm, practical craftsmanship but quite novel technique. At the age of 62 Szabelski had begun to compose innovatory pieces that put many younger Poles to shame. He embraced 'point'-type scoring and 12-note serialism, together with their formal consequences, as well as introducing new procedures of his own. Most of these late compositions are chamber-like in scoring and tend to develop perfectly finished motifs (often serial) throughout the whole form. One exception is the single-movement Fifth Symphony for chorus (treated instrumentally), organ and orchestra.

WORKS
(*selective list*)

ORCHESTRAL
Sym. no.1, 1926; Sym. no.2 (trad.), S, chorus, orch, 1934; Suite, 1938, incl. Toccata; Etiuda, 1939; Pf Concertino, 1946; Sinfonietta, str, perc, 1946; Sym. no.3, 1951; Uwertura uroczysta [Solemn ov.], 1953; Conc. grosso, 1954; Pf Concertino no.2, 1955; Sym. no.4, 1956; [3] sonety, 1958; Wiersze [Verses], pf, orch, 1961; Preludia, 1963; Conc., fl, small orch, 1964; Sym. no.5, chorus, org, orch, 1968

OTHER WORKS
Choral: Cantata (A. Mickiewicz), 1928; Magnificat, S, chorus, 1942; Marsz żołnierski [Soldiers' march] (W. Broniewski), chorus, brass, 1948; Heroic Poem (A. Bezymieński), 1952; Improwizacje, chorus, chamber orch, 1959
Chamber: Str Qt no.1, 1924, lost; Str Qt no.2, 1956; Aforyzmy '9', fl, ob, cl, tpt, trbn, perc, vn, va, vc, 1962
Kbd: Variations, pf, 1923, lost; Passacaglia, org, 1930; Org Sonata, 1943

Principal publisher: Polskie Wydawnictwo Muzyczne

BIBLIOGRAPHY
A. Sutkowski: 'III symfonia Szabelskiego', *Przegląd kulturalny* (1955), no.23
Z. Lissa: 'III symfonia Bolesława Szabelskiego', *Muzyka*, i/1 (1956), 34–72
B. Pociej: 'IV symfonia Bolesława Szabelskiego', *Ruch muzyczny*, ii/19 (1958), 16
L. Markiewicz: 'Trzy sonety na orkiestre', *Ruch muzyczny*, iii/8 (1959), 11
T. Zieliński: ' "Sonety" Bolesława Szabelskiego', *Ruch muzyczny*, iv/21 (1960), 8
Z. Wachowicz: 'Stare i nowe w twórczości Bolesława Szabelskiego' [Old and new in the work of Szabelski], *Muzyka*, ix/3–4 (1964), 16
L. Markiewicz: 'Bolesław Szabelski on his 70th birthday', *Polish Music* (1967), no.1, p.10
——: 'Ostatnie utwory Bolesława Szabelskiego', *Res facta* (1969), no.36

BOGUSŁAW SCHÄFFER

Szabó, Csaba (*b* Acăţari-Mureş, 19 April 1936). Romanian composer and critic of Hungarian descent. He studied at the music college in Tîrgu-Mureş (1949–53) and at the Cluj Conservatory (1953–9). He has served as conductor of the Tîrgu-Mureş Song and Dance Ensemble (1959–67) and as lecturer at the drama institute in the same city (from 1964). In 1969 he received the Culture Order.

WORKS
(selective list)
Stage: Aranyszőrü bárány [The lambkin with golden hair] (ballet, 1), 1958; Bokréta [Garland] (choreographic scene), 1962; Kis épitők [Little builder] (children's opera), 1963; A betyár balladája (ballet, 1), 1964; Törökbúza hántás (choreographic scene), 1964; incidental music
Orch: Concert-rondo, vn, orch, 1963; Naenie, pf, cel, xyl, str, tape, 1966
Vocal: Királyfalvi szőlőhegyen [Vintage at Királyhegy], S, T, B, chorus, orch, 1971; choruses, mass songs, children's choruses, songs
Chamber: Str Qt, for young players, 1958; 4 Miniatures, pf, 1961; Sonata con ritmo di ballo, fl, pf, 1964; Parlando giusto e coral, 1974

ISTVÁN LAKATOS

Szabó, Ferenc (*b* Budapest, 27 Dec 1902; *d* Budapest, 4 Nov 1969). Hungarian composer. Between 1921 and 1926 he studied composition with Weiner, Siklós and then Kodály. He received surprisingly quick recognition in Hungarian musical life with the chamber works of 1926–31, in which he reinterpreted Kodály's folk style in a manner uniting lyrical reflection and sharp polytonal contrasts within strict and complex structures. Committed to left-wing politics from early youth, he joined the Communist Party, then illegal, in 1927. He took part with enthusiasm in leading workers' choirs and writing music for performance by the masses, seeking new types of mediation between high art and popular culture. In this he condensed his style into small, readily practicable forms and achieved through reduced means a quality of terse contrast and complexity, while maintaining the individual character of his music. The fertility of this approach was demonstrated by the success of the *a cappella* cycle *Farkasok dala* ('Song of the wolves'), performed at the 1931 ISCM Festival in London with the text by Petőfi translated by Dent.

As a communist, Szabó was obliged to emigrate through Berlin (1931) to the USSR (1932). He became a respected figure in Soviet musical life, and found the opportunities to explore common ground between the concert hall and mass music-making on a far higher level. Besides composing a number of mass songs and film scores (notably for Piscator's *The Fisher's Revolt*, 1934), he transcribed the Sinfonietta, originally for chamber orchestra, for an orchestra of *domrï* (plucked folk instruments). He strongly resisted making any sim-

plification in his style, and yet he was able to arrive at a positive human viewpoint through expressionist tension, somewhat in the manner of Bartók, Honegger or even Schoenberg, at a time when intellectuals internationally were taking an anti-fascist stance.

A new period in Szabó's work was fully revealed, and with decisive success, in the Lyric Suite for orchestra, introduced by Szenkár at Moscow in 1937. Szabó returned to Hungary in 1944 as a Red Army officer, and in 1945 he was appointed professor of composition at the Budapest Academy of Music, of which he was made director-general in 1958. He retained both posts until his retirement in 1967, and was also president of the Association of Hungarian Musicians (1949–51). Twice recipient of the Kossuth Prize (1951, 1954), he was named Eminent Artist of the Hungarian People's Republic in 1962. In the 'folk epic' approach of his later years, most fully displayed in the triptych made up of the orchestral suite *Ludas Matyi* (1950), the symphony *Memento* (1952) and the oratorio *Föltámadott a tenger* ('In fury rose the ocean', 1955), he confirmed his individual style in music that is monumental but also deeply critical and analytical in treating his country's history. This is, however, no mere applied art: the music is on a high level, as are the late chamber works, which are full of polytonal antinomies yet moulded in a seemingly natural melodic style, their masterly complexity having the face of simplicity. Szabó's last work, an almost finished opera on autobiographical themes, is a summary of these qualities.

WORKS
(selective list)

STAGE AND VOCAL
Stage: Ludas Matyi (ballet, G. Harangozó, after M. Fazekas), 1960; Légy jó mindhalálig [Be good until your death] (opera, J. Romhányi, after Z. Móricz), 1969, completed A. Borgulya
Choral orch: Aufbau der Stadt Traktorostroy (J. R. Becher), solo vv, chorus, brass, perc, 1931; Meghalt Lenin! [Lenin has died!] (A. Komját), chorus, orch, 1933; Kolkhoznaya syuita (A. Hidas), solo vv, chorus, orch, 1934; Nótaszó [Singing songs], 1v/chorus, small orch, 1950; Föltámadott a tenger [In fury rose the ocean] (Petőfi), oratorio, 1955; Vallomás [Confession] (Petőfi), chorus, brass, perc, 1967
Unacc. choral: Magyar parasztdalok [Hungarian peasant songs], male vv, 1929; Farkasok dala [Song of the wolves] (Petőfi), 1929–30; Kitartás! Agitáció kórusra [Hold on! Agitation for chorus] (A. Tamás), ?1930; Der 7-te November (Komját), ?1931–2; Die Fahne (Becher), male vv, ?1934; Grabschrift (Becher), male/female/mixed vv, ?1935; Velikiy Stalinskiy Zakon (Dzhambul), T, mixed vv, 1939; 3 Little Choruses (A. József), 1948; Petőfi Songs, male/female/mixed vv, ?1950–51; Hajnali nóta [Dawn song], 1953
Songs for 1v, pf: Still, mein Herz! (Becher), 1938; 3 Songs (M. Radnóti), 1964
*c*50 mass songs and smaller choral works, 1927–64

INSTRUMENTAL
Orch: Suite, small orch, 1926; Musik für Streichorchester, 1930; Klassovaya bor'ba, sym., 1932; Ov., brass, 1934; Rhapsody, brass, 1935; Sinfonietta, chamber orch, arr. domrï orch, 1935; Lyric Suite, str, 1936; Moldavian Rhapsody, 1941; Hazatérés [Returning home], conc., 1948; Számadás [Accounting], 1949; Ludas Matyi, suite, 1950; Memento, sym., 1952; Felszabadult melódiák [Liberated melodies], 1955; Ballet Music, 1961; Sérénade oubliée, 1964
Chamber: 2 str qts, 1926, 1962; Serenade, fl, va, ?1926–7; Trio, 2 vn, va, 1927; Hungarian Peasant Songs, str qt, 1929; Sonata, vc, 1929; Sonata, vc, pf, ?1930; 2 sonatas, vn, 1930–31; Trio, vn, va, pf, 1931; Sonata (alla rapsodia), cl, pf, 1964
Pf: Toccata, 1928; Sonatina, 1929; 5 Light Pieces, ?1929; Suite, 1930; 3 sonatas, 1940–41, 1947, 1957–61; Felszabadult melódiák, 1949
Film scores, 1920s–59; several smaller inst pieces; arrs.

Principal publishers: Editio Musica, Gosudarstvennoye Muzïkal'noye Izdatel'stvo

BIBLIOGRAPHY
A. Pernye: *Szabó Ferenc* (Budapest, 1965)
J. Maróthy: *Szabó Ferenc indulása* (Budapest, 1970)

——: *Zene, forradalom, szocializmus: Szabó Ferenc útja* (Budapest, 1975)

JÁNOS MARÓTHY

Szabolcsi, Bence (*b* Budapest, 2 Aug 1899; *d* Budapest, 21 Jan 1973). Hungarian musicologist. He studied law, literary history and philosophy at Budapest University (1917–20), musicology, history and art history at Leipzig University (1921–3) and composition at the Budapest Academy of Music with Kodály, Weiner and Siklós (1917–21) and in Leipzig with Karg-Elert (1921–3), taking the doctorate in 1923 under Abert with a dissertation on Benedetti and Saracini. From the 1920s he worked in Budapest as a publisher's reader, editor and music critic, and as co-editor of the journal *Zenei szemle* (1926–9) and (with Tóth) of the Hungarian *Zenei lexikon* (1930–31). From 1945 until his death he was professor of music history at the Budapest Academy of Music, where he founded the faculty of musicology (1951), serving as its professor and head until his death. He was on the editorial committees of the periodicals *Új zenei szemle* (1950–56), *Magyar zene* (1960–73) and *Studia musicologica Academiae scientiarum hungaricae* (1961–7, editor 1967–73) and co-editor with Bartha of the series *Zenetudományi tanulmányok* (1953–62). In 1961 he founded the Budapest Bartók Archives, which he directed until his death, and which in 1969 became the Musicological Institute of the Hungarian Academy of Sciences. His awards included the Baumgarten Literary Prize (1933), the Kossuth Prize (1951, 1965), the Hungarian Golden Order of Labour (1969) and the Gottfried Herder Prize (1971). He was a member of the Royal Asiatic Society, London (1936), the International Society for Musicology (1938), the International Folk Music Council (1940), the Hungarian Academy of Sciences (1948) and the Finnish Kalevala Society (1960) and president (1951–6, 1959–61) of the Association of Hungarian Musicians.

Szabolcsi belonged among that generation of Hungarians born between about 1890 and 1900 (Molnár, Tóth, Major) who took upon themselves the task of creating a contemporary musicology in their own country. Szabolcsi's work centred on his aim to create a Hungarian literature of musical history which would fulfil 20th-century requirements, to establish publishers and a readership for it and to train others to continue his initiative. It was through him that music history, as a specialized branch of literature, became a matter of common knowledge in Hungary. His scholarship was informed by the thoroughness and highly developed methodology of German research, the historical and stylistic standards of such French scholars as Taine and Rolland, and the principles of Hungarian comparative musical research inspired by Bartók and Kodály, whose example he followed in linking East and West – his first Hungarian publications were on Mozart and his first German ones on Kodály and the problems of early Hungarian music history.

Szabolcsi's collection of early Hungarian music from the Danube region in the 1920s and 1930s led to ten central studies (1928–54) of Hungarian music history from the Middle Ages to the 19th century, united as *A magyar zene évszázadai* ('Centuries of Hungarian music', 1959–61) and in the 1930s and 1940s he made fundamental contributions to Hungarian musicology with a number of works on general musical history: *A*

zene története ('A history of music'), a monograph on Beethoven and *Európai virradat* ('Daybreak over Europe'). His chief work, *A melódia története* ('A history of melody'), is a synthesis of his dual interest in research of eastern and western European music. His research of phenomena of music in Hungarian literature and poetry was widely acclaimed. He was a pioneer of the literature on Bartók and Kodály and the author of the first Hungarian scholarly biography of Bartók. He also contributed to the spread of their vocal compositions by translating into German the texts of Bartók's *Cantata profana*, *Village Scenes* and *20 Hungarian Folksongs* and Kodály's *Psalmus hungaricus*, *The Transylvanian Spinning-room*, choral works and songs. He compiled two record anthologies: *Musica hungarica* (1965, 2/1970), a chronological survey of Hungarian music, and the posthumous *Musica mundana* (1975), an anthology of general music history arranged by type of melody.

WRITINGS

Mozart: kísérlet [Mozart: an experiment] (Budapest, 1921)

'Die Instrumentalmusik Zoltán Kodálys', *Musikblätter des Anbruch*, iv (1922), 270

Benedetti und Saracini: Beiträge zur Geschichte der Monodie (diss., U. of Leipzig, 1923; partial Hung. trans., *Magyar zene*, xiv (1973), 233)

'Probleme der alten ungarischen Musikgeschichte', *ZMw*, vii (1924–5), 647; viii (1925–6), 140, 342, 485

'Maróthi György magyar zeneelmélete' [Treatise on music by Maróthi], *Magyar könyvszemle*, xxxiv (1927), 154

'Pálóczi Horváth Ádám ötödfélszáz énekének töredékes kézirata' [The fragmentary MS of Pálóczi Horváth's collection of 450 songs], *Irodalomtörténeti közlemények*, xxxvii (1927), 99

Zoltán Kodály: Chormusik (Vienna, 1927)

Zoltán Kodály, ein Meister des Liedes (Vienna, 1927)

'Egy kurucdallam régi feljegyzései' [Old notations of a Kuruc melody], *Zenei szemle*, xii (1928), 61

Mozart: Szöktetés a szerályból [Mozart's *Entführung*] (Budapest, 1928)

'Öt régi magyar tánc' [5 old Hungarian dances], *Zenei szemle*, xii (1928), 118

'Ungarische Chorpartituren des 18. Jahrhunderts', *ZMw*, xi (1928–9), 306

'Die metrische Odensammlung des Johannes Honterus', *ZMw*, xiii (1930–31), 338

'A zsidó zenetörténet problémái' [Problems of the history of Jewish music], *Magyar-zsidó szemle*, xlviii (1931), 185

Mozart: Varázsfuvola [Mozart's *Zauberflöte*] (Budapest, 1932)

'Osztják hősdalok – magyar siratók melódiái: néhány ázsiai adalék a magyar népzene keleti kapcsolataihoz' [Ostiak saga songs – Hungarian dirges: some data on the Eastern relations of Hungarian folk music], *Ethnographia*, xliv (1933), 71

'A keleti ugorok, mint előázsiai kultúrhatás közvetítői a zenetörténetben' [Eastern Ugrians as mediators in music between western Asia and Europe], *Emlékkönyv Balassa József 70. születése napjára* (Budapest, 1934), 139

A magyar zene története rövid összefoglalásban [A short history of Hungarian music] (Budapest, 1934)

'Népvándorláskori elemek a magyar népzenében' [Rudiments of the migration period in Hungarian folk music], *Ethnographia*, xlv (1934), 138

'Über Kulturkreise der musikalischen Ornamentik in Europa', *ZMw*, xvii (1935), 65

'Adatok a keleteurópai zenestílus kialakulásához' [Some data on the development of an eastern European musical style], *Libanon*, i (1936), 16

Bevezetés a zenetörténetbe [Introduction to the history of music] (Budapest, 1936)

'Egyetemes művelődéstörténet és ötfokú hangsorok' [Universal history of civilization and five-note scales], *Ethnographia*, xlvii (1936), 233; Eng. trans., *AcM*, xv (1943), 24

'Osztyák és vogul dallamok: újabb adalékok a magyar népi siratódallam problémájához' [Ostiak and Vogul melodies: some new data on the problems of Hungarian dirges], *Ethnographia*, xlviii (1937), 340

'A zenei földrajz alapjai' [The outlines of a geography of music], *Ethnographia*, xlix (1938), 1

'Egy régi zsidó hangsorról' [An old Jewish scale], *Libanon*, iii (1938), 1

'Adatok a középázsiai dallamtípus elterjedéséhez' [Data on the diffusion of a type of melody from Central Asia], *Ethnographia*, li (1940), 242

A zene története [The history of music] (Budapest, 1940, 5/1974; Slovak trans., 1962)

'A zsidó liturgia rövid zenetörténete' [A concise history of Jewish liturgical music], *Emlékkönyv Heller Bernát professzor 70. születésnapjára* (Budapest, 1941), 276
with A. Tóth: *Mozart élete és művei* [Mozart: his life and works] (Budapest, 1941)
'Zsidó zenei nyelvemlék: a legrégibb kótázott bibliadallam', *Libanon*, vi (1941), 67; Eng. trans. in *Semitic Studies in Memory of Immanuel Löw* (Budapest, 1947), 131, as 'A Jewish Musical Document of the Middle Ages: the Most Ancient Noted Biblical Melody'
'A Survey of Hungarian Music', *A Companion to Hungarian Studies* (Budapest, 1943), 468; Fr. and Ger. trans., *Corvina* (1949), no.6, p.1
A magyar zenetörténet kézikönyve [Handbook of the history of Hungarian music] (Budapest, 1947, 3/1977; Eng. trans., 1964, 2/1965, as *A Concise History of Hungarian Music*; Ger. trans., 1964, 3/1975)
Beethoven: művész és műalkotás két korszak határán [Beethoven: the artist and his work between two eras] (Budapest, 1947, 5/1976)
ed.: *Régi muzsika kertje* [The garden of music from bygone days] (Budapest, 1947, 2/1957)
'Tre composizioni sconosciute di Antonio Vivaldi', *Quaderno dell'Accademia Chigiana*, xv (Siena, 1947), 23
'About Five-tone Scales in the Early Hebrew Melodies', *Ignaz Goldzieher Memorial Volume* (Budapest, 1948), i, 309
'Egy XVII. századi zsidó muzsikus: Salomone Rossi és kora' [A Jewish musician from the 17th century: Rossi and his age], *IMIT Yearbook*, lxvi (1948), 58
Európai virradat: a klasszikus zene kialakulása Vivalditól Mozartig [Daybreak over Europe: the development of Classical music from Vivaldi to Mozart] (Budapest, 1948, 2/1961)
'Írott hagyomány – élő hagyomány: makámelv a népi és művészi zenében' [Written and unwritten tradition: maqām as principle of both folk and art music], *Ethnographia*, lx (1949), 71
A melódia története: vázlatok a zenei stílus múltjából (Budapest, 1950, 2/1957; Eng. trans., 1965, as *A History of Melody*; Ger. trans., 1959, as *Bausteine zu einer Geschichte der Melodie*)
'Bartók és a népzene' [Bartók and folk music], *Új zenei szemle*, i/4 (1950), 39; Fr. trans. in *Bartók: sa vie et son oeuvre* (Budapest, 1956), 75; Ger. trans. in *Béla Bartók: Weg und Werk* (Budapest, 1957, 2/1972), 93
A művész és közönsége: zeneszerző, társadalom és zenei köznyelv a polgári társadalom küszöbén [The artist and his public: the composer, society and the common musical language at the beginning of the bourgeois era] (Budapest, 1952, 2/1954; Fr. trans., *Europe revue mensuelle*, xxxiv (1956), 35
'Új kínai népdalgyűjtemények' [New collections of Chinese folksongs], *Zenetudományi tanulmányok*, i (1953), 758
Népzene és történelem [Folk music and history] (Budapest, 1954, 2/1955)
'Bartók Béla élete' [The life of Bartók], *Csillag*, ix (1955), 1855; as introduction to F. Bónis: *Bartók élete képekben* [Bartók's life in pictures] (Budapest, 1956, 3/1961; Eng. trans., 1964); Fr. trans. in *Bartók: sa vie et son oeuvre* (Budapest, 1956), 9–42; Ger. trans. in *Béla Bartók: Weg und Werk* (Budapest, 1957, 2/1972), 11–65, and as *Béla Bartók: Leben und Werk* (Leipzig, 1961, 2/1968)
ed.: *Bartók: sa vie et son oeuvre* (Budapest, 1956, 2/1968; Ger. trans., 1957, 2/1972, as *Béla Bartók: Weg und Werk: Schriften und Briefe*)
'Exoticism in Mozart', *ML*, xxxvii (1956), 323; Ger. trans., *Internationale Mozartkonferenz: Prag 1956*, 181
Liszt Ferenc estéje (Budapest, 1956; Eng. trans., 1959, as *The Twilight of Ferenc Liszt*; Ger. trans., 1959)
'Mozart und die Volksbühne', *Kongressbericht: Wien Mozartjahr 1956*, 623; Fr. trans., *SM*, i (1961), 66
'Über Form und Improvisation in der Kunst- und Volksmusik', *IMSCR*, vii *Cologne 1958*, 257
'A búcsúzó klasszicizmus: Haydn utolsó kamaraművei' [Farewell to Classicism: Haydn's last chamber works], *MTA nyelv- és irodalomtudományi osztályának közleményei*, xv (1959), 7; Slovak trans., *SH*, iii (1959), 275
'Bartók és a világirodalom' [Bartók and world literature], *Nagyvilág*, iv (1959), 265; Fr. trans., *Europe revue mensuelle*, xli (1963), 221; Eng. trans., *International Musicological Conference in Commemoration of Béla Bartók: Budapest 1971*, 103
'Das Naturbild bei Händel und Haydn', *Händel-Ehrung der Deutschen Demokratischen Republik: Leipzig 1959*, 88
'Haydn és a magyar zene' [Haydn and Hungarian music], *Magyar tudomány*, iv (1959), 631; also in *Zenetudományi tanulmányok*, viii (1960), 481; Ger. trans., *BMw*, i/2 (1959), 62, *Internationale Konferenz zum Andenken Joseph Haydns: Budapest 1959*, 159, and *ÖMz*, xxi (1966), 589; Russ. trans., *SovM* (1959), no.6, p.77
Vers és dallam [Verse and melody] (Budapest, 1959, 2/1972) [15 studies on Hungarian literature]
A magyar zene évszázadai [Centuries of Hungarian music], ed. F. Bónis (Budapest, 1959–61) [10 studies from the Middle Ages to the 19th century]
ed., with B. Rajeczky: *Bartók Béla kézírása* [Bartók's handwriting] (Budapest, 1961, 2/1964)

'La situation de la musicologie hongroise', *SM*, i (1961), 9
ed.: *Liszt–Bartók: 2nd International Musicological Conference: Budapest 1961* [*SM*, v (1963)] [incl. 'Mensch und Natur in Bartóks Geisteswelt', 525]
'Man and Nature in Bartók's World', *New Hungarian Quarterly*, ii (1961), 147; Ger. trans., *ÖMz*, xvi (1961), 577, and *SM*, v (1963), 525
'Über das Fortleben antiker Metren in der ungarischen Lied- und Tanzmusik', *Festschrift Heinrich Besseler* (Leipzig, 1961), 15
A válaszút és egyéb tanulmányok [The crossroads and other essays] (Budapest, 1963)
'Keleti dallamproblémák' [On the problem of oriental melodies], *Magyar zene*, iii (1962), 213
'Kleine Beiträge zur Melodiegeschichte des 18. Jahrhunderts, i: Zwei Zitate bei Mozart; ii: Eine deutsch-ungarische Weise: das "Hussitenlied" ', *SMw*, xxv (1962), 532
'Folk Music – Art Music – History of Music', *Notes*, xxi (1963–4), 503; also in *SM*, vii (1965), 171; Hung. orig., *MTA nyelv- és irodalomtudományi osztályának közleményei*, xxii (1965), 9
'Die Anfänge der nationalen Oper im XIX. Jahrhundert', *IMSCR*, ix *Salzburg 1964*, 57
'Die Handschrift von Appony (Oponice)', *SM*, vi (1964), 3
'Mozarts faustische Dramaturgie', *Festschrift zum 80. Geburtstag von Georg Lukács* (Neuwied and Berlin, 1965), 535; also in *ÖMz*, xxiii (1968), 393
'Musicology', *Science in Hungary* (Budapest, 1965), 246
'Osteuropäische Züge in der italienischen Monodie des 17. Jahrhunderts', *Sbornik prací filosofické fakulty brněnské university*, F9 (1965), 319
'Zoltán Kodály (1882–1967)', *SM*, ix (1967), 1
A zenei köznyelv problémái: a romantika felbomlása [Problems of musical everyday language: the decline of Romanticism] (Budapest, 1968) [2 essays; Eng. trans. of no.2, *SM*, xii (1970), 263]
'The "Proclamation Style" in Hebrew Music', *Yuval*, i (1968), 38, 249
'Über metrische Melodien in Beethovens und Bartóks Musik', *Musamens–musici: im Gedenken an Walther Vetter* (Leipzig, 1969), 255
Tanzmusik aus Ungarn im 16. und 17. Jahrhundert (Budapest and Kassel, 1970)
'A Biblia és a zenetörténet' [The Bible and the history of music], *A Biblia világa* (Budapest, 1972, 2/1973), 249
Úton Kodályhoz [On the way to Kodály] (Budapest, 1972) [7 essays]
'Két adalék a magyar zene XVIII. századi történetéhez' [Contributions to the history of Hungarian music in the 18th century]; 'Bertha Sándor levelei Bartalus Istvánhoz' [S. Bertha's letters to Bartalus], *Magyar zenetörténeti tanulmányok* (1973), 9; 129

BIBLIOGRAPHY

ZL
B. Bartók: 'Szabolcsi, Bence (Benedict)', *The Universal Jewish Encyclopedia* (New York, 1943)
J. Maróthy: 'Eine kurzgefasste Bibliographie der musikwissenschaftlichen Werke von Bence Szabolcsi', *BMw*, ii/1 (1960), 43
D. Bartha, ed.: *Studia musicologica Bence Szabolcsi septuagenario* (Budapest, 1969) [incl. 'On Bence Szabolcsi's 70th Birthday', 5; complete list of writings compiled by M. Berlász and I. Homolya, 7]
F. Bónis, ed.: *Magyar zenetörténeti tanulmányok Szabolcsi Bence 70. születésnapjára* [Hungarian musicological studies for Szabolcsi's 70th birthday] (Budapest, 1969) [incl. complete list of writings compiled by M. Berlász and I. Homolya, 7–42]
Obituary: F. Bónis, *Muzsika*, xvi/4 (1973), 6; F. Bónis, *Népszabadság*, xxxi (23 Jan 1973); I. Kecskeméti and others, *Muzsika*, xvi/4 (1973), 1 [as educator]; G. Kroó, J. Ujfalussy and B. Köpeczi, *Hungarian Music News*, nos.2–3 (1973), 1; B. Rajeczky, *SM*, xiv (1972), 3
F. Bónis: 'The Magnum Opus of Bence Szabolcsi', *New Hungarian Quarterly*, xv/53 (1974), 218

FERENC BÓNIS

Szadek, Tomasz [Thoma a Szadek] (*d* Kraków, 1612). Polish composer, singer and priest. On 25 June 1569, already a bachelor in the liberal arts, he was appointed a singer in the royal chapel in Kraków. He remained there until 1574, when he was most likely ordained and became a curate of Kraków Cathedral. From 1575 to 1578 he was a member of a group of singers called the Chapel of the Rorantists (of Kraków Cathedral) and subsequently held some non-musical posts at the cathedral, including that of a penitentiary.

All his extant compositions were written to meet the requirements of the Chapel of the Rorantists (an ensemble of male voices). They are in the late Netherlands style, each based on a plainsong cantus firmus. The two masses for four voices in the Kraków town archive are of the parody type: the *Officium Dies est laetitiae* (ed. in WDMP, xxx, 1957) is modelled on the song *Pieśń o narodzeniu Pańskim* ('Song of our Lord's Nativity') by Wacław z Szamotuł; the other, *Officium in melodiam motetae 'Pisneme'* (ed. in Monumenta musicae sacrae in Polonia, i, 1885), is based on Crecquillon's chanson *Puis ne me peult venir.* There are three incomplete antiphons in the Kraków Cathedral library: the gradual *Haec dies*; the communion *Pascha nostrum*; and the introit *Vultum tuum.*

BIBLIOGRAPHY
A. Chybiński: 'Trzy przyczynki do historii muzyki w Krakowie w pierwszej połowie XVII wieku' [3 contributions on music history in Kraków in the first half of the 17th century], *Prace polonistyczne ofiarowane Janowi Łosiowi* (Warsaw, 1927), 24
——: 'Msza pastoralna Tomasza Szadka' [The pastoral mass of Tomasz Szadek], *Muzyka kościelna*, iii (1928), nos.1–9, 11–12; iv (1929), nos.1–3
H. Feicht: Preface to: *T. Szadek: Officium Dies est laetitiae*, WDMP, xxx (1957)

ZYGMUNT M. SZWEYKOWSKI

Szalonek, Witold (*b* Czechowice, 2 March 1927). Polish composer and teacher. He studied composition with Woytowicz at the Katowice Conservatory, where he was later appointed professor of composition. Among the awards he has received are the music prize of the city of Katowice (1964) and a prize from the Polish Ministry of Culture (1967). In 1974 he was appointed professor of composition at the Hochschule für Musik, West Berlin. His early works, such as the *Suita kurpiowska* ('Kurpie suite'), draw on the modality of Polish folk music; in later years he has followed other composers in developing new techniques. At first he took Lutosławski as a model, but he went on to incorporate impressionist and pointilliste sonorities. Whatever the style, however, Szalonek displays high purpose and expressive intensity.

WORKS
(selective list)

Orch: Pastorale, ob, pf/orch, 1952; Suita polifoniczna, str, 1955; Satyra symfoniczna, 1956; Concertino, fl, chamber orch, 1962; Les sons, sym. ens, 1965; Mutazioni, chamber orch, 1966
Vocal: Nokturn (L. Staff), Bar, harp, str orch, 1955; Suita kurpiowska [Kurpie suite], A, wind qnt, pf, str trio, 1955; Wyznania [Confessions] (K. Iłłakowicz), speaker, chorus, orch, 1959; Ziemio miła [O pleasant earth] (cantata, A. Gołubiew), 1v, orch, 1969; solo and choral songs, incidental music, Silesian folksong arrs.
Inst: Sonata, vc, pf, 1958; Arabeski, vn, pf, 1963; Proporzioni, fl, va, harp, 1967; Improvisations sonoristiques, cl, trbn, vc, pf, 1968; Mutanza, pf, 1968; 5 małych utworów [5 little pieces], fls/recs, other insts, 1969; 1 + 1 + 1 + 1, 1–4 str, 1969; Aarhus Music, wind qnt. 1970; Proporzioni no.2, fl, vc, pf/harp, 1970; 3 sketches, harp, 1972; Connections, 10 insts, 1972; Conc., str, 1971–5; Proporzioni no.3, vn, vc, pf/harp, 1977; Piernikiana, tuba, 1977; Trio, ob, cl, bn, 1978

Principal publishers: Chester, Moeck, Polskie Wydawnictwo Muzyczne

BIBLIOGRAPHY
H. Schiller: ' "Concertino" Witolda Szalonka', *Ruch muzyczny*, vii/22 (1963), 12
L. Markiewicz: ' "Les sons" Witolda Szalonka', *Ruch muzyczny*, ix/17 (1965), 13
R. Gabryś: 'Nad utworem Witolda Szalonka "Proporzioni" ', *Ruch muzyczny*, xiii/17 (1969), 11
T. Kaczyński: ' "Monologhi" Szalonka', *Ruch muzyczny*, xiii/4 (1969), 6
M. Kondracki: 'Witold Szalonek: 1 + 1 + 1 + 1 per 1–4 strumenti ad arco', *Ruch muzyczny*, xiv/14 (1970), 13

BOGUSŁAW SCHÄFFER

Szałowski, Antoni (*b* Warsaw, 21 April 1907; *d* Paris, 21 March 1973). Polish composer. He received his first music lessons from his father, a distinguished violinist and teacher. In 1930 he graduated from the Warsaw Conservatory, where his teachers had included Lewiecki (piano), Sikorski (composition) and Fitelberg (conducting). He then studied with Boulanger in Paris (1931–6), where he remained for the rest of his life. From 1936 to 1948 he was president of the Association of Young Polish Musicians in Paris. Among the many awards he received was a first prize from the ORTF in 1960 for *La femme têtue.*

An outstanding representative of the inter-war Paris school, Szałowski was one of the leading Polish neoclassicists. He preferred strict, established forms and he employed all the contrapuntal arts, yet he succeeded in writing music that is easy on the ear, full of Parisian elegance but linked to the emotional and colourful Polish symphonic tradition. His finest achievements were the celebrated Overture, the Sinfonietta and the Music for Strings (he composed very little vocal music, most of it for the radio). In Poland he was little known except during a few years after World War II, and then principally for the Overture, whose success led other Poles, among them Lutosławski and Malawski, to compose similar works, but without reaching the distinction of their model. This, probably Szałowski's only composition of international stature, is written with such verve and skill that, within its Classical mould, it gives the impression of inevitability. It was composed in 1936 and the next year received the Gold Medal at the Paris International Exhibition. One of the very few contemporary works to be published and recorded in Warsaw shortly after the war, the Overture was Szałowski's greatest success, but this very success proved a burden. Unable to repeat it and unwilling to keep up with new developments, he proceeded to compose firmly traditional works – well crafted, straightforward, vital and motoric in rhythm, and amusing (his humour was his strongest point), but ultimately of little interest. There is great value, however, in some of the later chamber works, such as the Sonatina for oboe and piano and the Allegretto for bassoon and piano.

WORKS
(selective list)

ORCHESTRAL

Sym. Variations, 1928, withdrawn; Kaprys, 1930, withdrawn; Pf Conc., 1930, withdrawn; Ov., 1936; Sym., 1939; Sinfonietta, 1940; Concertino, chamber orch, 1942; Partita, 1942, withdrawn; Zaczarowana oberża [The enchanted inn] (ballet, 1), 1945, also concert version; Divertissement de ballet, 1950, withdrawn; Concertino, fl, str, 1951; Suite, 1952; Partita, chamber orch, 1954; Vn Conc., 1954
Aria and Toccata, chamber orch, 1957; Conc., ob, cl, bn, orch, 1958; Wskrzeszenie Łazarza [Lazarus's resurrection], sym. picture, 1960; Allegretto, bn, orch, 1962; Music for Str, 1970; 6 szkiców [6 sketches], 1972
Popular pieces: Radio-music, 1955; Dance, 1957; Mazurka, 1959; Intermezzo, 1961; Berceuse pour Clémentine, 1964

CHAMBER AND INSTRUMENTAL

For 3–5 insts: Pf Trio, 1926, withdrawn; Str Qt no.1, 1928, withdrawn; Str Qt no.2, 1934, withdrawn; Str Qt no.3, 1936; Trio, ob, cl, bn, 1936; 4 pastorales, fl, str trio, 1947; Wind Qnt, 1954; Divertimento, ob, cl, bn, 1955; Str Qt no.4, 1956
For 2 insts: Prelude, vn, pf, 1928; Suite, vn, pf, 1931; Andante, vn, pf, 1934; Aria and Burleska, vc, pf, 1936; Sonatina, cl, pf, 1936; Duo, fl, cl, 1939; Duo, vn, vc, 1941, withdrawn; Sonatina, ob, pf, 1946; Allegretto, bn, pf, 1962, orchd
Pf: Sonata, 1932; 2 sonatinas, 1933, 1957; Mélodie, 1935; Mała humoreska [Little humoresque], 1935; Perpetuum mobile, 1937; Study, 1950
Other solo inst: Partita, vc, 1933; 3 Pieces, harmonium, 1943; Suite, hpd, 1951; 2 Pieces, ondes martenot, 1968

VOCAL

2 mélodies, 1v, orch, 1927, withdrawn; Sonet, S, chamber orch, 1931, withdrawn; 3 pieśni ludowe [3 folksongs], 1v, pf, 1942; Polskie

melodie ludowe, 1v, pf, 1950, 1956, 1966; Cantata, female vv, chamber orch, 1960; Pater noster, vv, org, 1968
Radio scores: L'autre, chorus, chamber orch, 1954; La femme tétue (J. Lescure), reciter, 15 insts, 1958; Le merveilleux voyage de Susanne Michel (J. Pivin), 1962

Principal publisher: Polskie Wydawnictwo Muzyczne

BIBLIOGRAPHY
W. Malinowski: 'Technika orkiestrowa a forma w "Uwerturze" Szałowskiego', *Muzyka*, iii/1–2 (1958), 33
Ruch muzyczny, xvii/10 (1973) [Szałowski issue, work-list in xvii/13]
BOGUSŁAW SCHÄFFER

Szamotuł [Szamotulczyk, Szamotulski], **Wacław z** [Samotulinus, Schamotulinus, Shamotulinus, Venceslaus] (*b* Szamotuły, nr. Poznań, *c*1524; *d* ?Pińczów, nr. Kielce, probably in 1560). Polish composer and poet. He studied first at the Collegium Lubranscianum at Poznań and afterwards, in 1538, at Kraków University. From 1545 to 1547 he was secretary to Hieronim Chodkiewicz, governor of Troki, Lithuania. During this period he published a number of Latin panegyrics celebrating events in the royal family. On 6 May 1547 he was appointed a composer at the court of King Sigismund II August, his duties being to provide sacred music for the chapel choir. From about 1550 he was involved with the Polish Protestant movement, and seven Polish four-part pieces by him intended for the Protestant service are extant. From 1555 until his death he worked at the Calvinist court of the great Lithuanian potentate Duke Mikołaj Radziwiłł and now maintained only tenuous relations with the royal court. He was a typical many-sided Renaissance figure. Much of his music has been lost. Although he composed simple pieces of popular cast in a simple note-against-note style he is more important for his sacred polyphony: indeed his mastery of late Netherlands techniques is considered a culminating point in the development of Polish *a cappella* music.

WORKS
SACRED VOCAL
Quatuor parium vocum lamentationes Hieremiae Prophetae . . . quibus adiunctae sunt exclamationes passionum, 4vv (Kraków, 1553)
2 Lat. motets, 4vv, 1554[11], 1564[5]; 1 ed. in WDMP, ix (1930, 3/1971), 1 ed. Z. M. Szweykowski, *Muzyka w dawnym Krakowie* (Kraków, 1964)
3 Lat. songs, 1v, in J. Seclucian: Pieśni chrześcijańskie (Königsberg, 1559)
3 Pol. psalms, 4vv (Kraków, 1558–64); 4 Pol. hymns, 4vv (printed Kraków): ed. in WDMP, xxviii (1956, 3/1972)
Sacred work, 3vv, in J. Zaremba: Pieśni chwał boskich (Brest Litovsk, 1558)

LOST WORKS
Nunc scio vere, motet in org transcr., lost (photographs of MS survive); ed. H. Feicht, *Muzyka staropolska* (Kraków, 1966)
Mass, 8vv, 2 Offitia, 4vv, Exclamationes et lamentationes, 4vv, Exclamationes secundae, 5vv, wedding piece, 6vv, 1553: cited in inventory of Kraków royal chapel, 1572

BIBLIOGRAPHY
SMP [incl. fuller bibliography]
S. Tomkowicz: *Materiały do historii stosunków kulturalnych w XVI wieku* [Sources for the history of cultural relations in the 16th century] (Kraków, 1915)
A. Chybiński: 'Wacław z Szamotuł (XVI w.)', *KM*, vi (1948), nos.21–2, pp.11–34; no.23, pp.7–22; no.24, pp.100–31
A. and Z. Szweykowscy: 'Wacław z Szamotuł – renesansowy muzyk i poeta', *Muzyka*, ix/1–2 (1964), 3
ZYGMUNT M. SZWEYKOWSKI

Szarfenberg [Szarffenberck, Scharpfenberg, Szarfenberger, Szarffemberg, Ostrowski, Ostrogórski], **Maciej** (*b* Liebenthal, nr. Jelenia Góra; *d* Kraków, between 21 March and 15 June 1547). Polish printer active in Kraków. He established his printing house in 1530. Among his music publications are secular and religious partsongs, liturgical books, and music treatises by Jerzy Liban (*De accentuum ecclesiasticorum exquisita ratione*, *c*1539) and Jan Spanenberg (*Questiones musicae in usum Scholae Northusianae*, 1544) which contain numerous musical examples, including some complete compositions. He used exclusively woodblock printing.

His relative Marek Szarfenberg (*b* Liebenthal; *d* Kraków, 1545) was a Kraków bookseller who first started printing in about 1543. He mainly published liturgical books with Gothic notation, using movable type in a double-impression technique, as well as woodblock printing.

Marek's grandson Mateusz Siebeneicher [Siebeneich, Sybeneycher, Zybenaicher] (*b* Liebenthal; *d* Kraków, 1582) married the widow of Maciej's son Hieronim and thus became the owner of the Szarfenberg printing house in 1557. He was one of the most eminent Polish publishers of his time and specialized in the printing of textbooks and Catholic devotional literature. He also issued many popular partsongs and psalms of Cyprian Bazylik z Sieradza, Wacław z Szamotuł and others (mostly published singly), and Krzysztof Klabon's collection, *Pieśni Kalliopy slowienskiey* ('Songs of the Slavonic Calliope', 1588), all printed from movable mensural type. After his death the firm continued until 1627.

BIBLIOGRAPHY
M. Przywecka-Samecka: *Drukarstwo muzyczne w Polsce do końca XVIII wieku* (Kraków, 1969)
——: *Słownik pracowników książki polskiej* [Dictionary of Polish workers] (Warsaw and Łódź, 1972)
TERESA CHYLIŃSKA

Szarth, Georg. See ZARTH, GEORG.

Szarzyński, Stanisław Sylwester (*fl* late 17th century). Polish composer and Cistercian monk. Extant copies of his works bear dates ranging from 1692 to 1713. His vocal music is exclusively sacred. His solo motets (with violin and continuo) are distinguished by their notably expressive melody and high technical level; the choral compositions, with the accompaniment of a large instrumental ensemble, show some carelessness in the part-writing. In these compositions Szarzyński made extensive use of melodies from popular religious songs, either as strict quotations or in stylized form. All his sacred works are in the concertato style, some of them resembling the church cantata in form. His only extant instrumental composition, a *sonata da chiesa* with some features of the canzona, is marked by its technical skill and melodic attractiveness.

WORKS
Ad hymnos ad cantus, S, S, A, T, B, 2 vn, 2 va, vc, bc, ed. in WDMP, xxvi (2/1964)
Ave regina, S, 3 vn, va, bc, ed. in WDMP, xxv (1953)
Gloria in excelsis Deo, S, S, A, T, B, 2 vn, 3 trbn, bc, ed. in ZHMP, xii (1968)
Jesu spes mea, S, 2 vn, bc, ed. in WDMP, x (3/1971)
Litania cursoria, S, A, T, B, 2 vn, va da gamba, bc, ed. in WDMP, lxxii (1974)
Pariendo non gravaris, T, 2 vn, bc, ed. in WDMP, v (2/1960)
Veni Sancte Spiritus, S, 2 vn, bc, ed. in WDMP, l (1963)
Sonata, 2 vn, org, ed. in WDMP, i (2/1958)

BIBLIOGRAPHY
A. Chybiński: 'Przyczynki bibliograficzne do dawnej muzyki polskiej, i: Stanisław Sylwester Szarzyński', *Przegląd muzyczny* (1926), no.1, p.2
——: 'Sonata triowa Stanisława Sylwestra Szarzyńskiego', *Śpiewak*, ix/1–3 (Katowice, 1928), 1, 16, 26
Z. M. Szweykowski: 'Niespodziewane zasoby Sandomierskie: Stanisław Sylwester Szarzyński', *Ruch muzyczny*, iii/1 (1959), 17

——: Prefaces to WDMP, xxvi (2/1964), and WDMP, x (3/1971)
ZYGMUNT M. SZWEYKOWSKI

Szczawiński, Henryk Melcer-. *See* MELCER-SZCZAWIŃSKI, HENRYK.

Szczecin (Ger. Stettin). Town on the river Oder in Poland, formerly (1713–1945) capital of the German (Prussian) province of Pomerania. The beginnings of the town's musical life were linked with the introduction of Christianity by Bishop Otto of Bamberg and Prince Bolesław Krzywousty, ruler of the area from 1102 to 1138. Music was cultivated in monasteries, particularly those of the Benedictines and Franciscans. In 1390 and 1399 two municipal schools were opened, and after the Reformation (1524–34) Duke Barnim XI founded a school, the Pedagogium, for the children of the aristocracy (1543). A combined school and poorhouse was also founded (1540). Each school had cantors responsible for the standard of singing and for giving music lessons. In the first half of the 17th century the activities of the schools reached a peak. Polyphonic and frequently polychoral sacred works were heard in the churches, and much music was performed in the schools themselves. Organ music also flourished, Michil Schuwarth being the earliest known organist (1475). The finest organ, in the Cathedral of St Jakub, was destroyed in 1677 during a siege; later in the 17th century it was rebuilt by Schurich and Heldt, and completed by Arp Schnitger. Many new organs were constructed in the 18th century, including four by Peter Migendt in 1751–64. In the 18th century church and school music declined.

The ruling Slavonic Pomeranian princes did not influence the town's music significantly, although they employed English and Polish violinists. The princes' musicians entertained the court, played in the castle chapel, at St Mary's church and during school ceremonies. In 1630 the town fell to the Swedes and in 1637 the Pomeranian dynasty came to an end; in 1713 Szczecin became part of Prussia. Conditions for musicians, generally poor, worsened considerably in the 18th century, and for financial reasons it was often necessary for them to hold two or even three posts. Nevertheless the town produced a number of distinguished figures, including Philipp Dulichius and Andreas Fromm, both cantors at the Pedagogium. Lesser figures active in the town were P. Praetorius (1520–97), P. Luetkemann (1588–1606), F. G. Klingenberg (1699–1720), M. Rhode (1706–38), Tobias Volckmar (1707–12), G. Klingenberg (1721–46), Friedrich Haack (1789–1827) and S. F. Brede (1792–8).

In the 19th century the leading local composer was Carl Loewe, who taught at the Gymnasium and was organist of the cathedral. He organized concert life in the town between 1820 and 1864, during which period it reached a peak; in 1827 Mendelssohn's overture *A Midsummer Night's Dream* had its première there, and Bach's *St Matthew Passion* was performed in 1831, only two years after its revival by Mendelssohn in Leipzig. After Loewe, the town's musical life declined. Before World War II there was no permanent opera company, symphony orchestra or choir; directors, actors and musicians changed each season (in 1913 Webern was conductor at the theatre), and symphony concerts were organized only sporadically.

After World War II, during which the town was very badly damaged, the Polish Broadcasting Service became active, and musical education was improved by the foundation in 1946 of two musical schools, nationalized in 1950. Following the development of school music, a department of the Poznań Conservatory was established (1961). Concert life revived through the activities of the broadcasting orchestra under W. Górzyński. The Szczecin PO was founded in 1948 and nationalized in 1954; conductors have included F. Lasota (1948–51), M. Lewandowski (1952–7), W. Pawłowski (1954–), J. Wiłkomirski (1957–71) and S. Marczyk (1971–). In 1957 an opera house was founded by J. Nieżychowski; it mainly performs operetta and occasionally modern works. The Szczecin Musical Association, founded in 1962, organizes concerts and master classes; since 1964 it has helped to organize an annual festival of organ and chamber music in nearby Kamień Pomorski. Several local choirs have been formed, the best known being the Technical University Choir, the Hejnał, Hasło and Halka choirs, the Szczecin Boys' Choir and the Teachers' Chamber Choir. The composer Ryszard Kwiatkowski is active in Szczecin.

BIBLIOGRAPHY

R. Schwartz: *Zur Geschichte der Musikantenzunft im alten Stettin* (Leipzig, 1898)

H. Engel: 'Spielleute und Hofmusiker im alten Stettin zu Anfang des 17. Jahrhunderts', *Musik in Pommern*, i (Greifswald, 1932)

W. Freytag: *Musikgeschichte der Stadt Stettin im 18. Jahrhundert* (Greifswald, 1936)

B. M. Jankowski and M. Misiorny: *Muzyka i życie muzyczne na ziemiach zachodnich i północnych 1945–1965* [Music and musical life in western and northern territories, 1945–1965] (Poznań, 1968)
PAWEŁ PODEJKO

Szczepanowski, Stanisław (*b* Kraków, 1814; *d* Lwów, 16 Sept 1877). Polish guitarist, cellist and composer. He studied the guitar with Horecki in Edinburgh and Sor in Paris. In 1840 he began giving concert tours in England, Spain, France, Germany, Russia and Turkey. In Paris his admirers included the greatest musicians, among them Chopin, Liszt, Habeneck and Kalkbrenner, who listened to him with 'great pleasure'. Adam Mickiewicz declared himself 'charmed' by Szczepanowski's playing. In Poland his playing of his compositions based on national themes was received with patriotic enthusiasm. He composed fantasies, variations and pieces in Spanish style, such as *Jota aragonesa*.

CZESŁAW R. HALSKI/JÓZEF POWROŹNIAK

Szczepańska, Maria (Klementyna) (*b* Złoczów, nr. Lwów, 13 May 1902; *d* Poznań, 18 Oct 1962). Polish musicologist. After piano studies at the Lwów Conservatory, she studied musicology with Chybiński at Lwów University (1922–6), where she took her doctorate in 1926 with a dissertation on Manuscript 52 in the Krasiński Library, Warsaw. From 1926 to 1939 she was a lecturer in the musicology department at Lwów University; she also lectured in theoretical subjects at the Paderewski Music School (1929–31) and at the Lwów Conservatory (1931–5). In 1940–41 and 1944–5 she was successively senior lecturer, professor and dean of the theory department of the conservatory. From 1946 until her death she worked in the musicology department at Poznań University, becoming senior lecturer in 1956 and head of the department in 1957. She also lectured at the State Music School, Poznań (1948–51).

Szczepańska's main achievement was her work on

basic sources of Polish polyphonic music of the 15th to 17th centuries (MS 52 Krasiński Library, Warsaw, *PL-Wn* 378, the Gosławski Hymnbook in the Kraków Cathedral chapter archives and Kraków lute tablatures of the 16th century, etc). She devoted considerable attention to the works of the leading Polish composer of the 15th century, Nicolaus de Radom. Her work has formed the basis for further research on the evolution of polyphony in Poland.

WRITINGS

Rękopis 52 Biblioteki Krasińskich w Warszawie i jego znaczenie dla historii muzyki średniowiecznej w Polsce [MS 52 in the Krasiński Library, Warsaw, and its significance for the history of medieval Polish music] (diss., U. of Lwów, 1926; extracts in *Sprawozdania Towarzystwa Naukowego we Lwowie* (1928), 3)

'Do historii polskiej pieśni z XV wieku' [The history of Polish song of the 15th century], *Przegląd muzyczny* (1927), no.5, p.6; (1927), no.6, p.1

'Hymn ku czci św. Stanisława z XV wieku' [A hymn in honour of St Stanisław from the 15th century], *Przegląd muzyczny* (1928), no.7, p.1; (1928), no.8, p.3; (1928), nos.9–10, p.18; (1928), no.12, p.5

'Wielogłosowe opracowanie hymnów mariańskich w rękopisach polskich XV wieku' [Polyphonic arrangements of Marian hymns in Polish 15th-century MSS], *KM* (1928), no.1, p.1; (1929), no.2, p.107; (1929), no.3, p.219; (1929), no.4, p.339

'Do historii polskiej muzyki świeckiej w XV stuleciu' [The history of Polish secular music of the 15th century], *KM* (1929), no.5, p.1

'Do historii muzyki wielogłosowej w Polsce z końca XV wieku' [The history of polyphonic music in Poland up to the end of the 15th century], *KM* (1930), no.8, pp.275–306

'Z folkloru muzycznego w XVII wieku' [Musical folklore of the 17th century], *KM* (1933), nos.17–18, p.27

'O dwunastogłosowym "Magnificat" Mikołaja Zieleńskiego z r.1611' [Mikołaj Zieleński's 12-part Magnificat (1611)], *PRM*, i (1935), 28

'Nieznana krakowska tabulatura lutniowa z drugiej połowy XVI stulecia' [The unknown Kraków lute tablature of the second half of the 16th century], *Księga pamiątkowa ku czci Prof. Adolfa Chybińskiego w 70-lecie urodzin* (Kraków, 1950), 198

'Nowe źródło do historii muzyki średniowiecznej w Polsce' [New sources for the history of medieval music in Poland], *Księga pamiątkowa ku czci profesora Dr. Adolfa Chybińskiego* (Kraków, 1950), 15–56

'Studia o utworach Mikołaja Radomskiego' [Studies on Nicolaus de Radom's works], *KM* (1949), no.25, pp.7–54; (1950), nos.29–30, p.64

'Zabytki muzyki wielogłosowej XV wieku' [Documents of polyphonic music from the 15th century], *Z dziejów polskiej kultury muzycznej*, ed. Z. M. Szweykowski, i (Kraków, 1958), 56

'Niektóre zagadnienia polskiej muzyki lutniowej XVI wieku' [Some problems of Polish lute music of the 16th century], *Chopin Congress: Warszawa 1960*, 630

EDITIONS

A. Jarzębski: *Chromatica*, WDMP, xxi (1950); *Bentrovata*, WDMP, xxvii (1955); *Sentinella*, WDMP, xxxii (1956); *Canzoni*, WDMP, xxxix (1958); *Tamburetta*, WDMP, xi (2/1960); *Nova casa*, WDMP, xv (2/1962); *Concerti a 2 voci*, WDMP, li, lvii (1964–5); *Concerti a 3 voci*, WDMP, lix (1965)

J. Polak: *Preludia, fantazje i tańce na lutnię* [Preludes, fantasies and dances for lute], WDMP, xxii (1951)

D. Cato: *Preludia, fantazje, tańce i madrygały na lutnię* [Preludes, fantasies, dances and madrigals for lute], WDMP, xxiv (1953)

W. Długoraj: *Fantazje i wilanele na lutnię* [Fantasies and villanellas for lute], WDMP, xxiii (1953)

B. Pękiel: *40 utworów na lutnię* [40 pieces for lute], WDMP, xxx (1955)

M. Zieleński: *Domus mea: communio*, WDMP, xxxi (1956); *Exiit sermo inter fratres, Si consurrexistis cum Christo: communiones*, WDMP, xxxvi (1957); *Communiones*, WDMP, xlv (1961)

Wacław z Szamotul: In te Domine speravi, WDMP, ix (1930, 3/1971)

BIBLIOGRAPHY

C. Sikorski: 'Doc.dr Maria Szczepańska: wspomnienie pośmiertne', *Ruch muzyczny*, vii/20 (1963), 7 [obituary]

ZOFIA HELMAN

Szczurowski, Jacek [Hyacinthus] (*b* 1716–21; *d* after 1773). Polish composer and monk. He probably came from south-eastern Poland. He entered a Jesuit monastery as a novice on 19 September 1735 and took minor orders on 24 November 1737. During his novitiate he was a member of the excellent Kraków musical college run by the Jesuits. His notable gift for composition

came to light when he was still a youth; in 1741 the inventories of the Jesuit college mention 38 of his works. Szczurowski did not continue his education and as a monk served as assistant to the prefect of the musical college and as sacristan at Kalisz, Krosno, Gdańsk, Toruń, Kraków, Jarosław, Poznań and Wałcz (near Poznań). The last record concerning him comes from Wałcz.

Only a few of his vocal compositions are extant, although Szczurowski was one of the most prolific Polish composers of the 18th century. They do not exhibit consummate technical elaboration; Szczurowski composed in a style typical of the late Italian Baroque, which he handled in a stereotyped manner, though often making considerable virtuoso demands (thus suggesting that high executive standards were possible in the Jesuit chapels of the time). Some of his compositions are particularly valuable as records of the 18th-century folk motifs (for example his *Missa Emmanuelis*). Szczurowski was also one of the first Polish writers of symphonies (1740, lost).

WORKS

(MSS in PL-SA unless otherwise stated)

Memento rerum conditor, SATB, 2 vn, 2 hn, bc

Dziecino Boża [The infant Christ], S, 2 ob, bc; ed. in ZHMP, xii (Kraków, 1968)

Mass, D, S, B, 2 vn, 2 clarinos, bc

Vesperae pro sanctis, S, B, 2 vn, 2 clarinos, bc

Missa Emmanuelis, SATB, 2 vn, 2 hn, bc, *Pu*

Caeli cives occurite, SATB, 2 vn, 2 clarinos, bc, *CZp*

BIBLIOGRAPHY

A. Chybiński: 'Z dziejów muzyki krakowskiej', *KM*, ii/1 (1913), 24–62

——: 'Przyczynki bio- i bibliograficzne do dawnej muzyki polskiej, vi: Jacek Szczurowski', *Przegląd muzyczny* (1929), no.11, p.2

J. J. Dunicz: 'Z badań nad muzyką polską XVIII wieku, ii: Jacek Szczurowski', *PRM*, ii (1936), 122

ZYGMUNT M. SZWEYKOWSKI

Szczurowski, Jan Nepomucen (*b* Pińczów, 18 May 1771; *d* Kielce, 30 Oct 1849). Polish bass, actor, and cellist. He came from Sierakowski's school in Kraków, where in 1789–92 he was a singer in Jacek Kluszewski's theatre. In 1793 he settled permanently in Warsaw, where he belonged to Bogusławski's theatre company. During his engagement with the Warsaw Opera (until 1839) he enjoyed great success as an outstanding creator of bass roles. In 1840 he moved to Kielce, where he organized concerts for charity. In 1806–7 he and his wife Joanna Gamalska (1776–1851), an actress and singer, toured Poland playing duodramas, including those of Elsner.

ALINA NOWAK-ROMANOWICZ

Székely, Endre (*b* Budapest, 6 April 1912). Hungarian composer. He taught himself to compose before taking lessons with Siklós at the Budapest Academy of Music, from which he graduated in 1937. Subsequently he joined the illegal Communist Party and took part as composer and conductor in the workers' choral movement. After World War II he exercised important functions in Hungarian musical life: he was secretary-general of the Hungarian Musicians' Union and the Béla Bartók Association, and he edited the periodicals *Éneklő nép* and *Éneklő munkás*. From 1952 to 1956 he directed musical life in Sztálinváros, and in 1960 he was appointed professor of methodology and theory at the teachers' training college in Budapest.

Székely's earlier works (up to 1952) are principally choral pieces and cantatas. These show at first the strong influence of Kodály; the later ones are characteristic products of the schematic social realism of the early 1950s. Later in that decade he made a gradual assimilation of the Bartók tradition and of the 12-note serialism of Schoenberg, Berg and Webern. This led to a period (c1957–64) of serial works emulating Schoenbergian expressive intensity within traditional formal patterns, but also including other features, such as Honegger-like choral tableaux. He then began to admit more novel elements, including clusters (in the Concerto of 1964) and Pendereckian string effects (in the Partita, 1965), these being associated with an abandonment of 12-note serialism. The Wind Quintet no.3 (1966), for example, is non-serially based on a three-note motif and is indicative of the direction Székely's music was taking at this time in that it alternates strict canonic movements with partly improvisatory ones. This broadening of style was summarized in the *Musica notturna* for chamber ensemble (1968), which accomodates static or mobile clusters and expansive melodies, free and motor rhythm, and aleatory and strict forms.

WORKS
(selective list)

STAGE AND VOCAL

Stage: Aranycsillag [Golden star] (operetta), 1950; Vizirózsa [Waterlily] (opera), 1958–61
Choral orch: Petőfi-kantáta, 1952; József Attila-kantáta, 1954; Dózsa György, oratorio, 1959; Nenia, oratorio, 1968–9
Solo vocal: 3 Sketches, S, gui, 1967; Maqamat, S, ens, 1970; Solokantate, S, ens, 1972

INSTRUMENTAL

Orch: 2 suites, 1947, 1958; Sym., 1956; Conc., pf, str, perc, 1957–8; Sinfonia concertante, vn, pf, orch, 1960–61; Conc., 8 insts, orch, 1964; Partita, 1965; Fantasma, 1969; Tpt Conc., 1971; Riflessioni, vc, orch, 1973
Chamber: 3 wind qnts, 1952, 1961, 1966; 4 str qts, 1954, 1961, 1962–3, 1972; Musica da camera, 8 insts, 1963; Musica da camera, 6 insts, 1965; Musica notturna, wind qnt, pf, str qnt, 1968; Trio, perc, pf, vc, 1968–9
Pf: 2 sonatas, 1952, 1963

Principal publisher: Editio Musica

F. ANDRÁS WILHEIM

Székely, Mihály (*b* Jászberény, 8 May 1901; *d* Budapest, 6 March 1963). Hungarian bass. He studied with Géza László, and made his début at the Budapest Municipal Theatre in 1923 as the Hermit (*Der Freischütz*). He joined the Budapest Opera the same year, making his début there as Ferrando in *Il trovatore*, and was soon singing leading bass roles such as Cardinal Brogni (*La juive*), Mephistopheles (*Faust*), Sarastro and King Marke; he was later made a life member of the opera house. An international career developed after World War II: his Metropolitan début (17 January 1946) was as Hunding, after which he sang many Wagner and other bass roles in New York until 1949. At Glyndebourne, from 1957 to 1961, his Sarastro, Osmin, Bartolo (*Figaro*) and Rocco were greatly admired. He played Boris in Paris (1957), and Bluebeard throughout Europe, partly transposed for his bass range by the composer (he also recorded the part). Székely was one of the greatest figures in the history of Hungarian opera, with a voice of intrinsically beautiful quality and wide range (his lowest notes were of particularly powerful 'black' timbre), and outstanding acting ability in many parts. In addition to those already mentioned, his Philip (*Don Carlos*), Fiesco (*Simon Boccanegra*), Dosifey (*Khovanshchina*) and Khan Konchak (*Prince Igor*) were all memorable portrayals.

BIBLIOGRAPHY
P. Várnai: *Székely Mihály* (Budapest, 1967)

PÉTER P. VÁRNAI

Székely, Zoltán (*b* Kocs, 8 Dec 1903). Hungarian violinist and composer. He studied the violin under Hubay and composition under Kodály in Budapest. He toured widely as a soloist and became the leader of the Hungarian String Quartet shortly after its foundation in 1935, a position that he held until the quartet disbanded. Székely was closely associated with Bartók both as his partner in sonata recitals and as an interpreter of his works; Bartók composed his Second Violin Concerto for Székely who gave the first performance in Amsterdam with the Concertgebouw Orchestra under Mengelberg in March 1939. In 1950 Székely moved to the USA. His compositions, mainly chamber music, include a string quartet, a duo for violin and cello and a sonata for unaccompanied violin. His arrangement for violin and piano of Bartók's *Romanian Dances* has become popular.

BIBLIOGRAPHY
J. Creighton: *Discopaedia of the Violin, 1889–1971* (Toronto, 1974), 747

RONALD KINLOCH ANDERSON

Székelyhidy, Ferenc (*b* Tövis, 4 April 1885; *d* Budapest, 27 June 1954). Hungarian tenor. He studied singing in Kolozsvár while practising as a lawyer. After joining the Budapest Opera House in 1909, he appeared in a wide range of roles both lyric and dramatic, from Tamino, Belmonte and Ottavio to Lohengrin, Parsifal and Radamès. He distinguished himself less by his voice alone, which lacked power, than by his stylistic understanding and interpretative force. A leading oratorio singer and exponent of new Hungarian music, he was the first tenor soloist in Kodály's *Psalmus hungaricus*. Kodály dedicated volumes six and seven of his *Magyar népzene* ('Hungarian folk music') to Székelyhidy, who recorded several arrangements with Bartók's piano accompaniment.

BIBLIOGRAPHY
Z. Kodály: 'Székelyhidy Ferenc koporsójánál' [At the grave of Ferenc Székelyhidy], *Visszatekintés* [In retrospect], ed. F. Bónis, Magyar zenetudományi, v–vi (Budapest, 1964, enlarged 2/1974)

PÉTER P. VÁRNAI

Szelényi, István (*b* Zólyom, 8 Aug 1904; *d* Budapest, 31 Jan 1972). Hungarian composer and musicologist. He studied at the Budapest Academy of Music with Kodály (composition) and Laub and Székely (piano). After a period of piano teaching at the Fodor Music School (1926–30), he lived in Paris and London as music director of a ballet company (1930–32). In 1945 he was appointed professor at the Budapest Conservatory, of which he later became director. He was also editor-in-chief of the *Uj zenei szemle* (1951–6) and a theory teacher at the Budapest Academy of Music (1956–72). In 1969 he received the Erkel Prize.

The 1920s and 1930s were Szelényi's best creative period. At the very beginning of his career he provoked a press attack because of his 'incomprehensibility', a charge which prompted a lengthy defence from Kodály in support of the young composers who were his pupils. As a pianist Szelényi introduced into Hungary works by Schoenberg, Hindemith and others, and this involvement with new music, together with his contacts with the 'activist-constructivist' circle around the poet and painter Lajos Kassák, was of decisive influence. His style at that time owed nothing to Bartók or Kodály: the shrill, vivid quality of his *Ouverture activiste* and the monomotivic structures of his songs and chamber music were entirely individual. In the years around and after World War II, however, his music became increasingly diatonic and he came under the influence of Kodály. His research on Liszt also left its mark, and only in his last years did he return to his constructivist style.

WORKS
(selective list)

Pantomimes: A tékozló fiu [The prodigal son], 1931; Babiloni vásár [Babylon fair], 1931

Orch: Sym. no.1, 1926; Vn Conc., 1930; Ouverture activiste, 1931; Triple Conc., pf trio, wind, 1933; Géptánc–munkatánc [Machine dance–work dance], 1942; Az ősök nyomában [In the footsteps of the ancestors] [after old Hebrew melodies], sym., str, 1946; Egy gyár szimfóniája [Sym. of a factory], 1946; Hommage à Bartók, 1947; Summa vitae [after Liszt], pf, orch, 1956; Conc. da camera, 1963; Pf Conc., 1969

Choral: Absolute Choral Sym. ('text' of vowel sounds), unacc., 1925; Virata (Zweig), oratorio, 1935; Programme Suite ('text' of vowel sounds), unacc., 1940; Jewish Folk Choruses, arrs., 1948; Spartacus, oratorio, 1960; Tiz nap, amely megrengette a világot [Ten days that shook the world], oratorio, 1964; Pro pace, oratorio, 1968

Chamber: A gyász órájában] [In the hour of mourning] (L. Kassák), Bar, hn, tpt, perc, pf, 1936; Vocalise, S, vc, 1939; 5 str qts, other works

Pf: 7 sonatas, 2 sonatinas; Colorit, 4 hands

Principal publisher: Editio Musica

WRITINGS

Rendszeres modulációtan [Methodical theory of modulation] (Budapest, 1927, 2/1960)

A zenetörténet és bölcselettörténet kapcsolatai [The interrelations of the history of music and that of philosophy] (Budapest, 1944)

Liszt élete képekben [Liszt's life in pictures] (Budapest, 1956)

A romantikus zene harmóniavilága [The harmonic realm of Romantic music] (Budapest, 1959)

A magyar zene története [The history of Hungarian music] (Budapest, 1965)

A népdalharmonizálás alapelvei [Principles of folksong harmonization] (Budapest, 1967)

BIBLIOGRAPHY

Z. Kodály: 'Tizenhárom fiatal zeneszerző' [13 young composers], *Budapesti hirlap* (14 June 1925)

L. Pollatsek: 'Jungungarische Musik', *Der Auftakt*, viii (1928), 45

J. S. Weissmann: 'The Contemporary Movement in Hungary', *Music Today* (London, 1949), 81

PÉTER P. VÁRNAI

Szeligowski, Tadeusz (*b* Lwów, 15 Sept 1896; *d* Poznań, 10 Jan 1963). Polish composer and teacher. He attended Kurz's piano classes at the conservatory of the Polish Musical Society in Lwów (1910–14), studied composition with Wallek-Walewski in Kraków, and took a law doctorate at Kraków University. From 1929 to 1931 he lived in Paris, where he had lessons with Boulanger. He taught composition in Poznań and Vilnius from 1932, and in Poznań and Warsaw after the war. In addition, he was president of the Polish Composers' Union (1951–4). Among the awards he received were a prize at the Chopin Competition (1949 for the Piano Sonata), second prize in the Polish radio competition (1949 for *Paw i dziewczyna*, 'The peacock and the maiden'), State Prize Second Class (1950), State Prize First Class (1951 for the opera *Bunt żaków*, 'The scholars' revolt') and a prize from the president of the council of ministers (1957 for his work with children and the young).

Szeligowski's development as a composer was long and full of sudden changes of direction. The technique at which he eventually arrived combined, in a somewhat loose manner, an abundance of stylistic borrowings, but with an often excessive tendency to conventionality. Though his work is rich, expansive and technically ac-

complished, revealing a definite talent, it is marked by a 'synthetic' eclecticism, drawing on such diverse sources as contemporary French music, Prokofiev, medieval music (evident in many pre-war 'archaic' works) and Polish folklore (which he arranged, as well as making stylizations for independent works). His chamber and vocal music shows a clear inability to keep up with new developments, while the eclectic character of his piano writing (in the Concerto and the Sonata, for example) blurred the virtuosity of his instrumental technique and the breadth of his emotional range. In *The Scholars' Revolt*, which is based on a 16th-century subject, he again attempted a synthesis of techniques from the 11th to the 18th century, together with more recent 'archaizing' methods. But, despite this variety of resources, the opera is saved from any disjunct stylistic variation by Szeligowski's skilful ability to bridge the old and the new.

WORKS
(selective list)

STAGE AND ORCHESTRAL

Operas: Bunt żaków [The scholars' revolt] (4, R. Brandstaetter), 1951; Krakatuk (Dziadek do orzechów) (3, K. Niyńska, after Hoffmann), 1955; Teodor Gentleman (2, C. Chruszczewski, P. Rewicz), 1960: Odys płaczący i opuszczono [Odysseus crying and abandoned] (opera-oratorio, Brandstaetter)

Ballets: Paw i dziewczyna [The peacock and the maiden] (W. Kubacki, after B. Leśmian), 1948; Mazepa (3, I. Turska, after J. Słowacki), 1957

Orch: Kaziuki, suite, 1928; Conc. for Orch, 1931; Cl Conc., 1932; Niebieski ptak [Blue bird], suite, after Maeterlinck, 1935; Epitafium na śmierć Karola Szymanowskiego, str, 1937; Pf Conc., 1941; Suita lubelska, small orch, 1945; Nocturne, 1952; Uwertura burleska, 1952; 4 Polish Dances

Incidental music

VOCAL

Choral: Kantata sportowa (K. Wierzyński), solo vv, chorus, orch, 1947; Karta serc [The charter of hearts] (J. Gisges), cantata, S, chorus, orch, 1952; Inclitus rex, oratorio, inc.; motets, folksong arrs., etc

Solo vocal orch: Rapsodia (Słowacki), S, orch, 1949; Renegat (A. Mickiewicz), B, orch, 1953; psalms, folksong arrs., etc

Songs for 1v, pf: 2 Songs (L. Staff), Bar, pf; 3 Songs (Pushkin); song (Lorca); etc

CHAMBER AND INSTRUMENTAL

Chamber: Pieśń litewska [Lithuanian song], vn, pf, 1928; 2 str qts, 1929, 1934; Fantazja, vn, pf, 1938; Nocturne, vc, pf, 1944; Orientale, vc, pf, 1945; Wind Qnt, 1950; Sonata, fl, pf, 1953; Air grave et air gai, eng hn, pf, 1954; Pf Trio, 1956; Suite, cl, vn, db

Pf: Mazurki, 1924; Album dziecięcy [Children's album], 1934; Romantyzm, study, 1937; Gitary z Zalamei [The guitars of Zalamea], 1939; Sonatina, 1940; Sonata, 1949; Drobne utwory [Little pieces], 1952; Suite, 2 pf, 1955; Na łące [On the meadow], suite, 2 pf, 1960

Principal publisher: Polskie Wydawnictwo Muzyczne

BIBLIOGRAPHY

T. Marek: 'Tadeusz Szeligowski', *Muzyka*, i/5 (1950), 28

Z. Lissa: 'Pierwsza opera w Polsce Ludowej – "Bunt żaków" Tadeusza Szeligowskiego i Romana Brandstaettera' [The first opera in People's Poland – *Bunt żaków* by Szeligowski and Brandstaetter], *Muzyka*, ii/10 (1951), 3

——: 'Bunt żaków' T. Szeligowskiego (Kraków, 1955, 2/1957)

J. Kański: ' "Mazepa" Tadeusza Szeligowskiego', *Ruch muzyczny*, iii/3 (1959), 10

Z. Mycielski: 'Tadeusz Szeligowski 1896–1963', *Ruch muzyczny*, vii/4 (1963), 4

Tadeusz Szeligowski: w 10 rocznice śmierci [On the 10th anniversary of Szeligowski's death] (Gdańsk, 1973)

BOGUSŁAW SCHÄFFER

Szell, George [Georg] (*b* Budapest, 7 June 1897; *d* Cleveland, 29 July 1970). American conductor of Hungarian birth. He grew up in Vienna, and studied with Mandyczewski (theory), J. B. Foerster and Reger (composition), and Richard Robert (piano). He made his début as a pianist in his own music at the age of 11 and as conductor of the Vienna SO at 16. After his début with the Berlin PO as composer, pianist and conductor, he was engaged by Richard Strauss for the staff of the Berlin Staatsoper in 1915. He held appointments at several German opera theatres (Darmstadt, 1921; Düsseldorf, 1922), then returning to Berlin (1924–9), where he was also professor at the Hochschule für Musik (1927–30). He was general musical director of the German Opera and Philharmonic in Prague (1929–37), then conductor of the Scottish Orchestra (1937–9). Meanwhile he had appeared widely with orchestras in the USA, Europe and the USSR. His London conducting début was in 1933. In 1939 he went to the USA; he conducted many American orchestras and at the Metropolitan Opera (1942–6).

As musical director of the Cleveland Orchestra (1946–70) he developed a superb ensemble that embodied his strict notions of discipline in producing an orchestral sound with the clarity and balance of chamber music. With that orchestra he appeared throughout the USA and Canada, visited Europe in 1957 and 1967, and toured the Far East shortly before his death. He also conducted extensively as a guest in Europe and was closely identified with the Amsterdam Concertgebouw Orchestra and the Salzburg Festival.

To the Austro-German tradition from Haydn to Richard Strauss he brought an extraordinary musical intelligence and a phenomenal memory; his approach was classical, for he shared with his idol Toscanini a dedicated respect for the composer's explicit intention, avoiding personalized emotion, showmanship and sentimentality. When chided for his reserved performance of Mozart, he replied, 'I cannot pour chocolate sauce over asparagus'. With his orchestra he was an exacting, frequently caustic, taskmaster, directing with precision and frequent indications to the players. He played relatively little contemporary music but did champion such composers as Bartók, Janáček and Walton.

Once established as a conductor, Szell composed little; among his youthful compositions were a Theme and Variations for orchestra, a Lyric Overture and various chamber and solo works for piano; he also arranged Smetana's String Quartet 'From my Life' for orchestra. His recordings with the Cleveland Orchestra, the Berlin PO, and London orchestras provide a good representation of his style and repertory.

BIBLIOGRAPHY
H. C. Schonberg: *The Great Conductors* (New York, 1967)
D. Wooldridge: *Conductor's World* (London, 1970)
H. J. Hirsh and J. Saul: 'George Szell Discography', *Grand baton*, ix (1972), 88

PHILIP HART

Szeluto, Apolinary (*b* St Petersburg, 23 July 1884; *d* Chodzież, 22 Aug 1966). Polish composer and pianist. He studied with Exner at the Saratov Conservatory, with Statkowski and Noskowski at the Warsaw Conservatory (1902–5) and with Godowsky (piano) in Berlin (1905–8); in addition he studied law in Warsaw and Dorpat (now Tartu). From 1909 to 1931 he was active as a pianist. As a composer he belonged with Szymanowski and Różycki to the group Młoda Polska. He produced an immense output – including 25 symphonies, several orchestral suites, five piano concertos, concertos for violin and cello, two masses, other choral music and songs, and chamber and instrumental works – but he had no great successes.

George Szell, c1968

BIBLIOGRAPHY
J. Kański: 'Apolinary Szeluto: 1884–1966', *Ruch muzyczny*, xi/2 (1967), 16

BOGUSŁAW SCHÄFFER

Szenci Molnár, Albert (*b* 1574; *d* 1634). Hungarian scholar and poet. He spent the greater part of his life abroad, mainly in Germany. His translation of the French Psalter with melodies, chiefly after Lobwasser's German version, was first published at Herborn in 1607 and has reappeared well over 100 times since. It is still in use, with slight modifications, in the Hungarian-speaking reformed churches in several countries and has exerted considerable influence on Hungarian folk and art music. It appears in *Régi Magyar költők tára: XVII század* ('Collection of early Hungarian poets: the 17th century'), vi, ed. B. Stoll (Budapest, 1971), the melodies having been edited, with an essay and notes, by K. Csomasz Tóth.

BIBLIOGRAPHY
L. Dézsi: *Szenczi Molnár Albert* (Budapest, 1897)
——: *Szenczi Molnár Albert naplója, levelezése, irományai* [Albert Szenci Molnár's correspondence and writings] (Budapest, 1898)
B. Árokháty: *Szenczi Molnár Albert és a genfi zsoltárok zenei ritmusa* [Albert Szenci Molnár and the musical rhythm of the Geneva Psalter] (Kecskemét, 1934)
K. Csomasz Tóth: *A református gyülekezeti éneklés* [The hymns of the reformed congregation] (Budapest, 1950)
——: *A humanista metrikus dallamok Magyarországon* [The humanist metrical tunes in Hungary] (Budapest, 1967)
G. Papp: 'Le psautier de Genève dans la Hongrie du XVIIe siècle', *SM*, ix (1967), 281

K. CSOMASZ TÓTH

Szendrei, Alfred. See SENDREY, ALFRED.

Szendy, Árpád (*b* Szarvas, 11 Aug 1863; *d* Budapest, 10 Sept 1922). Hungarian pianist, teacher and composer. He studied the piano with Henrik Gobbi and composition with Hans Koessler and in 1881 became a pupil of Liszt. From 1890 he taught the piano at the Budapest Academy of Music, where from 1911 he was professor of the master class. An excellent pianist in the Lisztian grand manner, his qualities as a teacher are indicated by the technical and cultural accomplishment of his pupils. Among his compositions are the opera *María* (1905) and orchestral and chamber works, characterized by a cultivated academicism rooted in the national idiom of the turn of the century. He also made noteworthy revisions and editions of the standard piano repertory.

BIBLIOGRAPHY

A. Tóth: 'Szendy Árpád', *Nyugat*, xv (1922), 1173

I. Molnár: 'A Szendy-iskola' [The Szendy school], *Zenei szemle*, ix (1925), 264

G. Kálmán: 'Szendy Árpád tanítói müködése' [Árpád Szendy's activity as teacher], *Zenei szemle*, xii (1928), 32

L. Veszprémi: *A magyar zongorapedagógia története* [History of Hungarian piano pedagogy] (Budapest, 1976)

JOHN S. WEISSMANN/PÉTER P. VÁRNAI

Szene (Ger.). SCENA.

Szenik, Ilona (*b* Gherla, 7 Sept 1927). Romanian-Hungarian ethnomusicologist. She studied music education at the Academy of Music in Cluj (now Cluj-Napoca), graduating in 1953; she held posts there as a part-time lecturer (1950–60), junior lecturer (1960–65) and lecturer (appointed 1965), teaching folklore in the musicology department and directing the students' teaching practice. She has collected about 3000 Hungarian and Romanian folksongs, her main research interests being the systematization of folk styles, folksong genres and methods of research.

WRITINGS

with I. Almási and I. Zsizsmann: *A lapádi erdő alatt* [Folksongs from Lopadea Nouă] (Bucharest, 1957)

with I. R. Nicola and T. Mîrza: *Curs de folclor muzical* [Lectures on musical folklore], i (Bucharest, 1963); ii (Cluj, 1969)

'Structura formei în cîntecul popular' [Formal structures in folksong], *LM*, i (1965), 141

'Amplificarea strofei melodice în unele tipuri ale cîntecului propriu-zis' [The expansion of melodic stanzas in certain types of folksong], *LM*, iii (1967), 105

'Înrudiri tipologice în cîntecul propriu-zis' [Related types in various folksongs], *LM*, iv (1968), 107

'Melodiile ritualului de înmormîntare din ținutul Năsăudului' [The melodies of ritual songs in the Năsăud district], *LM*, v (1969), 93

'Sistemul de educație muzicală Kodály', *Contribuții la educația muzicală preșcolară*, ed. A. Ivăscanu (Cluj, 1969), 131

'A balladák dallamáról' [Ballad melodies], *Háromszéki népballadák*, ed. F. Faragó (Bucharest, 1973), 52

'Kutatás és módszer' [Research and method], *Bartók-dolgozatok*, ed. F. László (Bucharest, 1974), 111

ANDRÁS BENKŐ

Szervánszky, Endre (*b* Budatétény, 1 Jan 1911). Hungarian composer and teacher. He studied the clarinet at the Budapest Academy of Music (1922–7) and then played in various orchestras before returning to the academy for composition studies with Siklós (1931–6). Until 1941 he worked as an orchestrator for Hungarian Radio and as a theory teacher in music schools. He then taught at the secondary music school in Budapest (1941–8) and was in 1948 appointed professor of composition at the Budapest Academy.

Szervánszky first came to public attention with the First String Quartet (1936–8), but he did not follow up this achievement with anything of similar importance until after World War II, when he produced a group of works influenced by Kodály and Bartók. But the works of this period (*c*1945–53) are not merely imitative: they include some of the best examples of Hungarian music of the time, such as the Clarinet Serenade (1950) and the Flute Concerto (1952–3). The latter is among his most successful compositions, typically Hungarian in its melodic writing, and rhythmically and formally irregular. A new phase opened in 1954 when Szervánszky composed a work of grander scope than any hitherto, the Concerto for Orchestra in memory of Attila József. Each of the concerto's five movements is based on a quotation from József, the freely formed music responding in a highly expressive manner to the emotional ambit of the poetry, whether meditative, desolate or frenzied. Notably, only the fourth movement is explicitly folklike in style. The odd-numbered movements show that Szervánszky was turning in the direction of Bartók, a trend confirmed by the String Quartet no.2 (1956–7) and the Wind Quintet no.2 (1957). The quartet's first ten bars expose the material for the whole work, which shows a Bartókian concern for tight thematic unity; the quintet is more calm and simple, although it clearly shows a tendency towards serialism.

With the Six Orchestral Pieces (1959) Szervánszky produced a work that marks a significant point in not only his own development but that of Hungarian music as a whole. In these pieces he employed 12-note serialism and 'point'-type scoring, but the heritage of Bartók is still evident. The work enjoyed an enormous popular success and provided the impetus for younger composers to pursue the ideas it opened up. If its historical importance appears particularly remarkable, the work's inherent qualities are equally noteworthy: it displays a mastery of new techniques, especially in the scoring for percussion (important throughout and heard alone in the first movement) and strings, and the six pieces are sharply characterized by means of texture, colour and idea. Szervánszky subsequently composed relatively little; it was not until 1963 that he produced another work of any stature, the oratorio *Requiem*, in which the immensely difficult choral music conveys the dark chaos of Pilinszky's text on the subject of Auschwitz. The Variations (1964) and the Clarinet Concerto (1965) are more direct successors to the Six Orchestral Pieces, in matters of virtuoso scoring and in their embracing of new developments within a specifically Hungarian tradition.

WORKS
(*selective list*)

STAGE AND VOCAL

Dance play: Napkeleti mese [Oriental tale], 1948–9

Choral: Folksong Suite, 1949; Honvédkantáta [Soldier's cantata], 1949; Tavaszi szél [Spring breeze], cantata, 1950; 3 Petőfi Choruses, 1953; 3 Male Choruses (ancient Chinese), 1958; Requiem (Dark Heaven) (J. Pilinszky), oratorio, 1963

Songs: 8 Petőfi Songs, 1951; 3 Songs, 1956–7

INSTRUMENTAL

Orch: 3 divertimentos, 1939, 1942, 1943; Serenade, str, 1947–8; Rhapsody, 1950; Serenade, cl, orch, 1950; Fl Conc., 1952–3; Conc. for Orch, 1954; 6 Pieces, 1959; Variations, 1964; Cl Conc., 1965

Chamber: 2 str qts, 1936–8, 1956–7; 20 Little Duets, 2 vn, 1941; Sonata, vn, pf, 1945; 25 Duos, 2 vn, 1946; Trio, fl, vn, va, 1951; Sonatina, fl, pf, 1952; 2 wind qnts, 1953, 1957; 5 Concert Etudes, fl, 1956; Suite, 2 fl, 1956; 2 Duos, 2 fl, 1972

Pf: Folksong Suite, 4 hands, 1935; Little Suite, 1939; Sonatina, 1941; Sonatina, 4 hands, 1950

Principal publisher: Editio Musica

BIBLIOGRAPHY

I. Barna: *Szervánszky Endre* (Budapest, 1965)

F. ANDRÁS WILHEIM

Szeryng, Henryk (*b* Warsaw, 22 Sept 1918). Mexican violinist of Polish birth. He was given childhood piano lessons by his mother, but turned instead to the violin. On the advice of Bronisław Huberman he was sent to

Henryk Szeryng

Berlin in 1928 to study with Flesch, and in 1933 he made his débuts in four European capitals. An interest in composition led him to spend six years until 1939 as a student of Nadia Boulanger in Paris. After the Nazi invasion of Poland his fluent command of seven languages brought about his appointment to the staff of General Sikorski, head of the Polish government in exile, with whom he travelled to Mexico to find homes for refugees; and during the war years he also gave more than 300 concerts for Allied troops in Europe, Asia, Africa and the Americas.

In 1946 Szeryng began teaching at the University of Mexico; he made his home there and took Mexican nationality. It was due mainly to the encouragement of Artur Rubinstein that he resumed concert touring on an international scale from 1954, gaining widespread admiration for his technical command, stylistic versatility and patrician elegance in established works of the concerto repertory. Among his gramophone records are the complete Mozart works for violin and orchestra. He has strongly advocated the merits of native Mexican composers by performing their music, and over a dozen major works have been written for him. He continues to teach regularly in Mexico, and also has about 50 pupils in 26 other countries.

BIBLIOGRAPHY

A. Blyth: 'Henryk Szeryng Talks', *Gramophone*, xlvii (1969), 547
J. Creighton: *Discopaedia of the Violin, 1889–1971* (Toronto, 1974)
NOËL GOODWIN

Joseph Szigeti

Szigeti, Joseph (*b* Budapest, 5 Sept 1892; *d* Lucerne, 19 Feb 1973). American violinist of Hungarian birth. He was given lessons by his father and uncle, both professional musicians, until he became a pupil of Jenő Hubay at the Budapest Academy. He began to play in public at the age of ten, and made his formal début in Berlin in 1905. He earned praise from Joachim but did not accept an offer to study with him. After his London début in 1907, Szigeti remained in Britain until 1913, giving numerous concerts, including the première in 1909 of the concerto written for him by Hamilton Harty. He also appeared with Melba and Blanche Marchesi, and played sonatas with Myra Hess, Lengyel and Busoni (the last-named was a strong influence on his musical development). His career was interrupted by World War I, and from 1917 to 1924 he gave master classes at the Geneva Conservatory. He then resumed his concert career, which expanded rapidly. He visited the USSR 11 times between 1924 and 1927, introducing Prokofiev's Concerto no.1 in Leningrad in 1924 after its Paris première the year before (and his own performance of it at the 1924 ISCM Festival in Prague). Equally successful was his American début in Philadelphia in 1925 under Stokowski.

During the 1930s Szigeti toured the Far East, Australia and New Zealand, South America and South Africa, and in 1938 he gave the world première of Bloch's concerto in Cleveland. He renewed an earlier friendship with Bartók when the latter went to the USA, appeared with him at a memorable concert in the Library of Congress in Washington, DC, in 1940, and gave many outstanding performances of his Concerto no.2, as well as the première of *Contrasts*. Szigeti settled in the USA in 1940 and became a citizen in 1951. After World War II he took part in the 1950 Casals Festival at Prades, and in 1952 gave the first performances of Frank Martin's concerto in Europe and the USA. After further tours he made his home in Switzerland in 1960 and gradually withdrew from concert activities. He turned to writing, published works on the violin and its repertory, and expanded his autobiography, first published in 1947. He accepted a few pupils and served on the juries of many international violin competitions, where his wise counsel and consistent musical integrity were an example to others.

Although Szigeti began as a child prodigy, his career did not flourish until he was in his 30s. His was a talent that needed time to mature, and he gradually abandoned all the trappings of the virtuoso repertory. By avoiding showmanship he made virtuosity seem easy. His unaccompanied Bach playing was exemplary (and inspired Ysaÿe to write his solo sonatas, of which the first is dedicated to Szigeti). Although his playing of Mozart was somewhat lacking in charm, he fully conveyed the impassioned grandeur of Beethoven and Brahms. He played contemporary music with enormous conviction and persuaded concert managers and recording companies to accept a repertory that stressed contemporary works. Many composers dedicated works to him; these include Bartók's Rhapsody no.1 and *Contrasts*, Rawsthorne's sonata, Bloch's *La nuit exotique* and Prokofiev's *Melody* op.35*bis* no.5, as well as the concertos by Casella, Harty and Frank Martin. He revived Busoni's concerto, and was a tireless advocate of Berg, Milhaud, Ravel, Roussel, Stravinsky and others. Among his numerous transcriptions for violin and piano are Elgar's Serenade for Strings and movements from the

Capriol Suite by Warlock; he also wrote cadenzas and edited a number of concertos and sonatas.

Szigeti's performing technique was not always flawless and his tone lacked sensuous beauty, although it acquired a spiritual quality in moments of inspiration. He played a Guarneri violin that previously belonged to Henri Petri. Szigeti held the bow in an old-fashioned way, with the elbow close to the body, and produced much emphatic power, but not without extraneous sounds. Minor reservations, however, were swept aside by the force of his musical personality.

WRITINGS

With Strings Attached (New York, 1947/*R*1979, 2/1967) [with discography]
A Violinist's Notebook (London, 1964)
ed. P. Roland: *The Ten Beethoven Sonatas for Piano and Violin* (Urbana, Ill., 1965)
Beethovens Violinwerke (Zurich, 1965)
Szigeti on the Violin (London, 1969, 2/1979)

BIBLIOGRAPHY

C. Flesch: *Memoirs* (London, 1957, 2/1958; Ger. orig., Freiburg, 1960, 2/1961)
J. Hartnack: *Grosse Geiger unserer Zeit* (Gütersloh, 1968)
J. Soroker: *Szigeti* (Moscow, 1968)
L. N. Raaben: *Zhizn' zamechatel'nïkh skripachey i violonchelistov* [The lives of famous violinists and cellists] (Leningrad, 1969)
J. Creighton: *Discopaedia of the Violin, 1889–1971* (Toronto, 1974)

BORIS SCHWARZ

Sziklay, Erika (*b* Budapest, 4 March 1936). Hungarian soprano. She studied in Budapest, at the Bartók Conservatory (1952–7) and the Academy (1957–60). After making her concert début in 1960, she studied with Heinz Rehfuss in Darmstadt (1963) and with Glettenberg in Cologne (1966). An outstanding singer of contemporary music, she has given the first performances of many Hungarian works, and the Hungarian premières of music by Schoenberg, Berg, Webern, Boulez, Lutosławski and Dallapiccola. She first sang abroad at Cologne in 1966, appearing later at Darmstadt, Warsaw, Zagreb and Lucerne. Her recording of *Pierrot lunaire* won a Grand Prix in Paris in 1972. A singer of impeccable musicianship and intonation, she is capable of great expressiveness and has a lively sense of humour. Sziklay was appointed a professor at the Budapest Academy in 1964, was awarded the Liszt Prize in 1969 and named Artist of Merit in 1975.

PÉTER P. VÁRNAI

Szirmai [Sirmay], **Albert** (*b* Budapest, 2 July 1880; *d* New York, 15 Jan 1967). American composer and publisher of Hungarian origin. Until 1906 he studied the piano with Árpád Szendy and composition with Hans Koessler at the Budapest Academy of Music, where he received the Volkmann Prize for composition, and at the same time he read political science at the university. While still a student he was second music critic of the Budapest German newspaper *Pester Lloyd*, and later he held a similar post on the Hungarian newspaper *Polgár*. In 1907 he took over the musical direction of the Budapest theatre Modern Szinpad, for which he wrote some 300 songs and the music for 12 one-act plays. After the success of his first operetta (1907) he remained faithful to that genre. From 1926 until his death he lived in New York as musical director for Chappell.

Szirmai belonged, with Kálmán and Jacobi, to the trio of composers who at the beginning of the 20th century raised Hungarian operetta to international status. He was influenced chiefly by the music of Schumann and Mendelssohn. From the former he learnt depth of expression, from the latter elegant lightness of touch. The influence of German Romanticism was combined in his operettas with those of Hungarian popular music and the French chanson of the turn of the century. The resulting idiosyncrasy of style remained even in his late works: jazz was not reflected in his music, although in America he was one of Gershwin's best friends and the editor of his musical estate.

WORKS
(*selective list*)
STAGE

A sárga dominó [The yellow domino] (operetta, 3, A. Mérei), Budapest, Népszínház-Vígopera, 4 Oct 1907
Bálkirályné [The belle of the ball] (operetta, 2, Á. Pásztor), Budapest, Népszínház-Vígopera, 16 Nov 1907
Naftalin [Naphthalene] (musical comedy, 3, J. Heltai), Budapest, Vígszínház, 6 June 1908
Táncos huszárok [Dancing hussars] (operetta, 3, F. Rajna, E. Szép), Budapest, Király, 7 Jan 1909
A mexikói lány [The Mexican girl] (operetta, 3, Rajna, A. Gábor), Budapest, Király, 11 Dec 1912
The Girl on the Film (operetta, 3, T. Tanner, A. Ross), London, Gaiety, 5 April 1913
Ezüstpille [Silver butterfly] (musical comedy, 3, Gábor), Budapest, Vígszínház, 9 May 1914
Mágnás Miska [Magnate Miska] (operetta, 3, K. Bakonyi, Gábor), Budapest, Király, 12 Feb 1916
Harangvirág [Bellflower] (ballad, 2 tableaux, T. Emőd, F. Karinthy), Budapest, Royal Opera, 11 March 1918
Gróf Rinaldo [Count Rinaldo] (operetta, 3, Bakonyi, Gábor), Budapest, Király, 7 Nov 1918
Mézeskalács [Honey cake] (musical comedy, 3, Emőd), Budapest, Király, 15 Dec 1923
The Bamboula (operetta, 3, H. M. Vernon, G. Bolton), London, His Majesty's, 24 March 1925
Alexandra (operetta, 3, F. Martos), Budapest, Király, 25 Nov 1925
Éva grófnő [Countess Éva] (operetta, 3, Martos), Budapest, Király, 3 Feb 1928
Lady Mary (operetta, 3, F. Lonsdale, J. H. Turner, H. Graham), London, Daly's, March 1928
Ripples (musical comedy, 2, W. A. Meguire), New York, New Amsterdam, 1930
A ballerina [The ballerina] (operetta, 3, Martos), Budapest, Király, 7 March 1931
Tabáni legenda [The legend of Tabán] (operetta, 3, K. Kristóf), Budapest, Déryné, Jan 1957
A Tündérlaki lányok [The Tündérlaki sisters] (operetta, 3, E. Innocent-Vincze, after Heltai), Budapest, Operetta, 29 Jan 1964

BIBLIOGRAPHY

G. S. Gál: *Weiner Leó életműve* [The life-work of Weiner] (Budapest, 1959)
F. Bónis: 'Szirmai Alberttal, emlékeiről' [Szirmai and his recollections], *Magyar zene*, iv (1963), 503
——: 'Szirmai Albert 1880–1967', *Magyar zene*, viii (1967), 286

FERENC BÓNIS

Szokolay, Sándor (*b* Kúnágota, 30 March 1931). Hungarian composer. Born into a musical family, he began music studies early and continued them at the Békéstarhos Music College, a type of primary school which followed Kodály's ideas. He then studied composition with Szabó and Farkas at the Budapest Academy of Music, receiving his diploma in 1957. After a short period with Hungarian Radio he joined the staff of the academy in 1966. He has won two Erkel Prizes and the Kossuth Prize in 1966 for his opera *Vérnász* ('Blood wedding'), and was named Artist of Merit in 1976.

From the earliest years of his studies Szokolay composed works for young musicians, combining his needs as a young composer with those of the young performer or listener. In the late 1950s he wrote a number of instrumental pieces, notably a sonata for solo violin and concertos for piano and violin, but he soon found his métier in vocal and dramatic music. He gained an impressive success with the oratorio *A tűz márciusa* ('Fiery march', 1957–8) on revolutionary poems by Ady. The same ardent tone and a similar ideological involvement distinguish his one-act ballet *Az iszonyat balladája* ('The ballad of horror', 1960), whose subject was taken from the World War II period. Parallel with this 'committed' attitude a definite inclination towards the cults of primitive peoples developed in his work, revealed successively in the oratorio *Istár pokoljárása* ('Isthar's descent into hell', 1960), the cycle for voice and chamber orchestra *Mágikus dalok* ('Magic songs') on ancient folk poetry, and the *Néger kantáta* ('Negro cantata', 1962). In these compositions, though he did not move far from Hungarian national intonation, Szokolay made reference to the ecstatic rhythms and instinctive expression of certain African peoples, so creating an individual style that shows certain affinities with the work of Bartók, Stravinsky and Orff.

But all this was only a preparation for a major operatic undertaking, *Blood Wedding*, completed in 1964 and based on Lorca's play. By excluding the colouristic elements present in the subject Szokolay succeeded in bringing the dark and tense ambience of the drama to the music. After its première in Budapest it was quickly taken up by opera houses in Wuppertal, Zagreb, Košice, Brno, Helsinki and Tallinn. His second opera, *Hamlet*, presented in Budapest (1968) and Cologne (1970), marks a clear departure in his creative path. After the gripping and almost brutal effects of *Blood Wedding* he apparently felt it necessary to search for a more introverted style, befitting Shakespeare's drama. The manner is more limpid, the cohesive force of dodecaphonic structures (based on a fairly liberal serialism) and the refined instrumentation underlying the complexity of the action. However, Szokolay's true gifts are displayed in the bold images and frenetic dynamism of his music. It is in these that the attractive and suggestive power of his third opera, *Sámson*, resides. The 1973 production in Budapest demonstrated the very personal conception of the biblical story contained in László Németh's drama, as well as the striking musical language of the composer.

WORKS
(selective list)
STAGE

op.
8 Orbán és az ördög [Urban and the devil] (ballet, 1, after J. Arany), 1958
12 Az iszonyat balladája [The ballad of horror] (ballet, 1), 1960
19 Vérnász [Blood wedding] (opera, 3, after Lorca), 1962–4
25 Hamlet (opera, 3, after Shakespeare, trans. Arany), 1965–8
27a Extázis (ballet, 1), 1970
31 Az áldozat [The sacrifice] (oratorio-ballet, 1), 1970–71
34 Sámson (opera, 2, after L. Németh), 1971–3
Csalóka Peter [Deluded Peter] (radio opera, 1, S. Weöres), 1978

ORCHESTRAL AND VOCAL ORCHESTRAL
4 Violin Concerto, 1956–7
5 Vízimesék [Children's cantata], 1957
7 Piano Concerto, 1958
9 A tűz márciusa [Fiery march] (Ady), oratorio, 1957–8
10 Mesteremberek [Artisans], cantata, 1958
11 Világok vetélkedése [Rivalry of worlds] (Bartók), cantata, 1959
13 Istár pokoljárása [Isthar's descent into hell] (Weöres), oratorio, 1960
14 Mágikus dalok [Magic songs] (G. Kulifay, after ancient folk poetry), S, chamber orch, 1962
16 Néger kantáta [Negro cantata] (N. Guillén, trans. E. Gáspár), 1962
17 Déploration, requiem for Poulenc, pf, chorus, chamber orch, 1964

26 Trumpet Concerto, 1968
27 Magyar kórus-szimfónia (Ady), 1970
30 Apokalipszis (after Dürer), cantata, 1971
Hommage à Kodály (G. Illyés), cantata, 1975

OTHER WORKS
Choral: Révélation, op.20 (Musset), vv, org/6 wind, 1966; other pieces
Radio operas, incidental music, film scores, songs, inst pieces, educational music
Principal publisher: Editio Musica

BIBLIOGRAPHY
I. Földes: *Harmincasok* [30-year-old generation] (Budapest, 1969) [interview]
G. Kroó: *A magyar zeneszerzés harminc éve* [30 years of Hungarian music] (Budapest, 1975)

JÁNOS KÁRPÁTI

Szőllősy, András (*b* Szászváros, Transylvania, 27 Feb 1921). Hungarian composer and musicologist. He studied at Budapest University, at the High School of Musical Art under Kodály and Viski, and in Rome at the Accademia di S Cecilia under Petrassi (1947–8). In 1950 he was appointed to teach history and theory at the Budapest Academy of Music. His music uses some new techniques within a traditional manner that shows no trace of a specifically Hungarian style. The classification employed in his Bartók catalogue (a supplement to his edition of 1966) is widely accepted and is indicated by the abbreviation SZ.

WORKS
(selective list)
Ballets: Oly korban éltem [Improvisations on fright], perf. 1962; A tűz fiai [Sons of fire], 1977
Orch: Conc. I, pf, brass, perc, str, 1957; Conc. II, destroyed; Conc. III, 16 str, 1968; Conc. IV, 1970; Transfigurazioni, 1972; Musica da camera, chamber orch, 1973; Musica per orchestra, 1973; Sonorità, 1974; Conc. V 'Lehellet', 1975; Conc., hpd, str, 1978
Vocal: Nyugtalan ősz [Restless autumn] (cantata, M. Radnóti), 1v, ens, 1954; Kolozsvári éjjel [Cluj elegy] (Jékely), 1v, wind qnt, 1955; Nehéz szerelem [Difficult love] (József), song cycle
Chamber: 3 pezzi, fl, pf, 1964; Musiche per ottoni, brass, 1975
Principal publisher: Zeneműkiadó Vállalat

WRITINGS
Kodály művészete [The art of Kodály] (diss., U. of Budapest, 1943; Budapest, 1943)
ed.: *Bartók válogatott zenei írásai* [Bartók's selected writings on music] (Budapest, 1948)
ed.: Z. Kodály: *A zene mindenkié* [Music belongs to everyone] (Budapest, 1954)
ed.: *Bartók Béla válogatott írásai* [Bartók's selected writings] (Budapest, 1956)
Arthur Honegger, Kis zenei könyvtár, xvi (Budapest, 1960)
ed.: *Bartók Béla összegyűjtött írásai* [Bartók's collected writings], i (Budapest, 1966)
'Vázlatok Stravinskyról' [Stravinsky's Variations], *In memoriam Igor Stravinsky*, ed. D. Révész (Budapest, 1972), 5

JOHN S. WEISSMANN

Szomjas-Schiffert, György (*b* Dunakeszi, 25 April 1910). Hungarian ethnomusicologist. He studied composition and singing at Szeged Conservatory (graduated 1934) and law at Szeged University (doctorate 1934); he also attended Kodály's folk music lectures at the Budapest Academy (1937–8) and qualified as a librarian (1940). After working as librarian of the Central Office for Statistics (1936–44) and head of the music department of the Ministry of Culture (1945–9) he joined the folk music research group at the Hungarian Academy of Sciences (1954–73); in 1974 this became the Institute of Musicology, of which he became a member. He has collected folk music in Hungary, among Czechoslovak Hungarians (from 1957) and among Lapps in Finland (1966).

WRITINGS
'Parasztdaltól a szimfóniáig' [From the peasant song to the symphony], *Szép szó* (1936), no.8, p.43
'Liszt Ferenc es az európai kultúra' [Liszt and European culture], *Korunk szava* (1937), no.7, p.11

'Csallóközi gyüjtés' [Folk music collections in Csallóköz], *MTA nyelv-és irodalomtudományi osztályának közleményei*, xiii (1959), 215–45
'Die finnisch-ugrische Abstammung der ungarischen Regös-Gesänge und der Kalewala-Melodien', *Musik des Ostens*, ii (1963), 126–56
'Der Kalevala-Typ in den gemeinsamen Melodien der finno-ugrischen Völker', *II. congressus internationalis fenno-ugristarum: Helsinki 1965*, ii, 31
'A finnugorság ősi zenéje nyomában' [Tracing the ancestral music of Finno-Ugrians], *Magvető* (1965), no.3, pp.357–420
'Les traditions communes des peuples finno-ougriens dans leurs mélodies de danse', *Etudes finno-ougriennes*, iii (1966), 105
'Népzenegyüjtő útam a Lappföldön' [My field trip collecting folk music in Lappland], *MTA nyelv- és irodalomtudományi osztályának közleményei*, xxvi (1969), 355
Hajnal vagyon, szép piros . . . énekes várvirrasztók és órakiáltók [Nightwatcher's cries] (Budapest, 1972)
'Traditional Singing Style of the Lapps', *YIFMC*, v (1973), 51
'Melodienverwandtschaft unter den tschechisch-mährischen und ungarischen Volksliedern', *Acta ethnographica*, xxiii (Budapest, 1974)
'Geschichte und Ergebnisse der finnisch-ugrischen vergleichenden Volksmusikforschung', *IV. congressus internationalis fenno-ugristarum: Budapest 1975*, 141

BÁLINT SÁROSI

Szönyi, Erzsébet [Elisabeth] (*b* Budapest, 25 April 1924). Hungarian composer and educationist. She studied at the Budapest Academy (teacher's diploma 1947) and the Paris Conservatoire (1948) under Aubin and Messiaen; she also studied privately with Boulanger. In 1948 she became lecturer at the Budapest Academy, becoming head of the teacher-training department in 1960. Having worked with Kodály, she has played an important part in implementing his teaching methods in Hungarian schools and abroad. Her compositions include four operas (*Dalma*, 1952; *A makrancos királylány*, 'The stubborn princess', 1955; *Firenzei tragédie*, after Wilde's *A Florentine Tragedy*, 1957; and *Az aranyszárnyú méhecske*, 'The little bee with the golden wing', 1974) and other stage works, as well as several choral, orchestral, instrumental and piano pieces. Among her most important writings are the four-volume *A zenei írás-olvasás módszertana* ('Methods of musical reading and writing', Budapest, 1953–65; Eng. trans., 1972) and a book on Kodály's teaching methods (Budapest, 1973), which has been translated into many languages.

Szopski, Felicjan (*b* Krzeszowice, nr. Kraków, 5 May 1865; *d* Warsaw, 28 Sept 1939). Polish composer, teacher and critic. He read philosophy at the University of Kraków, where concurrently he studied the piano and theory with Domaniewski and composition with Żeleński (1885–92). Later he was a pupil of Noskowski in Warsaw, Urban in Berlin and Riemann in Leipzig. He was a professor at the Kraków Conservatory (1893–1907) and then in Warsaw, being active as a music critic in both cities. His works, cast in a Romantic style, include the opera *Lilie* ('Lilies', three acts, libretto by H. Zbierzchowski and Szopski after A. Mickiewicz), a *Preludium symfoniczne* for orchestra, piano pieces, choruses and songs. He also wrote a monograph on his teacher, *Władysław Żeleński* (Warsaw, 1928).

MIECZYSŁAWA HANUSZEWSKA

Szostek-Radkowa, Krystyna (*b* Katowice, 14 March 1933). Polish mezzo-soprano. She studied at the State Music High School, Katowice (1955–9), with Argasińska, Lenczewska and Łozińska, and was a prizewinner at the Geneva (1958), Vercelli (1960) and Sofia (1961) competitions. She was a soloist at the Bytom State Opera (1957–62) and, from 1962, at the Wielki Theatre, Warsaw. In Poland she is ranked among the finest performers of oratorio, opera and contemporary

music (among other roles, she created the lead in Tadeusz Baird's *Conrad* opera *Jutro*). Her many European appearances include those during the Polish National Opera's 1976 visit to Lisbon, as Sister Jeanne in Penderecki's *The Devils of Loudun*.

MIECZYSŁAWA HANUSZEWSKA

Sztompka, Henryk (*b* Bogusławce, nr. Łuck, 4 April 1901; *d* Kraków, 21 June 1964). Polish pianist and teacher. He studied at the Warsaw Conservatory under Turczyński (diploma 1926) and later under Paderewski in Morges, Switzerland (1928–32). He also studied at the philosophy department of Warsaw University. In 1927 he won a prize for the best performance of mazurkas at the Chopin International Competition in Warsaw. He gave concerts in many countries, including Britain, Austria, Belgium, Czechoslovakia, France, Holland, Germany, Switzerland, the USSR and Turkey, and also in South America. From 1945 he taught at the State Music High School in Kraków, where Regina Smendzianka was among his pupils. He served on the juries of many international piano competitions, and in 1956 in Leipzig he gave a course on the interpretation of Chopin. He received many state awards, including the Cavalier Cross of the Order of Polonia Restituta, the Gold Cross of Merit and the Cross of the Hungarian Republic. He wrote a monograph on Artur Rubinstein (Kraków, 1966).

BIBLIOGRAPHY
K. Tarnowski: 'Artysta i cztowiek: Henryk Sztompka' [Artists and men], *Ruch muzyczny*, viii (1964)

MIECZYSŁAWA HANUSZEWSKA

Szulc. Polish family of musicians.

(1) **Henryk Szulc** (*b* Warsaw, 31 Jan 1836; *d* Warsaw, 11 Feb 1903). Violinist and composer. He led the Warsaw Opera orchestra and taught the violin at the conservatory. At his silver jubilee concert in the Reduta Hall, Warsaw, he and his six sons played the Beethoven Septet. He was renowned for his memory, knowing by heart almost all the parts of any chamber work in which he had ever played.

(2) **Józef Zygmunt** [Joseph Sigismond] **Szulc** (*b* Warsaw, 4 April 1875; *d* Paris, 10 April 1956). Pianist and composer, son of (1) Henryk Szulc. He studied at the Warsaw Conservatory, where Noskowski was his composition teacher, and continued his piano studies with Moszkowski. Although he established himself as a pianist, he soon withdrew from the concert platform and turned successfully to composition. His works include many *opérettes-bouffes* (listed in *Grove 5*) written for the interwar Paris theatre, a ballet, overtures, chamber music and piano pieces.

(3) **Bronisław Szulc** (*b* Warsaw, 24 Dec 1881; *d* Tel-Aviv, 17 July 1955). Conductor and composer, son of (1) Henryk Szulc. He studied composition with Noskowski at the Warsaw Conservatory and played the horn in the opera-house orchestra (1899–1908). In 1909 he went to Germany to continue his studies with Riemann (theory) and Nikisch (conducting). Two years later he returned to Poland and began to make a reputation as a conductor both there and abroad. Subsequently he emigrated to Israel and directed an orchestra in Tel-Aviv. His works include two symphonic poems and chamber music.

(4) **Józef Szulc** (*b* Warsaw, 1893). Pianist and composer, grandson of (1) Henryk Szulc. He studied at the Warsaw Conservatory and with Busoni (piano) at the

Stern Conservatory, Berlin. His début was with the Warsaw PO in Mozart's D minor Concerto (1903). After World War I he was appointed to teach piano at the Strasbourg Conservatory, whence he moved to Switzerland and then to Cairo, where he founded the Szulc Conservatory. He composed many songs and works for solo piano and for cello.

CZESŁAW R. HALSKI/R

Szweykowski, Zygmunt Marian (*b* Kraków, 12 May 1929). Polish musicologist. He studied musicology at Poznań University under Chybiński, graduating in 1951, and under Chomiński at Kraków University, where he took his doctorate in 1964 with a dissertation on concertato technique in the Polish Baroque. He was Chybiński's assistant at the musicology faculty of Poznań University (1950–53) before moving to Kraków, where he was appointed editor of the Polish music publishers, Polskie Wydawnictwo Muzyczne (1954–61), as well as lecturer (1954–69), reader (1970–71) and director (1971–4) of the musicology faculty of Kraków University.

Szweykowski is one of the leading Polish musicologists of his generation. His interests are mainly in the historical aspects of music (especially Polish) and Italian cultural history. He worked first on the Renaissance and did intensive research into Baroque music, especially that of the 17th century. His editions of early Polish music are highly regarded; he has also initiated and edited a number of established journals. He developed Wydawnictwo Dawnej Muzyki Polskiej, which from volume li (1964) he co-edited with Feicht, and founded Źródła do Historii Muzyki Polskiej (1960), Symfonie Polskie (1964) and the *Katalog tematyczny rękopiśmiennych zabytków dawnej muzyki w Polsce* ('Thematic catalogue of early music manuscripts in Poland', 1969). He has also edited important individual anthologies, such as *Muzyka w dawnym Krakowie* ('Music in ancient Kraków'; Kraków, 1964) and such comprehensive works as *Z dziejów polskiej kultury muzycznej* ('From the history of Polish musical culture'; Kraków, 1958).

WRITINGS

Kultura wokalna XVI-wiecznej Polski [The vocal culture of 16th-century Poland] (Kraków, 1957)
ed.: *Z dziejów polskiej kultury muzycznej* (Kraków, 1958) [incl. 'Rozkwit wielogłosowości w XVI-w.' [The development of polyphony in the 16th century], 79–156]
'Franciszek Lilius i jego twórczość na tle współczesnego baroku w Polsce' [Franciszek Lilius and his work in the context of contemporary Baroque in Poland], *Muzyka*, v/1 (1960), 78; vii/4 (1962), 51
'Proces przemian stylistycznych w muzyce wokalno–instrumentalnej epoki saskiej' [The process of stylistic change in vocal–instrumental music of the Saxon era], *Chopin Congress: Warszawa 1960*, 633
'Z zagadnień melodyki w polskiej muzyce wokalno–instrumentalnej późnego baroku' [Problems of melody in Polish vocal–instrumental music of the late Baroque], *Muzyka*, vi/2 (1961), 53
'Sylwetka kompozytorska Damiana Stachowicza (1658–1699)' [An outline of the compositions of Damian Stachowicz (1658–1699)], *Muzyka*, vii/1 (1962), 14
'Eliasz karmelita, nieznany staropolski kompozytor' [Elias the Carmelite, an unknown early Polish composer], *Z dziejów muzyki polskiej*, vii (1964), 110
Technika koncertująca w polskiej muzyce wokalno–instrumentalnej okresu baroku [Concertato technique in Polish vocal–instrumental music of the Baroque] (diss., U. of Kraków, 1964); extracts in *Muzyka*, xv/1 (1970), 3; Eng. trans. in *Polish Musicological Studies*, i (1977) and in *Studia Hieronymo Feicht septuagenario dedicata* (Kraków, 1967), 220
with A. Szweykowska: 'Wacław z Szamotuł – renesansowy muzyk i poeta' [Wacław of Szamotuł – Renaissance musician and poet], *Muzyka*, ix/1–2 (1964), 3
with J. Buba and A. Szweykowska: 'Kultura muzyczna pijarów polskich

w XVII i XVIII wieku' [Music culture of the Polish Piarists in the 16th and 17th centuries], *Muzyka*, x (1965), no.2, p.15; no.3, p.20
'Próba periodyzacji okresu baroku w Polsce' [An attempt at the periodization of the Polish Baroque], *Muzyka*, xi/1 (1966), 17
'Some Problems of Baroque Music in Poland', *Musica antiqua Europae orientalis I: Bydgoszcz 1966*, 294
'The Choice of Means of Performance in Seventeenth-century Polish Vocal–Instrumental Music', *Musica antiqua: Brno II 1967*, 82
' "Missa sub concerto" Adama Jarzębskiego', *Muzyka*, xiii/4 (1968), 28
'Problem przełomu stylistycznego między renesansem i barokiem w muzyce polskiej', *Musica antiqua Europae orientalis II: Bydgoszcz 1969*, 209
'Tradition and Popular Elements in Polish Music of the Baroque Era', *MQ*, lvi (1970), 99
' "Ah dolente partita": Monteverdi – Scacchi', *Quadrivium*, xii/2 (1971), 59
'Praktyka wykonawcza jako przedmiot badania muzykologicznego' [Performing practice as a subject of musicological research], *Muzyka*, xvi/3 (1971), 38
'Muzyczne poszukiwania w bibliotekach szwedzkich' [Musical searches in Swedish libraries], *Muzyka*, xvi/4 (1971), 97
'Tańce polskie w zbiorze "Delitiae musicae" Mikołaja Hassego' [Polish dances in Nikolaus Hasse's collection *Delitiae musicae*], *Muzyka*, xvi/4 (1971), 91
'Kilka uwag o twórczości mszalnej Giovanni Francesco Aneria związanej z Polska' [Some thoughts on the masses of Giovanni Francesco Anerio and their links with Poland], *Muzyka*, xvii/4 (1972), 53
'Poglądy Scacchiego na muzykę jako sztukę' [Scacchi's views on music as art], *Pagine*, i (Warsaw, 1972), 17
'Unikalne druki utworow Asprilia Pacellego' [Unique prints of the works of Asprilio Pacelli], *Muzyka*, xvii/1 (1972), 74
'Czy istnieje manieryzm, jako okres w historii muzyki?' [Does mannerism exist as a period in music history?], *Muzyka*, xviii/1 (1973), 32
'Jan Brant (1544–1602) i jego nowoodkryta twórczość muzyczna' [Jan Brant and his newly discovered music], *Muzyka*, xviii/2 (1973), 43
'Stile imbastardito i stile rappresentativo w systemie teoretycznym Marka Scacchiego', *Muzyka*, xix/1 (1974), 11
Problematyka stylistyczna polskiego baroku (Kraków, in preparation)
Musica moderna w ujęciu Marka Scacchiego [Scacchi's defence of modern music] (Habilitationsschrift, U. of Kraków; in preparation)

EDITIONS

S. S. Szarzyński: *Ad hymnos ad cantus*, WDMP, xxvi (1954, 2/1964); *Ave regina*, WDMP, xxv (1954, 2/1964); *Litania cursoria*, WDMP, lxxii (1974)
Wacław z Szamotuł: *Pieśni*, WDMP, xxviii (1956, 4/1973)
T. Szadek: *Officium 'Dies est laetitiae'*, WDMP, xxxiii (1957)
C. Bazylik: *Pieśni*, WDMP, xxxiv (1958)
M. Mielczewski: *Veni Domine*, WDMP, xxxviii (1958, 2/1972); *Vesperae dominicales*, WDMP, xlii (1962); *Canzoni a 2*, WDMP, xxix (1963); *Canzoni a 3*, WDMP, lxi (1966); *Triumphalis dies*, Muzyka staropolska (1966); *Benedictio et claritas*, WDMP, lxvi (1969)
F. Lilius: *Iubilate Deo*, WDMP, xl (1959, 2/1964); *Tua Jesu dilectio*, WDMP, lvi (1965)
J. Różycki: *Exsultemus omnes*, WDMP, xliv (1961, 2/1966); *Magnificat*, WDMP, liv (1964); *Confitebor*, WDMP, lx (1966); *Iste sanctus*, Muzyka staropolska (1966)
Muzyka w dawnym Krakowie [Music in ancient Kraków] (Kraków, 1964)
M. Zieleński: *In Monte Oliveti*, WDMP, liii (1964, 2/1974); *Communiones a 3*, I, WDMP, lxx (1973)
J. Kobierkowicz: *Ego mater*, WDMP, lv (1965)
M. Wronowicz: *Koncerty wokalno–instrumentalne*, ZHMP, viii (1965)
J. P. Habermann: *Utwory wokalno–instrumentalne*, ZHMP, x (1966)
B. Pękiel: *Audite mortales*, WDMP, iv (1968); *Missa a 14*, WDMP, lxix (1971)
Muzyka wokalno–instrumentalna, muzyka a cappella, MAP, 3rd ser., Barok, i (1969); *Muzyka instrumentalna, tance i piesni*, ibid, ii (1969); *Noty*, ibid, iii (1969)
J. Brant: *Utwory zebrane* [Collected works], ZHMP, xxiv (1975)

MIROSŁAW PERZ

Szydłowita [Szydłovita]. Polish 15th-century music theorist. His surname is derived from the town of Szydłów or Szydłowiec (Feicht, *MGG*) in central Poland. He was the author of the treatise *Musica magistri Szydlovite* (in *PL-GNd* 200, a manuscript originating in the Benedictine monastery in Lubiń, Great Poland; ed. in Gieburowski). He may be identifiable with one of four 'De Szydlov' associated with Kraków University in the 15th century. These were

Johannes (*artium baccalarius* connected with the Collegium Jerusalem, 1414; copyist of the treatise by Jehan des Murs), Johannes (*magister*, 1475), Jacobus (*artium baccalarius*, 1480) and Matthias (*magister et senior domus Jerusalem*, 1469; *decretorum doctor, cantor ecclesiae S. Floriani et plebanus* at Ilkusz, 1486; *s. theologiae professor et doctor, rector Universitatis, decanus S. Floriani, canonicus ecclesiae cathedralis Cracoviensis*, 1489; *ratione inoboedientie excommunicata*, 1513). The author of the treatise is usually thought to be the first of the above (Jachimecki, Feicht), but the manuscript tradition to which *Musica magistri Szydlovite* belongs indicates one of the later figures.

The treatise is concerned with Gregorian chant; it contains 14 chapters and its 'intencio est scolarum in musica minus perfectorum erudicio'. Szydłowita used two chief models: a lost treatise by Theogerus, a Benedictine monk from Metz (not the text *Musica* published by Gerbert); and the work of Joannes Olendrinus (called Hollandrinus in other sources), surely identifiable with Valendrinus, author of *Opusculum monocordale* (in *WRu* IV Qn 81, from Głogów, *c*1450; edn. by Feldmann). Szydłowita's *Musica* displays numerous connections with *Opusculum*. Quotations from Valendrinus appear in seven texts (including Anonymous XI, *CS*, iii, 416–75) written in the second half of the 15th century in areas around Poland – Bohemia, Hungary and southern Germany. It is most probable that Szydłowita's *Musica* – the oldest Polish musical treatise whose author is known – was written at this time.

BIBLIOGRAPHY
SMP
E. Nikel: *Geschichte der katholischen Kirchenmusik*, i (Breslau, 1908), 249, 369
W. Gieburowski: *Die 'Musica Magistri Szydlovite', ein polnischer Choraltraktat des XV. Jahrhunderts und seine Stellung in der Choraltheorie des Mittelalters, mit Berücksichtigung der Choraltheorie und -Praxis des XV. Jahrhunderts in Polen, sowie der nachtridentinischen Choralreform* (Posen, 1915)
——: *Choral gregorjański w Polsce od XV do XVII wieku* (Poznań, 1922)
F. Feldmann: *Musik und Musikpflege im mittelalterlichen Schlesien* (Breslau, 1938)
Z. Jachimecki: *Muzyka polska w rozwoju historycznym* [Polish music in its historical development], i/1 (Kraków, 1948), 40
A. Chybiński: *Słownik muzyków dawnej Polski* [Dictionary of early Polish musicians] (Kraków, 1949), 162
F. Merlan: 'Music in Poland: the Fifteenth Century', in G. Reese: *Music in the Renaissance* (New York, 1954, rev. 2/1959), 741
H. Feicht: 'Muzyka liturgiczna w polskim średniowieczu', *Musica medii aevi*, i (Kraków, 1965), 9–52
——: 'Szydłowita', *MGG*
E. Witkowska: 'Anonimowy traktat chorałowy ze zbiorów Biblioteki Ossolineum' [An anonymous plainchant treatise from the Ossolineum Library Collection], *Muzyka*, xx/2 (1975)
MIROSŁAW PERZ

Szymanowska [née Wołowska], **Maria Agata** (*b* Warsaw, 14 Dec 1789; *d* St Petersburg, 24 July 1831). Polish pianist and composer. She studied in Warsaw with Antoni Lisowski (1798–1800) and Tomasz Gremm (1800–04). In 1810 she made her début as a concert pianist in Warsaw and Paris; there she won the admiration of Cherubini, who dedicated to her his Fantasia in C major for piano. From 1815 until 1828 she gave concerts in Poland, Austria, France, England, Belgium, Holland, Italy and Russia, and in 1822 received the title of First Pianist to the Russian court. During her concert tours she enjoyed enormous success everywhere, gaining the highest approbation and the respect of all the eminent people of the day: Goethe

wrote his *Aussöhnung* verses for her, and in Berlin and London the royal courts attended her concerts. In 1828 she settled in St Petersburg, ending her performing career and devoting herself to teaching. Her salon was frequented by the social and artistic élite of the capital, among them Mickiewicz, Pushkin and Glinka.

Szymanowska's compositions for piano, particularly her studies (*Vingt exercices et préludes*), nocturnes and dance miniatures, herald Romanticism in style, and demonstrate new technical and colouristic possibilities for the instrument; they occupy an important position in the history of Polish music before Chopin.

WORKS

Chamber: Divertissement, vn, pf (Leipzig, 1820); Sérénade, vc, pf (Leipzig, 1820); Fanfara dwugołosowa [2-pt. fanfare], 2 hn, 2 tpt, *PL-Kj*; Thème varié, pf, fl/vn, lost
Pf: 20 exercices et préludes (Leipzig, 1820); Caprice sur la romance de Joconde (Leipzig, 1820); 6 Marches (Leipzig, 1820); Grande valse, pf 4 hands (Leipzig, 1820); 6 Minuets (Leipzig, 1820); 18 Danses (Leipzig, 1820); Romance (Leipzig, 1820); Polonaise sur l'air national favori du feu Prince Joseph Poniatowsky (Leipzig, 1820); Fantaisie, F (Leipzig, 1820); 4 valses, pf 3 hands (Warsaw, 1822); Danse polonaise (Paris, 1824); Cotillon ou valse figurée (Paris, 1824); Nocturne 'Le murmure' (Paris, 1825); 24 Mazurkas (Leipzig, 1826); Nocturne, B♭ (St Petersburg, 1826); Preludium, B♭, *Kj*; Valse, d, *Kj*; Temat wariacji [Theme for variations], b♭, *Kj*
Vocal: [5] śpiewów historycznych [Historic songs], 3 pubd (Warsaw, 1816), 2 in *Kj*; Le départ (Cervantes) (Leipzig, 1820); 6 Romances (Shakespeare, Saint-Onge, F. de Berni) (Leipzig, 1820); Śpiewka na powrót wojsk polskich [Song on the return of the Polish armies] (L. Dmuszewski) (Warsaw, 1822); Mazurek (A. Gorecki) (Warsaw, 1822); Świtezianka [The water sprite] (Mickiewicz) (Moscow, 1828); 3 pieśni (Mickiewicz) (Kiev and Odessa, 1828); Romance à Joséphine, *Kj*
BIBLIOGRAPHY
M. Iwanejko: *Maria Szymanowska* (Kraków, 1959)
ALINA NOWAK-ROMANOWICZ

Szymanowski, Karol (Maciej) (*b* Tymoszówka, Ukraine, 6 Oct 1882; *d* Lausanne, 29 March 1937). Polish composer. He was a central figure in Polish music in the first half of the 20th century.

1. Background and early career. 2. The World War I period. 3. The 1920s. 4. The 1930s. 5. Music.

1. BACKGROUND AND EARLY CAREER. At the time of Szymanowski's birth, Tymoszówka was in that part of the former kingdom of Poland which had been annexed to the Russian Empire. The Szymanowski family, like most of the other landed gentry of the region, were of long-established Polish extraction, and the composer's father, Stanisław Korwin-Szymanowski, was a convinced Polish patriot as well as an ardent connoisseur of the arts. The cultural atmosphere of the house was further sustained by contacts with the Szymanowskis' numerous relations, particularly with the musical families of Blumenfeld and Neuhaus, and all four of Karol Szymanowski's siblings followed artistic pursuits: Feliks was a pianist and composer, Stanisława a singer, Zofia a talented poet and Nula (Anna) a painter. Karol began his music education with his father and continued at Neuhaus's school in Elisavetgrad (two of Neuhaus's children, Natalia and Harry, were excellent pianists and close friends of Szymanowski). At the age of 13, in Vienna, he first heard the music of Wagner. The impressions he received were so strong that they not only gave the impulse to his first compositions but shaped his aesthetic personality for many years.

In 1901 Szymanowski went to Warsaw for more regular studies in music. From that year until 1904 he had private lessons with Zawirski for harmony and with Noskowski for counterpoint and composition. Warsaw was then, by European standards, an isolated and backward musical centre: the development of music schools was slow; there were opera theatres but no professional orchestras or chamber groups; the critics were conservative and the audiences apathetic. As a result, there was little to stimulate the aspirations of Polish composers. Even Moniuszko, in Szymanowski's view, 'lacked that inner greatness . . . which alone can give birth to truly universal great art', and he considered the achievement of Moniuszko's followers, perhaps referring to Żeleński and Noskowski, 'markedly lower' ('Uwagi w sprawie współczesnej opinii muzycznej w Polsce', 1920, reprinted in *Z pism*, 1958). It was thus natural for Szymanowski and his ambitious associates to turn to the major European centres for help in promoting their work. In 1905 Fitelberg, Różycki, Szymanowski and Szeluta founded the Young Polish Composers' Publishing Co. in Berlin under the patronage of Prince Władysław Lubomirski; its aim was to encourage new Polish music through publications and performances. The group is also referred to as 'Young Poland in Music', but it was not a community of shared artistic ideals. It was active for almost six years, from its first concert (Warsaw, 6 February 1906) until Różycki and Szymanowski found publishers of their own and Fitelberg gave his attention to conducting. The company was active in Warsaw, Lwów, Kraków, Berlin, Leipzig, Vienna and Dresden, and it was supported by the pianists Artur Rubinstein and Harry Neuhaus and the violinist Paweł Kochański.

Szymanowski's earliest compositions were piano pieces, the Preludes op.1 and the Studies op.4, which are stylistically akin to the music of Chopin, Schumann and Skryabin, and also some songs of a distinctly late Romantic character. Between 1909 and 1911 came the first great works of his maturity: the Concert Overture op.12, the Second Symphony op.19, the Second Piano Sonata op.21 and the opera *Hagith* op.25. These were the pieces that took Szymanowski's name to London and the large German cities, but all of his music before 1914 belongs to the current of Germanic Romanticism. The orchestral works are close to Wagner and Strauss in melodic shaping and in their markedly chromatic harmony; the treatment of sonata, variation and fugue forms is similar to that of Reger (but independent). Yet these features do not entirely obscure Szymanowski's individuality. Despite a predilection for dense, massive sound and expanded structures with polyphonic elements, there is already a foreshadowing of Szymanowski's distinctive tone and expression in the melody that dominates the music. His fully mature style is foreshadowed in its character, full and intense.

2. THE WORLD WAR I PERIOD. The first important stage in the development of Szymanowski's music was his departure from the sphere of late Romantic aesthetics. The links he retained with the post-Wagner tradition were principally of a technical rather than philosophical nature. His reading of Nietzsche had at first accompanied a fascination with Wagner's music, but there came a time when, following the philosopher, Szymanowski began to regard Wagner as a 'gesticulating actor' who smothered his music under the 'enormous weight of his personal experience' ('O romantyzmie w muzyce', 1929, reprinted in *Z pism*, 1958). Strauss he saw as the last gleam of Romanticism, illuminating the 'deep abyss before which contemporary German music stood, an abyss which had at any cost to be bridged if we were to go onwards' ('W sprawie "muzyki współczesnej" ', reprinted in *Z pism*, 1958). His own answer was to seek quite other foundations for a new aesthetic, and here the erotic Dionysiac element was to be of primary importance.

Most of 1911 and 1912 Szymanowski spent in Vienna, where the artistic milieu bored and oppressed him. But he made journeys to Italy (1909), Sicily (1910) and north Africa (1914, visiting Algiers, Constantine, Biskra and Tunis), and direct contacts with ancient, Arab and early Christian cultures formed a strong stimulus to his psychological transformation, or rather to the crystallization of a new poetics and a new musical idiom. Some more purely musical experiences were also to be decisive: during this period he saw *Pelléas et Mélisande* and, most significantly, *The Firebird* and *Petrushka* in the Dyagilev productions. On the way back from Italy he made the acquaintance of Stravinsky in London, and his letters emphasize that the two composers were on excellent terms.

Szymanowski reached home by the last trains in the summer of 1914. He remained in Tymoszówka until 1917, sometimes visiting Kiev in the winter months or travelling to St Petersburg and Moscow on his affairs as a composer. Cut off from active life by the war, he studied and composed with all the more intensity. He read the antiquarian Zieliński, the Byzantine scholar Diehl, the Greek tragedies, Plato, Da Vinci, Taine's *Philosophie de l'art*, Muratov's *Pictures of Italy*; he studied the histories and cultures of Islam, ancient Rome and early Christendom. Among the works of this period of greatest creative activity, when Szymanowski was composing tirelessly in the most diverse styles, are the Symphony no.3 'Pieśń o nocy' ('The song of the night') to words by the 13th-century Persian poet Jalāl ad-Dīn ar-Rūmī, the Violin Concerto no.1, the *Mity* ('Myths') for violin and piano, the Nocturne and Tarantella for violin and piano, the cantatas *Agave* and *Demeter*, the piano cycles *Metopy* ('Metopes') and *Maski* ('Masques'), the Piano Sonata no.3, the *Pieśni księżniczki z baśni* ('Songs of a fairy-tale princess'), the Tagore songs, the *Pieśni muezina szalonego* ('Songs of the infatuated muezzin') and the String Quartet no.1.

The seeds of Szymanowski's individual idiom, which had been present from the first, had by now developed into a style of great originality. Established forms are much less important, tonal harmony is relinquished in favour of polar centres, emphatic dynamics are exchanged for a more differentiated and generally softer treatment, and new means of articulation are used. These changes were all at the service of the new colouristic approach to sound. Szymanowski's music of this period combines the techniques of Debussian impressionism with those of Skryabinesque expressionism, but on the basis of late Romantic orchestration, still in evidence, for example, in the Third Symphony. Another special quality of Szymanowski's synthesis is the retention of the expressive function of melody, though its character and structure are changed. Almost all of the works written at this time share qualities of ecstasy and fervour, maintaining the utmost intensity of expression.

In autumn 1917 the Szymanowskis' house at Tymoszówka was destroyed and the family moved to Elisavetgrad. For nearly two years Szymanowski exchanged music for literature, perhaps because he required a more precise and unambiguous medium in which to formulate and clarify the philosophical and moral problems that were consuming him. He wrote a long novel, *Efebos*, on the subject of love and eroticism, to him a most essential question; the manuscript was lost in the Warsaw fires of 1939, but Iwaszkiewicz (1947) gives some account of its content. When Szymanowski returned to composition it was to begin work on the opera *Król Roger* ('King Roger'), which originated in his Sicilian experiences (the subject is Roger II of Sicily). The text, written jointly with Iwaszkiewicz, is based, broadly speaking, on the Dionysian thesis that only through bodily love can the mysteries of divine love be approached or creative work accomplished.

3. THE 1920S. Towards the end of 1919 the Szymanowski family left Elisavetgrad for Poland, now an independent state. After a short stay in Bydgoszcz they settled in Warsaw. Together with Kochański and Rubinstein, Szymanowski twice travelled to the USA by way of London in 1920–21, giving concerts that met with critical and popular success. In spite of this, and of the insistence of his two friends, Szymanowski would not be persuaded to remain abroad, although the conditions for the development of musical life in Poland were by no means favourable. For the liberation of his native country had had a profound effect on Szymanowski: his ruling principle became, as he said, a 'fanatic love of the idea of Poland', which gave him a sense of responsibility not just for his own work but for the fate of Polish music. In essay, manifesto and argument he fought for its rebirth, insistent that it should be worthy of the mantle of Chopin and also achieve international standards of quality and modernity. For Szymanowski, the composition of national music required the composer to take his stimulus from the deepest 'racial' element, by which he understood the qualities inherent in folk music (it should be emphasized that he never identified national music with directly folk-based music). Szymanowski's ideal was the thorough deployment of ethnic characteristics that Stravinsky had managed in *Petrushka*, *The Rite of Spring* and *The Wedding*, preserving national features in music of far wider range.

The changes wrought in Szymanowski's own music can be seen in the song cycle *Słopiewnie* (1921), the first work written after his return to Poland. Here he tried to reconstruct an imaginary primitive Polish music, using cries, shrieks, and other sounds drawn from nature. This was the first deliberate attempt since Chopin to create a Polish national style on so high an artistic level. Szymanowski found his richest source in the music of the Tatra mountain people, and from 1922 he spent much of his time in their 'capital', Zakopane. There was born the idea of the ballet *Harnasie* (1923–31); the piano Mazurkas and the Second Quartet were also Tatra works. He turned to the music of the plainsmen of Kurpie when writing the solo and choral sets of *Pieśni kurpiowskie* ('Kurpie songs'). In the *Stabat mater* for solo voices, chorus and orchestra (1925–6), he welded together folk material and stylized versions of early church music, producing one of his greatest compositions – a work of monumental proportions, but one which pursues the ideological direction of *Słopiewnie*.

During the years 1924–6 Szymanowski received increasing recognition at home, despite the opposition of conservative sections of musical society, and abroad. He spent a lot of time in Paris, chiefly for the many per-

formances there of his compositions. The First Violin Concerto, the Third Symphony, the *Myths* and the piano pieces and songs were taken up by many of the leading performers of the day and performed throughout Europe and the USA. The opera *Hagith* was given its first performance in Warsaw (1922) and repeated in Darmstadt (1923); *King Roger* was also introduced in Warsaw (1926) and then staged in Duisburg (1928). Szymanowski received many high distinctions and was appointed to numerous international societies. In 1927 he was offered the directorships of the conservatories of Cairo and Warsaw. He chose Warsaw, despite the much better terms of the Egyptian invitation and the opportunity of living in a climate which would have benefited his health, threatened since early childhood by tuberculosis.

Szymanowski saw the Warsaw post as an opportunity to re-invigorate Polish music education, neglected during the years of partition, and to form a new generation of Polish composers. He expounded something of his attitude in an interview published in the *Kurier czerwony* (24 Feb 1927): 'I recognize artistic traditionalism most sincerely as the starting-point, ... yet our aim is not "yesterday", but "today" and "tomorrow" '. Such a creed could hardly fail to evoke reaction from the conservative elements among the critics and conservatory staff. The years 1927–9 were entirely taken up by his campaign to establish a new model of training, to open wide horizons to the young and to equip them with a thorough knowledge of composition. He achieved his aim, but at a very high cost: these were years of creative stagnation and of great physical and nervous stress, which led to a serious crisis in his health. His pulmon-

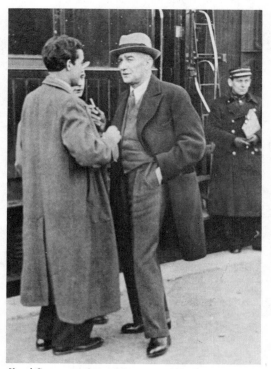

Karol Szymanowski in 1935

ary tuberculosis was found to be advanced, and he had to give up his duties and go to a sanatorium in Davos. There he remained for almost a year, writing a treatise, *Wychowawcza rola kultury muzycznej w społeczeństwie* ('The educational role of musical culture in society'), which gives a most interesting, original and broad treatment of a whole complex of sociological, aesthetic and musical questions.

4. THE 1930S. The next two years (1930–31) were the period of Szymanowski's greatest stability, success and prosperity. He rented a house, 'Atma', in Zakopane, his first real home since the 1917 revolution. In 1930 he was appointed rector of the Warsaw Academy of Music (which had replaced the conservatory) and made an honorary doctor of Kraków University. He was elected to the highly select group of honorary members of the ISCM. The *Stabat mater* brought him widespread renown, and in 1932 *King Roger* was presented in Prague. There was a return to his creative energy, and he composed two works for solo voices, chorus and orchestra, *Veni Creator* and *Litania do Marii Panny* ('Litany to the Virgin Mary'), and completed the ballet *Harnasie*.

New troubles in the academy, again provoked by conservative factions, forced Szymanowski to resign in 1932. Lacking a regular income, he decided to make public appearances as a pianist in his own compositions, but since such pieces as the Sonatas, *Metopes* and *Masques* were beyond his technique, he composed a Fourth Symphony with a concertante piano part. This was followed by his last large-scale work, the Second Violin Concerto; after the Two Mazurkas of 1933–4 he wrote no more. External circumstances had a decisive effect in inhibiting his creativity during these last years. The need to provide for his family, a need exacerbated by the current economic crisis, was a burden on his weakening health; the effort he put into performing (he appeared in all the major musical centres of Europe) left little energy for composition.

In April 1936 he experienced his greatest popular success when *Harnasie*, which had received its première in Prague in the previous year, was presented at the Paris Opéra and was highly praised by critics and public alike. But there were no offers of further performances, and in mid-1936 Szymanowski had to give up the rented house in Zakopane. His illness advanced rapidly, but he continued to attempt to work. He corresponded with Rodziński about a possible production of *Harnasie* in New York; he planned a visit to Italy. Contributions from friends and from a state bursary enabled him to travel to Grasse, yet, unable to afford the fees of a good sanatorium, he continued to decline. He died shortly after a move to a sanatorium in Lausanne.

The works composed after 1920 are usually described as belonging to Szymanowski's 'national' period, whose sources lay deep in his ideological development, his conscious attempt to capture the national element. Technically, however, this attempt was not undertaken so single-mindedly as it was in the sphere of ideas. The language formed during the years 1914–17 had been enlarged but not essentially changed by the ethnic and archaic influences he absorbed during the 1920s; by the 1930s, however, he had become convinced of the limitations of folk music. All the major late pieces – *Veni Creator*, the *Litany to the Virgin Mary*, the Symphony no.4 and the Violin Concerto no.2 – are closely linked with folk music as regards material, yet

the *Litany* contains sound and colour effects that stem directly from the Symphony no.3 and the Violin Concerto no.1, while the Symphony no.4 resorts to a neo-Baroque sinfonia concertante form, though Szymanowski had little in common with Stravinskian neo-classicism. In his last months he planned a ballet, *Powrót Odyssa* ('The return of Odysseus'), of which a vague outline had been sketched in 1933.

5. MUSIC. Szymanowski's oeuvre, though not very large (62 opus numbers), is highly varied in genre and form. Two-thirds of his output consists of settings of or reactions to literary texts: his talent was a pre-eminently lyrical one, stimulated and intensified by words. The piano cycle *Metopes* took subjects from the *Odyssey* – 'The Isle of Sirens', 'Calypso' and 'Nausicaa' – interpreting them in a manner suggested by the sculptural metopes of Sicily. Another set of piano pieces, the *Masques*, presents parody portraits of figures from literature: 'Scheherazade', 'Tantris the Jester' (after Ernst Hardt's play, a travesty of the tale of Tristan and Isolde) and 'Don Juan's Serenade'. The First Violin Concerto follows the programme of Tadeusz Miciński's poem *A Night in May*, and the *Myths* for violin and piano are again linked with scenes from Greek mythology: 'Arethusa's Spring', 'Narcissus' and 'Dryads and Pan'.

The conception of artistic creation as a complex, comprehensive synthesizing of human culture is perhaps one of the foundations of Szymanowski's aesthetic, and one essential to an understanding of his work. His interests embraced the life and arts of cultures from the Tatra mountains of Poland to the most exotic. In this light, his deeply penetrating approach to Arabic–Persian culture is particularly significant. The Third Symphony, parts of the opera *King Roger*, the *Love-songs of Hafiz*, the *Pieśni księżniczki z baśni* ('Songs of a fairy-tale princess') and the *Songs of the Infatuated Muezzin* are his musical testimony. Unlike most European composers who have interested themselves in the orient, Szymanowski did not attempt to give his music an eastern colour, nor did he ever use Arab or Persian melodies or scales. Rather, his unerring intuition succeeded in extracting and generalizing the most basic qualities of oriental music: coloratura melody reflecting the voice in emotion, sequential chromatic patterns (in imitation of micro-intervals), melodic, harmonic and rhythmic ground basses, certain percussion sounds and, finally, its characteristic expressive qualities of ecstasy, fervour and passion. Sorabji (1947) wrote of one of the Hafiz settings as 'music of a radiant purity of spirit, of an elevated ecstasy of expression', going on to describe the score as glowing 'with gorgeous colour, rich, yet never garish nor crude, like a Persian painting or silk rug'. This is not, again in Sorabji's words, the product of a 'European in fancy dress' but the achievement of 'an astonishing kinship of spirit [which] succeeds in giving us in musical terms what we instinctively know and recognize as the essence of Persian art'. Szymanowski's need for the exotic led him not only to models from the east but also to the invented archaic–church–folk style of *Słopiewnie* and the *Stabat mater*, absolutely original and supremely beautiful.

His less common, 'abstract' works – such as the Symphony no.2, the Second and Third Piano Sonatas, the Piano Variations in B♭ minor and B minor and the Studies op.33 – show Szymanowski's success in building a structural totality, in solving the problems of combining established forms with new modes of thought. In this he sometimes achieved more interesting results than Reger in fugues and variations, or than Skryabin in sonatas. But Szymanowski's greatest contributions to the piano literature, the *Metopes* and *Masques*, are frankly improvisatory in form. They are based on transformations of small cells, dense and stratified textures descending from late Romanticism, a rich and colourful harmony without tonal function, and a subtle treatment of dynamics, timbre and articulation. Both sets are imbued with Szymanowski's characteristic intensity of expression. Several works with violin solo – the Nocturne and Tarantella, the *Myths* and the Violin Concerto no.1 – give the fullest evidence of Szymanowski's development of a new kind of musical imagination. Individual sounds generate the forms, displacing conventional thematic working, and the enriched range of colouristic effect is joined by an attempted new rhythmic organization, freed from the rigidity of beat and bar. The violin writing in these pieces is in the highest degree refined and exploratory.

Szymanowski's contact with Polish folk music gave complex and varied results. The *Kurpie Songs* are very straightforward elaborations of authentic folksongs; at the other extreme the mazurkas are a link with Chopin modified by ethnic elements from Podhale (the rhythm is duple throughout), a very advanced harmonic idiom (which has drawn importance from the melody) and an extremely subjective expression. *Harnasie*, a splendid fresco, uses direct quotations from folk music, ideas framed on folk models and supported by autochthonous features, and completely original material no more than tinged by Tatra mountain music. In the 1930s Szymanowski retreated from the use of folk music, though indigenous rhythmic patterns occur. Despite the fact that several of his finest works were written in the 1920s, when he was closest to folk music, it may be that the shared quality of folk culture was inimical to his exuberant subjectivity and to his lyrical talent.

The evolutionary progress of Szymanowski's work suggests that, had he lived, he might have reached a new period of synthesis. He was, at any event, opposed to eclecticism or imitation, intent on transforming any influence to produce a characteristic personal tone: a polished, subtle, simple phrase with an ardent, spiritual expression.

WORKS

Edition: *K. Szymanowski: Dzieła*, ed. T. Chylińska (Kraków, Paris and Vienna, 1973–) [S]

op.

STAGE

— Loteria na mężów [The lottery for men] (operetta, 3, J. Krzewiński-Maszyński), 1908–9; unperf., S D/17
25 Hagith (opera, 1, after F. Dörmann), 1913; Warsaw, 13 May 1922; S D/13
43 Mandragora (pantomime, 3 scenes, R. Bogusławski, L. Schiller, after Molière: Le bourgeois gentilhomme, Act 3), 1920; Warsaw, 15 June 1920; S D/16
46 Król Roger [King Roger] (opera, 3, Szymanowski, J. Iwaszkiewicz), 1918–24; Warsaw, 19 June 1926; S D/14
51 Kniaź Patiomkin [Prince Potemkin] (music for Act 5 of play by T. Miciński), 1925; Warsaw, 6 March 1925; S D/16
55 Harnasie (ballet-pantomime, 3, Iwaszkiewicz, J. M. Rytard), 1923–31; Prague, 11 May 1935; S D/15

ORCHESTRAL AND VOCAL ORCHESTRAL

6 Salome (J. Kasprowicz), S, orch, c1907, reorchd 1912; S A/5
12 Concert Overture, E, 1904–5; Warsaw, 6 Feb 1906; reorchd 1912–13; S A/1
15 Symphony no.1, f, 1906–7; Warsaw, 26 March 1909; S A/1
18 Penthesilea (S. Wyspiański), S, orch, 1908; Warsaw, 18 March 1910; reorchd 1912; S A/5
19 Symphony no.2, Bb, 1909–10; Warsaw, 7 April 1911; reorchd 1936, collab. G. Fitelberg; S A/1

26 Pieśni miłosne Hafiza [Love-songs of Hafiz] (trans. Bethge) [incl. op.24/1, 4, 5, orchd], 1v, orch, 1914; Paris, 23 June 1925; S A/5
27 Symphony no.3 'Pieśń o nocy' [The song of the night] (Jalāl ad-Dīn ar-Rūmī), T/S, chorus, orch, 1914–16; London, 24 Nov 1921; S A/2
31 Pieśni księżniczki z baśni [Songs of a fairy-tale princess] (Z. Szymanowska), 1v, orch, 1933; Warsaw, 7 April 1933; S A/5
35 Violin Concerto no.1, 1916; Warsaw, 1 Nov 1922; S A/3
37b Demeter (Szymanowska, after Euripides: Bacchae), A, female chorus, orch, 1917, reorchd 1924; Warsaw, 17 April 1931; S A/4
39 Agave, A, female chorus, orch, 1917; S A/4
42 Pieśni muezina szalonego [Songs of the infatuated muezzin] (Iwaszkiewicz), 1v, orch, 1934; S A/5
46b Słopiewnie (J. Tuwim), 1v, orch, 1928; S A/5
53 Stabat mater (medieval sequence, trans. J. Jankowski), solo vv, chorus, orch, 1925–6; Warsaw, 11 Jan 1929; S A/4
57 Veni Creator (Wyspiański), S, chorus, orch, org, 1930; Warsaw, 7 Nov 1930; S A/4
59 Litania do Marii Panny [Litany to the Virgin Mary] (J. Liebert), S, female chorus, orch, 1930–33; Warsaw, 13 Oct 1933; S A/4
60 Symphony no.4 (Symphonie concertante), pf, orch, 1932; Poznań, 9 Oct 1932; S A/2
61 Violin Concerto no.2, 1933; Warsaw, 6 Oct 1933; S A/3

CHAMBER

9 Sonata, d, vn, pf, 1904; Warsaw, 19 April 1909; S B/9
16 Piano Trio, 1907; destroyed
23 Romance, D, vn, pf, 1910; Warsaw, 8 April 1913; S B/9
28 Nocturne and Tarantella, vn, pf, 1915; S B/9
30 Mity [Myths], vn, pf, 1915; S B/9
37 String Quartet no.1, C, 1917; Warsaw, April 1924; S B/6
40 Three Paganini Caprices, vn, pf, 1918; Elisavetgrad, 25 April 1918; S B/9
52 Kołysanka [Lullaby] (La berceuse d'Aïtacho Enia), vn, pf, 1925; S B/9
56 String Quartet no.2, 1927; Paris, aut. 1929; S B/6

SONGS AND CHORUSES
(for 1v, pf unless otherwise stated)

— Pieśni polskie [arr. soldiers' songs], collab. F. Szymanowski; S C/11
2 Six Songs (K. Tetmajer), 1900–02; S C/10
5 Three Fragments from Poems by Jan Kasprowicz, 1902; S C/10
7 Łabędź [The swan] (W. Berent), 1904; S C/10
11 Four Songs (Miciński), 1904–5; S C/10
13 Five Songs (Dehmel, F. Bodenstedt, O. J. Bierbaum), 1905–7; S C/10
17 Twelve Songs (Dehmel, Mombert, G. Falke, M. Greif), 1907; S C/10
20 Six Songs (Miciński), 1909; S C/10
22 Barwne pieśni (Buntelieder) (K. Bulcke, A. Paquet, E. Faktor, A. Ritter, Huch), 1910; S C/10
24 Pieśni miłosne Hafiza [Love-songs of Hafiz] (trans. Bethge), 1911; S C/10
31 Pieśni księżniczki z baśni [Songs of a fairy-tale princess] (Z. Szymanowska), 1915; S C/11
32 Three Songs (D. Davidov), 1915; S C/11
41 Four Songs (Tagore), 1918; S C/11
42 Pieśni muezina szalonego [Songs of the infatuated muezzin] (Iwaszkiewicz), 1918; S C/11
44 Two Basque Songs, c1920; S C/11
46b Słopiewnie (J. Tuwim), 1921; S C/11
48 Three Lullabies (Iwaszkiewicz), 1922; S C/11
49 Rymy dziecięce [Children's rhymes] (Iłłakowicz), 1922–3; S C/11
54 Four Songs (Joyce), 1926; S C/11
— Vocalise-étude, 1928; S C/11
— Pieśni kurpiowskie [Kurpie songs], chorus, 1928–9; S C/12
58 Pieśni kurpiowskie, 1930–33; S C/11

PIANO

1 Nine Preludes, 1900; S B/7
3 Variations, bb, 1903; S B/7
4 Four Studies, 1902; S B/7
8 Sonata no.1, c, 1904; Warsaw, 19 April 1907; S B/7
10 Wariacje na polski temat ludowy [Variations on a Polish folk theme], b, 1904; Warsaw, 6 Feb 1906; S B/7
14 Fantasy, 1905; Warsaw, 9 Feb 1906; S B/7
— Prelude and Fugue, c#, 1905, 1909; S B/7
21 Sonata no.2, A, 1911; Berlin, 1 Dec 1911; S B/7
29 Metopy [Metopes], 1915; S B/8
33 Twelve Studies, 1916; S B/8
34 Maski [Masques], 1916; St Petersburg, 12 Oct 1916; S B/8
36 Sonata no.3, 1917; S B/8

50   Twenty Mazurkas, 1924–5; S B/8
—   Four Polish Dances, 1926; S B/8
62   Two Mazurkas, 1933–4; London, Nov 1934; S B/8

Principal publishers: Eschig, Polskie Wydawnictwo Muzyczne, Universal

WRITINGS

'Uwagi w sprawie współczesnej opinii muzycznej w Polsce' [Some observations concerning contemporary musical opinion in Poland], *Nowy przegląd literatury i sztuki* (1920), July [repr. in *Z pism*]
'Fryderyk Chopin', *Skamander* (1923), no.28
'Drogi i bezdroża muzyki współczesnej' [The highways and pathless tracts of contemporary music], *Muzyka* (1926), no.5
'O romantyzmie w muzyce', *Droga* (1929), no.1 [repr. in *Z pism*]
'Frédéric Chopin et la musique polonaise moderne', *ReM* (1931), no.121, p.30
Wychowawcza rola kultury muzycznej w społeczeństwie [The educational role of musical culture in society] (Warsaw, 1931)
'Wstęp do pamiętnika' [Introduction to memoirs], *Wiadomości literackie* (1938), no.1
ed. T. Bronowicz-Chylińska: *Z pism* [From the writings] (Kraków, 1958) [selection of essays]

BIBLIOGRAPHY

LETTERS, MEMOIRS AND ICONOGRAPHY

J. Iwaszkiewicz: *Spotkania z Szymanowskim* [Meetings with Szymanowski] (Kraków, 1947)
J. R. Mieczysław: *Wspomnienia o Karolu Szymanowskim* [Reminiscences of Szymanowski] (Kraków, 1947)
T. Bronowicz-Chylińska, ed.: *Szymanowski Karol: z listów* [From the letters] (Kraków, 1957)
T. Chylińska: *Szymanowski* (Kraków, 1962, 3/1973; Eng. trans., 1973) [iconographical album]
B. M. Maciejewski and F. Aprahamian, eds. and trans.: *Karol Szymanowski and Jan Smeterlin: Correspondence and Essays* (London, ?1970)
T. Chylińska, ed.: *Dzieje przyjaźni: korespondencja Karola Szymanowskiego z Pawłem i Zofią Kochańskimi* [The story of a friendship: the correspondence of Szymanowski and Paweł and Zofia Kochański] (Kraków, 1971)
A. Rubinstein: *My Young Years* (London, 1973), esp. 116ff, 371ff
J. M. Smoter, ed.: *Wspomnienia o Karolu Szymanowskim* (Kraków, 1974)
T. Chylińska, ed.: *Zakopianskie dni Karola Szymanowskiego* (Kraków, 1976)

MONOGRAPHS AND THEMATIC CATALOGUE

Z. Jachimecki: *Karol Szymanowski: rys dotychczasowej twórczości* [Szymanowski: an outline of his output] (Kraków, 1927)
——: *Karol Szymanowski* (London, 1938)
S. Szymanowska-Korwin: *Jak należy śpiewać utwory Karola Szymanowskiego* [How to sing Szymanowski's works] (Warsaw, 1938, 3/1957)
S. Golachowski: *Karol Szymanowski* (Warsaw, 1948, 2/1956)
S. Łobaczewska: *Karol Szymanowski: życie i twórczość (1882–1937)* [Szymanowski: life and work] (Kraków, 1950)
J. M. Chomiński, ed.: *Z życia i twórczości Karola Szymanowskiego* (Kraków, 1960)
Karol Szymanowski: Warszawa 1962
J. Iwaszkiewicz: *"Harnasie" Karola Szymanowskiego* (Kraków, 1964)
B. M. Maciejewski: *Karol Szymanowski: his Life and Music* (London, 1967)
K. Michałowski: *Karol Szymanowski: katalog tematyczny dzieł i bibliografia* (Kraków, 1967)
J. M. Chomiński: *Studia nad twórczością Karola Szymanowskiego* (Kraków, 1969)
T. Chylińska: *Szymanowski i jego muzyka* (Warsaw, 1971)
A. Wightman: *The Music of Karol Szymanowski* (diss., U. of York, 1972)

OTHER REFERENCES

M. Draper: *Music at Midnight* (London, 1929)
K. S. Sorabji: *Around Music* (London, 1932), 57f
——: *Mi contra fa* (London, 1947), 178ff

TERESA CHYLIŃSKA

T

T. *See* TUTTI.

Ta. The flattened leading note of the prevailing key (or, if this is minor, its relative major), in TONIC SOL-FA.

Tabachnik, Michel (*b* Geneva, 10 Nov 1942). Swiss composer and conductor. He received diplomas in theory and conducting at the Geneva Conservatory and attended the 1964 Darmstadt summer courses. In 1965 he was a member of Boulez's class at the Basle Musikakademie, and he then became Boulez's assistant until 1971. His earliest published compositions follow his mentor quite directly: *Supernovae* has many points in common with *Eclat*, and the mobile-form *Frise* takes up the more elaborately ornamented piano writing of *Structures II*. The première of his *Fresque* at the 1970 Royan Festival initiated Tabachnik's independent career as a conductor (he had already taken part with Boulez in performances of *Gruppen*). Specializing in 20th-century music, he has given the first performances of Xenakis's *Synaphaï*, *Aroura*, *Linaia*, *Eridanos* and *Cendrées*. His later works have remained under the influence of Boulez – as is most evident in his orchestration and his conception of 'harmonic fields' which may be combined in various ways – but the association with Xenakis has also left a mark. Besides these predecessors, his biggest work, *Mondes* for two orchestras, recalls Stockhausen's *Carré*, though Tabachnik's interest is not so much in moving sounds through space as in distinguishing 'modulating' from 'modulated' sonorities, these terms being understood to apply to rhythm, density, register or duration. Tabachnik has been conductor of the Gulbenkian Foundation Orchestra of Lisbon, 1973–5, of the Ensemble Européen de Musique Contemporaine of Paris, 1976–7, and of the Lorraine PO in Metz from 1975.

WORKS
Supernovae, 19 insts, 1967; Frise, pf, 1968; Pastel I, fl, hn, cel, harp, 2 perc, vc, 1968; Pastel II, orch, 1969; Fresque, 33 insts, 1970; Mondes, 2 orchs, 1970–72; Sillages, 32 str, 1972; D'autres sillages, 8 timp, 4-track tape, 1972; Invention à 16 voix, 23 insts, 1972; Movimenti, 51 insts, 1973; Eclipses, pf, 1974; Les imaginaires, orch, 1974; Argile, 4 perc, 1975; Les perseïdes, 1976

Principal publishers: Fairfield/Novello, Ricordi

PAUL GRIFFITHS

Tabakov, Mikhail Innokent'yevich (*b* Odessa, 6 Jan 1877; *d* Moscow, 9 March 1956). Ukrainian trumpeter. He studied at the Odessa Music Academy (1889–90) and performed in various orchestras between 1891 and 1896. From 1897 to 1938, with interruptions, he was a member of the Bol'shoy Theatre Orchestra, becoming first trumpet in 1903. From 1910 to 1917 he was the manager of Koussevitzky's virtuoso symphony orchestra, in which he played first trumpet, and he was a founder-member and manager of the Persimfans Orchestra (1922–32), an orchestra without a conductor. Siegfried Wagner invited him to perform in the Bayreuth Festival Orchestra, an honour only once accorded a Russian musician. From 1914 until his death, Tabakov taught the trumpet at the Academy of Music and Drama (later combined with the Moscow Conservatory), where he also taught military band conducting from 1928; from 1943 he was in charge of the department of specialist orchestration (later of military band orchestration). He left these two posts in 1947 to become head of the department of wind instruments at the Gnesin Institute, where he remained until his death.

Tabakov is regarded as the founder of the Russian school of trumpet playing. His tone was highly praised; as a teacher he emphasized the importance of good tone, calling it 'the valuable capital of the artist'. In 1947 he was named an Honoured Art Worker of the RSFSR. He wrote *Progressivnaya shkola dlya trubi* ('Systematic guide to trumpet playing') (Moscow, 1946).

BIBLIOGRAPHY
S. Bolotin: *Biograficheskiy slovar' muzïkantov-ispolniteley na dukhovïkh instrumentakh* [Biographical dictionary of musicians and wind instrument players] (Leningrad, 1969), 104, 177
EDWARD H. TARR

Tabart [Tabaret], Pierre (*b* Chinon, mid-17th century; *d* after 1711). French composer. He was a choirboy at Tours and then choirmaster at the cathedrals of Orleans and Senlis. He was defeated in the competition for the four positions of *sous-maître* at the royal chapel in 1683, but he did succeed Nicolas Goupillet, one of the winners, as choirmaster of Meaux Cathedral. He resigned from this post in 1698 but remained at Meaux as titular head of a *grande chapelle*. Brossard, his successor at Meaux, thought highly of him and consulted him about the selection of a choirmaster for Evreux Cathedral in 1711. A mass, requiem, *Te Deum*, *Magnificat* and three motets by him survive in *F-Pn* Vm¹.948–948*bis* and 1643–7.

BIBLIOGRAPHY
EitnerQ
Mercure galant (April 1683), 310
M. Brenet: 'Sébastien de Brossard', *Mémoires de la Société de l'histoire de Paris et de l'Ile de France*, xxiii (1896); also pubd separately (Paris, 1896)
WILLIAM HAYS

Tabel [Table], **Hermann** (*b* Low Countries; *d* London, before 8 May 1738). Netherlands harpsichord maker. He may have learnt from the Couchets, successors to the Ruckers of Antwerp. Probably about 1700 he settled in London, where both Shudi and Kirckman worked for him. In 1738 Kirckman married Tabel's widow. Only one of Tabel's instruments survives, and is now in the County Museum, Warwick; the top key of the lower manual is inscribed 'No. 43 Herm Tabel Fecit Londini 1721' (see Mould).

Tabel's one surviving harpsichord caused Russell to think it 'likely that the standard large harpsichord made in this country derived from his designs', Hubbard to suggest it 'likely that the traditional role ascribed to Tabel and his posthumous fame were the fabrication of both Kirckman and Shudi in their dotage' and Mould to point out that in any case 'there is no element of this disposition which is not found elsewhere on earlier English harpsichords'. Nonetheless, the 1721 instrument is one of the few extant English double harpsichords to have been built before 1730, and its dogleg upper-manual jacks and original lute arrangement (perhaps both familiar in Flanders by 1720) did become normal. Burney called him 'the celebrated Tabel', and an advertisement in the *Evening Post* for 30 May 1723 noted that he had three harpsichords for sale, 'which are and will be the last of his making'. Nevertheless, on 8 May 1738, Kirckman advertised 'several fine harpsichords', made by 'Mr Hermann Tabel . . . the famous harpsichord maker, dead'. In short, his historical position is uncertain, as are the details of his work, known from one, much altered instrument.

BIBLIOGRAPHY

R. Russell: *The Harpsichord and Clavichord* (London, 1959, rev. 2/1973)

F. Hubbard: *Three Centuries of Harpsichord Making* (Cambridge, Mass., 1965)

C. M. Mould: 'The Tabel Harpsichord', *Keyboard Instruments*, ed. E. M. Ripin (Edinburgh, 1971), 57

DONALD HOWARD BOALCH, PETER WILLIAMS

Tabīra. Sassanid drum; *see* PERSIA, §3(ii).

Ṭabl. A generic term for drums in the Islamic Near East and north Africa. It usually refers to a double-headed cylindrical drum whose heads are stretched over hoops and then laced to each other around a shallow wooden cylinder (*see* IRAQ, fig.4). The two principal types are *ṭabl baladī* and *ṭabl turkī*. The *ṭabl baladī*, the smaller, is the ancestor of the European side drum or tenor drum. The *ṭabl turkī* is the ancestor of the European bass drum: its name is related to the Turkish DAVUL (a similar type of drum). It is played slung from one shoulder, although smaller instruments are sometimes held between the knees. Both types of *ṭabl* are beaten with a pair of flexible beaters, either sticks or, as in Egypt, a stick and a bundle of thongs. The *ṭabl* is frequently played in ensemble with shawms to accompany dancing at weddings and in processions. The term 'tabl' used in combination with other terms, can also refer to types of shallow kettledrum such as *ṭabl šāmī*, *ṭabl al-ġāwīġ* and *ṭabl migrī*, all of which are played singly.

See also the entry 'Ṭabl' in Appendix A.

BIBLIOGRAPHY

'Ṭābl Khāna', *The Encyclopaedia of Islam* (Leiden and London, 1913–38, rev. 2/1960–)

C. Sachs: *The History of Musical Instruments* (New York, 1940), 249ff

J. Jenkins and P. Rovsing Olsen: *Music and Musical Instruments in the World of Islam* (London, 1976), 73ff

WILLIAM J. CONNER, MILFIE HOWELL

Tablā (from Perso-Arabic *ṭabl*: 'drum'). A pair of single-headed drums, played by one person, used in vocal and instrumental Hindustani music. The right-hand drum, itself also called *tablā* or *dāyā* ('right'), is a small, thong-tensioned wooden barrel drum about 15 cm in diameter; the left is a slightly larger clay or copper kettledrum called *bāyā* ('left'). For a discussion of its history, playing technique and associated rhythmic theory *see* INDIA, SUBCONTINENT OF, §II, 6(iii), and fig.15*d*. European composers who have made use of the *tablā* include Berio (*Circles*, 1960), Cowell (Concerto for percussion and orchestra, 1961) and John Mayer (*Talas* for *tablā*, *tamburā*, *mṛdaṅgam* and Western percussion, 1968). A variety of drums with similar names are widely diffused throughout south and west Asia and north Africa.

See also AFGHANISTAN, §4; BANGLADESH, §5; EGYPT, §II; IMPROVISATION, §II, 2; IRAQ, §§4, 5; KASHMIR; PAKISTAN, §4.

JAMES BLADES

Tablature (Fr. *tablature*; Ger. *Tabulatur*; It. *intavolatura*). Any notational system of the last 650 years that uses letters, numbers or other signs as an alternative to conventional staff notation. Such systems were chiefly used for instrumental music; dance tablatures are beyond the scope of this article. For a discussion of tablature in its historical context, *see* NOTATION, §III, 5(i).

1. General. 2. Keyboard. 3. Lute. 4. Guitar. 5. Other string instruments. 6. Wind instruments. 7. Figured bass and similar chordal notations. 8. Vocal music.

1. GENERAL. Systems of tablature have been in use in western European music since at least the early 14th century, most of them deriving from the playing technique of a particular instrument. Whereas staff notation shows in one symbol both the pitch and duration of a note, tablature systems in general use one symbol to show how to produce a sound of the required pitch from the instrument in question (which string to pluck, which fret to stop, which key to press, which holes to cover etc) and another to show its duration. Staff notation was developed for, and is primarily associated with, single-line music, whereas tablature's speciality is part-music. Each was originally at its maximum effectiveness in its own field. Although staff notation has now superseded most tablatures, it gained much from its long contact with its rivals, and many of its most valuable features derive ultimately from one or other of them. In tablature systems, for instance, each note or rest was worth two of the next smaller value, and a dot after a note had only one meaning: that it increased the note's duration by half its original value. Regular barring, too, was frequently adopted, especially in lute tablatures. The simplicity, clarity and logic of such common features of tablatures were considerably in advance of staff notation. The most important categories of tablature are those for keyboard (usually organ) and lute. A large proportion of the keyboard pieces copied between 1320 and 1520, many of which are of German origin, survive in tablature form. The various types of lute tablature, on the other hand, represent a more direct form of instruction to the player, and these have been used for virtually all lute music from the early 16th century to the present day.

1. The earliest known example of keyboard tablature: the Robertsbridge Codex, c1320 (GB-Lbm Add.28550, f.43v, detail)

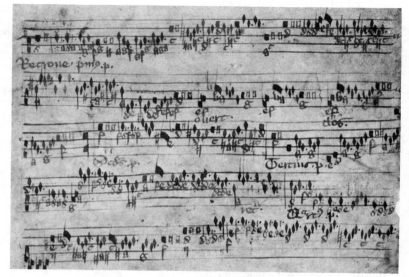

2. Old German keyboard tablature: Preambulum in C from the Ileborgh tablature, 1448 (US-PHci, p.2); the letters below the first system (C, G, D, F♯, etc) may indicate two-note chords in the pedal

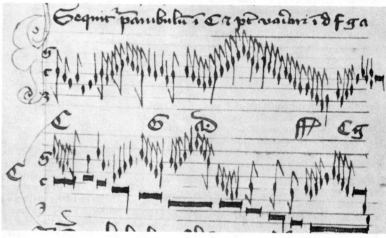

3. Spanish keyboard tablature with numerals for diatonic notes in each octave: 'Susana un jur' from Antonio de Cabezón, 'Obras de música' (1578)

2. KEYBOARD.

(*i*) *Germany, 14th century*. The earliest known example, the Robertsbridge Codex (*GB-Lbm* Add.28550; fig.1), dates from about 1320 and was almost certainly intended for the organ, but some scholars consider that it may have been for clavichord. Although some of its contents are French, and the manuscript itself comes from an English abbey, its rightful place in a discussion of tablatures is under German keyboard tablature since many of its characteristics are, in embryo, those of later German ones. It is a part-tablature only, however, since the top voice of the music is notated on a five-line staff (no explanation has been suggested for this illogical feature of early German tablature). The notes of the lower voices are written in letter notation beneath the notes on the staff; their length and the beat on which they are to be played is determined by their position with respect to the staff-notes and their octave by considerations of part-writing. The word 'sine' (or simply the letter 's') denotes a rest. The black notes of the keyboard are regarded as belonging to the white note on their left (B♭ and B♮ taking the normal forms of ♭ and ♯ however): thus the black note between C and D is regarded as 'the black note of C' or, for short, 'of-C' and, in vulgar Latin, 'Cis'. A common medieval abbreviation for '-is' was a wavy line at the top right-hand corner of a word. The chromatic scale thus appears as in ex.1. Although the

Ex.1

compass of these pieces does not exceed *c–e″*, it is interesting that, in the middle octave at least, all 12 notes of the octave are in use, even at this early date. Organ pedals were in existence in Germany by the time the manuscript was written, yet these six pieces do not appear to require their use.

(*ii*) *Germany, 1432–1570*. The above system of tablature had been considerably improved in many respects by the time it is next encountered, over a century later. The top part was written on a six-, seven- or eight-line staff (a retrograde step, perhaps: five-line staves were not in general use again for keyboard music until the 17th century); a downward stem, with or without a dash through it, indicated chromatic alteration (♭ or ♯ as appropriate), and a loop to such a stem denoted a mordent. Each lower voice was shown as a row of letters, the sharp affix now taking the form of a loop; the letters b and h signified B♭ and B♮ respectively. The middle octave consisted of plain letters, the ones above it of doubled letters or letters with a dash or dashes above them (cc, c , c̄) and the one below it of capital letters or letters with a dash beneath them (C, c̜). Each letter had a rhythm sign above it to show its duration; these signs were derived from their staff notation equivalents as in ex.2. For rests, staff notation signs or slight variants of

Ex.2

them were used. Many of the tablatures dating from this period were barred regularly. Some, such as the 'Ileborgh' tablature (*US-PHci*), contain what appear to be indications for two-note chords in the pedals, although not all scholars agree with this interpretation (see fig.2). When possible, notes and rhythm signs of like value were grouped together, as in ex.3. The extract of music which in staff notation would appear as in ex.4*a* would have been shown in this tablature as in ex.4*b* (all the music examples in this article show the first two bars of Dowland's ayre *Flow my tears*).

Ex.3

Ex.4

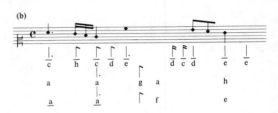

(*iii*) *Germany, 1570–1750*. From about 1570 the above system continued in use, but with two substantial changes: the top part no longer used staff notation but was written in letter notation like the other parts; and the value of the rhythm signs was doubled in conformity with contemporary lute tablature. The modern tie sign appeared for the first time, although its use in staff-notation keyboard scores was already well established. This modified form of the earlier German keyboard tablature remained in widespread use, especially in northern Germany, until the mid-18th century, and it is last mentioned in Johann Samuel Petri's *Anleitung zur praktischen Musik* (Leipzig, 2/1782). J. S. Bach used it occasionally in the *Orgel-Büchlein* as a space-saving device when insufficient allowance had been made for the length of a chorale prelude (*see* BACH, fig.7). An example of this later German keyboard tablature is shown in ex.5.

Ex.5

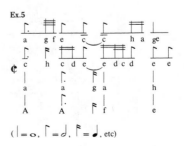

(iv) Spain, 1550–1700. Nothing is known of Spanish keyboard music before 1555, when Juan Bermudo explained two new systems of notation in his *Declaración de instrumentos musicales*; the systems he proposed may well have been his own inventions. The first assigned a number, from 1 to 42, to each key of the organ, the numbers proceeding in unbroken sequence from left to right of the keyboard (*C–a″*, but fully chromatic *A–a″* only). The number of lines to a 'staff' in the resulting tablature corresponded to the number of voices in the composition, and the music was barred regularly. The apparent suitability of this system for contrapuntal music was more than outweighed by the ambiguities that inevitably resulted from the absence of rhythm signs and from the inability to indicate ties in the inner parts (see ex.6). This system was quite unsuited to music that

Ex.6

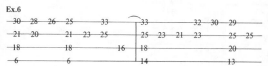

included cross-rhythms, considerable independence of parts, or a free-voiced texture; moreover, it was awkward and difficult to memorize. Its use was apparently confined to Bermudo's book.

Bermudo's second system, also used for certain Italian publications, assigned a number, from 1 to 23, to each white note of the keyboard (the existence of the 'short octave' meant that although the number 1 was used for *C*, numbers 2 to 23 represented *F* to *f″*). The black notes were all considered as sharps, and were shown by a sharp sign above the appropriate number. Thus a sharp over a 6 was *c♯*, a sharp above a 10 was *a♭* or *g♯*, according to context, and so on; the letter 't' above a figure denoted an ornament. The right-hand and left-hand parts were shown above and below a horizontal line; note values were indicated as in lute tablature by signs above the right-hand part, sometimes supplemented by additional signs (; : and ?) placed after the figure to which they refer. Each rhythm sign above the staff applied to all the figures in the column immediately below it and remained valid until contradicted by another sign. Although the indications of rhythm represented a considerable advance over Bermudo's first system it was still not always possible to establish the exact intended duration of each note (see ex.7).

Ex.7

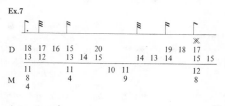

$(\bvert = o, \; \Gamma = d \;, \text{etc})$

A third numerical system of Spanish keyboard tablature was used also for the harp or the vihuela. It was first used by Venegas de Henestrosa in his *Libro de cifra nueva* (Alcalá, 1557), and later in Cabezón's *Obras de música* (Madrid, 1578) among others; it emphasized the division of the scale into a repeating octave pattern of seven white notes (the middle octave from *f* to *e′* is

Ex.8

assigned the numbers 1 to 7). Pitches one or two octaves lower were shown by one or two dashes through the number, pitches one or two octaves higher by a superscript dot or comma (fig.3). Each voice (from two to six) had a line of its own, chromatic alteration was indicated by sharps or flats placed after the note they affected, and rhythm signs of staff notation were added where required. Since these rhythm signs were valid for all the figures in the column below, the value of only the shortest of the notes to be played simultaneously could be precisely notated. A comma by itself indicated a tie from the preceding note, an oblique stroke or the letter 'p' a rest, and the letter 'R' an embellishment. Time and key signatures were given before the beginning of the piece, with B and ♮ standing for B♭ and B♮ respectively (see ex.8). An early 17th-century extension of this tablature for vocal music is discussed in §8 below.

All these numerical systems, *cifras* ('ciphers') as they were called in Spanish, had the great advantage that they could be set up in any printer's shop from standard or near-standard founts of type by unskilled compositors. Founts of music type were expensive; they could be adapted to keyboard music only with great difficulty and labour and they needed experienced and skilled typesetters. The engraving and punching of plates was ultimately to prove the best method of printing music, but it was still in its infancy when these numerical systems were flourishing. Derivations of them were in use for psaltery and dulcimer music as late as 1752 (in Pablo Minguet's *Academia musical*). Many variants have been put forward by a legion of theorists from the 13th century (*GB-Ob* Marsh 161) to the present day (see Wolf).

(v) Other forms of keyboard notation from 1500. Words like 'intavolatura' and 'tabulatura' were loosely used in many 16th- and 17th-century sources to describe music in staff notation or (at a slightly later date) in keyboard partitura. In Italy this can be seen in two of the earliest surviving printed sources of keyboard music, Andrea Antico's *Frottole intabulate da sonare organi, libro primo* (Rome, 1517) and Girolamo Cavazzoni's *Intavolatura cioè recercari, canzoni, himni, Magnificat* (Venice, 1543). In France a parallel can be seen in the *Dixneuf chansons musicales reduictes en la tablature des orgues espinettes manicordions* (Paris, 1530), the first of several such collections of keyboard music published by Pierre Attaingnant in the 1530s. In the early 17th century the use of the term 'tabulatura' to describe staff notation spread to Germany, an early example being Johann Ulrich Steigleder's *Ricercar tabulatura* (Stuttgart, 1624). Some early 17th-century German sources of keyboard music use words such as 'Tabulatur' or 'Tabulaturbuch' to describe the form of notation more properly known as keyboard partitura. These include Samuel Scheidt's *Tabulatura nova* (Hamburg, 1624) and Johann Ulrich Steigleder's *Tabulatur Buch darinnen dass Vater Unser* (Strasbourg, 1627). (*See* INTAVOLATURA and PARTITURA.)

4. The earliest known printed example of German lute tablature: Sebastian Virdung, 'Musica getutscht' (1511); each numeral refers to an open string and each letter or other symbol refers to one position on the fingerboard (each is given a rhythm sign)

5. Italian lute tablature: Francesco Spinacino, 'Intabolature de lauto, libro secondo' (1507); the lowest line of the 'staff' corresponds to the course highest in pitch

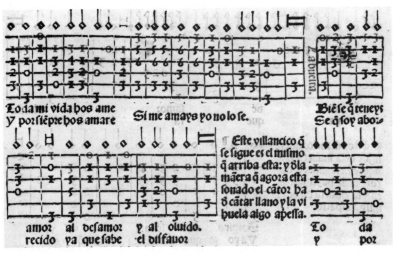

6. Spanish vihuela tablature: Luis de Milán, 'El maestro' (1536); the lowest line of the 'staff' corresponds to the course lowest in pitch, and the top line carries the vocal melody printed in red

7. French lute tablature: a presto by Silvius Leopold Weiss in Telemann, 'Der getreue Music-Meister' (1728–9); the lowest line of the 'staff' corresponds to the course lowest in pitch, and extra diapasons are indicated by ||a, |||a etc

3. LUTE. Although the German system of notating lute music is possibly the oldest it appears that the three principal systems of lute tablature were developed almost simultaneously in the second half of the 15th century. Their basic principle was to guide the fingers of the player's left hand over the lattice, formed by courses and frets crossing them at right angles, on the fingerboard. (In the following explanations 'course' will have its standard meaning. The usual 16th-century lute had seven frets and six courses of strings, usually tuned *G–c–f–a–d′–g′* or *A–d–g–b–e′–a′*. Each course consisted of either a single string or a pair of strings, the strings of a pair being tuned either in unison or at the octave; later instruments acquired extra frets and more strings: *see* LUTE). Each intersection of fret and course corresponded to a specific note, and an efficient system of notation therefore needed to identify each such intersection clearly and unmistakably. Even on a 15th-century lute with only five courses and five frets there were 30 such intersections (including the open strings) and on an early 17th-century theorbo-lute there might have been seven courses, up to 12 frets, and also six or seven 'diapasons' (open strings running clear of the fingerboard). The tablature for such an instrument needed to be capable of directing the player to form almost 100 notes. Moreover, the lute was required to give the impression of polyphonic part movement, so the tablature symbols needed to be capable of being grouped together two, three or four at a time. One area of inadequacy that lute tablatures share with Spanish keyboard tablatures is that the value of only the shortest of the notes to be played simultaneously could be notated precisely.

(i) Germany, 1511–1620. Although the earliest known printed example of the cumbersome German tablature, in Sebastian Virdung's *Musica getutscht* (fig.4), dates from 1511, the fact that the system was clearly designed for a five-course lute with five frets shows that it must have been invented considerably earlier. According to Virdung the system was attributed to the blind organist Conrad Paumann (1410–73). The open courses are numbered 1 to 5, with 1 corresponding to the bottom course, and each intersection of fret and course is denoted by a letter of the alphabet running across the fingerboard from bottom course to top. In order to provide the 25 symbols required, the common abbreviations for 'et' and 'con' were added to the 23 letters of the German alphabet; for higher frets the alphabet was repeated either in doubled letters or in letters with a dash above them (aa or ā, bb or b̄ etc). When a sixth course was added below the original five it was not possible to extend this closed system in any logical way, and several compromise solutions were used. The German tablature, with the most important of its alternative forms, is given in the diagram shown as ex.9. In practice, symbols intended to be played simultaneously were grouped in vertical columns; rhythm signs were placed above each note or group of notes, often grouped in twos or fours. The music was usually barred regularly (see ex.10).

The German tablature was strongly criticized as early as 1528 by Martin Agricola, although the alternative system he proposed was not adopted anywhere. Melchior Neusidler tried to introduce Italian lute tablature into Germany in the mid-16th century, but he met with much opposition.

Ex.9

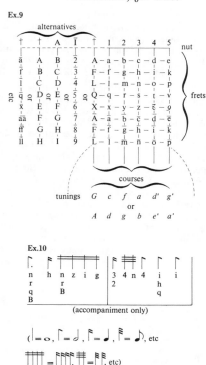

Ex.10

(accompaniment only)

$(\downarrow = \circ , \Gamma = \downarrow , \Gamma = \downarrow , \Gamma = \uparrow$, etc

$\dagger\dagger\dagger\dagger = \Gamma\Gamma\Gamma\Gamma , \dagger\dagger = \Gamma\Gamma$, etc)

(ii) Italy, 1500–1650. The Italian system was more logical than German lute tablature since it was a visual representation of the fingerboard. Its clarity and ease of application remained, however many courses or frets the instrument possessed. Each course was represented by a horizontal line, the bottom course corresponding to the top line (fig.5; in the playing position the bottom course of the lute is uppermost to the player's eye). The 'staff' formed in this way normally had six lines (i.e. as many as there were courses). The open course was represented by a figure 0 on the appropriate line, the first fret by 1, the second by 2 and so on, the 10th, 11th and 12th frets being represented by the special single symbols x, ẋ and x̄, since a double symbol like 10 might be confused with the two separate symbols 1 and 0. Rhythm signs were shown above the notes; at first they were repeated for each note or chord (see ex.11),

Ex.11

(accompaniment only)

$(\downarrow = \circ , \Gamma = \downarrow$, etc; in the earliest sources the following also occur:

$\Gamma = \Gamma\Gamma = \frac{3}{2}\circ ; \lnot = \lnot\lnot = \frac{3}{2}\circ)$

but from about 1530 onwards a more economical system prevailed whereby each rhythm sign remained valid until it was replaced by another. In later sources, both printed and manuscript, the normal staff notation rhythm signs tended to replace the traditional lute ones.

Diapasons were shown as numbers (from 7 to 14) set between the 'staff' and the rhythm signs. Italian tablature was used for some books printed in Kraków, Lyons and Strasbourg in the second half of the 16th century, and a few English and Austrian manuscripts are known (e.g. *GB-Lbm* Add.29246–7 and 31992); but it was mainly confined to Italy.

(*iii*) *Spain, 1530–80*. The indigenous Spanish instrument of the lute family was the vihuela, tuned and played like a lute, but shaped and strung slightly differently. Spanish tablature closely resembled Italian, although exceptionally, as in Milán's *El maestro* (1536), the six-line 'staff' was inverted so that the top line represented the highest course of the vihuela (fig.6). Occasionally a vocal line was included in staff notation above the tablature, as in Germany and Italy; or it might be incorporated in the tablature itself in red numerals. In some collections of Spanish lute music the compositions are barred in units of one semibreve, a system of barring that differs from that of most barred lute sources. Ordinary staff notation rhythm signs were used (see ex.12).

Ex.12

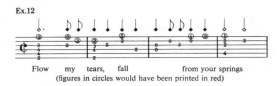

Flow   my   tears,   fall   from your springs
(figures in circles would have been printed in red)

(*iv*) *France, 1500–1815*. The French form of lute notation, adopted by English composers, was the most successful of all lute tablatures, and it eventually superseded the others. It used a five- or six-line 'staff' in which, as in Milán's book, the top line represented the highest course. The frets, however, were lettered and not numbered, the open string being 'a' or 'A', the first fret 'b' or 'B', and so on. To assist the eye in distinguishing between similar letters these were soon given special forms; the commonest lute alphabet is shown in ex.13.

Ex.13

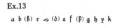

low   my   tears,   fall   from your springs

The letters were placed either on or above the line to which they referred. Lute and, later, staff notation rhythm signs were used, placed as usual above the 'staff'. Letters or figures beneath it denoted diapasons (fig.7); their tuning sometimes varied according to the key of the piece, but they usually descended diatonically (a, /a, //a, ///a, ////a . . .; 7, 8, 9, 10 or X, 11. . .). In English lute music plain letters below the 'staff' often denoted a seventh course running over the fingerboard and tuned a 4th below the sixth course.

(*v*) *Supplementary signs*. Many of the niceties of lute playing were indicated by special signs, the most important of which are listed here. A dot beneath a symbol sometimes meant that the chord was to be struck from above instead of, as normally, from below; it was more likely, however, to have been a fingering indication for the right hand (· = 1st, ·· = 2nd, ∴ or ·.· = 3rd, ···· = little finger). A vertical line facilitated orientation when the components of a chord were widely spaced. An asterisk, cross or oblique stroke by the side of a symbol showed that the stopping finger must be held down on its fret for as long as possible, thus sustaining the note or notes in question. A numeral by a symbol showed left-hand fingering. Slurs joining two symbols indicated a special kind of legato playing, only the first of the two notes being plucked. A wide variety of special signs was used to indicate trills and ornaments (see Dodge).

4. GUITAR.

(*i*) *Tablature proper, 1549–1741*. Throughout this period a certain amount of contrapuntal guitar music was written and published using French, Italian or Spanish lute tablature, and it needs no special discussion. Music for gittern or for five-string guitar can be identified by its tunings and the number of 'staff' lines – four for the gittern, five for the guitar. The first steps towards a new type of notation were made by Joan Carlos Amat in his *Guitarra española* (Barcelona, 1586, and later edns.); he assigned a single arabic numeral to each of the most frequently used chords (i.e. positions of the left hand), arranging them in a systematic order.

(*ii*) *'Alphabets', 1606–1752*. An important innovation was introduced by Girolamo Montesardo in his *Nuova inventione d'intavolatura* (Florence, 1606; fig.8). It was a new shorthand notation for *rasgueado* playing, sweeping the hand back and forth over all the strings at once, as distinct from *punteado* playing, in which the strings were plucked individually according to the lute technique. In Montesardo's system each left-hand finger position for the 27 usual chords was denoted by a single letter. Thus 'A' stood for the finger position which in five-line Italian tablature would have been shown as in ex.14 according to the tuning *A–d–g–b–e'*. These symbols were arranged above or below a horizontal line according to one of the following plans: a symbol above

> *Il Balletto della Pauaniglia sopra tre lettere si costuma sonare, e più vsato da Sonatori, cioè sopra la O, principalmente sopra la Ɛ, e sopra la L, e prima sopra la O, come vedete qui sotto.*
>
>   o   σ   o   g   g   A b
>   o Cc CC Co OO Gg G B Gg GG A Bb
>
>   a
>   C   H   B   C Ɑ a   Ɑ   C   Ɑ

8. *Abbreviated alphabetic notation for 'rasgueado' in guitar tablature introduced by Montesardo: Girolamo Montesardo, 'Nuova inventione d'intavolatura' (1606)*

Ex.14

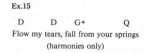

A =

(alphabet A–Z used, omitting J, U, and W,
but including +, &, $\mathcal{J}$ and R$_6$)

a line meant a chord struck upwards, below the line a chord struck downwards, and note values were shown by capital or small letters; or upward and downward dashes above or below the line showed the direction in which a chord was to be struck, and note values were shown by rests and staff notation notes or by the spacings between the dashes. Sometimes bar-lines were used, sometimes the horizontal line was broken up into a number of short equal segments, each representing a bar of music. Numerous modifications, additions and improvements were made to this primitive but adequate shorthand by the leading 17th-century guitar players such as Foscarini and Millioni (most are given in Wolf). Their most important single feature was the introduction of symbols for discords. The system was obviously easy to learn and extremely cheap to print, and a considerable amount of music in these 'alphabets' is still extant, most of it dating from the 17th century. Many manuscript collections of popular Italian poems of this period have 'alphabets' above the words as in ex.15, so that they may be sung to a strummed guitar.

Ex.15

D   D   G+   Q

Flow my tears, fall from your springs

(harmonies only)

Combinations of 'alphabets' and staff notation are found in some sources of the period. However, the most worthwhile guitar music of the period, for example Foscarini's and Corbetta's, is written in an unusual combination of conventional tablature and 'alphabet'; once the principles of each have been grasped it is not difficult to transcribe (see ex.16).

Ex.16

(accompaniment only)

After about 1750 guitar music was written in conventional staff notation an octave above the sounding pitch, the guitar like the double bass being regarded as a transposing instrument.

5. OTHER STRING INSTRUMENTS.
(*i*) *Plucked instruments*. Most plucked instruments (angelica, chitarrone, cittern, colascione, gittern, mandolin, orpharion, pandora, theorbo) used either French or Italian lute tablature, and once the tuning is known the transcription presents few difficulties. It is often impossible to tell for which instrument a tablature was intended until, by process of elimination, the tuning has been discovered, and this can sometimes be a lengthy process. Special harp tablatures were used in Ireland and Wales during the Middle Ages, and some features of their notation show surprising analogies with neumatic or ancient Greek notation; one of them (*GB-Lbm* Add.14905) purports to be a 17th-century copy of music played at a bardic congress of the late 11th

century, but the music itself and its notation make this extremely unlikely (*see* AP HUW, ROBERT, and NOTATION, fig.121). The surviving sources are too few and too meagre to deserve detailed description of their tablature systems. The Spanish keyboard tablature used by Arauxo, Cabezón, Venegas and Ribayaz was also suitable for the guitar, harp and vihuela (perhaps bowed), according to the title-pages of many of their works. 17th-century sources containing tuning instructions such as '(high) harpway sharp' or 'ton de la harpe par b mol' are for lyra viol or perhaps lute, but not for harp.

(*ii*) *Bowed instruments*. Much 17th-century lyra viol (*viola bastarda*) music was written in French lute tablature, and since some of the many lyra viol tunings were identical with contemporary lute tunings the question sometimes arises as to the instrument for which a certain composition was intended. There are usually two clues: in lyra viol music there are no gaps between the component letters of a chord, since it is impossible on a bowed instrument to omit one string when playing those on both sides of it; and all lyra viol music uses staff notation rhythm signs. Lyra viol tuning is often indicated at the beginning of a piece, the first letter of a pair shown for a string being the fret required to be stopped for that string to be in unison with the string above (see ex.17).

Ex.17

High harpway flat   (accompaniment only)

A certain amount of early viol and violin music is found in Italian tablature and there is a little 16th-century viol music in German tablature. Its mainly homophonic texture readily distinguishes it from lute music. *Lira da gamba* and baryton (*viola di bordone*) music is occasionally found in French tablature; as with music for lyra viol it may be identified by its tuning and by the disposition of the chords. A number of systems using figures have been used during the last two centuries for instruments such as the English guitar, zither, autoharp, balalaika, guitar and accordion, none of great interest or importance. One rather unexpected modern example of true tablature should be mentioned, however; it is for the ukelele, and is a schematic representation of the strings and frets of the instrument, with dots marking the position of the left-hand fingertips (*see* NOTATION, fig.119).

6. WIND INSTRUMENTS. Diagrams representing the finger-holes of wind instruments such as the clarinet, fife, flageolet, galoubet, oboe, recorder etc, showing which holes should remain open and which should be closed to produce certain notes and trills, have been a common feature of instrumental tutors since 1535 and have never lost their value and appeal. Mersenne's *Harmonie universelle* (1636–7) is a valuable source of a wide variety of such diagrams. Many tablatures of this nature ought more accurately to be described as 'fingering charts', since their use for the notation of music was at best limited, and mainly confined to late 17th-century music. Sufficient pictorial evidence exists to suggest that, for players of such instruments, the use of staff notation was very much the rule rather than the excep-

tion. Even so, 'dot-way' notation, as it was called, was in widespread use among English enthusiasts of the flageolet, and it survived into the 18th century. Six lines represented the six finger-holes of the instrument; a short vertical stroke on a line indicated that the hole in question was to be closed, a horizontal line through a stroke that it was to be played an octave higher, and a large comma that a grace note was called for. Rhythm signs, one to each note, were placed above the 'staff', and the music was barred regularly. Articulation, when shown, was notated by slurs (see ex.18).

Ex.18

(tune only)

Another tablature, for recorder, is found in Sebastian Virdung's *Musica getutscht* (1511), but as it was apparently not used for practical music it does not justify detailed explanation; a dot in a circle indicated that all the holes were closed, 1 that the bottom hole was open, the figure 2 with a diagonal stroke through it that the second was open, 2 that the bottom two holes were open and so on. A derivative of this system was in use in 17th-century music for the musette, but at no time did it completely replace staff notation. A special system of tablature was used by the Russian horn bands of the late 18th century; a band consisted of ten to 50 players, and as each was required to produce a note of only a single pitch all he needed to know was the rhythm and dynamic markings of his part. This was shown in staff notation on a single line with special signs for rests (fig.9). Other systems for notating rhythms alone have

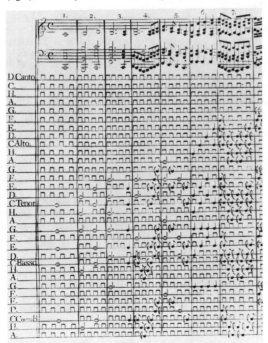

9. Russian horn band notation in score: J. C. Hinricks, 'Entstehung, Fortgang und . . . russ. Jagdmusik' (1796)

been used for hunting horns, trumpets and drums, but since they ignore the element of pitch they do not rank as true tablatures.

7. FIGURED BASS AND SIMILAR CHORDAL NOTATIONS. A distinction must be drawn between the accumulations of figures found in textbooks on figured bass and harmony, and those found in actual musical practice. The latter may be considered as a part-tablature, since their use constituted a valuable system of musical shorthand, conveying a great deal of information clearly and succinctly. The figured bass principle still fell short of a true tablature in two important respects: it required the retention of staff notation for the bass line; and a figured bass part was never intended to convey the detail of a continuo part but merely its most important harmonic and melodic features – only in exceptional cases, for instance, did the figures delineate the octave in which the various intervals above the bass were to be placed. Even so, it probably remains the only tablature which, although long since discarded for the notation of music, is still used in performance (for a full discussion *see* THOROUGHBASS). Certain other systems of chordal notation must be classed as true tablatures, for example Gottfried Weber's system of upper- and lower-case letters to indicate major and minor chords, or roman numerals to indicate root-position chords on various degrees of the diatonic major scale; this system was first expounded in his *Versuch einer geordneten Theorie der Tonsetzkunst* (1817–21). Hugo Riemann's functional harmony notation, proposed in his *Vereinfachte Harmonielehre* (1893), is another important tablature and is of great value in the analysis of classical harmony. It uses a combination of capital letters and signs of various kinds to denote the principal chords of a key and their variants.

Numerous new systems of musical notation and shorthand have been proposed during the last three centuries, but only those that dispense completely with the conventional five-line staff can be classed as true tablatures. Most, in any case, were too short-lived or too fanciful to be dealt with in detail here (but *see* NOTATION, §III, 5(iv), 6). The Braille system of musical notation for the blind (1829–34) must be mentioned, however. Its basis is a frame of six dots grouped as a rectangle; a large number of different and distinguishable symbols are available by embossing any dot or combination of dots on the paper, and by the use of various ingenious contractions and abbreviations both melody and harmony can be speedily notated and equally quickly deciphered (*see* BRAILLE NOTATION).

8. VOCAL MUSIC. Attempts at devising vocal tablatures had been made as early as 1600 or so, but none of them was very successful or important, nor were they true tablatures, since they did not completely dispense with the five-line staff. An extension of Venegas's system of Spanish keyboard tablature (see §2(iv), above) was used for vocal music in William Braythwaite's *Siren coelestis* (London, 1638), an illegally printed English edition of Catholic motets by Georg Victorinus which had first been issued in Munich in 1616. Braythwaite's system (see ex.19) was both complex and unattractive,

Ex.19

ↄ 6·5 4 3 1 7 6ª 5

(Treble   Flow my   tears, fall from your springs
clef)

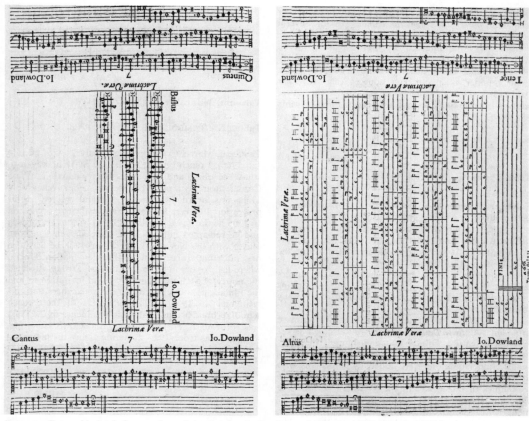

Pavan no.7, in table-book format, from John Dowland's 'Lachrimae' (London: John Windet, 1604)

being based predominantly on minor modifications of a single typographical fount of the numerals 1 to 7; the system required no fewer than 231 symbols, and must have proved extremely unpopular with singers if it was ever used for music-making. Its only advantage was that it required no music type and nothing that an adventurous jobbing printer would not have had in stock.

Tonic Sol-fa, which dates from 1812, is the only other vocal tablature of any importance (*see* TONIC SOL-FA).

BIBLIOGRAPHY

E. Gasparini: *Storia della semiografia musicale* (Milan, 1905)
J. Dodge: 'Ornamentation as Indicated by Signs in Lute Tablature', *SIMG*, ix (1907–8), 318
J. Wolf: *Handbuch der Notationskunde*, ii (Leipzig, 1919/R1963) [exhaustive study with comprehensive lists of sources, numerous facs. and exx.]
O. Chilesotti: 'Notes sur les tablatures de luth et de guitare', *EMDC*, I/ii (1921), 636–84
L. Schrade: *Die ältesten Denkmäler der Orgelmusik* (Münster, 1928)
W. Apel: *The Notation of Polyphonic Music, 900–1600* (Cambridge, Mass., 1942, rev. 5/1961)
K. Dorfmüller: 'La tablature de luth allemande et les problèmes d'édition', *Le luth et sa musique: CNRS Neuilly-sur-Seine 1957*, 245
A. Woodford: 'Music for Viol in Tablature: Manuscript Sources in the British Museum', *Chelys*, ii (1970), 23
H. Ducasse: 'Un problème de saisie de l'information: le traitement des tablatures', *Journées d'étude informatique musicale: ERATTO Paris 1973*, 48
J. Eppelsheim: 'Buchstaben, Notation, Tabulatur und Klaviatur', *AMw*, xxxi (1974), 57
For further bibliography *see* SOURCES OF INSTRUMENTAL ENSEMBLE MUSIC TO 1630; SOURCES OF KEYBOARD MUSIC TO 1600; SOURCES OF LUTE MUSIC.

THURSTON DART/JOHN MOREHEN

Table (Fr.). BELLY.

Table, Hermann. *See* TABEL, HERMANN.

Table-book. A manuscript or printed book of the 16th or 17th century in which the vocal or instrumental parts of an ensemble composition are displayed in such a way that the performers can read their parts while seated across or around a table. It is an extension of the choirbook system in which one volume suffices for all the performers, as opposed to the partbook system in which each performer is allocated an individual book. The Lyons printer Jacques Moderne was probably the first to issue a collection in which parts were disposed in inverted positions on the upper half of each side, *recto* and *verso*, of an opening (*Le parangon des chansons*, 1538). A similar system, but with the complete *recto* page inverted, was adopted by Pierre Phalèse for lute duets (1568). These systems were later modified so as to cater for as many as eight performers, although the obvious practical difficulties of performing music under such conditions suggest that this manner of performance was not normal practice. The table-book format was used for most collections of English lute airs and for such works as Dowland's *Lachrimae* (1604; see illustration) and Sir William Leighton's *The Teares or Lamentacions of a sorrowfull Soule* (1614). Several continental sources are in table-book format; they are considerably outnumbered by the English sources. Although printed music books account for the majority of table-books this principle was also adopted for a small number of manuscript sources (e.g. *GB-Lbm* Add.31390, *Och* 45 and *B-Br* II.4109). The latest sources in table-book format are certain English prints of the 1630s.

BIBLIOGRAPHY
S. F. Pogue: *Jacques Moderne* (Geneva, 1969), 46, 74, 77
D. W. Krummel: *English Music Printing: 1553–1700* (London, 1975), 104
JOHN MOREHEN

Table d'harmonie (Fr.). SOUNDBOARD.

Table entertainment. A peculiarly British species of performance, consisting generally of a mixture of narration and singing delivered by a single individual seated behind a table facing the audience. The material was often satirical. It seems to have originated about the middle of the 18th century. G. A. Steevens gave table entertainments in Dublin in 1752 and actors and singers such as R. Baddeley, G. S. Carey and J. Collins mounted them with great success in 1775–6 at many towns in Britain.

From 1789 to 1809 Charles Dibdin gave a series of table entertainments in London in which song was the prominent feature. Dibdin united in himself the functions of author, composer, narrator, singer and accompanist. Impersonations were added by comedians who took up the genre, which had much in common with the techniques of music hall in the Victorian period. The Edinburgh singer John Wilson gave table entertainments with a Scottish flavour from 1841 to his death, the first of which was entitled 'A Nicht wi' Burns'. The solo performances of Joyce Grenfell and others may be seen essentially as a modern survival of the tradition.

MICHAEL TILMOUTH

Tabor. A small side drum with one or more snares; see PIPE AND TABOR and DRUM, §3.

Taborowski, Stanisław (*b* nr. Krzemieniec, Volhynia, 1830). Polish violinist and composer. He studied music under Fenz and Billi at Odessa; he was also a student at St Petersburg University from 1847. He played his own compositions with success at a concert in Odessa in 1853, and then undertook a concert tour of Poland, Volhynia, Podolia and the Ukraine. From 1854 he studied in Brussels with Léonard (violin) and Damcke (composition), and returned to St Petersburg in 1859. He gave concerts in Warsaw in 1860, Kiev and Zhitomir in 1861, Kraków and Poznań in 1871–2, Wrocław, the spa of Ciechocinek, as well as many European cities, including Berlin and Paris. He was also a professor at the Freie Deutsche Hochschule der Musik, founded in Berlin in 1872 by Tyszkiewicz, and from 1878 he was in charge of the music school of Kronstadt in Transylvania.

WORKS
Stage: Une paire de bottes (opera buffa)
Orch: Ov.; Ov. intermezzo; Titan, ov.; Pas redoublé, military band; Vn Conc. (Berlin, 1860); Wisła mazur, vn, orch (Berlin, 1860); Aux bords de la Neva, vn, orch; Tarantella, vn, orch

Chamber: Str Qt; Elégie, vn, pf (Berlin, 1860); Les clochettes, vn, pf (Berlin, 1860); Śpiew łabędzi [The swan-song], vn, pf (Berlin, 1860); Skarga dziewczęcia [The maiden's lament], vn, pf; Barcarolle, vn, pf (St Petersburg, n.d.); studies, polkas and mazurkas, vn, pf

BIBLIOGRAPHY
SMP
Ruch muzyczny, v (1861), 240
IRENA PONIATOWSKA

Tabourot, Jehan. See ARBEAU, THOINOT.

Tabret. See TAMBOURINE; see also FRAME DRUM.

Tabuteau, Marcel (*b* Compiègne, 2 July 1887; *d* Nice, 4 Jan 1966). French oboist. At the age of 11 he began to study the oboe, and two years later entered the Paris Conservatoire as a pupil of Georges Gillet. When only 17 he was awarded a *premier prix* and entered on his professional career, first in a French theatre orchestra. In 1905 he was invited to the USA by Walter Damrosch and he remained until 1914 as oboe and english horn player with the New York SO. From 1908 he was also first oboe under Toscanini at the Metropolitan Opera, where his playing in a performance of *Tristan* attracted the notice of Stokowski and led to an invitation to join the Philadelphia Orchestra. He remained there until his retirement in 1954. As an exponent of the French school of oboe playing Tabuteau's influence in the USA was profound. He taught at the Curtis Institute, Philadelphia, from 1924, fostering many distinguished pupils, including John de Lancie who succeeded him in the Philadelphia Orchestra. His recordings include a 'master class' with his own illustrations and commentary, under the title *The Art of the Oboe*.

PHILIP BATE

Tacchinardi, Nicola [Niccolò] (*b* Livorno, 3 Sept 1772; *d* Florence, 14 March 1859). Italian tenor and singing teacher. Although his parents wanted him to become a priest, he gave up religious studies to study painting, sculpture and music. At the age of 17 he joined the orchestra of the Teatro della Pergola in Florence as a cellist, remaining there until 1797. He then studied singing and, after an apprenticeship in church choirs, sang in Livorno, Pisa, Florence and Venice in 1804. In the spring of the following year he appeared at La Scala in Paer's *Elisa e Griselda* and Farinelli's *Odoardo e Carlotta* for the celebration of the coronation of Napoleon I as King of Italy, and during Carnival 1805–6 sang at the Teatro Carcano, Milan, in Gnecco's *Le nozze di Lauretta*. From then until 1811 he established himself in Rome, in Bergamo, at the Teatro Comunale in Bologna (summer 1809) and at the Teatro Regio in Turin (Carnival 1810–11); he achieved his greatest success in Rome, at the Teatro Valle (1806–7) and the Teatro Argentina (1809–10) in Morlacchi's *Le Danaidi*, Nicolini's *Il traiano in Dacia* and Zingarelli's *La distruzione di Gerusalemme*.

His performance of *La distruzione di Gerusalemme* brought him tumultuous applause at the Paris Odéon on 4 May 1811, and he remained in Paris until 1814 at the Théâtre-Italien, singing in Paer's *Didone*, *Don Giovanni* (with the title role transposed), Cimarosa's *Gli Orazi ed i Curiazi* and Pucitta's *Adolfo e Chiara*, and winning his greatest success in Paisiello's *La bella molinara*. He sang in Spain from 1815 to 1817 and appeared in

Vienna in 1816. In 1818–19 he sang at the Teatro Argentina as well as in Bologna, Modena, Venice and Ravenna, performing in Mayr's *Danao*, Nicolini's *Cesare nelle gallie* and Rossini's *Ciro in Babilonia* and *Aureliano in Palmira*. In April 1820 he sang Othello in Rossini's *Otello* at the Teatro del Giglio in Lucca (an opera that became his warhorse), and in 1820–21 he appeared in *Il barbiere di Siviglia* and *La donna del lago*; Rossini, who had met Tacchinardi in Bologna in 1809, had a high regard for him as a singer.

Tacchinardi was made principal singer of the Grand Ducal Chapel in Florence in 1822, but was free to continue his operatic career, which brought him back successfully to Vienna in 1823 and to Barcelona in 1826, as well as to Ravenna, Turin, Trieste, Bergamo, Venice (1827–8) and Parma (1825), where he sang at the Teatro Ducale in *Il crociato in Egitto*, which Meyerbeer composed for him. He retired from the stage in 1831 and became a singing teacher; among his pupils were his daughter Fanny, E. Frezzolini and R. Mirate. He composed vocal exercises for his pupils and wrote an essay on contemporary opera in Italy (*Dell'opera in musica sul teatro italiano e de' suoi difetti*, Florence, 2/1833).

Short and stocky, though with a noble expressive face, Tacchinardi had a voice that was mellow, powerful, extensive in compass and almost baritone in colouring. His technique was masterly, especially with regard to breathing, phrasing, agility in vocal flourishes and ease in passing from chest voice to head voice. As an actor he was more controversial, probably modifying his approach with time as part of the transition from the 18th-century florid style to the expressiveness of the Romantic era. A marble bust of him by Canova is in the Museo della Scala in Milan.

Tacchinardi's son Guido (*b* Florence, 10 March 1840; *d* Florence, 6 Dec 1917), a conductor, a critic and a composer of theatrical, sacred choral and orchestral music, was the director of the Istituto Musicale in Florence from 1891 to 1917.

BIBLIOGRAPHY

FétisB
N. Jarro: *Le memorie di un impresario fiorentino* (Florence, 1892)
A. Bonaventura: *Musicisti livornesi* (Livorno, 1930)
A. Rapetti and C. Censi: *Un maestro di musica piacentino: Giuseppe Nicolini* (Piacenza, 1944)
A. Della Corte: *L'interpretazione musicale e gli interpreti* (Turin, 1951)
R. Celletti: 'Tacchinardi, Nicola', *ES*

FRANCESCO BUSSI

Tacchinardi-Persiani, Fanny (*b* Rome, 4 Oct 1812; *d* Neuilly-sur-Seine, 3 May 1867). Italian soprano and singing teacher. She was the second daughter of Nicola Tacchinardi, who taught her singing and made her perform at a very early age at the little theatre he ran for students near Florence. In 1830 she married the composer Giuseppe Persiani; she made her début in Livorno two years later in the title role of Giuseppe Fournier-Gorre's *Francesca da Rimini*. Singing in Venice in *Tancredi*, *La gazza ladra*, *Il pirata* and *L'elisir d'amore* (Carnival season 1832–3) and in Milan in *L'elisir*, *Beatrice di Tenda* and *La sonnambula* (summer 1833), she made a deep impression as an interpreter of Bellini and particularly of Donizetti, who wrote for her the title roles of *Rosmonda d'Inghilterra* (Florence, 1834), *Lucia di Lammermoor* (Naples, 1835) and *Pia de' Tolomei* (Venice, 1837). She scored further triumphs in

1834 at the Teatro del Fondo in Naples in Valentino Fioravanti's *Le cantatrici villane* and again in *L'elisir* and *Beatrice*, and in 1836 at the Teatro Comunale in Bologna in her husband's *Ines de Castro*; her frequent appearances in her husband's operas contributed to the success of these works.

She first sang in Paris at the Théâtre-Italien in the autumn of 1837 in *La sonnambula* and *Lucia*, and distinguished herself particularly as Carolina in *Il matrimonio segreto*. She remained there 13 years, appearing also in *Le nozze di Figaro*, *Don Giovanni* (as Zerlina), *Il barbiere di Siviglia*, *Linda di Chamounix* (1842) and her husband's *Il fantasma*. She sang in London almost every year from 1838 until 1849, first at the King's Theatre (where she made her début in *La sonnambula*) and later at Covent Garden, where her husband was manager and where she won distinction despite the public's recollections of Maria Malibran and Giulia Grisi; among other operas, she sang in *Lucia* with Giovanni Rubini. She also appeared in Vienna (1837 and 1844) in such works as *Torquato Tasso*, *Lucrezia Borgia*, *I due Foscari* and *Ernani*, in Holland (1850) and at the Italian Opera in St Petersburg (1850–52). In her last performances of *L'elisir* at St Petersburg, she showed signs of decline with a kind of 'hoarseness' which, according to Fétis, had already been noticeable in London in 1843. She retired from the stage and returned to Paris, managing the Théâtre-Italien briefly and unsuccessfully, and teaching singing jointly with her husband.

Called 'la piccola Pasta', she had a small and delicate voice that was sweet, polished, distinct by virtue of good placement, and had a compass of two octaves and a 5th ($b\flat$–f'''). Her technique was almost impeccable, with an extraordinary agility in embellishing (though apparently her trill was less satisfactory). Donizetti described it as 'ben precisa e intonatissima', and its lack of fullness of tone and passion was compensated for by its exceptional bel canto purity and near-instrumental virtuosity. Tacchinardi-Persiani's singularly ethereal presence – diaphanous, dreamy, pathetic – together with a fragile figure, a charming pale face and flaxen hair, fitted her for a complete identification with her roles of the early Romantic 'amorosa angelicata'. She was less effective in comic roles (in which she nevertheless triumphed) than as a lovelorn, dejected, tremulous heroine of a gloomy Romantic tragedy, idealized in chaste and innocent passion.

BIBLIOGRAPHY

FétisB
Chaudesaigues: *Madame Persiani* (Paris, 1839)
T. Gautier: *Histoire de l'art dramatique*, i (Paris, 1858)
E. Creathorn Clayton: *Queens of Song* (New York, 1865)
G. Tebaldini: 'Giuseppe Persiani e Fanny Tacchinardi, memorie e appunti', *RMI*, xii (1905), 579
G. Monaldi: *Cantanti celebri* (Rome, 1929)
A. Della Corte: *L'interpretazione musicale e gli interpreti* (Turin, 1951)
R. Celletti: 'Persiani, Fanny', *ES*

FRANCESCO BUSSI

Tacchino, Gabriel (*b* Cannes, 4 Aug 1934). French pianist. He graduated from the Paris Conservatoire in 1953, having won a *premier prix* for piano, and made his début the same year. He competed in various international competitions, winning the first prizes at Vercelli (1953), Geneva (1955) and Naples (1956), and then pursued an international concert career. He is a pianist of a gentle but disciplined temperament, praised especially for his fresh and stylish re-creations of the standard Classical and Romantic repertory. He has made a number of records, notably a recital of solo music by Poulenc, as well as Poulenc's Piano Concerto and *Aubade*, and concertos by Rakhmaninov and Beethoven.

DOMINIC GILL

Tacet (Lat.: 'he is silent'). An indication found in vocal and instrumental parts, mainly when a performer is silent for a whole movement. *Tacet al fine* shows that the performer is not required for the rest of the piece.

Tachezi, Herbert (*b* Wiener Neustadt, nr. Vienna, 12 Feb 1930). Austrian organist and harpsichordist. He studied at the Vienna Academy of Music under Karl Wolleitner (piano), Alois Forer (organ), Ernst Tittel, Alfred Uhl and Karl Schiske (composition) and Otto Siegl (musicology), while doing a course of German studies at Vienna University. From 1952 to 1967 he taught music in secondary schools in Vienna. In 1958 he began teaching the organ and composition at the Vienna Academy of Music (now the Musikhochschule), where in 1972 he became a professor. After taking harpsichord lessons from Fritz Neumeyer, in 1960 he began to play with the Vienna Soloists and the Zagreb Soloists. In 1964 he became permanent organist and harpsichordist with the Viennese ensemble Concentus Musicus, and in 1974 organist of the Hofmusikkapelle in Vienna. His many awards include first prize in the 1958 Innsbruck International Organ Competition and the Viennese Theodor Körner prize in 1965. He has given concerts in many European countries and in the USA, and made records and broadcasts, often with the Concentus Musicus. His repertory is based on European organ music, especially that of Bach, contemporary works and improvisation. He is also known as a composer of lieder, chamber music, and piano, organ, orchestral and vocal works (including choruses and masses). He has written an introduction to the playing of contemporary organ music entitled *Ludus organi contemporarii* (Vienna, 1973); he edits early music and contributes to Austrian music journals.

GERHARD WIENKE

Tactus. (1) The 15th- and 16th-century term for a beat, i.e. a unit of time measured by a movement of the hand, first discussed in detail by Adam von Fulda (1490). One *tactus* actually comprised two hand motions, a downbeat and an upbeat (*positio* and *elevatio*, or thesis and arsis). Each motion was equal in length in duple time (*tempus imperfectum*); in triple time (*tempus perfectum*) the downbeat was twice as long as the upbeat.

In theory the *tactus* in 16th-century music measured a semibreve of normal length (*integer valor notarum*), a breve in diminution (*proportio dupla*), and a minim in augmentation. Gaffurius (1496) wrote that one *tactus* equalled the pulse of a man breathing normally, suggesting that there was an invariable tempo then of MM = c60–70 for a semibreve in *integer valor*. Dahlhaus pointed out, however, that the length of the *tactus* did change in the 16th century; in *tempus perfectum diminutum* (ϕ), for example, the time value of the notes was reduced by one third and not one half so that the *tactus* was in fact faster. Moreover in isolated cases, for example in Luis de Milán's *vihuela* book, *El maestro*

(1536), tempo changes are indicated by verbal instructions (Milán wrote *apriessa* for quick and *espacio* for slow), a circumstance that naturally affects the length of the *tactus*.
See also CONDUCTING and PERFORMING PRACTICE, §4.

(2) The verb *tangere* was used from the Middle Ages onwards to mean 'to play on an organ' or, more generally, on any keyboard instrument. From this, *tactus* came to mean a short musical formula incorporated by organists into their improvisations. Various 15th-century German treatises on organ playing call their sample improvisations *tactus* while the Buxheimer Orgelbuch even gives the name to several entire compositions.

(3) Giorgio Anselmi, *De musica* (1434), used the word to mean the FRET on a lute or clavichord, and also the keys of a clavichord or organ (*see* KEY (ii)). Gaffurius, *De harmonia musicorum instrumentorum opus* (1518), followed Anselmi's example.

BIBLIOGRAPHY

G. Schünemann: 'Zur Geschichte des Taktschlagens', *SIMG*, x (1908–9), 73–114
——: *Geschichte des Dirigierens* (Leipzig, 1913)
W. Apel: *The Notation of Polyphonic Music, 900–1600* (Cambridge, Mass., 1942, rev. 5/1961)
A. Auda: 'Le "tactus" dans la messe "L'homme armé" de Palestrina', *AcM*, xiv (1942), 27–67
——: 'Le tactus, principe générateur de l'interprétation de la musique polyphonique classique', *Scriptorium*, iv (1950), 44
C. van den Borren and S. Cape: 'Autour du "tactus"', *RBM*, viii (1954), 41
C. Dahlhaus: 'Zur Theorie des Tactus im 16. Jahrhundert', *AMw*, xvii (1960), 22
——: 'Zur Entstehung des modernen Taktsystems im 17. Jahrhundert', *AMw*, xviii (1961), 223
H. O. Hiekel: '"Tactus" und Tempo', *GfMKB, Kassel 1962*, 145
A. Auda: *Théorie et pratique du tactus* (Brussels, 1965)
J. A. Bank: *Tactus, Tempo and Notation in Mensural Music from the 13th to the 17th Century* (Amsterdam, 1972)

HOWARD MAYER BROWN

Taddei, Giuseppe (*b* Genoa, 26 June 1916). Italian baritone. He studied in Rome and made his début there at the Teatro Reale dell'Opera in 1936, as the Herald in *Lohengrin*. He sang regularly in Rome until 1942, when he was conscripted into the army. His repertory at that time included Alberich, Germont and Rivière in Dallapiccola's *Volo di notte*. Taddei was imprisoned by the Germans but after his release he gave a concert for the American forces in Vienna, the success of which led to his engagement in 1946 for two seasons at the Vienna Staatsoper; he scored particular successes in the Verdi repertory. In 1947 he sang Scarpia and Rigoletto at the Cambridge Theatre, London, and in 1948 Mozart's Figaro at the Salzburg Festival. He resumed his Italian career that year, singing at La Scala (1948–51 and 1955–61); his roles there included Pizarro, Malatesta, the three villains in *Les contes d'Hoffmann*, and parts in operas by Sanzogno and Ferrari Trecate. Elsewhere in Italy he made a name for himself as Hans Sachs, Gunther, Wolfram and the Dutchman, all of which he sang in Italian. He began to specialize in Mozart, singing Papageno under Klemperer and Karajan, as well as Figaro and Leporello. He appeared at Covent Garden between 1960 and 1967 as Macbeth, Rigoletto, Iago and Scarpia, and was also heard in San Francisco, Chicago and, with notable success, at the Bregenz Festival (1968–9, 1971) as Falstaff, Dulcamara and Sulpice (*La fille du régiment*). Taddei was one of the most versatile and gifted Italian baritones of the postwar period, as successful in dramatic as in comic roles.

HAROLD ROSENTHAL

Tadei, Alessandro (*b* ?Graz, *c*1585; *d* Gandria, nr. Lugano, 1667). Italian composer and organist, possibly Austrian-born. From 16 March 1604 to 16 September 1606, at the expense of Archduke Ferdinand of Inner Austria, he studied in Venice with Giovanni Gabrieli, whom he visited again in 1610. At the end of 1606 he was appointed court organist at Graz. When the archduke became emperor as Ferdinand II in 1619, Tadei moved to Vienna with other musicians of the Graz court, and there is evidence that he was organist to the imperial court until 1628. From 11 November 1628 to 20 May 1629 he acted as Kapellmeister at the abbey of Kremsmünster in Upper Austria. It may well have been soon after this, as he was then a widower, that he entered the Carmelite monastery in Venice; he was certainly there in 1640. On 22 May 1642 he became second organist at Udine Cathedral, but his successor was appointed on 29 May 1647. He may then have retired to Gandria, though nothing is heard of him until his death.

Like his predecessors at Graz, Annibale Perini and Francesco Stivori, Tadei transplanted to Austria elements of Gabrieli's style, including polychoral techniques, as in his *Missa sine nomine* for 16 voices (*A-Wn*; Lugano, 1937) and the motet *Hodie beata virgo* for 10 voices (*A-KR* Cod. Lechler 12). His only known collection is the *Psalmi vespertini integri* for eight voices and continuo (Venice, 1628). There is also a motet for three voices and continuo, *O beatum Carolum*, in G. B. Bonometti's anthology *Parnassus musicus Ferdinandaeus* (*RISM* 1615[13]). According to Gerber, Tadei was 'a famous contrapuntist and composer of church music' in Italy, which may indicate that he continued to compose after 1630 although no music by him from his later years is known.

BIBLIOGRAPHY

GerberL

H. Federhofer: 'Alessandro Tadei, a Pupil of Giovanni Gabrieli', *MD*, vi (1952), 115

——: 'Graz Court Musicians and their Contributions to the *Parnassus musicus Ferdinandaeus* (1615)', *MD*, ix (1955), 167–244

——: *Musikpflege und Musiker am Grazer Habsburgerhof der Erzherzöge Karl und Ferdinand von Innerösterreich (1564–1619)* (Mainz, 1967), 216ff

D. Arnold: 'Gli allievi di Giovanni Gabrieli', *NRMI*, v (1971), 943–72

S. Schmalzriedt: *Heinrich Schütz und andere zeitgenössische Musiker in der Lehre Gabrielis* (Neuhausen, nr. Stuttgart, 1972)

HELLMUT FEDERHOFER

Tadolini [née Savonari], **Eugenia** (*b* Forlì, 1809; *d* Naples). Italian soprano. She studied with her husband, Giovanni Tadolini, and made her début in Florence in 1828, afterwards singing in Venice and Trieste. She first appeared in Paris at the Théâtre-Italien in Rossini's *Ricciardo e Zoraide* (23 October 1830). The following year she sang Donna Elvira in *Don Giovanni* and Jane Seymour in Donizetti's *Anna Bolena*, and in 1832 was heard as Amina in Bellini's *La sonnambula*. She appeared in Donizetti's *Il furioso all'isola di San Domingo* at La Scala on 1 October 1833 and the following February sang Jane Seymour at La Fenice. A single performance as Rosina in Rossini's *Il barbiere di Siviglia* at the Teatro Carcano, Milan, in spring 1834 was followed by appearances in Vienna as Adina in Donizetti's *L'elisir d'amore* and at Sinigaglia in the title

Eugenia Tadolini: lithograph (1844) by J. Carlo after Dolfino

role of Bellini's *Norma*. In 1836 she sang Antonina in Donizetti's *Belisario* both in Vienna and at La Scala, where she also appeared in Rossini's *Armida*. The following year she was engaged in Florence to sing Donizetti's *Lucia di Lammermoor*, and in 1838 she returned to Sinigaglia for Bellini's *I puritani*. In 1838–9 she sang at La Scala in Ricci's *La prigione d'Edimburgo* and Mercadante's *Il bravo*.

For the next few years she concentrated mainly on operas by Donizetti, singing in *Parisina* in Genoa, *L'esule di Roma* and *Fausta* in Bergamo and *Maria Padilla* in Naples. In 1842 she sang the title role in *Anna Bolena* in Vienna and appeared there in the first performance of *Linda di Chamounix* (19 May), rehearsed and conducted by the composer. The following year she sang Norina in *Don Pasquale* and the title role at the first performance of *Maria di Rohan* (5 June), with Donizetti conducting once again. One of the first sopranos to take up the cause of Verdi, she sang Elvira in *Ernani* in Vienna in 1844, and then created the title role of *Alzira* in Naples on 12 August 1845. She sang Odabella in *Attila* at La Scala in December 1846 and appeared in *Macbeth* at the Teatro S Carlo, Naples, in 1848, though Verdi considered her voice too beautiful and her personality not sufficiently violent for the part of Lady Macbeth.

She made her London début at Her Majesty's Theatre on 20 May 1848 in *Linda di Chamounix*, and later in the season she also sang in *Don Pasquale*. The same year she appeared in two more Donizetti operas, as Leonora in *La favorita* and as Paolina in the Italian première of *Poliuto*, both given at the Teatro S Carlo. She retired in 1851.

BIBLIOGRAPHY

G. Zavadini: *Donizetti: vita, musiche, epistolario* (Bergamo, 1948)

H. Weinstock: *Donizetti and the World of Opera in Italy, Paris and Vienna in the First Half of the 19th Century* (New York, 1963)

J. Budden: *The Operas of Verdi: from Oberto to Rigoletto* (London, 1973)

ELIZABETH FORBES

Tadolini, Giovanni (*b* Bologna, 18 Oct ?1789; *d* Bologna, 29 Nov 1872). Italian composer and singing teacher, husband of Eugenia Tadolini. He studied with Mattei and Babini at the Liceo Musicale in Bologna, and went to Paris to become *répétiteur* and later chorusmaster at the Théâtre-Italien (1811–14). He returned to Italy, where eight of his operas were produced between 1815 and 1827; he was made a member of the Accademia Filarmonica in Bologna, and was named *maestro di cappella* of the city's cathedral in 1825. In 1829 he returned to Paris to become the musical director of the Théâtre-Italien. He is said to have composed six sections of the *Stabat mater* commissioned from Rossini by the Spanish priest Varela, which received a single performance in Madrid on Easter Saturday, 1833. He returned once again to Bologna in 1848, where he founded and taught in a singing school.

WORKS

STAGE

La fata Alcina (dramma giocoso, 2), Venice, 1815
Le bestie in uomini (dramma, 2, A. Anelli), Venice, 1815
La principessa di Navarra ossia Il Gianni di Parigi (dramma serio, 5), Bologna, 1816
Il credulo deluso (dramma giocoso, 2, C. Sterbini), Rome, 1817; given as Il finto molinaro, Rome, 1820
Tamerlano, Bologna, 1818
Moctar, Gran Visir di Adrianopoli (dramma serio, 2), Bologna, 1824
Mitridate (melodramma eroico, 2, G. Rossi), Venice, 1827
Almanzor (melodramma serio, 2, F. Romani), Trieste, 1827

OTHER WORKS

Numerous cantatas and other sacred vocal works, many with orch acc.; arias; songs
2 sinfonie, orch; Concertone, ob, bn, orch; chamber music for wind insts

BIBLIOGRAPHY

L. Sgargi: 'I professori principali dei tre pubblici stabilimenti di musica in Bologna', *Miscellanea musicale*, ed. G. Gaspari (MS, *I-Bc*), i, 236
G. Radiciotti: *Gioachino Rossini* (Tivoli, 1927–9)

ELIZABETH FORBES

Taegio [Taeggio]. *See* ROGNONI family.

Tafall y Miguel, Mariano (*b* *c*1813; *d* Santiago de Compostela, 26 Sept 1874). Spanish organist, organ maker and composer. Tafall began his career as an instrumentalist. In 1836 he was already conductor of an important military band, but resigned the post within a year to become an instrumentalist at the Cathedral of Burgos. In 1854 he went to Santiago as an instrumentalist for the cathedral there; he was later appointed organist and made and repaired organs. As an organ maker Tafall was active in the provinces of Galicia, repairing and constructing organs in various cathedrals and churches. By 1855, he had fully repaired one of the two main organs of the Cathedral of Santiago.

In his last years, he assembled the knowledge gained from his long experience as an organ maker in his four-volume treatise: *Arte completo del constructor de órganos, o sea guía manual del organero* (Santiago de Compostela, 1872–6). This book is still valuable, for it is extraordinarily clear, practical and complete, although Tafall was more an artisan than a theoretician.

Tafall left some fine compositions. Both his sons, Rafael and Santiago Tafall Abad, were good organists and composers.

BIBLIOGRAPHY

J. López-Calo: *Catálogo musical del Archivo de la Santa Iglesia Catedral de Santiago* (Cuenca, 1972)

JOSÉ LÓPEZ-CALO

Tafelklavier (Ger.). SQUARE PIANOFORTE.

Tafelmusik (Ger.: 'table music'; Fr. *musique de table*). A term used since the 16th century for music at feasts and banquets, both in noble and middle-class circles, and as a title for printed and manuscript music anthologies. Musical presentations at feasts were common in antiquity, and written and pictorial accounts of musical compositions and performances *in conviviis et festis* survive from the Middle Ages. However, the expression 'Musik zur Tafel', 'Tafelmusik' or 'musique de table' (with related compounds) came into use only in the mid-16th century, when it delimited a genre equivalent in stature to sacred or chamber music. Appointment records and descriptions of duties in chapel archives from the second half of the century frequently refer to vocal and instrumental performance *zur Taffel* ('at the table').

Michael Praetorius (*Syntagma musicum*, iii (2/1619), 130 [*recte* 110]) reported that vocal and instrumental music was performed at feasts as at intermezzos ('Also und dergestalt kan man es mit anordnung einer guten Music vor grosser Herrn Taffel oder bey andern frölichen conventibus auch halten'). In 1617 Samuel

Tafelmusik: panel entitled 'Feast of Ahasuerus' from a retable (1494) by ? Wilm Dedeke in the St Annen-Museum, Lübeck; two shawms and a sackbut can be seen in the musicians' gallery (see also NUREMBERG, fig.2)

Schein published his *Banchetto musicale*, and paraphrases of the expression 'Tafelmusik' soon became common, for example in Isaac Posch's *Musicalische Tafelfreudt* and Thomas Simpson's *Taffel Consort erster Theil* (both 1621). During the 17th century vocal works (often with continuo) and instrumental suites alike were published under the title 'Tafelmusik' or 'Musique de table'. In J. V. Rathgeber's collections (1733–46) instrumental works in several genres appear alongside songs and polyphonic vocal pieces; Telemann's three sets (1733, published as *Musique de table*) each consist of an overture and suite, a quartet, a concerto, a trio sonata, a solo sonata and a 'conclusion'. In the second half of the 18th century *Tafelmusik*, which had always tended to be light and entertaining, approached the character of the DIVERTIMENTO and was given such alternative titles as *Musicalische Blumenlese*, *Musikalisches Magazin* or *Musikalischer Blumenkranz*. The importance of the genre soon diminished and even the purpose met with disapproval. Zelter's *Liedertafel*, although based on nationalist political elements, partly restored the original function of *Tafelmusik* to the 19th century.

BIBLIOGRAPHY

M. Ruhnke: *Beiträge zu einer Geschichte der deutschen Hofmusikkollegien im 16. Jahrhundert* (Berlin, 1963)
G. Hausswald: *Die Orchesterserenade*, Mw, xxxiv (1970)
E. Reimer: 'Tafelmusik', *HMT* (1972)

HUBERT UNVERRICHT

Taffanel, (Claude) Paul (*b* Bordeaux, 16 Sept 1844; *d* Paris, 22 Nov 1908). French flautist. Taffanel may be regarded as the father of the modern French school of flute playing. The son of a music teacher, he played the flute in local concerts at the age of ten. In 1858 he was accepted as a pupil by Dorus and when in 1860 the latter became professor at the Paris Conservatoire, Taffanel joined his class. This association was of great importance, for it was under Dorus that the Boehm flute was first recognized and taught officially in France. While still studying harmony, counterpoint and fugue at the Conservatoire, Taffanel's professional career began, first at the Opéra Comique, and from 1864 at the Opéra. In 1870 he became solo flautist there, and from 1890 conductor. In this same year he was appointed conductor to the brilliant Société des Concerts du Conservatoire, in which he had formerly played. Taffanel's concern for polished wind playing led in 1879 to the foundation of the Société des Instruments à Vent, which for 14 years exerted tremendous influence throughout Europe.

With the resignation of Altes, successor to Dorus, Taffanel was appointed to the Conservatoire vacancy in 1893 and quickly attracted a brilliant group of pupils who, in turn, passed on his methods. As professor he is recorded as being less rigid in the application of official rules than were his predecessors and to have been flexible in his teaching practice, suiting his instruction to the individual capacity and temperament of the student. His performing style was pure and devoid of all meretricious effects such as excessive use of vibrato. Taffanel's teaching remains embodied in a *Méthode complète* produced in association with Gaubert, and some excellent chamber music for wind and arrangements for flute and piano.

PHILIP BATE

Tag, Christian Gotthilf (*b* Beierfeld, 2 April 1735; *d* Niederzwönitz, nr. Zwönitz, 19 July 1811). German Kantor and composer. In 1749, through the assistance of G. A. Homilius, he was awarded a scholarship to the Dresden Kreuzschule, where he studied for six years. In 1755 he became Kantor and schoolteacher in Hohenstein-Ernstthal, where he remained until his retirement in 1808, having established an outstanding reputation as a Kantor and organist.

Tag was a prolific composer of *Kantorenmusik* in a style combining elements of the Baroque and *Empfindsamkeit*. At the centre of his creative output were his sacred cantatas; written between 1760 and 1780, predominantly to Pietist texts, they reflect the influence of Hasse and J. G. Naumann (a personal friend of Tag's) and are particularly striking for their conservative adherence to fugue and their penchant for tone-painting and symbolism. The masses, of the two-movement *missa brevis* type with recitatives and arias, closely resemble the cantatas. After 1780 Tag emerged as a fashionable composer of lieder and keyboard pieces in a style heavily indebted to J. A. Hiller and the Berlin lied school. In his organ compositions he applied Rococo and *empfindsamer Stil* orchestral and keyboard music techniques. An *Orgelprobe* and a series of 26 letters formerly in the archives of Breitkopf & Härtel (1795–1806) are now lost.

WORKS

Sacred: 106 cantatas [3 with only texts extant], solo vv, chorus, insts, most in *PL-GD*, some in *D-ABG*, *Bds*, *CR*, *HOE*, *LST*, *ZE* and elsewhere [details in Vieweg (1933)]; 6 masses, 4vv, 3 with insts, *Bds*; Mass, 4vv, insts, *HOE*; motets, hymns, other sacred works, *ABG*, *Bds*, *BIT*, *HOE*, *LÜh*, *MLHb*, *USSR-KAu*; Melodie zum Vaterunser und zu den Einsetzungsworten des Abendmahls, org acc. (Penig, n.d.)
Lieder collections: [17] Lieder beim Clavier zu singen (Leipzig, 1783); [16] Lieder beim Clavier zu singen nebst einer melodramatischen Scene, ii (Leipzig, 1785); [3] Lieder der Beruhigung (F. von Matthisson, S. G. Bürde) (Leipzig, 1793); 24 Lieder nebst einer 4-stimmigen Hymne . . . beim Klavier zu singen, iii (Dresden, 1798)
Other vocal: Auf den Borschberg bei Pillnitz (Leipzig, 1783); Pilgerlied (C. Overbeck) (Leipzig, 1787); Volksgesang an die Chursächsische Armee (J. F. Dietrich) (Dresden, 2/1795); Urians Reise um die Welt . . . und Urians Nachricht von der neuen Aufklärung (Leipzig, 1797); Wörlitz, eine Ode . . . nebst einem Vorbereitung des Dichters (Dietrich) (Berlin, 1802); Todtenopfer unserm vollendeten Naumann (Dresden, n.d.); many lieder in contemporary anthologies; secular cantatas, incl. 3 in *D-Dlb*, 1 in *Bds*, 4 in *A-Wn*; 2 arias, S, orch, *PL-GD*; miscellaneous lieder, *A-Wn*, *D-Dlb*
Kbd: 6 Choralvorspiele nebst einem Trio und Allabreve, org (Leipzig and Dessau, 1783); 70 Veränderungen über ein Andantino fürs Klavier (Leipzig and Dessau, 1784); Der Glaube, mit einer neuen Melodie für die Orgel (Leipzig, 1793); 12 kurze und leichte Orgelvorspiele nebst einer Orgelsinfonie, org, pf, i (Leipzig, 1794); 6 kurze und leichte Parthien für kleine Anfänger . . . mit darüber gesetzter Applikatur und einer Ausführung der Manierung nach Bachischen Grundsätzen, i (Meisser, 1804); several pieces in contemporary anthologies; chorale preludes and arrs., org, 11 in *LEm*, 2 in *Bds*; Kurtze und leichte Clavier Stücken durch alle Tone Dur und Moll, *LEm*; Divertimento II, hpd, *LEm*

Sym., qt, other kbd sonatas and divertimentos, other works, lost, mentioned in Tag's letters, *GerberNL* and Vieweg (1933)

BIBLIOGRAPHY

EitnerQ; *GerberL*; *GerberNL*
R. [? F. Rochlitz]: 'Christian Gotthilf Tag', *AMZ*, xvii (1815), col.681
F. Rochlitz: *Für Freunde der Tonkunst*, iii (Leipzig, 1830), 143
H. J. Vieweg: *Christian Gotthilf Tag (1735–1811) als Meister der nachbachischen Kantate* (diss., U. of Leipzig, 1933; Leipzig, 1933) [with index of works]
G. Frotscher: *Geschichte des Orgel-Spiels und der Orgel-Komposition* (Berlin, 2/1959)

DIETER HÄRTWIG

Tag, Christian Traugott (*b* Hohenstein-Ernstthal, 2 June 1777; *d* Glauchau, 12 July 1839). German Kantor and composer, nephew of Christian Gotthilf Tag. He received his early education from his uncle, then attended the Leipzig Thomasschule for eight years, where he was encouraged by J. A. Hiller. After studying philosophy and theology at Leipzig University he became Kantor in Jessen (1803). In 1805 he went to Glauchau as Kantor, director of music and schoolteacher. Unlike his uncle, he composed few works; his known publications include two sacred choral pieces (*Worte der Beruhigung bey unverschuldeten Schicksalen*, 1813, and the litany *Ewiger, erbarme dich*, 1815) and 12 variations on *Gaudeamus igitur* for keyboard and flute. A Gloria for chorus and instruments survives in manuscript, and his *Hosianna! Davids Sohn* for Advent was transmitted orally until its publication in W. Hüttel's *Volkslieder aus der Glauchauer Pflege*.

BIBLIOGRAPHY

B. F. Jäneke: 'Christian Traugott Tag', *Neuer Nekrolog der Deutschen 1839*, xvii (1841), 628

H. J. Vieweg: *Christian Gotthilf Tag (1735–1811) als Meister der nachbachischen Kantate* (diss., U. of Leipzig, 1933; Leipzig, 1933)

DIETER HÄRTWIG

Tagelied (Ger.: 'day song'). A German strophic song announcing or praising the break of day, cultivated notably by Minnesinger in the late Middle Ages and strongly influenced by the Provençal ALBA, which dealt with similar subjects. Early polyphonic examples include one attributed to Hermann von Salzburg in the Mondsee-Wiener Liederhandschrift, in which the lower part is the song of a nightwatchman while the upper part is a trumpet prelude followed by a dialogue between parting lovers. Wolfram von Eschenbach and Oswald von Wolkenstein are other important composers of *Tagelieder*. The tradition of the *Tagelied* was eventually incorporated into German folksong and especially into popular hymns, as in Philip Nicolai's 16th-century chorale *Wachet auf, ruft uns die Stimme*. It was revived by Wagner in the warning 'Habet acht! Schon weicht dem Tag die Nacht', with which Brangäne wakes the lovers in Act 2 of *Tristan und Isolde*.

See LIED, §I.

BIBLIOGRAPHY

H. Ohling: *Das deutsche Tagelied vom Mittelalter bis zum Ausgang der Renaissance* (diss., U. of Cologne, 1938)

B. Stäblein: 'Eine Hymnusmelodie als Vorlage einer provenzalischen Alba', *Miscelánea en homenaje a Monseñor Higinio Anglés*, ii (Barcelona, 1961), 889

A. T. Hatto: 'Das Tagelied in der Weltliteratur', *Deutsche Vierteljahrsschrift für Literaturwissenschaft und Geistesgeschichte*, xxxvi (1962), 489

Tagh. (1) A type of hymn of the Armenian Church, collected in a book known as the *tagharan*; *see* ARMENIAN RITE, MUSIC OF THE. For discussion of the relationship between the *tagh* and Armenian folksong, *see* UNION OF SOVIET SOCIALIST REPUBLICS, §I, 2(v).

Tagi-zade-Hajibeyov, Nijazi Zul'fagarovich. *See* NIJAZI.

Taglia, Pietro (*fl* Milan, 2nd half of the 16th century). Italian composer. He was a madrigalist of cultivated taste, a member of the circle of noble connoisseurs who, during the period when Milan was reduced to a province of Spain and was dominated by the spirit of the Counter-Reformation, nevertheless kept alive the love of secular music. In his two books of madrigals Taglia followed the new and daring harmonic technique of Cipriano de Rore; indeed, one of his madrigals is included in the *Quarto libro di madrigali* (*RISM* 1557[23]) by de Rore. The texts he set are taken from some of the finest writers: Petrarch, Ariosto, Boiardo, Sannazaro and G. B. Giraldi. Taglia's style is rich in harmonic and rhythmic alternations and contrasts, but he could adapt it to the direct and the popular when the text so required. The extent to which his compositions were appreciated is demonstrated by the large number of collections in which they appear. The greater part of these anthology pieces are new compositions as distinct from those included in the three books published by Taglia himself. He had, apparently, an extremely original personality: Einstein referred to him as 'a genius of high order'.

WORKS

Il primo libro de madrigali, 4vv (Milan, 1555); 1 ed. in Einstein, iii, 120
Il primo libro de madrigali, 5vv (Milan, 1557)
Il secondo libro di madrigali, 5vv (Venice, 1564)
Further vocal works, 1557[23]; 1559[16]; 1564[16], ed. S. Cisilino, Celebri raccolte musicali venete del Cinquecento, i (Padua, 1974); 1567[13]; 1569[25]; 1575[4]; 1579[4]; 1600[5]
3 madrigals, 4vv, *I-CMs*; several madrigals, 5–8vv, *VEaf*

BIBLIOGRAPHY

A. Einstein: *The Italian Madrigal*, i (Princeton, 1949/R1971), 425

MARIANGELA DONÀ

Tagliabue, Carlo (*b* Mariano Comense, 13 Jan 1898; *d* Monza, 5 April 1978). Italian baritone. He studied with Gennai and Guidotti and made his début at the Teatro Verdi, Lodi, in 1922 as Amonasro. After appearances in provincial theatres and in Florence, Palermo and the Verona Arena, where he first sang in 1930, he was engaged for La Scala in 1930 and appeared there regularly until 1943 and between 1946 and 1953. As well as singing in the Italian repertory, he was heard as Telramund, Wolfram, Gunther and Kurwenal. At the Rome Opera he created Basilio in Respighi's *La fiamma* (1934), and he sang Scedeùr in the first performances at La Scala of Pizzetti's *Lo straniero*. He sang at the Metropolitan Opera, where he made his début as Amonasro (1937–9), in San Francisco (1938) and at the Teatro Colón, Buenos Aires (1934). He made his Covent Garden début in 1938 as Rigoletto and returned in 1946, as Germont, with the San Carlo company from Naples, which gave the first opera performance there after the war. In 1953 he sang Carlo in *La forza del destino* at the Stoll Theatre. He continued to sing until 1960. Tagliabue possessed a warm, beautifully produced lyric baritone voice, and he rarely made an ugly sound. But his acting was limited and his performances were reliable rather than inspired.

BIBLIOGRAPHY

G. Lauri-Volpi: *Voci parallele* (Milan, 1955)
R. Celletti: 'Tagliabue, Carlo', *Le grandi voci* (Rome, 1964) [with opera discography by R. Vegeto]

HAROLD ROSENTHAL

Tagliafico, Joseph (Dieudonné) (*b* Toulon, 1 Jan 1821; *d* Nice, 27 Jan 1900). French bass of Italian parentage. He studied in Paris and made his début there in 1844 at the Théâtre-Italien. On 6 April 1847 he sang Oroe in the performance of *Semiramide* that inaugurated the Royal Italian Opera at Covent Garden, and he appeared there every season until 1876. He sang Oberthal in *Le prophète* (1849), Sparafucile in *Rigoletto* and Fieramosca in *Benvenuto Cellini* (1853), Ferrando in *Il trovatore* (1855), the High Priest of Brahma in *L'africaine* (1865) and Friar Lawrence in *Roméo et*

Juliette (1867), all first London performances. Although his voice was neither large nor remarkable in quality, his extreme versatility made him one of the most highly valued singers of his day. His enormous repertory included many other roles in the operas of Mozart, Rossini, Bellini, Donizetti, Halévy, Meyerbeer, Gounod and Verdi. He was the stage manager at Covent Garden from 1877 to 1882, composed some songs, and wrote criticism for *Le ménestrel* under the name of De Retz.

BIBLIOGRAPHY
H. Rosenthal: *Two Centuries of Opera at Covent Garden* (London, 1958)
ELIZABETH FORBES

Tagliapietra, Gino (*b* Ljubljana, 30 May 1887; *d* Venice, 8 Aug 1954). Italian composer, pianist and musicologist. He studied in Vienna and under Busoni in Berlin, and taught the piano at the Liceo Musicale, Venice (1906–40). A promising career as a concert pianist was soon undermined by recurrent neuritis in his right arm. As a composer Tagliapietra has attracted little attention, even in Italy, though his piano music has remarkable qualities. A loyal disciple of Busoni, he showed in his best pieces (e.g. the two sets of *Tre pezzi* listed below, or the tough, uncompromising *Otto preludi*) that he could use a basically Busonian language with a vitality that is not merely second-hand: these pieces sometimes have a distinctive, rugged hardness that has led one writer to see aptness in Tagliapietra's name ('stone cutter'). Similar qualities may be found even in his didactic works, notably the *40 studii di perfezionamento*: technical exercises whose musical intensity and exceptional harmonic enterprise call to mind those in Busoni's *Klavierübung*.

WORKS
(*selective list*)

Stage: La bella addormentata, fiaba musicale, textless, H. Tagliapietra, Venice, 1926, unpubd

Orch and vocal orch: Pf Conc., pf, chorus, orch, 1913, unpubd; Pf Concertino, 1922; Parafrasi, pf, orch, 1922; Requiem, 1923, unpubd; Variazioni a fantasia, pf, str, 1930

Pf: 3 pezzi, 1910; Per la gioventù, 24 bagatelles, 1914; Ad heroum majorem gloriam, 2 pf, 1914–18; 3 pezzi, 1918; 40 studii di perfezionamento, 2 vols., 1922; 3 esercizii, una toccata e fughetta, 1924; 3 esercizii e 20 variazioni, 1925; Rapsodia armena, 1932; 8 preludi, 1937

Other works: Sonata, vn, 1937; songs, choral pieces

Edns.: *Antologia di musica antica e moderna per il pianoforte* (Milan, 1931–2), *Raccolta di composizioni dei secoli XVI e XVII* (Milan, 1937)

Principal publishers: Carisch, Giuliana (Trieste), Ricordi, Sanzin (Venice)/Zanibon (Padua)

MSS in *I-Vnm* [principal collection], *US-Wc*, *NYp*

BIBLIOGRAPHY
R. Stevenson: 'Busoni: the Legend of a Prodigal', *Score* (1956), no.15, p.28
J. C. G. Waterhouse: *The Emergence of Modern Italian Music* (*up to 1940*) (diss., U. of Oxford, 1968), 611ff
F. M. Vadalà: *Gino Tagliapietra* (diss., U. of Messina, 1976)
JOHN C. G. WATERHOUSE

Tagliato (It.). CUT TIME.

Tagliavini, Ferruccio (*b* Reggio Emilia, 14 Aug 1913). Italian tenor. He studied in Parma with Brancucci and in Florence with Amadeo Bassi. He made his début in October 1938 in Florence as Rodolfo in *La bohème* and by the end of World War II had established himself as one of the leading tenors of the Italian stage; he then appeared successfully at the Metropolitan (1947–54 and 1961–2). During the Scala's 1950 visit to Covent

Garden, he sang Nemorino in *L'elisir d'amore*, revealing his vocal achievements as well as a considerable talent as a comic actor. He made further appearances in London as Cavaradossi and as Nadir in *Les pêcheurs de perles*.

Essentially a *tenore di grazia*, Tagliavini excelled in the bel canto operas of Bellini and Donizetti and in the title role of Mascagni's *L'amico Fritz*, which he recorded under the composer's direction, with his wife, the soprano Pia Tassinari, as Suzel. Many regarded him as the successor of Tito Schipa; Tagliavini's style, however, was less dependable. He could spin out a sustained note until it became a mere thread of tone, and he sang florid passages more accurately than was usual in the postwar period; but he also relied on abrupt transitions between *fortissimo* and *pianissimo* to the neglect of the intermediate shades, and in later years permitted his louder tones to develop a harsh quality.

BIBLIOGRAPHY
C. Tedeschi: *Ferruccio Tagliavini* (Rome, 1942)
A. Natan: 'Tagliavini, Ferruccio', *Primo uomo* (Basle, 1963) [with LP discography]
G. Gualerzi: 'Tagliavini, Ferruccio', *Le grandi voci* (Rome, 1964) [with opera discography by R. Vegeto]
H. Rosenthal: 'Ferruccio Tagliavini', *Great Singers of Today* (London, 1966), 193
DESMOND SHAWE-TAYLOR/HAROLD ROSENTHAL

Tagliavini, Luigi Ferdinando (*b* Bologna, 7 Oct 1929). Italian organist, harpsichordist and musicologist. He studied at the conservatories of Bologna and Paris (1947–52) under Ireneo Fuser and Marcel Dupré (organ), Napoleone Fanti (piano) and Riccardo Nielsen (composition). He took the PhD at the University of Padua in 1951 with a dissertation on the texts of Bach cantatas. From 1952 to 1954 he taught the organ at the G. B. Martini Conservatory in Bologna and had charge of the conservatory library from 1953 to 1960. In 1954 he became organ professor at the Monteverdi Conservatory in Bolzano and taught there until 1964, when he was appointed organ professor at the Boito Conservatory in Parma. Since 1959 he has taught regularly at the summer organ courses in Haarlem.

Tagliavini's academic career began in 1959 with his appointment as *Privatdozent* in music history at the University of Bologna. He was visiting professor at Cornell University in the summer of 1963 and at the State University of New York at Buffalo in the autumn of 1969. In 1965 he became reader in music history and director of the Institute of Musicology at the University of Fribourg, and in 1971 was appointed professor there. Since then he has divided his time between Bologna, where he has made a fine collection of old instruments, and Fribourg.

Tagliavini has taken a pioneering interest in organ restoration based on historical research, and in his official capacity on Italian and Swiss state commissions he has rescued a number of valuable organs from neglect and destruction. He has also contributed three volumes to the Neue Mozart-Ausgabe and is editor of Monumenti di Musica Italiana and of *L'organo*, which he founded in 1960 with R. Lunelli. He is a well-known and widely recorded performer on the organ and harpsichord; his concerts have taken him to nearly every European country and to North America. His performances of older music, particularly Italian, combine his talents as musicologist and practical musician to produce lively, yet authentic interpretations. Taking advantage of the Italian placement of organs in the choir, he has frequently explored the two-organ repertory and has made several such recordings with Marie-Claire Alain.

WRITINGS

Studi sui testi delle cantate sacre di J. S. Bach (diss., U. of Padua, 1951; Padua, 1956)

'Glorioso passato e problemi presenti della Biblioteca Musicale "G. B. Martini" di Bologna', *FAM*, ii (1955), 62

'La scuola musicale bolognese', *Musicisti della scuola emiliana*, Chigiana, xiii (1956), 9

'L'ópera italien du jeune Mozart', *Les influences étrangères dans l'oeuvre de Mozart: CNRS Paris 1956*, 125–56

'Primo contatto bolognese [di Mozart]' and '[Mozart] accademico filarmonico', *Mozart in Italia*, ed. A. Della Corte and G. Barblan (Milan, 1956), 76, 108

'Un musicista cremonese dimenticato: ritornano alla luce i Ricercari a quattro voci di Niccoló Corradini', *CHM*, ii (1956), 413

with O. Mischiati: 'Prefazione', *T. Merula: Composizioni per organo e cembalo*, ed. A. Curtis (Brescia, 1961)

——: 'Prefazione', *G. Frescobaldi: Nove toccate inedite*, ed. S. Dalla Libera (Brescia, 1962)

'Un oratorio sconosciuto di Leopoldo Mozart', *Festschrift Otto Erich Deutsch* (Kassel, 1963), 187

'Prassi esecutiva e metodo musicologico', *IMSCR, ix Salzburg 1964*, i, 19

'Un importante fonte per la musica cembalo-organistica di Johann Kaspar Kerll: Il Ms. DD/53 della Biblioteca Musicale "G. B. Martini" di Bologna', *CHM*, iv (1966), 283

'Registrazione organistiche nel Magnificat dei "Vespri" monteverdiani', *RIM*, ii (1967), 365

'Ideali sonori e criteri costruttivi nell'organo della basilica di S. Maria dei Servi in Bologna', *L'organo di S. Maria dei Servi in Bologna nella tradizione musicale dell'ordine* (Bologna, 1967), 23

'Problemi di prassi esecutiva', *Studi Corelliani: 1° congresso internazionale: Fusignano 1968*, 151

'Quirino Gasparini and Mozart', *New Looks at Italian Opera: Essays in Honor of Donald J. Grout* (Ithaca, NY, 1968), 151

with O. Mischiati: 'La situazione degli antichi organi in Italia: problemi di censimento e di tutela', *L'organo*, vii (1969), 3–61

'Johann Gottfried Walther trascrittore', *AnMc*, no.7 (1969), 113

'Orgel und Orgelmusik', *Geschichte der katholischen Kirchenmusik*, ed. K. G. Fellerer, i (Kassel, 1972), 464

ed. with O. Mischiati: *Un anonimo trattato francese di arte organaria del sec. XVIII* (Bologna, 1974)

'L'arte di "non lasciar vuoto lo strumento": appunti sulla prassi cembalistica italiana nel cinque- e seicento', *RIM*, x (1975), 360

Numerous articles in *L'organo* and in *MGG, RicordiE, LaMusicaD, LaMusicaE, Larousse de la musique* and *DBI*

EDITIONS

W. A. Mozart: Ascanio in Alba, Neue Ausgabe sämtlicher Werke, ii/5/5 (Kassel, 1956); *Betulia liberata*, ibid, i/4/2 (Kassel, 1960); *Mitridate, re di Ponto*, ibid, ii/5/4 (Kassel, 1966)

ETIENNE DARBELLAY

Täglichsbeck, Thomas (*b* Ansbach, 31 Dec 1799; *d* Baden-Baden, 5 Oct 1867). German violinist and composer. He received his first violin lessons from his father, Johann Täglichsbeck, who settled in Voigtland, Lower Saxony, in 1800. In 1816 he was a fellow student of Molique with Rovelli in Munich; a mass of his, written under the supervision of Josef Gratz, was performed in 1817. That year Täglichsbeck became a violinist in the Isarthortheater orchestra, and, despite his youth, succeeded Lindpaintner as music director two years later. In 1822 he became a solo violinist at the Munich court, a post which allowed him more time to give concert tours and to compose; his first opera, *Webers Bild*, and the variations on *La gazza ladra* date from this period. In 1824 he made an extensive tour of Germany, Switzerland and northern Italy; he joined the Philharmonic Society of Bergamo, where Rovelli then lived. Reviews of his concerts in the *Allgemeine musikalische Zeitung* (1825–32) are laudatory, although his playing in Munich in 1832 was described as 'more charming than exceptional'.

In 1827 Täglichsbeck became the Kapellmeister to Prince Hohenlohe-Hechingen. Under Prince Constantine (1838–48) the court became a well-known musical centre which was visited by Berlioz (1842) and Liszt (1848). When political changes in 1848 eliminated the principality Täglichsbeck was pensioned and the musicians were given paid leave. Constantine recalled Täglichsbeck from Stuttgart in 1852 and reconstituted his orchestra at Löwenberg. Five years later Täglichsbeck was pensioned and succeeded by Max Seyfriz. He subsequently taught composition at the Dresden Conservatory for two years, then lived for a while in Munich before retiring to Baden-Baden in 1866.

The climax of Täglichsbeck's career as a composer came with the performance of his Symphony no.1 in E♭ at the Paris Conservatoire in 1836. It was a popular success, though Berlioz dismissed it as 'academic music, and nothing more'; reviewing a performance a year later, Berlioz wrote more graciously: 'works of this kind gain 100% on rehearing'. The opera *König Enzio*, produced in Karlsruhe in 1843, did not establish itself in the repertory. Täglichsbeck was an excellent Kapellmeister, a good if not brilliant violinist and a skilled if not very original composer.

WORKS

OPERAS

Webers Bild (1, A. Lewald), Munich, Court Opera, 24 Aug 1823
König Enzio (2, G. Schilling), Karlsruhe, 14 May 1843
Guido oder Das Jägerhaus im Walde Sila (2, F. Ellmenreich), unperf.

OTHER WORKS

Orch: 2 syms.; 2 concertinos, fantasia, variations: all vn, orch
Chamber: Qnt, cl, str; 3 str qts; Pf Trio; 3 sonatas, vn, pf; Concert Piece, va, pf; 5 duets, 2 vn
Vocal: Mass, solo vv, chorus, orch, org; 6 songs, 4vv; 6 songs, 1v, pf

BIBLIOGRAPHY

FétisB
AMZ, xxxviii (1836), 417–19
Revue et gazette musicale, lvi (1839), 441f
R. Eitner: 'Täglichsbeck, Thomas', *ADB*
E. Burmester: *Thomas Täglichsbeck und seine Instrumental-Kompositionen* (diss., U. of Munich, 1936)
E. Flad: 'Thomas Täglichsbeck', *Zollernheimat*, vi (Hechingen, 1937), nos.8–9

ALBERT MELL

Taglietti, Giulio (*b* Brescia, *c*1660; *d* Brescia, 1718). Italian composer, violinist and violin teacher, probably brother of Luigi Taglietti. He taught at the Jesuit Collegio dei Nobili, Brescia, at least from 1702. His music was very popular in the first decades of the 18th century and was published in Italy at a time when the printing of instrumental music there was becoming comparatively rare. The Amsterdam publisher Pierre Mortier, in a 1709 list of his publications, placed him and Luigi Taglietti second only to Corelli, and they were indeed important in the development of the concerto and sonata. His concertos have more in common with the concerto grosso than with the solo type, though his op.8 features four solo violins, antedating by a few years the publication of Vivaldi's op.3, which contains some concertos for the same scoring. Occasional solo passages, including some for the viola, do, however, occur. He was among the first composers regularly to limit his concertos to three or four movements only. He shows a marked preference for only one solo treble line in his non-concerto works, witness his numerous instrumental arias (opp.3, 6 and 10) and the powerful melodic lines of his op.13 sonatas.

WORKS

[10] Sonate da camera, 2 vn, bc (vle/spinet), op.1 (Bologna, 1695)
[6] Concerti e [4] Sinfonie, 2 vn, bc (vle/hpd), op.2 (Venice, 1696)
[30] Arie cantabile, vn, vc/bc (vle/spinet), op.3 (Amsterdam, 1709); lost, probably not 1st edn.
[8] Concerti, 2 vn, alto va, bc, op.4 (Amsterdam, 1709)
Sonate da camera, 2 vn, vle/bc, op.5 (Amsterdam, 1709–10), lost
Pensieri musicali (24 arie) vn, vc, bc, op.6 (Venice, 1707)
Divertimenti, vn, vc, bc (vle/hpd), op.7 (Venice, c1708), lost
Concerti, 4 vn, va, vc, vle, bc, op.8 (Venice, c1709), lost
Sonate da camera, 2 vn, vc, bc (vle/hpd), op.9 (Venice, c1710), lost
Arie da sonare, vn, vc, bc (vle/hpd), op.10 (Venice, c1711), lost
[10] Concerti, 4 vn, alto va, vle, org, op.11 (Bologna, 1713)
Pensieri da camera, 2 vn, bc, op.12 (Venice, c1714), lost
[10] Sonate per camera, vn, bc, op.13 (Bologna, 1715)

BIBLIOGRAPHY

L. Torchi: 'La musica strumentale in Italia nei secoli XVI, XVII e XVIII', *RMI*, v (1898), 311; vi (1899), 271; pubd separately (Turin, 1901)
G. Gaspari: *Catalogo della biblioteca del Liceo musicale di Bologna*, iv (Bologna, 1905/*R*1961), 150f
A. Schering: *Geschichte des Instrumental-Konzerts* (Leipzig, 1905, 2/1927/*R*1965)
P. Guerrini: 'Per la storia della musica a Brescia', *NA*, xi (1934), 25f
F. Lesure: 'Estienne Roger et Pierre Mortier', *RdM*, xxxviii (1956), 35
C. Sartori: 'Un catalogo di Giuseppe Sala del 1715', *FAM*, xiii (1956), 112
W. S. Newman: *The Sonata in the Baroque Era* (Chapel Hill, 1959, rev. 2/1966/*R*1972)

ROBIN BOWMAN

Taglietti, Luigi (*b* 1668; *d* ?Brescia, 1715). Italian composer and trumpet marine player and teacher, probably brother of Giulio Taglietti. He was associated with the Jesuit Collegio dei Nobili, Brescia, from at least 1697; in 1702 he was recorded as 'maestro di tromba marina' there. Like that of Giulio Taglietti, his music was very popular in the early 18th century and was published in Italy at a time when the printing of instrumental music was becoming comparatively rare. The Amsterdam publisher Pierre Mortier, in a list of his publications dated 1709, placed the two composers second only to Corelli, and they were indeed important in the development of the concerto and sonata. Like Giulio's, his concertos have more in common with the concerto grosso than with the solo type, and he too was among the first composers to write concertos with only three or four movements. Some of his movements show a remarkably clearcut and enterprising ritornello structure.

WORKS

[10] Suonate da camera, 2 vn, bc (vle/spinet), op.1 (Bologna, 1697)
Sonate a 3 e basso, op.2 (Venice, c1700), lost
Concerti a 4 e basso, op. 3 (Venice, c1702), lost
Sonate, vn, vc, bc (hpd), op.4 (Venice, 1705), lost
Concertini e preludi con diversi pensieri e divertimenti a cinque, op.5 (Venice, 1708), lost
[5] Concerti, 2 vn, va, vc, org, [5] sinfonie, 2 vn, vc, org, e 2 sonate, 3 viols, org, 4 viols, org, op.6 (Amsterdam, 1709)

For bibliography see TAGLIETTI, GIULIO.

ROBIN BOWMAN

Taglioni, Marie (1804–84). Italian dancer, daughter of Filippo Taglioni (1777–1871); *see* DANCE, §VI, 1(ii).

Tagore, Rabindranath (*b* Calcutta, 7 May 1861; *d* Calcutta, 7 Aug 1941). Bengali poet and composer. Though primarily a poet (he won the Nobel Prize for Literature, 1913), Tagore was also a prolific composer of more than 2500 songs popularly known as *Rabindrasangīt* ('Songs of Rabindranath'). Melodically they are related to raga of Indian classical music as well as to the folk music of Bangladesh. Some of Tagore's early songs were also inspired by popular 19th-century Irish, Scottish and English songs. The *Rabindrasangīt* were notated by Tagore's musical associates during his lifetime and in 1942 were published in more than 60 volumes of *svarabitan* (scores in Bengali notation) by Visva Bharati University. Both India and Bangladesh have adapted Tagore's compositions as their national anthems.

Tagore also introduced a new kind of sophisticated musical drama known as *nṛtya-nāṭya* ('dance-drama'); *see* BANGLADESH, §4). He is the author of several works on music and aesthetics which are important in the understanding of musics of both India and Bangladesh. Some Western composers have included translations of Tagore's poems in their compositions, e.g. John Alden Carpenter (*Gitanjali*, 1914) and Arthur Shepherd (*Triptych* for high voice and string quartet, 1927).

BIBLIOGRAPHY

R. Tagore: *My Reminiscences* (New York, 1917)
A. A. Bake: *Chansons de Rabindranath Tagore* (Paris, 1935)
S. Ghosh: *Rabindrasangīt* [Songs of Rabindranath] (Calcutta, 1942, rev. 4/1962/*R*1969)
F. K. Ghosh: 'The Voice of Tagore', HMV India EALP 1256 [disc notes]
D. P. Mukerji, ed.: *Anthology of One Hundred Songs of Rabindranath Tagore in Staff Notation* (New Delhi, 1961–7)
'Tagore Centenary Number', *Bulletin of the Sangeet Natak Akademi*, (1961)
Tagore Centenary Volume 1961, ed. Singapore Centenary Celebration Committee (Singapore, 1961)
A. H. Saaduddin: *A Study of the Prakriti-Sangeet of Rabindranath Tagore with Reference to their Rhythm, Melody and Form* (diss., U. of Hawaii, 1966)

ABUL H. SAADUDDIN

Tagore, Sir Sourindro Mohun [Ṣaurīndramohana Ṭhākura] (*b* Calcutta, 1840; *d* Calcutta, 5 June 1914). Indian musicologist, educationist and patron of Indian music. His grandfather, father and elder brother were all connoisseurs of music. (Rabindranath Tagore belonged to another branch of the family.) As a boy he attended Hindu College, Calcutta, and studied Sanskrit; subsequently he made an intensive study of Indian music with K. M. Goswami and L. P. Misra, specializing in the sitar (1856–8), and then, in order to prepare himself for studies in comparative musicology, engaged two Europeans as his instructors in Western music. He maintained a worldwide correspondence and collected a fine music library; his main achievements were in education, publishing and the collection of instruments.

In 1868 Tagore sponsored publication of Goswami's *Sangīta Sāra* ('The essence of music'), a musical treatise in Bengali; with K. P. Banerjea he produced the *Yantra Kshetra Dipika* ('Treatise on instruments'), a sitar instruction book. These and similar books on singing, drumming and on violin and harmonium playing, prepared by Tagore and his staff, were used in the Bengal Music School, which he founded in 1871. His advocacy of one- or three-line syllabic notation for teaching led to disputes with a British school inspector and a rival group of Bengali educators, who advocated staff notation. Tagore supplied music teachers and books to public and private schools at his own cost and organized classes in theory and Vedic chanting at Sanskrit College, Calcutta. In 1882 he opened a second institution, the Bengal Academy of Music. Of his extremely varied output, *Hindu Music from Various Authors* has proved especially useful. This compilation of English writings on Indian music has kept scarce items, such as Willard's *Music of Hindoostan* (1834), available to scholars. In his work to disseminate Indian music Tagore became known to several Western scholars and monarchs, to whom he donated sets of his books and instruments. In recognition he was frequently decorated and honoured, being knighted and receiving an honorary doctorate from Oxford (1896). Parts of his instrument collections are dispersed in European and American museums.

WRITINGS

with K. P. Banerjea: *Yantra Kshetra Dipika, or a Treatise on the Setar* (Calcutta, 1872, 3/1890) [in Bengali]

Aektana, or the Indian Concert, containing Elementary Rules for the Hindu Musical Notation (Calcutta, 1875)

Hindu Music from Various Authors (Calcutta, 1875, enlarged 2/1882/R1965)

Saṅgīta-Sāra-Saṅgraha, or Theory of Sanskrit Music, compiled from the Ancient Authorities, with Various Criticisms and Remarks by the Author (Calcutta, 1875) [in Sanskrit]

Yantra Kosha, or a Treasury of the Musical Instruments of Ancient and of Modern India, and of Various Other Countries (Calcutta, 1875/R1976) [in Bengali, with Eng. notes]

Six Principal Rāgas, with a Brief View of Hindu Music (Calcutta, 1876, 3/1884)

Victoria Saṃrājyan, or Sanskrit Stanzas on the Various Dependencies (Calcutta, 1876, 3/1887) [in Sanskrit and Eng.]

A Few Lyrics of Owen Meredith set to Hindu Music (Calcutta, 1877)

Short Notices of Hindu Musical Instruments (Calcutta, 1877)

Gīta Praveśa: a Manual of Hindu Vocal Music in Bengali (Calcutta, 1883)

The 22 Musical Srutis of the Hindus (Calcutta, 1886/R1967, 2/1887)

List of Titles, Distinctions and Works of Raja Sir Sourindro Mohun Tagore (Calcutta, 1895)

Universal History of Music, together with Various Original Notes on Hindu Music (Calcutta, 1896/R1963)

BIBLIOGRAPHY

C. B. Clarke: 'Bengali Music', *Calcutta Review*, lviii (1874), 243; see also Tagore's reply in 'Hindu Music', *Hindu Music from Various Authors* (1875), 338–87

Bengal Music School: *Public Opinion and Official Communications about the Bengal Music School and its President* (Calcutta, 1876; partial Ger. trans. by F. Chrysander as 'Das bengalische Conservatorium in Calcutta', *AMz*, xiv (1879), 737, 753, with notes)

A. Weber: 'Elf Werke über indische Musik', *Jenaer Literaturzeitung* (1877), no.31, p.487 [incl. discussion of 10 of Tagore's works]; see also F. Chrysander: 'A. Weber über Dr. Tagore's indische musikalische Schriften', *AMz*, xiv (1879), 540 [repr. with commentary]

M. Fürstenau: 'Die königliche Musikaliensammlung in Dresden', *MMg*, x (1878), 113 [on Tagore's gifts to the King of Saxony; repr. from *Dresdener Journal*]

F. Chrysander: 'Dr. Tagore's Streitschrift gegen C. B. Clarke', *AMz*, xiv (1879), 561, 577, 657, 689, 705, 721

——: 'Prof. G. B. Vecchiotti über Rajah Sourindro Mohun Tagore und indische Musik', *AMz*, xiv (1879) [Ger. trans. of article in It. by Vecchiotti in *Rafaello* (1877), nos.21–4]

——: 'Verzeichnis der Werke und Publikationen von Dr. S. M. Tagore', *AMz*, xiv (1879), 537

F. Vogt: 'Sourindro Mohun Tagore, ein indischer Dichter-Componist', *AMz*, xvii (1882), 465, 481

A. J. Ellis: 'On the Musical Scales of Various Nations', *Journal of the Society of Arts*, xxxiii (1885), 485–527 [section vii, 'India', on Tagore's *The Musical Scales of the Hindus*]

——: 'Description of Rajah Sir S. M. Tagore's Sruti Vina', appx to C. R. Day: *The Music and Musical Instruments of Southern India and the Deccan* (London, 1891)

Viśvapati Čaudhuri: Songs and Addresses in Memory of the Late Raja Sir Ṣaurīndramohana Thākura (Calcutta, 1919)

MICHAEL D. ROSSE

Tahiti. *See* POLYNESIA, §4(v).

Tahourdin, Peter Richard (*b* Bramdenn, Hants., 27 Aug 1928). British composer and educationist. He studied composition with Richard Arnell and trumpet with Rowland Dyson at Trinity College of Music, London (1949–52), and for the next 12 years he worked as a freelance composer, mainly in films and television. His first important premières were those of the overture *Hyperion* in Leeds in 1952, the First Sinfonietta (Holland and Canada, 1955) and his first television ballet, *Pierrot the Wanderer*, broadcast by CBC in Toronto in 1955. In 1965 he was appointed visiting composer at the University of Adelaide, and then he took a course in electronic music at the University of Toronto, graduating MMus in 1967. He returned to Adelaide in 1969 as teaching fellow in electronic music; in 1973 he was appointed lecturer in electronic music at Melbourne University Conservatory. He is interested in electronic music both for the dramatic possibilities exploited in his stage pieces and for its educational value as a bridge between technology and the arts.

WORKS
(*selective list*)

Pierrot the Wanderer, television ballet, 1955; Illyria, ballet, 1966; Riders in Paradise, monodrama, A, ww qt, str qt, tape, 1968; Pacific Rape, music-theatre, tape, 1970; Parrot Pie (children's opera, B. K. Wilson), 4 solo vv, pf, tape, 1972

Hyperion, ov., 1952; 2 sinfoniettas, 1955, 1961; 2 syms., 1960, 1968–9; Clarinet Sonata, 1962; Dialogue, vn, pf, 1972

Principal publisher: Hinrichsen

WRITINGS

'Composers in Australia', *Composer* no.25, (1967), p.29

'Electronic Music in the Classroom', *ASME Journal*, ii (1968), 25

'Professional Opportunities for the Australian Composer', *Report of the Seminar on Contemporary Australian Composers and Society* (Perth, 1971)

'The Role of an Electronic Studio within a University', *Report of the Seminar on the State of the Art of Electronic Music in Australia* (Melbourne, 1972)

ELIZABETH WOOD

Taiber. *See* TEYBER family.

Tailer, Daniel. *See* TAYLOR, DANIEL.

Tailer, John (*d* after 1569). English choirmaster and ?composer. He was probably master of the singing boys of St Anthony's Hospital, London, in 1557, and certainly, from 1561 to 1569, master of 'the children of the grammer schoole in the colledge of Westminster', where he succeeded Robert Lamkyns at an annual salary of £10. During the years of his association with the college the choristers engaged in occasional dramatic activities for which they and their master received monetary rewards: singing and playing in a Lord Mayor's Day pageant, 1561; providing 'speches and songes' for the Ironmongers' pageant, 1566; and presenting plays, including pieces by Plautus and Terence, at court in 1564, during Shrovetide 1566 and at Christmas 1568. Tailer not only trained the boys but may on occasion have taken part in the entertainments himself: when the boys played at Putney before Bishop Grindal in 1567, the choirmaster received 2s. to pay 'for the conveiance of . . . his attyre fro London to puttneie and from thence to London againe'; another time the payment was for conveying the 'Masters apparell and instrumentes'. Some time after 18 June 1569 Tailer left Westminster and appears to have moved to Salisbury where, in July of that year, a John Tailer is listed in the cathedral records as lay vicar and in September as master of the choristers. Whether the choirmaster is the same 'mastyre taylere' to whom a pavan is ascribed in the Dublin Virginal Manuscript (ed. in WE, iii, 1954, rev. 2/1964) or the 'Mr Tayler' to whom a motet, *Christus resurgens*, is ascribed in *GB-Och* 948–88, is an open question.

BIBLIOGRAPHY
Westminster Abbey Muniments, 33618, 33620, 33623–9, 33198G, 38667, 38684–5, Minute Book I
J. Nicholl: *Some Account of the Worshipful Company of Ironmongers* (London, 1851, 2/1866)
C. M. Clode: *The Early History of the Guild of Merchant Taylors* (London, 1888)
H. Baillie: 'Some Biographical Notes on English Church Musicians, Chiefly Working in London (1485–1569)', *RMARC*, ii (1962), 18–57

JOHN M. WARD

Tailhandier [Talhenderius, Taillandier], **Pierre** (*fl* c1390). Composer and theorist. He wrote a three-voice Credo, which survives in many manuscripts with only the upper part texted and with two different contratenors. He compiled a theoretical work *Lectura per Petrum Talhanderii ordinata, tam super cantu mensurabili, quam super immensurabili* (in *I-Rvat* 5129; 18th-century copy in *Bc*). He probably also composed the rhythmically very complex three-voice ballade *Se Dedalus* (in *F-CH* 564, ascribed 'Taillandier') which is often attributed to Mossen Borra, alias Antoni Taillandier (1360–1446), the famous French court jester to several kings of Aragon, although there is no proof of any musical activity on the part of the latter. Another possibility is that the ballade may have been composed by Antoni's brother Leonardus, who was a *clericus* in the royal chapel of Martin I and is often incorrectly described as Antoni's son.

BIBLIOGRAPHY
G. Gaspari: *Catalogo della Biblioteca del Liceo musicale di Bologna*, i (Bologna, 1890/R1961)
A. Pagès: *La poésie française en Catalogne du XIIIᵉ siècle à la fin du XVᵉ* (Toulouse, 1936)
G. Reaney: 'The Manuscript Chantilly, Musée Condé 1047', *MD*, viii (1954), 78
H. Harder and B. Stäblein: 'Neue Fragmente mehrstimmiger Musik aus spanischen Bibliotheken,' *Festschrift Joseph Schmidt-Görg zum 60. Geburtstag* (Bonn, 1957), 131
H. Stäblein-Harder, ed.: *Fourteenth-century Mass Music in France*, CMM, xxix (1962)
——: *Fourteenth-century Mass Music in France*, MSD, vii (1962)
W. Apel, ed.: *French Secular Compositions of the Fourteenth Century*, CMM, liii/1 (1970)

URSULA GÜNTHER

Thaillandier, Antoni. French court jester (1360–1446), often confused with the composer PIERRE TAILHANDIER.

Taille (Fr.: 'tenor'). A middle part (usually a tenor) of a vocal or instrumental piece of music. The origins of the word in this sense are obscure. 'Taille' was used to mean a tenor voice by the mid-16th century, though in published partbooks of both vocal and instrumental music in France the nomenclature was almost invariably Latin. Philibert Jambe de Fer, in his *Epitome musical* (1556), named the four voices *dessus*, *contrehaut*, *teneur* and *bas*, but he switched from 'teneur' to 'taille' in describing instruments of the viol, violin and flute families. The first published partbooks to use French nomenclature were those of the *Dodécacorde* (1598) by Claude Le Jeune, the foremost composer of the Académie de Poésie et Musique, whose goal was to elevate the status of the French language. Mersenne (*Harmonie universelle*, 1636–7) used French terminology in describing musical instruments, equating 'taille' with 'ténor' 'because it holds the plainchant'.

'Taille' remained the standard term in France for a tenor instrument throughout the 17th and 18th centuries. In Bach's scores it refers to an oboe in F or an oboe da caccia. In Baroque opera it was most often used to refer to chorus tenors, leading male roles being assigned to the *haute-contre*; Rousseau remarked in his *Dictionnaire* (1768) that 'almost no *taille* roles are used in French operas'. Towards the end of the 18th century both 'taille' and 'haute-contre' were superseded by the word 'ténor', and one of the last mentions of 'taille' as a contemporary term is in Gilbert Duprez's *L'art du chant* (1845). Duprez equated 'taille' with 'ténor limité' (range *c* to *g'*, with a falsetto extension to *b♭'*), contrasting this with the new 'ténor élevé' (range *e* to *b♭'*, with a falsetto extension to *d'*).

French organ composers of the Baroque era frequently used the term 'en taille' for pieces that featured a particular stop (e.g. Tierce, Trompette or Cromorne) for a solo melody in the middle of the texture. Among numerous examples is the 'Tierce en taille' from the *Messe à l'usage ordinaire des paroisses* by François Couperin (ii).

BIBLIOGRAPHY
C. S. Terry: *Bach's Orchestra* (London, 1932), chap.5
F. Reckow: 'Taille', *MGG*

OWEN JANDER

Tailleferre, Germaine (*b* Parc-St-Maur, nr. Paris, 19 April 1892). French composer. Despite her parents' strong objection to a musical career, she entered the Paris Conservatoire in 1904 and won first prizes in harmony and solfège (1913, under H. Dallier), counterpoint (1914, under G. Caussade) and accompaniment (under Estyle). At the Conservatoire she met Auric, Honegger and Milhaud, who introduced her to Satie. In 1918 a String Quartet of hers was included in one of the concerts given by the Nouveaux Jeunes, a group which two years later became Les Six, of which she was one. She quickly escaped from academic constraints to employ new musical techniques: she essayed polytonality and later serialism (in the Clarinet Sonata of 1958) and explored new sound combinations, although without leaving the traditions of Fauré and of Ravel, whom she admired and with whom she studied orchestration. The style she developed has the concision, incisiveness and mobility of Couperin or Domenico Scarlatti, together with a tenderness and humour exemplified in the *Six chansons françaises*. Her spontaneity, freshness and fantasy have remained as links with Satie and the original aesthetic of Les Six. Cocteau described her as 'a Marie Laurencin for the ear', and her music has always been gracious and feminine, qualities well displayed in the First Violin Sonata, the ballet *Marchand d'oiseaux* and the sparkling orchestral *Ouverture* which recaptures something of Chabrier's verve.

For photograph *see* SIX, LES.

WORKS
(selective list)

Stage: Les mariés de la tour Eiffel (Cocteau), 1921, collab. Les Six; Marchand d'oiseaux, ballet, 1923; Sous les remparts d'Athènes (incidental music, Claudel), 1927; Paris-magie, ballet, 1949; Dolorès, operetta, 1950; Il était un petit navire (opéra comique, Jeanson), 1951; Parisiana, ballet, 1955; La petite sirène (opera, 3, Soupault, after Andersen), 1958; Mémoires d'une bergère, opéra bouffe, 1959; Le maître (chamber opera, Ionesco), 1961

Instrumental pieces incl. Str Qt, 1918; Jeux de plein air, 2 pf, 1918; Ballade, pf, orch, 1922; Pf Conc. no.1, 1924; Vn Sonata no.1, 1924; Fleurs de France, pf, 1930; Ouverture, orch, 1932; Partita, pf, 1951; Concertino, fl, pf, str, 1953; Vn Sonata no.2, 1956; Sonata, harp, 1957; Sonata, cl, 1958; Partita, 2 pf, perc, 1964; Sonatine, vn, pf, 1973; 4 Pieces, fl, ob, cl, tpt, pf, 1973

Vocal works incl. 6 chansons françaises, 1v, pf, 1930; Concerto, 2 pf, chorus, orch, 1934; La cantate du Narcisse (Valéry), solo vv, female chorus, orch, 1937; Concertino, S, orch, 1957; Concerto des vaines paroles (Tardieu), 1958

Principal publishers: Durand, Heugel

WRITINGS

Mémoires à l'emporte pièce (Paris, 1974)

BIBLIOGRAPHY

Roland-Manuel: 'Esquisse pour un portrait de Germaine Tailleferre', *Revue Pleyel* (1926), Nov
P. Landormy: *La musique française après Debussy* (Paris, 1943)
J. Bruyr: 'Germaine Tailleferre', *Musica*, xxxvi (1957), March, 29
C. Chamfray: 'Hommage à Germaine Tailleferre', *Courrier musical* (1972), no.39, p.119

ARTHUR HOÉRÉE

Tailler [Taillerus, Taylor], **Simon** [Symon] (*fl* ? c1230–40). ?Irish or Scottish musical theorist and reformer of church music. According to Dempster, he was one of the first Dominicans to enter Scotland, and he wrote numerous treatises, of which *De cantu ecclesiastico corrigendo, De tenore musicali, Tetrachordorum* and *Pentachordorum* were the best. Dempster had himself not seen the treatises but claimed to have drawn his information from the *Historia* of George Newtoun, an early 16th-century Archdeacon of Dunblane. (This claim is unverifiable, since the work, if it ever existed, is not known to survive.) Tailler has been mentioned surprisingly often without question by modern authors, whose accounts derive from authorities such as Mackenzie, Quetif and Echard, and Fabricius, or more recently Placid Conway OP (in an unsigned article in *Analecta sacri ordinis fratrum Praedicatorum*, ii, 1896, 485), Fétis, and Farmer (articles 'Tailler' in *Grove 5* and *MGG*). All known accounts of Tailler seem, nevertheless, ultimately to be dependent on Dempster; the varying details of Tailler's life and output they give probably all stem from rationalizations and miscopyings of Dempster's account.

Dempster was a patriotic Catholic controversialist anxious to re-create a glorious past for the Scottish Church, and to represent the 'haeretici' of the reformed Church as responsible for the wholesale destruction of ancient learning. His work is a vast compilation of biographical material, in which hundreds of figures, Scottish, English, Irish and others, are made into Scottish authors. Some of these (e.g. Sedulius and Aeneas Sylvius Piccolomini) are incredible in this role, and others appear to have had their importance exaggerated. Among these authors, genuine and spurious, Dempster included some seven 'musical theorists' and some 25 'hymnographers', but no thorough investigation of the evidence has yet been made to find whether Dempster was drawing on sound sources for any of them; his work, in the words of a sympathetic modern evaluation, has to be used 'with caution amounting almost to constant suspicion' (Ross). The lack of good evidence for Tailler makes it very doubtful that he existed, or that there were any early Dominican musical treatises of Scottish origin.

BIBLIOGRAPHY

FétisB
T. Dempster: *Historia ecclesiastica gentis scotorum* (Bologna, 1627, 2/1829), ii, 617
G. Mackenzie: *The Lives and Characters of the Most Eminent Writers of the Scots Nation* (Edinburgh, 1708–22), i, 187ff
J. Quetif and J. Echard: *Scriptores ordinis Praedicatorum recensiti*, i (Paris, 1719–21/R1961), 111
J. A. Fabricius: *Bibliotheca latina mediae et infimae aetatis*, vi (Hamburg, 1734–46, rev. and enlarged 3/1858–99), 487

H. G. Farmer: *A History of Music in Scotland* (London, 1947/R1970), 58f
A. Ross: 'Some Scottish Catholic Historians', *Innes Review*, i (1950), 5

GEOFFREY CHEW

Tailour [Taylour, Taylor], **Robert** (*fl* 1613; *d* ?London, by 1637). English composer. There seems little doubt that the 'Robert Taylour' who appears in the Lord Chamberlain's accounts under 'Musicians' for the funeral of James I in 1625, is the 'Robert Taylor' who was a city wait from 1620 to 1637. In the latter year the court musician was described as 'deceased'. 'Taylor' is first heard of as one of the lutenists who played in Chapman's *Masque of the Inner Temple and Lincoln's Inn* in February 1613. When he first joined the waits in 1620, he was hired for one year at £10, on condition he should not ask for more, should his services be required for a further period. He served a second year at the same rate of pay, but subsequently he received £40 a year. It is likely that the Robert Tailour who wrote *Sacred Hymns, consisting of Fifti Select Psalms* (London, 1615), for five voices, 'as also to the Viole [i.e. Lyra viol], and Lute or Orph-arion' was the same as the court musician and city wait known to have played these instruments. In *Sacred Hymns* 12 tunes are provided for the 50 psalms: they are in the English consort song tradition, elaborately scored in a stiff and busy style. Songs and consort music by him are extant in *EIRE-Dtc* D.I.21, *GB-Lbm* Add.10444, 31423, *Ob* Mus.Sch.D.247, *Och* 439, *Mp* Lyra Viol MS). 'A pavyn by mr Robert Taylor: the devisions sett by mr Thos Greaves' appears in *GB-Ctc* O.16.2., ff.122–119.

BIBLIOGRAPHY

W. L. Woodfill: *Musicians in English Society from Elizabeth to Charles I* (Princeton, 1953/R1969)
R. T. Daniel and P. le Huray: *The Sources of English Church Music, 1549–1660*, EECM, suppl.i (1972) [lists contents of *Sacred Hymns*]

DIANA POULTON

Tailpiece (Fr. *cordier, tirechordes*; Ger. *Saitenhalter*; It. *cordiera*). A string-holder to which the strings are attached at the lower end of a string instrument. It consists of a piece of wood (generally ebony, sometimes boxwood) or, for high-tension metal strings, metal, secured by a piece of gut (or wire) looped over a button projecting from the ribs at the bottom of the instrument (*see* VIOLIN, fig.1). In viols the tailpiece is secured by a kind of spike that runs up the back of the lower part.

DAVID D. BOYDEN

Tailpin. An ambiguous term, infrequently used, sometimes meaning the ENDPIN of the cello and double bass, and sometimes the 'button' that is let into the bottom block of instruments of the violin family to which the tailpiece is attached by a gut or wire loop.

Tait, Andrew (*b* c1710; *d* Aberdeen, 11 June 1778). Scottish organist and church musician. He was for many years a leading figure in Aberdeen's musical life. He was organist of St Paul's Episcopal Chapel, c1735 to c1775, master of the Aberdeen music school from 1740 until its closure c1755, and a founder of the Aberdeen Musical Society in 1748. He collaborated with the printer James Chalmers over *A New and Correct Set of Church Tunes* (1749), contributing a manual on choir-training and a psalm tune 'Aberdeen, or St Paul's' of his own composition, which has survived to the present day (e.g. in *English Hymnal*, 1933, no.561). Samuel Johnson praised Tait's organ playing during his visit to Scotland in 1775.

BIBLIOGRAPHY

H. G. Farmer: *Music Making in the Olden Days* (London, 1950), 19f
D. Johnson: *Music and Society in Lowland Scotland in the 18th Century* (London, 1972)

DAVID JOHNSON

Taiwan. East Asian island off the Chinese mainland (formerly called Formosa). Its music can be divided into two major categories: the music of the aboriginal tribes and that of the Han people (ethnically Chinese immigrants). The aboriginal peoples, Taiwan's earliest inhabitants, belong linguistically to the Malayo-Polynesian group and physically to the Proto-Malaysian type. Scholars have speculated that migrations took place from 1200 BC or 1300 BC to between the 9th and 12th century AD. The tribes can be subdivided into three groups: the mountain or Shan-ti tribes, including the Tayal, Saisiat, Bunun, Tsou, Rukai, Paiwan, Puyuma, Ami and Yami; the plain or P'ing-p'u tribes, which include nine linguistic groups and which have assimilated many cultural elements of the Han people since the 16th century; and the Thao, a very small tribe whose classification remains uncertain. The Han people (originally from mainland China) can also be divided into two groups, Hokkien and Hakka. The Chinese had made frequent contacts with Taiwan by the 12th century, although the mass migration of the Han people to Taiwan did not begin until the late 16th century, the Hokkien group coming from Fukien province and the Hakka from Kwangtung province. The last migration took place after World War II, when Chinese came to Taiwan from all provinces. The population of Taiwan is now about 16 million: aborigines, 2%; Hokkien, 70%; Hakkah, 13%; and other Chinese, 15%. Since the 17th century Taiwan has been a colony of many nations: the Dutch (1624–62, in the south), the Spanish (1626–42, in the north), the Chinese (1662–1895) and the Japanese (1895–1945); it became a province of the Republic of China in 1945.

The music of Taiwan is first referred to in 'Tung fan chi' ('The accounts of the savages of the East') by Ch'en Ti in Shen Yu-jung's *Min hai tseng yen* (1603), a work which mentions instruments and musical activities among the tribes. Many other historical accounts have also recorded similar activities (see Lü Ping-ch'uan, *Shinchō bunken ni yoru Taiwan Takasagozoku no gakki ni tsuite no kōsatsu* ('A study of Taiwan aborigines' musical instruments based upon Ch'ing dynasty documents', 1973). The first brief description of tribal instruments in a scholarly journal was by Ten Kate (1903); several Japanese anthropologists have written papers on tribal instruments (see Lü Ping-ch'uan, 1974). Chang Fu-hsing was the first Taiwanese to publish on tribal music (1922), and Kurosawa Takatomo the first to do extensive research on tribal music (1943, 26 volumes of recordings and documentary films, of which all copies except his personal set of records were destroyed during World War II). There are few historical accounts of Han music in Taiwan, apart from Lü Su-shang's book which describes the history and practice of *koa-a-hi* (Taiwanese opera) and other related entertainment music (1961).

1. Music in society. 2. Vocal music. 3. Instrumental and dance music.

1. MUSIC IN SOCIETY. Music is an integral part of almost all aspects of tribal life. It complements planting, harvesting, weaving, rice pounding, fishing and hunting, as well as religious ceremonies: prayers, invocation and dismissal of spirits, thanksgiving, supplication for rain, head sacrifice, exorcism and healing. Music and dance also serve as entertainment at weddings, New Year ceremonies and harvest festivals. Love-songs, epic legends and songs expressing joy and sorrow are mostly sung as solos.

The Han people use music largely for religious and social purposes and as entertainment. *Koa-a-hi* (Taiwanese opera), which originated locally in the second decade of the century, is their major source of entertainment. *Nan-kuan* ensembles perform at birthdays, weddings and other festivities. Small ensembles of *ku* (drum) and *lo* (gong) are frequently used to accompany dragon and lion dances. The same combination with the addition of the *so-na* (shawm) is used in funeral processions and to escort deities in religious parades.

Most of the tribes retain some animistic beliefs despite mass conversion to Christianity during the mid-20th century. Although Christian hymnody has been widely accepted, a number of tribal songs have also been adapted for Christian use. The Saisiat, Tsou and P'ing-p'u have certain songs which are restricted to particular cults, and their performance is prohibited out of context.

The Han people continue to be markedly influenced by Buddhism, Taoism and folk religions. Traditional Buddhist religious music has almost disappeared. Sutra chanting with the accompaniment of *mu-yü* ('wooden fish', a percussion idiophone) and *yin-ch'ing* (hemispheric brass gong) can occasionally be heard in remote mountain monasteries. Few urban monks practise traditional Buddhist chant, taped chanting being used instead. Taoist music is usually performed during funeral services, when the priest chants for the dead, accompanying himself with a small handbell. Well-to-do families sometimes hire an ensemble of *so-na*, *ti* (flute), *ku* and *hu-ch'in* (two-string fiddle) on special occasions or for funeral processions, in which the Western brass band is also indispensable. The annual *chiao* (ritual of renewal) and *p'u-tu* (mass for the souls in Purgatory), both belonging to community rites, which may last up to a week, generally incorporate larger ensembles with *so-na*, *san-hsien*, *ti*, *ku*, *ling* (bell) and other percussion instruments. At the Confucian Temple in Tainan only one ceremony is performed annually, commemorating the sage's birthday (28 September). Six hymns of equal length are sung and danced, one in each of the six sections of the ritual. The main instruments used to lead and accompany singing are *pien-ch'ing* (stone-chime), *ke-chung* (song bell-chime), *pien-chung* (bell-chime), *yün-lo* (cloud gong), *ch'in* (seven-string zither), *se* (25-string zither), *p'ai-hsiao* (panpipes), *ti-tzǔ* (transverse flute), *kuan* (oboe) and *sheng* (mouth organ).

In Taiwanese tribal society singing is an integral part of everyday life, and children acquire singing skills without formal training. Among the Han, however, although musicians are informally trained, they traditionally have a low position on the social scale. Professional musicians are associated mostly with troupes and opera companies; semi-professionals are usually called on to perform for specific occasions. Musicians are taught by rote or learn by observation and by participation in rehearsals. Most of the *nan-kuan*

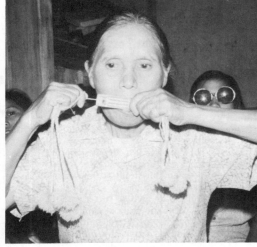

2.

1. Group of women with bamboo stamping tubes

2. Tubu sepatz (three-tongue jew's harp) of the Seedeq (Tayal) tribe, Ch'ing-liu, 1973

3. Nan-kuan ensemble with (front row, left to right) san-hsien (lute), p'i-p'a (lute), p'ai-pan (woodblock), hsiao (end-blown flute), erh-hsien (fiddle); (second row) san-hsien (lute), two ti (flutes), so-na (shawm), hsiao (end-blown flute), to-hsien (fiddle); (third row, centre) hsiang-chan (clappers); Taipei, 1965

1.

3.

music is taught according to the *kung-ch'e* notation while the theatrical or folk repertory is mostly transmitted orally; some teachers use cipher notation as a memory aid. In *nan-kuan* style the instrumental portions are learned vocally as solfège before being studied on instruments. Five universities and several junior colleges now have music departments; of these only the College of Chinese Culture, Tung-hai University and the National Academy of Arts (a junior college) offer extensive courses in classical Chinese music. Western music, including theory, harmony, composition, analysis, history and performance, is widely taught.

2. VOCAL MUSIC. The rich vocal traditions of the Taiwanese tribal peoples (apart from those of the Yami tribe which are unique in incorporating microtones, parallel 3rds and tone clusters) can be categorized into various forms of monophonic, chordal harmonic and polyphonic singing. Monophonic singing takes the form of responsorial singing between soloist and chorus (Tsou tribe); narration of stories in recitative style within a narrow melodic range (the Tayal); and simple song with repetition of complete phrases (e.g. *AABA*), which is common among most tribes. Members of the Bunun tribe sing in a strict chordal harmonic style (closely resembling Western triadic harmony) in three to six parts within the framework of the pitch series *doh–mi–sol*; *re* is used cadentially in a descending terminal glide to *doh*. Ex.1 illustrates the beginning and

Ex.1 *Song of loneliness*, Bunun tribe, Wang-hsiang; rec. and transcr. I-To Loh

end of a song of this type; the concluding open 5th is typical of final cadences in this type of music. The same tribe is fond of two-part singing with frequent open 4ths and 5ths (see ex.2). A style of unison singing with

Ex.2 *Pasi pot-pot*, song for ceremony at first sowing of millet, Bunun tribe, Rilansan (Takatomo, 1973)

occasional harmonic passages may be derived from the chordal singing style and is practised by the Tsou, Ami and Thao (see ex.3, taken from the last two phrases of

Ex.3 *Toisoh*, Tsou tribe, Tapang; rec. and transcr. I-To Loh

the song *Toisoh*). Saisiat and Tsou women practise a style of polyphonic singing in strict parallel 4ths or 5ths above men's voices. Canonic singing in two or more parts is a favourite practice of the Tayal, the Saisiat and the Puyuma. In a type of melody with drone popular among the Rukai a freely ornamented solo melody is set against a reiterated choral pattern which frequently centres on a drone (see ex.4). Contrapuntal singing, one

Ex.4 *Song of joy*, Rukai tribe, Wu-t'an; rec. and transcr. I-To Loh

of the most complicated indigenous styles, is found among the Rukai, the Paiwan and especially the Ami; the melody is sung against two or more contrapuntal lines (see ex.5).

Ex.5 Prayer for rain, *Pakaraw*, Ami tribe, Ma-lan (Takatomo, 1973)

Treatment of texts varies among tribes. The Ami and Puyuma use non-lexical syllables (e.g. 'O-hai-yan'), a practice which has begun to be adopted by other tribes. According to Kurosawa a significant feature of Saisiat song is that poems are metrical, rhymed, and have repeated sections. In some types of Puyuma song the text rhymes at both beginning and end of symmetrical lines (e.g. 'A i ru ba *no li ni*, A de to ka *no li ni*').

The vocal music of the Han people is usually solo, with or without instrumental accompaniment; group singing is rare. The anhemitonic pentatonic scale (particularly *la–doh–re–mi–sol*) is preferred by most Han people. Although *fa* and *ti* are occasionally used, semitone progressions using them are found most frequently in the descending lines of melodies. Ornamentation varies according to genre, style and personal preference. The Hokkien vocal repertory can be classified as folksong, theatrical song, ballad, children's song and song associated with folkdance (the last two being somewhat rare). A large number of love-songs and wailing songs from different localities have been adapted for theatrical use. Hakka songs are called *chiu-ch'iang shih-pa tiao* ('9 styles and 18 tunes'), an ambiguous term which needs further investigation. *Lao Shan-ko* ('Old mountain song') is among the most popular of these songs. The Hakka and Hokkien have some common songs, but the differences in tonal inflections of the two groups' languages can result in differing versions. Hakka songs generally tend to be more ornamental, with skips of 4ths or 5ths and vocal slides. They also emphasize a heterophonic relationship between the solo voice and the instrumental accompaniment.

3. INSTRUMENTAL AND DANCE MUSIC. The instruments used by Taiwanese tribes include a number of idiophones: the jew's harp (one to eight tongues), stamping pestle, stamping tube (see fig.1), bell, rattle, slit-drum and three-keyed xylophone (no longer used); a drum (membranophone) is played by the P'ing-p'u only; chordophones include the musical bow and five-string plucked zither (no longer used); and aerophones include the end-blown flute, nose flute (one or two pipes with two and four holes respectively) and transverse flute (six to eight holes). All the idiophones except the xylophone are used to accompany dances; stamping pestles have a melodic as well as a rhythmic function. The jew's harps and musical bows were used by men to serenade their lovers at night; a typical tuning of a four-tongue jew's harp is c'–d'–f'–g' (see fig.2). End-blown flutes were previously associated with head-hunting and could only be played by men. The remote Yami tribe has no instrumental tradition.

The main instruments of the Han people include among the idiophones the *lo* (gong), *pa* (cymbal), *p'ai-pan* (woodblock) and *mu-yü* ('wooden fish'); among the membranophones, the *t'ang-ku* and *pan-ku* (tall and short drums); among the chordophones, the *hu-ch'in* (two-string fiddle), *yeh-hu* (two-string coconut-shell fiddle), *yüeh-ch'in* (long-necked, round-bellied plucked lute with two strings), *san-hsien* (three-string plucked lute) and *p'i-p'a* (four-string plucked lute); and, among the aerophones, the *hsiao* (end-blown flute), *ti-tzŭ* (transverse flute), *kuan* (double-reed oboe) and *so-na* (shawm with flaring bell). The Han people brought the *pei-kuan* ('north pipe') and *nan-kuan* ('south pipe') musical traditions from China to Taiwan. *Pei-kuan* music including Peking opera is popular in urban areas. Some *pei-kuan* music has been adapted to reflect local stylistic preferences, for use in theatre and in Taoist rituals.

Nan-kuan (the traditional music of Amoy on the Chinese mainland) is a combination of classical literature and music, a type of chamber music which has been practised with little change since about the 10th century. It is popular among the Amoy- (i.e. Hokkien-) speaking Chinese communities in Taiwan, in the Philippines and in Singapore. The basic ensemble (*shang ssu-kuan*) consists of *hsiao*, *p'i-p'a*, *erh-hsien* (like the mainland *erh-hu*, a two-string fiddle), *san-hsien* and *p'ai-pan*, and the larger ensemble (see fig.3) also includes *so-na* (substituting for *hsiao*) and several percussion instruments (*hsia ssu-kuan*): *hsiang-chan* and *ssu-pao* (types of clapper), *lo* and *mu-yü*, *shuang-ling* (double bell), and *pien-ku* (thin drum). The *nan-kuan* repertory can be divided into three categories. *Ch'i-tsou ch'ü* ('pieces played in unison') or *chih* comprises over 40 sets of elegant songs organized in sections, with instrumental accompaniment and with texts set according to a strictly organized melodic formula (*ch'ü-p'ai*). *Ch'i-yüeh ch'ü* ('instrumental piece') or *p'u* consists of 16 sets of purely instrumental pieces which emphasize various playing techniques. The third genre, *ch'ang-tz'u* ('aria') or *ch'ü*, consists of short lyric songs without distinct sections, in which clarity of diction is emphasized. Approximately 1000 songs of this type survive; the *ch'ang-tz'u* genre is considered the most important one in *nan-kuan* music.

Tribal people perform a variety of dances at wed-dings, harvest and New Year festivals. Dance-steps are highly repetitive. The human voice, metal and shell rattles and (sometimes) the jew's harp are used to give rhythmic support. Except for the festival lion and dragon dances, folk dances seem to be rare among the Han people, although this area is yet to be investigated.

Western music has gradually come to dominate musical life since its introduction to Taiwan in the late 19th century. Compositions by Taiwanese composers in traditional style, both sacred and secular, are however gradually gaining recognition. Composers such as Hsu Tsang-houei have begun to adapt the local melodic idioms and scale systems with considerable skill in modern works, creating a mixture of Eastern and Western elements, and an attempt has been made to reconstruct ancient Chinese ritual music for modern use. But although the Han music of *pei-kuan*, *nan-kuan* and folk traditions is enjoying wider popularity, rapid acculturation may cause tribal music to disappear.

See also CHINA.

BIBLIOGRAPHY

Ch'en Ti: 'Tung-fan chi' [The accounts on the savages of the East], in Shen Yu-jung: *Min-hai tseng-yen*, ii (n.p., 1603, ed. Bank of Taiwan, Taipei, 1959), 24

H. ten Kate: 'The Musical Bow in Formosa', *American Anthropologist*, new ser., v (1903), 581

Chang Fu-hsing: *Shui-she Hua-fan ch'u-yin chi ko-yao* [Music of the stamping tubes and songs of the Plain Tribe in Shui-She] (Taipei, 1922)

Li Huei: 'Chi pen-hsi so ts'ang T'ai-wan t'u-chu tsu k'ou-ch'in piao-pen' [The specimens of jew's harp of the Taiwan aborigines in the National Taiwan University], *T'ai Ta Journal of Archaeology*, v (1955), 63

——: 'T'ai-wan chi Tung-nan-ya ke ti t'u-chu min-tsu ti k'ou-ch'in chih pi-chiao yen-chiu' [A comparative study of jew's harps among the aborigines of Formosa and Asia], *Bulletin of the Institute of Ethnology, Taipei*, i (1956), 85–140

Lin Heng-li: 'Sai-hsia tsu ai-ling chi ko-tz'ŭ' [The songs of the 'Pastaai'], *Bulletin of the Institute of Ethnology, Taipei*, ii (1956), 31–107

Ling Man-li: 'T'ai-wan A-mei tsu ti yüeh-ch'i' [Musical instruments of the Ami tribe in Taiwan], *Bulletin of the Institute of Ethnology, Taipei*, xi (1961), 185–220

Lü Su-shang: *T'ai-wan tien-ying hsi-chü shih* [The history of motion picture and drama in Taiwan] (Taipei, 1961)

Chang Tsai-hsing: *Nan-kuan ming-ch'ü chi* [Anthology of famous Nan-kuan music] (T'ai-nan, 1962)

Shih Wei-liang: 'A-mei min-ko fen-hsi' [An analysis of the Ami folksong], *Yin-yüeh hsüeh-pao*, v (1966), 17

F. J. Lenherr: 'The Musical Instruments of the Taiwan Aborigines', *Bulletin of the Institute of Ethnology, Taipei*, xxiii (1967), 109

Yen Wen-hsung: *T'ai-wan min-yao* [Folksongs of Taiwan] (Taipei, 1967–9)

H. Tanabe: *Taiwan to Amoy: Nanyō, Taiwan, Okinawa ongaku kikō* [Taiwan and Amoy: musical journey to the South Pacific, Taiwan and Okinawa] (Tokyo, 1968)

Hsu Tsang-houei: *T'ai-wan min-yao chih yen-chiu* [Study on Taiwanese folksong] (Taipei, 1969)

F. Lieberman: 'The Music of China, ii: Traditional Music of Amoy' AST 4002 [disc notes]

W. Eberhard: *Taiwanese Ballads: a Catalogue* (Taipei, 1972)

Chang Hsüen-wen: *Ko-tsai-hsi ti yin-yüeh yen-chiu* [Study on the music of Koa-a-hi] (diss., College of Chinese Culture, 1973)

Lao Hong-kio: *Min-nan yin-yüeh chih-p'u ch'uang-tso ch'üan-chi* [Complete collection of notation books and creations of Amoy music] (Taipei, 1973)

Lü Ping-ch'uan: *Shinchō bunken ni yoru Taiwan Takasagozuku no gakki ni tsuite no kōsatsu* [A study of Taiwan aborigines' musical instruments based on Ch'ing dynasty documents] (Tokyo, 1973)

——: *Taiwan Dochaku zoku no ongaku: hikaku ongakugaku teki kō-satsu* [Music of the Taiwan aborigines: a comparative study] (diss., U. of Tokyo, 1973)

Kurosawa Takatomo: *Taiwan Takasagozoku no ongaku* [Music of the Takasago tribes in Taiwan] (Tokyo, 1973)

Hsu Tsang-houei: 'Heng-ch'un min-yao 'su-siang-ki' ti yen-chiu' [A comparative study of a Heng-ch'un melody 'Su-siang-ki'], *Tunghai Ethnomusicological Journal, Taichung*, i (1974), 1–54

I-To Loh: 'P'ing-p'u tsu A-li-chu chih chi-tien chi ch'i shih-ko chih yen-chiu' [A study of the P'ing-p'u Arit festival and its songs], *Tughai Ethnomusicological Journal, Taichung*, i (1974), 55

——: *T'ai-wan min-tsu yin-yüeh yen-chiu chih yu-kuan ts'an-k'ao wen-hsien* [Reference materials in Taiwan ethnomusicological studies], *Tunghai Ethnomusicological Journal, Taichung*, i (1974), 204

Lü Ping-ch'uan: 'T'ai-wan t'u-chu tsu chih yüeh-ch'i' [Musical instruments of the Taiwan aborigines], *Tunghai Ethnomusicological Journal, Taichung*, i (1974), 85–203

Hsu Tsang-houei: *Kuan-yü T'ai-wan ti min-chien yin-yüeh* [On the folk music of Taiwan] (Taipei, 1975)

Hsu Tsang-houei: 'T'ai-wan min-yao ti yen-chiu: i-pai shou min-ke ti fen-hsi' [Studies on Taiwanese folksong: an analysis of 100 folksongs], *Tunghai Ethnomusicological Journal, Taichung*, ii (1976)

Yang Chao-chen: 'K'o-chia min-yao chiu ch'iang shih-pa tiau ti yen-chiu' [A study on Hakka folksong] (1976)

I-TO LOH

Tajčević, Marko (*b* Osijek, 29 Jan 1900). Yugoslav composer, writer on music and conductor. He studied in Zagreb with Lhotka, D. Dugan and Bersa, in Prague with Štepán and in Vienna with Marx. During the years 1924–40 he taught at many schools in Zagreb, where he founded the Lisinski Music School; he then taught in Belgrade at the secondary music school and at the academy as professor of theory and composition (1945–66). In Zagreb he conducted several choirs, and he wrote music criticism for reviews and daily papers in Zagreb and Belgrade (1921–55). Tajčević is an outstanding representative of the Yugoslav national school; his music either employs folk motifs in a refined manner or else creates a popular spirit with original material. He has never written in large forms, but has concentrated rather on piano and choral miniatures in a style of polished technique, formal elegance and direct expression. The work with which he made his reputation, the *Sedam balkanskih igara* ('Seven Balkan dances'), became a classic of Yugoslav piano music. His choral music shows a mastery of polyphonic technique, with melodies arising from spoken inflections, as they do in the solo songs.

WORKS
(selective list)

Sacred choral: Liturgija; 4 duhovna stiha [4 spiritual verses] (Psalms)

Secular choral: 20 srpskih narodnih pesama [20 Serbian folksongs], chorus/female chorus; Pesme od kola, male chorus; Komitske pesme, male chorus; Pesme iz Gradišća, male chorus; Makedonske pesme; 3 madrigala; pieces for children's chorus

Songs: Priča [Story], Balade Petrice Kerempuha, 2 soneta Michelangela, Iz ruske lirike [From Russian lyrics]

Piano: 7 balkanskih igara [7 Balkan dances], 1927; Srpske igre; 5 preludiuma, 1948; 2 male svite [2 little suites], n.d.; educational pieces

Principal publishers: Hrvatski Glazbeni Zavod, Muzgiz, Prosveta, Schott

WRITINGS

Kontrapunkt (Belgrade, 1958)

Opšta nauka o muzici [The general science of music] (Belgrade, 3/1963)

Osnovi muzičke pismenosti [Elements of musical literacy] (Belgrade, 8/1967)

Osnovna teorija muzike (Belgrade, 5/1968)

Nauka o harmoniji (Belgrade, 1972)

BIBLIOGRAPHY
D. Despić: *Marko Tajčević* (Belgrade, 1972)

STANA ĐURIĆ-KLAJN

Tajikistan. A constituent republic of the USSR; *see* UNION OF SOVIET SOCIALIST REPUBLICS, §XI, 6.

Tajo, Italo (*b* Pinerolo, Piedmont, 25 April 1915). Italian bass. He studied with Nilde Stinchi Bertozzi in Turin (1932–4), and in March 1935 made his début there at the Teatro Regio, as Fafner in *Das Rheingold* under Fritz Busch. Busch took him to Glyndebourne that summer to understudy Mozart roles and to sing in the chorus; Tajo sang Bartolo's Act 1 aria in the first Glyndebourne recording of *Le nozze di Figaro* because

Norman Allin was not available. During the war he appeared regularly at the Rome Opera in a wide variety of roles, including the Doctor in the Italian première of *Wozzeck* (1942), and at La Scala, where he returned in the first postwar season (1946) as Don Magnifico (*La Cenerentola*) and Baron Ochs, and where he continued to appear until 1956. Tajo's British career, which began at the 1947 Edinburgh Festival, when he was heard as Figaro and Banquo with the Glyndebourne company, continued in London at the Cambridge Theatre, 1947–8, as Don Basilio, Leporello and Don Pasquale, and at Covent Garden with the Scala company in September 1950 when, as Dulcamara, he revealed his outstanding gifts as a *buffo* artist. He made his American début in Chicago in 1946, as Ramfis, and sang at the San Francisco Opera (1948–56) and at the Metropolitan (1948–50). During the 1956–7 season he sang on Broadway in the musical *Fanny*. In Italy Tajo created roles in operas by Bucchi, Malipiero, Nono, Berio, Lualdi and Tosatti; he was Samuel in the first performances at La Scala of Milhaud's *David* (1955), Calchas in the Italian première of Walton's *Troilus and Cressida* (1956), and Ivan in the Italian première of Shostakovich's *The Nose* (1964); he made three films. In 1966 he was appointed to teach singing at the Cincinnati Conservatory. During the 1970s he continued to make occasional guest appearances in the USA as the Sacristan and Benoit and in other character roles.

BIBLIOGRAPHY
R. Hastings: 'Italo Tajo', *Opera Annual*, vii (London, 1960)

HAROLD ROSENTHAL

Takács, Jenő [Eugene] (*b* Cinfalva [now Siegendorf], 25 Sept 1902). Austrian composer, pianist, ethnomusicologist and teacher of Hungarian origin. He studied composition with Gál and Marx and the piano with Weingartner in Vienna, where he was also in contact with the Schoenberg school. From 1927 to 1932 he taught at the Cairo Conservatory, taking an interest in Arab music; at the 1932 Cairo congress on Arab music he met Bartók, whom he had come to know in 1926 in Budapest. He then taught at the University of the Philippines in Manila (1932–4), from where he made ethnomusicological expeditions to the tribes of north Luzon. Between 1934 and 1936 he again taught in Cairo, and served as music adviser to Egyptian Radio. Apart from making concert tours of Europe he has visited the Near and Far East (he played his Piano Concerto for Radio Tokyo), and in 1938 he gave his first series of concerts in the USA. In 1939 he lived in Sopron, the next year he taught in the music school at Szombathely, and he was then director of the Pécs Conservatory (1942–8). He was visiting professor at the conservatories of Geneva and Lausanne in 1949, living meanwhile in Grundlsee, Styria. In 1952 he was appointed to teach at the University of Cincinnati, where in 1970 he was made emeritus professor and fellow of the graduate school. While based in the USA he has made frequent visits to Europe as a pianist and conductor in performances of his own works; he established a home in his native town and also accepted the post of music adviser to the Eisenstadt Liszt Centre. His honours include an Austrian State Prize (1963) and the freedom of Siegendorf. In his works he has made use of Hungarian and other folk musics in a contemporary tonal style which, over the years, has become more wide-ranging and involved.

WORKS
(selective list)

Ballets: Nile Legend (K. Tüdős, after Gautier), 1937–9; Narcissus, 1939; The Songs of Silence, 1967

Orch: Tarantella, pf, orch, 1937; Antiqua hungarica, 1941; Ländliches Barock, 1941; Partita, gui/hpd, orch, 1949–50; Volkstänze aus dem Burgenland, 1952; Overtura semiseria, 1958–9; Passacaglia, 1960; Serenade nach Alt-Grazer Kontratänzen, 1966

Vocal: 5 Fragments of Jade, SSA, 1938; The Chant of the Creation (Weöres), 1v, orch, 1943–4; Shepherds Hark, SATB, 1961; Let Nothing Disturb Thee, SATB, 1964; 3 Japanese Tanka, SATB, 1965; Meditation, SATB, 1968; Toccata mistica, SATB, org, 1968

Chamber: Goumbri, vn, pf, 1931; 8 kleine Stücke, vn, pf, 1949–50; Sonata concertante, vn, pf, 1956; Sonata missoulana, ob/bn, pf, 1958; Wind Qnt, 1961–2; Sonata capricciosa, tuba, pf, 1965; Späte Gedanken, vn, gui, 1969; 2 Fantastics, a sax, pf, 1969; Musica reservata, db, pf, 1969; Monologue, vc, 1973–4; Octet, 1974–5

Pf: Von fremden Ländern und Menschen, 20 easy pieces, 1936–7; Toccata und Fuge, left hand, 1950; Double Dozen for Little Fingers, 1958; For Me, 21 easy pieces, 1963; 4 Epitaphe, 1964; Sons et silences, 1963–4; Twilight Music, 6 pieces, 1970–71; Klänge und Farben, 15 pieces, 1973–4; Tagebuch-Fragmente, 2 pf, 1973

Principal publishers: Doblinger, SIDEM (Geneva), Universal

WRITINGS

'Arabische Musik in Ägypten', *Der Auftakt*, ix (1929), 241

'Music of the Philippines', *Philippine Touring Topics* (1933), Nov; (1934), July

'Tune and Chant in Egypt', *Africa* (Johannesburg, 1936), Feb

Several articles on Bartók

BIBLIOGRAPHY

W. Suppan: 'Jenő Takács', *Mitteilungen des steirischen Tonkünstlerbundes*, nos.21–2 (1965)

JÁNOS DEMÉNY

Takahashi, Yuji (*b* Tokyo, 21 Sept 1938). Japanese composer and pianist. He studied at the Toho School with Shibata and Ogura for composition (1954–8) and first drew public attention in 1961 when he deputized at a Japanese radio contemporary music concert. Under a Ford Foundation grant he lived in Berlin (1963–5), the only composition pupil at that time of Xenakis. In 1966 a grant from the Rockefeller Fund took him to New York for work on computer composition, and he attended the Tanglewood courses of 1966–8. He has been internationally active as a pianist able to make a brilliant effect with difficult avant-garde works: he gave the first performance of Xenakis's *Herma* and has recorded pieces by Brown, Cage, Reynolds, Takemitsu, Xenakis and himself. His occasional performances of works from the standard piano repertory have been unremarkable. As a composer he has been one of the few to take up the stochastic and other methods introduced by Xenakis.

WORKS
(selective list)

Orch: Prajnâ pâramitâ, 4 ens (each of Mez, 9 insts), 1969; Orphika, 1969; Kaga-i, pf, chamber orch, 1971

Chamber: Chromamorphe I, vn, db, fl, tpt, hn, trbn, vib, 1963; 6 stocheia, 4 vn, 1965; Bridges I, elec hpd/pf, b drum, castanets, amp vc, 1967; Operation Euler, 2/3 ob, 1967; Rosace I, amp vn, 1967; Bridges II, 2 ob, 2 cl, 2 tpt, 3 va, 1968; Corona borealis, pic, ob, cl, bn, hn, 1971; Nikite, ob, cl, tpt, trbn, vc, db, 1971

Pf: Chromamorphe II, 1964; Rosace II, 1967; Metatheses, 1968

Tape: Ye-guen, 18-track, laser beams, 1970; Tadori, 1972

Principal publisher: Peters

MICHAEL STEINBERG

Takata, Saburō (*b* Nagoya, 18 Dec 1913). Japanese composer. He was a pupil of Nobutoki and Pringsheim, and graduated from the Tokyo Music School in 1939. For some time he was active as a composer and conductor (of the Central SO), but after World War II he gave up conducting. In 1947 he joined the Japanese Society for Contemporary Music, of which he was president from 1963 to 1968, and in 1953 he was appointed professor of composition at the Kunitachi Music College. His style draws principally on the German Romantic tradition, though some works show the influence of impressionism, particularly of Debussy.

WORKS
(selective list)

Opera: Aoki ōkami [The dark blue wolf], 1970–72, Tokyo, 1972

Orch: Yamagata min'yō ni yoru fantazī to nijū-fūga [Fantasy and double fugue on a Yamagata folksong], 1941; 2 rhapsodies, 1945, 1946

Choral: Kisetsu to ashiato [Seasons and footprints], male vv, 1958; Musei dōkoku [Wordless tears], cantata, solo vv, chorus, orch, 1956–64; Mizu no inochi [The soul of water], vv, pf, 1964; Hana no no [Flowered fields], 1969; 2 masses, psalms, sequences, hymns

Songs: 8 Songs (Takuboku), 1956; Pari ryojō [Feelings in Paris], 1963; Kodoku na taiwa [Solitary dialogue], 1971; c50 others

Inst: Pf Preludes, 1947; Sonata, vn, pf, 1949; Suite, wind qnt, 1952; Marionette, suite, str qt, 1954; org pieces

Principal publishers: Kawai-Gakufu, Ongaku-no-Tomo Sha

MASAKATA KANAZAWA

Takemitsu, Tōru (*b* Tokyo, 8 Oct 1930). Japanese composer. In 1948 he became a private pupil of Kiyose, with whom he studied intermittently for a few years; otherwise he is self-taught, which may partly explain the originality of his approach and style. From the first he was ready to experiment with newly developed means and methods, including unusual combinations, unconventional performing techniques, *musique concrète* and other kinds of tape music, free improvisation, graphic notation, aleatory music and the incorporation of visual elements. Although some of his earlier works may show the influences of the expressionism of Schoenberg, Berg and Webern or of melodic and harmonic features of French music from Debussy to Messiaen, Takemitsu's work is essentially independent; there is almost no reliance on traditional theory, functional harmony, regular metre and rhythm, or conventional structures. Takemitsu's primary preoccupations are with timbre and texture – and with silence, which is often as important as sound in his works. His music often gives an impression of spatial experience and of materials evolving freely of their own accord: each composition appears to fill its own acoustic space with a variety of sounds, which may be conventional, performed through some new device or recorded from everyday life, but always establishing a certain unity. In general the feeling is grave, intense and dynamic, yet also natural and well balanced. To quote his own words, composition is 'to give a proper meaning to the "streams of sounds" which penetrate the world which surrounds us' (see Funayama).

In 1948 Takemitsu met two other composers (besides Kiyose) who later exerted some influence on him, Hayasaka and Matsudaira, both of whom shared a deep interest in the traditional musics of Japan and the rest of Asia. Between 1950 and 1952 he belonged to the Shin Sakkyokuha Kyōkai, a group headed by Kiyose, and it was at one of their regular concerts (December 1950) that he had his first performance. The piece was *Futatsu no rento* ('Lento for two') for piano, whose abundant dissonances already showed Takemitsu's unorthodox attitude to musical structure. Although the première was received rather coldly, there were two enthusiastic supporters in the audience, Yuasa and Akiyama, who were to remain his friends; in 1951, together with other musicians and artists, the three founded a new group, the Jikken Kōbō (Experimental Workshop), for collaboration in mixed media. For this association Takemitsu composed *Saegirarenai kyūsoku no.1* ('Pause uninterrupted no.1') for piano (1952), written in irregular rhythm without bar-lines, and the *Shitsunai kyōsōkyoku* ('Chamber concerto') for 13 wind instruments (1955), which displays his sensitive handling of sonority. He then turned to electronic music in *Relief statique* (1955) and *Vocalism A·I* (1956); the latter uses only the phonemes 'a' and 'i' ('ai' being the Japanese for 'love'), pronounced in various ways by two actors. Material is similarly restricted in *Mizu no kyoku* ('Water music', 1960), formed exclusively from recorded water sounds.

Takemitsu's first composition on a larger scale, *Requiem* for strings (1957, dedicated to the memory of Hayasaka), was heard in 1959 by Stravinsky, who declared it a masterpiece, commenting on the music's intensity; it has become one of Takemitsu's most frequently performed works. In 1958 he composed three prizewinning pieces, *Le son-calligraphie no.1*, a mere 31 bars for two string quartets, *Kuroi kaiga* ('Black painting') for reciter and small orchestra, and the orchestral *Solitude sonore*. He also began to take an active part in concerts and festivals of modern music, including those sponsored by the Institute for Twentieth-century Music after 1959. For the institute's summer festival of 1961 he composed *Ring* for flute, guitar and lute; the work takes its title from the initial letters of its four sections ('General theme', 'Retrograde', 'Inversion' and 'Noise'), which may be performed in any order; between two of them an interlude with improvisation, notated in graphic score, is played. *Kanshō* ('Coral island'), an orchestral composition with unconventionally employed solo voice and again partly in graphic notation, received favourable mention at the 1962 ISCM Festival, and *Textures* for orchestra was named best work of the year at the 1965 festival.

In 1964 Takemitsu was invited by the East–West Center of Hawaii to give a series of lectures in conjunction with Cage; later in the same year he staged 'events' with Cage and Ichiyanagi in Tokyo. Meanwhile he had developed a fresh interest in traditional Japanese instruments, particularly the *biwa*, which he used for the first time in his music for the film *Seppuku* (1962), honoured as the best film score at the Mainichi Music Festival. From then he employed Japanese instruments frequently in music for the cinema, radio and television. His first concert work for such forces was *Eclipse* for *biwa* and *shakuhachi* (1966), which was widely performed by the virtuosos Kinshi Tsuruta and Katsuya Yokoyama to great acclaim. Takemitsu has been more successful than anyone else in composing for Japanese instruments in a European manner, largely because his formal and rhythmic notions are close to the aesthetic aims of traditional Japanese music; at the same time it should be noted that, unlike others, he has not attempted any combination of Japanese and European features, but instead has created a quite new sound world with materials from both regions. When he was commissioned in 1967 to write a piece for the 125th anniversary of the New York PO, he again turned to the *biwa* and *shakuhachi*, this time for a sort of double concerto, *November Steps*. Introduced at the Lincoln Center on 9 November 1967, with Tsuruta and Yokoyama as soloists, *November Steps* scored an immediate success and brought Takemitsu to public attention throughout the world. Numerous commissions have followed: *Asterism* for piano and orchestra (1968) was composed for RCA and *Stanza I* (1969) for Deutsche Grammophon, to cite two examples. Takemitsu was director of the Space Theatre in the Steel Pavilion at Expo '70, Osaka.

WORKS

(*selective list*)

ORCHESTRAL

Ikiru yorokobi [The joy to live] (ballet), 1951
Shitsunai kyōsōkyoku [Chamber concerto], 13 wind, 1955
Requiem, str, 1957
Solitude sonore, 1958
Ki no kyoku [Tree music], 1961
Arc, pf, orch: Pile, 1963; Solitude, 1966; Your Love and the Crossing, 1963; Textures, 1964; Reflection, 1966; Coda, 1966 [6 movts may be played independently]
Chiheisen no dōria [Dorian horizon], 17 str, 1966
November Steps, biwa, shakuhachi, orch, 1967
Green (November Steps II), 1967
Asterism, pf, orch, 1968
Crossing, 1969
Cassiopea, perc, orch, 1971
Gemeaux, ob, trbn, 2 orchs, 1972
Aki [Autumn], biwa, shakuhachi, orch, 1973
Gitimalya, orch, 1975
Quatraine, cl, vn, vc, pf, orch, 1975
Marginalia, 1976
Mar Conc., 1976

VOCAL

Kuroi kaiga [Black painting], reciter, small orch, 1958
Kanshō [Coral island], S, orch, 1962
Kaze no uma [Horse in the wind], female chorus, 1962
Stanza I, female v, pf, gui, harp, vib, 1969

CHAMBER AND INSTRUMENTAL

Ens: Yōsei no kyori [Distance of fairy], vn, pf, 1951; Le son-calligraphie nos.1–3, 2 str qts, 1958–60; Mask, 2 fl, 1960; Landscape, str qt, 1960; Ring, fl, gui, lute, 1961; Corona no.2, 1962; Sacrifice, fl, lute, vib, 1962; Valeria (Sonant), 2 fl, 2 bandoneons, gui, vn, vc, 1965; Eclipse, biwa, shakuhachi, 1966; Ring no.2, vn, pf, 1966; Crosstalk, 2 bandoneons, tape, 1968; Eucalypts, fl, ob, harp, str, 1970; Eucalypts II, fl, ob, harp, 1970; Distance, shō, ob, 1972; Shūteika [In an autumn garden], gagaku ens, 1973; Tabi, 3 biwa, 1973; Garden Rain, brass, 1974; Bryce, fl, 2 harp, mar, perc, 1976; Waves, cl, hn, 2 trbn, perc, 1976
Solo inst: Seasons, perc, 1970; Koe [Voice], fl, 1971; Stanza II, harp, tape, 1971; Folios, gui, 1974
Pf: Futatsu no rento [Lento for 2], 1950; Saegirarenai kyūsoku [Pause uninterrupted] nos.1–3, 1952–9; Piano Distance, 1961; Corona, 1962; The Crossing, 1962; Far Away, 1973

OTHER WORKS

Tape: Relief statique, 1955; Yuridis [Euridice], 1956; Vocalism A·I, 1956; Sora, uma soshite shi [Sky, horse and death], 1958; Quiet Design, 1960; Mizu no kyoku [Water music], 1960; Kwaidan [after film score], 1966; Armanac, 1970; Toward, 1970
Events: Time Perspective, Tokyo, May 1964, collab. Ichiyanagi, Akiyama and others; Blue Aurora, Tokyo, 27 Nov 1964, collab. Cage; Seven Hills Event, Tokyo, 1966
Film scores: Seppuku, 1962; Suna no onna [Woman in the dune], 1964; Kwaidan, 1964; Tanin no kao [The face of another], 1966; Dodosuka den; many others

Principal publishers: Ongaku-no-Tomo Sha, Peters, Salabert, Universal

WRITINGS

Takemitsu Tōru⊆1930 · · · · · ∞ (Tokyo, 1964)
Oto, chinmoku to hakariaeru hodo ni [As much as can be measured with sounds and silence] (Tokyo, 1971)

BIBLIOGRAPHY

K. Akiyama: 'Takemitsu Tōru', *Record geijutsu* (1973), Sept, 95
T. Funayama: *Gendai ongaku* [Contemporary music] (Tokyo, 1973), 9ff

MASAKATA KANAZAWA

Taki, Rentarō (*b* Tokyo, 24 Aug 1879; *d* Ōita, 29 June 1903). Japanese composer and pianist. In 1894 he was admitted to the Tokyo Music School where he studied with Aya Kōda. Four years later he began to teach at the school and made his début as a pianist. In June 1900 the Japanese government sent him to study at the Leipzig Conservatory, but after a year of study he fell ill; he was sent home in October 1902 and was confined to bed for the remaining months of his life. He left only a few piano pieces, choral works and songs, in which he attempted to handle traditional Japanese melodies with the techniques of German Romanticism. As a composer and as a pianist he did not reach maturity, but he is remembered as a leading advocate of European music at the earliest stage of its introduction into Japan, and his song *Kōjō no tsuki* ('Moon at a desolate castle', 1901) became the best known of early Japanese songs in a European style.

MASAKATA KANAZAWA

Takt (Ger.). (1) METRE or time, as in *Dreivierteltakt* (3/4 time), *im Takt* (in strict tempo), *Taktart* (metre), *taktieren* (to indicate the beat), *Taktmesser* (metronome), *Taktstock* (baton), *Taktvorzeichnung* or *Taktzeichen* (time signature), *Taktwechsel* (change of metre), and so on.

(2) BAR, as in *Taktstrich* (bar-line). *Taktteil* means beat (i.e. a part of the bar; *see* BEAT (i)), as in *guter Taktteil* (good, i.e. strong, beat).

Taktakishvili, Otar Vasil'yevich (*b* Tbilisi, 27 July 1924). Soviet composer, teacher, conductor and writer on music. He graduated from Barkhudaryan's composition class at the Tbilisi Conservatory in 1947 and then did postgraduate work at the same institution, where he taught choral literature (from 1947), counterpoint and instrumentation (from 1959) and served as rector (1962–5). In addition, he was appointed artistic director of the State Choral Kapella of Georgia in 1952, having previously worked as a choirmaster and conductor. He also served as a deputy to the Supreme Soviet of the USSR (fourth to sixth convocations), a deputy to the Supreme Soviet of the Georgian SSR and a member of the Presidium of the International Music Council of UNESCO. In 1965 he was appointed minister of culture of the Georgian SSR, and in 1966 was made a professor. He is the secretary of the Composers' Union of the USSR, a People's Artist of the Georgian SSR (1961) and a People's Artist of the USSR (1974); he holds three State Prizes (1951, 1952, 1967) and the orders of Lenin, the October Revolution and the Red Banner of Labour.

Taktakishvili's output embraces almost all genres and, despite its variety, it displays a consistency of intention and thematic working. He achieved wide recognition right from his earliest creative years, from the mid-1940s to the early 1950s. The best works of this period, the two symphonies and the First Piano Concerto, are marked by technical mastery, the creative use of folk material and a reliance on international symphonic traditions. They also share a lyric–dramatic narrative quality and a loftiness of sentiment, which at times mutates into pathos. In his subsequent development Taktakishvili has turned increasingly to vocal music and concrete images; his deployment of the expressive possibilities of the voice has been significantly affected by his continuing interest in folk choral singing, as well as by his early work as a choirmaster. This evolution led him naturally to opera, by way of a programmatic symphonic poem (*Mtsïri*, 1956), songs to words by Pshavela and Pushkin, and vocal orchestral cycles on texts by Tabidze and other Georgian poets

(1957–9), works distinguished by an ever more noticeable social element. *Mindiya* (1961) was the culminating opera, an organic solution of new problems, glorifying the wisdom of a harmonious union between man and nature. It is built on the transformation of folk intonations and marked by a singing, melodious character; dramatically it relies on the alternation of epic narration with lyric–dramatic scenes. A creative response to the traditions of the ancient theatre can be detected in the principles of plot development and in the endowment of each of the main characters with a distinctive philosophical symbolism.

Subsequent works testify to Taktakishvili's continuing development of this tendency. The oratorio *Rustavelis nakvalevze* ('In the steps of Rustaveli', 1964) creates an image of the great poet of the 12th-century Georgian renaissance through the epic strength of its choral frescoes, which draw on folk choral polyphony, and it also raises the question of the place of the past in the present. Another oratorio from the same year, *Tsotskhali kera* ('The living hearth'), addresses the theme of war and peace, extolling the value of the latter and the immortality of the people. Taktakishvili's third such work, *Nikoloz Baratashvili* (1970), is deeply imbued with the spirit and words of the outstanding Georgian Romantic poet of the first half of the 19th century; its underlying theme is the inseparable link which binds the creative artist to the history and fate of his country, and this theme is developed on three planes: those of the poet himself, his world view and his relationship with the composer. The scoring of the work supports quasi-dramatic functions: a tenor soloist expounds the lyrical and philosophical burden, an octet of male voices symbolizes time arising (the proximity of their music to an ancient chorale assists this) and the chorus is used in an epic and dramatic role, commenting and summarizing.

The trilogy of one-act operas *Sami novela* ('Three stories', 1967) marked a new development in the Georgian musical theatre. Set in pre-revolutionary Georgia, the pieces concern the tragic fate of the country's simple people, employing a wide range of expressive means from developments of banal urban street songs to parodies of genre music and the music of everyday life; the result is a musical narrative of poster-like boldness. The cantata *Guruli simgerebi* ('Gurian songs', named after a region of western Georgia having a particularly highly developed tradition of folk choral polyphony) extended Taktakishvili's expressive use of folk materials, employing as it does quite specific folksong features in music that contrasts characteristic, lyrical and heroic ideas.

Taktakishvili has written a number of articles in *Sovetskaya muzïka* and *Sabchota khelovneba*.

WORKS
(selective list)

Operas: Mindiya (2, R. Tabukashvili, after V. Pshavela), 1961, Tbilisi, 1961; Sami novela [3 stories] (Taktakishvili): Ori ganacheni [2 verdicts] (after M. Dzhavakhishvili), Dzhariskatsi [The soldier] (after Dzhavakhishvili), Droshebi chkara [Hold the banners high] (G. Tabidze), 1967, Tbilisi, 1967, rev. as Tri zhizni [3 lives] with new no.3: Chikor (S. Tsenin, after Dzhavakhishvili), 1972, Moscow, 1972; Mtvaris Motatseba [The abduction of the moon] (after K. Gamsakhurdia), 1976

Vocal orch: O Tbilisi, cantata, 1958; Klde da nakaduli [Rock and stream], vocal sym. poem, 1962; Rustavelis nakvalevze [In the steps of Rustaveli] (I. Abashidze), oratorio, B, chorus, orch, org, 1964; Tsotskhali kera [The living hearth] (S. Chikovani), oratorio, speaker, solo vv, chorus, orch, 1964; Nikoloz Baratashvili, oratorio, T, 8 solo male vv, chorus, orch, 1970; Guruli simgerebi [Gurian songs], can-

tata, 8 solo male vv, chorus, orch, 1971; Megruli simgerebi ['Megrel' songs], suite, 1v, 8 solo male vv, chamber orch, 1972
Orch: 2 syms., 1949, 1953; Samgori, sym. poem, 1950; 2 pf concs., 1951, 1973; Vn Concertino, 1955; Mtsïri, sym. poem, 1956; Humoresque, chamber orch, 1963; ovs. and other works
Inst: Sonata, fl, pf; pf suites
Choruses, songs, incidental music, film scores

Principal publishers: Muzfond Gruzii (Tbilisi), Muzgiz, Muzïka, Sovetskiy Kompozitor (Moscow and Leningrad)

BIBLIOGRAPHY

V. Kukharsky: 'Slushaya vremya' [Listening to time], SovM (1952), no.4, p.9
V. Belïy and V. Vanslov: 'Novoye v gruzinskom simfonizme' [Something new in Georgian symphonism], SovM (1954), no.9, p.9
L. Polyakova: O. Taktakishvili (Moscow, 1956)
N. Shumskaya: 'Kontsertino O. Taktakishvili', SovM (1956), no.12, p.10
M. Sabinina: 'Mtsïri: simfonicheskaya poema O. Taktakishvili', SovM (1957), no.5, p.61
O. Geronimus: Kontsert dlya fortepiano s orkestrom O. Taktakishvili (Leningrad, 1959)
G. Toradze: 'Geroi Vasha Pshavela v opere', SovM (1961), no.9, p.22
D. Romadinova: Opera 'Mindiya' O. Taktakishvili (Moscow, 1963)
G. Ordzhonikidze: 'Oratoria "Zhivoj ochag" ' [The oratorio The living hearth], Literaturnaja gruzja (Tbilisi, 1965), no.7, p.88
A. Tsulukidze: 'Droshebi chkara' [Hold the banners high], Sabchota khelovneba (Tbilisi, 1967), no.10, p.23
G. Toradze: 'Po sledam Baratashvili' [In the steps of Baratashvili], SovM (1971), no.10, p.9
A. Shaverzashvili: ' "Guriyskiye pesni" O. Taktakishvili', SovM (1973), no.7, p.32
M. Achmeteli: 'Otar Taktakishvili', Sabchota khelovneba (1974), no.12, p.21
L. V. Polyakova: Otar Taktakishvili (Moscow, 1979)

EVGENY MACHAVARIANI

Taktakishvili, Shalva Mikhailovich (b Kvemo Khviti, 14 Aug 1900; d Tbilisi, 18 July 1965). Soviet composer and conductor. He studied at the Tbilisi Conservatory (1920–28, composition with Sergey Barkhudaryan), and then helped to found a music school at Batum where he was both director and teacher of music theory. From the 1930s he held a number of posts in Tbilisi: teacher of the opera class at the conservatory (1937–9) and director of its opera studio (from 1951); conductor of the radio chorus (1934–8); and conductor of the Georgian State Orchestra (from 1952). He composed the operas Rassvet (1923), Deputat (1939; both performed in Tbilisi) and Otarova vdova (1942), a sinfonietta, overtures and other pieces for orchestra, a cello concerto (1932), chamber music and many choruses and songs, some to verse by Pushkin. He also published writings on Rimsky-Korsakov and Shalyapin and studies of several operas.

BIBLIOGRAPHY

G. Bernandt and A. N. Dolzhansky: Sovetskiye kompozitorï (Moscow, 1957), 557f
P. V. Hukua: Shalva Taktakishvili (Tbilisi, 1962)
S. D. Krebs: Soviet Composers and the Development of Soviet Music (London, 1970)

Taktmesser (Ger.). METRONOME.

Taktstrich (Ger.). Bar-line; see STRICH.

Tal, Josef (b Pinne, nr. Poznań, 18 Sept 1910). Israeli composer, pianist and teacher. He graduated in composition and music teaching from the Berlin Hochschule für Musik, where his teachers included Tiessen, Trapp, Hindemith, Sachs, Kreutzer and Saal, and left for Palestine in 1934. After two years of agricultural work as a member of Kibbutz Gesher, he became a teacher of piano and composition at the Jerusalem Conservatory. Following the establishment of the state of Israel, the conservatory was reorganized as the Israel Academy of Music, with Tal as director from 1948 to 1952. In 1950 Tal joined the staff of the Hebrew University and eventually served as the first chairman of its department of musicology. As associate professor he has taken charge of the University Centre for Electronic Music, which he founded in 1961 as an independent institution. He has represented his country at ISCM festivals, IMC meetings and countless specialized conferences in Europe, Asia and elsewhere. Awards made to him include the ISCM Festival Award (1954), a UNESCO research fellowship in electronic music (1957–8), and two Israel State Prizes. From 1965 to 1968 Tal was a member of the Israel Broadcasting Authority and chairman of its music committee. After serving as a corresponding member for two years, he was appointed an ordinary member of the Berlin Academy of Arts in 1971.

Unlike some members of the neo-impressionist 'Mediterranean school' (which, in the years just before and after the establishment of Israel, tried to infuse Israeli music with a regional, often distinctly pastoral flavour), Tal has never denied his central European past. While drawing on the history and philosophy of the Old Testament, as well as on the rhythm and intonation of modern Hebrew, he has remained opposed to any parochialism, and from the 1960s has been his country's foremost composer for electronic media. Such successful earlier works as his First Symphony (1952), the two string quartets and the Cello Concerto freely use 12-note materials while avoiding strict serial procedures. On the other hand, his Five Methodical Piano Pieces are sophisticated didactic exercises in dodecaphonic technique. In his electronic work Tal has been both liberal and practical, convinced that 'financial feasibility and aesthetically satisfying projects' are compatible. He manages to produce a rich diversity of sounds from relatively limited electronic resources, and it is his firm conviction that the future of electronic music lies in partnership with live performers. This practicality is evident in the series of 'portable' or 'instant' concertos for piano and tape. Through his theoretical work and his teaching, Tal has also had a substantial effect on Israeli musical life.

The characteristic features of Tal's music are broad dramatic gestures and driving bursts of energy generated, for example, by various types of ostinato or sustained textural accumulations. Complex rhythmic patterning is typical of the widely performed Second Symphony and of a number of notable dance scores. But Tal's marked dramatic and philosophical propensities find total expression only in opera, particularly in the large-scale, 12-note opera Ashmedai, commissioned and first performed by the Hamburg Opera. The libretto, originally in Hebrew, relates a post-biblical Jewish legend in the form of a morality play, with allusions to the perversion of power in Nazi Germany. It is a profoundly expressive work, drawing on a wide range of media and styles. Ashmedai represents the creative world of Tal, central European by birth and upbringing, dedicated Israeli by choice. Massada 967, the electronic opera that followed, was written in honour of the 25th anniversary of the state of Israel.

WORKS
OPERAS
Saul at Ein Dor (opera concertante, 1 Samuel: xxv, xviii), 1957; Ramat Gan Chamber Orch, cond. M. Taube, Tel-Aviv, 1957
Amnon and Tamar (1, R. Freier), 1961; Kol Israel Orch, cond. H. Freudenthal, Jerusalem, 1961

Ashmedai (2, I. Eliraz), 1968–9; cond. Bertini, Hamburg, Oct 1971
Massada 967 (15 scenes, Eliraz), solo vv, chorus, elec, 1972; cond. Bertini, Jerusalem, July 1973
Die Versuchung (2, Eliraz), solo vv, chorus, elec, orch, 1973–4; cond. Bertini, Munich, 1976
Else (chamber scene, Eliraz), 1v, narrator, 4 insts, 1975; Tel-Aviv, July 1975

ORCHESTRAL

Piano Concerto no.1, 1944; Tal, Palestine PO, cond. G. Singer, Tel-Aviv, 1947
Reflections, str, 1950; Israel PO, cond. Taube, Tel-Aviv, 1950
Piano Concerto no.2, 1953; Tal, Kol Israel Orch, cond. Taube, Jerusalem, 1953
Symphony no.1, 1953; Israel PO, cond. Freudenthal, Tel-Aviv, 1953
Viola Concerto, 1954; G. Roehr, Kol Israel Orch, cond. Freudenthal, Haifa, 1954
Piano Concerto no.3 (E. Hakalir), T, pf, orch, 1956; C. Flaschner, Tal, Kol Israel Orch, cond. Taube, Jerusalem, 1956
Festive Vision, 1959; Israel PO, cond. I. Solomon, Tel-Aviv, 1960
Symphony no.2, 1960; Kol Israel Orch, cond. S. Ronly-Riklis, Jerusalem, 1961
Concerto, vc, str, 1961; U. Wiesel, Kol Israel Orch, cond. Ronly-Riklis, Jerusalem, 1961
Double Concerto, vn, vc, chamber orch, 1970; Zuckerman, Wiesel, Israel Chamber Ens, cond. Bertini, Tel-Aviv, April 1970
Shape, chamber orch, 1975; cond. R. Shapey, Chicago, 1976
Concerto, fl, chamber orch, 1976; A. Nicolet, Tel-Aviv, 1976
Symphony no.3, 1978; Israel PO, cond. Mehta, Tel-Aviv, 3 July 1978

VOCAL

Exodus (choreographic poem, Bible), Bar, orch, 1946; K. Salmon, Palestine PO, cond. Molinari, Tel-Aviv, 1947
The Mother Rejoices (sym. cantata, 2 Maccabees: vii), chorus, pf, orch, 1949; M. Harnick, Kol Israel Orch, cond. Tal, Jerusalem 1950
3 Songs (trad.), chorus, 1953; Kol Israel Choir, Jerusalem, 1954
Succoth Cantata, 1955; Kol Israel Orch, cond. Tal, Jerusalem, 1955
The Death of Moses (oratorio, legends arr. J. Jaari), 1967; Kol Israel Orch, cond. Bertini, Jerusalem, 1967
Misdar hanoflim [Parade of the Fallen] (cantata, H. Hefer), 1968; Kol Israel Orch, cond. M. Rodan, Jerusalem, 1968
Song on Verses by Heine, A/Bar, fl, hn, tom-tom, pf, 1971; Angervo, Blau, Seifert, Müller, Broddack, Berlin, 1972
The Wooden Horse (cantata, N. Sach), solo vv, chorus, elec, 1973
Na'ari (N. Yonathan), S, cl, 1975; A. Etzion, Tel-Aviv, 1975

INSTRUMENTAL

3 Preludes, pf, 1942; Tal, Jerusalem, 1944
6 Sonnets, pf, 1946; Tal, Jerusalem, 1946
Lament, vc, harp, 1950; B. Weissgerber, C. Szarvas, Tel-Aviv, 1950
Piano Sonata no.1, 1950; Tal, Jerusalem, 1951
Sonata, vn, pf, 1951; L. Fenyvesz, Tal, Jerusalem, 1951
Sonata, ob, pf, 1952; G. Haas, Tal, Jerusalem, 1954
Inventions, pf, 1956; Tal, Jerusalem, 1957
Intrada, harp, 1959; Szarvas, Jerusalem, 1959
String Quartet no.1, 1959; Tel-Aviv Qt, Tel-Aviv, 1959
Sonata, va, pf, 1960; O. Partos, Tal, Warsaw, 1962
From the life of a 12-tone row, pf, 1962; Tal, Jerusalem, 1963
Structure, harp, 1962; Szarvas, Jerusalem, 1962
String Quartet no.2, 1964; New Israel Str Qt, Jerusalem, 1966
Duet, va, pf, 1965; Lehmann, Tal, Hamburg, 1968
Wind Quintet, 1966; Danzi Qnt, Holland, 1968
Piano Trio, 1973
Treatise, vc, 1973; U. Wiesel, Jerusalem, 1974
String Quartet no.3, 1976

WORKS WITH TAPE

Exodus II, ballet, tape, 1954; Jerusalem, 1954
Piano Concerto no.4, pf, tape, 1962; Tal, Tel-Aviv, 1962
Ranges of Energy, ballet, tape, 1963; Holland, 1963
Piano Concerto no.5, pf, tape, 1964; G. Herzog, Berlin, 1964
Concerto, hpd, tape, 1964; F. Pelleg, Tel-Aviv, 1964
Piano Concerto no.6, pf, tape, 1970; Tal, Jerusalem, 1970
Variations, ballet, tape, 1970; USA, 1973
Concerto, harp, tape, 1971; Zabaleta, Munich, 1972
Min hameitzar [From the depths] (Psalm cxxix), ballet, tape, 1971; New York 1975
Overture to an Opera, ballet, tape, 1973; Tel-Aviv, 1973
Frequencies 440–462 (Hommage à Boris Blacher), tape, 1973

Principal publishers: Israel Music Institute, Israeli Music Publications, Merkaz Letarbut Ulechinuch

WRITINGS

Jessodot hateoria hamusikalit [Elementary musical theory] (Jerusalem, 1944)
Mavo letorat hatsura hamusikalit [Introduction to musical form] (Tel-Aviv, 1951)
'Synthetic Means', The Modern Composer and his World, ed. J. Beckwith (Toronto, 1961), 116
'Gedanken zur Oper "Ashmedai"', Ariel, xv (1972), 89
'Rationale und sensitive Komponenten des Verstehens in Musik',

Aufsätze zur semantischen Theorie, Aesthetik und Soziologie der musikalischen Kommunikation, ed. H. P. Reinecke (Cologne, 1973)

BIBLIOGRAPHY
A. L. Ringer: 'Musical Composition in Israel', MQ, li (1965), 282
S. Kaufman: 'Josef Tal: a Composer of his Time', Tarbut, xxvi (1973), 10
Y. W. Cohen: Werden und Entwicklung der Musik in Israel (Kassel, 1976 [pt.ii of rev. ed. of M. Brod: Die Musik Israels]
W. Elias: The Music of Israel: a Bibliography of Israeli Art Music since 1920 (Tel-Aviv, in preparation)

ALEXANDER L. RINGER

Tala. An Indian term often translated as 'rhythm'. Tala is a fixed and cyclically repeated time-span for music, articulated into segments by beats of the hand or a percussion idiophone, or by a drum pattern; see INDIA, SUBCONTINENT OF, §§I, 2(iii), II, 3(ii–iii), 5.

Talbot [Munkittrick], Howard (b Yonkers, NY, 9 March 1865; d Reigate, 12 Sept 1928). English composer. He came to England as a child; he was a medical student at King's College, London and studied at the RCM under Parry, Bridge and Gladstone. A few early songs were published before he turned his attention to the popular theatre, composing the comic-opera scores Wapping Old Stairs (1894) and Monte Carlo (1896), and achieving fame with the musical comedy A Chinese Honeymoon (1899) which ran for over 1000 performances in London. From 1900 he conducted at various London theatres for George Edwardes, and his further musical comedy scores included The White Chrysanthemum (1905), The Girl behind the Counter (1906), The Three Kisses (1907) and The Belle of Brittany (1908). Talbot also composed music for several other works in collaboration with Monckton, Rubens, Felix, Finck and Novello, the best known being The Arcadians (1909, with Monckton), from which such numbers as the opening chorus, 'I like London', 'My Motter' and 'Half-past Two' testify to Talbot's inventiveness and craftsmanship.

ANDREW LAMB

Talbot, James (b London, 1665; d Cambridge, 1708). English writer on music. He was educated at Westminster School and Trinity College, Cambridge (matriculated 1683), and was Regius Professor of Hebrew at Cambridge from 1689 to 1704. His importance to music history derives from his manuscript GB-Och Music MS 1187 (formerly owned by Henry Aldrich) which provides copious information on instruments. The manuscript, for which an approximate date of 1695 has been suggested, consists mainly of numbered sheets on which are recorded details of instruments; the information was obtained first-hand from leading players and makers in London, and from Talbot's examination and measurement of instruments provided by these men. Other pages record tunings and tablatures, or quotations from Praetorius, Mersenne and Kircher. Most of the information is published in the Galpin Society Journal: i (1948), 9 (wind); iii (1950), 27 (bowed strings); v (1952), 44 (bagpipes); xiv (1961), 52 (lutes); xv (1962), 60 (other plucked strings); xvi (1963), 63 (harps); xxi (1968), 40 (harpsichord). The remainder of the manuscript, including sections on ancient Greek music etc, seems to be of less value and has not been published.

ANTHONY C. BAINES

Talea (Lat.: 'a cutting'). A medieval term usually understood to denote a freely invented rhythmic configuration, several statements of which constitute the note values of the tenor of an isorhythmic motet (or of its first section, if diminution is later applied to the tenor).

While medieval writers were far from unanimous in their use of 'talea' and 'color', modern musicology has been influenced by the definitions that Jehan des Murs, the first to mention talea (c1340–50), ascribed to 'some musicians': 'A configuration of pitches and its repetitions are called "color"; a rhythmic configuration and its repetitions are called "talea" ' (CS, iii, 58b; cf also 99a). Even more precise are the statements of the anonymous author (late 14th century) of an Ars cantus mensurabilis (Anonymous V of CS, iii, 397b): 'When the same note shapes [i.e. rhythms] are repeated, but with different pitches, this is called "talla". . . . When the same pitches are repeated, but with different note shapes, that is "color" '.

While most medieval writers defined 'talea' as a process of repetition, for the anonymous author of the Notitia del valore (late 14th century) it denoted the entity ('cutting') to be repeated, which the composer devised by 'dividing [cutting] the tenor into parts'. He therefore referred to two particular motet tenors as 'a tre taglie di valore' (CSM, v, 57). This meaning is consistent with the original sense of the word, and has been adopted by musicologists (the modern usage of 'color' is analogous). It is possible that the large strophes produced by the lengthy taleae of isorhythmic motet tenors account for the appearance of the term, by analogy with the rhetorical term 'taille'.

The differences in medieval opinions are more apparent in the definitions of color (evidently the older term) than in those of talea. 'Color' as the more generic term meant any process of repetition, including purely rhythmic reiteration. Hence Jehan des Murs began his definitions with the statement that 'color in music is the rhythmic identity of a section (passage) repeated several times in the same voice part'. Since rhythmic recurrence is the governing structural principle affecting, to varying degrees, all the voices of an isorhythmic motet, 'color' was the obvious traditional term to apply to it. Only in the tenor does melodic repetition play a role, and even there a subordinate one. Jehan therefore added that while the difference between color and talea 'applied to a good many motet tenors, it does not apply to the upper voices [ipsis motettis]', where only the term 'color' is needed. Moreover, the origins of the musical use of 'color' are evidently connected with the upper voices of Notre Dame polyphony.

All the medieval authors cited so far wrote in the 14th century. The two 15th-century authors to mention color and talea were Prosdocimus de Beldemandis and Tinctoris. The latter, writing several decades after the demise of the isorhythmic motet, reversed the above definition; he identified color as rhythmic identity and equated talea with both rhythmic and melodic identity in one voice part (CS, iv, 180a, 189b). But as early as the beginning of the century Prosdocimus found it necessary in his Tractatus practice de musica mensurabili to report elaborately on three different understandings of the two terms, for two of which he cited Jehan des Murs as authority. According to the first opinion 'there is no difference between color and talea; rather, they are the same, and therefore [Jehan des Murs] defined color and not talea in his treatise' (see the beginning of the latter's definitions cited in the preceding paragraph). Secondly there is the opinion attributed by Jehan des Murs to 'some musicians', which according to Prosdocimus was the most common of the three. The third opinion was the result of intentional compromise: color is identical repetition of rhythms as well as pitches, while talea concerns rhythmic repetition only (CS, iii, 225ff). Four years later Prosdocimus again mentioned the third definition, but otherwise simply stated that 'color or talea in music is the repetition of like rhythms or like pitches' (CS, iii, 247b). The mention of the possibility of repeating the pitches as well as the rhythms of phrases reflects the appearance of isomelic passages in the upper voices of motets written in the early 15th century, especially those by composers resident in northern Italy.

See also Color, §(1); Isorhythm; Motet, §I.

ERNEST H. SANDERS

Taler, Daniel. See TAYLOR, DANIEL.

Talesio, Pedro. See THALESIO, PEDRO.

Talhanderius, Pierre. See TAILHANDIER, PIERRE.

Talich, Václav (b Kroměříž, 28 May 1883; d Beroun, 16 March 1961). Czech conductor. The son of a choirmaster and music teacher, Jan Talich (1851–1915), he played the violin from his youth. Dvořák's recommendation secured him financial support at the Prague Conservatory (1897–1903), where he was a pupil of Mařák and Ševčík, took chamber music in Kàan's classes and with the New Czech Quartet, and conducted the Academic Choir. In 1903 he joined the Berlin PO and soon became leader. There he got to know Nikisch, whose example determined Talich's future career. A serious lung infection ended his Berlin engagement, and in 1904 he became leader in the Municipal Opera in Odessa, which he left to become professor of music at Tbilisi. In 1906 the stormy political events took him back to Bohemia and he began working in Prague as a répétiteur at a singing school and as conductor of the amateur orchestral association. Talich's friendship with Suk, Vítězslav Novák and members of the Czech Quartet dates from this time; occasionally he played with the quartet as second violist. During his years (1908–12) as conductor of the Slovenian PO in Ljubljana (where he also conducted Rusalka with great success), he studied briefly at the Leipzig Conservatory with Reger and Sitt, attending Nikisch's lectures and, in Milan, those of Arturo Vigna. After working in Plzeň theatres (1912–15), he was without a permanent engagement during World War I, appearing only occasionally with the National Theatre orchestra and the Czech PO in 1917. His presentation of Suk's Ripening in 1918 led to his appointment as second conductor of the Czech PO.

In September 1919 Talich was appointed chief conductor of the Czech PO, which, except in 1931–2, he directed until 1941. In addition he was head of opera at the National Theatre from 1935 and conducted there until the theatre was closed by the Nazis in 1944. After Liberation he conducted the opera only briefly, in the 1947–8 season. At the beginning of 1946 he founded the Czech Chamber Orchestra; though it lasted less than two seasons Talich demonstrated his ability to inspire young players to outstanding performances. In the autumn of 1949 he became chief conductor of the newly formed Slovak PO in Bratislava. He returned to Prague in 1952 as artistic adviser of the Prague radio orchestras and the Czech Philharmonic, and made some gramophone recordings. In March 1954 he appeared again publicly in Prague with the Czech PO but in 1956 his health forced him to retire. His exceptional gifts as a teacher made themselves felt not only in training his orchestral players, but also at the Prague Conservatory Master School (from 1933) and the Bratislava

Academy, and in training young conductors (Ančerl, Krombholc, Iša Krejčí, Rudolf Vašata, Ladislav Slovák and Charles Mackerras).

Talich was one of the great Czech conductors of modern times. His sensitivity, imagination and exceptional feeling for orchestral colour placed him in the forefront of international conductors between the wars. In an uncommonly wide symphonic repertory he gave preference to the works of Dvořák, Smetana's *Má vlast* and the best works of his contemporaries, Suk and Novák. He also felt an affinity with the French impressionists and the music of Mozart, and devoted time to younger composers. He brought Janáček's works into the standard operatic repertory. Though coming to the Czech PO at a time of artistic and economic crisis, he enlarged it and, through his untiring hard work, stringent demands and methodical approach, brought it rapidly to world standard. In the 1920s and 1930s he appeared in leading European centres, and from 1924 he conducted regularly in England, Scotland and Sweden (where he was chief conductor of the Konsertföreningen in Stockholm, 1931–3). A polished writer, he often published, in the daily and scholarly press, introductions to and analyses of the works he was studying. His personal views often evoked polemics, especially in operatic productions, where they were frequently connected with his far-reaching dramaturgical changes. He recorded *Má vlast* as early as 1929; in the years 1935–7 he made recordings in London. He was a member of the Royal Music Academy in Stockholm (1928) and the Czech Academy of Arts and Sciences (1936), and held decorations from Bologna, Romania, Yugoslavia, Sweden and France. In 1957 he was made National Artist. Suk dedicated his *Epilog* to him, Novák his *Signorina Gioventù* and Martinů his *Julietta*. His publications include *Sukova Stezka* ('Suk's path') (Prague, 1944).

BIBLIOGRAPHY
J. Hutter: 'Talichovo slohové dirigentství' [Talich's style of conducting], *Hudební věstník*, xxxvi (1943), 50
O. Šourek, ed.: *Václav Talich* (Prague, 1943) [incl. bibliography, discography, repertory and a selection of Talich's articles]
J. Procházka: *Generace za Hilarem a Ostrčilem* [The generation of Hilar and Ostrčil] (Prague, 1947)
J. Pauer: 'Václavu Talichovi, národnímu umělci' [To Talich, National Artist], *HRo*, x (1957), 488
V. Pospíšil: *Václav Talich: několik kapitol o díle a životě českého umělce* [Some chapters on the life and work of a Czech artist] (Prague, 1961)
V. Holzknecht: *Česká filharmonie: příběh orchestru* [Czech PO: story of the orchestra] (Prague, 1963)
J. Burghauser: *Slavní čeští dirigenti* [Famous Czech conductors] (Prague, 1963), 60
V. Pospíšil: 'O Václavu Talichovi s Josefem Vlachem', *HRo*, xvi (1963), 450
J. Krombholc: 'Za Václavem Talichem', *HRo*, xvi (1963), 225 [obituary]
H. Masaryk, ed.: *Václav Talich: dokument života a díla* [A document of his life and work] (Prague, 1967) [incl. selection of Talich's articles, speeches and correspondence]
M. Kuna: 'Bankrot samozřejmosti I' [The bankruptcy of self-evident truths], *HRo*, xxi (1968), 609
M. Kuna, ed.: 'Josef Suk Václavu Talichovi' [Suk to Talich], *HV*, vii (1970), 356–89
——: 'Korespondence Bohuslava Martinů Václavu Talichovi', *HV*, vii (1970), 212–47
——: 'Torzo vztahu lidského a uměleckého: korespondence Al. Háby–V. Talichovi' [The torso of a human and artistic relationship: Hába–Talich correspondence], *HV*, viii (1971), 94
M. Kuna: 'Vaclav Talich a SSSR' [Talich and the USSR], *HV*, xiv (1977), 301 [with Ger. summary]
ALENA NĚMCOVÁ

Talking drum. In general any drum (including the SLIT-DRUM) that is beaten in such a way that certain features of an unvocalized text can be recognized by a listener, these features acting as clues to the meaning of the words being drummed. The two main instances in which a drum is used in this way are in signalling and in music performances especially in parts of Africa (for illustration, *see* GHANA, fig.2). The textual features most commonly reproduced on a drum are syllabic tone, stress and quantity, and phrase or sentence intonation and rhythm, but not all of these are used in any one culture or on any one occasion.

Because of its great tonal flexibility, the hourglass pressure drum is sometimes referred to as 'the talking drum', but in many parts of Africa not only do all kinds of drum 'talk', but so also do various wind instruments, string instruments, and certain rattles and other idiophones.

See also HOURGLASS DRUM.

BIBLIOGRAPHY
J. F. Carrington: 'The Drum Language of the Lokele Tribe', *African Studies*, ii/2 (1944), 75
——: *Talking Drums of Africa* (London, 1949)
R. G. Armstrong: 'Talking Drums in the Benue-Cross River Region of Nigeria', *Phylon*, xv (1954), 355
H. U. Beier: 'The Talking Drums of the Yoruba', *Journal of the African Music Society*, i (1954), 29
R. G. Armstrong: 'Talking Instruments in West Africa', *Exploration*, iv (1955), 140
J. H. K. Nketia: *Drumming in Akan Communities of Ghana* (London, 1963)
D. W. Ames, E. A. Gregersen and T. Neugebauer: '*Taaken samaarii*: a Drum Language of Hausa Youth', *Africa*, xli/1 (1971), 12
ANTHONY KING

Tallafangi Calabr., Andreas (*fl* 1440–50). Italian composer. He is known through a brief textless work for four voices in *I-TRmn* 89 and is sometimes credited with a three-voice Sanctus found in *I-TRmn* 92 attributed to 'Magister Andreas'. In the section beginning 'Pleni' the tenor is silent, but a fourth voice, perhaps added by a later hand, enters for this section only. All four voices are low, using tenor and bass clefs.

TOM R. WARD

Tallat-Kelpša, Juozas (*b* Kalnujai, 1 Jan 1889; *d* Vilnius, 5 Feb 1949). Lithuanian composer and conductor. After studying the cello at the Vilnius Music School he attended the St Petersburg Conservatory (1907–16). In 1919 he worked in Vilnius and in 1920 he settled in Kaunas, teaching at the music school and, from 1933, directing the opera class at the conservatory. He founded the Kaunas Opera in 1920 and was its conductor during the years 1920–41 and 1944–8. The most popular of his works are the choral songs and folksong arrangements, mostly written before 1920, though he also wrote piano pieces and other instrumental music. He won the Stalin Prize in 1948. His works are published by Muzgiz and Vaga.

BIBLIOGRAPHY
J. Gaudrimas: *Muzikal'naya kul'tura Sovetskoy Litvï* (Leningrad, 1961)
——: *Tarybu lietuvos kompozitoriai ir muzikologai* (Vilnius, 1971)
Encyclopedia Lituanica, v (Boston, 1976), 359
JOACHIM BRAUN

Tallinn (Ger. Reval). Capital of the Estonian SSR. Founded by the Danes in 1219, it became a seat of the Teutonic Order in 1346. It was taken over by Sweden in 1561 and by Russia in 1710. With Estonian independence (1918) it became the capital. The Danes founded monasteries and church schools; by the 14th century there were church organs and travelling players were superseded by town Stadtmusikanten. When the city became Protestant after the Reformation, the church repertory consisted mainly of Lutheran hymns. Later in the 16th century the Nikolaikirche had a choir of some 50 singers and the Stadtmusikanten were employed in the churches. Musicians active in Tallinn at this time included the organist Bartholomäus Busbetzki (d 1701) and J. V. Meder (Kantor, 1674–83). Travelling players performed religious plays, and, by the end of the century, opera and ballet.

Musical activity had increased by the end of the 18th century. C. C. Agthe was music director of the Hündelberg theatrical company, 1776–82, and his Singspiels, *Martin Velten* (1778), *Aconcius und Cydippe* (c1780) and *Das Milchmädchen* (c1780), were first performed there. C. F. Agthe was active as organist at various churches, 1760–86. The city's inhabitants formed musical societies for private concerts. In 1784 A. von Kotzebue founded the Revaler Liebhaber-Theater (a permanent institution since 1809) which included in its repertory performances by Mme Tilly's troupe of Singspiels and Mozart's operas (*Die Zauberflöte*, c1795; *Don Giovanni*, 1797).

Early in the 19th century symphonies and oratorios by Haydn and Mozart were performed. Gertrud Elisabeth Mara was active as a singing teacher in Tallinn from 1812 until her death in 1833. In 1819 and 1821 the first Estonian-language stage works, which included Estonian folksongs and dances, were produced by P. A. J. Steinsberg. Karl Friedrich Karell (1791–1857) was organist at the Church of the Holy Spirit (1817–20) as well as working in various musical posts in the orchestra and other ensembles. J. A. Hagen (1786–1877) taught singing at the grammar school from 1815 and was organist at the Olaikirche, 1827–54. In 1823 he founded a German and an Estonian choir. In 1841 the pianist Theodor Stein (1819–93), F. J. Wiedermann and others founded the Musikverein, which performed vocal and orchestral works; Stein himself gave many concerts and arranged musical entertainments until he left for St Petersburg in 1872. Societies founded in the mid-19th century include the Revaler Männergesang-Verein (1849), the Revaler Liedertafel (1854), Eintracht (1858), the Jäkelscher Gesang-Verein (1859), and the Russian group Gusli (1864). In 1857 and 1866 German–Baltic song festivals were held in Tallinn. The conductor A. F. Krüger (1810–83) made a significant contribution to the city's musical life: from 1848 he conducted the Städtliche Kapelle, later directed the Männergesang-Verein and Liedertafel choirs, worked as Kapellmeister at the theatre and arranged symphony concerts (programmes included works by Viennese Classical composers as well as Wagner, Liszt and Glinka). Spitta taught at the grammar school and lectured on Bach, Beethoven, Schubert and Schumann at the Estonian Provincial Museum. In 1863 the first Estonian choral society, Revalia, was founded, followed by Estonia in 1865. In 1869 the German Instrumentalverein was founded; this organization was responsible for the celebrations of the centenary of Beethoven's birth. In 1888 the Kammermusik-Verein was founded, whose members included a string quartet and a string orchestra. Outstanding choral organizations include the mixed choir, conducted by H. F. D. Stiehl, who gave the first performance of Bach's *St Matthew Passion* in the Russian Empire in 1882, and the St Nikolai Gesangverein, led by the gifted Estonian composer and conductor Konstantin Türnpu (1865–1927). Türnpu assumed the direction of the Liedertafel in 1894 and took the group to St Petersburg and Germany. In 1880 the third Estonian song festival took place, with more than 900 singers and instrumentalists; at the sixth festival (1896) there were more than 5000. These song festivals are still held in Tallinn every five years.

With the rise of nationalism, Estonian musical activity expanded. In 1906 the club Estonia became a professional theatre, where symphony concerts, operettas and Singspiels were given. At the seventh song festival (1910) most of the works performed were Estonian. In 1912 Raimund Kull (1882–1942) became music director of the theatre; August Topman (1882–1968) took over the choir. Folk music concerts were introduced, and in 1916 the Tallinna Meestelaulu Selts (Male Voice Choir) was founded. In 1919 the Music School (from 1923, Conservatory) was established, and in 1921 the Eesti Lauljate Liit (Federation of Estonian Singers) was formed. This was concerned with the development of choral music; it planned and administered the song festivals, 1923–38, and published a periodical, *Muusikaleht* (1924–40). In 1924 a music museum club was founded and in 1934 the museum was inaugurated. The Akadeemiline Helikunstnikkude Selts (Academic Artists' Society) was formed in 1924, with a string quartet and a wind quintet. The state established a fund in 1925 to support cultural and musical establishments, including the purchase and publication of works and provision of scholarships to composers and performers. In 1929 Töölismuusika Ühing (Workers' Music Club) was formed to arrange symphony concerts. The Tallinn Radio Orchestra was established in 1930 and from 1934 gave symphony concerts with the United Estonia Orchestra. The Estonia Theatre performed operas, operettas and ballets. Around 1930 the first Estonian nationalist operas were performed: Evald Aav's *Vikerlasad* (1920), Artur Lemba's *Kalmuneid* (1929) and Adolf Vedro's *Kaupo* (1932); resident conductors were R. Kull, J. Aavik and O. Roots. After 1940 the State Philharmonic and the Composers' Union Committee were formed. The number of choirs was reduced during World War II and the German occupation, but concerts and opera performances continued. In 1944 Gustav Erneskas established the Eesti NSV Riiklik Akadeemiline Meeskoor (National Professional Male Chorus), and the Eesti Televisioni ja Raadio Segakoor (Estonian Radio Mixed Chorus) was founded in 1945. The Tallinn Jazz Festival was inaugurated in 1949. Other postwar organizations include the Tallinna Kammerkoor (1966) under the direction of Neeme Järvi, and the chamber orchestra (1961). In 1975 the radio orchestra was renamed the Eesti NSV Riiklik Sünfonia Orkester.

See also UNION OF SOVIET SOCIALIST REPUBLIC, §IV.

based on *MGG* (xvi, 1549–54) by permission of Bärenreiter
KARL LEICHTER

Tallis [Tallys, Talles], **Thomas** (*b* c1505; *d* Greenwich, 23 Nov 1585). English composer.

1. Life. 2. Latin polyphony before 1559. 3. Elizabethan motets. 4. English church music. 5. Secular and instrumental music. 6. Conclusion.

1. LIFE. Although no record of his childhood has been found, Tallis must have been born in the earliest years of the 16th century, possibly in Kent, with which county he later had various connections. His first recorded appointment was as organist of the Benedictine Priory of Dover in 1532. The next known reference to him is in

THE EXTRACT AND EFFECT OF THE QVENES
Maiesties letters patents to Thomas Tallis and VVilliam Birde,
for the printing of musicke.

ELIZABETH *by the grace of God Quene of Englande Fraunce and Irelande defender of the faith &c. To all
printers bokesellers and other officers ministers and subiects greting, Knowe ye, that we for the especiall affection and
good wil that we haue and beare to the science of musicke and for the aduauncement thereof, by our letters patents
dated the xx i i. of Ianuary in the xv i i. yere of our raigne, haue graunted full priuiledge and licence vnto our welbeloued
seruaunts Thomas Tallis and VVilliam Birde Gent. of our Chappell, and to the ouerlyuer of them, & to the assignes of them
and of the suruiuer of them, for xx i. yeares next ensuing, to imprint any and so many as they will of set songe or songes in
partes, either in English, Latine, French, Italian, or other tongues that may serue for musicke either in Churche or
chamber, or otherwise to be either plaid or soonge, And that they may rule and cause to be ruled by impression any paper to
serue for printing or pricking of any songe or songes, and may sell and vtter any printed bokes or papers of any songe or
songes, or any bookes or quieres of such ruled paper imprinted, Also we straightly by the same forbid all printers booke-
sellers subiects & strangers, other then as is aforesaid, to do any the premisses, or to bring or cause to be brought out of any
forren Realmes into any our dominions any songe or songes made and printed in any forren countrie, to sell or put to sale, vp-
pon paine of our high displeasure, And the offender in any of the premisses for euery time to forfet to vs our heires and successors fortie shillings, and to the said Thomas Tallis & VVilliam Birde or to their assignes & to the assignes of the suruiuer of
the, all & euery the said bokes papers songe or songes, VVe haue also by the same willed & commaunded our printers, maisters
& wardens of the misterie of stacioners, to assist the said Thomas Tallis and VVilliam Birde & their assignes for the dewe executing of the premisses.*

Letters-patent granted to Tallis and Byrd from the 'Cantiones sacrae' (London: Vautrollier, 1575)

London, where his name appears on the payroll for 1537 and 1538 of the church of St Mary-at-Hill; again, probably he was organist, although this is not specifically stated. Close to this church stood the London house of the abbot of Holy Cross, Waltham, which may explain Tallis's move to Waltham Abbey in about 1538. An inventory of the abbey dated 24 March 1540 shows that it had at least three organs of various sizes, and a choir of five boys and an unspecified number of men, of whom Tallis was one of the most senior. On the dissolution of the abbey in 1540 Tallis was not granted a pension, but received 20s. in wages and 20s. 'reward'; he also seems to have acquired a volume of musical treatises copied by John Wilde, a former precentor of the abbey, which has the autograph 'Thomas Tallys' on its last page (*GB-Lbm* Lansdowne 763).

Tallis then found new employment at Canterbury Cathedral, where he is listed as lay clerk in 1541 and 1542. His name does not appear in 1543, from which year he probably served full-time at the court as a Gentleman of the Chapel Royal. There is no record of his formal enrolment there, but in a document of around 1545 (*Lbm* Stowe 571) his name is 16th in a list of 32. In a petition of 1577 Tallis claimed to have 'served yo[u]r Ma[jes]tie and yo[u]r Royall ancestors these fortie yeres', implying that his association with the court may have begun even during his employment at St Mary-at-Hill. His career up to this point also suggests that he may have been personally known to Archbishop Cranmer.

Tallis remained in the royal household until his death, serving under Henry VIII, Edward VI, Mary Tudor, and finally for more than half of the reign of Elizabeth I. He undoubtedly acted as an organist throughout this period, but was not so designated until after 1570. However, he had always been active as a composer as well, and in the middle decades of the century the provision of new vocal polyphony for the royal chapels must have occupied much of his time, and earned him the greatest prestige. In 1557 Queen Mary granted to Tallis and Richard Bowyer jointly a 21-year lease of the manor of Minster in Kent, with the considerable annual income of £91 12s. The royal household accounts for the first year of Elizabeth's reign contain the entry 'In bonis Thomas Talys ... 40li', which has been thought to record a gift of this amount, but which is more likely to represent an assessment for the purposes of a subsidy or forced loan

to the queen, and confirms that Tallis was living in fairly comfortable circumstances at the time. Rapid inflation had evidently changed that situation by the time Byrd joined the Chapel Royal in 1572, for in 1573 the two men petitioned the queen for some source of additional income. On 22 January 1575, she responded by granting them an exclusive licence to print and publish music, the letters-patent issued for this purpose being among the first of their kind in the country (printed in full in E. H. Fellowes, *William Byrd*, 2/1948, p.7). Later that year there duly appeared the *Cantiones sacrae*, an anthology of Latin motets to which Tallis and Byrd each contributed 17 compositions, perhaps in reference to the 17th year of the reign. Financially the undertaking was a failure, for a second petition followed in 1577 resulting in the grant of a joint lease to the two composers, with an annual value of £30.

In or around 1552 Tallis had married a woman named Joan, who survived him by nearly four years. At the time of his death he owned a house in Greenwich, where he was buried in the chancel of the parish church of St Alphege. His epitaph, lost in the subsequent rebuilding of the church, was recorded by Strype in his *Continuation of Stowe's Survey of London*. The wills are extant of both Tallis (PCC 52 Brudenell) and his wife (PCC 54 Leicester), and give details of their numerous household possessions and legacies but little clue to Tallis's family connections, except that he had a 'cozen' named John Sayer living in the Isle of Thanet. (The texts of the epitaph, and of both wills, are printed in TCM, vi (1928), pp.xv ff.)

2. LATIN POLYPHONY BEFORE 1559. The votive antiphon of the Virgin Mary, a devotional composition used outside the formal liturgy, was strongly cultivated in England up to about 1530, but then largely disappeared with the fall of Wolsey and the pressures for reform exerted by Cromwell and Cranmer. Three such pieces by Tallis, all in five parts, are probably his earliest surviving works. *Salve intemerata virgo* and *Ave rosa sine spinis* are associated in the Henrician Partbooks at Peterhouse, Cambridge, with music composed before 1530; the first is, surprisingly, also found in *Lbm* Harl. 1709, the sole survivor of a set of partbooks which seem to have been copied no later than about 1525. The third, *Ave Dei patris filia*, survives only in much later sources. All display the traditional votive antiphon structure with

its division into two halves (in perfect and imperfect time respectively) and the schematic layout of sections in reduced and full textures. Much of the writing is, however, somewhat awkward, with neither the florid exuberance of the previous generation nor the compelling logic of Ludford and Taverner. Although handicapped by a long and shapeless text, *Salve intemerata virgo* is in many ways the most accomplished and adventurous of the three, with a well-judged mixture of imitative techniques and older procedures. Most of its material, extensively reordered and with some additions, was incorporated into a parody mass of the same title, which is also early in date. Despite some incongruity between old and new material, this mass is a workman-like demonstration of a technique otherwise little known in England. Another votive antiphon, *Sancte Deus*, is in honour of Jesus rather than the Virgin Mary, and reflects both the doctrine and musical style of about 1540. There is also a *Magnificat* whose style and use of a faburden tenor suggest that it, too, belongs to this early period. Both these works are in four parts and apparently for men's voices.

The inclination away from the florid composition of the first quarter of the century, already observable in Tallis's early music, was sharply accentuated late in Henry VIII's reign, probably through the direct influence of Cranmer and other reformers. It is particularly marked in a group of four-voice masses by Taverner, Tallis, Sheppard and others, which set the Gloria and Credo in an almost wholly syllabic and often chordal style, using extended melisma only in parts of the Sanctus and Agnus Dei. Some are entitled 'Plain song', probably because the rhythmic style employed is similar to that of plainsong sung in mensural faburden. Tallis's own mass of this type has no title, but shares with the others an obvious concern for clear declamation of the text.

After six years of protestant liturgy under Edward VI (1547–53) the Catholic rite was restored on the accession of Mary Tudor, producing a brief revival of the large-scale manner of composition typical of her childhood years. Two of Tallis's most sumptuous works, the six-voice antiphon *Gaude gloriosa Dei mater* and the seven-voice Mass '*Puer natus est nobis*', must both date from this period and are probably the most extended examples of their respective genres by any English composer. *Gaude gloriosa*, ostensibly in honour of the Virgin Mary, is really addressed to Queen Mary herself, extolling her as the restorer of the true faith. Some significant phrases of text are emphasized by pointed musical imagery of a kind rarely found earlier: for example, the words 'a potestate diabolica' are tersely enunciated, but the next word, 'liberati', takes wing with some huge soaring melismas. However, the formal design is that of the old antiphon, and rigorous imitative entries embedded in the full choral sections do little to soften the effect of archaic splendour so redolent of the late medieval world of Cardinal Wolsey. The mass, on the other hand, is an entirely 'modern' work in a Renaissance manner. Probably composed for the combined English and Spanish royal chapels during Philip II's residence in London, it shows an astonishingly resourceful handling of current imperial techniques of structural imitation and choral antiphony, all laid out on a slow-moving, symbolic cantus firmus. The latter, the Christmas introit *Puer natus est nobis*, may well be connected with the announcement (which later proved unfounded) that the queen was expecting an heir. Only

fragments of the mass were printed in Tudor Church Music (vol.vi, pp.49–61), but the discovery of a new source (*Lbm* Madrigal Society G9–26) has since permitted all but the Credo to be satisfactorily reconstructed.

Several further groups of Latin church music by Tallis must have been written for the chapel of Henry VIII or Mary Tudor, but cannot yet be safely allocated to either reign because their manner of composition is determined more by liturgical function than by the musical style of any one decade. The largest consists of the six settings of responsories of major feasts which, viewed in conjunction with those of Sheppard, suggest that the two composers had in mind some sort of joint annual cycle of such works. The choral plainsong is set as an equal-note cantus firmus, normally in the tenor, leaving incipit and verse(s) to be chanted; the polyphony, richly sonorous and solemn, nevertheless subtly reflects the general sense of the text by its choice of vocal scoring or musical idea. Indeed the technical and imaginative powers brought to bear on such a severely ritual design place the best of these responsories (such as *Videte miraculum* and *Candidi facti sunt*) among Tallis's finest works. The seven Office hymns are similar in principle but inevitably more functional in effect: they set the even-numbered verses in five parts, with the plainsong clearly audible in the highest voice. There are also three smaller responsories which set only the solo parts of the liturgical text: *Hodie* does not use the plainsong at all, but *Audivi vocem* and *In pace in idipsum* treat the Sarum chant in a masterly imitative-paraphrase fashion.

3. ELIZABETHAN MOTETS. The Act of Settlement of 1559 finally abolished the Sarum rite in favour of the Protestant prayer book. The composers at the court continued to set Latin texts, and their music may have been used in a somewhat peripheral way in the queen's private services; but some of these 'motets' appear to have been conceived primarily as studies in composition, for no more than recreational singing. A few of Byrd's earlier contrapuntal exercises, for example, may even have had their texts fitted after composition, including *Laudate pueri* and possibly *Memento homo* and *Diliges Dominum*. The last of these, the famous crab canon, is paralleled by Tallis in the seven-voice *Miserere nostri*, a brief but complex essay in simultaneous canons. The second *Salvator mundi* may also have begun life as a two-voice canon above a free bass, later being adapted, with added voices, to both English and Latin words.

However, contrapuntal ingenuity is an unusual feature in Tallis's late motets. Nor, apparently, did he take much interest in the early Elizabethan fashion for cantus firmus writing: he had already explored this technique, and after 1560 seems to have confined it entirely to a handful of experimental keyboard pieces. His late vocal music is characterized chiefly by a mature, restrained and often sombre handling of the all-purpose imitative techniques imported from the Continent. In the mass for Mary Tudor he had already applied such methods to a long ceremonial work, using elaborate imitative expositions. *Suscipe quaeso* is a motet in the same manner, set to a long, penitential non-liturgical text of a type also used by Tye (*Peccavimus cum patribus*) and Byrd (*Tribue, Domine*). Much shorter motets in a more streamlined imitative style are *Mihi autem nimis* and the extraordinarily accomplished first setting of *Salvator mundi*. Another, *In manus tuas*, brings to mind one of Lassus's techniques: that of using very brief and adaptable imitative points in quick succession to build up sonority rapidly. Two substantial works with considerable variety of texture are the psalm settings *Laudate Dominum* and *Domine quis habitabit*.

It is perhaps the element of restraint that chiefly distinguishes Tallis's Elizabethan motets from those of his younger contemporaries, for not even in *Laudate Dominum* – which includes the doxology – did he show much interest in the florid and exuberant writing sometimes found in Robert White or Byrd. He adhered to a 'norm' of syllabic word-setting, developed during the mid-century Protestant years, and seems to have deliberately avoided reverting to the routine melismatic writing of his earliest works. Where melisma occurs in his late music, it is sparingly and very expressively used for a key word like 'auxilium', or a pleading reference to God, such as 'Deus meus' or 'Dominus Deus noster'. *Absterge Domine* illustrates this particularly clearly, as also do the two sets of Lamentations, which are possibly his best-known works. They form part of a long European tradition of settings of the Holy Week readings from Jeremiah. Each begins with the announcement (e.g. 'Incipit Lamentatio . . .'), treated as a formal imitative exposition, and ends with the response 'Ierusalem convertere ad Dominum Deum tuum' set in a simple chordal style. Within this frame are two or three of the biblical verses, each prefaced by its Hebrew letter, the soulful melismas of the latter providing the perfect foil to the richly varied syllabic music of the verses. These two works (which are independent compositions, even though they set successive readings) demonstrate Tallis's ability to transcend any preoccupation with technical problems as such, and to produce large musical designs which integrate, with supreme mastery and control, most of the available resources of composition. Nevertheless he was evidently willing, in his old age, to explore at least some new styles and techniques. Two respond motets, *Derelinquat impius* and *In jejunio et fletu*, show him using technical resources for depictive purposes: the first has a highly irregular set of imitative entries, to suggest the errant ways of the ungodly; in the second the mood of extreme penitence is conveyed by using simple triadic harmony to effect rapid and poignant 'modulation'. These are two remarkable works, which must have been written in association with Byrd in or about 1572, for together with Byrd's *Emendemus in melius* they form the third Nocturn of (Roman) Matins for the first Sunday in Lent. Such a close liturgical dependence was exceptional at the time, and suggests a somewhat emotionally charged observance of Lent at the court – a not unlikely supposition in view of the recent Ridolphi plot and the threat of imminent invasion by the Catholic powers of Europe.

One further work, the 40-voice motet *Spem in alium*, is such an astonishing technical achievement, and so completely without precedent anywhere in Europe, that to call it 'experimental' seems an absurd understatement. So far as is known English composers had previously used no more than simple decani–cantoris antiphony, in a manner analogous to the double-choir techniques of psalm singing in northern Italy. What significance there may be in a composition for eight five-voice choirs can at present only be a matter for conjecture. The text is a respond from the liturgical *historia* of Judith, and one suggestion is that it may have been set as part of a dramatic enactment of the apocryphal story presented at the court on Queen Elizabeth's 40th birthday in 1573. If this is so, it would have effectively complemented the petition submitted to her by Tallis and Byrd in the same year. Whatever its date, *Spem in alium* may well have been Tallis's only major choral composition in the last ten or twelve years of his life. By this time Byrd, following the elder Ferrabosco, was beginning to develop new methods of motet composition not found in Tallis, including the construction of complex expositions of subjects and countersubjects, and the compilation of texts conflated from separate biblical extracts. He was developing the 'personal' voice of the Renaissance humanist, spurred by religious oppression and a more turbulent private life, whereas Tallis was content to draw his texts from liturgical sources and to remain essentially a craftsman in the service of the queen, voicing the mood of the community in which he worked.

4. ENGLISH CHURCH MUSIC. Tallis was clearly one of the first musicians to write for the new Anglican liturgy of 1547–53, and he again composed to English words in the reign of Elizabeth. Four pieces are found in manuscripts dating from 1547–8: the anthems *Hear the voice and prayer* and *If ye love me* in the Wanley Partbooks, and *Remember not* and a setting of the Benedictus in the Lumley Books. (The first three of these, together with *O Lord in thee is all my trust*, were also printed in John Day's *Certaine Notes*.) Many of the remaining English compositions, however, cannot safely be assigned to one period or the other. Some occur only in much later sources – including the Dorian Service, which has no source earlier than around 1620. Moreover, internal evidence is a very unsafe guide, for there is some relatively elaborate music that must have been written under Edward VI (notably by Sheppard), whereas certain Elizabethan music, such as Tallis's psalm tunes, is in a simple chordal style.

The four works of Tallis that are known to be early do reflect, on the whole, the express wish of Cranmer and other reformers for clear syllabic word-setting. *Remember not* is a particularly ascetic piece, almost entirely chordal and in effect deeply penitential. (In Day's later printed version it was, interestingly, somewhat expanded and elaborated.) *Hear the voice and prayer* and *If ye love me*, however, represent in every way the prototype of the early Anglican anthem: they are cast in an *ABB* form, and mix homophony with rather formal imitation in a succinct and neatly turned manner, somewhat reminiscent of certain French chansons. The most extended of the four, the Benedictus, is possibly the earliest of all, but nevertheless has the greatest variety of texture and thematic resource. The Dorian Service, which is likely to date from this period, is for the most part heavily chordal and incantatory, but does use limited imitation in its longer movements. It consists of the five morning and evening canticles, together with Gloria, Creed and Sanctus for the Communion; other items are probably later accretions.

This music is all in four parts. The Chapel Royal, however, evidently used some in five or six, and occasionally even more where decani and cantoris voices divided. An entire five-voice service by Tallis, probably with two canonic voices, has been lost except for the bass. An indication of his richer manner can, however, be gained from the isolated five-voice *Te Deum*, almost 200 bars long in a modern edition, and astonishingly well shaped and varied for a piece with so little melismatic writing. In both these works textual archaisms suggest that they are Edwardian, although this evidence is not conclusive.

In the first half of Elizabeth's reign the country as a whole, now fairly strongly puritanical, seems to have had little interest in liturgical polyphony except for various simple forms of psalm singing. Tallis contributed nine four-voice psalm tunes (one of which has since been made famous by Vaughan Williams) for one of the many metrical psalters published at this time, that of Archbishop Parker in 1567. Otherwise, however, his English music of this period was almost entirely for five voices and was probably written for routine use in the Chapel Royal. It includes the litany, the preces and responses, and some simple polyphonic treatments of prayer book psalms for the Christmas season (called 'festal' psalms). Rather curiously two canticles, a paired *Magnificat* and *Nunc dimittis*, were set in Latin: they are for Walter Haddon's Latin translation of the English prayer book, which was published in 1560 but apparently used very little, if at all, outside the royal chapels. Of the more elaborate anthems that must have been produced by the queen's composers scarcely one by Tallis is known. A bold setting of *Christ rising*, sometimes attributed to Tallis, is more likely to be by Byrd. *Blessed are those*, which uses antiphony between high and low voices in a smooth continental style, may be an adaptation from a Latin psalm setting. Several of Tallis's best motets were certainly fitted with English words, for use as anthems: *Absterge Domine*, for example, had at least three such adaptations by 1600. However, the work published in the *Cantiones sacrae* with the Latin text *O sacrum convivium* reveals, on close examination, that it was probably originally composed to the English text *I call and cry*: not only does the English text fit better, but the music also has the *ABB* structure typical of the early anthem.

5. SECULAR AND INSTRUMENTAL MUSIC. The Mulliner Book contains keyboard arrangements of four partsongs by Tallis, of which only *When shall my sorrowful sighing slake* is found with its text in contemporary vocal sources. It uses imitation and expressive melisma in a manner very similar to that of the Elizabethan consort songs, and was clearly widely known and popular. Text has been found for *O ye tender babes* and *Like as the doleful dove*, both of which are much more chordal in texture. The fourth, *Fond youth is a bubble*, has the same music as the anthem *Purge me, O Lord*.

Tallis's relatively small contribution to the rich repertory of consort music of around 1550–70 includes two fine and well-contrasted In Nomine settings. A third piece, interestingly, is composed not on the usual *Gloria tibi Trinitas* plainsong but on that of a different Trinity Sunday antiphon, *Libera nos, salva nos*: although very vocal in style, the setting is clearly instrumental because

the cantus firmus includes the incipit.

As Tallis apparently spent at least 50 years as an active organist, it must be assumed that his surviving keyboard compositions represent no more than a fraction of his output. Most are in the Mulliner Book (MB, i, 1951, rev. 2/1954) and consist of hymn verses and other short liturgical items which set imitative points against a plainsong cantus firmus, presumably for service use before 1559. The contrapuntal working is skilful, but shows somewhat less concern for idiomatic keyboard writing than is found in Redford and others. A small group of later pieces, however, displays a developed virtuoso manner that has no known parallel anywhere in Europe during Tallis's lifetime. They include, most conspicuously, the two extended treatments of the *Felix namque* plainsong found in the Fitzwilliam Virginal Book, where they are dated 1562 and 1564 respectively. In each the plainsong is, for the most part, presented as an equal-note cantus firmus against which the composer explored a succession of highly resourceful keyboard idioms and textures.

6. CONCLUSION. By 16th-century standards Tallis seems to have been a slow developer. His early music, as a whole, is relatively undistinguished, with neither Taverner's consummate mastery of the festal style nor the modernisms of Tye; and the mid-century ritual music is a shade less sumptuous and exuberant than that of Sheppard. Thereafter, however, he was able to produce occasional works as fine as anything by his European contemporaries. In a few instances, such as *Spem in alium* and the *Felix namque* settings, he easily outstripped them; but for the most part he was content to compose in an unostentatious manner, relying not on technical display but on the mastery and control born of long experience. His late works in an imitative style are infused with the penitential mood of his own generation, rather than the humanistic spirit of Byrd's. To modern listeners his best work may seem to lie in the restrained pathos of the Lamentations and similar late motets, but the large responds of his mid-career are in many ways no less fine, while the artless perfection of his short, functional anthems must have done much to set the pattern for this new genre. John Day, and later Barnard and Boyce, placed his work first in their anthologies of English church music, tacitly accepting his primacy among its earliest composers. A couplet from his epitaph:

As he dyd lyve, so also did he dy,
In myld and quyet Sort (O! happy Man)

points to a humble, unassuming man, who avoided religious controversy, and who was undoubtedly deeply respected, both by the four monarchs for whom he worked and by many generations of church musicians.

WORKS

Editions: *T. Tallis*, ed. P. C. Buck and others, TCM, vi (1928); TCM Appendix (1948) [TCM vi; Appx]
The Mulliner Book, ed. D. Stevens, MB, i (1951, rev. 2/1954) [Smb]
T. Tallis: Complete Keyboard Works, ed. D. Stevens (London, 1953) [S]
T. Tallis: English Sacred Music: I Anthems, ed. L. Ellinwood, rev. P. Doe, EECM, xii (2/1974) [D i]
T. Tallis: English Sacred Music: II Service Music, ed. L. Ellinwood, rev. P. Doe, EECM, xiii (2/1974) [D ii]
LATIN CHURCH MUSIC
Only those sources not in TCM vi are listed; * – composed probably after 1559; Willmott – Willmott MS, Spetchley Park, Braikenridge; C – Cantiones quae ab argumento sacrae vocantur, 5–7vv (London, 1575), with Byrd

Title	No. of vv	Source	P.no. in TCM vi	Remarks
*Absterge Domine [=Discomfort them, O Lord; Forgive me, Lord, my sin; O God, be merciful; Wipe away my sins]	5	C; *GB-Lbm* Add.3 1390, *T* 1464, 1486, Willmot, *US-NYp* Drexel 4180–85	180	—
Alleluia, Ora pro nobis	4	—	88	C.f. chant; for Lady Mass

Title	No. of vv	Source	P.no. in TCM vi	Remarks
Audivi vocem	4	—	90	Re for Matins, All Saints Day
Ave Dei patris filia	5	*GB-CF* D/DP.Z/6.1, *Lbm* Add.34049, *T* 1469–71, 1486, Willmott	162, Appx 43	Votive ant, lacks T in 4 sections
Ave rosa sine spinis	5	*CF* D/DP.Z/6.1, *T* 342, 354–8, 1486, Willmott	169, Appx 49	Votive ant; now complete
[Candidi] facti sunt Nazarei	5	C	186	C.f. chant; re for 1st Vespers, Apostles
*Derelinquat impius	5	C	189	Roman re, 1st Sunday in Lent
Domine quis habitabit	5	*Ckc* 316, *CF* D/DP.Z/6.1, *T* 1464, 1486, Willmott	246	Ps xiv
[Dum transisset] Sabbatum	5	C; *Ckc* 316, *Lbm* Add.31390, Add.32377	257	C.f. chant; re for Matins, Easter Day
Euge caeli porta	4	—	179	V. of seq Ave praeclara for Lady Mass
Gaude gloriosa Dei mater	6	*Lbm* Add.18936	123	Votive ant
Haec dies	?	*Lbm* Add.32377	—	Single voice; textless
Hodie nobis caelorum Rex	4	—	92	1st re for Matins, Christmas Day
[Homo] quidam fecit coenam	6	*US-NYp* Drexel 4180–85	282	C.f. chant; re for 1st Vespers, Corpus Christi; new source supplies T
[Honor] virtus et potestas	5	C	237	C.f. chant; re for Matins, Trinity Sunday
*In jejunio et fletu	5	C	198	Roman re, 1st Sunday in Lent
*In manus tuas	5	C; *GB-Lbm* Add.30480–84, Mad.Soc.A6–11, *Y* 5	202	Re for Compline
In pace in idipsum	4	—	94	Re for Compline, 1st 5 Sundays in Lent
[Jam Christus astra ascenderat . . .] Solemnis urgebat dies	5	*T* 1464	285	Even-numbered verses only; c.f. chant; hymn for 1st Vespers, Pentecost
[Jesu salvator saeculi . . .] Tu fabricator omnium	5	*T* 1464	289	Even-numbered verses only; c.f. chant; hymn for Compline, Sunday after Easter to Ascension
*Lamentations	5	*CF* D/DP.Z/6.1, *US-NYp* Drexel 4180–85	102	1st Lectio at Matins, Maundy Thursday
*Lamentations	5	*GB-CF* D/DP.Z/6.1, *T* 369–73, 1464, 1469–71	110	2nd Lectio at Matins, Maundy Thursday
*Laudate Dominum	5	*CF* DP.Z/6.1, *Lcm* 2089, *T* 369–73, 1486, Willmott	266	Ps cxvi
[Loquebantur] variis linguis	7	—	272	C.f. chant; re for 1st Vespers, Pentecost
Magnificat	4	—	64	On faburden, 1st tone
Magnificat and Nunc Dimittis	5	—	73	Evensong of Latin prayer book
Mass	4	—	31	
Mass 'Puer natus est nobis'	7	*Lbm* Mad.Soc.	49	Probably composed in 1554; new source extensively supplements TCM vi
Gloria		*Lbm* Mad.Soc.G9–15, G16–20, G21–6	49	Now complete
Credo		—	56	Fragment
Sanctus		*Lbm* Mad.Soc.G21–6	—	Complete except for beginning of T
Pleni sunt		*Lbm* Mad.Soc.G9–15, G16–20	—	
Benedictus		*Lbm* Mad.Soc.G9–15, G16–20	58	
Agnus Dei		*Lbm* Mad.Soc.G9–15, G16–20	—	Lacks T and 1 B
Mass 'Salve intemerata'	5	—	3	On his own motet; T missing but partly restorable from motet
*Mihi autem nimis [= Blessed be thy name]	5	C	204	Introit, Feast of the Apostles
*Miserere nostri	7	C; *Lbm* Mad.Soc.A52–6 (attrib. Byrd)	207	? Adapted from psalm-ant Miserere mei
*O nata lux de lumine	5	C	209	Hymn for Lauds, Transfiguration
O sacrum convivium [= I call and cry to thee; O sacred and holy banquet]	5	C; *Ckc* 316, *Lbm* Add.30480–84, Add.31390, *T* 1464, *US-NYp* Drexel 4180–85	210	Mag ant for 2nd Vespers, Corpus Christi; probably Latin adaptation of I call and cry
*O salutaris hostia [= O praise the Lord]	5	—	—	Roman ant, Corpus Christi
(1st version)		*GB-Ckc* 316	276	—
(2nd version)		*CF* D/DP.Z/6.1, *Lbm* Add.22597, Add.31390, *Lcm* 2089, *T* 1464, 1469–71	279	—
[Quod chorus vatum . . .] Haec Deum coeli	5	*Lbm* Add.32377, *T* 1464	261	Even-numbered verses only; c.f. chant; hymn for 1st Vespers Purification
Rex sanctorum	3	—	298	Fragment; textless
[Salvator mundi Domine . . .] Adesto nunc propitius	5	*T* 1464	242	Even-numbered verses only; c.f. chant; hymn for Compline, Vigil of Nativity and various other seasons
*Salvator mundi (i) [= Arise, O Lord, and hear; With all our hearts]	5	C; *Lbm* Add.29247, Mad.Soc.A52–6, *US-NYp* Drexel 4180–85	216	Ant for Matins, Exaltation of the Cross

Title	No. of vv	Source	P.no. in TCM vi	Remarks
Salvator mundi (ii) [= When Jesus went]	5	C	219	Ant for Matins, Exaltation of the Cross
Salve intemerata virgo	5	GB-CF D/DP.Z/6.1, Lbm Add.30513, Add.41156–8, Ob Mus.Sch.E.423, T 1464, 1469–71, 1486, Willmott	144	Votive ant, parodied in Mass 'Salve intemerata'
Sancte Deus, sancte fortis	4	—	98	Jesus ant
[Sermone blando angelus . . .] Illae dum pergunt concitae	5	C; Lbm Add.30480, T 341–4	193	Even-numbered verses only; c.f. chant; hymn for Lauds, Sunday after Easter to Ascension
*Spem in alium [= Sing and glorify]	40	—	299	Re for Sunday Matins, History of Judith
*Suscipe quaeso	7	C; Lbm Add.29247, Mad.Soc.G16–20, G21–6	222	Non liturgical prayer; possibly composed in 1554 with Mass 'Puer natus'
[Te lucis ante terminum . . .] Procul recedant somnia (i)	5	C; Lbm Add.31822	214	Even-numbered verses only; c.f. chant; hymn for Compline (except Easter)
[Te lucis ante terminum . . .] Procul recedant somnia (ii)	5	C	215	Even-numbered verses only; c.f. chant; hymn for Compline (except Easter)
[Videte] miraculum	6	EIRE-Dtc B.1.32	293	C.f. chant; re for 1st Vespers, Purification

ENGLISH SERVICE MUSIC

For sources see R. T. Daniel and P. le Huray: *The Sources of English Church Music 1549–1660*, EECM, suppl.i (1972)
Short Service (Dorian Service), 4vv, D ii, 1
Service 'of five parts, two in one', 5vv, D ii, 179 (B only)
Service, 5vv, *SHR* 356.2 (B only)
Benedictus, 4vv, D ii, 102 (text earlier than 1549)
Te Deum, 5vv, D ii, 78 (defective but restorable)
Preces and Responses (i), 5vv, D ii, 120, 144 (first preces printed with second responses in 1641⁵)
Preces and Responses (ii), 5vv, D ii, 122, 147 (second responses printed with first preces in 1641⁵)
Litany, 5vv, D ii, 150 (ends at Lord's prayer)
Psalm sequence for Christmas, 5vv: 24 Dec: Blessed are those (B only), D ii, 189; Wherewithal shall a young man cleanse his way, D ii, 125; O do well, D ii, 131; My soul cleaveth, D ii, 138; 25 Dec: The Lord saith (B only), D ii, 189; Lord, remember David (B only), D ii, 189; 26 Dec: I call with my whole heart (B only), D ii, 189; O consider mine adversity (B only), D ii, 189; Princes have persecuted me (B only), D ii, 189; Let my complaint (B only), D ii, 189
9 psalm tunes, 4vv, for M. Parker, The Whole Psalter translated into English Metre (London, 1567): Come, Holy Ghost ('Tallis's Ordinal'), D ii, 177; E'en like the hunted hind, D ii, 168; Expend, O Lord, D ii, 171; God grant we grace ('Tallis's canon'), D ii, 175; Let God arise, D ii, 162; Man blest no doubt, D ii, 160; O come in one, D ii, 166; Why brag'st in malice high, D ii, 173; Why fum'th in sight, D ii, 164

ENGLISH ANTHEMS AND MOTET ADAPTATIONS

For full details of sources see R. T. Daniel and P. le Huray: *The Sources of English Church Music 1549–1660*, EECM, suppl.i (1972)
A new commandment, 4vv, D i, 19 (lacks B but restorable)
Arise, O Lord, and hear [= Salvator mundi (i)], 5vv
Blessed are those, 5vv, D i, 1 (?adaptation of psalm, Beati immaculati)
Blessed be thy name [= Mihi autem nimis], 5vv, D i, 55
Discomfort them, O Lord [= Absterge Domine], 5vv
Forgive me, Lord, my sin [= Absterge Domine], 5vv (inc.; only in kbd scores)
Hear the voice and prayer, 4vv, D i, 11
I call and cry to thee [= O sacrum convivium], 5vv, D i, 60 (printed in C, 1575, with Latin text, but English anthem probably earliest version)
If ye love me, 4vv, D ii, 16
O give thanks unto the Lord, D ii, 189 (single voice)
O God, be merciful [= Absterge Domine], 5vv
O Lord, give thy Holy Spirit, 4vv, D i, 25
O Lord, in thee is all my trust, 4vv, D i, 29
O praise the Lord [= O salutaris hostia], 5vv
O sacred and holy banquet [= O sacrum convivium], 5vv
Purge me, O Lord [= Fond youth is a bubble], 4vv, D i, 40
Remember not, O Lord God, 4vv, D i, 111 (earlier version)
Remember not, O Lord God, 4vv, D i, 43 (later expanded version)
Sing and glorify [= Spem in alium], 40vv
Teach me thy way, D ii, 178 (Tr only)
Verily, verily, I say unto you, 4vv, D i, 51
When Jesus went [= Salvator mundi (ii)], 5vv, D i, 68
Wipe away my sins [= Absterge Domine], 5vv, D i, 73
With all our hearts [= Salvator mundi (i)], 5vv, D i, 88

SECULAR PARTSONGS

Fond youth is a bubble [= Purge me, O Lord], 4vv, Smb 21, D i, 95
Like as the doleful dove (text: W. Hunnis), 4vv, Smb 84, D i, 98
O ye tender babes (text: W. Lyly), Smb 61, D i, 102
When shall my sorrowful sighing slake, 4vv, Smb 63, D i, 106

KEYBOARD MUSIC

(liturgical)

Clarifica me pater (i), S 10 (Mag ant for 1st Vespers, Palm Sunday)
Clarifica me pater (ii), S 10 (Mag ant for 1st Vespers, Palm Sunday)
Clarifica me pater (iii), S 11 (Mag ant for 1st Vespers, Palm Sunday)
Ecce tempus idoneum (i), S 12 (hymn for 1st Vespers, 3rd Sunday in Lent)
Ecce tempus idoneum (ii), S 13 (hymn for 1st Vespers, 3rd Sunday in Lent)
Ex more docti mistico, S 14 (hymn for 1st Vespers, 1st Sunday in Lent)
Gloria tibi Trinitas, S 38 (ant for 1st Vespers, Trinity Sunday)
Iste confessor Domini sacratus, S 40 (hymn for 1st Vespers, Commemoration of a Confessor Bishop)
Jam lucis orto sidere, S 39 (hymn for Prime, Sundays)
Natus est nobis hodie, S 46 (ant for Compline, Christmas Day; possibly non-liturgical)
Veni Redemptor gentium (i), S 47 (hymn for 1st Vespers, Vigil of Nativity)
Veni Redemptor gentium (ii), S 48 (hymn for 1st Vespers, Vigil of Nativity)

(non-liturgical)

Fantasy, S 14
Felix namque (i), S 16
Felix namque (ii), S 26
Lesson 'Two parts in one', S 41 (also attrib. Bull)
Poyncte for the Virginals, S 46

CONSORT MUSIC

In Nomine (i), a 4, Ob Mus.Sch.D.212–16 no.3
In Nomine (ii), a 4, Ob Mus.Sch.D.212–16 no.18 (a 5 in Lbm Add.31390, ƒ93)
Libera [nos, salva nos], Lbm Add.37402–6

FALSE OR DOUBTFUL ATTRIBUTIONS

All people that on earth do dwell, 5vv, Och 1220–24 (17th-century composer)
Arise, O Lord, why sleepest thou, 5vv, Cp 35, 42, 44 (Byrd, Exsurge Domine)
Christ rising, 5vv US-BE M2.C645, D ii, 63 (probably Byrd, as in NYp Chirk)
Domine Deus, 3vv, GB-Lbm Add.18936–9, TCM vi, 62 (Tye)
[Deus tuorum militum . . .] Hic nempe mundi gloria, 5vv, T 341–4, TCM vi, 264 (probably Sheppard, as in Och 979–83)
Dum transisset Sabbatum, 6vv, US-NYp Drexel 4180–85 (Roose)
How long shall mine enemies, 5vv, GB-Lbm Add.29247 (Byrd)
I give you a new commandment, Lbm Add.30513 (attrib. Sheppard in 1560²⁶ and various MSS)
If that a sinner's sighs, 5vv, Grove 5 in error (Byrd)
In trouble and adversity, TCM vi, p.xviii in error (Taverner, In Nomine)
Lord, for thy tender mercy's sake, J. Clifford, The Divine Services and Anthems (London, 2/1664) (?Hilton or Farrant)
Not every one that saith, Och 6, US-NYp Chirk, D ii, 190
O God, be merciful, Grove 5 in error (Tye)
O Lord God God of Hosts, GB-Lbm Add.29289 (17th-century composer)
O Lord, I bow the knees, Cpc Mus.6.1–6 (W. Mundy)
O sing unto the Lord, attrib. Tallis in Ob Mus.Sch.E.423, attrib. Sheppard in T 791, Y M.29 (S)
O thou God almighty, Och 1001 (Hooper)

Out from the deep, *Och* 6, *US-NYp* Chirk, D i, 35 (probably W. Parsons)

Pange lingua, *Grove 5* (not in source quoted, *GB-Lbm* Add.30513)

Submit yourselves to one another, *Och* 6, *US-NYp* Chirk (Sheppard)

The simple sheep that went astray, *GB-Lbm* Harl.6346 (text only)

This is my commandment, *DRc* A1, A3 (probably W. Mundy)

BIBLIOGRAPHY
GENERAL

E. F. Rimbault: *The Old Cheque-book, or Book of Remembrance of the Chapel Royal*, Camden Society, new ser., iii (London, 1872/*R*1966)

H. C. de Lafontaine: *The King's Musick* (London, 1909/*R*1973)

H. B. Collins: 'Thomas Tallis', *ML*, x (1929), 152

E. Walker: *A History of Music in England*, (Oxford, 1907, rev. 3/1952 by J. A. Westrup)

D. Stevens: *Tudor Church Music* (New York, 1955, 2/1966)

F. Ll. Harrison: *Music in Medieval Britain* (London, 1958, 2/1963)

——: 'Church Music in England', *NOHM*, iv (1965), 465

A. Smith: *The Practice of Music . . . during the Reign of Elizabeth I* (diss., U. of Birmingham, 1967)

——: 'The Cultivation of Music in English Cathedrals in the Reign of Elizabeth I', *PRMA*, xciv (1967–8), 37

P. Doe: *Tallis* (London, 1968, rev. 2/1976)

A. Smith: 'Elizabethan Music at Ludlow: a New Source', *ML*, xlix (1968), 108

LATIN CHURCH MUSIC

W. G. Whittaker: *Collected Essays* (London, 1940), chap. 'An Adventure'

B. Schofield: 'The Manuscripts of Tallis's Forty-part Motet', *MQ*, xxxvii (1951), 176

J. Kerman: 'An Elizabethan Edition of Lassus', *AcM*, xxvii (1955), 71

——: 'Byrd's Motets: Chronology and Canon', *JAMS*, xiv (1961), 359

——: 'The Elizabethan Motet: a Study of Texts for Music', *Studies in the Renaissance*, ix (1962), 273

F. Ll. Harrison: 'Faburden in Practice', *MD*, xvi (1962), 11

J. Kerman: 'Byrd, Tallis, and the Art of Imitation', *Aspects of Medieval and Renaissance Music: a Birthday Offering to Gustave Reese* (New York, 1966), 519

P. Doe: 'Latin Polyphony under Henry VIII', *PRMA*, xcv (1968–9), 81

——: 'Tallis's *Spem in alium* and the Elizabethan Respond-motet', *ML*, li (1970), 1

P. Brett: 'Tallis and Byrd: Cantiones Sacrae (1575)', *MQ*, lviii (1972), 149 [record review]

N. Davison: 'Structure and Unity in Four Free-composed Tudor Masses', *MR*, xxxiv (1973), 328

ENGLISH CHURCH MUSIC

W. H. Frere: 'Edwardine Vernacular Services before the First Prayer Book', *Walter Howard Frere: a Collection of his Papers on Liturgical and Historical Subjects*, ed. J. H. Arnold and E. G. P. Wyatt (London, 1940)

L. Ellinwood: 'Tallis's Tunes and Tudor Psalmody', *MD*, ii (1948), 189

M. Frost: *English and Scottish Psalm and Hymn Tunes c.1543–1677* (London, 1953)

P. le Huray: 'Towards a Definitive Study of Pre-Restoration Anglican Service Music', *MD*, xiv (1960), 167

——: *Music and the Reformation in England, 1549–1660* (London, 1967)

R. H. Illing: 'Tallis's Psalm-tunes', *MMA*, ii (1967), 21

C. W. Warren: 'Music at Nonesuch', *MQ*, liv (1968), 47

R. T. Daniel: 'Contrafacta and Polyglot Texts in the Early English Anthem', *Essays in Musicology: a Birthday Offering for Willi Apel* (Bloomington, 1968), 101

E. H. Fellowes: *English Cathedral Music* (London, 1941, rev. 5/1969 by J. A. Westrup)

J. Blezzard: 'The Lumley Books', *MT*, cxii (1971), 128

——: *The Sacred Music of the Lumley Books* [Lbm Roy.App.74–6] (diss., U. of Leeds, 1972)

SECULAR AND INSTRUMENTAL MUSIC

E. H. Meyer: *English Chamber Music* (London, 1946)

B. Pattison: *Music and Poetry of the English Renaissance* (London, 1948)

D. Stevens: *The Mulliner Book: a Commentary* (London, 1952)

——: 'The Keyboard Music of Thomas Tallis', *MT*, xciii (1952), 303

——: 'The Background of the *In Nomine*', *MMR*, lxxxiv (1954), 199

J. J. Noble: 'Le répertoire instrumental anglais: 1550–85', *La musique instrumentale de la Renaissance: CNRS Paris 1954*, 91

D. Stevens: 'A Musical Admonition for Tudor Schoolboys', *ML*, xxxvii (1957), 49

J. Stevens: *Music and Poetry in the Early Tudor Court* (London, 1961)

P. Brett: 'The English Consort Song', *PRMA*, cxxxviii (1961–2), 73

J. Kerman: *The Elizabethan Madrigal* (New York, 1962)

J. Caldwell: 'Keyboard Plainsong Settings in England, 1500–1660', *MD*, xix (1965), 129

——: *English Keyboard Music before the Nineteenth Century* (Oxford, 1973)

PAUL DOE

Tallone (It.). FROG.

Talma, Louise (*b* Arcachon, 31 Oct 1906). American composer. She studied theory and composition at the Institute of Musical Art from 1922 to 1930, the piano with Isidore Philipp and harmony, counterpoint, fugue, composition and the organ with Nadia Boulanger at Fontainebleau every summer from 1926 to 1939. She received the BMus from New York University in 1931 and the MA from Columbia University in 1933. She began teaching at Hunter College of the City University of New York, where she later became professor of music. Among the awards which she has received are two Guggenheim Fellowships (1946 and 1947), a Senior Fulbright Research Grant to compose *The Alcestiad* (1955–6), the Koussevitzky Music Foundation Commission for a chamber work (1959), the Marjorie Peabody Waite Award from the National Institute of Arts and Letters (1960), the Sibelius Medal for Composition from the Harriet Cohen International Awards, London (1963), and a grant from the National Endowment for the Arts of the National Foundation on the Arts and the Humanities, Washington (DC), in 1966. In 1974 she became the first woman composer to be elected to the National Institute of Arts and Letters.

Until 1952 her music was neo-classical in style, but in the Six Etudes for piano (1953–4) she began to use serial procedures, and since the opera *The Alcestiad* she has combined tonal and serial elements. Frequent residence at the MacDowell Colony has played a major role in her production.

WORKS
(*selective list*)

Vocal: The Divine Flame (oratorio, Bible, missal), Mez, Bar, chorus, orch, 1948; Let's Touch the Sky (Cummings), 3 poems, chorus, fl, ob, bn, 1952; La Corona (Donne), chorus, 1955; The Alcestiad (opera, 3, Wilder), 1955–8; All the Days of My Life (cantata, Bible), T, cl, vc, pf, perc, 1965; A Time to Remember (J. F. Kennedy), chorus, orch, 1967; The Tolling Bell (Shakespeare, Marlowe, Donne), Bar, orch, 1969; Voices of Peace, vv, str, 1973

Inst: Pf Sonata no.1, 1943; Toccata, orch, 1944; Alleluia in Form of Toccata, pf, 1944; 6 Etudes, pf, 1954; Str Qt, 1954; Pf Sonata no.2, 1955; Vn Sonata, 1962; Dialogues, pf, orch, 1964; 3 Duologues, cl, pf, 1967; Summer Sounds, cl, str qt, 1973; Textures, pf, 1978

Principal publisher: G. Schirmer

BIBLIOGRAPHY

M. Goss: 'Louise Talma', *Modern Music-Makers* (New York, 1952), 382ff

R. Berges: 'The German Scene: "Alcestiad" in Frankfurt; Hamburg and Munich Seasons', *Musical Courier*, clxiv (1962), 33

P. Moor: 'Louise Talma's "The Alcestiad" in Première at Frankfurt Opera', *New York Times* (2 March 1962), 25

E. Barkin: 'Louise Talma: "The Tolling Bell"', *PNM*, x/2 (1972), 142

DOROTHY REGINA HOLCOMB

Talon (Fr.). FROG.

Talon, Pierre (*b* Rheims, 25 Oct 1721; *d* Paris, 25 June 1785). French cellist and composer. He probably arrived in Paris from Rheims before 1753, when he was granted a privilege to publish instrumental music. His *Six symphonies* op.1, dedicated to the Marquise de Ségur, were published that year in Paris by Vernadé. On 29 March 1755, described as coming from the diocese of Rouen, he entered the Sainte Chapelle as 'gagiste'. By 1763 he had entered the service of the king as a cellist; announcements of his works in 1765 refer to him as 'ordinaire de la musique du roi', and those of 1767 as 'ordinaire de la chambre du roi'. The contemporary almanacs do not record any solo performances, nor is he listed as a member of any Parisian orchestra or as a teacher. He was retired from the king's service in 1782.

Talon was a moderately gifted musician typical of those of his time who chose to work within the patronage system in Paris. His known works are all dedicated to minor nobility. The op.1 symphonies (1753), all in three movements, combine older French Baroque traits such as rapid harmonic movement and occasional passages in dotted rhythm with Italian influences from Sammartini and Brioschi, particularly in the fast triple-metre finales. The op.5 symphonies (1767), also in three movements, are longer and more orchestrally conceived. A substantial viola part replaces the third violin, and the string writing is expert, with careful and frequent expression markings. They are in a clear early Classical style. Unlike the earlier symphonies, their first movements are bi-thematic and in sonata-allegro form; the slow movements show more flexibility in choice of key, and the finales are all in double rather than triple metre. Talon's predilection for his own instrument is apparent in his chamber works (opp.2 and 4) which feature a cello obbligato in addition to a figured bass.

WORKS
(partial thematic catalogue in Brook)

op.
1 Six simphonies, 3 vn, b (Paris, 1753)
[2] Six quatuors, vn, ob, vc/other insts, bc (Paris, 1761), lost; as Six symphonies à quatre, op.2 (Paris, 1767)
2 Six trio, vn, vc, b (Paris, c1761)
4 Six trio, vn, vc/bn, b (Paris, 1765)
5 Six simphonies à quatre parties ou à grand orchestre (Versailles, 1767)
Op.3 not located, see Johansson

BIBLIOGRAPHY
GerberL
Etat actuel de la musique du Roi (Paris, 1763)
M. Brenet: *Les musiciens de la Sainte-Chapelle du Palais: documents inédits, recueillis et annotés par Michel Brenet* (Paris, 1910/R1973), 297
L. de La Laurencie and G. de St-Foix: 'Contribution à l'histoire de la symphonie française vers 1750', *Année musicale*, i (1911), 1–123
C. Johansson: *French Music Publishers' Catalogues of the Second Half of the Eighteenth Century* (Stockholm, 1955), i, 160
B. S. Brook: *La symphonie française dans la seconde moitié du XVIIIe siècle* (Paris, 1962)
BARRY S. BROOK, RICHARD VIANO

Talvela, Martti (Olavi) (*b* Hiitola, 4 Feb 1935). Finnish bass. A schoolteacher by profession, he entered the Lahti Academy of Music in 1958. After winning a lieder competition in 1960, he continued his studies in Stockholm, making his début at the Royal Opera House there in 1961, as Sparafucile; shortly afterwards, an audition with Wieland Wagner resulted in his being engaged as Titurel at the 1962 Bayreuth Festival (the year he joined the Deutsche Oper, Berlin). A voice of immense size and wide range, capable of thundering grandeur and great gentleness, allied to a giant's physique and an impressive stage presence, has won him international fame in Musorgsky, Verdi and all the principal Wagner bass roles. He was Boris Godunov in New York's first 'original version' of the opera, at the Metropolitan (1974); his first Gurnemanz, at Covent Garden in 1973, although uncertain in places, was remarkable for its natural nobility (he had made his house début in 1970). In recital and on record, he is a devoted advocate of the songs of Sibelius and Kilpinen. He became director of the Savonlinna Festival in 1972, the first opera under his aegis being, in 1973, *Die Zauberflöte*, in which he was Sarastro.

MAX LOPPERT

Tamagno, Francesco (*b* Turin, 28 Dec 1850; *d* Varese, 31 Aug 1905). Italian tenor. A pupil of Pedrotti in Turin, he began his career in 1870 in the chorus of the Teatro Regio and made his solo début as Nearco in Donizetti's *Poliuto*. From 1874, when he sang Riccardo in Verdi's *Un ballo in maschera* at Palermo, he was in constant demand as a leading tenor throughout Italy. In 1875, at La Fenice, he sang the title role of *Poliuto* and Edgardo in *Lucia di Lammermoor*. He made his La Scala début in December 1877 as Vasco da Gama in *L'africaine*, and the following season appeared there in the title role of Verdi's *Don Carlos*, as Alim in Massenet's *Le roi de Lahore*, and as Fabiano in the first performance of *Maria Tudor* by Gomes. On 26 December 1880 he created the role of Azaele in Ponchielli's *Il figliuol prodigo* and on 24 March 1881 he sang Gabriele Adorno in the first performance of the revised version of *Simon Boccanegra*. He also made several visits to Buenos Aires.

At La Scala, Tamagno took part in another Ponchielli première, singing Didier in *Marion Delorme* on 17 March 1885, and on the opening night of the following season he sang Radames in *Aida*. His greatest triumph came on 5 February 1887, when he created Verdi's Othello; he repeated the role in *Otello*'s first London performance (Lyceum Theatre) in July 1889, at Chicago (where he had made his American début a few days previously as Arnold in *Guillaume Tell*) in January 1890, at the Metropolitan in March 1890 and at Nice in 1891. He appeared in Puccini's *Edgar* at Madrid (1892) and in the first performance of Leoncavallo's *I Medici* at the Teatro dal Verme, Milan (1893). He returned to the Metropolitan for the 1894–5 season, and made his Covent Garden début on 13 May 1895 as Othello. After creating the role of Helion in De Lara's *Messaline* at Monte Carlo on 21 March 1899, he sang it at La Scala and at Covent Garden, where he returned for a final season in 1901.

Tamagno's heroic voice, with its brazen, trumpet-like top notes, was heard to best advantage in Verdi roles, especially Othello, which displayed the magnificent strength and security of its upper register. He was a forceful, convincing actor, and though not a subtle

Francesco Tamagno in the title role of Verdi's 'Otello'

artist, he brought great vocal and dramatic excitement to all his performances.

BIBLIOGRAPHY

B. Roosevelt: *Verdi: Milan and 'Otello'* (London, 1887)
H. Klein: *Thirty Years of Musical Life in London* (London, 1903)
M. Corsi: *Francesco Tamagno* (Milan, 1937/*R*1977 with discography)
W. H. Seltsam: *Metropolitan Opera Annals* (New York, 1949)
H. Rosenthal: *Two Centuries of Opera at Covent Garden* (London, 1958)
C. Gatti: *Il Teatro alla Scala nella storia e nell'arte: 1778–1963* (Milan, 1964)

ELIZABETH FORBES

Set of Hausa tambura from Nigeria, 1972

Tambari (pl. *tambura*). The commonest name for the kettledrum used in sets as part of the regalia of many traditional savannah states of west Africa. Its association with royalty in, for instance, the Hausa states of Nigeria is chronicled in the 17th century, and in its form, usage and name the *tambari* is related to the 16th-century court *ṭabl* at Fez in the Maghrib.

The individual drums in a set vary considerably in size so that the membranes may measure from 23 cm to 65 cm in diameter, and the height of the drum bodies from 20 cm to 60 cm. The *tambari* is beaten with two heavy thongs of hippopotamus hide, producing a deep and resonant sound. In performances the drums may be mounted singly or in pairs on heavy stakes driven into the ground (see illustration), or in pairs on the backs of camels for use in royal cavalcades.

See also HAUSA MUSIC, NIGERIA.

ANTHONY KING

Tamberg, Eino (*b* Tallinn, 27 May 1930). Estonian composer. In 1953 he graduated from Kapp's composition class at the Tallinn Conservatory. He then worked as a sound director for Estonian radio and as a consultant to the Estonian Composers' Union; in 1967 he was appointed to the staff of the Tallinn Conservatory. At the Sixth World Festival of Youth and Students (1957) he received a gold medal for the Concerto grosso; later awards were won by the *Ballet-sümfoonia* (first prize at the All-Union Young Composers' Competition, 1962) and the opera *Raudne kodu* ('Iron house') (second prize at the All-Union Musical Stage Works Competition, 1967). This through-composed work treats a sailors' uprising; the solo parts are principally in recitative or arioso, and the choral episodes show the influence of Estonian folksong. The three-act ballet *Joanna tentata* ('Joanna the possessed') is a tense psychological drama, set off by pastoral scenes. Tamberg's stage works have a primary posi-

tion in his oeuvre, and his orchestral pieces are also dramatic in their handling of dynamics, rhythm, orchestration and virtuoso writing. In 1960 he was made an Honoured Art worker of the Estonian SSR.

WORKS
(selective list)

Dramatic: Ballet-sümfoonia, 1959; Poiss ja liblik [The boy and the butterfly], ballet, 1963; Raudne kodu [Iron house] (opera, U. Laht after E. Tammlaan), 1965; Joanna tentata [Joanna the possessed], ballet, 1971; Cyrano de Bergerac (opera, J. Kross), 1974; incidental music for the theatre and cinema

Orch: Vürst Gabriel [Prince Gabriel], sym. suite, 1955; Conc. grosso, 1956; Sümfoonilised tantsud, 1957; Tocatta, 1967; Tpt Conc., 1972

Vocal: Rahva vabaduse eest [For the freedom of the people] (oratorio, K. Sküvalep), 1953; Tsar' Edip, suite, chorus, orch, 1959; Aafrika laul (L. Mikaya), male chorus, perc, 1961; Kuupaiste-oratoorium (oratorio, Kross), 1962; *c*70 songs incl. 5 romances (Petöfi), 1955

Inst: Str Qt, 1958; Partita, pf, 1971

Educational: 17 pale lastele [17 children's pieces], pf, 1960; Prelüüdja metamorfoos, vn, hn, pf, 1960; other inst pieces and songs

Principal publishers: Muzfond (Estonian department), Muzïka, Sovetskiy kompozitor

BIBLIOGRAPHY

O. Tuisk: *Eino Tamberg* (Moscow, 1961)
P. Kuusk: 'Eino Tamberg', *Kuus eesti tänase muusika loojat* [Six Estonian creators of modern music], ed. L. Normet (Tallinn, 1970)

MARINA NESTYEVA

Tamberlik [Tamberlick], Enrico (*b* Rome, 16 March 1820; *d* Paris, 13 March 1889). Italian tenor. He studied in Rome, Naples and Bologna with Zirilli, Borgna, Guglielmi and de Abella. When he was 18 he sang Gennaro at a semi-private performance of Donizetti's *Lucrezia Borgia* in Rome, but his official début, under the name of Danieli, was at the Teatro del Fondo, Naples, as Tybalt in Bellini's *I Capuleti e i Montecchi* in 1841. At the S Carlo the following year, he appeared (as Tamberlik) in Bordese's *I quindici* and Sarmiento's *Il tramonto del sole*; in 1843 he sang in Battista's *Anna la Prie* and Nicolai's *Il templario*. He made his London début on 4 April 1850 as Masaniello in Auber's *La muette de Portici* at Covent Garden, where he appeared regularly until 1864. In his first London season he also sang leading tenor roles by Rossini, Bellini, Donizetti, Verdi, Halévy and Meyerbeer, and the following year he added Don Ottavio in *Don Giovanni*, Max in *Der Freischütz*, Florestan in *Fidelio*, Alphonse (a baritone role) in *La favorite* and Phaon in Gounod's *Sapho* to his repertory. His many other roles included Hugo in Spohr's *Faust* (15 July 1852), Berlioz's Benvenuto Cellini (25 June 1853) and Manrico in *Il trovatore* (10 May 1855), all first London performances.

Tamberlik appeared at St Petersburg for several seasons between 1850 and 1863, and sang Don Alvaro in the first performance of *La forza del destino* (10 November 1862). He also appeared at Buenos Aires, Paris, Madrid and Moscow; after the early years of his career, he rarely sang in Italy. In 1877 he sang at Her Majesty's Theatre, London, and in 1881, when over 60, he embarked on a tour of the Spanish provinces in *I puritani*, *Poliuto*, *Ernani*, *Il trovatore*, *Rigoletto* and *Faust*. His robust voice, with its ringing top notes, was marked by a fast vibrato, but his musicianship, and handsome, exciting stage presence made him a superb interpreter of Florestan, Othello, Arnold and Manrico. Rossini is said to have asked him, when he came to call, to leave his *c♯''* from the chest on the coat-rack.

BIBLIOGRAPHY

H. F. Chorley: *Thirty Years Musical Recollections* (London, 1862)

H. Rosenthal: *Two Centuries of Opera at Covent Garden* (London, 1958)
H. Weinstock: *Donizetti and the World of Opera in Italy, Paris and London* (New York, 1963)

ELIZABETH FORBES

Tambor (Sp.). Drum; also an ORGAN STOP (*Pauke*).

Tamborito. An Afro-Hispanic recreational dance of Panama. It is sung responsorially by women, solo or in chorus. It is accompanied by hand-clapping in duple metre and a drum ensemble including *repicador, llamador, pujador, tambor, almirez* and the small *tamborito* from which the dance gets its name. Song texts are often in *copla* (four-line stanza) form and express the exuberance of the Panamanian *costeño*, serving also as a vehicle for socio-political commentary.

WILLIAM GRADANTE

Tambour (Fr.: 'drum'). Originally used to denote a side drum, kettledrum or tambourine. In French the word is usually modified in some way, for example, *tambour militaire, tambour roulant*, etc. In junior school percussion 'tambour' denotes a small single-headed frame drum (resembling a tambourine without jingles) with a head of parchment or plastic material. This instrument is used as a timekeeper in a percussion and instrumental groups. It is held in the hand and struck with the fingers or a soft-headed drumstick, and in some cases is sufficiently deep in tone to be used instead of a bass drum.

JAMES BLADES

Tambour à cordes (Fr.). STRING DRUM.

Enrico Tamberlik (left) as Manrico in Verdi's 'Il trovatore', with Francesco Graziani as Di Luna (centre, with plumed helmet) and Jenny Ney as Leonora (right): lithograph by John Brandard

Tambour d'acciaio (It.; Fr. *tambour d'acier*: 'steel drum'). *See* STEEL BAND.

Tambour de basque (Fr.). TAMBOURINE.

Tambourin (i). An 18th-century French character-piece supposedly based on a Provençal folkdance accompanied by pipe and tabor. The bass part simulates a drum by sharply accentuating the rhythm and by the repetition of a single note, usually the tonic, while an upper voice imitates the pipe with a fast-moving melody. The metre is usually 2/4 and the tempo lively. Rousseau described it as 'a kind of dance much in style today in the French theatre', adding that it must be lively and well accented, or 'swinging' ('sautillant et bien cadencé').

The most famous tambourins are in Rameau's operas and ballets, where they usually occur in pairs, one in a major key and one in the minor, with the first repeated da capo; rondeau form is also used. Ex.1 shows a keyboard version of the tambourin in *Les fêtes d'Hébé*

Ex.1 Rameau: Tambourin, *Pièces de clavecin*, 1724

(Entrée 3 scene vii). Rameau also composed two tambourins in his third *concert* for harpsichord and two melody instruments (1741). François Couperin's harpsichord works contain a short piece entitled *Les tambourins* (20th Ordre), in 3/4 metre and marked 'tres legerement' and 'notes égales'. Other examples are in J. M. Leclair's violin sonatas op.5 no.10 (1734) and op.9 no.3 (1738), Piccinni's opera *Roland*, Act 2 (1778), and Maurice Duruflé's Three Dances for orchestra, op.6 (1936). A 'tamburino' occurs at the end of Handel's opera *Alcina* (1735).

MEREDITH ELLIS LITTLE

Tambourin (ii) (de Provence) (Fr.). A double-headed drum from Provence in the form of a large tabor with a long cylindrical body and a single snare on the upper head. It is often referred to as *tambourin à corde* or *tambourin provençal*. The depth of its shell is approximately 70 cm and the width 35 cm. It was known in the 15th century and is still played together with the *galoubet*. Characteristically this species of tabor is struck in simple rhythmic sequences, with a single drumstick.

The tambourin was scored for by Rameau (*Les fêtes d'Hébé*, 1739), Berton (*Aline*, 1803) and later by Bizet (*L'arlésienne*, second suite, 1872). 20th-century composers who have scored for *tambourin de Provence* include Milhaud (*Suite française*, 1944), Copland (*Appalachian Spring*, 1945) and Roger Sessions (Third Symphony, 1962).

'Tambourin' is occasionally used in German and Italian to denote tambourine.

JAMES BLADES

see illustration overleaf

Tambourin de Béarn [tambourin de Gascogne, tambourin à cordes] (Fr.). A string drum in the form of a simple dulcimer, used primarily in southern France, as

1. Tambourines: detail from marble bas-relief (c1430) by Luca della Robbia, in the Museo dell'Opera del Duomo, Florence

Tambourin (de Provence) (with galoubet and drumstick), 19th century (Conservatoire Royal de Musique, Brussels) [see article, p.551]

Tambourin de Béarn (right): detail of 'Danse pastorale' by Nicolas Lancret (1690–1743) in the Museum Boymans van Beuningen, Rotterdam

an accompaniment to the pipe (*see* PIPE AND TABOR). It was commonly used to accompany dancing during the Renaissance; La Borde in the late 18th century mentioned it as still popular in the Gascogne and Béarn regions of France. The 18th-century vogue for the pastoral created a fashion for it in French court circles, and produced numerous keyboard pieces featuring bass drones, often entitled 'Tambourin'. It continues to flourish in and around the Basque country, where it is known by such local names as *bertz*, *soinu*, *tuntun* and *toutouna*. In Aragon it is known as *chicotén* or *salterio* ('psaltery'), and elsewhere in Spain as *salmo*. In its earlier history it was known in Germany, Italy and Switzerland.

The drum consists of six thick gut strings stretched over a wooden soundbox some 90 cm long and tuned to the key note and 5th of the pipe. The strings are struck with a stick (*baguette*), held in the player's right hand, and provide a rhythmic bass to the pipe – the three-holed flute, or *galoubet* – played by the left hand. Both instruments are shown being played in Lancret's painting *Danse pastorale* (see illustration) and in a fresco (dated 1487) by Filippino Lippi in the chapel of S Maria sopra Minerva, Rome. Examples of the *tambourin de Béarn* survive in the Stearns Collection and the Paris Conservatoire. A string drum is mentioned by Altenburg (1795) – the *trombe*, a wooden chest with a gut string stretched over a bridge. A two-string drum is depicted in the Angers Tapestry (1380).

BIBLIOGRAPHY

J.-B. de La Borde: *Essai sur la musique ancienne et moderne*, i (Paris, 1780/*R*1972), 288
A. Jacquot: *Dictionnaire pratique et raisonné des instruments de musique anciens et modernes* (Paris, 1886)
C. Sachs: *Real-Lexikon der Musikinstrumente* (Berlin, 1913/*R*1962)
A. A. Stanley: *Catalogue of the Stearns Collection of Musical Instruments* (Ann Arbor, 1921)
R. Wright: *Dictionnaire des instruments de musique* (London, 1941)
J. A. de Donostia and J. Tomás: 'Instrumentos de música popular española', *AnM*, ii (1947), 105–50
J. A. de Donostia: 'Instrumentos musicales del pueblo vasco', *AnM*, vii (1952), 3–49

JAMES BLADES, MARY CYR, DAVID KETTLEWELL

Tambourin de Gascogne. *See* TAMBOURIN DE BÉARN.

Tambourin de Provence [tambourin provençal]. *See* TAMBOURIN (ii).

Tambourine [timbrel] (Fr. *tambour de Basque*; Ger. *Tamburin*, *Schellentrommel*; It. *tamburino*, *tamburello*; Sp. *panderete*). A small single-headed frame drum of Near Eastern origin that has changed little over a long period of time. It consists of a shallow ring of wood, covered on one side with parchment (or today a plastic material). With isolated exceptions small metal discs called jingles (and occasionally small bells), arranged singly or in pairs, hang loosely in openings in the shell. In the modern European form the head is nailed to the shell (see fig.1). Rod-tensioning is occasionally applied. In many Near Eastern instruments, the heads are glued to the frame. The diameter of the present-day instrument (varying from 20 to 30 cm) seems to correspond with early representations, though certain 18th-and 19th-century specimens reach a diameter of about 50 cm.

The ancestry of this simple instrument is most remote, for the timbrel is found in use among the most ancient nations of the world, such as those of Assyria and Egypt; its distribution too seems to be world-wide, the hoop-drums of China, the rectangular *daff* of India, the *chilchiles* of the Peruvian Incas and the *aelyau* of Greenland being but varied forms of the timbrel. Its introduction into Britain is certainly prehistoric, for not only did the Gauls use it, but the advent of the Romans must have increased its popularity, as, with little bells or jingles attached, it marked the rhythm of the dance or roused to frenzy the devotees of Bacchic rites. Under the Hebrew name *toph* it was presumably the instrument used by Miriam and her maidens to celebrate Israel's triumph over the Egyptian foe. The numerous Old Testament references (from *Genesis* to *Ezekiel*) to the *toph* (translated as tabret or timbrel) are considered to indicate small hand drums. There is little proof however at this period of the jingling contrivance. In these biblical references the word 'tinkling' or 'metal' is used in connection with bells and cymbals, and not with tabret or timbrel.

Reliefs depicting small frame drums give no indication of jingling contrivances, though considering the manner in which the instrument sometimes appears to be held aloft and shaken, it is possible that a jingling contrivance was known. It was essentially a woman's instrument, though not absolutely so. In Sumerian and Babylonian art works, instruments of this type are portrayed in processions. On occasion the instrument is held on the left shoulder, while the player strikes it with the right hand. In Egypt it served in a similar capacity. It was one of the chief instruments used during funeral lamentations. In contrast, the Israelites associated it with processions, and with joy, feasting and mirth. There is one exception however, when tabrets are said to have been used to drown the cries of human sacrifices, or of those who passed through the fire in the valley of Hinnom. A small hand drum appears on one of the most remarkable portrayals of musicians of ancient times discovered to date: the royal Elamite orchestra and choir delineated on an Assyrian bas-relief (*c*660 BC) in the British Museum. In Egypt, a large tambourine measuring about 61 cm was used at the time of Osorkon II (*c*800 BC). A rectangular frame drum excavated at Thebes, from the 18th dynasty, is in the Cairo Museum.

The tambourine was certainly known to the Greeks and the Romans, and from the evidence of a 2nd-century Roman relief the instrument was very much as it is known today. In Arabia and Iran frame drums (*duff*), round and rectangular, appear as early as pre-Islamic times. These were hand drums of moderate dimension used for accompanying dance and song, and were associated with mirth and mourning. The largest of the round drums was the *ghirbal*, a frame drum with no jingles but equipped with snares (gut strings) stretched across the inside of the head. During a period of musical inactivity enforced in the 7th century by the prophet Mohammed, approval was given to the *ghirbal* and the tambourine, the latter (according to some legists) without jingles, since the instrument with jingles was forbidden.

The tambourine was popular throughout the Middle Ages in all parts of Europe, and was frequently depicted in ecclesiastical carvings and MSS. The commonest medieval type was similar to the tambourine known today, and even closer to the Turkish instruments of the 19th century, which usually had three or more sets of jingles arranged equidistantly in groups of two pairs. This is the form that appears more often in paintings and carvings in churches, and in illuminated MSS from the 11th century and throughout the Middle Ages. Some instruments have numerous sets of jingles, as in the

2. *Ways of playing the tambourine*

painting *The Assumption of the Virgin* by Matteo de'
Giovanni; and some have small pellet bells as well as, or
instead of, the ordinary jingles. Usually the instrument
is held aloft and struck with the fingers. Occasionally it
is depicted with a snare or snares running either above
or below the head. A few instruments have no jingles of
any description. An early instance of a tambourine
equipped with jingles is seen on a 2nd-century Roman
relief, *The Triumph of Bacchus*. Though the tambourine
is so often illustrated in the hands of angels, it was in
many respects a rustic instrument, associated with wandering minstrels, showmen and jugglers. In the late
Middle Ages it was given a part in concerted music
(Henry VIII had four tambourines in his musical ensemble of 79 musicians).

Mozart was one of the earliest composers to make
orchestral use of the tambourine (German Dances
K571, 1787); Gluck used it a little earlier (*Echo et
Narcisse*, 1779). By the early 19th century the tambourine was, as Berlioz said, 'in considerable use'. Its firm
introduction into orchestral works was occasioned by
the need for special effects of a Spanish or gypsy character, as for instance in Weber's overture to *Preciosa*
(1821). Berlioz, who in his *Traité d'instrumentation*
dealt to some extent with technical details concerning
the instrument, often used the tambourine. He occasionally called for two tambourines, as in *Benvenuto*

Cellini (two players), and for three in *Harold en Italie*.
20th-century composers have used the tambourine in a
variety of ways. In addition to providing local colour,
the instrument is used to mark rhythms and supply a
particular background. Exemplary scoring for the tambourine is found in Rimsky-Korsakov's Spanish
Capriccio and *Sheherazade*, and in Stravinsky's
Petrushka. In *Petrushka* (Gypsies and a Rake Vendor)
Stravinsky wrote for the tremolo by means of a shake
and a thumb roll (see ex.1). Composers make frequent

Ex.1

use of the thumb roll to ensure a quiet tremolo; it is
produced by rubbing the moistened ball of the thumb in
an upward direction along the surface of the vellum near
the rim. This vibrating of the jingles by means of friction
is by no means a simple matter, and at times may elude
the most skilful. (In the case of a *pp* tremolo, if not
marked as a thumb roll, the player will use his discretion as to whether to use a shake or a friction roll.) One
of the most generally known examples of the use of
the thumb roll occurs in the Arabian Dance in
Tchaikovsky's *Nutcracker Suite*. In the same work
(Trepak) there is a vigorous part for the tambourine,

calling for an extremely deft wrist, or the use of two tambourines (or the striking of the instrument back and forth on the knee and the hand). For a normal tremolo the tambourine is held aloft and shaken, and for the normal stroke the head (calfskin or plastic) is struck with the fingertips, knuckles, palm or closed fist, according to the composer's instructions or the player's discretion. For a series of quiet strokes the rim may be struck with the fingertips or drumsticks. To ensure a *pp* or *ppp* many orchestral players use a jingle-ring – a tambourine with the head removed. (The jingle-ring (*Schellenreif*) is occasionally referred to and illustrated in medieval MSS.) More unusual methods of playing the tambourine include flicking the jingles (Walton, *Façade*) and brushing the jingles (Lambert, *Rio Grande*). Possibly the most unusual request came from Stravinsky, who (in *Petrushka*: The Scuffle) asked for the instrument to be held close to the floor and dropped. A tambourine without jingles is occasionally used in the modern orchestra, e.g. in Stravinsky's *Renard* and Falla's *El retablo de Maese Pedro*.

The notation of the tambourine is on a single line or, more often today, on a staff. It is indicated as above and occasionally illustrated pictographically.

BIBLIOGRAPHY
F. W. Galpin: *Old English Instruments of Music* (London, 1910, rev. 4/1965 by T. Dart)
——: *Textbook of European Musical Instruments* (London, 1937)
R. Donington: *The Instruments of Music* (London, 1949)
F. Ll. Harrison and J. Rimmer: *European Musical Instruments* (London, 1964)
J. Blades: *Percussion Instruments and their History* (London, 1970, 2/1974)
J. Blades and J. Montagu: *Early Percussion Instruments from the Middle Ages to the Baroque* (London, 1976)

JAMES BLADES

Tambour militaire (Fr.). Side drum; *see* DRUM, §3.

Tamburā [tanburā, tānpura]. In India, a long-necked lute used as a drone accompaniment in the *dhrupad* and *khayāl* genres. It usually has a movable bridge and four wire strings tuned to the tonic and the 4th, 5th or occasionally the 7th, depending on the particular raga. The strings are plucked with the forefinger and are never stopped (*see* INDIA, SUBCONTINENT OF, §§II, 3 (iii), 6 (i), III, 1, V, 1, and fig.11, and PAKISTAN, §4). Long-necked lutes with related names are distributed throughout eastern Europe, the Middle East and central Asia. These include the *tanbur* (*see* AFGHANISTAN, §3; IRAN, §§I, 1, and II, 5; IRAQ, §§2, 5, and figs. 2, 5; ISLAMIC RELIGIOUS MUSIC, §3 (ii); KURDISH MUSIC, §§2 (ii), 4, and fig.3; TURKEY, §4 (ii)), and the eastern European fretted *tambura* (*see* BULGARIA, §II, 7; GYPSY MUSIC, §2; YUGOSLAVIA, §II, 2 (v), 3 (viii), 4 (iv)). Also related is the Arabic *ṭunbūr*, mentioned by al-Fārābī in the 10th century (*see* ARAB MUSIC, §I, 2 (i), and RABĀB).

Tamburello (It.). TAMBOURINE.

Tamburi. *See* TAMBARI.

Tamburin (Ger.). TAMBOURINE.

Tamburini. Italian firm of organ builders. Giovanni Tamburini (*b* Bagnacavallo, 25 June 1857; *d* Crema, 23 Nov 1942) was apprenticed to Trice and Pietro Anelli

of Codogna before joining Pacifico Inzoli of Crema (1887), where he invented the Tamburini wind-chest with double compartments. In November 1893 he established his own business in Crema: direction later passed to his sons Anselmi Umberto Tamburini and Severgnini Luigi Tamburini, and later still to his grandsons Franco and Luciano Anselmi Tamburini. The firm makes both slider-chests and spring-chests, more usually the former because of cost, but it has constructed spring-chests of the type used by Serassi and prefers these for the sound they produce, their stability and durability. Wind pressure is between 40 and 50 mm. Voicing is carried out without ears, beards or bridges. The pipework has a tin content of between 40 and 85%, and is polished, left dull or hammered; casework is designed with the collaboration of specialist architects.

The most important new Tamburini organs include those at Montebelluna; Stresa; Conservatorio Monteverdi, Bolzano (1965; three manuals, 33 stops); Basilica of S Maria dei Servi, Bologna (1967; three manuals, 59 stops); S Maria della Mercede, Rome (1971; three manuals, 54 stops); Bologna Conservatory (1971; three manuals, 60 stops); Conservatory of L'Aquila (1972; three manuals, 56 stops); Cassa di Risparmio, Florence (1974, three manuals, 48 stops). Organs (also with mechanical action) are under construction at the Bari Conservatory (three manuals), Piacenza Conservatory (four manuals, 65 stops), Basilica of S Miniato al Monte, Florence (four manuals; planned by Luigi F. Tagliavini), and Pesaro Conservatory (three manuals, 59 stops). Important restorations include organs of the Basilica of S Petronio, Bologna, two organs at S Alessandro in Colonna, Bergamo (by Carlo and Andrea Serassi, 1793; they are situated in opposite *cantorie* and connected by an original mechanism, devised by Serassi, which passes through a subterranean gallery for a distance of about 30 metres), the organ at Serravalle Scrivia (Serassi, three manuals), and that of S Maria della Scala, Siena (16th-century wind-chest, metal pipes and case).

In 1970 the firm restored the Vito Trasuntino harpsichord of 1571 in the Museo Civico in Milan, and it has since made copies differing from the original only in the extension of the compass in the bass from *C* short octave to *G'* short octave.

GUY OLDHAM

Tamburini, Antonio (*b* Faenza, 28 March 1800; *d* Nice, 8 Nov 1876). Italian baritone. He made his début in Cento at the age of 18 in Generali's *La contessa di colle erbose*, and then sang in Piacenza, Naples, Livorno and Turin. In 1822 he appeared at La Scala in Rossini's *Matilde di Shabran*, Mercadante's *Adele e Emerico* and in the first performance of Donizetti's *Chiara e Serafin*. After singing in Trieste and Vienna, he took part in another Donizetti première, *L'ajo nell'imbarazzo*, at the Teatro Valle, Rome (4 February 1824). Engagements in Naples and Venice followed, then he went to Palermo for the 1825–6 season, appearing in Rossini's *L'italiana in Algeri*, *Il barbiere di Siviglia*, *Aureliano in Palmira*, *L'inganno felice* and *Tancredi* and Mercadante's *Elisa e Claudio*. On 7 January 1826 he sang in the first performance of Donizetti's *Alahor di Granata*.

The following year at La Scala he sang the part of Ernesto in the première of Bellini's *Il pirata* (27

October), repeating it in Vienna at the Kärntnerthor Theatre (25 February 1828). He appeared in the revised version of Bellini's *Bianca e Fernando* at the opening of the Teatro Carlo Felice in Genoa (7 April 1828) and in the first performance of Donizetti's *Alina, regina di Golconda* at the same theatre a month later. During the next four years he took part in five more premières of Donizetti operas, all produced in Naples: *Gianni di Calais* (1828), *Imelda de' Lambertazzi* (1830), *Francesca di Foix* (1831), *La romanziera* (1831) and *Fausta* (1832). He also sang Valdeburgo in the first performance of Bellini's *La straniera* at La Scala (14 February 1829), a part he repeated at the Teatro S Carlo (December 1830) and at the King's Theatre, London (23 June 1832).

In 1832 he appeared for the first time at the Théâtre-Italien, Paris, in three operas by Rossini, singing Dandini in *La cenerentola*, Assur in *Semiramide* and the title role in *Mosè in Egitto*; that year he also sang in *La straniera*. For the remainder of the decade he sang alternately in London and Paris, appearing in the title role of *Don Giovanni* and as Count Almaviva in *Le nozze di Figaro*, as well as in Rossini's *La gazza ladra*, *Otello*, *La donna del lago*, *L'assiedo di Corinto* and *Guillaume Tell*. He created the part of Sir Richard Forth in the first performance of Bellini's *I puritani* at the Théâtre-Italien (24 January 1835) and Israele in Donizetti's *Marino Faliero* at the same theatre (12 March 1835). Other Donizetti operas in which he sang included *Lucia di Lammermoor*, *Parisina*, *Roberto Devereux* and *Lucrezia Borgia*. In 1840 he was not engaged by Her Majesty's Theatre, and the so-called Tamburini riots resulted in his hasty recall. He sang in the first Paris performance of Donizetti's *Linda di Chamounix* (1842) and sang Malatesta in the première of *Don Pasquale* at the Théâtre-Italien (3 January

Antonio Tamburini as Sir Richard Forth in Bellini's 'I puritani': lithograph by R. J. Lane after A. E. Chalon

1843). He was engaged in St Petersburg the following winter, and after an absence from London of five years, sang Assur in the performance of *Semiramide* for the opening of the Royal Italian Opera at Covent Garden (6 April 1847).

He retired in 1855, but five years later, at the age of 60, he was still capable of singing Figaro in *Il barbiere di Siviglia* in a performance at Nice. His voice, having a range of two octaves, *F–f'*, was unusually flexible for a baritone, and was rich and solid throughout.

BIBLIOGRAPHY
J. de Biez: *Tamburini et la musique italienne* (Paris, 1877)
H. Gelli-Ferraris: *Antonio Tambarini nel ricordo d'una nipote* (Livorno, 1934).

ELIZABETH FORBES

Tamburini, Giuseppe [Bagnacavallo, Giuseppe da] (*b* Bagnacavallo, nr. Ravenna). Italian composer and organist. He was a minorite. He was made *maestro di cappella* of the Accademia della Morte, Ferrara, in 1668 and of Urbino Cathedral from 1669 to 1674, when he resigned because of ill-health. Later he was an organist at Assisi. A small amount of sacred music by him survives in manuscript, and a manuscript note on a copy of the volume of four-part masses published at Bologna in 1678 as the work of BARTOLOMEO BALDRATI states that Tamburini was their composer.

BIBLIOGRAPHY
B. Ligi: 'La cappella musicale del duomo di Urbino', *NA*, ii (1925), 115

Tamburini, Pietro Antonio (*b* Bologna, baptized 10 Aug 1589; *d* Rome, 22 July 1635). Italian composer and singer. He sang at S Petronio, Bologna, from 1601 to 1613. He then moved to Rome, where from 1619 until his death he sang alto in the papal chapel. Ten masses by him for four to six voices survive in manuscript (all in *I-Rvat* C.S., except one, which is in *I-Bc*). There are also an eight-part *Te Deum* and three motets for four and eight voices (all in *I-Rvat* C.S., the first-named also in *A-Wn*).

Tamburino (It.). TAMBOURINE.

Tamburo (It.). DRUM.

Tamburo militare [tamburo piccolo] (It.). Side drum; *see* DRUM, §3.

Tamias, Dimitrios. Composer of Byzantine chant; *see* GREECE, §II.

Tamir, Alexander. *See* EDEN–TAMIR DUO.

Tammerinpfeife (Ger.). The pipe of the PIPE AND TABOR.

Tampon [mailloche double] (Fr.). A double-headed drumstick originally used for playing rolls on the bass drum. This type of drumstick is still used in the military band and occasionally in the orchestra when the bass drum and cymbals are played by one performer. The roll (which today is normally played with two soft-headed drumsticks) is produced by a rapid oscillating movement of the wrist bringing the heads of the stick into contact with the drumhead. Dukas scored for this effect in *L'apprenti sorcier*, Stravinsky in *The Firebird*, and Britten in *The Burning Fiery Furnace*.

JAMES BLADES

Tam-tam. *See* GONG.

Tanabe, Hisao (*b* Tokyo, 16 Aug 1883). Japanese musicologist. His mother was a music teacher and performer on Japanese instruments and he himself began to learn the violin at the Tokyo Music School in 1903. As a physics student at Tokyo University (1904–7) he began studying composition with Noël Peri, and while continuing postgraduate studies in acoustics at the university (1907–10) he studied Japanese music and dance with Shōhei Tanaka. He taught acoustics and music history at Tōyō Music School (1907–35), mathematics and physics at Waseda Junior High School (1908–18), and music history and theory at the Imperial Music Bureau (1919–23). He also made frequent field studies, working on Korean court music (1921) and visiting Formosa and the Ryūkyū Islands (1922), north China (1923) and the Pacific islands (1934). He was successively professor in Japanese music history at Kokugakuin University (1923), lecturer in Japanese music history at Tokyo University (1930), lecturer in acoustics and Japanese music history at Tokyo Music School (1934), lecturer in music history at Waseda University (1947) and professor of acoustics at Musashino College of Music (1949). When the Society for Research in Asiatic Music was founded in 1936, Tanabe became the president, and a Festschrift for his 60th birthday was published in 1943. For his contribution to Japanese music he has received the Imperial Academy Prize (1929), the Medal of Honour with Purple Ribbon (1957) and the Fourth Order of Merit (1964).

Tanabe can be regarded as a pioneer among modern Japanese music scholars. Although he is primarily known as an authority on oriental music and acoustics, his interest covers broader fields including European music, dance, mathematics and physics. In the early years of the 20th century he had already become active as a leading promoter of European music in Japan through his writings and lectures. He performed both European and Japanese music – *gagaku* performance, noh singing and *shamisen* and violin playing – and composed many school songs in European style, and some orchestral works including *Takiguchi Nyūdō* (1927) and *Geijutsu no hikari* ('Light of the arts') for chorus and orchestra (1929). His first publication on Japanese music, *Nihon ongaku kōwa* ('Lectures on Japanese music', 1919) was followed by several other versions of Japanese music history, each with a slightly different title and emphasis.

WRITINGS

Seiyō ongaku annai [Introduction to western music] (Osaka, 1906)
Onkyō to ongaku [Accoustics and music] (Tokyo, 1908)
Seiyō ongakushi taiyō [An outline of western music history] (Tokyo, 1913)
Seiyō ongaku kōwa [Lectures on western music] (Tokyo, 1915)
Ongaku no genri [Principles of music] (Tokyo, 1916)
Nihon ongaku kōwa [Lectures on Japanese music] (Tokyo, 1919)
Gagaku tsūkai [Commentaries on *gagaku*] (Tokyo, 1921)
Daiichi ongaku kikō [The first musical trip] (Tokyo, 1923)
Ongaku gairon [Introduction to music] (Tokyo, 1925)
Nihon ongaku no kenkyū [Study of Japanese music] (Tokyo, 1926)
Gendai Shina no ongaku [Music in modern China] (Tokyo, 1927)
Shimaguni no uta to odori [Songs and dances in an insular country] (Tokyo, 1927)
Edo jidai no ongaku [Music in the Edo period] (Tokyo, 1928)
Tōyō ongaku ron [Discussion on oriental music] (Tokyo, 1929)
Nihon ongaku tsū [A survey of Japanese music] (Tokyo, 1930)
Tōyō ongaku shi [A history of oriental music] (Tokyo, 1930)
Ongaku riron [Music theory] (Tokyo, 1931)
Hōgaku kenkyūsha no tameni [For students of Japanese music] (Tokyo, 1932)

Nihon ongaku shi [A history of Japanese music] (Tokyo, 1932)
Ongaku genron [Principles of music] (Tokyo, 1935)
Nihon ongaku gaisetsu [Introduction to Japanese music] (Tokyo, 1940)
Daitōa to ongaku [East Asia and music] (Tokyo, 1942)
Daitōa on ongaku [Music in East Asia] (Tokyo, 1943)
Fue [Flute] (Tokyo, 1947)
Nihon on ongaku [Japanese music] (Tokyo, 1947)
Nihon ongaku gairon [Introduction to Japanese music] (Tokyo, 1951)
Ongaku onkyōgaku [Acoustics of music] (Tokyo, 1951)
Ongaku geijutsu gaku [Study of the art of music] (Tokyo, 1954, rev. 2/1960)
Ongaku riron [Music theory] (Tokyo, 1956)
Seiyō ongaku shi [History of western music] (Tokyo, 1957)
Japanese Music (Tokyo, 1959)
Ongaku tsūron [General survey of music] (Tokyo, 1959)
Shamisen ongaku shi [History of *shamisen* music] (Tokyo, 1963)
Nihon ongaku shi [History of Japanese music] (Tokyo, 1963)
Nihon no gakki [Japanese instruments] (Tokyo, 1964)
Meiji ongaku monogatari [Story of music in the Meiji era] (Tokyo, 1965)
Nan'yō Taiwan Okinawa ongaku Kikō [Expeditions in Micronesia, Formosa and Ryukyu], Tōyō ongaku sensho, v (Tokyo, 1968)
Chūgoku Chōsen ongaku chōsa Kikō [The expedition in China and Korea], Tōyō ongaku sensho, xi (Tokyo, 1970)

EDITIONS

Nihon ongaku shū [Anthology of Japanese music] (Tokyo, 1931)
Kinsei nihon ongaku shū [Anthology of Japanese music in recent years] (Tokyo, 1931)
Nihon zokkyoku shū [Anthology of Japanese popular music] (Tokyo, 1932)

BIBLIOGRAPHY

Tanabe sensei kanreki kinen: tōa ongaku ronsō [To celebrate the birthday of Prof. Tanabe: a collection of articles on the music of east Asia = *Tanabe Festschrift*] (Tokyo, 1943) [with outline of life and list of works]

MASAKATA KANAZAWA

Tanaglia [Tanaglino], Antonio Francesco. *See* TENAGLIA, ANTONIO FRANCESCO.

Tanburā. *See* TAMBURĀ.

Tanel (*fl* late 14th century). Composer, probably French. His name, clearly incomplete, appears at the head of a simple two-voice virelai, *Nulle pitié, ma dame*, in the Bolognese fragment *I-Bu* 596 (no.2).

BIBLIOGRAPHY

H. Besseler: 'Studien zur Musik des Mittelalters', *AMw*, vii (1925), 206

KURT VON FISCHER

Tañer (Sp.). *See* TOCCATA, §1.

Tanev, Alexander (*b* Budapest, 23 Oct 1928). Bulgarian composer. He graduated first in law from Sofia University and then in music from the Sofia State Academy (1957). From that time he worked as music editor at the Centre of Amateur Art, Sofia. He was appointed to teach composition at the Bulgarian State Conservatory in 1970, and from 1972–6 was secretary of the Bulgarian Composers Union. His music, which draws on Bulgarian folksong, shows a predilection for humour.

WORKS

(*selective list*)

Choral: c200 songs incl. Suite, 1967; Theme and Variations nos.1, 2, 1969; Prabalgarski napevi [Old Bulgarian dances], male chorus, perc, 1974; Letopis na svobodata [Chronicle of freedom], oratorio, Bar, reader, mixed chorus, orch, 1975
Inst: Pf Sonatine, 1959; Sinfonietta, orch, 1959; Pf Sonata, 1966; Youth Concerto, vn, str, 1970; Rondo concertante, trbn, orch, 1971; Conc., brass, perc, 1972; Stroitelna musika [Builders' music], 2 pf, perc or orch, 1976; Pf Conc., 1976
Stage: Prasnik v Tsaravets [Festival in Tsaravets], ballet, 1968; incidental music

Principal publisher: Nauka i izkustvo

LADA BRASHOVANOVA

Taneyev, Alexander Sergeyevich (*b* St Petersburg, 17
Jan 1850; *d* Petrograd, 7 Feb 1918). Russian composer.
He was an uncle of S. I. Taneyev. On graduating
from St Petersburg University, he entered the civil
service and rose to become director of the imperial
chancellery. He also found time to compose; it is said
that he used to hide the score on which he was working
under his official papers and write a few bars between
appointments. He studied music with Reichel in
Dresden, and with Rimsky-Korsakov and A. A. Petrov.
Through his friendship with members of the Balakirev
circle, he became interested in musical nationalism. His
Second Symphony is a not particularly successful
attempt to write a 'truly Russian' work. Many of his
songs and piano pieces, and his lighter orchestral works,
are pleasing.

WORKS

(selective list; published in Leipzig, n.d., unless otherwise stated)

Stage: Mest' Amura [Cupid's revenge] (opera, 1, T. N. Shchepkina-
Kupernik), op.13, concert perf., St Petersburg, 19 May 1899; Metel'
[The snowstorm] (opera, Svetlov, after D. Tsertelev), Petrograd, 11
Feb 1916 (Moscow, n.d.)

Orch: Suite no.1, A, op.9 (Hamburg, n.d.); Alyosha Popovich, ballade,
after A. K. Tolstoy, op.11 (Moscow, n.d.); Festive March, op.12;
Suite no.2, F, op.14; 2 Mazurkas, A, F, op.15; Sym. no.2, b♭, op.21;
Rêverie, vn, orch, op.23; Hamlet, ov., op.31; Sym. no.3, E, op.36
(Moscow, n.d.)

Inst: Bagatelle and Serenade, vc, pf, op.10; Mazurka no.3 (Souvenir de
Bade), pf, op.20; Bluette, pf, op.22; Arabesque, cl, pf, op.24; 3 str qts,
no.1, G. op.25, no.2, C, op.28, no.3, A, op.30; Valse de concert, pf,
op.32; Feuillet d'album, va, pf, op.33 (Moscow, n.d.)

Vocal: 2 Duets, op.17; 3 Songs, op.18; 13 Songs, op.34 (Moscow, n.d.);
7 Songs, op.37 (Moscow, n.d.)

JENNIFER SPENCER

Sergey Ivanovich Taneyev

Taneyev, Sergey Ivanovich (*b* Vladimir-na-Klyaz'me,
25 Nov 1856; *d* Dyud'kovo, nr. Moscow, 19 June
1915). Russian composer. He was the nephew of
Alexander Sergeyevich Taneyev, who as a composer was
inclined to the nationalist school. By contrast, Sergey
Taneyev's works reveal a far more cosmopolitan outlook.

1. 1856–89. 2. 1889–1915. 3. Works.

1. 1856–89. Taneyev was the son of a government official, a cultured and intelligent man with aristocratic
connections. He had his first piano lessons when he was
five, and in September 1866 he entered the Moscow
Conservatory, even though he was not yet ten years old.
In the following year his course was interrupted, but in
1869 he resumed his piano studies with Eduard Langer,
also joining the theory class of Nikolay Hubert and,
most important, Tchaikovsky's composition class. In
1871 his piano tuition was undertaken by Nikolay
Rubinstein. Taneyev's official début was on 29 January
1875, when he played Brahms's D minor Concerto at a
concert of the Russian Musical Society, and on 3
December he gave the first performance in Moscow of
Tchaikovsky's First Piano Concerto. Subsequently
Taneyev was to play the solo part in the premières of all
Tchaikovsky's works for piano and orchestra. A firm
friendship between them had begun while Taneyev was
still a student, and it continued until Tchaikovsky's
death, despite the frankness with which Taneyev was
prepared (and, uniquely among Tchaikovsky's circle,
encouraged) to criticize Tchaikovsky's work.

In May 1875 Taneyev graduated from the conservatory, being the first student to receive a gold medal for
performance and composition. During the summer he
travelled abroad with Nikolay Rubinstein, and in

February and March 1876 he toured Russia with the
violinist Leopold Auer. In October he went abroad again,
visiting Paris for a year and meeting Turgenev and leading
French musicians. In 1878, on Tchaikovsky's resignation
from the Moscow Conservatory, Taneyev was persuaded
to take his place, though he consented to direct only the
harmony and orchestration classes. So far, Taneyev had
kept his own music a secret confined almost exclusively
to Tchaikovsky and himself. He had already written one
symphony while still a student, and after his Paris visit
he started upon a second, though this was interrupted by
his conservatory appointment. His self-criticism was
severe, and it was not until June 1880 that he at last
made his début as a composer with the cantata for the
unveiling of the Pushkin memorial in Moscow. An
eclectic and conservative at heart, Taneyev had early
been drawn to the music of Bach, and subsequently he
was to extend his studies to the great contrapuntists of
the Renaissance such as Ockeghem, Josquin Desprez
and Lassus. This interest is demonstrated not only in the
considerable number of contrapuntal exercises which
survive in manuscript, even from his mature years
(including attempts to use Russian folksongs as the basis
of contrapuntal pieces), but also in the powerful contrapuntal element in his own independent work. Taneyev's unpublished works also reveal, by contrast, a
strong humorous streak, engagingly displayed particularly in a variety of musical greetings to friends.

The next few years saw Taneyev being increasingly
drawn into the work of the conservatory. After a further
visit to Paris in 1880 he returned to take over the piano
class of Nikolay Rubinstein, who had died in March
1881, and, when Hubert resigned in 1883, he undertook
the composition class. Then in May 1885 he reluctantly

became director of the conservatory. Meanwhile his list of compositions had been growing slowly. Quite apart from his arduous conservatory duties, Taneyev was interested in a wide range of intellectual pursuits. During the 1890s these included Esperanto, and his vocal works include settings of texts in that language. Because of such distractions composition was normally confined to the summer months spent on the estate of his friends, the Maslovs. On 23 March 1884 he conducted his cantata *Ioann Damaskin* ('John of Damascus'), published as his op.1, and in January 1885 he directed the première of his D minor Symphony. During the summer he visited the Caucasus, noting down folksongs, and in 1886 he began what was to be his first published string quartet. The following year he started upon his most ambitious work, the opera *Oresteya* ('The Oresteia'), a task which occupied him for the next seven years. In May 1889, finding that the work at the conservatory was distracting him from composition, he resigned the directorship (which he had held very successfully), though he continued to teach counterpoint. Taneyev was one of the best and most influential Russian teachers of his period, his pupils including Skryabin, Rakhmaninov, Lyapunov and Glier.

2. 1889–1915.
Having now more free time, Taneyev embarked systematically upon a book on counterpoint, finishing it in 1906; in addition he pressed ahead with *The Oresteia* and completed it in July 1894. It was first given in St Petersburg on 29 October 1895, but despite initial success, it never established itself in the repertory. During the summer of 1895 Taneyev became friendly with Tolstoy, and subsequently often visited the Tolstoys' estate at Yasnaya Polyana. It is known that Tolstoy's wife became infatuated with Taneyev, though it appears that he himself was quite unaware of this. During Tchaikovsky's last years Taneyev had some contact with Rimsky-Korsakov, and acquaintance now developed into a firm friendship which lasted until the latter's death. Taneyev also became more sympathetic to other members of the nationalist school, conceding at last Borodin's gifts, and in 1898 dedicating his C minor Symphony to Glazunov.

Taneyev was a man of marked integrity and openness, and seems to have had a gift for arousing respect and even affection in people who could not share his musical outlook. In 1905, when the revolutionary movement in Russia sparked off disturbances at the conservatory, his principles led him to resign from the staff in protest at the director's repressive disciplining of some students. Being now free from teaching, he resumed his career as a concert pianist, both as soloist and participant in chamber music. Since completing *The Oresteia* 11 years earlier he had centred his creative attentions upon chamber music. By 1905 he had composed six string quartets and two quintets, and now he was able to pursue this line of composition more intensively, composing in particular chamber works with a piano part which he could play in concerts. He also wrote some choruses and a substantial number of songs. His book on counterpoint appeared in 1909, and he then turned his attention to a study of canon, though this work remained unfinished. In 1913 he was elected an honorary member of the Russian Musical Society. Taneyev's last completed work was the cantata *Po prochtenii psalma* ('At the reading of a psalm'), completed at the very beginning of 1915, and universally acclaimed

at its first performance in March. On 27 April his former pupil Skryabin died and Taneyev, after attending the funeral, developed pneumonia. He rallied, but soon succumbed to a heart attack.

3. WORKS.
The Russian scholar Boris Asaf'yev observed that Taneyev, 'like no other Russian composer, lived and worked immersed in the world of ideas, in the development of abstract concepts'. Taneyev is, in fact, a lone figure in late 19th-century Russian music, owing nothing to the indigenous Russian tradition established by Glinka, and openly disapproving of contemporary nationalist composers. He was the antithesis of Glinka, for whereas the latter was possessed of a powerful and vivid imagination but was deficient in technique, Taneyev had little imaginative endowment but commanded a compositional skill unsurpassed by any Russian composer of his period. The patient diligence which marked his approach to composition was the very opposite of the capricious bursts of energy which characterized the work habits of many of his contemporaries. It was his normal practice to do extensive preliminary work on his basic materials, such as working out contrapuntal possibilities, before setting about the main task of composition. His creative mentality is clearly exposed in a letter written to Tchaikovsky when he was working on his opera *The Oresteia*:

[My approach] means that not one number is written in its final form until the outline of the whole work is prepared. It is written, you might say, concentrically, not by composing the whole out of the separate, successive parts, but by going from the whole to the details: from the opera to the acts, from the acts to the scenes, from the scenes to the separate numbers . . . Thus one may perceive the most important points in the drama on which the attention of the composer must be most concentrated, determine the length of scenes and numbers according to their importance, plan the modulatory scheme of the acts, define the orchestral sounds, and such like.

Because of this painstaking approach Taneyev's scores are among the most orderly and polished in Russian music. His inclination to contrapuntal techniques attracted him to the great contrapuntists of the past, and these studies in their turn fortified his skill, resulting in textures which, however complex, are always engineered with precision and polish. He often used contrapuntal procedures as an enrichment of his harmonic palette, and despite the lack of individuality in his melodic fund, his skill in building melodic paragraphs and in devising interesting phrase structures is admirable. In an early work like the Canzona for clarinet and strings (1883) the lyricism and waltz proclivities of his teacher, Tchaikovsky, are clearly reflected, but Taneyev's style was to develop a more broadly based eclecticism which ultimately achieved an illusion of individuality through its constant capacity to avoid commitment to the style of any one composer, however close certain passages may be to the sound worlds of masters like Tchaikovsky and Brahms (whose music, however, Taneyev claimed to dislike).

The fastidiousness of Taneyev's craftsmanship is evident in his songs, many of which are admirable compositions, but his gifts are seen to better advantage in his accomplished handling of large-scale forms, particularly in his fluent sonata structures, as in the first movement of his C minor Symphony (1898), usually considered his finest instrumental work. The slow movement is also an impressive piece, revealing a warm lyricism deployed on an impressive scale, while the scherzo shows his capacity for delightful, if restrained, capriciousness. It was natural that a composer of Taneyev's leanings should be drawn increasingly to chamber music. Nor is it surprising that one who thrived on counterpoint should wish to augment the linear resources of the string quartet, and in addition to his six numbered string quartets, he composed three string quintets. The first of these (1901, revised 1903) is typical of his chamber music, opening with a vast sonata structure which exhibits a thoroughly Germanic handling of thematic and tonal mechanisms. Nevertheless, Taneyev's penchant for contrapuntal thinking is revealed in the constant thematic interactions of the first movement, and even more explicitly in the variation finale, which concludes with a parade of contrapuntal expertise in a fugue on three subjects. Taneyev's contrapuntalism reaches its apogee in his last work, the choral–orchestral *At the Reading of a Psalm*, a cantata which some regard as his masterpiece.

Taneyev's most ambitious work was *The Oresteia*, which, despite the retention of the original designation 'trilogy', is in fact an opera in three acts. Being attracted neither to the graphic realism nor the fairy-tale fantasy which dominated contemporary Russian opera, Taneyev turned to classical mythology. Except for Musorgsky's abortive *Oedipus rex*, this was the first Russian opera to use such a subject. It has the stage-picture manner typical of the Russian tradition, but this comes less from commitment to the principles that guided Glinka or Musorgsky than from Taneyev's lack of interest in the actual events of the plot (significantly, for instance, the offstage murders of Aegisthus and Clytemnestra have no effect upon the musical flow), which are purely incidental to the broader themes of fate, revenge and expiation that are the fundamentals of Aeschylus's drama. Taneyev employed musical styles and dramatic conventions deriving from French grand opera, but overlaid these with an epic vein which makes his loftier musical intentions clear. The care with which he composed the piece is reflected in the final result, which is a splendidly efficient score. Nevertheless, the conventional character and inequality of his musical invention causes the achievement to fall short of the intent. Taneyev had none of Tchaikovsky's gift for full-blooded melody, and his lyrical passages sound like his master's at their weakest; nor had he any trace of Musorgsky's ability to capture a character or action within an unforgettable musical invention. His music envelops the tale in a noble aura instead of illuminating it by uncovering the souls and feelings of human beings caught in a train of events which is their destiny. In *The Oresteia* he was usually at his best when composing a passage in which his resourcefulness as a composer was exercised (as in some of the chromatic sections which avoid stock progressions and combinations), or when the dramatic situation demanded the construction of a large musical span. On such occasions he sometimes produced music that has real distinctiveness, though it rarely lodges for long in the memory.

WORKS

(many MSS of unpublished works in USSR-Mk)

STAGE

Oresteya [The Oresteia] (musical trilogy, Venkstern, after Aeschylus), 1887–94, St Petersburg, Mariinsky, 29 Oct 1895 (Leipzig, 1900)

ORCHESTRAL

(for full orch unless otherwise stated)

Quadrille, D, small orch, 1872–3
Sym. [no.1], e, 1873–4 (Moscow, 1948)
2 ovs., g, 1874–5, d, 1875
Pf Conc., E♭, 1876 (Moscow, 1957) [2 movts only]

Sym. [no.2], b♭, 1877–8 [3 movts only]
Ov. on a Russian theme, C, 1882 (Moscow, 1948) [based on no.10 in Rimsky-Korsakov's folksong collection, op.24]
Canzona, f, cl, str, 1883 (Moscow, 1947)
Sym. [no.3], d, 1884 (Moscow, 1947)
Adagio, C, ?1885 (Moscow, 1950)
Ov. to Oresteya, op.6 (Leipzig, 1897)
Sym. for children's insts, ?1895
Sym. no.4, c, op.12 (Leipzig, 1901) [orig. pubd as no.1]
Suite de concert, vn, orch, op.28, 1909 (Berlin and Moscow, 1910)

CHAMBER

Str Qt, d, 1874–6 [2 movts only]
March, 2 pf, harmonium, 3 trbn, vc, ob, glock, 1 other inst, 1877
Str Trio, D, 1879–80
Str Qt, E♭, 1880
Str Qt, C, 1882–3
Str Qt, A, 1883
Str Qt no.1, b♭, op.4, 1890 (Moscow, 1892)
Sonatina, A, vn, pf, 1895 [1st movt only; other 3 movts by Morozov, Koreshchenko and Konyus; for I. V. Grzhimali's silver jubilee]
Str Qt no.2, C, op.5, 1895 (Leipzig, 1896)
Str Qt no.3, d, op.7, 1886, rev. 1896 (Leipzig, 1898)
Variations on a favourite theme, mand, vn, pf, 1897
Str Qt no.4, a, op.11, 1899 (Leipzig, 1900)
Str Qt no.5, A, op.13, 1903 (Leipzig, 1903)
Str Qnt no.1, G, op.14, 1901, rev. 1903 (Leipzig, 1904)
Str Qnt no.2, C, op.16, 1904 (Leipzig, 1905)
Str Qt no.6, B♭, op.19, 1905 (Leipzig, 1906)
Pf Qt, E, op.20, 1906 (Moscow, 1908)
Trio, D, 2 vn, va, op.21, 1907 (Moscow, 1908)
Pf Trio, D, op.22, 1907 (Moscow, 1908)
Trio, E♭, vn, va, tenor va, op.31, 1910 (Moscow, 1911)
Pf Qnt, g, op.30, 1911 (Moscow, 1912)
Vn Sonata, a, 1911 (Moscow, 1948)
Str Qt, c, 1911 [2 movts only]
Str Trio, b [2 movts only]

KEYBOARD

(for solo pf unless otherwise stated)

Scherzo, e♭, 1873–4 (Moscow, 1953)
Theme and variations, c, 1874 (Moscow, 1953)
Pf Sonata, E♭, 1874–5 [1st movt only]
4 scherzos, F, C, g, d, 1875 (Moscow, 1953)
4 pieces (Moscow, 1953): Quadrille, A, 1879; March, d, 1879; Repose, 1880; Slumber song, 1881
Variations on a theme of Mozart, E♭, 2 pf, 1880
March, C, pf 4 hands, 1881
Den' rozhdeniya kompozitora [The composer's birthday], 1892 [a joke for Tchaikovsky's birthday, based on themes from his ballets]
Prelude, F, 1894–5 (Moscow, 1904), arr. pf 4 hands, 1896
Improvisation, 1896 (Moscow, 1923) [for a set, collab. Arensky, Glazunov and Rakhmaninov]
Prelude and fugue, g♯, op.29, 1910 (Moscow, 1911), arr. 2 pf (Moscow, 1914)
Choral varié, org (Paris, n.d.)
Andante semplice (Moscow, 1953)

CHORAL

Bozhe! bud milostiv k nam [God be merciful unto us], 1874–5
Slava N. G. Rubinshteynu [Glory to N. G. Rubinstein] (Samarin), 4 solo vv, chorus, orch, 1874 [based on the Russian folksong Slava Bogu na nebe]
3 choruses, SATB, 1877: Serenada [Serenade] (Fet); Venetsiya noch'yu [Venice at night] (Fet), rev.1880; Sosna [The pine] (Lermontov)
Kvartet chinovnikov [Civil servants' qt], 1v, chorus, str qt, 1879
Fugue on a Russian folksong, 1879
Netherlandish fantasia on a Russian theme, chorus/? 12 solo vv, 1880 [based on no.12 in Balakirev's folksong collection; no text]
Cantata for the unveiling of the Moscow Pushkin Memorial in 1880 (Pushkin), E♭, chorus, orch, 1880 (Moscow, 1937)
Kheruvimskaya [Cherubim's song], SSATBB, 1880
Lech' bï v krovati [I want to lie in bed] (Taneyev), comic canon, 1880
Ceremonial chorus for the arrival of guests, STBB, 1880
2 comic fugues (Prutkov), 3vv, 1880: Spetsialist podoben flyusu [A specialist is like a gumboil], ATB; Fontan [The fountain], ABarB
3 choruses, male vv (Moscow, 1881): Venetsiya noch'yu [Venice at night] (Fet), 1877, rev.1880; Noktyurn [Nocturne] (Fet), 1880; Vesolïy chas [A happy hour] (Kol'tsov), 1880
Irmos [1st verse] from the first hymn of Epiphany, SATB, 1881
Apofeoz khudozhnika [Apotheosis of the artist] (Taneyev), cantata, B, chorus, pf, 1881
Vechernyaya pesnya [Evening song] (Khomyakov), 1881, ?pubd
Fugue, c, SATB/?solo vv, 1883
3 sacred pieces, 1883: Khvalite imya Gospodne [Praise the name of the Lord], 5vv; Tvoryay angelï svoya [He who makes his angels], 4vv; Spaseniya sodelal esi [Thou hast brought salvation], on a theme

from the Ordinary, 6vv
Madrigal (Taneyev), SAB/?solo vv, 1884
Ioann Damaskin [John of Damascus] (A. K. Tolstoy), cantata, chorus, orch, op.1, 1884 (Moscow, 1886)
Slava Kirillu i Mefodiyu [Glory to SS Cyril and Methodius], 1885
Syadu zavtra ya k okoshechku [Yesterday I sat by the little window] (Taneyev), romance, chorus/4 solo vv, 1887
Ekho [The echo] (Pushkin), SATBB, 1888
3 comic canons for Leonid Sabaneyev (Esperanto texts), chorus/?solo vv, 1895
Voskhod solntsa [Sunrise] (Tyutchev), op.8, by 1897 (Leipzig, 1898)
Iz kray v kray [From border to border] (Tyutchev), double chorus, op.10, by 1897 (Leipzig, 1899)
2 Choruses, op.15, 1903 (Leipzig, 1904): Zvyozdï [Stars] (Khomyakov); Alpï [The Alps] (Tyutchev)
2 Choruses, SATBB: Tï konchil zhizni put', geroy [You have finished life's journey, O hero], ?1909; Solntse nespyashchikh [Sun of the sleepless], ?1910
12 Choruses (Polonsky), op.27, by 1909 (Moscow, 1910): Na mogile [On the tomb]; Vecher [Evening]; Razvalinï bashni [The tower's ruins]; Posmotri, kakaya mgla [Behold, what darkness]; Na korable [On the boat]; Molitva [Prayer]; Iz vechnosti muzïka vdrug razdalas' [Music suddenly sounded from eternity]; Prometey [Prometheus]; Uvidal iz-za tuchi utyos [From behind the cloud I saw a rock]; Zvyozdï [Stars]; Po goram dve khmurïkh tuchi [Two sullen clouds among the mountains]; V dni, kogda nad sonnïm morem [On a day when over the sunny sea]
16 Choruses (Bal'mont), male vv, op.35, 1912–13 (Moscow, 1914): Tishina [Stillness]; Priznaki [Visions]; Sfinks [Sphinx]; Zarya [Dawn]; Molitva [Prayer]; V prostranstvakh efira [In the spaces of the ether]; I son i smert' [Both sleep and death]; Nebesnaya rosa [The dew of heaven]; Myortvïye korabli [Dead ships]; Zvuki proboya [Sounds of the surf]; Morskoye dno [The sea bed]; Morskaya pesnya [Sea song]; Tishina [Stillness]; Gibel' [The wreck]; Belïy lebed' [The white swan]; Lebed' [The swan]
Po prochtenii psalma [At the reading of a psalm] (Khomyakov), cantata, 4 solo vv, chorus, orch, op.36, 1915 (vocal score (Moscow, 1923), full score (Moscow, 1960)

VOCAL
(with pf acc. unless otherwise stated)

Luna na nebe golubom [The moon in a blue sky] (?Yazïkov), S, 1876
Chto tebe v imeni moyom? [What's in my name for you?] (N.), eclogue, S, 1877
3 Duets, S, A, c1870–80: Gornïye vershinï [Mountain summits] (Lermontov); Blizost' vesnï [Spring's nearness] (Zhukovsky); Sosna [The pine] (Lermontov)
Starïy rïtsar' [The old knight] (Zhukovsky), ballad, S, c1870–80
2 Duets (Fet), 2 B, 1879: Vecher u vzmor'ya [Evening by the seashore]; Rastut, rastut prichudlivïye teni [The fantastic shadows grow and grow]
Netherlandish fantasia on a Russian theme, 12vv/?chorus, 1880 [based on no.12 in Balakirev's folksong collection; no text]
2 Trios (Maykov), T, B, B, 1880: O chom v tishi nochi tainstvenno mechtayu? [Of what do I secretly dream in the quiet of the night?]; Ya v grote zhdal tebya [I waited for you in the grotto]
Golos v lesu [A voice in the wood] (Maykov), T, 1880
Iz Shillera [From Schiller] (Tyutchev), T, B, 1881
Polden' [Noon] (Tyutchev), A, B, 1881
Fugue, c, S, A, T, B/?chorus, 1883
Kak nezhish' tï! [How luxurious you are!] (Fet), T, B, 1883
2 Duets (Pushkin), 2 B, 1884: Bakhicheskaya pesnya [Bacchic song] [1st version of op.18 no.2]; Solovey [The nightingale]
Serenade on the departure of the Marquise de Fige (A. K. Tolstoy), B, 1884 [1st version of op.17 no.5]
Kolïshetsya more [The sea heaves] (A. K. Tolstoy), B, 1884
Madrigal (Taneyev), S, A, B/?chorus, 1884
2 Duets, 2 B, 1886: Nochnoy zefir [The night zephyr] (Pushkin); Vesnoy, volshebnoyu vesnoy [In enchanted spring] (Grekov)
Iz Gafiz [From Gafiz] (Maslov), Bar, 1886
Adeli [To Adèle] (Pushkin), 4 B [1st version of op.24 no.2]
Syadu zavtra ya k okoshechku [Yesterday I sat by the little window] (Taneyev), 4vv/chorus, 1887
Iz Shelli [From Shelley] (Bal'mont, after Shelley), 1895: Mechtï v odinochestve vyanut [Dreams wither in solitude]; Pust' otzvuchit [Let it sound no more] [1st versions of op.17 nos. 2 and 3]
3 comic canons for Leonid Sabaneyev (Esperanto texts), solo vv/?chorus, 1895
Kolïbel'naya pesnya [Cradle song] (Bal'mont), 1v, 1896, rev. version (Moscow, 1916)
Sonoriloi di vespero [The evening bell] (Esperanto text), 1v, ?1894–6
Se premas min dolore (Esperanto text, after Lermontov: Molitva [Prayer]), 1v, 1896
2 Romances, 1v, pf, mand, op.9, 1899 (Leipzig, 1899): Venetsiya noch'yu [Venice at night] (Fet); Serenada [Serenade] (Khomyakov)
10 Romances, 1v, op.17 (Leipzig, 1905): Ostrovok [The island]

(Bal'mont, after Shelley), 1905; Mechtï v odinochestve vyanut [Dreams wither in solitude] (Bal'mont, after Shelley), 1895, rev.1905; Pust' otzvuchit [Let it sound no more] (Bal'mont, after Shelley), 1895, rev.1905; Blazhennïkh snov ushla zvezda [The star of the blessed ones again disappears] (Bal'mont, after Shelley), 1905; Ne veter veya s vïsotï [Not the wind blowing from the heights] (Tolstoy), 1884, rev. 1905; Kogda, kruzhas', osenniye listï [When the whirling autumn leaves] (Ellis, after Stecchetti), 1905; Noktyurn: Aromatnoy vesenneyu noch'yu [Nocturne: In the scented autumn night] (Shcherbina), 1905; V dïmke nevidimke [In the invisible mist] (Fet), 1905; B'yotsya serdtse bespokoynoye [The restless heart is beating] (Nekrasov), 1905; Lyudi spit [The world sleeps] (Fet), 1905
2 Duets, 2 vv, orch/pf, op.18 (Leipzig, 1906): Kak nezhish' tï! [How luxurious you are!] (Fet), Mez, T, 1905; Bakhicheskaya pesnya [Bacchic song] (Pushkin), T, B, 1884, rev. 1905
Neostïvshaya ot znogi [Still sweltering from the heat] (Tyutchev), S, A, T, 1907 [orig. no.3 in a cycle of 4 terzettos, of which nos.1, 2 and 4 were pubd as op.23]
3 Terzettos (Tyutchev), S, A, T, op.23, 1907 (Moscow, 1908): Sonet Mikel-Andzhelo [Sonnet by Michelangelo]; Rim noch'yu [Rome at night]; Tikhoy noch'yu [In the silent night]
2 Quartets (Pushkin), S, A, T, op.24 (Moscow, 1908): Monastïr na Kazbeke [The monastery on the Kazbek], 1907; Adeli [To Adèle], rev. 1907
S ozera veyet [It blows from the lake] (Tyutchev, after Schiller), S, A, T, orch, op.25, 1907 (Moscow, 1908)
10 Romances from Ellis's Immortelles, 1v, op.26, 1908 (Moscow, 1909): Rozhdeniye arfï [The birth of the harp] (after Moore); Canzone XXXII (after Dante) [later arr. with acc. for vn, vc and pf]; Otsvetï [Reflections] (after Maeterlinck); Muzïka [Music] (after Baudelaire); Lesa dremuchiye [Thick woods] (after Baudelaire); Stalaktitï [Stalactites] (after Sully-Prudhomme); Fontanï [Fountains] (after Rodenbach); I drognuli vragi [And the enemy trembled] (after Heredia); Menuet [Minuet] (after d'Orias); Sredi vragov [Among the foe] (after Nietzsche)
4 Songs (Polonsky), 1v, op.32, 1911 (Moscow, 1911): V godinu utratï [In time of loss]; Angel [The angel]; Moy um podavlen bïl toskoy [My mind was crushed by melancholy]; Zimnïy put' [The winter road]
5 Songs (Polonsky), 1v, op.33, 1911 (Moscow, 1912): Noch' v gorakh Shotlandiy [Night in the mountains of Scotland]; Svet voskhodyashchikh zvyozd [The light of the rising stars]; Potseluy [The kiss]; Chto mne ona? [What is she to me?]; Uznik [The prisoner]
7 Songs (Polonsky), 1v, op.34, 1911 (Moscow, 1912): Posledniy razgovor [The last talk]; Ne moy li strasti? [Are they not my passions?]; Maska [The mask]; Lyubya kolos'yev myagkiy shorakh [Loving the soft rustle of the ears of corn]; Posledniy vzdokh [The last sigh]; Noch' v Krïmu [Night in the Crimea]; Moyo serdtse – rodnik [My heart is a spring]
Kolïbel'naya pesnya [Cradle song] (Bal'mont), 1v, 1915
Nakhodka [The windfall] (Kolomizev, after Goethe), 1v

WORK ON TCHAIKOVSKY'S COMPOSITIONS
Pf arrangements: Sym. no.4 arr. pf 4 hands (Moscow, 1879); Sym. no.5 arr. pf 4 hands, 1888; Iolanta, vocal score (Moscow, 1892); The Nutcracker, arr. solo pf, ?1892; Count Almaviva's couplets from The Barber of Seville, vocal score, 1905
Orchestrations: Ni slova, o drug moy [Not a word, O my friend], op.6 no.2; Ne otkhodi ot menya [Do not leave me], op.27 no.3, 1891; Strashnaya minuta [The fearful minute], op.28 no.6, 1891; V ogorode, vozle brodu [In the garden, near the ford], op.46 no.4; Pesn' tsïganki [Gypsy's song], op.60 no.7, 1891; Serenada [Serenade], op.63 no.6; Noch' [Night]
Completions: Duet for Romeo and Juliet, completed and orchd (Moscow, 1894); Andante and Finale, pf, orch, op.79, completed and orchd (Moscow, 1897); Impromptu, A♭, pf, completed (Moscow, 1898)

OTHER ARRANGEMENTS
2 Italian songs: Voca, voca, arr. SATB, pf, 1880; Addio, mia bella Napoli, arr. SAB, pf, 1880
Transcrs. of 20 Caucasian folktunes, 1885
1st movt of Arensky's orch Suite, op.7, arr. pf 4 hands, ?1886
Transcrs. of folksongs, 27 Ukrainian and 1 Russian, c1880–90
2 Belorussian spring songs arr. ob, harp, ?1907
Vocal score of Arensky's Gimn iskusstvu [Hymn to art], 1913

For further details of sketches, very fragmentary pieces and student exercises see Popov; for details of projected operas see Belza

WRITINGS
['O muzïke gorskikh tatar'], *Vestnik Evropï*, xxi/1 (1886), 94
Podvizhnoy kontrapunkt strogovo pis'ma [Invertible counterpoint in the strict style] (Leipzig and Moscow, 1909; Eng. trans., 1962)
ed. V. M. Belyayev: *Ucheniye o kanone* [The study of canon] (Moscow, 1929)

BIBLIOGRAPHY
N. A. Rimsky-Korsakov: *Letopis' moyey muzïkal'noy zhizni* [Chronicle of my musical life] (St Petersburg, 1909, 3/1928; Eng. trans., 1942)

I. Glebov [B. V. Asaf'yev]: *Oresteya . . .: analiza muzïkal'novo soderzhaniya* [The Oresteia: analysis of its musical content] (Moscow, 1916)

V. Karatïgin: 'Neizdannïye simfonii S. I. Taneyeva' [Taneyev's unpublished symphonies], *MS* (1916), no.2, p.104

M. Tchaikovsky, ed.: *Pis'ma P. I. Chaykovskovo i S. I. Taneyeva* [Letters of Tchaikovsky and Taneyev] (Moscow, 1916)

K. A. Kuznetsov, ed.: *Sergey Ivanovich Taneyev* (Moscow and Leningrad, 1925)

S. S. Popov: 'Neizdannïye sochineniya i rabotï S. I. Taneyeva: arkheograficheskiy ocherk' [Taneyev's unpublished compositions and works], *Sergey Ivanovich Taneyev*, ed. K. A. Kuznetsov (Moscow and Leningrad, 1925), 113

V. V. Yakovlev: *Sergey Ivanovich Taneyev: evo muzïkal'naya zhizn'* [Taneyev's musical life] (Moscow, 1927)

B. V. Asaf'yev: *Russkaya muzïka ot nachala XIX stoletiya* [Russian music from the beginning of the 19th century] (Moscow and Leningrad, 1930; Eng. trans., 1953)

L. L. Sabaneyev: *S. I. Taneyev: mïsli o tvorchestve i vospominaniya o zhizni* [Thoughts about his work and reminiscences of his life] (Paris, 1930)

G. Abraham: 'Sergeï Taneïef', in M. D. Calvocoressi and G. Abraham: *Masters of Russian Music* (London, 1936), 439

A. Al'shvang: 'Perepiska S. I. Taneyeva i N. N. Amani' [Correspondence between Taneyev and Amani], *SovM* (1940), no.7, p.61

I. F. Belza, ed.: *S. I. Taneyev i russkaya opera: sbornik statey* [Taneyev and Russian opera: collection of articles] (Moscow, 1946)

V. V. Protopopov, ed.: *Pamyati Sergeya Ivanovicha Taneyeva 1856–1946: sbornik statey i materialov k 90-letiyu so dnya rozhdeniya* [In memory of Taneyev: a collection of articles and materials for the 90th anniversary of his birth] (Moscow and Leningrad, 1947)

G. Bernandt: *S. I. Taneyev* (Moscow and Leningrad, 1950)

V. A. Zhdanov, ed.: *P. I. Chaykovsky, S. I. Taneyev: pis'ma* [Letters] (Moscow, 1951)

V. A. Kiselyov and others, eds.: *S. I. Taneyev: materialï i dokumentï* (Moscow, 1952)

Yu. Keldïsh: *Istoriya russkoy muzïki*, iii (Moscow, 1954)

T. de Hartmann: 'Sergeii Ivanovitch Taneieff', *Tempo* (1956), no.39, p.8

J. Weinberg: 'Sergei Ivanovitch Taneiev', *MQ*, xliv (1958), 19

L. Korabel'nikova, ed.: 'Novïye materialï o S. Taneyeve' [New material on Taneyev], *SovM* (1959), no.9, p.70

M. Velimirović: 'Russian Autographs at Harvard', *Notes*, xvii (1959–60), 555

A. Alexandrov: 'Iz vospominaniy o Taneyeve' [From reminiscences about Taneyev], *SovM* (1963), no.5, p.28; no.8, p.50

F. G. Arzamanov: *S. I. Taneyev: prepodavatel' kursa muzïkal'nïkh form* [Teacher of a course in musical form] (Moscow, 1963)

S. V. Evseyev: *Narodnïye i natsional'nïye korni muzïkal'novo yazïka S. I. Taneyeva* (Moscow, 1963)

M. I. Fikhtengolts: *Kontsertnaya syuita dlya skripki i orkestra S. I. Taneyeva* [Taneyev's Concert Suite for violin and orchestra] (Moscow, 1963)

A. Alexandrov and F. Gartmann: 'Vospominaniya o S. I. Taneyeve' [Reminiscences about Taneyev], *SovM* (1965), no.6, p.64

J. Gardner: 'A Russian Contrapuntist', *Composer* (1965), no.17, p.6

T. A. Khoprova: *S. I. Taneyev* (Leningrad, 1968)

N. Bazhanov: *Taneyev* (Moscow, 1971)

V. Blok: 'Nezaverchennaya simfoniya Taneyeva' [The unfinished symphony of Taneyev], *SovM* (1974), no.4, p.84

L. Korabel'nikova: *S. I. Taneyev v Moskovskoy konservatorii* (Moscow, 1974)

DAVID BROWN

Tangent. (1) The brass blade at the back of a clavichord key which strikes the string when the front of the key is depressed (*see* CLAVICHORD, fig.1).

(2) In some 17th- and 18th-century writings from Germany and the Low Countries, a JACK.

Tangent piano (Ger. *Tangentenflügel*). A keyboard instrument whose strings are struck by freely moving slips of wood resembling harpsichord jacks rather than by hinged or pivoted hammers. The most important instrument of this type was the *Tangentenflügel* said to have been invented in 1751 by Franz Jakob Späth the younger and made by him (in partnership with his son-in-law Christoph Friedrich Schmahl after 1774) in Regensburg. The tangent piano principle was, however, incorporated in a number of other designs both earlier and later, none of which can be shown to have had any direct connection with Späth's. It is embodied in the actions devised by Jean Marius in 1716 and Christoph Gottlied Schröter in 1739 but not published until 1763; and a grand piano action patented in England in 1787 by Humphrey Walton (no.1607) altered the ordinary square piano action by making the hammer propel a padded jack-like striking element towards the strings. In addition, a number of surviving harpsichords and virginals were converted to instruments of the tangent piano type simply by replacing their jacks with shorter slips of wood and then shifting either these or the strings so that the short jack-like pieces would strike the strings from below when the keys were depressed.

None of these converted instruments, however, includes the refinements found in Späth and Schmahl's instruments, of which all the surviving examples seem to

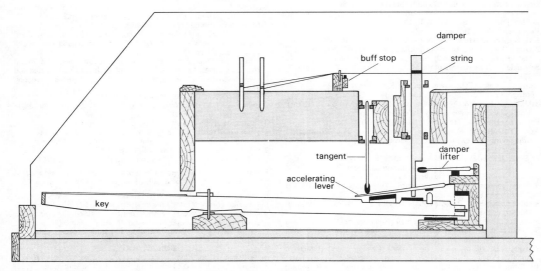

Diagram of the action of a tangent piano (1800) by Christoph Friedrich Schmahl

have been made after 1790. The action of these instruments includes an intermediate lever to increase the velocity with which the jack-like striking element is propelled towards the strings, as well as a large assortment of tone-altering devices, including means for raising the dampers, for introducing a strip of cloth between the striking elements and the strings, for shifting the striking elements sideways so that they strike only one of the two strings provided for each note, and a buff stop that mutes the strings by pressing a piece of leather or cloth against them at the nut; moreover, in several of the surviving examples one or more of these devices can be used separately in the treble and bass. These instruments look very like grand pianos of the period and, as in pianos, the loudness of their sound is determined by the force with which the keys are struck, although the action is far less complicated. Their sound is very beautiful, especially when one of the muting devices tempers the somewhat metallic sound of the bare wooden striking elements against the strings.

The conversions from quilled instruments must be thought of as makeshifts and the tangent piano actions of Marius and Schröter were experimental constructions, each employed in only a single instrument (if, indeed, any instruments employing them were ever built), but the developed tangent piano is neither an experiment nor a compromise. Rather, it is a valuable instrument in its own right, and is the only one of many short-lived 18th-century keyboard instruments to survive in sufficient numbers for it to be judged on its merits. The rest, including two developed by Johann Andreas Stein and a number produced by the highly inventive Parisian makers of the period, have vanished entirely, leaving nothing but the enthusiastic claims of their inventors on which to speculate.

BIBLIOGRAPHY

H. Herrmann: *Die Regensburger Klavierbauer Späth und Schmahl und ihr Tangentenflügel* (Erlangen, 1928)

R. E. M. Harding: *The Piano-forte: its History Traced to the Great Exhibition of 1851* (Cambridge, 1933, rev. 2/1978), 48ff

E. M. Ripin: 'En Route to the Piano', *Metropolitan Museum Journal*, x (1976)

EDWIN M. RIPIN

Tanglewood. Estate where the BERKSHIRE FESTIVAL is held.

Tango. A Latin American song and dance genre. The etymology of the word 'tango' is still much debated. During the 19th century in Spain and several Latin American countries the term designated various types of dances, songs and communal festivities. Fernando Ortiz and others claim the word is of African origin with the general meaning 'African dance'. Others believe it is of Castilian origin, derived from the old Spanish word *tañer* (*taño*; 'to play' an instrument). Rossi and Vega stated that the term 'tango' was used by black slaves in the La Plata area (Argentina and Uruguay) from colonial times to designate their percussion instruments (particularly drums), the locale of the dance and the dance itself. By the first decades of the 19th century the meaning was extended to black *comparsas*, festive carnival groups in Montevideo also known as *candombe*. As late as 1900 the Cuban *comparsas* (a type of carnival parade) were designated as tangos. From the mid-19th century there are references to the Spanish Andalusian or gypsy ('flamenco') tango. From a musical viewpoint (particularly as regards rhythm), however, there is little doubt that the internationally known tango – the fore-

most Argentine and Uruguayan urban popular song and dance – is related to the Cuban *contradanza*, habanera and Cuban tango. The latter, together with the habanera, had spread throughout Latin America by the 1850s. In Brazil as well as in the Río de la Plata area 'tango' was the name given to the habanera itself during the latter part of the 19th century. The *tango brasileiro* was at first nothing more than a local adaptation of the Cuban habanera. Several popular genres including the MAXIXE developed from the habanera. All of these dances have in common the prevailing duple metre (2/4), the accompanimental patterns shown in ex.1*a* and *b*, and the formal sectional designs of the European polka.

Ex.1 Accompaniment patterns

(a)   (b)

Despite its many meanings 'tango' primarily designates the most popular Argentine urban dance of the 20th century: it is one of the most expressive and nationalistic symbols of the Argentine character. The tango is said to have developed in the *arrabal* or *orillas* (poor slum areas) on the outskirts of Buenos Aires. The *arrabal* or suburban culture consisted of elements introduced after 1870 by millions of frustrated European immigrants, and aspects of urbanized pampa (or gaucho) traditions. Gaucho musical traditions were especially represented by the *payada* and the MILONGA. The improvised song texts of the *payada* often referred to current events, and frequently voiced social protest. The *milonga*, a dance of alleged African origin in duple metre and syncopated rhythm, contributed to the rhythmic structure of the tango. Most tango scholars, however, interpret the dance as being at first an adaptation of the Andalusian tango, and the Cuban DANZÓN and habanera. Until after 1915 the tango maintained the duple metre (2/4) of the habanera and *milonga*, after which 4/4 or 4/8 became more frequent; after 1955 new rhythmic complexities developed. Three types of tango may be distinguished: the *tango-milonga*, the *tango-romanza* and the *tango-canción*. The *tango-milonga* is strictly instrumental (for popular orchestras) and has a strong rhythmic character; the most 'classic' example is the tango *Boedo* (1928) by Julio De Caro (although it originally included lyrics by Dante Linyera, these were rarely used in performance). The *tango-romanza*, either instrumental or vocal, is more lyrical and melodic, and has a strongly romantic text; one of the best known is *Flores negras* (1928) by Francisco De Caro, considered a model of refined lyricism in tango style. The *tango-canción*, as its qualification indicates, is always vocal with instrumental accompaniment and has a strong sentimental character. This type represented, particularly in the 1930s, the tango's transformation into a wider urban popular genre no longer associated primarily with the underworld of the *arrabal*. The lyrics of the 'tango-song', however, continued to express views of love and life in highly pessimistic, fatalistic and often pathologically dramatic terms, as was the case in the intensely bitter, ill-humoured and introverted songs of the *arrabal*. During the same period social protest themes appeared in numerous tango-songs. Some of the best examples of tango-songs include Samuel Castriota's *Mi noche triste* (c1915), Julio César Sanders's *Adiós muchachos* (1928), Enrique Delfino's *Milonguita* (1920) and Anibal Troilo's *Sur* (1948).

From a structural viewpoint the first tangos tended to have a tripartite form, but after about 1915 the two-part form began to predominate. Delfino (1895–1967) is considered the first composer to have established the standard form of the tango: two parts of equal length (14 to 20 bars), the second generally in the dominant or the relative minor of the main key. The first instrumental ensembles performing tangos were *tercetos* (trios), generally including violin, guitar and flute, with accordion frequently replacing the guitar. Numerous pieces were also written for piano solo, and voice with piano accompaniment. About 1900 the new trio included piano, violin and *bandoneón* (diatonic accordion with 38 keys or buttons for the high and medium registers and 33 for the low register, in the most classic size adopted by *bandoneón* tango players). Vicente Greco (1888–1924), a famous composer and band-leader, is generally credited as the first to standardize the ensemble which he called Orquesta Típica Criolla, and which initially included violin, flute, guitar and *bandoneón*. Greco's ensemble was first recorded in 1911 (with two violins and two *bandoneones*). After that, larger bands were formed, culminating with ensembles of up to four *bandoneones*, a sizable string section, with violins, a cello, a double bass, and a piano. Often during the 1930s and 1940s vocal duets were added to the instrumental groups. Ensembles that gained great popularity included those of Juan Maglio ('Pacho'), Roberto Firpo, Francisco Canaros and Eduardo Arelas. Some of the best-known bands included the Orquesta Típica 'Select' (established in 1919), the Orquesta Típica 'Victor' (1925) formed to record for RCA, the Orquesta Típica 'Novel' (1934) and the Orquesta Típica 'Los Provincianos' under the famous *bandoneón* player and composer, Ciriaco Ortiz (*b* 1908). Under the influence of Astor Piazzolla (*b* 1921) the large orchestral arrangements with percussion instruments and other additional colours appeared in the 1940s, breaking away from the *orquesta típica* arrangement. In the 1960s Piazzolla introduced the electric guitar in smaller ensembles, for example in his Quinteto 'Tango Nuevo'.

The internationalization of the tango took place during the first 15 years of the 20th century. It became fashionable in Parisian society after 1907 when Camille de Rhynal (or 'Tod Cams'), a dancer, dance teacher and producer of dance competitions, modified the abrupt movements which were considered too crude for the ballroom. In England it became popular from 1912, when it was danced by George Grossmith and Phyllis Dare in *The Sunshine Girl* (Gaiety Theatre), and soon was being danced in restaurants and at tango parties or 'tango teas'. After World War I it became the most popular ballroom dance with many bands and featured in most dance competitions. The extraordinary figure Carlos Gardel (1887–1935) was particularly influential in making it fashionable throughout Europe and the western hemisphere; in the 1920s he became an Argentine popular idol whose legend still continues. Himself a product of the *arrabal*, Gardel came to symbolize the fulfilment of the dreams of the poor *porteño*. One of his major contributions to the history of the tango was to transform it from its strictly dancing character to a song type of socio-cultural significance, and a type with which Argentines of different social classes could identify. Besides his own recordings of well-known tangos and his numerous appearances in classic films, his best-known compositions include *El día que me quieras, Mi Buenos Aires querido, Por una cabeza, Volver, Silencio* and *Cuesta abajo*. Perhaps the most popular tango ever written was Gerardo Matos Rodríguez's *La cumparsita* (1917). Other representative pieces of the international repertory are Sanders's *Adiós muchachos* (1928), Enrique Santos Discépolo's *Yira, yira* (1930), Juan Carlos Cobián's *Nostalgia* (*c*1930), Francisco Canaro's *Adiós, pampa mía* and Edgardo Donato's *A media luz*.

The choreography of the tango is also symbolic of the *arrabal* culture, in that dance figures, postures and gestures reflect some of the mannerisms and style of the *compadrito*, a popular hero similar to Don Juan, and a pimp in the early Buenos Aires *barrios* (districts). Mafud (1966) interpreted the straight, immobile upper body of the male dancer as a reflection of the characteristic posture of the *compadrito*; he related the smooth pattern of steps to the same patterns in the creole knife duels, and the forward tilt of the spine to the use of elegant high-heeled shoes. The major theme of the tango as a dance for embracing couples is the obvious domination of the male over the female, in a series of steps and a very close embrace highly suggestive of the sexual act. Characteristic of the dance is the contrast between the very active male and the apparently passive female. Taylor (1976) interpreted this as a danced statement of *machismo* (manly assertion), confidence and sexual optimism.

The tango lost some of its earlier popularity in the late 1940s and 1950s but it was revived in the 1960s and 1970s. In Argentina, however, the socio-cultural

The 'pas oriental à gauche' from 'The Tango and How to Dance It' (1913) by Gladys Beattie Crozier

complex of the tango has always attracted the attention of both intellectuals and other social strata, including the younger generation of the 1970s.

BIBLIOGRAPHY

F. Ortiz: *Hampa afro-cubana: glosario de afronegrismos* (Havana, 1924)
V. Rossi: *Cosas de negros* (Buenos Aires, 1926)
C. Vega: *Danzas y canciones argentinas* (Buenos Aires, 1936)
I. Carella: *El tango* (Buenos Aires, 1956)
H. Ferrer: *El tango: su historia y su evolución* (Buenos Aires, 1960)
T. de Lara: *El tema del tango en la literatura argentina* (Buenos Aires, 1961)
J. de Caro: *El tango en mis recuerdos* (Buenos Aires, 1964)
F. García Jiménez: *El tango: historia de medio siglo, 1880–1930* (Buenos Aires, 1964)
H. Milkewitz: *Psicología del tango* (Montevideo, 1964)
D. D. Vidart: *Teoría del tango* (Montevideo, 1964)
A. Chinarro: *El tango y su rebelión* (Buenos Aires, 1965)
F. Diego Astigueta: 'La mentalidad argentina en el tango y sus modismos', *Journal of Inter-American Studies*, vii/1 (1965), 67
F. García Jiménez: *Así nacieron los tangos* (Buenos Aires, 1965)
E. Sábato: *El tango: discusión y clave* (Buenos Aires, 1965)
I. Vilariño: *Las letras del tango* (Buenos Aires, 1965)
C. Castillo, ed.: *Buenos Aires: tiempo Gardel* (Buenos Aires, 1966)
J. Mafud: *La sociología del tango* (Buenos Aires, 1966)
L. A. Sierra: *Historia de la orquesta típica: evolución instrumental del tango* (Buenos Aires, 1966)
R. O. Cerrutti: *El tango* (Resistencia, 1967)
N. Ulla: *Tango, rebelión y nostalgia* (Buenos Aires, 1967)
C. Vega: 'Las especies homónimas y afines de "Los orígenes del tango Argentino" ', *Revista musical chilena* (1967), no.101, p.49
D. Vidart: *El tango y su mundo* (Montevideo, 1967)
D. Canton: 'El mundo de los tangos de Gardel', *Revista latinoamericana de sociología*, iv (1968), 341
A. Defino: *Carlos Gardel: la verdad de una vida* (Buenos Aires, 1968)
F. García Jiménez: *Estampas de tango* (Buenos Aires, 1968)
R. Cavadini: *¿Tango o nueva expresión de Buenos Aires?* (Buenos Aires, 1969)
B. Matamoro: *La ciudad del tango* (Buenos Aires, 1969)
H. Ferrer: *El libro del tango* (Buenos Aires, 1970)
J. Barcia: *Discepolín* (Buenos Aires, 1971)
B. Matamoro: *Carlos Gardel* (Buenos Aires, 1971)
——: *Historia del tango* (Buenos Aires, 1971)
C. Sobrino: *Diccionario del tango* (Buenos Aires, 1971)
O. Bozzarelli: *Ochenta años de tango platense* (La Plata, 1972)
R. Briand: *Crónicas del tango alegre* (Buenos Aires, 1972)
J. Portogalo: *Buenos Aires: tango y literatura* (Buenos Aires, 1972)
J. M. Taylor: 'Tango: Theme of Class and Nation', *EM*, xx (1976), 273

GERARD BÉHAGUE

T'an Hsin-p'ei (*b* Hupeh, 23 April 1847; *d* Peking, 10 May 1917). Chinese opera actor. He began training for the stage at the age of ten and was for a time the disciple of Ch'eng Chang-keng and a member of the latter's San-ch'ing company. Later he founded his own troupe, the T'ung-ch'ing, and became a distinguished *lao-sheng* actor of Peking opera (*see* CHINA, §III, 2(i)). He spent most of his life in Peking but travelled frequently to Tientsin and four times to Shanghai, the last being in 1913. His greatest social success was to become the favourite actor of the Empress Dowager Tz'u-hsi. T'an had a powerful voice but as a performer he was better known for his capacity to absorb and transmit the best features of earlier masters than for his creativity. Five of his 11 children became actors.

BIBLIOGRAPHY

K. Hatano: *Shina geki to sono meiyu* [Chinese opera and its famous actors] (Tokyo, 1925; Chin. trans., 1926, as *Ching-chü erh-pai nien chih li-shih* [The history of Peking opera over 200 years]), 39ff

COLIN MACKERRAS

Tanhûser, Der. *See* TANNHÄUSER, DER.

Tannenberg [Tanneberg, Tanneberger], **David** (*b* Berthelsdorf, Upper Lusatia, 21 March 1728; *d* York, Pennsylvania, 19 May 1804). Moravian–American organ builder. Brought up in Count Zinzendorf's religious community of Herrnhut, he went to America with a group of Moravian colonists in 1749, settling in Bethlehem, Pennsylvania. At first he worked as a joiner both there and in nearby Nazareth, but in 1757 the organ builder J. G. Klemm went to Bethlehem, and shortly afterwards Tannenberg became his assistant. Tannenberg worked with Klemm until the latter's death in 1762. Continuing his new occupation, he moved to Lititz, Pennsylvania, in 1765. There the majority of his organs were built, at an average of one a year until his death (he also built some harpsichords and virginals).

Although Tannenberg occasionally travelled as far as North Carolina or northern New York in his work he was at heart a provincial; very few outside influences can be found in the almost pure South German idiom of his work which was his legacy from Klemm. His organ cases were well-proportioned, with handsome, carved decorations. All are said to have been originally painted white with gold trimming. Many of his instruments were for small churches, with only one manual; his largest were built for Holy Trinity Lutheran Church, Lancaster, Pennsylvania (1774), and Zion Lutheran Church, Philadelphia (1790). In his later years Tannenberg was assisted by Philip Bachmann (1762–1837), who succeeded him on his death.

BARBARA OWEN

Tannhäuser [Danhuser, Don heusser, Tanvser, Tanhûser], **Der** (*b* c1205; *d* c1270). German Minnesinger. He was of noble birth, and probably came from Bavaria. Six Leiche and ten lieder survive in the Manesse manuscript (*D-HEu* cpg 848, without music). They show his life as one of adventurous travel: he participated in the fifth crusade (1228–33) and the Cypriot war as well as spending time at the court of Friedrich II 'der Streitbare' in Vienna (*see also* WALTHER VON DER VOGELWEIDE), that of Otto II of Bavaria in Landshut, and elsewhere. In his lyric verse there is a mixture of seriousness and humour, of courtliness and satirical parody. The dance-songs depict the joys of life and of courtly love with a new and realistic spontaneity which reveals above all the influence of Neidhart von Reuental.

There is some doubt as to which melodies are actually by Tannhäuser and which were merely ascribed to him later. The Tannhäuser legend of the knight who paid court to Venus and sought papal absolution developed as early as the 14th century, so for the Meistersinger he was counted among the 12 *alte Meister*, and several spurious melodies and *Töne* (*see* TON (i)) were considered his. The *Tannhäuserlied* (c1520) was reprinted by Achim von Arnim and Clemens Brentano in their collection *Des Knaben Wunderhorn* (1806) and was extensively reworked in 19th-century German literature: Tieck's *Novelle* entitled *Der getreue Eckart und der Tannhäuser* (1800), the ballades of Heine (1836), Geibel (1838) and Brentano (*Romanzen vom Rosenkranz*, published posthumously in 1852), the operas of Wagner (1845) and C. A. Mangold (1846, later revived as *Der getreue Eckart*) and the epic poem of Grisebach (*Der neue Tannhäuser*, 1869). In most of these the character of Tannhäuser was conflated with that of HEINRICH VON OFTERDINGEN.

WORKS

Editions: *Der Dichter Tannhäuser: Leben – Gedichte – Sage*, ed. J. Siebert (Halle, 1934) [S] [standard complete text edn.]
      Tannhäuser, ed. H. Lomnitzer and U. Müller, Litterae, xiii (Göppingen, 1973) [LM] [complete edn. of authentic texts and melodies, incl. facs. and comprehensive bibliography]

Hie vor do stuont min Dinc also (text only), S xii, ? text for the 'Hofton' in several Meistersinger MSS (*D-Ju* El.fol.100, f.138, *WRtl* Q576.l, f.71*v*, *PL-WRu* 356 [lost: Adam Puschman's *Singebuch*]) with different texts and modified melody; ed. G. Münzer, *Das Singebuch des Adam Puschman* (Leipzig, 1906/*R*1970), 70

Ich lobe ein Wîp, diu ist noch bezzer danne guot (text only), S iv, model for conductus 'Syon egredere nunc de cubilibus' (*D-Mbs* clm 5539, f.161); ed. in Kuhn, 111ff, and LM 59–70

Staeter dienest der ist guot (text only), S ix, ? text for 'Des Danhusers luode Leich' (*D-Mbs* cgm 4997 (Colmar MS), ff.72–73*v*, with inc. melody and the text 'Mir tet gar wol ein lieber Won'); LM 46ff (facs.) and 72 (edn.)

MELODIES OF DOUBTFUL AUTHORSHIP
Ez ist hivte eyn wunnychlicher Tac ('Busslied'), S p.207, in the Jena MS (*D-Ju* El.f.101), f.42*v*–43, ascribed 'Der Tanvser' but text and music doubtful; LM 29ff (facs.) and 71 (edn.)

Tanhusers heupt Ton oder gulden Ton', *D-Mbs* cgm 4997, f.785 with text 'Gelückes waer mir Nôt', ? spurious; text is 14th- or 15th-century Meistersinger Spruch; melody probably also later; variants in other 15th- and 16th-century MSS; ed. P. Runge, *Die Sangesweisen der Colmarer Handschrift* (Leipzig, 1896/*R*1965), 169

'Langer Ton', unauthentic; in several 16th- and 17th-century Meistersinger MSS

BIBLIOGRAPHY
H. Spanke: 'Eine neue Leich-melodie', *ZMw*, xiv (1931–2), 385 [on S iv]

J. Siebert: *Der Dichter Tannhäuser: Leben – Gedichte – Sage* (Halle, 1934)

M. Lang: *Tannhäuser*, Von deutscher Poeterey, xvii (Leipzig, 1936)

M. Lang and J. Müller-Blattau, eds.: *Zwischen Minnesang und Volkslied: die Lieder der Berliner Handschrift Germ. fol. 922* (Berlin, 1941) [on S ix, pp.27–9, 58f, 90]

H. Kuhn: *Minnesangs Wende* (Tübingen, 1952, 2/1967) [on S iv]

H. de Boor: *Geschichte der deutschen Literatur*, ii (Munich, 1953, rev. 5/1962, 9/1974), 370ff, 509

K. H. Bertau: *Sangverslyrik: über Gestalt und Geschichtlichkeit mittelhochdeutscher Lyrik am Beispiel des Leichs*, Palaestra, ccxl (Göttingen, 1964) [on S iv]

M. Wis: 'Ursprünge der deutschen Tannhäuserlegende', *Neuphilologische Mitteilungen*, lxi (1966), 8–58

R. J. Taylor: *The Art of the Minnesinger* (Cardiff, 1968)

H. Lomnitzer and U. Müller, eds.: *Tannhäuser*, Litterae, xiii (Göppingen, 1973) [with bibliography]

For further bibliography *see* MINNESANG.

BURKHARD KIPPENBERG

Tanpurā. See TAMBURĀ.

Tansman, Alexandre [Aleksander] (*b* Łódź, 12 June 1897). French composer, conductor and pianist of Polish origin. Having begun to compose at the age of eight, he studied the piano, harmony and counterpoint at the Łódź Conservatory (1902–14), and then followed courses in law and philosophy at Warsaw University, taking lessons in counterpoint, form and composition with Rytel. In 1919 he sent in two works, under different pseudonyms, to the Polish National Music Competition: the *Fantaisie* for violin and piano won first prize and the Piano Sonata second prize. This success enabled him to move to Paris, where he arrived in October 1919. He became acquainted with Ravel, Roland-Manuel, Milhaud, Honegger and Golschmann, who conducted his *Intermezzo sinfonico* in 1920. After Koussevitzky directed the First Piano Concerto with Tansman as soloist, his music was taken up by Stokowski, Toscanini and Mengelberg. Tansman made his first tour as a pianist in 1927 with the Boston SO under Koussevitzky; later he toured extensively in Europe, Canada and Palestine. He began to conduct his own works and in 1932–3 travelled to the Far East. During World War II he lived in the USA, where he associated with Stravinsky, wrote film music and gave concerts; he was awarded the Coolidge Medal in 1941. He returned to France in 1946 and continued his work as a composer and his annual European concert tours.

Tansman's earliest Parisian music was composed under the influences of Chopin, Stravinsky and Ravel,

but by the early 1920s he was writing pieces of a more individual lyricism and melancholy, such as the Flute Sonata and the orchestral *Danse de la sorcière*. At this time he was close to the ideas of Les Six; Tansman may be compared to Milhaud in his use of folk materials and his ready response to different instrumental combinations. His music also has affinities with that of Stravinsky (to whom Tansman was linked in almost fraternal friendship) in its employment of divergent styles: Tansman is as adept at writing in C major as he is at composing serially and he has made use at different times of atonality and polytonality. The death of Stravinsky stimulated one of his most deeply moving works, the *Stèle* of 1972. Tansman is the author of *Stravinsky* (Paris, 1948; Eng. trans., 1949).

WORKS
(selective list)

STAGE
Sextuor, ballet, 1, 1922; La nuit kurde (opera, 3, prologue, after J.-R. Bloch), 1925, orch suite, 1927; Lumières, ballet, 4 scenes, 1928; La grande ville, ballet, 3 scenes, 2 pf, 1932; Bric à brac, ballet, 3 scenes, 1936; La toison d'or (opéra bouffe, 3, S. de Madariaga), 1938; Ballet mexico américain, 1945; Le roi qui jouait le fou, ballet, 1947; Sabbataï zévi, le faux messie (opera, 4, prologue, N. Bistritzky), 1953; Le serment, opera, 1954; Résurrection, ballet, 4 scenes, 1961; L'usignolo di Boboli (opera, M. Lambroca), 1962; Georges Dandin (opéra comique, 3, Molière), 1974

ORCHESTRAL
Intermezzo sinfonico, 1920; Légende, 1923; Danse de la sorcière, 1923; Sinfonietta, 1924; Sym. no.1, 1925; Ouverture symphonique, 1926; Sym. no.2, a, 1926; 2 pf concs., 1926, 1927; Toccata, 1926; Suite, 2 pf, orch, 1928; Triptyque, str, 1930; 2 intermezzi, 1930; 4 danses polonaises, 1931; Pf Concertino, 1931; Sym. no.3 (Symphonie concertante), pf qt, orch, 1931; 2 mouvements symphoniques, 1932; Partita, str, 1933; Rapsodie hébraïque, 1933; Adagio, str, 1934

Va Conc., 1936; Fantaisie, vc, orch, 1937; Vn Conc., 1937; Variations sur un thème de Frescobaldi, 1938; Sym. no.4, 1939; Rapsodie polonaise, 1941; Etudes symphoniques, 1941; Serenade no.3, 1942; Sym. no.5, d, 1942; Sym. no.7, 1944; Musique pour cordes, 1948; Musique pour orchestre, 1948; Ricercari, 1949; Conc. for Orch, 1954; Cl Conc., 1958; 6 études, 1962; Vc Conc., 1963; Suite concertante, ob, orch, 1967; 4 mouvements, 1968; Concertino, fl, str orch, 1969; Diptyque, 1969; Hommage à Erasme, 1969; Elégie (à la mémoire de Darius Milhaud), 1976

OTHER WORKS
Vocal: 6 mélodies japonaises, 1v, orch, 1919; 6 Songs (N. de Bragança), 1v, orch, 1936; Sym. no.6 'In memoriam', chorus, orch, 1943; Ponctuation française (C. Oulmont), 1v, orch, 1947; Isaïe, le prophète, oratorio, T, chorus, orch, 1951; Prologue et cantate, female chorus, orch, 1956; Psaumes, T, chorus, orch, 1961; Stèle (in memoriam Stravinski), 1v, insts, 1972; many songs

Inst: 8 str qts, 2 str trios, 2 pf trios; Pf Sonata, 1919; Fantaisie, vn, pf, 1919; Sonata, fl, pf, 1925; Suite divertissement, pf qt, 1929; Septet, ob, cl, bn, hn, va, vc, db, 1930; Sonata, vc, pf, 1930; 2 mouvements, 4 vc, 1938; Divertimento, ob, cl, tpt, vc, pf, 1944; Etude concertante, pf, 1968; Hommage à Chopin, gui, 1969; Variations sur un thème de Scriabine, gui, 1972; Musique à six, cl, str qt, pf, 1977; many other chamber and pf works

Incidental music for the theatre, cinema and radio

Principal publishers: Editions françaises de musique, Eschig, Senart, Schott, Universal

BIBLIOGRAPHY
I. Schwerke: *Alexandre Tansman, compositeur polonais* (Paris, 1931)

ANNE GIRARDOT

Tans'ur [Tansur, le Tansur, Tanzer], **William** (*b* Dunchurch, Warwicks., 1700, baptized 6 Nov 1706; *d* St Neots, Hunts., 7 Oct 1783). English psalmodist and theorist. He was the son of a labourer named Edward Tanzer, but generally used the spelling Tans'ur. The main facts of his life emerge from the prefaces to his publications. For many years he travelled to various parts of England as a teacher of psalmody, sometimes working also as an organist. Later he settled at St Neots as a stationer, bookseller and music teacher; surprisingly he seems to have played no part in the music of the local parish church. His son, also named William Tans'ur, was a chorister at Trinity College, Cambridge, on which flimsy pretext the father signed some of his prefaces 'University of Cambridge'. In reality he had no links with the upper strata of English musical life. His field was country music, and here he established a dominance that extended as far as the American colonies.

In 1734 Tans'ur published his first psalmody collection, *A Compleat Melody: or, The Harmony of Sion*, consisting of metrical psalms, hymns and anthems, chiefly of his own composition. The music was in two to four parts without accompaniment, but so contrived that it could be sung throughout in two parts (tenor and bass). The text of the metrical psalms was the Old Version of Sternhold and Hopkins, with revisions by Tans'ur. In 1735 he produced a similar collection, *The Melody of the Heart*, but using the New Version of Tate and Brady. The two books together appeared as *The Works of Mr William Tans'ur* and went into several editions. There were several later compilations, of which the most important was *The Royal Melody Compleat* (1754–5), containing revised versions of earlier pieces and some new compositions as well. It was later printed in revised form as *The American Harmony* (Newburyport, 1771).

Tans'ur was one of the most successful exponents of the elaborate hymn tune of the time, with repeating last lines, solo sections and heavily ornamented melodies. From 1755 he introduced fully 'fuging' tunes, taking care to design them so that the contrapuntal sections could be left out. At least three of his simpler tunes ('Bangor', 'Colchester', 'St Andrew') survived into the 20th century. His anthems are remarkable for their freedom of rhythm, often following the rhythms of speech at the expense of regular musical accent. The basis of his harmony is the two-part combination of tune and bass: the upper parts often produce meaningless clashes, and breaches of the very rules of counterpoint that he laboured in his introductions. His style, as composer and as writer, was pretentious. In the preface to *The Royal Melody Compleat* he lamented that

there are many in this *Age*, that assume the Shape of a *Master*, or *Tutor*, who are so very ignorant, as not to say their *Gamut*; and much less to understand it . . . Many of these will set up for *Composers*, which neither know *Tune*, *Time*, nor *Concord*: And, for all they cut so *ridiculous a Figure* in the Eyes of the *Learned*, yet they gain *Proselytes* luckily amongst the Ignorant.

Unfortunately this comes close to a description of Tans'ur himself.

His principal work of theory, *A New Musical Grammar* (1746), went into several editions, and appeared in revised form as *The Elements of Musick Display'd* (1772); it was still in use in the 19th century (another revised version was published in 1829). Beneath its rather grandiose manner it is a sound treatise of a conservative type, based on the medieval gamut and deriving much from Playford's *Brief Introduction*, but well designed for the aspiring country church musician.

WORKS
(published in London unless otherwise stated)
A Compleat Melody: or, The Harmony of Sion (1734)
The Melody of the Heart (1735)
Heaven on Earth: or, The Beauty of Holiness (1738)
Sacred Mirth: or, The Pious Soul's Daily Delight (1739)
The Royal Psalmodist: or, The New Universal Harmony (Ewell, 1748)
The Royal Melody Compleat: or, The New Harmony of Zion (1754–5); later pubd as The American Harmony (Newburyport, 1771)
The Psalm-singer's Jewel: or, Useful Companion to the Singing-psalms (1760)
The Psalmist's Jewel (1766)
Melodia sacra: or, The Devout Psalmist's New Musical Companion (3/1772)
These collections include 39 anthems, a Te Deum and 2 Magnificat, some responses and chants, and over 100 psalm and hymn tunes, claimed as Tans'ur's own. Daniel (p.54) lists 15 anthems published in New England, but one, Sing ye merrily, is by James Green.

WRITINGS
A New Musical Grammar: or, The Harmonical Spectator, with Philosophical Demonstrations on the Nature of Sound (London, 1746) [5/1772 as *The Elements of Musick Display'd*, 7/1829 as *A Musical Grammar*]
The Life of Holy David (Cambridge, 1770)
The Beauties of Poetry (Cambridge, 1776)

BIBLIOGRAPHY
J. Rix: 'William Tansur', *Notes & Queries*, 4th ser., ii (1868), 257
E. F. Rimbault: 'William Tansur', ibid, 401
A. H. Mann: *Huntingdonshire Musicians* (MS, *GB-NWr* 450)
O. G. T. Sonneck: *Francis Hopkinson and James Lyon* (Washington, 1905/R1967), 166ff
R. T. Daniel: *The Anthem in New England before 1800* (Evanston, 1966), 52ff

NICHOLAS TEMPERLEY

Tanto (It.: 'so much'). In a tempo mark such as *allegro ma non tanto* ('*allegro* but not so much') it should presumably suggest something a little slower than *allegro*; but there is no evidence that this is always the case, and for many composers it is barely distinguishable from *allegro ma non troppo* ('*allegro* but not too much', i.e. do not let it run away, keep it steady).

Tanvser, Der. *See* TANNHÄUSER, DER.

Tanymarian. The bardic name of EDWARD STEPHEN.

Tanz (Ger.). DANCE; *see also* BALLO.

Tanzania. East African republic (formerly Tanganyika, Zanzibar and Pemba). The population is mainly Bantu-speaking with the exception of a number of peoples who live in the northern part of the Rift Valley, including the Kindiga (or Hadzapi) and Sandawe, remnant hunters and gatherers who speak Khoisan languages; the Iraqw, Gorowa (or Goroa) and Burunge, who speak Southern Cushitic languages; and the Masai, who speak an Eastern Sudanic language of the Nilotic family (see fig.1).

1. Historical background. 2. The coastal region and islands. 3. The Nyamwezi and Sukuma area. 4. North-western Tanzania. 5. Central region. 6. The Ruvuma region. 7. The southern highlands and Lake Rukwa region.

1. HISTORICAL BACKGROUND. The Tanzanian coast, like the rest of the east African coast, has had intensive contact with the outside world from the earliest times. The *Periplus of the Erythraean Sea*, written by a Greek merchant in 120, relates how Arab traders settled among the people of the east African coast. About the year 300, sailors from Indonesia visited this part of Africa. Some scholars maintain that, besides bananas and the outrigger canoe, they introduced such instruments as the box-resonated xylophone (*see* MARIMBA) and the *zeze* (flat-bar zither). Box-resonated xylophones are not found in the interior of Tanzania but in the north-eastern parts of the coastal strip, a small area of coastal Kenya and on the islands of Zanzibar and Pemba.

From about 700 onwards Indian Ocean trade increased through the activities of Muslim merchants. In the following centuries the influence of Islam slowly increased. Trade created some cultural separation between the Islamic coast and the interior which had little contact with the Indian Ocean trading network in the

1. Map of Tanzania showing the distribution of major ethnic groups

period from 1000 to 1500. But not all influences were one-sided. Coastal music was also exported. A popular dance of east African minorities now living in Bahrain on the Persian Gulf is called *leiwah*. Its source is probably to be found in Zanzibar or on the coast of Mombasa, and its introduction dates from the political union of Muscat and Zanzibar (c1690–1861).

After 1700 the Nyamwezi, a Bantu people who had settled in central Tanzania, became the leaders in the long-distance ivory trade with the interior. The trade route was from Bagamoyo to Ujiji on Lake Tanganyika, a second route leading from Tabora northwards towards Buganda and Bunyoro. Traditional ivory trumpets, still in good condition, can be seen in villages near Bagamoyo. The power of the Nyamwezi chieftains grew with the increase in trade, so that occasional and ceremonial music became necessary. Large drums were built; perhaps the largest in Tanzania are those in the palace of the Nyamwezi paramount chief at Tabora, at the junction of the trade routes. Wachsmann described this type as 'Uganda drums' (i.e. double-headed drums with the skins laced to cylindro-conical bodies; *see* UGANDA, §§I, 4(iv), II, 1). They have been found among the Nyamwezi, Haya, Sukuma, and even as far south as the Nyakyusa on the northern shore of Lake Malawi, where there were several highly organized kingdom-states (Buganda, Bunyoro etc) in the inter-lacustrine area. These 'royal drums' played an important role as the kings' regalia.

In the 19th century the Ngoni, who are related to the Zulu (*see* NGUNI MUSIC), moved up from what is now South Africa, and some groups finally settled east of Lake Malawi in the present Songea district; they influenced the south-western peoples such as the Pangwa of the Livingstone mountains. The Pangwa mouth-resonated musical bow, the *mtyángala*, played exclusively by young women, derives from the *nqangala* musical bow introduced by the Ngoni. During the 1830s the Nilotic Masai entered Tanzania from Kenya. Their advance was finally halted by the Gogo of Central Province who became culturally influenced by

them. The Masai have had an important influence on the dance decoration and hairstyle of most of their neighbours. Cattle-breeding and -raiding were part of their economic organization, and many of their songs deal with these subjects.

In the colonial and post-colonial periods new musical trends made their mark. Before World War I German military music, and afterwards British army music, had some impact, as did church hymns, particularly in the southern highlands province where Catholic missions had a strong foothold. Later the Christian liturgy became more African in character, as in Stephan Mbunga's *Misa baba yetu* (1959), which is based on traditional songs of the Lake Malawi area. After World War II modern Swahili guitar music had a strong influence, starting when soldiers who had learnt to play rumba music overseas returned from the army. Latin American music on records and later the music of Congolese and Kenyan guitar groups have been the dominating influences on many young guitarists and groups.

2. THE COASTAL REGION AND ISLANDS. Arab influence is particularly strong in music, notably in Zanzibar and Pemba, as can be seen in the playing of the unfretted Swahili *udi* lute (from the Arabic *'ūd*) by musicians such as Ali Othmani of Zanzibar, and Rajabu Madua of Dar es Salaam. In the 1950s a popular centre for this kind of music was the Egyptian Music Club in Dar es Salaam; its leader Bom Amberon established a small orchestra of violins and *udi* which played in the *taarab* style.

Further Arab influence is found in certain aspects of Swahili verse and song. It is difficult to distinguish between song and poetry, for most pieces were intended to be sung or recited. The verb -*som*- ('to read') describes the recitation of certain types, and the verb -*imb*- ('to sing') refers to the performance of a *wimbo* (plural *nyimbo*, 'song'). The main recited forms are the *shairi*, a piece of moderate length on a topic such as love or war, and the *utenzi*, a long, often epic narrative on a religious or historical subject such as the life of the Prophet.

The formal distinction between *nyimbo*, *shairi* and *utenzi* is often blurred. The celebrated Swahili writer and scholar Shaaban Robert thought their difference lay largely in length or elaboration: 'a song is a short *shairi*; a *shairi* is a long song; and a *utenzi* is a *shairi* taken to its extreme'. The recited forms and some of the songs share certain structural features: they can be divided into verses or *beti* (Arabic *bait*); verses can be divided into lines marked by a final rhyming pattern or *kina*; lines can be divided into two hemistichs or *vipande* (singular *kipande*), with the end of the first *kipande* marked by another rhyming pattern or *kituo*; and the hemistich or *kipande* can be measured by the number of its constituent syllables, or *mizani* (from Arabic). In a common *shairi* pattern each of some 40 verses consists of four lines or eight *vipande*, each *kipande* containing eight syllables; and the rhymes at the half line (*vituo*, singular *kituo*) and the full line (*vina*, singular *kina*) form the pattern: *ab, ab, ab, ba*. A common pattern for a *utenzi* is one in which each of some 1000 verses or more consists of two lines or four *vipande*, each *kipande* having a fixed number of syllables (often six or eight), and a rhyme scheme of *aaab* for each verse. Other recited forms include the *tathlitha* with three lines to a verse, the *tarbiya* with four lines to a verse (sometimes considered to be the original model for the *shairi*) and the *takhamisi* with five lines to a verse.

While some *nyimbo* fit the patterns of the recited forms, many have a much less regular line and verse structure and rhyme scheme, with little or no sign of Arab influence. One of the main sung forms is the *taarab*, an essentially urban piece, originally developed as a courtly entertainment for the Sultans and based on Arab and Indian models; it is accompanied by a small ensemble which may include the *udi* lute, the harmonium, the piano accordion and drums. Among other important sung forms are the *gungu*, a praise song sung for traditional rulers or at weddings and other festivities, and the *nyimbo za pungwa*, songs associated with spirits which possess humans and protect many of the coastal communities from their enemies. There is also a large variety of more occasional songs sung by various classes of people on various occasions or at different times of the year.

Other coastal music shows less sign of Arab or Indian influence. Xylophone music, for instance, contrasts with Arab-influenced instrumental styles, as does the Zaramo use of drums and flutes (*viyanzi*) in the *mbeta* dance in which the flute ensemble is accompanied with sticks and rattles. Kwere initiation dances for girls are famous along the coast while among the Zigua, who are also influenced by Indo-Arab culture, the *sero*, *bigilia*, *kinzalia*, *silanga*, *ndekule*, *beni* and *madogoli* dances retain their African traits.

3. THE NYAMWEZI AND SUKUMA AREA. This part of central Tanzania has felt the influence of Islam from the coast and more specifically African cultures from the Ugandan kingdoms. The adoption and adaptation of 'coastal traits' in Nyamwezi music resulted from trade. Unlike the neighbouring Gogo and Kimbu, whose music is pentatonic, the Nyamwezi are the only people of central Tanzania who use a heptatonic system of the kind that occurs on the coast and in Zanzibar. Their vocal style makes much use of melisma.

During the month of Ramadan small groups of singers parade the streets of Tabora at about midnight, waking up the inhabitants for their last meal. Initiation ceremonies and didactic songs play a large part in the secret and semi-secret societies of the Sukuma, at which large double-headed cylindrical drums are used. The zither, one-string fiddle (similar to the Ugandan type) and the *endono*, a gourd-resonated braced musical bow, are also found further south.

4. NORTH-WESTERN TANZANIA. Among the Haya, the Zinza and the Ha, music is stylistically linked to that of the former kingdoms of Uganda, in particular to Bunyoro and Butoro, and was also influenced by that of Rwanda and Burundi. The seven-string *enanga* zither is associated with high social status among the wealthy Haya. Trough zithers have entered Tanzania from Rwanda, Burundi and western Uganda, where they are important instruments; in Tanzania there are several varieties, found as far south as among the Safwa and the Hehe.

Haya zithers are deep-toned and are used to accompany the singing of legends which tell of the Spirit of the Wind on Lake Victoria, and how the Haya once emerged from the lake. They are also used to accompany songs about local history and praise songs for the chiefs. As in Bunyoro the Haya use ensembles based on sets of *makondere* (composite gourd trumpets). Each trumpet produces two notes which interlock with the pairs of notes produced on the other instruments to give an elaborate resultant melody; these ensembles are accompanied by drums.

The Kerebe on the island of Bukerebe on Lake Victoria are linguistically and culturally closely related to the Haya and the Zinza. G. W. Hartwig made a comprehensive survey of the social context of earlier music on the island of Bukerebe, in which he stated that the seven-string trough zither was the only Kerebe string instrument before 1900. The zither first appeared when the eight clans of the Kerebe, including the royal clan, arrived from Buhaya in the late 17th century; traditions connect it with Bunyoro and it apparently spread from there first into Buhaya and then to Bukerebe. It was to the music of this instrument that the elders of the Kerebe drank their beer. The royal drums in Bukerebe were made by Haya and Ganda slaves. Horns for hunting, including the animal-horn *enzomba* and the wooden *omwomba*, were formerly used a great deal. The *omwomba* was made from a hollowed-out branch of a tree 4 to 6 cm in diameter; one end was closed and the horn was side-blown. The songs used by buffalo hunters were called *obwaso*.

5. CENTRAL REGION. This is perhaps the most musically active area of Tanzania. Musicians are often both players and dancers, as when a dancer holds and shakes a *kayamba* (raft rattle) in time to his movements. Some of the music of this region is associated with secret societies, such as the *mandabaha* society of old men among the Cushitic Gorowa, in which a sacred horn plays an important part. Music is also used in the initiation of the young. Among the Gogo there are three dances for circumcision: the *chasi*, sung by old people, the *chipande* for boys, and the *chaluko*, sung by girls. The *chipande* is danced in the hot season (August to October) during the *jando* (circumcision) feasts. It is accompanied by large cowbells played by the girls, and is danced by men and women and, at a distance, the boys who await circumcision.

Before 1960 the Gogo used to come in thousands to the old town of Dodoma to take part in annual dance festivals; their dances included the *nindo*, *msunyunho* (or *msunyuntho*), *saigwa*, *ng'oma*, *chiganda*, *mpendo*, *chasi*, *chipande*, *chaluko*, *saigweda* and the *sero*. The Kimbu appear to have similar dances.

The *nindo* used to be performed on the death of a chief before the installation of his successor, but is now often performed during an official visit. It consists mostly of praise songs: the dance movements are slow and solemn; the men and women form two lines; the male dancers wear bells strapped to their legs, and they jump and grunt the syllables *hra hra*; the male and female choruses sing alternately; the composer or his assistant continually guides the singers by calling out the first line of each stanza or phrase of text as a cue, as the praise poems and recitals are very long, and one piece may consist of many stanzas. The instruments used in the *nindo* dance are the *ndulele* (a side-blown animal horn) and the *mlanzi* (a transverse flute). The performance often begins with whistle signals, then the flute enters followed by the horn. The flute and horn do not play in the pentatonic scale of the *nindo* chants, but play patterns which are signals and are not tonally related to the vocal parts.

The *msunyunho* is danced when the millet and maize are ripe for harvest, usually in May. Sometimes

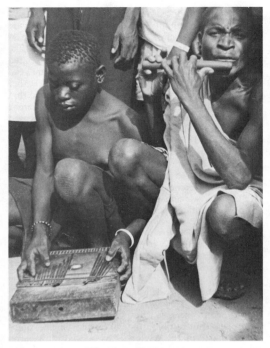

2. Marimba lamellaphone and mlanzi (transverse flute) played by Gogo musicians for the dance chiganda

hundreds of people take part, but men and women do so separately, the men holding shepherds' sticks. It is also danced in January when the rain has stopped, when it becomes a 'cry for rain'. The *msunyunho* is in two parts: the first consists of a long chorus; the second is in a faster tempo and the men vocalize syllabic patterns called *kilumi*, mainly on *hra hra*. In another type of *msunyunho*, *ndualala* (small bells) may be struck with

3. The Pangwa ngwaya dance with ng'oma (hourglass drums), 1960

crossing accents, often in a rhythm of three against two. There is also a form of *msunyunho* for young boys, who form a duo or trio: one boy sings evenly spaced *u–u–u–u* sounds on a single note, while the other two sing phrases in polyphony to such yodel syllables as *he he* or *hoi gbe*, each boy producing a short melodic fragment starting at a different point from his partner's. A similar type of polyphony occurs in the *saigwa* dance in which men and women join in chorus to sing in hocket fashion.

In the *ng'oma* dance women hold hourglass-shaped drums between their legs and drum with the hands in triple rhythms, the main accents of which cross and interlock. While drumming they shake their shoulders which are specially decorated; they also play European whistles, bought locally, in hocket style. One or two *kayamba* (raft rattles) are played by men to accompany the group. The drums, which are played exclusively by women, are single-headed and open-ended. The big drum played by the group leader is called the *ng'oma fúmbwa* and is about 55 to 60 cm high; the smaller drums are called *nyanyúlua*. *Ng'oma* is danced when a boy is taken for circumcision, at the end of a girl's first menstrual period and at weddings.

The *chiganda*, formerly danced before an elephant hunt, is a very popular Gogo dance. The instruments used are one to three marimba lamellaphones, a *chizeze* fiddle, a transverse flute, and rattles, usually shaken by women. The marimba lamellaphone (fig.2) is known almost throughout Tanzania. The Gogo instruments are particularly large (19 to 36 lamellae) and are colourfully decorated with brass nails, beads and pieces of animal skin. They are also used as solo instruments. The *chizeze* or *nzeze* is a two-string fiddle with tuning-pegs, about 50 to 70 cm long, whose strings are tuned a minor 3rd apart. The tuning of Gogo musical instruments coincides exactly with the 4th to 10th partials of the harmonic series, with a diminished 5th occurring between the 5th and 7th partials. This tuning is also the foundation of Gogo vocal polyphony and accounts for the characteristic chordal patterns of Gogo singing.

6. THE RUVUMA REGION. Makonde traditional circumcision dances in the south-east of Tanzania are well known. The *mapiku* (singular *lipiku*, masked dancer) are accompanied by a set of drums peculiar to the Makonde: the bodies of the smaller, single-headed instruments end in thin extensions, so that each instrument looks like a giant nail. Before starting to play, the musician pushes the thin end of his drum into the sand. The Makua are known for their *isinyago* dancers, who dance inside the masks which are large structures made of bamboo thatched with grass and covered with rags. Another group of masks among the Makua are called *midimu* (singular *n'dimu*); these are face masks, each one worn by an individual dancer. A special Makonde variant occurs in the masked dancers on stilts, the *midimu ya muha*, in which the mask is usually smaller than the dancer's face and is worn on the forehead.

Musical instruments in this area are varied. The Makonde use the *chityatya*, a small gourd-resonated eight-note lamellaphone, the *akanyembe* (one-string fiddle) and the *dimbila* (log xylophone). The *dimbila* usually has six keys placed over two hard stems of wood or soft banana stalks. Bundles of grass are placed on the two stems to give the keys a soft base, and the rather light and flat keys are pegged at one end with small sticks. The other end is left loose, but at both sides of each key small sticks are pressed into the grass bundles. This instrument is played by two musicians sitting obliquely opposite each other. Log xylophones of a slightly different type also occur among the Makua and Yao.

7. THE SOUTHERN HIGHLANDS AND LAKE RUKWA REGION. In the southern highlands, especially at Lake Malawi, there is considerable musical influence from the other side of the lake. In the 1950s and early 1960s several songs about Chikanga, a famous prophet, herbalist and healer by witchcraft who operated near Rumpi (Malawi), were famous among the Pangwa and Kisi. Thousands of supposed *wachawi* (wizards and witches) were forced by their communities to go on a pilgrimage to Chikanga, so that he could establish whether or not they possessed evil magic. Chikanga's songs in the Tumbuka language of Malawi were known all over the Tanzanian side of the lake. Another example of musical influence from Malawi in the south-west is the presence of the *malipenga* and *ingoma* dances among the Nyakyusa, and the *mganda* dance among the Kisi settled along the north-east shore of the lake (*see* MALAWI, §4); the *kihoda*, a girls' and women's dance, derived from the *chiwoda* of Malawi.

At Manda, which was one of the terminals of the Arab trade routes from Kilwa to Lake Malawi, much Islamic music can be heard, particularly during the Muslim New Year festival; this, however, is limited to certain sections of the population and to certain places, and is not characteristic of south-western Tanzania as a whole. A much more penetrating musical influence, especially among the Pangwa and Ndendeule, was introduced by the Ngoni settlers. The Pangwa retain a few early dances, such as the *ngwaya* performed with large hourglass-shaped drums (fig.3). The men drummers sit astride these instruments, striking the single skin with their right hand only, while women hold the small hourglass-shaped *fimkhang'u* drums and beat them above their heads. Another Pangwa dance is the *matuli*; this is a circle-dance with drums in the centre, performed at beer parties. The Safwa frequently play trough zithers. The Hehe *ligombo* (trough zither) is used to accompany legends and heroic songs about chieftainship. In the 1940s and 1950s Pancras Mkwawa, the uncle of the paramount chief of that time, was widely known as an outstanding performer. The *ligombo* is about 1 metre long, with a broad gourd resonator with a hole only 10 cm in diameter; the instrument has six strings and is tuned to a low pitch.

BIBLIOGRAPHY

E. M. von Hornbostel: 'Wanyamwezi-Gesänge', *Anthropos*, iv (1909), 781, 1033

——: 'Wasukuma-Melodie, nach der Aufnahme von Dr. J. Czekanowski', *Bulletin international de l'Académie des sciences de Cracovie*, series B, *Sciences naturelles*, ii (1910), 11

R. Skene: 'Arab and Swahili Dances and Ceremonies', *Journal of the Royal Anthropological Institute*, xlvii (1917), 413

A. C. Hollis: 'Dance of Sagara Women, Tanganyika Territory', *Man*, xxiv (1924), 5

A. T. Culwick: 'A Pogoro Flute', *Man*, xxxv (1935), 39

R. de Z. Hall: 'The Dance Societies of the Wasukuma, as Seen in the Maswa District', *Tanganyika Notes and Records*, i (1936), 94

H. Tracey: 'Recording Tour, May to November 1950 – East Africa', *African Music Society Newsletter*, i/4 (1951), 38

G. Hunter: 'Hidden Drums in Singida District', *Tanganyika Notes and Records*, xxxiv (1953), 28

V. E. Johnson: 'Africa Harvest Dance', *Tanganyika Notes and Records*, xxxvii (1954), 138

R. H. W. Pakenham: 'Two Zanzibar Ngomas', *Tanganyika Notes and Records*, lii (1959), 111

G. Kubik: 'Musikinstrumente und Tänze bei den Wapanga in Tanganyika', *Mitteilungen der Anthropologischen Gesellschaft in Wien*, xci (1961), 144

W. F. E. R. Tenraa: 'Sandawe Musical and other Sound Producing Instruments', *Tanganyika Notes and Records*, lx (1963), 23; see also 'Supplementary Notes', lxii (1964), 91

G. Kubik: 'The Traditional Music of Tanzania', *Afrika*, viii/2 (1967), 29

J. H. Nketia: 'Multi-part Organization in the Music of the Gogo of Tanzania', *JIFMC*, xix (1967), 79

P. R. Olsen: 'La musique africaine dans le Golfe persique', *JIFMC*, xix (1967), 28

G. Kubik: *Mehrstimmigkeit und Tonsysteme in Zentral- und Ostafrika* (Vienna, 1968)

S. Mbunga: 'Music Reform in Tanzania', *African Ecclesiastical Review*, x/1 (Masaka, 1968)

G. W. Hartwig: 'The Historical and Social Role of Kerebe Music', *Tanzania Notes and Records*, lxx (1969), 41

M. Mluanda: 'The Luguru Traditional Moral Schools', *Review of Ethnology*, iii (1971), 57

J. A. R. Wembah-Rashid: 'Isinyago and Midimu: Masked Dancers of Tanzania and Mozambique', *African Arts*, iv/2 (1971), 38

GERHARD KUBIK

Tanzer, William. *See* TANS'UR, WILLIAM.

Tanzmeistergeige (Ger.). KIT.

Tapada [Tapadillo] (Sp.). An ORGAN STOP.

Tapales, Ramón (*b* Baybay, Leyte, 17 Feb 1906). Filipino composer and conductor. He had his first training in solfège and the violin from his father; and continued violin lessons at the age of 12 with Abdon. In 1923 he went to Europe for further studies at the Milan Conservatory (from which he graduated in 1929), with Flesch at the Berlin Hochschule and with Kaplan at the Klindworth–Scharwenka Conservatory; he also studied composition with Butting and conducting with Robitsok. In Riga he appeared as guest conductor of the National Opera. After returning to the Philippines in 1937, he conducted opera and orchestral concerts in many parts of the country. He was appointed director of the Silliman University Conservatory (1939–41), a teacher at the Philippine Women's University, and director, then dean, of the Conservatory of the University of the Philippines (1967–70). Founder-president of the National Music Council of the Philippines and the Regional Music Commission of south-east Asia (both 1953), he served on the executive board of the International Music Council for several years. Later he became commissioner for culture in Makati, Rizal. His orchestral works include the ballet *Mariang Makiling* ('Legendary Marifa of Mount Makiling', 1934), the *Philippine Suite* and *The Last Trial* (1946); among other compositions are the *Sonata satirica* for solo violin (1971) and the songs *Luha, masaklap na luha* ('Tears, bitter tears'), *Ave Maria, Stranger at the Gate* and *Carnations* (1953). His textbook *Singing and Growing* (Manila, 1952), is used in Philippine primary education.

LUCRECIA R. KASILAG

Tap dance. A stage dance in which rhythmic patterns are sounded by the toes and heels striking the floor. The style developed in the USA and England in the mid-19th century from the steps of the jig and the clog dance and in imitation of blacks in minstrel shows. The steps were sometimes performed without musical accompaniment. In the 1910s the tap dance was influenced by the new glide styles of ballroom dance (e.g. the foxtrot) and by the less restrained torso movements of the shimmy and other negro-derived dances. In the early 20th century the dance was performed most often in music halls and vaudeville theatres, and in the 1930s to 1950s in revues, musicals and films, usually as a solo or by a chorus line. A variant is the 'soft shoe', deriving from the negro 'shuffle' of the minstrels; it was danced in leather soles, with graceful, gliding motions without lifting the feet, to a slower tempo and often with only a staccato chordal or light percussion accompaniment.

BIBLIOGRAPHY

M. and J. Stearns: *Jazz Dance* (New York, 1968)

Taperay [Taperet], **Jean-François**. *See* TAPRAY, JEAN-FRANÇOIS.

Tape recording. *See* SOUND RECORDING, TRANSMISSION AND REPRODUCTION, §9.

Taphouse, Thomas William (*b* Oxford, 11 Feb 1838; *d* Oxford, 8 Jan 1905). English music and instrument dealer and collector. He was the son of Charles Taphouse (*c*1816–1881), the founder of the firm of Charles Taphouse & Son Ltd, first established in 1857 at 10 Broad Street, Oxford, shortly after at 33 St Giles, and since 1859 at 3 Magdalen Street, where it is still flourishing. Taphouse held various local appointments as organist, and made the music shop into a lively musical centre, having added a piano warehouse and several music rooms to the premises – one of which was for many years the home of the Oxford University Music Club. His collection of early music and instruments, which contained numerous rare and some unique printed and manuscript items (including the only contemporary source of the Violin Sonata by Henry Purcell), became one of the finest in the country. The library was sold by auction at Sotheby, Wilkinson & Hodge's on 3 and 4 July 1905, for a total of £1062. He held several civic appointments in the City of Oxford, becoming mayor in 1904; in the same year Oxford University conferred on him an honorary MA.

His only son, Charles Milner Taphouse (1863–1928), organist, pianist and double bass player, took over the firm in 1897 and, from 1913, in new and larger premises, expanded its scope to include instrument hire, gramophones, records, radio, and concert management. Further developments in all departments took place under the management of his two sons John Milner Taphouse (*b* 1907) and Charles Trevor Taphouse (*b* 1913), which reflects the greatly increased musical activities in the University and City of Oxford.

BIBLIOGRAPHY

Anon.: 'The Musical Library of Mr. T. W. Taphouse, M.A.', *MT*, xlv (1904), 629

Catalogue of the Valuable and Interesting Musical Library . . . of the late T. W. Taphouse [Sotheby, Wilkinson & Hodge sale catalogue, 3–4 July 1905]

Anon.: *The Story of a Music Shop 1857–1957* (Oxford, 1957)

A. H. King: *Some British Collectors of Music c1600–1960* (Cambridge, 1963), 71

F. B. Zimmerman: *Henry Purcell 1659–1695: an Analytical Catalogue* (London, 1963), 385f

ALBI ROSENTHAL

Tapia [Numantino], **Martín de** (*fl* 1559–70). Spanish theorist. He came from the province of Soria, in which the ancient Iberian city of Numantia was located. He is thought to have been a 'bachiller' of Salamanca University and a musician in the Cathedral of Burgo de Osma. Tapia's one publication was completed in 1559,

11 years before publication. This treatise, *Vergel de música spiritual, speculativa y activa, del qual muchas, diversas y suaves flores se pueden coger* (Burgo de Osma, 1570), was held in high regard both by later Spanish theorists and by recent music historians, earning him a reputation for erudition and originality. The respect was misplaced, as has been shown by Stevenson and León Tello, who discovered independently that Tapia plagiarized in its entirety, including even the dedication and prologue, Bermudo's *Libro primero de la declaración de instrumentos* (1549). The trifling alterations made by Tapia, chiefly consisting of added sentences at the beginnings and ends of chapters, were designed to conceal the deception.

BIBLIOGRAPHY

J. Subirá: *Joyas bibliográphicas* (Madrid, 1954) [includes edn. of *Vergel de música*]

R. Stevenson: *Juan Bermudo* (The Hague, 1960)

F. J. León Tello: *Estudios de historia de la teoria musical* (Madrid, 1962)

ALMONTE HOWELL

Tapissier, Johannes [Jean de Noyers] (*b* *c*1370; *d* before Aug 1410). French composer and pedagogue. Tapissier, whose true name was Jean de Noyers, is named along with the composers Jean de Suzay and Jehan Vaillant in the anonymous *Règles de la seconde rhétorique* (*c*1400) as one of the principal French poet-musicians of the day. By 1391 he had been engaged as a chamber valet and court composer to Philip the Bold, Duke of Burgundy. That same year he accompanied Philip and his court on a journey to Milan and Avignon; in the spring of 1395 he made a second visit to Avignon in the ducal service; and in the summer of 1399 he was with Duke Philip in Flanders. The Burgundian court records reveal that Tapissier maintained an 'escole de chant' in Paris and that in 1406 three choirboys of the court were sent to his school 'to learn how to sing'. In 1408 Tapissier was ordered to bring his choirboys from Paris to Amiens to sing before the new Duke of Burgundy, John the Fearless, and later the same year he was rewarded for having helped perform the divine service before Duke John when the Burgundian court was in Paris. Although the accounts show that Tapissier died before August 1410, his name was known well enough several decades later to be mentioned in Martin le Franc's poem *Le champion des dames* (the citation is given in the article JOHANNES CARMEN).

Johannes Tapissier's extant compositions are a three-voice Credo, a three-voice Sanctus and a four-voice isorhythmic motet. The motet, *Eya dulcis adque vernans rosa/Vale placens peroratrix*, laments that the church was then divided by the Great Schism. His Credo appears with two different concluding amens, one in the Apt MS and a second in the more recent *I-Bc* Q15. In the latter source the Credo is preceded by a Gloria composed by THOMAS FABRI, one of Tapissier's pupils in Paris. *See* BAUDE CORDIER for a Gloria which possibly forms a pair with the Credo. Tapissier's three compositions are published in *Early Fifteenth-Century Music*, ed. G. Reaney, CMM, xi/1 (1955).

BIBLIOGRAPHY

C. van den Borren: *Guillaume Dufay* (Brussels, 1925), 330f

E. Dannemann: *Die spätgotische Musiktradition in Frankreich und Burgund vor dem Auftreten Dufays* (Strasbourg, 1936), 67f

C. Wright: *Music at the Court of Burgundy, 1364–1419* (diss., Harvard U., 1972), 295ff

——: 'Tapissier and Cordier: New Documents and Conjectures', *MQ*, lix (1973), 177

CRAIG WRIGHT

Tapkov, Dimiter (*b* Sofia, 12 July 1929). Bulgarian composer. Until 1955 he studied composition with Goleminov at the Sofia State Academy of Music. He was head of the music department of Sofia Radio (1956–62), general secretary of the Bulgarian Composers Union (1962–5) and director of the National Opera, Sofia (1967–70). In addition he taught orchestration from 1962 at the Bulgarian State Conservatory (lecturer 1971, professor 1975). His witty music makes use of new techniques and is often directed to children or young people.

WORKS
(*selective list*)

Orch: Prelude, str, 1953; Fl Conc., 1956; Suite of sym. marches, 1956; Belassitsa, ov., 1957; 2 sinfoniettas, str, 1966, 1967; Conc. for Orch, 1969; Suite, chamber orch, 1970; Harp Conc., 1971
Chamber: 2 trios, fl, cl, bn, 1952, 1953; Sonata, tpt, pf, 1952; Variations, str qt, 1954; Skizzen nos.1, 2, str qt, 1957; 2 str qts, 1957, 1972; Samonadeyanata zhaba [The conceited frog], fl, cl, bn, 1959; Pf Pieces, 1960; 3 Pieces, str qt, 1963; Sonata, db, 1969; Basnya [Fable], wind qnt, 1970; Qt, va, harp, fl, pf, 1973
Vocal: Conc., S, str qt, 1955; 4 songs, S, orch, 1958; Requiem for Song Mi, 1970; Kantata za mira [Peace cantata], 1975

Principal publisher: Gerig, Leduc, Nauka i izkustvo, Sovyetskaya muzika

LADA BRASHOVANOVA

Tappato (It.). An ORGAN STOP (*Tapada*).

Tappert, Wilhelm (*b* Ober-Thomaswaldau, Silesia, 19 Feb 1830; *d* Berlin, 27 Oct 1907). German critic and writer on music. He began his career as a schoolmaster, but in 1856 turned to music, studying under Dehn and Adolph Kullak. From 1858 he was a music critic and teacher in Glogau. In 1866 he returned to Berlin and settled there, becoming well known as a teacher and writer on music, and as an able and enthusiastic partisan of Wagner. He edited the *Allgemeine deutsche Musikzeitung* from 1866 to 1880, contributed to the *Musikalisches Wochenblatt* and published several pamphlets. His *Wagner-Lexikon* (1887) contains a collection of the abuse lavished on Wagner and his circle; more important are his researches into notation and lute tablatures. His valuable library was bought in 1908 by the Royal Library in Berlin.

WRITINGS
Musik und musikalische Erziehung (Berlin, 1866)
Musikalische Studien (Berlin, 1868)
Wandernde Melodien (Leipzig, 1868, 2/1890)
Das Verbot der Quintenparallelen (Berlin, 1869)
Richard Wagner (Elberfeld, 1883)
Geschichte der alten deutschen Lauten-Tablatur (MS, *D-Bds*, 1885)
Wagner-Lexikon: Wörterbuch der Unhöflichkeit, enthaltend grobe, höhnende, gehässige und verleumderische Ausdrücke, welche gegen den Meister Richard Wagner, seine Werke und seine Anhänger von den Feinden und Spöttern gebraucht worden sind (Leipzig, 1887, 2/1903)
54 Erlkönig-Kompositionen (Berlin, 1898, 2/1906)
Katalog der Spezialausstellung von Wilhelm Tappert: die Entwicklung der Notenschrift (Berlin, 1898)
900 bis 1900: tausend Jahre Entwicklungsgeschichte der musikalischen Zeichenschrift (MS, *D-Bds*, 1901, enlarged 1903)
Sang und Klang aus alter Zeit (Berlin, 1906) [100 lute pieces]
Essays, chiefly on lute music and tablature, in *Allgemeine deutsche Musikzeitung*, *MMg*, *Musikalisches Wochenblatt*, *NZM* and others

BIBLIOGRAPHY
R. Schaal: 'Tappert, Wilhelm', *MGG*

GEORGE GROVE/R

Tappolet, Willy (*b* Lindau, nr. Zurich, 6 Aug 1890). Swiss musicologist. After studying literature, psychology and musicology he took his doctorate at Zurich University in 1917 with a dissertation on Heinrich Weber. In 1938, after teaching in Geneva, he completed his *Habilitation* in musicology at Geneva University

with a study of musical notation and its practical influence. He was appointed reader at Geneva University in 1955 and, following his retirement, honorary professor in 1960. His writings are mainly concerned with new music, notably French music, whose cause in the German-speaking world he took up with success. In this connection his Honegger biography occupies a particularly important place and remains a standard work on the composer.

WRITINGS
Heinrich Weber (diss., U. of Zurich, 1917; Zurich, 1918)
Arthur Honegger (Zurich, 1933, enlarged 2/1954; Fr. trans., 1939, 2/1957)
La notation musicale et son influence sur la pratique de la musique au moyen-âge à nos jours (Habilitationsschrift, U. of Geneva, 1938; Neuchâtel, 1945; enlarged Ger. trans., 1967)
Maurice Ravel: Leben und Werk (Olten, 1950)
'Le séjour de W.-A. Mozart à Genève en 1766', *Kongressbericht: Wien Mozartjahr 1956*, 637
'Einige prinzipielle Bemerkungen zur Frage der Improvisation', *IMSCR, vii Cologne 1958*, 287
'Georges Becker, 24. Juli 1834 bis 18. Juli 1928', *SMw*, xxv (1962), 539
'Johann Kaspar Weiss: ein Beitrag zur Musikgeschichte Genfs im 18. Jahrhundert', *Karl Gustav Fellerer zum 60. Geburtstag* (Regensburg, 1962), 530
Notenschrift und Musizieren: das Problem ihrer Beziehungen vom Frühmittelalter bis ins 20. Jahrhundert (Berlin, 1967)
'Haydn in unserer Zeit', *SMz*, cx (1970), 285
Begegnungen mit der Musik in Goethes Leben und Werk (Berne, 1975)

BIBLIOGRAPHY
SML
Schweizer Musikbuch (Zurich, 1939), ii, 203

JÜRG STENZL

Tappy, Eric (*b* Lausanne, 19 May 1931). Swiss tenor. He studied at the Geneva Conservatory with Fernando Carpi (1951–8), at the Salzburg Mozarteum with Ernst Reichert, in Hilversum with Eva Liebenberg, and in Paris with Nadia Boulanger. He made his début in 1959 at Strasbourg as the Evangelist in the *St Matthew Passion* and later that season appeared in Zurich in Milhaud's *Les malheurs d'Orphée* under Paul Sacher. His musicianship and intelligence commended him to Frank Martin and Ernest Ansermet, and under the latter he sang in the first performances of Martin's *Le mystère de la Nativité* (1959) and *Monsieur de Pourceaugnac* (1963). Tappy's first operatic appearance was in the title role of Rameau's *Zoroastre* at the Paris Opéra-Comique in 1964, during the 200th anniversary commemorations of Rameau's death. At Herrenhausen in 1966 he sang Monteverdi's Orpheus and the following year he played Nero in *L'incoronazione di Poppea* at Hanover. From 1963 he has appeared regularly at the Grand Théâtre, Geneva, distinguishing himself especially in the Mozart repertory. He made his Covent Garden début in 1974 in the title role of Mozart's *La clemenza di Tito*, and the same year made his American début as Don Ottavio in San Francisco. His operatic repertory also includes Aaron (*Moses and Aron*), Pelléas, Idomeneus and Lysander (*A Midsummer Night's Dream*). His concert repertory includes choral works of Bach, Berlioz, Handel, Haydn, Mozart, Schütz and Stravinsky, as well as lesser-known music by Campra, Carissimi, Nono, Scarlatti and Vivaldi.

HAROLD ROSENTHAL

Tapray [Taperay, Taperet], **Jean-François** (*b* Gray, Haute Saône, 1738; *d* Fontainebleau, *c*1819). French organist, composer and keyboard teacher. He first studied music with his father, Jean Tapray, organist at the collegiate church of Gray, and with a Monsieur Dancier who had been a pupil of Domenico Scarlatti for the harpsichord and composition. When he was ten he gave an organ concert at the Jesuit church of Dôle, Franche-Comté. From the age of 14 he was organist and *maître de musique* at the collegiate church of Dôle, a position that his father had also held. On 30 April 1756 he performed at Versailles in the presence of Mme Victoire, daughter of the king. In 1763 he became organist at Besançon Cathedral; five years later he settled in Paris, where in addition to performing and composing he established an excellent reputation as a teacher of harpsichord and piano (the names of many of his pupils, mostly noblewomen, appear in the dedications of his published works up to 1781). In 1776 he was *maître de clavecin* and organist at the Ecole Royale Militaire. By 1780 he had acquired the titles of organist 'des Ordres Royaux, Militaires et Hospitaliers de Notre Dame de Mont Carmel et de St Lazard'. On 10 April 1778 he performed in a *symphonie concertante* by Navoigille at the Concert Spirituel, one of his few appearances as a keyboard virtuoso (Servières' claim that Tapray frequently performed his own works there is not substantiated by press accounts). In 1786 he left his position at the Ecole Militaire and soon afterwards retired to Fontainebleau, where in the 1790s he played the organ at the church of St Louis and directed the orchestra.

Tapray was a composer of limited gifts; except for a few moments, his music lacks imagination and organic unity. Most of his works are in two movements: Allegro and Minuet or Rondo. When there are three movements, they are often in the same key, a practice largely abandoned by this time. His keyboard pieces, methods and arrangements were designed for use by his pupils. He sometimes wrote for unusual instrumental groupings (the *Quatuor concertant* op.19 is for keyboard, flute, viola and bassoon) and was one of the first composers in France to write specifically for the piano, though he made little distinction in idiom between that instrument and the harpsichord. Of particular interest are his four *symphonies concertantes*, which have solo parts for both harpsichord and piano. A didactic work, *Abrégé de l'accompagnement du clavecin* (Paris, 1775), which appeared under the name of Tapray without the added *fils*, is probably by Tapray's father.

WORKS
(all printed works published in Paris)

INSTRUMENTAL

Orch: 6 concertos, hpd/org, 3 vn, vc obbl, op.1 (1758); Concerto, hpd, orch, op.3 (1771); Symphonie concertante, hpd, pf, orch, op.8 (1778); Simphonie concertante, hpd, pf, vn, orch, op.9 (1778); Symphonie, hpd, orch, op.12 (1780); Symphonie concertante, hpd, pf, orch, op.13 (1781); Simphonie concertante, hpd, pf, orch ad lib, op.15 (c1782–3); 2 simphonies, hpd, orch, op.21 (1784)

Chamber: 4 sonates en trio, hpd, vn, va, op.5 (1776); 3 sonates en trio, hpd/pf, vn, va, op.6 (1777); 3 sonates, hpd/pf, vn, va, op.7 (1778); 2 quatuors, hpd/pf, cl/vn, va, b/vc, op.18 (1784) [sometimes listed as op.17 or 21]; Quatuor concertant, hpd/pf, fl/vn, va, bn/vc, op.19, in *Journal de clavecin*, i/6 (1784); Quatuor concertante, op.20 (1784); 2 sonates, hpd/pf, vn, vc, op.23 (1788)

KEYBOARD

6 sonates, hpd, vn ad lib, op.1 (1770); 3 sonates, hpd, vn ad lib, op.2 (1770); 4 sonates, hpd/pf, op.4 (1773), nos.1–3 with other insts; 6 sonates, hpd/pf, vn acc., op.10 (1779); 3 sonates, hpd/pf, op.11 (1780); 3 sonates, hpd/pf, 2 vn ad lib, op.16 (1784); 6 sonates, pf, op.17 (1784); Sonate, hpd, in *Journal de clavecin*, iii/10 (1784)

3 sonates, hpd/pf, op.22 (1785); 3 sonates, hpd/pf, vn ad lib, op.24 (1788); 6 sonates très faciles, hpd, vn ad lib (?1789); 3 sonates, pf, op.28 (?1800); Sonate, pf 4 hands, op.29 (1800); arrs. of opera ovs. and airs by Monsigny, Grétry, Paisiello etc; numerous other pieces in

contemporary anthologies; 6 [*recte* 3] sonnattes, hpd, vn ad lib, *F-Pn*

Pedagogical works: Premiers éléments du clavecin ou de piano avec des observations préliminaires (c1789); 12 pièces d'une difficulté graduele, hpd/pf, suite de l'oeuvre 25e (c1789); Complément non gravé de l'oeuvre 25, *F-Pn*, incl. exercises, definitions, preludes, 30 études

VOCAL

1er [–3e] recueil d'ariettes, 1v, hpd (1771)

Opp.14, 26–7 not known

BIBLIOGRAPHY

FétisB; *GerberL*; *GerberNL*

J.-B. de La Borde: *Essai sur la musique ancienne et moderne* (Paris, 1780/*R*1972)

A. Choron and F. Fayolle: *Dictionnaire historique des musiciens* (Paris, 1810–11/*R*1971)

G. de Saint-Foix: 'Les premiers pianistes parisiens: N. J. Hüllmandel', *ReM*, iv/6 (1923), 193

G. Servières: *Documents inédits sur les organistes français des XVIIe et XVIIIe siècles* (Paris, 1924)

G. Favre: 'Les organistes parisiens à la fin du XVIIIe siècle', *Petite maîtrise* (1936), April

——: *La musique française de piano avant 1830* (Paris, 1953)

B. S. Brook: *La symphonie française dans la seconde moitié du XVIIIe siècle* (Paris, 1962)

BARRY S. BROOK, RICHARD VIANO

Tār (Iranian: 'string'). Fretted long-necked lute, descended from the *tumbur* of Sassanian Iran and known in various forms throughout the Middle East and in parts of Asia. Its name traditionally varied according to the number of strings used: hence, for example, *dutar* ('two strings') of Iran and Afghanistan; *setār* ('three strings') etc. This is no longer true, however, as in many cases instruments retained their earlier names after they were given more strings, examples being the sitar of north India (with up to seven strings) and the Afghan *dutar* (with two, three or fourteen strings).

For illustration, *see* IRAN, figs. 5a and d.

Tār. Arabic frame drum with jingles used in classical and folk music in north Africa, Egypt, the Arabian Gulf and as far east as Malaysia. See ARAB MUSIC, §§I, 5(ii), II, 4.

See also the entry 'Ṭār' in Appendix A.

Tarade, Théodore-Jean (*b* Paris, 1 Nov 1731; *d* La Flèche, 14 Sept 1788). French violinist and composer. He may have been a pupil of Jean-Marie Leclair. He played for the balls at the Paris Opéra in 1750–51 and was a member of the Opéra orchestra from 1751 until he was pensioned in 1776. Between 1754 and 1757 he appeared as soloist at the Concert Spirituel on four occasions, and he played in the orchestra there from 1755 to 1772. His operetta *La réconciliation villageoise* (1765) was well received, the *Mercure de France* finding its music 'agreeable, and extremely well suited to the light kind of spectacle to which it is adapted'. Its success was reflected by the two published editions of the score (dedicated to Papillon de la Ferté, *Intendant des menus plaisirs du roy*) and by the appearance of its airs in several anthologies. From the 1760s to the early 1780s he ran a music shop with his wife, the former Françoise-Madeleine Dutartre, *graveuse de la reine*, who during these years published works under the name Mme Tarade. In 1783 the couple moved to La Flèche, where Tarade taught violin at the Collège Royal.

Apart from preserving Gaviniès's famous *Romance* and demonstrating contemporary taste, Tarade's music is of slight worth. More important are his two violin treatises. The first of these is known only from excerpts published in Cartier's *L'art du violon* (1798). The second, a reworking of the first published around 1778, offers an excellent formulation of the basic French violin technique of an earlier generation (Anet, Senaillé, Leclair, Mondonville, Guignon). Although the technique of his own day had already been handled in the better-known, more forward-looking treatise of L'Abbé le fils (1761), Tarade's *Traité* remains an important document for the study of performing practice.

WORKS

OPERAS

La reconnaissance (comédie, 1), 1765; score, *F-Pc*, according to *EitnerQ*

La réconciliation villageoise (comédie, 1, Poinsinet, after La Ribardière), Comédie-Italienne, 15 July 1765; scores (Paris, 1765)

OTHER WORKS

Le triomphe de l'amour, premier cantatille (de la Hogue), 1v, insts (Paris, 1760–61)

6 sonate, vn, b, op.1 (Paris, 1761)

Premier recueil des plus beaux airs et la Romance de M. Gaviniès variés (Paris, 1773)

Symphonie concertante, 2 vn, va, orch (Paris, 1778), lost

Les amusements d'un violon seul, ou 2ᵉ recueil d'airs connus et autres variés (Paris, n.d.)

THEORETICAL WORKS

Nouveaux principes de musique & de violon beaucoup plus instructifs que ceux qui ont paru jusqu'à présent (Paris, 1774) [lost; extracts in J.-B. Cartier: *L'art du violon* (Paris, 1798)]

Traité du violon, ou Règles de cet instrument à l'usage de ceux qui veulent en jouer avec la parfaite connaissance du ton dans lequel on est (Paris, c1774 [lost], 2/?1777–9/*R*1972)

BIBLIOGRAPHY

L. de La Laurencie: *L'école française de violon de Lully à Viotti* (Paris, 1922–4/*R*1971), ii, 441ff

C. Hopkinson: *A Dictionary of Parisian Music Publishers, 1770–1950* (London, 1954)

A. Wirsta: *Ecoles de violon au XVIIIᵉ siècle d'après les ouvrages didactiques* (diss., U. of Paris, 1955)

B. S. Brook: *La symphonie française dans la seconde moitié du XVIIIe siècle* (Paris, 1962), ii, 689

B. Gérard: 'Inventaire alphabétique des documents répertoiriés relatifs aux musiciens parisiens conservés aux Archives de Paris', *RMFC*, xiii (1973), 181

NEAL ZASLAW

Tarakanov, Mikhail Evgen'yevich (*b* Rostov-na-Donu, 20 Feb 1928). Soviet musicologist. From 1948 until 1952 he studied in the department of theory and composition at the Moscow Conservatory with Igor' Vladimirovich Sposobin, Sergey Sergeyevich Skrebkov and Viktor Abramovich Tsukkerman. He completed his postgraduate studies in 1955, and in 1957 took his *kandidat* degree with a dissertation on the thematic development of Myaskovsky's first six symphonies. He was awarded a doctorate in 1970 for his book on the style of Prokofiev's symphonies. He taught music theory at the Moscow Conservatory (1955–60), and in 1960 became a research fellow at the Institute for the History of the Arts. Tarakanov's work is concerned mainly with 20th-century music and general problems of music theory.

WRITINGS

'Novïye obrazï, novïye sredstva' [New forms, new means], *SovM* (1966), no.1, p.9; no.2, p.5

'Muzïkal'noy kritike – konets?!' [Is this the end of music criticism?!], *SovM* (1967), no.3, p.26

'Novaya zhizn' staroy formï' [New life for an old form], *SovM* (1968), no.6, p.54

Stil' simfoniy Prokof'yeva [The style of Prokofiev's symphonies] (diss., Institute for the History of the Arts, Moscow, 1970; Moscow, 1968)

with V. A. Vasina-Grossman: 'Tvorchestvo russkikh sovetskikh kompozitorov 1917–32' [The work of Soviet Russian composers 1917–32], *Istoriya muzïki narodov SSSR*, i, ed. Yu. V. Keldïsh (Moscow, 1970), 62

'Tvorchestvo russkikh kompozitorov: simfonicheskaya i kamerno-instrumental'naya muzïka 1932–41' [The work of Russian composers: symphonic and instrumental chamber music 1932–41], *Istoriya muzïki narodov SSSR*, ii, ed. Yu. V. Keldïsh (Moscow, 1970), 156–96

'RSFSR: kamernaya instrumental'naya muzïka 1941–5' [The RSFSR:

instrumental chamber music 1941–5], *Istoriya muzïki narodov SSSR*, iii, ed. Yu. V. Keldïsh (Moscow, 1972), 146

'RSFSR: kamernaya instrumental'naya muzïka 1946–56' [The RSFSR: instrumental chamber music 1946–56], *Istoriya muzïki narodov SSSR*, iv, ed. Yu. V. Keldïsh (Moscow, 1973), 256

'RSFSR: kamernaya instrumental'naya muzïka 1956–67' [The RSFSR: instrumental chamber music 1956–67], *Istoriya muzïki narodov SSSR*, v/1, ed. Yu. V. Keldïsh (Moscow, 1974), 239

'Novaya tonal'nost'' v muzïke XX veka' [New tonality in 20th-century music], *Problemï muzïkal'noy nauki*, i, ed. G. A. Orlov and others (Moscow, 1972), 5–35

Muzïkal'niy teatr Al'bana Berga [The musical theatre of Alban Berg] (Moscow, 1976)

YURY KELDÏSH

Taranta. A Flamenco-type song of Andalusian origin; see FLAMENCO, Table 1.

Tarantella [tarandla, tarantela, tarantelle]. A folkdance of southern Italy also used in art music. It derives its name from Taranto (the ancient Tarantum) in Apulia. It is now a kind of mimed courtship dance, usually performed by one couple surrounded by a circle of others, accompanied by castanets and tambourines held by the dancers; occasionally the onlookers sing during the dance, usually a regularly phrased tune in 3/8 or 6/8 that alternates between major and minor mode and gradually increases in speed. Ex.1 shows a traditional Italian tarantella.

Ex.1 Traditional

The tarantula (*lycosa tarentula*) also derived its name from the town of Taranto, a coincidence that may have given rise to the popular but repeatedly discredited legend that the dance (sometimes called 'tarantula' in literary references) was a cure for the mildly toxic bite of the spider. A disease known as tarantism, prevalent in southern Italy from the 15th century to the 17th, seems to have been more a form of hysteria than a consequence of the bite. Athanasius Kircher included eight songs used to cure tarantism in the early 17th century in his *Magnes* (1641; iii, chap.8), remarking that these tarantellas were ordinarily 'rustic extemporizations'. All

Ex.2 Athanasius Kircher: *Magnes* (Rome, 1641) p. 875

but one are in simple duple metre, unlike the traditional tarantella, and all have regular phrases made up of eight beats with a caesura after the fourth and a point of repose on the seventh or eighth. Melodic figures characteristic of the tarantella include repeated notes, the alternation of a note with its upper or lower auxiliary, scalic motion, leaps and arpeggios. Like some early 17th-century correntes which are notated in simple duple metre, Kircher's tarantellas might have been altered in performance to accommodate the dance's characteristic patterns; in fact, the music of Kircher's compound duple tarantella (ex.2) is similar to the typical early 17th-century corrente. Seven 18th-century tarantellas, both Spanish and Italian, are reprinted by Schneider, all in compound metres and all structurally similar to Kircher's examples (for a further 18th-century example, said to have been used to cure a case of tarantism in Torre dell'Annunziata near Naples, see 'Tarantella' in Grove 5).

The tarantella was revived as a concert piece in the 19th and 20th centuries, perhaps because of the enthusiasm for its frenzied energy evinced by such writers as Goethe and Rilke. Tarantellas for piano, normally in 6/8, are marked 'Presto', 'Prestissimo' or 'Vivace', and are often virtuoso showpieces. The salient features of the folkdance music are reflected in the piano tarantella: phrase structure tends to be regular, and the melodic devices are like those of the dance, although the dance's diatonic scales are frequently replaced by virtuoso chromatic scales. Sectionality is emphasized by modulation and by the use of contrasting tempos. Good examples of the concert tarantella are those by Chopin (op.43) and Liszt (Années de pèlerinage, première année, 'Suisse', 3); less virtuoso are those by L. M. Gottschalk (op.67), Stephen Heller (op.85), Anton Rubinstein (op.82), Rakhmaninov (op.17) and Mario Castelnuovo-Tedesco (op.156).

A tarantella-like movement may also appear as the final movement of a sonata, symphony or suite. Weber used the driving rhythm of the tarantella in his Piano Sonata op.70; Richard Strauss introduced Italian themes, including a tarantella, in Aus Italien op.16. Mendelssohn headed the finale of his Italian Symphony op.90 'Saltarello', but Tovey quoted Rockstro as saying that the legato running theme so prominent in the development is a tarantella; the saltarello and tarantella rhythms of the finale are differentiated by their melodic styles and qualities of movement (ex.3). The concert tarantella has also been parodied: the finest is Rossini's Tarantelle pur sang (avec traversée de la procession), where the furious tarantella is twice interrupted by a religious procession featuring bells and a harmonium. William Albright's Gothic Suite (1973) for organ, strings and percussion closes with a 'Tarantella demente' marked 'Presto furioso'.

BIBLIOGRAPHY
A. Kircher: Magnes sive de arte magnetica (Rome, 1641)
S. Storace: 'A Genuine Letter from an Italian Gentleman, Concerning the Bite of the Tarantula', Gentleman's Magazine, xxiii (1753), 433
H. Mendel: 'Tarantella', Musikalisches Conversations-Lexikon (Leipzig, 1870–79, 3/1890–91/R1969)
M. Schneider: La danza de espadas y la tarantela (Barcelona, 1948)
A. G. Bragaglia: Danze popolari italiane (Rome, 1950)
B. Galanti: Dances of Italy (New York, 1950)
M. Schneider and A. Würz: 'Tarantella', MGG

ERICH SCHWANDT

Ṭăranu, Cornel (b Cluj, 20 June 1934). Romanian composer and conductor. After studying theory with I. Mureşianu and composition with Toduță at the Cluj Conservatory (1951–7), he went on to study in Paris (1966–7) and at the Darmstadt summer courses (1968, 1969, 1972) with Ligeti, Stockhausen, Xenakis and Maderna. He was appointed senior lecturer in composition at the Cluj Conservatory in 1957 and in 1968 he became conductor of the Ars Nova ensemble. In his music he has employed the parlando rubato cantilena and the rhythmic freedom and the folk-whistle sounds of Romanian peasant music; he has been particularly influenced by the innovations of Enescu. Ṭăranu's instrumental works use improvisation and aleatory ideas, together with harshly acid harmonies and other material of a folklike modality. The experience of several cantatas and incidental scores for the Cluj National Theatre resulted in the comic opera Secretul lui Don Giovanni ('Don Giovanni's secret'), a piece that achieves a surprising stylistic unity although it includes collages of Renaissance, Baroque, serial and jazz elements.

WORKS
(selective list)
Secretul lui Don Giovanni [Don Giovanni's secret], opera, 1970
Orch: 2 syms., 1957, 1962; Secvenţe [Sequences], str, 1960; Simetrii, 1964; Incantaţii, 1965; Pf Conc., 1966; Intercalări, 1967; Sinfonietta giocosa, 1968; Alternanţe, 1968; Racorduri [Connections], 1971
Chamber: Str Trio, 1952; Sonatas: cl, pf, 1954; vc, pf, 1956; fl, pf, 1960; ob, pf, 1963; Sonata ostinato, pf, 1961; Contrasts I–II, 1964; Dialoguri, 1966
Vocal: 2 cantatas, 1962–3; 3 elegii bacoviene, 1958–62; Odă în metru antic, 1972

Principal publisher: ESPLA (Bucharest)

WRITINGS
Enescu in conştiinţa prezentului [Enescu in present consciousness] (Bucharest, 1969)

BIBLIOGRAPHY
V. Cosma: Muzicieni români (Bucharest, 1970), 431ff
T. Albescu: 'Opera "Secretul lui Don Giovanni" de Cornel Ṭăranu', Muzica, viii (Bucharest, 1970), 32

VIOREL COSMA

Tarchi, Angelo [Angiolo] (b Naples, c1760; d Paris, 19 Aug 1814). Italian composer. He is said to have entered the Pietà dei Turchini conservatory, Naples, in 1771, studying under Lorenzo Fago and Sala. In 1778 his first opera, a Neapolitan dialect comedy, was performed so successfully at the conservatory that the king commanded a performance at the palace in Caserta. This was followed by three comic operas for Neapolitan theatres in 1778–80, his last for that city except for one in 1790. From 1781 to Carnival 1785 he worked mostly in Rome and then farther north, centring his activities on Florence in 1785 and Milan in 1787–8.

Ex.3 Mendelssohn: Italian Symphony, op.90, 4th movt
(a) saltarello theme.

(b) tarantella theme.

He produced his first *opera seria*, the successful *Ademira*, at Milan in 1783, and from Carnival 1785 most of his work was in that genre. A remarkably fertile composer, even for the time, he usually produced from four to six operas each year; perhaps his most successful work of this period was *Ariarate* (Milan, 1786), also performed at Naples and elsewhere. The quick growth of his reputation is shown by his appointment as music director and composer at the King's Theatre in the Haymarket, London, for the seasons December 1787 to June 1788 and January to June 1789 (he had earlier composed the music for the castrato Rubinelli's part in a pasticcio, *Virginia*, performed at the King's Theatre for Rubinelli's début there on 4 May 1786, but it is not clear whether he went to London then). In 1790 his earlier opera *Il conte de Saldagna* (1787) was performed in Paris and two new comic works were given there in 1790–91. Continuing his career in Italy, he is said by Fétis to have fallen ill on a visit to Naples in 1793, making a long recovery and not producing a new opera until Carnival 1794–5. His output of operas had slowed somewhat in the early 1790s and now it did so still more. His last Italian works were performed early in 1797. He then went to Paris and attempted to establish himself as an *opéra comique* composer, having seven works performed between late 1798 and early 1802. However, he never found the formula for success in that genre. Although some Italian influence was not distasteful to *opéra comique* audiences at this time, Tarchi's music seems to have remained too Italianate to please completely. Several of his attempts were failures (Fétis called *D'auberge en auberge*, 1800, his best), and he finally abandoned the stage, remaining in Paris as a fashionable singing teacher.

Tarchi's great popularity in his day is evident from the large number of excerpts from his operas still extant in manuscript. The source of his popularity almost certainly lay in his talent for extremely grateful vocal writing set against accompaniments skilfully contrived to show off the voice without obscuring it. Perhaps largely because of this smoothness and facile effectiveness of his style, however, his music now seems rather bland and lacking in character and dramatic strength (manuscript scores of whole operas by him are much rarer than excerpts, suggesting that even in his day they were more admired in excerpted form). According to Gervasoni, Villarosa and other early writers, Tarchi composed considerable church music. The mass in the British Library is a grandiose work based on the spatial effects produced by two choirs and groups of instruments in alternation and together (there are also contrasting solo movements). Again, the musical ideas are somewhat neutral in character, but this may have been partly the result of acoustical considerations.

WORKS

DRAMATIC

ML – *Milan, La Scala*   c – *commedia or opéra comique*
FP – *Florence, Pergola*   d – *dramma per musica*
PO – *Paris, Opéra-Comique*   i – *intermezzo*

L'archetiello (c), Naples, Conservatorio della Pietà dei Turchini, carn. 1778
I viluppi amorosi (c, G. Mililotti), Naples, Nuovo, spr. 1778
Il barbiere di Arpino (farsa), Naples, Fondo, aut. 1779
Il rè alla caccia (c, P. Mililotti), Naples, Nuovo, aut. 1780; ? also as La caccia di Enrico IV
Le disgrazie fortunate (i), Rome, Capranica, carn. 1781
Don Fallopio (i), Rome, Valle, carn. 1782
Il guerriero immaginario (i), Rome, Valle, carn. 1783
Ademira (d, F. Moretti), ML, 27 Dec 1783, ?*F-Pc*, *GB-Lbm*

I fratelli Pappamosca (c, S. Zini), Rome, Valle, carn. 1784
Bacco ed Arianna (festa teatrale or cantata, C. Oliveri), Turin, Regio, spr. 1784, *I-Gi(l)*
Le cose d'oggi giorno divise in trenta tomi, tomo primo, parte prima (i), Rome, Capranica, 26 Dec 1784
Il matrimonio per contrattempo (c), Livorno, Nuovo, carn. 1785
Mitridate rè di Ponto (d), Rome, Dame, carn. 1785; ? also as La morte di Mitridate
L'Arminio (d, Moretti), Mantua, Nuovo Regio-Ducale, 8 May 1785, *D-Mbs*
Ifigenia in Aulide (d, Zeno), Padua, Nuovo, June 1785, *P-La*
La Virginia (d), FP, aut. 1785
Ifigenia in Tauride (d, B. Pasqualigo), FP, aut. 1785, *D-Bds*, ?*F-Pc*, *I-Fc*, (?Ifigenia in Aulide)
Ariarate (d, Moretti), ML, Jan 1786, ?*F-Pc*, *P-La*, *US-Bp*
Publio (d, A. Piovene), FP, spr. 1786
Demofoonte (d, Metastasio), Crema, Nuovo, 24 Sept 1786, or ML, 1786
Il trionfo di Clelia (d, Metastasio), Turin, Regio, 26 Dec 1786, ?*F-Pc*, *P-La*
Demetrio (d, Metastasio), ML, 1787
Melite riconosciuta (d, G. Roccaforte), Rome, Dame, 3 Feb 1787
Il conte di Saldagna (tragedia, Moretti), ML, 10 June 1787, ?*F-Pc*
Le nozze di Figaro (c, after Da Ponte), Monza, Villa Reale, aut. 1787 [new Acts 3, 4 to Mozart's work]
Antioco (d, Moretti), ML, 26 Dec 1787, *Pc*, *I-Gi(l)*
Le due rivali (c), Rome, Dame, 1788, or spr. 1787
Alessandro nelle Indie (d, Metastasio), Milan, 1788, *Fc*; rev. as La generosità di Alessandro (C. F. Badini, after Metastasio), London, 1789, 2 arias, trio (London, 1789); ? new setting, Turin, Regio, carn. 1798
Artaserse (d, Metastasio), Mantua, Ducale, spr. 1788, *D-Mbs*, ?*F-Pc*
Ezio (d, Metastasio), Vicenza, Eretenio, 1789, ? *Pc*, *I-Fc*; ? new setting, Vicenza, Nuovo, sum. 1792
Il disertore francese (c, B. Benincasa, ? after J. M. Sedaine: Le déserteur), London, Haymarket, 28 Feb 1789, ?*F-Pc*, *I-Fc*
La finta baronessa (c, F. Livigni), Naples, Fiorentini, 1790
Giulio Sabino (d, P. Giovannini), Turin, Regio, carn. 1790, *P-La*
Il cavaliere errante (dramma eroicomico), Paris, Monsieur, sum. 1790
Lo spazzacamino principe (c, G. Carpani, after La ramoneur prince), Monza, Villa Reale, aut. 1790, *I-MOe*
L'apoteosi d'Ercole (d, M. Butturini), Venice, S Benedetto, 26 Dec 1790
Don Chisciotte (c), Paris, 1791
Tito Manlio (d, Roccaforte), Rome, Argentina, carn. 1791
La morte di Nerone (d), Milan or Florence, 1792
L'Olimpiade (d, Metastasio), Rome, Argentina, carn. 1792
Adrasto rè d'Egitto (d, G. de Gamerra), ML, ?4 Feb 1792
Dorval e Virginia (dramma prosa e musica, G. M. Foppa), Venice, S Benedetto, 8 Jan 1793; also as Paolo e Virginia
Lo stravagante (c, L. Lantini), Bergamo, Nuovo, Fair 1793
Le Danaidi (d, G. Sertor), ML, 26 Dec 1794
L'impostura poco dura (c, ? after G. B. Neri: Le vicende d'amore), ML, 10 Oct 1795, *Mr*
Ciro riconosciuto (d, Metastasio), Piacenza, Ducale, carn. 1796
Isacco (oratorio), Mantua, ?Lent 1796, *Bc*, *Fc*
La congiura pisoniana (d, F. Salfi), ML, Jan 1797
Ester (azione sacra), FP, Lent 1797, ?autograph *I-Fc*
Le cabriolet jaune, ou Le phénix d'Angoulême (c, J. A. de Ségur), PO, 7 Nov 1798, excerpts (Paris, n.d.)
Aurore de Gusman (c), PO, spr. 1799
Le général suédois (c, T. Favart), PO, 5 May 1799
Le trente et quarante (c, A. Duval), PO, 18 May 1799, *B-Bc*, *F-Lm*, *US-Bp*, excerpts (Paris, 1799)
D'auberge en auberge, ou Les préventions (c, E. Mercier-Dupaty), PO, 26 April 1800, *A-Wgm*, *D-Bds*, excerpts (Paris, 1800); as Zwei Posten, *I-Fc*, excerpts (Vienna, n.d.)
Une aventure de M. de Sainte-Foix, ou Le coup d'épée (c, Duval), PO, 20 or 28 Jan or 27 Feb 1802, *B-Bc*
Astolphe et Alba, ou A quoi la fortune (c, De Ségur), PO, spr. 1802
?Il Pimmaglione, *D-Dlb*

Miscellaneous excerpts: *A-Wgm*; *B-Bc*, *Br*; *CH-Zz*; *D-Bds*, *Dlb*; *E-Mp*; *F-Lm*, *Pc*; *GB-Cfm*, *Lbm*, *Lcm*, *T*; *I-Bc*, *Bsf*, *Fc*, *Gi(l)*, *Mc*, *Nc*, *Pca*, *PAc*, *Plbottini*

OTHER WORKS

Sacred: Missa per la Domenica Laetare, d, 4vv, orch, autograph *I-Nc*, copy *Mc*; Mass (Ky–Gl), solo vv, double choir, double orch, *GB-Lbm*; Credo, C, 4vv, str, b, autograph *I-Nc*, copy *Mc*; Stabat mater, 2S, orch, *PAc*
Secular: Intrattimento musicale (Sempre di verdi allori), solo v, chorus, orch, for Duke Ernst of Saxe-Gotha Altenburg, *GB-Lbm*

BIBLIOGRAPHY

EitnerQ; *FétisB*; *GerberL*; *GerberNL*
C. Gervasoni: *Nuova teoria di musica* (Parma, 1812/*R*)
C. A. di Rosa [Marchese di Villarosa]: *Memorie dei compositori di*

musica del regno di Napoli (Naples, 1840)
F. Florimo: *La scuola musicale di Napoli ed i suoi conservatorii*, iii (Naples, 1883/*R*1969), 55
A. Einstein: 'Mozart and Tarchi', *MMR*, lxv (1935), 127; repr. in *Essays on Music* (New York, 1956), 187
C. Sartori: 'Lo "Zeffiretto" di A. Tarchi', *RMI*, lvi (1954), 233

DENNIS LIBBY (text), JAMES L. JACKMAN (work-list)

Tardando (It.: 'delaying'). *See* RITARDANDO.

Tarditi, Orazio (*b* Rome, 1602; *d* Forlì, 18 Jan 1677). Italian composer and organist. He became a brother in the Camaldolite order. In the first part of his career he was an organist: at Arezzo Cathedral from 23 December 1624 to 21 August 1628, at S Michele, Murano, near Venice, in 1629 and at Volterra Cathedral in 1637. For the remainder of his career he was a *maestro di cappella*: at Forlì Cathedral in 1639 and Jesi Cathedral in 1644–5 and lastly at Faenza Cathedral, where he went in 1647, remaining until 1670.

As well as being one of the most travelled Italian church composers of his time Tarditi was also one of the most prolific. His output is mainly of sacred music, including many volumes of concertato motets, solo motets with or without violins, small and large concertato masses and psalm settings. He tended generally to write for increasingly intimate scorings: thus a fair number of his early works are for up to five voices and organ, whereas, entirely in accord with changes in north Italian church music at this period, the later ones are dominated by duet and trio textures. As early as 1629 he had a fine grasp of the declamatory solo motet writing of the Venetians, and the duet *Dulcis et suavissime Jesu* (1637) is a particularly fine example of spontaneous, emotionally charged melody; the two voices come together only at the end of each exposition, by way of climax. On a grander scale some of Tarditi's masses are impressive in their use of dramatic tuttis, especially at the openings of movements; they have extended solo episodes, which tend to be a trifle repetitive when treated in sequences. This judgment applies perhaps to Tarditi's largest work, the third of his 1648 collection of masses, which is for five voices, two violins, trombone and organ and is thus a ceremonial mass in the Venetian manner.

Tarditi's secular works are less interesting, though the arias of 1628, all unassuming strophic songs, include some agreeable tunes (e.g. that of *Gioisca pur contento*), the canzonets have a certain charm, and the duets resemble his better sacred ones in their combination of declamatory and contrapuntal interest.

WORKS

(all published in Venice unless otherwise stated)

SACRED

Sacri concentus, 1–5vv . . . cum Litaniis . . . BVM, 5vv, bc (org) [libro I] (1622)
Il secondo libro de [12] motetti, 1–5vv, con una messa e salmi, 5vv, bc (1625)
Il terzo libro de motetti, 2, 3vv, bc, op.7 (1628)
Celesti fiori musicali di [12] varii concerti sacri, 1v, bc (org/chit/harp/lute/spinet/other inst), libro II, op.8 (1629)
Il quarto libro de motetti, 2–4vv, con le Letanie della madonna, 4vv, bc, op.13 (1637)
Messe, 4, 5vv, con un Laudate . . . 3vv, 2 vn, bc (chit), op.15 (1639)
Messe e salmi, 4vv, bc, op.16 (1640)
Missa et psalmi in vespertinis laudibus, 3vv, bc (org) . . . cum Litaniis . . . BMV, op.17 (1640)
Concerto il XVIII: [19] musiche da chiesa, motetti, 2–5vv, 2 de quali . . . con 2 vn, . . . salmi, . . . doi, 3vv, 2 vn, e doi altri, 5vv, Lettanie della madonna, 5vv, bc (1641)
Il secondo libro de [11] salmi, 3vv, bc, con le Litanie della madonna, op.20 (1643)
Letanie della BVM, 3–5vv, con le 4 Antifone dell'istessa vergine santis-

sima, 2vv, alcuni motetti, 3vv, bc, et il Te Deum laudamus, 4vv, bc, ed. A. Vincenti (1644)
Motetti e salmi, 2, 3vv, bc, op.22 (1645)
[18] Motetti, 1v, bc (org/hpd/theorbo/other inst), libro III, op.23 (1646)
Psalmi ad Completorium et Litaniae beatae virginis, 4vv, cum 4 Antiphonis eiusdem virginis sanctissima, 3vv, . . . psalmo . . . et himno . . . vv/insts, op.24 (1647)
Concerto il XXV: [15] musiche da chiesa diverse, cioè motetti, è salmi, 3, 4vv, con una messa, 4vv, bc (1647)
[11] Motetti, 1v, bc (org/hpd/theorbo/other insts), libro IV (1648)
[3] Messe, 5vv, parte con insts . . . [5] salmi, 3–5vv, con insts e senza, bc, op.27 (1648)
Salmi, 8vv, bc (org), op.28 (1649)
[3] Messe, 3, 4vv, bc, libro III, op.30 (1650)
Concerto [23] musiche varie da chiesa, motetti, salmi, è hinni, 1–3vv, bc, parte con vns, theorbo, e parte senza, op.30 (1650)
Motetti, 2, 3vv, libro X, op.31 (1651)
Concerto il XXXIII: motetti e [3] salmi, 3, 4vv, parte con vns e parte senza, con una messa, 4vv, el et un Laudate pueri, 1v, 2 vn, bc (1652)
Il terzo libro de salmi, 3vv, bc, op.34 (1654)
Sacri concentus, 2, 3vv, bc, op.35 (1655)
Concerto il XXXV, di motetti, 2, 3vv, alcuni con vns, et una messa, 3vv, bc, op.36 (1663[3])
Messa e salmi, 2vv, bc, op.39 (Bologna, 1668)
Motetti, 2vv, bc (org) (Bologna, 1670)
Motetti, 1v, 2 vn, bc, libri [I], II, op.41–2 (Bologna, 1670)

9 motets in 1629[5], 1641[2], 1656[1], 1668[2], 1670[1]; 2 masses in 1641[3], 1642[4]; Magnificat in 1646[4]; psalm in 1642[4]
Kyrie, Gloria, 8vv, bc; Magnificat, 4vv, bc (org); Elevazione, org: *D-Bds*
4 sacred vocal works: *S-Uu*

SECULAR

Amorosa schiera d'arie, 1v, bc (hpd/chit/lute) con le lettere et intavolatura per gui, op.6 (1634)
[17] Madrigali, 2–4vv . . . con una lettera amorosa in stile recitativo, 1v, bc (hpd/chit/spinet/other inst) libro II, op.10 (1633)
[15] Madrigali, 3, 5vv, bc, op.14 . . . libro III (1639)
[19] Canzonette amorose, 2, 3vv, bc (hpd/theorbo), ed. A. Vincenti (1642)
[13] Arie, 1v, gui, bc (spinet/chit/other inst), A. Vincenti (1646[9])
[24] Canzonette amorose, libro II, 2, 3vv, bc (hpd/spinet/theorbo/other inst) (1647[5])
Il terzo libro di [14] canzonette e madrigaletti, 2, 3vv, bc (hpd/theorbo/other inst), op.32 (1652)

3 madrigals, 3, 4vv, in 1624[11]; 6 arias in 1634[7], 1656[4]; toccata in *D-Bds*
Cited in A. Vincenti: *Indice di tutte le opere di musica* (Venice, 1622): Arie, 1v, bc, libro IV and Scherzi recitativi, 1v, bc; in the *Indice* of 1649: vocal music, 2–4vv, bc, libro III and Arie, vv, insts, bc, libro II

BIBLIOGRAPHY
H. A. Sander: 'Beiträge zur Geschichte der Barockmesse', *KJb*, xxviii (1933), 77–129
F. Coradini: 'La cappella musicale del duomo di Arezzo dal secolo XV a tutto il secolo XIX', *NA*, xviii (1941), 93
J. L. A. Roche: *North Italian Liturgical Music in the Early 17th Century* (diss., U. of Cambridge, 1968)

JEROME ROCHE

Tarditi, Paolo (*b* 2nd half of the 16th century; *d* after 1649). Italian composer. There is no evidence that he was related to Orazio Tarditi. He seems to have spent his entire career in Rome. From 1597 he appears to have been a member of the Vertuosa Compagnia dei Musici di Roma. On 23 March 1601 he took part in a procession to the church of S Biagio, and on several occasions between 1602 and 1623 he was in charge of the choir of the Arciconfraternità di Ss Crocifisso at S Marcello. Early on he was organist of S Giovanni dei Fiorentini. He refused the post of *maestro di cappella* at S Maria Maggiore when it was offered to him in 1610 on the departure of Vincenzo Ugolini. He was *maestro di cappella* of SS Giacomo e Ildefonso degli Spagnuoli about 1619–20, of S Maria Maggiore from 1629 to 1640 and of the church of the Madonna dei Monti from 1649.

Tarditi's most interesting works are those in his collection of 1620. This consists of music for double choir – five psalms and a *Magnificat* for voices alone and nine psalms, a *Magnificat* and four Marian antiphons in the concertato style with instrumental accompaniment; together with G. F. Anerio's *Il teatro armonico spirituale* (1619), this last-named group of 14 works affords the earliest instance of the use of obbligato instruments in works by Roman composers. There is usually a close motivic connection between the voice parts and the instrumental accompaniment (lute and theorbo with the first choir, cornett and violin with the second). Tarditi frequently transferred parts of his vocal themes, especially their first few notes, to the instrumental introductions and interludes, which are mostly composed in motet style. The same procedure is found in monodic sections with continuo; the solo part here is usually interspersed with instrumental imitations, both preceding and following it. In the concertato psalms the instrumental and vocal textures change with every new verse. This creates a continuous series of contrasts, to which the obbligato instruments make a telling contribution: it is an element in Tarditi's style that points to later developments, with formal anticipations of the sacred concerto and even of the later cantata. Traditional components are nevertheless still very pronounced. The conservatism in Tarditi's style is clearest in the monodic psalm verses with continuo. Even here there is imitative writing; the melodies owe much to the nature of motet themes of the early 17th century, and their metre is governed by that of the text. In his polyphonic compositions, too, there is an obvious preference for imitation. This predilection is symptomatic of the change of style that took place after 1600, as are also the melodic shapes rising to climactic points, and the occasional replacement of the freely flowing melody which was characteristic of earlier, classical vocal polyphony, by melody with periodically recurring sections. Tarditi's works do not reveal the identification with the content of the text and the representation of emotions which characterize the genuine monodic style: they are at once typical of an age of transition and of the Roman tradition.

WORKS

Motecta, 1–6vv, bc (Rome, 1619)

Psalmi, Magnificat cum 4 antiphonis ad vesperas . . . liber II, 8vv, bc (Rome, 1620)

Motets in 1615¹, 1616¹, 1618³, 1621³, 1623², 1639², 1642¹, 1649², 1650¹, 1656²

Beatus vir, psalm, 8vv, bc, in F

Costantini: Salmi, himni et Magnificat concertati, op.11 (Venice, 1630)

Messa intitolata Hieronymi Cardinalis Columnae (Rome, 1630); lost, mentioned in Pitoni

1 mass, 8vv, bc, in Diversorum autorum misse quinque (Rome, 1623), authenticity doubtful

BIBLIOGRAPHY

G. O. Pitoni: *Notitia de contrapuntisti e de compositori di musica* (MS, *I-Rvat* C.G., I/1–2, c1725), 652

R. Giazotto: *Quattro secoli di storia dell'Accademia Nazionale di S. Cecilia* (Rome, 1970), i, 37, 54, 59

KLAUS FISCHER

Tardo (It.: 'slow'). One of the earliest tempo marks in music. Perhaps it came into early favour because of being cognate with the Latin adverb *tarde* which has a long history of appearances in musical theory: Augustine and Aribo Scolasticus both contrasted *tarditas* with *celeritas*; and Aribo added that these were the correct interpretations of the Romanus letters *t* and *c*. So when tempo marks began to be used it initially had some prominence. Michael Praetorius gave *tarde* as the Latin equivalent of the Italian *lento* and the German *langsam* (e.g. in *Syntagma musicum*, iii, 2/1619). Monte-

verdi marked at one point in the organ part of his 1610 collection 'va sonata tardo perchè li doi tenori cantano di semicroma' ('should be slow because the two tenors sing quavers'). It was used as the designation for a slow tempo by Priuli (1618), Jelich (1622), Marini (op.1, 1626), Schütz and several other composers in the 17th century. But its career was thwarted, so to speak, by the sheer plethora of slow tempo marks: *adagio*, *grave*, *lento* and *largo* left little room for yet a fifth word meaning essentially the same thing. And though the word was still defined in Brossard's *Dictionaire* (1703) and the anonymous *A Short Explication* (1724), examples of its use after Schütz are hard to find. For the gerund, *tardando*, see RITARDANDO.

See also TEMPO AND EXPRESSION MARKS, §5.

DAVID FALLOWS

Tardos, Béla (*b* Budapest, 21 June 1910; *d* Budapest, 18 Nov 1966). Hungarian composer. He studied the piano at the National Conservatory in Budapest (1926–9) and composition with Kodály at the Budapest Academy of Music (1932–7), earning his living in an insurance company between 1930 and 1945. A printworker's son, he had early connections with the Hungarian labour movement; from 1933 to 1945 he conducted workers' choirs, notably the Vándor Chorus, which performed several of his works. Later he held appointments as music editor of the Szikra publishing house (1945–8), general manager of the National Philharmonic Concert Bureau (1950–52) and director of Editio Musica (1955–66).

The most important works from Tardos's first creative period, up to 1945, are the Divertimento for wind octet (1935), the Piano Quartet (1939–41) and *Német zsoldosdal* ('German mercenary song', 1942); many other pieces, such as the first version of the cantata *A város peremén* ('At the outskirts of the city', 1944), were lost during the war. In 1948 Tardos won the first prize at the Bartók International Competition in Budapest for his String Quartet no.1. The major part of his output of the early 1950s consists of cantatas, choruses, film music, songs and mass music. It was in his last decade that he produced his best work, whose quality was recognized by the award of two Erkel Prizes, one, in 1960, for the second version of *At the Outskirts of the City*, the other, in 1966, for his whole oeuvre.

WORKS

(selective list)

VOCAL

Opera: Laura (M. Gyárfás, Tardos), 1958, rev. 1964

Cantatas: A város peremén [At the outskirts of the city] (A. József), 1st version 1944, lost, 2nd version 1958; Rólad susog a lomb [The leaves whisper about you] (G. Képes), 1949; Májusi kantáta [May cantata] (Zs. Gál), 1950; A béke napja alatt [Under the sun of peace] (I. Raics), 1953; Hajnali dal [Morning song] (F. Juhász), 1953; Dózsa feje [Dózsa's head] (Gy. Juhász), 1958; Szabadság született [Liberty has been born] (Gál), 1960; Az új isten [The new god] (Á. Tóth), 1966

Choral: Német zsoldosdal [German mercenary song] (Gy. Faludy), vv, wind/ens, 1942; 3 Choruses (József), 1942–3; 3 Choruses (Gy. Juhász), 1943; 2 Choruses (Ady), 1943; Pillantás előre [A glance forwards] (A. Gábor), 1945; Muzsikásláda [Music box] (S. Weöres), 1954; Magyar tájak [Hungarian landscapes] (A. Károlyi), 1955; Keserű esztendők [Bitter years], suite, 1959; Tiszta szigorúság [Pure severity] (G. Garai), 1964; Rendért kiáltunk [We cry for order] (Garai), vv, pf, 1966; 4 Michelangelo Sonnets, male vv, 1966

Songs: Dalok régről [Songs of olden times], 1v, pf, 1931–43; Dalok kínai versekre [Songs on Chin. poems], 1v, pf, 1937–41; Songs (József), 1v, pf, 1943; 6 kuruc dal [6 Kuruts songs] (S. Erdődy), 1v, pf, 1943; 5 Songs (József), 1v, pf, 1955; Edes rózsám [My sweetheart] (Weöres), 1v, orch, 1963; 4 Songs (Gy. Illyés), T, orch, 1964

INSTRUMENTAL

Orch: Suite, 1949; Ov., 1949; Pf Conc., 1954; Mesejáték nyitány [Ov. to a fairy tale], 1955; Sym. 'In memoriam martyrum', 1960; Fantasy, pf, orch, 1961; Variation on a Theme of Kodály, 1962; Vn Conc., 1962; Evocation, 1964; Pezzo per violino, vn, orch, 1965
Chamber: Variations, str qt, 1935; Divertimento, 8 ww, 1935; Pf Qt, 1939, rev. 1941; 3 str qts, 1947, 1949, 1963; [3] Improvisations, cl, pf, 1960, arr. va, pf, 1965; Prelude and Rondo, fl, pf, 1962; Quartettino, wind, 1963; Divertimento, 4 wind, 1963; Cassazione, harp trio, 1964; Sonata, vn, pf, 1965; Meditation, vn, harp, 1966
Pf: 5 Bagatelles, 1955; Szivárvány [Rainbow], 7 pieces, 1957; 2 Little Pieces, 1960; Miniatures, 1961; Suite, 1961; Sonatina, 1961; 6 Little Studies, 1963; 4 études, 4 hands, 1966
Educational pieces, incidental music, film scores

Principal publishers: Boosey & Hawkes, Editio Musica

BIBLIOGRAPHY
P. Várnai: *Tardos Béla* (Budapest, 1966)

MARIA PÁRKAI-ECKHARDT

Ṭarīqa. Syllabic recitation of hymn melodies in the MUSIC OF THE COPTIC RITE.

Tarisio, Luigi (*b* Fontaneto, nr. Novaro, Piedmont, *c*1790, *d* Milan, Oct 1854). Italian violin dealer and collector. He was born of humble parents and is said to have trained as a carpenter, with violin playing as a hobby. He developed an interest in violins themselves, and with a natural talent both as a connoisseur and for business he began to acquire and resell some of the many fine instruments that were lying unused in the towns and villages of northern Italy. His first journey to Paris (in 1827) was evidently profitable for him and for the dealers there, who gave him every encouragement. In the same year he made his greatest coup, acquiring a number of violins from Count Cozio di Salabue, including a 1716 Stradivari in unused condition. This violin was Tarisio's treasure, and as he spoke of it on every visit to Paris but never actually brought it with him it came to be known as the 'Messiah'.

Tarisio searched indefatigably for violins and had a true love of them. The novelist Charles Reade, who knew Tarisio, wrote of him: 'The man's whole soul was in fiddles. He was a great dealer, but a greater amateur, for he had gems by him no money would buy'. An insatiable demand in northern Europe for what nobody wanted or appreciated in the south, and the absence of much competition, gave him unique opportunities; and by bringing his stock to Paris, the only place where the art of restoration was at all advanced, he rescued many great instruments for posterity. After his death it was the turn of Vuillaume, the leading Parisian dealer, to make the greatest purchase of his life. At a small farm near Fontaneto, where Tarisio's relatives lived, were the six finest violins of the collection, including the celebrated 'Messiah'; and in a dingy attic in Milan, where Tarisio's body had been found, were no fewer than 24 Stradivaris and 120 other Italian masterpieces.

BIBLIOGRAPHY
W. E. Hill: *The Salabue Stradivari* (London, 1891)
F. Farga: *Violins and Violinists* (London, 1950)

CHARLES BEARE

Tarjáni, Ferenc (*b* Dorog, 11 Sept 1938). Hungarian horn player. He studied with János Onozó at the Liszt Academy of Music (1959–64), having already made his début in 1958. He became principal horn in the Budapest Radio and Television SO in 1958. A notable virtuoso with a flawless technique, he is also a natural musician, who has a special feeling for melody. He was highly praised in the USA (with the Budapest SO) in 1971 and 1973, in Germany, and wherever he has ap-

peared as a member of the Budapest Chamber Ensemble. His recordings include all the horn concertos of Haydn and Mozart, Beethoven's sonata, and many contemporary Hungarian works, most of them dedicated to him. He was awarded the Liszt Prize in 1965, and named Artist of Merit in 1975.

PÉTER P. VÁRNAI

Tarnowski, Count Władysław (*b* Wróblewice, Galicia, 1841; *d* at sea nr. California, 19 April 1878). Polish pianist, composer and poet. He studied in Lwów and Kraków, then under Auber at the Paris Conservatoire (until 1863), in Leipzig under Moscheles (piano) and Richter (composition), and in Rome with Liszt. He performed in Vienna, Venice, Florence and Paris, and undertook concert tours in the Middle and Far East; for long periods he lived in India, China and Japan. His instrumental works enjoyed considerable success, and he also wrote poetry under the pseudonym Ernest Buława. He died while returning on the *SS Pacific* from a concert tour.

WORKS

Stage: Achmed, czyli Pielgrzym miłości [Ahmed, or The pilgrim of love] (opera, 2, Tarnowski, after W. Irving: Alhambra), vocal score (Leipzig, *c*1875); Joanna Grey (incidental music, Tarnowski)
Chamber: Str Qt; Fantasia quasi una sonata, pf, vn
Pf: Nocturne dédié à sa soeur Marie (Vienna, n.d.); Sonata à son ami Zawadzki (Vienna, n.d.); Grande polonaise quasi rapsodie symphonique (Vienna, n.d.); Chants sans paroles; Extases au Bosphor, fantasy on oriental melodies, op.10; Grande sonate; Nocturnes; Romanze; 2 morceaux: Fantaisie, Impromptu; Valse poème
Vocal: Songs, incl. Jak to na wojence ładnie [Isn't the war fun] (Warsaw, 1917)

BIBLIOGRAPHY
SMP
I. J. Kraszewski: 'Władysław Tarnowski', *Kłosy* (1877), no.630, p.60
Tygodnik illustrowany (1878), no.132, p.1

IRENA PONIATOWSKA

Tárogató. A woodwind instrument usually associated with Hungarian music. It was generally between 30 and 40 cm in length, and had a slightly tapered body, seven to nine finger-holes, and a double reed usually inserted in a forked, tubular mouthpiece. In the era of the Rákóczy struggles at the beginning of the 18th century the instrument was very popular with the adherents of the movement; it later became a symbol of freedom to the Hungarians. When the Rákóczy movement was defeated the instrument was prohibited, in consequence of which it disappeared from public use, reappearing only at the time of the war of independence against the Austrian Habsburg rule. A number of attempts were made at reconstruction: András Szuk produced a type in 1859 which, however, was based on an early form of the english horn rather than the ancient tárogató. Towards the end of the century V. J. Schunda, another instrument builder, on the advice of Gyula Káldy, designed its present form (see illustration). It consists of a straight body of wood with a conical bore and a clarinet (single-reed) mouthpiece. Its keywork resembles that of the oboe and the compass runs from $b\flat$ to c''. The quality of its tone is dark and penetrating in character, resembling that of the english horn. In its present-day form it is built in three pitches: $B\flat$, $E\flat$, $A\flat$. Following the directions of Mahler the instrument has been used for the shepherd's tune in Act 3 of *Tristan und Isolde* in performances at the Budapest Opera House; on the advice of Hans Richter it was also introduced at Bayreuth. Today it is used by folk musicians in Hungary and Romania.

Tárogató (clarinet) player from Hungary

The ancient tárogató is a variant of the Eastern oboe; it may have been introduced to Europe by the Arabs through Spain in the 13th century, or by the Magyars (Lajtha). Of this original form three types are distinguishable: the Arab–Persian–Turkish, the Mongol and the Indian. Their distinguishing characteristics are respectively: straight wooden body without finger-holes; curved body in the shape of successively increasing beads at the finger-holes, increasing in size towards the bell, which resembles that of a trumpet; and straight body with a flat bell of bronze.

The Magyar tárogató can be traced in an unbroken line from the earliest times until the 18th century. Following the conquest of Hungary by the Magyars it fell into disuse until the invasion and occupation by the Turks again brought it to light; its reappearance may have been stimulated by the Turkish instrument, to judge from its name *töröksip* ('Turkish pipe'). From the 16th century to the 18th, descriptions of contemporary life and manners at princely and aristocratic residences made frequent allusions to its appearance. The double reed of the tárogató was placed in the mouth of the player, following Eastern practice, and a small disc at the end of the mouthpiece supported his lips; this manner of playing made its tone harsh and shrieking. It was principally a military signal instrument, but was also employed at funerals, weddings and out of doors generally. As a cavalry instrument it appeared almost always in conjunction with drums.

The first known appearance of the tárogató in symphonic music was in Károly Thern's opera *Svatopluc* (1839). In more recent times Antal Molnár used the instrument in his *Kuruc muzsika* for small orchestra and four tárogatós (1936).

BIBLIOGRAPHY

L. Lajtha: 'A tárogató vándorutja Perzsiából Európába' [The route of the tárogató from Persia to Europe], *Magyarország* (Budapest, 22 July 1923)

B. Szabolcsi: *A xvii század magyar főúri zenéje* [Hungarian aristocratic music in the 17th century] (Budapest, 1928)

H. Welsh: 'The Tárogató: its History and Details', *Leading Note*, i/2 (1929), 46

G. Gábry: 'Le "tárogató", ancien chalumeau hongrois', *SM*, xiii (1971), 61

JOHN S. WEISSMANN

Tarompet. Shawm of west Java with seven finger-holes and a narrow, slightly conical bore which widens towards the lower end into a large bell. Its double reed is held entirely within the musician's mouth and vibrates freely there; a crescent-shaped piece of coconut-shell attached to the mouthpiece serves as a cheek support (for illustration, *see* INDONESIA, fig.25). The player employs circular breathing to produce a continuous tone. The instrument has a piercing sound and is not played in the usual gamelan but in smaller outdoor ensembles, mainly those which accompany the combat dance, *pěnca*, for which one or two *tarompet*, one or two sets of drums and a small gong are used. Other ensembles in which the *tarompet* plays the leading melodic role are those of the *ujungan* stick-fights (*tarompet* with gong, drum and iron clappers), and of the *kuda lumping* hobby-horse trance-dance (*tarompet* with bamboo *angklung* and four single-headed *dogdog* drums). The *tarompet* (like its central Javanese parallel *sělompret*) is derived from the musical culture of Islamic south-western and southern Asia but the name is derived from the Dutch word 'trompet'.

ERNST HEINS

Taroni [Tarroni], **Antonio** (*b* ?Mantua; *fl* 1604–46). Italian composer. His earliest recorded association with composers of the Mantuan *cappella* is the appearance of his *Eran ninfe e pastori* in Gastoldi's popular *Concenti musicali* (*RISM* 1604²¹). Between July and April 1609 and in August and September 1612 he served temporarily as *maestro di cappella* of the ducal chapel of S Barbara, Mantua. From July 1610 to September 1612 he also held the less important post of *maestro di cantofermo* with responsibility for instructing the choristers in 'canto figurato e contrappunto'. His abilities as a composer seem to have been highly valued by his Mantuan colleagues. His *Ardo mia vita* appeared together with works by Gastoldi, Virchi and Monteverdi in 1608 in Wert's posthumous *Il duodecimo libro de madrigali a 5, 6 & 7*. In 1610 G. B. Sacchi, a singer and composer employed at S Barbara, sent madrigals by him to Cardinal Ferdinando Gonzaga, a noted patron of music and a composer, who succeeded to the Duchy of Mantua in 1612. Cagnani included Taroni in the lists of Mantuan composers in his *Lettera cronologica*, though he mistakenly stated that he contributed to *L'amorosa caccia de diversi eccellentissimi musici mantovani nativi* (*RISM* 1588¹⁴); his absence from that volume possibly signifies that he was not born in Mantua, though it may have been because he was too young at the time. Despite the support of distinguished contemporaries and the efforts of Sacchi, he seems not to have held an important musical post, at least at Mantua. In 1614 he was a canon at S Barbara. According to a letter from Monteverdi, dated 13 June 1627, Taroni was in Poland at that time. Nothing is heard of him between that date and the appearance 19 years later of his *Messe da capella*, which according to the conservatory catalogue is a reprint with basso continuo of *Il primo libro di messe*.

WORKS
(all printed works published in Venice)

SACRED

Il primo libro di messe, 5vv, ed. P. E. Gonzaga (1614)
Messe da capella, 5vv, bc (1646)

Missa in contrapuncto, 5vv, org, 1614, *D-Rp*
1 mass, *A-Kr*
3 settings of Ps cxviii, *I-Mc*

SECULAR

Il primo libro de madrigali, 5vv, con due nel fine, 8vv (1612)
Il secondo libro de madrigali, 5vv, con due nel fine, 8vv (1612)

1 madrigal, 8vv, 1604[21]; 1 in G. de Wert: Il duodecimo libro de madrigali (1608)

BIBLIOGRAPHY

E. Cagnani: *Lettera cronologica*, foreword to *Raccolta d'alcune rime di scrittori mantovani* (Mantua, 1612)
P. Canal: 'Della musica in Mantova', *Memorie del R. istituto veneto di scienze, lettere e arti*, xxi (1881)
A. Bertolotti: *Musici alla corte dei Gonzaga dal secolo XV al XVIII* (Milan, 1890/R1969)
P. M. Tagmann: 'La cappella dei maestri cantori della basilica palatina di Santa Barbara a Mantova (1565–1630)', *Civiltà mantovana*, xxiv (1970), 376
Conservatorio di musica Giuseppe Verdi in Milano: catalogo della Biblioteca: fondi speciali, i; *Musiche della cappella di S. Barbara in Mantova* (Florence, 1972)

IAIN FENLON

Tarp, Svend Erik (*b* Thisted, 6 Aug 1908). Danish composer. He began his music studies at the University of Copenhagen and with Elof Nielsen for the piano. At the Copenhagen Conservatory he was taught theory by Jeppesen and the history of music by Simonsen. After graduation he studied in Germany, Holland and Austria (1933 and 1937). He taught intermittently during the 1930s and 1940s at the opera school of the Royal Theatre (1936–40), the Copenhagen Conservatory (1936–42), the Statens Lærerhøjskole (1941–5) and the University of Copenhagen (1939–47), but gradually became completely involved in administrative tasks, especially for Koda, of which he was administrative director from 1960 to 1974. He was also an administrator for Edition Dania (1941–60) and chairman of Samfundet til Udgivelse af Dansk Musik (1961–4). These and other organizational posts have been responsible for a diminished later output.

Starting from the style of Nielsen, and in emphasizing a clearly arranged and entertaining concertante musical progression, Tarp represents the French-orientated neo-classical modernism of Denmark in the interwar years. He composes music that is equally approachable and acceptable to listener and performer alike, without lapsing into banality and cliché. Rhythmic suppleness, polyphony on a tonal basis and ostinato formations are important elements in his style. With his ability to limit himself, Tarp has mostly concentrated on works for smaller ensembles and on easily playable piano music; but his Symphony no.2, for example, is an expressive and brilliantly conceived work on a larger scale. Also, Danish film music has acquired a serious composer in Tarp, who has discussed this functional form of art in several articles.

WORKS
(*selective list*)

DRAMATIC AND VOCAL

Stage: Den detroniserede dyretæmmer (ballet, B. Bartholin), Copenhagen, 1944; Prinsessen i det fjærne (lyric comedy, E. Hjejle), Copenhagen, 1953; Hæsblæs fra Husum (school opera), 1954; Skyggen (ballet, Bartholin), Copenhagen, 1960
Film and television: music for c40 films, incl. Gården hedder Vikagardur, 1946; Qivitoq, 1956; 9.90 (comic opera for television, 1, Soya), 1962
Radio: incidental music, incl. Blodbryllup (Lorca), 1951; Leonce og Lena (Büchner), 1955
Choral: Amatørmusik no.1, op.6, 2vv, bc, 1930; Te Deum, op.33, solo vv, chorus, orch, 1938; Julens budskab, op.44, cantata, reciter, Bar, chorus, orch, org, 1945; Missa juvenalis, op.82 (1979); Requiem, op.83 (1980); unacc. songs
Solo songs: Her har hjertet hjemme, 1940; Over et meget yndeligt sted i skoven strax ved Colding (1942)

ORCHESTRAL

Dansk ouverture, 1926; Sørgemarch og koral, 1928; Concertino, pf,

chamber orch, 1930; Concertino, va, str, 1931; Festmarch, 1931; Sinfonietta, op.11, chamber orch, 1931; Vn Concertino (Vn Conc.), op.13, 1932; Concertino, sax, str, 1932; Suite over danske folke-visemotiver, op.17, 1933; Conc. for Orch, op.18, 1933–4; Ov., op.25, str, 1932; Russisk dans, 1934; Cimbrernes tog, op.26, 1936; Dansk folketone, str (1936); Fl Concertino, C, op.30, 1937; Orania, suite, 1938; Pezzo sinfonico, op.34, 1940; Mosaik, op.35 (1942); Lystspilouverture no.1, op.36, 1940; Pf Conc., C, op.39, 1942–3
Sym. no.1 (Sinfonia divertente), op.42, 1945; Pro defunctis, 1945; Sym. no.2, E♭, op.50, 1949; Lystspilouverture no.2 'Til mit Dukketeater', op.53, 1949; Divertimento, op.58, 1954; Lyrisk suite, op.67, 1956; Sym. no.3 (Quasi una fantasia), op.66, 1958; Burlesk ouverture (1958); Rhapsodisk ouverture (1963); Lille festouverture, op.75 (1969); Sym. no.4, op.77 (1976); Sym. no.5, op.78 (1976); Sym. no.6, op.80 (1977); Sym. no.7, op.81 (1977)

CHAMBER AND INSTRUMENTAL

Chamber: Pf Trio, g, 1925; Serenade, fl, cl, str trio, op.8, 1930; Str trios nos.1–2, op.3, 1930; Taffelmusik, fl, cl, bn, 1932; Divertimento og serenade, fl, pf qt, op.28, 1934; Morgenserenade, ob, cl, bn, hn, 1941; 12 bagateller, vn, pf (1970); Str Qt, op.76, 1971
Pf: Romantisk ouverture, 1928; Suite, 1928; 3 improvisations, op.21, 1934; 3 danses, op.41, 1944; Tema med variationer 'Carillon', op.43, 1944; 3 sonatiner, op.48 (1947); Sonata, op.60, 1954
Educational works for pf: Mosaik, op.31, 1938; Snap-shots, op.45 (1947); Cirkus, op.47 (1947); Konfetti, op.52 (1950)

BIBLIOGRAPHY

J. Balzer: 'Svend Erik Tarp', *Dansk musiktidsskrift*, ix (1934), 18

NIELS MARTIN JENSEN

Tarr, Edward H(ankins) (*b* Norwich, Conn., 15 June 1936). American trumpeter and musicologist. He studied the trumpet under Roger Voisin in Boston (1953), Adolph Herseth in Chicago (1958–9); and, after leaving the USA, he studied musicology in Basle under Leo Schrade (1959–64). His main interest is in reviving early trumpet music on modern and old instruments and on present-day reconstructions, on which he has collaborated with the German makers Meinl & Lauber. He cultivates a brilliant and resonant tone on these instruments to match the sound described by contemporary writers. His repertory includes many solo Baroque works (from Italy, Germany, England and France), Classical concertos and a number of modern works, including *Atem* and *Morceau de concours* by Kagel (dedicated to and recorded by him) and pieces by Berio and Stockhausen. He has received enthusiastic acclaim for his recordings and public performances, particularly on his annual tours of the USA. In 1967 he founded the Edward Tarr Brass Ensemble to perform Renaissance and Baroque music on authentic instruments, as well as contemporary music on modern ones. He taught the trumpet at the Rheinische Musikschule, Cologne, 1968–70, and in 1972 started teaching the cornett at the Schola Cantorum Basiliensis. As an author and editor, Tarr has been equally adventurous, contributing much to the history of the trumpet and making much Baroque music available for the first time in modern performing editions, as notable for their scholarship as for their practical advice in authentic playing. Particularly noteworthy are many Italian Baroque works, including the complete trumpet works of Torelli.

WRITINGS

'Monteverdi, Bach und die Trompetenmusik ihrer Zeit', *GfMKB, Bonn 1970*, 592
'Original Italian Baroque Compositions for Trumpet and Organ', *Diapason*, lxi (1970), 27
'The Baroque Trumpet, the High Trumpet, and the So-called Bach Trumpet', *Brass Bulletin* (1972), no.2, p.25; no.3, pp.44, 54
Die Trompete (Berne, 1977, rev. 2/1978)
with B. Dickey and P. Leonards: 'The Discussion of Wind Instruments in Bartolomeo Bismantova's *Compendio musicale* (1677): Translation and Commentary', *Basler Jb für historische Musik-praxis*, ii (1978), 143
with T. Walker: 'Bellici carmi, festivo fragor: die Verwendung der Trompete in der italienischen Oper des 17. Jahrhunderts', *Hambur-*

ger Jb für Musikwissenschaft, iii (1978), 143
with B. Dickey: Articulation in Early Wind Music: a Source Book, i
(Nashville, in preparation)

NIALL O'LOUGHLIN

Tárrega (y Eixea), Francisco (b Villarreal, Castellón, 21 Nov 1852; d Barcelona, 15 Dec 1909). Spanish guitarist and composer. When he began the study of the classical guitar with Julian Arcas in 1862, the instrument was at a low ebb throughout Europe, overshadowed by the ever louder and more resonant guitar. Tárrega's father insisted that the boy study the piano as well, which was practical advice at the time; he became accomplished on both instruments at an early age. In 1869 he had the good fortune to acquire an unusually loud and resonant guitar designed and constructed by Antonio Torres, the famous luthier, then living in Seville. With this superior instrument Tárrega was to prepare the way for the rebirth of the guitar in the 20th century. He entered the Madrid Conservatory in 1874, and received a thorough grounding in theory, harmony and the piano. By 1877 he was earning his living as a music teacher and concert guitarist; he gave recitals in Paris and London in 1880, and was hailed as 'the Sarasate of the guitar'. He married María Josepha Rizo in 1881 and they settled in Barcelona in 1885. Within a few years he displayed a repertory that included, besides his own compositions in the smaller forms, piano works by Mendelssohn, Gottschalk, Thalberg and others arranged for the guitar. The Spanish 'nationalist' composers, Albéniz and Granados, were his friends; many of their works were first transcribed for the guitar by him. He also adapted movements from Beethoven's piano sonatas (including the Largo of op.7, the Adagio and Allegretto from the 'Moonlight' Sonata) and half a dozen preludes of Chopin. During the years 1885–1903, Tárrega gave concerts throughout Spain. He toured Italy in 1903. At the height of his fame, in 1906, he suffered a paralysis of the right side from which he never fully recovered. He did, however, appear publicly, and to loud applause, in 1909.

Tárrega's influence on the 20th century, through pupils who included Emilio Pujol, Maria Rita Brondi and Josefina Robledo, has been tremendous. His compositions for solo guitar, not all of which have been published, comprise approximately 78 original works and 120 transcriptions; he also made 21 transcriptions for two guitars. Among his most famous solos are *Recuerdos de la Alhambra* (a tremolo study), *Capricho árabe* and *Danza mora*.

BIBLIOGRAPHY
F. Buek: 'Franzisko Tarrega', Der Gitarrefreund, xxv (1924), 18
M. Llobet, E. Pujol and others: 'Tarrega als Mensch und Künstler im
  Urteil seiner Zeitgenossen', Die Gitarre, xi (1930), 5
E. Schwarz-Reiflingen: 'Tarregas Gitarrentechnik', Die Gitarre, xi
  (1930), 9
E. Pujol: Tárrega: ensayo biográfico (Lisbon, 1960)
T. Heck: 'Historical notes to a Tárrega recital of 1888', Guitar News
  (1970), no.107, p.24

THOMAS F. HECK

Tarreria, Francesco. See TERRIERIA, FRANCESCO.

Tarroni, Antonio. See TARONI, ANTONIO.

Tartaglino, Hippolito (b ?Modena, ?1539; d Naples, 1582). Italian composer and organist. He was probably in Rome by 1574; he was named *maestro di cappella* of S Maria Maggiore, Rome, on 10 October 1575. He was organist of St Peter's in February 1577, and during Holy Week and Easter he performed for the Arciconfraternità del Santissimo Crocifisso at S Marcello, Rome, where there are still some of his motets or parts of motets. Some time between January 1580, when his name appears in the archives of the Annunziata in Naples, and June 1581, when he was officially replaced at St Peter's, he moved to Naples, where he was organist at the Church of the Annunciation until his death. Fétis asserted that he had been made a Roman citizen and Knight of the Golden Spur through the influence of Cardinal Farnese, and Prota-Giurleo (in *MGG*) mentioned that he received the patronage of Cardinal Burali of Arezzo. Giovanni d'Avella, in his *Regole di musica* (Rome, 1657), treated Tartaglino among Neapolitan composers, although he is not listed as such in Scipione Cerreto's *Prattica musica* (Naples, 1601, 157ff).

Tartaglino's surviving music is less ambitious in scope than the masses and motets for three and four choruses which Eitner, without giving details, claimed for him. His *Motettorum quinque & sex vocum liber primus* (Rome, 1574), his only motet publication, constitutes the entire known musical production of the printer Giovanni Osmarino Gigliotti (Liliotus). Tartaglino's madrigal for five voices, *Celeste donna*, was included among the *Dolci affetti* collected by a Roman academician from works by Roman composers (*RISM* 1582⁴). Two of his madrigals for four voices were printed in Rodio's *Secondo libro di madrigali a quattro* (*RISM* 1587¹²). One of the two, *Hor le tue forz' adopra*, was reprinted in the five Neapolitan editions of Arcadelt's *Primo libro di madrigali a quattro* (*RISM* 1608¹⁴ etc). Prota-Giurleo reported the existence, as yet unconfirmed, of a book of *Madrigali a cinque voci* (Rome, 1576). Two *canzoni francesi* attributed to 'Ippolito' are in *GB-Lbm* Add.30491.

BIBLIOGRAPHY
EitnerQ; FétisB
G. Baini: Memorie storico-critiche della vita e delle opere di Giovanni
  Pierluigi da Palestrina (Rome, 1828/R1966), i, 364; ii, 31
G. Gaspari: Catalogo della Biblioteca del Liceo Musicale di Bologna
  (Bologna, 1890–1905/R1961), ii, 503; iii, 28
D. Alaleona: Storia dell'oratorio musicale in Italia (Milan, 1908, 2/
  1945), 166, 331f
A. Ducrot: 'Histoire de la Cappella Giulia au XVIe siècle', Ecole
  française de Rome: Meslanges d'archéologie et d'histoire, lxxv (1963),
  504
R. Jackson, ed.: Neapolitan Keyboard Composers circa 1600, CEKM,
  xxiv (1967), pp.ix–x, 1ff
L. Cammarota: Gian Domenico del Giovane (Rome, 1973), i, 39

THOMAS W. BRIDGES

Tartini, Giuseppe (b Pirano, Istria, 8 April 1692; d Padua, 26 Feb 1770). Italian composer, violinist, teacher and theorist. He was a principal contributor to the virtuoso concerto and sonata literature for violin, and to a north Italian synthesis of *galant* and *empfindsam* stylistic qualities during the middle of the 18th century. He was the teacher of several prominent violinists and composers of the succeeding generation, including J. G. Graun, Nardini, J. G. Naumann, Paganelli and Pagin, and author of a noteworthy work on violin playing and ornamentation, as well as two major treatises and numerous unpublished writings on the acoustical foundations of harmony.

1. Life 2. Works. 3. Theory, acoustics.

1. LIFE. As Petrobelli has shown, the principal source of biographical information about Tartini's youth is a manuscript compiled at the time of the composer's death,

probably by his friend and colleague of many years, the cellist Antonio Vandini. Original documents from the period before 1721 are scarce and relatively uninformative. The fourth child of Giovanni Antonio Tartini, a native of Florence and minor public official in Pirano, he was schooled under clerics at Pirano and Capodistria, and destined by his parents for a monastic career. Apart from one passing reference to violin instruction received at Capodistria, nothing is known about the circumstances that led him, against parental wishes, to pursue music seriously. In 1708, having renounced the cloister but still nominally a candidate for the priesthood, he was permitted to travel to Padua. Somewhat incongruously, his name appears in 1709 among those of students enrolled at the law faculty of the university. He appears to have led a kind of double life, becoming known principally for his prowess as a swordsman. In 1710 he came into serious conflict with church authority through his marriage to Elisabetta Premazore, permission for which he may have obtained by concealing his clerical status. Threatened by the personal displeasure of the Bishop of Padua, Cardinal Giorgio Cornaro, Tartini took up secret asylum in the monastery of the Friars Minor Conventual at Assisi. Here he is said to have studied music (?composition) under a certain Padre Boemo, probably Bohuslav Černohorský, who later held various organist's posts as Tartini's colleague at St Anthony's in Padua.

By 1714 at the latest, Tartini was dividing his time between Assisi and Ancona, where he found employ-

ment in the opera orchestra. It was at Ancona, in that year, that he later claimed to have discovered the phenomenon of the 'third sound' (difference tone) which played so central a role in his acoustical theories and the polemics surrounding them. After being pardoned by the Paduan authorities and reunited with his wife about 1715, he lived alternately in Venice and Padua for about a year before returning alone to the Marche (Ancona, Fano and perhaps elsewhere). His biographers explain this renewed separation from his wife as the result of Tartini's having heard Veracini play at a private concert in Venice (probably in July 1716, though Hill has suggested a date of 1712; see VERACINI, FRANCESCO MARIA): awed by the prowess of the renowned virtuoso, he is said to have resolved to perfect his own technique in solitary self-exile. By c1720, in any case, he had returned to Venice. His by now considerable reputation as violinist is reflected by the extremely favourable terms of his employment on 16 April 1721 as 'primo violino e capo di concerto' at St Anthony's Basilica ('Il Santo') in Padua. These included the freedom to accept outside engagements, a privilege of which Tartini clearly made liberal use until about 1740, when he sustained an arm injury of an unknown nature while at Bergamo; thereafter his outside concert activity declined progressively.

Capri suggested that Tartini's longest known absence from Padua – his stay in Prague, from 1723 to 1726 – may have been occasioned by the threat of a paternity suit by a Venetian landlady (whose son, as late as 1767, was still importuning Tartini to be declared his offspring and heir). In any case, Prague did not lack strong inducements. Tartini performed in an unknown solo capacity at the coronation festivities of Emperor Charles VI (June–September 1723) and remained in the lucrative employment of the Bohemian court chancellor, Count Kinsky. His return to Padua during 1726 is at least partly accounted for by two surviving letters to his family in Pirano in which he complains of ill-health from the northern climate.

We know almost nothing of Tartini's activity as a composer up to this time. One of his early concertos (D89, published in 1728) survives in a Dresden manuscript dated 1724; though a few other works may go back to the Prague period, the main flow of compositions does not appear to begin much before 1728. Certainly little credence attaches to the claim, attributed to Tartini by Lalande, that the 'Devil's Trill' was composed in 1713; stylistically, the sonata as we now know it can scarcely be earlier than 1745 (no autograph is extant).

The only publications of his music known to have been supervised by the composer at any stage of their preparation are the sonata prints of 1734 and 1745 and, according to their title-page, the trios published in London in 1750. Several letters record his consternation on learning of works published without his knowledge or assent. This state of affairs, compounded by the relative scarcity of surviving autographs (particularly among the sonatas) and the almost total absence of dated manuscripts, has prevented a detailed and accurate chronology of his output: the time that elapsed between composition and publication is in most cases still unknown. Tentative classifications of the sonatas and concertos according to period (Brainard, Dounias) have had to rely too heavily on stylistic judgments to be more than a

1. Giuseppe Tartini: engraving by Carolus Calcinoto

2. *The first page (Adagio and opening of the Allegro) from a violin sonata in A minor, in Tartini's autograph (I-Pca 1888.D.VI, p.18)*

rough guide. Tartini's concertos in particular are, of course, to be regarded primarily as vehicles for his own performances at 'Il Santo', whose orchestra was among the leading ones in Europe. Dounias's assignment of only a relatively small number of works (about 10%) to the period after 1750 is thus entirely plausible, considering the reduced scale of Tartini's concert activity and his increasing preoccupation with harmonic-acoustic theory.

According to Tartini's own later recollections, he founded his 'school' of violin instruction in either 1727 or 1728. Continued into his last years, it was to become a magnet for aspiring violinists from most of Europe. Doubtless his precepts on violin playing, published shortly after his death as *Traité des agréments*, were a considerably earlier outgrowth of this teaching activity; they must in any case antedate 1756, for they are freely pirated by Leopold Mozart in his *Violinschule*. Jacobi suggests that they may never have been written down in their surviving form by Tartini, but transmitted as a compilation of lesson materials by his pupils.

Clearly Tartini's instruction encompassed considerably more than instrumental technique alone. A preserved fragment of a copybook of J. G. Naumann's (c1762) contains counterpoint and modulation exercises corrected by Tartini, rules concerning cadence types, dissonance treatment, chord inversions, etc, and a 'Regola del terzo suono', confirming the close connections between Tartini's didactic and theoretical pursuits.

Despite his lack of formal training, Tartini seems to have been strongly inclined towards speculative musical thinking both by his own temperament and by the nature of his associations at Padua. Among those most influential upon him as a theorist were his colleague and fellow theorist F. A. Vallotti, the Paduan astronomer Gianrinaldo Carli and G. B. Martini in Bologna, with whom Tartini corresponded regularly during his last 40 years. The *Trattato di musica* (1754) was written at the instigation of Count Decio Agostino Trento, a member of a circle of Paduan university acquaintances, who became Tartini's pupil in 1748. Tartini sent a preliminary version of the text to Bologna in 1751 for scrutiny by Martini and the mathematician Balbi. Their apparently unfavourable judgment was but a foretaste of the criticisms of Serre, Rousseau and others which were to cause him evident mental anguish throughout his declining years. Extensive responses to his critics are found in manuscripts and in his two publications of 1767. Most are highly defensive in character and marked by an attitude of great (possibly assumed) deference towards persons of learning: the expression 'i Dotti' occurs repeatedly in his writings, often invoking the notion of a kind of entrenched opposition arrayed against him.

The composer's known correspondence extends from 1725 until his death and is widely scattered. It deals (apart from theoretical subjects) with employment recommendations and other concerns of his students; with occasional musical events (mentioned, unfortunately, only in passing), both in Padua and on Tartini's concert trips up to 1740; with the continually recurring pecuniary worries of his family in Pirano and his attempts (and occasional refusals) to provide assistance; with the deteriorating health of his childless wife after a severe illness in 1745 (although her death was to precede his by only a year); and with Tartini's own complaints of failing strength from at least 1747. The letters reveal a personality of great warmth, tenderness, extreme sensibility, and a fastidiousness and personal modesty that verge on the obsessive. The composer's anger, expressed in a letter to Padre Martini in 1761, over the unauthorized circulation of copies of a portrait which he had reluctantly consented to have engraved, is so excessive as to seem disingenuous; but the truth of this is by no means certain in the light of the character traits displayed elsewhere.

One of the most revealing expressions of his personality is Tartini's unique custom of appending poetic mottoes to his instrumental works, and of couching them in a secret cipher in those cases (apparently) where a manuscript was intended for use outside his own circle of intimates, or where the predominantly secular texts might run foul of church strictures. Dounias, who deciphered the rather primitive 'code' in 1935, also discovered that the bulk of the mottoes are drawn from the dramas of Metastasio; their pronounced pathetic-dramatic cast is often strangely appropriate to that of Tartini's effusive musical language.

Tartini was not formally relieved of his duties as leading violinist at St Anthony's until 1765, when he was succeeded by his pupil Giulio Meneghini. He was still actively teaching, however, until at least 1767 and continued to pursue the elusive goal of recognition for his system of harmony. In 1768 he suffered a mild stroke, the effects of which are clearly visible in the autograph of a sonata movement preserved in Paris. His death in 1770 is attributed to gangrene from an ulcerated foot. A small group of sacred vocal pieces, his only known works in this genre, derives apparently from the last year or so of his life.

2. WORKS. In the majority of his sonatas, Tartini followed a three-movement plan in which a slow opening movement is succeeded by a principal Allegro and a metrically contrasting finale that is either quicker than the preceding, or more relaxed (and frequently dance-like); all three movements are in the same key. Standard mid-century binary structures, with a central double bar framed by repeat signs, prevail. The amount of 'exposition' material reappearing in the second half of the movement varies from one or two concluding phrases to a full-scale 'recapitulation'. The principal departures from this normal arrangement are a handful of early church sonatas (including the first six works of the 1734 Amsterdam print), the largely unaccompanied 'piccole sonate' with their varying successions of three, four and five movements, and the strangely unprepossessing trio sonatas of the 1740s, many of which have come down to us with only two movements, usually of very brief duration.

Tartini's concertos generally conform to the Vivaldian fast–slow–fast scheme, with the middle movement in a contrasting key. For the most part the outer movements have the standard four tutti-ritornello statements, interspersed with extensive solo passages whose point of departure is generally the ritornello itself instead of a contrasting idea. More frequent alternation between solo and tutti instrumentation is found in the earliest concertos. During the 1740s Tartini began to employ a synthesis of ritornello structure and binary form in which a lengthy, multi-phrase opening ritornello form (in the tonic) and an even more extensive solo passage (quoting the opening, then establishing and reinforcing the dominant) are repeated in toto in place of the middle tutti and solo passages of the earlier form.

Despite the limitations of chronological information that were described earlier, one can discern in Tartini's music the general tendencies of the early phases of 'pre-Classicism': growing upper-voice supremacy; decreasing linearity and increasing harmonic-support function of bass lines; gradual transfer of syntactical interest from the single motif-unit to the complete phrase; growing regularity of period structure, extending in Tartini's case to the employment of one new four-bar phrase after another in almost unbroken succession in the majority of works written after about 1743. It is nonetheless far from a routine or colourless style. Its peculiar blend of lyricism, pathos and virtuosity, its violinistically conceived mannerisms, frequent echo effects, occasional harmonic boldnesses and (in particular) elaborate cadence formulae are not mistakable for the work of any other composer.

Burney said of Tartini: 'He changed his style in 1744, from extreme difficult, to graceful and expressive'. Though it is hard to reconcile this statement with the technically very demanding sonatas that appeared in Rome a year later, there is no doubt that it is true of much of Tartini's music. A long passage in the Trattato devoted to 'buon gusto' and several other utterances by the composer reveal that he had become an enthusiastic convert to the neo-humanistic and 'nature-imitation' aesthetics of the 1740s, and in particular to the notion that the true power of emotional expression resides in the human voice. That he paid this idea more than lip-service is confirmed by Dounias's discovery that many of Tartini's themes are actual settings of the Metastasian and other texts that accompany them in the manuscripts.

3. THEORY, ACOUSTICS. Tartini's theoretical system, as expounded in the Trattato of 1754, is a curiously flawed attempt to reconcile empirical observation with classical harmonics and the laws of physics and geometry. Like the exponents of harmonic dualism since Zarlino, Tartini derived the major system from the harmonic series, the minor from the arithmetic sextuplum 1, 2, 3 . . . 6; but he parted company with the dualists in maintaining that both major and minor harmony are products of the same fundamental law. This he explained as a set of properties of the geometric figure of a circle enclosed by a tangential square: a succession of radii, chords and chord extensions is used to 'prove' the common origin of the harmonic, arithmetic and geometric series. A unique aspect is Tartini's incorporation into his system of the difference tone ('terzo suono') which he regarded as the physical foundation of harmonics and the empirical proof of the existence of a single, all-encompassing set of musical-physical-mathematical relationships. Planchart has recently provided the most lucid summary of the serious mathematical inaccuracies that underlie the entire system.

Not limiting himself to acoustics, Tartini also dealt in the Trattato with melody, cadence types, dissonance, scale structure and harmonization, metre, and the Greek chromatic and enharmonic genera, all treated in relationship to one or more corollaries of his system. The later and much briefer *De' principi* (1767) confines itself to a defence of Tartini's central thesis, now stripped of the geometric paraphernalia and lengthy calculations that had drawn the particular censure of his critics. His late writings all lay special stress on the importance of difference tones in both system and practice, and are particularly concerned with reasserting his claim to have been the first discoverer of the phenomenon.

WORKS

Editions: *Le opere di Giuseppe Tartini*, 1st ser., ed. E. Farina and C. Scimone (Milan, 1971–) [FS]

   25 piccole sonate per violino e violoncello e per violino solo, ed. G. Guglielmo (Padua, 1970) [see *Notes*, xxviii (1971–2), 299]

   Numerous individual edns., many highly unreliable; for partial lists see *MGG* and *La MusicaE*

   D – *no. in Dounias* (1935)

   B – *no. in Brainard* (1975) (*incorporating keys*)

SACRED VOCAL

Canzoncine sacre, 1–3vv (some in more than one version): Alma contrita; Alma pentita; Amare lacrime; Caro Signor amato; Chi cerca un'innocenza; Crocifisso mio Signor; Dio ti salvi regina; Dolce mio Dio; E m'ami ancor; Iddio ti salvi; Infrangiti mio cor; Mio Gesù con tutto il cuore; No, che terreno fallo; O peccator che sai; Rimira, o peccatore; Ti voglio amar Gesù; Vedi, Signor, ch'io piango; Vergine bella del ciel regina; Vergine bella e pietosa; Voglio amar Gesù anch'io: all *I-Pca*; 5 ed. in *Musica sacra*, lxxxiii (1959), suppl.

Stabat mater, 3vv, copy, 1769; Pange lingua, 3vv; 2 Tantum ergo, 3vv; 3 Miserere, 3vv, 4vv, 5vv, copy, 1770 (additional copies, *F-Pc, GB-T*); Salve regina, 4vv, copy, 1773 ('ultima composizione del . . . Tartini'): all *I-Pca*

INSTRUMENTAL (MS)

*c*135 vn concertos (vn, str a 4, bc), thematic catalogue by Dounias, supplemented by Duckles and others; principal MS collections in *I-Pca* (incl. 55 complete autographs), *F-Pc, GB-Mp, US-BE* (first publications listed below); 6 ed. in FS: D125, i; D12, x; D83, xi; D117, xiii; D21, xiv; D115, xv

Concertos for other insts (str a 4, bc): vc/va da gamba, A, *I-Pca*, autograph; va (va da gamba), 2 hn, D, *A-Wgm*, autograph; fl, G, *S-Skma*, dubious; fl, F, *I-Nc*, dubious

Sinfonie and sonatas a 4 (str qt, bc): D (autograph), G, A, D, *I-Pca*; 11 (some a 5, one with 2 clarini), dubious

*c*40 trio sonatas (2 vn, bc), mostly 1745–9, *I-Pca, F-Pc* (thematic catalogue by Brainard)

*c*135 sonatas, 40 dubious sonatas (vn, bc), mostly *I-Pca, F-Pc, US-BE* (thematic catalogue by Brainard); 3 ed. in FS, xvi

*c*30 sonatas, many single movts (vn, without acc. or with optional bc), probably *c*1745–60, mostly *I-Pca, A-Wgm* (thematic catalogue by Brainard)

INSTRUMENTAL (PUBLISHED)

op.

1 lib.1. Sei concerti a 5: D85, 55, 60, 15, 58, 89 (g, e, F, D, F, A) (Amsterdam, 1728)

1 lib.3. Sei concerti a 5 del . . . Tartini a G. Visconti: D Anh.III–VI (B♭, D, F, a), 2 others unlisted (Amsterdam, *c*1728); none definitely attributable (Dounias); date derived from Le Cène's publishing numbers

1 lib.2. Sei concerti a 5: D111, 91, 59, 71, 88, 18 (a, A, F, G, A, D) (Amsterdam, 1730); date derived from Le Cène's publishing numbers

1 VI sonate vn, bc: B B♭7, a9, b5, g9, A3, B♭8 (Amsterdam, 1732)

1 (12) Sonate e una pastorale: B A14, F9, C11, G17, e6, D12, D6, c2, A15, g10, E5, F4, A16 (Amsterdam, 1734); nos.1–6 church sonatas, nos.7–12 chamber sonatas; A16, 'Pastorale', uses scordatura; the nickname of g10, 'Didone abbandonata', is of 19th-century origin; ed. in FS, vii–viii, xii

2 VI concerti a 8: D73, 2, 124, 62, 3, 46 (G, C, b, F, C, E) (Amsterdam, *c*1734)

– VI concerti . . . d'alcuni famosi maestri, lib.2 (no.5): D1 (C) (Amsterdam, *c*1740)

2 VI sonate, vn, bc: B g4, A5, d4, e7, F5, E6 (Amsterdam, 1743)

2 (12) Sonate, vn, bc: B D13, G18, A17, b6, a10, C12, g11, D14, B♭9, F8, e8, G19 (Rome, 1745); pubd as op.3 (Paris, *c*1747)

– Nouvelle étude . . . par Mr. Pétronio Pinelli: B F11 (17 variations on Gavotte from Corelli's op.5 no.10) (Paris, *c*1747); see L'arte del arco

4 (6) Sonates: B E3, G20, B♭10, A3, D15, c5 (Paris, 1747); no.6 probably by Mauro D'Alay

5 (6) Sonates: B a11, B♭11, A18, G21, F10, B♭12 (Paris, *c*1747); some dubious; ed. E. Bonnelli (Padua, 1951)

6 Sei sonate: B G8, A19, D8, A6, B5, G10 (Paris, *c*1748)

7 (6) Sonate: B D11, B♭7, G9, E4, g3, F7 (Paris, 1748)

8 Sei sonate a tre: Trios A5, D7, G4, D10, A10, D11, some with movts added (Paris, 1749)

– XII Sonatas, 2 vn, b: Trios G4, D11, A5, D10, G3, F2, D7, A8, A9, D12, A10, A7 (London, 1750)

– VI [and VI] sonate, 2 vn, bc, lib. [I], II: Trios D8, C4, D6, F2, D5, D2, D12, C5, D4, C3, D3, D9 (Amsterdam, *c*1755), as op.3 (London, 1756)

– L'arte del arco: B F11 (38 variations on Gavotte from Corelli's op.5 no.10) (Paris, 1758); attrib. of both this and the earlier print is questionable

9 Sei sonate: B E♭1, G6, G22, A20, F6, D16 (Paris, *c*1763)

– J. B. Cartier: L'art du violon: B g4, A14, F11 (expanded to 50 variations), g5 (first appearance in print of 'Le trille du diable'), and Adagio varié (17 variations on B F5, 1st movt) (Paris, 1798); the Adagio, probably spurious, *R* in H.-P. Schmitz: *Die Kunst der Verzierung im 18. Jahrhundert* (Kassel, 1955)

WRITINGS

Regole per arrivare a saper ben suonar il violino (MS compiled by G. F. Nicolai, *I-Vc*); ed. in Jacobi (1961); variant versions: *Libro de regoli, ed esempi necessari per ben sonare, US-BE*; and *Traité des éréments de la musique* (Paris, 1771); Petrobelli (*I fonti*, 1968) reports the recent discovery of a further Italian MS version

Trattato di musica secondo la vera scienza dell'armonia (Padua, 1754/*R*1966 and 1973; Ger. trans., 1966)

De' principi dell'armonia musicale contenuta nel diatonico genere (Padua, 1767/*R*1970)

Risposta di Giuseppe Tartini alla critica del di lui trattato di musica di Mons. Le Serre di Ginevra (Venice, 1767)

'Lettera [dated 1760] del defonto Sig. Giuseppe Tartini alla Signora Maddalena Lombardini', *L'Europa letteraria*, v/2 (Venice, 1770; Eng. trans., 1771/*R*1967)

For a list of principal unpublished writings see Capri and *MGG*.

BIBLIOGRAPHY

WORKS CONTAINING CATALOGUES, SUBSTANTIAL BIBLIOGRAPHIES, ETC

G. Tebaldini: *L'archivio musicale della Capella antoniana* (Padua, 1895)

A. Bachmann: *Les grands violonistes du passé* (Paris, 1913)

M. Dounias: *Die Violinkonzerte Giuseppe Tartinis* (Wolfenbüttel, 1935, 2/1966)

A. Capri: *Giuseppe Tartini* (Milan, 1945)

P. Brainard: *Die Violinsonaten Giuseppe Tartinis* (diss., U. of Göttingen, 1959)

V. Duckles, M. Elmer and P. Petrobelli: *Thematic Catalog of a Manuscript Collection of 18th-century Italian Instrumental Music* (Berkeley, 1963)

P. Petrobelli: 'Tartini, Giuseppe', *La MusicaE*

P. Brainard: 'Tartini, Giuseppe', *MGG*

——: 'Le Sonate a tre di Giuseppe Tartini: un sunto bibliografico', *RIM*, vi (1969), 102

——: *Le sonate per violino di Giuseppe Tartini: catalogo tematico* (Milan, 1975)

DOCUMENTS, LETTERS, ETC

Anon.: *Regole, e capitoli della pia Aggregazione delli signori professori, e dilettanti di musica eretta in Padoa l'anno 1726* (Padua, 1727)

A. Hortis: 'Lettere di G. Tartini', *Archeografo triestino*, new ser., x (1884), 209–43

Anon.: *Per le nobili nozze Tattara–Persicini* (Bassano, 1884)

F. Parisini: *Carteggio inedito del Padre G. B. Martini*, i (Bologna, 1888)

M. Tamaro and G. Wieselberger: *Nel giorno della inaugurazione del monumento a Giuseppe Tartini a Pirano* (Trieste, 1896)

B. Ziliotto: 'Gianrinaldo Carli e G. Tartini', *Pagine istriane*, ii (1904), 8

F. Pasini: 'Il Tartini a G. V. Vannetti', *Pagine istriane*, iv (1906), 1

V. Fedeli: 'Lettere di musicisti italiani', *RMI*, xix (1912), 696

L. Weinhold: 'Musikerautographen aus fünf Jahrhunderten', *Philobiblon*, xii (1940), 52

H. Nathan: 'Autograph Letters of Musicians at Harvard', *Notes*, v (1947–8), 461

P. Petrobelli: 'Tartini, Algarotti e la corte di Dresda', *AnMc*, no.2 (1965), 72

——: 'Una presenza di Tartini a Parma nel 1728', *Aurea Parma*, l (1966), 109

——: *Giuseppe Tartini: le fonti biografiche* (Vienna, Milan and London, 1968)

——: critical edition of Tartini's letters (in preparation)

LIFE, WORKS AND RELATED STUDIES

(*see also first section of bibliography*)

J. le R. d'Alembert: *Elémens de musique théorique et pratique* (Lyons, 1762)

J. A. Serre: *Observations sur les principes de l'harmonie* (Geneva, 1763)

J. J. Rousseau: *Dictionnaire de musique* (Paris, 1768)

Anon.: *Risposta di un anonimo al celebre Signor Rousseau circa al suo sentimento in proposito d'alcune proposizioni del Sig. Giuseppe Tartini* (Venice, 1769)

J. G. de Lalande: *Voyage d'un françois en Italie*, viii (Paris, 1769)

[G. Gennari]: 'Elogio del defonto Sig. Tartini', *L'Europa letteraria*, iv/1 (1770), 94

F. Fanzago: *Orazione . . . delle lodi di Giuseppe Tartini* (Padua, 1770, enlarged 2/1792)

B. Stillingfleet: *Principles and Power of Harmony* (London, 1771)

[A. Neumayr]: *Illustrazione del Prato della Valle* (Padua, 1807)

F. Fayolle: *Notices sur Corelli, Tartini, Gaviniès, Pugnani et Viotti* (Paris, 1810)

G. Benedetti: 'Giuseppe Tartini', *Archeografo triestino*, new ser., xxi (1896), 1

M. Goldin: *The Violinistic Innovations of G. Tartini* (diss., New York U., 1955)

D. D. Boyden: 'The Missing Italian Manuscript of Tartini's *Traité des agrémens*', *MQ*, xlvi (1960), 315

A. Planchart: 'A Study of the Theories of G. Tartini', *JMT*, iv (1960), 32

P. Brainard: 'Tartini and the Sonata for Unaccompanied Violin', *JAMS*, xiv (1961), 383

E. R. Jacobi: 'G. F. Nicolai's MS of Tartini's *Regole per ben suonar il violino*', *MQ*, xlvii (1961), 207 [with facs. and Ger. trans.; reviewed in *L'organo*, iv (1963), 224, and *Mf*, xvi (1963), 309]

M. Elmer: *Tartini's Improvised Ornamentation* (diss., U. of California, Berkeley, 1962)

P. Petrobelli: 'Per l'edizione critica di un concerto tartiniano (D. 21)', *Musiche italiane rare e vive da Giovanni Gabrieli a Giuseppe Verdi*, Chigiana, xix (Siena, 1962), 97–128

A. Dunning: 'Die De Geer'schen Musikalien in Leufsta', *STMf*, xlviii (1966), 187

P. Petrobelli: 'Tartini, le sue idee e il suo tempo', *NRMI*, i (1967), 651

——: 'La scuola di Tartini in Germania e la sua influenza', *AnMc*, no.5 (1968), 1

——: 'Tartini e Corelli – preliminari per l'impostazione di un problema', *Studi corelliani: I° congresso internazionale: Fusignano 1968*, 99

L. Ginzburg: *Giuseppe Tartini* (Moscow, 1969; Ger. trans., 1976)

P. Petrobelli: 'Tartini e la musica popolare', *Chigiana*, xxvi–xxvii (1969–70), 443

M. Abbado: 'Presenza di Tartini nel nostro secolo', *NRMI*, iv (1970), 1087

A. Garbelotto: 'Tartini nei ricordi di un turista inglese', *Padova*, xii/11–12 (1970), 14

L. Frasson: *Giuseppe Tartini, primo violino e capo concerto nella Basilica del Santo* (Padua, 1974); orig. in *Il Santo*, xii (Padua, 1972), 65–152, 273–389; xiii (1973), 280–434

PAUL BRAINARD

Tartöld. A 16th-century RACKET with a metal body brightly painted to resemble a dragon; it is a relatively squat double-reed instrument with a cylindrical coiled metal tube pierced by seven finger-holes and a thumb-hole. The crook forms a twisted dragon's tail, and the bell is the dragon's mouth with a trembling tongue, made of iron. Only one set of five *Tartölden* or *Tartölten* – two trebles, two tenors and a bass – are known to exist (see illustration); they are named in the 1596 inventory of the collection at that time in Archduke Ferdinand's castle of Ambras near Innsbruck. The word 'Tartöld' may be derived either from KORTHOLT (that is, a short wind instrument) or from *torto* (It.: 'crooked'). The instrument may have been used for theatrical events; similarly disguised instruments were often described in reports of 16th-century Italian *intermedii*. The *Tartölden* from Vienna are illustrated in E. Winternitz: *Musical Instruments of the Western World* (London, 1966), no.17; and more fully described in J. von Schlosser: *Die Sammlung alter Musikinstrumente* (Vienna, Kunsthistorisches Museum, 1920).

HOWARD MAYER BROWN

Tartu. Estonian city; *see* UNION OF SOVIET SOCIALIST REPUBLICS, §IV, 1.

Tās. Sassanid small drums; see PERSIA, §3(ii).

Tasbiḥa. Office of the Coptic Church; *see* COPTIC RITE, MUSIC OF THE.

Taschengeige (Ger.). KIT.

Taskin, Pascal(-Joseph) (*b* Theux, nr. Liège, 1723; *d* Paris, 9 Feb 1793). Flemish harpsichord maker. He is the most important of a family of makers active in the Low Countries in the 18th century. He worked for François Etienne Blanchet the younger (*d* 1761), whose business he took over on his marriage to Blanchet's widow in 1766. In 1774 he became court instrument maker and keeper of the king's instruments, deputing some of the work of the post to his nephew Pascal Joseph the younger. Although he later made pianos, he continued to make harpsichords, with the assistance of his nephews Henry and Lambert Taskin and his stepson Armand François Nicholas Taskin.

Three particular features of Taskin's work have been influential on modern harpsichord making: the characteristic French tone (deep, round, with a booming bass), the musical advantages of the sliding coupler (no dogleg jacks), and the lacquered or painted casework (for illustration *see* HARPSICHORD, fig.10). In addition, Taskin's French tone is more attractive to those builders and players reacting against the sound of extant English harpsichords and their modern 'copies'. Taskin's original keyboard actions are light and easy (too much so for prolonged playing on the upper manual); his scaling is very like that of the Ruckers' instruments (allowing for the longer compass and wider dimensions), and his frame is 'better worked out in detail' than theirs (Hubbard). But how many features can be attributed to Taskin, to his master Blanchet, or to his many Parisian contemporaries, is uncertain; for example, the light action of various French harpsichords was frequently

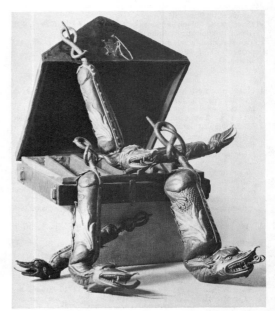

Five Tartölden, German, 16th century, from Ambras (Sammlung alter Musikinstrumente, Kunsthistorisches Museum, Vienna)

commented on at the time (e.g. by Hüllmandel and Burney). His celebrated 'invention' of the *peau de buffle* registration (in 1768) was accredited in the *Encyclopédie méthodique* (compendium volume, 1785, 'Le clavecin') with greater powers of dynamic expression than its capabilities allow, and his pianos (first made 1776, new action 1787) were relatively old-fashioned in their lack of escapement, despite the patented device for special screw-regulated wrest pins. His gut-strung, keyboardless *armandine* of 1789 was a kind of harp-psaltery, no more successful than others of the type.

Nevertheless, Taskin can be regarded as the prime exponent of the developed French harpsichord of 1770, a most able member of the Blanchet dynasty that lasted from at least 1686 to the 19th century. Inventories of 1777, 1783 and 1793 show a prosperous firm – now concerned more with pianos, but their two main harpsichord activities were no less important. These were the making of new instruments of fine, uniform tone (8′, 8′, 4′, one or two buffs, three registers, F′ to f′′′) and the rebuilding of old Flemish harpsichords and virginals, particularly those by the Ruckers, into large, comparable, splendidly decorated instruments (8′, 8′, 4′, buff, four registers including *peau de buffle*, often *genouillères* or knee-levers). It is not clear where such makers as Taskin obtained all the bits and pieces of old Flemish instruments, documented in numerous inventories; nor were all the ascriptions genuine, since the value of such rebuilt instruments (which included an occasional old French harpsichord, for example a Dumont of 1693) was much higher than the new. In this particular craft Blanchet had been renowned, 'yet he has been surpassed by M. Pascal Taskin, his pupil' turning out instruments 'which, all considered, keep of their original state only the soundboard and about two and a half feet of the original right side' (*Encyclopédie méthodique*). The *peau de buffle*, a soft colour or echo effect, was applied to the fourth register of a Ruckers two-manual instrument, for which the knee-levers were also useful, allowing the player to change timbre 'without removing the hands from the keyboard; these produce *pianos*, *fortes* and crescendos in the clearest and most sensitive manner' (claimed an advertisement of 1777) and were known in France from at least 1759. Five and sometimes six such knee-levers were applied, thus giving more variety than the English machine stops, which seem to have been geared more towards gradual crescendos.

Taskin's nephew Pascal-Joseph Taskin (1750–1829) was keeper of the instruments to Louis XV from 1772 until the Revolution. His son Henri-Joseph (1779–1852) was an organist and the composer of piano music, operas and songs. Henri-Joseph's grandson Alexandre Taskin (1853–97), after training with Ponchard and Bussine, made his début as a baritone in Amiens in 1875; he sang at the Opéra-Comique from 1879 until his retirement in 1894 and then taught at the Conservatoire.

BIBLIOGRAPHY

D. H. Boalch: *Makers of the Harpsichord and Clavichord, 1440–1840* (London, 1956, rev. 2/1974)

R. Russell: *The Harpsichord and Clavichord* (London, 1959, rev. 2/1973)

F. Hubbard: *Three Centuries of Harpsichord Making* (Cambridge, Mass., 1965)

E. M. Ripin: 'Expressive Devices applied to the Eighteenth-century Harpsichord', *Organ Yearbook*, i (1970), 65

DONALD HOWARD BOALCH, PETER WILLIAMS

Tasso, Gioan Maria. Italian composer, who published at least 15 duets together with works by BERNARDINO LUPACCHINO.

Tasso, Torquato (*b* Sorrento, 11 March 1544; *d* Rome, 25 April 1595). Italian poet and courtier. He was one of those rare literary figures whose works held an immediate and continuing fascination for musicians and writers alike and whose life became a legend that survived his death by three centuries.

1. LIFE. Tasso was the son of Bernardo Tasso (*d* 1569), a court poet well known in his day. His early years were marred by political difficulties that caused his father to be expelled from Naples and the boy himself to be separated from his mother. These events caused his lifelong financial insecurity, since, deprived of his father's land and his mother's dowry, he became completely dependent on – and increasingly bitter about – court patronage. His early education was that of a courtier: literature (including Latin and Greek), mathematics, music and riding. In Venice, under the constant threat of Turkish invasion, he wrote *Gierusalemme*, a first draft of his great epic on the liberation of Jerusalem. He was sent to Padua in 1560 to study law but soon switched to philosophy and rhetoric. There he continued to write poetry: the chivalrous romance *Rinaldo* and a series of love lyrics, first to LUCREZIA BENDIDIO and then to LAURA PEVERARA, both of whom became famous singers at the court of Ferrara. However, these years were also marred by brawls and escapades which can possibly be seen in retrospect as early manifestations of an unstable temperament. Before leaving Padua in 1565 he joined the newly formed Accademia degli Eterei, taking the name 'Il Pentito' ('The Repentant One').

Tasso's long association with Ferrara began in October 1565. He was first a member of the household of Cardinal Luigi d'Este and from 1572 a 'gentleman' in the service of Duke Alfonso II. The splendour and luxury of the Este court provided him with a stimulating environment, and the knowledge that Boiardo and Ariosto had written their poems there must have spurred him on. Encouraged by Leonora and Lucrezia d'Este, he wrote more lyrics and some dialogues and theoretical works and began his *Gerusalemme liberata*, which was to occupy him for a decade. Except for visits to Mantua, Urbino, Rome and Paris (in 1570–71) he remained at Ferrara until spring 1577.

Although Tasso won great favour with the performance of his pastoral drama *Aminta* (1573), he was plagued by unauthorized editions of it and of *Gerusalemme liberata*. Those of the latter had been circulating among his friends before the first complete edition was published in 1581, thereby sparking off one of the great literary debates of the century. Anxious about piratical publishers, fearful that his work would incur the wrath of the Inquisition and worried about his ill-health, Tasso revealed in his letters an increasing tendency towards paranoia. He was imprisoned in June 1577 after attacking a servant who, he thought, was spying on him, but in July he escaped and fled the court. Although he was reconciled with the duke in April 1578, his mental agitation did not allow him to remain in Ferrara for long nor to find a satisfactory patron in Mantua, Padua, Venice, Florence, Urbino, Pesaro or Turin. In February 1579 he returned to Ferrara, where, amid preparations for the reception of Duke Alfonso's third bride, he felt ignored and humiliated. Within a month his angry outbursts and denunciations caused him to be arrested again and taken to the hospital of S Anna, where he was confined for seven years. Although he suffered hallucinations and fits of melancholy, his writings from this period – lyrics, dialogues, letters, even a comedy *Intrichi d'amore* – do not appear to be the work of a madman.

Tasso was released in 1586 at the request of Duke Vincenzo I of Mantua, where he completed his tragedy *Il Rè Torrismondo*. But his sense of persecution and dissatisfaction with his material benefits continued to make him restless. In April 1590, at the invitation of Jacopo Corsi, he was in Florence, where he may have witnessed a performance of his *Aminta*, with music composed by Emilio de' Cavalieri. He divided his last years between Naples and Rome, writing prose and poetry of a religious nature, including his less successful revision of *Gerusalemme liberata* known as *Gerusalemme conquistata*.

2. WORKS. In his lyrics Tasso, like many 16th-century Italian poets, displayed a partiality for the madrigal; unlike them, however, he wrote some of his best verse in the genre and brought it to a point of unsurpassed technical perfection. His madrigals were set by almost all the important composers, both madrigalists and monodists, of his own and the next few generations (there is a list of settings in *Le rime di Torquato Tasso*, ed. A. Solerti, Bologna, 1898–1902). At Ferrara and Mantua he knew Luzzaschi, Wert and Alessandro Striggio (i), whose styles he praised in his dialogue *La Cavalletta* (Venice, 1587), contrasting them with 'degenerate music which has become soft and effeminate'. His Aristotelian studies had persuaded him that all types of poetry purge the passions (see his *Del giudizio sovra la sua Gerusalemme*, Rome, 1666; edn. in *Torquato Tasso: Prose diverse*, ed. G. Guasti, Florence, 1875, i), and the new affective madrigal of the 1580s and 1590s was possibly prompted in part by his influence.

Written in the traditional *ottava rima* of the epic, *Gerusalemme liberata* soon surpassed Ariosto's *Orlando furioso* as a popular source of texts for composers (see Einstein, 1950–51). Wert gave portions of Armida's monologue (canto xvi) their first setting in his eighth book of madrigals (1586). Monteverdi's second and third books (1590–92) reflect Tasso's influence, the latter including two cycles drawn from cantos xii and xvi respectively. His *Combattimento di Tancredi e Clorinda* (1624; published in the eighth book of madrigals, 1638) is taken from canto xii, and his lost *Armida* (1627) is the first of the numerous operas based on Tasso's epic, which was a prime source of Italian operas in the 17th century. Composers who wrote operas based on it include Michelangelo Rossi (*Erminia sul Giordano*, 1633), Lully (*Armide*, 1686), Handel (*Rinaldo*, 1711) and Dvořák (*Armida*, 1902–3). *Aminta* was also significant for the history of opera. It is written principally in hendecasyllabic verse in which assonance and refrain, rather than rhyme, assume structural importance. This flexible style, particularly apparent in the concluding choruses of Acts 2, 3 and 5, was adopted by Rinuccini for the recitative sections of the first opera librettos.

The standard edition of Tasso's works is that edited by B. T. Sozzi (Turin, 1955–6).

BIBLIOGRAPHY
A. Solerti: *Vita di Torquato Tasso* (Turin, 1895)
——: *Gli albori del melodramma* (Milan, 1904–5/*R*1969), i
B. Pennacchietti: 'Le pastorali del Tasso e del Guarini e la prima maniera di P. Metastasio', *Studi di letteratura italiana*, xi (1915), 175
R. Rolland: 'L'opéra avant l'opéra', *Musiciens d'autrefois* (Paris, rev. 3/1912; Eng. trans., 1915)
A. Einstein: *The Italian Madrigal* (Princeton, 1949/*R*1971)
——: '*Orlando furioso* and *La Gerusalemme liberata* as Set to Music during the Sixteenth and Seventeenth Centuries', *Notes*, viii (1950–51), 623
C. Calcaterra: *Poesia e canto: studi sulla poesia melica italiana e sulla favola per musica* (Bologna, 1951), 41ff
B. Weinberg: *A History of Literary Criticism in the Italian Renaissance* (Chicago, 1961), ii, 646ff, 954ff
B. Hathaway: *The Age of Criticism: the Late Renaissance in Italy* (Ithaca, NY, 1962), 140ff, 390ff
C. P. Brand: *Torquato Tasso: a Study of the Poet and his Contribution to English Literature* (Cambridge, 1965)
N. Pirrotta: 'Scelte poetiche di Monteverdi', *NRMI*, ii (1968), 10
B. RUSSANO HANNING

Tastar, tastar de corde (It.: 'testing of the strings'). A 16th-century term for a preludial style of lute writing, often chordal, designed to test the tuning of the strings and set the mode for the pieces that followed (e.g. HAM, i, no.99*a*). The term first appeared in print in the fourth part of J. A. Dalza's *Intabolatura de lauto* (1508). *See* PRELUDE, §1, and TOCCATA, §1.

Tastatur (Ger.; It. *tastatura*). KEYBOARD.

Tastavin, Geronimo (*fl* ?1560–80). Italian composer. By 1569 he had probably entered the service of Cardinal Flavio Orsini, to whom he dedicated his only extant publication, *Il primo libro de madrigali a cinque voci* (Venice, 1569; only the cantus partbook survives). Orsini had been Bishop of Muro Lucano, Basilicata, from 1560 to 1565, and it is possible that Tastavin lived in that region and made his acquaintance at that time. Ten of his 19 madrigals are settings of poems from Petrarch's *Canzoniere*. The collection opens with a setting of a canzone by Sannazaro, *Amor, tu voi ch'io dica*, which he truncated and carved into six *partes* that do not correspond to the stanzaic structure of the poem. Among the settings of Bembo are two ottavas from the sequence *Nell'odorato e lucido oriente*. All the pieces are set in the old-fashioned *misura comune*. A *napolitana* by Tastavin, *Se mai pianser per te quess' occhi miei*, was included in an anthology full of references to Ferrara, prepared by Gioseffo Policretto: *Il primo libro delle napolitane a tre voci* (Venice, 1571). He is called here 'Hieronimo Tast.', which probably influenced Fétis wrongly to describe him in *FétisB* as 'Jérome Tast, allemande'.

DONNA G. CARDAMONE

Tastiera (It.). (1) FINGERBOARD.
(2) KEYBOARD.

Tastiera per luce (It.). Colour organ; *see* COLOUR AND MUSIC.

Tasto (It.: 'fret'). The key of a keyboard instrument; or the fingerboard of a bowed string instrument. *See also* FRET; SUL TASTO; TASTO SOLO.

Tasto solo (It.: 'single key'). A phrase used by composers to instruct the keyboard player of a continuo part to play the bass note(s) alone, without chords above. The phrase seems to occur in music (e.g. Corelli op.5) before it is described in theory books (Heinichen, 1728, Pasquali, Albrechtsberger), where the player is directed to play only those notes, singly (Heinichen) or with their octave (Adlung) or (if long) restruck (C. P. E. Bach, etc). C. P. E. Bach noted that the Italians did not in practice ever play *tasto solo*. Many composers also gave figures for passages marked *tasto solo* and in this case the figures may merely indicate the harmony implied or stated above by other instruments; these are either for the continuo player to fill in if necessary or, as in the case of Bach's cantata bass parts, for the sake of the copyist writing out a part from the full score. To distinguish single notes from those doubled at the octave above or below, C. P. E. Bach applied the phrases *all'unisono* and *all'ottava*, but only theorists and composers under his influence (e.g. G. S. Löhlein, 1791) made any use of them.

PETER WILLIAMS

Tate, Henry (*b* Prahran, Victoria, 27 Oct 1873; *d* Melbourne, 6 June 1926). Australian writer and composer. His first musical experience was as a chorister at St Kilda Anglican Church and a piano student under local teachers. On leaving high school, he was employed in clerical work while studying composition and the piano under G. W. L. Marshall-Hall at the Melbourne University Conservatorium, a post which lasted most of his life, until his appointment as music critic to the Melbourne *Age* (1924–6) finally brought his musical insight to attention. Contributions to journals, a weekly chess column and several books of verse gave meagre supplements to his income while he pursued his unique and visionary theories for the foundation of a national school of Australian music. Noting the absence of traditional folk sources, he advocated a musical vocabulary derived from characteristic natural sounds, birdsong and Aboriginal song and dance. For example, he devised a 'deflected scale pattern' (corresponding to the major scale but with a flattened 2nd and 6th) as an alternative to the diatonic system and suggested techniques of adapting rhythms and motives from bush sounds, which he then illustrated in his compositions for piano, songs and orchestral tone poems (many of which remain unpublished). A generous champion of contemporary composers (Alfred Hill, Fritz Hart and Percy Grainger), his ideas for an Australian mythology and musical identity were underrated in musical circles but welcomed by leading nationalist writers and dramatists in Melbourne who encouraged him to lecture and present his music. His lyrical programmatic music has been overtaken by a growing professionalism in Australian music and his writings have gained a historical rather than practical value.

WRITINGS

Australian Musical Resources: some Suggestions (Melbourne, 1917)
Australian Musical Possibilities (Melbourne, 1924)

BIBLIOGRAPHY

K. S. Prichard: 'A Reverie in Memory of Henry Tate', *Manuscripts* (1932), no.3, p.46
R. Covell: *Australia's Music: Themes of a New Society* (Melbourne, 1967), 4, 104ff, 142

ELIZABETH WOOD

Tate, James W(illiam) (*b* Wolverhampton, 30 July 1875; *d* Stoke on Trent, 5 Feb 1922). English composer and accompanist, elder brother of the soprano Maggie Teyte. He gained varied theatrical experience as an actor, in management, and as musical director for the Carl Rosa Opera Company and at Wyndham's Theatre. In 1902 he married the music-hall singer Lottie [Charlotte Louisa] Collins (1865–1910) for whom he conducted; in 1912 he married another singer, Clarice Mayne (Clarice Mabel Dulley, 1886–1966), with whom he formed a highly successful music-hall act. He wrote many songs for pantomimes, the music-hall and revues, among them 'I was a good little girl till I met you', 'A Broken Doll' (for André Charlot's revue *Samples*, 1915) and 'Give me a little cosy corner'. His additional numbers for Fraser-Simson's musical play *The Maid of the Mountains* (1915), in which his step-daughter José [Josephine] Collins (1887–1958) took the leading role, provided much of the score's romantic appeal. In his last years he produced touring revues and pantomimes in partnership with Julian M. Wylie.

BIBLIOGRAPHY

J. Collins: *The Maid of the Mountains: her Story* (London, 1932)
Valentine [pseud. of A. T. Pechey]: *Leaves of Memory* (London, 1939)
W. Macqueen-Pope: *Shirtfronts and Sables* (London, 1953)

ANDREW LAMB

Tate, Maggie. *See* TEYTE, MAGGIE.

Tate, Nahum (*b* 1652; *d* London, 30 July 1715). English poet and playwright. He was educated in Dublin and had settled in London by 1678, when his first play, *Brutus of Alba*, was produced. Seven other plays, mostly adaptations, followed during the 1680s. In 1689 he provided the libretto for Purcell's opera *Dido and Aeneas*, performed at a boarding-school for gentlewomen in Chelsea run by JOSIAS PRIEST, a dancing-master, probably in celebration of the coronation of William and Mary. Tate took the outlines of his plot from *Brutus of Alba* but so compressed it that the motivation of the witches was lost. Nevertheless the libretto shows considerable dramatic sense; the character of Dido is convincingly portrayed and the necessary chorus skilfully used, both to comment upon and to participate in the action. The poetry is undistinguished, but the language is direct and very suitable for setting to music. In the original libretto the main opera is preceded by a sung allegorical prologue, the music for which has been lost. Charles Gildon inserted both opera and prologue into his adaptation of Shakespeare's *Measure for Measure*, performed at Lincoln's Inn Fields in 1700.

Tate was appointed poet laureate on 8 December 1692 and in this capacity provided the texts of a number of birthday, New Year and other celebratory odes. He also collaborated with Nicholas Brady in producing in 1696 a metrical version of the psalms. A few of these, together with Tate's Christmas hymn *While shepherds watched*, are still included in modern hymnbooks.

BIBLIOGRAPHY

E. K. Broadus: *The Laureateship* (Oxford, 1921), 88ff
I. Holst, ed.: *Henry Purcell, 1659–1695: Essays on his Music* (London, 1959), 35ff
A. M. Laurie: *Purcell's Stage Works* (diss., U. of Cambridge, 1962)
J. Buttrey: 'Dating Purcell's "Dido and Aeneas" ', *PRMA*, xciv (1967–8), 51

MARGARET LAURIE

Tate, Phyllis (Margaret) (*b* Gerrards Cross, 6 April 1911). English composer. She studied composition with Farjeon at the RAM (1928–32). While there she had an operetta, *The Policeman's Serenade*, performed by students, but this – like other works written before the war – has been discarded. She first attracted public attention with the performances of her Sonata for clarinet and cello in London in 1947 and at the 1952 ISCM Festival. Further critical acclaim followed the production of her opera *The Lodger* in 1960. Tate is not a prolific composer. She has preferred the more modest genres, and her best works have been those for small ensemble, often with voice or voices. Within these limits, she has been concerned primarily with the resolution of problems of texture and sonority; unusual combinations often result in fascinating and highly individual effects. She is aware of a need to communicate with a wide public, and her children's music stems naturally from her other creative work.

WORKS
(*selective list*)

Operas: The Lodger (D. Franklin), 1960; Dark Pilgrimage (television opera, Franklin), 1963, unpubd
Choral: Choral Scene from 'The Bacchae' of Euripides, double chorus, 1953; 7 Lincolnshire Folksongs, chorus, insts, 1966; A Secular Requiem, chorus, insts, 1967; Christmas Ale, 1v, chorus, orch, 1967; To Words by Joseph Beaumont, SSA, pf, 1970; Serenade to Christmas, Mez, chorus, orch, 1971–2; St Martha and the Dragon, narrator, S, T, chorus, children's chorus, chamber orch, 1976; All the World's a Stage (Shakespeare), SATB, orch, 1976
Solo vocal: Nocturne for Four Voices (S. Keyes), Mez, T, Bar, B, insts, 1945; The Lady of Shalott (Tennyson), T, insts, 1956; A Victorian Garland (Arnold), S, A, hn, pf, 1965; Apparitions, T, insts, 1968; Gaelic Ballads, 1v, pf, 1968; 3 Northumbrian Coastal Ballads, arr., Bar, insts, 1969; 2 Ballads, 1v, gui, 1972; Songs of Sundrie Kindes, T, lute, 1976
Inst: Conc., a sax, str, 1944; Sonata, cl, vc, 1947; Str Qt, F, 1952; Air and Variations, vn, cl, pf, 1958; Pf Sonatina no.2, 1959; Illustrations, brass band, 1969; Variegations, va, 1970; Explorations around a Troubadour Song, pf, 1973; Lyric Suite, pf 4 hands, 1973–4; The Rainbow and the Cuckoo, ob qt, 1974; Sonatina pastorale, harmonica, hpd, 1974; Songs without Words, orch, 1976
Educational music

Principal publisher: Oxford University Press

BIBLIOGRAPHY
M. Carner: 'The Music of Phyllis Tate', *ML*, xxxv (1954), 128
H. Searle: 'Phyllis Tate', *MT*, xcvi (1955), 244
M. Carner: 'Phyllis Tate', *MT*, cv (1964), 20
N. Kay: 'Phyllis Tate', *MT*, cxvi (1975), 429

RICHARD COOKE

Tátrai String Quartet. Hungarian string quartet. It was formed in 1946 from soloists of the Budapest Municipal Orchestra (which became the Hungarian State Concert Orchestra). The original members were Vilmos Tátrai and Albert Rényi, violins, József Iványi, viola, and Vera Dénes, cello. It won the 1948 Bartók Competition for quartets, and quickly became the foremost Hungarian string quartet. It began touring widely in Europe from 1952, and has appeared at leading international festivals including those of Dubrovnik, Edinburgh, Salzburg and Vienna. The first violinist has remained unchanged, but other changes in membership have brought Mihály Szücs as second violin from 1955, György Konrád, viola, from 1959, and Ede Banda, cello, from 1952. The players have sought to maintain the best Hungarian traditions of quartet performance; being the only quartet in Hungary for some time, they introduced the Classical and Romantic repertory to many audiences. Contemporary Hungarian composers have been commissioned to write for the quartet, which has also introduced new works from other countries (the ensemble had given about 70 first performances by the mid-1970s). Its numerous records include complete cycles of Beethoven's and Bartók's quartets (the latter for the complete recorded edition). The quartet was awarded the Kossuth Prize in 1958.

PÉTER P. VÁRNAI

Tattersall, William Dechair (*b* 1752; *d* Wotton-under-Edge, Gloucs., 26 May 1829). English amateur musician. He was rector of Westbourne, Sussex, from 1778, and from 1779 also vicar of Wotton-under-Edge, Gloucestershire, where he lived. He devoted much energy to improving psalmody in the church at Wotton-under-Edge. His first step was to take control of the choir. He then introduced Merrick's metrical translation of the psalms in place of the Old and New versions. His first printed collection, *Psalms selected from the version of the Revd Jas Merrick* (London, *c*1790), uses mostly traditional tunes. *Improved Psalmody* (1794), however, includes a large number of tunes specially composed or adapted for the work, by many prominent composers such as Shield, Callcott, Samuel Arnold, Webbe, Stevens and even Haydn, who contributed six cantata-like pieces. The music is in three parts (SSB or TTB) and is for the most part too elaborate for congregational singing. Tattersall's aim was to 'excite a laudable Zeal throughout the lower Orders' by providing examples of the most elegant music available: 'the serious Glees which consist only of three Parts, seem to present a perfect Model for this Species of Divine Harmony'. The list of subscribers is impressive evidence of Tattersall's social connections: it includes most of the royal family, both archbishops, heads of colleges, peers and ladies of title, as well as prominent musicians. Perhaps for this reason *Improved Psalmody* was widely used throughout the south of England for 40 years or more, occupying a position similar to that of Edward Miller's *Psalms of David* in the north. In 1802 he published a third collection, *Improved Psalmody; sanctioned by the King at Weymouth*. Merrick's version was again used: but in deference to the taste of George III the music was entirely 'adapted from the sacred compositions of Handel'.

BIBLIOGRAPHY
J. D. Brown and S. S. Stratton: *British Musical Biography* (Birmingham, 1897)
R. Hughes: *Haydn* (London, 1950), 94, 222

NICHOLAS TEMPERLEY

Tattoo. A musical ceremonial practised in most armies at about 10 p.m., at the end of the soldier's day. It dates from 1625 at the latest when it was a simple drum call, although its predecessor, 'Setting the Watch', is traceable in the 16th century. Besides this purpose it had another significance. In early days soldiers were either encamped regimentally or billeted in towns, and the call or sounding of the tattoo warned them that it was time for 'retiring' to camp or billet, hence the call played at this time was named Retreat. An order of William III, dated 1694, demands that the drum-major and drummers shall beat 'this call named Retreat' through the main streets of the town for this purpose. Indeed the ceremony is termed 'Retreat or Tattoo' in W. B. Bland's *Military Discipline* (London, 1727).

When fifes were restored to the British army about 1745 a melody was set for them to the older and fun-

Ex.1

damental drumbeats of the call, and soon the Tattoo became one of the most spectacular parades of the British army, as it already was with the Prussians; ex.1 shows the Prussian *Zapfenstreich* of about 1720. At the time of the Crimean War it was being used in the British army as the 'Officers' Mess Call'.

The earliest British specimens are to be found in *A Complete Tutor for the Fife* (London, c1750), which contains the Tattoo of both 'English Duty' and 'Scottish Duty'. They are extremely quaint and consist of two nine-bar strains, both being clearly derived from some common original (see ex.2). The parading of the drums

Ex.2

and fifes at Tattoo was described by Thomas Simes (*The Military Guide*, 1781):

It is performed by the Drum-major and all the drummers and fifers of that regiment which gives a captain to the main-guard that day. They begin at the main-guard, beat round the grand parade, and return back and finish where they began. . . . They are answered by the drummers and fifers of all the other guards.

This is identical with what Bland wrote in 1757, except that fifes have been added.

At the close of the 18th century, however, when the bugle was adopted for infantry calls, two calls were adapted for watch-setting so as to coincide with cavalry procedure, and the Tattoo of the drums and fifes then found a place between the two calls known as 'Setting the Watch' (now 'First Post') and 'Second Post'. In 1815 Samuel Potter's two books of fife calls and drum calls were published. These were the soundings used in the Foot Guards, and they became so popular with the army authorities that they were made compulsory throughout the army, ousting the old 'English Duty' and 'Scottish Duty'. The result of this was that a new Tattoo appeared which was simply the 'Retreat' with a special feature in the 'doublings'. Before half a century had passed even this was no longer *de rigueur*, since it was agreed that 'the tunes to be played at Tattoo time may be chosen optionally'.

Modern conditions have driven out most of the old drum and fife calls, and the Retreat and the Tattoo are all that remain. Even these have a precarious existence and are preserved by only a few regiments in an attempt to hold on to these old and treasured customs. In the heyday of the Tattoo, after the First Post had been sounded, the drums and fifes made ready for their Tattoo, opening with the traditional three cadences or pauses (possibly a tribute to the Trinity – certainly it is observed in other army practices) when they marched off to the Tattoo call (ex.3). Other tunes were also used;

Ex.3

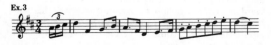

but they always finished with the coda in ex.4. To all this music the performers (accompanied in the old days by a file from the main guard) marched and countermarched up and down the parade ground. At the com-

Ex.4

pletion of this (about 15 minutes later) the national anthem was played, followed by the Last Post on the bugle or bugles.

Beethoven is said to have composed three 'tattoos' for military band; in Austria tattoos were played by the regular military band as well as the drums and fifes. In Britain the military band also takes part in a grandiose form of the old ceremony in what is called a 'Torchlight Tattoo' or a 'Grand Military Tattoo', but in such displays the simplicity of the music and the quaintness of the ceremony is lost entirely. A particularly spectacular one is enacted each year at the Edinburgh Festival.

BIBLIOGRAPHY

A Complete Tutor for the Fife (London, c1750)
The Compleat Tutor for the Fife (London, c1760)
The Young Drummer's Assistant (London, 1785)
S. Potter: *The Art of Beating the Drum* (London, 1815)
——: *The Art of Playing the Fife* (London, 1815)
Drum, Flute and Bugle Tutor (London, 1817)
G. Tamplini: *The Fife Major* (London, c1862)
Drum and Flute Duty (London, 1887)
G. R. Howe: *Drums and Drummers* (London, 1893)
Manual for the Corps of Drums of the 22nd (Cheshire) Regiment (c1921)

H. G. FARMER/JAMES BLADES

Tatum, Art [Arthur] (*b* Toledo, Ohio, 13 Oct 1910; *d* Los Angeles, 5 Nov 1956). Black American jazz pianist. He was almost totally blind from early childhood, and played in local Ohio nightclubs and on radio before going to New York in 1932 as accompanist to the singer Adelaide Hall. He made his first solo recordings in 1933 and continued to record throughout his life, prolifically during the last few years. Briefly in the bands of Speed Webb, Milton Senior and in McKinney's Cotton Pickers, he had his own trio during the 1940s, but usually appeared as a soloist in clubs, principally around New York, Chicago and in California. By the late 1930s his reputation had spread far beyond the USA; he played in London in 1938, but despite being universally respected by the international jazz community, was never offered a tour abroad and always worked in relative obscurity.

Tatum's earliest recorded performances are excessively decorative, but through the 1930s he gradually transformed external filigree into necessary detail, as on *Willow, weep for me* (1949). In the process he absorbed a range of keyboard devices that was exceptional even by the standards of 19th-century virtuoso pianism, a tradition to which he had considerable affinities, as is obliquely confirmed by Godowsky's and Horowitz's praise of him. His contribution to jazz was a final sophistication of the New York 'stride' piano school, and he always acknowledged Fats Waller as an influence. He often used a popular song as a cantus firmus, evolving round it a structure of constantly shifting textures rich in inner voices; he might fragment the melody into basic motifs which he then remodelled and reharmonized over various intensifications of stride bass patterns. Despite the refinement and extreme elaboration of his textures, harmony and rhythm were the chief areas of Tatum's originality, leading him to anticipate many of the supposed innovations of bop. Yet his work could equally be said to synthesize all the resources of jazz pianism as he found it, so that a recording such as *St*

Louis Blues (1940), opening with boogie-woogie tremolos and closing with bop triplets, is almost a miniature history of the art.

BIBLIOGRAPHY

E. Barksdale: 'Art Tatum', *Melody Maker*, xxx (11 Aug 1956), 3
J. Mehegan: 'Art Tatum', *Down Beat*, xxiii (12 Dec 1956), 15
M. Edey: 'Art Tatum', *Jazz Review*, ii (1959), June, 28
D. Katz: 'Art Tatum', *Jazz Review*, ii (1959), Sept, 28
M. Edey: 'Art Tatum', *Jazz Review*, iii (1960), Aug, 4
A. Hodeir: *Toward Jazz* (New York, 1962), 127ff
W. Mellers: *Music in a New Found Land* (London, 1964), 376ff
M. Harrison: 'Art Tatum', *Jazz on Record*, ed. A. McCarthy (London, 1968), 279

MAX HARRISON

Taube. *See* TEYBER family.

Taube, Michael (*b* Łódź, 13 March 1890; *d* Tel-Aviv, 23 Feb 1972). Israeli conductor and composer of Polish birth. After childhood studies in the violin, flute, piano and cello, he attended the Leipzig Conservatory, then moved to Cologne to study the piano with Neitzel, composition with Strässer and conducting with Hermann Abendroth. In 1918 he founded the Concert Society at Bad Godesberg and in 1920 was invited as a guest conductor to Frankfurt, Berlin and Cologne. At Leo Blech's instigation he joined the Berlin Städtische Oper (now the Deutsche Oper) in 1924, and when Bruno Walter took over the direction of the company Taube remained with him for five years. At Berlin in 1926 he founded a chamber orchestra and choir, with which he presented rarely performed or little-known works, and some written for the ensemble. In 1935 he settled in Israel where he helped to build the orchestra that later became the Israel PO; together with Toscanini, Dobrowen and Steinberg, he was one of its principal conductors from its inception in 1936. Taube founded the Ramat Gan Chamber Orchestra and several times toured with it to Europe; concurrently he appeared with the Israel Radio SO and was a regular guest in Italy, Austria, Switzerland and West Germany, giving numerous concerts with the Berlin PO. He also taught voice training and conducting and soon after his arrival in Israel founded the Taube Conservatory (now defunct). He wrote some orchestral and chamber works, and made several arrangements.

WILLIAM Y. ELIAS

Taubel, Christian Gottlieb. German printer who worked with FRANZ ANTON HOFFMEISTER.

Tauber [Taube], Maria Anna (*fl* 1777–9). Austrian soprano, not identifiable with either of the sisters Elisabeth and Therese Teyber; *see* TEYBER family.

Tauber, Richard (*b* Linz, 16 May 1891; *d* London, 8 Jan 1948). Austrian tenor, naturalized British. As he was illegitimate, he was christened Richard Denemy (after his mother's maiden name), and was sometimes known as Richard Seiffert (after her married name). Frau Seiffert was the soubrette of the local theatre; the boy's father was an actor, Richard Anton Tauber. To distinguish himself from his father the young tenor at first adopted the additional name of Carl which is often found as an initial on his early gramophone records. He studied with Carl Beines at Freiburg and made his début on 2 March 1913, as Tamino in Mozart's *Die Zauberflöte*, at the Chemnitz Neues Stadt-Theater, of which his father was the director. His success was im-

mediate, and he was engaged on a five-year contract with the Dresden Opera, where he sang all the leading lyrical tenor parts. In 1915 he appeared for the first time at the German Opera House in Berlin, singing Bacchus in Strauss's *Ariadne auf Naxos*; by the end of 1919 he was well known throughout the German-speaking countries. Both at Munich and at Salzburg he was enormously, and justly, popular during the Mozart festivals in the parts of Tamino, Belmonte and Don Ottavio.

Richard Tauber

It was in lighter music, however, that he made his name with the general public. From about 1925 he began to appear with increasing frequency in the operettas of Lehár and others, charming thousands by his true tenor quality, sympathetic and somewhat 'nutty' in timbre, and by the grace and variety of his vocal inflections. England also succumbed (in 1931) when Lehár's *Das Land des Lächelns* repeated its universal success at Drury Lane, making Tauber the idol of a not too discriminating public. The strain of singing long parts eight times a week left its mark on his vocal cords, and some dubious stylistic elements became discernible on the occasions of his return to lieder and opera. A tendency to distort vowel sounds on high notes could perhaps be traced to a natural desire to husband his voice during the many encores which were always demanded after he sang a favourite piece. When Covent Garden first heard him he was no longer at his very best; in 1938 he sang Tamino and Belmonte, in 1939 Don Ottavio, and Hans in the German version of *The Bartered Bride*. After the war, however, he surprised his warmest admirers by the excellence of his Don Ottavio during the 1947 visit of the Vienna Staatsoper to Covent Garden. Tauber's first marriage was dissolved, and he married the actress Diana Napier in 1936. He was naturalized British in 1940.

BIBLIOGRAPHY

H. Ludwig: *Richard Tauber* (Berlin, 1928) [foreword by L. Blech]

D. N. Tauber: *Richard Tauber* (London, 1949)

W. Korb: *Richard Tauber* (Vienna, 1966)

J. Dennis and others: 'Richard Tauber', *Record Collector*, xviii (1969), 171–272 [with discography]

C. Castle and D. N. Tauber: *This was Richard Tauber* (London, 1971)
DESMOND SHAWE-TAYLOR

Taubert, Gottfried (*b* Ronneburg, Meissen; *fl* 1717). German dancing-master. He was the author of the dance treatise *Rechtschaffener Tanzmeister* (Leipzig, 1717/ *R*1976). The work is divided into three sections: a history of dance; a didactic description of French court dance practices, including the technique of individual steps and many varieties of three main dances, the courante, the minuet and the bourrée; and miscellaneous matters such as qualities desirable in a dancing-master and in his pupils, and the actual use of dances in a court ball.

This treatise is the longest (1176 pages) and most comprehensive description of 18th-century French court dance ever written. Although an invaluable source of information, it has been little used by dance historians because of its ponderous and flowery style, difficult even for those whose native language is German.

Little is known of Taubert's life other than that he was a dancing-master specializing in French dances at Leipzig. His treatise is dedicated to Friedrich Augusto, Duke of Saxony, Julich, Cleve and Berg, also Engern and Westphalia.

BIBLIOGRAPHY

A. Gerbes: *Gottfried Taubert on Social and Theatrical Dance of the Early Eighteenth Century* (diss., Ohio State U., 1972)

K. Petermann: introduction to facs. of *Rechtschaffener Tanzmeister*, Documenta choreologica, xxii (Leipzig, 1976)
MEREDITH ELLIS LITTLE

Taubert, (Carl Gottfried) Wilhelm (*b* Berlin, 23 March 1811; *d* Berlin, 7 Jan 1891). German conductor, composer and pianist. He studied under Ludwig Berger (piano) and Bernhard Klein (composition) and by 1831 had become assistant conductor and accompanist of the Berlin court concerts. During the 1840s he was associated with the Berlin Royal Opera under Mendelssohn and Meyerbeer, and served as Generalmusikdirektor there from 1845 until 1848. At that time he also held the appointment of court Kapellmeister, a position he retained until 1869. As chief Kapellmeister, Taubert continued to conduct the royal orchestra until 1883. Highly thought of as a teacher, he taught at the Royal Academy of Arts from 1865, Theodor Kullak being one of his pupils. Among his first compositions were small instrumental pieces and sets of songs which attracted the favourable notice of Mendelssohn and led to a correspondence, including Mendelssohn's long letter of 27 August 1831. In these letters Mendelssohn seems to put his finger on the lack of impetus and spirit which, with all his real musicianship, refined taste and immense industry, hindered Taubert from achieving real importance as a composer. His larger works suffer particularly, but his graceful, almost popular style was well suited to the short character-pieces so much in vogue at the time. The *Minnelieder* op.16 for piano, sometimes misleadingly compared with Mendelssohn's *Lieder ohne Worte*, are still occasionally performed, as are the vocal *Kinderlieder*, which include the best known of Taubert's 300 songs, opp.145 and 160. His works comprise over 200 opus numbers and also include six operas produced

in Berlin, incidental music for eight plays, four symphonies and three orchestral overtures, two piano concertos, a cello concerto, a concertino for violin, four string quartets, two piano trios, violin sonatas, choral music, six sonatas and numerous character-pieces for piano.

BIBLIOGRAPHY

R. Schumann: *Gesammelte Schriften* (Leipzig, 1854, 5/1914/*R*1968)

W. Neumann: *Wilhelm Taubert und Ferdinand Hiller* (Kassel, 1857)

E. Glusman: 'Taubert and Mendelssohn: Opposing Attitudes toward Poetry and Music', *MQ*, lvii (1971), 628

R. Sietz: 'Taubert, Carl Gottfried Wilhelm', *MGG* [with complete list of works]

Taubman, Howard (*b* New York, 4 July 1907). American music and drama critic. He took the AB at Columbia University in 1929 and that year joined the staff of the *New York Times*. He became the paper's music editor (1935–55), its music critic (1955–60) and its drama critic (1960–66). As the *New York Times*'s critic-at-large, until his retirement in 1972, Taubman travelled throughout the USA and Europe, contributing articles on the complex growth and economic problems of the arts. In this capacity, he made particular use of the breadth of interests and sympathies that had been the most notable features of his more specialized earlier writings.

WRITINGS

Opera Front and Back (New York, 1938)

Music as a Profession (New York, 1939)

ed.: G. Gatti-Casazza: *Memories of Opera* (New York, 1941)

Maestro: The Life of Toscanini (New York, 1951)

How to Build a Record Library (New York, 1953)

ed.: M. Anderson: *My Lord, What a Morning* (New York, 1956)

The Making of the American Theater (New York, 1965; rev. in *Musical Comedy*, xii, 1967, 822)

ed.: *The New York Times Guide to Listening Pleasure* (New York, 1968)

BIBLIOGRAPHY

L. Weldy: *Music Criticism of Olin Downes and Howard Taubman in 'The New York Times', Sunday Edition, 1924–29 and 1955–60* (diss., U. of Southern California, 1962)
PATRICK J. SMITH

Taubmann, Otto (*b* Hamburg, 8 March 1859; *d* Berlin, 4 July 1929). German conductor, critic and composer. He studied the piano, the cello and composition at the Dresden Conservatory and then went to Paris and Vienna for further instruction. After experience as an opera conductor, he became the director of the Wiesbaden Conservatory in 1886, remaining there until 1889. He conducted in St Petersburg from 1891 to 1892 before becoming conductor of the Cäcilienverein in Ludingshafen. From 1895 he was active in Berlin as a composer and also as critic for the *Börsenkurier*. He became professor in 1910 and senator of the Academy of the Arts in 1923. From 1920 to 1925 he taught at the Hochschule für Musik. His works include the opera *Porzia*, based on *The Merchant of Venice* and produced in Frankfurt am Main in 1916, the choral drama *Sängerweihe* (1904), the cantata *Kampf und Friede* (1915), the *Deutsche Messe* (1899), the Symphony in A minor and String Quartet in E minor, as well as choruses and psalm settings. He also published a number of piano reductions, of works by Sibelius among others, and was a contributor to the Liszt *Gesamtausgabe*.

BIBLIOGRAPHY

H. Kretzschmar: *Führer durch den Konzertsaal* (Leipzig, 1921)

Obituaries: *Die Musik*, xxi (1928–9), 942; *ZfM*, Jg.96 (1929), 506

P. Schwers: 'Der 70jährige O. Taubmann', *AMz*, lvi/10 (1929)

G. Schünemann: *Die Singakademie zu Berlin 1791–1941* (Regensburg, 1941)
ERIC BLOM/GAYNOR G. JONES

Tauranth, Johannes. *See* TOURONT, JOHANNES.

Tauriello, Antonio (*b* Buenos Aires, 20 March 1931). Argentinian composer and conductor. His piano studies were begun with Raul Spivak and completed with Gieseking; at the same time he studied composition under Ginastera. In 1958 he began his career as a conductor when an Interamerican Festival was held in Argentina under the auspices of the Buenos Aires Chamber Concerts Association. Shortly after he was appointed conductor of the Teatro Colón, and he also conducted the percussion ensemble Ritmus. He moved to the Chicago Lyric Opera as assistant director in 1965, later conducting for the Washington Opera Society, the New York City Opera and the American Opera Center. Concurrently he was conducting orchestral concerts, notably for the Inter-American Music Festivals in Washington, DC. These festivals saw first performances of his own *Obertura sinfónica* (1961), *Transparencias* (1965) and the Piano Concerto (1968). His music has also been heard in Spain at festivals of Spanish and South American music (*Canti* in 1967, *Mansión de Tlaloc* in 1970), and at the 1970 ISCM Festival (*Serenata II*). In 1969 he received a Guggenheim Scholarship and the International Composition Prize of Bowdoin College, Brunswick, Maine (for *Signos de los tiempos*). As a composer Tauriello belongs to the Argentinian avant garde. The Piano Concerto is notable for the extraordinary freedom of its solo part, which, at certain moments, is quite independent of the orchestra; sometimes durations and intensities are to be chosen by the soloist.

WORKS
(*selective list*)

Obertura sinfónica, 1961; Ricercari I–VI, orch, 1963; Transparencias, 6 inst groups, 1964; Música III, pf, orch, 1965; Escorial, opera, 1, 1966; Serenata II, 7 insts, 1966; Canti, vn, orch, 1967; Pf Conc., 1968; Signos de los tiempos, ens, 1969; Mansión de Tlaloc, orch, 1970

SUSANA SALGADO

Tausch, Franz (Wilhelm) (*b* Heidelberg, 26 Dec 1762; *d* Berlin, 9 Feb 1817). German clarinettist, basset-horn player and composer. He founded the German playing style, which put beauty of tone above technique. He was a child prodigy: at the age of eight he played in the Mannheim orchestra with his father Jacob, who taught him. Moving with his father to Munich, Franz became a notable soloist and made several concert tours. In 1789 he became chamber musician to the dowager Queen of Prussia and from 1797 to Friedrich Wilhelm III. In 1805 Tausch opened a conservatory for wind players in Berlin, where Heinrich Baermann and Crusell were among his pupils. His compositions are noteworthy, and make considerable demands on the player. They include a number of clarinet concertos, six quartets for two basset-horns and two bassoons (with two horns ad lib), duos for violin and viola and for two clarinets, and other chamber music for wind. After his death the conservatory continued under the direction of his son Friedrich Wilhelm (1790–1845), himself a fine player.

BIBLIOGRAPHY
P. Weston: *Clarinet Virtuosi of the Past* (London, 1971)

PAMELA WESTON

Tausch, Julius (*b* Dessau, 15 April 1827; *d* Bonn, 11 Nov 1895). German conductor and composer. He was a pupil of F. Schneider at Dessau. In 1844 he entered the Leipzig Conservatory, then in the second year of its existence, and on leaving in 1846 settled at Düsseldorf.

There he gradually advanced, taking the direction of the artists' *Liedertafel* on Julius Rietz's departure in 1847, and succeeding Schumann as conductor of the music society, temporarily in 1853 and permanently in 1855. He was associated with the direction of the Lower Rhine Festivals from 1853 to 1887. In the winter of 1878 he conducted the orchestral concerts at the Glasgow Festival. He retired to Bonn in 1890.

WORKS
(*complete list in du Mont*)

Music to Shakespeare's Twelfth Night, op.4 (Düsseldorf, 1863)
Festouvertüre, E♭, orch, op.9, pf score (Hamburg, c1875)
Der Blumenklage auf den Tod des Sängers, S, female vv, orch, op.10 (Berlin, ?1877)
Germanenzug (A. Silberstein: Trutz-Nachtigall), S, 4vv, orch, op.16, pf score (Leipzig, c1833)
Mirjams Siegesgesang (W. Hosäus), S, 4vv, orch, 1877, not pubd
The Conzertstück for 6 timpani and orch cited in *Grove 5* is not mentioned by du Mont.

BIBLIOGRAPHY
W. du Mont: 'Tausch, Julius', *Rheinischer Musiker*, ii, ed. K.G. Fellerer (Cologne, 1962), 104

GEORGE GROVE/BRUCE CARR

Tausig, Carl [Karol] (*b* Warsaw, 4 Nov 1841; *d* Leipzig, 17 July 1871). Polish pianist and composer. He was first taught by his father, Aloys Tausig (*b* Prague, 1820; *d* Warsaw, 14 March 1885), a good professional pianist, pupil of Thalberg and the composer of many brilliant piano pieces. When Carl was 14 his father took him to Liszt at Weimar, where he quickly became Liszt's favourite, accompanying him on concert tours and studying counterpoint, composition and instrumentation, as well as the piano. In 1858 he made his public début at a concert in Berlin conducted by Bülow. Opinion was divided: his technical feats were extraordinary, but the most severe critics talked of noise and rant, and even those who might have been ready to sympathize with his 'Lisztian eccentricities' thought he would play better when his period of 'Sturm und Drang' was over. In 1859–60 Tausig gave concerts in various German towns, making Dresden his base. In 1862 he went to live in Vienna where, following Bülow's example in Berlin, he gave orchestral concerts with very 'advanced' programmes; they were artistically only partly successful, and financially were failures. Thereafter he stayed out of the public eye for a few years. In 1864 he married the fine pianist Seraphine von Vrabely (1841–1931) and the next year they settled in Berlin; they were later divorced. The 'Sturm und Drang' was finished and Tausig was now recognized as a fine pianist. He had achieved self-possession, breadth and dignity of style, while his technique was, as Liszt described it, 'infallible'. He opened a school of advanced piano instruction but soon gave it up as he was not much interested in teaching; there is a vivid account of his methods by Amy Fay. Continued tours weakened his health, which had never been robust, and he died of typhoid at 29.

Tausig was the most gifted and most famous of the first generation of Liszt pupils. His manner of playing at its best was grand, impulsive and impassioned, yet no longer with a trace of eccentricity. His tone was superb, his touch exquisite, and his technical dexterity and endurance astonished even experts: Liszt said he had 'fingers of steel'. He made a point of executing his tours de force with perfect composure and took pains to hide every trace of physical effort. His repertory was varied and extensive, and he could play from memory any representative piece by any composer of importance from Scarlatti to Liszt. A virtuoso of the highest rank,

Carl Tausig

During the 1950s he followed the aesthetics of socialist realism, but later turned to folklore and adopted a more romantic approach. About 1965 he became acquainted with the new music of western Europe, and from then he was much influenced by recent techniques. His most important contributions are in small-scale genres, though the ballet and the opera are notable exceptions.

WORKS
(selective list)

Stage: Noc [Night], ballet, 1967; Ošklivá příhoda [Nasty event] (comic opera, after Dostoyevsky), 1969

Chamber: 2 krátké úvahy [2 brief reflections], b cl, pf, 1967; Str Qt no.3, 1967; Brass Qnt, 1968; Prelude, Sarabande and Postlude, wind, perc, pf, 1968; Concertino meditazione, va, ens, 1969; Canto di speranza, pf qnt, 1969; 2 apostrofy, wind qnt, 1969; Kruhy [Circles], fl, pf, 1969; 7 microchromophones, pf, va, cl, 1973; Trio, str, 1973; On revient toujours, suite, vn, pf, 1974; Hukvaldy, nonet, 1974

Orch: Improvisation, pf, orch, 1970; Sinfonia bohemica, B, male vv, tpt, hpd, orch, 1973–5

Pf: Circonvolutions, prepared pf, 1971; 10 Dodecaphonic Studies, 1972

Songs: Čmáranice po nebi [Scrawls across the sky] (cycle, V. Chlebnikov), 1v, pf, 1967; Konstelace, cycle, S, pf, 1968

Principal publishers: Český hudební fond, Panton

BIBLIOGRAPHY
ČSHS
I. Stolařík and B. Štědroň: 'K dějinám hudby v Ostravském kraji' [History of music in the Ostrava region], *Slezský sborník*, liii (1955), 224
M. Navrátil: 'Skladatelské znovuzrození Jana Tausingra' [Tausinger's compositional rebirth], *HRo*, xxiv (1971), 221
A. Košťál: 'Rozhovor s Janem Tausingrem', *OM*, iv (1972), 310
OLDŘICH PUKL

he was also an accomplished musician, familiar with scores old and new. Tausig composed a few pieces for piano: they include an impromptu, *Das Geisterschiff* and *Etudes de concert*, all published as op.1; *Tarantelle* and *Réminiscences de Hallka de Moniuszko*, both as op.2; a nocturne with variations entitled *L'espérance* op.3; *Rêverie* op.5; and an étude, *Le ruisseau* op.6. He also arranged, transcribed and fingered many more works, including a piano score of Wagner's *Die Meistersinger*, six Beethoven string quartets and three Scarlatti sonatas. His arrangements are extremely effective but at times very tasteless; his transcriptions of Berlioz and Wagner are brilliant, but Weber and Schubert are over-arranged and the Scarlatti pieces show him deficient in any stylistic sense. However, Tausig's *Tägliche Studien*, transposing chromatic finger exercises, posthumously revised and edited by Heinrich Ehrlich, remain invaluable.

BIBLIOGRAPHY
C. F. Weitzmann: *Der Letzte der Virtuosen* (Leipzig, 1868)
W. von Lenz: *Die grossen Pianoforte-Virtuosen unserer Zeit* (Berlin, 1872, Eng. trans., 1899/R1973)
A. Fay: *Music Study in Germany* (Chicago, 1880/R1965)
EDWARD DANNREUTHER/R

Tausinger, Jan (*b* Piatra Neamt, Romania, 1 Nov 1921). Czech composer, conductor and teacher. He studied at the Bucharest Conservatory with Ducline and, after settling in Czechoslovakia, he continued his studies with Hába and Bořkovec at the Prague Academy (1948–52). He conducted the radio orchestras in Bucharest, Ostrava and Plzeň, and from 1954 to 1958 he was head of the Ostrava Conservatory. Afterwards he spent two years as director of the artistic ensemble of the ministry of the interior, leaving this position to devote his time to composition. He was a member of the Prague music staff of Czech radio (1969–70) and was then appointed head of the Prague State Conservatory.

Tavener, John (Kenneth) (*b* London, 28 Jan 1944). English composer. Tavener was educated at Highgate School, London, and at the Royal Academy of Music (1961–5), studying with Berkeley and Lumsdaine. While still at the RAM Tavener composed his dramatic cantata *Cain and Abel*, which won the Prince Rainier of Monaco Prize in 1965 and was the first work to bring him to prominence in Britain. It was followed by another biblical cantata, *The Whale* (1965–6). This had its first performance at the inaugural concert of the London Sinfonietta in January 1968, and subsequently enjoyed something of a vogue, to the extent of being recorded in 1970 by Apple Records, the company formed by the Beatles.

Tavener's early bias towards religious subjects has continued, explicitly and implicitly, in most of his works since *The Whale*. These include three Requiems, of which the first, *A Celtic Requiem*, draws a comparison between children's games and the ritual celebration of death, while the *Little Requiem for Father Malachy Lynch* amounts to a study for the complete setting in the *Requiem for Father Malachy*. Tavener has also been drawn towards mysticism, particularly to the writings of St John of the Cross, whose visions are the subject of *Nomine Jesu* and *Coplas*. In 1972 *Ultimos ritos*, a further setting of texts by St John of the Cross and Tavener's largest completed work up to that time, won the prize for religious composition in the international contest of the Italian Society for Contemporary Music at Perugia.

From the beginning Tavener's style has been eclectic to a degree, and yet the general effect of his music is completely individual. The strongest early influence was late Stravinsky. There is an evident parallel between *Cain and Abel* and the Stravinsky of *A Sermon, a Narrative and a Prayer*, and the influence persists through *The Whale*, the Chamber Concerto and the

Introit for the Feast of St John Damascene. But while Stravinsky's religiosity was of an ascetic, formal cast, Tavener's is transcendental, associative and nostalgic. A taste for plain Romantic harmony betrays the influence of Victorian hymn tunes, while the use of repetition and long-held chords to create a mood of ecstatic contemplation suggests Messiaen.

Many of Tavener's mature works are collages, with a generous helping of simple pictorialism. *The Whale* opens with a long spoken extract from *Collins' Encyclopedia* and later offers a kind of musical picture-book of the story of Jonah (including a graphic account of his emission from the whale's stomach). On the other hand the Vulgate text rather oddly recalls Stravinsky's preference for Latin as a vehicle for monumental, 'incantatory' drama. The many-layered *Celtic Requiem* incorporates children's singing-games alongside poems by Vaughan, Newman and the early Irish poet, Blathmac. Direct musical allusions occur infrequently (although the Introit and *Coplas* both borrow from Bach's B minor Mass). Tavener generally prefers to compose his own versions of familiar types, like the hymn tune in *In alium*, which is a variant of the work's main theme.

For some years Tavener has been organist in a Presbyterian church. But the main direction of his thought appears to be Catholic, mystical and literary – high rather than low. Recent works show a preoccupation with Catholic funeral rites, always coloured, however, with that peculiar revivalist sentimentality which enables him to fulfil such daunting commissions as the writing of music for Barrie's *Mary Rose*. Criticism of his work for its inclusiveness and lack of intellectual rigour ignores the predominantly reflective rather than dialectical cast of his mind. His best works are undoubtedly all of a piece, even when their density of thematic argument is low.

WORKS

Three Holy Sonnets (Donne), Bar, chamber orch, 1962; J. Noble, ECO, cond. Steinitz, July 1964
Concerto, pf, chamber orch, 1962–3
Three Sections from T. S. Eliot's Four Quartets, T, pf, 1963–4
The Cappemakers, dramatic cantata, 2 narrators, 10 solo vv, male chorus, chamber orch, 1964, rev. for stage 1965
Cain and Abel (dramatic cantata, York Mystery Plays, Vulgate), S, A, T, Bar, chamber orch, 1965
Little Concerto, orch, 1965; rev. as Chamber Concerto, small orch, 1966, rev. 1968; London Sinfonietta, cond. Atherton, Queen Elizabeth Hall, June 1968
The Whale (dramatic cantata, Collins' Encyclopedia, Vulgate), narrator, Mez, Bar, chorus, orch, 1965–6; A. Lidell, A. Reynolds, R. Herincx, London Sinfonietta, cond. Atherton, Queen Elizabeth Hall, 24 Jan 1968
Birthday Bells, pf, 1967; for Stravinsky's 85th birthday
Grandma's Footsteps, ens, 1967–8; Morley College Chamber Ens, Camden, 14 March 1968
Introit for the Feast of St John Damascene (Introit for March 27th), S, A, chorus, orch, 1967–8; H. Harper, M. Cable, London Bach Society, ECO, cond. Steinitz, Queen Elizabeth Hall, 27 March 1968
The Amphis-Baena, S/T, pf, 1968
Concerto for Orchestra, 1968
Three Surrealist Songs (Lucie-Smith), Mez, pf + bongos, tape, 1968
In alium (Péguy, Vulgate), high S, orch, tape, 1968; R. Bruce, BBC SO, cond. Del Mar, Albert Hall, 12 Aug 1968
Celtic Requiem (Requiem Mass, H. Vaughan, Newman, Blathmac, trans. J. Carney, children's games), S, children's chorus, chorus, orch, 1969; Little Missenden Village School Choir, London Sinfonietta, cond. Atherton, Festival Hall, 16 July 1969
Ultimos ritos (St John of the Cross, Crucifixum from Nicene creed), S, A, T, B, 5 male speakers, chorus, large brass ens, orch, 1969–72; BBC Chorus, Netherlands RPO, cond. John Poole, Haarlem, St Bavokerk, 22 June 1974
Coplas (St John of the Cross), S, A, T, B, chorus, tape, 1970; Louis Halsey Singers, Cheltenham, 9 July 1970
Nomine Jesu (St John of the Cross, Bible), Mez, 5 male speakers, chorus, 2 a fl, org (2 players)/org, hpd, 1970; Dartington, Aug 1970

Canciones españolas, 1/2 Mez/Ct, fls, chamber org, hpd, perc, 1971; J. Bowman, London Sinfonietta, cond. Atherton, Queen Elizabeth Hall, 8 June 1972
In memoriam Igor Stravinsky, 2 a fl, org, bells, 1971
Ma fin est mon commencement, T chorus, 4 vc, 4 trbn, perc, 1972; Exultate Singers, London Sinfonietta, cond. Tavener, Southwark Cathedral, 23 April 1972
Responsorium in memory of Annon Lee Silver, 2 solo vv, 2 fl, chorus, 1972
Little Requiem for Father Malachy Lynch, chorus, chamber orch, 1972; Southern Cathedrals' Festival Choir, Bournemouth Sinfonietta, cond. M. Neary, Winchester Cathedral, 29 July 1972
Mary Rose (incidental music, Barrie), 1972
Variations on Three Blind Mice, chamber orch, 1972
Requiem for Father Malachy, 6 solo vv, tpt, trbn, chamber org, perc, pf, str, 1973; King's Singers, Nash Ensemble, cond. Tavener, Queen Elizabeth Hall, 10 June 1973
Thérèse (opera, G. McLarnon), 1973–6; Royal Opera, cond. Downes, Covent Garden, 1 Oct 1979
A Gentle Spirit, S, T, ens, 1976
Canticle of the Mother of God, S, SATB, 1976
Kyklike kinesis, S, SATB, vc solo, orch, 1977
Lamentation, Last Prayer and Exaltation, S, handbells/pf, 1977
Palin, pf, 1977
Palintropos, pf, orch, 1977
The Last Prayer of Mary Queen of Scots, S, handbells, 1977
6 Russian Folksongs, S, ens, 1978
The Immurement of Antigone (monodrama, G. McLarnon), S, orch, 1978; V. Townley, RPO, cond. W. Rennert, Festival Hall, 30 March 1979
Greek Interlude, fl, pf, 1979
6 Abbasid Songs, T, 3 fl + a fl, perc, 1979
Akhmatova: rekviem, S, B, ens, 1979–80

Principal publisher: Chester

WRITINGS
'Cain and Abel', *MT*, cvii (1966), 867
'Celtic Requiem', *MT*, cx (1969), 736

BIBLIOGRAPHY
A. Payne: 'Tavener's *In alium*', *Tempo* (1968), no.86, p.19
B. Dennis: 'John Tavener's *Celtic Requiem*', *Tempo* (1969), no.90, p.31
P. Griffiths: 'Tavener and "Ultimos ritos" ', *MT*, cxv (1974), 468
——: 'Thérèse: a Saint in Hell', *MT*, cxx (1979), 814
STEPHEN WALSH

Taverna, Gianpiero (*b* Bibbiena, 26 June 1932). Italian conductor. He studied the piano, composition and conducting at the Florence Conservatory, graduating in 1954, and took further conducting studies with Markevich in Salzburg and Berlin in 1955, and with Scherchen, working as the latter's assistant on concert tours (1956–60) and at his studio for electro-acoustical research at Gravesano, Switzerland. Since 1962 Taverna has been active as a conductor in Italy and abroad, including appearances at the Spoleto, Venice and Warsaw festivals, specializing in contemporary Italian works. Among the numerous premières he has given are Petrassi's *Beatitudines* (1969), Bussotti's *I semi di Gramsci* and *Lorenzaccio* (both 1972) and Sciarrino's *Amore e Psiche* (1973). Taverna has translated Webern's lectures and a volume of his letters into Italian (Milan, 1963), and served as music critic of *La nazione*, Florence (1963–4), and *Paese sera*, Rome (1967–9). In 1971 he became director of the instrumental ensemble at the Pesaro Conservatory, and he was a panellist at the 1974 International Conference on New Musical Notation at Ghent. In 1976 he was appointed artistic director of the Teatro Regio, Turin.

ELVIDIO SURIAN

Taverner, John (*b* south Lincs., *c*1490; *d* Boston, Lincs., 18 Oct 1545). English composer. He was the most important English composer of the first part of the 16th century, and is known chiefly for his sacred music.

1. LIFE. Taverner has been singularly maltreated by his modern biographers, and the following account of his

life relies on an entirely new examination of the sources. The date of his birth is unknown; some point around the year 1490 would seem to be most consistent with the other known facts of his biography; the region in which his family was rooted lay somewhere in the vicinity of Boston, Lincolnshire. There is no evidence whatever to support the usual assertion that in boyhood he served as a chorister of the choir of the collegiate church of Tattershall, Lincolnshire. A good deal of this college's archival material still survives for the period 1492–1507, which reveals the names of several choristers, but no John Taverner appears among them.

It has been further asserted that as a young man Taverner worked in London, and in 1514–15 joined the Fraternity of St Nicholas, the guild of the parish clerks and choir clerks of the London parish churches. This does not bear close examination. The nature of the fraternity has been somewhat misunderstood: only a small proportion of its members were musicians; and although a certain John Tavernar was indeed admitted to membership of the guild in 1514–15, his name appears in a section of the record reserved for new members who were not active parish clerks or church musicians. Consequently there are no grounds at all for identifying this John Tavernar with the composer. Similarly, there is no justification for the claim that Taverner may have had associations with Henry VIII's court and Chapel Royal at this period.

The earliest unequivocal references to the composer occur in 1524 and 1525, when he was a lay clerk of the choir of the collegiate church of Tattershall. The archives of this college show it to have maintained a lively and enterprising musical tradition, with a large and expert choir consisting of six chaplains, ten lay clerks and ten choristers. The statutes provided for one of the chaplains or clerks to act as instructor of the choristers, but it is not known if Taverner ever served there in this capacity.

Apparently his outstanding abilities were already well known, for in the autumn of 1525 John Longland, Bishop of Lincoln, invited him to move to Oxford to become first instructor of the choristers of the choir of Cardinal College (now Christ Church), Cardinal Wolsey's magnificent new foundation there. Taverner at first declined, on the grounds that by moving from Tattershall he would lose the opportunity of a favourable marriage. However, by early 1526 he had changed his mind and had accepted the job, and by Whitsuntide he was already actively recruiting singers for his new and very large choir, which was to consist of 12 chaplains, 12 lay clerks and 16 choristers. In October 1526 Cardinal College was formally opened, and Taverner's duties there began in earnest.

His career at Cardinal College was brief. Wolsey fell from grace as Henry VIII's chief minister in October 1529, and his colleges at Oxford and Ipswich soon began to be run down. By April 1530 provision for the choral service in the chapel of Cardinal College was already becoming sufficiently attenuated for Taverner to make the decision to leave. Although the evidence is far from conclusive, it appears that he now returned to his native Lincolnshire. He became a lay clerk of the choir maintained in the parish church of St Botolph, Boston, and probably took up the post of instructor of the choristers there. In this church the Gild of St Mary, an organization of enormous wealth, maintained a choir of almost cathedral proportions – ten chaplains, ten to 12 lay clerks and eight to ten choristers – and spent lavishly on the provision of music and musical expertise. However Taverner's membership of this choir too was cut short. Legislation enacted in 1534–5 had the effect of depriving the guild of its major sources of revenue, and it must then have ceased to be able to pay Taverner his probably very generous salary. Certainly by 1537 he had ended his direct association with this choir, and indeed, he seems at this point to have retired altogether from full-time employment in church music.

He continued to live in Boston, but from then on he appears in the records less as a musician than as a local worthy, of some considerable wealth and local stature. He seems to have known personally Thomas Cromwell, then Henry VIII's chief minister, and in 1538 Taverner was entrusted with supervising the demolition and burning of the rood screen in Boston parish church, evidently in execution of the government's current policy towards shrines and other objects of 'superstitious' veneration. In 1537 he was admitted a member of the Gild of Corpus Christi established in the parish church of Boston, and during 1541–3 served as one of its two treasurers. Soon after the town received its first charter of incorporation in 1545 Taverner was selected

Autograph letter (1538) from John Taverner to Thomas Cromwell concerning the burning of the rood screen in Boston parish church (GB-Lpro SP1/136)

as one of its 12 aldermen. He died soon afterwards and was buried in Boston parish church, survived by his wife Rose (née Parrowe) and her two daughters by a previous marriage.

In 1528, during his career at Cardinal College, Oxford, Taverner had briefly become embroiled in an outbreak of Lutheran heresy among certain members of the college. Two of those concerned were members of Taverner's choir whom he had himself recruited from Boston two years earlier. However, Wolsey made light of Taverner's own part in this incident, and no suspicion need be entertained that the composer ever seriously pursued deeply-held views in conflict with the Catholic orthodoxy of the time. The Boston Gild of Corpus Christi, to which he later belonged, existed 'to honour the transubstantiation of the body of Christ', and to maintain priests to pray for the souls of deceased members – two functions embodying doctrines totally incompatible with any sympathy for Protestant opinions. Further, Taverner's courteous and generous demeanour towards the Boston friars before the dissolution of their houses in 1538–9 similarly belies an impression that he felt any hostility towards the old order, although his readiness to deal in the landed property of the dissolved friaries certainly bespeaks a conventional acquiescence in at least the economic consequences of the Henrician Reformation of the 1530s.

There seem to be few grounds, therefore, for granting any credence to the well-known statement by the martyrologist John Foxe (written more than a generation after the composer's death) that at some point in his career Taverner became sufficiently influenced by Protestant doctrine as to 'repent him very much that he had made songs to popish ditties in the time of his blindness'. Consequently there are no foundations for the assertion that he ceased composition on leaving Cardinal College in 1530; indeed, he might well have continued composing until the day of his death. Allegations that he served as a paid agent of Thomas Cromwell, and devoted the last years of his life to the fanatical persecution and dissolution of religious houses, are totally without any foundation, and have no value except as dramatic fiction. The only respect in which Taverner's career departed from that of any conventional church musician of his period lies in the way in which he achieved sufficient wealth and esteem to be able eventually to retire from a career in active music, and spend the last years of his life as a respected burgher of his adopted town.

2. WORKS. It is, however, likely that the greater part of Taverner's known music was composed during his employment at Tattershall and at Cardinal College in the decade 1520–30, when Wolsey was at the height of his power, and English church music still showed little inclination to depart from its well-established late medieval practices. His most substantial works are those in the three traditional forms of large-scale writing: the mass, *Magnificat* and votive antiphon.

The three six-voice masses are all composed on cantus firmi, and illustrate clearly the culmination of nearly a century of development of the English festal mass. In most movements the cantus firmus is stated three times, in progressively shorter note values at each statement, and laid out in accordance with a carefully planned scheme of sections for full or reduced choir. There are certain other archaic features, such as the frequent huge spans of melisma, some hollow scoring

for high and low voices, and the occasional use of conflicting mensurations as a climactic device. At the same time Taverner integrated, with remarkable fluency, many of the distinctive features of the music of his predecessors, such as the expressive melodic lines of Fayrfax, the rhythmic tensions of William Cornysh, and the purposeful (often scalic) vocal part-writing of Ludford. His own most characteristic habit, perhaps, was to develop a selected rhythmic or melodic fragment by means of imitation or canon, or – more often – as a sequential ostinato within a single voice or pair of voices, giving many of his long melismatic sections a cogency and sense of direction less apparent in those of earlier composers. The masses are remarkable for their inventiveness and variety as much as for their extraordinary contrapuntal skill and the unerring control of a very large design. The three *Magnificat* settings are similar in style, with some exceptionally florid writing in the six-voice work. This and the four-voice setting are among the few English *Magnificat* settings to use the chant itself as a cantus firmus; that for five voices, of which the tenor is lost, was probably based on the older faburden technique.

Wolsey's statutes for Cardinal College required three polyphonic votive antiphons to be sung daily after Compline: one to the Trinity, one to St William of York, and finally one to the Virgin Mary. This lengthy procedure may have prompted some economy of method, for Taverner's antiphons are markedly less melismatic and more declamatory than had previously been normal. The Marian antiphons *Ave Dei patris* and *Gaude plurimum* and the Trinity antiphon *O splendor gloriae* are all set to long prose texts, the first being also one of the few 16th-century English antiphons to incorporate a cantus firmus. Two others, *Mater Christi sanctissima* and *O Wilhelme, pastor bone* (which survives only as *Christe Jesu, pastor bone*) are settings of much shorter metrical texts, and seem clearly to show the influence of Josquin and his pupils in their use of succinct, rounded phrases repeated in high–low antiphonal groupings. Taverner used both as material for parody masses (the second called 'Small Devotion', 'small' being probably a scribe's misreading of 'S[ancti] wil[helmi]'), and both masses, because of their syllabic style and lucid phrase structure, were even adapted to English translations for use in Communion services after 1547.

Ritual polyphony, in which plainsong is mostly treated as an equal-note cantus firmus, is scarcely found among the surviving music of Fayrfax's generation, but reappears increasingly from about 1520 onwards, eventually to form a major part of the output of, for example, Sheppard. Taverner composed settings of the two ceremonial matins responds, *Audivi vocem* and *Hodie nobis caelorum Rex* (beginning with the verse *Gloria in excelsis*), as well as the Compline respond *In pace in idipsum* (all three were later set by both Tallis and Sheppard). Of larger responds, with the polyphony clothing the choral rather than the solo chant, there are only the two settings of *Dum transisset Sabbatum* for Matins on Easter Sunday. Other pieces in this ritual category are a *Te Deum* (which sets the even-numbered verses only, as in the *Magnificat* settings), the *prosa Sospitati dedit aegros* for the Feast of St Nicholas, and a handful of items for the Lady Mass, including two alleluias, and also a Kyrie and three Christes in each of which the cantus firmus is not a plainsong but a square. Unfortunately several sequences and similar works are now known only from isolated verses in three parts, extracted by Elizabethan anthologists for instrumental playing.

Taverner himself may have contributed to the beginning of the Tudor fashion for playing viols in consort, for a six-part piece entitled *Quemadmodum* has no text in any source, and uses throughout an elaborately wrought texture that seems to have been instrumentally conceived. It should be made clear, however, that the In Nomine which became the prototype of this English genre is quite clearly a direct transcription of the 'In nomine Domini' section of his *Missa 'Gloria tibi Trinitas'*, and there is no evidence that Taverner himself was responsible for any of the instrumental versions. He also composed at least four secular songs. In *XX Songes* of 1530 there survives a single bass voice of three such pieces (one of which, *The Bella the bella*, has fragmentary concordances elsewhere). A fourth, *In women is rest*, is in Baldwin's commonplace-book: it is not clear whether the two voices there represent the complete texture, but they are enough to reveal a vigorously florid and very subtle setting of a witty text.

With the possible exception of *Quemadmodum* and the *Dum transisset* settings, all the music discussed so far seems reasonably characteristic of the period up to 1530, when Taverner left Cardinal College. There remain, however, three masses whose musical style is markedly different, and whose novel features are easier to explain in the context of the changed religious conditions of the last ten or 12 years of the composer's lifetime. By this time Henry VIII had rejected the papacy and all 'superstitions', including the veneration of most medieval (as distinct from biblical) saints; but he adhered staunchly to what he saw as an orthodox Catholic faith and to the Sarum rite, resisting the pressures of Cranmer and Cromwell towards Lutheran doctrines and a vernacular liturgy. The normal observance of Mass certainly continued; but there is no reason why such pressures should not have affected the musical style of settings of the Ordinary. Thus Taverner's *'Western Wynde'* mass, for example, has an SATB vocal layout and consists of a series of contrapuntal variations on a secular tune, in a manner that has more affinity with Lutheran methods than with the hallowed English traditions of Wolsey's lifetime. (A recent attempt to date this work as early as c1515 is almost entirely without foundation.) The masses of Tye and Sheppard based on the same tune are so similar to Taverner's as to suggest that the three composers may have worked in close association at some time between 1530 and 1543, perhaps at the Chapel Royal or in Lincolnshire. Three other masses by the same composers also have curiously close parallels, not in any common cantus firmus but in their novel mensural structure and use of very similar melodic material: namely Sheppard's *Frencis Mass*, Tye's five-voice mass in the Peterhouse Partbooks, and Taverner's *Missa sine nomine*. Finally, there is the group of *Playn Song* masses by Taverner, Sheppard and others, which set the Ordinary in a deliberately simple rhythmic style modelled on that of plainsong when sung in improvised polyphony (as in faburden). This method does have much earlier antecedents, but it is nevertheless tempting to see its revival as an embodiment of Cranmer's 'one syllable, one note' principle.

Conjectural though they must remain, such observations do tend to confirm the career pattern suggested by biographical evidence: namely, that of a church musician who composed intensively within the rigid

traditions of the period up to 1530, and perhaps more sporadically in the musically experimental climate that followed it, and who was in no sense wilful or rebellious. That he was pre-eminent among English musicians of his day is beyond question. Fayrfax and Cornysh had died soon after 1520; the younger generation of Tallis, Tye and Sheppard emerged after 1530; and only Ludford, probably some ten years his senior, even approached his stature. It was Taverner who enriched and transformed the English florid style by drawing on its best qualities, as well as on some continental techniques, and who later, when ideological considerations so dictated, was able to use his experience and maturity to produce simpler works of the greatest poise and refinement.

WORKS

Principal sources: *GB-Cjc, Cp, Cu, Lbm, Lcm, Ob, Och, T*
Editions: *J. Taverner c. 1495–1545, I*, ed. P. C. Buck and others, TCM, i (1923) [B i]

J. *Taverner c. 1495–1545, II*, ed. P. C. Buck and others, TCM, iii (1924) [B ii]

J. *Taverner: I, The Six-part Masses*, ed. H. J. Benham, EECM, xx (1978)

J. *Taverner: II, The Votive Antiphons*, ed. H. J. Benham, EECM, xxv (in preparation)

MASSES AND MASS SECTIONS

Missa 'Christe Jesu' [Small Devotion; In all Devotion], 5vv, B i, 70 (parody of ant; lacks T)
Missa 'Corona spinea', 6vv, B i, 157
Missa 'Gloria tibi Trinitas', 6vv, B i, 126 (c.f. ant at 1st Vespers, Trinity Sunday)
Missa 'Mater Christi', 5vv, B i, 99 (parody of ant; lacks T)
Missa 'O Michaell', 6vv, B i, 194 (c.f. Archangeli Michaelis interventione, re at Matins, Feast of St Michael in Monte Tumba)
Missa sine nomine [Meane mass], 5vv, B i, 50
Playn Song mass, 4vv, B i, 30
'Western Wynde' mass, 4vv, B i, 3 (c.f. popular song)
Kyrie 'Leroy', 4vv, B ii, 54 (c.f. square)
Kyrie, 1v, MS addn to printed processional (1545), *GB-Lbm* c.35, f.14 (apparently a counter to a chant)
Christe eleison (i), 3vv, B ii, 56 (c.f. square)
Christe eleison (ii), 3vv, B ii, 56 (c.f. square)
Christe eleison (iii), 3vv, B ii, 57 (c.f. square)
Sanctus, 3vv, B ii 58 [= frag. of Gaude plurimum]
Osanna in excelsis, 3vv, *Lbm* Add.18936
Benedictus, 3vv, B ii, 59 [= Traditur militibus]
Agnus Dei, 3vv, B ii, 60

MAGNIFICAT SETTINGS

Magnificat (primi toni), 6vv, B ii, 17
Magnificat (sexti toni), 4vv, B ii, 3
Magnificat (?octavi toni), 5vv, B ii, 9 (lacks T, which was probably faburden of 8th tone)

MOTETS

Alleluia, Salve virgo, 4vv, B ii, 52 (for Lady Mass)
Alleluia, Veni electa mea, 4vv, B ii, 53 (for Lady Mass)
Audivi vocem, 4vv, B ii, 35 (re at Matins, All Saints' Day; 1 voice described in source as 'pars ad placitum' by Whitbroke)
Ave Dei patris filia, 5vv, B ii, 61 (votive ant of BVM; c.f. chant of Te Deum)
Ave Maria, 5vv, B ii, 134 (votive ant of BVM; lacks Tr and T)
Christe Jesu, pastor bone, 5vv, B ii, 73 (votive ant of Jesus, adapted from lost ant O Wilhelme, pastor bone, of St William of York; lacks T)
Dum transisset Sabbatum (i), 5vv, B ii, 37 (re at Matins, Easter Sunday; c.f. chant; 1 source contains version for 4 men's vv, ed. in B ii, 40)
Dum transisset Sabbatum (ii), 5vv, B ii, 43 (re as preces, c.f. chant)
Ecce mater nostra, 5vv, B ii, 122 (verse of Ecce carissima dies, processional ant for Lent)
Fac nobis, 5vv, B ii, 135 (votive ant of Jesus; lacks Tr and T)
Gaude plurimum, 5vv, B ii, 78 (votive ant of BVM)
Gloria in excelsis, 4vv, B ii, 46 (verse of Hodie nobis caelorum Rex; re at Matins, Christmas Day)
Gloria tua, 2vv, *Lbm* Add.29246, f.12 (textless extract in lute tablature)
In pace in idipsum, 4vv, B ii, 48 (re at Compline, first 5 Sundays in Lent)
Jesu spes penitentibus, 3vv, B ii, 123 (3rd verse of seq Jesu dulcis memoria, for Mass of Holy Name of Jesus)
Mater Christi sanctissima, 5vv, B ii, 92
O splendor gloriae, 5vv, B ii, 99 (votive ant of Trinity; attrib. 'Taverner and Tye' in Baldwin's MSS *Och* 979–83 and *Lbm* R.M.24.d.2)
O Wilhelme, pastor bone [= Christe Jesu]

Prudens virgo, 3vv, B ii, 124 (section of lost votive ant)
Sancte Deus, 5vv, B ii, 139 (votive ant of Jesus; lacks Tr and T)
Sospitati dedit aegros, 5vv, B ii, 110 (prosa for 9th re at Matins, Feast of St Nicholas)
Sub tuum praesidium, 5vv, B ii, 141 (votive ant of BVM; lacks Tr and T)
[Te Deum laudamus] . . . Te aeternem Patrem, 5vv, B ii, 26 (c.f. chant of Te Deum except in 1 verse; lacks T)
Tam peccatum, 3vv, B ii, 126 (verse of tr Dulce nomen, for Jesus Mass)
Traditur militibus, 3vv, B ii, 132 (6th verse of seq Caenam cum discipulis, for Mass of the Five Wounds of Jesus)
Virgo pura, 3vv, B ii, 131 (?section of lost votive ant)

ENGLISH ADAPTATIONS

Communion Service, from Missa 'Christe Jesu', 5vv, B ii, 169 (lacks T)
Communion Service, from Missa sine nomine, 5vv, B ii, 143
In trouble and adversity, 4vv, B ii, 199 (from inst In Nomine)
I will magnify thee, Ckc Rowe 316 (from Gaude plurimum; single voice)
O give thanks, 4vv, Lbm Add.30480–83 (from inst In Nomine)
O most holy and mighty Lord, Ckc Rowe 316 (from Mater Christi; single voice)

SECULAR PARTSONGS

In women is rest peas and pacience, 2vv, Lbm R.M.24.d.2
Love wyll I and leve, 1530⁶ (B only)
Mi hart mi mynde, 1530⁶ (B only)
The Bella the bella, 4vv, 1530⁶ (B only), US-NYp Drexel 4184, 4185 (frags.)

INSTRUMENTAL

In Nomine, a 4, ed. in HM, cxxxiv (1956) (consort), MB, i (1951, rev. 2/1966) (kbd) (inst arr. of 'In nomine Domini' from Missa 'Gloria tibi Trinitas')
Quemadmodum, a 6, B ii, 117 (?viols)

MISATTRIBUTED WORKS

Ave regina caelorum, referred to in TCM, appx (1948), 6, 56, cannot be traced in sources named
Esto nobis is part of Tallis's Ave Dei patris filia
Rex amabilis is part of Fayrfax's Maria plena virtute
Tu ad liberandum is part of Aston's Te matrem Dei laudamus
Tu angelorum is part of Aston's Te matrem Dei laudamus

BIBLIOGRAPHY

H. B. Collins: 'John Taverner's Masses', ML, v (1924), 322
——: 'John Taverner – Part II', ML, vi (1925), 314
W. H. G. Flood: Early Tudor Composers (Oxford, 1925), 49
R. Donington and T. Dart: 'The Origin of the In Nomine', ML, xxx (1949), 101
G. Reese: 'The Origins of the English In Nomine', JAMS, ii (1949), 7
D. Stevens: The Mulliner Book: a Commentary (London, 1952)
——: 'The Background of the In Nomine', MMR, lxxxiv (1954), 199
——: Tudor Church Music (New York, 1955, 2/1966)
H. Baillie: 'A London Gild of Musicians', PRMA, lxxxiii (1956–7), 15
F. Ll. Harrison: Music in Medieval Britain (London, 1958, 2/1963)
H. Baillie: 'Squares', AcM, xxxii (1960), 178
J. D. Bergsagel: 'An Introduction to Ludford', MD, xiv (1960), 105
F. Ll. Harrison: 'John Taverner', NOHM, iii (1960), 339
J. Stevens: Music and Poetry in the Early Tudor Court (London, 1961)
J. D. Bergsagel: 'The Date and Provenance of the Forrest–Heyther Collection of Tudor Masses', ML, xliv (1963), 240
R. Bray: 'British Museum Additional Mss 17802–5 (the Gyffard Part-books): an Index and Commentary', RMARC, vii (1967), 31
D. S. Josephson: 'John Taverner: an English Renaissance Master', American Choral Review, ix/2 (1967), 6
——: 'The Festal Masses of John Taverner', American Choral Review, ix/3 (1967), 10
——: 'John Taverner: Smaller Liturgical Works', American Choral Review, ix/4 (1967), 26
P. M. Doe: 'Latin Polyphony under Henry VIII', PRMA, xcv (1968–9), 81
D. Stevens: 'John Taverner', Essays in Musicology in Honor of Dragan Plamenac (Pittsburgh, 1969), 331
T. Messenger: 'Texture and Form in Taverner's Western Wind Mass', JAMS, xxii (1969), 504; repr. in MR, xxxiii (1972), 167
H. J. Benham: The Music of John Taverner: a Study and Assessment (diss., U. of Southampton, 1970)
R. Bray: 'The Part-books Oxford, Christ Church, Mss 979–983: an Index and Commentary', MD, xxv (1971), 179
N. Davison: 'The Western Wind Masses', MQ, lvii (1971), 427
H. J. Benham: 'The Formal Design and Construction of Taverner's Works', MD, xxvi (1972), 189
——: 'The Music of Taverner: a Liturgical Study', MR, xxxiii (1972), 251
D. S. Josephson: 'In Search of the Historical Taverner', Tempo (1972), no.101, p.40
N. Davison: 'Structure and Unity in Four Free-composed Tudor Masses', MR, xxxiv (1973), 328
E. H. Sanders: 'England . . . the Early Sixteenth Century', Music from the Middle Ages to the Renaissance, ed. F. W. Sternfeld (New York, 1973), 304
N. Sandon: 'The Henrician Partbooks at Peterhouse, Cambridge', PRMA, ciii (1976–7), 106
D. S. Josephson: John Taverner, Tudor Composer (Ann Arbor, 1979)
ROGER BOWERS (1), PAUL DOE (2, work-list, bibliography)

Tavola (It.). BELLY.

Tavola, Antonio dalla. See DALLA TAVOLA, ANTONIO.

Tavola armonica (It.). SOUNDBOARD.

Tavoletta (It.). A board or table struck with a hammer. Respighi used two *tavolette* in his *Feste romane* (1928).

Tavrizian, Mikhail Arsen'yevich (b Baku, 27 May 1907; d Erevan, 17 Oct 1957). Armenian conductor. He graduated from the Leningrad Conservatory as a violist in 1932 and from the conducting class of Alexander Gauk in 1934. He became leader of the viola section at the conservatory's opera studio in 1926, and in the orchestra of the Malïy Opera, Leningrad, in 1928. In 1935 he turned to conducting and in 1938 was appointed principal conductor at the Erevan Opera and Ballet Theatre, where he played an important part in the development of Armenian national opera. An outstanding conductor with a fine instinct for music drama and operatic character, he aimed at blending all the constituent elements of opera, so that the stage and musical characterizations were closely linked. Among the operas he conducted were Chukhadjian's *Arshak II* (1945), *Lusabatsin* (1938) and *Geroinya* (1950) by Haro Step'anyan, *David-Bek* (1956) by Armen Tigranyan and *Aruvaberd* (1957) by Andrey Babayev. Tavrizian was also a talented symphonic conductor, particularly noted for his interpretations of Khachaturian's Symphony no.2 and Shostakovich's Symphony no.7. He was made People's Artist of the USSR in 1956.

BIBLIOGRAPHY

E. Grosheva: 'Dirizhor M. Tavrizian', SovM (1956), no.9, p.101
G. Vorian: 'Zhizn' posvyashchennaya iskusstvu' [A life dedicated to art], Literaturnaya Armeniya (1959), no.6
I. M. YAMPOL'SKY

Tawaststjerna, Erik (Werner) (b Mikkeli, 10 Oct 1916). Finnish musicologist. He studied the piano at Helsinki Conservatory with I. Hannikainen (1934–7) and K. Bernhard (1937–44), in Stockholm with H. Leygraf and Moscow with H. Neuhaus (1946), and in Paris with Cortot and Gentil (1947); he made his début in Helsinki in 1943. His concert career was limited to a period of recitals in Scandinavia, Vienna and the USSR, but he continued his interest in the piano as a highly esteemed private teacher, essayist and member of juries of international piano competitions (Tchaikovsky Competition 1970 and 1974, Rio de Janeiro Competition 1973, Ravel Competition 1975). He also studied at Helsinki University (MagPhil 1958), where in 1960 he took his doctorate with a dissertation on Sibelius's piano works and became professor of musicology. He has also held appointments at the press and cultural affairs department of the Finnish Foreign Ministry (1948–60), as music critic (from 1957) of *Helsingin sanomat*, the leading Finnish daily paper, and as chairman of the boards of the Finnish Musicological Society (from 1968) and the Sibelius Academy (from 1971).

Tawaststjerna is the most widely known Finnish

musicologist of his generation, having given lectures at many European and American universities and at musicological congresses. He is the leading authority on Sibelius: his five-volume monograph is based on exceptionally comprehensive and hitherto largely unexplored source materials (e.g. Sibelius's diaries and private letters). Besides providing new information on his life and insights on his music, it affords useful comparisons with many of his contemporaries – Busoni, Debussy, Mahler and Schoenberg as well as Scandinavian composers, writers and artists – and gives a full account of the general cultural trends of Sibelius's time and the political context as it affected the composer. Its scope, style and understanding of Sibelius's creative imagination make the book an outstanding work of its kind.

WRITINGS

Sibeliuksen pianosävellykset ja muita esseitä [Sibelius's piano works] (Helsinki, 1955; Eng. trans., 1957; Swed. trans., 1957, as *Ton och tolkning: Sibelius-studier*)
'Shostakovitsh soittaa' [Shostakovich's piano playing], *Uusi musiikkilehti* (1956), no.7, p.10
'Prokofjevin jäljillä' [Following Prokofiev's path], *Uusi musiikkilehti* (1956), no.8, p.13
Sibeliuksen pianoteokset säveltäjän kehityslinjan kuvastajina [The evolution of Sibelius's piano works] (diss., U. of Helsinki, 1960; Helsinki, 1960)
Sergei Prokofjevin ooppera Sota ja rauha [Prokofiev's *War and Peace*] (Helsinki, 1960)
Jean Sibelius, i–iii (Helsinki, 1965–72; Swed. trans., i–ii, 1968; Eng. trans., i, 1976) [vols. iv and v in preparation]
'Jean Sibelius und Claude Debussy (eine Begegnung in London 1909)', *Leoš Janáček et musica Europaea: Brno III 1970*, 307
'Sibelius und Bartók: einige Parallelen', *International Musicological Conference in Commemoration of Béla Bartók: Budapest 1971*, 121
'Sibelius' 4. Sinfonie – Schlussphase und Vollendung', *BMw*, xvi (1974), 97
Esseitä ja arvosteluja [Essays and criticism] (Helsinki, 1976)

BIBLIOGRAPHY

P. Suhonen: 'Erik Tawaststjerna', *Delfiini ja muita esseitä* (Helsinki, 1973), 59
E. Salmenhaara, ed.: *Juhlakirja Erik Tawaststjernalle* (Helsinki, 1976) [incl. list of writings]

ERKKI SALMENHAARA

Tayber. *See* TEYBER family.

Tayler, Simon. *See* TAILLER, SIMON.

Taylor, Brook [Brooke] (*b* Edmonton, London, 18 Aug 1685; *d* London, 29 Dec 1731). English mathematician and amateur musician. He was first educated at home. His upbringing is described by Sir William Young (his grandson). According to this account Taylor's father treated his large family very strictly and had a morose temper that 'would yield only to the powers of music'. The young Taylor was musically the most proficient member of the family, and in a large family picture he is represented at the age of 13 sitting in the centre of his brothers and sisters, the two eldest of whom crown him with a laurel bearing the insignia of harmony. Young mentioned frequent musical parties at the family's country home in Kent and reported that Geminiani, Babell and Louis Lully were among the musicians welcomed there. Taylor entered St John's College, Cambridge, in 1701 as a Fellow-commoner; he graduated LlB in 1709 and became an LlD in 1714. In 1712 he was admitted a Fellow of the Royal Society. On 14 January 1714 he was appointed its first secretary, but he resigned for health reasons on 21 October 1718 and went to France for a year.

From 1708 Taylor occupied himself with the problems of transverse vibrations of strings and with the centre of oscillation. These matters formed the subject

Brook Taylor: miniature by J. or L. Goupy in the National Portrait Gallery, London

of two of the three papers that he read to the Royal Society in 1712, 'De inventione centri oscillationis' and 'De motu nervi tensi' (both published in *Philosophical Transactions of the Royal Society*, xxviii, 1713). In his *Methodus incrementorum directa et inversa* (London, 1715), which was the first treatise on the calculus of finite differences and which contained 'Taylor's theorem' (though Lyons considered this to have been discovered 40 years previously by James Gregory), he applied the theorem to a number of problems, including those concerning the vibrations of strings. On 18 January 1727 he read to the Royal Society a paper called 'A Summary Account of a New System of Music by M. Rameau, formerly Organist of the Cathedral Church of Clermont in Auvergne' (in *Register Book of the Royal Society*, copy xiii, p.19). It appears from this paper that the society had asked him to investigate Rameau's new theory of music but that he did not consider himself sufficiently acquainted with

the Maximi received by the most eminent Professors of this Art, to judge whether our Author is right in everything he advances: the principal part of his System appears to be reasonable and natural and it deserves to be esteem'd a valuable Improvement to have been able so far as this Author has done, to reduce the confus'd Variety of intricate and difficult Rules in this Art to so few and simple Principles.

Taylor's exceptional mathematical and artistic gifts attracted the attention of mathematicians and philosophers both in England and abroad. Young presented to the Royal Society a collection of his correspondence with eminent mathematicians. He also stated that Taylor had delivered before the society a paper on his favourite subject, 'Of Music', and added: 'probably an essay on that gentle art was not deemed congenial with the institution of that learned body, for it is not preserved in their Transactions'. Taylor was a close friend of Sir

Isaac Newton, the astronomer John Keill, Edmond Halley, Baron de Montmort and Lord Bolingbroke; he was one of the few of Newton's friends allowed to copy Newton's treatise *Of Music*. Hawkins wrote not only that 'besides being an excellent mathematician, [he] was eminently skilled in the theory of music' but that it was said that he assisted Pepusch with his *A Short Treatise on Harmony* (1731) by 'forming the diagrams'.

A portrait of Taylor painted by Amiconi and presented by Young is at the Royal Society; a gouache miniature by Goupy showing him three-quarter length, standing beside a two-manual harpsichord, is in the National Portrait Gallery, London (see illustration).

BIBLIOGRAPHY

FétisB; *HawkinsH*
W. Young: Biography prefixed to B. Taylor: *Contemplatio philosophica* (London, 1793)
Lord Rayleigh: *The Theory of Sound*, i (London, 1877)
W. W. Rouse Ball: *A Short Account of the History of Mathematics* (London, 1893)
E. I. Carlyle: 'Taylor, Brook', *DNB*
The Record of the Royal Society of London (London, 1901, rev. 3/1912)
H. Lyons: *The Royal Society 1660–1940* (Cambridge, 1944)
SUSI JEANS

Taylor, Cecil (Perceval) (*b* New York, 15 March 1933). Black American jazz pianist. He studied at the New England Conservatory for four years, then appeared in various groups around Boston before returning to New York. There he led a number of small groups from 1956, and performed in Jack Gelber's *The Connection*, a play that requires live jazz on stage. He also gave concerts at New York's Town Hall (1966), toured Europe in 1962 and 1969, was one of the organizers of the Jazz Composers' Guild in 1964–5 and taught at Antioch College, Ohio.

Taylor was a leading innovator of the 1960s, and shared with Ornette Coleman the task of freeing jazz from many earlier conventions, especially those of tonal harmony. Technically more sophisticated than Coleman or other 'free jazz' musicians, he commands great variety of rhythmic accent and keyboard texture, employing numerous tone clusters whose dissonance has no harmonic function, and accompanying right-hand lines with non-harmonic left-hand chords. Through obliterating tonal centres and dispensing with bar-lines and conventional phrase lengths, he improvised music that took on a multi-layered discontinuity, exemplified by his record *Unit Structures* (1966). Despite his own virtuosity Taylor directed his approach increasingly to ensemble playing, particularly with his long-term associates Jimmy Lyons (alto saxophone) and Sonny Murray (percussion). His handling of thematic material (chiefly written by himself) and the texture of his ensembles grew progressively more plastic, and at times he seemed to attempt to give each ensemble line an expressive density comparable to that of solos by Charlie Parker or 'Fats' Navarro. His recorded output traces a continuous and coherent musical growth unusual to jazz.

BIBLIOGRAPHY

G. Schuller: 'Cecil Taylor', *Jazz Review*, ii (1958), Jan, 28
L. Gushee: 'Cecil Taylor', *Jazz Review*, iii (1960), June, 28
R. Atkins: 'Jazz Piano: Present and Future', *Jazz Monthly*, viii (1962), Sept, 10
J. Goldberg: *Jazz Masters of the 50s* (New York, 1965), 213ff
A. Spellman: *Four Lives in the Bebop Business* (New York, 1966), 1ff
M. Harrison: 'Cecil Taylor', *Jazz on Record*, ed. A. McCarthy (London, 1968), 281f
E. Raben: *A Discography of Free Jazz* (Copenhagen, 1969)
V. Wilmer: *Jazz People* (London, 1970), 21ff
R. Atkins: 'Cecil Taylor', *Modern Jazz: the Essential Records*, ed. M. Harrison (London, 1975), 20
MAX HARRISON

Taylor, Charles (*fl c*1685). English composer. He was listed among the choir of Westminster Abbey at the coronation of King James II in 1685. Some pleasing songs by him are in *Choice Ayres and Songs* (1683) and *The Theater of Music* (1685). There is a motet by him in *GB-Och* 623–6.

IAN SPINK

Taylor [Tailer, Taler], **Daniel** (*d* London, April 1643). English musician and composer. By 1625 he was a 'singing-man' at Westminster Abbey and he apparently continued as such until his death. Two full anthems by him are known: *I will sing unto the Lord as long as I live* ('Mr Taylor of Westminster', *GB-Ob*) for five voices, and *Sing we merrily* (in *DRc*, *Lbm*, *Och*, *Y*) for six. A single part of a secular work, *Appollo did in musick's art*, survives (*Och*).

PETER LE HURAY

Taylor, (Joseph) Deems (*b* New York, 22 Dec 1885; *d* New York, 3 July 1966). American composer and critic. He began piano studies in 1895, and in 1906 took the BA at New York University. Victor Herbert, who in 1907 heard his music for a university show, *The Oracle*, advised him to study theory, and so he took harmony and counterpoint lessons with Oscar Coon, a bandsman of Oswego, New York (1908–11). After various jobs in publishing and journalism he became music critic of the *New York World* (1921–5), editor of *Musical America* (1927–9) and music critic of the *New York American* (1931–2). In addition, he was director (1933–66) and president (1942–8) of ASCAP, and he worked for NBS as opera commentator from 1931, also serving as interval commentator for the national broadcasts of the New York PO (1936–43). His books of 1937, 1940 and 1949 contain expanded versions of his radio talks. He received honorary doctorates from New York University (1927), the University of Rochester and Dartmouth College (1939), the Cincinnati Conservatory (1941) and Syracuse University (1944). His music, like his critical work, never bores and is often witty, always deftly constructed and well timed. So skilful was he in blending European influences that even at his most derivative he is not easily labelled. His number of Metropolitan Opera performances (14 for *The King's Henchman* in 1927–9 and 16 for *Peter Ibbetson* in 1931–5) surpasses that of any other American composer, and no native American of his time had more large works published.

WORKS

(selective list)

Operas: The King's Henchman, op.19 (3, E. St Vincent Millay), New York, 1927; Peter Ibbetson, op.20 (3, C. Collier, after du Maurier), New York, 1931; Ramuntcho, op.23 (3, Taylor), Philadelphia, 1942; The Dragon, 1, New York, 1958

Orch: The Siren Song, op.2, sym. poem, 1912; Through the Looking Glass, op.12, chamber orch, 1917–19, arr. full orch 1921–2; Jurgen, op.17, sym. poem, perf. 1925; Circus Day, op.18, jazz orch, 1925, orchestration by Grofé, arr. full orch, 1933; Ballet from Casanova, op.22, perf. 1937; Marco Takes a Walk, perf. 1942; A Christmas Ov., perf. 1943; Elégie, perf. 1945; Restoration Suite, perf. 1950

Choral: The Chambered Nautilus, op.7 (O. W. Holmes), cantata, chorus, orch, 1914; The Highwayman, op.8 (Noyes), cantata, Bar, mixed vv, orch, 1914

Other works: 2 Studies in Rhythm, op.5, pf, ?1913; Portrait of a Lady, op.14, 11 insts, 1918; Traditional Airs, op.15, female v, pf, ?1923; Lucrece, op.16, str qt

Principal publishers: Ditson, J. Fischer

WRITINGS
Of Men and Music (New York, 1937)
The Well Tempered Listener (New York, 1940)
Music to my Ears (New York, 1949)
Some Enchanted Evenings: the Story of Rodgers and Hammerstein (New York, 1953)

BIBLIOGRAPHY
J. F. Porte: 'Deems Taylor, an American Hope', *Sackbut*, ix (1929), 193
Current Biography, i (1940), 261
J. T. Howard: *Deems Taylor* (New York, 2/1940)
I. Kolodin: *The Metropolitan Opera* (New York, 1966)
ROBERT STEVENSON

Taylor, Edward (*b* Norwich, 22 Jan 1784; *d* Brentwood, 12 March 1863). English musician, lecturer and writer. He was the son of a music-loving Nonconformist minister, and a pupil of J. Beckwith of Norwich Cathedral. In Norwich, where he was celebrated as a choir trainer and as a fine bass singer, he took a leading part in organizing musical activities among fellow amateurs, and helped to establish the triennial Norwich Musical Festival in 1824. He moved to London in 1825 and became a successful professional singer, teacher and music journalist, attracting further notice in 1830 with his translation and adaptation of Spohr's *Die letzten Dinge* as *Last Judgment*. In 1837 he was appointed professor of music at Gresham College, a post which enabled him to continue encouraging amateur music, but among a wider circle. Taylor's early Gresham lectures, illustrated with performed examples and admirably suited to general audiences, were widely appreciated and influenced the growth of popular esteem for music in London, preparing the way for the sight-singing movement of the following decade.

Taylor published English versions of Mozart's *Requiem*, Haydn's *Jahreszeiten* and other choral works, wrote original English librettos for two of Spohr's later oratorios, compiled (with James Turle) *The People's Singing Book* (1844) and *The Singing Book* (1846); and edited Purcell's *King Arthur* for the Musical Antiquarian Society, an institution which he founded with Chappell and Rimbault. He also founded the Vocal Society and the Purcell Club, and was music critic of the *Spectator* for many years.

BERNARR RAINBOW

Taylor, Franklin (*b* Birmingham, 5 Feb 1843; *d* London, 19 March 1919). English pianist and teacher. He showed his musical talent very early, and when only 13 was appointed organist at the Old Meeting Place, Birmingham, having studied the organ with Bedsmore, organist at Lichfield Cathedral. His first piano teacher was Charles Flavell, and from 1859 to 1861 he studied at the Leipzig Conservatory, where he advanced steadily, studying the piano with Plaidy and Moscheles and harmony and composition with Hauptmann, E. F. E. Richter and Papperitz. But he was not particularly gifted as a composer; he was primarily an interpreter and teacher. In 1861 he went to Paris to work under Clara Schumann and became an enthusiastic exponent of her method and manner of playing. In the following year he returned to London, where he soon became renowned as a soloist and teacher. He often played at the Crystal Palace concerts (from 1865) and the Monday Popular Concerts (from 1866). Returning to

his early love of the organ, he held the post of organist in several London churches in succession.

In 1876 he was appointed as one of the first teachers in the new National Training School for Music, founded under the auspices of the Royal Society of Arts. When the school was amalgamated with the Royal College of Music (1882), Taylor was made professor of piano, and held this post until 1916. He was also president of the Academy for the Higher Development of Pianoforte Playing (founded by Oscar Beringer) during its 24 years (1873–97) and was director of the Philharmonic Society (1891–3). Pupils and colleagues regarded him with affection and respect.

Taylor contributed several articles to the earlier editions of *Grove's Dictionary*, and published a number of works on piano playing; his *Technique and Expression in Pianoforte Playing* (London, 1897) is still used, and his *Primer of Pianoforte Playing* (London, 1877) passed through numerous editions. He also collaborated with other writers on music. Today he is probably best remembered for the remarkable series of *Progressive Studies for the Pianoforte*, carefully selected and edited from the works of Bertini, Cramer, Czerny, etc (London, 1893–4). These are issued in groups, each group being designed to aid the player in overcoming one particular difficulty of technique. His fine musicianship is revealed in his choice of works.

BIBLIOGRAPHY
T. F. Dunhill: 'Franklin Taylor', *MT*, xl (1899), 798
——: Obituary, *MMR*, xlix (1919), 97
P. A. Scholes: *The Mirror of Music 1844–1944* (London, 1947)
Who was who 1916–1928 (London, 1967)
GEORGE GROVE/JEAN MARY ALLAN

Taylor, John (*fl* 1637–45). English composer. He became a member of the King's Musick in 1637 and presumably died before the Restoration (1660). An elegy he wrote on the death of 'his Friend and Fellow, Mr. William Lawes' was published in Henry Lawes's *Choice Psalmes* (1648), and several songs were printed by John Playford in *Select Musicall Ayres and Dialogues* (1652) and *Catch that Catch Can* (1663 and later editions). His songs are in *GB-Lbm* Add.29396, *US-NYp* Drexel 4257 and especially 4041, which, since it is an important source of pre-Commonwealth play songs, may indicate that the composer was a theatre musician some time before 1642. Two of his songs are printed in *MB*, xxxiii (1971). An ayre and saraband by him were included by Playford in *Court Ayres* (1655); there are also some instrumental pieces in *GB-Ob* Mus.Sch.D.220 and bass parts in *Och* 1022.

IAN SPINK

Taylor, John & Co. English firm of bellfounders. Its exports of carillons between World Wars I and II, with those of GILLETT & JOHNSTON, made the carillon widely known outside Europe for the first time. In the 19th century it contributed more than any other foundry to improvements in the tuning of tower bells.

The Taylor family began making bells at St Neots, Huntingdonshire, in the latter part of the 18th century, and after moving to Oxford and to Devon established their foundry at Loughborough, Leicestershire, in 1839. In the late 19th century two Taylor brothers, John William jr and Dennison, conducted research in fine tuning; consequently, from 1897 they were able to make properly tuned replacements for faulty and missing bells in Dutch carillons. Between 1911 and the end of World

War II (before the Dutch regenerated their own bell-tuning skills) they provided bells for ten new carillons in the Netherlands (only one of these, at Zwolle, survived World War II).

The firm now makes carillons, as well as bells for swinging peals. Its carillons include those at Rainbow Falls, Niagara Falls, Canada (55 bells, *e* to *a''''*), Mountain Lake Sanctuary, Lake Wales, Florida, the University of Michigan, Ann Arbor, and the Washington (Episcopal) Cathedral (each 53 bells, *d#* to *g#''''*), the University of Kansas, and the Carillon Tower, Canberra, Australia (each 53 bells, *f#* to *b''''*), and the War Memorial, Loughborough, Leicestershire (47 bells, *g#* to *g#''''*).

PERCIVAL PRICE

Taylor, Raynor (*b* London, 1747; *d* Philadelphia, 17 Aug 1825). English organist, teacher, composer and singer active in the USA. As a choirboy at the Chapel Royal he sang at Handel's funeral in 1759, and Parker (1822) reports that his hat dropped into the composer's grave. Taylor studied with Samuel Arnold in London; in 1765 he was appointed organist at Chelmsford as well as musical director and composer for Sadler's Wells and Marylebone Gardens. He emigrated to the USA in 1792, possibly at the suggestion of his pupil Alexander Reinagle. Taylor taught and gave evening extravaganzas or 'olios' in Baltimore and Annapolis, briefly served as organist at St Anne's Church in Annapolis, and was organist at St Peter's Church in Philadelphia from 1793 until his death. He was a major figure in the musical life of Philadelphia, active in the church, the theatre, as a teacher and as a friend and colleague of Benjamin Carr, Alexander Reinagle and J. G. Schetky. He helped found the Musical Fund Society in 1820 and served as one of its directors. As a performer he was noted for his organ improvisations as well as for his renditions of comic theatre songs. Taylor's extant instrumental works are chiefly pedagogical piano pieces. Of greater interest are his church anthems, glees and particularly the theatrical songs which show a gift for setting comic texts. His one extant opera, *The Ethiop*, has vocal and instrumental parts of great vitality.

WORKS

(selective list; full list in Sonneck (1905), Wolfe)

Stage: The Ethiop (opera, W. Diamond), vocal score (Philadelphia, 1814); incidental music, songs, arr. songs, marches, dances (for plays, operas, burlettas, pantomimes, melodramas etc), mostly performed Philadelphia, 1793–1822, some lost

Other vocal: 3 anthems, in *Cathedral Magazine*, ii–iii (London, ?1780s); 6 glees, 3 male vv, *c*1795–1800, *US-NY*p; Monody on the Death of Washington, Philadelphia, 1799, collab. A. Reinagle, lost; A Collection of [3] Favorite Songs (T. Moore: Lalla Rookh), 1v, pf (Philadelphia, ?1817); *c*33 songs, 1–2vv, pf, pubd Philadelphia, Baltimore, London (1770–1815); choruses, hymns, 3–4vv, a cappella/pf/org, some pubd; other songs, lost

Inst: 6 sonatas, hpd/pf, vn, op.2 (London, *c*1780); 6 sonatas, vc, bc, ?1780s; An easy and familiar lesson, pf 4 hands (Philadelphia, ?1797); Divertimenti . . . [with] Ground for the Improvement of Young Practitioners, pf (Philadelphia, 1797), lost; The Martial Music of Camp Dupont, arr. pf, 2 German fl/2 fifes/2 vn (Philadelphia, ?1816); *c*10 others, mostly marches, pf, pubd Philadelphia (*c*1800–1815)

BIBLIOGRAPHY

J. R. Parker: 'Musical Reminiscences', *The Euterpeiad*, ii/21 (5 Jan 1822), 162, abridged in *Musical Biography* (Boston, Mass., 1824), 179ff

O. G. T. Sonneck: *A Bibliography of Early Secular American Music* (Washington, DC, 1905; rev. 2/1945, ed. W. T. Upton, 3/1964)

——: *Early Concert-life in America* (Leipzig, 1907/*R*1969, 2/1949)

J. T. Howard: *Our American Music: Three Hundred Years of It* (New York, 1931, rev. 3/1946)

R. A. Gerson: *Music in Philadelphia* (Philadelphia, 1940), 26, 40ff, 52, 56, 81, 88f, 95

Church Music and Musical Life in Pennsylvania in the 18th Century (Philadelphia, 1947), 252, 254ff, 426, 436

J. Mates: *The American Musical Stage before 1800* (New Brunswick, NJ, 1962), 198f

R. J. Wolfe: *Secular Music in America, 1801–1825: a Bibliography* (New York, 1964)

ANNE SHAPIRO

Taylor, Robert. *See* TAILOUR, ROBERT.

Taylor [Domvill], **Silas** (*b* Harley, nr. Much Wenlock, Shropshire, 16 July 1624; *d* Harwich, 4 Nov 1678). English antiquarian and amateur musician, brother of Sylvanus Taylor. He was educated at Shrewsbury School and Westminster School, and subsequently entered New Inn Hall, Oxford, in 1641. He left the university without taking a degree and joined the Parliamentary Army, where he rose to the rank of captain. After the Civil War he was appointed sequestrator in Herefordshire and used the opportunity to appropriate MSS from Hereford and Worcester cathedrals. After the Restoration he was commissary for ammunition at Dunkirk until 1664 and keeper of naval stores at Harwich from 1665 to his death. He was one of the group that took part in chamber music at Oxford in the last years of the Commonwealth. In addition to his antiquarian works – *The History of Gavel-Kind* (1663) and *The History and Antiquities of Harwich and Dovercourt* (1730) – he composed anthems (lost), 30 sacred duets to Latin and English words for soprano, bass and continuo (*GB-Cfm*) and two dance suites for treble and bass (published in John Playford's *Court-Ayres*, 1655). Two MS pieces, apparently for four viols, marked 'Taylor' (*GB-Lbm* Add.31423), may be by his brother Sylvanus. He also made an MS *Collection of Rules in Musicke* (*GB-Lbm* Add.4910). Some of his anthems were sung in the Chapel Royal and according to Aubrey pleased Charles II. Pepys (29 July 1668) and the Duke of York took a less complimentary view.

JACK WESTRUP

Taylor, Sylvanus (*d* Dublin, Nov 1672). English amateur musician, younger brother of SILAS TAYLOR. He entered Wadham College, Oxford, in 1650 and graduated BA in 1654 and MA in 1657. He was later a Fellow of All Souls College. Like his brother he took part in chamber music at Oxford and probably wrote for the participants his *Ayres for Trebles and a Base* (*GB-Ob* Mus.Sch.E.429); he may also have composed the two pieces apparently for four viols mentioned above. A two-part glee was published in John Playford's *Musical Companion* (1667).

JACK WESTRUP

Taylour, Robert. *See* TAILOUR, ROBERT.

Tbārtā. A category of chant in SYRIAN CHURCH MUSIC.

Tchaikovsky [Tchaikowski], **Boris Alexandrovich.** *See* CHAYKOVSKY, BORIS ALEXANDROVICH.

Tchaikovsky, Pyotr Il'yich (*b* Kamsko-Votkinsk, Vyatka province, 7 May 1840; *d* St Petersburg, 6 Nov 1893). Russian composer. Standing outside the nationalist circle of composers around Balakirev, Tchaikovsky nevertheless dominates 19th-century Russian music as its greatest talent. His formal conservatory training instilled in him Western-orientated attitudes and techniques, but his essential nature, as he always insisted, was Russian, both in his actual use of folksong and in his deep absorption in Russian life and ways of thought. His natural gifts, especially his genius for what he called the 'lyrical idea', the beautiful, self-contained melody, give his music a permanent appeal; it was his hard-won but secure and professional technique, and his ability to use it for the expression of his emotional life, which enabled him to realize his potential more fully than any of his major Russian contemporaries.

1. Early years (1840–65). 2. Progress to maturity (1866–70). 3. High nationalism (1870–74). 4. Increasing problems (1874–7). 5. Marriage: crisis and aftermath (1877–8). 6. Creative trough (1878–84). 7. Creative renewal (1884–90). 8. Last years (1891–3). 9. Technique and style.

1. EARLY YEARS (1840–65). Tchaikovsky was the second son of Il'ya Petrovich Tchaikovsky, a mining engineer and manager of the metal works at Kamsko-Votkinsk; his second wife and the composer's mother, Alexandra Andreyevna (née Assier), was the granddaughter of a French émigré, Michel d'Assier, a fact that may have some relevance to Tchaikovsky's strong attraction to French music. Her father had been an epileptic, and she herself was of a nervous disposition: it was from his mother's side that Tchaikovsky inherited his morbid sensitivity. According to his brother Modest there is no evidence of any previous member of the family having been a professional musician.

What may be the first record of Tchaikovsky attempting composition dates from September 1844, when his father reported to his wife, who was in St Petersburg, that 'Sasha [the composer's 19-month-old sister, Alexandra] and Pyotr have composed a song, *Our mama in Petersburg*'. Certainly Tchaikovsky's musical interests and aptitudes revealed themselves clearly in the following year, when he started taking piano lessons with a local teacher, Mariya Palchikova, whose abilities he quickly outstripped. His musical experiences were supplemented by the family's orchestrion, which played excerpts from Mozart's *Don Giovanni* (a work that always retained a special aura for Tchaikovsky), as well as pieces by Bellini, Rossini and Donizetti. He also became familiar with some Chopin mazurkas. Between 1844 and 1848 he benefited greatly from the attention and kindness of Fanny Dürbach, a French governess engaged for his elder brother Nikolay and a cousin. Under her guidance he wrote some sentimental French verses, including a poem on Joan of Arc, and started to learn German.

In February 1848 Tchaikovsky's father resigned his post, and in November the family arrived in St Petersburg, where Tchaikovsky entered a miserable phase at the fashionable Schmelling School; he also started piano lessons with a teacher named Filippov, though these were curtailed in December when Tchaikovsky had a bad attack of measles and was ordered to rest for six months. In May 1849 the family moved to Alapayevsk where Il'ya had a new appointment. Tchaikovsky and his mother returned to St Petersburg in summer 1850, and in September he was enrolled in the preparatory class of the School of Jurisprudence. His mother also took him to a performance of Glinka's *A Life for the Tsar*, which made a deep and permanent impression on him. The parting

from his mother when she returned to Alapayevsk was remembered by Tchaikovsky as 'one of the most terrible days' of his life. Since Fanny Dürbach had left two years earlier he had been exceedingly moody and easily reduced to tears. His life had become unsettled, and this parting from a parent to whom he was emotionally very close was a shock he never forgot and whose effects were profoundly disturbing to his whole disposition. His distress was exacerbated by a sense of guilt at the death from scarlet fever of the eldest son of Modest Vakar, a family friend who had undertaken to lodge and look after him during an epidemic of the disease at Tchaikovsky's school. Despite all Vakar's assurances, he remained convinced that, since he had introduced the disease into the family, he was responsible for the boy's death.

Nevertheless, the nine years spent at the School of Jurisprudence did serve to introduce some stability into his existence, though the homosexual practices common in the school may well have served to reveal or to confirm his own tendencies. In 1852 his father resigned again, and in May the family returned to St Petersburg; Tchaikovsky's happiness was augmented by success in the entrance examination to the School of Jurisprudence itself. But in June 1854 there came a shattering blow in the death of his mother. For relief he turned to music. He had for some years found emotional release in improvisation; he now wrote down a piano waltz, and even thought of attempting an opera on Viktor Olkhovsky's *Hyperbole*. In the same year he went for singing lessons to Gavriil Lomakin, and in 1855 transferred for piano tuition to Rudolf Kündinger, a good teacher (whose brother gave Tchaikovsky some lessons in thoroughbass) but one who discouraged him from placing any hopes on a professional career. In 1856 Tchaikovsky met an Italian singing teacher, Luigi Piccioli, who widened his knowledge of Italian opera, and led him to compose a pallid Italianate canzonetta, *Mezza notte*; this was to become Tchaikovsky's first published work.

In May 1859 Tchaikovsky completed his course at the School of Jurisprudence and took a post as clerk in the Ministry of Justice, engaging in a lively social life in which music figured prominently. His father was no longer able to support him, and his idea of becoming a professional musician had to be shelved. Nevertheless, in autumn 1861 he began studying thoroughbass in Nikolay Zaremba's class at the recently founded Russian Musical Society, which in 1862 was transformed into the St Petersburg Conservatory. During summer 1861 he travelled in western Europe, acting as interpreter to a friend of his father and visiting Germany, Belgium, England and France. On his return he continued his technical studies with Zaremba twice weekly, and at the end of 1862 also joined the composition class of the conservatory's director, Anton Rubinstein, who gave him considerable encouragement. Finally, in 1863, he resigned from the Ministry of Justice and entered the conservatory as a full-time student, attending Zaremba's class in form and Rubinstein's in instrumentation. Although Tchaikovsky's father had already given moral support to his decision, his circumstances remained straitened; but Rubinstein was able to help by finding him piano and theory pupils. Modest recollected that, despite the privations of this new student life, Tchaikovsky was profoundly contented now that he had at last taken the step of devoting himself to music.

The next two and a half years were spent at the conservatory, where, having been excused the compulsory piano class, Tchaikovsky took up the flute and the organ. For summer 1864 he went to Alexey Golitsïn's estate near Khar'kov. In 1865 his father remarried, and Tchaikovsky and his younger twin brothers Modest and Anatoly, to whom he was devoted, spent a happy summer on the estate of their brother-in-law Lev Davïdov at Kamenka, near Kiev, where Tchaikovsky busied himself with translating Gevaert's *Traité général d'instrumentation* from the French. Rubinstein, who had set him this task, proved well pleased with the completed work. Tchaikovsky had hoped to familiarize himself with Ukrainian folksongs while at Kamenka, so as to gather material that he might use later in his own works; but his disenchantment with those that he heard grew with the feeling that they had been contaminated by contact with 'Western' music. In the end he noted down only one song, which he used first in the quartet movement in B♭, composed later that year, and then in the *Scherzo à la russe* for piano, published as his op.1 no.1. That September Johann Strauss conducted a public performance at Pavlovsk of the Characteristic Dances which Tchaikovsky had composed earlier that year. In November he made his own début as a conductor, directing the conservatory orchestra in a performance of his Overture in F.

Only one of Tchaikovsky's student compositions is of any permanent value: his overture to Ostrovsky's play *Groza* ('The storm'). Originally Tchaikovsky had thought of using the play for an opera, but he decided to channel his enthusiasm for it into the holiday task required of him by Rubinstein in 1864. He sketched out a programme, and composed the piece while staying on the Golitsïn estate. On completing it, he sent it to Hermann Laroche (a fellow student at the conservatory, who was the first critic to champion his music and who remained a lifelong friend), with instructions to hand it over to Rubinstein. The latter's tastes were idiosyncratic and highly conservative, and he condemned the piece which, though it incorporates a Russian folksong, reflects Tchaikovsky's growing command of Western musical techniques. There is a little influence from Liszt, and the admirable scoring is indebted to Berlioz. Yet most remarkable of all is the degree to which Tchaikovsky's own musical personality is already apparent in the attractive and sometimes striking invention. Nor did Rubinstein give any warmer approval to the setting of Schiller's *An die Freude* which Tchaikovsky presented as his graduation exercise. Tchaikovsky could not face the strain of the official public performance of the piece, and, to Rubinstein's further annoyance, absented himself. Nevertheless, despite the generally adverse critical comment on the cantata (including in due course a vitriolic review from Cui, the spokesman of The Five), the final report on Tchaikovsky as a student was very favourable, and he graduated with not only a diploma but also a silver medal.

2. PROGRESS TO MATURITY (1866–70). In September 1865, even before his graduation from the St Petersburg Conservatory, Tchaikovsky had been approached by Anton Rubinstein's brother Nikolay with an offer of a post as teacher of harmony at the classes of the Russian Musical Society's Moscow branch (which in September 1866 was to become, under Nikolay's direction, the Moscow Conservatory). Despite the low salary Tchaikovsky accepted and moved to Moscow in January 1866. Initially his awareness of his lack of qualification for teaching made these duties a strain, and he found the constant social attentions of Nikolay Rubinstein, who took him into his own home and pressed upon him his own convivial style of living, somewhat overpowering. Yet the transfer to Moscow was beneficial, despite his longing for St Petersburg, for here he met a whole range of new friends that included his future publisher, Pyotr Jurgenson. Nikolay himself, moreover, was to be a powerful advocate for Tchaikovsky's compositions, conducting or playing in the first performances of many of them over the next 15 years. Above all, Moscow provided a more liberal environment in which he could develop himself as a composer; furthermore, Nikolay, unlike his brother Anton, was favourable towards the new group of Russian composers that was forming in St Petersburg under the despotic guidance of Balakirev. In this freer environment Tchaikovsky completed the orchestration of a Concert Overture in C minor, which both Rubinsteins condemned and which remained unperformed. In March, however, Nikolay Rubinstein directed a successful performance of the revised Overture in F, and in consequence and at Nikolay's prompting Tchaikovsky embarked on a symphony.

The composition of the First Symphony proved a severe labour; no previous composition of his had demanded such sustained effort, and his confidence in his creative powers had been devastated by Cui's newly published review of his graduation cantata. The work proceeded sluggishly, though apparently the symphony was at least fully sketched by early June, when Tchaikovsky began its orchestration. By the end of July, however, overwork brought him to the verge of a breakdown, and the symphony's completion was delayed. Hoping to have it performed in St Petersburg, he showed the unfinished work to Zaremba and Anton Rubinstein, but they censured it heavily. During the autumn Tchaikovsky revised the piece, and in December Nikolay Rubinstein conducted the scherzo in Moscow. For this movement Tchaikovsky had adapted the Mendelssohnian scherzo of his Piano Sonata in C♯ minor, composed in 1865 while he was still a student, adding as a trio an orchestral waltz that was to be the first of a whole line of such compositions. The scherzo was coolly received, though it fared better in St Petersburg in February 1867 when it was coupled with the slow movement, which is largely an attractive rumination upon a folky tune in rich orchestral colouring, flanked by a string passage salvaged from *The Storm*. This slow movement was particularly successful with the audience; both it and the first movement bear descriptive titles. The symphony was given its first complete performance in February 1868, when it was well received.

The continuing influence of conservatory habits is less evident in the symphony's first movement than in the finale, with its selfconscious demonstrations of contrapuntal techniques. The theme of the introduction (also used as the second subject) is a Russian folktune, but this is the only national element in the music. Though Tchaikovsky could fabricate efficiently contrapuntal passages that are sometimes quite complex, he was incapable of the sort of contrapuntal thinking needed to generate a substantial and living musical organism.

Nevertheless, he found that if short contrapuntal passages were repeated sequentially in different keys, with or without modification, or if a new passage followed abruptly in a new key, an illusion of progress resulted. Thus in this finale Tchaikovsky paraded his contrapuntal expertise in modulatory contexts (the transitions and development). Inevitably such passages create a feeling of fabrication which is not dispelled by the extended chromatic lead to the coda, an undeniably original passage that must have displeased Zaremba and Anton Rubinstein. In the first movement even more remained to give them offence, such as Tchaikovsky's penchant

1. Pyotr Il'yich Tchaikovsky, c1864

for harmonic pungency. Nor are they likely to have approved of the tonal balance of this first movement, with its heavy gravitation to sharp keys, nor of the proportions of the exposition. Despite Tchaikovsky's modulatory facility, he had no more capacity for the organic tonal evolution of Classical symphonic practice than for the organic counterpoint of Baroque precedents, and the two subjects are gigantic, tonally enclosed paragraphs, joined by the briefest of transitions. Yet the exposition is acceptable, for what Tchaikovsky lacked in ability to evolve he made up for in capacity for straightforward statement. The fundamental contour of the opening phrase and its subsequent repetitiveness have a marked affinity with Russian folk music, but the spaciousness and generous emotion of the second subject are already unmistakably Tchaikovsky's own. Despite his lifelong deficiencies as an organic contrapuntist, Tchaikovsky had an innate flair for decorative counterpoint and for devising felicitous contrapuntal combinations; this is already evident in the development, while his gift for combining

themes contrapuntally and for neat, if shortwinded, imitative passages is demonstrated in the coda.

Between September and November 1866 Tchaikovsky was also occupied with a Festival Overture on the Danish national hymn, composed in connection with the wedding of the tsarevich to a Danish princess. Royal gratitude was expressed in the form of a pair of cufflinks, which Tchaikovsky promptly sold. At the same time his thoughts were turning towards an opera. He had been contemplating one within a month of his arrival in Moscow, but had dropped the idea when he became engrossed in his First Symphony; now he began to consider an opera based on Ostrovsky's melodrama *Voyevoda* ('The voyevoda'). Tchaikovsky persuaded the playwright himself to provide the libretto and started work in March 1867. However, Ostrovsky abandoned the project when Tchaikovsky lost what had been sent him, and the composer himself wrote the libretto of most of Act 2 and the whole of Act 3. The orchestration was completed while he was on a visit to Paris in summer 1868, and the first performance was early in 1869. Despite Tchaikovsky's own report of a great public success, the critics (including his friend Laroche) were unenthusiastic, and the work survived only five performances. Some years later Tchaikovsky came to agree with his critics, and destroyed the score after incorporating some material from it into *Oprichnik* ('The oprichnik'), though virtually the whole opera has been reconstructed from the surviving orchestral parts and other material. At the time he felt in a sufficiently buoyant mood to embark on another opera, and between January and July 1869 he composed a romantic fairytale opera, *Undina* ('Undine'). However, the theatre postponed production, and in the end the work never reached the stage. Like *The Voyevoda*, it was later destroyed by Tchaikovsky after some of its best music had been incorporated in other compositions. Work on a third opera, *Mandragora*, begun early in 1870, proceeded no further than a Chorus of Flowers and Insects, which won some approval in concert performances.

In 1866 Tchaikovsky's family organized a holiday in the company of Vera and Elizaveta Davïdova, the sisters-in-law of his own sister, Alexandra. The following year, after a holiday in Finland had had to be abandoned through lack of money, he and Modest again spent some six weeks with the Davïdovs at Hapsal; there Tchaikovsky composed three slight piano pieces, *Souvenir de Hapsal*, of which the third, *Chant sans paroles*, achieved much popularity. This second summer interlude also failed to rouse any romantic feeling for Vera Davïdova. The only woman who seems to have interested him at all was the singer Désirée Artôt, whom he met in September the following year, and in whose company he spent much time. For Artôt's benefit performance of Auber's *Le domino noir* he provided special choruses and recitatives. He wrote to his father that they wished to marry; but his own friends and Artôt's mother all opposed the match, and the affair was concluded when she suddenly married a Spanish baritone, Mario Padilla, early in 1869. Thereafter, until the desperate venture of his marriage in 1877, Tchaikovsky seems to have had no further direct emotional involvement with any woman.

The musical contacts of this period were far more fruitful. At the end of 1867 Tchaikovsky met Berlioz, then visiting Moscow to conduct some concerts.

Balakirev was in Moscow to attend them and three months later, on a visit to St Petersburg, Tchaikovsky met other members of Balakirev's circle. The contact with Balakirev was to have a profound effect on him. His dances from *The Voyevoda* had already been successfully performed in Moscow, and Balakirev requested them from Tchaikovsky, intending to give them in St Petersburg. The performance did not materialize, but on 29 March 1869 Balakirev conducted the first St Petersburg performance of Tchaikovsky's symphonic fantasia *Fatum* ('Fate'), composed in the last months of 1868. Balakirev, to whom the work was dedicated, had strong reservations about it, and subsequently communicated these to Tchaikovsky. Later Tchaikovsky destroyed the piece (though it has been reconstructed from the surviving orchestral parts). The relationship between the two men was always uneasy; clearly Balakirev, though suspicious of anyone with a formal conservatory training, recognized Tchaikovsky's great talents, and wanted him for his own circle. As for Tchaikovsky, he obviously wished passionately for acceptance and recognition by Balakirev and his group, recognizing the force of Balakirev's criticisms while deeply resenting their bluntness. In fact, Balakirev was the only man who ever persuaded Tchaikovsky to rewrite a work several times, and his quite extraordinary catalytic power is forcefully demonstrated in *Romeo and Juliet*. It proved to be Tchaikovsky's first masterpiece.

The idea of a work on this Shakespeare subject was probably first discussed between Balakirev and Tchaikovsky in summer 1869. When Tchaikovsky's creativity failed to stir, Balakirev wrote to him (16 October), outlining his own method of composition from a literary groundplan, and even including the four bars of music with which he would begin. The letter was productive, for within six weeks Tchaikovsky had completed the first version of the piece, which Nikolay Rubinstein conducted in March 1870. Even before this Balakirev had commented on Tchaikovsky's material, approving the first subject, judging the second part of the second subject to be a little overripe, but unreservedly endorsing the first theme. The introduction he found completely inadequate, recommending Tchaikovsky to compose something on the lines of a Lisztian chorale. After the first performance Tchaikovsky took this advice, not merely launching the piece with a modal hymn-like theme, but following Liszt's practice of repeating the whole introduction, starting in another key. This new material necessitated further revisions in the development and coda. A second revision, made in 1880, provided a still better climax to the recapitulation and reordered the coda.

Balakirev's curious obsession with keys of two sharps and five flats dictated to Tchaikovsky his choice of tonal relationships in the exposition (B minor and D♭ – in fact C♯). The prominent use of the harp is redolent of Liszt, while the influence of Glinka is unmistakable in the alternating, chromatically related chords suspended on a held note in the violins; this occurs twice in the development, and obviously derives from Chernomor's music in *Ruslan and Lyudmila*. Otherwise, *Romeo and Juliet* is thoroughly characteristic. Quite apart from the powerful stimulus of the play itself, the adaptation of sonata structure to the demands of the story created a situation that suited Tchaikovsky ideally, for it fully justified those very procedures that he had used with more questionable success in his First

Symphony. There he had been driven, through his deficiencies in organic transition, to make each subject a self-contained unit, with only the smallest of links between them; now, by using each subject and the introduction as an embodiment of three separate characters or elements from Shakespeare's play, he made the construction of such an exposition inevitable, and rendered strong contrasts between the subjects desirable. The shifting keys within the first subject and the canonic treatment it receives already foreshadow Tchaikovsky's tendency to become obsessed with his material in quasi-developmental manner, though as yet there is no question of it getting out of hand. Likewise, in the development and coda, where the drama itself is played out and fulfilled, it suited Tchaikovsky ideally to realize the clash between the chief characters either by simultaneous confrontation or by sharp juxtaposition of representative musical material, and the sense of dutiful contrivance from which the developments of the First Symphony do not escape is avoided in this piece. While being as vivid and emotionally powerful as any of Tchaikovsky's works, *Romeo and Juliet* has no excesses.

3. HIGH NATIONALISM (1870–74). From the beginning Tchaikovsky's interest in Russian folk music had been quite as strong as that of any member of The Five. Examples of his use or imitation of it have already been cited; to these may be added the intensely national idiom (and actual use of folksong) in the opera *The Voyevoda*, composed before he met Balakirev. After finishing this work he had started on the piano duet arrangements of 50 Russian folksongs (1868–9), further confirmation of his preoccupation with indigenous material, though he had no hesitation in 'improving' his material if he thought he could. What principally distinguished Tchaikovsky from The Five was his formal conservatory grounding in Western musical techniques, which entrenched in him concepts of harmonic propriety often inimical to folksong. He rarely succeeded in purging completely the manner in which he treated national material of elements that compromised its essential character. Each member of The Five, on the other hand, had acquired his technique empirically, and contact with such men and attitudes was bound to have a certain broadening, even liberating effect on Tchaikovsky's own technique. He was certainly delighted to have their interest and approval, and in the next few years his music often drew close to theirs in its ideals and procedures. Yet he had to apply such things in his own way, and he knew that Balakirev's direct guidance had to be shed. So when Balakirev proposed in October 1871 a plan for a cantata, *Night*, to absorb the Chorus of Flowers and Insects from the abortive opera *Mandragora*, Tchaikovsky tactfully evaded the suggestion. With the withdrawal of Balakirev from Russian concert life in 1872, contact between the two men was broken for some ten years.

Though Tchaikovsky had found himself in *Romeo and Juliet*, his subsequent creative career was certainly not a consistent further revelation of his own personality; for alongside works of unmistakable originality are others that mark out parallel but less individual lines. One such line is represented by his songs, many of which are hardly more than drawing-room pieces, sometimes almost indistinguishable from those that Glinka was purveying nearly half a century before Tchaikovsky composed his first set. These were the Six

Songs op.6, written immediately after the first version of *Romeo and Juliet* in 1869. The melodies of such songs are too often saturated in a sentimentality that thwarts any moment of truly passionate or dramatic utterance, and there is nothing remotely connected with folksong in the majority of them. Of these first songs the last is the best; in its English version, *None but the lonely heart*, it has remained one of his most popular short pieces.

Like this set of songs, Tchaikovsky's next extended composition, his First String Quartet, initiated a line of works in which his personality stands less than fully revealed. In February 1870, shortly after the completion of *Romeo and Juliet* and the op.6 songs, he set to work on a new tragic opera, *The Oprichnik*, drawing his own libretto from Lazhechnikov's drama. Work proceeded slowly and was interrupted in May by an urgent summons to Paris to visit a sick friend, Vladimir Shilovsky. June was spent in Germany, and after six weeks in Switzerland, where the first revision of *Romeo and Juliet* was made, he returned to Russia. By the end of the year he had resumed work on *The Oprichnik*, but in February 1871 it was again interrupted, this time by the composition of a string quartet which he planned to include in a concert of his own works from which he hoped to make some money. The concert took place successfully in March; in the audience was Turgenev. As a medium the string quartet offered Tchaikovsky no scope for the dramatic contrasts or grand rhetoric possible with the orchestra, and in his First Quartet he showed himself concerned to compose as absolute a piece as he could, attempting to think, in the sonata structures of the outer movements and in the scherzo, through the mind of a Classical composer. Individuality is inevitably sacrificed, and the opening of the quartet, for instance, might be taken for Schubert; the reward of this self-negation is a notable structural equilibrium and expressive poise. Only in the second movement, the famous Andante cantabile based on a folksong collected at Kamenka, is Tchaikovsky unmistakably himself.

In May Tchaikovsky was again hard at work on *The Oprichnik*, and after visits to Kamenka and to the estate of his friend Nikolay Kondrat'yev at Nizy near Khar'kov, during which he completed his textbook on harmony, he visited Shilovsky on his estate at Usovo, not far from Kiev, where he resumed the composition of his opera, actually permitting his host to compose and score the prelude to Act 2. On returning to Moscow he moved for the first time into his own flat. Because of the extra expense this involved, he had to supplement his earnings by undertaking some work as a music critic; he continued this part-time occupation until 1876. A holiday in Nice (at Shilovsky's expense) and a lucrative commission for a festival cantata again held up *The Oprichnik*, which was not completed until April 1872.

Abraham has described *The Oprichnik* as 'Meyerbeer translated into Russian', adding, however, that the translation is done thoroughly. The plot is a melodrama of love and conspiracy in which a crucial role is played by the oprichniks, the notorious bodyguard of Ivan the Terrible. A sizable portion of the music was transferred bodily from *The Voyevoda*, and the work was composed, following the precedent set by Glinka's *A Life for the Tsar*, as a succession of self-contained movements linked by a species of accompanied recitative or arioso. A certain musical integration is achieved by the modest use of leitmotifs. Much of the music with which Tchaikovsky supplemented his material from *The Voyevoda* is filled with the same kind of national flavour, and the opera uses a number of real folksongs. There is also an element in the music arising from the idiom of Slavonic church music. All this is supplemented by a liberal amount of that lyricism which, at its feeblest, is related to the manner of the drawing-room song, and at its best transmutes itself into the full-blooded cantilena which is unmistakably Tchaikovsky's. The work was successful when it reached the stage in April 1874; but Tchaikovsky himself turned against it, and it might have suffered the same fate as his first two operas had he not already sold the rights to Bessel.

Having completed *The Oprichnik*, Tchaikovsky spent summer 1872 in his customary round of the estates of his family and friends, starting work on his Second Symphony in June while at Kamenka. This work, together with the opera *Kuznets Vakula* ('Vakula the smith'), represents Tchaikovsky's nationalism at its strongest; it received its nickname 'Little Russian' after Tchaikovsky's death because of its incorporation of Ukrainian folktunes. It was completed in November, and when he visited St Petersburg at the end of the year, he played the finale to Rimsky-Korsakov and some friends: all were enraptured by it. Similar enthusiasm greeted the first performance in Moscow in February 1873. Yet Tchaikovsky was immediately dissatisfied with it, and in 1879–80 he provided a virtually new first movement, revised the scherzo, and made a substantial cut in the finale.

The authorized version of the first movement is notable for its economy. As in *Romeo and Juliet*, the theme of the slow introduction (the first of the Ukrainian folktunes) is drawn into the development; but the structure of the introduction itself is quite different, with the single Lisztian repetition of a large section in another key being replaced by a section built around the statement and three repetitions of the folktune, set against different backgrounds after the practice of Glinka. In the exposition, too, instead of a tonally closed first subject as in the First Symphony, Tchaikovsky devised a terser utterance that moves quickly to the dominant of the second subject, an extended paragraph. The theme of the introduction recurs to close the movement. The second movement had originally been the Bridal March in the opera *Undine*; here, again, the influence of Glinka is apparent in the changing backgrounds to which the central theme (another Ukrainian folksong) is treated. The scherzo is clearly conditioned by that of Borodin's First Symphony. It is the finale that is the most fully Russian. Here the third of Tchaikovsky's folksongs, *The Crane*, is first heard in a portentous introduction not unlike the 'promenade' manner of Musorgsky's *Pictures at an Exhibition*, and then in a swift series of repetitions against changing backgrounds to form the first subject, into which is incorporated a passage built over a whole-tone scale. To initiate the development Tchaikovsky, with scant regard for consonance, flung his folktune against a wide-stepping bass, furnished the second subject with an unstable chromatic support which slips it out of key in mid-phrase, and then led a mixture of these two elements through an orgy of modulation to fashion one of the most striking passages anywhere in his work. Nowhere did Tchaikovsky draw closer to Musorgsky at his most boldly imaginative.

At the end of 1872 Tchaikovsky composed a second

set of six songs, op.16, which continued the stylistic line of op.6 and was as far removed from any folk tradition; the last is an interesting experiment incorporating the *Dies irae* theme throughout as a kind of cantus firmus. During March and April 1873 he applied himself to the composition of incidental music for Ostrovsky's fairy-tale drama, *Snegurochka* ('The snow maiden'), providing a prelude and 18 separate pieces that incorporate 12 folksongs. As with his later music to *Hamlet*, he relied on some material from earlier works. The attractiveness of the music won it a considerable success with the public when the play was produced in May. Visits to Nizy and Kamenka, and a trip to the West, intervened before Tchaikovsky settled down at Usovo in August to compose a symphonic fantasia, *Burya* ('The tempest'), based on a plan that Vladimir Stasov had provided for him earlier in the year. Work went easily, and the composition was completed in 11 days. The orchestration was finished on his return to Moscow, and when the work was performed in December it enjoyed a success as great as that of the Second Symphony. *The Tempest* is not, however, one of Tchaikovsky's best orchestral pieces. It is a five-section mirror structure, with musical portrayals of Ariel and Caliban at the centre, flanked by love music for Ferdinand and Miranda, with the sea and Prospero surrounding all. Virtually no effort is made to engage musical material from the various sections, but this would scarcely have mattered if Tchaikovsky's material had been of sufficient quality. The heaving of the sea, depicted by undulating divided strings deployed on massive, slow-moving harmonies, was (according to Rimsky-Korsakov) modelled on the opening of Wagner's *Das Rheingold*. It is an effective enough formula, and the love music has much appeal, though it is not really a match for that of *Romeo and Juliet*. Nevertheless, in his portrayal of Caliban (though hardly Shakespearean and completely lacking the grotesque richness that Musorgsky might have bestowed on it) Tchaikovsky did not succumb to the rather facile creative attitude revealed in the rest of the piece.

Nor was the rapturous reception accorded the Second String Quartet justified by the quality of the piece itself. It was written in January 1874, and Tchaikovsky recorded that none of his works had ever been composed so effortlessly. Here lies a clue to the trouble, for, as with *The Tempest*, the piece has fluency, showing skilled craftsmanship but little of the freshness of invention that had marked the First Quartet. The chromaticism of the first movement's introduction promises well, but the ensuing movement has a blandness that Tchaikovsky's refined textural resourcefulness cannot conceal. The scherzo is the most interesting movement, with its free alternation of bars of two and three beats, and the slow movement contains some characteristic music, though a slender idea is repeated at excessive length. The material of the finale is second rate, too, and its cordiality culminates in a fugato that is as sterile expressively as it is skilful technically.

Tchaikovsky's next significant work contained some of the best music he wrote. This was the opera *Vakula the Smith*, set to a libretto based on Gogol's *Christmas Eve*. Polonsky had originally provided this for Serov, but on the latter's death in 1871 the Grand Duchess Helena Pavlovna had made it into a competition piece, offering two prizes and a guarantee of performance at the Mariinsky Theatre for the winning work. Helena

Pavlovna's own death in 1873 left the competition in the hands of the Russian Musical Society, who fixed the closing date as August 1875. Immediately after the première of *The Oprichnik* in April 1874, Tchaikovsky left for Italy in his capacity as music critic to review the first performance of *A Life for the Tsar* in Milan. Thoroughly riled that the Glinka première had been postponed so that adjustments could be made to suit Italian taste, he decided not to visit Milan. Late in May he arrived back in Russia. Under the impression that the closing date for the opera competition was January 1875 he withdrew to Nizy; only two and a half months later at Usovo he completed the scoring of his entry. Having submitted it under a pseudonym as required, he learnt of his mistake and forthwith negotiated to withdraw from the competition, hoping to get *Vakula* staged earlier. This request was summarily rejected, but it had revealed his identity to the committee, and the opera's overture was actually publicly performed. Despite these and other improprieties Tchaikovsky was subsequently awarded the prize, and in December 1876 the work was staged. It was not a great success, and nine years later Tchaikovsky revised it, renaming it *Cherevichki* ('The slippers'; in the West it became generally known as *Les caprices d'Oxane*). Even with these later additions that Tchaikovsky made when his most nationalist period was far behind him, the opera remains a thoroughly Russian work.

Unlike Lazhechnikov's *The Oprichnik*, Gogol's delightful fairy tale did not afford melodramatic situations that might all too easily have tempted Tchaikovsky into an exaggerated response in *Vakula the Smith*. Instead it offered a liberal measure of the fantastic which required (and drew) from him a matching musical fantasy that he never surpassed. It is not surprising that this work remained one of his own favourites. Of purely non-Russian music there is surprisingly little, really only the couplets and the minuet in Act 3: the latter is the first of a line of Rococo stylizations that were to appear in his work. Elsewhere in the opera the influence of Glinka is strong; the model for the polonaise in Act 3, and the style of the whole choral scene at the beginning of Act 2, are to be traced to *A Life for the Tsar*, while the influence of *Ruslan and Lyudmila* is even stronger. This is perhaps surprising, for while *Ruslan* held the greater attraction for Balakirev and his circle, it was Glinka's first opera that had the firmer hold on Tchaikovsky. In *Ruslan* Glinka had worked out his particular idiom for the treatment of magical and fantastic happenings, and this proved a rich source of suggestion to Tchaikovsky for his own handling of the supernatural and unearthly in this opera. There is a good deal that is indebted to *Ruslan* in the opening scene with the Devil (including one passage built on a whole-tone bass), and even more perhaps in the scene of Vakula with the *rusalki* at the beginning of Act 3. In addition to the Russianness arising from Glinka, there is that which came from folksong (especially Ukrainian), most obviously revealed in the number of gopak tunes in the opera. The intonations of folk music also infiltrate the music relating to human emotions rather than to supernatural happenings. On the whole the weakest passages are the more lyrical ones involving Vakula and Oxana. It is when the lyrical vein is subjected to high dramatic pressure that there is a danger of Tchaikovsky's invention taking refuge in routine operatic gestures. Nevertheless, such moments are minor blemishes in one of

Tchaikovsky's most inventive and imaginative scores; it is worth observing the marked gift for comedy that he was beginning to develop in his handling of the succession of little scenes between Solokha and her lovers at the beginning of Act 2.

4. INCREASING PROBLEMS (1874–7). Although there was to be a strong resurgence of a national character in parts of *Evgeny Onegin* ('Eugene Onegin'), *Mazepa* ('Mazeppa') and *Charodeyka* ('The sorceress'), Tchaikovsky's period of high nationalism was over with *Vakula the Smith*. Hitherto his music, however impassioned, full-blooded and dramatic, had been free of that emotional excess which spills over into morbidity or hysteria. Yet within three years these characteristics were to affect some of his works, revealing themselves forcefully in the Fourth Symphony. However, during these same years certain other lines that resist all overstatement become clearer in his output. What might, with some reservation, be called his neo-classical manner, begun in the First Quartet and confirmed in the Second, is extended in the Third and even manifests itself in parts of the Third Symphony; it must be added, however, that by this time the influence of Schumann had made itself evident above that of generalized Classical practice. Meanwhile an even more deliberate foraging into the past ushers in Tchaikovsky's line of Rococo pastiches, presaged in the minuet in *Vakula the Smith*, and firmly instituted by the Rococo Variations for cello and orchestra. In his neo-classical works Tchaikovsky had clearly been drawn to past styles because he thought he might solve certain structural problems more easily within them. In his Rococo pastiches, however, he sought refuge in a musical world that he felt to be purer than that into which his own personal style was being irresistibly drawn. The ballet, too, offered him escape by taking him into an elegant fairy-tale realm arising from a French tradition, where he could exercise freely his splendid gifts for composing memorable dance music.

During these three years there also appeared Tchaikovsky's first essays in composing for a solo instrument and orchestra. In September 1874 he composed the Six Songs op.25, writing an overtly Russian piece in the last, *Kak naladili: Durak* ('As they reiterated: Fool'), and in the fourth, *Kanareyka* ('The canary'), making one of his rare excursions into a pseudo-oriental idiom. Then, in November, he started work on his First Piano Concerto. At the beginning of 1875 he played it over to Nikolay Rubinstein who in a notorious incident summarily condemned it as ill-composed and unplayable. Tchaikovsky was badly hurt but completed the score as planned, ultimately dedicating it to Hans von Bülow, who greatly admired it and gave the first performance in October in Boston. Later Rubinstein recanted his opinion. The dramatic possibilities in the confrontation of heroic soloist and eloquent orchestra obviously fired Tchaikovsky. Structurally the concerto has been faulted for the huge tune which launches the first movement in the wrong key and never returns; yet one of the most admirable features of the first movement is a structural one, namely, Tchaikovsky's enterprising exploitation of tonal instability to enhance the tensions and restlessness that are such essential ingredients in the high drama of the late 19th-century concerto. His resourcefulness is maintained in the other two movements, the finale being an effective type of sonata rondo with a Ukrainian folksong

providing the first theme; in the second movement a flow of simple melody is supported by a characteristically Russian semitonal key relationship (D major against a D♭ tonic). The swift waltz theme in D in the middle of the movement is said to be based on a song from Désirée Artôt's repertory, *Il faut s'amuser et rire*.

During April Tchaikovsky completed two further sets of six songs, opp.27 and 28, of which *Korolki* ('The corals' op.28 no.2) is a notable dramatic ballad. Summer 1875 was spent at Usovo, Nizy and Verbovka (another of the Davïdov estates near Kamenka). Here he worked on his Third Symphony, a piece which in its first and last movements is far closer in nature to the Second String Quartet than to the Second Symphony. In the first movement Tchaikovsky was clearly deepening his preoccupations with the basic problems of sonata structure, taking his decisions on what he considered to be the grounds of good technique, unmolested by any imaginative impulse or powerful emotional pressure. Schumann is the prime influence. Though some of Schumann's harmonic practices provided enrichment of Tchaikovsky's resources, the influence of his more forceful and bluff utterances rarely proved beneficial; for what might possess dignity in Schumann too often degenerates into a foursquare sterility when processed by Tchaikovsky. The first subject of the Third Symphony demonstrates this cogently, and Tchaikovsky's endeavour to pare down his material to what he believed to be the bare essentials required for future development permits only a ghost of his real self to remain. The simple counterpoints of the second movement, Alla tedesca, are incomparably more attractive. Even the Tempo di polacca finale (from which the conductor August Manns later gave the symphony its irrelevant nickname 'Polish') does not escape a demonstration of academic expertise in a lengthy fugato. The delicate scherzo shows Tchaikovsky's fascination with light and varied orchestral textures which he was to exploit with greater mastery in the scherzo of the *Manfred* symphony; the trio of this movement was drawn from music composed for the cantata of 1872.

Despite the charm of the middle three movements, the Third Symphony is the dullest of the series; nevertheless, it was warmly received at its first performance in November. The same was not true of Tchaikovsky's next major work, his first ballet, *Lebedinoye ozero* ('Swan lake'), commissioned by the Imperial Theatres in Moscow. Tchaikovsky began work on the score in August 1875, using some music from a little domestic ballet of the same title composed for his sister Alexandra's children, evidently in 1871. The new work was not finished until the following April and was first performed in March 1877. The performance was poor, and Tchaikovsky's score, already heavily cut, was adulterated by the interpolation of some pieces by Pugni to make it more palatable to the impoverished taste of the audience and easier for the dancers. *Swan Lake* is, however, among the more satisfactory of Tchaikovsky's works. He admitted that he could write well in an opera only when he became personally involved with his characters, and all too often they remained puppet figures of little or no credibility, who drew from him music that was at best efficient. In ballet, however, characterization was of less significance: what was required was music that could establish atmosphere when necessary, and provide at all times a characteristic accompaniment to the movement on stage. With his rich gifts for melody

2. Autograph MS of the opening of the Act 1 finale from Tchaikovsky's 'Swan Lake', composed 1875–6

and special flair for writing memorable dance-tunes, with his ready response to the atmosphere of a theatrical situation and his masterly orchestration, Tchaikovsky was ideally equipped as a ballet composer.

Not that *Swan Lake* is a consistently successful piece. In those passages where Tchaikovsky was concerned with dramatic action he showed his aptitude for producing music which, if rarely revealing that vivid pantomimic quality in which Musorgsky excelled, nevertheless felicitously supports the stage action in movements of considerable musical substance and scale, far weightier than anything in earlier Russian ballet. Yet the expectations of the Russian public for decorative spectacle had to be satisfied; thus Act 1 contains a lengthy divertissement quite unrelated to the main plot, and though Act 3 initially contrives to combine such formal dancing with dramatic movement as various characters or groups enter in turn, it subsequently slides into decorative dancing, culminating in five charmingly characterful but irrelevant national stylizations. However, the suite of dances for the swans and the *pas d'action* for the lovers in Act 2 are dramatically justifiable, and the final act is purged of all extraneous matter to grow from its briefly relaxed opening into an organism as purposefully dramatic as it is concise. Warrack has drawn attention to Tchaikovsky's use of key structure as an agent of dramatic articulation, the music for Siegfried and Odette being set mainly in sharper keys, that of Rotbart and the force of evil gravitating towards flat keys. It was with the revival of *Swan Lake* in 1895, with choreography by Petipa and Ivanov, that it received the appreciation that it merited and that has subsequently endured.

At the end of 1875 Tchaikovsky began what was to prove his best-known piano work, the set of 12 pieces, *Les saisons*, composed for publication in the monthly parts of a periodical during 1876. All his piano music is of only minor importance, and despite the popularity subsequently achieved by some of *Les saisons*, this set of salon pieces is of slender value. It was also towards the end of 1875 that Tchaikovsky made the acquaintance of Saint-Saëns, who was visiting Moscow. Then, at the beginning of 1876, cheered by the successful Russian performances of the Third Symphony and First Piano Concerto and by the welcome news of his success with *Vakula the Smith* in the opera competition, he left for Paris. There he attended a performance of Bizet's *Carmen*, a work that made a profound and lasting impression on him, and also started his Third String Quartet. He completed it on his return to Russia, and it was well received at its first performance in March. It is strange that Tchaikovsky, who nine months after the first hearing of his Second Quartet could still judge it to be his best work, should have had immediate reservations about the new piece, fearing that he was repeating himself; for the Third Quartet is far more characteristic than its predecessor. Dedicated to the memory of his violinist friend Ferdinand Laub, the work makes its elegiac function explicit in the third movement, Andante funèbre e doloroso. It may be that in the earlier part of this movement the intensity of feeling is stronger than its musical material, but the music's relative austerity provides a splendid foil for the G♭ cantilena that follows. Neither the scherzo nor the finale is as weighty or as consistently characteristic; nevertheless, the former has some effervescent wit, the latter a vigour of the kind displayed in the finale of the First Piano Concerto.

The impact of *Carmen* impelled Tchaikovsky to seek an opera libretto on a similar subject for himself, and in February Laroche sent him one by Zvantsev based on the tale of Francesca da Rimini from Dante's *Inferno*. The need to complete *Swan Lake* prevented Tchaikovsky from undertaking anything else for the moment, and a subsequent recurring ailment drove him to seek a cure in Vichy. There, in early July, he received from Modest some suggestions for an orchestral work. Besides Hamlet, Othello and Lermontov's Tamar, Modest proposed Francesca da Rimini, and a subsequent reading of Dante persuaded Tchaikovsky that he would compose an orchestral piece and not an opera. In August he visited Bayreuth to attend, as a critic, the first complete cycle of the *Ring*; he was warmly received by Liszt, though Wagner was unable to see him. The *Ring* proved not at all to Tchaikovsky's taste, despite his recognition of some remarkably beautiful and striking moments in it. Returning to Russia in late August he composed, at Nikolay Rubinstein's request, his Slavonic March, which provoked a storm of patriotic feeling at its first performance in November; then he settled down to *Francesca da Rimini*, sketching it in full in less than three weeks, and completing it in November. Its first performance in Moscow in March 1877 was warmly greeted by both the public and the critics.

In *Francesca da Rimini* there are already signs of those excesses that were to mark many of Tchaikovsky's works from the Fourth Symphony onwards. Here, however, they arise not so much from an almost hysterical need to find a personal emotional outlet as from a straining after effects to compensate for the work's lack of organic development. The subject of *Francesca da Rimini* did not offer a variety of characters locked in drama, as did *Romeo and Juliet*, but a single individual narrating a sad tale. The evolving conflict of sonata procedures was therefore inappropriate, and Tchaikovsky chose instead a simple ternary scheme whose sections are built through literal or decorated repetition. Francesca's pathetic narration forms the centre of the work, flanked by an Allegro vivo that graphically depicts the buffeting winds of the Second Circle of the Inferno, all of which is preceded by an introduction saturated with plangent diminished 7ths and wailing chromaticism that owe a good deal to Liszt. The absence of any genuine thematic development is matched by the restricted tonal range, most of the piece centring on E or A. The virtuosity of the craftsmanship is more conspicuous than in *Romeo and Juliet*, but *Francesca da Rimini* lacks that work's cogent sense of evolution. The winds of Hell tempt Tchaikovsky into a vivid but facile chromaticism; too many bars are spent in preparing great climaxes that do not match expectations. As for Francesca herself, she is prolix almost to the point of tedium. Set beside the intense subjectivity of the Fourth Symphony's first movement, *Francesca da Rimini* comes to seem an objective piece; yet there is already, in the seemingly interminable alternation of two themes in the central section, a foretaste of the obsessiveness that was to mark some of Tchaikovsky's later music.

There could hardly be a greater contrast between the fervent dramatic expression of *Francesca da Rimini* and the poised elegance of the Variations on a Rococo Theme for cello and orchestra, which followed immediately in December 1876. The former had been an emotional torrent; the latter revealed a world of order and calm in beautifully wrought music, as gracious and as slight as an 18th-century divertimento. In turning to such music of the past as a basis for his own compositions, Tchaikovsky had a purpose the very opposite of that which later impelled Stravinsky; for whereas the latter, in his neo-classical works, subjected styles from the past to his Russian flair for creative caricature as a means of further self-discovery, Tchaikovsky turned to the 18th century as a means of escape from himself. It is highly significant that in his own life he was already preparing desperately for the ultimate step through which he hoped he would gain release from his homosexuality. In his self-loathing, and in order to escape the shame he felt at any public suspicion of his abnormality, he decided on marriage. In the West earlier in the year he had declared his intention of marrying, and before the year was out he had resolved to go through with it.

5. MARRIAGE: CRISIS AND AFTERMATH (1877–8). In December 1876 Tchaikovsky met Tolstoy who, having been reduced to tears by the Andante cantabile of the First Quartet, furnished him with some folksongs that Tchaikovsky promised to use. Of greater consequence, however, was his first contact at much the same time with the wealthy widow Nadezhda von Meck. Her interest in him had been first aroused by his orchestral piece *The Tempest*, and was stimulated further when the violinist Yosif Kotek, one of Tchaikovsky's former pupils, was engaged by her as resident violinist. Small but handsomely rewarded commissions for violin and piano arrangements of some of Tchaikovsky's own smaller pieces initiated an extraordinary relationship that was to last for 14 years. It was maintained entirely by correspondence, and all personal contact was deliberately avoided; on the two occasions when they accidentally met, they hurried past each other without speaking. For each the other thus remained a fantasy figure, unspoilt by the disenchantment of reality. The root of the relationship for Mme von Meck, as for Tchaikovsky, appears to have been a revulsion against physical relations with the opposite sex. The death of her husband in 1876 had released her from sexual demands, and, now evidently frigid, she could idealize Tchaikovsky as revealed in his music, find emotional nourishment and fulfilment in responding to that music, and in correspondence pour out to him her thoughts and feelings without risking the pressures of a more personal relationship. The growing confirmation of his homosexuality was already leaving its marks on Tchaikovsky's music. From the beginning his musical language had been generous in its emotional power, but the element of overstatement, shown both in the inflated gestures of *Francesca da Rimini* and in the heightened emotional temperature of the Fourth Symphony, must surely arise from the need to find an outlet for emotional drives that could not be channelled into a full physical relationship. The advent of Mme von Meck could hardly have been more timely: for him she remained a depersonalized woman, making no physical demands, but longing for the confidences of his most personal thoughts and feelings. When, after the stunning blow of his attempted marriage, an emotional blockage came between Tchaikovsky and his own music (perhaps because his music would have too publicly revealed the feelings of which, after the humiliation of his disastrous marriage,

he felt ashamed) the privacy of his written confidences with Mme von Meck became of even more crucial importance. The intensity of feeling within this curious relationship is confirmed by the vicarious physical union which Mme von Meck (with Tchaikovsky's full approval) sought and achieved when, on 23 January 1884, her son Nikolay married Tchaikovsky's niece Anna Davïdova.

Tchaikovsky's marriage was the rash and hasty act of a desperate man. In late April or early May 1877, while working on his Fourth Symphony, he received a written declaration of love from a certain Antonina Milyukova, who claimed she had met him at the conservatory, though Tchaikovsky himself could not recollect her. Further letters followed, including a threat of suicide if he would not see her. On 1 June Tchaikovsky visited her and told her firmly but not unkindly that he could not love her. There the matter might have rested, had not a coincidence in his creative life at that moment impelled him to reconsider his attitude. A week before their meeting, with the first three movements of the Fourth Symphony now sketched in full, his attention had been drawn to Pushkin's *Eugene Onegin* as a possible opera subject. He was quickly fired by it and set about working out his own scenario, abandoning plans for an opera on *Othello* or De Vigny's *Cinq-mars*. With Onegin's heartless spurning of Tatyana now firmly in his mind, Tchaikovsky was driven to reconsider his own rejection of Antonina. As a result, within a week of their first meeting he had proposed and, though he tried to make it clear that there could be no physical relationship between them, been accepted. With the last movement of the Fourth Symphony now also finished, he departed for Shilovsky's home at Glebovo, where he settled down to composing *Eugene Onegin* (he had started with Tatyana's Letter Scene which, he perceived, had a remarkable parallel with Antonina's first declaration to him). Before returning to Moscow to prepare for the wedding he had already sketched about two-thirds of the opera. Now at last he informed his family and Mme von Meck of his intention. He married Antonina on 18 July. His nightmare began immediately. After making some family visits he escaped from his wife to Kamenka, pretending that he was taking a cure in the Caucasus. During August he scored some of the Fourth Symphony and resumed work on *Eugene Onegin*. The beginning of the conservatory term on 24 September forced him to return to Moscow and his wife. Unable to stand the strain, he had within days made a pathetic attempt at suicide. When it failed he engineered an urgent summons to St Petersburg, where he arrived on 7 October in a state of complete nervous collapse. A specialist was consulted who, pronouncing his reason to be threatened, ordered a complete change; he was further recommended never to see his wife again. His brother Anatoly promptly left for Moscow to arrange a separation from Antonina, returning to St Petersburg to bear his brother off to western Europe.

With the worst horrors of this most critical event in his life now behind him, Tchaikovsky began to recover. After nearly a month at Clarens in Switzerland, he briefly visited Paris and then moved on to Italy. His personal condition, though still not normal, had further improved, and his financial worries had been removed by news from Nikolay Rubinstein that his conservatory stipend would be paid in full for the session. Moreover, Mme von Meck, from whom he had already requested

loans, declared that she would settle on him an annuity of 6000 rubles. Thus, when he was nominated Russian delegate to the Paris Exhibition of 1878, he felt able to decline this appointment which earlier he had agreed to accept. During a visit to Vienna he saw Delibes' ballet *Sylvia*, which he admired greatly, declaring that his own *Swan Lake* was not fit to hold a candle to it. In January 1878 he completed the scoring of his Fourth Symphony, and in February *Eugene Onegin* was completed.

Both the symphony and the opera bear unmistakable marks of the events in Tchaikovsky's private life at the time of their creation. In 1878, after the symphony was completed, Mme von Meck, the work's dedicatee, elicited from him the programme on which he alleged the work to be based. While it is impossible to take the whole programme seriously, it is certainly easy to believe that the opening theme does symbolize fate, for although it engages briefly with the main material during the first movement's development and coda, its chief function is to intrude peremptorily and inexorably, sweeping aside all other material. On a purely musical level it provides some powerful dramatic moments, while its strategic insertion, first between the exposition and development, then between the recapitulation and coda, aids structural clarity. Its return before the coda of the finale tightens the whole four-movement structure. The first movement, with its enormous expressive range

3. Part of Tchaikovsky's autograph letter (15 July 1877, old style) to Madame von Meck describing his return to Moscow after his wedding, and asking for a loan of money to allow him to escape (Tchaikovsky-House Museum, Klin)

and ruthless climaxes, is one of the most fascinating in all Tchaikovsky's works, generated as it is by the interaction of a normal sonata structure and a thoroughly unorthodox key scheme founded on a circle of minor 3rds (F, A♭, C♭ (= B), D, F). The first subject, a melancholy waltz with a constant hesitant cross-rhythm, is, like that of *Romeo and Juliet*, a tonally enclosed section encompassing a development, here expanded to substantial proportions. The use in the exposition of the first three keys in the cycle creates a problem that Tchaikovsky solved by treating A♭, the conventional key centre for the second subject, as a transitional key. Thus, having reached A♭ minor and introduced a new clarinet theme, he quickly probed a minor 3rd higher, devised a simple counter-melody to this clarinet tune, and then quickly settled into C♭ for the main second subject, in which he combined material from the preceding A♭ and F minor (first subject) sections. The recapitulation resumes the circle of keys, entering in D minor, a key that is retained for the restatement of the former clarinet tune, thus ensuring that the main part of the second subject will recur in the tonic, F. A hectic coda confirms this as the most nakedly emotional movement that Tchaikovsky had yet composed.

Taneyev censured Tchaikovsky for adopting a style reminiscent of ballet for his middle two movements. This stylistic perception is hardly valid as an objection, for they provide a much needed relief after the first movement, functioning as they do as intermezzos. In the second, the scherzo, Tchaikovsky deliberately exploited the colour contrasts between groups of instruments, scoring the flanks of the ternary structure for pizzicato strings, and allotting the trio first to woodwind, then to brass and timpani, before combining them. All three sections are used in the coda. The finale cannot match the first movement. It uses a folktune as its second theme, badly compromising its national character by expanding its natural three-bar phrases (written by Tchaikovsky as one and a half bars) into ones of four bars; much of the movement is built around this tune, which is either repeated with changing backgrounds after the example of Glinka, or else used for quasi-developmental passages.

The secret of Tchaikovsky's success in *Eugene Onegin* lies in the passionate sympathy he conceived for Tatyana, heightened obviously by the analogies of the tale to current events in his own life. He drew his libretto from Pushkin's verse novel, using the poet's own lines as far as possible. From the beginning he was aware of the problem of translating this story into operatic form, realizing that, while it ran deep in feeling, it offered few opportunities for conventional scenic effects. He can have been little surprised, therefore, that at its first performance by students of the Moscow Conservatory in March 1879 it made little impression. Nevertheless, these 'lyrical scenes' comprise his finest opera. Their thematic integration is striking. The short orchestral prelude is founded on a four-note germ (probably conditioned by the fate motif from Bizet's *Carmen*) which haunts much of the first two scenes, permeating the opening ensemble, playing a large part in the exchanges between the women, tinging the first encounter between Tatyana and Onegin, and figuring prominently in the beautifully sensitive scene between Tatyana and the Nurse. In contrast to the highly charged feelings associated with this phrase is the fresh, unsophisticated music of the peasants' chorus and

4. Nadezhda von Meck

dance. The four-note motif persists in the first part of the Letter Scene, and is rhythmically echoed in the horn answer to the descending oboe phrase of the Andante, which itself generates further motifs in the opera, and which here distils the very essence of Tatyana's feelings. Strangely, however, both elements of this theme seem to have a clear relationship with the duet 'Tu l'as dit' from Meyerbeer's *Les Huguenots*.

Tatyana's long agitated monologue in the Letter Scene is Tchaikovsky's finest operatic scene. Little of the rest of the work quite matches the best that Tchaikovsky put into the first act. The balls at the Larins' and Gremins', which open Acts 2 and 3 respectively, gave Tchaikovsky opportunities both to compensate for the lack of scenic effect elsewhere and also to indulge his gift for ballet music. There can be a certain bitter irony in the unfolding of catastrophic events against the background of cheerful dance music, but there is perhaps too much decorative music, and the incorporation into the Gremin scene of a trivial écossaise, composed for the Bol'shoy Theatre's production in 1885, only exacerbates the situation. Tchaikovsky was uncertain how to complete the opera, and the ending of the definitive version is certainly different from that heard at the first student performance.

Before returning to Russia, Tchaikovsky composed his Violin Concerto. On 9 March he had settled down in Clarens again; stimulated by the arrival of Kotek, and especially by their playing of Lalo's *Symphonie espagnole*, Tchaikovsky launched himself into the concerto, sketching it in 11 days and completing the scoring within a fortnight. At the same time he replaced the original slow movement with another (immediately using the first piece as the *Méditation* for violin and piano op.42 no.1). Despite Kotek's collaboration, Tchaikovsky offered the dedication to Leopold Auer; Kotek was recompensed by the dedication of the *Valse-scherzo* for violin and orchestra, composed the previous

5. Autograph MS of the opening of Tchaikovsky's 'Eugene Onegin', composed 1877–8; Tchaikovsky's own piano reduction for the vocal score can be seen at the foot of the page

year. But, to Tchaikovsky's dismay, Auer refused to give the concerto its first performance on the grounds that the violin writing was impracticable. Consequently its première was delayed until 1881, when it was performed in Vienna by Adolf Brodsky (who in 1876 had also given the first performance of another work intended for Auer, the *Sérénade mélancolique* for violin and orchestra). The concerto was not well received, drawing from Hanslick a damning review which hurt the composer deeply. Yet it is one of the least pretentious and freshest of Tchaikovsky's works, in which a simple concerto pattern is filled with appealing melody that might have spilt over from one of his ballets. The melodic flow and sense of creative delight emanating from it reflect, unusually in a large-scale work, the degree to which he was able for the moment to detach himself from his emotional problems.

6. CREATIVE TROUGH (1878–84). On returning to Kamenka on 23 April 1878, Tchaikovsky found himself embroiled in troubles (concerning his marriage) from which he was not to escape for three years. Antonina tormented him by alternately accepting and refusing a divorce, at one stage making life intolerable by moving into the flat above his own. At last, in 1881, it was discovered that she had given birth to an illegitimate child, and Tchaikovsky had the grounds he needed to divorce her. Yet this did not remove the misery of knowing that his abnormality must now be common knowledge, or that Antonina could at any time choose to publicize it. It is not surprising, then, that from this time he seems as far as possible to have avoided contact with anyone except his family and a few close friends, spending as much time as he could in the country or abroad. On returning to Russia, he spent four months at Kamenka and other estates (including two visits to Braïlov, one of Mme von Meck's estates, in her absence). In September he had to return to Moscow; in October he resigned from the conservatory.

In these circumstances his work suffered in quality. His sterility is painfully demonstrated in the Piano Sonata, started just before the Violin Concerto but not completed until August. In this piece, as arid as the concerto is fresh, Tchaikovsky's neo-classical manner sinks to its most inglorious level. In May and June he escaped from larger compositional tasks by compiling a collection of children's pieces for piano, by making his first attempt at church music in setting the Liturgy of St John Chrysostom, and by working on the Six Songs op.38, which he had started in Switzerland and which include *Serenada Don-Zhuana* ('Don Juan's serenade'), one of his most appealing songs. During August he worked on the first of his orchestral suites.

Tchaikovsky's three original orchestral suites are one of the most explicit reflections of his state in these difficult years. It seems that the experience of his marriage had raised a barrier between him and his own music, and his best work of this period is to be found in those genres that did not depend upon too much in the way of personal expression. In the ten years from 1877 it was only in the Piano Trio (1881–2), where an event outside his inner life (the death of Nikolay Rubinstein) stimulated him to a formal expression of grief, and in the *Manfred* symphony (1885), where he could pour out his feelings vicariously through a musical projection of Byron's hero, that he achieved something of the emotional fullness of the Fourth Symphony. In this inhibited condition the suite suited him ideally, for here he could relax in a series of amiable movements without the expressive or structural responsibilities of the symphony. The result is always second-rate Tchaikovsky, which sometimes dips towards the level of the salon

piece (as in the intermezzo of this First Suite), sometimes raises the level of musical respectability, if not of interest, with a fugue (as in the first movement), and at best enchants the listener with orchestral piquancy (as in the Miniature March) or with a flow of that facile melody which it seems Tchaikovsky could always command (as in the Divertimento). For some of these reasons the suites enjoyed a ready success in Tchaikovsky's lifetime.

The personal void is even more evident in Tchaikovsky's next opera, *Orleanskaya deva* ('The maid of Orleans'), which he began in December 1878 in Florence during an extended visit to the West. The composition went easily, and was completed less than three months later in Paris. Tchaikovsky had compiled his own libretto, planning situations which would allow for crowd spectacle, dramatic climaxes and a large ballet; he even invented a romantic interlude between the main character, Joan of Arc, and a Burgundian knight, Lionel, to afford an opportunity for some love music and to transform Joan into a tragic romantic heroine. In providing these ingredients he produced an unworthy plot which deprived his characters of any real life that might have sparked off his musical imagination. As in *The Oprichnik*, the influence of Meyerbeer and French grand opera is evident, but without the leaven of any significant Russian character. Perhaps there is a hint in the Minstrels' Chorus that opens Act 2, and there is more in the opening Chorus of Maidens; but this latter is merely a dilution of its obvious model, the women's choruses in Glinka's *Ruslan and Lyudmila*. Tchaikovsky had started composition with the scene of Joan's recognition in the latter part of Act 2, and this contains some of the best music in the opera; but even here attractive and sometimes touching passages are embedded in other music of patchy invention. When Joan really engaged his sympathy, Tchaikovsky's inspiration was roused at least a little, though neither the hymn nor Joan's farewell (the latter unmistakably Slavonic in complexion) in Act 1 represents Tchaikovsky at his best; nor does the love-duet in Act 4, though it does offer a more distinctive melodic fund. The faceless music with which the other characters are provided fails to raise them above the level of mere ciphers. Only in the ballet of Act 2, where Tchaikovsky could exercise his natural gift for dance music, did he succeed in producing an extensive stretch of music that rises above the efficiently routine. For the rest, the opera unfolds mostly in vast vistas of undistinguished music, with a liberal amount of pallid and sometimes shortwinded melody supported by conventional harmonic progressions, often artificially animated by mechanical accompaniment patterns. The large solo–choral ensembles that erupt on any pretext are adequately handled, but, compared with the models set in Musorgsky's *Boris Godunov*, are at best glib, at worst banal. With such flatulence and limp lyricism it is not surprising that *The Maid of Orleans* was not successful when it reached the stage in 1881, though it was the first of Tchaikovsky's operas ever to be produced abroad.

Back in Russia in March 1879 Tchaikovsky spent as much as he could of the next eight months on estates in the country. The scoring of *The Maid of Orleans* and the completion of the First Suite occupied him until late summer, and at Kamenka in October he started on his Second Piano Concerto. He undertook the task out of boredom from creative inactivity, working at it deliberately and without hurrying, and pronouncing himself well satisfied with it when he had worked on it in Paris during December (it was completed in Russia the following May). Immediately afterwards he left for Rome, where he spent three months and began his *Italian Capriccio*. This was a conscious attempt to emulate Glinka's evocation of a Mediterranean world in his Spanish Overtures, and its debt to the second of these, *Recollection of a Summer Night in Madrid*, is patent in its succession of independent sections loosely patched together, each conjuring up some unspecified aspect of Italian life or scenery. The orchestration, too, shows a good deal of Glinka's fastidious ear for clean and well-contrasted sonorities. Nevertheless, Tchaikovsky's material is inferior to Glinka's, and his fantasy less rich. However, the capriccio does possess a genuine vitality absent from the Second Piano Concerto. Whereas Tchaikovsky could relax in the untroubled, kaleidoscopic world of the *Italian Capriccio*, the heavy hand of duty seems to have rested on the concerto, and his creativity was little stirred. As in the Third Symphony and the Piano Sonata, the ghost of Schumann looms large in the squarely chordal first subject, while the second is a trivial little tune. Unable to strike any inventive fire from these indifferent materials, Tchaikovsky fabricated a movement in which the piano pours out hollow rhetoric or meanders in long solo stretches. The banality of some of the material in the slow movement, with its concertante parts for solo violin and cello, is merely emphasized by the scale on which Tchaikovsky deployed it; later he himself authorized some cuts, and others are occasionally made in performances. The finale, though far from the best of Tchaikovsky's last movements, is the least unsatisfactory part of the concerto.

Returning to St Petersburg in March 1880, Tchaikovsky met the young Grand Duke Konstantin Romanov, a great admirer of his music. (Subsequently the two men corresponded, and in 1887 Tchaikovsky set some of the grand duke's verses.) He did not stay long in St Petersburg or Moscow, however, but escaped to the country for the rest of the year. During the summer the Six Duets op.46 and the Seven Songs op.47 were written, and in the autumn at Kamenka the overture *1812* was composed for the Moscow Exhibition. Tchaikovsky felt no enthusiasm for the work while composing it, and reasonably enough doubted its value when it was completed. But the Serenade for strings, composed at exactly the same time, was written from inner compulsion. Here at last Tchaikovsky composed a piece to which Anton Rubinstein found himself able to give wholehearted approval. It is Tchaikovsky's equivalent of an 18th-century divertimento, inhabiting a world not so far removed from that of his Rococo pastiches.

Tchaikovsky remained in Russia until the première of *The Maid of Orleans* in February 1881; the next day, 26 February, he left for the West. At Nice he heard of the sudden death on 23 March in Paris of Nikolay Rubinstein. After attending Rubinstein's funeral he returned to Kamenka on 11 May, making this his headquarters until November. As his sister and her husband were away, he found himself in charge of their children, whom he adored. Some progress was made on his Vesper Service, but his main effort was directed into editing the complete church music of Bortnyansky for Jurgenson. With his poor opinion of Bortnyansky he found this an

uncongenial task. By August he had already started work on a new opera, *Mazeppa*, which was to occupy him off and on for the next two years. In November he was back in the West, staying in Rome where he began work on his Piano Trio in December. The medium was not one he liked, but he wished to write a memorial work for Rubinstein incorporating an elaborate piano part, and Mme von Meck had been pressing for such a piece for her resident piano trio, whose current pianist was the young Debussy. The trio is in two movements, of which the second is a long set of variations on a simple tune which had some particular association with Rubinstein, just as each variation was a portrayal of some incident in his life. Like the corresponding movement of the Fourth Symphony, this first movement sets some of the thematic events of a sonata structure against an unorthodox tonal background, thus drastically modifying their functions within the movement. Though not equalling the achievement of the Fourth Symphony, this 'Pezzo elegiaco', as Tchaikovsky labelled it, displays a musical quality and personal voice that remained unmatched in his music of 1878–85.

In April 1882 Tchaikovsky returned to Russia, soon resuming work on *Mazeppa*, which he finished composing in September. In the first act of this opera there is a resurgence of some national colouring, as in the first scene with its admirable and Glinka-like opening chorus in 5/4, and in the last scene of Act 2, actually described as a 'folk scene'. Elsewhere, however, the work is rarely more Russian than *The Maid of Orleans*. This tale, drawn from Pushkin, of an elderly hetman who is capable of tender love, yet who can be utterly ruthless in the pursuit of that love and of his personal ambition, offered better material than *The Maid of Orleans*. Tchaikovsky began composition with the love scene for Mazeppa and Mariya in Act 2, and this drew from him some agreeable, if less than first-rate, music. The execution scene has plenty of conventional theatrical power, and the incorporation of material from the opera's opening chorus into Mariya's demented lullaby at the end of the opera touchingly enhances the undeniable pathos of this conclusion. Yet Tchaikovsky remained unstirred by his characters and, despite some good moments, *Mazeppa* is little more than an opera of 'strong' situations efficiently handled. Just before Tchaikovsky returned to Russia the scoring of the work was completed in Paris, where he had spent the first four months of 1883; during this period he fulfilled three commissions in connection with the coronation of Alexander III. Back in Russia, he started working on his Second Suite in July, completing it in October. This five-movement work is notable chiefly for its use of accordions ad lib in the third movement, and for its alleged imitation of Dargomïzhsky in the kazachok finale. During October and November he composed 15 of the 16 Children's Songs op.54. This set includes the famous *Legenda* ('Legend'), whose popularity later caused Tchaikovsky both to orchestrate it and arrange it for unaccompanied mixed chorus.

By this time Tchaikovsky's reputation and the enthusiasm of the tsar for his music were such that *Mazeppa* was given concurrent productions in St Petersburg and Moscow. Tchaikovsky attended the one in Moscow on 15 February 1884, but left for the West the next day, neither waiting for the première of his Second Suite that evening, nor passing through St Petersburg to attend the first performance there of the opera three

6. *The Tchaikovsky brothers* (left to right): *Anatoly, Nikolay, Ippolit, Pyotr and Modest*

days later. His absence occasioned an expression of surprise from the tsar, who nevertheless did not withhold the Order of St Vladimir (fourth class); Tchaikovsky was obliged to return from Paris to receive the decoration in March. The early summer of 1884 saw the completion of the four-movement Third Suite. The last movement, theme and variations, is the one movement in all Tchaikovsky's suites that has found a place in the repertory. Having abandoned his original idea of making the work a symphony, Tchaikovsky used the first movement as the second movement of the Concert Fantasia for piano and orchestra, which dates from about the same time. To 1884 also belong the Six Songs op.57.

7. CREATIVE RENEWAL (1884–90). With the exception of the Piano Trio, none of Tchaikovsky's works since the Violin Concerto can be ranked among his better compositions. During 1884, however, he began to shed that unsociability and restlessness which had driven him to retreat to country estates or to wander over Europe. The tsar's decoration was a visible seal of official approval that helped his social rehabilitation, and the great popular success of *Eugene Onegin* in St Petersburg later in the year bolstered his social confidence. In addition he was elected head of the Moscow branch of the Russian Musical Society. When in November he was urgently summoned to Switzerland to visit Kotek, who was dying of tuberculosis, he suffered acutely from homesickness and from the longing for a real home of his own. In February 1885 he settled just outside Moscow, at Maidanovo near Klin; this house, and others nearby, were to be his homes for the rest of his life.

At this period, too, his contact with Balakirev was renewed, with fruitful consequences. Early in 1878 he had written to Mme von Meck an unsparing verdict on members of The Five, condemning Balakirev especially for what he considered to be his musical misguidance of the group. For some years Tchaikovsky had had no contact with his former mentor, but in 1882 Balakirev wrote to him and elicited a warm response. Balakirev's suggestion that Tchaikovsky should compose a work on Byron's *Manfred* was firmly rejected at that stage, but when two years later Balakirev sent him a modified plan for the work, he agreed to compose it. Quite apart from the older man's extraordinary powers of musical persuasion, it is obvious that Tchaikovsky hoped Balakirev's strong Christian convictions might also provide for him an escape from earthly guilt. Certainly the two men drew close together for a while. In October 1885 the *Manfred* symphony was finished.

The original plan for this work had been devised in the 1860s by Vladimir Stasov for Balakirev who, feeling that it was not congenial to him, proposed it to the ailing Berlioz in 1868. When Balakirev presented it to Tchaikovsky, he drew his attention to Berlioz's *Symphonie fantastique* and *Harold en Italie*, and even specified various works that might provide 'helpful materials' for Tchaikovsky's separate movements. Among those Balakirev suggested for the first and last movements were the 'Orgie de brigands' from Berlioz's *Harold en Italie*, and Tchaikovsky's own *Francesca da Rimini* (which Balakirev considered Tchaikovsky's best work); for the scherzo he proposed the Queen Mab scherzo from Berlioz's *Roméo et Juliette* and the scherzo from Tchaikovsky's Third Symphony. For the slow movement he suggested the 'Scène aux champs' from Berlioz's *Symphonie fantastique*. Tchaikovsky's music in his middle two movements shows how respectfully he heeded Balakirev's suggestions, though the Berlioz models are transmuted into two of Tchaikovsky's most delightful creations, the one bewitching, the other of a radiant freshness. Berlioz's practice of an *idée fixe* was accepted, too, the symphony's opening theme intruding (as in *Harold en Italie*) rather than integrating with the scene in each of the middle movements, and confronting new material in the finale. The first movement, a musical picture of Manfred haunted by memories of his beloved Astarte, is a unique organism, though features both of sonata practice and of the explicitly ternary structure of *Francesca da Rimini* are detectable in it. The endless chromatic swirls of the earlier piece are here replaced by sturdier harmonic language, abounding in 7th chords and strong dissonance presented with a particularly dark orchestral palette. The gloomy, rugged blocks that embody Manfred contain some of Tchaikovsky's toughest music, just as his personification of Astarte's shade elicits some of his tenderest invention. In the finale liberal quotations from this movement are pitted against the Bacchanalian forces of Arimanes. While the wholesale parading of familiar material from the first movement certainly binds the ends of the symphony together, this is achieved at the cost of musical integrity within the finale itself. The burden of the programme lies too heavily upon this movement, marring a symphony that is otherwise one of Tchaikovsky's most characteristic and fully realized conceptions.

While finishing the scoring of the *Manfred* symphony, Tchaikovsky embarked on another opera, *Charodeyka* ('The sorceress'). In his more settled life and regular daily routine at Maidanovo he worked steadily on the opera until early April 1886; he then set out to join Anatoly for a month at Tbilisi, where he was fêted by the local musicians. In May he visited Paris, travelling by sea from Batum to Marseilles. The whole expedition proved very pleasant, and back at Maidanovo in June he resumed work on *The Sorceress*, completing the composition in August (though the orchestration was not finished for another nine months). The next day he set to work on the 12 Songs op.60. In January 1887 he conducted *The Slippers* (the revision of *Vakula the Smith*, made two years earlier), and in March directed an entire concert of his own works. After these hard-won victories over his nerves he felt able to embark on concert tours abroad, conducting mostly his own compositions. With the scoring of *The Sorceress* finished, June was spent with Modest and Anatoly at Borzhom in the Caucasus, where he scored the four pieces by Mozart which make up his Fourth Suite, 'Mozartiana'. In July a sudden summons took him to Aachen to visit the dying Kondrat'yev. During this visit, in August, he composed the *Pezzo capriccioso* for cello and orchestra. Back in Russia in September, he conducted the première of *The Sorceress* in November, and before the year was out had composed the Six Songs op.63, to words by the Grand Duke Konstantin.

The Sorceress proved a failure, and one that hurt Tchaikovsky deeply, though the adverse verdict was not undeserved. Shpazhinsky's tale of an innkeeper's daughter who is courted by two princes (father and son), with

7. Principals in the first production of 'The Sleeping Beauty', first performed at the Mariinsky Theatre, St Petersburg, on 15 January 1890, with Carlotta Brianza (centre) as Aurora

melodramatic consequences, is poor stuff, and far too involved to provide a satisfactory scenario. Realizing this, Tchaikovsky cut both Shpazhinsky's libretto and, subsequently, his own music. But the real trouble was that yet again his characters had failed to engage his sympathy, and only the first act, in which there is a strong national flavour, is of any real quality. This is largely concerned with setting the scene, placing Nastasya, the heroine, in a rustic world, and prompting Tchaikovsky to reopen that national vein that he had so profitably mined in the earlier 1870s. The result is an abundance of racy music, the repetitiveness of many of the folky melodies eliciting from him a variety of felicitous accompaniments. But with Act 2, where the conventional passions and contrived melodramatic happenings begin, the invention loses character, and the treatment becomes, characteristically, no more than efficient. Occasionally the level rises, as in the earlier part of the love scene between the heroine and Prince Yuri at the end of Act 3. Nastasya was the one character who really engaged Tchaikovsky's interest, and in this scene her urgent wish to convince Yuri of her innocence and detain him is substantiated by some appealing and tender phrases. But at the end, when the conventional expressions of mutual love are reached, the defined musical character slips away into a generalized amorous aura that prompted no more than a routine response from Tchaikovsky. As in *The Maid of Orleans*, the more melodramatic incidents are served with a generous allowance of hectic sequential tumults, laden with diminished 7ths. In spite of its first act *The Sorceress* must rank among the weaker of Tchaikovsky's works.

Tchaikovsky himself conducted the first four performances of *The Sorceress*, as well as a further concert of his own works in November, and in December set out on his first foreign tour as a conductor. In Germany he met Brahms, Grieg, Ethel Smyth and – a reunion that seems to have touched them both – Désirée Artôt. In December 1877 he had made the acquaintance of Brahms's First Symphony, and had disliked it. When the two men now met face to face there was at first some constraint between them, though Brahms did his best to be friendly and succeeded in breaking down his somewhat embarrassed colleague's reserve. Tchaikovsky conducted in Leipzig, Hamburg, Berlin and Prague, where he was rapturously received. Concerts in Paris and London followed. On his return to Russia in April 1888 he revisited Tbilisi, and then moved into a new house at Frolovskoye. Though at this time he evidently felt more pleasure in his garden than in composition, he set about his Fifth Symphony in May, finding that inspiration came as the work progressed. Before completing it in August he had started the fantasy overture *Hamlet* which was finished in October. Three days later the last of the Six Songs op.65, composed to French texts, was completed.

Though Tchaikovsky did jot down an embryonic programme for his Fifth Symphony, he reverted to a more traditional structure with little evidence of the influence of external factors; the exception is that the principle of a motto theme, established in the Fourth Symphony, is here extended to all four movements, as in the *Manfred* symphony. The only irregular feature of the first movement is the three-stage exposition, somewhat similar to that of the Fourth Symphony, in which the string theme of the second stage (in B minor)

becomes the accelerated answering phrase to the new two-bar woodwind motif ushering in the third stage, which is the true second subject set in D major. Thus Tchaikovsky established the same tonal relationship between his subjects as in the First Piano Concerto's first movement. The waltz-conditioning of much of the thematic material of this movement prepares for the explicit waltz which does duty as the scherzo. Between these two movements is one of the composer's most personal utterances, an extended flow of yearning melody that is quintessential Tchaikovsky. As in the two preceding symphonies, it is the finale that is the weakest part, especially the peroration from which almost all trace of tonal tension is gone, and which brazenly restates the motto theme in a blatant attempt to synthesize extra power. The motto theme, as Abraham has pointed out, is derived from the trio in Act 1 of Glinka's *A Life for the Tsar*, where it had set the words 'Turn not into sorrow'. In a notebook Tchaikovsky had specified the motto theme as signifying 'complete resignation before fate', and the emphatic reiterations that it receives at the conclusion of this finale might be interpreted as a firm riposte to the inexorable, peremptorily intrusive fate as embodied in the motto theme of the Fourth Symphony. However, Tchaikovsky himself later sensed the musical insincerity of such overstatement as at the end of the Fifth Symphony. Certainly it provides a crude end to a work which, if not Tchaikovsky's most enterprising, resounds in every bar with his individual voice, speaking in those heightened emotional accents already heard in the Fourth Symphony and *Manfred* symphony.

Hamlet differs from *Romeo and Juliet* in that Tchaikovsky was not concerned with diverse characters and the musical realization of dramatic tensions; instead, like *Francesca da Rimini*, it centres on one person. Not requiring dramatic clashes, Tchaikovsky dispensed with a development section, articulating instead a series of psychological or emotional states, though presumably the march section which concludes both the exposition and recapitulation conveniently signals Fortinbras's two arrivals. Despite the absence of dramatic confrontations, *Hamlet* is a better piece than *Francesca da Rimini*, not least because Shakespeare's hero provides a diversity of traits which Tchaikovsky's invention builds into a figure as Byronic as Manfred.

Tchaikovsky himself conducted the first performances of both the Fifth Symphony and *Hamlet*, also directing the former in Prague during a visit in November to conduct *Eugene Onegin*. Back home in December he set to work on a new three-act ballet, *Spyashchaya krasavitsa* ('The sleeping beauty'), completing sketches of the prologue and first two acts by the end of January 1889. A further concert tour followed when Tchaikovsky conducted in Cologne, Frankfurt, Dresden, Berlin, Geneva and Hamburg. In Hamburg he had a second meeting with Brahms who delayed his own departure for a day to hear Tchaikovsky's Fifth Symphony: he approved of all of it except the finale. Tchaikovsky invited Brahms to conduct a concert of the Russian Musical Society, without success. During the last part of the tour, which took him to Paris and London, he worked on the third act of *The Sleeping Beauty*. After returning to Russia by sea to Batum he visited Anatoly at Tbilisi, and at Frolovskoye started orchestrating the ballet. This task, which caused him a good deal of trouble, occupied much of the summer.

Tchaikovsky rightly rated *The Sleeping Beauty* as one of his best works. The scenario was precisely designed by Petipa from Perrault's fairy tale, and its structure proved far more satisfactory than that of *Swan Lake*, for while the prologue and first two acts, in which the main plot unfolds, contain a certain number of set dances, they are well scaled; they are not merely gratuitous choreographic decoration, but have some marginal relevance to the drama itself. The formal divertissement element is reserved for the last act, in which set decorative dances could be dramatically excused as part of the wedding entertainment. In any case these dances are far more striking than most such pieces in *Swan Lake*, for a number of them are character-pieces for figures from fairy stories (Puss-in-Boots, Little Red Riding Hood etc), and this elicited from Tchaikovsky a far more individual type of invention, and some display of a pantomimic gift. Likewise in the prologue and first two acts the musical ideas are more striking and pointed, the characterization more precise, and the music excellently paced to the sequence of dramatic events. Tchaikovsky's gift for evoking atmosphere is even more splendidly revealed in this score than in *Swan Lake*, whether he was required to suggest bustling activity, as at the beginning of Act 1, or the magically haunted world of the forest and the night, as in Act 2. This conjunction of characterful musical invention, structural fluency and sure sense of atmosphere, all framed within an admirably structured plot, makes *The Sleeping Beauty* his most consistently successful theatre piece, and one of the peaks of the ballet repertory.

Tchaikovsky's next stage work, also one of his best known, was less satisfactory, though it enjoyed a far greater initial success. Soon after the first performance of *The Sleeping Beauty* in January 1890 he left for Florence, where he settled down to a new opera, *Pikovaya dama* ('The queen of spades'), commissioned for the famous tenor Nikolay Figner and his wife Medea. Tchaikovsky became so bound up in the work that the whole was sketched in six weeks. Three weeks later he left for Rome, where he stayed about a fortnight, returning to St Petersburg on 4 May. During the next six weeks the scoring of the opera was completed at Frolovskoye.

Pushkin's original story of *The Queen of Spades* has a spare simplicity which gives its ghoulishness and wry humour a particular edge. Modest, however, turned it into a romantic melodrama, adding a fair amount of love interest, and inflaming the end by making Liza throw herself into a canal (a scene added at his brother's request) and Hermann die at the gaming table. Though the general level of musical invention is not his best, *The Queen of Spades* is Tchaikovsky's most conventionally effective opera. He responded strongly to the character of Hermann (recording that he actually wept while composing the last scene), and especially to any opportunity for underlining the macabre or chilling, or simply for conjuring up some sort of musical atmosphere. His style had evolved to a condition that particularly suited it to such purposes, as is most powerfully demonstrated in the great scene in the Countess's bedroom (scene iv), the most consistent in the whole opera. To offset – or enhance – the emotional tension or morbidity of a good part of the music, Tchaikovsky incorporated into the opera the largest amount of Rococo material to appear

in any of his works, as part of his evocation of the bygone Russia of Catherine the Great; there is not only a complete pastoral cantata in scene iii, but also a setting of some words by 18th-century poets and the quotation of an aria from Grétry's *Richard Coeur de Lion* in scene iv. A tiny echo of national music is heard in the Russian Song with Chorus in scene ii. Tchaikovsky himself devised the effective idea of ending the ballroom scene by building up towards a grand entry of the Empress herself with all awaiting her as the curtain falls. As part of the supernatural vocabulary in the later scenes Tchaikovsky followed Glinka's example in using the whole-tone scale. It is not surprising that such a skilfully theatrical opera was an immediate success.

In June, immediately after finishing *The Queen of Spades*, Tchaikovsky composed the string sextet, *Souvenir de Florence*, whose untroubled world is in complete contrast to that of the opera. In this sextet his neo-classical line reaches its end. During its 19 years this succession of works had changed its character much. The First Quartet is the closest to true Classical precedents, the line later developing a strong bias towards Schumann which sapped its life and drew it into the earnest banality of the Piano Sonata. Subsequently it found renewal in the Serenade for Strings, whose more relaxed world (which owes something to that of Tchaikovsky's Rococo pastiches) is also inhabited by the pleasantly urbane *Souvenir de Florence*. Tchaikovsky's next large work, the symphonic ballad *Voyevoda* ('The voyevoda'), was sketched during the early autumn while he was visiting Anatoly at Tbilisi for six weeks (the piece has no connection with the earlier opera of the same title). At Tbilisi also, on 6 October, he suddenly received from Mme von Meck a letter announcing that she was bankrupt, and that his allowance would have to be discontinued. By now Tchaikovsky was no longer dependent upon her financially, for in addition to his royalties he had the life pension of 3000 rubles a year granted to him by the tsar in 1888. His increased income in the next three years in fact more than made up the loss. He might have been relatively unaffected by the news, had she been prepared to continue the correspondence and had her story of bankruptcy been true; but, as Tchaikovsky soon discovered, it was false, and when he wrote to her she made no reply. In fact it seems that his last letter never reached her and that the complete rift between them was the result of misunderstanding. According to Galina von Meck, a month or so before his death Tchaikovsky endeavoured to heal the breach, and died believing he had done so. Nevertheless, at the time of the rupture his pride was deeply wounded by the conclusion that for 14 years he had been merely a pleasant diversion for her. Disenchanted by the shattering of this image of his fantasy friend, and deprived of a correspondent in whose precious confidences he could find emotional release, he became profoundly embittered.

8. LAST YEARS (1891–3). Tchaikovsky's last years were marked by increasing outer success and deepening inner gloom. The triumph of *The Queen of Spades* led to a commission from the Imperial Theatre for two one-act pieces, an opera and a ballet. Before settling down to these, Tchaikovsky composed incidental music for a production of *Hamlet*, completing it in three weeks during January and February 1891. To finish the work

8. Tchaikovsky (centre) with Nikolay and Medea Figner, who created the roles of Hermann and Liza in 'The Queen of Spades' in 1890

easily he fell back on material from his earlier works, drawing on *The Snow Maiden*, the Third Symphony, the string Elegy in honour of Ivan Samarin (1884) and, of course, his own fantasy overture *Hamlet*, which he shortened and rescored as the overture. Having finished this chore he set to work in February on the new ballet, *Shchelkunchik* ('The nutcracker'), before leaving in March for another conducting tour, this time to the USA. In Paris he was enchanted by a new instrument, the celesta, and resolved to use it both in *The Voyevoda* and in the new ballet. After conducting a concert, he embarked for New York in a thoroughly depressed, homesick state that was increased by news of his sister Alexandra's death. His deplorable nervous condition was relieved by the kindness and respect shown to him by the Americans, and the tour, which included concerts in Baltimore and Philadelphia after four in New York (and also visits to Niagara Falls and Washington), was a great success with both the public and the press. Leaving the USA on 21 May he returned to Russia via Hamburg. To his dismay the woods at Frolovskoye had been cut down; but he settled back into his old house at Maidanovo, and began work on the one-act opera, *Iolanta* ('Iolanthe'), and *The Nutcracker*.

Although the ballet subject had been prescribed for him, Tchaikovsky had himself chosen that for the opera. Yet the romantic story of a blind princess, set in Provence, obviously failed to stir much of a response in him, and the result is a pretty but rather characterless piece, though there are premonitions of the dark world of the Sixth Symphony. Tchaikovsky did not think highly of the music he wrote for *The Nutcracker*, rightly rating it below that of *The Sleeping Beauty*. Certainly *The Nutcracker* is the least important of Tchaikovsky's three ballets. Nevertheless, the criticisms that are habitually levelled against it should be tempered by consideration of the restrictions it imposed on Tchaikovsky. The rigorous scenario that Petipa devised (and expanded into two acts) from the fairy tale by Dumas *père* from Hoffmann provided no opportunity for the expression of human feelings beyond the most trivial, confining him

mostly within a world of tinsel, sweets and fantasy, peopled by wedding-cake fairy figures engaged in inconsequential acts or in mere choreographic divertissement. In view of the lack of real dramatic or human motivation, Tchaikovsky's treatment of the subject is as good as could be expected. It is true that much of the harmonic language is essentially simple, even trite, and some of the melodic material is naive almost to the point of banality. There is no really strong tune anywhere in the work, and what had been characterful in the preceding two ballets has now sometimes become merely cute. Yet at its best the melodic invention is charming and pretty, and by this time Tchaikovsky's virtuosity in devising varied orchestral colours and his mastery of contrapuntal devices, whether sparkling counterpoints or patterned figurations, was such as to ensure endless fascination in the surface attractiveness of the score.

Early in 1892 Tchaikovsky compiled a suite from the ballet, creating what was to become one of his most frequently heard compositions. The suite was a hurriedly devised replacement for the symphonic ballad, *The Voyevoda*, against which he had turned so violently after its first performance in November 1891 that he had destroyed the score. Of all Tchaikovsky's works that have subsequently been restored from the orchestral parts, *The Voyevoda* is perhaps the most valuable. Pushkin's ballad (after Mickiewicz) concerns a voyevoda, or warrior, who returns home to find his wife engaged in a romantic interlude; his servant, told to shoot the unfaithful wife, misses his aim and kills his master instead. Tchaikovsky planned *The Voyevoda*, like *Francesca da Rimini*, as a ternary structure, the voyevoda's appearance and subsequent death forming the flanks, the centre unfolding as a love scene centring on E♭, thus creating the maximum tonal tension with the voyevoda's portrayal in A minor (it is worth noting that Tchaikovsky had used the same tonal tension between the two subjects of the fantasy overture *Hamlet*, and also in *The Nutcracker*, beginning and ending it in B♭, but concluding the first and beginning the second act in E major). The music with which Tchaikovsky filled this

9. *Tchaikovsky in his doctoral robes, Cambridge, 1893*

scheme in *The Voyevoda* contains some first-rate, if not consistent, invention and a notable range of colour in the orchestration, which is less remarkable, perhaps, in the opulent sounds of the love scene than in the sinister portrayal of the voyevoda, and in the dark, deep sounds that signify his death, and that look forward to the world of the Sixth Symphony.

At the beginning of 1892 Tchaikovsky embarked on yet another foreign tour, conducting in Warsaw, hearing a fine performance of *Eugene Onegin* under Mahler in Hamburg, but feeling so homesick in Paris that he cut short the tour and hurried back to Russia. In May, shortly before taking a three-week cure in Vichy, he moved to a new (and his last) home near Klin, where he began work on a Symphony in E♭. It was virtually completed, but in December his dissatisfaction with it led him to convert the first movement into a concert piece for piano and orchestra (the indifferent Piano Concerto no.3), and to start a similar metamorphosis of the Andante and finale. The reception of *Iolanthe* and *The Nutcracker* was disappointing, but the revised *Souvenir de Florence* was warmly received. Meanwhile proof of Tchaikovsky's international reputation came from France, where he was elected a corresponding member of the Académie Française, and from England, where he was nominated for an honorary MusD by Cambridge University. In late December he left for the West, meeting in her home near Basle his old governess, Fanny Dürbach, whom he had not seen for over 40 years; he visited Paris, conducted successfully in Brussels, and on his return to Russia was continuously fêted for nearly a fortnight in Odessa. On his way back to Klin, where he arrived on 15 February 1893, a scheme for a new symphony came to him.

The idea for this new 'Programme Symphony' (as Tchaikovsky called it at this stage) seems to go back to a document that he evidently scribbled in 1892. 'The ultimate essence of the plan of the symphony is LIFE. First movement – all impulsive passion, confidence, thirst for activity. Must be short. (Finale DEATH – result of collapse.) Second movement love; third disap-

pointments; fourth ends dying away (also short).' By February 1893 the plan was obviously much modified, and Tchaikovsky had decided that among the numerous structural modifications within this symphony the finale would be a long-drawn Adagio. The work was fully sketched by April, but the composition of his last group of songs (op.73) and final set of piano pieces (op.72) intervened before the scoring was undertaken. Furthermore, in May Tchaikovsky had to go to England, where he shared a Royal Philharmonic concert with Saint-Saëns, rather eclipsing the Frenchman with a triumphant performance of his own Fourth Symphony. In Cambridge he conducted *Francesca da Rimini*, and received the MusD along with Saint-Saëns, Boito, Bruch (whom he found insufferable) and (*in absentia*) Grieg. Nearly a month of the summer was spent scoring the symphony; as so often in his later works, this caused him a good deal of trouble. In August it was completed, and was first performed on 28 October. The title 'Pathétique' was proposed by Modest on the day after the première.

Tchaikovsky's Sixth Symphony was both his last work and his most profoundly pessimistic. Its expressive extremes are great, the dynamic range stretching from *ffff* to *ppppp*. The first subject emerges from the lowest depths of the introduction, and the opposition of character between the two subjects is the strongest in all Tchaikovsky's sonata structures. The scale of this exposition is huge, and is compensated by telescoping the development and recapitulation, the latter being gathered up into the ferocious activity of the former (which includes a quotation from the music of the Russian Orthodox Requiem) so that the final catharsis is achieved in the middle of the recapitulation. By shortening the ensuing second subject and concluding with an economical coda, a notable sense of progressive compression is achieved as the movement advances. As in the Fifth Symphony, one of the middle movements is a waltz, this time given a curious but charming limp by being written in 5/4. The trio, *con dolcezza e flebile*, exploits some of the harmonic tensions that also appear in the outer movements. The march grows into a substantial third movement whose fertile ornamentation and sparkling sound provide an ideal background for the agonies of the finale, with its obsessive clinging to two descending melodic ideas supported by some of Tchaikovsky's most plangent harmonies. The result is the most explicit emotional declaration in all Tchaikovsky's works, a mixture of anguish, brooding and sorrow, which finally retreats into the subterranean gloom in which the whole symphony had started, fading into oblivion. It is not surprising that Tchaikovsky rated the Sixth Symphony as among the most sincere of his works.

Nine days later Tchaikovsky died. That he committed suicide cannot be doubted, but what precipitated this has not been conclusively established. In 1978 the Soviet scholar, Alexandra Orlova, revealed a narrative dictated to her in 1966 by the aged Alexander Voitov of the Russian Museum in Leningrad. According to this, a member of the Russian aristocracy had written a letter accusing the composer of a liaison with his nephew, and had entrusted it to Nikolay Jacobi, a high-ranking civil servant, for transmission to the tsar. Jacobi, like Tchaikovsky a former pupil of the School of Jurisprudence, feared the dishonour with which this disclosure would tarnish the 'school uniform', and hastily instituted a

10. Tchaikovsky's autograph sketches for the opening of the Allegro non troppo from the first movement of his Sixth Symphony ('Pathétique'), composed 1893 (USSR-Mcm)

court of honour (which included six of Tchaikovsky's contemporaries from the school) to decide how the scandal might be averted. Tchaikovsky was summoned to appear before this court on 31 October which, after more than five hours of deliberations, decreed that the composer should kill himself. Two days later the composer was mortally ill, almost certainly from arsenic poisoning. The story that he died of cholera from drinking unboiled water is fabrication.

Tchaikovsky was buried in the Alexander Nevsky cemetery in St Petersburg. A second performance of the Sixth Symphony on 18 November made a deep impression, the work being seen in retrospect as a premonition of the composer's own end.

9. TECHNIQUE AND STYLE. In spite of the heavy conditioning of his conservatory training, Tchaikovsky's innate Russianness and his love of his own country's folk music ensured that he could never become a mere imitator of Western practices and styles. In consequence, his work shows a remarkable range of character and technique, and this breadth was fostered further by the diverse expressive purposes he sought in his compositions, whether it was to fashion a poised 'Classical' form, simulate the elegance of the 18th-century Rococo, plunge into the bold, emancipated world of the Russian nationalists, or forge a musical language that might be a vehicle for his own overwrought emotions. Thus his fund of melody ranges from efficient, if not first-rate, inventions of a Western cast to folksong stylizations. On occasions he used folksongs themselves, and the influence of modal practices is heard repeatedly, if not very strongly, in his original tunes. Yet Tchaikovsky's most characteristic melodic types are the dance-tunes (especially waltzes) which fill not only his ballets, but spill over in profusion into all his other genres except church music, and the impassioned cantilenas, often of considerable strength of contour, whose full-blooded emotion is often heightened by harmonic support containing complementary expressive tensions. Tchaikovsky knew well and sometimes employed the characteristic repetitive trait of certain Russian folktunes that extend themselves by constant variations on a single motif. Yet the repetitions in his own tunes are normally sequential, thus reflecting Western practices, and may be extended at immense length. Clearly this almost obsessive dwelling on a single phrase was frequently conditioned by Tchaikovsky's emotional identification with the expressive properties of that phrase, and the release it afforded through such repetitions; so, too, the relentless reiteration to which he subjected certain of his tunes fulfilled a similar purpose. At times such repetitions result in expressive surfeit, but they can build into an emotional experience of almost unbearable intensity.

Though Tchaikovsky did experiment in unusual metres, his very Russian sense for dynamic rhythm was usually applied to provide a firm, essentially regular metre, as shown in his innumerable dance-tunes, where it is occasionally used with such elemental vigour that it becomes the main expressive agent. A strong metrical drive may also be used as a means of synthetic propulsion in a large-scale symphonic movement. Tchaikovsky also revealed a wide range of practice in his harmony. His first two quartets in particular show how thoroughly he was grounded in Western harmonic and textural procedures. At the opposite extreme are such unor-

thodox progressions as fill the centre of the finale to the Second Symphony, a movement that also includes one of the few applications in his work of the whole-tone scale in the bass. These last practices are not typical, however, and show the explicit influence of the Russian nationalists. Tchaikovsky's more normal harmonic language is based on relatively conventional progressions (the first love theme of *Romeo and Juliet*, for instance, is built over a circle of 5ths), though frequently such progressions involve a typically Russian liberality in the use of pedals, and also some sort of decorative chromaticism which gives it its individuality. Tchaikovsky's most favoured chromatic chord is the major triad on the flattened submediant in a major-key context, an elevation to the status of harmonic support of a note which had been, since Glinka, the favoured chromatic degree of the scale for Russian composers. But usually Tchaikovsky's chromaticism, like Glinka's, arises from contrapuntal decoration, ranging from single chromatic passing notes or dissonances to extended scales that may be set quite abrasively against the melody. A rare example of fundamental chromaticism occurs at the opening of the Second Quartet, the effect of which is, nevertheless, less close to that which Wagner was currently exploiting than to that to which Bartók came some 35 years later at the opening of his First Quartet. The harmonic palette of Tchaikovsky's later works is increasingly enriched by 7th chords and trenchant dissonance.

Most of Tchaikovsky's music involves the orchestra, and his textural practices become increasingly conditioned by considerations of orchestral colour. In spite of his grounding in Western orchestral practices, Tchaikovsky from the beginning showed a typically Russian disposition for bright and sharply differentiated orchestral colouring in the tradition initiated by Glinka. The mastery and resourcefulness with which he handled the orchestra is occasionally compromised by an excess and even brashness which disfigures the music as acutely as the overblown emotions that it is sometimes forced to bear. A tendency for the musical fabric itself to be conditioned by the orchestral sound envisaged by Tchaikovsky can be heard in the scherzo of the Third Symphony and in *Francesca da Rimini*, not only in the conventional tempest textures of the outer sections, but more significantly in certain of the accompaniment figurations of the central passage. In the scherzo of the *Manfred* symphony the process is carried much further, the result being a kaleidoscopic web of delicate sound of remarkable virtuosity. Much of the life of *The Nutcracker* ballet stems from the fascination of the orchestral textures and accompaniments. In the pieces mentioned it is primarily the fleet delicacy of the treble instruments that Tchaikovsky exploited, but this is balanced in the later music by a matching exploration of the darker, even gloomy sounds of the bass instruments.

Since his death Tchaikovsky has gained remarkable popularity. Yet the very directness of his utterance, founded primarily on his ability to fashion themes of remarkable eloquence and emotional power supported by matching harmony and rich orchestral resource, has often been interpreted as a sign of essential shallowness. Likewise the way in which his world of strong emotions has been freely plundered by composers of lower intentions has proved detrimental to his reputation. But when popular adulation and critical prejudice are set aside

Tchaikovsky can be seen as a composer who toiled unceasingly over creative problems, whose range was wide both in genre and in type of expression, who could bring to the solution of a structural problem a quite notable enterprise, and whose professional competence was of the highest.

WORKS

Edition: *P. I. Tchaikovsky: Polnoye sobraniye sochineniy* [Complete edition of compositions] (Moscow and Leningrad, 1940–71) [T]

(printed works published in Moscow unless otherwise stated)

STAGE

(* – full score; † – vocal score)

Op.	Title	Libretto	Composed	Published	First performance	T
—	Boris Godunov, music for Fountain Scene	Pushkin	?1863–4	lost	—	—
—	Dmitry Samozvanets i Vasily Shuysky [Dmitry the Pretender and Vasily Shuysky], 2 pieces, small orch:	Ostrovsky	by 11 Feb 1867	—	—	—
	Introduction			1955		xiv, 3
	Mazurka			1962		xiv, 8
—	Putanitsa [The tangle], couplets for the vaudeville	P. Fyodorov	Dec 1867	lost	Moscow, Dec 1867	
3	Voyevoda [The voyevoda], opera, 3 [destroyed by Tchaikovsky, reconstructed by Pavel Lamm; material used in Characteristic Dances, orch, 1864–5, and Potpourri, pf, 1868]	Ostrovsky and Tchaikovsky, after Ostrovsky: Son po Volge [A dream on the Volga]	20 March 1867–sum. 1868	1953	Moscow, Bol'shoy, 11 Feb 1869	*ia, b, v, †i suppl.
—	Recitatives and choruses for Auber's Le domino noir	—	Oct 1868	lost	Moscow, 1868	—
—	Undina [Undine], opera, 3 [destroyed by Tchaikovsky, 1873; frags. only]:	V. Sollogub, after Zhukovsky's trans. of F. de la Motte Fouqué	Jan–July 1869	Moscow and Leningrad, 1950	Moscow, 28 March 1870, excerpts only	
	Undine's aria					*ii, 3, †ii, 161
	Act 1 finale					*ii, 44, †ii, 169
—	Mandragora, opera, Chorus of Flowers and Insects only, mixed and children's vv, pf; orchd later	S. Rachinsky	8 Jan 1870; orchd by 25 Jan 1870	Moscow and Leningrad, 1950	Moscow, 30 Dec 1870	*ii. 92, †ii, 191
—	Oprichnik [The oprichnik], opera, 4	Tchaikovsky, after I. Lazhechnikov: Oprichniki [The oprichniks]	Feb 1870– April 1872	*St Petersburg, 1896, †St Petersburg, 1874	St Petersburg, Mariinsky, 24 April 1874	*iiia, b, †xxxiv
—	Le barbier de Séville, couplets 'Vous l'ordonnez' for Almaviva, 1v, 2 vn	Beaumarchais, trans. M. Sadovsky	by 24 Feb 1872	1906	Moscow, Conservatory, 24 Feb 1872	*xiv, 19
12	Snegurochka [The snow maiden], incidental music, solo vv, chorus, small orch	Ostrovsky	March–April 1873	*1895, †1873	Moscow, Bol'shoy (by Malïy Company), 23 May 1873	*xiv, 23
—	Kuznets Vakula [Vakula the smith], opera, 3 [rev. as Cherevichki]	Ya. Polonsky, after Gogol: Noch' pered rozhdestvom [Christmas eve]	June–2 Sept 1874	†1876	St Petersburg, Mariinsky, 6 Dec 1876	—
—	Recitatives for Mozart's Le nozze di Figaro	—	1875	†1884	Moscow, Conservatory, 17 May 1876	—
20	Lebedinoye ozero [Swan lake], ballet, 4	V. Begichev and V. Heltser	Aug 1875–22 April 1876	*1895, †1877	Moscow, Bol'shoy, 4 March 1877	*xi, †lvi
—	Evgeny Onegin [Eugene Onegin], lyric scenes, 3	K. Shilovsky and Tchaikovsky, after Pushkin	May 1877–1 Feb 1878	*1880, †1878	Moscow, Malïy, 29 March 1879	*iv, †xxxvi
—	Orleanskaya deva [The maid of Orleans], opera, 4	Tchaikovsky, after Zhukovsky's trans. of Schiller: Die Jungfrau von Orleans	17 Dec 1878–4 Sept 1879; rev. 1882	*1902, †1880	St Petersburg, Mariinsky, 25 Feb 1881	*va, b, †xxxvii
—	La fée, cradle song for the play Montenegrins receiving the news of Russia's declaration of war on Turkey, music for tableau, small orch	O. Feuillet	13 July 1879 8–11 Feb 1880	lost lost	Kamenka	—
—	Mazepa [Mazeppa], opera, 3	V. Burenin, rev. Tchaikovsky, after Pushkin: Poltava	sum. 1881–10 May 1883	*1899, †1883	Moscow, Bol'shoy, 15 Feb 1884	*via, b, †xxxviii
—	Cherevichki [The slippers] (Les caprices d'Oxane), comic–fantastic opera, 4 [rev. of Kuznets Vakula]	Ya. Polonsky, after Gogol: Noch' pered rozhdestvom [Christmas eve]	Feb–3 April 1885	*1898, †1885	Moscow, Bol'shoy, 31 Jan 1887	*viia, b, †xxxix
—	Charodeyka [The sorceress], opera, 4	I. Shpazhinsky	Sept 1885–18 May 1887	*1901, †1887	St Petersburg, Mariinsky, 1 Nov 1887	*viiia, b, †xla, b
—	Voyevoda, Domovoy's monologue, melodrama for the play	Ostrovsky	25–9 Jan 1886	1940	Moscow, Malïy, 31 Jan 1886	*xiv, 277
66	Spyashchaya krasavitsa [The sleeping beauty], ballet, prol, 3	M. Petipa and I. Vsevolozhsky, after C. Perrault: La belle au bois dormant	Dec 1888–1 Sept 1889	*1952, †1889	St Petersburg, Mariinsky, 15 Jan 1890	*xiia, b, v, g, †lvii

Op.	Title	Libretto	Composed	Published	First performance	T
68	Pikovaya dama [The queen of spades], opera, 3	M. and P. Tchaikovsky, after Pushkin	31 Jan–20 June 1890	*1891 †1890	St Petersburg, Mariinsky, 19 Dec 1890	*ix*a, b, v,* †xli
67a	Hamlet, incidental music, solo vv, small orch	Shakespeare	13 Jan–3 Feb 1891	*1896	St Petersburg, Mikhaylovsky, 21 Feb 1891	*xiv, 320
69	Iolanta [Iolanthe], lyric opera, 1	M. Tchaikovsky, after V. Zotov's trans. of H. Hertz's King René's Daughter	22 July–27 Dec 1891	*1892, †1892	St Petersburg, Mariinsky, 18 Dec 1892	*x, †xlii
71	Shchelkunchik [The nutcracker], fairy ballet, 2	M. Petipa, after A. Dumas *père*'s version of E. T. A. Hoffmann's Nussknacker und Mausekönig	Feb 1891–4 April 1892	*1892, †1892	St Petersburg, Mariinsky, 18 Dec 1892	*xiii*a, b,* †liv
—	Romeo and Juliet, duet, S, T, orch [partly based on orch fantasy ov.; incomplete, completed by Taneyev]	Shakespeare, trans. A. Sokolovsky	1893	1894	—	—

ORCHESTRAL
(for full orchestra unless otherwise stated)

Op.	Title, forces	Composed	Published/MS	First performance	T
—	Allegro ma non tanto, G, str	1863–4	—	—	—
—	Little Allegro, with introduction, D, 2 fl, str	1863–4	—	—	—
—	Andante ma non troppo, A, small orch	1863–4	—	—	—
—	Agitato and allegro, e, small orch	1863–4	—	—	—
—	Allegro vivo, c	1863–4	—	—	—
—	The Romans in the Coliseum, orch	1863–4	lost	—	—
76	Groza [The storm], ov., E, to Ostrovsky's play	sum. 1864	St Petersburg, 1896	St Petersburg, 7 March 1896	xxi, 3
—	Characteristic Dances [rev. as Dances of the Hay Maidens in opera Voyevoda]	wint. 1864–5	—	Pavlovsk, 11 Sept 1865	—
—	Overture, F				
	1st version for small orch	begun 27 Aug 1865	1952	St Petersburg, 26 Nov 1865	xxi, 85
	2nd version for full orch	Feb 1866	1952	Moscow, 16 March 1866	xxi, 121
—	Concert Overture, c	sum. 1865–?31 Jan 1866	1952	Voronezh, 1931	xxi, 213
13	Symphony no.1, g ('Winter daydreams')				
	1st version	March–Aug 1866	—	—	—
	2nd version	Nov–Dec 1866	—	Moscow, 15 Feb 1868	xv*a*
	3rd version	1874	1875	Moscow, 1 Dec 1883	—
15	Festival Ov., D, on the Danish national hymn [arr. pf 4 hands (1878), T l*a*]	22 Sept–24 Nov 1866	1892	Moscow, 11 Feb 1867	xxii, 1
77	Fatum [Fate], sym. poem, c [destroyed by Tchaikovsky, reconstructed 1896]	22 Sept–Dec 1868	St Petersburg, 1896	Moscow, 27 Feb 1869	xxii, 81
—	Romeo and Juliet, fantasy ov., b, after Shakespeare				
	1st version	7 Oct–27 Nov 1869	Moscow and Leningrad, 1950	Moscow, 16 March 1870	xxiii, 3
	2nd version	sum. 1870	Berlin, 1871	St Petersburg, 17 Feb 1872	xxiii, 199, frag. only
	3rd version	completed 10 Sept 1880	Berlin, 1881	Tbilisi, 1 May 1886	xxiii, 89
—	Serenade for Nikolay Rubinstein's name day, small orch	13 Dec 1872	1961	Moscow, 18 Dec 1872	xxiv, 3
17	Symphony no.2, c ('Little Russian')				
	1st version [arr. pf 4 hands (St Petersburg, 1874), T xlvii]	June–Nov 1872	1954	Moscow, 7 Feb 1873	xv*b*, 169
	2nd version [arr. pf 4 hands (St Petersburg, 1880), T xlvii]	Dec 1879–Jan 1880	St Petersburg, 1880	St Petersburg, 12 Feb 1881	xv*b*, 9
18	Burya [The tempest], sym. fantasia, f, after Shakespeare	19 Aug–22 Oct 1873	1877	Moscow, 19 Dec 1873	xxiv, 13
29	Symphony no.3, D ('Polish')	17 June–13 Aug 1875	1877	Moscow, 19 Nov 1875	xvi*a*
31	Slavonic March, B♭ [arr. pf 4 hands (1876)]	completed 7 Oct 1876	1880	Moscow, 17 Nov 1876	xxiv, 117
32	Francesca da Rimini, sym. fantasia, e, after Dante	7 Oct–17 Nov 1876	1878	Moscow, 9 March 1877	xxiv, 187
36	Symphony no.4, f	May 1877–7 Jan 1878	1880	Moscow, 22 Feb 1878	xvi*b*
43	Suite no.1, D [arr. pf 4 hands (1879)]	27 Aug 1878–Aug 1879	1879	Moscow, 23 Nov 1879	xix*a*
45	Italian Capriccio, A [arr. pf 4 hands (1880), T l*a*, 41]	16 Jan–27 May 1880	1880	Moscow, 18 Dec 1880	xxv, 3
48	Serenade, C, str [arr. pf 4 hands (1881)]	21 Sept–4 Nov 1880	1881	St Petersburg, 30 Oct 1881	xx, 301
49	1812, festival ov., E♭ [arr. pf, and pf 4 hands (1882)]	12 Oct–19 Nov 1880	1882	Moscow, 20 Aug 1882	xxv, 97
—	Festival Coronation March, D [arr. pf (1883)]	21 March–1 April 1883	1883	Moscow, 4 June 1883	xxv, 187
53	Suite no.2, C [movts 2–5 arr. pf 4 hands (1884)]	9 July–25 Oct 1883	1884	Moscow, 16 Feb 1884	xix*b*
55	Suite no.3, G [arr. pf 4 hands (1885)]	April–31 July 1884	1885	St Petersburg, 24 Jan 1885	xx, 3
—	Elegy, G, in honour of Ivan Samarin, str [used as Act 4 entr'acte, Hamlet, 1891]	18 Nov 1884	1890	Moscow, 28 Dec 1884	—

Op.	Title, forces	Composed	Published/MS	First performance	T
58	Manfred, sym., after Byron, b [arr. pf 4 hands, collab. A. Hubert (1886)]	April–4 Oct 1885	1886	Moscow, 23 March 1886	xviii
—	Jurists' March, D	completed 17 Nov 1885	1894		—
61	Suite no.4, G ('Mozartiana') [based on works by Mozart]	29 June–9 Aug 1887	—	Moscow, 26 Nov 1887	xx, 225
64	Symphony no.5, e	May–26 Aug 1888	1888	St Petersburg, 17 Nov 1888	—
67	Hamlet, fantasy ov., f, after Shakespeare	June–19 Oct 1888	1890	St Petersburg, 24 Nov 1888	xviia
78	Voyevoda [The voyevoda], sym. ballad, a, after Mickiewicz	Sept 1890–4 Oct 1891	St Petersburg, 1897	Moscow, 18 Nov 1891	xiv, 285
71a	Shchelkunchik [The nutcracker], suite from the ballet [arr. pf (1897)]	Jan–21 Feb 1892	1892	St Petersburg, 19 March 1892	—
—	Symphony no.7, E♭ [unfinished; sketches used for Pf Conc. no.3, and for Andante and Finale, pf, orch]	May–Dec 1892			—
74	Symphony no.6, b ('Pathétique') [arr. pf 4 hands (1893)]	16 Feb–31 Aug 1893	1894	St Petersburg, 28 Oct 1893	xviib

		SOLO INSTRUMENT AND ORCHESTRA			
23	Piano Concerto no.1, b♭	Nov 1874–21 Feb 1875	1879	Boston, 25 Oct 1875	xxviii, 5
	arr. 2 pf		1875		xlvia, 5
26	Sérénade mélancolique, b, vn, orch	Jan 1875	1879	Moscow, 28 Jan 1876	xxxa, 3
	arr. vn, pf		1876		—
33	Variations on a Rococo Theme, A, vc, orch	Dec 1876	1889	Moscow, 30 Nov 1877	—
	arr. vc, pf		1878		lvb, 5
34	Valse-scherzo, C, vn, orch	1877	1895	Paris, 20 Sept 1878	xxxa, 19
	arr. vn, pf		1878		—
35	Violin Concerto, D	17 March–11 April 1878	1888	Vienna, 4 Dec 1881	xxxa, 49
	arr. vn, pf		1878		—
44	Piano Concerto no.2, G	22 Oct 1879–10 May 1880	1881	New York, 12 Nov 1881	xxviii, 167
	arr. 2 pf		1880		xlvia, 131
56	Concert Fantasia, G, pf, orch	June–6 Oct 1884	1893	Moscow, 6 March 1885	xxix, 5
	arr. 2 pf		1884		xlvib, 5
62	Pezzo capriccioso, b, vc, orch	24–31 Aug 1887	1888	Moscow, 7 Dec 1889	—
	arr. vc, pf		1888		lvb, 43
75	Piano Concerto no.3, E♭ [1 movt; also named Allegro de concert and Konzertstück]	5 July–15 Oct 1893	1894	St Petersburg, 19 Jan 1895	xxix, 161
	arr. 2 pf		1894		xlvib, 73
79	Andante, B♭, Finale, E♭, pf, orch [unfinished; completed and orchd Taneyev]	begun after 15 Oct 1893	St Petersburg, 1897	St Petersburg, 20 Feb 1896	lxii, 3
	arr. 2 pf		St Petersburg, 1897		lxii, 137

		CHORAL			
—	[oratorio]	?1863–4	lost	—	
—	Na son gryadushchiy [At bedtime] (N. Ogaryov), unacc. chorus [arr. mixed chorus, orch (1960), T xxvii, 455]	1863–4	1941 [unacc.]	—	
—	K radosti (Ode to joy) (Schiller: An die Freude, trans. K. Axakov and others), cantata, S, A, T, B, chorus, orch	Nov–Dec 1865	1960	St Petersburg Conservatory, 10 Jan 1866	xxvii, 3
—	Priroda i lyubov [Nature and love] (Tchaikovsky), SSA, pf	Dec 1870	1894	Moscow, 28 March 1871	—
—	Cantata (Ya. Polonsky) in commemoration of the bicentenary of the birth of Peter the Great, T, chorus, orch	Feb–March 1872	1960	Moscow, 12 June 1872	xxvii, 189
—	Cantata (hymn) (N. Nekrasov) in celebration of the golden jubilee of Osip Petrov, T, chorus, orch	by 29 Dec 1875	1960	St Petersburg Conservatory, 6 May 1876	xxvii, 341
41	Liturgy of St John Chrysostom, unacc. chorus [arr. pf, 1879]	May–July 1878	1879	—	
—	Cantata, unacc. 4-pt. women's chorus	?Dec 1881	lost	—	
—	Vecher [Evening] (?Tchaikovsky), unacc. 3-pt. men's chorus	by 25 Dec 1881	1881	—	
52	Vesper Service, unacc. chorus (17 harmonizations of liturgical songs) [also with pf acc., 1882]	May 1881–7 Dec 1882	1882	—	
—	Couplets on a theme from Glinka's A Life for the Tsar, linked with the Russian National Anthem of A. Lvov	9–16 Feb 1883	after 1897	Moscow, Red Square, 22 May 1883	—
—	Moskva [Moscow] (A. Maykov), coronation cantata, Mez, Bar, chorus, orch	21 March–5 April 1883	score 1888; vocal score 1885	Moscow, Kremlin, 27 May 1883	xxvii, 361
—	9 sacred pieces, unacc. mixed chorus [also with pf acc., 1885]:				
	Kheruvimskaya pesnya [Cherubim's song], F	Nov 1884	1885		

Op.	Title, forces	Composed	Published/MS	First performance	T
	Kheruvimskaya pesnya, D				
	Kheruvimskaya pesnya, C				
	Tebe poyom [We sing to thee] (tune taken from the Ordinary)	April 1885			
	Dostoyno est' [It is very meet]				
	Otche nash [Our Father]				
	Blazhenni yazhe izbral [I, a blessed one, chose]				
	Da ispravitsya [Let my prayer ascend], 3vv, chorus				
	Nïne sili nebesnïye [Today the heavenly powers]				
—	Hymn in honour of SS Cyril and Methodius (Tchaikovsky), unacc. chorus, based on a Cz. hymn [arr. pf, 1885]	18–20 March 1885	1885	Moscow Conservatory, 18 April 1885	—
—	Song (Tchaikovsky) for the golden jubilee of the Imperial School of Jurisprudence, unacc. chorus	by 9 Oct 1885	1885	—	—
—	Blazhen, kto ulïbayetsya [Blessed is he who smiles] (Grand Duke Konstantin Romanov), unacc. 4-pt. men's chorus	19 Dec 1887	1889	Moscow, 20 March 1892	—
—	Angel vopiyashe [An angel crying], unacc. chorus	2 March 1887	1906	—	—
—	Nochevala tuchka zolotaya [The golden cloud has slept] (Lermontov), unacc. chorus	17 July 1887	1922	—	—
—	A greeting (Ya. Polonsky) to Anton Rubinstein for his golden jubilee as an artist, unacc. chorus	2–12 Oct 1889	1889	St Petersburg, Hall of the Court Assembly, 30 Nov 1889	—
54/5	Legenda [Legend] (Pleshcheyev), unacc. chorus [arr. of solo song]	by 27 Dec 1889	1890	—	—
—	Solovushka [The nightingale] (Tchaikovsky), unacc. chorus	by 27 Dec 1889	1890	Moscow, 25 Dec 1892	—
—	Ne kukushechka vo sirom boru ['Tis not the cuckoo in the damp pinewood] (N. Tsïganov), unacc. chorus	by 26 Feb 1891	1894	—	—
—	Bez porï, da bez vremeni [Without time, without season] (Tsïganov), unacc. 4-pt. women's chorus	by 26 Feb 1891	1894	—	—
—	Shto smolknul veseliya glas [The voice of mirth grew silent] (Pushkin), unacc. 4-pt. male chorus	by 26 Feb 1891	1894	—	—
—	Noch' [Night] (Tchaikovsky), SATB, pf [reworking of part of Mozart's Fantasia in c к475]	13–15 March 1893	1893	Moscow Conservatory, 21 Oct 1893	—
—	Vesna [Spring], unacc. women's chorus	—	lost	—	—

CHAMBER MUSIC

op.
— Adagio, C, 4 hn, 1863–4
— Adagio, F, 2 fl, 2 ob, 2 cl, eng hn, b cl, 1863–4
— Adagio molto, Eb, str qt, harp, 1863–4
— Allegretto, E, str qt, 1863–4
— Allegretto molto, D, str trio, 1863–4
— Allegro, c, pf sextet (pf, 2 vn, va, vc, db), 1863–4
— Allegro vivace, Bb, str qt, 1863–4
— Andante ma non troppo, e, prelude, str qt, 1863–4
— Andante molto, G, str qt, 1863–4
— String Quartet, Bb [1 movt only], begun 27 Aug 1865, completed by 11 Nov 1865 (1940), T xxxi, 3
11 String Quartet no.1, D [Andante cantabile arr. vc, str orch by Tchaikovsky, ?1886–8], Feb 1871 (1872), T xxxi, 25
22 String Quartet no.2, F, completed by 30 Jan 1874 (1876), T xxxi, 63
30 String Quartet no.3, eb [Andante funèbre arr. vn, pf by Tchaikovsky, 1877 (1877)], early Jan–1 March 1876 (1876), T xxxi, 115
42 Souvenir d'un lieu cher, vn, pf, March–May 1878 (1879):
  1 Méditation, d
  2 Scherzo, c
  3 Mélodie, Eb
50 Piano Trio, a, Dec 1881–9 Feb 1882 (1882), T xxxiia
70 Souvenir de Florence, str sextet, D, 24 June–Aug 1890 (opening sketched in 1887); rev. Dec 1891–Jan 1892 (1892), T xxxiib

PIANO

(for solo pf unless otherwise stated)

op.
— Valse, 1854, lost
— Piece on the tune Vozle rechki, vozle mostu [By the river, by the bridge], musical joke after Konstantin Lyadov, Sept–Dec 1862, lost
— Allegro, f, 1863–4, inc.
— Theme and variations, a, 1863–4 (1909), T lia, 3
80 Sonata, c#, 1865 (1900), T lia, 27
1 Two pieces, March 1867 (1867), T lia, 81:

1 Scherzo à la russe, Bb, on Ukrainian folktune (first called Capriccio)
2 Impromptu, eb, 1863–4
2 Souvenir de Hapsal, June–July 1867 (1868), T lia, 105:
  1 Ruines d'un château, e
  2 Scherzo, F
  3 Chant sans paroles, F
— Potpourri on themes from the opera Voyevoda, 1868 (1868) [pubd under pseud. Cramer], T lib, 197
4 Valse caprice, D, Oct 1868 (1868), T lib, 3
5 Romance, f, Nov 1868 (1868), T lib, 23
7 Valse-scherzo [no.1], A, by 15 Feb 1870 (1870), T lib, 31
8 Capriccio, Gb, by 15 Feb 1870 (1870), T lib, 43
9 Trois morceaux, by 7 Nov 1870 (1871), T lib, 57:
  1 Rêverie, D
  2 Polka de salon, Bb
  3 Mazurka de salon, d
10 Deux morceaux, Dec 1871 (1876), T lib, 81:
  1 Nocturne, F, also (1874)
  2 Humoresque, e [arr. vn, pf by Tchaikovsky, 1877]
19 Six morceaux, by 8 Nov 1873 (1874), T lib, 91:
  1 Rêverie du soir, g
  2 Scherzo humoristique, D
  3 Feuillet d'album, D
  4 Nocturne, c# [transcr. vc, small orch by Tchaikovsky, c1888]
  5 Capriccioso, Bb
  6 Thème original et variations, F
21 Six morceaux, composés sur un seul thème, by 12 Dec 1873 (St Petersburg, 1873), T lib, 139:
  1 Prélude, B
  2 Fugue à 4 voix, g#
  3 Impromptu, c#
  4 Marche funèbre, ab
  5 Mazurque, ab
  6 Scherzo, Ab
37b Les saisons, Dec 1875–Nov 1876 (1876), T liii, 3:
  1 Janvier: Au coin du feu, A

2   Février: Carnaval, D
3   Mars: Chant de l'alouette, g
4   Avril: Perce-neige, B♭
5   Mai: Les nuits de mai, G
6   Juin: Barcarolle, g
7   Juillet: Chant de faucheur, E♭
8   Août: La moisson, b
9   Septembre: La chasse, G
10 Octobre: Chant d'automne, d
11 Novembre: Troika, E
12 Décembre: Noël, A♭
—   Funeral March on themes from opera The Oprichnik, 19–28
    March 1877, lost
—   March for the Volunteer Fleet, C, 6 May 1878 (1878) [pubd under
    pseud. P. Sinopov], T lii, 65
39 Album pour enfants: 24 pièces faciles (à la Schumann), ?26 Feb–
    Oct 1878 (1878), T lii, 139 [Tchaikovsky's orig. sequence;
    nos. in brackets indicate Jürgenson's pubd order]:
    1 (1)   Prière de matin, G
    2 (2)   Le matin en hiver, D
    3 (4)   Maman, G
    4 (3)   Le petit cavalier, D
    5 (5)   Marches des soldats de bois, D
    6 (9)   La nouvelle poupée, B♭
    7 (6)   La poupée malade, g
    8 (7)   Enterrement de la poupée, c
    9 (8)   Valse, E♭
    10 (14) Polka, B♭
    11 (10) Mazurka, d
    12 (11) Chanson russe, F
    13 (12) Le paysan prélude, B♭
    14 (13) Chanson populaire (Kamarinskaya), D
    15 (15) Chanson italienne, D
    16 (16) Mélodie antique française, D
    17 (17) Chanson allemande, E♭
    18 (18) Chanson napolitaine, E♭
    19 (19) Conte de la vieille bonne, C
    20 (20) La sorcière (Baba Yaga), e
    21 (21) Douce rêverie, C
    22 (22) Chant de l'alouette, G
    23 (24) A l'église, e
    24 (23) L'orgue de barberie, G
40 Douze morceaux (difficulté moyenne), 24 Feb–12 May 1878
    (1879), T lii, 73
    1 Etude, g
    2 Chanson triste, g
    3 Marche funèbre, c
    4 Mazurka, C
    5 Mazurka, D
    6 Chant sans paroles, a
    7 Au village, a
    8 Valse, A♭
    9 Valse, f♯ [1st version, 16 July 1876; rev. 1878]
    10 Danse russe, a
    11 Scherzo, d
    12 Rêverie interrompue, f
37 Sonata, G, 13 March–7 Aug 1878 (1879), T lii, 173
51 Six morceaux, Aug–22 Sept 1882 (1889), T liii, 3:
    1 Valse de salon, A♭
    2 Polka peu dansante, b
    3 Menuetto scherzoso, E♭
    4 Natha-valse, A [1st version, 17 Aug 1878]
    5 Romance, F
    6 Valse sentimentale, f
—   Impromptu-caprice, G, 2 Oct 1884 (Paris, 1885), T liii, 57
59 Dumka: Russian rustic scene, c, 27 Feb–5 March 1886 (1886), T
    liii, 63
—   Valse-scherzo [no.2], A, by 28 Aug 1889 (1889), T liii, 77
—   Impromptu, A♭, 2–12 Oct 1889 (1897), T liii, 85
—   Aveu passioni, e, ?1892 (Moscow and Leningrad, 1949), T liii,
    229 [largely a transcr. of an episode in the sym. ballad The
    Voyevoda, 1890–91]
—   Military march [for the Yurevsky Regiment], B♭, 5 April–17 May
    1893 (1894), T liii, 91
72 Dix-huit morceaux, 19 April–4 May 1893 (1893), T liii, 97:
    1 Impromptu, f
    2 Berceuse, A♭
    3 Tendres reproches, c♯
    4 Danse caractéristique, D
    5 Méditation, D
    6 Mazurque pour danser, B♭
    7 Polacca de concert, E♭
    8 Dialogue, B
    9 Un poco di Schumann, D♭
    10 Scherzo-fantaisie, e♭
    11 Valse bleuette, E♭
    12 L'espiègle, E

13 Echo rustique, E♭
14 Chant élégiaque, D♭
15 Un poco di Chopin, c♯
16 Valse à cinq temps, D
17 Passé lointain, E♭
18 Scène dansante (invitation au trépak), C
—   Impromptu (Momento lirico), A♭, ?1893 (1898), T lxii, 295
    [inc.; completed by Taneyev]

SONGS AND DUETS
(all in T xliv–xlv)

op.
—   Pesnya Zemfirï [Zemfira's song] (Pushkin: Tsïganï) c1855–60, ed.
    in SovM (1940)
—   Moy geniy, moy angel, moy drug [My genius, my angel, my
    friend] (A. Fet: K Ofeliy [To Ophelia]), c1855–60, ed. in SovM
    (1940)
—   Mezza notte, c1855–60 (St Petersburg, c1865)
6   Six Songs, 27 Nov–29 Dec 1869 (1870): Ne ver, moy drug [Do
    not believe, my friend] (A. K. Tolstoy); Ni slova, o moy drug
    [Not a word, O my friend] (A. Pleshcheyev, after M. Hartmann:
    Molchaniye [Silence]); I bol'no, i sladko [Both painfully and
    sweetly] (E. Rostopchina: Slova dlya muzïki [Words for
    music]); Slyoza drozhit [A tear trembles] (A. K. Tolstoy);
    Otchevo? [Why?] (L. Mey, after Heine: Warum sind dann die
    Rosen so blas? from Lyrisches Intermezzo); Net, tolko tot, kto
    znal [No, only he who has known] (L. Mey, after Goethe: Nur
    wer die Sehnsucht kennt, Mignon's song from Wilhelm Meister,
    usually known in Eng. as None but the lonely heart
—   Zabït tak skoro [To forget so soon] (A. Apukhtin), 1870 (1873)
16 Six Songs, ?Dec 1872 (St Petersburg, 1873): Kolïbel'naya pesnya
    [Cradle song] (A. Maykov, from cycle Novogrecheskiye pesni
    [New Greek songs]), arr. pf, 1873; Pogodi [Wait] (N. Grekov);
    Poymi khotraz [Accept just one] (A. Fet); O, spoy zhe tu
    pesnyu [O sing that song] (A. Pleshcheyev, after Felicity
    Hemans: Mother O sing me to rest), arr. pf, and vn, pf, 1873;
    Tvoy obraz svetlïy [Thy radiant image] (Tchaikovsky), arr. pf,
    1872; Novogrecheskaya pesnya (V tyomnom ade) [In dark
    Hell] (A. Maykov, from cycle Novogrecheskiye pesni [New
    Greek songs])
—   Unosi moyo serdtse [Take my heart away] (Fet: Pevitse [The
    singer]), by 11 Oct 1873, ed. in Nouvelliste (1873)
—   Glazki vesnï golubïye [Blue eyes of spring] (M. Mikhaylov, after a
    poem from Heine's Die blauen Frühlingsaugen), by 11 Oct
    1873, ed. in Nouvelliste (1874)
25 Six Songs, Sept 1874–early 1875 (St Petersburg, 1875): Primireniye
    [Reconciliation] (N. Shcherbina); Kak nad goryacheyu zoloy
    [As o'er the burning ashes] (F. Tyutchev); Pesnya Minonï
    [Mignon's song] (F. Tyutchev, after Goethe's Kennst du das
    Land, from Wilhelm Meister); Kanareyka [The canary] (L.
    Mey); Ya s neyu nikogda ne govoril [I never spoke to her] (L.
    Mey, from cycle Oktavï [Octaves]); Kak naladili: Durak [As
    they reiterated: 'Fool'] (Mey: Pesnya [Song])
27 Six Songs, by 20 April 1875 (1875): Na son gryadushchiy [At
    bedtime] (N. Ogaryov); Smotri, von oblako [Look, yonder
    cloud] (Grekov; Stansï [Stanzas]); Ne otkhodi ot menya [Do
    not leave me] (Fet, from cycle, Melodii [Melodies]); Vecher
    [Evening] (Mey, after Shevchenko); Ali mat menya sozhala?
    [Was it the mother who bore me?] (Mey, after Mickiewicz);
    Moya balovnitsa [My spoilt darling] (Mey, after Mickiewicz);
    rev. later
28 Six Songs, by 23 April 1875 (1875): Net, nikogda ne nazovu [No,
    I shall never tell] (Grekov, after Musset: Chanson de fortunio);
    Korolki [The corals] (Mey, after L.-V. Kondratowicz); Zachem?
    [Why did I dream of you?] (Mey); On tak menya lyubil [He
    loved me so much] (?A. Apukhtin); Ni otzïva, ni slova, ni
    priveta [No response, or word, or greeting] (Apukhtin);
    Strashnaya minuta [The fearful minute] (Tchaikovsky)
—   Khotel bï v edinoye slovo [I should like in a single word] (Mey,
    after a poem in Heine's Die Heimkehr), by 10 July 1875, ed. in
    Nouvelliste (1875)
—   Ne dolgo nam gulyat [We have not far to walk] (Grekov), by 10
    July 1875, ed. in Nouvelliste (1875–6)
38 Six Songs, 23 Feb–8 June 1878 (1878): Serenada Don-Zhuana
    [Don Juan's serenade] (A. K. Tolstoy); To bïlo ranneyu vesnoy
    [It was in the early spring] (A. K. Tolstoy); Sred shumnovo bala
    [Amid the din of the ball] (A. K. Tolstoy); O, esli b tï mogla [O,
    if only you could for one moment] (A. K. Tolstoy); Lyubov
    mertvetsa [The love of a dead man] (Lermontov); Pimpinella
    (Tchaikovsky, from a Florentine popular song)
46 Six Duets, 16 June–5 Sept 1880 (1881): Vecher [Evening] (I.
    Surikov), S, Mez; Shotlandskaya ballada [Scottish ballad:
    Edward] (trans. A. K. Tolstoy), S, Bar; Slyozï [Tears] (F.
    Tyutchev), S, Mez; V ogorode, vozle brodu [In the garden, near
    the ford] (Surikov, after Shevchenko), S, Mez; Minula strast
    [Passion spent] (A. K. Tolstoy), S, T; Rassvet [Dawn]
    (Surikov), S, Mez, orchd, T xxvii
47 Seven Songs, July–Aug 1880 (1881): Kabï znala ya [If only I had

known] (A. K. Tolstoy); Gornimi tikho letala dusha nebesami [Softly the spirit flew up to heaven] (A. K. Tolstoy); Na zemlyu sumrak pal [Dusk fell on the earth] (N. Berg, after Mickiewicz); Usni, pechalnïy drug [Sleep, poor friend] (A. K. Tolstoy); Blagoslavlyayu vas, lesa [I bless you, forests] (A. K. Tolstoy, from John Damascene); Den li tsarit? [Does the day reign?] (Apukhtin), orchd 24 Feb 1888, lost; Ya li v pole da ne travushka bïla? [Was I not a little blade of grass?] (Surikov; Malorossïyskaya pesnya [Ukrainian song]), orchd by 7 Oct 1884, T xxvii

54   Sixteen Children's Songs, nos.1–15, 28 Oct–15 Nov 1883, no.16, 19 Jan 1881; nos.1–16 (1884): Babushka i vnuchek [Granny and grandson] (Pleshcheyev); Ptichka [The little bird] (Pleshcheyev: Podsnezhnik [The snowdrop], from a Pol. source); Vesna [Spring] (Pleshcheyev, from a Pol. source); Moy sadik [My little garden] (Pleshcheyev); Legenda [Legend] (When Jesus Christ was but a child) (Pleshcheyev, from an Eng. source), orchd 14 April 1884 (1890), T xxvii, 501, arr. unacc. mixed chorus by 27 Dec 1889; Na beregu [On the bank] (Pleshcheyev, from an Eng. source); Zimniy vecher [Winter evening] (Pleshcheyev); Kukushka [The cuckoo] (Pleshcheyev, after C. Gellert); Vesna (Uzh tayet sneg) [Spring (The snow is already melting)] (Pleshcheyev); Kolïbel'naya pesnya v buryu [Lullaby in a storm] (Pleshcheyev); Tsvetok [The flower] (Pleshcheyev, after L. Ratisbonne); Zima [Winter] (Pleshcheyev); Vesennyaya pesnya [Spring song] (Pleshcheyev); Osen [Autumn] (Pleshcheyev); Lastochka [The swallow] (Surikov, after T. Lenartowicz); Detskaya pesnya [Child's song] (K. Axakov) (1881)

57   Six Songs, no.1, ?early 1884; nos.2–6, Nov 1884; nos.1–6 (1885): Skazhi, o chom v teni vetvey [Tell me, what in the shade of the branches] (V. Sollogub); Na nivï zhyoltïye [On the golden cornfields] (A. K. Tolstoy); Ne sprashivay [Do not ask] (A. Strugovshchikov, after Goethe's Heiss mich nicht reden, from Wilhelm Meister); Usni [Sleep] (D. Merezhkovsky); Smert' [Death] (Merezhkovsky); Lish tï odin [Only thou alone] (Pleshcheyev, after A. Kristen)

60   Twelve Songs, 31 Aug–20 Sept 1886; nos. 1–6 (1886), nos. 7–12 (1887): Vcherashnyaya noch' [Last night] (A. Khomyakov: Nachtstück); Ya tebe nichevo ne skazhu [I'll tell you nothing] (Fet, from cycle Melodiy [Melodies]); O, esli b znali vï [O, if only you knew] (Pleshcheyev); Solovey [The nightingale] (Pushkin, after V. Stefanović Karadžić: Songs of the western Slavs); Prostïye slova [Simple words] (Tchaikovsky); Nochi bezumnïye [Frenzied nights] (Apukhtin); Pesn' tsïganki [Gypsy's song] (Ya. Polonsky); Prosti [Forgive] (N. Nekrasov); Noch' [Night] (Polonsky); Za oknom v teni melkayet [Behind the window in the shadow] (Polonsky: Vïzov [Challenge]); Podvig [Exploit] (A. Khomyakov); Nam zvezdï krotkiye siyali [The mild stars shone for us] (Pleshcheyev: Slova dlya muzïki [Words for music])

63   Six Songs (Grand Duke Konstantin Romanov), Nov–Dec 1887 (1888): Ya snachala tebya ne lyubila [I did not love you at first]; Rastvoril ya okno [I opened the window]; Ya vam ne navlyus [I do not please you]; Pervoye svidaniye [The first meeting]; Uzh gasli v komnatakh ogni [The fires in the rooms were already out]; Serenada [O ditya, pod okoshkom tvoim) [Serenade (O child, beneath thy window)]

65   Six Songs (Fr. texts, trans. A. Gorchakova), sum.–22 Oct 1888 (1889): Sérénade (Où vas-tu, souffle d'aurore) (E. Turquéty: Aurore); Déception (P. Collin); Sérénade (J'aime dans le rayon de la limpide aurore) (Collin); Qu'importe que l'hiver (Collin); Les larmes (A.-M. Blanchecotte); Rondel (Collin)

73   Six Songs (D. Rathaus), 5–17 May 1893 (1893): Mï sideli s toboy [We sat together] (from cycle Romansï [Songs]); Noch' [Night]; V etu lunnuyu noch' [In this moonlight]; Zakatilos solntse [The sun has set]; Sred mrachnïkh dnei ['Mid sombre days] (from cycle Romansï [Songs]); Snova, kak prezhde, odin [Again, as before, alone]

—   Kto idyot? [Who goes?] (Apukhtin), lost

ARRANGEMENTS AND EDITIONS

Weber: Scherzo, Pf Sonata, op.39 (J199), orchd 1863
Beethoven: 1st movt, Pf Sonata, op.31 no.2, orchd ?1863; 4 versions
Beethoven: 1st movt, Vn Sonata, op.47 ('Kreutzer'), orchd 1863–4
Gung'l: Valse: Le retour, pf, orchd 1863–4
Schumann: Adagio and Allegro brillante from Etudes symphoniques, op.13, orchd 1864
K. Kral: Triumphal March, pf, orchd May 1867
Dargomïzhsky: Malorossïyskiy kazachok [Little Russian kazachok], fantasia, arr. pf 1868
E. Tarnovskaya: Ya pomnyu vsyo [I remember all], song transcr. pf by Dubuque, arr. pf 4 hands 1868
50 Russ. folksongs, arr. pf 4 hands, ?aut. 1868 (nos.1–25), and by 7 Oct 1869 (nos.26–50) [1–25 taken mostly from the collection of K. Villebois; 25–50 taken from Balakirev's collection, except no.47, collected by Tchaikovsky], T lxi, 3

A. Rubinstein: Ivan Groznïy [Ivan the Terrible], musical picture, orch, arr. pf 4 hands 8 Oct–11 Nov 1869
A. Dubuque: Maria-Dagmar, polka, pf, orchd 1869
Dargomïzhsky: Nochevala tuchka zolotaya [The golden cloud has slept], 3vv, pf, pf pt. orchd 1870
A. Rubinstein: Don Quixote, musical picture, orch, arr. pf 4 hands 1870
Stradella: O del mio dolce, aria, 1v, pf, orchd 10 Nov 1870
Cimarosa: Trio Le faccio un inchino from Il matrimonio segreto, orch from vocal score 1870
Weber: Finale (Perpetuum mobile) from Pf Sonata, op.24 (J138), transcr. pf L.H. only 1871
V. Prokunin: 66 Russ. folksongs, ed. 1872, T lxi, 61
M. A. Mamontova: A Collection of Children's Songs on Russ. and Ukrainian Melodies, harmonized by 7 Sept 1872 (1st issue of 24 songs), and by May 1877 (2nd issue of 19 songs), T lxi, 169
Anon.: Gaudeamus igitur, arr. for 4-pt. men's chorus, pf 1874
Haydn: Gott erhalte, Austrian national anthem, orchd by 24 Feb 1874
Schumann: Ballade vom Haideknaben, op.121 no.1, declamation, 1v, pf, orchd 11 March 1874
Liszt: Der König in Thule, 1v, pf, orchd 3 Nov 1874
Bortnyansky: Complete church music, ed. 3 July–8 Nov 1881
Mozart: 4 pieces, usually known as Suite no.4 ('Mozartiana'): Gigue (K574); Minuet (K355); Ave verum corpus (K618); Theme and 10 variations on a theme of Gluck from La rencontre imprévue (K455), orchd 29 June–9 Aug 1887, T xx, 225
H. Laroche: Karmozina: fantasy ov., pf, orchd 27 Aug–27 Sept 1888
S. Menter: Ungarische Zigeunerweisen, pf, arr. pf, orch 1893

WRITINGS

Diaries, 1858–9 (destroyed by accident, 1866), 1873, 1882 (lost), 1884–91 (1885 lost; 1888 pubd as 'Avtobiograficheskoye opisaniye puteshestviya za granitsu v 1888 godu', 1894 [see below])
57 reviews or critical articles pubd in journals, 1868–76; first pubd collectively in 1898 [see Bibliography, 'Source material']; full list in Dombayev
Rukovodstvo k prakticheskomu izucheniyu garmoniy [Guide to the practical study of harmony], completed 14 Aug 1871 (1872)
Kratkiy uchebnik garmoniy, prisposoblennïy k chteniyu dukhovno-muzïkal'nïkh sochineniy v Rossiy [A short manual of harmony, adapted to the study of religious music in Russia], 1874 (1875)
'Avtobiograficheskoye opisaniye puteshestviya za granitsu v 1888 godu' [Autobiographical description of a journey abroad in 1888], *Russkiy vestnik* (1894), no.2, pp.165–203
Autobiography, 1889, lost
'Vagner i evo muzïka' [Wagner and his music], *Morning Journal* (New York, 3 May 1891)
'Beseda s Chaykovskim v noyabre 1892 g. v Peterburge' [A conversation with Tchaikovsky in November 1892 in St Petersburg], *Peterburgskaya zhizn'* (24 Nov 1892)
Editing and correcting of musical terms in *Slovar' russkovo yazïka* [Dictionary of the Russian language], ii–iii, Oct 1892–3 (1892 and 1895)

TRANSLATIONS

F.-A. Gevaert: *Traité général d'instrumentation* (1863), sum. 1865 (1866)
Meyerbeer: *Les Huguenots*: Urbain's cavatina 'Une dame noble et sage', by 17 June 1868 (1868)
Schumann: *Musikalische Haus- und Lebensregeln* (1850), by 1 Aug 1868 (1869)
J. C. Lobe: *Katechismus der Musik* (1851), completed 20 Nov 1869 (1870)
Trans. from the Ger. of texts used by A. Rubinstein:
12 persische Lieder, op.34 (F. von Bodenstedt, after Mirza Shafi), by 24 Dec 1869 (1870)
4 songs, op.32 nos.1 and 6 and op.33 nos.2 and 4, ?1870–71 (?1871)
6 romances, op.72, ?1870–71 (?1871)
6 romances, op.76, ?1871 (?1872)
3 songs, op.83 nos.1, 5 and 9, ?1871 (?1872)
Mozart: Le nozze di Figaro, trans. of da Ponte's lib, 1875 (1884)
Trans. from the It. of 6 texts used by Glinka, by 27 Dec 1877 (1878): Mio ben, ricordati; Ho perduto il mio tesoro; Mi sento il cor traffigere; Pur nel sonno; Tu sei figlia; Molitva [Prayer] (vocal qt)
Handel: Israel in Egypt, trans. of text (collab. Taneyev), 1886 (1912)

BIBLIOGRAPHY

CATALOGUES AND BIBLIOGRAPHIES

B. Jürgenson, ed.: *Catalogue thématique des oeuvres de P. Tschaikowsky* (Moscow, 1897/R1965)
M. Shemanin: 'Literatura o P. I. Chaykovskom za 17 let (1917–34)' [Literature about Tchaikovsky, 1917–34], *Muzïkal'noye nasledstvo* (Moscow, 1935)
Z. V. Korotkova-Leviton and others, eds.: *Avtografï P. I. Chaykovskovo v arkhive Doma-Muzeya v Klinu: spravochnik* [Tchaikovsky: autographs in the House Museum, Klin: a guide] (Moscow and Leningrad, 1950)
V. A. Kiselyov, ed.: *Avtografï P. I. Chaykovskovo v fondakh Gosudarstvennovo tsentralnovo muzeya muzïkal'novo kulturï imeni*

M. I. Glinki: katalog-spravochnik [Tchaikovsky's autographs in the State Central Glinka Museum of Musical Culture: catalogue] (Moscow, 1956)

G. S. Dombayev: *Tvorchestvo P. I. Chaykovskovo* [Tchaikovsky's works] (Moscow, 1958)

SOURCE MATERIAL

H. Laroche, ed.: *P. I. Chaykovsky: muzïkal'noye feletonï i zametki* (Moscow, 1898; Ger. trans., 1899, as *Musikalische Erinnerungen und Feuilletons*)

P. I. Tchaikovsky: *Guide to the Practical Study of Harmony* (Leipzig, 1900)

S. M. Lyapunov, ed.: *Perepiska M. A. Balakireva s P. I. Chaykovskim* [Balakirev's correspondence with Tchaikovsky] (St Petersburg, 1913); repr. in *M. A. Balakirev: vospominaniya i pis'ma*, ed. A. Orlova (Leningrad, 1962), 115–203

M. Tchaikovsky, ed.: *Pis'ma P. I. Chaykovskovo i S. I. Taneyeva* [Letters of Tchaikovsky and Taneyev] (Moscow, 1916); ed. V. A. Zhdanov (Moscow, 1951)

I. I. Tchaikovsky, ed.: *P. Chaykovsky: dnevniki (1873–1891)* [Diaries 1873–91] (Moscow and Petrograd, 1923; Eng. trans., 1945)

V. A. Zhdanov and N. T. Zhegin, eds.: *P. Chaykovsky: perepiska s N. F. von Meck* [Correspondence with Nadezhda von Meck] (Moscow and Leningrad, 1934–6)

——: *P. Chaykovsky: perepiska s P. I. Yurgensonom* [Correspondence with Jürgenson] (Moscow, 1938–52)

V. Yakovlev, ed.: *Dni i godï P. I. Chaykovskovo* [The days and years of Tchaikovsky] (Moscow and Leningrad, 1940)

T. Sokolova, ed.: *P. Chaykovsky: muzïkal'no-kriticheskiye stat'i* (Moscow, 1953)

P. Chaykovsky: literaturnïye proizvedeniya i perepiska [Literary works and correspondence] (Moscow, 1953–)

V. A. Zhdanov, ed.: *P. Chaykovsky: pis'ma k blizkim* [Letters to relatives] (Moscow, 1955)

K. Klindworth: 'Unveröffentlichte Briefe an Tschaikowsky', *Musik und Geschichte*, xv (1965), 547

L. Atanova, ed.: 'Pis'ma k P. I. Chaykovskomu' [Letters to Tchaikovsky], *SovM* (1966), no.5, p.112

BIOGRAPHIES AND STUDIES

H. A. Laroche: *Na pamyat' o P. I. Chaykovskom* [In memory of Tchaikovsky] (St Petersburg, 1894)

——: *Pamyati Chaykovskovo* [Memories of Tchaikovsky] (St Petersburg, 1894)

V. V. Stasov: *Sobraniye sochineny* [Collected works], iii (St Petersburg, 1894)

V. S. Baskin: *P. I. Chaykovsky* (St Petersburg, 1895)

H. A. Laroche: *Chaykovsky kak dramaticheskiy kompozitor* [Tchaikovsky as a dramatic composer] (St Petersburg, 1895); orig. in *EIT 1893–4*

N. D. Kashkin: *Vospominaniya o P. I. Chaykovskom* [Reminiscences of Tchaikovsky] (Moscow, 1896, 2/1954)

I. Pryashnikov: 'P. I. Chaykovsky v role muzïkal'novo kritika', *RMG* (1896), 1001

V. V. Bessel: 'Moi vospominaniya o P. I. Chaykovskom' [My reminiscences of Tchaikovsky], *EIT 1896–7*

G. Timofeyev: *P. I. Chaykovsky v role muzïkal'novo kritika* [Tchaikovsky in the role of music critic] (St Petersburg, 1899)

I. Knorr: *Peter Jljitsch Tschaikowsky* (Berlin, 1900)

K. de-Lazari: 'Vospominaniya o P. I. Chaykovskom' [Reminiscences of Tchaikovsky], *Rossiya* (1900), nos.388, 393, 405, 441

R. Newmarch: *Tchaikovsky: his Life and Works* (London, 1900)

M. I. Tchaikovsky: *P. I. Chaykovsky* [Tchaikovsky's life] (Moscow, 1900–02; Eng. trans., abridged, 1906)

E. Newman: 'The Essential Tchaikovsky', *Contemporary Review*, lxxix (1901), 887

D. G. Mason: *From Grieg to Brahms: Studies in some Modern Composers* (New York, 1902)

E. Evans: *Tchaikovsky* (London, 1906, rev. 2/1935)

R. Genik: 'Fortepiannoye tvorchestvo Chaykovskovo' [Tchaikovsky's piano works], *RMG* (1908)

I. A. Klimenko: *Moi vospominaniya o P. I. Chaykovskom* [My reminiscences of Tchaikovsky] (Ryazan, 1908)

N. A. Rimsky-Korsakov: *Letopis' moyey muzïkal'noy zhizni* (St Petersburg, 1909; Eng. trans., 1942)

A. Tchaikovskaya: 'Vospominaniya vdovï P. I. Chaykovskovo' [Reminiscences of Tchaikovsky's widow] (1913)

R. Newmarch: 'Tchaikovsky', *The Russian Opera* (London, 1914), 334

I. Glebov and V. Yakovlev: *Proshloye russkoy muzïki ... I. P. I. Chaykovsky* [The past of Russian music: 1. Tchaikovsky] (Petrograd, 1920)

I. Glebov: *P. I. Chaykovsky: evo zhizn' i tvorchestvo* [Life and works] (Petrograd, 1922)

——: *Instrumental'noye tvorchestvo Chaykovskovo* [Tchaikovsky's instrumental works] (Petrograd, 1922)

H. A. Laroche: *Sobraniye muzïkal'no-kriticheskikh statey* [Collected critical articles on music] (Moscow, 1922–4)

I. Glebov: *Chaykovsky: opït kharakteristiki* [An attempt at a description] (Petrograd and Berlin, 1923)

E. Blom: 'The Early Tchaikovsky Symphonies', *The Stepchildren of Music* (London, 1925), 153

——: *Tchaikovsky: Orchestral Works* (London, 1927)

N. F. Findeizen: *Kamernaya muzïka Chaykovskovo* [Tchaikovsky's chamber music] (Moscow, 1930)

R. Felber: 'Tchaikovsky and Tolstoy', *The Chesterian*, xci (1931), 65

G. Abraham: 'Tchaikovsky Revalued', *Studies in Russian Music* (London, 1935), 334

A. Budyakovsky: *P. I. Chaykovsky: simfonicheskaya muzïka* [Symphonic music] (Leningrad, 1935)

D. F. Tovey: *Essays in Musical Analysis* (London, 1935–9) [vols.ii and vi incl. studies of Tchaikovsky's Syms. nos.5 and 6]

G. Abraham and M. D. Calvocoressi: *Masters of Russian Music* (London, 1936) [incl. G. Abraham: 'Tchaikovsky', 249–334; rev. and repr. 1944 as *Tchaikovsky: a Short Biography*]

R. Fiske: 'Tchaikovsky's Later Piano Concertos', *MO*, lxii (1938), 17, 114, 209

G. Abraham: *On Russian Music* (London, 1939) [incl. 'The Programme of the *Pathétique* Symphony', 143; '*Eugene Onegin* and Tchaikovsky's Marriage', 225]

——: 'Tchaikovsky: some Centennial Reflections', *ML*, xxi (1940), 110

V. M. Bogdanov-Berezovsky: *Opernoye i baletnoye tvorchestvo Chaykovskovo* [Tchaikovsky's operas and ballets] (Leningrad and Moscow, 1940)

I. Glebov: *Pamyati P. I. Chaykovskovo* [Memories of Tchaikovsky] (Leningrad and Moscow, 1940)

I. Kolodin, ed.: *The Critical Composer: the Musical Writings of Berlioz, Wagner, Schumann, Tchaikovsky and Others* (New York, 1940)

A. I. Shaverdyan, ed.: *Chaykovsky i teatr* [Tchaikovsky and the theatre] (Moscow, 1940)

J. Westrup: 'Tchaikovsky and the Symphony', *MT*, lxxxi (1940), 249

V. V. Yakovlev: *Chaykovsky na moskovskoy stsene: pervïye postanovki v godï evo zhizni* [Tchaikovsky on the Moscow stage: first performances during his life] (Moscow and Leningrad, 1940)

SovM (1940), nos.5–6 [special Tchaikovsky issue]

B. V. Asaf'yev: '*Evgeny Onegin*': opït intonatsionnovo analiza stilya i muzïkal'noy dramaturgii [An attempt at intonation analysis of style and musical dramaturgy] (Moscow and Leningrad, 1944)

G. Abraham, ed.: *Tchaikovsky: a Symposium* (London, 1945)

H. Weinstock: *Tchaikovsky* (London, 1946)

D. Shostakovich and others: *Russian Symphony: Thoughts about Tchaikovsky* (New York, 1947)

B. Yarustovsky: *Opernaya dramaturgiya Chaykovskovo* [Tchaikovsky's operatic dramaturgy] (Moscow and Leningrad, 1947)

E. Orlova: *Romansï Chaykovskovo* [Tchaikovsky's songs] (Moscow and Leningrad, 1948)

A. A. Nikolayev: *Fortepianovye naslediye Chaykovskovo* [Tchaikovsky's piano legacy] (Moscow and Leningrad, 1949, 2/1958)

D. V. Zhitomirsky: *Baletï P. I. Chaykovskovo* [Tchaikovsky's ballets] (Moscow and Leningrad, 1950, 2/1958)

A. A. Al'shvang: *Opït analiza tvorchestva P. I. Chaykovskovo* [An attempt to analyse Tchaikovsky's works] (Moscow and Leningrad, 1951)

B. V. Asaf'yev: *Izbrannïye rabotï o P. I. Chaykovskom* [Selected works on Tchaikovsky], *Izbrannïye trudï*, ii, ed. E. Orlova (Moscow, 1952)

V. Ferman: '*Cherevichki* (*Kuznets Vakula*) Chaykovskovo i *Noch' pered rozhdestvom* Rimskovo-Korsakova: opït sravneniya' [Tchaikovsky's *The Slippers* and Rimsky-Korsakov's *Christmas Eve*: an attempt at comparison], *Voprosï muzïkoznaniya*, i, ed. A. S. Ogolevets (1953–4), 205

A. A. Nikolayev: *Fortepiannoye proizvedeniya P. I. Chaykovskovo* [Tchaikovsky's piano works] (Moscow, 1957)

V. V. Protopopov and N. V. Tumanina: *Opernoye tvorchestvo Chaykovskovo* [Tchaikovsky's operas] (Moscow, 1957)

K. Yu. Davïdova and V. V. Protopopov: *Muzïkal'noye naslediye Chaykovskovo* [Tchaikovsky's musical legacy] (Moscow, 1958)

G. S. Dombayev: *P. I. Chaykovsky i mirovaya kul'tura* [Tchaikovsky and world culture] (Moscow, 1958)

N. S. Nikolayeva: *Simfonii P. I. Chaykovskovo* [Tchaikovsky's symphonies] (Moscow, 1958)

L. N. Raaben: *Skripichnïye i violonchel'nïye proizvedeniya P. I. Chaykovskovo* [Tchaikovsky's violin and cello works] (Moscow, 1958)

A. A. Al'shvang: *P. I. Chaykovsky* (Moscow, 1959)

E. Gershkovich: 'Novïye materialï o P. I. Chaykovskom' [New material on Tchaikovsky], *SovM* (1959), no.1, p.73

G. Abraham: 'Russia', *A History of Song*, ed. D. Stevens (London, 1960), 338

A. N. Dol'zhansky: *Muzïka Chaykovskovo: simfonicheskiye proizvedeniya* [Symphonic works] (Leningrad, 1960)

D. Brown: 'Balakirev, Tchaikovsky and Nationalism', *ML*, xlii (1961), 227

A. Dol'zhansky: *Simfonicheskaya muzïka Chaykovskovo* [Tchaikovsky's symphonic music] (Moscow, 1961, 2/1965)

G. V. Krauklis: *Skripichnïye proizvedeniya P. I. Chaykovskovo* [Tchaikovsky's violin works] (Moscow, 1961)

G. Abraham: 'Tchaikovsky's First Opera', *Festschrift Karl Gustav*

Fellerer (Regensburg, 1962), 12

E. E. Bortnikova and others, eds.: *Vospominaniya o P. I. Chaykovskom* [Reminiscences of Tchaikovsky] (Moscow, 1962)

Yu. L. Davïdov: *Zapiski o P. I. Chaykovskom* [Notes on Tchaikovsky] (Moscow, 1962)

N. Tumanina: *Chaykovsky: put' k masterstvu* [Path to mastery] (Moscow, 1962)

——: *Chaykovsky* (Moscow, 1962–8)

I. F. Kunin, ed.: *P. I. Chaykovsky o simfonicheskoy muzïke* [Tchaikovsky on symphonic music] (Moscow, 1963)

B. I. Rabinovich, ed.: *P. I. Chaykovsky i narodnaya pesnya* [Tchaikovsky and folksong] (Moscow, 1963)

K. E. von Mühlendahl: *Die Psychose Tschaikowskis und der Einfluss seiner Musik auf gleichartige Psychotiker* (diss., U. of Munich, 1964)

A. Yakovlev: *Izbrannïye trudï o muzïke* [Selected works on music], ed. D. Zhitomirsky and T. Sokolova (Moscow, 1964)

J. Clapham: 'Dvorak's Visit to Russia', *MQ*, li (1965), 493

K. Davïdov: *Klinskiye godï tvorchestva Chaykovskovo* [Tchaikovsky's works in his Klin years] (Moscow, 1965)

A. Al'shvang: *P. I. Chaykovsky* (Moscow, 1967)

R. Thomas: 'Tschaikowskys Es-Dur-Sinfonie und Idee einer Sinfonie "Das Leben"', *NZM*, Jg.128 (1967), 160

G. Abraham: *Slavonic and Romantic Music* (London, 1968)

V. Fédorov: 'Tchaikovsky et la France', *RdM*, liv/1 (1968), 16

D. Lloyd-Jones: 'A Background to Iolanta', *MT*, cix (1968), 225

J. Friskin: 'The Text of Tchaikovsky's B flat minor Concerto', *ML*, l (1969), 246

L. Koniskaya: *Chaykovsky v Peterburge* [Tchaikovsky in St Petersburg] (Leningrad, 1969)

J. Warrack: *Tchaikovsky Symphonies and Concertos* (London, 1969)

Chaykovsky i zarubyozhnïye muzïkantï: izbrannïye pis'ma inostrannïkh korrespondentov [Tchaikovsky and foreign musicians: selected letters from foreign correspondents] (Leningrad, 1970)

V. Blok: 'Na puti k Pateticheskoy' [On the path to the *Pathétique*], *SovM* (1970), no.9, p.78

E. Balabanovich: *Chekhov i Chaykovsky* (Moscow, 1973)

E. Garden: *Tchaikovsky* (London, 1973)

G. von Meck: *As I Remember them* (London, 1973)

J. Warrack: *Tchaikovsky* (London, 1973)

E. Garden: 'Tchaikovsky and Tolstoy', *ML*, lv (1974), 307

U. Niebuhr: 'Der Einfluss Anton Rubinsteins auf die Klavierkonzerte Peter Tschaikovskys', *Mf*, xxvii (1974), 412

V. Volkoff: *Tchaikovsky* (Boston and London, 1974)

D. Brown: *Tchaikovsky: a Biographical and Critical Study*, i: *The Early Years (1840–1874)* (London, 1978)

E. Garden: 'Three Russian Piano Concertos', *ML*, lx (1979), 166

J. Warrack: *Tchaikovsky Ballet Music* (London, 1979)

A. Orlova: 'Tchaikovsky: the Last Chapter', *ML*, lx (1979)

DAVID BROWN

Tchaikowsky, André (*b* Warsaw, 1 Nov 1935). British pianist of Polish birth. Having lost his parents during the Nazi occupation, he was smuggled from Poland to Paris, but returned at the age of ten to enter the State Music School in Łódz. In 1948 the Polish government allowed him two years at the Paris Conservatoire, after which he studied the piano and composition at the Warsaw Conservatory (1950–56). In 1957 he attended the American Conservatory at Fontainebleau for further tuition in composition with Nadia Boulanger, and also had private piano lessons from Stefan Askenase. He made his American début in 1957, and introduced himself to London in 1958, settling in England soon afterwards. His repertory extends from Bach to 20th-century music (excluding the avant garde) with Mozart as a favourite. Though sometimes over-subjective and romantically pliable in music requiring a firm backbone, he is an exuberant natural musician with an intimate understanding of what a keyboard can yield. Composition interests him as much as the piano, and among his main works are a sonata for clarinet and piano (1959), a string quartet (1967), a cycle of Inventions for piano (1960–61), a piano concerto (1966–71) and two song cycles.

JOAN CHISSELL

Tcherepnin [Cherepnin]. Russo-Franco-American family of composers.

(1) Nikolay (Nikolayevich) Tcherepnin (*b* St Petersburg, 15 May 1873; *d* Paris, 26 June 1945). Conductor and composer. He was a pupil at the St Petersburg Conservatory of Rimsky-Korsakov, by whom his own early music was much influenced and the Parisian première of whose *Golden Cockerel* he supervised in 1908. Before leaving the conservatory in 1898 he had already appeared as a pianist and conductor in the capital and the provinces. Appointments with the Belyayev Symphony Concerts, at the Mariinsky Theatre and the Imperial Opera (1908) followed, and in 1909 he was engaged by Dyagilev to conduct the celebrated first season of the Ballets Russes in Paris, where his own ballet *Le pavillon d'Armide* was notably successful; the 1911 season featured his *Narcisse et Echo*. In 1918 he was appointed director of the National Conservatory of Tbilisi, where for three years he was also conductor at the Opera. In 1921 he took his family to Paris, where Pavlova commissioned ballets from him, among them *L'oiseau enchanté* and *Romance of the Mummy*; he also assumed control of the Russian Conservatory in Paris. The French capital remained his home for the rest of his life, although he made many conducting tours of Europe and in 1923 prepared and directed in Monte Carlo the first performance of *Sorochintsy Fair*, for which he completed Musorgsky's score. In 1932 he appeared as guest conductor with the Boston SO in a programme of his own compositions.

Tcherepnin's music is basically traditionalist. The faery fantasy world of Rimsky-Korsakov dominates such orchestral works as the *Prélude pour la princesse lointaine* op.4 and *Le royaume enchanté*, while the ballet *Narcisse et Echo*, and other compositions which postdate his encounter with modern French music, contain elements of impressionism: two works inspired by Poe, the ballet *Le masque de la mort rouge* and the orchestral *Trois fragments symphoniques*, are couched in a Franco-Russian idiom similar to that employed by Florent Schmitt. However, the Russian note asserted itself increasingly during Tcherepnin's years of exile, particularly in the operas *Swat* (1930) and *Vanka* (1932), both of which are more strongly nationalist in character than anything he had composed previously. Later works, such as the orchestral suite *Chants sacrés*, the three liturgies for unaccompanied chorus and, most importantly, the oratorio *La descente de la Sainte Vierge à l'enfer*, all reflect his long-standing interest in church music. His memoirs were published posthumously (Leningrad, 1976).

WORKS
(selective list)

Operas: Swat (after Ostrovsky), 1930; Vanka (after Sologub), 1932, Belgrade, 1935

Ballets: Le pavillon d'Armide, St Petersburg, 1908; Narcisse et Echo, Monte Carlo, 1911; Le masque de la mort rouge (after Poe) Moscow, 1922; Dionysus, London, 1922; Russian Fairy Tale, London, 1923; Romance of the Mummy, London, 1924; L'oiseau enchanté

Orch: Prélude pour la princesse lointaine, op.4; Le royaume enchanté; 3 fragments symphoniques; Chants sacrés

Vocal orch: Le chant de Sappho, S, female vv, orch; Joyselle au jardin, 1v, orch; La descente de la Sainte Vierge à l'enfer, oratorio

Other works: choral music, songs, chamber pieces, pf music

Principal publishers: Belyayev/Belaieff, Bessel, Jürgenson, Schirmer

(2) Alexander (Nikolayevich) Tcherepnin (*b* St Petersburg, 21 Jan 1899; *d* Paris, 29 Sept 1977). Composer, pianist and conductor, son of (1) Nikolay Tcherepnin. He played the piano and composed prolifically from a precociously early age, stimulated by the atmosphere of his home, which was a rallying point for many well-known musicians and artists of the day. Also, he travelled with his father on many of his pre-war European concert tours and gained much valuable experience. In 1918 the family fled St Petersburg and settled for a while in Tbilisi, where Alexander continued his studies at the conservatory, gave concerts as both pianist and conductor and wrote music for the Kamerny Theatre, of which he was musical director. In 1921 the increasingly hostile political climate forced the Tcherepnins to leave Russia permanently. They settled in Paris, where Alexander completed his studies with Vidal and Philipp and became associated with the group of composers including Martinů, Mihalovici and Conrad Beck. From Paris he launched an international career as a pianist-composer. He made his Western début in London in 1922, and in 1923 his ballet *Ajanta's Frescoes*, written for Pavlova, was performed at Covent Garden. In 1926 he toured the USA, and the next year completed his Symphony no.1, which achieved a *succès de scandale* at its first performance in Paris. In 1934–7 his travels in the Far East brought him into direct contact with Chinese and Japanese musical ideas that were to have far-reaching consequences in his creative work. He taught in these countries and founded a publishing house in Tokyo to promote the work of his pupils; in Shanghai he met the young Chinese pianist Lee Hsien Ming, whom he later married. They settled in Paris, but the war put a temporary stop to their musical activities. The immediate postwar period however brought a resurgence of Tcherepnin's creative energies, and he produced a number of important works. In 1948 he returned to the USA on a concert tour, after which he and his wife were invited to teach at De Paul University, Chicago; in 1950 the family settled in that city. In 1958 he became a citizen of the USA, and in 1964 moved to New York. From then on he divided his time between Europe and the USA. In 1967 he was invited by the Soviet government to return to Russia on a concert tour.

Many elements contributed to the formation of Tcherepnin's quicksilver, egregiously cosmopolitan musical personality, which, though recognizably Russian at base, conspicuously lacked the nostalgia and melancholy of other expatriate Slavs. He had the free-ranging open-mindedness of St Petersburg as opposed to the intensely nationalist introversion of Moscow. The keenly speculative nature of his mind was in evidence as early as 1913 in the fourth of his *Pièces sans titres* op.7 for piano, a piece which is frankly bitonal. Later, in the Symphony no.1, he incorporated a startling movement for pitchless percussion. In this and other representative early works, such as the Second Piano Concerto (1923), the influence of Prokofiev is discernible (motor rhythms and a mordant though fundamentally good-tempered wit), as is that of contemporary French music (a sophisticated clarity and simplicity of texture); but Tcherepnin was also experimenting with new scales and a new species of counterpoint. The scale which bears his name in the compendia of Riemann and Slonimsky consists of nine notes in the form of three conjunct tetrachords, each containing a whole tone and two semitones (ex.1). The new contrapuntal species, 'interpoint', allows one self-contained set of two contrapuntal voices to enter the cavity in another similar set, provided no overlapping takes place; this second set may then enter a third, again with the same proviso, and so on.

Ex.1 The Tcherepnin Scale

Other important constituents of Tcherepnin's musical language are those deriving from the various folk cultures which his travels enabled him to assimilate and through which he sought 'to escape from the mousetrap of cultural music into the world of natural art'. The Georgia sojourn yielded several compositions based on its folklore, while important works that attest to the influence of oriental music are the Piano Concerto no.4 (*Fantaisie*), the *Cinq études de concert* for piano, the Piano Studies on the Chinese Scale, *The Lost Flute* for narrator and orchestra and the opera *The Farmer and the Nymph*. After this literal and metaphorical 'journey to the East' came a return to the West: the American period was one of synthesis and consummation, as represented by the Symphonies nos.2 and 4, the *Symphonic Prayer* and the Fifth Piano Concerto (1963). Although he remained unaffected by both serialism and jazz, Tcherepnin incorporated electronic elements in his radio score for the BBC, *The Story of Ivan the Fool*.

WORKS
(selective list)
DRAMATIC

Operas: 01–01, op.35 (L. Andreyev), 1925, Weimar, 1928, rev. 1930, New York, 1934; Die Hochzeit der Sobeide, op.45 (after Hofmannsthal), 1930, Vienna, 1933; Die Heirat, op.53 [completion of Musorgsky work], 1933–5, Essen, 1937; The Farmer and the Nymph, op.72 (Siao Yu), Aspen, Colorado, 1952
Ballets: Ajanta's Frescoes, op.32, London, 1923; Der fahrende Schüler mit dem Teufelbannen, op.54 (after H. Sachs), 1937, orch score lost, reorchd, Kiel, 1965; Trepak, New York, 1938; La légende de Razine, Paris, 1941; Le déjeuner sur l'herbe [after Lanner], Paris, 1945; Chota Rostaveli (3, Lifar), Act 2 only, other acts by Honegger and Harsányi, Monte Carlo, 1946; La femme et son ombre, op.79 (Claudel), Paris, 1948; Le gouffre (after Andreyev), 1953, Nuremberg, 1969
Radio score: The Story of Ivan the Fool (Tolstoy), BBC, 24 Dec 1968

ORCHESTRAL

Pf Conc. no.1, op.12, 1919–20; Rhapsodie géorgienne, op.25, vc, orch, 1922; Pf Conc. no.2, op.26, 1923; Conc. da camera, op.33, fl, vn, chamber orch, 1924; Magna mater, op.41, 1926–7; Sym. no.1, op.42, 1927; Pf Conc. no.3, op.48, 1931–2; Suite géorgienne, op.57, pf, str, 1938; Sym. no.2, op.77, 1947–51; Pf Conc. no.4 (Fantaisie), op.78, 1947; Sym. no.3, op.83, 1952; Harmonica Conc., op.86, 1953; Suite, op.87, 1953; Divertimento, op.90, 1955–7; Sym. no.4, op.91, 1957; Georgiana, op.92, suite [from Chota Rostaveli], 1959; Sym. Prayer, op.93, 1959; Pf Conc. no.5, op.96, 1963; Pf Conc. no.6, op.99, 1965; Russian Sketches, op.106, 1971

OTHER WORKS

Vocal: Les douze, op.73 (Blok), speaker, chamber orch, 1945; Le jeu de la Nativité, op.74, solo vv, chorus, perc, str, 1945; 7 Chinese Folksongs, op.95, 1v, pf, 1962; Vom Spass und Ernst, op.98, cantata, A/B, str orch, 1964; Mass, op.102, 3 female vv, 1966; 6 Liturgical Songs, op.103, chorus, 1967; 4 Russian Folksongs, op.104, chorus, 1967; The Lost Flute, speaker, (fl, harp, pf, str qt)/orch, op.89; Baptism Cantata, chorus, orch, 1972
Chamber: Str Qt no.1, op.36, 1922; Str Qt no.2, op.40, 1926; Pf Qnt, op.44, 1927; Duo, op.49, vn, vc, 1932; Sonatine sportive, op.63, sax, pf, 1939; Sonata da chiesa, op.101, va da gamba, org/(fl, str, hpd), 1966; Qnt, op.105, 2 tpt, hn, trbn, tuba, 1972; Qnt, op.107, ww, 1976; Duo, op.108, 2 fl, 1977
Kbd etc: Bagatelles, op.5, pf, 1913–18, also with orch; Pf Sonata no.1, op.22, 1918; Showcase, op.75, pf, 1946; 12 Preludes, op.85, pf, 1952–3; Partita, accordion, 1961; Pf Sonata no.2, op.94, 1961; Processional and Recessional, org, 1962; Suite, op.100, hpd, 1966; Tzigane, accordion, 1966; Invention, accordion, 1967; Caprices diatoniques, Celtic harp, 1973

Principal publishers: Associated, Belaieff, Boosey & Hawkes, Chester, Durand, Eschig, Gerig, Heugel, Marks, MCA, Peters, Presser, Schirmer, Schott, Templeton, Universal

BIBLIOGRAPHY
W. Reich: *Alexander Tscherepnine* (Bonn, 1959, rev. 2/1970; Fr. trans., *ReM* (1962), no.252)

A. Tcherepnin: 'A Short Autobiography', *Tempo* (1979), no.130, p.12

(3) Serge (Alexandrovich) Tcherepnin (*b* Paris, 2 Feb 1941). Composer, son of (2) Alexander Tcherepnin. As a violinist he played professionally with his father while in his teens. He later studied composition with his father (after tuition in harmony from Boulanger), at Harvard (1958–63) with Billy Jim Layton and Leon Kirchner, at Princeton (1963–4) and finally in Europe with Eimert, Stockhausen, Nono, Earle Brown and Boulez. A naturalized American, he directed the electronic music studio at New York University (1968–70) and in 1970 was appointed to teach composition and electronic music at the Valencia (California) School of Music. He designs electronic instruments for his company Serge Modular. He collaborated with his father on the tape part of *The Story of Ivan the Fool*.

WORKS
(*selective list*)
Str Trio, 1960; Str Qt, 1961; Kaddish (Ginsberg), speaker, fl, ob, cl, pf, 2 perc, vn, 1962; Figures-Grounds, 7–77 insts, 1964; Background Music I–II, 4-track tape, 1966; Morning After Piece, sax, pf, 1966; Piece of Wood, actors, musicians, stage hands, 1967; Film (mixed-media piece), 1967; 'Hat' for Joseph Beuys, actor, tape, 1968; Paysages électriques, 1977; Samba in an Aviary, 1978; film scores

Principal publishers: Belaieff, Boosey & Hawkes

(4) Ivan (Alexandrovich) Tcherepnin (*b* Paris, 5 Feb 1943). Composer, son of (2) Alexander Tcherepnin. He studied the piano with his mother and composition initially with his father, whose classes he also attended at the Académie Internationale de Musique in Nice. At Harvard (1960–64) he studied with Randall Thompson and Leon Kirchner, and in Europe (1965) he was a pupil of Pousseur and Stockhausen for electronic music and Boulez for conducting. A naturalized American, he has taught at Harvard (1967) and, as professor of composition from 1969, at the San Francisco Conservatory and Stanford University; he returned to Harvard in 1972 as associate professor and head of the electronic studio.

WORKS
(*selective list*)
2 entourages pour un thème russe, hn/ondes martenot, pf, perc, 1961; Reciprocals, fl, cl, bn, 1962; Beginnings, pf, 1963; Cadenzas in Transition, fl, cl, pf, 1963; Sombres lumières, fl, gui, vc, 1965; Work Music, elec gui, cl, hn, vc, 1965; Rings, str qt, tape, 1966; Grand Fire Music, tape, 1966; Wheelwinds, 9 wind, 1966; Alternating Currents 1, 8 perc. elec, 1967; Film Music, tape, 1967; Light Music with Water, insts, elec, 1970; Summer Brass, 6 brass, 1970; Les adieux, 3vv, 15 insts, elec, 1972; Globose floccose, 9 insts, elec, 1973; 3 Pieces, 2 pf, 1974; Fêtes, pf, 1975; Set, hold, squelch and clear, ob, synth, 1976, rev. 1978 as Le va et le vient, orch; Santur opera, santur, synth, 1977

Principal publishers: Belaieff, Boosey & Hawkes, Schott
CHRISTOPHER PALMER

Tchicai, John (Martin) (*b* Copenhagen, 28 April 1936). Danish jazz saxophonist, composer and band-leader. His father was a Congolese diplomat, his mother Danish. He first studied the violin, then at the age of 16 took up the alto saxophone and clarinet. He attended conservatories in Århus and Copenhagen. Influenced at first by the alto saxophonist Lee Konitz, notably in his dry instrumental sound and melodic line, Tchicai made his first international appearance at a youth festival in Helsinki (1962), where he met the American avant-garde saxophonist Archie Shepp. Later that year he played at the Warsaw Jazz Festival with his own group, and there recorded his first LP. Shortly afterwards he went to New York and soon became a leading member of the New York avant garde and one of the most important young alto saxophonists of the 1960s. Together with Shepp and the trumpeter Don Cherry he organized the New York Contemporary Five; later he collaborated with the trombonist Roswell Rudd and the drummer Milford Graves in the New York Art Quartet. These groups toured Europe and made recordings. During these years he also recorded with the Jazz Composer's Guild, Archie Shepp, John Coltrane and Albert Ayler. In 1966 he returned to Denmark where he has led the group Cadentia Nova Danica. Since 1970 he has worked in different groups with leading players of the European avant garde, and has found inspiration in non-European music (Tibet, Korea, India and Africa) and in recent European and American art music.

BIBLIOGRAPHY
A. Barnett: 'John Tchicai: of Three Continents', *Jazz Monthly*, xiv (1968), Oct, 2
J. Cooke: 'John Tchicai', *Modern Jazz: the Essential Records*, ed. M. Harrison (London, 1975), 110
OLE MATTHIESSEN

Tchoung-tou. Chinese CLAPPERS.

Te. The leading note of the prevailing key (or, if this is minor, its relative major), in TONIC SOL-FA.

Teagarden, Jack [Weldon Leo] (*b* Vernon, Texas, 20 Aug 1905; *d* New Orleans, 15 Jan 1964). American jazz trombonist and singer. After touring with various bands in the South-west and northern Mexico he moved in 1927 to New York, where he began recording on a freelance basis. He worked regularly with Ben Pollack's orchestra (1928–33), Paul Whiteman's, and from 1939 to 1947 with his own orchestra in Chicago. He then became a member of Louis Armstrong's 'All Stars', but by 1951 he was leading his own small ensembles, sometimes with his brother Charlie ('Little T') as trumpeter. In 1957–9 he toured widely in Europe and Asia. Teagarden was one of the most prominent of a generation of jazz trombonists who, guided by Louis Armstrong's accomplishments as a brass player, raised the level of the trombone to that of a precise, melodic solo voice. His calm, deceptively lazy manner of playing was particularly suited to paraphrases of a given melody, but he was also noted for his playing and singing of the blues. His recording career (documented by Watters, 1960) was extensive; his version of *Rockin' Chair* (1947), recorded with Armstrong at Town Hall, New York, might best serve to express his artistry as a performer.

BIBLIOGRAPHY
C. Smith: 'Jack Teagarden', *Jazz Monthly*, iii (1957), Oct, 2
J. D. Smith and L. Guttridge: *Jack Teagarden: the Story of a Jazz Maverick* (London, 1960/*R*1977)
H. Watters jr: *Jack Teagarden's Music* (Stanhope, NJ, 1960)
R. Hadlock: *Jazz Masters of the 20s* (New York, 1965), 172ff
H. Woodfin: 'Jack Teagarden', *Jazz Monthly*, xii (1966), Nov, 7
A. McCarthy: *Jazz on Record* (London, 1968), 282f
M. Williams: *Jazz Masters in Transition* (New York, 1970), 174ff
MARTIN WILLIAMS

Tear, Robert (*b* Barry, 8 March 1939). Welsh tenor. He studied at King's College, Cambridge, where he was a choral scholar from 1957, and in 1961 joined the St Paul's Cathedral Choir. He sang with the English Opera Group, 1963–71, first as Quint in Britten's *The Turn of the Screw*, then creating Meshach in *The Burning Fiery Furnace* and the Younger Son in *The Prodigal Son*, as well as sharing many of the roles created for Peter Pears, whose voice and manner Tear's rather resembled at that time. At Covent Garden he sang Dov in the first performance of Tippett's *The Knot Garden* (1970) and his parts there since have included Lensky, Paris (*King Priam*), Jaquino, Prince Khovansky, Jack (*The Midsummer Marriage*), Matteo (*Arabella*) and Froh. He returned to the English Opera Group in 1973 as Idomeneus at Aldeburgh. He has also sung Nero with the Netherlands Opera, Alfredo with Scottish Opera, and Loge at the Paris Opéra (1976). In concerts he has performed widely in Europe and North America: in the *Missa solemnis* under Giulini, *Das Lied von der Erde* under Solti, and Verdi's Requiem under Bernstein. He has made many records, notably anthologies of English song, and music by Rakhmaninov, Tchaikovsky and Weber; his recital repertory is similarly wide-ranging. Tear's keen mind is always evident directing his clear, expressive voice, which has developed considerably in character and become capable of the delicate articulation needed for the Evangelist in Bach's Passions and (though the heavier roles put some strain on his resources) the almost heroic quality for Lensky.

ALAN BLYTH

Tebaldi, Renata (*b* Pesaro, 1 Feb 1922). Italian soprano. She was brought up at Parma where she studied the piano, but her teacher, Passani, was so amazed by the richness and range of her voice that he suggested she should have an audition as a singer. Thus at 18 she entered the Arrigo Boito Conservatory at Parma, and became a pupil of Carmen Melis. She made her début in May 1944 as Elena in Boito's *Mefistofele* at Rovigo. In 1946 Toscanini, who was auditioning for the reopening of La Scala, chose her to sing under him on the opening night, 11 May 1946, as soprano soloist in the *preghiera* from Rossini's *Mosè in Egitto* and in Verdi's *Te Deum*. In the first winter opera season at the rebuilt Scala (1946–7) she sang Mimì and Eva. Other appearances in Italy followed, and from 1949 to 1954 she sang regularly at La Scala, where her roles included Madeleine in *Andrea Chénier*, Adriana Lecouvreur, Tosca, Desdemona and the title role of Catalani's *La Wally*.

Tebaldi was a great favourite at the San Carlo, Naples, and both there and in South America was compared with Claudia Muzio, especially for her interpretation of Violetta. Tebaldi's London début was at Covent Garden as Desdemona on the opening night of the Scala company's London season in 1950; she was also heard in Verdi's Requiem. She returned to London in summer 1955 to sing Tosca. Her American début was in San Francisco in 1950. She also sang in Chicago, and was a member of the Metropolitan Opera after 1954. Besides the usual *lirico-spinto* repertory, she sang the title role of Spontini's *Olympia* (Florence, 1950), Pamira in Rossini's *Le siège de Corinthe* (Florence, 1949), Cleopatra in Handel's *Giulio Cesare* (Naples, 1950) and the title role of Verdi's *Giovanna d'Arco* (Naples and Paris, 1950). In 1973 she was awarded the Verdi d'Oro.

Tebaldi possessed one of the most beautiful Italian voices of this century; she did not indulge in the overabundance of chest notes so dear to many Italian sopranos, and her *mezza voce* singing was a joy to hear. Early in her career her interpretations lacked dramatic conviction, but later they gave evidence of a heightened sense of drama, and the voice, which, in the years following her first London appearances, began to show

Renata Tebaldi in the title role of Puccini's Tosca

some strain and lose a little of its beauty and steadiness, again became as lovely as it originally was.

BIBLIOGRAPHY

H. Rosenthal: 'Renata Tebaldi', *Sopranos of Today* (London, 1956)
F. F. Clough and G. J. Cuming: 'Renata Tebaldi Discography', *Gramophone Record Review*, new ser. (1957), no.46, p.789
W. Panofsky: *Renata Tebaldi* (Berlin, 1961)
V. Seroff: *Renata Tebaldi: the Woman or the Diva* (New York, 1961)
H. Rosenthal: 'Renata Tebaldi', *Great Singers of Today* (London, 1966)
K. Harris: *Renata Tebaldi: an Authorised Biography* (New York, 1975)

HAROLD ROSENTHAL

Tebaldini, Giovanni (*b* Brescia, 7 Sept 1864; *d* S Benedetto del Tronto, Ascoli Piceno, 11 May 1952). Italian scholar, composer and conductor. He studied at the Milan Conservatory with Panzini and Ponchielli (1883–5) and with Haller and Haberl at the Kirchenmusikschule, Regensburg (1888). He was *maestro* of the Schola Cantorum of St Mark's, Venice (1889–93), *maestro di cappella* of the Basilica of St Anthony, Padua (from 1894), director of the Parma Conservatory (1897–1902) and music director at the Santa Casa of Loreto (1902–24). In 1925 he took charge of the courses in Palestrina interpretation at the Naples Conservatory and in 1931 became director of the Ateneo Musicale, Genoa.

Although Tebaldini was active as a historian, conductor and composer (most notably of sacred works, but also of much orchestral and chamber music), he was most important for his long and devoted scholarly research and his promotion of the Cecilian movement for the reform of church music. (He was probably among those who inspired the *Motu proprio* of Pius X on church music in 1903.) He actively supported Gregorian societies and concerts of 16th- and 17th-century sacred and secular music, for which he often prepared performing editions. He gave numerous lectures in Italy and abroad, especially on Palestrina, and contributed to many newspapers and journals, founding one himself, *La scuola veneta di musica sacra* (1892).

WRITINGS

'G. P. da Palestrina', *RMI*, i (1892), 213

La musica sacra in Italia (Milan, 1893)

L'archivio musicale della Cappella antoniana in Padova (Padua, 1895)

'Il "motu Proprio" di Pio X sulla musica sacra', *RMI*, xi (1904), 578–619

La musica sacra nella storia e nella liturgia (Macerata, 1904)

'Telepatia musicale: a proposito dell'Elettra di Strauss', *RMI*, xvi (1909), 400

L'archivio musicale della Cappella lauretana (Loreto, 1921)

BIBLIOGRAPHY

A. Untersteiner: 'Giovanni Tebaldini e la riforma della musica da chiesa', *Gazzetta musicale di Milano*, 1 (1895), 425

M. Pilati: 'Giovanni Tebaldini', *Bollettino bibliografico musicale*, iv (1929)

M. Horwath: 'Tebaldini, Gnecchi and Strauss', *CMc* (1970), no.16, p.74

SERGIO LATTES

Tebaldini, Nicolò (*fl* Bologna, 1620–46). Italian publisher. Between 1627 and 1639 he printed four music publications: Costanzo Fabrizio's *Fior novello, libro primo di concerti* (1627); Bartolomeo Guerra's *Il diletto del notturno* (1634; the publication, however, is without the intended music); two books of Ascanio Trombetti's *Intavolatura di sonate per chitarra* (1639). The last-named uses an unusual kind of tablature notation, which, as the author explained in his advice to the reader, incorporates letters of the alphabet and celestial symbols such as the sun to indicate repetitions. The same letter notation but without celestial signs is employed in the *Fior novello*; in this publication each page is printed half in the normal way and half upside-down so that it may be read by a person facing the first performer. All the pages are enclosed in an ornamental frame and every canzona finishes with an elegant frieze. Tebaldini also published Adriano Banchieri's *Lettere scritte a diversi patroni ed amici* (1636).

BIBLIOGRAPHY

F. Vatielli: 'Editori musicali dei secoli XVII e XVIII', *Arte e vita musicale a Bologna* (Bologna, 1927/R1969), 239

A. Sorbelli: *Storia della stampa a Bologna* (Bologna, 1929)

L. Gottardi: *La stampa musicale in Bologna dagli inizi fino al 1700* (diss., U. of Bologna, 1951)

C. Sartori: *Dizionario degli editori musicali italiani* (Florence, 1958)

ANNE SCHNOEBELEN

Tebir. Sign used in Hebrew EKPHONETIC NOTATION.

Tecchler, David (*b* Augsburg, *c*1666; *d* Rome, after 1747). Italian violin maker of German birth. The leading violin and cello maker of the Roman school, he is thought to have learnt the rudiments of his craft in Augsburg before moving to Rome some years before the end of the 17th century. Once settled there he became a prolific instrument maker, particularly of cellos. There had been no significant maker of bowed instruments before him, though a number of German-born craftsmen had moved to Rome during the previous 100 years to make chitarroni and other plucked instruments. In Rome as in other Italian cities, the last quarter of the 17th century saw a sudden demand for violins and cellos, and Tecchler's productions would have found a ready market.

Tecchler was no copyist of Stainer, though the great Austrian maker's work was without doubt a powerful influence in Rome as elsewhere. He seems to have taken the Cremonese as his main example, though from the beginning he gave a distinct and appealing personal touch to his instruments. In particular the scrolls are handsome in design and deeply and emphatically carved. He is known chiefly for his cellos, many of which are used by leading professional players. With few exceptions they were originally of very large dimensions, and have had to be reduced in size to suit the players of the 19th and 20th centuries. He also made some excellent violins, and others which are perhaps less admirable, made in the style of Stainer. He made almost no violas, noting on the label of one made in 1730 that it was only the third he had constructed. His productivity had begun to decline by that time, as he gave way to his pupils Michael Platner and Francesco Emiliani.

BIBLIOGRAPHY

W. H., A. F. and A. E. Hill: *Antonio Stradivari: his Life and Work (1644–1737)* (London, 1902/R1963)

CHARLES BEARE

Tech a Curia, Nikolaus. See DECIUS, NIKOLAUS.

Techelmann, Franz Matthias (*b* Hof, Moravia [now Dvorce na Mor, Czechoslovakia], *c*1649; *d* Vienna, 26 Feb 1714). Austrian composer of Moravian birth. By 1678 he was active in Vienna, apparently at St Michael. From May 1685 until his retirement in 1713 he held the post of second organist at the Hofkapelle. Together with his colleague F. T. Richter he represents the next generation of court organists in Vienna after Kerll and Poglietti, and his music belongs to the Viennese keyboard tradition passed down from Froberger. Two sets of keyboard pieces by him survive in an autograph manuscript (*A-Wn* 19167; ed. in DTÖ, cxv, 1966) dedicated to the Emperor Leopold I; the title-page describes him as organist at St Michael, and the allemand in the second set is sub-titled 'Dell'allegrezze alla liberazione di Vienna', evidently referring to the Turkish siege of 1683. The dances from the second set recur among 14 anonymous suites in another source (*A-GÖ* Kerll 2), but there is no evidence that the other 13 suites are by him. The two authentic sets resemble Poglietti's *Rossignolo* in format. Each is unified by key, opening with a toccata followed by a canzona and ricercare and ending with a dance suite. The first set also contains an *Aria semplice* with variations. Techelmann used traditional procedures such as sectional design in the canzonas, thematic linking of allemand and courante, and fugato treatment of the gigue. Although the dances are generally simple in style, there is considerable virtuosity in the allemand of the second set as well as in the toccatas and variations.

BIBLIOGRAPHY

L. von Köchel: *Die kaiserliche Hof-Musikkapelle in Wien von 1543 bis 1867* (Vienna, 1869), 116

H. Knaus: *Franz Matthias Techelmann, sein Leben und seine Werke* (diss., U. of Vienna, 1958)

——: 'Franz Matthias Techelmann (1649–1714), kaiserliche Hoforganist in Wien', *SMw*, xxvii (1966), 186

——: Introduction to DTÖ, cxv (1966)

C. D. Harris: *Keyboard Music in Vienna during the Reign of Leopold I, 1658–1705* (diss., U. of Michigan, 1967)

H. Knaus: *Die Musiker im Archivbestand des kaiserlichen Obersthofmeisteramtes (1637–1705)*, ii–iii (Vienna, 1968–9)

SUSAN WOLLENBERG

Technitai [synoditai, synodeitai] (Gk.: 'artists', 'craftsmen'; Lat. *artifices*). In antiquity, professional artists incorporated in guilds (*koinon*, later *synodos*), beginning at Athens in the 3rd century BC. They included actors, members of the choruses, solo singers, instrumentalists, dancers, *choregoi* and others concerned with the production and performance of *agones*, tragedy, comedy, epic and other musical genres. The term *technitai* (pl. of *technitēs*) was used in antiquity as an abbreviation of *hoi peri ton Dionyson technitai* (literally 'the artists around Dionysus'; Lat. *Dionysiaci artifices*: 'Dionysiac artists'); these *technitai* were religious associations led by a priest of Dionysus. Their members enjoyed substantial privileges such as exemption from taxation and military duty and unusual freedom to travel. With the expansion of musical activity in the Hellenistic period, their importance increased, and they must have played an important part in the spread of Greek music throughout the Hellenistic world – for example, 3000 artists are reported to have attended the wedding of Alexander the Great at Ecbatana (*see* HELLENISTIC STATES and ROME, §I). At first confined to single cities such as Athens, *technitai* later enjoyed royal and imperial patronage and played a part in the state cults of various provinces, notably Ptolemaic Egypt and Pergamum. Comparable guilds at Rome included the so-called *parasiti Apollinis*; for the various types of musicians' guilds at Rome see Fleischhauer, and Wille (pp.357ff). *See also* LIMENIUS.

BIBLIOGRAPHY
F. J. F. A. L. Poland: *Geschichte des griechischen Vereinswesens* (Leipzig, 1909)
——: 'Technitai', *Paulys Realencyclopädie der classischen Altertumswissenschaft*, 2nd ser., v (Stuttgart, 1934), 2473–558 [with references to earlier literature]
M. Bieber: *The History of the Greek and Roman Theater* (Princeton, 1939, 2/1961), esp. 84
G. Fleischhauer: *Die Musikergenossenschaften im hellenistisch-römischen Altertum: Beiträge zum Musikleben der Römer* (diss., U. of Halle, 1960)
G. Wille: *Musica romana: die Bedeutung der Musik im Leben der Römer* (Amsterdam, 1967)
W. H. Gross: 'Technitai', *Der kleine Pauly*, v (Munich, 1975), 553

Tedesca (It.; Ger. *Teutscher*, *Deutscher*). A term meaning 'German' or 'in the German style'. It is found applied to dances from the end of the 15th century. In the late 16th century, madrigal-like compositions of a light character with texts mimicking a German accent in Italian were called *tedesche*. In the Baroque period the word was sometimes used as an alternative name for the allemande, an association still evident in Beethoven's use of the term, since the 'Alla danza tedesca' of the Quartet in B♭ op.130 is marked 'Allemande Allegro' in one of the sketches. Beethoven's 'Presto alla tedesca' in the Piano Sonata in G op.79 furnishes another instance. By this time, however, as Beethoven's Bagatelle 'A l'allemande' from op.119 also suggests, the term 'allemande' was associated with quick dances in triple time of which the deutscher Tanz, ländler and waltz were the chief types. Beethoven's 'Alla danza tedesca' therefore means 'in the style of a deutscher Tanz'. *See* GERMAN DANCE.

MAURICE J. E. BROWN

Tedeschi, Luigi Maurizio (*b* Turin, 7 June 1867; *d* Cairate, Varese, 1944). Italian harpist and composer. Tedeschi received a degree in natural science but turned to the harp and studied under Angelo Bovio in Milan, and later under Félix Godefroid in Paris. As a composer he was self-taught. From 1890 he toured Europe as a soloist and in 1899 was appointed professor at the conservatory in Venice. In 1902 he became professor at Milan, where he gained an outstanding reputation as a teacher; among his pupils were Maria Grossi, Marguerita Hazon and Maria Giulia Scimeca. Ricordi commissioned him to revise the teaching repertory of the harp. Tedeschi became a member of the Commission of Italian and Foreign Artists and received honours from both the Italian and French governments. He composed an opera *Jocely* produced at St Remo in 1908, and about 50 pieces for the harp.

BIBLIOGRAPHY
B. Bagatti: *Arpa e arpisti* (Piacenza, 1932), 75
M. G. Scimeca: *L'arpa nella storia* (Bari, 1938), 171
A. N. Schirinzi: *L'arpa* (Milan, 1961), 142
H. Charnassé and F. Vernillat: *Les instruments à cordes pincées* (Paris, 1970), 49

ALICE LAWSON ABER

Tedeschi [Tedesco], **Simplicio**. *See* TODESCHI, SIMPLICIO.

Tedeschino, Il. Nickname of GIOVANNI BATTISTA GIGLI.

Te Deum. A chant in praise of God sung at the end of Matins on Sundays and feast days, either after the last responsory (the medieval practice) or in its stead (the modern one). It has also been used as a processional chant, the conclusion for a liturgical drama, a song of thanksgiving on an occasion such as the consecration of a bishop and a hymn of victory on the battlefield. During the Middle Ages it was widely believed that St Ambrose and St Augustine composed the *Te Deum* as an improvised prayer at the baptism of St Augustine. Some studies have named Nicetas of Remesiana the probable author, but the matter remains unsettled.

1. Text. 2. Melody. 3. Polyphonic settings.

1. TEXT. The text of the *Te Deum* consists of 29 verses of prose (or 30, depending on how the last verse is treated). In the first ten, which praise God the Father, parallel construction is the rule: 'Te Deum laudamus, te Dominum confitemur'. The Sanctus of the Mass is quoted in verses 5 and 6; elsewhere the vocabulary and sequence of ideas suggest a connection with the popular hymnody of the 2nd century. Verses 11 to 13 are a doxology and are thought to be a later addition to the basic text. A second section, in praise of Christ, begins with verse 14, 'Tu rex gloriae Christe', and continues to verse 23. (Two verses in this section appear to be later additions – verse 15, 'Tu Patris sempiternus es filius', and verse 19, 'Judex crederis esse venturus'.) The last four verses of this section are a prayer (verses 22 and 23 are borrowed from Psalm xxviii.9 and form the conclusion of what is now regarded as the principal part of the text, about which the manuscript sources are in substantial agreement). Kähler's exhaustive analysis of the text reveals important similarities between this principal part and the formulae of the Gallican and Mozarabic liturgies. His conclusion is that the *Te Deum* originated before the middle of the 4th century as the preface, the Sanctus and the prayer following the Sanctus of an old Latin Mass of the Easter vigil, a Mass of baptism. The final section, from verse 24 to the end, consists almost entirely of psalm verses that adapt what has preceded them to daily recitation: 'Per singulos dies benedicimus te', etc (Psalm cxliv.2).

2. MELODY. The regular place for the *Te Deum* in medieval manuscripts is among the canticles of the Divine Office that are written without musical notation in the appendix to the liturgical psalter. Early manuscripts containing the *Te Deum* melody written precisely are still urgently sought; the earliest source indicated for any of the published transcriptions cur-

Ex.1

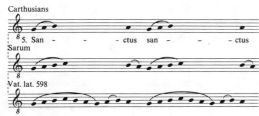

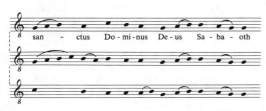

begin like verse 5).

Most of the text is chanted to a 4th-mode formula in which the principal reciting note is A. Two versions of the formula are used, the first in verses 1–10 (except for verse 5), the second in verses 14–20. (Omitted from consideration for the present are verses 24–9.) Ex.2 shows these two versions in the *Te Deum* melody of a 12th-century north Italian Carthusian gradual. In a 13th-century manuscript written in France (the musical supplement to *I-Rvat* lat.598, quoted by Wagner, 1907, p.67), the beginning of formula A is simplified as in ex.3, though the rest remains essentially the same. In formula B the intonation of the second half of the line is frequently omitted or condensed, but not that of the first half.

Ex.3 *I-Rvat* lat. 598

It is interesting to consider the treatment of the second degree of the scale in formula B (it does not appear in formula A). Wagner's Carthusian source gives it as F♮. The Solesmes editions and the Sarum version of the chant (Harrison, p.66) avoid it, substituting G, the third degree. Other sources, including an important early one, the *Musica enchiriadis* (which quotes only one verse of the *Te Deum*), clearly indicate a pattern of intervals that would require either notating the second degree of formula B as F♯, or else transposing this part of the chant down a tone, with D as the final and B♭ in the key signature. The 13th-century Worcester Antiphoner (*GB-WO* F.160; PalMus, xii, 5–6) opts for the latter solution, but runs into difficulties after verse 20. Verses 21–3 are rather like antiphons in style; if Kähler's conclusions concerning the text can be applied also to the music, then they form the original ending of the chant. In the Carthusian version, and in both Solesmes editions, there is reciting on G in verses 21 and 23, which have similar melodies, and in verse 22 the reciting is on F. To preserve these relationships, the Worcester Antiphoner would have had to write E♭ for

rently available is of the 12th century. (The transcriptions in the Solesmes editions, the *Liber usualis* and the *Antiphonale monasticum*, are from unspecified sources; Huglo has implied that in at least one respect the version of the *Antiphonale monasticum* is the 'original' one.) There is only one chant melody for the *Te Deum*, and no significant disagreement among the manuscripts concerning its broad outlines up to the end of verse 20. There are discrepancies of detail, such as differentiate the 'solemn tone' and the 'simple tone' of the *Liber usualis*; ex.1 shows how different sources treat the beginning and verse 5 (verses 11 and 13, later additions,

Ex.2 Formulae A and B for the *Te Deum* of a 12th-century north Italian Carthusian gradual (Jacques Rosenthal, Kat. 7, Nr. 933; present whereabouts unknown) published by P. Wagner (*Einführung*, iii, 225–7).

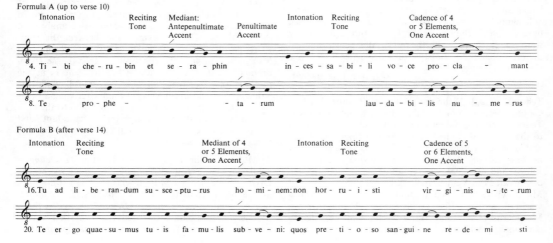

Ex.4

(a) Carthusians

[20] quos pre - ti - o - so san-gui-ne   re - de - mi-sti. 21. Ae -ter - na

(b) Worcester

fac   cum san-ctis tu - is in glo-ri - a mu-ne - ra - ri.

22. Sal-vum fac po-pu-lum .... he-re - di-ta-ti   tu - ae, 23. Et re -

- ge   e - os   et ex - tol - le il-los us-que in ae-

- ter - num. 24. Per sin - gu-los di - es be-ne - di - ci - mus te.

the reciting note of verse 22; rather than do this it made several changes (see ex.4).

Verse 24 marks the beginning of the later supplement to the chant. It opens with the melody of 'Te Deum laudamus', blending it into formula B, and this continues until the end of verse 28. The final verse is sung to a more elaborate form of the melody of verse 22. The second degree of formula B of the Te Deum melody posed a difficult problem for notators and analysts of Gregorian chant during the Middle Ages and the Renaissance, and it was not until the late 17th century, in Paris, that chant books offered the simple, precise solution of ex.5.

Ex.5

[28.] . Do-mi - ne su - per nos: quem - ad - mo-dum spe - ra - vi - mus

in   te. 29. In te Do-mi - ne

3. POLYPHONIC SETTINGS. The earliest known setting of a part of the Te Deum is in the Musica enchiriadis (c900), where the verse 'Tu Patris sempiternus es filius' is used to illustrate various kinds of parallel organum. A number of references from the 10th to 14th cen-

turies suggest that a festive performance of the Te Deum was normally accompanied by instruments (in particular organ and bells), the normal concomitant of which would be polyphony of some kind. Nevertheless, such polyphony was essentially improvised; no written settings of the Te Deum, apart from the verse just mentioned, are known to have survived from before the early 14th century. From this period comes an isolated setting from an English manuscript (GB-Cgc 334) of the final verse, 'In te Domine speravi' with the plainsong in the bass surmounted by two upper parts mostly in parallel movement (Reese, 1940, p.339). The harmonies are largely a succession of 6-3 chords, interspersed with 8-5 chords at cadences and elsewhere, and an occasional 10-5 and 5-3 also. Such parallel movement is clearly descended from the earliest forms of organum, and may represent in written form a type of singing more readily improvised (see FABURDEN).

15th-century settings are rare. The work by Binchois sets every verse in fauxbourdon, the plainsong paraphrased in the upper part throughout (J. Marix: Les musiciens de la cour de Bourgogne, Paris, 1937, pp.219ff). From England there are early 16th-century settings by Taverner, Sheppard and an anonymous work based on the faburden of the chant (GB-Lbm Add.17802–5). Aston set a variant of the text, Te matrem Dei laudamus, together with a Te Deum Mass based on the plainsong. Another English work based on the plainsong was Taverner's antiphon Ave Dei Patris Filia. There are alternatim organ settings by Burton, Redford (two) and Blitheman, and from the Continent a setting in Attaingnant's sixth collection of keyboard music (1531). Continental liturgical settings of the polyphonic period include works by G. F. Anerio (two), Festa, Kerle (two), Lassus, Morago, Resinarius, Handl and Vaet; and there is the Te Deum Mass by Palestrina. Like the contemporary hymn and Magnificat, the Te Deum was frequently performed in alternatim fashion, plainchant or organ versets alternating with choral polyphony. There are also reports of instrumental ensembles used antiphonally, particularly on festive occasions. At the coronation of Pius III, for example, 'tibia una et tribus tubis contortis quos trombones vulgo appelant' responded in turn to the intonations of the Te Deum (C. Mazzi: La Congrega dei Rossi di Siena del secolo XVI, Florence, 1882, p.44).

A new tradition of festive settings was inaugurated in the Baroque era with the large-scale works of Benevoli, Lully, Carl Heinrich Graun and others, and continued in the later 18th century with the settings by Sarti, Michael Haydn (who wrote six) and the two by Joseph Haydn. Joseph Haydn's second work is a remarkably fine piece from 1800 or shortly before, the first of a number of striking compositions of the 19th and 20th centuries. These include works by Berlioz (written for the Paris Exhibition, 1855), Bruckner (Vienna, 1885), Dvořák (1896), Verdi (Paris, 1898) and Kodály (1936, written to celebrate the 250th anniversary of the relief of Buda from Turkish occupation).

After the Reformation, settings of the Te Deum in English occupied a regular place in the Anglican SERVICE; there is a modified version of its melody in Merbecke's Book of Common Prayer. Luther's version, Herr Gott dich loben wir, also based on the Gregorian melody, gave rise to such widely diverse settings as the six by Michael Praetorius, the organ settings of Scheidt (Tabulaturbuch, 1650), Buxtehude and J. S. Bach, and

Bach's four-part chorale version in the edition of C. P. E. Bach.

The tradition of festal settings in English begins with Purcell's of 1694 (for St Cecilia's Day, with *Jubilate*) and continues with those of Handel ('Utrecht', 1713, and 'Dettingen', 1743), Sullivan (1897), Parry (1911), Stanford (1918) and Walton (1953). Parry and Stanford also wrote Latin works (1898, 1900) and Parry revised his to English words for performance in 1913. Walton's piece, a distinguished contribution to the genre, was written for the coronation of Queen Elizabeth II.

BIBLIOGRAPHY

J. Julian: *Dictionary of Hymnology* (London, 1892, rev. 2/1907)
A. Gastoué: 'Le "Te Deum"', *Revue de chant grégorien*, xiv (1906), 129
P. Wagner: 'Das Te Deum', *Gregorianische Rundschau*, vi (1907), 49, 65, 81, 98, 114
——: *Einführung in die gregorianischen Melodien*, iii: *Gregorianische Formenlehre* (Leipzig, 1921/*R*1962)
G. Reese: *Music in the Middle Ages* (New York, 1940)
M. Righetti: *Manuale di storia liturgica*, i (Milan, 1945, 3/1964)
G. Reese: *Music in the Renaissance* (New York, 1954, rev. 2/1959)
F. Ll. Harrison: *Music in Medieval Britain* (London, 1958, 2/1963)
E. Kähler: *Studien zum Te Deum* (Göttingen, 1958)
W. Kirsch: *Die Quellen der mehrstimmigen Magnificat- und Te Deum-Vertonungen bis zur Mitte des 16. Jahrhunderts* (Tutzing, 1966)
K.-H. Schlager: 'Te Deum', *MGG*
B. Blackburn: 'Te Matrem Dei laudamus: a Study in the Musical Veneration of Mary', *MQ*, liii (1967), 53
M. Huglo: 'Te Deum', *New Catholic Encyclopedia* (New York, 1967), 954
J. Aplin: 'The Survival of Plainsong in Anglican Music: Some Early English Te-Deum Settings', *JAMS*, xxxii (1979), 247
RUTH STEINER (1, 2), JOHN CALDWELL (3)

Teeus. *See* THEEUWES family.

Teghi, Pietro (*b* Padua; *fl* mid-16th century). Italian lutenist. His only publisher, Pierre Phalèse, indicated in the titles of his publications that Teghi was a Paduan. His entire contribution to lute music appears to consist of intabulations of chansons and motets (described in H. M. Brown, *Instrumental Music Printed before 1600: a Bibliography* (Cambridge, Mass., 1965, item 1547⁹). Teghi's first published collection was *Des chansons & motetz reductz en tablature de luc, a quatre, cinque et six parties, livre troixiesme* (Louvain, 1547). Most references state that the publisher reissued the collection in that same year with the title *Carminum ad testudinis usum compositorum liber tertius*. Only the chanson *Je prens en gre* by Clemens non Papa is common to both publications, and the rest of the later volume is made up of dances and fantasias by Francesco da Milano and other Italians. In 1573 the first collection was again reprinted as *Cantionum gallicarum, et motettarum liber*. The copy described by Brown (1573⁵) is incomplete and cannot be checked against the parent volume.

ELWYN A. WIENANDT

Teiber. *See* TEYBER family.

Teike, Carl (Albert Hermann) (*b* Altdamm, nr. Szczecin, 5 Feb 1864; *d* Landsberg an der Warthe, 28 May 1922). German composer. From the age of 14 he took instruction on several wind instruments from Paul Böttcher, bandmaster at Wollin, and for four summers he played in Böttcher's band at the Baltic resort of Misdroy. In 1883 he became oboist in the band of the 123rd Rifle Regiment stationed at Ulm, where he also played in the town's opera orchestra. At this time he composed his first marches, including *Alte Kameraden* which brought him international fame. From 1890 he was a policeman until ill-health forced his retirement to Landsberg an der Warthe in 1909. Besides *Alte Kameraden* Teike composed about 100 marches, including *In Treue fest, Treue um Treue* and *Graf Zeppelin*, and also a number of dances.

BIBLIOGRAPHY

K. A. Döll: *Alte Kameraden* (Bad Homburg, c1965; Eng. trans., 1971)
ANDREW LAMB

Teiler (Ger.). In Schenkerian analysis (*see* ANALYSIS, §III) the first occurrence of the dominant in a period, movement or piece that marks a temporary resting-point in the progression of the bass towards a perfect cadence (hence also *Quintteiler, Oberquintteiler, teilende Dominante*); it is so called because it divides this progression into two parts, I–V and I–V–I. For works in the minor mode, the *Teiler* may be a minor dominant; the raised 3rd is then introduced later, in preparation of

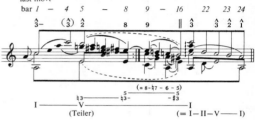

Ex.1 Schenker's analysis of Mozart: Sonata in A K331/300*i*, theme of last movt

the final V–I cadence. Thus in Schenker's analysis of the last movement of Mozart's Sonata in A K331/300*i* (*Der freie Satz*, 2/1956, fig.35/2), given in ex.1, the *Teiler* occurs in bar 5 though the raised 3rd of the dominant does not appear until bars 14 and 16.

See also UNTERBRECHUNG.

WILLIAM DRABKIN

Teilich, Philipp. *See* DULICHIUS, PHILIPP.

Teinturier, Johannes. *See* TINCTORIS, JOHANNES.

Teixeira, António (baptized Lisbon, 14 May 1707; *d* ?Lisbon, after 1759). Portuguese composer. Aided by a royal grant he studied counterpoint, composition and keyboard playing at Rome, c1717–28. On returning home he became diocesan examiner in plainchant and chaplain singer in the Lisbon Patriarchal Cathedral on 11 June 1728; at Carnival 1732 his cantata *Gli sposi fortunati* was sung and his 20-voice *Te Deum* was given in S Roque Church on 31 December 1734. Apart from an allegorical cantata for three voices and orchestra (*P-Ln*), much sacred music by him (or another composer of the same name) survives (*P-Lf* and the ducal palace, Vila Viçosa). He composed at least two masses, in eight and four voices, a set of four-voice vesper psalms for the Portuguese church at Rome, offertories, Lamentations, and motets with and without instruments, and an *a cappella* eight-voice *Miserere*.

BIBLIOGRAPHY

D. Barbosa Machado: *Bibliotheca lusitana*, iv (Lisbon, 1759), 61
M. de Sampayo Ribeiro: *A música em Portugal nos séculos XVIII e XIX* (Lisbon, 1936), 28f, 64
ROBERT STEVENSON

Tejeda, Alonso de (*b* Zamora, c1556; *d* Zamora, 7 Feb 1628). Spanish composer. He was the son of Benito de la Torre, but used the name of his maternal grandfather, a royal councillor. After studying at Salamanca, he held successive appointments as *maestro de capilla* at Ciudad Rodrigo, León (8 February 1591), Salamanca (11 November 1593), Zamora (3 December 1601), Toledo (3 August 1604, confirmed 12 November), Burgos (18 April 1618) and Zamora (1623–8).

He also won the post of *maestro* of the royal chapel at Granada on 12 March 1601, but withdrew in favour of returning to Zamora. At Toledo he argued with the singers whose insults eventually caused him to resign on 27 May 1617; he then briefly dallied with the idea of becoming an Augustinian friar in Madrid. At Burgos too he fell foul of the singers, who complained that his compositions lacked brilliance, and who deliberately made mistakes while singing them. His surviving 81 motets, extant at Zamora Cathedral, are well written but at times conservative, reminiscent of the style of Morales.

BIBLIOGRAPHY

D. Preciado: 'Alonso de Tejeda (†1628) Pequeña biografía', *Tesoro sacro musical*, liii (1970), 81

——: 'Cantus firmus "ostinati" de Alonso de Tejeda', *Tesoro sacro musical*, lv (1972), 48

I. Fernández de la Cuesta: 'Cantorales polifónicos de la Abadía de Santo Domingo de Silos', *Tesoro sacro musical*, lvii (1974), 36f

D. Preciado, ed.: *A. de Tejeda: Obras completas* (Madrid, 1974–) [incl. important introduction]

ROBERT STEVENSON

Te Kanawa, Kiri (*b* Gisborne, Auckland, 6 March 1944). New Zealand soprano. Winner of many prizes in New Zealand and Australia, she later studied at the London Opera Centre and with Vera Rosza. After appearances with Northern Opera and the Chelsea Opera Group, she joined the Royal Opera Company, making her Covent Garden début in 1970 as a Flower Maiden. Her first major role, Mozart's Countess, marked her as a singer of exceptional promise, and was repeated at the Lyons Opera (1971), in San Francisco (1972) and at Glyndebourne (1973). Her other roles at Covent Garden have included Amelia (*Simon Boccanegra*), Donna Elvira, Desdemona, Marguerite, Mimì and Fiordiligi. Purity of voice and a noble simplicity of style made her Micaela outstanding in a cast (1973) that included Verrett and Domingo. In 1974 she made her New York début at the Metropolitan Opera as Desdemona, again to great public and critical acclaim. At the Paris Opéra (1974, 1976) she has sung Elvira and Pamina, and she has also returned to Australia (as Amelia and Mimì in 1976) and New Zealand (appearing, in 1969, as Carmen). Her recordings include the role of Elvira in *Don Giovanni* and she has sung at concerts in the Holland Festival and at the Festival Hall in London. Her voice, vibrant but mellow, ample but unforced, impressed from the first by its freshness and warmth. With a touching dignity and beauty in her stage presence, she is one of the finest lyric sopranos to have been heard regularly at Covent Garden since World War II.

BIBLIOGRAPHY

M. Barichella: 'Kiri te Kanawa', *Opéra* (1975), no.106, p.64

J. B. STEANE

Tel-Aviv. Israeli city. It was founded in 1909 with the aim of building a Jewish colony from the early migrations of Jews from the Diaspora, especially that which began in the early 20th century, mostly from Russia and eastern Europe. Tel-Aviv expanded and in 1950 absorbed the ancient city of Jaffa; it is now Israel's largest city and centre of the country's musical life.

In 1910 the city's first music school was founded by Shulamit Ruppin and the violinist and conductor Moshe Hopenko, and for some time the Shulamit Conservatory was the centre of musical life in Tel-Aviv; the conservatory orchestra was particularly active under Hopenko's direction. In 1914 the Beit Leviyim music school was founded by Miriam Levitt; it was active until 1934. In 1923 the Israel Opera was founded with a performance of *La traviata* in Hebrew under the conductor Mordechai Golinkin; the company existed until 1927. In 1924 Joel Engel left Russia to settle in Israel; one of the pioneers of Jewish music, he arranged a series of concerts, wrote music for Jewish plays, and founded the Ohel Choir, which he conducted from 1925 until his death in 1927. Almost all composers in Tel-Aviv before the rise of the Nazis wrote in the lighter genres: songs, incidental music and popular or folkloristic music. Plays with incidental music were of special importance, particularly those given in the Ohel Theatre (1925–70) and the Matateh ('Broom') satirical theatre.

In 1927 Fordhaus ben Zyssi founded the Eretz Israel SO, the first independent orchestra of its kind in Israel; in the same year he founded and conducted the Oratorio Choir, and for many years also conducted the orchestra of the Habima Theatre. The Concert Ensemble (founded 1928) gave concert series for a short period under the direction of Zvi Kampaneietz. In 1930 Golinkin founded a choir with which he toured the country; with Solomon Rosowsky and David Shore he also founded the Institute for Music Studies (1931), a music school with a student chamber ensemble later enlarged to a symphony orchestra of 54 players which gave concerts under Golinkin. Recitals were also given by visiting artists, including Heifetz (1926), Godowsky (1926) and Huberman (1929).

With the rise of the Nazi regime a large immigration began and several composers, performers and scholars already established in their countries of origin settled in Tel-Aviv. 1936 was an important year for Israel's musical life in general and for Tel-Aviv's in particular; the Broadcasting Authority was inaugurated, and the Israel PO (later the Palestine SO, the Palestine PO from 1946 and the Israel PO again from 1948) was founded by Huberman, giving its first concert in the Levant Fair Hall under Toscanini. For much of its existence it did not have a permanent conductor, but in 1968 Zubin Mehta became musical director; under him more contemporary works were included in the repertory. The orchestra has also played under numerous leading conductors and with many outstanding soloists, making regular tours abroad from 1951. By its 40th season (1976) the orchestra, with 110 members, was giving 12 performances (nine in Tel-Aviv) of each programme in a season. Since its foundation the orchestra has also given special youth concerts, and from 1958 presented Jeunesses Musicales concerts with the same soloists as at the regular subscription series. It performed initially in the Levant Fair Hall, from 1947 to 1957 at the Ohel-Shem Hall, and from 1957 at the Mann Auditorium. In 1959 the orchestra introduced staged opera of the standard repertory to the city, starting with *Falstaff* under Giulini. In the same year the New Israel Quartet was formed by members of the orchestra. From the late 1960s the orchestra held several Rubinstein Festivals. Several other orchestras are active in the Tel-Aviv area: the IPO Youth Orchestra, the municipal, police and fire brigade orchestras, and the Kiryat Ono Symphonic Band.

In the pre-war period concerts of Jewish music were revived by Joachim Stutschewsky; their highlight was the première of Seter's *Sabbath Cantata* in 1940. The Israel String Quartet (1939–54) gave regular concerts of the standard and contemporary repertory, including the première of Partos's First String Quartet. The Eretz Israel Popular Opera (1940–47), conducted by Lavry, Singer and Golinkin, gave the première of Lavry's *Dan the Guard* (1945). The Israel Academy of Music was founded in 1945 and in 1965 was incorporated into the University of Tel-Aviv as the Rubin Academy of Music under the directorship of Partos and from 1973 under Vardi. Besides the Shulamit Conservatory there were several others active in the 1930s and some in the 1940s: the Taube and Buch conservatories, Ravina's Hebrew Conservatory, the Ebenstein and Ginzburg conservatories and the Tel-Aviv Conservatory. Some of these amalgamated to form the Tel-Aviv Conservatory and Academy of Music. In 1945 the Music Teachers' Seminary was founded by Kestenberg (its first director) and Amiran; it was later directed by Shmueli (1955–66) and Tuvya (from 1966).

In 1939 four young composers (Avidom, Jacoby, Pelleg and Seter) formed the '1939 group' to encourage performances of contemporary (especially Israeli) music, but only one chamber music concert was given. Bracha Zefira, who had an expert knowledge of Sephardic and Eastern Jewish folksong, greatly influenced such Tel-Aviv composers as Ben-Haim, Partos and Jacoby. With the establishment of the state of Israel in 1948 many new musical establishments developed in the city: the opera was revived as the Israel National Opera (it closed in 1953 but was revived again in the late 1950s); the Inbal Dance Theatre, founded in 1949 by Sara Levi-Tanai; the Histadrut Centre for Culture and Education (1949); the Israel Defence Army Symphonic Band (1949); Israeli Music Publications (1950); the League of Composers in Israel (1950); the AMLI Central Music Library (1950); the America–Israel Cultural Foundation (1950); the Israel Defence Army SO (1951, amalgamated with the Gadna Youth Orchestra of 1952 in 1957); and a branch of Jeunesses Musicales founded by Gary Bertini (1954). The acclaimed Rinat–Israel Chamber Choir was founded by Bertini in 1955 and became semi-professional in 1974; apart from its unaccompanied appearances it performs regularly at the Israel Festival and sometimes also with the Israel PO and other orchestras. It has had a significant influence on choral activity in Israel, and many similar choirs were formed.

Since 1945 the Tel-Aviv municipality has awarded an annual prize in memory of Joel Engel to an Israeli composer or performer. From 1960 to 1964 musical evenings emphasizing contemporary and Israeli music were given by the Chamber Music Association, established by Batsheva de Rothschild and directed by Bertini. The music section of the National Council for Culture and Art was set up in 1960 by the Ministry of Education and Culture. In 1961 the ISRAEL FESTIVAL was inaugurated, and in the same year the Israel Music Institute was founded to publish and promote Israeli music, being an active member of the IAML International Music Information Centres from 1969; the institute's Centre for Israeli Music was founded in 1968. The Israel Chamber Ensemble was founded in 1965 to perform chamber works and chamber opera; it was inaugurated with Menotti's *The Medium* and Bizet's *Le docteur miracle* under its musical director Bertini. The ensemble has become a large chamber orchestra and performs much contemporary music. Berio was appointed musical director in 1975, succeeded by Rudolph Barshai in 1977.

The musicology department of Tel-Aviv University opened in 1966, and the Bar Ilan University musicology department was founded in 1969; from the early 1970s it had a composer-in-residence. The Tel-Aviv Choir (founded 1941) was enlarged to form the Philharmonic Choir in 1971. With the foundation of the new Tel-Aviv Museum in 1970 and the opening of the Kaufman and Recanati halls (1971), regular chamber music activity was transferred there from the old Tel-Aviv Museum, for many years the focus of chamber music events. Recitals also take place in numerous other halls in the city. In 1974 the triennial Rubenstein International Piano Master Competition began. Musically, modern Tel-Aviv is remarkably active for its size; in season there are often up to a dozen concerts in a week, given both by Israeli groups and by leading foreign ensembles.

BIBLIOGRAPHY

M. Golinkin: *Meheichalei Yefet Leoholei Shem* (Tel-Aviv, 1948)
M. Ravina: *Joel Engel and Jewish Music* (Tel-Aviv, 1957)
I. Ibbeken: *An Orchestra is Born* (Tel-Aviv, 1969)

WILLIAM Y. ELIAS

Tel-Aviv Quartet. Israeli string quartet. It was founded in 1962 and the original members were Chaim Taub (*b* Tel-Aviv, 1 Aug 1925), Uri Pianka, Daniel Benyamini (*b* Tel-Aviv, 17 April 1925) and Uzi Wiesel (*b* Tel-Aviv, 8 Jan 1927). Pianka was replaced in 1963 by Menahem Breuer, and then in 1971 by Yefim Boyko (*b* Kishinev, Moldavia, 27 Jan 1947). Taub was educated in Israel, studying the violin under Oedoen Partos, then at the Juilliard School, New York, under Galamian, 1947–51. After an engagement with the Pittsburgh SO he joined the Israel PO in 1959, and soon became its leader. He teaches at the Rubin Academy of Music, Tel-Aviv. Boyko studied in the USSR with Bondarenko. In 1967 he settled in Israel and joined the Israel PO as leader of the second violins. Benyamini studied at the Shulamit Conservatory, Tel-Aviv, and then at the Jerusalem Academy. He joined the Israel PO in 1950 and became its principal viola in 1960. Wiesel studied at the Tel-Aviv Academy, in New York, and with Casals in Prades (1954–5). He won the 1953 Piatigorsky Prize. Since his return to Israel in the mid-1950s he has frequently appeared as a soloist and recitalist, and has given the premières of works by Tal, Partos, Sheriff and others. In 1955 he began teaching in Tel-Aviv. In the year of its formation the quartet toured the Far East and since then has toured internationally every year, appearing at leading festivals and making many broadcasts. It has recorded much of the standard quartet repertory, including works by Mozart, Schubert, Brahms and Reger, and often appears with the clarinettist Yona Ettlinger. Its repertory also includes works by Prokofiev, Britten, Bartók and Shostakovich, and it has given the first performances of Tal's String Quartet no.1, Seter's *Ricercar*, Elegy (with Ettlinger) and String Quartet (1975), and quartets by Tzvi Avni, Zeev Steinberg and Yardena Alotin. The ensemble plays with remarkable unanimity of style and approach, particularly in works of dramatic character. In 1976 it was awarded the Performers Prize of the Israeli National Council for Culture and Art.

WILLIAM Y. ELIAS

Teleia. A sign used as the second of a pair with the *oxeia*, *syrmatikē*, *paraklitikē* or *synemba* in Greek EKPHONETIC NOTATION.

Telemann, Georg Michael (*b* Plön, 20 April 1748; *d* Riga, 4 March 1831). German composer, grandson of Georg Philipp Telemann. When his father, G. P. Telemann's eldest son Andreas, who had been a clergyman at Plön, died in 1755 at the age of 40, his grandfather took him to Hamburg, where he brought him up and gave him a musical education. While he was still at school he played accompaniments under his grandfather, and after the old man died he took temporary charge of church music until C. P. E. Bach took over as Kantor in March 1768. In 1770 Telemann matriculated at the University of Kiel. On the title-page of his treatise on thoroughbass (1773) he described himself as a divinity student although by then he had abandoned his university course. After a short spell as a teacher at the Nicolaischule in Hamburg he was appointed as Kantor and teacher at the cathedral school in Riga. He took with him many of his grandfather's sacred vocal works in manuscript, studied them closely, and prepared them for performance; during the period 1776–1827 he was responsible for at least 21 performances of Passions by G. P. Telemann, though he made alterations to both texts and scores. He modified some of the more colourful lines in the librettos and shortened the evangelist's role; to compensate, he added instrumental interludes, designed to give the audience the opportunity to reflect on the relevant passages in the Gospel text and adopt the correct mental attitude. He also arranged performances of some of his grandfather's funeral cantatas, consecration music and other occasional compositions. Telemann was always careful to acknowledge any alterations, and added his reasons for making them in explanatory notes which accompanied the manuscripts.

Telemann's own compositions are relatively undistinguished. In the preface to his *Beytrag zur Kirchenmusik* (1785) he defends his scoring of only two to three vocal lines with purely supporting scoring for the instrumental accompaniment on the grounds that, first, he had only a small choir at his disposal, and second, he felt it right to make a virtue of necessity, suggesting that over-elaborate middle parts might overshadow the melodic line. The foreword to his *Unterricht im Generalbass-Spielen* hints at an ambitious programme of modernization for the rules of thoroughbass, but the content is based on the textbooks of C. P. E. Bach and Marpurg and is confined to explanatory commentary.

WORKS

Beytrag zur Kirchenmusik (Königsberg and Leipzig, 1785) [10 choral anthems, 2–4vv, 2 ob, 2 tpt, hn, timp, str, bc; 10 chorale preludes and 2 fugues, org]
Auferstehn, ja auferstehn (Klopstock), chorus (Riga, 1809)
Sammlung alter und neuer Choralmelodien für das seit 1810 in . . . Riga eingeführte Neue Gesangbuch (Mitau, 1811–12)
6 chorale preludes, org, 1766, *D-Bds*; Hamburg, Deutschlands Pflegerin, cantata, for installation of C.P.E. Bach as Kantor, 1768, *B*; Ruhe sanft, chorus, *B*

WRITINGS

Unterricht im Generalbass-Spielen (Hamburg, 1773)
Beurteilung der im 23. Bande der Allgemeinen deutschen Bibliothek befindlichen Recension seines Unterrichts (Riga, 1775)
Über die Wahl der Melodie eines Kirchenliedes (Riga, 1821)

BIBLIOGRAPHY
F. Chrysander: 'Briefe von Ph. E. Bach und G. M. Telemann', *AMZ*, new ser., iv (1869), 177
H. Miesner: 'Die Lebensskizze des jüngeren Telemann und seine Werke', *Zeitschrift des Vereins für Hamburgische Geschichte*, xxxiii (1932), 143
H. Hörner: *G. Ph. Telemanns Passionsmusiken* (Leipzig, 1933), 134ff
MARTIN RUHNKE

Telemann, Georg Philipp (*b* Magdeburg, 14 March 1681; *d* Hamburg, 25 June 1767). German composer. The most prolific composer of his day, Telemann was widely regarded as Germany's leading composer in the early and middle 18th century; his fluent command of melody and uncomplicated textures show him as an important link between the late Baroque and the new Classical style. He was also highly influential in concert organization, music education and theory.

1. Sources, ancestry, school years. 2. Leipzig, Sorau. 3. Eisenach, Frankfurt. 4. Hamburg. 5. Influence on musical life. 6. Reputation. 7. Sacred music. 8. Secular vocal music. 9. Instrumental music. 10. Theory.

1. SOURCES, ANCESTRY, SCHOOL YEARS. Telemann left three autobiographies, in which he described his career, his artistic development and to some extent his attitude to music. The first was written in 1718, at the request of Mattheson, who had intended to publish a series of biographies of the best-known musicians. The second, which is shorter, is in the form of a letter from Telemann to Walther in 1729, giving him information for inclusion in his *Lexicon*. The third, the most comprehensive, dates from 1739, and was published by Mattheson in his *Grundlage einer Ehren-Pforte* (1740). A biographical study, published in both German and French in *c*1745, draws heavily on the *Ehren-Pforte* but includes additional material and information that the editor, B. Schmid, can have obtained only from Telemann himself. Although the autobiographies and the biography provide a wealth of background for an evaluation of Telemann's character and his approach to music, they contain a number of contradictions.

Telemann's forebears belonged to the upper middle class; there were no musicians among them. His father's family came from the area of Nordhausen, near Erfurt. His grandfather was vicar of Cochstedt, near Aschersleben, and his grandmother was a clergyman's daughter. His father, Heinrich Telemann (1646–85), went to school in Halberstadt and Quedlinburg, studied at the University of Helmstedt from 1664, and in 1668 was appointed headmaster of a school before becoming a parish priest in 1669 and subsequently, in 1676, a deacon in Magdeburg. In 1669 he married Maria Haltmeier (1642–1711), daughter of a Protestant clergyman from Regensburg, who, having been dismissed from his living in Freistadt, near Linz, in 1624, had found a new appointment near Magdeburg. Although Telemann claimed that his musical talent was inherited from his mother, there is no evidence that her family showed any musical talent except for her nephew, Joachim Friedrich Haltmeier (1668–1720), who became Kantor at Verden after spending some time at university. His son Carl, author of a treatise on thoroughbass published by Telemann in 1737, was an organist in Hanover.

Almost all Telemann's ancestors had received a university education, and most of them had entered the church. When his father died in 1685 his mother was left with the task of guiding her two sons along the same path. The elder studied theology and became a clergyman. The younger, Georg Philipp, attended two schools in Magdeburg, the Altstädtisches Gymnasium and the Domschule, where he received instruction in Latin, rhetoric and dialectic, and became interested in German poetry. Although he had no special coaching, by the time he was ten he had learnt to play the violin, the flute, the zither and keyboard instruments, studied the compositions of his music master the Kantor Benedikt Christiani, transcribed other compositions, and tried his hand at writing arias, motets and instrumental pieces. When at the age of 12 he embarked on the composition of an opera, *Sigismundus* (to a libretto by Postel), his mother and her advisers are said to have forbidden him any further involvement with music and taken away all his musical instruments. It was felt that in different surroundings he would find his way back to his true vocation; and to that end he was sent in late 1693 or early 1694 to school at Zellerfeld, where he was placed in the care of the superintendent Caspar Calvoer, who had apparently become acquainted with the family while studying at Helmstedt. Calvoer did more than guide Telemann's academic progress: an informed devotee of theoretical music studies, he taught his pupil the relationship between music and mathematics; with Calvoer's approval, Telemann continued to complement his general education by teaching himself composition and thoroughbass, and from time to time he seems to have composed symphonies for the local Stadtpfeifer. After four years he moved to Hildesheim, where he became a scholar at the famous Gymnasium Andreanum. The Rektor of the school, J. C. Losius, had been educated in Magdeburg and Helmstedt, and he too did more than simply supervise Telemann's general education, encouraging him to compose incidental songs for his numerous Latin school dramas (texts of four have survived in their entirety; six more are known by name). This music is no longer extant; but it is possible that it was also Telemann who wrote the anonymous songs for the collection *Singende Geographie*, in which Losius recorded his geography syllabus in verse form. Father Crispus, in charge of Roman Catholic church music, also made use of Telemann's talents in the Catholic Godehardi church, where Telemann and some of his Protestant fellow students gave performances of German cantatas. On visits to Hanover and Brunswick he had his first taste of French instrumental music and Italian opera, and in his private studies in composition he modelled his writing on the music of Steffani, Rosenmüller, Corelli and Caldara.

2. LEIPZIG, SORAU. In autumn 1701 Telemann embarked on his university studies, not in Helmstedt, where his ancestors and his teachers had been students, but in Leipzig. By his own account (in the autobiographies of 1718 and 1739) he started out with the firm intention of studying law, in accordance with his mother's wishes. He had allegedly left behind in Magdeburg all his instruments, compositions and notes, and contrived for a time to conceal his musical gifts from the music lovers among his fellow students. The story goes, however, that one day a room-mate happened to discover one of Telemann's compositions, which he arranged to have performed in the Thomaskirche. When as a result of this Telemann was commissioned by the mayor of Leipzig to write a cantata every two weeks for performance there, the stage was set for a musical career. Telemann had the gift of attracting musical students to himself and of engaging them in pleasurable activities. In 1702 he founded a student collegium musicum; the regular public concerts he organized began a new chapter in the history of the collegia musica. While in the 17th century student music-making was a casual, leisure-time activity, Telemann and his collegium musicum were orientated towards public performance. In 1702 he became musical director of the Leipzig Opera, whose founder, N. A. Strungk, had died two years before; here he was able to employ students as singers and instrumentalists. Within three years he had composed at least four operas, and he later continued to supply operas for Leipzig from Sorau, Eisenach and Frankfurt – more than 20, according to the 1739 autobiography, though evidence of no more than five is available. When in 1704 a new organ was installed in the Neue Kirche, which until 1710 was also the university church, Telemann applied for the post of organist, supporting his application with the promise that, with no increase in stipend, he would also act as musical director and that he and his collegium musicum would give concerts of sacred music in the church on feast days and fair days. On these terms he was offered the appointment.

Telemann's many activities offended against the existing order of Leipzig's musical life, and encroached on the territory of Kuhnau, then Kantor at the Thomaskirche. As the city director of music, Kuhnau was responsible for the music in all the Leipzig churches, and until this time he had been able to decide what was or was not possible with the available resources. The choristers and Stadtpfeifer could take it in turn to perform cantatas on alternate Sundays in the Thomaskirche and the Nicolaikirche, while the second choir, conducted by a prefect, sang traditional motets and German chorales in the Neukirche. More money would have been needed to augment this programme. But Telemann achieved what had hitherto seemed out of reach. In the Thomaskirche cantatas were now sung every Sunday instead of in alternate weeks, and university church services no longer had to forgo performances of fine church music. On several occasions Kuhnau petitioned against Telemann's infringement of his rights and tried to discredit him as an 'opera musician'; the only result was that the city fathers forbade Telemann to appear on the operatic stage. Kuhnau complained bitterly about the students' 'rush to opera', for they had flocked to join Telemann and no longer supported Kuhnau in providing music for the church services. Even after Telemann had left Leipzig, the leaders of the students' collegium musicum still held on to the organist's post at the Neukirche; and to the end of his life Kuhnau inveighed against what he considered to be the illegal activities of the students, trying in vain to reassert his original rights.

In 1705 Telemann was summoned to the court of Count Erdmann II of Promnitz at Sorau, Lower Lusatia (now Żary, in Poland), where he became Kapellmeister. According to the autobiographies of 1718 and 1739, the invitation had been issued in 1704; but Telemann was still in receipt of his organist's stipend in Leipzig on 22 April 1705, and the 1729 autobiography states that he spent four years at Leipzig University. Before taking up the reins of government in 1703, the Count of Promnitz had travelled through Italy and France, and had acquired a taste for excessive displays of courtly splendour. In particular he had become enamoured of French instrumental music, and his new Kapellmeister was required to provide French overtures in the style of Lully and Campra. When the court spent six months at Pless, one of the count's domains in Upper Silesia, Telemann came into contact with Polish folk music, and visits to Kraków helped to develop his admiration for this fascinating form of art, whose 'barbaric beauty' captivated him. He made several journeys from Sorau to Berlin, where he became familiar with the court instrumental music and court opera. Controversies with the Sorau Kantor and theorist W. C. Printz brought him to grips with problems relating to musical theory. It was also in Sorau that Telemann met the reformer Erdmann Neumeister, who wrote cantata texts and since 1706 had been superintendent and court chaplain. In 1711 Neumeister stood godfather at the baptism of Telemann's first daughter; ten years later, in Hamburg, he successfully supported Telemann's appointment to a post in that city.

3. EISENACH, FRANKFURT. The date of Telemann's move from Sorau to the court at Eisenach has long been disputed. In the autobiographies of 1718 and 1739 he gave the year as 1708; the published biography gives 1709. C. Freyse (*MGG*, 'Eisenach') suggested that the document recording Telemann's appointment as court Kapellmeister was drawn up as early as 11 March 1707; this would be corroborated by what Telemann said in his poem on the death of his first wife (DDT, xxviii) – that he and others fled before the Swedish troops sweeping through Saxony from the east. This document however is a ratification on 11 March 1717 of Telemann's appointment as visiting Kapellmeister; and nowhere in the poem does Telemann say that it was to Eisenach that he fled. In fact he was initially appointed to take charge of the newly formed musical establishment at the court on 24 December 1708. Before that he had been Konzertmeister of the court orchestra under Pantaleon Hebenstreit, and eventually he had been given the task of recruiting singers for the proposed establishment. It seems that 1708 may have been the date of his actual move to Eisenach. For the orchestra, of which he evidently thought highly, Telemann began to compose overtures, concertos and chamber works. When the new Hofkapelle was established he was also required to compose church cantatas and music for special occasions. While he was at Eisenach he must have met J. S. Bach, whose cousin Johann Bernhard Bach was town organist there and was involved in the musical life at court; in 1714 Telemann was to stand godfather to C. P. E. Bach. In autumn 1709, on his solemn undertaking that he would return to Eisenach and refuse all other offers of employment, Telemann was granted leave of absence. He returned to Sorau, where he married Louise Eberlin, a lady-in-waiting to the Countess of Promnitz and daughter of the musician Daniel Eberlin – only to lose her in January 1711 after the birth of his first daughter. Looking back in 1718, he was to claim that in Eisenach he not only came of age musically but that as a Christian he became a different man.

In February 1712, a year after his wife's death, Telemann accepted an invitation to Frankfurt am Main, where he became the city director of music and Kapellmeister at the Barfüsserkirche. No school appointment was connected with this post; Telemann merely supervised such singing instruction as was given in the schools. His six to eight choristers, personally selected from the schoolboys, had to be trained privately by him. He composed at least five cycles of cantatas in Frankfurt, each of them spanning the liturgical year. In addition he was expected to write and arrange performances of special works for civic celebrations. Though at court he was relatively restricted as a musician and composer by the demands of his official duties, his civic appointment allowed him a much greater degree of freedom to influence and reshape the city's musical life. He assumed the directorship of the collegium musicum of the Frauenstein Society, an association of the aristocracy and the bourgeoisie, who immediately made him their secretary and administrator. In conjunction with the collegium musicum he organized weekly public concerts for which he composed chamber and orchestral music and oratorios. At one special concert he arranged a performance of his setting of the Brockes Passion in the Barfüsserkirche, in the presence of the Landgrave of Hesse, whose own court musicians took part (1716).

In 1714 he married Maria Katharina Textor, daughter of a Frankfurt council clerk: from this union were born eight sons (none became a musician) and two daughters. Through his marriage Telemann became a citizen of Frankfurt, a privilege that he retained even after he left for Hamburg, by promising to continue to write church cantatas for Frankfurt.

In September 1716 Telemann visited Eisenach, where he conducted a special concert in honour of the duchess's birthday. Shortly afterwards he was made visiting Kapellmeister at Eisenach. In 1717 he was offered the post of Kapellmeister in Gotha, and there were moves to have him appointed Kapellmeister to all the courts of Duke Ernst's line. Telemann, however, took advantage of the offer from Gotha to strengthen his position in Frankfurt, and he obtained not only better conditions for himself but also the employment of extra musicians. In his application Telemann stressed that he had been active as a singer and instrumentalist as well as a composer and conductor. In 1719 he went to Dresden for the celebrations on the marriage of the Prince Elector of Saxony, Friedrich August II. During this visit he had the opportunity to hear, among other things, several operas by Lotti, and he dedicated a violin concerto to the Dresden Konzertmeister J. G. Pisendel, a pupil of Vivaldi. From Frankfurt he sent his own operas to Leipzig and to Hamburg.

4. HAMBURG. On 10 July 1721 Telemann was invited by the city of Hamburg to succeed Joachim Gerstenbüttel as Kantor of the Johanneum and musical director of Hamburg's five main churches. In his letter to the Frankfurt authorities asking to be released from his contract he explained that he had not applied for the post and so regarded the offer as an act of God. He must, however, have had some exploratory contacts with Hamburg, for in January 1721 his opera *Der geduldige Socrates* was given there; he had also contributed pieces to the performance of Keiser's opera *Ulysses* on 7 July 1721. Presumably the prospect of finding an outlet for his compositions at the Hamburg Opera was a key factor in his decision to move. A definite disadvantage, however, was that the director of music was obliged to act as school Kantor. At his installation on 16 October 1721 Telemann delivered a Latin panegyric on the '*excellentia*' of church music.

Telemann's new post demanded unprecedented productivity. For each Sunday he was expected to write two cantatas and for each year a new Passion. Special cantatas were required for induction ceremonies, and oratorios for the consecration of churches. Still more cantatas had to be written and performed to mark civic celebrations, of which there were many; and, once a year, to entertain the guests of the commandant of the city's militia, Telemann had to provide the 'Kapitänsmusik', consisting of an oratorio and a serenata. The demands of his official duties did not, however, prevent Telemann from once again conducting a col-

1. Georg Philipp Telemann: engraving by G. Lichtensteger

legium musicum in public concerts, or from participating in operatic productions. At first he met strong opposition, and in July 1722 a group of city councillors tabled a motion forbidding the Kantor to take part in public performances of theatrical or operatic music. Telemann reacted by applying for the post of Kantor at the Thomaskirche, Leipzig, which conveniently had fallen vacant on Kuhnau's death. Having been chosen by the Leipzig authorities, he wrote asking to be released from his Hamburg contract, stating that he had decided to accept the Leipzig invitation because the post there was materially more advantageous and because the Hamburg public were not favourably disposed towards him. After lengthy deliberations the council refused to release Telemann. But his stipend was increased, and no further objections were raised to his public concerts or his involvement with the opera. In July 1723 Telemann told J. F. A. von Uffenbach that his public concerts were patronized by many high-ranking people, the most prominent citizens and the entire council. He was entirely responsible for the establishment of public concerts in the city. In 1722 he was appointed musical director of the Hamburg Opera, of which he had charge until it closed in 1738. As well as many operas by Telemann

himself, works by Handel and Keiser were prominent in the programmes; for these he often provided additional material.

Telemann had published a number of his chamber works while he was still in Frankfurt; and in Hamburg, between 1725 and 1740, he brought out a further 44 publications, 43 of them under his own imprint. In this group an entire cycle of 72 sacred cantatas for the church year constitutes one published item, as does the three-part *Musique de table*, comprising 18 separate compositions. Telemann himself usually engraved the plates. Further, he was largely responsible for advertising the editions in the press and for soliciting subscriptions. In Berlin, Leipzig, Jena, Nuremberg, Frankfurt, Amsterdam and London, distribution was arranged through booksellers; elsewhere friends undertook this responsibility.

In autumn 1737 Telemann went to Paris, where he remained for eight months. The 1739 autobiography suggests that a group of musicians familiar with his music had invited him there and arranged performances of his works. One reason for the visit may have been Telemann's desire to forestall the printing of pirated editions of his music. Before 1734, Boivin had brought out six of his trio sonatas from a pirated manuscript, and in April 1736 Le Clerc was granted a royal warrant authorizing him to reprint five of Telemann's publications without the composer's consent. When Telemann arrived in Paris these had already appeared. He was given his own warrant, and during his stay he brought out two new editions, although he was powerless to prevent a further five pirated editions from Le Clerc after 1740. Performances of his works at court and in the Concert Spirituel seem to have won him great acclaim.

On 14 October 1740 Telemann offered for sale the plates of all his own editions of his works. In his biography this step is explained as a consequence of his decision to issue no more of his compositions but rather to devote the rest of his life to compiling books on musical theory. Certainly his musical output fell sharply between 1740 and 1755, though he continued to write Passions, Kapitänsmusiken and music for church consecrations, inductions, memorial services and civic occasions. Few church cantatas of this period have survived, apart from the two series published in 1744 and 1748 (which may have been written before 1740); and the Hamburg Opera was now closed.

1755 marks the beginning of a new phase in Telemann's creativity. Influenced perhaps by Handel, whom he had known since 1701 and with whom he still corresponded in old age, he turned once more, at the age of 74, to writing oratorios, choosing texts by the younger generation of poets, such as K. W. Ramler, F. G. Klopstock, J. A. Cramer, J. F. W. Zachariä and J. J. D. Zimmermann. Some of these late works were still frequently performed in Hamburg decades after Telemann's death.

5. INFLUENCE ON MUSICAL LIFE. Telemann not only lived through a great change in the history of German musical life; he actively helped to bring it about. Until the 18th century a composer's output was largely dictated by the nature of the post he held, and the various spheres of musical activity were strictly defined. A Kantor did not write operas; public performances of music were generally connected with some institution.

But Telemann refused to be fettered, as a composer, by the chains of his official duties; and he broke down the barriers between sacred and secular music. By organizing public concerts, he was trying to give music lovers the opportunity to hear all kinds of music, including some which had originally been composed to lend atmosphere to some special occasion and might otherwise have been heard by only a limited number of people. His concerts might thus include operatic excerpts as well as festive or funeral music. The Passion oratorios which he composed in addition to the liturgical Passions were sung not only in the city's smaller churches but even before paying audiences at public concerts. At a time when music publishing in Germany was still in its infancy, music lovers and self-taught musicians had great difficulty in obtaining printed scores. Telemann's eagerness to publish was prompted by a desire to ease this situation and provide a service to his fellow men. He not only increased sales, but also increased the possibilities for the performance of his music by reducing the scoring in the printed editions of his cantatas or by providing alternative instrumentation in his chamber music. Wherever possible, he avoided technical difficulties, for his constant aim was to achieve a wide dissemination and to foster the spread of music in the home as well as in the collegia musica. In some editions there are traces of Telemann the pedagogue, as when in the *Sonate metodiche* and the *Trietti methodici* he demonstrated the art of ornamentation in an instrumental line; or when, in the vocal *Singe-, Spiel- und Generalbass-Übungen*, the rules of continuo realization are given; or when, in the *Harmonischer Gottes-Dienst*, the principles of performing practice in recitative are elucidated. In the protracted struggle between Telemann and the Hamburg book publishers, the issue in dispute was not only the retailing of the textbooks but the composer's rights regarding the performance of his own works. Telemann's great achievement, through his public concerts, was to establish the composer's prerogative to do as he thought fit with his own compositions, even when they had originally been intended for some special occasion. He gave a new meaning to the post of civic director of music. By refusing to be confined to his contractual obligations, he reorganized the city's music to suit his own forward-looking ideas, and in so doing made his influence felt on musical life throughout Germany.

6. REPUTATION. In the decades between 1720 and 1760, long regarded by musicologists as having been dominated by J. S. Bach, it was not he but Telemann who played the leading role and ranked as one of the most famous and most important German composers. Even in his youth, as director of the Leipzig collegium musicum, he was an inspiration to the music lovers among his fellow students and stimulated the most gifted of them to become professional musicians. Graupner, Pisendel and Heinichen all made music under his direction and were involved in his opera productions. Younger composers such as Fasch and Stölzel, who joined the collegium musicum under Telemann's successor and thus became familiar with some of his compositions, modelled their music on his. In Frankfurt and Hamburg the various civic musical events and the performances by the collegium musicum delighted visitors as well as the local audiences. But it was above all by publishing so many of his compositions that Telemann

made them generally accessible; among the leading theorists of the day, not only Mattheson and Scheibe (who were in constant touch with him in Hamburg and directly influenced by him) but also Quantz and Marpurg could cite his works when setting out rules of composition and principles of style. Scheibe ranked Hasse, C. H. Graun, Telemann and Handel as the most advanced of the German composers, and praised their good taste and their achievement in bringing German music into high esteem. In his *Lexicon* J. G. Walther devoted four times as much space to Telemann as he did to his own kinsman J. S. Bach; while the poet Gottsched, in his *Ode zum Lobe Germaniens*, hailed Telemann and Handel as the most distinguished of German composers although as a resident of Leipzig he must have been familiar with the music of J. S. Bach. The subscription lists for some of Telemann's published works indicate that his compositions were also known and loved outside Germany. For the *Musique de table* (1733), 52 of the 206 subscriptions came from abroad, 33 of them from France. Handel sent an order from London, and in several subsequent compositions (for example the Organ Concerto op.7 no.4) he borrowed and reworked many themes from the *Musique de table*. Another subscription list, that for the *Nouveaux quatuors* (Paris, 1738), attracted 237 orders, no fewer than 138 of them from France. Scheibe admired Telemann's compositions for their artlessness and unforced ease by comparison with the exaggerated contrapuntal artificiality and 'eye music' of the older composers. Telemann, in fact, was praised for not composing like Bach.

When the 19th century rediscovered Bach, it was Bach's concept of his official position and style of composing that were adopted as the criteria. A Kantor who had written operas came to be looked down on as merely a 'fashionable' composer, lacking in religious fervour. Although his works were hardly known, Telemann was criticized as superficial and excessively prolific. His output surpassed Bach's not only because he refused to be restricted by his official duties. Bach was content to produce no more than five cantata cycles during his 27 years in Leipzig; Telemann is known to have written at least 31. Clearly he believed that, because of his desire to reorganize the city's musical life in accordance with his own ideas, he must be seen to be all the more wholehearted in fulfilling his prescribed tasks. It was not until the 20th century, when he had long been written off as too facile, that research began to give a more general view of his creativity, to make the works more widely known, and to seek a more rational evaluation of him. This trend originated in the contentions of Max Schneider and Romain Rolland, which argue that Telemann's musical ideas were entirely different from those of Bach, that it is pointless to compare the two, and that Telemann should be seen as a forerunner of the Classical style. This clearly does not hold good for all the works or categories; but the present state of research allows for more detailed distinctions of judgment.

7. SACRED MUSIC. Church cantatas were rarely published in the 18th century. Telemann, however, brought out four complete annual cycles and the arias from a further cycle, reducing the scoring so as to make them suitable for smaller church choirs and domestic worship. In 1752 Quantz could ironically claim that, until a

2. *The title-page of Telemann's 'Harmonischer Gottes-Dienst'* (Hamburg, 1725–6) *with the opening of the cantata 'Am Feste der Heiligen Drey Einigkeit'*

few years before, there had still been some Kantors who could not bring themselves to perform one of Telemann's sacred works. The style of his cantatas met the demands of the music theorists. When he was still at Sorau, Telemann had met Erdmann Neumeister, originator of the modern 'madrigal' type of church cantata, designed to resemble nothing more or less than 'an operatic piece, combining recitatives and arias'. Mattheson thought that church music should aim to arouse the emotions in a specific way and to interpret the finer points of the text dramatically. To achieve this, the most appropriate style was that of the theatre, for even in church we are only human beings, susceptible to human representations. Both Mattheson and Scheibe expressed their admiration for the expression and harmony of Telemann's sacred music. Scheibe felt that sacred music demanded an elevated style the more vividly to bring out the imagery and 'affect' of the text. As an experienced opera composer Telemann was a master of the art of interpreting in musical terms the words and the sense of his text, and was quick to respond to any cue offered to him by his librettist. Although the edition of the cycle *Harmonischer Gottes-Dienst* requires one voice, one melody instrument and continuo, it demonstrates the broad range of possibilities inherent in theatrical church music. Words like 'hell', 'terror', 'revenge', 'torment',

'fear' etc are treated dramatically; but when the text speaks of 'grace', 'quiet enjoyment' or 'innocent trust', the music conveys the mood in smooth cantabile lines with the simplest of accompaniments. Here Telemann is a more straightforward composer than Bach. With its simple scoring and the restricted scope of each of its cantatas, *Harmonischer Gottes-Dienst* is exceptional in Telemann's cantata output. In each cycle his treatment of text, form and scoring are different. About 90 per cent of the surviving cantatas are for four or more voices, and about 60 per cent are accompanied by strings and woodwind; the cantatas for special feast days also have brass. When Scheibe called for harmony as well as expression, he meant that in the larger-scale works the middle parts should be unobtrusive, free from unvocal ornamentation and too frequent dissonances; overelaborate counterpoint should be avoided, since it made the music obscure and unnatural. Telemann's cantatas fulfilled all these conditions.

In Hamburg one of Telemann's obligations was to write each year a new Passion, to be performed in turn in each of the five principal churches. In 46 years he only twice parodied Passions from previous years, and not until he was an old man did he occasionally re-use older recitatives and turba choruses. His Passions, too, clearly reflect the development of the genre in the 18th century. The Gospel text is increasingly filled out with contemplative interpolations, and eventually even parts of the biblical text are altered and dramatized, with Christ's words rewritten as the texts for bravura arias. In the light of this development, Telemann's *St Luke Passion* of 1728 has a special historical significance: here he and his librettist (M. A. Wilkens) attempted to distinguish between the liturgical Passion and the Passion oratorio. The interruptions of the action of the Passion are neither random nor formless – a criticism levelled at Bach's Passions by M. Hauptmann in the 19th century. Before each of the five sections of the Passion story a parallel passage from the Old Testament is inserted, to act as a 'preparation', and is interpreted as an 'application of faith'. Da capo arias are found only in these sections. In the Gospel text only contemplative congregational chorales are interpolated. The turba choruses show concise rhythms and striking word interpretations. Unlike Bach, with his idiosyncratic recitative lines, Telemann, in his Passion recitatives and particularly in the 1728 *St Luke Passion*, kept to the rules laid down by the theorists and modelled on Italian opera recitative: rhythm and melodic line had to be subordinate to speech declamation. Only when the recitative was mostly in quavers could faster or slower declamation or the lengthening of individual notes give point to the text; and only when the melodic line consisted mainly of stepwise movement and repetition could melodic leaps and unusual intervals stand out and become significant. Where the recitative accompaniment generally pursued an uneventful course, the composer could at appropriate points in the text create additional rhetorical accents harmonically. By adopting these basic principles in his recitatives, Telemann was able to achieve the maximum effect with the simplest means.

Apart from the liturgical Passions with biblical texts, Telemann composed six Passion oratorios on freely written librettos. As early as 1716 he set the text by B. H. Brockes, which also served as a model for *Seliges Erwägen*, written in Frankfurt to his own text. This oratorio, whose dramatic accents, contrasting 'affects' and colourful language called for all the resources of theatrical composition, was given almost every year in Hamburg from 1728 in the concert hall and in the smaller churches. After Telemann's death there were 17 performances between 1786 and 1799 alone, although in 1755 he had also written settings of two more modern texts, Ramler's *Der Tod Jesu* and Zimmermann's *Betrachtung der neunten Stunde*.

8. SECULAR VOCAL MUSIC. In Hamburg, Telemann's sacred and secular oratorios and his occasional compositions had many public performances, and their popularity did much towards establishing public concerts. In the oratorios and larger-scale cantatas Telemann followed traditional principles regarding the musical equivalents of rhetorical figures. He took as his starting-point a simple melodic line and easily accessible forms. His striking divergences from conventional musical language are always motivated by the text. Among the smaller secular cantatas of before 1740, some tend towards operatic virtuosity while others display a simple and folklike melodic line in their arias.

With his songs, Telemann revived a category which had fallen into oblivion during Germany's 'songless period'. He published his first songs earlier than Sperontes (*Singende Muse an der Pleisse*, from 1736)

and Gräfe (*Oden-Sammlungen*, from 1737). In the preface to 24 *Oden* (1741) he set out his theories about song composition in lighthearted terms: the melodic line of a song should be comfortable to sing, avoiding extremes of the vocal register and virtuoso ornamentation, it should accord with the sense of the text, and it should fit all the verses. To Telemann the greatest problem lay in determining the correct metric and periodic structure. His collection of *Oden* demonstrates this difficulty: the various texts (drinking-songs, comic songs, moral and pastoral songs) demand corresponding types of melody and accompaniment.

With his intermezzo *Pimpinone* Telemann was again a pioneer in a new development. In this work, written eight years before Pergolesi's *La serva padrona*, many elements of the *buffo* style are present, like the rapid 'babbling' on one note, the repetition of small motifs and the characterization by accompanying figuration in the orchestra. Telemann's surviving operas show that bourgeois German opera did not conform to any specific type. Apart from the intermezzos, he wrote both serious and light operas. The latter include the comic type (*Der geduldige Socrates*) and the satirical (*Der neumodische Liebhaber Damon*). His greatest success was undoubtedly achieved with *Socrates* (1721), whose text had been adapted by J. U. von König from the libretto by Nicolò Minato (1680); it shows many of the traits which later distinguished the *opera buffa* from the *opera seria*. There are 17 ensembles and choruses to 38 arias, the latter showing a diversity of formal structures. The four female singers appear more often in ensembles than in arias. A large-scale choral scene, comprising two choruses, an aria with chorus and a dance, opens the third act. The constant variety in the choice of accompanying instruments serves to highlight the characterization and the situations: a prince's opening aria is accompanied by a solo violin, and to mislead the audience as to which of the two leading ladies will finally prevail, the prima donna introduces herself in an aria with a modest accompaniment for continuo alone (her second aria has a flute obbligato). Changes in style are also used to convey character. When the rival ladies are pursuing the same end, they imitate one another in canon. Socrates' adversary is made ridiculous in a 'revenge' aria which is pushed to the extremes of parody. Such moments of comedy are repeatedly enhanced by effectively contrasting them with others of a more lyrical or seriously contemplative tone.

9. INSTRUMENTAL MUSIC. In evaluating Telemann's contribution to German music, Romain Rolland described him as having let in 'currents of fresh air'. This applies above all to instrumental music. Fresh air had already been added to Germany's musical life through the spread of amateur music-making and music in the home; and Telemann accelerated this process by publishing a great quantity of instrumental music which, though technically not too demanding, offered scope for spirited and lively playing. When Telemann once said that he was no great lover of concertos, he had in mind only the purely virtuoso concerto. He many times exploited the inherent possibilities of concertante techniques in ensemble playing. In his concertos there is no rigid scheme dictating the number, disposition or relationship of the movements, nor the structure of the first movement. When he popularized the French overture in Germany, he turned what had been typical court music into a new

3. Autograph MS from Telemann's opera 'Der geduldige Socrates', first performed in Hamburg, 1721 (D-Bds Mus.ms.autograph Telemann 1, f.39r)

form of light music, epitomized by the programme overture (for example *Don Quixote* and *Hamburger Ebb und Fluht*). But the fresh air was introduced above all in his rejection of the learned style and the formation of the *galant* style. Much (though not all) of Telemann's chamber and keyboard music shows *galant* characteristics: a simple melodic line with clear periodic divisions and transparent structure, in which the accompaniment occupies a purely subordinate role. He was particularly successful in developing a conversational style in his quartets, a form rarely used by other composers and employed by Telemann in each 'production' of the *Musique de table*. He was fond of using elements borrowed from folk music, such as rhythms and melodic phrases which he had first encountered in Polish and Hanakian (Moravian) music. His compositions of before 1740 are historically of particular interest. Side by side with their simple structure, the keyboard fantasias (published in 1732–3) show the beginnings of sonata form. Here Telemann used the technique of bringing together different motifs: some may be re-positioned in the reprise, while others fulfil a specific function as transitional, contrasting or epilogue motifs. The *Fugues légères*, also published before 1740 and described by Telemann as 'Galanterie-Fugen', show by their title the direction in which he was moving. A fugal but almost consistently two-part introduction is followed by a series of short fantasias and dance sections in which tremolando basses, bagpipe accompaniments, unison passages and Polish rhythms appear. This fugue cycle represents the antithesis of Bach's pattern of prelude and fugue. Following the sense of the requirements of Quantz and Marpurg, this is an illustration of the fact that residual traces of the contrapuntal style could still be used to enhance the *galant* style. Art should be combined with charm.

10. THEORY. Telemann's manifold official duties in no way hindered his activities as composer, editor and impresario. It was only in music theory that he was frustrated in his ambitious plans. Problems of theory preoccupied him all his life. In a letter to Mattheson, written in 1717, he announced his intention of writing a treatise on the most common instruments and the best ways of exploiting their individual characteristics. In 1728 a newspaper reported his plans for translating J. J. Fux's *Gradus ad Parnassum*, and a published catalogue of his printed works which appeared that year even listed its price. In the preface to *Der getreue Music-Meister* (1728–9) Telemann gave notice that, work permitting, he would publish theoretical analyses of some of his compositions in later fascicles. In 1731 another newspaper item stated that Telemann was writing a theoretical treatise on musical invention. The printed catalogue of 1733 lists a *Traité du récitatif* among his projected publications, while a treatise on composition was promised in 1735, combining the most important elements from the textbooks of Fux and Heinichen and including some discoveries of his own. After his visit to Paris, Telemann declared his intention of recording in print his impressions of French music and musical life. In the published biography a forthcoming treatise on composition (*Musicalischer Practicus*) is again referred to; and in the preface to the cantata cycle *Musicalisches Lob Gottes* Telemann said that he had intended to write at length on the application of the theatrical style to church music, on the composition of German recitative

and on the use of dissonance. But he then limited himself to a few observations on the figuring of thoroughbass, and referred again to the *Musicalischer Practicus*, which was to throw further light on the subject.

Telemann, a self-taught musician, intended through his theoretical writings to make performance and composition more accessible to the amateur. The basic rules for setting out continuo parts are laid down in his detailed comments on the songs in the *Singe-, Spiel- und Generalbass-Übungen*. The appendix to the 1730 songbook not only gives directions for setting out continuo parts; it also gives a first introduction to writing inner parts where upper and lower ones are given. Telemann dealt with the basic principles of recitative composition in the foreword to the *Fortsetzung des Harmonischen Gottesdienstes*; and important rules on the proper performance of recitative had already been given in the preface to *Harmonischer Gottes-Dienst*. In many of his prefaces, and in particular in the autobiographies, Telemann gave indications of his attitude to music and to questions of musical aesthetics. Surprisingly, his contribution to the Sozietät der Musikalischen Wissenschaften, founded by Mizler, touched neither on composition nor on performing practice; instead he gave them his *Neues musicalisches System*. Here he attempted a theoretical demonstration of chromatic and enharmonic relationships, and tried to show the difference between B♯ and C, F𝄪 and G etc. But he did not mention all the possible alternatives and limited himself for each interval to four degrees – smallest, small, large and largest 2nd (C–D♭♭, D♭, D and D♯; thus the use of the double flat would preclude that of the double sharp, and vice versa). The criticism of this thesis by some members of the society was unjustified. Intervallic relationships cannot be demonstrated on an equal-tempered keyboard, and it was not Telemann's intention to develop a new temperament; nor had he contemplated using occasional enharmonic changes in harmonizing simple chorales unless called for by the text. Later Scheibe claimed priority for his own discovery of the interval system, though he conceded that he had discussed with Telemann in advance the details of his *Abhandlung von den musikalischen Intervallen* (1739). Only after Telemann's death did Scheibe also reveal that the *Critischer Musikus* stemmed from a joint project with Telemann, who had originally intended to compose every other piece himself, and had indeed seen and approved the first 14 pieces before printing. Even if this belated recognition contradicts other statements by Scheibe, it is certain that Scheibe's discussions with Telemann in Hamburg greatly stimulated his work on the *Critischer Musikus* and that his whole musical philosophy was influenced and strengthened by Telemann.

WORKS

Editions: *G. P. Telemann: Musikalische Werke* (Kassel and Basle, 1950–) [T]
       G. P. Telemann: Orgelwerke, ed. T. Fedtke (Kassel, 1964) [F]

SACRED CANTATAS

Principal sources: *B-Bc, D-B/Bds, Bdhm, DS, F*, formerly Königsberg, *LEm, LEt, SHk, SWl, DK-Kk GB-Lbm*; all printed cycles contain 72 cantatas.
Harmonischer Gottes-Dienst, oder Geistliche Cantaten zum allgemeinen Gebrauche, 1v, 1 inst, bc (Hamburg, 1725–6); T ii–v
Auszug derjenigen musicalischen und auf die gewöhnlichen Evangelien gerichteten Arien, 1v, bc (Hamburg, 1727) [arias only]
Fortsetzung des Harmonischen Gottesdienstes, 1v, 2 insts, bc (Hamburg, 1731–2)

Musicalisches Lob Gottes in der Gemeine des Herrn, 2–3vv, 2 vn, bc [with tpts, timp for festivals] (Nuremberg, 1744)

Untitled cycle of cantatas for the church year, from 1st Sunday in Advent to 27th Sunday after Trinity, 1v, str, bc [4vv, str, tpt, timp, bc for festivals] (Hermsdorff, 1748)

1043 cantatas, incl. Das ist je gewisslich wahr [= BWV141], ed. in *J. S. Bach: Werke*, xxx (1884); Ich weiss, dass mein Erlöser lebt [= BWV160], ed. in *J. S. Bach: Werke*, xxxii (1886); Gott der Hoffnung erfülle euch [= BWV218], ed. in *J. S. Bach: Werke*, xli (1894); Siehe, es hat überwunden [= BWV219], ed. in *J. S. Bach: Werke*, xli (1894); So du mit deinem Munde (chorus) [= BWV145], ed. in *J. S. Bach: Werke*, xxxiv (1884) and in *J. S. Bach: Neue Ausgabe sämtlicher Werke*, i/10 (1955); Nun komm der Heiden Heiland, ed. R. Fricke (Hameln, 1930); Locke nur, Erde, ed. W. Bergmann (London, 1953); Lobt Gott, ihr Christen, ed. A. Adrio (Berlin, 1947); Gesegnet ist die Zuversicht, ed. A. Dürr (Kassel, 1954); In dulce jubilo, ed. F. Stein (Berlin, 1957); Uns ist ein Kind geboren, ed. H. Jaedtke (Wolfenbüttel and Zurich, 1963); Ein Kindelein so löbelich, ed. K. Schultz-Hauser (Berlin, 1963); Ihr Lieben, gläubet nicht (Kantate wider die falschen Propheten), ed. W. Bergmann (London, 1967); Ehre sei Gott in der Höhe, ed. G. Fock (Kassel, 1969); 9 cantatas ed. in *Die Kantate* (Stuttgart, 1963)

FESTAL CHURCH MUSIC

(*principal sources: A-Wn, B-Bc, D-B/Bds, Dlb, DS*)

Zwo geistliche Cantaten (Sei tausendmal willkommen, S, str, bc; Du bleibest dennoch unser Gott, S, B, str, bc) (Hamburg, 1731)

8 other cantatas for 200th anniversary of the Augsburg Confession (texts only)

Holder Friede, dich zu küssen (cantata, J. J. D. Zimmermann), thanksgiving ceremony for 200 years of religious peace, 1755

Inauguration music: Siehe da, eine Hütte Gottes, Billwerder, Nicolaikirche, 1739, ed. in Rhea; Ich halte mich, Herr, zu deinem Altar, Hamburg, inauguration of altar in Gertrudskirche, 1742; Kommt lasst uns anbeten, Hamburg, Hiobs-Hospitalkirche, 1745; Heilig ist Gott, Hamburg, Georgkirche, 1747; Zerschmettert die Götzen, Neuenstetten, 1751; Singet Gott, lobsinget seinem Namen, Rellingen, 1756; Komm wieder, Herr, Hamburg, Michaeliskirche, 1762

Music for miscellaneous ceremonies: music for the afternoon catechism sermon as perf. in Hamm and Horn, near Hamburg, 1726; 7 cantatas, incl. 5 with frags. only; 74 cantatas (texts only) for prayer introductions; 10 Veni Sancte Spiritus; 3 Komm heiliger Geist

Funeral music: Du aber, Daniel, gehe hin, ed. G. Fock (Kassel, 1968); 11 other funeral cantatas, incl. 3 with frags. only; 7 funeral cantatas (texts only)

OTHER OCCASIONAL VOCAL

(*principal sources: A-Wn, DS, Hs, SWl*)

Wedding music: Auf, ihr art'gen Liebesgötter (wedding entertainment with dancing); O erhabnes Glück der Ehe (serenata, M. Richey), 1732, for golden wedding of Hamburg councillor M. Mutzenbecher; 10 cantatas and 1 cantata frag.; 15 cantatas (texts only)

Music for political ceremonies: De danske, norske og tydske undersaatters glaede, for birthday of Frederik V of Denmark (Hamburg, 1757); Auf, Christenheit, begeh' ein Freudenfest, for birthday of an imperial prince, 1717; Ich will dem Herrn singen, for prince's birthday, Eisenach, 1730; Ich hoffete aufs Licht, funeral music for Karl VII, 1745; Hallelujah, Amen, Lob und Ehre, thanksgiving for victory at Lobositz, 1756; Hannover siegt, der Franzmann liegt, 1758 or 1761; Bleibe, lieber König, leben, 1760; Liebster König, du bist tot, 1760; Grossmächtiger Monarch der Briten, birthday of King of England; Herr, wir danken deiner Gnade, ceremony for the victory of the allies in Hesse; 12 other cantatas (texts only)

Music for academic ceremonies: 2 cantatas (Gebeut, du Vater der Gnade; Geschlagene Pauken, auf auf), for inauguration of a Gymnasium, 1744; 4 cantatas, 5 duets, 4 arias, 1 chorus; 2 frags. of arias; 4 cantatas (texts only)

Kapitänsmusiken, sacred oratorio and secular serenata for the yearly celebrations of the city militia commandant: 9 complete pieces, for 1724, 1730, 1736, 1738, 1742, 1744, 1755, 1760, 1763; serenade only for 1728; oratorio frags. for 1756 and 1761; 9 others (texts only)

PASSIONS, PASSION ORATORIOS

Principal sources: B-Bc, D-B/Bds, Bdhm, LEm, SWl, DK-Kk; thematic catalogue in Hörner.

Music vom Leiden und Sterben des Welt Erlösers (Nuremberg, 1745–9) [from St John Passion, 1745]

46 Passions, 1 for each year 1722–67, incl. St Matthew: 1730, ed. K. Redel (Vaduz, n.d.), 1746, 1750, 1758, 1762, 1766; St Mark: 1759, ed. K. Redel (Vaduz, 1963), 1767; St Luke: 1728, ed. in T xv, 1744, ed. F. Schroeder (Stuttgart, 1966), 1748, 1760, 1764; St John: 1733, 1737, 1745, 1749, 1757, 1761, 1765; remainder lost

Der für die Sünden der Welt gemarterte und sterbende Jesus (B. H.

Brockes), 1716, rev. 1722, ed. H. Winschermann and F. Buck (Hamburg, 1964)

Seliges Erwägen des Leidens und Sterbens Jesu Christi (text: Telemann), 1728

Der bekehrte Hauptmann Cornelius, 1731 (text only)

Die gekreutzigte Liebe, oder Tränen über das Leyden und Sterben unsers Heilandes (J. U. von König), 1731

Der Tod Jesu (K. W. Ramler), solo vv, chorus, orch, 1755

Betrachtung der neunten Stunde an dem Todes-Tage Jesu (Zimmermann), 1755

ORATORIOS

(*principal sources: A-Wn, B-Bc, D-B/Bds, SWl*)

Donnerode (J. A. Cramer), pt.1, 1756, pt.2, 1760; T xxii

Sing, unsterbliche Seele und Mirjam und deine Wehmut, from *Der Messias* (F. G. Klopstock), 1759; ed. G. Godehart (Celle, n.d.)

Das befreite Israel (J. F. W. Zachariä), 1759; T xxii

Die Hirten bei der Krippe zu Bethlehem (Ramler), 1759

Die Auferstehung und Himmelfahrt Jesu (Ramler), soli, chorus, orch, 1760

Die Auferstehung (Zachariä), 1761; ed. W. Menke (Hamburg, 1967)

Der Tag des Gerichts (C. W. Alers), 1762; ed. in DDT, xxviii (1907/R)

Der königliche Prophet David als ein Fürbild unseres Heilands Jesu (König), 1718; Freundschaft gehet über Liebe, 1720: both lost

MASSES, ETC

(*principal sources: B-Bc, D-B/Bds, F*)

Missa sopra 'Ein Kindelein so löbelich', ed. K. Schultz-Hauser (Heidelberg, 1964)

Missa sopra 'Allein Gott in der Höh' sei Ehr', ed. W. Menke (Stuttgart, 1967)

9 other masses on chorale tunes: Ach Gott, vom Himmel sieh darein, Christ lag in Todesbanden, Durch Adams Fall, Erbarm' dich mein, Es woll' uns Gott genädig sein, Gott der Vater wohn' uns bei, Komm heiliger Geist (2 settings), Es wird schier der letzte Tag kommen

Missa brevis, 4vv, bc; Missa alla siciliana, 4vv, chorus, vn, bc; 2 short masses (Ky–Gl)

Sanctus, Pleni sunt coeli, 4vv, 2 ob, 3 tpt, timp, str, bc

Heilig ist der Herr, unacc. male voice chorus 2vv

Magnificat (Lat.), 4vv, 3 tpt, timp, str, bc, ed. K. Redel (Vaduz, n.d.); Magnificat (Ger.), 4vv, 2 fl, 2 ob, str, bc; Kleines Magnificat (Ger.), S, vn, va, fl, vc [= BWV Anh.21]

PSALMS, MOTETS

(*principal sources: A-Wgm, D-B, Dlb, F, Hs, formerly Königsberg, SWl*)

Der 117. Psalm, 4vv, 2 vn, bc, ed. E. Valentin (Kassel, 1936)

Ach Herr, straf mich nicht (Ps vi), A, 2 vn, bc, ed. W. Steude (Leipzig, 1966)

15 psalms, 4vv, insts; 3 psalms, 3vv, insts; 5 psalms, 2vv, insts; 4 psalms, 1v, insts

Werfet Panier auf (motet), 4vv, ed. in DDT, xlix-l (1915/R)

7 motets: Amen, Lob und Ehre und Weisheit; Es segne uns Gott; Ein feste Burg; Der Gott unsers Herrn; Halt, was du hast; Der Herr ist König; Und das Wort ward Fleisch: ed. W. Menke (Stuttgart, 1967)

Danket dem Herrn (motet), 2 choirs, ed. W. Hobohm (Wolfenbüttel, 1967)

Jauchzet dem Herrn alle Welt, 2 choirs [= BWV Anh.160]

4 motets, ed. in Cw, civ (1967)

12 other motets

MISCELLANEOUS SACRED VOCAL

(*principal sources: A-Wgm, B-Bc, CH-E, D-B/Bds, DS, F, SWl*)

Fast allgemeines evangelisch-musicalisches Lieder-Buch, 4vv, bc (Hamburg, 1730)

[12] Canones, 2–4vv (Hamburg, 1735–6); ed. F. Stein (Berlin and Darmstadt, 1954)

Die Begnadung (Kaum wag' ich es, dir Richter), 1v, bc, in *Unterhaltungen*, ii (Hamburg, 1766), 328

XI dicta biblica, 2vv, 2 vn, bc; 4 duets, incl. 2 a cappella; 8 choruses, 4vv, insts; 2 choruses, 3vv, insts

OPERAS

(*principal sources: A-Wn, D-B/Bds, F, LEm, Mbs, SWl, S-Skma*)

Adonis, 1708, 1 aria extant

Narcissus, 1709, 3 arias extant

Mario, 1709, 2 arias extant

Die Satyren in Arcadien, Leipzig, 1719, rev. 1724, as Der neumodische Liebhaber Damon; T xxi

Der geduldige Socrates (J. U. von König, after Minato), Hamburg, 1721; T xx

Sieg der Schönheit, 1722, rev. 1725 and 1732, as Genserich

Belsazar, 1723, 3 arias extant; 1 in Der getreue Music-Meister (Hamburg, 1728–9)

Pimpinone (intermezzo), 1725 (Hamburg, 1728); ed. in EDM, 1st ser., vi (1936)

La capricciosa e il credulo (intermezzo), 1725, 4 arias extant

Sancio, 1727, 3 arias in Der getreue Music-Meister (Hamburg, 1728–9); 1 ed. in HM, xii (1949)

Calypso, 1727, 1 chorus in Der getreue Music-Meister (Hamburg, 1728–9)

Miriways, 1728

Die Last-tragende Liebe, oder Emma und Eginhard, 1728, destroyed, 1907 copy in US-Wc, 5 arias and 1 duet in Der getreue Music-Meister (Hamburg, 1728–9); 3 arias, 1 duet ed. in HM, xii (1949)

Die verkehrte Welt, 1728, 1 aria and 1 scene in Der getreue Music-Meister (Hamburg, 1728–9)

Flavius Bertaridus, 1729

Aesopus, 1729, 3 arias in Der getreue Music-Meister (Hamburg, 1728–9), 1 ed. in HM, xii (1949)

Don Quichotte der Löwenritter, 1761

Other frags. etc: Lustige Arien aus der Opera Adelheid (Hamburg, 1727–8); Adam und Eva (7 pieces); Hercules und Alceste (4 pieces); Herodes und Mariamne (2 pieces); recit. and aria from unnamed opera in Der getreue Music-Meister (Hamburg, 1728–9); 7 other operas, 2 intermezzos (texts only)

SECULAR CANTATAS

Principal sources: A-Wgm, B-Bc, D-B/Bds, DS, LEm, SHk, SWl, DK-Kk.

Ich kann lachen, ich kann scherzen (M. von Ziegler), in Der getreue Music-Meister (Hamburg, 1728–9)

Sechs Cantaten, 1v, 2 vn, va, vc, rec, fl, ob (Hamburg, 1731)

VI moralische Cantaten, 1v, bc (Hamburg, 1735–6)

6 moralische Cantaten, 1v, vn/fl, bc (Hamburg, 1736–7)

37 cantatas and 2 cantata frags. incl.: Ino, ed. in DDT, xxviii (1907/R); Lustig bei dem Hochzeitsschmause, ed. in Deutsche Hausmusik aus vier Jahrhunderten (Berlin, 1905); Trauer-Music eines kunsterfahrenen Canarienvogels, Die Hoffnung ist mein Leben, Süsse Hoffnung, wenn ich frage, Alles redet jetzt und singet, ed. W. Menke (Kassel, n.d.); Der Schulmeister, ed. F. Stein (Kassel, 1956); Die Tageszeiten, ed. A. Heilmann (Kassel, 1934); Kleine Kantate von Wald und Au, ed. R. Ermeler (Kassel, 1943); Der Weiberorden, ed. W. Hobohm (Leipzig, 1966); Ha ha! Wo will wi hüt noch danzen, ed. W. Hobohm (Leipzig, 1971)

SERENADES, OCCASIONAL MUSIC

(principal sources: D-B/Bds, F)

Serenades: Unsre Freude wohnt in dir; Willkommen, schöner Freudentag; Erklinget durch gedoppelt; Kommt mit mir, ihr süssen Freuden; Ihr lieblichen Täler, annehmliche Felder; 24 others (texts only)

Music for the Admiralty jubilee: Unschätzbarer Vorwurf, 1723

Music for the jubilee of the Hamburg College of Commerce, 1765 (sinfonia only)

Serenade to the Petrimahl, 1724 (text only)

Music for the jubilee of the aldermen, 1728 (text only)

SONGS

2 songs in Der getreue Music-Meister (Hamburg, 1728–9); incl. Das Frauenzimmer verstimmt sich immer, ed. in HM, xii (1949)

48 songs in Singe-, Spiel- und Generalbass-Übungen (Hamburg, 1733–4); ed. M. Seiffert (Kassel, n.d.)

24 Theils ernsthafte, theils scherzende Oden (Hamburg, 1741), ed. in DDT, lvii (1917/R)

3 songs in F. W. Birnstiel: Oden mit Melodien (Berlin, 1753)

Other songs etc pubd in 18th-century anthologies

Bartholomaeus (quodlibet), 3vv, bc, D-B/Bds

35 songs in J. C. Losius: Singende Geographie (Hildesheim, 1708) [handwritten anon. adds.]; ed. in Hoffmann (1962)

OVERTURES, ETC

Principal sources: B-Bc, D-B/Bds, Dlb, DS, KA, MÜu, ROu, SWl, DK-Kk; thematic catalogue and editions in Hoffmann (1969).

3 ovs. (e, D, B♭) in Musique de table (Hamburg, 1733); T xii–xiv; ed. in DDT, lxi–lxii (1927/R)

Six ouvertures à 4 ou 6 (Hamburg, 1736), destroyed; incl. 2 (g, a) ed. in Perlen alter Kammermusik (Leipzig, n.d.)

122 ovs.; 3 frags of ovs.; 1 ov. destroyed

4 syms.; 2 divertimentos, ed. in Musikschätze der Vergangenheit (Berlin, 1936–7)

CONCERTOS

Principal sources: A-Wgm, B-Bc, D-B/Bds, Dlb, Ds, MÜu, PA, ROu, SWl, S-Skma, US-Wc; thematic catalogue in Kross (1969).

Conc., A, fl, vn, str; conc., F, 3 vn, str; conc., E♭, 2 hn, str: all in Musique de table (Hamburg, 1733), T xii–xiv, ed. in DDT, lxi–lxii (1927/R)

47 concs. for 1 solo inst, str: 21 for vn, 12 in T xxiii, 1 (G) ed. F. Schroeder and F. Rübart (Zurich, 1965), 1 (a) ed. K. Grebe (Hamburg, 1967), 12 ed. S. Kross (Kassel, 1973); 11 for fl; 8 for ob; 2 for rec; 2 for ob d'amore; 2 for va; 1 for hn; 1 for tpt

25 concs. for 2 solo insts, str: 8 for 2 vn, 1 (G) ed. W. Lebermann

(Mainz, 1970); 4 for 2 hn; 3 for 2 fl; 2 for 2 chalumeaux; 2 for rec, va da gamba; 1 for 2 va; 1 for 2 ob d'amore; 1 for rec, fl; 1 for rec, bn; 1 for ob, vn; 1 for vn, vc

9 concs. for 3 solo insts, incl. conc., D, 3 tpt, ed. G. Fleischhauer (Leipzig, 1968); conc., D, vn, tpt, vc, ed. H. Töttcher and K. Grebe (Hamburg, 1965)

6 concs. for 4 solo insts, incl. conc., B♭, 2 fl, ob, vn; ed. G. Fleischhauer (Leipzig, 1974)

8 concerti grossi, incl. conc., F, a 7, ed. F. Brüggen and W. Bergmann (London, 1967), conc., F, rec, ob, 2 hn, bn, ed. F. Schroeder (Adliswil, 1972)

CHAMBER MUSIC

Principal sources: A-Wgm, Wn; B-Bc; D-B/Bds, BMs, Dlb, DS, F, Gs, LEm, PA, ROu, Sl, SWl; DK-Kk; F-Pn; GB-Lbm; S-Skma; catalogue in Graeser (1924).

(without bc)

Sonates sans basse, 2 fl/vn/rec (Hamburg, 1727); T viii

Sonata, D, va da gamba; Sonata, B♭, 2 fl/va da gamba, ed. in HM, xi (1949); Suite, D, 2 vn, ed. in HM, xi (1949); Carillon, F, chalumeau, chalumeau/rec/fl; Menuett, 2 hn; Sonata, B♭, 2 insts, ed. in HM, xi (1949): all in Der getreue Music-Meister (Hamburg, 1728–9)

12 fantaisies, fl (Hamburg, 1732–3); T vi

[12] Fantaisie, vn (Hamburg, 1735); T vi

12 fantasies, b viol (Hamburg, 1735)

XIIX Canons mélodieux, ou VI Sonates en duo (Paris, 1738); T viii

3 sonatas, D, e, b, 3 insts, in Sonates en trio, fls, vns etc (Paris, 1738–42) [only fl II extant]

Duo, 2 vn/fl/ob, livre II (Paris, 1752); T vii

Sei duetti, 2 fl; T vii

3 concertos, C, D, G, 4 vn; T vi

2 sonatas, e, f♯, 2 fl

(for 1 instrument and bc)

Six sonates, vn, bc (Frankfurt, 1715); ed. in Moecks Kammermusik, nos.101–3 (Celle, 1948)

Kleine Cammer-Music, bestehend aus VI Partien (Frankfurt, 1716); ed. in HM, xlvii (1949)

Sei suonatine, vn, hpd (Frankfurt, 1718); ed. K. Schweickert (Mainz, 1938)

Solos, vn, bc, op.2 (London, c1725)

Sonate metodiche, vn/fl, bc (Hamburg, 1728); T i

10 Sonatas, 7 other pieces in Der getreue Music-Meister (Hamburg, 1728–9); ed. in HM, vi–viii (1949), xiii (1949), clxxv (1961) clxxxix (1966), ed. in NM, viii (1966), ed. H. Ruf (Mainz, 1966); 4 sonatas ed. W. Bergmann (London, 1974)

[6] Nouvelles sonatines, hpd/vn/fl, 2 for rec, bc (Hamburg, 1730–31) [only 1 inst pt. extant]

Continuation des Sonates methodiques (Hamburg, 1732); T i

3 solo sonatas, fl, vn, ob, in Musique de table (Hamburg, 1733); T xii–xiv, ed. in DDT, lxi–lxii (1927/R)

XII Solos, vn/fl, bc (Hamburg, 1734); 2 ed. F. Brüggen (Amsterdam, n.d.)

10 Sonatas in Essercizii musici (Hamburg, 1739–40); 1 ed. W. Woehl (New York, 1939), 1 ed. in NM, clxiii (1953), 2 ed. R. Lauschmann (Hamburg, 1954), 4 ed. H. Ruf (Mainz, 1964–5)

17 other solo sonatas

(for 2 instruments and bc)

6 trio, vn, ob, bc (Frankfurt, 1718), ed. K. Schultz-Hauser (Berlin, 1969)

Musique héroïque, ou XII marches (Hamburg, 1728); ed. E. Pätzold (Berlin, n.d.)

Sonata in Der getreue Music-Meister (Hamburg, 1728–9); ed in HM, x (1949)

III trietti methodici e III scherzi (Hamburg, 1731); ed. M. Schneider (Leipzig, 1948)

Sonates en trio, fl, vns, obs (Paris, 1731–3)

3 sonatas in Musique de table (Hamburg, 1733); T xii–xiv, ed. in DDT, lxi–lxii (1927/R)

Six concerts et six suites (Hamburg, 1734); T ix, xi

Scherzi melodichi (Hamburg, 1734); T xxiv

Sonates Corellisantes (Hamburg, 1735); T xxiv

12 trio sonatas in Essercizii musici (Hamburg, 1739–40); 2 ed. in NM, xlvii (1930), cxxxi (1937); 1 ed. R. Lauschmann (Leipzig, 1925); 1 ed. W. Woehl (Leipzig, 1954); 2 ed. H. Töttcher (Hamburg, 1962); 3 ed. H. Ruf (Mainz, 1964–7); 1 ed. W. Woehl (New York, n.d.)

3 trio sonatas, in Sonates en trio, fls, vns etc (Paris, 1738–42) [only fl II extant]

82 other sonatas; for edns. see Petzoldt (1967)

(quartets and quintets)

Quadri, vn, fl, va da gamba/vc, bc (Hamburg, 1730); T xviii

3 quartets in Musique de table (Hamburg, 1733); T xii–xiv, ed. in DDT, lxi–lxii (1927/R)

Six quatuors ou trios, 2 fl/vn, 2 vc/bn (Hamburg, 1733); T xxv

Nouveaux quatuors en six suites (Paris, 1738); T xix

Quatrieme livre de quatuors, fl, vn, va, bc (Paris, c1752)

23 other quartets; 9 quintets: for edns. see Petzoldt (1967)

KEYBOARD, LUTE

Principal sources: *B-Bc, D-B/Bds, Dlb, LEm, Mbs, GB-Lbm*; thematic catalogue of keyboard music in Schäfer-Schmuck.

Sept fois sept et un menuet (Hamburg, 1728); ed. I. Amster (Wolfenbüttel and Berlin, 1930)

Partia a cembalo solo, G; Ouverture à la polonaise, d; Marche pour M. le Capitaine Weber, F; Retraite, F; La poste, B♭: all in *Der getreue Music-Meister* (Hamburg, 1728–9); ed. in HM, ix (1949)

Zweytes sieben mal sieben und ein Menuet (Hamburg, 1730)

XX kleine Fugen…nach besonderen Modis verfasset, org/hpd (Hamburg, 1731); F ii; ed. in NM, xiii (1928)

[36] Fantaisies pour le clavessin (Hamburg, 1732–3); ed. M. Seiffert (Kassel, 4/1955)

Fugirende und veraendernde Choraele (Hamburg, 1735); F i; ed. A. Thaler (New Haven, Conn., 1965)

Fugues légères et petits jeux, hpd (Hamburg, 1738–9); ed. M. Lange (Kassel, 1929)

2 solos, F, C, hpd, in Essercizii musici (Hamburg, 1739–40); ed. H. Ruf (Mainz, 1964)

VI Ouverturen nebst zween Folgesätzen (Nuremberg, before 1750); ed. in *Deutsche Klaviermusik des 17. und 18. Jahrhunderts*, iv–v (Berlin, n.d.); ed. A. Hoffmann (Wolfenbüttel and Zurich, 1964)

2 fughettas, D, F; F ii

5 chorale preludes; 2 in F i

7 suites; 1 ed. in *Unbekannte Meisterwerke der Klaviermusik* (Kassel, 1930), 1 [= BWV824] ed. in *J. S. Bach: Werke*, xxxvi (1890), 1 [= BWV832] ed. in *J. S. Bach: Werke*, xlii (1894)

Neue auserlesene Arien, Menuetten und Märsche [168 pieces, incl. only 4 authentic], *D-Mbs*

Concerto, b; ed. in *Unbekannte Meisterwerke der Klaviermusik* (Kassel, 1930) [?transcr. of vn conc.]

Lute music: Partie polonaise, B♭, ed. as kbd transcr. in Florilegium musicae antiquae, xi (Kraków, 1963); Partie, G, 2 lutes; 1 suite, formerly W. Wolffheim library, lost; Galanteries pour le luth, cited in catalogue of 1733, ?lost

WRITINGS

Beschreibung der Augen-Orgel (Hamburg, 1739)

Neues musicalisches System, in L. C. Mizler, Musikalische Bibliothek, iii/4 (Leipzig, 1752/R1966), 713; rev. as Letzte Beschäftigung G. Ph. Telemanns im 86. Lebensjahre, bestehend in einer musikalischen Klang- und Intervallentafel, in Unterhaltungen, iii (Hamburg, 1767)

EDITIONS BY TELEMANN

MUSIC

Johann Ernst of Saxe-Weimar: 6 concerts, solo vn, 2 vn, va, hpd/bass viol (Leipzig and Halle, 1718)

Works by 13 composers in Der getreue Music-Meister (Hamburg, 1728–9)

J. Graf: 6 soli, vn, bc (Hamburg and Rudolstadt, 1737)

C. Förster: Sei duetti, 2 vn, bc, op.1 (Paris, 1737)

J. Hövet: Musikalische Probe eines Concerts vors Clavier (Hamburg, 1741)

WRITINGS

C. J. F. Haltmeier: Anleitung, wie man einen General-Bass…in alle Tone transponieren könne (Hamburg, 1737)

D. Kellner: Treulicher Unterricht im General-Bass (Hamburg, 2/1737)

G. A. Sorge: Anweisung zur Stimmung und Temperatur (Hamburg, 1744); Gründliche Untersuchung, ob die…Schröterische Clavier-Temperaturen für gleichschwebend passiren können oder nicht (Hamburg, 1754)

BIBLIOGRAPHY

SPECIALIST STUDIES

1. Magdeburger Telemann-Festtage: Magdeburg 1962

R. Petzoldt: *Telemann und seine Zeitgenossen* (Magdeburg, 1966)

3. Magdeburger Telemann-Festtage: Magdeburg 1967

C. C. J. von Gleich: *Herdenkingstentoonstelling G. Ph. Telemann* (The Hague, 1967) [Gemeentemuseum catalogue]

K. Zauft: *Telemanns Liedschaffen* (Magdeburg, 1967)

G. Ph. Telemann, Leben und Werk: Beiträge zur gleichnamigen Ausstellung (Magdeburg, 1967)

I. Allihn: *G. Ph. Telemann und J. J. Quantz* (Magdeburg, 1971)

5. Magdeburger Telemann-Festtage: Magdeburg 1973

Telemann-Renaissance: Werk- und Wiedergabe (Magdeburg, 1973)

BIBLIOGRAPHICAL STUDIES

W. Menke: 'Das Vokalwerk Georg Philipp Telemanns: eine bibliographische Zwischenbilanz', *Mf*, i (1948), 192

M. Ruhnke: 'Zum Stand der Telemann-Forschung', *GfMKB, Kassel 1962*, 161

——: 'Telemann-Forschung 1967', *Musica*, xxi (1967), 6

A. Thaler: 'Der getreue Music-Meister, a "Forgotten" Periodical', *The Consort* (1967), no.24, p.280

M. Ruhnke: 'Telemann als Musikverleger', *Musik und Verlag: Karl Vötterle zum 65. Geburtstag* (Kassel, 1968), 502

——: 'Die Pariser Telemann-Drucke und die Brüder Le Clerc', *Quellenstudien zur Musik: Wolfgang Schmieder zum 70. Geburtstag* (Frankfurt am Main, 1972), 149

LIFE AND WORKS: GENERAL

WaltherML

J. Mattheson: *Grosse Generalbassschule* (Hamburg, 1731) [incl. Telemann's autobiography, 1718]

——: *Grundlage einer Ehren-Pforte* (Hamburg, 1740); ed. M. Schneider (Berlin, 1910/R1969) [incl. Telemann's autobiography, 1739]

Herr G Ph. Telemann: Lebenslauf, ed. B. Schmid (Nuremberg, c1745)

J. D. Winckler: 'G. Ph. Telemann', *Nachrichten von niedersächsischen berühmten Leuten und Familien*, i (Hamburg, 1768), 342

J. Sittard: *Geschichte des Musik- und Concertwesens in Hamburg* (Altona and Leipzig, 1890)

C. Valentin: *Geschichte der Musik in Frankfurt am Main vom Anfange des XIV. bis zum Anfange des XVIII. Jahrhunderts* (Frankfurt am Main, 1906/R1972)

M. Schneider: Preface to DDT, xxviii (1907/R)

A. Schering: *Musikgeschichte Leipzigs*, ii (Leipzig, 1926)

E. Valentin: *Georg Philipp Telemann* (Burg, 1931, 3/1952)

W. Kahl: *Selbstbiographien deutscher Musiker des 18. Jahrhunderts* (Cologne and Krefeld, 1948/R1970)

A. Hoffmann: *Die Lieder der Singenden Geographie* (Hildesheim, 1962)

H. Grosse: 'Telemanns Aufenthalt in Paris', *HJb 1964–5*, 113

W. Hobohm: 'Telemann und seine Schüler', *GfMKB, Leipzig 1966*, 260

W. Bergmann: 'Telemann in Paris', *MT*, cviii (1967), 1101

O. Büthe: 'Das Frankfurt Telemanns', *Frankfurt, Lebendige Stadt*, xii (1967)

R. Petzoldt: *Georg Philipp Telemann: Leben und Werk* (Leipzig, 1967; Eng. trans., 1974 [with list of edns.])

M. Ruhnke: 'Relationships between the Life and Work of Georg Philipp Telemann', *The Consort* (1967), no.24, p.271

W. Hobohm: 'Zwei Kondolenzschreiben zum Tode Georg Philipp Telemanns', *DJbM*, xiv (1969), 117

K. Grebe: *Georg Philipp Telemann in Selbstzeugnissen und Bilddokumenten* (Reinbeck bei Hamburg, 1970)

L. Füredi and D. Vulpe: *Telemann* (Bucharest, 1971)

H. Grosse and H. R. Jung, eds.: *Georg Philipp Telemann, Briefwechsel* (Leipzig, 1972)

W. Hobohm: 'Drei Telemann-Miszellen', *BMw*, xiv (1972), 237

WORKS

M. W. Frey: *Georg Philipp Telemanns Singe-, Spiel- und Generalbass-Übungen* (Zurich, 1922)

H. Graeser: *Georg Philipp Telemanns Instrumental-Kammermusik* (diss., U. of Munich, 1924)

M. Seiffert: 'Georg Philipp Telemanns "Musique de Table" als Quelle für Händel', DDT, *Beihefte*, ii (1927)

H. Hörner: *Georg Philipp Telemanns Passionsmusiken* (Leipzig, 1933)

K. Schäfer-Schmuck: *Georg Philipp Telemann als Klavierkomponist* (diss., U. of Kiel, 1934)

H. Büttner: *Das Konzert in den Orchestersuiten Georg Philipp Telemanns* (Wolfenbüttel and Berlin, 1935)

W. Menke: *Das Vokalwerk Georg Philipp Telemanns* (Kassel, 1942)

A. Dürr: 'Zur Echtheit einiger Bach zugeschriebener Kantaten', *BJb*, xxxix (1951–2), 30

F. D. Funk: *The Trio Sonatas of Georg Philipp Telemann* (diss., George Peabody College, Nashville, 1954)

L. Hoffmann-Erbrecht: *Deutsche und italienische Klaviermusik zur Bachzeit* (Leipzig, 1954)

W. Braun: 'B. H. Brockes' "Irdisches Vergnügen" in Gott in den Vertonungen G. Ph. Telemanns und G. F. Händels', *HJb 1955*, 42

G. Hausswald: Prefaces to *G. P. Telemann: Musikalische Werke*, vi–viii (Kassel and Basle, 1955)

F. Stein: 'Eine komische Schulmeister-Kantate', *Festschrift Max Schneider* (Leipzig, 1955), 183

H. C. Wolff: *Die Barockoper in Hamburg* (Wolfenbüttel, 1957)

C. H. Rhea: *The Sacred Oratorios of Georg Philipp Telemann* (diss., Florida State U., 1958)

W. S. Newman: *The Sonata in the Baroque Era* (Chapel Hill, 1959, rev. 2/1966/R1972)

P. Sisk: *Telemann's Menuet Collection of 1728* (diss., U. of Texas, 1960)

G. Godehart: 'Telemanns Messias', *Mf*, xiv (1961), 139

J. Birke: 'J. Hübners Text zu einer unbekannten Festmusik Telemanns', *Mf*, xvii (1964), 402

M. Ruhnke: 'G. Ph. Telemanns Klavierfugen', *Musica*, xviii (1964), suppl., 103

——: Preface to *G. P. Telemann: Musikalische Werke*, xv (Kassel and Basle, 1964)

W. Bergmann: Prefaces to *G. P. Telemann: Musikalische Werke*, xviii–xix (Kassel and Basle, 1965)

A. Briner: 'Die neuentdeckte Matthäuspassion von Telemann', *SMz*, cv

B. Baselt: 'Georg Philipp Telemann und die protestantische Kirchenmusik', *Musik und Kirche*, xxxvii (1967), 196

——: Preface to *G. P. Telemann: Musikalische Werke*, xx (Kassel and Basle, 1967)

C. P. Gilbertson: *The Methodical Sonatas of Georg Philipp Telemann* (diss., U. of Kentucky, 1967)

W. Maertens: 'Georg Philipp Telemanns Hamburger Kapitänsmusiken', *Festschrift für Walter Wiora* (Kassel, 1967), 335

W. C. Metcalfe: 'The Recorder Cantatas of Telemann's Harmonischer Gottesdienst', *American Recorder*, viii/4 (1967), 113

K. Zauft: *Telemanns Liedschaffen und seine Bedeutung für die Entwicklung des deutschen Liedes in der 1. Hälfte des 18. Jahrhunderts* (Magdeburg, 1967)

T. Nishi: 'Georg Philipp Telemann no Junankyoku ni tsuite' [G. P. Telemann's St John Passion], *Ongaku gaku*, xiv/3 (1968)

H.-J. Schulze: 'Das "Kleine Magnificat" BWV Anh.21 und sein Komponist', *Mf*, xxi (1968), 44

C. Annibaldi: 'L'ultimo oratorio di Telemann', *NRMI*, iii (1969), 221

B. Baselt: Preface to *G. P. Telemann: Musikalische Werke*, xxi (Kassel and Basle, 1969)

G. Frum: *The Dramatic-dualistic Style Element in Keyboard Music Published before 1750* (diss., Columbia U., 1969)

A. Hoffmann: *Die Orchestersuiten Georg Philipp Telemanns* (Wolfenbüttel and Zurich, 1969)

S. Kross: *Das Instrumentalkonzert bei Georg Philipp Telemann* (Tutzing, 1969)

M. A. Peckham: *The Operas of Georg Philipp Telemann* (diss., Columbia U., 1969)

L. Finscher: 'Corelli und die "Corellisierenden" Sonaten Telemanns', *Studi corelliani* (Florence, 1972)

G. Fleischhauer: 'Zum Konzertschaffen Georg Philipp Telemanns', *Telemann-Renaissance: Werk- und Wiedergabe* (Magdeburg, 1973), 21

——: 'Telemann, G. Ph.: Orchestersuiten und Instrumentalkonzerte', *Konzertbuch*, iii, ed. H. J. Schaefer (Leipzig, 1974), 469

A. Hoffmann: Preface to *G. P. Telemann: Musikalische Werke*, xxiv (Kassel and Basle, 1974)

W. Maertens: *Telemanns Kapitänsmusiken* (diss., U. of Halle, 1975)

STYLE

R. Rolland: *Voyage musical au pays du passé* (Paris, 1919)

W. Serauky: 'Bach-Händel-Telemann in ihrem musikalischen Verhältnis', *HJb 1955*, 72

E. Valentin: *Telemann in seiner Zeit* (Hamburg, 1960)

H. Pohlmann: *Die Frühgeschichte des musikalischen Urheberrechts* (Kassel, 1962)

M. Ruhnke: 'Telemann im Schatten von Bach?', *Hans Albrecht in memoriam* (Kassel, 1962), 143

W. Maertens: 'Georg Philipp Telemann und die Musikerziehung', *Musik in der Schule*, xv (1964), 498

P. Beaussant: 'Situation de Telemann', *La table ronde* (1965), no.207, p.121; (1966), no.208, p.115

G. Carleberg: *Buxtehude, Telemann och Roman, Mus. och biogr. skisser* (Stockholm, 1965)

G. C. Ballola: 'Telemann dotto e galante', *Lo spettatore musicale*, ii (1967)

G. Fleischhauer: 'Die Musik Georg Philipp Telemanns im Urteil seiner Zeit', *HJb 1967–8*, 173; *HJb 1969–70*, 23–73

A. Dürr: 'Eine Handschriftensammlung des 18. Jahrhunderts', *AMw*, xxv (1968), 308

G. von Dadelsen: 'Telemann und die sogenannte Barockmusik', *Musik und Verlag: Karl Vötterle zum 65. Geburtstag* (Kassel, 1968), 197

A. Dekker: 'J. S. Bach en G. P. Telemann', *Mens en melodie*, xxiv (1969), 304

L. Finscher: 'Der angepasste Komponist', *Musica*, xxiii (1969), 549

H. C. Wolff: 'Das Tempo bei Telemann', *BMw*, xi (1969), 41

M. Ruhnke: 'Zu L. Finschers neuestem Telemann-Bild', *Musica*, xxiv (1970), 340

S. Kross: 'Telemann und die Aufklärung', *Musicae scientiae collectanea: Festschrift Karl Gustav Fellerer* (Cologne, 1973), 284

C. Wolff: 'Ein Gelehrten-Stammbuch aus dem 18. Jahrhundert', *Mf*, xxvi (1973), 217

G. Fleischhauer: 'Einflüsse polnischer Musik im Schaffen Georg Philipp Telemanns', *Wissenschaftliche Zeitschrift der Martin-Luther-Universität*, xxv/3 (1976), 77

MARTIN RUHNKE

Tellefsen, Thomas (Dyke Acland) (*b* Trondheim, 26 Nov 1823; *d* Paris, 6 Oct 1874). Norwegian pianist and composer. He studied in Trondheim with his father, the organist Johan Christian Tellefsen, and with O. A. Lindeman, and gave his first public concert in his home town when he was 18. In the following year he went to Paris, where he became the pupil of his compatriot Charlotte Thygeson, and later attended some of Kalkbrenner's classes. During the years 1844 to 1847 he was taught periodically by Chopin (approximately two years in all), who also became his personal friend and had considerable influence on his musical taste, style of playing and compositions.

After his extremely successful Paris début in 1851 Tellefsen soon became regarded as one of the outstanding pianists of his time, and was especially admired as an interpreter of Chopin's music. He attracted many pupils, particularly among the upper classes, and after Chopin's death also took over some of his teacher's pupils, including Jane Sterling. Until the early 1860s he gave a number of concerts in Paris, Honfleur, London, Stockholm, Christiania, Bergen, Trondheim and other cities. He stayed in London on several occasions both for concerts and teaching. When not travelling he lived mostly in Paris, where he taught, composed and held frequent concerts and social gatherings in his large house. From the early 1860s his declining health gradually forced him to reduce his activities.

Tellefsen composed chiefly for the piano; among his most important works are two concertos (1852, 1854), 16 mazurkas, Norwegian dances, a piano trio (1861), a sonata for two pianos (1870) and two violin sonatas (1856). Although there is an obvious resemblance to the music of Chopin, Tellefsen's is generally more conservative, having mostly diatonic melodies, with only occasional chromatic interjections. His use of ornamentation is far less prominent than with Chopin, but his harmony is typically Romantic in its sudden modulations and harmonic shifts. The mazurkas contain some of his most original ideas, as well as the frequent borrowing of material from Norwegian folk music also found in his other works.

Tellefsen's published output comprises 44 works, most of them first published by Richautt in Paris. There are also some manuscript compositions in the Oslo University Library and in the Ringve Museum in Trondheim.

BIBLIOGRAPHY
T. S. Tellefsen, ed.: *Thomas Tellefsens familiebreve* (Christiania, 1923)

H. Huldt-Nystrøm: 'Thomas Dyke Acland Tellefsen', *Norsk musikkgranskning årbok 1956–8*, 80–198

KARI MICHELSEN

Teller, Florian Johann. *See* DELLER, FLORIAN JOHANN.

Teller, Marcus (*fl* 1715–27). Netherlands composer. The only record of his life is found in the list of priests at St Servais, Maastricht, where his name appears between 1715 and 1727. He published much small-scale Catholic church music in Augsburg – one of few composers from northern Europe to do so – whose simple, tuneful style is typical of that adopted by Bavarian church composers.

WORKS
(all published in Augsburg)

Novem motetta, 4vv, 3 insts, op.1 (*c*1720)
Trois messes, 4vv, 4 insts, op.2 (*c*1720)
Quatre motets, 2vv, 4 insts (*c*1720)
Missae solennes, 4vv, 3 insts (*c*1720)
Messe de Requiem, c, 2vv, 4 insts, op.2 (*c*1725)
Musica sacra, stylo plane italico et cromatico, 4vv, insts (1726), incl. 6 masses, 13 motets
3 masses, 1 requiem, 4 motets, for 4vv, 2 vn, va, bn, bc (*c*1730), lost
Missa pro defunctis à 10, Missa solemnis à 10, *B-Bc*

ELIZABETH ROCHE

Tellern (Ger.). CYMBALS.

Telmányi, Emil (*b* Arad, Hungary [now Oradea, Romania], 22 June 1892). Hungarian violinist and conductor. He made his début at the age of ten and studied the violin (with Hubay) and composition at the Budapest Academy, winning the Reményi Prize in 1906. He began a professional career in 1911, and attracted international attention with his Berlin début that year, when he gave the first German performance of Elgar's Concerto. Admired for the fluency and vitality of his playing, he also acquired a reputation as a conductor after his début in 1919 at Copenhagen, where he later formed and conducted a chamber orchestra.

Telmányi married Anne Marie, younger daughter of Nielsen, in 1918, and eventually settled in Denmark. He made his London début in 1923 on a visit with Nielsen, of some of whose works he has given premières as a soloist or conductor. He was assistant conductor with the Göteborg SO (1925–6) and in 1926 conducted *Don Giovanni* and *Il trovatore* at the Budapest Royal Opera. His second marriage in 1936 was to the pianist Annette Schiøler and from 1956 they have performed and recorded with their three children as a quintet. Telmányi has also been active as a teacher, arranger and a writer.

Telmányi's interest in problems of performing Baroque music led him to bring about the construction of a special violin bow (named the 'Vega' bow in 1954) with a curved back and a mechanism for instantly tightening or loosening the hairs. He used this in his recordings of Bach's solo violin music, and demonstrated it widely in 1955 (in two London recitals, among others). It was favourably received as a means of playing true chords across the strings softly as well as loudly, avoiding the usual arpeggio effect, but its use has not become widespread.

WRITINGS

'Akkordteknikken i Bach's sonater for solo-violin', *Dansk musiktidsskrift*, xxvi/6 (1951)
'Some Problems in Bach's Unaccompanied Violin Music', *MT*, xcvi (1955), 14
'The Purpose of the Vega Bach Bow', *MT*, xcvi (1955), 371
'The Bach Bow', *The Strad*, lxvii (1956), 144
'Introduktion til Carl Nielsens violinvaerker', *Oplevelser og studier omkring Carl Nielsen* (Århus, 1966)
'Koncersal kontra mikrofon', *Dansk musiktidsskrift*, xliii/7–8 (1970)

BIBLIOGRAPHY

V. Papp: *Arcképek a zenevilágból* [Portraits from musical life] (Budapest, 1918–25)
A. Tóth: 'Telmányi, Emil', *Nyugat*, xiv (Budapest, 1921), 80
J. Creighton: *Discopaedia of the Violin, 1889–1971* (Toronto, 1974)
NOËL GOODWIN

Temianka, Henri (*b* Greenock, 19 Nov 1906). American violinist and conductor of Scottish birth. He studied with Blitz in Rotterdam (1915–23), with Hess at the Berlin Hochschule (1923–4), with Boucherit in Paris (1924–6), and with Flesch and Rodzinski (conducting) at the Curtis Institute, Philadelphia, from which he graduated in 1930. He made his début in New York in 1928, followed by recitals in Paris and London in 1932. He was leader of the Scottish Orchestra (1937–8) and the Pittsburgh SO (1941–2), but he devoted himself mainly to an expanding career as a soloist. In 1935 he was a prizewinner at the Wieniawski Competition in Warsaw and was invited to play in the USSR, where he returned in 1936 and 1937. In 1946 he founded the Paganini String Quartet, so named because the four instruments used by the players were once owned by Paganini, and under his leadership the quartet

achieved international success until it disbanded in 1966; it gave premières of works by Castelnuovo-Tedesco, Milhaud and Lees, among others. In 1960 Temianka founded the California Chamber SO which is widely acclaimed for its polished performances. He has held master classes at state universities, and among his professorial appointments were those at the University of California at Santa Barbara (1960–64) and California State University at Long Beach (1964–76). He has made a number of educational films and has published *Facing the Music* (New York, 1973) and numerous articles; he has also edited several quartets in collaboration with members of the Paganini Quartet. As a violinist Temianka is known for his flawless mastery of his instrument, a pure and expressive tone, and forceful yet elegant interpretations. His temperament is controlled by intellect, and he combines the best elements of the French tradition and the Flesch school. His quartet performances were distinguished by strong leadership and a modern approach, projecting with brilliance while preserving musical values. Among his finest recorded performances are Beethoven's Razumovsky Quartets.

BIBLIOGRAPHY

J. Creighton: *Discopaedia of the Violin, 1889–1971* (Toronto, 1974)
BORIS SCHWARZ

Tempérament égal (Fr.; It. *temperamento equabile*). EQUAL TEMPERAMENT.

Temperaments. Tunings of the scale in which most or all of the concords are made slightly impure in order that few or none will be left distastefully so. Equal temperament, in which the octave is divided into 12 uniform semitones, is the standard Western temperament today except among specialists in Renaissance or Baroque music. This article traces the history of temperaments in performing practice; for additional technical details *see* INTERVAL, TUNING, PYTHAGOREAN INTONATION, JUST INTONATION, MEAN-TONE, WELL-TEMPERED CLAVIER and EQUAL TEMPERAMENT.

1. Introduction. 2. Regular mean-tone temperaments to 1600. 3. Irregular keyboard temperaments to 1680. 4. Equal temperament to 1735. 5. Regular mean-tone temperaments from 1600. 6. Irregular temperaments from 1680. 7. Equal temperament from 1735. 8. Fretted instruments.

1. INTRODUCTION. Since the mid-15th century, tempered tuning has characterized keyboard music and in Western culture the art music of fretted instruments such as the lute. Its prevalence is due mainly to the fact that the concords of triadic music – octaves, 5ths and 3rds – are in many cases incommensurate in their pure forms. Three pure major 3rds (e.g. A♭–C–E–G♯) fall short of a pure octave by approximately one fifth of a whole tone (lesser diesis); four pure minor 3rds (G♯–B–D–F–A♭) exceed an octave by half as much again (greater diesis); the circle of 5ths, if the 5ths are pure, does not quite cumulate in a perfect unison; and, most important of all in the context of Renaissance and Baroque music, the whole tone produced by subtracting a pure minor 3rd from a pure 4th (C–F–D) is about 11% smaller than that produced by subtracting a pure 4th from a pure 5th (C–G–D). These discrepancies are summarized in Table 1.

Not all timbres, however, are equally conducive to temperament. In general, it is only when the component overtones of the timbre (together with the fundamental

TABLE 1

If each interval in this chain is tuned pure (untempered),	the last note will be lower than the first by about	The name of this discrepancy is
	41·1 cents.	lesser diesis.
	62·6 cents.	greater diesis.
	23·5 cents.	Pythagorean comma.
	21·5 cents.	syntonic comma.

tone of the note) form a virtually pure harmonic series that consonant intervals will sound sufficiently different in quality from dissonant ones for the need for tempering the concords to arise. A pronounced degree of inharmonicity in the timbre, as in a set of chimes or a xylophone, eliminates the qualitative difference, except in the case of a unison or octave, between the sound of a pure concord and that of a slightly impure or tempered one. (An artful exception to this general rule is mentioned in the last paragraph of §5 below.)

Moreover, theorists are obliged to contrive specific mathematical schemes for tempering the scale only when the medium of performance allows little or no flexibility of intonation, for only then does the incommensurability of pure concords have to be dealt with systematically by the tuner rather than ad hoc by the performer. A singer or violinist will inflect certain intervals depending on their immediate context; but he does not produce thereby a specific temperament because at different moments he will represent each note of the scale by different shades of pitch within a fairly narrow band (about half as wide again, perhaps, as his vibrato). On most keyboard instruments and the harp, however, the complete lack of such flexibility obliges the tuner to impose a specific temperament, while on fretted instruments, the clavichord, and many wind instruments the tuner or maker establishes a certain model of intonation, albeit one that an ingenious player can modify significantly during performance.

For present purposes three main types of temperaments may be distinguished: equal temperament, mean-tone temperament and irregular temperaments. This article will describe primarily the history of their use, but some plain and easy arithmetic is necessary here to distinguish one from another.

For a series of 12 5ths or 4ths to produce cumulatively a perfect unison and so comprise the 'circle of 5ths', each must be tempered by an average of $\frac{1}{12}$ of the Pythagorean comma (hence about two cents) – 4ths larger than pure, 5ths smaller. If three major 3rds are to reach a full octave they must average about 14 cents ($\frac{1}{3}$ of the lesser diesis) larger than pure, while four minor 3rds, in order not to exceed a pure octave, must average about 16 cents ($\frac{1}{4}$ of the greater diesis) smaller than pure. In equal temperament, which is modelled on these averages, the major 3rds are thus tempered seven times as much as the 5ths, and the minor 3rds and major 6ths eight times as much. Historically this is as important an aspect of equal temperament as the fact that, uniquely, it divides the octave into 12 equal semitones. As a harmonic interval the major 3rd f–a at modern concert pitch, for instance, beats seven times per second – too fast for the ear to trace, even subliminally, the rise and fall of each beat, and fast enough to cause an intermittence of tone that is likely to strike an unaccustomed ear as unpleasant in many contexts.

To avoid such heavily tempered 3rds and 6ths, Renaissance and Baroque keyboard musicians tempered their 5ths two or even three times as much as in equal temperament. This choice entailed 'breaking' the circle of 5ths, a fact reflected in traditional pitch notation and nomenclature with their enharmonic distinctions between flats and sharps. If all the good 5ths in such a tuning are diminished the same amount, the result may be called a regular mean-tone temperament, although some writers restrict the term 'mean-tone' to that scheme in which 5ths are tempered so as to produce exactly pure major 3rds. In any mean-tone temperament the diatonic semitones are larger than the chromatic (for instance, D♯ is lower in pitch than E♭).

Certain irregular keyboard temperaments, in which different 5ths are tuned differently but none rendered unserviceable, were favoured during the late 17th and 18th centuries because they enabled the more frequently used 3rds to be tempered less than those used infrequently, and because the various keys thereby gained a diversity of intonational shading that was highly valued by connoisseurs and formed a prominent aspect of 18th-century musical thought. In 17th-century France an irregular scheme midway between a regular mean-tone and a typical 18th-century irregular temperament seems to have played a role in the contemporaneous development of the French keyboard style.

The word 'temper' and its derivatives were originally applied to music in a broader context than they now denote. Carter's *Dictionary of Middle English Musical Terms* (1961) indicates that the adjective 'temperate' was once used in a general sense to mean 'musically controlled', as in a reference (1398) by John of Trevisa to a 'swete voys an temperate sowne'. But the verb 'temperen' and its past participle 'temperd' referred in Middle English unequivocally to tuning, albeit pure tuning as well as tempered tuning in the modern sense; and this meaning was still encountered in 1593: 'Whereupon M. Barleycap tempered up his fiddle, and began' ('Temper', *OED*). In the writings of Zarlino, the eminent 16th-century Italian theorist and musician, 'temperamento' was closely associated with the term 'participatio' by which, according to Gaffurius in 1496, Renaissance organists referred to their use of 5ths diminished 'by a very small and hidden and somewhat uncertain quantity'.

2. REGULAR MEAN-TONE TEMPERAMENTS TO 1600. In the last chapter of his *Musica practica* (Bologna, 1482) Bartolomeo Ramos de Pareia indicated that mean-tone temperament was in common use on keyboard instruments of his day. Earlier in the book he had presented a new, mathematically simple scheme which he said even young singers could use for a monochord to provide a model scale for plainchant. In that scheme the wolf 5th was ostensibly between G and D. But his elaborate and comprehensive rules, in the last chapter, for avoiding 'bad' intervals on fully chromatic instruments ('instrumenti perfecti') leave no doubt that

in general practice G–D was perfectly serviceable and the wolf 5th was between C♯ and A♭. This is corroborated by his lists of 'good' and 'bad' semitones, whole tones, and major and minor 3rds, and by the pattern of his nomenclature for the sharps and flats. Ramos expressed particular concern that only 'good' major 6ths and 3rds be used in cadential progressions. There is confirmation that 'good' did not mean 'Pythagorean' in a letter (published in 1518) from his disciple Giovanni Spataro to Franchinus Gaffurius. Criticizing Gaffurius for saying that the syntonic comma was an insignificant intervallic quantity, Spataro argued, on behalf of Ramos, that for practical music the harsh Pythagorean monochord had to be reduced and smoothed for the ear ('el duro monochordo pythagorico . . . riducto in molle al senso de lo audito'). Gaffurius, though a strict Pythagorean in his mathematical calculations of intervals, acknowledged in 1496 that organists tempered their 5ths, while his chromatic monochord of 1518 (reprinted in 1520) indicates that G♯ and D♯ differed from A♭ and E♭. Ramos's discussion of 'good' cadential 6ths and 3rds mentions the device, which later became widespread in Italy on keyboard instruments in mean-tone (see Barnes, 1971, and Dupont, 1935), of doubling the accidentals A♭ and E♭ to provide their enharmonic neighbours G♯ and D♯; and the 1480 contract for the cathedral organ at Lucca specifies the inclusion of such a device. The use of regular mean-tone temperaments had probably evolved from ad hoc alterations of certain earlier 15th-century untempered schemes in which, as in Ramos's own pedagogical monochord, the wolf 5th was placed ostensibly among the naturals (see Lindley, 1975–6). Perhaps the oldest known keyboard composer whose music requires a mean-tone temperament for its proper effect was Conrad Paumann. His use of triads, as in ex.1, suggests that he regarded them as solid vertical

Ex.1

sonorities, more so than they would in fact be in Pythagorean intonation. The use of triads in contemporary vocal music (e.g. Ockeghem, Busnois and late Dufay) is similar in this respect.

No particular shade of mean-tone temperament on keyboard instruments – such as $\frac{2}{7}$-comma, $\frac{1}{4}$-comma or $\frac{1}{5}$-comma (see MEAN-TONE) – was favoured exclusively at any time during the Renaissance. The earliest mathematically specific formula was Zarlino's scheme of 1558 for $\frac{2}{7}$-comma mean-tone, in which major 3rds are very slightly smaller than pure. But Lanfranco's keyboard tuning instructions of 1533 are unequivocally for some form of mean-tone, such as $\frac{1}{4}$- or $\frac{1}{5}$-comma, with major 3rds slightly larger than pure (and with the wolf 5th lying between G♯ and E♭ instead of between C♯ and A♭ as in Ramos). The same can be inferred from other writers, and not just those who cited Lanfranco. Schlick had implied in 1511 that some organists would prefer such a tuning to his own irregular scheme (see §3 below). The clavichord tuning instructions published by Tomás de Santa María in 1565, though clearly for some form of mean-tone, do not specify the exact quality of the major 3rds; but when

Pietro Cerone copied these instructions in 1613 he added a few words to specify major 3rds slightly larger than pure and declared that this was the method most used by master organ builders ('es manera mas usada de los Maestros de hazer Organos'). An approximation of $\frac{2}{9}$-comma mean-tone (with major 3rds very slightly larger than pure) was described in 1590 by Cyriacus Schneegass, who may have confused it with $\frac{1}{4}$-comma mean-tone.

Meanwhile Zarlino in 1571 described $\frac{1}{4}$-comma mean-tone, which has pure major 3rds, in mathematically clear terms. He said it was new ('un novo Temperamento & . . . una nova Participatione'); but Francisco de Salinas implied in 1577 that he had been using it in the 1530s. Many scholars attribute $\frac{1}{4}$-comma mean-tone to Aaron in his harpsichord tuning instructions of 1523, but an equally legitimate interpretation of Aaron's text suggests that while he would not have faulted regular $\frac{1}{4}$-comma mean-tone, neither did he specify it. Salinas's $\frac{1}{3}$-comma mean-tone (1577), with its pure minor 3rds at the expense of major 3rds distinctly smaller than pure, does not seem to have been used much, even though it is very easy to tune. Salinas himself expressed reservations; Zarlino described it in 1571 as less sonorous than $\frac{1}{4}$- or $\frac{2}{7}$-comma mean-tone, and added in 1588 that 'it seems to me a bit more languid' ('anzi al mio parere è un poco più languido'). Its intervals are virtually identical, however, with those produced by an equal division of the octave into 19 parts, and in that guise it may have been familiar to Guillaume Costeley (see Levy, 1955).

Evidently, then, all the forms of mean-tone described by Abraham Verheyen in his letter to Simon Stevin of about 1600 – namely $\frac{1}{3}$-, $\frac{2}{7}$-, $\frac{1}{4}$-, and $\frac{1}{5}$-comma mean-tone – had been in use, though $\frac{1}{3}$-comma probably least and $\frac{2}{7}$-comma, which is difficult to tune precisely, perhaps less than $\frac{1}{4}$-comma or some shade of mean-tone with major 3rds slightly larger than pure. No doubt most tuners, rather than trying to exemplify any particular mathematical model, merely sought to achieve sonorous 3rds and 6ths without making any 5th or 4th (other than the wolf) beat obstreperously. Yet some of the best may have sought a fairly precise regularity in the tempering of their intervals, if only for the sake of craftsmanship.

Musical evidence cannot show that any specific shade of regular mean-tone was exclusively favoured by any composer, but certain compositions benefit particularly from certain shades. The sprightliness of the sharps and B♮ in ex.2, the first strain of an alman by John Bull, is better served by $\frac{1}{5}$-comma than by $\frac{1}{4}$- or $\frac{2}{7}$-comma mean-tone. Ex.3, the opening of a toccata by Giovanni Gabrieli, gains a certain warmth and dignity in $\frac{2}{7}$-

Ex.2

Ex.3

comma mean-tone, while the relatively untuneful style of the entire toccata minimizes the dull melodic effect of the rather large diatonic semitones of $\frac{2}{7}$- or $\frac{1}{4}$-comma mean-tone. In $\frac{1}{4}$-comma mean-tone the contrast between pure major 3rds and tempered minor 3rds prevents that effect of banality which in equal temperament would afflict the middle bars of ex.4, the opening of an organ

Ex.4

verso by Antonio Valente; and in a more elaborate way the same kind of contrast – but involving tempered 5ths as well – is a positive delight when ex.5, the opening of a Cabezón tiento, is played in $\frac{1}{4}$-comma mean-tone.

Ex.5

The possible use of regular mean-tone on 16th-century fretted instruments is discussed in §8 below.

3. IRREGULAR KEYBOARD TEMPERAMENTS TO 1680. Perhaps the earliest suggestion of an irregular keyboard temperament is an anonymous English prescription for organ pipes of about 1373 ('Incipit mensura', transcribed by K.-J. Sachs, 1970) instructing the builder that the correct pipe length for a chromatic note will halve the difference between its diatonic neighbours that form a Pythagorean whole tone ('Ubicumque vis habere semitonium, semper fistulam inferiorem et superiorem in duas divides'). In the wake of the Renaissance revival of Euclidian geometry (see THEORY, THEORISTS, §8), Henricus Grammateus published in his arithmetic book of 1518 a simple diagram (see fig.1) showing how the geometrical mean between two pipe lengths in the ratio 9 : 8 could be determined by drawing a semicircle on the sum of the lengths 9 and 8 taken as diameter, and then measuring the perpendicular from the juncture of the two lengths. By this means the Pythagorean whole tone would be, in theory, divided into two musically

equal semitones. Grammateus referred to these as 'minor semitones', and other theorists later used that term to designate equal semitones on the lute (see §8 below); but the context of the prescription leaves no doubt that he intended his 'amusing reckoning' ('kurtz-weyllig rechnung') to be applied to organ pipes. Such a temperament would make both B–F♯ and B♭–F sour, however, and even Barbour (1951), though ideologically attracted to it, described it as an organ tuning which 'may have been used in practice but hardly by anyone who was accustomed, like Schlick, to tune by ear'. Nor does any extant Renaissance organ music avoid B♭–F as well as B–F♯.

The irregularities of a number of other schemes similarly deserve scant attention from the student of keyboard performing practice because they are only trivially different from regular schemes (e.g. Aaron, 1523), or quite incompetent (Reinhard, 1604) or of such limited historical and geographical scope (Douwes, 1699) as to be no more important for the history of musical style than the survival, to this day, of Pythagorean intonation as a provincial keyboard tuning method. Also relatively inconsequential, insofar as normal keyboard instruments are concerned, were expert and elaborate irregular schemes for the *arcicembalo* such as those of Vicentino (1555) and Trasuntino (instrument of 1606). However, irregular temperaments of musical consequence were published by Arnolt Schlick (1511) and Marin Mersenne (1635 and 1636).

Schlick's temperament was an artful variant of regular mean-tone with major 3rds slightly larger than pure. The ten 5ths forming a chain from E♭ to C♯ were tempered more or less alike yet not all quite the same, for the major 3rds among the naturals were to be tempered less than those involving an accidental. Implicitly, B–D♯ was not obliged to be serviceable at all, nor was the 5th from C♯ to G♯ or A♭. But to gain a G♯ that could be used (if camouflaged by ornamentation or treated warily as in ex.6) to cadence on A, Schlick

Ex.6

advised tempering the 5th A♭–E♭ larger than pure. The result was to render E–G♯ more or less Pythagorean and A♭–C (as in ex.7) more or less as in equal temperament (see Husmann, 1967, and Lindley, 1974). Schlick remarked that some patrons would prefer to have an unequivocally serviceable G♯ and no A♭ at all, but he considered that arrangement an impoverishment of the

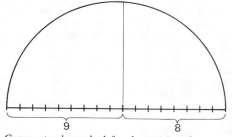

1. Grammateus's method for determining the geometrical mean between two pipe lengths in the ratio 9:8

Ex.7

Ex.8

Ex.9

harmonic resources of the organ; and he disapproved also of splitting accidentals to gain both enharmonic forms in a euphonious intonation. It is not known how widespread the use of Schlick's tuning ever became, but his intended readership encompassed the Holy Roman Empire under Maximilian I.

The context of Mersenne's step-by-step tuning procedure of 1635–6, and his subsequent acknowledgments of errors in the organ instructions, indicate that he had intended merely to prescribe regular ¼-comma mean-tone, for the organ on pp.364f and for the spinet on pp.108f where an ambiguity would allow an equivalent error to be inferred by a hasty reader. This error, concerning the 5ths down from F to B♭ and thence to E♭, was evidently due to the fact that Mersenne had not tuned a keyboard instrument himself but was transmitting instructions from someone else (perhaps Jean Denis): hence he did not adequately clarify the fact that when one tempers an ascending 5th, for instance by tuning G to C, one makes the note G lower than pure in order to make the interval C–G smaller than pure, but when one is tempering B♭ to F one must tune the note B♭ higher than pure in order to produce the same kind of interval, namely a 5th tempered smaller than pure. Virtually every set of step-by-step instructions for mean-tone temperament includes an awkward sentence or two about this point (Praetorius devoted nearly half a page to it). In Mersenne's treatise the awkwardness was aggravated into succinct confusion. At one point he did specify that 'il faut tenir la note de dessouz [B♭ or E♭] un peu forte'; but elsewhere he gave a contrary impression, and in the instructions for tuning the spinet he said ambiguously: 'Cette quinte doit estre augmentée au lieu que les precedentes ont esté diminuées'. The likelihood that some 17th-century readers – particularly musicians using the instructions without reading all the accompanying theory – interpreted this passage as a prescription for irregular temperament is shown by Chaumont's 'Méthode d'accorder le clavessin' (in his *Pièces d'orgue*, 1695) which indicates explicitly that E♭ and B♭ were treated, by various tuners, as 'foible ou forte'. It happens that Mersenne's inadvertent novelty was musically opportune because the cumulative lowering of E♭ would more than achieve, on behalf of D♯, that which Schlick's temperament had achieved on behalf of G♯, albeit at the cost of rendering E♭–G slightly 'darker' than the A♭–C of Schlick's temperament. It may further be argued that Louis Couperin's use of E♭ and even B♭ (as in ex.8) differs from that of his teacher Chambonnières (ex.9), the older man's music requiring a regular mean-tone temperament while the younger found an opportunity for chiaroscuro in the kind of tuning inadvertently implied by Mersenne. Thus Couperin's long G minor Passacaille, with its recurring bass line G–F–E♭–D, may gain a dimension of structure as well as expressiveness when G–B♭ beats about eight times per second but 'resolves' to a pure or nearly pure F–A, and then E♭–G, beating about ten times per second, likewise yields to a more euphonious D–F♯;

and this would represent a significant stylistic departure from Frescobaldi's music in the same genre, which was known to Couperin. But when inferences are thus drawn beyond what can be proved by documents, a careful assessment – in this case requiring the use of authentically reconstructed 17th-century instruments – must be supplied by impartial judges. An examination of the bulk of Couperin's extant organ music from this point of view cannot be undertaken until the surviving manuscript (see Oldham, 1960) becomes available to scholars.

In 1697 Andreas Werckmeister suggested that organists unwilling to adopt his circulating temperament (see §6 below) or to install a split key with separate pipes for E♭ and D♯ might compromise by tuning E♭ down to serve for both notes. Composers like Samuel Scheidt (1587–1654) and his contemporaries used D♯ enough to tempt any organist without the split key at his disposal perhaps to consider such a makeshift adjustment of the temperament.

4. EQUAL TEMPERAMENT TO 1735. Although no Renaissance keyboard musician is known to have advocated or adopted equal temperament, it appears to have been used on fretted instruments such as the lute and viol at least since the early 16th century (see §8 below). A line of theorists from Vicentino (1555) to Mersenne and beyond took for granted that fretted and keyboard instruments were incompatible because of their distinct styles of intonation. The development of methods for calculating or approximating the intervals of equal temperament has been traced in J. M. Barbour's dissertation (1932) and summarized in *Tuning and Temperament* (1951), where he wrote, 'The simplest way . . . is to choose a correct ratio for the semitone and then apply it twelve times'. The ratio 18:17, familiar to

theorists from well before the Renaissance and recommended by Vincenzo Galilei in 1581 for equal temperament on the lute, corresponds mathematically to a semitone of 99 cents, virtually indistinguishable from the 100-cent semitone of equal temperament. Therefore the theoretical refinements of a Zarlino (1588) or a Stevin (c1600) may have had less bearing than one might imagine on the historical status of equal temperament in musical practice: an essentially equal temperament was feasible in practice before those theoretical refinements were achieved, and such compositions as Willaert's famous *Quid non ebrietas* (published in 1530) or Francesco Orso's setting (1567) of Petrarch's *Il cantar nuovo* indicate that 16th-century composers appreciated the enharmonic advantages of equal temperament which its advocates have always emphasized. The practical history of equal temperament, then, is largely a matter of its refinement in various respects and its gradual acceptance by keyboard musicians from the late 1630s, when Frescobaldi endorsed it, to the 1870s, by which time even the conservative English cathedrals were won over.

Zarlino in 1588 attributed the following prophetic arguments to Girolamo Roselli, abbot of S Martino in Sicily:

This way of dividing the diapason or octave into 12 equal parts . . . could alleviate all the difficulties of singers, players and composers by enabling them generally . . . to sing or play . . . DO–RE–MI–FA–SOL–LA upon whichever of the 12 notes they wish, touring through all the notes, making, as he [Roselli] says, a circular music; hence all the instruments will be able to keep their tuning and be in unison, and organs, as he says, will be neither too high nor too low in pitch.

About 50 years later an 'old man in rags', who had spent most of his life in Sicily and Calabria and knew 'nothing except how to play the harpsichord', retired to Rome and made a stir by advocating equal temperament on the harpsichord and even inducing Frescobaldi, with the aid of 'frequent and gratuitous beverages', to recommend it for the organ in Bernini's new apse at S Lorenzo in Damaso. The malicious details of this story are due to G. B. Doni (in his book of 1647 and in a letter to Mersenne of February 1640), who prevailed upon Cardinal Francesco Barberini to ignore Frescobaldi's advice. The renovated apse, with 'doi bellissimi organi' (*see* ROME, fig.7) in mean-tone, was inaugurated in August 1640 (and witnessed, towards the end of the century, performances by Corelli under the patronage of Cardinal Ottoboni). But already in April 1638 Doni had written to Mersenne that Frescobaldi failed to grasp the difference between major and minor semitones ('ne scait pas ce que c'est semiton majeur ou mineur') – an unlikely accusation to make of a former pupil of Luzzaschi and yet perhaps a fair indication of Frescobaldi's attitude towards niceties of intonation. Whether his magnificent *Cento partite sopra gli passacagli* (1637) were intended for equal temperament or for a harpsichord with split accidentals for Db/C♯ as well as G♯/Ab and D♯/Eb, the influence of Frescobaldi's acceptance of equal temperament is apparent in the later keyboard music of Froberger, who was his pupil in Rome when the old Sicilian harpsichordist was there.

Froberger was not the first north European to use equal temperament on keyboard instruments. In 1626 the inventor Jean Gallé, later described by Mersenne (1636–7) as the only person known by him to have 'accommodated this tuning to the organ and spinet', contracted to teach the young Liège organ builder André Severin how to construct transposing keyboard instruments in equal temperament. There is no evidence that Severin ever used this knowledge, but by 1645 Gallé or some other man 'fort docte en Mathématiques' had gone to Paris advocating equal temperament, and the instrument maker Jean Denis had been told, to his dismay, that perhaps he would not disapprove of equal temperament on the harpsichord so vehemently if he were accustomed to the sound.

It was not mere conservatism that prompted most Baroque keyboard musicians to resist or ignore the suggestions of an Artusi (1600) or a Mersenne (1636–7) that they consider adopting equal temperament, but rather their appreciation of the virtues of the feasible alternatives: regular mean-tone in the early 17th century, certain irregular temperaments thereafter. The same interest in timbre and sonority that nourished the Baroque refining of wind and string instruments must also have nourished an interest in the sensuous qualities of relatively subtle tunings. Some representative early 18th-century views are summarized in the following passage from Neidhardt (1732):

Most people do not find in this tuning that which they seek. It lacks, they say, variety in the beating of its major 3rds and, consequently, a heightening of emotion. In a triad everything sounds bad enough; but if the major 3rds alone, or minor 3rds alone, are played, the former sound much too high, the latter much too low. . . . Yet if oboes, flutes & the like, and also violins, lutes, gambas & the rest, were all arranged in this same [tuning], then the inevitable church- and chamber-pitch would blend together throughout in the purest [way]. . . . Thus equal temperament brings with it its comfort and discomfort, like blessed matrimony.

In the late 17th century and early 18th, however, a circle of German theorists became very interested in equal temperament, including Werckmeister, Neidhardt, Meckenheuser, Sinn, Goldbach and Mattheson. The wave of interest that they represent never thereafter lost momentum, although most of the best German organ builders are said to have resisted until after the generation of Gottfried Silbermann and Wender (Mattheson, 1722–5). In England the builder Renatus Harris, wishing to discredit the use of split accidentals by his competitor 'Father' Bernard Smith, induced John Wallis to publish in the *Philosophical Transactions* of 1698 an article 'On the Imperfections of the Organ' (see Williams, 1968). Though admittedly 'little acquainted' with the instrument, Wallis asserted that equal temperament had been 'found necessary (if I do not mistake the practice)' on organs. This rather exaggerated claim appears to indicate that equal temperament in any case was no longer unthinkable for organs. And when Brossard in 1703 remarked on the existence of two schools of opinion regarding temperament in practice, he did not, as so many had done before him, associate equal temperament with fretted instruments and its alternatives with keyboard instruments.

Special comment is warranted by the fact that equal temperament is often particularly associated with the name of Werckmeister, or with John Bull's long *Ut–re–mi–fa–sol–la* in the Fitzwilliam Virginal Book (no.51). Bull's piece does use all five sharps in some sections and all five flats in others, but never both a sharp and a flat in the same section; it was most probably conceived for *arcicembalo*. Werckmeister's attitude at the end of his life is summarized in a book published posthumously (1707) where in effect he apologized for not having included equal temperament among the various circulating temperaments for which he had earlier published a monochord diagram. (The incompetent engraver, he said, had complained about dividing the narrow space of a comma into 12 parts.) He quite approved of equal temperament, yet was willing 'to have the diatonic 3rds left somewhat purer than the other, less often used ones', a procedure for which he had expressed clear preference in his earlier writings (see §6 below).

5. REGULAR MEAN-TONE TEMPERAMENTS FROM 1600. The late Renaissance system of church modes or tones was suited to the harmonic dimensions of a 12-note mean-tone palette (from E♭ to G♯ in the chain of 5ths) as long as V–I cadences were not required in the Phrygian mode (E minor) and as long as the Dorian, with its often flattened sixth degree, was not transposed more than one place down in the chain of 5ths to G minor. Cadences to E could be accommodated by the use of a split accidental on the keyboard to provide D♯ as well as E♭; and a split accidental for A♭ and G♯ was also often provided (*see*, for instance, COMPENIUS). But the growing popularity, from the late 17th century, of more expansive modulations rendered regular mean-tone temperaments musically problematical well before the end of the Baroque era, though the old tunings remained familiar on many organs.

Michael Praetorius in his *Organographia* (1618) prescribed exclusively $\frac{1}{4}$-comma mean-tone for keyboard instruments, a tuning later referred to by German theorists as the 'Praetorianische Temperatur'. In France Mersenne, relying heavily upon Salinas's *De musica*, also neglected to mention any shade with major 3rds larger than pure; he described $\frac{1}{4}$-comma mean-tone as 'la manière d'accorder perfaictment les Orgues ordinaires'. The pre-eminence of these authorities and Zarlino caused $\frac{1}{4}$-comma mean-tone to be regarded by many subsequent writers as the exemplary ideal of mean-tone temperament and even of Renaissance and Baroque keyboard tunings in general. An indication of its use on 17th-century German organs lies in Werckmeister's assertion (1697) that an instrument would be converted to his circulating temperament, in which the 5ths C–G–D–A are tempered $\frac{1}{4}$-comma, by resetting only some of the pipes. In the late 17th and 18th centuries the increasing popularity of tierce ranks in mixture stops promoted the brilliance of $\frac{1}{4}$-comma mean-tone, with its pure major 3rds, on the organ.

But mean-tone temperament with major 3rds larger than pure also flourished. Cerone attributed it in 1613 to master organ builders. Lemme Rossi (1666) described $\frac{1}{5}$-comma and mentioned $\frac{2}{9}$-comma mean-tone. The instructions of Jean Denis (1643), a professional harpsichord tuner, specify no particular shade of mean-tone, prescribing only 'good' 3rds together with 5ths tempered by 'un poinct'; but in 1707 and 1711 the acoustician Joseph Sauveur, using an elaborate monochord to compare $\frac{1}{4}$-, $\frac{1}{5}$- and $\frac{1}{6}$-comma mean-tone, reported that organ and harpsichord makers adhered more closely to $\frac{1}{5}$-comma mean-tone than to the other two forms, even though 'les musiciens ordinaires' used $\frac{1}{5}$-comma mean-tone. W. C. Printz in 1696 described the same three shadings and also $\frac{2}{9}$-comma mean-tone, which he said was 'even earlier' ('noch eher') than Zarlino's $\frac{2}{7}$-comma. Loulié in 1698 said that $\frac{1}{5}$-comma mean-tone was 'better and more in use' than any other temperament. Sorge in 1748 attributed the use of $\frac{1}{6}$-comma mean-tone to Gottfried Silbermann (and a posthumous book of Sorge (1773) confirmed the presence on two 'especially good' Silbermann organs of a 'horribly large beating 5th, G♯–D♯, along with four unbearably barbaric major 3rds'). J.-B. Romieu in 1758 expressed preference for $\frac{1}{6}$-comma mean-tone because he liked the relative amount of tempering that it allots to 5ths and 3rds. The same aesthetic criterion worked up into a mathematical formula led Giordano Riccati in 1762 to give preference to his own $\frac{3}{14}$-comma system (among regular temperaments).

Mean-tone with major 3rds smaller than pure seems to have disappeared from normal practice, although Cerone reproduced Zarlino's instructions of 1558, and Cima's instructions (1606) confused it (even more plainly than Aaron's of 1523) with $\frac{1}{4}$-comma mean-tone. Lemme Rossi, Mersenne and Printz described it, and in the 18th century Hensling (1710) and Smith (1748) advocated it as an innovation. More recently Kornerup sought to champion it in the 1930s, and in 1948 A. R. McClure published a good account of its sound. According to Mersenne, Titelouze had a harpsichord with 19 notes per octave tuned in equal microtones – the equivalent, as it happens, of $\frac{1}{3}$-comma mean-tone. It is not certain whether the 19-note harpsichord built by Pesarese for Zarlino or the one built by Elsasz for Luython and described by Praetorius were tuned thus, though Salinas had proposed using his $\frac{1}{3}$-comma scheme for a 19-note octave without realizing that it would form a virtually equal division. In the 20th century, interest in the 19-note equal division has been developed by, among others, Yasser (1932), Handschin (1927) and Mandelbaum (1961).

For various shades of mean-tone the corresponding schemes of dividing the octave into equal microtones were worked out during the 17th and 18th centuries (*see* INTERVAL, Table 1). When an 18th-century writer advocated one of these schemes he is much more likely to have been referring to a general theoretical model – a shade of mean-tone regarded as an ideal of intonation – than to an experimental keyboard instrument. In this sense the 55 division, corresponding to $\frac{1}{6}$-comma mean-tone, was particularly eminent. Not only did Sauveur attribute it to 'ordinary musicians', but Mattheson (1722–5) was familiar with it and Sorge (1748) labelled it 'Telemann's system'. In this scheme the whole tone comprises nine 'commas'; but not every reference to that feature necessarily implies the 55 division, as the same feature characterizes the nearly Pythagorean 53 division, which happens to contain virtually pure 3rds as well as 5ths and which had been referred to in a Pythagorean context by Italian theorists since the 15th century (e.g. Anselmi, 1434). Neither Praetorius (1618)

Ex.10

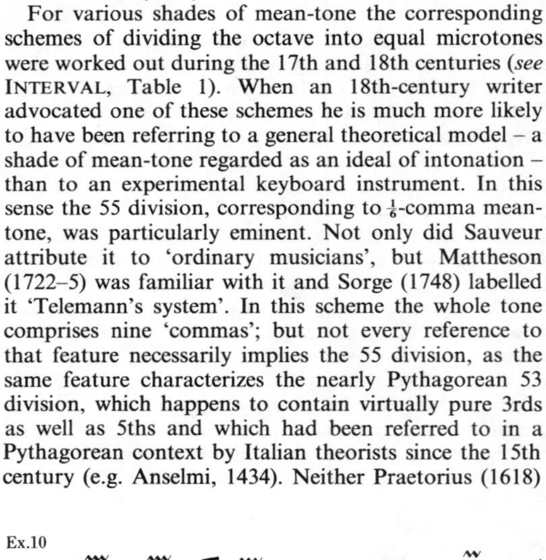

nor Nassarre (1723–4) had in mind $\frac{1}{6}$-comma mean-tone when referring to the whole tone as made up of nine commas, and one may entertain doubts in the case of other writers, like Brossard (1703) or Tosi (1723), who were not specialists in the theory of microtonal scales. The status of $\frac{1}{6}$-comma mean-tone in performing practice might better be confirmed by systematic research into 18th-century woodwind instruments that survive un-altered. And certainly the expressive semitones and harmonic 3rds and 6ths in ex.10, the opening of Lully's overture to *Bellérophon* in a 17th-century keyboard transcription, are ill-served by $\frac{1}{4}$-comma mean-tone.

Some scholars have assumed that Baroque harpsi-chordists habitually retuned wholesale the accidentals on their instruments in order to produce various disposi-tions of regular mean-tone for music in various keys (Barbour and Kuttner, 1958; Rayner, 1969). But no Baroque musician or theorist other than Cima (1606) is known to have described this procedure; and evidently the standard 17th-century 12-note disposition (E♭–G♯) was used by some late 17th- and 18th-century musicians as if it were a circulating temperament. References to this practice can be found in the writings of Christiaan Huygens (?1670s), Werckmeister (1700), Romieu (1758) and Bédos de Celles (1770), in the fourth edition of the *Encyclopaedia Britannica* (1810) and elsewhere. As late as 1847 I. F. Holton in New York wrote:

In Unequal Temperament some of the chords are very good, while the aggravated dissonance of others, called by tuners the WOLF, imparts a peculiarity to the keys in which it occurs, much admired by certain musicians. . . . These predilections . . . must be chiefly attributed to fancy and prejudice. Some inequality of temperament may be preferable, but no key ought to be made so bad as to give it a character for harshness.

Similar opinions had been expressed throughout the 18th century.

Extant specimens of Baroque carillon are said to be tuned to some form of mean-tone; in view of their inharmonic timbre this is a remarkable indication of the precision in tuning and control of timbre achieved by the Hemonys and other master bellfounders.

6. IRREGULAR TEMPERAMENTS FROM 1680. The most characteristic type of 18th-century keyboard tuning was an irregular temperament with no wolf 5th but with the 3rds in the C major scale tempered lightly as in some form of mean-tone temperament; most of the 3rds in 'modern' keys (such as B major, A♭ major or F minor) were thereby rendered distinctly more impure than in equal temperament. As a modulation of triadic har-monies moved about the circle of 5ths the amount of tempering in the 3rds would thus change, in a more or less unabrupt fashion, according to whether one was closer to the front or back of the circle as shown in fig.2. The degree and exact pattern of the differences might vary to suit taste and circumstance without forfeiting this principle; in fact different instruments require dif-ferent quantities to achieve equivalent results. But there was a tendency for the E major triad to be tuned approxi-mately as in equal temperament. Concomitant to vari-ously tempered 3rds were diverse sizes of semitone, the largest being E–F and B–C and the smallest C–D♭ and perhaps F–G♭ (or E♯–F♯). Hence the major keys with few sharps or flats had the most resonant and limpid triads but the least keenly inflected leading notes. In minor keys the effects were more intricate, E minor for instance having a sharper leading note but a less harsh

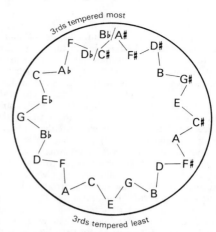

2. *Circle of 5ths indicating the relative amount of tempering of 3rds in characteristic 18th-century keyboard tuning*

tonic triad than F minor, a key often remarked on (e.g. by M.-A. Charpentier, c1695; Mattheson, 1713; Rousseau, 1768; Gervasoni, 1800) for its dark qualities.

Routine sequences as in ex.11 (from a sonata of G. B. Platti) gain savour in this kind of tuning, and more elaborate sequential manipulations are enhanced. In lieu

Ex.11

of an extensive discussion of key character, ex.12 (the opening of an organ prelude of J. C. F. Fischer) may represent the fact that in the key of A♭ major, D♭ is often a particularly tender note by virtue of its low intonation and its affinity in part-writing to C (which is inflected high in relation to A♭ and D♭). Shadings of this sort lend an unimaginable dimension of beauty to

Ex.12

such lavishly flat-laden pieces as J. S. Bach's chorale prelude *O Mensch, bewein'* or the Adagio of Beethoven's 'Pathétique' Sonata. Qualities of nuance in various keys created by this kind of tuning contributed much to the beauty of the Baroque French harpsichord and its music by such masters as D'Anglebert and François Couperin, who according to Jean-Jacques Rousseau 'proposed and abandoned' equal temperament ('Tempérament', in the *Encyclopédie*, 1748–9). Handel's harmonically daring recitatives are also brilliantly enhanced, and the static tendency of the harmony in some of his arias (compared with Bach's) is rendered more logical. William Croft (1700) was evidently the first English keyboard composer to exploit the resources of this type of intonation (see Meffen, 1978).

Except for Werckmeister's harpsichord tuning instructions of 1698 (summarized by F. T. Arnold, 1931), no Baroque prescription in German is known to have called for any 5ths larger than pure or, consequently, any 3rds less pure than Pythagorean 3rds. In German tunings the 5ths among the naturals averaged a heavier degree of tempering than those among the accidentals, the latter tending in fact to be pure. Some German writers characterized as 'good' any temperament without a wolf 5th, thereby including equal temperament; but others regarded equal temperament as distinctly less 'good' than irregular temperaments of the type described here (*see* WELL-TEMPERED CLAVIER).

French tuning instructions characteristically required two or three 5ths at the back of the circle of 5ths to be tempered slightly larger than pure (most probably Ab–Eb–Bb–F; see §3 above), thus producing a more pronounced difference in size and quality between the 3rds Db–F–Ab–C and the 3rds among the seven diatonic notes. This kind of tuning was often referred to by 18th-century French musicians as the 'ordinary' or 'common' temperament, though some occasionally confused it with regular mean-tone (e.g. Bédos de Celles, 1770) or with some tuning similar to the irregular temperament described in §3 above (e.g. M. Corrette, 1752). Hence it is difficult to be certain exactly what shade of temperament Ozanam had in mind when he wrote in 1691:

Whatever precaution we might take in tuning our instruments to render all the chords equal, there is always left therein some inequality that causes us to notice a je-ne-sais-quoi of sadness or gaiety, of the melodious or the harsh, which [in turn] makes us distinguish one key from another by ear.

Yet Ozanam's distinction between 'natural' and 'transposed' modes confirms that the inequalities in question were distributed not at random but in a pattern consistent enough to allow the keys to be identified by ear according to their intonational inflections. Rousseau also wrote, in 1748–9, that the keys could thus be identified by ear, in the course of discussing a circulating form of the 'ordinary' temperament as described by Rameau in 1726. Rameau's instructions were accompanied with the following remarks:

The excess of the last two 5ths and the last four or five major 3rds is tolerable, not only because it is almost insensible, but also because it occurs in modulations little used – except for when one might choose them on purpose to render the expression more keen etc. For it is good to note that we receive different impressions from intervals in keeping with their different [degree of] alteration. For example the major 3rd, which [in its] natural [state] excites us to joy, as we know from experience, impresses upon us ideas even of fury when it is too large; and the minor 3rd, which [in its] natural [state] transports us to sweetness and tenderness, saddens us when it is too small. Knowledgeable musicians know how to exploit these different effects of the intervals, and give value, by the expression they draw therefrom, to the alteration which one might [otherwise] condemn.

In 1737 Rameau changed his views (see §7 below); but in that respect d'Alembert (1752) took a neutral position in what had evidently become a controversial matter. Remarkably lucid comments on the relation between irregular temperaments and modulation (in virtually the modern classroom sense of the term) appeared in the *Histoire de l'Académie royale des sciences* at Paris in 1742. The preference of some composers for the 'transposed modes' had been discussed in an equally urbane article in the *Mémoires de Trevoux* (1718) which suggested that while it was arbitrary to give specific affective labels to particular keys, the key of Db major was, because of its tuning, comparable with a ragout with more vinegar and spice than an ordinary one or one conducive to good health. Mattheson in 1720 published a book of reflections on this article and mentioned favourably the work of Neidhardt, who soon became the most elaborate technician of subtle shades of 'good' temperament (1724 and 1732). Later French and English advocates of a fairly subtle irregular tuning included Mercadier de Belesta (1776), Suremain-Missery (1793), Thomas Young (1800) and Jean Jousse (1832). Sorge (*Anweisung zur Stimmung und Temperatur*, 1744, and *Vorgemach der musicalischen Composition*, 1745–7) and Lambert (1774) also described such tunings, but were themselves content with equal temperament. These finer tunings are usually the most appropriate for late 18th-century music. Tartini in 1754 approved of the chiaroscuro achieved by the moderately subtle organ tuning of his colleague Francesco Antonio Vallotti, *maestro* at S Antonio, Padua, from 1730 to 1779 and a highly regarded church composer in Italy. Vallotti's tuning (in which the 5ths F–C–G–D–A–E–B are each tempered by ⅙-comma) is one of the simplest of its type, though Werckmeister's equally simple scheme for the organ (in which the 5ths G–D–A–E and B–F♯ are each tempered by ¼-comma) sounds more fitting in some late 17th- and early 18th-century German organ music.

Among the late 18th- and early 19th-century Italian and English accounts of irregular temperaments may be mentioned those of Gervasoni (1800 and 1812), Serassi (1816), Asioli (1816), William Jones (i) (1784), Cavallo (1788 and 1803), Robison (1801), Stanhope (1806) and Callcott (1807). Of more central importance, however, is the evidence, which can be outlined here only briefly, that none of the masterworks of late Baroque and Classical German keyboard music was in fact created in a pervading ambience of equal-tempered intonational sameness among the various triads and keys, though some forward-looking composers did tend, like C. P. E. Bach (see §7 below), to think in such terms. In 1697 Werckmeister had written:

Now if all semitones, tones, 3rds, 5ths, etc, had the same size and [equivalent] beating, people would take little pleasure in transpositions: for example, if the Dorian is transposed a second into either C or E: such transpositions produce notable alterations and excitement. This is brought about not so much by the change in pitch level as by the reordering of the tones and semitones, and also the [varied] beating of the concords.

Heinichen in 1728, while ridiculing Mattheson's propensity to 'assign specifically to this or that key the affect of love, sadness, joy, etc', acknowledged that

in general it may well be said that one key is more fitting than another for expressing affects [at large]; and in today's good temperaments (I am not referring to old organs) the keys with two or three flats or sharps in their signatures emerge, especially in the theatrical style, as the most beautiful and expressive. For this reason I would not even support the invention of the long-sought clavier in just intonation were it to become practicable.

Kirnberger held that a good temperament 'must not injure the variegation of the keys' (1776–9), and his disciple Tempelhof in 1775, while acknowledging that any key could express any affect, held nonetheless that in a good temperament each key would do so in its own particular way ('auf eine ihnen angemessene Art') and that without such expressive resources music would be 'nothing more than a harmonious noise that tickles the ear but leaves the heart slumbering away in a disgusting indifference'. In 1780 the polymath J. J. Engel, in a book dedicated to Reichardt, placed the choice of key before melody and harmony as a resource of musical portrayal, adding that among the major keys, C and A♭ differed most since the steps of their scales differed most.

In 1784 Cramer's *Magazin der Musik* reported that Clementi used a tuning in which C–E was tempered 'ein klein wenig hoch schwebend' ('beating, slightly high'), E–G♯ 'sehr hoch' ('very high') and A♭–C 'noch höher' ('even higher'). In 1785 Mozart's pupil Thomas Attwood recorded in his notebook that G♭ was a note which 'the Harpsichord has not, but all other instruments have' (see Chesnut, 1977). Anton Schindler recalled (1840) that Beethoven in his last years maintained a keen interest in the expressive characteristics of different keys. It is not clear to what extent Beethoven may have attributed the differences to acoustical factors, but much of his piano music does in fact benefit from an 18th-century unequal tuning. In 1826 the leading champion of Viennese Classical music in Italy, Peter Lichtenthal, wrote that equal temperament 'cannot subsist' or else the keys would lose their character and 'one could equally [well] compose a nocturne in A minor or a military blare in A♭' – an opinion that was excised, however, in Dominique Mondo's French translation 13 years later. Yet the late Baroque associations of different qualities with different keys cast their shadows far into the 19th century. This legacy awaits investigation, which might take as a point of departure the curious fact that D minor, the most eminent of keys in Baroque keyboard music and one that to a large extent retained its old mean-tone-like sound in the 18th-century irregular temperaments, was the key least favoured by Chopin, except in the last and most magnificent of his 24 preludes.

Confusion has been wrought by the neglect of some scholars to distinguish adequately between the tunings actually used by a Werckmeister or a Neidhardt and theoretical schemes that represent little more than speculative calculations. When Werckmeister said that an organ could be retuned by adjusting only some of the pipes with the tuning cone, and that this temperament would require only about an hour for each rank (1697, p.32), he clearly allotted to a lesser practical status his own mathematical schemes involving 5ths tempered by the relatively unhealthy amount of $\frac{1}{3}$-comma; Sorge's description of Werckmeister's tuning (1748) confirms that in practice Werckmeister had favoured the one scheme in particular (*see* WELL-TEMPERED CLAVIER, fig.1c). Neidhardt's method of presentation was to describe a long series of speculative possibilities and then specify three or four as being of practical value. Marpurg, championing equal temperament and irritated by the inept $\frac{1}{2}$-comma temperaments of Kirnberger and

C. L. G. von Wiese, printed in 1790 a number of new irregular schemes none of which favoured the diatonic 3rds and none of which was intended for use. In short, the significant late Baroque and Classical irregular temperaments were those described above in connection with fig.2. Although some of the unduly large body of 18th-century writings on this topic may well represent mere decadence, a familiarity with the sound of this kind of tuning is vital for a proper understanding of 18th-century harmony and tonal structure insofar as the harpsichord and organ influenced them.

7. EQUAL TEMPERAMENT FROM 1735. In his *Génération harmonique* (1737) Rameau endorsed equal temperament and, by way of retracting his own views of 11 years before, introduced a new argument in its favour:

He who believes that the different impressions which he receives from the differences caused in each transposed mode by the temperament [now] in use heighten its character and draw greater variety from it, will permit me to tell him that he is mistaken. The sense of variety arises from the intertwining of the keys [*l'entrelacement des Modes*] and not at all from the alteration of the intervals, which can only displease the ear and consequently distract it from its functions.

Distracting the musical ear from its proper functions is an unpardonable fault in a tuning. Rameau's argument might well have applied more palpably in France than in Germany, if French unequal tunings were, as they generally appear to have been, less subtle than their German counterparts. Rameau's authority as a musician was such that the 1749 register of the Paris Académie Royale des Sciences could state, 'M. Rameau assures us that experience is not opposed to the temperament that he proposes; and in this regard he has earned the right to be taken at his word'. Equal temperament continued to be identified with his name throughout the 18th century in France and occasionally in Italy as well.

In Germany J. N. Ritter, perhaps the most important organ builder in Franconia at the middle of the century, used equal temperament. Among theorists advocating it Barthold Fritz is especially important, despite the crudeness of his tuning instructions, because in the preface to the second edition (1757) of his *Anweisung* (1756: the title may be translated as 'Method for tuning claviers, harpsichords and organs, in a mechanical way, equally pure in all keys'), he reported that C. P. E. Bach had found 'in my few pages everything ... that was necessary and possible' for a good tuning. C. P. E. Bach's own advice (1762) for improvising a fantasia mentioned temperaments: on the organ, he said, 'one must restrain oneself in chromatic passages; at least they should not be advanced sequentially, because organs are seldom well tempered. The clavichord and the piano are the most fitting instruments for our fantasia. Both of them *can*, and *must*, be tuned pure'. For Marpurg and others 'rein' ('pure'), which C. P. E. Bach himself here distinguished from 'gut' ('good' or 'well'), became a catchword in arguments favouring equal temperament. Fritz's title shows how it came to serve in that capacity; once equal-tempered 3rds were considered acceptable, then a tuning with certain 3rds tempered more heavily could be described as relatively impure. Since C. P. E. Bach was sufficiently concerned to give not only a warning about the limitations of mean-tone but also emphatic advice about the tuning of the clavichord and piano, the fact that he did not recommend exploiting the inflections of a circulating unequal temperament in a genre which, by his own definition, 'modulates into more keys than is customary in other pieces' suggests an indifference to those inflections. When C. P. E. Bach spoke of 'remote' keys, he meant keys remote from the tonic key, not keys remote from C major or D minor. His compositions, for instance the great rondos from the collections *für Kenner und Liebhaber*, reflect this neglect of the concept expressed in fig.2 above; and his favourite instrument, the clavichord, was the least likely of all normal keyboard instruments to display to much advantage the niceties of an irregular temperament. If the music of any leading 18th-century German composer ought to be performed in equal temperament, C. P. E. Bach is the best candidate.

No unequivocal conclusion can be established as to the attitude of his father, J. S. Bach, towards the relative merits of equal temperament and a mildly unequal one. On the basis of evidence such as applied above to C. P. E. Bach, Barbour showed (1932) that J. S. Bach would probably not have held a dogmatic opinion. Barbour's later statement (1951, p.196) that 'much of Bach's organ music would have been dreadfully dissonant in any sort of tuning except equal temperament' is an exaggeration (due perhaps to the fact, which he mentioned in a letter of 1948 to A. R. McClure, that Barbour had never heard any keyboard temperament other than equal temperament). During the 1960s John Barnes investigated the '48' in a fairly subtle type of 18th-century irregular temperament and found that the peculiarities of the various keys in that tuning were nicely suited to or accommodated by the music. According to Marpurg (1776), Kirnberger scrupulously reported that Bach, his teacher, had instructed him to tune all major 3rds larger than pure – thus ruling out any unsubtle irregular temperament (such as used by Kirnberger himself). One could readily believe that Bach sometimes exploited the qualities of a particular key as inflected in a typical irregular temperament, sometimes merely accommodated what he knew was likely to be the kind of tuning his published music would be played on, and sometimes – for instance, in the concluding ricercar of the *Musical Offering* – ignored completely the possibility of intonational shadings.

The most vigorous and articulate late 18th-century champion of equal temperament seems to have been F. W. Marpurg, whose *Versuch über die musikalische Temperatur* was published in 1776 but who had already advocated equal temperament in his *Principes du clavecin* (1756). Though capable of meretricious reasoning he presented, in greater detail than Rameau, numerous forceful arguments, some of which were rendered so valid by historical circumstance that during the 19th century equal temperament became the standard keyboard tuning and, in the West, a widely followed norm of intonation in general. Marpurg (1776) knew that a composer might select a key for reasons 'that have nothing to do with temperament'; and he perceived (as did Tiberius Cavallo in 1788) the advantages of equal temperament in ensemble music, where

so long as not all the instruments playing together, and the vocal parts as well, are intoned in the most perfect agreement in one kind of [irregular] temperament, the composer must obtain the character of his piece, the building up of an emotion, and the strength of expression, from sources quite other than the creative powers of the tuning hammer or cone.

His encounters with the tuning schemes of Kirnberger and von Wiese, as well as his knowledge of the writings of Werckmeister, Neidhardt, Lambert and others, showed him that:

There is only one kind of equal temperament but countless possible

types of unequal temperament. Thus the latter opens up to speculative musicians an unstinting source of modifications, and since every musician will readily invent one, the result will be that from time to time we shall be presented with a new type of unequal temperament, and everyone will declare his own the best.

In short, he gave equal temperament decisive preference on both of the counts envisaged by Fontanelle, who had written in 1711: 'After these motley combats, one system will become victorious. If fortune favours the best system, music will gain thereby a real advantage; and in any case it will at least profit from the convenience of having the same ideas and the same language accepted everywhere'.

D. G. Türk (1802) extended Rameau's argument of 1737 cited above by suggesting that a sameness of quality among the various keys would contribute to unity of character in a composition. Influential musicians supported equal temperament in Italy (Asioli, 1816) and England (Crotch, 1812 and, invoking J. S. Bach, 1833). Hummel's *Anweisung zum Piano-Forte Spiel* (1828) concluded with a discussion of tuning that justified ignoring the old, unequal temperaments on the grounds that they presented, particularly for the many novice tuners brought into the trade by the popularity of the piano, greater difficulties than equal temperament and that these difficulties were aggravated critically by the burden of tuning, on modern pianos, three heavy strings for each note instead of two thin ones as on older instruments. Jousse, in a book on piano tuning (1832) dedicated to W. F. Collard, expressed preference for a subtly unequal temperament, but Claude Montal (1834) gave instructions solely for equal temperament on the piano. In the 1840s A. J. Hipkins persuaded the Broadwood firm to tune their pianos in equal temperament, which he must have used when tuning for Chopin in London in 1848. Cavaillé-Coll and no doubt most German organ builders used it; almost all the English organ builders resisted until after the Great Exhibition of 1851, but their notebooks show that from the mid-1850s until the 1870s, rebuilt or reconditioned church organs were usually raised to the current concert pitch and converted to equal temperament (see Mackenzie).

The ideals of sonority in the acoustic design of the modern piano and in all but the more radical forms of modern pianism are as intimately bound to the acoustic qualities of equal temperament as any previous keyboard style ever was to its contemporary style of intonation. The enharmonic facility of Brahms or Fauré, the hovering sonorities of Debussy, the timbral poise of Webern, the slickness of urbane jazz and dance-band chord progressions, all rely implicitly on the hue of equal temperament as much as on the other normal characteristics of the instrument's tone. An 18th-century tuning usually sounds as inappropriate for this music as the piano would seem visually if its glossy black finish were replaced by an 18th-century décor.

8. FRETTED INSTRUMENTS. Insofar as the relation between performing practice and compositional style is concerned, the history of temperaments on fretted instruments in Western art music since the mid-16th century has been simpler than on keyboard instruments, for two reasons: the placing of the frets and tuning of the open strings does not impose an exact intonation of the scale on the player as definitively as the harpsichord or organ tuner's handiwork does; and the fact that each fret runs under all the strings is likely to render inconvenient

the use of distinctly unequal semitones in the fretting scheme.

Lute and viol strings were traditionally made of gut (though from the late 17th century the lowest strings were likely to be overspun). Inconsistencies in this material are greater than in carefully drawn wire for harpsichord strings. Even Hubert Le Blanc acknowledged, in his enthusiastic *Défense de la basse de viole* (1740), that 'the rules for gut strings are variable. Two strings of the same thickness [*grosseur*], as clear as rock crystal, make the 5th at a considerably different degree forward and back'. Practical considerations of this kind tend to overshadow the embodiment of any precise model of a tempered scale to a greater extent than on the harpsichord (where imperfections in the strings are less telling) or the organ. Moreover, all the mathematical schemes for determining the position of the frets were based on measuring off certain portions of the neck, as if an alteration in string length were the only effect produced when the player presses the string against the fret: but the concomitant increase in the string's tension is significant enough to reduce even the most precise geometrical division to a mere preliminary. Most Renaissance and Baroque musician–theorists who discussed fret placing remarked that one must make, or that players did make, further adjustments by ear.

Thus a mathematical procedure for determining the position of frets on a lute or viol had a rather different kind of significance from that of a monochord prescription. Monochord schemes often embodied a precise model of intonation which the performer or instrument maker or tuner was supposed to transfer into practice by whatever techniques were appropriate. The fact that Renaissance and Baroque theorists developed the use of irrational numbers in their monochord schemes is, in large part, evidence of this precise intention. Formulae for marking where to tie a fret on the neck of a lute or viol often involved exclusively rational numbers. The reason is not only that an accomplished player, a person often of quite different educational and social background from many music theorists, would be less likely to know or care about irrational numbers, but also that for him the numerical measuring was but the first stage in determining the intonation of his instrument. Its function was merely to help place the frets close enough to their final position so that he could go on to the next stage, that of tuning the open strings by ear and concurrently making slight adjustments in the frets. He might then further shade the intonation of the notes ad hoc during performance.

In this light one may distinguish four kinds of late Renaissance fretting prescriptions: those with exclusively Pythagorean ratios (e.g. Finé, 1530); those that embody a precise mathematical model of equal temperament but are too elaborate to be of much practical use (e.g. Salinas, 1577; Zarlino, 1588; Stevin, c1600); those that seem to betray by their complexity an erudite intention, but fail to embody precisely any feasible model of intonation (notably Dowland, 1610; see Poulton, 1972, appx 1); and those simplified for practicability. Among the last type equal temperament is best represented by Vincenzo Galilei's rule – that the ratio 18 : 17 should be used for placing each successive fret down the neck of the instrument – a rule that Mersenne said was used by many instrument makers. A less exact approximation, but adequate for its purpose, could be gained by dividing the 9 : 8 whole tones of a Pythagorean diatonic scheme into 18 : 17 and 17 : 16 semitones, a rule given by theorists as late as Nassarre (1723–4). Ganassi's equally simple viol prescription (1542–3) would have produced, from the nut to the eighth fret, the ratios 24 : 22⅔ : 21⅓ : 20 : 19 : 18 : 17 : 16 : 15, had he not specified that certain frets be shifted up or down by their own width or by half that amount. His accompanying remarks not only emphasize the need for refinements by ear but also refer to the tempering of 5ths for the sake of distinguishing major and minor semitones and for a better sound in chords and in ensemble music. There are corroborating indications that before the second half of the 16th century, approximations of mean-tone temperament may have competed with equal temperament on fretted instruments, and a distinguished modern lutenist (see Dombois, 1974) has found them musically advantageous in some instances. The historical evidence is inconsistent but suggestive.

In mean-tone temperament as in Pythagorean intonation there is a distinction in size between diatonic and chromatic semitones (A–B♭, for example, being larger than B♭–B♮ in mean-tone temperament, but smaller in Pythagorean intonation. The inconvenience of maintaining this distinction on fretted instruments is illustrated by the fact that most 16th-century lute music requires the first fret on the third lowest string to provide the note a chromatic semitone above the open string (F♯ on the F string or G♯ on the G string) but calls on the same fret to provide a diatonic semitone above the fourth open string (B♭ on the A string or C on the B string).

It would have been difficult for early Renaissance theorists to recognize or approve of the use of equal semitones because until the publication in Latin of Euclid's *Elements* in 1482, the myth that a whole tone could not be divided into two equal parts was virtually unchallenged among scholars. To demonstrate this premise, it was common for theorists to explain that if a whole tone of ratio 9 : 8 were divided into two semitones of ratio 18 : 17 and 17 : 16, then obviously one of the semitones (18 : 17) would be smaller than the other. The fact that an 18 : 17 semitone amounts to 99 cents, virtually the same as the semitone of equal temperament, might give particular significance, however, to certain early 16th-century assertions such as that of Spataro (1521) that 'the lute has minor semitones [for] all its frets' ('el leuto ha tuti li soi tasti semitonii minori'; see Lowinsky, 1956) or of Martin Agricola (1545) that 'almost the majority of lute and viol players make all the frets equal to one another . . . a fret produces the minor semitone':

> . . . fast das gröste part
> Der Lautnisten und Geiger art
> Alle bünd machen gleich von ein
>
> . . . ein bund
> Der semiton minus/thut kund

Yet Agricola's statement implies that in his day some players of fretted instruments did not use equal semitones. Arnolt Schlick (*Tablaturen etlicher Lobesang und Lidlein,* 1512) and, for the most part, Luis de Milán (*El maestro,* 1536) seem to have avoided those combinations of fingerings that would render inconvenient the use of unequal semitones. The only one of Schlick's 15 extant lute pieces that uses the first fret on the third string (*Nach lust hab ich*) does so on no other, while in other respects his music accommodates a fretting with the following succession of semitones as

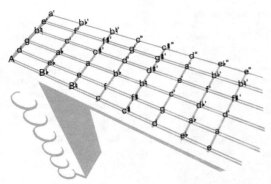

3. Partly schematic representation of a typical 16th-century lute fretting

one ascends from the open strings: diatonic, chromatic; diatonic, chromatic; diatonic; diatonic, chromatic; diatonic. (Above each string the intervals provided are: minor 2nd, whole tone, minor 3rd, major 3rd, perfect 4th, diminished 5th, perfect 5th, minor 6th; see fig.3.) To judge by his organ tuning instructions, Schlick's ear was probably extraordinarily perceptive of such intricacies; he might well have sought to accommodate the use of a mean-tone temperament in his lute compositions.

Luis de Milán did not avoid using the first fret to provide G♯ on the G string but he did exercise circumspection: whereas he would use the second fret for the A in ex.13a or the fourth fret for the G♯ in ex.13b, the first fret would not be required to provide G♯ in any context more conspicuous vertically than that shown in ex.13c. It is true that occasionally (see ex.13d) he required the fourth fret to provide not only the B shown in fig.3 but also an E♭ (instead of the D♯ in fig.3), and similarly with regard to C♯ and F at the sixth fret. Yet a rejection of equal temperament, in which major 3rds are the same size as diminished 4ths, is indicated by the prefatory instructions to one of his fantasias

(1536, p.30) to 'raise the fourth fret a little so that the note of that fret will be strong and not feeble'. It is difficult to be certain just what 'raise' and 'strong' meant in this instance; but a clearer inference can be drawn from the instruction to adjust the same fret 'up towards the pegs' in his setting of *Con pavor recordo el moro*, in which the fret is used exclusively for notes a major 3rd above the open string. This inference is confirmed obliquely by an instruction of Enríquez de Valderrábano (1547, fol.74v) to move the fourth fret 'slightly down towards the rose', indicating unequivocally that the pitch of the notes affected, which in this case are all a diminished 4th above the open string, was to be higher than if they had been a major 3rd above the open string: the major 3rd, one may thus infer, was a smaller interval than in equal temperament. Evidently, however, Valderrábano did not consistently reject the use of equal semitones, as some of his duets require the two vihuelas to be tuned a minor 3rd apart from each other, an arrangement for which the use of unequal semitones in the fretting would be bound to entail some sour unisons.

Bermudo's comments (1555, fols.103–9) on fret placement and intonation reflect a confusion – which is evident elsewhere in his book and which he shared with Gaffurius, Aaron, Lanfranco and a number of other early 16th-century theorists – between mean-tone temperaments in practice and Pythagorean intonation in theory. (In analysing Bermudo's discussion one must beware also of Ward's premise (1953, p.33) that in equal temperament itself 'the *mi* frets were a comma higher than the *fa* frets'.) Bermudo indicated unmistakably, however, that rather than using equal semitones many vihuelists would set some of the frets at a slant or else 'not press down the finger equally' when playing. The latter technique had been referred to ten years earlier by Aaron (1545, fol.35v): 'the [intonation of a] lute can be aided with the finger of the player, by the *intensione* and *remissione* of a minute space for the reintegration of its consonance'.

Well before the end of the 16th century it became a commonplace of Italian musical writings that the use of equal temperament was normal for fretted instruments while keyboard instruments were tuned with unequal semitones (i.e. in some form of regular mean-tone temperament); and this distinction was carried on through most of the 17th century. Mersenne wrote, when discussing the characteristics of equal temperament, that musicians called the lute the charlatan of instruments 'because it passes off as good [*il fait passer pour bon*] that which, on good instruments, is bad'. The legerdemain in question, however, may often have been of the kind referred to by Bermudo and Aaron: a matter of left-hand artfulness to draw chords more resonant than those of equal temperament from instruments fretted in equal semitones. Every modern viol consort of any degree of finesse does this, and Marin Marais (1689) implied the use of such a technique on the solo viol when he said that his compositions in F♯ or B minor would, to their detriment, sound less 'piercing' ('perçant') if the viol were tuned up a semitone (taking its F♯ from the harpsichord's G) for the benefit of an accompanist unfamiliar with those keys. In all probability equal temperament was, then as now, a theoretical norm from which players departed flexibly for acoustical reasons – much as Renaissance keyboard musicians, confronted with instruments of rigid intonation, departed

Ex.13

from the theoretical norm of just intonation for reasons of practicability.

Two potential sources of systematic data on the spacing of frets in old instruments are the surviving, unaltered specimens of the cittern and the like, in which the frets were usually inlaid as they are on a modern guitar; and depictions in works of art where the artist can be shown to have treated such minutiae with sufficient care to give his rendition documentary value.

BIBLIOGRAPHY

TO 1690

G. Anselmi: *De musica*, 1434; ed. G. Massera (Florence, 1961)

Euclid: *Elementa geometriae*, trans. Johannes Campanus (Venice, 1482)

B. Ramos de Pareia: *Musica practica* (Bologna, 1482, 2/1482); ed. G. Vecchi (Bologna, 1969) [facs.]

F. Gaffurius: *Practica musicae* (Milan, 1496; Eng. trans., 1968; MSD, xx, 1969; 2/1497; rev. It. trans., 1508 as *Angelicum ac divinum opus musicae*)

A. Schlick: *Spiegel der Orgelmacher und Organisten* (Speyer, 1511/R1959); ed. in *MMg*, i (1869), 77–114

H. Grammateus: *Ayn new kunstlich Buech* (Nuremberg, 1518)

F. Gaffurius: *Apologia adversum Ioannem Spatarium* (Turin, 1520)

G. Spataro: *Errori de Franchino Gafurio da Lodi* (Bologna, 1521)

P. Aaron: *Thoscanello de la musica* (Venice, 1523/R1969; rev. with suppl. as *Toscanello in musica*, 1529/R1969, 1539/R1971, 1562; Eng. trans. collating all edns., 1970)

O. Finé: *Epithoma musice instrumentalis* (Paris, 1530)

G. M. Lanfranco: *Scintille di musica* (Brescia, 1533/R); Eng. trans., B. Lee (diss., Cornell U., 1961)

S. di Ganassi dal Fontego: *Regola rubertina* (Venice, 1542–3/R1970)

P. Aaron: *Lucidario in musica* (Venice, 1545/R1969), fol.35v

M. Agricola: *Musica instrumentalis deudsch* (Wittenberg, 5/1545); facs. edn. (Leipzig, 1896)

J. Bermudo: *Declaración de instrumentos musicales* (Osuna, 1555); facs. edn. (Kassel, 1957)

N. Vicentino: *L'antica musica ridotta alla moderna prattica* (Rome, 1555/R1959, 2/1557)

G. Zarlino: *Le istitutioni harmoniche* (Venice, 1558/R1965, rev. 3/1573/R1966)

T. de Santa María: *Arte de tañer fantasia* (Valladolid, 1565)

G. Zarlino: *Dimostrationi harmoniche* (Venice, 1571/R1966, 2/1573, rev. 1588)

F. de Salinas: *De musica libri septum* (Salamanca, 1577, 2/1592)

V. Galilei: *Dialogo della musica antica et della moderna* (Florence, 1581/R1968)

G. Zarlino: *Sopplimenti musicali* (Venice, 1588/R1966)

C. Schneegass: *Nova & exquisita monochordi dimensio* (Erfurt, 1590)

G. M. Artusi: *L'Artusi, overo Delle imperfettioni della moderna musica ragionamenti dui* (Venice, 1600/R1969)

S. Stevin: *Van de spiegeling der singconst*, c1600, ed. D. Bierens de Haan (Amsterdam, 1884); ed. A. Fokker in *The Principal Works of Simon Stevin*, v (Amsterdam, 1955–66)

A. Reinhard: *Monochordum* (Leipzig, 1604)

G. P. Cima: *Partito di ricercari, canzoni alla francese* (Milan, 1606¹⁵); ed. C. G. Rayner, CEKM, xx (1969)

P. Cerone: *El melopeo y maestro* (Naples, 1613/R1969)

M. Praetorius: *Syntagma musicum*, ii: *De organographia* (Wolfenbüttel, 1618, 2/1619/R1958)

M. Mersenne: *Harmonicorum libri, in quibus agitur de sonorum natura* (Paris, 1635–6)

——: *Harmonie universelle* (Paris, 1636–7/R1963; Eng. trans., 1957)

——: *Letters*, ed. C. de Waard as *Correspondance du P. Marin Mersenne* (Paris, 1932–)

J. Denis: *Traité de l'accord de l'éspinette* (Paris, 1643, 2/1650/R1969)

G. B. Doni: *De praestantia musicae veteris libri tres* (Florence, 1647)

L. Rossi: *Sistema musico, overo Musica speculativa* (Perugia, 1666)

C. F. Milliet de Chales: *Cursus seu Mundus mathematicus* (Lyons, 1674)

A. Werckmeister: *Orgel-Probe* (Frankfurt am Main and Leipzig, 1681, 2/1698/R1970 as *Erweiterte und Verbesserte Orgel-Probe*, 5/1783)

C. Huygens: Writings on music, *Oeuvres complètes*, xx (The Hague, 1942)

1690–1800

J. Ozanam: *Dictionaire mathématique* (Amsterdam, 1691)

A. Werckmeister: *Musicalische Temperatur* (Frankfurt am Main and Leipzig, 2/1691)

M.-A. Charpentier: *Règles de composition*, ?c1692, *F-Pn*, nouv. acq fr.6355, 6356

L. Chaumont: *Pièces d'orgue sur les 8 tons* (Huy, 1695); ed. J. Ferrard, Le pupitre, xxv (Paris, 1970)

W. C. Printz: *Phrynis mitilenaeus* (Dresden and Leipzig, 1696)

A. Werckmeister: *Hypomnemata musica* (Quedlinburg, 1697/R1970)

E. Loulié: *Nouveau système de musique* (Paris, 1698)

J. Wallis: 'A Letter of Dr. John Wallis to Samuel Pepys Esquire, Relating to some Supposed Imperfections in an Organ', *Philosophical Transactions* (1698), no.242, p.249

A. Werckmeister: *Die nothwendigsten Anmerckungen und Regeln, wie der Bassus continuus oder General-Bass wol könne tractiret werden* (Aschersleben, 1698, 2/1715)

C. Douwes: *Grondig ondersoek van de toonen der musik* (Franeker, 1699/R1970)

A. Werckmeister: *Cribrum musicum* (Quedlinburg and Leipzig, 1700/R1970)

S. de Brossard: *Dictionaire de musique* (Paris, 1703/R1964, 2/1705)

J. Sauveur: 'Système general des intervalles des sons, et son application à tous les systèmes et à tous les instruments de musique', *Histoire de l'Académie royale des sciences* [1701] (Paris, 1704), *Mémoires*, 297–364

J. G. Neidhardt: *Beste und leichteste Temperatur des Monochordi* (Jena, 1706)

A. Werckmeister: *Musicalische Paradoxal-Discourse* (Quedlinburg, 1707/R1970)

J. Sauveur: 'Methode generale pour former les systèmes temperés de musique, et du choix de celui qu'on doit suivre', *Histoire de l'Académie royale des sciences* [1707] (Paris, 1708), *Mémoires*, 203

K. Hensling: 'Specimen de novo suo systemate musico', *Abhandlungen der Berliner Akademie* (Berlin, 1710)

J. Mattheson: *Das neu-eröffnete Orchestre* (Hamburg, 1713)

B. Le B. de Fontenelle, ed.: *Histoire de l'Académie royale des sciences* [1711] (Paris, 1714)

J. Sauveur: 'Table generale des sistemes temperez de musique', *Histoire de l'Académie royale des sciences* [1711] (Paris, 1714), *Mémoires*, 309

C. A. Sinn: *Die aus mathematischen Gründen richtig gestellete musicalische temperatura practica* (Wernigeroda, 1717)

'Eclaircissement d'un problème de musique practique', *Mémoires pour l'histoire des sciences et des beaux arts* (Trevoux, 1718), 310

J. Mattheson: *Réflexions sur l'éclaircissement d'un problème de musique pratique* (Hamburg, 1720)

——: *Critica musica* (Hamburg, 1722–5/R1964)

P. F. Tosi: *Opinioni de' cantori antichi e moderni* (Bologna, 1723/R1968; Eng. trans., 1742, 2/1743/R1969 as *Observations on the Florid Song*)

P. Nassarre: *Escuela música, según la práctica moderna* (Saragossa, 1723–4)

J. G. Neidhardt: *Sectio Canonis Harmonici, zur völligen Richtigkeit der Generum Modulandi* (Königsberg, 1724)

J.-P. Rameau: *Nouveau système de musique théorique* (Paris, 1726)

J. G. Meckenheuser: *Die sogenannte: Allerneuste, musicalische Temperatur* (Quedlinburg, 1727)

J. P. A. Fischer: *Kurt en grondig onderwys* (Utrecht, 1728)

J. D. Heinichen: *Der General-Bass in der Composition* (Dresden, 1728)

J. G. Neidhardt: *Gäntzlich erschöpfte mathematische Abtheilungen des diatonisch-chromatischen temperirten Canonis Monochordi* (Königsberg, 1732, 2/1734)

J.-P. Rameau: *Génération harmonique* (Paris, 1737); ed. and trans., D. Hayes (diss., Stanford U., 1974)

J.-J. Rousseau: *Dissertation sur la musique moderne* (Paris, 1743)

R. Smith (iii): *Harmonics, of the Philosophy of Musical Sounds* (London, 1748, 2/1768)

G. A. Sorge: *Gespräch zwischen einem musico theoretico und einem studioso musices* (Lobenstein, 1748)

Extraits des registres de l'Académie royale des sciences (10 Dec 1749)

J. le R. d'Alembert: *Elémens de musique* (Paris, 1752)

M. Corrette: *Le maître de clavecin pour l'accompagnement: méthode théorique et pratique* (Paris, 1752/R1970)

G. Tartini: *Trattato di musica secondo la vera scienza dell'armonia* (Padua, 1754/R1966; Ger. trans., 1966)

B. Fritz: *Anweisung, wie man Claviere, Clavecins, und Orgeln, nach ein mechanischen Art, in allen zwölf Tönen gleich rein stimmen könne* (Leipzig, 1756, 5/1829)

F. Marpurg: *Principes du clavecin* (Berlin, 1756)

J. B. Romieu: 'Mémoire théorique et pratique sur les systèmes tempérés de musique', *Histoire de l'Académie royale des sciences* [1758] (Paris, 1763), *Mémoires*, 483–519

C. P. E. Bach: *Versuch über die wahre Art das Clavier zu spielen*, ii (Berlin, 1762/R1969)

G. Riccati: *Saggio sopra le leggi del contrapunto* (Castelfranco, 1762)

J.-J. Rousseau: *Dictionnaire de musique* (Paris, 1768/R1969; Eng. trans., c1775, 2/1779/R1975)

F. Bédos de Celles: *L'art du facteur d'orgues*, ii–iii (Paris, 1770/R1965)

G. A. Sorge: *Der in der Rechen- und Messkunst wohlerfahrne Orgelbaumeister* (Lobenstein, 1773)

J. H. Lambert: 'Remarques sur les tempéraments en musique', *Nouveaux mémoires de l'Académie royale des sciences et belles-lettres* (Berlin, 1774)

G. F. Tempelhof: *Gedanken über die Temperatur des Herrn Kirnberger* (Berlin and Leipzig, 1775)

F. W. Marpurg: *Versuch über die musikalische Temperatur* (Breslau, 1776/*R*)

J. B. Mercadier de Belesta: *Nouveau système de musique théorique et pratique* (Paris, 1776)

J. P. Kirnberger: *Die Kunst des reinen Satzes in der Musik*, ii/3 (Berlin and Königsberg, 1776–9/*R*1968, 2/1793)

J. J. Engel: *Über die musikalische Malerey* (Berlin, 1780)

C. F. Cramer, ed.: *Magazin der Musik*, ii (Hamburg, 1784/*R*1975)

W. Jones [of Nayland]: *A Treatise on the Art of Music* (Colchester, 1784, 2/1827)

T. Cavallo: 'Of the Temperament of those Musical Instruments, in which the Tones, Keys, or Frets, are Fixed, as in the Harpsichord, Organ, Guitar, &c.', *Philosophical Transactions of the Royal Society of London*, lxxviii (1788), 238

F. W. Marpurg: *Neue Methode allerley Arten von Temperaturen dem Claviere aufs Bequemste mitzutheilen* (Berlin, 1790/*R*1970)

A. Suremain-Missery: *Théorie acoustico-musicale* (Paris, 1793)

1800–1900

C. Gervasoni: *La scuola della musica* (Piacenza, 1800)

T. Young: 'Outlines of Experiments and Inquiries Respecting Sound and Light', *Philosophical Transactions*, xc (1800), 106–50

J. Robison: 'Temperament', *Encyclopaedia Britannica* (Edinburgh, 3/1801)

D. G. Türk: *Clavierschule* (Leipzig and Halle, enlarged 2/1802/*R*1967)

T. Cavallo: *The Elements of Natural or Experimental Philosophy* (London, 1803)

C. Stanhope: 'Principles of the Science of Tuning Instruments with Fixed Tones', *Philosophical Magazine*, xxv (1806), 291

J. W. Callcott: *Plain Statement of Earl Stanhope's Temperament* (London, 1807)

W. Crotch: *Elements of Musical Composition* (London, 1812, 2/1833)

C. Gervasoni: *Nuova teoria di musica* (Parma, 1812)

H. Liston: *An Essay on Perfect Intonation* (Edinburgh, 1812), 23

B. Asioli: *Osservazioni sul temperamento proprio degl'istromenti stabili* (Milan, 1816)

G. Serassi: *Sugli organi, lettere a G. S. Mayr, P. Bonticli e C. Bigatti* (Bergamo, 1816)

P. Lichtenthal: *Dizionario e bibliografia della musica* (Milan, 1826; Fr. trans. by D. Mondo, 1839, as *Dictionnaire de musique*)

J. N. Hummel: *Ausführlich theoretisch-practische Anweisung zum Piano-Forte Spiel* (Vienna, 1828; Eng. trans., 1829)

J. Jousse: *An Essay on Temperament* (London, 1832)

C. Montal: *Abrégé de l'art d'accorder soi-même son piano* (Paris, 1834)

A. F. Schindler: *Biographie von Ludwig van Beethoven* (Münster, 1840, rev. 3/1860; Eng. trans., 1966, as *Beethoven as I Knew him*)

I. F. Holton: 'Essay on Musical Intonation and Temperament', *Annals of the Lyceum of Natural History, of New York*, iv (1847), 387

H. von Helmholtz: *Die Lehre von den Tonempfindungen, als physiologische Grundlage für die Theorie der Musik* (Brunswick, 1863, 4/1877; Eng. version by A. J. Ellis, as *On the Sensations of Tone*, rev. 2/1885)

W. Pole: *The Philosophy of Music* (London, 1879, 6/1924, ed. H. Hartridge)

T. Elliston: *Organs and Tuning* (London, 1894)

SINCE 1900

A. Pirro: *Descartes et la musique* (Paris, 1907/*R*1973–4)

E. P. L. Atkins: 'Ear-training and the Standardization of Equal Temperament', *PMA*, xli (1914–15), 91

S. Wolfenden: *A Treatise on the Art of Pianoforte Construction* (London and Woking, 1916/*R*1975)

W. B. White: *Modern Piano Tuning and Allied Arts* (New York, 1917, rev. and enlarged 5/1946 as *Piano Tuning and Allied Arts*)

J. S. Handschin: 'Über reine Harmonie und temperierte Tonleitern', *Schweizerisches Jb für Musikwissenschaft*, ii (1927), 145

P. Garnault: *Le tempérament, son application aux claviers, aux violes de gambe et guitars, son influence sur la musique du XVIIIe siècle* (Nice, 1929)

T. Kornerup: *Das Tonsystem des Italieners Zarlino* (Copenhagen, 1930)

F. T. Arnold: *The Art of Accompaniment from a Thorough-bass as Practised in the 17th and 18th Centuries* (London, 1931/*R*1965, 2/1961)

J. M. Barbour: *Equal Temperament: its History from Ramis (1482) to Rameau (1737)* (diss., Cornell U., 1932)

J. Yasser: *A Theory of Evolving Tonality* (New York, 1932)

W. Dupont: *Geschichte der musikalischen Temperatur* (Kassel, 1935)

T. Kornerup: *Das goldene Tonsystem* (Copenhagen, 1935)

J. M. Barbour: 'Bach and The Art of Temperament', *MQ*, xxxiii (1947), 64

A. R. McClure: 'Studies in Keyboard Temperaments', *GSJ*, i (1948), 28

J. M. Barbour: *Tuning and Temperament, a Historical Survey* (East Lansing, Mich., 1951, 2/1953/*R*1973)

J. M. Ward: *The Vihuela da Mano and its Music (1536–1576)* (diss., New York U., 1953)

K. J. Levy: 'Costeley's Chromatic Chanson', *AnnM*, iii (1955), 213–63

E. E. Lowinsky: 'Adrian Willaert's Chromatic "Duo" Re-examined', *TVNM*, xviii/1 (1956), 1–36

H. P. Reddick: *Johann Mattheson's Forty-eight Thorough-bass Textpieces: Translation and Commentary* (diss., U. of Michigan, 1956)

J. Wilson, ed.: *Roger North on Music* (London, 1959), 203

H. Kelletat: *Zur musikalischen Temperatur, in besondere bei Johann Sebastian Bach* (Kassel, 1960)

G. Oldham: 'Louis Couperin: a New Source of French Keyboard Music of the mid 17th Century', *RMFC*, i (1960), 56

H. H. Carter: *A Dictionary of Middle English Musical Terms* (Bloomington, Ind., 1961)

M. J. Mandelbaum: *Multiple Division of the Octave and the Tonal Resources of 19-tone Temperament* (diss., Indiana U., 1961)

G. Massera: 'Musica inspettiva e accordatura strumentale nelle "Scintille" di Lanfranco da Terenzo', *Quadrivium*, iv (1964), 85

H. Husmann: 'Zur Charakteristik der Schlickschen Temperatur', *AMw*, xxiv (1967), 253

P. Williams: 'Equal Temperament and the English Organ', *AcM*, xl (1968), 53

C. G. Rayner: 'The Enigmatic Cima: Meantone Tuning and Transpositions', *GSJ*, xxii (1969), 23

G. Sargent: 'Eighteenth-century Tuning Directions', *MR*, xxx (1969), 27

O. B. Billeter: 'Die Silbermann–Stimmungen', *AMw*, xxvii (1970), 73

H.-P. Reinecke: 'Zum Problem der musikalischen Temperatur in aussereuropäischen Tonsystemen', *Speculum musicae artis: Festgabe für Heinrich Husmann* (Munich, 1970), 271

K.-J. Sachs: *Mensura fistularum: die Mensurierung der Orgelpfeifen im Mittelalter* (Stuttgart, 1970–)

J. Barnes: 'The Specious Uniformity of Italian Harpsichords', *Keyboard Instruments: Studies in Keyboard Organology*, ed. E. M. Ripin (Edinburgh, 1971), 1

D. Poulton: *John Dowland* (London, 1972)

E. M. Dombois: 'Varieties of Meantone Temperament Realized on the Lute', *Journal of the Lute Society of America*, vii (1974), 82

M. Lindley: 'Early Sixteenth-century Keyboard Temperaments', *MD*, xxviii (1974), 129

R. Meylan: *La flûte* (Lausanne, 1974), 71

F. A. Kuttner: 'Chu Tsai-Yü's Life and Work: a Re-evaluation of his Contribution to Equal Temperament Theory', *EM*, xix (1975), 163–206

M. Lindley: 'Fifteenth-century Evidence for Meantone Temperament', *PRMA*, cii (1975–6), 37

J. Chesnut: 'Mozart's Teaching of Intonation', *JAMS*, xxx (1977), 258

M. Lindley: 'Instructions for the Clavier Diversely Tempered', *Early Music*, v (1977), 18

J. Meffen: 'A Question of Temperament: Purcell and Croft', *MT*, cxix (1978), 504

D. de Klerk: 'Equal Temperament', *AcM*, li (1979), 140

M. Lindley: 'Lutes, Viols and Temperaments', *LSJ* (in preparation)

——: 'Mersenne and the Well-tempered *Clavecin*', *JMT* (in preparation)

A. C. N. Mackenzie of Ord: *Keyboard Temperament in England during the Eighteenth and Nineteenth Centuries* (diss., U. of Bristol, in preparation)

MARK LINDLEY

Temperley, Nicholas (*b* Beaconsfield, 7 Aug 1932). English musicologist. After attending Eton College (1945–51), he studied for a year at the RCM, London (ARCM 1952), before reading music at King's College, Cambridge (BA 1955, MusB 1956). He took the PhD there in 1959 with a dissertation on 19th-century instrumental music in England. He was a postdoctoral Fellow at the University of Illinois (1959–61) and returned to Cambridge as an assistant lecturer (1961–6). He became successively assistant professor at Yale University (1966), associate professor at the University of Illinois (1967) and professor and chairman of the musicology department there (1972).

Temperley has done much to promote a reassessment of English 19th-century music in its social and historical context; and he has edited Loder's opera *Raymond and Agnes* (given at Cambridge, 1966), piano music, songs and liturgical pieces. He has worked on Anglican music of all periods, culminating in his substantial study of parish church music, as well as hymns, psalmody in Britain and the USA, especially the development of the English metrical psalm; his study on

Playford's publications of these psalms is valuable both for its insight into the musical climate of the time and for its masterly analysis of the publications. The same meticulous approach marks his edition of Berlioz's *Symphonie fantastique* (New Berlioz Edition, xvii, Kassel, 1972) in which 14 versions are collated.

WRITINGS

'Domestic Music in England, 1800–1860', *PRMA*, lxxxviii (1958–9), 31

Instrumental Music in England, 1800–1850 (diss., U. of Cambridge, 1959)

'Mendelssohn's Influence on English Music', *ML*, xliii (1962), 224

'Personal Tempo and Subjective Accentuation', *Journal of General Psychology*, lxviii (1963), 267

'George Frederick Pinto, 1785–1806', *MT*, cvi (1965), 265

'Tempo and Repeats in the Early 19th Century', *ML*, xlvii (1966), 323

'The English Romantic Opera', *Victorian Studies*, ix (1966), 293

'The *Symphonie fantastique* and its Program', *MQ*, lvii (1971), 593

'John Playford and the Metrical Psalms', *JAMS*, xxv (1972), 331–78

'Henry Hugo Pierson, 1815–73', *MT*, cxiv (1973), 1217; cxv (1974), 30

'John Field's Life and Music', *MT*, cxv (1974), 386

'John Field and the First Nocturne', *ML*, lvi (1975), 335

'Sterndale Bennett and the Lied', *MT*, cxvi (1975), 958, 1060

'Schubert and the Lied', *Of German Music: a Symposium*, ed. H.-H. Schönzeler (London and New York, 1976), 153

'Croft and the Charity Hymn', *MT*, cxix (1978), 539

The Music of the English Parish Church (Cambridge, 1979)

'Balfe, Michael William', 'Benedict, Julius', 'Bennett, William Sterndale', 'Birmingham', 'Chopin, Fryderyk Franciszek', §§7–14, 'Crotch, William', 'Field, John', 'Hymn', §IV, 'Loder', 'London', §I, 'Norwich', 'Psalmody (ii)', §I, 'Psalms, metrical', §§I, III, V, 'Symphony', §II, 'Wesley', *Grove 6*

EDITIONS

with G. Bush: *English Songs, 1800–1860*, MB, xliii (1979)

DAVID SCOTT

Temple block. See WOODBLOCK.

Templeton, John (*b* Riccarton, nr. Kilmarnock, 30 July 1802; *d* New Hampton, nr. London, 2 July 1886). Scottish tenor. He studied music theory with Blewitt and singing with Welsh, De Pinna and Tom Cooke. After appearances in the provinces (1828–30), he made his London début at Drury Lane on 13 October 1831 as Belville in *Rosina* (Shield). In February 1832 he sang Raimbaut in the first performance in England of Meyerbeer's *Robert le diable* and the following year scored a brilliant success as the first English Don Ottavio. In 1833 Malibran chose him as her leading tenor, which he remained until the end of her brief career. He also appeared with Malibran in *Fidelio* and Balfe's *Maid of Artois*; her coaching is said to have markedly improved his skill as an actor. He took the leading tenor roles in the first performances in English of Auber's *Le cheval de bronze* (1836), Hérold's *Zampa* (1836), Rossini's *Le siège de Corinthe* (1836), *Die Zauberflöte* (1838) and Donizetti's *La favorite* (1843). In 1842 he visited Paris with Balfe and received the attention of Auber. The last years of his professional career were chiefly devoted to the concert room; in the 1845–6 season he visited the principal American cities with his 'Templeton Entertainment', consisting of English, Scottish and Irish folksongs. He retired in 1852 and published his reminiscences and commentaries as *A Musical Entertainment* (Boston, Mass., 1845).

BIBLIOGRAPHY

W. H. Husk: *Templeton and Malibran* (London, 1880)

J. C. Hadden: 'Templeton, John', *DNB*

HAROLD ROSENTHAL

Temple University Music Festival. Festival held annually at Ambler, near Philadelphia, from 1967; *see* PHILADELPHIA, §1.

Templin, Procopius von. *See* PROCOPIUS VON TEMPLIN.

Tempo (It.). The 'time' of a musical composition; hence the speed at which its performance proceeds. (The French *temps* normally means either measure or, more usually, beat; *mouvement* is French for speed but, as in English and other languages, 'tempo' is an acclimatized and common term.)

The notation of tempo may be definite or indefinite. The definite notation of tempo is by stating the number of specified units (e.g. crotchets, dotted crotchets) to the minute. These may be rendered audible by coupling a clicking mechanism to the swinging of an adjustable pendulum, as in Maelzel's metronome, which improved on previous devices by using a compound in place of a simple pendulum, thus greatly reducing the length required. The notation 'M.M.60' means '60 units to the minute', the note value of the unit remaining to be inferred; the notation 'crotchet = 60' defines the unit and means '60 crotchets to the minute', and is now preferred, because it is more specific, and because Maelzel's metronome has been virtually replaced by handy electronic devices which can be of high precision.

There are schools of modern composition in which the precise determination and subdivision of tempo represent an integral component to be approximated as nearly as possible by human performers, or achieved with more than human accuracy by electronic means. In no other school of composition, perhaps, is it either feasible or desirable to determine or subdivide tempo with mathematical precision. There is no one right tempo in the absolute, but only a tempo which is more or less excellent in relation to other variables: the reverberation of the hall; the size of a choir or orchestra; and, especially, the disposition of the performance. To draw out most brilliance, quick tempos are appropriate; to draw out most expressiveness, slow ones may be: and both dispositions may lie within the valid implications of a piece of music as different performers (or the same performer in different moods) may fairly experience it.

These considerations greatly reduce the usefulness of the definite notation of tempo. Beethoven attached much importance to his metronome markings, but when some were lost he replaced them by others quite different, to his own incredulous irritation when the original ones were found. Brahms (in a letter to George Henschel, quoted in his *Personal Recollections of Johannes Brahms*, Boston, Mass., 1907, p.78f) concluded that:

. . . the metronome is of no value. As far at least as my experience goes, everybody has, sooner or later, withdrawn his metronome marks. Those which can be found in my works – good friends have talked me into putting them there, for I myself have never believed that my blood and a mechanical instrument go well together. The so-called 'elastic tempo' is moreover not a new invention. 'Con discrezione' should be added to that as to many other things.

Baroque writers used similar terms: J. J. Quantz (*Versuch*, 1752, chap.11, p.13), 'performance should be easy and flexible'; François Couperin (*L'art de toucher le clavecin*, Paris, 1716, 2/1717, p.38), 'measure defines the number and time value of beats; nuance [*cadence*] is properly the spirit, the soul which must be added to it'; Thomas Mace (*Musick's Monument*, London, 1676, p.81), 'sometimes Faster, and sometimes Slower, as we perceive, the Nature of the Thing Requires'.

The indefinite notation of tempo may be by time signatures, by tempo marks, or by a combination of these. Time signatures are (and have been since the very transition from Renaissance into early Baroque music) a confused and confusing legacy from the signs and conventions, themselves confused and inconsistent, of a quite different method of notating time values and (up to a point) tempos: the proportional system of mensural notation. The unit there was the *tactus*, shown by the up-and-down movement of the hand: even, for duple measure, and uneven, for triple measure. The tempo of the *tactus* was, by convention (and to some extent by muscular necessity), neither very fast nor very slow: within these limits, it was to be adapted to the requirements of the music, and not the music to the *tactus*. Thus it gave a very approximate measure of absolute tempo in accordance with the signs indicating the note values allotted to comprise the *tactus*. In theory, the signs gave a mathematical measure of relative tempos when changed in course of a composition; but in practice this relationship may also have been always approximate, and certainly was so in the decline of the proportional system which may be dated to the early Baroque period but was probably in progress as early as 1500, if not before. The system was strongly criticized by Zarlino (*Le istitutioni harmoniche*, Venice, 1558, 2/1562, p.278), by Pierre Maillart (*Les tons*, Tournai, 1610, p.348), who described 'the signs of imperfection' as 'superfluous and useless', and, a century after Zarlino, by Athanasius Kircher (*Musurgia*, Rome, 1650, p.676), who, after setting out the signs of proportion with exceptional completeness and detail, dismissed them entire as 'hanc confusissimam materiam' ('this most confused subject matter') and 'haec tota farrago' ('this utter jumble').

Proportional notation, however, was prolonged in its decay, and must still be taken into account during most of the 17th century, as an element of mystification rather than of clarification in determining not so much tempos (always primarily a matter for musicianly judgment) as changes of tempo. The following points are of some practical significance.

The half-circle C and the crossed half-circle ₵ stand in the theoretical proportion of 1:2. Other things being equal, a piece headed ₵ should in theory have a tempo twice as fast as a piece headed C; and a change in course of a piece from C to ₵ should cause a doubling of the tempo. But this theory has little bearing on the facts. As Kircher justly pointed out, 'a majority of the most excellent musicians and the most expert in theory of the present time' (i.e. about 1650) have 'taken them for one and the same sign' ('pro unico signo'). J. D. Heinichen (*General-Bass*, Dresden, 1728, pt.i, chap.4, p.48) confirmed for the generation of J. S. Bach, three-quarters of a century later, that C and ₵ were 'used without discrimination, sometimes for a naturally rapid piece and sometimes for a slow one'. The repeated statements of the conventional theory, copied from one another by inferior writers in popular textbooks, are therefore misleading.

Writers who, without being great theorists, were too musicianly merely to reiterate the conventional theory, gave the more realistic but still quite unreliable advice to take ₵ 'a little faster', and 𝄵 'quickest of all'. Those remarks appear in the editions from 1694 on, 'Corrected and Amended by Mr Henry Purcell', of John Playford's *Introduction to the Skill of Musick* (p.25); originally (1654 edition, p.15) no C but only ₵ is given; the 1672 edition has also 𝄵 'as swift again', i.e. twice as fast. Thus at the head of a piece the difference between C and ₵ may be slight or none; in course of a piece, a change from C to ₵ may need a somewhat faster tempo but not necessarily double. There is also a considerable possibility (though by no means a certainty) that C may hint at a pulse of four in the bar and ₵ a pulse of two in the bar.

A particular warning must be given for Baroque French recitative, in which changing time signatures including C and ₵ are extremely common, but where the tempo remains unaffected: i.e. crotchet equals crotchet throughout. Etienne Denis Delair (*Traité d'accompagnement*, Paris, 1690, p.48) has 'one crotchet . . . for each beat' in 'the measure of four beats'. Henri-Louis Choquel (*La musique rendue sensible*, Paris, 2/1762, p.109ff) described ₵ and 2 as equivalent 'when used in recitatives' to the 'measure with four beats', i.e. C, but elsewhere 'very much more quickly than in the measure with four beats'; moreover 'for recitatives, the speed is arbitrary and it is the words which decide it'. Thus in French recitatives changes of time signature may represent subtle adaptations of musical pulse to the verbal accents, but not changes of tempo. Crotchet equals crotchet, which is the same as to say beat equals beat.

Numerical time signatures have the appearance of being mathematically precise, but this appearance likewise is contrary to the facts. In early Baroque music, the tripla time signature 3 or (more specifically) 3/1 stands in the theoretical proportion 3:1 in relation either to an assumed *tactus* (if at the head of a piece) or to the previous tempo (if in course of a piece): i.e. three units (new) in the time of one unit (old), or three times as fast. And the sesquialtera time signature, which may also be notated 2 but should be notated (more specifically) 3/2, stands in the theoretical proportion 3:2, i.e. three units (new) in the time of two units (old), or half as fast again; in the 16th century it is often notated simply as 3.

In practice, these mathematical proportions do not necessarily obtain. Triple-time signatures in course of a piece can, however, ordinarily be relied upon to indicate some increase of speed, and commonly a great increase. More generally, passages or pieces with a triple-time signature are likely to need a much faster speed than their notation would suggest to a modern musician unacquainted with the proportional system and its Baroque transition.

The transition from proportional (relative) to modern (absolute) interpretations of time signatures, changed in meaning though not in appearance, may be seen as fairly well established by the late 17th century, and consolidated in late Baroque music. The transition was so gradual that it cannot be exactly documented; but in the music and the treatises of the later Baroque period we find our modern interpretation taken for granted, by which numerical signatures notate the relationship of numerator and denominator, so that 3/1 means three units of one semibreve to the bar, and 3/2 means three units of one minim to the bar. Neither at the head of a piece nor in course of a piece do modern time signatures convey any information concerning the tempo, except in so far as bars with a small number of notes of short value (e.g. 3/8 or three units of one quaver to the bar) suggest a higher speed of movement than bars with more notes or longer values to the bar.

Time-words were developed early in the Baroque period as indefinite indications of tempo and at the same time of mood (in the sense of the prevailing spirit or character of the piece or passage thus headed). These two connotations of tempo and mood were associated from the start, and properly so, since tempo is to a large extent a function of mood and governed thereby. Nevertheless the two functions, though always related, are not identical. Some time-words found in early Baroque music, such as the Italian *adagio* ('at ease') or *allegro* ('cheerful'), describe mood directly, tempo indirectly; others, such as *lento* ('slow') or *presto* ('quick'), describe tempo directly, mood indirectly. (In ordinary Italian parlance, *adagio* means 'slowly' but *allegro* does not mean 'fast'.) In the Baroque period particularly time-words may be used as indications of mood rather than of tempo; above all care should be taken not to take slow movements too slow, or fast movements too fast. That was the admirable advice of C. P. E. Bach (*Versuch über die wahre Art das Clavier zu spielen*, 1753, chap.3, p.10):

> The tempo of a piece, which is usually indicated by a variety of familiar Italian terms, is derived from its general mood together with the fastest notes and passages which it includes. Proper attention to these considerations will prevent an Allegro from being hurried and an Adagio from being dragged.

Many movements in compositions of different periods are in dance form or based upon dance forms. It is therefore helpful to have a practical acquaintance with the dance itself, of which the steps not only set limits (often very narrow limits) to the margins of tempo within which they can be executed, but also give clear indications about the phrasing, the articulation and the accentuation of the music designed for them. This can be invaluable for interpreting even those dance and dance-form movements which have been removed far from their ballroom origins; but in these cases it must be appreciated that the tempos may not necessarily be the same, though the phrasing and the general character probably will. It has also to be appreciated that a particular dance may vary greatly in tempo at different times and places: compare, for example, the quick English saraband of the 17th century with the moderate Italian and the slow French sarabande – at its slowest in the 18th century, when Bach used it with a degree of ornamental figuration which would be undesirable at too great a speed.

Tempo 'is a various and undetermined thing', wrote Alexander Malcolm (*Treatise of Musick*, Edinburgh, 1721, p.394), who did not specify the variations, 'and indeed the true Determination of them must be learnt by Experience from the Practice of Musicians'; from this, as Leopold Mozart commented (*Violinschule*, Augsburg, 1756, i, chap.3, p.7) 'the true worth of a musician can be recognized without fail'.

See also TEMPO AND EXPRESSION MARKS.

BIBLIOGRAPHY
H. Bellermann: *Die Mensuralnoten und Taktzeichen des 15. und 16. Jahrhunderts* (Berlin, 1858, 4/1963)
G. Schünemann: *Geschichte des Dirigierens* (Leipzig, 1913/*R*1965 and 1966)
C. Sachs: *Rhythm and Tempo* (New York, 1953)
I. Herrmann-Bengen: *Tempobezeichnungen: Ursprung; Wandel im 17. und 18. Jahrhundert* (Tutzing, 1959)
E. Barthe: *Takt und Tempo* (Hamburg, 1960)
C. Dahlhaus: 'Zur Entstehung des modernen Taktsystems im 17. Jahrhundert', *AMw*, xviii (1961), 223
R. Donington: *The Interpretation of Early Music* (London, 1963, rev. 3/1974)
S. Gullo: *Das Tempo in der Musik des XIII. und XIV. Jahrhunderts* (Berne, 1964)
A. Auda: *Théorie et pratique du tactus* (Brussels, 1965)
J. A. Bank: *Tactus, Tempo and Notation in Mensural Music from the 13th to the 17th Century* (Amsterdam, 1972)

ROBERT DONINGTON

Tempo and expression marks. Words and other instructions in musical scores used to amplify the notation and specify the manner of performance.

1. Introduction. 2. Taxonomy and taxonomies. 3. The language. 4. Considerations in establishing the tempo. 5. Early history of performance instructions.

1. INTRODUCTION. Tempo and expression marks are probably the most consistently ignored components of a musical score. Musicians who know the key, pitch, phrasing and perhaps even the first page or so of the precise scoring of the *Figaro* overture, for instance, are rarely able to name the tempo and opening dynamic of this most popular of all scores. The main reason is probably that the musician looks first at the music, and only then looks at the markings to see whether they agree with his initial impression; for the marking without the music would convey no information at all. To explore the further reasons with any pretence at rigour would be an enormous pursuit encompassing the nature of music, the nature of musical notation and the nature of the human brain; but for the present purposes it should perhaps be taken as axiomatic that staff notation is relatively precise for what it is equipped to express whereas verbal or implicitly verbal instructions are employed for the dimensions that cannot be expressed in such simple and unambiguous form. To distinguish between correct and incorrect performance of pitches and rhythms is a relatively simple matter whereas tempo and expression are largely subjective.

The responsibility lies less with physical qualities – musical volume and time can be analysed and defined with complete scientific objectivity – than with the nature of Western music and its instruments. Dynamics are contextual, not only within the musical gradation of a phrase and within the voicing of a chord (let alone the size of the room and of the ensemble) but also within the instrument itself: the difference between the loudest and softest tones on a trombone or a violin is far greater than on an oboe or a flute and suggests that some of the attempts in the 1950s to serialize dynamics may be a little out of touch with reality. And while the metronome has been available for nearly two centuries, there has been considerable resistance to its use, both among composers who have found that their metronome marks simply could not be made to work in all conditions and among performers who look with suspicion on anything that seems to reduce them to the level of an automaton. Part of the reason in both cases, as Rudolf Kolisch pointed out (1943), is that a musician rarely plays any two consecutive bars or even any two consecutive beats at precisely the same tempo, so metronome instructions are often difficult to give and even more difficult to follow; moreover, until recently the metronome was such a clumsy instrument that good metronome marks could be given only by composers who, like Bartók, had a kind of 'perfect tempo' and could instantly reproduce a tempo such as crotchet = 130 without reflection or any danger of inaccuracy.

But there is a further problem with tempo. Evidence suggests that increasing familiarity with a work leads audiences and musicians to prefer slower performances: the surviving early and apparently authoritative metronome marks, such as those by Beethoven for his own works (see Kolisch, 1943, and Stadlen, 1967) and those by Hummel for Mozart (see Münster, 1962–3), tend to be substantially faster than the fastest times taken today for the same works. Even if this is explained by the (improbable) theory that all early metronomes were inaccurate, there is the evidence of the regular timings of all operas performed at the Bayreuth Festival since 1882 which show that *Parsifal*, for instance, now usually takes an hour longer than at its earliest performances; and the three recordings Boulez has made of his own *Le marteau sans maître* over a mere 15 years show a remarkable slowing down as the work became more widely known and accepted as a classic.

This same imprecision and variability of meaning has led to a serious lack of musicological study. Metronome marks have been studied extensively, and with the increasing availability of recordings of the same work by different artists at widely divergent tempos this study will continue; but its bearing on the question of tempo marks is almost exhausted with the simple observation that it is impossible to provide as much as an approximate metronome equivalent for any tempo mark even within the works of a single composer, for many other considerations must be taken into account (see §4 below). As a historical study, tempo and expression marks present a front so slippery that few have ventured to tackle this area in which conclusions are so subjective, facts so difficult to establish or check, and the available data in many cases not at all carefully considered by the composer when he wrote them. Consequently the fullest studies of tempo and expression marks are still those in the dictionaries of the 18th and early 19th centuries: here there was an attempt to show how different composers had used a mark with different intentions and in different contexts at different parts of their lives. So the rigorous study of the subject today would (like Siegele, 1974) begin from there. The study of the early use and introduction of tempo marks in the 17th century has recently been outlined with remarkable thoroughness and perspicacity by Herrmann-Bengen (1959); but no attempt has yet been made to establish the traditions in which particular marks were used. Thus it has been shown that Beethoven normally used the word ASSAI to mean not 'very' but 'rather', and it has been shown that Brossard (1703), whom Beethoven is not likely to have read, gave that meaning for the word; but nobody has attempted to show a tradition of *allegro assai* running through the 18th century used in that way. Many similar examples could be given.

Study of the subject is made particularly difficult by the eagerness with which many 19th-century editors added tempo and expression marks to scores. Even today the nature of traditional music typography is such that it can be extremely difficult for even the most conscientious editor to indicate clearly which directions are original and which editorial; indeed, a consistent practice in this was really established only in the critical complete editions that have appeared since the 1950s (Mozart, Haydn, Schubert, etc). Anyone who has compared a few internationally orientated performing editions of the Schubert songs or Wagner's later operas will see how the original German directions were not merely translated but rejected and replaced with often thoroughly incompetent pseudo-Italian markings inserted by anonymous editors. This is just the most conspicuous tip of the iceberg which makes the whole study of tempo and expression marks extremely hazardous. Even in many of the collected editions it is impossible to tell which directions are the editor's and which the composer's.

In a sense, this is a function of a development most clearly visible in music since about 1800. In 1826 Beethoven wrote to Schott: 'We can hardly have any *tempi ordinari* any more, now that we must follow our free inspiration': the Romantic search for individuality had made the obvious tempo something to be despised. In 1817 he had written to Hofrat von Mosel saying that he wished to discard the 'four principal tempos' (*allegro*, *andante*, *adagio* and *presto*) and to use a metronome for tempo, but added: 'the words that indicate the character of a piece are another thing . . . these terms refer actually to its spirit, which is what I am interested in'. The individuality that he represented and that was to become the hallmark of 19th-century music led to an extraordinary proliferation of tempo and expression marks, a significant increase in a development which had been going on since the middle of the 17th century. Such words are rare in earlier music and entirely absent from all other music traditions in the world: in those a knowledge of the tradition was normally sufficient to establish the correct tempo and playing style. But of course the same is true for a fairly large proportion of 19th-century music in which, therefore, the tempo and expression marks are often fundamentally superfluous – which perhaps explains why they are so often ignored.

2. TAXONOMY AND TAXONOMIES. Although verbal instructions have several quite separate functions in scores it is difficult to establish a watertight division of these functions. *Spiccato* is not merely an instruction to use a particular bowing technique but also a request for a particular kind of sound; and it is, moreover, found in many contexts where such bowing would be impossible. *Vivace* in 19th-century scores can be a tempo designation, a modification of another tempo designation or an indication of mood alone. But a relatively simple and workable taxonomy is implied by the layout and typography of most published performing scores circulating today. It is offered here as being the current practice whose very familiarity and relative consistency solve many of the inevitable problems of rationalization.

(*a*) The tempo designation and similar instructions concerning the entire ensemble appear at the top in bold roman type.

(*b*) Dynamics are notated below each staff, separately for each performer or voice, in bold italic. Normally only the traditional letter-abbreviations are used: *p*, *mp*, *ff*, etc, together with *sfz* and similar accent marks. *Crescendo* and *diminuendo* cannot be expressed in this abbreviated form and are therefore taken in under category (*c*).

(*c*) Marks of expression are printed in normal italic: *espressivo*, *zart*, *markig*, *con voce cupa*, etc. In this category also belong qualifications to the dynamic (*cresc.*), or even sometimes to the tempo (*slentando*, *stringendo*, *accelerando*) – presumably because small adjustments to the tempo are constantly to be expected in music of the later 19th century.

(*d*) Technical instructions are printed in small roman: arco, senza sord., Schalltrichter auf!, getheilt, am Steg, baguettes de bois, etc.

There are obvious dangers in the conceptual use of such an analysis. Beethoven's letter to Hofrat von Mosel (cited above) shows that he saw clear and essential divisions within the first group; several of the terms appear in different categories in modern printed scores according to context or the whim of the editor; and the implicit application of the modern system to 18th-century scores in 20th-century editions has led to substantial misinformation. More important, terms have changed their functions over the years (*see* ANDANTE) or even between one composer and the next (*see* DOLCE). The early history of the whole topic is particularly fraught: there are suggestions that a *piano* section should also be slow, that in several cases ADAGIO is not a tempo but a style of playing (e.g. in Frescobaldi), and so on. This all makes the categorization of such marks seem hopeless; but the attempt seems necessary if any kind of conceptual order is to be brought to the subject.

A further division is important. Some marks have traditions associated with them and others do not. On the whole the dividing line here is between Italian and non-Italian, or perhaps between words used internationally (like *martelé* or *Flatterzunge*) and those whose use is confined to the vernacular. *Adagio*, for instance, has a history of its own, much more than *langsam* or *slow*; not that the vernacular forms never caught on (they did, often) but merely because their selfconsciously vernacular position tended to prevent their developing the kind of purely musical tradition that *adagio* acquired all over Europe. There is a long and respectable tradition of composers using their own vernacular in verbal directions, but the history to be drawn there would be of the fact of using the vernacular, not of the shades of musical meaning within the words themselves.

This raises a related matter: the distinction between traditional use and vernacular use of Italian by composers who happened to be fluent in Italian. At the beginning of *La bohème* Puccini marked all the parts *ruvidamente* ('roughly', 'harshly'), but its meaning here is simply its literal meaning, and it is most unlikely that Puccini would have had any earlier musical uses of the word in mind as he wrote it, even less that in doing so he was specifically recalling them. Nor should all the verbose markings of Vivaldi be so carefully categorized: he made free use of all kinds of fascinating instructions, but there is no reason to list them all or to think that their meanings went any further than the literal. The reader of such scores would be better equipped with a pocket Italian dictionary than a dictionary of musical terms.

3. THE LANGUAGE. Italian music – and indeed Italian culture in general – so strongly dominated the European scene during the years 1600 to 1750, the years in which tempo and expression marks were not only introduced but developed into a system, that the international vocabulary for these words inevitably became Italian. There is no evidence of any particular power struggle: German and English words appear occasionally in 17th-century music, and both Praetorius and Purcell implied a little frustration with the idea of such instructions being more acceptable when put in Italian, but they accepted the growing convention and nothing systematic developed in either language. In the early 18th century a system of French words evolved with almost as much range and coherence as the German-language system of the later 19th and early 20th centuries, but the influence of French music was not sufficient to present any significant challenge to the supremacy of Italian, the language known to most musicians. By the time the later German system evolved the Italian system had 300 years' advantage. So although most composers of the 19th and 20th centuries have at some point in their career preferred to use their own language for all tempo and expression marks, whether for reasons of precision, more direct communication with their anticipated readers or mere impatience with the assumption that Italian should dominate musical scores, many have subsequently regretted and reversed this decision both because the Italian terms are the only ones adequately understood by musicians all over the world and because usage and tradition have given the Italian markings depths of meaning or accrued implication far beyond their dictionary definitions.

Musicians' Italian is a kind of *lingua franca* several of whose central components have musical meanings only loosely related to their literal meanings (*adagio*, *andante*, *allegro*), many of whose commoner words do not appear in current spoken Italian (*adagietto*, *andantino*), and whose larger vocabulary is mostly current Italian but includes some weird byways, both in terms of improbable instructions (*andante ed innocentemente*, Haydn; *allegro cristiano*, Rossini, etc) and pseudo-Italian constructs (*glissando*, *leggieramente*). In a curious way this language has acquired at least a patina of precision, although the wide divergence of tempos on modern recordings hints at a much deeper problem which Beethoven had evidently taken to heart when he added longer and longer tempo designations to his works, such as the *Andante con moto assai vivace quasi Allegretto ma non troppo* with which he opened his C major Mass op.86.

A casual approach is also noticeable. The expanding range of instructions in the 19th century coupled with the receding general importance of Italian to the educated musician resulted in some extraordinary manifestations, especially among marks added by arrangers and editors. *Poco adagio* (literally 'rather uncomfortable'; *see* POCO) and *poco allegro* ('unhappy') acquired a currency sufficient to cause considerable alarm to Eric Blom, for instance, many of whose articles on tempo marks in *Grove 5* are entirely linguistic in content and framed with a view to correcting some of the more startling errors. The full study of the subject in the future will need to take account of these eccentric usages and concentrate on what they mean rather than whether they are correct: grammatical and illiterate alike, they belong to 'musicians' Italian'.

There are of course distinctive and important uses of languages other than Italian. 'Long', 'slow' and 'away' appear in English sources (the earliest being *GB-Och* 732–5, early 17th century) as do 'brisk' and 'drag' in the later years of the 17th century; and it is a measure of the influence of the Italian trio sonata that Purcell used Italian tempo marks for his *Sonnata's* of 1683. J. S. Bach's use of French in certain works has reasonably been construed as directing that a French performing style should be used. Liszt, Kodály and Bartók used the Hungarian *lassan* (slowly) and *friss* (fast) for music in the folk style, drawing attention, as tempo and expression marks generally do, to particular traditions within which the pieces belong.

Long and elaborate instructions have more recently been confined to prefaces which in some cases occupy more pages than the music; but they can still occasionally be found taking up rather more space than seems justifiable within the score itself. Schoenberg's instruction at bar 12 of his Prelude op.49 reads: 'Immer ohne Vibrato und Portamento nach Hollywood-Art; auch grosse Intervalle dürfen nicht durch Gleiten verbunden werden sondern, wenn nötig, durch Ausgreifen. Dieses Gleiten ist abscheulich sentimental', which is really less a performance instruction than a declaration of musical beliefs. Poulenc's instruction in the orchestral version (1962) of *L'histoire de Babar*, 'excessivement prétentieux alla Callas', combines the charms of topicality, entirely clear macaronic usage and totally superfluous irrelevance.

4. CONSIDERATIONS IN ESTABLISHING THE TEMPO. Before the advent of the metronome – a device whose very precision is often considered artistically counterproductive – there were several ways of indicating tempo without recourse to the Italian terms (*see also* TEMPO). They are enumerated here not only because they explain the late and slow development of the Italian terms within the history of Western music, but also because most of them remain valid for more recent scores.

(*i*) *Time signatures or mensuration signs*. From the mid-15th century on, ₵ was theoretically twice as fast as C: the stroke denoted diminution by half. But there is considerable evidence that in practice it was rarely taken so literally but merely implied a somewhat faster tempo. Binchois, for instance, would direct that a Kyrie movement (*c*1430) in O mensuration should be repeated in Φ, but it seems musically unlikely that the addition of a stroke here indicated a doubling of speed. If any sign was consistently used for a doubling of speed it was C 2 or O 2. Studies of the mensural practices of Dufay (Hamm) and Isaac (Gossett) seem to indicate that proportional relationships were not necessarily precise but that certain mensuration signs did indeed imply the use of a faster or a slower tempo. Michael Praetorius stated in 1612 (*Terpsichore*) that he had used mensuration signs to denote tempo; later he used the Italian words which 'bei den Italis im vollen Gebrauch seyn' (*Polyhymnia caduceatrix*, 1619), but finally (*Puericinium*, 1621) settled on an equivalence table:

C id est lento: tardè: langsam
₵ id est presto: velociter: geschwindt

He thereby placed more faith in time signatures than in tempo words. In 1752 Quantz still included the time signatures as a major consideration when defining the tempo implied by the various tempo marks. Zaslaw (1972) pointed out that when Mozart wrote to his father in 1783 describing Clementi as a charlatan for playing too slowly he had to quote both tempo mark and time signature to make his point clear: one without the other would have been insufficient.

(*ii*) *Note values*. Nicola Vicentino (*L'antica musica*, 1555, f.42) gave a characterization of the different note values, associating each with a tempo and making a special issue of the point that he was not discussing merely the relative lengths of the notes (which had been described earlier) but rather showing how different note values could be used to produce pieces of different speeds. The *maxima* was used for 'moto tardissimo', the *longa* for 'tardo', the *brevis* for 'moto naturale che non sarà ne presto ne tardo', the *semibrevis* for 'moto mediocre', the *minima* for 'più che mediocre', the *semiminima* for 'moto presto', the *croma* for 'veloce' and the *semicroma* for 'moto velocissimo'. In 1725 Fux (*Gradus ad Parnassum*) implied the same when he presented a single passage in two different note values labelling one *presto* and the other *adagio*. Still, after the earlier years of the 17th century the relationship be-

tween note value and tempo became complex, as it still is: its study belongs more in the realm of musical perception than in that of tempo marks. Suffice it to say here that note values obviously affect the musician's choice of tempo and that they do so most clearly when they bring to mind other pieces, particularly within a single tradition (such as certain kinds of 12/8 implying a gigue, and 3/2 sometimes implying a sarabande or a chaconne; see §(*v*) below). Logically this suggests that the reduction of note values in any modern edition is likely to obscure vital information.

(*iii*) *Physical considerations*. The shortest note value or the longest is obviously a relevant factor, whether in relation to the player's capabilities or the instrument's characteristics. Many Baroque treatises (and indeed more recent ones) instruct the performer to take note of these factors in selecting a tempo. But this consideration is a timeless commonplace and should perhaps not be given the importance attached to it by some writers (see Rothschild, 1953).

(*iv*) *'Tempo giusto'*. The concept of a normal or correct speed for music is surely the main reason why the Italian tempo marks arrived so late in history. As a concept it appears, defined or implied, throughout the early literature on the TACTUS (*see also* CONDUCTING, §1). To some extent the concepts of normal and correct tempo are separate. The normal is the main issue of tactus, whether it is defined in terms of the heartbeat (from Ramos de Pareia, 1482, through to Quantz, 1752), of walking (Buchner), of breathing (Gaffurius), of vegetable chopping (Hermann Finck), or whatever else. But the term TEMPO GIUSTO was used by Frescobaldi and many later writers down to Leopold Mozart, who included its understanding as one of the fundamental requirements for a complete musician: 'and it is this', he wrote, 'by which the true worth of a musician can be recognized without fail'. It should be borne in mind that he wrote this at a time when practically all music was provided with tempo marks: without an understanding of *tempo giusto*, he seems to have been saying, you will never understand the instructions written on the score. (*See also* TEMPO ORDINARIO.)

(*v*) *Traditions*. Obviously the identification of a piece as a gavotte or as a minuet directly affects the choice of tempo even if the information provided by such identification is neither precise nor accurate. Many Elizabethan galliards are of a complexity that makes the full dancing tempo impossible, but even so the mood and spring of a galliard can be retained at the slower tempo and remain relevant to the performance of the piece. At the other end of the scale, the symphonic minuet of the late 18th century departed from the court minuet; and even if the stateliness of the model was lost there was a rich tradition of fast minuet movements which would directly influence the choice of tempo even after composers had begun to give such movements the more rational title of 'scherzo'. Indeed to this day the reference to a particular musical tradition is often far more useful and precise than the use of one of the standard terms: 'in blues tempo' means far more than would *andante moderato* on the same piece.

(*vi*) *Text content*. Vicentino (1555, f.94*v*) stated that compositions should be performed 'with their *forte*, *presto* and *tarde* in accordance with the words'; Dahlhaus (1959) pointed to several examples of singers in the later 16th century being instructed to allow the meaning of the text to guide the ebb and flow of their performances; and the instructions given by Giulio Caccini (*Le nuove musiche*, 1601/2) may be construed in the same light. In general tempo marks were avoided in *stile antico* sacred music down to the end of the 17th century, partly of course because here there was a stronger tradition and the *tempo giusto* was more easily established, but also because the meaning of the words left less danger that the music might be misunderstood by the performer.

All these considerations continue to operate to some extent even when there is a tempo indication of some kind; and the addition of a metronome mark does not instantly wipe away all the accumulated tradition of European music and its codes. Musicians will continue to regard metronome marks with caution; and it is remarkable how rarely they will actually use a metronome to verify a tempo unless they are trying to demonstrate its correctness to somebody else. For the film composer to whom split-second timing is important, the metronome is indispensable; but for much of the musical profession it is a mixed blessing. Berlioz told the following story (*Memoirs*, trans. D. Cairns, 1969):

One day, when I spoke of the metronome and its usefulness, Mendelssohn said sharply, 'what on earth is the point of a metronome? It's a futile device. Any musician who cannot guess the tempo of a piece just by looking at it is a duffer'. I could have replied that in that case there were a good many duffers, but I held my peace.... One day he asked to see the score of the *King Lear* overture, which I had just composed in Nice. He read it through slowly and carefully, and was about to begin playing it on the piano (which he did, with incomparable skill) when he stopped and said, 'Give me the right tempo'.

But a surprisingly large proportion of the scholarly literature concerning tempo marks centres on metronome marks: absolute figures are rather less difficult to discuss than the vaguer (but infinitely more rich in meaning) Italian terms. Such discussions give rise to certain questions and doubts which may be expressed as follows.

(*a*) Did Beethoven's (or Schumann's) metronome work correctly? It now seems arrogant to assume that practically all early metronomes were deficient: the story of Schumann's incorrect metronome has now been thankfully discarded (see Kämper, 1964); musicians of the experience of Kolisch (1943) have declared Beethoven's metronome marks playable; and the timings of such figures as Hummel, George Smart and Crotch have been subjected to the most careful analysis. Very few practising musicians seem inclined to adopt those tempos today, but it is generally agreed that most of them were probably considered acceptable at the time.

(*b*) Did Beethoven (or whoever) know how to use a metronome accurately? Did he ever try playing or conducting those tempos with the metronome ticking at the same time? It is not always recognized that the very regularity of the metronome is so anti-musical that it is difficult to feel a piece of music sensitively or effectively while the machine is going; and there is much to be said for believing that many composers, even today, prefer to sit at their desk conducting a piece and then estimate the metronome mark from their own beat rather than from the metronome itself. This may explain some of Schoenberg's absurdly fast metronome marks; and only the advent of the synchronized film score has forced on composers a chronological accuracy which their forerunners did not find necessary.

(*c*) Did composers who used metronome marks for

some of their works and then either withdrew them or changed them do so because of a considered decision that it was counter-productive? There is substantial evidence that Beethoven reached that conclusion (see Rothschild, 1961); but this was not necessarily always the case. After all, tempo was not the only feature about which composers have allowed themselves second thoughts. Reorchestration, the cutting of a whole section, changes of harmony, and re-sequencing of events are among the revisions often made by the most professional of composers during rehearsals, after the first performance and in some cases even 20 or 30 years later. So it is perhaps in relation to Wagner's constant tampering with the *Tannhäuser* score until the very end of his life that one should interpret the following passage from his *Über das Dirigieren* (1869):

To speak from my very own experience, I should say that I filled my earlier publicly performed operas with really verbose tempo indications and fixed them precisely and infallibly (I thought) by adding metronome numbers. Consequently when I heard a stupid tempo in a performance, of my *Tannhäuser* for example, a conductor would protect himself against my recriminations by saying that he had followed my metronome indications most conscientiously. I understood from this how unsure mathematics must be in relation to music and thereafter not only omitted metronome numbers but also contented myself with giving the main tempos in very general indications, taking care only with modifications of this tempo.

That may have been a mistake, if one is to judge from the Bayreuth timings kept for all performances since 1882. But Wagner should not have been particularly surprised to learn that his works are now performed at quite different tempos, for he himself had observed in the preface to the first volume of *Bayreuther Blätter* (1878):

Why, only 18 years after Weber's death, and at the very place where for many years he himself had led their performance, I found the tempos in his operas so falsified that nothing but the faithful memory of the master's widow, then still living, could assist my feelings about it.

Yet the fear of killing his work with numbers kept Wagner from adding any precise indications. Brahms felt similarly, and there is some discussion of the point in his correspondence with Clara Schumann while they were preparing the complete works of Robert Schumann for the press. In February 1878 Brahms wrote:

To give metronome marks immediately for dozens of works, as you wish, seems to me not possible. In any case you must allow the work to lie for at least a year, and examine it periodically. You will then write in new numbers each time and finally have the best solution. Consider well also that nobody can have the choral and orchestral works played for this purpose – and on the piano, because of its lighter tone, everything happens faster, much livelier and lighter in tempo. I advise you to steer clear of this, because intelligent people will hardly respect or make use of your conscientious work.

But Clara Schumann's metronome numbers are helpful so long as it is remembered that they are not Robert Schumann's, nor necessarily more accurate than his, that Clara was noted as a pianist who liked to show off with extreme tempos, and that Robert had even expressed dissatisfaction with her performances for precisely that reason (see Kämper, 1964). Although they are in no sense definitive they do at least give some idea of how one great pianist played the pieces. Perhaps the sanest approach to metronome marks, however, is the healthy discontent of Schoenberg, who prefaced most of his scores after op.23 with the instruction: 'Die Metronomzahlen sind nicht wörtlich, sondern bloss als Andeutung zu nehmen' (the metronome marks should be taken not literally but merely as an indication) – a comment curiously reminiscent of that offered by

François Couperin in relation to his verbal indications two centuries earlier: 'So having not thought up signs or characters to communicate our particular ideas, we attempt to remedy this by marking at the beginning of our pieces by means of a few words, like *tendrement*, *vivement*, etc, more or less what we would like to be heard'.

Perhaps the fairest answer to the question would be in the observation that many composers (e.g. Chopin and Elgar) have been described as being quite unpredictable in the tempos they took for their own music, and in Wasielewski's testimony (1883) that Mendelssohn was far more consistent in the tempos he adopted for other people's works than he was for his own.

5. EARLY HISTORY OF PERFORMANCE INSTRUCTIONS. Verbal instructions in musical scores probably made their earliest appearance in the form of 'canons', directions for the interpretation of some obscure notational gimmick which was incomprehensible without instructions. The history of such devices includes the instructions on the Reading rota (13th century), on Baude Cordier's *Tout par compas* (c1400) and the most elaborate instructions on Lloyd's Mass *O quam suavis* (c1500). But these amount to no more than an attempt to make the performer's role more difficult by putting into words instructions that would far more easily have been expressed in notes.

The earliest performance instructions designed to help the performer took the form not of words but of letters. The Romanus letters (*litterae significativae*) found particularly in St Gall chant manuscripts of the 11th century are mentioned by Notker, Johannes Afflighemensis and Aribo: *c* is used to mean *cito* or *celeriter*, *t* for *trahere*, *tarde* or *tenere*, etc. But in each case the letters are placed above individual notes, never added to concern a whole piece: they may be considered part of the development of a mensural notation and no more belong in a category with tempo and expression marks than do the 'Guidonian letters' denoting pitch names.

Even though the 10th-century *Commemoratio brevis* (*GS*, i, 213), the *Musica enchiriadis* (*GS*, i, 166) and other treatises of the following years mention that some pieces should be performed *morosus* (sad), *cum modesta morositate* (fairly sadly), *cum celeritate* (with speed), etc, no tradition of specific instructions in musical scores began until the 16th century. The first serious attempt seems to be that of Luis de Milán, who in his vihuela book *El maestro* (Valencia, 1536) included a short paragraph of playing instructions immediately before each piece. He described the nature of the piece, its tonality, its place within his pedagogical pattern and its tempo, normally expressed in the form: 'se ha de tañer con el compas algo apresurado' (it must be played with a fairly hurried beat). Other tempo words used by Milán include *espacio* (slow), *apriessa* (swift) and *mesurado* (measured). He also gave more detailed instructions in his preface, that for certain fantasias the musician should 'play all *consonancias* [intervals or chords] with a slow tactus and all *redobles* [ornaments or diminutions] with a rapid *tactus* and pause a little in playing each *coronada* [high point]' (trans. Jacobs, 1964). But although similar hints also appear in the publications of Hans Neusidler (1536) and Luys de Narváez (1538) the idea took longer to catch on than might be expected. Dahlhaus (1959) has shown how theorists from the middle of the 16th century urged performers to introduce

freedoms similar to those mentioned by Milán and which today would be described as rubato; and the increasing need for affect in the age of mannerism in the figurative arts was perhaps the crucial stimulus for Giovanni Gabrieli to introduce the marks *piano* and *forte* into his instrumental pieces (1597); but even the prefaces of Caccini (*Le nuove musiche*, 1601/2) and Frescobaldi (*Toccate e partite*, 1615), while including much of the same matter as Luis de Milán, were exceptional in their precise instructions as to the manner of performance the composers thought appropriate for their works.

Early uses of tempo and expression marks in scores are isolated. Monteverdi used some in his 1610 vespers publication, and in the next year Banchieri included elaborate markings in the 'Battaglia' of his *L'organo suonarino*. Thereafter the words were used by Praetorius (1619), Jelić (1622), Priuli (1618), Marini (1617) and others. Schütz used them from 1629 on, as did Frescobaldi in his *Fiori musicali* of 1635, not to mention Carlo Farina in the elaborate 'Capriccio stravagante' from his *Paduanen* of 1627. The words very quickly became established, so that by the end of the century Corelli, for instance, marked everything he published though retaining a limited vocabulary; in the next generation Vivaldi and François Couperin made the most elaborate use of words and texts to make the expressive content of their music clearer. From then on, the degree of 'tempo and expression editing' (W. S. Newman's phrase) done by composers depended very much on their own preferences, the range of styles they used, the distance their music was expected to travel and their faith in other musicians; but the marks had become an integral part of every formal score.

By and large it is true to say that in the early years *lento*, *tarde* or *adagio* were introduced as interruptions to an assumed *tempo giusto* and that *allegro* or *presto* were used to denote a return to the normal speed (see Kolneder, 1958). So also, *piano* (or occasionally *echo*) was used for dynamic contrast whereas *forte* denoted a return to normal dynamics: even in Corelli *forte* does not appear except when preceded by *piano*. Two further considerations about the early use of these terms point towards the nature of their position. First, *adagio* and *piano* remarkably often appear together and are followed by *allegro* and *forte*, also together; that is, sudden slowness and quietness often went hand in hand, so in 17th-century music the appearance of the one may very often be taken to imply the other as well. Second, the indications are found most often in instrumental music where there is no text to hint at inherent moods and changes: repeated references in the theorists suggest that in vocal music, particularly in the madrigal, changes of tempo and dynamic were entrusted to the sensitivity of the performers.

It did not take long for the Italian words to be accepted in the other European countries. As early as 1619 Michael Praetorius (*Polyhymnia caduceatrix*) could write that *tutti*, *forte*, *piano*, *presto* and *lento* or *adagio* were 'bei den Italis im vollen Gebrauch' and introduced them into his own north German publications. In 1653 J. A. Herbst (*Musica moderna prattica*, Frankfurt) defined *largo*, *lento*, *adagio*, *tardo*, *presto* and *tutti* with the annotation 'Dieweilheutiges Tages, hin und wider die italienischen *termini musici*, bey den Componisten sehr gebräuchlich sind' (these days now and then the Italian musical terms are very common among composers). And in 1683 Purcell included them (with definitions) in his *Sonnata's of III Parts* because, he said, they were already international.

Historically speaking, dynamic instructions fall into two distinct categories: contrast and gradation. Of these the contrast was the simplest to identify and the first to be notated. Giovanni Gabrieli's introduction of *forte* and *piano* (1597) was merely a way of notating an echo effect and was just an outgrowth of the polychoral tradition found in northern Italy throughout the 16th century. Echo effects of this kind are written or implied in many works of Gabrieli's time and later: some are notated as such (because it was easy to do so); others are not (because it was superfluous).

More gradual changes of dynamic first appeared in prefaces and in theoretical works from the second half of the 16th century. Zarlino (*Le istitutioni harmoniche*, 1558) mentioned them with particular care, but they also appear in the earlier treatises of Vicentino (1555), Ganassi (1535) and even Petrus de Canuntiis (Florence, 1510). While it was once thought that Hermann Finck (1556) gave evidence of a 16th-century preference for unchanging dynamics, Meier (1977) has shown that the text should be construed in precisely the opposite way. Elaborate descriptions of *crescendo* and *decrescendo* appear in the preface to Caccini's *Le nuove musiche* (1601/2) and in Fantini's *Modo per imparare a sonare di tromba* (1628). So although terraced dynamics are perhaps appropriate on instruments such as the harpsichord or organ where nothing else was possible, this was by no means the general practice except in the case of echo effects. The famous crescendo of the Mannheim orchestra in the later 18th century may have seemed astonishing to its contemporaries, but there is very little in the scores that cannot also be found in those of Vivaldi: the novelty at Mannheim was probably rather more in unanimity of execution and a conscious striving for effect than in any new musical or conceptual basis. On the other hand it may be significant, as Cahn pointed out ('Retardatio, ritardando', *HMT*), that the late 18th century saw the introduction of gerund forms into verbal instruction: *ritardando*, *calando*, *smorzando*, all began at that time. Whether this is symptomatic of an actual new preference for gradual changes or of a desire to designate and rationalize existing practice more precisely is difficult to tell, but the words themselves seem curiously characteristic of *Empfindsamkeit*.

It seems that the earliest extensive listing of tempo and expression marks was that in Sébastien de Brossard's *Dictionaire* (1703) containing a wide range of internationally current Italian words which were from then on used liberally in scores all over Europe. Brossard also served as the prime source for the entries in many of the other 18th-century music dictionaries until that of Jean-Jacques Rousseau (1768), who still used Brossard heavily but made a serious attempt to establish a logical conceptual basis for such a study, particularly in the article 'Mouvement'. Longer discussions appear in the later dictionaries, particularly those of H. C. Koch (1802) and of Gustav Schilling (1835–42). After that tempo and expression marks almost ceased to be a topic for discussion (as opposed to brief definition) in dictionaries until the Sachteil of *Riemann Musiklexikon* (12/1967), which contains many thoughtful articles (mostly by Carl Dahlhaus and drawing, as do those in this dictionary, on the work of Herrmann-Bengen, 1959). Dictionaries of musical terms constitute an enormous and rather different category of literature stretching back, for these purposes, to the anonymous *A Short Explication* (London, 1724), but their entries are mostly little more than translations: their lists of words rarely provide information that would not more clearly be derived from a study of the scores; and although their graduated lists of tempo marks are usually provocative in some respect, these dictionaries are on the whole remarkably uninstructive and contain very little that could not be found in a pocket language dictionary.

BIBLIOGRAPHY
IMPORTANT SOURCE MATERIALS
N. Vicentino: *L'antica musica ridotta alla moderna prattica* (Rome, 1555/*R*1959, 2/1557)
G. Caccini: *Le nuove musiche* (Florence, 1601/2/*R*1973) [introduction]
B. Bottazzi: *Choro et organo* (Venice, 1614)
M. Praetorius: *Syntagma musicum*, iii: *Termini musici* (Wolfenbüttel, 1618, 2/1619/*R*1958), 50, 78, 88, 132
Composition Regeln (*c*1640), Werken van Jan Pieterszn. Sweelinck, x, ed. H. Gehrmann (1901), 56
T. B. Janovka: *Clavis ad thesaurum magnae artis musicae* (Prague, 1701/*R*1973, 2/1715 as *Clavis ad musicam*)
M. de Saint-Lambert: *Principes du clavecin* (Paris, 1702)
S. de Brossard: *Dictionaire de musique* (Paris, 1703, 3/1707)
F. E. Niedt: *Handleitung zur Variation* (Hamburg, 1706)
F. Couperin: *L'art de toucher le clavecin* (Paris, 1716, 2/1717/*R*1969), 40f
A Short Explication of Such Foreign Words as are Made Use of in Musicke Books (London, 1724)
J. G. Walther: *Musicalisches Lexicon* (Leipzig, 1732/*R*1953)
J. Grassineau: *A Musical Dictionary* (London, 1740/*R*1966)
J. J. Quantz: *Versuch einer Anweisung die Flöte traversiere zu spielen* (Berlin, 1752, 3/1789/*R*1953; Eng. trans., 1966)
C. P. E. Bach: *Versuch über die wahre Art das Clavier zu spielen* (Berlin, 1753–62, 2/1787–97/*R*1957; Eng. trans., 1949)
L. Mozart: *Versuch einer gründlichen Violinschule* (Augsburg, 1756/*R*1922; Eng. trans., 1948), 48ff
J.-J. Rousseau: *Dictionnaire de musique* (Paris, 1768/*R*1969) [esp. article 'Mouvement']
J. G. Sulzer: *Allgemeine Theorie der schönen Künste* (Leipzig, 1771–4, rev. 2/1786–7) [esp. articles 'Bewegung und Vortrag', 'Takt und Zeiten', 'Taktzeichen']
J. P. Kirnberger: *Die Kunst des reinen Satzes* (Berlin, 1771–6)
E. W. Wolf: *Musikalischer Unterricht* (Dresden, 1788)
D. G. Türk: *Klavierschule* (Leipzig, 1789, 2/1802)
W. Crotch: 'Remarks on the Terms, at Present used in Music, for Regulating the Time', *Monthly Magazine*, viii (1799–1800), 941
M. Clementi: *Introduction to the Art of Playing on the Piano Forte* (London, 1801/*R*1974), 13f
C. Mason: *Rules on the Times, Metres, Phrases & Accent of Composition* (London, *c*1801; copy in *US-NYp*)
H. C. Koch: *Musikalisches Lexikon* (Frankfurt, 1802/*R*1964)
W. Crotch: *Specimens of Various Styles of Music* (London, 1807–18)
Notice sur le métronome de J. Maelzel (Paris, 1816)
Castil-Blaze: *Dictionnaire de musique moderne* (Brussels, 1821, 3/1828)
J. N. Hummel: *Klavierschule* (Vienna, 1828)
G. Schilling: *Encyclopädie der gesammten musikalischen Wissenschaften oder Universal-Lexikon der Tonkunst* (Stuttgart, 1835–42/*R*1973) [major articles on 'Adagio', 'Andante', 'Allegro', 'Tempo', etc]
M. and L. Escudier: *Dictionnaire de la musique* (Paris, 1844, 5/1872)

DYNAMICS
A. Heuss: 'Einige grundlegende Begriffe für eine historische Darstellung der musikalischen Dynamik', *IMusSCR*, iii *Vienna 1909*, 144
——: 'Über die Dynamik der Mannheimer Schule', i, *Riemann-Festschrift* (Leipzig, 1909), 433; ii, *ZMw*, ii (1919–20), 44
——: 'Das Orchester-Crescendo bei Beethoven', *ZMw*, ix (1926–7), 361
R. E. M. Harding: *Origins of Musical Time and Expression* (London, 1938), 85ff
H. Hering: 'Die Dynamik in Joh. Seb. Bachs Klaviermusik', *BJb*, xxxviii (1949–50), 65
H.-H. Dräger: 'Begriff des Tonkörpers', *AMw*, ix (1952), 68
E. Kurth: *Studien zur Dynamik Max Regers* (diss., U. of W. Berlin, 1952)
H.-H. Dräger: 'Dynamik', §A: 'Systematisch', *MGG*
W. Gerstenberg: 'Dynamik', §B: 'Historisch', *MGG* [extensive study]
D. D. Boyden: 'Dynamics in Seventeenth- and Eighteenth-century Music', *Essays on Music in Honor of Archibald Thompson Davison* (Cambridge, Mass., 1957), 185
W. Kolneder: 'Dynamik und Agogik in der Musik des Barock', *IMSCR*, vii *Cologne 1958*, 343 [with panel discussion]
K. Marguerre: 'Forte und Piano bei Mozart', *NZM*, Jg.128 (1967), 153
B. Meier: 'Hermann Fincks Practica Musica als Quelle zur musikalischen Dynamik', *Mf*, xxx (1977), 43

METRONOME MARKS

E. F. Schmid: 'Joseph Haydn und die Flötenuhr', *ZMw*, xiv (1932–3), 193

H. Gál: 'The Right Tempo', *MMR*, lix (1939), 174

R. Kolisch: 'Tempo and Character in Beethoven's Music', *MQ*, xxix (1943), 169, 291

H. Beck: 'Bemerkungen zu Beethovens Tempi', *BeJb 1955–6*, 24–54

W. Gerstenberg: 'Authentische Tempi für Mozarts "Don Giovanni"?', *MJb 1960–61*, 58 [marks by W. J. Tomašek, 1839]

F. Goebels: 'Metronom', *MGG*

R. Münster: 'Authentische Tempi zu den sechs letzten Sinfonien W. A. Mozarts', *MJb 1962–3*, 185 [Hummel]

C. Bär: 'Zu einem Mozart'schen Andante-Tempo', *Acta Mozartiana*, x (1963), 78 [Gottfried Weber]

H. Beck: 'Die Proportionen der Beethovenschen Tempi', *Festschrift Walter Gerstenberg* (Wolfenbüttel, 1964), 6

D. Kämper: 'Zur Frage der Metronombezeichnungen Robert Schumanns', *AMw*, xxi (1964), 141

H. Diack Johnstone: 'Tempi in Corelli's Christmas Concerto', *MT*, cvii (1966), 956 [Pasquali]

N. Temperley: 'Tempo and Repeats in the Early Nineteenth Century', *ML*, xlvii (1966), 323 [George Smart]

P. Stadlen: 'Beethoven and the Metronome – I', *ML*, xlviii (1967), 330

MARKS AND INTERPRETATION

G. Schünemann: *Geschichte des Dirigierens* (Leipzig, 1913/*R*1965 and 1966)

R. Vannes: *Essai de terminologie musicale: dictionnaire universel* (Thaun, 1925)

R. Steglich: 'Das Tempo als Problem der Mozart-Interpretation', *Tagung der Internationalen Stiftung Mozarteum: Salzburg 1931*, 172

B. Simonds: 'Chopin's Use of the Term "con anima" ', *MTNA Proceedings*, xlii (1948), 515

H. Hofmann: 'Aufführungspraxis', *MGG*

S. Deas: 'Beethoven's "Allegro assai" ', *ML*, xxxi (1950), 333

L. Kunz: 'Die Romanusbuchstaben c und t', *KJb*, xxxiv (1950), 7

W. Gerstenberg: *Die Zeitmasse und ihre Ordnungen in Bachs Musik* (Einbeck, 1951)

R. Steglich: 'Über Mozarts Adagio-Takt', *MJb 1951*, 90

R. Elvers: *Untersuchungen zu den Tempi in Mozarts Instrumentalmusik* (diss., Free U. of Berlin, 1952)

F.-J. Machatius: *Die Tempi in der Musik um 1600: Fortwirkung und Auflösung einer Tradition* (diss., Free U. of Berlin, 1952)

F. Rothschild: *The Lost Tradition in Music: Rhythm and Tempo in J. S. Bach's Time* (London, 1953)

C. Sachs: *Rhythm and Tempo: a Study in Music History* (New York, 1953)

H. Beck: *Studien über das Tempoproblem bei Beethoven* (diss., U. of Erlangen, 1954)

T. Dart: *The Interpretation of Music* (London, 1954, 4/1967)

A. Gertler: 'Souvenirs sur Béla Bartók', *ReM* (1955), no.224, p.99

W. Kolneder: *Aufführungspraxis bei Vivaldi* (Leipzig, 1955)

F.-J. Machatius: 'Über mensurale und spielmännische Reduktion (der Integer valor und der Kanzonettenpuls)', *Mf*, viii (1955), 139

E. and P. Badura-Skoda: *Mozart-Interpretation* (Vienna and Stuttgart, 1957; Eng. trans., 1962, as *Interpreting Mozart on the Keyboard*)

A. Forte: 'The Structural Origins of Exact Tempi in the Brahms–Haydn Variations', *MR*, xviii (1957), 138

C. Raeburn: 'Das Zeitmass in Mozarts Opern', *ÖMz*, xii (1957), 329

A. G. Huber: *Takt, Rhythmus, Tempo in den Werken von Johann Sebastian Bach* (Zurich, 1958)

F.-J. Machatius: 'Die Tempo-Charaktere', *IMSCR, vii Cologne 1958*, 185

C. Dahlhaus: 'Über das Tempo in der Musik des späten 16. Jahrhunderts', *Musica*, xiii (1959), 767

I. Herrmann-Bengen: *Tempobezeichnungen: Ursprung; Wandel im 17. und 18. Jahrhundert* (Tutzing, 1959)

J. P. Larsen: 'Tempoprobleme bei Händel dargestellt am "Messias" ', *Händel-Ehrung der Deutschen Demokratischen Republik: Leipzig 1959*, 141

E. Barthe: *Takt und Tempo* (Hamburg, 1960)

F. Goebels: *Studien zur Tempoindikation in der Klaviermusik seit Ph. E. Bach* (diss., U. of Cologne, 1960)

G. Houle: *The Musical Measure as Discussed by Theorists from 1650 to 1800* (diss., Stanford U., 1960)

K. Reinhard: 'Zur Frage des Tempos bei Chopin', *Chopin Congress: Warszawa 1960*, 449

C. Dahlhaus: 'Zur Entstehung des modernen Taktsystems im 17. Jahrhundert', *AMw*, xviii (1961), 223

F. Rothschild: *Musical Performance in the Times of Mozart and Beethoven* (London, 1961)

I. Fellinger: 'Zum Problem der Zeitmasse in Brahms' Musik', *GfMKB, Kassel 1962*, 219

W. Gerstenberg: 'Andante', *GfMKB, Kassel 1962*, 156

H. O. Heikel: ' "Tactus" und Tempo', *GfMKB, Kassel 1962*, 145

U. Siegele: 'Bemerkungen zu Bachs Motetten', *BJb*, xlix (1962), 33

R. Steglich: 'Mozarts Mailied: Allegro Aperto?', *MJb 1962–3*, 96

R. Donington: *The Interpretation of Early Music* (London, 1963, rev. 3/1974) [esp. chap.35, 'Tempo in Early Music', and chap.49, 'Volume']

G. Frotscher: *Aufführungspraxis alter Musik* (Wilhelmshaven, 1963)

A. Geoffroy-Dechaume: *Les 'secrets' de la musique ancienne: recherches sur l'interprétation XVIe–XVIIe–XVIIIe siècles* (Paris, 1964), 111ff

C. Jacobs: *Tempo Notation in Renaissance Spain* (Brooklyn, 1964)

F.-J. Machatius: 'Dreiertakt und Zweiertakt als Eurhythmus und Ekrhythmus', *Festschrift Walter Gerstenberg* (Wolfenbüttel, 1964), 88

F. Rothschild: *Vergessene Traditionen in der Musik: zur Aufführungspraxis von Bach bis Beethoven* (Zurich, 1964) [reworking of books of 1953 and 1961]

D. D. Boyden: *The History of Violin Playing from its Origins to 1761* (London, 1965)

'Le tempo: séance de la Société française de musicologie, Fontenay, 1965', *FAM*, xii (1965), 161–206 [with contributions by G. Thibault, D. Launay, C. Cudworth, B. S. Brook, A. Verchaly and C. Marcel-Dubois; see esp. next two entries]

B. S. Brook: 'Le tempo dans l'exécution musicale à la fin du XVIIIe siècle: les contributions de C. Mason et William Crotch', *FAM*, xii (1965), 196

C. Cudworth: 'The Meaning of "Vivace" in Eighteenth Century England', *FAM*, xii (1965), 194

J. Troy Johnson: 'How to "Humour" John Jenkins' Three-part Dances: Performance Directions in a Newberry Library MS', *JAMS*, xx (1967), 197

A. Mendel: 'Some Ambiguities of the Mensural System', *Studies in Music History: Essays for Oliver Strunk* (Princeton, 1968), 137

U. Siegele: 'Vortrag', *MGG*

Z. Chechlińska: 'Rodzaje tempa w utworach Chopina' [Types of tempo in Chopin's compositions], *Muzyka*, xiv/2 (1969), 45

I. Saslav: *Tempos in the String Quartets of Joseph Haydn* (diss., Indiana U., 1969)

J. Tobin: *Handel's Messiah* (London, 1969), esp. 83, 85ff, 260ff

H. C. Wolff: 'Das Tempo bei Telemann', *BMw*, xi (1969), 41

W. Kolneder: *Georg Muffat zur Aufführungspraxis* (Strasbourg, 1970)

W. F. Kümmel: 'Zum Tempo in der italienischen Mensuralmusik des 15. Jahrhunderts', *AcM*, xlii (1970), 150

J. A. Bank: *Tactus, Tempo and Notation in Mensural Music from the 13th to the 17th Century* (Amsterdam, 1972)

R. Leibowitz: 'Tempo and Character in the Music of Verdi', *3° congresso internazionale di studi verdiani: Milano 1972*, 238

N. Zaslaw: 'Mozart's Tempo Conventions', *IMSCR, xi Copenhagen 1972*, 720

D. Charlton: *Orchestration and Orchestral Practice in Paris, 1789–1810* (diss., U. of Cambridge, 1973)

R. Donington: *A Performer's Guide to Baroque Music* (London, 1973)

U. Siegele: ' "La cadence est une qualité de la bonne musique" ', *Studies in Renaissance and Baroque Music in Honor of Arthur Mendel* (Kassel and Hackensack, 1974), 124 [on Rousseau]

H. Ferguson: *Keyboard Interpretation* (London, 1975), 40ff

W. S. Newman: 'Freedom of Tempo in Schubert's Instrumental Music', *MQ*, lxi (1975), 528

H. Cahn: 'Retardatio, ritardando', *HMT*

M. Rudolf: 'Ein Beitrag zur Geschichte der Temponahme bei Mozart', *MJb 1976–7*, 202

W. S. Newman: 'Das Tempo in Beethovens Instrumentalmusik – Tempowahl und Tempoflexibilität', *Mf*, xxxiii (1980), 161

DAVID FALLOWS

Tempo di gavotta. Title used for gavotte-style movements in instrumental works of the first half of the 18th century. James Grassineau wrote that the title means that 'the time or movement of a gavotte is imitated, without any regard had to the measure or number of bars or strains' (*A Musical Dictionary*, London, 1740; trans. from Brossard, *Dictionaire de musique*, Paris, 1703). A famous example is in J. S. Bach's Partita in E minor for keyboard which may be considered an improvisation on the 'gavotte idea', in a moderate tempo and with the predominant movement or beat in minims. Other examples may be seen in Corelli's sonatas opp.2, 4 and 5. *See* GAVOTTE.

MEREDITH ELLIS LITTLE

Tempo giusto (It.: 'just time', 'strict time'). (1) The

abstract concept of a 'correct' tempo for a piece. Frescobaldi (preface to *Toccate e partite*, 1615) wrote that 'Nelle partite si pigli il *tempo giusto* e *proportionato*'; Rousseau (1768, article 'Mouvement') stated that each basic measure had an ideal tempo called in Italy the *tempo giusto*; and Kirnberger (1776), following Rousseau's lead, explained all the tempo marks in relation to a *tempo giusto* which was 'determined by the time signature and by the shortest and longest note values contained in a piece'.

(2) As a tempo designation (also *a tempo giusto*) actually affixed to a piece it is rarer, but found particularly in Handel. 'Egypt was glad', 'He led them out of the deep', 'Thy right hand' and 'The horse and his rider' from *Israel in Egypt* are all *tempo giusto*; and Handel originally marked the *allegro moderato* in the *Messiah* overture as *a tempo giusto* before changing it to the present marking. It was presumably in the same sense that Stravinsky used *tempo giusto* to open his 'Dumbarton Oaks' Concerto. But when Chopin used it for some of his waltzes (though scarcely elsewhere in his work) he was indicating that the traditional waltz tempo should be adopted. In 1800 William Crotch wrote to the *Monthly Magazine* observing, among other things, that '[*tempo ordinario*] varies with the fashion of the age, [*tempo giusto*] with the fancy or judgement of the performers'.

(3) A direction to return to strict tempo after a deviation. It is found particularly often in Italian Baroque opera and described by Brossard (1703, article 'Tempo'); but its use continued through the 19th century, for instance in Liszt, who normally used it to mark the end of an *a piacere* section.

For bibliography *see* TEMPO AND EXPRESSION MARKS.

DAVID FALLOWS

Tempo ordinario (It.: 'common time'). (1) The Italian name for common time, 4/4, as explained by Brossard (1703, article 'Tempo') and many subsequent writers.

(2) As a tempo designation (also *a tempo ordinario*) it is found particularly in Handel, who used it, for instance, in 'Lift up your heads' and 'Their sound is gone out'. But, like TEMPO GIUSTO, it was evidently in fairly current use as a concept to describe the ordinary, non-committal tempo that required no tempo designation. It was presumably in this sense that Beethoven wrote to Schott on 18 December 1826 saying: 'We can hardly have any *tempi ordinari* any more, now that we must follow our free inspiration'.

For bibliography *see* TEMPO AND EXPRESSION MARKS.

DAVID FALLOWS

Tempo primo (It.: 'first pace'). After a change of tempo in the course of a composition the indication *tempo primo* directs that its opening pace is to be resumed.

Temporale (It.: 'storm'). (1) A term used to describe the storm scenes common in 19th-century Italian opera, in particular the operas of Rossini (for example *La Cenerentola* and *Il barbiere di Siviglia*). It is sometimes applied to Verdi's storm scenes (for example in *Rigoletto*) although he did not use the term. In musical style *temporali* appear to show a debt to the fourth movement of Beethoven's Pastoral Symphony.

(2) *See* PROPER OF THE TIME.

Temps (Fr.). BEAT.

Tempus (Lat.: 'time'). In the system of mensural notation of the late Middle Ages, the relationship between semibreve and breve: *see* NOTATION, §III.

Tenaglia [Tanaglia, Tanaglino], **Antonio Francesco** (*b* Florence, *c*1610–20; *d* Rome, after 1661). Italian composer, keyboard player and lutenist. By 1644 he was in Rome as a musician in the service of Donna Olimpia Aldobrandini, wife of Camillo Pamphili. In September of that year he became a musician in Cardinal Antonio Barberini's household and thus an associate of Giovanni Lotti (whose poetry he set), and Luigi Rossi, whom he emulated and whom he acknowledged in his cantata *Che volete ch'io canti*. By 1648 he had left Rome to work abroad. A letter dated 28 March 1648 from the castrato Giovanni Battista Mocchi to Carissimi reminds him of a previous letter that informed him of 'a certain Anton Francesco Tenaglia, who is going about complaining unjustly of this kind prince' (Count Palatine Philipp Wilhelm of Neuburg-Düsseldorf), and says that he has been ordered to write, presumably by the count, so that Carissimi may defend his kindness. It seems that Tenaglia had been connected in some way with the count and through him had suffered some injustice. Evidently his complaints were vehement and diffused enough for Philipp Wilhelm to have been troubled by them, but the facts behind this letter have yet to be uncovered. During 1648 Tenaglia was paid by Cardinal Barberini, whom he may have served during the cardinal's exile in Lyons; there is no evidence, however, that his affiliation with the Barberini family continued after that year.

In 1654 Tenaglia was in Rome where he was probably employed by one or more of the Roman aristocracy as a keyboard virtuoso and lutenist. In a letter to Cardinal Mazarin dated 26 October 1654 the agent Elpidio Benedetti described his rapture at the music he had heard performed the previous evening by a singer and two instrumentalists, one of them Tenaglia, and warmly recommended them for service at the French court. In another letter, written a week later, he suggested that if Mazarin should want to employ only one of the instrumentalists he should choose the other one rather than Tenaglia, 'even though in accompanying at the harpsichord Tenaglia has no equal and far surpasses poor Luigi' (Luigi Rossi, who had died the year before). There is no evidence that Tenaglia ever served at the French court. In 1656, when the Roman aristocracy organized splendid festivities in honour of Queen Christina of Sweden, Tenaglia seems to have been connected again with the Pamphili: *Il giudizio di Paride*, with music by him, was performed at the Palazzo Pamphili during Carnival in honour of the queen. Another theatrical work by him, the *favola musicale Il Clearco*, was performed in 1661. At some point in his life he was organist of St John Lateran, Rome, but precisely when is not known. Of his last years all that is recorded is that he died in poverty.

Tenaglia's cantatas, his only surviving compositions, seem to have been widely known and much appreciated in his day, for they are mentioned as prime examples of the genre, together with those of Carissimi and Luigi Rossi, by both Christoph Bernhard (*Tractatus compositionis*) and Angelo Berardi (*Ragionamenti musicali*, 1681). Far fewer can at present be attributed to him than to Rossi, Carissimi, Caproli, Marazzoli and Savioni: it is not unlikely, however, that a good many of the enormous number of anonymous MS cantatas are also his. The extant cantatas demonstrate how powerful and audacious was his creative imagination and how extraordinary his musicality. Among their impressive features are the intensity and freedom of their expression, the animation and humour of some of the arias (those in 6/8 and common time) and the tender lyricism of others, the eloquence of the recitatives and the remarkably active and melodic bass line: interplay between the vocal and continuo lines is more characteristic of his cantatas than of those of his contemporaries.

Among the 67 solo cantatas (all for soprano) and eight duets and trios one finds primarily works in a varying number of sections, with or without refrains and with no clear overall structure. There are works in binary, ternary and rondo form. The last is the most frequent, but not in its simple strophic form: Tenaglia preferred rondos with long, differing strophes between the recurrences of the refrain and/or with an abbreviated version of the refrain occurring within the cantata, the complete restatement being reserved for the close. Other characteristics of his style include the often improvisatory, virtuoso quality of the music, the sequential repetition of an opening phrase, the frequent change of metre and the bold use of unsynchronized cadences (the melodic line coming to a close on the tonic over a bass that is still continuing its motion toward it). Tenaglia also made beautiful use of the Phrygian cadence, closing a few cantatas with it in the manner of Rossi. He differed from Rossi, however, in his more frequent choice of major tonalities and common time and in his habit of beginning a cantata with a short phrase for continuo alone.

WORKS

OPERAS

Il giudizio di Paride (G. Lotti), Rome, Carnival 1656; music lost
Il Clearco (L. Cortesi), 1661; lib pubd., music lost

CANTATAS
(all for S, bc)

Affe, di mia vita mostrandoti, *I-Rc*; Begl'occhi, merce, ed. A. Parisotti, *Arie antiche*, iii (Milan, 1900); Begl'occhi, scoccate saette, *Rvat*; Bella cosa è l'inconstanza, *Nc*; Cangia, mio cor cangia pensiero, *Rc*; Cessate, o pensieri, d'affligermi, *MOe*; Che musica è questa, *Fc*; Che sarà, con tanti guai, *B-Bc*; Che volete ch'io canti, *I-Nc* [quotes the opening recitative of L. Rossi's Un ferito cavalier]

Che volete più da me, *B-Bc*; Chi ama che fa, *I-Nc*; Chi credete ch'havesse poi il vanto, *Nc*; Compatitemi, Zerbina, se disprezzo i vostri affetti, *Nc*; Cor mio, tu ti lamenti, *F-Pthibault*; Costanza, mio core, *I-Rc*; Crudele che chiamarti crudele, *Nc*; Dal suo bel sol lontano, *Nc*; Doppo che la magia di prieghi, *Rc*; Dove frondoso il bosco, *Nc*

Ecce torna a penar per te, *Nc*; E tu parti, mia vita, *I-Nc*; E tu resti, mia vita, *B-Bc*; E ve lo credereste che senza, *B-Bc*; Filla mia, tue luci belle, *I-Nc*; Il dolore ch'ogn hor mi tormenta, *Fc*; Il nocchier che torna al lido, *A-Wn*; In che da il cercar, *I-Rn*; In mare di sdegno il legno, *Rc*; Io non lo so, son tanto fuor di me, *B-Bc*; Io per me cosi l'intendo, *Bc*; Io vo morir per te, *Bc*

La mia dama arcibizzarra, *I-Fc*; Libertà, grida mio core, *Rc*; Maledetto sia quel dì, *B-Bc*; Manco male che nel mio cor, *I-Nc*; Mentre in seno a flutti, *Nc*; Mi fa rider la speranza, *Nc*; Misero chi si fida, *Rn*, excerpts ed. L. Torchi, *Eleganti canzoni* (Milan, 1894); Misero e con quai larve, *Rc*

Nel'atlantico Dori, *Nc*; No, che mai lo dirò (C. P. Mandosi), *F-Pthibault*; No, che non basta, no, *B-Bc*; Non diamo in barzellette, *GB-Och*; Non la finite mai, *B-Bc*; Non la saprò ben dire, *Bc*; Non si da il caso mai, *Bc*; Non si può vivere con questi amanti, *Bc*; Non voglio che alberghi nel core, *I-Nc*; ?Nova Cinthia africana, *Nc*

Occhi, lingue di bellezza, *Rc*; Ogni cosa è variabile, *Nc*; Oh, che bizzarro humor, *A-Wn*; O quante punture mi sento, *B-Bc*; O questa è gustosa, *Bc*; Pensieri, che dite, speranza mi chiama, *I-Rvat*; Perche aprite col bel riso, *Rc*; Quanto è meglio esser suo, *MOe*

Sappia o pianga ogni core, *Nc*; Se fosse cosi conforme, *I-Bc*; Sereno per me non è più, *Rc*; Su le spiaggie Tirrene, *Rvat*; Udite, o degli amanti, *Nc*; Una nova è giunta, amanti, *Rdp*; Un impazzito ciglio, un sguardo ardito, *Nc*; Un pensier dal cor m'è uscito, *Rvat*, ed. F.

Vatielli, *Antiche cantate d'amore* (Bologna, 1920); Vezzosa fanciulla ch'amore, *Rc*; Voglio parlar con voi, *Nc*

OTHER WORKS

A chi vive, ogn'hor contento, S, S, bc, *I-Nc*; Cor mio, ti credi tu, S, S, B, bc, *P-La*; Nel'alto rigore d'un volto, S, S, bc, *I-Rc*; O bell'onde fortunate, S, S, bc, *Nc*; Son disperato, abbandonato, S, S, bc, *GB-Lbm*; Sospiri, chi sete, messaggi del core, S, S, bc, *I-Nc*
Madrigals: Madonna udite come questa, A, T, B, bc; E cosi pur languendo me'n vo, A, T, B, bc; both in 1653[4]

DOUBTFUL WORKS

Che ti resta, o mio core, *B-Bc*; Con amor si pugna invano, *I-Nc*; Crederesti, o mio tesoro, *B-Bc*; Del bel Serbeto a i lidi, *I-Nc*; Due pensieri ho nel pensiero, *B-Bc*; E quando ve n'andate, speranze, ed. A Parisotti, *Arie antiche*, ii (Milan, 1900), attrib. C. Caproli in *GB-Ouf*; Mia fortuna trova quiete, *I-Nc*; O quanto più bella saresti, *B-Bc*; Quando sarà quel dì, *I-Rc*; Quanto vi costerà, occhi, *B-Bc*; Son fanciulla che d'amore, *I-Nc*

BIBLIOGRAPHY

A. Ademollo: *I teatri di Roma nel secolo decimosettimo* (Rome, 1888/ R1969)
L. Torchi: 'Canzoni ed arie Italiane', *RMI*, i (1894), 581–656
H. Prunières: *L'opéra en France avant Lulli* (Paris, 1913)
——: 'Les musiciens du Cardinal Antonio Barberini', *Mélanges de musicologie offerts à M. Lionel de la Laurencie* (Paris, 1933), 119
T. D. Culley: *Jesuits and Music*, i: *A Study of the Musicians Connected with the German College in Rome during the 17th Century* (Rome, 1970)
E. Caluori, ed.: *Antonio Francesco Tenaglia* [thematic catalogue], WECIS, vi (in preparation)

ELEANOR CALUORI

Tendre, tendrement (Fr.: 'tender', 'tenderly'). A designation often found in French Baroque music. François Couperin headed over 30 pieces *tendrement*, sometimes with the qualification *sans lenteur*. Rousseau (1768) defined it in terms of the Italian AMOROSO.

See also TEMPO AND EXPRESSION MARKS.

Giusto Ferdinando Tenducci: portrait by Thomas Gainsborough (1727–88) in the Barber Institute of Fine Arts, University of Birmingham

Tenducci, Giusto Ferdinando (*b* Siena, *c*1735; *d* Genoa, 1790). Italian castrato soprano and composer. After some success in Venice and Naples, he went to London in 1758 and sang for two seasons at the King's Theatre, most notably in Cocchi's *Il ciro riconosciuto* (though he was no more than *secondo uomo*). His extravagance led to his being in a debtors' prison for most of 1760, but by 1762 his growing command of English enabled him to create Arbaces in Arne's *Artaxerxes*, and in 1763 he won further admirers at Ranelagh Gardens. During three more seasons at the King's Theatre, Tenducci sang in the first performance of J. C. Bach's *Adriano in Siria*, became friendly with the Mozart family and paid a short visit to Dublin (1765) where he repeated his success in *Artaxerxes*. Harried again by bailiffs, he paid a longer visit to Ireland in 1766, and in Cork married a well-to-do Limerick girl, Dora Maunsell; Tenducci was jailed and his wife kidnapped by outraged relatives. They were soon reunited, and it has been stated, by Casanova among others, that they produced two children. *A True Genuine Narrative of Mr and Mrs Tenducci* (1768) is alleged to have been written by Dora.

On 11 July 1767 Tenducci announced in the *Public Advertiser* that he had 'renounced the Errors of Popery', and this gave him support when he spent a year or more in Edinburgh. Impressed by the 'Scotch' songs he now met with, he included three of them in *Artaxerxes*. After four years he returned to England (1770) and sang in the Worcester Three Choirs Festival of that year, as well as in a free adaptation of Gluck's *Orfeo*; it was Tenducci who made 'Che farò' popular in London. He then deepened his friendship with J. C. Bach, whom he persuaded to write accompaniments, mainly orchestral, for some half-dozen Scotch songs. Tenducci sang these at the Bach–Abel concerts. With the decline of continuo accompaniments, Scotch songs had fallen from favour, but Bach showed they would respond to *galant* treatment, and Tenducci sang them with an expressiveness previously unknown. Similarly arranged Scotch songs were soon introduced into nearly all English operas, notably *The Duenna*. 'It was in consequence of my hearing Tenducci and Signora Corri sing a number of our songs so charmingly', wrote the publisher George Thomson, who was later to commission arrangements from Haydn, Beethoven and others, 'that I conceived the idea of collecting all our best melodies and songs'. He added that of all the singers he had heard in 50 years, 'not one of them surpassed Tenducci for singing from the heart', and he was especially moved by his performance of Bach's arrangement of 'I'll never leave thee'.

By 1778 Tenducci was again pursued by his creditors, and on meeting Mozart again, this time in Paris, he persuaded Mozart to write for him an aria on the lines of some by J. C. Bach, with four concertante solo parts, one of them for piano. This is now lost. Tenducci had never been in the front rank as a singer of Italian opera, and by this time his voice was deteriorating. He paid further visits to Dublin, sang in the 1785 revival in London of Gluck's *Orfeo* (a version Gluck would barely have recognized), and wrote a singing tutor. It is stated in *RicordiE* that he died in Genoa in 1790.

Tenducci's operas, listed below, were all adaptations involving little composition, and none was successful; the failure of *Amintas* caused its publication to be abandoned before completion.

WORKS

OPERAS
(*all first performed in Dublin*)
Amintas (R. Rolt, after Metastasio), perf. July 1765 [all-sung adaptation of G. Rush: The Royal Shepherd]; with addns by S. Arnold, Covent Garden, 15 Dec 1769; Act 2 pubd (London, 1769)
The Revenge of Athridates, perf. 1767 [trans. and adaptation of D. Perez: Il Farnace]; some songs pubd
Il castello d'Andalusia, perf. 1783 [? adaptation of Arnold: The Castle of Andalusia], unpubd
The Campaign (Jephson), perf. 1784 [afterpiece with spoken dialogue]; arr. W. Shield, Covent Garden, 1785; lost
Single songs, incl. 1 for ballad opera Love at First Sight (1763)

OTHER WORKS
6 English Songs 'sung at Ranelagh' (London, 1763)
Lessons for the Harpsichord or Piano & Forte (Edinburgh, 1768)
6 French Songs (London, *c*1770)
A Collection of Favorite Airs in Score (London, *c*1775)
6 Italian Songs 'perform'd at Mr Bach's Concert' (London, 1778)
Instruction of Mr Tenducci to his Scholars (London, *c*1785; with portrait)
? Overture, lost

BIBLIOGRAPHY
J. C. Hadden: *George Thomson, Friend of Burns* (London, 1898)
C. S. Terry: *Johann Christian Bach* (London, 1929, rev. 2/1967)
A. Heriot: *The Castrati in Opera* (London, 1958)
C. B. Oldman: 'Mozart's scena for Tenducci', *ML*, xlii (1961), 44
T. J. Walsh: *Opera in Dublin, 1705–1797* (Dublin, 1973)
ROGER FISKE

Tenebrae (Lat.: 'darkness'). A name commonly applied to the combined Offices of Matins and Lauds on the Thursday, Friday and Saturday of Holy Week. The service is marked by the extinction of 15 candles, one after each psalm. At the end of the canticle *Benedictus Dominus* all the candles are extinguished and what follows is said or sung 'in tenebris'. The musically significant parts of the service are the first three of the nine lessons of Matins, taken from the Lamentations of Jeremiah, and the responsories that follow each lesson. The plainsong of the Lamentations is an elaborated psalm tone, and there is a continuous history of polyphonic settings from the 15th century to the early 19th (sometimes under different titles, as in Couperin's *Leçons de ténèbres* or Stravinsky's *Threni; see* LAMENTATIONS). The responsories were set with particular frequency after the Council of Trent (*see* RESPONSORY, §5). Other texts from Tenebrae set polyphonically include the BENEDICTUS (ii) and the MISERERE from Lauds. These two items, alone of the four psalms and two canticles of Lauds, are unchanged on each of the three days, which is no doubt why they alone were set. Composers of Tenebrae music (apart from the Lamentations) include G. M. Asola, Gesualdo, Jacob Handl, Lassus, Morales, Pomponio Nenna, Palestrina and Victoria. Although the Lamentations remained popular as a Baroque form, the attraction of other Holy Week texts appears to have been almost exclusively confined to the Counter-Reformation.

JOHN CALDWELL

Tēnella. The first word of a victory hymn by ARCHILOCHUS, supposedly imitative of the twang of a lyre string.

Teneramente (It.: 'tenderly'). A direction indicating a style of performance rather more sentimental than that called for by *dolce* (sweet), but on the whole having much the same meaning and use in music. A good instance of the distinction between the terms is found in the second movement of Beethoven's Sonata in E minor op.90, where the subject, at its first entry labelled *dolce*, is subsequently directed to be played *teneramente*, it being evidently intended that the music should become slightly more impassioned as it goes on. *Con tenerezza* ('with tenderness') is also found.

See also TEMPO AND EXPRESSION MARKS.   GEORGE GROVE/R

Teniers, Guillaume [Willem] **Albert** (*b* Louvain, baptized 20 April 1748; *d* Amsterdam, 12 Feb 1820). South Netherlands violinist and composer. The great-grandson of the painter David Teniers, he travelled for many years in the Netherlands, England and France as a violinist in theatre orchestras. In 1775 and 1776 he was a first violinist at the Théâtre des Spectacles at Brussels, and in 1780 he was a first violinist and *maître des simphonies* at The Hague Opera. From 1792 he was a member of the Théâtre de la Monnaie orchestra in Brussels. After an unsuccessful attempt to gain a place at the court he joined a travelling opera company. By 1800 he was a member of the Théâtre Français orchestra in Hamburg; he finally settled in Amsterdam as a music teacher and first violinist at the Théâtre Français. His compositions are primarily for the violin.

WORKS
3 concertos, vn, orch, op.1 (Amsterdam, n.d.)
3 sonates, va, va acc., op.6 (Hamburg, *c*1790)
Variations: 12 for vn, va acc., op.7 (Amsterdam, n.d.); Aria variée de l'opéra *Léonce* [?Isouard], 2 vn, pubd; 6 . . . sur la contredanse Hoep Marianetie, 2 vn, pubd; 6 . . . sur l'angloïse de Mlle Furioso la cadette, 2 vn, pubd
Andante avec le Roxolane de . . . [J.] Haydn, arr. vn, va (Berlin, n.d.)

BIBLIOGRAPHY
EitnerQ; *FétisB*; *GerberNL*
E. Gregoir: *Galerie biographique des artistes musiciens belges du XVIII*^e *et du XIX*^e *siècle* (Brussels, 1862)
——: *Panthéon musical populaire*, i (Brussels, 1876)
R. Vannes: *Dictionnaire des musiciens (compositeurs)* (Brussels, 1947)
                                                    JACQUES VAN DEUN

Tenney, Gena. *See* BRANSCOMBE, GENA.

Tennstedt, Klaus (*b* Merseburg, 6 June 1926). German conductor. He studied the piano, violin and theory at the Leipzig Conservatory, and from 1948 led the orchestra at the Halle Municipal Theatre, becoming principal conductor there. He later held appointments at the Dresden opera house and as conductor of the Schwerin orchestra, also appearing as a guest conductor within East Germany. He moved to Sweden in 1971, working at the Stora Theatre, Göteborg, and with the Swedish RSO, Stockholm. In 1972 he was appointed Generalmusikdirektor of the Kiel Opera. In 1974 he appeared in north America with the Toronto SO and the Boston SO; two years later he made his début in London, where he has been associated particularly with the LPO. He has conducted the Berlin PO and the Orchestre de Paris, and in 1979 became chief conductor of the Norddeutscher Rundfunk SO, Hamburg. The same year he was appointed chief guest conductor of the Minnesota Orchestra. Tennstedt conducts a substantial repertory, but has been especially praised for his interpretations of Mahler, where his command of form and clarity of texture, and the urgency and sincerity of his performances, have been noted.

Tenor (from Lat. *tenere*: 'to hold'). In polyphony between about 1250 and 1500, the structurally fundamental (or 'holding') voice, vocal or instrumental; by the 15th century it came to signify the male voice that sang such parts, and later it was applied not only to singers covering roughly *c* (called Tenor C) to *a'* but also instrumental parts occupying approximately that register (*see* TENOR VIOLIN, for example). In some 18th-century sources 'tenor' means 'viola'.

1. Early uses of the word. 2. Up to *c*1500. 3. *c*1500 to *c*1600. 4. The tenor in opera.

1. EARLY USES OF THE WORD. The word is found only once in Cicero but more often in Virgil, Livy and later writers with the meaning of 'a holding fast' and thence of 'an uninterrupted course' or 'a career'. Nor do its earlier musical uses have any particular consistency. But with the exception of Cassiodorus, who used it for string tension or pitch, and Guido, whose several uses include one where it apparently means the duration of a note, most of the early music theorists used the word only in discussions of chant modality.

Even there, however, usage varied from writer to writer and even from passage to passage. For Jacques de Liège *tenor* was the final or key note of a mode, whereas for Aurelian of Réôme 400 years earlier it seems to have been one reciting-note, more commonly called *tuba* and in modern discussions of modality often called the dominant. Yet another meaning, rather more common, is that of 'melodic formula': Aurelian, again, seems to have used *tenor* for a psalm tone, and many theorists up to the 16th century used it for the termination formula of a psalm tone. Indeed, as late as 1701, T. B. Janovka began his definition of tenor: 'in musica alicuius melodiae (ut Ariae, Sarabandae &c) significat processum, & quendam fluxum' ('in melodious music it means [melodic] progression or turn of phrase'); he then proceeded to define the word in terms of the high male voice.

2. UP TO *c*1500. Because high voices are almost universally considered to be most apt for virtuoso singing, and because female voices were for many centuries excluded from the church, the most prominent solo singers in the early history of Western music were almost certainly tenors. In the Middle Ages tenors would have been especially evident in the performance of such highly melismatic chants as the alleluia, the gradual and the tract, all of which are closely linked to the cantorial tradition of the synagogue (Werner, 1959, pp.500–45). The alleluia, for example, was by Jewish tradition and Christian exegesis understood to be 'a song performed by men and angels' (Werner, p.138). Because plainchant notation is not related to a fixed pitch it is impossible to say what range it was intended for, but most melismatic

Ex.1 Léonin: verse 'Sed sic eum volo' (W. G. Waite: *The Rhythm of Twelfth-century Polyphony, its Theory and Practice*, New Haven, Conn., 1954, pp.90–91)

(all over sustained C in tenor)

chants seem to suit best a tenor with a flexible voice, and in the judgment of Isidore of Seville (c559–636) 'the perfect voice is high, sweet, and loud' (*Etymologiarum sive originum libri xx*). Virtuoso display by high male voices became a distinct characteristic of early polyphony, and was brought to a high peak of cultivation in the florid lines of the Parisian school of the 12th and 13th centuries (see ex.1).

In medieval and Renaissance polyphony the counterpoint in all other voices was normally calculated in relation to the structurally fundamental tenor: if one voice was to proceed in longer note values that voice would be the tenor; if one voice was to carry a borrowed CANTUS FIRMUS that voice would nearly always be the tenor before 1400 and often thereafter; all writings about counterpoint were concerned primarily with the relation of the discanting voice (discantus) to the tenor; and during the 15th century all polyphony retained that firm 'discant' relationship between discantus and tenor even when there were several other voices, both above and below them.

Before 1300 such voices were labelled 'tenor' in the sources only when they were not taken from chants or when the chant was not known; and about 1300 Johannes de Grocheo specifically described tenors as those fundamental voices in polyphony that had not been taken from chant. But in 14th-century sources any such voice could be labelled 'tenor', and in the 15th century practically all such voices could be so labelled. In the 16th century the hegemony of the tenor–discant pair broke down as fully imitative polyphony developed its own requirements and rules; but it was still common to give the name 'tenor' to any voice carrying a cantus firmus, and there were several forms in which the old rules continued to hold sway.

The long-held assumption that 13th-century musicians called the bottom line of polyphony a 'tenor' (from Lat. *tenere*: 'to hold') because it 'held' the pre-existing chant melody has recently been called in question (Hoffmann-Axthelm, §II, 1). It was based on a passage in Johannes de Garlandia's *De mensurabili musica* (second quarter of the 13th century), where in reference to the two lines of polyphony, 'primus cantus' and 'secundus cantus', it is said that the 'tenor' part is the one called 'primus cantus' ('a parte tenoris, qui dicitur primus cantus'). The true meaning of this is probably that the first line the composer wrote in polyphony was called the tenor because it 'held up' or supported the harmonic structure of the counterpoint. Such is the meaning conveyed by two later treatises, Franco of Cologne's *Ars cantus mensurabilis* (c1250) and an anonymous treatise of about 30 years later from St Emmeram; the latter equates 'tenor' with the concept of a foundation, or 'fundamentum'. In view of the fact that almost all names for the voices in early polyphony derive from the actual process of composing music (cf the early 14th-century *contra-tenor*, a line composed against a tenor; or the late 15th-century *basis-tenor*, a tenor that acts as a foundation), this explanation of the original meaning of the word 'tenor' is entirely plausible.

In the late 14th and early 15th centuries any tenor line in polyphony was almost invariably paired with a CONTRATENOR part. These two lines, overlapping in range, shared the functions of providing both a harmonic foundation and a harmonizing part. (The contratenor, in fact, was occasionally called a 'concordans',

a word that lingered in French usage well into the 19th century as a term for the baritone voice.) With the late 15th-century progression from three- to four-voice composition a *contratenor bassus* was introduced, which assumed the role of providing a harmonic foundation. Tenor and contratenor then became more clearly distinguished from one another, and the old contratenor became known as the CONTRATENOR ALTUS. Although this 'altus' part was still sung by a male voice, it tended to lie slightly higher in range than the tenor – with the result that the word 'tenor' came more and more to refer to a vocal range.

In the late 14th and 15th centuries the French word 'tenoriste', or 'tenoristre', and the Italian 'tenorista' were used for a highly skilled singer able to perform the lower lines of polyphony, contratenor as well as tenor. (The singer of a top part was a 'discantista'.) Given the limited range of these lines, any good baritone, especially with skilful use of falsetto, could have performed all these parts and thus qualified as a 'tenoriste'. The word tended to be reserved, however, as a title for the most eminent singers, some of whom appear to have functioned also as choir directors. In the late 15th century, as four-voice polyphony became the norm, some singers were given such titles as 'tenorista basso', 'controriste', 'contro alto' or simply 'contro'. From this confusion of terminology, however, there gradually emerged the word 'tenore', and this term became clearly fixed with the publication of partbooks.

3. *c*1500 TO *c*1600. In the 16th century the tenor remained the most important voice for solo and virtuoso purposes (though it was joined in secular music by the soprano). The solo vocal repertory with instrumental accompaniment was published with the voice part mostly in either the treble or the soprano clef, but these clefs were the common property of all high voices, male or female, the tenor clef being reserved for the tenor voice in ensembles. The texts suggest that the bulk of the Renaissance lute-song repertory was most appropriate for male singers. Most of the performers of this repertory were probably amateurs, or musicians of only local reputation, since no singers appear to have enjoyed international reputations, as did various lutenists and keyboard players of the high Renaissance. In the second half of the century the art of vocal ornamentation was cultivated to a high degree. Although treatises on the subject make it clear that ornamentation was not limited to any particular voice range, most of the important writers were themselves tenors. Perhaps the most influential was Giulio Caccini (c1545–1618), whose *Le nuove musiche* (1601/2) contained the most elaborate description of this virtuoso art 'which admits of no mediocrity'; ornamentation is even more explicitly notated in his *Nuove musiche e nuova maniera di scriverle* (1614). Caccini became the first tenor to enjoy an international reputation as a soloist, and the first of a succession of Italian singers to attract attention at the French court, where he created a vogue for Italian singing which reached a climax in the career of the Italian-influenced Pierre de Nyert (c1597–1682). Luigi Rossi was another Italian tenor–composer who enjoyed success both in Italy and elsewhere.

4. THE TENOR IN OPERA. The growing importance of the castrato in Italian opera during the second half of the 17th century meant that the tenor, for the first time in history, was relegated to a secondary status among

virtuoso singers. In France, where the castrato was ill-tolerated, tenors trained their voices to perform comfortably in ever higher ranges, cultivating the HAUTE-CONTRE voice. Female singers, in intense competition with the castrato, brought their voices to a high peak of virtuoso development and became the prima donnas that they were to remain throughout the 18th and 19th centuries – with the result that tenors were never to reclaim the primary status that they had enjoyed since the Middle Ages. Vocal treatises of the 18th century are mostly concerned with the instruction of the castrato. The first chapter of P. F. Tosi's *Opinioni de' cantori antichi e moderni* (1723) is headed 'Per chi insegna ad un soprano' ('For one who teaches a soprano'), meaning a castrato. Galliard's English translation (1742) provides a footnote that says that 'the soprano is most apt to perform the things required by the author', and that the tenor presents 'less of the pathetick, but more of the volubility than the contr'alto, though not so much as the soprano'. While in early opera the tenor had been cast as Orpheus (the title part of Monteverdi's *Orfeo* was sung by the tenor Francesco Rasi), and later as the hero-lover, before the end of the 17th century these heroic roles were taken from the tenor and assigned to the castrato. In minor roles the tenor sometimes assumed the part of an old man (often with comic overtones), of a lighthearted adviser-companion of the hero, of a mischievous schemer or of a messenger. The castrato was only rarely cast in comic roles, and the 18th-century *tenore buffo* was therefore in competition only with the *basso buffo*. In oratorio and Passion music the tenor was used for the important function of narrator.

Until the late 18th and even early 19th centuries most tenors in the Italian tradition emphasized the lyrical quality of their top range and, when required, carried their voices with ease into the falsetto register (treatises of the 18th century and earlier call the falsetto range the *voce di testa*). During the first half of the 19th century, however, this traditional Italian manner of singing in the top range fell into disuse, and the expression *voce di testa* came to refer to the normal, much stronger head voice, falsetto being reserved as a special effect only for the very highest notes. In this period of transition towards a more powerful and dramatic tenor voice the most significant figures were Domenico Donzelli (1790–1873), Adolphe Nourrit (1802–39) and Gilbert Duprez (1806–96). Duprez, one of the most controversial figures in the history of singing, was the first tenor to carry the chest tone up to a high *c″*. Rossini was one of the composers who induced tenors to use greater volume in the top register, though he deplored the fundamental change in singing style that went hand in hand with the production of clarion high notes.

The second half of the 19th century witnessed the development of such voices as the HELDENTENOR (the heroic tenor called for by Wagner and others; Siegfried in the *Ring* is the outstanding example), as well as the *tenore robusto* and the *tenore di forza*, a lyrical voice that, like the female *lirico spinto*, can be pushed to occasional climaxes of some power. The *tenore robusto* is an operatic tenor with a powerful, baritone-like voice particularly suited to such heroic roles as Manrico, Radamès and Othello. An early instance of a *tenore robusto* part is the title role in Verdi's *Ernani* (1844), in which the singer is required to produce high *a′* (often 'con forza') many times, but is never taken above *b♭′* (this being characteristic of Verdi's writing for such a

voice). The tenor voice, with its new strength and its suggestion of youth and vigour, was more than ever called upon to play the hero-lover, always in a dramatic and often in a tragic context. It was in such roles as Manrico in Verdi's *Il trovatore* (1853), Andrea in Giordano's *Andrea Chénier* (1896) and Rodolfo in Puccini's *La bohème* (also 1896) that Enrico Caruso, Beniamino Gigli and other Italian tenors earned their enormous reputations.

The cultivation of such weightier voices did not lead entirely to the demise of the lyric tenor, who was particularly prized in French opera. The roles of Nadir in Bizet's *Les pêcheurs de perles* (1863), for example, and of Don José in the same composer's *Carmen* (1875) call for a lighter type of voice than the big Wagner and Verdi tenor roles. A highly specialized type of tenor voice is the *tenor altino* (or *tenore-contraltino*), which extends into the treble region in true head tone (i.e. without breaking into falsetto). The part of the Astrologer in Rimsky-Korsakov's *The Golden Cockerel* is for *tenor altino*, though in this case the composer did foresee some use of falsetto. Another type of light tenor voice was known in the 19th century as the 'tenorino'; such singers were often amateurs who made a speciality of performing love-songs to salon audiences.

Among leading tenors of the 20th century have been Giovanni Martinelli, who with Gigli succeeded Caruso as a chief exponent of dramatic and heroic roles; Lauritz Melchior, remembered chiefly for his singing of Wagner; Jussi Björling, who brought to the Romantic Italian repertory a purity and refinement that the Italians themselves were rarely interested in cultivating; Peter Pears, whose close collaboration with Benjamin Britten has resulted in a new concert and operatic repertory for the tenor voice; and Jon Vickers, widely regarded as the leading interpreter of many heroic roles, German and Italian (Florestan, Tristan, Othello).

BIBLIOGRAPHY

RicordiE
M. Kunath: 'Die Charakterologie der stimmlichen Einheiten in der Oper', *ZMw*, viii (1925–6), 403
J. Arger: 'Evolution de la technique vocale', *EMDC*, II/ii (1926), 966–1049
A. de Martini: 'Histoire du chant', *EMDC*, II/ii (1926), 871
H. Killer: *Die Tenor-Partien in Mozarts Opern* (Kassel, 1929)
E. Werner: *The Sacred Bridge* (London and New York, 1959)
K. Gudewill: 'Tenor', *MGG*
D. Hoffmann-Axthelm: 'Tenor', *HMT*
For further bibliography *see* SINGING.

DAVID FALLOWS (1, 2), OWEN JANDER (2–4)

Tenor altino. A type of TENOR voice.

Tenor bassoon. *See* TENOROON.

Tenor C. The note *c*.

Tenor cor (Fr. *cor alto*; It. *genis corno*; Port. *clavicorno*). A valved brass instrument, distinct from the TENOR HORN, introduced by Besson in Paris about 1860 and modified by Henry Distin in London a few years later. It is circular in shape, being designed to resemble the horn (see illustration). It is pitched in F but has half the tube length of a horn in F, so that its series of harmonics lies an octave higher than that of a horn. Hence, where a horn player uses high, closely grouped harmonics, the tenor cor player, with the same part before him, uses low, widely separated harmonics, which enormously simplifies the lip technique. The conical bore tapers less finely towards the mouthpiece than that of the horn, and the mouthpiece is wider than a

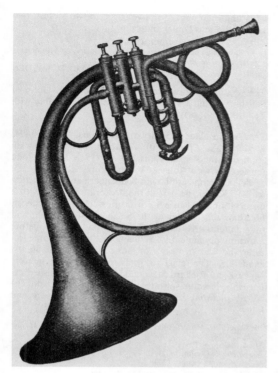

Tenor cor from a Rudall, Carte & Co. catalogue of 1931

horn mouthpiece, allowing readier emission of the notes. The valves are worked by the right hand as in other brass instruments. The tenor cor is thus a kind of hybrid between the horn and the Eb tenor horn, and has been widely used as a substitute for the horn, especially in military bands. It shares sufficiently the technical simplicity of the tenor horn to enable it to be quickly mastered by any bandsman, while with skilful use of the left hand (which rests in the bell) something of the musical effect of the true horn can be reproduced. Since some military band horn parts are in Eb, the tenor cor is supplied with a crook or a slide to transpose the instrument's pitch. In the USA the instrument has usually been called a 'mellophone'. It was very popular in American bands in the early 1900s, and is still manufactured in limited numbers and used by some school groups. A version with the bell pointed forwards (called the 'mellophonium') was introduced in the 1950s by C. G. Conn Ltd (Elkhart, Indiana) with the intention of appealing to jazz musicians.

An earlier instrument designed to serve the same purposes as the tenor cor was Červený's Cornon (Hradec Kralové, 1844). This was succeeded by various Austrian and German models, some of which are still made (e.g. the Altkorno, by Alexander, Mainz). However, the wide popularity and improved teaching of the modern German orchestral horn in all countries, and its greater facility and power of sound as against models previously in use, have now made the tenor cor and equivalent instruments largely obsolete.

ANTHONY C. BAINES

Tenor drum. *See* DRUM, §4.

Tenore robusto. A type of TENOR voice.

Tenorfagott (Ger.). TENOROON.

Tenor horn (Fr. *bugle alto*; Ger. *Althorn*; It. *genis*). A valved brass instrument of alto pitch, like a small euphonium in shape; in brass band scores it is usually referred to as 'Eb horn'. It has as its fundamental Eb (though this note is not used) and is thus intermediate in pitch between the cornet and the euphonium. It is a transposing instrument, its music being written a 6th above sounding pitch. The full compass is from (written) f♯ to c''', but in the band it is used mostly between a and a'', sounding c and c''.

Although used as an alto instrument in many continental military bands, it is not used by British ones; it is an essential component in the brass band, however, three tenor horns being required by the rules of the National Festival of Brass Bands (their parts generally described as 'solo horn', 'first horn' and 'second horn').

Historically, the tenor horn is the modern form of the Eb alto saxhorn, which in its early days in France, England and the USA was also termed 'tenor'; thus, in a catalogue (c1850) of Henry Distin, London, it appears as 'Saxhorn, tenor, Eb'. The instrument of the brass band that stands in Bb, a 4th below the tenor horn, is known in England and the USA as the 'baritone' and in Germany as *Tenorhorn* (*see* BARITONE (ii)).

See also ALTHORN (i); BRASS BAND; SAXHORN.

ANTHONY C. BAINES

Tenori (It.). An ORGAN STOP.

Tenorino. A type of TENOR voice.

Tenorlied (Ger.: 'tenor song'). The principal type of German polyphonic lied during the period from c1450 to c1550. The texture of such a piece consists of a pre-existing lied melody as a cantus firmus, or tenor (hence the name of the genre), with two or three independent contrapuntal parts accompanying it. In sources before 1536, only the tenor is underlaid with the complete text. This was presumably because it was the only sung part: it was indeed performed by a solo singer, while the rhythmic and generally more animated accompanying parts were played on instruments. It must be stressed that the word 'tenor' is here used, in the medieval sense, synonymously with 'cantus firmus': that the tenor should sound within the compass of the male tenor voice became the rule only in four-part Tenorlieder dating from after c1500. In earlier Tenorlieder, most of which are in three parts, the tenor is often the highest part.

See also HOFWEISE and LIED, §I, 2–3.

NORBERT BÖKER-HEIL

Tenor mass. A setting of the five sections making up the Ordinary of the Roman Catholic Mass in which the same borrowed material appears as a cantus firmus in the tenor of each section. This technique of unifying a mass cycle was particularly important in the late 15th century and early 16th; it was eventually superseded by the 'imitation' or 'parody' mass. Prominent examples of tenor masses include Dunstable's *Missa 'Rex seculorum'*, Dufay's *Missa 'Ecce ancilla'* (both using liturgical melodies), Ockeghem's *Missa 'Malheur me bat'* and Josquin's *Missa 'L'homme armé' super voces musicales* (both using secular melodies).

See also MASS, §II.

Tenoroon [tenor bassoon] (Fr. *basson quinte*; Ger. *Hochquintfagott*, *Tenorfagott*; It. *fagottino*). A small BASSOON pitched a 5th above the normal bassoon.

See also ORGAN STOP.

Tenor tuba. *See* TUBA (i).

Tenor violin. A term for a string instrument, most often denoting a type of viola or a small cello. From the 16th century onwards the term was most commonly applied to a large viola with four strings tuned like a modern viola in 5ths upwards from *c*. By 1556 Jambe de Fer was using 'tenor-contralto' (*taille/haute-contre*) in this sense. In its earliest uses, however, 'tenor violin' must have referred to a three-string viola tuned upwards in 5ths from *c*, according to theorists such as Ganassi (1543) and M. Agricola (1545).

Sometimes 'tenor violin' refers to an instrument resembling and played like a small cello, with four strings tuned upwards in 5ths from *F* or *G* (i.e. a tuning between that of the modern viola and cello). This instrument never attained the status of a principal member of the violin family; although its 'banishment' was regretted by Arnold Dolmetsch, Gerald Hayes and others, its use was peripheral and sporadic, and it was hardly noticed by the theorists or explicitly called for in music after the mid-17th century. It was a victim of the clear historical tendency, in the violin family, to keep the number of members to a minimum (i.e. three) and at the same time to increase the playing range and variety of colour of which each member was capable.

The *c*-tuned 'tenor violin' was actually a regular *c*-tuned viola, but the term implied a viola of large size, normally used to play in the lower part of the viola register. In contrast, the 'alto' (or 'contralto') viola was smaller and favoured a higher tessitura. This explains why Stradivari referred to his 'Tuscan' tenor viola as 'T.V.' and the contralto of the same set as 'C.V.'. Some of these early 'tenors', especially before 1700, were very large instruments whose body lengths extended the player's arm to the limit – one reason most of them were later cut down in size. The Stradivari 'Tuscan' tenor (now in Florence) has a body length of 47·9 cm, and the magnificent viola of Andrea Amati, made for Charles IX of France and dated 1574 (now in the Hill Collection, in the Ashmolean Museum, Oxford), measures 47 cm. Some instrument makers continued to construct very large violas intended to be played on the arm (e.g. the Ritter *viola-alta* in the 19th century), but all these instruments almost immediately disappeared owing to the physical difficulty of playing them.

In the 16th and 17th centuries the four parts of an ensemble, corresponding to soprano, alto, tenor and bass ranges, were typically assigned to one violin, two violas (one being larger than the other) and cello. According to Mersenne (1636–7), the five parts of a string ensemble were allotted to one violin, three (*c*-tuned) violas of differing sizes and cello. In Mersenne's 'ordinary ensemble' the three violas were called *quinte* or *cinquiesme*, *haute-contre* (contralto) and *taille* (tenor). In this typical ensemble there was no 'tenor' between the range of the viola and cello. Around 1700 partbooks labelled 'tenor viola' and 'alto viola' were both intended to be played on the *c*-tuned viola, but one part was in a lower range of the viola than the other. In Italian music and most other music after 1700 the four parts of an ensemble were more generally allocated to two violins, viola and cello; and, if in five parts, to two violins, two violas (alto and tenor) and cello.

BIBLIOGRAPHY
D. D. Boyden: 'The Tenor Violin: Myth, Mystery, or Misnomer?', *Festschrift Otto Erich Deutsch* (Kassel, 1963), 273

DAVID D. BOYDEN

Tenredus. A 12th-century monk mentioned by John of Salisbury in his *Metalogicon*, probably identifiable with THEINRED OF DOVER.

Tenschert, Roland (*b* Podersam, Bohemia, 5 April 1894; *d* Vienna, 3 April 1970). Austrian musicologist. He studied at the Leipzig Conservatory (1913–15) and then musicology with Adler at Vienna University (1917–21), as well as composition with Schoenberg and conducting with L. Kaiser; he gained the doctorate in 1921 with a dissertation on Mozart's overtures. He was archivist, librarian and teacher at the Salzburg Mozarteum, and then taught privately in Salzburg and Vienna before returning permanently to Vienna in 1945 to become lecturer and later professor of music history at the Staatsakademie. The chief subjects of his research were Mozart and Richard Strauss on whom he published extensively; in addition to the monographs listed below he edited pictorial biographies of Mozart, Haydn and Gluck.

WRITINGS
Die Ouvertüren Mozarts (diss., U. of Vienna, 1921; pubd in *Mozart-Jb*, ii, 1924)
Mozart (Leipzig, 1931)
Joseph Haydn (Berlin, 1932)
Musikerbrevier (Vienna, 1940)
Mozart: ein Leben für die Oper (Vienna, 1941)
Dreimal sieben Variationen über das Thema Richard Strauss (Vienna, 1944)
Frauen um Haydn (Vienna, 1946)
Salzburg und seine Festspiele (Vienna, 1947)
Vater Hellmesberger: ein Kapitel Wiener Musikerhumor (Vienna, 1947)
Richard Strauss und Wien: eine Wahlverwandtschaft (Vienna, 1949)
Wolfgang Amadeus Mozart (Salzburg, 1951; Eng. trans., 1952; Fr. trans., 1954)
Christoph Willibald Gluck: der grosse Reformer der Oper (Olten and Freiburg, 1951)
ed.: *Richard Strauss und Joseph Gregor: Briefwechsel 1934–1949* (Salzburg, 1955)
Franz Schubert (Vienna, 1971)

BIBLIOGRAPHY
H. Boese: 'Roland Tenschert', *ÖMz*, xiv (1959), 65
E. Tenschert: *Musik als Lebensinhalt* (Vienna, 1971) [incl. list of writings]

Tenso [tenson]. A debate between two or more troubadours or trouvères in the form of a poem. According to Guilhem Molinier, in *Las leys d'amors* (1328, rev. 1337), there is a clear difference between a *tenso* and a *partimen* (*see* JEU-PARTI). The *tenso*, supposedly, was used for a debate in which each participant presented his own opinion or conviction on a topic 'as in a trial' whereas in the *partimen* the participants seem to have chosen sides for the sake of discussion only. Consequently the *tenso* could be rather free in form, each participant contributing as much text as he saw fit. However Molinier ruefully admitted that the two terms were often used the wrong way and often a *tenso* was called *partimen* and vice versa. In the poems there is almost complete corroboration of this remark; furthermore, in manuscripts that separate the poems by genre, debates may be separated from other poems, but there is no clear distinction between the various kinds of debates.

For bibliography *see* TROUBADOURS, TROUVÈRES.

HENDRIK VANDERWERF

Tenth (Fr. *dixième*; Ger. *Dezime*; It. *decima*). The interval of a compound THIRD, i.e. the sum of an octave and a 3rd.

Tento (Port.). TIENTO.

Tenuto (It.: 'held'; past participle of *tenere*, to hold, hold back, restrain). A performance instruction normally applied to single notes or groups of notes, also abbreviated to *ten*. It can denote either a holding of individual notes to their full length or a complete interruption of the metre. C. P. E. Bach (1753) stated that 'Notes which are neither staccato nor legato nor sostenuto are held for half their value unless the word "ten." is placed over them, in which case they have to be sustained'; D. G. Türk (*Clavierschule*, 1789) wrote that 'When playing notes in the ordinary manner, that is, neither staccato nor legato, the finger should be lifted shortly before the written value of the note requires it ... Where single notes are supposed to be held for their full value they have to be marked *ten.* or *tenuto*'. The predominantly detached style of playing which made this necessary seems to have gone out of favour around 1800; but it is presumably in this sense that the first note of each of the repeated-note patterns in the second movement of Beethoven's Seventh Symphony is marked *ten*. In the second sense it is often used for a delay of the metre in bravura operatic lines, particularly to indicate that the upbeat must be held back; there are many instances in Verdi. The term has a distinguished position as one of the first to be used in music: according to Notker's letter to Lambertus (*GS*, i, 95f) the Romanus letter *t* meant 'trahere vel tenere debere', though Aribo asserted that it meant 'tarditas'.

For bibliography *see* TEMPO AND EXPRESSION MARKS.

DAVID FALLOWS

Teodorini, Elena (*b* Craiova, 25 March 1857; *d* Bucharest, 27 Feb 1926). Romanian singer. She studied the piano and theory in Craiova and Milan, and singing with George Stephănescu at the Bucharest Conservatory. At the age of 20 she made her operatic début in Italy, where after three years of provincial performances she played Gounod's Marguerite at La Scala (1880), the first Romanian ever to sing there. In the next 25 years she toured throughout Europe, Africa and South America in more than 40 operas and operettas, in several of whose premières she had participated. She was also a leading singer in both the Italian Opera and the National Opera of Bucharest. A singer with an exceptional range, she undertook various roles in *Norma*, *Gioconda*, Gounod's *Faust*, *Aida*, *Il trovatore* and *Un ballo in maschera*, being equally at ease in the lyric and dramatic soprano, mezzo and contralto repertories; her stage presence was imbued with her passionate dramatic temperament. After her retirement in 1904 she taught in Europe and South America.

BIBLIOGRAPHY
V. Cosma: *Cîtăreaţa Elena Teodorini* (Bucharest, 1962)
R. Celletti: 'Teodorini, Elena', *Le grandi voci* (Rome, 1964) [with opera discography]
V. Cosma: *Interpreţi români* (Bucharest, 1977)

VIOREL COSMA

Teodoro del Carmine. *See* BACCHINI, GIROLAMO M.

Terascon, Albertet de. *See* ALBERTET DE SESTARO.

Terce (Lat. *tertia, hora tertia, ad tertiam*). One of the LITTLE HOURS of the DIVINE OFFICE, recited about midmorning, or at the 'third hour'. *See also* LITURGY OF THE HOURS.

Terence [Publius Terentius Afer] (*b* north Africa, *c*190 BC; *d* ?159 BC). Roman comic playwright. Only six plays survive, all *fabulae palliatae* (i.e. with Greek settings; *see* PLAUTUS, TITUS MACCIUS). Like Plautus, he adapted specimens of Greek New Comedy, but with far less lyric diversity (only 25 lyric lines out of 6000) and a heavy preponderance of spoken dialogue. The musical element was nevertheless more important than appears from the text; a considerable portion of the plays is recitative *cantica*, lines recited or intoned to an accompaniment on the pipes. (See Beare for a dissenting view.)

The *didascalia* (prefatory information) to each of Terence's works names a slave or freedman, Flaccus, as composer of the music (*modi*) and mentions the kinds of double reedpipe used. These are 'equal' in length, 'unequal', 'right', 'left' or, for one play, 'Sarranian'. Commentaries by the 4th-century grammarian Aelius Donatus also specify them for each play, and identify equal pipes as Lydian and unequal as Phrygian, but the connections he suggested between these terms and the ethos or mood of the piece seem arbitrary and should be treated with caution (Wille, 169ff).

According to Donatus, some recitative portions of the plays were marked 'M.M.C.' (*mutatis modis cantica*), *cantica* with a change of *modi*. *Modi* could mean either 'melodies' (*Weisen*: Wille, 164) or 'measures' (Duckworth, 362); the metres in these passages do not differ radically from those of other recitative *cantica*.

References to music in Terence are rare. The adjective *musicus* occurs in three prologues (*Heautontimorumenos*, 1.23; *Phormio*, 1.17; *Hecyra*, ll.23, 46), referring to poetry and specifically to comic drama. The plural substantive *musica* denotes 'music' as a main part of the Hellenistic curriculum once (*Eunuchus*, ll.476f; *see* EDUCATION IN MUSIC, §I). *Fidicinae* and *psaltriae*, girls skilled in playing the lyre or psaltery, occur as characters in the plays (*Eunuchus*, 1.985; *Adelphoe*, ll.842, 967); they are little more than concubines.

BIBLIOGRAPHY
S. G. Ashmore, ed.: *The Comedies of Terence* (New York, 1908, 2/1910), esp. 54f
J. Sargeaunt, ed. and trans.: *Terence* (London and Cambridge, Mass., 1912/R1964–5)
R. Kauer and W. M. Lindsay, eds.: *Terenti comoediae* (Oxford, 1926/R1973; suppl. by O. Skutsch, 1958)
W. Beare: *The Roman Stage* (London, 1950, 3/1964), 91ff, 219ff
G. E. Duckworth: *The Nature of Roman Comedy* (Princeton, 1952/R1967), esp. 361ff
G. Wille: *Musica romana* (Amsterdam, 1967), 158ff, 308ff
E. Pöhlmann: *Denkmäler altgriechischer Musik* (Nuremberg, 1970), 41f

WARREN ANDERSON

Terényi, Ede (*b* Tîrgu-Mureş, 12 March 1935). Romanian composer and musicologist of Hungarian descent. He studied at the music college in Tîrgu-Mureş (1942–52) and at the Cluj Conservatory (1952–8), where he has served as assistant lecturer (from 1962) and lecturer (from 1970) in harmony and counterpoint.

WORKS
(*selective list*)

Orch: Concertino, str, org, elec, 1958, rev. 1969; Pasărea maistră, sym. poem, 1965; Pf Conc., 1968
Chamber: Sonatina, vn, pf, 1955, rev. 1965; 4 Pieces, pf, 1958; Prelude no.1, fl, 1963; 3 Pieces, prepared pf, 1968; Prelude, Toccata, Fantasia and Fugue, org, 1968; Str Qt no.1, 1973; Sonatina, va, pf,

1974; 18th-century Dances, vn, pf/orch, 1974; Variations on a Theme, org, 1974

Vocal: Terzine di Dante, Bar, trbn, pf, 1972; cantatas, choruses, mass songs, songs

WRITINGS

'Problema polivalenţei în armonizarea modernă', *LM*, i (1965)

'Unele aspecte ale intrebuinţării octavei micşorate' [Some aspects of the diminished octave], *LM*, ii (1966)

'Tipuri de cadenţe finale în muzica contemporană', *LM*, iv (1968)

'Succesiuni acordice specifice muzicii moderne', *LM*, v (1969)

'Structuri de straturi acordice în muzica contemporană', *LM*, vi (1970)

'Tipuri de clustersuri', *LM*, vii (1971)

ISTVÁN LAKATOS

Teretismata. Meaningless syllables such as te re re, ti ri ri, to ro ro, etc, which first appear in Byzantine musical manuscripts of the 14th century. *See* KRATĒMA.

Terian, Mikhail (Nikitovich) (*b* Moscow, 14 July 1905). Soviet viola player, conductor and teacher. He studied at the Moscow Conservatory until 1929 under Konstantin Mostras, and from 1924 to 1946 was a member of the Komitas String Quartet. From 1926 he also taught at the conservatory, and from 1935 directed special quartet and viola classes. He conducted the conservatory's student symphony orchestra until 1972, and in 1961 formed and conducted its chamber orchestra with a mixed membership of students, graduates and teachers. After touring in eastern Europe and Cuba, the chamber orchestra won the 1970 Karajan Orchestral Competition in West Berlin. Terian has published instructional works for the viola including *Shest' etyudov virtuoznoy trudnosti* ('Six studies of virtuoso standard', Moscow, 1936) and *Shest' etyudov dlya detskikh shkol* ('Six studies for children's schools', Moscow, 1939). He was made People's Artist of the Armenian SSR in 1945.

I. M. YAMPOL'SKY

Ternaria (Lat.). A *ligatura ternaria* or ligature comprising three notes. *See* LIGATURE (i).

Ternary form. A tripartite musical form designated symbolically as *ABA*. The two elements *A* and *B* are often thematically independent and each is generally a 'closed' structure tonally, so that the interdependence of the two sections characteristic of binary form is not necessarily evident in ternary. The recurrence of *A* is sometimes modified by added ornamentation or more radically by a redevelopment of the same material, and in such cases *ABA'* better represents the result; a coda based on either *A* or *B* may also be subjoined.

Schemes of this kind are evident in the respond–verse–respond structure of responsories and graduals in Gregorian chant, and certain liturgical texts such as the Kyrie (Kyrie–Christe–Kyrie) invite treatment of this kind, though many composers have in fact set the two Kyries to different music. However, the value of such an obvious means of achieving both the variety implied in a form with a contrasting central section and the sense of unity which results from a return to the opening material was grasped early in the history of Western music. At its simplest, ternary form is found in German song from the 12th century to the 16th in the work of the Minnesinger and in chorale melodies, and it occurs in some Italian *laude* of the 13th century (e.g. HAM no.21*a*). Other comparatively early instances, the more interesting in that the musical shape is not conditioned by a textual repetition, occur in Josquin's chanson *Faulte d'argent* (HAM no.91) and in a number of

basses danses such as *La volonté* set by Claude Gervaise (HAM no.137, 1).

Ternary form, however, is a more natural outcome of a primarily homophonic idiom than of polyphony. Rare during the Renaissance, it inevitably became a scheme of great importance during the Baroque period, being discussed as early as 1676 in Printz's *Phrynis* and receiving theoretical recognition by such critics as Mattheson (*Das neu-eröffnete Orchestre*, 1713). Monteverdi used it for the shepherd's song at the beginning of Act 1 of *Orfeo* ('In questo lieto e fortunato giorno') and in the closing duet of *L'incoronazione di Poppea* ('Pur ti miro'). During the course of the 17th century arias and duets were increasingly often cast in da capo form, and in the late Baroque period choruses were often written in this form too (e.g. the opening chorus of J. S. Bach's *St John Passion*).

Early examples of ternary form tend to emphasize contrasts between the *A* and *B* sections. The ground bass at the opening of Monteverdi's 'Pur ti miro' is dropped for the middle section, and in Steffani's aria 'Un balen' from *Henrico Leone* (HAM no.244) a new texture and movement are established at this point. Later, composers often cast the *A* section in binary form, drawing material from it for the *B* section which began in a related key but was tonally an 'open' structure leading back naturally to the reprise, often lavishly decorated, of *A*. In Handel's music the middle section is generally much shorter than the first, and usually differentiated from it in texture: a continuo accompaniment may replace that of the full string band, or an obbligato wind instrument present in the *A* section may be discarded for the *B*. Handel also achieved striking dramatic effects by curtailing the da capo or abandoning it altogether (e.g. 'Why do the nations' in *Messiah*, 'A serpent in my bosom warm'd' in *Saul*, or the duet 'Prendi da questo mano' in *Ariodante*), but such effects derive their force from the fact that a full da capo was usual and therefore expected.

Ternary form was sometimes applied to instrumental polyphony: a number of canzonas of the 17th century have a clearly marked return of the opening section, and Bach's 'Wedge' Fugue for organ has a middle section constructed by the interposition of toccata-like flourishes between statements of the fugue subject (which itself is treated in more conventional polyphonic terms in the outer parts of the movement). Those rondeaux of the French harpsichord composers which have only one couplet, such as the Menuet en rondeau in Rameau's *Pièces de clavecin* (1724), provide further examples of ternary instrumental pieces, as do the innumerable paired dances (generally the *Galanterien*) of the Baroque suite where the second of a pair of minuets, for example, may be labelled 'Alternativo', 'Trio', or simply 'Minuet II'. In collections such as J. C. F. Fischer's *Musicalischer Parnassus* or J. S. Bach's French Suites *alternativements* have no thematic identity, merely an appropriate continuity of style; in the Gavotte and

Ex.1

second Gavotte (or Musette) of Bach's English Suite no.6 in D minor, on the other hand, the two are clearly related (see ex.1).

During the 18th century the increasing tendency to introduce an element of recapitulation into binary structures gave them certain of the characteristics of ternary form and led to the rise of sonata form (*see* BINARY FORM, SONATA FORM). Ternary structures varying in their degree of complexity were sometimes used in the slow movements of sonatas and symphonies of the Classical period. The Andante of Mozart's Piano Sonata K330/300*h* is a simple example. The Largo of Beethoven's Piano Sonata op.7 shows how the form was expanded and given a lengthy coda to produce a lyrical movement of generous proportions. In the Andante of Beethoven's Piano Sonata op.28 both *A* and *B* sections are themselves in rounded binary form; at its return *A* has 'varied reprises' in a manner recalling the division technique of the Baroque period, and the coda is compounded of elements from *A* and *B*.

The minuet (or scherzo) and trio as a ternary movement continued in use throughout the 19th century. As early as Haydn both principal elements were often miniature sonata forms. In his quartets Haydn secured contrast of texture by such devices as using only two or three of the instruments in the trio (e.g. op.20 no.6, op.33 no.3). Occasionally he allowed the trio to pick up a thematic detail from the minuet, a device more fully exploited in Mozart's G minor String Quintet K516. Key relationships between *A* and *B* sections had been fairly limited during the Baroque period but, as might be expected, Haydn expanded the possibilities to include the submediant and flat submediant tonalities (op.74 no.1, op.77 no.2) as well as the usual change from tonic major to minor or vice versa; even in late works, however, he was prepared, as earlier composers had been, to use the same key for both sections (op.76 nos.1 and 4).

Beethoven added codas to many of his scherzos; these were usually very terse and often contained a humorous reference to the trio section (the piano sonatas op.2 no.3 and op.106; the Third and Ninth Symphonies). His expansion of ternary form was more concerned with the full-scale exploitation of a sonata form scheme within one section, as in the scherzo of the Ninth Symphony, and the extension of the *ABA* pattern to *ABABA* exemplified in the Fourth and Seventh Symphonies and several chamber works. Such an extension gives the movement the character of a rondo (*ABACA*) when the trios are different, a device earlier used by Bach (Brandenburg Concerto no.1) and Mozart (Serenades K361/370*a* and 375, String Trio K563, Clarinet Quintet K581) and subsequently by a number of Romantic composers, including Schumann (in the Piano Quintet and Piano Quartet).

The ease and effectiveness with which strongly contrasted, predominantly lyrical, ideas may be accommodated to a ternary scheme made it particularly suitable for the character pieces of the 19th century. Mendelssohn's *Lieder ohne Worte*, Brahms's fantasias and intermezzos, and Chopin's waltzes, the nocturnes op.15 and other pieces, contain many examples, some extended with introductions or codas or both. Thematic transformation, an important device in Romantic music, is responsible in some cases for a close relationship between *A* and *B* sections which may initially seem to be of extreme diversity, as in Brahms's Intermezzo op.119

no.2 (see ex.2). Songs like Schumann's *Widmung*, where the central stanza is sharply differentiated in texture and key, provide many further instances of the use of the form. In the 20th century the neo-classical movement

Ex.2

and its associated tendency to view musical form not necessarily as something dynamic but equally as something capable of being handled in terms of the straightforward juxtaposition of sharply contrasted blocks of material, have given simple ternary and rondo forms a new relevance (e.g. the Fuga quarta in A of Hindemith's *Ludus tonalis* and the Allegretto of Stravinsky's 'Dumbarton Oaks' Concerto).

BIBLIOGRAPHY
R. O. Morris: *The Structure of Music* (London, 1935)
E. J. Dent: 'Binary and Ternary Form', *ML*, xvii (1936), 309
W. S. Newman: *The Sonata in the Classic Era* (Chapel Hill, 1963)
I. Spink: *An Historical Approach to Musical Form* (London, 1968)
MICHAEL TILMOUTH

Ternaux, Victoire. See STOLTZ, ROSINE.

Ternina [Trnina], Milka (*b* Doljnji, Moslavina, 19 Dec 1863; *d* Zagreb, 18 May 1941). Croatian soprano. She studied in Zagreb with Ida Winterberg and at the Vienna Conservatory with Gänzbacher and, while still a student, made her début in 1882 at Zagreb as Amelia in *Un ballo in maschera*. In the following year she was engaged at Leipzig, where she sang Elisabeth in *Tannhäuser*. After performances at Graz and Bremen, in 1889 she made guest appearances in Munich as Valentine in *Les Huguenots*, Amelia and Elisabeth, and in 1890 she inaugurated her engagement as a member of the company singing Leonore in *Fidelio*. She made her Covent Garden début as Isolde on 3 June 1898, later appearing as Sieglinde in *Die Walküre*, Brünnhilde in *Siegfried* and *Götterdämmerung* and as Leonore. In 1899 she sang Kundry in *Parsifal* at Bayreuth, and returning to Covent Garden the following year, she sang both Elsa and Ortrud in *Lohengrin* and Tosca in the first London performance of Puccini's opera (12 July 1900). Her American début was at Boston in 1896, singing Brünnhilde and Isolde with the Damrosch Opera Company, and she first appeared at the Metropolitan, New York, on 27 January 1900 as Elisabeth. Her later Metropolitan roles included Tosca, which she sang in the American première of the opera (4 February 1901) and Kundry (24 December 1903) in the first staged performance of *Parsifal* outside Bayreuth. In 1906 she made her Covent Garden farewell as Elisabeth on 28 May, and her final stage appearance at Munich on 19 August, as Sieglinde. She had a superb voice whose 'overwhelming plentitude of warm, mellow tone' (*New York Times*) was heard to best advantage in the great Wagner roles, while her dramatic gifts were magnificently displayed in such parts as Leonore and Tosca. After her retirement, she taught singing, first at the Institute of Musical Art, New York, and then in Zagreb, where Zinka Milanov was among her pupils.

BIBLIOGRAPHY
H. Klein: *Thirty Years of Musical Life in London* (London, 1903)

W. H. Seltsam: *Metropolitan Opera Annals* (New York, 1949)
I. Kolodin: *The Story of the Metropolitan Opera* (New York, 1951)
H. Rosenthal: *Two Centuries of Opera at Covent Garden* (London, 1958)
H. Wagner: *200 Jahre Münchner Theaterchronik* (Munich, 1958)

ELIZABETH FORBES

Terpander (*fl c*675 BC). Lyric poet of Lesbos. He became famous in the musical life of Sparta during its brief period of brilliance. According to a late tradition, he had been brought to Sparta at a time of public discontent, which he quieted through his music. Only this minor episode links him with the Greek belief in the power of musical ethos. His importance consists rather in having been an innovator, the first significant and credible figure in the early history of Greek music.

Apollo, playing the seven-string lyre introduced by Terpander, enters Delos in a chariot accompanied by two women (? Muses): detail of an amphora (late 7th century BC) from Melos (National Archaeological Museum, Athens)

Terpander's most remarkable achievement was the successful introduction of the seven-stringed lyre. In one fragment of his verse (Edmonds, frag.5), he proudly described the revolutionary change by which it supplanted the four-stringed phorminx, familiar since the Homeric period. In another (frag.6), he ranked Sparta's music equally with her valour, as did Alcman a generation later. The authenticity of all six surviving fragments, however, has been called into question. He was further credited with having introduced a new type of composition, the lyric *nomos* or nome. As in the case of aulos nomes, to which an even earlier origin was ascribed, later generations remembered the melody rather than the sung text. Supposedly Terpander was also the first to make lyric settings (almost certainly monodic, like the nome) of epic hexameters, not only those of Homer but his own as well. These, with their settings for lyre, constituted the prooimion or prelude prefacing recitations of Homer.

EDITIONS

Lyra graeca, ed. and trans. J. M. Edmonds (London and New York, 1922–7, 2/1928–40)
Poetae melici graeci, ed. D. L. Page (Oxford, 1963)
Lyrica graeca selecta, ed. D. L. Page (Oxford, 1965), 204

BIBLIOGRAPHY

O. J. Gombosi: *Tonarten und Stimmungen der antiken Musik* (Copenhagen, 1939/*R*1950), 40ff, 73ff
B. A. van Groningen: 'A propos de Terpandre', *Mnemosyne*, iv (1955), 177

J. Lohmann: *Musikē und Logos* (Stuttgart, ?1971), 68ff
For further bibliography *see* GREECE, §I.

WARREN ANDERSON

Terpodion. An ORGAN STOP.

Terpsichore. The Muse of the choral lyric and dance, represented with the lyre; *see* MUSES.

Terradellas, Domingo Miguel Bernabe [Terradeglias, Domenico] (*b* Barcelona, baptized 13 Feb 1713; *d* Rome, 20 May 1751). Spanish composer. He probably received part of his musical instruction from Francisco Valls, choirmaster of Barcelona Cathedral. In 1732 he moved to Italy. Sponsored by the Prince of Belmonte, he registered as a student at the music conservatory Poveri di Gesù Cristo in Naples on 23 May, at the same time committing himself to stay in the conservatory and contribute to its music for a period of six years. His first important work, the oratorio *Giuseppe riconosciuto*, was written in 1736 while he was still a student. His professional career as a dramatic composer opened in Carnival 1739 with the production in Rome of his heroic opera *Astarto*. He then returned to Naples where he wrote his second oratorio, *Ermenegildo martire* (performed 1739), and his single comic opera, *Gli intrighi delle cantarine* (performed 1740).

In 1743 he achieved his first outstanding success with the presentation in Rome of his opera *Merope*. The Neapolitan envoy at the papal court, Cardinal Acquaviva, was so impressed that he wrote a strong recommendation for the composer to the court authorities in Naples, claiming that *Merope* had obtained a success in Rome 'the like of which no one can remember for many years'. But the Neapolitan court took no interest, and Terradellas stayed in Rome where he secured an appointment at the Spanish church of Santiago y S Ildefonso. During his years in this post (1743–5) he wrote many church compositions. According to Carreras, he left S Ildefonso in 1745 because of differences with his colleagues. In 1746 he went to London where, in the course of a winter season, he composed two operas and arranged a pasticcio, all for the King's Theatre. In the spring or early summer of 1747 he returned to the Continent by way of Paris. By 1750 he was back in Italy. During Carnival that year he was at Turin for the production of his new opera *Didone*, and in May he was at Venice for the production of another new opera, *Imeneo in Atene*. *Sesostri re d'Egitto*, his last opera, was performed with great success in Rome in Carnival 1751. The following May he died; how he died is still a mystery. The lurid report in the *Allgemeine musikalische Zeitung* of 12 March 1800 (cols.430–31) that, after a period of intense rivalry between him and another composer, Nicolò Jommelli, he was murdered and his body thrown into the Tiber, is nowadays discounted.

Though Terradellas was Spanish by birth, his taste and musical style were thoroughly Italianate. His reputation rests primarily on his Italian *opere serie*. The structure of these operas was the usual one of the period: recitatives alternate with lyrical items, most of which are da capo arias. Terradellas used accompanied recitative sparingly but always to good advantage in moments of heightened dramatic intensity, and often increased its effectiveness by introducing wind instruments; before the 1740s composers had usually supported accompanied recitative with strings and continuo alone, and Terradellas was one of the first to popularize the use of the wind in this situation. Ferocity of expression, caused primarily by the vigorous orchestral accompaniment, marks many of his arias in fast time. His arias are generally distinguished by their strong contrasts, created by such means as changes of colour and texture, of key (from major to minor and back again), of time signature and of speed. Such features are among the advanced elements of Terradellas's music. The Italian aria of his period was gradually developing into a variegated piece, characterized by variety rather than by uniformity of texture and style, and Terradellas contributed to the course of this development.

His church music contains the same degree of vigour and the same elements of contrast. Here he demonstrated his skill in composing for large choir, often divided into two or four groups which might themselves be doubled in loud passages. Well-developed choral fugues occur in some of his masses. At the end of his career he is said to have reacted against these types of technique. Following a meeting with Terradellas, which presumably occurred in Paris in about 1747, Rousseau reported in his *Lettre sur la musique française* (Paris, 1753) that the composer expressed himself ashamed of his earlier motets with their 'laboured' choruses. 'Once upon a time', Rousseau quotes him as saying, 'I loved to create noise; now I try to make music'.

WORKS

STAGE

(all operas unless otherwise stated)

Astarto (heroic opera, Zeno and P. Pariati), Rome, Delle Dame, carn. 1739
Cerere (componimento per musica), Rome, 20 Jan 1740
Gli intrighi delle cantarine (comic opera, A. Palomba), Naples, Fiorentini, 1740
Issipile (? Metastasio), Florence, 1741 or 1742
Merope (Zeno), Rome, Delle Dame, 3 Jan 1743; *A-Wn*; 2 copies *I-Bc* [1 entitled Epitide]; ov., 13 arias and 3 recits *GB-Cfm*
Artaserse (Metastasio), Venice, S Giovanni Grisostomo, carn. 1744; *I-Vnm*, 7 arias *Vqs*
Semiramide riconosciuta (Metastasio), Florence, Pergola, carn. 1746
Annibale in Capua (pasticcio, F. Vanneschi), London, King's, 4 Nov 1746, other music by Hasse, Lampugnani, Malegiac and Paradies; Favourite Songs (London, 1746)
Mitridate (Vanneschi), London, King's, 2 Dec 1746; Favourite Songs (London, 1746–7)
Bellerofonte (Vanneschi), London, King's, 24 March 1747; Favourite Songs (London, 1747)
Didone abbandonata (Metastasio), Turin, Regio, carn. 1750; ov., 10 arias *I-Rsc*
Imeneo in Atene (S. Stampiglia), Venice, S Samuele, 6 May 1750
Sesostri re d'Egitto (Zeno and Pariati), Rome, Delle Dame, carn. 1751; *D-MÜs, I-Rsc*

SACRED VOCAL

Giuseppe riconosciuto (oratorio, Metastasio), Naples, Oratory of S Filippo, 1736, *D-MÜs*
Ermenegildo martire (oratorio), Naples, Oratory of S Chiara, 1739, music lost
Missa solemnis, *B-Bc*; Mass, SATB, insts, *D-MÜs*; Mass, 5vv, insts, *E-V*; Kyrie–Gloria, 8vv, insts; Messa Lucina [Ky–Gl], SSATB, insts; Credo, SATB, insts: last 3 in S Maria di Monserrato, Rome
Confitebor di Napoli, *B-Bc*; Dixit Dominus, SATB, insts, *D-MÜs*; Te Deum, SATB, insts, *I-MOe*
Laudate, S, SATB, insts; Confitebor, SSATB, insts, 1743; Credidi, S, A, SATB, insts, 1744; Dixit Dominus, S, A, SATB, insts; Laetatus sum, S, A, SATB, insts, 1743; Debellato duce ingrato, SATB, insts, 1743; Domine me festina, SATB, insts, 1743; O diem fortunatum, SATB, insts, 1743; Praestantissime stellae, SSATB, insts, 1744: all in S Maria di Monserrato, Rome
Nocturna procella, *B-Bc*; Gloria patri, SATB, insts, *E-Mn*; Luminosa consurgit, SATB, insts, *GB-Lcm* and S Maria di Monserrato, Rome

OTHER WORKS

Dal oriente non nasce il sole, cantata, *I-Rsc*; Tradita sprezzata, cantata, *D-B*; Ov., D, *B-Bc*
Numerous arias, some from operas, in *A-Wn, B-Bc, D-B, Dlb, SWl, W,*

GB-Cfm, Lbm, I-Mc, Nc
Arias and other pieces in 18th-century anthologies

BIBLIOGRAPHY

BurneyH
J. R. Carreras i Bulbena: *Domènech Terradellas, compositor de la xviii centuria* (Barcelona, 1908)
H. Volkmann: 'Domenico Terradellas', *ZIMG*, xiii (1911–12), 306
U. Prota-Giurleo: *Nicola Logroscino 'il dio dell'opera buffa'* (Naples, 1927)
S. di Giacomo: *I quattro antichi conservatorii musicali di Napoli*, ii (Palermo, 1928)
J. Roca: 'La producció musical de Domènec Terradellas, deixeble de Durante', *Revista musical catalana*, xxxi (1934), 305
J. Subirá: *Història de la música* (Barcelona, 1947–58)

MICHAEL F. ROBINSON

Terrasse, Claude (Antoine) (*b* Grand-Lemps, Isère, 27 Jan 1867; *d* Paris, 30 June 1923). French composer. He studied the organ at the Lyons Conservatory and then entered the Ecole Niedermeyer in Paris. His teacher was Eugène Gigout, organist of St Augustin, with whom his studies continued privately after Gigout left the Niedermeyer in 1883. After a period in the army and as a piano teacher at Arcachon (Gironde), Terrasse returned to Paris in 1895. He began to compose incidental music for the theatre, notably for Alfred Jarry's *Ubu-Roi* (1896) and Ferdinand Hérold's *Savitri* (1898). He had previously written only piano music and a few religious works, but he now found his métier in *opéra bouffe*; his works formed a conspicuous part of the renaissance of this genre which followed the last examples by Audran and Strauss, and was contemporary with Lecocq's last pieces. Debussy, reviewing *Le sire de Vergy* (1903), acknowledged Terrasse's success and praised his invention and orchestration.

The appeal of Terrasse's works in over 30 years came partly from the distinction of his librettists, who were active contributors to a vintage period of French light comedy; they included De Flers and De Caillavet, Tristan Bernard and Franc-Nohain. Jarry himself was a co-librettist. Terrasse also wrote incidental music for Georges Courteline's *Godefroy*, *L'expulsion d'Antoine* and *Panthéon-Courcelles*.

WORKS

(printed works published in Paris)

c28 operettas, first perf. in Paris unless otherwise indicated, and pubd in same year, incl.: Les travaux d'Hercule (3 acts, R. de Flers, G. A. de Caillavet), 7 March 1901; Le sire de Vergy (3, Flers, Caillavet), 16 April 1903; M. de la Palisse (3, Flers, Caillavet), 2 Nov 1904; Le mariage de Télémaque (5, M. Donnay, after J. Lemaître), 4 May 1910; Pantagruel (5, E. Demolder, A. Jarry), Lyons, 30 Jan 1911
Incidental music to several plays incl. Ubu-Roi (Jarry), 1896, pubd (pf and vocal score) in Répertoire des pantins (1898)
Les lucioles (ballet), Paris, Opéra-Comique, 28 Dec 1910
Songs, incl. 3 chansons à la charcutière (Franc-Nohain) and 3 others, pubd in Répertoire des pantins (1898)
[19] Petites scènes familières, pf (1895); other pf and inst music
2 masses; motets

BIBLIOGRAPHY

R. Dumesnil: *Portraits de musiciens* (Paris, 1938)
A. Jarry: *Oeuvres complètes* (Lausanne, 1948), viii
C. Debussy: *Monsieur Croche et autres écrits*, ed. F. Lesure (Paris, 1971)

DAVID CHARLTON

Terrieria [Tarreria, Tarriera, Terriera], **Francesco** (*b* Conegliano, nr. Treviso; *fl* 1596–1606). Italian composer. The dedication of *Madrigali . . . libro primo* states that these are early works. He probably died young.

WORKS

[18] Madrigali . . . libro primo, 5vv (Venice, 1596)
Messa, salmi per i vesperi, et motetti . . . libro primo, 8vv, org (Venice, 1601)
Il secondo libro de [17] madrigali, 5vv (Venice, 1606)

Magnificat, 7vv, 1600[1]
Vespri, libro 1 e 2, 7vv, lost, cited in Giunta catalogue (see Kast)

BIBLIOGRAPHY

G. O. Pitoni: *Notitia de contrapuntisti e de compositori di musica* (MS, *I-Rvat* C.G., 1/1–2, c1725)
N. Bridgman: 'Musique profane italienne des 16e et 17e siècles', *FAM*, ii (1955), 54
P. Kast: 'Die Musikdrucke des Katalogs Giunta von 1604', *AnMc*, no.2 (1965), 41

PIER PAOLO SCATTOLIN

Terry, Charles Sanford (*b* Newport Pagnell, 24 Oct 1864; *d* Westerton of Pitfodels, nr. Aberdeen, 5 Nov 1936). English historian and Bach scholar. Descended from a line of doctors, he was educated at St Paul's Cathedral Choir School, where he was a solo boy under Stainer, and later at King's College School (then in the Strand) and Lancing. From 1883 to 1886 he read history at Clare College, Cambridge, devoting his spare time to music. In 1890 he went to Newcastle upon Tyne as lecturer in history at what was then the Durham College of Science, and founded the College Choral Society. In 1898 he took a similar post at the University of Aberdeen; here he set up a choral society of 150, with an orchestra of 70, which he conducted himself. In 1903 he was appointed to the newly founded Burnett-Fletcher Chair of History at Aberdeen, and held the post until he retired in 1930. In that year he lectured on Bach in America and Canada, and in 1935 he became an Hon. PhD of Leipzig. He received several other honorary degrees and distinctions, and in 1914 Elgar dedicated a partsong to him.

As a historian, he contributed to the Cambridge Medieval and Modern Histories, dealing chiefly with Scottish affairs. He was particularly successful with the involved and obscure problems of the 17th and 18th centuries, all the more because he was able to treat them from a broad European point of view – thanks partly to the lifelong interest in German culture that presumably led him to study the Bachs from about 1915 onwards. In musical matters he sometimes made elementary mistakes, which is strange, considering his wide practical experience; he never knew the difference between Bach's writing and his wife's; and his original ideas – such as his attempt to show that Bach wrote the *Orgel-Büchlein* in prison – were not always sound. But he was excellent at collecting and organizing information. He was the first to take J. C. Bach seriously as a subject for general research. His biography of J. S. Bach remains the only one that is both detailed and readable; its merits were immediately recognized, and a German translation appeared within a year. His complete edition of the chorales (adequately supplied with German and English words), his translations of Forkel (London, 1920) and of cantata texts, with his studies of the Leipzig liturgy, the origins of the chorales, and the instruments of the period, are all easy to consult, and still valuable if used with caution. He also helped to popularize the major choral works by producing booklets that served as superior programme notes. In his time, he probably did as much as any man to advance the study of Bach. His widow gave his Bach library to the RCM; with it is a pencil portrait of Terry by J. B. Souter.

WRITINGS

Articles on the whole Bach family and related subjects in *Grove 3–5*
Bach's Mass in B minor: a Study (Glasgow, 1915)
Bach's Chorals (Cambridge, 1915–21)
Bach: the Mass in B minor (London, 1924, rev. 2/1931, 7/1958)
Bach: the Cantatas and Oratorios (London, 1925)
Bach: the Passions (London, 1926)
Joh. Seb. Bach: Cantata Texts, sacred and secular, with a Reconstruction of the Leipzig Liturgy of his Period (London, 1926)
Bach: a Biography (London, 1928, rev. 2/1933, 6/1967)
Bach: the Magnificat, Lutheran Masses, and Motets (London, 1929)
John Christian Bach (London, 1929/R1980, rev. 2/1967 by. H. C. R. Landon)
The Origin of the Family of Bach Musicians (London, 1929)
Bach: the Historical Approach (London, 1930)
Bach's Orchestra (London, 1932, 4/1966)
The Music of Bach (London, 1933/R1963)

EDITIONS

Coffee and Cupid (*The Coffee Cantata*): *an Operetta by Johann Sebastian Bach* (London, 1924)
The Four-part Chorals of J. S. Bach (London, 1929, 2/1964)

BIBLIOGRAPHY

A. M. Mackenzie: 'Terry, Charles Sanford', *DNB*
Obituary, *MT*, lxxvii (1936), 1137
A. Schering: Obituary, *BJb*, xxxiii (1936), 115
M. Campbell: *Dolmetsch: the Man and his Work* (London, 1975)

WALTER EMERY

Terry, Sir **R(ichard) R(unciman)** (*b* Ellington, Northumberland, 3 Jan 1865; *d* London, 18 April 1938). English organist and musical scholar. He became organist and music master at Elstow School in 1890, organist and choirmaster of St John's Cathedral, Antigua, in 1892, and in 1896 was appointed to a similar post at Downside Abbey, Somerset, where he began his work of reviving the music written for the Latin ritual by early English composers. He was the first to perform liturgically the three- and five-part masses by Byrd, Tye's *Euge bone*, Tallis's four-part Mass and Lamentations, Mundy's Mass *Upon the Square* and motets by Morley, Parsons, White and others. When Westminster Cathedral was built he was appointed organist and director of music, a post which he held with great distinction from 1901 until 1924, when he resigned after increasing criticism of his bold choice of works. Terry was able to establish at Westminster Cathedral a tradition of musical treatment for the whole of the Roman liturgy in England based on the principles laid down in the *Motu proprio*, so that the Use of Westminster offered an example to Roman Catholic church musicians unequalled anywhere outside Rome itself. He set a high standard of performance and demonstrated the great wealth of English liturgical music of the finest period. He revived Peter Philips's *Cantiones sacrae*, Byrd's *Gradualia* and *Cantiones sacrae*, the *Cantiones* of Tallis and Byrd, White's Lamentations, and motets by Dering, Fayrfax, Sheppard, Tye and others. He also performed the fourth volume of Jacob Handl's *Opus musicum*.

Terry did much editorial work, especially of early English church music (e.g. Byrd's Mass for five voices, London, 1935; 24 motets in Novello's series of Tudor motets, London, 1937). He also published modern editions of Calvin's first psalter of 1539 (London, 1932) and the Scottish Psalter of 1635 (London, 1935). He was the first chairman of the Carnegie Trust's editorial committee for Tudor Church Music, and his *Westminster Hymnal* (London, 1912, rev. 3/1916, 7/1937) was for many years the standard hymnal for Roman Catholic use in Britain. He was awarded an honorary MusD by Durham in 1911 and knighted in 1922.

WRITINGS

Catholic Church Music (London, 1907, enlarged 2/1931 as *The Music of the Roman Rite*)
'The Music of the Byzantine Liturgy', *PMA*, xxxv (1908–9), 53
'Sea Songs and Shanties', *PMA*, xli (1914–15), 135
'John Merbecke (1523(?)–1585)', *PMA*, xlv (1918–19), 75

'Giovanni de Palestrina (1525–1594)', *The Heritage of Music*, ed. H. J. Foss, i (London, 1927), 3
On Music's Borders (London, 1927)
A Forgotten Psalter and other Essays (London, 1929) [Scottish Psalter, 1635]
'Calvin's First Psalter, 1539', *PMA*, lvii (1930–31), 1
Voodooism in Music and other Essays (London, 1934)
'Byrd'; 'Palestrina', *Lives of the Great Composers*, ed. A. L. Bacharach (London, 1935), 131; 423; repr. in *The Music Masters*, ed. A. L. Bacharach (London, 1948–54), i, 79; 291

BIBLIOGRAPHY
W. H. Hadow: Speech given at Terry's MusD conferment, *MT*, lii (1911), 525
H. F. Andrews: *Westminster Retrospect: a Memoir of Sir Richard Terry* (London, 1948)

J. A. FULLER MAITLAND/H. C. COLLES/PETER PLATT

Ter-T'at'evosyan, Hovhannes Gurgeni (*b* Erevan, 14 Sept 1926). Armenian composer. He graduated from Boghdanyan's violin class at the Erevan Conservatory in 1952, and from Mirzoyan's composition class in 1957. His music combines national traditions with new techniques; the individuality of this style was evident in his earliest works, despite the debts to Shostakovich and Mirzoyan. Two features are particularly characteristic: an emphasis on the linear, sometimes leading to polytonality, and a predilection for monothematic variation. Expressive force is sometimes enhanced by the construction in vast planes, or by the clash of contrasting thematic areas. The use of a single germinal motif is exemplified by the First Symphony; the integrity of the Second Quartet is assured by means of 12-note serialism.

WORKS
(*selective list*)
Liricheskaya, sym. poem, 1955; 2 str qts, 1955, 1967; Sym. no.1, 1957; Sym. no.2 (Sholokhov: Sud'ba cheloveka [The fate of a man]), 1960; Pamyati E. Charentsa [In memory of E. Charents], sym. poem, 1962; O revolyutsii i partii [Revolution and the party] (Mayakovsky), speaker, orch, 1965; Vn Conc, 1973
Inst pieces, songs, film scores

SVETLANA SARKISIAN

Terteryan, Avet (*b* Baku, 29 July 1929). Armenian composer. In 1957 he studied with Mirzoyan at the Erevan Conservatory, where he was later appointed to the staff. His confidently written music is formed in a synthetic manner from diverse materials: Armenian *sharakan* (hymns), free 12-note music, aleatory devices and Xenakis-like blocks, sometimes including parts for non-tempered folk instruments.

WORKS
(*selective list*)
Stage: Ring of Fire (opera, after Lavrenyov, Charents), 1967, Erevan, Opera, 1972; Richard III (ballet, after Shakespeare), 1977–
Vocal orch: The Motherland (Shiraz), 1957; The Revolution (Charents), 1960
Orch: Sym. no.1, 1969; Sym. no.2, 1972; Sym. no.3, 1975; Sym. no.4, 1976
Chamber: Str Qt, 1963

BIBLIOGRAPHY
K. Khudabashyan: 'Romanticheskaya epopeya', *SovM* (1967), no.9, p.32
S. Sarkisian: 'O stile sovremennoy armyanskoy operi', *Muzïka v sotsialisticheskom obshchestve*, iii (Leningrad, 1977)
R. Step'anyan: *Avet Terteryan* (Erevan, 1978)

SVETLANA SARKISIAN

Tertia. (1) (Ger.) An ORGAN STOP (*Tierce*).
(2) (Lat.) TERCE.

Tertian (Ger.). An ORGAN STOP.

Tertiary [tertian] **harmony.** A term for a harmonic system based on the interval of a 3rd (as in the major–minor tonal system), as opposed to the QUARTAL HARMONY of the Middle Ages.

Tertis, Lionel (*b* West Hartlepool, 29 Dec 1876; *d* London, 22 Feb 1975). English viola player. He studied violin at the Hochschule für Musik in Leipzig and at the RAM, London, where the principal, Alexander Mackenzie, urged him to specialize in viola playing. Following this sound advice he became the foremost player of his instrument and toured Europe and the USA as a soloist. He had to overcome much prejudice before the public accepted the viola as a solo instrument, and to do a great deal of pioneer work to find music to play. Many British composers wrote specially for him: McEwen, Bax, Benjamin Dale, Bowen, Bridge and Harry Farjeon. Although much of this music failed to maintain a permanent place, it served the double purpose of providing an immediate repertory and an inspiration to such later composers as Walton, Vaughan Williams and Bliss.

Tertis produced a big powerful tone of much beauty and intensity. He played on a large viola to achieve his aim of a rich and resonant C-string tone which bordered on the quality of a cello and avoided the characteristic nasal quality of the smaller viola. So keen was he on this depth of tone that he designed a large viola in collaboration with the English maker, Arthur Richardson; through his enthusiasm he inspired players and instrument makers to adopt his ideal (*see* VIOLA, fig.1*b*). On similar principles, he designed a cello in 1960 and a violin in 1962. In 1936 Tertis retired, and spent his time teaching and encouraging interest in the viola. He continued to play for special occasions, the last being when he was 87. He made numerous transcriptions, many of which filled gaps in the scanty repertory; others, like those of Mozart's Clarinet Concerto and Elgar's Cello Concerto, were criticized as concert pieces but are valuable to students. In 1950 he was made a CBE. On his 90th birthday EMI reissued on LP some of his cele-

Lionel Tertis

brated 78s, including his performance with Sammons of Mozart's Sinfonia concertante.

WRITINGS

Beauty of Tone in String Playing (London, 1938)
'Introduction to an English Viola', *ML*, xxviii (1947), 214 [with diagram]

BIBLIOGRAPHY

L. Tertis: *Cinderella No More* (London, 1953, rev. and enlarged, 1974, as *My Viola and I*, incl. *Beauty of Tone* and other writings) [autobiography, with discography by M. Walker]

WATSON FORBES

Terz (Ger.). An ORGAN STOP (*Tierce*).

Terzago [Terzagus, Terzagi], **Bernardinus** [Bernardino] (*b* Rome, *fl* 1623–5). Italian composer and singer, resident in Poland. He worked at Kraków Cathedral from September 1623 to August 1625. He went to Poland from Rome, where he had probably been born, since in the cathedral records he is sometimes described as 'Romanus'. He was a member both of the Cappella Rorantistarum, which sang in the so-called Sigismund Chapel, and of the cathedral's main vocal and instrumental forces. Three four-part compositions by him are known: *Patrem omnipotentem* (dated 25 December 1623); an antiphon of St Martin, *O beatum pontificem* (dated 1624); and *Sancte Sebastiane* (written on 18 January 1624). All are in the Kraków Municipal Archive (they were formerly in *PL-Kk*). The first two are for boys' and men's voices and must therefore have been intended for the main cathedral chapel, while the third, which is for low voices, must have been written for the Cappella Rorantistarum, which consisted only of natural men's voices. Despite some rhythmically interesting polyphony in *O beatum pontificem*, the pieces are stereotyped and conservative, an impression reinforced by the even note values of the cantus firmi. The title of *Patrem omnipotentem* continues 'na augment Bernardyńskie'. It is not clear what this means, though it probably suggests that the cantus firmus was derived from the melody of a pseudo-chorale.

BIBLIOGRAPHY

SMP

A. Chybiński: 'Muzycy w kapelach katedralnych krakowskich, 1619–1657' [Musicians of Kraków Cathedral chapel, 1619–1657], *Przegląd muzyczny* (1926), nos.11–12; (1927), nos.1–5, 7, 8; also pubd separately (Kraków, 1927)

——: *Słownik muzyków dawnej Polski* [Dictionary of early Polish musicians] (Kraków, 1948–9), 129

E. Głuszcz-Zwolińska: *Zbiory muzyczne proweniencji wawelskiej* [The collection of music originally from Wawel Castle archives], *Musicalia vetera: katalog tematyczny rękopiśmiennych zabytków dawnej muzyki w Polsce* [Musicalia vetera: thematic catalogue of early Polish music], ed. Z. M. Szweykowski, i/2 (Kraków, 1972)

E. Głuszcz-Zwolińska: *Twórczość kompozytorów włoskich z I połowy XVII wieku dla kapeli rorantystów wawelskich* [The work of Italian composers of the first half of the 17th century for the Cappella Rorantistarum at Wawel] (Warsaw, 1974), 204ff

MIROSŁAW PERZ

Terzakis, Dimitri (*b* Athens, 12 March 1938). Greek composer. He studied the piano under Thurneissen and theory and composition under Yannis Papaioannou at the Hellenic Conservatory, Athens (1959–64). Then he spent the years 1965–9 at the Musikhochschule in Cologne, where he studied composition with Zimmermann and electronic music with Eimert. His music has developed from an expanded tonality (*Prelude* and *Legend*) through 12-note serialism (e.g. the Sinfonietta) to a fruitful exploration of micro-intervals, principally in his melody, based on Byzantine music. This interest began with *Ikos* (1968) and has continued to

preoccupy Terzakis. Works by him have been performed at the ISCM Festival in Basle (1970), the Darmstadt summer courses (1970) and the Hamburg Das Neue Werk series (1972). In 1974 he was appointed to teach counterpoint and fugue and, later, Byzantine music and composition at the Musikhochschule of Düsseldorf.

WORKS
(*selective list*)

STAGE

Circus Universal (chamber opera, 1, A. Terzakis), 1974–5
Thomas Torquemada (opera, 1, A. Terzakis), 1974–6

VOCAL

Medea (Euripides), S, ens, 1966; Oceanides (Aeschylus: Prometheus), 2 S, Mez, orch, 1967; Clytaemnestra (Aeschylus: Eumenides), S, ens, 1967; Ikos (Romanos the Melode), chorus, 1968; Nuances (textless), Mez, va, perc, tape, 1970; X (textless), Bar, chorus, ens, tapes, 1971; 3 Pieces, 1v, 1972; Katavassia (Romanos), 2 S, Mez, Ct, T, Bar, 1972; Stichiron (St John Damascene), chorus, ob, cl, hn, trbn, tuba, perc, 1972; Ethos B (textless), Mez, fl, vc, 1973; Von Feuer und Finsternis (J. Böhme, St John of the Cross, Heraclitus), 16vv chorus, 1974; Ethos C I (textless), Bar/Mez. 1975; Nomoi (Heraclitus), psaltis, 1v, cl, vc, santouri, perc, 1975; Notturni (Sappho), 6 solo vv, cl, vn, perc, 1976; Ethos C ii (papyrus W. Leiden), Bar, pf, 1977; Liturgia profana (Song of Songs, Sappho, Egyptian Book of the Dead), psaltis, T, mixed vv, 2 vc, santouri, perc, 1977; Odyssey (Homer), S, T, Bar, mixed vv, chamber orch, 1977–; Sappho Fragmente, S, 1978

ORCHESTRAL

Divertimento, 1961; Prelude, 1961; Picture, str, 1963; Legend, 1964; Sinfonietta, 1965; Echochronos II, 9 insts, 1968, rev. 1974; Chroai, 1970; Echochronos III, 1970; Hommage à Morse, 1971; Transcriptions télégraphiques, 1971; Ethos A, ens, tapes, 1972; Kosmogramm, 1973–4; Schatten (Tropoi), 1975

OTHER WORKS

Aphorisms, pf, 1964; Septet, 7 fl, 1965; Trio, gui, vc, perc, 1966; Echochronos I, tape, 1968; Str Qt, 1969–70; Stixis I, ob, 1970; 3 Pieces, vn, 1972; Stixis II, cl, 1973; Duo, vc, perc, 1973; Stixis III, tuba, 1974; To alloithoro psari [The squint-eyed fish], tape, 1974; Str Qt no.2, 1976; Omega I, vc, 1978; incidental music for 22 plays

Principal publishers: Bärenreiter, Gerig

WRITINGS

'Auf der Such nach neuem Tonhöhenmaterial', *Melos*, xxxviii (1971), 190
'Die byzantinische Musik', *Musik und Bildung* (1971), no.10, p.467

GEORGE S. LEOTSAKOS

Terza mano (It.). An ORGAN STOP.

Terzet (Ger. *Terzett*; It. *terzetto*). A composition for three voices with or without accompaniment. The term was defined by J. G. Walther (*Musicalisches Lexicon*, 1732) and occasionally appears in scores from the first half of the 18th century (e.g. Handel's *Solomon*, 1748, and J. S. Bach's Cantata no.38). Many compositions for three voices were written before then, however, in the forms of the TRICINIUM, the madrigal and the villanella in the Renaissance; accompanied pieces for three similar voices were not infrequent in 17th-century opera and oratorio, for example the three *famigliari* in Monteverdi's *L'incoronazione di Poppea* (1642) and the interludes for the three shepherds and three wise men in Schütz's *Weihnachts-historie* (1664).

In the Classical period the 'terzett' (so named in the scores) frequently appears. Mozart's *Le nozze di Figaro* and *Die Zauberflöte* contain celebrated examples. In the latter work that for the three boys, 'Seid uns zum zweitenmal willkommen', continues the earlier operatic tradition of trios for similar voices (which survived to Wagner's time in the three Norns and three Rhinemaidens of the *Ring*), though in general the name implies no limitation of voices of this kind nor any particular style of treatment. For the little trio 'Soave sia il vento' in *Così fan tutte* Mozart used the diminutive, 'terzettino'. The terzetts in Weber's *Der Freischütz* include one with a choral conclusion; that from Mendelssohn's *Elijah* for the three angels, 'Lift thine eyes to the mountains', is in every feature simply an unaccompanied partsong. Dvořák called his op.74 trio for two violins and viola 'Terzetto', but the use of the term for instrumental music in the sense of 'Trio' is uncommon.

MICHAEL TILMOUTH

Terzi, Giovanni Antonio (*fl* Bergamo, *c*1580–1620). Italian lutenist and composer. The title of his *Gagliarda nova del padre dell'auttore* indicates that his father was a musician. He was apparently an accomplished singer as well as a lutenist. Donato Calvi, a literary man of Bergamo, wrote that 'he loved vocal music, but even more that of instruments; and if with his voice he emulated the harmony of the heavens, with the sound of his lute he vied with that of the angels'. His two surviving lutebooks show him to have been a virtuoso player. Both contain intabulations ranging from madrigals, canzonas and motets to instrumental pieces and dances of all kinds. The first book includes 17 compositions with two lute parts; they may be played as duos, or each part may be performed separately, as a solo. 11 other pieces 'per suonar in concerti...& solo' have only one lute part, and are presumably intended for ensemble performance in unison. The later collection offers a similar repertory, including pieces for two lutes, one for four lutes and one for a viola bastarda to play with a 'liutto grande' (theorbo). Of the numerous dances and purely instrumental pieces, very few are by Terzi. Several of the intabulations include texts, but the voice part is not indicated. Both collections draw on popular repertory, and are interesting reflections of contemporary taste.

Terzi was an extraordinarily skilful intabulator; his arrangements never obscure the original compositions, but it is clear that he was chiefly concerned with solo performance in a brilliant, virtuoso style. He delighted in rapid figurations and arabesques.

WORKS

Intavolatura di liutto, accomodata con diversi passaggi per suonar in concerti a duoi liutti, & solo, libro primo (Venice, 1593/*R*1964); 15 pieces transcr. for gui in O. Chilesotti: *Lautenspieler des 16. Jahrhunderts* (Leipzig, 1891, repr. 1926)

Il secondo libro de intavolatura di liuto (Venice, 1599)

BIBLIOGRAPHY

BrownI

D. Calvi: *Scena letteraria* (Bergamo, 1664)

C. MacClintock: 'Two Lute Intabulations of Wert's *Cara la vita*', *Essays in Musicology: a Birthday Offering for Willi Apel* (Bloomington, Ind., 1968)

CAROL MacCLINTOCK

Terzian (Ger.). An ORGAN STOP (*Tertian*).

Terziani, Eugenio (*b* Rome, 30 July 1824; *d* Rome, 30 June 1889). Italian conductor, teacher and composer, son of Pietro Terziani. He studied under Mercadante at the Naples Conservatory and later under Baini in Rome. He became a member of the Filarmonica in Rome (1842) and in 1843 conducted then for the first time, though in a private rehearsal. His first opera, *Giovanna I*, was performed at Ferrara in Carnival 1844. He fought as a volunteer in the Garibaldi brigade (Legion Lipari, 1848). From 1847 to 1868 he was the conductor of the Teatro Apollo in Rome, where his *Alfredo* was given in 1852, and from 1867 to 1871 at La Scala. The Milanese did not like him, but Verdi admired him and entrusted him with the revised *La forza del destino* in

1869. From 1871 to 1875 he was again at the Apollo in Rome, but his stay was continually marred by critical opprobrium. Nevertheless, he was considered by many one of the most illustrious and learned of Roman musicians. From 1875 he held the composition chair at the Liceo Musicale di S Cecilia; he also taught singing (according to Schmidl, he was vice-president there). One of his last concerts (1887) was a benefit for a monument to Rossini in Santa Croce.

The last of Terziani's three operas, *L'assedio di Firenze* (1883), published in vocal score by Lucca in Milan, is a four-act *dramma lirico* which owes much to Verdi: the short Prelude with two motifs; the texture of tremolo chords under a melody doubled by voice and orchestra, as in *Aida*; a scena and monologue for the tenor. The musical style is more interesting than that of most Italian operas of the day. Among his other works are two ballets (both early), several sacred pieces, including a Requiem (1882), an *Inno sinfonico* (1882) and various occasional items.

Terziani's son Raffaele (1860–1928) was artistic director of the Reale Filarmonica Romana (1890–95), a singing teacher at the Accademia di S Cecilia, and later its acting director (1915–16) and vice-director (1917–23). He composed sacred music, instrumental pieces and an opera, *Aman*; although never performed, it won a prize in the first Sonzogno competition (1889).

MARVIN TARTAK

Terziani, Pietro (*b* Rome, 1765; *d* Rome, 5 Oct 1831). Italian composer. A pupil of G. B. Casali in Rome, in 1780 he entered the Conservatorio di S Onofrio, Naples, where Carlo Cotumacci and Giacomo Insanguine were his teachers. He afterwards returned to Rome to study the strict *a cappella* style of composition, again under Casali. In 1784 he was admitted to the Bologna Accademia Filarmonica, composing a four-part antiphon as his test piece, and at about the same time also became a member of the Rome Accademia di S Cecilia, of which he was an officer from 1797 to 1803. In the early years of his career he composed two operas, *Il geloso imprudente* (Rome, 1785) and *Creso* (Venice, 1788), and some oratorios. After the French invasion of Italy at the end of the century he went to Vienna, where he remained until the end of the Napoleonic wars, composing an opera there (*I campi d'Ivri*, 1805). He then returned to Rome and in 1816 became *maestro di cappella* at St John Lateran and later at the churches of Il Gesù, S Ignazio and S Silvestro. In this period he devoted himself exclusively to sacred music. He composed in both the strict and free accompanied styles and was highly regarded as a contrapuntist, although Schilling regarded his works as insufficiently powerful for performance in large churches. A large number of masses, graduals, offertories, antiphons, psalms, hymns, motets and other sacred pieces survive in libraries and church archives in Italy and elsewhere (*A-Wgm*, *Wn*, *B-Bc*, *D-Mbs*, *MÜs*, *I-Baf*, *Bc*, *Bsf*, *Mcap*(*d*), *MOe*, *Nc*, *Rsc*, *US-NYp*); some were published.

Terziani's sons Gustavo and Eugenio both became musicians; Gustavo (*b* Vienna, 17 Feb 1813; *d* Rome, 31 Aug 1837) was a pupil of his father and Baini, but died before establishing a reputation as a composer.

BIBLIOGRAPHY

EitnerQ; *FétisB*

G. Schilling: 'Terziano, Pietro', *Encyclopädie der gesammten musikalischen Wissenschaften oder Universal-Lexikon der Tonkunst*, vi (Stuttgart, 1838/*R*1973)

P. Alfieri: *Brevi notizie storiche sulla congregazione ed accademia de' maestri e professori di musica di Roma sotto l'invocazione di Santa Cecilia* (Rome, 1845), 61

SIEGFRIED GMEINWIESER

Terzina (It.). TRIPLET.

Terzposaune (Ger.). A trombone pitched a 3rd below the ordinary trombone. *See* QUARTPOSAUNE.

Terzzimbel (Ger.). An ORGAN STOP (*Zimbel*).

Terzzug (Ger.). In Schenkerian analysis a diatonic melodic progression encompassing the interval of a 3rd, e.g. $f'-g'-a'$, $e\flat-d-c$ (*see* ZUG (i)).

Teschemacher, Frank (*b* Kansas City, Missouri, 14 March 1906; *d* Chicago, 1 March 1932). American jazz clarinettist, alto saxophonist and violinist. He spent his childhood in Chicago, where he studied various instruments and around 1922 helped to found the 'Austin High School Gang' of young Chicago jazz musicians. He played with Jimmy McPartland and other members of this group in various bands, and from 1926 performed mainly in commercial dance orchestras in Chicago, though he continued to record in small jazz groups. In summer 1928 he performed with Red Nichols in New York. Teschemacher's importance to jazz rests primarily in his performing style as a clarinettist, though he played regularly only from 1925 to about 1930. He was strongly influenced by Bix Beiderbecke, and his best playing makes telling use of the distinctive articulation and accented 9ths and 11ths of Beiderbecke's cornet style. His 'dirty' tone resembles (and may have influenced) that of PeeWee Russell and the young Benny Goodman. His low-register solo on *Darktown Strutters Ball* was frequently copied, but poor intonation and insecure technique mar many of his recordings, of which he made about two dozen before his early death.

BIBLIOGRAPHY
N. Shapiro and N. Hentoff, eds.: *Hear me Talkin' to ya* (New York, 1955), 118ff
R. Hadlock: *Jazz Masters of the Twenties* (New York, 1965), 106ff
B. Rust: *Jazz Records: 1897–1942* (London, 1965, rev. 2/1969)

J. R. TAYLOR

Teschemacher, Margarete (*b* Cologne, 3 March 1903; *d* Bad Wiessee, 19 May 1959). German soprano. She studied in Cologne where she made her début in 1924 as Micaela. Engagements followed at Aachen (1925–7), Dortmund (1927–8), Mannheim (1928–31), Stuttgart (1931–4), Dresden (1935–46) and Düsseldorf (1947–52). At Dresden she created the title role in Strauss's *Daphne* (1938) and Miranda in Sutermeister's *Zauberinsel* (1942); she was also the first Dresden Countess in *Capriccio* (1944). She sang Pamina and Elsa at Covent Garden in 1931 and Countess Almaviva and Donna Elvira during the Dresden Staatsoper's London visit in 1936. In 1934 she appeared at the Teatro Colón, Buenos Aires, where she sang the title role in *Arabella*, Senta, Sieglinde and Mařenka. Teschemacher's roles also included Jenůfa, Minnie (*La fanciulla del West*), and Zandonai's Francesca da Rimini. Her warm lyric–dramatic voice was one of the best of its kind, especially during her Dresden days.

HAROLD ROSENTHAL

Teschner, Gustav Wilhelm (*b* Magdeburg, 26 Dec 1800; *d* Dresden, 7 May 1883). German singer, teacher and music editor. He studied singing and composition with C. F. Zelter and Klein, then went to Italy, where he studied with Ronconi, Bianchi and Crescentini. Through his acquaintance with Fortunato Santini he became interested in old Latin and German church music. Returning to Germany, he studied singing in Dresden with Miksch, and then settled in Berlin as a singing teacher using Italian principles. In 1873 he was appointed Royal Prussian Professor. His numerous editions of old church music include H. L. Hassler's *Psalmen und christliche Gesänge*, Eccard's *Geistliche Lieder auf den Choral* and *Preussiche Festlieder* by Eccard and Stobaeus. He also published several collections of solfèges by Minoja, Crescentini, Zingarelli and Clari, as well as some of his own vocal exercises. His collection of early music is in the Deutsche Staatsbibliothek, Berlin.

BIBLIOGRAPHY
R. Schaal: 'Teschner, Gustav Wilhelm', *MGG*

ELIZABETH FORBES

Teschner, Melchior (*b* Fraustadt [now Wschowa], Silesia, 29 April 1584; *d* Oberpritschen [now Przyczyna Górna], nr. Fraustadt, 1 Dec 1635). German clergyman and composer. From 1602 he studied theology, philosophy and music at Frankfurt an der Oder; Bartholomäus Gesius was among those who taught him music. In 1605 he became Kantor at Schmiegel (now Smigiel). After further study, at the universities of Helmstedt and Wittenberg, he became Kantor of the Protestant Kirche zum Kripplein Christi at Fraustadt in 1609. From 1614 until his death he was pastor of the church at Oberpritschen. The pastor with whom he worked at Fraustadt from 1609 was Valerius Herberger, who wrote the text of the hymn *Valet will ich dir geben* in 1613 after surviving a plague. Teschner made two five-part settings of it, which were published at Leipzig in 1615. The second of them (in Winterfeld), which is modelled on the Geneva psalm *O Seigneur, que de gens* by Loys Bourgeois (1550), is still popular and has been reprinted in hymnals up to the present day, often with different words; with some modification it appears in English hymnbooks as the Palm Sunday hymn *All glory, laud and honour*. Teschner is otherwise known as a composer only by two wedding songs published respectively at Liegnitz in 1614 and at Leipzig in 1619.

BIBLIOGRAPHY
EitnerQ
S. F. Lauterbach: *Fraustädtisches Zion* (Leipzig, 1711)
C. von Winterfeld: *Der evangelische Kirchengesang*, iii (Leipzig, 1847/*R*1966), xviii f, 276
J. Zahn: *Die Melodien der deutschen evangelischen Kirchenlieder* (Gütersloh, 1889–93/*R*1963), iii, 406f; v, 411
S. Fornaçon: 'Melchior Teschner', *Musik und Kirche*, xvii (1957), 231
S. Büchner: 'Das Kirchenlied in Schlesien und der Oberlausitz', *Das evangelische Schlesien*, ed. G. Hultsch (Düsseldorf, 1971), 65

FRITZ FELDMANN

Teshbohtā. A category of chant in SYRIAN CHURCH MUSIC.

Tesi (Tramontini), Vittoria ['La Moretta'] (*b* Florence, 13 Feb 1700; *d* Vienna, 9 May 1775). Italian contralto. She received her first instruction from Francesco Redi in Florence and from Campeggi in Bologna. (An alleged meeting with Handel in Florence, in connection with the performance there of his opera *Rodrigo* in 1707, rests on a confusion between Tesi and Vittoria Tarquini.) She first appeared as an opera singer in 1716, in Parma (*Dafni*) and Bologna (*Il sogno avverato*). In the 1718–19 season she was in Venice as *virtuosa di camera* to Prince Antonio of Parma. By 1719 she was in Dresden, where she sang in Lotti's *Giove in Argo* for the opening of the new opera house on 3 September, and ten days later appeared as Matilda in his *Teofano*, thereby numbering (along with the singers Coralli, Durastanti, Santa Stella Lotti and the castrato Senesino) among the most prominent performers in the musical festivities surrounding the marriage of the Saxon electoral prince to the Archduchess Maria Josepha. With the dissolution of the Italian Opera Tesi left Dresden to return to Italy; in Carnival 1721 she sang in Florence and from there travelled until 1747, visiting all the great theatres of Italy between Naples, Venice and Milan, with a guest appearance in Madrid (1739–40) and perhaps a trip to Frankfurt in 1741–2 for the emperor's coronation. Her career reached a peak at the opening of the Teatro S Carlo in Naples (1737) and again ten years later when she appeared there with Caffarelli, Gizziello, Manzuoli and others in Calzabigi's serenata *Il sogno d'Olimpia*, with music by Majo.

In 1748 she appeared in Vienna, taking the title role in Gluck's setting of Metastasio's *Semiramide riconosciuta*. Details of who arranged her appearance there remain uncertain; Gluck had met her in Venice in 1744, when she sang the title role in his *Ipermestra*, but Metastasio had also known her previously, although he had no high opinion of her abilities (calling her a 'grandissima nullità') until her appearance in *Semiramide* convinced him to the contrary. Further successful stage appearances in Vienna included the title roles in Jommelli's settings of Metastasio's *Achille in Sciro* and *Didone abbandonata* (1749) and her later appearance as Lisinga in Metastasio's *Le cinesi*, set by Gluck for the famous Schlosshof festival of 24 September 1754. In the early 1750s she began her retirement from the stage. She was not engaged for the 1751–2 season in Naples because of her age; Metastasio, who shortly before had found her 'rejuvenated by 20 years', mentioned in autumn 1751 that Tesi was 'costume director' for the Vienna court theatre. After retiring from the stage Tesi devoted herself to the education of younger talent with considerable success; among her pupils were Catterina Gabrielli, Anna Lucia de Amicis and Elisabeth Teyber. In Vienna she enjoyed the special patronage of Maria Theresia and of Prince Joseph Friedrich of Hildburghausen, in whose palace (the present Palais Auersperg) she resided. Among those who met her there were Casanova (1753) and Leopold and W. A. Mozart (13 December 1762). Towards the end of her life she was given the honorary title *virtuosa della corte imperiale* and her husband was made an honorary *consigliere del commercio*. Two years before her death Ange and Sarah Goudar, apostrophizing her personality and achievement, called her 'perhaps the first actress who recited well while singing badly'. Many of her contemporaries, including Quantz, Mancini, Metastasio, Dittersdorf and Burney, found her incomparable in expression and stage bearing, and to Gerber (1792) she was one of the greatest singers of the century.

A Faustini Tesi, who combined the names of the famous singers Faustina Bordoni and Vittoria Tesi, may possibly be related to the latter; she was active from 1765 at various Italian theatres, including Venice

(1765), Piacenza (1775) and Naples (1777). Zinzendorf in 1778 mentioned 'cette Tesi vieille et laide' in Trieste.

BIBLIOGRAPHY
GerberL
A. Ademollo: 'Le cantanti italiane celebri del secolo decimottavo: Vittoria Tesi', *Nuova antologia di scienze, lettere ed arti*, 32nd ser., xxii (1889), 308
B. Croce: *Un prelato e una cantante del secolo XVIII* (Bari, 1946)
G. Zechmeister: *Die Wiener Theater nächst der Burg und nächst dem Kärntnerthor von 1747 bis 1776* (Vienna, 1971), 194ff
GERHARD CROLL

Tess, Giulia (*b* Milan, 19 Feb 1889; *d* Milan, 17 March 1976). Italian soprano, producer and teacher. She studied with Bottagisio in Verona, making her début at Venice in 1908, in the mezzo role of Mignon. After appearances in Prague, Vienna, St Petersburg and other centres, as Adalgisa, Leonora (*La favorite*), Amneris and Charlotte (*Werther*) she was advised by Battistini, opposite whom she had been singing, to become a soprano. After further study she established herself as a leading exponent of the *verismo* repertory. She created Jael in Pizzetti's *Debora e Jaele* (1922) at La Scala under Toscanini, and continued to appear in Milan until 1936, in such roles as Salome, Electra, and Orsola in the première of Wolf-Ferrari's *Il campiello*. She was the first Italian Ariadne (Turin, 1925), and sang the title role in the Italian première of Honegger's *Judith* (Naples, 1937). After her retirement in 1940 Tess became director of stagecraft at the Centro di Avviamento al Teatro Lirico, Florence. In 1942 she was appointed to a similar position at the Bologna Conservatory and in 1946 at La Scala's school. She produced *La Cenerentola* (La Scala, 1946), and later *I quattro rusteghi* and *L'elisir d'amore* at Florence; she came out of retirement to sing Orsola in her own production of *Il campiello* in Cagliari and Palermo in 1949 and 1950. She married the conductor Giacomo Armani (1868–1954).

HAROLD ROSENTHAL

Tessarini, Carlo (*b* Rimini, *c*1690; *d* ?Amsterdam, after 15 Dec 1766). Italian violinist and composer. The earliest known reference to him is in a charter of 15 December 1720, where he is mentioned as a violinist at St Mark's Cathedral, Venice. From 1729 he was also leader of the concerts of the Venetian Conservatory SS Giovanni e Paolo. At the end of 1731 he applied for a post in the chapel of Urbino Cathedral, and he probably worked there from about 1733 (he tried in the same year to obtain a substitute). The dedication of his op.4 (1735) to Cardinal Wolfgang Schrattenbach of Brno suggests that he stayed at the latter's court. Three years later, after the cardinal's death, he returned to Urbino, but in April 1739 he again asked for leave so that he could undertake concert tours. At the end of the year he returned and his contract was renewed until 1744. In 1740 and 1742 he visited Rome. In 1743 he called himself 'direttore perpetuo' of the Accademia degli Anarconti of Fano, a town near Urbino. He was also engaged (with Giovanni Francesco Tessarini, possibly his brother) in publishing; he issued works of his own and of others, including Joseph Canavas. From 1744, however, many of his works were published by Boivin in Paris and dedicated to members of the Parisian nobility, which suggests that he lived there for a time (his name disappears from the Urbino records briefly from 1743). In 1747 he gave concerts in the Netherlands, beginning with one at Arnheim (now

Arnhem) on 17 February. He was back at Urbino Cathedral from 1750 to 1757, though often away on concert tours. He returned to Arnheim in 1761 and probably spent the following years in Holland until his death; his final appearance was at the Arnheim Collegium Musicum on 15 December 1766. According to Lustig's description in Marpurg's *Kritische Briefe* (December 1762), Tessarini had lately settled in the Netherlands; 'despite his grey hairs and his 72 years he reads without spectacles like a young man ... I call out to all our musicians, who are getting slower in their middle life, "Sancte Tessarini, ora pro nobis" '.

During his last years Tessarini published several works in the Netherlands, many of which were in unauthorized reprints. His compositions, which are almost exclusively for strings, show the influence of Vivaldi, although there is no more documentary evidence for his being a pupil of Vivaldi than for Fétis's assertion that he was a pupil of Corelli. Tessarini's works show some progressive traits: he used concerto form in his violin sonatas op.1 (1729), and his op.3 concertos (?1740) follow the three-movement structure of the Italian sinfonia. *Galant* gestures are also found in his sonatas, which contain themes of clear phrase structure and dance-like character. It is clear from his music that he must have been an accomplished player; his works demand a highly developed technique. His only theoretical work, his violin school *Gramatica di musica* (1741), is of special interest for its discussion of high-position playing and of cadenzas and other performing practices of the 18th century.

WORKS

op.
1 [12] Sonate ... parte I e II, vn, vc/hpd (Venice, 1729)
2 Il maestro e discepolo, divertimenti da camera, 2 vn (Urbino, 1734)
3 [6] Allettamenti da camera, vn, vc (Rome, ?1740)
4 [6] Trattenimenti, vn, bc (Rome and Urbino, c1743)
5 Il piacer del amator di musica, [5] facile sonatine da camera ... con [1] canone al fine, 2 vn, bc (Paris, c1744)
6 Sei trio, 2 vn, bc (Paris, c1744)
7 [6] Sinfonie, 2 vn, bc/hpd (Paris, c1744)
– [12] Concerti a 5 con violino obligato [bks 1–4] (Paris, c1745)
– Il piacer delle dame, facile ariete instrumentali, vn, fl, viol, bc (Paris, c1745)
8 [6] Sonate, vn, bc (Paris, c1747)
9 [6] Sonate da camera e chiesa ... con pastoralle, 2 vn, bc (Paris, c1747)
10 Contrasto armonico ... con suoi rinforzi, 3 vn, bc (Paris, c1748)
11 [12] Introducioni a 4, 2 vn, va, vc, hpd [bks 1–4] (Paris, 1748)
12 [6] Sonate, 2 fl/vn, bc (Paris, c1749), as op.3 (London, 1752)
13 [6] Aletamenti armonici a 4, 2 vn, va, bc, hpd (Paris, c1749)
14 Sei sonate, vn/fl, hpd (Paris, c1749)
15 Trattenimento musicale, [6] dueti, 2 vn/tr viols (Paris, c1750)
16 [6] Sonate, vn, vc, hpd (Paris, c1753)
– L'arte di nuova modulacione, capricio musicale a 7 partie (Paris, c1762)
– VI Sonates, vn, bc (Paris and Amsterdam, 1763)
18 VI grand ouverture a 4, 2 vn, va, bc (Paris, c1764)
20 VI grand sinfonie a 4, 2 vn, va, bc (Paris, c1765)
MSS, ? duplicating printed works, in *A-Wn, D-Dlb, KA, SWl, F-Pn, GB-Lbm, I-Mc, S-L, Skma, Uu*

THEORETICAL WORK
Gramatica di musica: insegna il modo facile e breve per bene imparare di sonare il violino sù la parte (Rome, 1741; Eng. trans., 1765)

BIBLIOGRAPHY
L. de La Laurencie: *L'école française de violon de Lully à Viotti* (Paris, 1922–4/R1971)
A. Pougin: *Le violon, les violonistes et la musique du violon du XVIe au XVIIIe siècle* (Paris, 1924)
B. Ligi: 'La cappella musicale di Urbino', *NA*, ii (1925), 1–369
W. S. Newman: *The Sonata in the Baroque Era* (Chapel Hill, 1959, rev. 2/1966/R1972)
A. Dunning: 'Some Notes on the Biography of Carlo Tessarini and his Musical Grammar', *SMw*, xxv (1962), 115

AREND KOOLE

Tessier, André (*b* Paris, 8 March 1886; *d* Paris, 2 July 1931). French musicologist. He studied law and literature at the Ecole de Droit and the Ecole de Langues Orientales but later became interested in art history, studying at the Ecole du Louvre, where he took a diploma in 1921 with a dissertation on the painter and stage designer Jean Berain; on the basis of this he was appointed archivist of the Ministry of Fine Arts in the same year. However he had also attended Romain Rolland's lectures on musicology at the Sorbonne (1919) and this discipline began to take precedence, although his special interest remained the history of music and painting in Italy and France during the 17th and 18th centuries. As secretary of the Société Française de Musicologie (1927–31) Tessier was closely associated with the preparation of the third French edition of Riemann's *Lexikon* (Paris, 1931). He contributed a volume on Couperin to the series Les Musiciens Célèbres and numerous articles to *Echo musicale, Rassegna musicale, Revue musicale* and *Revue de musicologie*, of which he was editorial secretary; he also produced a complete edition of Chambonnières (in collaboration with Paul Brunold) and editions of Lully's ballet music (for the complete edition by Prunières) and of a volume of Gaultier's lute music. He initiated a complete edition of Couperin, but had prepared only a single volume of secular vocal music before his death; Maurice Cauchie succeeded him as editor of that project.

WRITINGS
Essai sur les Berain, décorateurs de la Chambre et du Cabinet du Roi (diss., Ecole du Louvre, 1921; extracts in *ReM*, vi/3 (1925), 56 as 'Berain créateur du pays d'opéra')
'Un document sur les répétitions du "Triomphe de l'Amour" à Saint-Germain-en-Laye (1681)', *Congrès d'histoire de l'art: Paris 1921*, 874
'Attribution à Couperin le Grand d'une pièce anonyme d'un recueil de Ballard', *RdM*, iii (1922), 69
'Les deux styles de Monteverde', *ReM*, iii/8 (1922), 223–54
'L'oeuvre de clavecin de Nicolas Le Bègue: notes bibliographiques', *RdM*, iv (1923), 106
'Quelques portraits de musiciens français du XVIIe siècle', *Bulletin de la Société d'histoire de l'art français* (1924), 244
'Un claveciniste français: Gaspard Le Roux', *ReM*, v/5 (1924), 230
Couperin (Paris, 1926)
'Les habits d'opéra au XVIIIe siècle: Louis Boquet, dessinateur et inspecteur général des menus-plaisirs', *Revue de l'art*, xlix (1926), 15, 89, 173
ed.: *Exposition internationale: la musique dans la vie des nations: catalogue de la section française* (Paris, 1927)
'Giacomo Torelli a Parigi e la messa in scena delle "Nozze di Peleo e Teti" di Carlo Caproli', *RaM*, i (1928), 573
'Monteverdi e la filosofia dell'arte', *RaM*, ii (1929), 459
'Quelques sources de l'école française de luth du XVIIe siècle', *IMSCR, i Liège 1930*, 217
'Une pièce inédite de Froberger', *Studien zur Musikgeschichte: Festschrift für Guido Adler* (Vienna, 1930/R1971), 147
ed., with A. Schaeffner and others: H. Riemann: *Dictionnaire de musique* (Paris, enlarged Fr. trans., 3/1931) [incl. articles on Agrément, Ballet, Caccini, Cavalieri, Couperin, Handel, Opera, Peri, Purcell, Rameau, Scarlatti]
'Ennemond Gaultier, sieur de Nève', *Mélanges de musicologie offerts à M. Lionel de la Laurencie* (Paris, 1933), 97
'Contribution à un fichier musical des archives photographiques des beaux-arts', *RdM*, xvii (1936), 161
ed. N. Dufourcq: *La vie musicale en France sous les rois bourbons: notes et références pour servir à une histoire de M.-R. Delalande* (Paris, 1957)

EDITIONS
with P. Brunold: *J. C. Chambonnières: Oeuvres complètes* (Paris, 1925/R1967)
J.-B. Lully: Les ballets, I–II, Oeuvres complètes (Paris, 1931–3)
with J. Cordey: *La rhétorique des dieux et autres pièces de luth de Denis Gaultier*, PSFM, 1st ser., i/6–7 (1932–3)
with P. Brunold: *F. Couperin: Musique vocale profane*, Oeuvres complètes, xi (Paris, 1932)

BIBLIOGRAPHY

P. Brunold: 'Quelques souvenirs sur André Tessier', *RdM*, xii (1931), 214

H. Prunières: 'André Tessier', *RdM*, xiii (1932)

A. Schaeffner: 'Bibliographie des travaux de André Tessier', *RdM*, xxxii (1953), 150

JOHN TREVITT

Tessier [Tessiery, Thessier], **Charles** [Carles] (*fl* c1600). French lutenist and composer. He was probably related to the Breton composer Guillaume Tessier, and perhaps to Valère Tessier, a lutenist active in Paris in 1609. Fétis claimed that Charles was born at Pézenas in about 1550, but no confirmation has been found. His *Premier livre de chansons et airs de cour tant en français qu'en italien et en gascon à 4 et 5 parties* appeared in London in 1597; the title-page refers to Charles as *musitien de la chambre du roy* (i.e. Henri IV of France). The dedication of the volume and two of the songs is to Lady Penelope Rich, sister of Robert Devereux, 2nd Earl of Essex; the texts praise her beauty, voice and lute playing. Eight of the pieces from the book appear in arrangements for solo voice and lute in an undated manuscript (*GB-Ob* Mus.Sch.D.237) dedicated to George Brouc (or Brooke), which contains a total of 28 *airs* signed by Tessier.

These signatures match those of three letters Tessier wrote in 1597 to Anthony Bacon, secretary of foreign affairs to the Earl of Essex, seeking his patronage or support in finding employment with some suitable English gentleman, and mentioning newly composed chansonnettes and *airs de cour*. The tenor of one of the chansonnettes is now among the Cecil Papers (200/84) in the library of Lord Salisbury at Hatfield House, Hertfordshire. Some of the pieces from the *Premier livre de chansons* (1597) reappeared in the *Airs et villanelles français, espagnols, suices et turcqs ... à 3, 4 et 5 parties*, published in Paris in 1604. This set was dedicated to the Protestant Moritz, Landgrave of Hessen-Kassel (Dowland's patron until 1597), who had been impressed by Tessier's lute playing at Poitiers in 1602–3. Tessier travelled to Marburg to present his new work to the landgrave but in June 1604 wrote to Ludwig, Landgrave of Hessen-Darmstadt, still seeking employment. The second edition of the *Airs et villanelles* (1610) was dedicated to King Matthias of Hungary, but Tessier continued to refer to himself as *musitien de la chambre du roy*.

Nearly all the pieces in both publications are strophic *airs* with the tune in the superius, equally suitable for performance by voices or solo voice and lute (several ed. in Verchaly, 1953 and 1961). A few such arrangements survive in the collections of Mangeant (1608 and 1615) and of Bataille (*RISM* 1611[10]).

BIBLIOGRAPHY

FétisB

E. Zulauf: *Beiträge zur Geschichte der Landgräflich-Hessischen Hofkapelle zu Cassel bis auf die Zeit Moritz des Gelehrten* (Kassel, 1902), 94

A. Verchaly, ed.: *Anthologie de la chanson parisienne* (Monaco, 1953), 20

F. Lesure: 'Tessier, Charles', *MGG*

A. Verchaly: *Airs de cour pour voix et luth* (Paris, 1961), 18

G. Ungerer: 'The French Lutenist Charles Tessier and the Essex Circle', *Renaissance Quarterly*, xxviii (1975), 190

J. M. Ward: 'Tessier and the Essex Circle', *Renaissance Quarterly*, xxix (1976), 378

N. McBride: *The Chansons of Charles Tessier: a Transcription and Commentary* (diss., Queen's U., Belfast, 1977)

F. Dobbins: 'The Lute Airs of Charles Tessier', *LSJ*, xx (1978), 23

FRANK DOBBINS

Tessier [Thessier], **Guillaume** (*fl* c1582). French composer. He may be the 'Guillaume Tixier musicien' active at Lyons in 1575. His only publication, a collection of four- and five-voice *airs* in French, Italian and Spanish, entitled *Premier livre d'airs tant francois, italien, qu'espaignol* (Paris, 1582), appeared in two editions (the second as *Il primo libro dell' arie*, also 1582) and was reprinted in 1585. The first piece is a five-voice 'madrigale all Sereniss[ima] and Sacratiss[ima] Regina d'Inghilterra'; since this is clearly addressed to Elizabeth I the preceding dedication in Italian signed 'Devotissimo servo et schiovo G. Tessieri, Brettone' at Paris on 10 May 1582 was probably also addressed to the queen. The fact that Robert Dowland's *Musicall Banquet* (London, 1610) includes Tessier's setting of Ronsard's *Le petit enfant amour* in a version for voice and lute as *In a grove most rich of shade* (the words are from Sidney's *Astrophel and Stella*) suggests similar English contacts (e.g. Lady Penelope Rich, John Dowland) to those of Charles Tessier, whose *Premier livre de chansons* was published in London by Thomas East in 1597.

Most of the 34 French pieces are short strophic *airs* by contemporary poets (Baïf, Bussy d'Amboise, Jacques de Constans, Desportes, Catherine and Madelaine des Roches, Amadis Jamin and Ronsard) set in the new rhythmically flexible, syllabic homophony of La Grotte, Courville, Caietain and Le Blanc: Tessier however composed entirely new music for the four texts (three by Jamin) which had appeared in four-voice settings by Le Blanc in 1579. The influence of the Académie de Poésie et de Musique is reflected in two successive *chansonnettes mesurées* – *Lesse moy osu* and *Cruelle sçais-tu pourquoy?* – which faithfully adhere to Baïf's metrical patterns. Although the dance-like rhythms with frequent syncopation and alternation of simple and compound metres prevail as in the four-voice *airs* of Courville and Caietain, Tessier occasionally adopted the freer style of dramatic *récit*, involving the use of melismatic diminutions, that had been employed the previous year in the *Balet comique de la Royne* – (e.g. *Pressé d'ennuis*, the monodic character of which is even more marked in the arrangement for superius and lute in *RISM* 1609[13]). The three 'espagnolles' and five 'napolitanes' at the end are like those in Caietain's second book of *airs*, lively ditties using dance rhythms with varied metre; all but the final two more madrigalian pieces (the last – like the opening piece – adding a second superius) are cast in clear binary form with one or both sections repeated.

BIBLIOGRAPHY

F. Lesure and G. Thibault: *Bibliographie des éditions d'Adrian le Roy et Robert Ballard (1551–1598)* (Paris, 1955), 212f

FRANK DOBBINS

Tessitura [testura] (It.: 'texture'). A term used to describe the part of a vocal (or less often instrumental) compass in which a piece of music lies – whether high or low, etc. The tessitura of a piece is not decided by the extremes of its range, but rather by which part of the range is most used. The role of Siegfried in Wagner's *Ring*, for example, ranges from $c\sharp$ to c'', but its tessitura would be described as high (and very demanding) because the tenor is required to sing phrases in the range c' to a' with great frequency (and often at high volume).

OWEN JANDER

Testagrossa, Giovanni [Gian, Zoan.] **Angelo** (*b* Pavia, 9 April 1470; *d* ?Urbino, Dec 1530). Italian lutenist, singer and teacher. In Milan in 1492 he provided improvised accompaniments for *ottava rima* recitations, a manner of *strambotto* performance that was later cultivated at Mantua. By 1495 or 1496 Testagrossa had succeeded Girolamo Sextula at the Gonzaga court in Mantua as lute teacher to Isabella d'Este; he remained there until about 1500. A number of letters between Isabella and Testagrossa exist. His travels away from the court are not known until 1506, when he reported in January from Parma about a viol and wrote from Busseto in December that he had obtained a lucrative post under the patronage of Galeazzo Pallavicino. It may have been between 1500 and 1506 that Testagrossa returned to Milan, where he taught Francesco Canova da Milano. By early 1510 Testagrossa had returned to Mantua to teach Isabella's son, Prince Federico. Later that year he entertained Francesco Gonzaga, then captive in Venice, and travelled with Federico to Rome, pausing briefly at the Duke of Urbino's court, where he was offered a post and where he met Leo X's lutenist Gian Maria Alemanni. Testagrossa remained at Mantua, however, until 1513, when he moved to Ferrara as lutenist to Isabella's brother, Cardinal Ippolito d'Este. In November 1517 Isabella, recommending him to the Marchioness Anna of Casale Monferrato as teacher for her daughter, wrote that 'he has sensitive fingers and an unexcelled method of teaching'. Testagrossa remained in Casale, somewhat dissatisfied with his situation, until he had to seek new employment in October 1518, when the marquis died. He received an offer from the Queen of France, but pleaded with Isabella for a return to Mantua, promising to bring a 'bona compagnia' of viol and lute players, singers and composers, and a remarkable collection of instruments: his 'old lute', two large lutes, five 'violoni', a chest of 'flauti', a crumhorn and 'an instrument called a "fagot"'; but it was only after Francesco Gonzaga's death in 1519 that Testagrossa was invited to return. He received Mantuan citizenship in 1525, but that year accepted a position at the court of Eleanora Gonzaga in Urbino. Although none of Testagrossa's music has survived, his style of playing may be reflected in Petrucci's publications of lute music and in the compositions of Francesco Canova da Milano. Francesco Marcolini, in his *Intabolatura di liuto* (*RISM* 1536[11]) ranked him with Josquin and Alemanni among the most eminent musicians of the Petrucci generation.

BIBLIOGRAPHY

P. Canal: *Della musica in Mantova* (Venice, 1881)

A. Bertolotti: *Artisti in relazione coi Gonzaga Duchi di Mantova, nei secoli XVI e XVII* (Modena, 1885/*R*1970), 112

S. Davari: 'La musica a Mantova', *Rivista storica mantovana*, i (1885), 67

A. Luzio: 'Federico Gonzaga ostaggio alla corte di Giulio II', *Archivio della R. società romana di storia patria*, ix (1886), 513

E. Motta: 'Musici alla corte degli Sforza: ricerche e documenti milanesi', *Archivio storico Lombardo*, xiv (1887), 514–61, esp. 546

A. Bertolotti: *Musici alla corte dei Gonzaga in Mantova dal secolo XV al XVIII* (Milan, 1890/*R*1969), 17, 23f

L. Dorez: *La cour du Pape Paul III d'après les registres de la trésorerie secrète* (Paris, 1932), i, 231, n.1

R. Giazotto: *Musurgia nova* (Milan, 1959), 7

ARTHUR J. NESS

Testi, Flavio (*b* Florence, 4 Jan 1923). Italian composer and musicologist. He studied with Gedda and Perrachio at the Turin Conservatory and then continued music studies on his own account while reading literature at Milan University. After working for Suvini Zerboni (1952–4) and Ricordi (1955–65) he was appointed to lecture in music history at the Padua Conservatory (1972) and at the Milan Conservatory (1974). In his music a poetic temperament is immediately revealed in a tendency towards eloquence, seeking expression more in discursive impulses than in the development of a musical argument, the emphasis being on the qualities of the moment. He uses a terse, gritty, polyphonically sparse language on the borders of atonality, though in later works he has moved to a denser style showing a greater awareness of timbre.

WORKS
(selective list)

Operas: Il furore di Oreste (after Aeschylus), Bergamo, 1956; La celestina (R. Prinzhofer, after F. de Rojas), Florence, 1963; L'albergo dei poveri (after Gorky), Milan, 1966

Orch: Conc. for Orch, 1954; Divertimento, 1956; Musica da concerto no.1, vn, orch, 1957; Musica da concerto no.2, str, 1957; 2 Pieces, 1958; Double Conc., vn, pf, orch, 1959; Musica da concerto no.3, pf, orch, 1961; Musica da concerto no.4, fl, orch, 1962; Opus 21, 1971; Opus 23, 2 pf, 2 chamber orchs, tpts, trbns, timp, 1972

Vocal: Crocifissione, male chorus, str, brass, timp, 3 pf, 1953; Stabat mater, S, chorus, insts, 1957; Mottetti, 4vv, insts, 1963; Il dolore (Ungaretti), 3 madrigals, small chorus, insts, 1963; New York: oficina y denuncia (Lorca), chorus, orch, 1964; Canto a las madres de los milicianos muertos (Neruda), S, chorus, orch, 1967; Passio Domini Nostri Jesu Christi secundum Marcum, SATTBB, insts, 1969; Cantata no.1 (Shakespeare), 1v, insts, 1970; Cantata no.2 (Shakespeare), T, cl, tpt, trbn, pf, vn, 1972; Cantata no.3 (Alberti), 1v, insts, 1974; Cantata no.4 (Baudelaire), Bar, 2 cl, 1974; Cori di Santiago, solo vv, chorus, orch, 1975

Chamber: Musica da concerto no.5, pf trio, 1969; Cielo, fl, 1974; Jubilus I, cl, 1974; Jubilus II, cl, 9 insts, 1975, Tempo, str qt, 1976

Principal publisher: Ricordi

WRITINGS

Introduzione alla musica (Milan, 1963)
Storia della musica italiana (Milan, 1969)

BIBLIOGRAPHY

P. Rattalino: 'Flavio Testi', *Ricordiana*, viii/3 (1963), 6

G. Ugolini: 'Profili: Flavio Testi', *Rassegna a cura del Centro istruzione musicale Anzaghi* (1964)

P. Santi: *Flavio Testi* (Milan, n.d.)

PIERO SANTI

Testo (It.: 'text'). A term commonly used in 17th-century Italian *oratorio volgare* and Passion settings for the narrative portions of the text and, by extension, the role of the narrator; it corresponds to the 'historicus' in the Latin oratorio and to the Evangelist in German Passion settings. In the 18th century, when narrative was almost entirely dropped from oratorio in favour of continuous dramatic dialogue, the term fell into disuse. The *testo* part was normally set as recitative with continuo accompaniment and sung either by one or more soloists or (less often) by a group of soloists forming a *coro*.

In secular music the term was occasionally used for the narrator in dramatic dialogues and similar works. Monteverdi used a solo tenor for the *testo* in his dramatic madrigal, *Il combattimento di Tancredi e Clorinda* (1624).

See also DIALOGUE.

Testore. Italian family of violin makers who worked in Milan from 1690 until the middle of the 18th century. Once even derided as the 'Milanese cheapjacks', the Testores were an industrious family of makers whose instruments are far more appreciated today than they can have been at the time of their manufacture. The demand of time and place was evidently for something inexpensive, so that hasty construction from commonplace materials was most often the rule of the day. They worked 'Al segno dell'Aquila', and often branded their work with an eagle emblem.

(1) **Carlo Giuseppe Testore** (*fl* 1690–*c*1720). He was the most skilled of the family, having been, according to his earliest labels, a pupil of Grancino. His violins are often mistaken for those of his teacher, the chief differences being that Carlo Testore's had slightly longer, more sweeping corners and less distinctive soundholes. The volute of the scroll tends to bulge diagonally in contrast to the perfect roundness of a Grancino, a feature unique to the Testore family, whose later makers copied and even exaggerated it. Carlo Giuseppe's varnish, like that of Grancino, varied from a rich, dark orange-brown to pale yellow, and there is little that distinguishes the two makers tonally.

(2) **Carlo Antonio Testore** (*fl* *c*1720–after 1760). The elder son of (1) Carlo Giuseppe Testore, whose style he followed closely, but with less charm, using a more brittle, light-coloured varnish. He almost always scratched a double line on the backs of his violins instead of inlaying the purfling, a feature occasionally seen in the work of Grancino and Carlo Giuseppe Testore. Another sign of haste was a flat back to the pegbox, in place of the normal fluting. Late in his working life he had the assistance of a son, Giovanni Testore.

(3) **Paolo Antonio Testore** (*fl* *c*1725–60). The younger son of (1) Carlo Giuseppe Testore. Although his working habits were the same as those of his brother, he had independent ideas of outline and modelling, not always as successful. His least inspired instruments appear awkward, if not crude, but where the situation demanded he would purchase handsome wood, work it with talent and character, and abandon the dull brown or yellow varnish for a soft orange of real quality.

(4) **Pietro Testore** (*fl* *c*1750–60). Son of (3) Paolo Antonio Testore. He had possibly the clumsiest pair of hands that ever made a violin, and more often than not made an equally clumsy choice of wood. Pietro's work demonstrates to modern ears the unique acoustical properties of Italian violin varnish. Several of his violas exist and are quite equal in tone to those of his relatives.

CHARLES BEARE

Testori, Carlo Giovanni (*b* Vercelli, 24 March 1714; *d* Vercelli, 20 May 1782). Italian theorist and composer. His father was a violinist and Testori himself studied the violin and composition in Milan. He returned to Vercelli and remained there for the rest of his life as a violin teacher. His compositions, all now lost, included sacred music and trio sonatas; but he is chiefly remembered for his *La musica ragionata* (1767; 3 suppls., 1771–82), a treatise based on Rameau's theories and dealing with composition in up to eight parts as well as the fundamentals of keyboard playing.

BIBLIOGRAPHY
C. Negri: *Brevi considerazioni sull'evoluzione storica ed estetica della musica: biografie di musicisti vercellesi* (Vercelli, 1909)
R. Allorto: 'La musica ragionata di Carlo Giovanni Testori', *RMI*, liii (1951), 242

Testori [Testore, Textoris], **Guglielmo** (*fl* 1566–71). ?Italian composer and singer. The existence of his name in a Latinized form may indicate that he was of French or possibly Netherlands origins. He was employed as a singer at the Gonzaga court at Mantua between 1566 and 1571; he was also responsible to the duke or to the *maestro di cappella*, Wert, for hiring new singers. His only known printed works are *Il primo libro de madrigali* (Venice, 1566) for five voices and a *laude spirituale* in Giovanni Arascione's *Nuove laudi ariose* (*RISM* 1600⁵). His two five-voice masses (in *I-Mc*), *In festis semiduplicibus minoribus* and *In festis apostolorum* were probably written for the Gonzaga *cappella*.

BIBLIOGRAPHY
P. Canal: *Della musica in Mantova* (Venice, 1881)
A. Bertolotti: *Musici alla corte dei Gonzaga in Mantova dal secolo XV al XVIII* (Milan, 1890/*R*1969)

PIERRE M. TAGMANN

Testorius, Johann. *See* WIRCKER, JOHANN.

Testudo (Lat.: 'tortoise'). The Latin name for the Greek lyre, the body of which was sometimes made from the shell of a tortoise, though the word could also mean any arched structure. In medieval Latin it came to be used for LUTE, since no specific term existed for that instrument. Another word so used, CHELYS, is borrowed direct from the Greek for tortoise. Both these words are of feminine gender, yet all the derivations from the Arabic *el 'ūd* are masculine.
See also LYRE.

IAN HARWOOD

Tetrachord (from Gk. *tetra*: 'four'; *chordē*: 'lyre string'). A system of four notes, contained within the limits of a perfect 4th. In ancient Greek music theory (*see* GREECE, §I) it serves as a basis for melodic construction, in much the same way as the HEXACHORD functions in modal music, and the major and minor scales in tonal music. Essentially tetrachords fall into three types, or genera, according to the size of the intervals between their notes: diatonic, chromatic and enharmonic. Reckoned upwards, the diatonic genus comprises the intervals semitone–tone–tone; the chromatic genus is based on the succession semitone–semitone–minor 3rd; the enharmonic genus is built on the intervals quarter-tone–quarter-tone–major 3rd. In medieval theory (for example in *Musica enchiriadis*) the form tone–semitone–tone was common.

The tetrachord was also used to define a particular register within the general notational systems as set forth by Aristoxenus, the Greater and Lesser Perfect Systems. The lowest of these tetrachords, the *hypaton*, consisted of the interval from *B* to *e*; the *meson* extended from *e* to *a*. The *diezeugmenon* was an octave higher than the *hypaton* (*b* to *e'*); the highest tetrachord, called the *hyperbolaion*, was an octave higher than the *meson* (*e'* to *a'*).

Tetrazzini, Luisa (*b* Florence, 29 June 1871; *d* Milan, 28 April 1940). Italian soprano. She studied at the Istituto Musicale of her native city and with her elder sister Eva (1862–1938), who was herself a soprano and had married the conductor Cleofonte Campanini. In 1890 Luisa made a surprise début at the Teatro Pagliano in Florence, as Inès in *L'africaine*. She next sang in Rome, and toured with growing success throughout Italy, adding to her repertory all the more famous roles for coloratura soprano; she also made a reputation abroad, notably in St Petersburg, Madrid, Buenos Aires and Mexico. The English-speaking world was slower to discover her merits, but made ample amends when her unheralded Covent Garden début on 2 November 1907, as Violetta, caused a sensation. She returned to London for every summer season from 1908 to 1912, singing also Lucia, Gilda, Rosina, Amina, Lakmé, Leïla in *Les pêcheurs de perles* and the Queen in *Les Huguenots* – the last three of these, like all her performances of French opera, in Italian versions. Her enormous success was the more welcome at a time when Melba had begun to relinquish her more brilliant parts.

Immediately after her London début she was engaged by Hammerstein for his Manhattan Opera House, where, on 15 January 1908, she repeated her London triumph, again in the role of Violetta. In three consecutive seasons there, in 1911–12 at the Metropolitan and 1911–12 and 1912–13 in Chicago, she appeared in most of her London roles, as well as in others in which London was never to hear her: Rossini's Mathilde (*Guillaume Tell*), Bellini's Elvira, Donizetti's Linda, Adina and Marie (*La fille du régiment*), Thomas' Ophélie and Philine, and Annetta in *Crispino e la comare* by the brothers Ricci. These pre-war years were the climax of her career. Thereafter, she made numerous and very lucrative concert tours, appearing for the last time in New York in 1931, and in London in 1934.

Tetrazzini possessed technical gifts of the highest order, and could dazzle audiences with the ease and agility of her chromatic scales, both ascending and descending, and with her staccato, trills and florid effects of every kind, especially above the staff; around the high B♭ and C, where most Italian sopranos of her type begin to thin out and become acid, her tonal emission remained as round and full as ever. A pallid, somewhat childish quality in the lower-middle register, which may have been the result of vocal overwork in early days, was felt to impair the absolute consistency of her tone, which was otherwise of a warm, clarinet-like beauty. Her cantilena was shapely, spontaneous and flowing.

In later years Tetrazzini taught in Milan, and produced at least one excellent pupil in Lina Pagliughi; but at the time of her death she had exhausted her resources and had to be buried at the expense of the state. It was a melancholy end for one who had been truly a queen of song, perhaps the last of the older breed. Between 1908 and 1914, the years of her prime, Tetrazzini recorded extensively. Her records of such pieces as 'Una voce poco fa', the Polonaise from *Mignon* or 'Ah non giunge' from *La sonnambula*, rank among the most brilliant ever made; while her skill and taste in the delivery of a simple melody show to admiration in her account of Tosti's *Aprile*.

WRITINGS
My Life of Song (London, 1921/R1977)
How to Sing (New York, 1923/R1975)

BIBLIOGRAPHY
J. B. Richards: 'Luisa Tetrazzini', *Record Collector*, iv (1949), 123 [with discography by P. H. Wade]
D. Shawe-Taylor: 'A Gallery of Great Singers: Luisa Tetrazzini', *Opera*, xiv (1963), 593
ALEXIS CHITTY/DESMOND SHAWE-TAYLOR

Tetz. *See* TITZ.

Teuber. *See* TEYBER family.

Teutscher (Ger.). TEDESCA.

Tevo, Zaccaria (*b* Piove di Sacco, nr. Padua, 16 March 1651; *d* Treviso, ? between May 1709 and March

Luisa Tetrazzini

1712). Italian theorist and composer. On 18 March 1665 he entered the Franciscan monastery at Treviso as a pupil, and in 1667 he took holy orders there; after further study he obtained a bachelor's degree. He appears to have been taught composition by one of the Franciscan fathers. In a statement written in 1692 he recorded that he was a music teacher and described his years of study and the periods he had spent at Fermo, Macerata, Padua and Venice. By 1677 he had returned to Treviso, and the records show that he became organist of the monastery church on 25 May 1688 and its *maestro di cappella* on 8 May 1689; he apparently held that post until 1705. Between 3 July 1705 and 21 May 1706 he seems to have been absent from Treviso, and his name next occurs in the records on 30 June 1706. He is last mentioned in the entry for 1 May 1709.

Although none of his musical works survives, Tevo is known to have been a composer; the title *maestro di musica* by which the monastery records refer to him was conferred by the Franciscan order only on composers who had published four or more works. The Venetian printer Giuseppe Sala published some psalms by him, and Sbaralea mentioned further musical works also published in Venice. His only known extant work is the treatise *Il musico testore* (Venice, 1706), a compendium of contemporary theories of composition; it includes a portrait of him.

BIBLIOGRAPHY
G. B. Candotti: 'L'anno di nascita del Tevo', *Gazzetta musicale di Milano*, xxxii (1854), 253
G. Gaspari: *Catalogo della Biblioteca del Liceo musicale di Bologna*, i (Bologna, 1890/R1961), 260
G. Marcolin and D. Libertini: *Storia popolare di Piove di Sacco* (Piove di Sacco, 1891)
D. M. Sparacio: 'Musicisti minori conventuali', *Miscellanea francescana*, xxv (1925), 13, 33, 81–112
J. H. Sbaralea: *Supplementum et castigatio ad scriptores trium ordinum S Francisci a Waddingo aliisve descriptos* (Rome, 1936), 302
F. Corradini: 'La cappella del duomo di Arezzo', *NA*, xv (1938), 49, 161, 248

P. Salviucci: 'Musicisti dell'ordine francescano dei minori conventuali', *NA*, xvi (1939), 187, 238, 274

A. Sartori: *La provincia del santo dei frati minori conventuali* (Padua, 1958)

C. Sartori: *Dizionario degli editori musicali italiani* (Florence, 1958), 137

based on *MGG* (xiii, 267–8) by permission of Bärenreiter

GIOVANNI D'ALESSI

Textbuch (Ger.). LIBRETTO.

Textoris, Guglielmo. *See* TESTORI, GUGLIELMO.

Texture. A term used loosely when referring to any of the vertical aspects of a musical structure, usually with regard to the way in which individual parts or voices are put together. In discussions of texture a distinction is generally made between homophony, in which all the parts are rhythmically dependent on one another or there is a clearcut distinction between the melodic part and the accompanying parts carrying the harmonic progression (e.g. most solo song with piano accompaniment), and polyphonic (or contrapuntal) treatment, in which several parts move independently in or imitation of one another (e.g. fugue, canon). Between these two extremes is a free-part style (Ger. *Freistimmigkeit*), characteristic of much 19th-century writing for the piano, in which the number of parts can vary within a single phrase. The spacing of chords may also be considered an aspect of texture; so may the 'thickness' of a sonority as determined by the number of parts, the amount of doubling at the unison or octave, the 'lightness' or 'heaviness' of the performing forces involved and the arrangement of instrumental lines in an orchestral work.

The word does not have an exact equivalent in any other language; the etymologically related Italian 'testura' and 'tessitura' refer to the register of a single part, usually vocal. Only the German SATZ, which in certain contexts denotes contrapuntal organization (*Dezimensatz* – counterpoint round the interval of a 10th) or part-writing style (*Kantilenensatz* – in the style of 14th- and 15th-century solo song with one- to three-part instrumental accompaniment), approaches the meaning of texture.

The term has occasionally been applied to non-vertical aspects of music: 'melodic texture' for example may refer to changes of pace or density in a melody, 'harmonic texture' to the rate of harmonic change.

Teyber [Deiber, Taiber, Taube, Tauber, Täuber, Tayber, Teiber, Teuber]. Austrian family of musicians.

(1) **Matthäus Teyber** (*b* Weinzettel, *c*1711; *d* Vienna, 6 Sept 1785). Violinist and, from 1757, court musician in Vienna. He became a violinist in the Empress Elisabeth Christine's Kapelle on 1 March 1741 and on 13 June married Therese Riedel in Vienna (F. I. A. Tůma and Giuseppe Bonno were witnesses at the wedding); four of their children attained distinction as musicians. He and his family were on friendly terms with the Mozart family by 1773, as Leopold's letters to his wife of August that year indicate. Apart from the four most important members of the family (their dates and even their names are subject to considerable variation in musical literature), another son, Friedrich (*b* Vienna, baptized 13 June 1748; *d* Vienna, 8 Jan 1829), was a talented amateur violinist who became a senior civil servant and was ennobled, and another daughter

Barbara (*b* Vienna, ?1750; *d* Vienna, 30 Jan 1832) sang Sara in the première of Haydn's *Il ritorno di Tobia* on 2 and 4 April 1775 in the Kärntnertor-Theater. Clemens Tauber, a cellist in the Esterházy orchestra early in 1788, was probably no relation.

(2) **Elisabeth Teyber** (*b* Vienna, baptized 16 Sept 1744; *d* Vienna, 9 May 1816). Soprano, daughter of (1) Matthäus Teyber. After study with Hasse and Tesi, she made her career mainly in Italy, following a series of Vienna performances in the 1760s, including the production of Hasse's *Partenope* in 1767 (Leopold Mozart was not particularly impressed by her – see his letter of 29 September 1767; for Hasse's own more favourable opinion, see Mennicke). She then sang with great success in Italy, appearing at Naples, Bologna, Milan and Turin. She married a Marchese Venier but was early widowed. She is said to have sung in Russia in the 1770s but to have been obliged for health reasons to return to Italy, but was not able to resume singing there until 1784. It is by no means certain that she appeared in Vienna again in 1788, as is sometimes stated, or even that she gave a solitary guest appearance there ten years earlier, on 8 September 1778. On this date Ulbrich's *Frühling und Liebe* was given for the first time. The playbill includes 'Mlle. Teyberin' (i.e. Therese Teyber) as Fiametta, and 'Mlle. Tauber' in the role of her stepmother, Markesinn Bellavita. It seems almost certain that this 'Mlle. Tauber' was in fact not Elisabeth Teyber but the unrelated Maria Anna (or Marianne) Tauber (or Taube), a soprano of the Esterházy company who in March of that year had impressed the Emperor Joseph II in Starzer's oratorio *La passione del Redentore*, but was less successful in subsequent appearances and left Vienna at the end of September.

(3) **Anton Teyber** (*b* Vienna, baptized 8 Sept 1756; *d* Vienna, 18 Nov 1822). Composer, pianist, organist and cellist, son of (1) Matthäus Teyber. After early education in Vienna he studied for some years in Bologna with Padre Martini, being there almost certainly as late as 1775. He then appeared in several Italian musical centres, touring with his sister Elisabeth, and in Spain and Portugal (also Germany and Russia, according to a biographical sketch in *A-Wgm*), before returning to Vienna about 1781. He was admitted to the Viennese Tonkünstler-Sozietät in 1784, and in 1787 entered the Hofkapelle at Dresden as first organist. At the end of 1791 he returned to Vienna and on 1 December took up a post as deputy to Joseph Weigl at the National-Hoftheater. However, cuts in the musical establishment under Franz II led to his losing his post, though he was successful in petitioning the emperor for help and was in 1793 appointed court composer (a post that had not been filled after Mozart's death) and instructor in keyboard to the imperial children. A *Missa solemnis* in C minor was written for and performed on the occasion of Archduke Rudolph's ordination as priest in 1819 (the archduke was a pupil of both Teyber and Beethoven), and he is recorded as having conducted other large works in the imperial chapel in 1820 and 1821; a mass by him was performed with great success at Olomouc Cathedral on Easter Sunday 1822. He also wrote a melodrama *Zermes* (or *Zerbes*) *und Mirabelle* (1779), two oratorios, *Gioas, rè di Giuda* and *La passione di Gesù Cristo* (performed in 1805 for Teyber's benefit at the Tonkünstler-Sozietät), and a quantity of orchestral, chamber and church music, most of which was bought from his widow by Archduke Rudolph and

later passed with his estate into the possession of the Gesellschaft der Musikfreunde.

WORKS

(for fuller list see Pfannhauser, MGG)

VOCAL

Stage: Zermes [Zerbes] und Mirabelle (melodrama), Vienna, Kärntnertor, 15 July 1779

Oratorios: Gioas, rè di Giuda (Metastasio), Dec 1786, *A-Wgm*; La Passione di Gesù Cristo, c1790, perf. 1805, *Wgm*

Sacred: 11 masses, 4vv, orch, *Wgm, D-Dlb*; Requiem pro defuncta Imperatrice Ludovica, 4vv, orch, *A-Wgm*; Dixit Dominus, 1778, Salve regina, 1v, insts, *Wgm*; mass sections, graduals, antiphons, motets, fugues, *Wgm, Wn, Wst*

Other vocal: [7] Gesänge für Musikkenner beim Clavier (Vienna, 1797), 1 ed. in DTÖ, lxxix, Jg.xlii/2 (1935/R); 12 lieder in C. F. Kriegel: Lieder beym Clavier zu singen, i–ii (Dresden, 1790–93); further lieder in contemporary anthologies; occasional works, lieder, arias, in MS

INSTRUMENTAL

Orch: Grande sinfonie, op.1 (Offenbach, 1799); 35 further syms., 16 in *Wgm*; 6 vn concs., 5 in *Wgm*; 4 kbd concs., *Wgm*; 2 hn concs., *Wgm*; double conc., vn, kbd

Chamber (mostly in *Wgm*): 3 octets, 4 str, 2 ob, 2 hn; 2 sextets, 4 str, 2 ob; 3 str qts, op.1 (Vienna, 1788); 3 str qts, op.2 (Dresden, n.d.); 23 further str qts, ?6 lost; 14 qts, kbd, str; 3 pf trios; 6 str trios; 12 minuets, 2 vn, b (Vienna, c1808); vn sonata (Vienna, 1786); 2 cassations

Kbd: 3 sonatas, *Wgm*; XII Menuetten aus dem . . . Redoutensaal (Vienna, 1796); XIII deutsche Tänze (Vienna, 1796); 3 nocturnes, 4 hands; further dances, incl. minuets, marches (Vienna, 1797–1808), also in MS, incl. *Wgm, Wn, D-Bds*

Various pedagogical works, *A-Wgm*

(4) Franz Teyber (*b* Vienna, baptized 25 Aug 1758; *d* Vienna, 21 or 22 Oct 1810). Composer, organist, bass singer and conductor, son of (1) Matthäus Teyber. After receiving musical instruction from his father and Wagenseil he undertook extensive tours of Swabia, Switzerland and Baden, and then in or about 1786 he joined Schikaneder's travelling troupe as conductor and composer, having been in Vienna again the previous season. Leopold Mozart, discussing the company's Salzburg season of 1786, refers to Teyber as 'my very good acquaintance from Vienna; a thorough, excellent musician, good composer, organist, and violoncellist' (letter of 5 May 1786). In 1788–9 Teyber was in Karlsruhe, in 1791–3 in Cologne, and then in Regensburg and Augsburg. From 1796 until 1798 he was at Berne and then returned to Vienna. He was honoured with the task of writing the opera for the opening performance at the new Theater an der Wien on 13 June 1801: *Alexander*, to a libretto by Schikaneder, which was given 44 times in less than three years. None of his later works for this theatre enjoyed much success, and his name disappears from the repertory list after a setting of Huber's *Der Zerstreute* in January 1805. He moved to the Leopoldstadt Theatre in 1807, and on 13 August 1810 was appointed court organist (from the previous year he had been organist at St Stephen's Cathedral). Despite his honours and successes, he died in penury. Wurzbach related that one of his last works was an oratorio, *Der sterbende Jesus*, performed in the Leopoldstadt Theatre for the musicians' benefit fund; this is presumably identical with the oratorio *Die sieben Worte des Heilands* (no composer named) that was given on 25 March 1810.

WORKS

DRAMATIC

(all first performed in Vienna unless otherwise stated)

Laura Rosetti (opera, 3, ? G. Stephanie the Younger), Pressburg, Aug 1785, *A-Wgm*

Die Dorfdeputierten (comic opera, 3, G. E. Heermann, after Goldoni), Kärntnertor, 18 Dec 1785, *Wn*

Adelheid von Veltheim (Singspiel, 3, G. F. Grossmann), Karlsruhe, 1788

Fernando und Jariko oder Die Indianer (Singspiel, 3, K. von Eckartshausen), Freihaus, 5 Sept 1789; ov., arr. kbd (Vienna, 1802)

Alexander (grand opera, 2, E. Schikaneder), an der Wien, 13 June 1801

Der Schlaftrunk (Singspiel, 2, C. F. Bretzner), an der Wien, 12 Nov 1801

Der Neuigkeitskrämer oder Der Telegraph (Singspiel, 2, F. Gewey), an der Wien, 12 May 1802

Pfändung und Personalarrest (Singspiel, Schikaneder), an der Wien, 7 Dec 1803

Der Zerstreute (comic opera, 3, F. X. Huber), an der Wien, 29 Jan 1805

Andrassek und Jurassek (pantomime, 2, F. Kees), Leopoldstadt, 20 Feb 1807

Ruthards Abenteuer oder Die beiden Sänger (comic opera, 3, W. Neubauer), Leopoldstadt, 26 July 1808

Pumphia und Kulikan (caricature opera, 2, J. Perinet, after J. F. von Kurz), Leopoldstadt, 8 Oct 1808

Der bezauberte Blumenstrauss (pantomime, 2, J. Worelly), Leopoldstadt, 29 Aug 1809

Der lebendige Postillonstiefel oder Die Luftreise des Arlequin und der Columbina (pantomime, 2, Kees), Leopoldstadt, 7 July 1810

Plays with songs: Scheredin und Almanzor oder Die Unsterblichkeit auf der Probe (4, I. Castelli), 1804; Der Schiffmeister von Straubing (3, K. Schikaneder), 1807; Aragis von Benevent (3, J. A. Gleich), 1807; Der Lohn der Nachwelt (4, Gleich), 1807; Die Vermählungsfeier Alberts von Oesterreich (4, Gleich), 1808; Die beiden Marillo (3, Gleich), 1808; Eppo von Gailingen (3, Gleich), 1809; Das Strafgericht (4, J. S. von Menner), 1809; Das Spinner-Kreuz am Wienerberge (3), 1811

OTHER WORKS

(MSS in A-Wgm, Wn, Wst)

Vocal: Missa de sanctissima Trinitate, vv, orch, 1806; Kyrie, 17 Aug 1766; Lamentations and Benedictus for Holy Week, 2–3vv, str; Der sterbende Jesus, oratorio, ?1810, lost; Die Entführung oder Ritter Karl von Eichenhorst (G. A. Bürger), narrative song, pf acc., 1793

Inst: 3 qts, kbd, str (Mannheim, c1789); 6 str qts; 3 sonatas, pf, vn acc. (Vienna, after 1803); sonata, pf, vn, vc (Vienna, c1808); preludes, org, 1809–10; dances, marches (Vienna, 1803–9), also in MS

(5) Therese Teyber (*b* Vienna, baptized 15 Oct 1760; *d* Vienna, 15 April 1830). Soprano, daughter of (1) Matthäus Teyber. She was a pupil of Bonno and Tesi. She made her début at the Vienna court theatre on 8 September 1778 as Fiametta in Ulbrich's *Frühling und Liebe*. (A letter of 8 February 1778 from Gebler to Nicolai mentions a 'Mlle Teuberin, until now at Prince Esterházy's Opera' among future attractions, but this doubtless refers to Maria Anna Tauber, who had probably already been engaged to sing in Starzer's *La passione del Redentore* in March, and who also sang in *Frühling und Liebe* in September; she is the only singer in the Esterházy records with that or a similar name. This information is corroborated by the *Wiener Diarium* of 1778, no.87.) Teyber was a popular portrayer of young lovers and artless girls, and in the early 1780s she also appeared in the concerts of the Tonkünstler-Sozietät. Her last appearance at one of these concerts seems to have been in March 1784, when she sang Sara in Haydn's *Il ritorno di Tobia* (her sister Barbara had sung this part in the first performances in 1775). She created the role of Blonde in *Die Entführung aus dem Serail* on 16 July 1782 and appeared with success in many other operas and Singspiels; contemporary reviews praised the charm of her acting ('the best of the women') and singing, though one critic accused her of letting her tongue run away with her in dialogue. She was always one of the lower-paid singers (in 1783 she was drawing 800 florins, less than a quarter of the salary of Nancy Storace). In 1787 (possibly 1785) she married the tenor Ferdinand Arnold, who had also sung in *Frühling und Liebe* in 1778 though he did not reappear with the court opera company between that year and 1786. The Arnolds are reported to have performed together with much success at Hamburg, Berlin, Warsaw and Riga, though the chronology of these appearances is confused. It seems reasonable to assume that it was Therese (and not, as is often stated, Elisabeth) who replaced Mombelli as Zerlina in the later Viennese performances of *Don Giovanni* in 1788. Therese is certainly the 'Mad:selle Täuber' ('Teyber') referred to in Mozart's letters of 29 March and 12 April 1783; they took part in each other's benefit concerts that Lent. Therese Teyber occurs in the court exchequer records of 1792 (the year after her retirement) as 'Arnoldin vormalige Sängerin' with a pension of 466·40 florins.

BIBLIOGRAPHY

EitnerQ; *GerberL*; *GerberNL*
A. Tauber: [autobiographical sketch] (MS, *A-Wgm*)
F. Teyber: [autobiographical sketch] (MS, *A-Wgm*)
J. H. F. Müller: *Abschied von der k. k. Hof- und Nationalschaubühne* (Vienna, 1802)
Allgemeine musikalische Zeitung mit besonderer Rücksicht auf den österreichischen Kaiserstaat, vii/14 (Vienna, 1823), col.111
A. Schmidt: *Denksteine* (Vienna, 1848)
L. von Köchel: *Die kaiserliche Hof-Musikkapelle in Wien* (Vienna, 1869/*R*1974)
C. F. Pohl and H. Botstiber: *Joseph Haydn* (Leipzig, 1875–1927)
C. von Wurzbach: *Biographisches Lexikon des Kaiserthums Oesterreich*, xliv (Vienna, 1882), 107
R. M. Werner: *Aus dem Josephinischen Wien* (Berlin, 1888)
C. Mennicke: *Hasse und die Brüder Graun als Symphoniker* (Leipzig, 1906), 427
R. Haas: *Wiener Musiker vor und um Beethoven* (Vienna, 1927)
F. Hadamowsky: *Das Theater in der Wiener Leopoldstadt* (Vienna, 1934)
O. E. Deutsch: *Das Freihaus-Theater auf der Wieden* (Vienna, 1937)
E. Komorzynski: *Emanuel Schikaneder: ein Beitrag zur Geschichte des deutschen Theaters* (Vienna, 2/1951)
H. Vogg: *Franz Tuma (1704–1774) als Instrumentalkomponist nebst Beiträgen zur Wiener Musikgeschichte des 18. Jahrhunderts* (*Die Hofkapelle der Kaiserin-Witwe Elisabeth Christine*) (diss., U. of Vienna, 1951), esp. pp.58–87
A. Bauer: *150 Jahre Theater an der Wien* (Zurich, 1952)
——: *Opern und Operetten in Wien* (Graz, 1955)
K. Pfannhauser: 'Wer war Mozarts Amtsnachfolger?', *Acta mozartiana*,
iii/3 (Augsburg, 1956), 6
O. E. Deutsch, ed.: *Mozart: die Dokumente seines Lebens* (Kassel, 1961; Eng. trans. as *Mozart: a Documentary Biography*, London, 1965, 2/1966)
W. A. Bauer and O. E. Deutsch, eds.: *Mozart: Briefe und Aufzeichnungen* (Kassel, 1962–75)
F. Hadamowsky: *Die Wiener Hoftheater (Staatstheater), 1776–1966*, i (Vienna, 1966)
K. Pfannhauser: 'Teyber', *MGG*
O. Michtner: *Das alte Burgtheater als Opernbühne* (Vienna, 1970)

PETER BRANSCOMBE

Té y Sagau, Jayme de la (*b* Barcelona, *c*1680; *d* Lisbon, 1736). Portuguese poet, printer and composer of Catalan birth. His father was a singer. The Jesuit diplomat Álvaro Cienfuegos, who assisted in arranging John V's marriage in 1708 to Marianna, daughter of Leopold I of Austria, took him to Lisbon and supported him from 1708 to 1715. In the year of his arrival he began composing up-to-date Italian-style cantatas in the new queen's honour (*P-Ln* Pombalina 82, ff.19*v*–21). During the next decade he continued writing music for palace festivities, such as the zarzuela *El poder de la armonía* (text by Luís Calisto da Costa e Faria) sung on John V's birthday, 22 October 1713. On 12 October 1715 he obtained a ten-year exclusive royal music printing privilege. Despite his humble origins, he was admitted to the Order of Santiago in 1716 through the queen's favour.

Apart from singly issued cantatas, he published three collections: *Cantatas a solo al Nacimiento*, 1721 (37 cantatas, solo voice with continuo, each consisting of a recitative, aria and *coplas*; copy in *P-EVp*); *Cantatas humanas a solo* (40 cantatas, solo and continuo; copies in *Ln*, *La*); *Cantatas humanas a duo* (copy at Mafra Palace). Despite being dismissed as trivial by various Portuguese critics, several of them continued to be sung as far away as Guatemala as late as 1788. In addition, he wrote the music of an oratorio sung in Lisbon Cathedral on 22 January 1719 and for various villancicos sung in the cathedral at S Vincent's Matins, 1719–23; in S Justa Church, Lisbon, at S Cecilia's feast, 1719–22; and for Christmas and S Gonçalo's Matins in Esperança royal convent, 1721–2. He bequeathed his press to his son Jayme Domingos de la Té y Sagau.

BIBLIOGRAPHY

F. X. de Oliveira: *Mémoires historiques, politiques et littéraires concernant le Portugal*, ii (The Hague, 1743), 317
F. M. Sousa Viterbo: *A litteratura hespanhola em Portugal* (Lisbon, 1915), 399ff
——: 'Subsídios para história da música em Portugal', *O Instituto*, lxxxiii (1932), 242ff
R. E. Horch: *Vilancicos da Coleção Barbosa Machado* (Rio de Janeiro, 1969), 129, 159
R. Stevenson: *Renaissance and Baroque Musical Sources in the Americas* (Washington, 1970), 100

ROBERT STEVENSON

Teyte [Tate], Dame **Maggie** (*b* Wolverhampton, 17 April 1888; *d* London, 26 May 1976). English soprano. She studied in London, then with Jean de Reszke in Paris. Her first public appearances, while not yet 18, were in a Mozart Festival organized in 1906 by Reynaldo Hahn and Lilli Lehmann, at which she sang in scenes from *Le nozze di Figaro* (as Cherubino) and *Don Giovanni* (as Zerlina), still using the original spelling of her surname, which she was to change in order to secure a correct pronunciation in France. In the following year she appeared at Monte Carlo, notably as Zerlina, and in various roles at the Opéra-Comique in Paris. Her big chance came in 1908, when Debussy selected her to succeed Mary Garden in the role of Mélisande; besides

Maggie Teyte as Mélisande in Debussy's 'Pelléas et Mélisande'

coaching her, he accompanied her in recitals of his songs, and from that time French song in general, and Debussy in particular, played a prominent part in her career. On her return to England she sang Mélisande and many other roles, including Cherubino, Blonde, Butterfly, Marguerite and Offenbach's Antonia, with the Beecham Opera Company and in later years with its successor, the British National Opera Company, besides appearing frequently in concert.

Teyte sang for three consecutive seasons (1911–14) with the Chicago Opera Company, both in Chicago and in Philadelphia and New York. Among her parts with this company was the title role of Massenet's *Cendrillon*, with Mary Garden as Prince Charming. At Boston, where she was a member of the Opera Company from 1914 to 1917, her Mimì and Nedda were specially admired; but her Mélisande was not heard in the USA until as late as 1948 (New York City Center). In England, between the wars, she appeared a good deal in operetta and musical comedy (*Monsieur Beaucaire, A Little Dutch Girl, Tantivy Towers*) and was even in some danger of being regarded as a lightweight artist, when, in 1937, her career received a fresh impetus. The occasion was a commissioned record album of Debussy songs, with Cortot as pianist, followed in 1940 by a second album of French song from Berlioz to Debussy, some with orchestral accompaniment (Leslie Heward) and some with piano (Gerald Moore). During the next eight years she made many further records of Fauré and other French songs with Moore, and her London recitals became notable events. In 1951 she appeared at the Mermaid Theatre as Purcell's Belinda to the Dido of Kirsten Flagstad; and in 1955 she made a final concert appearance at the Festival Hall. The exquisite purity and perfect placement of her tone, together with her spontaneity and distinction as an interpreter, secured for her a unique position, which was recognized when she was made a Chevalier of the Légion d'honneur in 1957 and DBE in 1958. Her voice recorded ideally, and her records of the French repertory have set a standard.

BIBLIOGRAPHY

D. Tron: 'Maggie Teyte', *Record Collector*, ix (1954), 129 [with discography by J. Dennis]

M. Teyte: *Star on the Door* (London, 1958) [with discography by D. Tron]

[D. Shawe-Taylor]: Obituary, *The Times* (28 May 1976)

G. O'Connor: *The Pursuit of Perfection: a Life of Maggie Teyte* (London, 1979)

DESMOND SHAWE-TAYLOR

Thackray, Thomas (*fl* 1770–80). English guitarist and composer. He seems to have come from York, but Gerber (1814) referred to him as still living in London. Since his first volume of six guitar lessons was printed 'for the author' in York *c*1770 and the second 'for the author' in London *c*1772, he may have moved to London about that time. His music has charm, especially the op.3 divertimentos for two guitars or guitar and violin (*c*1775), in which the upper part is considerably more difficult than the lower. He also published a collection of airs for guitars.

Thailand. Country in south-east Asia (formerly Siam). The music of Thailand (one of the 'gong-chime' cultures) and its music system are related to those of Burma, Laos, Kampuchea (formerly Khmer Republic, Cambodia), Indonesia (Java and Bali) and the Philippines.

1. History and introduction. 2. Instruments: (i) Melodic percussion (ii) Rhythmic percussion (iii) Wind instruments (iv) String instruments (v) Ensembles. 3. Fundamentals of the music system: (i) Ensemble music (ii) Tuning (iii) Melody (iv) Styles (v) Metre, rhythm and tempo. 4. Modal practice. 5. Form. 6. Vocal music.

1. HISTORY AND INTRODUCTION. The Thai claim their original homeland to be somewhere in southern China, perhaps in Kuang Tung (Canton) province, south-west of the present city of Canton. By AD 600 the city of Nan-chiao (now Meng-che) in Yunnan province, said to be a Thai city, was flourishing. Thai means 'free', and until the Mongols conquered the area during the second half of the 13th century, the Thai were more or less independent of the Chinese-held regions to the north. At times the area was under the direct control of the Chinese or was closely allied to them through royal intermarriage and political treaties. There are signs that the Thai were musical during this period, but how much was Thai and how much part of the culture of the Chinese Sung dynasty (960–1279) it is impossible to say. Elements in the existing Thai traditional music system suggest a close relationship, if, in fact, the music of this whole southern area of China was not at that time a single system.

As the Mongols pushed the Chinese southward, the Thai began migrating into what are now Thailand, Laos and northern Burma. The last great migration was in 1253 with the fall of southern China to the Mongols. As early as 1238, however, the Thai had wrested the city of Sukhothai from the Cambodians and made it the first Thai capital. From about 1250 to 1350 the Thai established themselves in their new surroundings and resumed their cultural development. One of the Sukhothai rulers created the Thai writing system, based on Cambodian and Sanskrit models. Carved on an extant stone tablet is the information that much music was to be heard in the city. Other Thai pushed farther southward and established the city of Ayutthaya. The two cities were friendly but Ayutthaya finally became the stronger, peacefully superseding Sukhothai as the capital in 1350, which it remained until 1767.

For much of this 400-year period, there was constant warfare with the Cambodians to the east and the Burmese to the west. The Thai finally conquered the Cambodians, destroying their capital city of Angkor in 1431. Whenever the Thai seized Cambodian territory, they took captives back to Ayutthaya and in the process were themselves civilized, it is said, by the Cambodians – much, perhaps, as the Romans were by the Greeks. The conflicts with the Burmese came to a head in 1767 when the Burmese in a surprise attack destroyed Ayutthaya, but the Thais rallied, and a new general (Rama I) assumed the leadership and moved the capital across the river to Bangkok where it has remained. This was the foundation of the Chakri dynasty; at least three of its kings and many princes were musically inclined and did much for Thai music.

Contact with the West started during the Ayutthaya period with the arrival of Western merchants and political figures, but Thailand never became a colony of a Western power; rather, it remained an independent buffer state between British-held Burma and French-dominated Indo-China. Few if any Western musical influences have penetrated the traditional Thai music system, probably because Thai musicians were protected within the court and isolated from Western music. The only Western music to have been heard in

Thailand in early times was that of an occasional military band. Since the mid-19th century, Western church music has been imported by missionaries, but has had no appreciable impact on traditional music. By nature the Thai music system is not of a kind to absorb Western musical elements, and by the time Western music began to be heard to any extent, the traditional system was already firmly established.

What is known of the Thai music system is primarily that of the Bangkok period. Only some half-dozen court annals and documents refer to music in the early periods, and these references are either lists of instruments or general comments: they tell nothing about the music itself. The relatively slow pace of cultural change in Asia, however, might allow the speculation that the music of the early Bangkok period hardly differed from that of the Ayutthaya period. The Thai music system is probably an amalgamation of essentially Chinese elements, with perhaps Indian elements that came through the Cambodians, and Indonesian elements received either indirectly via the Cambodians or directly by sea, up river to the capital cities.

Thai music itself is basically Chinese-derived, while the instruments of the gong-chime ensemble are southeast Asian. It is possible that Indian elements caused the evolution of the equidistant tuning system, and that when the Chinese pentatonic system (based on the first five pitches in the cycle of 5ths) clashed with an Indian-derived system of pitches used by the Cambodians, the resulting blend was shaped into an equidistant system. On the other hand, it cannot be proved that the equidistant system was not an independent creation of the Thai

(or perhaps an earlier creation of the Cambodians adopted by the Thai), evolved to accommodate a system of 'modulation', a procedure similar to that followed in the West. It is clear that Thai culture in general has borrowed elements from all the surrounding cultures. These elements have been adapted and combined by the Thai with their own original culture to produce a blend that is unique and not to be confused with any of the neighbouring cultures.

Thai traditional music, always under the patronage of the royal courts, fell into disfavour after 1932, when a form of democracy supplanted the absolute monarchy; this was probably because music was so closely connected with the old regime. With the creation of the Department of Fine Arts, National Archives Division, Bangkok, in 1952, a certain amount of protection and preservation was given to the traditional arts, but the music will probably never again reach the heights it once did at the royal courts. This is to be expected from the music system itself, which has evolved centripetally within narrow restrictions. Everything that could be done within these limits would seem to have been done, and 'new' creations have for some time been merely reworkings of already overworked material. Indeed, it has never been the custom in Thai music to create 'original' compositions but rather to arrange pre-existing material according to specific principles. This has undoubtedly restricted musical growth and there is no evidence of any new generation of experimental composers arising to develop traditional music in new directions.

Music has apparently always been held in high regard

1. *Wall painting at Wat Phragāeo, Bangkok, showing a pī phāt ensemble* (left), *and a fanfare ensemble* (right) *with conch-shell trumpets, curved horns* (derived from Indian models) *and trumpets*

by the Thai, and good musicians, if not excessively honoured in the Western sense, have always been respected, and even, exceptionally, given titles by the king. But because it existed and flourished in the courts, traditional music has probably played no great part in the life of the Thai people. It was not their music and this may be another reason why, after 1932, with the disappearance of the royal households, the people did not foster it. No appreciable amount of research has yet been done on Thai folk music: what little is known of it suggests that it consists mostly of simple songs in a melodic style similar to that of the simplest traditional melodies. Where the text is more important the style is more chantlike, since the Thai language, like the Chinese dialects, is tonal and therefore precludes a use of free melodies with texts.

sist of tuned horizontal gongs placed in diatonic order in a circular frame, open at the back, which rests on the floor. The player sits in the centre and uses two beaters made of circular heads with handles. The range of the instruments is just over two octaves (see figs.5, 6 and 7, pp.716–17).

The two Thai metallophones (ranāt ēk lek – high-pitched, and ranāt thum lek – low-pitched) were adopted by the Thai in the 19th century and were probably copied from the Indonesian metallophones, saron and gěnder. They both have rectangular, box-shaped resonators and rectangular iron keys, and duplicate the xylophones in pitch and range.

(ii) Rhythmic percussion. This category includes ching (small hand cymbals of thick metal); chāp lek (hand

2. Part of a mǫn ensemble with khǫng mǫn (gong-chime, centre), ranāt ēk (xylophone, rear) and pī mǫn (double-reed instrument, left)

Music is much used with theatre and dance, but this is in the same style as non-theatrical music, and uses the same instruments (see SOUTH-EAST ASIA, §II, 4).

2. INSTRUMENTS.
(i) Melodic percussion. Two sizes of xylophone are used, high-pitched (ranāt ēk) and low-pitched (ranāt thum). The ranāt ēk has a boat-shaped wooden resonator mounted on a pedestal; the ranāt thum has a rectangular, box-shaped resonator. The wooden keys on both instruments are strung on cords which are hung over hooks on the end-boards. The range of the ranāt ēk is three octaves, that of the ranāt thum is just over two octaves. The player uses two padded playing sticks.

Two sizes of gong-chimes (gong circles or sets of kettle-gongs) are played, high-pitched (khǫng wong lek) and low-pitched (khǫng wong yai). The instruments con-

cymbals of thin metal between about 6 and 7·5 cm in diameter); and mōng (a medium-sized, wide-flanged gong, usually hung on a metal stand and played with a padded beater), as well as several types of drum. The taphōn, a barrel-shaped drum mounted on a stand, has laced heads and a body completely covered with strips of thong. It is played with the hands (figs.5 and 6 below). The klǫng that, a large barrel-shaped drum with pegged heads, is played with sticks and used in pairs (fig.6 below). The klǫng khāek, a long, narrow cylindrical drum with laced heads, is played with the hands and also used in pairs. The thōn (goblet- or vase-shaped single-headed drum; fig.7 below) is probably derived from similar drums of the Near East, and is played with the hands. The rammanā (a shallow frame drum with one pegged head; fig.7 below), probably derived from Chinese models, is also played with the hands. The thōn and rammanā are often played by the same player.

(iii) *Wind instruments*. The *khlui* (bamboo flute; fig.5 below) is made in three sizes: the medium-sized is the one now usually used. The instrument has seven finger-holes and a membrane-covered hole in the side: the air is directed through the pegged mouthpiece against a sharp edge of a rectangular hole in the back.

The *pī* is a double-reed instrument in which both sides of the reed are made from two layers, thereby making it in fact a quadruple reed. The wooden body is flared out at each end and bulges slightly in the centre; it has a cylindrical bore and six finger-holes. Three sizes are made: small, medium and large; the largest, the *pī nai*, is the one now generally used (fig.3). The player uses circular breathing.

The *khāen* is not a member of any traditional ensemble but is widely used in northern Thailand, Burma and Laos. It consists of free-beating metal reeds placed inside long bamboo tubes which are placed in two rows having a common mouthpiece. Holes in the sides of the tubes allow the air to pass through: when they are covered by the fingers, the air is forced through the tubes, setting the reeds in motion. The instrument varies in size, some models being as long as 2·1 metres. Although different in shape, the *khāen* is related to the Chinese *sheng* and the Japanese *shō*.

(iv) *String instruments*. Plucked string instruments include the *jakhē* and the *krajappī*. The former is a zither with three strings, plucked with an ivory plectrum. The body is a stylized version of what was originally a carved head of a crocodile, from which the instrument gets its name. It rests on three short legs on the floor (fig.7 below). Although little used today, the *krajappī* was once an important instrument. It is a plucked lute with a resonating box shaped somewhat like a tortoise-shell (from which the instrument gets its name), a long, narrow neck and four strings in two courses. It is played with a plectrum.

Of the bowed instruments, the *sǫ duang* consists of a round resonating box, covered with leather at one end and open at the other, a long cylindrical neck that goes through the resonator, and two strings attached to two pegs. The hair of the bow is fixed permanently behind the strings (fig.4). The instrument is analogous to Chinese fiddles of this type (*hu-ch'in*). The *sǫ ū* is similar to the *sǫ duang*, but with a resonating chamber of half a coconut shell (see fig.7). The *sǫ sām saī* (fig.7) is a spike fiddle with three strings and a bow separate from the instrument, probably derived from a Near Eastern model; it is similar to the two-string Javanese *rĕbab*. It is usually played solo or to accompany the voice. It is not a regular member of any ensemble but may be added to one if there is singing.

(v) *Ensembles*. There are three main ensembles used to perform Thai music, and each may be small, medium or large. Only the essential instruments are found in the small ensemble. The medium-sized ensemble usually has one of each of the principal instruments, and the large ensemble generally has two of all the instruments that lend themselves to doubling, together with some extra instruments that are not essential to the medium-sized ensemble.

The *pī phāt* is the standard Thai ensemble (figs.5 and 6) and consists of the melodic percussion instruments, the hand cymbals and gong, and the *taphōn* and *klǫng that* drums. The *pī* is the only wind instrument included and gives the ensemble its name. The *mahōrī* ensemble includes smaller models of the melodic percussion in-

3. *Pī nai (double-reed instrument)*

4. *Sǫ duang (fiddle)*

struments, the hand cymbals and gong (frequently omitted), and the *thōn* and *rammanā* drums (fig.7). The flute is the wind instrument, and the string instruments include the *sǭ duang*, *sǭ ū* and *jakhē*.

The *khrῠang saī* is the ensemble of string instruments: *sǭ duang*, *sǭ ū* and *jakhē*. The *sǭ sām saī* may occasionally be added, particularly if there is to be much singing. The flute, *thōn*, *rammanā* and hand cymbals are used, and the gong is optional.

Substitutes and additions are often made if the ensemble or the event for which it is playing is informal: a pair of *klǭng khāek* will often be substituted for the other drums, and the flute may replace the *pī* in a *pī phāt* ensemble if the music is played indoors, in a small room.

Another set of instruments, similar to the regular facets (the rest of the parts), presenting many simultaneous views of the same object. The parts for the *khǭng wong lek*, *ranāt ēk*, *ranāt ēk lek*, *khlui*, *pī* and the string instruments generally proceed at a faster pace than the main melody, played by the *khǭng wong yai*. The parts for the *ranāt thum* and *ranāt thum lek* are at a slower pace. The faster-moving parts add passing notes and ornaments to the main melody, while the slower-moving parts are extractions from it. This can be seen in ex.1, which shows part of the score of a composition for the *pī phāt* ensemble.

Thai music has no notation system of its own but can easily be shown in Western notation: the written notes of a conventional Western scale or mode may represent the seven pitches of any octave series in Thai tuning.

5. *Small indoor pī phāt ensemble: front row* (left to right), *khlui* (flute), *ranāt ēk* (xylophone), *thōn chatri* (vase-shaped drums), *ranāt thum* (xylophone); *back row* (left to right), *klǭng that* (barrel drums, not being played), *ching* (cymbals), *khǭng wong yai* (gong-chime), *klǭng khāek* (cylindrical drum) and *taphōn* (barrel drum)

Thai melodic percussion instruments, form the *mǭn* (Môn people) ensemble, which plays for funerals and cremations. In this, the *khǭng* instruments have heavy wooden frames that stand upright, and the *pī mǭn* and *taphōn mǭn* are larger than the Thai models. The melodic percussion instruments are highly ornamented and decorated in red and gold. The ensemble is otherwise basically the same as the *pī phāt* ensemble.

3. FUNDAMENTALS OF THE MUSIC SYSTEM.

(i) *Ensemble music*. Thai traditional music has a linear, non-harmonic system: its texture derives from the technique of polyphonic stratification (a term first used by Mantle Hood in Indonesian studies), which may be likened to a gemstone (the main melody) with many

It must be noted, however, that the intervals are equidistant, not tones and semitones as in Western tuning. As the instruments cannot produce a wide variety of dynamics, Thai ensemble music is not characterized by dynamic variations, although the ensembles themselves have a certain basic dynamic characteristic: the *pī phāt* ensemble is relatively loud, the *mahōrī* ensemble less so, and the *khrῠang saī* ensemble is the softest. Apparent dynamics vary, of course, with the distance of the listener from the ensemble. Because of the lack of dynamic differentiation and the repetitive metrical structure of its compositions, Thai music sounds to a listener unfamiliar with the style like one long unbroken pattern.

(ii) *Tuning*. Thai instruments of fixed pitch are tuned to

6. *Large pī phāt ensemble: front row (left to right), ranāt ēk lek (metallophone), ranāt ēk, ranāt thum (xylophones), ranāt thum lek (metallophone); centre (left to right), taphōn (barrel drum), pī nai (double-reed instrument), khǭng wong yai, khǭng wong lek (gong-chimes), pī nǭk (double-reed instrument), klǭng that (barrel drums); back row (left to right), ching and chāp lek (cymbals), mōng (gong) and chāp yai (cymbals)*

seven equidistant pitches to an octave, the interval between any two pitches being ideally 171·4 cents, which is about 28 cents (about one seventh of a tone) less than the Western whole tone. In practice, intervals vary between 165 and 180 cents. The 4th and 5th are relatively close to the comparable tempered intervals; the other intervals do not correspond to any in the Western system. The 3rd and 6th are called 'neutral', occurring approximately halfway between the corresponding Western major and minor intervals. Each of the seven pitches has a name which in general corresponds to the style of music for which that pitch is a tonal centre or tonic, or to the instrument commonly associated with

that style. A simple comparison of Thai and Western divisions of the octave is shown in Table 1.

TABLE 1: Comparison of Thai and Western octave divisions

Thai	1	2	3	4	5	6	7	1
Western	C	C♯ D	E♭ E	F	F♯ G	A♭ A	B♭ B	C

Most intervals in the Thai system do not correspond to simple, whole-number acoustical ratios, but the musicians are keenly aware of their tuning system; they

7. *Large mahōrī ensemble: back row (left to right), ching (cymbals), two sǭ duang (fiddles), khǭng wong yai (gong-chime), thōn and rammanā (goblet and frame drums), khǭng wong lek (gong-chime), two sǭ ū (fiddles), chāp lek (cymbals); centre, khlui phiang ǭ and khlui ū (flutes); centre row, jakhē (zithers, extreme left and right), ranāt ēk, ranāt thum (xylophones); front row, two sǭ sām sāi (spike fiddles)*

Ex.1 from *Sāthukān, pī phāt* ensemble

Special *ching* pattern of four strokes per bar.

can tune their instruments accurately by ear with little effort and take great care to do so before playing. Although there is no standard tuning level among different ensembles, most are fairly similar; the range of difference is perhaps 10–15 cycles per second in the region of Western *c'*. The instruments of one ensemble are, of course, carefully tuned to each other.

(*iii*) *Melody*. The main melodies of traditional compositions are of two types: those of the older compositions are simpler and based on motifs, the newer ones are more lyrical. In ex.1 the *khǫng wong yai* part is a motivic type of main melody; further examples may be seen in ex.2 below. Examples of lyrical melodies will be found in exx.3, 4 and 5 below. Thai melodies are generally diatonic within the basically pentatonic framework. Leaps may occur, but they are restricted by definite principles, the main one being that after a leap of an acoustical 4th or more, the melody changes direction. Leaps may also sometimes occur when a portion of the melodic line is shifted an octave upwards or downwards, usually owing to the limited range of the instruments.

(*iv*) *Styles*. Two main musical styles may be said to be prominent. 'Thai' style, which is related to Chinese music, is basically pentatonic. (In speaking of the pentatonic in Thai and Chinese music, the anhemitonic or

minor 3rd, gapped genus is meant, which is often indicated in ciphers as 123 56 1.) The other style, referred to as the *mǫn* style, although generally confined to the five pitches of the pentatonic scale at basic structural points, uses the other two available pitches of the octave to a much greater extent in the melody, and 'modulation' to other pitch levels is more frequent than in Thai style. Ex.5 is a section of a composition in Thai style; examples of *mǫn* style may be seen in exx.3*b* and 4.

(*v*) *Metre, rhythm and tempo*. With few exceptions, Thai traditional music is in duple metre, which is traditionally notated in 2/4 time. Within the duple metre, rhythmic procedures are relatively simple. Three basic tempos are used: slow, medium and fast. The slow tempo is approximately andante (crotchet = 50–60), the medium tempo twice as fast, and the fast tempo twice as fast again.

The strokes of the small hand cymbals, the *ching*, which mark the structure of all traditional compositions, corresponds to these tempos – there is a pattern for each. Certain strokes of the *ching* are reinforced by the gong, if it is present. (The colotomic structure of Thai music is far less elaborate than that of the Javanese and Balinese systems, but it seems definitely related to them.) The slow tempo has one *ching* stroke to a bar, alternating open (i.e. ringing, unaccented) strokes and damped (accented) strokes. The medium tempo has two *ching* strokes to a bar, and the fast tempo has four. In other words, increases in tempo involve a doubling and quadrupling of the number of *ching* strokes.

TABLE 2: Pulse groupings

1 bar	1	2	3	4			
2 bars	1		2	3	4		
4 bars		1		2	3		4
8 bars			1 3		2 4		
16 bars				1 2 3			4
etc							

The system of emphasis in traditional music is similar to that of Indonesia: groups of four pulses have a secondary emphasis on the second pulse and a strong emphasis on the fourth. There are several types of pulse-groupings, as shown in Table 2. Motifs and phrases drive towards the final beat or pulse of the group. In Western music notation the final (strongest) beat or pulse of a group occurs on the first beat of the bar: when notating Thai music, for convenience, the Western pattern of emphasis is followed. The two methods of notating pulse-groupings can be seen clearly in the two charts of the *ching* patterns. Table 3*a* shows three *ching* patterns according to the Western system, ending the pattern on the downbeat of the final bar – this necessitates beginning the new pattern in that same final bar as an anacrusis. Table 3*b* shows the same patterns notated according to the Thai (and south-east Asian) system of emphasis in which each pattern ends on the fourth pulse or beat of a bar.

TABLE 3

(a) Ching patterns according to Western notation

	(final bar)
	1 2 3 4 1 2 3 4 1 2 3 4 1 2 3 4
prop kai and sām chan }	|o |+ |o |x∥ o ∥
sōng mai and sōng chan }	|× o |× o |× o |×∥o × o∥
phlēng reo and chan dio }	|× o × o|× o × o|× o × o|×∥ʔ ↯ ∥

(end of composition)

(b) Ching patterns according to the Thai system

	(final bar)
	1 2 3 4 1 2 3 4 1 2 3 4 1 2 3 4
prop kai and sām chan }	| o| +| o| ×∥
sōng mai and sōng chan }	| o ×| o ×| o ×| o ×∥
phlēng reo and chan dio }	|o × o ×|o × o ×|o × o ×|o × o ×∥

KEY:
= strong emphasis
– secondary emphasis
o open (i.e. ringing), unaccented ching stroke
+ damped, accented ching stroke
× ching and gong together

4. MODAL PRACTICE. There is no Thai word comparable to 'mode'. Modal practice in Thai traditional music seems to be derived from and related to modal procedures in Chinese music: each pitch of the pentatonic scale may serve as the tonic of a mode. Thus there are five basic modes: mode 1, mode 2, mode 3, mode 5 and mode 6. Theoretically each of these could begin on any of the seven pitches in the octave tuning, but in practice this is not the case. Four pitch levels only are used to any great extent. Little musical terminology is used by the Thai, and for purposes of analysis and discussion the following scheme has been devised: the pitch at which the *pī* is said to play or be 'at home' is labelled pitch level I; the *khlui* is 'at home' one pitch level lower at pitch level VII (both instruments can, of course, play at any pitch level); the other pitches are labelled accordingly in order. The pitch levels IV and III are the other two levels most frequently used. Levels II, V and VI rarely occur as tonal centres of an entire composition, although occasionally a section or frequently a temporary 'modulation' may lie in one of these areas.

Pitch level I is called *kruat* which means 'gravel' or 'pebbles' and aesthetically means 'hard' and 'bright'. This would seem to describe well the complex tone quality of the sound of the *pī*. Pitch level VII is referred to as *phiang q̄*, part of the full name of the medium-sized flute (*khlui phiang q̄*), and can be considered aesthetically to mean 'soft', like the tone quality of the flute. Because the pitch levels a 5th apart (levels I and IV, levels VII and III) often work together in 'modulations' and because the two strings of the *sǭ duang* and *sǭ ū* are tuned to these pitches, it is convenient to refer to levels I and VII as 'high' pitch levels and to levels IV and III as 'low' pitch levels. The other three pitches are referred to simply by number.

Pitches have different functions in different pitch levels, just as in Western music, and these are shown in diagram form in Table 4.

TABLE 4

I	(high *kruat*):			5 6	1 2 3	5 6 1
VII	(high *phiang q̄*):	1 2 3	5 6	1 2 3	5 6 1	
IV	(low *kruat*):		1 2 3	5 6	1	
III	(low *phiang q̄*)		1 2 3	5 6	1	

Pitch level I is traditionally notated as in the key of G, level VII as F, level IV as C, and level III as B♭. Thus pitch 3 in pitch level I (G) is B, while in pitch level III (B♭) it is D; pitch 1 in VII (F) is F, while pitch 3 in V (D) is F♯.

The pitches that coincide with the *ching* strokes in a composition give the modal implications of that composition. Those pitches that coincide with the damped, accented strokes, and those that coincide with every fourth pulse of a group of four pulses or multiple of four, are modally more important than other pitches.

Another aspect of Thai music is the special emphasis on 5th relationships. The main melody of compositions is made up of a number of motifs or 'phrase-units' generally two or four bars long. The pitches at the middle and end of such phrase-units are frequently 5ths, which have been termed 'pivotal 5ths'. In the Thai pentatonic system the pivotal 5ths are 1–5 and 5–1, 5–2 and 2–5, 2–6 and 6–2, 6–3 and 3–6. Since a 5th above pitch 3 is pitch 7, which does not occur in the pentatonic series (123 56 1), it appears that pitch 1 may be substituted for pitch 7; likewise, a 5th below pitch 1 is pitch 4, which does not occur in the pentatonic series, for which pitch 3 is substituted. This assumption is supported by the frequent occurrence of 1–3 and 3–1 at the middle and end of phrase-units. Some of these pivotal 5ths are illustrated in ex.2; others may be seen in the other examples.

Ex.2 Pivotal 5ths in four-bar phrase-units

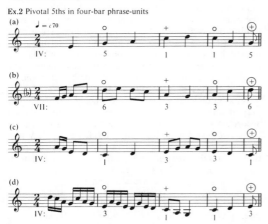

The final notes of a section and of a composition are very important pitches; in fact, the final note in Thai compositions (as in a great many Chinese compositions) is perhaps the most important factor in defining the mode, because final cadences (usually four descending pitches, e.g. 5–3–2–1) almost without exception end on the final *ching* stroke. The two most used modes in Thai music are those on 1 and 6, in which the final cadences are 5–3–2–1 and 3–2–1–6. Pitch 1 in both cases is the same, and therefore the pitch level will be the same, the arrangement being as shown in Table 5.

TABLE 5

Mode 1 (VII):		1 2 3	5 6 1
Mode 6 (VII):	6	1 2 3	5 6

The parallel Western major–minor concept does not occur in Thai music. These two modes can be heard as comparable to Western major and relative minor modes, but since modes 1 and 6 have always been prominent in Chinese music, this would not seem to be a Western influence. The mode on 2 is frequent in *mǫn* style. Modes 3 and 5 are rarely used except in passing.

Thai music has great variety in spite of the restrictions within which it operates, and often more than one mode occurs in a composition, or the mode is transferred to another pitch level. In a linear style of music this latter procedure (called 'modulation' in Western music) has been called 'metabole' (an ancient Greek term) by Brăiloiu and Trân Van Khê (in his writings on Vietnamese music) and it is also appropriate to Thai music. Metabole may be accomplished by a 'pivotal pitch' method in which a principal pitch in one mode becomes a principal pitch of the mode on another level: for example, pitch 5 in VII is pitch 2 in III (see ex.3a). In other cases one of the non-modal pitches (pitch 4 or 7), often used for decoration or as a passing note, may become a principal pitch of a mode on another pitch level: for example, pitch 4 in IV may become pitch 1 in VII (see ex.3b). The shift of pitch in metabole is usually to a 5th above or below, but occasionally a 5th may be

Ex.3

(a) from *Ton nāng nāk*, metabole, Thai style

(b) from *Jin tharāhū, mǫn* style

elided, and the new level may be two 5ths away, the result of which is a diatonic movement. A possible instance of this may be seen in ex.4 from the second to the third line; if the third line is considered to be in level IV, then the metabole is from level V in the second line to level IV in the third, a diatonic movement, proceeding to the intermediate level (I) in the fourth line.

With so much allowable variety within the restrictions of the system, it is often the general mood of a composition, rather than the strict adherence to a modal procedure (as in Indian raga and Indonesian *paṭēt*), that prevails in Thai music. This mood is conveyed by the frequency with which certain pitches occur on the

Ex.4 from *Phrayā khruan, mǫn* style

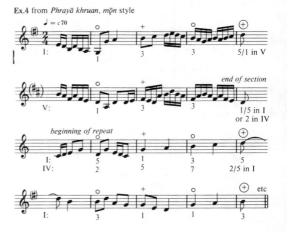

damped *ching* strokes. It can be readily seen that a composition in which pitches 1, 3 and 5 are emphasized will have a very different 'mood' from one in which pitches 3, 6 and 2 are emphasized, even though both may end on pitch 1 with a 5–3–2–1 cadence. This may be seen by examining the outline of structural pitches shown in Table 6.

TABLE 6: Outline of structural pitches in *Khruan hā*

Section 1	Section 3
0 + 0 X	0 + 0 X
1 3 3 1	2 6 6 2
3 5 1 5	5 2 2 6
5 5 1 5	3 1 1 3
1 5 5 3	6 3 3 1
3 1 1 3	2 6 2 5
6 3 3 1	2 6 3 1

The total length of each section is 24 bars. Each section ends with a 5–3–2–1 cadence. A comparison of the pitches occurring on all *ching* strokes, on the accented *ching* strokes only, and on the strokes played simultaneously by *ching* and gong, reveals the decided difference in pitch emphasis, and consequently in 'mood', of each section.

5. FORM. Few forms exist in Thai traditional music. Form may basically be equated with the three *ching* patterns illustrated in Table 2.

The oldest body of extant Thai compositions is that of the *Rŭang*, medleys or suites of compositions which share a similar name, form (i.e. *ching* pattern) or style, or combination of these. These compositions have motivic main melodies, generally through-composed, and each section is usually repeated. Some *Rŭang* are as short as ten minutes, others last up to 40 minutes. The same motivic material and phrase-units (i.e. 'melodic species') are frequently found in more than one composition.

Many of the compositions in the *Rŭang*, or portions of them, served as the basis of new compositions in a style or form that arose in the second half of the 19th century and reached its peak of development in the first quarter of the 20th century. This form, called *thao*, is a variation form (the word *thao* means 'a set of something in graduated sizes'). To create a *thao*, a composer took a piece of existing material, the sections of which were usually 16 bars long, extended this material to twice its length, and shortened it to half its length. Compositions usually have two or three sections. Each division uses one of the *ching* patterns: the original version is in the *sŏng mai* or *sŏng chan* pattern, the extended version in the *prop kai* or *sām chan* pattern, and the short version in the *phlēng reo* or *chan dio* pattern.

The method of extending the original material is to put the pitches that occur on the *ching*-and-gong strokes in the original version on the accented *ching* strokes of the *sām chan* pattern; the pitches that occur on the unaccented strokes of the original may also be transferred to the unaccented strokes of the extended version, but this is optional. Table 7 shows this in diagram form. The composer then composes new material in the style of the original, arranging the new melody so that the proper pitches occur in it at the correct places. For the short version the composer reverses the process and contracts the original version to half its length, following the same procedure of keeping the essential pitches

TABLE 7

extended version sām chan (4 bars)	|○	|+	|○	|×
original version sōng chan (2 bars)	| ○	|×	○	|×
short version chan dio (1 bar)	○	×	○	|×

in the proper places (Table 7). The 'telescopic variations' are then played in the order: extended version, middle version (i.e. the original version) and short version. If vocal sections are used, they precede the comparable instrumental section.

To illustrate this, the outline of structural pitches of the composition *Khamēn phuang* is shown in Table 8. An examination of the pitches reveals where principles are adhered to and where deviations (for aesthetic and artistic reasons) occur; the pitches in the right-hand column (primary accents) in each version rarely vary, those in the second column of the extended version will sometimes vary from those in the comparable column in the middle version, and those in the columns showing unaccented strokes frequently vary, sometimes because melody pitches are sounded slightly before or after the beat and sometimes because the pivotal 5th of the original pitch is substituted. For the short version only the primary accented pitches are given, since to contract the melody usually involves a good deal of manipulation and often only the essential pitches are retained. The last phrase-unit may appear different in all three versions as the cadential unit of the middle version is sometimes transferred intact to the extended and short versions, which often causes different pitches to fall on the *ching* strokes in the last line. Or, as in *Khamēn phuang*, the direction of the cadence may be reversed from the middle to the extended version. Ex.5 shows the last four lines of section 1 of *Khamēn phuang* in open score, the three versions being given one under the other for purposes of comparison. The composition is by Luang Pradit Phairǫ, a notable 20th-century Thai

TABLE 8: Outline of structural pitches in *Khamēn phuang*

	Extended version	Middle version	Short version
Section 1	32 bars	16 bars	8 bars
		0 X 0 X	X X
	1 1 2 1	1 1 1 1	1 1
	6 3 3 6	2 3 5 6	3 6
	6 2 6 6	5 1 1 6	1 6
	6 5 3 5	3 5 3 5	3 5
	5 5 6 1	5 5 1 1	1 1
	1 1 1 3	6 1 2 3	1 3
	3 2 1 6	3 3 2 6	2 6
	6 3 2 1	6 6 5 1	6 1
Section 2	48 bars	24 bars	12 bars
	0 + 0 X	0 X 0 X	X X
	1 1 2 1	1 1 1 1	1 1
	3 1 1 1	6 1 2 3	1 3
	3 3 3 6	3 5 5 6	3 6
	6 6 3 2	6 3 3 2	3 2
	2 2 2 6	2 2 2 6	3 6
	6 3 6 6	6 6 6 6	6 6
	1 2 1 6	5 7 2 6	3 5
	6 3 3 1	1 5 5 1	1 1
	1 3 2 6	1 2 2 6	5 5
	6 3 2 1	2 5 5 1	1 1
	1 3 2 6	1 2 2 6	3 2
	6 3 2 1	2 5 5 1	6 1

Ex.5 from *Khamēn phuang*, section 1

composer.

There are hundreds of *thao* compositions in the Thai repertory. Frequently only the extended or *sām chan* version was written or preserved, and many compositions are found only in that form. There are a few well-known compositions originally created in the *sǒng chan* form, a rather unusual occurrence. The *phlēng reo* compositions of the *Rǔang* and the *chan dio* section of the *thao* are never performed separately.

6. VOCAL MUSIC. Vocal sections are accompanied by the *ching* and drums only, and occasionally by a string instrument. There are no vocal sections in the *Rǔang*. *Thao* compositions and those in *sām chan* and *sǒng chan* have vocal sections alternating with the instrumental sections, although the instrumental sections may be performed alone. The vocal sections have essentially the same pitch structure as the instrumental sections that follow, but the frequent complex ornaments tend to obscure this.

The Thai language is tonal, and at some time in the past this was felt to restrict the melodic scope of the instruments, and so the two were separated. In most styles the vocal line adheres to the pitches of the fixed-pitch system at structural points. Intricate ornaments are often used which involve pitches and inflections not in the fixed-pitch system. The vocal quality of singers is fairly complex acoustically, and the tone is straight, without vibrato. Characteristic of Thai vocal style is the increase in volume of sound towards the end of a held pitch, and the use of the glottal sound, particularly a kind of glottal falsetto ornament at the end of a held pitch, often a 4th higher than the principal pitch.

See also LAOS.

BIBLIOGRAPHY

A. J. Ellis: 'Tonometrical Observations on some Existing Non-harmonic Scales', *Proceedings of the Society of Arts*, xxvii (1884), 368
——: 'On the Musical Scales of Various Nations', *Journal of the Society of Arts*, xxxiii (1885), 485–527; appx, p.1102
F. W. Verney: *Notes on Siamese Musical Instruments* (London, 1885)
C. Stumpf: 'Tonsystem und Musik der Siamesen', *Beiträge zur Akustik und Musikwissenschaft*, iii (1901), 69–138 [pubd separately Leipzig, 1901; also in *Sammelbände für vergleichende Musikwissenschaft*, i (1922), 122–77]
E. M. von Hornbostel: 'Formanalysen an siamesischen Orchesterstücken', *AMw*, ii (1919–20), 306
J. Kunst: 'Een overwalsche bloed verwant van den Javaanschen gamelan: geschiedenis van het Siameesche orkest' [A relative of the Javanese gamelan: history of the Siamese orchestra], *Nederlandsch-Indië oud en nieuw*, xiv (1929–30), 79, 354
Damrong Rajanubhab: *Thamnān khrǔang mahōrī pīphāt: Siamese Musical Instruments* (Bangkok, 2/1931)
L. Strickland: 'Music and Dancing in Siam', *Etude*, lvi (1938), 440
X. Zarina: 'The Thai Royal Ballet', *Asia*, xli (1941), 285
D. Morton: 'Thailand', *Harvard Dictionary of Music* (Cambridge, Mass., 1944, rev. 2/1969)
K. Pringsheim: 'Music of Thailand', *Contemporary Japan*, xiii (1944), 745
Phra Chen Duriyanga: *Siamese Music* (Bangkok, 1948, 2/1953, 4/1956 as *Thai Music*)
D. Yupho: *Atibāiyanāt silpa Thai* [On classical Siamese theatre] (Bangkok, 1951; Eng. trans., 1952)
——: *The Preliminary Course of Training in Siamese Theatrical Art* (Bangkok, 1952, rev. 2/1954)
V. Vichitr-Vadakarn: 'The Evolution of Thai Music', *Thai Digest*, i (1957), 8 Feb, p.42; 15 Feb, p.12
D. Yupho: *Khrǔang dontri Thai* [Thai musical instruments] (Bangkok, 1957, 2/1967; Eng. trans., 1960, 2/1971)
W. Blanchard and others, eds.: *Thailand: its People, its Society, its Culture* (New Haven, 1958)
Thai Classical Music, ed. Dept. of Fine Arts, i (Bangkok, 1961)
D. Yupho: *The Khon and Lakon* (Bangkok, 1963)
D. Morton: 'The Traditional Instrumental Music of Thailand', *The Musics of Asia: Manila 1966*, 90
—— 'The Traditional Music of Thailand', IER 7502/A-D [disc notes]
S. Moore: 'Thai Songs in 7/4 Meter', *EM*, xiii (1969), 309
D. Morton: 'Thai Traditional Music: Hot-house Plant or Sturdy Stock', *Journal of the Siam Society*, lviii/2 (1970), 1–44
——: 'An American Discovers Thai Music', *Arts of Asia*, i/5 (1971), 11
——: 'Polyphonic Stratification in Traditional Thai Music: a Study in Multiple Tone Color', *Asian and Pacific Council Quarterly of Cultural and Social Affairs*, iii/1 (1971), 70
——: 'Music in Thailand: the Traditional System and Foreign Influences', *Musikkulturen Asiens, Afrikas und Ozeaniens im 19. Jahrhundert*, ed. R. Guenther (Regensburg, 1973), 185
——: 'Vocal Tones in Traditional Thai Music', *Selected Reports*, ii/1 (1974), 89
Selected Reports, ii/2 (1975) [special issue, incl. articles on Thai music by G. P. Dyck, M. Hood, S. P. Mendenhall, P. Silapabanleng, D. Morton]
D. Morton: *The Traditional Music of Thailand* (Berkeley, 1976)

DAVID MORTON

Ṭhākura, Ṣaurīndramohana. *See* TAGORE, SOURINDRO MOHUN.

Thalben-Ball, George (Thomas) (*b* Sydney, 18 June 1896). British organist. He was a leading performer, with musical roots going back to Stanford and Parry, and was in the forefront of international recitalists for more than half a century. He studied at the Royal College of Music and became a Fellow of the Royal College of Organists at 16. He was appointed organist of the Temple Church, London, in 1923 and civic and university organist, Birmingham, in 1949 (being awarded an honorary doctorate in December 1972). He inaugurated many important organs, including those in the Royal Albert Hall and the BBC Concert Hall, London, and was for many years a regular performer and broadcaster at the Henry Wood Promenade Concerts. He was a member of the BBC music department from 1939 to 1946, and adviser until 1970, during which time he set his stamp on the daily religious service, and composed a variety of organ and choral music. Thalben-Ball firmly believes that the resources of the modern organ should be fully exploited; some of his exuberant and intensely romantic interpretations of music of all periods have come to sound a little dated although they have uniquely inspired succeeding generations of organists.

BIBLIOGRAPHY
D. Lewer: *A Spiritual Song: the Story of the Temple Choir* (London, 1961)
J. Rennert: *George Thalben-Ball* (Newton Abbot and London, 1979)
STANLEY WEBB

Thalberg, Sigismond (Fortuné François) (*b* Pâquis, nr. Geneva, 8 Jan 1812; *d* Posillipo, nr. Naples, 27 April 1871). German or Austrian pianist and composer. He was said to be the illegitimate son of Count Moritz Dietrichstein and the Baroness von Wetzlar, but his birth certificate states that his parents were Joseph Thalberg and Fortunée Stein, both of Frankfurt am Main. Although the certificate describes them as 'mariés', the wording rather suggests that each was married to someone else. It seems possible that Dietrichstein induced Joseph Thalberg to assume paternity and that the mother was a baroness in disguise; but the circumstances remain mysterious.

At the age of ten Thalberg was sent to Vienna to prepare for a career in the diplomatic service, but he studied music at the same time, receiving a rudimentary training from Mittag, the first bassoonist at the Court Opera, and then studying theory with Simon Sechter and the piano with Hummel. From the age of 14 he appeared with great success as a salon pianist, and two years later his first works were published. His international career began in 1830 when he toured in England and Germany and later in other European countries. He continued his studies with J. P. Pixis and Frédéric Kalkbrenner in Paris and Moscheles in London. In 1836 he won considerable success and renown in Paris, and this was further increased the following year when Liszt, returning from Switzerland to challenge Thalberg's position as the leading virtuoso in Paris, wrote an article in the *Revue et gazette musicale* harshly criticizing his compositions. This article was the start of an animated controversy between Liszt and Fétis, who considered Thalberg the greatest living pianist and defended his compositions in the *Revue et gazette*

Sigismond Thalberg: lithograph by F. Grevedon

musicale; Berlioz joined the controversy on the side of Liszt, who pressed his claim in some very forthright articles and gave numerous concerts. The rivalry came to an end with a concert the two pianists gave jointly for the Princess de Belgiojoso; this symbolic reconciliation was sealed by their agreeing to cooperate with other famous virtuosos in composing one variation each for *Hexaméron*, as a tribute to the princess (the other composers were Pixis, Herz, Czerny and Chopin). From that time Thalberg enjoyed enormous popularity throughout Europe. In 1855 he travelled as far as Brazil and Havana, and he then lived for several years in the USA, where he gave successful concerts, taught and organized opera productions. He married the daughter of the opera singer Luigi Lablache in 1844, and in 1858 he bought a villa in Posillipo, near Naples. He continued to tour during the next five years, though with less frequency, and then retired to Posillipo, where he spent his last years as a vintner.

Together with Liszt, Thalberg must be ranked as the greatest virtuoso pianist of the mid-19th century, a view endorsed by Mendelssohn in a letter of 30 March 1840. In keeping with the virtuoso tradition he played almost exclusively music of his own composition, which consisted mainly of fantasias on favourite opera arias by Rossini, Meyerbeer, Donizetti, Verdi and sometimes Weber and Mozart. His Fantasia op.33, on themes from Rossini's *Moïse*, brought him wide recognition, and the dazzling technique it demanded aroused admiration. Later it was realized that Thalberg's basic compositional method was relatively simple, consisting of placing the melody in the centre of the keyboard first in one hand, then in the other (the thumbs and the sustaining pedal used in particular to prolong the sound), and ornamenting it with florid counterpoint and chords above and below. Nevertheless, an image of Thalberg as a stupendous virtuoso composer had been created, and the cartoonist Dantan portrayed him as having ten hands.

Fétis admired Thalberg for his ability to combine the merits of 'brilliant' technique, derived from Clementi, and of the singing style of Hummel and Mozart; in Thalberg's art, regard for phrasing and expression did not conflict with sparkling passage-work, but the two techniques were superimposed on each other; he combined dash and power with unfailing care for bel canto. In this context one of his most significant works is *L'art du chant appliqué au piano*, in which arrangements of opera arias are used as teaching pieces for the piano.

With regard to Thalberg's merits as a composer Schumann, who was not at all favourably disposed towards virtuosos, made an exception in this case; in his reviews for the *Neue Zeitschrift für Musik* he gave high praise to the Fantasia and Variations op.12 on themes from *Norma*, the E minor Caprice op.15, the Nocturnes op.16, the Variations op.17 and the Scherzo op.31. Nevertheless, Thalberg's compositions are of questionable value, and neither the Concerto op.5 nor the Sonata op.56 is worthy of attention. A few minor pieces, such as the nocturnes, the *Romances sans paroles*, the studies and the Ballade op.76 are more appealing. The most interesting works are the long fantasias: though they give the impression of a potpourri method more often than of genuine invention on well-known themes, they are skilfully and effectively written. Using popular operas as their basis, they helped to bring to the art of piano playing the same kind of emotional feeling which the great singers aroused. Neither of Thalberg's own operas, however, enjoyed any success.

WORKS

PIANO WORKS BASED ON OPERA THEMES
(many with orch accompaniment ad lib)

Fantasias and variations: on Euryanthe, op.1; on Robert le diable, op.6; on La straniera, op.9; on I Montecchi ed i Capuleti, op.10; on Norma, op.12; on Don Giovanni, op.14; 2 on Les Huguenots, opp.20 and 43; on Moïse, op.33; on Benedict's The Gipsy, op.34; on Oberon, op.37; on La donna del lago, op.40bis; on the Serenade and Minuet from Don Giovanni, op.42; on the Andante finale from Lucia di Lammermoor; on Beatrice di Tenda, op.49; on Lucrezia Borgia, op.50; on Semiramide, op.51; on Auber's La muette de Portici, op.52; on Hérold's Zampa, op.53; on the Triumphal March from Berlioz's L'apothéose, op.58; on Il barbiere di Siviglia, op.63; on Don Pasquale, op.67; on La fille du régiment, op.68; on Il trovatore, op.77; on La traviata, op.78; 1 variation in Hexaméron, variations on a theme from I puritani (1837), collab. Liszt and others

Other works: Impromptu, on Le siège de Corinthe, op.3; Mélange on Guillaume Tell, op.5bis; Les soirées musicales, divertimento on favourite themes by Rossini, op.18; Caprice, on La sonnambula, op.46; Caprice, on Halévy's Charles VI, op.48; Decaméron, 10 pieces [based on opera themes], op.57; Souvenir de Un ballo in maschera, op.81; Souvenir de Rigoletto, op.82

OTHER PIANO WORKS

2 caprices, e, op.15, E♭, op.19; 8 nocturnes, F♯, B, op.16, A♭, D♭, a, op.21, E, op.28, 'Le trémolo' op.35, B, op.51bis; over 15 waltzes, 12 as op.4, others as op.47, op.62, 'Les capricieuses' op.64; 16 studies, 12 as op.26, 1 in op.38, 1 in op.40, 1 in op.45, 'Le départ' op.55; 5 romances, 1 in op.38, 3 'sans paroles', E, F♯, g, op.41, 'dramatique' op.79bis

7 variation sets: on a Scottish theme, op.2, 2 on Russian themes, op.17, on a funeral march, op.59, on 'Home, Sweet Home', op.72, on 'The Last Rose of Summer', op.73, on 'Lilly Dale', op.74

5 fantasias: op.22, on 'God Save the Queen', op.27, 'Souvenir de Beethoven' op.39, on Styrian melodies, op.61, on 3 melodies by Schubert, op.79

Miscellaneous: Divertimento, f, op.7; Deux âmes, melody, op.26bis; Scherzo, C♯, op.31; Andante, D♭, op.32; 10 Pieces, op.36; Sonata, c, op.56; Tarantelle, op.65; Les soirées de Pausilippe: hommage à Rossini, 24 pensées musicales, op.75, Ballade, g, op.76; La napolitaine, dance, op.80

OTHER WORKS

Operas: Florinda (Scribe, trans Giannone), London, 1851; Cristina di Svezia, Vienna, 1855

Orch: Pf Conc., f, op.5

Chamber: Duo concertant, on themes from Semiramide, vn, pf, op.54, collab. Bériot; Pf Trio, op.69

Vocal: lieder, 1v, pf, opp.8, 11, 13, 23–5, 29–30

Pedagogical: L'art du chant appliqué au piano, op.70

BIBLIOGRAPHY

FétisB

A. Marmontel: *Les pianistes célèbres* (Paris, 1878)
L. Ramann: *Franz Liszt als Künstler und Mensch* (Leipzig, 1880)
R. Schumann: *Gesammelte Schriften über Musik und Musiker* (Leipzig, 1914/*R*)
A. Kullak: *Die Ästhetik des Klavierspiels* (Leipzig, 1916)
H. Engel: *Die Entwicklung des deutschen Klavierkonzertes von Mozart bis Liszt* (Leipzig, 1927)
L. Plantinga: *Schumann as Critic* (New Haven and London, 1967)
G. Puchelt: *Verlorene Klänge: Studien zur deutschen Klaviermusik 1830–1880* (Berlin, 1969)
V. Vitale: 'Sigismondo Thalberg a Posillipo', *NRMI*, vi (1972), 503
C. R. Suttoni: *Piano and Opera: a Study of the Piano Fantasies Written on Opera Themes in the Romantic Era* (diss., New York U., 1973)

ROBERT WANGERMÉE

Thalberg, Zaré [Western, Ethel] (*b* Derbys., 16 April 1858; *d* London, 1915). English soprano. Contrary to popular belief, she was not the daughter of the pianist Sigismond Thalberg, but a pupil who adopted his name professionally. After studying in Paris and Milan, she made her début at Covent Garden on 10 April 1875 as Zerlina in *Don Giovanni*. During the five seasons that she appeared in London, she also sang Cherubino in *Le nozze di Figaro*, Zerlina in *Fra Diavolo*, Adina in *L'elisir d'amore*, Lady Harriet in *Martha*, Frau Fluth in *Die lustigen Weiber von Windsor* and Elvira in *Ernani*. After a promising start to her career, at the age of 22 she lost her singing voice and became an actress under her real name of Ethel Western, touring the USA with Edwin Booth's Shakespearean company.

BIBLIOGRAPHY

H. Rosenthal: *Two Centuries of Opera at Covent Garden* (London, 1958)

ELIZABETH FORBES

Thalesio, Pedro (*b c*1563; *d* Coimbra, *c*1629). Portuguese (or possibly Spanish) theorist and composer. He was appointed *mestre de capela* of the hospital of Todos-os-Santos at Lisbon on 30 June 1593, at an annual salary of 16,000 réis with other benefits. While at Lisbon he claimed to have been the first to introduce polychoral singing. In 1603 he helped to found the Confraria de S Cecilia, a protective association for musicians. He became *mestre de capela* of Guarda Cathedral in 1610, and in 1612 professor of music at Coimbra University, at a salary of 60,000 réis, raised in 1616 to 70,000. In 1618 Thalesio published *Arte de canto chão* (Coimbra, revised 2/1628), a text on plainchant; he received financial aid for its publication from his protector, Bishop Furtado de Mendonça. Although heavily indebted to Cerone, the manual is a work of individual merit which goes far beyond its announced subject and is particularly valuable for its allusions to the use of plainchant in Renaissance polyphony. An MS treatise on counterpoint, fugue and composition, and a polychoral motet *Iam de somno* were in the library of King John IV of Portugal. Three vesper psalms with alternate verses set survive in *P-VV* choirbook 11.

BIBLIOGRAPHY

DBP

Primeira parte do index da livraria de musica do muyto alto, e poderoso Rey Dom João o IV. nosso senhor (Lisbon, 1649/*R*1967), 115, 121, 452; ed. J. de Vasconcellos (Oporto, 1874–6)
C. Pérez Pastor: *Noticias y documentos relativos a la historia y literatura españolas*, i (Madrid, 1914), 146, 152
J. Mazza: *Dicionário biográfico de músicos portugueses* (Lisbon, 1945), 38, 98f
M. Joaquim: *Vinte livros de música polifónica do Paço Ducal de Vila Viçosa* (Lisbon, 1953), 120ff
R. Stevenson: *Spanish Music in the Age of Columbus* (The Hague, 1960), 95f

——: *Renaissance and Baroque Musical Sources in the Americas* (Washington, DC, 1970), 296

ROBERT STEVENSON

Thalia. The Muse of comedy, light poetry and the idyll; *see* MUSES.

Thaller, Johann Babtist (*b* Röhrmoos, 10 Dec 1872; *d* Endorf, Bavaria, 2 Feb 1952). German composer and church musician. He studied in Freising at the Royal Gymnasium, the Klerikalseminar and the Royal Lyceum, and was ordained in 1897. A particularly gifted organist, he held appointments as a vicar and church musician in Munich and elsewhere before settling in Endorf in 1934. His compositional style, which during his formative years was of a Romantic cast, became gradually closer to that of Reger, and he used varied vocal and instrumental forces while allowing for the capacities of the small congregations he served. Several unpublished scores are held by the monasteries of Schönbrunn and St Konrad, Altötting, Bavaria, where they were still being performed some 20 years after his death.

WORKS
(selective list)
Masses: C, F, op.1, 2vv, org, 1896; Ab, op.2, 2vv, org, 1897; Missa pro defunctis, Eb, chorus, org/4 brass, 1902; Deutsche Messe, op.40, unison, org, 1929; d, op.50, 2vv, org; Requiem, d, chorus, orch, org, unpubd
Other choral works: 2 cantatas, 3 hymns, 32 offertories, many other sacred pieces
Org: 2 educational works

Principal publishers: Boehm, Coppenrath, Feuchtinger & Gleichauf

MOSHE THALLER

Thamant, Johannes. German 16th-century composer. He contributed seven duos to Rotenbucher's extensive bicinium collection *Diphona amoena et florida* (*RISM* 1549¹⁶). Thamant's pieces are: *Agnus Dei, Benedictus, Is facile extinget, Omnis qui invocaverit, Pleni sunt coeli, Qui propter* and *Una salus servire.*

RICHARD MARLOW

Thames Chamber Orchestra. London orchestra founded in 1962: *see* LONDON, §VI, 2(ii).

Tharpe, 'Sister' Rosetta (*b* Cotton Plant, Arkansas, 20 March 1915; *d* ?1973). Black American gospel singer and guitarist. She was brought up in Chicago, where she was influenced by her mother's spiritual singing and was attracted to blues guitar techniques and to the ecstatic religion of the Sanctified Church. She gained a reputation as a singer–evangelist in Chicago and then moved to Harlem, where she became known for her compositions and her electrifying performances at the Holy Roller Church. In 1938 she appeared in the 'From Spirituals to Swing' concerts at the Carnegie Hall and sang with Cab Calloway. Later she sang with the swing orchestras of Benny Goodman and Count Basie and made recordings with Lucky Millinder. The solo recording *Rock me* (1938), with its surging rhythm and secularized title (she also sang it as 'Feed me dear Jesus until I want no more'), was followed by many successes, including *God don't like it* and *I looked down the line and I wondered* (1939). She recorded several outstanding vocal duets in 1949 with her mother, Katie Bell Nubin, and with 'Sister' Marie Knight. Later she used choirs and accompanists, including the Richmond Harmonizing Four and the Sally Jenkins Singers of the Church of God in Christ, New York (e.g. *I have good news to bring*, 1960). Tharpe's vocal technique was closest to that of the blues singer Big Bill Broonzy; accompanying groups tended to cloud the bright sound of her voice and the brilliance of her guitar playing, which she offset by using an electric guitar. In the 1960s she made two European tours.

PAUL OLIVER

Thayer, Alexander Wheelock (*b* South Natick, Mass., 22 Oct 1817; *d* Trieste, 15 July 1897). American writer, biographer of Beethoven. After graduating from Harvard College in 1843, Thayer combined five years of graduate work at the Harvard University Law School with the posts of proctor and assistant librarian, during which time he developed as a bibliophile and researcher. The discrepancies between Schindler's biography of Beethoven and the biographical notices of Ries and Wegeler spurred him to investigate the known evidence concerning Beethoven's life and he spent 1849–51 in Europe assembling material. After two years as editorial writer for the *New York Tribune*, he was able to devote two more years to research. Based in Berlin, he made his central task the deciphering of the conversation books. His funds soon ran out, and it was not until 1858, with support from two benefactors, that he was able to move to Europe permanently and begin his visits to all important persons who had been associated with Beethoven. Krehbiel (1917) wrote: 'His industry, zeal, keen power of analysis, candor and fairmindedness won the confidence and help of all with whom he came in contact except the literary charlatans whose romances he was bent on destroying in the interest of the verities of history'. From 1865 to 1882 he was United States Consul in Trieste. Three volumes of a German edition of the biography – edited, revised and translated by Bonn Court Councillor Hermann Deiters – appeared between 1866 and 1879. Thayer planned to follow the completion of this edition with a condensed biography in English, but in the 1880s, having completed the work as far as 1816, he found himself unable to pursue it. From Thayer's notes Deiters (and on Deiters's death Hugo Riemann) completed the last two volumes of the German edition.

Thayer's exhaustive search for source material and objective presentation established a new standard for musical biography; his *Life* is still definitive. In a letter to Deiters in 1865 he stated his principle: 'I fight for no theories and cherish no prejudices: my sole point of view is the truth . . . It appears to me that Beethoven the *composer* is amply known through his works and in this assumption the long and wearisome labors of so many years were devoted to Beethoven the *man*'. Deiters and Riemann added passages concerning the characteristics of certain compositions; Thayer asked that these interpolations be clearly identified. In preparing the two subsequent editions in English, Krehbiel and Forbes eliminated all musical description in order to preserve Thayer's original concept. The revised English edition (1964) incorporated new biographical knowledge, removed what had become redundant exposure of false information, and reorganized Krehbiel's presentation of the last ten years of Beethoven's life to conform to that established by Thayer for the earlier years.

WRITINGS
Chronologisches Verzeichnis der Werke Ludwig van Beethovens (Berlin, 1865)
Ludwig van Beethoven's Leben, ed. and trans. H. Deiters, i (Berlin, 1866; rev. 2/1901; rev. 3/1917 by H. Riemann); ii–iii (Berlin, 1872–9; rev. 2/1910–11 by H. Riemann); iv–v, ed. H. Riemann (Leipzig, 1907–8) [Eng. edns. by H. Krehbiel (New York, 1921) and E. Forbes (Princeton, 1964, rev. 2/1967)]

Ein kritischer Beitrag zur Beethoven-Literatur (Berlin, 1877) [Eng. edn.
in *Dwight's Journal of Music*, xxxvii–xxxviii (1877–8), 121, 129,
137, 145
Numerous articles for *Grove 1*, *The Musical Review and Gazette* and
Dwight's Journal of Music

BIBLIOGRAPHY
J. Geddes jr: 'Memories of E. L. Pierce and A. W. Thayer', *Boston
University Beacon*, xxiii (1897); repr. in *Memories of a College
Professor*, ed. S. M. Waxman (Boston, 1945), 19
H. E. Krehbiel: 'A. W. Thayer and his "Life of Beethoven" ', *MQ*, iii
(1917), 629
C. Hatch: 'The Education of A. W. Thayer', *MQ*, xlii (1956), 355
E. Forbes: Preface and Note to *Thayer's Life of Beethoven* (Princeton,
2/1967)

ELLIOT FORBES

Thayer, (Whitney) Eugene (*b* Mendon, Mass., 11 Dec
1838; *d* Burlington, Vermont, 27 June 1889). American
organist and composer. He studied the piano and the
guitar and, from the age of 14, the organ. His first post
was as organist in Worcester, Mass. In 1865 he went to
Europe to study and gave recitals in Berlin, London and
elsewhere. He then lived in Boston, and in 1881 moved
to New York, where he remained until 1889 when he
moved to Yantic, Connecticut, the month before his
death. Thayer established the custom of giving free
organ recitals in the USA; he was also active as a
teacher and lecturer.

BIBLIOGRAPHY
L. F. Thayer: 'Eugene Thayer: a Biographical Sketch and List of
Compositions', *American Organist*, xvi/8 (1933)
E. A. Kriege: 'Eugene Thayer', *The Tracker*, xxi (1976), 172

Theatre organ. The organ as used in theatrical entertainments, operas, oratorios and concerts during the
17th and 18th centuries, and fulfilling the function of a
substitute for the orchestra in the 19th century. For a
different, specifically American usage of the term, *see*
CINEMA ORGAN.

1. General. 2. Use in Italian entertainments, intermedi and operas. 3. Use
in London oratorios and concerts.

1. GENERAL. Although the structure, history and repertory of the organ are usually traced through instruments
made for the church, other kinds of organ have had their
own development and function, notably the smaller por-
tatives, table positives and regals. During the 15th, 16th
and 17th centuries such instruments had a part in
courtly entertainments, and were played in private
theatres (often makeshift) and concert rooms. During
the later 17th and 18th centuries they were used in
public theatres, concert rooms and pleasure gardens,
and during the 19th and 20th centuries organs were
built in large concert halls.

Today the last are usually indistinguishable from
church organs, except sometimes in appearance. Earlier
in the 20th century they were often very different, containing more solo stops, swells, etc, suitable for the
orchestral arrangements which were played on them (a
tradition as old as the organ recital itself). In 1850
concert hall organs were generally much more advanced
than contemporary church organs in mechanism, case-
design, specification and tonal concept. As distinct from
such instruments, the theatre organ has its own history
and function, though neither history nor function was
continuous. Certain parts of Europe at certain times had
a tradition of theatre organs, which in many cases led to
a distinct and important repertory.

2. USE IN ITALIAN ENTERTAINMENTS, INTERMEDI AND
OPERAS. Secular documents concerning organs being
inevitably rarer than ecclesiastical, it can only be assumed that the 'bellissimo organo che sonava a festa'
during a play given at wedding celebrations at Pesaro in
1475 was typical at such courtly entertainments. There
are similar accounts of Vatican court activities in the
early 16th century, as later of the Medici court in
Florence where, indeed, the tradition appears to have
been unbroken until after the heyday of the *intermedi*.
During the *intermedi* of 1565 there were three *organi di
legno*, two at 8′ pitch, one at 16′ (? 'due all'unisono, &
uno all'ottava bassa'), used for different accompanimental purposes, such as the 'heavenly music' for flutes,
large lute and organ. In the same way Monteverdi's
Orfeo (Mantua, 1607) called for *duoi organi di legno*,
used in one instance for a pair of echoing continuo
groups. The preface to Cavalieri's *Rappresentatione*
(1600) notes that an *organo soave* goes well with chitarrone, confirming a tradition of organ with lute that was
to last until well into the 18th century, in many countries, within or outside the church. The term *organo di
legno* occurs now and then in the sources (e.g. Francesca Caccini's *Liberazione di Ruggiero*, Florence,
1625) but not often enough for its meaning to be quite
clear. Was it a small table positive with stopped wooden
pipes? If so, it was intended to give a totally different
effect from the Italian church organ of the time, in
which (*a*) wooden pipes and (*b*) stopped pipes were rare.
The largest it could have been as an instrumental type is
the kind of organ now in the Silberne Kapelle,
Hofkirche, Innsbruck (Roman, *c*1550), with pipes of
wood (except for a few top trebles) having the following
specification:

Principals	8′, 4′, 2′, 1⅓′, 1′
Flute	4′
Voce umana	8′ (treble)

This is the kind of 'organum quoddam totum ligneum'
that was given to Archduke Ferdinand II in 1571.
Antonio Barcotto (MS, *c*1650; cited in R. Lunelli:
'Un trattatello di Antonio Barcotto colma le lacune,
dell'Arte organica', *CHM*, i, 1953, p.135) thought such
'istrumenti dolci' useful in private chambers, larger
rooms and especially in the *accademie* or concert
societies. In court theatre performances influenced by
the northern Italian orchestras, such as that of Cesti's *Il
pomo d'oro* (Vienna, 1668), there is still a clear distinction between the regals and the positive organ in the
continuo grouping. While some Italian theatres may
have continued to bring in small organs for certain
productions, the Teatro la Fenice, Venice, had a large
one-manual organ made as late as 1881, containing a
12-rank manual chorus and a four-rank pedal.

3. USE IN LONDON ORATORIOS AND CONCERTS. As in
cities elsewhere, London theatres occasionally put on a
concert by a showman-organist, such as 'the famous Mr
Clinch of Barnet' at the Theatre Royal in 1702. At the
farther end of this tradition can be seen the secular
organ recitals given later in the century by J. C. Bach,
Mozart, Hässler and Vogler in such places as the
Ranelagh Gardens, or earlier in the next century by
Samuel Wesley in the Hanover Square Rooms. The
organ at Ranelagh was built in 1746 by Byfield, with a
12′ front more in the chinoiserie-gothick style than any
church would then have allowed. At least 17 of the
London and provincial pleasure gardens are known to
have had an organ of some kind, two in the case of
Vauxhall where the bandstand organ (?1728) had the
following specification:

The New Drury Lane Theatre, showing the organ by W. & J. Gray: sketch from 'Organographia', early 19th century (GB-Lcm 1161, f.167)

Open Diapason	8′
Stopped Diapason	8′
Principal	4′
Flute	4′
Twelfth	2⅔′
Fifteenth	2′
Sesquialtera	IV

To all appearances, such organs were similar to those in the more permanently respectable concert rooms, such as St Cecilia's Hall, Edinburgh, for whose musical society Snetzler made an organ of seven stops in 1775, the whole contained in a Swell box. Such organs were suitable both for continuo playing and for their own repertory of organ concertos, quartets, etc, many of which seem to have been written either for the pleasure gardens (Henry Burgess, James Hook), or for concert rooms of a private or public kind in London (Charles Wesley, Philip Hayes, William Hayes) and in the provinces (Chilcot, Dupuis, Avison). As such, the English organ concerto can be seen as a much more versatile form than it appears to have been in the hands of the theatre composers (Stanley, Arne, J. C. Bach) or Handel imitators (Felton, Mudge).

In some of the theatres themselves, small organs of a box-like shape seem to have been part of the equipment, as in the Royalty Theatre, c1785. They may well have been 'Organized Piano Fortes' (i.e. square pianos with one or more sets of pipes lying horizontally below the piano) of the type heard by R. J. S. Stevens in a concerto played by Michael Arne at the Little Theatre, Haymarket, during April 1784. The bigger theatres had much more important instruments, chiefly for performances of oratorios. New oratorio organs were built as late as 1810 (Allen's for the Covent Garden Oratorios) and 1815 (Gray's for New Drury Lane Theatre): organs of seven to ten full-scaled stops. By then they were much smaller than, for example, the two-manual organ with pedals made in 1804 for the Hanover Square Concert Room, which itself was a very lowly start to the new tradition for concert and town hall organs.

In March 1735 Handel began advertising organ concertos as part of the evening's music in the theatres at Covent Garden and Lincoln's Inn Fields, and at the King's in the Haymarket. These served as interludes between the acts of such oratorios as *Esther*. There were other organs later (e.g. Arne's concertos at Drury Lane Theatre Royal in 1755), and in 1769 a new organ was built for the Drury Lane Theatre oratorios of Stanley and J. C. Smith. To some extent, the practice seems to have been reflected in the Concert Spirituel, Paris, where interlude concertos in the 1750s often included one for organ. At Lincoln's Inn, Handel may well have had an organ of two manuals and pedal pull-downs for a performance of his concerto op.7 no.1 and perhaps others. For *Esther* (1732), *Deborah* (1738) and *Saul* (1738) he probably had two organs, at least one of which was no doubt a small chamber organ specially brought in. For *Saul*, moreover, the major organ on the stage behind the choir had keys of communication with the harpsichord in front, so that the composer could variously accompany arias and choruses; this was probably achieved by trackers dropping to and running in a special box along the floor beneath the singers. The Old Theatre Royal, Covent Garden, burnt in 1800, had an organ built by Jordan in about 1730, with a specification as noted by Henry Leffler (MS, *c*1810) of:

$G'-d'''$

Open Diapason	8′
Stopped Diapason	8′
Principal	4′
Twelfth	2⅔′
Fifteenth	2′
Tierce	1⅗′
Trumpet	8′

This would of course allow varied registration for the episodes in the organ concertos, but does not contain a Flute 4′ as registered by Handel in op.4 no.4; perhaps the registration was for a performance elsewhere, later than (but similar to) the one he gave on a visit to Oxford in 1733. In most respects, the specification resembles that suggested by Handel to Jennens in 1749; although the instrument was a house organ he recommended it to be made as 'Church Work', i.e. with full-size metal scaling. In this way, the instrument would have been quite different from the putative small chamber organ of Italian make that Handel had for the 1708 performance of *Il trionfo del Tempo*, where the organ concerto as it became familiar in England had its particular origin. The theatre organ built in Drury Lane for Stanley and Smith was considerably bigger:

Byfield & Green, 1769
$G'-e'''$, one set of keys, detached console
(?'long communication')

Great		*Swell* (from *c*)	
Open Diapason (from *G*)	8′	Open Diapason	8′
Stopped Diapason	8′	Principal	4′
Principal	4′	Cornet	III
Flute	4′	Hautboy	8′
Fifteenth	2′		
Sesquialtera	III		
Trumpet	8′		

Although the Swell was played from the same keyboard as the Great, certain expressive solos for the right hand were possible, and the slow movements of organ concertos often contained melodies aiming at such expressiveness. Presumably these theatre organs were moved out each year after Lent, but the sources of information are poor.   PETER WILLIAMS

Theatre Royal. London theatre built in 1720 and known as the Little Theatre in the Haymarket until 1766; *see* LONDON, §IV, 3.

Theatre Royal, Drury Lane. London theatre; the first on the site was opened in 1663 and the present one in 1812. *See* LONDON, §IV, 3.

Théâtres de la Foire (Fr.: 'fair theatres'). The two Paris fairs, the Foire St Germain and the Foire St Laurent, were important in the history of the musical stage in the late 17th century as the sites for the *comédie en vaudevilles*, out of which grew the musically more elaborate *opéra comique*. The Foire St Germain was located about where the Hôtel des Examens and the Marché St Germain are now; by the end of the 17th century it always opened on 3 February and ended on Palm Sunday. The Gare de l'Est now occupies the approximate site of the Foire St Laurent, whose season was somewhat variable, generally lasting from mid-June to the end of September.

The fairs had been the scene of popular farces, acrobatic displays and animal shows since the Middle Ages and, after 1642, of marionette plays. Before the 1670s, when they were limited by the restrictive patents granted to Lully, these spectacles made extensive use of accompanying musical instruments, as appears from Scarron's poem *La Foire St Germain* (1643):

Le bruit des pénétrants sifflets,
Des flûtes et des flageolets,
Des cornets, hautbois et musettes . . .

In 1678 the Foire St Germain came under the direction of the acrobats Claude and Pierre Alard and Maurice van der Beeck. Their first theatrical production, *Les forces de l'amour et de la magie*, pleased the king, and they were granted a patent to present 'jumping acts accompanied by some discourse . . . with the condition that there be no singing or dancing' (4 February 1679).

In 1697, when the Comédie-Italienne was suppressed and its actors expelled from France, the Théâtres de la Foire quickly appropriated its large repertory (published in 1694 by Evaristo Gherardi as *Théâtre italien*), thereby filling the gap left by Arlequin and Scaramouche. The musical content of these comedies consisted of original compositions (overtures, dances, dramatic *symphonies*), vaudevilles and extended parodies of the most popular Lully operas. In 1699 (20 and 27 February) the Théâtres de la Foire felt the full force of their main antagonist, the Comédie-Française. The *forains* were forbidden to perform entire comedies or farces, but they circumvented this by performing fragments; when all dialogues were forbidden in 1707, the *forains* converted to monologues. In 1708 Guyenet, director of the Opéra, gave them permission to use songs, dances and scenery changes, but in 1710 this privilege was revoked, and the *forains* were reduced to using large placards displaying each performer's text, at first in prose and later in *couplets* (stanzas in French poetry). With the Opéra's permission these *couplets* were set to popular vaudeville tunes. The orchestra, which by 1714 consisted of nine or ten instruments, played the tunes, the audience sang the words and the actors performed in mime. In 1716, in return for an annual payment of 35,000 livres, the Opéra permitted the Théâtres de la Foire to give 'spectacles mixed with music, dance and *symphonies* under the name of Opéra-Comique' (this term had first appeared on publicity notices in 1715). On the opening day of the Opéra-Comique at the Foire St Laurent (25 July 1715) 'the Comédie and the Opéra were deserted', according to the *Mercure de France*. The Comédie-Française retaliated;

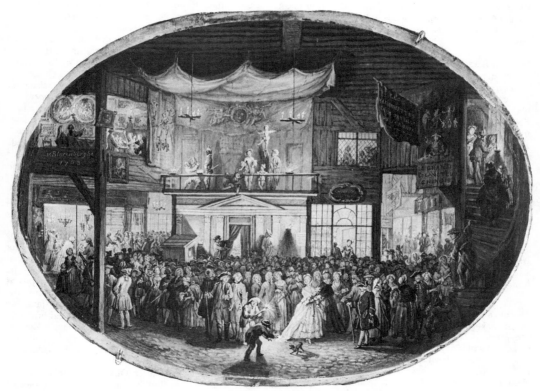

Scene at the Foire St Germain: miniature (1763) by Nicholas van Blarenberghe in the Wallace Collection, London

from November 1718 to 1724 only marionette shows and tight-rope dancers were allowed at the Théâtres de la Foire (from 1721 to 1723 the Italian comedians, who had been recalled to Paris by the regent in 1716, took over the Foire St Laurent for their productions).

The most productive years of the early Opéra-Comique began after its return to the Foire St Germain in 1724. Its repertory from 1724 to 1737 appears in the ten volumes of Le Sage and d'Orneval's *Le Théâtre de la Foire ou l'opéra comique*. These plays continued to depend heavily on vaudevilles, although descriptive *symphonies*, dances, overtures and vaudeville finales were common. In addition to supplying original music, the most important task of the first generation of *opéra comique* composers (including Mouret, Gillier, Aubert and Rameau) was to arrange the vaudevilles and to provide them with orchestral accompaniments. The playwrights (chiefly Le Sage, d'Orneval, Fuzelier, Piron and, later, Favart) selected the vaudeville tunes from the large number available and often used the same tune repeatedly for a specific situation until it became associated with that situation from play to play. Parfaict, in his *Dictionnaire*, noted that the 'vaudevilles translate with minute exactitude successive degrees of the same sentiment and the most rapid, minute shifts within one action. Thus . . . the pursuit of a kiss could scarcely be posed'.

The Opéra-Comique flourished until 1744, the second year of Jean Monnet's directorship, when it was again suppressed by the Comédie-Française. In 1752 it reopened, remaining under Monnet until 1758, when the privilege passed to a group including Favart and Delresse. In 1762 the Opéra-Comique merged with the Comédie-Italienne, transferring its operations to the Hôtel de Bourgogne.

BIBLIOGRAPHY

A. Le Sage and d'Orneval: *Le Théâtre de la Foire ou l'opéra comique* (Paris, 1721–37)

C. and F. Parfaict: *Histoire du théâtre françois depuis son origine jusqu'à présent* (Amsterdam, 1734–49)

C. Parfaict and G. d'Abguerbe: *Dictionnaire des théâtres de Paris* (Paris, 1756)

J. Bonnaissies: *Les spectacles forains et la Comédie française* (Paris, 1874)

E. Campardon: *Les spectacles de la foire* (Paris, 1877)

V. Barberet: *Lesage et le Théâtre de la Foire* (Nancy, 1887)

A. Font: *Favart: l'opéra comique et la comédie-vaudeville au XVIIᵉ et XVIIIᵉ siècles* (Paris, 1894/R1970)

G. Cucuel: *Les créateurs de l'opéra comique français* (Paris, 1914)

F. J. Carmody: *Le répertoire de l'opéra-comique en vaudevilles de 1708 à 1764* (Berkeley, 1933)

D. J. Grout: *The Origins of the Opéra-Comique* (diss., Harvard U., 1939)

C. Barnes: *The 'Théâtre de la Foire' (Paris, 1697–1762): its Music and Composers* (diss., U. of Southern California, 1965)

——: 'Instruments and Instrumental Music at the "Théâtres de la Foire" ', *RMFC*, v (1965), 142

N. Wild: 'Aspects de la musique sous la régence. Les Foires: naissance de l'Opéra-Comique', *RMFC*, v (1965), 129

C. Barnes: 'Vocal Music at the "Théâtres de la Foire" 1697–1762', *RMFC*, viii (1968), 141

H. Lagrave: *Le théâtre et le public à Paris de 1715 à 1750* (Paris, 1972)

J. R. Anthony: *French Baroque Music from Beaujoyeulx to Rameau* (London, 1973, rev. 2/1978)

G. Sadler: 'Rameau, Piron and the Parisian Fair Theatres', *Soundings*, iv (1974), 13

JAMES R. ANTHONY

Theatron [theëtron] (Lat. *cavea*). The auditorium in an ancient Greek or Roman theatre: this and the *orchēstra*, or area for the chorus, formed its two essential components.

Thebom, Blanche (*b* Monessen, Penn., 19 Sept 1918). American mezzo-soprano of Swedish parentage. In New York she studied with Margarete Matzenauer and Edyth Walker, then made her début as a concert singer in 1941. She made her Metropolitan Opera début in New York as Fricka in *Die Walküre*, on 14 December 1944, and remained at that house until the 1966–7 season, singing much Wagner and a variety of other leading roles. In 1950 she sang Dorabella in Glyndebourne's *Così fan tutte*, and in 1957 she had considerable success at Covent Garden as Dido in the first English professional staged performance of *Les troyens*. She retired about 1970. Thebom had a rangy mezzo-soprano of generally fine quality, not a great voice, but one capable of most pleasing effect. Her handsome presence and gracious manner served her as well as her secure musicianship. She was also a most satisfying concert artist; her recitals brought her deserved respect. Her article 'Singing or Acting?' was published in *Opera News*, xxix/21 (1965), 9.

MAX DE SCHAUENSEE

Theeuwes [Theewes, Teeus]. Flemish family of harpsichord makers of the second half of the 16th century. Three members of the family are known as instrument makers, Jacob (*fl* 1533–57), Lodewijk (i) (*fl* 1557) and Jacob's son, Lodewijk (ii) (*fl* 1561–85). Jacob and Lodewijk (i) may have been brothers, but little is known about them except that both were members of the group of ten instrument makers who applied for guild recognition of harpsichord making in Antwerp in 1557; no instrument made by either has survived. Lodewijk (ii) was admitted into the Antwerp Guild of St Luke in 1561 but subsequently emigrated to England, where he is listed in 1568 as 'Lodewyke Tyves, virginall maker, a Dutchman' living in the parish of St Martin-le-Grand, London. In 1579 he built the earliest surviving harpsichord made in England, part of a CLAVIORGAN painted with the arms of the Roper family, now in the Victoria and Albert Museum. This important instrument has features that are probably characteristically English (oak casework, embossed paper decoration around the soundboard, chromatic compass from *C*), in addition to being the only surviving instrument giving evidence of the nature of Flemish harpsichord building practice before Ruckers.

BIBLIOGRAPHY

D. H. Boalch: *Makers of the Harpsichord and Clavichord 1440–1840* (London, 1956, 2/1974)
R. Russell: *Victoria and Albert Museum Catalogue of Musical Instruments* (London, 1968), 48f

EDWIN M. RIPIN

Theile, Johann (*b* Naumburg, 29 July 1646; *d* Naumburg, buried 24 June 1724). German composer, theorist and teacher. He is noted particularly for his sacred music, and he was a specially skilful contrapuntist.

1. LIFE. Theile received his first musical training from Johann Scheffler, Kantor of Magdeburg, and had attained enough skill to support himself as a law student at the University of Leipzig from 1666. Friends helped to pay for his first publication, *Weltliche Arien . . .* (1667), a set of student songs. Membership of the university's collegium musicum gave him musical experience and contacts, and some time between 1666 and 1672 he studied with Schütz. It is doubtful whether he completed his legal studies. He may have taught in Stettin before moving to Lübeck, where he was living in 1673, numbering among his friends Reincken and Buxtehude.

In 1673 Theile was appointed Kapellmeister at Gottorf. There he may have written his first operas or opera-like works, as Duke Christian Albrecht spent money on 'musical entertainments' as well as plays. Political developments soon interrupted the duke's promising reign: he was kidnapped and forced to cede territory, and in 1675 he fled to Hamburg. Theile was released from service when the Kapelle was dissolved but went with his patron to Hamburg. There his first opera inaugurated the new opera house in the Gänsemarkt on 2 January 1678. Though he remained on good terms with Christian Albrecht he probably considered the duke's unstable situation a strong enough reason to take a new position. He served as Kapellmeister at Wolfenbüttel from 1685 to 1691, after which he entered the service of Duke Christian I at Merseburg. As he had done in previous positions he continued to teach at both places. One of his pupils at Wolfenbüttel, Georg Oesterreich, 'moved into the Kapellmeister's house and lodged with him, [and he] instructed him . . . quite untiringly and faithfully in composition'. A pupil at Merseburg, Johann Ziegler, 'studied composition with various teachers . . . [until he] finally found more satisfaction with Kapellmeister Theile'.

Where Theile lived after Duke Christian's death in 1694 is not certain, but he may have been connected with the Prussian court in Berlin: dedicating his *Andächtige Kirchen-Music* to King Friedrich I, he stated 'I taught Your Majesty the oboe'. He spent his last years in Naumburg; he had moved there by 1718. Mattheson paid him this simple tribute in *Critica musica*, ii: 'he was a specially pious, honest man and thoroughly understood the harmonious arts'.

2. WORKS. Much of Theile's music survives in manuscript; many works have been lost. The first of his few extant published works is *Weltliche Arien* (1667), a collection of 24 secular solos, five duets and a quartet, with instrumental ritornellos. In his St Matthew Passion (1673), which was also published, he followed the traditions of the turba, a 'halo' of sound for the words of Jesus, and a closing chorus of thanksgiving. The most progressive aspect of the work was the addition of four strophic arias, to words not taken from biblical or chorale texts, commenting on the crucial parts of the story; this is one of the first instances of such interpolations in Passion music.

It is in his concerted sacred music that Theile made his most important contribution. Of 34 extant works, 22 are settings of Latin or German psalms; other pieces are settings of other biblical texts, Luther's Litany and independent verses. The words of six works consist of an introductory scriptural verse followed by a poem expanding its central ideas; five of these works are in the *Andächtige Kirchen-Music*, Theile's last collection. This type of cantata may have resulted from a desire for a compromise between the orthodox preference for scripture and the Pietistic desire for devotional poetry in services. Theile presented each verse of his text as a short movement, with new thematic material, changes of key, metre and texture, and alternation between soloists and chorus; while such movements do not of course constitute full-scale compositions, they are a step in that direction. The forces for which Theile wrote range from solo soprano, two strings and continuo to five-part chorus with two violins, two violas, bassoon, two clarinos, timpani, two cornetts and three trombones; he included parts for oboes in the *Andächtige Kirchen-Music*. The instruments strongly support the vocal line; in choral works the first violin plays a higher contrapuntal line, while the other instruments double the vocal parts.

Among his contemporaries Theile was called 'the father of contrapuntists', and polyphonic textures indeed assume a paramount role in his music. His six treatises also deal with counterpoint. The most important, *Musikalisches Kunst-Buch*, contains compositions illustrating various contrapuntal techniques and may have given Bach the idea of writing *Die Kunst der Fuge*. Two of the compositions are masses, in which invertible counterpoint is employed to produce two more masses; like all but one of Theile's other eight masses they are in the *stile antico*. In general he wrote simple imitative passages, inverted or transposed parts as the basis of varied repetition and set entire sections as fugues, dominated by inversion at the octave between two subjects, one for each half of the text. He provided as movements of his sacred works some of the earliest examples of full-scale vocal fugues, with two subjects, tonic and dominant entries and a complete thematic reliance on the subjects. While others were content with brief sections of imitation, Theile made a unique contribution to the development of the choral fugue.

In other aspects of composition Theile was conservative. Traditional dissonance treatment, careful text-setting (with some word-painting) and moderate ranges are all characteristic. His harmony consists of simple basic progressions, enlivened by frequent changes of key and intensified by occasional chromatic alterations. Although reprises and ritornellos appear, he preferred varied repetition of his material. In his motets he took great care over contrasts of texture and the placing of climaxes. The quality and style of his output are remarkably uniform; with deference to the traditions of his time and with skill and sensitivity, he remained faithful throughout his career to a personal means of expression.

WORKS
OPERAS
(*known only from librettos in D-Hs unless otherwise stated*)
Der erschaffene, gefallene und auffgerichtete Mensch (Adam und Eva), Hamburg, 1678
Orontes, Hamburg, 1678; 7 arias, *D-Bds*, some ed. in Wolff
Die Geburth Christi, Hamburg, 1681

MASSES, PSALMS, PASSIONS
Pars prima [6] missarum, 4vv, bc (Wismar, 1673)
Passio nach dem Heiligen Evangelisten Matthäo, 4vv, 4 viols, bc (Lübeck, 1673); ed. in DDT, xvii (1904)
Mass, 5vv, 2 vn, 2 va, 2 cornetts, bc, *D-Bds*
Mass, 5vv, bc, *B*; ed. in Cw, xvi (1932/*R*)
2 masses in *Musikalisches Kunst-Buch*, see 'Writings'
7 psalms: Beatus vir, 4vv, 5 insts; Benedicam Domino, 4vv, 6 insts; Cum invocarem, 4vv, 5 insts; Dixit Dominus, 4vv, 6 insts; Domine ne in furore, 4vv, 5 insts; Jubilate Deo, 4vv, 5 insts, anon., MS 30243; Laudate Dominum, 4vv, 6 insts: *B*

MOTETS
Ach dass ich hören sollte, 1v, 4 insts, bc, *D-B*, *S-Uu*; Daran ist erschienen die Liebe Gottes, 4vv, 6 insts, bc, *Uu*; Die Seele Christi heilige mich, 1v, 3 insts, bc, *Uu*; Gott hilf mir, 1v, 2 insts, bc, *D-B*; Gott hilf mir, 5vv, 5 insts, bc, *S-Uu*; Gott, sei mir gnädig, 4vv, 5 insts, bc, *D-B*; Herr, unser Herrscher, 5vv, 13 insts, bc, *B*; Ich habe

den Herrn allezeit vor Augen, 4vv, 4 insts, bc, *B*; Ich preise dich Herr, 5vv, 4 insts, bc, *B*; Ich will den Herrn loben allezeit, 2vv, 3 insts, bc, *B*; Ich will den Herrn loben allezeit, 5vv, 5 insts, bc, *B*; Jauchzet Gott, alle Lande, 5vv, 7 insts, bc, *B*; Jesu, mein Herr und Gott allein, 1v, 3 insts, bc, *S-Uu*; Litaney, 5vv, 5 insts, bc, *D-B*; Schaffe in mir Gott, 4vv, 5 insts, bc, *B*; Triumpff, alleluja, 3vv, 2 insts, bc, *B*; Tröstet mein Volk, 5vv, 7 insts, bc, *B*; Warum toben die Heiden, 5vv, 8 insts, bc, *B*; Wirf dein Anliegen, 4vv, 4 insts, bc, *B*
Andächtige Kirchen-Music, 4vv, insts, bc, *B*
Opus musicalis compositionis (Merseburg, 1708) [a catalogue of Theile's sacred works from printed works and MSS]

SECULAR
Weltlicher Arien und Canzonetten erstes, anderes und drittes Zehen, 1, 2, 4vv, 4 viols, bc (Leipzig, 1667); 1 ed. in GMB
1 madrigal, Unser Matz hat einen grossen langen Bart, 3vv, bc, *S-Uu*; ed. H. J. Moser, Corydon, ii (Brunswick, 1933)
Sonata, 2 vn, trbn, bn, bc, *Uu*
Sonata, vn, 2 viols, vle, bc, *Uu*; ed. in Organum, iii/19 (Leipzig, 1929)
Many lost works, listed in *MGG*

WRITINGS
(*all in D-Bds*)
Musikalisches Kunst-Buch; incl. 2 masses, ed. in C. Dahlhaus, Denkmäler norddeutscher Musik, i (Kassel, 1965)
Curieuser Unterricht von den gedoppelten Contrapuncten
Contrapuncta praecepta
Von den dreifachten Contrapuncten
Gründlicher Unterricht von den gedoppelten Contrapuncten
Von dem vierfachen Contrapunct alla octava

BIBLIOGRAPHY
J. Mattheson: *Critica musica*, ii (Hamburg, 1725), 57f, 282f
——: *Grundlage einer Ehren-Pforte* (Hamburg, 1740); ed. M. Schneider (Berlin, 1910/*R*1969)
W. Maxton: *Johann Theile* (diss., U. of Tübingen, 1927)
B. Engelke: 'Die Gottorfer Hofkapelle unter Joh. Theile und M. Colerus', *Kieler Blätter* (1943), 93
B. Smallman: *The Background of Passion Music* (London, 1957, rev. and enlarged 2/1970)
H. C. Wolff: *Die Barockoper in Hamburg* (Wolfenbüttel, 1957)
J. Mackey: *The Sacred Music of Johann Theile* (diss., U. of Michigan, 1968)

JOCELYN MACKEY

Theinred of Dover. English 12th-century theorist. Although his treatise, *Breviarium regulare musice*, exists only in a single manuscript of the late 14th century (*GB-Ob* 842, ff.1–44*v*), Theinred is probably to be identified with the monk Tenredus, a contemporary mentioned by John of Salisbury in his *Metalogicon*. The work is addressed to Aluredus (Ailred) of Canterbury. At the end is written, in a somewhat less formal script, 'Explicit informacio juvenum', indicating the pedagogical purpose of the work. Comprehensive and meticulously detailed in its description of proportions, intervals, species and the mathematical ratios underlying music, the treatise explains fundamental theory at great length and with numerous diagrams and circles showing the intervals and cycles of transposition. But, as Theinred's introduction states, his purpose was not to supersede Guidonian theory, but rather to extend it to account for the additional chromatic notes not rendered by the Guidonian hand. This purpose Theinred achieved in a table (see illustration), in which the following gamuts appear: the normal Guidonian gamut and solmization syllables; the so-called organ scale in which the letters *A–a* represent the Guidonian *C–c*; a second organ scale extending from *F* to *f* but again with its *A* representing the Guidonian *C*; a set of solmization syllables – not Guidonian – beginning from five different pitches; the Boethian letters *a–p* extending over two octaves and including the low B♭, E♭ and F♯ shown by special signs; the letters *a–g*, repeated at the octave, and including in the lower octave *b* for B♭, *h* for B♮ and *F* for F♯. These different alphabetic notations and syllables are interlined with alphabetic symbols: a long *s* for

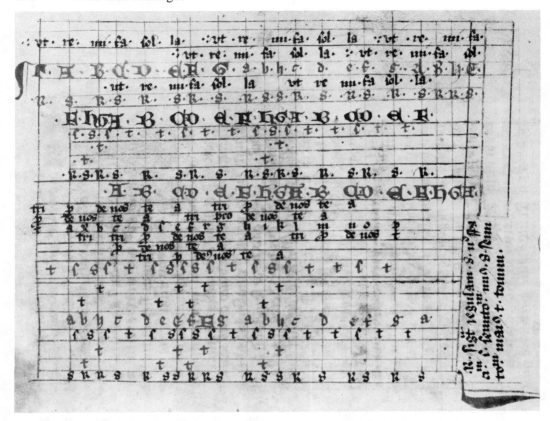

Table of gamuts from the treatise 'Breviarium regulare musice' by Theinred of Dover (GB-Ob 842, f.23r)

the small semitone, *s* for the larger semitone, *t* for the tone, *r* for *regulam* (line) and *s* for *spatium* (space).

The solmization syllables are *tri*, *pro*, *de*, *nos*, *te* and *a*, beginning on *G*, *C* and *F* to give the normal Guidonian hexachords, and on low *B♭* and *D* to give the chromatic notes *E♭* and *F♯* which are shown also in some of the alphabetic notations. The important sections of the treatise describe the transpositions which can be achieved by means of these additional hexachords.

BIBLIOGRAPHY

H. Davey: 'Theinred', *DNB*
G. Reaney: 'The *Breviarium regulare musice* of Ms. Oxford Bodley 842', *MD*, xi (1957), 31

ANDREW HUGHES

Thematic catalogue.

1. Definition and organization. 2. History and function. 3. Historiography.

1. DEFINITION AND ORGANIZATION. A thematic catalogue is an index to a group of musical compositions that incorporates citations of their opening notes (incipits), or principal melodic features (themes), or both. These citations may be given in various forms, such as conventional notes, neumes, tablatures, syllables, numbers, letters or computer codes. This broad definition must be qualified, however, for in practice, defying etymology, most thematic catalogues are concerned with incipits rather than with themes as such.

The semantic confusion arose in the late 18th century, when the terms 'theme' and 'thematic catalogue' were first regularly used. Because compositions almost always began with their main theme, the words 'theme' or 'themata' were treated as synonymous with what has only recently come to be called 'incipit'. In the 18th century, they were used interchangeably with 'initia', 'beginnings', 'commencements', 'Anfänge', 'subjects' or 'first few bars'. The combined term 'thematic catalogue' was first used in print by J. J. Hummel in 1768 for what was really an incipit index (but not the earliest: see §2(i) and (iii) below). In this century, in the relatively few instances where true themes rather than incipits are catalogued, the adjective 'thematic' is avoided in the title (e.g. H. Barlow and S. Morgenstern: *Dictionary of Musical Themes*, 1949, and H. Schiegl and E. Schwarzmaier: *Themensammlung musicalischer Meisterwerke*, 1967).

The thematic catalogue is far superior to the non-thematic one as a research aid since it not only presents a body of music arranged in systematic order, but, by its incipits, provides positive identification in a minimum of space and symbols. For most music an incipit of about a dozen pitches suffices. When rhythmic values accompany the pitches, the incipit is likely to be unique. While the non-thematic list may identify a work by its composer, title, opus number, key, instrumentation, movement headings, first line of text, date, publisher, dedicatee, plate number etc, no one of these, indeed no combination of these, can normally provide as certain an identification as an incipit. Even transposed works can be readily identified in properly organized incipit files. In dealing with works that are anonymous or of disputed authorship, incipits become indispensable.

The organization of a thematic catalogue will vary in accordance with what it covers and should ideally include (as suggested by A. Hyatt King) the following elements: (*a*) title, opus or other identification numbers, references to standard and complete editions, author or other source of text, date and place of composition; (*b*) incipits of each movement, noting the number of bars in each movement where applicable and indicating variants among sources; (*c*) full description, location and shelf-mark of autographs; (*d*) description of significant copies, their shelf-marks, dates and important differences or special markings; (*e*) bibliographical description of first editions, including date, imprint, price and plate number, and of all subsequent editions or arrangements published in the composer's lifetime or reflecting changes made or sanctioned by him; (*f*) references to contemporary diaries, memoirs and newspapers, thematic and non-thematic catalogues; and (*g*) references to significant citations in scholarly studies.

While the few notes of an incipit may be sufficient for the recognition of a particular work, their presentation must take into account the requirements of the genre from which they are quoted. Two incipits for a single piece may often be required, for example, a vocal entry after an orchestral ritornello, or the beginning of an aria following a recitative. Furthermore, the practice of quoting only the uppermost voice may be misleading in polyphonic works when that voice is not the first to enter. In such cases, it may be useful to quote the opening of the piece in short score, with indication of vocal disposition or instrumentation. The original clefs, tempo, expression, phrasing and dynamic indications should normally be included, following the chosen (and specified) source. In certain repertories, reproduction of the original notation may be advantageous.

2. HISTORY AND FUNCTION. The history of thematic catalogues may best be outlined in terms of their functions, nine of which may be specified.

(*i*) *Mnemonic aid.* This type of thematic catalogue helps the performer recall the beginnings of well-known tunes or melodic formulae. Some tonaries of the 10th and 11th centuries (e.g. those by Odo of Cluny, *d* 942, or Guido of Arezzo, *d* after 1033) belong to this type and must be considered the earliest examples of thematic catalogues. These treatises contain musical incipits to guide the reader in choosing the proper tone or formula to connect the end of the psalm verse with the antiphon. Interestingly enough, the first printed thematic catalogue had a similar function. In 1645 William Barton published *The Book of Psalms in Metre*, a 304-page collection of psalm texts, which contains an incipit index of 'The beginnings of [22] G[eneral] and P[articular] tunes now used in London'. Most of the book's psalm texts are marked with one, two or three asterisks so they can be sung to one or more of the popular 'common tunes' represented by similarly marked incipits. This practice survives in the handwritten incipit lists used by some song leaders and café pianists.

(*ii*) *Table of contents.* This is an incipit index appearing in a printed or manuscript volume of musical pieces as a guide to its use. The first known thematic index of this

type was prepared by Heinrich Lübeck in 1598 for King Christian of Denmark as the index to a volume containing 202 trumpet sonatas and fanfares (*DK-Kk*, Gl.kgl.S.1874.4). Thematic tables of contents are common in 19th- and 20th-century editions, such as the Beethoven sonatas or Chopin mazurkas.

(*iii*) *Guide to a composer's output.* The earliest catalogues of this type were compiled by composers themselves as a means of organizing their works or protecting their authorship against counterfeiters before copyright laws were established. In 1686 J. K. Kerll published a set of *Magnificat* versets for organ, *Modulatio organica super Magnificat*, to which he attached a ten-page thematic index entitled 'Subnecto initia aliarum compositionum'. It contained 32 incipits for 22 of his other keyboard works (not included in the *Modulatio*) which, he said, he had seen 'in more than one place ... ascribed to someone else'; with this catalogue, Kerll was asserting his authorship and publicizing his wares at the same time. It was not until almost a century later that similar catalogues by other composers began to appear (e.g. J. G. Schürer, *Catalogo della musica di chiesa*, *c*1765, *D-Dlb*; Haydn, the 'Entwurf Katalog', *c*1765–*c*1805, *D-Bds* mus.607; and Mozart, *Verzeichnüss aller meiner Werke vom Monath Febraio 1784 bis* [*15 Nov 1791*]). After 1800 the increasing tendency to use chronologically ordered opus numbers (Beethoven being the first great composer to do so systematically) reduced the need for composers to prepare their own thematic catalogues. During the 19th century the compilation of such catalogues was taken over largely by publishers and scholars (see (vi) and (ix)), the latter led by a famous collector of musical manuscripts, Aloys Fuchs (1799–1853). From around 1830 to shortly before his death Fuchs prepared over 20 thematic catalogues of the works of 17th- and 18th-century composers, from Albrechtsberger to Vivaldi (now in *D-Bs*). His work on Mozart, for example, served as an important starting-point for Köchel. Some of his catalogues have not been superseded.

For illustrations *see* HAYDN, JOSEPH, fig.10 and MOZART, fig.11.

(*iv*) *Inventory of a library's holdings.* In the 18th century the contents of many large church, court and private music collections were catalogued thematically for the purpose of facilitating the location and identification of works. Such catalogues could be arranged by date of acquisition, by composer's name, or by storage shelf. The earliest known example of a thematic library catalogue (*Des Herren General Major Frey Herrn von SonsFeldt musicalisches Cathallogium*, *c*1728–60, in Schloss Herdringen, Germany, Fü 3720*a*) was compiled for the Prussian general, Friedrich Otto von Wittenhorst-Sonsfeld. Other manuscript catalogues include those of the Rheda library (*Catalogi musici*, *D-MÜu*), the library of Maria Anna of Bavaria (*Catalogo de libri di musica*, *c*1750–90, *D-Mbs* mus.1648), the Abbey of Herzogenburg (*Catalogus selectiorum musicalium*, 1751–?, *A-H*), and the library of the Italian flautist Filippo Ruge (*Catalogue de la collection symphonique*, *c*1757, in the San Francisco State College Library). When such catalogues list works that have since been lost, as they often do, they may prove useful in the identification of anonymous works or those of disputed authorship and in tracing patterns of music dissemination.

Among the earliest printed thematic library

catalogues are those by Coussemaker of the anonymous masses in Cambrai (in *Notice sur les collections musicales de la Bibliothèque de Cambrai*, 1843), by Haberl of sacred works in the Cappella Sistina at the Vatican Library (in *Bibliographischer und thematischer Musikkatalog des päpstlichen Kapellarchives zu Rom*, 1888), and by Kade of the great collections in Schwerin (*Die Musikalien-Sammlung des grossherzoglich Mecklenburg-Schweriner Fürstenhauses aus den letzten zwei Jahrhunderten*, 1893–9). The considerable growth, in recent years, in thematic cataloguing of library holdings, including that for *RISM*, represents a major advance for musicological research.

(*v*) *Copying firm advertisement*. Such catalogues display incipits of the works, manuscript or printed, that the establishment has on hand; copies of these works were made on demand at so much per page. There is evidence of the existence of only three such catalogues: the famous Breitkopf *Catalogo delle sinfonie, partite, overture, soli, duetti, trii, quattri e concerti per il violino, flauto traverso, cembalo ed altri stromenti*, published between 1762 and 1787 in six parts and 16 supplements, with 888 pages and over 14,000 incipits; Ringmacher's *Catalogo de' soli, duetti, trii, quadri, quintetti, partito, de' concerti e delle sinfonie*, published in 1773, 628 incipits; and the lost *Der grosse thematische Catalogus* of Christian Gottfried Thomas, which was issued in Leipzig in manuscript copies from 1778 onwards. Despite their rarity, the significance of such catalogues is great. The Breitkopf catalogue, by virtue of its size, breadth of coverage and sociological import (discussed in the introduction to the 1966 reprint), may well be the most useful single bibliographic aid to 18th-century research, for despite its inaccuracies it remains indispensable for dating and attribution. Catalogues of published works are inventories of compositions once existing in multiple prints, one of which can usually be located; but catalogues like Breitkopf's, containing incipits mainly of manuscripts, often cite rare and even unique works, and the incipits may be the only evidence of a composition's existence or the sole means of identifying anonymous and doubtful works (*see* BREITKOPF & HÄRTEL for illustration).

(*vi*) *Publishing firm advertisement*. These catalogues present incipits of a firm's own publications. They may be devoted to one or several composers and may be issued either as part of a musical edition (e.g. a single leaf added to a violin part) or in a self-contained volume. The earliest example of such a catalogue appears to be that of J. J. and B. Hummel: *Catalogue thématique, ou Commencement de touttes les oeuvres de musique qui sont du propre fond de J. J. & B. Hummel, publié à la commodité des amateurs, par où ils pourront voir, si les pièces qu'on leur présente pour original, n'ont pas déjà été imprimées* (published with six supplements, Amsterdam, 1768–74: this is the first time the term 'thematic catalogue' appears in print). Others were subsequently published by Corri in Edinburgh (*A Select Collection of the Most Admired Songs, Duetts, etc. from Operas of the Highest Esteem*, c1779), Bland in London (*Catalogues of Subjects or Beginnings of the Several Works ... which are Printed and Sold by J. Bland*, 1790–?1793), Bossler in Speyer (1790–94), Imbault in Paris (*Catalogue thématique des ouvrages de musique mis au jour par Imbault M^d de musique*, c1792) and Artaria in Vienna (*Catalogue thématique de Haydn,*

Mozart, Clementi, et Pleyel, 1798). The earliest publishers' catalogues of the works of individual composers include Forster's 'Catalogue of the works of Giuseppe Haydn' in his edition of op.50 (London, ?1785) and Artaria's *Catalogue thématique* of Pleyel's chamber works (Vienna, 1789).

The 19th century saw a great flowering of catalogues of this type, such as those of Mozart (published by Monzani, c1805), Mauro Giuliani (Steiner, 1815), Beethoven (Hofmeister, 1819), Gelinek (André, ?1820), Czerny (Diabelli, ?1827), Mendelssohn (Breitkopf & Härtel, 1843), Schubert (Diabelli, 1852), Schumann (Schuberth, 1850s), Chopin (Breitkopf & Härtel, 1855) and Schumann (Dörffel, 1860). In some instances the catalogues were prepared or corrected by the composers themselves, like those of Moscheles (published by Probst, 1825) and Liszt (Breitkopf & Härtel, 1855). The high season of publishers' sales catalogues was reached in the mid-19th century, and similar ones continue to be produced.

(*vii*) *Legal documents*. Contracts, bills of sale, *inventaires après decès*, and similar documents have included incipits for positive identification. Two such by Haydn are known, one of which declares: 'I acknowledge to have received seventy pounds [from William Forster, London publisher] for 20 symphonies, sonatas ... composed by me' (1786, *GB-Lbm* Eg.2380, f.12). There are five by Boccherini, including his *Catalogo della opere da me ... cedute in tutta proprieta al Sig^r Ignazio Pleyel* (1796). Similar documents exist concerning Michael Haydn (1808, *A-Wn* 2103) and Mayseder (1819, *A-Wst* MH 9171/c). A famous example of an estate inventory containing incipits is the *Verzeichniss des musicalischen Nachlasses des vestorbenen Capellmeisters C. P. E. Bach* (1790).

(*viii*) *Index of themes*. Such catalogues will usually quote complete themes or leitmotifs (as distinct from incipits) and may serve (*a*) for analysis of musical works (E. Tanzberger: *Jean Sibelius: eine Monographie mit einem Werk-Verzeichnis*, 1962); (*b*) as guides for the music lover (E. M. Terry: 'Leading Motives of the Operas', *A Richard Wagner Dictionary*, 1939; R. Burrows and B. C. Redmond: *Symphony Themes*, 1942); and (*c*) as pedagogical tools (D. J. Echelhard: *A Thematic Dictionary and Planning Guide of Selected Solo Literature for Trumpet*, diss., U. of Montana, 1969, which contains solo trumpet passages 'grouped into various levels of metric, rhythmic, ornamental, and miscellaneous problems').

(*ix*) *Musicological documentation*. Thematic catalogues prepared with scholarly thoroughness and accuracy represent a new direction in cataloguing that began about 1850. Such catalogues may be related in function to some of those previously mentioned, but primarily they serve as the essential, initial step in the answering of historical, analytical and musico-sociological questions. They may be based on a genre, form, period, country, region, publishing house, library, a specific monumental or complete works edition, an individual composer or group of composers. They may either be buried in the supplement to an unpublished dissertation or represent the efforts of many scholars working collectively on a substantial union-cataloguing project.

The model for this scientific approach was Ludwig Ritter von Köchel's *Chronologisch-thematisches Verzeichnis* of Mozart's works. He began research on his great catalogue in the early 1850s and published it with Breitkopf & Härtel in 1862. Köchel went far beyond the mere listing of a work's title, date, instrumentation and opening bars by providing such additional information as location of autographs, lists of early editions, references to literature about the work, and multiple-staff incipits for all movements.

This new direction in cataloguing coincided with the 19th-century development of musicology as a discipline and the publication, especially in Germany, of the great complete editions. The stream of catalogues that appeared during the second half of the century, often prepared in conjunction with such editions, included those for Beethoven, Spohr, Saint-Saëns, Tchaikovsky, Brahms, Gluck, C. P. E. Bach and Dvořák. These rarely, however, approached the Köchel catalogue in scholarship, and remained closer in purpose and coverage to publishers' sales catalogues (F. W. Jähns's detailed work on C. M. von Weber is a notable exception).

After a lapse following World War I, publication gained momentum in the 1930s and 1940s with catalogues for Reger, Kreisler, Volkmann and Domenico Scarlatti, as well as a number of facsimiles of 18th-century manuscript catalogues (especially Larsen's invaluable *Drei Haydn Kataloge in Facsimile*, 1941). It was not until the 1950s and the postwar resurgence of musicological activity that the full impact of Köchel's innovations began to be felt. At last there appeared definitive, scholarly thematic catalogues of the works of Bach (W. Schmieder: *Thematisch-systematisches Verzeichnis der musikalischen Werke*, 1950), Beethoven (G. Kinsky: *Das Werk Beethovens: thematisch-bibliographisches Verzeichnis seiner sämtlichen vollendeten Kompositionen*, 1955), Schubert (O. E. Deutsch and D. R. Wakeling: *Schubert: Thematic Catalogue of All his Works in Chronological Order*, 1951), Couperin (M. Cauchie: *Thematic Index of the Works*, 1949), Haydn (A. van Hoboken: *Joseph Haydn: thematisch-bibliographisches Werkverzeichnis*, 1957–71), Boccherini (Y. Gérard: *Catalogue of the Works*, 1969) and others. Many more are in progress.

3. HISTORIOGRAPHY. Too few studies have been made of the different methods of catalogue organization and incipit classification, of the problems of inclusion and exclusion of information and of the use of non-conventional, machine-readable notational codes. Among the few classic articles contributing to an understanding of the history and function of the thematic index are those by Wilhelm Altmann, O. E. Deutsch, Wolfgang Schmieder, A. Hyatt King and Nanie Bridgman. In folk music classification and thematic indexing, Scheurleer's famous article of 1899 launched an important discussion, still continuing, to which such scholars as Koller, Krohn, Heinitz, Elschek and Stockmann have contributed.

A number of effective non-conventional, typewriter and machine-readable codes have been developed in recent years to simplify the control of data. Among those in extensive use are Nanie Bridgman's intervallic system, Ingmar Bengtsson's 'Numericode', Barry Brook's 'Simplified Plaine and Easie Code', Stefan Bauer-Mengelberg's Ford–Columbia language, and the melodic code used by Franklin B. Zimmerman.

Broad interest in the machine processing of musical data developed in the early 1960s, but unfortunately the enormous potential of computerization for thematic cataloguing has not yet been realized. What are needed are not merely successful pilot projects, of which there have been many, but rather full-scale bibliographical and analytical systems capable of dealing with quantities of data, and able to transform coded notation into inexpensive photo-composed pages and transpose and extract parts automatically. (Computer applications have been discussed by Lawrence Bernstein, Barry Brook, Jiří Fukač, Jan LaRue, Harry Lincoln, Alfons Ott, F. W. Riedel and Franklin B. Zimmerman.) With computer assistance, thematic cataloguing should be able to play a central role in providing a complete and accurate distillation of available musical, analytical, literary, contextual and chronological information for any given topic.

BIBLIOGRAPHY

D. Scheurleer: 'Preisfrage: welches ist die beste Methode, um Volks- und volksmässige Lieder nach ihrer melodischen (nicht textlichen) Beschaffenheit lexikalisch zu ordnen', *ZIMG*, i (1899–1900), 219

O. Koller: 'Die beste Methode, Volks- und volksmässige Lieder nach ihrer melodischen Beschaffenheit lexikalisch zu ordnen', *SIMG*, iv (1902–3), 1

I. Krohn: 'Welches ist die beste Methode, um Volks- und volksmässige Lieder nach ihrer melodischen (nicht textlichen) Beschaffenheit lexikalisch zu ordnen?', *SIMG*, iv (1902–3), 643

W. Heinitz: 'Eine lexikalische Ordnung für die vergleichende Betrachtung von Melodien', *AMw*, iii (1921), 247

W. Altmann: 'Über thematische Kataloge', *Beethoven-Zentenarfeier: Wien 1927*, 283

N. Bridgman: 'L'établissement d'un catalogue par incipit musicaux', *MD*, iv (1950), 65

O. E. Deutsch: 'Theme and Variations, with Bibliographical Notes on Pleyel's Haydn Editions', *MR*, xii (1951), 68

N. Bridgman: 'A propos d'un catalogue central d'incipits musicaux', *FAM*, i (1954), 2

A. H. King: 'The Past, Present, and Future of the Thematic Catalogue', *MMR*, lxxxiv (1954), 10, 39

O. E. Deutsch: 'Thematische Katalcge', *FAM*, v (1958), 73

N. Bridgman: 'Le classement par incipit musicaux, histoire d'un catalogue', *Bulletin des bibliothèques de France*, iv (1959), 303

J. Fukač: *Inventarien böhmischer oder mährischer Provenienz* (Brno, 1959)

J. LaRue: 'A Union Thematic Catalogue of 18th Century Symphonies', *FAM*, vi (1959), 18

——: 'Major and Minor Mysteries of Identification in the 18th Century Symphony', *JAMS*, xiii (1960), 181

——: 'Union Thematic Catalogues for 18th Century Chamber Music and Concertos', *FAM*, vii (1960), 64

N. Bridgman: 'Nouvelle visite aux incipit musicaux', *AcM*, xxxiii (1961), 193

J. Fukač: 'Inventáře hudební', *Československý hudební slovník osob a institucí*, i (1963), 550

R. Schaal: 'Quellen zur Musiksammlung Aloys Fuchs', *Mf*, xvi (1963), 67

W. Schmieder: '"Menschliches-Allzumenschliches", oder einige unparteiische Gedanken über thematische Verzeichnisse', *Festschrift Otto Erich Deutsch* (Kassel, 1963), 309

L. F. Bernstein: 'Data Processing and the Thematic Index', *FAM*, xi (1964), 159

B. S. Brook and M. Gould: 'Notating Music with Ordinary Typewriter Characters (a Plaine and Easie Code System for Musicke)', *FAM*, xi (1964), 142

B. S. Brook: 'The Simplified Plaine and Easie Code System for Notating Music: a Proposal for International Adoption', *FAM*, xii (1965), 156

——: 'Utilization of Data Processing Techniques in Musical Documentation', *FAM*, xii (1965), 112

J. LaRue and G. W. Logemann: 'E[lectronic] D[ata] P[rocessing] for Thematic Catalogues', *Notes*, xxii (1965–6), 1179

F. B. Zimmerman: 'Melodic Indexing for General and Specialized Use', *Notes*, xxii (1965–6), 1187

A. Ott: 'Thematische Verzeichnisse', *MGG*

J. Fukač: 'Tschechische Musikinventare', *Tschechische Musikwissenschaft: Geschichtliches* (Prague, 1966), 1–64

O. Pulkert: *Souborný hudební katalog: pokyny ke katalogizaci hudebnin* (Prague, 1966)

F. W. Riedel: 'Zur Geschichte der musikalischen Quellenüberlieferung und Quellenkunde', *AcM*, xxxviii (1966), 3

B. S. Brook: 'Music Bibliography and the Computer', *West Virginia University Conference on Computer Applications in Music: Morgantown 1966*, 9

I. Bengtsson: 'Numericode: a Code System for Thematic Incipits', *STMf*, xlix (1967), 5–40

H. Heckmann, ed.: *Electronische Datenverarbeitung in der Musikwissenschaft* (Regensburg, 1967) [incl. H. B. Lincoln: 'Some Criteria and Techniques for Developing Thematic Indices']

H. B. Lincoln: 'Musicology and the Computer: the Thematic Index', *Computers in Humanistic Research: Readings and Perspectives* (Englewood Cliffs, NJ, 1967), 184

——: 'The Thematic Index: a Computer Application to Musicology', *Computers and the Humanities*, ii (1968), 215

O. Elschek and D. Stockmann: *Methoden der Klassifikation von Volksliedweisen* (Bratislava, 1969)

K. Gofferje: 'Über lexikalisch geordnete Melodieverzeichnisse zum mehrstimmigen deutschen Lied des 15. und 16. Jahrhunderts: ein neuer Versuch', *Musa–mens–musici: im Gedenken an Walther Vetter* (Leipzig, 1969), 37

S. Bauer-Mengelberg: 'The Ford–Columbia Input Language', *Musicology and the Computer: Musicology 1966–2000: Three Symposia*, ed. B. S. Brook (New York, 1970), 48

F. B. Zimmerman: 'Musical Biography and Thematic Cataloguing: Two Opposing Aspects of Musicology in the 21st Century', ibid, 216

B. S. Brook: 'The First Printed Thematic Catalogues', *Festskrift Jens Peter Larsen* (Copenhagen, 1972), 103

——: *Thematic Catalogues in Music: an Annotated Bibliography* (Hillsdale, NY, 1972)

BARRY S. BROOK

Thematic transformation. *See* TRANSFORMATION, THEMATIC.

Thematik (Ger.). The approach to THEME and MOTIF as musical resources; the characteristic use of themes and motifs by a composer or school, piece or set of pieces etc.

Thematische Arbeit (Ger.). A term used to describe the process of musical development whereby thematic material is expanded, broken into its motivic elements, regrouped, rhythmically reinterpreted or subjected to transformation in some other way; it seems to have been in use by the end of the 18th century, for it is mentioned in Koch's *Musikalisches Lexikon* (1802). *See* DEVELOPMENT; FORTSPINNUNG; PERIOD; SONATA FORM; TRANSFORMATION, THEMATIC.

Theme. The musical material on which part or all of a work is based, usually having a recognizable melody and sometimes perceivable as a complete musical expression in itself, independent of the work to which it belongs. It gives a work its identity even when (as is frequently the case with a theme and variations) it is not original to the work.

The Greek *thema* (from the verb *tithēmi*: 'to set or place'), as it was used in ancient rhetoric and composition, generally referred to a proposed idea or argument (i.e. a subject for discussion). It was first used as a musical term by Zarlino in *Le istitutioni harmoniche* (1558), where it denoted a melody that was repeated and subjected to variation in the course of a work. 'Thema' thus meant much the same as 'punto', which was then the standard term among Italian theorists; Thomas Morley was later to call this 'point', in *A Plaine and Easie Introduction to Practicall Musicke* (1597). Zarlino also contrasted 'thema' with 'soggetto', which was a fixed line that underlay the structure of a piece but did not interact with the other voices – hence a cantus firmus. This distinction was not, however, maintained in the 17th and early 18th centuries, when many writers used the vernacular equivalents of 'theme', 'subject' and 'invention' synonymously. Bach seems to have preferred 'thema' for his fugue subjects, though he often used the Latin *subjectum* for the second subject of a double fugue, or for a counter-subject maintained rigorously in the course of a fugue. The definition of 'Thema' in J. G. Walther's *Musicalisches Lexicon* (1732) as 'the subject [*Satz*] of a fugue' is characteristic of the use of the term in the 18th century, namely for a melodic line worked out contrapuntally. Towards the end of the century, however, it connoted the leading section or phrase (Ger. *Hauptsatz*) of a sonata movement; for Koch (*Musikalisches Lexikon*, 1802) it referred specifically to the first four-bar phrase of the initial eight-bar PERIOD.

By the mid-19th century 'theme' had taken on three important attributes which it has retained: it was no longer restricted to the very beginning of a work but might appear in any part of a composition (hence the notions of 'first theme', 'second theme'); it had a certain completeness, a roundedness, which distinguished it from the shorter and more elemental MOTIF (theme and motif had often been treated synonymously in the early 19th century); and a theme was a recognizable entity, something that could be used to identify a work – thus it was not until the 19th century that the now pervasive requisite of originality in theme writing became a significant part of composition. But the most important aspect of theme remained that which Zarlino had discussed three centuries before, its repetition and variation in the course of a work. As early as 1802 Koch discussed *thematische Arbeit*, the development of thematic materials. The related idea of THEMATIC TRANSFORMATION (sometimes 'transformation of themes') has been current in English writings for some time, denoting the interrelatedness of many themes (particularly by their melodic shape) in a single composition, that is their derivation from a common source. The process of thematic transformation is encountered frequently in the works of Liszt, appearing ubiquitously in his symphonic poem *Les préludes*.

In much contemporary music it is difficult to draw a line between what is proposed (i.e. a theme) and what is worked out from the proposal. Writers have increasingly turned away from using 'theme' in any but a formal sense, for example to show the first and second 'themes' of a work clearly modelled on the sonata form of the Classical–Romantic period. Thus the theme of, say, a 12-note instrumental composition by Schoenberg might well be viewed conceptually as the 12-note set on which it is based; in a descriptive analysis of the work, however, the 'first theme' might be indicated by its opening bars. As applied to earlier music 'theme' has taken on one new characteristic, namely that it can be viewed as polyphonic in design. A distinction between 'subject' and 'theme' has yet to be worked out rigorously, although the former has maintained its supremacy in discussions of fugue, while the latter has begun to be more widely accepted in its polyphonic totality, instead of merely being thought of as a leading melody.

See also SUBJECT; SUBJECT GROUP; MELODY.

WILLIAM DRABKIN

Theme group. *See* SUBJECT GROUP.

Théobalde. *See* GATTI, THEOBALDO DI.

Theobaldus [Hofacker, Andreas] (*fl* 1694–1704). German friar and poet. His original name is known through the solution of a riddle in the preface to the *Marianische Einöde*. His sacred odes were widely circulated in southern Germany. The most important settings of them are by JOHANN WILHELM SCHEFFER who is named in the appendix to *Chorus Marianus*, which was published anonymously. The four collections are unified in several ways, a feature that is typical of such volumes of Catholic music for devotional and domestic use about 1700: the titles are not dissimilar, each volume includes emblematic engravings, each contains 24 pieces, with similar melodies, and ritornellos for two violins and continuo.

WORKS

Chorus Marianus, oder Marianischer Rayen (Überlingen, 1694) [music by J. W. Scheffer in appx]
Schmertzhaffte Marianische Einöde, also die irrende Polymnia ... Arien und Ritornellen, 2 vn (Konstanz, 1698)
Petra deserti, das ist Felsen der schmertzhafften Marianischen Einöde ... Arien und Ritornellen, 2 vn, bc (Augsburg, 1703)
Marianischer Baum-Garten, allwo die in der schmertzhafften Marianischen Einöde herumb gewanderte Polymnia (Konstanz, 1704)

BIBLIOGRAPHY

W. Bäumker: *Das katholische deutsche Kirchenlied in seinen Singweisen*, iii (Freiburg, 1891), nos.97, 99, 100, 107 [contains several melodies]

WALTHER LIPPHARDT

Theobaldus Gallicus (*fl* early or mid-13th century). Composer or scribe, working probably in Paris between the time of Robertus de Sabilone and that of Franco. He is mentioned only by the theorist Anonymous IV (ed. Reckow, 1967, i, 50) writing about 1275.

See ORGANUM AND DISCANT: BIBLIOGRAPHY.

IAN D. BENT

Theocritus [Theokritos] (*b* Syracuse, *c*308 BC; *d* ?Syracuse, *c*240 BC). Greek poet. A Sicilian by birth, he apparently spent most of his life outside Sicily, and much of it in Alexandria. His surviving works (including some false ascriptions) consist of 27 epigrams and 30 longer poems; the latter, composed almost entirely in hexameters, came to be called idylls (*eidyllia*) and contain some of the first and most perfect surviving specimens of 'pastoral poetry', later imitated in Virgil's *Eclogues*. The shepherds of the *Idylls* usually play the syrinx (panpipes). This was rectangular, with the individual pipes (*kalamoi*) stopped with wax in graduated amounts; it thus differed from the triangular fistula of the Romans. When Theocritean shepherds play any other instrument it is a single reed, pierced with finger-holes but lacking a mouthpiece (e.g. Idyll v, 1.7). This was probably a simple form of the *syrinx monokalamos*, like the oat-straw *avena* in Italy (*see* VIRGIL). The mention of a double aulos and of a transverse flute (*plagiaulos*) in Idyll xx (l.29) is one of many indications that this poem is not Theocritean.

The professional performance of music is illustrated in the *Idylls* by the singing of an elaborate lament (*ialemos*) for Adonis (xv, ll.100–144), and by several references to playing on the double reedpipes by an *aulētris*, a flute-girl. Theocritus reserved his most detailed comments for the sphere of amateur music-making, as in the description of fine panpipes (i, ll.128f) and the praise of a singing harvester who 'skilfully measured out the [?]shape of the tune' (*idean harmonias* x, l.39). Singing and piping do not occur simultaneously in the *Idylls*; this apparent assumption of alternation was a literary convention that did not correspond to reality, as Homer's description of the LINUS song shows.

Impromptu singing matches between shepherds are the most celebrated element of Theocritean pastoral; such 'flyting' has been noted even in the 20th century as a feature of gatherings of Greek and Sicilian country people. However, the evidence of ethnomusicology and details of the *Idylls* suggest that Theocritus was not describing a universal folk practice, but drawing on a specific and strong local tradition. *See also* GREECE, §I.

BIBLIOGRAPHY

J. M. Edmonds, ed. and trans.: *The Greek Bucolic Poets* (London and Cambridge, Mass., 1912, 9/1970)
A. S. F. Gow, ed.: *Theocritus* (Cambridge, 1950, rev. 2/1952)
R. Merkelbach: '*Boukoliastai* (der Wettgesang der Hirten)', *Rheinisches Museum für Philologie*, xcix (1956), 97–133
G. Lawall: *Theocritus' Coan Pastorals* (Cambridge, Mass., 1967), 54
A. Holden, trans.: *Greek Pastoral Poetry* (Harmondsworth, 1974)

WARREN ANDERSON

Theodericus [Theodorici], **Sixt.** *See* DIETRICH, SIXT.

Theodonus de Caprio (*b* ?Sant'Agata; *d* Capua, 1434). Italian theorist. He was a Benedictine at the monastery of Montevergine (Avellino), and prior of the abbey of Capua. His treatise *Regule contrapuncti*, in an addition to the manuscript *I-Rvat* Barberini lat.307, is dated 13 July 1431. It begins with a description of the nine consonances, five perfect (unison, 5th, octave, 12th, 15th) and four imperfect (3rd, 6th [major and minor], 10th, 13th), and continues with illustrations of their possible combinations in compositions for two voices. At the end of the same manuscript, under the date 31 March 1432, Theodonus had begun to copy the *Libellus cantus mensurabilis* of Jehan des Murs.

BIBLIOGRAPHY

R. Casimiri: 'Teodono de Caprio non Teodorico de Campo teorico musicale italiano del secolo XV: un suo trattato inedito', *NA*, xix (1942), 38, 93

F. ALBERTO GALLO

Theodorakis, Mikis (*b* Khios, 29 July 1925). Greek composer. Circumstances prevented his receiving much formal musical training in Greece, but he was early influenced by Byzantine music and Cretan folk music. In 1954, after unhappy years of military service, he went to Paris, where he enrolled at the Conservatoire. His ballet *Antigone* was produced at Covent Garden in 1959, in which year he returned to Greece and issued a manifesto that subjected the Greek musical establishment and the National School of Music to scathing attack. In the 1960s his revolutionary doctrines expanded to embrace poetry, film and drama as well as national music, and his influence was such that, when Greece fell under right-wing rule in 1967, his music was banned and he was imprisoned. He was released in 1970 in response to worldwide appeals. His large output includes many oratorios, ballets, film scores and song cycles with pop orchestra, almost all based on historical or contemporary Greek subject matter.

BIBLIOGRAPHY

G. Giannaris: *Mikis Theodorakis: Music and Social Change* (London, 1973)
M. Theodorakis: *Les fiancés de Pénélope: conversations avec Denis Bourgeois* (Paris, 1975)

CHRISTOPHER PALMER

Theodoricus. *See* GERARDE, DERICK.

Theodoricus, Georg. *See* DIETRICH, GEORG.

Theodoricus de Campo. Supposed author of the mid-14th-century treatise on mensural notation preserved anonymously in *I-Rvat* Barberini lat.307, ff.21–27. The attribution was due to Coussemaker's error in reading the name THEODONUS DE CAPRIO or Capua, as well as linking the name with a treatise quite different from those bearing it in the MS. The short set of counterpoint rules and the fragment of JEHAN DES MURS' *Libellus cantus mensurabilis* attributed to Theodonus, no doubt as copyist, are in fact a later addition. The value of the anonymous work is that it bridges the gap in our knowledge of mensural theory between Franco of Cologne and the later 14th century. Both the French and Italian Ars Nova notational methods of Vitry and Marchetto are discussed, and there is valuable information about the value of the various lengths of semibreve used immediately preceding the period of the Ars Nova. Even so, newer note forms such as the semiminim and dragma are also treated.

BIBLIOGRAPHY
R. Casimiri: 'Teodono de Caprio non Teodorico de Campo teorico musicale italiano del secolo XV: un suo trattato inedito', *NA*, xix (1942), 38, 93
W. Apel: *The Notation of Polyphonic Music 900–1600* (Cambridge, Mass., 1942, 4/1949), 320, 324, 384, 392
G. Reaney: 'The Question of Authorship in the Medieval Treatises on Music', *MD*, xviii (1964), 8
C. Sweeney, ed.: *Anonymus: De musica mensurabili*, CSM, xiii (1971) [with important introduction]

GILBERT REANEY

Theodoricus Petri Nylandensis [Ruutha, Didrik Persson; Rwtha, Didrik Persson] (*b* near Borgå, [Porvoo, Nyland, Finland], *c*1560; *d* ?Poland, probably before 1617). Swedish government official and music editor. His family originally came from Denmark and he seems to have attended the cathedral school at Viborg (then part of Sweden, now in the USSR). He studied at the University of Rostock from 1581 to 1584, during which years he published a few poems in Latin and had his song collection *Piae cantiones* printed in Greifswald (1582). He then entered the service of the King of Sweden and was governor of Västerbotten in the north of the country in 1598–9. After the revolution against the Catholic King Sigismund (also King of Poland), he left Sweden, and is believed to have died in Poland. His family was ennobled by King Gustav Vasa.

Theodoricus's famous songbook is entitled *Piae cantiones ecclesiasticae et scholasticae veterum episcoporum, in inclyto regno sueciae passim usurpatae, nuper studio viri cuiusdam reverendissimi de ecclesia Dei et schola Aböensi in Finlandia optime meriti accurate a mendis correctae, et nunc typis commissae, opera Theodorici Petri Nylandensis: his adiecti sunt aliquot ex psalmis recentioribus* (Greifswald, 1582/*R*1967; ed. G. R. Woodward, London, 1910). The clergyman at the cathedral school of Åbo (Turku) mentioned in this title was Jacobus Finno. It has been suggested that he was the true editor of the collection and that it contains the medieval repertory of the Åbo school, but Finno's part in the anthology was probably no more than the granting of a Lutheran imprimatur. The volume contains 74 songs, 12 of which are for two to four voices. As the title indicates, some of the songs are intended for use in church services, while the Christmas songs are for church or school use. Fewer than 40 are known in earlier sources from other countries. An enlarged and revised edition, *Cantiones piae et antiquae*, was printed in Rostock in 1625, but later only parts of the collection were reissued, mostly in Finland and often with changes in the melodies that are typical of an oral tradition. 17 songs were reprinted in J. Lindell's *Cantilenarum selec-*

tiorum editio nova (1776) and Sibelius made three arrangements in *Carminalia* (1899). In the mid-19th century a copy of the original edition was brought from Stockholm to England, where it came into the hands of J. M. Neale, through whose carols several of the *Piae cantiones* melodies have become widely familiar (e.g. 'Good King Wenceslas looked out'), as has Holst's fine setting of 'Personent hodie'.

BIBLIOGRAPHY
T. Norlind: 'Schwedische Schullieder im Mittelalter und in der Reformationszeit', *SIMG*, ii (1900–01), 566ff
——: *Latinska skolsånger i Sverige och Finland* (Lund, 1909)
T. Mäkinen: *Die aus frühen böhmischen Quellen überlieferten Piae Cantiones-Melodien* (Pieksämäki, 1964)
——: 'Piae cantiones: über die Geschichte und Zusammensetzung der Liedersammlung', *SM*, ix (1967), 371
F. Bohlin: 'Piae cantiones', *Kulturhistoriskt lexikon för nordisk medeltid*, xiii (Malmö, 1968), col. 268

FOLKE BOHLIN

Theodoricus Sistinus. Latinized name of TRUID AAGESEN.

Theodorus Petrejus. See PERS, DIRCK PIETERSZOON.

Theogerus of Metz (*b* *c*1050; *d* Cluny, 29 April 1120). German Benedictine abbot, bishop and musical theorist. Educated by Manegold of Lautenbach, Theogerus entered the abbey of Hirsau and studied under its abbot WILHELM OF HIRSAU, who in 1088 appointed him Abbot of St Georgen in the Black Forest. In 1117 he was elected Bishop of Metz, and consecrated in 1118, but he was never able to occupy the see, and he retired to Cluny as an ordinary monk.

Theogerus is credited with one treatise, *Musica* (*GS*, ii, 182–96; *PL*, clxiii, 777; MS sources listed by H. Hüschen in *MGG*, 'Theogerus von Metz'), which drew heavily on the work of Wilhelm of Hirsau. It contains a description of the monochord (including 'monochords' with as many as eight strings) and discussions of intervals, tetrachords, species of 4ths, 5ths and octaves, and the modes. The last were listed as *protus*, *deuterus*, etc, and also divided into authentic and plagal groups. Theogerus, unlike his contemporaries, admitted the theoretical existence of B♭ in the lowest tetrachord.

BIBLIOGRAPHY
P. Wagner: *Einführung in die gregorianischen Melodien*, i (Leipzig, 3/1911/*R*1970), 243
G. Reese: *Music in the Middle Ages* (New York, 1940), 383
H.-J. Wollasch: *Die Anfänge des Klosters St. Georgen im Schwarzwald*, Forschungen zur oberrheinischen Landesgeschichte, ed. C. Bauer and others, xiv (Freiburg, 1964)

RICHARD SHERR

Theokritos. See THEOCRITUS.

Theon of Smyrna (*fl* Smyrna [now Izmir], early 2nd century AD). Greek philosopher and mathematician. His work was dependent on that of Tiberius's court astrologer, Thrasyllus of Alexandria (*d* AD 36), and Adrastus, a member of the (Aristotelian) Peripatetic School (*fl* 1st–2nd century AD), but not on the *Almagest* (i.e. the *Syntaxis*) of Ptolemy. Besides two treatises about Plato, now lost, Theon wrote a dissertation on 'mathematical questions necessary to the understanding of Plato' (*Ta kata to mathēmatikon chrēsima eis tēn Platōna anagnōsin*).

This mathematical introduction to the study of Platonic philosophy survives in two separate sections: one is concerned with the study of numbers and harmony, and the other with astronomy. Part of the work seems to have been lost, for Theon in his preamble promised discussions of five numerical sciences: arithmetic, geometry, stereometry, astronomy and music (ed. Hiller, i.15ff; xvi.24ff).

The second main section of this work is devoted to music. In it, music is divided into three main categories: the 'noetic', or intelligible, music of numbers (*hē en arithmois mousikē*), deduced from arithmetical theorems; the 'aesthetic' music of instruments (*hē en organois mousikē*), perceived through the senses; and the music of the cosmos (*hē en kosmō harmonia kai hē en toutō harmonia*), or harmony of the spheres. Although Theon regarded the music of the cosmos, rather than the music of instruments, as the proper subject for consideration, he dealt with instrumental music first; he sought to justify this procedure by arguing that it made the music of numbers easier to grasp.

Theon's section on instrumental music represents chapters from a mathematical treatise on musical intervals, in the tradition of the Pythagoreans, rather than a discussion of melody or scale in the manner of the followers of Aristoxenus. In it he quoted Thrasyllus (xlvii.18ff) concerning notes, harmonic sounds, intervals and *harmonia*. The consonances (*symphōniai*) are graded according to the simplicity of their ratios, or their ability to blend, first as *antiphōnia* (the octave or double octave) and *paraphōnia* (4th and 5th) – the cornerstones of the tonal system, and then as consonances 'according to proximity', i.e. indirectly related (whole tone, *diesis*). Theon quoted Adrastus (xlix.6ff; lxi.18ff), also using excerpts from Thrasyllus dealing with physical experiments (lvi.9ff), concerning the analogy between speech and music; the requirements for the production of notes; the principal consonances, whole tones and semitones; the three *genera*; and the *diesis*, the combination and categorization of the consonances, the whole tone and the *leimma*.

His section on the music of numbers, or computable music, is purely arithmological, and again draws on Thrasyllus and Adrastus. It gives an account of ratios (lxxiv.15ff), proportions, with a digression on the division of the monochord (lxxxii.16ff), and finally of means (cvi ff).

Only in the third main section, on astronomy (cxx–ccv), did Theon touch upon the music of the cosmos.

There are striking correspondences between Theon's sources and those parts of the writings of the Latin neo-Platonists Chalcidius, Favonius and Macrobius which deal with the theory of number, even discounting the Pythagorean and Platonic tradition common to all of them. Possible connections between Theon's musical classification and that of Boethius, which was to become authoritative in the Latin Middle Ages, have yet to be investigated; but Theon's categorization of the intervals according to their degree of consonance, which he derived from Thrasyllus, like the similar categorization of Ptolemy, exerted an influence on Byzantine theorists such as Psellus and Bryennius, and through their work survived for a millennium after Theon's lifetime.

WRITINGS

ed. E. Hiller: *Expositio rerum mathematicarum ad legendum Platonem utilium* (Leipzig, 1878)

ed. and Fr. trans. J. Dupuis: *Théon de Smyrne: Exposition des connaissances mathématiques utiles pour la lecture de Platon* (Paris, 1892)

BIBLIOGRAPHY
(*only works concerned with music*)

C. Stumpf: 'Geschichte des Consonanzbegriffes: I', *Abhandlungen der Bayerischen Akademie der Wissenschaften, Philosophisch-philologische Klasse*, xxi (Munich, 1901), 49

L. Schönberger: *Studien zum 1. Buch der Harmonik des Claudius Ptolemäus* (Augsburg, 1914)

F. E. Robbins: 'Posidonius and the Sources of Pythagorean Arithmology', *Classical Philology*, xv (1920), 309

——: 'The Tradition of Greek Arithmology', *Classical Philology*, xvi (1921), 97

K. von Fritz: 'Theon 14', *Paulys Real-Encyclopädie der classischen Altertumswissenschaft*, 2nd ser., x (1934), 2067

L. Richter: *Zur Wissenschaftlehre von der Musik bei Platon und Aristoteles* (Berlin, 1961), 74f

LUKAS RICHTER

Theorbe (Ger.). An ORGAN STOP.

Theorbo [theorbo lute] (Fr. *téorbe, théorbe, tuorbe*; Ger. *Theorb*; It. *tiorba, tuorba*). An instrument of the Western lute family with stopped courses considerably longer than those of a lute and with a separate nut and pegbox for a set of longer, unstopped bass strings (diapasons). During the 17th century and part of the 18th the theorbo was popular as an accompanying instrument, and in the 17th century a certain amount of solo music in tablature was published for it.

The pegbox for the stopped strings of a theorbo is

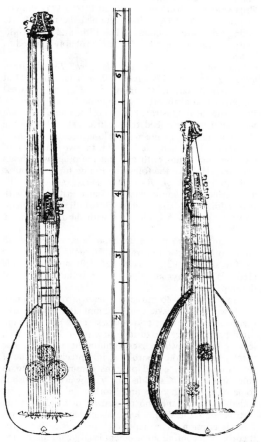

1. Lang romanische Theorba: Chitarron (left), and paduanische Theorba (right): woodcuts from Praetorius, 'Syntagma musicum', ii (2/1619); 1 Brunswick foot = 28 cm

nearly aligned with the neck, not bent back sharply as on a lute. Beyond the upper end of this pegbox the neck extends to an additional pegbox for the additional bass strings. The extension is of the same piece of wood as the first pegbox, and the bass strings are kept from crossing the stopped courses by setting the extensions at a slight angle off centre. Later a second, more Baroque type of design was developed, involving an S-like kink in the extension above the first pegbox. This type of instrument had 13 courses of strings tuned $A'–B'–C–D–E–F–G–A–d–f–a–d'–f'$, the same tuning as for solo lute music after $c1700$ when the lowest two courses were added to the 11-course Baroque lute.

The stopped courses of the theorbo are much longer than those of the ordinary tenor lute – too long for the highest strings to withstand the tension necessary to tune them as they would be tuned on the lute. Consequently the first course, and sometimes the second, was tuned down an octave. The third course was thus the highest in pitch and in solo music became the melody course. (Mace advocated in 1676, however, that if the second course could withstand the higher tuning only the first course should be tuned down.) The octave displacement of the upper course or courses is an important factor distinguishing the theorbo – and the CHITARRONE – from the lute-sized LIUTO ATTIORBATO (see also ARCHLUTE), which retained the normal lute tuning for its fretted courses. The 17th- and early 18th-century English term 'theorbo lute' probably referred to a theorbo.

Praetorius distinguished a *paduanische Theorba* from a *lang romanische Theorba: Chitarron* (see fig.1), but Cavalieri, Agazzari, Piccinini and Kapsberger used 'chitarrone' and 'theorbo' synonymously (see Spencer). Praetorius also illustrated a 'theorboed lute' (*testudo theorbata*) but described that instrument in his tuning charts as merely a 'lute with a long neck', i.e. a *liuto attiorbato*. Elsewhere he alluded to two varieties of theorbo, one strung with gut and the other with brass and steel. He gave the following tuning for a 14-course theorbo: $F'–G'–A'–B'–C–D–E–F–G–c–f–a–d–g$; he also included a tuning for a 16-course instrument with two additional bass strings. Most Italian sources, however, give an A tuning (i.e. with the note names a step higher).

The invention of the theorbo was attributed to Antonio Naldi (also known as 'Il Bardella') in Florence by Cavalieri (1592), Caccini (1601/2) and Mersenne (1636–7). It is certain that the instrument was first developed in Italy.

Tablatures of solo music for theorbo were idiomatically written to take into account the octave displacement of the first two courses. Thus the left hand often has to finger the third course up to the 12th fret, leaving the first two courses to fill in the harmony. The greater length of the theorbo's strings precluded some of the more difficult chord patterns commonly found in solo lute music. Castaldi (1622), however, published some duets for theorbo and 'tiorbino al ottava', presumably a small theorbo pitched an octave above; an instrument in the Vienna Kunsthistorisches Museum fits this description. The repertory of music using the theorbo as a continuo instrument is large; it requires the theorbo player to read from a bass line and devise his own accompaniment (like a keyboard continuo player). In this role the instrument was used in large-scale ensembles as well as to accompany solo songs.

2. Mary Sidney, Lady Wroth, holding a theorbo: portrait (c1620) attributed to John de Critz, at Penshurst Place, Kent

TABLATURE SOURCES

1614   P. P. Melli: *Intavolatura di liuto attiorbato, libro secondo* (Venice, 1614)
1620   P. P. Melli: *Intavolatura di liuto attiorbato e di tiorba, libro quinto* (Venice, 1620)
1622   B. Castaldi: *Capricci a due stromenti cioè tiorba e tiorbino* (Modena, 1622)
1645   *Conserto vago di balletti, volte, corrente, et gagliarde per sonare con liuto, tiorba, et chitarrino* (Rome, 1645)
1668   H. Grenerin: *Livre de théorbe* (Paris, 1668)
1668   V. Strobel (ii): *Conzerten für 2 angeliken und 1 theorbe* (Strasbourg, 1668), lost
1669   A. M. Bartolotti: *Table pour apprendre facilement à toucher le théorbe* (Paris, 1669)
1669   G. Pitoni: *Intabolatura di tiorba nella quale si contengono dodici sonate da camera* (Bologna, 1669)
1669   G. Pitoni: *Intabolatura di tiorba nella quale si contengono dodici sonate da chiesa* (Bologna, 1669)
1676   T. Mace: *Musick's Monument* (London, 1676/R1966)
MS, late 17th century, US-NYpm 17524 (music by Hurel)
MS, late 17th century, F-Pn Rés.Vm⁷ 6265 ('Tablature de theorbe')

BIBLIOGRAPHY

M. Praetorius: *Syntagma musicum*, ii (Wolfenbüttel, 1618, 2/1619/R1958)
M. Mersenne: *Harmonie universelle* (Paris, 1636–7/R1963; Eng. trans., 1957)
T. Mace: *Musick's Monument* (London, 1676/R1966)
N. Fortune: 'Giustiniani on Instruments', *GSJ*, v (1952), 48
——: 'Continuo Instruments in Italian Monodies', *GSJ*, vi (1953), 10
M. Morrow and M. Graubart: 'Lutes and Theorboes: their Use as Continuo Instruments, described by Praetorius in his *Syntagma musicum*, 1619', *LSJ*, ii (1960), 26
M. Prynne: 'James Talbot's Manuscript, IV: Plucked Strings – the Lute

Family', *GSJ*, xiv (1961), 52

E. Pohlmann: *Laute, Theorbe, Chitarrone: die Instrumente, ihre Musik und Literatur von 1500 bis zur Gegenwart* (Bremen, 1968, enlarged 4/1976) [lists publications where theorbo is mentioned as continuo inst]

R. Spencer: 'Chitarrone, Theorbo and Archlute', *Early Music*, iv (1976), 407

IAN HARWOOD, JAMES TYLER, ROBERT SPENCER

Theory, theorists. Theory is now understood as principally the study of the structure of music. This can be divided into melody, rhythm, counterpoint, harmony and form, but these elements are difficult to distinguish from each other and to separate from their contexts. At a more fundamental level theory includes considerations of tonal systems, scales, tuning, intervals, consonance, dissonance, durational proportions and the acoustics of pitch systems. A body of theory exists also about other aspects of music, such as composition, performance, orchestration, ornamentation, improvisation and electronic sound production. (There are separate articles on most of these subjects, but for more detailed treatment of the most fundamental of them *see* in particular ACOUSTICS; ANALYSIS; COUNTERPOINT; HARMONY; IMPROVISATION; MELODY; MODE; NOTATION; RHYTHM.)

The Western art music tradition is remarkable for the quantity and scope of its theory. The Byzantine, Arabic, Hebrew, Chinese and Indian traditions are also notable in possessing significant bodies of theoretical literature. Recently there has also been some theoretical treatment of jazz and other genres of popular music. This article, however, will deal exclusively with the Western art music tradition. (For these other traditions *see* particularly ARAB MUSIC, §I; CHINA, §IV; INDIA, SUBCONTINENT OF, §II; IRAN, §I; JAPAN, §I; JEWISH MUSIC, §I, 13; *see also* BYZANTINE RITE, MUSIC OF THE; GREECE, §I; MODE; JAZZ; POPULAR MUSIC.)

1. Introduction. 2. Definitions. 3. Antiquity. 4. Hellenic period. 5. Early Middle Ages. 6. Early polyphony and mensural music. 7. 14th century. 8. 15th century. 9. 16th century. 10. The Baroque period. 11. The Classical–Romantic period. 12. Theory of genres: 16th to 18th centuries. 13. Theory of rhythm: 17th to 19th centuries. 14. 20th century.

1. INTRODUCTION. Treatises as disparate as *De institutione musica* (*c*500) by Boethius, *L'arte del controponto ridotta in tavole* (1586–9) by Giovanni Maria Artusi, *L'armonico pratico al cimbalo* (1708) by Francesco Gasparini, and *Der freie Satz* (1935) by Heinrich Schenker are all commonly subsumed under the category of thought called music theory. Yet these four books have little in common. That of Boethius was totally divorced from the music of his time and probably not intended to be read by musicians or composers. In it a student of the liberal arts sums up the speculations about music of a number of Greek authors, mainly from the 2nd century. Artusi's book was a text for the training of musicians and composers in counterpoint as practised and taught by his, then older, generation. Gasparini's is a manual for harpsichordists on the art of accompanying from a thoroughbass. Schenker's expounds some fundamental hypotheses about masterpieces of 18th- and 19th-century music through an analysis of their tonal and harmonic content.

Even allowing for the span of time encompassing them – from about 500 to 1935 – and the changing practice of music, the absence of any significant overlap in these four books, whether of content, purpose or intended audience, demonstrates at once the diffuseness and richness of the concept of theory. The term can be given an inclusive or an exclusive definition; in the one case it will embrace all of these works, in the other only one or two of them. It is useful to begin with an attempt at an inclusive definition.

2. DEFINITIONS. The word 'theory' itself has broad implications. Its Greek root *theōria* is the noun form of the verb *theōreō*, meaning to inspect, look at, behold, observe, contemplate, consider. A *theōros* is a spectator, as at a festival or game. Etymologically, then, theory is an act of contemplation. It is observing and speculating upon as opposed to doing something.

Aristides Quintilianus, who understood the concept in this way, in the 2nd century constructed a plan of musical knowledge that may be outlined as follows:

I. Theoretical (*theoretikon*)
  A. Natural (*physikon*): 1. arithmetical (*arithmetikon*), 2. natural (*physikon*)
  B. Artificial (*technikon*): 1. harmonic (*harmonikon*), 2. rhythmic (*rhythmikon*), 3. metric (*metrikon*)
II. Practical (*praktikon*)
  A. Creative (*chrestikon*): 1. melo-poetic (*melopoiia*) (pertaining to song making), 2. temporal (*rhythmopoiia*), 3. poetic (*poiēsis*) (composition of music and poetry)
  B. Executive (*exangeltikon*): 1. instrumental (*organikon*), 2. vocal (*ōdikon*), 3. dramatic (*hypokritikon*)

Although Aristides separated the purely theoretical from the practical, the entire field that he ordered is theoretical in a broad sense, the division under 'Theoretical' being what might now be called precompositional theory, while the category 'Practical' deals with compositional theory and the theory of performance. He was not so much dividing music as what can be said about music, consequently musical knowledge and thought.

Not much needs to be added to this outline to embrace all modern musical knowledge. Certain of the categories need to be broadened; for example the 'arithmetical' ought to include mathematics in general, communications theory and artificial intelligence; 'natural' theory should include psychological and physiological as well as physical acoustics. Under 'Theoretical' one would add history, aesthetics, psychology, anthropology and sociology of music. Among the 'Artificial' categories, the 'harmonic' as understood by Aristides applied to tonal relations in terms of successive pitches and would have to be extended to simultaneous relations. Another technical category that one would add is that of 'timbre', comprehending instrumentation, orchestration and electronic media. Similarly under 'Practical', 'melodic' would be complemented by 'harmonic', while 'poetic' would, as in Aristides' day, embrace both written and improvised composition.

A modern version of Aristides' plan might then look as follows:

I. Theoretical
  A. Scientific: 1. mathematical, 2. physical, 3. psychological, 4. physiological, 5. anthropological, 6. sociological
  B. Technical: parameters: 1. pitch, 2. duration, 3. timbre
  C. Critical: 1. analytical, 2. aesthetic, 3. evaluative
  D. Historical
II. Practical
  A. Creative: 1. written composition, 2. improvisational, 3. synthetic (tape, computer etc)
  B. Pedagogical: 1. melody, 2. harmony, 3. counterpoint, 4. orchestration etc
  C. Executive: 1. instrumental, 2. vocal, 3. electronic or mechanical, 4. dramatic and choreographic
  D. Functional: 1. pedagogical (e.g. children's songs), 2. therapeutic, 3. political, 4. military, 5. recreational

This entire field has sometimes been called *Musikwissenschaft*, the science of music, or musicology.

Although it is all 'theoretical' in the sense that its method is thoughtful observation, only a relatively small part of this scheme is acknowledged as the province of the modern working theorist, namely the Theoretical–Technical (I.B), the Theoretical–Critical–Analytical (I.C.1), the Practical–Creative (II.A) and the Practical–Pedagogical (II.B) categories, which may be assumed under the catchwords 'theoretical', 'analytical', 'creative' and 'practical'. Yet many of the books from earlier times that are commonly referred to as 'theoretical treatises' address themselves to the whole area represented by the above outline. In this survey it will be important, therefore, to keep in mind three things: the conception of the theoretical function prevailing at a particular time, the audience for which a treatise was written, and the philosophical or practical goals of the author.

3. ANTIQUITY. This article cannot be a complete historical survey; it aims only to illustrate the variety of music theory through the ages, particularly its changing scope and methodology, although the central problem of tonal systems will be given special attention.

The earliest theorist for whom a significant body of writing has survived is Aristoxenus (4th century BC; *see also* GREECE, §I); much of his *Harmonics* and fragments of his *Rhythmics* are extant. The *Harmonics* concerns pitches as audible phenomena and their relationships to each other in melody; consequently it is dominated by the theory – he used the word *theōria* – of scales (*systēmatē*) and keys (*tonoi*). If one goes beyond the theory of scales and keys to their use in the service of composition (*poiētikē*), he contended, one passes outside the science of harmonics to the science of music. He who possesses this larger science is a musician. The theory of music contained a number of components that Aristoxenus did not specifically enumerate; so far as poetics or composition is concerned, it comprised melody and, one assumes, versification. His scheme of the science of music may be partly reconstructed as shown in Table 1.

TABLE 1

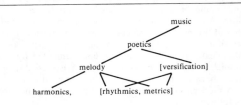

Among the topics considered by Aristoxenus are high and low pitch, intervals, scales, keys, species of motion – diastematic and continuous – the nature of diastematic melody, concords, species of consonances, tetrachords, the genera and the shades of tuning. These are studied through the hearing and intellect: by hearing one judges the magnitude of intervals, by intellect one contemplates the functions of notes. Aristoxenus eschewed questions such as that which asks what makes a good melody, because he was concerned with describing exhaustively the medium – the materials from which melody is made. His motive was at least in part to counteract the theories of the Pythagoreans, who based their harmonic science on numerical ratios, and the 'harmonists', who dealt exclusively with the enharmonic scale. As a scientific tract the *Harmonics* was unique in completely excluding mathematical speculation. It is unlikely that Aristoxenus reached musicians, though it would have pleased him; rather he was studied by those who aspired to be philosophers.

4. HELLENIC PERIOD. The scope of music theory widened with the Hellenistic writers of the 2nd and 3rd centuries. Claudius Ptolemy, the most systematic of these writers, took theory from the narrow sphere of tonal relationships to the larger one of natural philosophy. Musical observations were for him only one facet of the total natural universe. As an astronomer he recognized parallels between the order of planetary measurements and that inherent in musical ratios. Cosmology, human and world harmony, and aesthetics were all manifestations of musical organization.

Ptolemy fundamentally revised the methodology of musical investigation. Whereas Aristoxenus began with sense-experience of musical sounds and built a theory on it through dialectical analysis, Ptolemy saw a further function of reason as an aid to sense-observation itself. It was not enough to experience two sounding strings as consonant; it was necessary to measure their length numerically. Particularly in dealing with the smaller intervals, the imperfection of the senses demanded the aid of the intellect and of scientific instruments. For example, he was dissatisfied with the kanōn – i.e. the monochord – as a device for investigation. He recognized that Didymus made an improvement when he plucked and measured the string of the monochord from both left- and right-hand sides of the bridge, facilitating comparison of sounds. But this did not go far enough. Ptolemy constructed a 15-string 'polychord' that permitted comparison of like strings of different tension or length. While the first two books of Ptolemy's *Harmonics* differ little in content from the treatise of Aristoxenus (they are mainly about scales and tunings) the third book goes beyond these considerations to the relationship between observed sounds and other natural facts, and to the relationship of music to human needs. Thus music involves judgment of good form, which does not reside in the natural material but in the artist's choices; and 'the power of melody applies as a tool or servant the highest and most wonderful of our senses, sight and hearing, which among all the leading parts of the soul, perceive and judge an object not according to desire but rather according to beauty' (*Harmonics* iii, 3). The genera of music are analogous to the virtues, the tetrachords to the aspects of the planets, and the greater perfect system is a microcosm for the ecliptic – the great circle formed by the intersection of the plane of the earth's orbit with the celestial sphere.

Aristides Quintilianus, who wrote *Peri mousikēs* ('On music') in the 3rd century, continued the expansion of the subject of music theory. As is evident from the outline of his division of the field (given above), he was concerned not only with the purely theoretical or speculative, but also the practical. The science of music includes both. 'Theory defines the principles and rules of the art as well as its parts, and beyond that goes back to the origins and natural causes of the concord of all things. Practice, by following the rules of the art, aims to realize a goal, namely an edifying one [*paideutikon*].' Aristides' first book was concerned with the classic

TABLE 2

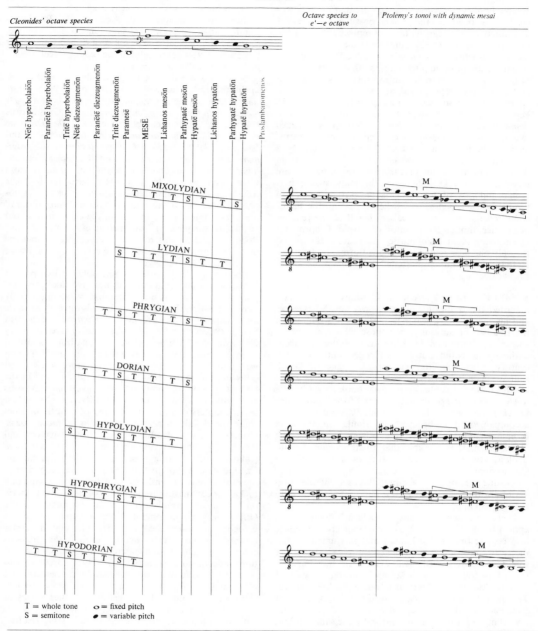

Cleonides' octave species

Octave species to e'—e octave

Ptolemy's tonoi with dynamic mesai

T = whole tone   ○ = fixed pitch
S = semitone   ● = variable pitch

triad: harmonics, rhythmics and metrics. In the second book he proceeded to the practice of music, which for him meant education through music, developing right feeling in children as a preparation for right thinking. In the third book music is treated as an art of numerical relationships allied with other numerical arts; there is much speculation, for example, on masculine and feminine principles, temperance and beauty. Thus practical theory came to include pedagogical, aesthetic and psychological aspects of music. Both Ptolemy's and Aristides' treatises seem to have been directed towards a learned audience, the same readers who would have studied the *Almagest*. Whereas Aristoxenus had a message for the musicians of his time, the two Hellenistic authors give the impression of being aloof from contemporary musical practice.

The tonal systems described by the post-classical Greek authors differ in details, as might be expected for theoretical constructions made over a period of seven centuries. Cleonides (2nd century) attributed to Aristoxenus 13 keys or *tonoi*, one on each semitone step of the octave, and to his followers 15 keys, thereby extending the range by two more semitones. Ptolemy accepted only seven keys, because only that number was needed to produce the seven possible varieties of diatonic octave species within the central octave of the male vocal range. He also considered the boundaries of the double-octave *systēma teleion* or 'perfect system' to constitute an absolute pitch limit, so that transpositions of the 'natural' Dorian system to other keys would lose at the top the steps gained at the bottom (Table 2). Alypius (3rd or 4th century) adopted the system of 15 keys, each with 15 steps from dynamic *proslambanomenos* to *nētē hyperbolaiōn*. Each step is assigned two notational symbols, one vocal, the other instrumental. The total range exceeds the double octave by a 3rd below and a 9th above. All the systems, from Aristoxenus on, assume that three genres of melody are possible in each key: diatonic, chromatic and enharmonic; and most of them also assume various 'shades' of tuning for each genre. It is believed that all the theoretical schemes represent ideals rather than the realities of practice, though the notation of Alypius is borne out by surviving examples of music. The neatest scheme and the only one propagated in western Europe by Boethius is that of Ptolemy represented in Table 2. *See also* GREECE, §I.

5. EARLY MIDDLE AGES. Boethius (*c*480–*c*524) inherited the tradition of the learned musical treatise, and his theory was a watershed. He knew a number of the treatises of antiquity, but those who read him in succeeding centuries did not. As a transmitter of ancient authority he could not be challenged until the 15th century, when scholars began reading ancient Greek sources again. The *De institutione musica* (*c*500) was a youthful effort. Like his even earlier book on arithmetic it was based principally on the work of the 2nd-century Greek Nicomachus. The two manuals were originally accompanied, it is believed, by similar manuals on geometry and astronomy, the other sciences of the Quadrivium. It is possible that Boethius intended his book as a teaching text for the study of music within the Quadrivium as part of the liberal arts curriculum, for St Augustine of Hippo had accepted this as a suitable foundation for the study of theology; but it may have had no pedagogical aim.

There were some elements in Boethius's doctrine that appear to be original, such as the classification of music into cosmic (*mundana*), human and instrumental, and the rather thorough treatment of the physical basis of sound (*see* MUSIC OF THE SPHERES). But the first four of the five books were largely based on the work of Nicomachus, whom Boethius frequently acknowledged. The first book was based on the brief *Manual* of Nicomachus, while the second to the fourth books are reworkings of a lost major treatise by the same author; the fifth book is a compendium, so far as it goes, and not without some misreadings, of the first book of Ptolemy's *Harmonics*. At no point, not even in an aside, did Boethius reveal the slightest interest in the musical practice of his time, which in any case would have been irrelevant to his purpose. Book 1 is a brief outline of the science of harmonics; book 2 concentrates on the arithmetical theory of proportions and the exposition of the intervals; book 3 is on semitones and other small intervals, particularly the comma; book 4 describes the Greek notation, derives the scale through the division of the monochord and briefly describes the system of *tonoi*, which Boethius called 'modes' (*modi*); book 5 goes over

the foundations of harmonics again, this time as seen through Ptolemy, with his polemics against such ancient authors as Archytas and Aristoxenus. Boethius's treatise, however unoriginal and limited, is a concise, studious and dedicated exposition of difficult matter. If there were better compendia of the best of Greek theory in Latin, they did not survive.

Boethius was not, of course, the only source of Greek music theory for the writers of the Middle Ages. Martianus Mineus Felix Capella (4th to 5th century; *De nuptiis Philologiae et Mercurii libri ix*), Cassiodorus (*c*485–*c*580; 'De musica', chap.5 of bk 2 *De artibus ac disciplinis liberalium artium* of his *Institutiones*) and Isidore of Seville (*c*559–636; *Etymologiarum sive originum libri xx*), among others, supplied topical, etymological, and occasionally technical information from Greek sources; and John Scotus Erigena (*c*810–77), a translator and commentator on Dionysius the Areopagite, in whose writings music is divided into 'natural' (*naturalis*), music praising God in the eight modes, and 'artificial' (*artificialis*), or instrumental music. But Boethius, and he was not unworthy of it, became the principal fount and methodological model of music theory in the Middle Ages.

Boethius could provide a model only for that part of theory which underlies but does not give rules for composition or performance. The first surviving strictly musical treatise of Carolingian times is directed towards musical practice, the *Musica disciplina* of Aurelian of Réôme (9th century), but it bolsters this practical theory with concepts, definitions and rationalizations drawn from Boethius, Cassiodorus and Isidore. Aurelian's aim was to make the *cantor* – the singer – more of a *musicus* – the literate connoisseur whom Boethius placed in the highest class of musicians, one who investigated reasons and could make judgments of quality. Aurelian's first seven chapters contain a miscellany of traditional doctrine: the definition and classification of music, basic terminology, an introduction to the consonances and their ratios, and an enumeration of the Greek *tonoi* (called *toni*), the latter based not on Boethius but on Cassiodorus. Although these chapters are preparatory, they relate only distantly to what follows in chapters 8 to 17, concerning the eight modes of plainchant, in 19, on the psalm formulae, and in 20, on chants of the Office and Mass in general. As an attempt to arrive at guidelines for usage, the portion from the eighth chapter onwards is more truly theoretical than the previous chapters, which, though based on traditional speculations, add up to no theory at all. Thus Aurelian pioneered a new kind of theory concerning the performance of plainchant. But because he did not use a nomenclature for the notes of the gamut, whether letters or Greek string names, he was forced to make his points with the utmost circuitousness, straining his readers' memories for countless passages of chant in order to fix his meaning concretely.

Hucbald (*c*840–930), writing at the end of the same century, saw that it was essential to establish a gamut, a pitch notation and a nomenclature if any meaningful discourse were to be carried on regarding plainchant. His *De harmonica institutione* has a cyclical form, proceeding three times through the elementary principles of music. First he explained melodic intervals and simultaneous consonances and the distinction between these without reference to pitch names or a gamut by recalling, as Aurelian did, segments of chant (*GS*, i, pp.104*a*–109*b*). Then he developed the gamut

1. *Tables from Hucbald's 'De harmonica institutione', GS, i, p.111a, showing (above) the tetrachord structure of the Boethian gamut, each tetrachord having the interval series, descending, tone–tone–semitone, which, with syllables adapted from the Byzantine solmization system would be sung No–ne–no–o, and (below) the same system starting at the bottom, sung o–no–ne–No, and accompanied by neumatic notation (B-Br fonds générale 10078–95, f.85r)*

through Daseia-like interval notation and spatial diagrams supplemented by the Byzantine Noneane syllables (pp.109b–114b) and organized in ascending tone–semitone–tone tetrachords (see fig.1). Finally he used the Greek string names to locate the system within a pitch framework, this time organized according to the Greek–Boethian descending tone–tone–semitone tetrachords. In the course of this, he introduced letter signs, i, m, p, c, f, for the descending series *mesē* to *lichanos hypatōn* (our a to d) in order to make the existing neumes more specific in their pitch reference while retaining the temporal and vocal subtleties communicated by neumes.

Thus Hucbald used Greek theoretical concepts as transmitted by Boethius to organize a gamut previously carried in the memory, registered only in the keys of hydraulic organs. In so doing he revealed a dichotomy between the Greek-based A system and a 21-note keyboard system starting with C, though he never referred to these letters but only to tone–semitone complexes. Whereas Boethius used the letters A to O and in another place A to P as geometrical points in monochord measurement, Hucbald and certain other medieval writers (not to mention modern commentators) took these to be an alternative system for the Greek string names or even a letter notation. Indirectly the Boethian letters may have inspired the gamut A to $\overset{a}{a}$ that must have predated that of Pseudo-Odo, Γ to $\overset{a}{a}$ (see Table 3).

Hucbald's treatise is practical without being addressed to either performance or composition, and puts forward a system that made discourse about these possible. Thus it is purely theoretical in the modern sense of being concerned with pre-compositional tonal systems; at the same time it does not give the impression of being a primer, because it assumes a wide acquaintance with chant. It is the essay of an author who had something significant and fundamental to communicate to his colleagues, and, having accomplished this, went no farther.

What relationship there may be between Hucbald's treatise and the two anonymous works once attributed to him, *Musica enchiriadis* and *Scolica enchiriadis*, is uncertain, but they appear together in four of the seven theoretical manuscript anthologies that contain the *enchiriadis* texts (*see* MUSICA ENCHIRIADIS). Hucbald's treatise seems almost to prepare the way for the *enchiriadis* tracts, but not altogether, because both their notation and their gamut depart from those of Hucbald, and they cover intervals, consonances, and modes again. *Musica enchiriadis* broke new ground in providing the earliest instruction in the improvisation of organum, using the intervallically precise if cumbersome Daseian notation. Whereas *Musica enchiriadis* is entirely practical in its thrust, the *Scolica*, a dialogue between master and disciple, proceeds from instruction in organum to definitions of mathematics (the Quadrivium) and a consideration of the ratios of intervals, classes of proportions, and the various types of mean. *Scolica enchiriadis* is thus the first of a genre of treatise in which complementary practical and theoretical approaches are merged; the first approach was obviously intended to train singers, the second to invite them to become educated in the Quadrivium.

The real successors to Hucbald's treatise were not the *enchiriadis* tracts but the *Dialogus* attributed to Odo and the *Micrologus* of Guido. Michel Huglo (1971) showed that the *Dialogus* attributed to Odo is probably by an anonymous Italian from the Milan area, and that the Prologue attached to it in some manuscripts was written later by a different anonymous author as a preface to an antiphoner. The *Dialogus* tackles the same question that Hucbald confronted: how to help singers learn new chants quickly and correctly. Again a letter notation is part of the solution, with the letters Γ (*gamma*) followed by the double octave A–a–$\overset{a}{a}$ (Table 3). To locate these letters in a diatonic system the author proposed a new method, which involved learning to sing the intervals by imitating the sounds of the monochord. The monochord was carefully divided according to a new set of rules, starting with two ninefold divisions to get the first two Pythagorean whole tones whose ratios are 9:8, namely Γ–A and A–B. Thanks to an easily accessible gamut, the author was able to give the clearest exposition so far of the determination of the modality of chant, including that of chants ending on the co-finals or transposed to B♭.

Guido of Arezzo's *Micrologus* deserves its fame, because its independence and originality of thought, breadth and clarity have rarely been equalled; it is also one of the few manuals whose context can be precisely established. It was written about 1026 to train a choir, probably that of Arezzo Cathedral, and includes some topics of traditional theory – intervals, scales, species of consonances, and the division of the monochord – but only insofar as they meet the needs of the choir singer. Guido explored several new areas: the emotional qualities of the various modes, the internal phrase structure of plainchant, the temporal meaning of the neumes, various types of repetition in chant composition,

TABLE 3: Letters for steps in the gamut and monochord

Modern	Ptolemy ('Harmonics', ii, 3)	Boethius ('De institutione musica', iv, 14)	Boethius ('De institutione musica', iv, 17)	Hucbald (vocal-no letters)	Hucbald (organ)	Pseudo-Odo
d''						
				T		
c''					*P	
				S		
b'					O	
				T		
a'	A	O	A		N	aa
				T		
g'	B	N	B		M	g
				T		
f'	Γ	M	C		L	f
				S		
e'	Δ	L	D		K	e
				T		
d'	E	K	E		I	d
				T		
c'	Z	I	F		H	c
				S		
b	H	H	G		G	♮
				T		
a	Θ	G	H		F	a
				T		
g	K	F	I		E	G
				T		
f	Λ	E	J		D	F
				S		
e	M	D	K		C	E
				T		
d	N	C	L		B	D
				T		
c	Ξ	B	M		A	C
				S		
B	O	A	N			B
				T		
A			O			A
						Γ

*this column probably represents a scribal addition to Hucbald's treatise

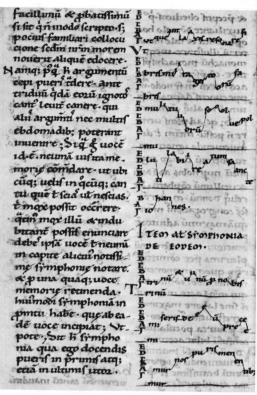

2. Passage from Guido's 'Epistola de ignoto cantu' in which he introduced the syllables, ut, re, mi, fa, sol, la, derived from the hymn to St John, 'Ut queant laxis' (right-hand column), with (below) the same melody set to an alternative text, 'Trinum et unum', which appears in a number of 11th- and 12th-century MSS and yields the syllables tri, pro, de, nos, te, ad (F-Pn lat.7211, f.99v)

considerations underlying the composition of new chant, and a mechanical method of inventing melodies for a given text using the vowels *a, e, i, o, u* (*see* GUIDO OF AREZZO, fig.3). Two chapters on *diaphonia*, or organum, come closer to describing and illustrating real music than any previous account. In the last chapter, almost as an afterthought, Guido recounted the story of the hammers of Pythagoras and finally gave the numerical ratios of the consonances, using the values 12, 9, 8, 6.

The system of hexachords with which Guido is usually credited does not appear in any of his extant works. In the *Epistola de ignoto cantu* he proposed the syllables, *ut, re, mi, fa, sol, la*, derived from the hymn *Ut queant laxis*, as a mnemonic aid for locating the semitones in the central part of the gamut, *C–D–E–F–G–a* (see fig.2). He probably used the hand for the same reason, but neither the fully developed Guidonian hand nor the system of natural, hard and soft hexachords (*see* HEXACHORD and SOLMIZATION, §I) can be securely attributed to him. Both systems, though, are true to this method, for his theorizing was eminently practical. And there is hardly a trace of Boethius, whose book, he said, was 'not useful to singers, only to philosophers' (*GS*, ii, p.50*b*).

To reconcile the exigencies of practice with the Boethian tradition was the tendency, on the other hand, of a group of theorists from the Rhineland, among them Berno of Reichenau (*d* 1048), Hermannus Contractus (1013–54), Wilhelm of Hirsau (*d* 1091), Aribo Scholasticus and John Cotton, or as he has more recently been called JOHANNES AFFLIGHEMENSIS. Whereas Guido tended towards the octave and hexachord as tonally organizing structures, these men were fond of speculating with the antique species of 4ths, 5ths and of octaves and of dividing their gamut into tetrachords. These they named in imitation of the Greeks; the two conjunct lower tetrachords were of the *graves* and *finales*, then after a tone of disjunction the upper two conjunct tetrachords were of the *superiores* and *excellentes*. But instead of starting from B, working upwards semitone–tone–tone, they started from A, working upwards tone–semitone–tone. This gamut is compared in a chart (Table 3) with the Greek system and other solutions before and after.

Berno in the *Prologus in tonarium* adopted the methodology of the ancient species of consonances but announced that modern authors counted the species differently, as shown in Table 4. His seven modern octave species were combinations of the species of 4ths and 5ths (first four), then of 5ths and 4ths (next three). These species agreed with the formation of the modes. Hermannus developed more explicitly the rationale for this arrangement: the first species of 4th was formed from the first step of the tetrachord of the *graves* and the first of the *finales*; the first species of 5th from the first of the *finales* and the first of the *superiores*; the first species of octave from the first of the *graves* and the first of the *superiores* etc. Similarly the first authentic mode was built from the first of the *finales* to the first of the *excellentes*, and so on. Hermannus assigned the names Hypodorian, Hypophrygian etc., to the octaves *A–a*, *B–b* etc, this being in agreement with the anonymous author of the commentary to the first 'Quidam' in the *Alia musica* (ed. Chailley, pp.121ff). In explaining why there should be two modal octaves *d–d'*, one Dorian, the other Mixolydian, Hermannus pointed out several important characteristics of modes: the Dorian made frequent use of its final *d* and middle pitch *a* for colons, commas and conclusions and emphasized by melodic contour its species of 4th and 5th, *a–d'* and *d–a*, while the Hypermixolydian was marked by returns to *g* and *d'* and the species of 4th *d–g* and 5th *g–d'*.

TABLE 4
Berno of Reichenau's comparison of ancient and modern consonance species

Ancient theory	Modern theory
species of 4th – descending	species of 4th – ascending
1. *G–D* TST	1. *A–d* TTST
2. *A–E* TTS	2. *B–e* STT
3. *c–G* STT	3. *c–f* TTS
species of 5th – descending	species of 5th – ascending
1. *A–D* TTST	1. *d–a* TSTT
2. *B–E* TTTS	2. *e–b* STTT
3. *c–F* STTT	3. *f–c'* TTTS
4. *d–G* TSTT	4. *g–d'* TTST

The most scholastic author of the group is Aribo, who dedicated his *De musica* to Ellenhard, Bishop of Freising (*d* 1078), and probably wrote it in Freising between 1068 and 1078. He included much of Hermannus's material in a more elaborately argued and

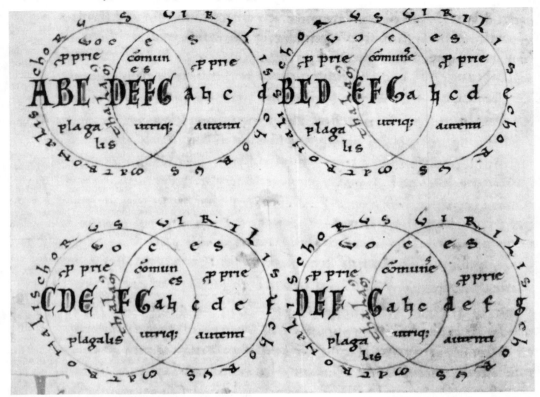

3. *The intersection of the authentic and plagal ranges of the four modes, showing which notes are exclusively plagal, which authentic and which common to both, from the 'De musica' of Johannes Afflighemensis* (D-LEu 79, f.103v)

minutely and didactically subdivided format, including many arresting and cogent diagrams. It clothed what was previously informally presented in an erudite and correct academic garb. Of particular significance is the great attention paid not only to the division of the monochord but to the measurement of organ pipes, a new topic for a general treatise. As a commentary and critique perhaps of Boethius's famous threefold classification, of players of instruments, inventors of songs and the true musicians (those who can judge and reason about music), Aribo divided musicians into 'natural' (*naturalis*) and 'artful' (*artificialis*). The 'natural' were mere minstrels (*histriones*), while the 'artful' understood all the intervals, modes and steps, knew by heart the qualities of hexachords, and could distinguish worthy melodies and correct corrupt chants. His treatise ends with a series of glosses on difficult passages in Guido's *Micrologus*.

A more extensive gloss on Guido, with many original comments, is the *De musica* of Johannes Afflighemensis. The manuscript tradition, the repertory of chants quoted, little-known notational devices described, the geographical distribution of the authors he used, and other circumstances suggest that it was produced about 1100 by a monk in the St Gall region to educate the boys of a cathedral or choir school. Casually unsystematic about such matters as the gamut and prone to technical errors, Johannes displayed great competence in the plainchant repertory, and his views about the correction of the readings and performance of chants

and the norms of the modes reveal more about the practice of composition, notation, transcription and performance in his time than any other book of its age.

6: EARLY POLYPHONY AND MENSURAL MUSIC. With the 12th century, writing about music entered a new phase dominated by the problems of improvising and writing organum and discant. The consonances recognized by Greek theory – the unison, octave, 5th and 4th – remained the cornerstones of note-against-note concurrences, but with the preference for contrary motion other intervals, particularly 3rds and 6ths, were tolerated, as in *Quiconques veut deschanter*. In melismatic organum, the instructions and examples of the Vatican organum treatise (*I-Rvat* Ottoboni, lat.3025; ed. Zaminer) showed that a framework of note-against-note organum existed as a middleground behind the improvised melismas; indeed each word of text in the examples ends on a unison, 4th, 5th or octave (*see* DISCANT, §2, and ORGANUM, §§6, 7).

It was only about the second quarter of the 13th century, with Johannes de Garlandia's treatise *De mensurabili musica*, that a new consonance theory appeared. Perfect consonances were now the unison and octave, imperfect were the major and minor 3rds, while the 4th and 5th were intermediate (*medie*), being partly perfect, partly imperfect. The dissonances were also classified; imperfect: major 6th, minor 7th; intermediate: whole tone, minor 6th; perfect: semitone, tritone, major 7th (the terms used are *diapason, ditonus, ditonus cum diapente* etc). Intervals compounded with the octave were classed together with their corresponding simple intervals. Johannes de Garlandia's symmetrical classification of consonances and dissonances into perfect, intermediate and imperfect is one of many instances of his application of the scholastic method taught in the universities; indeed his book is believed to have been intended as a text for the University of Paris. Each genre of music is defined by dividing it into species, and each of the species is then defined by further division. For example, in his first chapter the genus mensural music (*musica mensurabilis*) or organum is divided into three species: discant, copula and organum. Discant is then divided into six *maneries* (the rhythmic modes), of which the first, second and sixth are measurable (*mensurabiles*), and the third, fourth and fifth are beyond measure (*ultra mensurabiles*). These are then identified more concretely with music examples. In subsequent chapters Johannes de Garlandia applied a similar method to the description of the notes and ligatures that underlie certain rhythmic modes. Thus the *longa* may be *recta*, *duplex* or *plicata* and the ligature may be *cum proprietate* or *sine proprietate*. By this method he realized a clear exposition of a potentially confusing subject, even if many of its points now seem obscure because of his language. The result is a highly theoretical exposition, independent in great part of previous writing, and exhaustive beyond the possibilities of practical application.

Johannes de Garlandia's disciplined focus on enumeration, definition and classification is all the more striking when compared with the treatise of Anonymous IV (*c*1275), which is clearly prescriptive as well as descriptive, at once a guide to composition and a commentary on existing compositions, excerpts from some of which are actually quoted. It includes an elementary introduction to arithmetical proportions and to the rules of discant, and was perhaps meant for the training of singers at Bury St Edmunds, where the author worked. The *Ars cantus mensurabilis* (*c*1250) of Franco of Cologne, for all its insistence on innovation and the importance of his step to unequivocal rhythmic reading of ligatures, broke no new ground either in re-defining the nature of theory or in methodology. This can be said also for the St Emmeram (Regensburg) Anonymous (*c*1279; ed. Sowa).

Deserving closer attention as a new type of treatise is Jerome of Moravia's *Tractatus de musica*. Written in Paris shortly after 1272, possibly in the monastery of the rue St-Jacques, it sums up the contemporary state of music theory, or at least as much as the compiler thought relevant. It is made up largely of carefully extracted and identified passages, and a few entire treatises, by authors from Boethius right up to immediate contemporaries, such as the Aristotelian commentary by Thomas Aquinas, *De coelo et mundo*, completed in 1272 (hence the earliest probable date for Jerome's compilation). The first chapter, for example, compares definitions of music and the musician by Boethius, al-Fārābī, Richard of St Victor, Isidore, Hugh of St Victor, Guido, Johannes Afflighemensis and Johannes de Garlandia. Its theoretical topics include the etymology of 'music', its inventors, its parts, instruments (the latter two based on Isidore), the classification of music according to al-Fārābī (*activa* and *speculativa*), Boethius, Richard of St Victor and Aristotle, its effect and its subject. The technical aspects begin with the tenth chapter, surveying the gamut, solmization, mutation, the intervals, the consonances (Nicomachus, Philolaus and Ptolemy, whom he knew through Boethius), the species of arithmetical proportions and means, the ratios of intervals (Boethius), monochord division (Johannes Afflighemensis), the Greek *tonoi* (Boethius), the modern modes (Johannes), the psalm tones, composition of new chants (Johannes, with apparently original commentary), the duration of notes and rests, voice quality and ornaments in the performance and notation of plainchant (original), discant (full text of four treatises: Anon., *Discantus positio vulgaris*, Johannes de Garlandia, *De musica mensurabili positio*, Johannes de Burgundia (or Franco), *Ars cantus mensurabilis* and Petrus de Picardia, *Musica mensurabilis*), Greek notation (Boethius), and finally the construction, tuning and technique of the vielle and rebec (original). Jerome thus discussed almost all that in this article has been defined as theory: the precompositional, compositional, executive and critical.

7. 14TH CENTURY. Jerome of Moravia's treatise must not lead one to conclude that the 14th century inherited this broad curriculum. Only one manuscript is known of the treatise, left to the Sorbonne by Petrus of Limoges in 1304 (*F-Pn* lat.16663). It was not an isolated example of the musical summa or encyclopedic compilation of learning. Walter Odington's *Summa de speculatione musice* (again only one complete copy, two fragmentary; early 14th century) is another such work, with greater emphasis than Jerome's on the mathematical side, more summary and synthetic on the practical. The most remarkable example of the summa is the *Speculum musice* of Jacques, believed to have been written in Liège in his old age, not before 1330, after he had spent most of his life perhaps in Paris. It is the biggest and most complete theoretical work of the Middle Ages. The critical edition by Roger Bragard (1955–73) occupies eight volumes. Jacques de Liège divided music into *theorica*, whose subdivisions were heavenly (*celestis*), cosmic (*mundana*), human, and sonorous or instrumental; and *practica*, whose subspecies are *plana* and *mensurabilis*. He spent little time on the non-sonorous categories and devoted most of the first five books to the theory of the sonorous realm, the sixth book mainly to the modes – ancient, intermediate and modern – the seventh book to measured music. Jacques de Liège's normal method was to cite one or more authorities and to make an extensive gloss on each. He displayed broad erudition; among the Greek sources he cited were Plato's *Timaeus*, Aristotle's *Physics*, *Nicomachean Ethics*, *Politics*, *On the Soul*, *Categories*, *De coelo*, Euclid's *De arte geometria* in Boethius's translation; among the Roman writers, Virgil, Lucanus, Seneca, Persius, Priscianus; among medieval writers, Augustine, *De musica*, Simplicius, Macrobius, Boethius, Gregory the Great, Jordanus Nemorarius, Petrus Comestor, Robert Kilwardby, Avverroes, al-Fārābī. Among the musical theorists he credited some by name; others he honoured only by quotation or paraphrase. They include Guido, Hermannus, Johannes Afflighemensis, Franco, Pseudo-Aristotle, Philippe de Vitry and Prosdocimus de Beldemandis. Some of the questions he proposed yielded to his method; others, such as 'Why does a diatessaron sound more consonant above a diapente than below?' (vii,8), elude his dialectics. Jacques was not just a dispassionate scholar, however; perhaps the best-known

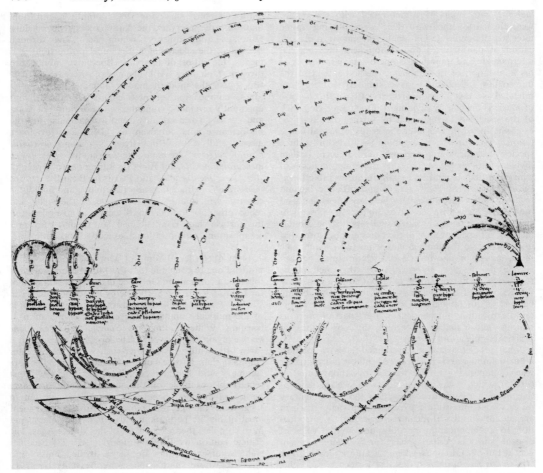

4. *Monochord division of the two-octave system, A–aa, with the entire string given the value 9216: diagram from the 'Speculum musice' of Jacques de Liège, v, chap.44 (F-Pn lat.7207, f.199r)*

chapters (vii,9ff) are his angry diatribes against the mensural practices of the 'moderni', the composers and theorists of the Ars Nova.

More characteristic of the 14th century than Jacques de Liège's encyclopedic approach are the fundamental revisions of practical theory by Jehan des Murs, Johannes de Grocheo, Marchetto da Padova and Philippe de Vitry. Jehan des Murs, a *magister artium* of the University of Paris, left a *Musica speculativa secundum Boetium* (*GS*, iii, 249–83; completed 1323), known to have been used in university curricula, for example at Kraków, Prague, Vienna, Leipzig and Erfurt. Jehan was not content with repeating the traditional numerical theory, but applied his mathematical skills to the observation of contemporary musical practices, as he also did to the observation of eclipses. His *Ars nova musice* (1319 or 1321), a youthful work, takes an objective stance on the controversial question of the duple versus triple division of note values. 'Time belongs to the genus of continuous things, therefore may be divided in any number of equal parts' (*GS*, iii, p.300b = CSM, xvii, *Notitia artis musice*, chap.13, p.104). He showed that the option between duple and triple operated at four levels or *gradus: maximodus,*

modus, tempus, and *prolatio* (*see* NOTATION, §III, 3). The relation of the shortest note, the minim, to the longest, the triplex long, was in the ratio of $1:3^4$ or $1:81$. Jehan des Murs may have derived the concept of four levels of musical time from his friend Philippe de Vitry, although the latter apparently did not complete his own *Ars nova* until 1320. There he implied a fifth level, at which the minim was divided into semiminims. Philippe's major innovation was the proposal of four signs whereby the singer could recognize immediately the way in which long and breve were to be divided (Table 5).

TABLE 5

◯ – perfect tempus	◖ – imperfect tempus
⊙ – perfect modus with perfect tempus	⊙ – imperfect modus with imperfect tempus

Philippe de Vitry accepted the division of music into *mundana, humana* and *instrumentalis,* even though at the outset he said he would deal only with the last. Johannes de Grocheo, on the other hand, in his untitled treatise of about 1300 rejected the Boethian classification altogether, noting that Aristotle denied the existence of celestial music; he also rejected the dichotomy between the immeasurable and the measured, because all music and art depend on measurement. Every region, linguistic culture and city should have its own classification; for Paris he proposed three genres: common (*vulgaris*) music of the city; measured (*mensurata*), composed, regular or regulated music; and ecclesiastical (*genus ecclesiasticum*), made up of the other two brought to their highest perfection for the praise of the Creator. Thus the study of music was the taxonomy of compositional genres. In the first category he distinguished between song (*cantus*) and melody (*cantilena*), the former including *cantus gestualis* (epic poems), *cantus coronatus*, monophonic conductus and *cantus versualis* (popular songs), while within *cantilena* he cited the rondeau (*rotundellus*), *estampie* (*stantipes*), and *ductia*. For each type he discussed the function, versification, form and manner of composition, but his descriptions are subject to a variety of interpretations. Measured music includes the motet, organum and hocket. Among the genres of ecclesiastical music, which he admitted varied with local custom, he named hymns, responsories, versicles, antiphons and parts of the Ordinary and Proper of the Mass.

The growing interaction of folk, popular and other secular music with church music documented by Johannes de Grocheo was bound to arouse discussion of the conflicting musical systems that existed side by side; even within church polyphony the favourite cadence form, that of major 6th progressing to octave, made it necessary to recognize the alteration of the gamut of the Guidonian hand, or *musica vera*. Magister Lambertus (*c*1270) argued that the practice of *falsa musica* or *falsa mutatione* was 'necessary, because of the search for good consonance' (*CS*, i, p.258*a*) and defined it as making a semitone out of a whole tone or vice versa. Odington recognized in his gamut E♭, F♯ and C♯ as well as B♭ (ed. Hammond, pp.97f). Johannes de Grocheo associated the need for *musica falsa* with the *estampie* and *ductia* and claimed that any tone could be made into a semitone through the rounded flat sign known as *b rotundum*, and any semitone into a tone through the square-shaped sign known as *b quadratum*.

Jehan des Murs is reported in *Ars discantus secundum Johannem de Muris* (*CS*, iii, p.72) to have taught that a minor 6th followed by an octave should be made major through the *b quadratum*, a major 6th contracting to a 5th should be made minor through a *b rotundum*, and whenever *la sol la* is to be sung in a single voice the *sol* should be raised to be sung *mi* in the sequence *fa mi fa*, and similar alterations (*see* MUSICA FICTA).

In his *Lucidarium* (1326–7) Marchetto da Padova began to confront the theoretical implications of this usage by dividing the whole tone into five *dieses* (*Tractatus*, ii, chap.5; *GS*, iii) of which two, or on some occasions only one, would comprise the melodic semitone from *mi* to *fa*. He also implied, as indicated in ex.1, that the ratio for a semitone comprising two *dieses* was 18:17. While these formulae are mathematically incompatible with each other and with Pythagorean

calculations, they indicate clearly enough that Marchetto preferred a melodic semitone to amount to less than half of a whole tone. Marchetto's calculations aroused objections from his Paduan compatriot Prosdocimus de Beldemandis, who adhered to the ratios of PYTHAGOREAN INTONATION and applied them to two chromatic monochords: in one the minor semitone preceded the major, in the second the opposite. Then he merged the two to provide both a flat and a sharp between each note of the regular monochord (*Tractatus de monochordum dividendi*, 1413; *CS*, iii, pp.251ff). In his *Tractatus de contrapuncto* (1412; *CS*, iii, p.198*a*) he had shown that any note could become a *mi* by placing the *b quadratum* before it, or a *fa* by placing the *b rotundum* before it.

8. 15TH CENTURY. The 15th century inherited several theoretical difficulties that had not been squarely faced; one was the definition of consonance. The 3rds and 6ths were accepted in counterpoint as imperfect consonances: the major 6th somewhat reluctantly by Anonymous IV and fully by the *Ars contrapuncti secundum Johannem de Muris* (*CS*, iii, p.60), Anonymous II (13th century; *CS*, i, p.312), and Anonymous XIII (*c*1300; *CS*, iii, p.496); the minor 6th was admitted by the *Ars contrapunctus secundum Phillippum de Vitriaco* (*CS*, iii, p.27) and the *Ars discantus secundum Johannem de Muris* (*CS*, iii, p.70); while the 4ths were rejected. Yet no theoretical justification had yet appeared. Walter Odington was on the verge of one when he called the 3rds and major 6th 'concordant discords' (*concordes discordiae*: ed. Hammond, CSM, xiv, p.75), and recognized that since the 3rds are close to the sesquiquarta and sesquiquinta ratios (in which the difference is one) many considered them consonant; and, he added, 'if in numbers they are not found consonant, the voices of men with its subtlety leads them into a smooth mixture and full consonance' (CSM, xiv, pp.70f).

Allied to the problem of consonance was that of tuning. The theoretically accepted tuning, even for Odington, was the Pythagorean, in which the ditone was 81:64 and the semiditone 96:81, both harsh-sounding. Also associated with the use of imperfect consonances was the use of *musica ficta*, which demanded potentially a full chromatic octave. Boethius provided no model for the division of the octave into semitones, whether equal or unequal.

While the problems just mentioned all involved mathematics in one way or another, conflicts also arose between traditional pedagogy and the realities of musical practice. Polyphony had inherited from plainchant a system of modes; but composers, even when basing their work on chant melodies, could not reconcile the purity of the modes with the desire for sweet and full concordance and smooth linear flow. The primacy of the modal octave *d–d′*, inherited from Byzantine music, conflicted with the C orientation apparent in several keyboard gamuts as early as the 10th century. The mutations of the hexachord system defied the limits of the octave and destroyed modal consistency, often going beyond the single flat of the Guidonian gamut to as many as three flats and three sharps, requiring hexachords starting on B♭, E♭, D and A. Moreover the single species of hexachord, *ut–la*, rendered meaningless the traditional species of 4ths, 5ths and octaves, and it was not clear how the modular tetrachord fitted into the

Ex.1

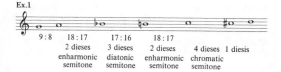

9:8	18:17	17:16	18:17	
	2 dieses	3 dieses	2 dieses	4 dieses 1 diesis
	enharmonic	diatonic	enharmonic	chromatic
	semitone	semitone	semitone	semitone

modern systems, which now descended below Γ (*see also* SOLMIZATION, §I). The admission of the duple division of time into written art music in the 14th century opened the gates to combinations of duple and triple divisions at several levels and to questions of relation of duration to speed of performance. This subject was becoming so complex, it was tempting to subject it to mathematical analysis.

Ugolino of Orvieto, author of the *Declaratio musice discipline* (c1430; CSM, vii), was on the threshold of the recognition of these problems. He discarded the tetrachordal gamuts, extended the normal range down one step to *F*, and alternatively recognized a further extension down to *C*, a 4th below Γ (ii, p.34). He permitted hexachords to begin on D, E, A and B♭, as well as C, F and G. Appended to his treatise in several of the manuscripts was a *Tractatus monochordi* that developed, in an elaborate and musicianly fashion, the three monochords described by Prosdocimus – of which the third was, according to Ugolino, more useful for organs than for singing (*see* TEMPERAMENTS and ENHARMONIC KEYBOARD). A fourth monochord added notes midway between B and C and E and F respectively, which Ugolino said were not sung by the moderns but had been by the ancients; this was a reference to the enharmonic genre of classical Greece.

Ugolino was in step with his age also in reviving the Quadrivial aspect of music, for the Boethian curriculum of arithmetical proportions of intervals and the metaphysics and physics of music are thoroughly explained in the fourth and fifth books, with many new insights drawn from the works of Aristotle and an otherwise unknown author cited as Petrus Hispanus. Ugolino anticipated the early Renaissance also in separating *musica theorica* from *musica practica*. The first two books cover the Guidonian curriculum of the choir school brought up to date by Johannes Afflighemensis and the discant and counterpoint tutors. The third book is a commentary on the mensural music treatise of Jehan des Murs. These three books constitute a summa of *musica practica*; the last two are a summa of *musica theorica*.

Reading the treatises of the 13th and 14th centuries leads one to question how much of Boethius was studied or understood during those years of swiftly changing musical practices or how relevant the book was considered. Only Jacques de Liège gave evidence of having studied all of it. Though Jacques admitted that he came on it late in his studies, it must have been available in every major monastic library. For a practising musician there was no compelling incentive for studying it. Careful study of Boethius was a phenomenon of the Italian Renaissance, and led to a search for the texts and authors whom Boethius mentioned, sometimes with praise as he did Nicomachus and Ptolemy, often deprecatingly, as Aristoxenus and Archytas.

The revival of Boethius elicited two opposite reactions: it led to his adulation, as in the writings of John Hothby, Johannes Legrense, Nicolaus Burtius, Giorgio Anselmi, and in his youth Franchinus Gaffurius; it also started an anti-theoretical movement. The latter was personified in Bartolomeo Ramos de Pareia, a Spanish mathematician who settled and lectured in Bologna. The title of his *Musica practica*, published there in 1482, is misleading, because the first of three parts is virtually all *musica theorica*, but conclusions are reached empirically rather than through citation and explanation of authorities. It is not lacking in citations, for the book gives evidence of wide reading, but more often than not Ramos cited other authors only to disagree with them. He discarded both tetrachordal gamut structure and hexachordal solmization, replacing them with an octave system of eight syllables, *psal-li-tur per vo-ces is-tas*, based on *C*, from where his gamut started, a 5th below Γ, to accommodate the range of contemporary organs and 'polichorda'. Mutation was accomplished by substituting *psal* for any of the other syllables.

Ramos revised Boethius's monochord division, which in any case he found too laborious and subtle for young musicians, to yield most of the imperfect consonances of diatonic music in their simple ratios: 5:4 (major 3rd), 6:5 (minor 3rd), 5:3 (major 6th) and 8:5 (minor 6th), and he constructed out of this division a new chromatic monochord (*see* TEMPERAMENTS, §2, and JUST INTONATION), which, like his other innovations, caused him to be attacked by his fellow theorists, Hothby, Burtius and Gaffurius. Although only Giovanni Spataro took up his defence at that time, many echoes of his theories, tempered in the forge of debate, found acceptance in the 16th century.

Johannes Tinctoris, in a series of 12 treatises (c1472–84) that exhausted current knowledge of musical practice, continued the empirical trend. His scepticism of the wisdom of the past was not confined to such mirages as *musica mundana* but to the entire repertory and foundation of older music, which he found inept and unworthy of performance. If he was fond of quoting the ancient Greek theorists and philosophers and even Boethius, the citations were more rhetorical ornaments than underpinning for his theories, which were founded squarely on the realities of everyday performance, composition and improvisation. Thus his citation of authorities is rendered pointless, as when he preferred Ptolemy's opinion reported by Boethius, that the 11th is a consonance, to that of Boethius himself, who considered it a dissonance, but finally rejected it from counterpoint as 'intolerably harsh' (*Liber de arte contrapuncti*, 1477, i, p.10). Tinctoris's great merit was not erudition but acute observation and analytical description. Thus his penetrating dissection of how the dissonant suspension, for which he had no word, works on various levels of time value and in different proportions and prolations, and his recommendations for when to use or avoid it, represents theorizing of the highest order (ibid, ii, pp.23ff). His important distinction between the standards of consonance and dissonance treatment in improvisation, *super librum cantare*, and written composition, *res factae*, was an important step in removing the art of counterpoint from trial and error. The *Proportionale musices* (c1473–4) was an exhaustive statement of the system of temporal relationships and their notation that reached the ultimate point of exploitation about that time. But the *Liber de natura et proprietate tonorum* (1476) said little that was new and did not come to terms with the nature of modality in polyphonic music.

It was Tinctoris who inspired Gaffurius to deepen his theoretical studies. From 1480 for 20 years Gaffurius was engaged in a constant search for the best truths of the past and tried to reconcile these with the most advanced knowledge and practices of his time. From almost complete dependence on Boethius in his

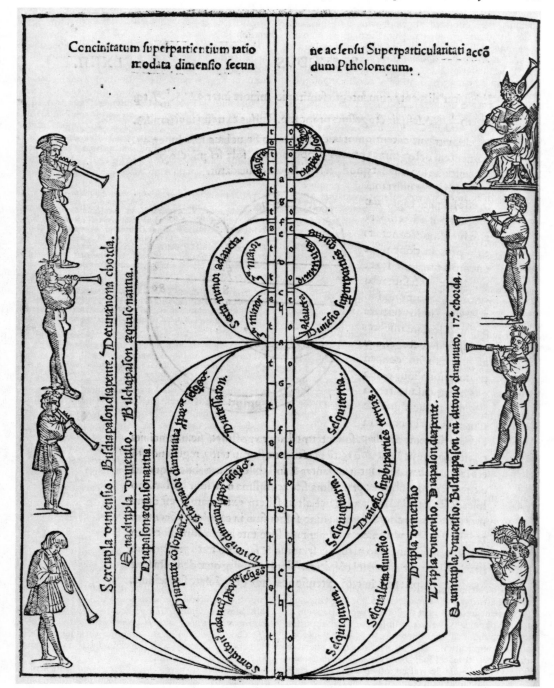

5. *Diagram showing justly tuned 3rds and 6ths according to Ptolemy's syntonic diatonic rediscovered by Gaffurius, from his 'De harmonia musicorum instrumentorum opus' (1518)*

Theoricum opus, he progressed in the *Theorica musicae* of 1492 to the use of several previously unknown Greek treatises in Latin translation. He profited most from Francesco Burana's Latin version of the musical treatise of Bacchius, Ficino's Latin translation of Plato, Ermolao Barbaro's Latin translation of Themistius's *Paraphrases* on the *De anima* of Aristotle, and Pietro d'Abano's translation and commentaries on Aristotle's

Problems. Added to his careful and critical reading of Boethius, they informed his work with a freshness of thought that merits our calling him the first real humanist in music. In preparation for his final speculative work, *De harmonia musicorum instrumentorum opus* (1518), he had translated for him the *Harmonics* of Ptolemy and the musical treatises of Aristides Quintilianus, Manuel Bryennius and the author now known as Bellerman's Anonymous. He also used Giorgio Valla's translation of Cleonides and Valguglio's of Plutarch. To cite only a few examples of the fruits of his studies, Gaffurius was able to communicate to Western musical readers for the first time Themistius's sophisticated theory of sound, the shades of tuning described by Ptolemy, including the syntonic diatonic soon to be championed by Spataro (see fig.5), and a glimmer of how the Greek tonal system differed from that of the medieval modes. The dynasty of Boethius was finally broken.

9. 16TH CENTURY. Hardly an author on music in Italy after 1500 escaped the powerful tides of the revival of ancient learning. The first half of the century was particularly swayed by Ptolemy's argument that, since sound is sensation, judgments concerning sounds should be made by the sense of hearing with the assistance of the reasoning faculty. The Pythagorean view, which had dominated earlier speculative theory, was that only the reason could make a final judgment, because the senses are easily corrupted. This principle had a particularly profound effect in the investigation of tuning. Even Gaffurius, who never departed from his advocacy of the Pythagorean tuning, recognized that keyboards were tempered by flattening the 5ths (*Practica musica*, 1496, ii, chap.3). Spataro, a disciple of Ramos, upbraided Gaffurius for saying that the major and minor 3rds in the ratios 81:64 and 32:27 were inaudibly different from 5:4 and 6:5 (*Errori de Franchino Gafurio*, 1521). He maintained that singers used only the latter, because they were 'softer' (Error 19, f.20*v*; Error 23, f.22*v*). Indeed Spataro identified the syntonic diatonic tuning of Ptolemy as 'that which is applied in musical practice today' (Error 16, f.21*v*).

Lodovico Fogliano, without citing either Ptolemy or Spataro, defended a similar tuning on the grounds that the ear is the natural judge of consonance and dissonance and esteems the 3rds and 6ths as consonances no less than octaves and 5ths; therefore it demanded that these intervals be in their best intonation (*Musica theorica*, 1529).

Gioseffo Zarlino too advocated the syntonic diatonic tuning (*Le istitutioni harmoniche*, 1558), but Giovanni Battista Benedetti soon proved that it was impossible to sing polyphonically with this intonation without the pitch slipping, and that therefore the tuning had no practical application in modern music (letter to Cipriano de Rore, *c*1563; *Diversarum speculationum*, 1585). Vincenzo Galilei raised other objections, and, convinced that equal temperament was the only solution for instrumental music, proposed a uniform semitone of 18:17 for placing the frets on a lute (*Dialogo della musica antica et della moderna*, 1581, p.49); voices, he admitted, strove for a juster intonation that, however, could not be defined. Giovanni Maria Artusi, although a disciple of Zarlino, later came to a similar conclusion (*L'Artusi*, i, 1600, f.34*r*). Both Galilei and Artusi supported their theories with the authority of Aristoxenus,

whose *Harmonics*, translated in 1562 by Antonio Gogava, described an octave divided into equal semitones.

However much they believed in equal division, one of the practical problems that defied theorists schooled in Boethius was that no integer could be found between the terms of a superparticular ratio that would divide it equally. So the Pythagorean whole tone, 9:8, could only be split into a lesser and greater but not two equal semitones. Euclid's *Elements*, printed in 1482 in a 13th-century Latin translation by Jan Campanus, offered geometrical constructions to make this division, and these were applied to this musical problem by Erasmus of Höritz (*Musica*, *I-Rvat* reg.lat.1245, *c*1504–8) and Henricus Grammateus in *Ayn new kunstlich Buech* (1518).

At the moment when *musica ficta* hexachords became accepted on almost every step (Pietro Aaron in *Lucidario in musica*, 1545, recognized them on A, B, D and E), the nature of modality in polyphonic music began to be clarified, first by Aaron (*Trattato della natura e cognizioni di tutti gli toni di canto figurato*, 1525), then by Heinrich Glarean (*Dodecachordon*, 1547). Leaning on the tradition that in ancient times there had been as many as 13 or 15 'modes', Glarean finally faced the problem of the finals on A and C. Although he claimed to understand it, he lacked the dimmest notion of the Greek tonal system. This did not prevent him from constructing a well-ordered system of 12 practicable modes, and showing how the great composer Josquin could endow them with every variety of emotion and musical fantasy.

Only when Girolamo Mei circulated his treatise *De modis musicis* (completed 1573) among a small circle in Florence did the truth, that the plainchant modes and those of Glarean bore no resemblance to the Greek 'modes' or *tonoi*, begin to penetrate musical, literary and scientific circles. Mei had studied in Greek every surviving ancient piece of writing on music and had concluded that the Greek *tonoi* were transpositions of one system higher or lower than the normal or 'Dorian' range. Francisco de Salinas (*De musica libri vii*, 1577), who also read Ptolemy in the original Greek, clearly showed that the *tonoi* were not modes, but reproductions of the same system at different levels of pitch, though he attributed to the octave species a modal function.

Zarlino first accepted the 12 modes of Glarean (*Le istitutioni harmoniche*, 1558); later he renumbered them (*Dimostrationi harmoniche*, 1571) so that the series started on C. But the removal of an antique precedent tended to discredit the modes towards the end of the 16th century. Galilei (*Il primo libro della prattica del contrapunto intorno all'uso delle consonanze*, 1588–91, *I-Fn* Gal.1, f.100) with rare candour proclaimed that the plainchant modes were meaningless in modern polyphonic composition.

If humanism deprived the modes of one of their main props, it gave legitimacy to the technique that helped destroy them – chromaticism. The medieval tradition was that the chromatic and enharmonic were abandoned by the ancients because they were difficult and ungratifying to the ear. But anyone reading Plutarch's *De musica* would have gathered the opposite. The enharmonic, he said, was the most beautiful of the genera, practised by the ancients because of its nobility but later undeservedly neglected (ed. Lasserre, chap.38). Gaffurius, taking his cue from this source, said it was the most artful of the genera, favoured by the most distinguished musicians but unknown to the common class of them, who could not discern the small intervals (*De harmonia*, ii, 8, f.xiv). The principal champion of the chromatic and enharmonic was Nicola Vicentino (*L'antica musica ridotta alla moderna prattica*, 1555), who modernized the two 'dense' genres by dividing the entire octave, not merely the dense segments or *pycna* of the tetrachords as the ancients did, into semitones and microtones. Salinas followed a similar procedure. The special instruments that Vicentino built and that were used by several distinguished musicians, notably Luzzasco Luzzaschi and Carlo Gesualdo, translated the exotic genres from theory into practice.

As has been seen, 3rds and 6ths and their compounds were considered consonances in the practical handbooks for some time. But in *musica theorica* the 3rds and 6ths were still in a no-man's-land, because they were outside the accepted Pythagorean ratios, those whose terms were made up of the numbers 1 to 4. Gaffurius, for example, although he admitted that the 3rds and 6ths were excellent in sound, attributed to them no perfection of ratio, indeed no determinable ratio, and, therefore, they were irrational (*De harmonia*, i, 3, f.5r). Fogliano was able to surmount the difficulty by proving that sound had no material existence but was an 'accident' of violent motion and therefore not subject to mathematical, only to aural, judgment (*Musica theorica*, 1529, ii, 1–3, ff.12ff). What the community of musicians and composers considered consonant was indeed so.

Zarlino took a step backwards, however, by reinstating the dominance of *ratio* over *sensus*, rationalizing a new numerical limit for consonance: the *senario*, or numbers 1 to 6, which took in the 3rds and the major 6th. This required that he hypothesize a 'natural' tuning in which these imperfect consonances were 'just' or 5:4, 6:5 and 5:3. When this was shown to be impractical, the *senario* theory too had to fall. Galilei opposed any limits, arguing that all musical intervals, whether within or outside the *senario*, were natural. He contended that there was theoretically an infinity of consonances (*Discorso intorno all'opere di Messer G. Zarlino*, 1589, pp.92f). Zarlino's practical theory of counterpoint, based on the premise of the *senario*, severely limited the introduction of dissonances to suspensions and passing notes; Galilei was much more pragmatic about them, opening the way to the free uses of the *seconda prattica* (*Discorso intorno all'uso delle dissonanze*, 1589–91). Thus Zarlino's heroic effort to bring *musica practica* and *musica theorica* together again was a failure because he bent theory to suit practice and misrepresented practice to fit the theory.

The aspect of the theory of music that was most affected by humanism was concerned with the goals and effects of music. Hardly a book on music failed to recount some of the stories that the ancient philosophers told about its miraculous therapeutic, moral or corrupting effects. The late 15th and early 16th centuries were dominated by the Platonically inspired judgment that only music that strengthened moral character was desirable. But those who followed Aristotle, and particularly commentators on the *Poetics* after 1550, emphasized the positive value of all kinds of music, particularly that which could induce the catharsis of the passions and could move listeners to feel the affections of a poem or a dramatic character. Mei condemned polyphonic music as impotent for this, because the different vocal parts pulled in opposing directions; only monodic music could have the power that Greek music possessed. Galilei, who espoused Mei's ideas, wrote a vehement critique of polyphonic music (*Dialogo della musica antica et della moderna*, 1581) but was rather vague about what should take its place. More than at any time in the past, practical theory became prescriptive, the cutting edge of innovation.

10. THE BAROQUE PERIOD. In the first half of the 17th century musical practice caught up with the aesthetic ideals proclaimed in the second half of the previous century and practical theory caught up with improvised practice. The ideal of moving the affections was realized in the *seconda prattica*. Claudio Monteverdi (Preface, *Quinto libro de madrigali*, 1605) used this term to distinguish his own freer approach to contrapuntal writing, particularly dissonance treatment, from the practice taught in Zarlino's *Istitutioni* in which dissonances were very strictly controlled (*see* PRIMA PRATTICA). His brother, Giulio Cesare Monteverdi, in commenting on this statement ('Dichiaratione', *Scherzi musicali*, 1607), explained that in the *seconda prattica* harmony is a servant of the text, while in the *prima prattica* the harmony is mistress over the text. The two prefaces were written in response to the criticisms of Giovanni Maria Artusi (*L'Artusi*, 1600), who enumerated some of the new style's characteristics more explicitly than its defenders: unprepared or improperly prepared suspensions, unprepared diminished 5ths and 7ths, false relations, difficult melodic intervals, incorrect part-writing after a flat or sharp, abuse of note-against-note chordal style, and other departures from the learned manner of writing counterpoint. Although Artusi described the style in negative terms he made the astute observation in his dialogue that a number of these departures were characteristic of improvised music or improvised elaborations of written music. Thus some of the freely introduced dissonances were *accenti* and other grace notes normally added by the singer. Several singing teachers had written tutors for embellishing written music, for example Girolamo dalla Casa (*Il vero modo di diminuir*, 1584). Other dissonances resulted from following the rules of counterpoint *a mente* or *supra librum* rather than the rules of *res facta*, or from imitating the free clashes allowed in instrumental figurations and runs. Thus many of the innovations of Monteverdi had been frequently heard before, but seldom written. In this sense the theory of written counterpoint was simply adjusting to the realities of performing practice.

In due time a theory developed to account for the new licences, but the *prima prattica* remained a viable option. Thus Girolamo Diruta (*Seconda parte del transilvano*, 1609) considered *contrapunto osservato* (strict counterpoint) and *contrapunto commune* (the free modern style) as alternatives for the modern composer. Adriano Banchieri (*Cartella musicale*, 1614) and Marco Scacchi (*Epistola* to Werner, c1648; *Breve discorso sopra la musica moderna*, 1649) specified some of the norms by which these two co-existent styles were to be distinguished. Scacchi, his pupil Angelo Berardi, and Cristoph Bernhard who also came under Scacchi's influence, developed a system of stylistic classification that represents the first efforts at a theory of musical style. Bernhard was the most assiduous of these in detailing the licences of the various styles, the freest of which was the recitative. Since the devices, like the figures of rhetoric, were at once a form of embellishment and of forceful expression, he gave them names derived from rhetorical theory, as Jacob Burmeister had done earlier in arriving at a terminology for the technical and expressive devices of polyphonic writing (*Musica autoschediastike*, 1601; *Musica poetica*, 1606).

Although the *prima prattica* continued to be applied in composition, particularly of sacred music, it became mainly a pedagogical style known as *stile antico* in which the pupil was expected to become proficient before attempting the modern style. Diruta taught five species of 'observed' or strict counterpoint, types that were later adopted, with modifications by Banchieri, Lodovico Zacconi (*Prattica di musica, seconda parte*, 1622), Berardi (*Ragionamenti musicali*, 1681, *Miscellanea musicale*, 1689) and Johann Joseph Fux (*Gradus ad Parnassum*, 1725). The *prima prattica* is thus the first example of a historical style that became the basis of a pedagogical theory, a phenomenon that was to mark the teaching of theory throughout the 19th and 20th centuries.

Another improvisatory practice that was annexed by written theory is that of florid elaboration, embellishment and variation on a written line or harmonic scheme. Throughout the 16th century musicians were taking melodic schemes or *arie* for singing poetry, and performing impromptu arrangements and variations on them, whether in reciting strophic poems or in playing variations or dances on a lute or other instrument. When performing the top line of frottolas and madrigals written in simple chordal style singers would supply runs and other embellishments, especially in approaching the cadence. Some handbooks were published in the 16th century to guide the improviser, for example *Trattado de glosas sobre clausulas y otros generos de puntos en la musica de violones* (1553) by Diego Ortiz, and Tomás de Santa María, *Libro llamado* (*Arte de tañer fantasia*, 1565). Singing tutors, such as that of Dalla Casa mentioned above or of Giovanni Battista Bovicelli (*Regole, passaggi di musica*, 1594), provided sample runs, figurations and models for the embellishment of both sacred and secular polyphonic music. A more tasteful, expressive and dynamically nuanced kind of ornamentation was developed in Giulio Caccini's *Le nuove musiche* (1601/2), which became a model for French treatises, such as Marin Mersenne's 'L'art de bien chanter', the fifth book of *Harmonie universelle* (1636–7). (Mersenne's contributions to music theory are not discussed in detail in this article since they pertain to acoustics and organology rather than theory proper.)

Accompanying from a bass was also probably an unwritten practice for many years before a basso continuo with figures was first printed in the score of Emilio de' Cavalieri's *Rappresentatione di Anima et di Corpo* (1600). Earliest rules for playing from a bass appeared in prefaces, such as that to Cavalieri's score or to Lodovico Viadana's *Cento concerti ecclesiastici* (1602). Soon it became the subject of short tracts, the most notable of which is Agostino Agazzari's *Del suonare sopra il basso con tutti stromenti & uso loro nel conserto* (1609). The usage and theorizing about it spread quickly to Germany (Michael Praetorius, *Syntagma musicum*, chap.6, 'De basso generali seu continuo', 1618), quite late to England (Matthew Locke, *Melothesia or Certain General Rules for Playing upon a Continued-bass*, 1673), and France (Michel de Saint-

Lambert's *Traité de l'accompagnement du clavecin, de l'orgue et de quelques autres instruments*, 1680).

The first phase of thoroughbass theory is best summed up by Lorenzo Penna's *Li primi albori musicali* (1672). Although this consisted largely of instructions for accompanying, its detailed rules, prescribing part-movement, interval content of chords, cadence formulae, rhythmic figures, and ornaments, make it by implication a book on composition; one section, indeed, showed how to supply a bass for an otherwise finished piece. The connection of thoroughbass with composition was made explicit in Johann David Heinichen's *Der General-Bass in der Composition* (1728). Though focussed on accompaniment, the book was invaluable for composers. One of its important contributions was that Heinichen clarified and expurgated the use of dissonances in the theatrical style in keeping with the renewed desire for correctness.

The chordal structure of Baroque music was obviously intuitively conceived and empirically understood by the thoroughbass theorists. But no theory had evolved that related the chords to a single goal or limited collection of pitches. The modes, through commonly used transpositions and accidentals, had been reduced in practice to just a few distinct octave species. Zarlino had already noted that the modes could be divided into two classes, those that began by rising a major 3rd, and those beginning with a minor 3rd. In England it became common to speak of 'sharp song' and 'flat song' for what in practice were the modes reduced to two (Christopher Simpson, *The Division-violist*, 1659). In 1683 Jean Rousseau took the radical step of proclaiming that there were only two modes, major and minor, although he still clung to the concept of 'natural' and 'transposed' keys (*Méthode claire, certaine et facile, pour apprendre à chanter*). Charles Masson went a step further and discarded the natural and transposed categories, accepting eight major and minor keys, omitting only the major keys on G♭, A♭, D♭ and E♭ and minor keys on G♭, A♭, B♭ and D♭ (*Nouveau traité des règles pour la composition de la musique*, 2/1699). He recognized in each key a 'final', a 'mediant' and a 'dominant', which he called the 'essential notes'.

These developments prepared the way for Rameau's conception of the notes and chords of a key as emanating from a single source pitch. Rameau acknowledged that the inspiration for this breakthrough came from Descartes' method, which was to build a system of natural law on a self-evident principle. In his *Traité de l'harmonie réduite à ses principes naturels* (1722) Rameau identified this first principle as the first six divisions of the string; these could be shown to generate all of the consonant and dissonant intervals and chords as well as the rules for their interconnection. But it was first necessary to recognize as an *a priori* fact that a note and its octave-replicates were identical. From this ensued the principle of inversion (see fig.6). Through inversion it was possible to incorporate the major 6th, 8:5, into the consonances of the *senario*, because it could now be explained as the inversion of the minor 3rd, 6:5. Thus Rameau marked a return to naturalism and rationalism after the pragmatic theory of the thoroughbass school.

By arithmetic manipulation of the ratios representing the primary division of the string, $\frac{1}{2}$ (octave), $\frac{1}{3}$ (octave-plus-5th, reducible to a 5th by the rule of octave equivalence), $\frac{1}{5}$ (double-octave-plus-3rd, reducible to a

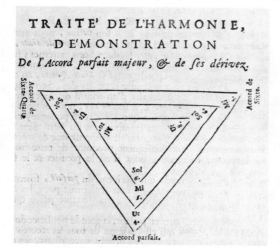

TRAITE' DE L'HARMONIE,

DEMONSTRATION

De l'Accord parfait majeur, & de ses dérivez.

6. *Diagram demonstrating the perfect major chord and its derivatives (i.e. inversions) from Rameau's 'Traité de l'harmonie réduite à ses principes naturels' (1722)*

3rd), he was able to generate the primary major triad. A triad, although it had three possible bass notes, had only one 'fundamental bass' note. A progression of chords could now be viewed as the movement of a fundamental bass line that may or not actually be sounded. The leaps or steps of the fundamental bass were controlled by a system of cadences having closing, evasive or interruptive functions, and all harmony could be viewed as an 'imitation of cadences'. Numerical ratios were used also to rationalize the elementary relationships of chords to the tonic and to each other. The triple proportion 1–3–9 represented the polarity of the subdominant (1) and the dominant (9) and their attraction to the tonic (3). This dominant he called the 'tonic dominant' (*dominante tonique*) to distinguish it from dominants on other than the fifth degree, which were simply 'dominants' (*dominantes*). The dominant chords normally carried a 7th, while the subdominant was normally accompanied by an added 6th, but this chord could also be interpreted as a 7th chord on the second degree, leading to the concept of 'double employment'. The diminished triads, diminished 7th chords and chords of the 9th, 11th and so on demanded a different explanation. For these Rameau invented the notion of assuming (*par supposition*) a fundamental bass note a 3rd or 5th above the actual lowest note of the chord.

While these general lines of his theory remained stable, many details, such as the derivation of the minor triad and the minor scale, experienced fluctuation in the course of a lifetime of publications. The most important change was his shift of the burden of the first principle from string division to the phenomenon of overtones in the *Nouveau système de musique théorique* (1726). Although Descartes had adumbrated the idea and Mersenne already reported observing the overtones in 1623 (*Quaestiones celeberrimae in Genesim*), and John Wallis had explained their physical origin (*Philosophical Transactions*, xii, 1677, April, 839ff), it was through the work of Joseph Sauveur ('Système général des intervalles des sons', 1701) that Rameau became aware of

the phenomenon. Sauveur had there given a detailed experimental and theoretical account of the partials that are heard in most vocal and instrumental sounds. This provided Rameau with an even more fundamental and natural first principle than string division, for the 3rd and 5th were actually generated by the fundamental pitch.

Rameau, while he clarified many aspects of harmonic practice, also left a legacy of unsolved problems – many of them in reality false issues – that occupied theorists long after him. The notion that the generation of each chord had to be explained led to a multitude of theories about the generation of the minor chord, the diminished triad, the diminished 7th chord, the augmented triad, and 7th chords on steps other than the dominant. The search to derive the minor and chromatic scale from some natural phenomenon exercised Rameau and many of his successors. How the fundamental bass should be permitted to move and how these movements were related to modulation raised other questions. Which was the primary dissonance, which dissonances could be attacked unprepared, and which had to be prepared were other problems seeking solution. There is hardly a theorist in the 18th or 19th centuries who did not engage in a dialogue across the years with Rameau on some of these and other issues first raised by him.

Rameau's most faithful interpreter, if also a severe critic, was Jean le Rond d'Alembert. While appreciating the great contribution he made to simplifying musical syntax, as a mathematician d'Alembert was shocked by Rameau's misuse of geometry and by his errors of method. He managed to compress the essence of Rameau's musical syntax in a little manual, *Eléments de musique, théorique et pratique suivant les principes de M. Rameau* (1752). Among other critics, Leonhard Euler (*Tentamen novae theoriae*, 1739) challenged the assumption that a pitch and its octave were identical and contested the validity of the principle of inversion.

Another attempt at a natural theory of music was Giuseppe Tartini's application of the difference tone or 'the third sound' that he had observed as being heard when two notes are sounded simultaneously (*Trattato di musica secondo la vera scienza dell'armonia*, 1754). Although Georg Andreas Sorge (*Vorgemach der musicalischen Composition*, 1745–7) and Romieu (*Nouvelle découverte des sons harmoniques graves*, 1751) had previously discovered the phenomenon, it was Tartini who showed that it corroborated six other fundamental observations previously made: string division; the notes of the trumpet marine, the trumpet, the hunting horn, and of organ mixtures; and notes derived by attaching weights to strings. All these produced the same series of notes, which added up to the diatonic system and supported the concept of the fundamental bass and the primacy of the triad. Tartini was not content with this deduction, but indulged in daring mathematical and geometric speculations, which two mathematicians soberly refuted: Benjamin Stillingfleet in *Principles and Power of Harmony* (1771) and Antonio Eximeno y Pujades in *Dell'origine e delle regole della musica* (1774).

11. THE CLASSICAL–ROMANTIC PERIOD. Rameau's theory spread to Germany through the efforts of Friedrich Wilhelm Marpurg, whose *Systematische Einleitung in die musikalische Setzkunst nach den Lehrsätzen des Herrn Rameau* is in great part a

translation of d'Alembert's handbook. Johann Philip Kirnberger (*Die Kunst des reinen Satzes in der Musick*, 1774–9) accepted many of Rameau's ideas, such as inversion, but he gave more importance to melodic functions. Thus he recognized two kinds of dissonance, the 'essential', as found in the 7th chord, and the 'incidental', as found in the suspension, which requires preparation. He united the study of counterpoint with harmony, counterpoint being given the subordinate role of arpeggiating the chordal harmony and colouring it through passing notes.

François-Joseph Fétis retained the main lines of Rameau's method, which he consecrated as 'the laws of tonality' (*Traité complet de la théorie et de la pratique de l'harmonie*, 1844). But he rejected mathematical and acoustical foundations for harmony, convinced by his study of history that the rules of composition were not dictated by nature but by feelings, needs and tastes of men in a given time and place. He identified four phases in the development of harmony: 'unitonic' (*unitonique*) or the unmodulating single tonality of plainchant; 'transitonic' (*transitonique*), in which through dissonance a tonality tended to expand outwards but was still held in check by a single centre as in plainchant; 'pluritonic' (*pluritonique*), the post-16th-century system in which the urge to express the passions led to a multiplying of the relationships one tonality had to others, so that any one harmony could now resolve in several ways; 'omnitonic' (*omnitonique*), the music of the future, in which any sound in a harmonic combination could progress to any other by a generalized application of the device of alteration.

Another theorist who put aside natural explanations was Moritz Hauptmann in *Die Natur der Harmonik und Metrik* (1853). Disturbed by explanations founded on the harmonic series because of its potentially infinite and all-inclusive nature – containing as it does both dissonant and consonant members – he preferred to construct a purely autonomous musical system by means of Hegelian logic. The intervals directly understood, the octave, 5th and major 3rd, were the fundamental building-blocks of all harmony. Chord succession depended not only on the progression of roots, which he adopted from Rameau, but on the joining together of chords that possess notes in common. These make the connecon intelligible as the other notes of the chord move on.

A return to natural theory is marked by Hermann von Helmholtz in *Die Lehre von den Tonempfindungen als physiologische Grundlage für die Theorie der Musik* (1863), which laid the foundation for modern physical and physiological acoustics. It is a book rich in new insights, among the most original being his explanation of dissonance through the intensity of beats, and of difference tones as subjective non-linear auditory responses to pitch. Helmholtz's forays into music theory were not productive of new theory so much as of authoritatively expressed syntheses, for example his definition of the principle of tonality (original italicized): 'the whole mass of tones and the connection of harmonies must stand in a close and always distinctly perceptible relationship to some arbitrarily selected tonic, and . . . the mass of tone which forms the whole composition must be developed from this tonic, and must finally return to it' (pt.iii, chap.13; Eng. trans., 1875, p.249). Hugo Riemann rehearsed a number of the problems arising from Rameau, and even revived his illusory undertone series to explain the minor triad and certain

dissonant chords. Of greater relevance to contemporary music was his attempt to explain altered chords as arising from melody. Indeed, he reversed the formula of Rameau and proclaimed that harmony had its roots in melody. Harmony, then, dominated theory in the 18th and 19th centuries, thanks to the impetus of Rameau. But notable contributions were also made in other areas.

12. THEORY OF GENRES: 16TH TO 18TH CENTURIES. The theory of genres and the norms for their composition received increasing attention. Its rather sketchy beginnings are to be seen in Pietro Pontio's *Ragionamento di musica* (1588), where the standards for composing motets, masses, madrigals, psalms and the like are discussed. Similar instructions occur in Pietro Cerone's *El melopeo y maestro* (1613) and in Michael Praetorius's (*Syntagma musicum*, iii, 1618). Johann Mattheson's *Vollkommene Capellmeister* (1739) and Johann Adolph Scheibe's *Der critische Musicus* (1737–40) are virtual textbooks of musical genres and forms. These instructions are symptomatic of the way in which the distinctive affective, compositional and associative traits attached to specific genres, each with its proper style and level of artfulness, came to be recognized during the Baroque period. Mattheson (pt.ii, chap.13) took up 16 such vocal genres, including the recitative, cavata, arioso, cantata, serenata etc, and 22 instrumental types, including 11 of the most common dances, and the sinfonia, overture and concerto grosso. Johann Adolph Scheibe was perhaps more typical of his time when he paid greater attention to technical method and formal structure than to affective character in describing such types as the sonata, symphony and concerto. Still, the descriptions are impressionistic, and it was only with Heinrich Christoph Koch (*Versuch einer Anleitung zur Composition*, pt.iii, 1793) that detailed enough models were presented to serve a composer embarking on a sonata or concerto movement. With Koch, too, the instrumental forms and genres occupied the foreground for the first time. They were not abstract, however, for he conceived of instrumental music as still bound up with feelings and emotions, if in a non-specific way.

The more this group of theorists focussed on the purely musical logic of genres of composition, the more they resorted to literary and visual models for both concepts and vocabulary. Burmeister had described a motet as having, like an oration, an *exordium*, a *confirmatio* and a conclusion. Mattheson named six parts in a well-developed composition, the *exordium*, *narratio*, *propositio*, *confirmatio*, *confutatio* and *peroratio* – that is, introduction, report, proposal, corroboration, refutation and conclusion (pt.ii, chap.14). Although the example he used was an aria of Benedetto Marcello, the text is never considered, only the musical continuity. Moreover, musical punctuation is seen as breaking the structure down into paragraphs, sentences, phrases etc.

Koch borrowed from visual art, and specifically from Johann G. Sulzer's *Allgemeine Theorie der schönen Künste* (1771–4), the concept of the *Anlage* or layout, a plan or sketch in which the most salient features of the final work are set down. Following this outline of the work, the artist proceeds to the *Ausführung* or execution, and finally the *Ausarbeitung*, or elaboration of details. Koch realized that the parallel was imperfect and he was forced into literary analogies to convey his formal ideas. For music, though amenable to spatial imagery, was a temporal art like literature. Thus, the musical *Anlage* is a statement of the principal ideas and an exposition of how they relate to each other within the main periods. When he went on to speak of the articulation of sections, he called upon grammatical terms such as *Redetheile* (parts of speech), periods, commas, semicolons, caesuras, periods and even subject and predicate. Koch's preoccupation with explaining every detail of the anatomy of a piece led him to consider both minute and large-scale temporal units.

13. THEORY OF RHYTHM: 17TH TO 19TH CENTURIES. Interest in temporal problems was awakening after the long hiatus brought on by the simplification of rhythm in the 16th and 17th centuries. Most of the texts during these centuries continued to repeat, sometimes dutifully, often with a tinge of scorn, traditional discussions of prolations and proportions. One of the treatises most attuned with the times was Agostino Pisa's *Battuta della musica dichiarata* (1611), a tutor for 'conductors' on beating time. As was conventional in the 16th century, he divided all metres into two parts, the *positione* and *elevatione*, the lowering and raising of the hand; but with uneven metres the downbeat marked the larger part, for example two beats down against one up in triple. The proportional signatures, such as 3/2, lost their precise meaning before theorists took note of the new practice of indicating tempo by adjectives of mood and gait, such as *allegro* and *andante*. Michel de Saint-Lambert (*Principes du clavecin*, 1702) claimed that the proportions still held in some cases – for example ₵ was twice as fast as C, though both were at a walking pace – but Thomas Morley (*Plaine and Easie Introduction*, 1597) a century earlier already found composers using the two indifferently.

A new approach to the organization of time is reflected in the dialogue by Joseph Riepel, *Anfangsgründe zur musicalischen Setzkunst* (1752–68). He was aware that the patterns of note values, their repetition in themes and their direction towards a cadence were subtly related to melodic and harmonic factors. In the first chapter, 'De rhythmopoeia oder Von der Tactordnung' (1752) the pupil is instructed to pay close attention to the length of phrases and the effect of adding them together. Although a preference is shown for four-bar modules, Riepel's preceptor shows that two-, three- and five-bar phrases (*Zweyer, Dreyer, Fünfer*) are also possible. Koch broke down temporal structure into even smaller units, which he called *Einschnitte* (incises), while at the level of the phrase or *Absatz* he differentiated those that tended towards the fifth degree from those that closed on the tonic. *Absätze* cumulated into periods and these into full compositions.

Riemann's theory of phraseology (*System der musikalischen Rhythmik und Metrik*, 1903) owed much to Koch, particularly the idea that phrases tend to extend over the bar (which Riemann applied in the rule that every phrase begins with an upbeat), and his belief in the universality of the four-bar phrase (*Vierhebigkeit*), departures from which he explained as elisions, extensions and truncations. Riemann also adopted the principle of antecedent–consequent symmetry developed by Jérôme-Joseph de Momigny (*Cours complet d'harmonie et de composition*, 1803–6).

14. 20TH CENTURY. The most crucial force in 20th-century theory was not Wagner's chromaticism, Debussy's non-functional harmony, or Schoenberg's 12-note system, but the historical perspective that made it inconceivable to try to explain music, past, present and future, by a single universal theory. Many 20th-century theories are deliberately limited in their applicability, as Alfred Lorenz's analyses of large-scale architecture in Wagner's music dramas (*Das Geheimnis der Form bei Richard Wagner*, 1924–33, 2/1966), or Heinrich Schenker's analytical system, which grew out of his studies of Beethoven.

Schenker's is probably the most original and influential retrospective analytical theory of the century. Developed over a period of 40 years (*Neue musikalische Theorien und Phantasien*, 1906–35), it revealed a new breadth of logic in tonal music. Although in a difficult style and accompanied by novel graphic representations, much of his writing was destined for the performer. As such it is parallel to the thoroughbass methods, such as C. P. E. Bach's *Versuch über die wahre Art das Clavier zu spielen* (1753), which Schenker greatly admired. It resembles them also in beginning with musical practice – that is actual compositions rather than abstract principles – and evolving general principles by an inductive process. The most radical aspect of Schenker's approach is probably his view that discrete musical forms, such as single movements, are explicable in the 18th and 19th centuries as structures within a single key; sections conventionally interpreted as modulations are seen as 'prolongations' of a chordal or harmonic scale-step (*Stufe*) within the central key. To apprehend the basic structure of a piece as entirely in the tonic requires that it be reduced to its basic melodic and harmonic movements, that is to the 'background' level. This level, in turn, is derived by converting the written music first to a 'foreground' sketch containing the most cogent linear movement noticed by the ear, then to a 'middleground'. As in Kirnberger's method, harmony and counterpoint are united. The synthesis thus reveals the interaction of a skeletal melody with a distilled harmonic progression. Schenker's theory (*see also* ANALYSIS, §III, 2) influenced a few German and Austrian theorists, such as Ernst Kurth (*Romantische Harmonik*, 1920) and Oswald Jonas (*Das Wesen des musikalischen Kunstwerks*, 1934), but his impact has been most pronounced among theorists and teachers in the USA: for example William J. Mitchell, who founded the journal *Music Forum* dedicated mainly to Schenkerian studies, Ernst Oster, Felix Salzer (*Structural Hearing*, 1952) and Allen Forte.

The search for a means of interpreting early 20th-century music led to a number of explanations based on the harmonic series. Schoenberg proposed that dissonances were not qualitatively distinguishable from consonances, since both could be found in the harmonic series (*Harmonielehre*, 1911, chap.2); he thus justified 'emancipating' dissonance from the restrictions of conventional counterpoint. Henry Cowell (*New Musical Resources*, 1930) applied the harmonics to rhythm by constructing a numerical series of durations analogous to the pitch numbers of the partials of a fundamental. Hindemith (*Unterweisung im Tonsatz*, 1937–9) used a synthesis of the harmonic series and the phenomenon of combination tones to classify chords according to the tension produced by their intervallic content. By this means he also determined the roots of chords and consequently, the relationships among them. Harmony, grounded in root progression – a kind of fundamental bass – and progressing through a 'fluctuation' of tension, lent directional meaning to free flights of melody, which could be broken down into chordal and nonharmonic notes. Hindemith's system was thus both analytical and compositionally prescriptive.

A different kind of scientism is evident in Joseph Schillinger's *The Schillinger System of Musical Composition* (1946), which is not so much a foundation of a music theory on scientific principles as the creation of a metalanguage of numbers, formulae, algebraic and other symbols to describe exhaustively and in the abstract existing and potential musical phenomena. While much of the book has been properly discredited for its lack of rigour and misuse of mathematical terminology, there are some interesting flashes, such as the concept of 'resultant rhythm' – the sum of all rhythmic events in a polyphonic fabric. More carefully rooted in science are a number of attempts to derive musical principles from information or communication theory. This involves the calculation of the quantity of 'information' (variety) and 'redundancy' (sameness) residing in a composition with respect to certain qualities or parameters. Lejaren Hiller (*JMT*, x, 1966), for example, compared the rate of information in stable and unstable sections by various composers, measured in terms of the occurrence of the 12 pitch classes; similarly Fritz Winckel (*MGG*, ix, 967ff) calculated the probability of consecutive intervals in a composition. The information model has been applied also in creative theory, as by Iannis Xenakis (*Musiques formelles*, 1963), who showed that 'stochastic' music can be composed at various levels of determinacy in which general and transitional probabilities are regulated according to the desired outcome.

Perhaps the most important theoretical development of the mid-20th century is the emergence of an objective theory in the work of Milton Babbitt and Allen Forte and their disciples. Babbitt insisted on rigorous scientific method and the precise and normal usage of mathematical and scientific terms and operations. He maintained that a theory should be 'statable as a connected set of axioms, definitions, and theorems, the proofs of which are derived by means of an appropriate logic' (*IMSCR*, viii *New York 1961*, i, p.399). Babbitt developed a theory of this kind for 12-note music in a series of articles (*Score*, 1955, no.12, p.53; *MQ*, xlvi, 1960, p.246; *JMT*, v, 1961, p.72). One of the axioms recognizes that pitches an octave apart belong to the same class – hence the term 'pitch class'; another that intervals of the same size are perceived as identical irrespective of pitch – hence the term 'interval class'. Using finite group theory, Babbitt developed theorems defining the variance and invariance of forms of the 12-note set. His theory has been extended by a number of other investigators: David Lewin, Donald Martino, John Rothgeb, Stefan Bauer-Mengelberg and Melvin Ferentz.

Allen Forte, influenced by Babbitt's method, developed a theory of set complexes that permits the analysis of predodecaphonic atonal music (*The Structure of Atonal Music*, 1973). Forte's set complexes are unordered collections of pitches (disregarding octave duplications) with certain arrangements of intervals. His theory permits the analysis of any music based on configurations of notes other than the major and minor scales and on chords not formed by the superposition of 3rds. Mathematical set and group theory are used to observe the behaviour of these set complexes, which in a piece of some length is greatly facilitated by storing the musical data in a computer and subjecting them to various analytical routines that Forte has developed.

The most formidable challenge that music theory has had to confront is to explain aleatory, electronic and colouristic music that exploits broad sound gestures rather than formal devices. It is apparent that informational, psychological, physiological, statistical, acoustical and even sociological approaches must figure prominently in theorizing concerning much new music. A growing reaction to some of the objective theories is also apparent; they are criticized for detecting micro-, macro- and hidden structures that are not apparent to the listener's hearing or related to his experience. This has led to an attempt to establish a phenomenological basis for analysis (Thomas Clifton, *JMT*, xiii, 1969; xix, 1975) and a critique of the use of verbal means to refer to non-verbal qualities (Benjamin Boretz, *PNM*, iv, 1966, viii, 1969).

A healthy trend is the recognition that music theory cannot be shielded from historical considerations, that analysis of structure divorced from stylistic, historical and sociological contexts falsifies the music it aims to describe. It is being recognized that only a multidimensional and pluralistic attack on the musical object can reveal its true nature and unique qualities.

BIBLIOGRAPHY
GENERAL

S. Wantzloeben: *Das Monochord als Instrument und als System* (Halle, 1911)

J. Gregory and O. G. Sonneck: *Catalogue of Early Books on Music* (Washington, DC, 1913); *Supplement, 1913–1942* (Washington, 1944)

M. Shirlaw: *The Theory of Harmony* (London, 1917/*R*1955 and 1969)

H. Riemann: *Geschichte der Musiktheorie im IX.–XIX. Jahrhundert* (Berlin, 2/1921; Eng. trans., 1967/*R*1974)

J. Wolf: 'Early English Musical Theorists from 1200 to the Death of Henry Purcell', *MQ*, xxv (1939), 420

G. Pietzsch: 'Zur Pflege der Musik an den deutschen Universitäten bis zur Mitte des 16. Jahrhunderts', *AMf*, v (1940), 65; vi (1941), 23–56; vii (1942), 90, 154; enlarged repr. 1971 with foreword

G. Reese: *Music in the Middle Ages* (New York, 1940)

G. Haydon: *Introduction to Musicology* (New York, 1941)

A. Mendel: 'Pitch in the 16th and Early 17th Centuries', *MQ*, xxiv (1948), 28, 199, 336, 575

O. Strunk: *Source Readings in Music History from Classical Antiquity through the Romantic Era* (New York, 1950)

J. M. Barbour: *Tuning and Temperament: a Historical Survey* (East Lansing, 1951, 2/1953)

Å. Davidson: *Catalogue critique et déscriptif des ouvrages théoriques dans les bibliothèques suédoises* (Uppsala, 1953)

C. Sachs: *Rhythm and Tempo: a Study in Music History* (New York, 1953)

G. Reese: *Music in the Renaissance* (New York, 1954, rev. 2/1959)

H. O. Rogers: *The Development of a Concept of Modulation in Theory from the 16th to the Early 18th Century* (diss. Indiana U., 1955)

H. Hüschen: 'Harmonie', *MGG*

J. Rohwer: 'Harmonielehre', *MGG*

F. B. Turrell: *Modulation: an Outline of its Prehistory from Aristoxenus to Henry Glarean* (diss., U. of Southern California, 1956)

G. Reese: *Fourscore Classics of Music Literature* (New York, 1957/*R*1970)

N. C. Carpenter: *Music in the Medieval and Renaissance Universities* (Norman, Oklahoma, 1958)

C. Palisca: 'Kontrapunkt', *MGG*

H. Powers: 'Mode and Raga', *MQ*, xliv (1958), 448

J. Coover: 'Music Theory in Translation: a Bibliography', *JMT*, iii (1959), 70; suppl., *JMT*, xiii (1969), 230

N. Cazden: 'Musical Intervals and Simple Ratios', *JRME*, vii (1959), 197

H. Zenck: *Numerus und Affectus*, ed. W. Gerstenberg (Kassel, 1959)

J. Backus: 'Pseudo-science in Music', *JMT*, iv (1960), 221

F. Crane: *A Study of Theoretical Writings on Musical Form to ca. 1460* (diss., U. of Iowa, 1960)

J. Haar: *Musica mundana: Variations on a Pythagorean Theme* (diss., Harvard U., 1960)

M. Babbitt: 'Past and Present Concepts of the Limits of Music', *IMSCR*, viii *New York 1961*, i, 398

C. Palisca: 'Scientific Empiricism in Musical Thought', *Seventeenth*

Century Science and the Arts, ed. H. H. Rhys (Princeton, 1961), 91–137

H. Eggebrecht: 'Musik als Tonsprache', AMw, xviii (1961), 73

J. Smits van Waesberghe: The Theory of Music from the Carolingian Era up to 1400, RISM, B III/1–2 (Munich and Duisburg, 1961–8)

F. J. León Tello: Estudios de historia de la teoría musical (Madrid, 1962)

W. Dürr and W. Gerstenberg: 'Rhythmus, Metrum, Takt', MGG

C. Palisca: 'American Scholarship in Western Music', in F. Harrison, C. Palisca and M. Hood: Musicology (Englewood Cliffs, 1963), 89–213

G. von Békésy: 'Hearing Theories and Complex Sounds', Journal of the Acoustical Society of America, xxxv (1963), 588

A. Machabey: 'De Ptolemée aux Carolingiens', Quadrivium, vi (1964), 37

M. Babbitt: 'The Structure and Function of Music Theory: I', College Music Symposium, v (1965), 49

C. Dahlhaus: 'Tonsysteme', MGG

I. Horsley: Fugue: History and Practice (New York, 1966)

A. Machabey: 'Teoria della musica', La MusicaE

L. Treitler: 'Music Analysis in an Historical Context', College Music Symposium, vi (1966), 75

F. Blume: Renaissance and Baroque Music (New York, 1967)

K. Meyer-Baer: Music of the Spheres and the Dance of Death (Princeton, 1968)

J. Backus: The Acoustical Foundations of Music (New York, 1969)

B. Boretz: 'Meta-variations: Studies in the Foundations of Musical Thought (I)', PNM, viii/1 (1969), 1–74

T. Clifton: 'Training in Music Theory: Process and Product', JMT, xiii (1969), 38

A. Mendel and A. J. Ellis: Studies in the History of Musical Pitch (Amsterdam, 1969)

B. Boretz: 'Sketch of a Musical System (Meta-variations, Part II)', PNM, viii/2 (1970), 49–111

D. Williams: A Bibliography of the History of Music Theory (Fairport, NY, 1970)

F. Zaminer: Über Musiktheorie: Referate der Arbeitstagung 1970 in Berlin (Cologne, 1970)

F. Lesure, ed.: Ecrits imprimés concernant la musique, RISM, B VI/1–2 (Munich and Duisburg, 1971)

C. Dahlhaus: 'Musiktheorie', Einführung in die systematische Musikwissenschaft (Cologne, 1971), 93–132

H. Eggebrecht: Handwörterbuch der musikalischen Terminologie (Wiesbaden, 1972–)

L. Gushee: 'Questions of Genre in Medieval Treatises on Music', Gattungen der Musik in Einzeldarstellungen: Gedenkschrift für Leo Schrade, i (Berne and Munich, 1973), 546–613

T. Clifton: 'Some Comparisons between Intuitive and Scientific Descriptions of Music', JMT, xix (1975), 66–110

C. Dahlhaus: 'Some Models of Unity in Musical Form', JMT, xix (1975), 2

M. Bielitz: Musik und Grammatik: Studien zur mittelalterlichen Musiktheorie (Munich, 1977)

ANTIQUITY AND HELLENIC PERIOD

A. Gogava: Aristoxeni musici antiquiss. harmonicorum elementorum (Venice, 1562) [collection of Gk. writings on music]

M. Meibom: Antiquae musicae auctores septem (Amsterdam, 1652/R1895)

R. Westphal: Die Fragmente und die Lehrsätze der griechischen Rhythmiker (Leipzig, 1861)

C. E. Ruelle: Collection des auteurs grecs relatifs à la musique (Paris, 1871–95)

F. Gevaert: Histoire et théorie de la musique de l'antiquité (Ghent, 1875–81)

D. B. Monro: The Modes of Ancient Greek Music (Oxford, 1894)

K. von Jan: Musici scriptores graeci et melodiarum veterum quidquid exstat (Leipzig, 1895); suppl. (Leipzig, 1899/R1962)

R. P. Winnington-Ingram: Mode in Ancient Greek Music (Cambridge, 1936/R1968)

I. Henderson: 'Ancient Greek Music', NOHM, i (1957), 336–403

R. Crocker: 'Pythagorean Mathematics and Music', Journal of Aesthetics and Art Criticism, xxii (1963–4), 189, 325

M. Vogel: Die Enharmonik der Griechen (Düsseldorf, 1963)

E. Lippman: Musical Thought in Ancient Greece (New York, 1964)

W. Anderson: Ethos and Education in Greek Music (Cambridge, 1966)

EARLY MIDDLE AGES, EARLY POLYPHONY, MENSURAL MUSIC

CS; GS

E. Coussemaker: Histoire de l'harmonie au moyen âge (Paris, 1852/R)

G. Gaspari: Catalogo della Biblioteca del Liceo musicale di Bologna, i (Bologna, 1890/R1961)

E. Steinhard: 'Zur Frühgeschichte der Mehrstimmigkeit', AMw, iii (1921), 220

H. Farmer: The Arabian Influence on Musical Theory (London, 1925)

J. Handschin: 'Zur Geschichte der Lehre von Organum', ZMw, viii (1925–6), 321

G. Pietzsch: Die Klassifikation der Musik von Boetius bis Ugolino von Orvieto (Halle, 1929)

O. Gombosi: Tonarten und Stimmungen der Antiken Musik (Copenhagen, 1939)

E. Werner and I. Sonne: 'The Philosophy and Theory of Music in Judaeo-Arabic Literature', Hebrew Union College Annual, xvi (1941), 265

O. Strunk: 'The Tonal System of Byzantine Music', MQ, xxviii (1942), 190

L. Spiess: Polyphony in Theory and Practice from the Ninth Century to the Close of the XIII Century (diss., Harvard U., 1947)

E. Werner: 'The Oldest Sources of Octave and Octoechos', AcM, xx (1948), 1

G. de Van: 'La pédagogie musicale à la fin du moyen âge', MD, ii (1948), 75

J. Smits van Waesberghe: 'Some Music Treatises and their Interrelation: a School of Liège (c. 1050–1200)?', MD, iii (1949), 25, 95

E. Wellesz: A History of Byzantine Music and Hymnography (Oxford, 1949; rev, enlarged 2/1961)

O. Gombosi: 'Key, Mode, Species', JAMS, iv (1951), 20

J. Smits van Waesberghe: 'La place exceptionelle de l'ars musica dans le développement des sciences au siècle des carolingiens', Revue gregorienne, xxxi (1952), 81

R. Crocker: 'Musica Rhythmica and Musica Metrica in Antique and Medieval Theory', JMT, ii (1958), 2

G. Reaney: 'The Greek Background of Medieval Musical Thought', MMR, lxxxvii (1959), 124

E. Apfel: 'Über das Verhältnis von Musiktheorie und Compositionspraxis im späteren Mittelalter (etwa 1200–1500)', GfMKB, Kassel 1962, 354

R. Crocker: 'Discant, Counterpoint, and Harmony', JAMS, xv (1962), 1

G. Möbius: Das Tonsystem aus der Zeit vor 1000 (Cologne, 1963)

G. Reaney: 'The Question of Authorship in the Medieval Treatises on Music', MD, xviii (1964), 7

U. Pizzani: 'Studi sulle fonti del "De Institutione Musica" di Boezio', Sacris erudiri, xvi (1965), 6–164

M. Vogel: 'Zur Entstehung der Kirchentonarten', Mf, xxi (1968), 199

F. A. Gallo: 'Tra Giovanni di Garlandia e Filippo da Vitry: note sulla tradizione di alcuni testi teorici', MD, xxiii (1969), 13

J. Smits van Waesberghe: Musikerziehung, Lehre und Theorie, Musikgeschichte in Bildern, iii/3 (Leipzig, 1969)

H. Eggebrecht and F. Zaminer: Ad organum faciendum: Lehrschriften der Mehrstimmigkeit in nachguidonischer Zeit (Mainz, 1970)

C. Bower: 'Natural and Artificial Music: the Origins and Development of an Aesthetic Concept', MD, xxv (1971), 17

M. Huglo: Les tonaires: inventaire, analyse, comparaison (Paris, 1971)

A. Gallo: 'Philological Works on Musical Treatises of the Middle Ages: a Bibliographical Report', AcM, xliv (1972), 78

S. Gut: 'La notion de consonance chez les théoriciens du moyen âge', AcM, xlviii (1976), 20

E. Ferrari Barassi: Strumenti musicali e testimonianze teoriche nel medio evo, IMa, viii (1979)

14TH AND 15TH CENTURIES

D. von Bartha: 'Studien zur musikalischen Schrifttum des 15. Jahrhunderts', AMf, i (1936), 59, 176

F. A. Gallo: 'Le traduzioni dal Greco per Fr. Gaffurio', AcM, xxxv (1963), 172

P. P. Scattolin: 'La regola del "grado" nella teoria medievale del contrappunto', RIM, xiv (1979), 1–74

16TH CENTURY

E. Praetorius: Die Mensuraltheorie des Franchinus Gafurius und der folgenden Zeit bis zur Mitte des 16. Jahrhunderts (Leipzig, 1905/R1970)

H. Collet: Le mysticisme musical espagnol au xvi siècle (Paris, 1913)

L. Schrade: 'Von der Maniera der Komposition in der Musik des 16. Jahrhunderts', ZMw, xvi (1934), 2, 98, 152

K. Jeppesen: 'Eine musiktheoretische Korrespondenz des früheren Cinquecento', AcM, xiii (1941), 3–39

D. P. Walker: 'Musical Humanism in the 16th and Early 17th Centuries', MR, ii (1941), 1, 111, 220, 288; iii (1942), 55; Ger. trans., 1949, as Der musikalische Humanismus im 16. und 17. Jahrhundert

E. Lowinsky: 'The Concept of Physical and Musical Space in the Renaissance', PAMS 1941, 57

H. Bush: 'The Recognition of Chordal Formation by Early Music Theorists', MQ, xxxii (1946), 227

F. Yates: French Academies of the 16th Century (London, 1947)

E. T. Ferand: '"Zufallsmusik" und "Komposition" in der Musiklehre der Renaissance', IMSCR, iv Basle 1949, 103

C. Palisca: The Beginnings of Baroque Music: its Roots in 16th Century Theory and Polemics (diss., Harvard U., 1954)

D. P. Walker: Spiritual and Demonic Magic from Ficino to Campanella (London, 1958)

E. Lowinsky: 'Renaissance Writings on Music Theory (1964)', RN, xviii (1965), 358

K. Fellerer: 'Zur Kontrapunkt-Literatur im 16. Jahrhundert', *FAM*, xiii (1966), 39

P. Bergquist: 'Mode and Polyphony around 1500: Theory and Practice', *Music Forum*, i (1967), 99–161

E. Lowinsky: 'The Musical Avant-garde of the Renaissance or: The Peril and Profit of Foresight', *Art, Science and History in the Renaissance*, ed. C. S. Singleton (Baltimore, 1968), 111–62

K. Fellerer: 'Die Kölner musiktheoretische Schule des 16. Jahrhunderts', *Renaissance-muziek 1400–1600: donum natalicium René Bernard Lenaerts* (Louvain, 1969)

S. Drake: 'Renaissance Music and Experimental Science', *Journal of the History of Ideas*, xxxi (1970), 483

BAROQUE PERIOD

H. Goldschmidt: *Die Lehre von der vokalen Ornamentik*, i: *Das 17. und 18. Jahrhundert bis in die Zeit Glucks* (Charlottenburg, 1907)

M. Schneider: *Die Anfänge des Basso Continuo und seiner Bezifferung* (Leipzig, 1918/R1971)

F. T. Arnold: *The Art of Accompaniment from a Thorough-bass* (Oxford, 1931/R1965)

R. Wienpahl: 'English Theorists and Evolving Tonality', *ML*, xxxvi (1955), 377

G. Houle: *The Musical Measure as Discussed by Theorists from 1650–1800* (diss., Stanford U., 1960)

E. Apfel: 'Satztechnische Grundlagen der neuen Musik des 17. Jahrhunderts', *AcM*, xxxiv (1962), 67

C. Palisca: 'The Artusi–Monteverdi Controversy', *The Monteverdi Companion*, ed. D. Arnold and N. Fortune (London, 1968), 133–66

A. Cohen: ' "La Supposition" and the Changing Concept of Dissonance in Baroque Theory', *JAMS*, xxiv (1971), 63

W. Atcherson: 'Key and Mode in 17th-century Music Theory Books', *JMT*, xvii (1973), 204–33

L. Tolkoff: 'French Modal Theory Before Rameau', *JMT*, xvii (1973), 150

CLASSICAL – ROMANTIC PERIOD

W. Newman: 'The Recognition of Sonata-form by Theorists of the 18th and 19th Centuries', *PAMS 1941*, 21

R. Rowen: 'Some 18th-century Classifications of Musical Style', *MQ*, xxxiii (1947), 90

L. Ratner: 'Harmonic Aspects of Classic Form', *JAMS*, ii (1949), 159

G. Fellerer: 'Vom "Stylo theatrali" in der Musiktheorie des 18. Jahrhunderts', *Mimus und Logos: eine Festgabe für Carl Niessen* (Emsdetten, 1952)

M. Hoffman: *A Study of German Theoretical Treatises of the 19th Century* (diss., U. of Rochester, 1953)

L. Ratner: '18th Century Theories of Musical Period Structure', *MQ*, xlii (1956), 439

C. Finney: *British Theorists of the 19th Century* (diss., U. of Rochester, 1957)

E. Jacobi: 'Harmonic Theory in England after the Time of Rameau', *JMT*, i (1957), 126

——: *Die Entwicklung der Musiktheorie in England nach der Zeit Jean-Philippe Rameau* (Strasbourg, 1957–60/R1971)

A. Mann: *The Study of Fugue* (New Brunswick, NJ, 1958/R1965)

P. Benary: *Die deutsche Kompositionslehre des 18. Jahrhunderts* (Leipzig, 1960)

20TH CENTURY

E. Coons and D. Kraehenbuehl: 'Information as a Measure of Structure in Music', *JMT*, ii (1958), 127–61

A. Berger: 'New Linguistic Modes and the New Theory', *PNM*, iii/1 (1964), 1

J. Tjulin: *Theoretical Problems of 20th-century Music* (Moscow, 1967)

B. Boretz and E. Cone, eds.: *Perspectives on Contemporary Music Theory* (New York, 1972)

A. Forte: 'Theory', *Dictionary of Twentieth Century Music*, ed. J. Vinton (New York, 1974)

CLAUDE V. PALISCA

Theotokion. A Byzantine hymn in which the mother of God ('theotokos') is addressed and invoked. In the Coptic rite the plural form 'theotokia' is used as a feminine singular.

Therache, Pierrequin de (*b* c1465; *d* after 1526). French composer. He was *maître des enfants* of the ducal chapel of the Duke of Lorraine at Nancy between 1492 and 1527. There is no evidence to support Fétis's suggestion that he was a singer in the French royal chapel at Paris. His music reflects his position as a provincial composer. Although showing connections with the style of Mouton and Févin, his contemporaries at Paris, it is less sophisticated, rhythmically less varied and tends to fall into clear-cut sections. In the motet *Senatus apostolorum*, for example, short routine motifs are passed apparently at random from voice to voice. The full four-voice texture is rarely used, and the piece appears to lack a formal structure. Nevertheless, his music was known and apparently admired at Paris; the motet *Verbum bonum et suave* exists in six sources, all of which contain music of the French court, and Mouton used it as the basis for a parody mass. This motet is more impressive, using chant melody and a simple rhythmic structure to build up a powerful movement. His music was also performed at the Portuguese court.

Although some of these pieces are simply ascribed to 'Pietrequin', he does not seem to be the same composer as the Pietrequin whose secular music is at Florence. A Loyset Therache was singer at the court of Philip the Good of Burgundy from 1496 to 1501.

WORKS

Missa 'Coment peult', 4vv, *E-TAc* 18; Missa 'Fortuna desparata', 4vv, *E-TAc* 3; Missa 'O vos omnes', 4vv, *A-Wkm* 5248
Gaude Maria virgo, 4vv, *Wn* 15941; Senatus apostolorum, 4vv, 1514[1]; Verbum bonum et suave, 4vv, ed. in MRM, iii–v (1968)
Magnificat, Fugger family library, Augsburg, lost; Magnificat, *E-Tc*, lost

BIBLIOGRAPHY

FétisB
A. Ambros: *Geschichte der Musik* (Leipzig, 1862–82; 3/1887–1911)
A. Jacquot: *La musique en Lorraine* (Paris, 1882)
W. Kirsch: *Die Quellen der mehrstimmigen Magnificat- und Te Deum-Vertonungen bis zur Mitte des 16. Jahrhunderts* (Tutzing, 1966)

STANLEY BOORMAN

Therapy. *See* MUSIC THERAPY.

Theremin. One of the earliest electronic musical instruments, named after its inventor Léon Thérémin (*b* St Petersburg, 15 Aug 1896), a Russian scientist of French descent. Thérémin studied physics at Petrograd University, and in 1919 he was placed in charge of the laboratory of electrical oscillations in the Physico-Technical Institute, where he combined his musical and research interests in the development of his instrument. In August 1920 he demonstrated this publicly for the first time, calling it the 'aetherophone'. In 1927 he went to the USA, gave a number of concert demonstrations and took out an American patent.

The first orchestral work with a solo electronic instrument seems to have been Andrey Pashchenko's *Symphonic Mystery* for theremin and orchestra, which received its first performance in Leningrad on 2 May 1924. Later composers for the instrument included Schillinger, whose *First Airphonic Suite* for theremin and orchestra was performed in Cleveland, Ohio, in November 1929; Varèse, who requested two special theremins for *Equatorial* (1934), although the revised score specifies ondes martenot; and Anis Fuleihan, whose concerto was performed by the New York SO under Stokowski in February 1945.

A notable feature of the theremin in its original form lies in its manner of performance, for the player does not actually touch it. The frequency of the single pitch emitted from its loudspeaker is dependent on the distance of the performer's hand from an antenna rising vertically from the instrument. Two radio-frequency oscillators are employed, one at a fixed frequency and the other controlled by the capacitance between the right hand and the antenna. When these two frequencies are heterodyned, the resulting frequency, lying within the audio range, is amplified and heard through the loudspeaker. Moving the hand back and forth can create pitch changes over the entire audio range. The volume is controlled by a similar procedure, with the left hand moving in relation to a metal loop. Different timbres can be chosen by setting a switch controlling a system of filters and varying the harmonics. The disadvantages of the theremin seem to have been in the difficulty of controlling the transition from one pitch to another, both because there was no gauge, such as a fingerboard, for the distance, and because (unless the left hand were used very cunningly to disguise it) a glissando invariably accompanied any move from note to note. Later versions of the instrument were devised with a fingerboard, rather like a cello in appearance, which alleviated some of these problems.

It is worth noting that an electronic system using the same principle as the theremin, that of capacitance between the human body and an antenna, was developed in 1965 by ROBERT A. MOOG for Cage's *Variations V*, which employs dancers moving between a number of antennae, thereby varying the sound.

BIBLIOGRAPHY

N. H. Crowhurst: *Electronic Musical Instruments* (Blue Ridge Summit, Penn., 1971), 78ff

RICHARD ORTON

Thern, Károly (*b* Iglau, 13 Aug 1817; *d* Vienna, 13 April 1886). Hungarian composer of German birth. He could not speak Hungarian fluently until the age of 13, but as early as 1832 he founded a musical society in Miskolc. In 1834 he formed an orchestra there, which he conducted and for which he composed. For a time he taught at a girls' boarding school in Balassagyarmat. In 1837 he entered the University of Pest and soon attracted the attention of Hungarian literary society with incidental music to József Gaál's *Peleskei notárius* ('The notary of Peleske', 1838), *Szvatopluk* (1839) and Szigligeti's *Rontó Pál* (1839). He was made assistant conductor of the National Theatre in 1841, and in this capacity wrote the operas *Gizul* (1841), *Tihany ostroma* ('The siege of Tihany', 1845) and *A képzelt beteg* ('The imaginary invalid', 1855). In 1853 he was appointed harmony and piano teacher at the National Conservatory.

In 1864 Thern moved with his sons Vilmos (1847–1911) and Lajos (1848–1920) to Leipzig to secure a more thorough education for them. They studied with Reinecke and Moscheles at the conservatory, later with Liszt, and won European renown with their concert tours of two-piano recitals from the mid-1860s. Vilmos later taught at the Horák music schools in Vienna, Lajos at the Vienna Conservatory. Their father returned to Pest in 1868 but spent his last years in Vienna.

Thern's music shows a sound theatrical inventiveness but does not rise above the level of most Hungarian operatic music of the time. He was most successful in adapting folksongs for use in popular stage works such as *Hortobágyi pusztán* ('On the Hortobágy puszta'). Although stage works dominate his output, he also published songs, piano music and chamber works (including a String Trio in F op.60), and composed a symphony (1871) and a few other orchestral works.

BIBLIOGRAPHY

Thesis. (1) A musical 'position' in Byzantine musical theory which is, in effect, a realization of subsidiary signs in the notation known as cheironomiai.

(2) *See* ARSIS, THESIS.

Thessaloniki (Gk.). Salonica, city in Greece, the country's second musical centre after Athens; *see* GREECE, §III, 2.

Thesselius, Johann (*fl* Aschach ob der Enns, nr. Linz, 1609). ?Austrian composer and musician. In the preface to his only surviving music, *Newe liebliche Paduanen, Intraden und Galliarden auff allerley Instrumenten zu gebrauchen fünff Stimmen componiert* (Nuremberg, 1609), he called himself a musician in the service of Baron Carl Jörger at the castle at Aschach ob der Enns. The castle actually belonged to the old Austrian noble family of Harrach, but Thesselius probably named Jörger as his employer because the head of the family at that time, Count Karl von Harrach, spent much of his time in Vienna as one of the Emperor Ferdinand II's leading counsellors. The fact that Thesselius is not heard of after 1609 may be connected with the fact that the Count's two daughters, to whom he perhaps taught music, married, respectively, Wallenstein, who rebelled against the emperor, and Count Adam Terzky, Wallenstein's most devoted supporter; this may have led to Thesselius being drawn into the Wallenstein intrigue. A similar explanation could account for the complete disappearance of a set of *Tricinia sacra* (Vienna, 1615), which Georg Draudius ascribed to him in his *Bibliotheca classica* (2/1625).

Thesselius's volume of 1609 consists of ten suites, which he explained were played as *Tafelmusik* at Schloss Aschach. In two significant respects they are similar to the important suites (published from 1611 onwards) of Paul Peuerl, who from no later than 1 November 1609 lived not far from him at Steyr and who may have got to know him. In the first place, each suite consists of a pavan, intrada and galliard, a sequence matched by Peuerl, who, however, added an extra movement between the last two. Thesselius thematically connected the beginning of the fourth suite with its end, a procedure anticipating the creation of the variation suite, with which Peuerl has for long been credited. The five-part texture of his suites is paralleled not only in those of Peuerl but in those of many other composers of the time. Thesselius wrote his suites in a wide range of keys and arranged them in pairs, in four of which the keys are a 5th apart: D/G, D minor/G minor, E major/A minor and C/F; the fourth pair, in C/B♭, is the exception. In such a scheme can be seen the hesitant beginnings of the principle of the cycle of 5ths, which became such a fundamental feature of Baroque music.

FRIEDRICH BASER

Thessier, Charles. *See* TESSIER, CHARLES.

Thessier, Guillaume. *See* TESSIER, GUILLAUME.

Thévenard, Gabriel-Vincent (*b* Orleans or Paris, 10 Aug 1669; *d* Paris, 24 Aug 1741). French singer. He went to Paris in 1690 and was a pupil of Destouches, who wrote several roles for him including Hylas in *Issé* (1698) and Amadis in *Amadis de Grèce* (1699). A member of the Académie Royale de Musique, he performed for over 30 years in some 80 *tragédies* and ballets, including premières of works by Campra, Collasse, Desmarets and Marais, as well as revivals of works by Lully. He frequently portrayed the role of a king, god or a grand priest (his *basse-taille* range was approximately *G* to *e′*) and was admired for the character and nobility which he imparted, and particularly for his ability to declaim recitative in a speech-like manner; in the words of Titon du Tillet:

Sa voix était sonore, moelleuse, étendue; il grasseyait un peu, mais, par son art, il trouvait moyen de faire un agrément de ce défaut. Jamais musicien n'a mieux entendu l'art de chanter. C'est à lui que l'on doit la manière naturelle et coulante de débiter le recitative, sans le faire languir en appuyant sur les tons pour faire valoir sa voix.

He excelled at tragic roles in which, especially in the works of Destouches, he often performed an emotional lament as a monologue. His duets with Mlle Journet, famous for her portrayal of tender roles, were much appreciated (such as 'Que j'éprouve un supplice horrible', the duet for Peleus and Alcyone in Marais' *Alcione*, 1706).

He was described as 'robust' (Noinville) and enjoyed drinking, which, he said, strengthened his voice. In 1729, when nearly 60, he married a young girl and retired from the opera. According to Campardon and others, his birthplace was Orleans, but an engraving of him by G. F. Schmidt after a painting by Geuslain gives Paris.

BIBLIOGRAPHY

[L. Travenol and J. B. Durey de Noinville]: *Histoire du Théâtre de l'Académie royale de musique en France* (Paris, 2/1757)

E. Campardon: *L'Académie royale de musique au XVIIIᵉ siècle* (Paris, 1884)

MARY CYR

Thiard, Pontus de. See TYARD, PONTUS DE.

Thibaud, Jacques (*b* Bordeaux, 27 Sept 1880; *d* Mont Cemet, nr. Barcelonette, 1 Sept 1953). French violinist. He was first taught the violin by his father, and appeared in public at Bordeaux when he was eight years old. At 13 his precocious talent took him to the Paris Conservatoire, where he studied with Marsick and graduated with a *premier prix* in 1896. Working at the Left Bank Café Rouge, he was heard and engaged by Edouard Colonne for the Concerts Colonne, in which he appeared some 54 times as a soloist in winter 1898–9, thereby establishing the basis of his reputation. He then began touring widely in Europe, making frequent appearances in Britain, and in the USA from 1903. He formed a trio with his brothers, a pianist and a cellist of ability, but it was as the partner of Cortot and Casals in a famous trio, chiefly active from 1930 to 1935, that he is remembered as an ensemble player. Their 1926 record of Schubert's Piano Trio in B♭ D898 has long been acknowledged a gramophone classic in its unanimity of musical thought and beauty of interpretation; it was reissued in 1972.

Thibaud was distinguished by the silvery purity of his tone and the exquisite polish of his technique, which combined with instinctive warmth of expression in performances that were refined rather than robust. He excelled in Mozart and in works from the French Romantic school. For some years he played a violin by Carlo Bergonzi, and later acquired the Baillot Stradivari. He remained in France throughout World War II, refusing to give concerts in Germany, but in 1943, with the pianist Marguerite Long, founded the

Marguerite Long–Jacques Thibaud Competition, which from 1946 has been a biennial international competition for violinists and pianists. Thibaud never retired; he appeared in London when he was over 70 and gave his last concert at Biarritz ten days before he was killed in an air crash on his way to a concert tour in the Far East.

BIBLIOGRAPHY

J.-P. Dorian, ed.: *Un violon parle: souvenirs de Jacques Thibaud* (Paris, 1947)

H. Jourdan-Morhange: 'Jacques Thibaud: souvenirs', *ReM* (1959), no.245, p.17 [special issue on the Concours Marguerite Long–Jacques Thibaud, with discography of 78-r.p.m. discs]

J. Creighton: *Discopaedia of the Violin, 1889–1971* (Toronto, 1974)

W. W. COBBETT/NOËL GOODWIN

Thibaud, Pierre (Jacques) (*b* Sarlat, Dordogne, 22 June 1929). French trumpeter. He studied the violin at the Bordeaux Conservatory and won a *premier prix* for the trumpet at the Paris Conservatoire at the age of 18, after only one year's study with Eugène Foveau. He joined the Israel PO as first trumpeter in 1960, played with the band of the Garde Républicaine from 1964 to 1966, and became first trumpeter of the Paris Opéra in 1966. He is also active as a soloist and has made a number of recordings. His method of playing is based on a particularly low breath support derived from the *hara* of karate, a head and throat position similar to the singer's falsetto, relaxed lips and precise articulation with the syllable 'ta'.

EDWARD H. TARR

Thibault, Geneviève [La Comtesse Hubert de Chambure] (*b* Neuilly-sur-Seine, 20 May 1902; *d* Strasbourg, 31 Aug 1975). French musicologist. She was a pupil of Lazare Lévy (piano, 1912–20), Eugène Cools (harmony and counterpoint, 1915–20) and Nadia Boulanger (fugue and organ, 1917–23) and also studied at the Sorbonne (1918–25, diplôme d'Etudes Supérieures 1920) and at the Ecole des Hautes Etudes (diploma 1952) and was supervised by Pirro. She did research on 15th-century French song for her dissertations: an edition of the *Chansonnier de Jean de Montchenu* with a historical introduction, and *La chanson française et la musique instrumentale de 1450 à 1550*. Many of her other publications deal with the same subject. From 1923 she also developed an interest in old instruments; in 1925, with Lionel de La Laurencie, Georges Le Cerf and Eugénie Droz she founded the Société de Musique d'Autrefois whose aim is to perform early music on authentic instruments and (from 1954) to publish Textes Musicaux and a review devoted to music of the Middle Ages and the Renaissance, *Annales musicologiques*. She succeeded Georges Migot as keeper of the instrument museum of the Paris Conservatoire (1961–73) and in 1968 became president of the Comité International des Musées et Collections d'Instruments de Musique (CIMCIM). She accumulated a fine collection of old instruments and an invaluable library of 15th- and 16th-century manuscripts and editions, and of works of music, which she kept at the disposal of musicians and scholars. She was a member of the Société Française de Musicologie and served as its president from 1968 to 1971.

WRITINGS

'Quelques chansons de Dufay', *RdM*, v (1924), 97

with E. Droz: 'Un chansonnier de Philippe le Bon', *RdM*, vii (1926), 2

'Un manuscrit de chansons françaises à la bibliothèque royale de La Haye', *Gedenkboek aangeboden aan Dr D. F. Scheurleer* (The Hague, 1926), 347

'Deux catalogues de libraires musicaux: Vincenti et Gardane (Venise 1591)', *RdM*, x (1929), 177; xi (1930), 7

'Les amours de P. de Ronsard mises en musique par Jehan de Maletty (1578)', *Mélanges de musicologie offerts à M. Lionel de La Laurencie* (Paris, 1933), 61

'Antoine de Bertrand, musicien de Ronsard, et ses amis toulousains', *Mélanges offerts à M. Abel Lefranc* (Paris, 1936), 282

with L. Perceau: *Bibliographie des poésies de P. de Ronsard mises en musique au XVIᵉ siècle* (Paris, 1941)

with F. Lesure: 'Bibliographie des éditions musicales publiées par Nicolas du Chemin (1549–1576)', *AnnM*, i (1953), 269; supplements in iv (1956), 251; vi (1958–63), 403

'Musique et poésie en France au XVIᵉ siècle avant les *Amours* de Ronsard', *Musique et poésie au XVIᵉ siècle: CRNS Paris 1953*, 79

'Le concert instrumental au XVᵉ siècle', *La musique instrumentale de la Renaissance I: CNRS Paris 1954*, 23

'Le concert instrumental dans l'art flamand au XVᵉ siècle et au début du XVIᵉ siècle', *La Renaissance dans les provinces du Nord: CNRS Entretiens d'Arras 1954*, 197

with F. Lesure: *Bibliographie des éditions d'Adrian Le Roy et Robert Ballard (1551–1598)* (Paris, 1955); suppl. in *RdM*, xl (1957), 166

'Un manuscrit italien pour luth des premières années du XVIᵉ siècle', *Le luth et sa musique: CNRS Neuilly-sur-Seine 1957*, 43

'Le XVᵉ siècle', *Précis de musicologie*, ed. J. Chailley (Paris, 1958), 152–90

'La chanson française au XVᵉ siècle de Dufay à Josquin des Prés (1420–1480)', 'La musique instrumentale au XVIᵉ siècle, Italie–Allemagne–France', *Histoire de la musique*, i, ed. Roland-Manuel [pseud. of R. A. M. Levy] (Paris, 1960), 890–944, 1196–1336

'Les collections privées de livres et d'instruments de musique d'autrefois et d'aujourd'hui', *HMYB*, xi (1961), 131

'L'ornementation dans la musique profane au Moyen-Age', *IMSCR, viii New York 1961*, 450

'Les instruments du Moyen-Age à la fin du XVIIIᵉ siècle', *La musique: les hommes, les instruments, les oeuvres* (Paris, 1965)

with A. Berner and J. H. van der Meer: *Preservation and Restoration of Musical Instruments* (London, 1967)

'Emblèmes et devises de Visconti dans les oeuvres musicales du Trecento', *L'ars nova italiana del Trecento II: Certaldo 1969*, 131

'Instrumental Transcriptions of Josquin's French Chansons', *Josquin des Prez: New York 1971*, 455

'Marc Pincherle (1888–1974)', *ReM*, lxi (1975), 169

EDITIONS

with E. Droz: *Poètes et musiciens du XVᵉ siècle* (Paris, 1924)

with E. Droz and Y. Rokseth: *Trois chansonniers français du XVᵉ siècle* (Paris, 1927/R1977)

with A. Maire and L. de La Laurencie: *Chansons au luth et airs de cour français du XVIᵉ siècle*, Société française de musicologie, i/3–4 (Paris, 1934)

with J. Porcher and D. Fallows: *Le chansonnier de Jean de Montchenu*, PSFM (in preparation)

BIBLIOGRAPHY

J. Jenkins: 'Geneviève Thibault, Madame H. de Chambure: an Appreciation', *Early Music*, iv (1976), 39

CHRISTIANE SPIETH-WEISSENBACHER

Thibault de Courville, Joachim. See COURVILLE, JOACHIM THIBAULT DE.

Thibaut IV (*b* Troyes, 30 May 1201; *d* Pamplona, 7 July 1253). Count of Champagne and Brie, King of Navarre. He was one of the most important of the northern French trouvères, with a larger surviving output of poetry and music than any other trouvère. His grandmother, Marie of France, patroness of Gace Brulé, Conon de Béthune, and Chrétien de Troyes, was a daughter of King Louis VII and Eleanor of Aquitaine. His mother, Blanche of Navarre, was the daughter of King Sancho VI. His father, Thibaut III, had been named head of the 4th crusade, but died suddenly on 24 May 1201, before departure. To obtain the protection of King Philippe Auguste, his mother contracted that Thibaut IV should spend four years at court and should pay homage to the king when he came of age. But because he was born only after his father's death, Thibaut's titles were twice challenged – in 1221 by Erard de Béthune and his wife Philippine, and in 1233 by Alix, Queen of Cyprus.

Thibaut was present at the battle of Bouvines (1214)

and took part in the siege of La Rochelle in 1224 in the war against the English. He fulfilled his duties as vassal at the siege of Avignon in 1226, but then left secretly against the wishes of Louis VIII. He refused to attend the coronation of Louis IX late that year, and joined a league of powerful nobles opposed to the regent, Queen Blanche of Castile. His submission and that of the Count of Bar was speedily enforced. This aroused the enmity of his former allies, who invaded Champagne and retired only after the threat of royal intervention. The bitter feelings were aired in sirventes by Hues de la Ferté.

Thibaut was crowned King of Navarre on 7 or 8 May 1234, after the death of his uncle, Sancho the Strong. His efforts to regain fiefs sold to the royal house to meet the settlement granted to Alix of Cyprus were frustrated.

In 1239 he left France for the Holy Land as the head of a crusade and, after visiting Jerusalem, returned the following year. He supported the French against the English in 1242, and in 1244 lost a battle in Gascony against English forces led by Nicolas de Molis. His headstrong, authoritarian attitudes led to quarrels with the clergy resulting in an interdiction, lifted after a 1248 pilgrimage to Rome. He married three times.

Thibaut's work was mentioned in the *Grandes chroniques de France*, and by Dante, by the theorist Johannes de Grocheo and by the Minnesinger Wahsmuot von Mülnhûsen. Quotations appear in Girardin d'Amiens' *Meliacin* and in Matfre Ermengau's *Perilhos tractat*.

Prolific and versatile, Thibaut wrote not only *chansons courtoises* but also *chansons de croisade*, jeux-partis, *débats*, pastourelles and religious works, including a lai, a serventois, and chansons to the Virgin. His poetry exhibits a wide variety of strophic structures, most strophes being isometric (many of them in decasyllables) but some having several different line lengths. His chansons normally contain five strophes, his jeux-partis six. Four works each use a fixed refrain and one has a variable refrain. The device of re-using the same strophic form for three pairs of chanson, and for one of these pairs using the same melody also (*Sire, loez moi a loisir*), is unusual for the period – parallels may be found in the work of Richart de Semilli and Moniot d'Arras. Most of the jeux-partis draw on poetic structures and melodies of older poems. It is possible that neither of the extant melodies to *Baudouin, il sont dui amant* was Thibaut's and that this jeu-parti was intended to use the melody to Bernart de Ventadorn's *Quan vei la lauzeta mover*. In turn, several of Thibaut's works (*De bone amour, Empereres ne rois, Tant ai Amours, Ausi com l'unicorne* and *Tuit mi desir*) served as models for later chansons, one of them being imitated three times.

Most of Thibaut's melodies are cast in bar form. However, some (*Une doulours enossee, A envis sent mal, Savés pour quoi Amors* and *Ausi com l'unicorne*) are non-repetitive, while others (*Li dous penser, Je ne puis pas bien metre, Li rossignous, Au tens plain de felonie*) contain unorthodox repetitions. *Pour mal tens* and *Robert, veez de Pieron* use forms characteristic of the rotrouenge. *Ausi com l'unicorne*, cited by Grocheo as 'cantus coronatus', begins near the peak of its range, defines the upper tetrachord in the first two phrases and the lower pentachord in the next two, cadencing on the ۔owest note and creating a momentary impression of finality. The remaining phrases explore primarily the upper tetrachord, ending on its lowest tone. *Chanter m'estuet*, cited by Grocheo as a *cantus versualis*, is a simpler, more symmetrical tune which moves primarily within the pentachord above the final. Like a large number of his melodies, these two are in the modes on G; Thibaut has in fact a clear preference for modes with a major 3rd above the final. (Except for melodies ending on F, he preferred authentic to plagal forms.) The nearly syllabic settings of these two songs, punctuated by brief cadential flourishes, are representative of many works. He normally began on or just above the final and expanded the melody upwards. Examples that descend from the 7th or octave (*De novel*, *Qui plus aime*, some versions of *En chantant veul*) are rare. Often the manuscript sources are divergent in essential features of modality. For example, the refrain of *Pour mal tens* ends on four different notes in five of its sources, and is lacking altogether in a sixth, causing still another note to appear as final. While most melodies by Thibaut make clear the importance of the final as the main tonal centre, some are ambiguous or even misleading. Most remain within the range of a 7th, 8th or 9th, but a few extend to an 11th. Mensural rhythm is indicated in about 20 melodies. *Dieus est ensi* is notated in first rhythmic mode in one source (*F-Pn* 12615). Many of the remaining examples, in *Pn* fr.846, show inconsistencies and contradictions in the notation. Disposition of patterns in some melodies sometimes hints that modal interpretation may be acceptable for other tunes.

WORKS

Edition: *Las canciones del Rey Teobaldo*, ed. H. Anglès (Pamplona, 1973)

(V) etc   MS (using Schwan sigla – *see* SOURCES, MS) in which a late setting of a poem occurs; when the letter appears in italics, the original setting cannot be identified with certainty.

A envis sent mal qui ne l'a apris, R.1521
Amours me fait comencier, R.1268
Ausi com l'unicorne sui, R.2075 [model for: Anon., 'De fin cuer et d'aigre talent', R.734; Jaque de Cambrai, 'Haute dame, com rose et lis', R.1563]; ed in Maillard
Au tens plain de felonie (chanson de croisade), R.1152 (written 1239)
Chancon ferai, que talent m'en est pris, R.1596
Chanter m'estuet, que ne m'en puis tenir, R.1476
Comencerai (lai), R.73a = 84; ed. in Maillard
Contre le tens qui debrise, R.1620
Costume est bien, quant on tient un prison, R.1880
Dame, ensi est qu'il m'en convient aler (chanson de croisade), R.757 (V)
Dame, l'on dit que l'on muert bien de joie, R.1727 (V)
De bone amour vient science et bonté, R.407 [model for: Anon., 'Vivre tous tens et chascun jor morir', R.1431]; ed. in Mw, ii, 33
De chanter ne me puis tenir (chanson à la vierge), R.1475 [modelled on: Thibaut de Blaison, 'Amours, que pora devenir', R.1402] (V)
De grant joie me sui tout esmeüs, R.2126
De grant travail et de petit esploit (chanson à la vierge), R.1843
De ma dame souvenir, R.1467
De novel m'estuet chanter, R.808
De tous maus n'est nus plaisans, R.275
Dieus est ensi conme est li pelicans (religious serventois), R.273 (V); ed. in Vander Werf, 122
Douce dame, mal a autre pensement, R.714
Du tres douc nom a la vierge Marie (chanson à la vierge), R.1181
Empereres ne rois n'ont nul pooir/Encontre, R.1811 [model for: 'Empereor ne roi n'ont nul pooir', R.1811a]
En chantant veul ma dolor descovrir, R.1397
Fueille ne flour ne vaut riens en chantant, R.324 = 329 (V)
J'aloie l'autrier errant (pastourelle), R.342
Je me cuidoie partir, R.1440
Je ne puis pas bien metre en nonchaloir, R.1800 (a)
Je ne voi mais nului qui gieut ne chant, R.315
L'autrier par la matinee (pastourelle), R.529
Les douces douleurs, R.2032 (V)
Li dous penser et li dous souvenir (chanson de croisade), R.1469 (written 1239–40; both settings in R)
Li rossignous chante tant, R.360 (O, R f.72)
Mauvais arbres ne puet florir (chanson à la vierge), R.1410 [modelled on: 'Sire, loez moi a loisir', R.1423a = 1393]

Nus hon ne puet ami reconforter, R.884
Por ce se d'amer me deuil, R.996 (a)
Pour conforter ma pesance, R.237
Pour froidure ne pour iver felon, R.1865
Pour mal tens ne pour gelee/Ne pour, R.523
Qui plus aime, plus endure, R.2095
Savés pour quoi Amors a non 'amors', R.2026
Seignor, sachiés, qui or ne s'en ira (chanson de croisade), R.6 (written 1235–9)
Tant ai Amours servies longuement, R.711 [model for: Anon., 'Tant ai servi le monde longuement', R.709a; Adam de la Bassée, 'Ave gemma quae lucis copia', Analecta hymnica medii aevi, xlviii, 300] (A)
Tout autresi com fraint nois et ivers, R.906
Tout autresi con l'ente fait venir, R.1479 (R)
Tuit mi desir et tuit mi grief tourment, R.741 = 991 [model for: Anon., 'Quant je plus pens a comencier chanson', R.1856; model for music of: Jehan de Maisons, 'Lo clar tems vei brunezir', R.1902; Anon., 'Quant fine iver que cil arbre sont nu', R.2057] (R)
Une chancon encor veuil, R.1002
Une doulours enossee, R.510 (R, V)

WORKS OF JOINT AUTHORSHIP

Baudouin, il sont dui amant (jeu-parti), R.294 (*A*, *a*)
Bon rois Thibaut, en chantant respondés (jeu-parti), R.943 [modelled on: Chastelain de Couci, 'Merci clamant de mon fol errement', R.671 = 1823] (V); ed. in Vander Werf, 126
Bon rois Thibaut, sire, conseilliez moi (jeu-parti proposed by a 'clerc'), R.1666 [model for: Raoul de Soissons, 'Rois de Navare et sire de vertu', R.2063; Oede de la Couroierie, 'Ma derreniere veul fere en chantant', R.321] (V)
Cuens, je vous part un gieu par aatie (jeu-parti), R.1097 [modelled on: Blondel de Nesle, 'Quant je plus sui en paor de vie', R.1227]
Dame, merci, une rien vous demant (tenson), R.335 (V)
Girard d'Amiens, Amours qui a pooir (jeu-parti), R.1804 [text only]
L'autre jour en mon dormant (débat), R.339
Par Dieu, sire de Champaigne et de Brie (dialogue with Philipe de Nanteuil), R.1111 (V)
Phelipe, je vous demant/Ce qu'est (tenson), R.333 [modelled on: Raimon Jordan, 'Lo clar tems vei brunezir', PC 404.4; model for: Guillaume li Vinier, 'Vierge pucele roiaus', R.388; Anon., 'A la mere Deu servir', R.1459] (R, V)
Phelipe, je vous demant/Dui amant (débat), R.334 [modelled on: Moniot d'Arras, 'Ne me dones pas talent', R.739] (R, V)
Robert, veez de Pieron (tenson), R.1878 (V)
Sire, loez moi a loisir (jeu-parti), R.1423a = 1393 (with Raoul de Soissons) [model for: 'Mauvais arbres ne puet florir', R.1410] (V)
Sire, ne me celés mie (tenson), R.1185 (A, V)
Une chose, Baudouin, vous demant (jeu-parti), R.332 [modelled on: Chastelain de Couci, 'Je chantasse volontiers liement', R.700] [text only]

WORKS OF UNCERTAIN AUTHORSHIP

Dame, li vostres fins amis, R.1516 (also ascribed to Gace Brulé)
De bone Amour et de loial amie/Vaurai chanter, R.1102a [modelled on: Gace Brulé, 'De bone Amour et de loial amie/Me vient', R.1102]
Je n'os chanter trop tart ne trop souvent, R.733 (V) (also ascribed to Jehan de Braine)
Quant Amours vit que je li aloignoie (tenson), R.1684 [text only]
Tres haute Amours qui tant s'est abessie, R.1098 (also ascribed to Perrin d'Angicourt)

WORKS OF DOUBTFUL AUTHORSHIP

Bele et blonde est cele pour qui je chant, R.308 (also ascribed to Chastelain d'Arras)
Bone dame me prie de chanter, R.790a (also ascribed to Gace Brulé and Jehan de Trie)
Ne rose ne flour de lis, R.1562 (R)
Poine d'amours et li maus que j'en trai, R.106 (R)

BIBLIOGRAPHY

Lesveque de la Ravallière: *Les poésies du roi de Navarre, avec des notes et un glossaire françois* (Paris, 1742) [edn. of texts]
J. Stafford Smith: *Musica antiqua* (London, 1812)
P. Tarbé: *Chansons de Thibaut IV, comte de Champagne et de Brie, roi de Navarre* (Rheims, 1851) [edn. of texts]
J. Bédier and P. Aubry: *Les chansons de croisade* (Paris, 1909)
A. Wallensköld: *Les chansons de Thibaut de Champagne, roi de Navarre* (Paris, 1925)
F. Gennrich: 'Thibaut IV', *MGG*
J. Maillard: *Anthologie de chants de trouvères* (Paris, 1967)
H. Vander Werf: *The Chansons of the Troubadours and Trouvères: a Study of the Melodies and their Relation to the Poems* (Utrecht, 1972), 122ff

For further bibliography *see* TROUBADOURS, TROUVÈRES.

THEODORE KARP

Thibaut, Anton Friedrich Justus (*b* Hameln, 4 Jan 1772; *d* Heidelberg, 28 March 1840). German legal scholar and amateur musician. After leaving the Gymnasium in Hanover, he began to study law in 1792 at the University of Göttingen, where he may have heard Forkel lecture. In the next year he moved to Königsberg to hear Kant, and in 1794 went to Kiel where he took the doctorate in law (1796) and formed a lasting friendship with Niebuhr. He was appointed professor in 1798 and four years later was called to Jena, where he met Schiller and wrote his principal legal work, *System des Pandektenrechts*. He moved to Heidelberg in 1805 to assume a chair of law and remained there for the rest of his life. The War of Liberation inspired him to write a collection of essays in 1814 urging codification of German laws: he was challenged by Savigny in a treatise which formulated the leading ideas of the historical school of law.

While in Jena Thibaut began collecting sacred vocal music and folksongs; with Ett and Klein generously contributing copies of works from several European libraries, the collection became one of the largest of its kind in Germany and attracted the attention of Zelter and Kiesewetter. In 1811 Thibaut assumed the direction of a small Heidelberg amateur chorus with which he gave annually about four concerts of works from the 16th to 18th centuries, trying to stimulate an appreciation for earlier music. As the chorus grew in size and reputation its otherwise private weekly rehearsals were occasionally attended by such figures as Goethe, Tieck, Mendelssohn and Schumann. Thibaut's most influential musical achievement was his book *Über Reinheit der Tonkunst* (1825), which is comparable to the writings of Baini and Kiesewetter in the importance of its contribution to early 19th-century Cecilian reforms. In this work, which was criticized by Nägeli, Thibaut expressed ideas similar to those of Hoffmann and Reichardt, arguing that the declining contemporary musical tastes could best be refined through study of older sacred choral music, especially that of Palestrina and Handel and their contemporaries.

WRITINGS

Über Reinheit der Tonkunst (Heidelberg, 1825, rev., enlarged 2/1826, 8/1907, ed. R. Heuler; Eng. trans., 1877)

BIBLIOGRAPHY

E. Baumstark: *A. Fr. J. Thibaut* (Leipzig, 1841)
W. von Waldbrühl [pseud. of A. W. F. von Zuccalmaglio]: 'Thibaut', *ZfM*, Jg.108 (1941), 1, 5
W. Ehmann: 'Der Thibaut–Behagel-Kreis', *AMf*, iii (1938), 428–83; iv (1939), 21–67
——, ed.: 'Musikalische Briefe A. F. J. Thibauts', *Neue Heidelberger Jb*, new ser. (1939), 9–48

RICHARD D. GREEN

Thibaut, Jean-Baptiste (*b* St Etienne, Loire, 5 Oct 1872; *d* Lorques, Varennes, 7 April 1938). French writer on Byzantine music. In 1891 he joined the Assumptionists and began to study Byzantine music, an interest developed during his long residence in the east. In 1900 he was ordained priest in Constantinople; thereafter he lived in Jerusalem, several Turkish and Bulgarian cities, Odessa (1907–11) and St Petersburg (1911–14). During World War I he worked as an army chaplain, returning to Turkey in 1920. He retired to France in 1922.

Thibaut was the first scholar to make a systematic investigation of Byzantine musical notation and to try to deduce the origin of Latin neumes from Constantinople. He divided Byzantine notation from the 11th to the 18th centuries into three phases, of which the first originated in Constantinople, the second in Jerusalem and the third was invented by Koukouzeles. His studies were based on MSS from all periods of which he edited an impor-

tant collection. Together with J. B. Rebours he also edited several treatises on Byzantine musical theory, but he was unable to decipher the notation.

WRITINGS

'La notation de Saint Jean Damascene ou Hagiopolite', *Ruskiy arkheologicheskiy institut: Izvestiya*, iv (Constantinople, 1898), 138–79
'La musique byzantine et le chant liturgique des Grecs modernes', *Echos d'Orient*, ii (1898), 353
'Etude de musique byzantine: le chant ekphonétique', *Byzantinische Zeitschrift*, viii (1899), 122
'Les traités de musique byzantine', *Byzantinische Zeitschrift*, ix (1900), 479
'Etude de musique byzantine: la notation de Koukouzéles', *Ruskiy arkheologicheskiy institut: Izvestiya*, vi (Constantinople, 1900), 361–90
'Les orgues à Byzance', *RHCM*, i (1901), 17
'Les notations byzantines', *RHCM*, i (1901), 102
'Le système tonal de l'Eglise grecque', *RHCM*, ii (1902), 43
'La musique byzantine chez les Slaves', *Tribune de St. Gervais*, x (1904), 157
Origine byzantine de la notation neumatique de l'Eglise latine (Paris, 1907/R1975)
Monuments de la notation ekphonétique et neumatique de l'Eglise latine: exposé documentaire des manuscrits de Corbie, de S. Germain des Prés et de Cologne, conservés à la Bibliothèque Impériale de St. Petersbourg (St Petersburg, 1912/R1976)
Monuments de la notation ekphonétique et hagiopolite de l'Eglise grecque: exposé documentaire des manuscrits de Jérusalem, du Sinaï et de l'Athos, conservés à la Bibliothèque Impériale de S. Petersbourg (St Petersburg, 1913)
La liturgie romaine: la liturgie primitive et le grand Hallel: liturgie romaine-grecque: liturgie romaine-africaine: liturgie romaine-latine (Paris, 1924)

BIBLIOGRAPHY

E. Wellesz: *A History of Byzantine Music and Hymnography* (Oxford, rev. 2/1961) [includes bibliography]

NANNA SCHIØDT

Thibaut de Blaison [Blason, Blazon] (*d* after March 1229). French trouvère. He was Seneschal of Poitou, and of a noble family with holdings in Blason and Mirabel; his uncle, Maurice, was Bishop of Poitiers. Thibaut was among the negotiators of the truce of 1214 between King Philip Augustus of France and King John of England. Together with Hues de la Ferté, he was among the nobles at the coronation of Louis IX (St Louis). He took part in a crusade against the Moors in 1212, and participated in the siege of Toulouse in 1218 during the Albigensian crusade. His name appears with that of Amauri de Craon (also a trouvère) in a document of 1219. Thibaut IV, King of Navarre, dedicated a song, *De ma dame souvenir* (R.1467) to Thibaut de Blaison; he also based a religious poem (R.1475) on the structure and melody of Thibaut de Blaison's *Amours, que porra devenir*. The melody of Gautier d'Espinal's song (R.1059) is also taken from the latter. The rhythms of the polyphonic conductus *Quid frustra consumeris* and *Sol sub nube latuit* may perhaps have some validity as the basis for *Bien font amours lor talent* and *Chanter et renvoisier seuil*.

11 poems, including one of contested authorship and one spurious, have been ascribed to Thibaut de Blaison in trouvère and troubadour MSS; the anonymous items may also be his work. Thibaut's songs display a preference for simpler poetic constructions, containing at most one change in line length; *Bien font amours, Bon jour ait hui cele* and *Quant je voi esté venir* are nevertheless more varied. The use in three chansons of *ouvert* and *clos* endings within each *pes* and the use of earlier material or symmetrical repetition within the cauda are among the distinctive traits of Thibaut's melodic structures, all in bar form. *Amours que porra devenir*, *Chanter et renvoisier seuil* and *Huimain par un ajourant* remain within the range of a 6th; this interval is

exceeded only once in *Li miens chanters*. Other melodies move more freely. (The simple restricted movement of *Bien fait amours* accords with Thibaut's style, but is in contrast to the more flamboyant melodies of Gautier de Dargies, to whom the piece is also attributed.) In *F-Pn* fr.846 (Chansonnier Cangé), the first six lines of *Quant je voi esté venir* are notated in the first mode; however, mensural indications are lacking for all other pieces. Most melodies are comparatively syllabic, although *Li miens chanters* is moderately ornate.

See also TROUBADOURS, TROUVÈRES.

WORKS

Abbreviations:
(V) etc MS (using Schwan sigla – *see* SOURCES, MS) in which a late setting of a poem occurs
(nm) No music

Amours, que porra devenir, R.1402 [model for: Thibault IV', 'De chanter ne me puis tenir', R.1475; Gautier d'Espinal, 'Se par force de merci', R.1059 (different poetic structure)], Gennrich, *Die Kontrafaktur im Liedschaffen des Mittelalters*, 224 (V)
Bien font amours lor talent, R.738 [contrafactum: Anon., 'Quid frustra consumeris'; model for: Anon., 'C'est en mai, au mois d'esté', R.439a = 1979]
Bien voi que ne puis morir, R.1433(= 1418) (V)
Bon jour ait hui cele a cui sui amis, R.1519 (nm)
Chanter et renvoisier seuil, R.1001 [contrafacta: Anon., 'Sol sub nube latuit'; Gautier de Coinci, 'Pour mon chief reconforter', R.885], Chailley, *Les chansons à la vierge de Gautier de Coinci*, no.17 (V)
Chanter m'estuet, si crien morir, R.1430 (V)
Huimain par un ajourant, R.293 (V)
Li miens chanters ne puet mais remanoir, R.1813
Quant je voi esté venir, R.1477(= 1488) (V)
Quant se resjouissent oisel, R.584 (nm)

(anonymous, now attrib. Thibaut)

Avant ier me chevauchoi, Motet no.402
Avant ier me chevauchoie, R.1705 (nm)
En avril au tens nouvel, R.575

BIBLIOGRAPHY

A. Pinguet: *Les chansons et pastourelles de Thibaut de Blaison* (Angers, 1930)

For further bibliography *see* TROUBADOURS, TROUVÈRES.

THEODORE KARP

Thibouville. French family of instrument makers. The best-known member is (Louis Emile) Jérôme Thibouville-Lamy (*b* Mouettes, 1 Feb 1833; *d* after 1890), who from about 1857 had worked with the firm Husson, Buthod & Thibouville, forming his own firm eight years later. He was one of the first to recognize the importance of mechanization and mass-production, resulting in lower-priced instruments. In the Vienna exhibition of 1873 he presented violins for five, ten and 20 francs. At its height his firm had three factories, one for brass instruments at Grenelle (founded 1865), one for woodwind at La Couture and one for strings at Mirecourt, where it founded a trade school in 1890.

The firm's C trumpets gradually replaced the old orchestral F trumpet from about 1880. The leading C trumpets of the Paris Conservatoire, under the professorship of Merri Franquin, were made by Thibouville-Lamy until their monopoly passed to Couesnon, probably in the late 1920s. With Franquin the firm started experiments in 1905 on a four-valve trumpet (an unsatisfactory one was first brought out by Millereau in 1888) and presented it in 1912. The fourth valve was an ascending whole-tone valve which simplified the fingerings and improved the intonation of several notes; C trumpets on the same principle were built by Tottle (Boston) until his death in 1976. In 1916, after a year of testing, they presented a trumpet with a fifth valve, which put the instrument into A, but this was never generally adopted. The firm was also the first to manufacture horns in F/B♭ with an ascending third valve, as designed about 1928 by Louis Vuillermoz. The Thibouville-Lamy factory was disbanded in 1961 by its last president, A. E. Acoulon (*b* 1887); the firm continues in London, selling instrument accessories.

Other important makers of the Thibouville family include Martin Thibouville, who in 1820 founded a woodwind instrument factory in La Couture; he opened a Paris shop before 1848. Notable instruments made by him include a metal double bassoon and a wooden Boehm-system flute with a metal head (1888). His son, Martin Victor Gustave Thibouville (*b* Tilly, 1856), headed the Paris shop and was succeeded by E. Bercioux (1820–1914). Louis, Nicolas and Pierre Thibouville were partners in Thibouville Frères, woodwind instrument makers at La Couture. Their firm branched into two: under Pierre as Thibouville–Hérouard (1842) and under Nicolas as Thibouville–Buffet (before 1873). Pierre's eldest son remained at La Couture, and another, Jean-Baptiste Thibouville (*b* 4 May 1832), founded a shop in Paris and revived the name Thibouville Frères which still existed in 1950. Thibouville–Béranger was formed in 1864 when Pierre's eldest son died and was replaced by his cousin Béranger (a son-in-law of Nicolas Thibouville), but he died the following year. The firm became Thibouville–Cabart in 1869 and moved to Ezy about 1880, where its factory used steam power; the firm was famous for its clarinets and oboes, and about 1893 the quality instruments were given the abbreviated name 'Cabart'. The firm continued into the 1970s.

André Thibouville (*b* La Couture, 1831), a woodwind instrument maker, succeeded Paul Bié and François Lefèvre in 1886 as head of the firm A. Thibouville & Cie at La Couture. His two sons, Désiré (*b* 1861) and Henri (*b* 1863), were partners. Later Désiré took over the firm's Paris shop and Henri the La Couture factory. Two other firms run by members of the Thibouville family include Thibouville–Coudevillain, successors to Isidore Lot, who added extra trill keys to the Boehm flute in 1886 (they received a bronze medal in the Paris exhibition of 1889), and Eugène Thibouville & Fils, which, formerly at Ivry-la-Bataille, was in Paris in 1855 and moved to La Couture in 1863. Flutes with the attributions 'Thibouville père', 'Thibouville père et fils' and 'Thibouville frère aîné' (all from Paris) are also known, but the connection of these makers with members of the Thibouville family is not known.

BIBLIOGRAPHY

C. Pierre: *La facture instrumentale à l'Exposition universelle de 1889* (Paris, 1890)
——: *Les facteurs d'instruments de musique* (Paris, 1893)
L. Langwill: *An Index of Musical Wind Instrument Makers* (Edinburgh, 1960, rev. 4/1974)
M. Broils: 'The Acoulon Letters', *Trumpets through Time* (MS, New York, 1964), iii, 12

EDWARD H. TARR

Thick, Henricus. See TIK, HENRICUS.

Thiele, Siegfried (*b* Chemnitz, 28 March 1934). German composer. At the Leipzig Hochschule für Musik (1953–8) he studied composition with Wilhelm Weismann and Johannes Weyrauch, and conducting; his studies were completed in Leo Spies's master class at the German Academy of Arts in Berlin. He has lectured at the Leipzig Hochschule für Musik and conducted the Leipzig Youth Orchestra. Awards made to him have included the German Democratic Republic's Mendelssohn Scholarship. His music tends towards concertante writing, and employs tonalities coloured by 12-note procedures.

WORKS
(selective list)

3 Pf Pieces, 1958; Str Qt, 1959; Auferstehungsmusik, chorus, insts, 1961; Tpt Conc., 1961; Wind Qnt, 1962; Urworte-Orphisch (Goethe), chorus 6vv (1962); Pantomime, orch, 1962; Pf Conc., 1962; Sonatine, youth orch (1964); Sym., 1965; Apokalypse, S, chorus, brass, timp, 1966; Octet, 1966; Tokkata, Intermezzo, Perpetuum mobile, pf, 1966; Sonata, str qt, orch, 1967; Introduktion und Tokkata, orch, 1969; Konzertante Etüden, org, 1972; Proportionen, ob, vc, pf (1975); 4 pieces, vc, pf (1977)

Principal publishers: Deutscher Verlag für Musik, Peters (Leipzig)

BIBLIOGRAPHY
E. Kneipel: 'Polarität und Metamorphose: Anmerkungen zu Siegfried Thieles Sinfonie in fünf Sätzen', *Musik und Gesellschaft*, xix (1969), 322

Thielo, Carl August (*b* Copenhagen, 7 Feb 1707; *d* Høsterkøb, 2 Dec 1763). Danish composer, theatre director and writer, of German descent. His father was Johann Hiob Thielo from Erfurt (*c*1685–1735), who as a young man settled in Copenhagen where in 1708 he became organist of the church of Our Saviour. According to his own account (*Grund-Regeln*), the younger Thielo was sent to Germany to learn music; from the age of eight until 12 he was taught keyboard and thoroughbass playing in Saxony but not until he became a pupil of J. G. Walther in Weimar did he really make progress. He returned to Copenhagen in 1726 and set himself up as a music teacher. He married in 1733 and in 1735 a daughter, Caroline Amalie, was born; she made her stage début at an early age and by the time of her death under mysterious circumstances at the age of 19 was the most admired actress of her day.

Thielo was organist of the Citadel Church in Copenhagen from 1739 to 1743, where in the latter year he composed and produced a Passion oratorio. In 1744 a musical society was founded and Thielo was asked to provide a book of musical instruction for the members as required by the society's statutes. The result was *Tanker og regler fra grunden af om musik for dem, som vil laere musiken til sindets fornøjelse, saa og for dem, som vil gjøre fait af klaver, general-bassen og synge-kunsten* ('Thoughts and rules providing an introduction for those who wish to learn music to delight the mind, as well as for those who wish to learn keyboard playing, thoroughbass and the art of singing'; Copenhagen, 1746). This book, the first about music in Danish to be published in Copenhagen, provides in addition to its practical information a lively picture of the Copenhagen musical scene in the mid-18th century.

An active member of the musical society was the distinguished dramatist Ludvig Holberg, on whose recommendation Thielo was granted at the end of 1746 a royal privilege to establish a Danish theatre. He gathered a company and in April 1747 the 'Danish Comedy' gave its first performance. Thielo now turned his hand to playwriting as well but with so little success that Holberg condemned his efforts and his actors refused to perform them. He was forced to assign his rights to the actors in return for which he was pensioned at a salary equal to that of the best actors. He continued to be actively associated with the theatre in a variety of capacities: music adviser, arranger, accompanist, copy-

ist and composer. This connection provided him with the material for the enterprise for which his name is most remembered today – the publication of a number of collections of theatre music from the first period of 'Syngespil' and opera in Danish. Between 1751 and 1754 he published four collections of *De oder, som paa den Danske Skue-Plads udi Kiøbenhavn ere blevne opførte* ('The odes which have been performed at the Danish Theatre in Copenhagen'). The contents of the first three were to a large extent reprinted in 1755 in three volumes under the title *Musikaliske comødie-stykker* ('Pieces from the musical comedies'), of which a fourth appeared in 1761. In addition Thielo published a collection of German *Oden mit Melodien* (1754), not composed for the theatre, and numerous other pieces of vocal and instrumental music, most of which are now lost. He also published other pedagogical works including a textbook in German, *Grund-Regeln wie man bey weniger Information sich selbst die Fundamenta der Music und des Claviers lernen kan* (1753); a weekly musical magazine containing music by famous foreign composers, as well as himself, together with instructions in playing and singing, of which four issues were advertised in 1756; and a book to teach pastors to chant properly, *Musikalisk underretning at messe for altret* (1762). His literary activities included a series of novels and a weekly paper *Spionen* ('The spy'; 1758), in which he included two of his 'Syngespil'. He applied to the university in 1757 for the title of professor and to Roskilde Cathedral in 1759 for the position of organist, but was unsuccessful in both applications. These disappointments, together with the temporary failure of the Danish opera, apparently decided him to abandon the ungrateful life of musician in the capital city. In 1762 he bought a farm north of Copenhagen, but before he could try this new career, while waiting for a house to be built, he died in Høsterkøb Inn.

BIBLIOGRAPHY
T. Krogh: 'De første forsøg paa at skabe en opera i det danske sprog', *Aarbog for musik 1922*, 123–58
——: 'Aeldre dansk teatermusik', *Musikhistorisk arkiv*, i (Copenhagen, 1931), 1–100
——: 'Thielo, Carl August', *DBL*

JOHN BERGSAGEL

Thieme [Thiem, Thime, Tieme, Time], **Clemens** (*b* Grossdittmannsdorf, nr. Dresden, 7 Sept 1631; *d* Zeitz, 27 March 1668). German composer and instrumentalist. He studied under Philipp Stolle in Dresden, then in 1642 was taken by Schütz to Copenhagen, where he was a choirboy at the court. He returned to Dresden after his voice broke, and began studying various instruments at the expense of the Elector of Saxony. On Schütz's recommendation he joined the elector's Kapelle in 1651. In 1663, after unsuccessfully seeking a post at Hamburg and again with Schütz's help, he entered the Kapelle of Duke Moritz of Saxony at Zeitz, where he rose to become Konzertmeister. Although none of his music was ever published, it enjoyed great popularity in and around Zeitz. Well over 100 titles are known by name, but only 18 have been located. The sonatas are among the best composed in the wake of Rosenmüller's. They are in a pseudo-polyphonic style, as can be seen in the alternation of lively homophony and fugal writing over a firm bass. The structure of the sacred works depends on the alternation of equally balanced choral and solo sections; homophonic, polyphonic and fugal elements again complement each other. The style of these works lies midway between the older contrapuntal style and the more expressive Italianate manner that informs the church music of Schütz's time.

WORKS

1 mass (Ky, Gl), 10vv, 4 vn, bc, *D-B*
1 mass (Ky, Gl), 5vv, 4 va, bn, bc, *S-Uu*
German Magnificat, 6vv, 2 vn, 5 va, 2 clarini, 3 trbn, timp, bc, *D-B*
Nunc dimittis, 4vv, 4 va, bn, bc, *S-Uu*
8 psalm settings: Befiehl dem Herren deine Wege; Danksaget dem Vater; Lobe den Herren; Schaffe in mir, Gott, ein reines Herz: 3vv, insts, *D-B*, *S-Uu*; Beatus vir qui timet Dominum; Laetatus sum in his; Laudate pueri Dominum; Lobe den Herren: several vv, *D-B*, *S-Uu*
1 suite, 2 vn, 2 va, bn/vle, bc, *Uu*
1 sonata, 5 viols, hpd; 1 sonata, 5 va, bc; 1 sonata, 2 vn, 4 va, bc; 1 sonata, 2 vn, 3 va, db, bc: *D-Kl*
1 sonata, 2 vn, 4 va, 2 trombetti/clarini, *S-Uu*

For details of lost works, incl. masses, psalm settings, sonatas, see Buch.

BIBLIOGRAPHY
EitnerQ
W. C. Printz: *Historische Beschreibung der edelen Sing- und Kling-Kunst* (Dresden, 1690), 148
P. Spitta: 'Leichensermon', *MMg*, iii (1871), 38
A. Werner: *Städtische und fürstliche Musikpflege in Zeitz* (Bückeburg and Leipzig, 1922)
E. H. Müller von Asow, ed.: *H. Schütz: Gesammelte Briefe und Schriften* (Regensburg, 1931)
E. H. Meyer: *Die mehrstimmige Spielmusik des 17. Jahrhunderts in Nord- und Mitteleuropa* (Kassel, 1934)
E. Schild: *Die Geschichte der protestantischen Messenkompositionen im 17. und 18. Jahrhundert* (Giessen, 1934)
H. J. Moser: *Heinrich Schütz: sein Leben und Werk* (Kassel, 1936, rev. 2/1954; Eng. trans., 1959)
H. J. Buch: 'Bestandsaufnahme der Kompositionen Clemens Thiemes', *Mf*, xvi (1963), 367

HANS-JOACHIM BUCH

Thiéme, Frédéric [Thieme, Friedrich] (*b* Rheims, 3 June 1750; *d* Rouen, 29 March 1802). French theorist and composer of German origin. From 1780 until the Revolution he taught music in Paris, becoming known both there and in Germany for his pedagogical publications. In 1792 he moved to Rouen where he continued to teach. His writings include *Eléments de musique pratique et solfèges nouveaux* (2/1784), *Eléments de musique . . . avec une basse chiffrée suivant . . . l'abbé Roussier* (n.d.) and *Nouvelle théorie sur les différens mouvemens des airs* (1800–01) as well as didactic works for aspiring pianists and violinists. His only surviving compositions are violin duos.

Thienen, Marcel van (*b* Paris, 3 Oct 1922). French composer. Between 1929 and 1939 he studied in Paris at the Ecole Normale (violin) and the Conservatoire Russe (composition); his violin studies were completed at the Paris Conservatoire (1940). He joined the Resistance in 1941 and his first works were not heard until after the war. In 1954 he was appointed director of the Haiti National Conservatory; on his return to France in 1957 he established a private electronic studio. He won the Italia Prize (1962) for his music for Obaldia's *Le damné*, and shortly thereafter he abandoned music to devote himself to sculpture.

WORKS
(*selective list*)

Conc. grosso, tpt, str orch, 1944; Petite symphonie sur le temps, orch, 1944; Le bal des pendus (Villon), Bar, speaker, str qt, 1945; Sonata à Tortilla Flat, vn, pf, 1948; La ralentie (Michaux), 3 insts, noise generator, 1952; De profundis, vn, tape, 1957; Le damné (Obaldia), S, Bar, actors, male chorus, orch, tape, 1962

DOMINIQUE AMY

Thierri de Soissons (*fl* 1230–60). French trouvère. Four songs (R.1267, R.1978, 2063 and 2107) survive with attributions to both RAOUL DE SOISSONS and Thierri de Soissons, the former being undoubtedly correct. Whether the two men are identical, the name Thierri being an error, is the subject of debate. No 'Thierri' has as yet been traced among the family of the counts of Soissons, but such relationship is perhaps not obligatory. Ascriptions to Thierri appear in *F-Pn* fr.845, which does not make mention of Raoul, and in *F-Pa* 5198, which does. The latter circumstance would argue against the presumed identity were it not for the fact that mention of Thierri occurs as part of a larger series of attributions to trouvères also presented earlier in the MS, precisely in the place where the recurrence of Raoul might be expected. One song attributable to Raoul (R.1154), together with *Destrece de trop amer* and *Quant avril* are all dedicated to Charles, Count of Anjou. *Se j'ai lonc tens* presents an unusual musical structure, *ABCC¹DEFC²C³* (phrase *D* containing some elements of *C*), in the setting of a poem that opens with an *ABBA* rhyme scheme. The disregard in *Sens et raison* of the *pedes*-plus-cauda structure in a non-repetitive musical setting is also noteworthy. The melody for *Destrece de trop amer* has a seldom-used final, *b*, located in the upper portion of a range *d–e'*. It would seem, however, that the number of works known under the names of the two trouvères is too few to permit firm conclusions regarding the existence of two different artistic personalities.

WORKS

(V) etc   MS (using Schwan sigla – *see* SOURCES, MS) in which a late setting of a poem occurs

A la plus sage et a la mieus vaillant, R.363
Amis Harchier, cil autre chanteour, R.1970
Chancon legiere a chanter, R.778 (V)
Chanter m'estuet pour faire contenance, R.211 (V)
Destrece de trop amer, R.767 (V)
Se j'ai lonc tens esté en Romanie, R.1204 (V)
Sens et raison et mesure, R.2106 (V)

DOUBTFUL WORKS
Helas, or ai je trop duré, R.429 (V)
Quant avril et li biaus estés, R.929 (V)

BIBLIOGRAPHY
E. Winkler: *Die Lieder Raouls von Soissons* (Halle, 1914)
For further bibliography *see* TROUBADOURS, TROUVÈRES.

THEODORE KARP

Thierry [Thiéry]. French family of organ builders.

(1) Pierre Thierry (*b* Paris, late 1604; *d* Paris, 28 Oct 1665). He studied music with Florent Bienvenu, organist of the Sainte-Chapelle, and was apprenticed to Valeran de Héman in 1623. Between 1634 and 1636 he worked with Crespin Carlier at St Nicholas-des-Champs. Later he set up on his own and worked at Notre Dame, St Jean and St Gervais, Paris. He added a 4′ stop to the Pedal of the St Gervais organ in 1649; in 1659–60, under the supervision of Louis Couperin, he added to the *Positif* a new 8′ Bourdon, a 4′ Flûte made out of the old Bourdon, a Nazard and a Tierce, as well as a fourth manual (an *Eccho* of three octaves from *c*) placed between those of the *Grand orgue* and the *Cornet séparé* and containing Bourdon et octave, Doublette, Nazard et tierce, Cromhorne and Cimballe. He added the *A* to all the stops of the *Positif* and Pedal, and arranged that the *Grand orgue* to Pedal coupler could be engaged at the discretion of the organist (these changes presumably according to the instructions of Louis Couperin as well).

Thierry's most important work was at the Hôtel-Dieu at Pontoise (1637–41), St Paul, Paris (1644–6), and Les Mathurins (containing the first combined wind-chest for the *Grand orgue* and *Récit*). In 1657, with Desenclos, he introduced a *Grand écho* division of seven stops on the organ at Rouen Cathedral. His masterpiece was the St Germain-des-Prés organ (1661; the *Récit* borrowed several stops from the *Grand orgue* by communication). On the death of Desenclos in 1664 he became *facteur du roi*. In addition to (2) Alexandre Thierry, two of his sons became organ builders: Jean (*b* c1638; *d* Paris, Oct 1689), who built the organ at St Père, Chartres; and Charles (*b* Paris, 15 Nov 1641), whose signature is on a *Trompette* pipe from the St Germain organ (now in the organ at St Merry).

(2) **Alexandre Thierry** (*b* 1646 or 1647; *d* Paris, Dec 1699). Son of (1) Pierre Thierry. With the completion of the organ at St Séverin in 1675, he established himself as the leading French organ builder of his time. The following year he made a new Cornet for the St Gervais *Cornet séparé* manual, replacing the mechanism for borrowing by communication the Cornet of the *Grand orgue*; between 1678 and 1684, he replaced the chorus tierce on the *Grand orgue* by a Quarte de nazard, and the Flageolet on the Positif by a Larigot (soon after used by François Couperin in his famous *Dialogue sur les trompettes . . . et le bourdon avec le larigot du positif*). Other organs by him in Paris include: St Cyr (1685); St Louis-des-Invalides (1679–87: specification in Williams, p.179; survives in part); and St Eustache (1681–9: his masterpiece, incorporating a 16′ *Bombarde*). Towards the end of his life, he worked with Robert Clicquot. His second wife, Marguerite, composed a volume of organ pieces.

(3) **François Thierry** (*b* Paris, late 1677; *d* Paris, 22 May 1749). Son of (2) Alexandre Thierry. He built the organ for Les Innocents, Paris (1723; part now at St Nicholas-du-Chardonnet), and completely reconstructed the organ at Notre Dame, Paris (1730–33; with apparently the first *Bombarde* manual, of Bombarde 16′, two Trompettes 8′ and Clairon 4′, with a coupler to the *Grand orgue*). Andreas Silbermann worked for him between 1704 and 1706.

BIBLIOGRAPHY
F. Raugel: *Les grandes orgues des églises de Paris et du département de la Seine* (Paris, 1927)
P. Brunold: *Le grand orgue de St. Gervais* (Paris, 1934) [incl. transcrs. of detailed contracts with (1) Pierre Thierry, 1649 and 1659; (2) Alexandre Thierry, 1676 and 1692; and (3) François Thierry, 1714]
N. Dufourcq: *Documents inédits relatifs à l'orgue français* (Paris, 1935)
P. Hardouin: *Le grand orgue de Saint Gervais à Paris* (Paris, 1955)
——: 'Le grand orgue de Notre-Dame', *L'orgue* (1958), no.78
P. Williams: *The European Organ 1450–1850* (London, 1966)
GUY OLDHAM

Thiéry. See THIERRY family.

Thies, Albert Christoph. See DIES, ALBERT CHRISTOPH.

Thijs, Johan. See THYSIUS, JOHAN.

Thill, Georges (*b* Paris, 14 Dec 1897). French tenor. After two years' study at the Paris Conservatoire, and two more in Naples with De Lucia, he sang Don José and other roles at the Opéra-Comique before making his début as Nicias in *Thaïs* on 4 February 1924 at the Opéra. There he stayed for 16 years, graduating from the lighter French repertory to Admetus (*Alceste*) and

Aeneas, Parsifal and Tannhäuser, and later Samson. At La Scala and Verona he sang Calaf; Buenos Aires invited him for Don Carlos, Calaf and Boito's Faust. He also sang at the Metropolitan Opera in 1931 and 1932, in Vienna and at Covent Garden. He bade farewell to the stage at the Opéra-Comique as Canio, as late as 1953. With his brilliant, robust tone, his spirited phrasing and aristocratic enunciation, Thill was the most distinguished exponent of the French style in his time. He appeared in several films, the most interesting of which is Abel Gance's *Louise*, with Grace Moore and Pernet.

BIBLIOGRAPHY
R. Celletti: 'Thill, Georges', *Le grandi voci* (Rome, 1964) [with opera discography by T. Kaufmann and R. Vegeto]
R. Mancini: *Georges Thill* (Paris, 1966) [with discography]
ANDRÉ TUBEUF

Thillière, Joseph Bonaventure. See TILLIÈRE, JOSEPH BONAVENTURE.

Thillon [née Hunt], **Sophie Anne** [Anna] (*b* Calcutta or London, 1819; *d* Torquay, 5 May 1903). English soprano. She studied in France with Bordogni, Tadolini and Claude Thomas Thillon, conductor of the Havre Philharmonic Society, whom she married. After appearances in Le Havre, Clermont and Nantes, she was engaged for the Théâtre de la Renaissance, Paris (Salle Ventadour), making her début there in the title role of Grisar's *Lady Melvil* on 15 November 1838. On 11 August 1840 she first appeared at the Opéra-Comique as Mathilde in Auber's *La neige*; she created Catarina in his *Les diamants de la couronne* (6 March 1841) and sang in operas by Balfe, Adam and Monfort. She made her English début on 2 May 1844 as Catarina at the Princess's Theatre, London, and in 1845 and 1846 was at Drury Lane, where she created Stella in Balfe's *The Enchantress*. From 1851 to 1854 she sang in the first San Francisco opera seasons. Her last stage appearance was in 1855 at the Lyceum Theatre, London, and she last sang in public at the Brighton Festival of 1867.

ALEXIS CHITTY/HAROLD ROSENTHAL

Thilman, Johannes Paul (*b* Dresden, 11 Jan 1906; *d* Dresden, 29 Jan 1973). German composer and teacher. He pursued music studies independently while attending a teacher training college. Hindemith admired his early Viola Sonata and performed it at the 1926 Donaueschingen Festival; Thilman subsequently studied with Hindemith (until 1927) and with Grabner and Scherchen (1929–31). At the same time he continued his general education at Dresden Technical University. During the years of fascist rule he was classed as an 'undesirable composer' (Böhm was one of the few to perform his music at this period) and so his artistic development was interrupted until 1945. He then organized a series of 40 concerts under the title 'New Music in Dresden' (1947–51), directed adult education courses and lectured at Dresden University. In 1965 he was appointed professor of composition at the Dresden Musikhochschule, and in 1960 he received the Martin-Andersen-Nexö Prize and the National Prize of the German Democratic Republic for his work in popular education. He wrote numerous articles and essays for *Musik und Gesellschaft*, most of them on socialist cultural politics.

WORKS
(selective list)

Ballet: Peter Schlemihl (after Chamisso), 1965, Brandenburg, 29 April 1966

Orch: Theme and Variations, op.42; Partita piccola, op.43; Concertino giocoso, op.47, trbn, chamber orch; Sonatine, op.51, bn, chamber orch; Die 7 Tänze, op.52; Sinfonietta, op.56; 3 little syms., G, op.56 no.2, F, op.60, D, op.63; Vn Conc., op.59; Sym. no.4, d, op.64; Lefthand Pf Concertino, op.65; Concertino, op.66, tpt, chamber orch; Sinfonische Variationen über ein tragisches Thema, op.76; Sinfonische Inventionen, op.77; Sym. no.5, 1 movt, op.79; Feierlicher Vorspruch, op.88; Sym. no.6, E, op.92, 1959; Sinfonischer Prolog, op.94; Huldigung für Robert Schumann, op.100, 1961; Sym. no.7, A, 1962; Rhapsodie, 1965; Ode, 1968–70; Impulse, 1971; Ornamente, 1972; Conc., vn, chamber orch, 1972

Chamber: Choralduo, op.26, vn, pf; Fl Sonatine, op.31; Ob Sonata, op.31 no.2; Eng hn Sonata, op.34; Wind Qnt, op.44a; Sonatine, op.49, str qt; 2 sonatines, opp.50, 82, vn, pf; Str Qt No.2, op.62; Cl Qnt, op.73; Sonata, op.80, vn, pf; Str Qt, D, op.81; Str Qt, A, op.84, 1 movt; Trio piccolo, op.90, a fl, b cl, va; Little Sonata, op.96, vc, pf; Das 7-Bläser-Stück, 2 hn, 2 tpt, 2 trbn, tuba; Dramatische Szenen, str qt, 1970; Elegie, str qnt, 1972

Pf: Sonatina patetica, op.39; 10 neue Inventionen, op.86; Wandlungen, 4 studies, 1963; 5 Praeludien, 1971

Vocal: Die Sage unseres Tages (G. Maurer), A, chamber ens, 1970; choral works

Numerous works for school/amateur orch, domestic music

Principal publishers: Breitkopf & Härtel, Dresdner Verlag, Hofmeister, Peters, Süddeutscher Musikverlag, Verlag Neue Musik

WRITINGS

Probleme der neuen Polyphonie (Dresden, 1949)
Neue Musik: polemische Beiträge (Dresden, 1950)
Musikalische Formenlehre in unserer Zeit (Dresden, 1952)

BIBLIOGRAPHY

K. Laux: 'J. P. Thilman', *Komponisten der DDR* (Berlin, 1969)
H. Böhm: 'J. P. Thilman 65', *Musik und Gesellschaft*, xxi (1971), 2, 283
H. J. Schaefer: 'Kunst ist Sorgfalt: in memoriam J. P. Thilman', *Musik und Gesellschaft*, xxiii (1973), 162
D. Uhrig: 'Johannes Paul Thilman: Persönlichkeit und Werk', *Sammelbände zur Musikgeschichte der Deutschen Demokratischen Republik*, iii (1973), 82   HELLMUT KÜHN

Thiman, Eric (Harding) (*b* Ashford, Kent, 12 Sept 1900; *d* London, 13 Feb 1975). English composer and organist. After childhood lessons at Trinity College of Music he was largely self-taught. He obtained the FRCO diploma in 1921 (Turpin Prize) and in 1927, after coaching from Harold Darke, the degree of DMus at London University. He was appointed professor to teach harmony and other subjects at the RAM in 1932, and he became examiner to the Royal Schools of Music in 1938. In 1952 he was appointed examiner to the Faculty of Music at London University, where he was for some time dean of the faculty. He was appointed organist and director of music to the City Temple, London, in 1957.

Thiman made extensive examination and recital tours, both in England and elsewhere (South Africa in 1940 and 1941, Australia and New Zealand in 1952, etc). In 1962 and 1964 he was adjudicator to the Hong Kong Schools Music Festival. He was a prolific composer in the best Kapellmeister tradition, writing sacred and secular cantatas, anthems and services, unison songs and partsongs, and piano and organ music, all of which have proved enormously popular with the less ambitious school and amateur musicians. Chief among his extended choral works are *The Last Supper* (1930), *The Parables* (1931), *The High Tide on the Coast of Lincolnshire* (1932) and *The Temptations of Christ* (1952). Such titles accurately reflect the line of musical descent from Stainer, Stanford and Parry. He wrote several orchestral pieces, but these have not enjoyed the widespread popularity of his vocal music.

Thiman's work is distinguished by a neat, textbook craftsmanship and easy melodic flow, and a firm grasp of what is practical and effective for the amateur. A similar utilitarian outlook informs his many textbooks on harmony, counterpoint, musical form and fugue. His principal London music publishers are Novello, Curwen, Boosey & Hawkes, and Ascherberg.

BIBLIOGRAPHY

D. Cairns: 'Eric Thiman', *Music in Education*, xix (1955), 13
C. Regan: 'Eric Thiman 1900–1975', *RAM Magazine* (1975), no.208, p.15   MICHAEL HURD

Thime, Clemens. *See* THIEME, CLEMENS.

Thimus, Albert, Freiherr **von** (*b* Aachen, 23 May 1806; *d* Cologne, 6 Nov 1878). German scholar and philologist. He studied law in Bonn and Heidelberg, became a judge in Cologne and represented the centre party as a member of the Reichstag. In Heidelberg, Thibaut and G. F. Creuzer stimulated his interest in symbological studies, and together with music theory and mathematics he took up Chinese, Arabic, cuneiform writing and hieroglyphics, thus embracing philological disciplines. Convinced that the fundamentals of music – above all, intervallic proportions – were the basis of teaching in the ancient Chinese, Hebrew, Egyptian and Greek civilizations, he sought to establish a symbolic expression of these fundamentals as a formulating principle of the ancient cosmogonic theories. His results were set down in a three-volume work, *Die harmonikale Symbolik des Altherthums*, the first two volumes of which were published (Cologne, 1868–76/R1972) but found little acceptance until they were taken up again by Hans Kayser in 1926; the manuscript of the third volume no longer survives.

Thimus's primary goal was to shed light on the harmonical foundations of Pythagorean theory, the most important discovery in this area being the *lambdoma*, a numerical table with wide-ranging applicability (used today in crystallography and cybernetics). He was also responsible for a new interpretation of the 'Timaeus scale', discussed in the writings of Plato. He demonstrated the existence of analogous harmonical theorems in Chinese, Hebrew and Greek sources whose symbolic content was identical to that of ancient musical myths. Often, however, it is not clear what part of his work is based on philological research and what part is his own speculation.

BIBLIOGRAPHY

R. Hasenclever: *Die Grundzüge der esoterischen Harmonik des Alterthums* (Cologne, 1870/R1972)
P. Reichensperger: 'A. von Thimus und A. Reichensperger', *Blätter für harmonikale Forschung*, viii (Berne, 1935)
H. Kayser: 'Albert von Thimus', *Abhandlungen zur Ektypik harmonikaler Wertformen* (Zurich, 1938)
R. Haase: 'Der Aachener Albert von Thimus als Musiktheoretiker', *Beiträge zur rheinischen Musikgeschichte*, vi (Cologne, 1954), 21
——: 'Klang aus Wasser und Feuer', *AnM*, ix (1963), 92
A. Köster: 'Die unmittelbaren Auswirkungen der "Harmonikalen Symbolik" des Freiherrn Albert von Thimus', *Antaios*, viii (Stuttgart, 1966), 450
R. Haase: *Geschichte des harmonikalen Pythagoreismus* (Vienna, 1969)
——: 'Eine unbekannte pythagoreische Tafel', *Antaios*, xii (1970), 357
L. Spitzer: *Die harmonikale Symbolik des Albert von Thimus* (Vienna, 1977)   RUDOLF HAASE

Third (Fr. *tierce*; Ger. *Terz*; It. *terza*). The INTERVAL between any two notes that are two diatonic scale degrees apart (e.g. C–E, E♭–G, F♯–A); 3rds are the intervals formed when a perfect 5th is divided into two consonant intervals to make a TRIAD. A 3rd made up of two whole tones is called a major 3rd (the medieval Latin name was *ditonus*); if it is made up of a tone and a diatonic semitone it is called a minor 3rd. A major 3rd that has been increased by a chromatic semitone is called an augmented 3rd (e.g. C–E♯, B♭♭–D), and a minor 3rd that has been decreased by a chromatic semitone is called a diminished 3rd (e.g. C–E♭♭, C♯–E♭).

In JUST INTONATION major and minor 3rds are pure, that is, they are based on ratios of small integers (5:4 and 6:5 respectively), and therefore the unisons among their overtones do not beat (when the timbre is purely harmonic). In the Pythagorean tuning system, intervals are derived from the pure 5th (ratio 3:2). The major 3rd is normally reckoned as the difference between five 5ths and three octaves, which gives a ratio of 81:64; this is more than ⅛ of a semitone larger than the major 3rd in just intonation. The minor 3rd, the difference between three octaves and four 5ths, has a ratio of 32:27 and is more than ⅛ of a semitone smaller than the minor 3rd in just intonation. A paradoxical feature of Pythagorean intonation, however, is that its diminished 4th and augmented 2nd (i.e. the difference between eight and nine pure 4ths, respectively, and three octaves) differ from a pure major and minor 3rd by an almost imperceptible interval (less than ¹⁄₅₀ of a semitone), a fact exploited in a significant proportion of extant keyboard music from the early to mid-15th century.

Throughout the Middle Ages, 3rds were regarded as imperfect consonances. They occurred regularly and were even necessary in counterpoint in more than two parts, but they did not figure in the final chord at cadences. Not until about 1500 were they used at final cadences, and then only the major 3rd could occur above the final – even in a minor-mode piece (this raised 3rd was later called the TIERCE DE PICARDIE). The acceptance of the minor 3rd as a consonance as good as the major 3rd coincided with the recognition of all 3rds as the basic units of chord structure in the early 18th century. Since Rameau, the ROOT of a chord (in tonal music) is normally determined as the lowest of its notes when arranged in a series of 3rds. Even chords that are perceivable as being in root position are traditionally analysed only in terms of the 3rds they contain; thus, for instance, the root of the German 6th chord in ex.1*a* is F♯, since the notes of the chord can be

Ex.1

arranged in 3rds only as F♯–A♭–C–E♭. But when the chord of the Neapolitan 6th is introduced (as in ex.1*b*) the German 6th chord must be interpreted as an applied dominant and its spelling changed accordingly.

WILLIAM DRABKIN

Third stream. A term coined by Gunther Schuller in the late 1950s for a musical style which, through improvisation or written composition or both, synthesizes the essential characteristics and techniques of contemporary Western art music and various types of ethnic music. It was originally used for a style that had existed for some years and that attempted to fuse basic elements of jazz

and Western art music, these two mainstreams joining to make a 'third stream'. Since then application of the term has been broadened, particularly through the work of the American pianist Ran Blake, to incorporate fusions with other Afro-American music, and with other ethnic musical traditions such as Greek folk or popular music and Japanese traditional music. The movement attracted much controversy and has often erroneously been allied with the SYMPHONIC JAZZ movement of the 1920s which, however, lacked its essential element – improvisation. Other critics have seen the movement as an inevitable outcome of postwar eclecticism and stylistic and technical synthesis. Third stream, like all musical syntheses, courts the danger of being merely a superficial application of exotica to an established musical style, but real cross-fertilization has occurred in the work of musicians deeply rooted in dual traditions. Composers associated with the movement include Larry Austin, Ran Blake, Jimmy Giuffre, Werner Heider, André Hodeir, John Lewis, Bogusław Schäffer and Gunther Schuller.

GUNTHER SCHULLER

Thiriet, Maurice (*b* Meulan, 2 May 1906; *d* Puys, 28 Sept 1972). French composer. At the Paris Conservatoire (1925–30) he studied solfège with Schwartz, harmony with Silver, fugue and counterpoint with Koechlin, and composition, orchestration and aesthetics with Roland-Manuel. In his music, clearly and brilliantly orchestrated, bold and lyrical in feeling, he remained faithful to the orthodox standards of the Conservatoire. After World War II he devoted most of his attention to film music.

WORKS
(*selective list*)

16 ballets incl. La nuit vénitienne, 1938; L'oeuf à la coque, 1948; Psyché, 1950; Héraklès, 1953; Deuil en 24 heures, 1953; La reine des îles, 1955; Le maure de Vénise, 1959; La chaloupée, 1961; Les amants de Mayerling, 1961; La chambre noire, 1969
Orch: Le livre pour Jean, 1929; 6 chansons dans le caractère populaire français, 1933; Rapsodie sur des thèmes Incas, 1935; Introduction, chanson et ronde, harp, orch, 1936; Suite française [after Couperin], 1936; Poème, str, 1936; Musique de cour [after Lully], 1939; Oedipe-roi (Cocteau), speaker, orch, 1940–41
Film scores: La nuit fantastique, 1941; Les visiteurs du soir, 1942; L'idiot, 1946; Lucrèce Borgia, 1953; Thérèse Raquin, 1953; many others
Chamber music, many songs, choral pieces

Principal publishers: Ahn & Simrock, Eschig, Lemoine, Société Editions Musicales Internationales, Transatlantiques

DOMINIQUE AMY

Thirty-second-note. American term for DEMI-SEMIQUAVER. *See also* NOTE VALUES.

Thoinan, Ernest [Roquet, Antoine Ernest] (*b* Nantes, 23 Jan 1827; *d* Paris, 26 May 1894). French writer on music. A merchant by trade, he took the opportunities offered by business journeys to England, Italy and Russia to accumulate an extensive music library. He became a contributor to the periodicals *La France musicale* and *L'art musical*, and later published these articles and others as pamphlets. He worked exclusively on the history of French music, basing his research firmly on primary sources which often enabled him to correct the errors of other writers.

WRITINGS
(*all published in Paris*)

with A. de Lasalle: *La musique à Paris* (1863) [survey of Parisian musical life in 1862]

Déploration de Guillaume Crétin sur le trépas de Jehan Ockeghem (1864)
Les origines de la chapelle-musique des souverains de France (1864)
Antoine de Cousu et ... son livre rarissime 'La musique universelle' (1866)
Louis Constantin, roi des violons, 1624–1657 (1878)
Un Bisaïeul de Molière: recherches sur les Mazuel (1878)
Notes bibliographiques sur la guerre musicale des Gluckistes et Piccinistes (1878)
ed.: *A. Gantez: Entretien des musiciens* (1878)
with C. Nuitter: *Les origines de l'opéra français* (1886)
Les relieurs français (1500–1800) (1893)
Les Hotteterre et les Chédeville (1894)

Thollary, Jan Křtitel. *See* TOLAR, JAN KŘTITEL.

Thomán, István (*b* Homonna, 4 Nov 1862; *d* Budapest, 22 Sept 1940). Hungarian pianist and teacher. He studied with Erkel and Volkmann (1882–5) and later with Liszt at the Budapest Academy and in Weimar and Rome. From 1888 to 1906 he taught the piano at the Budapest Academy, where his pupils included Bartók, Székely and Dohnányi. Throughout his life he was greatly esteemed as a pianist and teacher, and played a large part in establishing recognized teaching methods based on those of Liszt. His compositions are mostly pedagogical piano pieces; they include six volumes of technical studies (*A zongorázás technikaja*), fantasias and other miniatures. Thomán also contributed articles on music to several Budapest periodicals.

His wife Valerie (*b* Budapest, 16 Aug 1878; *d* Budapest, 8 Sept 1948) had a successful career as a singer and gave early performances of works by Kodály and Bartók; their daughter Mária (*b* Budapest, 12 July 1899; *d* Budapest, 25 Feb 1948), a pupil of Hubay, Vecsey and Flesch, toured Europe as a solo violinist and chamber music player.

BIBLIOGRAPHY
I. Engel: 'Thomán István negyven éves müvészi jubileumára', *Crescendo*, i/4 (1926), 1
B. Bartók: 'Thomán István', *Zenei szemle*, ix (1927), 93; repr. in *Bartók Béla összegyüjött irásai* (Budapest, 1966)
A. Varannai: 'Egy nagy magyar zongoratanitó Thomán István: Liszt növendéke és Bartók mestere', *Muzsika*, ii (1959), 25

Thomas, (Charles Louis) Ambroise (*b* Metz, 5 Aug 1811; *d* Paris, 12 Feb 1896). French opera composer. While remaining firmly within the conventions of the *opéra comique*, he imbued the form with more lyricism and sentiment than it had possessed in the works of his predecessors Auber and Halévy. His *Mignon* received over 1000 performances at the Opéra-Comique between 1866 and 1894, thus becoming one of the most successful operas in history.

1. LIFE. The son of music teachers, Thomas was systematically prepared for a musical career, and by the age of nine was a good pianist and violinist. After his father's death his family moved to Paris, and in 1828 Thomas entered the Conservatoire, where he studied the piano with P.-J.-G. Zimmermann and harmony and accompaniment with Dourlen, winning the *premiers prix* in these subjects in 1829 and 1830 respectively. He also studied privately with Kalkbrenner (piano) and Barbereau (harmony). He later became a composition pupil of Le Sueur at the Conservatoire, and in 1832 won the Prix de Rome with his cantata *Hermann et Ketty*. During his subsequent stay in Rome he was encouraged by the friendship of Ingres, who shared his admiration for Mozart and Beethoven; while in Italy he composed

1. Ambroise Thomas

chamber and piano music and a requiem. He next spent a few months in Germany, but returned to Paris in December 1835 and began to compose industriously for the stage. Of Thomas' nine stage works produced in Paris between 1837 and 1843, the first and most promising was *La double échelle*, an *opéra comique* which won praise from Berlioz and enjoyed popularity abroad as well as in France. A more decisive success came in 1849 with *Le caïd*, an affectionate parody of Rossini's *L'italiana in Algeri* that pointed to the wilder farces of Offenbach.

Thomas' next compositions, a series of *opéras comiques*, marked a modest improvement on Auber in melodic invention, sentiment and delicacy of orchestration, but followed contemporary taste in their dependence on startlingly virtuoso coloratura soprano roles and in the absurdity of their librettos, which show a strange blend of romanticism and flippancy. The plot of the first and most successful of these works, *Le songe d'une nuit d'été*, is fairly representative. It has no connection with *A Midsummer Night's Dream*; the characters include Falstaff, Shakespeare and Elizabeth I; Shakespeare becomes drunk in the presence of the disguised queen, who has him conveyed to Richmond Park where, taking advantage of his impressionable condition, she appears as his muse and rouses him to resume his poetic mission for the glory of the nation. The success of *Le caïd* and *Le songe* secured Thomas' election to the French Academy on Spontini's death in 1851, and in 1856 he became a professor of composition at the Paris Conservatoire. Thoroughly eclectic, he now began to be influenced even by younger composers in his musical style and choice of operatic subjects. Thus, in *Psyché* he followed Gounod's *Sapho* in the choice of a classical theme, and in *Le carnaval de Venise* he echoed Victor Massé's *La reine Topaze* by capitalizing on the popularity of Paganini's variations on the Venetian tune from which the opera took its name.

After the success of Gounod's *Faust* in 1859 and the failure of his own *Le roman d'Elvire* early the following year, Thomas presented no new operas for over six years. *Faust*'s novel emphasis on simple lyricism and sentiment marked a partial abandonment of the Meyerbeerian conventions which had dominated French opera for a generation, and stimulated Thomas to emulate this opera in both subject matter and musical style. The result was *Mignon*. Thomas delayed its production until it was assured of a strong cast, but in 1866, with Galli-Marié (later to be the first Carmen) in the title role and Marie Cabel as Philine, *Mignon* won immediate approval. Having capped *Faust* with his own sentimental treatment of a Goethe heroine, Thomas next attempted to eclipse Gounod's *Roméo et Juliette* with his setting of a Shakespearean tragedy, *Hamlet*. The part of Hamlet was originally written for a tenor, but after the baritone J.-B. Faure emerged as the Opéra's leading male artist, Thomas rewrote the part for him. Thanks largely to Faure and the Swedish soprano Christine Nilsson (in the disproportionately expanded coloratura role of Ophelia), *Hamlet* was hailed in 1868 as the best new work to have been given at the Opéra since the days of Meyerbeer and Halévy. The success of *Mignon* and *Hamlet*, produced within a span of 16 months, soon became international, thus clinching Thomas' reputation and distinguishing him as the rightful successor to Auber as director of the Conservatoire.

Despite his age of nearly 60 years, Thomas' patriotism led him to volunteer for service in the Franco-Prussian war before taking up his new post in 1871. His official duties at the Conservatoire left him little time for composition and his last three stage works were comparative failures. *Gille et Gillotin*, a slight Italianate operetta written in 1859, was not produced until 1874 and then only after its librettist, T. M. F. Sauvage, had won a protracted legal tussle with Thomas, who wanted to suppress it. *Françoise de Rimini* (1882) and the ballet *La tempête* (1889) both met with indifference in the new musical climate that had succeeded the war, though the former enjoyed a brief *succès d'estime* when the Opéra revived it shortly before Thomas' death.

2. WORKS. Thomas was the last of a long line of French composers for whom success in opera was the ruling consideration; during most of his career the qualities necessary for this attitude were an uncritical acceptance of conventions and the desire to please a musically uncultivated public. The critical acclaim which *Mignon* and *Hamlet* received was due to their conventionality, for the chauvinistic French critics of the day were much cooler about Gounod's operas, which they considered insidiously Wagnerian. Nevertheless, the shortwinded melodiousness and dreamy sentiment of *Mignon*'s music ensure it a fitful existence in provincial continental repertories, and its vocal characterization remains effective: the superficiality of Philine's skittish polonaise aria 'Je suis Titania' is deliberate, and probably provided Puccini with a hint for Musetta in *La bohème*. Although Thomas considered *Hamlet* his masterpiece, his light musical style was quite unsuited to the subject, despite the lengths to which his librettists went to adapt such intractable material to French operatic taste. Act 4, to which the work owed much of its early success, consists of a *ballet-divertissement*, followed by a floridly inconsequential mad scene for Ophelia, who then drowns to the offstage accompaniment of harps and a wordless chorus of water-spirits. Still more absurd is the last act, in which the ghost appears at Ophelia's funeral and orders Hamlet to kill Claudius and ascend the throne. The stronger sections of the work, some of which were adversely criticized by contemporaries, include a sombrely atmospheric scene for the first appearance of the ghost on the battlements, the feverish recall of

Hamlet's drinking-song in the uproar after the players' scene and a dramatically powerful duet for Hamlet and his mother in Act 3. A number of 'Scandinavian' elements appear in the score, notably the 'Näckans polka' and the almost Griegian tinge of melancholy in some of Ophelia's music, particularly the A♭ minor section of her Act 2 aria, and her ballade in Act 4. *Hamlet* is also noteworthy as the first opera to include a part for the saxophone, which lends an ironic touch to the players' scene.

Complaisance, rather than artistic conviction, led Thomas to revise several of his operas to accommodate new singers, varying national tastes or changes in fashion. Thus, when *Mignon* was first performed in London in 1870, it was sung in Italian, recitatives replaced the dialogue, the title role was rewritten for coloratura soprano (Nilsson), the small tenor part of Frédéric became a breeches role for Zelia Trebelli, who was rewarded with a sung version of the popular gavotte entr'acte, and a new aria, 'Alerta, Filina', was added for Philine. In a belated attempt to soothe literary susceptibilities, German audiences were offered a tragic ending in which Mignon, stunned at hearing the offstage voice of Philine, expires in Wilhelm's arms. Later, for the revival of two of his earlier works at the Opéra-Comique, Thomas followed the lead of the new *opéras lyriques* by replacing spoken dialogue with recitative; he made further alterations to *Psyché* in 1878 by suppressing the element of Offenbachian parody adding a *ballet-divertissement*, and to *Le songe d'une nuit d'été* in 1886 by adapting the tenor role of Shakespeare for the baritone Victor Maurel.

Thomas was made a Chevalier of the Légion d'honneur in 1845, and in 1894, after the 1000th performance of *Mignon*, he became the first composer to receive the Grand Croix of this order. In his lifetime, he

2. J. Chéret's poster for the first production of 'Mignon' (1866)

enjoyed a status comparable with that of his close contemporary Verdi. Berlioz, Gounod, Bizet and Massenet all spoke well of his music, and Verdi abandoned his long-projected Hamlet opera out of respect for him (though he later expressed his disgust with the libretto).

Thomas proved a more conscientious director of the Conservatoire than Auber, and brought about several reforms, introducing lectures in the history of music, an orchestral class and a compulsory class for vocal sight-reading. He did his best to raise standards of tuition and increase the budget of the institution. Nevertheless his regime was conservative and unbending; he was troubled by the growing influence of Wagner, and showed little sympathy for the work of Bizet, Fauré, Debussy and other younger French composers, with the notable exception of Massenet, who, together with Théodore Dubois and Bourgault-Ducoudray, had been among his composition pupils. The war, the Commune and the activities of the Société Nationale de Musique (founded in 1871) had combined to weaken the overpowering predominance of opera in French musical life, with the result that, within a few years of Thomas' greatest triumphs, his music was regarded as anachronistic by a rising generation of French composers fired with enthusiasm for instrumental music and Wagner. Thomas' disappointment at his brutally sudden eclipse as a composer probably accounts for the notorious inflexibility of his attitudes in later years. Convinced that dramatic music was the highest expression of the art, when asked why the Prix de Rome should always be awarded on the basis of a cantata, he is said to have retorted that no musician would be willing to lower himself to teach instrumental composition. The violence of his refusal to consider appointing Fauré to the teaching staff of the Conservatoire provides further evidence of his artistic isolation.

Apart from *Mignon*, *Hamlet*, the palpably Rossinian overture to *Raymond* and a number of male voice choruses, little of Thomas' music is now performed, even in France. In most technical aspects, particularly rhythm, his music is often commonplace. Whether from reticence or lack of imagination he never established a distinctive personal style, such as those associated with Gounod or Massenet. Thomas' music at its best, however, as in the gavotte from *Mignon* with its clearcut, naively appealing melody, simple harmonizations and light scoring, has a pleasing, unpretentious elegance.

WORKS

(*printed works published in Paris unless otherwise stated*)

OPERAS

Unless otherwise stated, all are *opéras comiques*; all were first performed in Paris.

OC – *Opéra-Comique*; SN – *Salle des Nouveautés*; SF – *Salle Favart*

La double échelle (1, F. A. E. de Planard), OC, SN, 23 Aug 1837 (1837), excerpts pubd separately
Le perruquier de la régence (3, de Planard, P. Dupont), OC, SN, 30 March 1838 (n.d.), excerpts pubd separately
Le panier fleuri (1, A. de Leuven, L. L. Brunswick), OC, SN, 6 May 1839 (1839), excerpts pubd separately
Carline (3, de Leuven, Brunswick), OC, SN, 24 Feb 1840, vocal score (1840)
Le comte de Carmagnola (opera, 2, E. Scribe), Opéra, 19 April 1841 (1841)
Le guerillero (opera, 2, T. Anne), Opéra, 22 June 1842; vocal score (1842)
Angélique et Médor (1, T. M. F. Sauvage), OC, SF, 10 May 1843, vocal score (1843)
Mina, ou Le ménage à trois (3, de Planard), OC, SF, 10 Oct 1843, vocal score (1843), excerpts pubd separately
Le caïd (2, Sauvage), OC, SF, 3 Jan 1849 (1849), excerpts pubd separately

Le songe d'une nuit d'été (3, J. B. Rosier, de Leuven), OC, SN, 20 April 1850 (1850), excerpts pubd separately
Raymond, ou Le secret de la reine (3, Rosier, de Leuven), OC, SF, 5 June 1851 (c1851), excerpts pubd separately
La Tonelli (2, Sauvage), OC, SF, 30 March 1853 (c1853), excerpts pubd separately
La cour de Célimène (2, Rosier), OC, SF, 11 April 1855, vocal score (1855)
Psyché (3, J. Barbier, M. Carré), OC, SF, 26 Jan 1857, vocal score (1857) [rev. 21 May 1878], excerpts pubd separately
Le carnaval de Venise (3, Sauvage), OC, SF, 9 Dec 1857 (1857), excerpts pubd separately
Le roman d'Elvire (3, A. Dumas père, de Leuven), OC, SF, 4 Feb 1860 (1860)
Mignon (3, J. Barbier, Carré, after Goethe: Wilhelm Meister), OC, SF, 17 Nov 1866 (n.d.), vocal score (1866), excerpts pubd separately
Hamlet (opera, 5, J. Barbier, Carré, after Shakespeare), Opéra, 9 March 1868 (1869), vocal score (1868), excerpts pubd separately
Gille et Gillotin (opera, 1, Sauvage), OC, SF, 22 April 1874 (1874) [written in 1859 as Gillotin et son père, unperf.], excerpts pubd separately
Françoise de Rimini (opera, 5, J. Barbier, Carré, after Dante), Opéra, 14 April 1882 (1882), excerpts pubd separately

BALLETS

La gipsy (3, J. H. V. de Saint-Georges, after Cervantes: La gitanella), Opéra, 28 Jan 1839 (1839), collab. F. Benoist, M. A. Marliani [only Act 2 by Thomas]
Betty (2, N. Mazillier, after A. Duval: La jeunesse d'Henri V), Opéra, 10 July 1846, fragments, F-Pn
La tempête (ballet fantastique, 3, J. Barbier, J. Hansen, after Shakespeare), Opéra, 26 June 1889, arr. pf (1889), excerpts pubd separately

SONGS

(*1v, pf, unless otherwise indicated*)

Souvenirs d'Italie: 6 romances italiennes et venitiennes (E. Delcuse) (1835); Adieu les beaux jours (Mlle de La Besge) (c1835); Doux abri (La Besge) (c1835); La vierge Marie (Mme Godefroy) (c1840); Viens (H. Lesguillon) (c1840); Belle folle espagnole (R***) (Mainz, 1844); Ange et mortel (M. Constantin) (c1855); C'est vous (E. de Lonlay) (1860); Sérénade (A. Dumas fils) (c1861); Le petit chou (anon.) (c1861); Ah sur ma parole (c1862); Le soir (Carré) (1869)
Le berger de la Reuss (L. Escudier) (c1870); Fleur de neige (J. Barbier) (c1880); Croyance, 2vv (G. Boyer) (1885); Passiflore (Comtesse de Chambrun) (c1887); Chanson de Margyane (M. Barbier) (1896); Baissez les yeux (A. Grimault) (1897); Ainsi va le monde (E. Vienet) (1903); Belle, ayez pitié (Speranza) (n.d.); C'est le bonheur (Speranza) (n.d.); La folle d'Yarmouth (La Besge) (n.d.); L'aimable printemps (J. Barbier) (n.d.); La belle arène de Montigny, Le leçon de musique, Lisa, Mademoiselle de Fontanges, all Pn

OTHER VOCAL

Sacred: Requiem mass, chorus, orch (c1840), vocal score (Rome, 1833); O salutaris, motet, 3 female vv, org (c1836); Sub tuum praesidium, motet, 3 female vv, org (c1836); Veni sponsa Christi, motet, 4 male vv, org (c1836); Messe solennelle, chorus, orch, perf. Paris, St Eustache, 22 Nov 1857 (1858); Beati mortui, vv, org, perf. ?Paris, 9 May 1873, Pn; Agnus Dei (A. N.-D. de Pontifroy), 3vv, org (?c1895); Pie Jesu, T, org (1896); Ave verum, after Mozart, arr. Thomas, Pn; Messe de l'orphéon, 4 male vv (n.d.), collab. A. Adam, F. Halévy
Secular: Bianca Capello, scène lyrique, 1831, Pn; Hermann et Ketty (de Pastoret), scène lyrique (1832); Silvio Pellico (E. Legouvé), cantata, 1837, lost; La charité du couvent, cantata (1843); Hommage à Lesueur (E. Praron), cantata, vv, orch, perf. Abbeville, 10 Aug 1852, Pn; Hommage à Boieldieu, cantata, male vv, brass, ww, perf. Rouen, 13 June 1875 (c1875); Va via!, canzone veneziano, 4vv, pf (n.d.)
Scènes chorales, 2T, 2B, unacc., unless otherwise indicated: Le chant des amis (A. de Musset) (1852); La vapeur (F. Duchemin) (Arras, 1853); L'harmonie des peuples (A. Lefèvre) (c1855); Choeur des gardes-chasses, 2T (Metz, c1857), arr. 4vv (Nancy, 1881); Salut aux chanteurs de la France (J. F. Vaudin) (c1859); France (Vaudin) (c1860); Le forgeron (P. Delombre) (c1861); Le Tyrol (G. Chouquet) (c1862); Les archers de Bouvines (G. d'Orquaire) (c1863); Le carnaval de Rome (Chouquet) (c1864); Le temple de la paix (Chouquet) (c1867); Paris (Vaudin) (c1867); La nuit du sabbat (Chouquet) (1869); Les traîneaux (Chouquet) (n.d.); L'Atlantique, 8vv (Chouquet) (n.d.); Chant patriotique, Pn

INSTRUMENTAL

Orch: Fantaisie brillante, pf, orch/str qt, op.6 (n.d.), arr. pf (c1836); Marche religieuse, perf. Paris, Notre-Dame, 25 March 1865 (c1867); Chant du psaume laudate, vn, orch (n.d.)
Chamber: Str Qt, op.1 (1833); Pf Trio, op.3 (c1835); Str Qnt, 2 vn, va, vc, db/vc (Leipzig, 1835), also arr. 3 str, pf (Mainz, ?1839); Souvenir, pf, vn/va (n.d.); Barcarolla, fl/vn, pf, Pn

Pf: 6 caprices en forme de valses caractéristiques, op.4 (Leipzig, 1835); Fantaisie sur un air favori écossais, op.5 (1835); Absence, nocturne, op.8 (n.d.); Valse de salon (London, 1851); Rêverie (1888); La dérobée, fantaisie sur un air breton (c1888); Valse et mazurka, Tarantella, both Pn; others, incl. works, pf 4 hands

Org: Absoute, in La maîtrise, i, ed. L. Niedermeyer, J. d'Ortigue (1857–8); Off and Prière, in La maîtrise, ii (1858–9); 3 preludes, in La maîtrise, iii (1859–60); Off, in La maîtrise, iv (1860–61); Dirge (?1883); 10 pastorales (n.d.)

Pedagogical works: Recueil des leçons de solfège à changement de clef composées pour les examens et concours du Conservatoire de musique 1872–1885 (1885), 1872–1896 (1900)

BIBLIOGRAPHY

FétisB

L. Escudier: *Mes souvenirs* (Paris, 1863, 2/1863)
E. Hanslick: *Die moderne Oper*, ii: *Musikalische Stationen* (Berlin, 1880/R1971, 6/1911); viii: *Am Ende des Jahrhunderts* (Berlin, 1899/R1971, 3/1911)
H. Sutherland Edwards: *The Lyrical Drama* (London, 1881)
A. Jullien: *Musiciens d'aujourd'hui* (Paris, 1892–4)
A. Soubies and C. Malherbe: *Histoire de l'Opéra-Comique* (Paris, 1892–3)
A. Hervey: *Masters of French Music* (London, 1894)
H. Delaborde: *Notice sur la vie et les oeuvres de M. Ambroise Thomas* (Paris, 1896)
A. Jullien: 'Ambroise Thomas', *RMI*, iii (1896), 358
J. Simon: 'Ambroise Thomas', *Revue de Paris*, iii/2 (1896), 98
H. Berlioz: 'Le caïd', *Les musiciens et la musique* (Paris, 1903)
A. Pougin: *Musiciens du XIXᵉ siècle* (Paris, 1911)
J. Combarieu: *Histoire de la musique*, iii (Paris, 1919, 3/1947, rev. R. Dumesnil, 1955/R1961)
C. Le Senne: 'Période contemporaine: Ambroise Thomas (1811–1896)', *EMDC*, I/iii (1921), 1697
A. Luzio, ed.: *Carteggi Verdiani* (Rome, 1935–47)
P. Landormy: *La musique française* (Paris, 1943–8, 19/1948)
M. Cooper: 'Charles Louis Ambroise Thomas', *The Music Masters*, ed. A. L. Bacharach, ii (London, 1950); pubd separately (London, 1957–8)
M. Curtiss: *Bizet and his World* (London, 1959)
W. Dean: 'Shakespeare and Opera', *Shakespeare in Music*, ed. P. Hartnoll (London, 1964)

PHILIP ROBINSON

Thomas, Arthur Goring (*b* Ratton Park, Sussex, 20 Nov 1850; *d* London, 20 March 1892). English composer. He was educated for the civil service and did not study music seriously until 1873, when he went to Paris to work for two years under Emile Durand. This was a formative period and most of his compositions show strong traces of French influence. From 1877 to 1880 he studied with Sullivan and Prout at the RAM, London, where he twice won the Lucas Medal for composition; later he received orchestration lessons from Max Bruch. In 1879 his opera *The Light of the Harem* was performed in part at the RAM; the success of this performance led to a commission from Carl Rosa, which Thomas fulfilled with *Esmeralda* (1883). The libretto, based on Victor Hugo's *Notre-Dame de Paris*, was described as 'a flow of doggerel' which stripped the story of all drama and passion (following the example of Gounod's *Faust*, the librettists gave *Esmeralda* a happy ending). This emasculated libretto was well suited to Thomas's graceful and elegant music, which only occasionally achieved the degree of passion displayed in the climactic love duet in the third act. Complicated scenes with several principals and chorus severely taxed his powers of dramatic invention, but some of the single, lyrical numbers are more successful. Although Thomas felt that he had never mastered the art of setting English words, the recitatives were considered 'advanced' and praised for their naturalness and flexibility. *Esmeralda* was later given in a German version at Cologne, Hamburg and Berlin, and in a French version (with a tragic ending) at Covent Garden in July 1890.

In 1885 the Carl Rosa Company produced a second opera by Thomas, *Nadeshda*, with a libretto adapted

from a Russian story. The subject was more serious than that of *Esmeralda*, and Thomas found some difficulty in producing music of sufficient dramatic power. Critics remarked that the music did not grow naturally out of the drama, but merely accompanied it, although the recitatives were again singled out for praise and several of the more lyrical passages were commended. *Nadeshda* was also given in a German version, at Breslau in 1890. An unfinished comic opera, *The Golden Web*, was completed by S. P. Waddington and performed with some success in 1893. After Thomas's death, a choral work, *The Swan and the Skylark*, was discovered in piano score; it was orchestrated by Stanford and produced in 1894. Thomas never found an individual musical style; as Shaw said, he 'always seems to be dreaming of other men's music'. Turns of phrase or chord progressions, particularly in the operas, constantly recall pieces by Gounod, Bizet, Delibes or Ambroise Thomas. Yet much of his lighter music has an infectious sparkle or a refined charm that is worthy of the French school at its best.

In 1891, after a period of weak health and an accident, Thomas began to show signs of suicidal mania, and in the next year he took his own life.

WORKS

Selective list; MSS in *GB-Lbm, Lcm*; all printed works published in London; see list in programme of memorial concert, St James's Hall, 13 July 1892

OPERAS

Don Braggadocio (3, C. I. Thomas), unfinished
The Light of the Harem (3, C. Harrison, after T. Moore), London, RAM, 7 Nov 1879 (1913)
Esmeralda (4, T. Marzials, A. Randegger, after Hugo), London, Drury Lane, 26 March 1883 (1883), rev. Covent Garden, 12 July 1890
Nadeshda (4, J. Sturgis), London, Drury Lane, 16 April 1885 (1885)
The Golden Web (3, F. Corder, B. C. Stephenson), Liverpool, Royal Court, 15 Feb 1893 (1893), completed by S. P. Waddington

CHORAL AND ORCHESTRAL

Out of the Deep (anthem, Waddington, after Ps cxxx), S, 4vv, orch, London, 1878 (1878)
Hero and Leander (scena, G. Macfarren), London, 1880
The Sun-worshippers (choral ode, C. Delavigne, C. Newton-Scott), Norwich Festival, 1881 (1881)
Suite de ballet, orch, Cambridge, University Musical Society, 1887 (1892)
The Swan and the Skylark (cantata, Keats, Shelley, F. Hemans), Birmingham Festival, 1894 (1894), completed and orchd C. V. Stanford
3 other concert scenas

SONGS AND OTHER WORKS

Mélodies, 1v, pf acc. (c1885)
12 Lyrics (H. Boulton) (1889)
Album of 10 Songs, 1v, pf acc. (1893)
6 romances et 2 duos (C. Bingham) (1894)
Many separate songs and duets
Works for vn, pf, and for vc, pf

BIBLIOGRAPHY

R. H. Legge: 'Thomas, Arthur Goring', *DNB*
E. Walker: *A History of Music in England* (London, 1907, rev. 3/1952)
G. B. Shaw: *Music in London 1890–94* (London, 1932)
J. W. Klein: 'English Opera Abroad', *MO*, lxvi (1942–3), 44
——: 'Tragic, Forgotten Pioneer: Arthur Goring Thomas', *MR*, xxxvi (1975), 180

JENNIFER SPENCER

Thomas, Christian Gottfried (*b* Wehrsdorf, nr. Bautzen, 2 Feb 1748; *d* Leipzig, 12 Sept 1806). German impresario, composer, horn player, writer on music and publisher. He attended the Gymnasium in Bautzen for seven years; in 1770 he began studying law at Leipzig University but within a year turned to music, becoming first horn player for the Grosses Konzert in 1771. In

1776 he founded a music copying business and manuscript storehouse, producing a large thematic catalogue (rivalling Breitkopf's) that he sold in manuscript. He described this catalogue (of manuscript works available for copying) and his idealistic plans for the storehouse in a series of pamphlets published between 1778 and 1781. From 1782 he sponsored a series of independent concerts in Leipzig, later producing the Gewandhaus concerts, Dilettanten concerts and Stadtmusik, and undertaking concert tours as far as Dresden, Hamburg and Prague. In addition to works by Haydn, Mozart and others, he performed a number of his own compositions. In 1789 he tried unsuccessfully to become C. P. E. Bach's successor as Hamburg city Kantor. His attempts to establish a 'public singing school in the Italian manner' (1790) and a school of composition (1796) were also unsuccessful.

Thomas devoted three pages in his periodical, *Unpartheiische Kritik* (1798), to a description of his own compositions, most of which are lost. 'In my younger years between 1766 and 1770 in the Bautzen Gymasium I wrote several four-voice choral-arias and motets as "Secundaner"; and several occasional cantatas as "Primaner". In the ensuing years, I wrote two double concertos for Waldhorn ... plus several symphonies and "Parthien" for Mr Caffetier Richter's concerts – in return for ready cash'. He mentioned several other vocal pieces written for specific purposes, including test pieces used in seeking various posts such as the one in Hamburg. Six works performed in his own concerts (1789–98) are described in detail. Thomas also described a seventh, 'unusually large' work which he was then (1798) writing with the intention of directing it himself in 1800 at a jubilee of the 18th century. It was a setting of Psalm cxvii for orchestra, with quadruple *divisi* strings, seven choirs singing in seven languages, 'and what is more with 4-, 8-, 12- and 16-part fugal movements of various kinds, *a cappella*'.

In his role of impresario and propagator of new music, Thomas, as Schering pointed out, played a significant role in the concert life of Leipzig and other cities. More important to music history are his writings, including his periodical, biassed though it may have been, and especially his pamphlets about his copying business and music storehouse, which reveal much about the problems of the dissemination of manuscripts and printed music in the last third of the 18th century. In his *Praktische Beyträge* he first expounded his ambitious plans and delineated his method of combating musical piracy or 'Schleichhandel' – which he defined as the selling of copies or having them printed or engraved without paying the composer – and his scheme for protecting the rights of the composer, consumer and music dealer. In the second chapter he defined his business as follows: 'It is a place where composers of music store their works in manuscript, and, under my supervision and direction, permit copies to be sold both here and, on commission, elsewhere as well'. To protect this relationship he drew up a lengthy contract with his composer clients, providing for a clean manuscript copy of each work to be corrected by the composer himself and to be stored in the dealer's (Thomas's) musical storehouse; 75% of the price of each copy sold to go to the composer, and 25% plus copying fees to the dealer; each distributed copy to have an engraved title-page bearing the signature and seal of the composer; strict control of all copying rights; the contract to last for the lifetime of the composer and his widow, with works becoming the dealer's property when the composer's orphaned children came of age.

Thomas's *Bekantmachung* and *Kurzgefasster Entwurf* further describe his copying and distribution practices, proposing an ingenious manuscript subscription scheme and developing his grandiose but naive vision of a conservatory – not a music school, but the expansion of his musical storehouse idea – which would serve as a permanent musical depository for all of Europe for centuries to come. The non-thematic first supplement (Leipzig, 1779) to what Thomas called his 'great thematic catalogue' of works in the storehouse lists symphonies, partitas, harpsichord solos, duets, trios, quartets, concertos etc, as well as Italian and German operas in manuscript, but little church music and no printed or engraved works. The 'great thematic catalogue' itself, never printed but distributed in manuscript, is now lost, as are a 'second collection of practical contributions', which Thomas said were published in 1779, and two manuscript items relating to the thematic catalogue.

In 1798 Thomas founded the *Unpartheiische Kritik*, a music periodical which he himself edited, devoted mostly to concerts he had organized in Leipzig and elsewhere. According to Schering, without this journal it would be impossible today to have a clear understanding of the intricate contexts within Leipzig's musical life in the late 18th century. Typical of Thomas's projects, this was short-lived; he chose to begin publishing the journal the same year that G. C. Härtel, of the publishers Breitkopf & Härtel, began his famous *Allgemeine musikalische Zeitung* in Leipzig. Thomas, though a man of imagination, intellect and energy, was an impractical idealist, an inefficient administrator and a garrulous if amiable braggart. He was apparently undaunted by his string of failures. His writings give a picture of the burgeoning bourgeois musical life of the time, and of the highly competitive business practices in music that were replacing the patronage system as the musician's means of making a livelihood.

WORKS

(lost unless otherwise stated)

Gloria, 24 insts, 12vv (3 choirs), Hamburg, 18 Aug 1789
Psalm cxlix, double choir, incl.: canon, 8vv; fugue, 8vv, in circle of 12 keys; written Hamburg, 1789; perf. Brunswick, 1789, with addl. final movt, Leipzig, 1794
Cantata, 24 insts, 8vv (2 choirs), Prague, 13 Aug 1792
[2] Gedichte (1 text by Klopstock), 18 insts, S, T, Leipzig, 1792, *D-Bds, Dlb, DS*
Schlachtgesang (Klopstock), 30 insts, 8vv (2 choirs), Leipzig, 1795, *DS*
[4] Volksgesänge, 20 insts, choir 4vv, Leipzig, 1797, vocal score *LEm*
Psalm cxvii, orch, 7 choirs

WRITINGS

Praktische Beyträge zur Geschichte der Musik, musikalischen Litteratur und gemeinen Besten, i (Leipzig, 1778)
Des musikalischen summarischen Verzeichnisses Erster Nachtrag (Leipzig, 1779)
Praktische Beyträge, ii (Leipzig, 1779), lost
Das summarische Verzeichniss, des musikalischen thematischen grossen Catalogi, von den Jahren 1776–77 und 78 (MS, lost)
Der grosse thematische Catalogus (MS, lost)
Der erste Nachtrag des thematischen Catalogus (MS, lost)
Bekantmachung (Leipzig, 28 Feb 1781)
Kurzgefasster Entwurf des Plan's des zuerrichtenden öffentlichen Musik-Conservatoriums und Musikalienhandlung zu N.N. (nach der neuesten vorzunehmenden Einrichtung) (Leipzig, 1781)
Unpartheiische Kritik (Leipzig, 1798–?1800; continued as *Musikalische kritische Zeitschrift,* ?1800–06)
Nachricht an ein verehrungswürdiges Publikum: die Herausgabe einer kritischen musicalischen Zeitschrift in Vergleichung mit einem anderen ähnlichen Unternehmen betreffend (Leipzig, 11 July 1798)
Musikalisch-litterarische Anzeige (Leipzig, 15 Aug 1798)

BIBLIOGRAPHY

A. Schering: *Musikgeschichte Leipzigs von 1723–1800*, iii (Leipzig, 1941)

R. Eller: 'Thomas, Christian Gottfried', *MGG*

B. S. Brook: 'Piracy and Panacea: on the Dissemination of Music in the Late Eighteenth Century', *PRMA*, cii (1975–6), 13

BARRY S. BROOK

Thomas, David Wynne. *See* WYNNE, DAVID.

Thomas, Ernst (*b* Darmstadt, 21 Feb 1916). German administrator and writer on music. He studied the piano with Teichmüller, conducting with Abendroth and Hochkofler, theory with Ludwig and musicology with Oppel at the Leipzig Conservatory (1934–9). He then took up conducting with Clemens Krauss at the Salzburg Mozarteum; at the beginning of the war he held conducting appointments in Freiburg and Görlitz. He was music critic of the *Darmstädter Echo* (1947–56) and music editor of the *Frankfurter allgemeine Zeitung* (1956–62). In 1962 he was appointed head of the International Institute of Music in Darmstadt, where he is also director of the international summer courses in contemporary music, editor of the *Neue Zeitschrift für Musik* (1963–) and organizer of the concert series Musica Viva at Bavarian Radio, Munich. He is general editor of Darmstädter Beiträge zur Neuen Musik (1962–) and Neue Musik in der BRD (1962–71).

WRITINGS

ed.: K. A. Hartmann: *Kleine Schriften* (Mainz, 1965)

ed.: *Zeitgenössisches Musiktheater* (Hamburg, 1965)

Der neue Musikbericht (Cologne, 1967) [articles from broadcast series for West German Radio, 1961–6]

ed.: *Ferienkurse '72* (Mainz, 1973) [incl. 'Von der Notwendigkeit, Ferienkurse für neue Musik zu veranstalten', 6; also published in the Strecker Festschrift, 1973]

ALFRED GRANT GOODMAN

Thomas, Isaiah (*b* Boston, Mass., 1749; *d* Worcester, Mass., 1831). American music publisher. His first publications date from the 1780s, from his shop in Worcester, Massachussetts. These early editions include *Laus Deo* (1786), *The Worcester Collection of Sacred Harmony*, John Hubbard's *Harmonia selecta* (1789) and Abraham Wood's *Divine Songs* (1789). In 1792 Thomas moved to Boston, then the centre of American music publishing. Forming a partnership with Ebenezer T. Andrews, he published many religious works and hymn tune books. These included Samuel Babcock's *Middlesex Harmony* (1795), Supply Belcher's *Celebrated Ordination Anthem* (1797), Hans Gram's *Sacred Lines* (1793), William Cooper's *Anthem for Thanksgiving Day* (1792) and Oliver Holden's *Plain Psalmody and Sacred Dirges* (1800). The firm also produced six later editions of Thomas's *Worcester Collection*, the last one appearing in 1800. Thomas was the first to import movable type from England in 1785. He was probably the foremost American music printer and publisher of his day, and he issued more titles than any of his contemporaries or predecessors. The firm was dissolved in 1800.

BIBLIOGRAPHY

O. G. Sonneck: *Bibliography of Early American Secular Music* (Washington, DC, 1905, rev. 3/1964)

W. THOMAS MARROCCO, MARK JACOBS

Thomas, Jess (Floyd) (*b* Hot Springs, South Dakota, 4 Aug 1927). American tenor. After study at Stanford University for a psychology doctorate, he was encouraged by his singing teacher Otto Schulman to pursue an operatic career. He sang Fenton in a workshop production of *Falstaff*, and in 1957 undertook Malcolm in *Macbeth* with the San Francisco Opera. He then went to Germany; studying with Emmy Seiberlich, he accepted a contract in Karlsruhe, where he sang 38 roles in 38 months, starting with Lohengrin. He soon began to make guest appearances with larger German companies, including those of Stuttgart and Munich, both of which engaged him as Bacchus in *Ariadne auf Naxos* in 1960. The following year Wieland Wagner cast him as Parsifal in Bayreuth and Radamès in Berlin. He returned to the USA for Walther von Stolzing at the Metropolitan Opera in 1962, and made his Covent Garden début in that role in 1969. He has also sung frequently in San Francisco, Salzburg and Vienna. Although his repertory at first included such relatively lyrical parts as Lensky and Cavaradossi, he later began to concentrate on the heavy Wagner roles including Siegfried, Tannhäuser and Tristan. Some listeners have felt that the strain of these challenges has robbed his voice of freshness and ease; nevertheless, his intelligence and histrionic credibility remain uncommon assets. In addition to his Wagnerian specialities, he has continued to sing Samson, Florestan and the Emperor in *Die Frau ohne Schatten*. At the opening of the new Metropolitan Opera House at Lincoln Center, on 16 September 1966, he sang Octavius in the première of Barber's *Antony and Cleopatra*.

MARTIN BERNHEIMER

Thomas, John [Pencerdd, Gwalia] (*b* Ogmore, Glamorgan, 1 March 1826; *d* London, 19 March 1913). Welsh harpist and composer. He is said to have played the piccolo at four years of age. He studied the harp under his father and won the triple harp competition in 1838 in an eisteddfod at Abergavenny; two years later he entered the RAM sponsored by the Countess of Lovelace. He studied composition, the piano, and the harp under J. B. Chatterton, whom he succeeded in 1871 as harpist to Queen Victoria. He became an FRAM in 1846 and began to make his mark in London as a harpist of great virtuosity. In 1851 he was playing at the opera, and the following year performed a harp concerto of his own at a Philharmonic concert. For ten years he toured each winter, playing throughout Europe from Russia to Italy. He was admitted to membership of the Società di S Cecilia, Rome, the Società Filarmonica of Florence and the Philharmonic Society, London. He was also a member of the Royal Society of Musicians. He was invested with the bardic title 'Pencerdd Gwalia' at the Aberdare eisteddfod in 1861, and though he lived mostly in London visited Wales frequently, appearing at every major eisteddfod as a performer or adjudicator. In 1862 the first volume of his collection of 49 Welsh airs with Welsh and English texts by John Jones 'Talhaiarn' and Thomas Oliphant was published in London and he gave there the first of a long series of concerts of Welsh music. His cantata *Llywelyn* was performed at the Aberdare eisteddfod in 1863, and *The Bride of Neath Valley* at Chester in 1866. Five years later he founded and conducted the Welsh Choral Union in London and endowed a permanent scholarship at the RAM. In 1882 he was appointed an examiner at the RAM and also professor of harp at the RCM and the GSM. He was a popular lecturer on Welsh national music and wrote on the subject in *Grove 1*; he also published 'The Musical

Notation of the Ancient Britons' (in *Myvyrian Archaiology*, Denbigh, 2/1870).

WORKS
(selective list; printed works published in London; MSS at GB-AB)
The Bride of Neath Valley (cantata, H. F. Chorley) (1863)
Llywelyn, cantata, Aberdare, 1863
for 2 harps: Scenes of Childhood, Cambria, both (1863)
ed.: Welsh Melodies (1862–74)
48 Studies for the Harp (1895)
Sym., 2 harp concs., str qts
Arrs., harp, of music of Gounod, Handel, Mendelssohn, Meyerbeer, Schubert, Verdi and others

BIBLIOGRAPHY
R. D. Griffith: 'Thomas, John', *Dictionary of Welsh Biography* (London, 1959)

OWAIN EDWARDS

Thomas (Sabater), Juan María (*b* Palma, Majorca, 7 Dec 1896; *d* Palma, 4 May 1966). Spanish composer and organist. A pupil of Daniel, Mas y Serracant and Huré, he was appointed organist of Palma Cathedral in 1914. With the Capella Classica, which he founded in 1932, he gave concerts throughout the world. He was a close associate of the poet Jiménez and of Falla: he published *Don Manuel de Falla en la isla* (Palma, 1947).

WORKS
(selective list)
Choral: Cánticos de mayo a la Virgen, chorus, org, 1918; Adeste fideles, chorus, org, 1919; Campanas sobre el mar, 1936; Dípticos, 1944; Mass 'Ex ore infantium', 3vv, 1952; Villancicos españoles para un nacimiento barroco, 1953; Música para el festival de Bellver, chorus, small orch, 1953; Cantata de Santa María, 1954; Partita super 'Salve regina', 1956; Homenaje a Juan Ramón y a Zenobia, 1957
Solo vocal: El íntimo refugio, 1v, pf, 1943; Canciones españolas de instrumentos, 1v, pf, 1944; Canciones populares mallorquinas, 1v, gui
Org: Magnificat, 1919; Rosetón, 1939; Coral y plegaria; Prelude 'Parce Domine'; Toccata post 'Te Deum'
Pf: Noël triste, 1936; Canticum de Archa Noe, 1951; Le clavecin voyageur, 1952

Principal publisher: Unión Musical Española

BIBLIOGRAPHY
G. Bourligueux: 'Juan María Thomas (1896–1966)', *L'orgue* (1968), no.128, p.171

GUY BOURLIGUEUX

Thomas, Kurt (Georg Hugo) (*b* Tönning, 25 May 1904; *d* Bad Oeynhausen, 31 March 1973). German choral conductor and composer. He studied church music in Leipzig under Straube and Grabner, and composition in Darmstadt under Arnold Mendelssohn. At the age of 21 he was appointed lecturer in theory and composition at the Leipzig Conservatory, and in 1928 took charge of the choir at the Institute of Church Music in the city. Subsequently he held posts as professor at the Berlin Musikhochschule (from 1934), director of the Musisches Gymnasium in Frankfurt (1939–45), Kantor of the Frankfurt Dreikönigskirche (1945–56), professor at the North West German Music Academy, Detmold (1947–55), and director of the Thomaskantorei and the Thomasschule in Leipzig (1955–61). He then left abruptly for West Germany to become conductor of the Cologne Bach Society concerts and again of the choir in Frankfurt.

Thomas enjoyed a high reputation as a choir trainer and conductor; his *Lehrbuch der Chorleitung* (Leipzig, 1935–48) has remained an essential work in this subject. He also played a significant part from 1925 in the renewal of Protestant church music in Germany. His enthusiasm for youth work sometimes made him appear rash and unheeding of the ruling political forces, and after his final return from Leipzig he was no longer able to exert much influence in German musical life.

WORKS
(selective list)
Orch: Serenade, op.10; Spielmusik I–II, opp.18a, 22; Pf Conc., op.30
Choral: Mass, a, op.1, 1925; Passionsmusik nach den Evangelisten Markus, op.6; Weihnachts-Oratorium, op.17; Auferstehungs-Oratorium, op.24; Hohes Lied der Arbeit, op.26; Eichendorff-Kantate, op.37; other cantatas, motets, psalms, songs etc
Other works: chamber pieces, org music, lieder

Principal publisher: Breitkopf & Härtel

BIBLIOGRAPHY
W. Weismann: 'Eine moderne Motettenpassion von Kurt Thomas', *ZfM*, xciv (1927), 207
M. Schneider: 'Brief an Kurt Thomas zur Vollendung seines 50. Lebensjahres', *Musik und Kirche*, xxiv (1954), 98
J. G. Mehl: 'Kurt Thomas 60 Jahre', *Gottesdienst und Kirchenmusik* (1964), 87
A. Adrio: 'Erneuerung und Wiederbelebung', *Geschichte der evangelischen Kirchenmusik*, ed. F. Blume (Kassel, 1965), 271
M. Kluge, ed.: *Chorerziehung und neue Musik: für Kurt Thomas zum 65. Geburtstag* (Wiesbaden, 1969)

HANSPETER KRELLMANN

Thomas, Mansel (Treharne) (*b* Tylorstown, Rhondda Valley, 12 June 1909). Welsh composer and conductor. In 1925 he won a scholarship to the Royal Academy of Music, where he studied composition under Dale. He left the RAM in 1930 and in the same year gained the BMus at Durham University. After some years as a freelance conductor in London he was appointed music assistant in the BBC Welsh Region in 1936 and conductor of the BBC Revue Orchestra in 1941. Between 1943 and 1946 he served with the Royal Army Service Corps in Belgium where he also appeared as guest conductor of the Belgian National Orchestra. In 1946 he was made conductor of the reconstituted BBC Welsh Orchestra and also of the Cardiff Municipal Choir, and in 1950 he was appointed BBC head of music in Wales, a post he relinquished 15 years later to devote more time to composition. He was elected an honorary fellow of the RAM in 1959 and in 1970 he was awarded the OBE in recognition of his services to Welsh music. He was made an honorary professorial fellow of the University of Wales in 1972.

As a conductor Thomas has always been associated with choral music and he has on several occasions directed choirs at the National Eisteddfod. His own compositions, too, are predominantly choral; their style is much influenced by Dale and by the music of Dale's English contemporaries. Among the most important of the choral works are three psalm settings and two full-scale cantatas, but several of the shorter anthems and partsongs are distinguished by their sensitivity to verbal rhythms and by a judicious use of chromaticism within a fundamentally diatonic idiom. Among the solo songs the *Four Prayers from the Gaelic* have attracted wide attention. Thomas has contributed articles on Welsh music to various journals.

WORKS
CHORAL
Moonbeams (M. H. George), SS, 1935–6; The Triumph Song (Shelley), TTBB, 1935–6; Coronach (Scott), TTBB, 1935–8; Daffodils (Herrick), TTBB, 1935–8; My true love hath my heart (Sydney), 1935–8; The Fairies (W. Allingham), SSA, pf, 1935–8; One Generation Passeth (Bible), SATB, 1952; 3 Songs for Christmas, SATB, 1952; Psalm cxxxv, A, male chorus, orch/org, 1959; Love came down at Christmas (C. Rossetti), SATB, 1962; I will lift up mine eyes (Psalm cxxi), SATB, 1964; Carol for Christmas (P. Cobb), unison vv, pf, 1964–6
Anthem of Challenge and Comfort (Bible), S, TTBB, org, 1964–6; Blest are the Pure in Heart (J. Keble), SATB, org, 1964–6; Carol for a New-born King (D. Adams-Jeremiah), unison vv, pf, 1964–6; Rise, O my Soul, anthem, SATB, 1964–6; Songs of Enchantment (de la Mare), SSA, pf, 1965–6; Cân serch (trad.), SATB, pf, 1967; Psalm

xxiv, Bar, SATB, brass, 1967; Songs of Britain (trad.), SSA, pf, 1967; Fantasia on Famous Welsh Airs (trad.). TTBB, pf, 1967
Hen ferchetan (trad.), TTBB, pf, 1968; Gwas y Goruchaf (Servant of the Most High) (cantata, E. Cleaver), SATB, orch, 1968; Fantasia on Well-known Carols (trad.), SATB, org, 1969; In Praise of Wisdom (cantata, Cobb), A, SATB, orch, 1969–70; Rhapsody for a Prince (trad.), SATB, orch, 1969–70; Psalm cl, TTBB, pf, 1970; Fantasia on Welsh Hymn Tunes, TTBB, org, 1971; hymn tune and folksong arrs.

OTHER WORKS

Operetta: The White Rose (l, I. O. Williams), broadcast May 1941
Vocal: A Boy's Song (J. Hogg), S, pf (1936); Life (T. G. Jones), S/T, pf, 1940; Y bardd (R. W. Parry), S/T, pf, 1940; Caneuon grace a sian (trad.), S, pf, 1943; Hymn to God the Father (Donne), Bar, orch, 1950; 4 Prayers from the Gaelic (Carmichael), Mez, pf, 1962; Gwyn ap nudd (Elfed), 1v, pf, 1963; 3 Songs from Joanna (A. G. Prŷs-Jones), 1v, pf, 1963; In memoriam Hywel Davies (W. Williams), T, pf/orch, 1965; Welsh Heritage, song cycle, 1974; Raiders Dawn, song cycle, Bar, pf, 1975
Orch: Allegro, str, 1929; Variations, 1935–7; 2 Welsh Dances, 1947; Breton Suite, 1949; Mini-variations on a Welsh Theme, brass, 1969
Chamber: 2 pf trios, 1933; Str Qt, f, 1939; Suite, 2 cl, 1939; Sonata, a, vc, pf, 1949, withdrawn; Variants, vc, 1973; Variants no.2, vc, 1974; Variants on an Old Welsh Theme, harp, 1975; 3 Pieces, vc, pf, 1975; Suite, vc, 1975

Principal publishers: Novello, Oxford University Press, University of Wales Press

PETER CROSSLEY-HOLLAND/MALCOLM BOYD

Thomas [Holmes], **(Averil) Mary** (*b* Swansea, 2 Aug 1935). Welsh mezzo-soprano. She studied at the RAM and began her career singing music of all types, though she was most associated with Baroque opera and oratorio: she sang Dido in Deller's 1965 recording of Purcell's opera. In 1967 she was a founder-member of the Pierrot Players (later Fires of London), an ensemble directed by Birtwistle and Davies, and from that time she has concentrated on 20th-century music. Her histrionic appearance as a screaming red nun in Davies's *Revelation and Fall* (1968) brought immediate notoriety to composer and ensemble, and she took a leading part in many of the group's later successes. Some of these depended as much on her theatrical abilities as on her wide-ranging vocal technique, but none so much as *Miss Donnithorne's Maggot* (1974), in which she played a raving aged bride amid the debris of her unconsumed wedding breakfast. Thomas has recorded several works by Davies, as well as her grotesque and macabre version of *Pierrot lunaire*. She has also sung with other London ensembles (in Berio and Webern with the London Sinfonietta, for example) and appeared at major festivals in Europe and Australia.

PAUL GRIFFITHS

Thomas, Michael Tilson (*b* Hollywood, 21 Dec 1944). American conductor. He began his musical studies in Los Angeles and attended the University of Southern California. The composer Ingolf Dahl, the pianist John Crown and the harpsichordist Alice Ehlers were his principal teachers. He conducted the Young Musicians Foundation Debut Orchestra, was pianist and conductor at the Monday Evening Concerts, played for Piatigorsky's master classes, prepared the orchestra for the Heifetz–Piatigorsky concerts, and was assistant conductor to Boulez at the Ojai Festival in 1967, being conductor there in 1968, 1969 and 1973. He attended the Bayreuth Festival master classes in 1966, and was a conducting fellow at the Berkshire Music Center, Tanglewood, in 1968 and 1969, winning the Koussevitzky Conducting Prize in his first year there. In spring 1969 William Steinberg heard him conduct the Boston Philharmonia and recommended his appoint-

ment as assistant conductor of the Boston SO. Only days after his first concerts, he attained celebrity on 22 October when he took over for Steinberg, suddenly ill, during a concert in Philharmonic Hall, New York. Thomas conducted the orchestra more than 30 times the rest of that season and was named associate conductor in spring 1970. In 1971 he became music director of the Buffalo PO and in 1972 was appointed (with Colin Davis) principal guest conductor of the Boston SO. In his first Boston season he was also pianist of the Boston Symphony Chamber Players. He conducts widely as a guest (his London début was with the LSO in 1970) and has recorded both as a conductor and a pianist (making the first record, with Ralph Grierson, of Stravinsky's own four-hand version of *The Rite of Spring*).

Thomas has a remarkable breadth of musical, artistic and intellectual interests. His repertory stretches from Pérotin, Josquin and Schütz to Stockhausen and Steve Reich, and he has a knack for original but harmonious programme building. Theatre, especially musical theatre, is a particular interest of his – the Tomashefskys, his family, were important in Yiddish theatre for more than a generation – and he enthusiastically supports the use of electronic devices to aid musical performance. He has intelligence and temperament, an outgoing personality, a flamboyant platform manner, and articulate speech.

MICHAEL STEINBERG

Thomas, Theodore (Christian Friedrich) (*b* Esens, East Friesland, 11 Oct 1835; *d* Chicago, 4 Jan 1905). American conductor of German birth. His father was a *Stadtmusikus* in Esens. Thomas started playing the violin when he was two. Five years later he performed for the King of Hanover who offered him a place in the royal household, which he declined. In 1845 the family went to the USA. Thomas's formal education evidently ceased after his arrival in New York, his home for the next 46 years. Nor is there any record of his having studied the violin with a recognized teacher, although he did study harmony and counterpoint in his 20s. He served as a member and leader of many opera, theatre and concert orchestras and was a well-known and esteemed soloist and chamber player. In 1855 he and the pianist William Mason launched a series of monthly matinée chamber concerts at Dodworth Hall in New York; this series continued for 14 years, featuring works for string quartet and for piano and strings, and the standard of playing and repertory attracted admiration in Europe and North America.

Thomas began conducting in 1859. Three years later he conducted his first personally sponsored orchestral concerts at Irving Hall. He was then engaged as conductor by the Brooklyn Philharmonic Society, starting an association with the group which, except for a few years, continued until 1891. In 1864 he began his Irving Hall Symphonic Soirées, which were distinguished by an ever-increasing sophistication in choice of repertory, comparable to the best orchestral programmes of London, Paris, Vienna and Berlin. The works performed most frequently were by Beethoven, Schumann, Liszt and Wagner, in that order. Thomas began giving lighter summer programmes in 1865, the most notable being those held at the Central Park Gardens in New York from 1868 to 1875. He led 1227 concerts of great variety from May to September in these eight years. In 1869 the Theodore Thomas Orchestra gave the first of many tours over the legendary 'Thomas Highway' of the USA and Canada.

Thomas was musical director of the 1876 Philadelphia Centennial Exposition. His orchestra gave concerts almost daily but attendance was poor. At great expense he had commissioned Wagner to write a piece for the national celebration and the composer complied with a banal march. Thomas accepted the directorship of the new College of Music in Cincinnati in 1878 but, frustrated with the school's policy, left a year and a half later. He did, however, remain in contact with Cincinnati through its biennial May Festival: he had directed the first one in 1873 and retained artistic leadership of the event until his death. Thomas adapted the Cincinnati pattern of choral-orchestral concerts for other cities, the most notable example being for New York in 1882. A chorus of 3000 sang to the accompaniment of an orchestra of 300. The audience numbered approximately 8000 at each of the seven concerts in the 7th Regiment Armoury. In 1883 his 'Highway' tour, subtitled 'the March to the West', included 30 cities from coast to coast, 74 concerts in as many days, and 12 festivals.

In 1877 Thomas was elected conductor of the New York PO, a post he held, excluding his stay in Cincinnati, until 1891. It thrived under his direction. He subordinated his own orchestra to it and finally disbanded the group in 1888 after it completed its summer season at Chicago. Three years earlier he had unwisely accepted the musical leadership of the newly formed American Opera Company. Its policy was to encourage composition of American works and to perform opera in English only, with American singers and no stars. It presented nine works in New York and on tour in its first season in 1886, including works by Wagner and Mozart. Six more operas were added in 1887. The company, however, failed dismally through lack of money and support.

This setback, the rise in prominence of the conductor Anton Seidl, the persistent competition of the Damrosch family, the growing importance of opera at the new Metropolitan Opera House (in which Thomas had no role) and his consuming wish for a full-time permanent orchestra, which the New York PO was not, set the stage for an exciting invitation from Chicago. A group of businessmen there offered to sustain a resident orchestra of Thomas's choosing, similar to that which Boston already had. This pattern of widely based support by the rich was the first of similar schemes for organizing orchestras in many other North American cities. Thomas endured several crises in Chicago: a scandal, for which he was essentially blameless, concerning the use of pianos at the 1892 Columbian Exposition; an antagonistic public and press; unwanted but financially necessary tours by the orchestra which taxed severely the energy of the prematurely aging conductor; and the unrequited need for an appropriate Chicago concert hall. In December 1904, a few weeks before his death, the new Orchestra Hall opened as the permanent home of the Chicago SO.

Thomas did more than any other American musician of the 19th century to popularize music of the great European masters. He planted the seed for local symphony orchestras in cities throughout the land because of his concert and festival tours and hoped to educate the American people towards a greater appreciation of symphonic music. He was a brilliant organizer and an indefatigable worker. He not only directed his orchestra with total autonomy but also managed its business details. He devised the subscription plan for ticket sales and mapped out special 'pop' and children's programmes, and even concerts for working men. His knowledge and understanding of audiences, as expressed in his programming, was exemplary. He was an undemonstrative, often aloof, conductor, but an admirable disciplinarian who knew his instruments and scores, understood the technical and psychological aspects of orchestral leadership and had the respect of his players. Thomas was admired by those great soloists of Europe who appeared with him. At its height in 1875 the Thomas Orchestra was, by common consent, unsurpassed anywhere, as was the New York PO under his direction ten years later. The popularity of the symphony orchestra in the USA today is due in great part to the work of Thomas.

The Thomas Collection of the Newberry Library, Chicago, has 50 volumes of his programmes, autograph scores of his compositions and transcriptions, his personal library and 631 letters, clippings and photographs. The Library of Congress, Washington, has 46 Thomas MS notebooks, memoranda and letters. He published *A Musical Autobiography* (Chicago, 1905/*R*1964, vol. i only, with an introduction by Leon Stein), which was edited by G. P. Upton.

BIBLIOGRAPHY

W. Mason: *Memoirs of a Musical Life* (New York, 1901)
P. A. Otis: *The Chicago Symphony Orchestra: its Organization, Growth, and Development* (Chicago, 1908)
G. P. Upton: *Musical Memoirs: my Recollections of Celebrities of the Half Century, 1850–1900* (Chicago, 1908)
R. F. Thomas: *Memoirs of Theodore Thomas* (New York, 1911/*R*1971)
C. E. Russell: *The American Orchestra and Theodore Thomas* (Garden City, NY, 1927)
E. T. Rice: 'Thomas and Central Park Garden', *MQ*, xxvi (1940), 143
A. Loft: 'Richard Wagner, Theodore Thomas and the American Centennial', *MQ*, xxxvii (1951), 184
J. H. Mueller: *The American Symphony Orchestra* (Bloomington, 1951)
T. C. Russell: *Theodore Thomas: his Role in the Development of Musical Culture in the United States, 1835–1905* [includes bibliography] (diss., U. of Minnesota, Minneapolis, 1969)

EZRA SCHABAS

Thomas Aquinas. *See* AQUINAS, THOMAS.

Thomaschor. The choir of the Leipzig Thomaskirche; *see* LEIPZIG, §1.

Thomas de Sancto Juliano (*fl* early or mid-13th century). Musical scribe active in Paris. He was roughly contemporary with Robertus de Sabilone but was described by the theorist Anonymous IV (ed. Reckow, 1967, i, 50) as the 'elderly Parisian'. Anonymous IV said that he did not write music as the scribes of the Notre Dame books after Pérotin did, but 'was good by the standards of the older notators'. He has been suggested (by Dittmer, *MD*, xi, 9) as the scribe of the St Victor manuscript (*F-Pn* 15139), but purely on grounds of notational style.

See ORGANUM AND DISCANT: BIBLIOGRAPHY.

IAN D. BENT

Thomé, Francis [François Luc Joseph] (*b* Port Louis, Mauritius, 18 Oct 1850; *d* Paris, 16 Nov 1909). French composer and teacher. He was taken as a child to Paris, where he studied at the Conservatoire with A. F. Marmontel (piano), Jules Duprato (harmony) and Ambroise Thomas (composition). In 1870 he won a *premier prix* for counterpoint and fugue. Soon after leaving the Conservatoire he became well known as a composer of salon pieces and was in demand as a teacher. His music was particularly successful in the French provinces, and two of his operas were given outside Paris. His most popular compositions were the choral ode *Hymne à la nuit*, the *mystère L'enfant Jésus* and piano pieces such as *Gavotte-madrigal* and *Simple aveu*; the last mentioned was republished in England in 1966.

Thomé's works have generally fallen into oblivion. They betray no originality of harmony or melody, and are a depressing example of musical commercialism. Possibly their worst feature, apart from their fundamental sentimentality, is their slavish adherence to four-bar phrases.

WORKS

(*all printed works published in Paris*)

STAGE

(*first performances in Paris unless otherwise stated*)

Martin et Frontin (opéra comique), Eaux-Bonnes Casino, Aug 1877
Le caprice de la reine (opéra comique, 1, A. Brisson, C. Foley), Cannes, April 1892
Vieil air, jeune chanson (operetta, 1, A. Lenéka), Galerie Vivienne, 13 Dec 1893 (1894)
Le château de Koenigsberg (operetta, 3, A. Silvestre), Opéra-Comique, 22 April 1896
Le chaperon rouge (operetta, 3, H. Lefebvre), Odéon, 7 April 1900
Ballets: Les noces d'Arlequin (1885); Djemmah, Eden, 1886 (1886): Endymion et Phoebé, Opéra-Comique; La fée du rocher (1894); La bulle d'amour, Eden, 1898; La folie parisienne, Eden, 1900
Ballet-pantomimes: Barbe-Bluette (1, R. de Najac), perf. 1889 (1901); Mademoiselle Pygmalion (1911); Le papillon; Le trottin
Incidental music: Roméo et Juliette, Odéon, 30 Oct 1890; L'infidèle, Vaudeville, 1890; Quo vadis, Porte St-Martin, 1901; La belle au bois dormant; Les noces corinthiennes

OTHER WORKS

Chorus, orch: Hymne à la nuit, symphonic ode; La fiancée du timbalier (Hugo) (1890); L'enfant Jésus (mystère, 5, C. Grandmougin) (1891)
Vocal: many songs
Chamber: Pf trio (1893); Vn Sonata (1901); other works
Pf: waltzes, preludes, études, genre pieces; arrs. of 40 Schubert songs (1875)

BIBLIOGRAPHY

L. de Romain: *Essais de critique musicale* (Paris, 1890)
C. Pierre: *Le Conservatoire national de musique et de déclamation: documents historiques et administratifs* (Paris, 1900)
A. P[?ougin].: 'Nécrologie', *Le ménestrel*, lxxv/47 (1909), 375
N. Wild: 'Thomé, François-Luc-Joseph', *MGG*

DAVID CHARLTON

Thomelin [Thomolin], **Jacques-Denis** (*b c*1640; *d* Paris, 1693). French organist and composer. He was a member of a family of musicians active over several centuries – most of them as organists – and is the only one deserving of special mention. He was organist of St Germain-des-Prés in 1667 and of St Jacques-la-Boucherie in 1669; both of these Paris churches were crowded when he played on feast days. In 1667 he became one of the four court organists, together with Lebègue, Buterne and Nivers. He was the guardian and teacher of François Couperin, who succeeded him as royal organist. There is one allemande by him in J. Bonfils, ed.: *Les pré-classiques français*, L'organiste liturgique, xviii, 1957. An MS *Suplément aux livres de messes et de motets* (*à l'usage de St Cyr*) (*F-Pn* Rés. 1680) contains a *Domine, salvum fac regem* by 'Thomelin'; which member of the family is not specified, but it is quite likely to be Jacques-Denis.

G. B. SHARP

Thomish, František Václav. See TOMEŠ, FRANTIŠEK VÁCLAV.

Thommen, Johannes (*b* Basle, 6 Jan 1711; buried Basle, 7 Feb 1783). He was a tailor until *c*1743, and proprietor of an oilcloth factory until 1762. From 1738 he officiated as cantor of St Peter's in Basle for several decades although, because of official opposition, he was unable to reform singing instruction. From 1765 he also served as city councillor.

Thommen collected 500 sacred texts which, together with 275 'Melodien' for one to four voices, he published as *Erbaulicher Musicalischer Christen-Schatz* (Basle, 1745), modelled on collections published by J. L. Steiner and J. C. Bachofen. Although Thommen did not name the composers, the introduction cites the well-known *Christenschatz* and the *Cöthnische geistliche Lieder* as the sources for the texts. Refardt (1920, p.102) identified the musical sources and suggested that the editor composed about 20 of the solo songs, which also appear as practice examples in his *Musicalische ABC* (Basle, 1744, enlarged 2/1763, 3/1768), intended for 'beginners, and especially the young'. Thommen also published an *Auszug der Catechismus-Lieder des neuen Gesang-Büchleins* (Basle, 1748) for young singing students.

BIBLIOGRAPHY

T. Goldschmid: *Schweizerische Gesangbücher früherer Zeiten* (Zurich, 1917) [with transcriptions]
——: *Geistliche Sologesänge und Duette*, i (Zurich, 1917); ii (Zurich, 1942)
E. Refardt: *Biographische Beiträge zur Basler Musikgeschichte* (Basle, 1920)
——: *Historisch-Biographisches Musiker-Lexikon der Schweiz* (Leipzig, 1928)
H. P. Schanzlin: 'Thommen, Johannes', *MGG*

PETER ROSS

Thomolin, Jacques-Denis. See THOMELIN, JACQUES-DENIS.

Thompson. English 18th-century family of music publishers, printers and instrument makers, established in London. The business was founded about 1746 by Peter Thompson and was continued after his death (*c*1757) by his widow Ann and son Charles, sometimes under the imprint Thompson & Son. About 1761 they were joined by a second son, Samuel Thompson (*d* Aug 1795), to become Thompson & Sons. Ann left the firm in about 1763, and thereafter it was under the direction of various family members whose names appeared on its imprints: it was under the joint management of Charles and Samuel until about 1776, after which Samuel continued alone for a year; he was then joined by another Ann (whose relationship to the preceding Ann is not known), and these two remained with the firm until Samuel's death, on their own (*c*1777–9), then with Peter (*c*1779–93), with Peter and Henry (*c*1793–4) and finally with Henry (*c*1794–5). During the several changes of membership after 1792 the imprints frequently give 'Messrs Thompson' or 'Thompsons' Warehouse'. After Samuel's death Ann and Henry managed the firm together until about 1798, after which it continued under the sole ownership of Henry Thompson. About 1805 the business was taken over by Purday & Button (later Button & Whitaker).

The early publications of the firm were mostly of a minor character and included many tutors for violin, flute, harpsichord and other instruments. From 1751 Thompson published annual collections of *Twenty Four Country Dances*, which were continued throughout the whole period of the firm's existence and also collected into five cumulative volumes of 200 dances each; later the firm initiated a similar series of minuets. In 1764 the Thompsons acquired some plates at the auction of John Cox's stock and reissued a number of works from them.

From about 1765, while under the direction of Charles and Samuel, the firm gradually became one of the most important in London. Further advances took place under the direction of Samuel, Ann and Peter, who published yearly catalogues of their newly issued works (c1781–90). Many works by Arne, Arnold, Dibdin, Philip Hayes, James Hook, Thomas Linley the elder, F. X. Richter, Samuel Webbe the elder and others appeared with the firm's imprint. A large number of violins also bear the Thompson label and were probably built by makers in their employ.

Robert Thompson, probably a brother of Peter Thompson, had a music shop in London from 1748 until 1785. He was an instrument maker and published a number of single sheet songs.

BIBLIOGRAPHY
C. Humphries and W. C. Smith: *Music Publishing in the British Isles* (London, 1954, 2/1970)

FRANK KIDSON/WILLIAM C. SMITH/
PETER WARD JONES

Thompson, Herbert (*b* Leeds, 11 Aug 1856; *d* Leeds, 6 May 1945). English critic. He was educated at Wiesbaden and St John's College, Cambridge. Though he was called to the Bar in 1879, a strong interest in music, stimulated at Cambridge by Stanford, led him to become music critic of the *Yorkshire Post* in 1886. He held this position for 50 years, throughout which time he was also the newspaper's art critic. He wrote analytical notes for the Leeds Festival and a book on the historical background to *Die Meistersinger* entitled *Wagner and Wagenseil* (London, 1927). His diary and collected newspaper articles, now in Leeds University library, form a valuable source of information on music in Yorkshire and beyond during his period. At that time music in the north of England was strongly amateur in character, and to this he was sympathetically critical. His authority, discriminating standards and literary skill contributed to the intellectual and artistic life of Yorkshire. He received the honorary degree of DLitt (Leeds) in 1925.

BIBLIOGRAPHY
G. F. Linstead: 'Herbert Thompson', *MT*, lxxxvi (1945), 207

H. C. COLLES/WATKINS SHAW

Thompson, Oscar (*b* Crawfordsville, Ind., 10 Oct 1887; *d* New York, 3 July 1945). American critic and writer on music. He was educated at the University of Washington (Seattle), and studied music privately, making several appearances as a singer (about 1912) while following a career in journalism. After army service in World War I he joined the staff of *Musical America* as critic (1919), later serving as editor (1936–43). He was also music critic of the New York *Evening Post* (1928–34), the *New York Times* (1935) and the New York *Sun* (from 1937 until his death). He instituted a unique course in music criticism at the Curtis Institute in Philadelphia (1928); he also wrote a textbook on the subject, and taught at Columbia University and the New York College of Music. His *Cyclopedia* is perhaps the best one-volume general dictionary of music in English.

WRITINGS
Practical Musical Criticism (New York, 1934/R1979)
How to Understand Music (New York, 1935/R1972, enlarged 2/1958)
Tabulated Biographical History of Music (New York, 1936)
The American Singer (New York, 1937/R1969)
'An American School of Criticism', *MQ*, xxiii (1937), 428
Debussy: Man and Artist (New York, 1937/R1967)
ed: *The International Cyclopedia of Music and Musicians* (New York, 1939, rev. 3/1945, 9/1964 ed. R. Sabin, rev. 10/1974 ed. B. Bohle)

Great Modern Composers (New York, 1941) [from the *Cyclopedia*]
Plots of the Operas (New York, 1943) [from the *Cyclopedia*]
Articles in *Daily Telegraph*, *MT*, *Sackbut*, and *Spectator*

RAMONA H. MATTHEWS

Thompson, Randall (*b* New York, 21 April 1899). American composer and teacher. He received his schooling in Boston and graduated in 1920 from Harvard, where he had studied with Davison, Hill and Spalding. By the time he received his MA in 1922 he had also studied with Bloch. In that year he received a three-year fellowship at the American Academy in Rome. From 1927 to 1929 and again from 1936 to 1937 he taught at Wellesley College. In 1929 and in 1930 he was awarded Guggenheim fellowships. He was commissioned by the Association of American Colleges to make an investigation that resulted in the book *College Music* (New York, 1935). Thereafter teaching was an important part of his life. From 1937 to 1939 he was professor of music at the University of California, Berkeley; from 1939 to 1941 director of the Curtis Institute of Music, Philadelphia. From 1941 to 1946 he was head of the music division of the School of Fine Arts at the University of Virginia, Charlottesville; in 1946 he joined the music faculty at Princeton University. In 1948 he was appointed to the faculty of the music department at Harvard University; he served as chairman for four years and later was made the Walter Bigelow Rosen Professor of Music. In 1965 he retired from teaching, but continued to compose and conduct. He received the MusD degree from the University of Rochester in 1933 and from the University of Pennsylvania in 1969. In 1941 he received the Elizabeth Sprague Coolidge Award for Services to Chamber Music, and at Harvard he received medals from the Signet Society and the Harvard Glee Club. In 1959 the Italian Government named him 'Cavaliere ufficiale al merito della Repubblica Italiana'.

Thompson is best known for his choral music, almost all of which has been written for a commission or other specific need. With the *Five Odes of Horace* (1924) he established the qualities of vocal writing which distinguish all his music written for this medium: lines which by their shape are grateful and rewarding to sing, individual choral colours to serve the successive word sounds, care for the natural rhythm of the spoken word, and an exquisite sensitivity to literary organization reflected in his musical phraseology. Harmonically both his instrumental and choral music are prevailingly diatonic. After two deft humorous pieces (*Rosemary* and *Americana*), Thompson turned to serious texts, many secular but more sacred, including a mass, a requiem and a Passion. The first of his two operas, *Solomon and Balkis*, was written for radio; the second, *The Nativity according to St Luke*, for church performance. His best-known instrumental works are the three symphonies, the two string quartets, and the symphonic fantasy *A Trip to Nahant*.

WORKS

SECULAR VOCAL

Five Odes of Horace, 4 male vv (no.1 with pf/orch, no.4 4/5 vv), 1924; Lauro, 16 May 1925
Rosemary (S. V. Benét), 4 female vv, 1929; New York, 18 Dec 1930
Americana (from The American Mercury), 4vv, pf/orch, 1932; New York, 4 April 1932
Tarantella (H. Belloc), 1937; New Haven, Conn., 12 Nov 1937
The Testament of Freedom (T. Jefferson), 4 male vv, pf/orch/band, 1943; Charlottesville, Virginia, 13 April 1943
Ode to the Virginian Voyage (M. Drayton), 4vv, orch, 1956–7; Williamsburg, Virginia, 1 April 1957

Frostiana (R. Frost), 7 Country Songs for men's, women's and mixed vv, 1959; Amherst, Mass., 18 Oct 1959
Songs, 1v, 1922–7

Pueri Hebraeorum, 8 female vv, 1928; Wellesley, Mass., 5 Feb 1928
The Peaceable Kingdom (Isaiah), 4vv, 1936; Cambridge, Mass., 3 March 1936
Alleluia, 4vv, 1940; Lenox, Mass., 8 July 1940
The Last Words of David, 4vv, orch, 1949; Lenox, Mass., 12 Aug 1949
Felices Ter, Horace Ode for A. T. Davison, 4vv, 1953
Mass of the Holy Spirit, 4vv, 1955–6; Cambridge, Mass., 22 March 1957
Requiem, 4vv, also 8vv, 1957–8; Berkeley, Calif., 22 May 1958
Glory to God in the Highest (St Luke), 4vv, 1958
The Gate of Heaven, 4vv, 1959; Hollins College, Virginia, 22 Feb 1959
The Lord is my shepherd, 4vv, pf/org/hp, 1962; New York, 1 May 1964
The Best of Rooms (R. Herrick), 4vv, 1963
A Feast of Praise, 4vv, brass choir, hp/pf, 1963; Stanford U., Calif., 11 Aug 1963
The Passion according to St Luke (oratorio in 10 scenes), 1964–5; Boston, Mass., 28 March 1965
A Psalm of Thanksgiving, 4vv, 2 children's vv, orch/pf/org, 1967; Boston, Mass., 15 Nov 1967
The Eternal Dove (J. Beaumont), for G. Wallace Woodworth, 4vv, 1968; Cambridge, Mass., 17 May 1970
The Place of the Blest (R. Herrick, R. Wilbur), 4 female vv, orch, 1969; New York, 2 March 1969
Two Herbert Motets (G. Herbert), 1. Bitter-Sweet; 2. Antiphon, 1970–71

OPERAS
Solomon and Balkis (Kipling), 5 solo vv, female chorus, orch, 1942; New York, CBS, 29 March 1942; (stage) Cambridge, Mass., 14 April 1942; commissioned by League of Composers and CBS
The Nativity according to St Luke (St Luke, R. Rowlands), 8 solo vv, 4vv, 2 boys' vv, orch, 1961; Cambridge, Mass., 13 Dec 1961; composed for the 200th anniversary of the dedication of Christ Church, Cambridge

ORCHESTRAL
Pierrot and Cothurnus, prelude, 1922; Rome, 17 May 1923
The Piper at the Gates of Dawn, prelude, 1924; Rome, 29 May 1924
Jazz Poem, pf, orch, 1928; Rochester, NY, 27 Nov 1928
Symphony no.1, 1929; Rochester, 20 Feb 1930
Symphony no.2, e, 1931; Rochester, 24 March 1932
Symphony no.3, a, 1947–9; New York, 15 May 1949; commissioned by the Ditson Fund
A Trip to Nahant, symphonic fantasy, 1953–4; Philadelphia, 18 March 1955; commissioned by the Koussevitzky Foundation

INSTRUMENTAL
The Wind in the Willows, str qt, 1924
Suite, ob, vn, va, 1940; commissioned by League of Composers
Str Qt no.1, d, 1941; Washington, DC, 30 Oct 1941; commissioned by Elizabeth Sprague Coolidge
20 Chorale Preludes, 4 Inventions, Fugue, keyboard, 1947–59
Str Qt no.2, G, 1967; Boston, Mass., 17 April 1967
Wedding Music (for Randall Thompson jr and Delia Hayes), str qt, db ad lib, 1971; Rome, 27 March 1971

Principal publisher: E. C. Schirmer

BIBLIOGRAPHY
Q. Porter: 'American Composers, XVIII, Randall Thompson', *MM*, xix (1942), 237 [includes list of works 1919–42]
E. Forbes: 'The Music of Randall Thompson', *MQ*, xxxv (1949), 1 [includes list of works 1922–43]

ELLIOT FORBES

Thomson, César (*b* Liège, 17 or 18 March 1857; *d* Bissone, nr. Lugano, 21 Aug 1931). Belgian violinist. Revealing remarkable ability at an early age, he entered the Liège Conservatory in 1864 to study with Jacques Dupuis; subsequent teachers included Léonard, Vieuxtemps, Wieniawski and Massart. His travels in Italy in 1873 led to employment by Baron Derwies at Lugano. Later he toured in Germany and Italy, winning great fame, and in 1879 he became the leader of an orchestra in Berlin. He taught the violin at the Liège Conservatory from 1882 to 1897 and in 1898 succeeded Ysaÿe as professor at the Brussels Conservatory, where he founded a string quartet with Lamoureux, Vanhout and Jacobs. In 1914 he was ap-

pointed to the staff of the Paris Conservatoire; he taught at the Ithaca Conservatory, New York, and the Juilliard School of Music from 1924 to 1927. His playing was particularly admired for its technical perfection and expressiveness. He made violin arrangements of works by Corelli, Tartini and Vivaldi, and attempted to revive interest in the music of Paganini.

BIBLIOGRAPHY
H. Timerman: *How to Produce a Beautiful Tone on the Violin . . . in Accordance with the Principles of César Thomson* (New York, 1923)
PATRICK PEIRE

Thomson, George (*b* Limekilns, Fife, 4 March 1757; *d* Leith, 18 Feb 1851). Scottish amateur folksong editor and publisher. He spent his childhood in Turriff, northern Scotland, and then at the age of 17 settled in Edinburgh. In 1780 he took a clerical post with the Board of Trustees for the Encouragement of Art and Manufactures in Scotland for whom he worked for the next 59 years. Financially secure, he devoted his spare time to music. He joined the influential Edinburgh Musical Society about 1780, playing the violin in the orchestra and singing in the choir. He also developed a taste for Scots folksongs in 'classical' arrangements by hearing foreign singers, notably the castrato Tenducci, perform them at the Edinburgh Musical Society's weekly concerts. Folksongs in their unadorned state, such as he must have heard in his childhood, do not seem to have appealed to him.

About 1791 Thomson decided to publish a prestigious collection of Scottish folksongs arranged for voice and piano trio by the greatest living European composers. This collection was to occupy him until 1841 and to cost him a great deal of his own money. Haydn and Pleyel visited London in 1791 and the publisher WILLIAM NAPIER signed on Haydn to arrange folksongs (published in 1792 and 1795): Thomson then engaged Pleyel for the same purpose and issued the first part of his *Select Collection of Scottish Airs* in Edinburgh (1793).

In 1797 Pleyel stopped arranging for Thomson, who then turned to Kozeluch (1797–1809), Haydn himself (1799–1804), Beethoven (1803–*c*1820), Weber (briefly in 1825), Hummel (1826–*c*1835) and Bishop (1841). Beethoven wrote 126 settings for Thomson, and Haydn 187. (A thematic catalogue of Haydn's and Beethoven's contributions is given in Hopkinson and Oldman.) Haydn also made a further 221 Scots song settings for William Napier and for William Whyte, another Edinburgh publisher. Musically the collection is unsatisfactory. Most of Thomson's arrangers had never heard genuine Scottish folksongs and tried to accommodate the melodies to Viennese harmony. Thomson, moreover, infuriated Beethoven by simplifying his piano parts for the drawing-room market. The folktunes were largely culled from earlier printed collections, only a few being personally collected by Thomson and his correspondents.

Many distinguished Scottish poets, such as Burns, Scott, James Hogg and Joanna Baillie, also worked for Thomson, rewriting the words of the songs at Thomson's insistence to remove their bawdiness and subsitute a pathetic sensibility. The collection contained 300 songs in six folio volumes (1793–1841). Six octavo volumes of selections were issued in 1822. But the collection was not an artistic success; it was criticized even in its own time for its lack of national spirit and is now considered not the standard classic that Thomson intended but an historical curiosity.

Other significant publications of his included three volumes of *Welsh Airs* in 1809, 1811 and 1817, and two of *Irish Airs* in 1814 and 1816. In 1817 he commissioned a cantata from Sir Henry Bishop on Burns's poem, *The Jolly Beggars*. From 1803 he made several attempts to get Beethoven to write chamber works incorporating Scots folktunes, but negotiations were unsuccessful because Beethoven asked for too much money.

In 1847 Thomson wrote an amusing and informative account of the Edinburgh Musical Society's activities in the 1780s which was published in Robert Chambers's *Traditions of Edinburgh* (1868). A watercolour of Thomson is in the Scottish National Portrait Gallery. Thomson's daughter, Georgina, married the music critic George Hogarth in 1814; their daughter married Charles Dickens in 1836.

BIBLIOGRAPHY

J. C. Hadden: *George Thomson, the Friend of Burns* (London, 1898)

R. Aldrich: 'Beethoven and George Thomson', *ML*, viii (1927), 234

F. Lederer: *Beethovens Bearbeitungen schottischer und anderer Volkslieder* (Bonn, 1934)

C. Hopkinson and C. B. Oldman: 'Thomson's Collection of National Song', *Transactions of the Edinburgh Bibliographical Society*, ii (1940), 3–64

K. Geiringer: 'Haydn and the Folksong of the British Isles', *MQ*, xxxv (1949), 179

C. B. Oldman: 'Beethoven's Variations on National Themes', *MR*, xii (1951), 45

C. Hopkinson and C. B. Oldman: 'Haydn's Settings of Scottish Songs in the Collections of Napier and Whyte', *Transactions of the Edinburgh Bibliographical Society*, iii (1954), 87–120

D. Johnson: *Music and Society in Lowland Scotland in the 18th Century* (London, 1972), 41f, 142ff, 162

DAVID JOHNSON

Thomson, John (*b* Sprouston, Roxburgh, 28 Oct 1805; *d* Edinburgh, 6 May 1841). Scottish musical scholar and composer. He was the son of Andrew M. Thomson (1778–1831), an eminent clergyman who later became minister of St George, Edinburgh. He met Mendelssohn during the latter's visit to Edinburgh in summer 1829, and Mendelssohn praised a trio and some other compositions of his in a letter of introduction to his family in Berlin. During his visit to Germany Thomson studied at Leipzig, kept up his friendship with Mendelssohn and became well acquainted with Schumann, Moscheles and other musicians, and Schnyder von Wartensee, whose pupil he became. In October 1839, with a recommendation from Mendelssohn he was elected the first Reid Professor at Edinburgh University. He gave the first Reid concert on 12 February 1841, and the book of words contains analytical remarks by him on the principal pieces – an early instance of such commentary. The songs from his three stage works remained popular long after his death.

WORKS

(selective list; all MSS in GB-Er)

STAGE

The House of Aspen (drama, Scott), Edinburgh, 19 Dec 1829, vocal score (Edinburgh, 1829)

Hermann, or The Broken Spear (opera), London, Lyceum, 27 Oct 1834, vocal score (London, 1834)

The Shadow on the Wall (musical play, T. J. Serle), London, Lyceum, 20 April 1835, vocal score (London, 1835)

OTHER WORKS

Benedictus and Osanna, vv, insts, 1829

3 Lieder, 1v, pf (Byron, Schiller, Uhland) (Frankfurt am Main, *c*1838); several single glees and songs, incl. The Pirate's Serenade, Harold Harfager; various It. arias

Overture, c, orch, 1830; Allegro maestoso and allegro grazioso, fl, orch, *c*1830

Minuet, fl, pf (London, 1839); Capriccio, vn, pf

Divertimento, pf 4 hands

Pf solo: Rondo, 1828; Mazurka (London, 1828); Polonaise (London, 1829); Waltz (London, 1830); Bagatelle, 1831; Minuet

EDITIONS

Vocal Melodies of Scotland (Edinburgh, 2/1836), collab. F. Dun

WRITINGS

First Annual Concert in Memory of General Reid . . . with Brief Notices of the Music (Edinburgh, 1841)

BIBLIOGRAPHY

S. Hensel: *Die Familie Mendelssohn, 1729–1847*, i (Berlin, 1879), 243

D. Baptie: *Musical Scotland* (Edinburgh, 1894/*R*1972)

C. H. Smith: 'Thomson, John', *DNB*

GEORGE GROVE/R

Thomson, Virgil (*b* Kansas City, Missouri, 25 Nov 1896). American composer and critic. His collaboration with Gertrude Stein produced two highly unusual stage wor·s, and his career in journalism established him as one of the sharpest music critics in the USA.

1. Career. 2. Style.

1. CAREER. Thomson learnt to play the piano at the age of five and began lessons with local teachers when he was 12. He studied the organ from 1909 until 1917 and again in 1919; from the beginning of this period he also worked as organist in the family church (Calvary Baptist) and other churches in Kansas City. He attended Central High School (1908–13) and a local junior college (1915–17, 1919). During the American involvement in World War I he enlisted in the army and was in a field artillery unit; he was also trained in radio telephony at Columbia University and in aviation at a pilots' ground school in Texas. He was set for embarkation to France when the war ended.

In autumn 1919 Thomson entered Harvard, where he was decisively influenced from the start by three men: the French-trained composer Edward Burlingame Hill, with whom he studied orchestration and modern French music among other subjects; Archibald T. Davison (also French-trained), the conductor of the Harvard Glee Club, for whom he was assistant and accompanist for three years; and S. Foster Damon, a Blake scholar, poet and composer, who introduced him to the works of Satie and to *Tender Buttons*, Gertrude Stein's early collection of writings. Thomson began to compose at Harvard in 1920. In the summer of 1921 the Glee Club toured Europe, with Thomson occasionally conducting, and he stayed on for a year in Paris under a John Knowles Paine Traveling Fellowship. He chose to study the organ at the Ecole Normale with Boulanger, and he also studied counterpoint with her privately. During the year he met Cocteau and Les Six and was introduced to Satie. He composed and wrote music notices for the *Boston Transcript*, his first published critical work. Back in the USA he returned to Harvard and was made organist-choirmaster at King's Chapel, Boston. He gave the first American performance of Satie's *Socrate* with the Harvard Musical Club and graduated from the university in 1923. In New York, with a grant from the Juilliard School, he studied conducting with Chalmers Clifton and counterpoint with Rosario Scalero.

Thomson returned in autumn 1925 to Paris, where he lived, apart from visits to the USA, until 1940. His first composition from this period was the *Sonata da chiesa*, a neo-classical chamber work for five instruments completed in February 1926 and consisting of a Chorale, Tango and Fugue. The conception of the piece – chic, ironic and deliberately outrageous – derived from Stravinsky's recent works. Thomson later called it his 'graduation piece in the dissonant style of the time'; he consulted with Boulanger for the last time while the work was in progress. He also composed four organ pieces based on American Protestant hymns (the *Variations and Fugues on Sunday School Tunes*) and the *Symphony on a Hymn Tune*, his first symphony.

The meeting with Gertrude Stein took place in autumn 1926, and the two expatriates began to lay plans for an opera. They decided it would concern Spanish saints and the Spanish landscape. Meanwhile, Thomson composed settings of two Stein texts: the song *Preciosilla* and *Capital Capitals*, an unorthodox cantata-like piece for four male voices and piano. (He had set Stein's *Susie Asado* before their meeting.) Stein completed the libretto for the opera, *Four Saints in Three Acts*, in June 1927, and Thomson finished the piano score a year later (it was orchestrated in 1933). The original text was rambling, plotless, hermetic, with no clearcut division into scenes and acts and with little indication of which character was speaking at any given moment. Stein's saints, led by Teresa of Avila and Ignatius Loyola, are devoid of any real character; they are preoccupied with asking questions ('How many saints are there in it?', 'How many acts are there in it?'), counting, and repeating children's rhymes. The text does contain religious symbolism and private references to events in the writer's life, but these serve only as material for word games and random remarks. Thomson imposed order on the material, eventually deleting about a third of it, and fashioned a work consisting of a prologue and four acts. In the absence of a plot, Thomson's painter friend Maurice Grosser devised a scenario, or series of tableaux and processions, for staging the work. The score consists of elements that were to be characteristic of much of Thomson's subsequent work: simple diatonic harmony (with occasional bichordal clashes), short tunes in Protestant-hymn style, extended parlando and chant passages reminiscent of Anglican liturgy, quotations of familiar airs (e.g. *God Save the King* or *My Country, 'tis of thee*), popular dance rhythms (especially the waltz and the tango), and careful, highly polished prosody. When *Four Saints* received its initial performances in Hartford, New York, and Chicago (with Stein present), it was widely publicized and became something of a *succès de scandale*. Though it never took a permanent place in the repertory, it is the composer's most famous work.

For a period of about seven years after the opera Thomson worked at expanding his technical facility, especially in writing for string instruments. Almost all of his works featuring strings – the Violin Sonata, the two string quartets, etc – date from this period. He also composed the Symphony no.2 (adapted from the First Piano Sonata) and a series of 'portraits', the musical equivalents of Stein's word pictures of the same name. Thomson eventually composed dozens of these pieces, some of which he orchestrated and used as sections of larger works. None of the works of this period contains allusions to hymn-tune style or traditional material (though Thomson's waltz strain is still prominent); they are concerned, rather, with problems of 'pure' music making. Thomson returned to the nationalistic vein in earnest, however, with two film scores and a ballet in the later 1930s. For *The Plow that Broke the Plains* and *The River*, widely acclaimed documentary films directed

by Pare Lorentz and sponsored by an American government agency, he used cowboy songs, traditional southern spirituals, old popular tunes and (for *The River*) the finale of the *Symphony on a Hymn Tune*. The dance score *Filling Station* was commissioned by Kirstein for Ballet Caravan and was called (by Balanchin) 'the very oldest classic ballet with a specifically native American theme in the extant repertory'. It has waltzes, tangos (one reworked from the *Sonata da chiesa*) and suggestions of a Salvation Army band.

Virgil Thomson

In October 1940 Thomson was appointed music critic of the *New York Herald Tribune*. During 14 years at this post he established himself as one of the major critical writers of the era. His newspaper pieces – all stylish, bright, deliberately provocative and unshakeably opinionated – furnished material for three anthologies, *The Musical Scene*, *The Art of Judging Music* and *Music, Right and Left*. He also continued to compose, most notably a second opera on a Stein text, *The Mother of us all* (commissioned by the Alice M. Ditson Fund), and the score for another documentary film, *Louisiana Story*, directed by Robert Flaherty. Stein's libretto, begun in 1945 and completed by March 1946 (four months before her death), was less abstract than her *Four Saints*, though still unconventional; it again required a scenario by Maurice Grosser for staging. The theme of the piece is the women's suffrage movement as typified by Susan B. Anthony, and it is played against a tapestry of 19th-century Americana. With its homespun hymn tunes, waltzes and marches, Thomson's setting is similar in many respects to that of *Four Saints*, but he provided a richer palette and moments of greater sentiment and seriousness. The score for *Louisiana Story* is an adroit mixture of folk material and descriptive music cast in formal sections (Pastorale, Chorale, Fugue and

Passacaglia). Thomson subsequently fashioned from it two widely-performed suites, *Acadian Songs and Dances* and *Louisiana Story*. The film score itself won the 1948 Pulitzer Prize for music.

Throughout the 1950s and 1960s Thomson travelled widely, lecturing at universities and participating in conferences, writing articles, conducting in the USA and Europe (he conducted the first Paris performance of *Four Saints* in 1952), and continuing to compose. His numerous awards included appointment to the Légion d'honneur.

2. STYLE. During Thomson's long career as a composer he worked with several different styles. Cage, in his study (with Kathleen Hoover) of Thomson's music, referred to 'the great variety and all but intangible nature of [his] work'. He often took up a style (such as that of Gregorian chant and modal polyphony in the early choral pieces with Latin texts), and then dropped it or merged it with other elements. Baptist hymns were perhaps the major preoccupation, revealed initially in the ambivalent Sunday-school pieces, where the gentle home-grown source material is disposed in a tortuous patchwork of variations and the organ is treated like a giant calliope. In many later works, however, such as the *Symphony on a Hymn Tune* and the Cello Concerto, the tunes are treated with affection and humour. Other popular music of the 19th century is also prominent, being used as a model and also for straightforward setting and literal quotation.

Thomson's curious 'portraits' dabble in a variety of styles. Paul Bowles described a group of them in 1942 as giving 'the impression of having come from nowhere, [moving] airily in and out of the focus of consonance like breezes through a pagoda'. A kind of serial technique is used in *A Solemn Music*, which develops from a series of 12 chords, and three 'pictures' for orchestra (*The Seine at Night*, *Wheat Field at Noon*, *Sea Piece with Birds*) are painted in a nostalgic latterday impressionism.

The greatest influence on Thomson was the music of Satie, and the Satian ideals of clarity, simplicity, irony and humour underlie the diversity of his work. The words used by Thomson to define Satie's aesthetic could be used to describe his own:

It has eschewed the impressive, the heroic, the oratorical, everything that is aimed at moving mass audiences . . . it has directed its communication to the individual. It has valued in consequence, quietude, precision, acuteness of auditory observation, gentleness, sincerity and directness of statement.

The work which comes closest to drawing together the various stylistic facets into a cohesive and congenial unity is Thomson's third opera, *Lord Byron*. He and his librettist, Jack Larson, worked on the opera for seven years, and it is undoubtedly his most ambitious project. The Thomson wit and playfulness are here, as is the meticulous (if occasionally monotonous) prosody – a hallmark of his vocal writing. Yet there is a seriousness of tone, a comparative richness of texture and a lyrical expansiveness seldom encountered in his earlier works. There are the expected liturgical elements and the use of quotations (*Auld Lang Syne*, for instance, is worked into an impressive septet), but the style, in general, is not greatly dependent on the Baptist hymnbook. Thomson's 'classical' string-writing period is represented in an important ballet sequence which uses material from the String Quartet no.2. What finally sets *Lord Byron* apart from Thomson's previous work, however, is its emotional content: the opera rises to moments of real passion. This suggests a new dimension for a composer who frequently demonstrates his ability to entertain but whose expressive voice is always carefully muted.

WORKS

OPERAS AND BALLETS

Four Saints in Three Acts (opera, Stein), 1927–8, orchd 1933; Hartford, Conn., 8 Feb 1934

Filling Station (ballet, Christensen), 1937; Hartford, 6 Jan 1938

The Mother of us all (opera, Stein), 1947; New York, 7 May 1947

The Harvest According (ballet, de Mille) after the Sym. on a Hymn Tune, the Vc Conc. and the suite from The Mother of us all, 1952; New York, 1 Oct 1952

Lord Byron (opera, J. Larson), 1961–8; New York, 20 April 1972

ORCHESTRAL AND BAND

2 Sentimental Tangos, 1923; Sym. on a Hymn Tune, 1928; Sym. no.2, 1931, rev. 1941; The Plow that Broke the Plains, suite [from film score], 1936; Filling Station, suite [from ballet], 1937; The River, suite [from film score], 1937; Fugue and Chorale on Yankee Doodle [fr·m film score Tuesday in November], 1945, arr. band; The Seine at Night, 1947; Acadian Songs and Dances [from film score Louisiana Story], 1948; Louisiana Story, suite [from film score], 1948; Wheat Field at Noon, 1948; At the Beach, concert waltz, tpt, band, 1949

The Mother of us all, suite [from opera], 1949; A Solemn Music, band, 1949, orchd, perf. 1962; Vc Conc., 1950; Sea Piece with Birds, 1952; Conc., fl, harp, str, perc, 1954; 11 Chorale Preludes [arr. from Brahms], 1956; The Lively Arts Fugue, 1957; Fugues and Cantilenas [from film score Power Among Men], 1959; A Joyful Fugue, 1962, arr. band; Autumn [arr. pf piece Homage to Marya Freund and Pf Sonata no.2], concertino, harp, str, perc, 1964; Ode to the Wonders of Nature, brass, perc, 1965; Fantasy in Homage to an Earlier England, 1966; Pilgrims and Pioneers [from film score Journey to America], 1966, arr. band

Portraits, arr. pf pieces where noted: The John Mosher Waltzes, 1935, orchd 1937, used as no.6 in Filling Station; Canons for Dorothy Thompson, 1942; The Mayor LaGuardia Waltzes, 1942; Barcarolle for Woodwinds (Portrait of Georges Hugnet), 1940, orchd 1944; Bugles and Birds (Portrait of Pablo Picasso), 1940, orchd 1944; Cantabile for Strings (Portrait of Nicolas de Chatelain), 1940, orchd 1944; Fanfare for France (Portrait of Max Kahn), 1940, orchd 1944; Fugue (Portrait of Alexander Smallens), 1940, orchd 1944; Meditation (Portrait of Jere Abbott), 1935, orchd 1944; Percussion Piece (Portrait of Jessie K. Lasell), 1941, orchd 1944; Tango Lullaby (Portrait of Flavie Alvarez de Toledo), 1940, orchd 1944; Pastorale (Portrait of Aaron Copland), 1942, orchd 1945, used in Tuesday in November; Edges (Portrait of Robert Indiana), 1966, orchd 1969; Study Piece (Portrait of Louise Crane, Insistences), 1941, orchd 1969; Metropolitan Museum Fanfare: Portrait of an American Artist (Portrait of Florine Stettheimer, Parades), 1941, orchd 1970; Sym. no.3, orch of Str Qt no.2, 1972

CHORAL

Unacc.: De profundis, 1920, rev. 1951; Tribulationes civitatum, 1922; 3 Antiphonal Psalms, 1922–4; Missa brevis, male vv, 1924; My Shepherd will Supply my Need (Watts), 1937; Scenes from the Holy Infancy According to St Matthew, 1937; [3] Hymns from the Old South (anon., Newton, Watts), 1949; 4 Songs to Poems of Thomas Campion [from solo vocal work], 1955; Crossing Brooklyn Ferry (Whitman), 1958; 5 Auvergnat Folk Songs, arr. SATB, 1964, also for 1v, orch

Acc.: Capital Capitals (Stein), male 4vv, pf, 1927; 7 Choruses from the Medea of Euripides (trans. Cullen), female vv, perc, 1934; Missa brevis (female vv, perc)/SATB, 1934; Missa pro defunctis, chorus, orch, 1960; Dance in Praise (Gaudeamus igitur, trans. Symonds), chorus, orch, 1962; The Nativity, as Sung by the Shepherds (Crashaw), chorus, orch, 1966–7; Cantata on poems of Edward Lear, 2 S, 2 Bar, SATB, orch, 1973, rev. 1974

SOLO VOCAL

With orch: 5 Songs to Poems of William Blake, Bar, orch, 1951; Collected Poems (Koch), S, Bar, orch, 1959; Mass, 1v/unison chorus, pf, 1960, orchd 1962; The Feast of Love (from Pervigilium veneris, trans. Thomson), Bar, orch, 1964; Ship Wreck and Love Scene from Byron's Don Jua1, T, orch, 1967

With insts: Stabat mater, S, str qt/str orch, 1931, arr. 1v, pf, 1960

With pf: The Sunflower (Blake), S, pf, 1920; Vernal Equinox (Lowell), S, pf, 1920; 3 Sentences from the Song of Solomon, T, pf, 1924; Susie Asado (Stein), S, pf, 1926; The Tiger (Blake), S, pf, 1926; Une mélodie dite La valse grégorienne (Hugnet), S, pf, 1927; Preciosilla (Stein), S, pf, 1927; Le berceau de Gertrude Stein (Hugnet), S, pf, 1928; Commentaire sur St Jerome (de Sade), S, pf, 1928; Les soirées bagnolaises (Hugnet), S, pf, 1928; 3 poèmes de la duchesse de Rohan, S, pf, 1928; Portrait of F. B. (Stein), S, pf, 1929; Le singe et le léopard (La Fontaine), S, pf, 1930; Air de Phèdre (Racine), S, pf, 1930; Film: deux soeurs qui ne sont pas soeurs (Stein), S, pf, 1930; Oraison funèbre (Bossuet), T, pf, 1930; Chamber Music (Kreymborg), S, pf, 1931; Dirge (Webster), 1939; The Bugle Song (Tennyson), Mez/Bar, pf, 1941; 4 Songs to Poems of Thomas Campion, Mez, pf/(cl, harp, va), 1951; 5 Songs from William Blake, Bar/pf, 1951, orchd; [3] Old English Songs, S, pf, 1955, no.2 arr. SATB; [4] Old English Songs, Bar, pf, 1955; Take, o Take those Lips Away (Shakespeare), 1956; Pardon, Goddess of the Night (Shakespeare), 1957; Sigh no more Ladies (Shakespeare), 1957; Tell me where is Fancy Bred (Shakespeare), 1957; Was this Fair Face (Shakespeare), 1957; 3 estampas de Ninez (Rivas), S, pf, 1957; If thou a Reason dost Desire to Know (Kynaston), Bar, pf, 1958; Collected Poems (Koch), S, Bar, pf, 1959, orchd; Mostly about Love (Koch), 1959; My Shepherd will Supply my Need (Watts), 1959; 5 Praises and Prayers (St Francis, Crashaw, St Augustine), 1963; Two by Marianne Moore, 1963; From 'Sneeden's Landing Variations' (F. O'Hara), 1v, pf, 1972; The Courtship of the Yongly-bongly-bo (Lear), Mez/Bar, pf, 1973–4

CHAMBER AND INSTRUMENTAL

Sonata da chiesa, cl, hn, tpt, trbn, vn, 1926; [4] Portraits, vn, 1928, 1940; 5 Portraits, 4 cl, 1929; Le bains-bar, vn, pf, 1929, arr. tpt, pf as At the Beach, 1948, arr. tpt, band; [4] Portraits, vn, pf, 1930, 1940; Sonata, vn, pf, 1930; Serenade, fl, vn, 1931; 2 str qts, 1931, 1932; Sonata, fl, 1943; Lamentations, accordion, 1959; Etude, vc, pf, 1966; Family Portrait, brass qnt, 1972–5; Parson Weems and the Cherry Tree Etc, fl + pic, cl + b cl, tpt + flugelhorn, trbn, perc, vn, db, 1975
Pf: Synthetic Waltzes, 2 pf, 1925; 10 Easy Pieces and a Coda, 1926; 5 Inventions, 1926; 4 sonatas, 1929, 1929, 1930, 1940; 32 Portraits, 4 vols., 1929–45; 9 Etudes, 1940, 1951; 10 Etudes, 1943; Portrait of Willy Eisenhart, 1972
Org: Fanfare, 1922; Passacaglia, 1922, rev. 1974; Pastorale on a Christmas Plainsong, 1922; Prelude, 1922; Variations and Fugues on Sunday School Tunes, 1926; Church Organ Wedding Music, 2 pieces, 1940

FILM SCORES

The Plow that Broke the Plains, dir. P. Lorentz, 1936; The River, dir. Lorentz, 1937; The Spanish Earth [montage of Spanish folk music], dir. J. Ivens, 1937, collab. Blitzstein; Tuesday in November, dir. J. Houseman, 1945; Louisiana Story, dir. R. Flaherty, 1948; The Goddess, dir. J. Cromwell, 1958; Power Among Men, dir. T. Dickenson, 1958; Journey to America, dir. Houseman, 1964

INCIDENTAL MUSIC

Hamlet (Shakespeare), 1936; Horse Eats Hat (Labiche) [orchestration of music by P. Bowles], 1936; Injunction Granted, 1936; Macbeth (Shakespeare), 1936; Antony and Cleopatra (Shakespeare), 1937; Androcles and the Lion (Shaw), 1938; The Trojan Women (Euripides), 1940; Life of a Careful Man, 1941; Oedipus tyrannus (Sophocles), 1941; King Lear (Shakespeare), 1952; The Grass Harp (Capote), 1953; Ondine (Giraudoux), 1954
King John (Shakespeare), 1956; Measure for Measure (Shakespeare), 1956; The Merchant of Venice (Shakespeare), 1957; Much Ado about Nothing (Shakespeare), 1957; Othello (Shakespeare), 1957; Bertha (Koch), 1959

Principal publishers: Boosey & Hawkes, Colombo, Fischer, Gray, MCA, Presser, G. Schirmer, Southern, Weintraub

WRITINGS

The State of Music (New York, 1939/R1974, 2/1961)
The Musical Scene (New York, 1945)
The Art of Judging Music (New York, 1948)
Music, Right and Left (New York, 1951)
Virgil Thomson (New York, 1966/R1977)
Music Reviewed (New York, 1967)
American Music since 1910 (New York, 1971)

BIBLIOGRAPHY
S. Barlow: 'American Composers, XVII: Virgil Thomson', MM, xviii (1941), 242
P. Glanville-Hicks: 'Virgil Thomson', MQ, xxxv (1949), 209
K. Hoover and J. Cage: Virgil Thomson: his Life and Music (New York, 1959)
R. Jackson: The Operas of Gertrude Stein and Virgil Thomson (diss., Tulane U., 1962)
'A Tribute to Virgil Thomson on his 81st Birthday', Parnassus: Poetry in Review, v/2 (1977), 405–531
RICHARD JACKSON

Thomson, William (b ?Edinburgh, c1684; d ?London, c1760). Scottish singer and folksong collector. His father was Daniel Thomson, one of the king's trumpeters for Scotland. He sang solos as a boy at a Musical Society concert in Edinburgh on St Cecilia's Day 1695.

By 1722 he had settled in London, where he gave a benefit concert in February that year, including (according to Burney) a Scottish folksong as an encore.

Thomson published Orpheus Caledonius, a Collection of the Best Scotch Songs set to Musick (London, 1725), a lavishly produced volume dedicated to the Princess of Wales, with a subscription list of 300 notable people. It contains 50 Scottish folksongs, most of them taken from Allan Ramsay's Tea-table Miscellany (Edinburgh, 1723); the melodic ornaments and the figured bass accompaniments are Thomson's own. Hawkins described Thomson as 'a tradesman' and the collection as 'injudicious and very incorrect'; it is true that some of the song texts are in crude, oral versions and that the figured basses have grammatical mistakes. In 1733 a second edition was issued, expanded to 100 songs, with new, improved harmonizations for the original 50. Thomson was still living in 1753, though his biography is obscure.

BIBLIOGRAPHY
BurneyH; HawkinsH
W. Tytler: 'On the Fashionable Amusements and Entertainments in Edinburgh in the Last Century', Transactions of the Society of Antiquarians of Scotland, i (1792), 508
D. Johnson: Music and Society in Lowland Scotland in the 18th Century (London, 1972), 140f, 155f
FRANK KIDSON/DAVID JOHNSON

Thopul, Timolphus. Name to which is attributed a work possibly by Thomas and Theophilus Lupo; see LUPO family.

Thórarinsson, Jón (b farm in eastern Iceland, 13 Sept 1917). Icelandic teacher, conductor and composer. He studied at the Reykjavík College of Music, with Hindemith at Yale (MM 1947), at the Juilliard School (1945) and in Germany and Austria (1954–5). In 1947 he was appointed head of theory and composition at the Reykjavík College of Music, and he has also been on the music staff of Icelandic broadcasting (1947–56), manager of the Iceland SO (1956–61), and head of music and drama for the state television service. He published a biography of the Icelandic composer Sveinbjörn Sveinbjörnsson, Aevisaga (Reykjavík, 1969). His music shows a flare for drama in a tonal style with ventures into chromaticism.

WORKS
(selective list)

Vocal: Kubla Khan, cantata, B, chorus, orch, 1947; Of Love and Death (C. G. Rossetti), B, orch, 1966; Völuspa, chorus, orch, 1974; folksong arrs. for children
Inst: Movement, vn, pf, 1946; Pf Sonatina, 1946; Music for Org, 1962; Sonata, cl, pf, 1964; children's pf pieces

Principal publishers: Helgafell, Musica Islandica

BIBLIOGRAPHY
J. Gudnason and P. Haraldsson: Íslenzkir samtídarmenn (Reykjavik, 1965–), 421
O. Kristjánsson: Kennaratal á Íslandi, ii (Reykjavík, 1965), 415
A. Burt: Iceland's Twentieth-century Composers and a Listing of their Works (Fairfax, Virginia, in prepation)
AMANDA M. BURT

Thórarinsson, Leifur (b Reykjavík, 13 Aug 1934). Icelandic composer. He studied with Jón Thórarinsson at the Reykjavík College of Music, with Jelinek in Vienna and with Riegger and Schuller in New York. For a time, before moving to Denmark, he was a music critic for Vísir and Thjódviljinn. His compositions are in an intriguing abstract style; at first he used serial methods, but the later works show modal writing and an individual kind of tonality.

WORKS
(selective list)

Orch: 2 syms., 1964, 1975; Vn Conc., 1970, rev. 1976
Inst: Barnalagaflokkur, pf, 1957; Pf Trio, 1961; Mosaic, vn, pf, 1966; Afstaedur, pf trio, 1966; Str Qt, 1969

Principal publishers: Helgafell, Musica Islandica

BIBLIOGRAPHY
A. Burt: *Iceland's Twentieth-century Composers and a Listing of their Works* (Fairfax, Virginia, in preparation)
AMANDA M. BURT

Thorborg, Kerstin (*b* Venjan, 19 May 1896; *d* Falun, 12 April 1970). Swedish mezzo-soprano. She studied at the Royal Conservatory, Stockholm, making her début at the Royal Theatre in 1924, as Ortrud. A member of the company until 1930, she also made guest appearances elsewhere in Sweden, notably as Amneris in Göteborg to the Aida of Flagstad. Early engagements outside Scandinavia were in Dresden (in 1929 as Waltraute), Prague and Berlin. In 1935 she was engaged at Salzburg and Vienna, remaining at the Staatsoper until 1938. From 1936 to 1939 she made annual appearances at Covent Garden in the Wagner mezzo roles, being greatly acclaimed – Ernest Newman wrote of her Kundry that 'she walks like a goddess, sits like a statue; and not a single gesture is wasted throughout the whole evening. All in all, I would rank her as the greatest Wagnerian actress of the present day'. Also in 1936 she began a Metropolitan Opera career (her début there was as Fricka in *Die Walküre* on 21 December) which lasted 15 years. Although her rich and ample tones were most admired in Wagner, her repertory also included Gluck's Orpheus, Marina, Ulrica, Strauss's Herodias and Clytemnestra, and Delilah. She was appointed a Swedish court singer in 1944. Of her recordings *Das Lied von der Erde* under Walter is the most notable.

BIBLIOGRAPHY
E. H. Palatsky: 'Goddess in Retirement', *Opera News*, xxvii (1963), 32
B. Berthelson: 'Kerstin Thorborg', *Musikrevy*, xxii (1967), 345
CARL L. BRUUN

Thórdarson, Sigurdur (*b* Dýrafiri, 8 April 1895; *d* Reykjavík, 1968). Icelandic composer and conductor. He studied in Leipzig (1916–18) and in Germany and Austria (1927). For about 30 years he was manager of Icelandic broadcasting, and he also served as conductor of the Reykjavík Male Choir, with which he toured internationally. A popular conductor and composer, he wrote in a national Romantic style.

WORKS
(selective list)

Stage: Bewitched, op.24 (operetta); Sigurdur Fáfnisbani, op.28 (opera)
Orch: Grandmother's Tales, op.12
Vocal: 5 Songs, op.4; Psalms, op.19, solo vv, chorus, orch; A Solemn Mass, op.20, male chorus, pf; Althing Festival Cantata, op.25, solo vv, chorus, orch
Pf: Easy Pf Pieces, op.2

Principal publishers: Islandia, Musica Islandica

BIBLIOGRAPHY
B. Tobíasson: *Hver er madurinn?* (Reykjavík, 1944), 222
O. Kristjánsson: *Kennaratal á Islandi*, ii (Reykjavík, 1965), 147
J. Gudnason and P. Haraldsson: *Íslenzkir samtídarmenn* (Reykjavík, 1965–), 228
A. Burt: *Iceland's Twentieth-century Composers and a Listing of their Works* (Fairfax, Virginia, in preparation)
AMANDA M. BURT

Thorette, Pierre (*b* c1620; *d* Liège, 11 Oct 1684). South Netherlands musician. He was appointed second succentor at Liège Cathedral on 24 November 1664 and at the same time received a benefice which was replaced by a more important one on 7 December 1668. He was to be responsible for the musical instruction of the *duodeni*. In November 1669 he and the first succentor were involved in a lawsuit against Lambert Pietkin. The cathedral canons admonished Thorette again and again for negligence, and since he did not improve they dismissed him from his post as succentor on 8 April 1672. But he retained his benefice and probably remained as a singer until his death. Auda was mistaken in stating that he was made a canon of Ste Materne. There is (at *B-Lc*) a short *Chasse de St Hubert* by him for two violins, two cornetts (or flutes), two corni da caccia, bassoon and continuo (this last replaced in a 19th-century copy by two clarinets). It is based on brief fanfare motifs; the use of alternating sonorities would be pleasing if the piece were not unremittingly in G major.

BIBLIOGRAPHY
A. Auda: *La musique et les musiciens de l'ancien pays de Liège* (Liège, 1930)
R. Vannes: *Dictionnaire des musiciens (compositeurs)* (Brussels, 1947)
JOSÉ QUITIN

Thori, Hermogene da [Torrio, Ermogine] (*b* ?Salerno, ?1555–65; *d* ?Salerno, after 1623). Italian composer and professor of law. As a youth he studied civil, and later canon law, probably at Naples. On 20 February 1582 he dedicated his three-voice *Canzone* (Naples, 1582) to Horatio Ogeda, baron of Santa Arsiero. Each piece has three sections, usually beginning with triadic motifs or 4ths in sequences arranged in imitative patterns. At some time, probably before 1621, he lectured on civil institutions at Naples University. Before 1 January 1621 he had become a member of the Friars Minor Conventual of St Francis in Salerno; he later published a legal treatise, *De actionibus* (Naples, 1623), dedicated to Lucio Sanseverino, Archbishop of Salerno.

BIBLIOGRAPHY
L. Giustiniani: *Memorie istoriche degli scrittori legali del Regno di Napoli*, iii (Naples, 1787–8), 212
KEITH A. LARSON

Thorne, Francis (*b* Bay Shore, NY, 23 June 1922). American composer. A grandson of Kobbé, he studied composition at Yale University with Hindemith and Richard Donovan until 1942. He pursued a career in commerce (1946–54) and then worked as a jazz pianist in night clubs in the USA and Italy (1955–61). After further studies with Diamond in Florence (1959–61), he devoted his time to composition. His music reflects his jazz interests; *Six Set-pieces*, for example, uses jazz phrasing and complex rhythmic patterns, and the Third Symphony sets rhythmic polyphony against long, lyrical string lines. *Liebesrock* features electric guitars with 'fuzz tone' as a surrealistic element relating to rock music. Thorne received an award and citation from the National Institute of Arts and Letters in 1968, and even before his return to the USA in 1971, he was active in the support of American composers through the foundation of the Thorne Music Fund and his membership of other organizations.

WORKS
(selective list)

Sym. no.1, 1961; Elegy, 1962–3; Burlesque Ov., 1963–4; Sym. no.2, 1964; Rhapsodic Variations, pf, orch, 1964–5; Pf Conc., 1965–6; Lyric Variations, orch, 1966–7; 6 Set-pieces, 13 insts, 1967; Gemini Variations, orch, 1967–8; Song of the Carolina Low Country, chorus, orch, 1968; Sonar Plexus, elec gui, orch, 1968; Liebesrock, 3 elec gui, orch, 1968–9; Sym. no.3, perc, str, 1969; Songs and Dances, vc, kbds, perc, 1969; Antiphonies, wind, perc, 1969–70; Simultaneities, brass qnt, elec gui, perc, 1971; Quartessence, jazz qt, orch, 1971; Lyric Variations II, wind qnt, perc, 1971–2; Pf Sonata, 1972; Fanfare, Fugue and Funk, orch, 1972; Pf Conc. no.2, 1973; 9 Playful Ploys, pf, 1973; Vc Conc., 1974; 3 Dance Movts, cl, pf, 1976; Vn Conc., 1976; Sym. no.4, 1977

Principal publishers: Joshua, Marks

LESTER TRIMBLE

Thorne, John (*b c*1519; *d* York, 7 Dec 1573). English composer, poet and church musician. He was appointed organist of York Minster on 24 July 1542, having received payment the previous year as 'organist within the choir'. Following the Injunctions of Archbishop Holgate in 1552, the minster organs were silenced. Thorne's services as organist were therefore no longer required, though as Master of the Choristers he was ordered to 'helpe to singe Divyne service . . . within the quere of the churche'. He later became Clerk of the Fabric, a position he held for ten years from 1561. He died aged about 54, and was buried in the minster. His inscription, recorded by Drake in 1736, read:

Here lyeth Thorne, musitian most perfitt in art,
In logick's lore who did excell, all vice who set apart,
Whose lief and conversation did all men's love allure,
And now doth reign above the skyes in joyes most firm and pure.
Who dyed Decemb. 7, 1573.

In view of Morley's high opinion of him (he was cited in *A Plaine and Easie Introduction* along with Redford and Tallis as a composer particularly skilled in ways of breaking plainsong) it is unfortunate that so little of Thorne's music has survived. In *GB-Ob* there is a four-part In Nomine by him, and *Lbm* Add.29996 contains the organ score of a motet, *Exultabant sancti*. The tenor part only is extant (in *DRc*) of a setting of the *Te Deum*; to judge from the predominantly syllabic underlay, the work seems to have been written in accordance with Archbishop Holgate's requirement that every word should be 'playnelie and distinctlie undrestood'. The only composition by Thorne which can be positively dated is the three-part motet *Stella coeli*, included by John Baldwin in his commonplace-book of *c*1600 (*Lbm*) and later printed by Hawkins. This motet, composed in 1551 as a thanksgiving for deliverance from the plague, is hardly comparable to the best work of Tallis or Redford, but its rhythmic subtlety, ingenious cadential harmonic shifts and assured use of sequence mark it a work of considerable charm. Three poems by Thorne survive in *Lbm*.

BIBLIOGRAPHY

HawkinsH
F. Drake: *Eboracum* (London, 1736)
J. Raine: *The Fabric Rolls of York Minster*, Surtees Society (Durham, 1859)
W. H. G. Flood: 'New Light on Late Tudor Composers', *MT*, lxvi (1925), 28
J. W. Knowles: *Records of the Musicians and Musical Services in York Minster* (*GB-Y* Add.157/1–5, 1929)
J. A. Caldwell: *Additional Manuscript 29996: Transcription and Commentary* (diss., U. of Oxford, 1965)
P. le Huray: *Music and the Reformation in England 1549–1660* (London, 1967)
P. Aston: *The Music of York Minster* (London, 1972)

PETER ASTON

Thoroughbass. The Italian and more original term 'basso continuo' has now largely replaced 'thorough-bass' as (1) the English term for the art of accompaniment from a figured bass line, and (2) the name or label for such a bass line when issued as an instrumental part. It is uncertain when the term originated. Early treatises used other terms (e.g. M. Locke's *General Rules for playing upon a Continued-Bass*), though John Blow's MS rules are *'for playing of a Through Bass'* (sic). For the instrumental part itself, particularly of the Italianate sonatas, etc, published in London from the end of the 17th century onwards, 'basso', 'per l'organo', 'cimbalo' and other names are as likely as 'thoroughbass'. Like GENERALBASS, the term came to stand for the science of harmony in general; and like the word CONTINUO, it probably arose as a description of a bass part present all or most of the time throughout a composition, unlike optional or obbligato parts.

PETER WILLIAMS

Thorpe Davie, Cedric (*b* London, 30 May 1913). Scottish composer. He studied at the Royal Scottish Academy of Music, Glasgow, and at the RAM with Craxton, Thiman and Aubrey Brain; later he was a pupil of Morris, Vaughan Williams and Jacob at the RCM, where he won the Cobbett and Sullivan prizes for composition in 1935. He also studied the piano with Petri in London and composition with Kodály in Budapest and with Kilpinen in Helsinki. Thorpe Davie taught theory and composition at the RSAM (1936–45), and was at the same time organist of Queen's Park High Parish Church, Glasgow. In 1945 he was appointed master of music to St Andrews University, and in 1947 he founded the department of music there, becoming reader (1956) and professor (1973–8). He has also been active on behalf of Scottish music as chairman of the music panel of the Scottish Certificate of Education Examination Board (1966–71), chairman of the music committee of the Scottish Arts Council and a member of the Arts Council of Great Britain (1968–73). Dundee University awarded him the LlD in 1969.

Thorpe Davie's Symphony won a prize in a newspaper competition in 1945; the work received several performances in England and entered the Scottish repertory. In 1948 Thorpe Davie became more widely known through his music for the revival of Lyndesay's *Ane Satyre of the Thrie Estatis* at the Edinburgh Festival. For the next year's festival he made arrangements of folk music to accompany Allan Ramsay's *The Gentle Shepherd*, and he provided arrangements of a similar sort for Mitchell's ballad opera *The Highland Fair* (1952). He also made a setting of *The Beggar's Opera* for performance at St Andrews University. Much his most successful undertaking has been his realization of Burns's dramatic cantata *The Jolly Beggars*, which has been performed throughout Scotland, broadcast on radio and television, and commercially recorded. A great deal of his later music was written for young people or amateurs; such works include the *Diversions on a Tune by Dr Arne*, written for the National Youth Orchestra and first played by them at a Prom under Boult, the choral pieces *The Thistle and the Rose* and *By the River*, the suite *New Town* for the Edinburgh Schools' Orchestra and the Variations on a Theme of Lully for the National Youth Brass Band of Scotland. Thorpe Davie has published *Musical Structure and Design* (London, 1953).

WORKS
(*selective list*)

Dramatic: Gammer Gurton's Needle, opera, 1, 1936; several comic operas and operettas, some for children; many scores for the theatre, cinema and broadcasting
Orch: Elegy, 1932; Concert Ov., 1934; Fantasia no.1 on Four Scottish Tunes, 1937; Conc., pf, str, 1943; Sym., C, 1945; The Beggar's Benison, 1949; Variations on a Theme of A. C. Mackenzie, 1949; Festal Ov., 1950; Royal Mile, march, 1952; Diversions on a Tune by

Dr Arne, 1954; 2 Burns ovs., 1963; Fantasia no.2 on Four Scottish Tunes, 1964; New Town, suite, 1966; several works for brass band
Choral: Dirge for Cuthullin (Ossian), chorus, orch, 1935; 3 anthems, chorus, org, 1937; Ode for St Andrew's Night (M. Lindsay), T, chorus, orch, 1950; many partsongs and folksong arrs.
Vocal: 6 Poems of Violet Jacob, T, pf, 1948; Directions for a Map, S/T, str qt, 1955; many other songs and folksong arrs.
Inst: Pf Trio, 1932; Sonatina, vc, pf, 1934; Fantasy-Qt, str, 1935; Sonatina, fl, pf, 1939; Sonata, vn, pf, 1939
Edn of Oxford Scottish Song Book (London, 1968)

Principal publisher: Oxford University Press

MAURICE LINDSAY

Thorsteinsson, Bjarni (b Melur, Mýrasýsla, 14 Oct 1861; d Reykjavík, 2 Aug 1938). Icelandic composer and folksong collector. Apart from early studies in harmony with Jónas Helgason, organist of Reykjavík Cathedral, he was self-taught as a musician. He studied theology at Reykjavík and from 1888 to 1935 was a priest at Siglufjördur. Early in the 1880s he became interested in Icelandic folk music, made study trips to Copenhagen and Stockholm (1899, 1903–4) and edited many collections of folksongs, among which Íslenzk thjódhlög (Copenhagen, 1903–6, 2/1974) was influential in establishing a basis for the study of Icelandic national song. His own works, mainly solo and choral songs, also show the influence of Icelandic folk melody, and his writings, published in Icelandic and Scandinavian journals, are important introductions to the subject.

BIBLIOGRAPHY
H. Helgason: 'Bjarni Thorsteinsson', Íslands lag [The melodies of Iceland] (Reykjavík, 1973), 26

Thrane, (Wildenrath Christian) Carl (Boeck) (b Fredericia, 2 Sept 1837; d Copenhagen, 19 June 1916). Danish music historian. From his youth he was interested in music and was taught the piano by Johan Christian Gebauer and Edvard Helsted. He took a law degree in 1863, and from 1875 was a secretary at the Danish supreme court of justice. For many years he was active as a music critic for the journal Illustreret tidende, and from his research into the sources of Danish music, he produced a number of excellent books and treatises, the most important being Fra hofviolonernes tid, a history of the Royal Danish Orchestra from 1648 to 1848.

WRITINGS
Danske komponister (Copenhagen, 1875) [studies of C. E. F. Weyse, D. F. R. Kuhlau, J. P. E. Hartmann, N. W. Gade]
Rossini og operaen (Copenhagen, 1885)
Caeciliaforeningen og dens stifter [The Cecilian Society and its founder] (Copenhagen, 1901), 528
'Sarti i Kopenhagen', SIMG, iii (1901–2)
Fra hofviolonernes tid [From the time of the court violins] (Copenhagen, 1908)
Weyses minde (Copenhagen, 1916) [Remembrance of C. E. F. Weyse]

BIBLIOGRAPHY
S. Lunn: 'Thrane, Wildenrath Christian Carl Boeck', DBL

SIGURD BERG

Thrane, Waldemar (b Christiania [now Oslo], 8 Oct 1790; d Christiania, 30 Dec 1828). Norwegian composer, violinist and conductor. Thrane came from a musical family whose members were active in the musical life of Christiania. He was trained as a violinist under Henrik Groth in Christiania, under Claus Schall in Copenhagen (1814–15) and under F. Baillot in Paris (1817–18). In Paris he also studied theory and composition with Anton Reicha and F. A. Habeneck. Returning to Christiania in 1818 he became conductor of the orchestras of the Dramatical Society and the

Musical Lyceum; he also worked as a music teacher and established himself as a prominent violin virtuoso, giving recitals in various Norwegian towns and in Stockholm.

His musical output is small. His main works are a Concert Overture (1818) and the first Norwegian opera, Fjeldeventyret ('The mountain adventure', 1824). He also composed a Finale for large orchestra (1818) and a cantata (1827), both now lost, and several piano pieces and songs. Fjeldeventyret, which is an 'opera comique', is based on a libretto by the Norwegian poet H. A. Bjerregaard. It was first given on 9 February 1825 at the Musical Lyceum and immediately became a great success; it was shortly afterwards given both in Bergen and Trondheim. It has from time to time been taken up by various theatres and is part of the repertory of the Norwegian State Opera. It has a strong appeal for the Norvegians. The story is very simple, as in a folk comedy, and Thrane retained the spoken dialogue. The music conforms more or less to the taste of its time. It contains reminiscences from Mozart and Weber, but is still more in the popular style of the French light operas of the late 18th century. In some sections, however, Thrane shows a musical individuality, particularly in the scenes which are of a folkloristic nature, e.g. in 'Aagots Fjeldsang' ('Aagot's mountain song'). This beautiful melody became internationally known through Jenny Lind, who often performed it at her recitals. It has a strong national flavour, and it includes imitations of Norwegian folktunes, so convincing that later generations have considered them to be genuine. Thrane made use of specific intervals and motifs and also rhythmic peculiarities of the instrumental peasant dances. His use of folk music idioms in art music set the model for the next generations of Norwegian composers: this may be regarded as his greatest achievement.

BIBLIOGRAPHY
F. Benestad: Waldemar Thrane: en pionér i norsk musikk (Oslo, 1961)

FINN BENESTAD

Three Choirs Festival. An annual event, of six days' duration, substantially but not exclusively choral in character, based in turn on the cathedrals of Gloucester, Worcester and Hereford. Its precise origins are not documented. By 1719 it was already referred to as a 'yearly Musical Assembly' which had been held at Gloucester in 1718, and the now conventional reckoning of the festival from 1715 is not unreasonable. The suggestion that it began for the purposes of singing glees and madrigals has nothing to support it. The earliest events consisted of Morning Prayer in the cathedral with Te Deum and Jubilate in orchestral settings and extended anthems on two successive days, and secular concerts in the town in the evenings. In 1724 at Gloucester the practice was initiated of taking up a collection for the widows and orphans of the cathedral choir members and diocesan clergy. Soon this was limited to dependants of clergy and in this form has continued to the present day.

At first only liturgical music and anthems were admitted to the cathedrals. Purcell's Te Deum and Jubilate in D was staple fare, with the occasional use of Croft's setting in the same key. Later Handel's 'Utrecht' and 'Dettingen' settings took turns with Purcell's. After 1727 one or more of Handel's coronation anthems was in regular use during the rest of the 18th century, frequently supplemented by anthems of

Boyce or, less frequently, some other English composer of the period. In the early years oratorios were given at the evening secular concerts, but in 1759 at Hereford a third morning was introduced in the cathedral and devoted to *Messiah*. This was the first stage in a prolonged process of extending the number of cathedral performances and eliminating Morning Prayer. With unimportant exceptions the 18th-century programmes, both in and outside the cathedrals, were dominated by Handel.

The organization rested on an annually chosen 'steward' (from 1755 two stewards, one clerical, the other lay); the stewards, who each bore the inevitable deficit, were increased to six from 1798. The event itself was known as the 'Gloucester [Worcester, Hereford] Music Meeting', the expression 'festival' in the modern sense being unknown, while the term 'Three Choirs' only came into use (and then informally) from about the mid-19th century. The choral body was originally the combined cathedral choirs supplemented by a few local amateurs. By the early 19th century, if not earlier, male singers from choirs in Oxford, London and elsewhere were also used, and beginning in 1772 (following the practice of the Antient Concerts in London) 'female chorus singers from the North of England' were engaged. Nothing is known of the earliest conductors. In 1737 and 1755 (both years at Worcester), possibly also in other years, William Boyce conducted, and William Hayes conducted at Gloucester in 1757, 1760 and 1763. The earliest organist of one of the three cathedrals to be recorded as conductor is Richard Clack of Hereford, who first conducted there in 1759. Elias Isaac, organist of Worcester, not only conducted there from 1761 to 1791 but at Gloucester also from 1769 to 1787 and at Hereford in 1777. The practice of having the organist of the 'home' cathedral conduct the festival was established after 1790; from 1934 the other two organists have shared in the conducting.

From the 1830s the music meetings changed considerably in character. In 1834 and 1835 Hereford and Gloucester transferred the cathedral performances from the choir to the nave, and Worcester followed in 1845. There was a consequent enlargement of orchestra, chorus and audience. Beginning in 1840 the number of stewards was progressively increased, leading to the present usage whereby the holders of subscription tickets are termed stewards. Though Handel retained his popularity, the choral music of Spohr and Mendelssohn began to be firmly established. The liturgical services with orchestra were reduced to one, and in 1860 this was relegated to an early hour on the first morning in order to accommodate an additional oratorio; later it was replaced by the service with chorus and orchestra which has since opened the festival on the Sunday afternoon. On the other hand, from 1853 the combined cathedral choirs sang Matins (Evensong in later years) daily. By the mid-19th century the prestige of older music meetings had declined in favour of the newly established festivals at Norwich, Birmingham and elsewhere, the term 'Worcester [Gloucester, Hereford] Musical Festival' coming into common use. Moreover, being held in cathedrals, they were increasingly criticized by those who felt that they offended against religious use. This feeling reached a climax in 1875 with the refusal of the dean and chapter of Worcester to allow their church to be used for a festival of the usual kind; and a series of church services without soloists

and orchestra was held, derisively called the 'Mock Festival'. Local feeling was strong enough to ensure the resumption of the festivals on their former lines, but a much greater sense of decorum was established.

Along with other festivals the 'Three Choirs' began from the 1860s to encourage choral music by English composers. But, as elsewhere, the list of 19th-century works, composed in a derivative if not moribund idiom, now makes depressing reading. Nevertheless the performance of this body of now forgotten pieces by minor worthies – Cusins, Barnby, Armes, Garrett, Stainer and the like – forms a recognizable facet of festival history.

Among the 19th-century cathedral organists who served as festival conductors only S. S. Wesley (organist of Hereford Cathedral, 1832–5, and of Gloucester Cathedral, 1865–76) was of real distinction, but he was a poor conductor. C. H. Lloyd, who was organist of Gloucester Cathedral briefly (1876–82), was a cultivated musician if not a good conductor. But little could be done to improve standards of performance so long as the festival chorus, in addition to the cathedral choirs and bodies of local singers, included contingents from places as far afield as Bradford, Leeds and Huddersfield with only one combined rehearsal. The first festival since the early 18th century to rely entirely on a chorus drawn from the counties of Gloucester, Hereford and Worcester was at Gloucester in 1892 under C. Lee Williams. Wesley (while at Gloucester), Lloyd and Langdon Colborne (organist of Hereford, 1877–89) introduced the music of Bach and Brahms to the festival, and Dvořák conducted his *Stabat mater* at Worcester in 1884.

The modern history of the festival began in the 1890s following the appointment of three organist-conductors who carried it into the 20th century: G. R. Sinclair (organist of Hereford Cathedral, 1889–1917), A. Herbert Brewer (Gloucester Cathedral, 1897–1928) and Ivor Atkins (Worcester Cathedral, 1897–1950). These men trained their own choruses and established the practice whereby about half the festival choir is drawn from the 'home' locality and a quarter each from the other two localities. Their programmes were also more adventurous and drew on a less stereotyped repertory, introducing the music of Wagner and Verdi and laying more stress on Bach. Sinclair was succeeded by P. C. Hull (1918) and Brewer by H. W. Sumsion (1928), and under these five men, up to the outbreak of World War II, the festival enjoyed the most significant period of its history. By the time they came on the scene Parry was already established as a festival composer; *Scenes from Prometheus Unbound* and *Job* were given first performances in 1880 and 1892 respectively, both at Gloucester, and he continued to figure prominently up to World War I. Between 1910 and 1930 a number of compositions by Walford Davies and Bantock, among others, received first performances. Among first performances given at the festival were Vaughan Williams: *Fantasia on a theme of Thomas Tallis* (1910), *Five Mystical Songs* (1911), *Magnificat* (1932); Bliss: *A Colour Symphony* (1922); Holst: *Choral Fantasia* (1931); Bax: *The Morning Watch* (1935); and Lennox Berkeley: *Domini est terra* (1938).

The performance of Bach's *St Matthew Passion* at Worcester in 1911 initiated a new approach to the work in England. It was above all in this period that an important part was played by performances of Elgar's music under his own direction until his death in 1934.

Elgar, himself Worcestershire-born, had intimate connections with the festival, having played in the orchestra in 1878 and contributed his *Froissart* overture to the 1890 Worcester festival. The performance of *The Dream of Gerontius* at Worcester in 1902 contributed much to help the work recover from its unhappy première in Birmingham in 1900.

After the intermission of the war years the festival was revived at Hereford in 1946, and in 1950 the first performance of *Hymnus Paradisi* by Herbert Howells was given. But in the postwar years the position of the festival in English musical life seemed much less decided. The link with the Elgar tradition was broken by the retirement of Sumsion in 1967. Meanwhile recent younger organist-conductors, some of fairly short tenure, have done much to bring the festival into line with modern trends, partly by replanning the week to secure better rehearsal and more varied concerts, using not only the cathedrals, but other interesting buildings; partly by discarding types of music no longer called for and taking a dispassionate look at formerly unquestioned landmarks; partly by continuing to promote unfamiliar music old and new. Among British contemporary composers who have had works performed for the first time at festivals since the late 1950s are Richard Rodney Bennett, Lennox Berkeley, Philip Cannon, Gordon Crosse, Peter Maxwell Davies, Peter Dickinson, Jonathan Harvey, Alun Hoddinott, Wilfred Josephs, John Joubert, Kenneth Leighton, Nicholas Maw, John McCabe, Gerard Schurmann, Christopher Steel and Malcolm Williamson.

After Atkins, Hull and Sumsion the conductors have been David Willcocks (Worcester, 1951, 1954, 1957); Meredith Davies (Hereford, 1952, 1955); Melville Cook (Hereford, 1958, 1961, 1964); Douglas Guest (Worcester, 1960, 1963); Christopher Robinson (Worcester, from 1966); Richard Lloyd (Hereford, from 1967); and John Sanders (Gloucester, from 1968).

BIBLIOGRAPHY
D. Lysons, J. Amott, C. L. Williams and H. G. Chance: *Origin and Progress of the Meeting of the Three Choirs* (Gloucester, 1895)
C. L. Williams, H. G. Chance and T. Hannam-Clark: *Annals of the Three Choirs of Gloucester, Hereford, and Worcester . . . from 1895 to 1930* (Gloucester, 1931)
W. Shaw: *The Three Choirs Festival* (Worcester and London, 1954)
WATKINS SHAW

Threnody (from Gk. *thrēnōdia*: 'lamentation'). A poem, or its musical setting, expressing a strong feeling of grief for the dead; the term has much the same meaning as 'lament'. 'Threnody' has also been used as a title for purely instrumental compositions of an elegiac nature, such as Penderecki's *Trenofiarom Hiroszimy* ('Threnody for the victims of Hiroshima') for 52 solo strings (1959–61). For the tragi-comic threnody in the last act of his opera *Albert Herring* (1947) Britten used a structure similar to that of the classical *thrēnos*, which alternated a ritornello for chorus with solo passages.

MALCOLM BOYD

Thrēnos (Gk.: 'lamentation'). Ancient Greek lament for a dead person, analogous to the Roman NENIA; according to Maas, also the leader of such a lament. The term was also latinized in the title of the biblical book of *Lamentations* and is so used by Stravinsky in his setting of texts from that book (*Threni*, 1958); it occurs as the designation of a category of Mozarabic chant sung in Lent (*see* MOZARABIC RITE, MUSIC OF THE, §3(b), vii).

In ancient Greece the term *thrēnos* seems to have covered all the different types of Greek lament, but it refers particularly to that performed (normally by women) during the laying-out (*prothesis*) of the corpse, usually on the day after death. This was performed by a leader (*exarchos*) who was interrupted by choral refrains; the singers were sometimes professional. Legislation, by Solon in the first half of the 6th century BC and by others, restricted the performance of the *thrēnos*, but the effect of this legislation is unknown.

The aulos was the normal accompanying instrument, and was specially favoured during the *ekphora* (carrying-out); Karian women, famous as professional mourners, used the aulos during *thrēnoi*. The Sirens are depicted on gravestones and elsewhere, from the 4th century BC, as mourners, tearing their hair, beating their breasts or playing the aulos like human mourners. Laments were composed as aulos solos (here termed *nomoi thrēnētikoi*) from an early period. Lydian modality was favoured.

The distinctions to be drawn between 'thrēnos' and other terms for laments are not always clear. The *epikēdeion* was claimed even in antiquity to have been sung only at a burial (*kēdos*), but may be a simple synonym for *thrēnos*. The terms *goos* and (less commonly) *ialemos* may have referred to less sophisticated and less literary laments than the *thrēnos*, and the term KOMMOS referred (though perhaps not exclusively) to the literary laments of Attic tragedy.

Besides laments for the dead, Greek tradition included special laments for gods and heroes (e.g. Adonis and LINUS), perhaps still reflected in medieval *staurotheotokia* (laments of the Virgin Mary at the cross) and other Byzantine chants such as the *epitaphios thrēnos* (lament for Christ in Holy Week), and laments for the fall of cities.

BIBLIOGRAPHY
H. W. Smyth: *Greek Melic Poets* (London, 1900/*R*), p.cxx
C. M. Bowra: *Greek Lyric Poetry from Alcman to Simonides* (Oxford, 1936, rev. 2/1961)
P. Maas: 'Thrēnos', *Paulys Real-Encyclopädie der classischen Altertumswissenschaft*, 2nd ser., vi (Stuttgart, 1937), 596
E. Reiner: *Die rituelle Totenklage der Griechen*, Tübinger Beiträge zur Altertumswissenschaft, xxx (Stuttgart and Berlin, 1938)
M. Alexiou: *The Ritual Lament in Greek Tradition* (London, 1974)
GEOFFREY CHEW

Through-composed (Ger. *durchkomponiert*). A term generally applied to settings of songs in which the music for each stanza is different, not repeated from one stanza to the next as it is in strophic songs. The resulting musical form is thus not necessarily determined by the verse form of the poem, and a continuity can be achieved in which the music responds minutely to the flux of ideas, images and situations in the verse. The recurrence of thematic motifs is of course not precluded. Certain dramatic and narrative texts (e.g. Goethe's *Erlkönig*) are most appropriately treated in this manner. Since Schubert and Loewe through-composed songs have generally predominated over strophic settings. Even in the 18th century, however, there were many examples, such as Mozart's sensitive setting of Goethe's *Das Veilchen* K476.

MICHAEL TILMOUTH

Through imitation. See DURCHIMITATION.

Thuille, Ludwig (*b* Bozen [now Bolzano], the Tyrol, 30 Nov 1861; *d* Munich, 5 Feb 1907). Austrian composer of Savoyard ancestry. He received his first musical instruction from his father, an amateur musician. After his parents' death, he went in 1872 to live with his step-uncle in Kremsmünster, where he served as a chorister in the Benedictine Abbey, studied the violin, piano and organ, and received a good secondary education. In 1876 the generous widow of the conductor and composer Matthäus Nagiller took him to Innsbruck. She provided for his general education, his expenses, and for his theory, piano and organ studies with Joseph Pembauer, who in 1879 commended his brilliant student to Joseph Rheinberger at the Königliche Musikschule in Munich. There he also continued to study the piano (under Karl Bärmann, graduating with honours in 1882. As a composition student Thuille was musically conservative, an ardent admirer of Viennese Classicism and sternly disciplined by Rheinberger's academicism. However, a decisive change suddenly occurred in his style through his association with Alexander Ritter, a forceful figure who converted him and his boyhood friend Richard Strauss into rich orchestral colourists in the late Romantic vein. Ritter diverted Thuille's attention to opera of Wagnerian proportions and encouraged the young composer to cultivate bold harmonic ideas.

After a year of giving private lessons, in 1883 Thuille received an invitation to teach at the Königliche Musikschule as well as a composition stipend from the Frankfurt-am-Main Mozart Foundation. He soon began to win acclaim as a chamber pianist, accompanist and composer. In 1890 he was appointed professor in Munich and a year later conductor of the Munich Liederhort, an esteemed male choral society. By the turn of the century Thuille had become a leading figure in the city's musical life; as a professor of theory and composition at the Königliche Musikschule, he exerted a strong and healthy influence; Ernest Bloch, Walter Courvoisier, Walter Braunfels and Hermann Abendroth were among his many well-known students.

Thuille's distinction as a composer rests partly on his cultivation of chamber music at a time when most of his contemporaries were ignoring the genre. His early Sextet op.6 (1889), a rewarding vehicle for piano and wind ensembles with its expert instrumental balance and sweeping lyricism, was an immediate success; still more individual and intense is his mature Piano Quintet op.20 (1901). Unlike many of his contemporaries, he composed operas on whimsical subjects; although his first, *Theuerdank* (1895) using a text by Ritter, was unsuccessful, his second, *Lobetanz* (1896), was heard from Riga to Vienna and in New York. It is a mixture of melodrama, music drama and comedy, expertly composed in spite of a weak libretto by O. J. Bierbaum, and it led to another collaboration on a fairytale text, *Gugeline*, again with fresh lyrical music but burdened by an even worse libretto. A judicious moderation marks Thuille's style and distinguishes it from the music of his more famous contemporaries. Although his use of harmony was often adventurous, Thuille's innate conservatism restrained him from attempting the extreme experiments of Reger, and in his imaginative, sometimes radiant orchestration he avoided the radical innovations of Mahler. Nor was he attracted by the symphonic poem, as was Strauss; the most appealing traits of his music are its structural clarity and ingratiating melodic invention.

Thuille's *Harmonielehre* (1907), written jointly with Rudolf Louis, remained a standard work long after his death. The textbook is in two parts, the first devoted to diatonic and the other to chromatic and enharmonic harmony, and considers chords not merely in the conventional vertical harmonic sense but also as horizontal contrapuntal textures.

WORKS

(*selective list*)

STAGE

Theuerdank (opera, 3, A. Ritter), 1893–5, Munich, 12 Feb 1897
Lobetanz, op.10 (opera, 3, O. J. Bierbaum), 1896, Karlsruhe, 6 Feb 1898 (Berlin, 1897)
Gugeline, op.18 (opera, 5, O. J. Bierbaum), 1898–1900, Bremen, March 1901 (Mainz, 1900)
Die Tanzhexe (melodrama with dance, O. J. Bierbaum), 1899–1900

OTHER VOCAL

13 choral pieces incl. Weihnacht im Walde, op.14, 5 male vv, 1898 (Leipzig and Zurich, 1900); Traumsommernacht, op.25 (O. J. Bierbaum), 4 female vv, solo vn, harp, 1902 (Leipzig, 1902); 3 Soldatenlieder (from 'Des Knaben Wunderhorn'), op.35, male vv, 1905 (Leipzig and Zurich, 1906)
78 songs

INSTRUMENTAL

4 orch works incl. Sym., F, 1886; Romantische Ouvertüre (ov. to Theuerdank), op.16, 1896 (Leipzig, 1899)
6 chamber works inc. Sextet, B♭, fl, ob, cl, bn, hn, pf, op.6, 1886–8 (Leipzig, 1889); Pf Qnt, E♭, op.20, 1897–1901 (Leipzig, 1901); Sonata, d, vc, pf, op.22, 1901–2 (Strasbourg, 1902); Sonata, e, vn, pf, op.30, 1903–4 (Strasbourg, 1904)
4 works, solo pf; 13 arrs. of orig. works and works by R. Strauss and P. Cornelius, pf, pf 4 hands

WRITINGS

with R. Louis: *Harmonielehre* (Stuttgart, 1907, rev. 10/1933 by W. Courvoisier, R. G'schrey, G. Geierhaas and K. Blessinger)
Other harmony textbooks

BIBLIOGRAPHY

W. Mauke: *Gugeline*, Opernführer, liii (Leipzig, 1901)
E. Istel: 'Ludwig Thuille', *Monographien moderner Musiker*, i, ed. C. F. Kahnt (Leipzig, 1906), 35
R. Louis: *Die deutsche Musik der Gegenwart* (Munich, 1909)
E. Istel: *Lobetanz*, Opernführer, cxiv (Berlin, 1910)
F. Munter: *Ludwig Thuille* (Munich, 1923) [incl. complete list of works]
E. Istel: 'Ludwig Thuille', *MQ*, xviii (1932), 463
J. Lachner: 'Ludwig Thuille: ein Münchner aus Tirol', *Süddeutsche Zeitung* (30 Nov 1961)
R. Strauss and L. Thuille: *Briefe der Freundschaft 1877–1907*, ed. A. Ott (Munich, 1969) [incl. complete list of works]

EDWARD F. KRAVITT

Thuma, František Ignác Antonín. *See* TŮMA, FRANTIŠEK IGNÁC ANTONÍN.

Thumb piano. *See* LAMELLAPHONE.

Thümmler, David Gotthilf (*b* Zwickau, 14 Sept 1801; *d* Zwickau, 25 Aug 1847). German organ builder. After employment under E. F. Walcker in Ludwigsburg, Aloys Mooser (Fribourg) and Dreymann (Mainz), he became in 1833 a citizen of his native Zwickau. His craftsmanship follows in the tradition of Andreas and Gottfried Silbermann, but also shows originality. The façades are beautiful and impressive. The manuals (with compasses ranging up to *f'''*) are well-endowed with overtones and independent of each other; a characteristic of his carefully planned specifications is that the Cornett is usually on the upper manual. On the magnificent Tettau organ (1840–41) the 8′ Flauto traverso and quadruple Cornett are capable on their own of filling the church with resonance. Choice materials and careful construction guarantee the high quality of Thümmler's organs, whose tone unites strength and silvery clarity with charm and a warmth of timbre. Important contemporary evaluations, as well as the surviving notable instruments near Glauchau (Schönberg, 1838; Tettau, 1840–41; Remse, 1844) and one in Bad Brambach, Vogtland (1846; two manuals and pedal, 20 speaking stops, manual and pedal couplers), attest to Thümmler's position among the major craftsmen of the 19th century.

BIBLIOGRAPHY
E. Herzog: *Chronik der Kreisstadt Zwickau*, i (Zwickau, 1839)
F. Oehme: *Handbuch über ältere und neuere Orgelwerke im Königreiche Sachsen*, ii (Dresden, n.d.); iii (Dresden, 1897)
WALTER HÜTTEL

Thumoth [Thumont], **Burk** [Burke of Thomond] (*fl* 1739–50). Irish music editor, composer and instrumentalist. The earliest known references to him occur in Dublin newspapers in 1739 and 1740, when he appeared as a soloist playing concertos on the trumpet and the flute. He also performed in England as a flautist, appearing for instance at Ruckholt House, Leyton, on 14 May 1744.

About 1745–50 he issued two books which provide one of the earliest printed sources of Irish traditional airs. The first consisted of 12 Scots and 12 Irish airs, the second of 12 English and 12 Irish airs. Both books, which contain 'Variations, set for the German Flute, Violin or Harpsichord', were published for John Simpson of London, reprinted *c*1765, and re-engraved and published in one volume about 1785 by S., A. & P. Thompson of London under the title *Forty-eight English, Irish and Scotch airs*. Thumoth's only other known publication is *Six Solos for a German Flute, Violin or Harpsichord, the First Three composed by Mr Burk Thumoth, the Three Last by Sigr. Canaby* (London, *c*1746).

BRIAN BOYDELL

Thump. A little-used 17th-century term for a primitive left-hand pizzicato, limited to open strings (see J. Playford: *Musick's Recreation on the Viol Lyra-way*, London, 1669, and T. Ford: *Musicke of Sundrie Kindes*, London, 1607, where the last piece has the alternative title 'Mr Richard Martin's Thump'; the term is explained on sig.K2*v* and the thump is to be executed with the first or second finger of the left hand).

Thumrī. A popular north Indian urban vocal genre *see* INDIA, SUBCONTINENT OF, §§II, 4(ii); III, 1; SURINAM, §4.

Thunder machine. An instrument for special effects used to produce an imitation (or evocation) of thunder, in the form of a revolving drum partly filled with balls of hard material: a modification of the 'bronteron' used in theatres for thunder behind the scenes. In the bronteron, either pebbles were poured into a large metal vessel, or bags filled with stones were flung against a metal surface, or lead balls were dropped on a sheet of leather. A further effective imitation was produced by rolling a heavy stone or ball of lead down a slatted ramp. Today it is customary to use recorded sound effects or a thunder sheet, consisting of a large metal sheet which is suspended and shaken. The thunder machine or sheet is requested in many orchestral scores, notably in Strauss's *An Alpine Symphony* and in Havergal Brian's *Gothic Symphony* (1919–27) and Tenth Symphony (1953–4). In *First Construction* (1962) John Cage scored for five graduated thunder sheets.

JAMES BLADES

Suspended thunder sheet with bass drum for added resonance

Thuren, Hjalmar (*b* Copenhagen, 10 Sept 1873; *d* Copenhagen, 13 Jan 1912). Danish folklorist. After taking the state examination in theology (1898) he worked as a schoolteacher until 1905. His main area of research was the folk music of the Faeroe Islands, particularly their dance-song; in 1902 he collected material for over 200 recordings there. He also analysed Eskimo song from recordings made by William Thalbitzer in east Greenland. Illness prevented him from completing his work on medieval Danish ballads, which remains unpublished. His writings are notable for their originality and thoroughness, and include the following (all published in Copenhagen): *Dans og kvaddigtning på Faer Øerne* (1901); *Folkesangen på Faer Øerne* (1908); *Vore sanglege: danske studier* (1908); *The Eskimo Music – meddelelser fra Grønland* (with W. Thalbitzer, 1911); *Melodies from East Greenland* (1914); and *Faerøske melodier til danske kaempeviser* (1923, ed. H. Grüner-Nielsen).

Thüring, Johann (*b* ?Trebra, nr. Apolda; *d* Willerstedt, nr. Apolda, buried 13 July 1635). German composer, ?organist and schoolmaster. In his publication of 1634 he described himself as 'Trebrensis' (also 'Trebensis'), which most probably means that he was born at Trebra. From about 1603 or 1604 he was a schoolmaster at Willerstedt, where he apparently remained for the rest of his life. He was employed by the local church, probably as a Kantor and organist and was certainly active as a composer of Lutheran church music. His publications of 1621 and 1634 contain music for both choir and congregational use in a basically simple style that increasingly allowed for the often limited musical resources resulting from the hardships of the Thirty Years War. Indeed he was one of several lesser Thuringian musicians through whose work the traditions of Lutheran church music were maintained at a time of crisis. Some of his chorale melodies reappeared in later hymnbooks.

WORKS
10 geistliche Cantiones und Moteten, 5–8, 10vv (Jena, 1617), inc.
2 christliche Erndten-Gesänge (Jena, 1620); lost, according to *WaltherML*
15 geistliche Gesänge und Moteten beneben der Litania und Te Deum Laudamus, 4–8vv (Erfurt, 1621); 2, 4vv, ed. L. F. Schöberlein, Schatz des liturgischen Chor-und Gemeinde-Gesangs (Göttingen, 1865–72); 2 ed. J. Zahn, Die Melodien der deutschen evangelischen Kirchenlieder (Gütersloh, 1889–93/R1963), nos.515, 4537
Sertum spirituale musicale, geistliches musikalisches Kräntzlein . . . 30 lieblicher Cantionen, 3vv, bc (Erfurt, 1634)
1 motet, 8vv, *D-Bds*, inc.; 1 motet, 8vv, *Z*
4 motets, 6–8vv; 3 German songs: lost

BIBLIOGRAPHY
WaltherML
G. Kraft: *Die thüringische Musikkultur um 1600* (Würzburg, 1941), i
A. LINDSEY KIRWAN

Thuringus [Thüring], **Joachim** (*b* Fürstenberg, Mecklenburg, late 16th century). German theorist. He referred to himself as 'S. S. Theol. et Lib. Art. Studiosus et P[oeta] L[aureatus] C[aesareus]'. In 1622 he published in Berlin *Nucleus musicus de modis seu tonis, ex optimus . . . musicorum abstrusioribus scriptus*, which he revised and expanded as *Opusculum bipartitum de primordiis musicis* (Berlin, 1624, 2/1625). It is the latter treatise which establishes him as a significant contributor to German music theory in the 17th century.

The *Opusculum bipartitum* consists of two major parts, 'De tonis sive modis' and 'De compondendi regulis'. Thuringus provided a list of the authorities from which he obtained much of his material. Most of them were German; they include Alsted, Burmeister, Calvisius, Henning Dedekind, Eichmann, Heinrich Faber, Galliculus, Glarean, Eucharius Hoffmann, Listenius, Nucius, Rhau and the composers Josquin and Senfl. As Feldmann has shown, much of the volume comes from the treatise by Nucius, *Musices poeticae . . . praeceptiones* (Neisse, 1613), as well as from Burmeister's *Musica poetica* (Rostock, 1603); Feldmann also proved that sections of the treatise rely heavily on the works of Glarean, Hoffmann and Eichmann. But despite the derivative nature of what may be the work of a music student, the *Opusculum bipartitum* is an important document, especially for its presentation of the new German aesthetics of *musica poetica*. Thuringus gave definitions of many of the most significant musical figures and apparently helped to transmit the German interest in musical rhetoric to later generations, including J. G. Walther.

See also WORD-PAINTING.

BIBLIOGRAPHY
H. H. Unger: *Die Beziehungen zwischen Musik und Rhetorik im 16. Jahrhundert* (Würzburg, 1941)
A. Schmitz: 'Die Figurenlehre in den theoretischen Werken J. G. Walthers', *AMw*, ix (1952), 79
F. Feldmann: 'Das "Opusculum bipartitum" des J. Thuringus (1625) besonders in seinen Beziehungen zu Joh. Nucius (1613)', *AMw*, xv (1958), 123
GEORGE J. BUELOW

Thurinomarus [Thurnmaier, John; Thurnmayer, Jean]. *See* AVENTINUS, JOHANNES.

Thurn und Taxis. Family active as musical patrons, in the Low Countries, Frankfurt and especially in REGENSBURG (from 1748). Carl Alexander (prince, 1773–97) was the composer of a sinfonia and keyboard music, now in *D-Rtt*, where the Thurn und Taxis Hofkapelle and Hoftheater library are preserved.

Thürschmidt, Carl. *See* TÜRRSCHMIDT, CARL.

Thurston, Frederick (John) (*b* Lichfield, 21 Sept 1901; *d* London, 12 Dec 1953). English clarinettist. After being taught by his father, he won an open scholarship to the RCM, where he was a pupil of Charles Draper. During the 1920s he played in the Royal Philharmonic and Royal Opera House orchestras, and in the BBC's Wireless Orchestra. In 1930 he became principal clarinet of the new BBC SO, in which he played with great distinction until 1946. He then left to concentrate on chamber music. He gave the first performances of many new works, of which several were dedicated to him, including Bax's Sonata, Bliss's Clarinet Quintet (which he recorded with its original performers, the Griller Quartet) and works by Howells, Ireland and Rawsthorne. His tone, which like his teacher's was without vibrato, was admired for its firmness and clarity. He visited several European countries as a soloist and was known throughout Great Britain for his lecture-recitals. He was also renowned as a teacher, and taught at the RCM from 1930. His pupils included Thea King, whom he married.

WRITINGS
with A. Frank: *The Clarinet* (London, 1939)
'Clarinet Tone', *Woodwind Year Book 1940–41* (London, 1940), 47ff
Clarinet Technique (London, 1956)

BIBLIOGRAPHY
P. Weston: *Clarinet Virtuosi of the Past* (London, 1971)
ROBERT PHILIP

Thyard, Pontus de. *See* TYARD, PONTUS DE.

Thybo, Leif (*b* Holsterbro, 12 June 1922). Danish composer and organist. At the age of ten he began private piano lessons and he subsequently took up the cello. He began to study theory privately with Holmboe just before entering the Copenhagen Conservatory in 1940. There he studied under Sigurdsson (piano), Bangert (organ), Høffding (theory) and Schierbeck (instrumentation). He completed the conservatory examinations in theory, history and the organ in 1944, and the following year he gained his teaching diploma. From 1945 to 1948 he continued music studies at the University of Copenhagen. He developed an interest in organ building as well as performance, and this was stimulated by extensive travel in England, France, Germany and the Netherlands. He was organist at the churches of Vedbaek (1948–56), Søllerød (1956–61) and Naerum (from 1971). From 1949 to 1965 he taught harmony and counterpoint at the University of Copenhagen, and he has taught theory (from 1952) and the organ (from 1960) at the Copenhagen Conservatory, where he was appointed lecturer (1961) and professor (1965). He served as head of the teachers' association at the conservatory between 1963 and 1968. The award of the Anckerske Legat in 1961 enabled him to spend a period of time in Italy composing, and he has made recital tours throughout Scandinavia and northern Europe as well as in the USA.

In his early compositions Thybo sought to exploit the

improved resources made available by recent organ-building developments. With technical assistance from the Danish builders Erik and Walther Frobenius, in 1952 he transcribed Stravinsky's *Dumbarton Oaks Concerto*, taking advantage of the latest refinements in tracker action. In 1952 and 1956 he composed two concertos for solo organ, still showing an appreciation of the idiom of Stravinsky. For Thybo the central problem of composing is the continual search for a new kind of tonality. Just as Stravinsky's influence may be found in the organ works and in such a piece as the Concerto for String Orchestra (1958), the pianistic style of the Piano Concerto (1961–2) shows the influence of Bartók. Many of Thybo's vocal works display the influence of Britten; the *Tre Baudelaire sange* (1974) are an example of what Thybo calls 'new impressionism'. He seeks the refinement of tonal aspects and a simplification of tonality, and is particularly concerned with finding a style most appropriate to a particular voice or instrument.

WORKS
(*selective list*)

Opera: Den udødelige historie [The immortal story] (Blixen, after Ostman), 1971; Vadstena, Sweden, 1971
Orch: Conc., str, 1958; Vc Conc., 1959; Conc., org, chamber orch, 1960; Pf Conc., 1961–2; Conc., fl, chamber orch, 1965; Vn Conc., 1969; Va Conc., 1972
Choral: Te Deum, S, chorus, wind/org, 1965; Prophetia, S, B, chorus, org, 1966; Amabo, chorus, 1968; Bier hoster sjaeldent (B. Andersen), chorus, 1971; Rosa rorans, 2 female vv, insts, 1973; The Fairy [from '(Blake)',] 3 female vv, 1974
Solo vocal: On his blindness (Milton), Mez, org, 1954; O gloriosa vergine Marie, Mez, vn, org, 1955; 3 sonnets (Labé), S, rec, ob, lute, vle, spinet, 1974; 3 Baudelaire sange, S, pf, 1974; Stemmer (Stuckenberg), reciter, S, wind qnt, 1974; The Token (Donne), 1v, pf, 1974; 2 Shakespeare Sonnets, 1v, fl, vc, pf, 1975; 2 Choral Phantasies, 1v, org, 1975; Camino de Santiago, S, org, 1975
Chamber and pf: Theme and Variations, pf, 1945; Elementi concertanti, sonata, pf, 1955; Non si levava ancor', rec, eng hn, bn, hn, 1964; Str Trio, 1964; Etudes, 1965; Hommage à Benjamin Britten, fl, 3 str, 1968; Engels nachtegaltje, rec, fl, org, 1974; Concertino, 2 tpt, org, 1976; Pf Trio, 1976
Org: Preludio, pastorale e fugato, 1948; Praeludium, 1950; Dumbarton Oaks [arr. from Stravinsky], 1952; Conc. I 'St James', 1952; 4 Chorales, 1953; Conc. II 'St Andrew', 1956; Passacaglia con intermedios, 1961; Contrasti, 1965; Liber organi, 1967; Compenius-suite, 1968

Principal publishers: Hansen, Musikhøjskolens Forlag, Samfundet tu Udgivelse af Dansk Musik

BIBLIOGRAPHY
L. Thybo: 'Carl Nielsen', *Musikrevy*, iv (1950), 127
K. Baekkelund: 'God musik vil altid slå an i menneskets sinn', *Musikrevy*, xvi (1961)
F. Høffding: 'Leif Thybos "Marcus-passion" ', *Dansk musiktidsskrift*, xxxix (1964), 145
'Thybo, Leif', *Kraks blå bog* (Copenhagen, 1974), 1056

WILLIAM H. REYNOLDS

Thyiades. See MAENADS.

Thysius [Thijs], **Johan** (*b* Amsterdam, 13–21 Aug 1621; *d* Leiden, buried 8 Oct 1653). Dutch lawyer. His father was Anthony Thijs, a merchant in Amsterdam. Thysius enrolled at the University of Leiden on 13 August 1635 and read philology and law. Between 1646 and 1648 he travelled in France and England to further his studies. Returning to Leiden he registered again on 27 August 1648 and graduated in law on 21 August 1652.

He owned an important library and founded the Bibliotheca Thysiana. In it is preserved an MS lutebook in French seven-line tablature. This volume was compiled by the Amsterdam minister Adrian Joriszoon Smout (as a reference 'Johan Thijs wt d'Auctie van Smoutius' in the MS suggests), while Smout was a student in Leiden (1595–1601). With some 452 pieces it is the richest Dutch collection of lute music and one which shows the international aspect of musical taste in the Netherlands at that time. The MS contains intabulations of Dutch, English, French and Italian songs, Reformation psalms, motets and some 164 dances, mainly French, English, Italian and Dutch in origin, as well as six fantasias, including one by Francesco da Milano. Claude le Jeune, Claude Goudimel, Orlande de Lassus, Peter Philips and Jan Pieterszoon Sweelinck may be singled out among the composers of the songs on which the lute intabulations are based, and John Dowland, Robert Jones and Thomas Robinson are among the composers of the dances. A few pieces come from collections by E. Adriaensen published in Antwerp in 1584 and 1592. Interestingly, many of the numerous English song and dance tunes are also found in the Fitzwilliam Virginal Book. The pavan by 'Signor Thysio' in Rude's *Flores musicae*, ii (Heidelberg, 1600) is not by Johan Thysius, as Eitner supposed.

BIBLIOGRAPHY
J. P. N. Land: 'Het Luitboek van Thysius beschreven en toegelicht', *TVNM*, i/3 (1884), 129–95; i/4 (1885), 205–64; ii/1 (1885), 1–56; ii/2 (1886), 109–74; ii/3 (1887), 177; ii/4 (1887), 278–350; iii/1 (1888), 1–57; also repr. (Amsterdam, 1889) [includes edition of the 6 fantasias and for the majority of the pieces, the basic melody]
R. Eitner: 'Besprechung der Arbeit Land's', *MMg*, xviii (1886), 39; xix (1887), 11
F. Kossmann: 'Die Melodie des "Wilhelmus von Nassouwe" in den Lautenbearbeitungen des XVII. Jahrhunderts', *AMw*, v (1923), 329 [includes edition of 5 pieces]
L. de La Laurencie: *Les luthistes* (Paris, 1928)

HANS RADKE

Tibaldi, Giuseppe (Luigi) (*b* Bologna, 22 Jan 1729; *d c*1790). Italian tenor and composer. He studied singing with Domenico Zanardi and composition with Martini (his counterpoint exercises are in the Bologna Conservatory library). In 1747 he was admitted to the Accademia Filarmonica as a singer and in 1750 as a composer; he served as *principe* in 1759, 1777 and 1783. In 1751 he succeeded Giuseppe Alberti as *maestro di cappella* at S Giovanni in Monte of Bologna, but after a few years decided to devote himself entirely to a career as an operatic tenor, becoming one of the few leading opera singers who had a disciplined training in counterpoint. He sang in the most important European opera houses, taking leading roles in the premières of Gluck's *Alceste* (Vienna, 1767) and Mozart's *Ascanio in Alba* (Milan, 1771). His few extant compositions (in *I-Bc*, one in *Bsp*) are sacred pieces dating from the time of his study with Martini, except for a later set of *Duetti notturni* for two sopranos and continuo (in *I-Bsp*).

His son, Ferdinando Tibaldi (*c*1750–1785), was also a singer and composer.

HOWARD BROFSKY

Tibbett [Tibbet], **Lawrence** (*b* Bakersfield, Calif., 16 Nov 1896; *d* New York, 15 July 1960). American baritone. After beginning his career as an actor and as a singer in church and light operas, he turned to Frank La Forge and Basil Ruysdael for more serious study, which led to his Metropolitan Opera début in the minor role of Lovitsky in *Boris Godunov* (November 1923). A week later he sang Valentin in *Faust*, but widespread recognition did not come to him until January 1925 when he sang Ford in *Falstaff* and eclipsed Antonio Scotti (who sang the title role). He eventually succeeded Scotti in the leading Italian roles and remained a principal singer with the company for

27 seasons, noted, in his prime, for his command of legato together with his vivid acting. He sang in the premières of Gruenberg's *The Emperor Jones* (1932), Taylor's *The King's Henchman* (1926) and *Peter Ibbetson* (1930), Hanson's *Merry Mount* (1933) and Seymour's *In the Pasha's Garden* (1934). At Covent Garden he created the title role in Goossens's *Don Juan de Mañara* (1937). He also took part in the first performances at the Metropolitan Opera of *Jonny spielt auf*, *Peter Grimes*, Hageman's *Caponsacchi*, *Simon Boccanegra* and *Khovanshchina* (in which he made his last Metropolitan appearance on 24 March 1950). He also sang at Paris, Vienna and Prague. His dark, pliant baritone and matinée-idol appearance made him a popular figure in films (*The Rogue Song*, *The New Moon*) as well as light opera, and he was a significant force in the early days of American radio. In 1950 he appeared on Broadway in *The Barrier* and his last stage role was in the musical comedy *Fanny* (1956). He is perhaps best represented on recordings in scenes from *Otello* which reveal him as an Iago of sly wit, his ample fervour in the 'Credo' being counterbalanced by a silken *pianissimo* in 'Era la notte', the dream narrative. He published an autobiography *The Glory Road* (Brattleboro, 1933/*R*1977 with discography by W. R. Moran).

BIBLIOGRAPHY
G. Lauri-Volpi: *Voci parallele* (Milan, 1955)
R. Whelan: 'Lawrence Tibbett Discography', *Record News*, v (Toronto, 1961), 165
R. Celletti: 'Tibbett, Lawrence', *Le grandi voci* (Rome, 1964) [with opera discography by S. Smolian]
J. B. Steane: *The Grand Tradition* (London, 1974), 295ff
MARTIN BERNHEIMER

Tibbits, George (Richard) (*b* Boulder, Western Australia, 7 Nov 1933). Australian composer and architect. He studied at the University of Melbourne, where he became senior lecturer in urban studies and architectural history. Unusually among Australian composers, he has no professional musical connections and works in deliberate isolation from the country's intense musical politics. The early influences on his music included Indonesian music and later Schoenberg, Perle, Babbitt and Cage; then, in the late 1950s, he produced 'bruitiste' music based on urban life. By the early 1960s he had rejected this aesthetic for lyricism, and in 1965, while in England on an extensive town-planning project, he took an interest in European rock and pop groups. In later works he has turned to antique models. He prefers the stimulus of writing for special events and commissions, and his music in general is notable for intellectual humour and an avoidance of pretension.

WORKS
(selective list)
Orch: Pili, wind qnt, 2 str qt, 1966; Fanfare for the Great Hall, orch in groups, 1968; Neuronis Nephronius and his Lowly Queen, small orch, 1968; I Thought you were all Glittering with the Noblest of Carriage, 1969; Serenade, small orch, 1969; Beside the Rivering Waters of . . ., 1970; Antediluvia, str, 1971; The Rose Garden of the Queen of Navarre, mands, 1975; Vn Conc., 1975
Vocal: 5 Songs, A, pf, 1969; Golden Builders (V. Buckley), S, small chorus, ens, 1972; Five Bells (K. Slessor), S, str qt, 1972; Shadows, S, hpd, str orch, 1974; The Ice Fishermen–Lake Erie (A. Taylor), S, orch, 1974
Chamber and inst: Silop, fl, cel, 1963; Qnt, fl, cl, va, vc, pf, 1964; Trio, fl, va, hpd, 1964; Qashq, fl, cl, hn, pf, 1966; Homage to Stravinsky, fl va, pf, 1967; Str Qt, 1968; Variations, pf 4 hands, 1969; Stasis, pf, 1970; Macrame, fl, bn, gui, 1974; Fantasy on the ABC, org, 1975; Gateau, wind qnt, 1975; Str Qt, 1975

Principal publisher: Albert

MAUREEN THÉRÈSE RADIC

Tiberti, Giacomo (*b* 1631; *d* 1689). Italian composer. According to the published libretto (in *A-Wn* and elsewhere) of his opera *La forza della fortuna e della virtù, overo Gl'amori d'Irena* (Teofilo), written for Vienna in 1661 and performed on the nameday of the Empress Eleonora, he was *maestro di cappella* at Ravenna. His only surviving works are two cantatas for solo voice in *I-MOe*.

BIBLIOGRAPHY
EitnerQ; *RicordiE* ('Ravenna')
F. Hadamowsky: 'Barocktheater am Wiener Kaiserhof', *Jb der Gesellschaft für Wiener Theaterforschung, 1951–2* (Vienna, 1955), 72

Tibet. Autonomous region of China and the southernmost major country of eastern Central Asia. The study of Tibetan music is important for several reasons: it establishes Tibetan ritual as having a major independent Asian musical style; it shows that various genres perpetuate archaic Central Asian features; it enables us to recognize models of the traditional music of many classes before these become further hybridized or disappear. First-hand material has become increasingly available since 1959 and enables one to form a reasonable picture of Tibetan music for the first time. (Transliteration of Tibetan words follows the principles set forth by Snellgrove.)

1. Background. 2. Music and religion: (i) Bön (ii) The Buddhist liturgy (iii) The mystery dance-drama. 3. Musical arts: (i) The secular dramas (ii) Party music (iii) Drum and reed music. 4. Epic song. 5. Folk music. 6. Instruments.

1. BACKGROUND. Isolated by high altitudes, a severe climate and formidable mountain ranges, Tibet has developed a very original civilization and music culture. Its population of about 1.7 million represents a blend of archaic whites and fully evolved mongoloids and goes back to the Central Asian *Ch'iang* tribes who were herders in the 1st millennium BC. Hence the ancient way of life is one of nomadic pastoralism. Economically Tibet belongs to a belt of cattle-raising cultures, stretching from Central Asia through Arabia into Africa. Agriculture is also found in the valleys of the south and south-east.

In the prehistoric age the religion of Tibet was Shamanism of the northern and Central Asian type. From this, in primitive times, developed *Bön* (the native religion), forms of which survive today. Tibet became a dominant military power in Central Asia in the 8th century during the first historical period which was that of the early kings (7th–10th century). From northern India it gradually adopted Mahāyāna Buddhism intermixed with Tantrism. During the rule of King Srong-btsan-sgam-po (*c*627–49) the Indian Gupta alphabet was adapted to Tibetan (a Tibeto-Burman language). This made possible the Tibetan Buddhist scriptures, primarily through translation from Indian sources during the 7th to 13th centuries. The indigenous religion, however, remained strong. The Middle Ages saw a reworking of Indian Tantric Buddhism, which, blended with *Bön*, created highly syncretistic forms. An essentially independent Tibetan culture was created, based on a feudal theocracy, and its arts acquired distinctive forms and styles.

In the modern period (15th–20th century), the *dGe-lugs-pa* Order ('Yellow hats') became dominant as the established church. One of its spiritual heads in the 17th century, the 5th Dalai Lama, became ruler of Tibet in 1642. The period was one of religious stabilization and even of stereotyping. The contemporary period began in 1950 with the attack by Communist China. After the 14th Dalai Lama's flight to India in 1959, China replaced the Tibetan Government with a dictatorship, calling Tibet an autonomous region of the Chinese Democratic Republic. In 1967 the Red Guards completed the destruction of holy places, including over 3000 monasteries, thereby destroying the mainsprings of Tibetan civilization. Relics of the civilization are still found in peripheral regions, though much of what remains in Tibet, including its musical arts, is being manipulated to political ends.

Throughout the ages Tibet has accreted around its Central Asian core cultural influences from surrounding regions. The influence of India (especially during the 8th to 11th century) was profound in the spiritual sphere. That of China, occasionally overlord of Tibet since the 13th century, has been more limited and more superficial, confined largely to the social world of a wealthy minority. Tibet has also had contacts with pre-Muslim Persia, Mongolia (from the 13th century), Islam and the Christian world (from the 16th century or earlier), and with the west (from the 18th century).

Tibet is not confined culturally and musically to modern political Tibet where much of what is described in this article has already changed. The broader area of ethnic Tibet also includes, to the east, parts of the Chinese provinces of Szechwuan, Kansu and Yunnan; to the west, the now Indian regions of Ladakh, Lahul and Spiti; to the south, Bhutan, Sikkim, parts of northern Nepal, the Sherpa and Tamang regions of eastern Nepal and the extreme north-west of Assam.

Music is very important in the lives of all Tibetan peoples and has been stressed alike in religion, education and entertainment, as well as in everyday life. The monks make music for the Buddha and their divinities; the minstrels delight and instruct their patrons; the people sing to lighten their work and enrich their leisure. Such different contexts have created different musical forms. In most of them dance is a close partner of music, as is also drama in ritual and in education.

2. MUSIC AND RELIGION.

(i) *Bön*. There are still many *Bön-po* (adherents of *Bön*), especially in the east of Tibet. In its monastic forms it has been largely assimilated by Tantric Buddhism, though there are also many practices suggestive of the Shamanism of Central and northern Asia and of the music of their hunting societies. *Bön* has also borrowed many features from Buddhism; for example, of its 'nine ways' of realization, the seventh is 'the way of pure sound'.

In ritual music, both instrumental music and chanting are employed. In the course of its long history *Bön* appears to have used flutes and trumpets made from animal bones. However, the *phyed-rnga* (single-headed drum) and the *gshang* ('flat bell'), both traditionally of Tibetan origin, have become its chief instruments. When the *Bön* priest plays his drum he is thought of, according to old legends, as mounted on a flying steed, especially a horse or deer, the domesticated animals of earth (which are considered the middle level of the *Bön* universe). The steed carries the priest into the heavens or highest level (i.e. brings him religious ecstasy), where he may communicate with the heavenly spirits (eagle or sun-bird, and dragon or thunder-bird). The animal-head terminals (horse-, dragon- and occasionally eagle-head)

of the *sgra-snyan* and *pi-wang* (Tibetan lutes) used in the performance of secular music today probably originated in such symbolism. The *Bön* drum occupies a central place in the instrumental aspect of the ritual. Its music is notated by using a circle to represent a beat, and a larger circle to represent an accented beat. The traditional '300 ways of playing' associated with the instrument have roots in number symbolism.

Ex.1 *Dance of the Wild Yak* (Jest, 1966)

↑ = slightly sharp
↓ = slightly flat

BAM. LD. 104

By contrast, the chant, traditionally also of Tibetan origin, appears less complex, and within a song in strophic structure shows little variation of either text or music (see ex.1). However, the intensity of the chanting increases (crescendo, accelerando) as the ritual proceeds, and the limited number of available examples suggests the use of a wide variety of vocal techniques, e.g. rising initial glides, falling terminal glides, whistling, shouting, masking the voice. Some of these techniques are attributed to the voices of the spirits heard through the practitioner as medium. A similar interpretation may also be made of instrumental styles, such as that of the *rkang-gling* (thigh-bone trumpets). In a Buddhist source (which, however, describes what is evidently a pre-Buddhist myth), the sounds of the *rkang-gling* are referred to as the neighing of the horses which will carry the faithful to the western paradise. Otherwise, *Bön* music may be close to that of the Tibetan Buddhist tradition in its more syncretistic forms.

(ii) *The Buddhist liturgy*. Buddhism in Tibet is a form of *Mahāyāna*, syncretized through an early blend with Tantrism in India and with *Bön* in Tibet. Its monastic system, with Tibetan everywhere the liturgical language, has existed not only throughout the whole region of ethnic Tibet, but also in Mongolia, Buryat Siberia, the Caucasus, Manchuria, and parts of China and Turkestan (Sinkiang). In this religion, music, both vocal and instrumental, has always been an important way to spiritual enlightenment; it prepares the mind to receive that truth which alone can take man beyond wrong knowledge and the consequent sufferings of life and, ultimately, beyond the inevitable circle of death and rebirth which these are said to entail. The music at once reflects the formless transcendent truth and the transitory world of forms considered indivisible from it. It exists on many levels, helpful alike to meditation, devotional communication, and the cultivation of special insights and powers. The works on sacred theory await translation; however, traditionally, only 'perfect beings' are able to compose, as they are in constant communication with the divine world and therefore ever-hearing the *mantras* (names of divinities) upon which this music is based. Tradition further links the sounds of the sacred instruments with those heard in the human body when other sounds are stilled.

The musical practices of the various orders of Tibetan Buddhism show differences; however, many general observations may be made. The monastic routine centres on five daily assemblies in the monastery temple; these take place at intervals, from before sunrise to sunset. Annual festivals and services which are celebrated monthly may be included in this routine. The service sequences are not masses or prayers of the Western kind but consist predominantly of choral chants; the standard chant texts are drawn from the sacred scriptures, known as the *bKa'-'gyur* (doctrines attributed to the Buddha) and from *bsTan-'gyur* (commentaries). There are also 'invitations' to the deities to visit the place of worship; choral and instrumental 'offerings' to please their ears; hymns of thanksgiving; and poems of praise to the Buddha and his chief disciples, and for founders of orders and monasteries. There are also private rituals for monks and hermits, special services for the laity, and numerous rites accompanying exorcism, healing, weather-making, mediumism and divination.

Under the quiet diffused glow of butter-lamps, the monks, sitting cross-legged in rows facing each other, chant and play instruments for much of their lives. The music of the services proceeds under the direction of the *dbu-mdzas* (chant leader), who also trains the monks. In training them, he may use a *dbyangs-yig* (musical score); this is set in front of him during the services, although he does not use it then. The *dbyangs-yig* constitutes a scroll-like score of the chanting in its different styles and the techniques for the production of various timbres and other features. The syllables of the text are written under these signs, and sometimes indications for the playing of instruments as well. Although such notation is likely to have existed for many centuries in Tibet, and different orders and even monasteries have their own forms of it, studies of the nature and origins of this system have been undertaken comparatively recently (*see* NEUMATIC NOTATIONS, §VII and fig.31).

The standard rituals usually include unaccompanied choral chants, instrumental hymns, and services employing both choral and instrumental forces. The typical full service, lasting up to an hour or longer, is broadly antiphonal; sections played by the monastery orchestra alternate with choral chanting either unaccompanied or accompanied only by the time-beaters (cymbals and drum). The primary tonal centre of the choral sections may be the same as that of the instrumental sections but with a different modality; it may, however, be different and apparently unrelated.

The choral chant, ascribed to early Indian origins, is normally rendered in unison, though cases of pedal points and oblique organum occur, as well as relatively independent part-movement. Chant sections are usually restrained and thus relatively quiet. There are three main styles, all of which may be found in a full service: parlando recitative, *gdang* (hymn chanting) and *dbyangs* (sustained chant). The recitative, usually solo in short introductory passages, may be in free or measured time (see ex.2). The *gdang* is chanted in strict tempo though

Ex.2 from *Ritual for Spiritual Adepts* (Crossley-Holland, 1965)

BM. 30L. 2009

the tempos used cover a wide range. The sacred poetry, which is rhymeless, is often cast in stanzas of four lines, the lines having an uneven number of syllables. Seven- and nine-syllable lines are very common, with alternately stressed and unstressed syllables. A nine-syllable line may be set syllabically (sometimes with melismatic elements) in a ten-beat measure, the last beat being a rest. Similarly, a seven-syllable line may be set in an eight-beat measure and a five-syllable line in a five-and-a-half-beat measure (11/8 in Western notation). Thus duple, asymmetrical and, less frequently, triple schemes occur.

When the chant sections alternate with the full instrumental sections in a service, they are normally accompanied only by cymbals and/or a drum, whose function is simply to beat time by reinforcing the stressed beats. The characteristic melodic form is repetition, with little variation, of a single phrase or two linked phrases. The melody is often confined to the compass of a 3rd and rarely exceeds a 5th or minor 6th; it thus consists of a few pitches (often three or four) within a scale ranging from dichordal to hexatonic. Anhemitonic pentatonic elements are relatively rare. The chant may also be monotonal (reiterated drone) and the melodies either centric or non-centric in type.

Ex.3 First choral section, service inviting deity to place of worship
(Crossley-Holland, 1965)

BM. 30L. 2010

1. Orchestra in the monastery courtyard at Thami, north Nepal, with (left to right) two dung (trumpets), dril-bu (handbell), two rol-mo (loud cymbals), two rgya-gling (shawms) and rnga (double-headed frame drum with handle)

2. Masked characters of 'cham (mystery dance-drama) at the monastery of Hemis in Ladakh, with two rnga (double-headed drums), two dung (trumpets) and two rgya-gling (shawms)

Although some melodies are based on arpeggiated triads, the movement of the chant is predominantly conjunct, with a great variety of ornaments, glissandos (initial rise or fall and terminal fall), and relatively non-tonal sounds (see ex.3).

The term 'dbyangs', loosely used to include this type of hymn chanting, properly refers only to the sustained type of chanting in which the voices are exceedingly low, centring on *d* or lower, and masked through constricted voice production. The setting of the words is still syllabic, but the notes are of varying lengths and as they are expanded, often to great durations (e.g. 18 seconds), all ordinary sense of time division is lost. The chant consists basically of a sustained monotone which serves as a point of departure and return for a variety of glides, microtonal inflections, and occasional short phrases of two or three pitches (see ex.4). The sense of

Ex.4 from *Melody of the Eternal Voice* (Crossley-Holland, 1965)
  [Numbers refer to duration in seconds (approx.)]

BM. 30L. 2011

monotony disappears when attention is transferred from the domain of immediate contrast and focussed on that of micro- and macro-movements. Within this style, a specialized vocal technique has been cultivated by two monasteries of the *dGe-lugs-pa* order, namely the *rGyud-smad* or *rGyud-stod*, where each chanter simultaneously sings a deep fundamental and a clear harmonic (either the 5th or 6th harmonic, reinforced by others), so that a chordal effect is heard. In addition to the various styles of chanting mentioned above, there are also melismatic chants called *rta-dbyangs* ('horse' chants). These again suggest a Shamanistic background, which may also be true of many of the sounds imitative of animals occurring in various classes of Tibetan chant.

In contrast to the chanted sections of the services, the instrumental sections that alternate with them are much louder and more complex. The full orchestra, with a basic nucleus of eight or 12 instruments, consists exclusively of wind and percussion (see fig.1). The wind instruments which appear in various combinations invariably play in pairs: two *rgya-gling* (shawms) play the melody, one ornamenting or punctuating the line of the other, while two *dung* (deep-sounding trumpets of various sizes and lengths, often overlapping in sound) play pedals, dichordal ostinatos and two-note calls. Sometimes two *rkang-gling* (shorter trumpets of human thigh-bone or of metal) and/or two *dung-dkar* (conches) are added or substituted for the *dung*, playing similar inner pedals and calls. The wind instruments, when all played together, thus provide a complex texture of many parts with a heterophonically treated melody in the highest part.

The percussion instruments, all untuned, also number four. The *gsil-snyan* (a pair of quiet cymbals) and/or the *rol-mo* (a pair of loud cymbals), together with a *rnga* (double-headed drum, struck with a crook-shaped stick), serve not only as time-beaters, but also play rhythmical figures, including accelerating patterns. The *gsil-snyan* and the *rol-mo* lead the orchestra in the *dGe-lugs-pa* order, and the *rnga* in the other orders. The other two instruments, played by a single player, are a

dril-bu (handbell) and a *damaru* (rattle-drum). These act as signals, marking off the sections of the service, or may sound continuously in some passages. Sometimes a gong and/or a plaque is added. The resulting texture may thus have 12 parts or more, those of the wind being related in pairs.

As the basic melody of the *rgya-gling* and the calls of the other wind instruments are often highly ornamented with glides and microtonal inflections, while the percussion is played with a great variety of rhythmic nuances and timbres, the orchestral style is exceedingly subtle and complex. In ex.5, which uses two *rgya-gling* and four percussion instruments, the *rgya-gling* parts are

Ex.5 First orchestral section, service inviting deity to place of worship
(Crossley-Holland, 1965)

BM. 30L. 2010

3. Tibetan monk playing a rgya-gling (shawm), with a dril-bu (handbell) on his right

deeply interwoven, and their ultimate complexities defy transcription in Western notation. What is believed to be the part of the first shawm is given in this example, the basic notes of the theme being marked by a short stroke above the note. The intensity of the sound is also very considerable. These procedures stand in marked contrast to the restrained use of ritual instruments throughout the remainder of the Buddhist world.

The shawms provide the only melodic element in the ensemble. A service may have a single shawm melody, consisting of a short monothematic nucleus (as in ex.5), repeated with more or less variation in succeeding sections; or it may have a small number of such nuclei in successive sections or groups of sections. Where an instrument section is long, such a melodic type is continuously repeated and transformed. These melodies, played with an even, penetrating dynamic, in a rhythmically flexible style, are predominantly conjunct (though some have an arpeggiated minor triad as a basis). They rarely exceed the range of a minor 6th and are played on hexatonic scales or segments of these in the whole-note and quasi-diatonic series with the subtonic as lowest pitch. In the independent hymns for shawms (or for shawms and trumpets), more complex melodies may be found, including bithematic structures; these are often quicker and more rhythmically marked. Ex.6 shows the skeletal notes of an ornately treated

Ex.6 Skeletal notes of an independent hymn for shawms
(Crossley-Holland, 1965)

SHAWMS [musical notation] ♩ = c52

BM. 30L. 2009

melody; circular breathing is practised, so that the melodic line is continuous.

Thus the monastery music, alternating between the loud orchestra with its complex texture and the soft, restrained, unison chanting, creates the sense of passing

from time to the timeless, from melody to sounds-in-one, from sound to silence. It is the tonal expression for going beyond the world of names and forms to the Formless, which Buddhists hold to be the nature of the ultimate reality.

(*iii*) *The mystery dance-drama.* This is a para-liturgical ritual known as *'cham* (miscalled 'devil dance'). It is not in any sense entertainment, and is not to be confused with the *a-che lha-mo* (secular morality plays on Buddhist themes). It exists in various versions and is basically a ritual for driving out spiritual and human enemies, with consequent benefits to man and the state. Its basis is in the pre-Buddhist myth telling of the expulsion of the Old Year and its associated demons of ill-luck by means of a human scapegoat, and the propitiation of the war-gods and guardian spirits in order to bring good luck in the New Year. Buddhism gave the myth a new significance by making the plot centre upon the expulsion of *Bön* by the Indian Buddhist missionary Padmasambhava, and by using a dough effigy as a scapegoat. This version is still performed at the monastery of Hemis in Ladakh (see fig.2) and elsewhere, and underlies the Sikkimese 'Kanchenjunga War-Dance' given in Gangtok. In a later phase the expulsion of evil forces became linked with the last historical king of Tibet, the apostate Lang Darma. He was an enemy of Buddhism, and his ritual assassination by a Lama disguised as a Shamanistic dancer (whence the 'Black Hat Dance') was a great triumph for Buddhism.

This last version of the mystery play was presented by the monks at Tashilhunpo monastery and many other monasteries in Tibet. Presentations continue now in other parts of ethnic Tibet and in exile at the end of the reformed Old Year. It is directed by the *'cham-dpor* (dance-master). The forecourt of the monastery is used as a stage, where the mystery is danced and mimed by characters in elaborate costumes, including masks, accompanied by chanting and instrumental music. The choreography, for which there is a *'cham yig* ('score'), includes whirl-dances. The musicians, seated opposite the monastery steps, consist of chanters (for prayers and celestial and demonic choirs), and players of the necessary sacred instruments. The instruments are used in a more fragmentary and dramatic way than in the services, making much use of signals, calls, wails, booms and special timbres, which are supplemented by whistling and other sounds. Like the play itself, these styles preserve many pre-Buddhist features.

3. MUSICAL ARTS. Music, dance and drama, regarded as aspects of the personification of gods and mortals, are provided in advanced secular education and are learned orally.

(*i*) *The secular dramas.* The *a-che lha-mo* are designed to attract Tibetans to religion by presenting it in the form of entertainment and are believed to have originated in the 15th century. They are strictly secular entertainments on Buddhist themes even when, as sometimes happens, they are performed by monks; they are not to be confused with the *'cham* (ritual dance-drama). Each of the plays (opinions of their number vary between eight and 12) is essentially a narration of a historical or legendary moralistic tale using the techniques of recitation and chanting. The dialogue is acted (with mime), danced and sung, with instrumental accompaniment, and the moral is always the triumph of virtue. Some of the themes originated in the *Jatakas* (Indian

Buddhist fables), others in Tibetan legends, such as that named after the 7th-century King *Srong-btsan-sgam-po*. The structure of the play has Indian affinities, whereas the gesture and costume are more Chinese in character.

The dramas are usually played during a seven-week season in the summer. The principal patrons have been the Tibetan government, the officialdom of Lhasa, monasteries or groups of monks, and wealthy families or groups of wealthy individuals. The Tibetan government officially lists ten troupes who, as a form of tax, are required to take part in the *zho-ston* (annual drama festival) in Lhasa (mid-June). The *lha-mo-pa* (troupes), traditionally male actors, consist principally of male peasant farmers serving overlords (monastery farms, aristocrats or the government). Occasionally they consist of monks, who may be joined by secular male actors. In Lhasa and the surrounding region, there are troupes in which women may play a part; these include the troupes of local trades-people and the amateur troupes of officials who give impromptu performances at parties. The dramas are usually staged in the open air or in tents, in settings such as Jewel Park, Lhasa, monastery forecourts, or sheltered gardens and willow groves. The audience, which comes from far and wide to see a play lasting one or two days, surrounds the 'stage'.

Each troupe compiles its own *khrub-ghzung* (book of plays), drawing material from the great collection of *rnam-thar* ('biography') or from historical and legendary tales of kings. The compilation is free, though the dialogue sections are usually literal. Every performance, however, is unique, varying according to the time available, the different troupes, free use of the *khrub-ghzung*, the professionals' own concepts of their roles, producers' surprises and comic interludes. Most of the narration is incomprehensible to the audience, though the dialogue is understood, and includes many forms of honorific address. The action, however, is realistic as are the costumes and masks, and the characterization is faithful, even in the music.

In addition to the nucleus of eight players who act, dance and sing, there are two *zar-gdung* (musicians); the leader plays *sbub-chal* (cymbals) while the second *zar-gdung* plays the *rnga* (drum). During the play music is heard continuously both in the instrumental sections and in the performance of narration and dialogue. The instrumental sections are usually short preludes or passages using a variety of playing techniques designed to serve the needs of the drama. Apart from time-beating and creating a rhythmical framework for the chanting of the chorus, they have a number of conventional functions: they frame scenes (e.g. actor preparing to speak: slow fluttering); they characterize broadly the *dramatis personae* (e.g. old age: slow uncertain dance to hesitating drumbeats and light tinkling of cymbals); and they evoke moods or situations (e.g. danger threatens: fast and furious music). For the rest, the instruments accompany the dance sections and the singing.

The narration is in prose and verse. The prose, describing a scene, is recited rapidly in parlando style by an unaccompanied solo singer. The reciting pitch is varied occasionally, especially by descending to about a 4th below; the tempo is very rapid and even, the style vigorous, and the passage ends in a descending rhetorical phrase. The verses (the couplets of the *rnam-thar*) are chanted by the chorus, either accompanied or unaccompanied, in a tense throaty style. The slow-moving chant is given by a principal singer, accompanied by one

or more 'helpers' who sing antiphonally with him, overlapping the ends of his long phrases. The style is melismatic and subject to glottal interruptions, and employs upward initial glides and downward terminal glides. The melodies are basically anhemipentatonic, containing arpeggiated minor triads, and often drifting in pitch for several hours. The overlapping antiphony gives rise to a variety of harmonies (see ex.7). The *rnam-thar* songs may also be performed separately on social occasions.

Ex.7 from the play *bro-Ba Bzang-Mo*

⊤ indicates glottal stop

The dialogue of the play is performed in two styles. The first corresponds essentially to that of the verse narration, while the second takes the form of solo songs which are generally also danced. The voice-style here does not include special techniques of the *rnam-thar* songs and is non-melismatic, though not devoid of ornamentation. The melodies are measured and more formal in strophic structure. Ex.8 shows a stanza of a song performed by the name-part of the play *Snang-gsal*: 'O Lake, let me, poor girl, Be shown the road to religion . . .'.

Ex.8 Song from the play *Snang-gsal*

CH. TR. 75. 5.

(ii) Party music. The performances of lighter forms of vocal, instrumental and choreographic art music in Tibet are found at parties of all kinds including luncheons and banquets in important houses and on official occasions, festivities at the New Year, summer picnics in the parks and groves and as interlude music between the acts of the secular dramas. The performers are both professional and amateur. The professionals are often musicians from the *lha-mo* troupes or may belong to small itinerant troupes that exist on all levels, the lowest being street musicians. The musicians differ greatly in status: the best performers may enjoy a prominent place

in Lhasa society, though this depends on their artistry and personal qualities rather than on any predetermined requisites. Amateur musicians may be officials or members of high-class families, or musically accomplished servants sent from one house to another to entertain. They may even be monks who sometimes make such music when on holiday.

The party repertory, which appears to have grown particularly over the last half-century in Lhasa, ranges in mood from the serious to the very gay. Song types include auspicious songs (for happiness, welcome, good wishes, birthday greetings), *chang-glu* (humorous and drinking-songs), *glu* and *gzás* (dance-songs, which may also be sung without dancing) and a variety of songs from the different regions of Tibet. The themes are traditional and the composers anonymous, though the texts of some of the love songs currently found are attributed to the 6th Dalai Lama.

The songs are usually sung by an ensemble and are accompanied by instruments. String instruments are predominant, in contrast to the instruments of the religious services, and include the *sgra-snyan* (lute; fig.4b), *pi-wang* (fiddle; fig.4a) and *rgyud-mang* (dulcimer). The resulting sound is bright in timbre. The *ti-gling* (flute) and, as time-beaters, small dance-cymbals and sometimes a drum are often added. In addition to

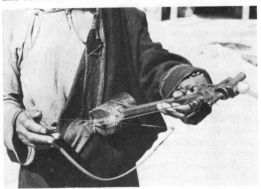

(a)

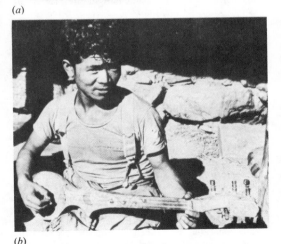

(b)

4. *Two Tibetan chordophones:* (a) *pi-wang* (fiddle), *Paro Bhutan;* (b) *sgra-snyan* (long-necked lute) *played by a sherpa, Nepal*

accompanying songs the instruments may play alone, either solo or in various combinations. These instrumental interludes are usually based on the material of the song, yet the music may create the impression of being essentially in an instrumental idiom in which the song element is incidental. There is indeed much flexibility in the use of musical resources. For instance, a piece may be sung or played or danced to, or all three. Similarly a piece may be played on the string instruments or on the flute; it may be heard solo, or in any combination of two, three or four instruments. Accordingly, the texture varies from strict monophony (flute, fiddle), or monophony with sparing use of chords (lute), to heterophony in various forms. An accompanying ostinato or reiterated drone may be added by the lute.

The musical forms owe much to the structure of the dance and to the background of words. They are basically either strophic with interludes, or in two-section forms with a slow followed by a quick section or with continued alternation of such sections; there are also suites. Antiphonal techniques are found in songs involving both sexes. The rhythms are influenced by the song-texts, which are mostly syllabically sung. Of the dance-songs, the *glu* have seven or eight syllables to a line, the *gzás* six syllables. The rhythmical schemes are duple though there is much syncopation and occasional variation, for instance, by the insertion of an extra half-beat. The melodic forms vary from sustained melody (voice, fiddle, flute) to more motivic material (lute, dulcimer). The most characteristic scale is hexatonic. A notable feature of closing sections is a well-controlled rise to a pitch a 4th higher. A number of elements in this music have some affinity with the lighter forms of Chinese music: the Tibetan *rgyud-mang* (dulcimer) was probably derived from the Chinese *yang-ch'in*, and some melodies in the Lhasa party repertory are known to have come from China more than a quarter of a century ago. A characteristically long phrase, using a heptatonic scale with pentatonic emphasis, is shown in ex.9.

Ex.9 The 'Luck' melody (Party repertory)

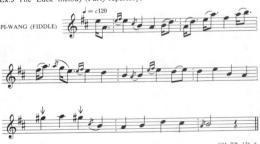

CH. TR. 126. 6.

(iii) *Drum and reed music.* Further forms of music-making are associated with an ensemble consisting of a pair (or pairs) of *lda-mán* (kettledrums) and one or more *sor-na* (shawms; fig.5). With its very penetrating sound it is essentially outdoor music, to which a voice (or voices) may be added as the occasion demands. Although only one of these ensembles comes strictly under the educational aspect of music in Tibet – the *gar-drug-pa*, a band accompanying a youths' dance for the Dalai Lama – the whole range of these ensembles must generally be regarded as belonging to art music. There

5. *Drum and reed ensemble of lda-mán (kettledrums) and sor-na (shawms), Ladakh*

Ex.10 from music played at polo matches (Crossley-Holland, 1965)

LL. 196

are three main groups: court bands, municipal bands (semi-professional) and bands of itinerant entertainers (professional and often hereditary).

The Sikkimese court band, which adds a *ding-ling* (percussion plaque) to the basic ensemble, plays for royal journeys, marriage ceremonies and for processions on important festival days. The municipal bands play for certain annual festivals, communal games and sport (polo, archery, horse-racing), rites of passage (births and marriages, including auspicious music and dance) and as a stimulus to labour. The itinerant minstrels have a varied repertory for social and communal occasions, consisting of descriptive, moralistic, historical and legendary songs, as well as love songs and songs for the harvest. In Ladakh, some of the *gLu* (popular art songs) are likely to be descended from those of the now vanished courts.

The rhythms employed in this music show greater variety than do those of the party music. Duple schemes are known, but triple and especially compound elements seem more frequent, and much freedom is found in the drum rhythms. The melodies, using scales varying from anhemipentatonic to complex chromatic structures, are sometimes very ornate and special forms of decoration are found in both voices and shawms. Characteristic of the purely instrumental music is that which is played at polo matches in Ladakh to work the crowd into a state of excitement. The following musical resources may be seen in ex.10: longer thematic sections framed by shorter motivic ones, a heptatonic scale with two auxiliary degrees, and pendular movement at different pitch levels. Ex.11 demonstrates further features, including the use of all four semitonal intervals within a major 3rd and a highly ornate type of melodic treatment. The form of the melodic cycle is *AA¹BC*.

The nature and origin of the drum and reed music is uncertain. It seems more specifically, though not exclusively, associated with the Himalayan regions of ethnic Tibet; more information is certainly available from these regions. The ensembles appear to be formed from minority ethnic groups, often from people called *Mon* which in Sikkim refers to the Lepchas. In Ladakh, how-

Ex.11 Sikkimese Court Music, introduction

CH. TR. 62. 1.

ever, it may refer to a people of Indo-European origin. Much of the rhythmic and tonal material of these bands is unlike any other music in Tibet. The antiphony between shawm and voice, with the drum continuing throughout, has a strong affinity with the Indian music known as *kachi kafi* which comes from near the Persian border. This, and the primary distribution of the drum and reed ensembles, as well as many of the contexts in which their music is found, suggests an early Near Eastern origin.

4. EPIC SONG. Various epic songs are found in ethnic Tibet. By far the most important of the epics is *Ge-sar sgrungs* ('The history of Gesar'). Sung in various forms as far north as Lake Baikal (Siberia) and Mongolia, it has been called 'the Iliad of Asia'. As manuscripts of it exist, it is often classed as secular literature. It is traditionally performed orally by *sgrung-pa*, 'wandering story-tellers of Gesar' or bards, who are illiterate. Monks are allowed to 'read' it but not to perform it.

The text concerns the great hero, Gesar of gLing (in Kham, eastern Tibet), or of Khrom, who slew many tyrannical rulers, demons and monsters. Regarded as Tibet's defender, protector and avenger, it is believed he will one day return. The historical core relates to a period around the 8th century when Tibet was a mighty empire in Central Asia and Gesar possibly a general of the time. Today he has become virtually deified and is celebrated in festivals (in Ladakh) and mystery plays (in Mongolian Buddhist monasteries). Many ancient elements of the epic seem to have appeared among the *Bön-po*; *gShen-rabs*, the traditional founder of *Bön*, is actually invoked in many of the songs. Thus *Bön*, and ultimately Shamanistic elements, seem deeply ingrained, for the bards sing in an entranced state, claiming to be directly inspired by Gesar or by some other personage who dictates their words. The performances are listened to with deep reverence for several hours a day over a period of many weeks. Each of the melodies, thought of as carrying the words like a steed, is referred to as a *rta* (horse).

Ge-sar sgrungs is sung unaccompanied and usually solo, though cases of dialogue are known. The short prose sections and longer verse sections of the text are set respectively in recitative and song, with added onomatopoeic effects, pious exclamations and interludes. The recitative to which the prose is set is strictly syllabic and is delivered in a parlando style with much upward and downward movement (compare prose passages in the secular plays). The verse sections consist of couplets, each of which have two long lines; they are set syllabically to a single melody with melismatic elements, and are sung over and over again with small variations for each couplet of a sequence. The melody is then changed for the next sequence. 14 different melodies have been reported for the epic as a whole. Ex.12 (from the hymn before the war episode) illustrates character-

istic features of these melodies: a cadence in which each line ends with long-short rhythmic values followed by a short breath; the occurrence of an anhemitetratonic or anhemipentatonic scale; the pitching of the final note of the second line a tone or minor 3rd lower than that of the first line. In this example, a syllabic structure of 5–6, 5–6 is set in a note-structure of 7–11, 7–11. In some performances the melody is treated more ornately.

5. FOLK MUSIC. Tibetan folk music is chiefly vocal, appearing in solo, choral, antiphonal and responsorial forms. It is usually unaccompanied, though a drum or a lute may accompany the dance-songs. The only widely found folk instrument proper is the *gling-bu* (shepherd's fipple flute), usually a seven-holed instrument of the recorder type. It also exists in the form of a double recorder, each tube of which has seven holes. Its melodies are mainly anhemipentatonic, and tend to be ornate (see ex.13).

Ex.13 Shepherd's flute tune, east Tibet

CH. TR. 75. 8.

Songs accompany a wide range of activities in everyday life – nomadic, pastoral, trading, agricultural, urban and domestic. The nomads, who are cattle-raisers and tradesmen, sing trekking songs to keep themselves company on their long journeys; they sing about the moon and about the horses on which their livelihood depends. In the evenings, the women sing as they dance, or young people of both sexes join hands and sing and dance in a circle. The numerous work songs include those for the work of the agricultural year, from seed-time to harvest, as well as songs for stone- and grass-cutting, log-carrying, building, washing clothes and carpet-making. More urban types of songs include street songs reflecting public opinion and lampoons on officials, and love songs and songs of consolation are widespread. There is a variety of songs on educational, moralistic, descriptive and even religious themes and in many of these a literary and Buddhist background may be detected. A certain reciprocity of musical ideas is found between folksong and other genres. This is not surprising in view of the existence of figures like Mi-la Ras-pa (c1053–c1135), the Yogi poet-saint who used folksong for religious teaching, and the 6th Dalai Lama (1681–1706), writer of many popular love songs.

The main verse form is that of the stanza; refrains are, however, often found. Stanzas are set strophically and are often paired antiphonally, sometimes responsorially. The lines are unrhymed but measured, and usually number four, although they may vary from two to eight. The melodic sections, corresponding to the lines of the stanza, may be of equal or unequal length. The number of syllables to a line is characteristically even, often six or eight. Of prior importance is not the number of

Ex.12 from *Ge-sar sgrungs*, epic song

Variations

CH. TR. 75. 9.

syllables or notes in a line, but the rhythmic values of the notes used to render those syllables. In Tibetan folk music, notes of unequal length predominate (usually at least three types in a song). Although the speech values of the syllables are not disregarded, the melody tends to be more important in itself. Rhythmical schemes include duple (most frequently used), triple and compound, and also the freer schemes of improvised nomadic song.

The tonal organization is often anhemipentatonic (all five modes). Hexatonic scales are also common, including those quasi-hexatonic scales generated from what is really a pentatonic scale through the natural transposition of melodic phrases by the singer. Initial ascending glides, terminal descending glides and intermediated ones are much used. The texture is normally monophonic, though heterophonic elements appear in nomadic songs and overlapping antiphony in stonecutters' songs. The cadence often entails the repetition of the final note. It is approached, from either above or below, by the interval of a tone, minor 3rd or occasionally a 4th. The ends of phrases are frequently characterized by a long-held note. On average, the melodic movement is equally conjunct and disjunct, and the number of different types of interval which appear in a song rarely exceeds four; of these the tone, minor 3rd and 4th are normally present. Melodic patterns include arpeggiated triads and 7ths, pendular minor 3rds and 4ths, and interlocking 4ths.

The differences in style found among songs may owe something to varying regional characteristics, in that eastern Tibet has a greater affinity with China, and southern Tibet with the Himalayan regions; styles, however, appear to be associated more naturally according to their context. Groupings of styles necessarily overlap as, indeed, do the activities of so many Tibetans. However, according to whether the music is rooted in nomadic pastoralism and agricultural and other occupations, or in urban and more literate backgrounds, three broadly different styles may be distinguished. The nomadic pastoral melodies have a wide range (9th to a 12th) and contain long descending phrases; they have a small number of sections based on a melody type which is subject to much variation and rhythmic freedom. The style is melismatic and ornate and the voice tense (see ex.14). The agricultural songs are generally narrower in range and the melodic line is consequently more even.

Ex.14 Horseback song, sung by two women

LL. 196

As might be expected, songs used to accompany particular forms of concerted work seek to describe that work and to convey its rhythms; they are therefore largely heterometric, with short phrases, a relatively small number of sections and an economy of thematic materials. Strophic antiphony and response are important features of this genre. The music is sung in a relaxed

voice, with parlando elements and a restrained use of ornament (see ex.15). The songs with urban and literate backgrounds are on the whole more formal in style. There is a greater variety of thematic material, often with a new section for each line. There is frequently a set rhythmic pattern (especially isometric) and a set melodic range (especially that of an octave and a 9th), with the use of a cantando (choral) style and a minimum use of grace notes.

Ex.15 Song for repairing water-channels, sung by two men

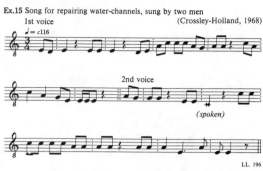

LL. 196

Since the early 1950s, Tibetan folksong has experienced new influences. Urban songs, in particular, are becoming more stereotyped in medium (uniform choral singing), with emphasis on a form consisting of sections of equal length which is mostly level or falling by a 5th. New melodic features include the use of a greater number of intervals (up to seven in a song), a change in the balance of these intervals within a song (more use of the major 3rd and the introduction of the semitone), and a breakdown of the old modal structure. In its music, as in its life, Tibet finds itself torn between age-old tradition and its wider modern situation.

6. INSTRUMENTS. More than 70 types of instrument have been found in Tibet. Many, however, seem to have existed for only a limited historical period, or, because of an overlap from surrounding cultures, only in particular regions; others are localized or very specialized. A list is given below of only the standard, widely distributed types, which are presented in the order of the Hornbostel–Sachs *Systematik*. Additional mention is made of special morphological or performance features, materials of manufacture and main uses of the instruments.

(i) Idiophones.

rol-mo: brass, cymbals with large central boss; loud (fig.1); called *sbub-chal* in Buddhist secular dramas;
gsil-snyan: brass, cymbals with small shallow boss, larger than *rol-mo*; soft; used by Buddhists;
ding-shag: metal, miniature cymbals, or cymbal struck with yak tine; formerly for solitary use by Buddhists;
ding-ling: metal, disc-shaped percussion plaque struck with mallet; used by Buddhists and in the court;
'khar-rnga: metal, gong; used by Buddhists;
gshang: metal, 'flat' bell with rim turned inwards; separate beater (horn); used in both *Bön* and Buddhist religions;
dril-bu: metal, tulip-shaped handbell with internal clapper; used by Buddhists (figs.1 and 3).

(ii) Membranophones.

lda-mán: pair of kettledrums mounted on metal or wooden frame; thick wooden beaters; used in drum and

6. *Damaru* (*rattle drum*) *and dril-bu* (*handbell*), *Paro, Bhutan*

reed bands (fig.5);
chos-rnga: double-skin frame drum, suspended and struck with beaters; used by Buddhists;
phyed-rnga: single-skin frame drum with handle; used in *Bön* religion;
rnga: double-skin frame drum with handle, struck with *yob* (crooked stick); used in Buddhist secular dramas (figs.1 and 2; for crooked beater, *see* DRUM, fig.1*h*);
damaru: wooden rattle-drum in shape of hourglass, struck by clappers suspended from median ligature (fig.6); called *thöd rnga* if constructed from two human half-crania; used by Buddhists.

(iii) *Chordophones.*
rgyud-mang: dulcimer with trapezoid box resonator; 25 strings stretched across two movable bridges; played with two soft-headed sticks; used in secular art music;
sgra-snyan: wooden long-necked lute, often with horse- or dragon-head terminal (fig.4*b*); unfretted, usually with six strings tuned in double courses (some forms may have three or five strings) played with plectrum; used in secular art music; sometimes known as *snyan-sgra*;
pi-wang or *hor-chin*: wooden long-necked lute often with horse- or dragon-head terminal; usually two strings (some forms may have four strings); usually played as fiddle with yak-tail bow which passes between strings (fig.4*a*); used in secular art music; sometimes known as *wang-pi*.

(iv) *Aerophones.*
ti-gling: bamboo side-blown flute; normally seven finger-holes; used in secular art music and folk music;

gling-bu: fipple flute of apricot-wood with internal or external ducts; normally seven finger-holes; single and double flutes are common; for secular and pastoral use;
rgya-gling: wooden shawm with disc-shaped pirouette and flared metal bell; seven finger-holes and thumb-hole; 60 cm long; used by Buddhists (fig.3);
sor-na: wooden shawm with disc-shaped pirouette and wooden bell; six finger-holes and thumb-hole; used in secular art music and in the court (fig.5);
rkang-gling: short trumpet of two types: (*a*) *yogins*, human leg-bone; used in Buddhist and *Bön* religions; (*b*) metal, with flared bell fashioned like the head of a *mā-kārā* (mythical water-creature); used by Buddhists;
dung-dkar: conch or whelk-shell trumpet, sometimes with mouthpiece; end-blown;
dung: copper or brass end-blown straight trumpet with mouthpiece; varies in length from 60 cm to 366 cm or more; most common forms are the medium-sized *rag-dung* and the large *dung-chen*; sections of the latter telescope, but not during performance; end-blown, used by Buddhists (figs.1 and 2).

BIBLIOGRAPHY
BOOKS AND ARTICLES

A. H. Francke: 'Musikalische Studien in Westtibet', *Zeitschrift der Deutschen morgenländischen Gesellschaft*, v (1905), 91
——: 'La musique au Thibet', *EMDC*, I/v (1922), 3084
T. H. Somervell: 'The Music of Tibet', *MT*, lxiv (1923), 107
G. Tucci: *Tibetan Folksongs* (Ascona, 1949, rev. 2/1966)
P. Crossley-Holland: 'Tibetan Music', *Grove 5*
D. L. Snellgrove: *Buddhist Himalaya* (Oxford, 1954)
L. E. R. Picken: 'Other Countries: "Tibet"', *NOHM*, i (1957), 137
P. Crossley-Holland: 'Tibet', *Pelican History of Music*, i (London, 1960, 2/1962), 71
W. Graf: 'Zur Ausführung der lamaistischen Gesangsnotation', *SM*, iii (1962), 133
E. Emsheimer: 'Tibet', *MGG*
P. Crossley-Holland: 'Form and Style in Tibetan Folksong Melody', *Jb für musikalische Volks- und Völker-Kunde*, iii (1967), 9–69, 109
——: 'The Religious Music of Tibet and its Cultural Background', *Centennial Workshop on Ethnomusicology: Vancouver 1967*, 79
——: 'The State of Research in Tibetan Folk Music', *EM*, xi (1967), 170
N. N. Dewang: 'Musical Tradition of the Tibetan People: Songs in Dance Measure', *Orientalia Romania: Essays and Lectures*, ii (1967), 205–347
W. Kaufman: 'The Notation of the Buddhist Chant (Tibet)', *Musical Notation of the Orient* (Bloomington, 1967), 355–417
W. P. Malm: 'East Asia: Tibet', *Music Cultures of the Pacific, the Near East and Asia* (Englewood Cliffs, 1967)
H. Smith and K. N. Stevens: 'Unique Vocal Abilities of Certain Tibetan Lamas', *American Anthropology*, lxix (1967), 209
H. Smith, K. N. Stevens and R. S. Tomlinson: 'On an Unusual Mode of Chanting by Certain Tibetan Lamas', *Journal of the Acoustical Society of America*, xli (1967), 1262
S. Kishibe: 'Lamaïsme thibétain', *Encyclopédie des musiques sacrées*, i (Paris, 1968), 190
L. P. Lhalungpa: 'Tibetan Music: Secular and Sacred', *Tibet Society Newsletter*, ii (1968), 8
P. Crossley-Holland: '*rGya-gling* Hymns of the Karma-Kagyu: the Rhythmitonal Architecture of some Tibetan Instrumental Airs', *Selected Reports*, i (1970), 79–114
A. M. Dauer: 'Tibeter (Zentralasien) Orchestermusik "Zla-Ba'i-gZhon-Nu'i-gZhas-Tshig"', *Encyclopaedia cinematographica* (Göttingen, 1970), 3
T. Ellingson: 'Some Techniques of Choral Chanting in the Tibetan Style', *American Anthropologist*, lxxii (1970), 826
P. Crossley-Holland: 'Musical Instruments in the Legends of Tibet', *A Tribute to Professor Liang Tsai-Ping on his 60th Birthday* (Taipeh, 1974)
T. Ellingson-Waugh: 'Musical Flight in Tibet', *Asian Music*, v/2 (1974), 3–44
Asian Music, vii/2 (1977) [Tibet–East Asia issue]

NOTES TO RECORDINGS, REVIEWS
G. Rouget: *Musique tibétaine du Sikkim*, Vogue MC.20.119, recorded by S. Bourguignon (Paris, 1955)
E. Wellesz, ed.: *The History of Music in Sound*, HMV HLP 1 (London, 1957)
W. Graf: *Lieder aus dem Land der Götter*, Athena 53134, recorded by René von Nebesky-Wojkowitz (Vienna, 1961)
H. Kaufman: *Songs and Music of Tibet*, Ethnic Folkways Library FE

4486 (New York, 1962)

G. Cronk and G. List: *Songs and Dances of Nepal*, Ethnic Folkways Library FE 4101 (New York, 1964)

P. Crossley-Holland: *The Music of Tibetan Buddhism* (UNESCO Collection: *A Musical Anthology of the Orient*), Bärenreiter Musicaphon BM 30L 2009–11 (Kassel, 1965)

C. Jest: *Tibet-Nepal: musique bouddhiste lamaïque – musique rituelle et profane*, La boîte à musique BAM.LD 104 (Paris, 1966)

A. Migot: *Musique religieuse chinoise et tibétaine*, La boîte à musique BAM.LD 383 (Paris, 1966)

P. Crossley-Holland: *Tibetan Folk and Minstrel Music*, Lyrichord LL 196 and LLST 7196 (New York, 1968)

——: *Tibetan Ritual Music*, Lyrichord LL 181 and LLST 7181 (New York, 1968)

——: 'The Music of the Tantric Rituals of Gyume and Gyutö', *The Music of Tibet*, Anthology AST-4005, recorded by H. Smith (New York, 1970), 3f

——: Review of *Musique rituelle tibétaine*, OCORA OCR.49, rec. G. Luneau (Paris, 1969), *EM*, xvi (1972), 310

——: Review of *Musique et théâtre populaires tibétains*, OCORA OCR.62 (Paris, 1972), *EM*, xvii (1973)

G. Luneau: *Musique religieuse tibétaine*, OCORA OCR.71 (Paris, 1973)

DRAMA, DANCE, EPIC

H. Siiger: 'Dancing Pilgrims from Tibet', *Geografisk tidskrift*, i (1877), 1

L. A. Waddell: 'The Motive of the Mystery Play of Tibet', *Xe congrès international des orientalistes: Genève 1894*, 169

A. H. Francke: *A Lower Ladakhi Version of the Gesar Saga* (Calcutta, 1905–41)

M. J. Bacot: 'Drimekundam', *Journal asiatique*, 2nd ser. (Paris, 1914)

G. N. Roerich: 'The Epic of Gesar of Ling', *Journal of the Royal Asiatic Society of Bengal*, viii (1942), 277–314

M. H. Duncan: *Harvest Festival Dramas of Tibet* (Hong Kong, 1955)

R. A. Stein: *L'épopée tibétaine de Gesar dans sa version lamaïque de Ling* (Paris, 1956)

J. Bacot: *Zugiñima* (Paris, 1957)

R. A. Stein: *Recherches sur l'épopée et le barde au Thibet* (Paris, 1959)

H. Lucas: *Lamaïstische Masken: der Tanz der Schrekensgötter* (Kassel, 1962)

M. H. Duncan: *More Festival Dramas of Tibet* (London, 1967)

L. G. Jerstad: *Mani Rimdu: Sherpa Dance Drama* (Seattle, 1969)

PETER CROSSLEY-HOLLAND

Tibia. An important ancient Roman wind instrument, substantially the same as the Greek AULOS in both construction and function. The existing differences resulted from the divergent histories of the two nations.

The tibia played a very prominent role in Etruscan and early Roman musical life. Ovid's verses which relate that 'the tibia sang in the temples, it sang in the games, it sang at mournful funeral rites' are corroborated by the abundant iconographic evidence which shows it playing in precisely those circumstances (see illustration) and also in wedding processions, at formal meals and as an accompaniment to manual work. Roman tibia players (*tibicines*) were organized during the republic in the guild-like *collegium tibicinum romanorum*. Plutarch listed the *tibicines* as the first of the trade groups organized by the ancient Roman king Numa. There is an element of myth about this but nevertheless it affirms the long-standing importance of the tibia, as does the legend of the tibia players' strike, told by both Ovid and Livy. In 309 BC the tibia players were discontented because certain of their privileges had been curtailed –in Livy's version, their ancient custom of eating in the Temple of Jupiter – and they therefore went into voluntary exile at Tibur. The Senate, distressed that the sacred rites might be unaccompanied by tibia playing, managed to get the players drunk, loaded them into a cart and returned them to Rome before they had recovered full consciousness. Their former privileges were restored and in addition they were permitted once a year to go about the city in full regalia playing their instruments; this was the origin of the mid-June festival called the *Quinquatrus minores*.

In 204 BC, during the second Punic War, the orgiastic cult of the Asiatic Magna Mater Cybele was introduced at Rome. A particular variation of the tibia was associated with the cult, a type in which one of the two pipes was longer than the other and terminated in an abrupt hook-like semicircle. (For illustration *see* CYMBALUM.) The Romans referred to it as the *tibia berecyntia* after a Phrygian mountain, sacred to Cybele. The instrument was prominent in Roman literature and iconography and appeared also in the cult of Dionysus and in the theatre.

During imperial times the tibia seems to have been used, outside religion, mostly in the theatre, where a prominent figure was the *scabillarius*, a kind of theatrical music director who played the tibia while beating time with his foot on the SCABELLUM. Meanwhile the tibia was developed in size and technical capacity like other Roman instruments: one illustration of a tibia shows pipes over a metre in length. Only one factor limited its role in comparison with the Greek aulos: the general richness and variety of Roman wind instruments, such as the tuba (*see* TUBA (ii)), CORNU and LITUUS with their obvious suitability for military and ceremonial functions, and the remarkable HYDRAULIS.

Since the Greek aulos had ethical connotations, one is bound to ask whether the Roman tibia had them also. There seems almost to have been a reversal of the Greek ideas. In republican Rome the memory of the ancient

Tibia players (bottom right), and above them two cornu players and a lituus player in a funeral procession: relief on a Roman sarcophagus (end of the 1st century AD) from Amiternum (Museo Civico, Aquileia)

and honourable history of the tibia gave it a quasi-sacred status whereas the KITHARA was looked upon by the conservative and agrarian Romans as a symbol of Greek refinement and luxury, recently imported along with the other spoils of war from the sacking of Corinth in 146 BC. However in time the Greek string instruments came to be generally accepted; Horace put it thus: 'And you, the tortoise [lyre], at one time neither welcome nor much heard, are now cherished in the temples and at the tables of the rich'. Roman authors even went as far as echoing the Greek preference for the lyre to the aulos: Horace called the sound of the lyre Dorian and the sound of the tibia barbaric. But this was a literary conceit rather than a description of contemporary attitudes. Just as Greek ethical ideas were firmly rooted in actual Greek experience, the central position the tibia occupied in Roman musical history prevented the development of any seriously negative ethical ideas concerning it.

See also ORGAN STOP.

For bibliography *see* ROME, §I.

JAMES W. Mc KINNON

Tibicen (Lat.). AULETE.

Tiburce, François. See TIBURTIUS VAN BRUSSEL.

Tiburtino, Giuliano [Giuliano Bonaugurio da Tivoli] (*b* *c*1510; *d* Rome, 16 Dec 1569). Italian instrumentalist and composer. He belonged to a family of professional men and landowners in Tivoli. Having acquired a reputation as an accomplished player of the violone, as Silvestro Ganassi pointed out, Tiburtino entered papal service; in 1545 he was listed as a 'musico' at the court of Paul III. By 1552 he had taken clerical orders and in 1564 he was still in the papal employ.

Two volumes containing music by Tiburtino were printed by Scotto in Venice in 1549. *Musica diversa a 3 voci* is a collection including a *Missa de beata virgine*, 11 motets (nearly all on Marian texts) and a dozen madrigals. Tiburtino's choice of three-voice texture for the whole of this somewhat unusual mixture of genres suggests that the pieces might be paraphrased reworkings of well-known compositions. Awkward spots in the counterpoint and the melodic angularity of the middle voice would seem to betray the hand of an arranger, and not a highly skilled one at that. For the sacred pieces no proof of this has yet been found. Among the madrigals (all written *a note nere* in the fashion of the 1540s), however, there are several confirmed instances of paraphrase; an example is *Quand'io pens'al martire*, a fussy but rather literal reworking of Arcadelt's madrigal of the same name.

To the second 1549 print, *Fantasie et recerchari a 3 voci*, Tiburtino contributed a fantasia and 12 ricercares, textless but described as 'suitable for singing or playing on any sort of instrument'. The volume also contains a few madrigals by Willaert, Rore and others, as well as a group of ricercares by Willaert. Willaert's ricercares were reprinted several times in *Fantasie, Recercari Contrapunti* (Venice, 1551, 3/1593), a collection similar in title to the 1549 print but omitting Tiburtino's pieces.

Tiburtino's ricercares are unlike those of Willaert and are closer in style and technique to the glosas and fantasias of Mudarra, Valderrábano and Pisador than to any Italian ricercares. All are based on hexachord themes, at least several of which are derived from well-known works such as Josquin masses and are mono-thematic, making use of rhythmic transformation, transposition and a variety of contrapuntal combinations of the theme. In general they show a more skilful hand at work than do Tiburtino's vocal works.

WORKS

Edition: *Italia musica sacra*, i, ed. K. Jeppesen (Copenhagen, 1962) [includes mass and six motets from *Musica diversa*]
Fantasie et recerchari a 3 voci, accomodate da cantare et sonare per ogni instrumento (Venice, 1549³⁴)
Musica diversa a 3 voci (Venice, 1549)
Madrigal, Madonna s'io potessi, 4vv, 1537¹¹

BIBLIOGRAPHY

S. Ganassi: *Regola rubertina* (Venice, 1542/*R*1970)
G. Radiciotti: *L'arte musicale in Tivoli nei secoli xvi, xvii, e xviii* (Tivoli, 1907)
H. C. Slim: *The Keyboard Ricercar and Fantasia in Italy ca. 1500–1550* (diss., Harvard U., 1961)
N. S Iosephson: *The Missa de Beata Virgine of the 16th Century* (diss., U. of California, Berkeley, 1970)
J. Haar: 'The *Fantasie et recerchari* of Giuliano Tiburtino', *MQ*, lix (1973), 223

JAMES HAAR

Tiburtius van Brussel [Bruxellensis] [Berghe, Frans van den] (*b* Brussels, *c*1605; *d* Lier, 5 Feb 1669). South Netherlands composer. Frans van den Berghe was his baptismal name; he is sometimes erroneously referred to as François Tiburce. He was admitted to the Capuchin order in Bruges in 1625 and was ordained priest some time after 1629. In 1660–61 he became father superior of the monastery at Hasselt. He died of the plague while tending victims of it at Lier. According to Miraeus he is the anonymous composer of the melodies for two sacred songbooks, the texts of which were written by two other Capuchins. The first, by Lucas van Mechelen, comprises *Den bliiden requiem* (1631), *Het cloosterken* (1639) and *Den droeven alleluia* (1674), all three being reprinted together in 1688–9. Music is found only in *Den bliiden requiem* of 1631, with a treble and bass for each text; in the 1688 reprint this music is contained in a separate volume. Moreover, as was usual at the time, each text was furnished with indications for one or more tunes from the widely known Dutch, French, Italian and Latin repertory of song and dance melodies. Both methods were also used in the other songbook, *De gheestelycke tortel-duyve* (1648) by Gabriël van Antwerpen.

WORKS

Den Boeck der gheesteliicke sanghen bedeelt in twee deelen: Den bliiden requiem & Cloosterken der gheestelijcke verryssenisse (Antwerp, 1631 and 1639) [2 vols.]
De gheestelycke tortel-duyve (Antwerp, 1648)
Den boeck der gheestelycke sanghen, bedeelt in dry deelen: Den blyden requiem, Den droeven alleluia ende Het cloosterken (Ghent, 1674; rev. 3/1688–9, incl. 142 musicale sangh-vooisen in superius en bassus, op dewelcke konnen gesongen werden alle de liederen, begreepen in drie deelen van het boeck der gheestelycke sangen)
Litaniae seraphicae BMV . . . in septem libris, 3–6, 8vv, bc (org) (Antwerp, n.d.), lost

BIBLIOGRAPHY

A. Miraeus: *Bibliotheca ecclesiastica*, ii (Antwerp, 1649), 262
W. Bäumker: 'Zur Geschichte der Volksliedermelodien', *MMg*, xvi (1884), 92
Pater Hildebrand: 'P. Lucas van Mechelen', *Ons geestelijk erf*, ix (1935), 238, 356, 371
R. Vannes: *Dictionnaire des musiciens (compositeurs)* (Brussels, 1947)
Pater Hildebrand: *De Kapucijnen in de Nederlanden en het Prinsbisdom Luik* (Antwerp), v (1950), 398; vii (1952), 603; viii (1954), 663; ix (1955), 366, 563
G. J. Helmer: *Den gheestelycke nachtegael: een liedboek uit de zeventiende eeuw* (Nijmegen, 1966)
G. Spiessens: 'Tiburtius van Brussel, Pater', *Nationaal biografisch woordenboek*, ii (Brussels, 1966), 868

K. Porteman: *De mystieke lyriek van Lucas van Mechelen* (*1595/96–1652*) (diss., U. of Louvain, 1972), i–ii, 18; iii, 534

GODELIEVE SPIESSENS

Tiby, Ottavio (*b* Palermo, 19 May 1891; *d* Palermo, 4 Dec 1955). Italian musicologist. He studied harmony with R. Storti in Rome and counterpoint and composition with Favara at Palermo, where he took a diploma at the conservatory in 1921. He worked as inspector general of music for the Direzione dello Spettacolo (1936–44) and taught organology and acoustics at the Rome Conservatory (1940–44). In 1939 and again in 1953 he was a member of the Italian delegation to London for the international conference on the determination of pitch and tuning. Although some of his earliest research concerned Greek, Roman and Byzantine music, Tiby's chief interest was the study of Sicilian musicians, such as Bellini and the Scarlattis, and Sicilian music history, particularly the polyphonic school. His work in this field includes an edition of Favara's *Corpus di musiche popolari siciliane* (Milan, 1957) and the third and fourth volumes of Favara's *Canti della terra e del mare di Sicilia* (Milan, 1954–9). Tiby was active in musicological circles; he took part in several conferences and organized the 1954 conference in Palermo on mediterranean music.

WRITINGS

Acustica musicale e organologia degli strumenti musicali (Palermo, 1933)
Antichi musicisti siciliani (Palermo, 1933)
'I codici musicali italo-greci di Messina', *Accademie e biblioteche d'Italia*, xi (1937), 64
L'incoronazione di Poppea di Monteverdi (Florence, 1937)
La musica bizantina: teoria e storia (Milan, 1938)
Vincenzo Bellini (Turin, 1938)
Carl Maria von Weber (Turin, 1941)
Claudio Monteverdi (Turin, 1942)
La musica in Grecia e a Roma (Florence, 1942)
I 50 anni del Teatro Massimo di Palermo (Palermo, 1947)
'La famiglia Scarlatti', *JRBM*, i (1946–7), 275
'Donizetti a Palermo', *Annuario dell'Accademia di Santa Cecilia* (1951)
'S. Raval, a 16th Century Spanish Musician in Italy', *MD*, ii (1951), 217
'Emanuele d'Astorga', *IMSCR, v Utrecht 1952*, 398
'La musica nella Real cappella palatina di Palermo', *Anuario de l'Instituto español de musicologia*, vii (Barcelona, 1952)
'L'origine popolare della "siciliana" ', *GfMKB, Bamberg 1953*, 194
'La tradizione del canto popolare in Sicilia e nelle regioni mediterranee', *Congresso internazionale di musiche popolari mediterranee: Palermo 1954*, 37
Il Real teatro Carolino e l'Ottocento musicale palermitano (Florence, 1957)
I polifonisti siciliani del XVI e XVII secolo (Palermo, 1969)
'La musique des civilisations gréco-latines', *Histoire de la musique*, ed. Roland-Manuel, i (Paris, 1960), 377–452

BIBLIOGRAPHY

G. Barblan: 'Ottavio Tiby', *Mf*, ix (1956), 296

FERRUCCIO TAMMARO

Tichatschek, Joseph (Aloys) [Ticháček, Josef] (*b* Ober-Weckelsdorf [now Teplice, nr. Broumov], 11 July 1807; *d* Blasewitz, nr. Dresden, 18 Jan 1886). Bohemian tenor. He had his first music lessons from his father Václav Ticháček, and sang in the choir at the Broumov Gymnasium. In 1827 he was sent to study medicine in Vienna, where he had singing lessons from G. Cicimera, and in 1830 he joined the chorus of the Kärntnerthor Theater. He soon progressed to comprimario parts, and made his début as a principal in Graz in 1837. He sang in Vienna that year, and also made his Dresden début on 11 August 1837 in the title role of Auber's *Gustavus III*; the following year he was appointed to the Dresden Court Opera. With Wilhelmine Schröder-Devrient, from whose friendship and advice

he greatly benefited, and the baritone Anton Mitterwurzer, Tichatschek helped the Dresden Opera set new standards of singing. In 1841 he sang at the Drury Lane Theatre (as Adolar, Tamino and Robert le diable), as well as in Manchester and Liverpool. He was pensioned in 1861 but continued to make appearances until 1870, his voice being remarkably well preserved. His repertory included the principal tenor parts of *Idomeneo, Die Zauberflöte, Fernand Cortez, I Capuleti, La muette de Portici* and *La dame blanche*. His range included lyric tenor and *Spieltenor* parts, but he was also the prototype of the Wagner *Heldentenor*, creating the title roles of *Rienzi* (20 October 1842) and *Tannhäuser* (19 October 1845).

All opinions agree on the beauty and brilliance of Tichatschek's voice. Sincerus praised his range of expression, even production, intonation and enunciation, although he had reservations about his coloratura. In 1840 Otto Nicolai called him the greatest German tenor, and Cornelius was deeply moved by his Lohengrin in 1867 (although King Ludwig II of Bavaria was in the same year distressed by his unromantic appearance in the part). Berlioz described him in the role of Rienzi as 'brilliant and irresistible . . . elegant, impassioned, heroic, his fine voice and great lustrous eyes marvellously effective'. Liszt thought he would be ideal for the role of Cellini and, in a letter to Wagner dated 20 February 1849, described him as 'an admirable artist and a charming comrade and friend'. Wagner, while also liking Tichatschek and admiring his singing ('a brisk and lively nature, a glorious voice and great musical

Joseph Tichatschek in the title role of Wagner's 'Rienzi'

talent'), found him childish and unable to portray 'the dark gloomy, demonic strain in Rienzi's character'. Tichatschek's simple devotion to his voice, his appearance and his costumes were exclusive of any fuller dramatic perception, and he horrified Wagner at the première of *Tannhäuser* by addressing his outburst in praise of Venus with great passion to Elisabeth.

BIBLIOGRAPHY

A. Sincerus: *Das Dresdner Hoftheater und seine gegenwärtigen Mitglieder* (Zerbst, 1852)
M. Fürstenau: *Joseph Tichatschek* (Dresden, 1868)
H. Berlioz: *Mémoires* (Paris, 1870; Eng. trans., 1969)
R. Wagner: 'Über Schauspieler und Sänger', *Gesammelte Schriften und Dichtungen*, ix (Leipzig, 1873; Eng. trans., 1896)
C. F. Glasenapp: *Wagner-Encyklopädie* (Leipzig, 1891)
E. Kloss: 'Joseph Tichatschek', *NMZ*, lxxiv (1907), 613
A. Kohut: 'Aus Joseph Tichatschek's Nachlass', *Bühne und Welt*, ix/2 (Berlin, 1907), 418
E. Newman: *The Life of Richard Wagner* (London, 1933–47)
M. Gregor-Dellin, ed.: *Richard Wagner: Mein Leben* (Munich, 1963), 943

JOHN WARRACK

Tie. A curved line between two notes of the same pitch indicating that they form a single note with their combined values. It is used to connect notes separated by a bar-line, and first appeared thus in the *Recerchari, Motetti, canzoni* of Marco Antonio Cavazzoni (1523 – a notable publication in many respects; *see also* LEGER LINE). The tie also facilitates the notation of values that cannot be written as a single note, such as seven quavers (which may be written as minim tied to dotted crotchet) or five crotchets (which may be written as dotted minim tied to minim). Occasionally a tie implies a subtle repetition of the second note. BEBUNG was indicated in clavichord music by a tie with dots below; and Beethoven's late piano sonatas contain several examples of repeated notes joined by a tie which demand gentle reiteration, as in the Adagio of the Sonata in B♭ op.106.

Tieck, (Johann) Ludwig (*b* Berlin, 31 May 1773; *d* Berlin, 28 April 1853). German poet, dramatist, translator and editor. Although he was not musically talented, his friendship with Wackenroder and acquaintance with Reichardt encouraged his awareness and understanding of music. After Wackenroder's death in 1798 Tieck edited and published his literary remains, adding to the *Phantasien über die Kunst* (1798–9) chapters on 'Unmusical Tolerance', 'Tones' and 'Symphonies'. For Reichardt, with whom he had become related by marriage, Tieck in 1798 wrote the libretto *Das Ungeheuer und der verzauberte Wald*, which however Reichardt failed to set; their later collaboration on another opera, *Sakuntula* (1811–12), was ended by the composer's death. In 1825 Tieck became friendly with Weber, following his appointment as dramatic adviser to the German theatre at Dresden (where he had settled in 1819). From 1842 he lived quietly at Potsdam and in Berlin, whither Frederick William IV had invited him as adviser to the Berlin theatre. Although illness prevented him from taking up Spohr's invitation to write him a libretto, his Berlin years witnessed some important stage productions and collaborations, including Mendelssohn's scores to Tieck's versions of *Antigone* and *Oedipus at Colonus*, and also his music for Tieck's production of *A Midsummer Night's Dream* (1843).

Apart from his writings in which music (especially song) plays an important part, Tieck's lyrics were frequently set to music by his contemporaries and by later composers. His editions of medieval Swabian *Minnelieder* and of versions of the Tannhäuser legend were also significant. In his highly individual plays *Der gestiefelte Kater* (1797), *Die verkehrte Welt* (1798) and *Prinz Zerbino* (1799) he at once satirized contemporary theatrical conditions and parodied its authors and styles, but also (*Die verkehrte Welt*) attempted to write verbal symphonies. His love for Mozart's operas is apparent in numerous direct and indirect references and quotations. His own lyrics, with their effective rhythm, assonances and usually simple imagery, appealed to several generations of composers: Brahms's *Die schöne Magelone*, Schumann's *Genoveva*, Spohr's *Pietro von Albano*, Bialas's *Der gestiefelte Kater*, and more than 300 songs by Reichardt, Hoffmann, Weber, Mendelssohn and others, are among the musical settings and arrangements of his works.

BIBLIOGRAPHY

K. Goedeke: *Grundriss zur Geschichte der deutschen Dichtung*, vi (Dresden, Leipzig and Berlin, 2/1898), 28ff; xi/1 (Düsseldorf, 2/1951), 333ff
M. Friedlaender: *Das deutsche Lied im 18. Jahrhundert*, ii (Stuttgart and Berlin, 1902/R1970) esp. 462ff
E. Challier: *Börsenblatt für den deutschen Buchhandel*, no.174 (Leipzig, 1912) [pp.8836–9 lists 349 Tieck settings]
K. Schönewolf: *Ludwig Tieck und die Musik* (diss., U. of Marburg, 1925)
A. H. Fox Strangways: 'Brahms and Tieck's "Magelone"', *ML*, xxi (1940), 211
R. Erny: *Entstehung und Bedeutung der romantischen Sprachmusikalität in Hinblick auf Tiecks Verhältnis zur Lyrik* (diss., U. of Heidelberg, 1957)
J. Trainer: *Ludwig Tieck: from Gothic to Romantic* (The Hague, 1964)

PETER BRANSCOMBE

Tieferlegung (Ger.). In Schenkerian analysis (*see* ANALYSIS, §III) the lowering of a melody or bass line by an octave, either by direct leap or in connection with one or more other methods of prolongation (e.g. arpeggiation). Often the bass line of a piece begins in a higher octave and is brought down by a *Tieferlegung* to its true or 'obligatory' register (*see* OBLIGATE LAGE) in order to emphasize the arrival of the first important cadence, the first tonic triad in the harmony (as in Chopin's Mazurka op.41 no.2, given in ex.1), or something else

Ex.1 Chopin: Mazurka in E minor op. 41 no. 2

of structural importance. In English-language writings *Tieferlegung*, like its counterpart HÖHERLEGUNG, is sometimes translated as 'octave transfer'.

WILLIAM DRABKIN

Tieffenbrucker [Dieffopruchar, Dieffoprukhar, Duiffoprugcar]. German family of string instrument makers. They originated in the small village of Tieffenbruck, near Rosshaupten in Bavaria, in the region of Füssen. The family split into two branches, one of which settled in Lyons and soon became naturalized French, specializing in viols and other bowed instruments. The larger

Gaspar Tieffenbrucker: engraving (1565) by Pierre Woeiriot

branch emigrated to Italy and became established principally in Venice and Padua, making mainly lutes.

Magno Tieffenbrucker the elder (*fl* ?mid-16th century) seems to the earliest known instrument maker in the family: although he is said to have been established in Venice by 1500, this must remain doubtful, as the sole supporting evidence is the date of a single label that some have read as 1560. The latest instrument attributed to him is dated 1575.

Gaspar Tieffenbrucker [Duiffoprugcar] the elder (*b* Tieffenbruck, 1514; *d* ?Lyons, 1571), probably the son of Magno the elder, was the most famous member of the French branch of the family; his name appears on labels in a number of French variants, of which 'Duiffoprugcar' is perhaps the most common. He settled in Lyons in 1533 and acquired French nationality in 1558. In 1564 his house and workshop were demolished to make way for the building of fortifications for the city and he was unable to get any compensation, a blow from which he never fully recovered. There is an engraved portrait of him by Woeiriot dated 1565 (see illustration). His eldest son, Gaspar Tieffenbrucker the younger (*fl* late 16th century), moved to Paris on the death of his father; he married Françoise, sister of the Parisian instrument maker Jacques Delamotte, and his workshop was established in the rue Pot-de-Feu in 1582. Johann [Jean] Tieffenbrucker (*fl* late 16th century), another son of Gaspar the elder, took over the remains of the business on his father's death and seems to have remained in Lyons until at least 1585, when he had settled the outstanding debts.

The other principal members of the family were all of the Italian branch. Magno Tieffenbrucker [Dieffoprukhar, Dieffopruchar] the younger (*fl* 1589–1621), probably the son of Magno the elder, also worked in Venice, and a number of his instruments survive. Leonardo Tieffenbrucker the elder (*fl* early 16th century), who probably came from Bavaria, lived and worked in Padua; Baron praised his work highly. Ulrich Tieffenbrucker (*fl* early 16th century), one of the earliest and least-known members of the family, is said to have worked both in Venice and Bologna; a label is cited dated 1521. Jacob Tieffenbrucker (*fl* ?mid-16th century) was apparently working in Genoa in about 1564. Michael Tieffenbrucker (*d* c1585) is mentioned as a lute maker in the Rosshaupten archives in 1554 and 1573. Leonardo Tieffenbrucker the younger (*fl* late 16th century), probably the son of Leonardo the elder, also worked in Padua before moving to Venice in about 1590; he, too, is mentioned by Baron, who wrote that he was the teacher and master of Michael Hartung. Another Johann Tieffenbrucker seems to have come from Rosshaupten and was apparently working in Venice in 1592.

Wendelin Tieffenbrucker (*fl* ?second half of the 16th century), probably a son of Leonardo the elder, is the most perplexing member of the family. He certainly worked in Padua, and a number of apparently genuine instruments by him survive. As their dates span an unusually long period, from 1551 to 1611, the question arises of whether or not there were two makers of this name. Only one surviving label has the expected 'In Padua Vendelinus Tieffenbrucker' (with date); from 1551 to about 1590 the labels read 'In Padoua Vvendelio Venere, de Leonardo Tieffenbrucker', and from 1591 until 1611 simply 'In Padoua Vvendelio Venere'. The initials 'WT' are found on one instrument, and 'WE' on two others, each time with an anchor. Various ingenious explanations, none entirely satisfactory, have been advanced to explain the use of the name 'Venere', the connection with Leonardo Tieffenbrucker and the significance of the initial 'E'.

Jachomo Tieffenbrucker seems to have worked in Milan in the 17th century, and to be distinct from the Jacob Tieffenbrucker mentioned above. Moises Tieffenbrucker is known to have worked in Venice in the 18th century, and was apparently the last maker to bear the family name.

BIBLIOGRAPHY
E. G. Baron: *Historisch-theoretische und practische Untersuchung des Instruments der Lauten* (Nuremberg, 1727/*R*1965)
H. Coutagne: *Gaspard Duiffoproucart* (Paris, 1893)
R. Vannes: *Essai d'un dictionnaire universel des luthiers* (Paris, 1932, 2/1951/*R*1972 as *Dictionnaire universel des luthiers*, suppl. 1959)
G. Hellwig: 'Tieffenbrucker', *MGG*
L. Cervelli: 'Brevi noti sui liutai tedeschi attivi in Italia dal secolo xvi° al xviii°', *AnMc*, no.5 (1968), 299–337
F. Hellwig: 'Makers' Marks on Plucked Instruments of the 16th and 17th Centuries', *GSJ*, xxiv (1971), 22

IAN HARWOOD

Tielke, Joachim (*b* Königsberg, 14 Oct 1641; *d* Hamburg, 19 Sept 1719). German string instrument maker. He possibly studied with Gottfried Tielke (who may have been his elder brother) in Italy in 1662. When he was about 25, he moved to Hamburg, where in 1667 he married the daughter of the instrument maker Christopher Fleischer. Nothing is known of Tielke's workshop in Hamburg: the only source of information on his life (a congratulatory work compiled by his friends on the occasion of his golden wedding) was destroyed in World War II, but it is clear that he was well known in musical circles there, since he and his wife were godparents to the children of several musicians. His instruments were much sought after by royalty and nobility in his lifetime.

A surprisingly large number of Tielke's instruments survive. There are nearly 100 in all: various kinds of lutes, guitars, citterns, violins and – especially – viols, which account for nearly half his extant output. His versatility is rare in makers of his time; his instruments, which are often lavishly decorated, are very fine musically (for illustration see GUITAR, fig.7).

BIBLIOGRAPHY

H. Nirrnheim: 'Hamburgische Instrumentenbauer, insbesondere Geigen- und Lautenmacher', *Mittheilungen des Vereins für Hamburgische Geschichte*, vii (1898–1901), 129
P. de Wit and H. Nirrnheim: 'Zur Geschichte des Musikinstrumentenbaues in Hamburg III: eine Zusammenstellung noch vorhandener Tielkscher Instrument', *Mittheilungen des Vereins für Hamburgische Geschichte*, vii (1898–1901), 449
G. Kinsky: *Katalog des Musikhistorischen Museums von Wilhelm Heyer in Cöln*, ii (Cologne, 1912), 275
——: 'Beiträge zur Tielke-Forschung', *ZMw*, iv (1921–2), 604
R. Vannes: *Essai d'un dictionnaire universel des luthiers* (Paris, 1932, 2/1951/R1972 as *Dictionnaire universel des luthiers*, suppl. 1959)
G. Hellwig: 'Joachim Tielke', *GSJ*, xvii (1964), 28
——: *Joachim Tielke, ein Hamburger Lauten- und Violenmacher der Barockzeit* (Frankfurt am Main, 1979)

IAN HARWOOD

Tieme, Clemens. See THIEME, CLEMENS.

Tiénot [Benvénisty, née Tiano], **Yvonne** (*b* Paris, 25 Jan 1897). French writer on music and pianist. After piano studies in Paris (1907–14) she became a pupil of Max Mayer at the Royal Manchester College of Music (1920–25), where she obtained the ARMCM in 1922. She also followed Cortot's public interpretation courses (1924–8). Since 1922 she has played in Manchester, London and Oslo and has broadcast for the BBC. From 1937 to 1940 she was general secretary of the Loisirs Musicaux de la Jeunesse. Since 1947 Tiénot has devoted herself to teaching the piano and music history, to acquainting the young with music, and to musicology. She instituted the 'Pour mieux connaître' series of popular monographs on great composers for Henry Lemoine Edition in Paris. She has written numerous articles in music reviews such as *Le guide du concert et du disque* and has occasionally broadcast for the ORTF.

WRITINGS

with P. Arma: *Nouveau dictionnaire de musique* (Paris, 1948)
Haydn (Paris, 1948)
Haendel (Paris, 1948)
Schubert (Paris, 1949)
Bach (Paris, 1951)
Berlioz (Paris, 1952)
Mozart (Paris, 1953)
Rameau (Paris, 1954)
Beethoven: l'homme à travers son oeuvre (Paris, 1956, enlarged 2/in preparation)
Schumann, l'homme à travers ses écrits (Paris, 1959)
with O. d'Estrade-Guerra: *Debussy: l'homme, son oeuvre, son milieu* (Paris, 1962)
Chabrier, par lui-même et par ses intimes (Paris, 1965)
Brahms: son vrai visage (Paris, 1968)
Mendelssohn, musicien complet (Paris, 1972)

CHRISTIANE SPIETH-WEISSENBACHER

Tiento (Sp.: 'touch'; Port. *tento*). In the 16th, and early 17th and 18th centuries, the term used for Spanish and Portuguese equivalents of the solo RICERCARE. The name indicates the purely instrumental origin of the form: the Spanish verb 'tentar' means to 'try out' or 'experiment', and the first known 'tientos' (for vihuela) seem to have been written with the intention of enabling the performer (or his pupil) to 'try out', or acquire a preliminary feeling for his instrument. The term 'tiento' (or 'tento') was often used interchangeably with *fantasía* (*see* FANTASIA).

It is in this respect that the growth of the Spanish tiento appears very similar to that of the Italian ricercare, which it closely resembles. In the fourth part of *Intabolatura de lauto* (1508), Dalza referred, in connection with some of his pieces, to a trying out or touching of the strings ('tastar de corde') with the ricercare that follows. In the same way Luis de Milán, in his vihuela manual *El maestro* (1536), wrote of some of his *fantasías* ('*fantasías* which should more precisely be called *tentos*') as being designed to enable the performer or pupil to try out the vihuela ('tentar la vihuela') with a mixture of chordal and instrumental passages. Alonso Mudarra (*Tres libros de música e cifra para vihuela*, 1546) also implied a didactic purpose in the manner in which he presented his tientos: a short tiento or prelude is given in each of the eight ecclesiastical modes, linked by way of introduction to one or more longer *fantasías* in the same mode and serving as a guide to their thematic content.

By the time of the appearance of Luis Venegas de Henestrosa's *Libro de cifra nueva para tecla, harpa y vihuela* (1557), the name tiento seems to have lost its earlier significance as a preliminary or introductory piece: Venegas used the term synonymously with the word *fantasía*. The form embodies the inventive idiom of the period, making free use of fugal entries and imitative counterpoint. Apart from two impressive tientos by Pedro Alberto Vila (whose *Libro de tientos* is lost) and one (possibly two) by Pedro Soto, the main body of tientos in Venegas's collection are contributed by 'Antonio', the blind court organist Antonio de Cabezón, who perhaps carried the tiento to its highest level of inspiration. Cabezón composed 29 tientos, 13 of which were published by his son Hernando in *Obras de música para tecla, harpa, y vihuela* (1578). Their range is impressive, and makes difficult any clear-cut definition of the form. All have the expressiveness and intensity characteristic of Cabezón's music. Some are short and meditative, with the calm of a spiritual verset; in others the form is extended to give ample opportunity, by means of diminution, ornamentation and the subtle use of imitation, for a more demonstrative exploration of the newly developing instrumental idiom. The keyboard tientos of Sebastián Aguilera de Heredia are notable for their conscious exploration of the harmonic effect of *falsas*, or false relations (in certain cases they are described as *tientos de falsas*). A different aspect of style is exploited in the 24 *tentos* included in the *Flores de música* (1620) by the Portuguese organist Rodrigues Coelho: the pieces are still arranged by mode (three to each mode), but the real interest of the music lies in the abundance of decorative effects.

After Cabezón, the tiento came to its fullest expression in the music of Correa de Arauxo whose *Libro de tientos y discursos de música práctica* (1626) for organ includes 62 tientos, graded by mode and difficulty. Apart from its didactic function, the tiento here serves as a vehicle of great affective power: phrases are still imitated between parts in the manner of the traditional tiento, but the mood is increasingly disturbed by sudden changes of timbre and improvisatory effects, in addition to the use of dissonance and ornamentation mentioned above.

Following Correa, the only composer of note to cultivate the form was the Valencian Cabanilles in whose music the pictorial and expressive effects of the early Spanish Baroque tiento are carried still further. Imitation is still present, but put to dramatic use. In his *Tiento de batalla*, for example, imitative phrases serve as illustrations of the rival trumpet-calls of conflicting factions (vividly portrayed by the brash trumpet-stops of the Spanish organ of the 17th and 18th centuries): the purely tactile quality of the tiento ('trying out the instrument') is seen raised to its highest degree.

BIBLIOGRAPHY

M. S. Kastner: *Música hispánica: O estilo musical de Padre Manuel R. Coelho* (Lisbon, 1936)

——: *Contribución al estudio de la música española y portuguesa* (Lisbon, 1941)

M. Bukofzer: *Music in the Baroque Era* (New York, 1947)

G. Reese: *Music in the Renaissance* (New York, 1954, rev. 2/1959)

W. Apel: 'Spanish Organ Music of the Early 17th Century', *JAMS*, xv (1962), 174

W. Apel, ed.: *Spanish Organ Masters after Antonio de Cabezón, CEKM*, xiv (1965)

W. Apel: 'Solo Instrumental Music', *NOHM*, iv (1968), 602–798

BEN RIDLER

Tierce (Fr.) (1) An obsolete name for the interval of a THIRD; it survives only as the technical name for the partial of a church bell that lies a 3rd above the fundamental (*see* BELL (i), §2).

(2) An open metal organ stop that sounds two octaves and a major 3rd above the note played, thus corresponding to the 5th harmonic partial of that note (*see* ORGAN STOP).

LL. S. LLOYD

Tierce de Picardie [Picardy 3rd]. The raised third degree of the tonic chord when it is used for the ending of a movement or composition in a minor mode, in order to give the ending a greater sense of 'finality'. The term was introduced by Rousseau in his *Dictionnaire de musique* (1767), though no explanation for its name is known. The use of the *tierce de Picardie* in the 16th century and throughout the Baroque era was common and, according to some writers, to be regarded as standard. In the Classical period it was used much less frequently, though it may be said to have found a replacement in the short section ending a minor-mode work in the parallel major, for example in the quartets of Haydn (op.64 no.2, op.74 no.3 and op.76 no.2) and Beethoven (opp.95 and 132).

Tierney, Harry (Austin) (*b* Perth Amboy, NJ, 21 May 1890; *d* New York, 22 March 1965). American songwriter and pianist. He studied at the Virgil School of Music, New York, and in 1911–13 toured the USA as a concert pianist. In 1915 he was in London as a staff pianist and composer for a music publisher, and he returned to the USA in 1916 in the same position for Remick's. From 1913 to 1930 he wrote songs for revues and musical comedies, including *Keep Smiling* (London, 1913), *The Passing Show of 1916* (New York), *Irene* (New York, 1919, filmed 1940; it includes 'Alice Blue Gown'), *The Broadway Whirl* (with George Gershwin, New York, 1921) and four versions of Ziegfeld's *Follies* (1916–24). His *Rio Rita* (New York, 1927) was one of the first musicals to be adapted to film (1929). From 1930 to the early 1940s he wrote songs for Hollywood films.

BIBLIOGRAPHY

R. D. Kinkle: *The Complete Encyclopedia of Popular Music and Jazz 1900–1950* (New Rochelle, NY, 1974)

DEANE L. ROOT

Tiersot, (Jean-Baptiste Elisée) Julien (*b* Bourg-en-Bresse, 5 July 1857; *d* Paris, 10 Aug 1936). French musicologist and folklorist. In 1876 he entered the Paris Conservatoire, where he became a pupil of Savard for harmony and Massenet for composition, and also studied the organ with Franck and music history with Bourgault-Ducoudray. He was appointed assistant to the Conservatoire librarian in 1883. Two years later he competed for the Bodin Prize of the Académie des Beaux-Arts with his *Histoire de la chanson populaire en France*; this work, which was published in 1889, brought him a commission from the government to collect folksongs in Savoy and the Dauphiné. The result was published in 1903 as *Chansons populaires recueillies dans les Alpes françaises*. With Charles Bordes, he supported the efforts of the Schola Cantorum to bring old music before a wider public, and he founded the Concerts Historiques du Cercle St Simon. He also contributed to the revival of interest in Berlioz and to the promotion of contemporary Scandinavian, Russian and Czech music in France. In 1909 he succeeded Weckerlin as head of the Conservatoire library, a position he held until 1921; he was also president of the Société Française de Musicologie. He edited the letters of Bach, Rameau, Mozart and Berlioz and a collection of *Lettres de musiciens écrites en français*. His own writings include books on French Revolutionary music, on music in the comedies of Molière and on Rousseau, but his chief importance rests in his work as a folklorist. Besides the French Alpine volume, parts of his collection of songs from Bresse and French Canada were also published, and his ten-volume *Mélodies populaires des provinces de France* has remained a classic.

WRITINGS

Histoire de la chanson populaire en France (Paris, 1889)

Musiques pittoresques: promenades musicales à l'Exposition de 1889 (Paris, 1889)

Rouget de Lisle (Paris, 1892)

ed.: 'Lettres inédites' [Mozart], *Le ménestrel*, lix (1893), 59

La messe Douce mémoire de Roland de Lassus (Paris, 1894)

Les types mélodiques dans la chanson populaire française (Paris, 1894)

Etude sur les Maîtres-Chanteurs de Nuremberg de Richard Wagner (Paris, 1899)

'Notes d'ethnographie musicale, i', *Le ménestrel*, lxvi–lxviii (1900–02); pubd separately (Paris, 1905)

ed.: 'Lettres inédites' [J. S. Bach], *Le ménestrel*, lxviii (1902), 243

'Ronsard et la musique de son temps', *SIMG*, iv (1902–3), 70; pubd separately (Paris, 1903)

ed.: [Berlioz correspondence], *Les années romantiques, 1819–42* (Paris, 1904); *Le musicien errant, 1842–52* (Paris, 1919); *Au milieu du chemin, 1852–5* (Paris, 1930)

Hector Berlioz et la société de son temps (Paris, 1904)

Les fêtes et les chants de la Révolution française (Paris, 1908)

'La musique chez les peuples indigènes de l'Amérique du nord', *SIMG*, xi (1909–10) [pt. ii of 'Notes d'ethnographie musicale']

Gluck (Paris, 1910)

Beethoven, musicien de la Révolution (Paris, 1910)

Jean-Jacques Rousseau (Paris, 1912, 2/1920/R1977)

Histoire de la Marseillaise (Paris, 1915)

ed.: 'Lettres, 1842–52' [Berlioz], *Revue de Paris*, xxiv (1917)

Un demi-siècle de musique française: entre deux guerres 1870–1917 (Paris, 1918, 2/1924)

La musique dans la comédie de Molière (Paris, 1922)

La damnation de Faust de Berlioz (Paris, 1924)

Les Couperin (Paris, 1926, 2/1933)

Smetana (Paris, 1926)

La musique aux temps romantiques (Paris, 1930)

La chanson populaire et les écrivains romantiques (Paris, 1931)

Don Juan de Mozart (Paris, 1933)

J. S. Bach (Paris, 1934)

ed.: 'Lettres inédites' [Rameau], *ReM*, xvi (1935), 15

ed.: *Lettres françaises* [Wagner] (Paris, 1935)

Articles on Beethoven, Franck, Saint-Saëns, Schumann, Voltaire and Rameau, French popular music etc, in *RdM*, *ReM*, *SIMG* and other journals

EDITIONS

Adam de la Halle: Le jeu de Robin et Marion (Paris, 1896)
A. *Campra: Daphné*, cantata (Paris, 1910); *Hébé*, cantata (Paris, 1910)
J. P. *Rameau: Thétis*, cantata (Paris, 1910)
J. J. *Rousseau: Ecce sedes hic tonantis*, motet, *BSIM*, viii (1912), 50
F. *Couperin: Suite no.3: L'impériale* (Paris, 1917); *Les nations, sonates . . . 1er ordre* (Paris, 1933)
C. W. *Gluck: Echo et Narcisse* (Paris, n.d.)

FOLKSONG EDITIONS

Mélodies populaires des provinces de France (Paris, 1888–1928); *Chansons populaires recueillies dans le Vivarais et le Vercors par V. d'Indy* (Paris, 1892); *Chants populaires pour les écoles* (Paris, 1896–1902); *Noëls français* (Grenoble, 1901); *Chansons populaires recueillies dans les Alpes françaises* (Grenoble, 1903); *Index musical pour le Romancéro populaire de la France par G. Doncieux* (Paris, 1904); *44 French folk songs and Variants from Canada, Normandy and Brittany* (New York, 1910); *Vieilles chansons pour les coeurs sensibles* (Paris, 1911); *50 chants populaires pour les écoles* (Paris, 1911); *60 Folksongs of France* (Boston, 1915); *Chansons populaires françaises* (Paris, 1921); *Montagnardes et bourrées* (Paris, 1930); *Chansons nègres* (Paris, 1933)

BIBLIOGRAPHY

D. C. Parker: 'The Work of Julien Tiersot', *Musical Standard* (1920), no.99, p.56
L. de La Laurencie: *Un musicien bressan: Julien Tiersot* (Bourg-en-Bresse, 1932)
C. Engel: 'Julien Tiersot', *MQ*, xxiii (1937), 238

SIMONE WALLON

Tiessen, Heinz (*b* Königsberg, 10 April 1887; *d* Berlin, 29 Nov 1971). German composer, teacher and critic. In 1905 he went to Berlin to study law but soon decided on a musical career. He studied theory and composition at the Stern Conservatory and took private composition lessons with Wilhelm Klatte until 1913. During this period he came under the influence of Strauss, whose assistant he became at the Berlin Hofoper in 1917. Strauss was responsible for arranging the performance of Tiessen's Second Symphony at the Essen Tonkünstlerfest in 1914. In addition to his activity at the Hofoper, Tiessen was critic for the *Allgemeine Musikzeitung* (1911–17). Following this he became a contributor to *Melos* and a member of Scherchen's circle. He affirmed his sympathy with the expressionist movement by serving as co-founder of the German division of the International Society for Contemporary Music from 1922 to 1933. Between 1918 and 1921 Tiessen was resident composer and conductor of the Berlin Volksbühne, in which capacity he wrote numerous musical plays. He directed the Academic Orchestra of the University of Berlin (1920–22) and the Jungen Chor (1922–33). The latter was grounded in the politically significant work-song movement for which Tiessen composed his *Aufmarsch* op.40 and the *Chorlieder* op.44. He was, however, censured by the Nazis in 1933 and a period of silence followed. During this time he managed to retain his post as teacher of composition at the Berlin Hochschule. Most of his published works were destroyed during the war. Tiessen was director of the Berlin Conservatory (1946–9) and later resumed his duties, as professor of composition, at the Hochschule (1949–55). In 1955 he was made director of the music division of the West Berlin Academy of Arts. He numbered among his pupils Erdmann, Vogel and Celibidache.

A committed advocate of new music, Tiessen also composed in a traditional vein; in his writings he acknowledged this dichotomy. His most nearly atonal work is the set of Six Piano Pieces op.37. The music written for the work-song movement falls into the tradition of Gebrauchsmusik, and his numerous musical plays are in a folklike idiom. Tiessen was one of the first composers to write film music (*Die 5 Frankfurter*, 1922, silent film). His love of nature led to his most famous hallmark – the use of birdcalls. Two early works, the *Natur-Trilogie* op.18 for piano and the *Amsel-Septett* op.20, are best known for this mannerism.

WORKS
(selective list)

Orch: Eine Ibsenfeier, op.7, n.d.; Sym. no.1, C, op.15, 1911; Sym. no.2 (Stirb und werde), f, op.17, 1912; Rondo, G, op.21, 1918; Ein Liebesgesang, op.25, 1917; Tanzstücke, op.27, n.d.; Ballett-Variationen, op.28, n.d.; Totentanz-Suite, op.29, vn, orch, 1918, rev. as Visionen, 1954; Hamlet-Suite, op.30, 1922; Musik, op.32a, str, n.d.; Vorspiel zu einem Revolutionsdrama, op.33, 1921–8; Salambo, op.34, ballet, 1924; Tanzstücke, op.39, n.d.; Ernste Hymne, op.50, wind, 1940; Konzertante Variationen über eine eigene Tanzmelodie, op.60, pf, orch, 1962

Chamber: Sonata, F, op.2, vn, pf, 1905–6; Trio, c, op.11, n.d.; Amsel-Septett, op.20, fl, cl, hn, str qt, 1915, rev. 1957; Str Qnt, op.32, 1919–22; Duo Sonata, op.35, vn, pf, 1925; Kleine Suite, op.42, 2 vn, n.d.; Kleine Schularbeit nach einem Amselmotiv, op.43, n.d.; Divertimento, op.51, 5 wind, 1942

Pf: Pieces, op.5, n.d.; Sonata, C, op.12, 1910; Natur-Trilogie, op.18, 1913; 3 Pieces, op.31, 1919; 6 Pieces, op.37, 1924–8; Pieces, op.43, 1930; Weltstadtrhythmus, op.45b, n.d.; 5 Pieces, op.52, 1944–5

Vocal: Ein Frühlingsmysterium (B. Schönlank), op.36, n.d.; Aufmarsch, op.40, chorus, wind, 1930; Chorlieder, op.44, n.d.; Der Kirschnein (incidental music, O. Hesse), n.d.; Pieces, chorus, op.54, n.d.; many musical plays

Lieder: opp.1, 3, 4, 6, 8–10, before 1910; opp.16, 22–3, 31, before 1918; opp.24, 26, 41, 44b, 47b, 48b, 49b, 53

WRITINGS

'Das Verhältnis zum heutigen Musikschaffen', *Melos*, iv (1924), 69
Zur Geschichte der jüngsten Musik (Mainz, 1928)
'Fragmente einer Autobiographie', *Musica*, ii (1948), 12
Musik der Natur: über den Gesang der Vögel, insbesondere über Tonsprache und Form des Amselgesanges (Zürich, 1953)
'Audiatur et altera pars: Selbstporträt eines Komponisten', *Musica*, x (1956), 52
'Erinnerungen an Richard Strauss in seinen Berliner Jahren', *Internationale Richard Strauss-Gesellschaft*, liv-lv (1967), 24

BIBLIOGRAPHY

E. Kroll: 'Heinz Tiessen', *Musica*, xi (1957), 191
H. Tiessen: *Wege eines Komponisten* (Berlin, 1962) [autobiography]
H. Stuckenschmidt: 'Tiessen, Heinz', *MGG*
H. Oesch: *Wladimir Vogel: sein Weg zu einer neuen musikalischen Wirklichkeit* (Berne, 1967)

CHARLOTTE ERWIN

Tietjens, Therese (Carolina Johanna Alexandra) (*b* Hamburg, 17 July 1831; *d* London, 3 Oct 1887). German soprano. She studied in Hamburg and Vienna, making her début at Altona in 1849 as Donizetti's Lucrezia Borgia, a role with which she was to be closely associated throughout her career. In 1850 she was engaged at Frankfurt; she sang Louise in the first performance of Lortzing's *Opernprobe* (20 January 1851). After appearances at Brno and Vienna, she made her London début at Her Majesty's Theatre on 13 April 1858 as Valentine in *Les Huguenots*, and then sang in London every year until her death. At Drury Lane she sang Elena in *Les vêpres siciliennes* (27 July 1859), at the Lyceum Theatre Amelia in *Un ballo in maschera* (15 June 1861), at Her Majesty's Marguerite in *Faust* (11 June 1863), Frau Fluth in *Die lustigen Weiber von Windsor* (3 May 1864), the title role of Gounod's *Mireille* (5 July 1864), Medea in Cherubini's *Médée* (6 June 1865) and Leonora in *La forza del destino* (22 June 1867), all first London performances. Her extensive repertory also included Iphigenia in Gluck's *Iphigénie en Tauride*, Mozart's Countess, Donna Anna, Constanze and Pamina, Leonore in *Fidelio*, Weber's Agathe and Reiza, Semiramide, Anna Bolena, Norma, Elvira in *Ernani*, Giselda in *I lombardi*, Leonora in *Il* *trovatore*, Meyerbeer's Alice and Fidès and Wagner's Ortrud.

She sang in Paris (1863) and at the Teatro S Carlo, Naples (1862–3, 1868–9), and made her Covent Garden début on 24 October 1868 as Lucrezia Borgia. In 1875, after laying the foundation-stone of Mapleson's ill-fated Grand National Opera House on the Victoria Embankment, she made a tour of the USA. She also travelled extensively with Mapleson's company in Great Britain and sang in oratorio at all the important English cathedral festivals. Her final appearance, at Her Majesty's on 19 May 1877, was appropriately in *Lucrezia Borgia*. Although in great pain from the cancer of which she was soon to die, she completed the performance, but then fainted and had to be carried from the stage.

Though ungainly in appearance, Tietjens was a magnificently dramatic artist, with a powerful but flexible voice that could overcome any technical difficulty. The authority of her stage presence and of her singing in such roles as Norma, Medea, Donna Anna, Lucrezia or Leonore (*Fidelio*) made her the true successor to Pasta, Malibran and Grisi, though she was also willing to undertake minor parts such as Queen Gertrude in Thomas' *Hamlet*, or to appear in operas of artistic merit but with small chance of success, such as Cherubini's *Les deux journées*.

BIBLIOGRAPHY
T. C. Cox: *Musical Recollections of the Last Half-century* (London, 1872)
J. H. Mapleson: *The Mapleson Memoirs* (London, 1888); ed. H. Rosenthal (London, 1966)

Therese Tietjens in the title role of Donizetti's Lucrezia Borgia

L. Arditi: *My Reminiscences* (London, 1896)
H. Klein: *Thirty Years of Musical Life in London* (London, 1903)
H. Rosenthal: *Two Centuries of Opera at Covent Garden* (London, 1958)

ELIZABETH FORBES

Tietz, Anton Ferdinand. *See* TITZ, ANTON FERDINAND.

Tifḥa. A sign used in Hebrew EKPHONETIC NOTATION.

Tigranyan, Armen Tigran (*b* Alexandropol [now Leninakan], 26 Dec 1879; *d* Tbilisi, 10 Feb 1950). Armenian composer, choirmaster and teacher. His early artistic character was strongly influenced by his home environment in an area steeped in the traditions of folk craft and of the *ashughner*, or *gusanner*, the Armenian folk minstrels. In 1894 he moved to Tbilisi, where he studied music at the Gymnasium, playing the flute, and then at the music college (1898–1902) as a pupil of Klenovsky (theory); he took lessons in harmony and composition with Ekmalyan. After returning to Armenia he worked as a school music teacher and choirmaster, played in public, staged his own dramatized arrangements of national songs, and wrote songs on Armenian texts. His first opera, *Anush*, was performed with success in amateur workshops in various Transcaucasian towns in 1912. In the next year he settled in Tbilisi, where he was a manager of the Tbilisi Armenian Music Society. *Anush* was republished in the 1930s and revived in Erevan.

With this work Tigranyan provided the foundations for an Armenian national operatic style. The lyrical, everyday nature of the text – concerning the love of Anush and Saro, who perish as a result of social prejudice – is matched in Tigranyan's music, which achieves its national qualities by approaching folksong intonation, though there is only one direct quotation, and using folksong forms (*ashugh* improvisations, ceremonial and wedding songs etc). The use of the chorus, important in *Anush*, was developed further in *David-Bek*, a heroic piece concerning the Armenians' struggle against Persian invaders in the 18th century; but the folklike melody remained, and here Tigranyan employed more quotations, notably from the song *I nnjmaned ark'ayakan* by the celebrated *ashugh* Paghtasar Dpir. Various nationalities presented in the opera – Russians, Georgians and Persians – are characterized by material approaching their respective folk music. On the large scale, *David-Bek* is organized along symphonic lines, which links it with Spendiaryan's *Almast*.

WORKS
(*selective list*)
Operas: Anush (Tigranyan), 1908–12, Alexandropol, 1912; David-Bek (5, Tigranyan), 1949, Erevan, 1950
Cantatas: K 15-letiyu sovetskoy Armendii [For the 15th anniversary of Soviet Armenia] (G. Saryan), 1935; Aryunot gisher [Bloody night] (V. Alazan), 1936
Inst: Haykakan parer [Armenian dances], pf suite, 1938; Parayin syuit [Dance suite], orch, 1946; 5 p'yes, pf, 1948
Songs, incidental music

BIBLIOGRAPHY
K. Melik-Vrtanesyan: *Armen Tigranian* (Moscow, 1939)
G. Tigranov: *Armyanskiy muzikal'nïy teatr* [The Armenian music theatre], i (Erevan, 1956), 221–70; ii (Erevan, 1960), 41ff
R. A'tayan and M. Muradyan: *Armen Tigranyan* (Moscow, 1966)

SVETLANA SARKISIAN

Tigranyan, Nikoghayos Fadeyi (*b* Alexandropol [now Leninakan], 31 Aug 1856; *d* Erevan, 17 Feb 1951). Armenian composer, ethnomusicologist and pianist. Blind from the age of nine, he was educated at the

Vienna Institute for the Blind (1873–80), where he studied the piano and compositional theory. After his return to Alexandropol, a town rich in folk culture, he embarked on a career as a composer and ethnomusicologist. He completed his studies in 1893 at the St Petersburg Conservatory under Rimsky-Korsakov and Solov'yov, and then returned to Armenia to collect Armenian, Azerbaijan, Georgian, Kurdish and Persian folksongs. In 1914 he visited St Petersburg, Vienna, Berlin and other cities, lecturing and playing his own compositions. He organized a school for the blind in Leninakan in 1922 and taught music there.

Tigranyan was the first to translate into orchestral terms the peasant music of the Caucasus and near east. His major contribution as a folk music collector was in the notation of the *mugam* (a vocal-instrumental rhapsodic genre) and the exposition of its characteristic features; many composers, among them Ippolitov-Ivanov and Spendiaryan, have drawn on Tigranyan's work in this field. His compositional work grew from his contact with the *ashughner* (folk minstrels) and *sazandars* (singers accompanying themselves on the *saz*), and in particular with the *t'ar* player Melik-Aghamalov. The results bear witness to his profound understanding of folk music; particularly important are the piano arrangements, which delicately underline the individuality of the song or dance. His harmonizations were based on folk modes, and he was able to use the facilities of pedal, ornamentation or rhythm to imitate peasant instruments. Among his best piano arrangements are *Kyandrbaz*, *Vard koshiks*, *Shavali*, *Duz par* and *Findjhan*; the vocal pieces include *Lusnakn gisher* and *Tun ari*.

WORKS

(selective list)

Pf: Kavkazskiye narodnïye pesni i plyaski [Caucasian folksongs and dances] (1887); 3 armyanskikh sol'nïkh tantsa [3 Armenian solo dances] (1897); Zakavkazskiye sol'nïye muzhskiye tantsï [Transcaucasian solo men's dances] (1900); Armyanskiye narodnïye tantsï [Armenian folkdances] (1935)

Mugam arrs.: Bayati-kurd, pf (1894); Bayati-shiraz, pf (1896); Eydari, pf (1897); Shakhnaz, pf (1899); Chargya, pf (1902); Nouruz arabi, pf (1907); Iranskiye mugamï, pf (1938); Shushtar, vn, pf (1933); Findjhan, orch (1937); Gyareyli, orch (1939)

Other folksong arrs., choruses, orch pieces

BIBLIOGRAPHY

Gumretsi: *N. F. Tigranov i muzïka Vostoka* [Tigranyan and the music of the East] (Leningrad, 1927)

SVETLANA SARKISIAN

Tigrini, Orazio (*b* ?Arezzo, *c*1535; *d* Arezzo, 15 Oct 1591). Italian theorist and composer. In 1560 he was *maestro di canto* at S Maria della Pieve, and in 1562 he moved to the cathedral there, holding various positions in one or other of these churches during the next few years. In 1571 he moved to Orvieto Cathedral, where he remained until he finally returned to Arezzo Cathedral in 1587 in the double position of *maestro di canto* and *di cappella*, which he held until his death.

Tigrini's most important contribution to music is a practical composition manual, *Il compendio della musica nel quale si tratta dell'arte del contrapunto*. Dedicated to Zarlino, whom he called the 'father and beginning of our age of music', it is based primarily on the third and fourth books of Zarlino's *Le istitutioni armoniche* (1558). Zarlino's approval of the *Compendio* is implied in his gracious reply to Tigrini's dedication printed at the beginning of it. Tigrini cited other treatises; much of the material in the *Compendio* comes

from Vicentino's *L'antica musica* (1555), and can therefore be considered a summary and extension of the teachings of Willaert. Tigrini's manual is a good introduction to the works of Zarlino and Vicentino, who presented much of their practical material in a discursive and rather disorganized manner; Tigrini extracted the essential details, presenting them in an orderly way. He showed how such different elements as modes, fugues and cadences are interrelated and in some cases he clarified ambiguities: Zarlino discussed cadence types only for two voices, using terms and defining forms and functions that are sometimes hard to understand or find in compositions for several voices; Tigrini explained that most of these were used only in duos (then becoming rare), and gave examples of cadences in music for three to six voices. Tigrini's small amount of extant music shows expert writing in a strict style. His madrigals for six voices, in particular, show contrapuntal mastery but little evidence of the new trends in text expression seen in the work of his more progressive contemporaries.

WORKS

Il I° libro de madrigali, 4vv (Venice, 1573)
Musica super psalmos libri primus et secundus (Venice, 1579)
Il I° libro de madrigali, 6vv (Venice, 1582)
Il II° libro de madrigali, 6vv (Venice, 1591[24])

WRITINGS

Il compendio della musica nel quale si tratta dell'arte del contrapunto (Venice, 1588)

IMOGENE HORSLEY

Tik, Henricus (*fl* mid-15th century). Composer. He was probably English. All that is known of him is the attribution, in the above form, of a three-voice mass cycle in Lucca (*I-La* 238). His name heads the untroped Kyrie (the mass survives imperfectly, with the Agnus incomplete). All five movements are unified by a head-motif, mensural scheme, and differently elaborated forms of (presumably) the same tenor cantus firmus, which is unidentified. The rate of tenor movement is assimilated to that of the upper voices.

The name could be a corruption of an English word such as Thick, which might permit an identification with Fich, one of the composers named in Hothby's *Dialogus in arte musica* (ed. A. Seay, CSM, x, 1964, p.65) in a garbled list with a strong English weighting, including at least two other composers represented in the Lucca manuscript.

BIBLIOGRAPHY

R. Strohm: 'Ein unbekanntes Chorbuch des 15. Jahrhunderts', *Mf*, xxi (1968), 40

MARGARET BENT

Tikotsky [Tsikotski], **Evgeny Karlovich** (*b* St Petersburg, 26 Dec 1893; *d* Minsk, 24 Nov 1970). Russian composer of Polish origin. His systematic music education was limited to private studies of the piano and theory with Volkova-Bonch-Bruyevich in St Petersburg (1912–14); in composition he was largely self-taught. He began to compose at the age of 14 (a symphony and some operas on Russian literary subjects), consulting with his friend, the composer Deshovov. At his father's insistence he entered the St Petersburg Psychoneurological Institute in 1911, leaving in 1914 without completing the course to study in the physics and mathematics department of St Petersburg University. After war service (1915–24) he found himself in Bobruysk, where he taught in a music school (1927–34), and where his first contacts with

Belorussian folk music stimulated more intensive creative activity. His earliest major works included the First Symphony (1924–7) on themes from revolutionary and Belorussian songs (one of the first Belorussian symphonies) and music for stage productions in Minsk. This work necessitated his removal to Minsk, where he taught at the music school (1934–41) and worked as a staff composer for Belorussian radio. During this period he wrote one of the first Belorussian operas, *Mikhas' Podgornïy* (1939). Evacuated during the war, he was subsequently artistic director of the Belorussian State PO (1944–5, 1953–7) and chairman of the board of the Composers' Union (1952–63). His honours included the Order of the Red Banner of Labour (1940, 1949), the Order of Lenin (1944), the titles People's Artist of the Belorussian SSR (1953) and of the USSR (1955), and the Badge of Honour (1963). Together with Churkin, Aladov and Turenkov, Tikotsky was a founder of Belorussian art music. He made wide use of the folk music of the region, treating it entirely in a 19th-century manner. His pioneering cultivation of the symphony and the opera was of particular importance in the development of music in Belorussia.

WORKS
(*selective list*)

Operas: Mikhas' Podgornïy, op.18 (P. Brovka), 1939; Alesya, op.31 (Brovka), 1942–8, rev. as Devushka iz Poles'ya [The girl from Poles'ye], op.46 (Brovka, E. Romanovich), 1952, rev. 1953

Musical comedy: Kukhnya svyatosti [Kitchen of sanctity], op.6 (G. Gradov, V. Orlov), 1931

Orch: 5 syms., op.5, 1927, op.19, 1941, op.36, 1948–59, op.53, 1958, op.65, 1963; Trbn Conc., op.9, 1934; Conc., op.47, pf, Belorussian folk orch, 1953, arr. pf, orch, 1954; Prazdnik na Poles'ye [Holiday in the Poles'ye], op.48, ov., 1954; Slava [Glory], op.59, ov., 1961

Belorussian folk orch: 2 suites, op.43, 1950, op.45, 1952

Inst: Pf Trio, op.8, 1934; other pieces

Songs, choruses, folksong arrs., incidental music, film scores

Principal publishers: Belgiz, Muzgiz

BIBLIOGRAPHY

G. Tsitovich and I. Nisnevich: *Belorusskaya SSR* (Moscow, 1957)
S. Nisnevich: *Belorusskaya simfonicheskaya muzïka* (Minsk, 1959)
B. Smol'sky: *Belorusskiy muzïkal'nïy teatr* (Minsk, 1963)
I. L. Gusin: *Evgeny Karlovich Tikotsky* (Moscow and Leningrad, 1965)
D. Zhuravlev: *Kompozitori sovetskoy belorussii* (Minsk, 1966), 156
Obituary, *SovM* (1971), no.3, p.34

L. M. BUTIR

Tilbury, Adelina. *See* DE LARA, ADELINA.

Tilbury, John (*b* London, 1 Feb 1936). English pianist. He studied at the RCM (1954–5, 1957–8), with James Gibb (1958–60) and with Zbigniew Drzewiecki at the Warsaw Conservatory from 1961. He spent three months studying electronic music in the experimental studio of Polish Radio before returning to England in 1965. A leading British exponent of indeterminate and experimental music, he has since 1958 introduced piano works by Cage, Feldman, Wolff, Brown and other American composers to European audiences. He has also made extensive use of electronics, audio-visual elements and accessory sound sources in his interpretations of indeterminate scores by Ashley, Brecht, Bryars, Cardew, Lucier and Young, and has given first performances of many works by younger English composers. A member of Cardew's Scratch Orchestra from 1969, he has since 1972 written critically on experimental music from a Marxist viewpoint, while continuing to perform it. In a penetrating analysis of Cage's *Music of Changes* he likened the chance processes used in its composition to the laws of supply and demand in capitalist economy, and described it as 'a pianistic mas-

terpiece rooted in bourgeois individualism, anarchism and reformism'.

WRITINGS

M. Parsons: 'The Contemporary Pianist', *MT*, cx (1969), 150 [interview]
'Introduction to Cage's *Music of Changes*', *Stockhausen Serves Imperialism*, ed. C. Cardew (London, 1974)

BIBLIOGRAPHY

M. Nyman: *Experimental Music: Cage and Beyond* (London, 1974)

MICHAEL PARSONS

Tilford Bach Society. An English society formed in 1952 to give an annual festival in the village of Tilford in Surrey; it was initiated by Denys Darlow, then organist of the parish church. The society, consisting of an amateur choir and a professional orchestra, was constituted in order to give stylish performances of the music of Bach, his contemporaries and immediate predecessors; however, later works for similar forces have also been performed, and the society has commissioned a number of new works, notably Stephen Dodgson's *Te Deum* (for the society's 21st anniversary) and *Magnificat*, Christopher Brown's *Woefully Arrayed*, Bryan Kelly's *Surrexit hodie* and *Stabat mater* and Rubbra's *Advent Cantata*. From its inception the society gave numerous broadcasts, including over 70 Bach cantatas for the BBC; it has also toured in Europe. The Tilford Bach Festival Choir and Orchestra has become independent of the society, giving concerts on the South Bank and, from 1973, an annual 'Bach in London' festival at St George's, Hanover Square; they were the first to give, from 1972, annual performances in English of Bach's *St Matthew Passion* within the context of Good Friday Vespers, first at the Lutheran Church of St Anne and St Agnes, Gresham Street, and subsequently at St George's.

Tilkin, Felix. *See* CARYLL, IVAN.

Till, Johann Christian (*b* 1762; *d* 1844). American Moravian composer; *see* MORAVIANS, AMERICAN.

Till, Maurice (*b* Christchurch, 22 Oct 1926). New Zealand pianist. The first of a generation of musicians who chose to train in New Zealand rather than go overseas, he studied with Ernest Empson (a pupil of Godowsky) in Christchurch. He has established a reputation as an accompanist, and has played for Victoria de los Angeles and Pierre Fournier, among others; he has also appeared as a soloist with the New Zealand SO. In the mid-1970s he began to teach the piano as senior lecturer at the University of Otago.

FREDERICK PAGE

Tillière [Tillier, Thillière], Joseph Bonaventure (*b* before 1750; *d* after 1790). Cellist and composer, active in France. He was a pupil of Berteau (as were Duport and Janson) and in 1760 played in the orchestras of Prince Conti. In 1770 he was a member of the Académie Royale de Musique and performed in the Paris Opéra orchestra. Tillière's *Méthode pour le violoncelle*, unlike the earlier cello tutor of Corrette, treats the cello mainly as a solo instrument. Beginning with scales, exercises for crossing strings, and fingerings of major and minor 3rds (extensions), he progressed to difficult technical problems: double stopping, holding a position, and the use of the thumb, which, he said, is often found in solo playing to facilitate difficult passages. He included only a few rules for proper bowing and articulation ('il faut employer l'archet et faire sentir la 1re de chaque mesure') and for beginning in the proper direction.

His sonatas are melodic in style and make full use of the cello's technical resources, employing double stopping, thumb position, the use of the upper register, arpeggios and string-crossings. Virtuoso figuration appears especially in the minuets with variations, and several sonatas have brief written-out cadenzas. Throughout he exploited the possibilities of resonance and contrasting tone colours of strings stopped in a high or low register and in combination with open strings.

WORKS
(all published in Paris)

Airs et 6 sonatas, vc (1760); 6 sonates, vc (1770); Recueil d'ariettes, menuettes, 2 vc (?1773); Recueil d'airs d'opéra-comique, 2 vc (1774); 4 sonates, vc, op.5 (n.d.); 6 duos, 2 vc (1777); 6 sonates, vc, b (1782), also incl. in later edns. of *Méthode*; 3 duos, op.8 (n.d.); Concerto, vc, 2 vn, va, b (1788)

Méthode pour le violoncelle contenant tous les principes nécessaires pour bien jouer de cet instrument (Paris, 1764; Eng. edn., London, c1795 as *New and Compleat Instruction*, rev. 4/1901, by I. Danbe) [1764 edn. reviewed in *Mercure de France* (Sept 1774), 213]

MARY CYR

Tillyard, H(enry) J(ulius) W(etenhall) (*b* Cambridge, 18 Nov 1881; *d* Saffron Walden, 2 Jan 1968). English scholar of Byzantine music. After studying at Gonville and Caius College, Cambridge (1900–04), he went to Athens in 1904 and stayed for three years at the British School of Archaeology, studying the modern phase (Chrysantine system) of Greek Church music under J. T. Sakellarides. His interest in the earlier phases of Byzantine music was aroused when he met Hugo Gaisser, and in 1907 he went to Mt Athos to study chant and the old manuscripts in its monasteries. He taught Greek at Edinburgh (1908–17), and held posts successively as professor of classics in Johannesburg (1919–21), professor of Russian in Birmingham, (1921–6), professor of Greek in Cardiff (1926–44) and lecturer in classics in Grahamstown, South Africa (1946–9). In the periods 1909–12 and 1922–50 he travelled extensively (to Athens, Moscow, Mt Athos, Mt Sinai, Patmos, Constantinople, Grottaferrata and Leningrad) to study Byzantine MSS. In 1931, with Carsten Høeg and Egon Wellesz, he founded Monumenta Musicae Byzantinae.

Because of his knowledge of modern as well as old Byzantine music Tillyard's ideas and theories about the problems in that field have remained valid to an unusual degree. As early as 1911 he stressed the importance of studying the music in the eastern church to determine its influence on Russian, Gregorian and other systems. To an extent rare for a single scholar he examined all periods of Byzantine music in some depth to prove the connection between them (from the 11th century to the present). As a result, he detected a basic continuity of the medieval system of neumatic notation in the centuries after the fall of Constantinople in 1453. He also refuted modern Greek theories (e.g. of Konstantine Psachos), asserting that the melodies used in the Greek Church have never changed, only the methods of notation. He made transcriptions from all the periods, starting in 1911 with the modern Chrysantine notation. In 1925 he found the connection between the signatures which indicated the starting-note of a melody, and the mode in which this melody has to be sung, making it possible at last to transcribe the repertory of hymns between 1175 and 1450 (Middle Byzantine notation).

He was one of the first to bring some order into the seemingly chaotic development of Byzantine notation before 1170. For notations before Middle Byzantine he invented the names 'Coislin' and 'Chartres', now used by all scholars.

WRITINGS

'Instrumental Music in the Roman Age', *Journal of Hellenic Studies*, xxvii (1907), 160
'Greek Church Music', *MA*, ii (1911), 80, 154 [with catalogue of the MSS in the British Museum]
'The Acclamation of Emperors in Byzantine Ritual', *Annual of the British School at Athens*, xviii (1911–12), 239
'Fragment of a Byzantine Musical Handbook in the Monastery of Laura on Mt. Athos', *Annual of the British School at Athens*, xix (1912–13), 95
'Studies in Byzantine Music', *MA*, iv (1913), 202
'Zur Entzifferung der byzantinischen Neumen', *ZIMG*, xv (1913), 31
'Rhythm in Byzantine Music', *Annual of the British School at Athens*, xxi (1914–16), 125
'The Modes in Byzantine Music', *Annual of the British School at Athens*, xxii (1916–18), 133
'The Problem of Byzantine Neumes', *American Journal of Archaeology*, xx (1916), 62
'The Problem of Byzantine Neumes', *Journal of Hellenic Studies*, xli (1921), 29
Byzantine Music and Hymnography (London, 1923)
'Byzantine Musical Notation: a Reply', *Byzantinische Zeitschrift*, xxiv (1923–4), 320
'The Stenographic Theory of Byzantine Music', *Laudate*, ii (1924), 216; iii (1925), 28
'Signatures and Cadences of the Byzantine Modes', *Annual of the British School at Athens*, xxvi (1923–5), 78
'Some New Specimens of Byzantine Music', *Annual of the British School at Athens*, xxvii (1925–6), 151
'A Byzantine Musical Handbook at Milan', *Journal of Hellenic Studies*, xlvi (1926), 219
'The Morning Hymns of the Emperor Leo', *Annual of the British School at Athens*, xxx (1928–30), 86; xxxi (1930–31), 115–47
'Early Byzantine Neumes', *Laudate*, viii (1930), 204
'Byzantine Music at the End of the Middle Ages', *Laudate*, xi (1933), 141
'Byzantine Neumes: the Coislin Notation', *Byzantinische Zeitschrift*, xxxvii (1937), 354
'Monumenta Musicae Byzantinae: a Reply', *MR*, iii (1942), 103
'The Stages of Early Byzantine Musical Notation', *Byzantinische Zeitschrift*, xlv (1952), 29
'Byzantine Music about AD 1100', *MQ*, xxxix (1953), 223
'The Byzantine Modes in the Twelfth Century', *Annual of the British School at Athens*, xlviii (1953), 182
'Gegenwärtiger Stand der byzantinischen Musikforschung', *Mf*, vii (1954), 142
'Recent Byzantine Studies', *ML*, xxxv (1954), 31
'The Rediscovery of Byzantine Music', *Essays Presented to Egon Wellesz* (Oxford, 1966), 3

EDITIONS

Handbook of the Middle Byzantine Notation, MMB, *Subsidia*, i (1935/R1971)
with C. Høeg and E. Wellesz: *Sticherarium* (*Codex Vindobonensis theol. graec. 181*), MMB, main ser., i (1935)
The Hymns of the Sticherarium for November, MMB, *Transcripta*, ii (1938)
The Hymns of the Octoechos, Part I, MMB, *Transcripta*, iii (1940)
The Hymns of the Octoechos, Part II, MMB, *Transcripta*, v (1949)
Twenty Canons from the Trinity Hirmologium, MMB, *Transcripta*, iv (1952)
The Hymns of the Pentecostarium, MMB, *Transcripta*, vii (1960)

BIBLIOGRAPHY

M. Velimirović, ed.: *Studies in Eastern Chant*, i (London, 1966) [contains almost complete bibliography, xv–xvi]
M. Velimirović: 'H. J. W. Tillyard, Patriarch of Byzantine Studies', *MQ*, liv (1968), 341
E. Wellesz: 'H. J. W. Tillyard: in memoriam', *Studies in Eastern Chant*, ii (1971), 1

NANNA SCHIØDT

Tilmant, Alexandre. French cellist, brother of THÉOPHILE TILMANT.

Tilmant, Théophile (Alexandre) (*b* Valenciennes, 8 July 1799; *d* Asnières, nr. Paris, 7 May 1878). French conductor and violinist. After studying the violin with

Rodolphe Kreutzer at the Paris Conservatoire (winning the *premier prix* in 1819), he played in the orchestras of the Théâtre-Italien and the Opéra (from 1825). He was deputy conductor of the Société des Concerts du Conservatoire from its establishment in 1828 until 1860. He conducted at the Gymnase Musical (1835) and was deputy conductor (1834–8) and chief conductor (1838–49) at the Théâtre-Italien. With his brother Alexandre Tilmant (*b* Valenciennes, 14 Oct 1808; *d* Paris, 13 June 1880), a cellist in the orchestras of the Théâtre-Italien and later the Opéra, he founded a chamber music society that played works by their contemporaries as well as Haydn, Mozart and Beethoven. As conductor of the Opéra-Comique (1849–68) he directed the premières of Thomas' *Le songe d'une nuit d'été* and *Mignon*, and Meyerbeer's *L'étoile du nord*. He was conductor of the Concerts du Conservatoire from 1860 (officially 1861) until 1863. His conducting was praised for its verve, precision, control, sensitivity in accompanying singers and conscientiousness.

BIBLIOGRAPHY
FétisB
Obituary, *Revue et gazette musicale de Paris*, xlv (1878), 150
A. Dandelot: *Le Société des concerts du Conservatoire* (Paris, 1898, enlarged 2/1923)
C. Pierre: *Le Conservatoire national de musique et de déclamation: documents historiques et administratifs* (Paris, 1900)
JEFFREY COOPER

Tilmouth, Michael (*b* Grimsby, Lincs., 30 Nov 1930). English musicologist. He was a scholar at Christ's College, Cambridge, studying under Dart, John Stevens and Orr (1951–8; BA 1954); he took the PhD in 1960 with a dissertation on English chamber music in the 17th and 18th centuries. He has published a number of useful editions of this music, including (among lesser-known works) two suites by John Banister the younger and a trio sonata by Sherard. He was appointed assistant lecturer at Glasgow University (1959), lecturer (1962) and Tovey Professor of Music at the University of Edinburgh (1971). From 1968 to 1976 he edited the *RMA Research Chronicle*, and in 1975 became a director of Scottish Opera. His research, largely confined to English music, shows a meticulous approach to source material, and his writing is marked by its clarity and directness.

WRITINGS
'Some Improvements in Music noted by William Turner in 1697', *GSJ*, x (1957), 57
'The Royal Academies of 1695', *ML*, xxxviii (1957), 327
'Some Early London Concerts and Music Clubs, 1670–1720', *PRMA*, lxxxiv (1957–8), 13
'Henry Purcell, Assistant Lexicographer', *MT*, c (1959), 325
'The Technique and Forms of Purcell's Sonatas', *ML*, xl (1959), 109
Chamber Music in England, 1675–1720 (diss., U. of Cambridge, 1959–60)
'A Calendar of References to Music in Newspapers published in London and the Provinces, 1660–1719', *RMARC*, i (1961), ii–vii, 1–107
'James Sherard, an English Amateur Composer', *ML*, xlvii (1966), 313
'Revisions in the Chamber Music of Matthew Locke', *PRMA*, xcviii (1971–2), 89
'York Minster MS.16(s) and Captain Prendcourt', *ML*, liv (1973), 302
'Music and British Travellers Abroad in the 17th and Early 18th Centuries', *Source Materials and the Interpretation of Music: a Memorial Volume to Thurston Dart* (London, in preparation)

EDITIONS
M. Locke: *Chamber Music*, MB, xxxi (1971); xxxii (1972)
H. Purcell: *Twelve Sonatas of Three Parts*, The Works of Henry Purcell, v (London, 1976); *Ten Sonatas of Four Parts*, ibid, vii (London, in preparation)
DAVID SCOTT

Tilney, Colin (*b* London, 31 Oct 1933). English harpsichordist. After studying the piano as a child, he read modern languages and music at King's College, Cambridge. While at Cambridge he began serious study of the harpsichord with Mary Potts, and later had lessons with Leonhardt in Amsterdam. From the early 1960s he has been active as a soloist and ensemble performer in Britain and on the Continent. He made his first appearances in the USA in 1971. Tilney's repertory is wide, embracing music of the principal European schools from the 16th century to the 18th, with particular emphasis on English music. His recordings include *Parthenia*, the complete keyboard works of Locke and the suites of Purcell and Handel. He is especially concerned with playing music on the most appropriate keyboard instrument, and has made use of a great variety of harpsichords, clavichords and early pianos, both historical instruments and modern replicas, in his concerts and recordings. He has edited the harpsichord music of Antoine Forqueray.

HOWARD SCHOTT

Timante, Bernardo delle Girandole. *See* BUONTALENTI, BERNARDO.

Timbales. Generally adopted name for a pair of single-headed, cylindrical drums. They are primarily associated with the Latin American dance orchestra but are also frequently used in modern orchestral music and rhythm ensembles. Their metal shells are of shallow diameter (usually between 30 and 50 cm); the screw-tensioned heads, invariably of plastic, produce definable notes that are normally tuned a certain distance apart. Timbales occasionally serve as unsnared membrane drums. Many modern composers have scored for them; Malcolm Lipkin's *Interplay* (1975) for recorder, harpsichord, viola da gamba and percussion uses six timbales tuned to G, $B\flat$, B, c, $d\flat$ *and* $e\flat$ instead of timpani.

See also KETTLEDRUM and TIMPANI.

JAMES BLADES

Timballo (It.). An ORGAN STOP (*Pauke*).

Timbre (i). A term describing the tonal quality of a sound; a clarinet and an oboe sounding the same note are said to produce different timbres. It is usually reserved for descriptions of steady notes and therefore the physical quantity with which it is most closely associated is the harmonic mixture, or the formant, or the spectrum. *See also* SOUND, §6.

Timbre (ii). A term of late 18th-century French origin widely applied by scholars of folklore and by musicologists to pre-existing *opéra comique* songs, vaudeville tunes, parody songs, 16th- and 17th-century chansons, and in a special sense to medieval monophony. A feature common to the later classes of French popular song was the adaptation of new words by the librettist or songwriter to well-known vocal or instrumental melodies; the 'timbre', a name identification tag taken from the refrain or first couplet of the original poem, was printed above the new text and served to identify the tune used to accompany the new words. During the 16th century these borrowed tunes were nearly always prefaced with the phrase 'Chanson sur le chant:'; later, this was replaced by a simpler form, 'Air:'. The term is closely associated with the large anthologies of *airs*, chansons and vaudeville songs edited during the early part of the 19th century by such collectors as Pierre Capelle, *Le clé du caveau* (Paris, 1807), Joseph Doche, *Musette du vaudeville* (Paris, c1822), Pierre Béranger, *Musique des chansons* (Paris, 1834) and others. The *airs* in these collections were arranged alphabetically according to the names of the 'timbres'. Jean-Jacques Rousseau in his *Dictionnaire de musique* (Paris, 1768) did not use the term in his definitions 'air', 'chanson', 'parodie', 'vaudeville', etc; nor did Pierre Nougaret in his extensive discussion of the vaudeville in *De l'art du théâtre* (Paris, 1769). A few years later, Pierre Laujon, apparently one of the earliest commentators to introduce the term, in *Les à propos de société* (Paris, 1776, vol.i, p.vii) carefully provided the reader with a succinct explanation of its meaning in a footnote: 'L'on appelle *Timbre*, en style de Chansonnier, le Refrain, où le Vers qui sert à rappeller l'Air d'une Chanson'. When a vaudeville was not particularly popular the first time it appeared, later songwriters would frequently adapt a second or even third set of lyrics to the original tune, but would retain the timbre of the superseded words. For the connoisseur of vaudeville singing, Capelle listed both the 'timbres originaux' or 'timbres primitifs' and these newer 'faux timbres'. In his essay on the *opéra comique*, La Laurencie carefully distinguished between the timbre (i.e. the name of a vaudeville tune) and the melody itself (*fredon*), with its inherent psychological and motivic features.

'Timbre' is sometimes used, particularly by French scholars, to characterize standard melodic themes, phrases or neumatic formulae in medieval monophony that recur in different musical compositions, and which are underlaid with different words. The general compositional techniques of direct borrowing, adaptation, and reorganization of textual and melodic fragments into new pieces during the Middle Ages are well known under such terms as 'centonization', 'contrafactum', 'migrating melismas' etc. The precise use of 'timbre', however, is closely linked with the Misset–Aubry edition of the proses of Adam of St Victor (*d* 1177 or 1192), based on a mid-13th-century gradual and troper (*F-Pn* lat.14452). Aubry, obviously adapting the folklorist's meaning of 'timbre' to an earlier corpus of music, identified and catalogued 183 'timbre adamiens', or recurring melodic phrases, among the 45 proses ascribed to Adam by Misset. Further, he hypothesized that these structurally simple timbres were derived from a body of popular medieval tunes ('les timbres populaires') now largely lost. Later, Spanke substantially revised Aubry's 'Catalogue des timbres' on the basis of a study by Franz Wellner, who ascribed 53 proses to Adam, and challenged Aubry's speculative theory regarding the secular origin of these phrases.

'Timbre' is also used by medievalists in other analytical contexts. Suñol (1925) used the term 'timbres grégoriens' to describe stereotype melodic and rhythmic groups of notes or stock neumatic formulae that often occur in certain classes of plainchant melodies. Chailley considered it highly probable that melodic phrases in the *versus* and *chansons de geste* found in early St Martial sources, which he labelled 'timbres', were influenced by pre-existing models. Hourlier used the term in his study of the Office antiphon to describe the adaptation of primitive melodic phrases into liturgical compositions of a much later date.

BIBLIOGRAPHY

A. Font: *Favart, l'opéra-comique et la comédie-vaudeville aux XVIIᵉ et XVIIIᵉ siècles* (Paris, 1894), 9ff

E. Misset and P. Aubry: *Les proses d'Adam de Saint-Victor* (Paris, 1900/R1969)

E. Picot: *Chants historiques français du seizième siècle* (Paris, 1903)

G. Cucuel: *Les créateurs de l'opéra-comique français* (Paris, 1914), 27ff

L. de La Laurencie: 'L'opéra-comique', *EMDC*, I/iii (1921), 1457

G. Suñol: *Introducció a la paleografia musical gregoriana* (Montserrat, 1925; Fr. trans., 1935)

F. Wellner: *Adam von Sankt Viktor: sämtliche Sequenzen, lateinisch und deutsch* (Munich, 1937)

D. J. Grout: *The Origins of the Opéra-comique* (diss., Harvard U., 1939)

H. Spanke: 'Die Kompositionskunst der Sequenzen Adams von St. Victor', *Studi medievali*, new ser., xiv (1941), 1

P. Coirault: *Notre chanson folklorique* (Paris, 1942), 458

——: *Formation de nos chansons folkloriques* (Paris, 1953–63)

J. Chailley: *L'école de Saint Martial de Limoges jusqu'à la fin du XIᵉ siècle* (Paris, 1960), 169, 270, 350, 354

D. J. Grout: 'Vaudeville', *ES*

H. Husmann: 'Notre-Dame and Saint-Victor: Repertoire-Studien zur Geschichte der gereimten Prosen', *AcM*, xxxvi (1964), 98, 191–221

C. Barnes: *The Théâtre de la Foire (Paris, 1697–1762), and its Music and Composers* (diss., U. of California, Los Angeles, 1965)

D. Heartz: 'Vaudeville', *MGG*

J. Hourlier: 'Notes sur l'antiphonie', *Gattungen der Musik in Einzeldarstellungen: Gedenkschrift für Leo Schrade* (Berne and Munich, 1973), 135

JOHN A. EMERSON

Timbrel. *See* TAMBOURINE.

Timbres (Fr.). GLOCKENSPIEL.

Time. A word loosely used as a synonym for METRE, as in the expression 'common time' (4/4 metre); it is sometimes applied in other senses concerning rhythm, TEMPO, duration etc.

Time, Clemens. *See* THIEME, CLEMENS.

Timer. *See* TIMMER family.

Time signature. A sign or signs placed at the beginning of a composition, after the clef and any key signature, or in the course of a composition. It indicates the METRE of the piece or a change in metre for a part of the piece. In modern usage two figures are usually given, one above the other: the lower indicates the unit of measurement, relative to the semibreve; the upper indicates the number of units in each bar. Thus a signature of 3/2 indicates that there are three minims ('half-notes') in each bar; a signature 9/8 indicates that there are nine quavers ('eighth-notes') in each bar.

Some signatures are survivors of the system of proportions and mensuration signs (*see* NOTATION, §III, 3(vii), 4(iii): C is used 4/4 and ¢ for 2/2 (also called *alla breve*). C is a relic of the medieval *tempus imperfectum cum prolatione minore*, a mensuration where each long contained two breves and each breve contained two semibreves. The sign ¢ is now used to indicate quick duple time, the beat falling on the minim rather than the crotchet. In medieval terms the *tactus* in C time fell on the semibreve; in ¢ time it fell on the breve. A diminution of note values in the ratio 2:1 was thus indicated by the introduction of the ¢ signature, so that any note was subsequently worth only half its previous value. In the Middle Ages, as in modern usage, it occasionally obviated the need to write notes such as the *fusa* and *semifusa* (the modern semi- and demisemiquaver).

Timm, Henry Christian (*b* Hamburg, 11 July 1811; *d* Hoboken, NJ, 5 Sept 1892). American pianist, organist and conductor of German birth. After studying with A.

G. Methfessel and Jacob Schmitt he emigrated to New York in 1835, making his début at the Park Theatre as a pianist on 19 July 1836. An extremely versatile musician, he doubled as chorus master and horn player in the American première of C. E. Horn's opera *The Pilgrim of Love* at the newly reopened National Theatre (12 October 1840); in the same year he married Sarah Archer, a leading actress in New York who later sang in opera and managed Vauxhall Gardens.

During the first season of the New York Philharmonic Society (1842–3) Timm doubled as trombone player and pianist, and at the inaugural concert (7 December 1842) conducted operatic scenes from Mozart, Beethoven, Rossini and Weber. While president of the Society (1848–63) he firmly set its tone as a servant of German music, receiving his best review as piano soloist (20 November 1852) in Hummel's Concerto op.90. 'Always reliable, and always equal to the emergency', he remained active as a performer in New York and as a church organist until 1882.

Together with Elam Ives (1802–64) he adapted the works of the Viennese Classicists in *The Beethoven Collection of Sacred Music* (Boston, 1857); for the use of his pupils he added a second piano part to the Cramer studies not already so provided by Henselt in *20 études célèbres* (Berlin, 1880). He left unpublished a Mass for soloists, chorus, orchestra and organ.

BIBLIOGRAPHY

R. O. Mason: *Sketches and Impressions Musical, Theatrical, and Social* (New York, 1887), 175, 179, 181f

G. C. D. Odell: *Annals of the New York Stage*, iv–v (New York, 1928–31)

J. T. Howard: 'Timm, Henry Christian', *DAB*

ROBERT STEVENSON

Timmer [Timer]. Austrian family of musicians. They were active in Vienna mainly in the first half of the 18th century. Five or six of the seven sons of Mathias Timmer (*b* c1662; *d* 15 Sept 1742), *regens chori* at St Dorothea and afterwards at St Stephen's Cathedral, were trained as musicians: (1) Joseph; Franz Joseph (*b* c1697; *d* 17 Nov 1731); Joseph Carl (*b* 1698; *d* 19 Nov 1785); (2) Leopold; (3) Joseph Ferdinand; and perhaps Anton (*b* 1706; *d* 8 Nov 1764). The frequency of the name Joseph has caused confusion and misattributions; the situation is further complicated by some of Mathias Timmer's grandchildren's also having become musicians. The Gesellschaft der Musikfreunde in Vienna owns a collection of violin variations by the Timmers in which each variation is composed by a different member of the family, the theme probably being by Leopold. The three most important members of the family are discussed below.

(1) Joseph Timmer (*b* Vienna, 1696; *d* Vienna, 27 Aug 1750). Composer, violinist and tenor. He may have been a choirboy in St Stephen's Cathedral and as such a pupil of J. M. Zächer or J. J. Fux before he became a *Hofscholar*, serving also as violinist. In 1719 he became a tenor in the court chapel on the recommendation of Fux, who later described him as 'not only a skilful singer but also a good violinist'. At the most splendid opera production of the century, the performance of Fux's *Costanza e Fortezza* in 1725 on the coronation of Charles VI in Prague, he sang a tenor part to great applause (according to Holzhauser's *Krönungsnachrichten*, ? Prague, c1726, p.318; some violin concertos attributed to (3) Joseph Ferdinand Timmer may be by him). The strong Italian influence, characteristic of

Viennese music of this period, dictated the form of his concertos; but their texture and melodic conception show more local traits. When Joseph Haydn was a choirboy at St Stephen's during the 1740s he heard and probably met Joseph Timmer who was one of the court musicians obliged to participate in cathedral performances.

(2) Leopold Timmer (*b* Vienna, 1701; *d* Vienna, 21 Oct 1757). Composer, brother of (1) Joseph Timmer. Nothing is known about his teachers or his apprenticeship years. In 1738, when he married, the court documents describe him as valet and director of the chamber music of Duke Franz Stephan of Lorraine (husband of Archduchess, later Empress, Maria Theresia). His surviving output consists mainly of chamber and orchestral music. He composed in a less virtuoso style than his brothers and is the most conservative of them. Nevertheless his compositions, though of variable quality, are by no means less appealing. His melodic invention shows a pleasing natural flow and his part-writing reveals a solid training in counterpoint.

WORKS

Amarilli e Nise, cantata pastorale, 2vv, orch, 1727, *D-MEll*

Concerto [grosso] a 4, G, vn solo, 2 vn, va, b; Intrada à 3, G, 2 vn, b; Parthia a 5, B♭, vn solo, 2 vn, va, b; 3 Parthie a 3, D, F, B♭, 2 vn, b: all *A-Wn*

Parthia, *Wm*; Parthia a 5, vn solo, vn, cl, hn, b, *WIL*

(3) Joseph Ferdinand Timmer (*b* Vienna, 1708; *d* Vienna, 11 June 1771). Composer and singer, brother of (1) Joseph Timmer. He became a member of the court chapel in 1728 as tenor, but at such a low salary that he exchanged this position in 1729 for that of royal valet. He later served Duke Franz Stephan of Lorraine in this capacity. Though he may have participated in performances arranged by his brother (2) Leopold Timmer, he was probably much less active as a musician and succeeded in making an official career, later becoming castellan in Castle Belvedere. His compositions are rather unattractive. Although he was the best-known member of the family, his music lacks the melodic charm and the other good qualities of (2) Leopold Timmer's works.

WORKS

(mostly ascribed 'Timmer'; some may be by (1) Joseph)

[12] Sonate, vn, b (Venice, n.d.)

12 solos, vn (Vienna, 1760), cited in *GerberL*, lost

3 sonatas, kbd, in Oeuvres melées, x (Nuremberg, 1764)

10 concertos à 5, vn solo, insts, 1733–43, *A-Wn* [Conc., A, *Wn* Sm 3782; and Conc., E♭, *Wn* 3778: ? both by (1) Joseph Timmer]; Concerto à 5, A, vn solo, insts, *Wgm* ix/2847 [? by (1) Joseph Timmer]; 24 Menuetts, 2 vn, b, 2 tpt, timp, *Wn*; Presto, kbd, *D-Bds*, cited in *EitnerQ*

Mass, 4vv, org, 1755; Mass, 4vv, vc, vle; Mass, 4vv, org, 1756: all *A-Wn*

BIBLIOGRAPHY

EitnerQ; GerberL

L. von Köchel: *Die Kaiserliche Hof-Musikkapelle in Wien, von 1543–1867* (Vienna, 1869), 74, 77, 82

H. Vogg: *Franz Tůma als Instrumentalkomponist nebst Beiträgen zur Wiener Musikgeschichte des 18. Jahrhunderts* (diss., U. of Vienna, 1951)

EVA BADURA-SKODA

Timotheus (*b* Miletus, c450 BC; *d* c360 BC). Greek composer and singer to the kithara. He represented the more extreme manifestations of the 'new music' that dominated the final decades of the 5th century BC and the succeeding period in Greece. He claimed to have introduced the use of 11 strings or notes (*chordē* may have either meaning) on the kithara (*Persae*, ll.241–3, Edmonds, frag.19). The contemporary evidence of the poet Pherecrates (in Pseudo-Plutarch, *De musica* 30) suggests that Timotheus's dithyrambic compositions, designed for accompanied chorus, were instrumentally conceived and forced the male voice as much as a 4th above its normal upper limit. They also appear to have lacked any stable basis of modality – a radical departure from tradition. As for solo writing, the considerable surviving portions of his nomes make clear the metrical and stylistic degeneration of the text, which had become subservient to a florid, amorphous melodic line. Traces of the same process are discernible at times in the lyrics of Euripides, a close associate of the composer.

The innovations of Timotheus came under sharp attack both in Athens and in Sparta. Although he actually proclaimed himself a champion of tradition (*Persae*, ll. 229–31, Edmonds, frag.19), another of his pronouncements (frag.24) contradicts this and comes much nearer the truth: 'I do not sing the old songs. . . . Away with the old music!'.

BIBLIOGRAPHY

J. M. Edmonds, ed. and trans.: *Lyra graeca* (London and New York, 1922–7, 2/1928–40), iii, 280–333
E. Diehl, ed.: *Anthologia lyrica graeca* (Leipzig, 1925, rev. 3/1949)
P. Maas: 'Timotheus 9', *Paulys Realencyclopädie der klassischen Altertumswissenschaft*, vi/A/2 (Stuttgart, 1937), 1331
O. J. Gombosi: *Tonarten und Stimmungen der antiken Musik* (Copenhagen, 1939/*R*1950), 65ff, 74ff
M. Wegner: *Das Musikleben der Griechen* (Berlin, 1949), 162ff
D. L. Page, ed.: *Poetae melici graeci* (Oxford, 1962), 399ff

For further bibliography *see* GREECE, §I.

WARREN ANDERSON

Timpán, tiompán. Timpán is the Middle Irish term (Middle English probably *timpe*) for what was probably a species of lyre (*see* CRWTH, ROTTE (i) and ROTTE (ii)). The Latin word 'tympanum' was used by Osbern (*fl* 1090) in his biography of St Dunstan, and by Giraldus Cambrensis (?1146–1220) in his *Topographia Hibernie*. The forms 'timpán' and 'tiompán' have occasionally been wrongly used to denote a drum-like instrument (a medieval Irish tract on Latin declension contains the gloss *timpánach* for *hic timpanista*); 'tiompán' is used in modern Irish, but only in a general sense to refer to any musical instrument.

The timpán mentioned in Irish literature between the 8th or 9th century and the late 17th is generally said to have had a body of willow (sometimes ornamented with metal), and three metal strings; two references suggest that one functioned as a melody string, the others as a drone. In its early period it was plucked with a long fingernail or plectrum; it was bowed after the early 11th century and has been described as sweet-stringed, light, pure and melancholy. The three old Irish categories of music (inducing weeping, laughter or sleep) are associated with it in the tale 'The Battle of Mag Mucrime' from the late 12th-century *Book of Leinster*. It was played in medieval Irish courts by both resident and travelling performers; the latter also played at fairs. Timpán players, like harpers, accompanied the declamation of Fenian epics and praise poetry. Eight players, said to have lived between the early 13th and late 15th centuries, and two individual patrons are named in the main collection of annals.

The decline of the timpán in Ireland (like that of the characteristically Irish harp) seems to have coincided with increasing anglicization in the 16th century, and the instrument was probably obsolete by the end of the 17th.

BIBLIOGRAPHY

A. Buckley: 'Notes on the Tiompán in Irish Literature', *Studia musicae instrumentorum popularis*, v, ed. E. Stockmann (Stockholm, 1977)

ANN BUCKLEY

Timpani (It.; Fr. *timbales*; Ger. *Pauken*). Kettledrums. The timpani are the most important of the orchestral instruments of percussion, mainly because they are capable of producing notes of definite pitch and so can take part in the harmony of the orchestra. They are tuned exactly, each to a given note, according to the composer's directions in his score, and these notes may be altered as required during the performance of a work, by tightening or slackening the drumhead by means of screws or other mechanisms.

1. Construction. 2. Technique. 3. History. 4. Repertory.

1. CONSTRUCTION. A kettledrum consists of a large bowl-shaped resonating chamber or shell, usually of copper, with a drumhead of specially prepared calfskin or of another material covering the open top of the shell, and a means of tightening or slackening the drumhead. Brass has been used for the shell, though rarely. The recently introduced fibreglass bowl, though not equalling a copper bowl tonally, has some advantages, chiefly durability and ease of transportation.

Kettledrums are divided into two distinct types: 'hand-screw' drums (fig.1) and 'machine' drums. There are three types of machine drums: pedal-operated (fig.2), with a single master screw (fig.3), and with rotating bowls (fig.4). In these three cases the whole counter-hoop is lowered or raised in a single operation. Hand-screw drums (which are supported either on a loose tripod stand or on three adjustable iron legs, which pass through sockets at the base of the shell and can be retracted inside the drum when not in use) have screws, each with its own handle, fitted round the counter-hoop. These engage with brackets on the shell. The counter-hoop conveys pressure to the flesh hoop on which the drumhead is mounted. The screws may be turned one or two at a time, the latter for preference in order to apply pressure on the drumhead as evenly as possible. In no instance is the correct tuning obtained by a consistent operation – a given number of turns on the handles, or a prescribed 'travel' on the foot-pedal; the amount of pressure is variable, and is governed by the condition and thickness of the drumhead and, in the case of calfskin, by atmospheric conditions.

The main factors determining the pitch of kettledrums are the diameter of their bowls and the tension on the drumheads. The effect of the depth and contour of the bowl – in which there remains a remarkable divergence in construction – has been a subject of discussion over a long period of time, and the theory of the shell remains controversial. Opinion is however fairly uniform in agreeing that the bowl of the kettledrum magnifies certain of the overtones in the harmonic series, rendering the note musical, and that a shallow bowl tends to clarify the principal note of the drum, and a deep shell to increase its resonance. The deeper the shell, however, the greater the tendency for the pitch of the note to flatten on impact. Modern makers prescribe that the bowl should be as deep as one half of its diameter. Some bowls are semicircular, others parabolic or with sloping sides. No final formula for timpani has yet been evolved, and a wide range of types is still encountered. Tonal differences are compensated for by

1. Hand-screw timpani by Premier, Leicester

2. Pedal-operated machine timpani with foot-operated fine-tuner, and tuning gauges, by Premier, Leicester

3. Machine timpani ('Dresden' model) with saw-tooth clutch locking pedal and master tuning handle by Ludwig Drum Co., Chicago

4. Rotary-tuned machine timpani by Murbach, Lucerne

the performer who can, for example, adjust the striking position to suit the depth of the bowl: reasonably close to the rim in the deeper bowl, and a little nearer the centre if the bowl is shallower.

The contention that the air trapped by the shell resonates in sympathy with the membrane is arguable, as there is no appreciable difference in tone when the hole in the bottom of the shell (for the release of air pressure) is open or plugged. Neither is there any appreciable difference in the volume of sound at a given point in the register, suggesting that the kettle acts less sympathetically than the XYLOPHONE resonator, where the air column corresponds to the frequency of the wooden bar. Experiments made on a shell-less kettledrum, similar to that patented by Adolphe Sax, support the contention that if the back wave were not contained, the front wave would be partially cancelled, resulting in a weak tone, and that a deep shell adds resonance to the drum because of the large column of air trapped by the shell, which determines the amount of restoring force on the membrane. It is only in the case of a closed 'double-skinned' cylindrical drum such as the 'long drum' that the depth of the shell affects the pitch of the drum. Rayleigh said in 1879: 'I am not in a position to decide the question as to the function of the shell; but I think it at least doubtful whether it introduces any really advantageous modification into the relations of the component tones . . .'. That the tone of the drumhead is most resonant at a given degree of tension supports the theory that the best tone production requires one drum for each note, but the impracticability of using 16 drums which would be needed to cover the orchestral range (at least one and a third octaves) is obvious. Arranged keyboard-fashion, the distance between two drums a 5th apart would be almost two metres.

To avoid a wide range of notes on each timpanum (i.e. to avoid a taut or slack drumhead) a minimum of three drums is required for orchestral purposes. The diameters of the once popular so-called 'symphonic set of three' hand-screw drums are approximately 75 cm, 66 cm and 61 cm, covering a compass of one and a third octaves: E♭ to B♭; G to d; c to g. Modern machine drums range from 81 cm to 27 cm, giving a musical range

from D to b♭. The diameters of the standard pair of timpani are 71 cm and 63 cm, covering a range of one octave, and allowing composers a choice of upper or lower dominant in the keys of F and B♭. Modern timpani produce well-sounding notes in the lower register and, through an improved mechanism, no loss in the higher register. There is also no appreciable loss of tone in modern machine timpani generally, because of the well engineered outer mechanism and bowl suspension.

The advantage of three or more drums is that in addition to the added voice and the extended range the tone quality is improved, since the drums are needed more frequently in their middle register. Thus with careful planning on the part of composers the wide range of the possible 5th on each drum can be avoided. A further important factor governing the tone quality of a kettledrum is the condition and texture of the drumhead. Until the introduction (c1950) of the plastic head – a form of polyethylene terephthalate – timpani heads were invariably of calfskin. The best quality calfskins are those prepared from the hides of young animals in prime condition when slaughtered. Thereafter the hide is skilfully treated to preserve the skin during the process of unhairing, after which it is strengthened in lime liquor and stretched on a wooden frame. It is then scraped by hand or equalized by machinery to a thickness of from 0·125 to 0·175 mm. In general, thin heads are preferable on large drums, but the inconsistency of animal skin permits no firm ruling. To mount a vellum on the wooden flesh hoop, it must first be soaked in cold water until pliable and then lapped completely round the hoop. The lapped head is placed on the bowl and the counter-hoop adjusted to draw the head slightly over the shell, giving a 'collar' to compensate for shrinkage in the head as it dries out, thus ensuring the lower notes. In the case of many hand-screw drums with flesh heads, the flesh hoop fits the top of the shell with no greater clearance than is necessary to allow the head to move when tuned. In machine drums the flesh hoop is of metal and fits the shell with a greater clearance, and the drum is then said to have a 'floating head'. The synthetic drumhead (approximately the thickness of a stout calfskin head) is mounted to a metal flesh hoop by the involved process of 'sealing'. The floating head is by no means an innovation. The heads of certain age-old Eastern hourglass drums are mounted in this way, as were the heads on the cavalry kettledrums used as orchestral timpani in the Baroque period.

Opinions remain divided regarding the relative tonal qualities of the calf and plastic heads. Players who at one time condemned the plastic head now speak highly of it; others who for some time found the synthetic head acceptable have reverted to calfskin. All however agree that under extreme atmospheric conditions the synthetic material is preferable. In contrast to the calf head, a plastic drumhead is almost unaffected by atmospheric conditions. The animal skin however is particularly susceptible to humidity, a moisture-laden atmosphere causing the membrane to expand and consequently to produce flatter notes. At times, as for example in a poorly heated hall on a damp night, conditions can render the upper notes in the drum's range unobtainable. Conversely, a dry atmosphere tends to shrink a drumhead, causing notes to be sharp. These conditions have led to the use of heating or moisture-carrying units, normally fitted inside the bowl.

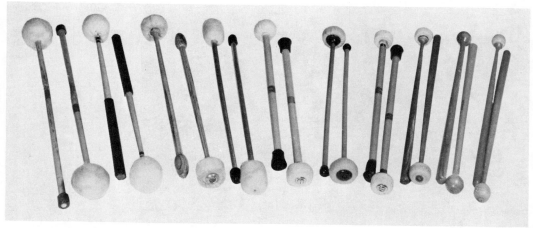

5. Some of the drumsticks used by a timpanist

2. TECHNIQUE. Timpani are played with a pair of drumsticks varying in design and texture according to the choice of the player, the work being played, and the instructions of the composer. To meet the demands of modern composers and to satisfy his own particular taste, the timpanist of today is equipped with a large variety of sticks ranging from those with large ends of soft felt to those with small ends of wood (fig.5). The length and thickness of the shaft, which is of hickory or similar straight-grained wood or malacca cane, varies according to the player's choice. The heads of the sticks vary in shape, size, weight and texture. In shape they vary from elliptical to pear-shaped, according to the area of contact and tone desired. The beating end of the normal timpani sticks consists of an inner core of hard felt, cork or balsa wood, which is covered with either one or two layers of felt (usually discs of white piano-damper felt, the discs being made into a small bag with drawn threads and fitting the core exactly). In general, the diameter of the heads ranges from about 2·5 to 5 cm. 'Hard' sticks have ends consisting of a small ball of wood or hard felt. 'Wooden' sticks are of two types: a small ball of wood fixed to the shaft, or the whole stick fashioned from suitable wood: ash, hickory or a similar wood. The sticks are held identically in each hand with the shaft nearly parallel with the drumhead and gripped firmly between the tip of the thumb and the first joint of the index finger at a point about 8 cm from the end of the stick – the precise distance being governed by its length and weight (see fig.6). In normal playing, the third and fourth fingers, which are clear of the shaft, act as a cushion.

In timpani playing alternate beating is the general rule. This is particularly applicable to the roll, which consists of a succession of single strokes of equal power. The speed of the roll is related to the tension on the drumhead, a greater speed being required to keep the head vibrating when tensioned to a high note. For musical purposes the correct striking point on the drumhead is approximately one eighth of the diameter of the shell from the rim; the exact position may be determined scientifically by the point of agitation of Lycopodium or similar powder on a vibrating drumhead. In orchestral performance a pair of timpani is placed side by side, the playing areas adjacent. Three or more drums are

placed in an arc. The arrangement of the drums varies according to the player's style, and in some respects to tradition. The majority of German, Russian, Austrian, Dutch and Czech timpanists position the large drum(s) to the right. With most American, British, Italian and French players, the large drum(s) are to the left. Those who adhere to the bass at the right hand quote the tradition of the cavalry kettledrums, this art being handed down for generations. It is argued by those who position the small drum(s) to the right hand, that this style of drumming has long existed, as for instance on the Indian *tablā*, and that timpani should be played in the same manner as the customary keyboard and mallet-played percussion instruments. Today, with the almost general use of pedal timpani, the drums are played from a seated position. The height of the drums is such that, in performance, the sticks lie horizontally.

The essentials of an orchestral timpanist are an accurate sense of pitch, the ability to produce a fine tone, an unerring sense of rhythm, and a fluent technique. The first requirement in the tuning of a kettledrum is the immediate recognition of the true pitch of the nominal or principal note of the drum. This note is one octave above the fundamental. Certain upper harmonics tend to register more strongly than the principal note until the ear is accustomed to the pitch of the drum, particularly

6. Normal grip for timpani sticks, demonstrated by James Blades

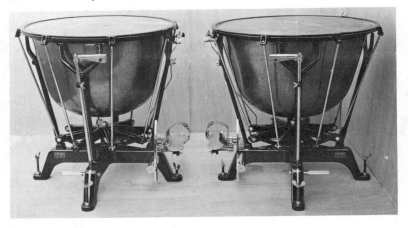

in view of the possibility of confusing pitch with tone, the brighter tone on the drumhead being mistaken for sharpness in pitch, while the duller-sounding places may be considered flat. To produce a true and resonant note the drumhead must be in good condition, even in texture and at the correct tension. In the initial tuning of a hand-tuned drum the opposite pairs of handles are turned simultaneously to ensure that the pressure is applied to the drumhead as evenly as possible. The head is then 'trued' by correcting the pitch at and between every tuning handle. In the case of machine drums, if the drumhead is even in texture and correctly tensioned, the raising and lowering of the counter-hoop in a single operation minimizes the 'trueing' process – one of the several advantages of this mechanism. The pitch of the drum is tested by flipping the drumhead at the playing spot with the fleshy part of the middle finger, or with a light touch of the drumstick. A further test – where time allows – is made by utilizing certain of the series of harmonics existing in an evenly tensioned drum. These harmonics are produced by humming the various tones into the drumhead close to the playing spot (a procedure which must be inaudible to all but the performer, and which has been responsible for the suggestion that the timpanist 'whispers to his drumskin'). The nominal and the 5th above (the second in the harmonic series from the fundamental) and the octave are particularly strong. In tuning, the 5th and the octave are the two harmonics most frequently used, the remainder of the series being the 10th, upper 5th, 7th and octave. The phenomenon of sympathetic resonance is also used advantageously by the timpanist in the process of tuning. With a pair of drums accurately tuned in 5ths the lower drum will 'sing' when the higher drum is struck.

The problem for the timpanist with the methods described above is how he can be certain that the process of tuning is audible to none but himself. To tune two or more drums in the silence of an empty concert hall, or while the orchestra is tuning up, is simple, but it is difficult to change pitch while the orchestra is playing in a key foreign to that to which the timpani are to be tuned. Instant recognition of the drum's note, however quietly elicited, and absolute or relative pitch are essential for good intonation. In performance the timpanist will compare the pitch of a drum with an identifiable or cued note in the orchestra. The pitch of forthcoming notes is often determined by using already

established notes as reference notes. Though the modern timpanist is obliged to cope with considerably more changes of pitch than were his predecessors, it must be said that his superbly engineered kettledrums have eased many problems that existed hitherto. When changing pitch, given favourable conditions, both atmospheric and mechanical, the player has his task relatively predetermined. The tuning gauges fitted to the majority of machine drums are a reasonable guide, particularly on instruments fitted with plastic heads. These gauges are controlled by the 'travel' on the foot pedal or the movement of the counter-hoop, and though by no means regarded as the ultimate in fine tuning, have certain advantages when making rapid changes on a number of drums. It is at such times that an approximation is necessary, for the player must strike the drum in performance before checking the pitch.

Good intonation also depends on correct tone production. Tone quality on the timpani is dependent on several factors: the construction of the drum; the quality and careful tuning of the drumhead; the type of sticks employed; and not least the skill of the player. To produce the best possible tone the stick must be immediately withdrawn from the drum after the blow has been delivered. If the blow is clumsy, loss of resonance and inaccuracy in pitch result from the slight lag and pressure of the drumstick on the head. In addition to the tonal differences produced with variously graded drumsticks, the drumhead is occasionally struck at varying distances from the rim, near the rim for a particularly soft tone, towards the centre for a 'thick' tone – the least resonant sound being produced towards the centre. In a crescendo roll the player may commence the roll near the rim of the drum, and with the increasing rise and fall of the sticks move them towards the 'playing spot', reversing the procedure in the case of a diminuendo roll. The careful player will ensure that the best register of each drum is used for the more important or solo passages, the positioning of such notes often requiring rapid changes on pedal-tuned timpani. Such expedients are but one of the several advantages of machine drums which the layman associates almost exclusively with glissandos.

The foundation of timpani technique is a fluent hand-to-hand performance, as wherever possible the drums are played with strokes from alternate hands. The double beat on the left or right hand is used only when necessary, perhaps to avoid a difficult crossover beat. At speed certain crossover beats are not practicable: there is the possibility of the drumsticks fouling each other (or the rim), or the danger of the drum being struck away from the correct playing spot. In the case of a cross-beat at a fast speed between two drums some distance apart the impetus of the movement adds strength to the stroke, which may result in an unintended *sforzando*. It is in such circumstances that the timpanist uses a double beat, often in the form of a 'paradiddle'. In the paradiddle the first two beats are struck by alternate sticks and the last two by one alone, as in ex.1. To prevent notes ringing on beyond their

Ex.1

time value and where there are *sec* effects, the vibrations are checked by a process known as 'damping'. In damping, the drumhead is touched lightly with the flattened second, third and fourth fingers (the stick being held between the thumb and forefinger). Where the speed of a series of short notes renders this method of damping impracticable, a small piece of felt is placed on the drumhead. The practice of damping or 'muting' the kettledrum is frequently met in orchestral scores. It is indicated by the words *coperti* (It.), *couvertes* or *voilé* (Fr.), or *Dämpfer* (Ger.). *Naturale* (or *scoperti*) is used when the muted effect is to cease. Composers utilize this muted quality of sound for clarifying certain passages, or to obtain a funereal effect. In contrast to the 'shortening' of certain notes, two drums may occasionally be tuned to the same note and struck simultaneously to ensure greater sonority. Grace notes on the timpani may be single, double or triple. Whether they are written before the bar or inside it but before the main note, the main stroke normally coincides with the music's accent. The use of the acciaccatura is rare, as is the striking of the drum with both sticks simultaneously. The latter is indicated by giving the note two tails.

3. HISTORY. The invention of the kettledrum goes back to remotest antiquity. Kettle-shaped hollow tree trunks, tortoise-shells, and clay bowls covered with hide were among the musical instruments of ancient people. Firm evidence of the early use of a kettledrum (shaped like a goblet) comes from a Babylonian plaque *c*700 BC (fig.8). Small kettledrums (*throph*) are considered to have been used by the Israelites. Kircher (*Musurgia universalis*, Rome, 1650/*R*1970) was of the opinion that the Hebrews took the kettledrum from the Egyptians. Greek vases from the 4th century BC are unanimous in representations of the *tympanon*. The instrument is portrayed in various sizes and is usually bowl-shaped. Plutarch (AD 46–120) referred to a certain big basin covered with leather used by the Persians as a war drum. Suidas wrote of the kettle-shaped drums (*dundubhi*) made of pine wood and covered with heads of bull hide, which were used by Indian tribes in battle. Use of a pair of kettledrums, one giving a higher note than the other, appeared in the Middle East in early Islamic times and was adopted in Europe for martial music in consort with trumpets and pipes during the

13th-century crusades. The drums were of the small, thong-tightened kind still in use among various peoples of the Middle East (*see* NAKERS, fig.1). Arabian kettledrums, hemispherical or egg-shaped, measuring approximately 50 cm and 60 cm in diameter, played mounted on camel or horse (see fig.9), reached the West from the Ottoman Empire during the 15th century, and inspired the European use of cavalry kettledrums, which in their turn began to be put to orchestral use in the 17th century. Larger kettledrums were also introduced to western Europe in the 15th century, the earliest known report of them being in the train of a Hungarian envoy to France in 1457. The size of these instruments prompted a Father Benoît to say that he had never before seen such drums 'like large cauldrons . . . carried on horseback'. Virdung (*Musica getutscht*, 1511) wrote

8. *Kettledrum and ?cymbals: detail from a Babylonian plaque (c700 BC) in the British Museum, London*

9. *Trumpets and kettledrums: miniature from the 'Al-Maqāmāt of Harīrī', Baghdad, 1237, illustrated by Yaḥyā ibn Maḥmūd al-Wāsiti (F-Pn arabe 5847, f.19v)*

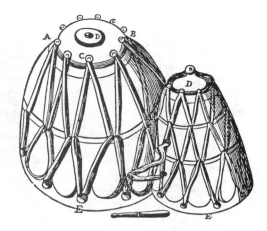

11(a)

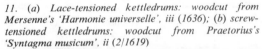

10. Artillery kettledrums: detail showing a grenadier furling a captured standard, from the Brussels tapestry 'The Battle of Blenheim' (c1710) at Blenheim Palace, Oxford

11. (a) Lace-tensioned kettledrums: woodcut from Mersenne's 'Harmonie universelle', iii (1636); (b) screw-tensioned kettledrums: woodcut from Praetorius's 'Syntagma musicum', ii (2/1619)

11(b)

12. Screw-tensioned kettledrums (left foreground) amongst the instruments of an 18th-century court: painting (1772) by Peter Jakob Horemans in the Bayerisches Nationalmuseum, Munich

disapprovingly of the big army kettledrums of copper, called *tympana*, which he believed to be the invention of the Devil. Kettledrums were already in use in certain English cavalry regiments in the 16th century, their novelty attracting the interest of Henry VIII, who ordered the purchase of a number of Viennese kettledrums for playing on horseback, and the hire of skilled performers. Almost invariably played in company with trumpets – usually 12 trumpets and one pair of drums – the drums constituted an ensemble that became a royal preserve and which remained so for a considerable time. In Germany similar ensembles were equally exalted and various imperial decrees had led in 1623 to the establishment of the Imperial Guild of Trumpeters and Kettledrummers. Kettledrums mounted on a carriage were known in England towards the close of the 17th century. Notable instruments of this type include the kettledrums in 'Marlborough's train of 1702' (the great kettledrums of the artillery, see fig.10), and the large drums (96 cm and 101 cm) in the Rotunda Museum, Woolwich, London, which, according to the museum's catalogue, were used in Strasbourg Cathedral before the French Revolution as an accompaniment to the organ in military music.

The earliest illustrations of kettledrums indicate various systems of laced and tensioned vellums, similar to the bracing of nakers and the larger Arabic kettledrums. This method of applying pressure to the head was used throughout the 16th century. Mersenne depicted laced kettledrums as late as 1636 (fig.11*a*). Screw-tensioning was adopted in Germany as early as the start of the 16th century. Throughout that century and onwards there are numerous representations of kettledrums with 'side screws' varying in number, and applying pressure directly to a flesh hoop, or indirectly to it through the medium of a counter-hoop (fig.11*b*). With these early kettledrums, which generally had bowls of copper, the screws in all cases were turned by means of a 'loose key'. In the majority of drums the screws are square-topped, though there are instances of the head of the screw being shaped to form a ring through which a short rod would have been passed. The diameter of the bowl varies. Arbeau referred to a width of 76 cm (Mersenne and Virdung said 60 cm). The instruments (*Heerpauken*) in the diagrams by Praetorius in his *Syntagma musicum*, ii (2/1619), are certainly smaller – 44·5 and 52 cm in diameter. A Russian kettledrum (*tulumbaz*), *c*1650, in the Leningrad Institute of Music measures 86 cm in diameter. It has eight square-topped tensioning screws and a floating head suspended over a copper bowl. Bowls of silver are used only on special presentation drums, such as the kettledrums presented to the 'Blues' by George III and those given to the Life Guards by William IV.

The sticks used on early kettledrums are represented in numerous styles, sometimes with round ends, sometimes oval or curved and quite often with narrow ends. There are literary references to wood and ivory ends. The heads of the beaters illustrated by Rembrandt, in his *Negro Commander and Kettle Drummer*, *c*1638, are large and suggest a lighter material than ivory or wood. In some instances kettledrum sticks are illustrated with straps for securing to the wrist. Certain types are grooved to give a secure grip. It has been said that no great amount of musicianship was demanded from the early cavalry kettledrummer, though it is un-

likely that 'one drum up and one drum down' was acceptable in all cases.

By the early part of the 17th century the kettledrums followed the trumpet into the orchestra in church music. The improvement in the construction of the drums and their constant association with cavalry trumpets had no doubt led to a more accurate tuning than hitherto, it being generally conceded that in the early stages the drums functioned much as their Arabian and Egyptian forebears, the large and small drums giving a difference in pitch, with such differentiation used only to distinguish between the pair of drums for rhythmical purposes. In Europe, tuning in 4ths was the general rule, a method derived from the technique of the trumpet. For the most part the drums were treated as transposing instruments and a pair notated as *c* and *G* (or occasionally *g*). For some time the lower drum of a pair was styled the 'G' drum and the higher-sounding instrument the 'C' drum.

4. REPERTORY. The introduction of the kettledrums into the orchestra has been generally attributed to Lully in his opera *Thésée* (1675). A festival mass (*c*1682), written for performance at Salzburg Cathedral and long wrongly attributed to Orazio Benevoli, calls for two combinations of trumpets and timpani. The drums were tuned in 4ths (*c* and *G*) and had individual parts for each pair. Three works by Malachias Siebenhaarm consisting of sacred vocal music with instrumental accompaniment, published *c*1600, specify on the title-page 'Heerpauken'. In the French military circles of this period substantial solo parts for the kettledrums appear. In 1685 a volume was published of *Pièces de trompettes et timbales à 2, 3, et 4 parties* by André Philidor. In the same year a march for two pairs of kettledrums was composed by André Philidor and his brother Jacques in which one pair of drums was tuned normally to *c* and *G* and the other to *e* and *g*, an unusual tuning for this period. Equally interesting are the *Marches de timbales* composed by Bablon, who was Louis XIV's *timbalier des plaisirs* (a highly-paid occupation, demanding private service at the king's pleasure). Bablon asked for two drums to be struck simultaneously to produce a chord, the earliest known written instance of this device, which has been attributed (as far as the orchestra is concerned) both to J. P. A. Martini in his opera *Sappho* (1793) and to Beethoven in his Ninth Symphony. Lully made interesting use of the timpani (*tymbales*) in his operas *Thésée*, *Achille et Polixène*, *Bellérophon* and *Proserpine*. In all cases a pair of drums was employed, tuned in 4ths with the dominant below the tonic. The Moravian composer Vejvanovský scored for timpani (*tamburini*) in his 23rd and 27th serenades (*c*1680). In the former the drums are tuned in 5ths, with the dominant (*g*) above the tonic (*c*) – a most unusual tuning at this period. By the close of the 17th century kettledrums were firmly established as orchestral instruments. Purcell, realizing their musical significance, entrusted them in the Symphony to Act 4 of his opera *The Fairy Queen* (1692) with what is considered to be their first orchestral solo passage (ex.2). Purcell also included the timpani in *The Indian Queen* and the Ode for St Cecilia's Day (1692).

Ex. 2

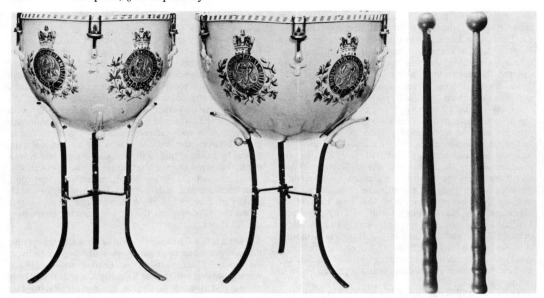

13. Screw-tensioned kettledrums by an unknown maker, English, c1810, and a pair of wooden drumsticks of approximately the same date (private collection)

Little is known about the use of the timpani in the orchestra between the music of Purcell and that of Bach and Handel. That kettledrums continued to be used in the orchestra is apparent from pictorial evidence concerning church and theatrical performances. In orchestras at the time of Bach and Handel the drums were cavalry kettledrums recruited for orchestral use; the range of well-sounding notes on these small drums (possibly 51 and 56 cm in diameter) may have restricted their common use to the trumpeter's keys of D and C. In the first key the drums were tuned in 4ths (to the tonic and dominant) to *d* and *A*, in the second to *c* and *G*. In the rare instances that Bach used the timpani in the key of G, the dominant is above the tonic. Where Bach used the drums in the key of B♭ the dominant is below the tonic (in their lowest possible register). This tuning occurs only in Cantata 143, here with three horns.

In general Bach treated the drums as transposing instruments, writing their parts in C in the bass clef with the actual notes indicated at the start of the work (ex.3).

Ex.3
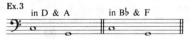

The pitch of the drums (never more than a pair) remained unchanged throughout an entire work. Where there was a change of key the drums were silent, awaiting the return of the original key. The timpani usually supported the brass or full choir, and it was only on rare occasions that Bach gave them a solo part or obbligato. Outstanding examples of his use of the timpani include *Vereinigte Zwietracht der wechselnden Saiten*, *Aeolus*, *Gott ist mein König*, the B minor Mass, *Tönet ihr Pauken!* and the *Christmas Oratorio*. At the beginning of the *Christmas Oratorio* (derived from *Tönet ihr Pauken!*)

the drums herald the choir's motif of rejoicing ('Jauchzet, frohlocket'). The then little-used roll is clearly indicated in this work. On many occasions in Bach's timpani parts (and those of subsequent composers), a closing note is indicated by a pause; a roll is occasionally employed at the discretion of the performer and conductor. The bulk of literary evidence refers to the 'dull thudding sound' or the 'harsh tone' of the orchestral drums at the time of Bach, due mainly to the frequent use of hard sticks. It could be argued, however, that Bach's timpanists produced a sufficiently musical tone to meet the demands of such a master, and that Bach would not have scored for the drums over a long period had he considered them unmusical. It is also unlikely that the timpanists of the 18th century (Bach's, Handel's and Haydn's included) would have rejected the aid afforded by covered sticks in the execution of certain tremolos and delicate passages.

Handel's use of drums was chiefly rhythmical, with no change of pitch throughout the entire work, and generally in company with trumpets and choir. In certain respects he differed from Bach; with the exception of *Il Parnasso in festa* (1734) he adhered rigidly to the interval of a 4th between a pair of drums. (In *Il Parnasso in festa* Handel used the drums in G and D – indicated 'scord' – in the key of B♭: presumably a special effect.) Like Bach, Handel was fully aware of the kettledrummer's craft. In *Semele* there occurs a series of semiquavers (*d–d–A–A*, *ċ–d–A–A*). These were known to timpanists of his day as 'double tonguing' – a technical term borrowed, with others, by German kettledrummers from the trumpeters a century or so earlier. Similar florid writing occurs in the overture to the *Music for the Royal Fireworks* where Handel prescribes 'Tymp 3 per parte'. The simpler scoring for the timpani in the

'Hallelujah chorus' of *Messiah* is generally recognized as one of the most thrilling and effective parts ever written for kettledrums. For his oratorios Handel constantly requested (and was granted) the use of the great kettledrums of the artillery – the Train Kettle Drums which were also known as the Tower Drums. These instruments, which are said to have been destroyed in a fire in 1841, are thought to have measured 76 and 96·5 cm. If so it is doubtful if the notes prescribed by Handel were heard in the written register.

Towards the middle of the 18th century a number of compositions introduced decided advances in the use of orchestral timpani. The first of these was a Concerto grosso written in 1743 by Francesco Barsanti. During the work the drums are heard in three keys: F, D and C. A further advance is seen in a Sinfonia for eight obbligato timpani with orchestra attributed to J. W. Hertel (*c*1748) in which there is a complete cadenza for the drums. In a work by J. M. Molter (Sinfonia no.99, written *c*1750) five kettledrums are used, the tuning being *F, G, A, B♭* and *c*. Unusual tunings are found in works by Salieri, whose treatment of the timpani could well have influenced his pupil Beethoven. In the opera *La grotta di Trofonio* (1785) Salieri used the unusual interval of C and G♭. In *Tarare* (1787) the drums are tuned a minor 3rd apart. Further unusual tunings are found in works by F. Gassmann and Sacchini. In his opera *L'Issipile* (1758) Gassmann used a drum in *a*, and in *Oedipe à Colone* (1786) Sacchini scored for four drums tuned to *B♭, b♭, F, f* (an early use of octaves).

Haydn, himself a timpanist, graced many of his symphonies and choral works with finely written parts for the timpani. The solo roll (on *e♭*) which opens Symphony no.103 (1795) was an effect new to the orchestra and gave the work its name: *Paukenwirbel*. In *The Creation* (1799) there are seven changes of tuning. In Symphony no.102 (1794) he prescribed covered kettledrums ('con sordini') with muted trumpets; an effect used earlier by Mozart and termed 'coperti' in *Idomeneo* (1781) and *Die Zauberflöte* (1791). (This effect was, and is still, applied to military kettledrums.)

Mozart made superb use of the timpani. Like Haydn and Bach he made no unusual demands on the timpanist. With only one exception he confined the tuning of the drums (a pair) to the interval of a 4th, with the tonic in its usual position above the dominant. This interval is so consistently observed that the timpani are omitted from works in the keys of G and A for instance where, because of the compass of the drums, the interval of a 5th with the dominant above the tonic would be necessary.

With such composers as Mozart and his predecessors the kettledrums had usually functioned in 4ths and 5ths. Beethoven made exemplary use of other intervals and so fully exploited the resources of the timpani that they became in every sense musical instruments. In *Fidelio* he employed (significantly) a pair a diminished 5th apart. Later, in the Scherzo of the Seventh Symphony the drums are a minor 6th apart, and in the Eighth and Ninth Symphonies they are tuned in octaves. Though Beethoven prescribed only two drums, he chose with consummate care the particular drum to be used at any given moment. He was equally careful in the manner by which he indicated the true roll: always with the tremolo sign. Where Beethoven wrote a note with its stem struck

through three times (frequently used today to denote a roll) he intended the demisemiquavers to be strictly observed. His important solo passages, his remarkable use of the roll, and the effect of his *pianissimo* (described as 'marvellous' by Berlioz), suggest that he, like Haydn, may have had a personal acquaintance with the instrument. Surprisingly, Beethoven (and his predecessors) specified no particular type of drumsticks, an omission which distressed Berlioz. Outstanding passages for the timpani in Beethoven's works include the use of chords and octave F's in the Ninth Symphony, the four solo notes to open the Violin Concerto, the remarkable roll covering 25 bars and the solo passage for two drums in the Fourth Symphony, the combination of timpani and soloist in the finale of the Fifth Piano Concerto, the transition from the Scherzo to the Finale of the Fifth Symphony and the recurring demisemiquavers in the first movement of the Ninth Symphony. Beethoven's works, though presenting occasional technical challenges, are so scrupulously planned that there is nothing beyond the ability of a competent timpanist.

With Beethoven and his predecessors, and such composers as Schubert, Mendelssohn and Rossini, there are occasional dissonances which suggest the lack of a third drum or the means of a 'quick change'. There are also many occasions where the drums are silent when, had it been practical to employ them, there seems little doubt that a part would have been given to them. The question of amendment is controversial. Owing no doubt to the demands of such composers as Beethoven and subsequent Romantic composers, the first half of the 19th century was a period of constant experiment and progress in the construction of orchestral timpani, particularly with an invention for instantaneous tuning. Innovators in almost every country in Europe made their contribution towards perfecting the mechanically tuned kettledrum. In 1812 Gerhard Cramer of Munich was responsible for a device whereby the turning of a central screw operated all screws simultaneously. In 1821, J. C. N. Stumpff of Amsterdam applied variable tension by rotating the bowl of the drum. Labbaye (a French postman) introduced a mechanically tuned drum with a regulated system indicating the pressure on the vellum as early as 1827. In 1837, Cornelius Ward of London patented a cable-tuned kettledrum in which a pitch indicator was incorporated (fig.14). 1840 saw a single-screw internal mechanism by Boracchi, an Italian, drawings of which resemble Ward's drum. Other experiments at this time included models operated by a hand-controlled crank, and those involving a series of foot-pedals operating on internal concentric rings. In 1855 Adolphe Sax constructed a species of *timbale* which he called *trompette-timbale*. In this instrument a vellum was stretched over a long conical resonator, and the pitch changed by adjusting the column of vibrated air by means of pedal-operated shutters. (Sax may have been influenced by the *tubo timpanite*, 'the drum with the far-carrying sound' suggested in the 17th century by Kircher and illustrated in Bonanni's *Gabinetto armonico*, 1723.) A further inspiration from Sax came in the form of *timbales chromatiques*, a series of kettledrums in which the normal bowl was replaced by a shallow cylinder. In 1856 H. J. Distin of London patented a drum with rod-tensioning on the exterior of the kettle, on the lines of a German model of 1851. A similar drum was patented by Henry Potter in 1884. Earlier (in 1862)

14. Cable-tuned kettledrum (with head removed) by Cornelius Ward, London, c1840 (Royal Military School of Music, Kneller Hall)

a system of tuning by means of cams operating on an internal ring was introduced by Köhler & Sons of London. In theory, this instrument was well engineered, but in practice, as with earlier systems, the proximity of the inner mechanism to the vellum impaired the tone of the drum. Improved continental inventions included models tuned by means of a single handle and rotary and foot-pedal tuning. Among the most advanced were the 19th-century instruments by Hudler of Vienna, Pfundt of Leipzig and Pittrich of Dresden. Advanced as these drums were in comparison with hand-tuned timpani, their limitations were such that composers made no significant demands on them until the 20th century.

Berlioz, who pioneered so successfully the use of other percussion instruments, made no mention of the use of machine timpani. From his remarks in his *Grand traité d'instrumentation* it seems that one pair of timpani was common in the majority of orchestras, though it is reasonably certain that he was not unaware of the use of three or more drums by certain of his predecessors, for instance, Molter, Salieri, Mozart, Weber, Auber and Reicha. Reicha (who taught Berlioz), in a setting of an ode by Schiller, employed eight drums in four pairs tuned chromatically. Weber used three drums in *Peter Schmoll* (1803) and *Der Beherrscher der Geister* (1811). Spohr in his oratorio *Calvary* (1833) scored for six timpani. In his *Grande messe des morts* (1837) Berlioz outstripped Reicha by using 16 kettledrums operated by ten players (the original manuscript specified 16 pairs of timpani). Berlioz made every effort to clarify his drum parts, giving constant instructions for the use of soft or hard sticks. In the *Symphonie fantastique* the rumble of thunder (played on four drums) is carefully marked 'with sponge-headed sticks'. In the March to the Scaffold there are instructions for both hard- and soft-ended sticks, and precise instructions as to how to perform certain figures.

The time of Berlioz was a period of considerable revolution in the orchestra (particularly in the use of percussion). Bellini made active use of the timpani in his

operas, and in 1831 in Meyerbeer's MS score of *Robert le diable*, a melody (solo) is given to four kettledrums. Wagner's scoring for the timpani throughout the *Ring* and elsewhere is typical of this masterly composer. Russian composers such as Glinka, Tchaikovsky, Rimsky-Korsakov, Stravinsky, Prokofiev and Shostakovich made heavy demands on the timpani. Glinka employed the *g* drum most effectively in the solo for the timpani in *Ruslan and Lyudmila* (1842), as did Rimsky-Korsakov in his *Russian Festival Overture* (1888). In the Finale of *Romeo and Juliet*, Tchaikovsky wrote the well-known 'heartbeat' and the awesome crescendo solo roll. Stravinsky's use of the timpani is exemplary, as is his use of other percussion. In *The Rite of Spring*, five drums including a piccolo drum tuned to *b* are struck simultaneously. In 1916 Stravinsky made use of glissandos on the timpani in *Renard* ('gliss pour le Timb a le·ier'). An exacting part for pedal drums occurs in his *Introitus* (1965), a work using two players. In *Peter and the Wolf*, Prokofiev used three timpani to create the effect of gunfire. Shostakovich gave a solo to three drums in the last movement of his First Symphony.

Mahler used three players in his Second Symphony (1894). In this work and in his Seventh Symphony (1906) he scored for a *D♭* drum. This was probably the first time the instrument was written for in this low register. In his Fourth and Eighth Symphonies he ensured forceful accents by stipulating that two sticks were to be used simultaneously on the same drum. Mahler seems not to have considered the use of machine timpani, for in the last movement of his First Symphony (1888), at a point during a tremolo when the pitch of one of the drums is lowered a semitone, instructions are given for the second timpanist to effect the change.

One of the earliest and clearest examples of the use of pedal timpani is the chromatic run in the second movement of d'Indy's *Jour d'été à la montagne* (1905), where d'Indy specified *timbales chromatiques*. In the same year Strauss called for machine drums in *Salome*; there is, for example, a rising passage in full tones in the Dance of the Seven Veils. Credit for the earliest use of the glissando on the timpani may well be due to Walford Davies who, in his *Conversations* for Piano and Orchestra (1914), wrote glissandos as well as chromatic and other passages. Nielsen's use of glissandos in his Fourth Symphony (1914–16) is unique. Here, Nielsen wrote for two timpanists, who play a passage in minor 3rds rising chromatically and marked 'gliss'.

While machine drums have made many effects possible on the timpani, a 'drum for each note' is vital in the case of sequences such as those in Strauss's *Burleske*, Elgar's 'Enigma' Variations ('Troyte') and Holst's *Beni Mora* Suite. Holst, like Elgar, requested many unique tone-colours. In *The Perfect Fool* (1923) he specified the use of one felt stick and one wooden stick. Elgar in the 'Enigma' Variations ('Romanza') asked for a roll with side drum sticks, though it became the custom, with Elgar's permission, to perform this tremolo with two coins. Other examples of a special timbre include Stanford's use of the tremolo with fingertips (*Songs of the Fleet*, 1910), and Britten's request for *ruthe* in his opera *Death in Venice* (1973). Requests for chords and extremely high notes requiring piccolo timpani are common, outstanding examples of the latter being found in *Lakmé* (where Delibes specified *petites timbales*), Milhaud's *La création du monde*, 1923 (*f♯'* and *d'*); Ravel's *L'enfant et les sortilèges* (*d'*); and works by Janáček. *D* and *D♭*

occur frequently today. In rare cases *timpani bassi* are requested. Stokowski in his arrangement of Bach's *Komm, süsser Tod* wrote for *C*, and Harsanyi in his *Suite pour orchestre* requested *B'*.

From 1930 onwards, with improved instruments and the influence of Bartók, the possibilities of pedal timpani were greatly exploited. In his *Cantata profana* (1930) Bartók frequently used glissandos, at times rising and falling simultaneously (as also in his Music for Strings, Percussion and Celesta (1937) and the Sonata for Two Pianos and Percussion (1937)). Britten also made extensive use of pedal timpani, a notable example being the decidedly challenging obbligato ('But that night') in his *Nocturne* for tenor solo, seven obbligato instruments and string orchestra (1958). In this work the ascending and descending passages are chromatic in all cases, and are carefully planned so that each drum restarts on the note on which it has been previously halted.

Further exacting requirements from the orchestral timpanist include Bliss's *Pastoral* 'Lie strewn the white flocks' (of 1928), Walton's First Symphony (1935), in which two timpanists each with three drums play in duet, Tippett's First Symphony (1945) and the opera *King Priam* (1962), Hartmann's Second Symphony (1960), Symphony no.7 (1968) by Egon Wellesz and Elliott Carter's Concerto for Orchestra (1969). Works for unaccompanied timpani include Daniel Jones's Sonata for three unaccompanied kettledrums (1953), Carter's *Recitative and Improvisation* (six pieces for kettledrums, 1966) and Sonatina for timpani (1967) by Alan Ridout. Concertos for timpani and orchestra include March and Polonaise for six timpani and orchestra by Julius Tausch (*c*1878), Tcherepnin's Sonatina for two (or three) timpani (1940, revised 1951), the Concerto for timpani and orchestra by Werner Thärichen (1954), Concerto for five kettledrums and orchestra by Robert Parris (1955), Concerto for timpani and orchestra by Harold Farbermann (1962) and *Mytho logica* (1962) by Karl Heinz Köper. The drums have a prominent part in Poulenc's Concerto in G minor for organ, strings and timpani (1939). The Dutch composer Henk Badings combined timpani and organ in his *Passacaglia* (1958) as did Elizabeth Poston in her choral work *Superest plebs pessima* (1961).

In orchestral music the part for the timpani is written in the bass clef. The required notes are frequently indicated at the start of a work. Directions to change pitch are indicated by 'change to' or 'muta in'.

BIBLIOGRAPHY

G. Kastner: *Instrumentation* (Paris, 1837)
V. de Pontigny: 'On Kettledrums', *PMA*, ii (1875–6), 48
P. R. Kirby: *The Kettle-drums* (Oxford, 1930)
C. S. Terry: *Bach's Orchestra* (Oxford, 1932)
J. Jeans: *Science and Music* (Cambridge, 1947)
S. Goodman: *Modern Method for Tympani* (New York, 1948)
H. Farmer: *Handel's Kettledrums* (London, 1950)
C. Titcomb: 'Baroque Court and Military Trumpets and Kettledrums', *GSJ*, ix (1956), 56
A. Shivas: *The Art of Tympanist and Drummer* (London, 1957)
G. Avgerinos: *Lexicon der Pauke* (Frankfurt am Main, 1964)
H. W. Taylor: *The Art and Science of the Timpani* (London, 1964)
J. Blades: *Percussion Instruments and their History* (London, 1970, 2/1974)
D. Charlton: 'Salieri's Timpani', *MT*, cxii (1971), 961
D. L. Smithers: 'The Hapsburg Imperial *Trompeter* and *Heerpaucker* Privileges of 1653', *GSJ*, xxiv (1971), 84
D. P. Charlton: *Orchestration and Orchestral Practice in Paris, 1789–1810* (diss., U. of Cambridge, 1973)

JAMES BLADES

Tímpano (Sp.). DULCIMER.

Timp-tom. See TOM-TOM.

Timre (Fr.). SNARES.

Tinazzoli, Agostino (*b* Bologna, 2nd half of the 17th century; *d* ?Pesaro, *c*1723). Italian composer and organist. He was an organist in Ferrara around 1690 and then went to Rome, where he was imprisoned for a time in the Castel Sant'Angelo for an unspecified offence. While there, he is said to have written a cantata, *In carcere penoso privo* (in *D-Bds, Mbs, I-Nc*), scratching it on the wall of his cell with a piece of charcoal. On his release he returned to his native Emilia-Romagna, but then moved to the Marches, where he was a *maestro di cappella* and opera director in Recanati in 1720 and at the Teatro del Sole in Pesaro in 1721–2. He apparently did not write any operas of his own, but he did compose numbers for insertion in those of others. A set of *Sonate e capricci per l'organo* (Rome, 1690), often listed among his works, may be wrongly attributed.

WORKS

Sacred: Il sacrificio di Gefte, oratorio, 1718; Mass, 4vv, 2 vn, bc, *A-Wn*; 4 requiem movts; Dixit Dominus, 4vv, 2 vn, va, bc, *D-Mbs*
Other vocal: madrigals, cantatas, 1–2vv, bc, *D-Mbs, GB-Lbm, I-Bc, Nc*; inserted nos. in operas: Orlandini's La costanza trionfante, Recanati, 1720, Gasparini's Il Sesostri, re d'egitto, Recanati, 1720, Orlandini's Lucio Papirio, Pesaro, 1721, C. F. Pollarolo's La Ginevra, Pesaro, 1721, Orlandini's L'amor tirannico, Pesaro, 1722
Inst: 13 sonatas, hpd, org, *D-MÜs*; Sonata da camera, hpd, org, *I-Bc*

BIBLIOGRAPHY

EitnerQ; *RicordiE*

MILTON SUTTER

Tinctoris [Tinctor, Teinturier, de Vaerwere, Färbers], **Johannes** (*b* Braine l'Alleud, nr. Nivelles, *c*1435; *d* ?1511). Franco-Flemish theorist and composer. He was one of the most important music theorists of his time; his writings are a valuable source of information on the music of the Renaissance, including instruments, performing practice and notation.

1. Life. 2. Treatises. 3. Music.

1. LIFE. His place of birth is taken from the matriculation registers of the German Nation of Orleans University, where he matriculated on 1 April 1463; at that time he was instructor of the choirboys (*choralium pedagogus*) at the Cathedral of Orleans. Elsewhere in the register he is described as 'venerabilis dominus magister' (see Ridderikhoff and Ridder-Symoens). Trithemius described him as 'doctor utriusque juris, maximus mathematicus, summus musicus' and 'archicapellanus et cantor Regis Ferdinandi Neapolitani' (*Catalogus illustrium virorum*, Mainz, *c*1495). According to *De inventione et usu musicae* Tinctoris taught music to the choirboys of Chartres Cathedral. Vander Straeten's opinion that he was one of two brothers born in Poperinge, west Flanders, in 1445, which is based on the matriculation registers of Louvain University for 1471 and 1475, must be regarded as untenable; it is doubtful whether Tinctoris was the Master of Arts registered there in 1471 (Reusens's register for that period cited several people of that name), but he may be identifiable with a singer at Cambrai Cathedral under Dufay in 1460. The alternative forms of his name are found only in later writings; in the sources he is always referred to as 'Tinctoris'.

Tinctoris entered the service of King Ferdinand I of Naples, probably about 1472, as tutor to the king's

Portrait from a late 15th-century source of Tinctoris's treatises, thought to represent him (E-VAu 835); as the manuscript was compiled during his time in Naples (the decoration of the first leaf of the text, including the portrait, appears to be the work of the Neapolitan artist Cristoforo Majorana), the portrait could have been taken from life

daughter Beatrice. It is known that he visited Ferrara for four days in May 1479. His presence is once again recorded at the Neapolitan court on 27 October 1480, and he must have known Gaffurius, who was teaching in Naples at this time. Tinctoris styled himself in various ways in his treatises, giving useful information about his positions at court: 'magister' and 'cappellanus'; 'inter cantores minimus' and 'inter musicae professores minimus'; 'in legibus licentiatus' and 'jurisconsultus'; 'legum artiumque professor' and 'inter legum et artium mathematicarum professores minimus'. In 1487 Ferdinand commissioned him to recruit singers from the French king, Charles VIII, and the King of the Romans, Maximilian. A poem that Tinctoris wrote in homage to Pope Alexander VI suggests that he spent some time in Rome in 1492. It is not known whether he died in Naples or in his home town of Nivelles, where he was a canon and prebendary. He probably died in 1511, for on 12 October of that year his prebend was transferred to Petrus de Coninck.

2. TREATISES. Only two of Tinctoris's surviving treatises were published during his lifetime, and only two can be dated precisely. Of the various attempts to date the others Schäfke's seem most plausible. Tinctoris's most important and best-known treatise is *Terminorum musicae diffinitorium*, which contains 299 definitions of the terms then current in *musica plana* and *musica mensurabilis*; it is the oldest printed music dictionary. The other treatises between them cover the principal subjects of theoretical writing of the period. The *Complexus effectuum musices* discusses the traditional powers ascribed to music: its ethical, educational and therapeutic uses, its aesthetic value and its role in religion (including exorcism). The *Proportionale musices*, the *Liber imperfectionum*, the

Tractatus de regulari valore notarum and the *Tractatus alterationum* deal with different aspects of mensural notation. The *Tractatus de notis et pausis* covers the symbols and values of various notes and rests, and the *Scriptum super punctis musicalibus* deals with the points of division, augmentation and perfection. The *Expositio manus* and the *De inventione et usu musicae* are concerned with practical music: the first covers in nine chapters the practices of solmization and mutation, and the extant sections of the second deal with the art of singing and flute and lute playing, with references to famous performers. The two remaining treatises are on the art of writing music. The *Liber de natura et proprietate tonorum* discusses in 51 chapters the characteristics of the system of church modes as applied to music. The *Liber de arte contrapuncti* is the most comprehensive treatise, comprising three books of 19, 34 and nine chapters respectively; the first and second books contain the principles of consonance and dissonance, while the third discusses the rules for writing using consonant intervals. The treatise also includes (book 2, chapter 19) a discussion of the difference between note-against-note counterpoint (*contrapunctus simplex*) and more florid writing (*contrapunctus diminutus vel floridus*), and (chapter 20) a discussion of the difference between composition (*res facta*) and improvisation (*super librum cantare*).

The treatises, apart from the first two, contain many music examples, and some cite a wide range of theorists and composers ranging from the traditional medieval authorities, including Plato, Aristotle, Aristoxenus, Plutarch, Ptolemy, Nicomachus, Ambrose, Augustine, Martianus Capella, Boethius, Isidore of Seville, Guido of Arezzo, Bernard of Clairvaux and Jehan des Murs, to later and contemporary composers such as Dunstable, Dufay, Binchois, Barbingant, Ockeghem, Busnois, Regis, Obrecht, Morton, Caron, Domarto and Faugues.

3. MUSIC. Apart from Tinctoris's surviving attributed music, there are some anonymous music examples in the treatises, especially those on counterpoint, which include a number of complete pieces, particularly motets. It is not known for certain whether he composed these pieces, but he named the composers of many of the other examples throughout his writings, leaving only a few unascribed. Tinctoris's style is marked by flowing polyphony of a complex nature, as might be expected from such a theorist. Two of the masses *sine nomine* are written for low voices, and both use head-motifs for each movement. The *Missa 'Cunctorum plasmator summus'*, named after the trope text, is a cantus firmus mass on *L'homme armé*.

Tinctoris has always been regarded as one of the leading musical figures of his time: as early as 1470 Compère's motet *Omnium bonorum plena* described him as one of the most notable musicians, and Ornithoparchus extolled him as one of the most important writers on music ('scriptor praeclarissimus') in his treatise *Musicae activae micrologus* (1517). Tinctoris had the humanist's wide range of interests: in addition to his musical work, he was also active as a cleric, tutor, lawyer and mathematician. His poetic skill can be seen in the poem which he wrote (and may also have set as a motet) in praise of Pope Alexander VI (1492), copied into Burckard's *Liber notarum*. The historian Ludovico Giucciardini, in his *Belgicum universum* (Antwerp, 1567), described Tinctoris as a prominent painter,

presumably on the evidence of Trithemius's reference that Tinctoris 'figuram unam depinxit'.

WRITINGS
(dates based on Schäfke)

Editions: *J. Tinctoris tractatus de musica*, ed. C.-E.-H. de Coussemaker (Lille, 1875) [C]

J. Tinctoris: Opera theoretica, ed. A. Seay, CSM, xxii (1975) [S]

Terminorum musicae diffinitorium (Treviso, 1495); C, *CS*, iv, 177–91; Ger. trans., *Jb für Musikwissenschaft*, i (1863), 61–114; Fr. trans. (Paris, 1951); Eng. trans. (London, 1964) [probably written c1472–3, before he had a position in Naples, for he is given no status on the title-page]

Complexus effectuum musices, B-Br (inc.), *Gu*, C, S ii, ed. in *CS*, iv, 191–200; ed. and It. trans. L. Zanoncelli (Bologna, 1979) [written c1473–4, for he is given his Naples titles]

Proportionale musices, *Br*, *Gu*, *E-VAu*; C, S ii, ed. in *CS*, iv, 153–77; Eng. trans., *JMT*, i (1957) [written c1473–4, mentioned in later books]

Liber imperfectionum notarum musicalium, B-Br, *Gu*, *E-VAu*, *I-Bc*; C, S i, ed. in *CS*, iv, 54–66 [written c1474–5]

Tractatus de regulari valore notarum, B-Br, *E-VAu*, *I-Bc*; C, S i, ed. in *CS*, iv, 46–53 [written c1474–5]

Tractatus de notis et pausis, B-Br, *Gu*, *E-VAu*, *I-Bc*; C, S i, ed. in *CS*, iv, 41–6 [written c1474–5, after *Tractatus de regulari valore notarum*]

Liber de natura et proprietate tonorum, B-Br, *E-VAu*, *I-Bc*; C, S i, ed. in *CS*, iv, 16–41; Eng. trans. (Colorado Springs, 1967, rev. 2/1976) [dated 6 Nov 1476]

Liber de arte contrapuncti, B-Br, *E-VAu*, *I-Bc*; C, S ii, ed. in *CS*, iv, 76–153; Eng. trans., *MSD*, v (1961) [dated 11 Oct 1477]

Tractatus alterationum, B-Br, *Gu*, *E-VAu*, *I-Bc*; C, S i, ed. in *CS*, iv, 66–70 [written after 1477]

Scriptum super punctis musicalibus, B-Br, *Gu*, *E-VAu*, *I-Bc*; C, S i, ed. in *CS*, iv, 70–76 [written after 1477]

Expositio manus, B-Br, *E-VAu*, *I-Bc*; C, S i, ed. in *CS*, iv, 1–16 [written after 1477]

De inventione et usu musicae (Naples, c1487), inc.; ed. in Weinmann (1909, 1917) [written after the Battle of Otranto, 1480]

Liber de origine musice, lost, mentioned by Trithemius [? = *De inventione et usu musicae*]

Epistolae, lost, mentioned by Trithemius

WORKS
Edition: *J. Tinctoris: Opera omnia*, ed. W. Melin, CMM, xviii (1976) [M]

SACRED
Missa 'Cunctorum plasmator summus', 4vv, *I-Rvat* C.S.35, M 74
Missa 'Nos amis', 3vv, *CS-Ppp* D.G.IV.47 (Ky, Gl in *I-TRmn* 89, Cr in *CS-HK* II A 7), unpubd (see Strohm) (on Adrien Basin chanson)
Missa sine nomine (i), 3vv, *I-VEcap* 755, M 1
Missa sine nomine (ii), 3vv, *VEcap* 759, M 33
Missa sine nomine, 4vv, *Md* 2268, M 55
Alleluia, 2vv, *E-SE* and *Liber de arte contrapuncti* (with different opening), M 128
Fecit potentiam, 2vv, *SE*, M 129
Lamentationes Jeremie, 4vv, 1506[1], M 115
O virgo miserere mei, 3vv, *US-NH* 91, M 125, also ed. in Perkins and Garey (1979), no.19
Virgo Dei throno digna, 3vv, 8 sources listed in M (to which add *I-VEcap* 757, ff.6v–7), M 126, also ed. in Perkins and Garey (1979), no.57
Credo attrib. Tinctoris in *CS-HK* II A 7 is from Josquin: Missa 'L'ami Baudichon'

SECULAR
Comme femme, 2vv, *E-SE*, M 144 (on tenor of Binchois chanson)
De tous biens playne, 2vv, *SE*, M 141 (on tenor of Hayne chanson)
D'ung aultre amer, 2vv, *SE*, M 143 (on tenor of Ockeghem chanson)
Helas le bon temps, 3vv, 7 sources listed in M, M 130
Le souvenir, 2vv, *SE*, M 137 (on tenor of Morton chanson)
Le souvenir, 4vv, *SE*, M 135 (on discantus of Morton chanson)
O invida Fortuna, 3vv, *I-Fn* Magl.XIX 176, M 133
Tout a par moy, 2vv, *E-SE*, M 138 (on tenor of chanson by Frye or Binchois)
Vostre regart, 3vv, 5 sources listed in M, M 131 (for full rondeau text see E. Droz and G. Thibault, eds.: *Trois chansonniers* (Paris, 1927/R1978), 46f)

BIBLIOGRAPHY
BurneyH; *FétisB*
J. N. Forkel: *Allgemeine Geschichte der Musik*, ii (Leipzig, 1801), 437ff, 502ff

E. A. Choron: *Rapport sur un manuscrit de Tinctoris* (Paris, 1813)

R. G. Kiesewetter: *Die Verdienste der Niederländer um die Tonkunst* (Amsterdam, 1828), 11ff

E. vander Straeten: *La musique aux Pays-Bas avant le XIXe siècle*, iv (Brussels, 1878/R1969)

F. Florimo: *La scuola musicale di Napoli e i suoi conservatorii, i* (Naples, 1880/R1969), 26

F. X. Haberl: 'Die römische "Schola cantorum" und die päpstlichen Kapellsänger bis zur Mitte des 16. Jahrhunderts', *VMw*, iii (1887), 189

A. W. Ambros: *Geschichte der Musik*, iii (Leipzig, rev. 2/1893 by O. Kade), 142ff

F. X. Haberl: 'Ein unbekanntes Werk des Johannes Tinctoris', *KJb*, xiv (1899), 69

L. Fökövi: 'Musik und musikalische Verhältnisse in Ungarn am Hofe von Matthias Corvinus', *KJb*, xv (1900), 1

U. Kornmüller: 'Die alten Musiktheoretiker: Johannes Tinctoris', *KJb*, xviii (1903), 1

E. de Reusens: *Matricule de l'Université de Louvain*, i (Louvain, 1903)

K. Weinmann: 'Ein unbekannter Traktat des Johannes Tinctoris', *Riemann-Festschrift* (Leipzig, 1909), 269

G. Pannain: *La teoria musicale di Giovanni Tinctoris* (Naples, 1913)

J. Wolf: *Handbuch der Notationskunde* (Leipzig, 1913/R1963), esp. 109, 385, 388

G. Pannain: *Le origini della scuola musicale napoletana* (Naples, 1914)

K. Weinmann: *Johannes Tinctoris und sein unbekannter Traktat 'De inventione et usu musicae'* (Regensburg, 1917/R1961)

H. Riemann: *Geschichte der Musiktheorie im IX.–XIX. Jahrhundert* (Berlin, 2/1920), esp. 310ff; (Eng. trans., 1962)

G. d'Alessi: *Il tipografo fiammingo Gerardo de Lisa* (Treviso, 1925), 9ff, 33

O. J. Gombosi: *La vita musicale alla corte di Re Mattia Corvino* (Budapest, 1929)

A. Schering: 'Musikalisches aus Johann Burckards "Liber notarum" (1483–1506)', *Musikwissenschaftliche Beiträge: Festschrift für Johannes Wolf* (Berlin, 1929/R1973), 171

A. Auda: *La musique et les musiciens de l'ancien pays de Liège* (Liège, 1930), 88ff

C. van den Borren: 'Tinctoris, Johannes', *BNB*

R. Schäfke: *Geschichte der Musikästhetik in Umrissen* (Berlin, 1934), 231ff

L. Balmer: *Tonsystem und Kirchentöne bei Johannes Tinctoris* (diss., U. of Berne, 1935)

H. Anglès: 'Un manuscrit inconnu avec polyphonie du XVe siècle conservé à la cathédrale de Ségovie', *AcM*, viii (1936), 6

E. T. Ferand: *Die Improvisation in der Musik* (Zurich, 1938), esp. 147ff, 155ff, 163ff

W. Apel: *The Notation of Polyphonic Music 900–1600* (Cambridge, Mass., 1942, rev. 5/1961), esp. 145, 153, 164

M. F. Bukofzer: 'An Unknown Chansonnier of the 15th Century (the Mellon Chansonnier)', *MQ*, xxviii (1942), 14

E. Krenek: *A Discussion of the Treatment of Dissonances in Ockeghem's Masses as Compared with the Contrapuntal Theory of Johannes Tinctoris* (St Paul, Minn., 1947)

C. van den Borren: *Geschiedenis van de muziek in de Nederlanden*, i (Antwerp, 1948), 223f

A. Baines: 'Fifteenth Century Instruments in Johannes Tinctoris' *De inventione et usu musicae*', *GSJ*, iii (1950), 19

D. Plamenac: 'A Reconstruction of the French Chansonnier in the Biblioteca Colombina, Seville', *MQ*, xxxvii (1951), 501; xxxviii (1952), 85, 245

J. Quitin: 'Les maîtres de chant de la cathédrale St. Lambert à Liège aux XVe et XVIe siècles', *RBM*, viii (1954), 14

G. Reese: *Music in the Renaissance* (New York, 1954, rev. 2/1959), esp. 137ff

F. Feldmann: 'Musiktheoretiker in eigenen Kompositionen: Untersuchungen am Werk des Tinctoris, Adam von Fulda und Nucius', *DJbM*, i (1956), 39

E. T. Ferand: 'What is Res facta?', *JAMS*, x (1957), 141

N. Bridgman: 'The Age of Ockeghem and Josquin', *NOHM*, iii (1960), 239–302

E. H. Sparks: *Cantus Firmus in Mass and Motet 1420–1520* (Berkeley and Los Angeles, 1963), esp. 98, 241

K.-J. Sachs: *Der Contrapunctus im 14. und 15. Jahrhundert: Untersuchungen zum Terminus, zur Systematik der Lehre und zu den Quellen* (diss., U. of Freiburg, 1967)

C. M. Ridderikhoff and H. de Ridder-Symoens, eds.: *Premier livre des procurateurs de la nation germanique de l'ancienne université d'Orléans, 1444–1546*, i (Leiden, 1971), 28ff

P. Carpenter: 'Tonal Coherence in a Motet of Dufay', *JMT*, xvii (1973), 2–64

W. E. Melin: *The Music of Johannes Tinctoris (c. 1435–1511): a Comparative Study of Theory and Practice* (diss., Ohio State U., 1973)

G. Gerritzen: *Untersuchungen zur Kontrapunktlehre des Johannes Tinctoris* (diss., U. of Cologne, 1974)

L. L. Perkins and H. Garey, eds.: *The Mellon Chansonnier* (New Haven, 1979)

R. Strohm: 'Die Missa super "Nos amis" von Johannes Tinctoris', *Mf*, xxxii (1979), 34

HEINRICH HÜSCHEN

Tindley, Charles Albert (*b* Berlin, Maryland, 7 July 1851; *d* Philadelphia, 26 July 1933). Black American minister and composer of gospel hymns. *See* GOSPEL MUSIC, §I.

Tinel, Edgar (Pierre Joseph) (*b* Sinaai, East Flanders, 27 March 1854; *d* Brussels, 28 Oct 1912). Belgian composer and pianist. After studies at the Brussels Conservatory with Brassin (piano) and Gevaert (composition), he began a career as a virtuoso, but soon abandoned this for composition. In 1877 his cantata *Klokke Roeland* won him the Belgian Prix de Rome, and in 1881 he succeeded Lemmens as director of the Ma⌐.ᵤes Institute of Religious Music. He devoted himself to a study of old church music, and his ideas gave rise to Pius X's *Motu proprio*. Appointed inspector of music education in 1889, he moved to the Brussels Conservatoire to become professor of counterpoint and fugue in 1896, and director at the end of 1908. He was made *maître de chapelle* to the king in 1910, having been elected to the Belgian Royal Academy in 1902. His liturgical music is polyphonic in the Palestrina style, but this technique conflicted with Tinel's lyrical and mystical temperament, and he had much greater success in his two concert settings of the *Te Deum*, the oratorio and the religious dramas. These works indicate his total admiration for Bach, but the orchestration, dominated by the strings, is Romantic. Tinel's piano pieces and songs recall Schumann, Mendelssohn and Brahms; the *Bunte Blätter* for piano are particularly spontaneous and touching, and his songs to melancholic texts have a most moving sincerity expressed through unexpected modulations (e.g. the *Adventlieder*). He published *Le chant grégorien* (Mechelen, 1890).

WORKS
(selective list)

Operas: Godelieve, op.43; Katharina, op.44

Choral: Klokke Roeland, op.17, cantata; Kollebloemen, op.20, cantata, 1879, rev. 1889–90; Vlaamsche stemme, op.25, 4 male vv; Te Deum, op.26, 4vv, org, 1883; Psalm vi, op.27, 4 male vv, 1891; Franciscus, op.36, oratorio, 1890; Aurora, op.37, 4 male vv (1885); Psalm xxix, op.39, 4 male vv; Missa in honorem BMV de Lourdes, op.41, 5vv, 1905; Cantique nuptial, op.45, S/T, org, pf/harp; Te Deum, op.46, 6vv, org, orch, 1905; Psalm cl, op.47, 4 male vv, 1907

Kbd: Pf Sonata, f, op.9; Org Sonata, g, op.29; Bunte Blätter, op.32, pf

Orch music, songs

Principal publishers: Breitkopf & Härtel, Schott (Brussels)

MSS in *B-Br*

BIBLIOGRAPHY

E. Closson: *Sainte Godelieve de E. Tinel* (Leipzig, 1879)

A. van der Elst: *Edgar Tinel* (Ghent, 1901)

P. Tinel: *Edgar Tinel: Le récit de sa vie et l'exégèse de son oeuvre de 1854 à 1886* (Brussels, 1923)

——: *Le 'Franciscus' d'Edgar Tinel* (Brussels, 1926)

——: *Edgar Tinel* (Brussels, 1946)

J. Ryelandt: 'Notice sur Edgar Tinel', *Annuaire de l'Académie royale de Belgique*, cxvi (1950), 207

C. van den Borren: *Geschiedenis van de muziek in de Nederlanden*, ii (Antwerp, 1951), 239ff, 287ff, 335f, 367f

F. van der Mueren: 'Edgar Tinel', *Musica sacra*, lxiii (1962), 113

J. Vyverman: 'Tinel, Edgar', *BNB*

HENRI VANHULST

Tini. Italian family of printers, in partnership with FILIPPO LOMAZZO.

Tinódi, Sebestyén ['Lantos'] (*b* between *c*1505 and *c*1510; *d* Sárvár, late Jan 1556). Hungarian poet, composer and bard. Early in life he spent some time at Szigetvár, and later he was at Nagyszombat, Kassa and Kolozsvár (now Cluj-Napoca). He seems to have been an itinerant musician for much of his life. At the time of his death he was employed at Tamás Nádasdy's court at Sárvár. 23 songs by Tinódi survive in his *Cronica* (Kolozsvár, 1554/*R*1959). His poetry is mostly either narrative (historical or biblical) or satirical, and the longer epics refer to the contemporary wars against the Turks. The texts were designed for musical performance and come to life only when sung to his clearly constructed melodies. These have obvious national characteristics, though they were probably not based on folk models. Their rhythmic range is limited, following one of three or four basic patterns. The songs were very influential, becoming (both in practice and by reputation) the seeds from which Hungarian folk music grew, and as a result they appear in hymnbooks as late as the 19th century.

BIBLIOGRAPHY

G. Mátray: *Történeti, bibliai és gúnyoros magyar énekek dallamai a XVI. századból* [Melodies of Hungarian historic, biblical and satirical songs from the 16th century] (Pest, 1859) [with editions]

L. Dézsi: *Sebestyén Tinódi* (Budapest, 1912)

B. Szabolcsi: 'Probleme der alten ungarischen Musikgeschichte', *ZMw*, vii (1924–5), 647

B. Pukánszky: 'Sebestyén Tinódi und der deutsche Zeitungsgesang', *Forschungsarbeiten des Collegium Hungaricum* (Berlin, 1927), 115

B. Szabolcsi: *Tinódi zenéje* [Tinódi's music] (Budapest, 1929; enlarged in *A magyar zene évszázadai*, Budapest, 1959, 61–100) [with editions]

K. C. Tóth: *A XVI. század magyar dallamai* [The Hungarian melodies of the 16th century] (Budapest, 1958) [with editions]

B. Szabolcsi: 'Tinódi, Sebestyén', *MGG*

K. CSOMASZ TÓTH

Tin Pan Alley. The popular songwriting and music-publishing industry, particularly that of New York from the late 19th century to the 1920s. At first it was centred on 28th Street and 6th Avenue, later round the Brill Building near 49th Street, where the most important publishers had offices. The term possibly referred to the 'tinny' sound of the office pianos used by the arrangers and songwriters.

See POPULAR MUSIC, §II, 11.

GUNTHER SCHULLER

Tinpanny. *See* STEEL BAND.

Tinsley, Pauline (*b* Salford, 23 Nov 1940). English soprano. She studied at the Northern School of Music, then with Joan Cross at the National School of Opera (later the London Opera Centre). Her stage début was at St Pancras Town Hall, as Desdemona in Rossini's *Otello* (12 May 1961); the following year her appearances included Elsa and Susanna with the Welsh National Opera. In 1963 she sang with the Handel Opera Society (Romilda in *Serse*), and made her Sadler's Wells début as Gilda. Among her many roles at Sadler's Wells and later at the Coliseum have been Elvira in *Ernani*, Mozart's Countess, Fiordiligi and Elvira, Leonora (*La forza del destino*), the title role in Beethoven's *Leonore*, and Donizetti's Elizabeth I in the 1973 English-language *Maria Stuarda* (a role she had earlier taken, in Italian, in New York). Santuzza in 1976 was her first important Covent Garden role (she had made her house début in 1965, in *Elektra*); other notable appearances have been at the Hamburg Staatsoper (Abigail in *Nabucco*, Leonora in *La forza del destino*), at the Santa Fe and Holland Festivals, and in Washington and New Orleans. Her bright dramatic soprano, not always pure or sweet of tone, can summon both flexibility and great brilliance for the Verdi heroines of *Nabucco*, *Ernani*, *I masnadieri* and *Macbeth*, and also the power for such roles as Turandot and the Kostelnička in *Jenůfa*. She is an imposing (if sometimes idiosyncratic) actress. She has recorded Electra in *Idomeneo* under Colin Davis.

ALAN BLYTH

Tintner, Georg (*b* Vienna, 22 May 1917). Australian conductor of Austrian birth. In 1927 he joined the Vienna Boys' Choir, with which he had his first opportunities to conduct. Later he studied composition with Joseph Marx and conducting with Weingartner at the Vienna Academy. In the late 1930s he went to Auckland. When the National Opera of New South Wales toured New Zealand he conducted for them, and in 1954 he went to Australia with the National Opera. Later he became resident conductor of the Elizabethan Trust Opera Company (now Australian Opera), and he pioneered television opera in Australia. Tintner's work abroad has included periods as musical director of the New Zealand Opera and Ballet Company and resident conductor of the Cape Town Municipal Orchestra; in Britain he has appeared with Sadler's Wells Opera, the LSO and the London Mozart Players. Returning to Australia in 1970, he became musical director of the Western Australia Opera Company and then resident conductor of Australian Opera. He has a large operatic and symphonic repertory, and specializes in the symphonies of Bruckner.

ANN CARR-BOYD

Tin whistle. A small high-pitched WHISTLE FLUTE, end-blown like a recorder, with six finger-holes and a small range, usually made of metal; also called 'penny whistle'.

Illustration Acknowledgments

We are grateful to those listed below for permission to reproduce copyright illustrative material, and those contributors who supplied or helped us obtain it. Every effort has been made to contact copyright holders; we apologize to anyone who may have been omitted. Brian and Constance Dear prepared the maps and technical diagrams, and Oxford Illustrators the typographic diagrams (except where otherwise stated). Photographs acknowledged to the following sources are Crown copyright: Her Majesty the Queen, the Victoria and Albert Museum (including the Theatre Museum), the Science Museum and the National Monuments Record. The following forms of acknowledgment are used where the copyright of an illustration is held by a contributor:

photo John Smith – John Smith is contributor and photographer
John Smith – John Smith is contributor and copyright holder
photo John Smith, London – John Smith is a contributor (not of the article concerned) and photographer
John Smith, London – John Smith is a contributor (not of the article concerned) and copyright holder.

Where illustrations are taken from books out of copyright, the full title and place and date of publication are given, unless in the caption.

Spiritual _1_ Paul Oliver, Oxford
Spohr, Louis _1_ Landesmuseum für Geschichte und Volkstum, Brunswick / photo Otto Hoppe
Spontini, Gaspare _1_ photo Archivio Fotografico dei Civici Musei, Milan; _2, 3_ Bibliothèque Nationale, Paris
Sri Lanka _1_ Popperfoto, London; _2_ photo Deben Bhattacharya, Paris; _3, 4_ Deben Battacharya, Paris / photo Giragama (_3_), Wevrukannala (_4_)
Stabile, Mariano Harold Rosenthal, London / photo Houston Rogers
Stadtpfeifer Staatsbibliothek Preussischer Kulturbesitz, Berlin
Staff _1_ Bibliothèque Municipale, Valenciennes; _2_ British Library, London
Stainer, Jacob W. E. Hill & Sons, Great Missenden / photo Desmond Hill
Stamitz _1_ British Library, London; _2_ Library of Congress, Washington, DC; _3_ Deutsche Staatsbibliothek. Berlin
Stanesby _1b_ Victoria and Albert Museum, London
Stanford, Charles Villiers National Portrait Gallery, London
Stanley, John Royal College of Music, London
Steel band Kensington News and Post, London
Steffani, Agostino _1_ British Library, London; _2_ Österreichische Nationalbibliothek, Vienna
Steibelt, Daniel Richard Macnutt, Tunbridge Wells
Stignani, Ebe Royal Opera House, Covent Garden, London
Stock-and-horn Glasgow Museums and Art Galleries
Stockhausen, Karlheinz _1_ Universal Edition (London) Ltd; _2_ photo Werner Scholz, Cologne; _3_ Karlheinz Stockhausen, Cologne
Stockholm _1_ Drottningholms Teatermuseum / photo Beata Bergstrom; _2_ Kungliga Biblioteket, Stockholm
Stokowski, Leopold CBS Records, London
Stolz, Teresa Stuart-Liff Collection, Tunbridge Wells
Storace _1_ British Library, London; _2_ Mander and Mitchenson, London
Stradivari, Antonio _2_ Ashmolean Museum, Oxford
Strauss _1, 4–6_ Österreichische Nationalbibliothek, Vienna; _2_ Archiv für Kunst und Geschichte, Berlin; _3_ Richard Macnutt, Tunbridge Wells
Strauss, Richard _1_ BBC Hulton Picture Library, London; _2_ Bibliothèque Nationale, Paris; _3_ Popperfoto, London; _4, 8_ Boosey & Hawkes Ltd, London (from E. Roth, ed., _Richard Strauss Bühnenwerke/Stage Works/Oeuvres lyriques_, 1954); _5, 6, 9_ Franz Strauss, Garmisch-Partenkirchen / (_5_) photo Archiv für Kunst und Geschichte, Berlin; _7_ Residenz Verlag, Salzburg: from F. Hadamowsky, _Richard Strauss und Salzburg_ (1964)
Stravinsky, Igor _2_ M. I. Glinka State Central Museum of Musical Culture, Moscow; _4_ Archives Théodore Strawinsky, Geneva, and Boosey & Hawkes Ltd, London: from T. Strawinsky, _Catherine and Igor Stravinsky, a Family Album_ (1973); _5_ Stravinsky Estate, New York, Meyer Collection, Paris, and Boosey & Hawkes Ltd, London; _7_ Victoria and Albert Museum, London; _8_ Museum of Modern Art, New York; _9_ photo Vera Stravinsky; _10_ photo Erich Auerbach, London; _11_ Stravinsky Estate, New York, Library of Congress, Washington, DC, and Boosey & Hawkes Ltd, London
Strepponi, Giuseppina Museo Teatrale alla Scala, Milan
Striggio, Alessandro (i) British Library, London
String quartet Fürstlich Oettingen-Wallerstein'sche Bibliothek und Kunstsammlung, Schloss Harburg
Strozzi, Giulio Ashmolean Museum, Oxford
Study Richard Macnutt, Tunbridge Wells
Stuttgart _1_ Victoria and Albert Museum, London / photo Eileen Tweedy; _2_ Württembergische Landesbibliothek, Stuttgart
Sudan _1–7_ Mahdi Ismail
Suite _1_ Bibliothèque Nationale, Paris / photo J. Colomb-Gérard; _2_ Richard Macnutt, Tunbridge Wells
Suk, Josef (i) Státní Pedagogické Nakladatelství, Prague: from E. Herzog, _Antonín Dvořák_ (1966)
Sullivan, Arthur _1_ National Portrait Gallery, London; _2, 3_ Mander and Mitchenson, London; _4_ Royal College of Music, London
Sumer is icumen in British Library, London
Sun Ra photo Valerie Wilmer, London
Supervia, Conchita Harold Rosenthal, London / photo Lassalle
Surinam _1, 2_ Terry Agerkop
Susato, Tylman Bayerische Staatsbibliothek, Munich
Sutherland, Joan Harold Rosenthal, London / photo Houston Rogers
Suzuki, Shin'ichi Minoa Shibata
Svanholm, Set Harold Rosenthal, London / photo Carmen
Svendsen, Johan Kongelige Teater, Copenhagen / photo Rigmor Mydtskov
Svetlanov, Evgeny Novosti Press Agency, London
Sweden _1_ Nordiska Museet, Stockholm; _2_ Alexandr Buchner, Prague
Sweelinck, Jan Pieterszoon _1_ Rijksmuseum, Amsterdam; _2_ British Library, London
Switzerland _1, 2_ Swiss National Tourist Office, London / (_2_) photo Philipp Giegel; _3_ Schweizerische Landesbibliothek, Berne
Sydney _1_ Max Dupain & Associates Pty Ltd, Sydney; _2_ Ove Arup & Partners, London / photo Michael Andrews, Sydney
Symphonie concertante Richard Macnutt, Tunbridge Wells
Symphony _1_ Kungliga Musikaliska Akademiens Bibliotek, Stockholm; _2_ Richard Macnutt, Tunbridge Wells
Synthesizer _1, 2_ Electronic Music Studios, London

Syrian church music *1* Musikalien Karl Dieter Wagner, Hamburg: from H. Husmann, 'Ein syrisches Sticherarion mit paläobyzantinischen Notation (Sinai Syr. 261)', *Hamburger Jahrbuch für Musikwissenschaft*, i (1975); *2* from J.-B. Thibaut, *Origine byzantine de la notation neumatique de l'église latine* (Paris, 1907)

Szell, George photo Erich Auerbach, London

Szeryng, Henryk Phonogram Ltd, London

Szigeti, Joseph EMI Ltd, London

Tablature *1, 3, 4, 6* British Library, London; *2* Curtis Institute of Music, Philadelphia; *5* Bibliothèque Nationale, Paris; *7* Deutsche Staatsbibliothek, Berlin; *8* Gesellschaft der Musikfreunde, Vienna; *9* Kurt Janetsky, Wiesloch

Table-book British Library, London

Tadolini, Eugenia Opera Rara Collection, London

Tafelmusik Museum für Kunst und Kulturgeschichte, Lübeck

Taiwan *1* Popperfoto, London; *2* photo I-to Loh; *3* Tsai-ping Liang

Tallis, Thomas Bodleian Library, Oxford

Tamagno, Francesco Museo Teatrale alla Scala, Milan

Tambari Anthony King, London

Tamberlik, Enrico Mander and Mitchenson, London

Tambourin Conservatoire Royal de Musique, Brussels / photo ACL

Tambourin de Béarn Museum Boymans van Beuningen, Rotterdam

Tambourine *1* Mansell Collection, London; *2* photo Colin Busby, London

Tamburini, Antonio Royal Opera House, Covent Garden, London

Taneyev, Sergey Ivanovich Novosti Press Agency, London

Tango British Library, London

Tanzania *2* Gerhard Kubik / photo Hillegeist; *3* photo Gerhard Kubik

Tárogató photo Bálint Sárosi, Budapest

Tartini, Giuseppe *2* Biblioteca Antoniana, Basilica del Santo, Padua

Tartöld Kunsthistorisches Museum, Vienna

Tauber, Richard Harold Rosenthal, London

Tausig, Carl Harry L. Anderson, San Diego, California

Taverner, John Public Record Office, London

Taylor, Brook National Portrait Gallery, London

Tchaikovsky, Pyotr Il'yich *1, 10* M. I. Glinka State Central Museum of Musical Culture, Moscow / photo (*1*) photo Tchaikovsky House Museum, Klin; *2, 5* Archiv für Kunst und Geschichte, Berlin; *3* AMH Printing Agency, Moscow / photo Tchaikovsky House Museum, Klin; *4, 6–8* Novosti Press Agency, London

Tebaldi, Renata Harold Rosenthal

Telemann, Georg Philipp *2* (left) Hessische Landes- und Hochschulbibliothek, Darmstadt; *2* (right) British Library, London; *3* Deutsche Staatsbibliothek, Berlin

Tenducci, Giusto Ferdinando Barber Institute of Fine Arts, University of Birmingham

Tenor cor Rudall, Carte & Co. Ltd, London

Terpander National Archaeological Museum, Athens

Tertis, Lionel Harvard Theatre Collection, Cambridge, Massachusetts / photo Angus McBean

Tetrazzini, Luisa Royal College of Music, London

Teyte, Maggie Harold Rosenthal

Thailand *1–5* David Morton; *6, 7* Department of Fine Arts, Bangkok

Thalberg, Sigismond Royal College of Music, London

Theatre organ Royal College of Music, London

Théâtres de la Foire Trustees of the Wallace Collection, London

Theinred of Dover Bodleian Library, Oxford

Theorbo *1* British Library, London; *2* The Viscount de l'Isle, Penshurst

Theory, theorists *1* Bibliothèque Royale Albert Ier, Brussels; *2, 4* Bibliothèque Nationale, Paris; *3* Universitätsbibliothek, Karl-Marx-Universität, Leipzig; *5, 6* British Library, London

Thomas, Ambroise *1* Archivio Storico Ricordi, Milan; *2* Bibliothèque Nationale, Paris

Thomson, Virgil G. Schirmer Inc., New York

Thunder machine Vienna Philharmonic Orchestra and Gustav Schuster, Vienna / photo Hans Wild

Tibet *1* Ocora Radio France, Paris: from record sleeve, *Musique rituelle tibetaine* (1969) / photo Georges Luneau; *2* Popperfoto, London; *3* photo D. L. Snellgrove, London; *4a, 5, 6* photo Gabrielle Yablonsky, Westfield, New Jersey; *4b* John Noxon and Indiana University Archives of Traditional Music, Bloomington

Tibia (i) Mansell Collection, London, and Alinari, Florence

Tichatschek, Joseph Mander and Mitchenson, London

Tieffenbrucker from G. Kinsky, ed., *Geschichte der Musik in Bildern* (Leipzig, 1929)

Tietjens, Therese Victoria and Albert Museum, London

Timpani *1, 2* Premier Drum Co. Ltd, Leicester; *3, 7* Ludwig Drum Co., Chicago; *8* Trustees of the British Museum, London; *9* Bibliothèque Nationale, Paris; *10* The Duke of Marlborough / photo Victoria and Albert Museum, London; *12* Bayerisches Nationalmuseum, Munich; *13* Edward Croft-Murray, Richmond, Surrey; *14* B. T. Batsford Ltd, London / photo L. G. Aubin

Tinctoris, Johannes Biblioteca Universitaria, Valencia